2001 / 2002

THE
WORLD
GUIDE

An alternative reference to the countries of our planet

General index

World Guide 2001/2002

The World Guide 2001/2002

CONTENTS
SECTION I:
Global issues

Theme

Article summary

Article text

Table
Statistics Figures

I. THE EARTH AND ITS PEOPLES

20. | **Rising death rates in the South**

21. | **Immigrants - indispensable to the North**

(Table) **Demography in figures**

Indicators: percentage of married women of childbearing age using contraceptives, 1990-99;
crude death rate per thousand people, 1998; crude birth rate per thousand people, 1998; children per woman, 1998.
Source: The State of the World's Children 2000 UNICEF, 2000.

23. | **WATER: Running out faster than ever**

WATER IS VITAL for human life and activities. Farming, mining and industry, electricity generation, transport and communications all soak up millions of gallons. However, only 3 per cent of the world's water is drinkable and there is an increasingly widening gap between demand and supply.

(Table) **Distribution of income and consumption**

Inequality in the distribution of income is reflected in the percentage share of either income or consumption accruing to segments of the population ranked by income or consumption levels. The segments ranked lowest by personal income receive the smallest share of total income. The Gini index provides a convenient summary measure of the degree of inequality (when Gini index is zero this represents perfect equality, while an index of 100 implies 'perfect' inequality). Source: World Development Indicators 2000, World Bank, 2000.

(Table) **Populaton Density**

Indicator: Population per sq km, 1999.
Source: Calculated from population, 1999 (United Nations Statistics Division - Web Site) and area (UNCTAD Handbook of Statistics, 2000).

II. SOCIETY

27. | **GLOBALIZATION: The diversification of economies**

IT'S BEEN HAMMERED into us that there's an entirely new phenomenon, a 'globalizing' economy, that we must obey. A 'driverless machine' assembles different parts from a dozen different countries to make a motorcar, or processes the bookings for European airlines in Bangalore. A new fuel — called 'market forces'— suddenly seems capable of bringing us close to perpetual motion.

28. | **GEOGRAPHY: Mapping humanity**

GEOGRAPHY, once called 'mother of the sciences', is nowadays seen by some to have lost its central importance. Some people say that, far from reaching the 'end of history', as late 20th-century theorists predicted, what we have reached is in fact the 'end of geography'.

29.

EDUCATION: The new illiterates

FOR INTERNATIONAL BODIES such as the United Nations or the World Bank, one of the greatest challenges is the eradication of illiteracy. There is wide agreement that people who cannot read will increasingly be left behind on the margins of society, employment and knowledge.

(table) **Educational imbalances**

Indicator: primary pupil to teacher ratio (1994/98).
Source: World Development Indicators 2000, World Bank, 2000.

(table) **Education enrolment in figures**

Indicators: percentage of students across the school-age population (gross enrolment rate is the number of children enrolled at a level - primary or secondary - regardless of age, divided by the population of that age group): male and female in primary and secondary level (1990/96) and total in tertiary level (1996/97).
Sources: The State of the World's Children 2000, UNICEF, 2000. World Development Indicators 2000, World Bank, 2000.

(table) **Literacy**

Indicator: adult literacy rate (total, female, male), 1995.
Source: The State of the World's Children 2000, UNICEF, 2000.

32.

PREDICTIONS: The new millennium

LEADING figures give their predictions for the new millennium

(table) **Women in work**

Indicators: percentage of women in labor force, 1998; percentage of administration and managerial posts occupied by women; percentage of professional women and women technicians; women's earned income share (data refers to 1995 or the latest available year).
Source: World Development Indicators 2000, World Bank, 2000; Human Development Report 1999, UNDP, 1999.

(table) **Women in political life**

Indicators: percentage of parliamentary seats occupied by women, 1999; percentage of governmental posts occupied by women (ministerial level and total), 1996.
Source: Human Development Report 1999, UNDP, 1999.

(table) **Breast is best**

Indicator: percentage of mothers breastfeeding at three months, 1990-99.
Source: The State of the World's Children 2000, UNICEF, 2000.

35.

WORK: Conditions for change

SOME TRADE UNIONISTS and socialist thinkers are optimistic about the new social dynamics generated by technological changes and the globalization of goods and services. But they also warn about the dangers of a society in which workers, regardless of the jobs they perform, simply become consumers with no rights at work.

(table) **Workers in figures**

Indicators: labor force (percentage of total population), 1995; percentage of the labor force in agriculture, industrial and services sectors, 1990; unemployment rate, 1994/97.
Sources: Human Development Report 1998, UNDP, 1998. World Development Indicators, 2000, World Bank 2000.

37.

FOOD: Tainted food

NEVER HAS HUMANITY had more scientific and technical achievements within its grasp - but never have issues of environmental and food pollution been raised as widely and seriously as they are now. For while cultural, medical and health improvements have helped prolong active human lives, we are witnessing a deterioration in the living conditions of broad sectors of the population.

(table) **Food in figures**

Indicators: food production per capita index (1989-91=100), 1997; food imports as a percentage of merchandise imports, 1997; cereal imports (1,000 metric tons), 1998.
Sources: Human Development Report 1999, UNDP, 1999; FAO Database - Web Site.

(table) **Health in figures**

Indicator: doctors and nurses per 100,000 people, 1993.
Source: Human Development Report 1999, UNDP, 1999.

40. CHILDHOOD: Mortgaging the future

THE WORD infant (infans) means "he/she who has no voice". In fact, until the beginning of the 20th century, children in many cultures were not even named until they were five years old. This was due to the uncertainty on the part of their parents and the community as to whether they would survive or not. Lacking a name, they could not be considered subjects.

(table) **Health services**

Indicators: percentage of population with access to safe water, 1990-98; percentage of population with access to health services, 1990-96.
Sources: The State of the World's Children 2000, UNICEF, 2000; The State of the World's Children 1997, UNICEF, 1997.

(table) **Children's health**

Indicators: percentage of births attended by health personnel, 1990-99; life expectancy at birth (years), 1998; percentage of low birth-weight babies (2,500 g), 1997; infant mortality rate (per 1,000 live births), 1998; underweight children under-five, percentage, 1990-98; maternal mortality rate (per 100,000 live births), 1990-98.
Source: The State of the World's Children 2000, UNICEF, 2000.

THE WORLD ACCORDING TO...

Different views of the world according to the World Bank, the UNDP and UNICEF.

III. SCIENCE AND TECHNOLOGY

44. SCIENCE: Where is the scientific society heading?

SCIENTIFIC development, as it arose within the framework of Western culture, has so permeated the world that present societies have been built on foundations created by that development and structured by its knowledge. This scientific knowledge which helped solve so many human problems has however created others which raise a question mark over where it will end.

(box) **Frankenstein fears**

(table) **Urban population**

Indicators: urban population as a percentage of total, 1997, and estimates to 2015.
Source: Human Development Report 1999, UNDP, 1999.

47. COMMUNICATIONS: Omnipresent, omniscient computers

IN AN INTERVIEW for the French newspaper *Le Monde*, Michael Dertouzos of the Massachusetts Institute of Technology, announced that in 20 years' time computers would be as popular and user-friendly as televisions. Meanwhile, the main source of information will be an extended Internet which will allow information to flow freely and more quickly than today.

47.

VEHICLES: The new species

THE ROBOT CAR, devised to overcome problems caused by the vehicles of the 20th century, will speed the mechanization of 21st century cities and so accelerate the robotization of city lifestyles.

(table) Communications in figures

Indicators: main telephone lines per thousand people, 1996; Personal computers per 1,000 people, 1996.
Source: Human Development Report 1999, UNDP, 1999.

49.

INTERNET: World wide web of companies

THE SHAKE-UP in the internet provider and entertainment industries produced by the merger between America Online and Time-Warner in early 2000 showed how entry into the commercial sphere and stock exchange speculation has put the internet at the heart of crucial disputes between the communications empires.

IV. ECONOMY

50.

EXCHANGE: New symbols of social exchange

ON THE BRINK of a crisis for civilization, where the key symbol - money - has lost its original meaning for millions of people, small groups and associations are creating new forms of exchange which revive old values of coexistence, respect for nature and human solidarity.

(box) Confession-time for IMF ideologues

(table) Aid in figures

Indicators: total net official development assistance (ODA) disbursed, in $ millions and as a percentage of donors' GNP, 1997.
Source: Human Development Report 1999, UNDP, 1999.

(table) GNP as indicator of wealth

Indicator: countries ranked by Gross National Product (GNP) per capita (US$), 1998. When calculating GNP in US dollars from GNP reported in national currencies, the World Bank follows its Atlas conversion method. This involves using a three-year average of exchange rates to smooth the effects of transitory exchange rate fluctuations.
Source: World Development Indicators 2000, World Bank, 2000.

(table) International trade

Indicators: exports and imports of goods and services by country (current $ millions), 1998.
Source: World Development Indicators 2000, World Bank, 2000.

55.

MONEY: You are your money

IN THE TIME OF the Trojan war (1250 BC), the worth of things was measured in oxen: a tripod could cost between ten and twelve oxen; a set of weapons and armour between nine and one hundred; a slave between ten and twenty. Later, coins prevailed, imposing the brilliance of the precious metals, with 'wealth accumulation' meaning piling up metals in jars and bags.

(box) Guidelines for the Global Barter Network

(table) The largest 100 companies

Indicators: the world's 100 largest corporations, revenues and employees.
Source: The Global 500, Fortune, 1999.

57.

TAXES: The mystery of the vanishing tax payers

RECENT FORECASTS suggest that states are facing problems in gathering sufficient taxes to guarantee the security and well-being of their citizens, for it is increasingly difficult to raise taxes from commercial transactions, personal income and even from goods and services.

(table) **Human Development Index**

Indicator: countries ranked by Human Development Index (HDI) value, 1997. The HDI value indicates how far a country has to go to attain certain goals: an average life span of 85 years, access to education for all and a decent income.
Source: Human Development Report 1999, UNDP, 1999. Methodological changes were made in the HDI calculation, thus HDI value from 1999 Human Development Report is not comparable with previous years.

(table) **Under 5 Mortality**

Indicator: countries ranked by under-five mortality rate (per 1,000 live births), 1998.
Source: The State of the World's Children 2000, UNICEF, 2000.

(table) **Official aid recipients**

Indicators: net official development assistance (ODA) received: total in $ millions and per capita $ (1997) and as a percentage of recipients' GNP, 1997.
Source: Human Development Report 1999, UNDP, 1999.

(table) **Debt in figures**

Indicators: total external debt ($ millions), 1998; debt service as percentage of exports of goods and services, 1998; external debt per capita ($) calculated from total external debt and total population, 1997.
Source: World Development Indicators 2000, World Bank, 2000; The State of the World's Children 2000, UNICEF, 2000.

V. INTERNATIONAL RELATIONS

62.

GLOBAL ORDER: The development of a global police force

THROUGHOUT MOST of the 20th century, communities organized in states assigned the task of maintaining public order to a group of officials. The indications are that the new century is preparing to open the era of a global police force which, free of the limits imposed by frontiers, will take on the task of making sure laws are obeyed and that offenders are punished.

63.

GLOBAL ETHIC: No new global order without a new global ethic

THE PARLIAMENT of the World's Religions issued a statement on the need for a new, global ethic to rule the world. Grounded in the conviction of the existence of an Ultimate Reality, it warns about the tensions that threaten the peaceful building of a better world and called for the full realization of the intrinsic dignity of the human person, the inalienable freedom and equality in principle of all people.

(table) **Arms in figures**

Indicators: Military expenditure as a percentage of GDP, 1996; imports of conventional weapons ($ millions, 1990 prices), 1997.
Source: Human Development Report 1999, UNDP, 1999.

SECTION II:

Countries

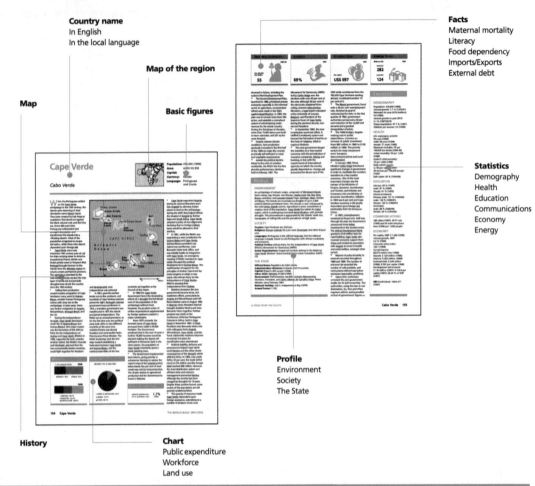

Country name
In English
In the local language

Map of the region

Map

Basic figures

Facts
Maternal mortality
Literacy
Food dependency
Imports/Exports
External debt

Statistics
Demography
Health
Education
Communications
Economy
Energy

Profile
Environment
Society
The State

History

Chart
Public expenditure
Workforce
Land use

INDEX TO COUNTRIES

225. Eritrea	357. Malaysia	239. St Pierre and Miquelon
226. Estonia	360. Maldives	469. St Vincent
228. Ethiopia	362. Mali	470. Samoa
202. Faeroe Is.	364. Malta	471. Samoa (American)
233. Fiji	89. Malvinas/Falkland Is.	232. San Marino
235. Finland	365. Marshall Is.	472. São Tomé and Príncipe
237. France	366. Martinique	474. Saudi Arabia
241. French Guiana	367. Mauritania	477. Senegal
242. French Polynesia	370. Mauritius	480. Seychelles
243. Gabon	178. Mayotte	482. Sierra Leone
245. Gambia	386. Melilla	484. Singapore
247. Georgia	373. Mexico	486. Slovakia
249. Germany	377. Micronesia	488. Slovenia
253. Ghana	378. Moldova	490. Solomon Is.
500. Gibraltar	231. Monaco	491. Somalia
256. Greece	380. Mongolia	493. South Africa
203. Greenland	383. Montserrat	326. South Korea
259. Grenada	384. Morocco	498. Spain
261. Guadeloupe	388. Mozambique	501. Sri Lanka
262. Guam	391. Myanmar/Burma	504. Sudan
263. Guatemala	393. Namibia	507. Suriname
267. Guinea	396. Nauru	509. Swaziland
269. Guinea-Bissau	397. Nepal	511. Sweden
271. Guyana	399. Netherlands	514. Switzerland
273. Haiti	402. Netherlands Antilles	517. Syria
276. Honduras	81. New Zealand (see Aotearoa)	520. Tajikistan
278. Hungary	404. Nicaragua	172. Taiwan
281. Iceland	407. Niger	522. Tanzania
283. India	410. Nigeria	525. Thailand
287. Indonesia	82. Niue	528. Togo
290. Iran	96. Norfolk Is.	84. Tokelau
293. Iraq	325. North Korea	530. Tonga
296. Ireland	413. Northern Marianas	531. Trinidad and Tobago
299. Israel	414. Norway	533. Tunisia
303. Italy	417. Oman	535. Turkey
306. Jamaica	419. Pakistan	538. Turkmenistan
308. Japan	422. Palau	540. Turks and Caicos
313. Jordan	423. Palestine	541. Tuvalu
315. Kanaky/New Caledonia	427. Panama	542. Uganda
317. Kazakhstan	430. Papua New Guinea	545. Ukraine
319. Kenya	432. Paraguay	547. United Arab Emirates
322. Kiribati	435. Peru	549. United Kingdom
323. Korea	438. Philippines	553. United States
328. Kuwait	441. Pitcairn	557. Uruguay
332. Kyrgyzstan	442. Poland	560. Uzbekistan
334. Laos	445. Portugal	562. Vanuatu
336. Latvia	448. Puerto Rico	232. Vatican City
338. Lebanon	450. Qatar	564. Venezuela
341. Lesotho	452. Réunion	567. Vietnam
344. Liberia	453. Romania	570. Virgin Is. (US)
346. Libya	456. Russia	571. Virgin Is. (Br)
231. Liechtenstein	461. Rwanda	240. Wallis and Futuna
348. Lithuania	464. Sahara (Western)	572. Yemen
350. Luxembourg	232. San Marino	575. Yugoslavia Fed. Rep.
351. Macedonia, TFYR	466. St Helena	579. Zambia
353. Madagascar	467. St Kitts-Nevis	581. Zimbabwe
355. Malawi	468. St Lucia	

Charts

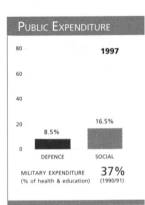

PUBLIC EXPENDITURE

1997

DEFENCE 8.5%
SOCIAL 16.5%

MILITARY EXPENDITURE (% of health & education) **37%** (1990/91)

Percentage of total social (including education, health, social security, housing and community amenities) and defence expenses (1994/97). The defence expenditure figure as percentage health and education expenditure (1990 /91).

Sources: **g, d**.

The male and female labour force, excluding caregivers at home and other unpaid workers (year 1998), and by activity sector (agriculture, industry and services, year 1990). Unemployment rate (1994/97).

Sources: **d, g**.

WORKERS

1996
UNEMPLOYMENT: 16.3%

% OF LABOUR FORCE **1998**

■ FEMALE: 45% ■ MALE: 55%

1990

■ SERVICES: 15.1%
■ INDUSTRY: 6.7%
■ AGRICULTURE: 78.2%

LAND USE

DEFORESTATION: 0.8% annual (1990/95)
IRRIGATED: 42.1% of arable (1993)

1993

■ FOREST & WOODLAND: 39.5%
■ ARABLE: 4.4%
■ OTHER: 56.1%

Forest and woodland as percentage of land area (1993). Arable land as percentage of land area (1993). Irrigated area as percentage of arable land area (1993). Annual rate of deforestation (1990/95, a positive number indicates a loss of forest area, a negative number a gain).

Source: **b, h**.

History

[1] A range of sources has been used to update the texts on each country. In many cases this meant checking with local sources and contributors, documentation centers linked to electronic mail networks and grass-roots organizations throughout the world. This input went into our database in Montevideo, where the final editing was done. Additional information, editing and checking was done by New Internationalist Publications Ltd, Oxford, UK.

[2] Efforts were made to avoid the most frequent bias of Western reference books, such as appearing to make history start with the arrival of the Europeans (particularly in the case of African and Latin American countries) or ignoring the role of women.

[3] The last overall updating of the database before printing was done in June 2000, but in several cases events as late as September were included.

Statistics

DEMOGRAPHY

Population:

Total population, according to 1999 United Nations Population Division. In some cases, figures have been corrected through consultation with other sources.
Source: **a**.

Annual growth:

Average annual rate of population growth during the period 1975/1997.
Source: **b**.

Estimates for the year 2015:

The population projections for the year 2015 are calculations based on current data on population, rates of growth, and trends of these rates to increase or decrease (1997-2015).
Source: **b**.

Annual growth to year 2015:

Average annual rate of population growth during the period 1997/2015.
Source: **b**.

Urban population:

Percentage of total population living in urban areas (1997). Figures are to be treated with care since definitions of "urban zones" differ from country to country.
Source: **b**.

Urban growth:

Average rate of annual growth of the urban population in the period 1980-1995.
Source: **i**.

Children per woman:

Total fertility rate - the number of children that would be born per woman were she to live to the end of her child-bearing years and bear children at each age in accordance with prevailing age-specific fertility rates (1998).
Source: **c**.

HEALTH

Life expectancy at birth:

The number of years a newborn infant (1998), male or female (1998), would live if prevailing patterns of mortality at the time of birth were to stay the same throughout child's life.
Source: **c, f**.

Infant mortality:

The annual number of deaths of infants under one year of age per 1,000 live births (1998).
Source: **c**.

Under-5 child mortality:

Number of children dying between birth and exactly five years of age per 1,000 live births (1998).
Source: **c**.

Calorie supply:

Daily per capita calorie supply (1996). Shown as a national average, though a country's income distribution may create a wide gap between the average, the highest and the lowest strata. Minimum calorie requirements vary in different countries, depending on climate and nature of the main activities.
Source: **b**.

Doctor per 100,000 people:

Traditional medicine and community health care practised by health personnel who are not officially recognised are not included in these statistics, although they may be the only health service available for the majority of the population in many countries (1993).
Source: **b**.

Safe water:

The United Nations includes the percentage of population with "reasonable" acces to safe water sources. They include treated surface waters and untreated but uncontaminated water from springs, wells and protected boreholes in the "reasonably safe water" category (1990/98).
Source: **c**.

EDUCATION

Literacy:

Indicates the estimated percentage of people, male or female, over the age of fifteen who can read and write (1995).
Source: **c**.

School enrolment:

Gross enrolment ratio by level of education. Number of people, male or female, enrolled in a schooling level (primary, secondary or tertiary), regardless of age, divided by the population of the age group officially corresponding to that level (1990/97).
Sources: **c, g**.

Primary school teachers:

Primary school teacher/students ratio (students per teacher, 1994/1998).
Source: **g**.

COMMUNICATIONS

Mass media:

Estimate of the number of copies of daily newspapers per 1,000 people (1994/96) and the number of radios (1996/97) and TV sets (1996) per 1,000 people. The latter figure may rely on the number of licences granted or the number of declared receivers.
Source: **b, g.**

Telephones:

Number of main telephone lines per 1,000 people (1996).
Source: **b.**

Books:

Number of new titles published in the given year per 100,000 people (1992/94).
Source: **h.**

ECONOMY

Per capita GNP:

GDP (Gross Domestic Product) is the value of the total production of goods and services of a country's economy within the national territory. GNP (Gross National Product) is GDP plus the income received from abroad by residents in the country (such as remittances from migrant workers and income from investments abroad), minus income obtained in the domestic economy which goes into the hands of persons abroad (such as profit remittances of foreign companies). The data is calculated in local currencies. Converting them into US dollars (or into any other currency) may lead to distortions. For example, if a country devalues its currency, conversion into US dollars would seem to cut its GDP or GNP while actual production was not reduced. The World Bank corrects such distortions by calculating per capita GNP on the basis of the purchasing power of the local currency and converting it into US dollar purchasing power (1998). This is the figure used.
Source: **g.**

Annual growth, GNP:

Average annual growth in GNP during 1998.
Source: **g.**

Annual inflation:

Annual inflation rate as GDP implicit deflator (average annual $ growth), measures the average annual rate of price change in the economy as a whole for the period 1990-1998.
Source: **g.**

Consumer price index:

Consumer price index (1995 = 100) reflects changes in the cost to the average consumer of acquiring a fixed basket of goods and services (1998).
Source: **g.**

Currency:

Name and exchange rate in relation to US dollar in 1998.
Source: **g.**

Cereal imports:

The cereals are wheat, flour, rice, unprocessed grains and the cereal components of combined foods. This figure includes cereals donated by other countries, and those distributed by international agencies (1998).
Source: **e.**

Food import dependency:

Imported food in relation to the food available for internal distribution (the total of food production, plus food imports, minus food exports), for 1997.
Source: **b.**

Fertilizer use:

Refers to purchases of nitrate, potassium and phosphate based fertilizers used on arable land (1996).
Source: **g.**

Imports & Exports:

Annual value in US dollars f.o.b. (free on board) for exports and c.i.f. (costs, insurance and freight) for imports (1998).
Source: **g.**

External debt (total and per capita):

Public state guaranteed and private foreign debt accumulated by 1998. Per capita debt was calculated from total external debt and total population (1998).
Source: **c, g.**

Debt service:

The service of a foreign debt is the sum of interest payments and repayment of principal (capital loaned, regardless of yield). The relation between debt service and exports of goods and services is a practical measurement commonly used to evaluate capacity to pay the debt or obtain new credits. These coefficients do not include private foreign debts without state guarantees - a considerable amount in some countries (1998).
Source: **g.**

Development aid received:

Official development assistance (ODA) consists of money flows from official governmental or international institutions for the purpose of promoting economic development or social welfare in developing countries. These funds are supplied in the form of grants or 'soft' loans, i.e. long-maturity loans at interest rates lower than those prevailing on the international market. We included the total and per capita net ODA received in dollars and as a percentage of recipient country's GNP (1997).
Source: **b.**

ENERGY

These statistics refer only to commercial energy, and do not include, for example, that which rural people in the poor countries produce by their own means (mainly firewood). Energy consumption of the country is measured in kilograms of 'oil-equivalent' per capita. Energy imports are given as a percentage of energy consumption. Figures are negative in those countries that are net exporters of energy products (1997).
Source: **g.**

Human Development Index

Since 1990 the UNDP has presented the HDI to capture as many aspects of human development as possible in one simple index. It is a composite index of archievements in basic human capabilities in three fundamental dimensions: a long and healthy life, knowledge and a decent standard of living. Three variables have been chosen to represent these three dimensions: life expectancy, educational attainment and income. Methodological changes were made in the HDI calculation, thus HDI value from the 1999 Human Development Report is not comparable with previous years.
Source: **b.**

Sources

a) Population Division, Web site, United Nations, 1999.

b) Human Development Report 1999, UNDP, 1999.

c) The State of the World's Children 2000, UNICEF, 2000.

d) Human Development Report 1998, UNDP, 1998.

e) FAOSTAT - FAO Statistical Database - Web Site.

f) World Health Report 1999.

g) World Development Indicators 2000, World Bank, 2000.

h) Human Development Report 1997, UNDP, 1997.

i) World Development Report 1997, World Bank, 1997.

j) Handbook of Statistics 2000, UNCTAD.

Index to Special Boxes

ENVIRONMENT

Estimates of area are based on UN official estimates according to internationally recognized borders; these include inland waters but not territorial ocean waters. Except where otherwise specified, territories claimed by certain countries but not under their effective jurisdiction are not taken into account, though this implies no judgement as to the validity of the claims. Geographical descriptions and data on environmental problems are based on the sources listed in the general bibliography at the end of this Guide.

SOCIETY

Peoples, Languages and Religions: Very few countries keep official ethnic and religious data, and UN-related institutions definitely do not do so. The ethnic and religious make-up of a society is a historical-cultural factor which is in constant change. Certain forces promote tribal or ethnic divisions to favour their own plans of domination, while others favour whatever makes for integration and national unity. In many countries the political and social problems cannot be grasped without reference to these factors. When including them here, we have sought to consult the most reliable sources (mentioned in the general bibliography) and to avoid the racist connotations often associated with such information.

Political parties and Social movements: It is practically impossible to make a complete listing of all parties and other movements of any country, since they are constantly changing

and in most cases would add up to several hundred names. Thus only major organizations are mentioned, even though 'major' is subjective when votes, parliamentary representation or number of members cannot be verified, where parties are outlawed or the right to associate is restricted.

THE STATE

Official Name: Complete name of the state in the official language.

Administrative divisions, the capital and other cities: Population figures are for the most recent available year. The legal limits of a city frequently do not match its real borders. Thus the information may refer only to the core area, which is a minor part of the whole city.

Government: Names of the major authorities and institutional bodies as of June 2000.

National Holiday: When more than one holiday is commemorated, Independence Day (if it is a holiday) is indicated.

Armed Forces and Others: The total number of personnel for the year indicated. 'Other' forces are those trained and equipped beyond the level of a Police Force (though some fulfill this role) and whose constitution and control means they can be used as regular troops. The source used is the most reliable available on military statistics, but the data is based on government information which is not always explicit as to the total number of troops and military expenditure.

SECTION III:

The world in figures

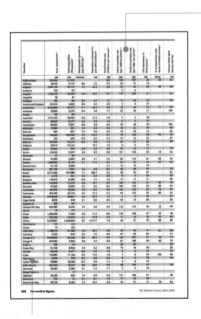

Indicators
Area
Population
Infant mortality
Health
Primary education
Communications
GNP
Inflation
Foreign Trade

Countries

Preface

If you knew the answers...

Many centuries ago, in the land of the Great Timur, the teacher Nasreddin Hodja wandered the streets shouting, desperate, because his donkey had been stolen.

"Who stole your donkey? How did they steal it from you?" asked a judge who was passing by.

"If I knew the answers," an irate Hodja responded, "they would not have stolen it!"

The curious reader (and we suppose that you are curious, or you would not be reading a preface) could deduce that the robbery probably occurred in the thirteenth or fourteenth century in Anatolia, now Turkey, because Timur Lenk is the same leader known in Europe as Tamerlane; that the robbery could have been an incident reflecting the instability caused by the migrations of peoples from the steppes toward the fertile lands of the Mediterranean; and that the presence of a concerned judge indicates the existence of a State authority and justice system, which is perhaps one of the keys to the rapid expansion of Islam over what was once the Eastern Roman Empire.

We will never know who stole the donkey, or if Hodja ever got it back, but the angry teacher leaves us a lesson in the value of knowing the answers. As with any good reference work, **The World Guide** is full of them. To ensure that the answers are precise, we dedicate ourselves year after year to compiling new statistics and current and reliable information, submitting the analyses to the correspondents and contributors (and to enthusiastic readers) in each of the countries for review. We also rewrite the articles in light of new research and meticulous re-readings in order to distinguish the relevant from the anecdotal, or to highlight an anecdote when it proves to be more illustrative than a cold, hard fact.

The World Guide's researchers and writers do not only utilize other books, news sources and the Internet in their work, they also rely on a dynamic network of people and non-profit institutions around the world engaged in studying reality and recording history day after day: organizations for human rights, women, the environment, labor and social development. The Third World Institute would not be able to produce **The World Guide** without this continuous flow of information, and the acknowledgements list only a portion of these important sources.

The people we could never thank enough are the readers, who encourage the efforts we began a quarter century ago. We are pleased when someone tells us they have found the answers they were looking for in **The World Guide**. What drives us to continue, however, is when a reader who was not born when the first edition was published says that reading the Guide has prompted even more questions. ∎

Roberto Bissio
DIRECTOR, ITeM, URUGUAY

THE WORLD GUIDE

INSTITUTO DEL TERCER MUNDO

Editor-in-Chief:
Roberto Bissio.

Managing Editors:
Roberto Elissalde and Víctor Bacchetta.

Research and editing:
Amir Hamed, Roberto Elissalde
and Santiago Gilles.

Contributors:
Jorge Barreiro, Levan Butkhuzi,
Mariana Cabrera, Ricardo Carrere,
Ricardo Cayssials, Mariela Farías, Alina González,
Alvaro González, Alexander Krylov,
Martha Long, Simone Lovera, Gustavo Nagy,
Andrew Nette, Katerina Oridjanska, Chakravarthi
Raghavan, Mikhail Roshchin, Susana Rostagnol,
Luis Sabini and Alexandre Sokolov.

Statistics:
Daniel Macadar.

Translators:
Álvaro Queiruga, Sarah Mason
and Linda Dorow.

Layout Design:
Ana Inés Piñeyro, Alejandro Sequeira
and Pablo Uribe [OBRA].

**Information and communication
technologies:**
Pablo Ramírez and Red Telemática Chasque.

Marketing:
Hersilia Fonseca.

Administration:
Ana Claudia Zeballos and Carmen Ridao.

E-mail:
guiatm@chasque.net

Home Page (Spanish):
http://www.guiadelmundo.org.uy/

NEW INTERNATIONALIST PUBLICATIONS LTD
(English language edition)

Editor:
Troth Wells.

Production:
Fran Harvey, Andy Kokotka, Dean Ryan, Ian Nixon,
Alan Hughes.

Marketing & Distribution:
Dexter Tiranti, Jo Lateu.

This book is the result of documentation, research, writing, editing and design work done by the Instituto del Tercer Mundo (Third World Institute), a non-profit institution devoted to information, communication and education, based in Montevideo, Uruguay.

The World Guide 2001/2002 is an updated, corrected and expanded edition of the World Guide 1999/2000. This reference book was published for the first time in Mexico in 1979, on the initiative of Neiva Moreira, to complement the dissemination work of the Third World magazine he had begun publishing. In 1980 the first Portuguese version of the Guide was published. The first English version was published in 1984. New Internationalist Publications Ltd, in Oxford, England, has been in charge of the English version and its distribution in English-speaking countries since 1996. In 1999, SERMIS-EMI (Editrice Missionaria Italiana), from Bologna, launched the Italian version of The World Guide. Since 1992, The World Guide has been published on CD-ROM. Since 1997, through the Internet and together with its updating service, Guía de la Semana, the Spanish version of the World Guide has been available in Web Pages.

The World Guide is a cumulative work, building on the efforts of former staff members. We would like to mention the contributions of: Mohiuddin Ahmad, Claude Alvares, Iván Alves, Juan José Argeriz, Maria Teresa Armas, Marcos Arruda, Iqbal Asaria, Gonzalo Abella, Susana de Avila, Edouard Balby, Artur Baptista, Roberto Bardini, Luis Barrios, Alicia Bidegaray, Beatriz Bissio, Ricardo de Bittencourt, Samuel Blixen, Gerardo Bocco, José Bottaro, José Cabral, Luis Caldera, Juan Cammá, Altair Campos, Paulo Cannabrava Filho, Carmen Canoura, Cristina Canoura, Gerónimo Cardozo, Diana Cariboni, Gustavo Carrier, Virgilio Caturra, Macário Costa, Carlos María Domínguez, Wáshington Estellano, Marta Etcheverrigaray, Carlos Fabião, Marcelo Falca, Helena Falcão, Wilson Fernández, Alejandro Flores, Lidia Freitas, Sonia Freitas, Marc Fried, Héctor García, José Carlos Gondim, Mario Handler, David Hathaway, Ann Heidenreich, Bill Hinchberger, Etevaldo Hipólito, Heraclio Labandera, Peter Lenny, Cecilia Lombardo, Linda Llosa, Geoffrey Lloyd Gilbert, Fernando López, Hakan Lundgren, Pablo Mazzini, Daniel Mazzone, Carol Milk, João Murteira, Abdul Naffey, Claudia Neiva, Ruben Olivera, Hattie Ortega, Pablo Piacentini, Ana Pérez, Christopher Peterson, Virginia Piera, Carlos Pinto Santos, Sieni C. Platino, Artur José Poerner, Graciela Pujol, Roberto Raposo, Felisberto Reigado, Maria da Gloria Rodrigues, Julio Rosiello, Ash Narain Roy, Ana Sadetzky, Alexandru Savulescu, John Sayer, Dieter Schonebohm, Irene Selser, Eunice H. Senna, Baptista da Silva, Yesse Jane V. de Souza, José Steinleger, Firiel Suijker, Carolina Trujillo, Pedro Velozo, Horacio Verbitsky, Amelia Villaverde, Anatoli Voronov and Asa Zatz.

We have received the help, encouragement and support of Carlos Abín, Carlos Afonso, Cedric Belfrage, Max van den Berg, Dirk-Jan Broertjes, Alberto Brusa, Anne-Pieter van Dijk, Rodrigo Egaña, Cecilia Ferraría, Goran Hammer, Mohammed Idris, Sytse Kujik, Arne Lindquist, Carlos Mañosa, Fernando Molina, Hans Pelgröm, Malva Rodríguez, John Schlanger, Gregorio Selser, Herbet de Souza, the late Sjef Theunis and Germán Wettstein. Leo van Grunsven gave us editorial suggestions, together with his confidence in the project.

The editorial staff acknowledges the valuable contributions made by the libraries of the following institutions: UNDE, UNESCO, CLASH, FE, the UN Information Center in Montevideo, Impala in Madrid and the UNCLAD in Geneva.

The Third World Network, Penang, Malaysia provided ideas, documents and links with many contributors.

To all of them we offer our thanks. Thanks are also due to the hundreds of readers who have given us their comments, suggestions and detailed information.

The judgements and values contained in this book are the exclusive responsibility of the editors and do not represent the opinion of any of the people or institutions listed, except for the Third World Institute. ▪

INSTITUTO DEL TERCER MUNDO
Juan D. Jackson 1136, Montevideo 11200, Uruguay
Phone: 598 2 4096192; Fax: 598 2 401 9222.
E-mail: item@chasque.apc.org.
Website: http://www.item.org.uy/

NEW INTERNATIONALIST PUBLICATIONS LTD
55 Rectory Road, Oxford OX4 1BW, United Kingdom
Tel: (44) 1865 728181; Fax: (44) 1865 793152
E-mail: ni@newint.org
Website: http://www.newint.org/

Global issues

A forecast
for the new century

I. The Earth and its peoples

THE INDIGENOUS peoples of the Americas are working together on a stronger, more organized campaign for the recognition of their history and cultures, with a view to building a new type of state where respect for and dialogue between the different nations and their traditions will help overcome the serious social and environmental problems of the present. Below is their proclamation.

Call for the rights of indigenous cultures

Representatives of the indigenous peoples of the Americas unanimously agree to declare that we always were, and continue to be, peoples with our own history, religion, culture, education, language and other elements which form an intrinsic part of being nations, nationalities and peoples.

Consequently, we urge all states and nations to recognise their plural composition considering the age-old presence of indigenous nations, nationalities and peoples, today included within State territories.

Our territories and lands are our life and lie at the heart of our millenarian cultures, governed by our legal systems, which establish internal and external relationships with these territories and lands, as manifested by our particular and communal behaviour.

Our territories and lands are non-transferable, and cannot be prescribed nor seized, as such is the case under each and every one of our legal systems, based on our cosmo-vision of the way these lands are integral to our indigenous nations, nationalities and peoples. This is so because the land is our mother and cannot be made private property, as, where the contrary occurs, we cannot ensure the collective future of our peoples.

The priority in such difficult times, is the demand for regional or local independence for our indigenous nations, nationalities and peoples, whenever these consider it suitable for this to be assumed in a concrete manner, in order to exercise our right to decide, resulting in a reinforcement of the unity of the current Nation States through constitutional recognition and the effective application of this in each of the cases.

Given the above, we condemn all action or intention to undermine our culture as a whole or any elements of these, and we reject all policies or impositions on every one of those.

Situations in the region

In Mexico the mass media has worked to change tradition and peoples are encouraged to migrate, uprooting them from their traditions and territory in order to make them part of the market economy.

One expression of this lies in the North American Free Trade Agreement and the changes to Article 27 of the Mexican Constitution. The indigenous people of today are used as a cheap workforce. Two concrete examples of this are the exploitation of women in Tehuacan, Puebla, and immigrants in California in the United States.

Meanwhile, the Western Shoshoni in the US have no voice in government nor in the media; they are also vulnerable to government cutbacks in health and education services. In addition they are subject to repression: in the state of Utah 10 per cent of the prison population are indigenous people, but they comprise less than 1 per cent of the population in the state. Around 8,000 nuclear tests have been carried out there, and the Shoshoni are exposed to contamination from chemicals used in gold extraction.

In Aztlan the Xicano movement has launched a campaign to recover its indigenous roots and they are also fighting for independence as a nation. One dimension of this struggle is the support of other indigenous nations for the protection of the mother earth. Ward Valley, California (considered the cradle of Aztlan), forms the territory of the Aha Macav Chemeheuvi nation, which is fighting plans to build a nuclear dump along the banks of the Colorado valley. This struggle has exposed links between governor Pete Wilson and the nuclear industry, exemplifying the bond forged between the government and the corporations under neoliberalism.

In Guatemala, around 85 per cent of the poor are indigenous people, suffering all aspects of exclusion, receiving no respect for their cosmo-vision and suffering cultural discrimination.

In Argentina, indigenous people are a very low percentage of the population, and their main problem is the lack of recognition of their land rights. The Wichis (free people), for example, have been forced into the neoliberal system as they were removed from their lands, undergoing the double injustice of suffering a lack of respect for their culture and then marginalisation within the new system imposed upon them.

Proposals

Our proposal is to recover and reinforce the way of life and values of the indigenous peoples, such as their communal labour, their cosmo-vision, philosophy, relationship with nature, their forms of justice and of resolving conflicts, their respect for the old, child-raising techniques, the fundamental role of women, their own organizational systems and the conscience of the collective. These are the weapons with which we can strike at the heart of the neoliberalism which oppresses all humanity, not only indigenous people.

These principles could form the basis of a more humane, worthy way of life. They are contributions these peoples have kept alive for centuries, despite persecution and attempts to destroy them, and which we now offer as a breath of life before the panorama of death offered by neoliberalism.

Our mere existence as peoples, with 80 million indigenous people on this continent, puts a brake on the neoliberal policies implemented by governments. And, to the lords of power and money, we are simply an impediment. But we will become the spearhead which will mortally wound them. In order to do this we need to strengthen our forms of political organization, the way the government and production of the indigenous peoples themselves are organized, putting collective interests first.

Far from seeking confrontation between people, between those of us who occupy the same geographical space, we promote respect for diversity, the respect and recognition of our differences. We will seek and discover the indigenous part in each one of us. The indigenous peoples alone cannot tame this monster. This is the task of everyone, indigenous or not.

No one is more respectful of the environment than the indigenous peoples. We even talk to plants. Our ancestral way of life was in harmony with the elements of nature. The cosmo-vision of our peoples considers that if we destroy nature we destroy ourselves. The voracious neoliberal quest for profit destroys nature and is leading us all to destruction. Transnational companies backed by governments destroy our forests and contaminate our air, soil, rivers and seas with toxic waste. The fight to stop this destruction means there should be no truce. We must remove them from wherever they are pillaging the resources. We must fight on, little by little, opposing every attempt at destruction. This is the task not only of the indigenous people but of all society. But indeed our ancestral respect for nature could offer the strength and moral authority to make this possible.

We must reinforce the natural and traditional medicine practised by our peoples and promote the transmission of this knowledge from one generation to the next, not overlooking the contributions of other healing systems. At present transnational companies are investigating our peoples' knowledge of natural resources in order to profit from the production of new medicines. This provides no benefit to our peoples and it must be denounced and stopped.

We demand that governments assign the resources necessary to improve or create basic services not only for health but also education, drinking water, electricity, telephone, and the communications media, transport and so on, but always with the peoples' participation in the decision-making process.

We call for

1. Indian peoples to have the right to decide on the use of their natural resources, and that this be made effective, making this not simply a case of consultation when the government has decided to exploit them.

2. Leaving behind 503 years of silence, creating spaces for the multiple sectors of society in the mass media. The indigenous peoples first.

3. The recognition of indigenous people as peoples and their full participation in decision-making, in the political, economic, social and cultural spheres, as a force to confront the objectives of neoliberalism.

4. Our peoples to have the obligation and right to write our own history until now twisted and changed to suit the interests of the oppressors.

We demand

1. That the states and government sign and ratify the following international pacts or agreements which protect the collective rights of the indigenous peoples.

   A) Convention 169 of the International Labor Organization, which recognises the indigenous as peoples with a right to a territory.

   B) The Charter of Rights of the Indigenous Peoples drawn up by the United Nations working group on indigenous peoples, based in Geneva, Switzerland.

   C) The Vienna Convention on human rights.

2. That the Guatemalan government fulfil the agreement on the identity and rights of the indigenous peoples signed in Mexico City in 1995 by the Government of the Republic of Guatemala and the Guatemalan National Revolutionary Unity (URNG).

3. That the Mexican government stop violating its own Law of Concordance and Pacification, ending military harassment and the invasion of Zapatista towns in Chiapas state, and that the agreements signed during the first month of dialogue between the Zapatistas (EZLN) and the federal government be implemented instead of being mere words.

Finally, we are convinced that the future of Indo-Latin America will be better and more lasting if, in a common effort between the nation states and indigenous nations, nationalities and peoples, we have dialogue and work together in respect for equality in diversity to find the principles on which to overcome problems and differences in order to achieve universal peace and development for all. ∎

Source: Continental Meeting for Humanity and Against Neoliberalism, Chiapas, Mexico (Encuentro Continental por la Humanidad y Contra el Neoliberalismo).

Demography

POPULATION in the North is declining; the more industrialized countries will have to allow more than 300 million new immigrants in their territories if they want their economies to avoid the effects of an ageing population. In the South, many countries with rapidly growing populations are headed for population stability in a matter of years because of rapidly rising death rates.

Rising death rates in the South

Many countries that have experienced rapid population growth for several decades will probably confront full-scale humanitarian crises. In fact, some developing countries with rapidly growing populations are headed for population stability in a matter of years - not because of falling birth rates, but because of rapidly rising death rates.

The United Nations projects world population to grow from 6.1 billion in 2000 to 9.4 billion in 2050, with all of that additional 3.3 billion occurring in the developing countries. However, this study raises doubts as to whether these projections will materialize.

Today, we find ourselves in a demographically divided world, one where national projections of population growth vary more widely than at any time in history. In some countries, population has stabilized or is declining; but in others, population is projected to double or even triple before stabilizing.

In 32 countries, containing 14 per cent of world population, population growth has stopped. By contrast, Ethiopia's population of 62 million is projected to more than triple to 213 million by 2050. Pakistan will go from 148 million to 357 million, surpassing the US total before 2050. Nigeria, meanwhile, is projected to go from 122 million today to 339 million, giving it more people in 2050 than there were in all of Africa in 1950. The largest absolute increase is anticipated for India, which is projected to add another 600 million by 2050, thus overtaking China as the most populous country.

To understand these widely varying population growth rates among countries, demographers use a three-stage model of how these rates change over time as modernization proceeds. In the first stage, there are high birth and high death rates, resulting in little or no population growth. In the second stage, as modernization begins, death rates fall while birth rates remain high, leading to rapid growth. In the third stage, birth rates fall to a low level, balancing low death rates and again leading to population stability, offering greater possibilities for comfort and dignity than in stage one.

It is assumed that countries will move gradually from stage one to stage three. Today there are no countries in stage one; all are either in stage two or stage three. However, this analysis concludes that instead of progressing to stage three as expected, some countries are in fact falling back into stage one as the historic fall in death rates is reversed, leading the world into a new demographic era.

After several decades of rapid population growth, many societies are showing signs of demographic 'fatigue', a result of the struggle to deal with the multiple stresses caused by high fertility. As recent experience with AIDS in Africa shows, some countries in stage two are simply overwhelmed when a new threat appears.

While industrial countries have held HIV infection rates among their adult populations at under 1 per cent or less, a 1998 World Health Organization survey reports that in Zimbabwe, for example, 26 per cent of the adult population is HIV-positive. In Botswana it is 25 per cent, Zambia 20 per cent, Namibia 19 per cent, and Swaziland 18 per cent.

Barring a miracle, these societies will lose one fifth or more of their adult population within the next decade from AIDS alone. These adult deaths, the deaths of infants infected with the virus, and high mortality among the millions of AIDS orphans, along with the usual deaths, will bring population growth to a halt or even into decline. With these high mortality trends, more reminiscent of the Dark Ages than the bright new millennium so many had hoped for, these countries are falling back to stage one.

New diseases are not the only threat to demographically-fatigued stage two countries. Because population growth affects so many aspects of a society, any of several different stresses can force a country back into stage one.

For example, in many developing countries food supplies are threatened by aquifer depletion. A forthcoming study by the International Water Management Institute (IWMI) reports that in India - a country heavily dependent on irrigation - recent growth in food production and population has been based partly on the unsustainable use of water. Nationwide, withdrawals of underground water are at least double the rate of recharge and water tables are falling by 1 to 3 meters per year. IWMI authors estimate that as India's aquifers are depleted, its grain harvest could fall by as much as one fifth.

In a country where food and population are precariously balanced and which is adding 18 million people per year, such a huge drop in food output could create economic chaos.

"The question is not whether population growth will slow in the developing countries", said Lester Brown, President of Worldwatch Institute, "but whether it will slow because societies quickly shift to smaller families or because ecological collapse and social disintegration cause death rates to rise." ∎

Source:
Extracted from a study of the Worldwatch Institute.

Immigrants indispensable to the North

From now until the year 2025, the more industrialized European countries will have to allow in 159 million new immigrants if they want their economies to avoid the effects of an ageing population. For the United States, the figure is 150 million.

The report called "Replacement migration: a solution to ageing populations" from the United Nations Population Division, estimates that only a massive migration of people from other continents will allow the European Union to sustain its current balance of 4/5:1 worker to pensioner ratio.

In order to sustain the number of active workers in 1995, the EU will have to admit 25 million immigrants. Joseph Chamie, director of the UN Population Division explains: "We are aware that these numbers are politically unacceptable for Europeans... Frankly, I see no other solution than looking at the problem straight in the face: the populations of all countries in the world are ageing at an alarming rate and it is becoming essential to consider the economic and social consequences of this fact."

The current birth rate (1.4 children per woman in the European Community) is clearly dropping throughout the industrialized world, while rising life expectancy rates complete the scenario of ageing populations in industrialized countries. Researchers also took into account for their analysis that those countries aim to sustain a rate of economic growth comparable to that of recent years and also that they will undergo equivalent increases in productivity. The late incorporation of youth into the job market, the rise in life expectancy and a decreasing birth rate would result in a 2:1 worker to pensioner ratio for Europeans in less than 50 years.

In order to avoid the upcoming crisis, the EU must allow some 159 million people willing to work into its territory, while the US will have to admit another 150 million. If everything remains as it is now, 47 per cent of the European population will be retired by the year 2050, while the number of people under 59 would have dropped by 11 per cent.

The relatively generous European social security institutions were designed for a 5:1 worker to pensioner ratio. Today they are undergoing difficulties; an even greater alteration would make the whole system collapse. The only proposed solution in order to maintain the immigration restrictions imposed by European community governments is to increase the retirement age, a measure that is also politically sensitive.

In addition to being an outright attack on the hard-won rights of those that have worked their whole lives, this would be a new source of increasing unemployment. Researchers analyzed four alternatives to the situation and took eight countries as their models (France, Germany, Italy, UK, United States, Japan and South Korea). Based on information from 1995 to the present, analysts applied four scenarios for periods running from 2025 to 2050.

In the first scenario, countries maintain the natural evolution in their population and keep immigration restrictions. In the second case, as many immigrants as are necessary to maintain current population levels are admitted. In the third case, as many are allowed in as would be necessary to sustain the 1995 level of the working population; while in the fourth scenario immigrants are allowed entry as needed to maintain the worker to pensioner ratio.

If current trends continue, the Italian population will decrease from 57 to 41 million in 2050, and the average age in Spain will be 54.3 years. The model currently operating in the United States, which allows up to one million immigrants per year, has been more realistic than the "zero immigration" approach of many European countries which seem to listen to the xenophobic outpourings of some population sectors rather than facing up to demographic and economic realities.

Europe would lose 30 million inhabitants by 2025 at the current fertility rate. In order to sustain the 1995 worker/pensioner ratio, the EU would have to admit 24 million immigrants by that date. But in order to sustain the current worker to pensioner ratio, the European Community would have to let another 123 million immigrants in. This would imply that 5.3 million people would come in on a yearly basis. In comparison, official French policy is to allow 30,000 people in each year until 2025; 20,000 annually in the following five years and 10,000, 5,000 and zero in the subsequent three five-year periods. ∎

DEMOGRAPHY IN FIGURES

A = Contraceptive prevalence %, 1990/99
B = Crude death rate per thousand people, 1998
C = Crude birth rate per thousand people, 1998
D = Children per woman, 1998

COUNTRIES	A	B	C	D	COUNTRIES	A	B	C	D	COUNTRIES	A	B	C	D
Afghanistan	2	21	52	6.8	Gambia	12	17	40	5.2	Norway	76	10	13	1.9
Albania	..	6	20	2.5	Georgia	..	9	14	1.9	Oman	40	4	35	5.8
Algeria	57	6	29	3.8	Germany	75	11	9	1.3	Pakistan	17	8	36	5.0
Angola	8	19	48	6.7	Ghana	22	9	37	5.1	Palau	38	..	..	..
Antigua	53	5	18	1.7	Greece	..	10	9	1.3	Palestine	..	..	..	6.0
Aotearoa/N.Zealand	70	8	15	2.0	Grenada	54	7	26	3.6	Panama	58	5	22	2.6
Argentina	74	8	20	2.6	Guatemala	31	7	36	4.9	Papua N. Guinea	26	10	32	4.6
Armenia	60	8	13	1.7	Guinea	29	17	42	5.5	Paraguay	59	5	31	4.1
Australia	76	8	13	1.8	Guinea-Bissau	1	20	42	5.7	Peru	64	6	25	2.9
Austria	71	10	10	1.4	Guyana	..	7	22	2.3	Philippines	47	6	28	3.6
Azerbaijan	..	7	16	2.0	Haiti	18	12	32	4.3	Poland	75	10	11	1.5
Bahamas	62	5	23	2.6	Honduras	50	5	33	4.2	Portugal	66	11	10	1.4
Bahrain	62	4	20	2.8	Hungary	73	14	10	1.4	Qatar	32	4	18	3.7
Bangladesh	49	10	28	3.1	Iceland	..	7	16	2.1	Romania	57	11	9	1.2
Barbados	55	8	12	1.5	India	41	9	25	3.1	Russia	..	14	10	1.3
Belarus	50	13	10	1.4	Indonesia	57	7	23	2.5	Rwanda	21	17	43	6.1
Belgium	79	10	11	1.6	Iran	73	5	21	2.8	Samoa	21	5	29	4.1
Belize	47	4	31	3.6	Iraq	18	8	36	5.2	S. Tomé and Príncipe	10	10	33	4.7
Benin	37	13	41	5.8	Ireland	..	8	14	1.9	Saudi Arabia	..	4	34	5.7
Bhutan	19	10	38	5.5	Israel	..	6	20	2.7	Senegal	13	13	40	5.5
Bolivia	48	9	33	4.3	Italy	78	10	9	1.2	Seychelles	..	7	21	2.1
Bosnia-Herz.	..	7	10	1.4	Jamaica	66	6	22	2.5	Sierra Leone	4	25	46	6.0
Botswana	48	16	34	4.3	Japan	59	8	10	1.4	Singapore	74	5	14	1.7
Brazil	77	7	20	2.3	Jordan	53	5	35	4.8	Slovakia	74	10	10	1.4
Brunei	..	3	22	2.8	Kazakhstan	59	9	18	2.3	Slovenia	..	10	9	1.3
Bulgaria	76	14	9	1.2	Kenya	39	12	34	4.4	Solomon Is.	25	4	35	4.8
Burkina Faso	12	19	46	6.5	Kiribati	28	8	32	4.5	Somalia	1	18	52	7.2
Burundi	9	20	42	6.2	Korea, North	..	5	21	2.0	South Africa	50	12	27	3.2
Cambodia	13	13	34	4.6	Korea, South	79	6	15	1.7	Spain	59	9	9	1.1
Cameroon	19	12	39	5.3	Kuwait	35	2	22	2.9	Sri Lanka	66	6	18	2.1
Canada	73	7	11	1.6	Kyrgyzstan	60	7	25	3.2	St Kitts-Nevis	41	12	21	2.4
Cape Verde	53	6	32	3.5	Laos	19	13	39	5.7	St Lucia	47	7	21	2.4
Cent. Afric. Rep.	15	19	37	4.9	Latvia	..	14	8	1.3	St Vincent	58	7	21	2.2
Chad	4	18	44	6.0	Lebanon	63	6	23	2.7	Sudan	8	11	33	4.6
Chile	43	6	20	2.4	Lesotho	23	12	35	4.7	Suriname	..	6	20	2.2
China	83	7	16	1.8	Liberia	6	15	44	6.3	Swaziland	21	9	38	4.7
Colombia	72	6	24	2.8	Libya	45	5	29	3.8	Sweden	78	11	10	1.6
Comoros	21	9	36	4.8	Lithuania	..	12	10	1.4	Switzerland	71	9	11	1.5
Congo D.R.	8	15	46	6.4	Luxembourg	..	9	12	1.7	Syria	36	5	30	4.0
Congo R.	..	16	44	6.0	Maced., TFYR	..	8	16	2.1	Tajikistan	..	7	32	4.1
Cook Is.	50	..	..	..	Madagascar	19	11	40	5.4	Tanzania	18	15	41	5.4
Costa Rica	75	4	23	2.8	Malawi	22	23	47	6.7	Thailand	74	7	17	1.7
Côte d'Ivoire	15	16	37	5.0	Malaysia	48	5	25	3.1	Togo	24	15	41	6.0
Croatia	..	11	11	1.6	Maldives	17	7	35	5.3	Tonga	39	6	28	3.6
Cuba	82	7	13	1.6	Mali	7	16	47	6.5	T. and Tobago	53	6	14	1.6
Cyprus	..	7	14	2.0	Malta	..	8	13	1.9	Tunisia	60	7	20	2.5
Czech Republic	69	11	9	1.2	Marshall Is.	37	..	..	..	Turkey	64	6	22	2.5
Denmark	78	12	12	1.7	Mauritania	4	13	40	5.5	Turkmenistan	..	7	28	3.6
Djibouti	..	15	37	5.3	Mauritius	75	6	16	1.9	Uganda	15	21	51	7.1
Dominica	50	6	22	1.9	Mexico	69	5	24	2.7	Ukraine	..	14	10	1.4
Dominican Rep.	64	5	24	2.8	Micronesia	..	6	28	4.0	U. A. Emirates	28	3	18	3.4
Ecuador	57	6	25	3.1	Moldova	74	11	13	1.7	United Kingdom	82	11	12	1.7
Egypt	55	7	26	3.3	Mongolia	..	6	23	2.6	United States	74	8	14	2.0
El Salvador	60	6	28	3.1	Morocco	59	7	26	3.0	Uruguay	84	9	18	2.4
Equatorial Guinea	..	16	41	5.5	Mozambique	10	19	43	6.2	Uzbekistan	56	7	28	3.4
Eritrea	8	14	40	5.7	Myanmar/Burma	33	9	21	2.4	Vanuatu	15	6	32	4.3
Estonia	70	14	9	1.3	Namibia	29	14	36	4.9	Venezuela	49	5	25	3.0
Ethiopia	4	20	44	6.3	Nepal	30	11	34	4.4	Vietnam	75	7	22	2.6
Fiji	32	4	22	2.7	Netherlands	80	9	11	1.5	Yemen	21	10	48	7.5
Finland	80	10	11	1.7	Nicaragua	60	6	36	4.4	Yugoslavia F. R.	..	10	13	1.8
France	75	9	12	1.7	Niger	8	17	48	6.8	Zambia	26	20	42	5.5
Gabon	..	16	38	5.4	Nigeria	6	15	39	5.1	Zimbabwe	66	18	31	3.8

Source: The State of the World's Children 2000, UNICEF, 2000.

SOME FACTS - 2000

Chemical Soup: Every human being harbors in his or her body about 500 synthetic chemicals that were non-existent before 1920.

Telephone Inequity: Just 23 countries account for 62 per cent of all phone lines, even though these countries are home to less than 15 per cent of the world's people.

Global Warming: The 3 parts per million increase in the atmospheric concentration of carbon dioxide in 1998 was the largest ever recorded.

Water Scarcity: Increasing water shortages threaten to reduce the global food supply by more than 10 per cent.

Malnutrition: Half the world's people, both rich and poor, are medically malnourished, suffering from either obesity or from diets with inadequate calories, vitamins, or minerals. A massive 55 per cent of American adults are overweight.

Trade in Animals: Each year 25-30,000 monkeys and other primates are shipped across international borders, along with some 2 to 5 million live birds, 3 million live farmed turtles, and 2 to 3 million other live reptiles.

Fast Food: The number of fast food restaurants per person in the United States has more than doubled since 1970; today there is one fast food joint for every 1,300 Americans.

WATER IS VITAL for human life and activities. Farming, mining and industry, electricity generation, transport and communications all soak up millions of gallons. However, only 3 per cent of the world's water is drinkable and there is an increasingly widening gap between demand and supply.

Running out faster than ever

Water is in short supply. Not only did the difference between water availability and demand multiply by five times during the 20th century, but also the pace of growth of this unbalance. In the second half of the 20th century demand for water tripled and forecasts state that from now on demand will double every 20 years.

If farming methods are not changed, the proportion of irrigated land would have to increase by a third by the year 2010 and by 50 per cent toward 2025 in order to satisfy demand for food. Similarly, industrial and domestic water use will increase at a rate ten times greater than that of the population.

On the other hand, despite the efforts made to increase the amount available (pumping out aquifers and wetlands), the total sum of renewable fresh water on the planet will be no more than 40,000 cubic kilometres.

Sources are shrinking

Whilst today there is more drinking water in the world than there was two thousand years ago (when the world population was not even 3 per cent of its present size), nonetheless towards the end of the 20th century, water reserves were shrinking in many locations around the globe.

In China, the Yellow River in China dried up before it reached the sea; Africa's Lake Chad shrank from an area of 10,000 square kilometres to barely 800 within a 30-year period, and the Aral sea in Asia lost 40 per cent of its surface area and 60 per cent of its volume of drinking water over a similar period.

At present, 500 million people around the globe suffer from an almost total lack of drinking water, and the figure is expected to reach 2.5 billion by the year 2025. If measures are not taken to reverse this trend, one in every three people will be living in a country with a drinking water shortage.

Similarly, even though the problem affects all countries, the most threatened are all in the South, where 95 per cent of the 80 million people added to the worlds population each year are living.

This shortage has a direct effect on people's health. Estimates suggest that 80 per cent of all illness and 33 per cent of deaths in the countries of the South are attribut-able to inadequate water quality. Six million children die each year from drinking contaminated water.

Similarly, four in every five endemic diseases in these countries are due to dirty water or the lack of health and hygiene facilities. In other words, practically half the world's population of 6 billion people today suffer from illnesses linked to water pollution and lack of hygiene.

While in the year 2000 there were 31 countries - mainly in Africa and the Middle East - affected by shortage of water, by 2025 demographic growth will add another 17 states to the list, including India, and China which by that date will probably have a population of 1.5 billion.

Diseases due to scarce or dirty water strike the countries of the South, while many homes in the rich countries manage to consume more than 2,000 litres of good quality water every day. The World Health Organization estimates that the basic requirement is 150 litres per day per household.

This squandering of a precious resource by the rich minority, and the problem of scarcity for the majority point up once more the differences between North and South. With increasingly serious environmental deterioration as well, the economic situation for most people in the poor countries has come to a standstill or worsened, widening the gap between rich and poor.

Whilst in the 1960s the difference in income between rich and poor was 30 to 1, by the year 2000 it stood at 60 to 1.

The circle of scarcity

Through the misuse of resources, the agro-industrial sectors - which consume 90 per cent of available water - have increased the damage. This is due not only to industrial pollution, but also to the lack of planning and badly designed irrigation schemes which have caused salinization, desertification and erosion, resulting in a loss of productive capacity in the soil and food shortages.

If we continue down this road, it will become necessary to irrigate in order to produce food which will sell for less than the cost of the water used to grow it. In addition, unless steps are taken now to manage water resources much more efficiently, water supplies will dwindle.

Water reserves will be affected even in countries where currently there is plenty. For example in the US, one of the six richest in terms of drinking water, the volume of water used is 25 per cent more than that recovered.

Pollution and misuse mean that large investments are required to boost the falling reserves. During the first decade of the new millennium, England like some other nations, will need to spend some $60,000 million to improve waste-water treatment plants to meet the standards for water quality demanded in Europe. Similarly, Hungary will have to spend around $3,500 million by the year 2020.

Eco-catastrophe

To date, the industrial and technological model applied across the globe by the Northern countries treats water as an unlimited resource rather than a finite element on which all the creatures of the planet depend.

Control over drinking water supplies will be a major cause of dispute and possible wars between states in the near future. In some parts of the world the ransacking of water sources has already triggered ecological disasters.

Since the 19th century, California in the US has lost 90 per cent of its wetlands, extinguishing or radically diminishing the population of fish species in the region. In Egypt, water extraction from the Nile killed off 30 of the 47 marketable species of fish. In Europe, the Rhine has seen 8 of its 44 fish species disappear, while a further 25 are in danger of extinction. In Colombia, the fish production of the Magdalena river fell from 72,000 to 23,000 tons over a period of 15 years - a decline similar to that experienced in the Mekong river in Southeast Asia.

If there is no change in our relationship to this vital element - change that requires major rethinking of the ecological, economical and political aspects - then life on this planet will end. It is as stark and as simple as that. Projections based on the current rate of consumption state that all surface waters will have been consumed by the year 2100 - only one hundred years from now. This is no longer the distant future. Without fresh water, the earth would continue to spin around the sun as part of the planetary system - but it would be a ghostly globe, devoid of life. ∎

DISTRIBUTION OF INCOME OR CONSUMPTION

COUNTRIES	SURVEY YEAR	GINI INDEX*	PERCENTAGE SHARE OF INCOME OR CONSUMPTION						
			LOWEST 10%	LOWEST 20%	SECOND 20%	THIRD 20%	FOURTH 20%	HIGHEST 20%	HIGHEST 10%
Algeria	1995 a,b	35.3	2.8	7.0	11.6	16.1	22.7	42.6	26.8
Australia	1994 c,d	35.2	2.0	5.9	12.0	17.2	23.6	41.3	25.4
Austria	1987 c,d	23.1	4.4	10.4	14.8	18.5	22.9	33.3	19.3
Bangladesh	1995-96 a,b	33.6	3.9	8.7	12.0	15.7	20.8	42.8	28.6
Belarus	1998 a,b	21.7	5.1	11.4	15.2	18.2	21.9	33.3	20.0
Belgium	1992 c,d	25.0	3.7	9.5	14.6	18.4	23.0	34.5	20.2
Bolivia	1990 c,d	42.0	2.3	5.6	9.7	14.5	22.0	48.2	31.7
Brazil	1996 c,d	60.0	0.9	2.5	5.5	10.0	18.3	63.8	47.6
Bulgaria	1995 a,b	28.3	3.4	8.5	13.8	17.9	22.7	37.0	22.5
Burkina Faso	1994 a,b	48.2	2.2	5.5	8.7	12.0	18.7	55.0	39.5
Burundi	1992 a,b	33.3	3.4	7.9	12.1	16.3	22.1	41.6	26.6
Cambodia	1997 a,b	40.4	2.9	6.9	10.7	14.7	20.1	47.6	33.8
Canada	1994 c,d	31.5	2.8	7.5	12.9	17.2	23.0	39.3	23.8
Central African Rep.	1993 a,b	61.3	0.7	2.0	4.9	9.6	18.5	65.0	47.7
Chile	1994 c,d	56.5	1.4	3.5	6.6	10.9	18.1	61.0	46.1
China	1998 c,d	40.3	2.4	5.9	10.2	15.1	22.2	46.6	30.4
Colombia	1996 c,d	57.1	1.1	3.0	6.6	11.1	18.4	60.9	46.1
Costa Rica	1996 c,d	47.0	1.3	4.0	8.8	13.7	21.7	51.8	34.7
Côte d'Ivoire	1995 a,b	36.7	3.1	7.1	11.2	15.6	21.9	44.3	28.8
Croatia	1998 a,b	26.8	4.0	9.3	13.8	17.8	22.9	36.2	21.6
Czech Republic	1996 c,d	25.4	4.3	10.3	14.5	17.7	21.7	35.9	22.4
Denmark	1992 c,d	24.7	3.6	9.6	14.9	18.3	22.7	34.5	20.5
Dominican Republic	1996 c,d	48.7	1.7	4.3	8.3	13.1	20.6	53.7	37.8
Ecuador	1995 a,b	43.7	2.2	5.4	9.4	14.2	21.3	49.7	33.8
Egypt	1995 a,b	28.9	4.4	9.8	13.2	16.6	21.4	39.0	25.0
El Salvador	1996 c,d	52.3	1.2	3.4	7.5	12.5	20.2	56.5	40.5
Estonia	1995 a,b	35.4	2.2	6.2	12.0	17.0	23.1	41.8	26.2
Ethiopia	1995 a,b	40.0	3.0	7.1	10.9	14.5	19.8	47.7	33.7
Finland	1991 c,d	25.6	4.2	10.0	14.2	17.6	22.3	35.8	21.6
France	1995 c,d	32.7	2.8	7.2	12.6	17.2	22.8	40.2	25.1
Gambia	1992 a,b	47.8	1.5	4.4	9.0	13.5	20.4	52.8	37.6
Germany	1994 c,d	30.0	3.3	8.2	13.2	17.5	22.7	38.5	23.7
Ghana	1997 a,b	32.7	3.6	8.4	12.2	15.8	21.9	41.7	26.1
Greece	1993 c,d	32.7	3.0	7.5	12.4	16.9	22.8	40.3	25.3
Guatemala	1989 c,d	59.6	0.6	2.1	5.8	10.5	18.6	63.0	46.6
Guinea	1994 a,b	40.3	2.6	6.4	10.4	14.8	21.2	47.2	32.0
Guinea-Bissau	1991 a,b	56.2	0.5	2.1	6.5	12.0	20.6	58.9	42.4
Guyana	1993 a,b	40.2	2.4	6.3	10.7	15.0	21.2	46.9	32.0
Honduras	1996 c,d	53.7	1.2	3.4	7.1	11.7	19.7	58.0	42.1
Hungary	1996 c,d	30.8	3.9	8.8	12.5	16.6	22.3	39.9	24.8
India	1997 a,b	37.8	3.5	8.1	11.6	15.0	19.3	46.1	33.5
Indonesia	1996 c,d	36.5	3.6	8.0	11.3	15.1	20.8	44.9	30.3
Ireland	1987 c,d	35.9	2.5	6.7	11.6	16.4	22.4	42.9	27.4
Israel	1992 c,d	35.5	2.8	6.9	11.4	16.3	22.9	42.5	26.9
Italy	1995 c,d	27.3	3.5	8.7	14.0	18.1	22.9	36.3	21.8
Jamaica	1996 a,b	36.4	2.9	7.0	11.5	15.8	21.8	43.9	28.9
Japan	1993 c,d	24.9	4.8	10.6	14.2	17.6	22.0	35.7	21.7
Jordan	1997 a,b	36.4	3.3	7.6	11.4	15.5	21.1	44.4	29.8
Kazakhstan	1996 a,b	35.4	2.7	6.7	11.5	16.4	23.1	42.3	26.3
Kenya	1994 a,b	44.5	1.8	5.0	9.7	14.2	20.9	50.2	34.9
Korea, South	1993 a,b	31.6	2.9	7.5	12.9	17.4	22.9	39.3	24.3
Kyrgyzstan	1997 c,d	40.5	2.7	6.3	10.2	14.7	21.4	47.4	31.7
Laos	1992 a,b	30.4	4.2	9.6	12.9	16.3	21.0	40.2	26.4
Latvia	1998 c,d	32.4	2.9	7.6	12.9	17.1	22.1	40.3	25.9
Lesotho	1986-87 a,b	56.0	0.9	2.8	6.5	11.2	19.4	60.1	43.4
Lithuania	1996 a,b	32.4	3.1	7.8	12.6	16.8	22.4	40.3	25.6
Luxembourg	1994 c,d	26.9	4.0	9.4	13.8	17.7	22.6	36.5	22.0

a. Refers to expenditure shares by percentiles of population.
b. Ranked by per capita expenditure.
c. Refers to income shares by percentiles of population.
d. Ranked by per capita income.

* The Gini index provides a convenient summary measure of the degree of inequality (when Gini index is zero this represents perfect equality, while an index of 100 implies 'perfect' inequality).

DISTRIBUTION OF INCOME OR CONSUMPTION

PERCENTAGE SHARE OF INCOME OR CONSUMPTION

COUNTRIES	SURVEY YEAR	GINI INDEX*	LOWEST 10%	LOWEST 20%	SECOND 20%	THIRD 20%	FOURTH 20%	HIGHEST 20%	HIGHEST 10%
Madagascar	1993 a,b	46.0	1.9	5.1	9.4	13.3	20.1	52.1	36.7
Malaysia	1995 c,d	48.5	1.8	4.5	8.3	13.0	20.4	53.8	37.9
Mali	1994 a,b	50.5	1.8	4.6	8.0	11.9	19.3	56.2	40.4
Mauritania	1995 a,b	38.9	2.3	6.2	10.8	15.4	22.0	45.6	29.9
Mexico	1995 c,d	53.7	1.4	3.6	7.2	11.8	19.2	58.2	42.8
Moldova	1992 c,d	34.4	2.7	6.9	11.9	16.7	23.1	41.5	25.8
Mongolia	1995 a,b	33.2	2.9	7.3	12.2	16.6	23.0	40.9	24.5
Morocco	1998-99 a,b	39.5	2.6	6.5	10.6	14.8	21.3	46.6	30.9
Mozambique	1996-97 a,b	39.6	2.5	6.5	10.8	15.1	21.1	46.5	31.7
Nepal	1995-96 a,b	36.7	3.2	7.6	11.5	15.1	21.0	44.8	29.8
Netherlands	1994 c,d	32.6	2.8	7.3	12.7	17.2	22.8	40.1	25.1
Aotearoa/New Zealand	1991 c,d	43.9	0.3	2.7	10.0	16.3	24.1	46.9	29.8
Nicaragua	1993 a,b	50.3	1.6	4.2	8.0	12.6	20.0	55.2	39.8
Niger	1995 a,b	50.5	0.8	2.6	7.1	13.9	23.1	53.3	35.4
Nigeria	1996-97 a,b	50.6	1.6	4.4	8.2	12.5	19.3	55.7	40.8
Norway	1995 c,d	25.8	4.1	9.7	14.3	17.9	22.2	35.8	21.8
Pakistan	1996-97 a,b	31.2	4.1	9.5	12.9	16.0	20.5	41.1	27.6
Panama	1997 a,b	48.5	1.2	3.6	8.1	13.6	21.9	52.8	35.7
Papua New Guinea	1996 a,b	50.9	1.7	4.5	7.9	11.9	19.2	56.5	40.5
Paraguay	1995 c,d	59.1	0.7	2.3	5.9	10.7	18.7	62.4	46.6
Peru	1996 c,d	46.2	1.6	4.4	9.1	14.1	21.3	51.2	35.4
Philippines	1997 a,b	46.2	2.3	5.4	8.8	13.2	20.3	52.3	36.6
Poland	1996 c,d	32.9	3.0	7.7	12.6	16.7	22.1	40.9	26.3
Portugal	1994-95 c,d	35.6	3.1	7.3	11.6	15.9	21.8	43.4	28.4
Romania	1994 c,d	28.2	3.7	8.9	13.6	17.6	22.6	37.3	22.7
Russia	1998 a,b	48.7	1.7	4.4	8.6	13.3	20.1	53.7	38.7
Rwanda	1983-85 a,b	28.9	4.2	9.7	13.2	16.5	21.6	39.1	24.2
Senegal	1995 a,b	41.3	2.6	6.4	10.3	14.5	20.6	48.2	33.5
Sierra Leone	1989 a,b	62.9	0.5	1.1	2.0	9.8	23.7	63.4	43.6
Slovakia	1992 c,d	19.5	5.1	11.9	15.8	18.8	22.2	31.4	18.2
Slovenia	1995 c,d	26.8	3.2	8.4	14.3	18.5	23.4	35.4	20.7
South Africa	1993-94 a,b	59.3	1.1	2.9	5.5	9.2	17.7	64.8	45.9
Spain	1990 c,d	32.5	2.8	7.5	12.6	17.0	22.6	40.3	25.2
Sri Lanka	1995 a,b	34.4	3.5	8.0	11.8	15.8	21.5	42.8	28.0
St Lucia	1995 c,d	42.6	2.0	5.2	9.9	14.8	21.8	48.3	32.5
Swaziland	1994 c,d	60.9	1.0	2.7	5.8	10.0	17.1	64.4	50.2
Sweden	1992 c,d	25.0	3.7	9.6	14.5	18.1	23.2	34.5	20.1
Switzerland	1992 c,d	33.1	2.6	6.9	12.7	17.3	22.9	40.3	25.2
Tanzania	1993 a,b	38.2	2.8	6.8	11.0	15.1	21.6	45.5	30.1
Thailand	1998 a,b	41.4	2.8	6.4	9.8	14.2	21.2	48.4	32.4
Trinidad and Tobago	1992 c,d	40.3	2.1	5.5	10.3	15.5	22.7	45.9	29.9
Tunisia	1990 a,b	40.2	2.3	5.9	10.4	15.3	22.1	46.3	30.7
Turkey	1994 a,b	41.5	2.3	5.8	10.2	14.8	21.6	47.7	32.3
Turkmenistan	1998 a,b	40.8	2.6	6.1	10.2	14.7	21.5	47.5	31.7
Uganda	1992-93 a,b	39.2	2.6	6.6	10.9	15.2	21.3	46.1	31.2
Ukraine	1996 a,b	32.5	3.9	8.6	12.0	16.2	22.0	41.2	26.4
United Kingdom	1991 c,d	36.1	2.6	6.6	11.5	16.3	22.7	43.0	27.3
United States	1997 c,d	40.8	1.8	5.2	10.5	15.6	22.4	46.4	30.5
Uruguay	1989 c,d	42.3	2.1	5.4	10.0	14.8	21.5	48.3	32.7
Uzbekistan	1993 c,d	33.3	3.1	7.4	12.0	16.7	23.0	40.9	25.2
Venezuela	1996 c,d	48.8	1.3	3.7	8.4	13.6	21.2	53.1	37.0
Vietnam	1998 a,b	36.1	3.6	8.0	11.4	15.2	20.9	44.5	29.9
Yemen	1992 a,b	39.5	2.3	6.1	10.9	15.3	21.6	46.1	30.8
Zambia	1996 a,b	49.8	1.6	4.2	8.2	12.8	20.1	54.8	39.2
Zimbabwe	1990-91 a,b	56.8	1.8	4.0	6.3	10.0	17.4	62.3	46.9

Inequality in the distribution of income is reflected in the percentage share of either income or consumption accruing to segments of the population ranked by income or consumption levels. The segments ranked lowest by personal income receive the smallest share of total income.

Source: World Development Indicators 2000, World Bank, 2000.

COUNTRY	DENSITY	COUNTRY	DENSITY	COUNTRY	DENSITY
Afghanistan	34	Ghana	82	Pakistan	191
Albania	108	Gibraltar	2,800	Palau	37
Algeria	13	Greece	81	Palestine	485
Andorra	142	Greenland	0,02	Panama	37
Angola	10	Grenada	250	Papua New Guinea	10
Anguilla	167	Guadeloupe	263	Paraguay	13
Antigua	157	Guam	300	Peru	20
Aotearoa/New Zealand	14	Guatemala	102	Philippines	248
Argentina	13	Guinea	30	Pitcairn	14
Armenia	118	Guinea-Bissau	33	Poland	120
Aruba	442	Guyana	4	Portugal	107
Australia	2	Haiti	291	Puerto Rico	431
Austria	98	Honduras	56	Qatar	54
Azerbaijan	89	Hungary	108	Reunion	275
Bahamas	22	Iceland	3	Romania	94
Bahrain	875	India	304	Russia	9
Bangladesh	882	Indonesia	111	Rwanda	275
Barbados	626	Iran	41	Sahara, Western	1
Belarus	49	Iraq	51	Samoa	62
Belgium	333	Ireland	53	Samoa, American	235
Belize	10	Israel	290	San Marino	417
Benin	53	Italy	190	São Tomé and Príncipe	10
Bermuda	1,132	Jamaica	233	Saudi Arabia	47
Bhutan	44	Japan	335	Senegal	169
Bolivia	7	Jordan	66	Seychelles	66
Bosnia-Herzegovina	75	Kanaky/New Caledonia	11	Sierra Leone	5,681
Botswana	3	Kazakhstan	6	Singapore	110
Brazil	20	Kenya	51	Slovakia	98
Brunei	56	Kiribati	105	Slovenia	15
Bulgaria	75	Korea, North	197	Solomon Is.	15
Burkina Faso	42	Korea, South	469	Somalia	33
Burundi	236	Kuwait	106	South Africa	79
Cambodia	60	Kyrgyzstan	24	Spain	284
Cameroon	31	Laos	22	Sri Lanka	29
Canada	3	Latvia	37	St Helena	117
Cape Verde	104	Lebanon	311	St Kitts-Nevis	219
Cayman Is.	131	Lesotho	69	St Lucia	29
Central African Rep.	6	Liberia	26	St Pierre and Miquelon	287
Ceuta	3,737	Libya	3	St Vincent	12
Chad	6	Liechtenstein	175	Sudan	3
Chile	20	Lithuania	56	Suriname	56
China	133	Luxembourg	165	Swaziland	20
Christmas Is.	18	Macedonia, TYFR	78	Sweden	178
Cocos	45	Madagascar	26	Switzerland	85
Colombia	36	Malawi	90	Syria	132
Comoros	303	Malaysia	66	Taiwan	606
Congo D.R.	21	Maldives	927	Tajikistan	43
Congo R.	8	Mali	9	Tanzania	37
Cook Is.	83	Malta	1,206	Thailand	119
Costa Rica	77	Malvinas/Falklands	0.2	Togo	79
Côte d'Ivoire	257	Marshall Is.	350	Tokelau	200
Croatia	40	Martinique	356	Tonga	131
Cuba	1,206	Mauritania	3	Trinidad and Tobago	251
Cyprus	10	Mauritius	563	Tunisia	58
Czech Republic	32	Mayotte Is.	398	Turkey	85
Denmark	123	Melilla	4,833	Turkmenistan	9
Diego García Is	19	Mexico	50	Turks and Caicos	37
Djibouti	27	Micronesia	151	Tuvalu	333
Dominica	100	Moldova	130	Uganda	88
Dominican Republic	172	Monaco	30,000	Ukraine	84
East Timor	59	Mongolia	2	United Arab Emirates	29
Ecuador	44	Montserrat	110	United Kingdom	241
Egypt	67	Morocco	62	United States	29
El Salvador	292	Mozambique	24	Uruguay	19
Equatorial Guinea	16	Myanmar/Burma	67	Uzbekistan	54
Eritrea	32	Namibia	2	Vanuatu	15
Estonia	31	Nauru	600	Vatican	1,977
Ethiopia	55	Nepal	166	Venezuela	26
Faeroe Is.	34	Netherlands	385	Vietnam	237
Fiji	44	Netherlands Antilles	269	Virgin Is. (Am.)	294
Finland	15	Nicaragua	38	Vírgin Is. (Br.)	133
France	107	Niger	8	Wallis and Futuna Is.	75
French Guiana	1	Nigeria	118	Yemen	33
French Polynesia	58	Niue	8	Yugoslavia Fed. Rep.	104
Gabon	4	Norfolk Is.	53	Zambia	12
Gambia	112	Northern Marianas	95	Zimbabwe	30
Georgia	72	Norway	14		
Germany	230	Oman	12		

Source: Calculated from population, 1999 (United Nations Statistics Division - Web Site) and area (UNCTAD-Handbook of Statistics, 2000).

II. Society

Globalization

IT'S BEEN HAMMERED into us that there's an entirely new phenomenon, a 'globalizing' economy, that we must adapt to. A 'driverless machine' assembles different parts from a dozen different countries to make a motorcar, or processes the bookings for European airlines in Bangalore. A new fuel called 'market forces' suddenly seems capable of bringing us close to perpetual motion.

The diversification of economies

The evidence on which all this fever relies is superficially convincing. The world's international trade has consistently grown faster than its economic output - more than twice as fast between 1985 and 1994. This means that an increasing proportion of what we consume is made somewhere else. The assumption here is that any kind of growth is good and that the cheaper things are the more efficiently they are being produced. Therefore an industrial machine that scours the world for the cheapest way of doing things is ultimately a boon to all. The only alternative is to revert to the kind of beggar-thy-neighbor protectionism that deepened the 1930s Great Depression and led to war - no alternative at all.

So what's gone wrong? The evidence is seriously misleading. The new 'global' economy is growing more slowly than the old 'Golden Age' economy did between 1945 and 1973 when there were widespread attempts to protect national economies and promote industrialization through 'import substitution'. In the end this did not work very well. But the globalizing, 'export-oriented' economy works no better. After the initial effect of removing trade barriers during the 1980s wore off, world trade began to slow down. So the benefits of being globalized seem short-lived at best. And economists already know that globalization will *never* solve the problems of unemployment in the North, poverty in the South or the North-South economic divide. It may even be responsible for aggravating them.

The 'driverless machine'[1] is industrial capitalism and its imperative is to maximize profits and minimize costs. The biggest of these costs is the toilers whom capitalism calls 'labor'. So it searches out the cheapest labor it can find: these days largely in the South. The irony is that the cheaper things are, the more they are produced but low wages and unemployment mean the less likely we are to be able to afford them. Capitalism, assisted by modern technology, has a predilection for what's called a 'crisis of over-production' ie waste. The global economy makes this worse. Leave aside the folly of 'over-producing' from non-renewable resources in vulnerable eco-systems. In strictly economic terms the gap between rich and poor widens and capital accumulates to the point

where it no longer quite knows what to do with itself.

The remainder of this excess capital swills around in 'finance houses' and banks, casting about for something more lucrative to do. That usually means gambling, 'speculation' on whatever comes to hand: commodities, foreign exchange, bonds, stocks, shares, all kinds of 'instruments' created for just this purpose. These days, the volatile 'emerging markets' of the South and former Soviet bloc have become speculative playgrounds. Foreign-exchange transactions now amount to more than a thousand billion dollars *a day*, with only a small proportion relating to any 'real' economic activity at all.

Two kinds of economic institution are key players in this bizarre game. The first is the Transnational Corporation (TNC). TNCs control two-thirds of world trade, and almost half of this share travels between different parts of the same TNC. So TNCs are quite logically the chief advocates of 'free trade' and globalization. Because many of them are richer and more powerful than mere national governments they usually get their way.

Second are the finance houses and banks, where so much surplus cash now sloshes around that they've become richer and more powerful than TNCs. They can bring catastrophe overnight to an entire country, like Mexico in 1995, or to the majority of the world's people through 'Third World' debt. They can even wipe the smile off the face of the Southeast Asian Tigers.

Because these institutions have grown so bloated, and because globalization is all about paying no taxes, states are becoming virtually bankrupt. The evidence of history suggests that when 'finance capital' gains the upper hand then the game is nearly up.

There are quite simple and obvious alternatives - it's just that the globalizers are opposed to every single one of them. The simplest would be to impose a tax on the transactions of foreign-exchange markets, which could generate maybe three trillion (thousand billion) dollars a year. Such a 'transaction tax' would be no more difficult to collect than profits, while having the entirely beneficial effect of calming feverish speculation and forcing governments to work together internationally.

But international paralysis is the order of the day. We have a dispiritingly broke and meek United Nations. We have a World Bank and an International Monetary Fund run like TNCs by a hierarchy of rich-state shareholders. More resources to this lot? First let them argue for a transaction tax.

We have a brand-new World Trade Organization (WTO) charged with refereeing the globalization game. Small groups of 'experts', against whom there can be no appeal, adjudicate on trade disputes. 'Distortions' of free trade could eventually include almost anything, from public health, to education or transport services. Things that are 'public' (ie that you don't pay for directly), are deemed not to be legitimate in the sense of being 'private' (ie you do pay for them). Other non-private matters, like decent air to breathe or reasonable conditions of work, are considered irrelevant to trade.

The truth is that our 'multilateral' regime is in a mess, totally ill-equipped to meet the challenges of our time. World government has to be reordered, or perhaps established for the first time. As this is done we should remind ourselves that democratic government is not the same thing as the state bureaucracy. The latter has, by and large, aligned itself with globalization, set itself against the people and lost all political credibility. The former has to represent the people's will or it is worthless.

Absolute poverty cannot be 'eradicated' by the judicious application of superior wisdom and cash from on high. The 'deep roots' of poverty lie in the depriving the landless of their land, the homeless of their homes, and the workless of their jobs. So the eradication of absolute poverty means that those communities where the poorest people live must have political power. In rural communities this almost always involves land reform, restoring local food production, restraining the power of landowning élites and showing 'agribusiness' the door. In urban communities it means forming trade unions, co-operatives, civic groups, and it means redefining the nature of work. In both it means strong, active *local* democratic control. ∎

1. The image is William Greider's in *One World, Ready or Not: the Manic Logic of Global Capitalism,* Simon and Schuster, New York, 1997.

David Ransom, New Internationalist

GEOGRAPHY, once called the mother of the sciences, is nowadays seen by some to have lost its central importance. Some people say that, far from reaching the end of history, as late 20th-century theorists predicted, what we have reached is in fact the 'end of geography'.

Mapping humanity

One goal of geography since ancient times was to keep people connected but, given the impact of modern media which allows for instant contact with all parts of the world without leaving home, the geographic dimension has perhaps been lost. In other words, once the need to travel for communication purposes is overcome, the notion of geography becomes, to some extent, obsolete.

In the opinion of French writer Paul Virilio, the disappearance of geography is a catastrophe since he considers it to be a vital aspect for individuals who will find themselves rootless without it. However, in order to agree or disagree with this view, it is necessary to add a few comments. In the first place, beyond the idea of uprootedness, what is at stake is the very notion of humanity which implies a collectivity where all members of the species participate.

Geography and necessity

The problem with geography, contrary to what Virilio believes, is whether it is still necessary or not since, as with any other knowledge, its value rests in its practical application. Thus, the first European contact with the continent cartographers would name America late in the 15th century, and the ensuing circumnavigation of the globe, confirmed the earth as being spherical, which was in doubt at the time. This fact - the roundness of the earth - took on great relevance for Europeans hungry to conquer, exploit and trade using military and merchant fleets.

Without doubt today, in order to travel to Timbuktu or communicate with somebody there, it is not necessary to know the location of the place on a map. All the person has to do is reach for the telephone or computer and get in touch with the place or book a ticket to the desired destination. In other words, we no longer need to guide ourselves by the stars or by a compass as in the old days, or even to ask how many kilometres away the destination is (and least of all the coordinates).

Clash of civilizations

In another sense, it could be argued that in order to reach practical conclusions about the world, excessive dependence on old cartographic criteria may lead to wrong conclusions. This is evident in works such as *The Clash of Civilizations* by Samuel T Huntington, in which this former US Defense advisor tried to delimit the conflicts of the 21st century.

Used to moving pieces on large maps, Huntington tried to solve his clash between civilizations according to obsolete military models, which have little in common with the reality of current times. The great migrations have resulted in the fact that, as far as civilization is concerned, 'China', 'India' or 'Pakistan' can develop in the big cities of the United States, Islam in European cities, while the West, with its economic and cultural expansionism is present in all the corners of the globe.

In other words, instead of the civilization clash that Huntington tries to impose on a differentiated physical and geopolitical plane, what we have in reality is an interaction - at times conflictual - throughout the world.

Geography as a discipline means much more than map-making and exploration and comprises a wide spectrum which allows it to cooperate in the study of biological, cultural and sociological principles. In order to gauge its capital importance for the study of human evolution in the 21st century it is enough to realize that human geography as a discipline includes cultural, social, demographic, political, urban and economic geography (the latter includes the study of agriculture, industry, trade and transportation).

Geography and humanity

The old maps still show in an impartial way that when it comes to reviewing the state of the world, how unequally its goods are distributed - despite rich natural resources the differences between North and South are stark. The areas of misery, hunger and disease are usually found below the Equator, while those areas that show the greatest comfort and technological development are in the North.

In this sense, the so-called end of the geographic dimension is closely linked to the denial of humanity as a basic right for all people. In order to conceive humanity we have to look at all parts of the globe and weigh up the conditions in which others live.

From this perspective, the argument that communications have made the world smaller loses credibility since the lack of attention to the existence of thousands of millions of people without means of communication opens up a huge information gap. It curtails the notion of humanity, understandable only if this incorporates all people.

Those who have access to telephones, the Internet and air travel are those who can allow themselves the luxury to decree the end of geography and ignore the fact that humanity is composed of the majority who live on the bottom half of maps made in the North, and who in many cases do not even have access to an education which would allow them to see a representation of the whole world.

The European civilization is the one which made the first world maps, reducing to a millimetric scale all the parts of the globe in the trail of its imperial expansion, thus placing itself at the centre of all its charts. This way of mapping the world was called eurocentrism, a concept which was fiercely challenged during the 20th century. In the same way, as seen next, it becomes feasible to say that our future will be linked to a new fashion of mapping.

Interactive maps

The 21st century will bring huge migrations, cultural changes and probably more than one ecological cataclism. The fact that maps will play an important role throughout the coming centuries will be of crucial importance in deciding what kind of future we want as a species.

It is easy to foresee that future maps (whether we look at them or not) will continue to show that the people who suffer most from hunger, violence and disease are in sub-Saharan Africa. If those of us who have received education continue to consult maps in order to locate our fellow humans on the planet and to understand their circumstances, we will have more opportunities to solve global problems.

The disappearance of the geographic dimension, by contrast, will be an indication that the culture (Western culture) which coined the term humanity chose to forget it. In other words, if people in the 21st century wish to keep talking about humanity, they will have to pay attention to maps.

And in order for us in the North to take a better look at the map of our world, it will be helpful if it is interactive, to allow us to change things around to show that what is on top can be at the bottom, the North can become the South, and that what is at the centre may be Asia, Africa or Latin America. They key point is that humanity should be at the centre. ∎

RELEVANT INSTITUTIONS have set themselves the aim of eradicating illiteracy by the year 2025. The figures indicate that while in 1970 only 48 per cent of adults in the world were literate, the percentage for 1997 had increased considerably, to a high of 72 per cent.

The new illiterates

Despite the percentage increase in literacy, at the end of the 20th century there were at least 1.5 billion illiterate people, of whom two thirds were women (even today women have a 6 per cent lower access rate to primary education than men). In addition, in line with demographic projections, these figures are set to double during the first three decades of the 21st century in some regions like southern Asia, where half of all adults do not know how to read, a quarter never had even minimal access to basic education and nearly 75 per cent did not complete primary school.

In addition these figures ignore the fact that the officials are operating with an anachronistic concept of "literacy". In the last analysis, reading and writing have been technological processes to facilitate communication and the production of knowledge, but they always depended on material support. First the printing press and then typewriters replaced formal hand-writing, and the development of e-mail and the Internet has meant that some people rarely now write on paper.

The problem, in this sense, is that our accelerating technological development - particularly the use of computers and the Internet - creates a new horizon in terms of access to communication and knowledge. The first decades of the 21st century will be marked by the fact that, strictly speaking, the literate - that is, those with access to the production and consumption of knowledge - will be the connected (to the electronic communication world). In other words, on a global scale, being disconnected will be the equivalent of illiteracy.

And among the disconnected of course are large numbers of women. Statistics have shown that the gender-based inequity of access to the Web not only replicates, but also amplifies the old model of literacy, as only 17 per cent of Internet users are women.

Meanwhile, even though the Internet is the fastest-growing communication tool ever, its growth has been very uneven between the North and South. The United States has more computers than the rest of the world put together while South Asia, home to 23 per cent of the world's population, has barely one per cent of the world's users.

Everywhere, access to the Internet reinforces and increases the division between the educated and the illiterate - in China for instance 60 per cent of users have a university degree. Other differences also become more

marked: between men and women and between rich and poor: someone earning the average salary in Bangladesh would have to work for eight years to buy a computer whereas the average US citizen could buy theirs in a month.

English has become the dominant language in the way that Latin was in the days before printing, when it was the only language which offered access to knowledge. For while less than 10 per cent of the world's population actually speaks or reads English, it is used on 80 per cent of all web sites. And if we add the fact that, world-wide, the typical Internet user is an urban male, under 35 years old, with

tertiary education and a high income, it becomes apparent that unless ways are found to democratize access to the new tools of literacy, the world will have characteristics reminiscent of medieval Europe, where a chosen few, mostly men, were privileged with knowledge.

And if access to the Internet and the digital world are considered in the same way as basic literacy, then we have to recognise that unless everyone in the world can have equal access then the number of 'unconnected illiterates' will have increased radically by the year 2025 regardless of the goals set by the international bodies. ∎

EDUCATION IMBALANCES

(PRIMARY PUPIL TO TEACHER RATIO) 1994 - 1998 (selected countries)

Country	Ratio	Year	Country	Ratio	Year	Country	Ratio	Year
Albania	18	(1995)	French Polynesia	14	(1995)	Niger	41	(1996)
Algeria	27	(1996)	Gabon	51	(1995)	Nigeria	37	(1994)
Aotearoa/N.Z.	18	(1997)	Gambia	30	(1995)	Oman	26	(1995)
Argentina	17	(1997)	Georgia	18	(1996)	Papua N.G.	38	(1995)
Armenia	19	(1996)	Germany	17	(1995)	Paraguay	21	(1996)
Australia	18	(1996)	Greece	14	(1996)	Peru	28	(1995)
Austria	12	(1996)	Guatemala	35	(1996)	Philippines	35	(1996)
Azerbaijan	20	(1996)	Guinea	49	(1997)	Poland	15	(1995)
Bahamas	22	(1996)	Guyana	29	(1996)	Romania	20	(1996)
Bahrain	20	(1994)	Honduras	35	(1994)	Russia	20	(1995)
Belarus	20	(1994)	Hungary	11	(1994)	Samoa	24	(1995)
Belize	26	(1994)	India	64	(1994)	Saudi Arabia	13	(1996)
Benin	52	(1995)	Indonesia	22	(1996)	Senegal	56	(1997)
Bermuda	12	(1996)	Iran	31	(1996)	Seychelles	17	(1996)
Botswana	25	(1996)	Iraq	20	(1995)	Singapore	22	(1995)
Brazil	23	(1994)	Ireland	22	(1996)	Slovakia	19	(1996)
Brunei	15	(1995)	Italy	11	(1995)	Slovenia	14	(1996)
Bulgaria	17	(1996)	Japan	19	(1994)	Solomon Is.	24	(1994)
Burkina Faso	50	(1995)	Jordan	21	(1995)	South Africa	36	(1995)
Burundi	50	(1995)	Kenya	30	(1995)	Spain	17	(1995)
Cambodia	46	(1997)	Kiribati	24	(1997)	Sri Lanka	28	(1996)
Canada	16	(1995)	Korea, South	31	(1996)	St Lucia	26	(1996)
Chad	67	(1996)	Kuwait	14	(1996)	Sudan	29	(1996)
Chile	30	(1996)	Kyrgyzstan	20	(1995)	Swaziland	34	(1997)
China	24	(1996)	Laos	30	(1996)	Sweden	1	(1996)
Colombia	25	(1996)	Latvia	13	(1996)	Syria	23	(1996)
Comoros	52	(1995)	Lesotho	47	(1996)	Tajikistan	24	(1996)
Congo D.R.	45	(1994)	Lithuania	16	(1996)	Tanzania	37	(1997)
Congo R.	70	(1995)	Maced., TFYR	19	(1996)	Togo	51	(1995)
Costa Rica	29	(1997)	Madagascar	37	(1995)	T. and Tobago	25	(1996)
Côte d'Ivoire	41	(1995)	Malawi	59	(1995)	Tunisia	24	(1996)
Croatia	19	(1996)	Malaysia	20	(1994)	Turkey	28	(1994)
Cuba	12	(1996)	Mali	80	(1996)	Uganda	35	(1995)
Cyprus	15	(1996)	Malta	19	(1995)	U. Arab Emirates	16	(1996)
Czech Republic	19	(1995)	Mauritania	50	(1996)	United Kingdom	19	(1995)
Djibouti	34	(1996)	Mauritius	24	(1996)	United States	16	(1995)
Ecuador	25	(1996)	Mexico	28	(1996)	Uruguay	20	(1996)
Egypt	23	(1996)	Moldova	23	(1996)	Uzbekistan	21	(1994)
El Salvador	33	(1996)	Monaco	19	(1995)	Venezuela	21	(1996)
Eritrea	44	(1996)	Mongolia	31	(1996)	Zambia	39	(1995)
Estonia	17	(1995)	Morocco	28	(1996)	Zimbabwe	39	(1997)
Ethiopia	43	(1996)	Mozambique	58	(1998)			
Finland	18	(1996)	Nicaragua	38	(1995)			

Source: World Development Indicators 2000, World Bank, 2000.

Percentage of students across the school-age population
(Gross enrolment rate is the number of children enrolled at a level - primary or secondary - regardless of age, divided by the population of that age group)

	PRIMARY (90-97)		SECONDARY (90-96)		TERTIARY (96-97)		PRIMARY (90-97)		SECONDARY (90-96)		TERTIARY (96-97)
	MALE	FEMALE	MALE	FEMALE	TOTAL		MALE	FEMALE	MALE	FEMALE	TOTAL
Afghanistan	64	32	32	11	2	Korea, North	108	101	..	..	..
Albania	100	102	35	35	11	Korea, South	94	94	102	102	68
Algeria	113	101	65	62	13	Kuwait	76	74	65	65	19
Angola	95	88	..	..	1	Kyrgyzstan	108	105	76	85	12
Aotearoa/N. Zealand	103	103	117	123	63	Laos	125	97	36	23	3
Argentina	114	113	73	81	42	Latvia	99	93	82	85	33
Armenia	86	90	85	91	12	Lebanon	113	108	78	85	27
Australia	103	103	153	153	80	Lesotho	92	102	23	34	2
Austria	100	101	105	101	48	Liberia	51	28	31	12	3
Azerbaijan	109	106	73	81	18	Libya	110	110	95	95	20
Bahamas	95	94	88	91	24	Lithuania	99	96	85	88	31
Bahrain	105	107	91	98	19	Luxembourg	88	94	72	76	10
Bangladesh	74	64	28	14	6	Macedonia, TFYR	90	87	58	58	20
Barbados	90	91	90	80	29	Madagascar	74	71	13	13	2
Belarus	101	96	91	95	44	Malawi	142	128	21	12	1
Belgium	103	102	141	151	57	Malaysia	90	92	58	66	11
Belize	124	118	47	52	1	Maldives	127	123	49	49	..
Benin	96	56	23	10	3	Mali	41	27	12	6	1
Bhutan	31	19	7	2	0	Malta	111	109	93	86	29
Bolivia	99	90	40	34	24	Mauritania	88	79	21	11	4
Botswana	111	112	63	69	6	Mauritius	107	106	63	66	6
Brazil	100	96	31	36	15	Mexico	116	113	61	61	16
Brunei	109	104	71	82	7	Moldova	96	95	78	81	27
Bulgaria	100	98	77	76	41	Mongolia	86	91	48	65	19
Burkina Faso	48	31	11	6	1	Morocco	95	72	44	34	11
Burundi	55	46	9	5	1	Mozambique	70	50	9	5	1
Cambodia	142	119	30	18	1	Myanmar/Burma	102	99	29	30	6
Cameroon	93	84	32	22	4	Namibia	130	132	56	66	9
Canada	103	101	107	106	90	Nepal	128	91	49	25	5
Cape Verde	132	129	28	26	..	Netherlands	108	106	141	133	47
Cent. African Rep.	71	46	15	6	1	Nicaragua	109	112	43	50	12
Chad	85	44	16	4	1	Niger	36	22	9	5	1
Chile	103	100	72	78	31	Nigeria	100	79	33	28	4
China	121	120	74	67	6	Norway	99	99	120	113	62
Colombia	119	118	70	75	17	Oman	80	75	68	65	8
Comoros	85	71	21	17	1	Pakistan	101	45	33	17	4
Congo D.R.	86	59	32	19	2	Panama	108	104	60	65	32
Congo R.	119	109	62	45	8	Papua New Guinea	87	74	17	11	3
Costa Rica	108	107	48	52	33	Paraguay	113	110	42	45	10
Côte d'Ivoire	81	60	33	16	..	Puerto Rico	..	..	..	..	42
Croatia	87	86	81	83	28	Qatar	87	85	81	79	27
Cuba	108	104	73	82	12	Romania	105	103	78	78	23
Cyprus	100	100	96	99	23	Russia	108	107	84	91	41
Czech Republic	105	104	97	100	24	Rwanda	83	81	12	9	1
Denmark	100	99	117	122	..	Samoa	111	103	59	66	5
Djibouti	44	32	17	12	0	Saudi Arabia	77	75	65	57	16
Dominican Rep.	103	104	34	47	23	Senegal	76	62	20	12	3
Ecuador	134	119	53	55	26	Sierra Leone	59	41	22	13	2
Egypt	109	94	80	70	23	Singapore	95	93	70	77	39
El Salvador	94	94	30	35	18	Slovakia	102	102	92	96	22
Equat. Guinea	..	..	..	..	2	Slovenia	106	105	92	94	36
Eritrea	59	49	24	17	1	Solomon Is.	104	90	21	14	..
Estonia	95	93	100	108	45	Somalia	15	8	9	5	2
Ethiopia	47	27	13	10	1	South Africa	117	115	76	91	..
Fiji	128	127	64	65	13	Spain	106	105	114	128	53
Finland	100	100	107	125	74	Sri Lanka	110	108	71	78	5
France	107	105	112	111	51	Switzerland	108	107	94	88	34
French Polynesia	..	..	..	..	3	Syria	106	96	45	40	15
Gabon	..	..	..	..	8	Tajikistan	95	92	81	72	20
Gambia	87	67	30	19	2	Tanzania	67	66	6	5	1
Georgia	85	84	74	72	41	Thailand	99	96	38	37	21
Germany	104	103	103	101	47	Togo	140	99	40	14	4
Ghana	83	70	45	29	1	Trinidad and Tobago	91	102	66	79	8
Greece	95	94	96	96	47	Tunisia	117	111	67	65	14
Guam	..	..	..	..	66	Turkey	107	102	67	45	21
Guatemala	90	79	26	24	8	Turkmenistan	..	..	..	..	20
Guinea	63	34	18	6	1	Uganda	79	67	15	9	2
Honduras	110	112	29	37	11	Ukraine	87	86	88	94	42
Hungary	105	103	97	100	25	United Arab Emirates	91	87	77	82	12
Iceland	99	97	105	102	36	United Kingdom	115	116	123	144	52
India	110	90	59	39	7	United States	102	101	98	97	81
Ireland	103	103	111	119	41	Uruguay	113	112	77	92	30
Israel	96	96	84	89	44	Uzbekistan	78	76	99	87	36
Italy	100	99	87	88	47	Vanuatu	105	107	23	18	..
Jamaica	107	107	62	70	8	Venezuela	90	93	33	46	25
Japan	101	102	98	100	43	Vietnam	106	100	44	41	7
Jordan	94	95	52	54	19	Yemen	100	40	53	14	4
Kanaky/N. Caledonia	..	..	..	..	5	Yugoslavia Fed. Rep.	71	72	62	66	22
Kazakhstan	95	96	80	89	32	Zambia	92	86	34	21	3
Kenya	85	85	26	22	2	Zimbabwe	115	111	52	44	7

Sources: The State of the World's Children 2000, UNICEF, 2000; World Development Indicators 2000, World Bank, 2000.

Adult literacy rate %, 1995

	TOTAL	MALE	FEMALE		TOTAL	MALE	FEMALE
Afghanistan	32	46	16	Libya	74	87	60
Algeria	58	71	45	Liechtenstein	100	100	100
Angola	42	56	29	Lithuania	99	100	99
Antigua	95	..	..	Madagascar	46	60	32
Argentina	96	96	96	Malawi	56	72	41
Armenia	100	100	99	Malaysia	84	89	79
Azerbaijan	100	100	99	Maldives	95	95	95
Bahamas	96	95	96	Mali	32	40	25
Bahrain	85	89	79	Malta	91	90	91
Bangladesh	38	49	26	Marshall Is.	91	..	90
Barbados	97	98	97	Mauritania	37	49	27
Belarus	99	100	98	Mauritius	82	86	78
Belize	70	70	70	Mexico	89	92	87
Benin	32	45	19	Micronesia	81	..	79
Bhutan	42	56	28	Moldova	98	99	97
Bolivia	82	90	75	Mongolia	83	89	77
Botswana	73	70	75	Morocco	44	58	31
Brazil	83	83	83	Mozambique	38	55	23
Brunei	89	93	85	Myanmar/Burma	83	88	78
Bulgaria	98	99	97	Namibia	78	80	77
Burkina Faso	19	29	10	Nepal	36	54	19
Burundi	42	52	33	Nicaragua	66	65	67
Cambodia	65	80	53	Niger	13	21	7
Cameroon	63	75	52	Nigeria	57	66	47
Canada	97	..	..	Niue	99	..	99
Cape Verde	69	81	61	Oman	64	75	51
Central African Rep.	40	54	27	Pakistan	39	54	24
Chad	48	62	35	Palau	98	..	97
Chile	95	95	95	Panama	91	91	90
China	80	89	71	Papua New Guinea	72	81	63
Colombia	90	91	90	Paraguay	92	93	90
Comoros	57	64	50	Peru	88	93	83
Congo D.R.	77	87	68	Philippines	94	94	94
Congo R.	74	83	67	Poland	100	100	100
Cook Is.	99	..	99	Portugal	90	93	87
Costa Rica	95	95	95	Qatar	79	79	80
Côte d'Ivoire	40	49	31	Romania	98	99	96
Croatia	97	99	96	Russia	99	100	99
Cuba	96	96	96	Rwanda	60	69	52
Cyprus	95	98	93	Samoa	98	..	98
Djibouti	46	60	33	São Tomé and Príncipe	57	..	..
Dominican Republic	82	82	81	Saudi Arabia	71	80	59
Ecuador	89	92	87	Senegal	33	43	23
Egypt	51	64	38	Seychelles	84	83	86
El Salvador	76	79	73	Sierra Leone	31	45	18
Equatorial Guinea	78	89	67	Singapore	91	96	86
Estonia	98	98	98	Slovenia	100	100	100
Ethiopia	33	40	26	Solomon Is.	62	..	56
Fiji	91	94	89	Somalia	24	36	14
Gabon	63	74	53	South Africa	83	84	82
Gambia	39	53	25	Spain	97	98	96
Georgia	99	100	99	Sri Lanka	90	94	87
Ghana	64	75	53	St Kitts-Nevis	90	..	..
Greece	96	98	94	St Vincent	82	..	..
Grenada	96	..	..	Sudan	51	63	38
Guatemala	65	73	58	Suriname	93	95	91
Guinea	36	50	22	Swaziland	76	78	75
Guinea-Bissau	31	48	16	Syria	70	85	54
Guyana	98	99	97	Tajikistan	99	99	98
Haiti	44	47	41	Tanzania	69	80	59
Honduras	70	70	69	Thailand	94	96	92
Hungary	99	99	99	Togo	51	67	35
India	50	64	35	Tonga	99	..	99
Indonesia	84	90	78	Trinidad and Tobago	98	99	97
Iran	71	79	63	Tunisia	65	76	53
Iraq	58	71	45	Turkey	82	92	72
Israel	95	97	93	Turkmenistan	98	99	97
Italy	98	99	98	Tuvalu	99	..	..
Jamaica	85	80	89	Uganda	62	74	50
Jordan	86	91	80	Ukraine	99	98	99
Kazakhstan	100	100	99	United Arab Emirates	79	79	80
Kenya	77	86	69	United States	99	..	..
Kiribati	93	..	92	Uruguay	97	97	98
Korea, South	97	99	95	Uzbekistan	100	100	100
Kuwait	79	82	76	Vanuatu	64	..	60
Kyrgyzstan	97	99	95	Venezuela	91	92	90
Laos	57	69	44	Vietnam	91	95	88
Latvia	100	100	99	Yemen	40	62	18
Lebanon	83	91	77	Yugoslavia Fed. Rep.	98	99	97
Lesotho	81	70	92	Zambia	78	86	71
Liberia	45	62	28	Zimbabwe	85	90	80

Source: The State of the World's Children 2000, UNICEF, 2000.

Predictions

LEADING FIGURES from different areas give their predictions for the near future. Some of them are optimistic, some show the dark side of the changes occurring in the world, but most acknowledge the difficulties that come with the new millennium.

The new millennium

THE THIRD MILLENNIUM
Sir John Maddox
British physicist and chemist, *Nature* magazine editor for 23 years and author of major books such as *The Revolution in Biology*, and *Beyond The Energy Crisis*. In the introduction to this special issue, Maddox admits that in the current world of fundamental sciences, many questions remain unanswered: "There are signs that we will be able to find out the characteristics of the common ancestor to all living organisms through the genetic analysis of present beings". For him, "the obvious black hole in our present knowledge lies in the fact that we still do not know how the human brain develops the functions we are most proud of, the ability to think, even over circumstances that can only be imagined, and the conscious decision-making process".

GROSS INEQUITIES
Gladys Acosta
Unicef director in Colombia: "There is no way of denying the gross inequities, the damaging and threatening wars in each one of our territories, besides all the manifestations of pain that nature is showing us. Many women will keep dying because they were not well taken care of during childbirth, or will lose their lives because of a jealous rage by those who never learnt to love. There is nowhere to hide your head and imagine that all will be well soon. All that being true, we cannot stop thinking that much of what is happening is avoidable, and that it would suffice to turn our wills in a different direction in order to defeat the almightiness derived from riches, weapons and authoritative power".

CLONING
Ian Wilmut
British biochemist and creator of Dolly the sheep, the first animal cloned from a grown cell. "The controversy goes beyond the strictly scientific", says the researcher, wholly convinced that medicine will one day cure diseases that we consider incurable today. "Cloning, by opening the door to the use of human embryos, has raised ethical considerations. There are some who grant an embryo the same status given to babies. However, I think it is quite inappropriate to consider it equivalent to a person".

ENVIRONMENT
Lester Brown and Christopher Flavin
Worldwatch Institute directors, a group established with funding from the Rockefeller Foundation which has become a point of reference for the environmental movement worldwide. "Maybe the most significant barometer reading on the state of the Earth's health is the decline of the number of species with whom we share the planet", they observe. "Unfortunately, we find ourselves on the brink of the greatest process of animal and plant extinction in the last 65 million years".

WATER
Elas Fereres
Agronomist, director of the CSIC Institute of Sustainable Agriculture and president of the Engineering Academy. Aware of the fact that today "more than one billion people lack direct access to drinking water", Fererer warns: "It is estimated that by 2025, we will use 70 per cent of the Earth's renewable resources compared to less than 50 per cent used today".

ENERGY
Guillermo Velarde
Director of the Nuclear Fusion Institute at Madrid's Universidad Politecnica. He argues that, "our planet, wholly immersed in the era of global industrialization and with a growing population, will need at an increasing rate more cost-competitive energy sources which reduce, almost to the point of disappearance, the biological damage caused by coal,uranium and natural gas". And adds, "this will be one of the great challenges we will have to face in the 21 st century".

RELIGION
Juan Mara Laboa
Spanish priest and Contemporary Church History professor at the Universidad Pontificia de Comillas. "In the multicultural society of the 21st century, we will need to know other religions better in order to have a better knowledge of our own and to fully respect our fellow citizens", states the author of, among other books, *Church and Intolerance*. "A society which respects other religious communities and collaborates with them on a regular basis is a more tolerant and democratic society". He adds, "inter-religious dialogue is an efficient means of promoting peace and social justice".

WOMEN
Irma Arriagada
Chilean sociologist from CEPAL's Social Affairs Division. "The 21st century must belong to women. We men and women survivors of the most violent century in history wish for new utopias. The millennium which begins with this 21st century grants us at least the right to imagine good and better times. May this new era be more humane and plural where gender will no longer be a category for classifying people but a culturally enriching criterion, with greater diversity, for all societies. Let us celebrate then, this century as our century".

LABOR
Michel Ickx
Belgian/Spanish consultant and expert on labor issues, currently coordinator of the European Telework Development Initiative, (ETD). "The webbing of labor relations will be different", he warns. "The new worker won't have just one boss, there will be shifting roles: sometimes he or she will be boss, sometimes a simple collaborator according to her or his capacity to undertake various tasks". Ickx explains that "professional, civic and scientific achievement will be valued more than wages. For instance, a researcher will place more value on her discovery than on its economic feasibility". This sociologist believes "future work will cover a more comprehensive space than traditional corporate labor: people will be more committed with commercial aspects, cultural, social and moral values. Their life will no longer be structured around well defined and consecutive stages: childhood, education, work and retirement. Work will alternate with life long education, with periods of rest and with social and civic activities".

COMMUNICATIONS
Nicholas Negroponte
US electronic commerce expert, co-founder and Director of the Media Lab Institute of Massachusetts. He assures us that "having access to all the libraries in the world, even at 4,800 bytes per second, is such a radical change that there is really no way of under-

standing it from our privileged First World standpoint". The author of the best-selling book *Being Digital* believes that "during the last five years, first world countries have fought for a place in the digital world. Finland and Sweden lead in Europe, while neighboring France and Germany have been left far behind. In other words, five years from now its possible that the Third World won't be where we currently think it is. Many "leap development" theories have been entertained, none of which have withstood the passage of time. That is about to change".

WAR
Wesley Clark

US General, supreme NATO commander in Europe and responsible for the military operation in Kosovo and the Dayton accords which put an end to the war in Bosnia. He states that "the Alliance and its member countries will need vision and dynamic political leadership to be part of the new human and technological potential which will integrate NATO's future military and systems organization". He adds that "adjusting to the dynamics of change will not be an easy task. The only real option is that the military arm of the Alliance turns into its beneficiary, or into its possible victim. NATO leaders have decided that it be their beneficiary". According to Clark, "The US has proven to be the backbone behind NATO's intelligence systems. There is no doubt that without the use of this country's national resources, NATO probably could not have generated the necessary intelligence to assign sufficiently detailed objectives". ■

Source:
Guía de las Mujeres (Women's Guide)

WOMEN IN WORK

A = % OF WOMEN IN LABOR FORCE 1998
B = % OF ADMINISTRATION AND MANAGERIAL POSTS OCCUPIED BY WOMEN [*]
C = % OF PROFESSIONAL AND TECHNICAL WORKERS [*]
D = WOMEN'S EARNED INCOME SHARE (%) [*]

COUNTRY	A	B	C	D	COUNTRY	A	B	C	D	COUNTRY	A	B	C	D
Afghanistan	35	..	..	..	Gambia	45	16	24	38	Nicaragua	35	..	..	..
Albania	41	..	..	..	Georgia	47	18	42	39	Niger	44	8	8	37
Algeria	26	6	28	19	Germany	42	27	49	35	Nigeria	36	..	..	..
Angola	46				Ghana	51	..	..	..	Norway	46	31	59	42
Aotearoa/N.Zeal.	44	24	50	39	Greece	37	12	44	32	Oman	15	..	..	..
Argentina	32	..	..	..	Guadeloupe	45	..	..	..	Pakistan	27	4	21	21
Armenia	48	..	..	..	Guatemala	27	32	45	21	Palestine	11	..	..	..
Australia	43	43	26	40	Guinea	47	..	..	..	Panama	34	28	49	28
Austria	40	22	50	34	Guinea-Bissau	40	..	..	..	Papua N.G.	42	12	30	35
Azerbaijan	44	..	..	..	Guyana	33	13	48	27	Paraguay	29	23	54	23
Bahamas	47	35	51	40	Haiti	43	..	..	36	Peru	30	20	39	24
Bahrain	20	..	..	..	Honduras	31	39	56	..	Philippines	37	35	65	35
Bangladesh	42	5	35	23	Hungary	45	33	61	39	Poland	46	34	61	39
Barbados	46	..	..	40	Iceland	45	23	53	42	Portugal	44	37	52	34
Belarus	49	..	..	..	India	32	2	21	25	Puerto Rico	36	..	..	..
Belgium	40	19	51	34	Indonesia	40	7	41	33	Qatar	14	..	..	..
Belize	23	37	39	18	Iran	25	4	33	19	Réunion	43	..	..	..
Benin	48	..	..	..	Iraq	19	..	..	..	Romania	44	28	56	37
Bhutan	40	..	..	..	Ireland	34	17	48	27	Russia	49	..	..	..
Bolivia	38	..	..	27	Israel	40	19	54	33	Rwanda	49	..	..	..
Bosnia-Herz.	38	..	..	..	Italy	38	54	18	31	Saudi Arabia	14	..	..	..
Botswana	46	26	53	39	Jamaica	46	..	..	..	Senegal	43	..	..	..
Brazil	35	17	63	29	Japan	41	9	44	34	Sierra Leone	36	..	..	..
Brunei	35	..	..	..	Jordan	23	5	29	19	Singapore	39	34	16	32
Bulgaria	48	29	57	41	Kazakhstan	47	..	..	..	Slovakia	48	31	60	41
Burkina Faso	47	14	26	40	Kenya	46	..	..	..	Slovenia	46	28	53	39
Burundi	49	..	..	..	Korea, North	43	..	..	..	Solomon Is.	47	..	..	..
Cambodia	52	..	..	..	Korea, South	41	4	45	29	Somalia	43	..	..	..
Cameroon	38	10	24	30	Kuwait	31	5	37	25	South Africa	38	17	47	31
Canada	45	42	51	38	Kyrgyzstan	47	..	..	..	Spain	36	12	48	30
Cape Verde	39	23	48	32	Laos	..	..	..	..	Sri Lanka	36	18	31	36
C. Afric. R.	..	9	19	39	Latvia	50	38	66	44	Sudan	29	2	29	22
Chad	45	..	..	..	Lebanon	29	..	..	..	Suriname	33	13	69	26
Chile	33	19	52	22	Lesotho	37	33	57	30	Swaziland	38	24	61	33
China	45	12	45	38	Liberia	39	..	..	..	Sweden	48	28	64	45
Colombia	38	39	46	33	Libya	22	..	..	..	Switzerland	40	29	23	32
Comoros	42	..	..	..	Lithuania	48	35	68	..	Syria	26	3	37	20
Congo D.R.	44	..	..	..	Luxembourg	37	9	38	29	Tajikistan	44	..	..	..
Congo R.	43	..	..	..	Maced., TFYR	41	..	..	..	Tanzania	49	..	..	..
Costa Rica	30	27	48	27	Madagascar	45	..	..	..	Thailand	46	20	55	37
Côte d'Ivoire	33	..	..	..	Malawi	49	5	35	42	Togo	40	8	21	32
Croatia	44	..	..	..	Malaysia	37	19	43	30	T. and Tobago	33	23	53	27
Cuba	39	19	48	31	Maldives	43	14	35	35	Tunisia	31	13	36	25
Cyprus	39	10	41	28	Mali	46	20	19	39	Turkey	37	9	33	36
Czech Republic	47	23	54	39	Malta	27	..	..	..	Turkmenistan	46	..	..	..
Denmark	46	20	63	42	Martinique	47	..	..	..	Uganda	48	..	..	..
Dominican R.	30	45	50	24	Mauritania	44	8	21	37	Ukraine	49	..	..	..
Ecuador	27	28	47	19	Mauritius	32	23	38	26	U. A. Emirates	14	2	25	10
Egypt	29	16	28	25	Mexico	32	20	45	26	United Kingdom	44	33	44	38
El Salvador	35	25	45	34	Moldova	49	..	..	..	United States	46	44	53	40
Eq. Guinea	35	2	27	29	Mongolia	47	..	..	..	Uruguay	41	28	64	34
Eritrea	47	17	30	..	Morocco	35	26	31	28	Uzbekistan	46	..	..	..
Estonia	49	37	67	42	Mozambique	48	11	20	42	Venezuela	34	23	57	27
Ethiopia	41	..	..	..	Myanmar/Burma	43	..	..	..	Vietnam	49	..	..	..
Fiji	29	48	11	22	Namibia	41	..	..	..	Yemen	28	..	..	..
Finland	48	27	63	42	Nepal	40	..	..	..	Yugoslavia F. R.	43	..	..	..
France	45	9	41	39	Netherlands	40	17	45	34	Zambia	45	6	32	39
Gabon	44	..	..	..	Neth.Antilles	43	..	..	..	Zimbabwe	44	15	40	38

[*] Data refers to 1995 or the latest available year.

Sources: Human Development Report 1999, UNDP, 1999; World Development Indicators 2000, World Bank, 2000.

A = % OF GOVERNMENTAL POSTS OCCUPIED BY WOMEN, TOTAL, 1996
B = % OF MINISTERIAL POSTS OCCUPIED BY WOMEN, 1996
C = % OF PARLIAMENTARY SEATS OCCUPIED BY WOMEN, 1999

	A	B	C		A	B	C		A	B	C
Albania	12	5	..	Gabon	8	3	10	Norway	24	29	36
Algeria	5	0	4	Gambia	19	19	2	Oman	4	0	..
Angola	5	11	16	Georgia	3	0	7	Pakistan	3	4	2
Antigua	27	0	11	Germany	6	11	30	Panama	9	17	10
Aotearoa/N.Zealand	26	9	29	Ghana	10	10	9	Papua New Guinea	4	0	2
Argentina	5	0	23	Greece	9	0	6	Paraguay	4	7	8
Armenia	2	0	6	Grenada	23	21	..	Peru	13	6	11
Australia	23	15	26	Guatemala	17	13	13	Philippines	23	5	13
Austria	7	24	25	Guinea	13	15	9	Poland	10	8	13
Azerbaijan	7	8	12	Guinea-Bissau	12	8	10	Portugal	17	12	13
Bahamas	30	19	20	Guyana	15	6	16	Qatar	0	0	..
Bahrain	0	0	..	Haiti	22	29	..	Romania	3	0	6
Bangladesh	2	8	9	Honduras	14	10	9	Russia	3	2	8
Barbados	26	31	..	Hungary	7	6	8	Rwanda	11	8	17
Belarus	7	5	..	Iceland	8	15	25	Samoa	9	8	4
Belgium	7	11	16	India	6	3	8	São Tomé and Príncipe	8	0	9
Belize	6	0	14	Indonesia	2	4	11	Saudi Arabia	0	0	..
Benin	15	19	7	Iran	0	0	5	Senegal	6	7	..
Bhutan	5	13	2	Iraq	0	0	6	Seychelles	21	33	24
Bolivia	7	0	..	Ireland	12	21	14	Sierra Leone	6	4	..
Botswana	14	8	9	Israel	11	13	8	Singapore	7	0	5
Brazil	14	4	6	Italy	7	4	10	Slovakia	16	15	13
Brunei	2	0	..	Jamaica	14	6	16	Slovenia	17	9	8
Bulgaria	15	5	11	Japan	9	6	9	Solomon Is.	0	0	2
Burkina Faso	12	9	11	Jordan	3	6	3	South Africa	7	1	28
Burundi	5	10	6	Kazakhstan	2	3	11	Spain	15	17	20
Cambodia	2	0	8	Kenya	6	3	4	Sri Lanka	10	13	5
Cameroon	5	3	6	Korea, South	1	3	4	St Kitts-Nevis	17	0	13
Canada	18	19	23	Kuwait	5	0	0	St Lucia	5	9	14
Cape Verde	11	13	11	Kyrgyzstan	11	11	5	St Vincent	19	20	5
Central African Rep.	5	8	6	Laos	4	0	21	Sudan	2	2	5
Chad	4	9	2	Latvia	18	11	17	Suriname	11	0	16
Chile	10	14	9	Lebanon	0	0	2	Swaziland	8	0	6
China	4	6	22	Lesotho	15	0	11	Sweden	31	38	43
Colombia	21	13	12	Libya	3	5	..	Switzerland	7	15	20
Comoros	3	6	0	Lithuania	7	0	18	Syria	4	7	10
Congo D.R.	3	8	..	Luxembourg	18	29	20	Tajikistan	4	4	3
Congo R.	7	7	12	Macedonia, TFYR	20	9	8	Tanzania	10	11	18
Costa Rica	27	11	19	Madagascar	2	0	8	Thailand	2	0	7
Côte d'Ivoire	7	8	8	Malawi	4	4	6	Togo	3	4	1
Croatia	19	12	7	Malaysia	8	6	10	Trinidad and Tobago	14	16	19
Cuba	9	3	28	Maldives	13	6	6	Tunisia	8	3	7
Cyprus	5	8	5	Mali	6	10	12	Turkey	5	3	2
Czech Republic	11	0	14	Malta	3	0	9	Turkmenistan	2	3	18
Denmark	14	29	37	Mauritania	5	4	2	Uganda	9	11	18
Djibouti	1	0	0	Mauritius	10	0	8	Ukraine	2	0	8
Dominica	25	18	9	Mexico	8	16	17	United Arab Emirates	0	0	0
Dominican Republic	10	4	15	Moldova	4	0	9	United Kingdom	7	8	12
Ecuador	3	6	17	Mongolia	2	0	8	United States	33	14	13
Egypt	4	3	2	Morocco	1	0	1	Uruguay	14	7	7
El Salvador	27	6	17	Mozambique	13	4	25	Uzbekistan	1	3	6
Equatorial Guinea	5	5	9	Myanmar/Burma	0	0	..	Vanuatu	0	0	0
Eritrea	8	19	21	Namibia	11	9	17	Venezuela	15	11	12
Estonia	14	0	11	Nepal	0	0	5	Vietnam	5	7	26
Ethiopia	9	7	2	Netherlands	17	24	32	Yemen	0	0	1
Fiji	15	5	6	Nicaragua	17	16	11	Zambia	8	8	10
Finland	20	36	34	Niger	11	14	1	Zimbabwe	12	8	15
France	11	15	9	Nigeria	6	8	..				

Source: Human Development Report 1999, UNDP, 1999.

BREAST IS BEST

% OF MOTHERS BREAST FEEDING AT 3 MONTHS (1990-99)

Mongolia	93	Turkmenistan	54	Swaziland	37	Central African Rep.	23	Kazakhstan	12
Rwanda	90	Azerbaijan	53	Laos	36	Namibia	22	Tunisia	12
Burundi	89	Egypt	53	Costa Rica	35	Armenia	21	Malawi	11
Nepal	83	Bangladesh	52	Congo D.R.	32	Cape Verde	18	Turkey	9
Chile	77	Guinea	52	Gabon	32	Kenya	17	Macedonia, TFYR	8
Cuba	76	Indonesia	52	Panama	32	Cameroon	16	Maldives	8
Papua New Guinea	75	India	51	Kyrgyzstan	31	Colombia	16	Paraguay	7
Ethiopia	74	Guatemala	50	Morocco	31	El Salvador	16	Yugoslavia Fed. Rep.	6
Uganda	70	Algeria	48	Ecuador	29	Mauritius	16	Burkina Faso	5
Eritrea	66	Philippines	47	Nicaragua	29	Pakistan	16	Comoros	5
Iran	66	Congo R.	43	Oman	28	Senegal	16	Côte d'Ivoire	4
China	64	Brazil	42	Zambia	26	Zimbabwe	16	Thailand	4
Peru	63	Honduras	42	Afghanistan	25	Benin	15	Uzbekistan	4
Bolivia	61	Tanzania	41	Dominican Republic	25	Jordan	15	Haiti	3
Madagascar	61	Botswana	39	Yemen	25	Togo	15	Chad	2
Cambodia	60	Mexico	38	Belize	24	Sudan	14	Nigeria	2
Mauritania	60	Mozambique	38	Croatia	24	Mali	13	Niger	1
Lesotho	54	Ghana	37	Sri Lanka	24	Angola	12		

Source: The State of the World's Children 2000, UNICEF, 2000.

Workers

SOME TRADE unionists and socialist thinkers are optimistic about the new social dynamics generated by technological changes and the globalization of goods and services. But they also warn about the dangers of a society in which workers, regardless of the jobs they perform, simply become consumers with no rights at work.

Conditions for change

The speed of scientific and technological development, its rapid impact on the means of production, and the resulting increase in productivity are fast eliminating manual jobs. This leads to changes in the social make-up, most noticeable so far in the Western industrialized world - the cradle of union and labor movements as social forces.

While some left thinkers believe that changes in technology will reduce the power and size of the working class, some union leaders wonder about how to organize effectively in the light of the almost total freedom of movement acquired by capital in recent decades. This freedom has resulted both in the reduction of hard-fought individual and collective rights and in increasing social inequality.

And globalization, which on the one hand threatens workers and society as a whole, could - with the proper approach - allow unions and civic organizations to participate in the creation of a new model for society. Wealth generated through new productive techniques could also create conditions for a world more open to promoting democracy, equality and justice.

New technologies are constantly developing robots and automated systems in production and services. These will add to the structural unemployment affecting some Western industrialized countries over the past years, and in turn will create a different model of society. The traditional definition of class or social sector will take into account not only the job or productive role, but also the standard of living and other social characteristics.

"The disappearance of the working class is certain", says Marxist philosopher Adam Schaff. "The capitalist class in its current form will disappear as a result. However, production of goods and services will remain, and will probably take on much greater significance. Who will produce and how will this process develop? The transformation of human knowledge, of science (…) into a basic instrument of production complicates things even more".

Schaff adds that the rural classes have practically disappeared in the industrial countries: only two or three per cent of the population is required to carry out agricultural work because so much is mechanised and industrialized.

Highly qualified personnel will replace the traditional proletariat in the automated production of goods and services. Although a great many workers in natural resource extraction and processing will do other useful activities for society, their number and influence will be greatly reduced.

Technically qualified social groups in charge of key tasks will be the new middle classes which, by virtue of being the most numerous and production-oriented, would play an unprecedented historical role.

The consequences of this scenario are clear: unions would no longer revolve around the "proletariat" but around a middle class in charge of productive tasks and basic services. The model of future society will depend on the organization and management capacity of these new classes in the process of technological and social change.

Antonio Gutiérrez, secretary general of the Spanish Comisiones Obreras (CCOO) trade union, tries to anticipate the future development of union, employers and state relations based on current trends of capitalism.

He says that the total freedom of movement of capital leads to widespread inequalities and to effective restrictions on individual and collective liberties. In his opinion, these liberties should be protected by social and civic rights guaranteed to citizens.

According to Gutiérrez, it is possible to effect change in the current globalizing trend as long as one doesn't get carried away by two tendencies which - although ideologically opposed - would have the same outcome. The one is leftist resistance anchored in past ideological paradigms, and the other a blind faith in the supposed benefits of unfettered market mechanisms: both lead to impotence. The former due to frustration, the latter to resignation.

The union movement is not immune to these trends. Unions have to renovate and adapt their ideas to the challenges of the evolving world, and rebuild their role as a driving force for democracy, equality and solidarity in a global environment which threatens these principles. If unions hold on to their traditional role as mediators between capital and labor under old models, then they will be mere guardians of the collective interests of the better employed but declining and less numerous labor groups.

In a world of open and interdependent economies, an all-out defense of the wealth redistribution systems of the past would lead to the overprotection of a few and to the neglect of the majority of workers. This conviction is based on the fact that the balance between primary distribution based on known labor costs in exchange for high rates of employment stability and the internalization of social costs by the na-

tion-states in the form of welfare has long been broken.

"Today the dispute is not between wages and benefits in a context of growing demand for employment", adds Gutiérrez. "The social conflict is rather between the quantity and quality of work and the excluded. This tends to increase with measures such as "labor optimization" - a euphemism which almost always translates into payroll reductions".

Because of this, in order to represent the overall interests of workers, unions have to adapt to the new organization of work, make space for sectoral collective bargaining, including operations abroad - an urgent challenge for European Union unions - and oversee their decentralization regarding the company.

But in order for unions to weave a new network of social solidarity, the leadership will have to abandon its defensive stance of the last decades in order to promote welfare reforms which primarily address the needs of the excluded and the worst-placed in the labor market, while at the same time increasing the benefits that the rest of society receive from the better-off sectors.

As proof that this is possible, Gutiérrez cites the examples of the two major Spanish union confederations (Comisiones Obreras and Unión General de Trabajadores) which in the last few years signed agreements with management in matters such as employment stability with positive labor flexibility, thus benefiting almost one and a half million unemployed or underemployed people.

Spanish unions also consider as victories the pacts that lead to sectoral collective bargaining and the agreement signed with the Government for the rationalization of the public pension plan.

The latter proves that it is possible to achieve reforms that, far from leading directly to customized pension plans based on private savings - for those who are able to save - it is possible to improve a state system to make it more efficient, solid and forward-looking.

Lastly, Gutiérrez asserts that this would require us to delve into political autonomy - which is neither being apolitical nor indifferent to politics - and into the unity of the great unions which are to grow even stronger promoting union enrollment, reforming their structures to reflect the increasing labor sector diversity, and more fluent in their dialogue with state powers of all territorial administrations. ∎

Sources: *Meditations on Socialism*, Adam Schaff, Siglo XXI Editores, Mexico 1998; Antonio Gutiérrez, for IPS news agency, 2000.

A = Labour force (% of total population), 1998
B = % agriculture, 1990

C = Industrial sector, 1990
D = Services sector, 1990
E = Unemployment (%)

COUNTRIES	A	B	C	D	E	COUNTRIES	A	B	C	D	E	COUNTRIES	A	B	C	D	E
Afghanistan	42	..	..	..	..	Gabon	46	52	16	33	..	Nigeria	40	43	7	50	..
Albania	49	55	23	22	..	Gambia	51	82	8	11		Norway	52	6	25	68	4
Algeria	33	26	31	43	26	Georgia	49	26	31	43	..	Oman	27	45	24	32	..
Angola	46	75	8	17	..	Germany	50	4	38	58	10	Pakistan	37	52	19	30	5
Aotearoa/N. Z.	50	10	25	65	7	Ghana	47	59	13	28	..	Palestine	..	12	39	50	12
Argentina	40	12	32	55	16	Greece	43	23	27	50	10	Panama	42	26	16	58	14
Armenia	49	18	43	39	..	Guatemala	36	52	17	30	..	Papua N. Gui.	49	..	..	..	..
Aruba	..	..	..	..	7	Guinea	48	87	2	11	..	Paraguay	37	39	22	39	8
Australia	51	6	26	68	8	Guinea-Bissau	47	85	2	13	..	Peru	37	36	18	47	8
Austria	..	40	8	38	55	Guyana	43	22	25	53	..	Philippines	42	46	15	39	7
Azerbaijan	44	31	29	40	1	Haiti	44	68	9	23	..	Poland	51	27	36	37	11
Bahamas	54	5	15	79	11	Honduras	37	41	20	39	3	Portugal	50	18	34	48	8
Bahrain	..	20	2	30	68	Hungary	48	15	38	47	9	Puerto Rico	37	..	..	..	14
Bangladesh	51	65	16	18	..	Iceland	56	11	27	63	4	Qatar	55	3	32	65	..
Barbados	53	7	23	70	20	India	44	64	16	20	..	Romania	47	24	47	29	6
Belarus	52	20	40	40	3	Indonesia	48	55	14	31	4	Russia	53	14	42	45	11
Belgium	41	3	28	70	9	Iran	30	32	25	43	..	Rwanda	54	..	..	..	..
Belize	34	34	19	48	14	Iraq	27	16	18	66	..	Saudi Arabia	33	..	..	..	..
Benin	45	64	8	28	..	Ireland	41	14	29	57	10	Senegal	45	77	8	16	..
Bhutan	48	94	1	5	..	Israel	43	4	29	67	8	Sierra Leone	37	67	15	17	..
Bolivia	40	47	18	36	4	Italy	44	9	31	60	13	Singapore	50	0	36	64	2
Bosnia-Herzeg.	46	..	..	..	..	Jamaica	52	25	23	52	16	Slovakia	54	12	33	55	12
Botswana	44	46	20	33	22	Japan	54	7	34	59	3	Slovenia	50	6	46	48	7
Brazil	46	23	23	54	7	Jordan	29	23	15	23	61	Solomon Is.	51	77	7	16	..
Brunei	44	2	24	74	..	Kazakhstan	48	22	32	46	4	Somalia	43	..	..	..	..
Bulgaria	51	13	48	38	14	Kenya	51	80	7	13	..	South Africa	39	14	32	55	5
Burkina Faso	50	92	2	6	..	Korea, North	53	38	32	30	..	Spain	44	12	33	55	21
Burundi	54	92	3	6	..	Korea, South	50	18	35	47	3	Sri Lanka	43	49	21	31	11
Cambodia	52	74	8	19	..	Kuwait	39	1	25	74	..	St Lucia	..	..	..	..	16
Cameroon	41	70	9	21	..	Kyrgyzstan	43	32	27	41	..	Sudan	39	69	8	22	..
Canada	54	3	25	71	9	Laos	..	78	6	16	..	Suriname	37	21	18	61	11
Cape Verde	40	31	30	40	..	Latvia	54	16	40	44	14	Swaziland	36	39	22	38	..
Cayman Is.	..	..	..	..	6	Lebanon	34	7	31	62	..	Sweden	54	4	30	66	8
Cent. Afric. R.	..	3	16	..	..	Lesotho	41	40	28	32	..	Switzerland	54	6	35	60	4
Chad	48	83	4	13	..	Liberia	41	..	..	..	..	Syria	31	33	24	43	
Chile	40	19	25	56	5	Libya	29	11	23	66	..	Tajikistan	38	41	23	36	3
China	60	72	15	13	3	Lithuania	52	18	41	41	7	Tanzania	51	84	5	11	..
Colombia	43	27	23	50	12	Luxembourg	43	4	27	69	3	Thailand	60	64	14	22	1
Comoros	45	77	9	13	..	Maced. TFYR	46	22	40	38	39	Togo	41	66	10	24	..
Congo D.R.	42	68	13	19	..	Madagascar	47	78	7	15	..	T. and Tobago	44	..	..	..	16
Congo R.	41	49	15	37	..	Malawi	48	87	5	8	..	Tunisia	39	28	33	39	..
Costa Rica	40	26	27	47	6	Malaysia	41	27	23	50	3	Turkey	47	54	18	28	6
Côte d'Ivoire	40	60	10	30	..	Maldives	41	32	31	37	..	Turkmenistan	43	37	23	40	..
Croatia	47	16	34	50	..	Mali	49	86	2	12	..	Uganda	49	85	5	11	..
Cuba	49	18	30	51	..	Malta	38	3	35	63	5	Ukraine	50	20	40	40	9
Cyprus	48	14	30	56	3	Mauritania	46	55	10	34	..	U. A. Emirates	50	8	27	65	..
Czech Republic	56	11	45	43	5	Mauritius	43	17	43	40	10	United Kingdom	50	2	29	69	7
Denmark	56	6	28	66	5	Mexico	40	28	24	48	4	United States	51	3	26	71	5
Dominican Rep.	43	25	29	46	16	Moldova	50	3	30	37	1	Uruguay	45	14	27	59	10
Ecuador	38	33	19	48	9	Mongolia	49	32	23	45	..	Uzbekistan	42	35	25	40	0
Egypt	37	40	22	38	11	Morocco	39	45	25	31	18	Venezuela	40	12	27	61	10
El Salvador	42	36	21	43	8	Mozambique	52	83	8	9	..	Vietnam	51	71	14	15	..
Equat. Guinea	42	..	..	..	..	Myanmar/Burma	53	73	10	17	..	Virgin Is. (Am.)	..	..	..	..	5
Eritrea	50	80	5	15	..	Namibia	41	49	15	36	..	Yemen	32	61	17	22	..
Estonia	55	14	41	44	10	Nepal	46	94	0	6	..	Yugos. Fed. R.	48	..	..	..	..
Ethiopia	43	86	2	12	..	Netherlands	47	5	26	70	6	Zambia	42	75	8	17	..
Fiji	39	46	15	39	5	Nether. Antilles	45	..	..	..	13	Zimbabwe	46	68	8	24	..
Finland	51	8	31	61	14	Nicaragua	40	29	26	45	..						
France	45	5	29	66	12	Niger	47	90	4	6	..						

Sources: Human Development Report 1998, UNDP, 1998; World Development Indicators 2000, World Bank, 2000.

NEVER HAS HUMANITY had more scientific and technical achievements within its grasp - but never have issues of environmental and food pollution been raised as widely and seriously as they are now. For while cultural, medical and health improvements have helped prolong active human lives, we are witnessing a deterioration in the living conditions of broad sectors of the population.

Tainted food

Humans, slowly and laboriously, learned to use containers for food. The basic design specification for a container was that it reliably contain food without affecting the contents.

Whether dealing with receptacles made of stone or leather, wood or glass, the packaging basically had to preserve the qualities of the contents, or even to improve them - whether it be water stored in obsidian (because minerals with silica were highly prized; and modern research recommends the presence of silicate salts in mineral water), or wine in oak casks. With this, tannins from the wood enhance the fermented grape juice. Heart specialists now recognise the benefits of these substances.

In the 20th century, the increasingly mass production of food led to the creation of new containers, distinguished by their industrial origin and their wide distribution. For instance, the United States of the 1930s spawned the eruption of tinned food, revolutionizing storage and provision for supplying the cities.

However, canned food may contain ten times more lead than average foods, from the solder used to seal the tins. And so this useful invention has a major drawback which is why we should not live on a daily diet of tinned food.

Plastic packaging also has disadvantages and on an incomparably larger scale. Some plastics contain pathogens and since plastic packaging is universal, many people are likely to be affected. What is of concern is that toxins can migrate from the plastic into the food itself.

This problem of toxic migrations has not been handled well by the food and packaging industry. Rather than address the issue at source and redirect the search toward inert packaging - a course of action which prioritises human health - the entrepreneurs have taken a second route, one characteristic of Western industrial civilisation. They have tried to work out how much of this contamination can be ingested before the consumer is patently endangered by these foods. Hence the PADI (Packaging Acceptable Daily Intake) levels. In this way, they have turned the problem to their advantage, with the adjective acceptable showing the way of thinking.

Just one characteristic of plastic is the source of most of its food toxicity. It is very sensitive to heat and, both in the production and sealing of packaging - where heat is a decisive factor - the plastic undergoes powerful molecular transformations with the resulting passage of tiny harmful plastic substances into the food.

The situation is even worse in packaging made of soft plastic materials, because the softening substances, generally *ptalates*, are particularly toxic and in this case carcinogenic.

Methods of preservation

People have been preserving foods since time immemorial. Given the obvious impossibility of always eating fresh foods, they have developed different techniques for preservation such as desiccation, salting, preservation in sugar, drying, smoking, cooking and freezing.

With the development of chemical products, a series of artificial preservatives arose. These were generally easy to use, and widely available. Initially, the aim of the food chemists was to find preservation methods suitable for the mass consumption in cities. These preservatives and colorants, known as food additives, share a unique characteristic among those ingredients which form part of the human diet: many of them are known to be toxic.

Their use is managed in the same way as the packaging intake. A limit is established above which ingestion of these substances is considered undesirable and dangerous - but at the same time ingestion below the limit is considered safe. In the jargon of their creators, this sacred limit also has a name: ALARA (As Low As Reasonably Achievable). As can be seen from that acronym, the limit does not establish criteria for health or toxicity but rather for commercial convenience.

The same treatment was given to other chemical additives including sweeteners (see box), gelling agents, aromatizers, flavour enhancers, colorants, antioxidants, acidifiers, thickeners, emulsifiers, anti-caking and aerating agents, and stabilisers. These are augmented by those not arising from mass food production but from earlier stages in the cycle - food growing. Here a cocktail of agrochemicals, insecticides, nematocides, mite killers, rodent poisons, pesticides, herbicides, as well as fertilizers, hormones and antibiotics are used - the latter fed to animals consumed by people.

The other modern preservation method is ionising irradiation. Foods thus treated no longer rot, they do not germinate, they lose all their bacterial flora and fauna (both bad and good). They are left as if they were everlasting fruits.

It is known that excessive irradiation changes the taste of food. And, of course, no one has been able to establish safe limits for this.

But the most significant element is, once again, the reasoning behind the new technique. "The aim (is) to extend shelf life", states a report from the 1989 Argentine National Commission for Atomic Energy. While extending the duration of fresh foods may sound convincing, the commercial aspect is uppermost where this technique is concerned.

This concern with the commercial is a common pattern running through the latest methods of chemical or radiation preservation, and it marks the distinction from classic methods of preservation: in the past, the aim was to prevent loss of food; now the aim is to prevent the loss of money, to maximise profits.

The Green Revolution

The end of World War II left many wartime research laboratories short of plans for the future. Enormous funds dedicated to the discovery of the most diverse bacterial weapons, to biological warfare, were coming to an end. The big laboratories took new paths, seeking new enemies, and Nature in the forms less desirable to humans provided new targets: parasites, predators and weeds. The chemicals underpinned the so-called green revolution.

The bellicose, aggressive nature of the new products showed in the trademark names used to market these agrochemicals in the United States: Round-up, Machete, Lasso, Pentagon, Prowl, Cetro, Squadron, Cadre, Lightning, Avenge, and the more recent One shot.

Traditional crop yields increased, but the true cost of the change appears increasingly excessive: the marginalisation of the smallest productive units and expulsion of the rural population, contamination of the soils, rivers and lakes, to the point where all the oceans are now tainted with pesticide and fertiliser run-off. The occupational illnesses of those working with agrotoxics have reached chilling figures at hundreds of thousands of victims each year.

Genetic engineering

The principle of transgenics consists of the implanting of one or more genes from one species into another in order to transfer desired attributes to specimens of the recipient species. For example, resistance to a pesticide or the incorporation of more desirable flavors

A = Food production per capita index (1989-91=100), 1997   **B** = Food imports (as % of merchandise imports), 1997   **C** = Cereal imports (metric tons), 1998

COUNTRY	A	B	C	COUNTRY	A	B	C	COUNTRY	A	B	C
Afghanistan	..	..	242,079	Georgia	73	..	423,097	Oman	101	17	509,292
Albania	..	27	278,067	Germany	93	9	2,672,677	Pakistan	134	19	2,527,375
Algeria	108	32	6,291,538	Ghana	148	..	458,995	Panama	103	10	371,387
Angola	133	..	445,255	Greece	96	15	1,220,578	Papua N.Guinea	107	..	320,101
Antigua	95	..	4,847	Greenland	..	..	2,503	Paraguay	119	21	141,669
Aotearoa/N.Z.	124	8	193,206	Grenada	96	26	28,184	Peru	139	14	2,797,788
Argentina	127	5	43,179	Guadeloupe	..	..	0	Philippines	123	8	4,569,803
Armenia	84	..	224,780	Guam	..	..	11,989	Poland	80	8	1,405,168
Aruba	..	..	10,959	Guatemala	118	13	702,649	Portugal	102	13	3,129,152
Australia	129	5	40,357	Guinea	133	..	288,179	Qatar	137	..	166,445
Austria	98	6	427,767	Guinea-Bissau	112	..	69,947	Réunion	..	..	0
Azerbaijan	58	..	655,321	Guyana	185	..	55,000	Romania	105	6	215,856
Bahamas	123	..	13,564	Haiti	92	..	481,009	Russia	71	19	2,016,659
Bahrain	117	12	185,080	Honduras	110	18	162,493	Rwanda	81	..	195,716
Bangladesh	111	17	3,684,072	Hungary	81	5	61,079	Samoa	94	..	17,489
Barbados	109	18	65,753	Iceland	93	10	60,789	Samoa, Amer.	..	..	5,084
Belarus	59	..	1,597,200	India	119	5	2,224,190	S. Tomé and Prínc.	122	..	9,445
Belize	148	20	19,220	Indonesia	124	9	2,691,499	Saudi Arabia	90	18	7,293,459
Benin	127	..	123,870	Iran	136	..	6,339,974	Senegal	112	..	856,168
Bermuda	..	..	2,434	Iraq	90	..	3,455,169	Seychelles	141	20	17,450
Bhutan	107	..	51,787	Ireland	108	8	719,451	Sierra Leone	97	..	311,529
Bolivia	134	9	194,421	Israel	116	7	2,734,762	Singapore	35	4	..
Bosnia-Herz.	..	..	422,516	Italy	97	11	..	Slovakia	73	8	107,308
Botswana	102	..	125,718	Jamaica	119	15	470,729	Slovenia	103	7	399,170
Brazil	128	9	10,013,807	Japan	96	15	26,996,997	Solomon Is.	107	16	31,342
Brunei	100	..	35,297	Jordan	151	..	1,766,139	Somalia	..	..	127,638
Bulgaria	59	..	54,646	Kanaky/N. Caled.	..	..	37,487	South Africa	100	6	1,316,828
Burkina Faso	123	..	202,113	Kazakhstan	72	..	18,591	Spain	104	12	6,708,592
Burundi	96	..	17,428	Kenya	105	17	931,998	Sri Lanka	115	..	1,131,842
Cambodia	126	..	38,455	Kiribati	..	..	10,458	St Helena	..	..	533
Cameroon	119	14	404,656	Korea, North	..	..	1,078,085	St Kitts-Nevis	127	19	4,180
Canada	113	6	1,644,422	Korea, South	123	6	11,993,181	St Lucia	75	26	20,068
Cape Verde	96	..	82,613	Kuwait	157	16	699,307	St Pierre and Miq.	..	..	1,038
Cayman Is.	..	..	905	Kyrgyzstan	124	21	154,532	St Vincent	81	..	31,268
Cent. African Rep.	124	12	41,883	Laos	113	..	100,104	Sudan	146	17	758,790
Chad	119	..	48,348	Latvia	45	13	49,862	Suriname	86	..	54,918
Chile	131	7	1,399,271	Lebanon	119	..	647,704	Swaziland	93	..	52,900
China	163	5	9,993,719	Lesotho	101	..	213,880	Sweden	97	7	211,917
Colombia	111	11	3,689,535	Liberia	..	..	204,471	Switzerland	96	6	360,027
Comoros	118	..	41,407	Libya	101	..	1,993,860	Syria	133	..	597,845
Congo D.R.	104	..	572,800	Lithuania	74	11	69,649	Tajikistan	68	..	..
Congo R.	116	..	210,779	Maced., TFYR	96	..	554,046	Tanzania	94	..	361,779
Cook Is.	..	..	924	Madagascar	107	15	148,298	Thailand	107	5	1,016,104
Costa Rica	130	13	594,977	Malawi	100	..	208,558	Togo	138	..	134,403
Côte d'Ivoire	115	17	824,434	Malaysia	127	5	3,569,469	Tonga	..	..	8,333
Croatia	59	10	65,320	Maldives	113	..	31,369	T. and Tobago	111	10	232,915
Cuba	64	..	1,592,794	Mali	127	..	115,437	Tunisia	105	11	1,953,172
Cyprus	107	27	626,557	Malta	136	11	173,755	Turkey	105	5	2,970,779
Czech Republic	81	7	328,324	Martinique	..	..	0	Turkmenistan	99	..	755,159
Denmark	102	13	554,748	Mauritania	105	..	801,448	Tuvalu	..	..	1,522
Djibouti	83	..	89,936	Mauritius	109	15	267,100	Uganda	110	..	138,400
Dominica	80	28	9,714	Mexico	120	6	11,621,226	Ukraine	68	..	201,907
Dominican Rep.	113	..	946,806	Micronesia	..	..	13,973	U. Arab Emirates	190	..	1,658,261
Ecuador	137	9	1,000,748	Moldova	57	..	80,584	United Kingdom	99	9	3,230,008
Egypt	133	26	10,589,395	Mongolia	82	14	91,633	United States	117	5	5,369,597
El Salvador	112	17	355,710	Montserrat	..	..	2,184	Uruguay	136	10	125,009
Equatorial Guinea	98	..	..	Morocco	95	17	3,340,314	Uzbekistan	96	..	1,564,893
Eritrea	107	..	323,813	Mozambique	133	22	523,317	Vanuatu	103	..	11,445
Estonia	48	16	156,111	Myanmar/Burma	131	..	69,771	Venezuela	121	16	2,347,907
Ethiopia	..	..	580,920	Namibia	126	..	68,000	Vietnam	135	..	697,580
Faeroe Is.	..	..	2,216	Nepal	116	14	37,973	Virgin Is. (Br.)	..	..	278
Fiji	108	..	113,445	Netherlands	108	11	5,818,419	Wall. and Futu. Is.	..	..	1,292
Finland	94	7	393,297	Nether. Antilles	..	..	195,155	Yemen	121	..	2,554,262
France	105	10	1,444,828	Nicaragua	128	14	180,724	Yugoslavia F. R.	..	..	342,708
French Guiana	..	..	0	Niger	121	..	98,798	Zambia	94	..	367,024
French Polynesia	..	..	36,024	Nigeria	136	..	2,955,325	Zimbabwe	106	7	294,435
Gabon	107	19	110,582	Norfolk Is.	..	..	118				
Gambia	84	..	127,690	Norway	100	7	441,719				

Sources: Human Development Report 1999, UNDP, 1999; FAO Statistical Data Base, FAOSTAT - Web Site.

(olive in rape for example). The same company may control all aspects of the operation, as with RR soy: the same company sells the genetically manipulated seeds and the pesticide.

In the transgenic process agents penetrate cell tissues carrying the foreign genes. These vehicles are pathogenic agents, specialists in this task. The method has been questioned by researchers such as Dr. Mae-Wan Ho, precisely because they introduce pathogenic factors which could become active at some future date.

Transgenics could bring with them a chain of modifications and even mutations as the action of genes may not only depend on characteristics isolated in laboratories but, for example, their relative position in chains of DNA. It is precisely these unforeseen modifications which form the basis of arguments by scientists sceptical of, or opposed to, genetically modified foods. Strictly speaking, the transgenic technique is as rigorously mechanistic as that postulated by Descartes in his clock analogy (see Science p 44). The name itself reveals this.

Dominant agricultural techniques aim to industrialise agriculture. But, what exactly is an industry of something? The nature of an industry is based on the production of identical units of an inert material, where the rendering uniform of measures and characteristics permits an extremely high level of productivity. Success in producing tiles or screws lies in them all being the same; any industry which does not fulfil this requisite would be failing.

But with living produce, with plants and animals, it is a different question because living organisms have what is called biological diversity. This is why we have different faces and fingers, different eyes, meaning we cannot be confused. The same applies to tomatoes, to basil plants, lambs and grains of corn.

The conceit of treating food industrially does away with a fundamental trait of plants and animals: the vital individuality, etymological indivisibility - this is the key characteristic of all living things that genetic engineering destroys.

Enormous transgenic salmon have been created, and their impressive size gives them preferential chances for reproduction as the females tend to go for the bigger males. This means that when the eggs are laid, the transgenic salmon are responsible for most of the offspring. But for a reason unknown by those dedicated to this engineering game, transgenic salmon have extremely short life spans. Estimates show that within tens of generations, any salmon population receiving the input from genetically modified individuals will become extinct.

So where does the faith of the technological optimists stem from? In material terms, certainly, it comes from the big transnational corporations and their bottomless funds, and they drive this research strictly for profit, but, there is another current.

Another eco-schizophrenia

There were always those who enjoyed abundant food whilst others died from lack of it: first class and second class foods. Agrotoxics and transgenic techniques appear to have simply exacerbated the gap between haves and have-nots.

"For, while advertising tries to persuade people that state-of-the-art technological foods are the best, the most modern, what they should be eating, the producers of such foods are saving a different diet for themselves. We currently have farmers, market gardeners, food producers, owners of large-scale orchards who would never consider eating their own produce. We are lucky, they say, that we have enough money to buy produce grown organically, without the use of poisons".

This quote, from E F Schumacher (in *Small is Beautiful*) dates from the 1970s. Today representatives of large rural unions say the same about the genetically modified products they have no problem at all in producing.

We are currently being offered increasingly processed foods, ever further from the freshness claimed in the advertisements. This diet is based on products increased in size artificially with chemicals or through specifically designed feeding, but which do not seem healthy. The question is: how long before this affects our health? It seems impossible that this increasingly unnatural path will lead to better health. ∎

HEALTH IN FIGURES

A = Doctors per 100,000 people, 1993*
B = Nurses per 100,000 people, 1993*

COUNTRY	A	B	COUNTRY	A	B
Albania	141	423	Kuwait	178	468
Algeria	83	..	Kyrgyzstan	310	879
Antigua	76	233	Latvia	303	628
Aotearoa/N.Z.	210	1,249	Lebanon	191	122
Argentina	268	54	Lesotho	5	33
Armenia	312	831	Libya	137	366
Austria	327	530	Lithuania	399	977
Azerbaijan	390	1,081	Luxembourg	213	..
Bahamas	141	258	Macedonia, TFYR	219	334
Bahrain	11	289	Madagascar	24	55
Bangladesh	18	5	Malawi	2	6
Barbados	113	323	Malaysia	43	160
Belarus	379	1,16	Maldives	19	13
Belgium	365	..	Mali	4	9
Belize	47	76	Malta	250	1,189
Benin	6	33	Mauritania	11	27
Bhutan	20	6	Mauritius	85	241
Bolivia	51	25	Mexico	107	40
Brazil	134	41	Moldova	356	1,02
Bulgaria	333	652	Mongolia	268	452
Burundi	6	17	Morocco	34	94
Cambodia	58	136	Myanmar/Burma	28	43
Cameroon	7	..	Namibia	23	81
Canada	221	958	Nepal	5	5
Cape Verde	29	57	Nicaragua	82	56
Central African Rep.	6	45	Niger	3	17
Chad	2	6	Nigeria	21	142
Chile	108	42	Oman	120	290
China	115	88	Pakistan	52	32
Colombia	105	49	Panama	119	98
Comoros	10	33	Papua New Guinea	18	97
Congo R.	27	49	Paraguay	67	10
Costa Rica	126	95	Peru	73	49
Croatia	201	470	Philippines	11	43
Cuba	518	752	Portugal	291	304
Cyprus	231	425	Qatar	143	354
Czech Republic	293	944	Romania	176	430
Denmark	283	..	Russia	380	659
Djibouti	20	..	Samoa	38	186
Dominica	46	263	São Tomé and Príncipe	32	..
Dominican Republic	77	20	Saudi Arabia	166	348
Ecuador	111	34	Senegal	7	35
Egypt	202	222	Seychelles	104	417
El Salvador	91	38	Singapore	147	416
Equatorial Guinea	21	34	Slovakia	325	..
Eritrea	2	..	Slovenia	219	686
Estonia	312	636	Solomon Is.	..	141
Ethiopia	4	8	South Africa	59	175
Fiji	38	215	Spain	400	..
Finland	269	2,184	Sri Lanka	23	112
France	280	392	St Kitts-Nevis	89	590
Gabon	19	56	St Lucia	35	177
Gambia	2	25	St Vincent	46	187
Georgia	436	863	Sudan	10	70
Germany	319	..	Suriname	40	227
Ghana	4	..	Sweden	299	1,048
Greece	387	278	Switzerland	301	..
Grenada	50	239	Syria	109	212
Guatemala	90	30	Tajikistan	210	738
Guinea	15	3	Tanzania	4	46
Guinea-Bissau	18	45	Thailand	24	99
Guyana	33	88	Togo	6	31
Haiti	16	13	Trinidad and Tobago	90	168
Honduras	22	17	Tunisia	67	283
Hungary	337	..	Turkey	103	151
India	48	..	Turkmenistan	353	1,195
Indonesia	12	67	Uganda	4	28
Iraq	51	64	Ukraine	429	1,211
Ireland	167	..	United Arab Emirates	168	321
Israel	459	671	United Kingdom	164	..
Jamaica	57	69	United States	245	878
Japan	177	641	Uruguay	309	61
Jordan	158	224	Uzbekistan	335	1,032
Kazakhstan	360	874	Venezuela	194	77
Kenya	15	23	Yemen	26	51
Korea, South	127	232	Zimbabwe	14	164

* Latest available data   Source: Human Development Report 1999, UNDP, 1999.

THE WORD infant (infans) means "he/she who has no voice". In fact, until the beginning of the twentieth century, children in many cultures were not even named until they were five years old. This was due to the uncertainty on the part of their parents and the community as to whether they would survive or not. Lacking a name, they could not be considered subjects.

Mortgaging the future

This situation seemed to have turned around, at least at the level of discourse, during the twentieth century. The 1924 Geneva Declaration on Children's Rights reflected this change by stating the need to offer special protection to minors. On 20 November 1959 the UN General Assembly recognized this declaration in the comprehensive Universal Declaration of Human Rights, the International Covenant of Political and Civil Rights, the International Covenant of Economic, Social and Cultural Rights, as well as in the relevant instruments and statutes of specialized agencies and international organizations interested in promoting the welfare of children. Finally, in 1989, almost all of the countries in the world signed and ratified the first legally binding international accord to incorporate an impressive array of human rights: civil, political, economic, social and cultural: The UN Convention on the Rights of the Child.

Declaration and realities
According to the Convention, all children the world over should be protected by law and so have the right to survival, to a full development, to protection against harmful influences, mistreatment and exploitation, and to participate fully in family, cultural and social life. The Convention stipulated specific measures related to health care, education and access to legal, social and civic services for children which were incorporated into the human development indicators collated by the United Nations Development Program (UNDP). According to what was signed, the states bound by the Convention have to establish and implement all measures and policies according to the superior interest of children.

One could argue that recognizing an illness is the first step towards trying to cure it, and by the same token, that to declare something as a right is also a necessary step towards its becoming a reality. In spite of this, the situation is that children are the ones who suffer most from hunger, displacement, slavery and exploitation. The Convention on children's rights established in 1989 that "the child, due to his/her lack of mental and physical maturity, needs special care and protection, including the proper legal protection, before and

after birth". The truth is that even today, hundreds of millions of children suffer all kinds of abuses of their rights.

Wars and children
Even though almost all of the world's countries have signed the children's rights Convention, the fact is that since it was written and signed, the impact of war on children has increased. According to a United Nations report, two million children died since then and another six million were left permanently disabled or seriously injured.

In addition, children not only make up 50 per cent of war refugees but they have become involuntary soldiers: some 300,000 minors are recruited as active combatants by rebel groups and armies, particularly in Africa and Asia. To make things worse, children are often the main targets of war. Many are used as mine sweepers, spies and for kamikaze attacks, besides taking part in other war related "chores" as cooks, messengers and lookouts.

Even more crudely, in many cases children fall victim to adults who want to eliminate the next generation of potential enemies. As it happens, a high percentage of states which have ratified the Convention are responsible for these abuses since children suffer the consequences of armed conflict in some 50 countries.

In addition, besides the wars which have left millions of orphaned children (who in turn have experienced permanent traumas caused by events they have seen or been involved in), the UN sanctions (as in the case of former Yugoslavia or Iraq) have also directly affected the most vulnerable population: children.

Work, slavery and prostitution
At least a million of the planet's children are forced into prostitution. Two thirds of them are in Asia and the rest in Europe and Latin America. However these numbers which are impressive per se, pale in comparison with the 400 million children who are forced to work full or part-time.

According to International Labour Organization (ILO) figures, more than 120 million 5-14 year-old Asian children work full time and another 250 million work part-time.

The mass publicity around issues of sex tourism and abuse have obscured the roots of the problem of child labour. In most cases, child labour is a direct result of socio-economic hardship. As a result the implementation of structural adjustment programs (SAPs) drawn up by organizations like the IMF or the World Bank for Southern countries have resulted in an increase in child labour.

Out of 400 million working children, 61 per cent are in Asia (mainly in South Asia) where they work in mines, plantations and brothels), 32 per cent in Africa and 7 per cent in Latin America. Some 250 million of these children work under conditions of "exploitation".

According to the International Labour Office (ILO), 128 million children of primary school age do not have access to any form of education. Without access to school, a great number of children are forced into work to contribute to their household and lose their opportunities of better employment in the future. Here one can also see how the increase in child labour, a result of extreme poverty, is a consequence of public spending cuts and measures imposed by international financial institutions on societies which cannot redistribute wealth and whose governments have dedicated themselves to rapidly privatising all sectors of the economy including education.

Children and the future
As has been noted, children have had a voice during the 20th century through institutions which have spoken on their behalf, to fight for their rights. Unfortunately, the facts show that despite that, a great number of the world's children are far from receiving even the most elementary rights granted them by the different institutional charters.

Lacking education and forced to work - these violations of their basic rights mean that in the immediate future tomorrow's adults will not be allowed to achieve, within their respective societies, even a minimum of social mobility. Neglected by their governments and their societies, they are doomed to be marginalized forever, especially as they are living in an age in which information becomes increasingly important.

The problem, which could be limited to some societies in particular, takes on a new dimension if it is seen from a global perspective. While it is the great majority of Southern countries that suffer from growing child poverty, it is the financial institutions guided by policies defined in the North which must carry major responsibility for this neglect. Nonetheless some Southern coun-

tries are as much to blame as their counterparts to the North for their contradictions regarding their children. For at the same time as paying lip-service to commitments such as the Convention, economic steps were being taken which had dire consequences for children of the South.

This hypocritical stance of governments directly affects children and also has a bear-

ing on the inmediate future, since the planet's next decades rest on these children. For a world which cannot protect its children is simply mortgaging its future. ∎

HEALTH SERVICES

A = % OF POPULATION WITH ACCESS TO SAFE WATER, 1990-98
B = % OF POPULATION WITH ACCESS TO HEALTH SERVICES, 1990-96

	A	B		A	B
Afghanistan	6	29	Liberia	46	39
Algeria	90	98	Libya	97	95
Angola	31	..	Madagascar	40	38
Aotearoa/New Zealand	97	..	Malawi	47	35
Argentina	71	71	Malaysia	78	..
Bahamas	94	..	Maldives	60	..
Bahrain	94	..	Mali	66	40
Bangladesh	95	45	Marshall Is.	82	..
Barbados	100	..	Mauritania	37	63
Belize	83	..	Mauritius	98	100
Benin	56	18	Mexico	85	93
Bhutan	58	65	Micronesia	22	..
Bolivia	80	67	Moldova	55	..
Botswana	90	..	Mongolia	45	95
Brazil	76	..	Morocco	65	70
Burkina Faso	42	90	Mozambique	46	39
Burundi	52	80	Myanmar/Burma	60	60
Cambodia	30	53	Namibia	83	59
Cameroon	54	80	Nepal	71	..
Cape Verde	65	..	Nicaragua	78	83
Central African Rep.	38	52	Niger	61	99
Chad	54	30	Nigeria	49	51
Chile	91	97	Niue	100	..
China	67	88	Oman	85	96
Colombia	85	81	Pakistan	79	55
Comoros	53	..	Palau	88	..
Congo D.R.	42	26	Panama	93	70
Congo R.	34	83	Papua New Guinea	41	96
Cook Is.	95	..	Paraguay	60	63
Costa Rica	96	..	Peru	67	44
Côte d'Ivoire	42	..	Philippines	85	71
Cuba	93	100	Rwanda	..	80
Cyprus	100	..	Samoa	68	..
Djibouti	90	..	São Tomé and Príncipe	82	..
Dominica	96	..	Saudi Arabia	95	97
Dominican Republic	79	78	Senegal	81	90
Ecuador	68	..	Sierra Leone	34	38
Egypt	87	99	Singapore	100	..
El Salvador	66	40	Somalia	31	..
Equatorial Guinea	95	..	South Africa	87	..
Eritrea	22	..	Sri Lanka	57	..
Ethiopia	25	46	St Kitts-Nevis	100	..
Fiji	77	..	St Lucia	85	..
Gabon	67	..	St Vincent	89	..
Gambia	69	93	Sudan	73	70
Ghana	65	60	Swaziland	50	..
Guatemala	68	57	Syria	86	90
Guinea	46	80	Tajikistan	60	..
Guinea-Bissau	43	40	Tanzania	66	42
Guyana	91	..	Thailand	81	90
Haiti	37	60	Togo	55	..
Honduras	78	69	Tonga	95	..
India	81	85	Trinidad and Tobago	97	100
Indonesia	74	93	Tunisia	98	..
Iran	95	88	Turkey	49	..
Iraq	81	93	Turkmenistan	74	100
Jamaica	86	90	Tuvalu	100	..
Japan	97	..	Uganda	46	49
Jordan	97	97	United Arab Emirates	97	99
Kazakhstan	93	..	Uruguay	..	82
Kenya	44	77	Uzbekistan	90	..
Korea, North	100	..	Vanuatu	77	..
Korea, South	93	100	Venezuela	79	..
Kuwait	..	100	Vietnam	45	90
Kyrgyzstan	79	..	Yemen	61	38
Laos	44	67	Yugoslavia Fed. Rep.	76	..
Lebanon	94	95	Zambia	38	..
Lesotho	62	80	Zimbabwe	79	85

Source: The State of the World's Children 2000, UNICEF, 2000; The State of the World's Children 1997, UNICEF, 1997.

A = Births attended by health personnel (%), 1990-99*
B = Life expectancy at birth (years), 1998
C = % of low birth weight babies (2,500 g), 1990, 1997*
D = Infant mortality (per 1,000 live births), 1998
E = Underweight children under-5, (%), 1990-98*
F = Maternal mortality (per 100,000 live births), 1990-98*

COUNTRIES	A	B	C	D	E	F	COUNTRIES	A	B	C	D	E	F	COUNTRIES	A	B	C	D	E	F
Afghanistan	8	46	20	165	48	..	Georgia	..	73	..	19	..	70	Niue	99	..	..	..	..	..
Albania	99	73	7	30	..	..	Germany	100	77	..	5	..	8	Norway	100	78	4	4	..	6
Algeria	77	69	9	35	13	220	Ghana	39	60	8	67	27	210	Oman	91	71	8	15	23	19
Andorra	..	..	..	5	..	..	Greece	99	78	6	6	..	1	Pakistan	18	64	25	95	38	..
Angola	..	47	19	170	42	..	Grenada	99	72	9	23	..	0	Palau	99	..	8	28	..	..
Antigua	100	76	8	17	10	150	Guatemala	35	64	15	41	27	190	Panama	86	74	8	18	7	85
Aotearoa/N.Z.	95	77	6	5	..	15	Guinea	31	47	13	124	..	670	Papua N. Guin.	53	58	23	79	30	370
Argentina	97	73	7	19	..	38	Guinea-Bissau	25	45	20	130	23	910	Paraguay	61	70	5	27	4	190
Armenia	96	71	7	25	..	35	Guyana	95	65	15	58	12	190	Peru	56	68	11	43	8	270
Australia	100	78	6	5	..	..	Haiti	21	54	15	91	28	..	Philippines	56	68	9	32	28	170
Austria	100	77	6	5	..	..	Honduras	55	70	9	33	18	220	Poland	99	73	..	10	..	8
Azerbaijan	99	70	6	36	10	37	Hungary	99	71	9	10	2	15	Portugal	98	75	5	8	..	8
Bahamas	100	74	..	18	..	..	Iceland	100	79	..	5	..	..	Qatar	98	72	..	15	6	10
Bahrain	98	73	6	16	9	46	India	34	63	33	69	53	410	Romania	99	70	7	21	6	41
Bangladesh	8	58	50	79	56	440	Indonesia	43	65	8	40	34	450	Russia	99	67	6	21	3	50
Barbados	100	76	10	13	5	0	Iran	86	69	10	29	16	37	Rwanda	26	41	17	105	27	..
Belarus	100	68	..	22	..	22	Iraq	54	63	15	103	23	..	Samoa	76	71	6	22	..	..
Belgium	100	77	6	6	..	..	Ireland	100	76	4	6	..	6	San Marino	..	..	..	6	..	..
Belize	77	75	4	35	6	140	Israel	99	78	7	6	..	5	S. Tomé and Prín.	86	64	7	60	16	..
Benin	60	53	..	101	29	500	Italy	100	78	5	6	..	7	Saudi Arabia	90	72	7	22	..	..
Bhutan	15	61	..	84	38	380	Jamaica	95	75	10	10	10	120	Senegal	47	53	4	70	22	560
Bolivia	59	62	5	66	10	390	Japan	100	80	7	4	..	8	Seychelles	99	71	10	14	6	..
Bosnia-Herz.	97	73	..	16	..	10	Jordan	97	70	10	30	5	41	Sierra Leone	..	38	11	182	29	..
Botswana	78	47	11	38	17	330	Kazakhstan	100	68	9	36	8	70	Singapore	100	77	7	4	..	6
Brazil	92	67	8	36	6	160	Kenya	44	52	16	75	22	590	Slovakia	..	73	..	9	..	9
Brunei	98	76	..	8	..	0	Kiribati	72	60	3	54	13	..	Slovenia	100	74	..	5	..	11
Bulgaria	100	71	6	14	..	15	Korea, North	100	72	..	23	60	110	Solomon Is.	85	72	20	22	21	550
Burkina Faso	27	45	21	109	30	..	Korea, South	98	73	9	5	..	20	Somalia	2	47	16	125	..	..
Burundi	24	43	..	106	37	..	Kuwait	98	76	7	12	6	5	South Africa	82	54	..	60	9	..
Cambodia	31	53	..	104	52	470	Kyrgyzstan	98	68	6	56	11	65	Spain	96	78	4	6	..	6
Cameroon	58	55	13	94	22	430	Laos	14	53	18	96	40	650	Sri Lanka	94	73	25	17	34	60
Canada	100	79	6	6	..	..	Latvia	100	69	..	18	..	45	St Kitts-Nevis	100	70	9	30	..	130
Cape Verde	54	69	9	54	14	55	Lebanon	89	70	10	29	3	100	St Lucia	100	70	8	18	..	30
Cent. Afric. Rep.	46	45	15	113	27	1,100	Lesotho	50	56	11	94	16	..	St Vincent	96	73	8	20	..	43
Chad	15	47	..	118	39	830	Liberia	58	48	..	157	..	..	Sudan	69	55	15	73	34	550
Chile	100	75	5	11	1	23	Libya	94	70	7	20	5	75	Suriname	91	70	13	28	..	110
China	89	70	9	38	16	65	Liechtenstein	..	..	..	10	..	..	Swaziland	56	60	10	64	10	230
Colombia	85	71	9	25	8	80	Lithuania	..	70	..	19	..	18	Sweden	100	79	5	4	..	5
Comoros	52	59	8	67	26	500	Luxembourg	100	77	..	5	..	0	Switzerland	99	79	5	5	..	5
Congo D.R.	..	51	15	128	34	..	Maced., TFYR	95	73	..	23	..	11	Syria	67	69	7	26	13	110
Congo R.	..	49	16	81	17	..	Madagascar	47	58	5	95	40	490	Tajikistan	79	67	..	55	..	65
Cook Is.	99	..	1	26	..	..	Malawi	55	39	20	134	30	620	Tanzania	38	48	14	91	27	530
Costa Rica	98	76	7	14	2	29	Malaysia	99	72	8	9	19	39	Thailand	71	69	6	30	19	44
Côte d'Ivoire	47	47	12	90	24	600	Maldives	90	65	13	62	43	350	Togo	51	49	20	81	25	480
Croatia	..	73	..	8	1	12	Mali	24	54	16	144	40	580	Tonga	92	71	2	19	..	..
Cuba	99	76	7	7	9	27	Malta	98	77	..	6	..	..	Trin. and Tob.	98	74	10	16	7	..
Cyprus	100	78	..	8	..	0	Marshall Is.	..	..	14	63	..	..	Tunisia	81	70	8	25	9	70
Czech Republic	99	74	6	5	1	9	Mauritania	40	54	11	120	23	550	Turkey	81	69	8	37	10	130
Denmark	100	76	6	5	..	10	Mauritius	97	72	13	19	16	50	Turkmenistan	96	66	5	53	..	110
Djibouti	79	51	11	111	18	..	Mexico	68	72	7	28	14	48	Tuvalu	100	..	3	40	..	..
Dominica	98	76	10	17	5	65	Micronesia	90	67	9	20	..	..	Uganda	38	40	13	84	26	510
Dom. Republic	99	71	13	43	6	230	Moldova	..	68	4	28	..	42	Ukraine	100	69	..	18	..	25
Ecuador	64	70	13	30	17	160	Mongolia	100	66	7	105	10	150	U. Arab Emir.	99	75	6	9	14	3
Egypt	56	67	10	51	12	170	Morocco	43	67	9	57	9	230	United Kingdom	98	77	7	6	..	7
El Salvador	87	69	11	30	11	160	Mozambique	44	44	20	129	26	1,100	United States	99	77	7	7	1	8
Equatorial Gui.	5	50	..	108	..	..	Myanmar/Burma	56	60	24	80	39	230	Uruguay	96	74	8	16	5	21
Eritrea	21	51	13	70	44	1,000	Namibia	68	51	16	57	26	230	Uzbekistan	98	68	..	45	19	21
Estonia	..	69	..	18	..	50	Nauru	..	..	..	25	..	..	Vanuatu	79	68	7	38	20	..
Ethiopia	8	43	16	110	48	..	Nepal	9	58	..	72	47	540	Venezuela	..	72	9	21	5	65
Fiji	..	73	12	19	8	38	Netherlands	100	78	..	5	..	7	Vietnam	77	68	17	31	41	160
Finland	100	77	4	4	..	6	Nether. Antilles	..	..	..	..	..	..	Yemen	22	58	19	87	46	350
France	99	78	5	5	..	10	Nicaragua	65	68	9	39	12	150	Yugos. Fed. Rep.	93	73	..	18	2	10
Gabon	80	52	..	85	..	600	Niger	18	49	15	166	50	590	Zambia	47	40	13	112	24	650
Gambia	44	47	..	64	26	..	Nigeria	31	50	16	112	36	..	Zimbabwe	69	44	10	59	15	400

* data refers to the most recent year available during 1990–99.

Source: The State of the World's Children 2000, UNICEF, 2000.

The world according to...

...The World Bank Ranked by income (GNP per capita). See page 53

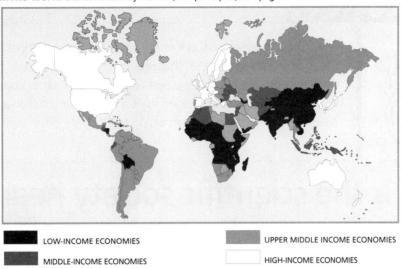

| | LOW-INCOME ECONOMIES | | UPPER MIDDLE INCOME ECONOMIES |
| | MIDDLE-INCOME ECONOMIES | | HIGH-INCOME ECONOMIES |

...UNDP (UN Development Program) Ranked by Human Development Index. See page 58

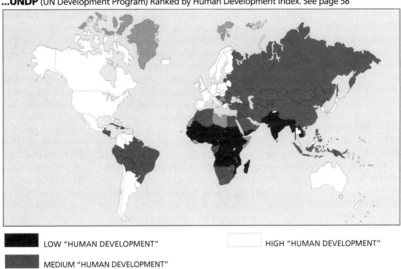

| | LOW "HUMAN DEVELOPMENT" | | HIGH "HUMAN DEVELOPMENT" |
| | MEDIUM "HUMAN DEVELOPMENT" | | |

...UNICEF (UN children's agency) Ranked by under-5 mortality rate. See page 59

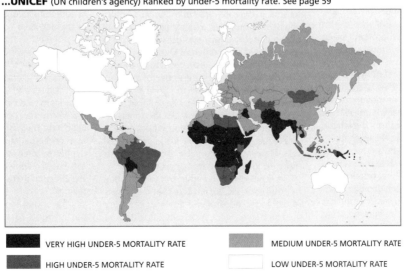

| | VERY HIGH UNDER-5 MORTALITY RATE | | MEDIUM UNDER-5 MORTALITY RATE |
| | HIGH UNDER-5 MORTALITY RATE | | LOW UNDER-5 MORTALITY RATE |

III. Science and technology

Science

SCIENTIFIC development, as it arose within the framework of Western culture, has so permeated the world that present societies have been built on foundations created by that development and structured by its knowledge. This scientific knowledge which helped solve so many human problems has however created others which raise a question mark over where it will end.

Where is the scientific society heading?

The current omnipresence of science immediately presents a problem. Modern scientific thought flourished in the infancy of the modern period - significantly, an era which coincided with the arrival of seaborne Europeans all over the world. This led to the Europeanization of world geography and economy through the twin processes of conquest and colonisation. Science was seen as a key which opened new areas of knowledge in a world where other forms of knowledge already existed, other ways of approaching reality and the position of the human being in nature and the cosmos.

Scientific knowledge demonstrated a great capacity for interpretation and transformation of the reality surrounding the humans themselves. And when this capacity was converted into practical successes, scientific know-how took off down the centuries, displacing and invading other dimensions of the human being.

Defining ethical values, what is beautiful and what ugly, is so arduous a task that it is understandable for people to leave these questions unresolved or, once resolved, for them to be reformulated in such a way that they have to be tackled over and over again. Scientific activity, meanwhile, based on methods developed by its pioneers, Francis Bacon and René Descartes, set out from the simplest problems to conquer vast fields.

Scientific activity has developed to such an extent that in the present cultural milieu science is expected to be the means and medium to solve *all* problems. Thus the scientific has been granted the stature of an absolute, scientific thought has been identified with valid thought, as though science could give us the instruments with which to solve all human problems; from the ethical, political, and existential to the aesthetic.

On being granted the status of absolute knowledge, science was co-opted by the state and, free from political or class trappings, it became the super-ideology legitimizing the exercise of power. Thus the ruling political class often fall back on scientific explanations for their actions. And thence the emergence of experts of all types, whom supposedly "scientifically" dominate each specific area.

The idea of "life" in crisis
What is the difference between a living body and a dead body? French philosopher René Descartes, in Article 6 of "The Passions of the Soul", wrote:

"We consider, then, to avoid this error [that the absence of soul is the cause of the lack of "movement" and "heat"] that death never takes place due to the absence of soul [...] and we think that the body of a living man differs from that of a dead man as a clock would differ [...] when mounted and having in it the bodily principle of the movements for which it was created, having all that necessary for it to function, from the same clock [...] when broken and when the principle of its motion has ceased to act."

The vision of the human being and nature which is summed up in this fragment of Cartesian thought shows another focus of scientific thought which is equally problematic - a focus which over the last centuries made a strong impression on our societies. Here are just two examples: computers and genetic engineering.

For many technicians and specialists, integrated circuits and electronics are bringing us closer to understanding the human brain. They believe that through these increasingly efficient computers, with the binary base which formed a keystone of current development, the human being is no more than copying its own characteristics, in this case those of the brain. Genetic engineering proposes, meanwhile, the creation of chimeras - organisms whose tissues are of two or more genetically different kinds.

So what do Cartesian reasoning on the human body and the clock, the notion of the computer-brain and the urge to create chimeras have in common? Or rather, what is it that none of the three has? They simply lack life, that is all.

For decades biologists, biochemists, geneticists, have been cultivating tissue, molecules, cells, filaments, to *create* life, that is to say, to make living organisms from inert tissue.

It is not certain whether this will one day be possible or not, but it is clear that the living is something so qualitatively dissimilar from the inert, and so complex even in its simplest form, that neither Descartes in the 1600s nor present-day biochemists know more than a tiny fraction of the factors needed for a living organism to exist.

Hence, while Descartes' reductionist pretension can be judged in retrospect as simplistic or foolish, that of the sorcerers' apprentices in present-day laboratories must qualify as pride - one of the seven deadly sins listed by our classical predecessors.

From traditional to modern science
Both Bacon and Descartes developed their trains of thought whilst struggling against the traditional knowledge of their era, in particular the thinking of the Catholic religion, which consisted to a large extent of prejudice and dogma increasingly removed from reality. Human knowledge was in this state when the first exponents of what we call modern thought rebelled. Bacon presented himself as "interpreter" of Nature, instead of accepting the "false idols" of prejudices and so on.

As very often happens, those who have the capacity and feel the need to renew tired contemporary notions produce a change of paradigms which does away with not only the out-dated parts of the old, but also some parts which are still applicable. In this process, modern thought lost its respect for life, indeed the notion of life itself was thrown into question, sifted and substituted with mechanisms.

This is how Carolyn Merchant sums up this change which constituted the mental revolution of modernity, the abandonment of the classical rationalism, imbued with pantheistic or spiritual ideas.

"The elimination of animist and organic hypotheses referring to the Cosmos constituted the death of Nature, the most far-reaching effect of the scientific revolution. As Nature was seen as a system of dead and inert particles moved by external, instead of internal, forces, the mechanical scheme itself could legitimate the manipulation of Nature. Also as a conceptual structure, the mechanical order had become associated with a values system based on power, totally compatible with the direction that commercial capitalism was taking."

It is of vital importance that the historical background to the shaping of modern thought be made clear, and Merchant puts her finger on it: it is when Europe "flooded" the whole planet that commercialism reached the first "globalization".

Yield to Nature or go without it

The development of a concept of Nature as a lapsed or dispensable thing, as disposable material, is patently obvious in the arguments of many current thinkers, in particular in some referring to the food question. Referring to the friction produced between agricultural and industrial activity, the former "seasonal, uncertain, risky" due to climate, the latter "continuous, repetitive and predictable", Argentina's Marcelo Posada wrote in *Ciclos* magazine in 1999: "another way to eliminate the constant friction consists of eliminating the interrelation of agro-industry through the substitution of the raw material of agricultural origin with some of a synthetic origin […] This tendency, known as "substitutionism", is strongly linked with biotechnological applications."

This is an example of what British economist EF Schumacher, author of *Small is Beautiful* classed as forms of work against Nature, instead of with it. And they are the flip-side of the message sent by Chief Seattle, of the Suwamich nation to the President of the United States in 1855:

"The Earth does not belong to Man, but He to the Earth. Man has not woven the web of life, he is only a thread in it […] The air is something precious […] because all things share the same breath: animals, trees and man […] If all the animals disappeared, man would die of a great loneliness of spirit."

We are thus presented with two different rationales, practically opposed in relation to Nature and the Universe in general: those who seek to follow the natural laws, bending to them with a specifically human creativity, and thus extracting benefits for the community - organic agriculture for example - and those who devalue the role of Nature in the specificity of life, who endeavour to reduce the living to the inert, for example farming and livestock raising to industrial activity (sheltering behind the commercial advantages this implies).

Science, public or private?

Scientific thought sought to set itself apart from other schools of thought, breaking secret codes, making verification a keystone of the scientific method, the repetition of experiments a guarantee of their quality as knowledge. Thus the first modern scientists stood in opposition to the alchemists, mystics, astrologers and other occultists, denying the validity of the esoteric.

But it is precisely this public nature of science which has begun to crack since the mid 20th century, and above all in the last few years. For centuries this development was centred on individual activity or the universities and centres of study. It was public and therefore exposed in the constant debates of the academic world. The transferral of ownership which has been produced is changing the basic nature of science.

In the United States since the 1950s half of all national scientific and technological research has been in the military sphere. Such volume gives scientific activity an inevitable focus and orientation, not only in the specific research undertaken but also in its method, changing for example the public nature of the activity.

Supporting the view of science as an activity largely harnessed for military purposes is the notion of the development of scientific research as private activity, promoted to make profits. The private laboratories of the transnational corporations are defining the direction of research and its technological applications.

In the last few years, it has become increasingly noticeable that the public research institutions are emptying, not now through closure or abandonment, but through seduction: the public laboratories, traditionally under-funded (but generally having the best staff), receive equipment, loans and offers from companies, all of which of course reinforce the scientific activity and technology of the companies themselves.

Science loses sense

Scientific and technological development has thus lost the objectivity normally attributed to them. Science has been co-opted, not because the business or military interests achieve their own science but, as recognised by Anglo-Argentine Nobel prize-winner Cesar Milstein, because "governments, money, can influence the greater or lesser growth of the various branches of science or even [growth] within any determined branch".

Scientific activity, pushed on by the basic human urge to know and understand has an immediate repercussion on us all, as it constitutes a privileged instrument for the permanent resiting of humans in the world. The same activity promoted by the drive for profit or power acts under an impulse outside of the individual.

There has been a radical change of purpose. The impulses for development stem from the technological applications, because it is these which make great dividends possible and it appears that all scientific activity is being towed along in their wake. Instead of the future of science as something always to be questioned, whose applications might be of uncertain benefit, today science appears to have a guaranteed future in the service of technological development and its increasingly sophisticated inventions.

Enslaved by the drive for success and generalised commercialisation, science has undergone development at an exponential speed of growth. But this has also raised the question again: what is the ultimate purpose of such science - a question which has prompted some to suggest that the time has come to turn away from it. ∎

Frankenstein fears

It is the age of atomic bombs, the age of information. Scientific knowledge has increased exponentially, especially in the last century. At the same time, the body of information in the world is also expanding. And yet, nobody can claim that these factors have led to an overall global improvement in education, or a cultural enrichment of our planetary society. Capitalism, allied to techno-science, has produced a situation bordering on chaos. Like Frankenstein, the invention has taken over the inventor. Scientists are among the few social groups that can put a stop to this.

Dark Ages

It is sometimes said that trying to halt progress would be like going back to the Dark Ages. But as typical scientists of today, surely our abysmal ignorance of everything that is not part of our tiny field of work amounts to obscurantism? Why does that not arouse the same protests that the mere suggestion of putting a halt to scientific research does? Such a moratorium would perhaps allow society to digest the colossal volume of information currently available in the world. But, of course, that is not sufficient reason. Such a motive has to be found in profit, companies, money and scientific careers. The acknowledgement of this difficulty by we scientists would seem impossible. Most of us do not even care. We do research devoid of values and responsibility and others take the blame. Nevertheless, we are dealing with a system. Everybody and nobody is responsible.

Human cloning

There are fields in which the economic and social consequences brought about by the explosion of knowledge are particularly important and perverse. In the human and social sciences, for example, we are generally dealing with just more papers. It should be possible to discuss which fields of research need to continue, which have to be slowed down and which probably have to be stopped. Genetics is without doubt among the latter. Cloned sheep can be nothing else but forerunners of cloned humans, and not simply in order to create an army to quell a rebellion in some far-off country. That would be useless and expensive. Rather, such human cloning would be to have perfect copies of organs which can be damaged during life. The clone is a spare part in a world in which we are all spare parts.

Discontinuing an area of investigation does not mean that scientists are left without a job. Our expertise is much too valuable for that to happen. Our tasks could be redefined and reoriented so that our accumulated knowledge can reach those social sectors in lack of it.

One last comment for local alarmists. A suspension of this kind could not be started [... from the South]. That would be nonsensical. But what could begin anywhere in the world is an attitude of resistance: the conviction that this crazy and impossible race towards a mind without a body should stop. And now is the time to start thinking really hard. ∎

Source: Alfonso Buch, Argentinian epistemologist

A = AS % OF TOTAL POPULATION, 1997
B = ESTIMATES TO 2015

COUNTRIES	A	B	COUNTRIES	A	B	COUNTRIES	A	B
Albania	37.9	47.6	Gabon	52.2	66.2	Norway	73.6	78.0
Algeria	57.2	67.5	Gambia	30.4	42.5	Oman	79.5	92.8
Angola	32.3	44.1	Georgia	59.3	67.7	Pakistan	35.4	46.7
Antigua	36.2	43.3	Germany	86.9	89.9	Panama	56.5	64.9
Aotearoa/N.Zealand	86.3	89.4	Ghana	36.8	47.8	Papua New Guinea	16.6	23.7
Argentina	88.6	91.9	Greece	59.5	65.1	Paraguay	53.9	65.0
Armenia	69.1	75.0	Grenada	36.6	47.2	Peru	71.6	77.9
Australia	84.6	86.0	Guatemala	39.4	48.3	Philippines	56.0	67.8
Austria	64.4	68.5	Guinea	30.6	42.9	Poland	64.4	71.4
Azerbaijan	56.3	64.0	Guinea-Bissau	22.5	31.7	Portugal	36.5	46.6
Bahamas	87.4	91.5	Guyana	36.4	48.0	Qatar	91.8	94.2
Bahrain	91.2	95.0	Haiti	33.0	44.8	Romania	56.8	65.4
Bangladesh	19.4	30.8	Honduras	45.0	56.1	Russia	76.6	82.0
Barbados	48.4	58.4	Hungary	65.5	73.2	Rwanda	5.8	8.9
Belarus	72.5	80.4	Iceland	91.9	93.8	Sahara, Western	21.1	26.7
Belgium	97.1	98.0	India	27.4	35.9	São Tomé and Príncipe	44.5	56.2
Belize	46.4	51.0	Indonesia	37.4	52.4	Saudi Arabia	84.1	89.7
Benin	39.9	53.0	Iran	60.0	68.8	Senegal	45.0	56.5
Bhutan	6.5	11.6	Iraq	75.5	81.6	Seychelles	56.1	67.3
Bolivia	62.3	73.7	Ireland	57.9	63.9	Sierra Leone	34.6	46.7
Botswana	66.1	88.7	Israel	90.9	92.6	Singapore	100	100
Brazil	79.6	86.5	Italy	66.7	70.7	Slovakia	59.7	68.0
Brunei	70.5	78.7	Jamaica	54.7	63.5	Slovenia	51.8	58.8
Bulgaria	69.0	75.4	Japan	78.4	82.0	Solomon Is.	18.0	28.6
Burkina Faso	16.9	27.4	Jordan	72.6	79.8	South Africa	49.7	56.3
Burundi	8.1	14.5	Kazakhstan	60.4	68.4	Spain	76.9	81.3
Cambodia	21.6	32.9	Kenya	30.4	44.5	Sri Lanka	22.6	32.0
Cameroon	46.4	58.9	Korea, South	83.5	92.2	St Kitts-Nevis	33.9	39.3
Canada	76.8	79.8	Kuwait	97.3	98.2	St Lucia	37.3	43.6
Cape Verde	57.7	73.5	Kyrgyzstan	39.2	47.9	St Vincent	50.9	68.0
Central African Rep.	39.9	49.7	Laos	21.8	32.7	Sudan	33.3	48.7
Chad	22.8	30.9	Latvia	73.4	78.9	Suriname	50.3	60.8
Chile	84.2	86.9	Lebanon	88.5	92.6	Swaziland	33.0	47.2
China	31.9	45.9	Lesotho	25.6	38.9	Sweden	83.2	85.2
Colombia	73.6	80.0	Libya	86.4	90.3	Switzerland	61.6	68.3
Comoros	31.5	42.6	Lithuania	73.1	80.1	Syria	53.1	62.1
Congo D.R.	29.2	39.3	Luxembourg	90.0	94.0	Tajikistan	32.4	40.1
Congo R.	60.2	70.1	Macedonia, TFYR	60.7	68.5	Tanzania	25.7	38.3
Costa Rica	50.3	60.3	Madagascar	27.6	39.3	Thailand	20.6	29.3
Côte d'Ivoire	44.7	55.7	Malawi	14.2	22.7	Togo	31.7	42.5
Croatia	56.5	64.4	Malaysia	55.1	66.2	Trinidad and Tobago	72.7	79.3
Cuba	76.7	82.7	Maldives	27.4	36.3	Tunisia	63.4	73.5
Cyprus	55.2	64.6	Mali	28.1	40.1	Turkey	71.9	84.5
Czech Republic	65.7	70.7	Malta	89.8	92.6	Turkmenistan	45.0	52.4
Denmark	85.4	87.8	Mauritania	54.0	68.6	Uganda	13.2	20.7
Djibouti	82.7	86.3	Mauritius	40.7	48.6	Ukraine	71.1	78.0
Dominica	70.0	76.0	Mexico	73.8	77.9	United Arab Emirates	84.8	88.8
Dominican Republic	63.3	72.8	Moldova	53.1	63.9	United Kingdom	89.3	90.8
Ecuador	60.4	70.6	Mongolia	61.9	70.5	United States	76.6	81.0
Egypt	45.1	53.5	Morocco	53.3	64.3	Uruguay	90.7	93.2
El Salvador	45.6	53.6	Mozambique	36.5	51.5	Uzbekistan	41.6	50.1
Equatorial Guinea	44.7	61.4	Myanmar/Burma	26.5	36.7	Vanuatu	19.3	27.0
Eritrea	17.7	26.2	Namibia	38.0	53.2	Venezuela	86.5	90.4
Estonia	73.5	78.7	Nepal	10.9	18.1	Vietnam	19.5	24.3
Ethiopia	16.3	25.8	Netherlands	89.1	90.9	Yemen	35.3	49.2
Fiji	41.2	50.5	Nicaragua	63.2	71.3	Zambia	43.6	51.5
Finland	63.9	70.9	Niger	19.1	29.1	Zimbabwe	33.2	45.9
France	75.0	79.4	Nigeria	41.3	55.4			

Source: Human Development Report 1999, UNDP, 1999.

IN AN INTERVIEW for the French newspaper *Le Monde*, Michael Dertouzos of the Massachusetts Institute of Technology announced that in 20 years' time computers would be as popular and user-friendly as televisions. Meanwhile, the main source of information will be an extended Internet which will allow information to flow freely and more quickly than today.

Omnipresent, omniscient computers

Dertouzos states that whilst the number of home computers will continue to grow, in 20 years' time we will no longer speak of cyberspace as we do now. By then it will be so commonplace that its presence will be as unremarked as refrigerator motors or washing machines are today.

He says there are four forces which will transform the world of the Internet and influence the domestic use of computers.

Firstly, the use of the spoken word will be increasingly common, allowing a certain "dialogue" between computers and people. Not that the machines will be able to speak to people and understand them, but that they will increasingly recognise basic orders and carry them out with precision. This new capacity will make the computer easier to use and increase the number of people who feel able to give it instructions.

A second change is automation. During the first industrial revolution, machines replaced people in the heaviest manual work and most unpleasant tasks. Computers are set to replace humans in the most repetitive and uncreative tasks.

The third change will be produced through "technological proximity", that is, the possibility of being close despite geographical distances between people. Here, what networked computers can perform simply is going to transform the world of work, freeing people from the need to be physically close to their work place. This move will fundamentally affect the tertiary sector, but will without doubt also influence the other sectors.

Meanwhile, where the technologies developed up until the present have been for general use, there is an increasing presence of specific tools to carry out various tasks through networks.

Lastly, entry into the "made to measure" world with increasing general access to systems adaptable to the needs of all users, will allow a less generic and more personalised use of networks and computers. The idea, already possible today, of a person exclusively receiving information important to themselves from the media they are interested in via electronic mail will be complemented with the possibility of ordering made to measure clothes or choosing the theatre seat they would prefer.

But for the Internet to be more than just a fashion, Dertouzos says the network must produce true value which serves the people, something which goes beyond the simple novelty of knowing the outcome of a baseball match or the lyrics of a song "right now."

The difficulties still limiting domestic computer use include band width, which, for example, prevents home users from requesting or viewing one of the 30,000 films available in the world. Other difficulties are of a cultural nature, like the growing gap between the world's two per cent of Internet users and those excluded from the new technologies.

Those connected have the chance to learn at speeds and volumes which increasingly separate them from those who only have access to information from books, or sometimes not even this. These cultural distances, compounded by the predominance of one language - English - and the non-existence of some others, prevent the formation of a truly global community of users. ∎

Source: Le Monde.

THE ROBOT CAR, devised to overcome problems caused by the vehicles of the 20th century, will speed the mechanization of 21st century cities and so accelerate the robotization of city lifestyles.

Vehicles: the new species

The 20th century, dubbed the era "of communication", spawned a novelty which first made itself a prerequisite of modern life and later turned into a nightmare: the car. In its day, it was a radical invention, an innovation whose very name stressed neither humans nor horses, oxen nor mules were needed to pull it along: the automobile, literally the "self-mover".

During the 20th century, this definition was misleading, for behind the wheel - forming an increasing threat to life and mental health as the automobile proliferated, was the human driver - more than a million people were killed or injured each year. Meanwhile, cities not designed to harbour millions of cars, saw themselves destroyed by the pollution produced, the din

of engines, horns and traffic jams. This overpopulation by cars slowed the pace of life they had initially accelerated.

In many ways, the car had become the antithesis of its initial aim: instead of serving humans, it had put people at its service; instead of offering a secure means of transport, it had converted a simple city journey into a mortifying entanglement; instead of leaving the driver right at their destination, it often forced them to walk long distances because of the lack of parking places and, instead of speeding up transport, in many cases the outcome was paralysis, making this accelerated life style even more traumatic.

Robotic car and city

In order to overcome these contradictory elements, by the end of the 20th century, designs had been drawn up for satellite-controlled cars. These vehicles could dominate the early decades of the 21st century.

The electronic circuitry in these cars will, at least hypothetically, put robotics at the service of drivers. They can be guided by satellite, receive signals telling them how far they are from the nearest petrol station and, also, be advised automatically on which is the least congested route to their destination. A verbal request from the driver can elicit information on how many spaces there are in the nearest car park, and the vehicles would also be able to go on auto-driver for long distances obeying signals sent up from the tarmac. The driver and passengers, freed from watching the road, will be offered a range of entertainment including television, video games or the Internet during the journey.

Of course, the ultimate aim behind the design of this new-style automobile is the same as that which spawned its predecessor in the 20th century: to make life faster and more economically productive. Much less time would be lost in travelling and more work could be done.

Just like the rattling, prototype T-Ford, these machines will demand a drastic rethink of our surroundings. Where the automobiles of the 20th century robbed space from pedestrians, led their owners into paroxysms of stress and brought with them, amongst other things, multi-storey car-parks - a necessity in order to keep going - the new species will introduce a new habitat: the robot city.

To a large extent, these vehicles will have achieved what their name 'automobile' proclaims: being able to move independently of any effort by or attention from their owners. But it still remains to be seen whether this robotization will spare those owners any of their alienation and provide them with a chance to catch up on lost leisure, or whether, as with most 20th century advances in transport and communication, it will merely contribute to the increasingly intense robotization of human society. ■

COMMUNICATIONS IN FIGURES

A = Main telephone lines per 1,000 people (1996)   **B =** Personal Computers per 1,000 people (1996)

COUNTRIES	A	B	COUNTRIES	A	B	COUNTRIES	A	B
Albania	17	..	Gabon	32	6.3	Nigeria	4	..
Algeria	44	3.4	Gambia	19	..	Norway	555	284.5
Angola	5	..	Georgia	105	..	Oman	86	10.9
Antigua	423	..	Germany	538	233.2	Pakistan	18	1.2
Aotearoa/New Zealand	499	266.1	Ghana	4	1.2	Panama	122	..
Argentina	174	34.1	Greece	509	35.3	Papua New Guinea	11	..
Armenia	154	..	Grenada	243	..	Paraguay	36	..
Australia	519	311.3	Guatemala	31	2.8	Peru	60	5.9
Austria	469	148.9	Guinea	2	0.3	Philippines	25	9.3
Azerbaijan	85	..	Guinea-Bissau	7	..	Poland	169	36.2
Bahamas	315	..	Guyana	60	..	Portugal	375	67.4
Bahrain	241	66.8	Haiti	8	..	Qatar	239	62.7
Bangladesh	3	..	Honduras	31	..	Romania	140	5.3
Barbados	370	57.5	Hungary	261	44.1	Russia	175	23.7
Belarus	208	..	Iceland	576	205.4	Samoa	50	..
Belgium	465	167.3	India	15	1.5	São Tomé and Príncipe	20	..
Belize	133	27.8	Indonesia	21	4.8	Saudi Arabia	106	37.2
Benin	6	..	Iran	95	32.7	Senegal	11	7.2
Bhutan	10	..	Iraq	33	..	Seychelles	196	..
Bolivia	43	..	Ireland	395	170.4	Sierra Leone	4	..
Botswana	48	6.7	Israel	441	116.3	Singapore	513	216.8
Brazil	96	18.4	Italy	440	92.3	Slovakia	232	186.1
Brunei	263	..	Jamaica	142	4.6	Slovenia	333	47.8
Bulgaria	313	29.8	Japan	489	128.0	Solomon Is.	18	..
Burkina Faso	3	..	Jordan	60	7.2	South Africa	100	37.7
Burundi	2	..	Kazakhstan	116	..	Spain	392	94.2
Cambodia	1	..	Kenya	8	1.6	Sri Lanka	14	3.3
Cameroon	5	1.5	Korea, South	430	..	St Kitts-Nevis	382	..
Canada	602	243.6	Korea, North	..	131.7	St Lucia	235	..
Cape Verde	64	..	Kuwait	232	74.1	St Vincent	171	..
Central African Rep.	3	..	Kyrgyzstan	75	..	Sudan	4	0.7
Chad	1	..	Laos	6	1.1	Suriname	132	..
Chile	156	45.1	Latvia	298	7.9	Swaziland	22	..
China	45	3.0	Lebanon	149	24.3	Sweden	682	214.9
Colombia	118	23.3	Lesotho	9	..	Switzerland	640	408.5
Comoros	8	..	Libya	68	..	Syria	82	1.4
Congo D.R.	1	..	Lithuania	268	6.5	Tajikistan	42	..
Congo R.	8	..	Luxembourg	592	..	Tanzania	3	..
Costa Rica	155	..	Macedonia, TFYR	170	..	Thailand	70	16.7
Côte d'Ivoire	9	1.4	Madagascar	3	..	Togo	6	..
Croatia	309	20.9	Malawi	4	..	Trinidad and Tobago	168	19.2
Cuba	32	..	Malaysia	183	42.8	Tunisia	64	6.7
Cyprus	485	40.9	Maldives	63	12.3	Turkey	224	13.8
Czech Republic	273	67.9	Mali	2	0.3	Turkmenistan	74	..
Denmark	618	304.1	Malta	483	80.6	Uganda	2	0.5
Djibouti	13	6.9	Mauritania	4	5.3	Ukraine	181	5.6
Dominica	264	..	Mauritius	162	31.9	United Arab Emirates	308	66.7
Dominican Republic	83	..	Mexico	95	29.0	United Kingdom	528	192.6
Ecuador	73	3.9	Moldova	140	2.6	United States	640	362.4
Egypt	50	5.8	Mongolia	39	..	Uruguay	209	22.0
El Salvador	56	..	Morocco	46	1.7	Uzbekistan	67	..
Equatorial Guinea	9	..	Mozambique	3	0.8	Vanuatu	26	..
Eritrea	5	..	Myanmar/Burma	4	..	Venezuela	117	21.1
Estonia	299	6.7	Namibia	54	12.7	Vietnam	16	3.3
Ethiopia	3	..	Nepal	5	..	Yemen	13	..
Fiji	88	..	Netherlands	543	232.0	Zambia	9	..
Finland	549	195.2	Nicaragua	26	..	Zimbabwe	15	6.7
France	564	150.7	Niger	2	..			

Source: Human Development Report 1999, UNDP, 1999.

THE SHAKE-UP in the internet provider and entertainment industries produced by the merger between America Online and Time-Warner in early 2000 showed how entry into the commercial sphere and stock exchange speculation has put the Internet at the heart of crucial disputes between the communications empires.

World wide web of companies

The sheer magnitude of the merger between the greatest private internet provider, US company America Online (AOL) with communications and media powerhouse Time-Warner (TW) shook the financial world. The impact was heightened by the fact that this two-headed giant represents a new era in relations between information and entertainment companies, and providers of the physical means of getting this to the consumer.

On the day after the merger was announced, the new company, AOL Time-Warner, had a joint value of more than $350,000 million. Wall Street analysts at the time stated that the final value of the company on the stock exchange would soar to $500,000 million when the deal was completed successfully.

At the time of the merger, AOL was the leading internet service provider in the United States and a strong player in Europe (with more than 3 million subscribers), Asia and Latin America. Its income totaled $4,800 million from three basic sources: subscribers' fees, advertising space and commissions on electronic sales - where AOL led the field.

Meanwhile Time-Warner, founded in 1990 from the merger of more traditional press, television, film and cable companies, was fully established as one of the leading concerns in the entertainment industry. Its two main elements of strategic value were its enormous flow of content (news, entertainment, music, films and others) and its cable network, the second largest in the country, serving 35 million users. This cable network allowed the company to offer wide-band (faster) internet access to 320,000 subscribers.

It was apparently just this added potential which precipitated the agreement between the two companies, with a view to building a new, invincible empire.

Fast access

The heart of AOL's business was the provision of access to the Internet, but it was up against two underlying problems which hampered the development of internet communication companies. Firstly, more and better content is needed each day - information of all types, on-line chat sites, games, things to see and to buy - in order for users to remain connected (hooked might be a better word).

In a country where local calls are charged within the fixed cost of a telephone call, and where the service works on a flat rate charge, the key to success is in getting the user to spend more hours connected, that is, reading or playing, but basically buying or soaking up the advertising. The number of users visiting each page is counted by the server and the advertisers pay according to how many view that page.

The other big drawback was the slow speed of the connections and the huge difficulty of transmitting good quality images or interactive content down the narrow-band telephone lines between the user and the server. These first few kilometers from the home modem to the local server where the system plugs in to wide-band lines are a bottle-neck which discourages users and inhibits downloading films.

In order to widen the range of goods sold or rented via the internet, a fast route had to be found into consumers' homes. At the same time, the products on sale needed to be practical and almost limitless in scope.

The TW cable network offered internet access on a far greater band width than was offered by the telephone network, making it both less congested and faster. With cable-style band width, plus the extra information and entertainment services on offer, AOL advanced to conquer a market it had powered for the last ten years.

The conventional media empires had been trying to join the new technological wave for several years and many of them today have mixed interests in one place and another. These have been crusading ventures which have sometimes formed the basis of strategic alliances, but at other times merely united competitors for investment in specific areas. Prior to the AOL Time-Warner merger, all attempts to link these empires to the new electronic realms had failed.

The change took place when big internet companies, hard pressed by the falling cost of network access, began to glimpse the advantages of the conventional media empires.

The power of two

There are at least three elements of corporations like TW which are of interest to their internet counterparts. The first of these is marketing: in order not to go unnoticed in the almost infinite web of internet sites, new companies spend an average 70 per cent of their budget on advertising. Their publicity is carried in the traditional media, transferring large sums of money from one business to another. Cable TV income from advertising increased by 15 per cent in 1998 and 21 per cent in the first nine months of 1999. A similar thing happened in the newspapers: 6 and 11 per cent growth in 1998 and 1999 respectively. Any company linking internet business and the traditional media would save enormously on advertising.

A second element is diffusion capacity. At first it was assumed that the Internet would resolve distribution problems, as the consumer would be able to travel anywhere from their own home But the enormous popularity of the system swiftly caused it to slow down and become clogged. Cable networks, controlled by the traditional companies, provide wide-band links to homes, which can rapidly carry videos, interactive games and other content.

Companies with communications satellites and cell-phone operators can also provide new access channels, freeing internet services from dependence on the traditional cables. These concerns are therefore potential allies for companies with content to sell. An alliance of this type would provide immediate access to new ways of reaching users, saving the generally costly initial investment.

The last element is that of content. The more content owned by an internet provider, the longer users will spend navigating within the companys own domain (web site), where the company alone charges for advertising on its pages.

AOL's buy-out of Netscape in 1998 clearly showed that AOL wanted to escape the control of Microsoft and its Internet Explorer, preferring to run its own web browser or navigator and avoid dependence on a potential competitor. On another front, AOL had tried several times to escape the grasp of companies like AT&T, owner of the main cable network and a thriving wide-band internet service.

The AOL Time-Warner alliance cleared the way, providing the company all the space it needed to grow within its own garden. It now has its own clients, its own internet provider and one of the largest stores of content in the world. It also owns a cable network and so can move confidently into a future dominated by wide band-width connections to bring speedy images from the ether. ∎

IV. Economy

ON THE BRINK of a crisis for civilization, where the key symbol - money - has lost its original meaning for millions of people, small groups and associations are creating new forms of exchange which revive old values of coexistence, respect for nature and human solidarity.

New symbols of social exchange

'War is so important we should not leave it in the hands of the military', said eighteenth-century French statesman Georges Clemenceau. Paraphrasing his words we could say that the economy is so important it should not be left in the hands of economists. We could say the same about banking and bankers. Society is forced by current circumstances to review and restructure its institutions based on first principles of coexistence, material and spiritual progress.

To some extent society can rely on fundamental ethical values of respect for life, coexistence and creative work, the gregarious instinct and common sense, as underpinning every individual and collective entity, the contributions of universal technology and lessons from history. We are on the brink of a crisis of civilization where money has lost its original value. Money today makes us vulnerable to a series of destructive phenomena - profiteering, speculation, inflation, devaluation, crime, opulence and marginalization - against which the forces of the state and market offer no real solutions. While money circulates at the speed of electrons and is concentrated in a few hands, natural values - vital and social - have continued to operate, at the margins, anonymously, without money or bank accounts. Good and sustainable lifestyles are still found based on the family, communities, villages and societies, where genuine values of solidarity, in the midst of all kinds of disasters, have not yet been destroyed by the dominant system.

For those of us who value the importance of this other economy, invisible - invisible to those who are only after money - this economy is immense to us. This invisible economy is basic (since without it the dominant one would not exist), and if one would want to calculate it in numbers, it would be infinitely greater than the dominant economy. Contact with reality has been lost.

The traditional economy

Many economists work with statistical indicators, certain measures and equations which are in themselves specious or can be manipulated. They ignore many other realities that do not fit into their calculations simply because they cannot measure them.

People themselves are an enormous pool of wealth. What is the true value of love and maternal care towards babies and children in every home? How can we put a price tag on taking care of the elderly in the Third World? What is the value of the respect and care that so many responsible peasants show for the land, jungles, rivers, lakes and all the flora and fauna despite the advances of a predatory civilization? What is the real contribution of a household economy that encompasses work, production and services that are not sold but provide subsistence to families? What is the worth of the symbolic wealth of thousands of different native cultures throughout the world? To some degree, this can be given some material value by commercial tourism, but it is the very essence of these cultures that is vital for the enrichment of human diversity. How do we truly reckon the contribution of the voluntary work of thousands and thousands of non-governmental social service organizations? And in terms of the planet's wellbeing, what is the value of underground oil supplies, the result of billions of years of cosmic knowledge, and how much are they worth when pumped out in order to squander them, polluting the environment and threatening ecological balance? How can we set a sum to account for the tropical forests that provide us with oxygen, today about to become extinct?

Taking on board these reflections implies an 180-degree shift in our thinking. Many poor people are in fact rich if we look at them from a different perspective. Many natural resources considered cheap today would be revalued in such a way they would be too precious to be squandered. And many of today's multimillionaires do not produce concrete things, just intangibles - films, internet or service industries. The current world economic system has transformed the most basic resources - labor, nature and means of exchange - into commodities that make money asocial and anti-social through the domination of exchange-value over use-value.

There is a proliferation of ambition, greed, selfishness, the law of the jungle, and above all a generalized fear at the advance of the mechanisms of social exclusion.

Surely it is necessary to tame the profit motive which today seems to drive every human activity. Some entrepreneurs seem to have reached a pitch where everything, even a smile, has a price. It is also necessary to go beyond a defensive, merely individualistic, and even opportunistic utilitarianism exclusively aimed at surviving.

In addition to exchange-value and use-value we must appreciate the value of relationships. Nowadays for example, the middle classes have to work even longer hours to get money in order to relate, it seems, purely with the cash register at the supermarket or shops.

Throughout history people have invented collective forms of social construction: taxes and redistribution; the market economy, and of major importance nowadays, the economy of giving and receiving.

Means and ends

Some 2,300 years ago, Aristotle knew of places where barter was predominant. In his ethical and philosophical reflections he distinguished between finance - to seek money for the sake of money, a source of wars - and the real economy, damaged by the former. In other words, he recognised the art of creating and acquiring the necessary means for the subsistence of the family and the state, that is, taking care of basic needs.

Industrial capitalism is only 300 years old and virtual capitalism just 30. We live in an age of fast changes that cause great uncertainty. Humanity must fight to overcome the current trend to make us into robots which leads us to condemn the vast majority of people to an economic oblivion in poverty and to the ecological destruction of the planet.

The loss of substance and meaning for the really important things in life leads us to a uniformity of behaviors. We need a genuine conversion to a set of universal human values and as yet undiscovered values through processes of socialization and deep self-analysis.

This implies a great transformation. As a symptom of this sea-change in many regions of the world, such as Mexico, there is a reconsideration of the concept of money. This phenomenon was already experienced in other critical times but was limited to particular countries or regions - as for example with bankruptcies, wars and revolutions, independence and emerging identities. Today, that phenomenon is global.

Meaning-less

Humanity as a whole seems to have lost the ability to communicate the symbols of its most cherished values and of how to achieve the subsistence and welfare of any social group. Nowadays there are symbols and messages, amplified by the super-technology of communication, which have turned out to be powerful signals from certain groups, sectors, corporations and criminal systems with exclusive and excluding faculties. We are dealing with the rule of money and image.

Finance and information, although intangible, are now more influential than the law and conventional authority, and are both transmitted through electronic screens. Stock exchanges and television throughout the world offer us scenarios where powerful messages are broadcast from a constellation of electronic screens: some with numbers, others with sex, violence, visual chaos and repeatedly, icons of all sorts mainly political although also informative, recreative and athletic.

It is the reign of the virtual world whose main achievement is the creation of passivity and addiction to the system, and consequently the voiding of autonomous content, the elimination of alternatives, the submission of the will. Money, like the wheel, is an original human invention. It was born as a symbolic resource, to facilitate communication and other problems, and as an aid to survival and welfare, individual as well as collective.

The roots of money

Money was invented at the dawn of history, replacing barter, to enable the exchange of goods, products and services. The barter system of exchange was limited by the difficulty of balancing demand and supply, by the proliferation of different goods, the discovery of distant communities and the increase in demand - all that is understood as progress. On the other hand, a space or commercial dimension was made possible which mediated between two poles: solidarity, generosity and moral indebtedness on the one hand; and pillage, plunder and war on the other.

Money implied the giving and receiving of useful and mutually beneficial specific values. It involved a debt, and it gave its owner the right to claim money or goods and services of equivalent value directly from the individual debtor or group concerned.

It was a token used to endow a uniform and accepted expression of value for products, and to project an obligation of reciprocity for the future. Money in itself was not only a symbol but also a useful object. History shows money or means of exchange developing from objects such as animals, valuable objects such as shells, cocoa seeds and feathers, and precious metals (gold, silver), until the invention of the bill or banknote. And so began the process of transformation from material to paper money, by way of checks and bank accounts, credit cards, and most recently, electronic accounts, including smart cards.

In tandem with the development of paper money, as three thousand years went by, money changed from being just the means (to purchase things or services) to becoming an end in itself: first with the accumulation of exquisite objects, and then with the creation of money itself through high interest rates. Nowadays, a major challenge is to learn once again to see and consider ourselves in relation to our intrinsic worth - something immeasurable - and appreciate all of that which each person, family, group, community or nation contributes towards the subsistence, welfare and social progress of others, on the basis of the principles of reciprocity and solidarity.

The purpose of the social issuing of symbols (bills, coins, checks, etc.) of the giving/receiving of a useful value-product, service, knowledge, by which a person or entity receives a benefit from another and thereby is obliged to reciprocate with that person or entity or with another similarly committed, is to facilitate a social market with its own currency as a factor of cohesion, commitment and equality.

Exchanging values

Given a totalitarian market where only the strongest and the most cunning survive to the detriment and exclusion of others, and to the detriment of the environment and planetary balance, there is the need to encourage mutually binding economic processes which will allow us to restore the social fabric and maintain the energy and vitality of the planet itself.

There is an urgent need to create information systems where various socioeconomic groupings and initiatives that are as yet unknown, marginalized or not fully exploited, could associate through useful mutual exchanges to better accomplish their goals. And in more ecological and economic terms, there could be an integration of disciplines which we could call ECO-sophy. An example of this is the Tianguis Tlaloc experience in Mexico City, which set up networks of labor associations and cooperatives of various levels of complexity: farms, workshops, small companies, cooperatives, local communities, service groups and so on, along with people, families and those affected by unemployment, poverty and lack of opportunities.

Each person in the Tianguis project has both a production and a consumer capacity - 'Prosumers'. This concept is clearly emphasized by the Global Barter Network and developed in various countries, with some 100,000 people in Argentina alone.

The unifying motive is to create a more humane economy based on basic social values. The identifying symbol is the Tlaloc receipt, equivalent to one hour of community work, which the members of the Tianguis have given an equivalent value in pesos. This value, due to the continuous devaluation of the official currency, is revised from time to time. The receipts are combined with the use of the official currency to complete payments and thus give more opportunities to those that have less resources. Receipts do not accumulate interest nor are they to be banked. On the contrary, they must circulate in order to invigorate the local economy with new members. The boards, data banks, mailings, subscriptions of those who take part in these exchanges, and their availability through different media, allow the interconnection and bilateral transactions among the interested parties.

Expos, fairs and meetings in different areas are held regularly to encourage personal contacts as well as concrete offers of each Tianguist. These meetings cement social relations, friendships and trust. They provide opportunities to share information and get to know each other, finding out who can do what and who has which skills.

Local experiences and global perspective

These experiences are not isolated. Networks, circuits and horizontal systems of information, communication, exchange and local, neighbourhood and workplace progress are emerging everywhere, and in differing degrees of organization and technology are mounting a challenge to the current monetary and banking system.

The LETS (Local Employment and Trade Systems) emerged over 15 years ago in Canada, initiated by Michael Linton. Today they are also thriving in Australia, New Zealand, the UK and the US. The ITHACA HOURS experience in New York state is another impressive example of local participation, in which already close to 1,500 establishments and small enterprises are involved. The SEL (Systems d'Emploi Local) also proliferate in France. Similar schemes are in place in Belgium, Switzerland, Germany and the Netherlands. In Latin America, the Argentinian example mentioned earlier - where the unit of exchange is called CREDITO - is also being tried in Uruguay. Also, there have been experiments in Ecuador and similar plans are afoot in Peru.

The ORALE experience, taken from a word from Mexicans in California, is being studied in Los Angeles. Even though these experiences take off almost from the social cell, they intend to integrate small rural and urban enterprises, trying to bridge the wide gap between the country and the city. A major step forward will be achieved when medium and large companies are incorporated, accepting these receipts in order to increase their sales, as well as the variety of products and services for prosumers.

In late 1998 in Helsinki, Finland, an international coalition of 100 regional processes including civil society, non-governmental organizations and grassroots groups from 40 countries, summoned by the IGGRI (International Group on Grass Roots Initiatives), outlined the importance of this symbolic and facultative factor which is the money of society, not of the states or of the banks. It is generating great interest from big corporations worried by the turn of events in the world today.

With a depressed economy it is not difficult to understand why established companies are prepared to slash prices by 20 to 40 per cent in exchange for circulation and social benefits receipts. A meso-economy (neither micro nor macro) would thus be created, which would be able to stem the mad dash for the concentration of power which is destroying society and also threatens to destroy the planet. ∎

Source: Extracted from an article from *La Otra Bolsa de Valores* (The other stock exchange), Mexico city.

Confession-time for IMF ideologues

Early in 2000, world financial institution bureaucrats admitted that the measures they had imposed for years on poor countries had seriously damaging effects for millions of people in debtor countries. In spite of this, the officials still insisted that the measures had been the right ones - and came up with a new set of arguments to back up their views.

Chief economist and outgoing Vice-President of the World Bank Joseph Stiglitz admitted at a Washington press conference that the response given by international financial institutions to the 1997 Asian crisis was designed to favor investors at the expense of workers. Stiglitz declared that a standard message was to "increase labor market flexibility" - in other words "lower salaries and fire workers".

The results included a spiralling of unemployment and severe deflation - the fall of prices due to decreasing economic activity - a combination that meant recession for 40 per cent of the world's economy. This happened in spite of the $100,000 million of emergency funds poured into countries affected by the financial crisis which devoured Asia and extended to Latin America.

At the same time, a department in the International Monetary Fund (IMF) acknowledged that controlling the inflow and outflow of capital in varying degrees helps countries protect themselves from crises. The overwhelming flood of capital into Asia had exacerbated the situation by encouraging speculative investments in projects of doubtful financial quality and economic merit.

In a report which summarized the conclusions from case studies of Brazil, Chile and Malaysia, IMF officials pointed out that experience of countries which tried to control the inflow of short-term investment revealed that in order to be effective, there has to be total coverage of the controls and these must be vigorously implemented.

IMF officials admitted that the measures applied by Malaysia to control the outflow of capital since 1998, first blocking it and then regulating investment withdrawals by foreigners, had apparently had good results. At the time it took these measures the country had been roundly condemned by international financial institutions. Doug Hellinger from the Alternative Policies Development group, a Washington-based NGO, says it is comforting to see this arrogant and scornful agency [IMF] admit that it was wrong to criticize Malaysia for introducing controls against the IMF's advice.

The IMF has insisted for years that countries open up their capital markets to foreign investment and even tried to modify its statutes in order to enforce compliance from member countries. Enthusiasm for that idea decreased during the financial crises of the late 20th century. During consecutive IMF and World Bank meetings an increasing number of debtor country delegates questioned the merits of withdrawing restrictions on speculative capital. The report proves them right.

Nevertheless, the conclusions did not lead to the IMF recanting. On the contrary, IMF officials reaffirmed their conviction that restrictions to the flow of capital are no substitute for solid macroeconomic measures. And the IMF analysts concluded that generally, countries with serious macroeconomic imbalances without prospect of improvement in the short term are unable to handle large-scale capital flows or their unwanted economic consequences through capital flow restrictions. Hellinger responds that now that they realize they were wrong, they produce arguments that were not raised before, when their position was to flatly reject the controls. ∎

Source: IPS

AID IN FIGURES

Total net official development assistance (ODA) disbursed, 1997

A = As % of GNP   B = Millions $

	A	B		A	B		A	B
Aotearoa/N. Zealand	0.26	154	France	0.45	6,307	Norway	0.86	1,306
Australia	0.28	1,061	Germany	0.28	5,857	Portugal	0.25	250
Austria	0.26	527	Ireland	0.31	187	Spain	0.23	1,234
Belgium	0.31	764	Italy	0.11	1,266	Sweden	0.79	1,731
Canada	0.34	2,045	Japan	0.22	9,358	Switzerland	0.34	911
Denmark	0.97	1,637	Luxembourg	0.55	95	United Kingdom	0.26	3,433
Finland	0.33	379	Netherlands	0.81	2,947	United States	0.09	6,878

Source: Human Development Report 1999, UNDP, 1999.

GROSS NATIONAL PRODUCT AS INDICATOR OF WEALTH

A = GNP PER CAPITA ($), 1998

	COUNTRIES	A		COUNTRIES	A		COUNTRIES	A
1	Luxembourg	45,100	58	Estonia	3,360	115	Solomon Is.	760
2	Switzerland	39,980	59	South Africa	3,310	116	China	750
3	Bermuda	35,590	60	Grenada	3,250	117	Honduras	740
4	Norway	34,310	61	Turkey	3,160	118	Congo R.	680
5	Denmark	33,040	62	Dominica	3,150	119	Turkmenistan	650
6	Japan	32,350	63	Botswana	3,070	120	Indonesia	640
7	Singapore	30,170	64	Panama	2,990	121	Zimbabwe	620
8	United States	29,240	65	Costa Rica	2,770	122	Cameroon	610
9	Iceland	27,830	66	Belize	2,660	123	Lesotho	570
10	Brunei	27,270	67	St Vincent	2,560	124	Guinea	530
11	Austria	26,830	68	Lithuania	2,540	125	Senegal	520
12	Germany	26,570	69	Colombia	2,470	126	Azerbaijan	480
13	Sweden	25,580	70	Peru	2,440	127	Pakistan	470
14	Belgium	25,380	71	Latvia	2,420	128	Bhutan	470
15	Netherlands	24,780	72	Russia	2,260	129	Armenia	460
16	Finland	24,280	73	Fiji	2,210	130	India	440
17	France	24,210	74	Belarus	2,180	131	Mauritania	410
18	United Kingdom	21,410	75	Thailand	2,160	132	Haiti	410
19	Australia	20,640	76	Tunisia	2,060	133	Ghana	390
20	Italy	20,090	77	Namibia	1,940	134	Mongolia	380
21	Canada	19,170	78	El Salvador	1,850	135	Moldova	380
22	Ireland	18,710	79	Micronesia	1,800	136	Kyrgyzstan	380
23	French Polynesia	18,050	80	Dominican Republic	1,770	137	Benin	380
24	United Arab Emirates	17,870	81	Paraguay	1,760	138	Angola	380
25	Israel	16,180	82	Tonga	1,750	139	Tajikistan	370
26	Aotearoa/New Zealand	14,600	83	Jamaica	1,740	140	Nicaragua	370
27	Spain	14,100	84	Suriname	1,660	141	Comoros	370
28	Qatar	12,000	85	Iran	1,650	142	Vietnam	350
29	Cyprus	11,920	86	Guatemala	1,640	143	Kenya	350
30	Greece	11,740	87	Algeria	1,550	144	Bangladesh	350
31	Portugal	10,670	88	Marshall Is.	1,540	145	Gambia	340
32	Malta	10,100	89	Palestine	1,537	146	Zambia	330
33	Slovenia	9,780	90	Ecuador	1,520	147	Togo	330
34	Korea, South	8,600	91	Swaziland	1,400	148	Laos	320
35	Antigua	8,450	92	Romania	1,360	149	Uganda	310
36	Puerto Rico	8,200	93	Kazakhstan	1,340	150	Nigeria	300
37	Argentina	8,030	94	Macedonia, TFYR	1,290	151	Central African Rep.	300
38	Bahrain	7,640	95	Egypt	1,290	152	Sudan	290
39	Saudi Arabia	6,910	96	Vanuatu	1,260	153	Yemen	280
40	Seychelles	6,420	97	Morocco	1,240	154	São Tomé and Príncipe	270
41	St Kitts-Nevis	6,190	98	Bulgaria	1,220	155	Madagascar	260
42	Uruguay	6,070	99	Cape Verde	1,200	156	Cambodia	260
43	Czech Republic	5,150	100	Kiribati	1,170	157	Mali	250
44	Chile	4,990	101	Jordan	1,150	158	Burkina Faso	240
45	Brazil	4,630	102	Maldives	1,130	159	Rwanda	230
46	Croatia	4,620	103	Equatorial Guinea	1,110	160	Chad	230
47	Trinidad and Tobago	4,520	104	Samoa	1,070	161	Tanzania	220
48	Hungary	4,510	105	Philippines	1,050	162	Nepal	210
49	Gabon	4,170	106	Syria	1,020	163	Mozambique	210
50	Poland	3,910	107	Bolivia	1,010	164	Malawi	210
51	Mexico	3,840	108	Ukraine	980	165	Niger	200
52	Mauritius	3,730	109	Georgia	970	166	Eritrea	200
53	Slovakia	3,700	110	Uzbekistan	950	167	Guinea-Bissau	160
54	Malaysia	3,670	111	Papua New Guinea	890	168	Sierra Leone	140
55	St Lucia	3,660	112	Sri Lanka	810	169	Burundi	140
56	Lebanon	3,560	113	Albania	810	170	Congo D.R.	110
57	Venezuela	3,530	114	Guyana	780	171	Ethiopia	100

Source: World Development Indicators 2000, World Bank, 2000.

A = EXPORTS (MILLIONS $), 1998

B = IMPORTS (MILLIONS $), 1998

COUNTRIES	A	B	COUNTRIES	A	B
Albania	289	980	Kazakhstan	6,735	7,716
Algeria	11,083	11,045	Kenya	2,851	3,742
Angola	3,874	3,113	Korea, South	156,330	114,879
Antigua	461	512	Kuwait	11,347	11,760
Aotearoa/New Zealand *	18,768	18,345	Kyrgyzstan	602	876
Argentina	31,019	38,494	Laos	47	61
Armenia	360	990	Latvia	3,053	3,899
Australia *	84,100	86,400	Lebanon	1,833	8,796
Austria *	87,234	88,418	Lesotho	265	988
Azerbaijan	963	2,312	Lithuania	5,071	6,348
Bahrain *	6,357	4,370	Luxembourg *	16,609	13,976
Bangladesh	5,885	8,058	Macedonia, TFYR	1,021	1,412
Barbados	1,484	1,475	Madagascar	796	1,094
Belarus	13,984	15,332	Malawi	515	740
Belgium *	176,844	165,856	Malaysia	82,899	67,098
Belize	330	363	Mali	636	928
Benin	537	740	Malta	3,071	3,259
Bhutan	132	170	Mauritania	407	536
Bolivia	1,693	2,480	Mauritius	2,723	2,727
Botswana	1,705	1,646	Mexico	122,956	130,668
Brazil	57,826	78,557	Moldova	752	1,216
Bulgaria	5,542	5,671	Mongolia	516	577
Burkina Faso	356	775	Morocco	6,421	9,251
Burundi	72	174	Mozambique	456	1,186
Cambodia	978	1,251	Namibia	1,951	1,956
Cameroon	2,305	2,176	Nepal	1,107	1,644
Canada *	247,047	237,088	Netherlands *	203,314	177,838
Cape Verde	124	282	Nicaragua	785	1,434
Central African Rep.	168	264	Niger	333	479
Chad	327	537	Nigeria	9,712	13,115
Chile	21,680	22,730	Norway *	63,277	52,453
China	207,595	165,906	Pakistan	10,017	12,818
Colombia	14,337	20,159	Palestine	693	2,532
Comoros	33	82	Panama	3,090	3,940
Congo D.R. *	1,463	1,350	Papua New Guinea	2,554	2,630
Congo R.	1,236	1,409	Paraguay	3,871	4,253
Costa Rica	5,132	5,326	Peru	7,506	10,483
Cote d'Ivoire	4,866	4,167	Philippines	36,232	39,008
Croatia	8,707	10,666	Poland *	36,718	42,931
Czech Republic	33,817	34,610	Portugal *	31,828	40,642
Denmark *	61,158	55,463	Romania	9,801	13,037
Djibouti *	207	285	Russia	87,734	74,078
Dominica	138	151	Rwanda	110	464
Dominican Republic	4,849	6,264	São Tomé and Príncipe	12	35
Ecuador	4,988	6,311	Saudi Arabia	46,275	39,546
Egypt	13,932	19,274	Senegal	1,559	1,780
El Salvador	2,738	4,239	Seychelles	376	468
Equatorial Guinea	465	791	Sierra Leone	142	203
Eritrea	129	583	Singapore	128,706	113,699
Estonia	4,149	4,651	Slovakia	12,965	15,239
Ethiopia	1,034	1,810	Slovenia	11,068	11,351
Fiji	1,041	1,021	South Africa	34,384	32,733
Finland *	47,709	37,106	Spain *	150,984	144,605
France *	371,529	316,618	Sri Lanka	5,648	6,661
Gabon	2,823	2,220	St Kitts-Nevis	149	224
Gambia	213	258	St Lucia	396	416
Georgia	720	1,437	St Vincent	159	226
Germany *	560,414	528,778	Swaziland	1,239	1,155
Ghana	2,004	2,732	Sweden *	99,727	83,758
Greece *	18,837	28,763	Switzerland *	101,826	90,492
Grenada	130	211	Syria	5,049	6,994
Guatemala	3,524	5,101	Tanzania	1,474	2,004
Guinea	777	841	Thailand	65,593	47,219
Guinea-Bissau	31	72	Togo	509	610
Guyana	690	774	Trinidad and Tobago	2,638	3,598
Haiti	445	1,128	Tunisia	8,464	9,103
Honduras	2,463	2,796	Turkey	49,229	56,129
Hungary	23,814	25,037	Uganda	697	1,335
Iceland *	2,693	2,647	Ukraine	17,365	18,687
India	47,419	59,138	United Kingdom *	367,971	374,045
Indonesia	50,755	41,250	United States *	948,600	1,058,800
Iran	14,927	16,750	Uruguay	4,512	4,620
Ireland *	61,457	47,739	Uzbekistan	4,529	4,578
Israel	32,105	43,278	Venezuela	19,030	19,083
Italy *	312,934	263,367	Vietnam *	11,480	13,625
Jamaica	3,166	4,007	Yemen	1,489	2,315
Japan *	465,591	415,867	Zambia	984	1,286
Jordan	3,636	5,200	Zimbabwe	2,911	3,027

* Data refers to 1997

Source: World Development Indicators 2000, World Bank, 2000.

In the time of the Trojan war (1250 BC), the worth of things was measured in oxen: a tripod could cost between ten and twelve oxen; a set of weapons and armour between nine and one hundred; a slave between ten and twenty. Later, coins prevailed, imposing the brilliance of the precious metals, with 'wealth accumulation' meaning piling up metals in jars and bags.

You are your money

During the Middle Ages, fear of thieves called for a new form of exchange. Traders and other travellers handed their jewels and coins to a moneychanger, who gave them a piece of paper (a bill) certifying that the said traveller had left whatever riches with them. Thus the cheque was born and with it the banks we still know today.

By the end of the 18th century, paper money and banker's notes became the norm in a world penetrated by the various European empires. This implied a radical change in transactions, as the sum of money in use no longer consisted of quantities of gold and silver, but in *fiduciary* money - promises of payment for specific quantities of silver and gold. These promissory notes were initially issued by individuals and companies as bankers notes or as transferable entries in a book which were called deposits. From the paper fiduciary money, promising to pay gold and silver, it was only a small step to paper money (guaranteed by the sovereign and later the State) specifying a determined amount of francs, reals, dollars, yen or pesos, which were valid in themselves and not as " promissory notes." Even though China had issued paper money centuries before, the current system as we know it was im-

posed following a massive print-run in post-revolutionary France between 1789 and 1796.

Forget PINs - it's the iris in your eye that counts

As the story moves on to the latter decades of the 20th century, a progressive loss of the "material" value of the coin can be seen. From oxen or solid coins, which make their value apparent in weight, shine, thickness, hardness and so on, we have passed on to increasingly indirect connection with actual cash relations. And since the introduction of the first credit cards at the end of the 1950s which allowed wealthier travellers to pay their hotel or restaurant bills with a piece of plastic, we have moved on again via automatic cash machines to electronic banks which receive deposits and release payment via the Internet. We have experienced an unstoppable dematerialization of money.

There are already designs for automatic bank tellers due to be introduced in the early decades of this 21st century, for which no code nor PIN (Personal Identification Number) number will be needed. These new models will use a camera to identify the individual by matching the pattern of the iris of their eye.

We are our money

Of course, while professional safe-breakers and forgers have mostly seen their livelihoods disappear, the increasingly volatile nature of capital has made tax fraud and the laundering of money from illegal deals even easier. We have also seen how global economic trade is increasingly entwined with the new technologies, as the model of production-based wealth (with the need for a material real backing) has already given way to one based on pure speculation. This means electronic flows of capital which move at the speed of sound, bursting onto stock exchanges world wide, carrying with them virtual figures which have left behind their material backing along the way.

At the same time, as the material underpinning of money becomes less tangible, its guarantee becomes more corporeal. In fact, whilst up until the 20th century a bank's customer was required first to register and use their signature, or more recently to create and memorise a personal code - this new century will impose a basically genetic guarantee. The genetic imprint of the individual (the owner of the money) is, like the fingerprint, something established at birth. And so the identification systems become more intimate, giving support to the notion that we are indeed our money. ∎

Guidelines for the Global Barter Network

I. Reaching our full potential as people should not be conditioned by money.

II. General welfare is a consequence of the progress of the greatest number of people in a society.

III. The Clubs as such shall have no other affiliation or formal organization. Their goal is self-management.

IV. Mutual assistance should replace futile competition, profit and speculation.

V. Our actions, products and services should respond to ethical and ecological standards, rather than market rules, consumerism, and the search for short-term gains.

VI. The only prerequisite for membership is being a producer and consumer (prosumer) of goods and/or services. All of this within the framework recommended by the Circles of Quality and Selfhelp (CCA.).

VII. Each member should pay attention to the nature of his/her actions, products and services, for which they are totally responsible.

VIII. Participation is free. Belonging to a Barter Club does not imply any dependency bond.

IX. Clubs should be totally autonomous with respect to their internal affairs.

X. As active members, we should not grant financial support, subsidize or sponsor any cause alien to our program that could deflect us from our original goals.

XI. It is best to lead by example, and also be discreet.

XII. We do not wish to promote any product or service but rather help each other reach a better quality of life through work, understanding and fair exchange.

A = Corporation name
B = Revenues $ millions
C = Employees
D = HQ Country

A	B	C	D	A	B	C	D
General Motors	161,315	594,000	United States	Sears, Roebuck and Co.	41,322	324,000	United States
DaimlerChrysler	154,615	441,502	Germany	Fujitsu Limited	41,018	188,000	Japan
Ford Motor	144,416	345,175	United States	Tokyo Electric Power	39,808	42,170	Japan
Wal-Mart Stores	139,208	910,000	United States	Deutsche Telekom AG	39,711	195,876	Germany
Mitsui	109,373	32,961	Japan	Sumitomo Life Insurance	39,535	66,858	Japan
Itochu	108,749	5,775	Japan	E.I. du Pont de Nemours	39,130	101,000	United States
Mitsubishi	107,184	36,000	Japan	Zurich Financial Services	39,115	68,876	Switzerland
Exxon	100,697	79,000	United States	Royal Philips Electronics	38,456	224,573	Netherlands
General Electric	100,469	293,000	United States	CGU	37,589	52,000	United Kingdom
Toyota Motor	99,740	183,879	Japan	Peugeot	37,540	156,500	France
Royal Dutch/Shell Group	93,692	102,000	U. Kingdom/Neth.	NEC	37,235	157,773	Japan
Marubeni	93,569	65,000	Japan	Procter & Gamble	37,154	110,000	United States
Sumitomo	89,021	30,700	Japan	Électricité De France	36,673	116,462	France
Intl. Business Machines	81,667	291,067	United States	Rwe Group	36,603	145,467	Germany
AXA	78,729	87,896	France	TIAA-CREF	35,889	5,229	United States
Citigroup, Inc.	76,431	170,100	United States	BMW	35,887	119,913	Germany
Volkswagen	76,307	297,916	Germany	Elf Aquitaine	35,864	85,000	France
Nippon Telegraph & Telephone	76,119	224,400	Japan	Merrill Lynch	35,853	63,800	United States
BP Amoco	68,304	96,650	United Kingdom	Munich Re Group	35,465	27,465	Germany
Nissho Iwai	67,742	19,461	Japan	Vivendi	35,292	235,610	France
Nippon Life Insurance	66,300	71,015	Japan	Suez Lyonnaise des Eaux	34,874	201,000	France
Siemens	66,038	416,000	Germany	Prudential Ins. Co. of America	34,427	77,806	United States
Allianz	64,875	105,676	Germany	ABN AMRO Holding	34,235	105,826	Netherlands
Hitachi	62,410	328,351	Japan	Sinopec	34,025	1,190,000	China
United States. Postal Service	60,072	904,636	United States	Prudential	33,677	22,834	United Kingdom
Matsushita Electric Industrial	59,771	282,153	Japan	Kmart Corporation	33,674	278,525	United States
Philip Morris	57,813	144,000	United States	American International Group	33,296	48,000	United States
ING Group	56,469	82,750	Netherlands	Crédit Agricole	33,022	86,100	France
The Boeing Company	56,154	227,000	United States	ENI	32,389	78,906	Italy
AT&T	53,588	107,800	United States	Chase Manhattan Corp.	32,379	72,683	United States
Sony Corporation	53,157	177,000	Japan	HypoVereinsbank	31,816	39,447	Germany
Metro AG	52,126	181,282	Germany	Texaco	31,707	24,628	United States
Nissan Motor	51,478	131,260	Japan	Bell Atlantic	31,566	140,439	United States
Fiat	50,999	220,549	Italy	Fannie Mae	31,499	3,800	United States
Bank of America Corp.	50,777	170,975	United States	Enron	31,260	17,800	United States
Nestlé S.A.	49,504	231,881	Switzerland	Bayer	31,197	145,100	Germany
Credit Suisse	49,143	62,296	Switzerland	Compaq Computer	31,169	80,500	United States
Honda Motor	48,748	112,200	Japan	Morgan Stanley Dean Witter	31,131	49,300	United States
Assicurazioni Generali	48,478	54,598	Italy	Dayton Hudson Corporation	30,951	165,750	United States
Mobil	47,678	41,500	United States	Tomen	30,935	10,409	Japan
Hewlett-Packard	47,061	124,600	United States	Bank of Tokyo-Mitsubishi	30,929	17,878	Japan
Deutsche Bank	45,165	75,306	Germany	ABB Asea Brown Boveri	30,872	199,232	Switzerland
Unilever N.V./ Unilever PLC	44,908	267,000	U. Kingdom/Neth.	BASF	30,732	105,945	Germany
State Farm Insurance Cos.	44,621	76,257	United States	J.C. Penney Company, Inc.	30,678	250,000	United States
Dai-ichi Mutual Life Insurance	44,486	63,427	Japan	Carrefour	30,479	144,142	France
Veba Group	43,408	116,774	Germany	Home Depot	30,219	140,000	United States
HSBC Holdings	43,338	144,521	United Kingdom	Lucent Technologies	30,147	141,600	United States
Fortis	43,200	59,481	Belgium	Société Générale	29,762	58,600	France
Toshiba	41,471	198,000	Japan	Mitsubishi Electric	29,682	116,479	Japan
Renault	41,353	138,321	France	Motorola	29,398	133,000	United States

Source: The Global 500, *Fortune*, 1999.

RECENT FORECASTS suggest that states are facing problems in gathering sufficient taxes to guarantee the security and the well-being of their citizens, for it is increasingly difficult to raise taxes from commercial transactions, personal income and even from goods and services.

The mystery of the vanishing tax payers

Two different tendencies - but with the same outcome - have turned this forecast into a visible threat at the opening of the new millennium. The first tendency is born of all the economic theories of the neo-liberal school: that in order to be truly free, trade must meet the least possible number of barriers, be these customs charges, tariffs or taxes.

The great reduction in taxes on international trade led to an explosion in the volumes of production earmarked for export. But this did not bring with it a parallel increase in taxes collected on imports.

Although international trade grew throughout the 20th century, and states received their share in the benefits of this growth, they also saw tariffs fall from an average of 20-40 per cent before World War I - with the exception of the United Kingdom - to nearly 5 per cent in recent decades.

The second tendency, still in full swing, is the one which raises more doubts for the future. One of the fruits of economic globalization is that formal trade barriers are becoming more blurred. The traditional agents of economic activity are increasingly volatile, increasingly mobile and as a result difficult to find when the time comes for paying their taxes.

Big companies act according to the logic of maximising their profits, and this includes incurring the lowest possible taxation. Entrepreneurs, scientists, independent professionals and artists also develop the capacity to seek new ways of furthering their work which cut out the tax collectors.

For example, in many cases physical transport is not needed; electronic advances mean work can be produced from remote places. And this implies that fees can be charged which do not pass through any tax office. Highly qualified staff, from management to technicians, have been acquiring elements for delocalization which were only previously enjoyed by the large investor.

Lastly, the development of electronic commerce via the Internet has created an opening which is difficult for governments to close, as they have no way of controlling the innumerable transactions carried out by this means.

In the new economic world, there are few taxable goods. Every time governments try to set a tax, they run the risk of the investors, qualified workers or traders changing direction in order to find a new "tax haven".

Modern international tax systems were developed after World War II when international movements of goods, capital and work were relatively small. Now, both companies and staff are more mobile and can rapidly exploit tax differences between countries. This is the heart of the problem faced by governments.

Impacts of globalization

To see more clearly how globalization adversely impacts on governments income from taxes look at these three scenarios.

The first and major impact occurs because companies have more freedom to choose where they want to locate their production, services, administration or marketing facilities. Activities which simply require a computer, telephone and modem can be established anywhere without this affecting the quality of work. Ease of transport and tax exemptions offered by many countries help attract large companies to set up shop. Any country which tries to charge higher taxes will see at least part of the business (and its staff) emigrate to find better tax breaks.

Corporate taxes still vary enormously from country to country (for example Germany charges double what Sweden does), but such differences persist because not all companies can move to follow the rhythm of tax highs and lows. But it is not beyond credibility that governments may show themselves willing to drop taxes on big business to near zero figures over the next few years.

Secondly, globalization makes it difficult to decide where a company should pay its taxes. Multinational firms design their product in one country, produce it in another and sell it in a third. This allows them to create accounting formulae and make transferrals on the prices of one or another activity, with the end aim of paying the least possible tax.

By paying inflated prices for components imported from a subsidiary in a country with low taxes, a firm can move its tax benefits to that country and thus reduce the amount to be paid. Foreign subsidiaries of US companies for example can declare higher profit margins in countries with lower tax rates than in those which charge high taxes.

The third reason why globalization increases tax problems is that even taxes on personal income are becoming a risk governments do not wish to assume. It is possible that in the near future it will become increasingly difficult to charge personal income tax as experts and professionals become more mobile than they were 20 years ago.

One illustration of this can be seen in Sweden, a country which towards the end of the last century charged personal income tax of up to 60 per cent for the higher brackets. The Ericsson company announced in 1999 that it was considering moving its headquarters to another country. The company did not complain of the taxes it had to pay but argued that the contributions its workers had to make were so high that it made it hard for them to find first-class staff. For whilst in Sweden an annual income of over $28,000 is taxed at 60 per cent, in the US only those earning $260,000 per year or more have to pay the upper bracket of 40 per cent.

But even if these qualified workers decide not to flee and become tax exiles as already happens in several rich countries, many earn an increasing proportion of their income abroad, from consultancy work or similar sources. Imposing taxes on these incomes is very complicated as the income may never enter the country.

Sales of shares to residents abroad increased from 3 per cent of GDP in 1970 to 136 per cent in 1995 in the United States. In these circumstances, governments have no way of knowing which of their citizens own such shares.

Cybertrade knows no barriers

Traditional forms of taxation appear to have a complicated future ahead. Even the Value Added Tax - the solution in the last decades of the 20th century - is undergoing drastic changes. The increasing popularity of electronic trade or e-commerce amongst consumers makes both governments and established traders tremble. A legal ruling on postal sales in the US Supreme Court in 1992 (Quill vs North Dakota) found that sales taxes were not applicable in operations carried out between different US states. Despite there being no actual law for electronic trade, jurisprudence applied exemption from sales taxes beyond state frontiers.

As the US has the largest internet market for goods and services and also because of the practical difficulties - not to mention the political upset - if they try to charge taxes on electronic transactions with other states - the rule acquired universal stature.

In 1999, US Congress approved the Internet Tax Freedom Act, guaranteeing investors in electronic trade freedom from taxes which might impede its development.

The study of possible forms of taxation was left until 2001, but most traditional traders believe this is just one more way of extending the deadline and thereby further discriminating against those who continue operating trading of this kind.

Neither does the contradiction between these two ways of doing business appear to have slowed the development of e-commerce. Many traditional traders such as bookstores were quick to climb aboard the bandwagon of the new form of business, finding it better to have a vast warehouse and deal exclusively with electronic requests, than to have a traditional store open to the public.

In the near future it is also probable that the less industrialized countries will be affected by the decline in tax income. Most of the trade in small goods with high added value - like electronic implements, jewels, books or records - could be done through the Internet tax free. It is also possible that whole branches of traditional commercial activity - a good source of local and national taxes - will be unable to compete with e-commerce and so will leave the regular market-place.

The difficulties of creating and maintaining a secure taxation framework sufficient to meet the responsibilities of national and local administrations are enormous and growing every day, while traditional formulae appear inadequate.

Against this backdrop, increasing numbers of analysts suggest that in a globalized economy the only viable solution for the maintenance of states (and also for multilateral and international bodies) must come from equally globalized taxes. But for the time being, no one has the least idea how to implement these. ■

HUMAN DEVELOPMENT INDEX

The HDI value indicates how far a country has to go to attain certain goals: an average life span of 85 years, access to education for all and a decent income. Methodological changes were made in the HDI calculation, thus HDI value from the 1999 Human Development Report is not comparable with previous years.

Countries ranked by HDI value, 1999

#	Country	HDI	#	Country	HDI	#	Country	HDI
1	Canada	0.932	60	Belarus	0.763	118	Solomon Is.	0.623
2	Norway	0.927	61	Fiji	0.763	119	Mongolia	0.618
3	United States	0.927	62	Lithuania	0.761	120	Egypt	0.616
4	Japan	0.924	63	Bulgaria	0.758	121	Nicaragua	0.616
5	Belgium	0.923	64	Suriname	0.757	122	Botswana	0.609
6	Sweden	0.923	65	Libya	0.756	123	São Tomé and Príncipe	0.609
7	Australia	0.922	66	Seychelles	0.755	124	Gabon	0.607
8	Netherlands	0.921	67	Thailand	0.753	125	Iraq	0.586
9	Iceland	0.919	68	Romania	0.752	126	Morocco	0.582
10	United Kingdom	0.918	69	Lebanon	0.749	127	Lesotho	0.582
11	France	0.918	70	Samoa	0.747	128	Myanmar/Burma	0.580
12	Switzerland	0.914	71	Russia	0.747	129	Papua New Guinea	0.570
13	Finland	0.913	72	Ecuador	0.747	130	Zimbabwe	0.560
14	Germany	0.906	73	Macedonia, TFYR	0.746	131	Equatorial Guinea	0.549
15	Denmark	0.905	74	Latvia	0.744	132	India	0.545
16	Austria	0.904	75	St Vincent	0.744	133	Ghana	0.544
17	Luxembourg	0.902	76	Kazakhstan	0.740	134	Cameroon	0.536
18	Aotearoa/New Zealand	0.901	77	Philippines	0.740	135	Congo R.	0.533
19	Italy	0.900	78	Saudi Arabia	0.740	136	Kenya	0.519
20	Ireland	0.900	79	Brazil	0.739	137	Cambodia	0.514
21	Spain	0.894	80	Peru	0.739	138	Pakistan	0.508
22	Singapore	0.888	81	St Lucia	0.737	139	Comoros	0.506
23	Israel	0.883	82	Jamaica	0.734	140	Laos	0.491
25	Brunei	0.878	83	Belize	0.732	141	Congo D.R.	0.479
26	Cyprus	0.870	84	Paraguay	0.730	142	Sudan	0.475
27	Greece	0.867	85	Georgia	0.729	143	Togo	0.469
28	Portugal	0.858	86	Turkey	0.728	144	Nepal	0.463
29	Barbados	0.857	87	Armenia	0.728	145	Bhutan	0.459
30	Korea, South	0.852	88	Dominican Republic	0.726	146	Nigeria	0.456
31	Bahamas	0.851	89	Oman	0.725	147	Madagascar	0.453
32	Malta	0.850	90	Sri Lanka	0.721	148	Yemen	0.449
33	Slovenia	0.845	91	Ukraine	0.721	149	Mauritania	0.447
34	Chile	0.844	92	Uzbekistan	0.720	150	Bangladesh	0.440
35	Kuwait	0.833	93	Maldives	0.716	151	Zambia	0.431
36	Czech Republic	0.833	94	Jordan	0.715	152	Haiti	0.430
37	Bahrain	0.832	95	Iran	0.715	153	Senegal	0.426
38	Antigua	0.828	96	Turkmenistan	0.712	154	Côte d'Ivoire	0.422
39	Argentina	0.827	97	Kyrgyzstan	0.702	155	Benin	0.421
40	Uruguay	0.826	98	China	0.701	156	Tanzania	0.421
41	Qatar	0.814	99	Guyana	0.701	157	Djibouti	0.412
42	Slovakia	0.813	100	Albania	0.699	158	Uganda	0.404
43	United Arab Emirates	0.812	101	South Africa	0.695	159	Malawi	0.399
44	Poland	0.802	102	Tunisia	0.695	160	Angola	0.398
45	Costa Rica	0.801	103	Azerbaijan	0.695	161	Guinea	0.398
46	Trinidad and Tobago	0.797	104	Moldova	0.683	162	Chad	0.393
47	Hungary	0.795	105	Indonesia	0.681	163	Gambia	0.391
48	Venezuela	0.792	106	Cape Verde	0.677	164	Rwanda	0.379
49	Panama	0.791	107	El Salvador	0.674	165	Central African Rep.	0.378
50	Mexico	0.786	108	Tajikistan	0.665	166	Mali	0.375
51	St Kitts-Nevis	0.781	109	Algeria	0.665	167	Eritrea	0.346
52	Grenada	0.777	110	Vietnam	0.664	168	Guinea-Bissau	0.343
53	Dominica	0.776	111	Syria	0.663	169	Mozambique	0.341
54	Estonia	0.773	112	Bolivia	0.652	170	Burundi	0.324
55	Croatia	0.773	113	Swaziland	0.644	171	Burkina Faso	0.304
56	Malaysia	0.768	114	Honduras	0.641	172	Ethiopia	0.298
57	Colombia	0.768	115	Namibia	0.638	173	Niger	0.298
58	Cuba	0.765	116	Vanuatu	0.627	174	Sierra Leone	0.254
59	Mauritius	0.764	117	Guatemala	0.624			

Source: Human Development Report 1999, UNDP, 1999.

UNDER FIVE MORTALITY

Under-5 mortality rate (per 1,000 live births), 1998
Under-5 mortality is an important economic indicator in that it measures the end result of the development process rather than an 'input' such as school enrolment.

RANK		MORTALITY RATE	RANK		MORTALITY RATE	RANK		MORTALITY RATE
1	Sierra Leone	316	68	Egypt	69	133	Dominica	20
2	Angola	292	69	Kyrgyzstan	66	133	Panama	20
3	Niger	280	70	Uzbekistan	58	137	Bosnia-Herzegovina	19
4	Afghanistan	257	71	Indonesia	56	137	Sri Lanka	19
5	Mali	237	71	Tuvalu	56	137	Uruguay	19
6	Liberia	235	73	Peru	54	140	Oman	18
7	Malawi	213	74	Guatemala	52	140	Qatar	18
8	Somalia	211	75	Dominican Republic	51	140	Seychelles	18
9	Congo D.R.	207	76	Vanuatu	49	140	Trinidad and Tobago	18
10	Mozambique	206	77	Botswana	48	144	Bulgaria	17
11	Guinea-Bissau	205	77	Nicaragua	48	145	Costa Rica	16
12	Zambia	202	79	China	47	146	Barbados	15
13	Chad	198	80	Azerbaijan	46	147	Kuwait	13
14	Guinea	197	81	Honduras	44	148	Chile	12
15	Nigeria	187	81	Philippines	44	149	Hungary	11
16	Mauritania	183	83	Belize	43	149	Jamaica	11
17	Burundi	176	83	Kazakhstan	43	149	Liechtenstein	11
18	Central African Rep.	173	85	Brazil	42	149	Poland	11
18	Ethiopia	173	85	Turkey	42	153	Malaysia	10
20	Equatorial Guinea	171	85	Vietnam	42	153	Slovakia	10
21	Rwanda	170	88	Algeria	40	153	United Arab Emirates	10
22	Benin	165	89	Ecuador	39	156	Brunei	9
22	Burkina Faso	165	90	Albania	37	156	Croatia	9
24	Cambodia	163	90	St Kitts-Nevis	37	156	Cyprus	9
25	Madagascar	157	90	Thailand	37	156	Portugal	9
26	Djibouti	156	93	Jordan	36	160	Cuba	8
27	Cameroon	153	94	Lebanon	35	160	United States	8
28	Côte d'Ivoire	150	94	Moldova	35	162	Greece	7
28	Mongolia	150	94	Suriname	35	162	Ireland	7
30	Gabon	144	97	El Salvador	34	162	Malta	7
30	Togo	144	97	Mexico	34	165	Andorra	6
32	Tanzania	142	97	Palau	34	165	Aotearoa/New Zealand	6
33	Lesotho	136	100	Iran	33	165	Belgium	6
33	Pakistan	136	100	Paraguay	33	165	Canada	6
35	Uganda	134	102	Syria	32	165	Czech Republic	6
36	Haiti	130	102	Tunisia	32	165	Israel	6
37	Iraq	125	104	Armenia	30	165	Italy	6
38	Senegal	121	104	Colombia	30	165	San Marino	6
38	Yemen	121	104	Cook Is.	30	165	Spain	6
40	Kenya	117	104	Korea, North	30	165	United Kingdom	6
41	Bhutan	116	104	Nauru	30	175	Australia	5
41	Laos	116	109	Grenada	28	175	Austria	5
43	Sudan	115	110	Belarus	27	175	Denmark	5
44	Myanmar/Burma	113	110	Macedonia, TFYR	27	175	Finland	5
45	Eritrea	112	110	Samoa	27	175	France	5
45	Papua New Guinea	112	113	Saudi Arabia	26	175	Germany	5
47	Congo R.	108	113	Solomon Is.	26	175	Iceland	5
48	Bangladesh	106	115	Russia	25	175	Korea, South	5
49	Ghana	105	115	Venezuela	25	175	Luxembourg	5
49	India	105	117	Libya	24	175	Monaco	5
51	Nepal	100	117	Micronesia	24	175	Netherlands	5
52	Marshall Is.	92	117	Romania	24	175	Singapore	5
53	Comoros	90	120	Fiji	23	175	Slovenia	5
53	Swaziland	90	120	Georgia	23	175	Switzerland	5
55	Zimbabwe	89	120	Lithuania	23	189	Japan	4
56	Maldives	87	120	Mauritius	23	189	Norway	4
57	Bolivia	85	120	St Vincent	23	189	Sweden	4
58	South Africa	83	120	Tonga	23			
59	Gambia	82	126	Argentina	22			
60	Guyana	79	126	Estonia	22			
61	São Tomé and Príncipe	77	126	Latvia	22			
62	Kiribati	74	126	Ukraine	22			
62	Namibia	74	130	Bahamas	21			
62	Tajikistan	74	130	St Lucia	21			
65	Cape Verde	73	130	Yugoslavia Fed. Rep.	21			
66	Turkmenistan	72	133	Antigua	20			
67	Morocco	70	133	Bahrain	20			

Source: The State of the World's Children 2000, UNICEF, 2000.

Total net official development assistance (ODA) received (net disbursements), 1997

A = As % of GNP　　B = Millions $　　C = Per capita $

Country	A	B	C	Country	A	B	C	Country	A	B	C
Albania	6.2	155	47.5	Gambia	10.0	40	41.6	Pakistan	1.0	597	5.4
Algeria	0.6	248	9.7	Georgia	4.7	246	45.0	Panama	1.5	124	50.7
Angola	9.9	436	45.5	Ghana	7.3	493	32.2	Papua New Guinea	8.6	349	88.9
Antigua	0.8	4	62.3	Grenada	2.7	8	85.5	Paraguay	1.2	116	26.7
Argentina	0.1	222	6.7	Guatemala	1.7	302	33.7	Peru	0.8	488	22.2
Armenia	9.6	168	46.5	Guinea	10.3	382	64.5	Philippines	0.8	689	10.8
Azerbaijan	4.2	182	25.1	Guinea-Bissau	49.7	125	126.0	Poland	0.5	641	16.8
Bahamas	..	3	11.6	Guyana	39.9	272	339.9	Qatar	..	1	2.0
Bahrain	1.6	84	165.4	Haiti	11.8	332	50.4	Romania	0.6	197	8.5
Bangladesh	2.3	1,009	9.0	Honduras	6.7	308	61.3	Russia	0.2	718	4.8
Barbados	..	3	11.5	Hungary	0.3	152	14.7	Rwanda	32.0	592	82.8
Belarus	0.2	43	4.2	India	0.4	1,678	1.9	Samoa	14.4	28	172.8
Belize	2.3	14	72.1	Indonesia	0.4	832	4.6	São Tomé and Prín.	87.5	34	287.3
Benin	10.7	225	46.1	Iran	0.2	196	3.5	Saudi Arabia	..	15	0.9
Bhutan	21.3	70	113.3	Iraq	..	281	15.1	Senegal	9.6	427	56.9
Bolivia	9.2	717	106.5	Israel	1.2	1,192	240.7	Seychelles	2.8	15	212.0
Botswana	2.6	125	95.1	Jamaica	1.8	71	29.3	Sierra Leone	16.0	130	31.8
Brazil	0.1	487	3.2	Jordan	6.8	462	130.3	Singapore	..	1	0.4
Brunei	..	..	1.1	Kazakhstan	0.6	131	8.0	Slovakia	0.3	67	12.7
Bulgaria	2.1	206	23.9	Kenya	4.6	457	18.8	Slovenia	0.5	97	48.5
Burkina Faso	15.5	370	40.7	Korea, South	..	-160	-3.7	Solomon Is.	11.4	42	126.3
Burundi	12.6	119	21.2	Kuwait	..	2	1.5	South Africa	0.4	497	13.8
Cambodia	12.2	372	41.7	Kyrgyzstan	14.1	240	53.9	Sri Lanka	2.3	345	20.0
Cameroon	5.9	501	42.5	Laos	19.5	341	82.4	St Kitts-Nevis	2.7	7	167.5
Cape Verde	26.2	110	316.6	Latvia	1.5	81	30.4	St Lucia	4.1	24	160.0
Central African Rep.	9.2	92	30.5	Lebanon	1.6	239	64.5	St Vincent	2.2	6	55.6
Chad	14.3	225	38.2	Lesotho	7.3	93	52.8	Sudan	2.1	187	7.6
Chile	0.2	136	10.2	Libya	..	9	2.0	Suriname	11.4	77	190.6
China	0.2	2,040	1.8	Lithuania	1.1	102	27.3	Swaziland	1.9	27	34.0
Colombia	0.3	274	7.7	Macedonia, TYFR	6.8	149	77.8	Syria	1.2	199	15.9
Comoros	14.5	28	63.1	Madagascar	24.3	838	70.5	Tajikistan	5.0	101	18.5
Congo D.R.	3.2	168	4.4	Malawi	14.1	350	40.0	Tanzania	13.0	963	36.6
Congo R.	14.7	268	117.3	Malaysia	-0.3	-241	-12.9	Thailand	0.4	626	11.1
Côte d'Ivoire	4.7	444	37.0	Maldives	8.4	26	118.8	Togo	8.6	124	34.1
Croatia	0.2	44	9.2	Mali	18.4	455	52.3	Trinidad and Tobago	0.6	33	26.5
Cuba	..	67	6.2	Malta	0.7	22	61.5	Tunisia	1.1	194	23.3
Cyprus	0.6	49	70.6	Mauritania	23.9	250	120.0	Turkey	..	-1	..
Czech Republic	0.2	107	10.4	Mauritius	1.0	42	39.4	Turkmenistan	0.4	11	2.9
Djibouti	17.5	87	163.3	Mexico	..	108	1.3	Uganda	12.8	840	49.7
Dominica	6.2	14	194.4	Moldova	3.5	63	14.5	Ukraine	0.4	176	3.4
Dominican Republic	0.5	76	10.5	Mongolia	25.2	248	109.7	United Arab Emirates	..	4	2.0
Ecuador	0.9	172	16.4	Morocco	1.4	462	18.8	Uruguay	0.3	57	18.2
Egypt	2.5	1,947	36.3	Mozambique	37.4	963	66.8	Uzbekistan	0.5	130	6.2
El Salvador	2.6	294	56.5	Myanmar/Burma	..	45	1.1	Vanuatu	11.6	27	178.2
Equatorial Guinea	4.9	24	66.6	Namibia	5.0	166	119.7	Venezuela	..	28	1.4
Eritrea	14.8	123	38.2	Nepal	8.4	414	21.5	Vietnam	4.1	997	14.7
Estonia	1.4	65	41.5	Nicaragua	..	421	..	Yemen	7.3	366	27.3
Ethiopia	10.1	637	12.0	Niger	18.4	341	86.5	Zambia	16.9	618	77.0
Fiji	2.2	44	59.0	Nigeria	11.0	202	25.3	Zimbabwe	3.9	327	32.6
Gabon	0.9	40	40.4	Oman	..	20	11.4				

Source: Human Development Report 1999, UNDP, 1999.

A = Total external debt (millions $), 1998
B = Debt service as % of exports, 1998
C = External debt $ per capita*, 1998

	A	B	C		A	B	C
Albania	821	4.5	263	Lesotho	692	8.4	336
Algeria	30,665	42.0	1,019	Liberia	2,103	..	789
Angola	12,173	34.4	1,007	Lithuania	1,950	3.3	528
Argentina	144,050	58.2	3,988	Macedonia, TFYR	2,392	13	..
Armenia	800	8.9	226	Madagascar	4,394	14.7	292
Azerbaijan	693	2.3	90	Malawi	2,444	14.7	236
Bangladesh	16,376	9.1	131	Malaysia	44,773	8.7	2,091
Barbados	608	..	2,268	Maldives	180	..	664
Belarus	1,120	2.0	109	Mali	3,201	12.6	299
Belize	338	..	1,468	Mauritania	2,589	27.7	1,024
Benin	1,647	10.6	285	Mauritius	2,482	11.3	2,175
Bhutan	120	..	60	Mexico	159,959	20.8	1,669
Bolivia	6,077	30.2	764	Moldova	1,035	18.5	236
Botswana	548	2.7	349	Mongolia	739	6.3	286
Brazil	232,004	74.1	1,399	Morocco	20,687	23.0	756
Bulgaria	9,907	22.1	1,188	Mozambique	8,208	18.0	435
Burkina Faso	1,399	10.7	124	Myanmar/Burma	5,680	5.3	128
Burundi	1,119	40.0	173	Nepal	2,646	7.0	116
Cambodia	2,210	1.5	206	Nicaragua	5,968	25.5	1,242
Cameroon	9,829	22.3	687	Niger	1,659	18.4	165
Cape Verde	244	..	597	Nigeria	30,315	11.2	285
Central African Rep.	921	20.9	264	Oman	3,629	..	1,523
Chad	1,091	10.6	150	Pakistan	32,229	23.6	218
Chile	36,302	22.3	2,449	Panama	6,689	7.6	2,417
China	154,599	8.6	123	Papua New Guinea	2,692	8.6	585
Colombia	33,263	30.7	815	Paraguay	2,304	5.3	441
Comoros	203	..	309	Peru	32,397	28.3	1,306
Congo D.R.	12,929	1.2	263	Philippines	47,817	11.8	656
Congo R.	5,119	3.3	1,838	Poland	47,708	9.7	1,232
Costa Rica	3,971	7.6	1,034	Romania	9,513	23.5	423
Côte d'Ivoire	..	26.1	..	Russia	183,601	12.1	1,245
Croatia	8,297	8.9	1,852	Rwanda	1,226	16.9	186
Czech Republic	25,301	15.2	2,461	Samoa	180	..	1,035
Djibouti	288	..	462	São Tomé and Príncipe	246	..	1,743
Dominica	109	..	1,534	Senegal	3,861	23.2	429
Dominican Republic	4,451	4.2	541	Seychelles	187	..	2,457
Ecuador	15,140	28.8	1,244	Sierra Leone	1,243	18.2	272
Egypt	31,964	9.5	484	Slovakia	9,893	15.9	1,840
El Salvador	3,633	10.4	602	Solomon Is.	152	..	365
Equatorial Guinea	306	..	710	Somalia	2,635	..	285
Eritrea	149	1.5	42	South Africa	24,711	12.2	628
Estonia	782	2.1	547	Sri Lanka	8,526	6.6	462
Ethiopia	10,352	11.3	174	St Kitts-Nevis	115	..	..
Fiji	193	..	242	St Lucia	184	..	..
Gabon	4,425	12.0	3,791	St Vincent	420	..	..
Gambia	477	9.7	388	Sudan	16,843	9.8	595
Georgia	1,674	7.6	331	Swaziland	251	..	263
Ghana	6,884	28.4	359	Syria	22,435	6.4	1,463
Grenada	183	..	1,966	Tajikistan	1,070	13.7	178
Guatemala	4,565	9.8	423	Tanzania	7,603	20.8	237
Guinea	3,546	19.5	483	Thailand	86,172	19.2	1,429
Guinea-Bissau	964	25.6	831	Togo	1,448	5.7	329
Guyana	1,653	..	1,944	Tonga	65	..	660
Haiti	1,048	8.2	132	Trinidad and Tobago	2,193	10.2	1,710
Honduras	5,002	18.7	814	Tunisia	11,078	15.1	1,187
Hungary	28,580	27.3	2,825	Turkey	102,074	21.2	1,583
India	98,232	20.6	100	Turkmenistan	2,266	42.0	526
Indonesia	150,875	33.0	731	Uganda	3,935	23.6	191
Iran	14,391	20.2	219	Ukraine	12,718	11.4	250
Jamaica	3,995	12.8	1,574	Uruguay	7,600	23.5	2,311
Jordan	8,484	16.4	1,346	Uzbekistan	3,162	13.2	134
Kazakhstan	5,714	13.0	350	Vanuatu	63	..	347
Kenya	7,010	18.8	242	Venezuela	37,003	27.4	1,592
Korea, South	139,097	12.9	5,958	Vietnam	22,359	8.9	288
Kyrgyzstan	1,148	9.4	247	Yemen	4,138	4.2	245
Laos	2,437	6.3	472	Yugoslavia Fed. Rep.	13,742	..	1,292
Latvia	756	2.5	312	Zambia	6,865	17.7	782
Lebanon	6,725	18.7	2,108	Zimbabwe	4,716	38.2	415

(*) Calculated from total 1998 external debt and total 1998 population.

Source: World Development Indicators 2000, World Bank, 2000; The State of the World's Children 2000, UNICEF, 2000.

V. International Relations

THROUGHOUT MOST of the 20th century, communities organised in states assigned the task of maintaining public order to a group of officials. The indications are that the new century is preparing to open the era of a global police force which, free of the limits imposed by frontiers, will take on the task of making sure laws are obeyed and that offenders are punished.

The development of a global police force

The traditional police forces of the last century were organised locally, made up of state or municipal public employees who, working on the basis of their country's laws, were responsible for the prevention of crime, for the capture of suspects and for handing them over to the legal authorities who would judge and apply sanctions where necessary.

These police forces had no extraterritorial function, some even being limited to internal administrative juridical boundaries, being answerable to the legal and, ultimately, political establishment for any excesses. For tasks beyond national frontiers - for defence - the army was normally used, specialised in warfare and not in dealing with civilians.

In the 20th century, driven by increasing world trade and imperialist developments, there was an increase in the phenomenon of foreign corrective intervention to regulate various parts of the world. But in the last decade of the 20th century there was exponential growth in the workload of the extraterritorial police. These years also gave rise to the notion of an "international community", replacing the old concept nurtured by European colonialism of "civilised nations", who took on civilisation as a task all of their own.

The "international community", on the other hand is a vague concept which includes - in general terms - the European Union (EU), Canada, the United States and also Japan, Australia and South Africa and other regional powers. By extension, it includes those countries who feel identified to join this group, offering their support to decisions made by the former group. When the international community deems it necessary to re-establish some order or other, the international political process comes into action.

Normally debate on the need for police mechanisms to monitor regional situations is informal and involves former colonial powers, local powers or countries more powerful than the recipient of the corrective action.

The great U-turn of 1999

But up until 1999, the executors of global policing had really been only two: either a regional organisation, generally spurred by a local power, or the UN which - through its Security Council - would decide the nature of the operation to be undertaken, along with the composition of the troops, the amount of time in which the conflict should be resolved and the monitoring mechanisms of the policing tasks themselves. This year, for the first time, the North Atlantic Treaty Organization (NATO) assumed police control in an area beyond its bounds: the Federal Republic of Yugoslavia.

The scenario in which the century opened will no doubt be repeated in the future. On the one hand, the constant growth of world trade, the productive and commercial interdependence of the world, along with the spectacular development in transport and communication media, increase the tendency to very strong supranational integration.

On the other hand the growth of activities considered criminal (drug-trafficking, industrial and intellectual piracy, ecological crimes) which also cross frontiers, allow us to forecast increasing intervention from the "international community" in the internal affairs of countries. The aim of these interventions can be presented as being to safeguard basic human rights. But the aim may also be seen as attempts to control regions of instability in a highly integrated and sensitive economic system.

Strategic forecasts from the large economic blocs, represented mainly by the Group of 8 countries (the United States, Canada, the United Kingdom, France, Italy, Germany and Japan plus Russia) mask the potential differences between their members - particularly between the Western powers and Japan, and within the EU states and the US - but set a course of action should this happen. As it is only these powers that could put into practice any form of global police control, it is interesting to see their forecasts for the future.

Some predictions

US economist Francis Fukuyama stands out amongst the optimistic ideologists, predicting the total triumph of Western representative democracy against socialism and of the market over economic planning, thus bringing an end to history and conflict as we knew them. Under his hypothesis, trade would replace war,

thus leaving little need for a global police force.

The pessimistic school of thought is led by authors like Robert Kaplan, whose prediction for the current century is for one zone of peace and prosperity, and another of chaos and poverty. In order to avoid the latter endangering the achievements of the former, mechanisms must be put in place to defend stability, and this naturally includes police surveillance of the chaos zone.

US thinker, Samuel Huntington, meanwhile believes that the end of the Cold War which marked the last century would open the way for confrontation between civilisations. The Islamic nations and China would be the next competitors to Western hegemony.

At the same time, in late 1999, the US National Security Council published a report entitled *The Coming World* suggesting four possible scenarios:

- The first, entitled "democratic peace" would have national identities persisting and collaborating - in the case of the most powerful nations - in order to ensure peace and freedom of trade. The main achievement of this scenario would be to integrate China and Russia into the heart of the "international community", the maintainer of order.

- The second scenario is that of "triumphant globalization", where national identities gradually disappear, leaving room for the multilateral institutions and particularly the transnational corporations to stimulate a growth of prosperity. The tasks of policing and defence would also fall back upon joint bodies.

- "Protectionist nationalism" is the third scenario. This envisages the disappearance of co-operation and the free market and shows the stronger powers competing militarily to maintain their markets and areas of influence.

- Finally comes the possibility of "chaos", caused by a global economic depression, environmental disaster or ethnic violence, leading to a world full of wars, mass migrations in search of better living conditions and waves of terrorism.

The future of the North Atlantic Treaty Organization (NATO)

With NATO's 50th birthday in 1999 hundreds of articles appeared on the organization's future. The influential Brookings Foundation stated that the alliance - created as a tool of defence against the growth of the communist bloc - would be maintained under a new concept: "NATO must abandon its emphasis on defending territories to move on to seeing itself as an instrument which defends common interests".

The abandonment of clearly defined territorial defence, and its replacement by the defence of interests, inevitably going beyond frontiers, is what enables NATO to set up policing functions. The main global enemies to be monitored, according to the Brookings Foundation, would be located in the Middle East, the Persian Gulf and Northeast Asia.

And there would most probably be intervention, not against groups of countries, but within zones of certain countries. To illustrate this, it is worth noting that of the 27 biggest armed conflicts of 1998, only two were between states: the face-off between India and Pakistan and the war between Eritrea and Ethiopia.

Analyst Johan Galtung predicted that given the eastern expansion of NATO into Turkey, it is highly probable that a Moscow-Beijing-New Delhi axis will emerge.

Meanwhile, Walter McDougall summed up the basic objectives of Washington's foreign policy for the future in four points:

1. Security for the territory, citizens and properties of the United States and security for those countries whose stability directly affects that of this nation;

2. To achieve the greatest extent of social and economic stability, in order to be prepared to anticipate difficulties there where they could arise;

3. To build a broad and transparent system of trade and commerce, both in order to increase the prosperity of the United States and to attract third countries to the system and

4. To promote respect for those values US citizens consider basic, "not only because it is just but because the more respect given to their own citizens, the more probable it is they will respect those of others."

It is evident that in order to carry out its objectives, the United States must have sufficient strength to avoid diversions; and many of these must be defused or taken care of by some type of global police force.

Sketching an outline

States which consider themselves representatives of the "international community" have planned preventive strategies and the foundations are laid for a world police force.

There are crimes defined on a global scale; all stand in the way of the normal circulation of goods and services. They include drug trafficking, conflicts which cause waves of immigration to the most industrialised countries, the violation of human rights established in the United Nations Charter and so on. There is also a dossier on the regular suspects - the countries which maintain economic and political sanctions on the United States: Syria, Iraq, Iran, Cuba, North Korea and Yugoslavia.

It is clear that the world police will not function on an official basis nor in an automatic manner. Rather, the force will seek at all times to legitimize its actions according to the interests of the "international community." For example, a crime committed by a friendly country would not be treated as harshly as one in one of the countries "with a record".

Policing tasks could be carried out at the request of governments - as in the case of Bolivia and Colombia - which have support to tackle drug trafficking. But policing could also be carried out without authorisation and even against the will of the authorities with jurisdiction in a region. Such was the case in Yugoslavia with the entry of NATO troops in the province of Kosovo.

The potential danger of a global police force is that once the UN loses its authority and recognition, there would be no body with sufficient legitimacy to provide a legal framework within which to regulate police action. There is no knowing which regulations will apply to the force, what sort of preventive and repressive powers it will have, what the sanctions will be for those who break international laws, and how the mechanism for implementing them will be invoked.

But above all, the project for a global police force lacks an appropriate system of *internal* regulation. Nobody knows who should judge its excesses or mistakes. And nobody knows which or what sort of body will judge its conduct and set fair objectives. To sum up, if the UN loses its role as the representative of the "international community", this right will remain in the hands of those who have the strongest interests and the greatest means to bring the global police under their own control. ∎

Global Ethic

THE PARLIAMENT of the World's Religions issued a statement on the need of a new, global ethic to rule the world. Grounded in the conviction of the existence of an Ultimate Reality, it warns about the tensions that threaten the peaceful building of a better world and called for the full realization of the intrinsic dignity of the human person, the inalienable freedom and equality in principle of all people.

No new global order without a new global ethic

We women and men of various religions and regions of Earth are addressing all people, religious and non-religious. We wish to express the following convictions which we hold in common:

- We all have a responsibility for a better global order.
- Our involvement for the sake of human rights, freedom, justice, peace and the preservation of Earth is absolutely necessary.

- Our different religious and cultural traditions must not prevent our common involvement in opposing all forms of inhumanity and working for greater humanity.
- The principles expressed in this Global Ethic can be affirmed by all persons with ethical convictions whether religiously grounded or not.
- As religious and spiritual people we base our lives on an Ultimate Reality and draw

spiritual power and hope therefrom in trust, in prayer or meditation, in word or silence. We have a special responsibility for the welfare of all humanity and care for the planet Earth. We do not consider ourselves better than other women and men, but we trust that the ancient wisdom of our religions can point the way for the future.

After two world wars and the end of the Cold War, the collapse of fascism and nazism, the shaking to the foundations of communism and colonialism, humanity has entered a new phase of its history.

Today we possess sufficient economic, cultural and spiritual resources to introduce a better global order. But old and new ethnic, national, social, economic and religious tensions threaten the peaceful building of a better world. We have experienced greater technological progress than ever before, yet we see that world-wide poverty, hunger, death of children, unemployment, misery and the destruction of nature have not diminished but rather have increased. Many peoples are threatened with economic ruin, social disarray, political marginalization, ecological catastrophe and national collapse.

In such a dramatic global situation humanity needs a vision of peoples living peacefully together, of ethnic and ethical groupings and of religions sharing responsibility for the care of Earth. A vision rests on hopes, goals, ideals, standards. But all over the world these have slipped from our hands.

Yet we are convinced that, despite their frequent abuses and failures, it is the communities of faith who bear a responsibility to demonstrate that such hopes, ideals and standards can be guarded, grounded and lived. This is especially true in the modern state. Guarantees of freedom of conscience and religion are necessary but they are no substitute for binding values, convictions, and norms which are valid for all humans regardless of their social origin, sex, skin color, language or religion.

We are convinced of the fundamental unity of the human family on Earth. We recall the 1948 Universal Declaration of Human Rights of the United Nations. What it formally proclaimed at the level of rights we wish to confirm and deepen here from the perspective of an ethic: the full realization of the intrinsic dignity of the human person, the inalienable freedom and equality in principle of all people and the necessary solidarity and interdependence of all people with each other.

On the basis of personal experiences and the burdensome history of our planet we have learned:

- that a better global order cannot be created or enforced by laws, prescriptions and conventions alone;

- that the realization of peace, justice and the protection of Earth depends on the insight and readiness of men and women to act justly;

- that action in favor of rights and freedoms presumes a consciousness of responsibility and duty, and that therefore both the minds and hearts of women and men must be addressed;

- that rights without morality cannot long endure, and that there will be no better global order without a global ethic.

By a global ethic we do not mean a global ideology or a single unified religion beyond all existing religions, and certainly not the domination of one religion over all others. By a global ethic we mean a fundamental consensus on binding values, irrevocable standards and personal attitudes. Without such a fundamental consensus on an ethic, sooner or later every community will be threatened by chaos or dictatorship, and individuals will despair. ■

Source: Parliament of the World's Religions, Cape Town, South Africa, December 1999.

ARMS IN FIGURES

A = Imports of conventional weapons ($ millions, 1990 prices), 1997
B = Military expenditure as % of GDP, 1996

COUNTRY	A	B	COUNTRY	A	B	COUNTRY	A	B
Albania	..	1.5	Guatemala	..	0.8	Panama	..	1.2
Algeria		3.4	Guyana	..	0.8	Paraguay	..	1.3
Aotearoa/New Zealand	343	1.2	Honduras	..	1.1	Peru	258	1.3
Argentina	148	1.2	Hungary	..	1.6	Philippines	47	1.6
Australia	215	2.3	India	1,085	2.5	Poland	..	2.8
Austria	139	0.9	Indonesia	171	1.3	Portugal	14	2.4
Bahrain	13	5.4	Iran	11	2.5	Qatar	286	..
Belarus	13	1.2	Ireland	..	1.1	Romania	12	3.5
Belgium	34	1.6	Israel	41	8.7	Russia	..	3.7
Bolivia	..	1.1	Italy	552	1.9	Saudi Arabia	2,370	13.2
Botswana	..	3.2	Japan	584	0.1	Seychelles	..	2.2
Brazil	384	1.9	Jordan	62	8.8	Sierra Leone	..	1.8
Bulgaria	40	1.8	Korea, South	1,077	3.2	Singapore	108	4.3
Burundi	..	4.9	Kuwait	411	11.9	Slovakia	..	2.3
Cambodia	..	4.7	Latvia	..	0.8	Slovenia	..	1.6
Canada	97	1.4	Lebanon	10	6.3	South Africa	8	2.1
Central African Rep.	..	1.1	Lithuania	..	0.5	Spain	316	1.5
Chile	180	1.6	Luxembourg	..	0.7	Sri Lanka	41	6.0
China	1,816	1.1	Madagascar	..	0.8	Sudan	..	1.6
Colombia	190	..	Malawi	..	0.8	Swaziland	..	2.3
Croatia	37	14.5	Malaysia	1,346	2.4	Sweden	123	2.4
Cyprus	110	3.4	Malta	..	0.1	Switzerland	391	1.5
Czech Republic	..	1.8	Mauritius	..	0.3	Syria	..	6.7
Denmark	46	1.8	Mexico	96	0.4	Thailand	1,031	1.9
Egypt	867	..	Moldova	..	0.8	Tunisia	37	1.8
El Salvador	..	0.9	Mongolia	..	2.2	Turkey	1,276	4.3
Eritrea	53	..	Morocco	104	3.9	Uganda	..	3.8
Estonia	..	1.2	Mozambique	..	3.4	Ukraine	..	4.5
Ethiopia	..	1.8	Myanmar/Burma	100		United Arab Emirates	808	4.5
Finland	492	..	Namibia	..	2.3	United Kingdom	71	3.0
Finland	..	1.6	Nepal	..	0.8	United States	656	3.6
France	160	3.0	Netherlands	93	2.0	Uruguay	..	1.5
Gambia	..	1.4	Nicaragua	..	1.6	Venezuela	..	1.0
Georgia	..	1.3	Nigeria	..	0.7	Vietnam	84	..
Germany	..	1.7	Norway	155	2.3	Zambia	..	1.1
Ghana	..	0.6	Oman	173	13.2	Zimbabwe	..	2.7
Greece	715	4.5	Pakistan	572	5.6			

Source: Human Development Report 1999, UNDP, 1999.

Countries of the world

Afghanistan

Afghanestan

Population: 21,923,000 (1999)
Area: 652,090 SQ KM
Capital: Kabul
Currency: Afghani
Language: Pushtu

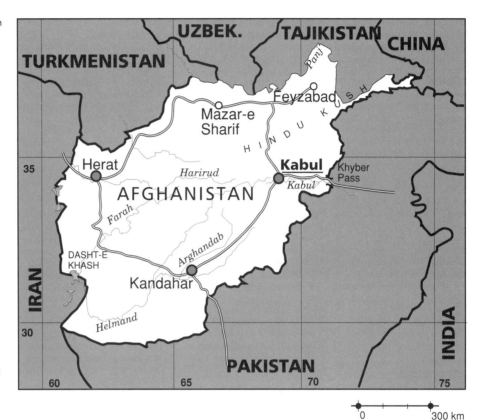

The group of mountains known as the Hindu Kush (called the Caucasus by the Greeks and Paropamisos by the Persians) were sparsely populated until the agricultural revolution. During this period the region was a passageway for frequent migrations of displaced peoples, and the Khyber Pass became the gateway to northern India.

[2] The Hindu Kush was incorporated into the Persian Empire of Cyrus the Great in the sixth century BC, and 300 years later became part of the Hellenic world, as a result of the military campaigns of Alexander of Macedonia who founded Alexandropolis (present-day Kandahar). An armistice between the Greeks and Indians made it a province of the Mauryan Empire, and unified all of northern India.

[3] Between the 1st century BC and the 3rd century AD, an invading nation of Scythian origin (speaking an Indo-European language) founded the state of Kusana, on the trade line between Rome, India and China, known as the "silk route". Following this trail, along the Tarim River basin, Buddhism found its way into China. In 240 AD, Kusana was annexed to the new Sassanian Persian Empire until the beginning of the 8th century and the succession of Caliph Walid, who extended his rule, and the Islamic faith, as far as the Indus.

[4] Towards the 13th century, the Mongol invasion caused great upheaval in the Old World. Afghanistan became part of the empire ruled by Genghis Khan from Karakoram. In 1360, the empire disintegrated as a result of constant dynastic strife and the Afghan region was ruled by Tamerlane, whose descendants governed until the beginning of the 16th century.

[5] With the rise of the third Persian Shi'a Empire (1502) and the Empire of the Great Mogul in India (1526), the region became the scene of constant battles between the Mongols of India who dominated Kabul, the Saffavid Persians who controlled the southern region, and the Uzbek descendants of Tamerlane who ruled the northwest.

[6] The unification of the country in 1747 came about through battles and political upheaval -

when an assembly of local chieftains elected Shah Ahmad Durrani, a military commander who previously served Persian sovereigns. Ruling by military might, the new shah consolidated the national borders. Nevertheless, due to its geopolitical relevance, the region was prone to attacks and its frontiers suffered radical transformations.

[7] Since the beginning of the 18th century the Russians had arrived in the area, eager to gain access to the sea ports of the Persian Gulf and the Arabian Sea in order to maintain a closer watch on their main enemy there, the Ottoman Empire. The British were also intent on controlling the Indus Valley area, where nomadic migrations and sanctuaries sheltering Indian rebels threatened their incipient colonial domain.

[8] Consequently, geopolitical conditions were as turbulent as they are today in Afghanistan, Iran and Pakistan. These regions held the geographic key to the colonial designs of both Russia and Britain. However, the two countries used divergent tactics: in Afghanistan, the Russians relied on diplomacy

and bribery whilst the British used force.

[9] The British defeat in the first British-Afghan War (1839-1842) reinforced Dost Muhammad Shah's slightly pro-Russian sympathies. He increased his influence in northern India by encouraging anti-British movements. His son Sher Ali Shah continued this policy, which led to a British invasion of the country once again.

[10] As a result of the second British-Afghan War (1878-1880), the Durrani dynasty was overthrown. Afghanistan lost its territories south of the Khyber (including the Pass itself) and under the rule of the British-imposed Emir, lost control over its foreign relations. Eventually, the British granted Afghanistan a narrow strip of land extending Afghan territory as far as the Chinese border. This closed off a common frontier between Russian and British territories.

[11] Afghanistan's borders, established artificially to create a buffer state between two empires, were never recognized by the peoples they were supposed to divide, who routinely crossed with their herds of cattle in search of

pastures. In 1919, after a third British-Afghan war, lasting four months, the country was free from British "protection". Independence leader Emir Amanullah Khan (the heir and grandson of the British-imposed ruler) came to power, modernized the country and became the first head of state to recognize the revolutionary government of the Soviet Union. He was overthrown in 1929 by the Mohammadzai clan (descendants of the dynasty ousted in 1879) which crowned Muhammad Nadir Shah. Constitutional guarantees in 1931 recognized the autonomy of local leaders and created a system which remained unchallenged until 1953.

[12] In that year, Muhammad Daud Khan, the Shah's cousin and brother-in-law, became Prime Minister and launched a new modernization process: he nationalized utilities, built roads, irrigation systems, schools and hydroelectric facilities (with US funding); he abolished the obligatory use of the *chador* (veil) by women; reorganized the armed forces (with Soviet assistance); and maintained neutrality throughout the Cold War. Unfortunately, land

reform was never attempted and he was forced to abdicate in 1963.

[13] The following period was dominated by traditional forces. The People's Democratic Party of Afghanistan (PDPA), founded as an underground organization, staged its first anti-government demonstrations in 1965, as Zahir Shah and his council were drawing up a new constitution. The PDPA split into two factions: the Khalk advocated revolution through a worker-peasant alliance, and the Parcham which sought to find a broad-based front involving the intellectuals, national bourgeoisie, urban middle class and military. The military finally overthrew the monarchy and Zahir Shah in 1973, installing Muhammad Daud as president with PDPA support.

[14] In April 1977, the murder of PDPA leader Mir Akhbar Khyber triggered a popular uprising. The Parcham military reacted by deposing President Daud, replacing him with Nur Muhammad Taraki. Hafizulah Amin and Babrak Karmal were appointed vice premiers but conflicts arose and in April 1979, Amin was appointed Prime minister, a position previously vacant. In September, Amin succeeded in a conspiracy to overthrow the President, who was subsequently murdered.

[15] As the new leader, Amin introduced reforms: a compulsory literacy campaign; abolition of the dowry system and other traditional customs; and radical land reforms. All of which brought predictable opposition from traditional local leaders and religious authorities. In February 1979, the US ambassador to Kabul was kidnapped and murdered; consequently the US withdrew economic assistance and increased hostilities towards what they considered a pro-Soviet government. The period between April 1978 and September 1979 saw 25 different cabinets. Amin survived several assassination attempts until in late 1979 he was finally murdered.

[16] He was replaced by Babrak Karmal, who had been placed in power by the Soviet troops that had entered the country in December 1979. Karmal himself had legitimized their presence, citing a treaty of friendship and cooperation between the two states. Soviet intervention served as a pretext for the intensification of the "Second Cold War", initiated several months earlier with the US decision to freeze SALT, the Strategic Arms Limitation Treaty. The presence of the Soviets also triggered a sense of solidarity among Islamic fundamentalists, who travelled into Afghan territory to fight "Satan", in volunteer expeditions financed by Saudi Arabia. Afghan peasants who supported the *mujahedin*, or Islamic guerrillas, migrated to the cities or to neighboring Pakistan or Iran.

[17] In April 1986, heavy fighting near the border with Pakistan left an estimated 2,000 insurgents and 200 Pakistani soldiers dead, and a combined Afghan-Soviet force captured the main opposition base. On May 4, President Babrak Karmal returned from several weeks of medical treatment in Moscow and asked to be relieved of his party post.

[18] New PDPA Secretary-General Najibullah, a 39 year old young doctor of Pushtu origin was made president. He announced a unilateral ceasefire in January 1987, with guarantees for guerrilla leaders willing to negotiate with the government, an amnesty for rebel prisoners, and the promise of a prompt withdrawal of Soviet troops.

[19] In 1988, after six years of negotiations, an Afghan-Pakistani accord was signed in Geneva, guaranteed by both the US and USSR. The agreement set the terms of mutual relations specifying the principles of non-interference and non-intervention, and guaranteeing the voluntary return of refugees. Another document, signed by Afghanistan and the USSR, provided for the withdrawal of Soviet troops a month later.

[20] Three thousand Jamiat-i-Islami fighters announced they would take advantage of the amnesty law, but turned the disarmament ceremony into an ambush, killing several members of the Kabul military high command. The PDPA was renamed the Watan Party, the Party of the Homeland.

[21] In September 1991, the US and USSR stopped sending arms to the Afghan guerrillas. The US-USSR pact sparked the confrontation between Saudi Arabia and Iran, countries that financed the Afghan *mujahedin* groups. The Kabul regime had no foreign support since the break-up of the USSR.

[22] President Najibullah was replaced in mid-April 1992, after he took refuge in the UN headquarters in Kabul. The Government remained in the hands of the four vice-presidents. The authorities immediately announced the Government's willingness to negotiate with the rebel groups and met commander Ahmed Shah Massud - of the Jamiat-i-Islami - at the city gates. Massud was a Tajik leader, known as the "Lion of Panjshir" because of the fierce battles he had waged in the northern region against the army and the Soviet occupation troops. Massud's presence in Kabul triggered demonstrations among the guerrilla groups who belonged to the Pushtu majority in the south and east of the country. From Pakistan, Gulbuddin Hekhmatyar, the head of fundamenstalist group Hezb-i-Islami, threatened to start bombing the capital if Massud did not surrender to the government. Provisional president Abdul Rahim Hatif stated that the Government would be transferred to a coalition of all the rebel groups and to none in particular. In the days that followed, the forces of Massud and Hekhmatyar fought in Kabul itself.

[23] In March, the president of the Central Bank fled the country, taking with him all the country's foreign reserves.

[24] An interim government under the leadership of Sibgatullah Mojadidi took power, toward the end of April. The alliance of moderate Muslim groups, under the leadership of Ahmed Shah Massud - the new minister of defence - gained control of the capital, expelling the Islamic fundamentalists led by Gulbuddin Hekhmatyar. Pakistan, Iran, Turkey and Russia were the first countries to recognize the new Afghan government.

[25] On May 6 1992, the Interim Council formally dissolved the communist Watan Party, whose

PROFILE

ENVIRONMENT

The country consists of a system of highland plains and plateaus, separated by east-west mountain ranges (principally the Hindu Kush) which converge on the Himalayan Pamir. The main cities are located in the eastern valleys. The country is dry and rocky though there are many fertile lowlands and valleys where cotton, fruit and grain are grown. Coal, natural gas and iron ore are the main mineral resources. The rapid increase in the rate of deforestation (which relates with desertification and soil degradation) constitutes the main environmental problem. The shortage of drinking water has contributed to the increase in infectious diseases.

SOCIETY

Peoples: The Pushtus (Pathans) are the majority of the population, the Tajiks one third; also Uzbeks, Hazaras and nomads of Mongol origin.
Religions: 99 per cent of the population is Muslim (Sunni and Shi'a).
Languages: Pushtu is the national language. Persian (Dari) is widely used; also Turkic and dozens of other languages.
Political Parties:
The Taliban party (whose name means "students") controls two thirds of the country and governs according to the party's interpretation of the Koran. Former Defence Minister, Ahmed Shah Massud, controls a strip in the north-east part of Afghanistan.

THE STATE

Official Name: Doulat i Islami-ye Afghánistan (Islamic State of Afghanistan).
Administrative divisions: 31 provinces.
Capital: Kabul 2,000,000 people (est 1997).
Other cities: Kandahar 225,500 people; Herat 177,300; Mazar-e-Sharif 130,600 (1988).
Government: Mohammed Omar Akhunzada was elected "Commandant of Believers" ("amir ol momumin").
National Holiday: May 27, Independence Day (1919).

various factions had governed the country since 1978. The Council set up a special court to try the former communist officials who had violated either Islamic or national laws. The KHAD, the country's secret police, and the National Assembly were also dissolved.

26 Some of the changes which were carried out showed the government's intention of imposing Islamic law: the sale of alcohol was outlawed, and an attempt was made to enforce new rules requiring women to cover their heads and wear traditional Islamic dress.

27 Towards the end of May 1992, most of the rebel Afghan groups, including the Hezb-i-Islami and the Jamiat-i-Islami, announced a peace agreement. The main points were the decision to hold elections within a year, and the withdrawal of some militia.

28 A few days after the agreement, interim president Modjadidi miraculously escaped an attempt on his life. On May 31, the truce between the two main factions of guerrillas was broken. During the first few days of June, the Afghan capital once again became a battleground for Hezb-i-Islami and Jamiat-i-Islami troops. In a week of fierce fighting, the death toll reached 5,000, and Kabul took on the look of a city devastated by war.

29 On June 28, Mojadidi turned over the presidency to the leader of Jamiat-i-Islami, Burhanuddin Rabbani. The latter declared, upon assuming the presidency, "We have only one condition in our program: unity. We will not take a single step without consensus".

30 Hekhmatyar continued fighting against Kabul, demanding the withdrawal of Massud, as well as the militia loyal to Abdel Rashid Dostam. The latter had been a member of the communist government, but had defected in order to join the Muslim guerrillas that took power.

31 The UN announced a $10 million aid program, to provide food and medication to the civilian population that had been forced to leave Kabul because of the violence. As a result of the war, the country's economy had come to a standstill and 60 per cent of its productive structure had been destroyed. Afghanistan had also become the world's largest producer of opium.

32 The Pakistani Government, a long-term supplier of the *mujahedin*, decided to put a stop to the arms and food contraband across its border with Afghanistan, in order to weaken Hekhmatyar, whom it accused of being responsible for a deterioration in relations between the two countries. The United Nations High Commissioner for Refugees declared the existence of 4.5 million Afghan war refugees. Almost 3 million of these were in Iran, and the Iranian Government announced its desire to expel the refugees. Most of these were Shi'ia Muslims, an Afghan minority.

33 In March 1993, the leaders of eight rival factions announced the signing of a peace agreement in Islamabad, Pakistan. The accord, sponsored by Pakistan's prime minister Nawaz Sharif, resulted in Rabbani and Hekhmatyar agreeing to share power for an 18-month period, until elections could be held. Rabbani was to continue as president, while Hekhmatyar was to be prime minister. Abdul Rashid Dostam, the powerful general whose militia controlled most of the northern part of the country, did not take part in the peace conference.

34 In June, Hekhmatyar became prime minister and Massud resigned from the Ministry of Defence. In September, Russian and Tajik government forces confronted Tajik rebels allied to Afghan fighters along the border with Tajikistan. In spite of accusations from Moscow and the Tajik capital, Dushanbe, Afghan authorities denied any participation in the conflict and demanded the withdrawal of Russian forces from their territory.

35 In January 1994, Dostam's militias, allied to prime minister Hekhmatyar, launched an offensive against the capital. Kabul remained divided in zones controlled by rival groups, while 75 per cent of the capital's 2 million population took refuge in other regions. In June, Rabbani refused to hand over the Government at the end of his term, which was finally extended by the supreme court.

36 The division of Afghanistan was partly a result of rivalry between various countries of the region, including Iran, Saudi Arabia, Uzbekistan, Pakistan and Russia, which intervened directly or indirectly in the civil war. In 1995,

the emergence of the armed Taliban group ("students" in Persian), in the south of Afghanistan, changed the course of the war. These guerrillas, trained in Pakistan, aimed to create a united Islamic government in Afghanistan and were supported by broad swathes of society.

37 In February, the Taliban occupied Hekhmatyar's general barracks in the centre of the country, while the Dostam militias continued reinforcing their positions in the north-west. Following the destruction of Kabul, some two thirds of the population resided in zones controlled by the Uzbek militias. At a time when no solution could be seen for the civil war, in mid-1996, some 8,000 Taliban guerrillas started to bombard the centre of Kabul from the suburbs, tightening the siege on the capital. In September, the capital fell into Taliban hands, while the Government headed to the north of the country.

38 During the first months of 1997, the situation remained unchanged but at the end of May, Dostam tried to break his alliance with the displaced president Burhanuddin Rabbani and join with the Taliban militia. The new alliance barely lasted two weeks and the gains made by the Kabul forces were rapidly lost. Ahmed Shah Massud, Rabbani's former military chief became the focal point of the new anti-Taliban alliance and took control of the north-east, which virtually started to function as an independent republic.

39 The Taliban were supported by Pakistan, Saudi Arabia and the US in taking over most of the Afghan territory. Once they had taken Kabul, the Taliban - following their decision to govern according to their interpretation of the Koran - banished women from the public sphere and from the education system. Meanwhile, they banned music and singing (except for hymns), cinema, theatre and alcohol, declaring them "non-Islamic". Following the taking of Kabul, the Taliban regime passed a series of decrees which sought to impose its form of Koranic law on sport. In October 1997, in commemoration of the fall of Kabul, a great sporting event was held with 3,000 participating male athletes covered from the neck to below the knees (women were also

banished from the sporting world). Applause was also prohibited, and the spectators were informed they were to encourage the athletes by shouting "Allah u Akbar" (God is great).

40 In early 1998, an earthquake shook Rustaq, a city controlled by opposition troops led by Massud. The government in Kabul considered this a "tragedy for all Afghanis", and sent dozens of lorries of medical supplies and food to help the thousands suffering cold and hunger as a result of the earthquake.

41 In July 1999, the opposition attempted unification under the leadership of Massud, who continued to control 10 per cent of the territory. But the government military offensive announced in August put the brakes on this process. The fighting brought little change, with advances and retreats on both sides. ∎

Albania

Shqipërí

Population: 3,113,000 (1999)
Area: 28,750 SQ KM
Capital: Tirana (Tiranë)
Currency: New lek
Language: Albanian

The Albanians are descendants of the ancient Illyrians, an Indo-European people who had migrated southward from Central Europe to the north of Greece by the beginning of the Iron Age. The southern Illyrians were much in contact with Greek colonies, while the northern Albanian tribes were united at various times under local kings. The most important of them was Argon, whose kingdom (second half of the 3rd century BC) expanded from Dalmatia in the north to the Vijose river in the south.

[2] By the year 168 BC the Romans conquered all of Illyria and then the Albanians became part of the prosperous Roman province of Illyricum. After 395 AD, with the decline of the Roman Empire, the area was administered from Constantinople. Despite the Hun incursions during the 3rd to 5th centuries, and the Slavic invasions during the 6th and 7th centuries, the Albanians were one of the few peoples in the Balkans who kept their own language and customs. In any case, with the passage of the years the impact of the Roman, Byzantine and Slavic influences changed the old Illyrian culture into the new Albanian one. Between the 8th and 11th centuries AD, even the name of Illyria changed to Albania. When the Christian church split in 1054, southern Albania maintained links with Constantinople, whilst the north fell under Roman jurisdiction, marking the first significant religious fragmentation of the country.

[3] When the Turks invaded in 1431, the Albanians put up stiff resistance, finally being occupied 47 years later. In the years which followed, the Ottomans imposed Islam upon the country, and they kept up the Islamic pressure over the following century. By the early 18th century, two thirds of the Albanian population had converted to Islam. More than twenty-five of the great Viziers of Turkey were of Albanian origin.

[4] The ideologists of the nationalist movement of the 19th century made great efforts to overcome the religious divisions and encourage national unity, adopting the slogan "The religion of the Albanians is Albania". The Albanian League - which had both political and cultural ends was

founded in 1878 in the Kosovan town of Pritzen. The League tried without success to bring the Albanian territories of Kosovo, Monastir, Shkodër and Jänina together as a single state within the framework of the Ottoman Empire. On a cultural front, the League worked hard to promote the language, literature and educational system which would foster nationalism.

[5] The Empire suppressed the League in 1881. In 1908, Albanian leaders met in Monastir (now in Macedonia) and adopted a national alphabet based mainly on Latin, which supplanted the Arabic and Greek versions which had been in use with others. Also that year, the "Young Turks" who took power in Istanbul ignored their promises of bringing in democratic reforms and guaranteeing Albanian autonomy, which led to three years of armed conflict. Turkey finally accepted the Albanian demands in 1912, and independence was declared.

[6] Due to pressure from Albania's neighbors, the European powers ceded Kosovo and Serbia when drawing up the borders of the new country, allowing Greece the bulk of Sameria and a portion of Epirus.

Half the Albanian population and territory was left beyond the Albanian borders.

[7] The international powers appointed German prince Wilhelm zu Wield as King of Albania. He arrived in the new nation in March 1914 but his lack of familiarity with the Albanians and the outset of World War I forced him to abandon the country six months later. During the War, Albania was occupied by the Austro-Hungarian, French, Italian, Greek, Montenegran and Serbian armies, and when the War ended the country would have disappeared had not US President Woodrow Wilson vetoed a plan by France, Britain and Italy, to divide the territory amongst its neighbors.

[8] A national congress, established in January 1920, set the bases for a new government. In December that year, Albanian was admitted to the League of Nations. In 1927, Ahmed Zogu, who had become president in 1925, signed a treaty with Italy's leader Mussolini, turning the country into a virtual Italian protectorate. A year later, Zogu proclaimed the country a monarchy.

[9] In April 1939, Italy occupied and formally annexed Albania to

the kingdom of Victor Emmanuel III. The Communists, under the leadership of Enver Hoxha, organized guerrilla resistance and a wide anti-Fascist front, receiving support from the Allies during World War II. The occupation forces withdrew on November 29 1944, and the People's Republic was declared on January 11 1945, with Hoxha at the helm.

[10] Despite its desire for independence, Albania matched its internal options to external events. When the neighboring Yugoslavian leader Tito and the Soviet Union's Josef Stalin split in 1948 (see Yugoslavia), the Albanian Workers' Party sided with the KOMINFORM (communist parties allied with the Soviet Union). Albania broke with Moscow after the "de-Stalinization" of the early 1970s. It established close ties with the People's Republic of China, with which it eventually broke in 1981, when the Cultural Revolution came to an end and the Maoists fell from power.

[11] The break with China became official at the Eighth Workers' Party Congress, where a party line was put forth "against US imperialism, Soviet socialist-imperialism, Chinese and Yugoslavian revisionism, Euro-Communism and social democracy", whilst condemning the policies of non-alignment and European detente, as set out in the Helsinki accords.

[12] Until Albania's liberation from Italian Fascist occupation in 1944, 85 per cent of the population lived in the countryside, and 53 per cent lacked even a place to grow their own vegetables. In 1967 collective farming was established. In 1977, Albania proclaimed self-sufficiency in wheat. According to official figures, between 1939 and 1992 industrial output increased over 100-fold, materials 250 times over, and electricity more than 300-fold.

[13] In 1989, Ramiz Alia, head of state since Hoxha's death in April 1985, initiated a process aimed at improving the economy, and breaking the country's international isolation. Border immigration procedures were simplified to encourage tourism; talks were initiated with the aim of resuming relations with both the US and the USSR; freedom of religion was declared; capital punishment was abolished for women; the number of crimes punishable by death was reduced from 34 to 11 and guidelines were established in the area of civil

rights allowing home ownership, opening up to foreign investment and the election of company directors by secret ballot.

[14] In February 1990, amnesty was granted to political and common prisoners. In November of the same year, Alia also announced that the constitution, in effect since 1976, would be revised. In December, independent political parties were authorized and general elections were announced - the first after 46 years of communist rule.

[15] The election had to be postponed due to the instability produced by a mass exodus of thousands of Albanians to Italy. However on 31 March almost two million voters chose from among one thousand candidates from 11 political parties, under the scrutiny of about 100 international observers and more than 250 foreign journalists. Amidst accusations of fraud the Communists won 156 of the 250 parliamentary seats.

[16] In May 1991, more than 300,000 workers went on strike demanding the resignation of the communist government, and also a 50 per cent salary increase. Prime Minister Fatos Nano dissolved his cabinet to form an alliance with the opposition. In full economic collapse, the parliamentary elections of March 1992 gave the Democratic Party (DP) a spectacular triumph (65. 6 per cent) over the Socialist Party (SP, 22.6 per cent). But 80 per cent of the two million voters abstained.

[17] In May, Sali Berisha, leader of the DP, replaced Ramiz Alia as president. He won the parliamentary vote 96 to 35, becoming the first non-Marxist president since the end of World War II. The following year, the Government began trials of the main political figures of the previous regime. Naxhmija Hoxha, widow of the autocratic communist leader Enver Hoxha, ex-President Ramiz Alia and ex-Premier Fatos Nano among others, were sent to prison convicted of misuse of public funds.

[18] Throughout 1995 and 1996, various media complained of censorship and intimidation, and relations amongst the political parties remained difficult. The so-called Verification Bill allowed for government discretion on assigning certain public posts, in accordance with the reports of Sigurimi, the communist regime's secret police. The Bill on Genocide and Communist Crimes barred notorious ex-political leaders from public office until the year 2002, and the new electoral law disallowed coalitions amongst the smaller parties.

[19] The parliamentary elections of 1996 took place but the main opposition leaders were barred from participation. The DP won 122 out of the 140 seats. In the following months, the legitimacy of the elections was challenged by the opposition, the US and several European countries interested in investing in Albania. In response to a recommendation by the European Council, the Parliament formed an ad hoc commission to investigate the accusations, particularly the violence against opposition leaders.

[20] In late January 1997, the collapse of a series of investment pyramid funds, guaranteed by the State, led to a bloody social and political uprising. One in six Albanians was left penniless and the biggest cities, including Tirana, rose in arms. This situation caused the virtual disintegration of the Albanian state. Eighty per cent of weapons were in the hands of civilians, after they sacked forts and barracks abandoned by the army and the police, who had joined the rebels. Armed confrontations caused 1,500 deaths. President Berisha was forced to bring forward parliamentary elections to June 1997. The SP, led by Fatos Nano, won the elections.

[21] Berisha resigned in July and the government was headed by Nano as prime minister. In September, due to a disagreement with a Socialist deputy, the National Council of the DP withdrew from the Parliament. By the end of the year, the Nano administration had resumed control over the country and was able to reduce inflation. The Socialist government pledged to carry out reforms which included the revitalization of the economy through an extensive privatization plan. In March 1998, the IMF praised Nano's management and promised funding for three years to support Albania's economic reforms.

[22] But in September an internal quarrel within the SP forced the Prime Minister to stand down. Government was passed on to Pandeli Majko, who in turn had to hand over to Ilir Meta, also from the Socialist Party.

[23] As troops advanced in the civil war in Yugoslavia, Albania called for NATO intervention to protect Albanian Kosovans. Local Mafias supplied weapons to the Kosovo Liberation Army (KLA). When NATO finally intervened, the country accepted tens of thousands of refugees and served as a base for NATO troops

[24] Ilir Meta became Prime Minister in October 1999. ∎

PROFILE

ENVIRONMENT

A Balkan state on the Adriatic Sea, Albania's coast is comprised of distinct regions. Alluvial plains, which become partially swampy in the winter, extend from the Yugoslavian border to the Bay of Vlöre. Further to the south, the coast is surrounded by mountains and has a Mediterranean climate. The soil of the mountainous inner region is very poor. Cattle-raising predominates there, while cotton, tobacco and corn are grown on the plains. Irrigated valleys produce rice, olives, grapes and wheat. The country has large areas of forest and is rich in mineral resources, including oil deposits.

SOCIETY

Peoples: Albanians are a homogeneous ethnic group; there is a Greek minority.
Languages: Albanian (official) and Albanian dialects.
Religions: Freedom of worship was authorized in 1989, having been banned since 1967. Pre-1967 estimates placed Islam as the largest religion (70 per cent), with the Albanian Orthodox Church in second place (20 per cent) and the Catholic Church (10 per cent) in third.
Political Parties: A multiparty system was established by the constitution which has been in effect since April 30 1991. Socialist Party (SP), formerly communist, it now advocates a democratic socialism within a free market economy. The Democratic Party (DP), a liberal democratic party, in favor of a free market economy.
Social Organizations: The Central Council of Albanian Trade Unions has 610,000 members.

THE STATE

Official Name: Republíka e Shqipërísë.
Administrative divisions: 26 districts.
Capital: Tiranë 350,000 people (1997).
Other cities: Durrës 170,000 people; Elbasan 120,000; Vlöre 88,000 (1997).
Government: Parliamentary republic. Rexhep Mejdani, President of the Popular Assembly since June 1997. Ilir Meta, Prime Minister and Head of Government, since October 1999. Single-chamber legislature: People's Assembly, made up of 140 deputies elected by universal suffrage every four years.
National Holiday: November 28, Liberation Day (1944).
Armed Forces: 73,000 (22,400 conscripts).
Other: 16,000: International Security Force: 5,000; People's Militia: 3,500.

Algeria

Algerie

Population: 30,774,000 (1999)
Area: 2,381,740 SQ KM
Capital: Algiers (Alger)
Currency: Dinar
Language: Arabic

From ancient times, the Numidians inhabited what now is Algeria. The Numidians, who were at first allies of Carthage and then clients of the Roman Empire, were Berbers - the name deriving from the Roman term for barbarians, as does the name Barbary, which formerly denoted the North African coastal area that is now Algeria. The Berbers resisted the Arab invasion of the 7th century AD, but were eventually converted to Islam, assimilated into the Arab community and played an important role in the Muslim conquest of Spain in the 8th century. In the 12th century a wave of invading Bedouin Arabs wrecked the Berbers' peasant economy in coastal North Africa and transformed many of the settled tribes into nomads.

2   With the downfall of the Almohad Empire, Yaglimorossen ibn Ziane founded a new state on the Algerian coast. Its borders were consolidated as economic prosperity and cultural development led nomadic peoples to settle. Ziane and his successors governed the country between 1235 and 1518. After the Christians had put an end to seven centuries of Muslim domination, in 1492 the Zianids were confronted with a series of Spanish military incursions in which various strategic sites, like Oran, were taken.

3   Algeria and Tunisia both became part of the Ottoman (Turkish) Empire in the 16th century. The Arroudj and Kheireddine brothers drove the Spanish from the Algerian coast and expanded the state's authority over a sizeable territory. Its mighty fleet won respect for the nation, and its sovereignty was acknowledged in a series of treaties (with the Low Countries in 1663, France in 1670, Britain in 1681 and the US in 1815).

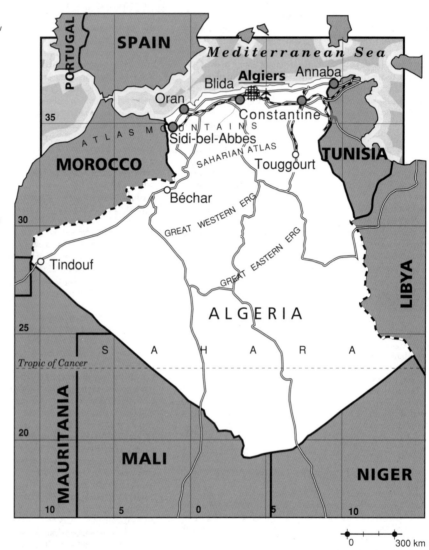

4   Wheat production gradually increased until it became an export crop once again, for the first time since the Hilalian invasion (see Mauritania). Wheat exports would eventually be the indirect cause of European intervention. At the end of the 18th century, the French revolutionary government bought large amounts of wheat from Algeria but failed to pay. Napoleon, and later the Restoration monarchy, delayed payment until the Dey of Algiers demanded that the debt be paid. Reacting to further excuses and delays, he slapped a perplexed French official in the face - a show of temper that would cost the Turkish Pasha dearly. 36,000 French soldiers disembarked to "avenge the offence", a pretext used by the French to carry out a long-standing project: to re-establish a colony on the African coast opposite their own shores. However, the French encountered heavy resistance, and were defeated.

5   In 1840, disembarking with 115,000 troops, the French set out once again to conquer Algeria. Successive rebellions were launched against the French. In the South however the nomadic groups remained virtually independent and fought the French until well into the 20th century (see Western Sahara). In 1873, France decided to expropriate land for French settlers, or *pieds-noirs* as they were known, who wished to remain in the colonies (they numbered 500,000 by 1900, and over a million after World

WORKERS

1997
UNEMPLOYMENT: 26.4%

% OF LABOUR FORCE   **1998**

■ FEMALE: 26%   ■ MALE: 74%

1990

■ SERVICES: 42.6%
■ INDUSTRY: 31.3%
■ AGRICULTURE: 26.1%

LAND USE

DEFORESTATION: 1.2% annual (1990/95)
IRRIGATED: 7.6% of arable (1993)

1993

■ FOREST & WOODLAND: 1.7%
■ ARABLE: 3.1%
■ OTHER: 95.2%

PUBLIC EXPENDITURE

DEFENCE EXPENDITURE   **12%**
(% of goverment exp.)   (1997)

MILITARY EXPENDITURE   **11%**
(% of health & education)   (1990/91)

War II). As a result, the French pieds-noirs came to monopolize the fertile land, and the country's economy was restructured to meet French interests.

[6] Nationalist resistance grew stronger from the 1920s until in 1945 it exploded when the celebration of the victory over Nazi-Fascism turned into a popular rebellion. The French forces tried to put down the rebellion and according to official French reports, 45,000 Algerians and 108 Europeans were killed in the ensuing massacre.

[7] Shortly thereafter, the Algerian People's Party, founded in 1937, was restructured as the Movement for the Triumph of Democratic Liberties (MTLD) which participated in the 1948 and 1951 elections called by the colonialists.

[8] Convinced of the futility of elections under colonial control, nine leaders of the OS (Special Organization, the military wing of the MTLD) founded the Revolutionary Committee for Unity and Action (CRUA). In November 1954, this committee became the National Liberation Front (FLN) that led the armed rebellion. Franz Fanon, a doctor from Martinique, who had fought in the liberation of France during World War II, joined the FLN and came to exert great theoretical influence not only in Algeria but also throughout the Sub-Saharan region.

[9] In order to maintain "French Algeria" and the pieds-noirs, the French colonial system destroyed 8,000 villages, eliminated more than a million civilians, made systematic use of torture and deployed more than 500,000 troops. Right-wing French residents of Algeria formed the feared Secret Army Organization (OAS), a terrorist group which blended Neo-Fascism with the demands of the French colonials, who resented the growing power of the Algerians. Finally, on March 18 1962, French President De Gaulle signed the Evian Agreement, agreeing to a cease-fire and a plebiscite on the proposal for self-determination.

[10] Independence was declared on July 5 1962, and a Constituent Assembly was elected later that year. Ahmed Ben Bella was named Prime Minister. Almost all foreign companies were nationalized, 600,000 French nationals abandoned the country taking everything they could with them, and 500,000 Algerians returned, to share the lot of 150,000 landless and hungry peasants. A system of local agricultural and industrial operations was introduced by the new government.

[11] However, Ben Bella's self-management program came up against the reality of a government with little administrative expertise. In June 1965 a revolutionary council headed by Houari Boumedienne took power and jailed Ben Bella. A new emphasis on organization, centralization, and state power began to prevail over Ben Bella's self-management notions. Under Boumedienne, there was further nationalization and a program of rapid industrialization based on revenues from oil and liquid natural gas. The country entered a period of economic expansion, which was not reflected in the countryside. Population grew more rapidly than agricultural production, and Algeria went from exporting to importing food.

[12] Houari Boumedienne died in December 1978, after a long illness, just as the country's political institutions were beginning to consolidate. In 1976, a new National Charter was approved and, in 1977, the new members of the National People's Assembly were elected, with Colonel Chadli Ben Jedid being designated president.

[13] The new president initiated a policy of reconciliation by releasing Ahmed Ben Bella, who had been imprisoned for 14 years. Restrictions on travel abroad were lifted, taxes reduced and prohibitions lifted on private housing. Over-large public enterprises gradually shrank and the restructuring of inefficient public enterprises gave an impulse to private companies.

[14] Ben Jedid was re-elected in January 1984. In October 1988, a wave of protests broke out in several cities due to the lack of water and basic consumer goods; the legitimacy of the FLN and the military was called into question. Among the main groups participating in these mass protests were militant Muslim fundamentalists. Some mosques - above all, those in poorer neighborhoods - became the site of political demonstrations, particularly on Friday afternoons, when mosque prayers ended in political declarations voicing economic and social demands.

[15] Some sectors of the most radical forms of Islam, influenced by Iran, began sending volunteers to fight in Afghanistan, to carry out the jihad or "holy war" against the Soviet-backed Kabul regime. In mid-1989, against a background of protest and upheaval, Ben Jedid presented a new constitution which introduced a modified multiparty system, breaking the monopoly which the FLN had held.

[16] More than 20 opposition groups - including Muslims - openly expressed their views. The most significant were the Islamic Salvation Front (FIS), the Da'wa Islamic League, the communist Socialist Avant Garde Party (PAGS) and the strongly Kabbyle (ethnic minority of Berber origin) Pro-Democracy and Culture Group (RDC). Mouloud Hamrouche, a leading reformer, was appointed Prime Minister. In the first multiparty elections since Algeria's independence from France in 1962, the FIS defeated the FLN in the June elections.

[17] Hamrouche and his cabinet resigned in June 1991, against a background of social agitation promoted by the *mullahs* (religious leaders). In early June, a state of siege was declared throughout the country in the face of massive protests.The country's military and police forces were pitted against FIS agitators who demanded that presidential elections be held ahead of schedule and that an Islamic state be proclaimed. Sid Ahmed Ghozali, an oil technician who had been Prime Minister during the previous administration, was designated as the new Prime Minister. Legislative and presidential elections were scheduled for later in the year, and

PROFILE

ENVIRONMENT

South of the fertile lands on the Mediterranean coast lie the Tellian and Saharan Atlas mountain ranges, with a plateau extending between them. Further south is the Sahara desert, rich in oil, natural gas and iron deposits. Different altitudes and climates in the north make for agricultural diversity, with Mediterranean-type crops (vines, citrus fruits, olives, etc.) predominating. The country's flora and fauna are seriously threatened. More than 30 mammal, 8 reptile and 70 bird species are in danger of extinction. Desertification affects primarily the pre-Saharan regions. However, erosion also poses a serious threat to 45 per cent of all agricultural land (12 million hectares).

SOCIETY

Peoples: Algerians are mostly Arab (80 per cent) and Berber (17 per cent). Nomadic groups linked to the Tuareg of Nigeria and Mali live in the south. Nearly a million Algerians live in France.
Religion: Islam
Languages: Arabic (official), and Berber in some areas. Many people speak French, but Arabic has gradually been replacing it in education and public administration.
Political Parties: National Liberation Front (FLN); Vanguard Socialist Party (PAGS); Front for Socialist Forces (FFS); Movement for Democracy in Algeria (MDA); Reunion of Culture and Democracy (RCD); Islamic Salvation Front (FIS); Hamas; Movement for a Peaceful Society.
Social Organizations: General Union of Algerian Workers (UGTA), National Union of Algerian Peasants, National Union of Algerian Women, National Youth Union.

THE STATE

Official Name: Al-Jumjuriya al-Jazairia ash-Shaabiya.
Capital: Algiers (Alger) 3,700.000 people (1998).
Other cities: Oran 609,823 people; Constantine 440,842; Annaba 348,322 (1987).
Government: Abdel-Aziz Bouteflika, President since 1999. Ahmed Benbitour, Prime Minister since December 1999.
National Holiday: November 1, Anniversary of the Revolution (1954).
Armed Forces: 121,700 (65,000 conscripts).
Other: 180,000 (Gendarmerie, National Security Forces, Republican Guard).

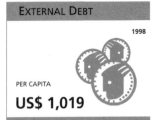
the FIS suspended its campaign of social and political agitation.

[18] The country requested loans from the IMF in order to palliate fluctuations in the price of oil. Ghozali proposed parliamentary reforms in order to ensure the transparency of the electoral system, but the proposals, which included the possibility of withdrawing a man's right to vote in the name of his wife, were boycotted by the FLN's parliamentary majority.

[19] In the December 1999 elections, 40 per cent of the 13 million registered voters abstained. The first round, for 430 seats in Parliament, gave the victory to the FIS, which took 188 seats. The anti-fundamentalists - alarmed by the FIS victory in the first round and headed by the Workers Centre, UGTA and the FFS - raised a demonstration of 100,000 in central Algiers. Women's, professional and intellectual movements also participated.

[20] President Chadli Ben Jedid resigned under strong pressure from the military and politicians fearful of a FIS victory. A Security Panel made up of three military leaders and the Prime Minister was put into power. Shortly after, the High Council of State was designated, headed by Mohamed Boudiaf, a dissident FLN leader in exile since 1964. The arresting of FIS leaders followed immediately and the election was annulled. In February, the High Council of State proclaimed a state of emergency throughout the nation, for a year. The army was opposed to any possibility of sharing power with the FIS.

[21] In March 1992, the FIS was outlawed. In early April, the Government dissolved nearly all local councils governed by FIS members since the municipal elections of June 1990. In late April, the Supreme Court ratified the illegality of the FIS.

[22] In June, Boudiaf was assassinated by one of his bodyguards whilst making a public speech. In September, the Government of Prime Minister Belaid Abdelsalam decreed a series of anti-terrorist measures, including extending the death penalty to various crimes.

[23] In February 1993, the High Council of State extended the State of Emergency indefinitely, imposed a curfew on Algiers and in five provinces and dissolved all associations linked to the FIS.

[24] From that moment, the army oscillated between the alternative of a negotiated outcome and the quest for a military defeat of the armed Islamic groups. Following a long series of failed negotiations, the product of disagreements between the various political sectors, the Government named Defense Minister Lamine Zeroual president of the country for three years.

[25] In a climate of increasing schism among all political groupings, the Islamic guerrillas split into the Armed Islamic Group (GIA) and the Armed Islamic Movement. In one of their most spectacular acts, the Fundamentalists allowed 1,000 prisoners to escape from the Tazoult high security prison.

[26] In early 1995, following a meeting in Rome, the FIS, FLN, FFS and some moderates from the Islamic group Hamas proposed an end to the violence, the liberation of the political prisoners and the formation of a national unity government to organize elections. Despite support from Spain, the United States, France and Italy, the proposal was not accepted by Zeroual, who countered by setting elections for November.

[27] The FIS, FLN and FFS boycotted the elections, which Zeroual won with 61 per cent of the votes against the moderate Islamic Mahfoud Nahnah's 25 per cent. Despite the presence of international observers, there were still strong doubts over whether the elections had truly been free and fair.

[28] In early 1996, Zeroual's government, apparently supported by the new leaders of the FLN, gained important military victories and followed an IMF-recommended structural adjustment plan which further increased impoverishment across a large section of the middle class and the most deprived sections of the population.

[29] As the June 1997 elections approached, the violence increased. The elections gave a relative majority to the ruling party, which took 155 of the 380 seats. The FIS, which had called for a boycott on the elections, declared itself satisfied with an abstention rate of 34 per cent.

[30] In August 1997, the recently freed FIS leader Abasi Mandana confirmed the desire of his movement to end the violence through dialogue with the Government. However, that same month, the massacre of some 300 people in a village south of Algiers - considered the most violent act by fundamentalist guerrillas since the beginning of the civil war in 1992 - once again reduced the possibility of bringing an end to the conflict. Witnesses of the event said members of the Algerian army could have prevented the event, but had preferred not to intervene. In October, the ruling party's victory in local and provincial elections ratified the governing coalition's mandate, but brought little or no hope for change.

[31] A group of Islamic Algerian militants was arrested in Belgium in March 1998 - a move which the Belgian authorities considered the first step towards the breaking up of the European supporters of the GIA.

[32] According to Amnesty International, the responsibility for the death and disappearance of hundreds of people lies both with government security forces as well as with armed opposition groups. The organization reported torture and ill-treatment of prisoners in 1997, as well as abuses of the legal detention period.

[33] In October, the ruling party triumph in municipal and provincial elections ratified the strength of the governing coalition, but brought little or no prospect of change. The arrest of a group of militant Algerian Muslims in Belgium, in March 1998, was classed as a first step toward the disbanding of the European GIA bases by the Belgian authorities. Amnesty International denounced the responsibility of government security forces and armed opposition groups in the death and disappearance of hundreds of people.

[34] A few months later, the President stood down and called new elections. In April 1999 Abdel-Aziz Bouteflika took over, immediately calling a referendum on a law of reconciliation. The response was hugely in favor (98.6 per cent), with overwhelming FIS participation and support. The President announced a general amnesty for those giving up their weapons and joining the legal political battle.

[35] Abdelkader Hachani, the number three in FIS, was murdered in a fundamentalist neighborhood of Algiers in November 1999. The murder was seen as an attack on the peace process by radical muslims opposed to Hachani's line of dialogue with the government. ■

Angola

Angola

Population: 12,478,000 (1999)
Area: 1,246,700 SQ KM
Capital: Luanda
Currency: New kwanza
Language: Portuguese

The original inhabitants of the current territory of Angola were Khoisan-speaking hunter-gatherers. The large-scale migrations of Bantu-speaking peoples in the first millennium AD made them dominant in the Khoisan area. The Khoisan - named Bushmen by the Europeans - still live in small groups in some zones of southern Angola.

[2] The Bantu-speakers were farming, hunting and gathering people who probably began their migration from the rainforest in what is the present-day frontier of Nigeria and Cameroon. Their expansion took place as small groups relocated in response to political and economic circumstances over an extended period of time. Between the 14th and 17th centuries, the Bantu set up a series of kingdoms. In Angola the most important one was the Kongo, covering the strip which today forms the frontier between Angola and Zaire, and reaching its apogee from the mid 13th to 14th centuries.

[3] In 1482, a Portuguese fleet commanded by Diogo Cao entered the Congo river mouth. He made the first contact with the Angolans of the old kingdom of Kongo and began the colonization process. This process was started by missionaries and traders, later giving way to military expeditions against the peoples of the Angolan interior.

[4] Various kingdoms within the country tenaciously opposed foreign occupation until the mid 18th century. Wars and slavery reduced the Angolan population from 18 million in 1450, to barely eight million in 1850. Even so, the Angolan people never ended their opposition to Portuguese colonization, with figures like Ngola Kiluange, Nzinga Mbandi, Ngola Kanini and Mandume leading the resistance.

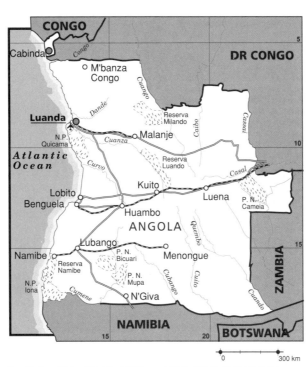

[5] Portugal intensified its military incursions following the 1884 Berlin Conference which divided Africa among the European colonial powers. Nonetheless, it took 30 years of military campaigns (1890-1921) to "pacify" the colony. From then on, Portuguese settlers arrived in ever-increasing numbers. In 1900, there were an estimated 10,000; in 1950, 50,000; and in 1974, less than a year before independence, 350,000. Only one per cent lived on farms inland. The colonial economy was parasitic, built upon the exploitation of mineral and agricultural wealth (diamonds and coffee), with the bulk of profits going to Portuguese merchants.

[6] On December 10 1956, several small nationalist groups joined together to form the Popular Movement for the Liberation of Angola (MPLA). Their aim was to pressure the Portuguese Government into recognizing the Angolan people's right to self-determination and independence. When Britain and France began to withdraw from their overseas colonies in the 1960s, Portugal did not follow suit and frustrated all Angolan attempts to win independence by peaceful means.

[7] On February 4 1961, a group of MPLA militants from the most underprivileged classes stormed Luanda's prisons and other strategic points in the capital. This spurred resistance in other Portuguese colonies. Their agenda was clear: they were fighting not just colonialism but also the international power system which sustained it. In addition, they were fighting racism and tribal chauvinism.

[8] In the years that followed, other independence movements with different regional origins sprang up: the National Front for the Liberation of Angola (FNLA) led

by Holden Roberto; the Cabinda Liberation Front (FLEC); and the Union for the Total Independence of Angola (UNITA) led by Jonas Savimbi.

[9] Under the direction of Agostinho Neto, the MPLA militants held a conference in January 1964 to discuss and define their strategy of a prolonged people's war.

[10] Portugal's domestic problems, coupled with military setbacks in Angola, Mozambique and Guinea-Bissau and repeated shows of international solidarity with the independence fighters, dashed Portuguese army hopes of a military solution. An uprising led by the Armed Forces Movement (MFA) overthrew the Portuguese regime of Oliveira Salazar and Marcelo Caetano on April 25 1974. The MFA expressly recognized the African colonies' right to self determination and independence.

[11] The MFA immediately invited the MPLA, FNLA and UNITA to participate with Portugal in a transitional government for Angola in the interim period, the mechanisms of which were established in the Alvor Accords, signed in January 1975. By this time, political and ideological divergences among the three groups had become irreconcilable; the FNLA was directly assisted by US intelligence services and received military aid from Zaire (now Democratic Republic of Congo). UNITA received overt backing from South Africa and Portuguese settlers while the MPLA was aligned ideologically with the socialist countries. The accords were never implemented.

[12] The FNLA and UNITA unleashed a series of attacks on MPLA strongholds in Luanda, and a bloody battle for control of the capital ensued. Between September and October 1975, Angola was attacked on all sides: Zaire invaded from the north while South Africa, with the complicity of UNITA, attacked from the south to prevent a Marxist government.

[13] On November 11 1975, the date agreed upon to end colonial rule, the MPLA unilaterally declared independence in Luanda, pre-empting the formal transfer of sovereignty. Some 15,000 Cuban troops aided the new government in fighting off the South African invasion. In 1976, the United Nations recognized the MPLA government as the legitimate representative of Angola.

[14] The Angolan economy was severely debilitated. The war had

WORKERS

% OF LABOUR FORCE **1998**

■ FEMALE: 46% ■ MALE: 54%

1990

■ SERVICES: 17.4%
■ INDUSTRY: 8.1%
■ AGRICULTURE: 74.5%

LAND USE

DEFORESTATION: 1.0% annual (1990/95)
IRRIGATED: 2.5% of arable (1993)

1993

■ FOREST & WOODLAND: 41.6%
■ ARABLE: 2.4%
■ OTHER: 56.0%

PUBLIC EXPENDITURE

DEFENCE EXPENDITURE
(% of central goverment) **36.3%** (1997)

MILITARY EXPENDITURE
(% of health & education) **208%** (1990/91)

paralyzed production in the far north and south of the country. The Europeans had emigrated en masse, taking all that they could with them and effectively destroying the productive capacity.

[15] Under these circumstances, the Angolan Government began to restore the chief production centres, and to train the largely unskilled and illiterate workforce. In this way, a large public sector emerged which was to become the economy's driving force, and banking and strategic activities were nationalized.

[16] In May 1977, Nito Alves led a faction of the MPLA committed to "active revolt", in a coup attempt. Six leading MPLA members were killed but the conspiracy was successfully put down within hours. Seven months later, at its first congress, the MPLA declared itself Marxist-Leninist and adopted the name of MPLA-Workers Party. In 1978, closer political and economic links were established with the countries of the socialist Council for Mutual Economic Assistance.

[17] The country's first president, Agostinho Neto, died of cancer in Moscow on September 10 1979 and was succeeded by Planning Minister José Eduardo dos Santos.

[18] In August 1981, South Africa launched Operation Smokeshell, in which 15,000 soldiers with tanks and air support advanced 200 kilometers into Cunene province. Pretoria justified this aggression as an operation against guerrilla bases belonging to the Namibian liberation movement, the South West African Peoples' Organization (SWAPO). The apparent aim was to establish a "liberated zone" where UNITA could install a parallel government inside Angolan territory capable of obtaining some degree of international recognition.

[19] This incursion and successive attacks in the years that followed were contained by effective Angolan and Cuban military resistance. The cost of the war, plus international pressure and the mounting anti-apartheid campaign at home, obliged South Africans to resume diplomatic discussions with the MPLA government. In December 1988, Angola, South Africa and Cuba signed a Tripartite Accord in New York which put an end to the war between Luanda and Pretoria, and provided for the independence of Namibia and withdrawal of South African and Cuban troops from Angola.

[20] In June 1989, UNITA signed a truce in the presence of 20 African heads of state at Gbadolite, Zaire. However, the ceasefire was broken barely two months later. At the end of April 1990, Angolan authorities announced in Lisbon, Portugal, that direct negotiations with UNITA would be resumed to achieve a lasting ceasefire. A month later, UNITA leader Jonas Savimbi officially recognized José Eduardo dos Santos as head of state.

[21] At the end of 1990, the MPLA announced the introduction of reforms geared towards democratic socialism. On May 11 1991, a law on political parties was published, which brought one-party rule (under the MPLA) to an end. In addition, the law banned political participation by active members of the armed forces, the police or the judiciary. On May 23, the last Cubans left Angola. After 16 years of civil war, a peace settlement was signed on May 31 by the Angolan Government and UNITA, in Estoril, Portugal. This agreement included an immediate cease-fire, as well as a promise to hold democratic elections in 1992 and the creation of a Joint Politico-Military Commission (CCPM), charged with establishing a national army made up of soldiers from both opposition groups. The governments of Portugal, the United States and the Soviet Union were involved in the discussion and drawing up of the agreement, as was the United Nations, which was put in charge of supervising compliance with the terms of the peace agreement.

[22] Holden Roberto and Jonas Savimbi, president of UNITA, returned to Luanda in August and September 1991 respectively - after 15 years of exile - to launch their election campaigns. The United States continued to support UNITA, and as a result tensions increased as the 1992 elections drew near.

[23] The changes of the 1990s went far beyond the agreements on a political and diplomatic level and were reflected in the mobilization and transformation of the Angolan society. The Organization of Angolan Women (OMA), founded in 1961, separated from the MPLA to become a non-governmental organisation (NGO). At its first Congress, in August 1991, the OMA established a common platform between church groups, intellectuals and professional associations.

[24] Plagued by a foreign debt of more than $6 billion, the Government appealed to the international community for economic aid. The US refused to

Congo and the Great Lakes

Behind the pain and bloodshed of the war in the Democratic Republic of Congo (DRC see p179) lies a revealing history. The countries involved have all been hungry for its wealth and territory.

In May 2000, the Democratic Republic of Congo (formerly Zaire) was again in the midst of civil war. The scale of the war has grown because of external causes and consequences. The fighting broke out over two years earlier in 1997 when veteran guerrilla Laurent Kabila proclaimed himself president and launched his dictatorial government. On coming to power in Kinshasa, Kabila and his Congolese Liberation Front brought an end to 30 years of another civil war, ousting former dictator Mobutu Sese Seko, who died days later in exile in Morocco. But the peace was too fragile to last.

BY THE RIVERS OF BABYLON

The latest conflict in the DRC operated on various fronts, with a wide range of causes and elements behind it. On the one hand, various rebel groups, with Ugandan and Rwandan military and economic backing tried to depose Kabila. On the other, government troops made no secret of the support offered them by Angola, Namibia and Zimbabwe.

These allied forces settled in the DRC, with large numbers of foreign troops digging trenches and setting up field camps - where they were joined by United Nations peace-keeping forces (MONUC), at that time consisting of 5,537 troops drawn from 20 or so African, Asian, European and South American countries. These soldiers, together with the occupying forces have turned the DRC into a kind of Babylon, a place inhabited by exiles. MONUC ranks also included Tanzanian and Kenyan "neutrals" - soldiers from countries implicitly involved in the earlier civil war in DRC as they had granted asylum to Laurent Kabila. Apart from Zambia, all the other countries of the Great Lakes region were involved in the DRC conflict: Uganda, Rwanda, Burundi, Kenya and Tanzania. The UN formation also included a South African contingent, and some from Angola, a country which had fought against Kabila and been his number one ally (although under another government at the time of the civil war in DRC).

THE MANY FACES OF THE CONFLICT

A first look at the DRC shows the country as the hinge between the north and south of the African continent. The vast country is bursting with gold, iron, copper, manganese, cobalt, diamonds, uranium and also oil, a seam of mineral wealth that reaches from Nigeria in the north to Angola in the south. The multiplicity of interests in play reflect the number of countries and foreign companies fighting for what they consider their share.

The scourge of internal and external conflict in the Great Lakes region, has been exacerbated by endemic famine, malaria and cholera, and pandemics of tuberculosis and HIV-AIDS. The most manifest result of these conflicts is the hundreds of thousands of refugees who form yet another battle front maintained by various human rights organizations such as Medecins Sans Frontières and some UN agencies. In an attempt to mitigate these diseases, the aid agencies - some funded by the World Bank - involuntarily provided another source of conflict as the refugee camps were frequently moved by the Congolese authorities to serve as a human shield against attacks from rebel groups or the enemy of the moment.

And in addition, in both the DRC and the rest of the Great Lakes region is the legacy of the thousands of people killed and maimed by so many years of civil war. The battelegrounds are littered by myriad tiny undetectable plastic antipersonnel mines, whose presence is only revealed when someone treads on them and they explode.

THE CIVIL WAR

The start of the DRC's civil war is usually put at 1960, when this countrty gained independence. But the origins of this conflict – like the others in the region – harks back to the colonial legacy.

In 1884 at the Berlin Conference, the European powers partitioned Africa. Using a ruler, they mapped out 48 new states, and they imposed their governors or regents to ride roughshod over the empires, kingdoms and ancient civilizations which messily straddled or stood in the way of these completely new and national borders. The earlier civilizations and relations between the various cultures had never need such boundaries. Once the decolonization processes began in earnest in the mid-20th century - although the former Portuguese colonies in Africa only became independent after the Carnation Revolution in Lisbon in 1975 - the African nations were forced to adopt systems of government alien to their historical traditions and centuries-old cosmologies.

In today's DRC and the Great Lakes nations it became imperative that there be a President, a two-chamber parliament and a Prime Minister. This move came from the West which pressed the countries to modernize along the lines of Western-style democracy.

Since independence these countries have spilled blood in civil wars often fed by ethnic differences exploited by the colonizers. Faced with disease and structural poverty, aid to the region came initially from the International Monetary Fund (IMF) and the World Bank, as well as from US interests at the height of the Cold War. Then came the first structural adjustment plans which ensured the countries would continue to hand over their birthright (their minerals, commodities, etc.) and open up their markets.

MOBUTU AND THE ALLIANCES

When army commander Mobutu came to power in a coup in 1965, he renamed the country Zaire and began to form alliances in order to shore up his position.

For France, Belgium and the US (and its Central Intelligence Agency, the CIA), the dictator Mobutu was their best defense against the advance of "communist" forces such as the Congolese Liberation Front led by Laurent Kabila. With military aid for arms and training, Mobuto was able to repel rebel advances for years and also cultivate friends and enemies. However, when the rebel advance could no longer be contained, international aid began to fall off or to change. Mobutu played the leading role in this complex tapestry of alliances. He requested help from Uganda and Rwanda, countries fighting in Zairean territory against Burundian and Rwandan Hutu and Tutsi refugees. With the support of these countries, Mobutu created a new dimension by allowing these soldiers and refugees to exploit and sell gold from the mining areas close to their frontiers. Slowly, the foreign armies occupied more territory and nobody was now going to get them out. The conflict in Zaire became more international, and the country was disempowered.

CONGO AND THE END OF APARTHEID

The Congo Liberation Front meanwhile, also wove alliances. During the 1960s and 1970s Laurent Kabila was in exile in Dar es Salaam, capital of Tanzania, shaping his plans and directing his troops from there. His forces were armed and trained by Cuba, which had sent the famous guerrilla fighter Ernesto Che Guevara to lend his support to the Congo in 1965. From exile, Kabila cemented a friendship with Agostinho Neto of Angola. Neto appeared to be the leader of Angolan independence, and the People's Movement for the Liberation of Angola (MPLA) was formed under his leadership. Mobutu meanwhile supported Jonas Savimbi's National Union for the Total Independence of Angola (UNITA), and Uganda did the same. The civil wars in both countries were closely related.

Kabila's troops - with backing from Cuba and the MPLA - helped to expel the South African Army from Angolan territory. The turning point for the South Africans, and therefore also for Angola and its allies, was the battle of Cuito Cuanavale. Until this, whites had not died in combat; their relatives had not received their loved ones back in body bags. In December 1988 South Africa signed an agreement to withdraw its forces from Angola, and also from Namibia. In this way, the victory for the MPLA, helped by Laurent Kabila and Cuba, was also significant in the struggles to end apartheid in South Africa, and to achieve Namibian independence. ∎

EXTERNAL DEBT

1998

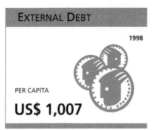

PER CAPITA

US$ 1,007

FOREIGN TRADE

Millions US$ 1998

IMPORTS

3,113

EXPORTS

3,874

suspend the economic and diplomatic blockade, alleging that Angola was a Marxist nation and announcing it would not grant diplomatic recognition until after the 1992 elections. Consequently, the US companies in Angola were unable to get loans from banks in their own country.

[25] Following intense negotiations between the Government and UNITA, elections were set for September 1992. The ruling MPLA took nearly 50 per cent of the vote, to UNITA's 40 per cent. Savimbi refused to recognise defeat and hostilities resumed. In their advance, the UNITA troops occupied the diamond mines of the interior, leaving the Government with oil as the only stable source of income (between $1.6 and $1.7 billion per year).

[26] In November 1993, peace talks were re-started in Lusaka, the capital of Zambia. A year later in November 1994 a peace agreement was signed. The main points - a ceasefire and constitutional changes so that Savimbi could become Vice-President - were not put into practice until late 1995 and the fighting continued.

[27] Some progress was seen during 1996. In May, an amnesty law was approved and UNITA soldiers began to be absorbed by the armed forces. Savimbi withdrew most of his troops to barracks and handed over some of the weapons. The civil war caused the most serious social and economic crisis in Angolan history. The adoption of IMF and World Bank economic liberalization measures did not improve matters for ordinary people.

[28] In April 1997, hard negotiating ended with UNITA's accepting to join the government at executive, legislative and military levels. Even though its position in the capital was weak, Savimbi's troops still controlled 40 per cent of the territory. The fall of Mobutu Sese Seko in Zaire (now DR Congo) in May weakened UNITA even further, and they were forced to abandon areas of the northern frontier. The Angolans wanted to avoid the infiltration of Mobutu's troops - formerly allied to Savimbi - into their territory. Mobutu's soldiers were fleeing from the government of the new DR Congo leader Laurent Kabila, a former ally of dos Santos.

[29] In March 1998, thousands of demobilised soldiers mostly with little or no education encountered serious difficulties in returning to their home villages, given the scarce employment possibilities there and the slow arrival of economic aid. Since 1994, only 300,000 of the 4.5 million people uprooted by the civil war had been able to resettle according to the United Nations figures. The presence of large numbers of land mines, spread across the entire territory increased the insecurity of the population.

[30] Renewed hostilities in the DR Congo also affected UNITA members. The government, which participated in the conflict by backing for Kabila, recovered territories previously controlled by the opposition or their Congolese allies.

[31] In April 1999, the Government announced the formation of a self-defence front with Zimbabwe, Namibia and the Democratic Republic of the Congo. This reflected the interconnected nature of regional conflicts which transcended frontiers established by former colonial powers. In late 1999, after winning back Andulo and Bailundo, the main cities under opposition control, and following a run of military victories the Government felt confident in announcing that the end of the war was in sight. ■

PROFILE

ENVIRONMENT

The 150 kilometre-wide strip of coastal plains is fertile and dry. The extensive inland plateaus, higher to the west, are covered by tropical rainforests in the north, grasslands at the center and dry plains in the south. In the more densely populated areas (the north and central west) diversified subsistence farming is practiced. Coffee, the main export crop, is grown in the north; sisal is cultivated on the Benguela and Huambo plateaus; sugarcane and oil palm along the coast. The country has abundant mineral reserves: diamonds in Luanda, petroleum in Cabinda and Luanda, iron ore in Cassinga and Cassala. The port of Lobito is linked by railway to the mining centers of Zaire and Zambia. There are a number of environmental problems aggravated by the civil war, the lack of drinking water (in 1987 there was a cholera epidemic in Luanda), soil erosion and deforestation as a result of the export of valuable timber.

SOCIETY

Peoples: As a consequence of centuries of slave trade the population density is still very low. To maintain control over the country, the Portuguese colonizers fostered local divisions between the various ethnic groups; Bakondo, Kimbundu, Ovimbundu and others.
Religions: The majority practise traditional African religions. 38 per cent Catholic, and 15 per cent Protestant. However, there are forms of syncretism which make it impossible to establish strict boundaries between one religion and another.
Languages: Portuguese (official) and African Bantu languages: Ovidumbo, Kimbundu, Kikongo and others.
Political Parties: The People's Movement for the Liberation of Angola (MPLA), founded by Agostinho Neto on December 10 1956; the National Union for the Total Independence of Angola (UNITA); and the National Front for the Liberation of Angola (FNLA).
Social Organizations: National Union of Angolan Workers (UNTA); Organization of Angolan Women (OMA).

THE STATE

Official Name: República Popular de Angola.
Administrative Divisions: 18 Districts. **Capital:** Luanda, 2,000.000 people (1998). **Other cities:** Huambo (Nova Lisboa), 203,000 people; Lobito, 150,000; Benguela, 155,000 (1988). **Government:** José Eduardo dos Santos, President; Fernando Franca Van Dunem, Prime Minister. Unicameral Legislature. 223-member National Assembly, elected by direct popular vote.
National Holiday: November 11, Independence Day (1975).
Armed Forces: 82,000. **Other:** 20,000 Internal Security Police.

STATISTICS

DEMOGRAPHY

Population: 12,478,000 (1999)
Annual growth: 3.0 % (1975/97)
Estimates for year 2015 (million): 19.7 (1999)
Annual growth to year 2015: 2.9 % (1997/2015)
Urban population: 32.3 % (1997)
Urban Growth: 5.9 % (1980/95)
Children per woman: 6.7 (1998)

HEALTH

Life expectancy at birth: 47 years (1998)
male: 45 years (1998)
female: 48 years (1998)
Infant mortality: 170 per 1,000 (1998)
Under-5 child mortality: 292 per 1,000 (1998)
Daily calorie supply: 1,983 per capita (1996)
Safe water: 31 % (1990/98)

EDUCATION

Literacy: 42 % (1995)
male: 56 % (1995)
female: 29 % (1995)
School enrolment:
Primary total: 88 % (1990/96)
male: 95 % (1990/97)
female: 88 % (1990/97)
Tertiary: 1 % (1996)

COMMUNICATIONS

11 newspapers (1996), 54 radios (1997), 51 TV sets (1996) and 5 main telephone lines (1996) per 1,000 people

ECONOMY

Per capita, GNP: $ 380 (1998)
Annual growth, GNP: 19.8 % (1998)
Annual inflation: 924.3 % (1990/98)
Consumer price index: 3,707.6 (1998)
Currency: 392,823.5 new kwanzas = $ 1 (1998)
Cereal imports: 445,255 metric tons (1998)
Fertilizer use: 2 kg per ha (1997)
Exports: $ 3,874 million (1998)
Imports: $ 3,113 million (1998)
External debt: $ 12,173 million (1998); $ 1,007 per capita (1998)
Debt service: 34.4 % of exports (1998)
Development aid received: $ 436 million (1997); $ 45.5 per capita (1997); 9.90 % of GNP (1997)

ENERGY

Consumption: 587.0 Kgs of Oil equivalent per capita yearly (1997); -505.0 % imported (1997)

HDI (rank/value): 160/0.398 (1997)Arable: 2.4 % of total (1993)
Other: 56.0 % of total (1993)

Anguilla

Anguilla

Population: 8,000 (1998)
Area: 96 SQ KM
Capital: The Valley
Currency: EC dollar
Language: English

Anguilla is the most northerly of the Leeward Islands. Its small size, barely 96 sq km including the neighboring Sombrero Island, and the lack of fresh water for agriculture, made the island unattractive to the British Empire. From 1816 to 1871 Anguilla, St Kitts-Nevis and the Virgin Islands were administered together as one colony. The Virgin Islands were split off in 1871, leaving the others as a colonial unit ruled from St Kitts.

[2] Colonialism lasted until the group became one of the five Caribbean "States in Association with the United Kingdom". Anguillans opposed the agreement and rebelled against the St Kitts government. Under the leadership of local entrepreneur Ronald Webster, Anguilla demanded a separate constitution. In March 1969, British troops disembarked on the island to supervise the installation of its colonial Commissioner, but the separatist movement continued its struggle.

[3] In 1976 a new constitution was approved by Britain, establishing a parliamentary system of government under the patronage of the British Commissioner. But it was not until 1980 that Anguilla was able formally to withdraw from the Associated State arrangement with St Kitts-Nevis, gaining the status of "British Dependent Territory".

[4] The 1976 constitution provided for a governor appointed by the British Crown, responsible for defense, foreign relations, internal security (including the police), utilities, justice and the public audit. The Governor presides over the Executive Council.

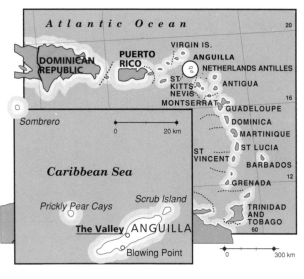

[5] The first legislative elections held in March 1976 voted in the Anguilla United Party leader, Ronald Webster, as Chief Minister. A year later he failed to win a vote of confidence and was replaced by opposition leader Emile Gumbs. In the 1980 general elections, the United Party of Anguilla, led by Webster, won by a landslide majority, obtaining six out of the seven seats. A year later, the Government suffered internal divisions and Webster created the Popular Party of Anguilla (PPA). In the elections of June 1981, he won 5 seats, while the remaining 2 went to the Anguilla National Alliance (ANA), led by Emile Gumbs.

[6] In September, the Constitution was changed leading to home rule on internal matters.

[7] On March 9 1984 in accordance with the new constitution of 1982 requiring a parliamentary government, elections were held and Emile Gumbs became Chief Minister once more. The ANA received 53.8 per cent of the vote.

[8] The new ANA government requested greater power for the Executive Council and an increase in British investment in the island's economic infrastructure. After the Council called for constitutional changes, particularly with reference to the situation of women and people born outside the island who had relatives there, the Governor appointed a Committee to review the Constitution.

[9] Through the 1980s the building industry for tourism reduced unemployment from 26 per cent to 1 per cent, but at the beginning of the 1990s this trend stopped and the US recession brought a reduction of tourists.

[10] In 1991 Prime Minister Gumbs tried to bring about closer cooperation between the British possessions and the Organization of East Caribbean States.

[11] The income generated by cattle-breeding, salt production, lobster fishing, boat building and the money sent by nationals working abroad (located mainly in the US), lost its former predominant role to the profit made by the building industry, tourism, and financial offshore services. In 1992 legislation gave then Governor Alan W Shave the task of granting permits to foreign firms, in an effort to control them more tightly.

[12] In March 1994, the legislative elections were won by Hubert Hughes, of the United Party of Anguilla. In November, the new legislative assembly proclaimed a law regulating the activities of transnational companies. In 1995, the economy suffered the effects of Hurricane Luis. Throughout 1997 and part of 1998, there was an average annual growth of 7 per cent as a result of increased tourism from the United States and Britain. ∎

PROFILE

ENVIRONMENT

Anguilla covers 91 sq km and its dependency, the island of Sombrero, is 5 sq km. They are part of the Leeward Islands of the Lesser Antilles. The climate is tropical with heavy rainfall. There are considerable salt deposits on the island.

SOCIETY

Peoples: Most inhabitants are descendants of African slaves integrated with European settlers. There is a British minority. Many Anguillans live permanently in the Virgin Islands or other US possessions.
Religions: Anglican 40 per cent; Methodist 33 per cent; Adventist 7 per cent; Baptist 5 per cent; Roman Catholic 3 per cent. Other 12 per cent.
Languages: English (official).
Political Parties: The Anguillan National Alliance; The Anguilla United Party; The Democratic Party of Anguilla.

THE STATE

Official Name: Anguilla.
Capital: The Valley, 1,600 people (est 1995).
Government: Osbourne Fleming, Chief Minister, since March 2000. Peter Johnstone, Governor-General appointed by the British Crown in February 2000. The single chamber Legislative Assembly has 11 members, 7 of them elected by direct vote.

DEMOGRAPHY

Population: 10,785 (est 1998).

LAND USE

1993

- FOREST & WOODLAND: 11.4%
- ARABLE: 18.2%
- OTHER: 10.4%

Antigua

Antigua and Barbuda

Population: 69,000 (1999)
Area: 440 SQ KM
Capital: St John's
Currency: EC dollar
Language: English

The Caribs inhabited most of the islands in the sea which took their name, but abandoned many of them, including Antigua, in the 16th century due to the lack of fresh water.

[2] In 1493 the name Antigua was given to one of the Antilles by Christopher Columbus in honor of a church in Seville. Other Europeans settled later (the Spanish in 1520, the French in 1629) but again left because of the scarcity of water. However, a few English were able to settle by using appropriate techniques to store rainwater. The nearby island of Barbuda was colonized in 1678 and granted by the crown granted to the Codrington family in 1685. Although it was planned as a slave-breeding colony but the slaves who were imported came to live self-reliantly in their own community

[3] By 1640, the number of English families on Antigua had increased to 30. The few indians who had dared to stay were eventually murdered by the settlers, who imported African slaves to work the tobacco plantations and later sugar plantations.

[4] In 1666, the French governor of Martinique invaded the island, kidnapping all the African slaves. When England regained control in 1676, a rich colonist from Barbuda, Colonel

Codrington, acquired large quantities of land and brought new African slaves. Thus sugar production was reinstated on the island.

[5] Slavery was abolished in the British colonies in 1838. The workers' situation did not noticeably change and quasi-slavery continued for several decades, until the early 20th century when trade unions began to appear.

[6] The first trade union, led by Vere Bird, was formed on January 16 1939.

The Antigua Labor Party (ALP), the first political party, originated within a trade union. It was also led by Vere Bird.

[7] In the elections of April 1960, Bird's party won and he became Prime Minister. In 1966, a new constitution introduced self-government with a Parliament elected by Antiguans and Barbudans. Britain remained responsible for defence and foreign relations. Bird was again successful in the 1967 elections.

[8] In 1979, opposition leader George Walter charged the Government with human rights abuses, citing brutal repression of a teachers' strike as an example. He claimed repression could only become worse with independence.

[9] On November 1 1981, Antigua and Barbuda became independent as a "sovereign, democratic and united state" and were admitted into the United Nations and the Caribbean Community (Caricom). Independence also gave the islands the right to become indebted to the IMF and the World Bank. The foreign debt grew dramatically and reached almost half of the GDP by the end of that year.

[10] The Prime Minister maintained close relations with the US, who rented part of the island's territory for military purposes. The alliance with the US was further consolidated in 1983, when Antigua participated in the US invasion of Grenada. Parliamentary elections were held in April 1984, and despite accusations during the electoral campaign, Bird was re-elected. His victory was attributed to approval of his stance on the Grenada issue.

[11] In 1987 opposition leaders demanded the Prime Minister's resignation, citing as one of the reasons the misappropriation of funds in the St John's Airport modernization project.

[12] Vere Bird retired from public life and his son Lester replaced him at the head of ALP in 1994. In the March elections, Labour lost 4 seats but retained an absolute majority at the Chamber of Representatives, with 11 seats out of 17.

[13] In September 1995, Hurricane Luis caused losses which amounted to $300 million, damaging 60 per cent of the country's buildings, whether partially or completely, including several main hotels, seriously affecting the country's tourism infrastructure.

[14] The catastrophic situation led the Government to apply an economic austerity programme in 1996, including severe spending cuts. Civil servants' pay was frozen for two years and government ministers lost 10 per cent of their income. The Government tried to raise money by privatizing some State assets.

[15] That year the Government in Barbuda was taken over by the People's Movement which took five seats in the local Council.

[16] In February 1997, the Government closed four banks, when irregularities were found in their accounts.

[17] Hurricanes lashed the island in two consecutive seasons (1998-1999). In 1998, Hurricane George killed more than 500 people in the Caribbean, and Hurricane Lenny caused massive damage in 1999.■

PROFILE

ENVIRONMENT

The islands - Antigua with 280 sq km and its dependencies Barbuda with 160 sq km and Redonda with 2 sq km - belong to the Leeward group of the Lesser Antilles. Antigua is endowed with beautiful coral reefs and large dunes. Its wide bays distinguish it from the rest of the Caribbean because they provide safe havens. Barbuda is a coral island with a large lagoon on the west side. It consists of a small volcano joined to a calcareous plain. Redonda is a small uninhabited rocky island, and is now a flora and fauna reserve. Sugar cane and cotton are grown along with tropical fruits; sea foods are exported. The reduction of habitats due to the reforestation of native forests with imported species is the main environmental problem of most of the Caribbean islands.

SOCIETY

Peoples: The majority of Antiguans and Barbudans are of African origin (91.3 per cent);

Europeans; Mestizo; Syrian-Lebanese; Indo-Pakistanis. **Religions:** Protestants 73.7 per cent (Anglicans 32.1 per cent, Moravians 12 per cent; Methodists 9.1 per cent; Adventists of the Seventh Day 8.8 per cent; Catholics 10.8 per cent; Jehova Witnesses 1.2 per cent). **Languages:** English is the official language, but in daily life a local Patois dialect is spoken. **Political Parties:** The Antigua Labour Party (ALP). The Antigua Caribbean Liberation Movement (ACLM). The United National Democratic Party (UNDP). The United Progressive Party (UPP). **Social Organizations:** The labour movement is divided into two groups: the Antigua Workers' Union, linked to the UNDP, and the Antigua Trades and Labour Union, with ALP leadership.

THE STATE

Official Name: Associated State of Antigua and Barbuda. **Capital:** St John's, 29,000 people (1997). **Other cities:** Parham, Cedar Grove. **Government:** James Carlisle, Governor-General, representative of Queen Elizabeth II (the Head of State); Prime Minister, Lester Bird, since March

1994. British-style bicameral legislature, composed of a 17-member Senate appointed by the Governor-General and a 17-member House of Representatives elected by universal suffrage for a 5-year term. **National Holiday:** November 1, Independence Day (1981).

DEMOGRAPHY

Population: 69,000 (1999). **Annual growth:** 0.5 % (1975/97). **Estimates for year 2015 (million):** 0.1 (1999). **Annual growth to year 2015:** 0.5 % (1997/2015). **Urban population:** 36.2 % (1997). **Children per woman:** 1.7 (1998)

HEALTH

Life expectancy at birth: 76 years (1998)
Maternal mortality: 150 per 100,000 live births (1990-98)
Infant mortality: 17 per 1,000 (1998) Under-5 child mortality: 20 per 1,000 (1998)
Daily calorie supply: 2,365 per capita (1996)
76 doctors per 100,000 people (1993)

Aotearoa/ New Zealand

Aotearoa/New Zealand

Population: 3,828,000 (1999)
Area: 270,534 SQ KM
Capital: Wellington
Currency: NZ dollar
Language: English and Maori

Aotearoa, "the land of the long white cloud", was settled around the 9th century by Maori, who arrived there from Polynesia. Over the years a distinct culture developed, based on tribal organisation and a strong affinity with the land. Maori saw themselves as guardians of the land for future generations.

[2] In 1642 Abel Tasman, from Holland, reached the South Island, the larger of Aotearoa's two main islands. However, a misunderstanding with the indigenous population prevented him from going ashore. It was not until 1769 that James Cook from England surveyed the shores of the two most important islands. This opened the door for a growing colonization of the country which Abel Tasman had named "New Zealand". Whalers, sealers and traders, along with a few deserters from the navy and fugitives from Australian jails, established themselves on the islands.

[3] In the early 19th century, colonization increased with the arrival of British immigrants and missionaries. They brought with them new diseases, values and beliefs, which affected the traditional Maori way of life. Trading with settlers initially bought wealth to many Maori communities, but these gains were reversed with interest once the settlers began to alienate significant amounts of Maori land.

[4] In 1840 the territory of New Zealand was formally annexed by the British crown as a colony. The two larger islands were occupied under different legal arrange-ments: the South Island was incorporated by virtue of the right of "discovery", and the North Island through the Treaty of Waitangi, signed in 1840 by Maori chiefs and representatives of the British Government. According to the text of the treaty - which is different in its English and Maori versions - Maori chiefs accepted the presence of British settlers and the establishment of a government by the Crown to rule the settlers. In exchange, Maori were assured absolute respect for their national sovereignty.

[5] However, 20 years after the signing of the Treaty an extremely violent process of expropriation of Maori lands began. The so-called "land wars" between Maori and the Europeans were essentially for sovereignty and guaranteed rights to the lands, forests, fisheries and other *taonga* (treasures).

[6] Massive immigration, land confiscation and legal decisions led to the gradual annexation of Maori land. The magnitude of their loss becomes clearer if one considers that, out of the 27 million hectares they owned in 1840, they now have a little over a million left.

[7] While the north of the country was involved in a series of wars, the South Island settlers went through a period of prosperity because of the discovery of gold. This discovery brought a massive flow of British, Chinese and Australian immigrants, which energized the region's economy.

[8] After 1840 colonization increased. The Pakeha (non-Maori) usurped the right to fish in the area, thus depriving Maori of one of their main activities.

[9] Maori opposition to Pakeha colonization found new expression by the end of the 19th century. They organized petitions, delegations and submitted their claims before local courts and even before the British Crown itself, demanding compliance with the Treaty of Waitangi. These efforts were fruitless. The lands that had once belonged to Maori were now used for farming, which had started to play a central role not only in the life of the settlers but also in the whole economy. New markets for dairy and meat products opened up in the 1880s, with the appearance of cold-storage systems which made long-distance shipping possible. These products constituted the basis of the country's economic development.

[10] For Maori, British rule also meant the beginning of a process of cultural assimilation, through the imposition of European language, religion, and customs. Thus, Maori language which was in theory protected by the Treaty of Waitangi, was given less and less importance.

[11] By the end of the century, the country's political scene was dominated by the Liberal government. They were the first in the world to grant the vote to women (1893) and to establish measures to protect the rights of industrial workers, a group which was growing parallel to the development of cities and manufacturing industries.

[12] In the 20th century new political movements appeared to oppose the power of the Liberals who had become a coherent, organized political party after 20 years in power. The Labour Party, with ample working-class and urban middle-class support, became one of the country's main political forces.

[13] During the 1930s, Maori demands acquired new strength thanks to an alliance between the groups representing Maori interests and the Labour Party, which came to power for the first time in 1935 with Maori support. But there was still no legislative recognition of the Treaty of Waitangi.

[14] World War II marked the beginning of a new era for the country. During the War Britain's inability to guarantee the security of its former colony led to closer ties between Aotearoa/New Zealand and the US. Through a series of political and military alliances, US presence was consolidated in the region. In the 1950s and 1960s Aotearoa had to pay the price for this relationship, particularly when it found itself involved in the Vietnam War, a conflict which touched the political life of the country very deeply.

[15] Legislation in the 1950s forced many Maori from their land and the 1960s saw their increasing urbanization. In conditions of economic prosperity and labor shortages, New Zealand's mono-cultural education system served to direct Maori into mainly unskilled labouring jobs.

[16] In the 1970s, Aotearoa/NZ's markets in the UK were shrinking as Britain moved closer to the (then) European Economic Community (EEC). Unemployment rose and inflation reached unprecedented levels due to the failure of the diversification scheme, the rise in the price of oil

and massive external loans to finance "think big" projects. 1975 saw a drastic fall in the purchasing power earned from primary exports. This fall, combined with the foreign loans, provoked a period of rising foreign debt. After 12 years in opposition, the Labour Party held power from 1972 until it was defeated by the conservative National Party in the 1975 elections. The new government closed the doors on Pacific immigrants, whom it blamed for increasing unemployment

[17] In 1975, growing Maori activism led to the formation of the Waitangi Tribunal to investigate Treaty claims. In 1986 the Labour Government gave it the power to hear claims dating back to the 1840 signing. The Tribunal had no binding powers over the Crown, and settlement of claims for compensation was slow and arbitrary.

[18] In 1984, the Labour Party regained office, and introduced a monetarist economic policy which included privatizating some public enterprises. These policies alienated many traditional Labour supporters.

[19] A 1987 law prohibited the entry of nuclear arms or vessels to the nation's ports, thus questioning the military presence of France and the United States, which used the South Pacific as a nuclear weapons testing ground. This decision ended the defence treaties between the US and Aotearoa/New Zealand.

[20] The National Party won the October 1990 elections, but the change in the governing team did not change the economic model of the country. There was an increase in privatizations, protectionism was dismantled even further, and there were large cut-backs in funding for health, education and contributions to social benefits. Legislation neutralizing trade unions was also introduced. The result was falling inflation, but unemployment also rose.

[21] The diminished popularity of the government was not reflected in the electoral results of 1993, when the National Party (NP) took 50 of the 99 seats in parliament and Jim Bolger was re-elected Prime Minister. The Labour Party (LP), the main opposition force, took 45 seats.

[22] Aotearoa achieved its first budget surplus in 17 years in 1994; the currency became more robust, unemployment fell and inflation settled at 2 per cent.

[23] Between 1994 and 1995, the Government compensated Tainui of the North Island both with NZ$180 million and 15,400 hectares of land, for their claims over land colonized in the previous century. Even Britain's Queen Elizabeth apologised for the loss of life during the colonization of the islands. In 1997, the Government reached an agreement with Ngai Tahu of the South Island to pay compensation of NZ$170 million and land.

[24] The general unemployment indices continued to fall, settling at 6 per cent in 1995. Young people, Maori and immigrants from other South Pacific islands constituted the bulk of the unemployed and nearly 10 per cent of the population received State subsidies. Citizen concern for the environment strengthened Bolger's position in the run-up to the October 1996 elections, as he was firmly opposed to the French nuclear trials on the Moruroa atoll.

[25] Bolger's National Party beat the Labour Party, although both majority parties lost seats to the minorities. The first parliament elected by proportional representation doubled the

Niue

Population: 2,000 (1998)
Area: 260 SQ KM
Capital: Alofi
Currency: NZ dollar
Language: English

Niue was settled by Samoans and Tongans. Captain James Cook named it "Savage Island" when he visited it in 1774. The indigenous peoples' reputation for fierceness kept missionaries away (the island's first permanent mission dates from 1861), and also the slave traders who caused much suffering in other areas of the Pacific. Emigration to the phosphate mines on other islands in the area initiated an outflow which has continued ever since. In 1900 the island was declared a British protectorate and was annexed by Aotearoa/New Zealand in 1901. It was administered along with the Cook Islands until 1904, when it seceded to form a separate possession. In 1974 it became an Autonomous Associated State of Aotearoa/New Zealand. The United Nations recognized this as a legitimate decision and eliminated the "Niue case" from the Decolonization Committee agenda. As well as economic support from Aotearoa, Niue also received help with defence and international affairs.

[2] In April 1989, questions arose over the management of economic aid received from Aotearoa by Prime Minister Robert Rex's government. Despite this, the opposition lacked the votes necessary to approve a parliamentary motion to censure Rex's administration.

[3] In 1991, Aotearoa announced a reduction of financial aid. Niue and Australia established diplomatic links during 1992. Prime Minister Roberto Rex died on December 12 and was substituted by Young Vivian, who was in turn defeated in the elections to be succeeded by Frank Lui in March 1993. In February 1996, Frank Lui was re-elected for a further three years.

ENVIRONMENT

Located in the South Pacific in southern Polynesia, 2,300 km northeast of Aotearoa, west of the Cook Islands and east of the Tonga Islands. Of coral origin, the island is flat and the soil relatively fertile. Its rainy, tropical climate is tempered by sea winds.

SOCIETY

Peoples: The people of Niue are of Polynesian origin.
Religions: Protestant.
Languages: English (official), local Niue language (national).
Political Parties: Niue People's Action Party (NPAP).

THE STATE

Official name: Niue. Capital: Alofi. Government: Autonomous associated state. Kurt Meyer, Representative of Aotearoa. Frank F Lui, Prime Minister, since March 9, 1993. Single-chamber legislature - National Assembly, made up of 20 members (14 village representatives). Since October 1974, the island has had an autonomous local government. There is a 20-member Legislative Assembly which is headed by the Prime Minister. Aotearoa/New Zealand controls defence and foreign affairs.

ENVIRONMENT

Aotearoa/New Zealand is situated in Oceania. Its two principal islands are relatively mountainous. The North Island is volcanic and has plateaus and geysers. The South Island is crossed by the Southern Alps, a mountain chain with peaks of over 3,000 metres. The climate is moderately rainy, with temperatures cooler in the south. The native rainforests have been devastated by early colonization, replaced by agricultural land and pastures. The economic base of the country is agricultural, with advanced techniques being used in pastoral and agricultural by-products. Tourism is becoming increasingly important.

SOCIETY

Peoples: Much of the population is descended from European settlers. 12.9 per cent are Maori (a figure rapidly increasing), and 3.5 per cent are from Pacific Islands descent. **Religions:** Anglican and other Protestant denominations dominate. There are also Catholic and various Maori church minorities. **Languages:** English and Maori are the official languages, with English dominant. **Political Parties:** A multi-party system in change due to the adoption of a proportional representation voting system. The major parties are National Party, Labour Party, New Zealand First, ACT and the Alliance Party. **Social Organizations:** The Trade Union Federation and the Council of Trade Unions.

THE STATE

Official Name: Aotearoa (Maori); New Zealand (English).
Administrative divisions: Divided into 15 town and 58 district authorities.
Capital: Wellington 414,048 people (1996). **Other cities:** Auckland 967,404 people; Christchurch 336,858; Dunedin 118,143; Hamilton 108,426; Palmerston North 73,095; Timaru 42,630; Nelson 40,242 (1996).
Government: A parliamentary monarchy and member of the British Commonwealth. Governor-General: Michael Hardie Boys. Jenny Shipley, Prime Minister and Head of Government (since December 1997). Aotearoa has a parliamentary system, with a unicameral legislative body of 120 members. The elected members of the Government form a cabinet chaired by the Prime Minister. On occasions this cabinet acts as the Executive Council presided over by the Governor-General. The Governor-General appoints cabinet on the recommendations of the Prime Minister, and has the power to dissolve Parliament. **National holiday:** February 6, Waitangi Day.
Armed Forces: 9,611 (1996)

number of Maori representatives and the number of women increased from 14 to 21 of the 120 seats.

[26] In December 1997, Bolger resigned after being challenged by members of his own caucus. Jenny Shipley, former transport minister, became the country's first woman Prime Minister, leading a weak coalition.

[27] The civil wars in Indonesia and Papua New Guinea led to increasing Australian participation in regional affairs. Aotearoa co-operated with Australian peacekeeping efforts in East Timor in 1999 and was waiting in the wings for events in Bougainville. In 1997, Wellington had hosted round-table talks between Bougainville rebels and the Papua New Guinean government.

[28] In the December 1999 elections, the Labour Party took 52 of the 120 seats and formed a coalition government. The new parliament included 16 Maori members, 2 gay activists, a transsexual (the first transsexual MP in the world) and 35 women. The latter included both the Prime Minister and the Leader of the Opposition.

[31] In coalition with the Alliance led by former Labour Party president leader Jim Anderton - who left the Party in protest against neo-liberal policies - the new government proposed to increase the minimum salary by 8 per cent, to adjust rents according to tenant income and raise the tax on personal incomes above $30,000 per year to 39 per cent. In April 2000 the Government announced that the knighthoods granted by the British crown would no longer be recognised by the NZ Government. In the same week, the Prime Minister ruled out a suggestion made by John Hewson, Liberal Party leader, of constituting a federation of sovereign states along with Australia. ■

Cook Islands

Population: 19,000 (1999)
Area: 230 SQ KM
Capital: Avarua
Currency: NZ dollar
Language: English

The islands, which had already been explored and settled by Polynesians and Spaniards, received their name from the English navigator Captain James Cook, who drew up the first map of the archipelago in 1770.

[2] In 1821, Tahitian missionaries were sent to the islands by the London Missionary Society; a Protestant theocracy was established and all "pagan" structures were destroyed, as were many of the traditional forms of social organization. The islands were declared a British Protectorate in 1888 and became part of Aotearoa/New Zealand in 1901. The land rights of the native Maori were recognized, and the sale of real estate to foreigners was prohibited. In 1965, the United Nations promoted and supervised a plebiscite, and the population voted against independence, and in favour of maintaining its ties to Aotearoa.

[3] Prime Minister Geoffrey Henry governed the country with an iron hand for 15 years before being replaced in 1978 by Thomas Davis, of the Democratic Party (DP), who gave incentives to private fruit planters. However he was dismissed from office by Parliament in 1987, being replaced by Pupuke Robati, also of the DP. In the 1990 elections, Geoffrey Henry's Cook Islands Party was returned to office, and re-elected in 1994.

[4] From 1991 on, when Aotearoa's economic injections to the Cook Islands fell to 17 per cent of the local budget, both governments decided that the auditors in the Cook Islands would take charge of the State finances in place of the Aotearoa office.

[5] The public debt stood at around $900 million as the second half of the 1990s began. Prime Minister, Geoffrey Henry announced a series of drastic measures including a 50 per cent reduction in State employees, a 15 per cent pay reduction for the remaining personnel and a privatization plan. In late 1997, some ministries were closed due to the lack of funds and the budget of the remaining entities was reduced by 10 per cent.

ENVIRONMENT:

Area: 236.6 sq km. Archipelago located in the South Pacific 2,700 km northeast of Aotearoa/New Zealand, made up of 15 islands which extend over an ocean area of 2 million sq km They are divided into 2 groups. The northern group is made up of 6 small coral atolls, which are low and arid, with a total area of 25.5 sq km. The southern group comprises 8 larger and more fertile volcanic islands (211 sq km). The capital, Avarua, is located on Rarotonga, the largest of the islands. Every 5 years, for the past 2 decades, the islands have suffered terrible droughts.

SOCIETY

Peoples: The people are of Polynesian origin. **Religions:** Christian. **Languages:** English (official), Cook Island Maori. Language and traditions similar to Maori in Aotearoa/New Zealand. **Political Parties:** The Cook Islands Party (CIP); the Democratic Party (DP), the main opposition force; the Tumu Democratic Party; the Alliance Party.

THE STATE

Official Name: The Cook Islands. **Capital:** Avarua. **Government:** Autonomous associated state. Tim Caughley, Representative of Aotearoa. Geoffrey Henry, Prime Minister since January 1990. Single-chamber legislature; there is a Legislative Assembly, with 25 members elected by direct vote every five years.

DEMOGRAPHY

Population: 19,000 (1999)

HEALTH

Infant mortality: 26 per 1,000 (1998). **Under-5 child mortality:** 30 per 1,000 (1998). **Safe water:** 95 % (1990/98)

EDUCATION

Literacy: 99 % (1995). **Female:** 99 % (1995). **School enrolment:** Primary total: 98 % (1990/96)

ECONOMY

Cereal imports: 924 metric tons (1998)

DEMOGRAPHY

Population: 3,828,000 (1999)
Annual growth: 0.9 % (1975/97)
Estimates for year 2015 (million): 4.4 (1999)
Annual growth to year 2015: 0.8 % (1997/2015)
Urban population: 86.3 % (1997)
Urban Growth: 1.0 % (1980/95)
Children per woman: 2.0 (1998)

HEALTH

Life expectancy at birth: 77 years (1998)
male: 74 years (1998)
female: 80 years (1998)
Maternal mortality: 15 per 100,000 live births (1990-98)
Infant mortality: 5 per 1,000 (1998)
Under-5 child mortality: 6 per 1,000 (1998)
Daily calorie supply: 3,405 per capita (1996)
210 doctors per 100,000 people (1993)
Safe water: 97 % (1990/98)

EDUCATION

School enrolment:
Primary total: 103 % (1990/96)
male: 103 % (1990/97)
female: 103 % (1990/97)
Secondary:
male: 117 % (1990/96)
female: 123 % (1990/96)
Tertiary: 63 % (1997)
Primary school teachers: one for every 18 (1997)

COMMUNICATIONS

216 newspapers (1996), 990 radios (1997), 517 TV sets (1996) and 499 main telephone lines (1996) per 1,000 people

ECONOMY

Per capita, GNP: $ 14,600 (1998)
Annual growth, GNP: -0.6 % (1998)
Annual inflation: 1.6 % (1990/98)
Consumer price index: 104.8 (1998)
Currency: 1.9 NZ dollars = $ 1 (1998)
Cereal imports: 193,206 metric tons (1998)
Food import dependency: 8 % (1997)
Fertilizer use: 4,444 kg per ha (1997)
Exports: $ 18,768 million (1997)
Imports: $ 18,345 million (1997)

ENERGY

Consumption: 4,435.0 Kgs of Oil equivalent per capita yearly (1997); 15.0 % imported (1997)

HDI (rank/value): 18/0.901 (1997)

Tokelau

Tokelau Islands

Population: 2,000 (1998)
Area: 12 SQ KM
Capital: Fakaofo
Currency: NZ dollar
Language: Tokelauan

From ancient times, the islands were inhabited by Polynesian peoples who lived by subsistence fishing and farming. The first European to set foot on the islands was English explorer John Byron, who arrived in 1765. However, the absence of great riches meant that the islands did not arouse the colonial interests of the British Crown.

[2] In 1877, the islands became a British protectorate. Britain annexed them in 1916, and included them as part of the colonial territory of the Gilbert and Ellice Islands (now Kiribati and Tuvalu). In 1925, Britain transferred administrative control of the islands to Aotearoa (New Zealand). In 1946, the group was officially designated the Tokelau Islands, and in 1958 full sovereignty passed to Aotearoa.

[3] Like the Cook Islands, Tokelau was claimed by the United States until 1980, when the US signed a Friendship Treaty with New Zealand/Aotearoa and dropped its claims.

[4] The Government of Aotearoa adopted policies intended to maintain traditional customs, institutions and communal relations in Tokelau. The population lives in relative isolation; with a single ship calling at the islands from Apia (Samoa) every two or three months. The ocean and lagoons provide fish and seafood which are the islanders' staple subsistence foods. There are no tourist facilities.

[5] In the 1980s, farming underwent a crisis due to a number of adverse climatic conditions. As a consequence, emigration to Aotearoa rose considerably. The New Zealand Government tried to encourage Tokelau immigrants to return to their homeland, but its policies have not been successful.

[6] In 1976 and 1981 the UN sent delegations to Tokelau. On both occasions the envoys reported that the inhabitants of the islands did not wish to change their relations with Aotearoa/NZ.

[7] In December 1984, the UN Assembly discussed Tokelau's situation and decided that Aotearoa should continue to administer the islands. However, in the report submitted to the UN Special Committee in June 1987, Tokelau expressed a wish to achieve greater political autonomy, while maintaining unchanged relations with Aotearoa.

[8] In 1989, Tokelau's motion to apply sanctions on those states fishing in its territorial waters was supported by the South Pacific Forum. In November of that year, Aotearoa banned fishing in a 200-nautical-mile exclusion zone, in order to protect the fishing reserves which constitute the islands' main wealth.

[9] In 1989, a UN report on the consequences of the greenhouse effect (the warming of the atmosphere as a result of pollution) included Tokelau among the islands which could disappear under the sea in the 21st century, unless drastic measures are taken to halt pollution.

[10] In February 1990, the three groups of islands which make up the country's territory were devastated by Hurricane Ofa, which destroyed all the banana trees and 80 per cent of the coconut plantations, as well as hospitals, schools, houses, and bridges. As a result, emigration to Aotearoa/NZ increased once again.

[11] Aotearoa established the first regular maritime transport service between the three atolls during 1991.

[12] In 1993, the Samoan Government announced an agreement with the Government of Samoa to transfer the Office of Tokelau Affairs, from Apia, Western Samoa, to the islands themselves.

[13] In May 1995, Aotearoa's parliament approved extended powers for the local assembly.

[14] In 1997, the island was linked to the satellite telephone system. ∎

PROFILE

ENVIRONMENT

A group of coral islands, comprising three atolls: Atafu 2,02 sq km and 577 people, Nakunono 5,46 sq km and 374 people, Fakaofo 2,63 sq km and 664 people. Geographically, Sivains atoll belongs to the group but is an administrative dependency of American Samoa. The group is located in Polynesia in the South Pacific, to the east of the Tuvalu islands. The islands are flat, with thin, not very fertile soil. Rainfall is erratic and there are frequent droughts. Fishing constitutes the traditional economic activity.

SOCIETY

Peoples: The population is of Polynesian origin.
Religions: Mostly Protestant, 70 per cent.
Languages: Tokelauan (official) and local dialects.

THE STATE

Official Name: Tokelau.
Capital: Fakaofo.
Other cities: Fenua Fala, and small villages on every island.
Government: The Governor-General of Aotearoa/NZ has legislative power over the islands, and their administration has been entrusted to the Aotearoan Secretary of Foreign Affairs. Brian Absolum, Administrator since 1994. Each atoll has a *Taupulega* (Council of Elders) formed by the heads of family groups, plus a *Faipule* (who represents the village in its dealings with the Aotearoan administration) and a *Pulenuku* (responsible for local administration). Twice a year, 15 delegates from each Taupulega attend the Fono.

DEMOGRAPHY

Population: 2,000 (1998)

Argentina

Argentina

Population: 36,577,000 (1999)
Area: 2,766,889 SQ KM
Capital: Buenos Aires
Currency: Peso
Language: Spanish

The Patagonians and the Andeans were the two largest groups living in what is now Argentina at the beginning of the 16th century. Patagonians included Tehuelch, Rehuelche, Rampa, Mataco and Guaycure peoples. The latter two were stable, agrarian civilizations, while the others were nomadic hunters and gatherers. They settled in the south, center and north of the country. The principal Andean groups were the Ancient Rehuenche, Algarrobero Rehuelche, Huerpe, Diaguita, Capayane, Omahuaca and Patama. Through contact with the Incas, they perfected their agricultural system introducing terracing and artificial irrigation. They raised llamas, and traded in the northwest and west of the country.

2   The Spanish explorations in the 16th century took Amerigo Vespuccio in 1502, and Juan Diaz de Solis in 1516, up the estuary they baptized the River Plate (Plata) in honor of the silver they were seeking - but did not find. In 1526, Sebastian Cabot founded a fort on the banks of the Carcarañá river which was the first settlement in present-day Argentina.

3   To check the Portuguese advance, Spain sent Pedro de Mendoza to the region on a contract granting the conquistador established political and economic privileges. In 1536, de Mendoza founded Santa Maria del Buen Ayre (Buenos Aires), a small town which was abandoned in 1541 after being besieged by the indigenous peoples.

4   Using Asuncion (in today's Paraguay) as a focus for colonization, the Spanish founded several cities in what is now Argentine territory

(Santiago de Estero, Córdoba, Santa Fé), until they came to the second founding of Buenos Aires in 1580. Under colonial administration, the region was

in principle subject to the Vice-Royalty of Peru. Three cities were predominant in succession. Tucumán, linked with gold exploitation in Upper Peru, was the centre during the 16th century. Córdoba, where the first university of the region was established in 1613, was the intellectual centre during the 17th and 18th centuries. And after the new administrative divisions in 1776, the port city of Buenos Aires became capital of the new Viceroyalty of the River Plate, which covered what are now Bolivia, Paraguay, Argentina and Uruguay.

5   In the 17th and 18th centuries, the Spanish conquest pushed the Mapuche - named Araucans by the Europeans - from Chile into the centre and south-east of present-day Argentina with the ensuing "Araucanisation" of the local inhabitants. The abundance of cattle, which provided the main product the viceroyalty sent to the metropolis, caused great ethnic and cultural changes. Outside the cities, vast plains of good pasture were ranged by horsemen, some of whom were indigenous people (who modified their diet to feed on beef). The rest were *gauchos* - mixed race cowboys who lived by working the cattle.

6   The strong bourgeoisie of the port area who favored free trade initiated the revolutionary movement of 1810, which created the United Provinces of the River Plate and overthrew the Viceroy, accusing him of a lack of loyalty to Spain, at that time occupied by Napoleon's troops. Gauchos and Indians swelled the ranks of armies organized in Buenos Aires to fight the Spanish crown beyond the frontiers of the Viceroyalty. General José de San Martín led the armies which defeated the royalists and contributed decisively to the independence of Chile and Peru.

7   Even though the Spanish were quickly expelled, discrepancies between Buenos Aires and the rest of the United Provinces of the River Plate (including the present-day Republic of Uruguay) kept the region in a permanent state of war. The Unionists defended the

WORKERS

1996
UNEMPLOYMENT: 16.3%

% OF LABOUR FORCE   **1998**

■ FEMALE: 32%   ■ MALE: 68%

1990

■ SERVICES: 55.4%
■ INDUSTRY: 32.4%
■ AGRICULTURE: 12.2%

LAND USE

DEFORESTATION: 0.3% annual (1990/95)
IRRIGATED: 6.8% of arable (1993)

1993

■ FOREST & WOODLAND: 18.4%
■ ARABLE: 9.0%
■ OTHER: 72.6%

PUBLIC EXPENDITURE

1997
63.6%

6.3%

DEFENCE   SOCIAL

MILITARY EXPENDITURE   **51%**
(% of health & education)   (1990/91)

PROFILE

ENVIRONMENT

Argentina claims sovereignty over the Malvinas (Falkland) Islands and a 1,250,000 sq km portion of Antarctica. There are four major geographical regions. The Andes mountain range marks the country's western limits. The sub-Andean region consists of a series of irrigated enclaves where sugarcane, citrus fruits (in the North) and grapes (central) are grown. A system of plains extends east of the Andes: in the North, the Chaco plain with sub-tropical vegetation and cotton farms; in the center, the Pampa with deep, fertile soil and a mild climate where cattle and sheep are raised, and wheat, corn, forage and soybeans are grown, and to the South stretches Patagonia, a low, arid, cold plateau with steppe vegetation where sheep are extensively raised and oil is extracted. Untreated domestic waste has raised the levels of contamination of many rivers, especially the Matanza-Riachuelo in Buenos Aires. Another problem is increasing soil erosion, especially in the damp northern Pampas.

SOCIETY

Peoples: Most Argentinians are descendants of European immigrants (mostly Spaniards and Italians) who arrived in large migrations between 1870 and 1950. Among them is the largest Jewish community in Latin America. According to unofficial figures, the indigenous population of 447,300 is made up of 15 indigenous and 3 mestizo peoples mainly in the north and southeast of the country, and in the marginal settlements around the major cities. Mapuche, Kolla, and Toba constitute the largest ethnic groups. The indigenous peoples in the east, center and southernmost tip are in decline.

Religions: Catholic (92 per cent, official); Protestant, Evangelical, Jewish and Islamic minorities.

Languages: Spanish. Minor groups maintain their languages: Quechua, Guarani and others.

Political Parties: Alliance, a coalition composed of the Radical Civic Union (UCR), and the Frepaso (a coalition made up of former communists, socialists, independents, members of the Intransigent Party and former Peronists, including the head of the alliance, Carlos Alvarez); "Justicialist" or "Peronist" Party (PJ), main opposition party; Socialist Unity; People's Socialist Party; Modin (nationalist); the Center Alliance, liberal, made up of the Progressive Democratic, Autonomist, Federal, Democratic and Union of the Democratic Center (UCeDé) parties; Republican Force, linked to the last military dictatorship.

Social Organizations: The General Labor Confederation (CGT), Peronist in orientation, founded in 1930. In reaction to the current Government's economic and labor policies, the confederation has split into three factions.

THE STATE

Official Name: República Argentina.

Administrative divisions: 5 Regions with 22 Provinces, Federal District of Buenos Aires, National Territory of Tierra del Fuego.

Capital: Greater Buenos Aires, 13,700,000 people (1997).

Other cities: Cordoba, 1,179,100 people; Rosario, 1,078.400; Mendoza, 801,900; La Plata, 542,560 (1991).

Government: Presidential system; Fernando de la Rúa, President since 1999. Legislature: made up of the Chamber of Deputies and the Senate. The 22 provinces, the Federal District and the National Territory of Tierra del Fuego have 3 seats each in the 72-member Senate.

National Holidays: May 25, Revolution (1810); July 9, Independence Day (1816).

Armed Forces: 67,300: army 60 per cent, navy 26.8 per cent, air force 13.2 per cent (18,100 conscripts).

Other: (Gendarmes) 18,000.

centralism of Buenos Aires, which threatened the economy of the interior, while the Federalists pursued a more equitable agreement for all the provinces.

[8] In 1829 Juan Manuel de Rosa, a land-owner from federal roots (opposed to Buenos Aires' centralism), took over as governor of Buenos Aires. Rosas, who had himself proclaimed Restorer of the Laws, gained fame in the "Desert Campaign" where Buenos Aires expelled the indigenous peoples from its surroundings. He used political means and force to pacify the interior, bringing most of the governors together and deploying troops from Buenos Aires as far as the frontiers with Bolivia and Chile.

[9] Since Buenos Aires was the gateway to the Paraná and Uruguay rivers - main arteries for French and British trade with the provinces of the interior and Paraguay - Rosas brought in a customs law which restricted access to foreign vessels and products. The Rosas government was attacked by armies from both powers, which blockaded the port of Buenos Aires intending to crush the government and support Rosas' more liberal rivals. During the campaign to put pressure on Rosas in 1833 Britain occupied the Malvinas (Falkland Islands).

[10] The "Great War" (waged in Argentina and Uruguay between 1839 and 1852) involved Argentina, Uruguay, Paraguay and Brazil, and saw direct intervention from Britain and France, bringing an end to Rosas' 20 years in power.

[11] Justo José de Urquiza, Governor of Entre Rios, then presided over the Argentine Confederation with its capital in Paraná in accordance with the federal constitution. However there was resistance from Buenos Aires, which proclaimed independence and declared itself a separate state, even having diplomatic representation abroad. After 10 years of fighting, in 1861 Buenos Aires got its own way.

[12] Bartolomé Mitre (president from 1862 to 1868) made an alliance with Pedro II, Emperor of Brazil, and Venancio Flores,

president of Uruguay, to wage the "War of the Triple Alliance" on Paraguay. The fighting started in 1865 and ended in 1870 with the death of Paraguayan president Francisco Solano López and most of the Paraguayan population. By the time "victory" came, Domingo Faustino Sarmiento had taken over from Mitre.

[13] Once the war was over, the rest of what is now Argentina was occupied through successive incursions against the indigenous peoples of Patagonia, the Chaco and the Andean regions of Río Negro. In 1879, General Julio Roca (president from 1880-86 and 1898-1904) ended Argentina's 60-year military campaign to exterminate the indigenous peoples. The railway, symbol of modernization, ensured the Buenos Aires government's control over the territory. The mass immigration of European workers, above all Spaniards and Italians, changed the face of the nation which underwent unprecedented industrial, agricultural and commercial growth. The population grew from less than a million people in 1869 to almost eight million in 1914.

[14] Up until the electoral law of President Roque Sáenz Peña in 1912, which guaranteed universal, secret and obligatory suffrage for adult men, political power had never been a matter of democratic elections, rather the product of permanent fraud. This was the cause of the 1874, 1890, 1893 and 1905 rebellions led by Mitre, Leandro Alem, Aristóbulo del Valle and Hipólito Irigoyen, respectively.

[15] The Sáenz Peña Law helped the Radical Party led by Irigoyen into power in 1916. During World War I, in which Argentina was neutral, the country experienced industrial growth. One result of this was that the unions became far stronger. In 1919, in the "Tragic Week", army troops machine-gunned striking workers while far-right activists opposed to the Government attacked the Jewish quarter to root out "Bolsheviks".

[16] Despite being re-elected by a margin of two to one in 1928,

Irigoyen was unable to ride the consequences of the world economic crisis of 1929, which drastically undermined the agro-exporter model. Irigoyen was ousted a year later in a military coup led by General José Félix Uriburu. The coup marked the end of a period of constitutional continuity which had lasted 68 years, as well as a long period of economic expansion based on the export of raw materials which had doubled between 1913 and 1928.

[17] During World War II, President Ramon S Castillo maintained Argentina's neutrality, provoking opposition. Another military coup ousted Castillo in 1943. Ensuing dissent within the army - which wanted neither to restore democracy nor to prolong an indefinite dictatorship - together with pressure from political groups and the United States (which wanted Argentina to support the Allies) brought Colonel Juan Domingo Perón to the presidency from his post in the Employment Ministry.

[18] Perón supported the unions and won the 1946 elections by a narrow margin. Backed by the General Labor Confederation (CGT), he declared a state of civil war, which allowed him to get round the opposition and extend his authoritarian power. He nationalized foreign trade, the banks, the railway, gas and telephones; extended the fleet and created the air force; increased the workers' share of the national income to 50 per cent and framed advanced social legislation. Furthermore, he organized workers and bosses into national confederations with whom he negotiated the economic and social policy. His wife Eva (Evita) formed an exceptionally charismatic nexus between Perón and the workers, whom she dubbed "the Shirtless Ones". It was Eva Perón who was largely responsible for Argentina giving women the vote in 1947. On a foreign front Perón took the "Third Position" between the two superpowers of the Cold War, which brought him into conflict with the US.

[19] Re-elected in 1951, Perón lost army support by confronting the Church. He was ousted in a coup in 1955 and forced into exile. A dictatorship headed by Pedro Aramburu replaced him, embracing the National Security Doctrine which passed responsibility for defending the region against "the enemies of democracy" to the US. The dictatorship imposed a regressive wealth distribution system and opponents from both army and civilian ranks were executed in the 1956 Operation Massacre, a precursor of decades of political violence.

[20] Peronism was outlawed, but it was the Peronist vote which brought the pro-development government of Arturo Fondizi to power in 1958, opening the country to oil and automobile transnationals, and implanting a model of growth and wealth concentration which fed serious social confrontations. Frondizi legalized Peronism, and in the 1962 parliamentary elections the Peronists won in 10 provinces. This provoked another coup from the army which toppled Frondizi. Following two serious confrontations between separate factions of the army, General Juan Carlos Onganía emerged as the new strongman.

[21] With Peronism banned once again, the Radical Party's Arturo Illia was elected in 1963 in the first administration for 40 years not to apply a State of Emergency nor other special measures for repression or cultural censorship. His term in office was marked by friction with the Peronist unions who organized strikes, demonstrations and occupations of factories.

[22] In June 1966, Illia was overthrown by the "Argentinian Revolution" of General Juan Carlos Onganía, who brought in a new authoritarian model, politically clerical and corporatist, economically liberal and defender of the "ideological borders" in foreign policy. Ongania consecrated the country to the Sacred Heart, banned political parties, intervened in the universities and the CGT and denationalised the economy: bankrupted companies were bought up extremely cheaply by US, British and German consortia.

[23] A succession of social uprisings, like the 1969 "Cordobazo", and the emergence of a guerrilla force, threatened to split the army. General Agustín Lanusse took over the presidency in 1971 and in order to preserve the military institution he announced elections, although he banned Perón, exiled in Madrid, from taking part.

[24] Héctor Cámpora, the "Justicialista" Liberation Front candidate - a Peronist electoral coalition - received 49 per cent of the vote in the March 1973 elections, taking office in May 1973, and resigning two months later to allow new elections after Perón's return to the country. On September 23, Perón was re-elected in a new contest with 62 per cent of the vote, and the vice-presidency went to María Estela ("Isabelita") Martínez de Perón, his third wife. He resumed diplomatic relations with Cuba, proposed a reorganization of the Organization of American States (OAS) to serve Latin America's interests, promoted Argentina's participation in the Non-Aligned Movement and increased trade with socialist countries. After the Ezeiza massacre on June 23 1973, the day Perón returned to Argentina, friction grew among various Peronist factions and a situation of open warfare broke out between the old-time labor leaders and the "special squads", as Perón used to call the guerrillas. When Perón died in 1974, his widow Isabelita took office. Her Social Welfare Minister (Perón's former secretary), José López Rega, set up the "Triple A" (Argentine Anticommunist Alliance), a paramilitary hit squad that murdered Marxist opponents and left-wing Peronists.

[25] On March 25 1976, a military coup put an end to Isabelita's inefficient and corrupt administration. A military junta led by General Jorge Videla suspended all civil liberties and set in motion a cycle of kidnapping, torture, betrayal and murder. The term "missing person" became ominously commonplace, and government priorities were dictated by the newly adopted "National Security" doctrine. Human rights organizations drew up a list of over 7,000 missing persons, 80 per cent of whom had been arrested by the police in front of witnesses. Their fate has never been determined with certainty, but a 1983 Armed Forces communiqué stated that the *desaparecidos* (disappeared) should be considered "killed in action" by counter-insurgency troops.

[26] The Junta encouraged imports to the point of liquidating a third of the country's productive capacity. Fifty years of labor gains were wiped out, real wages lost half their purchasing power, and regional economies were choked by high interest rates. The country's cattle herds decreased by 10 million head and the foreign debt climbed to $60 billion, a quarter of which had been spent on arms. It was the era of what Argentines called the *patria financiera* (financial fatherland), when governmental economic policies encouraged most of the country's productive sector to turn to speculation. In 1980, a wave of bankruptcies hit banks and financial institutions.

[27] In 1981, General Leopoldo Galtieri became president and Army Commander-in-Chief. He agreed on Argentinean military participation in the US intervention in Central America. Thinking that this was enough to secure US president Reagan's unconditional support, Galtieri decided to ward off the domestic crisis by recovering the Malvinas Islands, in British hands since 1833. His troops landed there on April 2 1982. Galtieri's error soon became evident. The UN Security Council opposed the invasion, Britain deployed a powerful fleet that included nuclear submarines, and the United States firmly supported its North Atlantic ally. After 45 days of fighting Argentina surrendered on June 15; 750 Argentineans and 250 British soldiers had been killed during the conflict. Two days later Galtieri was forced to resign from both his military and presidential posts.

DEMOGRAPHY

Population: 36,577,000 (1999)
Annual growth: 1.4 % (1975/97)
Estimates for year 2015 (million): 43.5 (1999)
Annual growth to year 2015: 1.1 % (1997/2015)
Urban population: 88.6 % (1997)
Urban Growth: 1.8 % (1980/95)
Children per woman: 2.6 (1998)

HEALTH

Life expectancy at birth: 73 years (1998)
male: 70 years (1998)
female: 77 years (1998)
Maternal mortality: 38 per 100,000 live births (1990-98)
Infant mortality: 19 per 1,000 (1998)
Under-5 child mortality: 22 per 1,000 (1998)
Daily calorie supply: 3,136 per capita (1996)
268 doctors per 100,000 people (1993)
Safe water: 71 % (1990/98)

EDUCATION

Literacy: 96 % (1995)
male: 96 % (1995)
female: 96 % (1995)
School enrolment:
Primary total: 113 % (1990/96)
male: 114 % (1990/97)
female: 113 % (1990/97)
Secondary:
male: 73 % (1990/96)
female: 81 % (1990/96)
Tertiary: 42 % (1996)
Primary school teachers: one for every 17 (1997)

COMMUNICATIONS

123 newspapers (1996), 681 radios (1997), 345 TV sets (1996) and 174 main telephone lines (1996) per 1,000 people
Books: 26 new titles per 100,000 people (1992/94)

ECONOMY

Per capita, GNP: $ 8,030 (1998)
Annual growth, GNP: 3.9 % (1998)
Annual inflation: 7.8 % (1990/98)
Consumer price index: 101.6 (1998)
Currency: 1.0 pesos = $ 1 (1998)
Cereal imports: 43,179 metric tons (1998)
Food import dependency: 5 % (1997)
Fertilizer use: 333 kg per ha (1997)
Exports: $ 31,019 million (1998)
Imports: $ 38,494 million (1998)
External debt: $ 144,050 million (1998); $ 3,988 per capita (1998)
Debt service: 58.2 % of exports (1998)
Development aid received: $ 222 million (1997); $ 6.7 per capita (1997); 0.10 % of GNP (1997)

ENERGY

Consumption: 1,730.0 Kgs of Oil equivalent per capita yearly (1997); -30.0 % imported (1997)

HDI (rank/value): 39/0.827 (1997)

---

28   Seventeen member countries in the OAS acknowledged Argentina's right to the Malvinas. They also voted against Washington for having violated the Interamerican Reciprocal Assistance Treaty by supporting Britain, a non-American nation, in acts of aggression against American territory.

29   Soon after Galtieri resigned, the upper echelons of the Armed Forces underwent a series of purges. The junta set elections for October 30 1983 and the Army, without consulting the Navy and the Air Force, appointed retired General Reynaldo Bignone acting president until January 30 1984.

30   The Radical Civic Union's new leader, Raul Alfonsín, won the election with 52 per cent of the vote, well ahead of the Peronists' 40 per cent. During his campaign, Alfonsín denounced the existence of a pact between the military and trade unions, and he offered himself as the candidate of law and life, standing against tyranny and death. This won him the election, even in the Greater Buenos Aires industrial belt, a traditional Peronist stronghold.

31   The new government, which started well, ended with the complete discrediting of Alfonsín. On the political front, the Government wanted to try the military leaders who had taken part in the "Dirty War", responsible for the disappearance of more than 30,000 people. On the economic front, it aimed to tackle inflation head on, as this had reached astronomical proportions - 688 per cent by the end of 1984 - by reducing public spending and launching the Austral Plan, which froze prices, fees for services and established a new currency, the Austral, initially worth more than the dollar.

32   On the basis of revelations made in CONADEP (National Commission of Missing Persons) studies nine Commanders in Chief of the dictatorship were put on public trial accused of having ordered the crimes of that period. The sentences meted out to several high-ranking army leaders - including former president Videla - and the later extension of the trials to lower ranking officers caused strong pressures amongst the military and between 1987 and 1989, Alfonsín had to put down four military uprisings. In 1987, the President sent Congress the "Due Obedience" bill, which was approved, exempting most

military personnel accused of human rights violations, claiming they were simply obeying orders from above.

33   The failure of the Austral Plan led to thousands of jobs being lost between December 1983 and April 1989, salaries were drastically reduced and some 10 million inhabitants, almost 30 per cent of the population - were virtually pushed out of the consumer market. In this period, the CGT organized 14 general strikes and shops were raided in various areas of the capital and some cities of the interior.

34   The May 1989 presidential elections brought the Peronist Carlos Saúl Menem to power, the man who was to govern until 1999. The magnitude of the economic troubles led to the assumption of the new president being advanced several months. Menem, who had been governor of La Rioja, established a program of privatizations based on the August 1989 State Reform Act. In his first year in power, the privatization of the state oil company was promoted. The economic liberalization policy caused a schism in the CGT between the sectors supporting the government and those opposing them. The split in the Army was repeated in the main political parties.

35   Menem re-established relations with the United Kingdom (leaving the key issue of sovereignty over the Malvinas under an ambiguous "protective umbrella") and in two stages pardoned all the army officers responsible for the "Dirty War". In 1991, Argentina announced it would be leaving the Non-Aligned Movement and in early 1992 the country joined the US in condemning the human rights situation in Cuba, breaking its traditional stance of non-interference.

36   Despite constant scandal and accusations of corruption, Menem maintained his image thanks to the economic stability achieved by the Convertibility Plan, which drastically reduced public spending and established parity between the new monetary unit - the peso - and the US dollar. Inflation fell and

reached a historical low: in 1993 it was 7.4 per cent.

37   Even though the Gross Domestic Product saw strong growth, industrial activity remained below 1987 indices. Unequal wealth distribution across the various regions worsened.

38   The big surprise of the 1994 constituent elections was the performance of the leftist "Frente Grande" (Broad Front), which became the third strongest political force in the nation and triumphed in the Federal Capital with 37.6 per cent of the vote. It also won in the southern province of Neuquén. In Buenos Aires it became the second political force with 16.4 per cent of the vote. However, Peronists and Radicals obtained the majority necessary to ensure the constitutional reform which allowed Menem to stand for re-election.

39   Shortly before Menem won the elections with 50 per cent of the vote in May 1995, scandal struck at the heart of his family. When Menem's son, Carlos Menem Junior was killed in a helicopter crash, the President's former wife, Zulema Yoma, claimed her son had been murdered despite the federal police classing the crash as an accident.

40   In August, Economy Minister Domingo Cavallo accused postal entrepreneur Alfredo Yabrán, a close ally of Menem, of being a "mafia chief" who aimed to monopolize the postal system and make million-dollar deals under cover of the State.

41   In mid-1996, unemployment topped two million and underemployment one and a half, according to official figures. Foreign debt saw growth of 57 per cent in relation to 1991, at the beginning of the anti-inflationary plan applied by the Government. In the first quarter of 1996, Menem sacked Cavallo. His replacement, Roque Fernández, with a doctorate in economics from Chicago, kept Cavallo's policies in place and promised to reduce the fiscal deficit, unemployment and the recession.

---

42 The murder of José Luis Cabezas, photographer for a magazine critical of the government, added to the tension in late January 1997, as the media blamed Yabrán for the murder. The guilty parties, tried in late 1999, were members of Yabrán's security forces. Yabrán himself committed suicide in mid-1998, as the police net closed in on him. In the elections for the lower house in August, the ruling Justicialista Party was beaten nationally for the first time in 51 years. It was pushed out by the Electoral Alliance (made up of the Radical Party and Frepaso).

43 In early 1998, public declarations by frigate captain Alfredo Astíz, a former torturer speaking under the protection of the Full Stop and Due Obedience Laws passed under Alfonsín, split the opposition Electoral Alliance. Following his declarations, Astíz was removed from his post by President Menem, and the military courts sentenced him to 60 days detention in civilian prison. A tent erected by the striking teachers' union provided the site for a rolling fast by union members and the structure was finally removed 1,000 days after the protest began (in late 1999), when the new government approved a budget which took their claims into consideration.

44 In the 1999 presidential elections, the Alliance candidate, the radical Fernando de la Rúa was victorious with almost 50 per cent of the vote in the first round. The Justicialist, Eduardo Duhalde was outdone, as was former minister Domingo Cavallo, in third place with around 10 per cent of the vote. In the Federal Capital, the biggest voting constituency in the country, the former vice president, Justicialist Carlos Ruckauf won by a narrow margin.

45 In the first two months of 2000, the new government tried to investigate the most flagrant cases of mismanagement and corruption in the wake of the Carlos Menem team. The most infamous of all was the ransacking of Pami, a pension fund, where the shortfall totalled tens of millions of dollars. ∎

Malvinas

Falkland Islands

When the islands were sighted for the first time in 1520 by a Spanish ship, they were uninhabited. In the 18th century, they were baptized the "Malouines" in honor of Saint Malo, port of origin of the French fishermen and seal hunters who settled there. In 1764, Louis Antoine Bougainville founded Port Louis on Soledad Island. This move brought Spanish protests, and France recognized Spain's prior claim. That same year the British, who since 1690 had called the islands "Falkland" (after the treasurer of the British Navy), founded Port Egmont. This was later returned to Spain in exchange for £24,000, and renamed Puerto Soledad.

2 In 1820, shortly after independence, Argentina appointed Daniel Jewit as first Governor of the Malvinas. In 1831, Governor Vernet impounded two US ships on charges of illegal fishing. A US fleet that was visiting South America avenged this act of "piracy" by destroying houses and military facilities at Port Soledad. On January 3, 1833, the English corvette Clio landed a contingent of settlers which the small local force was unable to repel.

3 After World War II, the United Nations Decolonization Committee included the Malvinas and their dependencies on the list of "non-autonomous" territories and established that, as the inhabitants were British, the principle of self-determination was not applicable. The only juridically valid solution to the problem was to recognize Argentinian sovereignty.

4 On April 2 1982, Argentinian forces occupied the Malvinas. Two months later, at the cost of more than 1,000 lives, the Union Jack was once again hoisted over the islands.

5 Diplomatic relations between Britain and Argentina were placed on hold. At the beginning of his administration, Menem renewed relations with London, but the intractable issue of the Malvinas' sovereignty was left pending. During his first official visit to the Malvinas, British Foreign Minister Douglas Hurd emphasized London's determination to maintain the islands under British sovereignty.

6 In November 1991 Britain authorized the Governor of the Malvinas to award contracts, for the exploration for and exploitation of possible underwater oil deposits around the islands.

7 In March 1994, the Argentinian Minister of Defence reported that in 1982, at least 9 Argentinian soldiers had died at the hands of British forces, in circumstances that violated the Geneva Convention on the treatment of prisoners of war. There were still some 15,000 live mines scattered across the islands.

8 Understanding agreed between President Carlos Menem and Prime Minister John Major at the United Nations, in September 1995, established that Argentina and the United Kingdom will explore and exploit jointly the west of the islands, where border lines overlap.

9 The giant US oil company Amerada Hess announced on May 1998 the presence of "minor hydrocarbons" while drilling a pilot well 120 miles off the north of the islands. ∎

Armenia

Hayastán

Population: 3,525,000 (1999)
Area: 29,800 SQ KM
Capital: Yerevan
Currency: Dram
Language: Armenian

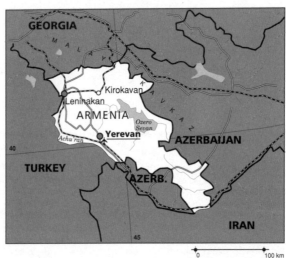

The first historical reference to the country "Armina" (Armenia) was made in the cuneiform writings from the era of King Darius I of Persia (6th-5th centuries BC). But the name Hayk, as the Armenians are called, comes from the name of the country, Hayasa, mentioned in the Hittite ceramic writings from the 12th century BC. The Urartians, direct ancestors of the Armenians, founded a powerful state in the 9th to 6th centuries BC; its capital was the city of Tushpa (today Van, in Turkey). In the year 782 BC, they founded the fortress of Erebuni, in the north of the country (today Yerevan, capital of Armenia).

[2] With the collapse of Ur, the ancient Kingdom of Armenia emerged in its territory. The first rulers were the *satraps* (viceroys) of the shahs of Persia. This period was recorded in the works of Xenophon and Herodotus. In "Anabasis", Xenophon described how the Armenians turned back 10,000 Greek mercenaries in 400 BC. His writings also describe Armenia's prosperous production, its wheat, fruit and delicious wines.

[3] After the expeditions of Alexander the Great and the rise of the Seleucid Empire, Armenia came under extensive Greek influence which had an important effect upon the cultural life of the country. The Seleucid State fell into the hands of the Romans in 190 BC, and Armenia became independent. The local government named Artashes (Artaxias) King of Greater Armenia.

[4] Armenia reached the pinnacle of its prosperity during the reign of Tigranes the Great (95-55 BC). King Tigranes united all Armenian-speaking regions and annexed several neighboring areas. Its borders extended as far as the Mediterranean to the south, the Black Sea to the north and the Caspian Sea to the east. Tigranes' empire soon fell, and Armenia was proclaimed "friend and ally of the Roman people", a euphemism for the vassals of Rome.

[5] Armenia began to disintegrate over a 400-year period until it finally disappeared as a state in the year 428, when the Roman Empire and the new kingdom of Persia divided it up between them.

[6] In 301, Armenia became the first country in the world officially to adopt Christianity as a state religion At that time, St Gregory the Illuminator, the first Armenian patriarch, founded the monastery at Echmiadzin, still extant as the headquarters for the patriarchs of the Armenian Church. Ever since the 4th century the Church has been identified with Armenian national feeling as religion made it possible to maintain the unity of the people over the long period during which the country lacked any actual state organization.

[7] In 405, the monk Mesrop Mashtots devised an alphabet which formed the basis of the Armenian writing system. The characters of this alphabet have remained unchanged, achieving a continuity which spans the centuries and links ancient, medieval and modern cultures. The 5th century was the golden age of religious and secular literature and of Armenian historiography; the natural sciences also developed during a later period. In the 7th century, Ananias Shirakatsi wrote that the world was round and formulated the hypothesis that there were several worlds inhabited by beings endowed with some form of intelligence.

[8] In the 5th and 6th centuries, Armenia was divided between Byzantium and Persia. The Persians tried to stamp out all traces of Christianity in the eastern Armenian regions triggering a massive rebellion. Prince Vartan Mamikonian, commander of the Armenian army, assumed the leadership of the rebellion. In the year 452, he led an army of 60,000 troops into battle against a vastly superior Persian force, in the Avaraev valley. The Armenians were defeated and Prince Vartan was killed, but the Persians also suffered heavy losses, and subsequently gave up their attempts to convert the Armenians to Islam. All those who lost their lives in this battle were later canonized by the Armenian Church.

[9] In the 7th century, Arab forces invaded Persia, bringing about the collapse of the Persian Empire. The new Muslim leaders also established control over the Armenian regions. The people resisted, fighting for their independence until the late 9th century, when Prince Ashot Bagratuni was named King of Armenia, and established an independent government. The epic novel "David of Sasun" describes this long struggle for independence.

[10] The prosperity of the Bagratids' reign was short-lived, for in the 11th century the Byzantines and Seleucids began bearing down on the Transcaucasian region from Central Asia. Many Armenian princes ceded their lands to the Byzantine Emperor, in exchange for lands in Cilicia. The inhabitants of other Armenian regions began flocking to Cilicia, fleeing the Turkish raids.

[11] At the end of the 11th century, the Rubenid dynasty founded a new Armenian state in Cilicia, which lasted 300 years. Cilicia had close ties to the western European states; Armenian troops took part in the Crusades, and intermarriage with other ruling dynasties introduced the Rubenids to the circle of European rulers. In 1375, Armenian Cilicia fell to the Mamelukes of Egypt, who retained Cilician science, culture and literature. In the meantime, the region that had originally been Armenia was devastated by invasions and wars.

[12] In the 13th century the Ottoman Turks replaced the Seleucids and began their conquest of Asia Minor. In 1453, they took Constantinople and marched eastwards, invading Persia. Armenia was the scene of numerous wars between Turkey and Persia, until the 17th century, when the country was divided between the two Islamic empires. During this period, the Church carried out secular functions and also called the attention of fellow-Christian European countries to the plight of the Armenians, who were forced to emigrate and settle far from their home country. Many of these expatriate Armenian "colonies" exist to this day.

[13] In 1722, Russian troops carried out an expedition to Transcaucasia, occupying the city of Baku and other territories belonging to Persia. Armenian princes in Nagorno-Karabakh and other neighboring areas seized the opportunity to join forces with the Russians, and organized a revolution against the Persians. The uprising was led by the Armenian national hero David-bek. However, Armenian hopes were dashed when the Russian Czar, Peter the Great, died. He had promised to support the Armenians, but on his death Russia signed a peace treaty with Persia. Another war between Russia and Persia, one hundred years later, ended in 1813 with the Treaty of Gulistan. According to the terms of this, Karabakh and other territories which had historically belonged to Armenia became part of the Russian Empire.

[14] Russia was at war with either Turkey or Persia during most of the 19th century; with each war, Russia annexed more and more Armenian territory. Finally, almost the entire eastern part - home to more than two million Armenians - was swallowed up. However, the major part of Armenia's historic lands - with a population of more than four million - belonged to Turkey.

[15] Protected by Russia against wars and invasions, Eastern Armenia prospered, while within the Ottoman Empire the Armenians were the object of abuse and persecution. There were frequent disturbances and riots, which were cruelly suppressed by the Turks in 1915. During World War I, citing the Armenians' pro-

Russian sympathies, the "Young Turk" government perpetrated the massacre that killed between 800,000-1,000,000 Armenians. While the men were executed in the villages, the women and children were sent to the Syrian deserts, where they starved to death. Survivors of these atrocities sought refuge in Armenian expatriate communities.

[16] On the fall of the Russian Empire, Armenia's independence was proclaimed in Yerevan. Turkey attacked Armenia in 1918 and again in 1920. In spite of some resounding victories on the part of the Armenian troops, the young republic's economy suffered and it also lost a significant part of its territory. In late 1920, a coalition of communists and nationalists proclaimed the Soviet Republic of Armenia. The nationalists were eased out of power and in February 1921 the Communist government was brought down. However, with the help of the Red Army - which came into Armenia from Azerbaijan - the Communists were back in power after three months of fighting.

[17] In 1922, Armenia, Georgia and Azerbaijan formed the Transcaucasian Soviet Federated Socialist Republic, which became a part of the USSR at the end of the year. In order to avoid ethnic friction between Christian Armenians and Muslim Azeris, the Soviet regime adopted the policy of the separation of nationalities into different political/administrative entities, which implied the relocation of large segments of the population. In 1923, the Nakhichevan (Nachicevan) Autonomous Soviet Socialist Republic was created as a dependency of Azerbaijan, from which the entire Armenian population had been removed. Azerbaijan was also given Upper Nagorno-Karabakh, a region which had historically been Armenian and which Azerbaijan had previously relinquished in 1920. In 1936, the Transcaucasian Federation was dissolved, and the republics joined the Soviet Union as separate constituent republics.

[18] In 1965, Armenians around the world commemorated the 1915 genocide for the first time. In the Armenian capital, demonstrators clamored for the return of their lands, referring to the region of Upper Karabakh. The first petition for the reunification of Nagorno-Karabakh and Armenia - signed by 2,500 inhabitants of the former - was submitted to the president of the USSR, Nikita Krushchev in May 1963. Since that time, there have been two diametrically opposed positions: Armenia, in favor of reunification, and Azerbaijan, against. In 1968, fighting broke out between Armenians and Azeris in Stepanakert, the capital of Nagorno-Karabakh.

[19] In February 1988, within the framework of *perestroika* (restructuring) in the USSR, Nagorno-Karabakh Armenians (80 per cent of the local population) decided to join Armenia. Karabakh's Regional soviet (Parliament) approved the resolution and in Armenia, the Karabakh petition for reunification was received enthusiastically. Moscow reacted violently and sent in troops to crush the demonstrations in Yerevan and Stepanakert.

[20] The National Pan-Armenian Movement won the Armenian elections of August 1990, determined to achieve independence by legal means. In the September 1991 referendum, 99.3 per cent of the electorate voted for separation from the USSR. The Armenian Soviet proclaimed independence and in October Levon Ter-Petrosian was elected president with 83 per cent of the vote.

[21] Nagorno-Karabakh also declared independence after 90 per cent of the voters approved the separation. Azerbaijan responded with an economic and military blockade around Nagorno-Karabakh, causing war between these republics. In December 1991 Armenia joined the Commonwealth of Independent States (CIS) and in February 1992 was admitted to the UN.

[22] From early 1993, while the pro-Armenian forces made important gains on the Nagorno-Karabakh front, Yerevan started to withdraw its unconditional support - at least officially. In September, Azerbaijan imposed an economic blockade on Armenia.

[23] The Armenian economy grew again in 1994 and 1995, partly because good relations with Iran cushioned the consequences of the Azerbaijani embargo. In May 1994 - when according to Azerbaijan the Armenian forces had taken 12,000 square kilometres of disputed territory - Russian pressure made a cease-fire possible in Nagorno-Karabakh. Some 20,000 people had been killed by the war and a million displaced. In 1995 and early 1996, negotiations continued between the warring parties.

[24] Ter-Petrosian started a second term in office after winning the elections in September 1996. Despite accusations of fraud, the President managed to remain in post but continuous protests over the social situation - unemployment affecting 20 per cent of the active population - forced him to resign in March 1998. In the elections to complete the period, Robert Kocharian, a native of Nagorno-Karabakh, took over from Karen Demirchian, who had been head of the Communist Party for 14 years during the Soviet era.

[25] Demirchian was avenged in the June 1999 parliamentary elections, when he was elected president of the legislative assembly with 43 per cent of the vote. His closest rival, the Communist Party, took only 12 per cent. But in October an armed group, unlinked to political organizations, stormed parliament killing Prime Minister Vazgen Sarkissian, Demirchian and other legislators, including two ministers. They held members of parliament hostage, until President Kocharian persuaded the attackers to give themselves up in return for his personal guarantee. In November the President appointed Aram Sarkissian prime minister. ■

PROFILE

ENVIRONMENT

Armenia is a mountainous country, bounded to the north by Georgia, in the east by Azerbaijan and in the south, by Turkey and Iran. With an average altitude of 1,800 meters, high Caucasian peaks - like Mount Aragats (4,095 meters) - alternate with volcanic plateaus and deep river valleys, where there are a number of important rivers. The most important of these is the Aras River, which is in turn a tributary of the Kura River, which forms a natural boundary with Turkey and Iran. The climate is dry and continental; the summers are long and hot and the winters, extremely cold. On the plains, wheat, grain, cotton, tobacco and sugar beets are grown. There are also vineyards, from which good-quality wine is made. Cattle-raising is generally limited to the mountains. There are important copper, aluminum and molybdenum deposits.

SOCIETY

Peoples: 93.3 per cent Armenian; 2.6 per cent Azeri; 2.3 per cent Russian; 1.7 per cent Kurd. **Religions:** Armenian Church (a branch of the Christian Orthodox Church), the vast majority. **Languages:** Armenian (official), Russian, Azerbaijani and Kurdish. **Political Parties:** Armenian National Movement (ANM); Dashnaktusiun Party (DP).

THE STATE

Capital: Yerevan (Jerevan) 1,500,000 people (est 1997). **Other cities:** Gyumri 163,000 people; Leninakan 218,000 people; Kirovakan 76,000 people; Alavrdi, Dilijan, Razdan, Kamo, Goris. **Government:** Robert Kocharian, President since April 1998, Aram Sarkissian Prime Minister since November 1999. **National Holiday:** May 28, Independence (1918). **Armed Forces:** 57,400 (1996).

Aruba

Aruba

Population: 84,000 (1999)
Area: 190 SQ KM
Capital: Oranjestad
Currency: Aruban florin
Language: Dutch

The Caiquetios were the first inhabitants of Aruba, one of the Lesser Antilles islands. In 1634, some European colonists settled on the island to raise horses, the only economically feasible activity in an archipelago that had been declared worthless by Spain. The Caiquetios were conquered by the Spaniards and sold to Hispaniola as slaves.

[2] According to the Treaty of Westfalia (1648), the Netherlands ruled over Aruba, Curaçao and Bonaire. Aruba required little labor to support its horse and cattle-raising industry, which explains why only 12 per cent of the population was of African origin by the time slavery was abolished.

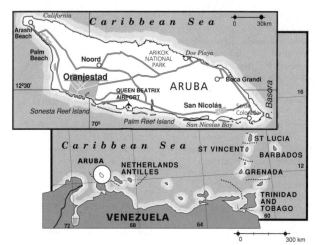

[3] The installation of large oil refineries on Aruba at the end of the 1920s generated a wave of immigration of specialized, high income workers, particularly from the US. Many Arubans began to resent the administrative dominance of Curaçao.

[4] In 1971, the Aruba People's Party (AVP), led by Prime Minister Henny Eman, an anti-Dutch, anti-Curaçao nationalist, split into two separate parties. One was the Aruban Patriotic Party (PPA), which opposed the separation of Aruba. The other was the People's Electoral Movement (MEP), radical wing, led by Gilberto "Betico" Croes, which supported each island's freedom to choose its own constitution and even become an autonomous republic. After the Netherlands' refusal to accept this proposal, Croes threatened a unilateral declaration of independence.

[5] In 1979 the Antiyas Nobo Movement (MAN), active on 16 islands, won a significant electoral victory in Curaçao. With the MEP and the Bonaire Patriotic Union (UPB), it established a left-of-center coalition government. But while MAN favored a federation with broad autonomy for each island, the MEP insisted on the secession of Aruba. These differences led to the disintegration of the governmental alliance in 1981.

[6] In 1983, the Dutch Government granted Aruba separate status, effective from January 1986, establishing a governor appointed by the Dutch queen, a single-chamber parliament with 21 members and its own national symbols. In the 1985 election, eight

seats were won by the MEP, seven by the AVP and the remaining six by three minor parties who entered a coalition with the AVP. Henny Eman was Prime Minister. Croes died in 1986 in suspicious circumstances.

[7] In the 1989 elections the MEP won 10 seats, the AVP won 8, and each of the 3 remaining parties, National Democratic Action (ADN), New Patriotic Party (PPN), and Aruban Patriotic Party (PPA), gained one seat. The new Prime Minister Nelson Odaber, defended continued association with the Netherlands.

[8] The economy of Aruba has the support of Dutch credit. It exports rum and tobacco, but 98.9 per cent of its exports came from refining Venezuelan oil. In 1985 Exxon, the owners of the refinery, withdrew from the country, leaving the island's economy in serious difficulties. With unemployment at 20 per cent, the Government turned to the tourist industry, which has provided 35 per cent of GDP. In recent years the authorities have tried to reduce the dependence on tourism by promoting industrial activities.

[9] In 1986 Aruba split off from the Netherlands Antilles as a first step towards what was to be total independence in 1996. The Netherlands revoked this resolution in 1990, but Aruba has autonomy over its internal affairs. After a faltering start, the economy grew at an average of 10 per cent annually between 1987 and 1993. Its strength was based on tourism, offshore finance and the resumption of oil refining.

[10] During 1990 the hotel capacity of Aruba doubled and the refinery was reopened in 1990-91. Unemployment fell to 0.6 per cent in 1992. However, the financial crisis led to the bankruptcy of many tourism related foreign companies.

[11] The MEP won the elections again in 1993 and started to implement an economic diversification policy, but the coalition faltered and was replaced in 1994 by the AVP.

[12] In September 1997, the legislative assembly was dissolved, due to disagreements between two of the main parties in the governing coalition. However, the December elections did not change the balance of power in the legislative body. ■

PROFILE

ENVIRONMENT

Located off the coast of Venezuela, the island of Aruba was until January 1986 one of the "ABC Islands", otherwise known as the Netherlands Antilles, together with Bonaire and Curaçao. The climate is tropical, moderated by ocean currents. Oil refineries, where Venezuelan petroleum is processed, and tourism are the main economic activities.

SOCIETY

Peoples: Predominantly of European and Carib origin, its inhabitants intermingled with Latin American and North American immigrants.
Religions: Mainly Catholic (82 per cent). There is also a Protestant (8 per cent) minority and small Jewish, Muslim and Hindu communities.
Languages: Dutch (official). The most widely spoken language, as on Curaçao and Bonaire, is *Papiamento*, a local dialect based on Spanish with elements of Dutch, Portuguese (spoken by the Jewish community), English and some African languages.
Political Parties: Aruba People's Party (AVP); People's Electoral Movement (MEP); Party of Curaçao; National Democratic Action (ADN); Aruban Patriotic Party (PPA); Aruban Liberal Organization (OLA).
Social Organizations: The Aruba Workers Federation.

THE STATE

Official Name: Aruba.
Capital: Oranjestad 26,000 people (est 1997).
Other city: St Nicolaas 17,000 people (1981).
Government: Olindo Koolman, Governor designated by Holland since1992. Jan Eman, Prime Minister and Minister of General Affairs since 1994. Holland continues to be in charge of defense and foreign relations. Single-chamber legislature; Parliament made up of 21 members elected for a 4-year term.

DEMOGRAPHY

Population: 84,000 (1999)

COMMUNICATIONS

552 radios (1997) per 1,000 people

ECONOMY

Consumer price index: 108.3 (1998)
Cereal imports: 10,959 metric tons (1998)

WORKERS

Unemployment: 6.5 % (1994)

Australia

Australia

Population: 18,705,000 (1999)
Area: 7,741,220 SQ KM
Capital: Canberra
Currency: Australian dollar
Language: English

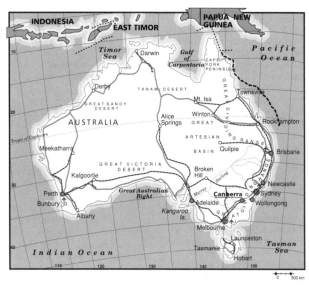

The first inhabitants of Australia came from Southeast Asia some 55,000 years ago, but whether or not they constituted one homogeneous ethnic group at the time of their arrival is not known.

² These peoples, named "Aborigines" by the Europeans, spoke over 260 different languages and had distinctive cultures, though they were all semi-nomadic hunters and gatherers. Their daily life was linked to a universal scheme through rituals which guaranteed the ordered changing of the seasons and the community's food supply.

³ Land was held in common, and there was no social stratification, other than the prestige gained by practising religious rites.

⁴ In 1606, the Spaniard Vaez de Torres explored the strait which today bears his name, located between Australia and Papua-New Guinea. Three years later, Fernández de Quirós, also Spanish, became the first European to set eyes on Australian territory. However, colonization did not begin until after the arrival of Captain James Cook in the late 18th century.

⁵ In 1788, the first British settlers arrived and established a penal colony. This was the beginning of an assault on the way of life and customs of the Aborigines, with the aim of taking over.

⁶ At first, the British settled in coastal areas, but the process of inland expansion soon began, with the settlers acting as though the land were uninhabited. While British and international law recognized the prior rights of indigenous peoples, Australia was simply declared *terra nullius* (uninhabited).

⁷ Gaining control of the land claimed the lives of 80 per cent of the Aborigines. The "Aborigine problem" was dealt with by genocide. Entire families were poisoned and others were forcibly removed from their lands onto reservations administered by the British.

⁸ In 1830 more than 58,000 convicts were "transported" to Australia, most of them petty thieves, deserters from the Royal Navy and members of Irish opposition groups. Known by the British as "the human refuse of the Thames", most of them served out their sentences by providing inexpensive labor for European landowners.

⁹ Australia served as a safety valve for social tensions generated by Britain's rapid industrialization. Most of the wealth accumulated in the colony returned to England, representing an important influx of capital. Finally, Australia's strategic location was important for British trade, in order to control its world-wide maritime network.

¹⁰ Australian society was controlled by the military, a legacy of its original function as a penal colony. Local government was normally limited to a high-ranking military officer, appointed by the Crown to oversee the prison population and take charge of the defence against possible attack by other European powers.

¹¹ Aboriginal religions, based on a strong spiritual link between each human being and the earth, was given no credence by the settlers. As a result, the religions and languages were debased and the people persecuted. The Aborigines lost lands rich in natural resources, fishing areas and any land that the settlers considered suitable for cultivation or grazing. Once the land was in the hands of settlers, it was stocked with sheep to provide the growing British textile industry with an abundant supply of raw materials and a cheap source of food for the industry's workforce.

¹² The development of the cattle industry and the subsequent discovery of gold and other precious metals boosted economic development between 1830 and 1860. The possibility of getting rich quickly led to increased European settlement. As resistance was broken, the Aborigines were progressively relegated to Australia's desert areas.

¹³ For many years, rural settlers had to deal with occasional armed Aboriginal resistance. Driven by their desire to free land from the Europeans, they fought the settlers and tried to disrupt their farming.

¹⁴ Once suppressed, Aborigines were forced to sign "work contracts" written in English. These contracts committed them to the status of unpaid workers, household slaves or concubines, often subject to extremely severe disciplinary measures.

¹⁵ In the meantime, a dynamic labor movement was beginning to appear in the cities, and it soon had a significant following. From the mid-19th century onwards, the unions obtained important victories and concessions which Europe's working classes were still a long way from obtaining.

¹⁶ In the latter part of the 19th century, Australia's growing urbanization process went hand-in-hand with an accelerated rate of industrial development, especially in Sydney and Melbourne, which took on the characteristics of any large urban centre.

¹⁷ Successive waves of immigration also helped change the face of Australian society. The low cost of land and a demand for Australia's products on the world market provided large numbers of mostly British immigrants with the means to increase their standard of living.

¹⁸ A vast middle class developed alongside a wealthy urban industrial bourgeoisie, utterly transforming Australian life. The liberal governments which dominated the country's political scene between 1860 and 1900 accelerated this political, social and economic transformation.

¹⁹ After an uneasy period of consolidation, in 1901 the six British colonies (New South Wales, Victoria, South Australia, Western Australia, Queensland and Tasmania) became independent states united in the "Commonwealth of Australia". The

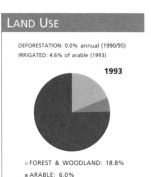

WORKERS

1997
UNEMPLOYMENT: 8.4%

% OF LABOUR FORCE **1998**

- FEMALE: 32%
- MALE: 68%

1990

- SERVICES: 68.2%
- INDUSTRY: 26.3%
- AGRICULTURE: 5.5%

LAND USE

DEFORESTATION: 0.0% annual (1990/95)
IRRIGATED: 4.6% of arable (1993)

1993

- FOREST & WOODLAND: 18.8%
- ARABLE: 6.0%
- OTHER: 75.2%

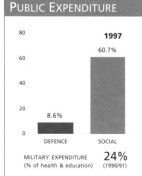

PUBLIC EXPENDITURE

1997
60.7%

8.6%

DEFENCE   SOCIAL

MILITARY EXPENDITURE **24%**
(% of health & education) (1990/91)

Northern Territory and the Australian Capital Territory did not join until 1911.

[20] A prolonged period of economic prosperity made it possible for the country to finance a series of social reforms. Australia was a relatively open society, in which social mobility was possible for certain sectors of the population, and there was protective legislation for workers before most European countries. In 1902, Australia became one of the first countries to grant women the right to vote.

[21] World War II loosened the ties between Britain and Australia, as Britain was unable to guarantee the security of its former colonies, in the face of the threat of Japanese attack. The US assumed the role of policing the region, as it has done ever since.

[22] The Korean War triggered a sharp increase in the price of wool on the world market, reinforcing Australia's economic growth. It also helped to avoid creating a gap between urban prosperity and the relative stagnation of the rural areas.

[23] With the onset of the Cold War, the ANZUS military assistance treaty was signed in 1951 by Australia, Aotearoa/New Zealand and the US. The aim of the treaty was to guarantee the security of US and allied interests in the region. This military alliance also committed the Australians to participate in the Vietnam War, which damaged the treaty's image internationally, and triggered an important anti-war movement.

[24] Japan became the main market for Australian minerals, financing coal exploration in Australia in the 1960s. The large coal deposits discovered have supplied local industry ever since, and have also met Japan's huge industrial needs.

[25] In the 1960s, the Labor Party became the platform for Aborigine groups, helping to publicize and sensitize public opinion to their grievances and demands.

[26] A plebiscite held in 1967 - supported by the Labor Party - granted Australian Aborigines full citizenship rights. The Aboriginal issue was also placed under the jurisdiction of the federal government. However, the Aborigines still did not gain recognition of their land rights.

[27] There are currently around 200,000 Aborigines in Australia, many retaining their original languages. Two-thirds of them no longer live in tribal groups, living instead in urban areas. A minority continues to live in areas which Europeans consider to be inhospitable, like the central desert or the wetlands which lie in the northern part of the country, where they have managed to keep their own religious and social traditions alive.

[28] In 1983, powerful transnational corporations interested in developing mineral resources launched a campaign aimed at convincing the population that the Aborigines' defence of their territorial claims compromised the country's economic growth. As a result of this campaign, the Government's promise of passing federal legislation on territorial rights of the Aborigines was shelved.

[29] In many cases the Aborigines found themselves forced to give in to pressure from mining companies and sign land use agreements, even though they knew that it could well adversely affect their sacred sites, the environment, and their traditional lifestyle.

[30] Although some aspects of the Aborigines' situation are uniform throughout the country, their legal status varies from one state to another. Some states, like Tasmania, put in practice proposals aimed at safeguarding some of the Aborigines' rights, as well as ways of combating the discrimination to which they were subjected.

[31] According to local and international human rights organizations, in 1987 the death rate of Aboriginal prisoners was two per month. In terms of the total prison population, this would be the equivalent of 100 deaths of prisoners of European descent, in the same amount of time.

[32] Australian Aborigines are probably the people with the largest prison population in the world. In 1981, the rate was 775 per 100,000 inhabitants. Among the

PROFILE

ENVIRONMENT

Australia occupies the continental part of Oceania and the island of Tasmania, and has a predominantly flat terrain. The Great Dividing Range runs along the eastern coast. Inland lies the Central Basin, a desert plateau surrounded by plains and savannahs. The desert region runs west to the huge Western Plateau. Rainfall is greatest in the north where the climate is tropical, with dense rainforests. 85 per cent of the population is concentrated in the southeast, which has a subtropical climate and year-round rainfall. Oats, rye, sugar cane and wheat are grown there; Australia is one of the world's largest producers of the latter. Australia has the largest number of sheep of any country in the world, located in the inland steppes and savannahs, and is also the world's largest exporter of wool. It also exports meat and dairy products and is one of the world's largest producers of minerals: iron ore, bauxite, coal, lead, zinc, copper, nickel and uranium. It is self-sufficient in oil and has a large industrial zone concentrated in the southeast. The soil has undergone increasing salinization. Many unique species, both plant and animal, are in danger of extinction due to the destruction of their habitats.

SOCIETY

Peoples: When the British "discovered" Australia in 1788, there were 250,000 Aborigines in approximately 500 different tribes. In 1901, only 66,000 of their descendants were still alive. Today, there are 200,000, representing just 1 per cent of the national population. Descendants of British immigrants make up two-thirds of the population. The rest are immigrants from Asia, Europe and Latin America, a process which continues today.
Religions: Christians 74 per cent (Catholic 27 per cent, Anglican 24 per cent, Methodist 8 per cent). Buddhist, Muslim, Confucian and other, 13 per cent. **Languages**: English.
Political Parties: Liberal (conservative) Party, a right-of-centre power (aligned with the National Party (NP), which represents the interests of pastoralists); Labor Party, a centre-left group; Australian Democrats (moderate); Party of the New Left, founded in 1989 after the dissolution of the Communist Party; Socialist Party; Marxist-Leninist Communist Party and Green Party.
Social Organizations: The Australian Council of Trade Unions (ACTU) is the largest labor confederation, with 133 union affiliates.

THE STATE

Official Name: Commonwealth of Australia.
Administrative divisions: 6 states and 2 territories.
Capital: Canberra 308,100 people (1999). **Other cities**: Sydney 3,986,700 people; Melbourne 3,371,300; Brisbane 1,574,600; Perth 1,341,900; Adelaide 1,088,400 (1999); Hobart 195,000; Darwin 86,000 (1999). **Government**: Parliamentary monarchy. William Deane, Governor General until July 2001, appointed by the Queen of England. John Howard, Prime Minister since March 1996. **National Holiday**: January 26, Australia Day. **Armed Forces**: 56,100 (7,500 women included). **Dependencies:** Cocos Islands, Coral Islands, Christmas Island, Norfolk Island.

population of European descent, the proportion was 67 per 100,000. In Queensland, in the northeast of the country, Aborigines make up only 2 per cent of the population, yet account for 35 per cent of the prison population. In Western Australia, where they also make up 2 per cent of the population, 44 per cent of the prison population are Aborigines.

[33] Given this situation, the federal government created a Royal Commission charged with investigating the deaths of Aborigines in prison. After several years of work and research, the Commission presented a provisional report which did not clearly establish what the actual causes of these events were, nor who was responsible for them. This report was harshly criticized by spokespersons of different groups, who called it a "sham" for all the country's citizens.

[34] In the area of health, the Aborigines are also at a clear disadvantage with relation to the rest of the population. They continue to contract diseases which have almost disappeared among the European population, and for which total immunization is available.

[35] Although Australia sided with Aotearoa/NZ in opposing British and French nuclear tests in the region, the virtual withdrawal of Aotearoa/NZ from ANZUS made it necessary for the Australian Government to redefine its role within this alliance, and within the region. The United States negotiated new agreements allowing the maintenance of troops and a telecommunications centre in Australian territory.

[36] In 1989, in order to meet this new international reality head-on, Australia proposed the creation of the Asian Pacific Economic Cooperation (APEC). The project proposed the formation of a common market among the countries of the region, with Australia taking a leading role. At the same time, Australia hoped to become the representative of food-exporting countries. To achieve this goal, it sponsored the creation of the so-called "Cairns Group", to

Christmas Island

Population: 2,373 (1999)
Area: 135 SQ KM
Currency: Australian dollar

The island, formerly a dependency of the British colony of Singapore, was transferred to Australia on October 1 1958. Nearly all the island's population work in the Phosphate Mining Commission.

[2] As of 1981, the residents of the island were granted the right to become Australian citizens. In 1984, the Australian Government extended social security, health and education benefits to the island, also granting the citizens political rights. There has been an income tax since 1985.

[3] In 1987, the authorities closed the mine, which was reopened in 1990 by private investors but under strict guidelines for the preservation of the environment. In 1991 investments were made to develop the island's tourist potential.

ENVIRONMENT

An island in the Indian Ocean, 2,500 km northeast of Perth, Australia, and 380 km south of Java, Indonesia. Mountainous and arid, it has a dry climate.

SOCIETY

Peoples: Nearly two-thirds of the population are of Chinese origin. There are some Malays and a minority of Australians. There are no native inhabitants. **Religions**: Christianity (Protestants), Confucianism and Taoism. **Languages**: English, Malay, Mandarin and Cantonese. **Capital**: Flying Fish Cove. **Government**: A.D. Taylor, Administrator appointed by the Australian Government.

DEMOGRAPHY

Population: 2,373 (1999)

Cocos Island

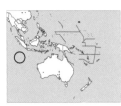

Population: 636 (1999)
Area: 14 SQ KM
Capital: West Island
Currency: Australian dollar
Language: English

The Clunies Ross Company, founded by John Clunies Ross in the early 1800s, was the real owner of the islands, despite their formal status as a British (1857) and later Australian (after 1955) colony. Clunies Ross brought in Malayan laborers to work the coconut groves.

[2] In 1978, after many years of negotiation, Australia bought the islands from the Company. However, the Company kept a monopoly on the production and commercialization of copra. The transfer was designed to give Home Island residents formal ownership of their plots of land in order to alleviate social tensions. On West Island, Australia also had a military base, purchased in 1951.

[3] In a 1984 referendum, the population voted in favor of Australian nationality for the islanders and full annexation of the territory to Australia. In December of that year the UN General Assembly validated the results of the plebiscite and Australia was freed from the obligation of reporting to the Decolonisation Committee.

ENVIRONMENT

A group of coral atolls in the Indian Ocean, southwest of Java, Indonesia. Of the 27 islets, only two are inhabited, West and Home. The climate is tropical and rainy, and the land is flat and covered with the coconut groves that give the islands their name.

SOCIETY

Peoples: The inhabitants of Home Island are descended from Malayan workers. Australians predominate on West Island. **Religions**: Mainly Protestant. **Languages**: English.

THE STATE

Capital: West Island 250 people. **Government**: D Lawrie, administrator appointed by the Australian Government.

DEMOGRAPHY

Population: 636 (1999)

include Argentina, Colombia, Thailand, Uruguay and other countries within the Uruguay Round of the GATT.

[37] In 1989, data supplied by Australian National University research damaged the Labor Government's image. The figures pointed to the fact that 1 per cent of all Australians owned more than 20 per cent of the total national wealth, and 13 per cent of all Australians live below the poverty line.

[38] The social and economic crisis worsened, with unemployment figures totalling more than a million in 1991. This put pressure on Bob Hawke's Labor government, which found itself under growing opposition from other political parties, and from within the party as well.

[39] Hawke had been elected Prime Minister in 1983, after 11 years as president of ACTU (the country's largest labor union), a fact which had given him a huge amount of popular support at the beginning of his term.

[40] Toward the end of the 1980s, with the support of the more conservative elements within his party, Hawke embarked on a series of economic reforms aimed at liberalizing the economy, including an accelerated program for privatizing public enterprises.

[41] There was growing discontent among the population at large, and opposition to the government began to emerge within the Labor Party itself. In addition, a power struggle developed between Hawke and his former Treasurer (Economics Minister), Paul Keating. In December 1991, the Labor Government held internal elections to resolve these conflicts once and for all, and also to open up the possibility of improving the government's image. Keating obtained a slim majority and became Prime Minister.

[42] Shortly after assuming his post as head of government, Keating announced that further measures would go into effect to liberalize the economy. He himself had initiated these measures between 1983 and June 1991, when he had been in charge of economic policy in Hawke's government. These measures were firmly rejected by the unions and the left wing of the Labor Party.

[43] In 1992, unemployment reached 11.1 per cent. The Government approved legislation aimed at increasing employment, by reducing immigration by 27 per cent.

[44] In the 1993 general elections, Labor won by a narrow margin, with 50.5 per cent of the vote. One of Keating's campaign promises was to give the rights of Indigenous Australians a high priority.

[45] An important decision on native land rights was made by the Australian High Court in June 1993. Known as the Mabo decision, it effectively overturned the notion of *terra nullius*, which had assumed that when the British colonists arrived in 1788 the Aborigines had neither right of law nor ownership of the land. Mabo was one of Australia's most significant legal decisions since federation in 1901. The decision drew on the history of Murray Island north of Queensland and to their Meriam people, whose rules of inheritance were crucial in the final judgement. Following the Mabo decision, the federal Labor government passed revised Native Title legislation. There are also concerns over other matters affecting Aborigines and Torres Strait Islanders, including infant mortality, health, education and the country's terrible record of black deaths in custody. Progress Australia had been making in multiculturalism also slowed, despite its being one of the most ethnically diverse countries in the world.

[46] The Government started to develop links with the Asian Pacific nations, through trade and dialogue with regional groups such as ASEAN. But its relations with Cambodia, North Korea, Vietnam, Indonesia, Malaysia and China advanced with greater difficulty.

[47] The republican debate intensified in 1995 when Prime Minister Keating announced that Sir William Deane, a Supreme Court judge, would replace Bill Hayden as Governor General. Keating's plans included replacing the post of governor with that of president (for the first time in the nation's history) before the year 2001.

[48] Privatization continued to be the government's main concern, with the sale of the Qantas airline, the Commonwealth Bank and the partial sale of telecommunications company Telstra.

[49] The French nuclear tests on Mururoa atoll caused public protests throughout Australia. The Keating and Chirac Governments were at loggerheads and broke off diplomatic relations. The Australian delegation which went to Europe with a South Pacific representative did not gain the support of the British Government, which refused to confront France. The British decision strengthened Australia's pro-republican stance.

[50] In the general elections held in March 1996, Liberal Party leader John Howard defeated his Labor rival. Howard became Prime Minister after pledging the "moralization" of his country's leadership.

[51] In early 1996, the High Court of Australia authorized Indigenous Australians to claim the use of land leased for grazing or mining activities. In August 1997, the start of new uranium mining activities in the north caused a strong sentiment of rejection among Aboriginal groups. The leaders of the protest claimed the mining would contaminate their land and the money would devastate their culture. By the end of the year, several Aboriginal groups filed suits for the recognition of their property over vast coast and sea areas. The issue of Aboriginal land rights remains politically controversial and undecided.

[52] In 1997 Amnesty International reported an increase in the death rate of indigenous peoples held in jails or in police detention operations, as well as ill treatment and intimidation in the enforcement of the law. In October, it was revealed that Victoria state police had spied, infiltrated and kept files on ethnic groups, journalists and organizations such as Greenpeace or groups fighting against AIDS. Although this shocked some Australians, senior Intelligence officials justified these proceedings and stressed it was an essential factor to maintain public order.

[53] Despite government opposition to union activity, the unions struggled to retain bargaining power. In April 1998, the Patrick Stevedores company dismissed 1,400 dockers with the implicit support of the Government. This led the Maritime Union of Australia to call a strike which became one of the biggest in the 1990s and it ended with the rehiring of the fired workers.

[54] Australian diplomacy participated in various ways in the crisis of its two biggest neighbors, Indonesia and Papua/New Guinea. Australia headed the UN peacekeeping force which intervened in East Timor, a former Portuguese colony annexed by Indonesia, in order to further the cause of independence forces and to put a halt to the violence between East Timor and Indonesia.

[55] The referendum held in November 1999 on whether Australia would become a republic was won by the monarchists who, with 54 per cent of the votes, maintained Elizabeth II of England as head of state. The opposition blamed Prime Minister Howard for the defeat since the proposed reform established that the head of state would be chosen by the Prime Minister in agreement with the opposition leader, with parliamentary approval. The inability to elect the head of state by direct ballot made many decide to vote against the reform. ■

Norfolk Island

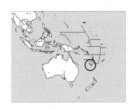

Population: 1,905 (1999)
Area: 36 SQ KM
Capital: Kingston
Currency: Australian dollar
Language: English

There are no records of the existence of a native population before the arrival of the Europeans. Captain Cook arrived in 1774, and then the island was used as a prison site between 1825 and 1855. It was transferred to Australia as an overseas territory in 1913. In November 1976, two thirds of the Norfolk electorate opposed annexation to Australia. Since 1979, the island has had internal autonomy.

In December 1991, the local population rejected a proposal to become part of Australia's federal electorate.

ENVIRONMENT

The island is located in Southern Melanesia, northwest of the North Island of Aotearoa/NZ. The subtropical climate is tempered by sea winds.

SOCIETY

Peoples: 1,905 inhabitants in 1999. A large part of the population are descended from the mutineers of the British vessel HMS Bounty, who came from Pitcairn Island in 1856.
Religions: Protestant.
Languages: English (official).

THE STATE

Official name: Norfolk Island.
Capital: Kingston.
Government: Commander John A Matthew, Administrator appointed by the Governor General of Australia. The office of Prime Minister was replaced by that of President of the Legislative Assembly. In the May 1992 elections, David Ernest Buffett was elected to this new office.

DEMOGRAPHY

Density: 59 people/sq km.

Coral Sea Islands

Created in 1969 as a separate administrative entity, the territory consists of several islets located east of Queensland (Eastern Australia). The major ones are Cato and Chilcott in the Coringa group, and the Willis archipelago. With the exception of a weather station on one of the Willis islands, the rest of the islands are uninhabited.

[2] The Constitutional Act by which the territory was created did not provide for Australian administration of the islands, but only for control over foreign visitors by the Canberra Government. However the discovery of oil fields and the expanding fishing industry may change this situation.

Austria

Österreich

Population: 8,177,000 (1999)
Area: 83,859 SQ KM
Vienna (Wien)
Currency: Schilling
Language: German

The first traces of human settlement in the Austrian Republic date back to the Early Paleolithic age. From then on, the territory was occupied by various ethnic groups. The Austrian region of Hallstat gave its name to the main culture in the Iron Age, from 800-450 BC.

2 Celtic tribes moved into the Eastern Alps in the 5th century BC, and it is thought that they founded the kingdom of Noricum, comprising modern central Austria and parts of Bavaria. Later, the Romans also settled here, attracted by the iron in the area and by its strategic military importance.

3 After peaceful invasion, the Roman troops conquered the whole of the country around the year 15 BC. Raetia, Noricum and Pannonia became Roman provinces, extending the Empire's dominions as far as the Danube. The provinces were subdivided into municipalities and a vast network of roads was built.

4 The Pax Romana ended with the arrival of the Germanic tribes between 166 and 180 AD. This invasion was repulsed, but the region did not recover its prosperity. Between the 4th and 6th centuries, the Huns and the Germans raided the area pushing back the Empire's borders on the Danube.

5 According to the only written records from the era, the Germanic tribes of the Rugii, Goths, Heruli and lastly the Langobardi (Lombards), settled in the territory and in the year 488, a part of the population of the devastated province of Noricum was forced to emigrate to Italy.

6 Following the departure of the Lombards to Italy, after successive battles with Slavic tribes, the Bavarians - Germans under the political influence of the Franks - reached as far as the Avar frontiers in the 6th century. When the Frankish king Dagobert I died, the Bavarian dukes were left virtually independent. Christianity spread in the region and was also practised by the Romans who remained in the territory. Under the protection of the Christian churches of Salzburg and Passau, which resisted the missions of the east, led by the Slav apostles Cyril and Methodius, during the 8th century the Bavarians expanded both militarily and economically.

7 Toward the end of the 8th century, Charlemagne, king of the Franks, led various attacks which broke down Avar control in the south, annexing these lands to his kingdom. The surviving Avars were forced to settle in the eastern part of Low Austria, between the Fischa and Leitha rivers and soon disappeared from the historical record, probably mixing in with the native population.

8 Charlemagne took over as Holy Roman Emperor in the year 800, becoming the model of Christian king and emperor. Even though the Empire disintegrated after his death, the German medieval monarchies - just like the French - derived their constitutional traditions from the Carolingian Empire.

9 The final years of the 9th century witnessed Bulgar incursions and the Magyar invasion, taking control of the low lands to the Rivers Enns and Styria to Koralpe. However, the Germans and Slavs continued to settle and after the German king Otto started expelling the Magyars in 955, the territory was predominantly German again.

10 Between the 10th and 13th centuries, during the period of Babenberg control, Austria was contested by the Pope and the Holy Roman Empire on several occasions in the battle for control of the German church. Meanwhile, the reformists gained ground, founding the monasteries of Gottweig, Lambach, and Admont in Styria.

11 Apart from brief interruptions, the Babenbergs maintained their sovereignty over the duchies of Austria and Styria, expanding them north and south. New settlements were made by clearing the forests and moving into mountain areas. The colonization process changed the distribution of the German-speaking population and apart from some Alpine regions, the Slavs were gradually assimilated, as were the remnants of Roman population in Salzburg and the northern Tyrol.

12 The expansion of the German language was also encouraged by the attraction the Babenburg court held for the leading German poets. Decorated texts proliferated in monasteries, and in the early 13th century, the saga of the Niebelungs was composed by and unknown Austrian poet. In this era Austria also saw the flowering of the best romanesque and early gothic architecture.

13 Following the death of Frederick II, the Babenbergs' dominions were coveted by their neighbors. The main beneficiary was Premysl Otakar II of Bohemia, until Rodolfo IV of Hapsburg came to the German throne in 1273 and pushed him out with the help of the Hungarians.

14 Even though they were initially rejected by the local nobility and their neighbors, the Hapsburgs managed to maintain control over their dominions. In 1322, the Hapsburgs' defeat by the Swiss, and in particular Frederick I at the hands of Louis IV of Bavaria, threatened the dominion of this royal house over the Rhine and Lake Constance. By passing the last years of his life on Austrian territory, and being buried in the Carthusian monastery of Mauerbach in 1330, Frederick was the first of his dynasty to consecrate Austria as a home for the Hapsburgs. From then on, the government and Hapsburg territories were known as *dominium austriae*, a term which would later be replaced by the concept of the House of Austria.

15 The consolidation of the House of Austria was achieved through inheritance and marriage alliances. Even though in 1490 following several crises, the Hapsburgs only controlled Lower Austria, Maximilian I, on the death of Frederick II, inherited the House of Austria and the German Empire. Similarly his son Phillip I, married in 1496 to the Infanta Juana, gained the throne of Spain. A famous saying of the time ran: "Let others make wars: you, fortunate Austria, get married".

16 By the end of the Middle Ages, the Hapsburg monarchy held an extent of Alpine land comparable in size to modern Austria. The House of Hapsburg had always wanted to rule over Bohemia and Hungary, an aspiration that Maximilian rekindled.

17 After unification, territories maintained their individuality and their own legal codes. Cities prospered, while rural settlement regressed, particularly in Lower Austria, because of the growing interest in mining.

18 Martin Luther's reforming ideas penetrated Austria, supported by the noble families, especially in the south and centre of the country. In 1521, Protestant pamphlets were printed in Vienna, and bans on their dissemination had no practical effect.

19 There were peasant revolts in Tyrol, Salzburg and Innerösterreich. Many peasants were joining the Anabaptists rather than the Lutherans. The name "Anabaptist" came from the Greek meaning "to baptize again", as they considered the christening of children ineffectual, and so subjected followers to a second christening. As they were more radical, and had no support from the powerful, they suffered greater persecution from the outset.

20 In 1528, in Vienna, Balthasar Hubmaier, leader of the Anabaptists in the Danube valley and southern Moravia, was burned at the stake. In 1536, in Innsbruck, Jakob Hutter, a Tyrolian, was sentenced to the same fate after he had led his followers into Moravia.

21 With the death of King Jagiellon of Bohemia and Hungary, Vienna took the chance to extend the power

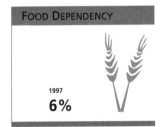

FOOD DEPENDENCY

1997

6%

FOREIGN TRADE

Millions US$ 1997

IMPORTS

88,418

EXPORTS

87,234

of the Hapsburgs. The union of Austria, Bohemia and Hungary became the driving idea behind Hapsburg policy. Ferdinand I was proclaimed King of Bohemia in 1526 but his troops were repelled with the help of the Turks when he tried to impose his choice on the Hungarians. The 1562 Constantinople Peace Treaty divided Hungary into three possessions: the north and west which went to the Hapsburgs; the centre held by the Turks; and Transylvannia, with its neighboring territories, to Hungary's Janos Zapolya and his successors.

22 In Austria, the Counter-Reformation started with the Jesuits, strong in Vienna, Graz and Innsbruck, and mainly with the impetus of Melchior Klesl, apostolic administrator in Vienna, who was to become Bishop and Cardinal and a key figure in Austrian politics. Even if Maximilian II - who succeeded Ferdinand I as Emperor of Bohemia, a part of Hungary and the Austrian Danube - had Protestant inclinations, he promised his father

he would keep the Catholic faith. His successor, Rudolf II, educated in Spain as a strict Catholic, expelled the Protestants from the court and put Klesl in charge of the conversion of the cities and markets. The implementation of the Counter-Reformation caused mass emigration, which included members of the nobility. Most of the emigrants headed to Protestant states and the imperial cities in southern Germany.

23 The Catholic-Protestant controversy continued in the House of Hapsburg until the death of Emperor Matthias in 1619, and the accession of Ferdinand II, who had been recognized a year earlier as king of Bohemia and Hungary and who tried to impose Catholicism on his subjects. While the states of Lower Austria fruitlessly proposed religious concessions for themselves, the Diet (Legislature) of Bohemia - predominantly Protestant in 1619 - unilaterally deposed Ferdinand, choosing to replace him with Frederick V on the Bohemian

throne. Two days after he was deposed, Ferdinand II was named Holy Roman Emperor; an investiture which gave him rights to that throne and committed him, as a secular branch of the church, to imposing Catholicism. The conflict, which ran beyond the borders of the Empire, led to a series of wars known as the Thirty Years War and changed the maps of Europe.

24 Bavaria and Saxony joined Ferdinand II, as did Spain - then at war with the Low Countries to sustain Catholicism. After five years, the Bohemian army was defeated, an imperial edict reduced the Diet to powerlessness and Catholicism was imposed by force. Protestants emigrated en masse to Germany, which was then invaded by imperial troops. The reaction came from the King of Switzerland, Adolf II, who invaded Germany in 1630 and won over many German princes to his anti-Catholic and anti-Roman cause. Although Germany was from then on the Gordian knot of the war, no throne in Europe was free of the conflict which drew in France, Poland and Denmark.

25 The Peace of Westfalia in 1648 brought an end to the war and marked a new order for Europe. Holland was recognized as an independent republic, and the member states of the Holy Roman Empire were granted complete sovereignty. The old notion of a Catholic empire of Europe, led spiritually by the Pope and secularly by the Emperor, was abandoned for good. The essential structure of the modern Europe was established as a community of sovereign states.

26 Though reluctant to participate in new conflicts, Ferdinand II's heir Leopold was threatened by Hungarian rebels and frontier disputes with the Ottoman Empire, which led to him form an alliance with Poland. In 1683, Vienna was besieged by the Turks, but the Austrians were rescued by Bavarian, Saxon, Frank and Polish forces, under the leadership of Polish king John III. Two years later a pact signed by the Emperor, Poland and the Republic of Venice established the Holy League.

27 Between the 17th and 19th centuries, the Hapsburgs were involved in all the European conflicts. The Napoleonic Wars virtually dismantled the Austrian Empire, and it was only after Napoleon's abdication in 1814 that the House of Austria recovered most of its territory.

28 The Austrian Chancellor Clemens Metternich was the creator of the Holy Alliance of the European powers in 1815. This upheld the principles of Christian authoritarianism and foreign intervention against the liberal and revolutionary movements of the time.

29 In 1848, a revolt broke out in Vienna, led by crowds demanding the liberalization of the regime. Metternich's resignation, rather than bringing peace, unleashed a revolution throughout the Empire.

30 In spite of their active presence in the street fights of Vienna, the workers had little muscle at that time due to Austria's lack of industrial development. The most important social consequence of the revolution was the liberation of the peasants, sanctioned by Emperor Franz Joseph in 1849.

31 At the same time the liberal government of Hungary demanded independence. In Germany the revolution installed a National Assembly in Frankfurt, which incorporated Austro-German liberals and conservatives interested in separation from the Hapsburg Empire.

32 The Emperor accepted the Budapest petitions, except on two key points: budget and military autonomy. The Hungarian Parliament declared the power of the Hapsburgs null and void, and proclaimed a republic in April 1849. The revolution was crushed four months later.

33 Counter-revolution also annulled the Frankfurt Assembly, but the dispute persisted. From then on, the Hapsburg Empire weakened inexorably. It lost, ceded and decentralized its dominions until its final disintegration in 1918, at the end of World War I.

34 In October of this year, a national assembly declared German Austria an independent state and, in November, following the abdication of the Emperor, the Austro-German republic was proclaimed a component of the Republic of Germany. The Socialist Karl Renner headed the first republican government, a coalition in which his deputy was the Social Democrat, Otto Bauer.

35 In the midst of economic chaos and hunger inherited from the war, the new government - without consulting the old regime - decided to use its own forces to confront the social unease and increasing communist activism. The communists had been inspired by the Russian revolution in 1917 and more especially by the Hungarian revolution of 1919. The personal prestige of Renner and Bauer helped them survive two attempted coups led by the communists.

36 Once political and social order were re-established in Vienna, the problem moved to the interior where some states were demanding secession. The 1920 Constitution guaranteed a loose federal system whereby the capital was governed by the Socialists and the rest of the country by the Conservatives.

37 The new Constitution granted women the vote, something which had been guaranteed from the time

PROFILE

ENVIRONMENT

Austria is a landlocked country in central Europe. The Alps stretch over most of its territory. Tourism, milk by-products and textiles are the main economic activities in the western mountain provinces of Vorarlberg and Tyrol. Rye and potatoes are farmed in the lower woodlands of the Eastern Alps. The rich agricultural basins of Klagenfurt and Styria, in the eastern Alps produce corn, wheat, fruit, cattle and poultry. Austria's iron ore and coal mines feed its large iron and steel industry. The Danube river valley runs across the northern foothills of the Alps and is a major route for river, highway and rail transportation. The gas emissions from industrial plants and cars in large cities, and the use of agrochemicals are the main causes of environmental degradation.

SOCIETY

Peoples: Mostly of Germanic origin. There are Slav, Polish and Hungarian minorities.
Religions: Mainly Catholic.
Languages: German.
Political Parties: The Austrian Social Democratic Party (SPÖ); the Liberal Party (FPÖ); the Austrian People's Party (ÖVP); the Green Alternative and the United Green Party of Austria; the Communist Party and the extreme-right National Democratic Party of Austria.
Social Movements: The Austrian Trade Union Federation.

THE STATE

Official Name: Republik Österreich.
Capital: Vienna (Wien), 1,540,000 people (1996).
Other cities: Graz, 237,000 people; Linz, 203,000; Salzburg, 143,000 (1991).
Government: Thomas Klestil, President, since May, 1992; Wolfgang Schüssel, Chancellor (Prime Minister), since February, 2000. A federal Republic of 9 provinces; bicameral parliamentary system.
Armed Forces: Around 52,000.

the Republic was proclaimed in 1918.

38 The Social Democrats had an indisputable majority in Vienna, where one-third of the population lived. Social Christians had guaranteed support among the peasants and the Conservatives, while German nationalism fed on popular discontent, with the support of the urban middle classes.

39 The League of Nations supported Austrian economic recovery during the postwar period, on the condition that the country would remain independent and would not join Germany. In 1922, the Government was granted a loan which enabled the country's finances to stabilize.

40 The great depression of 1929 brought the Austrian economy to the verge of collapse. The Government tried to arrange a customs agreement with Germany which was fiercely opposed by the rest of Europe. Together with the rise of Nazism under the leadership of Adolf Hitler, German nationalism in Austria was showing signs of strengthening.

41 In 1932, the Social Christian government of Engelbert Dollfuss attempted to take an authoritarian stance against the Social Democrats and the Nazis simultaneously. The Social Democrats rebelled and were declared illegal and in 1934 the Nazis murdered Dollfuss in a failed coup.

42 Taking advantage of the internal crisis and the government's weakness, German troops invaded Austria in 1938, unchallenged by the European powers. A plebiscite carried out that same year in greater Germany recorded a vote of more than 99 per cent in favor of Hitler.

43 In 1945 after Hitler's defeat in World War II, Austria was divided into 4 zones, occupied by US, French, British and Soviet troops. In the November elections, out of the 165 seats in the National Council, the Conservatives obtained 85 and the Social Democrats 76 seats.

44 The Austrian economy recovered with difficulty after the War, with the aid of the United Nations and the US, through the implementation of the Marshall Plan. Heavy industry and banking were nationalized in 1946, and inflation was controlled by price and salary agreements.

45 Conservatives and Socialists shared the government of the Second Austrian Republic, which only recovered full independence in 1955, with the Treaty of State and the withdrawal of the allied troops. The coalition held until 1966, when the People's Party was elected to govern alone.

46 During the postwar period, Austria did not become a member of international organizations. During the Cold War, the country was liberal in the acceptance of political refugees from Poland, and it was a transit station for Soviet Jewish émigrés.

47 Austria became a member of the United Nations in 1955 and of the Council of Europe in 1956. Since then, Austrian foreign policy has centered on the dispute with Italy over Sudtirol (Bolzano), resolved in 1969, and its association with the European Economic Community (EEC).

48 In 1958, Vienna joined the European Free Trade Association, establishing a special agreement with the EEC. It established negotiations with the neighboring countries belonging to the Common Economic Assistance Council. In this way it remained a neutral nation.

49 The Socialist Party (SPÖ) won a narrow victory in 1970 forming a minority government led by Bruno Kreisky. In 1971 and 1975, the SPÖ obtained an absolute majority and monopolized government, supported by great economic stability and a policy of moderate social reforms.

50 The Austrian Government was a guest at the meetings of the Movement of Non-Aligned Countries and acted as a bridge between the Palestine Liberation Organization (PLO) and Western Europe. Vienna was energetic in its condemnation of the Israeli invasion of Lebanon in 1982.

51 In 1978, the government lost a plebiscite on the installation of a nuclear plant, but the SPÖ confirmed its support of the prime minister and maintained control in the 1979 election. Kreisky resigned when the SPÖ lost its majority in 1983. In coalition with the Liberal Party (FPÖ), the SPÖ maintained its social welfare policy and active neutrality in the international plane.

52 The political force which grew most in the last decade of the century was the ultra-nationalist Liberal Party (FPÖ) headed by Joerg Haider. Even though he was removed from his post as governor of Carinthia in June 1991 for praising the full employment policy of the Third Reich, in the municipal elections of November that year - following a campaign in which he accused foreigners resident in Austria of "stealing" jobs from the Austrians - the FPÖ gained 22.6 per cent of the vote, becoming the second political force in Vienna.

53 In 1992, against a backdrop of increasing attacks against immigrants, the Government adopted a law which punished neo-Nazi activities. In May, Thomas Klestil of the ÖVP was elected President with almost 57 per cent of the vote.

54 In 1993, Haider stepped up his xenophobic rhetoric, attributing the increasing crime rate and unemployment to "uncontrolled" immigration, and backing a new bill to reduce the number of foreigners and their rights, but this did not gain enough support to be approved.

55 A referendum in 1994 decided that Austria would join the European Union, which in theory would not affect the country's neutrality, as stated by the Constitution. In the March regional elections, the FPÖ improved its electoral performance once again.

56 Although Haider officially condemned a series of attacks on immigrants, in a widely circulated book, Hans Henning Scharsach highlighted the similarities between Haider and Hitler - who "also came from populist origins". The rise of the FPÖ leader coincided with a debate on the Austria's role in World War II.

57 More than 1,600 companies went bust in the first nine months of 1996. This situation was associated with an increase in competitive pressure on the economy due to joining the European Union. The ensuing discontent favored the growth of the ultra-nationalist Freedom Alliance which gained the same number of seats (six) as the SPÖ in the European Parliament in June 1996. This signalled the rise of the so-called Freedom Alliance, headed by the FPÖ, towards becoming the main right wing party, overcoming the ÖVP.

58 The Foreign Minister Vranitsky resigned in January 1997 and was replaced by finance minister Viktor Klima, a sharp negotiator who masterminded an austerity plan for that year. On an official visit to Israel in March 1998, Klima promised to compensate Nazi victims and recognized the role of Austria in the massacre of millions of Jews. In April, a referendum called for the government to end genetic modification of food.

59 The October 1999 elections confirmed the decline of Social Democrats. Even though they came first with 33.4 per cent of the votes, it was their worst-ever turnout. Haider was re-elected in Carintia and managed to transform the FPÖ into the second political force with 27.2 per cent of the votes, beating the conservative ÖVP party by 400 votes. The Greens increased their number of legislators from nine to 13 with 7 per cent of the votes, which proved to be inadequate for an alliance with the SPÖ.

60 Klima's attempts to form a government failed and the President accepted an alliance between conservatives and liberals. Before the constitution of the new government, the presidency of the European Union warned that the incorporation of Haider and his party would jeopardise relations with the whole bloc. Although Haider did not form part of cabinet, the 14 remaining members of the EU decided to curtail diplomatic contacts and to withhold support for Austrian candidates within the European Union or other international bodies. Israel and other countries recalled their ambassadors from Vienna, increasing the isolation of the government headed by conservative Wolfgang Schüssel. ■

STATISTICS

DEMOGRAPHY

Population: 8,177,000 (1999)
Annual growth: 0.3 % (1975/97)
Estimates for year 2015 (million): 8.3 (1999)
Annual growth to year 2015: 0.2 % (1997/2015)
Urban population: 64.4 % (1997)
Urban Growth: 0.5 % (1980/95)
Children per woman: 1.4 (1998)

HEALTH

Life expectancy at birth: 77 years (1998)
male: 74 years (1998)
female: 80 years (1998)
Infant mortality: 5 per 1,000 (1998)
Under-5 child mortality: 5 per 1,000 (1998)
Daily calorie supply: 3,343 per capita (1996)
327 doctors per 100,000 people (1993)

EDUCATION

School enrolment:
Primary total: 100 % (1990/96)
male: 100 % (1990/97)
female: 101 % (1990/97)
Secondary:
male: 105 % (1990/96)
female: 101 % (1990/96)
Tertiary: 48 % (1996)
Primary school teachers: one for every 12 (1996)

COMMUNICATIONS

296 newspapers (1996), 753 radios (1997), 496 TV sets (1996) and 469 main telephone lines (1996) per 1,000 people
Books: 100 new titles per 100,000 people (1992/94)

ECONOMY

Per capita, GNP: $ 26,830 (1998)
Annual growth, GNP: 3.3 % (1998)
Annual inflation: 2.5 % (1990/98)
Consumer price index: 104.1 (1998)
Currency: 12.4 schillings = $ 1 (1998)
Cereal imports: 427,767 metric tons (1998)
Food import dependency: 6 % (1997)
Fertilizer use: 1,664 kg per ha (1997)
Exports: $ 87,234 million (1997)
Imports: $ 88,418 million (1997)

ENERGY

Consumption: 3,439.0 Kgs of Oil equivalent per capita yearly (1997); 71.0 % imported (1997)

HDI (rank/value): 16/0.904 (1997)

Azerbaijan

Population: 7,697,000 (1999)
Area: 86,600 SQ KM
Capital: Baku
Currency: Manat
Language: Azeri

Azerbaidzhan

The Azeris came from the mix of ancient peoples of eastern Caucasus. In the 9th century BC, the States of Mana, Media, Caucasian Albania and Atropatene (the name "Azerbaijan" being derived from the latter) emerged in the area corresponding to modern Azerbaijan. General Atropates proclaimed the independence of this province in the year 328 BC, when Persia was conquered by Alexander the Great.

[2] Later, these states were incorporated to the Persian Arsacid and Sassanid kingdoms. There were a number of anti-Sassanid revolts, such as the Mazdokite rebellion. In the year 642, the Arab caliphate conquered Azerbaijan, which was still inhabited by tribes of different ethnic groups. The Arabs united the country under Shi'a Islam, despite some resistance. Between 816 and 837, an anti-Arab revolt was led by Babek.

[3] Between the 7th and 10th centuries, an important trade route passed through Azerbaijan, united the Near East with Eastern Europe. From the 11th to the 14th centuries the Seleucid Turks occupied Transcaucasia and the north of Persia. All the peoples in the region adopted Turkish as their language, and the Azeris' ethnic identity was forged during this period. In the 15th and 16th centuries, the region of Sirvan in the north of Azerbaijan, became an independent State.

[4] Between the 15th and 16th centuries, the Setevid State emerged. Shah Ishmael I, founder of the dynasty, was supported by the nomadic Azeri tribes who became the main power behind the State. In the late 16th century, Azeri nobility transferred its support to the Iranians.

[5] In the 16th to 18th centuries, East Transcaucasia was the scene of Iranian-Turkish rivalry. In the 18th century, the Russian Empire began its expansion toward Azerbaijan and by the middle of this century more than 15 Azerbaijani Khanates were dependent upon Iran. After several Russian wars against Turkey and Persia, the peace treaties of Gulistan (1813) and Turkmenchai (1828) were signed, granting Russia Northern Azerbaijan (the provinces of Baku and Yelisavetpol, corresponding to modern Gyanja).

[6] The peasant reform carried out in Russia in 1879 accelerated the development of Azerbaijan, which

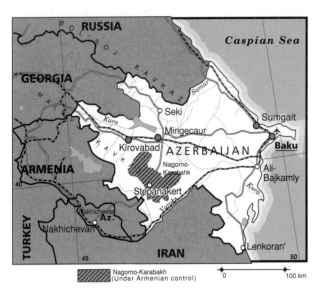

Nagorno-Karabakh
(Under Armenian control)   0   100 km

was attractive because of the abundance of oil in the region. After the Russian Revolution of 1905, the nationalist Musavat (Equality) Party was founded in Baku in 1911. Its base was the country's bourgeoisie, and it had a pan-Turkish, and pan-Islamic platform. After the triumph of the Bolsheviks in October 1917, Soviet power was established in Azerbaijan by the Commune of Baku.

[7] In the summer of 1918, joint Turkish-British intervention ousted the Commune of Baku and brought the Musavatists to power. However, two years later the Red Army reconquered Baku and re-established Soviet power throughout Azerbaijan. It was proclaimed the Soviet Socialist Republic (SSR) of Azerbaijan and in March 1922, became part of the Transcaucasian Federation of Soviet Socialist Republics, along with Armenia and Georgia.

[8] In the early 1920s, in an attempt to ease inter-ethnic tensions, Moscow decided to incorporate the regions of Upper Nagorno-Karabakh and Nakhichevan into Azerbaijan. These had previously belonged to Armenia as the ancient khanates of Karabakh and Nakhichevan. In July 1923, the Autonomous Region of Nagorno-Karabakh was founded, and in February of the following year, the Autonomous Region of Nakhichevan; both had formerly belonged to the SSR of Azerbaijan. In December 1936, the Transcaucasian Federation was

dissolved, and the SSR of Azerbaijan joined the USSR on its own. In 1929 an attempt was made to substitute the Latin alphabet for Azeri script, which used Arabic characters. In January 1940, the Cyrillic alphabet was introduced.

[9] Between 1969 and 1982, the leadership of the Communist Party of Azerbaijan was in the hands of Gueidar Aliev, a former KGB (Soviet secret police) agent who was known and trusted by the Secretary of the Soviet Communist Party, Leonid Brezhnev.

[10] By the end of the 1980s, socio-economic, political and ethnic problems exacerbated the feeling of discontent among the Azeris. In 1986, the new Soviet leader Mikhail Gorbachev initiated a period of economic reforms (*perestroika*) and openness in the administration of the country (glasnost) which channelled popular discontent throughout the Soviet Union.

[11] In the republic of Azerbaijan, there was a wave of strikes, political rallies and demonstrations. New political movements came into being, like the leading People's Front of Azerbaijan (PFA) with a platform stressing civil rights, free elections and political and economic independence for the country. The PFA opposed the long-standing aspiration of the Armenian population of Nagorno-Karabakh (90 per cent of that region's inhabitants) to rejoin the Armenian republic.

[12] On September 25 1989, Azerbaijan was proclaimed a

sovereign state within the USSR. The worsening of ethnic conflicts between Azeris and Armenians led to the formation of extremist groups. In 1989, Armenians were massacred in Sumgait and in 1990, in Baku. After the events in Baku, the Communist Government decreed a state of emergency and called in troops from the USSR to re-establish order; a total of 100 people were killed in the ensuing violence.

[13] The Nagorno-Karabakh issue increased friction with Armenia, triggering an escalation of conflicts between Armenian and Azerbaijani guerrilla groups. The Autonomous Region of Nagorno-Karabakh proclaimed its independence from Azerbaijan. In December 1989, Armenia's Soviet (Council) approved reunification with Nagorno-Karabakh and Azerbaijan denounced this decision as interference in its internal affairs. In September 1991, the Republic of Nagorno-Karabakh declared independence from both Azerbaijan and Armenia. In November 1991, the Azerbaijani Soviet annulled the status of Nagorno-Karabakh as an "autonomous region".

[14] On August 30 1991, the USSR's Soviet Presidium approved Azerbaijan's declaration of independence. The state of emergency was lifted in Baku and on September 8, presidential elections were held. The Communist Party of Azerbaijan was dissolved. Former Azeri Communist leader, Ayaz Mutalibov, who had supported the aborted coup against Gorbachev, was the only candidate, and was elected President. The PFA called the elections "undemocratic" because they were held under a state of emergency, and withdrew their candidate. The Autonomous Republic of Nakhichevan, with Gueidar Aliev, abstained from voting.

[15] On December 22 1991, Azerbaijan joined the new Commonwealth of Independent States (CIS) which replaced the Soviet Union, and on February 2 1992 it was admitted to the UN as a new member.

[16] On December 10 1991, besieged by Azeri troops and with bombs going off intermittently, the people of Nagorno-Karabakh participated in a plebiscite in which 99 per cent of the electorate voted for independence. The Azeri minority abstained from voting. CIS troops

began withdrawing from Nagorno-Karabakh, but fighting between Azeri and Armenian guerrillas intensified.

[17] The People's Front of Azerbaijan accused the Government of ineptitude in handling the Karabakh issue, and demanded that the Government speed up the creation of an Azeri national army. Baku, in turn, accused CIS troops of facilitating the union of Armenia and Nagorno-Karabakh. On March 6 1992, Ayaz Mutalibov resigned and Yuri Mamedov, the acting President of the Soviet, assumed presidential powers.

[18] In April, fighting between Armenians and Azeris extended to Nakhichevan. Turkey warned that it would not accept any changes in its borders, which have been in effect since 1921.

[19] On May 14 1992, Azerbaijan's Parliament, controlled by former communists, reinstated deposed President Ayaz Mutalibov. He subsequently suspended the June 7 presidential elections, banned all political activity, and imposed censorship of the press and a curfew. The leaders of the Popular Front, with the support of most of the leaders of the national militia, seized the Parliament building in Baku, declaring the reinstatement of Mutalibov illegal. After two days of street demonstrations and clashes in the capital between supporters of both factions, the opposition consolidated its position and ratified Mamedov as president. The Popular Front assumed key posts in the new government, such as the directorship of the security services and of the official media.

[20] In December 1992, President Mutalibov was forced to resign after the repeated defeat of Azeri troops and the forces of the Popular Front besieged Parliament. In the following weeks, Armenian attacks intensified and, in May 1993, an offensive was launched on Stepanakert, the administrative centre of Nagorno-Karabakh.

[21] In mid-May, Parliament reinstated Mutalibov as President but the Popular Front ousted him once again in an armed uprising. The fighting extended beyond Nagorno-Karabakh and after occupying Stepanakert, Armenian forces fanned out to several other Azerbaijani regions.

[22] In June, Albufaz Elchibei, leader of the Popular Front, won the presidential elections, facilitating the return of Heydar Aliev, former leader of the Communist Party of the Soviet Union, to a leading position. However, a new Armenian attack in Nagorno-Karabakh was followed by a coup. Its leader, Colonel Guseinov, seized control of five of the country's regions. When the attack on Baku began, Elchibei fled the country and Aliev remained as interim president.

[23] In September 1993, Parliament agreed to Azerbaijan joining the CIS. A month later, Aliev won the presidential elections and launched a successful attack on Nagorno-Karabakh. In May 1994, under pressure from Russia, a ceasefire was agreed and negotiations between rival parties began. These contacts continued throughout 1995 and the first months of 1996, but progress was not made toward a definite agreement.

[24] A coup attempt by followers of prime minister Surat Husseynov failed in October 1994. Major demonstrations of support for Aliev, who dismissed Husseynov, were held in Baku. The President decreed a two-month state of emergency and several members of government were arrested, accused of involvement in the failed coup.

[25] Parliamentary elections were held in November 1995, without the participation of the influential Musavat party or Communist or Islamic groups whose presence was banned by the Government. New Azerbaijan, Aliev's party, won the elections. The gross domestic product in 1995 fell 20 per cent, a reduction similar to the previous year, while inflation fell from 880 per cent to 790 per cent in the same period.

[26] In November 1996, Artur Rasizade replaced prime minister Fuad Guliyev, who left his post for "medical reasons" according to official explanations. Several ministers responsible for economic affairs, including privatizations, were sacked for their incompetence. Diplomatic relations with Iran and Russia deteriorated in 1994 due to the invasion of Chechnya and the arrest of members of the pro-Iranian Islamic Party of Azerbaijan. In the Russian case, collaboration with Armenia also weakened diplomatic ties.

[27] Political attention that year centered around the October 1998 elections. The main opposition leaders, including former president Abulfaz Elchibey, boycotted the elections and Aliev received 76 per cent of the votes. The opposition protested fraud with street demonstrations, while editors from 20 newspapers called for a hunger strike to ask for the annulment of the election results.

[28] Late that year, Azerbaijan celebrated the inauguration of its oil fields in the Caspian sea. The initiative was a result of a contract between the Azeri Government and a 12-company consortium with a 40 per cent stake by US capital. It is estimated Azerbaijan, Kazakhstan and Turkmenistan together possess the third largest oil reserve in the world. In December 1999, a Japanese company decided to invest $2.3 billion to exploit fields in a joint venture with capitals from Asia and Azerbaijan. ∎

Bahamas

Bahamas

Population: 301,000 (1999)
Area: 13,880 SQ KM
Capital: Nassau
Currency: Bahamian dollar
Language: English

The Bahamian archipelago was one of the few areas of the Caribbean from which the Arawak Indians were not displaced by the Caribs. These Americans were probably the first to "discover" the lost European navigators, on October 12 1492.

[2] Indeed Columbus probably first trod American soil on the Bahamian island of Guanahani or San Salvador, although he thought he was in Asia. "The Arawaks opened their hearts to us..". wrote the navigator to his Catholic sovereigns, "We have become great friends". Soon enough, the initial enthusiasm cooled to give way to less idealistic concerns: "From here, in the name of the Holy Trinity we can send all the slaves that can be sold... If Your Majesties so commanded, the entire population could be shipped to Castile or be enslaved on the island... as these people are totally ignorant of warfare."

[3] Only 300 out of 500 indians lived through the first voyage to Spain. Moreover, most of the survivors died within a few years for they lacked immunity to European diseases. But Columbus had also set out to find gold for himself and the royal family. As Spanish historian Francisco de Gomara has pointed out, "over a period of 20 years, the Spaniards enslaved 40,000 indians who were sent to work in mines on the other islands".

[4] The Spaniards did not colonize the islands that lacked mineral resources. Instead, British privateers and pirates sought refuge in these islands after seizing "Spanish" gold (or rather, gold appropriated by the Spanish with the heavy cost of indian lives

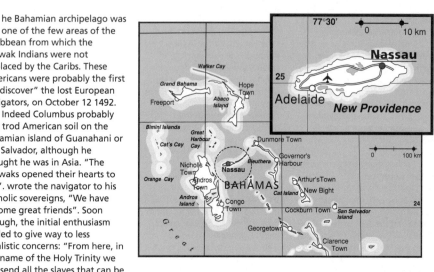

in different American territories). Both the Bahamas and the Bermudas were located in an area frequently hit by tropical storms, a fact that made buccaneers seek shelter in these islands. From 1640 the British began to settle the Bahamas. Sugarcane and other tropical crops were grown in plantations worked by African enslaved laborers whose descendants today make up most of the local population. In 1873, the Treaty of Madrid settled the dispute over control of the Bahamas in favor of the British.

[5] The British refused to accept the independence of this strategic archipelago, and it was not until 1973 that the Bahamas proclaimed their independence within the British Commonwealth. This change actually meant little to the islanders because in the meantime the country had become increasingly dependent on the United States.

[6] Most of the tourists who now visit the Bahamas come from the US, drawn to its beaches and casinos. The transnationals which use the Bahamas as their formal headquarters are also North American, taking advantage of the exemptions that make the country a "tax-haven". Also, US citizens are the chief buyers of lottery tickets, a source of fiscal revenues that contributes heavily to the state budget. In 1942, the US installed a naval base at Freeport, which helped control traffic from the Gulf of Mexico to the Atlantic, via the Florida Strait.

[7] While other Caribbean nations sought ways to bring about regional integration, the Bahamas preferred to take advantage of its proximity to the US, turning its back on regional co-operation. In times while other islands were founding regional organizations, the Bahamas did not join any of them.

[8] The first political party - the Progressive Liberal Party (PLP) - was formed in 1953, and in 1958 the United Party of the Bahamas was founded. In the 1954 elections the PLP obtained six seats out of a total 29. In 1956 the Assembly passed an anti-discriminatory resolution aimed at promoting ethnic equality. Thus, the Afro-Caribbean population was given access to places where they had never before been admitted.

[9] In the 1962 general elections the PLP won 8 of the 29 seats. Two years later the new Constitution was passed and a

ministerial form of Government was established. The number of representatives to the Assembly was increased to 38. Sir Roland Symonette was elected prime minister and Lynden Pindling became the leader of the opposition. In the January 10 1967 election, each party obtained 18 seats, and the representatives who won the 2 remaining seats joined the PLP, thus enabling this party to form a Government. Lynden Pindling became Prime Minister.

[10] In 1977, when the economic and social crisis started to bite, the Government decided to give even greater incentives to foreign capital. It promoted the use of the Bahamian flag by foreign ships as a "flag of convenience", to compete with Panama and Liberia. In an attempt to diminish the massive unemployment which threatened to create social tensions and changes in the archipelago, the Government opened an industrial estate of 1,200 hectares near a deep water port in Grand Bahama. It was meant to be used as a storage point for merchandise which was later to be re-exported after minimal local processing.

[11] During the 1977 electoral campaign the opposition parties - the Free National Movement, the Democratic Party of Bahamas, and the Vanguard Party - accused the Government of corruption and squandering public funds. Pindling promised to "Bahamize" the economy, to give more participation to domestic capital, emphasizing that he would not damage the country's image as a tax haven. Both left and right criticized the Government's policy towards transnationals, the former because they considered it complacent, the latter because they thought that excessive taxation was driving foreign investment away. However, Pindling again won by a landslide and promised to lower unemployment. He opened the country's coasts to the "seven sisters" (the seven companies controlling the world oil industry) which started oil prospecting in 1979.

[12] In 1984, the political scene was further upset when the US NBC Network News directly

WORKERS

1995
UNEMPLOYMENT: 11.1%

% OF LABOUR FORCE **1998**

■FEMALE: 32%   ■MALE: 68%

1990

■SERVICES: 79.3%
■INDUSTRY: 15.5%
■AGRICULTURE: 5.2%

LAND USE

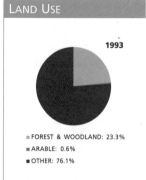

1993

■FOREST & WOODLAND: 23.3%
■ARABLE: 0.6%
■OTHER: 76.1%

ENVIRONMENT

The territory comprises over 750 islands, only 30 of them inhabited. The most important are: New Providence (where the capital is located), Grand Bahama and Andros. These islands, made of limestone and coral reefs, built up over a long period of time from the ocean floor. Despite the subtropical climate, the lack of rivers has prevented the favorable climatic conditions being fully exploited for agirculture. Farming is limited to small crops of cotton and sisal. The main economic activity is tourism, centered on New Providence. The effects of industrial development beyond their borders, the warming of the seas, the increasing frequency and intensity of tropical hurricanes and coastal erosion all pose a growing threat to the islands' environment.

SOCIETY

Peoples: Descendants of enslaved African workers, 85 per cent, plus North Americans, Canadians and British. **Religions:** Non-Anglican Protestants 55 per cent, of which 32 per cent are Baptists; Anglicans 20 per cent; Catholics 19 per cent. **Political Parties:** National Free Movement. Progressive Liberal Party (PLP) founded in 1953; bringing together the population of African origin, under a pro-independence banner. The Vanguard Party, socialist. The People's Democratic Force. **Social Organizations:** Trade Union Congress; trade unions such as the Bahamas Hotel Catering and Allied Workers Union, the Bahamas Union of Teachers, the Bahamas Public Service Union, the Airport & Allied Workers Union, the Musicians and Entertainers Union, the Taxi Cabs Union. **Languages:** English (official) and Creole.

THE STATE

Official Name: The Commonwealth of the Bahamas. **Capital:** Nassau 190,000 people (est 1997). **Other cities:** Adelaide, Freeport/Lucaya, Marsh Harbour. **Government:** Queen Elizabeth II is Head of State, represented by Orville Alton Turnquest since 1995. Prime Minister Hubert Ingraham, since 1992. There is a bicameral Legislative Power, with a 16-member Senate and a 49-member Assembly. **National Holiday:** July 10, Independence (1973). **Other:** 2,550: Police (1,700); Defence Force (850).

charged Prime Minister Pindling with receiving large sums of money for authorizing drug traffic through Bahamian territory. An investigation immediately confirmed that Government officials were involved in smuggling but cleared Pindling of any responsibility in the affair.

[13] In 1987, the unemployment rate was estimated to be above 18 per cent, with the under-25s and 35 per cent of women affected. With these figures in mind, public protests against the recruiting of Haitian refugees to the labor force became more understandable. Although they had strongly supported the Government in the past, labor unions now criticized the authorities for the lack of constructive, long-term programs aimed at solving the grave unemployment problem.

[14] After 20 years in office, Lynden Pindling won his sixth consecutive election on June 19 1987. His Progressive Liberal Party obtained 31 out of 49 seats for a 5-year term. The opposition Free National Movement (FNM), led by Cecil Wallace Whitfield (after lawyer Kendal Isaac's resignation following the electoral defeat) repeatedly asked Pindling to step down, charging him with fraud, corruption, and being "soft" towards drug dealers.

[15] In 1991, there was a sharp decrease in the number of tourists, estimated at three million per annum. This was attributed to the fact that there had been a rise in crime, compounded by the country's extremely high cocaine consumption rate. Although there had been a slow-down in inflation and a slight fiscal surplus, this did not prevent the people from taking to the streets, to voice discontent over economic conditions.

[16] US officials accused Pindling of allowing the Bahamas to be used as a transfer point for drugs. Testimony from the trial of the former Panamanian General, Manuel Antonio Noriega, alleged that Pindling had received at least $5 million in payments for this service.

[17] Tourism had generated over 65 per cent of the country's GDP, but in 1992 this fell by 10 per cent in relation to 1990 figures. Meanwhile the banking system lost customers to its competitors in the Cayman Islands. In addition, the Government was unable to increase agricultural production, making it necessary for the country to import 80 per cent of its food.

[18] Pindling's 25 years in office ended in 1992 when Hubert Ingraham, a former *protegé* of Pindling's and leader of the National Free Movement, won the parliamentary elections with 55 per cent of the vote. The new Government aimed to reduce unemployment through the liberalization of foreign investment laws and the re-establishment of the Bahamas as a major tourist destination.

[19] In February 1994, one of the prominent figures from Pindling's time, lawyer Nigel Bowe, was incarcerated in Miami for drug trafficking. That year, the Government appointed a commission to investigate Pindling, accused of having used the Hotel Corporation's funds to increase his wealth. Pindling denied the charges and sought protection in bank secrecy, which limited the Commission's progress.

[20] In 1995, foreign investors carried out the privatization of several hotels belonging to the Hotel Corporation. The most significant problems for the Government were unemployment and the presence of several thousands of Haitian and Cuban refugees. A repatriation agreement with Haiti was achieved, but the Cuban refugees refused to be sent back, and demanded to be transferred to the United States.

[21] In January the following year the conflict was resolved when the Bahamas signed an agreement with Cuba whereby Cubans living in Bahaman detention camps were returned to their home country. During 1996, 250 Cubans from the camps, and a further 70 living illegally with "sympathisers" were returned to Cuba. Under the agreement, the Bahamas Government had the Cuban Government's commitment that the deportees would be treated "fairly".

[22] The death penalty was applied in March 1997 for the first time in 12 years when two prisoners were hanged. The National Free Movement won the Parliamentary elections held that month with 35 seats. The Progressive Liberal Party won five seats. Hubert Ingraham was reelected as Prime Minister.

[23] In February 1998, religious leaders in the country publicly demonstrated against visits from homosexual tourists, prompting a British Government representative to say the United Kingdom would oppose any type of discriminatory practices in the Bahamas.

[24] The parliamentary elections of February 1998 won by the National Free Movement, with 34 seats, while the Progressive Liberals took six.

[25] The Bahamas were ravaged in September 1999 by hurricane Floyd, the worst storm in decades. Tens of thousands of people were evacuated, and the winds which came in 12-hour gusts reached speeds of 240 km per hour. They swept through whole villages, destroying boats and severing communications in Nassau. Prime Minister Hubert Ingraham, accompanied by US ambassador Arthur Schechter, flew over the affected areas.

[26] In spite of pleas for pardon from different human rights defense groups, a man was hanged in January 2000 for the murder of two German tourists. Amnesty International asked Bahamas governor Orville Alton Turnquest to abide by international treaties, stop the executions and consider abolishing the death penalty. ∎

STATISTICS

DEMOGRAPHY

Population: 301,000 (1999)
Annual growth: 2.0 % (1975/97)
Estimates for year 2015 (million): 0.4 (1999)
Annual growth to year 2015: 1.4 % (1997/2015)
Urban population: 87.4 % (1997)
Children per woman: 2.6 (1998)

HEALTH

Life expectancy at birth: 74 years (1998)
male: 71 years (1998)
female: 77 years (1998)
Infant mortality: 18 per 1,000 (1998)
Under-5 child mortality: 21 per 1,000 (1998)
Daily calorie supply: 2,443 per capita (1996)
141 doctors per 100,000 people (1993)
Safe water: 94 % (1990/98)

EDUCATION

Literacy: 96 % (1995)
male: 95 % (1995)
female: 96 % (1995)
School enrolment:
Primary total: 100 % (1990/96)
male: 95 % (1990/97)
female: 94 % (1990/97)
Secondary:
male: 88 % (1990/96)
female: 91 % (1990/96)
Tertiary: 24 % (1996)
Primary school teachers: one for every 22 (1996)

COMMUNICATIONS

99 newspapers (1996), 744 radios (1997), 233 TV sets (1996) and 315 main telephone lines (1996) per 1,000 people

ECONOMY

Annual growth, GNP: 3.0 % (1998)
Consumer price index: 103.3 (1998)
Cereal imports: 13,564 metric tons (1998)
Fertilizer use: 500 kg per ha (1997)
Development aid received: $ 3 million (1997); $ 11.6 per capita (1997)

HDI (rank/value): 31/0.851 (1997)

Bahrain

Bahrayn

Population: 607,000 (1999)
Area: 694 SQ KM
Capital: Manama (Al-Manamah)
Currency: Dinar
Language: Arabic

Since the time of the Sumerians, the area now called Bahrain was central to the intense maritime trade between Mesopotamia and India. This trade became particularly prosperous between the 11th and 15th centuries, as Islamic civilization expanded over all the territory from the Atlantic Ocean to the South Pacific.

[2] Portuguese sailors occupied the island in 1507 and stayed there for a century until the Persians expelled them. Iran's claim to sovereignty over this part of the Persian or Arab Gulf dates from this period. Sheikh al-Khalifah took power in 1782, displacing the Persians the following year; his descendants are still in power. Independence lasted until 1861, when another Khalifah, afraid of Persian annexation, agreed to declare a "protectorate" under the British.

[3] During the two World Wars Bahrain was an important British military base. In 1932 the first oil wells were opened. Nationalist movements demanding labor rights, democracy and independence grew during the 1950s, as they did in other parts of the Arab world.

[4] In 1954, a strike broke out in the oil fields and in 1956 colonial administrative offices were attacked. British troops were sent to quash the rebellion and opposition leaders were arrested and exiled. Slowly, some reforms were carried out and local participation in public administration increased.

[5] Finally, beginning in the early 1970s, the British decided to withdraw from their last colonies "east of Suez", though they maintained their economic and strategic interests in Bahrain. Bahrain and Qatar refused to join the United Arab Emirates, so in 1971 the country became independent under Sheikh Isa ibn-Sulman al-Khalifah.

[6] The new nation authorized the US to set up naval bases in its ports. These were dismantled in 1973

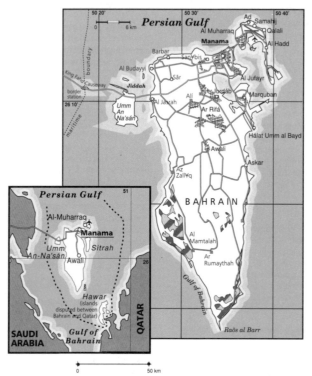

following the Arab-Israeli conflict. Local elections were held the same year and the National Assembly came under the control of progressive candidates calling for freedom to organize political parties and greater electoral representation. The British felt their interests were being threatened, and, in August 1975, they backed al-Khalifah's decision to dissolve Parliament.

[7] In the 1970s, Iran managed to eclipse Saudi control of the Emirates, forcing a virtual protectorate over them. Meanwhile, heavy migration into Bahrain threatened to create an Iranian majority, or at least a large Iranian minority on the islands.

[8] Shortly before his assassination in 1975, King Faisal of Saudi Arabia reacted against growing Iranian influence by embarking on a diplomatic campaign that his successors continued. He put pressure on Qatar, the only Emirate that was traditionally loyal to the

Saudis, to solve its dispute with Bahrain over territorial waters. Faisal appealed to the "Arab sentiment" that supposedly united them (Iran is Muslim but not Arab). This attempt at solidarity lost ground in 1976 when Saudi Arabia increased its oil prices less than the other OPEC countries, including Iran.

[9] The fall of the Shah of Iran in 1979 made matters worse, as the unofficial representatives of the new Islamic Republic declared publicly that Iran maintained its claim to the Gulf islands. The Emir retaliated by cracking down even harder on both Iranian (or Shi'a) immigrants and on all progressive movements. At the same time he drew closer to the other Arab governments, rejecting the Camp David agreement and signing mutual defense treaties with Kuwait and Saudi Arabia.

[10] Bahrain is the "least rich" oil producer in the Gulf. Its known total reserves (300 million barrels at the beginning of the 1990s) showed signs of exhaustion. Aware that dry oil wells, and competition to Bahrain's pearl-diving from Japanese oyster farms may leave this desert country with fishing as its only resource, the Government decided to slow down oil

production in 1980 taking advantage of the islands' strategic location to turn them into a trade and financial center.

[11] In May 1975, Bahrain obtained a controlling interest in its oil industry and in 1978 announced that all concessions to transnational companies would be cancelled.

[12] The State also promoted the establishment of industries, especially for copper and aluminium production. Generous tax exemptions and unrestricted facilities for profit remittance encouraged transnational corporations to set up subsidiaries. The country became a base for the re-export of all kinds of goods to other ports in the area. Bahrain also housed the second largest refinery in the Middle East, BAPCO, which processed local as well as a large part of Saudi crude oil.

[13] In 1981, the country joined the Gulf Cooperation Council (GCC). This was set up with US help to guarantee military and political control over the area, to counteract spreading Iranian influence, and to keep an eye on opposition groups in the member states.

[14] One of the most closely watched movements was the Bahrain National Liberation Front, supported mainly by oil workers, students and professionals. This group was a member of the Gulf Liberation Front until 1981.

[15] Toward the end of 1986, Bahrain bought ground-to-air missiles and warplanes from the US to defend itself in the event of Iranian aggression. In exchange, the US won authorization for the construction of a military airport and the right to use Bahrain's naval bases for its Gulf fleet, which patrolled the Gulf during the last few months of the Iran-Iraq war.

[16] In November 1986, a super-highway was opened between Saudi Arabia and Bahrain. As a result, Bahrain is no longer truly an island. During the first year alone, the highway was used by more than a million vehicles. The fall in world oil prices in the 1980s plunged the country into serious crisis and many of the grandiose building projects of the past were shelved.

[17] In 1989, Bahrain was forced to seek credit in order to balance its budget. Kuwait and Saudi Arabia contributed $100 million per year to ensure the stability of the Manama government.

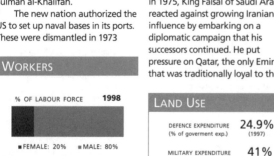

WORKERS

% OF LABOUR FORCE **1998**

■ FEMALE: 20% ■ MALE: 80%

LAND USE

DEFENCE EXPENDITURE (% of goverment exp.)	**24.9%**	(1997)
MILITARY EXPENDITURE (% of health & education)	**41%**	(1990/91)

18 In March 1991, after the Iraqi defeat in the Gulf War, the foreign ministers of Egypt, Syria and the six Arab member States of the GCC signed an agreement with the US in Riyadh in order to "preserve the regional security".

19 In July 1991, the Government announced that it would allow foreign companies to have full control of the local businesses they bought. Previously, all business interests on the island had to have a minimum of 51 per cent of national capital. The change in policy was aimed at attracting foreign investment to compensate for economic losses caused by the Gulf War.

20 After Kuwait, Bahrain was the emirate most affected by the conflict. The country was threatened by the oil slick, and Bahrain's skies were blackened for several months by Kuwait's burning oil wells. In the economic field, the effects of Kuwait's invasion and the subsequent war against Iraq were also felt. For instance, private bank deposits dropped by 30 to 40 per cent. The number of foreign banks fell from 75 in 1981 to 51 by the end of 1991.

21 As from 1992, foreign capital slowly began to return to Bahrain. Also that year, the country played an important role in the Middle East Peace Conference held in Moscow, which was attended by 10 Arab nations, as well as Israel.

22 In October 1994, Israeli Minister Yoosi Sarid's visit to Manama - the first high level public contact between Israel and a Gulf State - was a clear indication of the economic liberalization policy of the regime.

23 In December 1994, Shi'a leader Sheikh al-Jamri was arrested, after signing a claim for the restoration of the Constitution and the Parliament, dissolved in 1975. His arrest provoked anti-governmental demonstrations, in which two students and a police officer died. In April 1995, Emir Isa ibn-Sulman al-Khalifa met with 20 opposition leaders in an attempt to put an end to growing violence. In August, both parties reached an agreement which concluded with the liberation of 1,000 political prisoners.

24 In June, al-Jamri and another six opposition leaders denounced the lack of government commitment to the agreement reached and a hunger strike started which ended on November 1. A large opposition demonstration was countered by closing mosques, a measure which only heightened the tension.

25 In 1996, the demonstrations spread across the country, and some ended in violent confrontations with the police. The Government decided to use the death penalty to punish those "responsible", a measure endorsed by the Courts. The UN Working Group on Arbitrary Detentions issued three declarations on the situation of the inmates of Bahrain's prisons in September. The international organizations were not allowed to see the prisoners, who were in many cases denied the right to trial. In July, Amnesty International reported that many women and children suffered severe abuse in the nation's prisons.

26 Due to the situation of social conflict, some financial bodies like the Core State Bank of the United States, abandoned the country to set up in Dubai. In March 1998, Bahrain and the other five member nations of the Gulf Co-operation Council (Saudi Arabia, Oman, Kuwait, Qatar and the United Arab Emirates) looked into the possibility of freeing their currencies from the dollar to protect themselves from persistent fluctuations and to prevent greater losses in oil income.

27 In October 1999, while on a tour of the Middle East, US Defense Secretary William Cohen came to Bahrain with clear intentions: to ask the country for continued support for the US-imposed embargo on Iraq. However, no details of the conversations held by the Emir Sheikh Hamad bin Isa Al-Khalifa and his Defense Minister Khalifa bin Ahmad al-Khalifa were "leaked".

28 In December 1999, during his Independence Day speech, the Emir Sheikh Hamad bin Isa Al-Khalifa talked about a democratic opening and promised to reinstall municipal councils.

29 The Ministry of Foreign Affairs announced on 12 January 2000 that Bahrain would resume relations with the Vatican, a measure probably agreed upon months before, when the Emir Hamad bin Isa Al-Khalifa visited Pope John Paul II in November. The trial against Abdul Wahab Hussain, who is the second most important leader within the dissident Bahrain Liberation Movement, began a month later, in February. Hussain had been arrested in 1996 for signing a leaflet which demanded the restoration of democracy in the country. ■

MATERNAL MORTALITY

1990-98

Per 100,000 live births

46

LITERACY

1995

85%

FOOD DEPENDENCY

1997

12%

PROFILE

ENVIRONMENT

This flat, sandy archipelago consists of 33 islands in the Arab Gulf between Saudi Arabia and the Qatar Peninsula. The largest island, also called Bahrain, is 48 km long and 15 km wide. The climate is warm, moderately humid in summer and slightly dry in winter. Manama, the capital and main trade center, is located on the island of Bahrain. Bahrain has the same environmental problems that are characteristic of all the Gulf countries. The need to industrialize the country led to the occupation of what few fertile lands there were, in the northern part of the main island. In addition, industries were located very near residential areas. The extraction of oil in this region accounts for 4.7 per cent of all pollution caused by the oil industry.

SOCIETY

Peoples: The Bahrainis are Arab people. The petroleum industry has attracted a number of Iranian, Indian and Pakistani immigrants.
Religions: Islamic, predominantly of the Sunni sect in the urban areas and Shi'a in the rural areas. **Languages:** Arabic.
Political Parties: There are neither legal political parties nor trade unions. Some opposition forces are the Liberation Front of Bahrain, the Baath Arab Socialist Party and the Arab Nationalist Movement.

THE STATE

Official Name: Daulat al-Bahrayn. **Capital:** Manama (Al-Manamah) 360,000 people (1995). **Other cities:** Al-Muharraq, 45,000 people (1991). **Government:** Sheikh Hamad ibn Isa Al Khalifah, Emir since 6 March 1999; Khalifah ibn-Sulman Al-Khalifah, Prime Minister since December 1971, assisted by an 11-member cabinet. The National Assembly, partially elected by popular vote, was dissolved in August 1975. **National Holidays:** August 15, Independence (1971); December 16, National Day. **Armed Forces:** 10,700. **Other:** (Ministry of Interior): Coast Guard: 400; Police: 9,000.

Bangladesh

Bangladesh

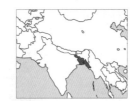

Population: 126,948,000 (1999)
Area: 144,000 SQ KM
Capital: Dhaka (Dacca)
Currency: Taka
Language: Bengali

Though Bangladesh is a relatively new state, it is an old nation, with roots in the ancient state of Banga. The country has a written history of several thousand years, dating back to the ancient epic, the Mahabharat.

2   The British East India Company called it "Bengal" in the 17th century. It was renamed East Bengal after the partition of Bengal and India in 1947, and then East Pakistan when it joined the newly created state of Pakistan in 1956. It emerged as an independent state in 1971, earning its current name (meaning "the land of the Bengali-speaking people") from the national language.

3   Hindu beliefs flourished in the region with the arrival of the Indo-Aryan peoples between 3,000 and 4,000 years ago. The country was subsequently occupied by Muslims during the 13th century, paving the way for a series of Afghan dynasties, which cut the ties with the ruling Muslim dynasties in Delhi. The country was periodically annexed by the Mughal empire, but these occupations were relatively brief. The Mughals conquered the territory in the 16th century and declared it an autonomous region. Later under Mughal rule, the country became virtually independent.

4   The Portuguese, Armenians, French and British came to the region in succession during the 17th and 18th centuries, establishing military and trade outposts. The British purchased three villages - Colikata, Sutanoti and Govindapur - from the landowners, and soon challenged the local authorities on trade and military issues. In June 1757, at the Battle of Plassy, 500 British soldiers led by Robert Clive defeated a much larger force under the command of local ruler Nawab Siraj-ud-Dwola. The defeat amounted to the British conquest of the country, marking the beginning of 190 years of British rule.

5   When the British partitioned India, transforming part of its territory into Pakistan in August 1947, Bengal was also partitioned. The Muslim majority areas, known as East Bengal, became part of Pakistan, and the Hindu majority areas became part of India. The people of East Pakistan became impatient when they became aware that many resources were being transferred from their part of the country to West Pakistan. They also lost patience with the bureaucratic military oligarchy in West Pakistan, and began to demand regional autonomy.

6   As a result, East Pakistan elected its own political leadership in 1970. The Pakistani Government refused to recognize this secession; the military blocked all attempts to form a government and began campaigns of aggression against East Pakistani civilians on March 25 1971.

7   The people of East Pakistan declared independence and launched an armed resistance movement. They formed a government-in-exile in India with Sheikh Mujibur Rahman as president, and finally succeeded in ousting the occupation forces. About 3 million lives were lost during the war and 10 million refugees were reported to have crossed the border into India.

8   On December 16 1972, Bangladesh adopted a constitution providing for parliamentary democracy. Large industries, banks and insurance companies were nationalized. Democracy, secularism, socialism and nationalism were declared as the state's basic principles.

9   But the task of reviving the war-torn economy proved too great a challenge for the inexperienced leadership of the ruling party, the Awami League. Nationalist fervor soon died down, giving way to widespread feelings of disappointment. Bangladeshi politics degenerated into confusion as insurgency and armed political movements erupted throughout the country.

10   In December 1974, the Government declared a state of National Emergency, and in January 1975 fundamental civil rights were suspended. All opposition political parties and trade unions were banned leaving a single party, Bakshal, mainly made up of Awami League members and pro-Moscow communists. Newspapers were banned - except for four national dailies controlled by the Government - and a new press and publication law suppressed all opposition views. On August 15 1975, against this backdrop, a group of active and retired army officers assassinated President Sheikh Mujibur Rahman and his family, and declared martial law.

11   On November 7 1975, General Zia ur Rahman emerged as the leading force in the opposition, following a series of coups and counter-coups. He founded the Bangladesh Nationalist Party (BNP) which included many members who had opposed Bangladesh's initial independence in 1971. The BNP won the 1978 and 1979 elections, and the Awami League went into opposition.

12   The country went through a brief period of relative stability. But in May 1981, Zia ur Rahman was killed in an abortive coup attempt. Almost a year later, on March 24

WORKERS

% OF LABOUR FORCE   **1998**

■ FEMALE: 42%   ■ MALE: 58%

1990

■ SERVICES: 18.4%
■ INDUSTRY: 16.4%
■ AGRICULTURE: 65.2%

LAND USE

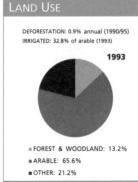

DEFORESTATION: 0.9% annual (1990/95)
IRRIGATED: 32.8% of arable (1993)

1993

■ FOREST & WOODLAND: 13.2%
■ ARABLE: 65.6%
■ OTHER: 21.2%

PUBLIC EXPENDITURE

DEFENCE EXPENDITURE (% of goverment exp.)	**10.7%**	(1997)
MILITARY EXPENDITURE (% of health & education)	**41%**	(1990/91)

MATERNAL MORTALITY 1990-98

Per 100,000 live births

440

LITERACY 1995

38%

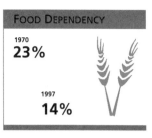

FOOD DEPENDENCY 1970

23%

1997

14%

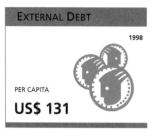

EXTERNAL DEBT 1998

PER CAPITA

US$ 131

1982, the army engineered a successful coup, placing General Ershad in the presidency.

[13] In 1985, General Ershad formed the Jatiya Party (JP), going on to win the 1986 general election with what the opposition saw as widespread fraud. As a result of this, massive popular uprisings forced Ershad to dissolve the parliament. Confidence in political integrity was so low that the 1988 elections, were boycotted by all the major political parties and a large percentage of the electorate as well.

[14] Since Sheikh Mujibur Rahman's death in 1975, socialism and secularism were discarded as state policy. Public sector budgets were gradually reduced and the military became a strong contender for political power.

[15] Bangladesh is one of the poorest and most densely populated countries in the world and has suffered many famines, an occurrence that seems hardly explicable in a country with extremely rich soil and plentiful water and sun - all the elements

necessary for agricultural production sufficient to feed the population. However, as most of the best land is concentrated in the hands of a few large landowners, the low productivity and enormous privations faced by the rural population are not altogether surprising.

[16] Prior to the "green revolution" of the 1970s and 1980s, over 7,000 varieties of rice were commonly cultivated in Bangladesh. More recently, only one is widely cultivated. This new high-yield variety promised to meet all the country's rice needs, but the only real achievement was to open a new market for the manufacturers of chemical fertilizers, upon which the production of this new variety of rice depends.

[17] In 1982, "administrative decentralization" was initiated, leading to huge unproductive spending in rural areas and a growing alliance between bureaucrats and the rural elite to control public resources.

[18] Economic performance has been very poor, complicated by indiscriminate privatization, increasing military expenditure, low growth rates in manufacturing, falling agricultural production and the material damage caused by recurrent floods.

[19] On April 30 1991, the worst storm to hit Bangladesh since 1970 killed nearly 100,000 people. Prime Minister Khaleda Zia reported that it had caused several million dollars' worth of damage and left millions of people homeless. The most devastated areas were along the coast and on islands of the Ganges delta.

[20] Bangladesh also suffered from man-made disasters. The Asian Development Bank had $5 million in aid reserved to end the pollution of Bangladesh's waters. Leaks from oil tankers and the disposal of industrial waste along the coast are destroying the coastal ecosystem. Marine life has been decimated, and it is believed that the sea here will soon be completely dead. Bangladeshi fisherfolk are having to go further out to sea to obtain a satisfactory catch. At this time fishing accounted for six per cent of the GNP, and the export of fish products earned over $150 million per year.

[21] The district of Khulna was among the world's most polluted areas, with the destruction in recent years of forest worth over $110 million. There were more than a thousand offending industries, known to the Government, which continued to operate in the knowledge that they cannot be closed without further aggravating an already serious unemployment situation.

[22] Bangladesh has always been a predominantly rural society. Agriculture accounts for about half of the gross domestic product, compared to just 10 per cent from manufacturing. About four-fifths of the labor force is employed in agriculture or related activities. Participation by women in the formal labor market is small: only around seven per cent of the work force is female.

[23] Women's social status remains very low, and under the fundamentalist-inspired constitution, a woman may inherit only half as much as her brother. In practice, this fraction goes to her husband or is saved as a dowry. Bengali feminists complain that women are treated as goods rather than individuals as they belong to their fathers in childhood, to their husbands in marriage (most marry at 13), and to their sons in old age. Their work in the home and the fields is not included in official production statistics, and divorce - a male prerogative under Islamic law - can be easily obtained if a woman's productivity drops. Unfortunately this frequently occurs as many women are seriously undernourished.

[24] Bangladesh joined the UN in 1974 after two earlier attempts were blocked by Chinese vetoes. It was a founding member of the Non-Aligned Movement and also of the Organization of the Islamic Conference. The country experimented a gradual Islamization of politics and in 1989 a constitutional amendment declared Islam the official religion.

[25] In 1991, Ershad was deposed, and elections were called, in which the Awami League (AL) opposed the Bangladesh Nationalist Party (BNP). Both political alliances had women as their major candidates; in both cases the widow of the former leader of the alliance.

PROFILE

ENVIRONMENT

Located on the Padma River Delta, formed by the confluence of the Meghna with the Ganges and the Brahmaputra, Bangladesh is a fertile, alluvial plain where rice, tea and jute are grown. There are vast rain forests and swamps. A tropical monsoon climate predominates, with heavy summer rains from June to September generally accompanied by hurricanes and floods of catastrophic consequences. Low-quality coal and natural gas are the only mineral resources. The increase in sea level poses a growing threat to the country. The coastal area along the Bay of Bengal has been severely affected by the discharge of sewage and industrial waste. This pollution, together with indiscriminate fishing to supply both internal and export markets, is leading to the destruction of one of the country's main resources with sea-borne pollution threatening to irreversibly damage the coastal ecosystem.

SOCIETY

Peoples: The people of Bangladesh are ethnically and culturally homogeneous, as a result of 25 centuries of integration between the local Bengali population and immigrants from Central Asia. There are small Urdu and Indian minorities. Of the present ethnic groups, the Chakma are known to have migrated from the hills of Chittagong to border states of India in 1981.

Religions: Mostly Islamic (83 per cent) and Hindu (16 per cent), with Buddhist and Christian minorities.

Languages: Bengali.

Political Parties: Awami League (AL), in favor of a socialist economy with the intervention of the private sector; Bangladesh Nationalist Party, right of center (Bangladesh Jatiyatabadi Dal, BNP); National Party (coalition), an Islamic-inspired alliance of five nationalist parties; Islamic Assembly; Jamaat-I-Islami, Islamic fundamentalists; Communist Party and other minor parties.

THE STATE

Official Name: Gana Prajatantri Bangladesh.

Capital: Dhaka (Dacca), 7,832,000 people (1995).

Other cities: Chittagong 2,040,663 people; Khulna 877,388; Rajshahi 517,136 people (1991).

Government: Parliamentary republic. Shahabuddin Ahmed, President and Head of State since Oct 1996. Sheikh Hasina Wajed, Prime Minister and Head of Government since June 1996. Single-chamber legislature: Parliament made up of 330 members (300 elected by direct vote and 30 reserved for women, nominated by Parliament, for 5-year terms).

National Holidays: March 26, Independence Day (1971); December 16, Victory Day (1971).

Armed Forces: 115,500 (1995).

Other: Bangladesh Rifles: 30,000 (border guard); Ansars (Security Guards): 20,000.

[26] On March 2 1991, Begum Khaleda Zia of the BNP was elected Prime Minister. Khaleda Zia declared that she supported the establishment of a parliamentary regime, thereby stripping the AL of one of its traditional platforms. Five months after her triumph in the general election, and with the unanimous approval of the legislative representatives of the two major parties, the Congress of Bangladesh replaced the country's presidential system with a parliamentary system.

[27] The previous president, Hussain Mohammad Ershad, had been sentenced in 1991 to 10 years in prison for abuse of power, unlawful wealth and possession of illegal weapons. However, he was able to run for the 1996 elections after appealing against the sentence.

[28] In mid-August 1991, the political reform was approved when, in a climate of great tension, President Shahabuddin Ahmed threatened to resign unless the system was modified.

[29] Bangladesh relied heavily upon international aid; 95 per cent of its development programs were financed from abroad. The United States, Japan, the Asian Development Bank (ADB) and the World Bank contributed $2.3 billion in 1991, 10 million more than the previous year. 95 per cent of the country's budget was taken up in interest payments on its foreign debt.

[30] In the early 1990s Bangladeshis had an average per capita annual income of $240. Fifty per cent of housing was of mud brick construction with no plumbing: one toilet may be shared by as many as 50 families. More than 13 million people lived in the shanty towns surrounding the cities, which continue to grow at a rapid rate.

[31] Among its measures to shore up the fragile economy, the Government declared all-out war against smuggling, in December 1991. Smuggling became big business in Bangladesh, involving important financial institutions, the nouveau riche, and corrupt political and government officials.

[32] The IMF- and World Bank-launched privatization scheme, which included the sale of 42 public enterprises, came to a standstill in 1991. Minister of Finance Saifur Rahman faced the opposition of organized labor, especially in the jute industry (one of the main sources of export earnings), as well as textile and railway unions that fear the loss of jobs. General strikes - demanding a national minimum wage - became commonplace.

[33] The Gulf War (1990-1991) prompted Bangladesh to reaffirm its identity as a Muslim community. This feeling was intensified in 1992, when the repatriation of Muslim refugees began. Early in that year, Bangladesh received several groups of some 250,000 Bihari Muslims, who had supported Pakistan in 1971. In June, another 270,000 Rohingya Muslims arrived, fleeing persecution in Burma, a predominantly Buddhist country. The repatriation agreements signed between the two countries in 1992 failed to stem the flow of refugees.

[34] In 1994, writer Taslima Nasrin became famous for her book *Shame* which condemned the alleged oppression of Hindus and other minorities by Muslims. Nasrin was detained for requesting a greater respect by Islamic law of women's rights: this was regarded as criticism against the Koran. Throughout 1994, some 154 MP's opposed to the Khaleda administration boycotted parliamentary activity and resigned en masse in December. Throughout 1994 and 1995 Sheikh Hasina, female leader of the Awani League (AL) led a series of protests by peasants demanding elections under a neutral administration: their protests paid off.

[35] In the 1996 general elections held on February 15, women voted for the first time. Prime Minister Khaleda Zia, from the PNB, kept her post but the elections, held under army control, were considered fraudulent. A general strike called by the AL was followed by confrontations between the police and opposition activists. Violence did not end with Khaleda's fall on March 30. On June 23, the former head of the Supreme Court of Justice, Mohammad Habibur Rahman, who had led the neutral government before the June elections, handed over the administration to Prime Minister Sheikh Hasina, chosen in the second elections over a four-month period.

[36] Social unrest continued throughout 1997 and increased in December with a string of strikes called by opposition parties, after the agreement signed by the Government to put an end to armed rebels in the southeast. For several days, those who supported the strikes and those who were against them held marches in cities - Dhaka, Chittagong, Barisal, Syleht and Rajsani, among others - and in many small towns, which almost paralyzed the country.

[37] In 1998, 15 million people were at risk from polluted wells, the main source of water supply for the population. The water, laced with naturally-occurring arsenic, had been dug in the last two decades after major mobilization campaigns. This contamination threatened to aggravate the situation of the poorest sectors of the population in a country where 50 per cent of newborn children were underweight.

[38] The Bangladesh Central Bank devaluated the *taka* by 3 per cent in November 1999 to improve competitiveness in the exporting sector. This had been recommended by the IMF, whose officials considered the currency overvalued. The main opposition party, the Nationalist Party of Bangladesh (PNA), warned that the measure went against the interests of the population, not least because it was the sixteenth currency devaluation since 1996. A month later, the Prime Minister extended her cabinet to 45 members, incorporating nine new Ministers. Hasina Wajid gave no reasons for the move other that it gave representation to regions of the country forgotten up to now. However, she was also accused of nepotism since three of the new members were her relatives.

[39] In an official visit to southern Asia in March 2000, US President Bill Clinton recognized the efforts Bangladesh was making to portray itself in a different light and for its battle against extreme poverty. However, this first visit of a US president in decades had its tense moments. As soon as he arrived in Bangladesh, Clinton declared this was "the most dangerous country in the world" – a reference to the strained relations between India and Pakistan, as well as to the conflict in the separatist Indian province of Kashmir. Separatist rebels received military training in Bangladesh until 1996. The Minister of Internal Affairs, Mohammad Nasima, admitted this a month later, saying that military assistance had been given by the previous administration through a foreign network of intelligence operations. Although he did not elaborate, everything pointed to Pakistani intelligence services.

[40] In April, two Supreme Court of Justice ministers rejected hearing the appeal presented by former army officers who in 1975 murdered then Prime Minister Sheikh Mujibur Rahman, the independence leader of Bangladesh and father of current Prime Minister Hasina Wajid. These officers had been sentenced to death in 1998. Before carrying out the death sentence, the Supreme Court has to ratify it and hear the appeals. ∎

DEMOGRAPHY

Population: 126,948,000 (1999)
Annual growth: 2.2 % (1975/97)
Estimates for year 2015 (million): 161.5 (1999)
Annual growth to year 2015: 1.5 % (1997/2015)
Urban population: 19.4 % (1997)
Urban Growth: 5.6 % (1980/95)
Children per woman: 3.1 (1998)

HEALTH

Life expectancy at birth: 58 years (1998)
male: 58 years (1998)
female: 58 years (1998)
Maternal mortality: 440 per 100,000 live births (1990-98)
Infant mortality: 79 per 1,000 (1998)
Under-5 child mortality: 106 per 1,000 (1998)
Daily calorie supply: 2,105 per capita (1996)
18 doctors per 100,000 people (1993)
Safe water: 95 % (1990/98)

EDUCATION

Literacy: 38 % (1995)
male: 49 % (1995)
female: 26 % (1995)
School enrolment:
Primary total: 69 % (1990/96)
male: 74 % (1990/97)
female: 64 % (1990/97)
Secondary:
male: 28 % (1990/96)
female: 14 % (1990/96)
Tertiary: 6 % (1996)

COMMUNICATIONS

9 newspapers (1996), 50 radios (1997), 7 TV sets (1996) and 3 main telephone lines (1996) per 1,000 people

ECONOMY

Per capita, GNP: $ 350 (1998)
Annual growth, GNP: 5.9 % (1998)
Annual inflation: 3.6 % (1990/98)
Consumer price index: 118.6 (1998)
Currency: 46.9 taka = $ 1 (1998)
Cereal imports: 3,684,072 metric tons (1998)
Food import dependency: 17 % (1997)
Fertilizer use: 1,355 kg per ha (1997)
Exports: $ 5,885 million (1998)
Imports: $ 8,058 million (1998)
External debt: $ 16,376 million (1998); $ 131 per capita (1998)
Debt service: 9.1 % of exports (1998)
Development aid received: $ 1,009 million (1997); $ 9.0 per capita (1997); 2.30 % of GNP (1997)

ENERGY

Consumption: 197.0 Kgs of Oil equivalent per capita yearly (1997); 10.0 % imported (1997)

HDI (rank/value): 150/0.440 (1997)

Barbados

Barbados

Population:** 269,000 (1999)
Area: 430 SQ KM
Capital: Bridgetown
Currency: Barbadian dollar
Language: English

The peaceful and nomadic Arawak people expanded throughout the Caribbean region, and although they were dislodged from many islands by the Caribs, they remained on others - as in the case of Barbados.

[2] The Spanish landed on the island early in the 16th century and christened it the "island of the bearded fig tree". Satisfied that there was no natural wealth they withdrew, but not before massacring the native population, taking a few survivors with them to amuse the Spanish court. In 1625 the British arrived and found a fertile, uninhabited territory.

[3] Around 1640 the island had close to 30,000 inhabitants. The majority were farmers and their families, and some were political and religious dissidents from Britain. The settlers grew tobacco, cotton, pepper and fruit on small plots, raising cattle, pigs and poultry.

[4] Sugarcane was introduced, with the support of the British, and caused extensive social change. Plantation owners purchased large plots which were required in order to be profitable, and small landowners - most of them in debt - sold off their land to the plantation owners. The importation of slaves from Africa to work the sugar plantations began during this period.

[5] In 1667, 12,000 farmers emigrated to other Caribbean islands or to the 13 colonies of North America. Nonetheless, the island had a commercial fleet of 600 vessels and, as recorded by a French traveller in 1696, was "the most powerful island colony in America".

[6] Towards the end of the 18th century, the island was one huge sugar-producing complex which included 745 plantations and over 80,000 African slaves. By that time there was no woodland left on an island described in a 16th century account as "entirely covered with trees". Its ecological balance seriously impaired, the island fell victim to drought in the early 19th century and parts of it suffered soil exhaustion.

[7] The pursuit of increased profitability and an economy oriented toward foreign trade resulted in underdevelopment. A different approach might have led to development along the lines of the other North American colonies.

[8] Slavery was abolished in 1834 but the plantation economy still dominated the island's fiscal system. European landowners controlled local politics until well into the 20th century.

[9] In 1938, following the gradual extension of political rights, the Barbados Labor Party (BLP) led by Grantley Adams developed from within the existing labor unions. Universal suffrage was declared in 1951, and Adams became leader of the local government.

[10] Internal autonomy was granted 1961, and in 1966 independence was proclaimed within the British Commonwealth. Errol Barrow was elected Prime Minister. Unlike the rest of the West Indies, Barbados never severed its links with the colonial capital in spite of its political independence.

[11] After 1966, Errol Barrow's Democratic Labor Party (DLP) contributed to the creation of the Caribbean Free Trade Association which became CARICOM in 1973, involving 12 islands of the region. Barrow showed great interest in the Non-Aligned Countries movement.

[12] Free education and new electoral laws were not followed by any significant change in DLP policies towards the owners of sugar refining plants. The rise in unemployment diminished DLP support and resulted in the Party's electoral defeat. In 1970, the country became a member of the International Monetary Fund (IMF).

[13] The BLP won 17 of the 24 available seats in 1976. Tom Adams, Grantley Adams' son, was elected Prime Minister. He promised to fight corruption and described himself as a social democrat (the BLP became a member of the Socialist International in 1978). However, the Government protected the interest of investors in sugar and tourism transnationals, while encouraging foreign investment.

[14] Adams pressured Washington to withdraw from its naval base on nearby St Lucia, which it did in 1979. In 1981, Adams was re-elected and consolidated relations with Washington. Barbados supported the US invasion of Grenada.

[15] In order to attract foreign capital, the Government passed new tax exemption laws and liberalized ship registration. In 1986, an agreement between the US and Barbados led to 650 new companies registering in the off-shore sector. Unemployment and inflation within Barbados continued to grow.

[16] The 1986 election was won by the DLP. Prime Minister Errol Barrow committed the Government to changing the policy toward the US which had been followed by the BLP Government in the preceding 10 years. In 1987, Barrow died of a heart attack and was succeeded as Prime Minister by Erskine Sandiford. Two years later, as a result of a split within the DLP, a new opposition group was founded, the right-wing National Democratic Party (NDP), under the leadership of Richard Heynes.

[17] Steadily falling sugar prices and rising interest rates fuelled inflation in 1989. The Government's resolve to cut its budget deficit roused fears of further unemployment and there

WORKERS

1995
UNEMPLOYMENT: 19.7%

% OF LABOUR FORCE **1998**

■ FEMALE: 46%   ■ MALE: 54%

1990

■ SERVICES: 69.9%
■ INDUSTRY: 23.4%
■ AGRICULTURE: 6.7%

LAND USE

1993

■ FOREST & WOODLAND: 11.6%
■ ARABLE: 37.2%
■ OTHER: 51.2%

PUBLIC EXPENDITURE

DEFENCE EXPENDITURE (% of goverment exp.)	**2.0%**	(1997)
MILITARY EXPENDITURE (% of health & education)	**5.0%**	(1990/91)

were several strikes. Nonetheless, industry recovered, exchange reserves increased, and about a hundred Panamanian offshore concerns expressed interest in Barbados. Japan signed agreements to invest in tourism on the island.

[18] That same year, Barbados requested a review of the CARICOM charter as it was felt that the constraints were too limiting. In order to favor local agriculture, Government import restrictions were introduced, particularly on vegetables from Guyana.

[19] In 1990, serious controversies arose over sugar cane prices between the sugar mills and the Government; demands from workers threatened to end in strike action. The tourist industry employed 15 per cent of the workforce of the island and 450,000 tourists had visited Barbados in 1988.

[20] The Government endorsed the use of solar power in 1990 as electricity was very expensive on the islands.

[21] According to the Inter-American Development Bank's report (1996), Barbados' economy registered a negative growth rate since 1990, although inflation has been reduced. While overall unemployment remained constant, there was an increase in unemployment among female workers in the garment, electronics and tourism industries, the country's main sources of foreign exchange. In the tourist sector, there was a 6.3 per cent decline in the number of tourists, as well as a reduction in the length of their stay on the island.

[22] In 1991, the DLP was re-elected with 49 per cent of the vote although it lost 2 of its 20 seats. In November, riots and protests due to an 8 per cent cutback on civil servants' wages led to a general strike. Despite this challenge, Sandiford remained in office.

[23] In 1992 the Government obtained an IMF loan amounting to $64.9 million and the Prime Minister announced further wage reductions in the public sector, a rise in interest rates and cutbacks in the social system, as well as the privatization of oil and cement production and the tourism industry.

[24] After two successive finance ministers resigned, Sandiford himself assumed the post in late 1992, attempting to transform the country into a financial center. Tourist activity has flourished since 1993. That year, tourism revenues reached $500 million, equivalent to one third of the country's GDP.

[25] In June 1994, the BLP withdrew its support for the Prime Minister and won the elections held on September 7. Owen Arthur, the new prime minister, cancelled planned wage reductions, and this became law in February 1995.

[26] Arthur introduced a deficit budget in April, arguing that expenditure was needed to tackle unemployment, which had reached 21.2 per cent. The IMF had advised caution in the management of public funds, but Arthur chose to overlook their prescriptions.

[27] The island's Governor General, Dame Nita Barrow, sister of former Prime Minister Errol Barrow, died on December 19 1995. She had held the post since June 1990.

[28] The legislative assembly voted in February 1996 for civil servant salaries to be brought back up over a two-year period. The measure, promoted by the BLP, was a response to the salary reduction policy applied in 1994 by the Democratic Labor Party.

[29] In May, the Government signed a contract with a US company to explore possible offshore oil fields.

[30] Tourism continued to be the main source of income for Barbados in 1997. The Government managed to further increase that income, even though the infrastructure was not considered the most adequate for large-scale expansion of the sector.

[31] In April 1998, during the summit of American Presidents in Santiago, Chile, Prime Minister of Barbados, Owen Arthur, said he was in favor of Cuba's inclusion at the next meeting.

[32] The January 1999 elections saw a broad victory for the BLP, which took 26 of the disputed seats, while the other two remained in DLP hands. Owen Arthur was returned to his post. ■

PROFILE

ENVIRONMENT

Of volcanic origin, it is the eastern-most island of the Lesser Antilles. The fertile soil and rainy tropical climate favor intensive farming of sugarcane, rotated with cotton and corn. The most serious environmental problems are the disposal of sewage and refuse, water consumption, and soil and coastal erosion. The Caribbean Sea is increasingly contaminated and its resources are over-exploited.

SOCIETY

Peoples: Most are of African origin (92.5 per cent), with a minority of Europeans (3.2 per cent) and mestizos (2.8 per cent). It is one of the most densely populated countries in the world, with an average of 616 people per square kilometer.
Religions: 33 per cent Anglican. There are also Catholics (4.4 per cent). Methodists and Moravians (29.8 per cent).
Languages: English (official). Creole is also spoken.
Political Parties: The Barbados Labor Party (BLP), in power since 1994. The Democratic Labor Party (DLP); the right-wing National Democratic Party (NDP).
Social Organizations: Barbados Workers' Trade Union.

THE STATE

Official Name: Barbados.
Capital: Bridgetown 10,000 people (est 1997).
Other cities: Speightstown; Holetown; Bathsheba.
Government: Owen Arthur, Prime Minister since September 7 1994; Sir Clifford Husbands, Governor-General, appointed in 1996. The bicameral Parliament has been shaped on the British model. The Legislative power is constituted by a Parliament, with a Lower Chamber, Senate and the post of Governor General.

National Holiday: November 30, Independence Day (1966).

STATISTICS

DEMOGRAPHY

Population: 269,000 (1999)
Annual growth: 0.4 % (1975/97)
Estimates for year 2015 (million): 0.3 (1999)
Annual growth to year 2015: 0.4 % (1997/2015)
Urban population: 48.4 % (1997)
Children per woman: 1.5 (1998)

HEALTH

Life expectancy at birth: 76 years (1998)
male: 74 years (1998)
female: 79 years (1998)
Maternal mortality: 0 per 100,000 live births (1990-98)
Infant mortality: 13 per 1,000 (1998)
Under-5 child mortality: 15 per 1,000 (1998)
Daily calorie supply: 3,207 per capita (1996)
113 doctors per 100,000 people (1993)
Safe water: 100 % (1990/98)

EDUCATION

Literacy: 97 % (1995)
male: 98 % (1995)
female: 97 % (1995)
School enrolment:
Primary total: 90 % (1990/96)
male: 90 % (1990/97)
female: 91 % (1990/97)
Secondary:
male: 90 % (1990/96)
female: 80 % (1990/96)
Tertiary: 29 % (1996)

COMMUNICATIONS

200 newspapers (1996), 891 radios (1997), 287 TV sets (1996) and 370 main telephone lines (1996) per 1,000 people

ECONOMY

Annual growth, GNP: 4.4 % (1998)
Consumer price index: 108.9 (1998)
Cereal imports: 65,753 metric tons (1998)
Food import dependency: 18 % (1997)
Fertilizer use: 2,000 kg per ha (1997)
Exports: $ 1,484 million (1998)
Imports: $ 1,475 million (1998)
External debt: $ 608 million (1998); $ 2,268 per capita (1998)
Development aid received: $ 3 million (1997); $ 11.5 per capita (1997)

HDI (rank/value): 29/0.857 (1997)

Belarus

Belarus

Population: 10,275,000 (1999)
Area: 207,600 SQ KM
Capital: Minsk (Mensk)
Currency: Rouble
Language: Belarusian

The territory known today as Belarus (formerly Belorussia) was inhabited from the 1st century AD by the Krivich, Radimich and Dregovich Slavic peoples. The first principalities were those of Polotsk and Turov-Pinsk. In the 9th century, Eastern Slav tribes belonging to the Western Rus joined other Eastern Slav peoples to form the Kiev Rus, the ancient Russian State (see history of Russia) which gave rise to modern Russia, Ukraine and Belarus. The major cities of the area, Polotsk, Turov, Brest, Vitebsk, Orsha, Pinsk and Minsk date from the 9th and 10th centuries.

2 In the 14th century, Lithuanian principalities annexed themselves to the Western Rus. As the Lithuanians lacked their own writing system, the language of the Belarusians (which was the only Russian language at the time) became the official language of the State.

3 Between the 14th and 16th centuries, the Belarusian culture began to differentiate itself from that of the Russians and the Ukrainians.

4 In 1569, according to the terms of the Union Treaty between Poland and Lithuania, Belarus became a part of Poland. The Belarusians resisted domination by the Catholic Poles, and maintained their linguistic and cultural identity.

5 With the first partition of Poland in 1772, Russia kept the eastern part of Belarus. Between 1793-95, the rest of Belarus became part of the Russian Empire. The abolition of serfdom in Russia in 1861 accelerated the development of Belarus. Important railways were built, including the Moscow-Brest and the Libava-Romni lines. By the end of the 19th century, Belarus had Russia's second most important railway system.

6 The Russian Czar's abolition of the serf system put an end to the peasants' feudal bondage to the landed nobility. However, this failed to solve the land tenure problem, as in Belarus only 35 per cent of the land was handed over to the peasants. This triggered a number of uprisings, the most important of which took place in 1863 under the leadership of Kalinovski.

7 In March 1899, the 1st Congress of the Social Democratic Workers' Party of Russia (SDWPR) was held secretly in Minsk. This group was inspired by Marxist socialism and was determined to bring down the Czar. Other sectors of the intelligentsia took their cue from the peasants' discontent, and founded an autonomous Belarusian movement in 1902, which sought to revive the nation's culture. During this period, the czarist regime deported Russian Jews to Belarus, where they came to account for a fifth of the local population.

8 During World War I (1914-1917) part of Belarus was occupied by German troops. After the Russian Revolution of February 1917, councils (soviets) made up of workers' representatives were formed in Minsk, Gomel, Vitebsk, Bobruisk and Orsha.

9 Soviet power began to be established at the end of 1917, and in February 1918 the large land holdings were nationalized. A few months later, land began to be distributed to the peasants. At the insistence of the Bolsheviks (socialist revolutionaries of the SDWPR), the first collective farms (*koljoses*) were set up. In reality, however, the land gradually went into State control.

10 The 6th Party Conference of the Russian Communists (Bolsheviks) - formerly the SDWPR - held in Smolensk, approved the decision to found the Soviet Socialist Republic of Belarus (SSRB). In January 1918, the decision to join Lithuania was made at the 1st Congress of the SSRB soviets. The Congress of the Soviets of Lithuania endorsed the same motion.

11 On February 28 1919 in the city of Vilno (today Vilnius, the capital of Lithuania) the Government of the Soviet Socialist Republic of Lithuania and Belarus was elected, with Mickevicius-Kapsukas as head of state.

12 In February 1919, Poland, which had become independent from Russia after the Bolsheviks had seized power in St Petersburg, occupied a large part of Belarus. According to the Treaty of Riga,

signed between Soviet Russia and Poland (1921), Western Belarus became part of Poland.

13 On August 1 1920 the Assembly of representatives of the Lithuanian and Belarusian Communist Parties and of labor organizations in Minsk and its surrounding areas approved the foundation of the independent Belarusian republic.

14 On December 30 1922, Belarus joined the Union of Soviet Socialist Republics (USSR) as one of its founders, along with the Russian Federation, Ukraine and the Transcaucasian Federation (Armenia, Georgia and Azerbaijan).

15 The industrialization and collectivization of agriculture began in the second half of the 1920s. On February 19 1937 the 12th Congress of the Soviets of Belarus approved the new constitution. In November 1939, as a result of the Molotov-Ribbentrop Pact - signed between the USSR and Germany - Western Belarus was reincorporated into the Soviet Union.

16 In June 1941 Belarus became the first of the Soviet republics to suffer Hitler's aggression. The fortress at Brest offered fierce resistance, becoming a symbol of Belarus' heroic defence. Guerrilla warfare extended throughout the country for the duration of the War, a conflict in which more than 2 million Belarusians lost their lives.

17 After Germany's defeat in 1945, Belarus' current borders were established. It became a charter member of the United Nations that same year; like Ukraine it had its own delegation, independent of the USSR.

18 It took Belarus almost two decades to restore its economy, becoming in the process an important producer of heavy trucks, electrical appliances, radios and television sets. Between the 1920s and the 1980s, Belarus ceased to be a rural country in which 90 per cent of the population lived from traditional farming and livestock raising becoming an urban, industrialized country with nearly 70 per cent of its population living in cities.

19 Belarus is one of the few republics that managed to maintain an ample majority of its local population - more than 80 per cent - with minimal influence from Russian or other immigration.

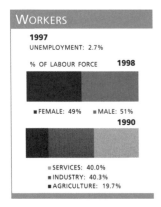

Workers

1997
UNEMPLOYMENT: 2.7%

% OF LABOUR FORCE **1998**

■ FEMALE: 49% ■ MALE: 51%

1990

■ SERVICES: 40.0%
■ INDUSTRY: 40.3%
■ AGRICULTURE: 19.7%

Public Expenditure

DEFENCE EXPENDITURE (% of goverment exp.)	**4.8%**	(1997)
MILITARY EXPENDITURE (% of health & education)	**45.7%**	(1990/91)

[20] Until 1985, the Communist Party and the Belarusian Government followed the course established by the Communist Party of the Soviet Union. Among the outstanding communist leaders of this period was Piotr Masherov.

[21] Because of the policies of glasnost (openness) and *perestroika* (restructuring) initiated by President Mikhail Gorbachev, there was no strong pressure within Belarus to secede immediately from the USSR, although there were movements favoring a multiparty political system, as well as protest demonstrations against high food prices.

[22] Belarus was the region outside Ukraine most affected by the 1986 catastrophe at the Chernobyl nuclear plant. According to foreign researchers, in the following years there was a rapid increase in cases of cancer, leukemia and birth defects in the areas affected by the disaster - Ukraine, Belarus and western Russia.

[23] In June 1991, Belarus declared independence and in October signed an economic integration agreement with Kazakhstan and Uzbekistan. On December 8, the presidents of the Russian Federation and Ukraine,

Boris Yeltsin and Leonid Kravchuk, and of the Belarus Parliament, Stanislav Sushkevich, signed an historic agreement which put an end to the USSR. Opposing President Gorbachev's idea of signing a new Union Treaty, the presidents decided to create an association of sovereign states. On the June 21, in Alma-Ata (Kazakhstan), 11 republics signed an agreement creating the Commonwealth of Independent States (CIS), whose members requested admission to the UN as separate countries. Belarus and 7 of the republics pledged to implement structural reforms which would convert them into market economies.

[24] In September 1993, tensions between the prime minister and the Parliamentary president came to a head amid rumors of a possible coup. In January 1994, Sushkevich was replaced by Mecheslav Grib. On March, Parliament passed the new Constitution, replacing the 1977 one when Belarus still belonged to the former USSR.

[25] The country became a presidential republic with a 260-seat Parliament. In July, Alexander Lukashenka obtained 80 per cent of the vote in the second round, after a campaign in which he lambasted the corruption of his predecessors.

[26] In spite of having criticized it in his electoral campaign, the President continued the policy of rapprochement which led to a monetary union with Russia on April 1994. In August, he met Russian President Boris Yeltsin and in November decreed a state of emergency, with the excuse of slowing down inflation.

[27] On February 1995, Minsk and Moscow signed a treaty of friendship and cooperation which enabled Russia to keep its troops deployed in the country. Insufficient participation in the May parliamentary elections, which Lukashenka held along with a referendum on his rapprochement policy toward Moscow, did not allow for the election of all deputies, which led to a second by-election in November.

[28] During the first months of 1996, opposition to Lukashenka and his pro-Russian policy, as well as the pressure he put on opposition groups such as the Popular Front, led to major demonstrations. In March, at the commemoration of the independent republic established in Belarus in 1917, tens of thousands protested against the union with the Russian Federation.

[29] In April, amid mass protests, Russia and Belarus strengthened their relations by signing a political and economic integration agreement. Several opposition leaders went into exile in the United States. By the end of the year, a constitutional reform granted more powers to Lukashenka. Among those arrested were the former Central Bank chairman and other senior officials. The opposition denounced the establishment of a dictatorship.

[30] The economy was in chaos in 1997. Over 70 per cent of the population was living below the poverty line. The value of the national currency, the rouble, fell against the dollar and inflation grew. Lukashenka dismissed foreign minister Vladimir Syanko and replaced him with Ivan Antanovich. Parliament confirmed the appointment of Syarhei Linh as prime minister.

[31] Amnesty International reported executions and arbitrary arrests and demanded the abolition of the death penalty. In February 1998, Belarus recalled its ambassador to Poland, amidst accusations of Polish interference in domestic affairs.

[32] In April 1999 Senate approval was given for integration with Russia. This caused some protests in the south of the country, but there was broad support in the north, where Russian influence is stronger. One issue agreed was that citizens of both countries would enjoy identical rights on either side of the border. ∎

PROFILE

ENVIRONMENT

Belarus is located between the Dnepr (Dnieper), Western Dvina, Niemen and Western Bug rivers. It is bounded in the west by Poland, in the northwest by Latvia and Lithuania, in the northeast by Russia and in the south by Ukraine. It is a flat country, with many swamps and lakes, and forests covering a third of its territory. Its climate is continental and cool, with an average summer temperature of 17-19 degrees, and 4-7 degrees below zero in winter. Due to its geographical proximity to Ukraine, Belarus received intense radioactive fall-out following the disaster at the Chernobyl nuclear plant in 1986. A quarter of the country's arable land shows signs of chemical pollution from the overuse of pesticides.

SOCIETY

Peoples: Belarusians, 77.9 per cent; Russians, 13.2 per cent; Poles, 4.1 per cent; Ukrainians, 4.1 per cent; Hebrew, 1.1 per cent (1989).
Religions: Christian Orthodox; in the west, Catholic.
Languages: Belarusian (official); Russian (spoken as a second language by most of the population) and Polish. **Political Parties:** Communist Party, Belarusian Popular Front, Agrarian Party.
Social Organizations: Labor Union Federation of Belarus; Free Union.

THE STATE

Official name: Respublika Belarus.
Administrative divisions: Six regions (Brest, Gomel, Grodno, Mensk, Moguiliov and Vitebsk).
Capital: Minsk (Mensk) 1,679,500 people (1997).
Other cities: Gomel 506,000 people; Mogilov 363,000; Vitebsk 373,000; Grodno 291,000; Brest 269,000 (1992).
Government: Executive power: President, Aleksander Lukashenka, since 1994; Prime Minister, Syarhei Linh, since 1996. The Supreme Soviet is the maximum legislative body; Myachaslau Hryb, President.
National Holiday: June 27, Independence (1991).
Armed Forces: 102,600.
Other: Border Guards (Ministry of Interior): 8,000. **Land use:** Forested 33.7 per cent; meadows and pastures 15.1 per cent; agricultural and under permanent cultivation 30.1 per cent; other 21.1 per cent.

Belgium

België / Belgique

Population: 10,152,000 (1999)
Area: 30,519 SQ KM
Capital: Brussels (Bruxelles/Brussel)
Currency: Belgian franc
Language: French, Dutch and German

Belgium, Holland, Luxembourg and a part of northern France make up the Low Countries, which had a common history until 1579 (see Netherlands). The linguistic separation which took place between the Roman and Germanic languages coincided with the borders of the Holy Roman Empire, which divided the Low Countries in two.

2   In 1519 Emperor Charles V who was born in Ghent ascended the throne, inheriting the Holy Roman Empire from his father and Spain from his mother. This was the beginning of 200 years of Spanish rule. In 1579, the creation of the Union of Arras (achieved by joining together the Catholic provinces of Artois and Hainaut) led Spain to resume its war against the Dutch Protestants. According to the terms of the 1713 Treaty of Utrecht the southern provinces and Luxembourg were left in the hands of Charles VI, head of the Holy Roman Empire and of the Austrian branch of the Hapsburgs.

3   The region's economy was based on the production of linen and textiles. Industrialization was facilitated by the fact that manufacturers and landowners were often one and the same, and that textile mills were concentrated in the hands of a few owners. Factories each employing more than 100 low-paid workers sprang up in Ghent, Antwerp, and Tournai.

4   Fearing the spread of the French Revolution, the House of Austria attempted some progressive reforms, but the conservative revolt of 1789 put an end to these. After French Republican troops invaded in 1794, France did away with the region's autonomy and the privileges of the local aristocracy, while encouraging the industrial revolution. After the fall of Napoleon in 1814, the European powers enforced reunification with the north. The southern provinces had already forged an identity of their own and were unwilling to accept Dutch authority.

5   In 1830, the Belgian bourgeoisie, along with urban labourers from Brussels and Lièges, took up arms against the Dutch authorities. When the conflict spread and proved substantial, European powers recognized the independence of the southern provinces, which were henceforth known as Belgium. Congress adopted a parliamentary monarchy, with an electing body made up of property owners. The duchies of Luxembourg and Limburg were divided between Belgium and Holland.

6   By the end of the 19th century, workers forced the Government to pass laws aimed at providing housing for working class people, and improving conditions in the workplace, especially for women and children. At the same time, Parliament changed the Constitution and in 1893, established limited male suffrage.

7   Between 1880 and 1885, Leopold II financed international expeditions to the Congo, making it effectively his "private" colony. Substantial losses and protests from several European nations against the severe repression and exploitation occurring in the Congo forced the Belgian Government to take it as a colony in 1908. With this, the worst excesses ended but the Belgian Government, businesses and the church increased their influence over the following years.

8   In 1914, Germany wanted to cross Belgian territory to invade France. Belgium refused to give way to the Germans and was drawn into war. The Treaty of Versailles granted the territories of Eupen and Malmedy to Belgium. In Africa, Belgium colonized the former German colonies of Rwanda and Burundi after the League of Nations granted them a mandate. But Belgium failed to realize any of its other territorial demands. In 1920 Belgium signed a military assistance treaty with France, and the following year, it formed an economic alliance with Luxembourg.

9   After the war, the Government established universal male suffrage. Parliament approved an eight-hour workday, a graduated income tax, and a retirement pension plan. From 1930, increased pressure was put on the Government to tackle discrimination against the Flemish people and the Dutch language. This resulted in several "linguistic laws" and two regions: Flanders and Wallonia. In the former, Dutch is the official language, while in the latter it is French.

10   During World War II Belgium remained neutral, but it was occupied by Germany in 1940 until liberation in 1944. The return of King Leopold III, who had been held prisoner by the Germans, unleashed a major controversy. In a plebiscite, 57 per cent of the population voted in favor of his return to the throne, but continuing tension in Wallonia forced Leopold to abdicate in favor of his son Baudouin (1950).

11   In 1947, Belgium, the Netherlands, and Luxembourg formed an economic association known as Benelux, still extant within the European Union. Belgium also became a member of NATO in 1949. In 1960 the Belgian Congo became independent, but soon had to deal with secessionist movements in the southern province of Katanga. Belgium tacitly took side with the secessionists, but UN troops eventually restored national unity. Later on Belgium and the western powers continued to intervene in the former colony (which became Zaire, and is now the Democratic Republic of Congo). In 1962 Rwanda and Burundi became independent.

12   Female suffrage was granted in 1949. In 1975, Belgian women gained the right to equal pay. During the 1960s and 1970s questions about linguistic communities became increasingly important. In 1970, they were granted autonomy in cultural matters. In 1980, a new federal structure was approved by Parliament, made up of Flanders, Wallonia, and Brussels as the bilingual capital district.

13   In 1983, hundreds of thousands gathered in the streets of Brussels to protest against the installation of NATO nuclear missiles on Belgian soil. The missiles were withdrawn in 1988, after an arms reduction agreement was signed between the United States and the USSR.

14   In April 1990, despite the opposition of Christian Democrats within the coalition government, Parliament approved an abortion law. In order to avoid having to sign

WORKERS

1997
UNEMPLOYMENT: 9.0%

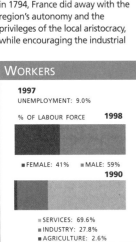

% OF LABOUR FORCE   **1998**

■ FEMALE: 41%   ■ MALE: 59%
                                1990

■ SERVICES: 69.6%
■ INDUSTRY: 27.8%
■ AGRICULTURE: 2.6%

MILITARY EXPENDITURE

DEFENCE EXPENDITURE (% of goverment exp.)	3.2%	(1997)
MILITARY EXPENDITURE (% of health & education)	20%	(1990/91)

the proposed legislation, King Baudouin stepped down temporarily from the throne, while the bill went through Parliament.

[15] Between 1983 and 1988, Belgium had an average unemployment rate of 11.3 per cent, the third highest in Western Europe, after Spain and Ireland. The economic situation improved in 1989, but after falling significantly in 1990, unemployment began to rise again in 1991. In October 1996 it stood at 13.8 per cent.

[16] In 1988, Belgium reaffirmed its support for the maintenance of NATO as a regional nuclear force, but extended support for its modernization until 1992, a position which was to be adopted by other Nato members. In the elections held in November 1991, the Vlaams Blok (Flemish Bloc), a xenophobic group which had geared its campaign around the expulsion of immigrants, experienced a six-fold increase in its parliamentary representation. The gains by the far Right and the Greens provoked the resignation of Prime Minister Wilfried Martens.

[17] Wilfried Martens, who had been premier for 10 years was succeeded by his party colleague Jean-Luc Dehaene, who formed a new government with the Christian Democrats and socialists in March 1992. Dehaene immediately announced a plan to reduce the national deficit in line with the requirements of the European Treaty of Maastricht. This included drastic curbs on public spending.

[18] On July 31 1993 King Baudouin died after a reign of 42 years. He was succeeded by his brother Albert who was crowned as Albert II. At the same time, Dehaene began negotiations with unions to produce a "comprehensive plan" against unemployment, which had reached 9.8 per cent in May 1994. Charges of corruption forced three leading socialist politicians to resign as ministers.

[19] The 1994 European elections reflected the population's lack of confidence towards the governing coalition. French-speaking socialists went from 38.5 per cent of the vote in 1989 to 30.4 per cent in 1994. In the municipal elections of October, the socialists lost votes once again, while the Vlaams Blok became the second party in Antwerp, by winning 18 out of the 55 seats at stake on the city council.

[20] Meanwhile Parliament had agreed on major constitutional changes that turned the country into a federal state. Therefore, on May 21 1995, voters not only elected their members of Parliament, but also three new regional assemblies of Brussels, Flanders and Wallonia. The government alliance led by Premier Dehaene reached clear victory in the national elections, allowing him to continue as head of government.

[21] The 1996 budget, which sought to limit the national deficit to 3 per cent of the GDP, was the cause of severe discussions between the Government and labor unions, which contested the reduction of public spending and purchasing-power. However, the unions' resistance gradually decreased, and supported by a significant economic growth and a resumption of private consumption, the Belgian Government managed to close the 1997 budget with a deficit of 2.7 per cent of the GDP. In spite of its enormous public debt, which clearly exceeded the criteria of the Maastricht Treaty, Belgium was allowed to join the European Monetary Union from its very beginning.

[22] The investigation of Marc Dutroux, accused of the kidnapping and murder of several children and teenagers, shifted attention to the judicial system. Questions were raised about incompetence, nepotism and rivalry among police forces and prosecutors. A parliamentary inquiry exposed serious faults and shortcomings, but failed to give evidence of any kind of deliberate protection of Dutroux or his fellows by politicians and prosecutors. In April 1998, there was further outrage when Dutroux escaped for a short time from a courthouse. Multi-party talks were held, in order to find the broadest possible agreement on substantial reforms of police and justice.

[23] A series of scandals which came to light in 1996, in addition to pressure from the Vlaams Blok, called into question the very existence of the country. A serious case of pornography trade and paedophilia cast major doubts on the political, judicial and police institutions since incompetence, rivalry and corruption were proved in various districts.

[24] The discovery of animal-derived foods contaminated with dioxins caused a shock in the population a few days before the 1999 elections. The scandal brought Dehaene down and allowed into the political arena a coalition headed by Guy Verhofstadt, leader of the liberal Walloons. Verhofstadt formed a coalition with socialists and greens from both linguistic communities, leaving the Christian Democrats out of office for the first time in 41 years. Magda Aelvoet, former green political chief in the European parliament was named Minister of Health, responsible for the control of food and for overcoming the crisis caused by the dioxin scandal. ■

PROFILE

ENVIRONMENT

Northwestern Belgium is a lowland, the Plains of Flanders, composed of sand and clay deposited by its rivers. In southern Belgium the southern highlands rise to 700 m on the Ardennes Plateau. One of the most densely populated European countries, its prosperity rests on trade, helped by its geography and by the transport network covering the northern plains, converging at the port of Antwerp. Belgium has highly intensive agriculture, and a major industrial center. Heavy industry was located near the coal fields of the Sambre-Meuse valley, and textiles were traditionally concentrated in Flanders, where new industries have developed since the late 1960s. Water protection laws were approved in 1971. However, the Meuse River, supplying 5 million people with drinking water, is contaminated by industrial waste. Pollution, by the excessive use of both animal wastes and chemical fertilizers, has increased the nitrate concentration in many rivers and accounts for the presence of algae. Belgian smokestack industries contribute to air pollution in Europe, and are responsible for acid rain in neighboring countries.

SOCIETY

Peoples: The country's two major language-based groups are the Flemish (55 per cent) and the Walloons (44 per cent). There is also a German minority (1 per cent). Many industrial workers are immigrants (Italian, Moroccan and, in lesser numbers, Turkish and African). Foreigners represent about 9 per cent of the whole population.
Religions: Mainly Catholic. **Languages:** French, Dutch and German are the official languages. French is the main language spoken in the south and east, and Dutch in the north and west, while German is spoken by 0.6 per cent of the population. Brussels is bilingual. **Political Parties:** Flemish Liberal Party (VLD); Flemish Christian People's Party (CVP); French-speaking Social Christians (PSC); French-speaking Socialists (PS); Flemish Socialists (SP); French-speaking Liberal Party (PRL); Green parties (AGALEV/ECOLO); Flemish nationalists (VU); and extreme right parties (Vlaams Blok, FN). **Social Organizations:** The General Labor Federation of Belgium (ABVV/FGTB), Confederation of Christian Labor Unions of Belgium (ACV/CSC).

THE STATE

Official Name: Royaume de Belgique/ Koninkrijk België.
Capital: Brussels (Bruxelles/Brussel) 1,840,000 people (1997). Brussels is also the capital of the European Union. **Other cities:** Antwerp 932,000 people; Liège 590,000; Charleroi 426,000; Ghent 228,000 (1997).
Government: Parliamentary monarchy. The Head of State is King Albert II, since August 1 1993. Prime Minister, Guy Verhofstadt, a Flemish Liberal (VDL), since July 1999. **National Holiday:** July 21, National Day (date King Leopold I came to the throne, 1831). **Armed Forces:** 53,000. Conscription was abolished in 1994 and there is now only the professional army.

Belize

Belize

Population: 235,000 (1999)
Area: 22,696 SQ KM
Capital: Belmopan
Currency: Belize dollar
Language: English

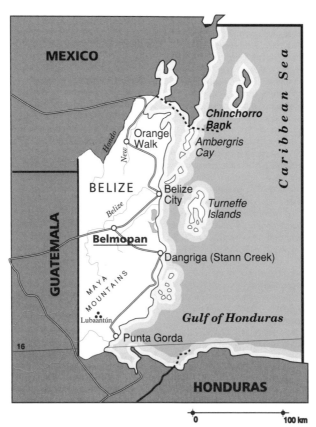

Native American people known as the Itzae were the original occupants of what is now Belize (formerly British Honduras). Belize, together with Guatemala and southern Mexico, formed part of the Mayan empire. In Belize, the Mayas built the cities of Lubaantún, Pusilhá, and a third which archaeologists call San José (its original name is unknown).

2 In 1504 Columbus sailed into the bay naming it the Gulf of Honduras. Spain was nominally the colonial power in the region, but never pushed further into Belize, because of tough resistance from the local people. According to the terms of the Treaty of Paris (1763) Spain allowed the British to start exploiting timber in the area. This authorization was later confirmed in the Treaty of Versailles (1783). From the Captaincy-General of Yucatan (now Mexico) the Spaniards tried on several occasions to drive out the British, many of whom were involved in piracy. In 1798 the British gained control of the colony, although Spain retained sovereignty until it became a British colony in 1862. As of 1871 the Crown took charge of local government with the territory administered by the governor of Jamaica until 1884.

3 By the second half of the 17th century, some British entrepreneurs attracted in particular by cedar, campeche wood, and timber, started establishing themselves in the depopulated coastal areas, importing African slaves to work their estates. Shortly afterwards, slaves outnumbered Europeans, and in 1784 only 10 per cent of the population was of European extraction, a ratio which has been steadily decreasing.

4 The ethnic base became more heterogeneous in the early 19th century. By that time, Garifuna migrants had settled on the Southern coast of Belize. The War of Castes in Yucatan between 1847 and 1853 displaced thousands of Spanish-speaking inhabitants to the northern coast of Belize, while several Maya communities re-settled in the northern and western areas of the country. These immigrants introduced changes in agricultural techniques which set the pattern for subsistence farming and set the basis of sugar, banana and citrus production. During the 1860s and 1870s, sugarcane

plantation owners sponsored the migration of several thousand workers from China and India. By the end of that century, Maya and Kekchi indigenous peoples, who had escaped oppression in Guatemala, established self-sufficient communities in the south and west of Belize.

5 By the early 20th century, this ethnic mix had become settled. However, the economy was stagnant and the British colonial administration prevented any democratic participation. In 1931, a hurricane destroyed a large part of Belize City. Strikes and demonstrations by workers and the unemployed gave rise to unions and increasing demands for democracy. Eligibility for voting was legally introduced in 1936, but it was heavily restricted by literacy, land titles and gender requirements. In 1949 when the Governor devalued the national currency, union leaders and the local middle class joined in a People's Committee which demanded constitutional changes.

6 In 1950 the People's United Party (PUP) was founded, led by

George Price. First organized as a "people's committee" to fight against arbitrary treatment by the colonial administration, the PUP won its first elections by a landslide majority. In 1954 universal suffrage was granted, and the majority of the legislative representatives were elected directly. In 1961 a ministerial system of government was established, and in 1964 the country was granted internal autonomy, with George Price becoming Prime Minister. On June 1 1973 the country changed its name from British Honduras to Belize.

7 Guatemala claimed to have inherited sovereignty over Belize from Spain, and did not recognize the Guatemala-Belize border. In March 1981, Guatemala and Britain signed a 16-point agreement. Britain assured the future independence of Belize in exchange for some concessions to the Guatemalan regime, such as free and permanent access to the Atlantic, joint exploitation of the marine resources, the building of a pipeline, and an "anti-terrorist" agreement.

8 Tourism brought in $4 million in 1983, but this was way behind the $36 million earned by sugar.

9 Price and the PUP were accused of partiality towards Cuba and Nicaragua, an issue exploited by the right-wing opposition, the United Democratic Party (UDP), which won 21 out of 28 seats in the December 1984 elections.

10 The new Prime Minister, Manuel Esquivel, a US-educated physics professor, adopted a liberal economic policy and supported the private import-export sector, which was in the hands of inexperienced family business ventures. He also encouraged foreign investment and sought to attract US, Jamaican, and Mexican investments in tourism, energy, and agriculture. The previous government had bequeathed Belize one of the most liberal set of laws concerning foreign investment in the Third World.

11 Sugarcane generated 50 per cent of the country's revenue, but a fall in international prices badly affected the economy. The industry only survived because of import quotas guaranteed by the US and EEC markets, which took 60 per cent of the sugar output, with the remainder being sold at a loss.

12 In March 1986, Prime Minister Esquivel proposed a plan for the sale of Belizean citizenship, aimed primarily at Hong Kong business people, as Hong Kong was due to revert to China in 1997. Anyone investing $25,000 in government bonds - really worth only $12,500 - would be granted instant citizenship of Belize.

13 During the 1980s, the country received approximately 40,000 Salvadoran, Guatemalan, Honduran and Nicaraguan refugees. In spite of official tolerance, some officials blamed immigrants for the dramatic rise in marijuana trafficking and crime.

14 When Vinicio Cerezo became President of Guatemala, relations between the countries changed substantially. In December 1986, Cerezo's government re-established diplomatic relations with Britain, broken off two decades earlier over Guatemalan claims to Belizean territory. A Permanent Joint Commission was formed with Belizean, Guatemalan and British representatives to find a peaceful solution to the issue.

15 In spite of the existence of the Commission, Belize feared a

STATISTICS

DEMOGRAPHY

Population: 235,000 (1999)
Annual growth: 2.4 % (1975/97)
Estimates for year 2015 (million): 0.3 (1999)
Annual growth to year 2015: 2.0 % (1997/2015)
Urban population: 46.4 % (1997)
Children per woman: 3.6 (1998)

HEALTH

Life expectancy at birth: 75 years (1998)
male: 73 years (1998)
female: 76 years (1998)
Maternal mortality: 140 per 100,000 live births (1990-98)
Infant mortality: 35 per 1,000 (1998)
Under-5 child mortality: 43 per 1,000 (1998)
Daily calorie supply: 2,862 per capita (1996)
47 doctors per 100,000 people (1993)
Safe water: 83 % (1990/98)

EDUCATION

Literacy: 70 % (1995)
male: 70 % (1995)
female: 70 % (1995)
School enrolment:
Primary total: 121 % (1990/96)
male: 124 % (1990/97)
female: 118 % (1990/97)
Secondary:
male: 47 % (1990/96)
female: 52 % (1990/96)
Tertiary: 1 % (1996)
Primary school teachers: one for every 26 (1994)

COMMUNICATIONS

594 radios (1997), 180 TV sets (1996) and 133 main telephone lines (1996) per 1,000 people
Books: 34 new titles per 100,000 people (1992/94)

ECONOMY

Per capita, GNP: $ 2,660 (1998)
Annual growth, GNP: 3.0 % (1998)
Consumer price index: 106.6 (1998)
Cereal imports: 19,220 metric tons (1998)
Food import dependency: 20 % (1997)
Fertilizer use: 750 kg per ha (1997)
Exports: $ 330 million (1998)
Imports: $ 363 million (1998)
External debt: $ 338 million (1998); $ 1,468 per capita (1998)
Development aid received: $ 14 million (1997); $ 72.1 per capita (1997); 2.30 % of GNP (1997)

HDI (rank/value): 83/0.732 (1997)

Guatemalan invasion and kept a standing army of 1,800 British troops. Esquivel declared in Mexico that he "would not allow the installation of US military bases", stressing that he did not wish to become involved in the Central American crisis.

[16] However, the number of US embassy personnel grew sixfold after independence and the number of Peace Corps volunteers was ten times higher. Dean Barrow, Minister of Foreign Affairs and Economic Development, admitted that he was aware of the country's dependence upon the US. But he also stated that Belize could defend its territorial integrity through the Non-Aligned Movement.

[17] Drug-trafficking - or the sale of "Belize breeze" as marijuana is known - showed spectacular growth. According to some foreign economists, it became the country's main export, and it was estimated that some 700 tons - worth at least $100 million had been taken into the US, where the resale price was at least ten times this sum. The area under cultivation increased by at least 20 per cent in spite of a US-sponsored herbicide-spraying campaign carried out with Mexican helicopters.

[18] George Price was returned to power when the PUP won the September 1989 elections with 15 of the 28 seats. The 13 remaining seats went to Esquivel's UDP.

[19] In September 1991 Guatemalan President Jorge Serrano Elias finally recognized Belize's sovereignty and right to self-determination. The Government of Belize in turn gave Guatemala free access to the Gulf of Honduras, thereby reducing its own territorial waters.

[20] At the end of the 1980s and early 1990s a large number of Haitians went to Belize as agricultural laborers, attracted by higher wages than at home. Lower inflation rates and more equal income distribution were incentives for immigration, and they also had access to health and education services. The social services consequently became overloaded, triggering a backlash from Belizeans who demanded that the Haitians be repatriated.

[21] A 1992 census revealed that the Spanish-speaking mestizo population had outgrown the English-speaking population of African origin who, together with the European descendants, had historically been the dominant group.

[22] Banana, sugar and citrus production increased, representing 40 per cent of the country's total production and four-fifths of its exports. Tourism became the sector with the greatest potential. Several environmental organizations cooperated in protecting nature

PROFILE

ENVIRONMENT

Belize covers the southeastern tip of the Yucatan Peninsula. The land is low, and the climate warm and rainy in the north. In southern Belize, the hillsides sustain a variety of crops. The northern coastline is marshy and flanked by low islands. In the south there are excellent natural harbors between reefs. Significant oil and gas deposits are believed to exist off the coast. The country shares many of the problems of the Caribbean region, including the deterioration of its water-quality and soil erosion. Close to the cities, the surface of the water is covered with residual wastes and by-products of sugar cane production. Industrial waste, dumped in the water, has generated public health problems and killed fish stocks.

SOCIETY

Peoples: Spanish-Indian descendants 43.6 per cent; Creole (predominantly black) 29.8 per cent; Mayan Indian 11.0 per cent; Garifuna (African-Carib Indian) 6.7 per cent; white 3.9 per cent; East Indian 3.5 per cent; other or not stated 1.5 per cent.
Religions: 60 per cent are Catholic, most of the rest are Protestant (34 per cent). **Languages:** English (official); Spanish; Mayan dialects are also spoken. **Political Parties:** The People's United Party (PUP), founded in 1950; The United Democratic Party (UDP); the National Alliance for the Rights of Belize, founded in 1992 by members of the UDP opposed to compromise with Guatemala. **Social Organizations:** The General Workers' Union, the Christian Workers' Union (CWU), the United General Federation, the General Federation of Workers and the Public Service Union of Belize.

THE STATE

Official Name: Belize. **Administrative divisions:** 6 districts.
Capital: Belmopan 3,900 people (est. 1996). **Other cities:** Belize City 47,700 people; Orange Walk 12,155; San Ignacio/Santa Elena 9,890; Corozal 8,158 (1996); Dangriga (formerly known as Stann Creek) 7,700 (1986). **Government:** Parliamentary monarchy, Queen Elizabeth II of England is Head of State. Colville Young, Governor-General since 1995. Said Wilbert Musa, Prime Minister since August 1998 (PUP). Legislative power lies with the House of Representatives, which has 28 members and is elected by universal suffrage, and an 8-member Senate appointed by the Governor-General. **National Holidays:** September 10, National Day; September 21, Independence Day (1981). **Armed Forces:** 1,065 (1995).

---

reserves and attempts to improve the quality of the Caribbean waters. Mayan archeological discoveries attracted many visitors.

[23] Hours after Guatemala's President Serrano was ousted on June 1 1993, Price brought the election date forward 15 months, counting on a new PUP victory to ratify agreements made with this neighbor. His opponent Manuel Esquivel questioned the validity of Price's concessions to Guatemala, and proposed that these be legitimized by a referendum.

[24] In the June 1993 elections the PUP was pushed out by the UDP, led by Esquivel's mestizo-dominated UDP. In March 1994, the UDP also won the elections for the nation's 7 local councils. The Government formed a group of economic advisors to look into establishing facilities for the capital and tourist markets, and the development of one or more free zones. The fear of new territorial demands from Guatemala and the withdrawal of British troops led to an increase in defence spending and new recruitment for the armed forces.

[25] In January 1995 Prime Minister Esquivel reshuffled his cabinet in an attempt to control the recession and the crime wave. The Government founded a committee to renew the economic citizenship programme (closed in June 1994) in order to attract investors and reduce the foreign debt. It also froze public sector salaries for the 1995-1996 period to reduce the fiscal deficit.

[26] In the March 1997 municipal elections, the opposition PUP took the majority of the seven local councils for the first time in the history of the country. In April, Esquivel made further changes to the cabinet; some ministers were given new portfolios and others were made ambassadors abroad.

[27] In late October, Hurricane Mitch, which killed thousands of people on its way through Central America, caused enormous damage to the economic infrastructure of the country.

[28] The August 1998 general elections were won by the PUP, which took 26 seats, with Said Wilbert Musa made Prime Minister. The Democratic Party was left with only 3 seats. ∎

Benin

Benin

Population: 5,937,000 (1999)
Area: 112,620 SQ KM
Capital: Porto Novo
Currency: CFA franc
Language: French

B enin (known as Dahomey until 1975) is among the poorest countries in the world. It lies in the region of the Yoruba culture, which developed at the ancient city of Ife. It was here that the Ewe peoples, who came from the same linguistic family developed into two distinct kingdoms during the 17th century: Hogbonu (today known as Porto Novo) and Abomey, further inland. These states developed around the booming slave trade, serving as intermediaries.

2 The traditional rulers of Abomey, the Fon, built a centralized state that extended east and west beyond Benin's present-day frontiers. A well-disciplined army, with European rifles and a large contingent of female soldiers enabled them to end the patronage of the Alafin of Oyo (Nigeria) and capture various Yoruba cities. After the 17th century, Ouidah became the main port for British, French and Portuguese slave traders receiving their human cargo.

3 The ruling group of Abomey suffered a setback in 1818 when Britain banned the slave trade, although Ghezo who ruled between 1818 and 1856 maintained a thriving clandestine traffic to Brazil and Cuba. He also promoted the development of agriculture and established a strict state monopoly on foreign trade.

4 In 1889, Ghezo's grandson Benhanzin inherited a prosperous state, but one already threatened by colonialism. In 1891, Fon troops resisted the French invasion only to be defeated a year later. The King and his army retreated to the forests, where they held out until 1894. Benhanzin, who became a symbol of anti-colonial resistance, died in exile in Martinique in 1906.

5 The colonists destroyed the centralized political structure of the ancient Fon state. Traditional Fon society was dismantled and replaced with a system based on the exploitation of farm labor. The French also declared a monopoly on the palm-oil trade and ruined families that had resisted foreign penetration for nearly a century.

6 By the beginning of the 20th century, the colony of Dahomey (as the French called it), was no longer self-sufficient. When it gained independence in August 1960, oil-seed exports stood at 1850 levels, while the population had tripled.

7 Independence came as a direct consequence both of France's weakness at the end of World War II and the activities of European-educated nationalists, led by Louis Hunkanrin, who waged a stubborn 20-year struggle against the compulsory labor imposed by the French. All forms of political organization were banned and in retaliation, Hunkanrin created the Human Rights League. A period of ruthless repression followed: hundreds of villages were burned down, nearly 5,000 people were killed, and Hunkanrin took refuge in Mauritania.

8 By 1960, Dahomey had become an unbearable economic burden and France agreed to independence. The new Government inherited a bankrupt economy and a corrupt infrastructure. A series of 12 military and civilian governments marked a 16-year period of instability.

9 The neocolonial elite collapsed in 1972 when then-Major Mathieu Kerekou headed a coup by a group of young officers opposed to political corruption and official despotism. Two years later, a Marxist-Leninist state was proclaimed and its name changed to Benin, with a communitarian political and economic system. All foreign property was nationalized, and a single-party system was introduced with the creation of the People's Revolutionary Party.

10 The revolutionary Government became the target of several conspiracies plotted abroad. There was an unsuccessful invasion in January 1977 with the participation of French mercenaries and the support of Gabon and Morocco.

11 In 1980, a new Revolutionary Assembly was elected through direct vote. The Government switched to a more pragmatic foreign policy and diplomatic relations with France were resumed. Although palm-oil production continued to drop as the trees grew older, cotton and sugar sales rose. High unemployment continued, but in 1982 offshore oil was discovered thus guaranteeing energy self-sufficiency. In addition large phosphate deposits were discovered in the Mekrou region.

12 Hopes of recovery dimmed as drought reached the northern provinces. Desertification was exacerbated, and the region was

WORKERS

% OF LABOUR FORCE **1998**

■ FEMALE: 48%   ■ MALE: 52%

1990

■ SERVICES: 28.4%
■ INDUSTRY: 8.1%
■ AGRICULTURE: 63.5%

LAND USE

DEFORESTATION: 1.2% annual (1990/95)
IRRIGATED: 0.7% of arable (1993)

1993

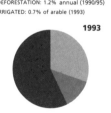

■ FOREST & WOODLAND: 30.2%
■ ARABLE: 12.7%
■ OTHER: 57.1%

PUBLIC EXPENDITURE

DEFENCE EXPENDITURE
(% of goverment exp.)   **6.8%** (1995)

MATERNAL MORTALITY

1990-98

Per 100,000 live births

500

LITERACY

1995

32%

unable to supply its own food even in traditional subsistence crops such as manioc, yams, corn and sorghum.

[13] To make matters worse, Nigeria cracked down on immigrants, expelling thousands back to Benin and closing the border.

[14] The economic crisis forced the Government to accept the terms of the International Monetary Fund, including a 10 per cent income tax and a 50 per cent reduction in non-wage social benefits. In January 1989 students, teachers and other educational bodies staged a strike demanding back pay and scholarship payments which had not been honored.

[15] On December 8 1989, disappointed with results and besieged by street demonstrations, President Kerekou announced that he was abandoning his Marxist-Leninism. A new constitution was drawn up, providing for a series of political and economic reforms, especially the promotion of free enterprise.

[16] On March 24 1991 Prime Minister Nicéphore Soglo defeated President Kerekou with 68 per cent of the votes in the country's first presidential election in 30 years. In 1992, former President Kerekou, prosecuted for his activities following the 1972 coup was granted an amnesty, and political prisoners were released.

[17] Soglo continued the economic liberalization and privatization policy initiated by Kerekou in 1986. Debt servicing still represented a high percentage of the resources annually obtained (in 1992 debt service was equivalent to 27 per cent of the country's income).

[18] The 100 per cent devaluation of the CFA franc decreed by France in January 1994 provoked contradictory effects in Benin's economy. GDP continued to grow at a 4 per cent annual rate and cotton exports increased. However, public expenditure cuts - aimed among other things at curbing inflation after the devaluation - brought about drastic reductions in social spending schemes.

[19] In July 1994, Soglo assumed the leadership of the Renaissance Party of Benin (RPB), founded by his wife Rosine in 1992. The RPB was defeated in the legislative and municipal elections of March 1995 by the opposition Democratic Renewal Party (DRP). In May 1995 the Government banned food exports to reduce local prices and curb inflation, at the same time that it refused to increase salaries.

[20] Soglo's "clannish" style and his tendency to rule together with his family not only angered the political class in Benin. In the general elections held in March 1996, Soglo suffered a narrow defeat by Kerekou, the former leader of the Marxist regime. In April, the World Bank stated that Benin's economic reform had made little progress and refused to renegotiate the $98 million loan which the National Assembly had rejected late in 1995.

[21] Between August and October 1997, disease killed around 60,000 pigs - 10 per cent of the country's stock of swine. The AIDS spread is likely to reduce life expectancy by ten years.

[22] In November, the unions called for a 72-hour strike protesting against the budget for the following year. The country's five unions called for a strike in February 1998 against "the antisocial budget for 1998, the dictates of the IMF, the World Bank and the European Union, as well as widespread corruption encouraged by Kérékou's government". The Government answered with a $10 million increase in public spending, a move deemed insufficient by the unions which called for a general strike. In January 1999 the IMF granted the country a $14 million loan at the lowest interest rates.

[23] The March parliamentary elections, in which 56 political parties took part, resulted in the victory of the president's party. Prime Minister Adrien Houngdedji resigned but was not replaced, his duties being taken over by Kérékou.

[24] In January 2000 the President denounced a conspiracy against his government by members of the army, specifically former members of regional peacekeeping forces. Former peacekeepers had staged a coup in Côte d'Ivoire in December 1999, while in Mali a similar attempt by former peacekeepers, demanding the payment of back wages, had just been put down. ∎

PROFILE

ENVIRONMENT

Benin is a narrow strip of land which extends north from the Gulf of Guinea. Its 120-km sandy coast lacks natural ports. Several natural regions cut across the country from south to north: the coastal belt where oil palms are cultivated; the tropical wooded lowlands; and the plateau which rises gradually towards the headwaters of the Queme, Mekrou, Alibori and Pendjari rivers, in a region of tropical hills. One of the major environmental problems is desertification, which has been aggravated in recent years by a significant decrease in rainfall.

SOCIETY

Peoples: Benin's people stem from 60 ethnic groups. The Fon (47 per cent), Adja, Yoruba and Bariba groups are the most numerous and before French colonization they had already developed very stable political institutions.
Religion: 70 per cent practise traditional African religions, 15 per cent are Muslim and 15 per cent Catholic.
Languages: French (official). Other widely-spoken languages are Fon, Fulani, Mine, Yoruba and Massi.
Political parties: Democratic Renewal Party (PRD); Renaissance Party of Benin (RPB).
Social organizations: The Benin Workers' National Trade Union (UNSTB).

THE STATE

Official name: République Populaire du Bénin.
Capital: Porto Novo 200,000 people (1998).
Other cities: Cotonou 533,000 people; Djougou 132,000; Abomey-Calavi 125,000; Parakou 106,000 (1992).
Government: Presidential republic. Mathieu Kérékou, President, elected in March 1996. Single chamber parliament.
National Holidays: July 1, Independence (1960); November 30, Revolution Day (1974).
Armed Forces: 4,800.
Other: Gendarmerie: 2,000; People's Militia: 1,500-2,000.

STATISTICS

DEMOGRAPHY

Population: 5,937,000 (1999)
Annual growth: 2.8 % (1975/97)
Estimates for year 2015 (million): 8.9 (1999)
Annual growth to year 2015: 2.6 % (1997/2015)
Urban population: 39.9 % (1997)
Urban Growth: 5.1 % (1980/95)
Children per woman: 5.8 (1998)

HEALTH

Life expectancy at birth: 53 years (1998)
male: 52 years (1998)
female: 55 years (1998)
Maternal mortality: 500 per 100,000 live births (1990-98)
Infant mortality: 101 per 1,000 (1998)
Under-5 child mortality: 165 per 1,000 (1998)
Daily calorie supply: 2,415 per capita (1996)
6 doctors per 100,000 people (1993)
Safe water: 56 % (1990/98)

EDUCATION

Literacy: 32 % (1995)
male: 45 % (1995)
female: 19 % (1995)
School enrolment:
Primary total: 76 % (1990/96)
male: 96 % (1990/97)
female: 56 % (1990/97)
Secondary:
male: 23 % (1990/96)
female: 10 % (1990/96)
Tertiary: 3 % (1996)
Primary school teachers: one for every 52 (1995)

COMMUNICATIONS

2 newspapers (1996), 108 radios (1997), 73 TV sets (1996) and 6 main telephone lines (1996) per 1,000 people
Books: 2 new titles per 100,000 people (1992/94)

ECONOMY

Per capita, GNP: $ 380 (1998)
Annual growth, GNP: 4.7 % (1998)
Annual inflation: 10.1 % (1990/98)
Consumer price index: 114.8 (1998)
Currency: 590.0 CFA francs = $ 1 (1998)
Cereal imports: 123,870 metric tons (1998)
Fertilizer use: 256 kg per ha (1997)
Exports: $ 537 million (1998)
Imports: $ 740 million (1998)
External debt: $ 1,647 million (1998); $ 285 per capita (1998)
Debt service: 10.6 % of exports (1998)
Development aid received: $ 225 million (1997); $ 46.1 per capita (1997); 10.70 % of GNP (1997)

ENERGY

Consumption: 377.0 Kgs of Oil equivalent per capita yearly (1997); 13.0 % imported (1997)

HDI (rank/value): 155/0.421 (1997)

Bermuda

Bermuda

Population: 60,000 (1999)
Area: 53 SQ KM
Capital: Hamilton
Currency: Bermuda dollar
Language: English

The Bermuda archipelago was the first colony of the British Empire. Sighted by the Spanish navigator Juan Bermúdez in 1503, it was settled in 1609 when British emigrants on their way to America were shipwrecked nearby.

[2] From 1612, the colony welcomed religious and political dissidents. In 1684, it began to be administrated by the British Crown, and the first parliament was installed. Even though African slaves formed the majority, only plantation owners could elect representatives.

[3] Agriculture almost disappeared in the 20th century, being replaced by tourism, gambling and transnational corporations lured by numerous tax exemptions. During the Prohibition (1919-1933) traffickers living in Bermuda smuggled rum into the United States. From 1941, Washington set up air and naval bases on the islands and has completely replaced the British military presence since 1957.

[4] After the creation of the Bermuda Industrial Union (BIU), in 1963 workers founded the Progressive Labor Party (PLP), which favored the country's total independence and the introduction of an income tax. The following year, the Right organized the United Bermuda Party (UBP).

[5] In 1968, Britain granted the islands greater administrative autonomy, and the majority party was given the right to name the prime minister. The period leading up to the elections was marked by racial and political violence. The assassination of the governor led to intervention by British troops. When the election was held, the UBP won by a large margin.

[6] In the 1976 election, the PLP increased its number of seats. From its position in opposition, the PLP continued to demand greater autonomy for the island.

[7] In 1977, two members of the "Black Cadre" were sentenced to death, for participating in armed anticolonial activities. Their execution unleashed a wave of protests, with British troops intervening once again. The Minister of Communal (Race) Relations was sacked, and his duties delegated to the Bermuda Regiment, responsible for putting down protest and discontent.

[8] In spite of charges of racism, the European population supported the Government, while the black population opted for the PLP or more radical organizations.

[9] The 1979 Bermuda Constitutional Convention failed to reach a consensus on representation and the minimum voting age. However, a reduction in the number of non-Bermudan voters went into effect that December.

[10] The UBP won both the 1980 and 1983 elections, although the opposition increased its representation. With the UBP in power, the country continued without self-determination as the Government claimed that the majority was against this.

[11] The islands' strategic location along North Atlantic routes explained the continued presence of British, Canadian and US troops.

[12] In 1989 Prime Minister John Swan of the UBP was re-elected and his party gained 23 seats . The PLP obtained 15 seats; one seat went to the National Liberal Party (NLP), a center party, and the Environmental Party won one seat.

[13] In 1989 and 1990, unemployment rose by 0.5 per cent and 2 per cent, respectively. Employment within the industrial sector was 3.1 per cent. The US recession continued to affect tourism in the first few months of 1992. London rejected plans for independence.

[14] In 1992, Sir John Waddington was nominated Governor-General.

[15] Intense drug-trafficking in 1993 resulted in a major diversion of investment away from Bermuda. That year, measures also went into effect to control offshore banking operations.

[16] In the October 5 1993 elections, J Irving Pearman was elected vice-premier. The UBP retained its majority in the Assembly with 22 seats while the PLP, led by Frederick Wade, confirmed its growth with 18 seats.

[17] In August 1995, a referendum was held regarding the Prime Minister's proposal on independence. The result was negative and so Bermuda remained a British colony.

[18] In March 1997, following the resignation of David Saul, Pamela Gordon took over as Prime Minister. In June, Thorold Masefield was appointed governor.

[19] The PLP won the November 1998 elections with 54 per cent of the votes (26 seats), while the UBP only managed to retain 44 per cent of the votes (14 seats). The remaining parties did not obtain one per cent of the total votes and were therefore left without parliamentary representation. ∎

PROFILE

ENVIRONMENT

This Atlantic archipelago is made up of 360 small coral islands, characterized by chalky, permeable soil. Bermuda includes 150 of these islands, of which 20 are uninhabited. The warm Gulf Stream current produces a mild climate which attracts tourists, mainly from the US.

SOCIETY

Peoples: Approximately 60 per cent are of African descent; there are also descendants of Portuguese from Madeira and the Azores; mixed European and Indian descendants and a minority of European origin.
Religions: Anglican majority (28 per cent), in addition to Methodists (12 per cent), Adventists (6 per cent), Catholics (15 per cent) and members of other religions.
Languages: English (official).
Political parties: The United Bermuda Party (UBP); Progressive Labor Party (PLP); National Liberal Party; Environmental Party.
Social organizations: Bermuda Industrial Union (5,202 members); Bermuda Public Service Association (2,300 members).

THE STATE

Official Name: Bermuda.
Capital: Hamilton, 6,000 people (1991).
Other cities: St George's, 3,000 people (1991).
Government: British dependency. Thorold Masefield, Governor since June 1997; nominated by Queen Elizabeth II. Prime Minister Jennifer Smith since November 1998. The Prime Minister appoints the cabinet on approval by the Governor. Bicameral parliament: Senate has 11 members, 5 elected by the Prime Minister, 3 by the opposition leader and 3 by the Governor. Assembly has 40 members elected for a 5-year term. **National Holiday:** May 24, Bermuda Day.

Bhutan

Druk Yul

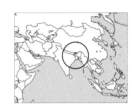

Population: 2,064,000 (1999)
Area: 47,000 SQ KM
Capital: Thimbu
Currency: Ngultrum
Language: Dzongkha

B hutan lies in the heart of the vast Himalayan mountains. Early explorers and envoys of the British colonial Government called it Bootan, land of the Booteas, or sometimes Bhotan. Wedged between giant neighbors China and India and cut off by some of the world's highest peaks, it was little known to the rest of the world. Even today, the origin of its name remains unknown. Perhaps it came from the Sanskrit Bhot'ante ("the end of Tibet") or from another Sanskrit word Bhu'nthan ("high land"). To the people of Bhutan it is Druk or Druk Yul, land of the Thunder Dragon. The name is derived from the Kargyud Sect of Mahayana Buddhism (Drukpa), now the state religion, which flourished in the 7th century.

[2] From the 12th century, the Drukpa Kargyud tradition became dominant. After a long period of rivalry among various groups, the country was united by a Drukpa Kargyud Lama named Ngawang Namgyal in the 17th century. Namgyal, popularly known as Shabdrung ("at whose feet one submits"), was both the country's spiritual and secular ruler. Factionalism gradually eroded the power of the subsequent Shabdrungs. On December 17 1907 Ugen Wangchuk united the country and established Bhutan's first hereditary monarchy.

[3] The British colonial administration in India signed important treaties with Bhutan in 1774 and 1865. The 1910 Treaty of Punakha stipulated that the British would not interfere in Bhutan's internal affairs, but made the country a British protectorate in terms of external relations. Similar provisions were included in the

1949 treaty signed between Bhutan and independent India.

[4] Bhutan emerged from its self-imposed isolation in the 1960s, by joining the Colombo Plan in 1962 and the Universal Postal Union in 1969. A department of foreign affairs established in 1970 was upgraded to ministerial rank in 1971. That same year, Bhutan became a member of the United Nations, opened a diplomatic mission in New Delhi and a permanent mission to the UN in New York. It also became a member of the Non-Aligned Movement.

[5] Present King Jigme Singye Wangchuk, fourth in line to the throne, was crowned in 1972. His father, the late King Jigme Dorji Wangchuk, was considered the architect of modern Bhutan. Under his rule, the political and administrative machinery were restructured and modernized, and successive 5-year development plans were initiated.

[6] Agriculture and animal husbandry are the predominant means of livelihood in the country. As Bhutan opened up, the development of an economic infrastructure became a priority. A road network, particularly important with the closure of the Tibetan border in 1960, is now in place across the country, with arterial routes heading south toward India.

[7] Many rivers and water falls have been exploited as sources of hydroelectric energy. The massive Chukha project lies on the main route between Phuntsholing and Thimbu. With a potential of 8,000 megawatts, it supplies electricity not only within Bhutan, but also to adjacent parts of India. Parts of southern Bhutan have been linked with the Indian grid system, but 80 per cent of the population lack electricity.

[8] The first chemical industry, Bhutan Carbide and Chemicals Ltd., started production in June 1988. The Bhutan Development Finance Corporation (BDFC) was also established in 1988 to encourage rapid expansion of the private sector. A rural credit scheme introduced in 1982 under the Royal Monetary Authority was brought under the auspices of the BDFC.

[9] The semblance of political stability which the Government attempts to project abroad has been seriously affected by the various opposition groups campaigning for the democratization of the country. The main agitator among these movements is a group representing

the Nepalese minority which has been extremely active in recent years.

[10] Ethnic friction has been on the increase since the 1988 census, when the King stepped up his "Bhutanization" campaign, prohibiting the public wearing of the national dress - the *ko* for men and the *kira* for women - as well as use of the Dzongkha language. Teaching in Nepalese was also forbidden, tourists were barred from sacred sites, and television signals from India were blocked. Work visas for foreigners were also outlawed.

[11] These measures infuriated the Nepalese minority (25 per cent of the population) who immediately rejected them. However, their demands were met with intransigence on the part of the monarchy, on various occasions.

[12] In September 1990, demonstrations and street protests by the banned Bhutan People's Party (BPP) were repressed by Government forces in Thimbu. Opposition groups claimed that 300 people were killed in the incidents.

[13] The BPP was founded by a group of students of Nepalese origin to represent the Nepalese minority and fight for an end to Drukpa domination (a sect of Tibetan Buddhism), to achieve a more democratic constitution, and legalization of the political parties.

[14] Since September 1990, social agitation has increased: Nepalese commandos set fire to schools and destroyed bridges, they also carried out kidnappings to raise money, and the Government blamed them for no fewer than 30 violent deaths.

[15] In the early 1990s Bhutan depended on India for its imports of consumer goods, fuel, grain, machinery, replacement parts, vehicles and exports with 93 per cent of its produce sold to India. The main Bhutanese exports are hydroelectric energy, cement, handcrafts, fruits and spices such as cardamoms.

[16] In the past few years, Bhutan tried to diversify foreign trade. India, Norway, Kuwait, Japan and Switzerland - amongst other countries - financed a number of development programs.

[17] Attempts to introduce a market economy constantly come up against the fact that Bhutan is among the world's 42 least developed countries. In addition,

WORKERS

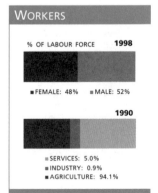

% OF LABOUR FORCE   **1998**

■FEMALE: 48%   ■MALE: 52%

1990

■SERVICES: 5.0%
■INDUSTRY: 0.9%
■AGRICULTURE: 94.1%

LAND USE

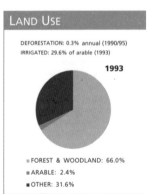

DEFORESTATION: 0.3% annual (1990/95)
IRRIGATED: 29.6% of arable (1993)

1993

■FOREST & WOODLAND: 66.0%
■ARABLE: 2.4%
■OTHER: 31.6%

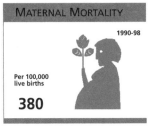

MATERNAL MORTALITY

1990-98

Per 100,000 live births

380

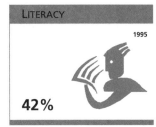

LITERACY

1995

42%

PROFILE

ENVIRONMENT

This Himalayan country is made up of three distinct climatic and geographical regions. The Duar plain in the south, humid and tropical, is densely wooded and ranges in height from 300 to 2,000 metres. At the centre lies a temperate region with heights of up to 3,000 metres. Finally, there are the great northern heights, with year-round snow and peaks that climb 8,000 metres high. Forests are the country's mainstay. Rivers and waterfalls have been exploited and they supply energy to the country and neighbouring areas. There are graphite, marble, granite and limestone deposits. Approximately half of the arable land lies on steep slopes; of this nearly 15 per cent is merely topsoil. The combination of these two factors makes the terrain very susceptible to erosion.

SOCIETY

Peoples: Bhutia (Ngalops) 50 per cent; Nepalese (Gurung) 35 per cent; Sharchops 15 per cent. There are also Lepchas, native people, and Santal, descended from Indian immigrants. 95 per cent of the teachers and 55 per cent of public servants are of Indian origin.
Religions: Buddhist 69.6 per cent; Hindu 24.6 per cent; Muslim 5.0 per cent; other 0.8 per cent (1980).
Languages: Dzongkha (official). Nepalese and other dialects are also spoken. **Political Parties:** The Bhutan People's Party (BPP), founded in Nepal in 1990; the National Bhutanese Congress founded in 1992, in Nepal and India; the People's Forum of Human Rights (PFHR), started in 1990, covering five refugee camps in Nepal; the United People's Liberation Front (UPLF), also founded in 1990.

THE STATE

Official Name: Druk Yul. **Administrative Divisions:** 18 Districts. **Capital:** Thimbu, 30,400 people (1993). **Government:** Jigme Singye Wangchuk, King since July 21 1972. The hereditary monarch is assisted by a council of 9 members, of whom 5 are elected by the people, 2 are appointed by the autocratic ruler and 2 by the Buddhist religious dignitaries whose 6,000 lamas (monks) are headed by the Je Khempo. Lyonpo Jigme Thimley was appointed as Prime Minister in August 1 1998. There is also a consultative assembly (*Tsogdu*) of 150 members 101 of whom are elected and 49 appointed, most being Buddhist monks. The ruler also dispenses justice. **National Holidays:** August 2, Buddhist Lent; October 30, end of Buddhist Lent.

---

the mountains make it difficult to build more highways and providing an adequate infrastructure is both costly and difficult. Peasants have been forced to work on such projects without remuneration.

[18] Despite these problems, the country's five-year plans have been followed and their timetables respected. As a result, the country's GNP grew in real terms by an annual average of 7.5 per cent between 1980 and 1990. Since 1992, the seventh plan has been implemented aiming to increase exports, conserve the environment, decentralize and promote women's rights. To achieve these aims the Government has encouraged foreign investment, receiving technical assistance from India. Likewise a cautious privatization

plan was introduced, with shares in state enterprises offered to the general public.

[19] Drastic cuts in public spending, the drive against nepotism and the voluntary reduction of the King's personal wealth - including moving from the royal palace into a modest home - encouraged international agencies to provide financing for development projects. Dependence upon foreign aid was consequently reduced from 50 per cent in 1982, to 20 per cent in 1992. The budget for 1994-95 revealed a new growth of international financial support: 41.6 per cent was contributions from the United Nations and other agencies and 21.2 per cent came from the Government of India.

[20] The country had frontier disputes with China and India. With

China the argument was over the sovereignty of the region of Arunachal Pradesh, while with India it concerned a small zone between Sarbhang and Gueyilegfug.

[21] In a country where neither political parties nor unions are permitted, the National Women's Association, one of the few social organizations, tried to encourage the "promotion" of Bhutanese women, seeking to make them branch out from their traditional agricultural activities into textile handcrafts.

[22] Up until 1996, the Nepalese Government had held seven fruitless meetings with the Bhutanese authorities about the 100,000 or so immigrants - Nepalese and Bhutanese of Nepalese origin - forced to flee or expelled from Bhutan, living in refugee camps. Since 1990, Bhutan has classed the refugees, called *Lhotsampas*, as having no nationality.

[23] In 1995, Nepalese activists claimed that over half the population of Bhutan was Nepalese, but government estimates said it was no more than a third. Most of the civil servants are of Indian origin.

[24] In 1996, the European Parliament condemned the Thimbu Government's human rights policies. Nepal proposed a survey to reveal the *Lhotsampas*' nationality, but Bhutan did not accept.

[25] On several occasions the government in New Delhi collaborated with Bhutan to keep opponents exiled in northern India under control, repressing several demonstrations against the Thimbu Government. Bhutan in turn supported India in international bodies. For example at the UN in September 1996 Bhutan voted against the suspension of nuclear tests alongside India and Libya.

[26] In early 1998, Amnesty International denounced a systematic government campaign against the opposition. Sympathizers of the National Bhutanese Congress (DNC), a party directed from exile in Nepal, had been illegally detained. According to Amnesty, most of these were Buddhist monks and religious teachers. The DNC was calling for democracy and respect for human rights.

[27] The King announced a series of changes during the latter half of that year. Parliament was granted the right to initiate legislation and to veto the King's decisions, as well as the right to ask the monarch to step down. The King named Lyonpo Jigme Thimley as Prime Minister. The opposition accused the King of presenting the reforms as a major advance - when in fact the legislation was introduced back in 1971 by his father and later revoked by the current king Jigme Singye Wangchuk. The opposition also claims that the King proposed the measure after placing his

followers in key parliamentary posts.

[28] When opposition groups decided to join forces in December 1998, Rongthong Kinley Torji, leader of the Druk National Congress, was elected leader of the movement. Hundreds of refugees who traveled to Nepal in January 1999 to join the pro-democracy demonstrations were retained in India, accused of illegally entering the country, and could not enter Bhutan. ∎

STATISTICS

DEMOGRAPHY

Population: 2,064,000 (1999)
Annual growth: 2.3 % (1975/97)
Estimates for year 2015 (million): 3.1 (1999)
Annual growth to year 2015: 2.6 % (1997/2015)
Urban population: 6.5 % (1997)
Children per woman: 5.5 (1998)

HEALTH

Life expectancy at birth: 61 years (1998)
male: 60 years (1998)
female: 62 years (1998)
Maternal mortality: 380 per 100,000 live births (1990-98)
Infant mortality: 84 per 1,000 (1998)
Under-5 child mortality: 116 per 1,000 (1998)
20 doctors per 100,000 people (1993)
Safe water: 58 % (1990/98)

EDUCATION

Literacy: 42 % (1995)
male: 56 % (1995)
female: 28 % (1995)
School enrolment:
Primary total: 25 % (1990/96)
male: 31 % (1990/97)
female: 19 % (1990/97)
Secondary:
male: 7 % (1990/96)
female: 2 % (1990/96)
Tertiary: 0 % (1996)

COMMUNICATIONS

60 radios (1997), 19 TV sets (1996) and 10 main telephone lines (1996) per 1,000 people

ECONOMY

Per capita, GNP: $ 470 (1998)
Annual growth, GNP: 5.5 % (1998)
Consumer price index: 115.9 (1997)
Cereal imports: 51,787 metric tons (1998)
Fertilizer use: 7 kg per ha (1997)
Exports: $ 132 million (1998)
Imports: $ 170 million (1998)
External debt: $ 120 million (1998); $ 60 per capita (1998)
Development aid received: $ 70 million (1997); $ 113.3 per capita (1997); 21.30 % of GNP (1997)

HDI (rank/value): 145/0.459 (1997)

Bolivia

Bolivia

Population: 8,142,000 (1999)
Area: 1,098,580 SQ KM
Capital: La Paz
Currency: Boliviano
Language: Spanish

I n 2000 BC the region of modern-day Bolivia was inhabited by farmers in the Andes, and forest hunter-gatherers in the east. Their terrain ranged from high mountain areas, *puna,* to hot valleys and forests. They raised livestock and grew potatoes, cotton, maize, and coca; they also fished and mined. This region, rich in natural resources, sustained several kingdoms and fiefdoms around Lake Titicaca, with the Tiahuanaco-Huari (600 BC-1000 AC) civilization at their center.

2   The basic social unit was the *ayllu* kinship group, in which there was no private land ownership. The society was stratified into farmers, artisans and the ruling *ayllu,* of priests and warriors, who appointed the *malku* (chief).

3   By 800 AD, Tiahuanaco formed the first Pan-Andean empire. By 1100, the *ayllu* of the Incas, from the Cusco Valley in Peru, had colonized the other Andean peoples and formed a confederation of states called the Tahuantinsuyo. Also known as the Inca empire, it adopted elements of Tiahuanaco culture, technology, religion and economics, particularly the *ayllu* social unit.

4   Through the mita, a mutual cooperation commitment between the different *ayllus,* each worker would render service to the centralized state; this system was later cruelly exploited by the Spaniards. The social structure was rigid; at the top was the Inca (son of the Sun), followed by the nobility and the priests. Then came the *capac,* governors of the regions into which the empire was divided, and lastly came the *curacas* (leaders of the *ayllus*) and the farmers. Social organization was based on self-sufficient, communal production.

5   When the Spaniards arrived at the beginning of the 16th century, the Tahuantinsuyo extended from southern Colombia, through Ecuador and Peru, to northern Chile, and from Lake Titicaca and the *altiplano* highlands to northern Argentina, embracing the mountain valleys and the eastern plains. One million people were estimated to have been living within the area of the present Bolivia, and from 12 to 13 million in the Tahuantinsuyo as a whole, making it the most densely populated area of South America. This society included a number of ethnic groups, predominantly Aymara (around Lake Titicaca) and Quechua. The eastern plains were inhabited by dispersed groups of Tupi and Guarani, with no central nucleus. To this day, Aymara and Quechua are the most widespread languages in Bolivia.

6   In 1545 the Spanish discovered silver at Potosi. They extracted immense quantities which contributed to the capital accumulation of several European powers. Millions of native Americans died there, cruelly exploited to the point of exhaustion. Potosi was one of the three largest cities of the 17th century, growing up at the foot of the hill. It became the economic nerve center for vast regions of Chile and Argentina, and nurtured a rich mining bourgeoisie, guilty of corruption, ostentation and squandering.

7   Decades of popular struggle against the Spanish reached their peak in the successive failed rebellions of Tupac Katari (1780-82), the Protective Board of La Paz (1809), headed by mestizo Pedro Domingo Murillo, and the "independence guerrillas". The pro-independence movement was subsequently taken up by the creoles (Spaniards born in America), who distorted it by advocating social, economic and political systems based not on native models but on those of emerging European capitalist powers. A British blockade interrupted the supply of mercury, essential for treating the silver, and the Bolivian mining industry went into decline. The Buenos Aires based trading bourgeoisie soon lost interest in Upper Peru (Bolivia) and offered little resistance when it fell under the influence of the independence leader Simon Bolivar. The country was renamed after him when the Assembly of Representatives proclaimed independence in Chuquisaca, in 1825.

8   Peru exerted great influence over the independent Bolivia until 1841. Bolivian president Marshall Andrés de Santa Cruz, tried to modernize Bolivia, founding universities and the Supreme Court of Justice, and compiling law codes.

9   A mine-owning oligarchy including Patiño, Aramayo and Hochschild worked with the politicians and generals, who were their associates, treating the Bolivian republic as if it were part of the tin business. British imperialist interests, initially in the saltpeter at Antofagasta and later in Bolivia's southern oil reserves, triggered two wars in South America: the Pacific War (Chile against Bolivia and Peru from 1879-83), and the Chaco War (Paraguay and Bolivia, from 1932-35). As a result of these conflicts, Bolivia lost its coast and three-quarters of its territory in the Chaco region. The ceding of Amazonian Acre to Brazil, in 1904, completed the country's dismemberment.

10   On July 21 1946 Bolivian president Gualberto Villaroel was overthrown, assassinated, and his body hung from a lamp-post in downtown La Paz. His predecessor, German Busch, from the military generation of the Chaco War, who had nationalized Bolivia's oil

WORKERS

1996
UNEMPLOYMENT: 4.2%

% OF LABOUR FORCE **1998**

■ FEMALE: 38%   ■ MALE: 62%

1990

■ SERVICES: 35.6%
■ INDUSTRY: 17.5%
■ AGRICULTURE: 46.8%

LAND USE

DEFORESTATION: 1.2% annual (1990/95)
IRRIGATED: 8.3% of arable (1993)

1993

■ FOREST & WOODLAND: 18.4%
■ ARABLE: 9.0%
■ OTHER: 72.6%

PUBLIC EXPENDITURE

1997

80 —
60 —   53.6%
40 —
20 —
6.7 %
0 —
DEFENCE   SOCIAL

MILITARY EXPENDITURE   **57%**
(% of health & education)   (1990/91)

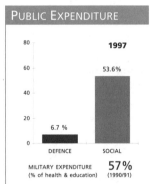

FOREIGN TRADE

Millions US$ 1998

IMPORTS
2,480

EXPORTS
1,693

reserves, had been accused of being a Nazi by US State Department propaganda.

[11] Nationwide frustration at these humiliations gave way to a powerful current of reformism and anti-imperialism. The Nationalist Revolutionary Movement (MNR) grew up alongside progressive labor and peasant movements. After several uprisings, and a 1951 electoral victory which was not honored, the MNR led a popular insurrection in 1952. Civilians defeated seven regular army regiments in the streets, and they carried first Victor Paz Estenssoro, and then Hernan Siles Zuazo, to the presidency. The Bolivian revolution nationalized the tin mines, carried out agrarian reform and proclaimed universal suffrage. Workers' and peasant militias were organized and, together with the Bolivian Workers' Confederation (COB), formed a coalition with the MNR. The army was eliminated after the insurrection, but was later reorganized under US pressure.

[12] Troubled by internal divisions, the MNR gradually lost its drive and was defeated in November 1964 by a military junta led by René Barrientos. Ernesto 'Che' Guevara tried to establish a guerrilla nucleus in the Andes to spread revolutionary war throughout South America, but he was caught by US-trained counter-insurgency troops, and assassinated on October 8 1967.

[13] Division within the army coupled with pressure from the grassroots level led to an anti-imperialist faction taking over government in 1969, with General Juan José Torres as the leader. During his short time in office, there was a significant increase in the number of grassroots organizations. The People's Assembly was formed, with links to the COB and the parties of the Left. In August 1971 he was ousted by Colonel Hugo Banzer Suarez, who formed a government with MNR support. The civilian-military coalition government remained in power until July 1978, with an authoritarian but development-oriented administration encouraging agribusiness and stressing infrastructure projects, bolstered by the high price of oil and other minerals.

[14] Military uprisings and disregard for election results occurred

repeatedly between 1978 and 1980. Juan Pereda Asbun, David Padilla Arancibia, Walter Guevara Arce, Alberto Natusch Busch and Lidia Gueiler all had fleeting presidencies, ended either by coups or parliamentary appointments. On June 29 1980, the elections were won by the Democratic Popular Union (UDP), a center-left coalition whose candidate, Hernan Siles Zuazo, was prevented from taking office by another bloody coup engineered by General Luis Garcia Meza.

[15] According to reports received by Amnesty International, thousands of people were killed or tortured, including Socialist leader Marcelo Quiroga Santa Cruz, Trotskyist parliamentary deputy Carlos Flores Bedregal, and miners' leader Gualberto Vega.

[16] By 1982, the army was seething with internal dissent. Government links with paramilitary groups and drug trafficking were eroding its international prestige, and it was facing dogged popular resistance led by the Bolivian Workers' Confederation (COB), leading to its destruction. In September, the military command decided to convene the Government which had been democratically elected in 1980. On October 10, after 18 years of military rule Hernan Siles Zuazo took office in a legal constitutional model that has continued ever since. Siles Zuazo, with a populist/nationalistic outlook, handed administration of the state-owned mines to the labor unions. He also announced the "non-payment" of Bolivia's foreign debt. The labor movement and the peasants exerted pressure on the government through demonstrations, and several laws passed by his administration allowed these groups to participate in the economic policy decisions of large businesses, and in local committees dealing with food, health and education issues. The Peasant Agricultural Corporation took partial control of the markets and set up collective machinery pools and work teams. In response to these measures, creditor banks, the IMF and the World Bank blocked credits to Bolivia placing an embargo on its international trade. These measures provoked a fiscal crisis and uncontrolled hyperinflation, with the average wage falling to $13 per month.

[17] Under heavy pressure from all social sectors, the Government cut short its term and called elections for July 14 1985. As neither candidate secured over 50 per cent of the vote, the decision was put to Congress, who elected Paz Estenssoro as constitutional president, though Hugo Banzer had marginally more votes.

[18] The Estenssoro Government decreed a program of neo-liberal measures to end subsidies and close down state enterprises. It eliminated price controls and the official listing of the dollar against the local currency. Mines were closed down, and others rented out, leaving thousands of miners jobless.

[19] There was a drastic cut in real wages, with high redundancies, while investment ground to a standstill. Inflation increased to four figures.

[20] In the 1989 national elections, Jaime Paz Zamora's Revolutionary

PROFILE

ENVIRONMENT

A landlocked country with three geographic regions. 70 per cent of the population live in the cold, dry climate of the *altiplano*, an Andean highland plateau with an average altitude of 4,000 meters. This region holds the country's mineral resources: tin (second largest producer in the world), silver, zinc, lead and copper. The subtropical valleys (*yungas*) of the eastern slopes of the Andes form the country's main farming area, where coffee, cocoa, sugar cane, coca and bananas are grown. The tropical plains of the East and North, a region of jungles and grasslands, produce cattle, rice, corn, and sugar cane. The area is also rich in oil. Bolivia is made up of three drainage basins which empty into Lake Titicaca, the Amazon and the Rio de la Plata. Unconstrained exploitation of lumber threatens the country's forest resources, as well as water supplies and fauna. In "El Alto" (a high district of La Paz), air pollution has risen in direct proportion to the number of motor vehicles.

SOCIETY

Peoples: 57 per cent of Bolivians belong to the Quechua and Aymara nations. *Mestizos* and *Cholos* account for 25 per cent of the population. A minority of European descent has ruled the country since the Spanish conquest. The Tupí and Guaraní peoples live in the eastern forests. **Religions:** Mainly Catholic. Freedom of religion. **Languages:** Spanish (official). More than half of the populatin speak native languages (Quechua, Guarani and Aymara); there are 33 ethnic-linguistic groups. **Political Parties:** The parties with parliamentary representation are the Nationalist Democratic Action (ADN; the Nationalist Revolutionary Movement; the new Patriotic Conscience Party (CONDEPA); the Solidary Civic Union (UCS); the Free Bolivia Movement; the Socialist Democratic Group (ASD); the Revolutionary Movement of the Left (MIR); the Pachacuti-Axis, supported by *campesinos* engaged in coca cultivation; and the MRTK-L (the political wing - albeit small in number - of the Tupac Katari Movement). **Social Organizations:** The Bolivian Workers' Confederation (COB); the Sole Labor Union Confederation of Farm Workers of Bolivia (CSUTCB). There are also important ethnic and environmental organizations like the Indigenous Confederation of the Eastern region, Chaco and Bolivian Amazon Area (CIDOB); the Guaraní People's Assembly (APG); the Federation of Campesino Women; the Federation of Neighborhood Commissions; and the Bolivian Forum on Environment and Development (FOBOMADE).

THE STATE

Official Name: República de Bolivia. **Administrative Divisions:** 9 Departments. **Capital:** La Paz 1,246,000 people (1995) - including El Alto (404,400 people) which became a separate city in 1988 - and functions as the seat of the Government. Sucre (150,000 people in 1997) is the constitutional capital, and seat of the judiciary. **Other cities:** Santa Cruz de la Sierra 697,000 people; Cochabamba 408,000 people (1992). **Government:** Hugo Bánzer Suárez, President and Head of the Government since June 1 1997. Bicameral legislature: Chamber of Deputies, made up of 130 members; Senate, 27 members. **National Holiday:** August 6, Independence Day (1825). **Armed Forces:** 25,000 (1993). **Other:** 23,000 Police.

MATERNAL MORTALITY	FOOD DEPENDENCY	EXTERNAL DEBT
1990-98	1970 **20%**	1996
Per 100,000 live births **390**	1997 **9%**	PER CAPITA **US$ 681**

Movement of the Left (MIR) proved itself a potent new political force, coming in third with 19 per cent of the votes (double that of previous elections). The MNR candidate, Gonzalo Sanchez de Losada, obtained 23 per cent and Banzer's Nationalist Democratic Action (ADN), 22.6 per cent. As no party had achieved a majority, an agreement known as the Patriotic Accord (AP) between the MIR and the ADN made it possible for Paz Zamora to be nominated president by the National Congress.

[21] The Patriotic Accord continued Paz Estenssoro's neo-liberal economic policy. In 1991, the Government embarked upon a transformation of the state, which entailed privatization. Congress passed a law permitting the state to sell off 22 of the existing 64 public enterprises, though the Supreme Court ruled it unconstitutional. The Government promoted joint ventures between the state-owned Mining Corporation (COMIBOL) and private companies. The Federation of Mining Workers (FSTMB) launched a series of hunger strikes and threatened to occupy the mines, defending the principle of continued state ownership.

[22] In April 1991, Bolivia's Congress authorized US military officers to come and train local personnel in the war against drugs. Despite military action and the policy of crop substitution - a program called "development for coca" - the area under coca cultivation increased. It was estimated that in 1992 there were some 463,000 people involved in coca-cocaine production, and that the national net earnings from this crop reached $950 million per year.

[23] The loss of power in the workers' movement was compensated for by new organizations of indigenous peoples and communities. In October 1991, the 9th Congress of the Confederation of Indigenous Peoples of the Eastern Region, the Chaco and the Bolivian Amazon Region (CIDOB) met in Santa Cruz. 340 representatives approved a series of demands, including claims to lands lost during the Spanish invasion, and the use of their native languages in the educational system.

[24] The population of Bolivia's eastern region includes 250,000 people of 10 linguistic groups and 35 ethnic groups. In September 1990, a group of peoples from this region carried out a 750 km march from the east to the capital with the slogan Land and Dignity. Paz Zamora's government approved a National Plan for the Defence and Development of the Indigenous Peoples, and in August 1991, recognized the Santa Ana de Horachi Mosetana Community's right to 8,000 hectares of land, which they consider collective property. These resolutions have been opposed by companies which have been exploiting the region's vast forestry resources.

[25] In January 1992, Presidents Paz Zamora and Alberto Fujimori (of Peru) signed an agreement whereby Peru ceded an area of 327 hectares to Bolivia for it to develop a free zone at the port of Ilo in southern Peru. In this way Bolivia gained access to the sea - a free port for its international trade.

[26] The MNR won the national elections of June 1993, with 36 per cent of the vote. Its presidential candidate was Gonzalo Sanchez Losada, and the vice-presidential candidate was Victor Hugo Cardenas, an Aymara sociologist and leader of the Tupac Katari Movement. While the ADN and MIR suffered significant losses, the new populist and nationalist movements, such as CONDEPA and UCS, led by Carlos Palenque and Max Fernandez retained their support among mestizos and the poorer neighborhoods.

[27] In its first year the Government established the right to education in the indian languages (Aymara, Quecha, Guarani). The Capitalization Bill aimed to privatize 50 per cent of the main public industries (telecommunications, electricity, oil, gas, railways, airlines) on the basis of transferring half the shares to the Bolivian citizens as pension funds. The aim was to attract foreign investment, reduce unemployment and increase GDP.

[28] Many local movements reacted importing toxic waste from Europe and the environmental deterioration caused by mining, while others protested against the closure of these same mines and the consequent job losses. The burning of coca plantations by the US led to continuous confrontations between the rural workers and the military. Meanwhile, the World Bank reported that 97 per cent of the rural population were living in poverty.

[29] In 1994, the YPBF oil corporation, on the brink of privatization, was made even more attractive by an agreement with Brazil for the construction of a $2 billion gas pipeline to join Santa Cruz de la Sierra with São Paulo. The Capitalization Bill, unpopular amongst workers fearful of losing their jobs, led to a series of strikes in 1995. The Government declared a state of emergency on two occasions, granting the police special powers and imposing a curfew. Public meetings were banned and more than 100 leaders were imprisoned.

[30] As part of its regional campaign to control the northward flow of cocaine, the US demanded that the Bolivian parliament approve a law against the drug-money laundering in February 1997. In January 1999 Washington stated the plan had been a success and that Bolivian coca production had been reduced by 50%.

[31] In the national elections in June, Nationalist Democratic Action (ADN) won with 22 per cent of the vote, followed by the MNR, MIR, UCS and Patriotic Conscience, with 18, 17, 16 and 16 per cent of the vote respectively. Hugo Banzer became president once again after complicated negotiation in Parliament between the parties, themselves divided.

[32] Throughout 1998 and 1999 the Bolivian Workers' Federation (COB) tried to challenge Banzer's policies, but internal division weakened it in early 2000.

[33] In the December 1999 local elections, ADN came third with 13 per cent of the vote, behind the opposition MNR which took 19.7 per cent, and the MIR with 14.7 per cent. But in general terms, the government alliance took all the major cities.

[34] While the 73-year-old Banzer was in the United States on a medical trip, vice-president Jorge Quiroga called on Washington to supply more funds for the eradication of illegal coca plantations. The Government considered that having eliminated three quarters of total plantations, the US should fulfil its part of the deal, by funding the changeover to legal produce for the farmers. ∎

DEMOGRAPHY

Population: 8,142,000 (1999)
Annual growth: 2.3 % (1975/97)
Estimates for year 2015 (million): 11.2 (1999)
Annual growth to year 2015: 2.1 % (1997/2015)
Urban population: 62.3 % (1997)
Urban Growth: 3.9 % (1980/95)
Children per woman: 4.3 (1998)

HEALTH

Life expectancy at birth: 62 years (1998)
male: 60 years (1998)
female: 63 years (1998)
Maternal mortality: 390 per 100,000 live births (1990-98)
Infant mortality: 66 per 1,000 (1998)
Under-5 child mortality: 85 per 1,000 (1998)
Daily calorie supply: 2,170 per capita (1996)
51 doctors per 100,000 people (1993)
Safe water: 80 % (1990/98)

EDUCATION

Literacy: 82 % (1995)
male: 90 % (1995)
female: 75 % (1995)
School enrolment:
Primary total: 95 % (1990/96)
male: 99 % (1990/97)
female: 90 % (1990/97)
Secondary:
male: 40 % (1990/96)
female: 34 % (1990/96)
Tertiary: 24 % (1996)

COMMUNICATIONS

55 newspapers (1996), 675 radios (1997), 202 TV sets (1996) and 43 main telephone lines (1996) per 1,000 people

ECONOMY

Per capita, GNP: $ 1,010 (1998)
Annual growth, GNP: 5.1 % (1998)
Annual inflation: 9.9 % (1990/98)
Consumer price index: 126.8 (1998)
Currency: 5.5 bolivianos = $ 1 (1998)
Cereal imports: 194,421 metric tons (1998)
Food import dependency: 9 % (1997)
Fertilizer use: 68 kg per ha (1997)
Exports: $ 1,693 million (1998)
Imports: $ 2,480 million (1998)
External debt: $ 6,077 million (1998); $ 764 per capita (1998)
Debt service: 30.2 % of exports (1998)
Development aid received: $ 717 million (1997); $ 106.5 per capita (1997); 9.20 % of GNP (1997)

ENERGY

Consumption: 548.0 Kgs of Oil equivalent per capita yearly (1997); -40.0 % imported (1997)

HDI (rank/value): 112/0.652 (1997)

Bosnia-Herzegovina

Bosna I Hercegovina

Population:	3,838,000 (1999)
Area:	51,130 SQ KM
Capital:	Sarajevo
Currency:	Dinar
Language:	Serb and Croatian

The earliest inhabitants of what is now Bosnia-Herzegovina were Illyrian tribes. After the Roman conquest in the mid-2nd century BC, this region became a part of the province of Illyria, although the Sava river basin remained within the province of Pannonia. Serbs settled in the area in the 7th century AD. Except for a brief interregnum (1081-1101), Bosnia remained politically separate from Serbia.

2   Hungarian control over Bosnia began in the mid-12th century. The combined efforts of the papacy and of the Hungarians to impose their religious authority over Bosnia gave rise to strong national resistance. Although war was avoided, the region came under the jurisdiction of the Hungarian archbishop of Kalocsa.

3   During this period, Bosnia was seen as a bastion of the Bogomils (or Cathari), one of southern Europe's main heretical movements, who found support among the local population, and from the State, as well. Neighboring Christians - both Orthodox Serbs and Catholic Croats - organized several crusades against this heresy. The Bogomils defeated the crusaders, but some parts of Bosnia were converted to Christianity

4   Ban Prijezda founded the Kotromanic dynasty (1254-1395) under which Bosnia conquered the province of Hum (Herzegovina). In 1377, Tvrtko crowned himself King of Serbia, Bosnia and the coastlands. With the Turkish invasion in 1386 the Serbs were defeated in Kosovo (1389), but Tvrtko carried out further conquests in the west, and in 1390 was crowned King of Rashka, Bosnia, Dalmatia, Croatia and the coastlands.

5   The Ottoman Empire occupied Serbia in 1459 and Bosnia became a province 1463. Hum resisted longer, but in 1482 the port of Novi fell, and Herzegovina too became a province of the Ottoman Empire.

6   After the Turkish conquest, a campaign began to convert Bosnian Bogomils to Islam. Thus, in addition to Catholic Slavs and Christian Orthodox Slavs, there were now Muslim Slavs. Ever since, relations between the three communities have been strained, and religion became the decisive social factor in the region.

7   At first, the Turkish governor (Pasha) had his headquarters in Banja Luka, but later transferred them to Sarajevo. In 1580, Bosnia was divided into 8 *sanjaks* (sub-regions), under the jurisdiction of 48 hereditary Kapetans, who exercised a feudal power over their territories. Mining and trade began to decline; only the manufacture of weapons and wrought metals survived.

8   In the 16th and 17th centuries, Bosnia played an important role in the Turkish wars against Austria and Venice. In 1697, Prince Eugene of Savoy captured Sarajevo. By the Treaty of Karlowitz (1699) the Sava river, which formed Bosnia's northern border, also became the northern boundary of the Ottoman Empire. Herzegovina and the part of Bosnia east of the Una river were ceded to Austria in 1718, and returned to Turkey in 1739.

9   In the 19th century, Bosnia's nobility resisted Turkish interference. In 1837, Herzegovina's regent declared independence. Uprisings became chronic, bringing Christians and Muslims together, despite their differences, against the bureaucracy and corruption of the Empire.

10   In 1875, a local Herzegovinian conflict unleashed a rebellion, which spilled over into Bosnia. Austria, Russia and Germany tried unsuccessfully to mediate between Turkey and the rebels. The Sultan's promise to reduce taxes, grant religious freedom and install a provincial assembly was also rejected.

11   By a secret agreement in 1877, Russia authorized Austria-Hungary to occupy Bosnia-Herzegovina, in exchange for its neutrality in Russia's upcoming war against Turkey. After the Russo-Turkish War of 1877-78, the Congress of Berlin disregarded Serbian wishes, and assigned Bosnia and Herzegovina to the Austro-Hungarian Empire (although nominally they continued to be under Turkish control).

WORKERS

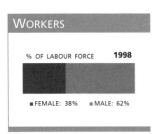

% OF LABOUR FORCE   **1998**

■ FEMALE: 38%   ■ MALE: 62%

PUBLIC EXPENDITURE

DEFENCE EXPENDITURE   **14.1%**
(% of goverment exp.)   (1997)

12 In 1878, Vienna put down armed resistance from Bosnia-Herzegovina. The revolution launched by the Young Turks in 1908 brought on a crisis within the Ottoman Empire.

13 The Turkish Government asked Bosnia-Herzegovina to participate in the new parliament at Istanbul but Austria-Hungary annexed the two provinces in 1908, with Russian consent. Vienna established a provincial assembly (*Sabor*) and special laws of association, without representation in Vienna or Budapest.

14 The 1910 Constitution consolidated social and religious differences by establishing three electoral colleges - Orthodox, Catholic and Muslim - each with a fixed number of seats in the *Sabor*.

15 The influence of the *Mlada Bosna* (Young Bosnia) movement and other revolutionary groups led the Empire's authorities to close Bosnia's Assembly, and dissolve several Serbian political groups. The assassination of Archduke Francis Ferdinand and his wife the Duchess of Hohenberg in Sarajevo in 1914 by a Bosnian Serb student triggered World War I.

16 After the collapse of the Austro-Hungarian Empire in the Balkans in 1918, Bosnia-Herzegovina became a part of Serbia.

17 During the Nazi occupation, Bosnia-Herzegovina was subjected to the puppet administration established in Croatia. In the two provinces, Croat *Ustashes* (Fascists) massacred the Serbs. The rivalry which had always existed between Muslim, Serb and Croat degenerated into deep hostility.

18 After the war, Bosnia-Herzegovina became a Yugoslav republic. The slogan of the Yugoslav federated socialists was "Brotherhood and Unity", but ethnic confrontation was visible in the arts, the humanities and literature.

19 In April 1990 the Yugoslav Communist League rescinded its total control, and in the first multiparty legislative elections to be held since the War, the nationalist parties elected 73 Serbs and 44 Croats. This resulted in heavy losses for the Democratic Reform Party (ex-Communist) candidates and the liberal technocrats.

20 The Muslims were represented by the Democratic Action Party (DAP) and its leader, Alija Izetbegovic, was elected President of the republic. The DAP held an absolute majority in 37 communities (administrative units) and a relative majority in 52 others. The Croatian Democratic Community, based in Zagreb, controlled 13 local communities and held a relative majority in 17 others.

21 In October 1991, Bosnia-Herzegovina's *Sabor* approved a declaration of independence from the Yugoslav federation. In January 1992, Parliament agreed to hold a plebiscite on the issue of separation. The Serbian communities of Bosnia wanted to remain within a Yugoslav federation, while the Croat and Muslim communities campaigned for independence.

22 Bosnian President Izetbegovic wanted to maintain the unity and integrity of the republic, promising that Bosnia-Herzegovina would not become a Muslim state, and guaranteeing that the rights of all nationalities would be respected. In early March, conflict broke out when the referendum was supported by 99.4 per cent of the Muslims and Croats, who ratified the republic's independence.

23 On April 7, the European Community and the US recognized the independence of Bosnia-Herzegovina. The Bosnian republic was accepted as a member state in the Conference of Security and Cooperation in Europe; in May it became a member of the UN.

24 At the same time, the Serbian community proclaimed the independence of the "Serbian Republic of Bosnia-Herzegovina" in the areas under Serbian control (Bosnian Krajina, with its center at Banja Luka). The conflict quickly extended throughout the entire region.

25 Local Croat forces also controlled certain areas of the Republic; there were sporadic confrontations with Bosnian government troops. In late July, Croatia and Bosnia signed a mutual recognition pact.

26 In January 1993, Serbian troops killed Bosnian deputy prime minister, Hakija Turajlic, in Sarajevo. In March the UN decreed a cease-fire in that city, which was under siege. There were numerous reports on the existence of Serbian concentration camps, as well as an "ethnic cleansing" campaign. The latter involved the expulsion of all members of rival ethnic groups, especially from the smaller villages.

27 According to Amnesty International, thousands of civilians, as well as soldiers that had been captured or wounded, were executed. In addition, prisoners were systematically submitted to torture and harsh treatment. According to UN figures, a total of 40,000 women had been raped. Although excesses were committed by all sides, the Serbians bore the major responsibility, while the Muslims were the main victims.

28 The UN Protection Forces (UNPROFOR) sent in some 20,000 peacekeeping troops. The US refused to send troops to Bosnia, despite pressure from the UN and European countries. Several security zones were decreed in such cities as Tuzla, Zepa, Gorazde, Bihac and Sarajevo. However, these were not always observed, just as successive cease-fires were consistently violated.

29 In October, Serbian occupation of Bosanki Brod opened up a corridor between Serbia and Bosnian Krajina. Serbians controlled 70 per cent of the territory, as a result of their superior artillery and armoured vehicles, as well as their control of the bridges over the Drina river - on the border between Serbia and Bosnia - which allowed them to receive arms and other supplies from the Yugoslav Federation. As a result of their support of the Serbians, the UN called for an economic blockade of the Federation, and an arms embargo aimed at Bosnians and Croats.

30 The Muslims found themselves cornered in Sarajevo and a few other minor sites, receiving what little financial and moral support they could from a few Islamic countries.

PROFILE

ENVIRONMENT

Bosnia-Herzegovina has a 20-kilometer coastline on the Adriatic Sea. In the west it is bounded by Croatia, Montenegro and Serbia. The major part of the country lies in the Dinaric Alps, with elevations of around 4,265 meters, making overland communication difficult. The country is drained by the Sava and Neretva rivers and their tributaries. The territory takes its name from the Bosna River, a tributary of the Sava. The main crops are grains, vegetables and grapes; there is also livestock rearing. There is a wealth of mineral resources, including coal, iron, copper and manganese. Because of air pollution, respiratory ailments are very common in urban areas. Barely half of the region's water supplies are considered safe, the Sava River being the most polluted of all.

SOCIETY

Peoples: Muslim-Slavs 49.2 per cent, Christian-Orthodox Serbs 31.3 per cent, Catholic-Croats 17.3 per cent. Ethnic differences stem from historical and religious factors. Serbs make up the majority in northeastern Bosnia, living in or around Banja Luka; Croats form the majority in western Herzegovina, Mostar being their main urban center. It is impossible to draw an "ethnic dividing line" in other regions. In the capital, Sarajevo, there is a Muslim majority, and also Serbs and Croats. There were 1,200 Jews until 1992.
Religions: The majority is Muslim. Other religions: Christian Orthodox and Roman Catholic.
Languages: Serb and Croatian.
Political Parties: Party of Democratic Action (Muslim); the Serbian Democratic Party; the Serbian Renaissance Movement; the Croatian Democratic Community; the Democratic Reforms Party (formerly the Communist Party).
Social Organizations: Currently in the process of being reorganized.

THE STATE

Official Name: Republika Bosna I Hercegovina.
Administrative Division: 50 Districts.
Capital: Sarajevo 390,600 people (est 1997), reduced to less than 50,000 in September 1995.
Other cities: Banja Luka 142,600 people; Tuzla 142,644; Mostar 110,377 (1991).
Government: As of the September 1996 elections, Bosnia has a three-member Presidency. Bosnia's Muslim President, Alija Izetbegovic, first chairman of the Presidency of the Republic since February 2000; the Serb nationalist Mirko Sarovic is the second chairman and the Croat leader, Ejup Ganic is the third. There are two co-prime ministers: Haris Silajdzic (since Jan 1997) and Svetozar Mihajlovic (since Feb 1999).
National Holiday: March 1, Independence (1992).
Armed Forces: approximately 60,000 troops. Reserves: 120,000, (1993). After the conflict, the United Nations sent in several thousand peace-implementation troops, replaced by a multinational force. There are more than 150,000 troops belonging to the Federal Yugoslavian Army, the Bosnian-Serb Army and the Serbian Nationalist Militia, among others.

31 In June 1993, Serbian President Slobodan Milosevic and his Croatian counterpart, Franjo Tudjman, announced the partition of Bosnia into three ethnic entities (Serbian, Croatian and Muslim), within the framework of a federal state.

32 The Croats, faced with the partition of Bosnia, sought to gain the upper hand, so as to negotiate from a position of strength. In July they launched an offensive against Mostar, capital of Herzegovina. The UN Human Rights Commission reported that 10,000 Muslims had been held in Croatian concentration camps, where they were submitted to torture and in some cases, to summary executions.

33 In the meantime, the situation in Sarajevo grew progressively worse: there was a lack of electricity, water and food. Besieged by a series of epidemics, the city's estimated 300,000 inhabitants managed to survive on minimal rations, while international aid agencies tried to reach the city despite mounting difficulties. In early 1994, the UN appealed to the Serbians to stop their attacks on Sarajevo and withdraw the heavy artillery surrounding the city. Despite resistance from the Russians, NATO threatened to bomb Serb positions. When the formal deadline expired, the Serbs withdrew.

34 The peace conference sponsored by the UN and the EU in 1994 proposed the territory be divided into Bosnian, Muslim and Croatian areas as ethnically homogeneous republics. This option called for the transfer of people from one sector to another. The UN's Human Rights Commission for the former Yugoslavia criticized the creation of ethnic boundaries and defended a reform of the democratic system.

35 In 1994, the US and Russia exerted growing pressure upon the Serbs to accept the proposal. Croatians and Muslims approved a federal agreement between the two communities: 51 per cent of the territory would remain among Bosnians and Croatians while Serbs would be in control of 49 per cent, without the need to divide Bosnia into three ethnically distinct states.

36 With support from the EU, Washington and Moscow, the federal agreement was signed by presidents Franjo Tudjman of Croatia and Alija Izetbegovic of Bosnia, but the Serbs rejected it. Negotiations were hampered because Serb president Slobodan Milosevic stated he had no authority over the self-proclaimed Bosnian-Serb Republic of Sprska.

37 In 1995, the Bosnian-Serbs held several UN troops hostage and took Bihac. In August, the situation was radically changed by NATO's bombing of Bosnian-Serb positions in the siege of Sarajevo. Almost at the same time, Croatia expelled Serb-Croat forces from the eastern side of the country forcing their delegates to negotiate.

38 According to the Dayton Accords of 1995, elections were to be held in September 1996, with the aim of promoting more tolerant leaders among each of the nationalities in conflict. The agreement was carried out under US military pressure with - some said - the underlying objective of influencing US President Clinton's campaign for re-election in November. The presence of American troops forced a peaceful settlement and, at the same time, froze the political situation.

39 The Dayton Accords acknowledged that the two ethnically based mini-states (the Bosnian-Serb Republic –Sprska - and the Croatian-Muslim Federation) resulted from the physical elimination or expulsion of ethnic minorities.

40 The International Criminal Tribunal for the Former Yugoslavia at the Hague convicted Radovan Karadzic, leader of the Sprska Republic and his military commander Ratko Mladic, for genocide. In spite of being convicted, neither was incarcerated. They retained great influence in the republic's political life even though the Dayton peace agreement had banned the electoral participation of individuals accused of war crimes.

41 In June 1996, power, water and transport services began to be reinstated and Sarajevo regained some of its former vitality. The environment of political tranquillity considered necessary for the run-up to the September elections was hindered by the refugees' inability to return to their homes unless their fellow citizens ruled over the area, the limitations of journalists' movements and the difficulties imposed on the activities of several NGOs.

42 After the September 1996 elections, Bosnia had a three-member presidency ranked according to their share of the vote. Bosnia's Muslim President, Alija Izetbegovic, is first chairman; the Serb nationalist Momcilo Krajisnik came second and the Croat leader, Kresimir Zubak was third. These three were the most nationalist among the candidates in each federated republic.

43 The Croatian and Bosnian presidents met in Split during August 1997 to relaunch the Muslim-Croatian federation, pledging once again to facilitate the return of the refugees. Karadzic questioned the December legislative elections, accusing Western representatives of having fixed the results in favour of the Muslim and Croatian parties.

44 The September 1998 elections confirmed the presidency in the hands of Izetbegovic. He won with 31 per cent of the vote (86.8 per cent of the Muslim votes), beating Iivko Radiciç who obtained 21.8 per cent (51.2 per cent of the Serbian poll) and Ante Jelavic, with11.5 per cent (52 per cent of the Croatian votes). The results confirmed the party of the Muslim president and of the ruling Croatian party, but placed Karadzic's party behind the nationalist Serbian Radical Party (SRP). Carlos Westendorp, the UN High Commissioner for the republic, promoted some unifying measures, like the creation of a flag and symbols common to all of Bosnia-Herzegovina, but these issues produced further clashes. Each group maintained its armed forces, and the federation between Croats and Muslims was confirmed as the sum of the two and not a separate entity. The main reason for this was the presence of Franjo Tudjman presiding over Croatia, giving strength to the more nationalist Croatian tendencies within the federation's territory.

45 The death of Tudjman in December 1999 and the electoral victory of the moderate left in Croatia in early 2000 were welcomed by Muslims and Bosnian Serbs alike. The April 2000 local elections gave a great boost to the multi-ethnic Social Democratic Party (SDP). The Muslim Social Democratic Action suffered considerable losses in Sarajevo and other cities. Some regions with Croatian majorities boycotted the elections for local reasons. The persistent power of the nationalist parties continued to make the return of tens of thousands of internal refugees difficult. ■

Botswana

Botswana

Population: 1,597,000 (1999)
Area: 581,730 SQ KM
Capital: Gaborone
Currency: Pula
Language: Setswana

In the course of its history "Bechuanaland" (the English corruption of *ba'tswana* - Tswana people) now Botswana, was also known as the "fatal crossroads" on account of its position in the heart of southern Africa, providing a passageway for pre-colonial movement and settlement. Later, the British used the "missionary route" from the south of Africa to Sudan and Egypt, whereas the Portuguese sought to unite their colonies of Angola and Mozambique by controlling Bechuanaland.

[2] Since the 18th century therefore this land has been a focal point for various strategic colonial interests, as well as for the Tswana who had lived in the area since the 17th century. Around 1830, the region was penetrated by Boer colonists (of Dutch origin), fleeing northward from the Cape to escape the British. These farmers fought with the local people for possession of the scant fertile lands, while the Tswana also clashed with Ndebele people who had been driven from Zululand by the Zulu kings (see South Africa). Tswanas and Boers united to withstand Ndebele invasion. In 1894, leaders of the three major kingdoms travelled to London to seek support. The British promptly complied, and Bechuanaland soon became a protectorate.

[3] British trusteeship prevented political absorption by South Africa but paved the way for white economic supremacy. Consequently, when the first nationalist movements arose they aimed at putting an end to both situations.

[4] Although Botswana has a large semi-arid area, it came to be one of southern Africa's major cattle and meat exporters. At the beginning of this century, 97 per cent of the population lived in rural areas, every family owned several cows, and the richest had oxen to plough their fields. By the 1960s, 15 per cent of the population had migrated to the cities and at least 40 per cent of the rural population had lost their cattle.

[5] The struggle for independence became entangled with the wedding of Seretse Khama, a leader of the major Bamagwato chiefdom who went to England to study law. He married Ruth Williams, a European white-collar worker. This upset both the British and the Afrikaners who prevented Seretse from returning home. He withstood every pressure including offers of money from the British and, firmly supported by his people, he retained leadership of the country's main ethnic group. Seretse finally returned home in 1956, nine years before the general elections in which his Botswana Democratic Party (BDP) polled 80 per cent of the vote.

[6] In September 1966, Botswana gained independence and Seretse was elected first president. A year later he was knighted by the British. The BDP pursued a conciliatory policy towards Europeans, who controlled many of the country's economic resources, and Botswana continued to be highly dependent upon South Africa. Almost all its imports came through Cape Town, and 60 per cent of its exports were purchased by South Africa. Nevertheless, in the political arena, Seretse maintained his distance from South Africa, and supported the region's anti-racist movements. Botswana was one of the "frontline nations" fighting apartheid, and a member of the SADCC (a grouping of the nine southern African countries seeking to end the economic dependence on South Africa).

[7] Seretse Khama died of cancer in July 1980 and was succeeded by the Vice-President, Quett Masire. Strong pressures were exerted on Masire by revolutionary socialist groups to limit the concentration of arable land in Tswana and white hands and to increase the area allotted to cooperatives. The rural poor accused large landowners of overgrazing, causing a deterioration in the quality of the land, and threatening their future. A movement also arose demanding the nationalization of rich diamond, iron, copper and nickel deposits exploited by South African companies.

[8] In 1982, the country faced balance of payments problems resulting from a drought that affected cattle farming and exports. By early 1983, and the end of the drought, the difficulties had subsided. Government austerity measures also contributed to increasing farm production and mineral exports grew. The deficit became a surplus in the first half of 1983, enabling the Government to ease the austerity program, giving wage increases and tax cuts.

[9] Between 1978 and 1988, Botswana became the third largest diamond producer in the world, behind Australia and the Democratic Republic of the Congo (then Zaire). The national economy grew at a record rate of 12 per cent a year. In any case, three fifths of the population lived on subsistence crops or "non-institutionalised" activities, that is, off the statistical record, beyond fiscal control and the commercial circuit.

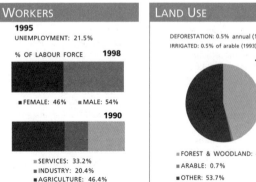

WORKERS

1995
UNEMPLOYMENT: 21.5%

% OF LABOUR FORCE **1998**

■ FEMALE: 46% ■ MALE: 54%

1990

■ SERVICES: 33.2%
■ INDUSTRY: 20.4%
■ AGRICULTURE: 46.4%

LAND USE

DEFORESTATION: 0.5% annual (1990/95)
IRRIGATED: 0.5% of arable (1993)

1993

■ FOREST & WOODLAND: 45.6%
■ ARABLE: 0.7%
■ OTHER: 53.7%

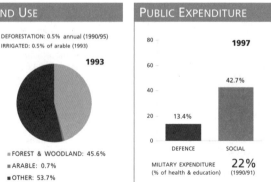

PUBLIC EXPENDITURE

1997

42.7%

13.4%

DEFENCE   SOCIAL

MILITARY EXPENDITURE   **22%**
(% of health & education)   (1990/91)

MATERNAL MORTALITY

1990-98

Per 100,000 live births

330

LITERACY

1995

73%

EXTERNAL DEBT

1998

PER CAPITA

US$ 349

DEMOGRAPHY

Population: 1,597,000 (1999)
Annual growth: 3.3 % (1975/97)
Estimates for year 2015 (million): 2.0 (1999)
Annual growth to year 2015: 1.4 % (1997/2015)
Urban population: 66.1 % (1997)
Urban Growth: 8.4 % (1980/95)
Children per woman: 4.3 (1998)

HEALTH

Life expectancy at birth: 47 years (1998)
male: 46 years (1998)
female: 48 years (1998)
Maternal mortality: 330 per 100,000 live births (1990-98)
Infant mortality: 38 per 1,000 (1998)
Under-5 child mortality: 48 per 1,000 (1998)
Daily calorie supply: 2,272 per capita (1996)
Safe water: 90 % (1990/98)

EDUCATION

Literacy: 73 % (1995)
male: 70 % (1995)
female: 75 % (1995)
School enrolment:
Primary total: 112 % (1990/96)
male: 111 % (1990/97)
female: 112 % (1990/97)
Secondary:
male: 63 % (1990/96)
female: 69 % (1990/96)
Tertiary: 6 % (1997)
Primary school teachers: one for every 25 (1996)

COMMUNICATIONS

27 newspapers (1996), 156 radios (1997), 27 TV sets (1996) and 48 main telephone lines (1996) per 1,000 people

ECONOMY

Per capita, GNP: $ 3,070 (1998)
Annual growth, GNP: 3.7 % (1998)
Annual inflation: 10.3 % (1990/98)
Consumer price index: 127.6 (1998)
Currency: 4.2 pula = $ 1 (1998)
Cereal imports: 125,718 metric tons (1998)
Fertilizer use: 109 kg per ha (1997)
Exports: $ 1,705 million (1998)
Imports: $ 1,646 million (1998)
External debt: $ 548 million (1998); $ 349 per capita (1998)
Debt service: 2.7 % of exports (1998)
Development aid received: $ 125 million (1997); $ 95.1 per capita (1997); 2.60 % of GNP (1997)

HDI (rank/value): 122/0.609 (1997)

---

[10] In 1985 there were repeated flare-ups along the frontier with South Africa due to Botswana government support for the African National Congress (ANC) anti-apartheid campaign. In 1987, South Africa applied pressure blocking the roads to Gaborone, the capital of Botswana.

[11] From 1989, the year Masire was re-elected President, the Government had to confront successive economic and political problems, fundamentally due to a fall in the international demand for diamonds. Increased unemployment and opposition criticism brought government corruption into the open, forcing several ministers to resign. During 1991, three of the seven opposition parties created the Peoples Progressive Front (PPF) in opposition to the governing Botswana Democratic Party (BDP).

[12] That same year, Botswana witnessed the biggest strikes since independence. Public sector workers demanded a 154 per cent pay increase and the Government responded by sacking 18,000 state employees. Despite having maintained economic growth for decades, some studies showed Botswana had the most severe social inequalities in the world.

[13] In 1992, unemployment came close to 25 per cent. In an attempt to increase employment and lift the flagging fortunes of the BDP, the Government initiated an incentive policy for non-mining industries. Severe drought forced the authorities to declare a state of emergency. Public spending was drastically reduced, which meant laying off more than a third of the workers employed directly or indirectly by the State.

[14] Despite the economic and social problems, the BDP kept its majority in the 1994 parliamentary elections, while losing nine seats. The country - now the second most important diamond exporter behind Russia - was still dependent on the export of its minerals. Tourism became the second largest foreign-exchange earner.

[15] Although the Government managed to keep the budget in the black, it failed to solve the most pressing problems of a population lacking, amongst other things, even the most basic medical attention. In 1998, 30 per cent of Botswana's adults were HIV-positive, according to the UN.

[16] In February of that year, an attempt by the Government to buy Belgian weapons brought German intervention to prevent the purchase. Two years previously, Germany had blocked Botswana's attempts to buy arms from the Netherlands. Despite these setbacks, Botswana appeared determined to acquire such weapons.

[17] Partly as a result of its diamond wealth, Botswana's economy has flourished over the last three decades. According to the World Bank, it had the fastest-growing economy in the world during the period 1965-1996, when per capita income grew at 9.2 per cent. The rapid growth led to increasing disparities between rich and poor people.

[18] The civil war in Namibia in the Caprivi Strip, a corridor 460 kilometres long and in some places 30 kilometres wide, affected Botswana's relations with its neighbor. In January 1999, some 2,000 residents of this area fled to Botswana. Many of them were separatists, and the decision to grant them asylum worsened relations with Windhoek. Both countries were also involved in a border dispute over an island in the Chobe river.

[19] The October 1999 elections once again gave victory to the BDP, which took 33 of the 40 seats open to direct vote. Its candidate, Festus Gontebanye Mogae was reconfirmed in the presidency he had held since Masire stood down in 1998. ∎

ENVIRONMENT

An extensive and sparsely populated country, Botswana is divided into three large regions. In the centre and southwest, the Kalahari basin is a desert steppe where grazing is only possible in certain seasons. The Okavango River basin in the northeast has a tropical climate suitable for agriculture. 80 per cent of the population lives within a strip in the east, stretching along the railroad. Traditionally pastoral, the country is beginning to exploit its mineral resources (manganese, copper, nickel and diamonds). Intensive cattle-raising has meant a reduction in the areas originally set aside for wildlife, and is also rapidly depleting the soil.

SOCIETY

Peoples: Tswana make up 90 per cent of the population.
Religions: Some are Catholic and Protestant, while the rest practice African religions.
Languages: Setswana (national) and English (official).
Political Parties: The Botswana Democratic Party (BDP), founded by Seretse Khama in 1961; the Botswana National Front (BNF) was founded in 1991 as a coalition of leftist and center-left parties.
Social Organizations: 5 of the 13 local trade unions form the Botswana Federation of Trade Unions, founded in 1976.

THE STATE

Official Name: Republic of Botswana.
Administrative Divisions: 4 Districts.
Capital: Gaborone, 180,000 people in 1994.
Other cities: Francistown, 65,026 people; Selebi-Pikwe, 39,769 (1994).
Government: Festus Gontebanye Mogae, President since April 1 1998, confirmed in October 1999 elections. The single chamber National Assembly has 46 members.
National Holiday: September 30, Independence Day (1966).
Armed Forces: 7,500 (1994).
Other: 1,000 Transport Police.

Brazil

Brasil

Population: 167,988,000 (1999)
Area: 8,511,969 SQ KM
Capital: Brasilia
Currency: Real
Language: Portuguese

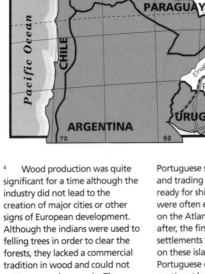

S mall tribal groups belonging mainly to the Tupi Guarani, Carib and Arawak linguistic groups initially inhabited the huge tracts of land that were to become today's Brazil. The indigenous peoples from the Amazon basin fished and cultivated while the inhabitants of the dry savannah were hunter-gatherers. When the first Portuguese ships arrived at the coast of what today is Bahia de todos os Santos in 1500, more than two million people inhabited these lands.

² Under the Tordesillas Treaty (1494) which divided the non-European world between Spain and Portugal, the latter was assured its rights over these lands. Sailing towards India, Pedro Alvarez Cabral landed at Bahia de todos os Santos in 1500 and christened the area the Island of Vera Cruz. Between 1501 and 1502 a naval expedition headed by Gaspar de Lemos covered the region between Rio Grande and the Río de la Plata. This is how Cabral's mistake (he thought he had reached an island) was corrected and the region came to be known by the Europeans as Santa Cruz Land.

³ For the Portuguese, these lands were far less lucrative than Africa and India. The strip of coast did not reveal major deposits of precious metals. It was inhabited by semi-sedentary indigenous peoples, the Tupis, related to the Guaranís, whom the Spanish would later find in Paraguay. At first the Portuguese crown only valued those lands as places to trade slaves or barter metals and trifles with the indians in exchange for brazilwood. The pulp from this tree, used to make a fire-colored dye, would give the country its final name - *brasa* in Portuguese means embers.

⁴ Wood production was quite significant for a time although the industry did not lead to the creation of major cities or other signs of European development. Although the indians were used to felling trees in order to clear the forests, they lacked a commercial tradition in wood and could not cut trees on a large scale. The

Portuguese supplied axes and saws and trading agents had the timber ready for shipment. Trading posts were often established on islands on the Atlantic ocean and, shortly after, the first Portuguese settlements were also established on these islands. Only a few Portuguese exiles inhabited the continent by that time, together with the indigenous communities. On several occasions, these exiles helped other mainland Portuguese make fruitful alliances with the natives.

⁵ Around 1530, the Portuguese were forced to increase their involvement with Brazil. Other European traders, particularly the

French, started to arrive. Commerce with India had slumped and the achievements of Spanish conquistadors in other parts of the continent represented both an incentive and a threat. The Portuguese sent an expedition to expel the French and establish its authority, along with some settlers. Thus, in 1532, the first official Portuguese settlement, São Vicente, was established on an island close to São Paulo.

⁶ The Spanish expanded their empire through the conquest of lands under the strict control of the Crown. The Portuguese however, in accordance with their maritime commercial tradition, divided the Brazilian coast into captaincies which were awarded to *donatarios*, prominent individuals who supposedly had the wealth required to carry out the occupation and exploitation of the lands. The captaincies were hereditary, with extensive judicial and administrative

WORKERS

1996
UNEMPLOYMENT: 6.9%

% OF LABOUR FORCE   **1998**

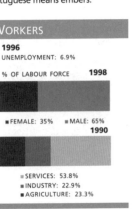

■ FEMALE: 35%   ■ MALE: 65%
1990

■ SERVICES: 53.8%
■ INDUSTRY: 22.9%
■ AGRICULTURE: 23.3%

LAND USE

DEFORESTATION: 0.5% annual (1990/95)
IRRIGATED: 6.7% of arable (1993)

1993

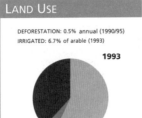

■ FOREST & WOODLAND: 57.3%
■ ARABLE: 4.9%
■ OTHER: 37.8%

PUBLIC EXPENDITURE

DEFENCE EXPENDITURE (% of goverment exp.)	**3.9%**	(1997)
MILITARY EXPENDITURE (% of health & education)	**23%**	(1990/91)

powers, although several were never occupied and others survived for a brief time. However, four of them became permanent settlements and two (Pernambuco to the north and São Vicente to the south) turned out to be viable and lucrative.

[7] As happened in the Spanish colonial outposts, the first Portuguese settlements had to be fortified to defend them from indian attacks. Procurement of supplies was difficult and for a while the Portuguese obtained most of their food by trading with the indigenous peoples and eating cassava instead of wheat, which was hard to grow in most of the region.

[8] Two agricultural systems developed, the *rozas* or farms and the large *fazendas*, given over to exports, mainly of sugarcane. In spite of favorable conditions, the *fazendas* took a long time to prosper, due to the lack of capital and labor. Agriculture and the discipline imposed on the plantations was foreign to the local peoples, whom the Portuguese forced to toil in exchange for European products. The settlers soon decided to obtain slave workers through expeditions which hunted for indians or through other indians acting as intermediaries.

[9] During the second half of the 16th century, many indians of the region had been decimated by illnesses (influenza, smallpox, measles) or had fled to other areas. African slaves were then imported to grow sugar. This trade grew and it is estimated that from 3 to 4 million Africans arrived in Brazil between the 16th and 17th century. In 1848, as a result of pressures similar to those of 1530, the Crown appointed a general governor, who with 1,000 men carried out an expedition to Brazil, establishing the capital in Bahia (now Salvador) on the north-eastern coast. A bishopric was created in 1551. Only 50 years after the first contact, Brazil had reached the same degree of European institutionalization which characterized the Spanish territories.

[10] The Jesuits had started coming to the country by that time, and soon became the strongest branch of the Catholic Church, unlike in Spanish America, where they arrived much later than other orders. The Jesuits were very active,

learnt the Guarani language to convert indians to Catholicism and established villages very similar to the missions in the Spanish areas. The main contacts between indians and Europeans (war, trade, slavery and missions) were the same as in the Spanish areas. Due to these contacts, Guaraní became the language used in that century for all kinds of exchanges.

[11] Brazil carried out major expansions towards the west of the Tordesillas line, whose meridian was drawn up 370 leagues to the west of Cape Verde. This expansion reached the slopes of the Andes mountain range and, from north to south, from the Amazon to the Río de la Plata. In the north, the movement was led by the Jesuits who established several missions along the Amazon. In the northeast, cattle farmers from the sugar areas of Pernambuco and Bahia ventured to the heart of the continent, looking for new grazing lands and reached today's Piauí, Goiás and Maranhao regions.

[12] The westward march was led by the *paulistas*, as São Paulo settlers were known. In the search for indian slaves, gold and precious stones, the paulistas set up major expeditions to the interior, known as *bandeiras*. The incorporation of Portugal into the Spanish kingdom in 1580 facilitated the *paulistas'* incursions, since inner borders were broken down and the Tordesillas division became ineffective. The *bandeiras* took the *paulistas* to Peru's mining regions and even to Bogota, Colombia. They also explored the region of Matto Grosso and to the south attacked local *reducciones* (missions), particularly those of Guaira. Here the guarani people were already relatively immune to disease and were accustomed to collective agricultural work. In most cases, the *paulistas* met resistance from the indians and from the Jesuits who protected them. The human hunts were so devastating that the missions were gradually pushed further and further south until they reached the "Seven Towns", in today's Rio Grande state.

[13] It was not just the *paulistas* who penetrated the dense forests. Thousands of Africans also sought refuge there, fleeing from the coastal plantations where they were kept as slaves. Africans, indigenous Americans and their mixed

ENVIRONMENT

There are five major regions in Brazil. The Amazon Basin, in the North, is the largest tropical rainforest in the world. It consists of lowlands covered with rainforest and rivers. The Carajás mountain range contains one of the world's largest mineral reserves, rich in iron, manganese, copper, nickel and bauxite. The economy is mainly extractive. The northeastern "sertao" consists of rocky plateaus with a semi-arid climate and scrub vegetation. Cattle raising is the main economic activity. The more humid coastal strip, situated on the "Serra do mar" (Coastal Sierra), has numerous sugarcane and cocoa plantations. In the southeast, the terrain consists of huge plateaus bordered in the east by the Serra do Mar mountain range. The main crops are coffee, cotton, corn and sugarcane. The southern plateau, with sub-tropical climate, is the country's main agricultural region, where coffee, soybeans, corn and wheat are grown. In the far south, on the Rio Grande do Sul plains, cattle raising is the main economic activity. Finally, the mid-west region is made up of vast plains where cattle raising predominates. With the devastation of the Amazon region, caused by unrestrained felling of trees and forest fires, the habitats of many species have been destroyed.

THE SOCIETY

Peoples: Brazilians come from the ethnic and cultural integration of native inhabitants (mainly Guaraní), African slaves and European (mostly Portuguese) immigrants. Arab and Japanese minorities have also settled in the Rio-Sao Paulo area. Contrary to what is commonly admitted, racial discrimination does exist and the groups fighting it are rapidly gaining strength.

Religion: Most are baptized Catholic; but there is considerable merging into syncretic Afro-Brazilian cults (*candomblé* and *umbanda*).

Language: Portuguese is the official and predominant language.

Political Parties: Brazilian Social Democratic Party (PSDB); Party of the Liberal Alliance (PFL); Party of the Brazilian Democratic Movement (PMDB); Worker's Party (PT); People's Reform Party (PPR); Democratic Labor Party (PDT); Brazilian Labor Party (PTB); the Communist Party split into many groups: Partido Comunista do Brasil (PC do B), Partido Comunista Brasileiro (PCB orthodox communists), and the People's Socialist Party. In addition, there are countless other minor national or provincial organizations.

Social Organizations: Workers are grouped together primarily in the Consolidated Union of Workers (CUT), the General Confederation of Workers (CGT) and the Labor Union Force. Many labor unions do not belong to any of these, preferring to remain independent. Movement of the Landless (MST), an association of workers without land whose agenda is agrarian reform in rural areas, and land for the construction of housing, in urban areas. National Union of Indigenous Peoples (UNI), an association of Brazil's different indigenous groups. Pastoral Commission of the Earth (CPT) and Indigenous Missionary Council (CIMI), pastoral groups of the Catholic Church involved in social action in these areas. Defence Network of the Human Race (REDEH), an eco-feminist organization. "Torture No More", state groups committed to the defence of human rights.

THE STATE

Official Name: República Federativa do Brasil.
Administrative Divisions: 26 States, 1 Federal District.
Capital: Brasilia, 1,492,500 people (1994).
Other cities: São Paulo 16,417,000 people (1995); Rio de Janeiro 5,473,900 (1994); Salvador 2,070,300; Belo Horizonte 3,000,000 (1994); Recife 1,297,000; Porto Alegre 1,500,000 (1994); Manaus 1,005,600 (1994). **Government:** Fernando Henrique Cardoso, President since 1995. Bicameral legislature. **National Holiday:** September 7, Independence Day (1822). **Armed Forces:** 295,000 troops (1995). **Other:** 243,000 Public Security Forces.

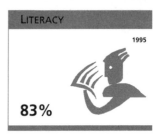

descendants joined forces in constant war against the colonial military expeditions. They also founded villages known by the African terms *quilombo* or *mokambo*, the most famous of which were at Palmares (1630-1695), in northeastern Brazil, where the legendary Zumbi led the struggle. The Brazilian anti-racist movement still commemorates the date of Zumbi's death in battle, November 20, as Black Consciousness Day.

[14] Meanwhile, Brazil found itself involved in a war of independence between the Netherlands and Spain. Flanders and the Netherlands had been "inherited" by the Spanish Crown. Between 1630 and 1654, the Dutch reasserted their control over Pernambuco after a failed attempt to conquer Bahia, which was repulsed by the joint efforts of native Americans, Africans and Portuguese.

[15] When Spain and Portugal were again separated in 1688, their colonial borders had shifted and the Tordesillas line could not be reinstated. In 1696, a bandeirantes expedition struck the first gold in what is now Minas Gerais. Gold mining peaked in the 18th century. The viceregal capital was transferred from Salvador to Rio de Janeiro in 1763 mostly due to the effect of these mines on the Brazilian economy.

[16] The local ruling class began to benefit from an expanding export economy and soon expressed a growing desire to dispense with the Portuguese role as intermediaries in their trade with Europe. The first moves towards independence came in the late 18th century and were rapidly crushed by the colonial power. Brazil's main freedom figure, Ensign Tiradentes, was executed in 1792 for his leading role in the Minas Conspiracy three years earlier.

[17] When Napoleon invaded the Iberian peninsula in 1808, Portuguese King Dom João VI had to transfer his court to Brazil, making the country semi-independent. Portugal ceased to be an intermediary and Brazil then dealt directly with its main customer, Britain. In this way, the Brazilian merchants prospered at the expense of other sectors linked to the Portuguese monopoly. The

1821 Oporto revolution in Portugal was an attempt to reinstate the old colonial system based on monopoly. When the King returned to Lisbon, the Brazilian merchants - determined to secure their gains - declared independence with British blessing. Brazil became an empire and Pedro I, formerly prince-regent, became its emperor in 1822..

[18] The following decade was one of the most turbulent in Brazilian history. From 1831 to 1835, a regency unsuccessfully tried to put an end to the civil war in the provinces and to the army's insubordination. In 1834, the Constitution was amended to decentralize the government, with the creation of provincial assemblies with considerable local powers, and to choose a regent for a period of four years. In 1835, Diego Antonio Feijóo, a priest, was elected and fought for two years against the break-up - with rebellions in the south, fought by the *gaúchos* of the State of Rio Grande, such as the Farrapos War (1835-1845). He was forced to resign in 1837. He was replaced by Pedro Araújo Lima. Impatient with the regency, Brazilians hoped to find in an Emperor the figurehead that would unite them. In 1840, Pedro de Alcántara - Pedro I's son - was declared of age and was enthroned with the name of Pedro II.

[19] The Empire lasted from 1822 to 1889. During this time Brazil consolidated its national unity and extended its borders over the areas settled by bandeirantes in the 17th and 18th centuries. This period of territorial expansion included the annexation of the Cisplatine Province (now Uruguay), the war of the Triple Alliance against Paraguay, in which Brazil annexed 90,000 square kilometers of Paraguayan territory; and, towards the end of the century, the annexation of Bolivia's Acre territory.

[20] Under the rule of Pedro II, the population grew from 4 to 14 million, but the economy continued to depend on large estates and the export of tropical agricultural products, mainly coffee. The abolition of slavery in 1888 accelerated the fall of the monarchy, but brought little change in the social and political conditions of blacks. As illiterate people, they were denied the right to vote and therefore political freedom.

[21] The gap between urban and rural areas widened in the last decades of the century. The urban middle class, the military and coffee growers pressed for the country's speedy modernization. For them, the monarchy was excessively linked to the old systems of production and to cattle-raising landowners. A republic was seen as a more convenient model for the modernization pursued by these three groups. In 1889, a conspiracy of modernists was supported by the army. Pedro II abdicated and was exiled in Europe.

[22] The consolidation and establishment of republican institutions experienced serious difficulties. Prudente de Morais was elected first civilian President in 1894. The Federal Republican Party had been founded in 1893, but the Navy rebelled both that year and the following. From 1893 to 1895, Brazil suffered a federalist rebellion in Rio Grande do Sul. From 1896 to 1897, the Canudos war, in which a religious community was wiped out by the republic's troops, took place in the northeastern provinces. This war was due to a clash between the interior - poor, illiterate and desperate - and the coast - literate, with a developed economy and seeking modernization.

[23] Uprisings, outbreaks of authoritarianism and fights among the regional oligarchies were frequent. Neither electoral justice nor the secret ballot were yet instituted and dissatisfaction with election results was widespread. Elections were rigged since the electoral rolls often included deceased voters.

[24] In the economic sphere, coffee remained the major export. Between 1914 and 1918, World War I brought an economic boom to Brazil, since the country was one of the main suppliers of commodities to the powers at war. Between 1920 and 1930, coffee prices slumped as international competition reduced sales and, in 1929, due to that year's world crisis, 29 million bags of coffee were left unsold.

[25] In 1930 a coup resulted in the appointment of Getulio Vargas as president. The Revolution of 1930 marked the end of the landowners' predominance, already weakened by the 1929 slump which had destroyed the coffee economy.

[26] Getulio Vargas introduced the "import substitution" model which

gave priority to national industrial development, especially in iron and steel during World War II. Vargas held power from 1937 to 1945 as dictator of the New State and in 1950 was elected constitutional president. Nationalism and reformist defence of workers' rights, *trabalhismo* (laborism), the name of his movement, were the two outstanding features of his government.

[27] In 1953 the state oil monopoly was created and social security laws were passed. Vargas committed suicide in August 1954 leaving a letter accusing "dark forces" (referring to imperialism and its local accomplices) of blocking his efforts to govern according to popular and national aspirations.

[28] Juscelino Kubitschek's administration (1956-61) promoted development and admitted transnationals to the Brazilian market, granting them exceptional privileges. Brasilia was built during his term in office to mark a new era in the country's economic development. In 1960, the federal capital, previously at Rio de Janeiro, was transferred to the new city. Kubitschek's successor, Janio Quadros, initiated some changes in foreign policy but resigned in unclear circumstances barely seven months after taking office.

[29] In September 1961, Vice-President João Goulart, the Labor Party leader and Getulio Vargas' political heir, assumed the presidency. High-ranking military officers opposed his appointment but the new President was backed by a civilian/military movement which wanted a legal government, led by Leonel Brizola, governor of Rio Grande do Sul. A compromise parliamentary solution was adopted, with Tancredo Neves becoming Prime Minister. The presidential system was reinstated in January 1963 after a national plebiscite. Goulart then tried to introduce a series of "basic reforms", including agrarian reform and legislation to regulate profit transfers abroad by foreign companies. A US-backed military coup deposed him on April 1 1964.

[30] The new government passed Institutional Act No. 1, which repealed the 1946 liberal constitution, allowing the revocation of parliamentary mandates and the suspension of political rights. A string of arrests all over the country forced major political leaders such as João

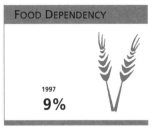

FOOD DEPENDENCY

1997
9%

EXTERNAL DEBT

1998

PER CAPITA
US$ 1,399

FOREIGN TRADE

Millions US$ 1998

IMPORTS
78,557

EXPORTS
57,826

Goulart, Leonel Brizola, Miguel Arraes and later even Juscelino Kubitschek into exile or to fight underground.

31   The military junta appointed General Humberto de Alencar Castello Branco head of government for the remainder of the constitutional period, but his mandate was later extended until 1967. In the October 1965 state elections, opposition candidates won in Rio de Janeiro and Minas Gerais. The military retaliated with Institutional Act No. 2, stating that the President would henceforth be appointed by an electoral college and banning existing political parties. A two-party system was created guaranteeing a majority to the pro-government National Renewal Alliance (ARENA), virtually excluding the opposition Party of the Brazilian Democratic Movement (PMDB) from power.

32   In January 1967, a new Constitution came into effect and two months later General Arthur da Costa e Silva was appointed President. In December 1968, to confront growing electoral support for the popular opposition, Institutional Act No. 5 was passed, granting full autocratic powers to the military regime. In August 1969, Costa e Silva was replaced by a Military Junta that remained in power until the following October, when another army general, Emilio Garrastazú Médici, former head of the National Information Services (SNI), became President. The Médici administration was marked by extreme repression of both the legal and illegal opposition, while his economic ministers fed middle class consumerism. In 1974, General Ernesto Geisel was appointed President by the Junta. He put an end to the state oil monopoly, signed a controversial nuclear agreement with West Germany and granted further prerogatives to foreign investors. Its arms industry placed Brazil fifth among the world's main arms exporters.

33   Under the Geisel administration there was a gradual relaxation of political controls, which allowed the democratic process to evolve. In 1974 and 1978, despite media censorship, the PMDB achieved significant victories at the polls. At the end of his mandate, Geisel delivered the reins of government to General João Baptista Figueiredo, also a former SNI head.

34   Figueiredo came to power in March 1979, announcing that he intended to complete the softening of political restrictions. A month later, a strike by 180,000 metalworkers in Sao Paulo led by Luis Inácio "Lula" da Silva was settled without violence, as a result of negotiations between the Labor Ministry and the Union. In November, the Brazilian Congress passed a bill granting a far broader amnesty to political opponents than the Executive had originally intended. As a result, political prisoners were released and exiles began to return.

35   In the economic-financial arena, the after-effects of the monetary policies applied by successive military governments were felt during the Figueiredo administration. Foreign debt spiralled and in the early 1980s, Brazil became an early exporter rather than importer of capital in its efforts to find funds to pay off the interest on its $100 billion debt.

36   In 1985, official statistics registered six million unemployed and 13 million under-employed, out of a population of more than 130 million, of which over 50 per cent lived below the poverty line and outside the formal economy, in cities alone. In July 1985, Ministry of Labor officials stated that "not even seven per cent growth per year for two consecutive decades would be enough to improve these peoples' living conditions".

37   The opposition's electoral victory in 1983 reflected enormous popular discontent. The central government held only 12 states while the opposition won 10, including the economically decisive states of São Paulo, Rio de Janeiro and Minas Gerais which accounted for 59 per cent of the population and 75 per cent of the country's GDP.

38   Tancredo de Almeida Neves, governor of Minas Gerais, was the chief co-ordinator of the opposition front. A popular campaign for direct elections in 1984 failed, but the opposition won the Electoral College due to divisions within the ruling party. Tancredo Neves was elected President and José Sarney, who a few weeks earlier had been president of the Government party, became Vice President. Tancredo announced plans for a new social order: the New Republic.

39   In this context, agrarian reform, renegotiation of the foreign debt and economic growth were seen as the most effective means towards modernization and democratization. The day before his inauguration, Tancredo Neves was hospitalized and rushed into surgery. José Sarney was sworn in as interim president but stayed on after Tancredo died on April 21 1985. Sarney legalized the Communist Party and other left-wing organizations, some after 20 or even 40 years of illegal existence. Democratization began to take place with the approval of direct election for President of the Republic and mayors of state capitals. A national assembly was convened for January 1987 to draft a new constitution and illiterate people were granted the right to vote.

40   In 1986 Sarney declared a moratorium on the foreign debt and launched the Cruzado Plan to fight inflation. The plan produced impressive short-term results: a boom in consumption and economic growth. This startling prosperity coincided with the November 1987 parliamentary and state governmental elections which the PMDB won by a landslide. The new Congress faced the task of drafting a new constitution which would formally inaugurate the return to democratic government. It set Sarney's term at five years, after considerable pressure from the Executive to ignore the groups who wanted to honor Tancredo's promise of reducing the term to four years.

41   But the Cruzado Plan could not be maintained without fighting financial speculation and halting pressure from the financial sector. Two days after the election, the price freeze came to an end and inflation leapt to a monthly rate in double figures. The planned agrarian reform was gradually reduced.

42   In the 1988 municipal elections, the left-wing and center-left PDT, PT, and PSDB parties began to make inroads on the PMDB's popularity.

43   In December 1988, landowners from the Acre region murdered Chico Mendes, leader of the *seringueiro* (rubber tappers) movement and the Amazonian indigenous peoples. They had organized an *empates* struggle (linking arms to prevent trees being felled) to prevent the clearing of the forests, and proposed the creation of reserves, to guarantee their right to live and work in the forest without destroying it.

44   Direct presidential elections - the first in 29 years - were held in November and December 1989. Nearly 80 million people voted and the final round was fought between conservative candidate Fernando Collor de Mello and Workers' Party leader, Luiz Inacio "Lula" da Silva. Collor de Mello, a young politician who had begun his career under the military regime, won the second round with 42.75 per cent to his opponent's 37.86 per cent of the vote.

45   On taking office, on March 16 1990, Collor de Mello announced the New Brazil Plan, an attempt to stem inflation by confiscating 80 per cent of the country's available financial assets.

46   Collor adopted the neo-liberal model of opening up the economy, with the privatization of state enterprises and the reduction of tariff barriers controlling the import of foreign products. However, he failed to control inflation, to hold off a recession and to reduce unemployment.

47   In this complex economic setting, the Government faced a critical social situation and the escalation of violence. In 1991, more than 350 street children were murdered in Rio de Janeiro. The parliamentary commission set up to investigate these murders estimated that over 5,000 children had been killed in this way over the past three years. The same commission reported that the persecution of homeless children - seven million according to estimates of the Brazilian Center for Childhood and Adolescence - was carried out by paramilitary groups financed by shop owners.

48   The indigenous peoples are under the constant threat of "progress". They have suffered epidemics, the degradation or loss of natural resources, pollution and a systematic fall in their standard of living. They are being decimated by disease, high suicide rates, murders and other violence committed by miners and by the police. Many also refrain from having children as they feel too threatened to do so.

49   The disappearance of indigenous cultures is linked to the accelerated destruction of the tropical forest in order to exploit its logging potential or to turn it into grassland or mining areas (especially

for gold, which pollutes the rivers with mercury). This predatory policy prevents the regeneration of natural resources and so they become depleted. The so-called "Amazonia Legal" is an area considered strategic by the army, which in 1995 began to invest several billions of dollars to monitor it by a satellite tracking system.

[50] In September 1991, thousands of people belonging to the Landless Movement of Brazil (MST) staged a march in the state of Rio Grande do Sul, where there were 150,000 families of landless farmers alongside 9 million hectares of land not in production. The protesters demanded settlements to work and that the 4,700 million cruzeiros earmarked for agrarian reform should be spent. Up till then, only 800 million had actually been used.

[51] Late in September 1991, a 400 per cent inflation rate and an increase in bank interest rates to almost 1,000 per cent a year, triggered wide-scale redundancies in the industrial sector which, in São Paulo alone, left more than one million jobless.

[52] In May 1992, a Parliamentary Investigating Commission was set up to study government corruption which took the form of influence-peddling in exchange for deposits made to the President's personal account. Demonstrations against corruption and the discovery of evidence implicating other government figures in these schemes led all the political parties to vote for the President's impeachment.

[53] In September, Congress voted to relieve the President of his duties, so that he could be put on trial. Vice-President Itamar Franco became interim President. In December 1992, Collor was found guilty by the Senate of "criminal responsibility" and sentenced. His presidential mandate was removed and his political rights suspended until the year 2000. Franco officially assumed the presidency until the end of that presidential term.

[54] The President tried to project an image of austerity and ethics onto the management of public affairs. After several changes in the Ministry of Economics, Fernando Henrique Cardoso was appointed to this cabinet position.

[55] According to figures provided by the Pastoral Commission of the Earth, in 1992 there were 15,042

rural slaves - triple the number recorded the previous year. According to data gathered by the Federal Bureau of Statistics, nearly four million people living in rural areas worked under conditions of virtual slavery. Collor's administration had zoned 20 million hectares as new land for indigenous peoples. This alleviated but did not fully solve the desperate situation of the indians.

[56] In late 1992, 111 inmates of São Paulo's Carandiru prison were killed by members of the Military Police who had entered the premises to deal with a dispute between rival groups of prisoners. Post-mortem examinations found that 85 of the prisoners had been executed after having surrendered. In July 1993, police members murdered 8 street children while they were sleeping on the doorsteps of the Church of the Candelaria, in Rio de Janeiro. The following month, 50 men entered the *favela* (shantytown) of Vigario Geral and killed 21 innocent people, to avenge the death of four military police who had been killed in a confrontation with drug dealers.

[57] The general outcry over these incidents led to some official response. In Rio de Janeiro, for the first time ever, a judge handed down prison sentences to the leaders of *jogo do bicho*, an illegal lottery linked to drug dealers and the police. In São Paulo, a police investigator received the maximum prison sentence (516 years) for causing the death of 18 prisoners who had died of asphyxiation in a police cell in 1992.

[58] The Citizens' Action Against Hunger and for Life group, founded in 1993 by Herbert de Souza, organized tens of thousands of committees throughout the country to collect and distribute food and obtain more jobs. Two million people, mostly women, priests and trade unions joined this grassroots movement. By August 1994, over four million families had received food aid.

[59] Towards the end of 1993, Economics Minister Cardoso presented the Plan Real, an economic stabilization project which ended index-linking and created a new currency, the Real, in July 1994. The success of this anti-inflationary policy rapidly made Cardoso the most popular candidate for the October elections. In the first round

he beat the previous favorite Luis Ignacio "Lula" da Silva, of the PT.

[60] Cardoso began the privatization of state companies, including part of the operations of Petrobras and the telecommunications sector, but economic recession rose along with stabilization which led to the rise of unemployment, urban labor conflicts, crime and land seizures by poor peasants.

[61] In September 1995, the President announced a government Multi-Year Plan with investments amounting to $153.39 billion, mainly focused on economic infrastructure. According to statistics issued in August, ten per cent of the population received 48 per cent of the income, four times the amount earned by the poor half of the country. According to the World Bank, 43 per cent of fertile land belonged to 0.83 per cent of land owners in 1997. These figures placed Brazil among countries with extreme social inequality. In June, Parliament passed a constitutional reform which enabled presidential re-election.

[62] In September, Cardoso issued a presidential decree which guaranteed indigenous peoples the exclusive use of 23 plots of land covering 8.4 million hectares, some 10 per cent of Brazilian territory. The marches and seizures of the Landless received the implicit support of the Vatican's Pontifical Council of Justice and Peace in February 1998, in the document "For better land distribution: the land reform challenge".

[63] The worst fires in the history of the Amazon displaced peasants and entire indigenous communities in the early part of 1998. By March, more than a quarter of the northern state of Roraima had been devastated by the fires.

[64] In 1999, former president Itamar Franco, then Governor of Minas Gerais, declared a moratorium on debt with the Federal Government. In January the Government freed the *real* against the dollar, resulting in a 10 per cent devaluation. The president of the Central Bank resigned but the *real* continued its slide with devaluation reaching 50 per cent in February. The *real* crisis hit consumption, industry working with imported resources and relations with Mercosur partners, but benefited the export sector.

[65] In August 2000, Brazil sent troops to its border with Colombia to prevent 'fallout' from its neighbour's US-backed blitz on drug traffickers.■

The Landless Movement and a new Brazil

The *Movimento dos Sem Terra* (MST-landless movement) has become a point of reference for social movements in Brazil and throughout Latin America because of its ongoing struggle for agrarian reform.

The MST arose in the early 1980s. This was a time of democratic flowering after 20 years of military dictatorship, and the capitalist system faced sharp internal contradictions. Broad sectors of the Brazilian population were struggling to make a living in rural areas. The land had historically been concentrated in the hands of a few and, as a result of agricultural modernization, tens of thousands of people were forced to leave the land and seek their fortunes in the large cities, worsening social conditions there.

The struggle for land is not new in Brazil. The MST is the most recent expression of the movement's history. Throughout the 19th century, indigenous communities and the Afro-Brazilians who had escaped slavery established free communities, or *quilombos* to work the land and protect it from bandits and white colonists, who were gaining ground and expanding landholdings of hundreds of thousands of hectares.

Early in 1900, several movements arose with messianic tendencies and charismatic leaders: Canudos (Antonio Conselheiro), Contestado (José María) and Cangazo (Lampiao). Even af-ter they were defeated, the fight for agrarian reform continued throughout the nation. With Marxist influences, some peasants formed class-based associations and founded the Peasant Leagues, the Union of Agricultural Labourers and Workers of Brazil (ULTAB) and the Movement of Landless Farmers (MASTER).

In 1964, the armed forces overthrew president Joao Goulart and the peasant movements were banned, their principal leaders were assassinated, imprisoned or exiled. Through the activities of MASTER in some southern states, which involved dozens of families who took over abandoned farmland, today's MST began to take shape, and was formally established in 1984. Since then, the movement has - through occupations - obtained land for some 200,000 families, while a similar number of families wait in settlements located in various parts of the country for their own land to farm.

A RESPONSE FOR EVERY CONFLICT

Tensions have hotted up between the government of President Fernando Henrique Cardoso and the MST in recent years. In 1996, police officers assassinated 19 "landless" peasants in Eldorado de Carajás, in Pará state. In an attempt to bolster its ranks, in April 1997 the MST organized a National March of the Landless, which brought some 100,000 people to Brasilia.

The peasants arrived in the capital from 15 states after walking as far as 1,000 km. The movement's representatives asked the President, "Why are we making this sacrifice?" The MST affirmed that the land must serve a social function, provide for everyone, and that widescale expropriations were necessary to fight land concentration in the hands of the few and the expansion of large landholdings.

The leaders maintained that Brazil must "reorganize agricultural production" to prioritize the internal market and supply the population in order to eliminate hunger. And the movement's objectives went even further. These affirm that agrarian reform must be linked to the issues of establishing agro-industry and co-operatives, and the landless settlements, in order to democratize rural Brazil and guarantee the population access to public services, especially education.

These measures, says the MST, would help combat the exodus of rural dwellers toward the cities because it would generate conditions for rural development, encouraging families to stay in their places of origin. The "landless" delegates exhorted the President to change his agricultural and economic policies and open the way for agricultural loans and insurance to make family farming viable, increase employment and improve the distribution of wealth.

Three years later, in April 2000, confrontations began to intensify again. The movement and other social organiztions (indigenous communities, Afro-Brazilians, feminists, environmentalists and human rights defenders) led the "counter-celebration" to mark the 500 years since the Portuguese arrival in Brazil. In the large urban centres, repression was severe and hundreds of the landless people were injured, some 70 arrested and one person killed.

The landless movements in Paraguay, Argentina and Chile condemned the incidents of repression, as did the indigenous communities in Chiapas, Mexico, united under the Zapatista National Liberation Army (EZLN). The Catholic Bishops' Conference of Brazil added its voice to the denunciation, maintaining that the tense situation was due to governmental authoritarianism, and defended the MST when the Government accused it of "turning political".

The bishops stated that "whatever is not political is not human. If a movement of this magnitude did not have a political dimension it would be a band of innocents dancing to find a way to survive ... agrarian reform is not possible without intervening in the broadest structure, which is politics, and as such is absolutely correct, legal and necessary". ∎

Brunei

Brunei

Population: 321,000 (1999)
Area: 5,770 SQ KM
Capital: Bandar Seri Begawan
Currency: Brunei dollar
Language: Behasa Malayu

B runei was known to be trading with and paying tribute to China in the 6th century AD. Today's Sultanate is what remains of a 13th century Islamic empire that once covered most of the island of Borneo, from which it derives its name. It then came under Hindu influence for a time through allegiance to the Majapahit kingdom in Java. When the ships of Ferdinand Magellan's expedition anchored off Brunei in 1521, the fifth sultan, the great Bolkiah, controlled practically the whole of Borneo, the Sulu Archipelago, and neighbouring islands.

[2] Toward the end of the 16th century, Brunei was torn by internal strife. A gradual decline in power continued through the 19th century, notably when in 1841, as payment for help in quelling a two-year long rebellion, the Sultan had to turn the province of Sarawak over to British adventurer James Brooke, a strange figure who became a European "Rajah" over a Malayan state. In 1846 the British annexed the strategic island of Labuan, and in following years paved the way for the secession of the province of Sabah. In 1888, the British consolidated their position and established separate protectorates over Brunei, Sarawak and Sabah.

[3] Following World War II, despite Britain's efforts, the island began the decolonization process. An agreement signed with Rajah Brooke in 1946 made Sarawak and Sabah into British colonies while Kalimantan (former Dutch Borneo) gained independence in 1954 as part of Indonesia.

[4] All that was left of the British protectorate was the Sultanate of Brunei, reduced to a tiny territorial enclave between two Malaysian provinces, scarcely 40 km from the

border with Indonesia. In 1929, the transnational company Shell discovered oil deposits in the area. In the following decades, drilling for oil and natural gas began, reaching current production rates of 175,000 barrels a day.

[5] In 1962, Sultan Omar Ali Saiffudin accepted a proposal from Malaysian Premier Abdul Rahman to join the Federation of Malaysia, which at the time included Sabah, Sarawak, Singapore, and the provinces of the Malayan peninsula.

The Brunei People's Party, (Rakyat) which held 16 seats in the 33-member Legislative Council, was not keen on the idea and opposed the move, proposing instead the creation of a unified state comprising Northern Borneo, Sarawak and Sabah, but excluding peninsular Malaya.

[6] A mass uprising broke out in December 1962, staged by the Rakyat, backed by the Barisan Sosialis (Socialist Party) of Singapore, with support from the anticolonialist Sukarno regime in Indonesia. The rebels opposed integration to the Federation of Malaysia, demanding participation in administration and the end of the autocratic regime. The rebellion was rapidly stifled, the party outlawed and the leaders arrested or forced into exile.

[7] Finally, in spite of ethnic, historical, and cultural ties with Malaya, Sultan Omar decided to keep his sultanate out of the Federation. He was not satisfied with arrangements for power-sharing with the other Malayan rulers and least of all with Federation hopes of a share in his territory's oil resources.

[8] In 1976, with Malaysian prompting and UN support, an opportunity arose to renegotiate the anachronistic colonial statute, when the newly-elected Malaysian Prime Minister Datuk Hussain Onn promised to respect Brunei's independence. In 1977, Brunei finally accepted independence, but postponed implementation until January 1 1984.

[9] Power was formally transferred on schedule but celebrations were postponed until February 23 1985, so that foreign guests could attend. One month later independence was formally proclaimed, and Hassanal Bokiah, son of Sultan Omar, who had abdicated in his favor in 1967, dissolved the Legislative Council and went on to govern by decree.

[10] Brunei embarked on independent existence in particularly favorable conditions for a Third World country. It had a relatively small population, a high per capita income, low unemployment, a generous social security system and considerable foreign exchange reserves. These reserves stood at $14 billion in 1984.

[11] The main sources of tension were the power struggle within the ruling family and the presence of foreigners in all the key positions of public office, the economy and the armed forces.

[12] Problems on the domestic front included poor basic education. In spite of advanced legislation for education, including a student transport allowance and free accommodation, the illiteracy rate kept climbing; it was estimated at 45 per cent in 1982, posing a serious obstacle to filling civil service posts with Brunei nationals.

[13] The Sultan was aware that the country depended on a non-renewable resource, and Brunei imported nearly 80 per cent of its food. Consequently, with a view to achieving self-sufficiency in food production, he attempted to diversify the economy and promote a new land-owning class. Only 10 per cent of the arable land was

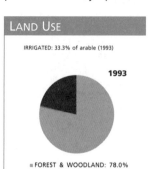

WORKERS

% OF LABOUR FORCE	**1998**

■ FEMALE: 35%   ■ MALE: 65%

1990

■ SERVICES: 73.6%
■ INDUSTRY: 24.3%
■ AGRICULTURE: 2.0%

LAND USE

IRRIGATED: 33.3% of arable (1993)

1993

■ FOREST & WOODLAND: 78.0%
■ ARABLE: 0.5%
■ OTHER: 21.5%

PUBLIC EXPENDITURE

DEFENCE EXPENDITURE (% of goverment exp.)	**13.8%** (1997)
MILITARY EXPENDITURE (% of health & education)	**125%** (1990/91)

cultivated, and small farmers, especially rubber-tree growers, tended to emigrate to the city where they believed a higher standard of living awaited for them.

[14] Economically, Brunei depended upon the complex interplay of transnational interests. The Government's partnership in exploiting natural gas reserves with Brunei Shell Petroleum and Mitsubishi, a shipping contract with Royal Dutch Shell and recent oil field concessions to Woods Petroleum and Sunray Borneo, introduced powerful new parties into the process of national decision-making.

[15] In March 1985, the Government announced the creation of an Energy Control Board to supervise the activities of the Brunei Shell Petroleum Company, a company funded equally by the Government and Shell.

[16] Membership of the Association of South East Asian Nations (ASEAN) and the UN, obtained in 1984, meant greater international support for the new nation.

[17] At this time 20 per cent of the population was living below the poverty line of $500 a month. Also, 90 per cent of all consumer goods - including basic foodstuffs - were still being imported, as the country produces little other than oil. The vast amount of imports explains the extremely high cost of living.

[18] In early 1987, it was reported that a request from US colonel Oliver North for "non-lethal" aid to the Nicaraguan contras led the Sultan of Brunei to deposit a $10 million donation in a Swiss bank account.

[19] The country's military dependence on Britain and the US increased. Under economic restructuring policies applied in recent years, only the military budget grew.

[20] While foreign investment in other areas remained unchanged or fallen, such investment in the military sector also increased. In August 1988, 3,000 British soldiers and Gurkhas based in Hong Kong carried out joint manoeuvres in the Sultanate's tropical forests

[21] In early 1991, Sultan Hassanal Bolkiah freed 6 political prisoners who had been detained after the failed 1962 revolt. The liberation was ascribed to political pressure by the British Government. This same year Brunei signed a contract for almost $150 million with the United Kingdom in order to modernize its army.

[22] In mid-1992, Brunei joined the Non-Aligned Movement, together with Vietnam and India. The commemoration of the 25th anniversary of Hassanal Bolkiah's reign stressed the role of the monarchy in affirming Brunei's national identity. Brunei's sultan, the only absolute monarch in the Far East, is also the richest person in the world.

[23] In September 1992, Brunei together with other members of ASEAN - Indonesia, Singapore, Thailand, Malaysia and Philippines - signed an agreement to create the first integrated market in Asia in 2007. This project stipulated the creation of "growth triangles" - association between some ASEAN members to deregulate trade in certain economic sectors, as a preparation for the overall liberalization planned for the year 2007. Thus, in March 1994, Brunei created - together with Philippines, Malaysia and Indonesia - a sub-regional market to intensify trade in tourism, fishing, and transport by sea and air.

[24] In February 1995, the Solidarity National Party of Brunei - the sole political organization in the country - organized its opening congress and declared its total support for the Sultan. Its leader, Abdul Latif Chuchu also spoke about a royal decree of 1984 which asserted that Brunei's nation-building was based on the principle of a democratic Malayan-Muslim monarchy. The Sultan qualified as a sign of "openness" his announcement that the state of emergency would be extended. In October 1995, Brunei joined the World Bank and the IMF.

[25] During 1996, the sultanate continued policies aimed at making Brunei an attractive proposition as a service economy country. Negotiations with Southeast Asian leaders were intensified following the regional stock market crisis in 1997, in order to co-ordinate policies to stabilize the regional economy and establish a recovery strategy. In the negotiations, the possibility was discussed of using local currencies instead of the US dollar for trade transactions within the area.

[26] In early 1998, uncontrollable fires in the Indonesian part of the Island of Borneo caused dense smoke clouds over Brunei. These affected daily life in the Sultanate and spread to several other nations of the region, affecting tourism.

[27] In August of that year, the Sultan named his eldest son, Al-Muhtadee Billah his successor - next in line in a 600 year-old Islamic dynasty which is the oldest in the region. The announcement was made in the midst of the worst economic crisis since independence. Construction and the export sector began a slow recovery during 1999. ∎

PROFILE

ENVIRONMENT

Brunei comprises two tracts of land located on the northwestern coast of Borneo, in the Indonesian Archipelago. It has a tropical, rainy climate slightly tempered by the sea. Rubber is harvested in the dense forests. There are major petroleum deposits along the coast. The country is one of the world's main exporters of liquid gas.

SOCIETY

Peoples: Malay 67 per cent; Chinese 15 per cent; Indian and other 18 per cent. **Religions:** Islam (official), Buddhism and Christianity. **Languages:** Behasa Malayu (official), Chinese and English. **Political Parties:** Brunei Solidarity National Party

THE STATE

Official Name: Islamic Sultanate of Brunei.
Administrative divisions: 4 districts. **Capital:** Bandar Seri Begawan, 65,000 people (1994). **Other Cities:** Kuala Belah 21,200 people; Seria 21,000 people; Tutong 13,000 people. **Government:** Hassanal Bolkiah Muizzaddin Waddaulah, Sultan and Prime Minister since 1967. **National Holiday:** January 1, Independence Day; July 16, the Sultan's birthday. **Armed Forces:** 4,900 (1995).

STATISTICS

DEMOGRAPHY

Population: 321,000 (1999)
Annual growth: 3.0 % (1975/97)
Estimates for year 2015 (million): 0.4 (1999)
Annual growth to year 2015: 1.6 % (1997/2015)
Urban population: 70.5 % (1997)
Children per woman: 2.8 (1998)

HEALTH

Life expectancy at birth: 76 years (1998)
male: 73 years (1998)
female: 78 years (1998)
Maternal mortality: 0 per 100,000 live births (1990-98)
Infant mortality: 8 per 1,000 (1998)
Under-5 child mortality: 9 per 1,000 (1998)
Daily calorie supply: 2,886 per capita (1996)

EDUCATION

Literacy: 89 % (1995)
male: 93 % (1995)
female: 85 % (1995)
School enrolment:
Primary total: 107 % (1990/96)
male: 109 % (1990/97)
female: 104 % (1990/97)
Secondary:
male: 71 % (1990/96)
female: 82 % (1990/96)
Tertiary: 7 % (1996)
Primary school teachers: one for every 15 (1995)

COMMUNICATIONS

70 newspapers (1996), 303 radios (1997), 417 TV sets (1996) and 263 main telephone lines (1996) per 1,000 people
Books: 16 new titles per 100,000 people (1992/94)

ECONOMY

Per capita, GNP: $ 27,270 (1997)
Annual growth, GNP: 0.4 % (1998)
Cereal imports: 35,297 metric tons (1998)

HDI (rank/value): 25/0.878 (1997)

Bulgaria

Balgarija

Population: 8,280,000 (1999)
Area: 110,910 SQ KM
Capital: Sofía (Sofija)
Currency: Leva
Language: Bulgarian

Bulgaria was occupied by the Slav people who spread across the area between the Danube and the Aegean Sea in the 7th and 6th centuries BC. Some of the old Thraco-Illyrian population were expelled, and the rest were assimilated by the invaders. The Slavs worked the land in small organized communities.

[2] The Bulgarians were among the non-European tribes who followed Attila. They were fierce warriors who lived by warfare and plunder. They first appeared in the region towards the end of the 5th century AD when they settled temporarily on the steppes north of the Black Sea and northeast of the Danube.

[3] Some tribes disappeared and others were enslaved by the Turks. Those tribes led by Kubrat remained in this region until the mid-7th century when the Kazars bore down on them, forcing them into crossing the Danube. They reached as far as Moesia, at that time a province of the Byzantine Empire. Emperor Constantine IV formally recognized the State of Bulgaria in the year 681.

[4] Constant invasions by foreign tribes, led to the new State consolidating its power in the center and southwest. Bulgarian leaders adopted the Slav language and culture. Prince Boris was initially baptized Roman Catholic, but in 870 he turned to the Orthodox Church.

[5] While the Patriarch of Byzantium recognized the independence of the Bulgarian Church, Rome refused to appoint a national patriarch. This support helped to consolidate the Kingdom's power. Under Simeon (893-927), the Bulgarian State extended its domain as far as the Adriatic, subduing the Serbs, and becoming the most powerful kingdom of Eastern Europe.

[6] Bulgaria's power declined after Simeon's death. Internal disputes among the nobility, the opposition of the peasants and renewed attacks from abroad led to its downfall. In 1014, Bulgaria lost all its territory to the Byzantine Empire, which kept control for more than 150 years. After a large uprising in 1185, the northern part of Bulgaria recovered its independence.

[7] During the reign of Ivan Asen II (1218-41) Bulgaria regained power and territory, including Albania, Epirus, Macedonia and Thracia. However, none of Ivan's successors managed to impose a central authority over these diverse areas where feudalism was the norm. By 1393 the whole of Bulgaria had fallen under Turkish rule.

[8] In the 17th and 18th centuries, after the wars with Austria and the unsuccessful siege of Vienna, the Ottoman Empire began to decline, though it still retained much of its territory. The former Bulgarian State was twice invaded by Russia in 1810 and 1828.

[9] Throughout the invasion period the Bulgarians maintained their cultural identity; keeping their language, music and folklore alive. Under Turkish domination, the Greek Orthodox Church assumed religious leadership, suppressing the independent patriarch. Hence, Bulgarian monks were among the precursors of the national liberation movement.

[10] The Bulgarian Church fought for 40 years to recover its independence. In 1870, the Sultan gave permission for the Church to create an exarchate with 15 dioceses. The first exarch (deputy patriarch) and his successors were declared schismatic and were excommunicated by the Greek patriarch; this further strengthened Bulgarian nationalism.

[11] From 1876 onwards, a series of revolts was cruelly put down. Some Bulgarian volunteers joined the ranks of the Serbian and Russian armies, who went to war against the Empire. One of Moscow's conditions for the Treaty of St Stephen, was the creation of a Bulgarian State. The European powers feared the creation of a Russian satellite in the Balkans so they blocked the motion.

[12] In the 1878 Berlin Congress, the "autonomous province" of Rumelia was created in the south, and the State of Bulgaria in the north. Rumelia was nominally under the Sultan's control, and Macedonia was to continue as part of the Ottoman Empire.

[13] The assembly approved a liberal Constitution, establishing a constitutional monarchy. Prince Alexander of Battenberg, grandson of Alexander II of Russia, was elected and assumed the Bulgarian throne in July 1878, swearing to uphold the Constitution. He suspended it two years later.

[14] The Prince set up a dictatorship, headed by Russian general LN Sobolev and other conservatives. The Russian Emperor's death modified Alexander's behavior, making him more attuned to Bulgarian issues. In 1885, he supported the liberal rebellion in Rumelia, the governor there was replaced and union with Bulgaria was proclaimed.

[15] The treaties of Bucharest and Top-Khane, signed in 1886, recognized Prince Alexander as the ruler of Rumelia and Bulgaria. However, he was subsequently taken to Russia against his will and forced to abdicate. Looking for someone who would be acceptable to Russia, as well as the rest of Europe, the Bulgarians finally appointed Ferdinand of Saxe-Coburg-Gotha as his replacement.

[16] Although initially distrusted, Ferdinand was able to gain the support of Vienna, London, Rome and Russia. He then concentrated on the reunification of the Bulgarians whose territory had been divided under the Treaty of Berlin. Prince Ferdinand proclaimed Bulgaria's independence in 1908, thereby breaking its nominal dependence upon Turkey.

[17] In 1912, Bulgaria signed secret military agreements with Greece and Serbia. In October of that year, Montenegro, accompanied by its Balkan allies, declared war on Istanbul. In May, Turkey ceded its European dominions, north of a line between Enos, in the Aegean Sea, and Midia, on the Black Sea.

[18] The allies did not agree with the distribution; Bulgaria confronted Greece and Serbia over the issue and Romania joined Serbia as its ally. The Second Balkan War quickly ended in Bulgarian defeat. In Bucharest, in August 1913, Macedonia was divided between Greece and Serbia, and Romania gained an area of northern Bulgaria, rich in natural resources.

[19] In 1913, the Bulgarian Government abandoned its traditionally pro-Russian stance, seeking closer ties with Germany. When World War I broke out the Bulgarian people and the army disapproved of the official policy, even though Serbia was beaten. Ferdinand surrendered to the Allies in 1918 and abdicated in favor of his son Boris.

LAND USE

IRRIGATED: 30.4% of arable (1993)

1993

- FOREST & WOODLAND: 35.0%
- ARABLE: 36.6%
- OTHER: 28.4%

PUBLIC EXPENDITURE

1997

80

60

42%

40

20

9.2 %

0

DEFENCE SOCIAL

MILITARY EXPENDITURE **29%**
(% of health & education) (1990/91)

20 Having lost much territory, Bulgaria was disarmed and forced to pay extensive war damages. With the restoration of the 1878 Constitution, elections were held in 1920. The anti-war reaction gave the Agrarian Party a wide margin. Working on a Soviet model, the Government started radical agrarian reforms. The Government was not pro-Soviet, however, and local Communists were persecuted.

21 Bulgaria joined the League of Nations and followed a conciliatory line of diplomacy for some time. However, its territorial losses and the pressure exerted by Bulgarians living abroad soon led to new tensions with its neighbors. Aleksandur Stamboliyski, the leader of the Agrarian Party and head of the Government, was ousted and assassinated by a conspiracy of Macedonians and opposition figures in 1923.

22 Aleksandur Tsankov assumed control of the Government, heading a multiparty alliance which excluded the Liberal, Communist and Agrarian parties. Uprisings and armed activity by the opposition led to hundreds of executions and assassinations. The Government declared martial law and reinforced the army in order to avoid outright rebellion.

23 In 1926, Tsankov resigned in favor of Andrei Liapchev, leader of the Democratic Party, to make way for more liberal policies. The Government approved a partial amnesty, and permitted a reorganization of the Agrarian Party. In 1932, Liapchev's cabinet was made up of members of the Democratic, Liberal and Agrarian parties, known as the National Bloc.

24 In 1934, fearing the effects of the worldwide economic depression and taking a cue from his neighbors, King Boris III supported the action of the conservative group, Zveno, which deposed Liapchev and set up a dictatorship. All political parties were proscribed, there was censorship of the press, the universities were closed and an ultra-right youth movement was established.

25 Tension with Turkey eased, and in 1937 a peace and friendship treaty was signed with Yugoslavia. The following year, Bulgaria signed a non-aggression pact with the Balkan alliance, in exchange for the rearmament of the Bulgarian army. While the King was once again seeking rapprochement with Germany, the Bulgarian dream of re-establishing its former borders was gathering strength.

26 In 1940, Germany made Romania return the parts of Bulgaria which it had won in the second Balkan War. Bulgaria signed the Anti-Komintern pact and German troops set up bases aimed at Greece and Yugoslavia on Bulgarian soil. In exchange, Bulgarian troops were allowed to occupy the part of Thrace belonging to Greece, and the part of Macedonia belonging to Yugoslavia, and part of Serbia.

27 When Bulgaria refused to declare war on the Soviet Union, King Boris was assassinated, and a new pro-German Government was formed. Growing anti-Nazi resistance, led by the Communists, contributed to the formation of the Patriotic Front in 1942. The Republicans, left-wing Agrarians, Democrats and independents all subsequently joined.

28 In May 1944, paralyzed by the civil war, the pro-German Boshilov resigned, and was replaced by Bagrianov. While Soviet troops advanced toward the Danube, Bagrianov sought an agreement with the Allies. In August, Bulgaria proclaimed its neutrality, and ordered the disarmament of the German troops on its soil.

29 Ignoring the Sofia Declaration, the Red Army entered Bulgarian territory. The resistance fanned local insurrection. On September 8, General Kyril Stanchev's troops took the capital, and the Patriotic Front formed a Government headed by the Republican Kimon Georgiev.

30 Sofia signed a treaty with the allies in October 1944. Bulgarian troops, under Soviet command, collaborated in the defeat of the German forces in Hungary, Yugoslavia and Austria. During 1945, war trials led to the imprisonment of 6,870 people and the execution of 2,680 others.

31 In March 1945, Communist leader Giorgi Dimitrov returned to Bulgaria after several years at the Komintern headquarters, in Moscow.

32 In a referendum held in September 1946, 92 per cent of the electorate approved of the creation of the Republic of Bulgaria. In the October election, the Patriotic Front won 364 seats with 70.8 per cent of the vote, 277 seats went to the Communist Party (BCP). In November, Dimitrov became Prime Minister.

33 In 1947, Britain and the US recognized the government. The National Assembly ratified the peace treaty with the Allies, the new Constitution went into effect and, at the end of the year, the Soviet troops withdrew from the country. After joining the BCP opposition, some of the Patriotic Front's former leaders were arrested and sentenced to death for conspiracy.

34 Under the leadership of the BCP, the Bulgarian State adopted the Soviet socio-economic model. A process of accelerated economic growth was set in motion, without taking into account the lack of raw materials or the technical preparation of the labor force. In the countryside, collective farming was enforced.

35 Dimitrov resigned from the administration in March 1949, and died a few months later. Vulko Chervenkov succeeded him, first as leader of the government, and then as party premier. In March 1954, Todor Zhivkov was named First Secretary of the BCP, becoming Prime Minister in 1962. Bulgaria was the USSR's closest ally among the Warsaw Pact countries, and in 1968 Bulgarian troops accompanied Soviet troops in the invasion of Czechoslovakia.

36 In the 1980s Bulgaria was accused of imposing a policy of forced assimilation, on the country's 10 per cent Turkish minority. In 1986, Sofia refuted Amnesty International's accusation that more than 250 Turks had been detained or imprisoned for refusing to accept new identity cards.

37 In 1988, Bulgaria and Turkey signed a protocol governing bilateral economic relations. The dialogue was interrupted in the following year, when it was revealed that the Bulgarian militia had used violence to put down a protest by 30,000 Turks, who had been demonstrating against the Government's policy of assimilation.

38 In June 1989, more than 80,000 Turks were expelled from Bulgaria. Turkey promised to accommodate them all, but towards the end of August, after receiving 310,000 Bulgarian Turks, it closed its borders. 30,000 of these refugees subsequently returned to Bulgaria.

39 The largest protest meeting since the War was held in November in front of the National Assembly. A group known as "Eco-glasnost" demonstrated against a proposed nuclear power plant on an island in the Danube, citing the fact that it lay in an earthquake-zone. They also protested against the construction of a reservoir in one of the country's largest nature reserves.

40 In December, some 6,000 members of the Pomak community - a Muslim minority group with an estimated 300,000 members - demanded religious and cultural freedom.

41 The Central Committee of the BCP replaced Zhivkov as Secretary General, a post he had held for 35 years. He was succeeded by Petur Mladenov, who had been Prime Minister since 1971 and was considered to be a proponent of liberalization of the regime. In December, Mladenov also replaced Zhivkov as president of the State Council.

42 The National Assembly lifted the ban on anti-government demonstrations, and granted amnesty to political prisoners. There was an immediate increase in the number of political demonstrations demanding reforms and elections.

43 In March 1990, the Union of Democratic Forces (UDF), made up of 16 opposition parties, and the official party agreed to the election of a Constitutional Assembly. The July election was won by the

PROFILE

ENVIRONMENT

Located in the Balkans, Bulgaria comprises four different natural regions. The fertile Danubian plains in the north are wheat and corn-producing areas. South of these lie the wooded Balkan Mountains, where cereals and potatoes are cultivated, cattle and sheep are raised, and the country's major mineral resources - iron ore, zinc and copper, are found. Cattle are also raised on the Rhodope Mountains in southern Bulgaria. South of the Balkan mountains there is a region of grassland, crossed by the Maritza River, where tobacco, cotton, rice, flowers and grapes are cultivated. Heavy metals, nitrates, petroleum derivatives and detergents have damaged the lower and mid-tributaries of the most important rivers. These flow into the Black Sea, which is highly polluted. About one quarter of the country's woodland is affected by air pollution.

SOCIETY

Peoples: Most of the Bulgarian population is of Slav origin, but there are also people of Turkish, Armenian and Greek origins.
Religions: Orthodox Christian and Muslim. **Languages:** Bulgarian (official); Turkish, Greek, and Armenian are also spoken. **Political Parties:** Union of Democratic Forces (a coalition made up of 16 parties); Bulgarian Socialist Party (formerly the Communist Party); Movement for Freedom and Human Rights (of the Turkish minority); Bulgarian Agrarian Party.

THE STATE

Official Name: Narodna Republika Balgarija. **Capital:** Sofia (Sofija) 1,200,000 people (1994). **Other cities:** Plovdiv 364,000 people; Varna 306,000 (1994). **Government:** Petar Stoyanov, President since January, 1997; Ivan Kostov, Prime Minister since 1997. **National Holiday:** March 3, National Liberation Day. **Armed Forces:** 102,000. **Other:** Border Guards (Ministry of Interior): 12,000; Security Police: 4,000; Railway and Construction Troops: 18,000.

Bulgarian Socialist Party, BSP (formerly BCP). In October, the BSP was forced to enter a new coalition, led by Yelio Yelev, a dissident during the 1970s and leader of the Social Democratic wing of the UDF.

[44] The new coalition government adopted a program of economic reforms in consultation with the IMF and the World Bank. They reached an agreement with the labor unions for a 200-day "social peace" until the reforms could go into effect.

[45] In July 1991, the new Constitution was approved, establishing a parliamentary system, allowing personal property, and freedom of expression. After the October election, Parliament named Filip Dimitrov as Prime Minister. Virtually alienated from the Social Democrats and the "Greens" - co-founders of the UDF - Dimitrov was chosen because of the support he had from the right-wing of the opposition coalition and the Movement for Freedom and Human Rights (of the Turkish minority).

[46] In the January 1992 election, in which 75 per cent of registered voters participated, Yelev was elected President of the Republic. As leader of the political transition period and author of the rapprochement toward the West, he received 54.4 per cent of the vote in the second round of voting, defeating the BSP candidate, Velko Valkanov.

[47] With a general strike protesting low wages and unemployment, the national labor union Podkrepa and the government parted company. The unemployment rate reached 17 per cent, and retirement pensions came to an average of $25 per month.

[48] In June 1992, Bulgaria joined the Council of Europe. During that year, former Communist leader Todor Zhivkov, three former Prime Ministers and another former member of government prior to 1991, were arrested charged with corruption in the exercise of their duties. The economic situation led the Movement for Rights and Freedoms (MRF) to withdraw its support of Dimitrov, which caused the downfall of his cabinet.

[49] Dimitrov was replaced by Liuben Berov from the MRF. The new Prime Minister stated he was willing to restore the lands confiscated by the Communists to the Turkish minority. Transition from a centralized planned economy to a free market economy continued to be difficult and caused paradoxical situations. For example, when agricultural cooperatives were dismantled, two million cattle were slaughtered as they could not be managed by the new private farms.

[50] When the former Soviet Union stopped buying two-thirds of Bulgarian exports, foreign trade was significantly reduced. UN sanctions imposed on neighboring former Yugoslavia caused losses of $1.5 million to Bulgaria. In 1993, Berov went on with the transition to a market economy at a rate considered excessively slow by the IMF, which caused a certain amount of tension between Sofia and the international organization.

[51] However, Berov held on to power until mid 1994, thanks to the support of the MDL, the BSP and the New Union for Democracy, a breakaway group from the UDF. Members of this opposition coalition frequently accused the Prime Minister of wanting to "restore socialism". Disagreements between Berov and the MDL in matters related to human rights and the social condition of Bulgarians of Turkish background, further weakened the Government.

[52] In June 1994, Berov was able to pass the privatization law and in September he presented his resignation. After three failed attempts to form a new Government, President Yelev dissolved Parliament and called new elections. The BSP won an absolute majority in the National Assembly - 125 seats out of a total of 240 - in the December elections, while the anti-Communist UDF gained 69 seats.

[53] In January 1995, socialist leader Zhan Videnov formed a new Government which included members from the BSP, the Bulgarian Agrarian National Union and the Eco-glasnost Political Club. His cabinet was the first in the history of post-Communist Bulgaria with an absolute majority at the National Assembly. Differences between the new Government and Yelev were frequent. In July, the President criticized the Government because he thought market reforms were not being implemented swiftly enough, suggesting the BSP was "genetically connected" to organized crime and that the Videnov administration was incapable of eliminating it.

[54] Petar Stoyanov's Union of Democratic Forces won the first round of the Presidential elections in November 1996 and one month later beat the Socialist candidate, Ivan Marazov in the final round with 59.7 per cent of the vote. Hounded by his political rivals, Prime Minister Zhan Videnov resigned in December. The conservative groups which supported Stoyanov called for the resignation of the Cabinet, bolstered by the parliamentary majority of Socialists and their allies. A series of large demonstrations in the capital and other cities pressed for new legislative elections. Stoyanov became President in January 1997, after vowing to bring forward the 1998 elections.

[55] The Union of Democratic Forces won the by-elections on April 1997 and obtained 137 seats in the National Assembly, compared to 58 for the Socialists and 19 for the Union of National Salvation, formed by the monarchists. The new government adopted a neoliberal economic policy, following the IMF guidelines with provision for the privatization of debt-ridden state companies and the scrapping of 60,000 jobs in the public sector. Services were also liberalized in order to reduce inflation.

[56] In late 1997, Bulgaria toughened its stance in the conflict with the Government of Macedonia. Sofia denied the nationhood of Macedonia and did not accept the use of Macedonian as a national language. For this reason, Bulgaria refused to sign any documents in that language. This attitude prevented the implementation of 20 economic and cultural agreements between the states.

[57] The new government applied all the IMF recommendations in order to gain its financial backing. In May 1998, agricultural sector subsidies were eliminated and the privatization of the state's telecommunications company, various banks and Bulgaria's national airline was announced. The Government declared that fiscal balance was its objective. A few weeks later the IMF agreed to a loan of $800 million.

[58] The parties of the left formed the Bulgarian Euroleft coalition, while four liberal parties created the Liberal Democratic Alliance. General Angel Marin, tough critic of the austerity measures in the armed forces, was dismissed by Stoyanov. In July, Commander in Chief Miho Mihov announced a reduction of a thousand officers over the following months.

[59] The EU announced in November 1999 that solutions would be sought for the replacement of the Kozloduy nuclear plant which produced 45 per cent of the country's electricity. According to the treaty, the Soviet-built reactors would be closed between 2003 and 2006. The measure was one of the conditions for access to the EU, although the Bulgarian Government requested compensation. Sofia asked for economic compensation for the damages caused by a cyanide spill into the Danube river from a Romanian mine which caused a general alert in the region.

[60] In March 2000 the UN accused Bulgaria - along with Togo, Rwanda and Burkina Faso - of violating the embargo on arms and equipment sales to Angola. According to the UN, Bulgaria was the main source of training and weapons for UNITA rebels fighting the Angolan Government. The rebels paid for the arms with diamonds and emeralds, whose trafficking is also banned by the UN. ∎

Burkina Faso

Burkina Faso

Population: 11,616,000 (1999)
Area: 274,000 SQ KM
Capital: Ouagadougou
Currency: CFA franc
Language: French

D uring the 11th century, the Mossi martial caste subdued the neighboring peoples in the region where the Volta rivers (Volta Noire, Volta Blanche and Volta Rouge) rise. In the following two centuries, they established a series of highly organized kingdoms, the most notable being Yatenga and Ouagadougou. In the latter group, rulers were chosen from the royal family by four officials with ministerial rank, whose role was to seek a balance between the Mossi aristocracy and the Mande base. This electoral system persisted into the 20th century.

2 The Mossi and Mande resisted attempts at annexation by the Mali and Songhai empires (see Mali and Guinea) and remained independent throughout the Fulah invasions of the 18th and 19th centuries. In a series of military incursions between 1896 and 1904, the French laid waste the central plains, burning houses, and slaughtering people and animals. The ensuing reign of terror finally sparked off an insurrection in 1916, which met with such violent repression that millions were forced to emigrate, mostly to Ghana.

3 By then the country had been incorporated into the colony of Haute Sénégal-Niger. It was reconstituted as the separate colony of Upper Volta in 1947.

4 Upper Volta had no directly productive role in the international division of labor. Its task was to produce people: forced labor on plantations in Côte d'Ivoire, or cannon fodder for French armies at war in Europe or the colonies.

5 Finally, in line with French neo-colonial strategy, the country was declared independent in 1960. That year's elections were won by the Voltanese Democratic Union (UDV),

a party backed by landowners and private enterprise. Maurice Yameogo was elected President and was re-elected in 1965 amidst intense trade-union agitation, which occurred in response to economic crisis, administrative chaos and austerity measures. Yameogo was overthrown a year later in a military coup led by army chief-of-staff, Colonel Sangoulé Lamizana.

6 The 1970s witnessed a succession of elections, military coups, and more or less fraudulent re-elections orchestrated by Colonel Lamizana. Starvation was widespread, herds were dwindling and an estimated quarter of the population had emigrated to neighboring states. In 1980 Lamizana was ousted in a coup by another colonel, Saye Zerbo, and there were further coups in November 1982, May 1983 and on August 4 1983.

7 The last of these changes was much more than just the latest game of musical chairs among the

military élite. The new leader, a young army captain called Thomas Sankara, saw it as a revolution. He launched into a program of radical change which aimed to chart an entirely new course for poor African countries, and this brought him to international notice. He was popular among soldiers and the rural poor as he brought in an anti-corruption campaign and organized brigades to assist victims of the prolonged drought and deforestation.

8 In the first year of Sankara's government Upper Volta was renamed Burkina Faso - "land of the incorruptible"; the national anthem was sung in African languages; land reform was carried out and popular courts were set up to dispense justice. Sankara set a target of two meals and 10 litres of water per person per day.

9 The implementation of such measures presented a considerable challenge in a country where 82 per cent of adults were illiterate and absolute poverty was the norm. There were practically no bank accounts held within the country. Kerosene was the energy source for lighting. Cutting wood, the main fuel, contributed some 50,000 to 100,000 hectares to the total annual deforestation. Encroachment by the Sahel arid area further aggravated the lack of firewood.

10 On December 15 1987, Sankara was overthrown and executed along with 12 of his supporters in a coup led by his second-in-command, Blaise Compaoré, who pledged to continue the Popular Front and "rectify" the regime internally.

11 Contrasting with the image of Sankara, a man of austere habits who shunned personal property, Compaoré built a government palace and purchased a presidential plane. His economic strategy included encouragement of private enterprise and foreign capital, and consideration of denationalization, deregulation and agreements with international lending institutions.

12 In September 1989, four high-ranking officers were accused of plotting to kill the head of state, and were shot.

13 The 4th Republic adopted a new constitution, which was approved by referendum on June 2 1991 (90 per cent voting in favor, with 50 per cent of registered voters participating). The new constitution, which was put into effect by de facto President Compaoré, re-established a multiparty system and the division of powers, while reducing presidential powers. The office of Prime Minister was created, and general elections were to be held every seven years.

14 In the May 1992 elections, the official party won 78 of the 107 National Assembly seats. The main opposition force, concentrated in the National Convention of Progressive Patriots-Social Democratic Party (CNPP-PSD) won 13 seats. Blaise Compaoré, who ran unopposed, became the first president of the 4th Republic, with 21.6 per cent of the vote.

15 Prime Minister Yussuf Ouedraogo promised to prioritize agriculture and provide incentives for the creation of small- and medium sized enterprises in order to create new jobs. International pressure made Ouedraogo pledge to reduce the country's bureaucracy; Burkina Faso had 36,000 public employees, most of them on pensions.

16 In December 1992 and March 1993 there were two general strikes against the implementation of the structural-adjustment plan recommended by the IMF. Devaluation of the CFA franc in January 1994 led to Ouedraogo's resignation and his replacement by

WORKERS

% OF LABOUR FORCE **1998**

■ FEMALE: 47%　■ MALE: 53%

1990

■ SERVICES: 5.8%
■ INDUSTRY: 1.8%
■ AGRICULTURE: 92.4%

LAND USE

DEFORESTATION: 0.7% annual (1990/95)
IRRIGATED: 0.6% of arable (1993)

1993

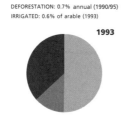

■ FOREST & WOODLAND: 50.4%
■ ARABLE: 13.0%
■ OTHER: 36.6%

PUBLIC EXPENDITURE

DEFENCE EXPENDITURE (% of goverment exp.)	**12.3%**	(1997)
MILITARY EXPENDITURE (% of health & education)	**30%**	(1990/91)

MATERNAL MORTALITY

1990-98

Per 100,000
live births

15

LITERACY

1995

98%

Marc-Christian Kabore in March that year. In July, in spite of protests from the opposition, Parliament passed a law which allowed the government to privatize 19 national companies.

[17] In February 1995, the opposition boycotted municipal elections since it considered they were being organized by a non-independent electoral commission. The ruling Organization for the People's Democracy-Workers' Movement won in 26 of the country's largest 33 cities. At a social level, conditions remained tense since indirect consequences from the 1994 devaluation led the cost of living to rise 30 per cent in the first half of 1995.

[18] The Government continued its policy of economic liberalization and officially took Burkina Faso into the World Trade Organization in June 1995. A project to restructure the recently privatized railways, resulting in 500 lay-offs, caused a new strike which led the country once again toward a tense situation, typical of the early 1990s.

[19] The economy grew 5 per cent in 1996. In June, the IMF approved a new $57 million loan to support the implementation of a structural-adjustment program in the subsequent three years. In 1997, a drought decimated food production and left the country in a critical situation. The deficit in food production, which added up to 32 per cent of the GDP and employed 90 per cent of the population, was estimated in 156,000 tonnes for the 1997-1998 period. In December 1997, Ouagadogou had to call on the international community for 67,000 tonnes of grain to tackle the crisis.

[20] Marijuana plantations grew swiftly in Burkina Faso, as well as in other countries of the region. It replaced some "traditional" cash crops whose price had fallen. The devaluation of the CFA franc caused a reduction in the import of medicines, which further complicated the fight against the two major diseases that ravage the population: malaria and Aids. In 1998, there was only one doctor for every 25,000 people in Burkina Faso.

[21] The 1998 elections were boycotted by the opposition granting the president-candidate victory. A series of protests led to the resignation of Kadré Ouedraogo's cabinet, but the president confirmed most of the ministers in their posts in January 1999. Yussuf Ouedraogo, another former prime minister was appointed to the cabinet.

[22] The murder of journalist Norbert Zongo brought the government under suspicion, as an independent investigation pointed the finger at the upper echelons of power. Zongo had made important revelations about another murder, where the President's brother was the main suspect. In order to get round the crisis, Compaoré called on the Green Party leader and former presidential candidate to join the government, but demonstrations calling for justice for Zongo erupted again in December. The Government rejected the accusations and made no effort to prosecute the six presidential guards accused of the murder.

[23] In February 2000, the National Reconciliation Commission called for the rehabilitation of former president Thomas Sankara, murdered in the 1987 Compaoré coup. The Commission had been established by the President himself in an effort to defuse tensions caused by the unresolved Zongo case.

[24] In March 2000 a UN report stated that Compaoré had been channeling arms from the former Soviet bloc to rebel groups such as UNITA in Angola and the RUF in Sierra Leone. This was in breach of an international arms embargo. Compaoré and his associates, the report claimed, were paid in diamonds for their services. Diamond trafficking is also prohibited. ∎

PROFILE

ENVIRONMENT

A landlocked country, Burkina Faso is one of the most densely populated areas of the African Sahel (the semi-arid southern rim of the Sahara). The Mossi plateau slopes gently southwards and is traversed by the valleys of the three Volta Rivers (Black Volta, White Volta and Red Volta). Though more fertile, these lands are plagued with tsetse flies. As in the whole Sahel region, this nation suffers from mounting aridity caused by inappropriate farming techniques introduced to produce peanuts and cotton for export. Wood, a popular energy source, is becoming scarce as a result of deforestation.

SOCIETY

Peoples: Over half of the population are Mossi. Pouhi herders and the Tamajek clans with their vassals, the Bellah, amount to around 20 per cent. Djula peasants and traders are indigenous minorities. The language of these three population groups is the linguistic bridge among the various regions. Senufo and Bobo-Fing cultures inhabit the western plains where the savannah merges into the forest. In the south, the predominant Lebi, Bobo-Ule, Gurunsi and Bisa cultures extend into several states. The savannah to the east holds the great Gurmantehé civilization, while the Sampo, Rurumba and Marko cultures live in the desert regions to the north and northeast.
Religions: The majority of the population profess traditional African religions; 30 per cent are Muslim and 10 per cent are Christian.
Languages: French (official); Mossi, Bobo and Gurma are the most widely spoken languages.
Political Parties: Organization for the People's Democracy-Workers' Movement (ODP/MT); National Convention of Progressive Patriots-Social Democrats (CNPP-PSD); Burkinabe Socialist Party (PSB).
Social organizations: Voltanese Free Unions Organization, Confederation of Voltanese Unions.

THE STATE

Official Name: République de Burkina Faso. **Administrative division:** 30 provinces, 300 departments and 7,200 villages. **Capital:** Ouagadougou 730,000 people (1994). **Other cities:** Bobo-Dioulasso 250,000 people; Koudougou 51,925; Ouahigouya 38,902 (1990).
Government: Republican parliamentary system, with a powerful head of state. Blaise Compaoré, President since 1987. Kadré Désiré Ouedraogo, Prime Minister since 1996. Single-chamber legislature: National Assembly (107 members elected by direct vote for a 7-year term). Judiciary: judges responsible to a Superior Council, under the authority of the President. **National Holiday:** August 5, Independence (1960). **Armed Forces:** 5,800 (1995). **Other:** Gendarmerie: 1,500; Security Company: 250; People's Militia: 45,000 trained.

Burundi

Burundi

Population: 6,565,000 (1999)
Area: 27,830 SQ KM
Capital: Bujumbura
Currency: Burundi franc
Language: Rundi, Kirundi and French

Burundi is one of the poorest countries in the world and one of the most densely populated in Africa. For five centuries it has been torn by ethnic and economic struggles involving the Hutu majority and the Tutsi (or Watusi). At least five major massacres affecting one or the other community have occurred since the 15th century.

[2] The Hutu, a Bantu group, were communal farmers. Five hundred years ago they were overrun by the Tutsi, who migrated south from Uganda and Ethiopia in search of fertile grazing land for their cattle. The Tutsis had more sophisticated weapons and were thus able to subdue the Hutus and enslave their people. Tutsi rulers held considerable power during the 17th and 18th centuries, but rivalry between the various local groups weakened the central power structure in the 19th century. This paved the way for German colonization around 1890. The Europeans upheld Tutsi domination and in turn forced the traditional ruler (Mwami) to accept German control. In 1899, Burundi and Rwanda (see Rwanda) were merged into a single colony, Rwanda-Urundi, which became famous for its ivory exports controlled by a German trade monopoly.

[3] Following the defeat of Germany in World War I, Belgium took over the colony and separated Burundi from Rwanda again only to merge the former with Zaire (now DR Congo). The Belgian system of indirect rule assigned Tutsi elites a privileged role and gave rise to nationalist movements in the 1950s. This process bred the Union for National Progress (UNAPRO) led by Louis Rwagasore, elected Prime Minister in 1960. The Belgians feared that Rwagasore might become a Burundian Lumumba (see DR Congo) and he was therefore assassinated before independence was granted. Burundi gained independence on July 1 1962, governed by a puppet Tutsi ruler under Belgian control.

[4] Violence marked the first four years of autonomous rule under five different Prime Ministers. Instability predominated until November 1966, when the Prime Minister Captain Michael Micombero, staged a coup and proclaimed the Republic of Burundi. The new president carried out a massive purge of all Hutu government officials. In 1971, 350,000 Hutus were killed through government repression and an additional 70,000 went into exile.

[5] In 1976, Lt-Col Jean Baptiste Bagaza took power promising to end ethnic persecution and set up a reformist government. Bagaza broadened UNAPRO, put a land reform program into practice, and rehabilitated labor unions, all in blatant defiance of the Tutsi elite and their foreign capitalist allies. In foreign policy, the new government drew closer to Tanzania, and China sent aid to develop Burundi's mineral resources.

[6] In 1979, the first post-independence congress of UNAPRO was held and a new constitution drafted, effective in 1981. The new constitution prevented the exploitation of the Hutu majority by the Tutsi minority, prompted the modernization of the political structure, and gave women equal rights. Reforms stirred up strong feelings between the Government and the conservative Catholic hierarchy, leading to confiscation of properties and deportation of 63 missionaries.

[7] Elections held in 1982, 20 years after independence, upheld President Bagaza's policies and brought about a swift stabilization of the young nation's political situation.

[8] Despite Burundi's established political independence, the country faced serious problems due mostly to economic dependence and its geographical location. Being a landlocked country raised the price of both imports and exports. Population density is high and unevenly distributed geographically; 70 per cent live in the north where overuse of the land has caused massive soil erosion. Wood is the main source of domestic fuel and unfortunately the high demand outstrips the forest production of the country. Ninety per cent of agricultural products were consumed by the domestic market. Burundi's economic hopes lay in the rich nickel deposits and in its hydroelectric potential. Belgian and US companies are currently developing the Musongati mines which also have large cobalt and uranium deposits.

[9] In September 1987, while attending a summit meeting of French-speaking countries in Quebec, Bagaza was overthrown by army major Pierre Buyoya in a bloodless coup.

[10] In August 1988, strife between Hutus and Tutsis broke out in Dtega and Marangana, in the north of the country, leaving several thousand dead, most of them Hutus. The rebellion against Tutsi landowners was cruelly dealt with by an army made up mostly of Tutsis. Over 60,000 Hutus sought refuge in Rwanda. The Government responded by designating a Hutu Prime Minister, Adrien Sibomana, with a new cabinet in which half the ministers were Hutus.

[11] In 1989, most refugees returned and there was reconciliation between the military government and the Catholic Church, who had regained their property. A structural adjustment program was initiated which included the privatization of public enterprises and the creation of a "watchdog" tribunal to combat corruption.

[12] Burundi depended largely on the export of its main crop, coffee, and on its fluctuating prices. Poverty and high population

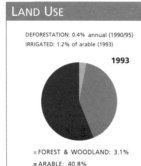

WORKERS

% OF LABOUR FORCE **1998**

- FEMALE: 49%   ■ MALE: 51%

1990

- ■ SERVICES: 5.6%
- ■ INDUSTRY: 2.7%
- ■ AGRICULTURE: 91.7%

LAND USE

DEFORESTATION: 0.4% annual (1990/95)
IRRIGATED: 1.2% of arable (1993)

1993

- ■ FOREST & WOODLAND: 3.1%
- ■ ARABLE: 40.8%
- ■ OTHER: 56.1%

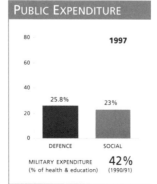

PUBLIC EXPENDITURE

1997

DEFENCE 25.8%   SOCIAL 23%

MILITARY EXPENDITURE **42%**
(% of health & education) (1990/91)

density added to the environment's degradation. The high rate of deforestation is in part due to the transformation of forests into farming lands for landless peasants.

[13] In 1992, Buyoya enacted a multiparty constitution and called elections to be held in 1993. Buyoya, leading UNAPRO - with a majority of Tutsi leaders - was defeated by Melchior Ndadaye, from the opposing Democratic Front of Burundi (DEFROBU) composed mainly of Hutus.

[14] On October 24 1993, three months after he was elected, Ndadaye was assassinated during an attempted coup. Prime Minister Sylvie Kinigi, who sought asylum in the French embassy, managed to keep the situation under control. The leaders of the rebellion were either arrested or fled to Zaire (now DR Congo). Cyprien Ntaryamira - a Hutu like Ndadaye - was appointed President by Parliament.

[15] In spite of the failed coup, Ndadaye's assassination led to one of the worst massacres in Burundi's history. Supporters of the former president attacked UNAPRO members - Tutsis or Hutus - causing the death of tens of thousands of people and the flight of some 700,000. The so-called "extremist armed militias" - hostile to living alongside the other ethnic groups - were consolidated by this time, as were the "Undefeated" Tutsis and the Intagohekas ("those who never sleep") Hutus. Violence spread.

[16] On April 6 1994, Ntaryamira died along with Rwandan president Juvenal Habyarimana when their plane was shot down in Kigali, capital of Rwanda. Another Hutu, Sylvestre Ntibantunganya, replaced the assassinated president. Violence intensified, especially between militias in favor of Hutu power and the army, controlled by Tutsi officers.

[17] In February 1995, UNAPRO left the government to force Prime Minister Anatole Kanyenkiko to resign. His resignation enabled the nomination of Tutsi Antoine Nduwayo and UNAPRO's return to the coalition government which it had been part of along with DEFROBU.

[18] The number of "domestic refugees" continued to rise in 1996. Many Tutsis fled to the cities, seeking protection from the army, while thousands of Hutu peasants - willingly or not - left with the guerrillas toward mountain or jungle regions.

[19] Fearing that the Burundian conflict would extend to neighboring countries, the UN and the Organization for African Unity decided to intervene. Pierre Buyoya, claiming the need to prevent an intervention by inter-African forces in the country, staged a successful coup in July 1996 and became the new president of Burundi. After this action, Ethiopia, Kenya, Rwanda, Tanzania, Uganda and Zaire (now DR Congo) imposed sanctions on Bujumbura. In mid-September, Hutu rebels reported the killing by the army of 10,000 civilians after the coup. A similar number was killed the following year, although Amnesty International considered it was very difficult to distinguish between government and rebel responsibility in these massacres.

[20] In late 1997, special UN monitor Sergio Pinheiro confirmed that international sanctions had had devastating effects, significantly degrading the life conditions of poor Burundians and requested the revision of the embargo's usefulness. Meanwhile, peace negotiations promoted by mediator Julius Nyerere, former Tanzanian president, had reached a stalemate. Relations between Burundi and Tanzania were significantly impaired and both accused each other of trespassing across their respective frontiers. In September, Buyoya accused Tanzania of protecting more than 200,000 Hutu rebels and of intending to "annex" Burundi. In October, Bujumbura reported the attacks of Tanzanian forces in the southern towns of Kubonga and Mugina. In February 1998, the number of victims of the civil war was estimated at more than 250,000.

[21] On July 16 1998, the National Assembly became the National Assembly in Transition (NAT) with the incorporation of 40 new representatives of the two political parties and the public. Until this point DEFROBU had 65 seats and UNAPRO 16.

[22] Several initiatives were taken to restart peace negotiations throughout 1999. Despite some reticence on the part of Burundi's political leaders, on 1 December former South African president Nelson Mandela was chosen as mediator, and Tanzania as host for the negotiations. The armed confrontations and massacres continued between Hutus and the (militarily superior) Tutsi minority, at war since 1994. Various leaders of eastern and southeastern Africa demanded the Government close down refugee camps within the conflict area. The nation's authorities stated these hundreds of thousands of people had been transferred to the camps for their own security. Meanwhile, the rebels stated the government camps prevented the civilian population from offering them help.

[23] In January 2000, US President Bill Clinton offered full personal backing to Nelson Mandela's mediation attempt. Several political analysts stated it was "highly unusual for a leader of the US to become involved in bringing a war in Africa to an end". On March 28, from the Tanzanian city of Arusha, a Mandela representative said the Burundi peace talks were "progressing" that there had been "great development" and that the objectives for peace had been "written in a single document" for the first time since the Peace Negotiations began in mid-1998. ■

PROFILE

ENVIRONMENT

Most of the land is made up of flat plateaus and relatively low hills covered with natural pastures. Located in the African zone of the Great Lakes (Tanganyika, Victoria), the Ruvubu River valley stretches through the country from north to south. Tropical forests are found in the low, western regions. Most inhabitants engage in subsistence agriculture (corn, cassava, sorghum, beans). Coffee is the main export product. Internal communications are hampered by natural barriers and the nearest sea outlet is 1,400 km beyond the border, a fact which makes foreign trade even more difficult. The forests are fundamental in maintaining climatic balance, and deforestation is one of the country's worst problems, aggravated by the growing incidence of farming on unsuitable lands.

SOCIETY

Peoples: Most Burundians (86 per cent) belong to the Hutu ethnic group, an agricultural people of Bantu origin. They were traditionally dominated by the Tutsi or Watusi (13 per cent), shepherds of Hamitic descent. There is a small minority (1 per cent) of Twa pygmies.
Religions: 67 per cent Christian; 32 per cent follow traditional African religions and 1 per cent are Muslim.
Languages: Rundi, Kirundi and French, official, with Swahili the business language.
Political Parties: Democratic Front of Burundi (DEFROBU); Union for National Progress (UNAPRO), led by President Pierre Buyoya.
Social Organizations: Workers' Union of Burundi (UTB)

THE STATE

Official Name: Républika y'Uburundi.
Administrative divisions: 15 Provinces.
Capital: Bujumbura 300,000 people (est 1995).
Other cities: Gitega 101,827 people (1994).
Government: Pierre Buyoya, President since July 1996. Pascal-Firmin Ndimira, Prime Minister since 1997.
National Holiday: July 1, Independence (1962).
Armed Forces: 12,600.

Cambodia

Cambodia

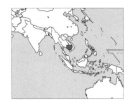

Population: 10,946,000 (1999)
Area: 181,040 SQ KM
Capital: Phnom Penh (Phnum Penh)
Currency: Riel
Language: Khmer

The land of Cambodia takes its name from a *rishi* (sage), for the first Cambodian kings proclaimed themselves descendants from the great sage Cambu Svayambhuva. The first kingdom of Cambodia was known in Chinese texts under the name of Funan and was founded by the Mon and Khmer peoples who migrated from the North in the first century AD. During these first centuries, there was strong Indian influence. By that time, Indian and Chinese pilgrims used to stop in today's Cambodian coasts to exchange silk and metals for spices and aromatic wood and gold.

2   During the 2nd and 3rd century Khmer rulers used to offer presents to Chinese emperors. Chinese sources reveal the scope of Indian influence by the example of the sage Kaundimnya, who married princess Soma, of Nagi origin (that is, semi-divine) and transformed the Khmer institutions along Indian lines. One of the modifications was probably the introduction of large-scale irrigation, which allowed the production of up to three rice harvests a year. Also the worship of the Indian god Shiva, who was considered a guardian ancestor and the spirit of land by the Khmer.

3   According to Chinese writings, the Funan created a centralized state machinery, headed by an absolute ruler. This ruler ran agricultural labor and used farming surpluses to maintain his lifestyle and that of a caste of priests, and also to build fortresses, palaces and temples.

4   The first Sanskrit writings date from the 6th century and the first ones found in the Khmer language are from the 7th century. The developments between the decline of Funan and the foundation, three

centuries later, of a new centralized state in the Cambodian north-eastern region (called Chenla in Chinese texts of that period) have not been fully documented as yet. Chinese sources cite the existence of at least two Cambodian Kingdoms, which - under the sovereignty of the Java Kingdom - requested recognition from China. In the meantime, Sanskrit and Khmer sources cite the existence, during the 7th, 8th and 9th century, of multiple Kingdoms that paid homage and fealty to the Java Kingdom.

5   In 790 AD, a Cambodian prince, born and raised in the Javanese court of the Sailendra dynasty,

proclaimed himself descendant of the Funan rulers. He declared the Khmer territory independent from Java and was crowned Prince Jayavarman II. During the following decade, Jayavarman extended his power north, controlling vassal states. In 802, he was named again, this time Chakravartin (a Sanskrit term meaning 'world ruler'). Jayavarman was the first "national" king of Cambodia.

6   In the year of 887 Indravarman I usurped the throne that belonged to his cousin Jayavarman III. During his reign, a large dam surrounding the capital city Roluos was built. This was the first of a vast system of dams, channels and irrigation canals that turned these lands productive and which would later allow the Khmer to maintain a densely populated and centralized State in the area, which otherwise would have resulted infertile. Two years later, Yasovarman I became king of Khmer and commenced the construction of Angkor city (then

called Yasodharapura), which turned into the capital of the Khmer Empire. In 1002, Suryavarman I usurped the throne and extended the Kingdom of Angkor to parts of today's territories of Thailand and Laos. In 1080, after Angkor had been conquered by the Kingdom of Champa, a Khmer ruler of a northern province proclaimed himself king under the name of Javayarman VI, ruling the Kingdom from his home province rather than from Angkor.

7   In 1177 Angkor was conquered once again by Champa forces. Jayavarman XII became king in 1181 and conquered Vijaya, capital of Champa (in present-day Vietnam). Under his rule, the Khmer Kingdom reached its height, virtually including the whole of today's Thailand and Laos and even reaching Myanmar/Burma, Malaysia and Vietnam. Jayavarman XII converted from Hinduism to Buddhism, which became the national religion.

8   In 1200, work began on building the new capital city of Angkor Thom. This undertaking depleted the royal coffers and the Kingdom experienced economic problems during the subsequent decades. The decline of Angkor coincided with the rise of the Thai Kingdom to the west and the Vietnamese one to the east. Turned into a small buffer state between both, the Khmer Kingdom alternately depended on the power of the Thais or the Vietnamese.

9   During more than 400 years, the Kingdom was alternately conquered by the Thai and Vietnamese forces. This changed in 1864, when Cambodian King Norodom accepted the status of French "protectorate" for his country, in the hope that the French would prevent further annexations. The French were not able to prevent the Siamese (Thais) from temporarily annexing some west Cambodian areas, including the city of Battambang. However, by recognizing the French authority, King Norodom managed to prevent the country from being divided and distributed between Vietnamese and Siam (Thailand). During the previous centuries, Vietnam had taken control of large tracts of Cambodia. The Mekong Delta and the area around Ho Chi Minh City (formerly Saigon) had been

---

WORKERS

% OF LABOUR FORCE   **1998**

■ FEMALE: 52%   ■ MALE: 48%

1990

■ SERVICES: 18.7%
■ INDUSTRY: 7.5%
■ AGRICULTURE: 73.8%

LAND USE

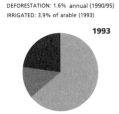

DEFORESTATION: 1.6% annual (1990/95)
IRRIGATED: 3.9% of arable (1993)

1993

■ FOREST & WOODLAND: 64.1%
■ ARABLE: 13%
■ OTHER: 22.9%

PUBLIC EXPENDITURE

DEFENCE EXPENDITURE   **25.8%**
(% of goverment exp.)   (1997)

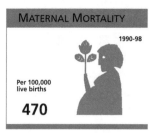

MATERNAL MORTALITY

1990-98

Per 100,000
live births

470

LITERACY

1995

65%

inhabited by Cambodians until the 18th century.

10   In 1884, with the consent of King Norodom, Cambodia became a French colony. France's political influence increased and, together with Vietnam and Laos, Cambodia became a part of the Indo-Chinese Union. During the following decades, the colonial empire installed a European administrative system in Cambodia and developed the country's infrastructure. However the economic development - or exploitation - of the French Indo-Chinese Union did not reach the levels attained by Burma or India under British rule.

11   After France was invaded by Germany during World War II, Japanese forces occupied Indochina in September 1940. What this actually meant was that the Japanese were able to use the military facilities in exchange for allowing France to maintain administrative control. As a result Cambodia suffered less damage during the War than the South Pacific islands, which were fiercely disputed by opposing forces.

12   In 1941, French authorities appointed the 18-year-old Prince Norodom Sihanouk as King of Cambodia, in the hope of easily controlling the politics of an inexperienced youngster. However, when the Japanese invaders withdrew, on March 12 1945, Norodom Sihanouk declared independence. But the French occupied Indochina again. While Vietnam began an anti-colonial war, in Cambodia the King managed to gain greater autonomy from France.

13   In 1947, a new constitution kept King Sihanouk on the throne. However his power was limited by parliament. In 1949, negotiations with France resulted in Cambodian independence "within the French union", with Paris retaining control over military and foreign affairs. In 1953, the Vietnamese offensive forced French troops to withdraw from Cambodia, leaving the country fully independent. In 1955, Sihanouk abdicated in favor of his father, changing his name to Prince Sihanouk so that he could participate in political life. From 1960 onwards, Sihanouk became head of state.

14   During the first years of US aggression against Vietnam, the Cambodian Government sought to maintain political and territorial neutrality. In 1965 however, following air raids by US-controlled South Vietnamese forces against North Vietnamese troop sanctuaries, Cambodia broke off relations with the US and moved closer towards the Chinese/Russian camp. Prince Sihanouk lost the 1966 elections to right-winger General Lon Nol who was later toppled during left-wing demonstrations. Sihanouk resumed power. In 1968 the US began launching regular air raids on the so-called Ho Chi Minh trail through Cambodian territory, allegedly supplying the Viet Cong from North Vietnam.

15   While taking diplomatic action abroad to protect his country's sovereignty, Sihanouk was ousted in a coup and replaced again by Lon Nol. During his five-year rule, Lon Nol received $1.6 billion in aid from Washington. During that period, US forces intervened in Cambodia to bomb the Communist Khmer Rouge guerrillas and Vietnamese sanctuaries. In four years of bombing about 50,000 were killed. Sihanouk went into exile in China.

16   From exile in Beijing, and supported by the Khmer Rouge, Sihanouk organized the National United Front of Kampuchea (NUFK) using the name of the country in Khmer language. By 1972, the NUFK was in control of 85 per cent of Cambodian territory, and its forces closed in on the capital, Phnom Penh (Phnum Pénh).

17   In 1975, the Khmer Rouge seized power. Lon Nol fled and the Kingdom became the Democratic Republic of Kampuchea with Sihanouk as head of government. In 1976, while a new Constitution was being approved, the People's Congress confirmed Khieu Sampham as head of state with Pol Pot as Prime Minister. However, on his return from exile, Sihanouk was forced to resign and kept under house arrest, while Pol Pot rose to the fore as the regime's new leading force.

18   Under Pol Pot, the country was completely sealed off from the outside world. Borders were closed and diplomats were not allowed to leave their embassies. Determined to build an unprecedented social system, Pol Pot set 1975 as Year Zero of a new era. He eliminated money and transferred large numbers of the urban population to the countryside, enforcing the return to an agricultural lifestyle. Mass purges and executions, hunger and illness, left at least a million people dead.

19   The Pol Pot regime strengthened ties with China, broke off diplomatic relations with Hanoi, refused to recognize borders "established by colonialism" and sent Khmer Rouge troops to invade Vietnamese territory in late 1977. The disputed borders had been established in 1973 by agreement between Vietnam and Sihanouk, as historical records could provide no exact basis for establishing boundaries.

20   The UN recognized the Khmer Rouge Government in 1978. The same year, Vietnam invaded to try and oust Pol Pot. In December 1978, when this border war was on the verge of being won by Vietnam, the United Front for the Salvation of Kampuchea was created under the presidency of General Heng Samrin. On January 11 1979, the Vietnamese forces and those of the United Front entered Phnom Penh and proclaimed the People's Republic of Kampuchea (PRK). A People's Revolutionary Council was established, and the Government began the enormous task of rebuilding a hungry and devastated nation.

21   Heng Samrin's government defined its policy as being one of "independence, non-alignment and democracy directed toward socialism". Pol Pot was tried in absentia for war crimes, and his forces turned to guerrilla warfare. With the support of China and the US, the Khmer Rouge managed to maintain UN recognition as the country's legitimate government. In 1982, Sihanouk and the Khmer Serei, led by Son Sann, joined former head of state Khieu Samphan's opposition government-in-exile.

22   One of the main goals of Heng Samrin's government was to reactivate the industrial, agricultural and transportation sectors. The Soviet Union, and other socialist countries gave aid which was focused on the reconstruction of power sources and the formation of a very basic industrial infrastructure.

23   In March and April 1981 municipal and legislative elections

PROFILE

ENVIRONMENT

The territory is mainly a plain surrounded by mountains, like the Cardamour Mountains in the southwest. In the north, the Dangrek range rises abruptly from the plain. The central basin of the country, occupied by the Tonle Sap (Great Lake) depression, is the point of confluence into the Mekong, one of the largest rivers in Asia. The country has a sub-tropical climate with monsoon rains. The population is concentrated in the central basin where rice, the mainstay of the diet and principal export crop, is grown. The country also exports rubber. The mineral reserves: phosphate, iron ore and limestone, are as yet unexploited. The main environmental problem is massive logging being carried out by foreign companies and the media, which if unchecked will destroy all the remaining forests in under a decade.

SOCIETY

Peoples: Mostly Khmers. The Khmers inhabit an area that extends beyond the present boundaries of Cambodia. There are Vietnamese and Chinese minorities.
Religions: In 1986 Buddhism - the religion of the majority - became the country's official religion. There is an Islamic minority (Cham).
Languages: Khmer, official and predominant.
Political Parties: United National Front for an Independent, Neutral, Peaceful and Cooperative Cambodia (Funcinpec); Cambodian People's Party; Liberal Democratic Buddhist Party; National Liberation Movement of Cambodia.

THE STATE

Official Name: Preach Reach Ana Pak Kampuchea
Administrative divisions: 22 provinces.
Capital: Phnom Penh (Phnum Pénh) 540,000 people (1994, est.).
Other cities: Battambang 45,000; Kompong Cham 33,000 (1989).
Government: Parliamentary monarchy. Norodom Sihanouk, King. Hun Sen, Prime Minister. The legislature is made up of a 120-member National Assembly, in which representatives hold 5-year terms.
National Holiday: November 9, Independence Day (1953).
Armed Forces: 88,500.

were held, with many candidates for each post. The Non-Aligned Movement summit meeting at the time in New Delhi did not support any of the contending groups. Faced with a wide set of electoral options, Cambodia's seat in the movement was left vacant.

24 In July 1985, the Vietnamese announced that their 150,000 troops would gradually be withdrawn from Cambodia over the following five years.

25 Difficulties stemming from the war affected the Phnom Penh Government, and it was only officially recognized by some 30 countries. Still, it managed to bring about a steady increase in the production of rice, cattle, pigs and poultry.

26 In 1986 the Government made overtures to Sihanouk within the context of a general agreement, offering him the position of head of state in a government from which the Khmer Rouge would be excluded. From the end of 1987 to mid-1989, Hun Sen, who had become Prime Minister, met with Sihanouk on six occasions. The main disagreement each time was whether the Khmer Rouge would be admitted to a new provisional government or not.

27 During the course of 1989, a curfew in effect since 1979 was lifted and private ownership of some "non-strategic" enterprises was permitted. In addition, collective farms passed into the hands of peasant families, with the assurance that the land could henceforth be passed from generation to generation, and transportation services were privatized. On June 1 1989, to complete the diplomatic offensive and improve its image, the country changed its name to the State of Cambodia. After a meeting between Hun Sen and the new Thai Prime Minister, Chatichai Choonhavan, the possibilities of regional agreement and economic relations between the countries improved.

28 The International Conference for Peace in Cambodia held in Paris in July 1989 ended in failure as the three factions of the armed opposition could not come to any agreement. The two main points of disagreement were UN monitoring of the Vietnamese withdrawal and Khmer Rouge participation in government. Even without this agreement, Vietnamese troops withdrew completely in September, as planned, followed by an advance in the position of rebel forces.

29 In April 1990, after a military offensive by Heng Samrin and Hun Sen's government soldiers, the opposition forces retreated to the Thai border. With this development the Thai premier Chatichai Choonhavan sponsored a new meeting between Sihanouk and

Hun Sen. In Bangkok, both leaders agreed to the installation of a supernational agency which would symbolize the sovereignty and national unity of Cambodia. An "adequate" UN presence was also agreed to by both parties.

30 In July 1990, the US announced they would recognize the State of Cambodia and would initiate negotiations with Vietnam over a peace settlement.

31 In October 1991, a peace treaty was signed. The Supreme National Council was created, with representatives of the Phnom Penh government and part of the opposition, it was chaired by Sihanouk and was to govern the country until elections in 1993. In 1992, the UN sent a peacekeeping force consisting of 20,000 troops to enforce the cease-fire and organize the elections. To many observers' horror, the Khmer Rouge was included in the UN operation as a legitimate "warring faction". This enabled them to gain respectability over time, rehabilitating their reputation.

32 In the constituent elections of May 1993, boycotted by the Khmer Rouge, the United National Front for an Independent, Neutral, Peaceful and Cooperative Cambodia (Funcinpec) party supporters led by Sihanouk's son Norodom Ranariddh won 58 seats. The former Cambodian People's Communist Party gained 51, the Liberal Democratic Party 10, and the National Liberation Movement of Cambodia, one. In the new government, Ranariddh and Hun Sen shared the post of Prime Minister.

33 In September 1993, a new Constitution was enacted. It turned the National Assembly into a Parliament and established a parliamentary monarchy. Sihanouk was appointed King, "independent" of all political parties. But he continued to advocate a "national reconciliation" government, with the inclusion of the Khmer Rouge.

34 In 1995, fighting intensified between the official army and the Khmer Rouge, which controlled about 15 per cent of the territory. The IMF expressed its faith in the country's economy, which grew 7 per cent in 1995 according to the government.

35 In 1996, the Khmer Rouge began to show signs of weakness. The rumours of Pol Pot's death in

June were construed as an indication of the existence of significant divisions within the guerrilla movement. Many defections - like Ieng Sary's (a leader of the armed group) in August - suggested that the government policy aim of splitting the Khmer Rouge was proving successful.

36 Accused of treason and of planning a civil war alongside the Khmer Rouge, Prince Ranariddh was ousted in July 1997 by Cambodian army officials loyal to the second Prime Minister Hun Sen. From China, King Sihanouk approved Hun Sen's proposal to appoint foreign minister Ung Huot, from Funcinpec, to the position of first Prime Minister, in place of Ranariddh. In March, 1998 the monarch pardoned his son - who had been sentenced to a 30-year prison term - a decision regarded as an attempt to delay the political chaos which followed Ranariddh's expulsion and as a means to secure international financial aid which had been interrupted since the July 1997 coup.

37 In spite of international efforts to rebuild Cambodian society, the lack of punishment of officials involved in serious human rights violations remained unchanged. Amnesty International reported the killing of hundreds of opposition members and the persistence of an incompetent, weak and corrupt judicial system.

38 A month after the death of Pol Pot in Thailand in April 1998, Ranariddh returned to Cambodia to run in an election. It was won by Hun Sen with a broad margin. Both Ranariddh's Funcinpec and Sam Rainsy's opposition party denounced irregularities in the elections, including the disappearance of voting lists, pressure on voters, errors in the count and an insufficient number of observers. The 600 international observers, however, said the process was sound.

39 In May 1999, when the effects of the 1997 Asian economic crisis were at their worst in Southeast Asia, ASEAN welcomed Cambodia as its tenth member. This caused upsets within ASEAN, for while some saw the event as the end of decades of instability caused by the Cold War in the region, others feared the economic crisis and differences in terms of democracy and human rights issues would lead to conflict as Phnom Penh would bring its

STATISTICS

DEMOGRAPHY

Population: 10,946,000 (1999)
Annual growth: 1.8 % (1975/97)
Estimates for year 2015 (million): 14.4 (1999)
Annual growth to year 2015: 1.8 % (1997/2015)
Urban population: 21.6 % (1997)
Urban Growth: 6.7 % (1980/95)
Children per woman: 4.6 (1998)

HEALTH

Life expectancy at birth: 53 years (1998)
male: 51 years (1998)
female: 55 years (1998)
Maternal mortality: 470 per 100,000 live births (1990-98)
Infant mortality: 104 per 1,000 (1998)
Under-5 child mortality: 163 per 1,000 (1998)
Daily calorie supply: 1,974 per capita (1996)
58 doctors per 100,000 people (1993)
Safe water: 30 % (1990/98)

EDUCATION

Literacy: 65 % (1995)
male: 80 % (1995)
female: 53 % (1995)
School enrolment:
Primary total: 131 % (1990/96)
male: 142 % (1990/97)
female: 119 % (1990/97)
Secondary:
male: 30 % (1990/96)
female: 18 % (1990/96)
Tertiary: 1 % (1997)
Primary school teachers: one for every 46 (1997)

COMMUNICATIONS

2 newspapers (1996), 127 radios (1997), 9 TV sets (1996) and 1 main telephone lines (1996) per 1,000 people

ECONOMY

Per capita, GNP: $ 260 (1998)
Annual growth, GNP: -0.1 % (1998)
Annual inflation: 32.8 % (1990/98)
Consumer price index: 130.3 (1998)
Currency: 3,744.4 riels = $ 1 (1998)
Cereal imports: 38,455 metric tons (1998)
Fertilizer use: 22 kg per ha (1997)
Exports: $ 978 million (1998)
Imports: $ 1,251 million (1998)
External debt: $ 2,210 million (1998); $ 206 per capita (1998)
Debt service: 1.5 % of exports (1998)
Development aid received: $ 372 million (1997); $ 41.7 per capita (1997); 12.20 % of GNP (1997)

HDI (rank/value): 137/0.514 (1997)central government expenditure: 25.8 % (1997)

internal problems to the forum. In Cambodia, opposition leader Sam Rainsy stated his fear that ASEAN would destroy Cambodian industry, making competition impossible and leaving the country reduced to the role of exporter of raw materials. ∎

Cameroon

Cameroun

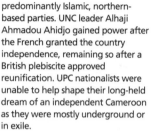

Population: 14,710,000 (1999)
Area: 475,440 SQ KM
Capital: Yaoundé
Currency: CFA franc
Language: French and English

The area known as Cameroon is the birthplace and original homeland of the Bantu ethnic group, which after 200 BC migrated east and south, spreading new crop varieties and methods for working iron. In 1472 Fernando Po named a river Camarones (Portuguese for shrimp) because of the crustaceans swarming at its mouth. The name eventually became Cameroon.

[2] The Fulah migration helped transform the local economies into part of a regional circuit which later gave rise to the Emirate of Adamaua in the north central region.

[3] German penetration began in June 1884 when German envoy Gustav Nachtigal signed an agreement with the ruler of the Doualas, a coastal group, making the region a protectorate. A year later, the Berlin Conference awarded Cameroon to Germany. But the Emirate of Adamaua, which the British wanted, was not given to the Germans until 1894.

[4] This protectorate did not survive very long. The Doualas dominated trade that the Germans wanted to control between the coast and Yaoundé, the trade center between Adamaua and the south. In 1897, the Doualas resisted German interference, and a bloody four-year war ensued.

[5] The Germans appropriated the most fertile lands, and the Africans began to die of hunger by the thousands, in an area where stable agriculture had existed for centuries. In 1918 France and Britain invaded Cameroon: the French taking three-fourths, and the English taking the rest. The pro-independence organizations found their cause was facilitated by the tensions between the colonial powers. In 1945, the People's Union

of Cameroon (UPC) was founded, headed by Rubem Um Nyobé. The UPC earned popular support and launched a series of legal campaigns between 1948 and 1956, when it was outlawed.

[6] Nationalist leaders fled to the British-held western sector and organized a guerrilla movement. The UPC established liberated zones in the southern forests where they set up their own administration - a

first for sub-Saharan Africa. The efficiency of the guerrillas made it possible for them to resist constant French attacks, until 1960. Two years later, Rubem Um Nyobé died, but the revolution continued.

[7] UPC resistance forced the French to adopt a new strategy, adding political manoeuvres to their repressive tactics. Paris created the National Union of Cameroon (UNC), merging two conservative,

predominantly Islamic, northern-based parties. UNC leader Alhaji Ahmadou Ahidjo gained power after the French granted the country independence, remaining so after a British plebiscite approved reunification. UPC nationalists were unable to help shape their long-held dream of an independent Cameroon as they were mostly underground or in exile.

[8] Ahidjo stepped up persecution of the opposition in the 1960s, developing one of sub-Saharan Africa's most efficient repressive systems. European human rights groups revealed the existence of thousands of political prisoners in the country. In 1982, Ahidjo suddenly resigned, and was succeeded by his former Prime Minister, Paul Biya.

[9] Biya maintained his predecessor's political and economic policies, though many of Adhidjo's followers supported a coup attempt by a group of military officers. Young people - especially students - resisted the coup attempt by taking to the streets.

[10] Growing unemployment and food shortages undermined Cameroon's traditionally prosperous image. Biya attempted to reinforce his control by calling early elections for April 1984. With democratic organizations prohibited, he was re-elected. Nevertheless, the overall instability of the country led to a new coup attempt, followed by a series of bloody incidents in which 200 people were killed.

[11] In the 1980s, the UNC changed its name to "Democratic Group of the People of Cameroon" (RDPC), but its political line remained the same.

[12] The UPC later adopted a more flexible stance in order to broaden its social scope, and Biya created new northern provinces to give the Muslims greater economic and political power. Disagreements over oil revenues aggravated inter-ethnic and inter-regional friction. Economic problems stemming from a drop in world prices for coffee, rubber and cotton were exacerbated by Cameroon's dependence on French companies which controlled almost 44 per cent of the export market.

[13] Biya was re-elected in 1988. Censorship increased, journalists were arrested and the post of Prime Minister was abolished.

[14] Faced with the fall in oil prices on the world market and foreign debt payments, the Government

WORKERS

% OF LABOUR FORCE **1998**

- FEMALE: 38% ■ MALE: 62%

1990

- SERVICES: 21.5%
- INDUSTRY: 8.8%
- AGRICULTURE: 69.7%

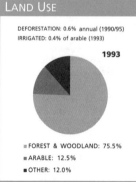

LAND USE

DEFORESTATION: 0.6% annual (1990/95)
IRRIGATED: 0.4% of arable (1993)

1993

- FOREST & WOODLAND: 75.5%
- ARABLE: 12.5%
- OTHER: 12.0%

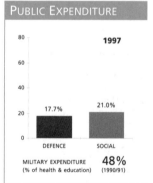

PUBLIC EXPENDITURE

1997

DEFENCE 17.7%   SOCIAL 21.0%

MILITARY EXPENDITURE **48%**
(% of health & education) (1990/91)

sought World Bank and IMF support for a structural adjustment program to stabilize its finances. By reducing imports and state expenditure, privatizing public enterprises and reorganizing the banking system, the country's debts were renegotiated with the Paris Club.

[15] In 1990, social and political organizations reported an increase in government repression of hundreds of citizens.

[16] A few months later, the Government authorized the creation of political parties: some 70 political organizations were granted legal recognition.

[17] In November 1991, opposition leaders demanded constitutional reform and a return to the federal system abolished in 1972. The political crisis deepened, strikes and pro-democracy demonstrations proliferated; 40 demonstrators were killed by the police.

[18] In December, the Government set the legislative elections for February 16 1992. The opposition wanted the constitution and electoral law be modified prior to the elections. Nonetheless, several parties participated in the elections on March 1 1992.

[19] The RDPC won 88 of the 180 parliamentary seats. The National Union for Democracy and Progress (UNDP) came in second, with 68 representatives. According to the official report, 61 per cent of the four million registered electorate voted.

[20] Biya brought forward the Presidential election to October 11 1992. Seven parties fielded candidates: among them, the Social Democratic Front (FSD) led by John Fru Ndi, the main opposition party representing the English-speaking community. Both the FSD and the Democratic Union of Cameroon, led by Adamu Ndam Njoya, had boycotted the March elections.

[21] Amid widespread accusations of fraud, the Government's narrow victory provoked incidents in the English-speaking Northwestern Province, Fru Ndi's territory.

[22] International observers confirmed the fraud, but the Supreme Court refused to annul the election. Fru Ndi proclaimed himself President, and the Government decreed a state of emergency in the Northwest. Fru Ndi and his supporters were immediately placed under house arrest.

[23] In November a "coalition" government of the RDPC and minor groups was formed. Government repression intensified, bringing international condemnation. In December, four members of the Bar Association were arrested for leading a protest, one dying after being tortured. When the US suspended foreign aid, Biya cancelled the state of emergency and freed Fru Ndi.

[24] In January 1993, Finance Minister Antoine Ntsimi announced the reduction of civil servants' pay by between 4 and 20 per cent in order, he said, to avoid job cuts for 50,000 employees.

[25] At that time, a third of the nation's foreign trade depended on France. The maintenance of this trade link led the opposition to propose a boycott on French products, stating that France supported Biya.

[26] Vice-president of the UDC Benjamin Menga was assassinated in January 1993. Several political leaders were imprisoned and press censorship was stepped up. In 1994, the schism in the opposition helped Biya's "firm hand" policy.

[27] On the economic front, Biya ignored opposition pleas against remaining in the CFA economic zone, despite the 100 per cent devaluation of the CFA imposed by Paris. Cameroon received funds from the IMF and the Paris Club after announcing far-reaching economic adjustment.

[28] In 1995, the opposition split again. In May, Siga Assanga, former secretary general of Fru Ndi's Social Democratic Front abandoned this group to found the Social Democratic Movement. Meanwhile the UNDP also divided following the expulsion of two members who had participated in Biya's governments.

[29] The results of the municipal elections in January 1996 consolidated Biya's power. In October 1997, he was re-elected in a poll challenged by the opposition parties, some of whom had called for a boycott of the election. Only three of the six million registered voters were called on to vote. The others had been excluded by the Government which insisted they were "foreigners".

[30] In late 1997, opposition increased to a World Bank project to extract oil in southern Chad and to transport it to the Atlantic through Cameroon. Dozens of Non-Governmental Organizations called on the Bank to back social development projects instead.

[31] In March 1998, Cameroon and Nigeria appeared before the International Court in the Hague in a dispute over the Bakassi peninsula, with its rich fishing resources and supposedly extensive oil fields. The disagreement between the two states had led to several armed confrontations.

[32] The economic crisis, exacerbated by the devaluation of the franc, dislocated Cameroon's society. In the 1990s, police corruption and the ineffective justice system led some of the population to vent their frustrations by beating up petty offenders, killing men and also causing serious injuries to women. On many occasions innocent people were killed. ■

PROFILE

ENVIRONMENT

The country is divided into three regions: the plains of the Lake Chad basin in the northern region (savanna where cattle are raised and corn and cotton are grown); the central part, made up of humid grasslands; and the southern part, an area with rich volcanic soil where the main cash crops (coffee, bananas, cocoa and palm oil) are grown. It is in the latter that most of the population lives. Drought and desertification are the main concerns in the southern region, which covers 25 per cent of the nation's land area, and houses over a quarter of the population.

SOCIETY

Peoples: There are some 200 ethnic groups, the main ones being the Dualas, Bamilekes, Tikars and Bamauns in the south; the Euondos and Fulbes in the west, and the Fulanis in the north. In the southeast live the Baka Pygmies, who live by hunting and fishing.
Religions: Half the population practice traditional African religions. Christians are a majority in the south while Muslims predominate in the north.
Languages: French and English are the official languages. There are nearly one hundred African languages and dialects.
Political Parties: Democratic Alliance of the People of Cameroon (RDPC); Movement for the Defense of the Republic; Social Democratic Front (FSD); National Union for Democracy and Progress (UNDP); Front of Allies for Change (FAC).
Social Organizations: National Workers' Union of Cameroon.

THE STATE

Official Name: République du Cameroun.
Capital: Yaoundé 800,000 people (1993).
Other cities: Douala 1,000,600 people; Garoua 102,000 (1993).
Government: Parliamentary republic. Paul Biya, President since 1982, re-elected in October 1997. Peter Musonge Mafani, Prime Minister since 1996.
National Holidays: January 1, Independence Day (1960); October 1, Reunification (1961), May 20, proclamation of the Republic (1972).
Armed Forces: 14,600.

Canada

Canada

Population: 30,857,000 (1999)
Area: 9,970,609 SQ KM
Capital: Ottawa
Currency: Canadian dollar
Language: English and French

The first inhabitants of present-day Canada were Inuit and other people that had come from the Asian continent across the Bering Strait. The European colonists who came to North America in the 16th century estimated the indigenous population of the entire continent to be between 10 and 12 million.

[2] Between the 17th and 19th centuries, these territories were colonized by Britain and France. Some areas changed hands several times until 1763 when the Peace of Paris which ended the Seven Years' War granted Canada to Britain. Colonization increased thanks to the profitable fur trade, with the local population growing to almost half a million by the end of the 19th century.

[3] The British North America Act of 1867 determined that the Canadian constitution would be similar to Britain's, with executive power vested in the King and delegated to a Governor General and Council. The legislative function would, meanwhile, be carried out by a Parliament composed of a Senate and a House of Commons.

[4] In 1931, the Statute of Westminster released Britain's dominions from the colonial laws under which they had been governed, giving Canada legislative autonomy. That same year, Norway recognized Canadian sovereignty over the Arctic regions to the north of the main part of its territory.

[5] In 1981, the Canadian Government reached an agreement with the British Parliament over constitutional transition. The following year, the 1867 Constitution was replaced by the Act of Canada, which granted Canada the autonomy to reform the constitution.

[6] The Constitution Act of 1982 included a Charter of Rights and Freedoms, which recognized the country's pluralistic heritage and the rights of its indigenous peoples. It set forth the principle of equal benefits among the country's ten provinces, and the sovereignty of each province over its own natural resources, though Quebec did not sign the agreement.

[7] When Quebec was occupied by English Protestants in 1760, its predominantly French population sought to maintain a separate Quebecois identity, marked by both religious and political nationalism. Quebec assumed a special role as guardian of the Catholic faith, the French language and the French heritage in North America. It was a role which it performed well. From a French population of 6,000 in 1769, the number of Québecois had increased to 6 million by 1960.

[8] In Quebec, four-fifths of the population speak French as a first language and are fiercely proud of their cultural identity, and provincial autonomy has always been a delicate issue. In 1977, the ruling separatist Parti Québecois (PQ), led by René Lévèsque, adopted French as the official language of education, business and local public administration.

[9] Lévèsque discarded the possibility of a unilateral separation proposing instead a concept of "sovereignty-association", with a monetary and customs union. However, voters rejected this proposal by 59.5 to 40.5 per cent in a plebiscite held in 1980. Fifteen years later, in a new plebiscite favoured by the Parti Québecois, the margin was narrowed with 50.4 per cent of voters opposing separation and 49.6 per cent approving it.

[10] Antiquated British law governed relations between the sexes in North America for a long time, and it was not until October 1929 that Canadian women obtained full legal rights, and it was only under the 1982 Constitution that true sexual equality in law was established.

[11] In addition to the federal law, each province has an equal rights law, guaranteeing access to housing, jobs, services and other facilities, without discrimination on the basis of race, religion, age, nationality or sex - though Quebec is the only province which prohibits discrimination on the basis of "sexual inversion", its terminology for homosexuality. A supreme court decision extended protection against discrimination based on sexual preference.

[12] Nevertheless as in other Western countries women are still discriminated against. Not all professions are open to them, and in many professional fields they have to accept lower salaries. Between 1969 and 1979, there was a 62 per cent increase in the number of women working outside the home. By 1981, this figure represented 49 per cent of all women, and 39 per cent of the economically active population.

[13] Liberal governments, led by Pierre Trudeau, were elected in 1968, 1972, 1974 and again in 1980, after a brief Conservative interlude. Trudeau loosened Canada's traditional ties with Western Europe and the US, and strengthened those with the Far East, Africa and Latin America. In addition, he refused to participate in the economic blockade against Cuba.

[14] Economic difficulties stemming from the worldwide recession triggered a sharp drop in the Liberal Party's popularity, in favour of the Conservative Party. In 1983, Conservative leader Brian Mulroney, a labour relations lawyer and businessman from Quebec became prime minister, replacing John Turner, who had succeeded Trudeau as head of the Liberal Party.

[15] Mulroney re-established a "special relationship" between Canada and the US, starting negotiations for a free trade agreement in 1985. This agreement, which went into effect in January 1989, provoked criticism from the Liberals and other members of the opposition, who claimed that the terms of the agreement were overly favourable to the US. Nevertheless, it received majority support from the voters in the 1988 election.

[16] The Conservative victory was made possible by the Québecois

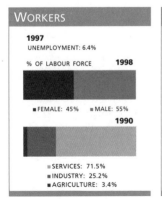

WORKERS

1997
UNEMPLOYMENT: 6.4%

% OF LABOUR FORCE **1998**

■ FEMALE: 45% ■ MALE: 55%

1990

■ SERVICES: 71.5%
■ INDUSTRY: 25.2%
■ AGRICULTURE: 3.4%

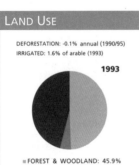

LAND USE

DEFORESTATION: -0.1% annual (1990/95)
IRRIGATED: 1.6% of arable (1993)

1993

■ FOREST & WOODLAND: 45.9%
■ ARABLE: 4.6%
■ OTHER: 45.9%

PUBLIC EXPENDITURE

DEFENCE EXPENDITURE (% of goverment exp.)	**7.1%**	(1994)
MILITARY EXPENDITURE (% of health & education)	**15%**	(1990/91)

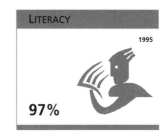
votes, reflecting the growing economic importance of French-speaking voters. The victory also reflected the impact of the Meech Lake Accord, initiated by Mulroney and signed in 1987, in which the Federal Government ceded important powers to the provinces, granting Quebec for the first time recognition of its unique cultural status, in order for it to accept the constitution and Charter of Rights and Freedoms.

[17] To be implemented, the Meech Lake Accord had to be ratified by the unanimous consent of each of the provinces, and it was blocked by Newfoundland and Manitoba. In Manitoba the one vote against came from a Native American who would not accept the "distinct society" clause for Quebec, saying native people were every bit as distinct.

[18] The Northwest Territories (NWT) - which make up one-third of the country's land area with only 52,000 inhabitants, half of whom are Inuit or members of other indigenous groups - were considering the possibility of splitting into two regions, Nunavut and Denendeh, each with an autonomous government. While this plan was approved by the provincial legislature in 1987, it was subject to ratification by a plebiscite of its residents, and the Federal Government.

[19] The Federal Government declared its willingness to accept the right of the Inuit and other native peoples of the NWT to self-government, incorporating this right into the Constitution if approved by the provincial governments and by organizations representing the interests of these peoples. In 1988, it transferred 673,000 sq km to the other native peoples and the Inuit. In 1992, representatives from the Federal and provincial governments signed an agreement on the land claims of 17,500 native peoples from the Northwest Territories. The way was paved for the creation of Nunavut ("Our Land" in Inuit), approved in a referendum held on April 4. Nunavut, which includes the area west of Hudson Bay and the Arctic archipelago, covers an area of 2.2 million sq km, equal to one fifth of the country. The agreement also included the transference of 350,000 sq km to the Inuit and the payment of $580 million as a

counterpart for the waiver of future land claims.

[20] The Inuit from northwestern Canada have been working with other indigenous groups of Greenland and Alaska to deal with ecological, cultural, social and political problems which affect their nation. The Fifth Circumpolar Conference of the Inuit (CCI) in 1989 reaffirmed Inuit rights to lands which Canada considered government property, and leased out to large mining interests.

[21] Canada's first trading partner is the US, and vice versa, but while the volume of Canada's sales to the US accounts for one-fifth of its total production, American exports to Canada represent less than 3 per cent. No other major Western economy maintains a trade imbalance of such magnitude. It is comparable only to the dependence of Southern countries in relation to the industrialized countries.

[22] With the free trade agreement which went into effect in 1989, Canada's integration with the American economy has been accentuated. Through trade, the extension of credit, and investments in Canada, the US secured ever greater control over Canadian natural resources and majority control over shares in some Canadian industries.

[23] A recession in the US means recession in Canada; Ottawa's monetary policy is essentially defined by its neighbour's. This degree of dependence has been labelled "colonial", despite the fact that Canada is the world's eighth largest industrial power, and that its standard of living is one of the highest in the world.

[24] The Canadian Armed Forces (CF) are charged with protecting national interests both inside and outside the country, with defending North America in cooperation with the US, and complying with its NATO commitments; in addition, it has participated in UN Peacekeeping Forces.

[25] The Canadian Forces Europe (CFE) supplied the NATO Supreme Command with troops which were permanently stationed in Germany, including four Mobile Command Brigades and an air division, all of which maintained maximum operational readiness. They also participated in the US intervention in Haiti in 1994.

PROFILE

ENVIRONMENT

Canada is the second largest country in the world in land area, divided into five natural regions. The Maritime Provinces along the Atlantic coast are a mixture of rich agricultural land and forests. The Canadian Shield is a rocky region which is covered with woods and is rich in minerals.

To the south, along the shores of the Great Lakes and the St Lawrence River, there is a large plain with fertile farmlands, where over 60 per cent of the population is concentrated, and the major urban centres are located. Farming (wheat, oats and rye), is the mainstay of the Central Prairie Provinces. The Pacific Coast is a mountainous region with vast forests. The "Great North" is almost uninhabited, with very cold climate and tundra. There are ten provinces, and two territories; the Yukon and Northwest. These are working towards provincial status, but this is complicated by Native Land claims. Canada has immense mineral resources; it is the world's largest producer of asbestos, nickel, zinc and silver and the second largest of uranium. There are also major lead, copper, gold, iron ore, gas and oil deposits. Its industry is highly developed. Industrial emissions from Canadian and US plants contribute to the "acid rain" which has affected thousands of lakes. The construction of a number of hydroelectric plants in Quebec is threatening to destroy the lands and livelihood of the indigenous population.

SOCIETY

Peoples: There are about 850,000 Native Americans, Métis (mixed race) and Inuit (Eskimos) ranging from highly acculturated city-dwellers to traditional hunters and trappers living in isolated northern communities. There are six distinct culture areas and ten language families; many native languages such as Cree and Ojibwa are still widely spoken. About 350,000 native people are classified as such: that is, they belong to one of 573 registered groups and can live on a federally protected reserve (though only about 70 per cent actually do so). Métis and those who do not have official status as "native people" have historically enjoyed no separate legal recognition, but attempts are now being made to secure them special rights under the law. The original European settlers came from France, England and Scotland. Today Canada is multicultural with many people from Asia, the Caribbean and southern Europe.

Languages: English and French, both official. 13 per cent of the population is bilingual, 67 per cent speak only English, 18 per cent only French, and 2 per cent speak other languages (Italian, German and Ukranian).

Religions: Roman Catholic 45.7 per cent; Protestant 36.3 per cent; Eastern Orthodox 1.5 per cent; Jewish 1.2 per cent; Muslim 1.0 per cent; Buddhist 0.7 per cent; Hindu 0.6 per cent; nonreligious 12.4 per cent; other 0.6 per cent.

Political Parties: The Liberal Party; the Conservative Party; Bloque Québécois; the New Democratic Party, and the Reform Party.

Social Organizations: The Canadian Labour Congress, with over two million members, is the largest trade union; The Assembly of First Nations; the Council of Canadians; National Status of Women Committee.

THE STATE

Official Name: Canada.
Administrative Divisions: 10 Provinces and 2 Territories.
Capital: Ottawa 1,056,000 people (1996).
Other cities: Toronto 4,263,757 people; Montreal 3,326,510; Vancouver 1,831,665 (1996).
Government: Adrienne Clarkson, Governor-General. Jean Chrétien, Prime Minister and Head of Government since November 1993. Canada is a federation of ten provinces and a member of the British Commonwealth, with a parliamentary system of government.
National Holiday: July 1, Canada Day (1867).

Quebec libre?

FOOD DEPENDENCY

1997
6%

FOREIGN TRADE

Millions US$ 1997

IMPORTS
237,088

EXPORTS
247,047

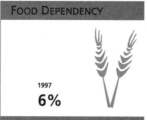

"**V**ive le Quebec *libre!*" exclaimed the French President, Charles de Gaulle, from the balcony of Montreal City Hall in 1967. His call was in open support of the province's separatists, awakening pro-independence demonstrations in the main cities.

[2] French nationalism in Quebec had taken shape in the late 1960s. Intellectuals and workers blamed the economic crisis in Quebec on the Canadian Federation and they proposed two alternatives: better relations with the other provinces and central government, or the independence of Quebec and its constitution as a sovereign state. Supporters of the second stance gathered around the recently created Parti Quebecois (PQ), led by René Lévèsque and made up of former left-wing militants from the unionist Liberal Party.

[3] However according to Canadian legislation, none of the provinces is allowed to separate and the pro-independence PQ would only be able to pursue the possibility by means of a referendum and the support of the international community.

[4] Two important events then occurred in three years, which projected Quebec onto the national and international scene. The first was De Gaulle's call in 1967. And then in October 1970, the extremist Quebec Liberation Front kidnapped Quebec's employment minister, Pierre Laporte, and British Trade Comissioner James Cross. Laporte was found dead days later, and Cross was freed. As a result of these events, Canadian Prime Minister, Pierre Trudeau, declared a state of emergency, sent in the troops and suspended civil rights.

[5] Once the economic problems were resolved, the separatist nationalists started to make other demands, like defending the French language from the Anglo and Protestant expansionism of the majority in Canada. To a certain degree, the separatists were running up the flag lost to Britain in 1759 when it took New France, the forerunner of Quebec, in the battle of the "Plains of Abraham".

[6] In the September 1994 provincial elections, the PQ was returned to power again, and its leader, Jacques Parizeau - who was elected Premier - promised a new referendum for independence - the first referendum had been held in 1980. The other separatist political force was the federalist Bloque Quebecois (BQ), led by Lucien Bouchard, the current Premier of Quebec. In the October 1995 referendum, the pro-independence parties just lost with 49 per cent of the vote, and certain things became clearer as a result.

[7] Firstly, that independence required a prior phase of new economic, political and military relationships with Canada. The separatist leaders, had they won, were under instructions to schedule negotiations with Canada and only to declare independence if their proposals were rejected. Secondly, it became obvious there are increasing numbers of separatists in Quebec, or at least that growing numbers of Quebecois feel less Canadian (separatists had only received 40 per cent of the vote in 1980).

[8] Since the failure of the most recent referendum on independence, many of the pro-independence movement have taken conservative stances - similar to those held by the Quebecois right in 1960. Today, Canada is structurally dependent on the US which does not want any split.

[9] Things have not been easy for the Quebecois since then. The BQ majority has shown itself to be less demanding although - always within its nationalist framework - it has claimed greater powers for Quebec. In October 1999, US President Bill Clinton said in Montreal, "think twice before separating, in these times of globalization". Of course, he would say that because 90 per cent of Canadian export earnings depend on the US. Bouchard believed Clinton had shown no preference for Canada. At the same time, he said his province should develop a relationship with Canada similar to that between the member states of the European Union (EU). Many Quebecois separatists are unhappy with this, as Bouchard's position is now little different from that held by the Liberal Party. ∎

[26] Relations between Canada and the US became tense in 1985, when a US Coast Guard vessel passed through the Northwest Passage without Canadian authorization. The US recognizes Canadian sovereignty over the Arctic islands but not over its waters; a similar dispute exists with relation to the waters surrounding the French islands of St Pierre and Miquelon.

[27] Canada made little headway in getting the US to control industrial gas emissions, which drift over Canadian territory, bringing with them acid rain, or in reaching agreement on catch limits for the shared west coast salmon fishery.

[28] The Canadian Government made a commitment to reduce its industrial emissions by half. This program anticipated a reduction in industrial pollution of 20 per cent by the year 2005.

[29] In 1991, Quebec's premier Robert Bourassa initiated the second phase of the huge James Bay Power Project, which involved damming or diverting nine rivers along 350,000 km of the northwestern part of the province, emptying into the James and Hudson Bays.

[30] The final capacity of 27,000 megawatts of hydro-electric power is far greater than the output of Itaipu Dam, in Brazil or that of Three Gorges Dam in China.

[31] The region affected by the projects is located in the hunting and fishing grounds of approximately 11,000 Cree and 7,000 Inuit, peoples who have lived in the area for over 5,000 years. This region contains the largest beluga whale population in the world, as well as the largest caribou herds and most of the world's fresh-water seals. Vast numbers of migratory birds make the extensive wetlands their home for several months each year.

[32] The second phase of the project involved flooding an additional 10,000 sq km of land. The dam enables Canada to sell electricity to the US, set up plants for aluminium production in Quebec and guarantee an energy supply for Canadian consumption, which is among the highest in the world. The ecological consequences of this project on the regional ecosystem are unforeseeable.

[33] In 1973, hunting and fishing provided two-thirds of the local population's food, with this

percentage dropping to one-fourth, 20 years later. A 1975 treaty allowed local people to retain a small part of their lands, granting some economic compensation for the loss of the rest of their territory. Even so, the chances of the local indigenous culture surviving the nationalistic ecocide of Quebec are severely limited.

[34] The Inuit, who inhabit the Belcher Islands in the Hudson Bay and navigate the frozen waters in search of fish and game, were not taken into account in these agreements, and they remain concerned about what effect these major changes will have upon the ecosystem and their way of life. The indigenous peoples are fighting for government respect of the treaties which affirm their rights to their land and resources. Those who live from hunting and fishing, like the Cree, the Dene, the Innu, the Inuit and the Haida are especially vulnerable facing multiple threats to their lands and livelihoods.

[35] Canada's original inhabitants have now organized more and between the 1960s and 1970s this culminated in the creation of the National Indian Brotherhood (NIB). The aim of this organization is to represent indigenous peoples to the general public and also to make their grievances known to the federal government. The NIB was subsequently renamed by the Assembly of First Nations.

[36] After World War II, the Government tried to restrict the Innu in Labrador to small reservations, and by the 1970s, most of them were living in areas designated for this purpose. Although Canada officially recognizes the claims of indigenous peoples over their lands, it has sought to reach agreements with individual groups, to set them up in smaller areas in exchange for economic compensation.

[37] The experience over one generation for the Innu people has demonstrated that they cannot accept government propositions. A 1984 report revealed that the suicide rate among the communities in the North of Labrador was five times the national average. In 1988, in retaliation, the Innu invaded the military base at Goose Bay, setting up a "peace camp".

[38] Four Innu charged with invading the base were

unexpectedly released under the argument that, since land ownership is a concept which is alien to Canada's original inhabitants, it was not reasonable for the court to consider evidence based on British or Canadian legal norms. The Canadian Government filed an immediate injunction, calling into question the validity of the judge's ruling, when it became obvious that this decision could set a precedent for land claims of the region's indigenous groups. In mid-1991, the International Task Force for Indian Affairs declared that the Canadian Government was not respecting the rights of the Mohawk people to practise their religion, and denounced specific acts of cultural aggression such as the construction of a golf course on their communal lands.

[39] In late 1990, the Federal Parliament approved restrictive legislation regarding refugee status, effective as of January 1991. The new legislation established that people fleeing persecution could be returned to their country of origin if that country was considered "safe". Both the opposition and humanitarian organizations accused the Government of going from one extreme to the other. The Government claimed it had not closed the borders completely, as it authorized the selection of 13,000 refugees by its embassies abroad and also allowed 10,000 family members of foreign residents to enter. Canada remains a major destination for political refugees.

[40] In October 1991 Ottawa announced the decision to earmark some $700 million for the agricultural sector; however, farmers were not satisfied with this amount, considering it insufficient to compensate for the losses of the previous year. Farm subsidies by the governments of the US and European countries left Canadian farmers disadvantaged in operating its policy of liberalizing trade under the GATT agreement.

[41] In December 1991, the Canadian Minister of Finance stated that the country had registered its first trade deficit in 15 years (in September, the trade deficit was $275 million). The year was characterized by economic recession, high taxes, corruption scandals, increasing separatism and a decline in Mulroney's popularity.

[42] In early 1992, there was intense debate over Quebec's growing demands for autonomy. In August, the province rejected the Government's scheme for granting it "special" status, as the terms were considered "insufficient".

[43] On August 12 1992, after 18 months of negotiations, Canada, the US and Mexico signed an agreement creating a free trade zone (North American Free Trade Agreement, NAFTA, see Box).

[44] In February 1993, Prime Minister Brian Mulroney resigned from the Conservative Party (and therefore from the Government) with the lowest popularity ratings ever. Earlier, in June, he had tried to take advantage of his 10-seat parliamentary majority to obtain ratification of NAFTA. But his resignation gave weight to the opposition's argument that key issues should be decided before new elections.

[45] In June of the same year, Parliament ratified the NAFTA treaty. Two months later Kim Campbell, the new Conservative Prime Minister travelled the country promoting the adoption of austerity measures to combat the budget deficit. In the meantime, her rival, Liberal Jean Chrétien, promised to give high priority to the creation of new jobs.

[46] In the October 1993 general elections, the Liberal Party (opposition) regained power after 9 years, with a landslide victory over the Conservative Party, whose representation in the House of Commons dropped from 155 seats to 2. The Liberals won 178 seats, against 79 in the previous legislature. The separatist Bloque Québecois (54 seats) and the right-of-center Reform Party (52 seats) both made significant gains. This was the worst defeat for a governing party in Canada's 126-year history.

[47] The new Prime Minister, Jean Chrétien, took office on November 4 1993. The following month, former prime minister Kim Campbell resigned from her post as leader of the Conservative Party.

[48] The reduction in the public deficit and State spending, the increase in unemployment to more than 10 per cent and the separatist tendencies in Quebec were the main Government concerns during 1994 and 1995.

[49] The Parti Québecois (PQ) again brought up the possible secession of Quebec from Canada in 1994. The popularity of Prime Minister Chrétien had increased 13 per cent since the 1993 elections, but the PQ triumphed in the province of Quebec. The new provincial Premier, Jacques Parizeau, promised to do everything possible to make Quebec a sovereign state.

[50] The geopolitical context of NAFTA, which came into force on January 1 1994, meant that the Quebec issue was followed with great attention in Mexico and the US, even though the PQ had promised that the province would meet the obligations assumed by Canada. However on October 30 1995, separation was rejected by 50.6 per cent of the electorate.

[51] The Quebec secession threat faded in 1996, despite the high number of votes received by the separatist option. The Federal Government transferred some powers to the provinces in an attempt to calm the nationalist movement. Lucien Bouchard, leader of the separatist forces, replaced Parizeau as Premier of Quebec when the latter resigned following the referendum defeat. Unemployment continued to rise in 1996, despite the economic growth. Disagreements continued throughout the year with the US over Canadian companies dealing with Cuba.

[52] In June 1997, Chrétien's party won the parliamentary elections, gaining 155 of the 301 seats, followed by the Reform Party and the PQ, then the New Democratic Party with 21 and the Conservatives with 20.

[53] In 1998 the Supreme Court ruled that Quebec could not separate without the consent of Federal Government. The Prime Minister, a native of Quebec and ardent opponent of secession, said the ruling supported the principal arguments of federal government, by establishing that Quebec lacked authority, within Canadian law, to execute unilateral independence.

[54] In 1999, a study by the David Suzuki Foundation stated Canada had the greatest per capita oil and gas consumption and that 16,000 people there die each year from air pollution. Furthermore, the study named Canada as the leading per capita producer of greenhouse gases. ∎

Cape Verde

Cabo Verde

Population: 418,000 (1999)
Area: 4,030 SQ KM
Capital: Praia
Currency: Escudo
Language: Portuguese and Creole

When the Portuguese settled on the Cape Verde archipelago in the 15th century, the islands were deserving of their descriptive name (Green Cape). They were covered by lush tropical vegetation that stood out against the black volcanic rock and the blue sea. Some 400 years later, Portuguese colonization had wrought devastation and transformed the islands into a "floating desert". Most of the population emigrated to escape starvation, while those who stayed depended upon foreign aid.

2   Cape Verde was a very important 16th century port of call for ships carrying slaves to America. Incursions by French, British and Dutch pirates were so frequent that Portugal brought farmers to the islands from the Alentejo region to ensure a more permanent presence. The agriculture practised by the new settlers quickly eroded the thin layer of fertile soil and periodic droughts have struck the country since the 18th century.

3   Falling farm production caused massive emigration of Cape Verdeans; many went to Guinea-Bissau, another former Portuguese colony with close ties to the archipelago. In later years, there was further emigration to Angola, Mozambique, Senegal, Brazil, and the US.

4   During the independence struggle, Cape Verde developed closer ties to Guinea-Bissau (see Guinea-Bissau). One major reason was the formation of the African Party for the Independence of Guinea and Cape Verde (PAIGC) in 1956, supported by both colonies. Amilcar Cabral, the PAIGC's founder and ideologist, planned that the two economically similar countries, could fight together for freedom and development, once independence was achieved.

5   In 1961, guerrilla warfare broke out on the continent, and hundreds of Cape Verdean patriots joined the fight. Portugal's colonial government was overthrown in 1974, a transition government was installed and in 1975 the islands proclaimed independence. The PAIGC set an unusual precedent, as for the first time ever one political party took office in two different countries at the same time. Aristides Pereira was elected President and commander Pedro Pires became Prime Minister. The PAIGC leadership took the first steps toward establishing a federation between Cape Verde and Guinea-Bissau, and the national assemblies of the two

countries sat together as the Council of the Union.

6   In 1968 the Cape Verde Government faced the devastating effects of a drought that left 80 per cent of the population of the archipelago without food. However, the prudent action of civilian organizations supplemented by foreign assistance averted a major catastrophe.

7   From 1975 onwards, the forested areas of Cape Verde increased from 3,000 to 45,000 hectares. The Government predicted that in the next 10 years a further 75,000 hectares would be planted making the islands self-sufficient in firewood. Early in the rainy season, the population of Cape Verde voluntarily spend a week planting trees.

8   The Government implemented land reform, giving priority to subsistence farming to replace the export crops of the colonial period, when barely five per cent of food needs was met by local production. The drastic decline in agricultural production led the Government to invest in fisheries.

9   Cape Verde supported Angola during its "second liberation war" (see Angola) by allowing Cuban planes to land on the archipelago during the airlift that helped defeat the invasion of Angola by former Zaire and South Africa. Cape Verde adopted a policy of non-alignment, declaring that no foreign military bases would be allowed in their territory.

10   In 1981, while the PAIGC was negotiating a new constitution for Guinea-Bissau and Cape Verde, Guinea-Bissau's president Luis Cabral was overthrown. João Bernardo Vieira took office, and was initially hostile to integration with Cape Verde. An emergency meeting of PAIGC members in Cape Verde discussed the political developments in Guinea-Bissau. This reaffirmation of support for the principles of Amílcar Cabral led the party congress to adopt a new name "the African Party for the Independence of Cape Verde" (PAICV) stressing their independence from Guinea.

11   Relations between the two governments became tense, but mediation efforts, particularly by Angola and Mozambique paid off. Reconciliation came in August 1982 in Maputo when President Machel brought Aristides Pereira and João Bernardo Vieira together. Further progress was made at the Conference of Former Portuguese Colonies in Africa, held in Cape Verde in November 1982. In Praia, President João Bernardo Vieira met with colleagues from Angola, Mozambique, Cape Verde, and São Tomé. Diplomatic relations returned to normal, but plans for reunification were abandoned.

12   Political stability, defiance and perseverance helped Cape Verde avoid famine and the other drastic consequences of the drought which afflicted Africa. In 1984, crop yields fell by 25 per cent, the trade deficit stood at $70 million and the foreign debt reached $98 million. However the food distribution system and efficient state and resource management prevented famine, although the country has been ravaged by droughts for 19 years. Despite these positive factors, some sectors of the population are still severely undernourished.

13   The paucity of resources made Cape Verde dependent upon foreign assistance, submitting to a number of projects which were

WORKERS

% OF LABOUR FORCE **1998**

- FEMALE: 39%   MALE: 61%

1990

- SERVICES: 39.7%
- INDUSTRY: 29.7%
- AGRICULTURE: 30.6%

LAND USE

IRRIGATED: 7.0% of arable (1993)

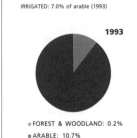

1993

- FOREST & WOODLAND: 0.2%
- ARABLE: 10.7%
- OTHER: 89.1%

PUBLIC EXPENDITURE

DEFENCE EXPENDITURE
(% of goverment exp.) **1.7%** (1994)

MATERNAL MORTALITY 1990-98

Per 100,000 live births

55

LITERACY 1995

69%

EXTERNAL DEBT 1998

Per capita

US$ 597

FOREIGN TRADE Millions US$ 1998

IMPORTS
282

EXPORTS
124

doomed to failure, including the nation's First Development Plan.

[14] The Second Development Plan, launched in 1986, prioritized private enterprise especially in the informal sector. In agriculture, concentrated efforts were made in the fight against desertification. In 1990, the plan was to recover more than 500 sq km, and establish a centralized system of administering water reserves for the whole country. During the first phase of the plan, more than 15,000 dams were built to store rainwater, and 231 sq km were forested.

[15] Despite adverse climatic conditions, farm production gradually increased in the first half of the 1990s to make the country practically self-sufficient in meat and vegetable requirements.

[16] Amidst the political decline linked to the crisis of socialism worldwide, the PAICV lost the first pluralist parliamentary elections, held in February 1991. The

Movement for Democracy (MPD) led by Carlos Veiga won the elections with over 65 per cent of the vote although 38 per cent of the electorate abstained from voting. Antonio Mascarenhas Monteiro, a legal expert educated at the University of Louvain, Belgium, and President of the Supreme Court of Cape Verde during the previous decade, was elected President.

[17] In September 1992, the new constitution went into effect. It ratified a multiparty system and banned the formation of parties on the basis of religious, tribal or regional divisions.

[18] The new government began the transition to a free-market economy with the privatization of insurance companies, fishing and banking, in line with the requirements of international agencies on which the country greatly depended on. Foreign aid accounted for 46 per cent of the

GDP, while remittances from the 700,000 Cape Verdeans residing abroad, constituted another 15 per cent of it.

[19] The liberal government, faced with a 25 per cent unemployment rate, declared its goal of restructuring the state. In the first quarter of 1993, government authorities announced a 50 per cent reduction of the 12,000 civil servants and a gradual deregulation of prices.

[20] The 1994 budget, despite making cuts in public expenditure, included an increase of public investment from $80 million in 1993 to $138 million in 1994. The priority sectors for state investment were transport, telecommunications and rural development.

[21] In January 1995, Prime Minister Carlos Veiga introduced significant changes in government in order to "facilitate the country's transition to a free-market economy". One of the most important changes was the merger of the Ministries of Finance, Economic Coordination and Tourism, and Industry and Commerce into one Ministry of Economic Coordination. Inflation in 1995 was 6 per cent and Cape Verdean economy is still greatly dependent upon foreign aid, particularly from the European Union.

[22] In 1997, unemployment remained at 25 per cent. Half way through the year, the Government announced more Italian investments in the tourism sector. The African Development Bank granted a $4.9 million loan for road-building. Cape Verde also received economic support from China and created an association with Angola to invest in health and social welfare, amongst other sectors.

[23] Reports of police brutality to prisoners recurred throughout 1998 and 1999. The number of prisoners far exceeded the number of cells available, and most prisons offered way below minimum reasonable conditions.

[24] Opposition politicians criticized the pro-government media for its self-censorship. The authorities, using the law to suit themselves, try, fine and often imprison editors and journalists critical of government figures. ∎

PROFILE

ENVIRONMENT

An archipelago of volcanic origin, composed of Windward Islands Santo Antao, Sao Vicente, Sao Nicolau, Santa Luzia, Sal, Boa Vista, Branco and Raso; and Leeward Islands Fogo, Santiago, Maio, Rombo and Brava. The islands are mountainous (heights of up to 2,800 meters) without permanent rivers. The climate is arid, influenced by the cold Canary Islands current. Agriculture is poor; nonetheless it employs most of the population. Cape Verde lies within the Sahel region, which is undergoing increased desertification, with periodic droughts. This phenomenon is aggravated by the islands' small size, topography of rolling hills and the prevalence of high winds.

SOCIETY

Peoples: Cape Verdeans are Africans.
Religions: Roman Catholic 93.2 per cent; Protestant and other 6.8 per cent.
Languages: Portuguese is the official language, but the national language is Creole, based on old Portuguese with African vocabulary and structures.
Political Parties: African Party for the Independence of Cape Verde (PAICV); Movement for Democracy (MPD).
Social Organizations: Organized workers belong to the National Cape Verde Workers' Union-Central Trade Union Committee (UNTC-CS).

THE STATE

Official Name: República do Cabo Verde.
Administrative divisions: 9 islands and 14 counties.
Capital: Praia 61,650 people (1998).
Other cities: Mindelo 47,000 (1990).
Government: Parliamentary republic. Antonio Mascarenhas Monteiro, President, and Carlos Alberto de Carvalho Veiga, Prime Minister, since February 1991.
National Holiday: July 5, Independence Day (1975).
Armed Forces: 1,100.

STATISTICS

DEMOGRAPHY

Population: 418,000 (1999)
Annual growth: 1.7 % (1975/97)
Estimates for year 2015 (million): 0.6 (1999)
Annual growth to year 2015: 2.1 % (1997/2015)
Urban population: 57.7 % (1997)
Children per woman: 3.5 (1998)

HEALTH

Life expectancy at birth: 69 years (1998)
male: 66 years (1998)
female: 71 years (1998)
Maternal mortality: 55 per 100,000 live births (1990-98)
Infant mortality: 54 per 1,000 (1998)
Under-5 child mortality: 73 per 1,000 (1998)
Daily calorie supply: 3,135 per capita (1996)
29 doctors per 100,000 people (1993)
Safe water: 65 % (1990/98)

EDUCATION

Literacy: 69 % (1995)
male: 81 % (1995)
female: 61 % (1995)
School enrolment:
Primary total: 131 % (1990/96)
male: 132 % (1990/97)
female: 129 % (1990/97)
Secondary:
male: 28 % (1990/96)
female: 26 % (1990/96)

COMMUNICATIONS

180 radios (1997), 45 TV sets (1996) and 64 main telephone lines (1996) per 1,000 people

ECONOMY

Per capita, GNP: $ 1,200 (1998)
Annual growth, GNP: 5.2 % (1998)
Consumer price index: 120.1 (1998)
Cereal imports: 82,613 metric tons (1998)
Exports: $ 124 million (1998)
Imports: $ 282 million (1998)
External debt: $ 244 million (1998); $ 597 per capita (1998)
Development aid received: $ 110 million (1997); $ 316.6 per capita (1997); 26.20 % of GNP (1997)

HDI (rank/value): 106/0.677 (1997)

Cayman Islands

Cayman Islands

Population: 34,000 (1998)
Area: 260 SQ KM
Capital: Georgetown
Currency: Cayman dollar
Language: English

In 1503, Christopher Columbus sighted the Cayman Islands and named them the "Turtles" because of the vast numbers of turtles, iguanas and alligators which were their sole inhabitants. The Cayman Islands include Grand Cayman, which is the largest, Cayman Brac and Little Cayman, and all three are surrounded by coral reefs.

[2] Shortly afterwards, the islands came under French control or more accurately, under the control of buccaneers and privateers: "the fathers of the French colonies in the West Indies". For a good part of the 17th century, the Caymans were the pirate headquarters of the Antilles.

[3] The first permanent colonial settlement was established in Grand Cayman and most of the settlers came from Jamaica. It was not until around the year 1833 that they started to live on the other two islands. The Antilles were all affected by power struggles between the European colonialists. When Jamaica was ceded to the British Crown in 1670, under the Treaty of Madrid, the Cayman Islands became a Jamaican dependency. In 1959 they were given the status of British dependent territory.

[4] In 1972, a new constitution was passed granting some local autonomy on domestic matters. The Governor is appointed by the Crown and is responsible for defence, foreign affairs, internal security, and some social services. There is also an Executive Council and Legislative Assembly. The new Executive Council, created after the 1988 general elections, has two new members and two who were already appointed.

[5] The Cayman Islands have few natural resources other than the sea and sand, which make them popular tourist resorts. With the exception of turtle farming, local industry and agriculture only meet domestic needs. The Caymanese are renowned schooner builders and sailors. One of the country's main sources of revenue is the money sent home by sailors.

[6] Their tax-exempt status has attracted a growing number of offshore banking and trust companies. In 1987, there were 515 banks in the Cayman Islands.

[7] By the end of the decade, a quarter of the economically active population worked in tourism. There island set a vast network of

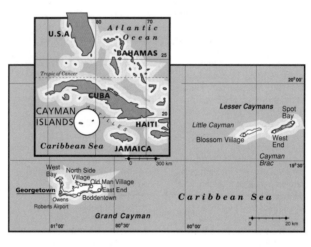

hotels throughout the islands, with a total of 5,200 beds. The influx of visitors has produced considerable immigration, which currently accounts for 35 per cent of the population. In 1989, the Caymans were visited by 618,000 tourists. Fishing declined seriously in the 1970s and has not recovered. Turtle farming is being developed to replace traditional turtle fishing.

[8] The Cayman issue is considered regularly by the UN Decolonization Committee, which asserts the legitimate right of the inhabitants to self-determination and independence. On the islands however the people do not seem anxious to sever links with Britain. In 1982, when the Malvinas/Falklands War broke out, the islands made a contribution of $1 million to the British forces.

[9] In August 1991, McKeeva Bush, a member of the Assembly, founded the first political party in the Caymans. The DPP (Democratic Progressive Party) aimed to change the legal status of the islands from being British dependencies. The DPP promoted constitutional reform, seeking the creation of a party system, a rise in the number of members of the Executive Council, the creation of the post of Prime Minister, and an increase in the number of seats in the Legislative Assembly. The Governor would become the President of the extended Executive Council.

[10] The Bank of Credit and Commerce International (BCCI) scandal disclosed the banking and speculation facilities in the Cayman Islands. In 1991 five countries took legal steps to close the BCCI, which they accused of systematic fraud. When the fraud was revealed, the Bank of England explained that the irregularities included the concealment of losses, the drawing up of false balance sheets and other serious alterations to documents. The two most important offices of the BCCI were in Luxembourg and on the Cayman Islands; both of which provided tax exemption and bank secrecy.

[11] In January 1996, the capture of a Mexican drug trafficker - the third largest cocaine supplier to the US - demonstrated the part played by the Cayman Islands in a money-laundering circuit between Texas and the final destination of Switzerland.

[12] In 1997, the Government was forced to abandon a series of tax increases planned in that year's budget, due to the strength of public objections.

[13] In January 1998, the Government denied a cruiser carrying 910 gay tourists, mostly US citizens, the right to dock on the islands, saying they "did not fulfil the behavior requirements". The British Government made it known they did not agree with these discriminatory practices.

[14] Peter Smith took over as governor on May 5 1999. ■

PROFILE

ENVIRONMENT

Located west of Jamaica and south of Cuba, this small archipelago is part of the Greater Antilles. It comprises the Grand Cayman islands, where most of the population live, Little Cayman, and Cayman Brac. The archipelago is of volcanic origin, and has rocky hills and considerable coral formations. The climate is tropical and rainy, tempered by oceanic influences.

SOCIETY

Peoples: 40 per cent of the population are of mixed European and indian descent; 20 per cent are of European descent; 20 per cent are of African origin.
Religions: Protestant.
Languages: English.
Political parties: Democratic Progressive Party (DPP). Groups of independent citizens are formed to elect the local government.

THE STATE

Official Name: Cayman Islands.
Administrative divisions: There are eight districts (Creek, Eastern, Midland, South Rown, Spot Bay, Stake Bay, West End, Western).
Capital: Georgetown, 16,923 people (1995).
Other cities: West Bay, 6,067 people, Bodden Town 5,109 (1995).
Government: Peter Smith, Governor since May 5,1999. There is an 18-member Legislative Assembly (15 elected by direct, popular vote and 3 named by the governor).

STATISTICS

DEMOGRAPHY

Population: 34,000 (1998)

COMMUNICATIONS

984 radios (1997)
per 1,000 people

ECONOMY

Cereal imports: 905 metric tons (1998)

Central African Republic

République Centrafricaine

Population: 3,549,000 (1999)
Area: 622,980 SQ KM
Capital: Bangui
Currency: CFA franc
Language: French

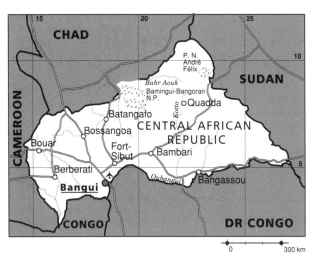

The old Ubangui-Chari empire was associated with other neighboring countries, such as Chad, Gabon and Congo during the colonial period. It has been ruled by tribal chiefs, a sultan, colonial traders, French civil servants, a president, a military dictator, an emperor, and corrupt politicians. This unstable leadership started late in the last century and has continued since the Central African Republic proclaimed independence in August 1960.

[2] The region suffered one of the most savage and devastating colonial regimes ever imposed by European powers in Africa. France took an interest in the Central African highlands in the late 19th century, when the coast had already been colonized. Occupation of the interior was begun by three military expeditions directed against Sultan Rabah, the governor of the territory now known as Sudan. The occupation provided an opening for about 40 trading companies which took over rubber and ivory operations in the region, later adding coffee, cotton and diamond mining to their production. This inaugurated a period of nearly 30 years in which the enslavement of native peoples, killings and persecution were widely used by the companies which controlled 70 per cent of the colonized area, renamed Ubangui-Chari in 1908.

[3] After World War II, France was short of the financial resources necessary for maintaining a full colonial administration, so it granted partial autonomy to the Bangui Government. The Europeanized local elite became an instrument of neocolonialism, by which the French retained control of foreign trade, defense and tax collection.

[4] Violence and oppression were on the increase in 1949 when a former minister, Barthelemy Boganda, founded the Movement for the Social Evolution of Black Africa (MESAN) to fight for the independence of the Central African Republic. Boganda's prestige grew enormously despite the French attempts to discredit him. In 1956, the French secret service infiltrated MESAN in an attempt to bribe two of Boganda's main advisers, David Dacko and Abel Goumba. Boganda died a year before independence in a suspicious airplane crash, in March 1959.

[5] David Dacko took over the post vacated by MESAN's founder, using the position to purge the party's more progressive elements. He drew increasingly closer to the French as the US began to show an interest in exploiting the country's uranium and cobalt reserves. Dacko lost the support he had inherited from Boganda, and his government became increasingly corrupt, while the country plunged into deep economic crisis.

[6] In December 1965, Dacko was ousted in a coup led by his cousin, Colonel Jean Bedel Bokassa who was pro-France, having served in the French Army for 22 years. Bokassa belonged to a small bourgeois group of M'Baka landowners from Lobaye, where France had recruited agents for its colonial administration. In 1972, he proclaimed himself president-for-life, later taking the rank of field marshal, and finally renaming the country the Central African Empire, crowning himself emperor. The coronation ceremony in December 1977 cost $28 million and was financed by France, Israel and South Africa.

[7] In 1978, Bokassa gave 30,000 sq km rich in diamonds to the Israeli army, hiring a notorious international arms dealer as his military adviser. He sent troops to Zaire (now DR Congo) to help Mobutu put down a rebellion in the province of Shaba (see DR Congo).

[8] Popular discontent finally erupted in a series of workers' and student rebellions, stifled with the help of Zairean troops. In April 1979, the students refused to comply with regulations specifying that uniforms had to be bought in stores owned by the emperor, and in the ensuing street demonstrations, 100 youths were arrested and taken to the infamous Ngaragba prison, where they were tortured and most of them killed under Bokassa's personal supervision.

[9] Resorting to neocolonial manoeuvring, France decided to depose the Emperor, attempting to erase the negative image it had created by supporting his crowning. On September 20 1979, while Bokassa was travelling in Libya, France sent a military plane to bring former president David Dacko back to Bangui. He took power, making no effort to hide his status as a colonial envoy, protected by 1,000 French troops. Dacko dissolved the Empire and reinstated a republic, granting France a 10-year lease on the enormous Bouar air base.

[10] Dacko's return amounted to no more than a change of name as corruption and repression continued. In 1980, the CAR Government broke off relations with the USSR and Libya, expelling all their technical advisers and diplomats. Political opposition was ruthlessly repressed and almost all opposition leaders were sent to prison or exiled. Amidst countless conspiracies, Dacko was overthrown by another military coup in September 1981, which brought General Kolingba to power.

[11] The new government's first measures were to ask the French to pay the salaries of 24,000 civil servants, and to grant new economic concessions to the US, allowing them to exploit uranium resources. Meanwhile, the return to normality, initially set for 1982, was postponed until 1986. On November 21 of that year, in an election barred to the opposition, Kolingba was elected President with the support of his CAR Party of Democratic Recovery (PCRD). A constitution was passed establishing a one-party system, and on July 21 1987, the members of the General Assembly were chosen from PCRD members.

[12] The Government launched a structural adjustment plan following IMF guidelines. Nevertheless, the economy as a whole showed no signs of recovery.

[13] In 1986 Bokassa returned from exile in France. Sentenced to death during his absence the former "emperor" was imprisoned.

[14] Within the framework of the democratization process, direct municipal elections were held in May 1988, with universal suffrage. It was hoped that this would help to improve trade relations with the developed countries. Seeking popular support for a return to democratic institutions, the Government tried to address the question of self-sufficiency in food production, although the country still figures among the world's poorest.

[15] Senegal, Côte d'Ivoire, Gabon, Djibouti and the Central African Republic (CAR) were the key areas of French foreign policy in Africa.

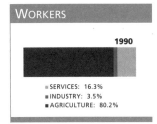

WORKERS

1990

- SERVICES: 16.3%
- INDUSTRY: 3.5%
- AGRICULTURE: 80.2%

LAND USE

DEFORESTATION: 0.4% annual (1990/95)

PUBLIC EXPENDITURE

DEFENCE EXPENDITURE (% of goverment exp.) **27.7%** (1997)

MILITARY EXPENDITURE (% of health & education) **33%** (1990/91)

[16] In July 1991 a plan was approved for Constitutional reform and for the adoption of a multiparty system. Elections were scheduled for October 1992, but shortly after the voting started Kolingba annulled the process claiming there had been irregularities. After the annulment a Provisional National Council of the Republic was formed, made up of the five presidential candidates. This council announced new elections for April 1993, but these were also postponed on several occasions.

[17] In May, a group of soldiers took the presidential palace and the Bangui radio station by force, demanding 8 months' back-pay. They agreed to return to barracks after two months' salaries were paid. The first round of the presidential elections finally took place on August 11 1993. Kolingba, who came fourth, annulled the result by decree once again. However, France threatened to suspend its military and financial aid, forcing him to allow the second round to go ahead.

[18] On September 1, Kolingba ordered the political prisoners to be freed, including former emperor Bokassa, who had been accused of cannibalism, murder and the misappropriation of public funds. On September 19, Ange-Felix Patassé, Bokassa's former Prime Minister, was returned as President with 52.47 per cent of the vote.

[19] In 1994, Patassé continued the rapprochement with Paris, which had supported the candidacy of former president Dacko in 1993. The economy remained weak. The payment of civil servants was resumed but the Government continued to owe large sums of back-pay. In August 1994, a parliamentary delegation from Kuwait visited Bangui to thank the CAR for its support during the Gulf War.

[20] On December 28 1994, a new Constitution was approved by referendum. However, the opposition considered this a defeat for Patassé, as only 46 per cent of the electorate turned out to vote. The increase in international prices for cotton and diamonds produced economic growth, estimated at seven per cent for 1995. Nonetheless, inflation caused by the French imposed 100 per cent devaluation of the CFA continued to affect a large part of the population.

[21] In May 1996, Patassé requested French military intervention to crush a new group of rebel soldiers. Direct involvement by French soldiers in street brawls led to a series of demonstrations against French intervention. Bangui was paralyzed after the rebellions, the looting and the French military action. The CAR economy became even more dependent on France.

[22] In June, the President announced a new government of national unity and named former ambassador in France, Jean Paul Ngoupande, Prime Minister. Social unrest was not appeased and caused the third rebellion in less than a year.

[23] In spite of a truce, in early 1997, France launched an offensive against rebel troops in Bangui in retaliation for the death of two French soldiers. This led Patassé and the rebel leader Anicet Saulet to agree the replacement of French troops by a guard from African countries, although funded by Paris.

[24] In January, Patassé appointed Michel Gbezera-Bria as Prime Minister. In February, a new Government was formed, including some opposition members. Most of the rebels returned to the barracks. In May, new armed confrontations caused a political crisis which led the opposition to leave the Government. New negotiations between the Government and rebel forces, with the mediation of foreign troops, settled the new crisis.

[25] Anti-France hostility was increasingly evident. In October, the CAR President demanded French withdrawal from the military bases. At the same time, he tried to strengthen links with the US, whose influence over the region had not stopped increasing at the expense of France.

[26] In March 1998, the UN Security Council authorized the sending of the United Nations Mission in the Central African Republic (MINURCA), made up of some 1,400 troops. In April the Inter-African security force was replaced by 1,350 UN troops. The day the international troops came in, France withdrew 1,400 troops. In May Patassé signed a mutual defense agreement with President of the Democratic Republic of the Congo, Laurent Kabila. This same month the Government announced the elimination of customs subsidies, as a way to fulfil IMF-imposed conditions. In July, the IMF granted a $66-million loan to support the economic reform plan.

[27] In the legislative elections of November and December that year, the ruling National Liberation Movement (NLM), led by Patassé, and his allies took 49 of the 109 seats. But after some negotiations, five independents and an opposition dissident joined the government group making an NLM majority. However, the nomination of the new cabinet sparked violent street demonstrations in Bangui in January 1999.

[28] The September elections had to be delayed a week following requests from the opposition and the threat of disturbances. Finally Patassé took 51 per cent of the vote, but the opposition called for the elections to be annulled, accusing the Government of fraud. Former president Andre Kolingba came second, with 19 per cent of the vote.

[29] Shots between the presidential guard and a military squadron which had been loyal to President Patassé through the two previous coup attempts caused panic in the capital in January 2000. The presidential force finally managed to subdue the squadron, which accused the President of not keeping promises made during the previous uprisings. ∎

PROFILE

ENVIRONMENT

This is a landlocked country in the heart of Africa. It is located on a plateau irrigated by tributaries of the Congo River, like the Ubangui, the main export route, and of Lake Chad. The southwestern part of the country is covered by a dense tropical forest. Cotton, coffee and tobacco are the basic cash crops. Diamond mining is a major source of revenue. Inadequate methods of cultivation have increased soil erosion and led to a loss of fertility. The scarcity of water and pollution of important rivers pose a serious problem.

SOCIETY

Peoples: Baya (Gbaya) 23.7 per cent; Banda 23.4 per cent; Mandjia 14.7 per cent; Sara 6.5 per cent; Mbum 6.3 per cent; Mbaka 4.3 per cent; Kare 2.4 per cent; other 18.6 per cent. **Religions:** Protestant 25.0 per cent; Roman Catholic 25.0 per cent; traditional African religions 24.0 per cent; Muslim 15.0 per cent.
Languages: French (official); Sango is the national language, used for intercommunication between the various ethnic groups. **Political Parties:** Central African People's Liberation Party; Democratic Movement for the Rebirth and Evolution of the Central African Republic (MDRERC).

THE STATE

Official Name: République Centrafricaine. **Administrative Divisions:** 16 Prefectures, 52 Sub-prefectures. **Capital:** Bangui 597,000 people (1995). **Other cities:** Bouar 43,000 people; Berberati 47,000; Bambari 41,000; Carnot 41,000 (1994). **Government:** Ange-Félix Patassé, President, elected in September, 1993. Anicet Georges Dologuele, Prime Minister since February 1999. Bicameral legislature. **National Holiday:** December 1, Independence Day (1960). **Armed Forces:** 2,650 (1996). **Other:** 2,700 Gendarmes.

Chad

Tchad

Population: 7,458,000 (1999)
Area: 1,284,000 SQ KM
Capital: N'Djamena
Currency: CFA franc
Language: Arabic and French

The Sahel region, of which the Republic of Chad is part, has been inhabited from time immemorial. Artefacts dating from 4,900 BC have been found in several tombs in the Tibesti mountain region, in the northern part of the country. The southern region around Chad has been under settlement since about 500 BC. In the 8th century AD, increased desiccation of Saharan borderlands stimulated Berber migrations into the area. At that time, the Kingdom of Kanem was founded; it converted to Islam in 1085. By the early 1200s the borders of Kanem had been expanded to Fezzan in the north, Quaddaï in the west, and north of Lake Chad into the Bornu kingdom. The new Kingdom of Kanem-Bornu was established through merger, its power and prosperity peaking in the sixteenth century because of its command of the southern terminus of the trans-Sahara route to Tripoli.

2   At this point the rival kingdoms of Baguirmi and Ouaddaï evolved in the south. At the height of their power in the 17th century, the Baguirmi made an unsuccessful attempt to expand their territory into Kanem-Bornu. Eventually, in the years 1883-93, all three kingdoms (Ouaddaï, Kanem-Bornu and Baguirmi) were to fall to the Sudanese adventurer Rabih az-Zubayr during 1883-1893.

3   Towards the end of the 18th century, European missionaries converted some of the southern Sara to Christianity and gave them a European-style education. These converts subsequently sided with the Europeans against the native peoples of the north and by 1900 Rabih az-Zubayr was overthrown. The French "acquired" Chad in 1885 during the Berlin Conference, but did not establish themselves in the territory until a 1920 invasion by the notorious French Foreign Legion which defeated the northern Muslim groups.

4   The colonizers introduced cotton farming in 1930, and small parcels of land were distributed to peasants to grow this crop, while the French monopolized its commercialization. In the south, forced changes in the land tenure system replaced a communal practice of self-sufficient agriculture with large-scale farming. The result was a cotton surplus and a food shortage, accompanied by famine.

5   In August 1960 when France granted Chad its independence, southern leaders who had been negotiating with the colonizers since 1956 assumed power. However Chad's first president, François Tombalbaye, leader of the Chad Progressive Party, was unable to unite the country whose frontiers reflected the arbitrary colonial divisions.

6   The Chad Liberation Front (FROLINAT), founded in 1966, was crushed by the French troops. The Front had become fully active about the time that southern peasants rebelled against a cotton marketing system introduced by the French company Cotonfran which controlled the cotton industry. Northerners provided FROLINAT's main political support.

7   In 1970, the Front controlled two-thirds of the national territory, and by 1972 FROLINAT guerrillas were within range of N'djamena, the capital. In 1975 Tombalbaye was ousted and killed in a French-staged coup which put General Felix Malloum in power. The guerrilla offensive continued, and France began to take advantage of the split within the Front, which had divided into more than 10 groups.

8   Paris supported Hissene Habré's faction because he opposed Goukouni Oueddei, FROLINAT's president, who was receiving support from Muammar Khaddafi's government in Libya. At the time, Habré was at the helm of the Armed Forces of the North (AFN), and Oueddei was the leader of the People's Armed Forces (PAF). Two years later, France dispatched an additional force of 3,000 soldiers, along with fighter planes.

9   The French announced that their troops would maintain neutrality in the struggle between FROLINAT factions, while Hissene Habré accepted the post of Prime Minister in Malloum's government.

10   Towards the end of 1979 Chad's 11 major political groups formed a Provisional Government of National Unity (PGNU). Habré was named Minister of Defence. However, the French were displeased with the make-up of the Cabinet because of their strategic interest in Chad - linked to the Maghreb and to the uranium and oil discoveries in the 1960s. In March 1980 Habré resigned, broke the alliance, and unleashed civil war that enabled him to consolidate his power in the south.

11   The ruling coalition split into three factions. In May 1980, Oueddei requested military aid from Libya, and Khaddafi sent 2,000 troops.

12   That same year, over 100,000 refugees fled the country, after the bombing of N'Djamena by Habré's forces. In October, Libyan troops reached the capital, mediation efforts by the Organization for African Unity (OAU) failed, and the defeated Habré fled to Cameroon in December 1980.

13   France led an international campaign against Libyan expansionism in Africa, with support from the United States, Egypt, Sudan, and other African countries, fearful that Khaddafi's revolutionary drive would eventually "infect" poor Islamic populations of the Sahel region, south of the Sahara.

14   Habré was accused of being opportunistic and corrupt; however, Libyan support made it possible for France to divide Oueddei's allies. In April 1981, backed by France, Habré reorganized his followers in Sudan.

Area claimed by Libya

0 — 300 km

WORKERS

% OF LABOUR FORCE — **1998**

■ FEMALE: 45%   ■ MALE: 55%

1990

■ SERVICES: 12.6%
■ INDUSTRY: 4.2%
■ AGRICULTURE: 83.2%

LAND USE

DEFORESTATION: 0.8% annual (1990/95)
IRRIGATED: 0.4% of arable (1993)

1993

■ FOREST & WOODLAND: 1.7%
■ ARABLE: 3.1%
■ OTHER: 95.2%

In July, in Nairobi, the OAU decided to send a peacekeeping force to Chad, with the help of the French and troops from six African countries. Oueddei, yielding to foreign pressure and tensions within the PGNU, requested the withdrawal of Khaddafi's troops in November.

[15] After his defeat by Habré's forces in June 1982, the exiled Oueddei set up a Provisional National Salvation Government in October with 8 of the 11 groups that had opposed Habré in the civil war. The new civil war practically split the country in two: northern Chad, under the control of a recently formed National Liberation Council with Libyan logistical support; and southern Chad, with the Habré Government dependent on French military support.

[16] When Habré seized power, bringing this phase of the civil war to an end, the country was in ruins. The population of the capital, N'Djamena, had dropped to 40,000, and half of its businesses and small enterprises had closed. Outside the cities, 2,000 wells and all the water towers had been destroyed, and the health and educational infrastructures were practically non-existent.

[17] An intense drought triggered widespread famine, despite French and American food aid. As hunger spread, massive protests and peasant uprisings occurred in the south. Repression by the Habré Government forced 25,000 Chadians to flee across the border into the Central African Republic.

[18] In 1987, the southern forces supported by France announced they had taken Fada, Faya Largeau and the frontier strip of Aozou, claimed by Libya. In 1989, Chad and Libya signed an agreement on this 114,000 sq km territory, which included the return of prisoners and the presentation of a territorial lawsuit before the International Court in The Hague.

[19] In 1990, Idriss Deby (leader of the Patriotic Salvation Movement, supported by France) defeated Habré after a three-month military campaign. During the deposed president's term in office in the 1980s, some 40,000 people were executed or "disappeared".

[20] Habré fled to Senegal, where he planned a new insurrection. Some 5,000 of his rebel supporters assembled in the N'Guigmi region near Lake Chad, from where they launched several offensives. In 1992, 400 rebels died and 100 were captured when government forces put down an uprising by troops loyal to Habré with French support.

[21] In 1993, Deby inaugurated a national conference to "democratize" Chad, with the participation of some 40 opposition parties, another 20 organizations and six armed rebel groups. Adoum Maurice El-Bongo was designated president of the conference. This meeting called a special court to judge Habré and selected Fidele Moungar as interim Prime Minister during the transition period.

[22] In February 1994, the International Court in The Hague ruled the Aozou strip belonged to Chad. In April, after Chad and the IMF signed an agreement to implement an annual growth program, the Transition High Council postponed the elections for one more year. In May, Libya officially returned the Aozou strip to N'Djamena.

[23] In March 1995, the Transition High Council once again postponed the elections for 12 months. At the same time, it considered as inadequate the Government measures to limit the impact of the devaluation of the CFA, decreed by France in 1994. In the Presidential elections, finally held in June and July 1996, Deby was elected constitutional President with 69 per cent of the vote.

[24] That was a year of "reconciliation", as in January the Government had signed a peace agreement with the Action of Union and Development, which was legalized as a party once it abandoned the armed struggle. In a meeting in Gabon, in March, several rebel groups signed peace agreements with the Government and in August, Deby signed an agreement with the armed forces of the south to establish a federal republic, and the fighting was brought to a close.

[25] The situation remained tense during 1997. At the end of the year, Amnesty International announced that there had been at least 80 people killed in confrontations between the Chad rebel forces and the regular army in the south of the country.

[26] Southern Chad was at the heart of an international controversy in December when the Campaign for the Reform of the World Bank, supported by dozens of NGOs, opposed a megaproject planned by the Bank in this zone. The project included digging 300 oil wells and transporting oil to the Atlantic Ocean through Cameroon. The NGOs considered that funds for fighting poverty should not be used for this type of project.

[27] In March 1998, the director and editor of the *N'Djamena Hebdo* newspaper were sentenced to two years' imprisonment for "slandering the President of Chad" in an article published in December of the previous year. However, the sentence remained suspended.

[28] In April, a new armed opposition group, the Renewed National Front (RNF), kidnapped a French citizen demanding the withdrawal of French troops and oil companies from the country.

[29] In 1999, Chad stepped up its contribution to the Democratic Republic of Congo regional war, supporting the Kabila regime with weapons and troops. ∎

PROFILE

ENVIRONMENT

The northern part of Chad is desert, and 40 per cent of its territory is part of the Sahara Desert, with the great Tibesti volcanic highlands. The central region, the Sahel, which stretches to the banks of Lake Chad, is a transition plain where nomadic pastoralism is common. The lake, only half of which lies within Chad's borders, is shallow and mostly covered with swamps. Thought to be the remnant of an ancient inland sea, its waters are fed by two rivers, the Logane and the Chari, which descend from the plateau that separates this basin from that of the Congo River. The banks of these rivers in southern Chad, fertilized by flooding, contain the country's richest agricultural lands and are the most densely populated areas. In colonial times, economic activity was concentrated there. Cotton is the main export product but subsistence agriculture, though hampered by droughts, still predominates. In recent years, mineral reserves of uranium, tungsten and oil have attracted the attention of the transnationals. Desertification and drought are endemic to the region and affect all aspects of daily life.

SOCIETY

Peoples: Northern Chadians are basically nomadic shepherds of Berber and Tuareg origin; Tubu, Quadainee, while southerners; Sara, Massa, Mundani and Hakka, are mainly traditional farmers. Famines have periodically driven people from the Sahel, in the north to the fertile southern regions. **Religions:** Around 50 per cent of are Muslim, 27 per cent practise traditional African religions and 23 per cent are Christian. **Languages:** Arabic and French are the official languages. There are many local languages, the most widely spoken being Sara (in the southern region). **Political Parties:** Patriotic Salvation Movement; National Union for Democracy and Socialism; Chad National Liberation Front (FROLINAT); National Front of Chad (FNT); Movement for Democracy and Development (MDD). **Social Organizations:** Chad Federation of Labor Unions.

THE STATE

Official Name: République du Tchad. **Administrative Divisions:** 14 Prefectures. **Capital:** N'Djamena 530,000 people (1993). **Other cities:** Sarh 198,000 people; Moundou 281,000; Abéché 187,000 (1993). **Government:** Idriss Deby, President, elected in July 1996. Nagoum Yamassoum, Prime Minister since December 1999. Council of the Republic with 31 members, appointed by the President. **Armed Forces:** 25,200. **Other:** 4,500 Gendarmes.

STATISTICS

DEMOGRAPHY

Population: 7,458,000 (1999)
Annual growth: 2.6 % (1975/97)
Estimates for year 2015 (million): 11.2 (1999)
Annual growth to year 2015: 2.6 % (1997/2015)
Urban population: 22.8 % (1997)
Urban Growth: 3.4 % (1980/95)
Children per woman: 6.0 (1998)

HEALTH

Life expectancy at birth: 47 years (1998)
male: 46 years (1998)
female: 49 years (1998)
Maternal mortality: 830 per 100,000 live births (1990-98)
Infant mortality: 118 per 1,000 (1998)
Under-5 child mortality: 198 per 1,000 (1998)
Daily calorie supply: 1,972 per capita (1996)
2 doctors per 100,000 people (1993)
Safe water: 54 % (1990/98)

EDUCATION

Literacy: 48 % (1995)
male: 62 % (1995)
female: 35 % (1995)
School enrolment:
Primary total: 65 % (1990/96)
male: 85 % (1990/97)
female: 44 % (1990/97)
Secondary:
male: 16 % (1990/96)
female: 4 % (1990/96)
Tertiary: 1 % (1996)
Primary school teachers: one for every 67 (1996)

COMMUNICATIONS

0 newspapers (1996), 242 radios (1997), 2 TV sets (1996) and 1 main telephone lines (1996) per 1,000 people

ECONOMY

Per capita, GNP: $ 230 (1998)
Annual growth, GNP: 8.4 % (1998)
Annual inflation: 8.3 % (1990/98)
Consumer price index: 133.1 (1998)
Currency: 590.0 CFA francs = $ 1 (1998)
Cereal imports: 48,348 metric tons (1998)
Fertilizer use: 37 kg per ha (1997)
Exports: $ 327 million (1998)
Imports: $ 537 million (1998)
External debt: $ 1,091 million (1998); $ 150 per capita (1998)
Debt service: 10.6 % of exports (1998)
Development aid received: $ 225 million (1997); $ 38.2 per capita (1997); 14.30 % of GNP (1997)

HDI (rank/value): 162/0.393 (1997)

Chile

Chile

Population: 15,019,000 (1999)
Area: 756,950 SQ KM
Capital: Santiago
Currency: Peso
Language: Spanish

At the beginning of the 16th Century, the north of Chile formed the southernmost part of the Inca empire (see: Peru, Bolivia and Ecuador). The area between Copiapo to the north and Puerto Montt to the south was populated by the Mapuche, later called Araucanians by the Europeans. Further south lived the fishing peoples: the Yamana and the Alacalufe.

[2] Diego de Almagro set off from Peru in 1536 to begin the conquest of Chile. With an expeditionary force of Spanish soldiers and enslaved native Americans he covered nearly 2,500 km, reaching central Chile when a mutiny in Lima forced him to turn back.

[3] Between 1540 and 1558, Pedro de Valdivia settled in what is now the port of Valparaiso and founded several cities including Santiago. The Mapuche, led by chief Lautaro, a capable military strategist, beat the invaders on several occasions, adapting their military tactics to changing conditions in the region. Valdivia died in one of these battles. His successor, Francisco de Villagra, defeated and killed Lautaro in 1557. And in a case unique in colonial America, the Mapuche maintained an independent territory on the Bio-bio river for more than 300 years, officially recognised by Spain as Araucaria. Creole-Spanish dominion only spread to all the territory in the second half of the 19th century.

[4] In 1811 the governing Junta headed by Jose Miguel Carrera instigated the independence process. General Bernardo O'Higgins, the son of a former viceroy in Peru, joined this movement. War broke out between the independence army and the royalist forces, with their strongholds in Valdivia and Concepción. Helped by the army of José de San Martín, which crossed the Andes to fight the royalists, the independence army finally defeated the Europeans on April 5 1818 in the Battle of Maipú.

[5] In 1817, O'Higgins was designated Supreme Head of State, while the royalist troops still maintained pockets of resistance. He lay the political foundations of the country, which were reinforced in the 1833 Constitution, during the Presidential term of Diego Portales. This "aristocratic republic", denied all forms of political expression to the new urban sectors, the middle class and the rising proletariat. English companies, in alliance with the creole oligarchy, organized an export economy based on the rich saltpeter deposits of the north along the maritime coast of Bolivia and reached as far as the southernmost regions of Peru. Soon the English controlled 49 per cent of Chile's foreign trade. Chilean and British capital also owned 33 per cent of Peru's saltpeter, but they wanted total control.

[6] The "Nitrate War" or Pacific War of 1879-1884 was caused by this Chilean-British alliance. Chilean territory increased by a third and left Bolivia in its present landlocked state. The victory brought about the rapid growth of the saltpetre industry and its labor force.

[7] Jose Manuel Balmaceda was elected President in 1886 and tried to break the oligarchic order. The nationalism fostered by war, economic growth, social diversification and the education of the wealthy helped to gain him support. He encouraged protectionism to develop national industry. The oligarchy reacted violently, supported by the English. The army defeated the President's partisans, and Balmaceda committed suicide in the Argentine embassy in 1891.

[8] In 1900, the first union was founded in Iquique. In 1904, 15 unions with 20,000 members joined to form a federation called the National Convention. That year the unions clashed with the military in Valparaíso and three years later automatic weapons supplied by the US were used to massacre 2,500 workers and their families in a school in Iquique

[9] Housing, railroads and new mines continued to expand, stimulating trade, new services and public administration. In 1920, populist politician Arturo Alessandri became the leader of the new social factions that sought to subvert the oligarchic order and achieve representation in politics. Alessandri's government promoted constitutional reform and welfare legislation with electoral rights for literate men over 21, direct presidential elections, an 8-hour working day, social security, and labor regulations.

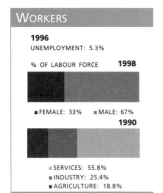

WORKERS

1996
UNEMPLOYMENT: 5.3%

% OF LABOUR FORCE **1998**

■ FEMALE: 33%   ■ MALE: 67%

1990

■ SERVICES: 55.8%
■ INDUSTRY: 25.4%
■ AGRICULTURE: 18.8%

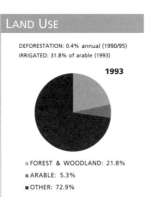

LAND USE

DEFORESTATION: 0.4% annual (1990/95)
IRRIGATED: 31.8% of arable (1993)

1993

■ FOREST & WOODLAND: 21.8%
■ ARABLE: 5.3%
■ OTHER: 72.9%

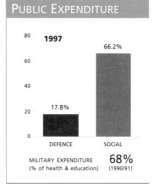

PUBLIC EXPENDITURE

1997
80
66.2%
60
40
20   17.8%
0
DEFENCE   SOCIAL

MILITARY EXPENDITURE **68%**
(% of health & education) (1990/91)

MATERNAL MORTALITY	LITERACY	FOOD DEPENDENCY
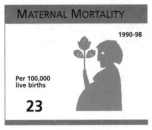 1990-98 Per 100,000 live births **23**	**95%** 1995	**15%** 1970 **7%** 1997 

[10]   Chile's economy, based on farm and mineral exports, was severely affected by the 1929-30 depression. Recovery did not come until the bourgeoisie was able to impose an industrialization program to produce previously imported goods. Their proposal served as a base for the 1936 Popular Front which marshalled support from Communists and Socialists. The front was led by Pedro Aguirre Cerda who later became President. The armed forces were purged and withdrew from the political scene for almost 40 years. Although the oligarchy was weakened, it made a pact with the Government on agrarian policies and Aguirre Cerda never allowed land reform or the formation of rural workers' unions.

[11]   The alliance worked out in the 1930s broke down during González Videla's term of office, 1946-1952. The climate created by the Cold War was used to legitimize the Law for the Permanent Defence of Democracy which banned the Communist Party and deprived its members of the vote. On January 9 1949, to compensate for these measures, the Government brought in female suffrage. The Radical Party's repressive and de-nationalizing policies, and the disabling of the left enabled the Populist Carlos Ibáñez to win the 1952 election.

[12]   Economic deterioration rapidly eroded the strength of the populist government. In 1957, offshoots from the National Falange (populist) and from the old Conservative Party (oligarchic), founded the Christian Democratic Party (PDC). The Communist Party was legalized and the Left rebuilt its alliances, forming the Popular Action Front. The people wanted change, but, sensitive to an aggressive anti-communist campaign, voted for Eduardo Frei's "revolution in freedom", which initiated agrarian reform in 1964.

[13]   The UP (Popular Unity) coalition led by Salvador Allende won the 1970 election, obtaining 35 per cent of the vote, while the rest of the electorate was split between the Christian Democrats and the conservative parties. The UP coalition included the Socialist Party, the Communist Party, the United Popular Action Movement (MAPU) and the Christian Left. The following year the UP won almost 50 per cent of the vote in the legislative elections, leading the right to fear a definitive loss of its majority.

[14]   Allende nationalized copper and other strategic sectors, together with private banks and foreign trade. He increased land reform, promoted collective production and created a "social sector" in the economy, managed by workers.

[15]   The traditional elite, now out of power, conspired with the Pentagon, the CIA and transnational corporations, particularly ITT, to topple the Government. The Christian Democrats were indecisive, but finally supported the coup. Inflation, a shortage of goods and internal differences within Popular Unity contributed to the climate of instability.

[16]   On September 11 1973 General Augusto Pinochet led a coup. The Presidential Palace at La Moneda was bombed by the air force, and President Allende died during the fighting. Violent repression ensued: people were shot without trial, sent to concentration camps, tortured, or simply "disappeared".

[17]   The Chilean military dictatorship was one of many that ravaged the Southern Cone of South America during the 1970s, inspired by the National Security Doctrine. This was supported by the Chilean oligarchy and the middle classes, as well as by transnational corporations who recovered the companies which had escaped their control.

[18]   After the coup, Chile's economic policy started to be based on neo-liberal doctrines. Inflation dropped below 10 per cent per year, unemployment practically disappeared and imported manufactured goods flooded the market. Alongside this ran a loss of earning power in workers' salaries and an overall impoverishment of the poorer classes.

[19]   The detrimental influence of these neo-liberal economic policies became evident in 1983, two years after a constitution containing a mandate for "continuity" was approved in a referendum by 60 per cent of the voters. Unemployment reached 30 per cent, 60 per cent of the population were malnourished, protein consumption had dropped by 30 per cent, real salaries had been reduced by 22 per cent in just two years and 55 per cent of all families were living below the poverty line. This situation provided the background for the violent popular uprising which took place in November 1983, led by the National Labor Co-ordination Board and the National Workers' Command.

[20]   In 1984 the Church started talks. To participate in these, the opposition formed the Democratic Alliance, led by the PDC. The talks with Home Minister Sergio Onofre Jarpa failed and from September 1984, the break with the Church became evident. After this date, the Vicarate for Solidarity of the Archbishopric of Santiago played a key role in defending human rights.

[21]   The political left joined together under the Popular Democratic Movement (MDP), vindicating all forms of struggle against the dictatorship. One faction formed the Manuel Rodriguez Patriotic Movement (MRPM), an armed group which carried out numerous attacks, the most important being an attempted assassination of Pinochet on September 7 1986.

[22]   The international isolation of Chilean Government during the US Carter administration eased a little with the election of Ronald Reagan, and Margaret Thatcher in the UK. In August 1985 Chile authorized US space shuttle landings on Easter Island. At the beginning of 1986 a US delegation proposed that Chile be condemned before the UN Human Rights Commission, thereby avoiding having to take more drastic action against the country.

[23]   On October 5 1988, an 8-year extension of Pinochet's rule was submitted to a referendum. Widespread opposition ended his government, bringing elections the following year.

PROFILE

ENVIRONMENT

Flanked by the Andes mountain range in the east and the Pacific in the west, the country is a thin strip of land 3,500 km long and never wider than 402 km. Its length explains its variety of climates and regions. Due to the cold ocean currents, the northern territory is a desert. The central region has a mild climate which makes it good for agriculture. The southern part of the country is colder and heavily wooded. The major salt and copper mines are located in northern Chile. 65 per cent of the population live in the central valleys. During the military regime, some 40 thousand hectares of native forests were cut down each year, and replaced by other tree species, causing the displacement and death of wildlife.

SOCIETY

Peoples: Chileans are descended from the native American population and European immigrants. 300,000 Mapuche indians live mainly in southern Chile.
Religions: Mainly Catholic (77 per cent), Protestant 13 per cent.
Languages: Spanish.
Political Parties: Concertación Democrática, a coalition of the Christian Democratic Party (PDC), the Socialist Party (PS), the Democratic Party (PPD) and the Radical Party (RP). The National Renovation Party (RN). The Independent Democratic Union (UDI). Democratic Alliance; Union of Center Center (UCC); National Party (PN); Communist Party of Chile (PCCh); Revolutionary Movement of the Left (MIR); the Manuel Rodríguez Patriotic Movement (MPMR); Humanistic Party (PH); the Green Party.
Social Organizations: The Central Workers' Union (CUT), the main labor organization until 1973, was banned during the dictatorship and became legal again in 1990. Other trade unions are: the Copper Workers' Confederation (CTC); the Confederation of Civil Servants of Chile (CEPCH); the National Association of Civil Servants; the United Workers' Front (FUT); the National Labor Co-ordination Board (CNS); the National Federation of Taxi Drivers, and unions representing artists, oil workers, professionals and truck drivers; the Democratic Workers' Union (UDT), and the National Union of Civil Servants.

THE STATE

Official Name: República de Chile.
Administrative divisions: 12 numbered Regions and the unnumbered Metropolitan Region of Santiago.
Capital: Santiago, 5,076,800 people (1995).
Other cities: Viña del Mar 322,220 people; Concepción 350,000; Valparaíso 282,000; Temuco 239,300 (1995).
Government: Ricardo Lagos, President since January 2000.
National Holiday: September 18, Independence Day (1810).
Armed Forces: 89,700 troops (1996).
Other: Carabineros, 31,000.

24 Facing up to the fact that change was inevitable, Pinochet negotiated constitutional reform. Proposed changes included further restrictions of the power of future governments, an increase in the number of senators, shortening the Presidential term from 8 years to 4 and a liberalization of the proscription of left-wing parties. The reform was approved by referendum on July 30 1989.

25 Elections were held on December 14 1989. Patricio Aylwin, leader of the Christian Democrats, gained 55.2 per cent of the vote, taking office on March 11, 1990.

26 In April, Aylwin appointed a Truth and Reconciliation Commission to investigate the issue of missing people. The Commission confirmed that there were at least 2,229 missing people, who were assumed dead. It also made a detailed study of repression during the dictatorship. When the facts were made public in March 1991 the President asked the nation for forgiveness in the name of the State. He announced that judicial procedures would follow and he requested the co-operation of the armed forces in these proceedings

27 Official recognition virtually brought about an institutional crisis. The armed forces and the Supreme Court justified their conduct during the Pinochet dictatorship, and denied the validity of the Government report - thus discrediting the President. The crisis was defused when the Government accepted the prerequisites of "Chilean transition", which included preserving the judicial system of the previous regime and guaranteeing impunity from charges of human rights violations.

28 On April 2, Senator Jaime Guzman, former adviser and ideologue of the military regime was murdered and the assassination attributed to radical left wing groups. This enabled the Right to raise the issue of terrorism once more. Political life was slowly brought back to normal. On April 23, the MRPM announced its decision to abandon armed struggle.

29 The Chilean economy maintained a 10-year expansion, with annual growth rates of over 6 per cent, mainly due to high levels of investment (especially fixed capital) and the expansion of the external sector. Direct foreign investment remained at significant levels: $3.5 and $2.9 billion in 1992 and 1993, respectively.

30 During Aylwin's presidency, social indicators improved. In 1993, real salaries increased 5 five per cent, the unemployment rate fell to 4.5 per cent, and social spending increased 14 per cent.

31 In August 1993, the Special Commission on Indigenous Peoples (a government agency) proposed introducing indigenous language instruction in Mapuche, Aymara and Rapa Nui at primary school level. This was considered vital by Mapuche educators to reduce the loss of cultural identity indigenous children experienced when put into a school system where Spanish is the sole medium of instruction.

32 In the 1993 elections, Eduardo Frei, candidate for the Christian Democratic Party and the *Concertación* (agreement) coalition, won the presidency with 58 per cent of the vote. However, he did not achieve the parliamentary majority required to do away completely with the old authoritarianism because of eight "designated" seats in the Senate which were a legacy from the Pinochet regime.

33 Shortly before handing over the presidency, President Aylwin pardoned four MRPM activists, sentenced to death for the assassination attempt against Pinochet in 1986.

34 The Frei Government announced a plan to reduce the poverty which affected nearly a quarter of the population. In May 1995, the minimum salary was increased 13 per cent. Taxes were introduced on the sale of cigarettes and motor vehicles to fund a 10 per cent increase in the lowest pensions and a 5 per cent increase in the education budget. In June, Chile requested associate membership of the Mercosur market and negotiated entry into the North American Free Trade Association (NAFTA).

35 Brigadier Pedro Espinoza and retired General Manuel Contreras were sentenced to imprisonment for their parts in the murder of former foreign minister Orlando Letelier in Washington in 1976. Pinochet reiterated his support for the sentenced officers, but then called for respect for the civil authorities. At the same time, the Government suspended investigations into corruption charges against the former dictator's son. In a later hearing, during February 1998, Contreras stated that the true leader of the DINA (the political police during the dictatorship) was Pinochet himself.

36 The Chamber of Deputies approved the trade agreement with Mercosur member nations by 76 votes to 26. Two right-wing parties the UDI and RN, came out against the agreement. The signing of the free trade agreement took place on June 25 1996, establishing the "four plus one" association between Argentina, Brazil, Paraguay, Uruguay and Chile. This formula was to remain in place until Chile became a full member of the agreement. The treaty with Mercosur came into operation on October 1 1996.

37 A report from the National Society of Farmers (SNA) said the agreement would mean annual losses of $460 million for the Chilean agricultural sector, but, balancing this, the country would become integrated into a market of more than 200 million people.

38 In the October municipal elections, the ruling Concertación Nacional took the majority of the votes. Representation of the Democratic Christians, the Socialist Party (PS), the Democratic Party (PPD) and the Radical Party (RP), increased in the municipal councils. However, the number of Concertación Nacional mayors fell compared with the previous elections in 1992.

39 Within Concertación, the Democratic Christians lost support to the increasingly popular PS and PPD, who were more successful in local councils and mayoralties. This political advantage allowed them to strengthen their position within the coalition.

40 Various studies in 1996 suggested the average economic growth of 6 per cent in the last 11 years had led to a reduction in "extreme poverty" - but not in social inequality. Thus 20 per cent of the population still controlled 57 per cent of the national wealth, while the poorest 20 per cent handled only 3.9 per cent. During the first half of 1996, military and civil tribunals closed 21 cases of disappearances and extra-judicial killings involving 56 victims, without finding anyone responsible.

41 In May 1997, demonstrations by the miners' union - a bastion of the union movement and the Communist Party - in central Santiago were put down violently.

42 Concertación retained the majority in the December 11 legislative elections, but lost ground to the right. The government coalition took 50.6 per cent of the vote (compared with 56.1 per cent in the 1996 municipal elections), while the right took 39 per cent (35 per cent in 1996).

43 After passing on the post of Commander-in-Chief of the armed forces to General Ricardo Izurieta, Pinochet entered the Senate on March 11 1998, amidst general indignation. During the former dictator's first appearance in the Senate, several senators carried photographs of people who had disappeared in the dictatorship. One member of Parliament hung a sign saying "murderers not admitted" on the window of his office.

44 After the President's plan for a plebiscite to eliminate the post of "senator for life" (Pinochet was one) was vetoed in the Senate, Frei again suggested a referendum. At the same time, 21 members of the Congress presented a document which stated the constitutional clause granting former presidents a seat in the Senate for life should not be applied to Pinochet, as he had not been an elected leader.

DEMOGRAPHY

Population: 15,019,000 (1999)
Annual growth: 1.6 % (1975/97)
Estimates for year 2015 (million): 17.9 (1999)
Annual growth to year 2015: 1.1 % (1997/2015)
Urban population: 84.2 % (1997)
Urban Growth: 2.0 % (1980/95)
Children per woman: 2.4 (1998)

HEALTH

Life expectancy at birth: 75 years (1998)
male: 72 years (1998)
female: 78 years (1998)
Maternal mortality: 23 per 100,000 live births (1990-98)
Infant mortality: 11 per 1,000 (1998)
Under-5 child mortality: 12 per 1,000 (1998)
Daily calorie supply: 2,810 per capita (1996)
108 doctors per 100,000 people (1993)
Safe water: 91 % (1990/98)

EDUCATION

Literacy: 95 % (1995)
male: 95 % (1995)
female: 95 % (1995)
School enrolment:
Primary total: 101 % (1990/96)
male: 103 % (1990/97)
female: 100 % (1990/97)
Secondary:
male: 72 % (1990/96)
female: 78 % (1990/96)
Tertiary: 31 % (1997)
Primary school teachers: one for every 30 (1996)

COMMUNICATIONS

98 newspapers (1996), 354 radios (1997), 277 TV sets (1996) and 156 main telephone lines (1996) per 1,000 people
Books: 13 new titles per 100,000 people (1992/94)

ECONOMY

Per capita, GNP: $ 4,990 (1998)
Annual growth, GNP: 8.7 % (1998)
Annual inflation: 9.3 % (1990/98)
Consumer price index: 119.8 (1998)
Currency: 460.3 pesos = $ 1 (1998)
Cereal imports: 1,399,271 metric tons (1998)
Food import dependency: 7 % (1997)
Fertilizer use: 2,195 kg per ha (1997)
Exports: $ 21,680 million (1998)
Imports: $ 22,730 million (1998)
External debt: $ 36,302 million (1998); $ 2,449 per capita (1998)
Debt service: 22.3 % of exports (1998)
Development aid received: $ 136 million (1997); $ 10.2 per capita (1997); 0.20 % of GNP (1997)

ENERGY

Consumption: 1,574.0 Kgs of Oil equivalent per capita yearly (1997); 65.0 % imported (1997)

HDI (rank/value): 34/0.844 (1997)

45 Pinochet's arrest in Britain in October 1998, following an extradition bid by Spanish judge Baltasar Garzon, deeply shook the Chilean political process. The Government and opposition united in calls for the General to be returned to Chile. But while the Right accused the government of only making luke-warm efforts, Concertación suffered internally from having to defend the former dictator under the guise of defending national sovereignty. The legal comings and goings in London were accompanied by often violent demonstrations in Santiago both for and against the arrest.

46 In November 1998, in a country where women only make up 32 per cent of the economically-active population, Mirella Perez was appointed the first female General in Chile after being promoted throught the ranks of the Carabineers.

47 There were confrontations between Mapuche indians and forestry planters in southern Chile in October 1999. These led to the mobilization of a special armed group of 200 police officers with helicopter backing who surrounded the village of Temucuicui. The Government announced a plan whereby Mapuche would receive $275 million for roads, technical agricultural aid, student grants, paying off the state agricultural agency debt and the establishment of bilingual schools. However, Mapuche leaders saw this as a collection of old unfulfilled promises dressed up as a new offer. The Chilean Constitution offers no special treatment to indigenous communities, unlike many other regional nations.

48 Ricardo Lagos, the socialist Concertación candidate won a slim victory in the January 2000 presidential elections leaving the new government with very little room for manoeuvre. The Right, which took a moral victory with 49 per cent of the vote, promised an attitude of "vigilant collaboration" with the president-elect.

49 Pinochet returned to Chile in March after British courts decided not to extradite him to Spain on grounds of "ill health". A week later, Chilean congress approved a constitutional amendment guaranteeing immunity to former presidents. But the Court of Appeals asked Parliament to strip Pinochet of his immunity in a ruling made public in May. Two weeks later representatives of the State (including the military) and civil society launched a committee for looking into human rights, aimed at finding the remains of the disappeared. In August the Supreme Court ruled that Senator Pinochet had lost his immunity. At the same time, the courts were considering more than 70 complaints of murder, torture and abduction committed by Pinochet during his 17 years in power. ■

The Mapuche and their struggle for land

The Mapuche of southern Chile have sought to democratize the country that has been in political transition since 1990, and where military prosecutors and courts still prevail.

2 For the last few years, the Mapuche communities living south of the Bío Bío River in Chile's Ninth region, have denounced the predation of their lands and destruction of their fields. They find especially galling the impunity with which the private logging and electricity companies help themselves to the 200,000 hectares plundered from the indigenous peoples during the military dictatorship of General Augusto Pinochet (1973-1989). Most of these companies are based on foreign capital, mainly from Spain.

3 The Mapuches staged peaceful demonstrations that were harshly repressed by the Carabineros - the military police force. The police force has increased its presence in the region since then, ultimately creating greater awareness among the Chilean population about the Mapuche situation. The media has given wide coverage on the indigenous group's social and political organizations and its worldview – in sharp contrast to these South American native peoples' earlier separation. The Mapuches belong to the Araucano linguistic group, and currently number some 300,000 people who are primarily involved in farming.

4 As the neo-liberal economic model strengthened its grip on Chile in the 1980s, the Mapuche communities lost 60 per cent of their lands practically overnight. Lawsuits over land ownership in the region are still pending in the civil court system; the communities charge that the national governments have lacked the political will to resolve the conflict. In 1997, the Mapuches created the Association of Mapuche Communities, which organized a march to Santiago in 1999, walking hundreds of kilometers to demand that the State return their lands and prevent the corporations from expanding activities in their territories.

5 Confrontations and repression led to the imprisonment of dozens of Mapuche leaders. They were tried by military prosecutors in military courts - which have jurisdiction over civilian issues - on charges of "illegal association" and other crimes established under the dictatorship to fight the leftist national liberation movements of that time. According to legal observers and various human rights organizations, under international humanitarian law, the Chilean military justice system cannot try civilians and it did not provide the defendants with appropriate guarantees of due process.

6 For 350 years, the Mapuche have resisted invasions, first by the Spanish colonists and later bu successive Chilean governments and the army. Led by Chief Lautaro, these indigenous peoples won several battles against the Spanish Army and nearly invaded Santiago, the capital. When Chile achieved its independence, in the early 19th century, the Government and the dominant class decided that the "Mapuche problem" must to be resolved, but it was not until 1881 that the Chilean Army "recovered" the indigenous Araucanía region by killing the native peoples. In 1883, after a series of treaties, the Mapuches were confined to 300,000 hectares. Previously they had held approximately five million hectares, and later under the Pinochet regime they lost the 200,000 hectares that are currently exploited by the Mininco forestry and Endesa hydro-electric firms. ■

China

Zhonghua

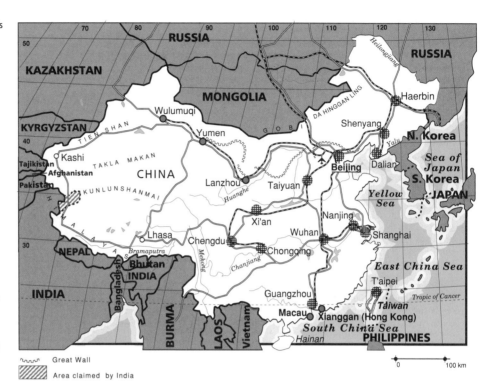

Population: 1,266,838,000 (1999)
Area: 9,559,867 SQ KM
Capital: Beijing
Currency: Renminbi yuan
Language: Chinese

〜〜〜 Great Wall

▨ Area claimed by India

0   100 km

C hina has one of the world's oldest civilizations, which achieved an unparalleled degree of cultural and social homogeneity several thousand years before most modern nations were formed.
2   Although the nation disintegrated into warring kingdoms at various points in its history, the development of Chinese civilization can be traced back 5,000 years to its emergence in the Yellow River (Huanghe) basin.
3   Territory was consolidated early on, and a single writing system was established by emperor Qin Shihuang some 2,200 years ago, in 221-206 BC; the same system is still in use today. In his determination to consolidate Chinese thinking he also ordered the burning of all previous books, and the execution of many scholars.
4   By the time of the Tang Dynasty, 618-907AD, China had developed a cultured civilization, and during the Song Dynasty, 960-1279 AD, the nation was more developed than Europe in every field.
5   Construction of the 5,000-km Great Wall of China was started in the third century BC in an attempt to repel invaders from the north. The wall ultimately failed, and China fell to Mongolian invaders; Genghis Khan and his grandson Kublai Khan ruled China from 1276 to 1368.
6   One of the most influential figures in Chinese culture was the scholar Confucius who lived about 2,500 years ago. As a philosopher, he emphasized

respect for one's elders, the importance of unquestioning loyalty and responsibility to superiors in the social hierarchy and the central role of the family. Other philosophers such as Lao Zi emphasized a more imaginative role for individuals in society, but Confucian thinking is most accurately reflected in the partially surviving social structures of China, Korea, Japan and Vietnam.
7   With their highly developed culture, the Chinese soon developed a disdain for

the "barbarians" beyond their borders. This attitude was often combined with the corruption of imperial dynasties, leading to eras of isolationism and social stagnation.
8   Regular contact with Europeans began when the Portuguese opened up maritime routes in the 15th century. The Chinese allowed Europeans to use a limited number of trading ports under strict conditions and granted the tiny enclave of Macau to the Portuguese in 1557. But the Chinese still refused to take foreign powers seriously.

9   The British eventually found a commodity that could be traded with China to pay for the Chinese silk, tea and porcelain products so fashionable in Europe. They began to import opium from India. When China tried to outlaw the drug trade, and later, to stop smuggling, Britain declared war in the name of free trade.
10   Modern European weapons easily defeated the Chinese imperial armies in the First Opium War, 1839-42. The victorious British demanded that five ports be opened to their trade, that low customs duties be imposed, and that the territory of Xianggang (Hong Kong) be given to them
11   The tottering Chinese Empire suffered another type of defeat with the Taiping rebellion in 1853. The rebel empire controlled much of southern China for 11 years before being crushed with the help of Western troops.
12   Massive imports of opium were then being paid for in Chinese silver, impoverishing the nation as it was weakened by widespread drug addiction.

WORKERS

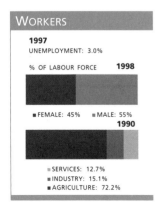

1997
UNEMPLOYMENT: 3.0%

% OF LABOUR FORCE   **1998**

▪ FEMALE: 45%   ▪ MALE: 55%

1990

▪ SERVICES: 12.7%
▪ INDUSTRY: 15.1%
▪ AGRICULTURE: 72.2%

LAND USE

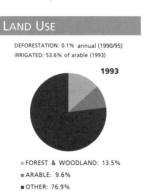

DEFORESTATION: 0.1% annual (1990/95)
IRRIGATED: 53.6% of arable (1993)

1993

▪ FOREST & WOODLAND: 13.5%
▪ ARABLE: 9.6%
▪ OTHER: 76.9%

PUBLIC EXPENDITURE

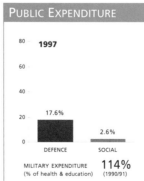

1997

17.6%

2.6%

DEFENCE   SOCIAL

MILITARY EXPENDITURE   **114%**
(% of health & education)   (1990/91)

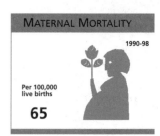
PROFILE

ENVIRONMENT

The terrain of the country is divided into three large areas. Central Asian China, comprising Lower Mongolia, Sin Kiang and Tibet, is made up of high plateaus, snow-covered in winter but sporting steppe and prairie vegetation in summer. North China has vast plains, such as those of Manchuria and Hoang-Ho, which boast large wheat, barley, sorghum, soybean and cotton plantations, and coal and iron ore deposits. Manchuria is the country's main metallurgical center. South China is a hilly area crossed by the Yangtse Kiang and Si-kiang rivers, this area has a hot, humid monsoon climate, and most of the nation's rice plantations. The country possesses great mineral wealth: coal, oil, iron ore and non-ferrous metals. The use of coal as the main source of energy produces acid rain. Less than 13 per cent of the land is covered by forest. The construction of the Three Gorges dam is considered a potential environmental disaster.

SOCIETY

Peoples: There are 56 official recognized nationalities. Han (91.96 per cent), Chuang (1.37 per cent), Manchu (0.87 per cent), Hui (0:76 per cent), Miao (0.65 per cent), Uighur (0.64 per cent), Yi (0.58 per cent), Tuchia (0.50 per cent), Mongol (0.42 per cent), Tibetan (0.41 per cent), Puyi (0.23 per cent), Tung (0.22 per cent), Yao (0.18 per cent), Korean (0.17 per cent), Pai (0,14 per cent), Hani (0.11 per cent), Kazak (0.1 per cent), Tai (0.09 per cent), Li (0.09 per cent), other (0.51 per cent).
Religions: No religion 59.2 per cent. Confucianism (a moral code, not a religion) combined with mystical elements from Taoism and Buddhism are what could be called the predominant "beliefs". Buddhist 6.0 per cent; Muslim 2.4 per cent; Christian 0.2 per cent; other 0.1 per cent.
Languages: Chinese (official), is a modernized version of northern Mandarin. Variants of this language can be found in the rest of the country, the most widespread being Cantonese, in the south. Ethnic minorities speak their own languages.
Political Parties: The Chinese constitution states that the Communist Party is "the leading nucleus of all the Chinese people".

THE STATE

Official name: Zhonghua Renmin Gongheguo.
Administrative divisions: 23 provinces, 5 autonomous regions and 3 municipalities.
Capital: Beijing 11,300,000 people (est 1996).
Other cities: Shanghai 14,500,000 people; Xianggang (Hong Kong), 5,574,000 (1995); Shenyang 4,500,000 people (est 1996).
Government: Jiang Zemin, President and General Secretary of the Communist Party since 1992, re-elected in March 1998. Zu Rongji, Prime Minister since March 1998. The 3,000-member National People's Congress (NPC) sits for about two weeks a year to ratify laws. NPC delegates are drawn from various geographical areas and social sectors (army, minorities, women, religious groups).
National Holiday: October 1 and 2, proclamation of the People's Republic.
Armed Forces: 2,930,000 (1995).
Other: 1,200,000 Armed Peoples' Police, Defense Department.

Another war from 1856-1860, this time against Anglo-French forces, ended with the capture of Beijing and a new round of concessions, including the admission of missionaries.

[13] In 1895, China suffered an even more humiliating defeat at the hands of its former tributary state Japan, which overran part of the Korean peninsula and the island of Taiwan.

[14] An anti-Western rebellion broke out in 1898 led by the Boxers, a secret society that attempted to drive foreigners out of China and to force Chinese converts to renounce Christianity. A joint British, Russian, German, French, Japanese and US expedition intervened to put down the uprising. The victorious armies divided the country into "zones of influence" and demanded that the Chinese pay huge war reparations.

[15] The most spectacular example of foreign involvement in China was in Shanghai, where the port was developed for trading, and foreign companies invested in hundreds of factories, located within foreign "concessions", to take advantage of cheap Chinese labor.

[16] Foreign exploitation also brought new ideas and concepts to China. The Government belatedly allowed small groups of students to study overseas. Nationalist groups emerged to focus and articulate the massive anti-foreign sentiment. In 1911, nationalists led by Sun Yat-sen, won the support of several imperial generals. A number of garrisons mutinied, and a Republic was proclaimed.

[17] Most of the generals who had joined the uprising wanted power and had no intention of instituting democratic reforms. Simmering rivalries soon burst into the open and China was thrust into an era of civil war as local "warlords", backed by various foreign powers, fought over the fragmented country.

[18] In 1921, 13 people from all over China gathered in a small house in the French concession of Shanghai to hold the first national congress of the Chinese Communist Party (CCP).

[19] The new party prioritized the organization of workers and it enjoyed considerable success. By 1926 it was involved with 700 trade unions representing 1.24 million members. They formed an alliance with Chiang Kai-Shek's Kuomintang (KMT) nationalist party to oppose the warlords. In 1927, the KMT turned on their allies and massacred some 40,000 communist labor leaders.

[20] In the face of such a defeat, a communist leader, Mao Zedong (Mao Tse Tung), argued that the Chinese peasantry should be mobilized as a revolutionary force. He led most of the Communist Party leadership into rural China, where they carried out political organizing and raised a peasant-based army.

[21] When the KMT armies tried to surround the CCP's remote bases in 1934, the communist army, their leaders and supporters began a march in search of an alternative site. They travelled for over a year, their numbers dwindling under frequent attacks and severe conditions, but they were eventually able to regroup. This legendary journey became known as the "long march".

[22] In 1937 a full-scale Japanese invasion of China forced the CCP and the KMT to set aside their differences and form a second United Front against the common enemy. While fighting against the Japanese, the Communists were also able to extend their influence among the workers in KMT-controlled areas. Chiang Kai-Shek showed more interest in fighting the Communists than the Japanese and broke the pact on several occasions. On one occasion, his own generals arrested him and forced him to negotiate with the CCP to continue joint resistance to the Japanese.

[23] When the allies defeated the Japanese in 1945, the CCP-KMT front collapsed into civil war. The corrupt and autocratic KMT proved no match for the highly-

LITERACY
1995
80%

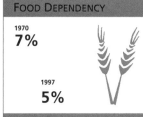

FOOD DEPENDENCY
1970
7%
1997
5%

EXTERNAL DEBT
1998
Per capita
US$ 123

FOREIGN TRADE
Millions US$ 1998
IMPORTS
165,906
EXPORTS
207,595

motivated CCP armies and their supporters. On October 1 1949, the communist leadership declared the foundation of the People's Republic of China.

[24] The remnants of the KMT Government and army fled to the island of Taiwan. There, under US protection, they claimed to represent all of China and laid plans to eventually "reconquer" the mainland.

[25] The Chinese Communists instituted far-reaching land reforms, adding to those already carried out in their own liberated zones before the final victory. They also nationalized all foreign-controlled property and initiated widespread education and health programs. In 1950 China invaded Tibet. Tibetan resistance was crushed in 1959 and the Dalai Lama (leader) fled to India where he still runs the government-in-exile.

[26] The first 5-year development plan incorporated many aspects of the Soviet model; the emphasis was on industrial investment rather than consumption, and heavy industry rather than light, all under a centralized economic plan. The creation of a strong industrial base could only be achieved by extracting a large surplus from rural areas, but by 1957 agricultural production was badly stagnating.

[27] In the name of open debate, and in search of solutions to the nation's problems, the party launched a campaign to "let a hundred flowers bloom, let a hundred schools of thought contend", inviting people to criticize the system and suggest alternatives. When citizens began to complain about the lack of democracy and question party rule, the leadership turned about-face and, cracked down on those who had spoken out.

[28] In 1958, Mao launched the Great Leap Forward, aimed at accelerating rural collectivization and urban industrialization. This heavy-handed, dogmatic and inflexible plan led the country down a disastrous path, sparking widespread famine in the countryside. The official Chinese figure for deaths between 1959 and 1961 is 20 million; one of the greatest human tragedies of the century, and one of the least widely reported.

[29] In 1962, Mao was forced to deliver a public self-criticism of his economic policies and was replaced by Liu Shaoqi as state chairman. Mao still enjoyed support among many radicals and, most importantly, from the People's Liberation Army.

[30] During this period, relations with the Soviet Union were souring due to ideological differences. This was highlighted in a 1956 speech by Soviet leader Nikita Khruschev. The split came in 1963, and USSR advisors left China taking plans and blueprints with them.

[31] In 1966, the army and young people, the "Red Guards", armed with the Little Red Book of Mao's thoughts, initiated campaigns throughout China attacking bureaucrats and university professors as reactionaries and "capitalist followers". The Great Proletarian Cultural Revolution had begun.

[32] There are many interpretations of the Cultural Revolution, and the upheaval occurred on many levels.

[33] At some stages during that period, with the internal "struggle between two lines" attaining civil war proportions, production suffered severely with many factories and universities closing altogether. An estimated 10 million people died during the years of turmoil, including Liu Shaoqi, Mao's chief opponent.

[34] At the same time, China took a leading role in founding the Non-Aligned Movement, and sent large numbers of workers abroad on high-profile development projects such as the Tanzam railway in Africa, linking Zambia to the coast via Tanzania. Liberation movements in many countries were inspired by China, adopting the peasant war strategies outlined in the works of Mao Zedong and Lin Piao.

[35] In the early 1970s Prime Minister Zhou Enlai started talks with the US, and Liu Shaoqi's protégé, Deng Xiaoping, was returned to power.

[36] In 1971 the mainland communist Government won sufficient support to replace Taiwan as the representative of China in the United Nations. Unlike earlier occasions, this time the US refrained from exercising its veto because it saw distinct advantages in improving relations with China. In 1976, the US and China re-established diplomatic relations.

[37] Internationally, China seemed to oppose all Soviet allies. This led to Chinese support for movements like UNITA in Angola and the PAC in South Africa. It also caused a growing rift with Vietnam after the defeat of the US in 1975. In 1979, China invaded Vietnam to "teach it a lesson" over its military contribution to the Khmer Rouge defeat in Cambodia.

[38] In 1975, Zhou and revolutionary veteran Zhu De both died, with Mao following in 1976. The pragmatists and reformists prevailed, taking advantage of support among party bureaucrats.

[39] The leaders of the Maoist faction - Mao's widow Jiang Qing, Zhang Chunqiao, Yao Wenyuan and Wang Hongwen, dubbed the "Gang of Four" - were arrested and charged with plotting to usurp state and party power. They became scapegoats for the failures and excesses of the Cultural Revolution. In 1981 they were put on public trial as a final symbolic gesture that the era of "revolutionary struggle" was over.

[40] Deng Xiaoping was rehabilitated by the new leadership, and he was universally acknowledged as its leading authority.

[41] The new leadership announced an ambitious economic development program. It envisioned significant advances in agriculture, industry, defense and science and technology.

[42] Government's acceptance of greater popular expression and criticism was apparent in 1978 and 1979. They knew that this would be directed against the turmoil of the Cultural Revolution and the radicals responsible for it. The "Beijing Spring" was centered on the "Democracy Wall", where ordinary citizens could display posters expressing their opinions. The wall also served as a spot where dissidents distributed unofficial magazines. When criticism began to focus on the country's core political structure, the leadership stopped the movement. The Democracy Wall, an institution throughout the Cultural Revolution, was discontinued. One dissident, Wei Jingshen, who published a magazine calling for a "Fifth Modernization" - democracy - was tried and sentenced to a 15-year prison sentence.

[43] In December 1978, at the 3rd plenary of the 11th Party Central Committee, Deng was fully rehabilitated and sweeping economic reforms were announced.

[44] In the countryside, the People's Communes were disbanded and land was redistributed into family-size units leased from the State. Production quotas were replaced by taxes, and peasants were permitted to sell their surpluses for cash in the towns and cities.

[45] China also announced a dramatic new openness to foreign trade, investment and borrowing. To attract foreign industry, Special Economic Zones were established near Hong Kong (Xianggang) and Macau, offering a range of incentives; such as tax breaks, and cheap land and labor, similar to free trade zones elsewhere.

[46] In industry, a good deal of decision-making power was

Mad about China

According to estimates, in a few years' time China will become the leading world economy. In the West it is believed the political changes will take place spontaneously. However, all indications point to pressure being lifted on this front to save rousing the "beast".

[2] For some Western economists - amongst them former World Bank economist and then US Secretary of the Treasury Department, Lawrence Summers - in the opening decades of the 21st century, China will match the US and Japanese economies. Once it overtakes these, the People's Republic will become the leading world economy. China currently ranks seventh on a global scale, with annual export earnings of $183 billion (1998) and an annual per capita Gross Domestic Product (GDP) of $750. On the world's economic league tables, the US comes first with export income of $630 billion and GDP of $29,340; Japan lies second with annual export earnings of $388 billion and the highest GDP of all at $32,380.

[3] For the last 20 years, the Chinese economy has been growing at 10 per cent per year, and although GDP is relatively lower than other economies, analysts state that in absolute terms it will out-perform British and French indicators within a few years. At the same time, it is twice the size of the Indian economy, the second largest country in terms of population.

[4] China is today a most alluring country. Since November 1999 when the country began trade talks with the US, the international community and particularly the US business sector have seen this "Communist" country as offering great opportunities. That's because China means a market of more than a billion potential consumers - a figure equivalent to one fifth of world population.

[5] For the larger economies, including the European Union (EU), China could be one step away from joining the World Trade Organization (WTO). With membership approved, China will become member 135 and the WTO will then become a truly world-wide organization. Chinese commitments within the WTO framework are many. Amongst other elements, it must guarantee all members no discrimination against investments from their companies, it must reduce tariffs as well as protection for its industries, mainly in the telecommunications field. The potential liberalization of the Chinese market, says the West, will enable all companies to compete in the telecommunications sector (with a similar-sized market of listeners and television viewers), services and agriculture.

For China, the WTO will ensure the favoring of some of its products, which are comparatively cheaper, like textiles, toys and electronic goods.

[6] In May 2000 when the US House of Representatives approved permanent trade relations with China for the first time in 13 years, many saw this gesture as definitive approval of Chinese entry to the WTO. For months, US President Bill Clinton constantly lobbied legislators - and world leaders - in an attempt to change some historical "prejudices".

[7] There was much discussion of the ideological contradiction harbored within this attitude in the US lower house, as it contrasts strongly with the line taken on another "Communist" country - Cuba. Considering that for the last decade the US has constantly tightened the embargo on the Caribbean island (although to little effect as the EU nations have invested millions of dollars in Cuba since then) then the new US policy - finally approved by legislators - shows that the market of 1.2 billion Chinese consumers is so attractive to capitalism that it forms a temptation big enough to overcome any ideological argument. ∎

passed from the ministries to individual plant managers, who were now free to plan production and distribution, and choose the sources of their raw materials. Young workers were offered a contract system of employment instead of lifetime assignment to a production unit. Individuals and families were given permission to start small businesses such as restaurants and shops.

[47] The Government began a phased program of removing price subsidies on consumer goods, allowing the market to determine the price of such basics as food and clothing, to spur economic growth and encourage consumption.

[48] As the changes took hold, more goods and foodstuffs appeared in shops, and wages increased for several years. The long-standing problem of unemployment and underemployment diminished as more people became self-employed. Restrictions on the freedom of travel inside and outside China were loosened, greater artistic diversity and expression were tolerated and a greater diversity of information was made available.

[49] These economic reforms began to accelerate inflation, especially on such basic items as food and clothing, and in the late 1980s, workers found that their buying power was falling.

[50] In the countryside, peasants with easy access to urban centers benefited as they were able to supply large markets. Those in more remote areas fell behind. The use of chemical pesticides and fertilizers soared, and production initially rose as well. But production levels began to fall, prompting farmers to apply greater quantities of chemicals, approaching danger levels. Pesticide and fertilizer prices rose sharply.

[51] Workers' welfare deteriorated, and the new employment systems generated insecurity. While managers were given more

power, even to hire and fire workers and set production targets, trade unions were not granted any corresponding freedom to act.

[52] High-level debate over the scale and pace of economic reforms included discussion of a clearer division between party and state.

[53] In 1986 students demonstrated in Shanghai, calling for freedom of the press and political reform. As a result, Hu Yaobang, then a relatively young Party General Secretary, was forced to step down, and a campaign against "bourgeois liberalism" was launched by hard-liners. This aimed to root out what they called "western" ideas; most importantly political pluralism, though consumerism and corruption were also mentioned. Many viewed this campaign as a veiled attack on Deng's economic reform policies, given that Hu Yaobang was one of Deng's protégés.

[54] In March 1989, police in what is known as Central Asian China fired on Tibetan demonstrators who were protesting against cultural and religious persecution and demanding greater political rights. The shooting triggered three days of widespread rioting which resulted in the imposition of Martial Law, lifted only in April 1990. Tibetan exiles reported the detention of many dissidents and several executions. Tibet had been officially annexed to China in 1950 and converted into an autonomous region in 1965.

[55] In April 1989, the death of Hu Yaobang served as a pretext for thousands of students to assemble in Tiananmen Square in downtown Beijing. In addition to mourning the death of the man who to them symbolized liberal reform, the students called for an end to corruption and changes in both society and the party.

[56] The students camped in the square and their numbers grew, buoyed by the anniversary of the student demonstrations of May 4 1919.

Hundreds of thousands of citizens and workers in Beijing began to demonstrate support for the reform movement, bringing food and other supplies to the students, marching, and blockading intersections when it seemed likely that troops would move against the students.

[57] Students, citizens and workers began similar demonstrations in other cities, and the banners of groups of workers from the official media, trade unions, and various party sections began to appear in the daily demonstrations. Various autonomous bodies were set up by demonstrators, challenging four decades of complete party control over all social organizations.

[58] Finally, on June 4 1989, the Government moved decisively and violently, sending troops into downtown Beijing to clear out the citizens and students. Many hundreds were killed and thousands wounded. Many Beijing residents and students were killed as the troops forced their way past barricades in armored vehicles and opened fire on the crowds. The pro-democracy demonstrations were smashed. The assault on Tiananmen was followed by a nationwide hunt for leaders of the autonomous student and workers movements, thousands were arrested and badly beaten; many others were executed. There were important political changes, and Li Peng became Prime Minister.

[59] The first Western government to send representatives to the capital after the Tiananmen massacre was Britain, in September 1991. They signed an agreement with Beijing on the construction of a new airport in Xianggang (Hong Kong), within the constraints of the negotiations to return the British colony to China in 1997.

[60] With one-third of all public enterprises operating at that time at a deficit, and less and less possibility of balancing the State budget, structural reforms seemed all

but inevitable in state enterprises. The Chinese Communist Party was paving the way for a return to the economic liberalization program initiated by Deng Xiaoping, who had reappeared on the political scene at the age of 87. At the same time, there were other indicators of changing attitudes: Jiang Zemin, Deng's successor as Communist Party Secretary, called for "free thinking", and charges against former Secretary Zhao Zhiyang were reduced. Shortly afterwards, however, he was blamed for events leading to the Tiananmen massacre, rendering impossible his chances of rehabilitation.

[61] The Paris Accords on Cambodia (see Cambodia), signed in October 1991, and the end of the Soviet Union accelerated a rapprochement between China and Vietnam. In November 1991, diplomatic relations between the two countries were re-established.

[62] In late November 1991 the Government freed the student leaders from the Tiananmen demonstrations. However, there were an estimated 70,000 political prisoners in various provinces of the the Xinjiang and Qinghai region.

[63] In 1992, China signed the Nuclear Non-Proliferation Treaty. At the annual session of the People's National Congress, Jiang Zemin was designated president of the republic, becoming the first person since Mao to combine the functions of head of state, the party and commander of the armed forces. Prime Minister Li Peng was confirmed in his post.

[64] In April 1992, the decision was made to build the giant Three Gorges dam on the Yangtse river. This controversial project was to be completed in 2009, flooding lands inhabited by 1.3 million people, drowning 10 cities and more than 800 towns. Ecologists immediately opposed the project, saying it would destroy the habitats of endangered species and

Hong Kong (Xianggang): One country, two systems

Hong Kong (Xianggang) island was ceded to Britain "in perpetuity" in 1842, when the British attacked China in the first Opium War. Eighteen years later, the British gained the rights over Kowloon, the mainland peninsula facing the island. In 1898, the British forced the Chinese to give them a 99-year lease on the rural zone north of Kowloon, known as the "New Territories".

2 Hong Kong was initially used as a trade centre, constituting a point of entry to China. But in the 1950s, following the Communist victory in China, the United States and Britain imposed a trade embargo. Deprived of its supplies, Hong Kong was forced to import all its basic goods from overseas, therefore having to develop exports, rapidly transforming itself into a light industry center, exporting textiles, clothing, plastic and electronic goods. Just as in Taiwan and South Korea, this development was generously supported by Western powers interested in these "bastions" of the Cold War.

3 Growth of trade and the export industry converted Hong Kong into a financial, communications and transport centre. The Government policy also contributed, setting low taxes and minimal customs tariffs, offering trustworthiness and freedom in movements of capital.

4 When China announced a stage of liberalization toward foreign trade and investment in the late 1970s, Hong Kong - with one of the best natural ports and port facilities in the world, sophisticated international investment and trade systems - was ready to take advantage of the situation. Between 30 and 50 per cent of China's foreign trade of was carried out through Hong Kong, which was also the source of nearly 90 per cent of foreign investment in the Chinese province of Kwangtung.

5 Almost the entire population of Chinese origin had settled in the enclave following successive migratory waves resulting from political and economic events in their Communist neighbor.

6 London and Beijing began negotiations on the future of the colony in the early 1980s, as the 99-year lease was due to end in 1997. The people of Hong Kong were not represented in these discussions.

7 Agreement was reached in 1984, giving China sovereignty over the entire territory, but allowing Hong Kong "a high degree of independence" as a Special Administrative Area.

8 In September 1991, the people of Hong Kong elected the members of the Legislative Council for the first time in 150 years. The United Democrats of Hong Kong (UDHK), candidates - critical of the colonial government of Hong Kong and of China and supporting stronger democracy - won most of the seats.

9 The last British Governor, Chris Patten, reformed the electoral system, totally separating the economic and legislative powers. China said this reform contradicted the principles of the Basic Law. In 1998, China appointed a Preparatory Committee for the Administrative Region of Hong Kong, made up of leading figures of Hong Kong, and consultants from the colonial government.

10 In 1994, Chris Patten proposed a plan to increase the number of voters in the 1995 elections, causing further confrontations with Beijing. In September 1995 the Democrat Party, opposed to the official Chinese interpretation of the Basic Law, triumphed in the Legislative Council elections. Beijing repeated its intention to dissolve the Council in 1997, alleging that it did not take the interests of all the social strata of Hong Kong into account.

11 The British Governor publicly upbraided the Chinese authorities for only negotiating with "multi-millionaires". Patten referred to the alliance made in 1996 between leading Hong Kong business people and the Government in Beijing.

12 On July 1 1997, China recovered control over Hong Kong after 155 years of British colonial dominion. Businessman Tung Chi Hua was appointed head of the new Executive with the support of a Legislative Council.

13 According to the new law, Hong Kong retains its rights and liberties, its legal independence and nature as an international financial and trade center, along with its way of life, for 50 years. The zone mints its own currency and is ruled by its own immigration and customs laws. Beijing will only handle defense and foreign relations during this period.

14 Reunification put China in a "one country, two systems" situation, combining the free market economy of Hong Kong with rigid political control over the rest of the country, a totally unprecedented situation.

15 The transfer took place against a backdrop of spectacular growth in the Chinese economy, which gave no signs of slowing. The Hong Kong economy, meanwhile, is considered the third most powerful in the world, and the former enclave is also the third most important international financial center behind New York and London.

16 Hong Kong was much more severely hit by the Asian financial crisis than the rest of China. Both imports and exports declined, the economy shrank 7 per cent in the third quarter of 1997 and unemployment rose to its highest level in 15 years. In a departure from previous laissez-faire practice, Hong Kong authorities intervened in currency markets to defend the Hong Kong dollar against currency speculators.

17 In May 1999 elections for the Legislative Council, voters expressed overwhelming support for the democratic parties and political leaders whom Beijing had excluded from the interim Hong Kong legislature it appointed in 1996. The electoral system, constructed to deny a popular majority, nevertheless delivered an equal number of seats to the Democratic Party, which garnered about 42 per cent of the vote, and to pro-Beijing parties, which gained 3 per cent. ∎

would leave millions of people exposed to the danger of earthquakes, avalanches and floods. They also considered the dam would not be profitable.

65   In September, the Government said the pro-independence action in Tibet would be "implacably repressed". On the economic front, an austerity plan was launched in the State apparatus and taxes on the rural population were increased. However, a series of protests and demonstrations forced the Government to remove the new charge from a sector of the population which totalled around 800 million people.

66   The GDP increased by 12.8 per cent in 1992, a figure unprecedented in the previous decade. However, this growth (the economy nearly doubled since 1990) had its first undesirable effects in 1993, when inflation hit 20 per cent in the first half year. In March 1994, Li Peng proposed limiting the economic expansion to 9 per cent in order to limit inflation despite protests from the coastal provinces like Guandong, the main beneficiaries of the Chinese "boom".

67   The social inequalities between the new rich in the cities and the vast majority of the workers and rural population continued to increase along with the migration of millions of people from the countryside to the cities. This led the Government to be cautious in closing and privatizing unprofitable State enterprises, as a sharp rise in unemployment would only worsen an already tense and precarious social situation.

68   However, another project which planned to limit the social effects of the economic reforms was postponed. The plan was to establish a redundancy payment for workers laid off from closed State companies, but the total lack of a State-run social security system in the nation - without so much as

unemployment benefit - made the Government back off from launching excessively radical reforms.

69   In 1995, Jiang Zemin consolidated his power to continue ruling the nation in the "post-Deng" era. The authorities still concerned about the social effects of the reforms, maintained the large subsidies for state enterprises.

70   In that year, inflation reached only 13 per cent, and the 1996-2000 five-year plan forecast annual growth of "only" 8-9 per cent. The number of corruption scandals increased dramatically. The CCP first secretary in Beijing, Chen Xitong, was forced to leave his post when it became clear he had been misappropriating funds along with important communal leaders and a large municipal metallurgical company. In April, the deputy-mayor of Beijing, Wang Daosen committed suicide, accused of having embezzled $37 million of government funds.

71   As in previous years, trade relations with the US strengthened, despite the constant public disagreements between the nations, like the situation provoked by military manoeuvres in the waters around Taiwan (see Taiwan) or the nuclear tests carried out by Beijing. In November, Jiang made the first ever visit of a Chinese president to South Korea, in another demonstration of the commercial and political rapprochement of China with countries it had classed as anti-Communist during the Cold War.

72   In May 1996 Amnesty International (AI) condemned the Chinese repression of Buddhist monks in Tibet. According to AI, 80 monks were injured for refusing to respect a ban on the public exhibition of pictures of the Dalai Lama.

73   Two student leaders of the 1989 uprising were sentenced to prison sentences of 11 and 3 years, accused of promoting the overthrow of the Government. Another

student gained political asylum in the United States. The regime continued on the psychological harassment of Taiwan, carrying out large-scale military exercises around the island.

74   Foreign investment, the dynamo of the great Chinese economic growth in these years, increased 20% in 1996. Several foreign companies operating in the country were authorised to convert local money into dollars or yen.

75   Following the death of Deng Xiaoping, in February 1997, the XV PC Congress confirmed Jiang Zemin as leader in October, reaffirming the present political system and reform policy, in particular with regard to the State companies

76   The 15th Communist Party Congress, in October of that year, consolidated reform policy, particularly as applied to the State companies, and reaffirmed the traditional political system.

77   In March 1998, the People's National Congress ratified the changes decided by the Communist Party. Jiang Zemin was re-elected head of State and commander of the armed forces, with 98 per cent of the vote. Some 2,882 deputies voted in favor, 36 against and 29 abstained.

78   Hu Jintao, mentioned as a possible successor to Zemin, was elected Vice-President, while outgoing Prime Minister, Li Peng, became Head of Parliament. The Constitution prevented him from serving a third term as Head of Government.

79   Zhu Rongji, former deputy Prime Minister in charge of the economy, was elected Prime Minister. The new cabinet, made up mostly of economic experts, faced the preparation of the 370,000 State companies for free market rules, a process which had already cost between 20 and 30 million jobs.

80   The Yangtse valley, home to some 400 million Chinese, suffered the worst flooding in decades in 1998, with a total of some 4,000 people killed

and damage worth $25 billion. The authorities tried to reinforce and modernize dykes, dams and sluices in order to handle the large swells. However, heavy rains overwhelmed these barriers and, in August 1999, the government once again declared a state of emergency in the valley. More than two million people were evacuated while another 60 million were affected. Harvests and housing were ruined throughout the valley.

81   In June 1999, the Government issued an arrest warrant on militants of the "exercise and meditation movement" Falun Gong and asked Interpol to arrest Li Hongzhi, the man who founded the sect in 1992 before emigrating to the United States. At the same time, the authorities destroyed more than one and a half million books on the group's beliefs. This confrontation with Falun Gong - seen by the Chinese leadership as the greatest threat since the demonstrations in 1989 - started after the group staged a silent protest against government hostility in April when 25,000 of its supporters demonstrated opposite Jiang Zemin's residence.

82   In a two-pronged move in November, China called for a reduction in global deployment of missiles in order to create a "favorable atmosphere" at the dawning of the new millennium. At the same time 100 new missiles were moved onto the south eastern coast facing Taiwan. This action aimed to pressure the US into limiting sales of advanced weapons to Taiwan.

83   In December 1999, for the first time in 442 years, China was complete again, as Europe lost its last remaining colonial possession in Asia when Portugal officially gave up Macau. On reunification, Macau, like Hong Kong, became a "special administrative region" with considerable independence, at least for the next 50 years. ∎

Taiwan

Taiwan

Population: 21,804,000 (1998)
Area: 36,000 SQ KM
Capital: Taipei
Currency: New dollar
Language: Chinese (Mandarin)

The island of Taiwan's government insists that it represents all of China. It calls itself the Republic of China, and for four decades has pledged itself to the cause of recovering the mainland, from which it is separated by the 200-km wide Taiwan Strait. In 1590 the Portuguese called it Ilha Formosa (Beautiful Island).

[2] China's Qing (Manchu) emperors incorporated Taiwan into the empire in 1683, and the island was proclaimed a separate province of China in 1887. During this time, the political and administrative systems of mainland China were extended to Taiwan, and many people migrated there from the mainland.

[3] After China's defeat in the 1895 Sino-Japanese war, Taiwan became a Japanese colony, but was returned to China after the defeat of Japan at the end of World War II. At first, the people of Taiwan rejoiced at the end of Japanese colonialism, but they soon discovered that life under the ruthlessly authoritarian, corrupt and vehemently anti-Communist Kuomintang (KMT) party led by Chiang Kai-shek resembled nothing less than a different kind of colonialism.

[4] On February 28 1947, there was a major demonstration against the KMT authorities. The KMT reacted at first by lifting martial law and inviting the opposition to form a Settlement Committee of politicians, trade unionists and student groups to discuss possible political reforms. Meanwhile, they drafted in 13,000 additional troops and when the opposition came forward, the KMT massacred large numbers of them, imprisoning others.

[5] In 1949, the entire KMT government, the remnants of its armies, and their relatives and supporters, fled to Taiwan after losing the mainland civil war to the Communist armies. From its refuge, backed by the United States, the KMT declared Taiwan to be the temporary base of the Republic of China pending recovery of the mainland. Most Western nations continued to recognize the KMT as the representatives of all China.

[6] When the Korean War erupted, with China supporting the North Koreans, the US redoubled its military and economic commitment to Taiwan, protecting it as a front-

line state in the battle to defend the "free world".

[7] Democracy disappeared. Human rights were violated, demonstrations, strikes and political parties banned, and Martial Law imposed - all in the name of the battle to reconquer the mainland. The KMT set up a governmental system which claimed to represent the whole of China, with legislators representing each mainland province.

[8] Taiwan's remarkable industrialization began in the 1960s, when World Bank and US technocrats helped the Government apply an export-oriented development strategy. The era of Japanese colonialism had left Taiwan with only partially-developed transport and an education system. The US granted ideologically-motivated financial, trade and aid advantages to bolster an authoritarian political regime which, in turn, hectored Taiwan's disenfranchised, and politically disorganized workforce.

[9] Taiwanese output grew at an average of 8.6 per cent each year between 1953 and 1985, and became one of the four newly-industrialized "tigers" of East Asia. Growth was entirely export-oriented, and the island developed the world's second-largest trade surplus with the US, following Japan. Today, Taiwan has highly developed plastics, chemical, ship-building, clothing and electronics industries.

[10] Sweatshop conditions were common in the 1960s and 1970s, and many workers put in long shifts, often exposed to toxic substances.

[11] In 1971, the US decided to seek closer ties with China, no longer vetoing the latter's admission to the UN. Taiwan therefore lost its representation in that world body. A few years later in 1979 the US officially broke off diplomatic relations with Taiwan.

[12] The country found itself at an economic crossroads. It was over-dependent on a few export markets

and labor-intensive industries, importing nations were pressuring for more balanced trade and Taiwan's labor was no longer as cheap as that of many of its Asian neighbors. Technocrats argued that in order to compete Taiwan should develop a more open political system. The KMT also faced an internal succession crisis as ageing politicians from the civil war era clung precariously to power.

[13] In that climate, social movements were proliferating, with ecological groups protesting against pollution and nuclear power, farmers' groups demanding higher prices, and students calling for more academic freedom and an end to human rights abuses.

[14] In addition, a significant portion of the population did not consider their country to be a part of China, and rejected both the authoritarian policies of the KMT and Deng Xiaoping's unification proposal of "one nation, two systems" with Taiwan becoming a Chinese dependency.

[15] In September 1986 the Democratic Progress Party (DPP) was formed as the first opposition party to challenge the KMT's political stranglehold. Although technically illegal, the party was allowed to survive, and Martial Law was formally lifted on July 15 1987.

[16] A huge upsurge in union activity took place in 1987. Strong independent sections were formed in the trade union system and supporters founded parallel political structures in the Labor Party and Workers' Party.

[17] Elections were held in December 1989. The KMT won 53 per cent of the vote, against the DPP's 38 per cent. The DPP also fared well in municipal and council elections, winning the mayoralty of Taipei.

[18] While the KMT was resolutely opposed to independence, some DPP members formed the New Wave group proposing that Taiwan declare self-rule. Other groups advocated a referendum for self-determination.

[19] The KMT achieved yet another victory over the opposition DPP in the National Assembly elections in December 1991. The results were regarded as a plebiscite on the independence issue. The DPP's electoral platform, favoring a definitive separation from China, was supported by just 21 per cent of the electorate, against the KMT's 71 per cent.

PROFILE

ENVIRONMENT

Located 160 km southeast of continental China, Taiwan is part of a chain of volcanic islands in the West Pacific which also includes the Japanese islands. A mountain range runs across Taiwan stretching from north to south along the centre of the country. A narrow plain along the island's western coast constitutes its main agricultural area where rice, sugar cane, bananas and tobacco are cultivated. More than two-thirds of the island's area is densely wooded. Taiwan has considerable mineral resources: coal, natural gas, marble, limestone and minor deposits of copper, gold, and oil. The country is suffering the consequences of its enormous industrial explosion, with high levels of water, air and land pollution.

SOCIETY

Peoples: Most inhabitants are Chinese who have migrated from the mainland since the 17th century and are known as "Taiwanese". Hundreds of thousands of Kuomintang Chinese fled to Taiwan during 1949-50. The island's indigenous inhabitants are of Malayo-Polynesian origin, and currently do not exceed 1.7 per cent of the population. They are concentrated on the east coast, where they make up 25 per cent of the population.
Religions: More than half of the population are Chinese Buddhist. There are also Muslim and Christian minorities.
Languages: Chinese (Mandarin), official. Taiwanese, a derivative of the Chinese dialect from Fujian province, is the language of the majority.
Political Parties: Democratic Progressive Party (DPP), formed in 1986 with a very broad platform to restore political democracy in Taiwan; Kuomintang (Chinese Nationalist Party/KMT) founded in China in 1919, took political monopoly of Taiwan when it fled from the continent in 1949 and ruled under Martial Law up to 1987; New Trend split from the DPP with claims for Taiwan independence; Labor Party, centrist, and Workers' Party, socialist, appeared after the resurgence of trade unions in 1987. Among the pro-independence groups there is the illegal World Union of Formosans for Independence.
Social Organizations: Every trade union has to be a member of the Chinese Federation of Labor, controlled by the Kuomintang, but in 1987 a few independent trade union appeared. These are organized in several federations, including the National Federation of Independent Unions and Tao-Chu-Miao Brotherhood.

THE STATE

Official name: Republic of China.
Administrative divisions: 7 municipalities and 16 counties.
Capital: Taipei (T'aipei) 2,595,699 people (1997).
Other cities: Kaohsiung 1,434,907 people; Taichung 881,870; Tainan 712,172 (1997).
Government: Chen Shui-bian, President elected in March 2000. Vincent Siew, Prime Minister since September 1 1997. The National Assembly has 720 members, is in charge of appointing the President for a six-year-period and is empowered to amend the Constitution. The President heads the legislative "Yuan", with 240 members, and appoints the Prime Minister who heads the executive "Yuan". Internal affairs are under the control of a Provincial Assembly of 77 members which deals with administrative matters.
National holiday: January 1, Day of the Republic; February 25, Constitution Day.
Armed Forces: 376,000 troops.
Other: Militarized police, 25,000.

DEMOGRAPHY

Population: 21,804,000 (1998)

[20] In 1992, fourteen members of the World Union of Formosans for Independence - a party which had been banned by the Government - were arrested. In addition, diplomatic ties were broken with South Korea, which established relations with China. In December, in the first open elections since 1949, the DPP obtained 31 per cent of the vote, and 50 of the 161 legislative seats.

[21] In early 1993, and as a direct consequence of the electoral results, there were two significant resignations by members of the KMT leadership: those of Prime Minister Hau Pei-tsu, and Secretary General James Sung, both of the conservative wing of the party. Lien Chan, the first government leader to have been born in Taiwan, was named Prime Minister. Shortly afterwards, the governing party experienced its first major division. Thirty deputies broke with the KMT to found the Party of the New Nationalist Alliance.

[22] From 1994, voices rose demanding an independent way for Taiwan, leaving behind the assumption of being a government representative of all Chinese. However, due to Beijing's opposition to any measure which could further lead the island toward independence, Taipei's efforts to be accepted into the United Nations were in vain.

[23] The first multiparty municipal elections were held in December. Most of the vote went to the ruling Kuomintang and the DPP. In spite of opposition from environmentalists and anti-nuclear activists and DPP objections, the KMT supported the construction of a fourth nuclear plant on the island.

[24] In 1995, economic relations with Beijing intensified. Taiwan became the second "foreign" investor in the People's Republic after Hong Kong, placing approximately $22 billion in China. In spite of this exchange, political relations between the two countries deteriorated after a private visit from Taiwanese president Lee Teng to the US in June. Heedless of US warnings, Beijing carried out a series of missile launchings in July and August on waters just 140 kilometers from Taiwan.

[25] In spite of losing ground in previous elections, the Kuomintang won the December legislative elections with 46 per cent of the vote and 33 per cent by the DPP. In the campaign prior to the March 1996 presidential elections, new Chinese military manoeuvres near the coast of Taiwan led Washington to send warships in defense of Taiwan's alleged threatened territorial integrity.

[26] Lee Teng, of the KMT, triumphed on March 20 in the first presidential elections with direct suffrage in the history of the island, taking 54 per cent of the vote. The defeated Peng Ming-min, of the Democratic Progressive Party, took 21 per cent. Lee repeated his decision to improve Taiwan's international profile through an energetic diplomatic offensive.

[27] In July, China made a show of military force off the coast of Taiwan, timed to coincide with the return of Hong Kong from British to Chinese control.

[28] In August the Government announced the closure of its embassy on the island of St Lucia, following the Caribbean island's decision to strengthen links with China. The severing of diplomatic relations reduced the number of countries recognizing the Taipei Government to 30. Also that month, Prime Minister Lien Chan handed in his resignation and was replaced by Vincent Siew from September 1.

[29] The triumph of the pro-independence movements in 12 towns, signaled clear defeat of the Nationalist Party in the October 1997 municipal elections. The result was poorly received by the Government party, in power since 1949, less than a year away from legislative elections.

[30] In April 1998, China and Taiwan decided to reopen direct negotiations, having broken off relations in June 1995. The KMT victory in the municipal and legislative elections in December appeared to support possibilities of dialogue with Beijing. However the opposition DPP maintained a more openly nationalist posture. Internally, increased representation in the legislature finally allowed the KMT to pass cut backs in provincial government.

[31] In the weeks running up to the presidential elections of 2000, Beijing repeatedly announced it could resort to force if Taipei refused unification. The announcement was made as a response to the DPP election campaign where candidate Chen Shui-bian, had stated he would hold a referendum to decide the future status of the island were he to win.

[32] This external pressure did the KMT no good, and on March 18 it lost power on the island for the first time in its history. The DPP won, followed by an independent candidate, James Soong, a former KMT leader who led a new faction which had split off. The KMT, which came in a poor third, immediately expelled more than 50 of its members, accusing them of supporting Soong instead of the ruling party candidate Lien Chan.

[33] Chen had been moderating his stance in the days running up to the election stating that there was no need to declare independence and that he was ready to discuss any sort of issue with Beijing, but once in power he announced that Tsai Ying-wen would be in charge of negotiating with China. However, both Chen and Tsai told their opponents to start negotiations on the platform of "a single China" proposed by Beijing. ∎

Colombia

Colombia

Population: 41,564,000 (1999)
Area: 1,138,910 SQ KM
Capital: Santa Fé de Bogotá
Currency: Peso
Language: Spanish

The best known of Colombia's indigenous cultures is that of the Chibchas or "Muiscas", as they called themselves. They lived in northern Colombia and Panama, farming and mining.

[2] In America, colonization resulted in the plundering of native wealth and the population was subjected to thinly disguised forms of slavery. After 300 years of colonialism, a large part of the indigenous population had disappeared.

[3] Spain conquered Colombia between 1536 and 1539. Gonzalo Giménez de Quesada decimated the Chibchas and founded the city of Santa Fé de Bogotá which became the center of the Viceroyalty of New Granada in 1718.

[4] Extensive, export-oriented agriculture (coffee, bananas, cotton and tobacco) replaced traditional crops (potatoes, cassava, corn, wood and medicinal plants) with African slaves replacing the more rebellious indigenous population.

[5] The Revolt of the Comuneros started the process leading to the declaration of independence in Cundinamarca, in 1813. The road to independence was marked by constant struggles between the advocates of centralized government and the federalists, headed by Camilo Torres. Antonio Nariño (who had drafted the declaration of independence) represented the urban bourgeoisie, linked to European interests, while Torres presided over the Congress of the United Provinces, representing the less privileged.

[6] In 1816, Pablo Morillo reconquered this territory, executing Torres. Three years later, Simon Bolívar counter-attacked from Venezuela, liberated

Colombia and founded the Republic of Greater Colombia, including Venezuela, Ecuador and the province of Panama. Regionalism and strong British pressure brought about the secession of Venezuela and Ecuador in 1829-30. The Republic of New Granada was then proclaimed and in 1886 Colombia adopted its current name.

[7] From 1830 to the early 20th century, the country went through civil wars, local wars (including two with Ecuador), three military uprisings and 11 constitutions. The Liberals and Conservatives have kept a permanent hold on the Colombian political situation, separated by a mutual hatred

passed down from generation to generation, despite having similar platforms for governing the country.

[8] Between 1921 and 1957, over-production of the country's oil reserves led to a depletion of this resource, leaving American oil companies with a profit of $1 billion, and Colombia with no oil. In those years American companies controlled 80 to 90 per cent of banana production and mining, and 98 per cent of energy production.

[9] In 1948, in Bogotá, Mayor Jorge Eliecer Gaitan of the Liberal Party was assassinated, and public indignation over his death triggered widespread riots, known as El Bogotázo. That same year, a Liberal mayor organized a guerrilla group, the first of 36 which were active during the presidencies of Ospina Pérez, Laureano Gómez and Rojas Pinilla. In 1957, a constitutional reform ensured the alternation of Liberals and Conservatives in the Government, every 12 years.

[10] The Revolutionary Armed Forces of Colombia (FARC), led by Manuel "Tiro Fijo" (Sure Shot) Marulanda and Jacobo Arenas, appeared on the scene in 1964. Guerrilla strategists included Camilo Torres Restrepo, a priest and co-founder of the National Liberation Army (ELN), who was killed in combat in 1965.

[11] Large landowners organized, armed and paid "self-defence" groups to fight these rural-based guerrilla movements. These were supported by members of the army and, in some cases, by foreign mercenaries. Closed out of official circles, the army also created paramilitary groups, later condemned by Amnesty International.

[12] From 1974, President Alfonso López Michelsen, a Liberal, tried to give greater attention to popular demands, but vested economic interests led to the failure of this policy. Figures for 1978 reveal that only 30 per cent of industrial workers and 11 per cent of the rural workforce had social security benefits. Colombia is dependent on international coffee prices on the US and German markets for its foreign exchange, as these countries consume 56 per cent of the Colombian product.

[13] Guerrilla movements, particularly FARC and the April 19 Revolutionary Movement (M-19), continued their activities into the late 1970s. Military repression grew during the Government of President Julio C Turbay Ayala (1978-82).

[14] In 1982, a divided Liberal Party nominated two candidates, thus handing the victory to the Conservative Party's Belisario Betancur, a journalist, poet and humanist, who had actively participated in the peace process in Central America. Betancur proposed that Colombia join the Non-Aligned Movement and reaffirmed the right of debtor nations to negotiate collectively with creditor banks. Also, in 1983 he entered into peace talks with leaders of the M-19.

[15] The M-19 had initiated the peace process in 1980, when guerrilla leader Jaime Bateman proposed a high-level meeting in Panama. Bateman subsequently died in a suspicious airline accident and talks were suspended. In the meantime, FARC and the

WORKERS

1997
UNEMPLOYMENT: 12.1%

% OF LABOUR FORCE   **1998**

■ FEMALE: 38%   ■ MALE: 62%

1990

■ SERVICES: 50.4%
■ INDUSTRY: 22.9%
■ AGRICULTURE: 26.6%

LAND USE

DEFORESTATION: 0.5% annual (1990/95)
IRRIGATED: 13.5% of arable (1993)

1993

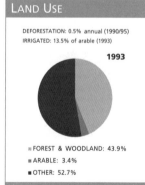

■ FOREST & WOODLAND: 43.9%
■ ARABLE: 3.4%
■ OTHER: 52.7%

PUBLIC EXPENDITURE

DEFENCE EXPENDITURE   **19.9%**
(% of goverment exp.)   (1997)

MILITARY EXPENDITURE   **57%**
(% of health & education)   (1990/91)

MATERNAL MORTALITY	LITERACY	FOOD DEPENDENCY	FOREIGN TRADE

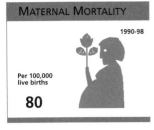

MATERNAL MORTALITY
1990-98
Per 100,000 live births
80

LITERACY
1995
90%

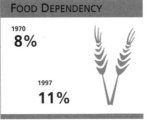

FOOD DEPENDENCY
1970
8%
1997
11%

FOREIGN TRADE
Millions US$ 1998
IMPORTS
20,159
EXPORTS
14,337

Government reached an agreement which led to a ceasefire between them and to the adoption of political, social and economic reforms.

16   Large landowners fiercely opposed talks between the Government and the guerrillas. The rural oligarchy, holding 67 per cent of the country's productive land, denounced the peace process as "a concession to subversion" and proposed the creation of private armies. Paramilitary action started up again; subsequent investigations revealed the hand of the *Muerte a los Secuestradores* (MAS - "death to the kidnappers"), which had opposed the withdrawal of the army from guerrilla-controlled areas. A one-year truce went into effect but M-19 withdrew five months later, claiming that the army had violated the ceasefire.

17   In January 1985, the Government passed a series of unpopular economic measures: drastic cuts in public spending, a salary freeze for civil servants, substantial fuel and transport price rises, increased taxes on over 200 products including some basic consumer goods, limited salary increases which lowered real purchasing power, and a currency devaluation. The object was to increase exports and reduce the $2 billion fiscal deficit by 30 per cent.

18   Rejected by the labor unions and the parties of the Left, the plan also failed to satisfy the country's creditors. A commission of 14 banks, presided over by the Chemical Bank, stated that the Government would have to sign a letter of intent and reach a formal agreement with the IMF, two steps which Betancur had wanted to avoid.

19   According to the Human Rights Commission, 80 prisoners had disappeared in one year, political prisoners had been tortured and 300 clandestine executions were confirmed. The number of political activists who had disappeared rose to 325.

20   On November 6 1985, 35 guerrillas from M-19 took over the Palace of Justice in Bogotá. The army attacked, causing a massacre. All the guerrillas were killed, along with 53 civilians, including magistrates and employees. A guerrilla commander known as Alonso insisted that those who had been killed "were deliberately sacrificed by the army".

21   Taking advantage of this panorama of violence, the drug lords and their traffickers have created a secure power base for themselves.

22   Over 2,000 left-wing activists were killed by terrorists, and in 1987 Jaime Pardo Leal, a member of the Patriotic Union, was assassinated. Liberal senator and presidential candidate in the 1990 election, Luis Carlos Galán - who had promised to dismantle the paramilitary groups and fight drugs - was assassinated in August 1989. War broke out between the Government and the drug mafia. In March 1990, Bernardo Jaramillo, the Patriotic Union's presidential candidate, was assassinated, with Carlos Pizarro (replacing Jaramillo) also killed 20 days later.

23   Official figures for the 1990s acknowledge the existence of more than 140 paramilitary groups, most financed by the drug mafia. Meanwhile, as part of its "War on Drugs", the United States Drug Enforcement Agency allegedly bombarded coca plantations with chemical herbicides.

24   Despite the huge profits generated by the planting, processing and export of drug products (which have given rise to an underground economy), agriculture continues to be the backbone of Colombia's legal economy. Despite using only 5 per cent of the land it represents 23 per cent of the GNP and in 1981 employed 21 per cent of the workforce.

25   The presidential elections of May 27 1990 were won by Liberal Party candidate Cesar Gaviria, who received 48 per cent of the vote in an election where the abstention rate was 58 per cent. The Movement for National Salvation obtained 23.7 per cent of the vote, the Democratic Alliance of the M-19 (ADM-19) 12.56 per cent, and the Conservative Party, 11.90 per cent.

26   In December 1990, elections were held to form a constituent assembly; there was a 65 per cent abstention rate. The number of votes received by ADM-19 was significant as they won 19 seats, 4 fewer than the Liberal Party (the party in power).

27   In June 1991, members of Gaviria's government met in Caracas with representatives of the Revolutionary Armed Forces of Colombia (FARC), the National Liberation Army (ELN) and the People's Liberation Army (EPL) - members of the Simón Bolívar Guerrilla Coordinating Committee, which controlled 35 per cent of the country. Talks dealt with the demobilization of guerrillas, the subordination of the armed forces to civilian authority, the dismantling of paramilitary groups and the reintegration of guerrilla fighters into areas where they could exert political influence.

28   On July 5 1991, the new constitution created the office of vice-president, eliminated the possibility of presidential re-election and included some major gains: civil divorce for Catholic marriages, direct election of local authorities, autonomy for indigenous peoples, the democratic tools of referendum and grassroots legislative initiatives, and guarantees of equal opportunities for women.

29   The Constitution met with criticism from the Left for failing to give civilian courts jurisdiction over members of the military accused of committing crimes against civilians and for granting judicial powers to State security agencies.

30   On October 27, an agreement between the President and the three major political forces participating in

PROFILE

ENVIRONMENT

The Andes cross the country from north to south, in three ranges: the western range on the Pacific coast, and further inland, the central and eastern ranges, separated by the large valleys of the Cauca and Magdalena Rivers. North of the Andes, the swampy delta of the Magdalena River opens up, leaving flat coastal lowlands to the west - along the Pacific coast- and to the east, plains covered by jungle and savannas extend downward to the Orinoco and Amazon Rivers. This diversity results in great climatic variety, from perpetual snows on Andean peaks to tropical Amazon rain forests. The country's Andean region houses most of the population. Coffee is the main export item, followed by bananas. Abundant mineral resources include petroleum, coal, gold, platinum, silver and emeralds. Intensive agriculture and mining have contributed to soil depletion. There is significant deforestation, and two-thirds of the country's bird species are in danger of extinction.

SOCIETY

Peoples: Colombians are descended from native Americans, Africans and Europeans.
Religions: 93 per cent are Catholic. Although this is the country's official religion, there is religious freedom.
Language: Spanish (official).
Political Parties: The New Democratic Force (NFD). The Liberal Party (LP); the Social Conservative Party (SCP); M-19 Democratic Alliance (ADM-19); National Salvation Movement (MSN), which broke away from the PSC; Patriotic Union, formed by the military.
Social Organizations: There are four major labor organizations: the Confederation of Colombian Workers; the Confederation of Workers' Unions of Colombia; and the General Labor Confederation. The Colombian United Labor Federation (CUT), founded on 26 September 1986, and 80 per cent of all salaried workers affiliated to trade unions are members.

THE STATE

Official Name: República de Colombia.
Administrative divisions: 32 departments and the capital district.
Capital: Santa Fé de Bogotá, 5,614,000 people (1995).
Other cities: Cali 1,718,900 people; Medellín 1,621,400; Barranquilla1,064,300; Cartagena 745,700 (1995).
Government: Andrés Pastrana, President since June 1998.
National Holiday: July 20, Independence Day (1810).
Armed Forces: 146,400 troops (1994).
Other: National Police Force, with 85,000 members. Coast Guard: 1,500 (1993).

the constituent assembly reduced the number of representatives. After the dissolution of Congress, parliamentary elections were held. The Liberal Party, split into several groups, obtained 60 per cent of the vote and support for the ADM-19 dropped to 10 per cent. In the March 1992 municipal elections, marked by a 70 per cent abstention rate, this trend was continued.

[31] The peace process reached a low point in 1992. After talks had been discontinued, the Government promoted its so-called "Integral War", which authorized intervention in civilian organizations with suspected links to rebel groups.

[32] The Simón Bolívar Coordinating Committee resisted the army offensive, continuing its campaign. In response, paramilitary groups resumed their activities, primarily in the Mid-Magdalena (River Valley) region, Boyaca and Medellín. Violence caused massive population displacement from conflict areas to other regions in the interior.

[33] In November, the Government decreed a state of emergency after Pablo Escobar Gaviria - head of the Medellín Cartel, a powerful drug-trafficking ring - had escaped from prison in mid-1992, stepping up the Cartel's violent actions. In January 1993 a group appeared known as "PEPES" - People Persecuted by Pablo Escobar. Within a two-month period, they killed 30 cartel members, destroyed several of Escobar's properties and harassed members of his family. The confrontation reached serious proportions, with car-bombs causing dozens of deaths.

[34] Finally, on December 2, Escobar was killed in a shoot-out with police forces in downtown Medellín. Although his death was a heavy blow to the political and social power of the Medellín Cartel, the drug-trafficking mafia still had many other operations, including the more discreet Cali Cartel, which emerged stronger.

[35] The Supreme Court of Justice decriminalized the use of cocaine, marijuana and other drugs, with the radical opposition of several political and religious circles, headed by President Gaviria.

[36] The coffee market crisis and the 1993 drought, as well as the reduction of banana quotas to the European Union, affected exports. However, with $2 billion per year from drug-trafficking and the discovery of oil in Casanare province, the country achieved a sustained growth of 2.8 per cent per capita. Construction grew 8 per cent in 1993, while both trade and transport increased by 5 per cent. Unemployment dipped below 9 per cent in the country's seven largest cities and wages maintained an upward trend. However, 45 per cent of the population were still living in abject poverty.

[37] President Gaviria was elected secretary-general of the Organization of American States (OAS), with the support of the United States, which welcomed the victory of Ernesto Samper, his party's candidate in the 1994 elections defeating Conservative Andrés Pastrana by 50 per cent to 48.6 per cent of the vote. Support for the ADM-19 dropped to 4 per cent of the vote, with abstentions slightly decreased to 65 per cent.

[38] The Samper Government began with a series of successful blows to drug-trafficking, but in September 1995 political scandal broke out when the Cali Cartel revealed details of that organization's contributions to both the Samper and Pastrana campaigns. Defense Minister Fernando Botero, Samper's former campaign director, was sent to prison for embezzling.

[39] In August 1996, Samper decreed a state of emergency to curb a wave of violence and kidnappings, a move considered an attempt to protect himself from drug-linked scandals. However, the murders of several opposition leaders and actions by FARC and the ELN, which attacked high-tension power lines, oil pipes, police and military facilities, continued. With fighting in almost 100 places, these two groups controlled growing areas in the economically powerful coffee region, the Caribbean and even in the vicinity of Bogotá and Medellín.

[40] Efforts to eradicate coca and opium poppy plantations continued, as well as armed operations against the Cartel's bases. Some of the Cali Cartel's main leaders, responsible for 70 per cent of cocaine traffic worldwide, gave themselves up. In March 1996 the US took Colombia off its list of countries which co-operate in the war on drugs. This measure ended bilateral aid to Colombia and blocked its access to foreign financial sources. Washington denied an entry visa to Samper, in an attempt to corner him diplomatically.

[41] Some 1,900 candidates decided not to run for the October 26 local elections because 49 mayors and city councillors had been killed and more than 180 kidnapped since the beginning of the year. In spite of the traditionally low turnout, over 5 million people enclosed symbolic "vote for peace" slogans onto their ballot papers.

[42] In November the Human Rights prosecutor revealed that since August 1995 his office had ordered disciplinary measures, including 50 dismissals, against 126 military and police officers for human rights abuses. In the same period, more than 600 cases were investigated against security forces members, related with 1,338 victims of murder, torture or disappearance. Some 500 kidnappings mainly by FARC and ELN were reported in the period.

[43] Several organizations estimated that since early 1997 one million Colombians had been displaced from their homes in conflict areas, mainly due to the activity of paramilitary groups. According to the Government, guerrilla groups obtained an annual net income $750 million, substantially more than that earned by coffee. The only sectors with higher earnings were the drug cartels of Medellín and Cali.

[44] US President Bill Clinton decided in February 1998 to reinstate Bogotá as a cooperating country in the drugs war , for "national interest" reasons. According to the World Bank, high homicide rates decreased the gross domestic product growth by 2 per cent per year.

[45] The worst defeat suffered by the armed forces in their 35-year fight against the guerrillas took place in March 1998, in Caqueta. Between 60 and 80 soldiers died in confrontation with FARC. The Government's military inferiority was revealed, causing the administration's worst crisis.

[46] In June 1998, former Bogotá Mayor Andrés Pastrana was elected President. The winner, from the conservative New Democratic Force party, obtained 50.4 per cent of the vote, ending the Liberal Party's 12-year hold on the presidency.

[47] In September, the Judicial Police carried out "Operation Infant" in several cities, raiding 250 houses and rescuing 255 children from a pedophile network and which trafficked children and produced pornographic videos. The ring was hidden behind a façade of off-licenses, video-bars and student residences.

[48] In November 1998, a cease-fire was proposed in order to show the world that all parties were committed to the peace process. However, as ratification of the truce was delayed the FARC intensified military operations in December and later that month attacked Jurado near the Panama border, killing several people. As a result of the attack, 23 marines, one police officer, one civilian and 42 guerrillas were killed, whilst 37 soldiers and police were wounded.

[49] In August 2000 US President Clinton visited to add $1.3 billion of support to the Government's Plan Colombia aimed at ending drug-trafficking and the 40-year-long civil war. ∎

Comoros

Comores

Population: 676,000 (1999)
Area: 2,230 SQ KM
Capital: Moroni
Currency: Comorian franc
Language: Arabic and French

Comoros was populated around the 5th century by one of the last Indonesian migrations (see Madagascar). The Comoros Islands remained isolated from the continent until the 12th century when Muslim traders from Kilwa settled on the islands, founded ports and reproduced the civilization of the eastern African coast (see Tanzania: The Zandj Culture in East Africa).

2   In the 16th century the Comoros had a prosperous economy but the Portuguese seized the islands and destroyed their active trade. When the Sultan of Oman finally drove the Portuguese from the region, the Comoros came under the influence of Zanzibar. The Bantu-speaking population, originally brought from the continent to work on the islands, increased considerably as a result of the slave trade.

3   In the 19th century, Zanzibar split from the sultanate of Oman and the French-occupied Mayotte in 1843. Colonial domination eventually spread to the entire archipelago as the islands' position on the Cape route gave them strategic value.

4   The Comoros National Liberation Movement (MOLINACO) was created in the context of successful anti-colonial struggles throughout Africa. It joined forces with the local Socialist Party (PASOCO) to form the United National Front (FNU) which pressured the French Government into holding a plebiscite in 1974. A large majority, 154,182 people, voted in favor of the islands' independence, and only 8,854 voted against.

5   Most of those who wished to remain under French rule were Mayotte residents (63 per cent of its voters). France had air and naval bases on Mayotte and the economy was controlled by a few dozen Catholic families, sympathetic to France and politically represented by the Mahorés People's Movement (MPM), led by Marcel Henry.

6   Ahmed Abdallah, the archipelago's leading rice exporter and Prime Minister of the semi-autonomous local government, proclaimed the independence of Comoros in July 1975, before the French announced the result of the referendum. Abdallah was afraid that his Udzima (Unity) Party would lose out to the FNU in a future assembly to draft a new constitution. The MPM took advantage of the situation to declare that Mayotte would continue under French rule. Paris supported the secession in order to maintain its military presence in the Indian Ocean, violating its previous commitment to respect the territorial integrity of Comoros and the result of the referendum. France did not oppose the islands' membership in the UN but vetoed specific Security Council resolutions to reincorporate Mayotte into the archipelago.

7   Less than a month before the declaration of independence, a small group of FNU youths seized the national palace in Moroni and appointed their leader, the socialist Ali Soilih, as president, in place of Ahmed Abdallah. France immediately reacted by sending a task force of three warships and 10,000 soldiers to Mayotte; one soldier for every three inhabitants.

8   In May 1978, a mercenary force, under the command of Ahmed Abdallah, in exile in Paris, landed on Grand Comoro (now Ndjazidja) overthrowing Ali Soilih, who was assassinated three days later. At the head of the operation was the notorious French mercenary Bob Denard, who had been tried in 1977 for mercenary acts of war against the Government of Benin. His presence in Comoros triggered international protests, to the point of the Comoros Islands' delegation being expelled from a ministerial meeting of the Organization for African Unity in Khartoum.

9   From then on, Denard became a key figure in the archipelago's politics, and Abdallah's control of the Government came to depend on support from Denard and his 650 troops.

10   On November 26 1989, a coup, led by Bob Denard succeeded in ousting President Ahmed Abdallah, who was killed in the fighting.

11   The European mercenaries were financed by South Africa. The Comoros were also said to have served as a supply base for RENAMO, the Mozambican South African-backed rebel group.

12   In the days following this coup, the French Government suspended all economic aid to the islands and initiated negotiations designed to

PROFILE

ENVIRONMENT

The Comoros Islands are located at the entrance of the strategic Mozambique Channel, on the oil tanker route between the Arab Gulf and western consumer nations. The four major islands of this volcanic archipelago are: Njazidja, formerly Grand Comoro; Nzwani, formerly Anjouan; Mwali, formerly Moheli; and Mahore, also known by its former name of Mayotte. Njazidja has an active volcano, Karthala, 2,500 meters in altitude. The mountainous island is covered by tropical forests. Only 37 per cent of the cultivated land is used to grow cash crops; vanilla and other spices, the rest is devoted to subsistence farming which is carried out without permanent rivers. The rainwater, which is stored in reservoirs, is easily polluted.

SOCIETY

Peoples: The original Malay-Polynesian inhabitants were absorbed by waves of Bantu and Arab migrations. Today, the latter groups predominate, co-existing with minor Indian and Malagasay communities.
Religions: Islam (official). There is one mosque for every 500 inhabitants.
Languages: Arabic and French are official. Most people speak Comoran, a Swahili dialect, and some groups speak Malagasay.
Political Parties: Comorian Union for Progress, formerly "Udzima"; National Union for Democracy in Comoros; Democratic Alliance; People's Democratic Movement; Comoros Party for Democracy and Progress; Socialist Party.
Social Organizations: The main organization is the Comoran Workers' Union.

THE STATE

Official Name: République Féderal et Islamique des Comores.
Capital: Moroni, 60,000 people (1995).
Other cities: Mutsamudu, 20,000 people; Domoni, 8,000; Fomboni, 5,600 (1991).
Government: Parliamentary republic. Col. Azzali Assoumani, President since April 1999. Tajidine Ben Said Massomde, Prime Minister since 1996.
National Holiday: July 6, Independence Day (1975).

WORKERS

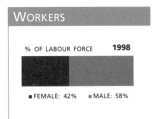

% OF LABOUR FORCE **1998**

■ FEMALE: 42%   ■ MALE: 58%

Mayotte

The Eighth Conference of Non-Aligned Countries, held in Harare (Zimbabwe), issued the following statement on France's failure to honor its commitment to respect Comoran territorial integrity: "The Heads of State or Government of the Non Aligned Countries reaffirmed the fact that the Comoran island of Mayotte, still under French occupation, is an integral part of the sovereign territory of the Federal Islamic Republic of the Comoros. They regret that the Government of France, despite repeated promises, has not, to date, adopted any measure or initiative that could lead to an acceptable solution of the problem of the Comoran Island of Mayotte".
In October 1991, the UN General Assembly reaffirmed the sovereignty of the Comoros over Mayotte by an overwhelming majority.

ENVIRONMENT

A mountainous island with tropical climate and heavy rainfall throughout the year. The island is of volcanic origin, has dense vegetation and is located at the entrance to the Mozambique Channel.

SOCIETY

Peoples: Native Mayotte inhabitants are of the same origin as Comorans. There is an influential community of French origin that controls the island's commerce.
Religions: 98 per cent Muslim. There is a Roman Catholic minority.
Languages: Arabic, Swahili, Comoran, and French (official).
Political Parties: the Mayotte Federation for the Organization of the Republic (RPR); the Mahoré People's Movement (MPM); the Party for the Democratic Organization of the Mahoré (PRDM), which seeks unification with the Comoros; the Union for French Democracy (UDF); the Social Democratic Center (CDS).

THE STATE

Official name: Collectivité Territoriale de Mayotte.
Capital: Dzaoudzi 22,000 people (est 1995).
Other cities: Mamoutzou 12,026 people (1985).
Government: Jean-Jaques Debacq, prefect, appointed by the French Government.

ECONOMY

Currency: CFA francs.

---

named Prime Minister, but less than a year later was forced to leave his position due to widespread protests.

[21] Denard attempted a new coup in September but - along with 1,000 followers - he ended up surrendering to French troops who arrived from Mayotte a few days later. The President was immediately freed. In October, when 80-year old Yohar had gone to Reunion for medical treatment, Prime Minister Caabi el Yachourtu Mohamed proclaimed himself "interim president", refusing to hand over the Government upon the head of state's return.

[22] Yohar recovered a "symbolic" presidency in January 1996 and general elections were held on March 6-17, won by Taki Abdoulkarim's National Union for Democracy in Comoros (NUDC).

[23] A month after becoming president, Taki Abdoulkarim dissolved the National Assembly and called for new elections to be held on October 6. The NUDC obtained 36 of the 43 seats at stake, in elections boycotted by the opposition.

[24] The 1996 Constitution, which replaced that of 1992, included among other innovations the creation of a Council of Ulemas to supervise respect of Islamic principles by future legislation. The death penalty, suspended in 1975, was restored.

[25] The World Bank financed a program to reduce communicable diseases. Malaria was the main cause of death in the country, affecting 20 per cent of children who died before their fifth birthday.

[26] In August 1997, a secessionist movement headed by Abdallah Ibrahim called for the independence of Anjouan island (now Nzwani), where half the population of Comoros lived. The intervention of the national army and a series of violent acts caused dozens of deaths in the following months.

[27] In March 1998, over 99 per cent of Anjouan (Nzwani) citizens voted for independence in a referendum. The vote was marred by the arrest in Moroni of a secession movement leader.

[28] Moheli (Mwali) island also demanded independence. The Organization of African Unity stated its wish that Comoros remain united and sent a delegation to both islands to monitor the situation.

[29] Three months before the planned elections, Taki Abdoulkarim died, at 62 years-old, from a heart attack. President of the Higher Council, Tadjidine Ben Said Massomde, took over as interim president.

[30] On April 23 1999, in Madagascar, an agreement was drafted granting greater

---

---

oust Denard and his mercenaries from the island. They left in mid-December, heading for South Africa, which allegedly had political and economic links to the former Comoran presidential guard. Prior to his departure, Denard is said to have turned over the responsibility for the armed forces to a French army contingent. The interim president of the Comoros permitted the French troops to stay on the islands for a further year or two.

[13] Legal restrictions on the formation of political parties ceased after Abdallah's death, and a number of opposition groups returned from exile.

[14] The IMF demanded a reduction of the number of civil servants. This instruction was carried out by the Government as of 1989 and has been extended in the last years. France was the main source of international credit, with Japan close behind.

[15] In August 1991, the Supreme Court of the Islamic Federal Republic of the Comoros found President Said Mohamed Yohar unfit to govern and guilty of serious negligence.

[16] An alliance of all the political parties of the Island of Mwali (25,000 inhabitants) demanded that central government divide civil service jobs and economic benefits, more fairly among the islands.

[17] After a failed attempt to oust the President in late 1991, the political parties and Yohar signed a national reconciliation pact. In January a new government was formed, headed by Mohammed Taki Abdoulkarim, leader of the National Union for Democracy in Comoros. At the same time, a National Conference drafted a new constitution, which was approved by referendum, in June 1992.

[18] In July 1992, President Yohar dismissed Taki Abdoulkarim and his government, accusing him of appointing a former French mercenary to his cabinet.

[19] In September, there was a failed coup against Yohar, led by two sons of former president Ahmed Abdallah. Several opposition leaders accused of conspiring against the Government were arrested and at least six civilians were killed.

[20] The first legislative elections were held between November and December. The opposition obtained 25 seats in the Assembly while the ruling party won 17. In June 1993, Ahmed Ben Cheikh Attoumane was

---

independence to Nzwami and Mwali, it established an interim government and a rotating presidency between the three islands. The Nzwami delegates declined to sign it, claiming they had to consult their electorate, and this action unleashed violent confrontations in both Ndjazdja and Nwani. The political instability precipitated a bloodless military coup on April 30. Colonel Azzali Assoumani took over as de facto president, promising to hold elections within 10 months. ■

Congo, Dem. Rep.

République Démocratique du Congo

Population: 50,336,000 (1999)
Area: 2,344,860 SQ KM
Capital: Kinshasa
Currency: Congolese franc
Language: French

The first known state to emerge in what is now DR Congo was the Luba kingdom, located in the Katanga (Shaba) region. The Luba Kingdom was created in the 16th century when a warrior named Kongolo subdued the small chiefdoms in the area and established a highly centralized state. To the northwest was the Kuba, a federation of numerous chiefdoms that reached its peak in the 18th century. Dr David Livingstone brought the region to the notice of the Western world through his explorations in Africa between 1840 and 1870. He met with Henry Stanley, a journalist and adventurer sent to seek him, in Ujiji in 1871. In 1876, King Leopold II of Belgium founded the International African Association (later, the International Association of Congo), a private organization that financed Henry Stanley's expeditions. Stanley succeeded in signing more than 400 trade and/ or protectorate agreements with local leaders along the Congo River. These treaties, and the Belgian trading posts established at the mouth of the river, were used to devise a system for the economic exploitation of the Congo. The Berlin Conference, 1884-1885, decided that the "Free State of Congo" was the Belgian King's personal property. Consequently, Leopold's "Compagnie du Katanga" stopped British colonialist Cecil Rhodes' northward expansion.

[2] The Congolese population was subjected to extremely harsh working conditions, which did not change when they formally became a Belgian colony in 1908. Military force was systematically employed to suppress anticolonial opposition and to protect the flourishing copper mining industry in Katanga (now Shaba).

[3] In 1957, liberalizing measures permitted the formation of African political parties. This led countless tribal-based movements to enter the political arena, all trying to benefit from the general discontent. Only the National Congolese Movement led by Patrice Lumumba had a national outlook, opposing secessionist tendencies and supporting independence claims.

[4] In 1959, the police suppressed a peaceful political rally triggering a series of bloody confrontations. King Baudouin of Belgium tried to appease the demonstrators by promising independence in the near future, but European residents of the Congo reacted with more oppressive measures. Independence was finally achieved in 1960, with Joseph Kasavubu as President and Lumumba as Prime Minister. A few days later, Moise Tshombe, then Premier of the Province of Katanga, initiated a secessionist movement.

[5] Belgium sent in paratroopers and the United Nations, acting under US influence, intervened with a "peacekeeping force". Kasavubu staged a coup and arrested Lumumba, delivering him to Belgian mercenaries in Katanga who killed him. The civil war continued until 1963. Secessionist activity ceased when Tshombe, who represented the neo-colonial interests, was appointed Prime Minister. With the help of mercenaries, Belgian troops and US logistical support, the Tshombe regime was able to stifle the nationalist opposition movement. In 1965, he was forced to resign by Kasavubu who was in turn overthrown by army commander Joseph Desiré Mobutu. For the transnationals, Mobutu was the only person in a position to restore the conditions required for them to continue operating there.

[6] Under the doctrine of "African authenticity", Mobutu changed the name of the country to Zaire and his own to Mobutu Sese Seko. However, his nationalism went little further than this, and the "Zairization" of copper, which he declared in 1975, only benefited an already wealthy economic elite and the state bureaucracy.

[7] Although these measures caused some discomfort among US diplomats, Mobutu offered Washington his services in the region.

[8] Zaire sheltered and actively supported the so-called National Front for the Liberation of Angola (FNLA). Mobutu encouraged secessionist groups in the oil-rich Angolan province of Cabinda, and Zaire's troops effectively cooperated with the South African racist forces in their war against the Angolan nationalists.

[9] Meanwhile, in Zaire guerrillas continued the struggle in the interior. In 1978 and 1979, the major offensive launched by the Congolese Liberation Front was checked with the aid of French and Belgian paratroopers and Moroccan and Egyptian troops, again with US logistical support.

[10] At the end of 1977, international pressure led to parliamentary elections being held for an institution which had been given limited legislative functions. This helped to divert international attention from human rights violations against students and intellectuals in the cities, the

WORKERS

% OF LABOUR FORCE **1998**

- FEMALE: 43%
- MALE: 57%

1990

- SERVICES: 18.8%
- INDUSTRY: 13.4%
- AGRICULTURE: 67.8%

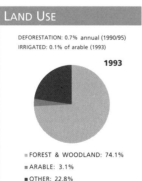

LAND USE

DEFORESTATION: 0.7% annual (1990/95)
IRRIGATED: 0.1% of arable (1993)

1993

- FOREST & WOODLAND: 74.1%
- ARABLE: 3.1%
- OTHER: 22.8%

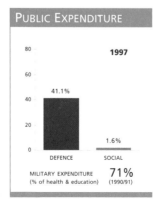

PUBLIC EXPENDITURE

1997

41.1% DEFENCE

1.6% SOCIAL

MILITARY EXPENDITURE
(% of health & education) **71%** (1990/91)

establishment of concentration camps for Mobutu's opponents and the brutal reception given to refugees who returned under an "amnesty" decreed in 1979.

[11] At this time Zaire was the world's largest cobalt exporter, the fourth biggest diamond exporter and ranked among the top ten world producers of uranium, copper, manganese and tin. But corruption was rampant throughout the country's administration, worsening the already unstable economic situation, and leading to soaring rates of unemployment.

[12] During 1980 and 1981, the major Western powers decided to seize direct control of the strategic mineral reserves in the country. The International Monetary Fund (IMF) took special interest in Zaire's economy, facilitating the renegotiation of its foreign debt, while at the same time imposing drastic measures against corruption. Zaire's economy was under direct IMF control, and the Fund's representatives in Kinshasa began to supervise the country's accounts personally.

[13] In April 1981, Prime Minister Nguza Karl I-Bond sought political asylum in Belgium; he presented himself to the western powers as a "decent alternative" to the official corruption in Zaire.

[14] The elections of June 1984 officially gave Mobutu 99.16 per cent of the vote.

[15] In February 1985, Zaire signed a security pact with Angola to improve relations between the two countries. These had deteriorated by the end of the previous decade because of Zaire's support of the FNLA and the Congolese Liberation Front, which operated from Angolan territory.

[16] In April 1990, anticipating the process of democratization which he considered imminent, Mobutu decided to take a bold step. He ended the one-party system, opened up the labor movement and promised to hold free elections within a year. A rapid process of political organization began. Hundreds of associations and political groups demanded legal recognition from the Government. The extent of the popular reaction frightened the authorities and on May 3, Mobutu issued a statement saying that no party had yet been legalized and that it would be necessary to modify the constitution before holding elections, because the head of state wished to "preserve his authority without exposing himself to criticism".

[17] Students initiated demonstrations throughout the country, especially at the university in Lubumbashi, capital of the province of Shaba. The students began calling for the resignation of Mobutu, who reacted by sending in his presidential guard to stifle the protests.

[18] The troops stormed the university campus at dawn on May 11. More than 100 students were killed and the terrified survivors fled to other provinces and Zambia, from where they condemned the massacre.

[19] The massacre at Lubumbashi University generated an anti-Mobutu wave which led to a series of strikes, like that at state-owned Gecamina, the country's most important mining company. In the United States there were repeated calls to end aid to Mobutu.

[20] In October 1990, under growing internal and external pressure, Mobutu decided to carry out a new political "democratization" process and he authorized the unrestricted creation of new political parties. In December, the opposition - grouped together under the Holy Union, a front made up of nine parties (including the four largest) - demanded Mobutu's resignation and called for a national conference to decide on the political future of Zaire without presidential intervention.

[21] In November 1991, the Holy Union formed a "shadow government", and appealed to the armed forces to depose Mobutu. The same month, the President appointed Nguza Karl I-Bond as his new Prime Minister - his fifth in that year. Nguza, a former opposition leader who had been Mobutu's head of government 10 years earlier, took office amidst a worsening economic crisis and growing international pressures, especially from the US.

[22] Early in 1992, the National Conference was set up. The opposition had long awaited this opportunity to press for constitutional reform and transition to democracy. In February of the same year, Prime Minister Nguza Karl-I Bond suspended the Conference, causing a faction of the army to rebel, taking over a state-run radio station and demanding President Mobutu's resignation. Some hours later the rebels were defeated by troops loyal to the Government. Thousands of demonstrators demanding the president's resignation and the reopening of the Conference were harshly repressed by the army, resulting in several deaths and many injuries.

[23] The European Community suspended financial aid to Zaire immediately, until the reinstatement of the National Conference. Meanwhile, representatives from the US, France and Belgium agreed to increase the pressure on the Mobutu government to speed up political change.

[24] In March 1992, after meetings with Conference president Archbishop Monsegwo Pasinya, President Mobutu appeared on radio and television to announce the reopening of the National Conference. Etienne Tshisekedi, leader of the Holy Union, was made Prime Minister, to replace Nguza Karl-I Bond. The delegates representing the Government and almost 160 groups resolved to return to the country's former name of the Congo Republic, which had been changed by Mobutu.

[25] Inter-ethnic strife erupted again in 1992. In Shaba there were outbreaks of violence after Karl-I Bond's dismissal. Lunda people, Karl-I Bond's group, attacked members of the Luba community, Tshisekedi's people. Some 2,000 people were killed, and thousands of Luba left Shaba as their homes had been destroyed. Security forces eventually intervened several weeks after the fighting broke out.

[26] The twelve commercial banks operating in Zaire closed indefinitely in 1992, due to a lack of funds. Inflation reached 16,500 per cent. According to a report by the Washington-based Population Crisis Committee, in 1992 Zaire was among the ten poorest countries in the world,

LITERACY	EXTERNAL DEBT	FOREIGN TRADE
1995	1998	Millions US$ 1997
 77%	Per capita **US$ 263**	IMPORTS **1,350** EXPORTS **1,463** 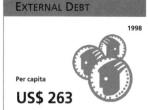

in 88th place on a scale of one to a hundred.

27   In December, galloping inflation prompted the Prime Minister to announce that the *zaire* would no longer be legal tender, placing a new currency in circulation. Regardless of this Mobutu ordered that troops receive their backpay in the old currency.

28   In early 1993, battles broke out between the soldiers, furious over having been paid in worthless bills, and Mobutu's personal guard. This confrontation caused over 1,000 deaths in Kinshasa, and the capital suffered looting, arson and attacks by irate soldiers.

29   On February 24, Mobutu's soldiers and tanks surrounded the building housing the High Council of the Republic, a transitional body formed by the National Conference, demanding that the 800 legislators approve the old currency which Mobutu had returned to circulation.

30   With the worsening situation, the US, Belgium and France sent a letter to Mobutu demanding that he resign in favor of a provisional government headed by Tshisekedi. Mobutu responded by dismissing Prime Minister Tshisekedi, in March 1993. Faustin Birindwa replaced him.

31   The economic and political uncertainty continued throughout 1994. The genocide in Rwanda and the arrival of masses of refugees - amongst whom were found thousands of members of the militias responsible for the massacre - created great tension in eastern Zaire.

32   When the Rwandan Patriotic Front (FPR) guerrillas came to power in Rwanda, several Western nations, including France, began to reduce the pressure on Mobutu - newly considered as a potential ally following the victory of "the English-speaking Tutsis" in the neighboring country. This reinforced the President's power, facilitating the nomination of Léon Kengo Wa Dondo as prime minister, though this was immediately challenged by the opposition.

33   At the end of 1995, the conflict between armed Tutsi groups and the remnants of the Rwandan army (mostly Hutu), assumed civil war proportions. The confrontation spread with government forces participating to put a stop to the advance of the Tutsi rebels, who had taken several cities in the east of the country. The Mobutu regime became seriously threatened when various opposition forces formed an alliance led by the veteran guerrilla leader Laurent Kabila. After convalescing in Switzerland for four months, Mobutu returned to face the situation in December. After a few weeks in the country during which he declared a general increase in army salaries, Mobutu returned to Switzerland.

34   In the first few months of 1997, opposition forces easily took over practically the whole country, and a group of states - South Africa, the US, France and Belgium included - attempted to mediate and seek a solution. South African president Nelson Mandela arranged a meeting between Mobutu and Kabila on a ship in international waters to negotiate the transition. However, the attempt was a failure, as Kabila demanded that Mobutu stand down as a pre-condition to the talks.

35   In March, Parliament sacked Prime Minister Kengo Wa Dondo, and a month later Étienne Tshisekedi was appointed as a replacement for his third term in office, with Mobutu's approval. Barely a week later, disagreements between the government parties led to Tshisekedi being replaced by Likulia Bolongo. Foreseeing the final outcome, the powerful mining companies began to negotiate with Kabila to protect their interests in Zaire.

36   On May 16, Mobutu fled to Morocco and opposition troops entered Kinshasa the following day. Kabila declared himself President. Mobutu died in Rabat on September 7 and the new strongman took over as President that month with full military, legislative and administrative powers. The new government changed the name of Zaire to the Democratic Republic of Congo and announced a series of economic recovery measures. Switzerland reopened an investigation into Mobutu's bank accounts there.

37   A study by Medecins Sans Frontières (MSF) in late 1997 revealed the massacrés committed by Kabila's troops and the Rwandan forces which supported him in defeating Mobutu. In April 1998, Kabila said he was prepared to allow United Nations inspectors back into the country to investigate the atrocities, although he disagreed with the procedures used by the international body. The UN had ordered the withdrawal of the previous mission after Kabila had accused the delegation of desecrating graves.

38   That month the nation was hit by the worst floods for 35 years, with large areas left under water and tens of thousands of people evacuated, mainly along the banks of the Congo river. The Government declared a state of emergency.

39   Under the leadership of intellectual Ernest Wamba dia Wamba, members of the Congolese Rally for Democracy (RCD, former members of the AFDL founded by Kabila himself), accused Kabila of returning to tribalism and set up an armed group made up of refugee Tutsis and demobilized Congolese soldiers. The Rwandan and Ugandan governments offered them support, providing weaponry and officers, and the group took control of half the country. Kabila, meanwhile, launched his resistance campaign under the banner "threat to Bantu civilization".

40   Conflict rapidly spread and other countries became involved. In response to an armed attack in April 1999, Kabila and the presidents of Angola, Zimbabwe and Namibia announced the formation of an alliance which would respond to an attack on any of the members. In this way, Angola, Zimbabwe and Namibia provided Kabila's army with troops and resources while Uganda and Rwanda increased their support for the rebels.

41   Two years after the outbreak of the civil war which brought Kabila to power, some provinces were under Ugandan and Rwandan control. ∎

STATISTICS

DEMOGRAPHY

Population: 50,336,000 (1999)
Annual growth: 3.3 % (1975/97)
Estimates for year 2015 (million):
80.3 (1999)
Annual growth to year 2015:
2.9 % (1997/2015)
Urban population: 29.2 % (1997)
Children per woman: 6.4 (1998)

HEALTH

Life expectancy at birth:
51 years (1998)
male: 49 years (1998)
female: 52 years (1998)
Infant mortality: 128 per 1,000 (1998)
Under-5 child mortality:
207 per 1,000 (1998)
Daily calorie supply:
1,815 per capita (1996)
Safe water: 42 % (1990/98)

EDUCATION

Literacy: 77 % (1995)
male: 87 % (1995)
female: 68 % (1995)
School enrolment:
Primary total: 72 % (1990/96)
male: 86 % (1990/97)
female: 59 % (1990/97)
Secondary:
male: 32 % (1990/96)
female: 19 % (1990/96)
Tertiary: 2 % (1996)
Primary school teachers:
one for every 45 (1994)

COMMUNICATIONS

3 newspapers (1996), 375 radios (1997), 41 TV sets (1996) and 1 main telephone lines (1996) per 1,000 people

ECONOMY

Per capita, GNP: $ 110 (1998)
Annual growth, GNP: 4.0 % (1998)
Annual inflation: 1,423.1 % (1990/98)
Consumer price index: 2,090.7 (1997)
Cereal imports: 572,800 metric tons (1998)
Fertilizer use: 9 kg per ha (1997)
Exports: $ 1,463 million (1997)
Imports: $ 1,350 million (1997)
External debt: $ 12,929 million (1998); $ 263 per capita (1998)
Debt service: 1.2 % of exports (1998)
Development aid received: $ 168 million (1997); $ 4.4 per capita (1997); 3.20 % of GNP (1997)

ENERGY

Consumption: 311.0 Kgs of Oil equivalent per capita yearly (1997); 1.0 % imported (1997)

HDI (rank/value): 141/0.479 (1997)

Congo Republic

République du Congo

Population: 2,864,000 (1999)
Area: 342,000 SQ KM
Capital: Brazzaville
Currency: CFA franc
Language: French

Today's Congo was originally populated by Pygmies and Bushmen (San). By the 16th century it comprised the Bantu states of Luango and Kacongo, for many years ruled by the Manicongo (see The Bantu States of the Congo). These nations managed to stave off early Portuguese attempts at colonization. Instead, for three centuries, under the Batekes of Anzico, they acted as suppliers and intermediaries of British and French slave dealers.

2 Towards the end of the 19th century, trade in rubber and palm oil replaced slave traffic. The new trade brought with it French colonization.

3 In 1880 French troops led by Savorgnan de Brazza began to colonize the Congo by force, and by the 1920s two-thirds of the local population had been killed. This genocide, along with the use of forced labor to build the Brazzaville-Pointe Noire railroad, resulted in the early emergence of independence movements with strong religious beliefs, under the leadership of Matswa.

4 After World War II, labor and student movements inspired by socialist ideas formed the backbone of resistance.

5 Sponsored by the French, Friar Fulbert Youlou led the Democratic Union for the Defence of African Interests and was the first president of independent Congo in 1960. Mass participation grew however and Youlu's neo-colonialist policies were rejected. A wave of demonstrations against corruption and the banning of trade unions ended in a popular uprising during the "three glorious days" (August 13-15) of 1963.

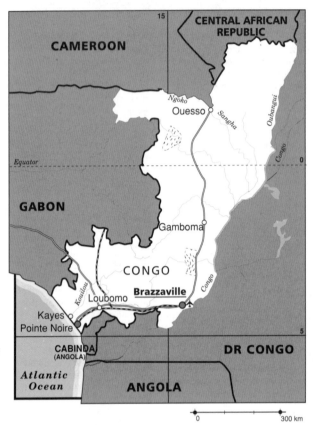

6 Youlou resigned and the President of the National Assembly, socialist Alphonse Massemba-Debat, took office and forced the French troops stationed in the country to withdraw. He then founded the National Movement of the Revolution (MNR) as the country's sole party.

7 This force could not coexist with the neo-colonial army, equipped and trained by the French, and the consequent crisis led Massemba-Debat to resign on January 1 1969. He was replaced by a young major, Marien N'Gouabi, backed by left-wing army officers. N'Gouabi founded a Marxist-Leninist party called the Congolese Worker's Party (PCT).

8 In 1973, a new constitution was approved, proclaiming the Congo a people's republic, and the State took control of energy, water, major industrial firms, and petroleum.

9 In December 1975, N'Gouabi made a public self-appraisal, issued a call "to extend the revolution", and launched a general review of party structures, the state apparatus and mass organizations.

10 To afford greater public participation in the running of the State, an ambitious educational reform was begun

and the structure of the Government was reformed. Until then all the school textbooks had come from France and were Eurocentric.

11 When Angola gained independence in 1975, Congo lost no time recognizing Agostinho Neto's government. His clear position on the problem of Cabinda was decisive in frustrating attempts to have this oil-rich province break away from Angola, a scheme which was being promoted by transnational companies with interests in the Congo.

12 On March 18 1977, N'Gouabi was assassinated by followers of ex-president Massemba-Debat. The conspirators failed in their efforts to seize power, however, and Massemba-Debat was executed.

13 The new president, Colonel Joachim Yombi Opango, did not maintain N'Gouabi's austere style and was forced to resign on February 6 1979, charged with corruption and abuse of power. Denis Sassou N'Guesso replaced him.

14 N'Guesso launched a campaign against corruption in the public sector, as well as a broad administrative and ministerial reform. Toward the end of 1981, the Congo faced foreign trade difficulties directly linked to inefficiency in state enterprises which the Government refused to close.

15 In 1982, the Congo's finances improved. Part of the recovery was attributed to oil exports, which financed 49.44 per cent of the budget.

16 Congolese oil was exploited in partnership with French, US and Italian firms. Annual exports approached eight million tons of crude in 1988.

17 President N'Guesso's foreign policy was pragmatic; he sought closer relations with Eastern Europe, while maintaining commercial ties with the United States and France. He played a leading role in negotiations between Angola, South Africa and Cuba, which culminated in the signing of a peace settlement for the region in December 1988, in Brazzaville, paving the way for Namibia's independence.

18 The fall of the Berlin Wall and the demise of the Soviet Union precipitated political and economic changes. In December 1990, the

WORKERS

% OF LABOUR FORCE **1998**

■ FEMALE: 43% ■ MALE: 57%

1990

■ SERVICES: 36.6%
■ INDUSTRY: 14.7%
■ AGRICULTURE: 48.7%

LAND USE

DEFORESTATION: 0.2% annual (1990/95)
IRRIGATED: 0.7% of arable (1993)

1993

■ FOREST & WOODLAND: 61.7%
■ ARABLE: 0.4%
■ OTHER: 37.9%

PUBLIC EXPENDITURE

DEFENCE EXPENDITURE (% of goverment exp.)	**12.3%**	(1997)
MILITARY EXPENDITURE (% of health & education)	**37%**	(1990/91)

LITERACY   1995

74%

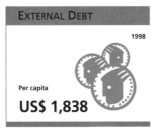

EXTERNAL DEBT   1998

Per capita

US$ 1,838

FOREIGN TRADE

Millions US$ 1998

IMPORTS

1,409

EXPORTS

1,236

country adopted a multiparty system. In July 1991, André Milongo took the post of Prime Minister until presidential elections could be held. This decision caused confrontation in the streets and the formation of a transition Government with army participation. Following elections in August 1992, Pascal Lissouba succeeded Sassou N'Guesso.

[19] In the early legislative elections of May 1993, the ruling party won 62 seats against the opposition coalition's 49. The opposition accused the Government of fraud and further clashes between demonstrators and the military left six people dead.

[20] President Pascal Lissouba named retired military officer, Jacques Yhombi-Opango, as Prime Minister, which led the opposition to form a parallel government led by Bernard Kolelas. In July and December, fresh disturbances caused the death of some 80 people. Meanwhile, the Government remained bankrupt and only paid civil servants 7 of their 12 pay packets in 1993.

[21] In January 1994, the army called in the artillery to counteract attacks from armed opposition groups. The disturbances caused the death of more than 100 people. An agreement between the opposition and the Government, in mid-March, marked the beginning of a cease-fire. Later, in July, the election of Kolelas as mayor of Brazzaville further calmed the situation, allowing for a public reconciliation ceremony the following month.

[22] During 1994 Lissouba accepted the IMF structural adjustment programme, including the reduction of the number of civil servants. Competition between various oil multinationals threatened the dominance of the French Elf in Congo, leading the company to increase the amount of profit reinvested in the country from 17 to 31 per cent.

[23] 1995 was dominated by the quest for a definitive agreement to disarm the anti-government urban militias and to eventually integrate them into the official army. On February 19 a general strike was started calling for the payment of overdue salaries. On March 1, an agreement was made including a reduction in salaries in return for a drop in working hours, but this was rejected by the civil servants.

[24] Fighting started in June 1997 when the Government aimed to disarm and arrest Denis Sassou N'Guesso and some of his followers. In November, following four months of civil war, the opposition forces defeated President Lissouba, with the help of Angolan troops, appointing N'Guesso in his place. The fighting often degenerated into pillaging from the local population.

[25] N'Guesso formed a new government in Brazzaville and prepared to stamp out the "ninja" militias, the self-proclaimed resistance forces led by Kolelas.

[26] In January 1998, Brazzaville and Kinshasa began negotiations to set the border for the two territories along the 2,410 km of common frontier. During that year, N'Guesso strengthened his army with weapons acquired from the "Russian mafia", and he put Israeli officers in charge of his personal guard.

[27] On November 16, 1999, a ceasefire agreement was signed between N'Guesso and the resistance forces, and this was confirmed on December 29, with the mediation of Gabon's president Omar Bongo. N'Guesso freed prisoners in line with the agreement, and during January 2000, thousands of rebels gave up their arms. In February, Kolelas ratified his recognition of N'Guesso as president. ∎

PROFILE

ENVIRONMENT

The country comprises four distinct regions: coastal plains; a central plateau (separated from the coast by a range of mountains rising to 800 meters); the Congo River basin in the northeast; and a large area of marshland. The central region is covered with dense rain forests and is sparsely populated. Two- thirds of the population live in the south, along the Brazzaville-Pointe Noire railroad. Lumber and agriculture employ more than one third of the population. The country has considerable mineral resources including oil, lead, gold, zinc, copper and diamonds. The environmental situation is characterized by haphazard urban development, the accumulation of refuse, a lack of sewage facilities, the proliferation of contagious diseases, pollution, deforestation and the disappearance of native fauna.

SOCIETY

Peoples: The Congolese are of Bantu origin; the Bakongo prevail in the South, the Teke (or Bateke) at the center; the Sanga and Vilil in the North.
Religions: The vast majority of the population practice traditional African cults. Christian elements are assimilated into these cults.
Languages: French (official), Kongo and various local dialects.
Political Parties: Pan-African Union for Social Democracy; Congolese Workers' Party (PCT); Congolese Movement for Democracy and Integral Development.
Social Organizations: The four existing labor organizations merged in 1964 to form the Congolese Labor Confederation (CSC).

THE STATE

Official Name: République du Congo.
Administrative divisions: 8 regions and 6 communes.
Capital: Brazzaville 1,009,000 people (1995).
Other cities: Pointe Noire 576,200 people; Loubomo 83,600 people (1992).
Government: Parliamentary republic. Denis Sassou N'Guesso, President since November 1997. Bernard Kolelas, Prime Minister since November 1997.
National Holiday: August 15, Independence Day (1960).
Armed Forces: 10,000.
Other: 6,100: Gendarmerie (1,400); People's Militia (4,700).

STATISTICS

DEMOGRAPHY

Population: 2,864,000 (1999)
Annual growth: 2.9 % (1975/97)
Estimates for year 2015 (million): 4.4 (1999)
Annual growth to year 2015: 2.8 % (1997/2015)
Urban population: 60.2 % (1997)
Urban Growth: 5.6 % (1980/95)
Children per woman: 6.0 (1998)

HEALTH

Life expectancy at birth: 49 years (1998)
male: 46 years (1998)
female: 51 years (1998)
Infant mortality: 81 per 1,000 (1998)
Under-5 child mortality: 108 per 1,000 (1998)
Daily calorie supply: 2,107 per capita (1996)
27 doctors per 100,000 people (1993)
Safe water: 34 % (1990/98)

EDUCATION

Literacy: 74 % (1995)
male: 83 % (1995)
female: 67 % (1995)
School enrolment:
Primary total: 114 % (1990/96)
male: 119 % (1990/97)
female: 109 % (1990/97)
Secondary:
male: 62 % (1990/96)
female: 45 % (1990/96)
Tertiary: 8 % (1996)
Primary school teachers: one for every 70 (1995)

COMMUNICATIONS

8 newspapers (1995), 124 radios (1997), 7 TV sets (1996) and 8 main telephone lines (1996) per 1,000 people

ECONOMY

Per capita, GNP: $ 680 (1998)
Annual growth, GNP: 11.4 % (1998)
Annual inflation: 7.1 % (1990/98)
Currency: 590.0 CFA francs = $ 1 (1998)
Cereal imports: 210,779 metric tons (1998)
Fertilizer use: 286 kg per ha (1997)
Exports: $ 1,236 million (1998)
Imports: $ 1,409 million (1998)
External debt: $ 5,119 million (1998); $ 1,838 per capita (1998)
Debt service: 3.3 % of exports (1998)
Development aid received: $ 268 million (1997); $ 117.3 per capita (1997); 14.70 % of GNP (1997)

ENERGY

Consumption: 459.0 Kgs of Oil equivalent per capita yearly (1997); -990.0 % imported (1997)

HDI (rank/value): 135 /0.533 (1997)

Slavery and sub-Saharan Africa

In the 13th century when the Europeans began to penetrate the region of Africa below the Sahara, lured by the promise of gold and ivory, they rediscovered slavery, which had become more or less obsolete in Catholic Europe. The practice, widespread in sub-Saharan Africa since pre-Islamic times, had expanded further with the arrival of Islam to the point that some 18 million black Africans were traded in the Islamic world between 865 and 1905. After this "rediscovery", in the second half of the 15th century, the Portuguese began to trade slaves from the west coast of Africa, taking first European slaves and later Berber slaves to the kingdom of Ghana.

But the scale and nature of slavery underwent major changes as the first wave of what we now call globalization began. After Europeans conquered the Americas and circumnavigated the world, "black Africa" was transformed by the wishes and needs of people living in far distant lands. The conquest of the Americas changed the status of slaves and how they were seen, as Europeans believed that Africans – like the Amerindians - were not "fully human". Once Spain sought African slaves in the early 16th century to replace the Amerindian workforce in its colonies, the "denial of humanity" was transferred from the indigenous people to the African slaves, with some 10 million brought to the New World by 1867.

LINES ON A MAP

The Europeans' contempt towards the African "savages" meant that they did not reach the interior of the continent until the mid-19th century, when the slave trade had already declined considerably. The European powers, requiring minerals and other raw materials to feed the industrial revolutions at home, parceled out the continent among themselves. In 1884 Africa was divided into 48 new states by the European powers at the Berlin Conference. The creation of this patchwork map did not respect local cultures or the geopolitical realities of the time: some peoples were divided and others, diverse and often ancestral enemies, were thrown together in order to meet the needs of the new European era.

The chaos and devastation that sub-Saharan Africa has suffered since the "decolonization" process begun after World War II is undoubtedly a product of that partition. But it is also the result of an even greater conceit: the assumption that herders and hunters could or should adapt to the dictates of the European cultures. And nowadays the assumption is that these countries can be inserted into the most recent globalization process - one that no longer requires colonies as such but feeds institutions that encourage the development of an ever-more enslaving capitalism.

NATION STATES

The first modern nation-states were in the Americas, an achievement bought at the price of genocide perpetrated by the "Creole" population (those of European origin) against the indigenous people who did not adapt to the demands of capitalism. Even among the European elite, this process sparked constant internal and external wars, both in "Anglo" and "Latin" America.

The sub-Saharan African countries were expected to become nation-states in a very short period of time. Lacking a European elite such as there had been in the Americas, the African countries had to establish states based on heterogeneous societies, while also taking on the demands of an interlinked world that called for modern and "globalized" behavior of its citizens. Paradoxically, these nations are at an historic moment at the global level, but internally some have been cursed with genocide. In response we have witnessed the horror expressed by countries like the US - which reinforced its own territorial and material wealth through the systematic extermination of its native peoples – and also the European countries which built their strength on the exploitation of slaves and natural wealth from Africa.

The plundering and exploitation the West inflicted on sub-Saharan Africa throughout the centuries, most notoriously through the slave trade, has left painful problems for the continent. Some seem to have no solution: for example, how will herders, hunters and gatherers escape or survive the fast-spinning wheels of Western capitalism. ∎

Costa Rica

Costa Rica

Population: 3,933,000 (1999)
Area: 51,100 SQ KM
Capital: San José
Currency: Colón
Language: Spanish

When the first Europeans arrived on its shores, the territory of present-day Costa Rica was populated by a number of small tribes of the Chorotega, Cobici, Carib and Boruca nations. Christopher Columbus reached the coast of Costa Rica - "the rich coast" - on his last voyage in 1502. Although the first contact was friendly, the local people were not easily dominated by the Europeans, and it took nearly 60 years for a permanent settlement to be established in the region.

2 Gaspar de Espinosa, Hernán Ponce de León and Juan de Castañeda travelled along the coast of the territory between 1514 and 1516. Between 1560 and 1564, they were followed by Juan de Cavallón, Juan de Estrada Rabago and Juan Vásquez de Coronado. The conquest of the territory was consolidated in the second half of the 16th century.

3 The Spanish established the first permanent settlement, the town of Cartago, on the central plain in 1564. This was assigned to the political jurisdiction of the Captaincy-General of Guatemala, while remaining under the spiritual guidance of the bishop of Nicaragua.

4 The indians' resistance kept the colonizers isolated for a long time. They were unable to establish a system of *encomiendas* - the virtual enslavement of the indian work force. In this way a patriarchal society of small landowners was formed, with no powerful land-owning oligarchy as in the neighboring countries. This might explain how, instead of becoming a nation scourged by civil wars and military dictatorships, modern Costa Rica maintained greater democratic

stability and has not established a regular army like the other countries in the region.

5 When Mexico declared independence from Spain in 1821, Costa Rica, along with other former Spanish colonies in Central America, formed part of the Mexican empire. In 1823, Costa Rica helped create the United Provinces of Central America and remained a part of this federation until its dissolution in 1840. A persistent opponent to the "Balkanization" brought about by British imperialism, Costa Rica's territory was used as a base for operations by Francisco Morazán - an advocate of Central American unity - until 1848, when Costa Rica became an independent state.

6 In the mid-19th century, William Walker - a US national who had taken control of Nicaragua - tried to extend his dominion over the Central American isthmus. He was defeated by forces commanded by the Costa Rican President Juan Rafael Mora. Material progress reached Costa Rica during the regime of General Tomás Guardia, who ruled the nation from 1870 to 1882. While his administration took away some liberties and increased foreign debt, coffee and sugar production rose and more schools were built. The constitution adopted in 1871 remained in place until 1949.

7 The last decades of the 19th century were marked by a gradual reduction of Church

influence in secular affairs. Cemeteries were secularized and the Jesuits expelled from the country for a few years. In 1886, primary education became obligatory and free. Schools were founded, along with a museum and a national library. In 1890, José Joaquín Rodríguez was elected President in what were considered the first free and fair elections in Central America.

8 In 1916, Nicaragua gave the US permission to use the San Juan river, which forms the frontier with Costa Rica. The San José Government protested that its rights had been overlooked and the complaint was taken to the Central American Court of Justice which ruled in favor of Costa Rica. Nicaragua rejected the verdict and withdrew from the Court. This was one of the main reasons for the dissolution of the Court a year later.

9 Costa Ricans had their first elections with direct voting in 1913. There was no outright winner and the Legislative Assembly designated Alfredo González Flores as President. General Federico Tinoco Granados, unhappy with the reforms proposed by González, led one of the few coups experienced by the nation, in 1917. But the lack of US recognition for his government and the threat of intervention forced Tinoco to resign in 1919.

10 Between 1940 and 1948 the Government was backed by coffee plantation owners and bankers. However in 1948 opposition leader Otilio Ulate, nominated by the National Unity Party, won a presidential election which was annulled by Congress. This unleashed civil war which ended with a junta seizing power, presided over by José Figueres. The junta issued a call for the election of new representatives, who in turn confirmed Ulate's victory. A year later, a new constitution was ratified, establishing a presidential system of government and prohibiting the formation of armies.

11 The populist revolution led by Figueres spread anti-dictatorial ideas throughout Central America.

WORKERS

1997
UNEMPLOYMENT: 5.7%

% OF LABOUR FORCE **1998**

■ FEMALE: 30% ■ MALE: 70%

1990

■ SERVICES: 47.2%
■ INDUSTRY: 26.8%
■ AGRICULTURE: 26.0%

LAND USE

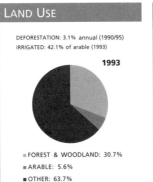

DEFORESTATION: 3.1% annual (1990/95)
IRRIGATED: 42.1% of arable (1993)

1993

■ FOREST & WOODLAND: 30.7%
■ ARABLE: 5.6%
■ OTHER: 63.7%

PUBLIC EXPENDITURE

1997

59.6%

3.1%

DEFENCE   SOCIAL

MILITARY EXPENDITURE **5%**
(% of health & education) (1990/91)

12   José Figueres was elected President in 1954 and during his administration Costa Rica became a strongly anti-communist welfare state. In 1958, the conservatives defeated Figueres and imposed an import-substitution development model.

13   The traditional antagonism between liberals and conservatives gave way to new tensions between the National Liberation Party (PLN), led by Figueres, and a heterogeneous group consisting of various small parties. In 1966, the opposition managed to form an electoral coalition, the United National Opposition which elected José Joaquín Trejos to the presidency.

14   After the 1970 election, the PLN returned to power with Figueres, who remained in office until 1974, when Daniel Odúber Quirós, co-founder of the Party in 1950, was elected President.

15   Odúber tried to restore unity to the Central American Common Market, left in a critical situation after the 1969 war between El Salvador and Honduras. However, his obvious pro-democracy stance did not meet with the approval of Somoza's regime in Nicaragua.

Costa Rica was constantly harassed by its neighbor and became a safe haven for thousands of political refugees.

16   1975 saw a rise in wages due to favorable conditions resulting from the nationalization of transnational oil companies and the rise in coffee prices on the world market .

17   In 1978, contrary to all expectations, presidential elections gave the victory to a conservative coalition which had been critical of the previous government's administration. The leftist bloc, grouped in the United People's Coalition, increased considerably and became the third most important political force. However they remained isolated and unable to propose social changes within the democratic and pluralist system favored by the majority.

18   The new President, Rodrigo Carazo Odio, imposed an unpopular economic policy prescribed by the International Monetary Fund (IMF), which resulted in growing confrontation with labor and left groups. In 1979 however, encouraged by popular sympathy towards the Sandinista rebels, and under threat of invasion by neighboring dictator Anastasio Somoza, the Costa Rican Government decided actively to support the Nicaraguan Sandinistas.

19   A radically different attitude was taken in 1980 with regard to El Salvador's insurgency. In spite of grave and continuous human rights violations in that country, the San José Government supported the Salvadoran military junta. In 1981 President Carazo broke off diplomatic relations with Cuba.

20   In January 1982, the US-backed Central American Democratic Community was set up in San José with the main objective of isolating revolutionary Nicaragua.

21   Luis Alberto Monge, a right-wing PLN candidate, became President in February 1982. When he took office in May, Monge proclaimed his alignment with Western democracies, and announced economic austerity measures. At the same time, he fostered closer ties with the governments of El Salvador, Guatemala and Honduras, thus aggravating relations with Nicaragua.

22   Costa Rica's hostile attitude towards its neighbor was clearly demonstrated when the US declared a commercial embargo on Nicaragua's revolutionary Government. A series of border incidents brought relations between the two countries to breaking point during July and August 1985. However, prompt action taken by the Contadora Group checked mounting tension in the area; both governments agreed to place neutral observers along the common frontier to arbitrate any further border clashes.

23   The winner of the February 1986 presidential election was Social Democrat Oscar Arias, who won a tight victory with 52 per cent of the vote.

24   Arias devoted himself to the task of designing a policy which would break both the logic of war and the escalating tension within the region. In August 1987 he presented a peace plan at a summit meeting held in Esquipulas, Guatemala. This was accepted and signed by the Presidents of El Salvador, Nicaragua, Guatemala and Honduras. The focal points of the plan were: a simultaneous cease-fire in Nicaragua and El Salvador, an immediate end to American aid to the Nicaraguan "contras", a democratization time-table for Nicaragua which included holding free elections and putting an end to the use of foreign territory as supply or attack bases.

25   The signing of this peace plan, known as "Esquipulas II", earned Costa Rica a special place in international relations, and constituted a personal triumph for President Arias, who received the Nobel Peace Prize in October 1987 in recognition of his efforts.

26   During his term, Arias instituted the first phase, and later the second, of a structural adjustment programme, with World Bank support. The objective of this programme was the transformation of

PROFILE

ENVIRONMENT

A mountain range with major volcanic peaks stretches across the country from northwest to southeast. Costa Rica has the highest rural population density in Latin America, with small and medium sized farmers who use modern agricultural techniques. Coffee is the main export crop. The lowlands along the Pacific and the Caribbean have different climate and vegetation. Along the Caribbean coast there is dense, tropical rainforest vegetation. Cocoa is grown in that region. The Pacific side is drier; extensive cattle raising is practiced along with artificially irrigated sugar cane and rice plantations. Deforestation has been partially responsible for soil erosion and reduced fertility.

SOCIETY

Peoples: Costa Ricans, usually called *ticos* in Central America, are descended from the integration between native Americans and European migrants, mainly Spanish. African descendants, who were brought in from Jamaica, make up 3 per cent of the population and are concentrated along the eastern coast. Indigenous peoples, 1 per cent.
Religions: 81.3 per cent of the population are Catholic; Evangelical Protestant 15 per cent.
Languages: Spanish is the official language, spoken by the majority. Mekaiteliu, a language derived from English, is spoken in the province of Limón (east coast). Several indigenous languages.
Political Parties: Social Christian Unity Party (PUSC); National Liberation Party (NLP), social democrat; Democratic Force, center-left coalition; "Cargagines" Agricultural Union, regional: the Agrarian Party.
Social Organizations: The Unitary Workers' Union (CUT); the 50,000-member CUT groups both workers and peasants from the National Federation of Civil Servants, the National Peasant Federation; the Federation of Industrial Workers, regional federations and smaller unions. 375 cooperatives.

THE STATE

Official Name: República de Costa Rica.
Administrative Divisions: 7 Provinces.
Capital: San José 1,450,000 people (1995).
Other cities: Limón 56,525 people; Alajuela 49,190; Cartago 109,000 (1992).
Government: Miguel Angel Rodríguez, president since January 1, 1998. Legislature, single-chamber Assembly, made up of 57 members.
National Holiday: September 15, Independence Day (1821).
Armed Forces: Abolished in 1949.
Paramilitaries: 7,500 Civil Guard, Frontier Guard and Rural Guard (1994). tw 26/11/99.

FOOD DEPENDENCY

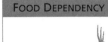

1997

13%

EXTERNAL DEBT

1998

Per capita

US$ 1,034

FOREIGN TRADE

Millions US$ 1998

IMPORTS

5,326

EXPORTS

5,132

DEMOGRAPHY

Population: 3,933,000 (1999)
Annual growth: 3.0 % (1975/97)
Estimates for year 2015 (million):
5.2 (1999)
Annual growth to year 2015:
1.9 % (1997/2015)
Urban population: 50.3 % (1997)
Urban Growth: 3.6 % (1980/95)
Children per woman: 2.8 (1998)

HEALTH

Life expectancy at birth: 76 years
(1998)
male: 74 years (1998)
female: 79 years (1998)
Maternal mortality: 29 per 100,000
live births (1990-98)
Infant mortality: 14 per 1,000
(1998)
Under-5 child mortality:
16 per 1,000 (1998)
Daily calorie supply: 2,822 per
capita (1996)
126 doctors per 100,000 people
(1993)
Safe water: 96 % (1990/98)

EDUCATION

Literacy: 95 % (1995)
male: 95 % (1995)
female: 95 % (1995)
School enrolment:
Primary total: 107 % (1990/96)
male: 108 % (1990/97)
female: 107 % (1990/97)
Secondary:
male: 48 % (1990/96)
female: 52 % (1990/96)
Tertiary: 33 % (1996)
Primary school teachers: one for
every 29 (1997)

COMMUNICATIONS

94 newspapers (1996), 271 radios
(1997), 221 TV sets (1996) and 155
main telephone lines (1996) per
1,000 people
Books: 29 new titles per 100,000
people (1992/94)

ECONOMY

Per capita, GNP: $ 2,770 (1998)
Annual growth, GNP: 4.7 % (1998)
Annual inflation: 17.6 % (1990/98)
Consumer price index: 148.6 (1998)
Currency: 257.2 colones = $ 1
(1998)
Cereal imports: 594,977 metric tons
(1998)
Food import dependency: 13 %
(1997)
Fertilizer use: 9,018 kg per ha
(1997)
Exports: $ 5,132 million (1998)
Imports: $ 5,326 million (1998)
External debt: $ 3,971 million
(1998); $ 1,034 per capita (1998)
Debt service: 7.6 % of exports
(1998)

ENERGY

Consumption: 769.0 Kgs of Oil
equivalent per capita yearly (1997);
57.0 % imported (1997)

HDI (rank/value): 45/0.801 (1997)

industry through technological modernization, increased efficiency and greater productivity. Neo-liberal formulas were applied, following the dictates of international financial organizations. However, according to the labor unions, these "prescriptions" were formulated without looking at their social repercussions.

27   In July 1989, an investigation into drug trafficking was carried out by a parliamentary commission. The report produced by the Commission found both of the main political parties (the PLN and the PUSC) guilty of receiving drug money during the 1986 electoral campaign. At the same time, another scandal broke out over the financing of electoral campaigns, with accusations that both parties - and Oscar Arias individually - had received money from Panamanian General Noriega in 1986.

28   Between March and July 1988 the structural adjustment policy of the Arias Government led to public discontent and demonstrations by many sectors of the population. Public employees protested against the concessions made to the IMF and the World Bank. The peasant unions staged a one-week strike to protest against the agrarian policy, and farmers went on strike several times.

29   The situation worsened throughout 1989 and in August a coalition of regional trade union federations, professional guilds, and citizens' groups called for a strike in the province of Limón. The strike paralyzed sea traffic on the Caribbean coast for four days. Some sectors on the Atlantic coast also joined the protests. In September, teachers staged a nationwide strike.

30   In 1990, women officially made up 29.9 per cent of the economically active population, but their number on the informal job market was estimated at 41 per cent. In the political arena women held only 15 per cent of posts. Women's organizations observed an increase in teenage prostitution through prostitution rings, which have become multi-million-dollar businesses for their owners.

31   Under the slogan of "change" and focusing specifically on low-income groups with lower educational levels, the social Christian candidate Rafael Angel Calderón won the election held in February 1990 by a wide margin. In addition, he obtained an absolute majority in the legislature.

32   The application of a severe economic adjustment program led to a reduction in the State apparatus as well as in the fiscal deficit, which had reached 3.3 per cent of GDP. As a result of these cuts, unemployment rose and popular discontent increased.

33   In the 1994 elections, social democrat candidate José María Figueres defeated government candidate Miguel Rodriguez by a narrow, after a campaign with few differences in their political positions but with notably harsh speeches from the rival parties.

34   A free trade agreement was signed with Mexico in January 1995. However, the deterioration of the economy, with rising inflation and a fiscal deficit led the Government to increase taxes in order to balance the budget. The World Bank rejected the economic plan and refused to finance the structural adjustment schedule.

35   In 1996, the governing PLN agreed a budget plan with the opposition which limited the Government deficit to 1 per cent of the Gross Domestic Product. In late July, Hurricane Caesar struck Costa Rica, especially the south, causing some 30 deaths. The damage was estimated at around $100 million. The kidnappings of one German and another Swiss tourist dealt a blow to the tourist industry. Both were freed two and a half months later. Many tourist operators preferred not to run the risk and took Costa Rica off their list of destinations.

36   In June 1997, San José ratified the Interamerican Convention on Forced Detentions. Amnesty International urged the Government to put an end to police abuse against prisoners and refugees, who were mostly Nicaraguans.

37   In February 1998, Miguel Angel Rodríguez, the Social Christian Unity Party (PUSC) candidate was elected president, with the PUSC also gaining the majority of seats in the parliamentary elections. Rodríguez stressed that during his administration Costa Rica would not adhere to political integration mechanisms like the Central American Parliament, but to economic ones.

38   In March, the US ambassador, Thomas Dodd, was accused by the Commission for the Defense of Human Rights in Central America (Codehuca) of interfering in the internal affairs of the country. Dodd had declared that his government might impose economic sanctions following the death of a US citizen in a private dispute.

39   A nutrition survey in March 1999 revealed that 75 per cent of infants aged from one to two years old had some degree of anaemia, a figure which fell to 26 per cent in pre-school children. Throughout the country, 33 per cent of people living in rural areas and 16 per cent of urban dwellers suffered the same problem.

40   In order to address the growing violence, and to avoid the country becoming a refuge for criminals operating in neighboring countries, in December the Government brought in the obligatory registration of weapons and offered a 12-month amnesty to those who gave up their arms.

41   Jewish activists accused the government of protecting Bodhan Koziy, a Ukrainian Nazi accused of war crimes who had been resident in Costa Rica for 15 years. In December, the Government began reconsideration of Koziy's case and announced that they would look into extradition.

42   In February 2000, San José suspended diplomatic relations with Vienna when the Austrian Liberty Party with neo-Nazi tendencies came to power. Foreign Minister Roberto Rojas stated his government would keep a close eye on whether the Austrian Government would retain the same level of tolerance as its predecessors. ∎

Côte d'Ivoire

Population: 14,527,000 (1999)
Area: 322,460 SQ KM
Capital: Abidjan
Currency: CFA franc
Language: French

Côte d'Ivoire

According to Baulé tradition, in 1730 Queen Aura Poka (sister of a defeated pretender to the Ashanti throne) emigrated westwards with her people. They founded a new state in the center of a territory known to Europeans since the 15th century as the Côte d'Ivoire (or Ivory Coast) because of the active trade in elephant tusks. This Ashanti state soon grew and became a threat to the small states of Aigini, on the coast, and Atokpora, inland. In 1843, these states requested French protection, thus enabling France to obtain exclusive rights over the coastal trade centres.

[2] Fifty years later, French troops moved up the coast aiming to join Côte d'Ivoire. to Guinea, Mali and Senegal. However, they met with stiff resistance from Samori Touré, a Fulani leader who had risen through the social ranks because of outstanding leadership ability. He had set up a state in the heart of the region which the Europeans were planning to unify under a central colonial administration (See Guinea).

[3] After three decades of bloody fighting (1870-1898), Touré was defeated and the leaders of the dominant Fulani groups were forced to sign colonial agreements with the French.

[4] In 1895 the area became known as French West Africa, comprising Senegal, French Sudan (now Mali), Guinea and Côte d'Ivoire. Later, what are now Chad, Burkina Faso and Mauritania were also annexed. The French hoped to balance the poorer regions of Chad and Burkina Faso with the better off Senegal and Côte d'Ivoire. This centralized administration failed after independence.

[5] Several attempts at economic integration were made, with different degrees of success, but real progress was made only recently with the creation of the Economic Community of West Africa, which includes 15 former colonies of France, Britain and Portugal.

[6] In French West Africa, modern political activities began in 1946 with the creation of the African Democratic Union (ADU), a political party with branches in Senegal, Mali and Guinea. The ADU promoted independence and unity for French colonies in the area. Felix Houphouët-Boigny, hereditary leader of the Baulé ethnic group, and also a physician and well-to-do farmer, was appointed party president, based on his experience leading a farmers' association which had fought against colonial policies.

[7] Tactically allied to the French Communist Party, the only anti-colonial French party at the time, the ADU staged strikes, demonstrations and boycotts of European businesses. The nationalist cause was savagely suppressed, leaving dozens of activists dead and thousands imprisoned, giving Houphouët-Boigny grounds for ending his alliance with the French communists in 1950. He soon reached a new agreement with François Mitterrand, then Minister for Overseas Territories. This move undermined the ADU's standing, and Houphouët-Boigny was only just able to maintain his prestige in his own land.

[8] Between 1958 and 1960 all of French West Africa became independent and the new states joined the UN. Aware of their meagre economic prospects, the political leaders proposed to form a federation. However Houphouët-Boigny, who became president in 1960, and confident in the relative prosperity of his country and his privileged neo-colonial relations with France, opposed the idea. "We are not saying 'goodbye' to France, but 'see you later'", he had declared when announcing independence.

[9] As a major producer of cocoa, coffee, rubber and diamonds, Côte d'Ivoire was able to attract transnational investors. In addition to the political stability produced by Houphouët-Boigny's paternalistic, authoritarian rule, the country. offered extremely cheap labor, mostly supplied by neighboring countries. In the 10-year period (1966-76) the economic growth rate remained between 8 and 10 per cent a year. But prosperity withered as the West went into a recession after 1979. Agricultural exports fell from $4 billion to barely $1 billion between 1980 and 1983. Half the industries set up between 1966 and 1976 closed down, pushing unemployment figures up to 45 per cent of the active population. By 1985, the foreign debt was five times that of 1981.

[10] Following International Monetary Fund recommendations, President Houphouët-Boigny made severe budget cuts, paralyzed nearly all public projects and slashed food subsidies. These decisions did not spark social unrest immediately, but only because of the weakness of the labor unions and the lack of fresh political leadership. The only groups which retained potential for opposition were students and liberal professionals, and they organized mass demonstrations and strikes.

[11] In May 1984, following negotiations with the Paris Club and other sources of financing, Côte d'Ivoire. was allowed to reschedule its foreign debt. The economy continued to deteriorate, particularly as coffee and cocoa export prices fell.

[12] In October 1985, the 8th congress of the Côte d'Ivoire Democratic Party (PDCI) issued a

LAND USE

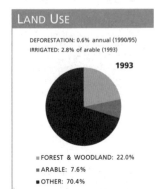

DEFORESTATION: 0.6% annual (1990/95)
IRRIGATED: 2.8% of arable (1993)

1993

- FOREST & WOODLAND: 22.0%
- ARABLE: 7.6%
- OTHER: 70.4%

WORKERS

1990

- SERVICES: 30.5%
- INDUSTRY: 9.6%
- AGRICULTURE: 60.0%

PUBLIC EXPENDITURE

MILITARY EXPENDITURE
(% of health & education) **14%** (1990/91)

MATERNAL MORTALITY	LITERACY
1990-98	1995

Per 100,000 live births
600

40%

resolution nominating octogenarian Houphouët-Boigny for a sixth presidential term. The appointment was confirmed that same month by 99 per cent of the electorate. In November, however, elections for the General Assembly were marked by a very low turnout of 25 per cent.

[13] President Houphouët-Boigny's grandiose building schemes stood in stark contrast to African realities. In the face of severe economic hardship, he built Africa's largest cathedral, a project offensive to many people, and also to the 23 per cent Muslim population.

[14] Côte d'Ivoire is one of the world's largest producer of cocoa and, like all Third World producers of raw materials, it suffered from falling commodity prices. From July to October 1987, the price of cocoa dropped 50 per cent on the world market.

[15] In 1990, a government austerity plan went into effect with IMF and World Bank support. The economic measures resulted in decreases in worker salaries in both public and private sectors.

[16] Public reaction, particularly by students, brought about a reduction in the price of staple goods. In the meantime, the Government decided not to carry out a planned 11 per cent wage cut, calling the measure a "contribution to national solidarity".

[17] In 1990, a multiparty system was established and presidential elections were held. Houphouët-Boigny was re-elected with 81 per cent of the vote.

[18] By 1991, the Government had not managed to fully apply its 3-year program to put the public finances in order, privatize some of the public companies and stimulate the "competitiveness" of the private corporations.

[19] The death of the President in December 1993 triggered a succession dispute. He was replaced by Henri Konan-Bédié, leader of the National Assembly, who consolidated his power within the ruling Democratic Party, despite the opposition of former Prime Minister Ouattara.

[20] In 1994, the Government faced a strong union movement demanding compensation after the 100 per cent devaluation of the CFA imposed by France and the IMF in January. In what was seen as a reward for having accepted the devaluation, half of Côte d'Ivoire's debt with the Paris Club was cancelled. However, the country continued to have the highest per capita foreign debt in the world.

[21] In October 1995, Bédié won a controversial presidential election, boycotted by the opposition. For the first time since the country's independence, residing foreigners were not allowed to vote, neither were those whose parents were not Ivorian. This allowed Bédié to dispose of Ouattara, whose father was from Burkina Faso. Prime Minister Daniel Kablan Duncan formed a new cabinet in January 1996, making no significant changes.

[22] The World Bank and the IMF granted Côte d'Ivoire loans worth $385 million to continue with its economic reform and privatisation plan. Public health care began to register enormous short-falls and life expectancy fell to less than 50 years. As well as AIDS, there were fresh outbreaks of yellow fever and tuberculosis.

[23] The opposition demanded the voting age be lowered from 21 to 18, an age at which men must do their military service. The President did not accept this, fearing that this segment of the population would swing against him in the elections planned for October 2000, because of his social policies.

[24] Between December of this year and February 1999, Bédié held talks with the two main opposition parties, the Republican Rally (RDR) and the Democratic Party of Côte d'Ivoire (PDCI), on the institutional regime of the country.

[25] Because of student protests, the Government closed educational establishments from May, but the situation became more violent. In the second half of the year there was conflict between transport unions and the police in various parts of the country. Most of the directors of the RDR were imprisoned in November, following a demonstration against presidential control over the state information bodies.

[26] A military coup led by General Robert Guéi ousted Bédié in December 1999 forcing him to flee the country. The United States and the European Union urged the military junta to regain the road to democracy. In January 2000, after declaring that the state coffers were empty, Guéi took over as interim president. A month later he announced a referendum on Constitutional change for April, and elections for October. The opposition candidates immediately started their pre-electoral campaigns. ∎

Croatia

Hrvatska

Population: 4,477,000 (1999)
Area: 56,540 SQ KM
Capital: Zagreb
Currency: Kuna
Language: Croatian

The Croats, a Slav tribe, emigrated in the 6th century AD from White Croatia, a region today in the Ukraine, toward the lower Danube valley. They moved on from there toward the Adriatic Sea, where they conquered the Roman stronghold of Salona, in 614. Once established in the former Roman provinces of Pannonia and Dalmatia, the Croats freed themselves from the Avars - a people of undetermined origin and language who had built an empire in the area between the Adriatic and the Baltic Sea - and began developing independently. Even though the territory was under the Byzantine empire, the Croats accepted the Roman Catholic Church, whilst preserving the Slav liturgy.

² The Croatians were a farming people, and maintained their old way of life, uniting under their tribal chieftains. In the 7th century, the Croats were converted to Roman Catholicism; a bishopric was established at Nin for this region, and the Croats obtained the right to use their own language in their religious services.

³ In the 9th century, an independent Croat State developed in Dalmatia. During the reign of Tomislav (910-928) this achieved great military development. Tomislav and his heirs defended themselves from the Bulgar Empire in Pannonia and the Venetian expansion along the Dalmatian coast. The Byzantine Empire helped Stjepan Drzislav (969-997) to defend himself from the Venetians, but re-established its influence in the Adriatic. King

Peter Kresimir (1058-1074) broke with Byzantium and strengthened links with the papacy. In that period, Croatia reached the peak of its power and territorial expansion.

⁴ However, during Kresimir's rule, the country split in two, with a Latin group favoring the king, and an opposition national group, backed up by broad popular support. When the Pope invited Dimitrije Zvonimir to involve the Kingdom in a war against the Seljuk Turks, the opposition accused him of being the Pope's vassal and assassinated him in 1089. The civil war which was then unleashed marked the beginning of the decline of the Croatian Kingdom.

⁵ The Byzantines recovered Dalmatia, and in the meantime, Lazlo I of Hungary conquered Pannonia in 1091, laying claim to the Croatian crown. Lazlo founded a bishopric at Zagreb in 1094, which became the center of the Church's power in the region. Petar Svacic was crowned King by the Dalmatians, but the Pope considered him a rebel, and turned to King Kalman of Hungary to unseat him. Kalman invaded the country; Svacic - the last king of Croat blood - fell in 1097.

⁶ After an extended war Kalman signed a treaty, the

Pacta Conventa, with the Croat representatives. Only Bosnia, then a part of the Croatian kingdom, refused to submit to a foreign monarch. For the next eight centuries, Croatia was linked to Hungary. In the 14th century, Dalmatia became a part of Venice, which ruled over it for 400 years.

⁷ After the defeat of the Croatian and Hungarian forces in the battles of Krbavsko Polje (1493) and Mohacs (1526), most of Pannonia and Hungary fell into Turkish hands.

⁸ Turkish domination altered the ethnic composition of Pannonia, as many Croats migrated northwards, some even going into Austria. In the meantime, the Turks brought in German and Hungarian settlers, and gave incentives for Serbians fleeing the Balkans to settle in the Vojna Krajina.

⁹ When the Turks were driven back in the 17th century, Austria tried to limit Croatia and Hungary's state rights, to make them mere provinces of the Austrian Empire. The Croatian and Hungarian nobility conspired together to organize an independence movement, which failed. The Croatian leaders were executed and their lands were distributed among foreign nobles.

¹⁰ After the annexation of Rijeka (Fiume) in the 1770s, Hungary tried to impose its language, but this triggered a nationalist reaction among the Croatians. In the meantime, the French Revolution and the Napoleonic Wars which had incorporated Dalmatia, Pannonia and the area south of the Sava river to the French Empire, further stimulated Croatian nationalism. Upon the fall of Napoleon, relations between Hungary and Croatia rapidly deteriorated.

¹¹ In April 1848, the Hungarian Parliament adopted a series of measures severely limiting Croatian autonomy. The Croatian Diet declared its separation from Hungary, abolishing serfdom and approving equal rights for all its citizens. Hungary's troops were weakened by this conflict, making it easier for the Hapsburgs to put down the

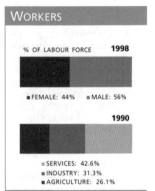

WORKERS

% OF LABOUR FORCE **1998**

■ FEMALE: 44% ■ MALE: 56%

1990

■ SERVICES: 42.6%
■ INDUSTRY: 31.3%
■ AGRICULTURE: 26.1%

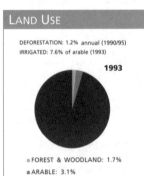

LAND USE

DEFORESTATION: 1.2% annual (1990/95)
IRRIGATED: 7.6% of arable (1993)

1993

■ FOREST & WOODLAND: 1.7%
■ ARABLE: 3.1%
■ OTHER: 95.2%

PUBLIC EXPENDITURE

DEFENCE EXPENDITURE (% of goverment exp.)	**12%**	(1997)
MILITARY EXPENDITURE (% of health & education)	**11%**	(1990/91)

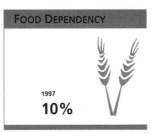
Hungarian Revolt and regain power later that year.

[12] The Croatian Diet was dissolved in 1865, and two years later, with the division of the crown, Germany and Hungary became the major nations of the Austro-Hungarian Empire. In 1868, Hungary accepted the union of Croatia, Slavonia and Dalmatia as a separate political entity, though Austria refused to relinquish its claim to Dalmatia.

[13] In the early 20th century, Croatian nationalist groups intensified their activity. An alliance of Croatian and Serbian leaders adopted the "Rijeka resolution", a plan of action which enabled them to win the 1906 elections. In the meantime, the Croatian Peasant Party began political activity among the peasants. The Crown responded by increasing repression.

[14] In 1915, Croatian, Serbian and Slovenian leaders organized the Yugoslav Committee in Paris to push for separation from the empire and union with an independent Serbia. Austria-Hungary's defeat in World War I accelerated the creation of the Yugoslav kingdom in 1918.

[15] The Serbian dynasty's policy of amalgamating the regions immediately came into conflict with Croatian desires for independence. Croatia demanded the creation of a Yugoslav federation. As of 1920, the Peasant Party, led by Stjepan Radic headed the Croatian opposition. The assassination of Radic and other members of the opposition, in 1928 provoked a serious crisis.

[16] When World War II broke out, Yugoslavia was divided internally, so it was easily occupied by Hitler in 1941. The German army set up a puppet regime made up of Croatia, Slavonia, parts of Dalmatia and Bosnia-Herzegovina. A racist campaign was launched in which Serbians, Jews, Gypsies and Croats opposed to Fascism were massacred in concentration camps or forced into exile.

[17] After the anti-Nazi guerrillas had occupied Zagreb in May 1945, the Anti-Fascist Council of National Liberation of Croatia assumed control of the Government. By the end of the year, Croatia was one of the constituent republics of the new People's Federated Republic of Yugoslavia.

[18] Within the Yugoslav socialist system (see Yugoslavia Federal Republic), Croatia maintained and strengthened its national independence, although this worked against its ethnic minorities. In 1972, a purge within the Croatian League of Communists led to the suspension of the Matica Hrvatska, the Croatian cultural organization.

[19] At the end of the 1980s, Yugoslavia modified its political system; the Yugoslav League of Communists (YLC) renounced the monopoly and leading role assigned to it by the constitution, and in April 1990, the first multiparty elections since World War II were held in the different regions.

[20] In Croatia, elections gave a majority to the Croatian Democratic Union (CDU), a center-right party which favored making Yugoslavia a confederation of sovereign states. The leader of the CDU, retired general Franjo Tudjman, was elected President of the republic. In December, Parliament ratified a new constitution which endorsed the right to separate from the federation.

[21] In June 1991, Croatia proclaimed its independence from the federation, while the Serbs in Krajina declared their intention of separating from Croatia. The US and the European Community held back from recognizing Croatia and Slovenia, which had also declared their independence. The federal army of Yugoslavia, whose officers answered mainly to Serbia, intervened in Croatia and Slovenia alleging that separation was a threat to the integrity of Yugoslavia. War broke out with many victims on both sides and accusations of "ethnic cleansing" - the systematic killing of an ethnic/religious group

[22] In November 1991, Tudjman's government arrested the leaders of the ultra-right wing Croatian *Ustasha* (Fascist) Party (CUP) and dissolved their militias, accused of conspiring against the legal authorities. Founded in February 1990, the CUP adopted the name of a nationalist party of the past, whose leader, Ante Pavelic, had headed the puppet government of Nazi-occupied Croatia in World War II.

[23] In December 1991, Germany recognized Croatian independence and encouraged the EC to do likewise. A few days earlier, the Serbs of Krajina (southern Croatia) and Slavonia, Baranja and western Serm (to the east), proclaimed the republic of Krajina, as a new federal Yugoslav unit or an alliance of Serb states.

[24] In January 1992, EC mediation enabled Serbia and Croatia to accept a peace plan and the stationing of 15,000 UN soldiers in the conflict zone. In May, the UN General Assembly meeting in New York formally allowed the former Yugoslav republics of Croatia, Slovenia, Bosnia-Herzegovina membership of the entity, increasing the number of members to 178.

[25] Following re-election on August 2 1992, President Tudjman worked on an agreement to reopen the main Zagreb-Belgrade road link. This was achieved in 1993, when former US Secretary of State

EXTERNAL DEBT		FOREIGN TRADE	
	1998	Millions US$	**1998**

EXTERNAL DEBT   1998

Per capita

US$ 1,852

FOREIGN TRADE   1998

Millions US$

IMPORTS

10,666

EXPORTS

8,707

Cyrus Vance, working as a UN negotiator, obtained a pact with the new Yugoslav Federation (Serbia and Montenegro).

[26] In October 1992 in Geneva, presidents Tudjman of Croatia and Cosic of the Yugoslav Federation, spoke out against ethnic cleansing and agreed that the refugees deserved humane treatment.

[27] In November 1992, Radovan Karadzic, the Bosnian Serb leader, announced the formation of the Confederation of his "Serbian Republic of Bosnia and Herzegovina" and the "Serbian Republic of Krajina" in Croatia, and the Serbs renewed hostilities.

[28] Although less bloody than the conflict in Bosnia and Herzegovina, the hostilities in Croatia caused tens of thousands of civilian deaths.

[29] In late 1993, Tudjman and President Izetbegovic of Bosnia-Herzegovina signed a cease-fire agreement and dismantled the prisoner of war camps.

[30] In Geneva, in January 1994, Croatia and Serbia agreed the full restoration of transport links and communications between the two republics. Similarly, they opened offices in Zagreb and Belgrade which operated as diplomatic missions.

[31] However, no solution was found for the enclave of Krajina, still under Serb control. In late January, Croatia attempted unsuccessfully to recover the enclave by force, which ended the cease-fire with Serbia. In February, the UN Security Council unanimously approved extending the term of the "blue helmets" stationed in Croatia.

[32] In June 1994, Croatia re-established the *kuna*, the currency used in the country during World War II by the German-backed government. This replaced the *dinar*, originally adopted following independence.

[33] Pope John Paul II's visit to Croatia in September contributed to improving the international profile of the country. The Serb rebels and the Croat Government agreed to open a Zagreb-Belgrade road, the Adria oil pipeline and to restore the supply of water and electricity to Serbs in occupied territories.

[34] On April 13 1995, Serb forces bombarded the airport at Dubrovnik and 10 days later once again blocked the Zagreb-Belgrade highway, in eastern Slavonia. The Croat army regained control of the area following a swift operation in May. Zagreb was immediately bombed by Serb troops.

[35] President of Serbia, Slobodan Milosevic, said that if the UN lifted sanctions on Yugoslavia, peace would return to the Balkans in a matter of months. An agreement between Franjo Tudjman and the US allowed the international forces to remain and to be gradually removed with the help of NATO troops.

[36] In early August, the Serbs suffered their worst defeat since the rupture of the former Yugoslavia. The Krajina region was taken by the Croats, forcing Serb troops and civilians to flee.

[37] Allegations of torture and pillaging were made against the Croats who occupied Krajina. Some 250,000 Serbs were added to the more than 700,000 refugees already displaced in the Balkans. The Croat occupation of Krajina was considered one of the biggest ethnic cleansing operations of the war in the former Yugoslavia. Up until May 1996, only eight Croats had been tried in their absence by the war crimes court in The Hague.

[38] In October, representatives of the Croat government and the Serb leaders of eastern Slavonia agreed the principles for the peaceful restructuring of this region. On October 29, Tudjman won the elections but did not get the two thirds of the vote needed to reform the Constitution and obtain more powers for the presidency.

[39] The signing of an agreement between the presidents of Croatia, Serbia and Bosnia-Herzegovina at Dayton airbase in the US marked the end of hostilities, although the population continued to attack UN and NATO forces throughout 1996.

[40] Negotiations between Zagreb and Belgrade from August 1996 allowed the refugees to return home, and set up elections in 1997. Tudjman, accused of obstructing the return of the refugees, allowed a limited number of Serbian Croats to settle again in his country. In June 1997, he was re-elected with 61.4 per cent of the vote. In late 1997 and early 1998, fresh reports emerged of abuses committed by the Croats in their counter-offensive to take Krajina.

[41] In April 1999, a court ruled there was insufficient evidence to convict six former Croat soldiers for war crimes against Serb rebels, even though one of the accused had admitted his guilt to the press. The court case was the first where the Croats, who generally viewed themselves as victims of Serb aggression, allowed themselves to be tried for their own crimes against the Serb minority.

[42] Tudjman was rushed into hospital in mid-November and died in December. As a result the elections planned for that month were deferred for a month later.

[43] In December the Supreme Court ruled that state television had violated the Constitution by refusing to show two party political slots by the recently-founded independent Voice 99. The Court said that the broadcasts were not calling for votes for Voice 99, but for the majority opposition party.

[44] The January 2000, Stipe Mesic became president in the elections, thus changing the political outlook. He represented a center-left alliance made up of liberals, social democrats and other groups. The new government prioritized entry into the European Union (EU) and NATO, elimination of corruption, army reform and limits on presidential powers. In order to achieve this, Mesic immediately proposed to clarify relations with Bosnia-Herzegovina, as Croatian funding of an army in a foreign country was barring the nation entry to the EU. ∎

STATISTICS

DEMOGRAPHY

Population: 4,477,000 (1999)
Annual growth: 0.2 % (1975/97)
Estimates for year 2015 (million): 4.3 (1999)
Annual growth to year 2015: -0.2 % (1997/2015)
Urban population: 56.5 % (1997)
Urban Growth: 2.0 % (1980/95)
Children per woman: 1.6 (1998)

HEALTH

Life expectancy at birth: 73 years (1998)
male: 69 years (1998)
female: 77 years (1998)
Maternal mortality: 12 per 100,000 live births (1990-98)
Infant mortality: 8 per 1,000 (1998)
Under-5 child mortality: 9 per 1,000 (1998)
Daily calorie supply: 2,458 per capita (1996)
201 doctors per 100,000 people (1993)

EDUCATION

Literacy: 97 % (1995)
male: 99 % (1995)
female: 96 % (1995)
School enrolment:
Primary total: 87 % (1990/96)
male: 87 % (1990/97)
female: 86 % (1990/97)
Secondary:
male: 81 % (1990/96)
female: 83 % (1990/96)
Tertiary: 28 % (1996)
Primary school teachers: one for every 19 (1996)

COMMUNICATIONS

115 newspapers (1996), 336 radios (1997), 267 TV sets (1996) and 309 main telephone lines (1996) per 1,000 people
Books: 59 new titles per 100,000 people (1992/94)

ECONOMY

Per capita, GNP: $ 4,620 (1998)
Annual growth, GNP: 1.8 % (1998)
Annual inflation: 131.2 % (1990/98)
Consumer price index: 115.6 (1998)
Currency: 6.4 dinars = $ 1 (1998)
Cereal imports: 65,320 metric tons (1998)
Food import dependency: 10 % (1997)
Fertilizer use: 1,776 kg per ha (1997)
Exports: $ 8,707 million (1998)
Imports: $ 10,666 million (1998)
External debt: $ 8,297 million (1998); $ 1,852 per capita (1998)
Debt service: 8.9 % of exports (1998)
Development aid received: $ 44 million (1997); $ 9.2 per capita (1997); 0.20 % of GNP (1997)

ENERGY

Consumption: 1,687.0 Kgs of Oil equivalent per capita yearly (1997); 48.0 % imported (1997)

HDI (rank/value): 55/0.773 (1997)

Cuba

Cuba

Population: 11,160,000 (1999)
Area: 110,860 SQ KM
Capital: Havana (La Habana)
Currency: Peso
Language: Spanish

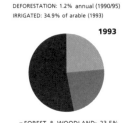

Until the 16th century the island of Cuba was inhabited by the Taino and Ciboney, a branch of the Arawak indians. In 1492, the Spanish emissary to the Indies arrived, but it was not until 1509 that a voyage was made around the coast proving that Cuba was an island. The conquest began in 1510 and Santiago de Cuba was founded in 1514 by Diego Velázquez. This was a violent period in the island's history, with a number of uprisings, like those led by native chieftains Hatuey and Guama.

2   The Spanish expeditions which would subsequently conquer a large part of the Caribbean, Mexico and Central America, departed from Cuba. It was described in mid-16th century document as "high and mountainous" with small rivers "rich in gold and fish". In 1511, colonists from Santo Domingo started mining Cuban gold. It was a short-lived economic cycle, probably because the indian population was rapidly exterminated. As the number of African enslaved workers on the island was insufficient, economic life soon declined and did not recover until the end of the 16th century, with the advent of sugar production.

3   As early as the 17th century, economic diversification was achieved through shipbuilding and the developing leather and copper industries. The economic center of the island gradually moved from Santiago, on the southern coast, to Havana, in the north, a port of great importance in the mid-17th century.

4   Sugarcane plantations in colonial America used slave labor and created economic dependence. There were periods, during 1840 for example, when slave labor represented 77 per cent of the total Cuban workforce. There is also evidence that there were *palenques*, settlements of escaped slaves (see Brazil) on the island, and there was an abortive slave revolt in 1843. It took a long, complex process to change this situation, comparable only with that of Brazil, the last American country to abolish slavery. British pressure against the slave contributed decisively to the abolition of slavery in 1886.

5   The struggle for independence began in the first few decades of the 19th century, but the decisive battle, with José Martí, Antonio Maceo and Máximo Gómez was not fought until 1895. In 1898, aware that the victory of the Cuban patriots was inevitable, the US declared war on Spain and invaded Cuba to guarantee their continued influence in the Caribbean.

6   US occupation forces ruled the country from 1899 to 1902, imposing a constitution including the so-called "Platt Amendment". This secured the US rights to intervene in Cuba and to retain a portion of its territory. Guantánamo became a powerful air and naval base that is still maintained. The "right" to intervene has been exercised on various occasions, with US Marines remaining on Cuban soil for extended periods of time.

7   With the fall of the dictator Machado in 1933, Carlos Manuel de Céspedes came to power. Several months later there was a military coup and the rebelling sergeants established a short-lived "Pentarchy". A few days later, Grau formed the "Government of a Hundred Days" with Fulgencio Batista and Antonio Guiteras, and several anti-imperialist measures were implemented. In January 1934, Batista led a reactionary counter-coup, and Guiteras was assassinated. Elections were held, ushering in a series of governments presided over by Batista's Authentic Party, dominating a period characterized by corruption and gangsterism under the auspices of the United States. On March 10 1952, Batista engineered yet another coup, establishing a dictatorial regime which was responsible for the death of 20,000 Cubans.

8   On July 26 1953, Fidel Castro and a group of revolutionaries attacked the Moncada Army Base in Santiago de Cuba. Although the attack itself failed, it marked the beginning of the revolution. After a short period of imprisonment, Castro went into exile in Mexico only to return in December 1956. Castro's revolutionary program had been defined during his trial after the failed initial uprising, ending with his well-known words: "History will absolve me".

9   On December 31 1958, Batista fled from Cuba as guerrilla columns led by Ernesto "Che" Guevara and Camilo Cienfuegos, closed on Havana. They were the vanguard of the Rebel Army. In just over two years, the guerrillas of the "26th of July" Movement, organized by Fidel Castro, broke the morale of Batista's corrupt army.

10   In 1961, counter-revolutionaries disembarked at Playa Giron (Giron Beach), in the

WORKERS

% OF LABOUR FORCE **1998**

- FEMALE: 39%   ■ MALE: 61%

1990

- SERVICES: 51.5%
- INDUSTRY: 30.4%
- AGRICULTURE: 18.1%

LAND USE

DEFORESTATION: 1.2% annual (1990/95)
IRRIGATED: 34.9% of arable (1993)

1993

- FOREST & WOODLAND: 23.5%
- ARABLE: 23.5%
- OTHER: 53.0%

PUBLIC EXPENDITURE

MILITARY EXPENDITURE **125%**
(% of health & education) (1990/91)

Bay of Pigs, in an attempt to bring down the regime which had carried out agrarian reforms and expropriated various American enterprises. They had counted on a popular uprising against the revolutionary government, but this did not materialize. After 72 hours of fierce fighting, the Bay of Pigs invasion ended in the defeat of the invading forces. Two days before the invasion, on April 15, while the victims of the Havana Airport bombing were being buried, Castro proclaimed the socialist nature of the revolution.

[11] Also in that year, all the pro-government organizations joined together in a common structure. This was initially known as the Integrated Revolutionary Organizations (ORI), and later became the United Party of the Socialist Cuban Revolution (PURSC). The United States had Cuba excluded from the Organization of American States (OAS). It also put pressure on other countries to sever diplomatic relations, engineering an economic blockade of the island. That year the October Crisis made the possibility of a third World War into a near-probability. The United

States photographed Soviet nuclear missile launching sites on the island, and began preparations for another invasion. However, a peaceful solution was reached as the Soviet Union and the United States came to an agreement. The US pledged not to invade Cuba, but disregarded the Cuban Government's demands for an end to the blockade, the withdrawal of US troops from Guantánamo and an end to US-managed terrorist activities.

[12] The literacy campaign during these years soon bore fruit, and by 1964, Cuba was free of illiteracy. Improvements in health were also one of the Government's priorities. In October 1965, the People's Socialist Party, the Revolutionary Directory and the 26 of July Movement (led by Castro himself) dropped the name PURSC and created the Cuban Communist Party (PCC). This was just one more step closer to the Soviet Union, a relationship which had been strengthened by the economic blockade.

[13] With the consolidation of the socialist regime, Cuba began lending technical assistance to like-minded peoples and governments of the Third World. It sent troops to countries like Ethiopia and Angola, who requested help to resist invading forces. In October 1967 Che Guevara was captured and killed in Bolivia, where he had been attempting to extend the revolution.

[14] The revolution began to be institutionalized after the first PCC congress in 1975. A new constitution was approved in 1976 and there were subsequent elections of representatives for the governing bodies at municipal, provincial and national levels. In 1979, Castro and the leaders of the PCC launched a campaign of revolutionary requirements to correct weaknesses in the administrative and political management areas of the revolutionary process.

[15] Tension between Cuba and the US increased when Ronald Reagan came to the White House in 1979.

[16] In the mid-1980s, some 120,000 people left Mariel bound for Florida taking advantage of a clause offering automatic US residency to any Cuban arriving in the United States - brought in when emigration from Cuba was practically impossible.

[17] Cuba's relations with many Latin American countries improved as a consequence of the Cuban attitude during the Malvinas/Falklands war. Anxious to put a halt to Cuban-Latin American rapprochement, the United States took a series of measures against Havana. In August 1982 the US Senate passed a resolution allowing its government to use the armed forces to halt "Marxist-Leninist subversion" in Central America.

[18] The results of the Third Congress were formalized in April 1986 and the so-called "process of the rectification of errors and negative tendencies" was initiated. This coincided with the changes which were taking place in the Soviet Union, but the Cubans avoided adopting the eastern European model.

[19] In June 1989, a high-ranking group of Army officers and officials of the Ministry of the Interior were brought to trial and executed for being involved in drug trafficking.

[20] From the time President George Bush there was an increase in US pressure on Cuba. In the first few months of 1990 there were important military manoeuvres at Guantánamo Base and in the Caribbean. The US also violated Cuban television airspace with transmissions by "Televisión Martí", which was supported by "The voice of America". However, this broadcast was only picked up on the island for one day, after which it was jammed.

[21] At this time, the last of Cuba's troops returned home from Zaire (now DR Congo) and Angola. More than 300,000 Cubans had served in Angola, with the loss of 2,016 lives.

[22] After a seven-month delay, the 4th PCC congress took place in October 1991. It was decided to reform the Constitution so that members of the National Assembly could be elected directly, a major ratification of the single-party system. People with religious beliefs were also admitted, and the Government recognized the need for joint ventures, especially with Latin American investors.

[23] With the changes in Eastern Europe, and the disappearance of its former Council for Mutual Economic Assistance allies, some of Cuba's basic supplies dropped to critical levels. To ease this crisis, the

PROFILE

ENVIRONMENT

The Cuban archipelago includes the island of Cuba, the Isle of Youth (formerly the Isle of Pines) and about 1,600 nearby keys and islets. Cuba, the largest island of the Antilles, has a rainy, tropical climate. With the exception of the southeastern Sierra Maestra highlands, wide and fertile plains predominate in the country. Sugarcane farming takes up over 60 per cent of the cultivated land, particularly in the northern plains. Nickel is the main mineral resource.

SOCIETY

Peoples: Cubans see themselves as Afro-Latin Americans on account of their mixed Afro-European-American ethnic background. There are also approximately 30,000 Asians, mainly Chinese.
Religions: Catholic 39.6 per cent; atheist 6.4 per cent; Protestant 3.3 per cent; and Afro-Cuban syncretists.
Languages: Spanish.
Political Parties: The Cuban Communist Party is defined by the constitution as the "supreme leading force of society and the state".
Social Organizations: Cuban Workers' Union (CTC). The CTC had 2,984,393 members in 1988, and represented more than 80 per cent of the Cuban labor force; the National Association of Small Farmers, 167.461 members (1988) with 3,500 grass roots organizations; the Federation of Cuban Women (FMC), 2,420,000 members; the University Student Federation (FEU) and the Federation of Secondary School Students (FEEM), 450,000 student members; the José Martí Pioneers' Union, 2,200,000 children and young people; the Revolution Defense Committees.

THE STATE

Official Name: República de Cuba.
Administrative Divisions: 14 Provinces, 169 Municipalities including the special municipality of Isla de Pinos.
Capital: Havana (La Habana) 2,300,000 people (1995).
Other cities: Santiago de Cuba 440,100 people; Camaguey 294,000; Holguín 242,100; Guantánamo 207,800 (1993).
Government: Fidel Castro Ruiz, President of the Council of State and the Council of Ministers. The 1976 constitution states that the power is exercised through the Assemblies of People's Power. The local Assemblies delegate power to successively more encompassing representative bodies until a pyramid is formed which peaks in the National Assembly. Representatives are subject to recall by the voters.
National Holidays: January 1, Liberation Day (1959); July 26, Assault on the Moncada military barracks (1953).
Armed Forces: 105,000 (1995).
Other: 1,369,000 Civil Defense Force, Territorial Militia, State Security, Border Guard.

Government strengthened its ties with China, Vietnam and North Korea, and looked for ways to capitalize on its recent technological advances.

24   Biotechnological research has made Cuba a Third World leader in this area; it recently developed an anti-meningitis vaccine.

25   The Government decided to ration fuel when the former USSR cut oil shipments by 25 per cent between 1989 and 1991. It also decided to strengthen the tourist industry. A further initiative was joint ventures with Spanish companies. The investors maintain 50 per cent ownership of the enterprise once it begins operation.

26   The loss of Cuba's main trading partners and the re-enforcement of the US blockade led to the creation of a Special Plan, aimed at distributing scarce resources equitably. In 1990, bread was rationed at 100 grams per person per day, three newspapers ceased publication, and the official newspaper, *Granma*, was forced to cut its circulation by more than two thirds. Alternative proposals included the possibility of offering more sugar, tobacco and coffee on the international market, an overall strengthening of the agricultural sector, and the possibility of oil purchase agreements with Mexico and Venezuela.

27   The severe shortage of food forced the authorities to carry out an emergency food program. This scheme sought to increase agricultural production rapidly, maximizing sugar production so that sugarcane derivatives could be used as animal feed. The emergency program also aimed to create new jobs.

28   With the break-up of the Soviet Union, the US urged Russia to take a tougher stand in its relations with the island, and this trend became evident during Mikhail Gorbachev's last months in power. Gorbachev's decision to withdraw 3,000 Soviet soldiers stationed in Cienfuegos and Havana, took the Cubans completely by surprise as the issue had not been discussed.

29   In August 1991, through its representative at the United Nations, Cuba presented a motion that the UN should debate ending the US economic blockade. The Cubans quickly withdrew the motion, when they realized what they were up against: the US had put pressure on all the other delegations.

30   In early 1993, National Assembly (parliament) elections were held, and deputies were elected directly for the first time. Ricardo Alarcón, foreign minister, was designated president of the National Assembly, and Roberto Robaina, secretary-general of the Communist Youth organization, became foreign minister.

31   On July 26 1993, in his speech for the commemoration of the 40th anniversary of the attack on Moncada Army Barracks, Castro announced that it would henceforth be legal for Cubans to possess and use foreign currency, and to be self-employed.

32   Towards the end of the same year, the National Assembly met to discuss the country's critical situation, especially its internal finances. The Assembly decided not to take any steps for the time being, but to discuss the issue and collect opinions and ideas in workplaces throughout the country. These "Workers' Parliaments" were held during the first quarter of 1994.

33   In April 1994, a meeting entitled "The Nation and Emigration" was held in Havana on the initiative of Foreign Minister Robaina, and it was attended by some groups of Cubans living abroad. Shortly afterwards, there were a series of incidents in Havana involving people who wanted to leave the country illegally in frail boats. When Cuba announced it would not stop the "boat people" from leaving, the United States started official negotiations to regulate the illegal departure of the immigrants.

34   In July, Cuba entered the Association of Caribbean States (ACS) as a full member. Its participation in the ACS, a group emerging as a new economic bloc, encouraged greater integration of the Cuban economy in the region, offering tariff benefits and trade facilities.

35   In 1995, the fiscal deficit fell for the third year running, due to the reduction of public services and cutbacks in subsidies. A system of convertibility of the peso with the dollar was introduced and holding US currency was legalized. The Cuban parliament approved a new investment law, allowing for totally foreign-owned companies to be established, including by Cuban residents abroad. US Congress approved the Helms-Burton law which penalized companies dealing with Cuba through third-party countries. The international community, especially the EU, harshly criticized this measure for violating the WTO and GATT agreements on free trade.

36   The Helms-Burton law barred Cuban access to loans from international institutions like the World Bank or the IMF. However the foreign companies continued to invest in Cuba by using various subterfuges such as pseudonyms, and the economic reforms continued to be implemented. Banks were allowed to extend their offer of services and tax-free trading areas were created by a

decree in June. In mid 1996, productivity was up 8 per cent on 1995 figures, while the GDP had increased 9.6 per cent.

37   In February 1996, the Cuban air force shot down two light aircraft flown by a group of Cuban exiles in Miami known as "Brothers to the Rescue". According to Havana, they had violated Cuban air space to drop anti-governmental leaflets on the island. Amnesty International denounced the imprisonment of several people linked to the Cuban Council. According to Amnesty, the Council included 140 groups of opponent journalists, professionals and union activists, while the Cuban government linked it with US intervention.

38   The Helms-Burton law barred Cuba from getting loans from the World Bank or the International Monetary Fund. However, foreign entrepreneurs continued to invest in Cuba, using various subterfuges, and the economic reforms continued. In mid-1996, productivity had grown 8 per cent on 1995 figures and the GDP had risen 9.6 per cent.

39   Cuban exiles in Miami suffered two "tough blows" in late 1997. The first was the death of its leader Más Canosa, on November 23, and second came Castro's political coup with Pope John Paul the Second's visit to the island. Following the CCP meeting in 1991 and constitutional amendments of 1992, relations between Cuba and the Vatican improved considerably. As a run up to the visit, the Pope condemned the US embargo on the island and Castro declared Christmas 1997 a national holiday.

40   In April 1998, Grenada and Cuba re-established diplomatic relations which had been suspended since the US invasion of the former in 1983. Grenada's prime minister Keith Mitchell made an official visit to Cuba where he signed an economic co-operation agreement.

41   In February, the UN Historical Verification Commission blamed the United States for backing the Guatemalan army in massacres of the population, whilst pointing out that Cuba's government had supported the left-wing guerrillas here, even sending supplies of weapons.

43   The constant tension between Castro and successive US administrations was revived in November 1999, when a young boy was the only survivor of a vessel carrying Cubans which sank just off Miami. Cuba claimed that Elián González should be returned to his father on the island, whilst various US political groups used the plight of the child as a ploy for the election in 2000. The Cuban exile community ignored rulings by

the US courts and the Attorney-General that the boy should be sent back to his country of origin. He was eventually returned to Cuba where he became a symbol of the fight against the US and its 40-year-long blockade on Cuba. ∎

STATISTICS

DEMOGRAPHY

Population: 11,160,000 (1999)
Annual growth: 0.8 % (1975/97)
Estimates for year 2015
(million): 11.6 (1999)
Annual growth to year 2015:
0.3 % (1997/2015)
Urban population: 76.7 %
(1997)
Children per woman: 1.6 (1998)

HEALTH

Life expectancy at birth: 76
years (1998)
male: 74 years (1998)
female: 78 years (1998)
Maternal mortality:
27 per 100,000 live births
(1990-98)
Infant mortality:
7 per 1,000 (1998)
Under-5 child mortality:
8 per 1,000 (1998)
Daily calorie supply:
2,357 per capita (1996)
518 doctors per 100,000 people
(1993)
Safe water: 93 % (1990/98)

EDUCATION

Literacy: 96 % (1995)
male: 96 % (1995)
female: 96 % (1995)
School enrolment:
Primary total: 106 % (1990/96)
male: 108 % (1990/97)
female: 104 % (1990/97)
Secondary:
male: 73 % (1990/96)
female: 82 % (1990/96)
Tertiary: 12 % (1996)
Primary school teachers: one for
every 12 (1996)

COMMUNICATIONS

118 newspapers (1996) , 353
radios (1997), 199 TV sets (1996)
and 32 main telephone lines
(1996) per 1,000 people
Books: 9 new titles per 100,000
people (1992/94)

ECONOMY

Cereal imports:
1,592,794 metric tons (1998)
Fertilizer use: 553 kg per ha
(1997)
Development aid received:
$ 67 million (1997);
$ 6.2 per capita (1997)

ENERGY

Consumption: 1,291.0 Kgs of Oil
equivalent per capita yearly
(1997); 49.0 % imported (1997)

HDI (rank/value): 58/0.765
(1997)

Cyprus

Kipros Kibris

Population: 779,000 (1999)
Area: 9,250 SQ KM
Capital: Nicosia (Levkosia)
Currency: Pound
Language: Greek and Turkish

The first civilization on Cyprus may be 3,000 years old. Hittites, Phoenicians, Greeks, Assyrians, Persians, Egyptians, Romans, Arabs and Turks trooped through its valleys and over its hills until 1878, when the British negotiated the island with Turkey in exchange for protection against Czarist Russia. Cyprus became a bridgehead of the British expansion eastward.

2   In 1930, movements favoring enosis (annexation) by Greece, gained ground stimulated by the incorporation of Crete to Greece in 1913. Enosis was promoted by the Greek Orthodox Church, the spiritual guide of Greek-Cypriots, who make up the majority of the island's population. But Turkey, Greece's perennial rival, was averse to being completely surrounded by a hostile neighbor on its Mediterranean coast. The British sent many Greek-Cypriot priests into exile. After World War II the country's most important political figure was Archbishop Vaneziz Makarios, who led the Cypriot anti-colonial movement from exile.

3   In 1959, representatives of the Greek and Turkish communities, of Makarios' Democratic Party and of British colonial interests, approved a plan whereby Cyprus was to become an independent republic with constitutional guarantees for the Turkish minority, and British sovereignty over the island's military bases. Independence was proclaimed on August 16 1960, and Makarios took office as president. An active supporter of anti-colonialism, the President played an important role in the Movement of Non-Aligned Countries. Makarios was re-elected in 1968 and 1973. Tensions between Greece and Turkey persisted and had frequent

repercussions in Cyprus where conflicts erupted between the Greek and Turkish communities.

4   The US Government was not friendly toward Makarios, either, considering him the "Fidel Castro of the Mediterranean". In 1963 there was an unsuccessful coup attempt by members of the radical right, who supported enosis. On July 15 1974, the crisis came to a head when the Cypriot National Guard, under the command of Greek army officers, ousted the President-Archbishop, who fled to Britain. Nikos Sampson, who favored annexation by Greece was appointed. Five days later, Turkey invaded northern Cyprus, bombed Nicosia, and drove 200,000 Greek Cypriots southward, under the pretext of protecting the Turkish minority.

5   Sampson turned the presidency over to the President of the Lower House, Glafkos Clerides, on July 23. That same day, the Greek military junta (in power since 1963) also stepped down, unable to face the prospect of a war with Turkey, domestic opposition, and world-wide repudiation.

6   The Turkish forces, who were occupying 40 per cent of the island, refused to return to the situation which had prevailed prior to the coup, and continued to occupy the north of the country. On August 16 1974 a Turkish-Cypriot Federal state was proclaimed in the northern part of the island - the part under Turkish control - under the presidency of Rauf Denktash.

7   Makarios returned to Cyprus in December 1974 and held the Presidential office until his death in 1977. Spyros Kyprianou succeeded Makarios and followed the same policy, refusing to recognize the division of Cyprus and retaining membership of the Non-Aligned Movement.

8   A pact between Makarios and Denktash had set four basic conditions for a negotiated settlement: the establishment of a communal, non-aligned, independent and federal republic; an exact delimitation of the

territories that each community would administrate; the discussion of internal restrictions on travelling, ownership rights and other important issues within the frame of a federal system with equal rights for both communities; and sufficient federal power to ensure unity.

9   The Turkish refusal to withdraw the troops meant that no substantial progress was made. On November 15 1983, the Turkish Republic of North Cyprus was proclaimed, but only Turkey recognized the new state.

10   In the 1980s, Cyprus enjoyed a period of economic prosperity brought by tourism, foreign aid, and international business that made the island a financial centre, replacing Beirut, whose money markets had been paralyzed by the Lebanese civil war. The main beneficiary of this was the Greek-Cypriot bourgeoisie. In the northern part of the island there had been an influx of 40,000 new Turkish immigrants. When added to the 35,000 Turkish soldiers stationed in the area, and the migration of 20,000 Turkish-Cypriots from the south, the Turkish population in the area tripled.

11   On May 5 1985, in northern Cyprus, a constitution for the Turkish-Cypriot Republic was submitted to a referendum. The turnout was 70 per cent, of which 65 per cent voted in favor.

12   In February 1987, the Greek premier cancelled a visit to the US, because the US had favorable relations with Turkey and installed US arms in the Turkish part of Cyprus.

13   Giorgis Vassiliu was elected President of Cyprus in 1988,. He re-established negotiations with Denktash which had been suspended in 1985. Political leaders on both sides and representatives of the 350,000 Cypriots in exile called for constructive flexibility on the part of both leaders. The Greek community - backed by their economic prosperity and the fact that they were numerically in the majority - wanted independence to be guaranteed by the United Nations. They also sought freedom of movement and property ownership throughout the island. The Turkish-Cypriots, on the other hand - based on the status quo and the superiority of the Turkish army - demanded a bi-national federation, under Ankara protection.

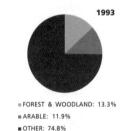

TERRITORY UNDER TURKISH CONTROL   0   50 km

WORKERS

1997
UNEMPLOYMENT: 26.4%

% OF LABOUR FORCE   **1998**

■ FEMALE: 45%   ■ MALE: 55%
    1990

■ SERVICES: 56.4%
■ INDUSTRY: 30.0%
■ AGRICULTURE: 13.6%

LAND USE

IRRIGATED: 35.5% of arable (1993)

    1993

■ FOREST & WOODLAND: 13.3%
■ ARABLE: 11.9%
■ OTHER: 74.8%

PUBLIC EXPENDITURE

DEFENCE EXPENDITURE (% of goverment exp.)	**16.2%** (1997)	
MILITARY EXPENDITURE (% of health & education)	**17%** (1990/91)	

95%

Millions US$ 1996

IMPORTS

4,703

EXPORTS

4,127

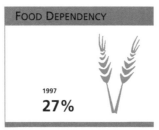

1997

27%

[14] The economy of the island grew by 6.9 per cent in 1989. In April 1990, Denktash was re-elected as President of the "Turkish Republic", in the north of the island. In 1991, with the support of US President George Bush, Turkey proposed a summit with representatives from Ankara, Athens and both Cypriot communities. Washington's support for the initiative was considered compensation for the help given to Turkey during the Gulf War by Greece and the Greek Cypriots.

[15] Nicosia demanded participation in the UN and the European Community, while rejecting the presence of Turkish Cypriot representatives. In April 1992, the UN declared Cyprus a bi-communitarian and bi-regional country, with equal political rights for both communities. In early 1993, Glafkos Klerides defeated Giorgis Vassiliu in the Presidential elections.

[16] In the north of the island, Denktash formed a new coalition government in December 1993. In 1994, the Cypriot courts ratified the "legitimacy" of the British military bases on the island, while the European Court ordered an embargo on Turkish Cypriot exports. Despite help from Ankara, this embargo seriously damaged the economy in the north of the island.

[17] In 1995, the idea of Cyprus joining the European Union began to be considered as a way of overcoming the division on the island. Meanwhile, the island received more than two million tourists and its economy continued to grow. Massive investments from Eastern Europe led to accusations of laundering money.

[18] In the May 1996 elections, the Workers' Party won a third of the votes, robbing parliamentary support from President Klerides' government. In August, a series of demonstrations along the internal frontier of the island left several people dead. Amnesty International accused the Turkish Cypriot police of being directly or indirectly responsible for at least two of these deaths.

[19] In attempts to join the European Union, Klerides and the Turkish Cypriot leader Denktash held meetings throughout 1997. These meetings, backed by the United Nations, aimed for the medium-term reunification of the island prior to entry into the EU. However, direct negotiations between the EU and Greek Cypriot authorities stalled dialogue within Cyprus and the reunification drive got nowhere.

[20] Given this impasse, the EU said if the island were not reunited, the Greek area could be admitted as an independent state, leaving the Turkish zone out.

[21] In March 1998, following three days of tough debate, the Foreign Ministers of the 15 EU member nations agreed to authorize the opening of negotiations for the incorporation of the Greek zone of Cyprus to the Union, leaving out the Turkish section.

[22] In the hard-fought February presidential elections, Klerides was re-elected Greek Cypriot President, with 50.8 per cent of the vote compared with the 49.2 per cent obtained by his rival George Iavacu, of the centre-right IKOS party.

[23] In 1999, the Greek decision to lift the veto on Turkish entry to the EU, plus aid offered to the Turkish Government in the wake of devastating earthquakes, indicated a change in the political atmosphere surrounding the situation in Cyprus.

[24] Negotiations were renewed between Clerides and Denktash within the UN framework, in February 2000. These were held as "proximity talks", avoiding all direct contact between the parties. ∎

PROFILE

ENVIRONMENT

Once part of continental Europe, the island of Cyprus is located in the eastern Mediterranean, close to Turkey. Two mountain ranges - the Troodos in the southwestern region, and the Kyrenia in northern Cyprus - enclose a fertile central plain. The temperate Mediterranean climate, with hot, dry summers and mild, rainy winters, is good for agriculture. The growing levels of atmospheric pollution rise even higher during peak hours of urban activity, with the combined effect of industrial pollution and traffic. However, though the quality of the air has been affected by pollution, it still lies within acceptable limits. Soil degradation is the result of natural causes and human abuse, particularly where there has been an excessive use of agrochemicals. The coastal ecosystem has felt the effects of tourism, particularly the construction of large hotels and high-rise apartment blocks.

SOCIETY

Peoples: Cypriots are divided into Greek (80 per cent) and Turkish (18 per cent) communities, within which they have separate political, cultural and religious organizations.
Religions: Greek Orthodox and Muslim.
Languages: Greek and Turkish (official).
Political Parties: Democratic Party (Greek sector) and National Unity (Turkish sector), are the main parties.
Social Organizations: There are two major labor organizations representing approximately 30 unions, the Pancyprian Federation of Labor, and the Cyprus Worker's Confederation.

THE STATE

Official Name: Kypriaki Dimokratia-Kibris Caemhuriyeti.
Capital: Levkosia (Nicosia) 178,000 people (1995).
Other cities: Limassol 137,000; Larnaca 61,000 (1992).
Government: Greek sector: presidential republic, constitution in effect since August 16 1960. Glafkos Klerides, Head of State and of the Government since January 28 1993, re-elected in February 1998. Single-chamber legislature: House of Representatives with 71 members (56 from the Greek community and 15 from the Turkish community). Turkish sector: parliamentary republic, constitution in effect since May 5 1985. Rauf Denktash, Head of State since February 13 1975. Single-chamber legislature: 50-member Assembly, elected every five years. The 'Turkish Federated State of Cyprus' based upon Turkish occupation and recognized only by Turkey, exercises an independent administration, including a judicial system and a Legislative Assembly.
National Holiday: October 1 Independence Day (1960).
Armed Forces: 10,000.
Other: Armed Police: 3,700.

STATISTICS

DEMOGRAPHY

Population: 779,000 (1999)
Annual growth: 1.0 % (1975/97)
Estimates for year 2015 (million): 0.9 (1999)
Annual growth to year 2015: 0.7 % (1997/2015)
Urban population: 55.2 % (1997)
Children per woman: 2.0 (1998)

HEALTH

Life expectancy at birth: 78 years (1998)
male: 76 years (1998)
female: 80 years (1998)
Maternal mortality: 0 per 100,000 live births (1990-98)
Infant mortality: 8 per 1,000 (1998)
Under-5 child mortality: 9 per 1,000 (1998)
Daily calorie supply: 3,341 per capita (1996)
231 doctors per 100,000 people (1993)
Safe water: 100 % (1990/98)

EDUCATION

Literacy: 95 % (1995)
male: 98 % (1995)
female: 93 % (1995)
School enrolment:
Primary total: 100 % (1990/96)
male: 100 % (1990/97)
female: 100 % (1990/97)
Secondary:
male: 96 % (1990/96)
female: 99 % (1990/96)
Tertiary: 23 % (1996)
Primary school teachers: one for every 15 (1996)

COMMUNICATIONS

114 newspapers (1996), 459 radios (1997), 146 TV sets (1996) and 485 main telephone lines (1996) per 1,000 people
Books: 142 new titles per 100,000 people (1992/94)

ECONOMY

Per capita, GNP: $ 11,920 (1998)
Annual growth, GNP: 5.0 % (1998)
Consumer price index: 109.1 (1998)
Cereal imports: 626,557 metric tons (1998)
Food import dependency: 27 % (1997)
Fertilizer use: 2,097 kg per ha (1997)
Exports: $ 4,127 million (1996)
Imports: $ 4,703 million (1996)
Development aid received: $ 49 million (1997); $ 70.6 per capita (1997); 0.60 % of GNP (1997)

HDI (rank/value): 26/0.870 (1997)

Czech Republic

Ceska Republika

Population: 10,263,000 (1999)
Area: 78,860 SQ KM
Capital: Prague
Currency: Koruny
Language: Czech

The exact origin of the first inhabitants of the Mid-Danube region remains uncertain, apart from the signs left by the Boii, a Celtic people whose name gave rise to the Latin name "Bohemia". The Celts were displaced without major conflict by Germanic tribes and later, in the 6th century, by the Slavs, while the Germans continued their migration southward.

[2] The inhabitants of mountain and forest areas had the natural protection of these areas. However, the lowlands were repeatedly invaded by the Avars. The Slavs were able to repel these invasions when they had leaders strong enough to unite the tribes. In the 8th century, calm was restored to Bohemia with the defeat of the Avars at the hands of Charlemagne.

[3] In the early 9th century, three potential political centers emerged: the plains of Nitra, the Lower Morava Basin and Central Bohemia. The Slavs of Bohemia gained the upper hand in most of the region. The first Moravian King was Mojmir I, who extended his realm as far as Nitra. His successor, Rostislav I, institutionalized the State and consolidated political relations with the Eastern Frankish empire, as a way of maintaining his own sovereignty.

[4] The Christian Franks organized the first missions at Nitra and in Bohemia, but Rostislav would not allow Latin to be taught, and asked the Byzantine emperor to send preachers who spoke the Slavic language. Religious texts were also translated into Slav. Constantine and Methodius

arrived in 863, leading a group of Greek missionaries.

[5] Methodius won recognition from Rome for his work in Moravia and in Panonia (Croatia), which became an ecclesiastical province linked to the Archbishop of Sirmium. The Franks came to consider Methodius an enemy; he was captured and kept prisoner until 873, when he returned to Moravia.

[6] Rostislav was the founder of Great Moravia, uniting the territories inhabited by the Slavs of the region for the first time. Slovakia, bordered by the northern ring of the Carpathian Mountains and by the Morava River, was a natural member of Great Moravia.

[7] Religious rivalry between the Latin and Slav languages continued throughout the period of expansion of the Bohemian principality. The death of Methodius in 885 strengthened the position of the Frankish Bishop Wiching, his life-long enemy. Wiching displaced

Methodius's disciples, and convinced the new Pope to outlaw the Slavic liturgy.

[8] Some years later the Czech expansion clashed with the kingdom of Germania. King Arnulf sent a military expedition to Moravia in 892, allying himself later with the Magyars to defeat the principality. Between 905 and 908, Great Moravia went through several foreign occupations, until an agreement was reached between Mojmir II and Arnulf.

[9] In the 10th century, between the strengthening of Germania and the restoration of the Holy Roman Empire, Bohemia lost the major part of its possessions. When Bfetislav I ascended the throne in 1034, the principality recovered part of Moravia and invaded Poland in 1039. However, King Henry III of Germania forced a retreat, and the Hungarian Crown kept Slovakia.

[10] In order to maintain its independence, Bohemia found it necessary to be actively involved in the campaigns of the Holy

Roman Empire. Thus, the situation arose whereby the Bohemian princes were being crowned king by both the rival powers.

[11] In the early 13th century the Church separated from the State, and the feudal lords began demanding greater political participation. At the same time, Germanic immigration was responsible for an increase in population. A series of incentives to build new urban centers and develop mineral resources gave rise to a new class of tradesmen and entrepreneurs.

[12] Under the Przemysl dynasty, which lasted until 1306, Bohemia controlled part of Austria and the Alps; at one point a single king ruled over Bohemia and Poland. This dynasty was succeeded by the Luxembourgs in 1310. With the coronation of Emperor Charles I in 1455, Bohemia and the Holy Roman Empire were joined together. As the capital of the Kingdom and the Empire, this was Prague's greatest moment.

[13] The high level of corruption among the clergy triggered a religious reform movement in the 14th century, which became even more radical under the influence of Father John Huss of Prague's Bethlehem Chapel. Excommunicated by the Pope, Huss was later tried for heresy and sedition by the Council of Constance, and was burned alive in 1415 after refusing to recant.

[14] The anger which followed Huss' execution marked the birth of the Hussite movement in Bohemia and Moravia. The Germanic peoples remained faithful to Rome, however, and in addition to these religious differences, the ethnic issue remained, triggering political conflict between them. The Holy Roman Empire, allied with the German princes, launched several military campaigns in Bohemia, but they were repulsed by the Hussites.

[15] Religious differences prevented political union between Bohemia and its former possessions for many years. Vladislav II reigned over Bohemia from 1471 but Moravia, Silesia and Lusacia were ruled by Mathias, of Hungary. Only when Vladislav II was elected king of

WORKERS

1997
UNEMPLOYMENT: 4.7%

% OF LABOUR FORCE   **1998**

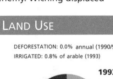

■ FEMALE: 47%   ■ MALE: 53%

1990

■ SERVICES: 43.4%
■ INDUSTRY: 45.4%
■ AGRICULTURE: 11.2%

LAND USE

DEFORESTATION: 0.0% annual (1990/95)
IRRIGATED: 0.8% of arable (1993)

1993

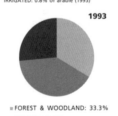

■ FOREST & WOODLAND: 33.3%
■ ARABLE: 40.2%
■ OTHER: 26.5%

PUBLIC EXPENDITURE

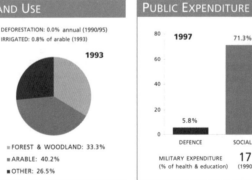

1997

DEFENCE 5.8%

SOCIAL 71.3%

MILITARY EXPENDITURE   **17%**
(% of health & education)   (1990/91)

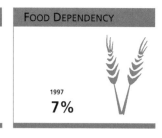

MATERNAL MORTALITY

1990-98

Per 100,000
live births

9

FOOD DEPENDENCY

1997

7%

Hungary, upon Mathias's death in 1490, were the territories reunited.

[16] The death of Vladislav II's son Louis II in 1526, paved the way for the rise of the Hapsburgs. Ferdinand I, Louis' brother-in-law, became king by currying favor with the nobility. Austria's victory over the Protestant Society of Schmalkaldica in 1547 permitted Ferdinand to impose the right of hereditary succession to the throne upon Bohemia and its states.

[17] The Hapsburgs strengthened the Counter-reformation throughout the region. Slovakia remained within its realm because the Hapsburgs had retained it when Hungary was invaded by the Ottoman Empire, in 1526.

[18] Rudolf II (1576-1612) transferred the seat of the empire to Prague, making it once again one of the continent's most important political and cultural centers. Many key positions of the kingdom were filled by Catholics during Rudolf's reign, as he himself was Catholic. However, this triggered a rebellion by the non-Catholic (Reformed church) majority, and the king was deposed in 1611.

[19] After a stormy succession, Ferdinand II of Styria, with the support of Maximilian I of Bavaria, defeated the Protestants and ruled with a strong hand. The Diet lost its power to initiate legislation, being reduced to merely approving the king's petitions. The Germanic language was added to the traditional use

of Czech, and only the Catholic religion was authorized.

[20] Unlike Bohemia, Moravia did not become involved in the fight against the Hapsburgs and therefore did not suffer the effects of civil and religious strife as severely. In Moravia there was religious tolerance allowing the growth of Protestantism in the state, which remained separate from the Austrian Crown until 1848.

[21] Despite the hegemony of the Germans and the prohibition of political activity, the Czechs conserved their ethnic identity, their language and their culture. Something similar had also occurred in the Hungarian counties inhabited by Slovaks. This set the scene for a resurgence of nationalism in the early 19th century, which strengthened the traditional ties between these two peoples.

[22] Czechs and Slovaks, together with the inhabitants of the German republics, helped put a stop to the absolutist doctrine, amidst a revolutionary wave which swept Europe in 1848. In 1867, the empire split in two: Austria, where ethnic Germans outnumbered the Czechs, Poles and other nationalities; and Hungary, where the Magyars subdued the Slovaks.

[23] With World War I the fall of the Austro-Hungarian Empire finally brought about the recognition of the Republic of Czechoslovakia. The new state's borders established in 1919 by the victorious powers included parts of Poland, Hungary and the Sudetenland, all home to ethnic minorities, and all sources of potential conflict.

[24] Czech and Slovak leaders charged the National Assembly with drawing up a Constitution. The Assembly opted for a strict parliamentary system, in which the President and his cabinet would be responsible to two legislative chambers. Women's right to vote or to be elected was granted for the first time.

[25] The 1930s world-wide depression affected the Sudetenland intensely, as it was a highly industrialized region. It also accentuated nationalistic feeling among the German people there, who developed a separatist movement alongside

Hitler's rise to power in 1933. Britain, France and Italy negotiated the ceding of the Sudetenland to Germany in 1938, thus paving the way for the German occupation of Czechoslovakia in 1939.

[26] After Hitler's defeat, Czechoslovakia recovered its 1919 borders, while the German population was almost entirely expelled from the country.

[27] The Communist Party (CKC) obtained 38 per cent of the vote in the 1946 election, increasing to 51 per cent in 1948. In June, a People's Republic was proclaimed, and the CKC applied the economic model in effect at the time in the USSR. Czechoslovakia joined the Council for Mutual Economic Assistance (CMEA) and the Warsaw Pact.

[28] In 1960, the People's Republic of Czechoslovakia added "socialist" to its name. In political terms, this decade was a turning point. Slovak leaders, expelled from the party in the 50s, were rehabilitated. The Slovak struggle for autonomy (which had been even further restricted by the new socialist constitution) together with the 1967 student strikes brought an end to Antony Novotny's leadership of the CKC.

[29] In early 1968, the election of Alexander Dubcek as Secretary of the CKC, and of Ludwik Svoboda as the country's president led to the implementation of a program to decentralize the economy, and affirm national sovereignty, against a background of broad popular support.

[30] Moscow viewed the possibility of Czechoslovakian reforms as a threat to the integrity of the socialist camp; in August 1968, it used Warsaw Pact Forces to intervene in the country and crush the movement. The leaders of the "Prague Spring" were expelled from the CKC and political alignment with the USSR was re-established.

[31] From the time Mikhail Gorbachev was named Communist Party Secretary in the USSR, the reform process there brought about changes in Czechoslovakia, with the CKC trying to keep its hold on power. In 1989, despite violent repression, anti-Government

PROFILE

ENVIRONMENT

The Bohemian massif occupies the western region, bounded to the southeast by the Moravian plains. Cereals and sugar beet are cultivated in the lowlands of Bohemia and Moravia, where cattle and pigs are also raised. Rye and potatoes are grown in the Bohemian valleys. The country has rich mineral deposits: coal, lignite, graphite and uranium in the Bohemian massif; coal in Moravia. Sulphur dioxide emissions-produced in the generation of electrical energy are very high, causing acid rain. Air pollution has destroyed or damaged large areas of forest. Approximately three-quarters of all the country's trees show a high degree of defoliation. Water pollution levels are also very high, especially in rural areas. Waste from industry, mining and intensive farms threaten the purity of the water, both above and below the ground.

SOCIETY

Peoples: Czechs, 81.2 per cent; Moravians, 13.2 per cent; Slovaks, 3 per cent.
Religions: Mainly Catholic.
Languages: Czech (official).
Political parties: Social Democratic Party; Civic Democratic Party; Communist Party of Bohemia and Moravia; Socialist Party; Agrarian Party, Green Party, Christian Democratic Union-Czechoslovakian People's Party, Association for the Republic-Republican Party, Democratic Civic Alliance; Movement for Autonomous Democracy of Moravia and Silesia.
Social Organizations: Central Trade Union Council

THE STATE

Official Name: Ceska Republika.
Administrative divisions: 8 regions subdivided into municipalities.
Capital: Prague 1,300,000 people (est 1996).
Other cities: Ostrava 326,000 people; Brno 390,000; Olomouc 106,000.
Government: Parliamentary republic. Vaclav Havel, President since January 1993; Milos Zeman, Prime Minister since July 1999.
National holiday: October 28, Independence Day.
Armed Forces: 92,900 in 1994.
Other: Border Guards: 7,000; Internal Security Forces: 2,000; Civil Defence Troops: 2,000.

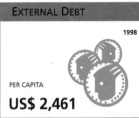

1998

PER CAPITA

US$ 2,461

Millions US$ 1998

IMPORTS

34,610

EXPORTS

33,817

DEMOGRAPHY

Population: 10,263,000 (1999)
Annual growth: 0.1 % (1975/97)
Estimates for year 2015 (million):
9.9 (1999)
Annual growth to year 2015: -0.2
% (1997/2015)
Urban population: 65.7 % (1997)
Urban Growth: 0.2 % (1980/95)
Children per woman: 1.2 (1998)

HEALTH

Life expectancy at birth: 74 years
(1998)
male: 70 years (1998)
female: 77 years (1998)
Maternal mortality: 9 per 100,000
live births (1990-98)
Infant mortality: 5 per 1,000
(1998)
Under-5 child mortality: 6 per
1,000 (1998)
Daily calorie supply: 3,177 per
capita (1996)
293 doctors per 100,000 people
(1993)

EDUCATION

School enrolment:
Primary total: 104 % (1990/96)
male: 105 % (1990/97)
female: 104 % (1990/97)
Secondary:
male: 97 % (1990/96)
female: 100 % (1990/96)
Tertiary: 24 % (1996)
Primary school teachers: one for
every 19 (1995)

COMMUNICATIONS

254 newspapers (1996), 803 radios
(1997), 406 TV sets (1996) and 273
main telephone lines (1996) per
1,000 people
Books: 91 new titles per 100,000
people (1992/94)

ECONOMY

Per capita, GNP: $ 5,150 (1998)
Annual growth, GNP: -2.2 %
(1998)
Annual inflation: 13.7 % (1990/98)
Consumer price index: 130.6
(1998)
Currency: 32.3 koruny = $ 1 (1998)
Cereal imports: 328,324 metric
tons (1998)
Food import dependency: 7 %
(1997)
Fertilizer use: 1,015 kg per ha
(1997)
Exports: $ 33,817 million (1998)
Imports: $ 34,610 million (1998)
External debt: $ 25,301 million
(1998); $ 2,461 per capita (1998)
Debt service: 15.2 % of exports
(1998)
Development aid received: $ 107
million (1997); $ 10.4 per capita
(1997); 0.20 % of GNP (1997)

ENERGY

Consumption: 3,938.0 Kgs of Oil
equivalent per capita yearly
(1997); 22.0 % imported (1997)

HDI (rank/value): 36/0.833 (1997)

protests continued, precipitating a crisis within the regime.

[32] The Government was forced to negotiate with the Civic Forum, an alliance of several opposition groups. Among other reforms, Parliament approved the elimination of the CKC's leadership role, issuing a condemnation of the 1968 Soviet intervention. In late 1989, a provisional Government was formed, with a non-communist majority.

[33] In December 1989, the Civic Forum declared that the CKC had redistributed cabinet positions in such a way as to keep its own people in the key positions. 200,000 people gathered in Prague to demand a greater opposition representation in the cabinet. Gustav Husak resigned the presidency of the federation and was replaced by Vaclav Havel, who immediately granted amnesty to all political prisoners and called elections for June 1990.

[34] In late 1989, the Soviet and Czech governments agreed on a gradual withdrawal of the 70,000 Red Army troops stationed within the country.. In October 1991, after the dissolution of the Warsaw Pact, president Havel and his Hungarian and Polish counterparts requested some kind of association with the Atlantic alliance.

[35] After the June 1990 elections Havel was confirmed in the presidency and the Czech and Slovak Federal Republic was proclaimed. In September, the Republic joined the World Bank and the IMF.

[36] Following the elections, the Forum divided into the Civic Democratic Party, the self-proclaimed "right with a conservative program", and the Civic Movement.

[37] In the June legislative elections, the Czech Civic Democratic Party and the Slovak group, Democratic Slovakia, won in their respective republics. When negotiations over the statutes of the new federation came to an impasse, Czech and Slovak leaders meeting in the Moravian city of Brno admitted that separation was inevitable.

[38] On July 17 1992, Czechoslovakian President Vaclav Havel announced his resignation after the declaration of sovereignty in the Slovakian National Assembly. Czechoslovakia disappeared from the world map, replaced by the Czech Republic, with its capital Prague (Praha), and the Republic of Slovakia, with its capital Bratislava.

[39] As soon as Slovakia became independent, in January 1993, the country began a rapid process of integration with Western Europe. On January 26, Vaclav Havel, the former president of Czechoslovakia, was elected President of the Czech Republic, with the support of a parliamentary majority led by the right wing Civic Party,

[40] As Prime Minister, the leader of the Civic Party, Vaclav Klaus, adopted a market economy with less negative results than the other former socialist republics. As for the rest of the region, the freeing of prices and the introduction of consumer taxes had limited inflationary effects: the price increase was 17 per cent in 1993. Unemployment remained at 2.5 per cent and per capita income continued to be one of the highest in Eastern Europe.

[41] The Czech Republic became the eleventh signatory of the Peace Association in March 1994, an organization which developed out of NATO to progressively include the nations of the former socialist bloc in the alliance.

[42] The national debt continued lower than that of other former communist countries of the region, while foreign investment was amongst the highest. Prime Minister Klaus planned an economic reform based on a rapid privatization campaign. In 1995, the banking system saw a high number of deposits, many of which came from illegal economic activities. This same year, the Czech Republic became the first former Communist OECD member.

[43] In June 1996, the electoral success of the Social Democrats left Klaus without an absolute majority in Parliament.

[44] In December, the Czech Republic and Germany signed a reconciliation document, in which Germany asked forgiveness for the behavior of the Nazi regime during World War II, while the Czech Government apologized for the expulsion of three million Germans from the Sudetenland following the War.

[45] During 1997, the devaluation of the national currency, the crown, brought political chaos. The Civic Party led by Klaus was accused of encouraging financial groups which bribed several of its members with "hidden commissions" during the privatization process. Havel publicly called for Klaus' resignation, which was received in November. Josef Tosovsky became the new Prime Minister.

[46] The economic crisis coincided with increasing in xenophobia, displayed in racist attacks against minority groups, like the Gypsies. This violence appeared to be supported by a large and increasing percentage of the population.

[47] In April 1998, the Czech Republic was admitted to NATO. The June elections were won by the Social Democratic Party. With 32.3 per cent of the vote, the SDP took 74 seats, while the CDP, with 27.7 per cent of the vote, retained 63. Given the difficulty in getting a majority, the CDP settled for giving the Social Democrats government in return for their leader, Klaus, being appointed parliamentary speaker. After the agreement, the SDP was to form the first left-wing government of the post-communist era. The objectives of the new minority government were the elimination of corruption, an increase in the national minimum salary and preventing the "devolution" of the property of the Catholic Church.

[48] The Government had problems approving the budget and in implementing its own program. Unemployment reached record levels at the end of 1998 and inflation exceeded 11.5 per cent. Economic problems dragged on throughout all 1999, and in December around 50,000 people took to the streets calling for the Government to resign. ∎

Denmark

Danmark

Population:	5,283,000 (1999)
Area:	43,090 SQ KM
Capital:	Copenhagen
Currency:	Kroner
Language:	Danish

The first hunters established themselves in Denmark in about 10,000 BC as the Neolithic period drew to a close. This was followed by a flourishing Bronze Age civilization, about 1000 BC Around the year 500 AD, northern Germanic peoples began settling on the islands as fishers and navigators. Certain placenames bear witness to the worship of Scandinavian gods, such as Odin, Thor and Frey.

² The first evidence of hierarchical society in Denmark comes from the Viking age, mostly from cemeteries and settlement sites. The Vikings were Scandinavian farmers, navigators, merchants and above all raiders who ruled the northern seas between the 8th and 10th centuries AD.

³ Archeological remains indicate that Roskilde on the island of Sjaeland Hedeby, south of Jutland, and Jelling in the center, were the most intensely populated areas. After the Danish victory over the Germans the Eider River became the final southern border. A huge wall was built to the south and west of Hedeby.

⁴ In the 10th century, after continuous conflict with rival kingdoms, the center of the kingdom's power was transferred to Jelling, where Gorm became king of Jutland. His son Harald Bluetooth (Blatand) is credited with uniting Denmark and conquering parts of Norway.

⁵ Subsequent Viking reigns extended Danish possessions as far as modern-day England and Sweden. In 1397 King Margrethe managed to unite Denmark, Norway, Iceland, Greenland, Sweden and Finland in the "Union of Kalmar".

⁶ The introduction and spread of Christianity and strengthening of the Hanseatic League went hand-in-hand with the weakening of Denmark's military power.

⁷ The Danish kings were involved in successive wars between themselves, campaigns which were interspersed with peasant rebellions and bourgeois revolts; a large and powerful middle class had developed as a result of growing mercantile activity. These conflicts ceased in the 17th century, when a weakened nobility gave the King power as absolute sovereign. He was then able to create laws to be imposed throughout the land.

⁸ During the 18th century, Denmark colonized the Virgin Islands. The Danish colonists organized local production using African slave labor and in 1917 the islands and their population were sold to the United States. (See US Virgin Islands)

⁹ Peace existed in Denmark and Norway from 1720 until the Napoleonic Wars. After Napoleon's defeat, Sweden attacked Denmark and, under the Kiel Peace Treaty, annexed Norway in 1814.

¹⁰ The loss of Norway, combined with British trading impositions brought on an economic collapse which worsened as a result of low wheat prices. The ensuing agricultural crisis forced land reform to a standstill. The situation later improved when agricultural prices stabilized, trade increased and industrialization began. In 1814 an educational reform made schooling obligatory.

¹¹ After the European revolutions of 1848, King Frederick VII called an assembly. A parliamentary monarchy was established and absolutism was abolished. The 1849 Constitution guaranteed freedom of the press, of religion and of association, as well as the right to hold public meetings. The main trends of the period were nationalism and liberalism.

¹² A territorial dispute with Germany over the Duchies of Schleswig and Holstein reinforced nationalistic sentiment. In 1864, when Denmark was defeated by Prussia and Austria, it lost its claim to these lands and the national-liberal government was brought down.

¹³ The 1866 Constitution maintained the monarchy. In 1871, Louis Pio, a former military officer, attempted to form a socialist party. A series of strikes and demonstrations organized by the socialists was put down by the army, and Pio was deported to the United States. The Social Democratic Party, mainly supported by intellectuals and workers, was formed in 1876.

¹⁴ The peasants and emerging middle class weakened the monarchy on three fronts: the farm co-operative movement, a liberal bourgeois party (popularly referred to as "leftist") and the social democrat party.

¹⁵ In 1901 the United Left (Liberal) came to power establishing a new government. The emergence of the UL and the Social Democrats as a leading force at the turn of the century was the result of agrarian reform, industrialization and the development of railroads. The growth of urbanization and overseas trade (accelerating the formation of labor unions throughout the country and the rise of co-operatives in the countryside) was the main reason for these changes.

¹⁶ In 1915, the Constitution was revised. The voting age of 35 was maintained, but the right to vote was extended to women, servants and farm hands. There were judicial reforms, bringing in trial by jury, and land distribution in the largest states.

¹⁷ Also in 1915 women were granted the right to stand for election. The first woman was appointed to the cabinet in 1924.

¹⁸ After the 1870-71 Franco-German War, Denmark adopted a neutral international stance. World War I provided Copenhagen with favorable trading opportunities with the warring nations, but at the same time affected its supplies. During World War II Denmark was invaded by Germany, although it

WORKERS

1997
UNEMPLOYMENT: 5.4%

% OF LABOUR FORCE **1998**

■ FEMALE: 46%   ■ MALE: 54%

1990

■ SERVICES: 66.2%
■ INDUSTRY: 28.2%
■ AGRICULTURE: 5.6%

LAND USE

DEFORESTATION: 0.0% annual (1990/95)
IRRIGATED: 17.1% of arable (1993)

1993

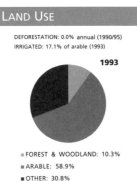

■ FOREST & WOODLAND: 10.3%
■ ARABLE: 58.9%
■ OTHER: 30.8%

PUBLIC EXPENDITURE

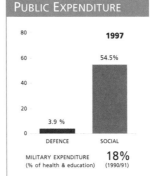

1997

54.5%

3.9 %

DEFENCE   SOCIAL

MILITARY EXPENDITURE   **18%**
(% of health & education)   (1990/91)

officially maintained its independence until 1943.

[19] When Hitler attacked the USSR, Denmark created a volunteer army and outlawed communist activity. The 1943 election was an anti-Nazi plebiscite, with the electorate throwing its support behind the democratic parties. Resistance to the Nazi regime, strikes, and the Government's refusal to enforce Nazi rule, led the German occupation forces to declare a state of emergency dissolving Denmark's police and armed forces.

[20] In September 1943, the Danish Freedom Council was created to co-ordinate the anti-Nazi opposition. When Germany finally surrendered, a transition government was formed, with representatives from the Council and the traditional parties. The 1945 election was won by the liberals.

[21] The Faeroe Islands, under Danish control since 1380, were occupied by Britain during the war and subsequently returned to Denmark. The 1948 Constitution gave the islands greater autonomy, though the Danish Parliament retained control of defense and foreign affairs.

[22] In Greenland, also controlled by the Danes since 1380, Denmark was responsible for foreign policy and justice. In 1979, the island obtained the right to have its own legislative assembly (*Landsting*), which has power over internal affairs. Other areas are dealt with by the Danish Parliament which has two representatives from the island.

[23] Since 1947, there has always been at least one woman in the cabinet. That same year, Protestant women achieved the right to be priests.

[24] In the post-war period, a proposed Nordic Defense Alliance did not come about, as Norway did not agree with Denmark and Sweden. Denmark joined NATO in 1949, increasing its military power with the help of the United States. A US proposal for setting up air bases on Danish soil was turned down.

Faeroe Islands

Population: 48,000 (1998)
Area: 1,400 SQ KM
Capital: Torshvn
Language: Danish

The climate is generally rainy and cloudy, with mild temperatures both in summer and winter. Only 6 per cent of the land is cultivated. Agricultural production mainly consists of vegetables as the land is not suitable for grain. Sheep are raised throughout the islands and there is mining in Suderoy. 20 per cent of the population are employed in handicraft production and 21 per cent in fisheries, which provide 90 per cent of the islands' exports.

SOCIETY

Peoples: The population is of Scandinavian origin.
Religions: Lutheran. There are a large number of Baptists and a small Catholic community.
Languages: Danish (official) and the Faeroese dialect.
Political Parties: Social Democratic and Union (liberal) parties, which favor ties with Denmark; the Republican "Left", Popular and Progressive parties, favor independence.

THE STATE

Capital: Thorshavn 16,000 people (1992).
Government: The parliament (*Lagtinget*) has up to 30 members, elected on a basis of proportional representation. Parliament names a national cabinet (*Landstyret*) of 6 ministers. After the 1990 elections, the latter was a coalition between the Social Democratic and Popular parties. A high commissioner (*Rigsombudsman*) represents the Crown. The islands elect 2 representatives to the Danish Parliament.
Diplomacy: In January 1974, the *Lagtinget* decided not to join the EEC. To protect the fishing industry, a 200-mile fishing zone was established in 1977. Modernization of the island's fishing fleet and methods was financed through a series of foreign loans, which totaled $839 million in 1990 - $18,000 per capita.

DEMOGRAPHY

Population: 48,000 (1998)

COMMUNICATIONS

594 radios (1997) per 1,000 people

ECONOMY

Cereal imports: 2,216 metric tons (1998).

[25] In 1953, the Constitution was amended reducing the Legislature to a single chamber (*Folketing*). In 1954 the post of "ombudsman" was created to ensure that municipal and national government complied with the law, and to protect "ordinary" citizens from the misuse of power on the part of government officials or agencies.

[26] In 1959, Denmark became the founding member of the European Free Trade Association (EFTA). In 1972, 63.7 per cent of the electorate voted yes in a referendum asking whether the country should join the European Economic Community. In 1973, the oil crisis seriously affected the Danish economy and unemployment rose to over 14 per cent.

[27] In the 1973 election, the traditional parties were ousted in favor of two new parties; the extreme right Progressive Party and the Democratic Center, the right-wing of the Social Democratic Party.

In 1975, the Social Democrats were voted back into power. They lost a significant number of votes in subsequent elections because of high unemployment and unpopular economic measures. In 1982 the Conservatives won office for the first time since 1894. Their victory was due to their alliance with the Liberals, the Democratic Center and the Christian People's Party.

[28] In the 1980s, 23 per cent of the seats in Parliament were held by women.

[29] In 1982, the Government appointed women as the ministers for Employment and Religious affairs. In that year 43.9 per cent of the economically-active population were women, and they were protected by specific legislation. Women can interrupt their careers for up to two years to raise their children.

[30] In 1986, Parliament approved a strict environmental protection law which proved costly for both the

MATERNAL MORTALITY

1990-98

Per 100,000 live births

10

FOOD DEPENDENCY

1997

13%

FOREIGN TRADE

Millions US$ 1997

IMPORTS

55,463

EXPORTS

61,158

STATISTICS

DEMOGRAPHY

Population: 5,283,000 (1999)
Annual growth: 0.2 % (1975/97)
Estimates for year 2015 (million): 5.3 (1999)
Annual growth to year 2015: 0.1 % (1997/2015)
Urban population: 85.4 % (1997)
Urban Growth: 0.2 % (1980/95)
Children per woman: 1.7 (1998)

HEALTH

Life expectancy at birth: 76 years (1998)
male: 73 years (1998)
female: 78 years (1998)
Maternal mortality: 10 per 100,000 live births (1990-98)
Infant mortality: 5 per 1,000 (1998)
Under-5 child mortality: 5 per 1,000 (1998)
Daily calorie supply: 3,808 per capita (1996)
283 doctors per 100,000 people (1993)

EDUCATION

School enrolment:
Primary total: 100 % (1990/96)
male: 100 % (1990/97)
female: 99 % (1990/97)
Secondary:
male: 117 % (1990/96)
female: 122 % (1990/96)

COMMUNICATIONS

309 newspapers (1996), 1,141 radios (1997), 533 TV sets (1996) and 618 main telephone lines (1996) per 1,000 people
Books: 230 new titles per 100,000 people (1992/94)

ECONOMY

Per capita, GNP: $ 33,040 (1998)
Annual growth, GNP: 2.7 % (1998)
Annual inflation: 1.6 % (1990/98)
Consumer price index: 106.3 (1998)
Currency: 6.7 kroner = $ 1 (1998)
Cereal imports: 554,748 metric tons (1998)
Food import dependency: 13 % (1997)
Fertilizer use: 1,882 kg per ha (1997)
Exports: $ 61,158 million (1997)
Imports: $ 55,463 million (1997)

ENERGY

Consumption: 3,994.0 Kgs of Oil equivalent per capita yearly (1997); 4.0 % imported (1997)

HDI (rank/value): 15/0.905 (1997)

industrial and agricultural sectors, in a country without nuclear plants.

[31] Denmark has been one of the few countries to comply with the UN's recommendation to contribute at least 0.7 per cent of the GNP to development. The country recycles around 72 per cent of all paper used and recovers more than 100,000 tons of industrial waste per year.

[32] Marriage between people of the same sex was authorized in 1989.

[33] In 1993, unemployment stood at 12.5 per cent of the economically-active population. The Progress Party demanded that foreigners no longer be allowed to enter the country. These account for a mere 3.3 per cent of the population, including 30,000 Turks, 30,000 Europeans from EU countries, 22,000 Scandinavians and other European nationalities, as well as Pakistanis and Sri Lankans.

[34] In 1993, the Danes finally approved the Maastricht Treaty, which formed the European Union, after rejecting it the previous year, on condition that the country would not join the Economic and Monetary Union.

[35] Social Democratic Prime Minister Poul Nyrup Rasmussen was reelected in 1994, after having been chosen for office the previous year as a result of the fall of the liberal-conservative government which broke refugee laws. Former Justice minister Erik Ninn Hansen was found guilty of having prevented the family reunion of Tamil refugees from Sri Lanka.

[36] Rasmussen achieved the majority in Parliament through alliances with center and left-wing parties. Economic growth reached its peak in 1994, with 4.4 per cent GDP growth and a 2 per cent rise in inflation. Economic expansion slowed down in 1995 and 1996. Reduction of extended social benefits enabled unemployment to fall from 12.5 per cent to 10 per cent in two years

[37] The country's domestic tranquillity was disturbed by a conflict between rival motorcycle bands in 1996. The bands attacked bars where their rivals met in urban areas with anti-tank missiles, causing panic and damage to private property. The Government decided to tackle the matter with emergency legislation. The same year, Denmark had a disagreement with Iceland over fishing rights in the strait located between Greenland and Iceland.

[38] The Danish People's Party (DPP) - now split from the Progress Party but both far right - obtained over 6 per cent of the vote in the Copenhagen local elections in November 1997. Its leader, Pia Kjaersgaard, based her campaign on the "threat" Third World immigrants posed to Denmark. However, the unemployment rate - 8 per cent of the economically active population - and the number of foreigners - 4.5 per cent of population - were the lowest in Western Europe.

[39] In legislative elections held on March 11 1998, the ruling Social Democratic coalition retained a majority, although it defeated the center-right coalition by only one seat, obtaining 90 of the 179 seats at stake, while the opposition received 89 seats.

[40] Early in 2000, surveys revealed that the DPP was ranked third in popularity with the public. Presenting a more bland front than the other similar European parties, the DPP adapted its xenophobic discourse to the liberal and tolerant tradition of the nation. It mainly targeted Muslims, stating "the Muslims are people as good as ourselves but present a problem for a Christian country". ∎

Greenland

Population: 59,000 (1998)
Area: 2,175,600 SQ KM
Capital: Nuuk (ex-Godhaab)
Currency: Kroner
Language: Greenlandic, Danish and Inuit

Located in the Arctic Ocean, the island is the second largest tract of frozen land on the planet. Nearly four fifths of its surface is covered by an ice cap. In the month of June, soon after the rapid thaw, moss and lichen vegetation appears on certain parts of the coast. Most of the population is concentrated in the western region, where the climate is less severe. Fishing forms the basis of the economy; whale oil and salted or frozen fish are exported. The country has lead, zinc, and tungsten deposits. Cryolite from the large reserves in Ivigtut is also exported.

SOCIETY

Peoples: 80 per cent are Inuit. The remaining 20 per cent are Danish or other short-term European residents.
Religions: Lutheran. The Greenlandic Church comes under the jurisdiction of the Bishop of Copenhagen and the minister of ecclesiastical affairs.
Languages: Greenlandic, Danish and Inuit

Political Parties: Siumut, Social Democratic; Atassut, liberal-conservative; Inuit Atgatigiit, nationalist federation.

THE STATE

Capital: Nuuk (formerly Godhaab) 12,217 people (1990).
Government: Jonathan Motsfeld, Prime Minister since 1997. Greenland elects two representatives to the Danish *Folketing*, and has one representative on the Nordic Council.
Diplomacy: On January 1 1985 the island withdrew from the European Economic Community. However, EEC countries can still fish in Greenland's territorial waters upon payment of $20 million.

DEMOGRAPHY

Population: 59,000 (1998)

COMMUNICATIONS

18 newspapers (1996) and 481 radios (1997) per 1,000 people

ECONOMY

Cereal imports: 2,503 metric tons (1998)

Djibouti

Djibouti

Population: 629,000 (1999)
Area: 23,200 SQ KM
Capital: Djibouti
Currency: Franc
Language: French

In about the 3rd century BC Ablé immigrants came from Arabia and settled in the north and parts of the south. The Afars, or Danakil, are descendants of these peoples. Later the Somali Issas pushed the Afars out of the south and settled in the coastal regions. In AD 825 Islam was brought to the area by missionaries. Arabs controlled the trade in this region until the 16th century, when the Portuguese competed for it. In 1862, Tadjoura, one of the Sultanates on the Somalian coast (see Somalia), sold the port of Obock and adjoining lands to the French for 52,000 francs and in 1888 French Somaliland (Côte Française des Somalis) was established.

[2] Djibouti became the official capital of this French territory in 1892. A treaty with Ethiopia in 1897 reduced the territory in size. A railway was built to connect Djibouti with the Ethiopian hinterland, reaching Dire Dawa in 1903 and Addis Ababa in 1917. The interior of the area was effectively opened up between 1924 and 1934 by the construction of roads and administrative posts. After World War II Djibouti port lost trade to the Ethiopian port of Asseb (now in Eritrea). In 1946 French Somaliland acquired the status of an overseas territory (from 1967 called the French Territory of the Afars and Issas), and in 1958 it voted to become an overseas territorial member of the French Community under the Fifth Republic.

[3] Independence and the reunification of neighboring Somalia stimulated the emergence of anti-colonialist movements such as the Somaliland Liberation Front and the African League for Independence, both of which used the legal and armed branches.

[4] During the 1970s, renewed resistance forced acting governor Ali Aref to resign. France called a plebiscite on May 8 1977, and 85 per cent of the population voted for independence. Hassan Gouled Aptidon, main leader of the African League for Independence, became President of the fledgling Republic.

[5] The Government of the new state had to deal with tension between the Afar and Issa peoples and with refugees from the war zones in Ethiopia and Somalia. In an attempt to overcome old ethnic divisions, Gouled granted governmental participation to various groups. He even appointed several Afar ministers. Though French remained the official language, Djibouti was admitted into the Arab League.

[6] Ethiopia and Somalia, its two neighbors, both had territorial designs on Djibouti. Ethiopia's interest in Djibouti was basically geopolitical. In the event of Eritrean nationalists achieving independence, Ethiopia would become a landlocked territory - if an agreement could not be reached for the use of Eritrean ports, Djibouti would be their only available harbor. For Somalia it was mainly a historical aim to unify the Somali nation.

[7] In mid-1979, President Hassan Gouled resumed relations with Ethiopia and Somalia, signing trade and transportation agreements with them. The participation of Afars in the Government and in the newly-formed army was encouraged as a way of securing some semblance of national unity.

[8] A ruling party was organized and municipal administrations were created to encourage political participation. Foreign aid was basically used for irrigation works and to improve the situation of refugees from the Ogaden war.

[9] The Gouled administration received aid from Saudi Arabia, Kuwait, Iraq and Libya. Gouled skilfully administered his country, playing upon its only valuable resource: its strategic position at the mouth of the Red Sea. Contrary to expectations which foretold a rapid annexation by Ethiopia or Somalia, Djibouti stressed its determination to remain independent.

[10] In spite of a successful performance in diplomatic relations, Gouled faced serious domestic problems, particularly ethnic rivalries between Afars and Issas. Afars, 35 per cent of the population, complained of political and economic discrimination. The Issas, 60 per cent of the population and hold key positions in the Government, refuted all accusations of favoritism, and supported Gouled's radical policies to neutralize the opposition. After the prohibition of the Popular Liberation Movement in 1979, the Afars tried to reorganize as the Djibouti Popular Party in 1981, but this was also banned.

[11] In October 1981, President Gouled amended the Constitution to introduce a single-party system. The official Popular Association for Progress (RPP) became the sole legal party and the other groups were banned. It was argued that they had racial or religious aims and in consequence were potentially harmful to national unity.

[12] During 1983, the first steps were taken in a project to radically alter Djibouti's economy. Incentives were to be given to transform the country into a financial center and free trading port, a sort of Middle Eastern Hong Kong. Six foreign banks opened offices in Djibouti, mainly attracted by a solid national currency backed by dollar deposits in the US.

[13] By the end of 1984, the first results were not encouraging: the number of passengers and goods in transit to Ethiopia and Somalia had dropped considerably and, therefore, customs revenues and bank activities had decreased. The continuing conflict in the area has been seen as the major cause for the withdrawal of European capital.

[14] With the support of the UN High Commissioner, the Government resumed the voluntary repatriation of more than a hundred thousand refugees, a process which had been interrupted in 1983.

[15] At the same time, bilateral agreements were signed with Ethiopia to combat contraband and promote peace in the border areas. These had been closed in 1977, at the outset of the conflict with Somalia over the Ogaden region.

[16] In August 1987, foreign military presence in Djibouti grew as French bases when used by US and British forces participating in manoeuvres in the Persian Gulf. Relations with the former colonial power were reinforced by President François Mitterand's visit, in December.

[17] Djibouti depended on French economic aid. Trying to avoid this dependence Prime Minister Barkad Gourad Hamadou signed an economic and technical aid agreement with Turkey in June 1989.

[18] In 1990 France wrote off Djibouti's debt by granting it $40,000,000 as public development aid. In 1991, confrontations between the Government and the Front for the Restoration of Unity and Democracy (FRUD) guerrillas were renewed. In November, Amnesty International accused the Government of the torture of 300 prisoners. Due to mounting pressure France pressed Gouled to begin talks with the opposition.

[19] In September 1992, amid combat against the FRUD, the Government introduced a constitutional reform which established a multiparty system. In the May 1993 presidential elections,

LITERACY

1995

46%

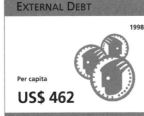

EXTERNAL DEBT

1998

Per capita

US$ 462

FOREIGN TRADE

Millions US$ 1997

IMPORTS

285

EXPORTS

207

Gouled was again re-elected, with over 60.8 per cent of the vote. However, encouraged by the FRUD, half of the electorate abstained from voting and the opposition considered the elections a "fraud". [20] Armed confrontations between government troops and guerrillas escalated in the weeks following the elections, which led thousands to seek refuge in Ethiopia. Acting as mediator, the French Government sought a cease-fire and negotiations began. Meanwhile, Gouled believed the rebellion was part of a plan orchestrated by Ethiopia. [21] In March 1994, the FRUD was divided due to a possible agreement with the Government. The movement's Politburo, led by Ahmad Dini Ahmad, who opposed the agreement, was replaced by an executive council headed by Ahmad Ougoureh Kible. In June, Gouled and the FRUD jointly decided to end the war. [22] In June, a demonstration of mostly Afar residents from the

Arhiba district, opposed to the demolition of their homes for "security" reasons, was quelled by government forces. Police intervention left four dead, 20 injured and 300 arrests, including that of Muhammad Ahmad Issa, United Opposition Front president. [23] In October, dissent within the FRUD had grown and the movement's leaders banned Ahmad Dini Ahmad and Muhammad Adoyta Yussuf, another breakaway leader, from holding any "activity or responsibility" in the FRUD. In 1995, after the Constitution was revised, a section of the FRUD formed an alliance with the ruling party. Ahmad Dini Ahmad said this alliance amounted to "treason". [24] In mid-1995 under pressure from the IMF, the Government substantially reduced public spending and took a series of measures to increase fiscal income. The following year, the IMF granted Djibouti a $6.7 million credit to support the Government reform programme. In March 1996,

President Gouled dismissed two ministers: defence and justice post-holder, Ahmed Boulaleh Barreh, and Moumin Bahon Farah of prisons and Islamic affairs. The departure of these ministers consolidated the position of Prime Minister Barkat Gourad Hamadou and the Head of Cabinet Ismael Omar Guelleh, a close relative of Gouled. [25] Farah, who had announced the formation of a new political party in April, was imprisoned for a month accused of having insulted Gouled. In August, Farah started a hunger strike protesting over his imprisonment. On September 26, in Addis Ababa, Ethiopia, 17 opponents to the Gouled regime were abducted and made prisoners of the Djibouti regime. The prisoners included human rights campaigner Aicha Debalé, who had moved to the Ethiopian capital on the request of the French NGO Mission Enfance, to help children fleeing the war and repression in Djibouti. [26] In December, legislative elections, classed as "a masquerade" by the opposition, were won by the People's Assembly for Progress (RPP) with 25 seats, followed by the Front for the Restoration of Unity and Democracy (FRUD) with 11 seats. [27] In February 1998, thanks to pressure from organizations like Women's Solidarity and the International Democratic Federation of Women, Debalé was freed. Her husband who had also been abducted, remained in prison. On February 17, despite Djibouti having signed the African Human Rights Charter, guaranteeing freedom of speech and information, director of the bi-monthly Al Wahda publication, Ahmed Abdi Farah, and a journalist on the paper, Kamil Hassan Ali, were arrested for an article which had criticized the Government a year earlier. [28] In April 1999, the first presidential elections since independence saw Ismail Omar Guelleh winning by a broad margin. Guelleh, the second president in the history of the nation, based his election campaign on promises to alleviate the poverty of the population. His political rivals accused him of having murdered opponents through the 20 years when he was the key advisor and director of the special police corps. ∎

PROFILE

ENVIRONMENT

Located in the Afar triangle, facing Yemen, Djibouti is one of the hottest countries in the world (average annual temperature 30°C). The land is mostly desert; its only green area is found in the basalt ranges of the northern region. Agriculture, confined to oases and to a few spots along the coast, satisfies only 25 per cent of the domestic food demand. Extensive cattle-raising is practised by nomads. Economic activity is concentrated around the port.

SOCIETY

Peoples: Djiboutians are divided into two major ethnic groups of equal size: the Afars, scattered throughout the country, and the Issas, of Somalian origin, who populate most of the southern territory and predominate in the capital. **Religions:** Muslim. There is a small Christian minority (5 per cent). **Languages:** Afar and Issa (Somali), French (official) and Arabic (religious). **Political Parties:** People's Assembly for Progress (RPP), which emerged in 1979 from the African People's League for Independence, founded in 1975 by Hassan Gouled. Democratic Renovation Party (PRD); Democratic Front for the Liberation of Djibouti; Movement for the Liberation of Djibouti and the Front for the Restoration of Unity and Democracy (FRUD).

THE STATE

Official Name: République de Djibouti. **Administrative divisions:** 5 districts. **Capital:** Djibouti 450,000 people (1989). **Other cities:** Ali-Sabieh 4,000 people; Tadjoura 3,500; Dikhil 3,000 (1989). **Government:** Ismail Omar Guelleh, President since May 1999. Barkad Gourad Hamadou, Prime Minister. **National Holiday:** June 27, Independence Day (1977). **Armed Forces:** Approximately 3,900. **Other:** Gendarmerie (Ministry of Defense): 600; National Security Force (Ministry of Interior): 3,000.

DEMOGRAPHY

Population: 629,000 (1999)
Annual growth: 5.1 % (1975/97)
Estimates for year 2015 (million): 0.9 (1999)
Annual growth to year 2015: 1.9 % (1997/2015)
Urban population: 82.7 % (1997)
Children per woman: 5.3 (1998)

HEALTH

Life expectancy at birth: 51 years (1998)
male: 49 years (1998)
female: 52 years (1998)
Infant mortality: 111 per 1,000 (1998)
Under-5 child mortality: 156 per 1,000 (1998)
Daily calorie supply: 1,920 per capita (1996)
20 doctors per 100,000 people (1993)
Safe water: 90 % (1990/98)

EDUCATION

Literacy: 46 % (1995)
male: 60 % (1995)
female: 33 % (1995)
School enrolment:
Primary total: 38 % (1990/96)
male: 44 % (1990/97)
female: 32 % (1990/97)
Secondary:
male: 17 % (1990/96)
female: 12 % (1990/96)
Tertiary: 0 % (1996)
Primary school teachers: one for every 34 (1996)

COMMUNICATIONS

84 radios (1997), 73 TV sets (1996) and 13 main telephone lines (1996) per 1,000 people

ECONOMY

Cereal imports: 89,936 metric tons (1998)
Exports: $ 207 million (1997)
Imports: $ 285 million (1997)
External debt: $ 288 million (1998); $ 462 per capita (1998)
Development aid received: $ 87 million (1997); $ 163.3 per capita (1997); 17.50 % of GNP (1997)

HDI (rank/value): 157/0.412 (1997)

Dominica

Dominica

Population: 75,000 (1999)
Area: 750 SQ KM
Capital: Roseau
Currency: EC dollar
Language: English

I n Sunday, November 3 1493, Italian navigator Christopher Columbus reached an island which he named Dominica. He planted a cross to claim Spanish sovereignty over the newly discovered territory in the name of Queen Isabella and King Ferdinand of Spain.

[2] This territory was actually already populated by Carib peoples, peaceful and friendly indigenous groups. They watched the claiming ceremony from a distance, but could not have fully understood its significance. Soon afterwards, the Spanish returned in a more aggressive frame of mind, searching for the vast stores of gold that they believed the Caribs were hiding from them. They rapidly exterminated all but a few of the island's people, a pattern of destruction and despoilment that would be repeated throughout the colonial possessions in the new continent.

[3] By 1632 there were only an estimated 1,000 Caribs on the island. Today, there are only 500 living in the reservations.

[4] The landscape of present-day Dominica has changed greatly since their ancestors' days. In colonial times, the forests were felled to clear the land for extensive sugar plantations. The Carib peoples could not provide a sufficiently robust and reliable workforce, so the plantations were worked by thousands of slaves transported from Africa.

[5] In the 17th century, the Spanish withdrew and the French took their place. They introduced cotton and coffee production to complement the sugar trade. In the following two centuries, frequent British attempts to seize the island from French hands culminated in Dominica becoming a British colony in 1805.

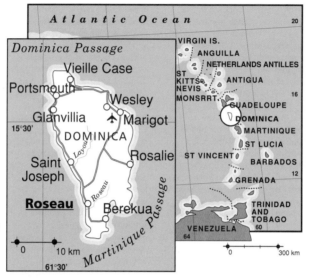

[6] French influence still persists. The Catholic religion predominates despite strong competition from well-financed Protestant sects, and Creole, the language spoken by the people is based on French mixed with African languages.

[7] After five centuries of colonization, the Dominicans inherited a rudimentary agrarian economy based on the mono-cultivation of bananas for export. These are the only significant export item, because most of the land went over to banana production when sugar cane became unprofitable at the end of the 19th century.

[8] The political system adopted on achieving internal autonomy in 1967 was a copy of the British model. The Constitution established the "free association" of the Associated States of the West Indies with Britain. Britain retained responsibility for defense and foreign relations and each member island elected its own state government. The seat of the federal government was in Barbados.

[9] From 1975, independence was negotiated separately by each State. In the case of Dominica the negotiations were conducted by Labor Party premier, Patrick John. In 1978, the British Parliament approved a new statute for the island and on November 3 1978, exactly 485 years after the arrival of Columbus, Dominica became an independent country once more.

[10] The protest rallies that took place during the celebrations were

an indication of the difficulties that lay ahead. Political division immediately became evident: a conservative group of veteran politicians opposed independence and a progressive sector supported by young people disagreed with the Labor Government which had done the negotiating.

[11] Since the island lacked the natural resources to attract transnationals and tourism, Dominica could not compete with its neighbors. Vast numbers of young people emigrated to neighboring Guadeloupe, while others who were more radical found political inspiration in the "black power" ideology of US black activists.

[12] In May 1979, the police fired at demonstrators protesting against two decrees limiting union activities and press freedom. At the same time, secret agreements between John and the South Africa were revealed. The Dominican premier had helped to plan a mercenary attack on Barbados and intended to supply Pretoria with oil refined in Dominica. Patrick John was forced to resign. His successor, Oliver Seraphine, from the progressive wing of the Labor Party, called elections and strengthened Dominica's ties with progressive neighboring governments. In September 1979, Hurricane David devastated the island. The Conservative opposition skillfully associated the catastrophe with the Labor administration and gained electoral support.

[13] In the July 1980 election, Mary Eugenia Charles won a landslide victory and became the first woman to head a Caribbean government. She was the daughter of a wealthy and influential landowner and described herself as "liberal, democratic and anti-communist".

[14] In the 1985 election, Charles' Dominican Freedom Party (DFP) obtained 15 of the 21 Parliamentary seats; the Labor Party, led by Michael Douglas, won only 5 seats and the United Dominican Labor Party (UDLP) won the remaining seat for its leader. During the electoral campaign, the opposition called for an investigation into a $100,000 donation made to the Government. It was believed that the donation had been made by the CIA to confirm Dominican collaboration in the US invasion of Grenada.

[15] In August 1986, Air Force commander Frederick Newton was sentenced to death by hanging for his participation in a plot to topple the conservative government in 1981. Former Prime Minister Patrick John and Michael Reid, captain of the Defense Forces, were found guilty of similar charges, and of involvement in a minor Ku Klux Klan conspiracy. They were sentenced to 12 years in prison.

[16] After the May 28 1990 parliamentary election, the third government since independence took office. Of the 21 seats up for election, Charles's DFP won by a slim majority of 11 seats, while the Labor Party (led by Douglas) won 4 and the United Labor Party, a newcomer in the electoral process and led by Edison James, won 6 seats. Leonard Baptist's Progressive Force did not win any seats.

[17] The day after the election, which gave the 71-year-old lawyer Charles her third consecutive term, Patrick John and Michael Reid were freed.

[18] In 1990, Prime Minister Charles signed an agreement with her counterparts James Mitchell of St Vincent, John Compton of St Lucia and Nicholas Braithwaite of Grenada, for the four islands to form a new state.

[19] In the same year the Regional Constitutional Assembly of the Eastern Caribbean was set up. It comprised government officials, religious authorities and representatives from social organizations. In a second meeting, in St Lucia in April 1991, the

LAND USE

1993

- FOREST & WOODLAND: 66.7%
- ARABLE: 9.3%
- OTHER: 24.0%

MATERNAL MORTALITY	FOOD DEPENDENCY	EXTERNAL DEBT
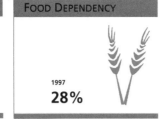 1990-98 Per 100,000 live births **65**	1997 **28%**	1998  Per capita **US$ 1,534**

Assembly studied various proposals for the establishment of the future State.

[20] This integration project was concordant with the Chaguaramas Treaty, which aimed at the unification of the entire English-speaking Caribbean community, although the three islands of St Kitts, Montserrat and Antigua refused to commit themselves to the process. The opposition parties of Grenada and St Lucia also stated they were against it. The seven mini-States of the Eastern Caribbean have a common Central Bank, which coins their shared currency.

[21] In 1991, the Government decided on a series of measures to stimulate the national economy, centering its efforts on the development of agriculture and communications.

[22] The Prime Minister narrowly escaped censure in April through a motion presented by the United Workers' Party. At the end of 1991, Charles attempted to enact legislation making it illegal for civil servants to protest against the Government.

[23] In 1993, Prime Minister Charles raised the rates on several services, suspended government investment and proposed a wage freeze, in an attempt to deal with the budget deficit. Thanks to her total support of US policies, the island obtained American foreign aid, earmarked for the revitalization of its agriculture.

[24] Charles proposed offering Dominican passports to 1,200 citizens of Hong Kong, on the condition that each one invested at least $35,000 in the country, but resistance to this idea increased during 1992-3. In mid-1993 the Prime Minister modified the project, raising the amount of the investment to $60,000 and imposing restrictions on the voting rights of the new citizens.

[25] In April 1994, the Government decision to increase the number of transport vehicle licenses caused protests and public disorder in Roseau. The Prime Minister accused the opposition of trying to bring forward the elections, and the crisis continued until an agreement was signed on May 6.

[26] In the same year, Dominica decided to vote against the establishment of a whale sanctuary in the South Atlantic. This attitude resulted in threatened tourism ban from the International Wildlife Coalition. This measure, which would have seriously affected a national economy heavily dependent on tourism, was not put into practice.

[27] In June 1995, the United Dominican Labor Party (UDLP) won the election, taking 11 of the 21 seats in Parliament. The Freedom Party and Liberal Party took five seats each. The new Prime Minister, Edison James, decided to promote the banana industry and privatize State enterprises in order to invest in the social infrastructure.

[28] In August and September 1995, Government plans were severely shaken as a succession of hurricanes and tropical storms destroyed the plantations and export projects. Houses, bridges, roads, hotels and public facilities were also destroyed and had to be rebuilt, absorbing vast amounts of resources.

[29] The external debt reached EC$ 320 million and the internal EC$ 80 million in January 1996. That year, the Government went ahead with a plan to privatize large public companies in an attempt to impose order on the financial sector. The Companies which passed into private hands were: Dominican Electricity Services, the Industrial and Agricultural Development Bank, the Import-Export Agency of Dominica and other services at the port of Roseau.

[30] Cuban Foreign Minister Roberto Robaina visited the country in May 1996, marking the re-establishment of diplomatic relations between Dominica and Cuba.

[31] In early 1997, the opposition parties severely criticized the privatizations, especially the sale of the Dominican Electricity Services to a British company, claiming the reasons behind this had not been sufficiently explained. On top of the $5 million received from the British Government for development projects, Dominica was awarded another million in April for a project to protect its coasts from erosion.

[32] Finance Minister Julius Timothy announced in 1998 that the international sector was going to be extended by enlarging the registration of foreign vessels and giving new incentives for the installation of insurance companies in the country.

[33] In October that year the Assembly appointed Vernon Lorden Shaw, a retired civil servant, seventh president of Dominica. Shaw promised recovery for the nation's sources of income which had been badly hit by climatic disasters and the global economic crisis.

[34] In February 2000, Rosie Douglas became Prime Minister. That same month, Dominica and Cuba signed a bilateral co-ordination and consultation agreement, including plans for annual meetings to strengthen cultural, social and political co-operation. Up until then, Cuban-Dominican co-operation had mainly concentrated on education, but now there were hopes for joint policies related to tourism. ∎

Dominican Republic

República Dominicana

Population: 8,365,000 (1999)
Area: 48,730 SQ KM
Capital: Santo Domingo
Currency: Peso
Language: Spanish

The island of Quisqueya was made up of two present-day countries: Haiti and the Dominican Republic. The first inhabitants belonged to several ethnic groups: the Lucayo, the Ciguayo, the Taino and the Carib. They were fishers and gatherers who practiced basic agriculture. There was always a great deal of contact between the Caribbean islands and trade between the groups.

[2] In December 1492 Christopher Columbus reached the island of Quisqueya, which he renamed Hispaniola. With the wood from one of his vessels he built a fort, initiating the European colonization of America. Within a few years, the Europeans had appropriated the whole island becoming owners of the land and the native Carib population. The terrible living and working conditions imposed by the Spaniards nearly exterminated the indians. Faced with this shameful situation, Bishop Bartolomé de Las Casas proposed that they replace local slave labor with Africans, millions of whom were distributed throughout the American continent.

[3] Dominican historical records show that in 1523 a group of rebel African slave workers, founded the first *quilombo* (former slave settlement) on the island. Subsequent rebel groups, in 1537 and 1548, set up their own quilombos. The replacement of native American labor with African labor accompanied a change in economic focus, from panning for gold to plantations of sugar cane and extensive cattle raising. As historian Pierre Vilar pointed out, the gold cycle in Hispaniola was "destructive, not of raw materials, but rather, of the labor force". During the colonial period the

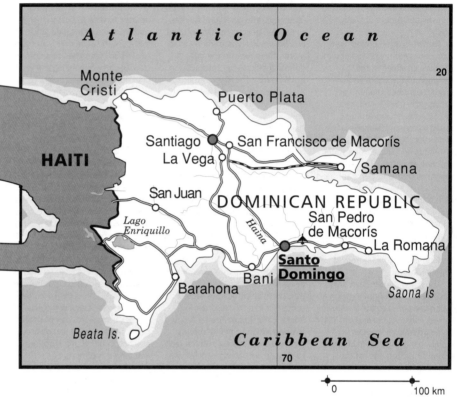

extraordinary economic potential of the Dominican Republic was comparable only with that of Brazil. The island was successively the greatest gold producer in the Antilles; one of the largest producers of sugar in the New World between 1570 and 1630; and finally, such an important cattle producer that there were 40 cattle per person on the island.

[4] As a major sugar producer with a key position on the trade route from Mexico and Peru to Spain, Hispaniola was coveted by the other colonial powers. In 1586, the English buccaneer Francis Drake

raided the capital and in 1697 the French occupied the island's western half. When they were given official ownership under the Treaty of Ryswick, they renamed it Haiti. Later, the whole island fell under French rule but was partially recovered by Spain in 1809, after the first Afro-American republic had been established (in Haiti).

[5] Haiti's government regained control over the whole island in 1822. The Spanish descendants' (*criollo*) resistance came to a head after an uprising in Santo Domingo. The independence of the Dominican Republic was

proclaimed, but in 1861 the Government asked Spain to reinstate colonial status, in an attempt to gain support for the *criollos*, whose dominance was threatened by the black and mulatto majorities.

[6] However, Spain did not defend its colony effectively and the Dominican Republic became independent again in 1865 after a mulatto uprising. The economic system remained unchanged.

[7] By that time the US, fully recovered from its civil war, began to gain influence in the West Indies (now called Caribbean). In 1907 the US imposed an economic and political treaty on the Dominican Republic prefiguring "dollar diplomacy". This treaty helped the US to invade the Dominican Republic and impose a protectorate that lasted until 1924.

[8] In 1930, when the country was autonomous again, Rafael Leónidas Trujillo seized power. He was Chief of Staff of the National Guard, elected and trained by the American occupation forces. He set up a dictatorial regime, with US backing, without nominally occupying the presidency. His crimes were so numerous and so apparent

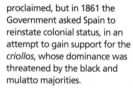

0   100 km

WORKERS

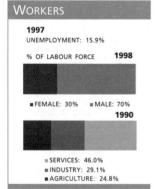

1997
UNEMPLOYMENT: 15.9%

% OF LABOUR FORCE **1998**

■ FEMALE: 30%   ■ MALE: 70%

1990

■ SERVICES: 46.0%
■ INDUSTRY: 29.1%
■ AGRICULTURE: 24.8%

LAND USE

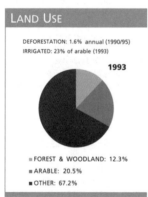

DEFORESTATION: 1.6% annual (1990/95)
IRRIGATED: 23% of arable (1993)

1993

■ FOREST & WOODLAND: 12.3%
■ ARABLE: 20.5%
■ OTHER: 67.2%

PUBLIC EXPENDITURE

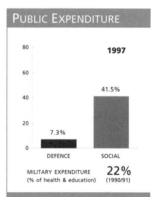

1997

41.5%

7.3%

DEFENCE   SOCIAL

MILITARY EXPENDITURE   **22%**
(% of health & education)   (1990/91)

MATERNAL MORTALITY		LITERACY	
	1990-98		1995
Per 100,000 live births			
230		82%	

that he finally became too embarrassing even for the US, and the CIA planned his assassination which was carried out in May 1961.

[9] One extreme example of his crimes was the case of Jesús de Galíndez, a Spanish Republican professor, labor leader, and member of the Basque Nationalist Party. He was kidnapped by assassins, on Trujillo's payroll and was subsequently killed, although his body was never found. Trujillo had the gunmen killed some time later. This proved to be a fatal mistake for among the assassins was an American with relatives in the CIA, and they settled the score by killing Trujillo. On his death, Trujillo owned 71 per cent of the country's arable land and 90 per cent of its industry.

[10] In 1963, following a popular rebellion, the first democratic elections were held and writer Juan Bosch was elected president. Seven months later, he was overthrown by military officers from the Trujillo regime. In April 1965, Colonel Francisco Cameo De led a constitutionals armed uprising. Accusing the nationalists of having "Pro-Castro/communist" sympathies, the US intervened once again, sending in 35,000 Marines who suppressed the insurgency.

[11] Before leaving the country, the US occupation force paved the way for an unconditional Trujillo supporter, Joaquín Balaguer, to rise to power. In return, he opened the country to transnationals, especially Gulf and Western. The sugar industry fell under Gulf control. The corporation also bought shares in local banking, agro-industry, hotels and cattle raising, consequently, becoming very influential in Dominican Republic.

[12] The nationalist opposition kept up its resistance and in 1973 Francisco Cameo was killed while leading a guerrilla group. The Dominican Revolutionary Party (PRD), originally led by Juan Bosch, split with the right wing (led by landowner Antonio Guzmán) eliminating the main reformist measures from its program. This action made it acceptable to the State Department and in 1978, when the PRD won the elections, the US used its influence - in the name of human rights - to ensure that the results would be respected.

[13] The PRD program promised to re-establish democratic freedoms and to follow an economic policy of income redistribution favoring the majority. The first promise was fulfilled and popular organizations took advantage of the new situation to reorganize their weakened structures after decades of harsh repression.

[14] New presidential elections were held on May 16 1981, and Salvador Jorge Blanco became president in the PRD's second successive victory. José Francisco Peña Gómez, one of the Latin American leaders in the Socialist International, was elected mayor of Santo Domingo. On July 4, departing president Antonio Guzmán killed himself, generating political tension which ended with the announcement of the electoral result.

[15] When President Blanco took office the trade deficit amounted to $562 million. In 1982, sugar prices fell and oil prices rose causing the foreign debt to climb to $2 billion. Unemployment affected 25 per cent of the active population.

[16] Blanco tried to tackle the situation by applying IMF-tailored austerity measures. But during 1983, the international price of sugar fell 50 per cent below the cost of production, and sugar accounted for 44 per cent of Dominican exports. In 1984, the Government withdrew the subsidies on several products, and imposed a 200 per cent price increase on staple and medical goods. These measures brought about protest rallies led by leftist organizations and labor unions. In return, the Union headquarters were occupied by soldiers leaving 100 dead, 400 injured and over 5,000 imprisoned.

[17] In 1985, the US reduced its Dominican sugar quota again, causing another decrease in exports. Unemployment rose abruptly, provoking yet another wave of social unrest. The Government continued to toe the IMF line, harshly repressing all the strikes and protests against its policies.

[18] In that year, the gravity of the economic crisis became evident. The judges went on strike and paralyzed the courts for three months. In May, the powerful Dominican Republic Medical Association began a new round of disputes, backed by the nurses, the Association of Agriculture Professionals and the Veterinary Association. In August, the Association of Engineers followed suit, supported by the architects and surveyors, who demanded a minimum wage of $260. The Dominican Association of Economists wrote that since 1980 poverty had been "initially limited to the low-income groups, (but) had spread to the point of affecting the middle classes".

[19] In the lower income categories, the situation was untenable. Committees for Popular Struggle began to appear and grass roots movements organized to resist price rises on basic goods and services. In April, dockworkers found 28 young Dominican Republic girls asphyxiated in a ship's container. They could not find work and had expected to find a way of making a living on another island. It was disclosed that every two weeks a "cargo" of young women from the Dominican Republic left for the Franco-Dutch island of St Martin, where a brothel manager sold them to other Caribbean islands for between 800 and 1,000 German marks.

[20] The circumstances surrounding Balaguer's inauguration were very difficult. Clearly a conservative, without a parliamentary majority and faced with highly organized social opposition, his hands were virtually tied. He did not even have the necessary power to impose a more restrictive economic program to get new loans from the IMF.

[21] The May 16 1990 general election went to President Joaquín Balaguer. His rival, Juan Bosch, leader of the PLD, accused him of an electoral fraud of monumental proportions. In the last opinion poll carried out before the election, Bosch was leading with 36 per cent of surveyed voters saying that they intended to vote for him, as opposed to the 26 per cent committed to Balaguer. The third candidate, PRD's Peña Gómez, suggested a recount which was held at the polling stations. This recount confirmed Balaguer's victory, with 35 per cent, to Bosch's 34 and Peña Gómez's 23.

PROFILE

ENVIRONMENT

The Dominican Republic comprises the eastern part of the island of Hispaniola, the second largest of the Antilles. The Cordillera Central, the central mountain range, crosses the territory from northwest to south east. Between the central and northern ranges, lies the fertile region of the Cibao. Sea winds and ocean currents contribute to the tropical, rainy climate. Between 1962 and 1990, the country lost a significant portion of its woodlands. Coral reefs are suffering the effects of pollution, which has harmed marine habitats and reduced fish populations.

SOCIETY

Peoples: Most Dominican Republicans are of Spanish and African descent, with a small native American component.
Languages: Spanish.
Religions: Roman Catholic 91.3 per cent; other 8.7 per cent.
Political Parties: Dominican Liberation Party (PLD); Social Christian Reformist Party (SCRP); Dominican Revolutionary Party (PRD).
Social Organizations: Most workers are represented by the General Workers' Union (CGT) and the Unity Workers' Union (CUT). In March 1991, 4 major labor groups, 57 federations and 366 labor unions merged within the CUT.

THE STATE

Official Name: República Dominicana.
Administrative Divisions: 26 Provinces, 1 National District.
Capital: Santo Domingo 2,400,000 people (1995).
Other cities: Santiago de Los Caballeros 690,000 people; La Vega 189,000; San Pedro de Marcorís 137,000 (1993).
Government: Leonel Fernández Reyna, President since August 1996.
National Holiday: February 27, Independence (1844).
Armed forces: 24,500 (1995). **Other:** National Police, 15,000.

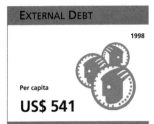
FOREIGN TRADE

Millions US$ 1998

IMPORTS

6,264

EXPORTS

4,849

STATISTICS

DEMOGRAPHY

Population: 8,365,000 (1999)
Annual growth: 2.2 % (1975/97)
Estimates for year 2015 (million): 10.3 (1999)
Annual growth to year 2015: 1.3 % (1997/2015)
Urban population: 63.3 % (1997)
Urban Growth: 3.8 % (1980/95)
Children per woman: 2.8 (1998)

HEALTH

Life expectancy at birth: 71 years (1998)
male: 69 years (1998)
female: 73 years (1998)
Maternal mortality: 230 per 100,000 live births (1990-98)
Infant mortality: 43 per 1,000 (1998)
Under-5 child mortality: 51 per 1,000 (1998)
Daily calorie supply: 2,316 per capita (1996)
77 doctors per 100,000 people (1993)
Safe water: 79 % (1990/98)

EDUCATION

Literacy: 82 % (1995)
male: 82 % (1995)
female: 81 % (1995)
School enrolment:
Primary total: 103 % (1990/96)
male: 103 % (1990/97)
female: 104 % (1990/97)
Secondary:
male: 34 % (1990/96)
female: 47 % (1990/96)
Tertiary: 23 % (1996)

COMMUNICATIONS

52 newspapers (1996), 178 radios (1997), 84 TV sets (1996) and 83 main telephone lines (1996) per 1,000 people

ECONOMY

Per capita, GNP: $ 1,770 (1998)
Annual growth, GNP: 6.8 % (1998)
Annual inflation: 10.6 % (1990/98)
Consumer price index: 119.3 (1998)
Currency: 15.3 pesos = $ 1 (1998)
Cereal imports: 946,806 metric tons (1998)
Fertilizer use: 956 kg per ha (1997)
Exports: $ 4,849 million (1998)
Imports: $ 6,264 million (1998)
External debt: $ 4,451 million (1998); $ 541 per capita (1998)
Debt service: 4.2 % of exports (1998)
Development aid received: $ 76 million (1997); $ 10.5 per capita (1997); 0.50 % of GNP (1997)

ENERGY

Consumption: 673.0 Kgs of Oil equivalent per capita yearly (1997); 74.0 % imported (1997)

HDI (rank/value): 88/0.726 (1997)

[22] From 1990 to 1991 there were hundreds of thousands of Haitian immigrants working as sugar cane cutters in the Dominican Republic sugar industry. In June 1991, Balaguer expelled illegal immigrants.

[23] Negotiations carried out by Balaguer made it possible to refinance the foreign debt. In 1933 tourism grew, making the country the fourth most important tourist destination in the Caribbean.

[24] As a result of the political crisis in neighboring Haiti, contraband goods were taken across the border from the Dominican Republic into Haiti. This practice foiled the international embargo against the Haitian regime. Oil was the main product smuggled into the country.

[25] Economic problems caused hundreds of Dominican Republicans to leave the country each year with forged visas and documents. Many sailed in unseaworthy vessels, bound for Puerto Rico, normally as a "stopover" on their way to New York.

[26] More than a million expatriates live in the United States, and half are illegal. There are also an estimated 20,000 in Spain, half of them illegal. The majority are women who work as domestics, while another 25,000 women work as prostitutes throughout Europe, most of them lured by false promises of employment.

[27] Although he had announced his retirement, Balaguer sought re-election. His perennial opponent Juan Bosch also ran in the 1994 election. According to opinion polls, José Francisco Peña Gómez, of the Dominican Revolutionary Party (PRD) held a slight lead over Balaguer. Intent upon avoiding another case of electoral fraud, four of the five participating parties signed a "civility pact", with the Catholic Church acting as guarantor. In spite of this, the electoral campaign turned violent, with hundreds of people injured and 12 people killed.

[28] International observers were called in to supervise the elections, denouncing irregularities, especially in the interior. The PRD condemned the election stating that some 200,000 voters were remained unable to vote as a result of official party manipulation. According to official figures, Balaguer obtained 43 per cent of the vote, leading Peña Gómez by 1.5 per cent, while Juan Bosch obtained 31.2 per cent.

[29] The US Government, anxious to win Balaguer's support in enforcing the trade embargo on Haiti, gave assurances that it would approve the final decision of the special commission set up to clarify the electoral results. However, three months after the August 1994 election, the special commission had still not reached a verdict. Finally, the Central Electoral Committee declared Balaguer the winner.

[30] But in mid-August, Peña Gomez and Balaguer agreed to hold elections on November 16 1995. Both leaders decided to reform the constitution in order to bar presidential re-election. In the meantime, Balaguer was proclaimed president. Official returns gave him a 22,281 vote lead.

[31] The Dominican Revolutionary Party (PRD) candidate, José Francisco Peña Gómez was the most popular candidate (48.75 per cent), but did not win an absolute majority. The ruling party candidate, Jacinto Peinaldo, did not reach the second round of voting. On June 30 1996, Leonel Fernández Reyna of the PLDP won the second round of elections after forming an alliance with the conservative PRSC On August 18 he succeeded Joaquín Balaguer, who had served seven terms as president.

[32] After the election, the PRSC signed an agreement with the PRD giving them control of the Senate, and the PRD dominated the Chamber of Deputies. The PLD remained in a minority in both chambers, preventing the President from implementing several of the initiatives announced in his electoral campaign.

[33] Increasing prices, unemployment of more than 30 per cent, and the poverty which affected 70 per cent of the population led to an increase in social tension. There were many demonstrations in the streets, some violent. Despite this, the economy in general saw exceptional growth of 6.9 per cent in the first half of the year.

[34] A law approved in June allowed private capital to invest in state companies, including the sugar and electricity sectors. The Government aimed to thus balance the state accounts.

[35] Towards the end of 1997, the Presidents of the Dominican Republic and Haiti agreed to stop the large-scale repatriation of Haitians and to respect human rights. The Haitians often worked in the worst conditions, and so the state sugar company had announced a plan to employ 16,000 Haitian cane-cutters. This cheap workforce was transported from the frontier to the various sugar plantations to work and then taken directly back to Haiti. However, pressure against the arrival of more Haitians did not stop: anti-immigrant protests led to the expulsion of some 2,500 undocumented Haitians and strengthened frontier controls.

[36] On April 16 1998, the Dominican Republic and Cuba restored diplomatic relations. The Government sent a consular representative to Havana, later followed by a delegation of ministers which formally inaugurated the diplomatic headquarters. The United States protested against the measure, deeming it "inappropriate".

[37] The May 1998 legislative and municipal elections gave a clear advantage to the opposition DRP, which took 83 seats in Parliament and 24 in the Senate. The DLP retained a mere 49 seats in parliament and 4 in the Senate (120 and 30 members respectively). In June, Fernández Reyna made a three day visit to the neighboring Haiti, the first official mission by a Dominican president since 1936, in order to set up a more effective joint border initiative, in order to stop the trafficking of weapons, drugs and immigrants between the two countries.

[38] Hurricane George, which left a total of more than 500 dead in September, also affected sugar cane production. Low nickel prices and poor sugar production hit the economy hard that year.

[39] Fresh disturbances shook the capital in January 1999 following the outcome of voting for the new president of the municipal league, an entity which handles a $100 million budget to aid local governments. In May, a widespread general strike demanded changes in government economic policy, but the demands were refused. In January 2000, at the age of 93, Joaquin Balaguer announced he would again stand for the presidency with the official approval of his party, the SCRP. ■

East Timor

Timor Leste

Population: 871,000 (1999)
Area: 14,870 SQ KM
Capital: Dili
Currency: Indonesian rupiah
Language: Tetum

Long before the arrival of the Portuguese, the Chinese and Arabs knew Timor as an "inexhaustible" source of precious woods which were exchanged for axes, pottery, lead and other goods of use to the local inhabitants.

2   Timor's traditional Maubere society consisted of five major categories: the Liurari (kings and chiefs), the Dato (lesser nobles and warriors), the Ema-reino (freemen) the Ata (slaves) and the Lutum (nomadic shepherds).

3   In 1859, Portugal and the Netherlands agreed to divide the territory between them. The Portuguese kept the eastern part, under an accord ratified in 1904. Resistance to colonialism included armed insurrections in 1719, 1895 and 1959, all of which were put down. Passive resistance by the Maubere enabled their culture to survive five centuries of colonialism. It fared better than the forests of precious woods: species like sandalwood were exhausted very early, or replaced with coffee plantations which are still Timor's economic mainstay.

4   The independence movement began later than in other Portuguese colonies, but in the mid-1970s a national liberation front was formed, bringing together nationalist forces and all sectors of society.

5   In April 1974, when the clandestine struggle against colonial rule had already grown and gained broad support, the "Carnation Revolution" took place in Lisbon. With the fall of the fascist colonial regime in the metropolis the political scene in Timor changed and the patriotic movement was legalized. In September, the Revolutionary Front for the Independence of East Timor (FRETILIN) was created.

6   The new Portuguese Government promised independence but the colonial administration favored the creation of the Democratic Union of Timor (UDT), which supported the colonial status quo and "federation" with Portugal. At the same time, the Indonesian consulate in Dili, Timor's capital, encouraged a group of Timorese to organize the Timor Popular Democratic Association (APODETI) which wanted full independence from Portugal, and supported integration with Indonesia.

7   A period of conflict ensued between Portuguese neocolonial interests, Indonesian annexationists and the independence movement. In August, the UDT attempted a coup causing FRETILIN to issue a call for general armed insurrection, and the Portuguese administration withdrew from the country. FRETILIN achieved territorial control and declared independence on November 28 1975, proclaiming the Democratic Republic of East Timor. Portugal's withholding of official recognition had important diplomatic and political implications.

8   On December 7 1975, Indonesia invaded the new republic. A few hours earlier, US President Gerald Ford had +visited Jakarta where he had probably learned of, and endorsed, Indonesian president General Suharto's expansionist plans. FRETILIN was forced to withdraw from the capital, Dili, and from the major ports. On June 2 1976, a so-called "People's Assembly", made up of UDT and APODETI members, approved Timor's annexation as a province of Indonesia. However, this illegal resolution was not recognized by the United Nations Decolonization Committee, which still regards Portugal as the colonial power responsible for Timor.

9   Meanwhile, the Democratic Republic of East Timor established diplomatic relations with numerous former Portuguese colonies and socialist states.

10   In December 1978, FRETILIN president Nicolau dos Reis Lobato died in combat. Despite this great loss, the liberation movement continued. According to reliable sources, Indonesia adopted a policy of extermination on the island, killing nearly 20 per cent of the population.

11   Tactics used in the war varied. In 1978, the Front organized the massive surrender of civilians, who then moved into the Indonesian-controlled cities. Young men were armed and trained by the Indonesian army in an attempt to "Timorize" the war and set the Maubere against each other. But acting on FRETILIN instructions, now well-armed and equipped recruits, rebelled and rejoined the revolutionary forces. The Front became active in both the countryside and the cities.

12   Indonesia's response to the war was erratic. In 1983, FRETILIN commander-in-chief, Xanana Gusmão, signed a cease-fire with the chief of the expeditionary force, Colonel Purwanto. However, President Suharto objected to this agreement and the guerrilla war continued.

13   The region is known for its mineral reserves and in April 1985, an international consortium was formed to explore oil and natural gas reserves in Timor territorial waters off the coast of Australia.

14   FRETILIN sought closer ties with the Democratic Union of Timor and in 1986 established a coordinating body, the National Convergence. This union helped Portugal to resume its active role. The internal structure of the nationalist movement was reorganized to become politically independent and more locally based. Gusmão was confirmed as commander-in-chief of Timor's liberation army.

15   Portugal won an important diplomatic victory when the European Parliament and the European Commission adopted a position on the East Timor issue. They defended the Maubere people's right to self-determination, recognized the need for a negotiated settlement, and condemned the Indonesian occupation.

16   In October 1989, the United Nations Human Rights sub-commission passed a motion condemning Indonesian occupation and repression in East Timor. The disturbances had spread throughout the island, above all in Dili where students took to the streets, burned cars and destroyed the houses of several Indonesian officers.

17   Repression increased after this. Foreign correspondents were forbidden entry, isolating Dili from the rest of the world. There were no telephone lines out of the country, nor any diplomatic representatives in the capital.

18   When Pope John Paul II visited Dili in October 1989, a group of young people unfurled a FRETILIN banner 20 meters from the altar where mass was celebrated. Of the 80,000 people who attended the ceremony, 13,000 were thought to have been members of the Indonesian security forces. The young protesters shouted independence slogans while the army waded in to prevent them. Reporters accompanying the Pope, some of whom had their cameras confiscated, witnessed at first hand the political oppression operating in East Timor, and were able to inform the rest of the world.

19   Repression continued: every house was required to hang a list on their door naming the family members living there. This list could be checked at any time by occupation forces. Thousands of Maubere women were compulsorily sterilized. Tetum, the national language, was banned from schools. The transmigration policy operated by the Indonesian authorities introduced about 100,000 pro-Indonesian settlers who held an economically privileged position in Timorese society.

20   In early November 1991, during a large peaceful funeral procession, the army opened fire on the crowd killing 271 people; countless more were injured. Media coverage of

this event caused the Portuguese Government to appeal to the EC countries to halt trade with Indonesia. Indonesia had a preferential trading agreement with the EC, being a member of the six countries of the Association of South East Asian Nations (ASEAN). Portugal requested a meeting of the UN Security Council, criticizing them for not responding to Indonesia as they had to Iraq over the invasion of Kuwait in August 1990.

[21] A visit to the island by Portuguese MPs scheduled for November 1991 was cancelled after the Indonesians refused to allow entry to an Australian journalist accompanying the delegation.

[22] Opposition leaders accused the US, Australia, the Netherlands, Japan and other countries with important economic interests in Indonesia, of co-operating with Jakarta in its attempt to play down the genocide and silence the international press.

[23] Late in 1991, Portugal reported that Jakarta and Canberra had signed a contract with 12 companies to extract around a billion barrels of oil from the sea around Timor. The list of companies was headed by Royal Dutch Shell (British and Dutch) and Chevron (US). They were followed by six Australian companies, Nippon Oil (Japan), Phillips Petroleum, Marathon, and the Enterprise Oil Company. Meanwhile, representatives of the Australian Government announced that they would not support the sanctions against Jakarta.

[24] In Timor, the leaders of Nationalist Convergence urged Portugal to break off negotiations with Indonesia and to take the stricter measures needed for a diplomatic solution to the conflict, through UN intervention. Nationalist Convergence hoped that conditions to put pressure on the Indonesian Government would be more favorable in 1992, when Portugal took up the EC presidency, both at EC and UN level. The Timorese demanded compliance with the UN resolutions: the withdrawal of occupation troops, and a referendum to decide on the country's political future.

[25] In March 1992, the ship "Lusitania Expresso" left Port Darwin in Australia. On board were human rights activists from over 23 countries and well-known Portuguese politicians including president Ramalho Eanes. "The Peace Boat", left with the aim of commemorating the Dili massacre of November 1991. The Indonesian authorities immediately announced that the ship would be diverted from its course to a nearby island; where the Government would decide which members of the committee would be authorized to enter Timor.

[26] Reports from the island in early 1994 indicated that the families of the dead, "disappeared" and prisoners met in the main square of Dili every Saturday to pray and protest. In November, some 100 people were arrested after a series of public demonstrations. The tension continued, and a year later in October 1995 between 50 and 100 people were arrested following three days of disturbances in Dili.

[27] In early 1996, shortly before the seventh meeting between the Indonesian and Portuguese foreign ministers to seek a solution, Amnesty International asked for free access to human rights observers to the occupied nation. Other specialist reports emphasized the social inequalities between the occupied and occupiers, despite the well-publicized investments made by the Indonesian Government in sectors like education.

[28] In December 1996, the exiled activist Jose Ramos Horta and the Catholic Bishop Carlos Felipe Ximenes Belo were awarded the Nobel Peace prize in Oslo. The Indonesian authorities tried to boycott the ceremony, but East Timor hit the headlines worldwide.

[29] In April 1997, Ramos Horta presented a documentary on the 20 years of Indonesian occupation to the UN Human Rights Commission in Geneva. In July while on a visit to Indonesia, South African president Nelson Mandela met with Xanama Gusmao, imprisoned leader of the Timorese resistance, and called for his release.

[30] In November, occupying army troops opened fire on university students holding a vigil in Dili in remembrance of the 1991 massacre there, killing one student and wounding another sixteen. Bishop Belo denounced the "outrageous brutality" of the military and stated the Indonesian occupation forces had entered the university campus without permission, breaking through windows and doors.

[31] In 1998, following unrest resulting from a serious slide in the value of the Indonesian currency, Indonesian President Suharto was overthrown. His successor, Jusuf Habibie, eventually capitulated to international pressure to institute a United Nations-supervised plebiscite in the territory. Voters were to be given a choice between continued rule from Jakarta or independence.

[32] The details of the vote and the drawing up of electoral lists defining who was entitled to vote led to great setbacks, and a few weeks before the election, pro-Indonesian paramilitary groups began a purging and terror war against independence supporters. When it became evident Habibie could no longer control the militia violence in East Timor, the new president announced the freeing of Gusmão and stated his commitment to respect the result of the vote. During the months of violence, thousands of Timorese were forced to flee, taking refuge in the mountainous interior; hundreds died.

[33] Eventually, the referendum was held on August 30 1999, in the midst of a violent campaign unleashed by pro-Indonesian paramilitaries with the support of the military. About 98 per cent of those registered to vote did so, of which 78.5 per cent voted for independence. The results caused a new wave of paramilitary violence. Massive destruction and the forced emigration of some 250,000 East Timorese to refugee camps in West Timor followed.

[33] After some hesitation and consultation with Jakarta, the UN decided to send a peace contingent headed by Australian soldiers. The force (called Interfet) reached Dili two weeks after the referendum and dislodged the paramilitaries from the capital and nearby areas, deploying itself throughout the border. The contingent, of more than 3,000 soldiers, was also made up of forces from the UK and Aotearoa/New Zealand. The implementation of sovereignty took place on October 25.

[34] The UN appointed Sergio Vieira de Melo as head of the Transitional Authority for East Timor. Vieira formed a 15-member Consultative Council which included Gusmão. On February 2000, Interfet handed over its control throughout large areas of the territory to the Transitional Authority. Most of the forces will be the same, but their command will change, being Vieira in charge.

[35] In March 2000 Indonesia and the UN claimed that those responsible for the violence committed in August and September 1999 would be brought to justice for their crimes. In late February, the leaders of Aitarak, one of the pro-Indonesian paramilitary groups, held a working meeting in Singapore with the military and political leaders of the pro-independence group Falintil. The way forward to reconciliation was addressed, as was the issue of the refugees - some 90,000 were still living in Indonesian territory. ∎

PROFILE

ENVIRONMENT

Located between Australia and Indonesia, East Timor comprises the eastern portion of Timor Island, the dependency of Oecusse, located on the northwestern part of the island, the island of Atauro to the North, and the islet of Yaco to the East. Of volcanic origin, the island is mountainous and covered with dense rainforest. The climate is tropical with heavy rainfall, which accounts for the extensive river system. The southern region is flat and suitable for farming. Agriculture is the basis of its export-oriented economy, and copra, coffee, rice, cotton, tobacco and sandalwood are its main crops. Marble is an important export.

SOCIETY

Peoples: The Maubere people are descended from Melanesian and Malayan populations. In 1975 there was a Chinese minority of 20,000 as well as 4,000 Portuguese. Amnesty International estimates that 210,000 people have died as a result of the Indonesian occupation. There are 6,000 Maubere refugees in Australia and 1,500 in Portugal.
Religions: Most of the population profess traditional religions. 50-75 per cent are Catholic.
Languages: Tetum is the national language. There are some forty dialects. Indonesian occupation has banned the use of these languages in education, and virtually all the teaching is done in Bahasa, the main Indonesian language. A minority also speaks Portuguese.
Political Parties: Roman, Arial">Socialist Party of Timor;Timorese Democratic Union; Roman, Arial">Revolutionary Front of a Independent East Timor

THE STATE

Official Name: República de Timor Leste.
Capital: Dili, 67,000 people (1980).
Government: Sergio Vieira de Melo, head of a 15-member Consultative Council.
National Holiday: November 28, Independence Day (1975).

Ecuador

Ecuador

Population: 12,411,000 (1999)
Area: 283,560 SQ KM
Capital: Quito
Currency: Sucre
Language: Spanish

I n 1478, Inka Topa Yupanqui united the agricultural peoples who had inhabited the territory that is now Ecuador since 2,000 BC, within the Tahuantinsuyu (Inka empire). Within a few years the northern region of the Quechua territory, of which Quito was the center, acquired great economic importance and became the commercial and cultural center of a great civilization. But the rivalry for succession between Atahualpa (from Quito) and Huascar (from Cuzco) weakened the power of the Empire.

2   The Spanish conquistadors commanded by Sebastián de Benalcázar took advantage of the situation to capture Quito in 1534. Indigenous South Americans, who had been free people working the land and living in communities characterized by a high level of social organization and mutual help (*ayllus*) were enslaved and cruelly exploited.

3   At first, the country formed part of the Viceroyalty of Peru as an administrative dependency known as the Real Audiencia de Quito (Royal District of Quito). In 1717, Quito was transferred by the Bourbons to the Viceroyalty of Nueva Granada, which also comprised present-day Colombia, Venezuela and Panama.

4   In 1822, General Antonio José de Sucre, Bolívar's deputy, defeated the royalist forces in the Battle of Pichincha, thus ending Spanish domination and incorporating Ecuador into Bolívar's Greater Colombia scheme.

5   The Royal District of Quito seceded from Greater Colombia in 1830 and adopted the name Republic of Ecuador. The change in name probably meant little to the peasant majority, as nothing changed with regard to the land tenure system.

6   In 1895, the Liberal Revolution led by Eloy Alfaro rekindled the people's hopes for real land reform. Church property was nationalized although large landowners were not affected. Alfaro was killed and the country, like other parts of the continent, came under the influence of British imperialism.

7   Ecuador successively lost one part of its territory after another, due to the ruling oligarchy's lack of political capacity. Under Spanish domination, Ecuador had covered 1,038,000 sq km, shrinking to 283,560 sq km by 1942 through successive agreements with external powers.

8   In 1944 a popular revolt ousted President Carlos Alberto Arroyo, ushering in a populist government headed by José María Velazco Ibarra and comprising conservatives, communists and socialists, under the common banner of the Democratic Alliance. The Cold War made it impossible for this alliance to continue, and the left began to be the object of repression. In 1962, under pressure from the United States, President Carlos Arosemena broke off diplomatic relations with Cuba.

9   In the early 1970s, bananas, coffee and cocoa exports were replaced by crude oil. That year the political situation also changed. Veteran populist leader, José María Velasco Ibarra was ousted for the fourth time by the armed forces. Under the government of General Guillermo Rodríguez Lara, the country joined OPEC. The Government purchased 25 per cent of the shares of Texaco-Gulf and affirmed its rights over 200 miles of territorial waters. The "tuna war" ensued when this claim was disputed by US fishing interests.

10   Jaime Roldós, nominated by the Convergence of People's Forces (CPF) and the People's Democratic Party, became president in August 1979. Ecuador renewed diplomatic relations with Cuba, China and Albania. The Government also initiated a program aimed at integrating marginalized rural and urban populations into the economy. However, it encountered a hostile Congress, as well as opposition from the United States, which did not take kindly to its human rights policies and its antagonism to the dictatorships in the southern cone.

11   Toward the end of January 1981, the Five Day War broke out between Ecuador and Peru, with skirmishes along borders which had not been clearly delineated by the 1942 Protocol.

12   In May of the same year, Roldós died in a suspicious airplane accident, whereupon Vice President, Osvaldo Hurtado took office. The following year was marked by the most severe social crisis since the military had left power. It was triggered, on the one hand, by the application of IMF formulas, and on the other, by an overt drive to build up military power to achieve parity with the Peruvian armed forces.

13   The 1984 election was won by conservative León Febres Cordero, of the Social Christian Party. For the most part, Febres Cordero was able to fulfil his campaign promises: to encourage free enterprise, develop agriculture and mining, attract foreign investment and establish relations with the IMF. The agreement with 400 creditor banks entailed assigning 34 per cent of estimated export revenues to meet new commitments.

14   Febres was an ardent defender of US President Reagan's Central American policy. In October 1985 he broke off diplomatic relations with Nicaragua, and on several occasions helped finance Nicaraguan "contra" leaders' travel and expenses.

15   The May 1988 election was won by Social Democrat Rodrigo Borja, inaugurated in August of that year with the support of a coalition made up of the Democratic Left, Osvaldo Hurtado's Christian Democrats and a dozen parties of the left.

16   From the time Borja took office, his government was confronted by high rates of inflation and a disastrous economic situation. Compounding a foreign debt of $11

WORKERS

1997
UNEMPLOYMENT: 9.2%

% OF LABOUR FORCE   **1998**

■ FEMALE: 27%   ■ MALE: 73%
                            1990

■ SERVICES: 47.6%
■ INDUSTRY: 19.1%
■ AGRICULTURE: 33.3%

LAND USE

DEFORESTATION: 1.6% annual (1990/95)
IRRIGATED: 34.1% of arable (1993)

1993

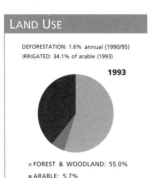

■ FOREST & WOODLAND: 55.0%
■ ARABLE: 5.7%
■ OTHER: 39.3%

PUBLIC EXPENDITURE

DEFENCE EXPENDITURE (% of goverment exp.)	**20.3%**	(1997)
MILITARY EXPENDITURE (% of health & education)	**26%**	(1990/91)

billion, was a fiscal deficit equalling 17 per cent of the GDP, negative monetary reserves of $330 million, and nearly 15 per cent unemployment.

[17] In 1990, the increase in international oil prices, accounting for 54 per cent of the country's exports, economic reform and the drastic limitation of public spending contributed to a mild economic recovery. The GDP rose 1.5 per cent, and inflation fell, as did the

country's balance of payments deficit; however, real wages declined. The foreign debt burden clearly had a negative effect upon Ecuador's economic recovery.

[18] Under Borja, important gains were made on the domestic front: the Taura Commandos, who had kidnapped Febres Cordero in January 1987, were deactivated and the guerrilla movement Alfaro Vive ("Alfaro Lives") was integrated into the political mainstream.

PROFILE

ENVIRONMENT

The country is divided into three natural regions: the coast, the mountains and the rainforest. Due to the influence of the cold Humboldt current, the climate of the coastal region is mild. More than half of the population lives along the coast, where cash crops of bananas, cocoa, rice and coffee are grown. In the highlands, extending between two separate ranges of the Andes, the climate varies according to altitude, and subsistence crops are grown. In the eastern Amazon region, recent oil finds supply internal demand, leaving a small surplus for export. The Colón or Galapagos archipelago belongs to Ecuador. The country also lays claim to 200,000 sq km of Amazon territory presently controlled by Peru, as well as the air space over its territory, where communication satellites are stationed. In the coastal region, 95 per cent of the woodlands have been felled. Soil depletion has increased by 30 per cent over the past 25 years.

SOCIETY

Peoples: Most Ecuadoreans descend from the Quechua people who made up the kingdom of Quito. The current population is mainly mestizos, the result of intermarriage with the Spaniards and their descendants, in addition to descendants of African slaves. There are nine indigenous nationalities: Huaorani, Shuar, Achar, Siona-Secoya, Cofan, Quechua, Tsachila and Chachi. There are over 1.5 million Quechua living in the inter-Andean valley. **Religions:** Mainly Catholic. **Languages:** Spanish (official), although 40 per cent of the population speaks Quechua. **Political Parties:** The Social Christian Party of Jaime Nebot; the United Republican Party, conservative; the Ecuadorean Roldosista Party; the Democratic Left, social democratic, affiliated to the Socialist International; the Conservative Party; People's Democracy; the Christian Democratic Union; the Democratic People's Movement; the Ecuadorean Socialist Party; the Convergence of Popular Forces; the Radical Liberal Party; the Broad Front of the Left; the Radical Alfarista Front; the National Patriotic Front, of Frank Vargas; the Ecuadorean People's Revolutionary Action; the National Liberation Party.
Social Organizations: The major union federations are the Ecuadorean Central Organization of Class Unions (CEDOC), and the Central Organization of Ecuadorean Workers (CTE) coordinated with the United Worker's Front (FUT). In the last few years the Confederation of Indigenous Nationalities of Ecuador (CONAIE) has gained importance; the National Federation of Small Producers (FNPA).

THE STATE

Official Name: República del Ecuador. **Administrative divisions:** 21 Provinces. **Capital:** Quito, 1,401,000 people (1995). **Other cities:** Guayaquil 1,877,000 people; Cuenca 329,000 (1995).
Government: Gustavo Noboa Bejarano, President since January 2000. The constitution approved by plebiscite in 1978 established a presidential system and granted the right to vote to illiterate people for the first time in 1984. **National Holiday:** August 10, Independence Day (1809). **Armed Forces:** 57,000 troops (conscripts). 100,000 reserves (1996). **Other:** 200 Coast Guard and 6 coastal patrol units (1993).

[19] On the international scene, under Borja, Ecuador participated actively in the different groups involved in subregional integration. In addition, it supported the Group of Eight, which replaced the Contadora Group (charged with mediating the Central American political crisis). In addition, it was a member of the Rio Group, it rejoined the Movement of Non-Aligned Countries, and became the site of numerous high-level international meetings and forums.

[20] In May 1990, the presidents of Bolivia, Colombia, Peru and Venezuela agreed to begin eliminating tariff barriers between their countries as of January 1 1992, as a first step toward the creation of an Andean Common Market by 1995. In addition, the Andean leaders underscored the importance of collective cooperation with the United States in the war against drugs.

[21] On May 28 1990, a group of Indians from the coast took over Santo Domingo Church in Quito, demanding that they be allowed to own land and that their human rights be respected. Shortly thereafter, several highways were closed by other indigenous groups from the highlands and the eastern part of the country.

[22] Dozens of middle-sized cities in the Andean region were symbolically taken over by tens of thousands of indigenous peoples from neighboring villages. Subsequently, native peoples from the Amazon region marched on Quito. In the ensuing police action, one person was killed and several injured, although the large-scale violence which had marked previous incidents was avoided.

[23] In the June 1990 legislative election, President Borja's party was badly defeated, with the winning share going to the conservatives, represented by the Social Christian Party, and the left, by the Socialist Party.

[24] On May 28 1991, more than a thousand indians peacefully occupied the assembly room of the National Congress, demanding amnesty for some thousand indians who had been tried in connection with the 1990 uprising.

[25] In the April 1992 elections, the Social Christian Party and the United Republican Party were the most successful participants. They obtained 19 and 13 of the 77 seats in Congress, respectively. The ex-president Febres Cordero was elected mayor of Guayaquil with 70 per cent of the returned votes. The turnout for the election was 73 per cent, six points higher than traditional level. None of the presidential candidates managed to achieve 50 per cent of the vote, so the election went to a second round between the two most

popular nominees. In the second ballot on July 5, Sixto Durán Ballén of the PUR gained 56 per cent of the vote over Jaime Nebot of the PSC who achieved 43 per cent.

[26] The left-of-center and the left contributed to the electoral victory of Sixto Durán, considered the "lesser of two evils", when compared with Nebot's authoritarianism.

[27] The new Government proposed a program based on the "modernization of the State", including a plan for privatizing state enterprises and a rigorous structural adjustment plan. This meant eliminating subsidies, increasing or floating the prices of basic goods (including gasoline and other hydrocarbon derivatives) and keeping wage adjustments below the accumulated inflation rate.

[28] After a year in office, Vice-President Dahik, considered the real power behind the throne, proclaimed the Government's adjustment policies to be a success. They had achieved a 60 per cent reduction of inflation in 1992 and 32 per cent in 1993, an increase in monetary reserves and a reduction of the fiscal deficit, especially in the public sector, and reduction of public spending to a mere 26 per cent of the GDP in 1993.

[29] The opposition, the Confederation of Indigenous Nationalities of Ecuador (CONAIE) and the United Workers' Front (FUT) questioned these policies, citing increased poverty and unemployment, and the total absence of social policies. In actual fact, the mean urban wage had continued to fall being worth only a fifth of the average 1980 value in 1993.

[30] The main conflict stemmed from privatization of the social security system, electricity, telecommunications and oil. The opposition was strengthened by the creation of a National Sovereignty Defense alliance, bringing together strategic labor unions, CONAIE and other social organizations.

[31] The legislative package authorizing the privatizations underwent several modifications. The attitude of the Social Christian Party, the main parliamentary force, proved decisive. Although the Party was ideologically in favor of privatization policies, it had to operate with an eye on its electoral prospects for 1996, so the Government proposals were eventually passed in much reduced versions to avoid having to pay a high political cost.

[32] Throughout this period the Government committed a number of faux pas, including the Ingenio Azucarero Aztra (a sugar mill) and Ecuatoriana de Aviación (the national airline) scandals. Both of these companies were allowed to go bankrupt before the privatization process began.

[33] The damage to the Government was extensive. In the May 1994

elections, the PUR did not obtain a single parliamentary seat, and the Conservative Party only won 6 of a total 77. Together, they obtained less than 10 per cent of the vote. The main beneficiary was the Social Christian Party, with 22 deputies, 25 per cent of the vote, and a candidate, Jaime Nebot, was the main contender for presidential succession.

34 The two left and left-of-center parties, the Democratic Left and Christian Democrats suffered serious setbacks, winning fewer than 15 legislative seats and 15 per cent of the vote. The surprise element was the increase in strength of the MPD - a party with a strong base in the educational sector - and the triumph in Quito of General Frank Vargas Pazzos, whose platform was marked by strong nationalism.

35 Meanwhile, the economy went through a period of deep recession. The PBI and exports decreased, specially banana exports, due to the restrictions of the European Community. The building industry and oil exports were the exceptions. The Government gave new licences for oil prospecting and planned the building of an oil pipeline. The measure was heavily criticised by the opposition, worried, so they said, about the possible exhaustion of the deposits.

36 In April 1994, a fire broke out on Isabela, one of the Galapagos islands, and destroyed 6,000 hectares of land and endangered the life and habitat of giant turtles. This led to a decree which restricted local tourism, immigration and illegal fishing. However, only in January 1998 did the country ban industrial fishing in the area as a way to protect the archipelago's fragile ecosystem.

37 In June 1994, President Durán Ballén reversed the land reform carried out in 1964 and 1973, which had put an end to large haciendas and turned land over to indigenous peoples and small-scale farmers. CONAIE reacted to the legislation by blocking roads in a number of cities and towns. The Government declared the state of emergency and sent the army to control the situation. Forty eight per cent of rural lands belonged to peasant communities, mostly indigenous, and 41 per cent belonged to individuals.

38 In early 1995, new armed struggles took place with Peru in the Condor mountain range. The border had never been precisely set in the area, which is thought to contain gold, uranium and oil reserves. Durán Ballén declared once again a state of emergency and, in spite of international mediation, the conflict caused dozens of victims, especially among the Peruvian army.

39 Late that year, many ministers were questioned by Congress for embezzling state funds. This led to the arrest of several ministers and the flight from the country of Vice-Ppresident Alberto Dahík.

40 After harsh debate, Congress passed the sale of 35 per cent of the telecommunications state company. The Government had been determined to arrange this first major privatization before ending its term in August 1996.

41 Populist Abdalá Bucaram won the elections with 54 per cent of the vote over his rival from the Social Christian Party, Jaime Nebot, who obtained 46 per cent. His first government task was to appease the fears of business and finance circles, worried about the fulfillment of his electoral promises to the poorer sectors of the population. Meanwhile, press stories which predicted a military coup in the event of Bucaram's electoral victory turned out to be without foundation.

42 The fiscal adjustment package imposed by the Government complicated Bucaram's situation. The labor movement called for a national strike day on February 5, 1997 and Bucaram responded by saying the initiative was just and had the Government's support. This unexpected political move did not stop the fall of the President's popularity, in part due to strong price increases: 1,000 per cent in telephone rates, 300 per cent in electricity, 245 per cent in gas and 60 per cent in urban transportation.

43 Parliament declared the president "insane" and did not recognize his authority, through a measure not included among its powers by the Constitution. After three days of uncertainty, with the coexistence of three presidents, Fabián Alarcón obtained the support of Parliament (and the opposition of the Government's seats) and the military to become president.

44 In late May, a plebiscite gave full support to president Alarcón and confirmed the legitimacy of his presidency with 65 per cent of the vote, against 28 per cent. Meanwhile, a National Assembly elected by universal suffrage was called to modify the Constitution.

45 The Supreme Court of Quito accused Bucaram of corruption and ordered his arrest. The former president, exiled in Panama, was sentenced in December to a two-year prison term for slander.

46 The Constituent Assembly elected in November 1997 started to draw up a new Constitution. The opposition Social Christian Party took most of the seats with a manifesto of decentralization, fighting corruption and the need for drastic economic reform. Meanwhile, elected members of indigenous organizations called for recognition of the multicultural and multi-ethnic nature of the country in the new Constitution.

47 With a broad margin of votes in his favor, in August 1998, Jamil Mahuad, a Harvard-trained economist from the People's Democracy party (DP), became president. In October, Mahuad signed an agreement with Fujimori in Brasilia to end the long-standing Peruvian-Ecuadoran frontier dispute.

48 Mahuad was backed by 63 per cent of public support when he came to power. In October he announced a series of measures to reduce inflation - then 14 per cent - and the budgetary deficit. The measures aimed at reduced public spending and increased taxes, were widely rejected by the population. Worker and indigenous protests heightened in several parts of the country as the economic crisis became more serious.

49 In January 1999 Mahuad announced new spending cuts, a salary freeze and delays in low priority public works. Annual inflation hit 60 per cent and the national currency, the *sucre* was devalued 200 per cent. By the end of that year, the political opposition and almost all the public was demanding the president stand down.

50 On January 5 2000, Mahuad declared a state of emergency in the face of a campaign of protest marches and road blocks by the United Workers' Front (FUT), calling for him to resign. The *sucre* fell to the all-time low of 26,000 to the dollar. The following Sunday, amidst nation-wide demonstrations and the threat of social uprisings from CONAIE, the President announced the economy would be linked to the dollar.

51 This decision was the last straw for the indigenous groups. They blocked highways, marched into Quito and invaded Parliament and the Government headquarters - aided by the troops deployed to block their way. Giving the presidency up, without a single shot being fired, a provisional government council was set up. This included representatives from the army, judicial power, indigenous groups and unions and was widely acclaimed by the public.

52 Pressure from abroad, especially the United States, led to the insurgent troops being arrested. Mahuad made an official resignation and was replaced by vice-president Gustavo Noboa. When taking up the post on January 22, Noboa said he would continue with his predecessor's economic policy. With the provisional government effectively dissolved, the indigenous groups withdrew from Quito, warning that they would be watching the new government. ∎

STATISTICS

DEMOGRAPHY

Population: 12,411,000 (1999)
Annual growth: 2.5 % (1975/97)
Estimates for year 2015 (million): 15.9 (1999)
Annual growth to year 2015: 1.6 % (1997/2015)
Urban population: 60.4 % (1997)
Urban Growth: 3.9 % (1980/95)
Children per woman: 3.1 (1998)

HEALTH

Life expectancy at birth: 70 years (1998)
male: 67 years (1998)
female: 72 years (1998)
Maternal mortality: 160 per 100,000 live births (1990-98)
Infant mortality: 30 per 1,000 (1998)
Under-5 child mortality: 39 per 1,000 (1998)
Daily calorie supply: 2,592 per capita (1996)
111 doctors per 100,000 people (1993)
Safe water: 68 % (1990/98)

EDUCATION

Literacy: 89 % (1995)
male: 92 % (1995)
female: 87 % (1995)
School enrolment:
Primary total: 127 % (1990/96)
male: 134 % (1990/97)
female: 119 % (1990/97)
Secondary:
male: 53 % (1990/96)
female: 55 % (1990/96)
Tertiary: 26 % (1996)
Primary school teachers: one for every 25 (1996)

COMMUNICATIONS

70 newspapers (1996), 419 radios (1997), 148 TV sets (1996) and 73 main telephone lines (1996) per 1,000 people

ECONOMY

Per capita, GNP: $ 1,520 (1998)
Annual growth, GNP: 4.2 % (1998)
Annual inflation: 32.0 % (1990/98)
Consumer price index: 221.1 (1998)
Currency: 5,446.6 sucres = $ 1 (1998)
Cereal imports: 1,000,748 metric tons (1998)
Food import dependency: 9 % (1997)
Fertilizer use: 1,065 kg per ha (1997)
Exports: $ 4,988 million (1998)
Imports: $ 6,311 million (1998)
External debt: $ 15,140 million (1998); $ 1,244 per capita (1998)
Debt service: 28.8 % of exports (1998)
Development aid received: $ 172 million (1997); $ 16.4 per capita (1997); 0.90 % of GNP (1997)

ENERGY

Consumption: 713.0 Kgs of Oil equivalent per capita yearly (1997); -168.0 % imported (1997)

HDI (rank/value): 72/0.747 (1997)

Tahuantinsuyo: the Inca empire

The Tahuantinsuyo or Inca empire had a brilliant, if brief, life - its evolution being interrupted by the Spanish invasion of 1532, at a time when it was weakened by in-fighting. The empire once covered almost all of the Andes region.

The beginning of Tahuantinsuyo is estimated around the year 1300, its expansion around 1450 and its end in 1532. Its founders, probably emigrants from Lake Titicaca led tribes from the Cuzco valley in order to unify all of the Andes region. If we refer to current political divisions, Tahuantinsuyo included a small part of southern Colombia, the high plateau and desert coast of Peru, the high plateau of Bolivia, northwest Argentina and all of the dry north and fertile lands of central Chile up to the Maule river.

The empire covered two major areas: the mountains or high plateau, where Tahuantinsuyo was founded, and the tropical, marshy and humid coast of Ecuador, as well as the deserted and rainless coast of Peru and Chile. The Incas failed to conquer the jungle.

Two north-south roads were the backbone of communications. The first, along the coast, measured 4,050 kilometers and the second, through the mountains, 5,180 kilometers. Estimates of the Empire's population vary. Most experts calculate it at between 10 and 16 million. Recent research has placed the figure at over 12 million inhabitants, which would give a population density of 13 inhabitants per square kilometer. By comparison, population density in the Roman Empire's Asian provinces under Augustus amounted to 30 and to 10 in the European provinces.

Some experts claim Tahuantinsuyo had organized armies of 200,000 to 300,000 soldiers, which does not seem far-fetched if we accept the 13 million population figure. The Roman empire had an army of 300,000 in the late second century.

QOZQO, THE CENTRE OF THE WORLD

Like other great empires, the Incas built upon knowledge acquired from previous cultures, such as the Chavin, Tiahuanaco-Huari, Nazca, Moche and Chimu. The Incas also stood out for their political and military efficiency, as well as their economic planning and social control. Cuzco (Qozqo to its founders), the capital of the Empire, had a population of 200,000 in 1532. At the time, only London and Naples in Europe were larger. Antwerp, Amsterdam, Lisbon, Rome and Seville had around 100,000 inhabitants each.

Located in an Andean valley blessed with fertile land and a beautiful landscape, Cuzco was specially developed to become a capital. With an area of some six square kilometers, the city had the shape of a puma, a sacred animal for the Incas. As centre of the empire, Cuzco was thought of as the intersection point of a sundial - Antisuyo was called the northeast quadrant, Contisuyo the southwest, Collasuyo the southeast and Chinchaysuyo the northwest, according to a tetramerous model.

A solar calendar was followed, which dictated agriculture and religious ceremonies, and which provided a mythical chronology.

It was believed history was ruled by a pattern of four pasts, each one with its own creation and a sudden violent end. The fifth age belonged to the time of Tahuantinsuyo and would also end in cosmic extermination.

SOCIAL STRUCTURE

The social structure of Tahuantinsuyo resembled a pyramid, with multiple rigid classes. Mobility from one class to another was exceptional and individual status was preordained. There were three distinct social classes.

The aristocracy included a reigning family group and descendants of monarchs, the clergy, military bosses, intellectuals and senior officials. At the summit was the Sapainka, Son of the Sun.

The middle class, the Jatunrunakuna, was a large mass of inhabitants which helped to support the state apparatus. Lastly, the Yanakuna, compared by some with Roman plebeians, who were relegated to menial jobs.

The monarch was not a mere autocrat, but a type of high priest and father, who had to conduct himself according to a code set down by tradition.

There were nine kinds of crimes: of status, high treason, against religion, against the administration and official duties, against taxes and property, and against life and health. Three principles were to be followed by everyone to prevent such crimes: *ama suwa*, *ama qella* and *ama llulla* (do not be a thief, a liar, or idle).

Everywhere, the empire was strictly organized. The population was ordered into communities (*ayllus*) according to the decimal system, ranging from smaller to larger units. Labour was divided into age categories, from childhood to old age, with an additional division for the disabled.

A TRULY AMERICAN ACHIEVEMENT

Capital was accumulated, mainly in the form of agricultural products, and its concentration enabled it to be used for social purposes. The system was based on the surplus production of the community.

The state and religious organization were maintained by this surplus. Planning was a key feature of the state.

One-third of arable land was allocated for religious purposes, another to the monarch and the rest to the community. The use of the land was distributed once a year among the members of the ayllu.

Artisanal production also had a significant role. The most important skills were weaving, metallurgy, pottery and woodcarving. State, communal and private property co-existed in a unique way.

Western observers have classified Tahuantinsuyo in different ways: primitive communism, socialism, totalitarianism, collectivism, paternalism, a softer version of oriental despotism, a mix of theocracy, monarchy and socialism, etc.

However, a close analysis shows that the Inca empire did not fit in with Old World paradigms because, although certain features were similar on the surface to those European contexts, it did not wholly resemble any of them.

In spite of its short existence and of the efforts to underrate it, Tahuantinsuyo was a vast and original achievement of the South American peoples, and has earned its place amongst the major human cultures. ∎

Egypt

Misr

Population: 67,226,000 (1999)
Area: 1,001,450 SQ KM
Capital: Cairo (Al-Qahirah)
Currency: Pound
Language: Arabic

Six thousand years ago, the inhabitants of the Nile valley, Nahr-an Nil, formed a civilization that eventually developed into a centralized state. While struggling to control the periodic flooding of the Nile, the Egyptians built the pyramids and created a culture which was used as an inspiration for the later "western civilization". They succeeded in feeding a large population for such a small area of land, and became a busy center of economic, diplomatic and cultural relations. In the last millennium BC, during the decline of this remarkable civilization, the country was ruled by Libyan and Sudanese Pharaohs and then directly by the Assyrian, Persian, Greek and Roman empires.

2   During the period of Greco-Roman domination, Alexandria (Al-Iskandariyah) was one of the most influential cultural centers in the classical world, and its famous library was the largest in existence until it was burned down under the Roman emperor Aurelian in the late 3rd century AD. It brought together the most outstanding philosophers, scientists and scholars of the era. In 642, when the Arabs conquered the country, little remained of its highly developed past and the Egyptians adopted Islam and the Arabian language.

3   Three centuries later, under the government of the Fatimid Caliphs, the new capital, Cairo (Al-Qahirah), became one of the major intellectual centres in the Islamic world and scholars, particularly African Muslims, were attracted by its university.

4   Between the 10th and 15th centuries, Egypt benefited from its geographic location, becoming the trade center between Asia and the

Mediterranean. The Venetians and Genoese came to trade here, and even the constant warfare provoked by the European Crusades in Palestine, in the 11th to 13th centuries, did not stop active trade.

5   Once the Crusaders were driven out, it seemed that Egypt would naturally become the center of the ancient Arab empire. However the Sultanate of the Ottoman Turks was the rising power in the Islamic world at the beginning of the 16th century, and it soon conquered Egypt. The opening of the sea route between Europe and the Far East had already put an end to Egypt's previous trade monopoly, reliant on its dominion over the Red Sea, and Egypt had begun its economic decline.

6   Until the 19th century, Turkish domination was little more than nominal and the real power lay in the hands of Mameluke leaders. In 1805, Muhammad Ali, an Albanian military leader, took power. He forcibly eliminated local Mameluke leaders, established a centralized regime, reorganized the army, declared a state monopoly on foreign trade of sugar cane and cotton and achieved increasing autonomy from the Sultan of Istanbul laying the foundations of a modern economy.

7   The economy was poorly managed by Muhammad Ali's successors, the crisis deepened and dependency on Europe increased. In 1874, Egypt was forced to sell all its shares in the Suez Canal, built as a joint Egyptian-French project between 1860 and 1870, to pay its debts to the British.

8   The situation continued to deteriorate, loans piled up and in 1879 the creditors imposed a Bureau of Public Debt formed by three ministers, one English, one French and one Egyptian. This bureau assumed the management of the country's finances.

9   This degree of interference awakened an intense nationalistic reaction, supported by the army. That year, the military overthrew Muhammad Ali's successor Khedive Ismail, forcing his son, Tawfiq, to

expel the foreign ministers and appoint a nationalist cabinet. The colonial power reacted promptly: in 1882 an Anglo-French fleet landed English troops in Alexandria, seizing military control of the country.

10   The occupation was "legalized" in 1914, when Egypt was formally declared a protectorate. This situation continued until 1922, when an Egyptian committee negotiated independence in London. This was negotiated in such a way that the resulting conditions really meant the continuation of the protectorate.

11   During World War II, Egypt was used as a British military base again. Anti-colonial feeling reached its height in 1948, when the state of Israel was created in Palestine.

12   Egypt and other Arab nations launched an unsuccessful war against the new state, and the frustration of defeat brought about massive demonstrations against the royal government.

13   Against a background of widespread government corruption, a nationalist group known as the "Free Officials" was formed within the Egyptian Army, led by General Mohammed Naguib and Colonel Gamal Abdel Nasser.

14   On July 23 1952 this group ousted King Faruk and, in June 1953, proclaimed a Republic. Three years later, Nasser became President.

15   The new regime declared itself nationalist and socialist, deciding to improve the living conditions of the *fellahin*, the country's impoverished peasants. Land reform was started, limiting the landowners' monopoly of the majority of the land.

16   Nasser gave priority to the construction of the Aswan dam, one of the world's largest dam projects. The construction was carried out by the Soviet Union, after the western powers had refused to take it on. The dam, which had been hailed as the key to the country's industrialization and "development", in fact caused serious environmental disruption.

17   In 1955, Nasser was one of the leading organizers of the Bandung Conference, a forerunner neutralist Afro-Asian movement which preceded the Movement of Non-Aligned Countries. Twenty-nine Afro-Asian countries condemned colonialism, racial discrimination and nuclear armament.

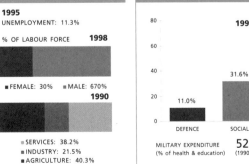

WORKERS

1995
UNEMPLOYMENT: 11.3%

% OF LABOUR FORCE   **1998**

■ FEMALE: 30%   ■ MALE: 670%
1990

■ SERVICES: 38.2%
■ INDUSTRY: 21.5%
■ AGRICULTURE: 40.3%

PUBLIC EXPENDITURE

1997

	DEFENCE	SOCIAL
80		
60		
40		31.6%
20	11.0%	
0		

MILITARY EXPENDITURE   **52%**
(% of health & education)   (1990/91)

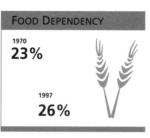
[18] In October 1956, after the nationalization of the Suez Canal, French, British and Israeli troops invaded Egypt. The Government responded by distributing weapons to civilians. A diplomatic battle was also launched; as a result of UN intervention and joint US-Soviet disapproval, France, Britain and Israel were forced to withdraw and the Canal finally came under Egyptian control.

[19] On February 1 1958, the union of Egypt and Syria was officially announced, under the name of the United Arab Republic (UAR). This lasted until September 1961, when Syria decided to separate from Egypt, although Egypt continued to call itself the United Arab Republic.

[20] After Nasser's re-election in 1965, Egypt gave high priority to the conflict with Israel. However, its attempt to economically paralyse Israel by blockading the Gulf of Aqaba failed during the Arab-Israeli conflict, the "Six-Day War" of June 1967. This ended in another defeat of the Arab countries - Egypt, Syria and Jordan - when Israeli forces occupied the Sinai Peninsula, the Gaza strip, the West Bank, and the Syrian Golan Heights. The cost of the war aggravated Egypt's financial problems and only Soviet aid prevented its total collapse.

[21] Nasser died in 1970, and Vice-President Anwar Sadat, a member of the right wing of Nasser's Arab Socialist Party, took his place. Sadat put the *infitah* into practice. This was a government plan which meant an opening to western influence, the de-nationalization of the Egyptian economy and the end of the single-party system. Furthermore, the new Government broke off relations with the Soviet Union and US economic and military aid flowed into Egypt.

[22] In 1973, Egyptian troops crossed the Suez Canal, beginning the fourth Arab-Israeli war. The Egyptians were not defeated, and their success resulted in OPEC substantially increasing oil prices. This move did not produce the desired effect, and Israel retained the rest of the occupied territories.

[23] Substantial price rises and unemployment worsened the living conditions of workers and resulted in massive anti-government demonstrations in 1976 and 1977. Peasants rebelled against the land redistribution of 1952, and the Islamic parties began to conspire openly against Sadat, accusing him of paving the road for a new period of foreign domination.

[24] Sadat's visit to Jerusalem in November 1977 raised a wave of protest in the Arab world. The process of rapprochement with Israel reached its apex in March 1979, with the signing of the Camp David Agreement, wherein the US negotiated the return of Sinai to Egypt. From then on, Egypt became the main beneficiary of US military aid, aimed at turning the country into the new US watchdog in the Arab World, as Shah Pahlevi of Iran had recently been deposed.

[25] In October 1981, Sadat was killed in a conspiracy organized by certain sectors of the military opposed to infitah and the repression of fundamentalist Islamic movements. Vice-President Hosni Mubarak became President on October 14.

[26] Repression, corruption and increasing poverty led to widespread popular discontent. To distract public attention Mubarak ordered an inquiry into the wealth accumulated by the Sadat family. He also extended further concessions to foreign companies.

[27] There were some improvements in Egyptian foreign affairs during 1984. Egyptian diplomacy managed to overcome the most adverse reactions to the Camp David agreements. Their new position on the Palestinian question argued that any fair settlement of the Middle East crisis had to contemplate the rights of the Palestinian people and that Arab solidarity was "the only way to recover the usurped rights".

[28] From early 1985 the economic situation became more difficult as revenues from the four economic pillars: oil, emigrants' repatriated pay, canal fees and tourism shrank considerably. Islamic Fundamentalism was very powerful in opposition and became increasingly so as the Government's popularity plummeted.

[29] Between 1980 and 1986 there was a dramatic increase in the role of foreign capital in the national economy and US aid continued to be a very important source of income. The Government received almost $3 billion per year, $1.3 billion of which was spent on defence. The IMF granted a further $1.5 billion loan in October 1986.

[30] The Egyptian foreign debt went from $2.4 billion in 1970 to $35 billion in 1986; the figure for military aid alone multiplying seven times. Military expenditure and losses caused by war had understandably negative effects upon the economy.

[31] Parliamentary elections, originally scheduled for 1989, were called two years early, and in April 1987 the National Democratic Party (NDP) was elected with 75 per cent of the vote.

[32] In September 1989, in the United Nations General Assembly, Mubarak, representing contact between the Arab countries and the United States, proposed arranging an Israeli-Palestinian dialogue, with no prior conditions. In October of that year relations with Libya were renewed.

[33] In the 1980s, Egyptian emigration to the Gulf countries reached very high levels. In some villages in the province of Sohag, in Upper Egypt, up to 60 per cent of the men left their homes, mainly to seek work in Kuwait and Lybia. This situation, which continues today, has forced Egyptian women to take sole responsibility for their families, generating conflict and tension between the mothers and their children. Emigrants manage to earn large amounts, but at the expense

PROFILE

ENVIRONMENT

99 per cent of the population live in the Nile valley and the delta although this constitutes only 30 per cent of the land. The remaining land is covered by desert except for a few isolated oases. The floods of the Nile set a pattern for the country's economic life thousands of years ago. There are several dams, the major one being the Aswan dam in the south. This has enabled farmers to add new crops such as cotton and sugar cane to the traditional crops; wheat, rice and corn. The hydroelectric power supply, together with the northeastern oil wells, in the Sinai Peninsula, favored industrial development and the disproportionate growth of the cities. Problems which remain unsolved include the unchecked growth of the cities, which have swallowed up fertile lands; erosion of the soil and the use of fertilizers; and water pollution.

SOCIETY

Peoples: Egyptians are Arabs of Hamite origin with East Asian communities in the north and central regions and African groups in the Upper Nile area.
Religions: Muslim, majority Sunni. There is a 10 per cent Coptic minority and other smaller Christian groups.
Languages: Arabic (official), English and French in business, Nubian and Oromo in daily use.
Political Parties: Liberal Party (LP), National Democratic Party (NDP); the New Delegation - Wafd - Party (NWP); National Union Progressive party (NPUP); Nasserist Party; the Muslim Brotherhood; Al Wasat.
Social Organizations: The Egyptian Labor Federation is the only central labor organization, and the Union of Egyptian Students represents the university students.

THE STATE

Official Name: Jumhuriyah Misr al-'Arabiyah.
Administrative divisions: 26 provinces.
Capital: Cairo (Al-Qahirah), 8,900,000 people (1995).
Other cities: Alexandria (Al-Iskandariyah) 3,382,000 people; El Giza (Al-Jizah), 2,144,000 (1994).
Government: Hosni Mubarak, President since 1981. Atef Ebeid, Prime Minister since October 1999. The Majlis (single-chamber legislature) has 454 members, of which 10 are named by the President.
National Holiday: July 23, Revolution Day (1952).
Armed Forces: 440,000 (incl. 270,000 conscripts).
Other: Coast Guard, National Guard and Border Guards, 74,000.

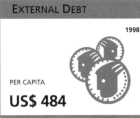

EXTERNAL DEBT

1998

PER CAPITA

US$ 484

FOREIGN TRADE

Millions US$ 1998

IMPORTS

19,274

EXPORTS

13,932

STATISTICS

DEMOGRAPHY

Population: 67,226,000 (1999)
Annual growth: 2.3 % (1975/97)
Estimates for year 2015 (million): 85.2 (1999)
Annual growth to year 2015: 1.5 % (1997/2015)
Urban population: 45.1 % (1997)
Urban Growth: 2.5 % (1980/95)
Children per woman: 3.3 (1998)

HEALTH

Life expectancy at birth: 67 years (1998)
male: 65 years (1998)
female: 68 years (1998)
Maternal mortality: 170 per 100,000 live births (1990-98)
Infant mortality: 51 per 1,000 (1998)
Under-5 child mortality: 69 per 1,000 (1998)
Daily calorie supply: 3,289 per capita (1996)
202 doctors per 100,000 people (1993)
Safe water: 87 % (1990/98)

EDUCATION

Literacy: 51 % (1995)
male: 64 % (1995)
female: 38 % (1995)
School enrolment:
Primary total: 102 % (1990/96)
male: 109 % (1990/97)
female: 94 % (1990/97)
Secondary:
male: 80 % (1990/96)
female: 70 % (1990/96)
Tertiary: 23 % (1996)
Primary school teachers: one for every 23 (1996)

COMMUNICATIONS

40 newspapers (1996), 324 radios (1997), 126 TV sets (1996) and 50 main telephone lines (1996) per 1,000 people
Books: 5 new titles per 100,000 people (1992/94)

ECONOMY

Per capita, GNP: $ 1,290 (1998)
Annual growth, GNP: 6.3 % (1998)
Annual inflation: 9.7 % (1990/98)
Consumer price index: 116.8 (1998)
Currency: 3.4 pounds = $ 1 (1998)
Cereal imports: 10,589,395 metric tons (1998)
Food import dependency: 26 % (1997)
Fertilizer use: 3,566 kg per ha (1997)
Exports: $ 13,932 million (1998)
Imports: $ 19,274 million (1998)
External debt: $ 31,964 million (1998); $ 484 per capita (1998)
Debt service: 9.5 % of exports (1998)
Development aid received: $ 1,947 million (1997); $ 36.3 per capita (1997); 2.50 % of GNP (1997)

ENERGY

Consumption: 656.0 Kgs of Oil equivalent per capita yearly (1997); -47.0 % imported (1997)

HDI (rank/value): 120/0.616 (1997)

---

of weakening the links with and unity of their families.

34   In August 1990 Iraqi troops invaded Kuwait; Egypt was among the first Arab countries to condemn the action, sending troops to the Gulf immediately.

35   When the land offensive started in January 1991, the US announced the cancellation of the Egyptian military debt, which amounted to $7 billion.

36   Egypt's alignment with the West in the war against Iraq was not supported by the majority of the country's population. In February 1991 a demonstration to end the hostilities and seek a peaceful solution to the war in the Persian Gulf was staged in Cairo.

37   There was great opposition to war against Iraq, despite the fact that Iraqi president Saddam Hussein had expelled nearly two million migrant workers from Iraq and Kuwait during the two previous years, and had attempted to forcibly recruit Egyptians to the army.

38   In 1990, the foreign debt reached a record $40 billion. Per capita income averaged some $600 per year, with over a third of the population living below the poverty line.

39   In May 1991, the IMF approved a stand-by loan of $372 million to Egypt, conditional on an economic "structural adjustment plan". Cairo committed itself to privatizing State-run companies, to eliminating controls on production and investment and to reducing the current fiscal deficit from 21 per cent to 6.5 per cent of the GNP. In order to achieve these goals the government decided to cut back subsidies on food and other staples and to reduce the program of aid for the needy.

40   On May 15 1991, foreign minister and deputy minister Esmat Abdel Meguid was named the new secretary- general of the Arab League. Coming upon the heels of the return of Arab League headquarters to Cairo (from Tunis) this appointment signified Egypt's recovery of its leadership role within the Arab world.

41   The escalation of violence from Islamic fundamentalists led the Government to enact an anti-terrorist law and extend for another three years the state of emergency which had been in effect for the past ten years. According to official

statistics, this violence caused 175 deaths between February 1992 and August 1993. Thousands of Islamic followers were arrested and in June and July 1993, 15 people were executed.

42   The Government continued its economic liberalization policies by facilitating foreign banks' operations. In March 1993, the IMF supported a privatization plan with the cancellation of $3 billion in foreign debt. In October, after being re-elected in a plebiscite, Mubarak continued his iron hand policy with Islamic fundamentalists. However, attempts against the lives of foreign tourists multiplied in 1994.

43   In April, lawyers' associations denounced the suspicious death in a police station of an Islamic activists' defender. After a week of demonstrations the movement concluded with a general strike which revealed the influence had by Islamic fundamentalists among lawyers' associations. In October, the number of dead reached 460 since March 1992 when the rebellion of Islamic fundamentalists against Mubarak began.

44   In May, the President formed a committee to organize political talks between the Government and opposition with the exclusion of communists, the Muslim Brotherhood and groups representing the Coptic minority. Simultaneously, relations with the IMF were hampered due to an alleged government slowness in implementing the planned economic liberalization.

45   In the international sphere, Egypt recovered its main role in the Middle East peace talks and in political exchanges between Arab countries. This was shown by a meeting held in Alexandria in December with the participation of leaders from Egypt, Saudi Arabia and Syria. In February 1995, a summit joined leaders in El Cairo from Egypt, Jordan, Israel and Palestine.

46   In 1995, Mubarak was unable to find a solution to the confrontation with Islamic fundamentalists. In January, secretary al-Alfi attended a meeting of Arab countries' interior ministers to attempt to coordinate the fight against violent Islamic movements.

47   In November, the ruling National Democratic Party won the parliamentary elections with the

participation of all the parties acknowledged by the Government. Elections, held amid a violent atmosphere, granted 416 of the 444 seats at stake to the ruling party which provoked several accusations of fraud. In January 1996, Mubarak appointed Kamal al-Ganzouri as Prime Minister, replacing Atef Sedki.

48   In July the Health Minister banned female circumcision - the removal of the clitoris or part of it and/or the sewing together of the vaginal labia - a practice common in some regions of the country.

49   Attacks by armed Islamic groups continued throughout 1996 and 1997, along with government repression of all such groups, including those opposed to the use of violence, like the Muslim Brotherhood. In early 1998 an estimated 1,251 people had fallen victim to attacks and political killings, whilst the estimated number of political prisoners was between 10,000 and 30,000.

50   In March 1999 there was heated debate in Parliament over decrees on female circumcision. Some argued that the present law protected the interests of circumcised women, for uncircumcised women have minimal chance of marriage. The decree provoked resistance in the traditionalist sectors as did other measures.

51   In October, the presidential bodyguards shot dead a man who injured Mubarak by attacking him with a knife.

52   In December, the Egyptian Foreign Ministry began mediation between the Sudanese Government and several opposition groups, in an attempt to end the war which had ravaged the country for nearly 20 years.

53   Parliamentary discussion on the status of women in Egyptian society was renewed in January 2000. The Government had proposed modifying family law to make divorce easier for women; they were also to be allowed to travel abroad without their husband's permission. There were high expectations that the reform would be passed either by the vote or through new presidential decrees. The proposal was considered "non-Islamic" by traditional sectors, whereas women's defense groups considered it too "limited". ∎

El Salvador

El Salvador

Population: 6,154,000 (1999)
Area: 21,040 SQ KM
Capital: San Salvador
Currency: Colón
Language: Spanish

The region of El Salvador was inhabited from early times by Chibcha people (muisca: see Colombia), most of whom were Pipile and Lenca. The Maya also lived within the region, but they were not very influential here.

[2] The Spaniards subdued the Aztecs in Mexico, and subsequently began the conquest of Central America under the leadership of Pedro de Alvarado. In 1525, Alvarado founded the city of El Salvador de Cuscatlan. The territory formed part of the Captaincy-General of Guatemala, a dependency of the Viceroyalty of Mexico. Central America became independent from Spain in 1821 and organized itself into a federation.

[3] In 1827, internal rivalries between "imperialists" and "republicans" led to civil war. In 1839, General Francisco Morazan, president of the Central American Republic, tried to prevent the break-up of the federation. From El Salvador, Morazan struggled to preserve the union with the support of some Nonulco natives, headed by Anastasio Aquino. Morazan was defeated in 1840 and sent into exile, and Anastasio Aquino was arrested and executed.

[4] When the federation was dissolved, Britain took advantage of the situation dominating the isthmus. In 1848, President Doroteo Vasconcelos refused to bow under British pressure, and the British blockaded Salvadoran ports. Over the last three decades of the 19th century, the US began to push the British out.

[5] At the end of the century, the invention of artificial coloring destroyed the demand for indigo - El Salvador's principal export

product - and its price fell to rock bottom. Indigo was replaced with coffee. Coffee required larger and more extensive farming areas, and the Liberal Revolution of 1880 drove thousands of peasants from their communal lands, forming a rural working class and a countryside full of anger and conflict. The coffee plantation owners became the dominant oligarchy and the ruling class of El Salvador.

[6] The 1929 financial crash caused the coffee market to collapse, crops were left unharvested, and thousands of sharecroppers and poor peasants starved. This led to a mass uprising headed by the Communist Party of El Salvador and Farabundo Martí, a former secretary of Augusto C Sandino in his campaign against the US invasion of Nicaragua.

[7] The January 1932 rebellion was ruthlessly crushed, around 30,000 Salvadorans were massacred by the troops of General Maximiliano Hernández Martínez, who had taken power in 1931. This started a series of military regimes which lasted half a century. Twelve thousand people died as a consequence of the repression.

[8] In 1960, the Alliance for Progress sponsored an industrialization program, within the Central American Common Market. High economic growth rates were attained without reducing the rampant unemployment which had caused 300,000 landless peasants to emigrate to neighboring Honduras. Population growth and competition between the local industrial interests, led to war between El Salvador and Honduras in June

1969. The regional common market collapsed after the 100-hour conflict, severely damaging Salvadoran industry.

[9] In the early 1970s unions and other civilian movements took on new life. Guerrilla fighters appeared in El Salvador and the legal opposition parties joined into a national front; the UNO, formed by the Christian Democrats (PDC), the Communists (UDN) and the Social Democrats (MNR). Colonel Arturo Molina, presidential candidate for the official National Conciliation Party, defeated the UNO's candidate Napoleón Duarte in a fixed election in 1972.

[10] In 1977, another fraudulent election made General Carlos Humberto Romero president. Mass riots broke out in protest but social unrest was suppressed leaving 7,000 dead.

[11] The elimination of the legal political opposition encouraged the growth of guerrilla organizations which began to co-ordinate their armed action with the democratic opposition. In response, the US State Department, afraid of a repeat of the Nicaraguan situation, supported a coup by reformist military officers.

[12] On October 15 1979, a civilian/military junta seized power. It included representatives of the social democrats and the Christian democrats. The Junta lacked real power and had no control over the ruthless repression campaigns

WORKERS

1997
UNEMPLOYMENT: 8.0%

% OF LABOUR FORCE **1998**

■ FEMALE: 36% ■ MALE: 64%

1990

■ SERVICES: 43.0%
■ INDUSTRY: 20.7%
■ AGRICULTURE: 36.3%

LAND USE

DEFORESTATION: 3.3% annual (1990/95)
IRRIGATED: 21.2% of arable (1993)

1993

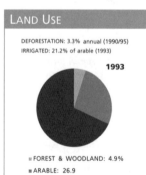

■ FOREST & WOODLAND: 4.9%
■ ARABLE: 26.9
■ OTHER: 68.2%

PUBLIC EXPENDITURE

1997

37.7%

6.7 %

DEFENCE   SOCIAL

MILITARY EXPENDITURE **66%**
(% of health & education) (1990/91)

MATERNAL MORTALITY	LITERACY	FOOD DEPENDENCY	EXTERNAL DEBT

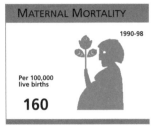

MATERNAL MORTALITY 1990-98
Per 100,000 live births
160

LITERACY 1995
76%

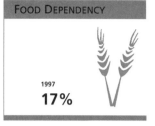

FOOD DEPENDENCY
1997
17%

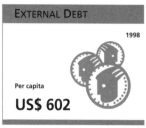

EXTERNAL DEBT 1998
Per capita
US$ 602

carried out by police and military forces. Civilian members resigned and were replaced by right-wing Christian democrats from Duarte's party.

[13] On March 24 1980, the Archbishop of San Salvador, Monsignor Oscar A Romero, was assassinated while performing mass in a clear reprisal for his constant defence of human rights. The leading guerrilla organizations, democratic parties and mass organizations united under the policy of a common program of "popular revolutionary democracy".

[14] In October 1980, the five anti-regime political-military organizations agreed to form the Farabundo Martí Front for National Liberation (FMLN). On January 10 1981 the FMLN launched a "general offensive" throughout most of the country. However, the Front was unable to seize power.

[15] In August 1981, the Mexican and French governments signed a joint agreement recognizing the FMLN and the Democratic Revolutionary Front (FDR) as "a representative political force".

[16] The US administration, led by President Ronald Reagan, saw the situation in El Salvador as a national security issue. The US became directly involved in the political and social conflict, and was the military and economic mainstay of the "counter-insurgency" war which the Salvadoran Army was unsuccessfully waging.

[17] On March 28 1982, as instructed by Washington, the regime held an election for a Constituent Assembly. In response, the rebels launched an offensive ending in a one-week siege of Usulatán, a provincial capital.

[18] After continuous internal tussling for power, the presidency of the constitutional convention went to Roberto D'Aubuisson, the main leader of the ultra-right Nationalist Republican Alliance (ARENA) and the power behind the assassination of Archbishop Romero.

[19] Against a background of an upsurge in fighting, general elections were held on March 25 1984. These were boycotted by the FDR-FMLN; the abstention rate by voters was 51 per cent. Ostensibly supported by the US, the PDC - led by Napoleon Duarte - obtained 43 per cent of the vote, against the 30 per cent won by ultra-right candidate Major Roberto D'Aubuisson.

[20] The extreme right parties disputed the election, but quick responses from the Minister of Defence and the High Command, in support of Duarte, quashed any further reaction. It was the first time that the armed forces had publicly supported the reformists

[21] In October 1986, a strong earthquake brought about a virtual cease-fire, which eventually led to the renewal of negotiations in October 1987. These talks took place within the new framework of regional peace making. The Central American governments had signed the Esquipulas agreements in August 1987, agreeing to strive for peace.

[22] Elections were held in October 1989; these were boycotted by some of the guerrillas, but civilian sectors of the FDR (members of the social democratic and Social Christian parties) participated, with Guillermo Ungo as their presidential candidate. Alfredo Cristiani, the ARENA (right-wing) party's candidate, won the election.

[23] In November 1989, the FMLN launched an offensive occupying several areas of the capital and surrounding regions. The Government responded by bombing several densely populated areas of the capital. Six Jesuits, including the rector of the University of Central America, Ignacio Ellacuria, were tortured and killed by heavily armed soldiers. This provoked a world-wide outcry, especially from the Catholic Church, and American economic aid was threatened.

[24] According to the El Salvador Human Rights Commission, women, students and members of labor unions were the people who suffered most from repression. During those years, the human rights movement was led by mothers, wives, daughters and relatives of the thousands of victims of repression, and by the National Union of Salvadoran Workers (UNTS).

[25] On March 10 1991, the legislative and local elections reflected a new spirit of negotiation. For the first time in 10 years the FMLN did not call for the boycott of the elections, instead they decreed a 3-day unilateral truce. Abstention was still above 50 per cent, and there were acts of paramilitary violence immediately prior to the polls. The voters narrowly elected the ruling party with 43 out of 84 seats.

[26] In Mexico on April 4 1991 delegates of the Cristiani Government and the FMLN started negotiations for a cease fire agreement. On April 19, 10,000 demonstrators, from 70 social organizations, gathered in the Permanent Committee for National Debate (CPDN), demanding that the Constitution be reformed.

[27] On April 27, after several attempts, representatives of the Government and the Farabundo Marti Front signed the "Mexico Agreements" restricting the function of the Armed Forces to the defence of national sovereignty and territorial integrity. The formation of paramilitary groups was banned, and it was agreed to reform article 83 of the constitution to say that sovereignty "resides in the people, and that it is from the people that public power emerges". In New York another agreement was reached in June. The Salvadoran Government committed itself to dismantling the National Guard and the Rural Police (Policia de Hacienda), replacing it with Civilian Police including FMLN-members.

[28] On November 16, new talks began in the UN headquarters. This time, the FMLN declared an indefinite unilateral truce until a new, definite, cease-fire was signed. A Spanish parliamentary delegation

PROFILE

ENVIRONMENT

It is the smallest and most densely populated country in Central America. A chain of volcanoes runs across the country from east to west and the altitude makes the climate mild. Coffee is the main cash crop in the highlands. Subsistence crops such as corn, beans and rice are also grown. Along the Pacific Coast, where the weather is warmer, there are sugar cane plantations. It is the country with the greatest problems of deforestation in Latin America.

SOCIETY

Peoples: 89 per cent of the Salvadoran population are mixed descendants of American natives and Spanish colonizers, 10 per cent are indigenous peoples, and 1 per cent are European.
Religions: Mainly Catholic (75 per cent), Protestant, Mormon, Jehovah's Witness. **Languages:** Spanish is the official and predominant language. Indigenous minority groups speak Nahuatl.
Political Parties: The Nationalist Republican Alliance (ARENA); the Christian Democratic Party; the left-wing Democratic Convergence, the Party of National Reconciliation (PCN). The Farabundo Martí; National Liberation Front (FMLN), founded in October 1980, is made up of five political-military organizations; the Farabundo Martí; People's Liberation Forces (FPL), the El Salvador Communist Party (PCS), the National Resistance Armed Forces (FARN), the People's Revolutionary Army (ERP) and the Central American Workers' Revolutionary Party (PRTC). **Social Organizations:** the National Union of Salvadoran Workers (UNTS), the United Union and Guild Movement (USIGES) and the National Confederation against Hunger and Repression (CNHR) created in 1988.

THE STATE

Official Name: República de El Salvador.
Administrative division: 14 Departments. **Capital:** San Salvador 422,600 people; 1,522,100 metropolitan area (1992).
Other cities: Soyapango 251,800 people; Santa Ana 202,300; San Miguel,182,800; Mejicanos 145,000 (1992). **Government:** Fernando Flores Pérez, President since June 1999. **National Holiday:** September 15, Independence Day (1821). **Armed Forces:** 30,700 troops (1994). Other: National Civilian Police, made up of former guerrillas, soldiers and police.

FOREIGN TRADE

Millions US$ 1998

IMPORTS
4,239

EXPORTS
2,738

wrote a report on the murders of the six Spanish Jesuits from the Central American University (UCA). The report, submitted to the Spanish, European, Salvadoran, and American parliaments, accused the Salvadoran government and the army of concealing evidence which could help to clarify the facts.

29   On January 1 1992, after 21 weeks of negotiation and 12 years of civil war, both parties met in New York to sign agreements and covenants establishing peace in El Salvador. The war left 75,000 people dead, 8,000 missing, and nearly one million in exile.

30   The final agreements were signed in the Mexican city of Chapultepec on January 16 1992. They included substantial modifications to the Constitution and to the structure, organization, regulation, and form of the Armed Forces. They guaranteed to change rural land tenure and to alter the terms of employee participation in the privatization of State companies; they established the creation of bodies for the protection of human rights, and guaranteed the legal status of the FMLN.

31   According to the peace accords the Government was to reduce its troops by half by 1994, bringing the number down to 30,000; in addition, it was to disband its intelligence service. As of March 3, a new civilian police was to be created, made up in part by former members of the FMLN. In January 1992, according to the terms of the Law of National Reconciliation, amnesty was granted to all political prisoners.

32   In addition, the Government pledged to turn over lands to the combatants and provide assistance to *campesinos* belonging to both bands. The FMLN became a political party as of April 30 1991, and held its first public meeting on February 1 1992. After years of being underground, it was presided over by guerrilla commanders Shafick Handal, Joaquin Villalobos, Fernan Cienfuegos, Francisco Jovel and Leonel Gonzalez.

33   In early March 1992, the first implementation difficulties began to be seen. Several leaders of the National Union of Salvadoran Workers accused the Government of violating the accords, and launching a propaganda campaign against grassroots organizations.

34   On February 15 1993, the last 1,700 armed rebels turned over their weapons in a ceremony which was attended by several Central American heads of State and by UN Secretary-General Boutros Boutros-Ghali. The National Civil Police was created, as well as a Human Rights Defense Commission and a Supreme Electoral Court.

35   The result of the investigation of human rights violations, carried out by the Truth Commission created by the UN, led to the resignation of Defence Minister General Rene Emilio Ponce, singled out in that investigation as being the one who ordered the assassination of six Jesuits at the University of San Salvador in 1989. According to the Commission's final document, the military, the death squads linked to these and the State were responsible for 85 per cent of the civil rights violations committed during the war.

36   The Truth Commission recommended the dismissal of 102 military leaders and that some former guerrilla leaders be deprived of their political rights. President Cristiani proposed a general amnesty for cases where excesses had been committed; this proposal was approved on March 20 1993, only 5 days after the document drawn up by the Truth Commission had been made public. With this measure, the most serious crimes committed during the war met with total impunity.

37   A year later on March 20 1994, the first elections since the civil war were held. The candidate of the left coalition, Democratic Convergence - made up of the FMLN and other groups - won 25.5 per cent in the first round of voting, against 49.2 per cent for the right-wing candidate, Armando Calderón Sol, from the ARENA party. After the elections, the FMLN faced an internal crisis triggered by discrepancies between the groups that make up the alliance.

38   According to ONUSAL, the peace accords did not bring an end to the violence. In addition to the existence of intelligence activities within the Armed Forces, members of the military were linked to organized crime. Likewise, the fact that nothing was done to create viable employment opportunities for discharged troops (from both bands) led to an increase in petty crime.

39   The long-promised award of land to demobilized fighters was slow and inefficient. By mid-1994, only one-third of the potential beneficiaries -12,000 of a total 37,000 former members of the army or the guerrillas - had obtained their plots. The rest remained inactive, living in substandard temporary housing and often drifting into organized crime.

40   According to official studies, 90 per cent of El Salvador's vegetation was depleted, two-thirds of the land was deeply eroded and subjected to inadequate agricultural techniques and a mere 2 per cent of the virgin forests remained intact. Also, 90 per cent of the rivers were polluted by sewage and chemical waste and more than half the population drank untreated water.

41   An agreement concluded on May 1995 between ARENA and the Democratic Party - split from the FMLN - enabled a 3 per cent rise of the valued added tax from 10 to 13 per cent. This raise was explained on the need to collect funds to finance land reform, infrastructure works and reconstruction of the country's electoral and judicial apparatus.

42   In August 1996 demonstrators who considered themselves affected by the slowness of the process, which included the transfer of plots of land and payment of retribution to war veterans, occupied streets and government buildings in downtown San Salvador. In May, the Democratic Party withdrew from its deal with ARENA, which left the Government without a parliamentary majority.

43   In March 1997, the opposition's FMLN obtained an important victory in municipal elections, after winning in the capital and dozens of provincial cities. In Parliament, ARENA, with 33.3 per cent of the vote, won 28 seats while FMLN with 32.1 per cent ended up with 27 deputies. Electoral turnout was just 40 per cent of those eligible to vote.

44   A study by the Interamerican Development Bank, issued in March 1998, estimated that 25 per cent of El Salvador's potential economic growth was lost every year due to political and criminal violence.

45   The March 1999 elections ratified ARENA's dominance. At the age of 39 Francisco Flores, a philosophy and political science graduate, became the youngest president in South America, providing an image of rejuvenation.

46   The day after Flores was sworn in as president, peasant farmers and environmental leaders marched through the main streets of San Salvador, calling for a plan to overcome the disasters caused by hurricane Mitch.

47   Flores's government program, "The New Alliance", had four priorities: work, social investment, citizen security and sustainable development. However the opposition, led by Schaffic Handal, thought the President would continue the policy of favoring the country's financial and business sectors. ∎

STATISTICS

DEMOGRAPHY

Population: 6,154,000 (1999)
Annual growth: 1.7 % (1975/97)
Estimates for year 2015 (million): 8.0 (1999)
Annual growth to year 2015: 1.7 % (1997/2015)
Urban population: 45.6 % (1997)
Urban Growth: 2.0 % (1980/95)
Children per woman: 3.1 (1998)

HEALTH

Life expectancy at birth: 69 years (1998)
male: 67 years (1998)
female: 73 years (1998)
Maternal mortality: 160 per 100,000 live births (1990-98)
Infant mortality: 30 per 1,000 (1998)
Under-5 child mortality: 34 per 1,000 (1998)
Daily calorie supply: 2,515 per capita (1996)
91 doctors per 100,000 people (1993)
Safe water: 66 % (1990/98)

EDUCATION

Literacy: 76 % (1995)
male: 79 % (1995)
female: 73 % (1995)
School enrolment:
Primary total: 94 % (1990/96)
male: 94 % (1990/97)
female: 94 % (1990/97)
Secondary:
male: 30 % (1990/96)
female: 35 % (1990/96)
Tertiary: 18 % (1996)
Primary school teachers: one for every 33 (1996)

COMMUNICATIONS

48 newspapers (1996), 464 radios (1997), 250 TV sets (1996) and 56 main telephone lines (1996) per 1,000 people

ECONOMY

Per capita, GNP: $ 1,850 (1998)
Annual growth, GNP: 3.3 % (1998)
Annual inflation: 8.9 % (1990/98)
Consumer price index: 117.6 (1998)
Currency: 8.8 colones = $ 1 (1998)
Cereal imports: 355,710 metric tons (1998)
Food import dependency: 17 % (1997)
Fertilizer use: 1,634 kg per ha (1997)
Exports: $ 2,738 million (1998)
Imports: $ 4,239 million (1998)
External debt: $ 3,633 million (1998); $ 602 per capita (1998)
Debt service: 10.4 % of exports (1998)
Development aid received: $ 294 million (1997); $ 56.5 per capita (1997); 2.60 % of GNP (1997)

ENERGY

Consumption: 691.0 Kgs of Oil equivalent per capita yearly (1997); 35.0 % imported (1997)

HDI (rank/value): 107/0.674 (1997)

Equatorial Guinea

Guinea Ecuatorial

Population: 442,000 (1999)
Area: 28,050 SQ KM
Capital: Malabo
Currency: CFA franc
Language: English

A round the 13th century, Fang and Ndowe people settled in the Rio Muni area, north of Gabon, subduing the Bayele pygmy population, who now only exist in a few isolated groups. From the continental coast, these nations expanded onto the nearby islands which were described as 'densely populated' in the 15th century. In the colonial division of Africa, the Rio Muni area and the islands received the name of Equatorial Guinea.

[2] The Ndowe became allies and intermediaries of Portuguese, Spanish, Dutch and English slave traders. The Fang, whose social organization did not include slavery, withdrew into the forests, convinced that the Europeans were cannibals.

[3] The kings of Portugal, proclaiming themselves the lords of Guinea, ceded the entire 'District of Biafra' to Spain under the treaties of San Ildefonso and Pardo in 1777 and 1778, in exchange for Spanish territory in southern Brazil. In 1778, an expedition sailed out from Montevideo to occupy the islands. They lost their commanding officer, Argelejos, in a battle against the Annoboneuses, and the survivors, under their new leader, Lieutenant Primo de Rivera, turned back. The French and British gradually took over sections of the territory, with the British finally occupying it, founding the first settlements. They used it as a base for their conquest of Nigeria and turned the freed slaves, or 'Fernandinos', into their agents, creating a ruling group that, in many aspects, still exists today.

[4] Between 1843 and 1858, the District was militarily reconquered by Spain, re-establishing their 'rights' over the area. At that time,

economic activity centred on cacao, coffee and timber, but the territory was ineffectively controlled from a distance

[5] In the 1936 Spanish Civil War the Spanish colonists led by Fernando Po supported Franco and were later granted almost full powers over the archipelago. Admiral Carrero Blanco, Franco's Prime Minister, owned the colony's largest cocoa plantations.

[6] In 1963, the colony obtained a degree of internal autonomy, and three legal political organizations were formed: MONALIGE (the Equatorial Guinean National Liberation Movement), MUNGE (the Equatorial Guinean National Unity Movement), and IPGE (the Equatorial Guinean Popular Ideal). Mounting international pressure forced Spain to grant the colony independence and this was officially proclaimed on October 12 1968.

[7] Francisco Macías Nguema assumed the presidency with the

support of Atanasio Ndongo, of MONALIGE and Edmundo Bosio, leader of the Bubi Union of Fernando Po. He headed a coalition government formed by IPGE and sizeable dissident groups from MUNGE and MONALIGE; movements that had emerged during the struggle for independence.

[8] Within a year, on the pretext of foiling an alleged coup attempt, Macías began a violent campaign to eliminate the opposition killing thousands of political prisoners, murdering opponents, causing disappearances and exiling 160,000 people. Amnesty International reported that two thirds of the National Assembly had mysteriously vanished.

[9] Continuing the repression, Macías Nguema dissolved all political parties and created the Sole Traditional Workers' Party (PUNT), proclaiming himself president for life and 'grand master of popular education, science and culture'. His reign of terror was kept going by the 'Youth on the March

with Macías' organization, who extended persecution to Catholic priests and Protestant missionaries.

[10] In August 1979, the rule of Macías Nguema ended in a coup led by his nephew, Lieutenant-Colonel Teodoro Obiang Mba Nzago. Macías was arrested, tried and executed for crimes against humanity.

[11] Persecution, indiscriminate arrests and corruption were soon rampant, reminiscent of the previous regime. In August 1982, legislative elections were held but the list of candidates was drawn up by the official party. The National Alliance for the Recovery of Democracy formed in exile, sought to negotiate with Obiang but accomplished little.

[12] A coup attempt in June 1986 sparked off another wave of arrests. Among those detained was the deputy Prime Minister, Fructuoso Mba Onana.

[13] In September 1984, Obiang joined the Customs and Economic Union of Central Africa (UDEAC), linking the *Ekwele* (then the national currency) to the central banks of the region. Stronger ties with the West resulted in a drastic reduction of facilities offered by the Soviet Union and East Germany. The US, France and Spain dominated the economy, controlling the extraction of oil, iron ore and timber. Meanwhile, Morocco sent troops to guarantee the stability of the new government.

[14] Teodoro Obiang was re-elected in June 1988 and he continued to apply IMF prescriptions, thus obtaining a $16 million loan to improve public investments, restructure the banking system, and accelerate growth. At a meeting of international loan agencies in November 1988, the regime obtained additional loans of $58 million to be spread over three years.

[15] Obiang's visit to France in September 1988 produced closer ties between the two countries and Equatorial Guinea later called for the integration of all French-speaking countries. At the same time, he obtained an amnesty for two-thirds of his country's foreign debt to Spain.

[16] There was no easing of the repression. Two members of the armed forces were executed in

LAND USE

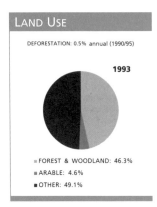

DEFORESTATION: 0.5% annual (1990/95)

1993

- FOREST & WOODLAND: 46.3%
- ARABLE: 4.6%
- OTHER: 49.1%

WORKERS

% OF LABOUR FORCE **1998**

- FEMALE: 35% ■ MALE: 65%

PUBLIC EXPENDITURE

DEFENCE EXPENDITURE (% of goverment exp.) **5.2%** (1996)

LITERACY

1995

78%

EXTERNAL DEBT

1998

Per capita

US$ 710

FOREIGN TRADE

Millions US$ 1998

IMPORTS

791

EXPORTS

465

September 1988 on the charge of conspiring against the Government. Around the same time, an opposition leader, José Luis Jones, was arrested on his return to the country, and condemned to a 17-year prison term. He was eventually pardoned.

[17] In June 1989, Obiang was re-elected in elections where the Democratic Party for Equatorial Guinea was the only legal party. After the elections the same political line was pursued.

[18] In early 1991, the Democratic Co-ordination of Opposition Parties (DCOP) was founded in Gabon and in May, Feliciano Moto, one of the main opposition leaders, was assassinated.

[19] In early 1992, the Government declared a general amnesty. The political parties law banned those based on 'tribal, regional or provincial' grounds, demanding the payment of $158,000 as a legalization fee. Presidential candidates were obliged to have 10 years' residence in the country, thus ruling out all those who had lived in exile.

[20] Despite the obstacles, ten political parties were legalized in early 1993. During this period the UN issued a report denouncing the systematic violation of the basic liberties of opposition politicians.

[21] At the same time, the UN accused the Obiang Government of involvement in the failed attack on US ambassador John Bennett, after the US State Department had criticized the regime for illegal imprisonment, torture and intimidation.

[22] In March, the Government and the Joint Opposition Platform (a coalition of ten legalized parties, formed in November 1992) signed the National Democratic Pact including a clause stating all political prisoners would be freed at the end of the month.

[23] The transparency of the legislative elections toward the end of 1993 was thrown into doubt by international observers. According to official results, the governing Democratic Party took 68 of the 80 seats in play. The expulsion of the Spanish consul-general from the city of Bata, in January 1994, prompted

Spain to reduce the amount of aid granted to Equatorial Guinea by half.

[24] In March 1995, Severo Moto, leader of the opposition Progressive Party, was sentenced to two and a half years in prison for allegedly bribing a police officer and for having 'damaged the reputation' of Obiang. In April, the regime invoked Western, especially Spanish, disapproval for sentencing Moto again - this time to 28 years in prison for treason and conspiracy.

[25] In July, several members of the Movement for the Self-Determination of Bioko, one of the islands belonging to Equatorial Guinea, were arrested. The Government set the presidential elections for early 1996 amidst accusations of arbitrary arrests and torture. In February the same year, just before the elections, the Government dissolved the Joint Opposition Platform and arrested several of its members. On February 25, Obiang won the elections - described as a 'farce' by the opposition - with 99 per cent of the vote.

[26] Amnesty received many complaints over arrests for political reasons, torture and murder, where the victims included Catholic priests and soldiers accused of conspiring against the Government.

[27] In January 1998 security forces arrested hundreds of members of the Bubi ethnic group on the island of Bioko. They were accused of having attacked military installations and of belonging to the Movement for the Self-Determination of Bioko. According to Amnesty, they were arrested only on ethnic grounds.

[28] Security forces arrested hundreds of members of the Bubi ethnic group on January 1998. These Bioko island natives were accused of attacking military installations and of belonging to the Movement for the Self-determination of Bioko Island. According to AI, they were arrested due to their ethnic origen. The Bubi are a minority in the country inhabited basically by people of Fang origin, although they are the majority on the island of Bioko.

[29] Angel Serafín Seriche Dougan, Prime Minister, resigned as was expected at the beginning of his mandate. The president formed a new cabinet early in 1998. The Secretary General of the opposition Convergence for Social Democracy (CFSD), Plácido Micó, was arrested in

September 1999 on the charge of conspiring against the government. He was later released on parole.

[30] Amnesty International announced in March 2000 that at least 50 of the Bubi prisoners on Bioko island, in Malabo, had been taken to an unknown destination. According to AI, the measure was adopted with the intent of inflicting physical and mental harm on the prisoners. ■

PROFILE

ENVIRONMENT

The country consists of mainland territory on the Gulf of Guinea (Rio Muni, 26,017 sq.km) and the islands of Bioko (formerly Fernando Po, and Macías Nguema) and Pigalu (formerly Annobon, Corisco, Greater Elobey and Lesser Elobey). The islands are of volcanic origin and extremely fertile; Rio Muni is a coastal plain covered with tropical rainforests but without natural harbors. It is one of the most humid and rainy countries of the world, a characteristic which limits the variety of possible crops.

SOCIETY

Peoples: The population is mostly of Bantu origin. In the islands there are also Ibo and Efik peoples who migrated from Nigeria, subduing the local Bubi population. In Rio Muni the inhabitants are mainly Fang and Ndowe. Nearly all of the Europeans and a third of the local population emigrated during the Macías regime.
Religions: Mainly Christian on the islands; traditional African beliefs in Rio Muni.
Languages: Spanish is the official and predominant language. In Rio Muni, Fang is also spoken, and on the islands, Bubi, Ibo and English.
Political Parties: Democratic Party for Equatorial Guinea (PDGE), Joint Opposition Platform, Movement for the Self-Determination of Bioko.

THE STATE

Official Name: República de Guinea Ecuatorial.
Administrative divisions: 4 continental and 3 island regions.
Capital: Malabo 50,000 people (est 1995).
Other cities: Bata 24,300 people (1983).
Government: Teodoro Obiang Mba Nzago, President since August 1979.
National Holiday: October 12, Independence Day (1968).
Armed Forces: 1,300.

Eritrea

Population: 3,720,000 (1999)
Area: 117,600 SQ KM
Capital: Asmara
Currency: Nafka
Language: Tigrinya

Eritrea

A s the site of the most important ports of the Aksumite empire (flourished 4th-6th century AD), Eritrea was linked to the beginnings of the Ethiopian kingdom, but it retained much of its independence until it fell under Ottoman rule in the 16th century. From the 17th to the 19th century control over the territory was disputed among Ethiopia, the Ottomans, the kingdom of Tigray, Egypt and Italy. In 1890, the treaty of Wichale between Italy and Menilek II of Ethiopia recognized Italian possessions on the Red Sea, and the colony, created on January 1 1890, was named by the Italians for the Mare Erythraeum ('Red Sea' in Latin) of the Romans.

2   Eritrea was used as the main base for the Italian invasions of Ethiopia (1896 and 1935-36) and it became one of the six provinces of Italian East Africa. During World War II, in 1941, the area came under British administration.

3   The common struggle against the Italians had brought a reasonable degree of unity to almost one million Eritreans. On December 2 1950, the United Nations declared that Eritrea should become a federated state within the Ethiopian Empire. The resolution rejected Ethiopian demands for outright incorporation, but also left the process of Eritrean self-determination undefined.

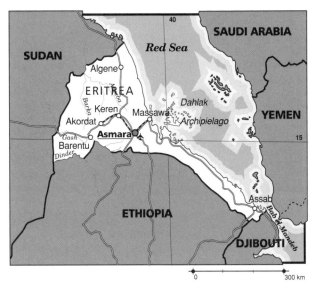

4   In Eritrea, a national assembly was elected which enjoyed some autonomy until 1962, when Ethiopian leader Haile Selassie forced a group of Eritrean politicians to vote for its complete incorporation into Ethiopia. The decision was contested by nationalist groups and immediately sparked a rebellion.

5   The oldest anti-Ethiopian resistance movement is the Eritrean Liberation Front (ELF) founded in 1958, in Cairo, by journalist and union leader Idris Mohamed Adem. It began guerrilla activities in September 1961. In 1966, a split produced the Eritrean Popular Liberation Front (EFPL). In 1974, with Sudanese mediation, the two groups agreed to coordinate their actions and in the next few years, the EFPL imposed its leadership upon the rebel movement.

6   During the pro-Soviet Mengistu government in Ethiopia, the Eritreans felt that the changes in Addis Ababa did not bring their self-determination closer, so they had no reason to stop fighting. The war against Ethiopia caused thousands of victims on both sides.

7   In February 1990, the EFPL captured the port of Massewa and nearly all of the Eritrean territory. The rebels entered Asmara on May 25 and the port of Aseb on the following day. The highway from Asseb to Addis Ababa is the only land supply route to the Ethiopian capital.

8   At the end of May, the EFPL announced the formation of a Provisional Government, and in July, in the Ethiopian capital, an agreement was reached to hold a UN supervised referendum within a two-year period.

9   From 1991, Asmara and Addis-Ababa started State to State relations. The Red Sea ports were reopened allowing international aid to enter. The rains also reappeared in Eritrea, ending two years of drought.

10   In a plebiscite in April 1993, 99.8 per cent of the voters were in favor of independence. The EPLF formed a provisional government led by Isaias Afeworki, charged with drawing up a new Constitution within four years and calling multiparty elections. In this year Eritrea joined the UN.

11   In February 1994, the EPLF held its third congress and became a political party, the Peoples Front for Democracy and Justice (PFDJ). Meanwhile, Eritrea joined the IMF.

12   In December 1994, deteriorating relations with Sudan obstructed the repatriation of 500,000 refugees. In October 1995, Afeworki declared his government would supply arms to any group prepared to overthrow the Khartoum regime.

13   In 1996, a project aiming to give land to foreign investors was obstructed by ownership disputes. That year, restrictions continued on the formation of opposition parties. The Government controlled the media and restricted press freedoms.

14   In late 1997, Eritrea abandoned the common currency and introduced the *nafka*, to replace the Ethiopian *birr*. As a counterpart measure, Ethiopia announced trade between the two nations should be carried out exclusively in US dollars.

15   The Government could not meet the political transition schedule and postponed the multiparty elections announced for 1997. Territorial disputes worsened with the neighboring Djibouti and Yemen. Against a backdrop of extreme poverty, tourism, mainly on the islands and coral reefs, gained greater importance as a source of hard currency.

16   The clashes with Ethiopia resumed in February 1999. The war expanded to include Nigeria, which provided arms to the Eritreans, and to Kenya, which mobilized forces along its Ethiopian border.

17   In June, Afeworki and his Prime Minister Meles Zenawi accepted the OAU proposal for an immediate ceasefire and withdrawal of troops along the disputed zones. Eritrean authorities demanded compensation for the deportation of thousands of its citizens who now had to live in Ethiopia and who had their possessions expropriated.

18   Eritrea accepted the UN peace plan in September while Ethiopia still harbored minor disagreements. Talks were intensified during the following months with the objective of both sides accepting the agreement. In spite of this, the situation remained tense and there were new clashes along the border between the two countries in February 2000. ∎

PROFILE

ENVIRONMENT

Eritrea is in the horn of Africa. The northeast coast, all 1,000 km. of it, is bordered by the Red Sea; to the northeast lies Sudan; to the south, Ethiopia and to the southeast, Djibouti. The dry plains and extremely hot desert steppes are inhabited by pastoralists. Deforestation and the consequent erosion are partly responsible for the frequent droughts.

SOCIETY

Peoples: The nine ethnic groups are the Tigrinya, Tigre, Bilen, Afar, Saho, Kunama, Nara, Hidareb and Rashaida. The majority are pastoralists or farmers; 20 per cent are urban workers. Half a million Eritrean refugees live in Sudan, 40,000 in Europe and 14,000 in the US. **Religions:** Almost half of all Eritreans are Coptic Christians; most of the rest are Muslim, although there are Catholic and Protestant minorities. **Languages:** Tigrinya and at least nine local languages. **Political Parties:** People's Front for Democracy and Justice (former Eritrean People's Liberation Front).

THE STATE

Capital: Asmara, 400,000 people (1992). **Other cities:** Asseb 50,000 people; Keren 40,000; Massaua (Mesewa) 80,000 (1996). **Government:** Parliamentary Republic. Isaias Afeworki, President since May 1993. **National holiday:** May 24, Independence (1993).

Estonia

Eesti

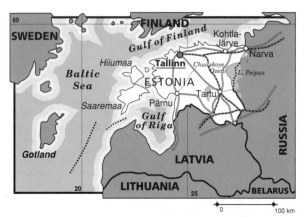

Population:	1,412,000 (1999)
Area:	45,100 SQ KM
Capital:	Tallinn
Currency:	Krona
Language:	Estonian

Despite historical and political links with their southern neighbors, Lithuania and Latvia, the Estonian people have always been known for their spiritual and cultural independence. Belonging to a branch of the Finno-Ugric nations, Estonians have greater cultural and linguistic ties with the Finns to the north than with the Indo-European Balts to the south.

[2] The region was settled some 6,000 years ago. Around the year 400 AD, the semi-nomadic peoples' hunting and fishing activity began to be replaced by agriculture and cattle raising. At the same time, navigation and trade with neighboring countries along the Baltic Sea intensified. In the 11th and 12th centuries, combined Estonian forces successfully repelled Russia's attempts to invade the territory.

[3] The Germans, Russians and Danes, invading Estonia in the 13th century, found a federation of states with a high level of social development and a strong sense of independence, keeping them united against foreign conquerors.

[4] In the 13th century, the Knights of the Sword, a Germanic order which was created during the Crusades, conquered the southern part of Estonia and the north of Latvia, creating the kingdom of Livonia and converting the inhabitants to Christianity. German traders and landowners brought the Protestant Reformation to Estonia in the first half of the 16th century.

[5] The northern part of Estonia remained under Danish control. Livonia was much disputed between 1558 and 1583; it was repeatedly attacked by Russia before being dismembered in 1561. Poland conquered Livonia in 1569; a hundred years later, it ceded the major part of the kingdom to Sweden. In the Nordic Wars (1700-1721), Russia took Livonia from Sweden, and kept these lands under the Treaty of Nystad.

[6] Russia received the Polish part of Livonia in 1772, with the first partition of Poland. The former kingdom of Livonia became a Russian province in 1783. Power was shared between the Czar of Russia and local German nobles, who owned most of the lands and the peasants lived in serfdom.

[7] The abolition of serfdom in Russia and peasant land ownership rights (1804), strengthened the Estonian national consciousness. During the second half of the 19th century, the Society of Estonian Literati developed the written language, and the preservation of national folklore, enabling the people to withstand the Czar's Russianisation campaigns.

[8] In 1904, Estonian nationalists seized control of Tallinn, ousting the German-Baltic rulers. After the fall of the Czar in February 1917, a demonstration by 40,000 Estonians in Petrograd forced the Provisional Government to grant them autonomy, maintained even after the Bolshevik Revolution.

[9] In November 1917, with the election of a constituent assembly, the Estonian Bolsheviks only obtained 35.5 per cent of the votes. On February 24 1918, Estonia declared its independence from the Soviet Union and set up a provisional government. The following day, German troops occupied Tallinn and the Estonian government was forced to go into exile.

[10] After World War I, the Estonians successfully fought both the Red Army and the Germans. On February 2 1920, the Soviet Union recognized Estonia's independence.

[11] Estonia, Latvia and Lithuania, joined the League of Nations in 1921. Following the Swiss model, the Estonian constitution established a parliamentary democracy. The Government began the reconstruction of the country and initiated agrarian reform. In the 1920s, Estonia established the world's first shale-oil distillery.

[12] Estonia passed legislation guaranteeing the rights of minorities, and ensuring that all ethnic groups had access to schools in their own languages. The economic depression of the 1930s led to a modification of the Estonian constitution; in 1933, it became a virtual dictatorship before adopting a presidential-parliamentary system in 1937.

[13] The secret protocols of the Molotov-Ribbentrop pact, signed in 1939, determined that Estonia - like its two Baltic neighbors - would remain within the Soviet sphere of influence. At the same time, Tallinn signed a mutual assistance treaty with Moscow giving the USSR the right to install naval bases on Estonian soil.

[14] In June 1940, after demanding the right for his troops to enter Estonian territory under the pretext of searching for missing soldiers, Stalin deposed the Tallinn Government and replaced it with members of the local Communist Party. Elections were held during the Soviet occupation, after which the Communist Party seized power.

[15] Following the examples of Latvia and Lithuania, the new Government adopted the name 'Soviet Socialist Republic of Estonia', joining the USSR. According to the official record, all three Baltic States voluntarily became a part of the USSR. In 1941, around 60,000 Estonians were deported to Siberia.

[16] When the German offensive against the USSR began in 1941, Nazi troops invaded Estonia, establishing a reign of terror which was especially directed against Jews, gypsies and Estonian nationalists. The USSR recovered the Baltic States in 1944; Estonian groups began pro-independence guerrilla activity, but had little impact against Soviet military might.

[17] Some 80,000 Estonians emigrated to the West, while Russian colonization gradually altered the traditional ethnic composition of the population .Around 20,000 Estonians were deported between 1945 and 1946. The third wave of mass deportations took place in 1949, when another 40,000 Estonians were sent to the farthest regions of the USSR, most of them farmers who refused to accept collectivization of the land, imposed by Soviet authorities.

[18] The reforms set in motion in 1985 by Soviet President, Mikhail Gorbachev stimulated social and political activity within Estonia. In August 1987, a demonstration in Tallinn demanded the publication of the Molotov-Ribbentrop pact. Latvians and Lithuanians also asked that the contents of the protocols be revealed.

[19] In January 1988, former Estonian political prisoners founded the Estonian Independence Party, defending the country's right to self-determination. In addition, this group called for the re-establishment of multiparty democracy, and the restoration of Estonian as the country's official language. Another group, the Estonian Heritage Society, began trying to locate and restore the country's historical monuments.

[20] The Popular Front of Estonia (FPE), founded in April by nationalists and communists, organized a rally in June 1988 which was attended by 150,000 people. The outlawed Estonian flag was displayed on this occasion. In September, some 300,000 Estonians held another rally; a few days later, the ban on the flag was lifted.

[21] In October, the first FPE congress reaffirmed Estonia's demand for autonomy, and asked Moscow for an admission of the fact that Estonia had been occupied against its will in 1940. The following month, Estonia's soviet (parliament) declared the country's sovereignty, and affirmed its right to veto laws imposed by Moscow without consent.

[22] In August 1989, some two million Estonians, Latvians and Lithuanians formed a 560-km human chain from Tallinn to Vilnius to demand the independence of the Baltic States. In February 1990, a convention of Estonian representatives approved the Declaration of Independence, based

on the 1920 Peace Treaty of Tartu between the Soviet Union and the newly independent Estonian republic.

23 In the May 1990 elections, the FPE and other nationalist groups won an ample majority within parliament. Moderate nationalist leader Edgar Savisaar was named as the leader of the first elected government since 1940. In August, parliament proclaimed the independence of Estonia, but Moscow did not consider it to be valid.

24 In late 1990-early 1991, Moscow threatened to impede Estonia's separation from the USSR, by force, and skirmishes took place between Soviet troops and nationalist groups. In September, the USSR recognized the independence of the three Baltic States, and that same month, they were admitted to the United Nations.

25 In January, Savisaar and his government resigned in the face of growing criticism over his economic policy. Parliament named former transportation minister Tiit Vahi to head the new government. Estonia had to ration food and fuel ever since the Russian Federation began restricting and raising the price of its products.

26 On June 20 1992, the new constitution (based on the 1938 Constitution) was ratified by referendum.

27 In September, the *Rligikogu* (parliament) of the 7th Legislature was elected. On October 7, it issued a declaration announcing the end of the transitional government, and re-invoking the constitution.

28 The following month, Estonia initiated negotiations with the Russian Government for the withdrawal of former Red Army troops. In addition, the Government has territorial claims over part of the Russian region of Pskov, with a land area of 2,000 sq km.

29 Lennart Meri, of the National Country Coalition Party, was elected President of Estonia by parliament on October 5 by 59 votes to 31.

30 In 1992, Estonia became the first Eastern European country to abandon the rouble, and create its own currency, the krona.

31 The privatization process came to a halt in December as a result of the resignation of the official in charge, accused of negligence and fraud. In early 1993, privatizations resumed, although these basically entailed returning properties and goods confiscated during the Communist regime to their former owners.

32 In June, a blatantly nationalistic law was approved, aimed at foreigners, especially those of Russian origin who make up 39 per cent of the total population. The law obliges foreigners to apply for a discretionary residence permit.

33 The March 1995 elections led to the defeat of the coalition which had ruled Estonia since the former Soviet republic broke away from the USSR. The new Prime Minister, Tiit Vahi, caused a controversy when he named a 'disproportionate' number of former communist ministers in his government. In October his cabinet was forced to resign due to corruption charges against the Minister of the Interior. The new government was formed with the inclusion of Reform Party members.

34 On September 20 1996, after a close vote from the Electoral College, Lennart Meri was re-elected as President. A report from the European Bank for Reconstruction and Development - created to favor the transition of former Socialist countries toward a market economy - estimated on December 1997 that reforms carried out by Estonia in its financial sector, which led to the highest foreign investment per capita in the region, favored its swift incorporation into the European Union.

35 In February 1998, Estonia, Latvia and Lithuania signed a Charter of Association with the United States, in which Washington vowed to support the entry of the three states into NATO. Immediately, Russia announced the normalization of relations with the Baltic nations, as long as they regularized the situation of the Russian-speaking minorities.

36 Mart Laar was appointed Prime Minister in March 1999. In order to compensate for the dismissal of Russian residents who did not speak Estonian, a program was started by which youth from the city of Narva are lodged by Estonian families in the Lake Peipus lake region which comprises a large part of the Russian border and where 95 per cent of its inhabitants speak Russian.

37 The repatriation and ceremonial funeral of an Estonian officer who commanded a Nazi unit during World War II caused controversy in Tallinn. Prime Minister Laar described him as one of the most outstanding soldiers of the nation and said it was the country's duty to honor him. But for the parties representing the Russian minority this was interpreted as support for fascism. ∎

Ethiopia

Yaitopya

Population: 61,095,000 (1999)
Area: 1,104,300 SQ KM
Capital: Addis Ababa (Adis Abeba)
Currency: Birr
Language: Amharic

In ancient times, the greek term 'Ethiopian', meaning 'burnt face' in Greek, was applied indiscriminately to all Africans. Ethiopia's other name, Abyssinia, came from the Arabic 'Habbashat', which was the name of one of the groups that emigrated from Yemen to Africa around 2000 BC.

[2] Axum, in the north of present-day Ethiopia, was the center of trade between the Upper Nile valley and the Red Sea ports which traded with Arabia and India, it reached its height in the first centuries AD. Ethiopia was a rich and prosperous state, which was able to subdue present-day Yemen, but which went through a crisis in the 7th century. Trade routes moved as Arab unification and expansion dominated the area, conquering Egypt. The Ethiopian ruling elite had converted to Christianity in the 4th century, further contributing to their isolation. Expansion towards the south, excessive growth of the clergy, and declining trade led to a process of social and economic stratification similar to that in feudal western Europe. By the 16th century, one third of the land belonged to the 'king of kings'; another third belonged to the monasteries and the rest was divided among the nobility and the rest of the population.

[3] The Muslim population that had developed a powerful trade economy on the coast of the Red Sea (see Tanzania: 'The Zandj Culture of East Africa'), instigated an insurrection, leading Ethiopia to resume its relations with Europe to request assistance. The aid took almost a century to arrive, but the Portuguese fleet, when it finally arrived in 1541, was decisive in destroying the Sultanate of Adal (See Somalia).

[4] For 150 years, Ethiopian emperors focused their efforts on the coast, giving Oromo (a nation akin to the Haussa) a chance to gradually penetrate from the west until they outnumbered the local population. Their influence grew so great that an Oromo became emperor, between 1755 and 1769; though the Amhara ruling elite took great pains to oust him.

[5] This state of affairs continued until 1889 when Menelik II came to power. Designated heir to the throne in 1869, he spent the next 20 years training an army (with British and Italian assistance) and organizing the administration of his own territory, the state of Shoa. His efficiency was fortunate; in 1895 his former allies, the Italians, invaded the country claiming that previous commitments had not been honored. The final battle was fought in Adua in 1896 where, 4,000 of the 10,000 Italian soldiers were killed. It was the most devastating defeat suffered by European troops on African soil until the Algerian War. In the diplomatic negotiations that followed their defeat, the Italians succeeded in obtaining two territories that Ethiopia did not really control: Eritrea and the southern Somalian coast. In 1906, the world powers recognized the independence and territorial integrity of what was then known as Abyssinia, in exchange for certain economic privileges.

[6] This arrangement saved Ethiopia from direct colonization until 1936, when Italian Fascist dictator Benito Mussolini invaded the country, taking advantage of internal strife among Menelik's would-be successors. Despite his pleas to the League of Nations, Haile Selassie, heir to the throne, got no concrete help. During the five-year occupation, several basic industries and coffee plantations were started, and a system of racial discrimination was installed, similar to that of apartheid in South Africa.

[7] In 1948, Ethiopians won their autonomy back from Britain, which had taken over the country after Mussolini's defeat in 1941. When Selassie returned to the throne, his country was floundering in unprecedented crisis: foreign occupation had disrupted production; nationalist political movements had strengthened in the struggle for autonomy and rejected a return to feudalism; and poverty in the interior had grown considerably.

[8] Selassie denounced colonialism, favored non-alignment and supported the creation of the Organization for African Unity, which finally set up headquarters in Addis Ababa. He also maintained close links with Israel. On the domestic front, the crisis deepened as his government was dominated by a corrupt oligarchy and the Orthodox Church, which between them held 80 percent of the country's fertile lands. The domestic crisis came to a head in 1956 when Eritrean separatist rebels intensified their attacks. In 1974, after a series of strikes, student rallies and widespread protests against absolutism and food shortages, Haile Selassie was overthrown.

[9] In 1975, an Armed Forces Coordination Committee, the *Dergue* ('committee' in Amharic), headed by General Aman Andom abolished the monarchy and proclaimed a republic, suspending the Constitution and dissolving Parliament.

[10] Popular movements became more radical, leading to a series of disputes among the military, and a subsequent crisis. Colonel Mengistu Haile Mariam rose to power in December 1977. He managed to hold the Dergue together and put an end to the military's internal struggles.

[11] The military government succeeded in carrying out agrarian reform, and nationalizing foreign banks and heavy industry. US military bases were closed down.

WORKERS

% OF LABOUR FORCE — **1998**

■ FEMALE: 41% ■ MALE: 59%

1990

■ SERVICES: 11.7%
■ INDUSTRY: 2.1%
■ AGRICULTURE: 86.2%

LAND USE

DEFORESTATION: 0.5% annual (1990/95)
IRRIGATED: 1.6% of arable (1993)

1993

■ FOREST & WOODLAND: 22.7%
■ ARABLE: 10.9%
■ OTHER: 66.4%

PUBLIC EXPENDITURE

1997

DEFENCE 7.9%
SOCIAL 30.8%

MILITARY EXPENDITURE **190%**
(% of health & education) (1990/91)

Right-wing groups carried out assassinations and bombings. Left-wing organizations retaliated by killing conspirators and monarchists on sight. Between December 1977 and April 1978, the violence left over 5,000 people dead.

[12] Once the military crisis was resolved, a struggle broke out for the control of grassroots organizations. At first the Dergue supported the Pan-Ethiopian Socialist Movement (Meison), which set up neighborhood committees (kebeles) as a basis for mass organization. The Meison grew stronger and proposed a system of self-controlled civilian units. This set them on a collision course with the Dergue, which rejected the creation of autonomous military groups.

[13] Mengistu declared the Meison illegal and backed the Revolutionary Flame, a group of officers and civilians who had studied in socialist Europe and were loyal to the president of the Dergue. After settling this latest crisis, the Government was able to confront the two separatist movements which had been gaining strength since 1977, in Eritrea and the Ogaden desert. The Eritrean rebels considered that their independence struggle was valid, regardless of the existence of a progressive government in Addis-Ababa, and the Somali population of the Ogaden desert (claimed by Somalia) took advantage of the domestic crisis in Addis-Ababa to further their own separatist cause.

[14] Mengistu rejected Eritrean separatist demands. He alleged that their struggle had only been reasonable when they had confronted the feudal monarchy, and not when they had opposed the pro-soviet regime.

[15] Faced with the Somalian intention of annexing the Ogaden, the Soviet Union broke its military treaties with Siad Barre. In this modern armed war, Soviet and Cuban support was decisive in his defeat. With the situation resolved on both battle fronts, Mengistu turned his attention back to domestic policy.

[16] In 1979 the Government set up the Ethiopian Workers' Party Organization Committee (COPWE), and their first general congress was held in 1980. In that year, there was a 15 per cent increase in cultivated land, which raised the GNP by 6 per cent.

[17] In 1984, the country was struggling under the effects of a prolonged drought which had begun in 1982, causing thousands of deaths from starvation. The drought affected twelve provinces, threatened five million lives and killed over half a million people.

[18] The Ethiopian Workers' Party (PWE) held their founding congress in 1984, approving a program to transform the country into a socialist state.

[19] The newly-elected Assembly (the Shengo, or parliament) proclaimed the People's Democratic Republic of Ethiopia on September 12, ratifying Mengistu Haile Mariam as head of state. Separatists extended operations in Eritrea and Tigray, as well as in Wollo, Gondar and Oromo in the south.

[20] The new constitution provided for the creation of five autonomous regions and 25 administrative regions. Eritrea was able to legislate on all matters except defense, national security, foreign relations and its legal status in relation to central government. The separatists rejected the proposal, calling it 'colonial'.

[21] In December 1987, after a bloody battle, the Eritreans took Af Abed. 18,000 Ethiopian troops, three Soviet advisors and the army commander of the northern region were taken prisoner.

[22] The Tigray People's Liberation Front (TPLF) captured important cities like Wukro, a distribution center for international aid to drought victims. Building on these victories, the rebels from Eritrea and Tigray signed cooperation agreements and began to plan joint military strategies.

[23] Increased rebel activity took a heavy toll on the Ethiopian army and in 1989 12 divisions (150,000 troops) stationed in the front line attempted a coup. Mengistu returned hastily from West Germany and managed to abort the coup. He executed dozens of officers, among them Generals Amha Desta, airforce commander-in-chief, and Merrid Negusie, chief-of-staff of the armed forces.

[24] By the end of the 1980s, the war was consuming 60 per cent of Ethiopia's national budget, and agricultural production was slumping. In 1989, former US President Jimmy Carter's mediation brought together delegations from the Government and Eritrean People's Liberation Front (EPLF) in Atlanta, in the US. The EPLF condensed its demands into one: a plebiscite for Eritrea's future. Mengistu refused.

[25] In September 1989, the last Cuban soldiers withdrew from Ethiopia. The Government had signed a peace agreement with

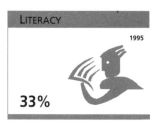
Somalia in April 1988, and no longer needed their services.

[26] Ethiopia re-established contact with Israel, as relations had been interrupted after the 1973 war. Mengistu looked to Tel Aviv for substantial military aid and facilities for 17,000 Ethiopian Jews to emigrate to Israel. Meanwhile in Eritrea and Tigray, where the drought had reduced the grain harvest by nearly 80 per cent, the situation of millions steadily worsened. International agencies warned of the danger of yet another famine.

[27] In 1990, the Central Committee of the Ethiopian Workers' Party decided to restructure the party and change its name to the Ethiopian Democratic Union Party (EDUP. While excluding the possibility of a multiparty system, the changes sought to lay the basis of 'a party of all Ethiopians', open to 'opposition groups'. The Marxist-Leninist tag was dropped. The Government established a mixed economy, including state enterprises, cooperatives and private businesses.

[28] Within one month, the former USSR withdrew its military advisors from Eritrea, and the EPLF took the port of Massawa, thus controlling all of Eritrea, except Asmara, which was totally cut off from the rest of Ethiopia by occupied land.

[29] In May 1991, after overwhelming guerrilla victories in the north, Mengistu Mariam's departure from Ethiopia was negotiated internationally. The Government was left in the hands of Vice-President Tesfaye Gabre Kidane, considered a moderate, who initiated his transitional government by negotiating a cease-fire with the Eritrean rebels.

[30] Kidane's government took part in peace talks, in London, presided over by the US, with the participation of the most important rebel groups. They aimed at reaching an agreement which would stave off civil war. Kidane resigned in late May, when the US advised the forces of the Ethiopian People's Revolutionary Democratic Front (EPRDF) to take control of Addis Ababa.

[31] Meles Zenawi, the 36-year-old leader of the EPRDF became interim president, until a multi-party conference could be held. He promised to bring the civil war to an end, re-establish democracy and referendum to decide the issue of independence (see Eritrea).

[33] The new government

PROFILE

ENVIRONMENT

A mountainous country with altitudes of over 4,000 meters. Ethiopia is isolated from neighboring regions by its geography. In the North, the Eritrean plain, a desert steppe, extends alongside the Red Sea. In the mountains and plateaus, vegetation and climate vary with altitude. The Dega are cool, rainy highlands, above 2,500 meters, where grain is grown and cattle raised. The deep valleys which traverse the highlands are warm and rainy with tropical vegetation, known as the Kolla (up to 1,500 m). The drier, cooler, medium-range plateaus where coffee and cotton are grown (1,500 to 2,500 m) are the most densely populated parts of the country. To the East lies the Ogaden, a semi-desert plateau inhabited by nomadic shepherds of Somali origin. Many regions which were once rich in vegetation are now rocky, desert areas. Desertification and erosion have increased within the past decade. Ethiopia is the home of Arabica coffee, and coffee accounts for over 60 per cent of Ethiopia's export income. Other exports are skins, meat, oil seeds and gum incense.

SOCIETY

Peoples: Two thirds are of Amhara or Oromo descent. There are many other ethnic groups including the Tigrai who speak Tigrigna; Gurage, Niloti, Somali and Afar from Danaki region.

Religions: There are roughly equal numbers of Christians and Muslims. About 40 per cent of the population is Christian, 40 per cent Islamic, and the rest, mainly in the South and South-west, practice local religions.

Languages: Amharic is the language of government, with all parliamentary documents also written in English. The second major language is Oromigna (the language of the Oromo). There are at least 100 local languages.

Political Parties: The are over 65 registered parties but the dominant one is the Ethiopian People's Revolutionary Democratic Front (EPRDF). Others include the All Amhara People's Organization (AAPO) and the Ogaden National Liberation Front (ONLF). The opposition Oromo Liberation Front is not registered.

THE STATE

Official Name: Federal Democratic Republic of Ethiopia.

Administrative Divisions: The are nine regional states (Tigray, Afar, Amhara, Oromia, Somali, Benishangul/Gumuz, Southern People's Region, Gambela and Harari). The are also two chartered cities (Addis Ababa and Dire Dawa).

Capital: Addis Ababa (Adis-Abeba), 2,209,000 people (1995).

Other city: Dire Dawa 117,700 people (1988).

Government: Negasso Gidada, President since August 1995; Meles Zenawi, Prime Minister since August 1995.

National Holidays: May 28, Overthrow of the Dergue (1991).

Armed Forces: 120,000 (1995).

EXTERNAL DEBT		1998

PER CAPITA

US$ 174

FOREIGN TRADE		1998

Millions US$

IMPORTS

1,810

EXPORTS

1,034

confronted two practically insoluble problems: reconciling the various guerrilla groups, and hunger. Ethiopia became one of the poorest countries in the world. In recent years it has been simultaneously confronted with severe drought and civil war on at least four fronts.

[34] It is estimated that within the past 20 years, more than a million Ethiopians have died of starvation, and another million have become refugees in neighboring countries. After an agreement was signed with the Eritreans, international aid was once more transported through the ports of Asseb and Massawa on the Red Sea.

[35] On July 9, for the first time in 17 years, residents of Addis Ababa elected their representatives to the *kebeles* which were outside the control of any political organization. The voters' main concerns were to achieve peace and security within the capital, and to elect a local administration.

[36] In March 1992, the minister of Insurance and Rehabilitation declared that if international aid did not arrive quickly, the transition to democracy would be jeopardized by the instability caused by the extreme poverty of a large number of Ethiopians. Population displacements and ethnic conflicts worsen the situation, events which are reminiscent of the 1984-85 famine.

[37] The transitional government promised to promote the market economy, stimulate agricultural production and reduce poverty, within a five year program coordinated by United Nations organizations and the World Bank. In January 1993, during a visit from the UN Secretary-General Boutros Boutros-Ghali, large student demonstrations once again reflected the tense social situation in the nation.

[38] In 1994, the delivery of the $1.2 billion in five years planned in the economic program, slowed down considerably as the international organizations decided the Ethiopian government was privatizing too slowly. In a criticism of the structural adjustment plan proposed by the IMF and the World Bank, humanitarian organizations supporting Ethiopia said there should be greater investment in seeds, tools and livestock in order to fight famine.

[39] Ten years after the 1984 famine, the situation became critical again in the first six months of 1994, with

5,000 deaths in the Wolayata district in the south of the country. In May, the Council of Representatives, a temporary 87-member body, approved a draft Constitution which created the Federal Democratic Republic of Ethiopia. This draft was based on the 'ethnic federalism' doctrine, which put an end to the previous official unified vision of the nation. According to the approved document, the 'sovereignty resides in the nations, nationalities and peoples of Ethiopia' and not the people as a whole.

[40] In June, elections were held for a Constituent Assembly, but were boycotted by main opposition parties, like the Oromo Liberation Front and the Ogaden National Liberation Front. In September, the police carried out mass arrests in the west of the country, a zone mainly inhabited by Oromos. Several human rights organizations, like Amnesty International, expressed concern over the situation of the country.

[41] In May and June 1995, parliamentary elections were held, also boycotted by most of the opposition parties. The new federal republic was officially established in August, when Negasso Gidada, a Christian Oromo from the Welega region in the west of Ethiopia, took over the presidency. The outgoing president, Meles Zenawi, became Prime Minister and the 17 members of government were carefully selected to reflect 'the ethnic balance' of the country.

[42] The trial of the old Mengistu regime members was proposed for the second time, and attempts to extradite the former president from Zimbabwe were unsuccessful. Amnesty condemned the Ethiopian government once again, following the arrest of five opposition politicians in June.

[43] The Government went ahead with the privatization of state companies - 144 were sold in 1995 - and the annual grain deficit stood at around a million tons. In 1996, there was an abortive assassination attempt against Mengistu in Zimbabwe. Many of his former supporters were still in prison. The rainy season started well and increased expectations of food self-sufficiency. The World Bank announced a large reduction in the Ethiopian debt. In 1997, Amnesty repeated its plea for the liberation of members of the opposition and called for an end to arbitrary arrests, torture and disappearances.

[44] In early 1998, food shortages

threatened millions of Ethiopians. Due to the price increases set by the Government (13 per cent between August and December 1997) the satisfaction of basic needs become increasingly difficult for the poorer sectors of society. The rains trailed off due to the climatic upset related to the El Niño phenomenon. The Ethiopian Disaster Prevention and Preparedness Commission (DPPC) formally called on the international bodies for help to avoid another famine.

[45] In May and June 1998 Ethiopia claimed that Eritrea had invaded northern Ethiopia, and Ethiopia began to rebuild the army, largely dismantled after the fall of Mengistu. Following fresh fighting in February 1999 Ethiopia reclaimed most of the land it had lost, but thousands were killed on both sides. The UN called for an immediate ceasefire, and the security council imposed an arms embargo until it was convinced the war was over.

[46] In March 1999, US President Bill Clinton proposed the cancellation of $70 billion of foreign aid paid to 46 African countries in a meeting of ministers there. At this time, Clinton was under pressure from Congress to approve its 'Trade initiative with Africa'.

[47] In July 1999, the World Health Organization (WHO) announced Ethiopia - as other African and Asian countries - would be offered a mass vaccination programme against polio, in an attempt to eradicate this disease by the year 2001.

[48] To regain all lost territory, Ethiopia staged a rapid advance behind Eritrean lines in May 2000. Again thousands were killed or taken prisoner, and UN ultimata for a ceasefire were ignored. In three weeks, Ethiopia occupied large tracts of Eritrea and regained all lost territory. Claiming that the losses were a result of "strategic withdrawal", the Eritreans accepted the position and Algeria brokered "proximity talks" to establish a peace plan. This required the Eritreans to withdraw all troops from along a 25-kilometre-wide zone inside its own territory until UN peacekeepers arrived, and a defined border negotiated. An advance UN mission was established, but countries have been slow to offer forces.

[49] In May a second round of five-year national elections was held, with opposition groups being funded by the Electoral Commission to get their message out. The Oromo Liberation Front still did not participate. The Opposition made small parliamentary gains and the Deputy Prime Minister lost his seat. The EPDRF maintained a strong hold. Food shortages again are critical as the entire Horn region is gripped by drought. ∎

STATISTICS

DEMOGRAPHY

Population: 61,095,000 (1999)
Annual growth: 2.7 % (1975/97)
Estimates for year 2015 (million): 90.9 (1999)
Annual growth to year 2015: 2.5 % (1997/2015)
Urban population: 16.3 % (1997)
Urban Growth: 4.5 % (1980/95)
Children per woman: 6.3 (1998)

HEALTH

Life expectancy at birth: 43 years (1998)
male: 42 years (1998)
female: 44 years (1998)
Infant mortality: 110 per 1,000 (1998)
Under-5 child mortality: 173 per 1,000 (1998)
Daily calorie supply: 1,845 per capita (1996)
4 doctors per 100,000 people (1993)
Safe water: 25 % (1990/98)

EDUCATION

Literacy: 33 % (1995)
male: 40 % (1995)
female: 26 % (1995)
School enrolment:
Primary total: 37 % (1990/96)
male: 47 % (1990/97)
female: 27 % (1990/97)
Secondary:
male: 13 % (1990/96)
female: 10 % (1990/96)
Tertiary: 1 % (1996)
Primary school teachers: one for every 43 (1996)

COMMUNICATIONS

1 newspapers (1996), 195 radios (1997), 4 TV sets (1996) and 3 main telephone lines (1996) per 1,000 people

ECONOMY

Per capita, GNP: $ 100 (1998)
Annual growth, GNP: -1.8 % (1998)
Annual inflation: 8.0 % (1990/98)
Consumer price index: 91.4 (1997)
Currency: 7.1 birr = $ 1 (1998)
Cereal imports: 580,920 metric tons (1998)
Fertilizer use: 134 kg per ha (1997)
Exports: $ 1,034 million (1998)
Imports: $ 1,810 million (1998)
External debt: $ 10,352 million (1998); $ 174 per capita (1998)
Debt service: 11.3 % of exports (1998)
Development aid received: $ 637 million (1997); $ 12.0 per capita (1997); 10.10 % of GNP (1997)

ENERGY

Consumption: 287.0 Kgs of Oil equivalent per capita yearly (1997); 5.0 % imported (1997)

HDI (rank/value): 172/0.298 (1997)

European Ministates

Andorra

Population: 64,000 (1999)
Area: 450 SQ KM
Capital: Andorra la Vella
Currency: Peseta, French franc
Language: Catalan

Located in the eastern Pyrenées, the co-principality of Andorra - it is ruled by two co-princes - is made up of deep ravines and narrow valleys surrounded by mountains with altitudes varying between 1,800 to 3,000 meters. The Valira de Ordino and Valira de Carrillo rivers join in Andorran territory under the name of the Valira river. Wheat is grown in the valleys, but livestock (especially sheep-raising) has given way to tourism as the primary economic activity.

SOCIETY

Peoples: Spanish 44.4 per cent; Andorran 20.2 per cent; Portuguese 10.7 per cent; French 6.8 per cent; other 6.6 per cent (1993).
Religions: Catholic 92 per cent; Protestant 0.5 per cent; Jewish 0.4 per cent: other 7.1 per cent (1992).
Languages: Catalan (official), French and Spanish.
Political Parties: Liberal Union Party (Unió Liberal, UL), Liberal Group (Grup Liberal), the National Andorran Coalition (Coalició Nacional Andorrana), and the Canillo-La Massana Grouping (Agrupació Canillo-La Massana). National Democratic Grouping.
Social Organizations: There are no organized trade unions. Many workers have joined French trade unions.

THE STATE

Official Name: Principat d'Andorra. **Administrative divisions:** 18 provinces. **Capital:** Andorra la Vella 21,984 people (1997). **Other cities:** Les Escaldes 15,182 people; Encamp 9,800 people (1997). **Government:** Parliamentary republic. Constitution in effect since March 14 1993. The Bishop of Urgel (Spanish jurisdiction) and the President of France, are 'co-princes' of the territory. Marc Forné Molné is President of the Executive Council and Head of Government. Single-chamber legislature (General Council), with 28 members elected by direct popular vote, every four years. At some point in the future, total independence from France and the Spanish bishopric is foreseen. **National Holiday:** September 8. ∎

Liechtenstein

Population: 28,000 (1999)
Area: 160 SQ KM
Capital: Vaduz
Currency: Swiss franc
Language: German

This small principality lies between Switzerland and Austria, in the Rhine valley. Wheat, oats, rye, corn, grapes and fruit are produced. 38 per cent of the land is pasture. In recent years, the principality has been transformed into a highly industrialized country, producing textiles, pharmaceutical products, precision instruments and refrigerators among other items.

SOCIETY

Peoples: German 95 per cent; Italian and other 5 per cent.
Capital: Vaduz 5,085 people (1996).
Religions: Catholic 80 per cent; Protestant 6.9 per cent; other 5.6 per cent.
Languages: German (official).
Political Parties: The Progressive Citizens' Party (FBP); Patriotic Union (VU); Free List, Green.
Social Organizations: The Trades Union Association (artisans and traders), and the Agricultural Union.

THE STATE

Official Name: Fürstentum Liechtenstein.
Administrative divisions: 11 communes.
Capital: Vaduz 5,067 people (1995).

Other cities: Schaan 5,143 people; Balzers,3,752 people; Triesen,3,586 people (1995).
Government: Liechtenstein is a constitutional monarchy. Prince Hans Adam II, Head of State since November 13 1989. Mario Frick, Prime Minister, Head of Government since December 1993. Government functions are carried out by a FBP and VU coalition. Cornelia Gassner (FBP), Minister of Construction, the first woman to be appointed to a cabinet post. Single-chamber legislature: Parliament with 25 members elected every four years.
Diplomacy: A member of the European Council, Liechtenstein has a customs and monetary alliance with Switzerland, which is its representative abroad.
National holiday: February 14. ∎

Monaco

Population: 30,000 (1999)
Area: 1 SQ KM
Currency: French franc
Language: French

A small principality on the Mediterranean coast, with a 3.5 km coastline, surrounded by the French department of the Maritime Alps. The territory is made up of three urban centers: Monaco-Ville, the capital, built upon an isolated cliff; Condamine, a residential center; and Monte Carlo, to the northeast of the port of Monaco, home of the famous casino and consequently the most visited location. Olives and citrus fruits are cultivated in the narrow inland strip. Tourism is the country's basic source of revenue.

SOCIETY

Peoples: 47 per cent French, 17 per cent Monacan, 16 per cent Italian, 4 per cent English, 2 per cent Belgian and 1 per cent Swiss.
Religions: 95 per cent Catholic (1997).
Languages: French and Monégasque (official), English, Italian.
Political Parties: There are no political parties. Candidates form lists to run for election in the National Council (CN). Until 1992, the CN was dominated by the National Democratic Union. In 1993, the main groups were the Cámpora List and the Médecin List. In the last CN election, in January 1997, Michel Leveque was elected Minister of State.

THE STATE

Official Name: Principauté de Monaco.
Administrative divisions: 1 commune.
Government: Parliamentary monarchy. Constitution in effect since December 17 1962. Prince Rainier III, sovereign since May 9 1949, Head of State and of the Government. Single-chamber legislature: National Council, with 18 members elected by direct vote every 5 years. ∎

San Marino

Population: 25,000 (1999)
Area: 60 SQ KM
Capital: San Marino
Currency: Lira
Language: Italian

The Republic of San Marino, founded in 1866 and located between the Italian provinces of Romana and Marca, is the world's smallest republican state. Its mountainous terrain is part of Mount Titano, an eastern branch of the Apennines; the La Rocca peak, 749 m, is the highest point in the city-state.

Grapes and grain are grown in the farmlands, and sheep are also raised. Tourism is the country's major source of income since the small republic is linked to the port of Rimini, on the Adriatic.

SOCIETY

Peoples: Sammarinesi 75.4 per cent; Italian 23.3 per cent; other 1.3 per cent (1996).

Religions: 95.2 per cent Catholic (1980).
Languages: Italian (official) and a local dialect.
Political Parties: Multiparty system. The Christian Democrat Party (PDC), 26 seats; Socialist Party (PS), 14 seats; Progressive Democratic Party (PDP) formerly communist, 11 seats; Popular Alliance (AP), 4 seats; Democratic Movement, (MD), 3 seats; Communist Refoundation (RC), 2 seats.
Social Organizations: The Unitarian Trade Union Central, the General Democratic Confederation of Workers and the General Confederation of Labor.

THE STATE

Official Name: Repubblica di San Marino.
Capital: San Marino 2,316 people (1996).
Other cities: Serravalle/Dogano 4,726 people; Borgo Maggiore 2,366 (1996).

Government: Presidential republic. The Executive of the Council of State, with ten members elected every six months (dominated by the PS and the PDC) is presided over by two regent Captains: Marino Bollini and Giuseppe Arzilli, head of State and head of Government since October 1999. Single-chamber legislature of the General Grand Council, with 60 members elected every five years by direct popular vote.
Diplomacy: At the beginning of 1992, San Marino joined the United Nations and the IMF. It has had a Friendship Treaty with Italy since 1862. As a neutral European country, it is a Non-Aligned Movement observer.

DEMOGRAPHY

Population: 25,000 (1999)

HEALTH

Infant mortality: 6 per 1,000 (1998)
Under-5 child mortality: 6 per 1,000 (1998). ∎

Vatican City

Population: 870 (1999)
Area: 0,44 SQ KM
Currency: Vatican lira
Language: Italian and Latin

The Vatican State dates back to the 9th century when Charlemagne, emperor of the Franks, legalized its existence. The Vatican ceased to exist in 1870 when the first king of Italy, Victor Emmanuel of Savoy, seeking national unification, formally occupied the territory and proclaimed Rome its capital. The 1871 Guarantees Law established the inviolability of the Pope and recognized his ownership of the Vatican, but the Roman pontiffs did not accept the situation until February 11 1929, when the Holy See signed the Treaty of Letran with Benito Mussolini, establishing the current State's borders and privileges.
[2]   Originally, the State's revenues derived from the financial investment of 1.75 billion lire indemnity established in the Treaty of Lateran as payment for the territories lost in 1870. Later they were increased by contributions and donations from all over the world,

especially from the United States and West Germany. At present, these resources are administered by the Institute for Religious Works - known popularly as the Vatican Bank - re-organized following banking scandals originated in the bankruptcy of the Ambrosiano Bank. Allegedly the Institute has reserves exceeding $11 billion, participates in numerous other banks and enterprises, and owns countless real-estate throughout the world.
[3]   In 1993 the Catholic Church's administration budget showed a $1.5 million profit (after years of deficits) – but this figure did not include capital reserves put at $900 million. That same year, Vatican workers organized the first ever protest, demanding wage increases and pensions. The commercialization of the Pope's image was authorized, during his visit to the United States in June, allowing the sale of posters and T-shirts. Two years later, the Vatican produced a compact disc of prayers recited by the Pope which sold more than 20

million copies. In 1995, the Vatican economy went back into the black, leaving the financial troubles behind. In January 1998 the Pope made a visit to Cuba.
[4]   In January 2000, the Catholics' jubilee year, the President of the German Episcopal Conference, Monsignor Karl Lehmann, shook the Catholic world by publicly stating his assurance that the Pope, then aged 79, would resign if he felt he could no longer continue in his post. Lehmann thus broke the taboo on the delicate issue of a Pope potentially standing down, a practice possible (authorized by the Code of Canon Law), but extremely rare in the millenarian history of the Vatican. Indeed the most recent case was in 1040, when Benedictine IX and Gregory VI resigned for different reasons.

ENVIRONMENT

Located within the city of Rome, not far from the banks of the Tiber river, the Vatican comprises St Peter's square and basilica, the palaces and gardens of the Vatican itself, the palace and basilica of St John Lateran, the papal villa at Castelgandolfo and another 13 off-limit buildings which enjoy diplomatic privileges because they house congregations of the Catholic Church.

SOCIETY

Peoples: Church members whose functions require residence, become Vatican citizens. Most permanent members are Italian, but there is also a large number of Swiss

residents, and some other nationalities.
Religions: Catholic.
Languages: Italian (official language of the State) and Latin (official language of the Church).

THE STATE

Official Name: Stato della Cittá del Vaticano.
Administrative divisions: Two parallel administrations: Holy See (supreme body of the Catholic Church) and Vatican City (site of the Church).
Capital: Vatican City 1,000 (1995)
Government: Elected lifelong monarchy. Monarch: John Paul II (Karol Wojtyla, of Polish origin), elected on October 16 1978 by the cardinals' conclave (secret meeting), the first non-Italian Pope in 456 years. Secretary of State (a position equivalent to Prime Minister): Cardinal Angelo Sodano. The state government is exercised by a 5-member pontifical commission appointed by the Pope and headed by the Secretary of State. The Pope is also the Bishop of Rome and the supreme ruler of the Catholic Church. In Church government, he is assisted by the College of Cardinals and the Synods of Bishops, which meet when so instructed by the Pope. The Church's administrative departments comprise 9 holy congregations, 3 Secretariats and several commissions, mayoralties and tribunals, known collectively as the Roman Curia. ∎

Fiji

Fiji

Population: 806,000 (1999)
Area: 18,270 SQ KM
Capital: Suva City
Currency: Fiji dollar
Language: English

Four thousand years ago the Fijian archipelago was already populated. Melanesian migrations first reached the islands in the 6th century BC, and the Fijians had one of the leading Pacific cultures. In 1789, British Captain William Bligh visited the islands, writing the first detailed account of Fijian life.

2 Social life on the islands was organized in families and clans which gradually formed larger communities. One of these, ruled by traditional leader Na Ulivau, extended its influence from Ngau over the rest of the islands, achieving unification.

3 Early in the 19th century, British adventurers and merchants exploited the forests of Fiji, rich in sandalwood and other aromatic species highly prized in China. To settle their rivalries, Europeans sought support from local leaders. In 1830, the first Christian missionaries arrived from Tonga and 24 years later achieved a major victory by christening ruler Thakombau, son of Na Ulivau. Contemporary accounts report a 'refined, courteous and honourable gentleman', and this 'king' (formerly reported to be a 'cannibal') became an enthusiastic admirer of the Western world. He offered to annex Fiji to the US, though this may have been more due to the Fijian ruler's heavy debts after prolonged wars with rival leaders. The White House, caught up in the turmoil of the Secession War, missed the opportunity to tack another star on the flag. The British, faced with a shortage of sugar, 'discovered' the archipelago's potential for growing cane and, with Thakombau's consent, officially annexed the islands on October 10 1874.

4 Fijian officials raised no objections to the purchase or expropriation of large tracts of land for the new crops, though the peasants were unwilling to leave their communal estates to work on the plantations. Consequently, a massive influx of bond workers were brought in, first from the Solomon islands, and then from India. Following the abolition of slavery, the British used this same system of transferring Indian workers to Africa and the Caribbean to curb the labor shortage and ease the population squeeze in India.

5 At the end of their contracts, the workers brought their families to Fiji and became small shop owners, craftspeople or bureaucrats in the colonial administration, and though far from India, they retained their language, religion and caste system. Colonial regulations meant that they were restricted from buying land from native Fijians; a law ostensibly designed to prevent inter-ethnic conflict.

6 Initial moves toward local autonomy resulted in a complicated electoral system securing political control by the 'natives' who were in the minority. Prime Minister Sir Kamisese Mara initiated an elaborate scheme of representation, where each electoral category was allotted a quota for governmental representation: Fijians 22; Indians 22 and General 8. The peculiar system that nonetheless proved useful in preventing major disruptions during the transition to independence in 1970. His Alliance Party claimed to be multiracial, and marshaled support from some Indians and other minor groups, in addition to the Fijian electorate.

7 In 1976, the Government turned down a constitutional reform project which would have required multi-group cooperation in the country's administration.

8 Inter-ethnic coexistence has been successful except for two fierce clashes in 1959 and 1968; however, potential conflict situations could still erupt. The recent 'back-to-the-roots' trend, centered mainly around the University of the Pacific in Suva, has encouraged young people to honor their Melanesian, Polynesian, Hindu, Islamic or Chinese cultural heritage, thus widening the existing gap between cultures. Indians predominate in trade and the liberal professions. Fijians, in turn, own the arable land and lease it on very advantageous terms to poor Indians.

9 In the 1970s economic difficulties forced thousands of Fijians to emigrate to Aotearoa/ New Zealand in search of jobs. Tourism, possibly the single industry which could improve the deficit balance of payments, required Melanesians to remain 'genuine' to satisfy Australian and Aotearoa's visitors' thirst for exoticism. Individualism and private land ownership were encouraged, seeking to bolster the economic situation of 'natives' over that of the Indians. However, under these conditions, the rural workers' gained few improvements; urban income increased by 3.5 per cent in 1978, but rural income increased only 0.3 per cent.

10 The difficult economic situation swelled the number of 'racist' groups such as the Nationalist Party, militant against the Indian majority, though Indians have been on the islands for four or five generations.

11 Former Prime Minister Kamisese Mara's conservative administration was deeply marked by racial and ideological trends. His government was the only one in the Commonwealth to maintain relations with the racist Rhodesian and South African regimes and to welcome Chilean dictator Augusto Pinochet on an official visit in early 1980. Mass demonstrations during Pinochet's visit demonstrated the growing progressive movement in Fiji.

12 In the 1982 election, the incumbent Alliance Party retained office with a small margin over the opposition NFP, which had united its two rival factions despite growing conflict within the party.

13 In the April 11 1987 election, the Indian majority won and Timoci Bavadra became premier, ending 16 years of government by Melanesians. In May, a few short weeks after the election, Bavadra's labor government was overthrown by a military coup led by Colonel Sitiveni Rabuka. The Colonel justified himself as 'attempting to solve the ethnic problem', though the real objective seemed to be the removal of the Indian Government, who believed in an independent foreign policy, and planned to join the treaty of Rarotonga. The treaty promoted regional denuclearization; endorsed by Australia and Aotearoa, but criticized by Britain and the US.

14 In 1987 Bavadra, who had been imprisoned by the military during the coup, was freed. He rejected the idea of new elections

WORKERS

1995
UNEMPLOYMENT: 5.4%

% OF LABOUR FORCE **1998**

■ FEMALE: 29%   ■ MALE: 71%
1990

■ SERVICES: 39.5%
■ INDUSTRY: 14.9%
■ AGRICULTURE: 45.6%

LAND USE

DEFORESTATION: 0.4% annual (1990/95)
IRRIGATED: 0.6% of arable (1993)

1993

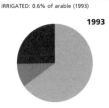

1990

■ FOREST & WOODLAND: 64.9%
■ ARABLE: 9.9%
■ OTHER: 25.2%

PUBLIC EXPENDITURE

DEFENCE EXPENDITURE (% of goverment exp.)	**6.4%**	(1997)
MILITARY EXPENDITURE (% of health & education)	**37%**	(1990/91)

proposed by the military for the end of 1988, ostensibly to draw up a new constitution. The main Indian and Melanesian political parties reached an agreement, with added pressure from the Commonwealth, which appeared to appease the military. However, on October 6 1987, Rabuka retaliated by proclaiming a Republic in a move intended to disavow the authority of the head of state, the British-appointed governor.

[15] In December 1987, Rabuka resigned as Head of State in an attempt to create an image of a joint civilian-military government, aimed at improving its foreign image. Penaia Ganilau was named President and Camisese Mara, Prime Minister, a regime never subjected to the approval of the electorate.

[16] In July 1990 a new constitutional decree based on apartheid went into effect, assuring the indigenous people 37 of the Chamber of Representatives' 70 seats and 24 of the Senate's 34 seats. A constitutional referendum announced for 1992 was finally cancelled. The following year, the apartheid model was denounced by the UN's General Assembly, Mauritius and India. In November, the Association of Fijian Young

People and Students organized a public burning of the new constitution's text. Demonstrators were harshly subdued.

[17] Rabuka founded the Fijian Political Party and in 1992, amid growing political and social strains, a military officer was named Prime Minister.

[18] Fiji was not able to overcome its chronic balance of payments deficit: almost all of its fuel and manufactured products were imported and its main sources of income - sugar exports and tourism - were not enough to balance the budget.

[19] In November 1993 six FPP members voted together with the opposition against the budget, forcing general elections. Rabuka retained power with 31 of the 37 Fijian seats and support from independent and General Vote Party members. Dissidents formed a Fijian Association obtaining only 5 seats.

[20] In November 1994, the Government began a timid revision of the racist constitution. In 1995, Rabuka had to reorganize his Cabinet several times due to internal divisions in the coalition. He took legal steps to challenge the findings of an independent prosecutor that which involved him in unlawful

management linked to the Central Bank's deficit. The Government's plan to allow 28,000 Chinese from Hong Kong to settle in the country also led to criticism. According to the official plan, each one of the future immigrants would have to pay $130,000 to legally reside in the country.

[21] In September 1996, a Commission completed a report on the new constitution, which created a 'multiracial council' and reserved a certain number of seats in Parliament for certain ethnic groups. The document was approved in July 1997, coming into operation a year later.

[22] In September 1997, Fiji was readmitted into the British Commonwealth, 10 years after the coup which took it out.

[23] The Asian crisis forced the Government to devalue the currency 20 per cent against the dollar and to lower customs barriers.

[24] At the end of that year, a study revealed that 40 per cent of women on Suva suffered from sexually transmitted diseases. In early 1998, the Government launched a health plan to combat an outbreak of dengue fever (similar to malaria) which had killed four children.

[25] In February 1998, Prime Minister Rabuka spoke publicly of his fear of being deposed in a new coup, accusing members of the clergy and army of plotting against him.

[26] The elections of May 1999, the first truly democratic since the coup, were won by Mahendra Chaudhry, of the Indian Party. The Fiji Party led by Rabuka won only 71 parliamentary seats, while its ally of the General Vote Party, belonging to the minority, did not win any seats.

[27] Despite the fact that many Fijians continued to consider the Indians a threat, the elections relegated the ethnic question to second place behind economic issues, unemployment, increasing crime and cutbacks in public services.

[28] However, ethnic tension exploded a year later, on May 19, 2000, when an armed group led by Fijian businessman George Speight, burst into parliament and abducted premier Mahendra along with thirty other people (including the daughter of President Kamisese Mara). The aim of this act of violence was that the constitution be reformulated in order to block Indian minority access to government.

[29] President Kamisese sacked the abducted prime minister, stating that this reduced the importance of Mahendra and forced Speight to give in. Nonetheless, the measure was also interpreted as firm backing for the kidnapper and his demands.

[30] Speight's sympathisers held demonstrations in the main towns of the country and there were confrontations in which several people were killed and injured.

Concluding that the conflict could not be resolved and that the President was weak and inoperative, Commodore Frank Bainarama led a fresh coup on May 29. After ousting the President, Bainarama announced martial law would be imposed and a military junta would be created to govern the country. ■

Finland

Süomi

Population: 5,165,000 (1999)
Area: 338,130 SQ KM
Capital: Helsinki
Currency: Markkaa
Language: Finnish

Finland was inhabited from 7500 BC onwards, and the first settlers were the Sami (later also called 'Lapps' by other people). The Sami were hunters, fishers and gatherers. Over the centuries they began domesticating animals and practising subsistence agriculture, remaining isolated from the rest of Europe. Much later - in the 1st century AD - descendants of the Finno-Ugrics entered from the south, and they pushed the Sami to the north, taking control of the major part of the territory. By 1000 years ago, the Finns had established many settlements in the south.

2   The ancestors of the *tavastlanders* came from the southwest across the Gulf of Finland, and the Carelians arrived from the southeast. Scandinavian peoples occupied the west coast, the archipelagos and also the Aland Islands (Ahvenanmaa).

3   From the 12th century onwards, Finland was claimed by both the Russian and Swedish empires. In 1172, the Pope advised the Swedes to control the Finns, to avoid their being proselytized by the Russian Orthodox Church. With the Protestant Reformation, Lutheranism became the official religion.

4   In 1809 Finland became a grand duchy of Imperial Russia, although it was allowed to maintain its own parliament, army and judicial system.

5   In 1889 the Social Democratic Party was founded, a party which was to play a leading role in Finnish political life from that moment onward. The presence of Lenin and other Bolshevik exiles also helped to strengthen the country's socialist leanings. In 1906 a single-chamber parliament was created, and universal suffrage was established.

Finland became the third country in the world to recognize female suffrage.

6   Independence was declared in December 1917. Spurred on by the example of the Russian Revolution, Finnish Socialists tried to seize power by means of a revolution. In January 1918, the Social Democratic Party (SDP) took Helsinki and the major industrial centres. The Government counterattacked, backed by the White Army and German troops under the command of General Mannerheim. In May, the civil war came to an end and the Socialist leaders were tried and given harsh sentences.

7   The country became a monarchy, and German Prince Frederick Charles of Hessen was elected king. After Germany's defeat in World War I, the monarchy collapsed and General Mannerheim was appointed regent, while new republican institutions were established.

8   The 1919 Constitution established a parliamentary system with a strong presidential figure. In addition, it made the Prime Minister the head of the government, and the President head of state. Although the constitution recognized both Finnish and Swedish as official languages, nationalist youth groups later demanded that Finnish be given priority. This led to the creation of the Swedish People's Party. Subsequent constitutional reforms maintained the right of the Swedish minority to its own language.

9   In 1918, 70 per cent of all Finns depended upon agriculture and forestry for a living. The importance of this segment of the population led to the formation of the Rural Party, which became the Center Party.

10   The country was ruled almost uninterruptedly since independence by alliances between the Social Democrats and the Centrists. From 1920 to 1930, these two political forces backed an ambitious program of social and economic reforms. Agricultural production was modernized, and the exploitation of the country's lumber resources was intensified. Likewise, the Government fostered industrialization in the cities, and sponsored progressive legislation, aimed at protecting the emerging working class and agricultural workers.

11   The growth of the Communist Party (FCP) gave rise to the ultra-right-wing Lapua (Lappo) Movement, whose terrorist acts and mass protests were supported by conservative groups and by some Rural Party members. In 1930, the FCP was banned by law, with the support of these parties. In 1931 the Lappo movement began to carry out attacks against the Social Democrats. After an attempted coup the following year, they were finally arrested by the Government.

12   After the German invasion of Poland, the USSR demanded part of the Karelian Islands, a naval base on the Hanko peninsula and other islands of the Gulf of Finland, as a means of defending themselves against imminent German attack. Given the refusal of the Finns to cede the lands, the USSR seized them by force, giving rise to a brief conflict. The 1940 Treaty of Moscow forced Finland to cede these territories.

13   Finland had declared its neutrality at the beginning of World War II, but since it had become involved in a conflict with the USSR, it permitted German troops to use its territory to launch an attack again

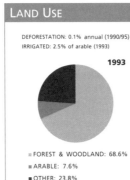

WORKERS

1997
UNEMPLOYMENT: 14.4%

% OF LABOUR FORCE   **1998**

■ FEMALE: 48%   ■ MALE: 52%
                            1990

■ SERVICES: 61.0%
■ INDUSTRY: 30.6%
■ AGRICULTURE: 8.4%

LAND USE

DEFORESTATION: 0.1% annual (1990/95)
IRRIGATED: 2.5% of arable (1993)

1993

■ FOREST & WOODLAND: 68.6%
■ ARABLE: 7.6%
■ OTHER: 23.8%

PUBLIC EXPENDITURE

DEFENCE (1996)	4.3%
SOCIAL (1997)	53.6%

MILITARY EXPENDITURE **15%**
(% of health & education) (1990/91)

their mutual enemy. Thus, Finland was briefly able to recover the territories lost in 1940.

[14] The 1944 Soviet counter-offensive and subsequent German retreat strengthened the Finnish peace movement. The Karelian Islands once again came under the control of the Red Army, causing the resignation of President Retie, the architect of the alliance with Germany. He was succeeded by General Mannerheim, who negotiated an armistice with Moscow, recognized the 1940 Treaty of Moscow and organized the fight to expel German troops from the country. During the war nearly 500,000 Finns had died.

[15] When the War ended, the country's political life was once again controlled by the Social Democratic-Finnish Rural Party alliance and the leader of the Finnish Rural Party, Urho Kekkonen, occupied the presidency from 1956-1982. The office of Prime Minister was also held by SDP figures for most of that same period.

[16] During the post-war period, Finland was faced with a critical social and economic situation. Production had come to a standstill, there were thousands of unemployed and more than 300,000 refugees from the occupied areas.

[17] Neutrality became the cornerstone of Finnish foreign policy. In 1948, Helsinki and Moscow signed the Finno-Soviet Pact of Friendship, Cooperation and Mutual Assistance. Seven years later, the USSR returned the naval base at Porkkala and the treaty was again ratified in 1970 and 1983. In 1955, Finland joined the European Free Trade Association (EFTA), the United Nations and the Nordic Council, but blocked the creation of a customs union within the framework of the Council. Finland was the only member of the OECD which simultaneously maintained relations with the EC and the CMEA (organization established in January 1949 to facilitate and coordinate the economic development of the eastern European countries belonging to the Soviet bloc). This situation helps explain the country's relatively rapid economic recovery.

[18] The Finnish Government offered incentives to develop the lumber industry, axis of the economy. It promoted industrialization and took advantage of the profits generated by its lucrative foreign trade.

[19] However, with the disintegration of the USSR which had provided the market for over 25 per cent of Finland's exports, economic growth came to a standstill.

[20] In 1991, Prime Minister Esko Aho, politically moderate, launched a drastic structural adjustment program which was resisted by workers. Economic stagnation caused a decline in Finnish standards of living, and unemployment went from 3.5 to over 20 per cent.

[21] Finland requested EU membership in 1992. A plebiscite in 1994 supported the initiative, which was confirmed in early 1995. The internal impact of this measure was softened by special subsidies for the farming sector, disadvantaged compared with its community partners, because of the cold climate. Part of the State monopoly on public health and the sale of alcoholic beverages was also maintained.

[22] Once the nation had effectively entered the EU, President Ahtisaari declared Finland would not enter the Western European Union, which could have been a step toward NATO membership. The Finnish Government considered a common defense policy should be based on consensus and that their traditional neutrality was obsolete since the fall of the Iron Curtain. It also warned the West of the risk of isolating Russia and of the environmental danger posed by the nuclear plants and industries in that country.

[23] In the March elections the Social Democratic Party, led by Paavo Lipponen, pushed out the rural-based Centre Party, which had been the ruling force in Parliament up until then. In October, the Government proposed a plan to reduce unemployment, which hovered at around 17 per cent. Lipponen was designated Prime Minister, replacing Esko Aho. The Finnish paper industry reduced its emissions of sulphur dioxide, but more than half the pollution continued to come from the neighboring countries.

[24] In 1996, the Government reiterated its policy of non-alliance on military matters, although it repeated its interest in the EU's economic and monetary union planned for 1999. Inflation stood at just under 1 per cent throughout 1997. The growth in industrial production was amongst the highest in the European Union at 3.2 per cent. In October, unemployment fell to 12.6 per cent.

[25] In early 1998, Lipponen increased contacts with his Western partners in efforts to gain greater economic support for Russian development.

[26] The Global Corruption Perception Index, issued by Transparency International based on the reports of investors, financial risk and public opinion analysts, placed Finland among the five countries with a lower index of perception of corruption in the world for 1998.

[27] Former Foreign Affairs Minister Tarja Halonen became the first Finnish woman to be head of state after she won the February 2000 elections. The social democratic candidate beat Esho Aho of the Center Party in the second round by a slim margin (51.6 against 48.4 per cent).

[28] However since the last constitutional reform introduced a parliamentary system the President now only performs representative functions and does not influence the formation of government or foreign policy. ∎

PROFILE

ENVIRONMENT

Finland is a flat country (the average altitude is 150 meters above sea level) with vast marine clay plains, low plateaus, numerous hills and lakes formed by glaciers. The population is concentrated mainly on the coastal plains, the country's main farming area. Lumbering of coniferous forests is the central economic activity and provides the main export products: lumber, paper pulp and paper. Sulfur dioxide emissions and the dumping of contaminated water into the Baltic Sea pose serious threats to the environment.

SOCIETY

Peoples: 92.1 per cent of the population is Finnish and 7.5 per cent Swedish. There are gypsy and Sami minorities. **Religions:** 86 per cent of the population are Lutherans and 1 per cent Finnish Orthodox Church (official churches). 12 per cent are non-religious.
Languages: Finnish (official and spoken by 93.2 per cent). Swedish, spoken by 6 per cent of the population, is also an official language. Lapp is spoken by a minority of around 1,700 people.
Political Parties: The Social Democratic Party (SDP), center-left; Center Party (KP), formerly the Finnish Rural Party; the People's Democratic League; the National Coalition Party (KOK), moderate conservative; the People's Liberal Party; the People's Swedish Party, liberal, represents interests of the Swedish-speaking minority; the Green Party; the Christian League of Finland; the Rural Party.
Social Organizations: Central Organization of Finnish Unions, with 1,086,000 members and 28 member unions.

THE STATE

Official Name: Suomen Tasavalta. **Administrative divisions:** 12 provinces. **Capital:** Helsinki 546,000 people (1998) metropolitan area 940,000 people (1995). **Other cities:** Espoo 186,500 people, Tampere 179,200; Vantaa 164,400; Turku (Abo) 162,400 (1995). **Government:** Unicameral parliamentary democracy. Tarja Halonen, President since February 2000; Paavo Lipponen, Prime Minister since April 1995. **National holiday:** December 6 (Proclamation of independence). **Armed Forces:** Total: 31,200 (1994). **Other:** Border guards: 4,400.

France

France

Population: 58,886,000 (1999)
Area: 551,500 SQ KM
Capital: Paris
Currency: French franc
Language: French

The two regions occupied by the Celts were known to the Romans as Gaul. The region between the Alps and Rome was Cisalpine Gaul, and beyond the Alps was Transalpine Gaul. With natural borders on all sides; the Alps, the Pyrénées, the Atlantic Ocean and the Rhine, Gaul occupied not only what is now France, but also Belgium, Switzerland and the western banks of the Rhine.

2 Gallic society was essentially agricultural, with almost no urban life. The few cities, were used as fortresses, where the peasants sought refuge when under attack. Society was divided into the nobles (who were also warriors), the people and the Druids, keepers of Celtic wisdom and religious traditions.

3 The Romans came to Gaul in 125 BC. They conquered the area along the Mediterranean, the Rhone valley and Languedoc, calling the combined area 'Provincia'. Caesar divided Gaul into two regions; Provincia and Free Gaul. Free Gaul was subdivided into Belgian Gaul in the north, between the Rhine and the Seine; Celtic Gaul in the center, between the Seine, the Garonne and the lower Rhine; and Aquitaine, in the southwest.

4 In 27 BC, Augustus Caesar set up administrative centres in Gaul, to manage Rome's affairs encouraging urbanization. Bridges and an extensive road network were built throughout the region, facilitating an increase in trade. Wheat production was increased and vineyards were planted, with wine replacing beer as the traditional beverage. After a series of invasions by the Visigoths in the south and the Burgundians along the Saone and the Rhone, the northern Gauls conquered the rest of Gaul under the leadership of Clovis, adopting the name, 'Franks'.

5 Between the 5th and the 9th centuries France emerged as the Merovingian and Carolingian dynasties brought the entire region under the influence of Christianity. With the Islamic expansion and the fall of the Roman Empire, trade ceased, urban civilization was almost completely wiped out, population decreased and the culture fell into decadence.

6 By the 9th century, feudalism had become firmly established. Centralized authority practically disappeared, as local people were unable to repel the Scandinavians, Hungarians, Saracens, and other invaders of this era. By the end of the century, the previously united land was a conglomerate of more than 300 independent counties.

7 From the 10th century onward, the royal dynasties slowly recovered their power. They established hereditary succession to the throne, they shared power with the Church and became the main feudal landowners.

8 In the 13th century, an increase in commercial activity led to a remarkable rebirth of the cities, and agricultural techniques were improved, as the population increased. The Crusades led to a greater circulation of people and goods, and the gradual disappearance of serfdom gave rise to greater social mobility. This was the 'Golden Age' of the French Middle Ages, when France had great power over, and influence upon Western civilization.

9 Paris was one of Europe's most important cities, and the prestige of its University was linked to its cultural pre-eminence. The University trained lawyers in Roman law, and their influence helped form a new concept of the State where the king was no longer a feudal lord, but rather the embodiment of the law. Over a period of time, nationalistic feelings began to develop.

10 Before the 18th century, France suffered from the Hundred Years' War with England, the Thirty Years' War with Spain, several wars with Italy, over a hundred revolts, wars between Catholics and Protestants, and the Black Death which scoured the country in the 14th and 15th centuries. Over the following century, the social and economic structures of the country changed, making conditions ripe for revolution.

11 All forms of servitude disappeared and many feudal lords had to sell their property. The country's mercantile structures stabilized with the rise of manufacturing and trade, triggering population growth and urbanization.

12 Louis XIV, the 'Sun King', personified the concept of absolute monarchy. He came to the throne in 1661, and established the 'Divine Right of Kings'. He consolidated the unity of France, giving rise to the concept of the modern State. During his reign, French cultural influence reached its apogee.

13 The 1789 Revolution opened up a new era in the history of France. The National Assembly, convened in July of that year, replaced the absolute monarch with a constitutional monarchy. The fall of the Bastille on July 14 and the Declaration of the Rights of Man, on August 27, brought the old regime to an end, thus paving the way for the rise of the bourgeoisie - the prevailing class of the towns - whose reforms came into direct conflict with the Church and the King. Finally, the Assembly overthrew the monarchy and proclaimed the First French Republic.

14 The rest of Europe joined forces against revolutionary France. Danton and Robespierre declared the nation 'to be in peril' and formed a citizen army. This Committee of Public Salvation was able to forestall foreign invasion but internal confrontations resulted in the 'Reign of Terror'. Robespierre and his companions were

---

WORKERS

1997
UNEMPLOYMENT: 12.3%

% OF LABOUR FORCE **1998**

■ FEMALE: 45%   ■ MALE: 55%

1990

■ SERVICES: 65.7%
■ INDUSTRY: 28.8%
■ AGRICULTURE: 5.5%

LAND USE

DEFORESTATION: -1.1% annual (1990/95)
IRRIGATED: 8.1% of arable (1993)

1993

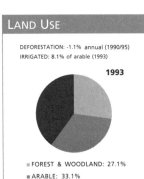

■ FOREST & WOODLAND: 27.1%
■ ARABLE: 33.1%
■ OTHER: 39.8%

PUBLIC EXPENDITURE

DEFENCE EXPENDITURE (% of goverment exp.)	**6.4%**	(1997)
MILITARY EXPENDITURE (% of health & education)	**29%**	(1990/91)

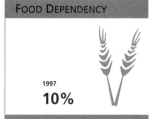
overthrown and executed by the liberal, more moderate bourgeoisie in July 1794.

[15] For the next five years, the revolutionaries tried to regain control of the country, which had fallen victim to corruption, internal strife and instability. Napoleon Bonaparte's coup (1799) brought an end to the dying regime. Seizing power, he had himself named Consul for Life in 1802 and then Emperor in 1804.

[16] Although Napoleon's reign represented a return to absolutism, it preserved the main achievements of the Revolution. Legal, administrative, religious, financial and educational reorganization changed the country irrevocably. Napoleon strove hard to bring the rest of Europe under his control and his armies occupied the whole of the continent from Madrid to the outskirts of Moscow. Finally, exhausted by war, France was defeated at Waterloo, in 1815.

[17] France was rocked by rebellions in 1830, 1848 and 1871, and constant disturbance. In spite of this, the Industrial Revolution brought factories, railroads, large companies and credit institutions to France. The Third Republic, beginning in 1870, was to be France's longest-lasting regime in almost a century and a half.

[18] With the establishment of universal male suffrage in 1848, the peasants and the urban middle class had the greatest electoral power. The Government managed to win their support by protectionism and the establishment of free, secular and mandatory primary education, which raised aspirations of greater social mobility.

[19] Under the Republic, France had a period of colonial expansion, beginning with the conquest of Algeria in 1830, and continuing with other territories in Africa and the Far East. A large empire was built, with colonies in the Caribbean, Africa, the Middle East, the Indochinese peninsula and the Pacific.

[20] World War I enabled France to recover Alsace and Lorraine, which had been annexed by Germany in 1870. The War left France devastated. More than 1.5 million people had been killed. Property damage coupled with the internal and foreign debt added up to more than 150 billion gold francs, and the nation's currency lost its traditional stability. Neither the right-wing bloc nor the radical party was able to bring the economic and political situation under control.

[21] The world-wide recession reached France in 1931. In 1936, the parties of the left, who had joined together to form the Popular Front, had won the legislative elections. They had carried out important social reforms, such as paid vacations and the 40-hour working week, but they were unable to hold back unemployment or the looming economic crisis. Government became polarized between supporters of Italian Fascism and those of Communism. This split led to an impasse until 1939, when Germany invaded Poland.

[22] Germany went on to occupy almost one-third of France. In 1940, Marshall Pétain signed an armistice proclaiming the 'national revolution' transforming non-occupied France into a satellite of Berlin. From London, General de Gaulle urged the French people to continue the fight.

[23] France was liberated in 1944. The French participated in the liberation and the invasion of Germany, with the resistance movement (especially the communists and socialists), the Free French Forces (liberal nationalists) and French troops fighting alongside the Allies. In October 1946, the Fourth Republic was proclaimed. This period was characterized by political instability and bitter opposition between the French Communist Party (PCF) and General de Gaulle's party.

[24] Funds from the US Marshall Plan, led to the economic and social reconstruction of the country. Production reached a six per cent annual growth rate. Per capita income increased 47 per cent between 1949 and 1959; women were granted the right to vote; the banks were nationalized and a social security program went into effect. In 1957 France was one of the six signatories of the Treaty of Rome, which created the European Economic Community (EEC).

[25] After 1945, France was unable to re-establish its pre-war control over its colonies. The spirit of democracy and increasing awareness of universal human rights, was consolidated by the anti-Fascist alliance and the creation of the United Nations. Colonization had not allowed local identity to influence policy, so decolonization took place through fierce pro-independence movements, with little room for negotiation.

[26] In 1945, Syria and Libya were the first countries to become independent, followed by Morocco, Tunisia and Madagascar. Vietnam, Laos and Cambodia became independent only in 1954, after a long and bloody war. In May 1958, four years after the Algerian revolution began, the pieds-noirs - French people residing in the colony - revolted. They made the army promise not to leave the country. This dealt a mortal blow to the Fourth Republic, and the Government called in General de Gaulle to deal with the crisis.

[27] The establishment of the Fifth Republic in 1958 and the 1962 decision to elect the President by direct universal suffrage laid the foundation for a regime with

PROFILE

ENVIRONMENT

In the north is the Paris Basin, which spreads out into fields and plains. The Massif Central, in the center of France, is made up of vast plateaus. In the southeast, the Alps rise up. The southern region includes the Mediterranean coast, with mountain ranges, like the Pyrénées, and plains. Grain farming is the main agricultural activity; wheat is grown all over the country, especially in the north. Grapes are grown in various regions for wine exports. The main mineral resources are coal, iron ore and bauxite. Dependence on nuclear energy poses a serious problem. Nuclear reactors operating in the country generate three quarters of the national consumption of electricity, making France the second largest producer of nuclear energy, after the United States. There is also a nuclear reprocessing plant, as well as one which generates plutonium.

SOCIETY

Peoples: Most of the population stem from the integration of three basic European groups: Nordic, Alpine and Mediterranean. Approximately 7 per cent of the population has a foreign descent. Portuguese 1.1 per cent; Algerian 1.1 per cent; Moroccan 1.0 per cent; Italian 0.4 per cent; Spanish 0.4 per cent; Turkish 0.3 per cent; other 2.1 per cent.
Religions: Mainly Catholic (76 per cent); Calvinism 2 per cent; Muslim 2 per cent, Judaism 1 per cent.
Languages: French is the official and predominant language. There are also regional languages: Breton in Brittany, a German dialect in Alsace and Lorraine, Flemish in the northeast, Catalan and Basque in the Southwest, Provençal in the South-East, Corsican on the island of Corsica. Immigrants speak their own languages, particularly Portuguese, Arab, Berber, Spanish, Italian and diverse African languages.
Political Parties: Socialist Party; Rally for the Republic (RPR); Union for French Democracy (UDF); National Front; Communist Party; the Greens.
Social Organizations: General Labor Confederation (CGT); French Democratic Labor Confederation (CFDT); Workers' Force (FO); French Confederation of Christian Workers (CFTC). France has the lowest level of unionization in the European Community (8 per cent in 1990).

THE STATE

Official Name: République Française.
Administrative divisions: 22 Regions with 96 Departments in France and 5 possessions, called 'Overseas Departments'.
Capital: Paris 9,800,000 people (est 1996).
Other cities: Marseille 1,230,000 people; Lyon,1,260,000; Toulouse 608,000; Nice 1,300,000.
Government: President: Jacques Chirac, since May 1995. Lionel Jospin, Prime Minister since June 1997. Bicameral legislature: Chamber of Deputies, 577 members; Senate, 317 members.
Armed Forces: 409,000 (1995) **Other:** 96,300 Gendarmes.

strong presidential powers. After the independence of Algeria and the last remaining African colonies, the country sought to achieve greater stability. With national independence as the primary aim of their foreign policy, France made use of 'deterrent' atomic power and withdrew from the military structure of the North Atlantic Treaty Organization (NATO), in 1966.

[28] France continued to be a member of the Atlantic alliance, and maintained enormous economic, cultural and political influence over its former African colonies, south of the Sahara. Diplomatic relations with Algeria, Vietnam, and other countries that had fought bloody wars for independence were not restored until 1982.

[29] In May 1968, the greatest social and political crisis of the Fifth Republic took place. Huge student protests and labor strikes throughout the country were brought on by the regime's growing authoritarianism in the educational and social sectors. For a whole month, the Government seemed to be seriously threatened. Apart from the student leaders, however, there were no other political forces capable of toppling the government, and the general strike was called off when a salary increase was promised.

[30] The years which followed saw the birth of other groups based around social issues, such as the feminist, ecological and antinuclear movements. In 1972 the Socialist Party and the Communist Party created the Union of the Left, and François Mitterand, the Socialist candidate, was elected President in 1981 because of the Communist votes; his was the first left-wing cabinet since 1958.

[31] The new government carried out reforms: the nationalization of important industrial and banking groups, new labor rights for workers, the 39-hour working week, an increase in social benefits, retirement at the age of 60 and a decentralization of power. However, unemployment, the economic crisis and an increase in imports led the Government to enforce a harsh economic policy and to carry out restructuring of the industrial sector. This led communist ministers to resign from the Government, in 1984. In 1981, a Ministry of Women's Rights had been created, charged to enforce existing legislation.

[32] In mid-1994, Prime Minister Pierre Maurois, a symbol of the Left's union, was replaced by Laurent Fabius, a young technocrat, considered a loyal friend of Mitterrand's. Fabius formed a more centrist government than Mauroy's, in which the communists refused to take part.

[33] In 1985, relations between France and several South Pacific countries like Australia and New Zealand were deteriorated when it was discovered the French were responsible for sinking a Greenpeace ship which caused the death of a militant ecologist when it was headed for the Mururoa atoll to demonstrate against French nuclear tests.

[34] In 1986, expecting a defeat of the Left, Mitterrand substituted the majority electoral system by a proportional system which gave more seats to the losers than the previous one. In March, a right-wing coalition made up mainly of the Group for the Republic (RPR), a party led by neo-Gaullist Jacques Chirac and by former president (1974-1981) Valery Giscard D'Estaing's Union for the French Democracy (UDF), defeated the Left in the legislative elections. The elections confirmed a clear progress of Jean Marie Le Pen's ultra-right National Front. Chirac had to form a new government and for two years the country experienced its first 'cohabitation' between a left-wing president and a conservative council of ministers.

[35] Chirac's government wiped out some of the 1981 and 1982 reforms with the privatization of several companies nationalized by the left but kept most of the social gains. In the meantime, it continued a liberalization policy of the economy and finances begun in the socialist government's last years. In the field of individual liberties, the strong hand of Interior minister Charles Pasqua, especially regarding legislation concerning foreigners living in France, was criticized by several humanitarian organizations.

[36] In 1988, Mitterrand defeated Chirac in presidential elections. The elected President called for new legislative elections. After a new victory of the Socialist Party, socialist Michel Rocard was appointed Prime Minister.

[37] The Socialist economic policy did not differ substantially from that of the right. Unemployment kept on the rise, with a 9.5 per cent rate of the economically active population in 1991. That year, Rocard was replaced by Edith Cresson, who was the first woman to become head of government in modern France. Nine months later, Mitterrand replaced Cresson with former Economy minister Pierre Bérégovoy, with the backing of industrial and financial circles.

[38] In 1993, the Left was defeated in legislative elections once again and Mitterrand named conservative Edouard Balladur as Prime Minister. The corruption scandals, whose main targets had been socialist leaders, affected this time renowned right-wing politicians and caused three of Balladur's ministers to resign in 1994.

[39] In the April 1995 presidential elections Chirac defeated socialist Lionel Jospin and appointed conservative Alain Juppé as Prime Minister.

[40] In December, the largest civil servants' strike since 1968 paralyzed the country for over three weeks. The social situation remained tense in 1996, which some observers linked with unfair income distribution - 20 per cent of the population received 44 per cent of total personal income - and property distribution, since 20 per cent of the French owned 69 per cent of national wealth.

[41] The Juppé administration continued its austerity policy which caused confrontation with labor unions in 1996. A new law was passed in 1997 to restrict the entrance and residence of immigrants in the country. In February there were demonstrations against the measure which mobilized over 150,000 people in one day.

[42] Unexpectedly, Chirac called for early legislative elections. In the second round, on May 25, the leftist opposition obtained an important victory after running united in the elections. The Socialist Party obtained 241 deputies and became the country's largest party once more. Together with the Communists, with 38 seats, the Greens, with seven, and other 33 deputies from the left, the Socialist

---

OVERSEAS DEPARTMENTS:

Mayotte (see Comoros), St Pierre and Miquelon (see box);

New Caledonia (see Kanaky); Wallis and Futuna (text follows); French Polynesia (see corresponding section).

Southern and Antarctic Territories:
Comprising two archipelagos: Kerguelen (7,000 sq.km, with 80 people in Port-Aux-Français) and Crozet (500 sq km, with 20 people); two islands: New Amsterdam (60 sq km, with 35 inhabitants.) and St Paul (7 sq km, uninhabited), located in the southern Indian Ocean; the Land of Adélie (500,000 sq km with 27 people at the Dumont Durville Base), in Antarctica. The Territories are governed by an Administrator-General advised by a seven-member Consultative Council appointed by the French government. Technical personnel at weather stations are the only inhabitants. ■

St Pierre and Miquelon

Population: 7,000 (1998)
Area: 242 SQ KM
Capital: St Pierre
Currency: French franc
Language: French

An archipelago of 8 small islands, near the Canadian coast, in the north Atlantic, economically dependent on fishing.

SOCIETY

The People: The majority are descendants of French settlers.
Religion: Catholic.
Language: French.

THE STATE

Capital: St Pierre 5,900 people (1996).
Other towns: Miquelon 750 people (1996).

Government: A French overseas department administered by a 19-member Conseil Général elected a 6-year term, and a Commissioner appointed by the French Government. In the French National Assembly, the area is represented by one deputy and has one senator and one representative in the European Parliament.

DEMOGRAPHY

Population: 7,000 (1998)

ECONOMY

Cereal imports: 1,038 metric tons (1998)

Party achieved a comfortable majority in parliament. The right wing coalition obtained 256 deputies, while the National Front only got only one seat.

[43] Lionel Jospin became the new Prime Minister and the Communists had two ministries while former presidential candidate Dominique Voynet held one for the Greens.

[44] In 1997, in order to address unemployment, Jospin proposed the reduction of the working week to 35 hours. Many demonstrations, both by workers and unemployed, which continued through to 1998, demanded the immediate adoption of this measure.

[45] The announcement that year of a law that would limit the entrance and permanence of immigrants in the country caused protests which mobilized more than 150,000 peolple in just one day. Jospin proposed to shorten the working week to 35 hours in order to alleviate unemployment. Workers and unemployed activists demonstrated asking for, among other things, the immediate application of this measure.

[46] Several studies and surveys done in 1998 and published by *Le Monde*, showed that two out of every five French citizens openly admitted having racist sentiments. The country was at the top of racism in the European Union, closely followed by Belgium. These figures were surprising to the researchers due to the fact that, second to Luxembourg, France is the most ethnically mixed country in the EU.

[47] In March 1999 the National Assembly approved a law giving legal status to unmarried couples, by 300 to 253 votes. Tens of thousands of citizens opposing the legislation demonstrated in the streets, fearing the law would allow gay couples to adopt children.

[48] The white-collar unions unleashed an offensive against the government in January 2000. In particular they were protesting about the 35-hour maximum work week initiative. They organized demonstrations, road blocks and in December announced they were pulling out of the joint committees, breaking with a tradition dating back to the first years after the War.

[49] The 35-hour week law came into effect on 1 February. The truckers began a strike along the French highways that same day. Unlike the previous month, the measures were taken by the workers - and not their employers. While employers opposed the reduction in hours, most workers supported it, but without pay cuts. ∎

Wallis and Futuna

Population: 15,000 (1998)
Area: 200 SQ KM
Capital: Mata-Utu
Currency: CFP franc
Language: French

Wallis was named after Samuel Wallis, a navigator who 'discovered' it in 1767. Marist missionaries arrived in the archipelago in 1837 and converted the inhabitants to Catholicism. It became a French protectorate in 1888, and in December 1959, after a referendum, the country adopted the status of French Overseas Territory.

[2] Unlike other French dependencies in the Pacific, there are no pro-independence movements on the islands. In 1983, the two kingdoms of Futuna achieved separation from Wallis, but maintained their relationship with France. The islands' economic prospects are poor: in addition to the devastating effect of cyclones which periodically hit the islands, the only bank on the islands was closed. Wallis and Futuna received FF55 million in aid from France in 1987. Approximately 50 per cent of the economically active population has had to emigrate to other parts of Polynesia in search of work. Their remittances, together with public works projects, constitute the main source of income for the islands.

[3] In the 1992 elections for the Territorial Assembly, the left managed to defeat the neo-Gaullist RPR, a party of the right, for the first time in twenty years. In 1997, the neo-Gaullist candidate Victor Brial gained the bench of deputy for Wallis in the French National Assembly.

ENVIRONMENT

The territory consists of the Wallis archipelago (159 sq km), formed by Uvea Island - where the capital is located - and 22 islets, plus the Futuna (64 sq km) and Alofi Islands (51 sq km). This group is located in western Polynesia, surrounded by Tuvalu to the north, Fiji to the south and the Samoa archipelago to the east. With a rainy and tropical climate, the major commercial activities are copra and fishing.

SOCIETY

Peoples: Of Polynesian origin. Approximately two thirds of the population live on Wallis and the rest on Futuna. Nearly 12,000 inhabitants live in Kanaky and Vanuatu.
Religions: Catholic.
Languages: French (official) and Polynesian languages.

THE STATE

Capital: Mata-Utu (located on Uvea) 1,137 people (1996).
Government: Overseas territory administered by a French-appointed Chief Administrator, Robert Pommies since 1990, assisted by a 20-member Assembly elected for a 5-year term. The kingdoms of Wallis and Futuna (in Sigave and Alo) from which the country was formed, have very limited powers. They send one deputy to the French National Assembly, and another to the Senate.
Currency: CFP francs.

DEMOGRAPHY

Population: 15,000 (1998)

ECONOMY

Cereal imports: 1,292 metric tons (1998)

DEMOGRAPHY

Population: 58,886,000 (1999)
Annual growth: 0.5 % (1975/97)
Estimates for year 2015 (million): 61.1 (1999)
Annual growth to year 2015: 0.2 % (1997/2015)
Urban population: 75.0 % (1997)
Urban Growth: 0.5 % (1980/95)
Children per woman: 1.7 (1998)

HEALTH

Life expectancy at birth: 78 years (1998)
male: 74 years (1998)
female: 82 years (1998)
Maternal mortality: 10 per 100,000 live births (1990-98)
Infant mortality: 5 per 1,000 (1998)
Under-5 child mortality: 5 per 1,000 (1998)
Daily calorie supply: 3,551 per capita (1996)
280 doctors per 100,000 people (1993)

EDUCATION

School enrolment:
Primary total: 106 % (1990/96)
male: 107 % (1990/97)
female: 105 % (1990/97)
Secondary:
male: 112 % (1990/96)
female: 111 % (1990/96)
Tertiary: 51 % (1996)

COMMUNICATIONS

218 newspapers (1996), 937 radios (1997), 598 TV sets (1996) and 564 main telephone lines (1996) per 1,000 people
Books: 78 new titles per 100,000 people (1992/94)

ECONOMY

Per capita, GNP: $ 24,210 (1998)
Annual growth, GNP: 3.2 % (1998)
Annual inflation: 1.7 % (1990/98)
Consumer price index: 103.9 (1998)
Currency: 5.9 French francs = $ 1 (1998)
Cereal imports: 1,444,828 metric tons (1998)
Food import dependency: 10 % (1997)
Fertilizer use: 2,771 kg per ha (1997)
Exports: $ 371,529 million (1997)
Imports: $ 316,618 million (1997)

ENERGY

Consumption: 4,224.0 Kgs of Oil equivalent per capita yearly (1997); 48.0 % imported (1997)

HDI (rank/value): 11/0.918 (1997)

French Guiana

Guyane Française

Population: 115,000 (1999)
Area: 90,000 SQ KM
Capital: Cayenne
Currency: French franc
Language: French

The Arawaks were short, copper-skinned people with straight, black hair. They grew corn, cotton, yams and sweet potatoes. They built round huts with thatched, cone-shaped roofs, and slept in hammocks - an Arawak word which survived the culture which gave rise to it. The Caribs displaced them from the area and later resisted the Spaniards who began to arrive toward the beginning of the 16th century.

2 In 1604 the French occupied Guiana, despite Carib resistance. The colony passed successively into Dutch, English and Portuguese hands, until the beginning of French domination in 1676. Towards the end of the 18th century, France sent more than 3,000 colonists to settle the interior. Few survived the tropical diseases, but those who did sought refuge in a group of islands off the coast which they named Health Islands. After a brief period of prosperity brought about by the discovery of gold in the Appranage River basin, the colony gradually fell into decline.

3 In 1946, Guiana became a French 'Overseas Department'. Nine-tenths of the country is covered by forests, and although the country is fertile, most of the food is imported. The creole (African and mestizo) 80 per cent of the population are limited to minor positions in the local bureaucracy or police. The country is heavily reliant on French funding which provided 70 per cent of the GNP in 1989. Imports are worth ten times the exports of wood, rum, coffee and gold.

4 In 1967, the National Center for Space Studies was established. Over 1,300 foreign technicians work there, earning First World salaries, as well as 1,500 French Guyanan nationals. Thirty Ariane voyages have been launched from the base at Kourou, with all the satellites sent into space financed by European consortia.

5 During the 1970s, the autonomist Socialist Party of Guiana (PSG) became the majority party at the local level. Early in the 1980s, armed groups attacked 'colonialist' targets, but tensions were defused with the victory in France of the French Socialist Party in 1981.

6 At the 'First Conference of the Last French Colonies' held in Guadeloupe in 1985, there was severe criticism of the availability of French visas and citizenship for east

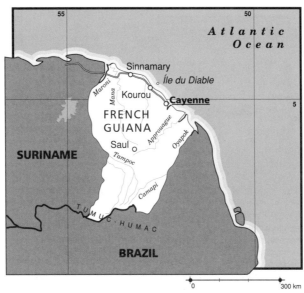

Asians, while Haitians, Brazilians and Guyanans, with closer cultural ties, underwent persecution and discrimination.

7 In 1986, Guyana's representation in the French National Assembly increased to two members. In the 1989 municipal elections, Cayenne and 12 other districts, out of the 19 at stake, were won by the Left. Georges Othily, a PSG dissident was elected for the French Senate.

8 In 1990, France announced a regional co-operation plan with the Caribbean, including aid of only $2.8 million.

9 In 1992, the persistent economic crisis caused a week-long general strike, called by unions and the business sector. As a result, Paris agreed to fund a plan to improve infrastructure and education. In 1994, French Guiana entered the Association of Caribbean States as an associate member.

10 The true situation of the people of French Guiana was far worse than the figures showed. Per capita income remains the highest in South America, but the economy is dependent on income generated by the space studies center in Kourou, French subsidies and imports of food from France.

11 In November 1997, French President Jacques Chirac announced a development plan for French Guiana, after recognizing critical economic situation. The announcement did not raise many expectations, with the local authorities let down by previous promises. Guiana, like Martinique, Guadeloupe and Réunion, was still considered a French Overseas Department. However, this status was resisted by broad sections of the population and, particularly, by

increasingly influential pro-independence groups.

12 On April 1 1998 André Lecante was designated president of the Guiana General Council, one of the two main legislative bodies in French Guiana. The growth of the independence movements was reflected in March in the elections for the Regional Council, the other legislative body. The governing Socialist party suffered a serious setback, losing its absolute majority when its representation shrank from 16 to 11 members, while the De-Colonization Movement of Guiana took three seats.

13 During an official visit to the department, Overseas Territories under-secretary Jean-Jacques Queyranne refused to meet with a delegation of separatists. This caused a wave of street demonstrations in which several policemen and demonstrators were wounded. The independent Workers of Guiana union called for a strike in order to protest against the behavior of Queyranne and police repression. ■

PROFILE

ENVIRONMENT

Guyana is located slightly north of the Equator. Due to its hot and rainy climate, only the coastal alluvial lowlands are suitable for agriculture (cocoa, bananas, sugar cane, rice and corn). The hinterland mountains are covered with rainforests. The country has large reserves of bauxite and gold.

SOCIETY

Peoples: Mostly from indian and European roots. There are Carib and Tupi Guarani ethnic groups, and Cimarrones, descendants of African slaves. In the cities there are Chinese, Indian and French minorities.
Religions: Mainly Catholic, also Hindu.
Languages: French (official), Creole.
Political Parties: The Union for the Republic (RPR); the Socialist Party of Guyana (PSG); the De-Colonization Movement of Guyana; the Union for French Democracy (UDF).

THE STATE

Official Name: Département d'Outre-Mer de la Guyane française.
Administrative Divisions: 2 Districts. **Capital:** Cayenne 55,000 people (est 1995). **Other Cities:** Kourou 135,000 people; St Laurent-du-Maroni 14,000 people.
Government: Jacques Chirac, Chief of State since May, 1995. Pierre Dartout, Prefect appointed by France. Regional parliament (consultative body): General Council, made up of 19 members, and Regional Council, with 31 members. The department has 2 representatives in the National Assembly and 2 in the French Senate. **National Holiday:** All French holidays. **Armed Forces:** 8,400 French troops.

DEMOGRAPHY

Population: 115,000 (1999)

French Polynesia

Polynésie Française

Population: 231,000 (1999)
Area: 4,000 SQ KM
Capital: Papeete
Currency: CFP franc
Language: French

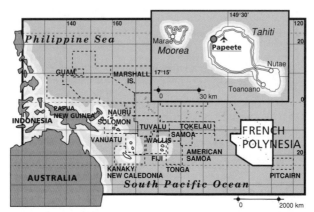

Polynesia's first inhabitants either came from America or Indonesia, but the evidence is inconclusive.

2   In 1840 the islands were occupied by France and in 1880, despite native resistance, the archipelago was officially made a colony under the name of 'the French Establishments of Oceania'. In 1958, they became an Overseas Territory.

3   Except for some concessions on the domestic front, France continued to maintain its control over the islands, with a hard-line policy because of the strategic location of the islands and the atomic tests which have taken place on the Mururoa atoll since 1966. In 1975 France also carried out tests on the Fangataufa atoll, despite strong opposition to the growing militarization of the islands from the population of the territory and other countries in the area, especially New Zealand,.

4   In the face of French intransigence, there was increasing resistance from separatist groups,

who took their case to the UN Decolonization Committee, though few concrete resolutions were made.

5   The 'nuclearization' of the area rapidly resulted in the destruction of French Polynesia's traditional economic base, as the island was currently dependent upon the French military budget. In less than one generation, the economy went from self-sufficiency to dependence

upon imported goods. By the end of 1980, 80 per cent of basic foodstuffs were imported.

6   Both the environment and the health of the islands' inhabitants has deteriorated over the last decades, and there were dramatic increases in the incidence of brain tumors, leukemia and thyroid cancer. The scale of these illnesses is hard to evaluate, as the French Government refused to divulge

medical statistics in recent years.

7   In 1985, the explosion of a bomb planted by two French secret agents killed an ecology activist and destroyed a Greenpeace ship that was heading for Mururoa in order to protest against nuclear testing. In 1992, French President François Mitterrand decided on a temporary suspension of nuclear tests and Paris began negotiations with Papeete for an economic plan to be carried out after the permanent closure of the experiment centers in Mururoa and Fangataufa.

8   The 'Progress Pact' between Paris and 'French' Polynesia was based on assumptions similar to those in structural adjustment programs advocated by the IMF, i.e. economic liberalization, privatization and 'major balancing' in public finance. For the 1994-1998 period, Paris planned a slight increase in financial contributions for the pact to attain its goals. However, the main pro-autonomy political party, Tavini Uiraatira (that means 'serving the people' in the Polynesian language) led by Oscar Temaru and representing 15 per cent of the voters, proposed nationalization and the extension of free services.

9   French President Chirac carried out further nuclear tests in 1995. After the first one of these explosions, there were disturbances and fighting in French Polynesia. In January 1996, he announced the permanent suspension of nuclear tests.

10   In May 1997, the legislative elections were won by the conservative candidates of the Tahoeraa Huiraatira-RPR, followed by the pro-independence tendencies.

11   In February 1998, it was revealed that tourism, above all from Japan and Italy, had increased 35 per cent during 1997. This was partly due to the suspension of nuclear tests.

12   Gaston Flosse, the President of Polynesia and a member of the French Senate, was prosecuted and found guilty of corruption by a French court of law. He received a two-year suspended prison sentence in November 1999 for having accepted tens of thousands of dollars in exchange for illegal gambling permits in Tahiti. Flosse refused to resign and stated he intended to appeal. ■

PROFILE

ENVIRONMENT

The territory is located in the southeast portion of Polynesia. Most of the French Polynesian islands are of volcanic origin but they also have major coral formations. The islands are largely mountainous, with tropical climate and heavy rainfall. Relatively fertile soils favor agricultural development. The Windward and Leeward Islands form the Society Archipelago. Nuclear tests carried out by France over a 26-year period have caused damage to the environment and people that is difficult to evaluate.

SOCIETY

Peoples: Polynesian 78 per cent, Chinese 12 per cent, French descendants 6 per cent. **Religions:** Mostly Christian, 54 per cent Protestant, 30 per cent Catholic. **Languages:** French (official), Tahitian (national). **Political Parties:** Tahoeraa Huiraatira (RPR), conservative; Pupu Here Ai'a, pro autonomy; Ai'a Api, a coalition of parties; Tavini Huiraatira, an anti-nuclear and independence movement. **Social Organizations:** The Pacific Christian Workers Central (CTCP), the Federation of French Polynesian Unions (FSPF) and the Territorial Union of the General Labor Confederation 'Workers' Force' (UTSCGT).

THE STATE

Official Name: Territoire d'Outre-Mer de la Polynésie française.
Administrative Divisions: Windward Islands, which include Tahiti, Murea, Maio; Papeete

constitutes the center of the district. Leeward Islands, with the capital in Utoroa on Ralatea island. It also includes the islands of Huahine, Tahaa, Bora-Bora and Maupiti. Tuamotu and Gambier Archipelagos, the Austral Islands and the Marquesas Islands.
Capital: Papeete 115,000 people (1994).
Government: The French Government is represented by a High Commissioner, who controls defense, foreign relations and justice. President of the Council of Ministers: Gaston Flosse. A local 41-member Territorial Assembly is elected by universal suffrage for a 5-year term. This assembly elects the President of the Council of Ministers, an executive body which is made up of 5 to 10 members of the Territorial Assembly, selected by the President.

DEMOGRAPHY

Population: 231,000 (1999)

EDUCATION

Tertiary: 3 % (1996). **Primary school teachers:** one for every 14 (1995)

COMMUNICATIONS

109 newspapers (1996) and 564 radios (1997) per 1,000 people

ECONOMY

Per capita, GNP: $ 18,050 (1997).**Annual growth, GNP:** 2.5 % (1997)
Cereal imports: 36,024 metric tons (1998). **Fertilizer use:** 1,667 kg per ha (1997)

Gabon

Gabon

Population: 1,197,000 (1999)
Area: 267,670 SQ KM
Capital: Libreville
Currency: CFA franc
Language: French

Tools found in the Gabon forests indicate that this region has been inhabited since the Palaeolithic age. Little else is known about life in the area until the 16th century, when the migrations that triggered the crisis in the ancient state of Congo brought the Myene and, in the 17th century, the Fang to Gabon. Thereafter, they monopolized the slave and ivory trade together with the Europeans.

2   The Portuguese arrived in 1472. Around the middle of the 19th century, the French, Dutch and British established a permanent trade of ivory, precious woods and slaves. In 1849, Libreville was founded and established as a settlement for freed slaves from other French colonies. The territory was of little economic interest to the French, who used it as a base for expeditions into the heart of the continent.

3   The quest for independence was relatively uneventful because the two local parties (the Joint Mixed Gabonese Movement of Leon M'Ba and the Democratic and Social Union of Jean-Hillaire Aubame) were willing to accept neo-colonialism.

4   Gabon has abundant resources: iron ore, uranium, manganese, timber and oil. The transnational oil company Shell discovered oil in Rabikuna, near Port Gentil. These oil reserves contain enough crude to last for 50 years and the oil wells are already in operation. Shell holds an 80 per cent interest in the wells already in operation and French company ELF the remaining 20 per cent; Amoco (an American company) and Braspetro (Brazilian) have been authorized to continue oil exploration in the Port Gentil area.

5   Until recently, timber mills were the only local industry of any size, but a few years ago, French and US transnationals discovered that Gabon could serve as a spearhead to penetrate the markets of central Africa, and they initiated its industrialization. This 'development', relying on foreign capital has only exacerbated social conflicts and the promise of jobs in the cities has encouraged urban migration. Gabon's social structure is changing as independent producers become suppliers of cheap labor for transnational industries. Economically, the breakdown of the rural economy has completely blocked the way to food self-sufficiency, destroying the only social sector which remained independent of foreign capital.

6   The neo-colonial system has been guaranteed by a military treaty signed between Libreville and Paris in 1960. Its effectiveness was proved in 1964 when M'Ba was deposed by a group of progressive officers.

7   When M'Ba died in 1967, he was succeeded by Omar Bongo, head of cabinet, who faithfully followed and even refined his predecessor's style, becoming French President Giscard D'Estaing's 'privileged spokesman' in Africa. Applying the US thesis of 'sub-imperialisms' to French interests, Bongo became its watchdog in central Africa, with Gabon a base for aggression against neighboring progressive regimes. In January 1977, Gabon provided the planes and arms used by a mercenary group in an unsuccessful attack on Benin.

8   Bongo's foreign policy maintained good relations with several states in the region, without altering the country's privileged relationship with France. Like Senegal, Ivory Coast, Chad, and the

Central African Republic, Gabon also had French troops on its soil.

9   In 1979 and again in 1986, Bongo was re-elected with 99 per cent of the vote, in presidential elections in which he was the only candidate.

10   His squandering of the country's income led to violent protests in the early 1980s. The revolt spread to the police who in 1982 organized an unprecedented demonstration, demanding an increase in wages and the withdrawal of French advisors. The protests were brutally repressed by Gabon's secret police, officially known as the 'Documentation Center'.

11   The Government repressed the National Reorientation Movement (MORENA), formed by intellectuals, workers, students and nationalist politicians. The movement was accused of having expropriated 30 tons of weapons in October 1982. At that time, the Bongo family and French military installations were the target of armed attacks. At least 28 top MORENA leaders were sentenced to 15 years' imprisonment. The French Socialist Party criticized the rulings, thus seriously upsetting Bongo's relations with French President Mitterrand.

12   This episode did not stop Bongo from visiting France in March 1984. The friendly greeting at the presidential palace received as much criticism as the decision to allow the French government to build a nuclear plant in Gabon.

13   In late 1989 there were signs of democratic participation for Gabon's opposition forces. After violent confrontations in the streets the President had the constitution amended, introducing a multiparty system and lifting censorship of the press. In the meantime, he invited six opposition leaders to join the cabinet.

14   There was a period of calm after all this social upheaval. However in May, Joseph Redjambe, president of the Gabonese Progressive Party was murdered in a Libreville hotel. His death provoked strong reactions against the Government, thought to be associated with the murder. A state of rebellion through the entire Port Gentil region lasted ten days and the French Government evacuated 5,000 French residents, charging the presidential guard

WORKERS

1997
UNEMPLOYMENT: 12.3%

% OF LABOUR FORCE   **1998**

■ FEMALE: 45%   ■ MALE: 55%

1990

■ SERVICES: 65.7%
■ INDUSTRY: 28.8%
■ AGRICULTURE: 5.5%

LAND USE

DEFORESTATION: -1.1% annual (1990/95)
IRRIGATED: 8.1% of arable (1993)

1993

■ FOREST & WOODLAND: 27.1%
■ ARABLE: 33.1%
■ OTHER: 39.8%

PUBLIC EXPENDITURE

DEFENCE EXPENDITURE (% of goverment exp.)	**6.4%**	(1997)
MILITARY EXPENDITURE (% of health & education)	**29%**	(1990/91)

MATERNAL MORTALITY

1990-98

Per 100.000 live births

600

LITERACY

1995

63%

EXTERNAL DEBT

1998

Per capita

US$ 3,791

STATISTICS

DEMOGRAPHY

Population: 1,197,000 (1999)
Annual growth: 3.0 % (1975/97)
Estimates for year 2015 (million): 1.7 (1999)
Annual growth to year 2015: 2.1 % (1997/2015)
Urban population: 52.2 % (1997)
Urban Growth: 5.4 % (1980/95)
Children per woman: 5.4 (1998)

HEALTH

Life expectancy at birth: 52 years (1998)
male: 51 years (1998)
female: 54 years (1998)
Maternal mortality: 600 per 100,000 live births (1990-98)
Infant mortality: 85 per 1,000 (1998)
Under-5 child mortality: 144 per 1,000 (1998)
Daily calorie supply: 2,517 per capita (1996)
19 doctors per 100,000 people (1993)
Safe water: 67 % (1990/98)

EDUCATION

Literacy: 63 % (1995)
male: 74 % (1995)
female: 53 % (1995)
Tertiary: 8 % (1996)
Primary school teachers: one for every 51 (1995)

COMMUNICATIONS

29 newspapers (1996), 183 radios (1997), 76 TV sets (1996) and 32 main telephone lines (1996) per 1,000 people

ECONOMY

Per capita, GNP: $ 4,170 (1998)
Annual growth, GNP: 5.7 % (1998)
Annual inflation: 7.2 % (1990/98)
Consumer price index: 104.7 (1997)
Currency: 590.0 CFA francs = $ 1 (1998)
Cereal imports: 110,582 metric tons (1998)
Food import dependency: 19 % (1997)
Fertilizer use: 6 kg per ha (1997)
Exports: $ 2,823 million (1998)
Imports: $ 2,220 million (1998)
External debt: $ 4,425 million (1998); $ 3,791 per capita (1998)
Debt service: 12.0 % of exports (1998)
Development aid received: $ 40 million (1997); $ 40.4 per capita (1997); 0.90 % of GNP (1997)

ENERGY

Consumption: 1,419.0 Kgs of Oil equivalent per capita yearly (1997); -1,110.0 % imported (1997)

HDI (rank/value): 124/0.607 (1997)

---

with re-establishing order. According to information confirmed by Amnesty International, the incidents left a toll of six dead and a hundred wounded.

[15] Once calm had been restored, the political and social groups met on June 6, in a National Conference and an agreement was reached whereby presidential elections would be held. This was undoubtedly a major victory for the opposition, who extracted promises of multiparty elections from the President. But Bongo advanced the election date from 1992 to late 1990, a tactic meaning that he could use the power base he had built up over the past 20 years in office to carry out his campaign, while the opposition had no time to organize itself adequately or overcome its internal divisions.

[16] In September 1990, President Bongo's Gabonese Democratic Party (PDG), obtained a majority in the National Assembly. The new constitution, approved in March 1991, formally established a multiparty system.

[17] In 1991, the country was rocked by a new outbreak of political and social violence. The economic crisis continued to worsen. The stabilization program launched in September under IMF guidelines and the structural adjustment plan promoted by the World Bank failed to generate much hope.

[18] The absence of an electoral timetable and student agitation demanding greater resources for the university increased tension even further. The President closed the university, called off the elections and banned all political meetings. The opposition called a general strike, which paralyzed Port Gentil, the center of the oil industry. Concerned by the extent of the protests, Bongo reopened the university and lifted the ban on demonstrations.

[19] The presidential elections of December 1993, which returned Bongo to power again, were questioned by the opposition. In February, the protests continued and were harshly repressed leaving 30 dead. In negotiations in Paris between September and November 1994, a coalition government was formed until new elections could be held.

[20] In July 1995, the President gained the support of 96 per cent of the voters in a referendum for constitutional reform in order for presidential and legislative elections to be held. The National Assembly elections in December 1996 gave the Democratic Party led by Bongo 47 of the 55 seats. Meanwhile, the opposition leader Paul Mba-Abessole, scored a sizeable victory in the municipal elections, becoming mayor of the capital Libreville.

[21] Despite the fact Gabon had per capita income of $3,490 per year due to the oil income, the poverty indicators provided an alarming picture. In 1997, life expectancy was less than 55years, literacy barely reached 63 per cent of adults and the infant mortality rate stood at 87 per thousand.

[22] Early in 1998, Mayor Mba-Abessole requested the United Nations to supervise presidential elections that were to be held later that year in order to avoid the 'fraudulent reelection of Omar Bongo'. The elections were in fact won by the president, who defeated Mba Abessole and Pierre-Andre Kombila, former deputy of Abessole in the Party of Timberworkers.

[23] The President appointed Jean-François Ntoutoume-Emane as Prime Minister on January 1999 in the midst of strong protests which led his government to close schools and the Libreville University to avoid demonstrations.

[24] The authorities asked the UN for humanitarian assistance to help with the continuous inflow of refugees. In October 1999, international organizations estimated the number of refugees in Gabon amounted to 10,000. ■

PROFILE

ENVIRONMENT

Irrigated by the Ogooué River basin, the country has an equatorial climate with year-round rainfall. The land is covered by dense rainforest and a large part of the population work in the local timber industry. The country has manganese, uranium, iron and petroleum reserves. Deforestation is one of the most serious environmental problems, together with the depredation of the country's wildlife.

SOCIETY

Peoples: Gabon was populated by pygmy hunters. In the 16th century it was invaded by Myene and other ethnic groups. Today over half of the population are Bantu, divided into more than 40 different groups including Galoa, Nkomi, and Irungu. One third of the population are Fang and Kwele, while in the northern and southern parts of Gabon there are Punu and Nzabi minorities.
Religions: Mainly Christian. More than one third practice traditional African religions and there is a small Muslim minority.
Languages: French (official). Bantu languages are spoken along the coast; Fang is used in northern Gabon; local languages and dialects are used in the rest of the country.
Political Parties: Gabonese Democratic Party (PDG), pro- government. Gabonese Progress Party and National Union of Timberworkers, in the opposition.

THE STATE

Official Name: République Gabonaise.
Administrative divisions: 9 provinces and 37 prefectures.
Capital: Libreville 420,000 people (1995).
Other cities: Port Gentil 178,200 people (1993); Franceville 75,000 people (1988).
Government: Parliamentary republic with strong head of State. Omar (Albert-Bernard) Bongo, President and head of State since December 1967. Jean-François Ntoutoume-Emane, Head of Government and Prime Minister since January 1999. Single-chamber legislature: National Assembly, with 120 members elected every five years.
National Holiday: July 17, Independence Day (1960).
Armed Forces: 4,700 (1995). **Other:** Coast Guard: 2,800; Gendarmerie: 2,000.

Gambia

Gambia

Population: 1,268,000 (1999)
Area: 11,300 SQ KM
Capital: Banjul
Currency: Dalasi
Language: English

The earliest settlers of the Gambia river valley came from what is now Senegal. Attracted by Gambia's coast, which lent itself to trade and navigation, they settled along the river, carrying out subsistence farming.

[2] In the 15th century, the region was colonized by the Mandingo who, together with the Mali Empire established their authority in the Gambia Valley. They also founded several kingdoms in the area, which controlled coastal trade and enabled them to develop economically and culturally.

[3] With the arrival of the Portuguese in 1455, most of the region's domestic trade was displaced toward the Atlantic coast, bringing about the decline of the local kingdoms which had prospered under this trade. For the Portuguese, Gambia became the point of departure for a large quantity of precious metals.

[4] Gambia was also important to them as a prosperous port of call on their route to the Orient. However, in 1618 the Portuguese Crown sold its commercial and territorial rights to the British Empire which at the height of its naval prowess was trying to assert its dominance as a colonial power by acquiring a foothold in Africa.

[5] At that time, a war began between Britain and France (controlling all of what is now Senegal) which was to last for more than 200 years. From 1644, the British used this coastal area as a source of slaves, setting up alliances with inland tribal princes to provide them with human merchandise.

[6] Throughout the 17th century, Gambia was nothing more than a source of slave labor for Britain's colonies and for its slave trade with other colonial powers. The British

therefore limited themselves to establishing a rudimentary trading post in the area, founded in 1660. Border disputes between the British and French increased during the 18th century.

[7] Throughout the 19th century a series of religious wars in the interior resulted in the complete Islamization of the country, with an increase in Muslim immigration from other parts of Africa. In the meantime, the region lost its international economic significance when the slave trade was abolished in Britain.

[8] It did however gain strategic importance by being a British enclave inserted into the heart of Senegal, a region instrumental in France's designs on sub-Saharan Africa. Slavery actually continued within the colony until the 20th century, not being outlawed until 1906.

[9] In 1889, France and Britain reached an agreement as to the boundaries of their respective colonies, ensuring peace in the region and the formal recognition of British sovereignty over Gambia by other European powers.

[10] Gambia's status as a British colony remained unchanged throughout the first half of the 20th century. Although the decolonization process in Africa began after World War II - resulting in the creation of a number of independent states in what had formerly been European colonies - Gambia did not receive administrative autonomy from Britain until 1963. Two years later, Gambia obtained full independence and joined the British Commonwealth. At the time of its independence, Gambia did not seem to constitute a nation as such because of its ethnic, cultural and economic complexity.

[11] After independence, the territory's social and economic structures remained unchanged. Exports continued to be based on a single crop, peanuts, while traditional social structures remained so unassailable that they were finally legitimized by the 1970 constitution. Thus, although some

legislative seats were determined by the election of deputies, others were assigned to the 5 regional leaders.

[12] Dawda Jawara, founder of the People's Progressive Party (PPP), dominated Gambian politics since the 1960s. He won the 1962 elections, but failed to assume office because of a vote of no-confidence from the opposition. However, he won the election in 1970 when the country was proclaimed a republic, with a presidential system of government.

[13] Around 1975, the success of Alex Haley's book 'Roots' turned Gambia into an important tourism center; but alongside this, prostitution and drug trafficking also increased while organized Islamic opposition emerged.

[14] The lack of border controls in Gambia led to it becoming a paradise for West African smuggling and a large part of Senegal's agricultural produce was illegally shipped through the port of Banjul.

[15] The close economic relationship between the countries led the Government of Dawda Jawara to accept a project for union with Senegal in 1973.

[16] In July 1981, Muslim dissidents attempted to overthrow Jawara, aiming to end official corruption through the establishment of a revolutionary Islamic regime. The revolt was crushed by Senegalese troops who entered Gambia at the request of President Dawda, who was in London at the time.

[17] The proposed union with Senegal had been planned for 1982,

WORKERS

% OF LABOUR FORCE **1998**

■ FEMALE: 45%   ■ MALE: 55%

1990

■ SERVICES: 32.5%
■ INDUSTRY: 15.9%
■ AGRICULTURE: 51.5%

LAND USE

DEFORESTATION: 0.5% annual (1990/95)
IRRIGATED: 1.4% of arable (1993)

1993

■ FOREST & WOODLAND: 74.3%
■ ARABLE: 1.1%
■ OTHER: 24.6%

PUBLIC EXPENDITURE

DEFENCE EXPENDITURE (% of goverment exp.) **7.0%** (1997)

MILITARY EXPENDITURE (% of health & education) **51%** (1990/91)

but the coup attempt against Gambia's government accelerated plans for creating the Senegambian federation.

[18] The 1980s were marked by a worsening of the country's economic situation, and a severe drought led to a sudden drop in the production of agricultural exports. The most obvious consequences were an increase in unemployment, migration from rural areas to the capital and increasing foreign debt to finance food imports.

[19] Senegambia was officially established in February 1982 with Abdou Diouf of Senegal as its first president, assisted by a council of ministers and a bi-national parliament. The federation did not totally unite Senegal and Gambia, as both states retained their autonomous character and internal organization. The treaty ensured that Dawda Jawara gained protection against internal rebellions and Senegal gained greater control over the leak of export tax revenues through smuggling.

[20] Gambia became unhappy with this alliance and its dissatisfaction became apparent in mid-1985, with its reluctance to sign the treaties aimed at strengthening ties with Senegal. Jawara subsequently failed to comply with the terms of the agreements promising Senegal military and diplomatic support in case of external or internal conflicts.

[21] In the 1991-92 budget, the Minister of Finance announced a 6 per cent increase in the salaries of civil servants and reinstated a series of benefits eliminated when a structural adjustment program went into effect.

[22] In May 1991, Gambia and Senegal took the first step toward reconciliation by signing a good-will and cooperation treaty. The agreement foresaw an annual meeting between the two heads of state and the creation of a joint commission presided over by the Foreign Ministers of both countries.

[23] In 1993, agriculture and tourism were hit by the consequences of the European economic crisis. Gambia's trade with Senegal was damaged when the Central Bank of the Western Africa States decided to stop financing trade based upon the African franc (CFA) outside the area comprised by countries using this monetary system.

[24] The Government took measures to initiate a national reconciliation process, including an amnesty granted to rebel movements fighting to oust the regime.

[25] In July 1994, a military coup overthrew President Dawda Jawara who sought asylum in Senegal after taking refuge in a US warship visiting the country. The presence of this ship in Banjul suggested complicity of the United States with the military. The coup, headed by Yahya Jammeh, began with the protests of soldiers who demanded payment for their peace mission carried out in Liberia.

[26] Two members of the Provisional Armed Forces Council were arrested in January 1995 after trying to hand the Government over to civilians. In March, Jammeh also arrested the former Justice minister and general prosecutor for promoting the return of civilian rule. In November, the military junta expanded the powers of the security forces.

[27] The Government announced legislative and presidential elections would be held in June 1996, but the vote was postponed. In August, after a referendum, a new Constitution was approved. Jammeh described this event as the first step toward the restoration of national political life. In September 1996, Jammeh, up to then chief of the Armed Forces Government Junta, became Gambia's second elected President.

[28] In August 1997, the Government lifted other restrictions which limited political activity since the 1994 military coup. Arrests of Islamic leaders were common in 1998. In August, Jammeh travelled to Mauritania and met with president Moaouia Ould Sidi Mohammed Taya to 'find a solution to the two month conflict in Guinea-Bissau'.

[29] In May 1999, the opposition Ousainou Darboe (UDP) accused the Government of maintaining a democracy with 'untruthful' laws. On June 9, Jammeh accused Western 'donor' countries of making aid conditional on human rights and democracy. Days later, rebel leaders of Casamance, Senegal, met in Gambia to draw up a common strategy for peace talks.

[30] On September 25, before the UN in New York, Jammeh criticized 'the sloth and irresponsibility of this body in the conflicts facing Africa'. A month later, the Press Union denounced a new 'governmental measure to regulate press freedom', with annual raids on their buildings and the power of the minister of information to confiscate their records. The security forces prevented an 'attempted coup d'état' in January 2000 and arrested the two officers allegedly responsible for the uprising.

[31] Gambia, in conjunction with another 44 countries - mostly African - lost its right to vote in the UN National Assembly on February 2000, for 'falling behind in debt payments'.

[32] The Community of States of the Sahel-Sahara (Comessa), meeting in Chad on February 5 accepted Gambia, Senegal and Djibouti as new members. The countries agreed not to 'interfere in the internal affairs of members, not to offer their territories to forces in opposition to any member, not to aid hostile forces in any of the countries'.

PROFILE

ENVIRONMENT

One of the smallest African countries, Gambia stretches 320 km along the Gambia River, which is fully navigable and one of the main waterways in the area. The climate is tropical; there are rainforests along the river-banks and wooded savannah further inland. The economy is based on peanut exports and tourism. Because of the use of firewood as a main energy source and the production of export crops, large areas of forest have been felled.

SOCIETY

Peoples: The majority of Gambians belong to the Mandingo ethnic group, 40 per cent; 14 per cent are Futa, 13 per cent are Wolof who belong to the same root and 7 per cent are Diula. There are minor ethnic groups inland (Serahuilis, Akus). Five to ten thousand laborers migrate from Mali, Senegal and Guinea-Bissau every year only to return home after the harvest. **Religions:** The majority of Gambians follow the Islamic faith; a minority practice traditional religions and Christianity, mostly Protestant. **Languages:** English (official); the most widespread local languages are Mandingo, Fulani and Wolof (the Wolof form a majority in the main trade center). **Political Parties:** The People's Progressive Party (PPP), founded by Dawda Jawara in the 1960s; the National Convention Party (NCP) from a PPP split in the 1970s; the People's Party of Gambia (PPG). **Social Organizations:** There are three trade union federations: the Gambia Workers' Union (linked to the PPP); the Gambia Labor Union; and the Gambia Salesmen's and Merchants' Union.

THE STATE

Official Name: Republic of The Gambia. **Administrative Divisions:** 5 Provinces and the Capital. **Capital:** Banjul 240,000 people (1995). **Other cities:** Brikama 24,300 people; Bakau 23,600 people (1986). **Government:** Presidential republic. Yahya Jammeh, President since September 1996. Legislature. Single-chamber Parliament: Chamber of Deputies, with 50 members, 36 of whom are elected by universal suffrage, 9 special members and 5 tribal chieftains. **National Holiday:** February 18, Independence (1965). **Armed Forces:** 800 troops (1994).

[33] On April 11, students and police clashed in the streets of Banjul while the former claimed to be 'victims of illegal arrests'. Six people died in the confrontations and the police declared they were on red alert. The International Red Cross claimed one of its helpers who died had been shot despite showing appropriate identification. ∎

Georgia

Sakartvelo

Population: 5,005,000 (1999)
Area: 69,700 SQ KM
Capital: Tbilisi
Currency: Kupon
Language: Georgian

The peoples of the Caucasian Isthmus, thought to be the inventors of metallurgy, entered the Bronze Age around 2000 BC. The ancestors of modern Georgians are thought to have formed the first tribes in that region about this time. The kingdom of Kolkhida - which dates back to the 6th century BC - is mentioned in Homer's poems and in traditional Greek mythology.

[2] Two centuries later, legendary chieftain Farnavaz created the kingdom of Iberia, in what is now eastern Georgia. These two kingdoms were the first Georgian States, the result of a fusion of ancient agricultural and iron-smelting tribes of the region.

[3] Kolkhida and Iberia were subdued by Greece and then by Rome, as the result of Pompey's campaigns, in the 1st century BC. In the year 337 AD, King Mirian of Iberia adopted Christianity, making it the country's official religion. Like the Armenian church, the Georgian church separated from Rome in 506, to form the national Church of St George, with its headquarters at Tiflis (today Tbilisi).

[4] From a minor city, Tiflis became first the capital of Iberia, and later of all Georgia, after the unification of the 8th and 9th centuries. Both kingdoms fell under Iranian (Sasanid), then Byzantine and finally Arab control, between the 6th and 10th centuries. Feudal Georgia prospered under King David 'the Builder', 1089-1125 and Queen Tamara, 1184-1213.

[5] In the 13th and 14th centuries Georgia was invaded by the Tatars and Tamerlane. In the 15th century it dissolved into small fiefdoms, becoming the object of territorial disputes between Turkey and Iran from the 16th to the 18th centuries and there were a number of anti-Turkish and anti-Iranian revolts.

[6] Through the Treaty of Georgievsk (1783) Russia established its protection over eastern Georgia, annexing it in 1801. In the second half of the 19th century, Western Georgia (Tiblisi and Kutaisi) met the same fate. The Georgian provinces were incorporated into Transcaucasia, where the Government was in the hands of a viceroy designated by the Czar.

[7] Annexation to Russia had a number of negative effects on Georgian life. The local language was eliminated from administrative documents, and it was replaced by Russian in literature and in schools. The Catholic Church of St George was outlawed and its patriarchs deported, to be replaced by Russian Orthodox bishops and Russians were encouraged to come and settle in all of Georgia's cities, a fact which explains why the revolutionary movement was so strong in Georgia, in all of its Marxist, nationalist, populist and social democratic forms. It was here that Josef Dzhugashvili, known as Stalin, began his political career. After frequent rebellions during this period, Georgians played an important part in the revolution which shook the empire in 1905.

[8] When World War I broke out, the Caucasus saw fighting between Russia and Turkey. The Georgians formed a legion to fight alongside the Turks. In February 1917, a new wave of uprisings was unleashed by war policies and by hunger, and the peoples of the Caucasus brought down the czarist regime.

[9] In November, after the Bolshevik triumph in Petrograd, power in Transcaucasia fell into the hands of the Mensheviks (who wanted gradual change rather than revolution). Confronted with this situation, Stalin's group allowed the Caucasus to join the Bolsheviks led by Lenin. In April 1918, in Tbilisi, the United Government of Transcaucasia announced its separation from Soviet Russia. On May 26, 1918, Georgia proclaimed independence, which was recognized by Moscow two years later.

[10] Between 1918 and 1920, German, Turkish and British troops entered Georgia, all intent upon bringing down the socialist regime. In February 1921 the Red Army occupied Georgia and established Soviet power. On February 25, 1921, the Soviet Socialist Republic of Georgia was proclaimed, with the Abkhaz Autonomous Region as an administrative division of this republic. In March 1921, a peace treaty between the Russian Federation and Turkey was finalized, with the latter ceding Batumi and the northern part of Adzharistan, which became an autonomous republic within the Georgian SSR.

[11] In March 1922, Georgia, Azerbaijan and Armenia were reorganized as the Transcaucasian Federation. The following month, the South Ossetian Autonomous Region was formed, as a part of Georgia. On December 5 1936 the federation was dissolved and Georgia became one of the 15 republics of the Soviet Union (USSR).

[12] Stalin became Secretary General of the Communist Party of the Soviet Union in 1922, and after Lenin's death he became party leader. From 1928, he was leader of the USSR. Georgia witnessed many purges and suffered the effects of centralization and the repression of Stalinism, although to a lesser degree than other republics. In 1924, the Red Army intervened to put down a peasant uprising against forced land collectivization.

[13] In the following years the country benefited from the cultural and economic development promoted by the Soviet Union. Many Georgians - apart from Stalin - were in the leadership circle of the Soviet Union's CP, including Sergo Ordzhonikidzegv, the USSR's Minister of Heavy Industry, and Lavrenti Beria, head of the secret police (NKVD) who was executed after Stalin's death, in 1953. When Krushchev denounced his predecessor's crimes at the 20th Party Congress in 1956, it hurt Georgian national pride.

[14] In 1953, Moscow made Eduard Shevardnadze chief of police in Tbilisi. Implicated in cases of corruption and fraud, Mzhavanadze was replaced by Shevardnadze in 1972. A new nationalist feeling began to emerge with declarations in defense of the Georgian language and violent acts of sabotage.

[15] In 1978, the new constitution of the USSR triggered a wave of protest, as it made Russian the official language of the Soviet Union. However, Shevardnadze managed to have the measure abolished and allowed an anti-Stalin movie, 'Repent', to be screened. This marked the development of glasnost (openness) and perestroika (restructuring) process in Georgia.

[16] Shevardnadze remained at the head of Georgia's Communist Party and government until 1985, when he was made Foreign Minister of the Soviet Union. After the political changes made by Mikhail Gorbachev, several movements and parties emerged in Georgia, clamoring for the independence which Georgia claimed to have lost in 1921, with the establishment of Soviet power. On April 9 1989 in Tbilisi, Red Army units dispersed a crowd meeting in the main square to demand the secession of Georgia, citing Article 72 of the Constitution of the USSR. Nineteen people were killed, most of them women or adolescents.

[17] In the mid-1980s, a Green Party emerged in Georgia amid the first ever open debates on the country's ecological problems. The Greens combined their concern for the environment with a defense of non-violence, democracy and human rights. Georgia was the second former Soviet republic - after Estonia - to join the European 'Green' Parliament.

[18] On October 28 1990, elections were held for the Soviet (parliament) of the Georgian SSR, and the 'Free Georgia Round Table' coalition won. Zviad Gamsakhurdia, a well-known political dissident who had been proscribed during the Soviet regime, became the leader of the coalition. The Georgian Soviet decided to change the country's name to the Republic of Georgia.

[19] Ethnic tensions increased, and the South Ossetian Autonomous Region claimed republican status.

Georgia's Soviet annulled this decision, declared a state of emergency in South Ossetia and organized a blockade of this region. In April 1991, after fighting broke out between Ossetian guerrillas and Georgian troops, the Soviet approved the region's independence.

[20] On May 27, Gamsakhurdia was elected President. In September, a struggle began between Gamsakhurdia's supporters and the opposition, led by Dzhaba Ioseliani and Tenguiz Kitovani, commander of the National Guard. Repeated demonstrations ended in violence on January 6 1992, when government forces (following Kitovani's orders) stormed government headquarters. Gamsakhurdia fled first to Armenia, and then to the Chechen Autonomous Republic.

[21] A Military Council led by Kitovani seized power in Tbilisi and suspended the constitution. Gamsakhurdia loyalists continued to fight against the new regime's forces in western Georgia.

[22] In March, former USSR foreign minister, Eduard Shevardnadze, returned to Georgia to take charge of the presidency of the Council of State, the most powerful governing body. Chosen by the Military Council, he held this post until democratic elections took place. Shevardnadze declared that his country would normalize relations with the international community, giving preference to relations with the former USSR republics, though for the moment not joining the Commonwealth of Independent States (CIS).

[23] On June 28 that year, a cease-fire was called in South Ossetia, supervised by a peacekeeping force of Russians, Georgians and Ossetians. From their capital in Sukhumi, the Abkhazian authorities resolved to limit the jurisdiction of Georgia's central government within the autonomous region. On August 14, government troops entered Abkhazia and occupied Sukhumi. Local authorities fled to the city of Gudauta, which became a center of resistance.

[24] In early October, with the support of Russian volunteers and army regulars, they managed to extend their control over a large part of Abkhazia, coming close to Sukhumi.

[25] Early in 1993, the Russian air force began regular bombing of Sukhumi, and by mid-March fighting had reached the outskirts of the city. On June 28, a Russian-mediated armistice went into effect, with both parties agreeing to demobilize their troops.

[26] In mid-September 1993, a strong Abkhazian offensive began, taking the Georgians by surprise and culminating in the capture of Sukhumi by the Abkhazian army. Eduard Shevardnadze remained in Sukhumi, leaving on the last flight out of the city.

[27] In November, supporters of former president Gamsakhurdia launched a broad offensive, but were defeated with the help of Russian troops. In the same month, Georgia joined the CIS. In early 1994, Gamsakhurdia died in a suicide attempt, according to official reports. In February, Georgia signed a friendship treaty with Russia, and in April a peace treaty was signed with the Abkhazian rebels in Moscow.

[28] In spite of its rapprochement with Russia, Tbilisi joined the Association for Peace, sponsored by NATO. The non-payment of a debt to the Government of Turkmenistan led to a reduction in gas sales, the main source of revenues in Georgia. Ignoring Russian protests, Georgia and Azerbaijan agreed to build an oil pipeline on Georgian territory to facilitate the export of Azerbaijani petroleum. Production increased in Georgia during the latter half of the decade, but inflation and unemployment levels remained high.

[29] Parliament approved a new constitution defining Georgia as a presidential republic in August 1995. In November, Shevardnadze won the presidential elections and his party, Citizens Alliance, obtained an overall majority in Parliament. In November 1997 the country became the first former Soviet republic to abolish capital punishment.

[30] President Shevardnadze narrowly escaped death in two assassination attempts in February 1998 and May 1999. There were rumors of Moscow's involvement in both cases, linked to the construction of the pipeline to carry Azerbaijani oil across Georgian territory (finished in April 1999). A senior military officer was accused of organizing the conspiracy inside Georgia.

[31] A few days after the May assassination attempt, Washington agreed to give the Georgian Government ten military helicopters and $3 million to finance pilot training. During the previous months, Russia had complained about increasing US influence in the region.

[32] The parliament of the separatist republic of Abkhaz declared its independence in October 1999, after a referendum in which the separatist option obtained 98 per cent of the ballot. Tbilisi condemned the declaration as illegal and did not recognize the new state. During parliamentary elections that year, President Shevardnadze's party, Citizens Alliance, won 40 per cent of the vote. The Renovation Movement, a coalition comprising groups from a wide political range, including populists, right-wing nationalists, socialists and monarchists, took 27 per cent. The turn-out for the election was below 70 per cent of registered voters. Shevardnadze declared that the excellent results would allow Georgia to join NATO in 2005.

[33] Tension with Russia increased again in late 1999 and early 2000 due to Chechen rebel activities. Moscow accused Tbilisi of giving support and refuge to Chechen separatists, something the Shevardnadze government strongly denied. ■

PROFILE

ENVIRONMENT

Located in the central western part of Transcaucasia, Georgia is bordered in the north by Russia, in the east by Azerbaijan and in the south by Armenia and Turkey, with the Black Sea to the west. Most of its territory is occupied by mountains. Between the Little and the Great Caucasus lies the Kolkhida lowland and the Kartalinian Plain; the Alazan Valley lies to the east. Subtropical climate in the west, moderate in the east; there is heavy rainfall in the western area, along the shores of the Black Sea. Principal rivers are the Kura and Rioni. 40 per cent of the republic is covered by forests. Georgia is famous for its wine. Bacterial pollution of 70 per cent of the Black Sea constitutes a serious problem. Only 18 per cent of the residual waters in the main port of Batumi undergo adequate treatment. The abuse of pesticides has resulted in a high level of chemical toxicity in the soil.

SOCIETY

Peoples: Georgians, 70 per cent; Armenians, 8.1 per cent; Russians, 6.3 per cent; Azeris, 5.7 per cent; Ossetians, Abkhazians and Adzharians. **Religions:** Georgian Orthodox (65 per cent), Muslims (11 per cent), Russian Orthodox (10 per cent), and Armenian Orthodox (8 per cent). **Languages:** Georgian (official), Russian and Abkhazian. **Political Parties:** Union of Citizens of Georgia, Georgian Communist Party, National Democratic Party, Aidguilara (national movement of the Abkhazians), Admon Nyjas (national movement of the South Ossetians).

THE STATE

Official Name: Sakartvelos Respublika. **Capital:** Tbilisi 1,500,000 people (est 1995). **Other cities:** Batumi 137,000 people; Sukhumi 122,000; Kutaisi 240,000; Rustavi 160,000 (1994). **Government:** Eduard Shevardnadze, President of Parliament and Head of State 1992-1995 and President since 1995 (re-elected in 1999); Vazha Lordkipanidze, Secretary of State. **National Holiday:** May 26, Independence (1918). **Armed Forces** 13,000.

Germany

Deutschland

Population: 82,177,000 (1999)
Area: 356,733 SQ KM
Capital: Berlin
Currency: Mark
Language: German

The first reference to the Germanic tribes comes from between 58 and 51 BC when the Romans under Julius Caesar invaded a part of Gaul north of the Alps and west of the Rhine. The Germans descended from the Teutoni and the Cimbri, who had in turn descended from the Danes. Between 113 and 101 BC. Teutoni and Cimbri tribes invaded the Mediterranean regions including the Italian peninsula.

2 In 9 AD Arminius, a Germanic chief and the earliest national hero, led a revolt which defeated three Roman legions in the Teutoburger Wald. By the second half of the 3rd century, the Germanic tribes had fused into larger political units; the Saxons, Franks and Germans.

3 The Romans found it increasingly difficult to keep their dominion over the region and withdrew gradually. In the 4th century Attila's Huns invaded, and a long period of Migrations followed throughout Europe. In 455, the Germans defeated the Mongols at the battle of the river Nedao and the Mongol Empire subsequently collapsed. Clovis and Charlemagne later subjected the Germanic and Saxon tribes to the Frankish Empire.

4 After the Treaty of Verdun and the division of the Carolingian empire in 843, the first entirely Germanic kingdom was established under Louis the German. Under Otto I, crowned in Rome in 936, Germania became Europe's most powerful kingdom.

5 During the 12th and 13th centuries Germany experienced a rapid growth in population, and continuous expansion.

6 The instability of royal dynasties encouraged the strengthening of secular and religious principalities. Princes were free to build fortresses, exploit natural resources and administer justice in their dominions.

7 In 1356, the authority of the king in relation to the papacy was consolidated in the Golden Bull of Charles IV (1346-1378) establishing the right to appoint the King without the Pope's approval, and strengthened the hand of the principalities, on whose support the king depended.

8 During the 15th and 16th centuries internal instability persisted. In 1517 Martin Luther led the Protestant Reformation, which, coupled with political rivalries, frustrated reunification efforts.

9 The Reformation provided a forum for criticisms of secularisation and corruption in the German Church, which had become an increasingly prosperous economic and financial institution. It owned a third of the land in some districts and profited from selling indulgences - one of the contributory factors to its downfall. After a succession of internal wars, including peasant uprisings, the Peace of Augsburg was reached in 1555, giving equal rights to both Catholics and Lutherans.

10 Political and religious factions combined their strengths; in 1608 the Protestant Union was created, and the Catholic League a year later. The Bohemian rebellion triggered the Thirty Year War (1618-1648),

which spread to the entire continent, and ultimately reduced the population of central Europe by around 30 per cent, ending with the Peace of Westfalia (1648).

11 In the 18th century, the Kingdom of Prussia emerged as a dynamic economic and political unit, responsible for creating tensions among the German states. Napoleon's victories over Prussia in 1806 and the formation of the Confederation of the Rhine put an end to the Holy Roman Empire.

12 In Central Europe during the 18th century, culture formed an outlet for intellectual energies which could not be expressed through politics, as political life itself was dominated by the autocratic rulers. Philosophers like Kant and Herder, and writers like Goethe and Schiller, expressed the idealism and spiritualism which characterized German art and literature of this time.

13 When Napoleon fell, the German princes created a confederation of 39 states, which were independent except for foreign policy. Austrian and Prussian opposition to broader forms of representation increased popular unrest, leading to the 1830 revolts and increased repression.

14 In 1834, Prussia threw its growing economic weight into the political realm, with the establishment of the German Customs Union, from which Austria was excluded. The main consequences of the Union were the duplication of trade among its members over the next ten years, as well as the formation of industrial centres and the emergence of a working class. Due to the rapid growth of the urban population, the supply of labour greatly exceeded the demand. The resulting impoverishment of industrial workers and artisans served as a breeding ground for the rebellions of subsequent years, culminating in the revolutionary wave of 1848-49.

15 A National Assembly first met in Frankfurt on May 18 1848; its representatives belonged mostly to liberal democratic sectors. They campaigned for German unity, and guarantees of

WORKERS

1997
UNEMPLOYMENT: 9.8%

% OF LABOUR FORCE **1998**

▪ FEMALE: 42%   ▪ MALE: 58%

1990

▪ SERVICES: 57.9%
▪ INDUSTRY: 38.1%
▪ AGRICULTURE: 4.0%

LAND USE

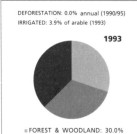

DEFORESTATION: 0.0% annual (1990/95)
IRRIGATED: 3.9% of arable (1993)

1993

▪ FOREST & WOODLAND: 30.0%
▪ ARABLE: 32.7%
▪ OTHER: 37.3%

PUBLIC EXPENDITURE

DEFENCE EXPENDITURE (% of goverment exp.)   **4.7%** (1997)

MILITARY EXPENDITURE (% of health & education)   **29%** (1990/91)

MATERNAL MORTALITY	FOOD DEPENDENCY	FOREIGN TRADE

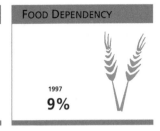

MATERNAL MORTALITY
1990-98

Per 100,000
live births

8

FOOD DEPENDENCY

1997

9%

FOREIGN TRADE

Millions US$ 1998

IMPORTS

528,778

EXPORTS

560,414

PROFILE

ENVIRONMENT

The northern part of the country is a vast plain. The Baltic coast is jagged, with deep, narrow gulfs. The center of the country is made up of very old mountain ranges, plateaus and sedimentary river basins. Of the ancient massifs, the most important are the Black Forest region and the Rhineland. The southern region begins in the Danube Valley, and is made up of plateaus (the Bavarian Plateau), bordered to the south by the Bavarian Alps. There are large deposits of coal and lignite along the banks of the Ruhr and Ens rivers, which provided the backbone of Germany's industrial development. Heavy industry is concentrated in the Ruhr Valley, mid-Rhineland and Lower Saxony. The south of the former German Democratic Republic is rich in coal, lignite, lead, tin, silver and uranium deposits. The chemical, electrochemical, metallurgical and steel industries are concentrated there. This region suffers severe air pollution as a result of the carbon output of the industries. The emission of sulphur dioxide in eastern Germany is 15 times that in the west, compounding the problem of acid rain. Untreated industrial effluents carrying heavy metals and toxic chemicals have contaminated many east German rivers, ending up in the highly polluted Baltic Sea.

SOCIETY

Peoples: German 93.4 per cent; Turkish 2.1 per cent, of which Kurdish 0.5 per cent; Yugoslav 0.8 per cent; Italian 0.7 per cent; Greek 0.4 per cent; Polish 0.4 per cent; Spanish 0.2 per cent; other 2.0 per cent.
Religions: Christian; a Catholic majority in the South and Protestant in the North. There are approximately 27 million Catholics and, before reunification, Catholics constituted a majority in West Germany.
Languages: German (official) and local dialects which, in spite of restrictions, are regaining popularity. Turkish, Kurdish.
Political Parties: Christian Democratic Union (CDU); Christian Social Union (CSU), Liberal Party (FDP), Social Democratic Party (SPD); the Greens/Alliance-90; Democratic Socialist Party (PDS), the Republicans (REP).
Social Organizations: Workers' Federation (DGB).

THE STATE

Official Name: Bundesrepublik Deutschland.
Administrative divisions: Federal parliamentary State made up of 16 *Länder* (federated states), as of October 3, 1990. 11 *Länder* made up what was formerly West Germany (Schleswig-Holstein, Hamburg, Bremen, Niedersachsen, Nordrhein-Westfalen, Hessen, Rheinland-Pfalz, Saarland, Baden-Wuettemberg, Bavaria and Berlin) while the former German Democratic Republic was divided into five *Länder* (Mecklenburg-Vorpommern, Brandenburg, Sachsen-Anhalt, Sachsen and Thueringen).
Capital: Berlin 3,471,418 people (1995).
Other cities: Hamburg 1,707,901 people; München (Munich) 1,244,676; Köln (Cologne) 963,817; Frankfurt am Main 652,412; Dresden 500,000; Leipzig 481,112 (1995).
Government: Johannes Rau, President; Gerhard Schröder, Chancellor, appointed by the federal parliament.
Armed Forces 340,000.
Other: Federal Border Guard (Ministry of Interior) 24,800; Coast Guard 535.

political freedom. However, internal divisions facilitated the regrouping of the forces of the former regime, leading finally to the dissolution of Parliament in June 1849 and the repression of opposition organizations.

[16] With the revolutionary tendencies crushed, Austria and Prussia were free to dispute their respective roles in German unification. The issue was settled in 1866 with Prussia's victory in the Seven Weeks' War. The union was forged around the North German Confederation, a creation of the Prussian chancellor, Otto von Bismarck, that aimed to halt liberalism. The Parliament (Reichstag) was inaugurated in February 1867.

[17] Three years later, war broke out with France. Prussia's victory in 1871 was the last step in Bismarck's scheme to unite Germany under a single monarch, and Prussian domination.

[18] The Empire had to deal with opposing internal forces - the Church and social democracy. Bismarck passed the May Laws, secularising education and some other activities. He later reversed this, securing the Church as an ally against socialism. Alarmed at the growth of social democracy, the regime used repression and social reform to neutralize the latter's potential.

[19] Bismarck's government introduced commercial protectionism to increase domestic income and foster national industry and the German economy grew substantially, especially in heavy industry, chemicals, the electro-technical area and production. The creation of the Triple Alliance with Austria and Italy, and the acquisition of colonies in Africa and Asia after 1884 made the German Empire a leading world power.

[20] German rivalry with France and Britain in the west, and Russia and Serbia in the east, triggered World War I. The capitulation of the Austro-Hungarian Empire and Turkey in November 1918 led to Germany's final defeat. The crisis was aggravated by an internal revolution which led to

the abdication of the Emperor. Government was handed over to the socialist Friedrich Ebert, who was to call a National Constituent Assembly.

[21] German social democracy split into a moderate tendency favouring a gradual evolution to socialism, and a radical tendency favouring revolutionary change. The radical group, the Spartacists, headed by Karl Liebknecht and Rosa Luxemburg, identified with the Russian revolution of October 1917 and wanted to set up a system similar to that of the Soviets. The Spartacist leaders were executed in January 1919 following a failed coup attempt. A few days later, the electorate returned a moderate socialist majority to power in the Constituent Assembly.

[22] Formally proclaimed in August of that year, the Weimar Constitution was welcomed as the most democratic of its time. The president elect had power to nominate the Chancellor, whose government needed approval of the lower chamber of parliament, or the Reichstag. It also provided for the constitution of an upper house or Länder, formed by delegates designate by the governments of the liberal states.

[23] The Weimar Republic had a short and hazardous life. Despite the virtues attributed to the Constitution, various factors came together to undermine it. One of the main destabilising elements for the Republic was the conditions imposed on the country in Versailles by the victorious powers after World War I. These affected not only the economy but also the morale of the population, which could not allow Germany to be considered 'guilty' of having caused the war in 1914 and was unable to accept the stipulations of the treaty that judged any German, from the Kaiser down, as a war criminal.

[24] Germany was declared bankrupt by the Commission of Reparations and in January 1923 Belgian and French troops occupied the industrial Ruhr region. Economic instability

caused hyperinflation. Even though the Republican government managed to weather the serious economic crises, as in 1920-23 and events following the Wall Street crash in 1929, the destabilising influence of the Communists and the National Socialist Party, led by Adolf Hitler were set to topple it. The National Socialist or Nazi party had attempted a coup in 1923. Although this failed, the party saw a sustained increase in its popularity throughout the decade, with rocketing support after the crisis in 1929. While there were barely 170,000 members in 1929, the number grew to 1,378,000 by 1932.

[25] Marshall Paul Hindenburg, elected president in 1925, dissolved parliament in 1930. In the elections later that year, Communists and Nazis both saw a great increase in votes. The Nazis' promises to rebuild Greater Germany following the humiliation of the post-war treaties, and their campaign to blame the Jews and Communists for the economic crisis were ratified when the Nazi party doubled its share of the vote in the 1932 elections, gaining 37 per cent of the total.

[26] The rise of Hitler and the National Socialist party proved unstoppable. Despite the fact that Hitler's demands to become head of government had been refused in principle, in January 1933 - as unemployment topped six million - Hindenberg was forced to hand him the reins of power.

[27] In Potsdam in March 1933, the new parliament granted Hitler the power to issue decrees outside the Constitution without the approval of the legislative body or the President for four years. He had the power to set the annual budget, request loans and sign agreements with other countries, reorganize both his cabinet and the supreme ranks of the armed forces, and proclaim martial law. In July, Hitler abolished the German Federation and set up absolute central power. He outlawed trade unions and strikes, and all parties except his own.

Germany also withdrew from the Disarmament Conference and the League of Nations. The Nazis dubbed their government the 'Third Reich' (Third Empire).

[28] After the death of President Hindenburg in August 1934, the cabinet was forced to swear personal allegiance to the Chancellor, Adolf Hitler. In 1935, in open violation of the Treaty of Versailles, he began to re-arm Germany. The European powers protested, but were unable to stop him. With the 1935 'Nuremberg Laws', the regime provided a legal framework for its racist ideology, laying the foundation for its subsequent policies of ethnic and religious extermination.

[29] Germany and Italy signed a co-operation agreement in October 1936 which included support for General Franco in the Spanish Civil War. The following month Germany and Japan (the Axis powers) agreed to set up a military exchange, and in November 1937 Germany, Italy and Japan signed the Anti-communist Pact in Rome.

[30] In March 1938, German troops invaded Austria, and Hitler annexed it. That same year, the pressure of Hitler and German nationalism on the Sudetenland forced the European powers to cede this Czechoslovakian region to Germany. On 'Kristallnacht', November 9-10, the Government carried out a systematic destruction of Jewish commercial property and religious and cultural institutions.

[31] In 1939, taking advantage of the disagreements between Czechs and Slovaks, German troops advanced into Prague; Bohemia, Moravia, and Slovakia became protectorates.

[32] Britain assured Poland, Romania, Greece and Turkey that it would protect their independence, and Britain and France attempted to establish an alliance with the Soviet Union. In August 1939, however, the USSR signed a non-aggression treaty with Germany. On September 1, German troops invaded Poland. Britain and France issued

Germany an ultimatum which was disregarded. World War II broke out.

[33] By 1940, Germany had invaded Norway, Denmark, Belgium, the Netherlands, Luxembourg and France. In 1941 Hitler started his offensive against the USSR, but German troops were halted a few miles outside Moscow. They were finally defeated after the siege of Stalingrad (Volgograd) in 1943.

[34] From the outset, German aggression against its neighbors was accompanied by the systematic extermination of the Jewish population in concentration camps, primarily in Poland. Over six million Jews, and a million other people were killed.

[35] The advance of the Red Army on the eastern front - culminating in the capture of Berlin - and the 1944 Allied landing in Normandy on the Western Front forced Germany to surrender in May 1945.

[36] Four million Germans from neighboring countries, and from the territories annexed by Poland and the USSR, were forced to move to the four zones that Germany was now divided into. The country remained occupied by the United States, France, Britain and the USSR. In 1949, discord between the former Allies over the future governance of Germany led to the creation of the Federal Republic of Germany (FRG), in the West, and the German Democratic Republic (GDR), in the East. The issue of the two Germanies became a bone of contention in post-war relations between the USSR and the US.

[37] In 1955, the sovereignty of both Germanies was recognized by their occupying forces. During the Cold War, West Germany became a member of NATO (the North Atlantic Treaty Organization) while East Germany joined the Warsaw Pact. Foreign forces continued to be based in their territories and the two republics were still subject to limitations on their armed forces and a ban on nuclear weapons.

[38] The United Socialist Party

STATISTICS

DEMOGRAPHY

Population: 82,177,000 (1999)
Annual growth: 0.2 % (1975/97)
Estimates for year 2015 (million): 81.6 (1999)
Urban population: 86.9 % (1997)
Urban Growth: 0.6 % (1980/95)
Children per woman: 1.3 (1998)

HEALTH

Life expectancy at birth: 77 years (1998)
male: 74 years (1998)
female: 80 years (1998)
Maternal mortality: 8 per 100,000 live births (1990-98)
Infant mortality: 5 per 1,000 (1998)
Under-5 child mortality: 5 per 1,000 (1998)
Daily calorie supply: 3,330 per capita (1996)
319 doctors per 100,000 people (1993)

EDUCATION

School enrolment:
Primary total: 103 % (1990/96)
male: 104 % (1990/97)
female: 103 % (1990/97)
Secondary:
male: 103 % (1990/96)
female: 101 % (1990/96)
Tertiary: 47 % (1996)
Primary school teachers: one for every 17 (1995)

COMMUNICATIONS

311 newspapers (1996), 948 radios (1997), 493 TV sets (1996) and 538 main telephone lines (1996) per 1,000 people
Books: 87 new titles per 100,000 people (1992/94)

ECONOMY

Per capita, GNP: $ 26,570 (1998)
Annual growth, GNP: 2.8 % (1998)
Annual inflation: 2.2 % (1990/98)
Consumer price index: 104.3 (1998)
Currency: 1.8 marks = $ 1 (1998)
Cereal imports: 2,672,677 metric tons (1998)
Food import dependency: 9 % (1997)
Fertilizer use: 2,415 kg per ha (1997)
Exports: $ 560,414 million (1997)
Imports: $ 528,778 million (1997)

ENERGY

Consumption: 4,231.0 Kgs of Oil equivalent per capita yearly (1997); 60.0 % imported (1997)

HDI (rank/value): 14/0.906 (1997)

(SED), formed from the union of Communists and Social Democrats in 1946, took over the government of East Germany. The USSR partly compensated them for war losses with money, equipment and cattle, and a social system similar to that of the USSR was set up. In 1953, the political and economic situation of East Germany led to a series of protests, which were put down by Soviet troops. In the meantime, emigration to the Federal Republic of Germany (FRG) increased.

[39] Between the state's formation and 1961, when the East German Government forbade all emigration to the West, some three million East Germans emigrated to West Germany. To enforce their resolution, the East closed its borders and built the Berlin Wall between the eastern and the western sections of the city. In 1971, Erich Honecker took over the leadership of the SED party, and later the GDR Government.

[40] Between 1949 and 1963, Chancellor Konrad Adenauer, a conservative Christian Democrat, oversaw the reconstruction of West Germany/FRG, under the slogan '[establishing] a social market economy'. With US support (the Marshall Plan) and huge amounts of foreign capital, the FRG became one of the most developed capitalist economies, playing a key role in the founding of the European Community (EC).

[41] With the victory of the Social Democratic Party (SPD) in the 1969 elections, the government of Chancellor Willy Brandt launched a policy of rapprochement toward Eastern Europe and the German Democratic Republic. In 1970 the first formal talks between the FRG and the GDR began, and in 1971 the occupying powers agreed to free access of FRG citizens to the GDR. A Basic Treaty of bilateral relations was signed by both Germanies in 1973; in September they were admitted to the United Nations.

[42] In the 1970s, the number of power stations producing nuclear energy increased. In response to this, a strong environmental movement was formed, with a network of hundreds of grassroots groups throughout the country.

[43] In 1974, after the discovery that his private secretary was an East German spy, Brandt resigned as Chancellor and was succeeded by Helmut Schmidt. The modernization of Soviet medium-range missiles in East Germany, and the December 1979 NATO decision to do the same with its arsenal in West Germany, gave a strong impetus to the anti-nuclear movement in both states, with massive protests in the FRG.

[44] In 1982, the SPD had to leave power when the Liberal Party withdrew from the government alliance after 13 years. It was succeeded by the liberal-conservative alliance (CDU/CSU, FDP) led by Chancellor Helmut Kohl (CDU).

[45] In mid-1989, Hungary liberalized regulations regarding transit across the border with Austria. Within a few weeks, some 350,000 Germans from the GDR had emigrated to the FRG. Street demonstrations demanding change brought on a crisis in the GDR. In August, Honecker resigned and was replaced by Egon Krenz. On November 9, the GDR opened up its borders and the Berlin Wall fell. Kohl immediately proposed the creation of a confederation of East and West Germany.

[46] In February 1990, the East German Government agreed to German unification and the withdrawal of all foreign troops from its territory. The fusion of the two states was officially recognized in August 1990, as the Federal Republic of Germany. Political union was made possible when the USSR accepted the East German entry into NATO. The only important difference between the two Germanies over the next two years was the East's preservation of a more liberal abortion law.

[47] In the first parliamentary elections of the new Federal Republic, in December 1990, the governing coalition of Social Christians and Liberals obtained 54 per cent of the vote and stayed in power. From 1991, the extreme right made important gains at a local level, like in Bremen, where they increased their share of the vote by 7 per cent.. During 1992, there were 2,280 attacks on foreigners and Jewish monuments, which left 17 people dead. After one incident which caused the death of a Turkish woman and two children, the Government outlawed three neo-Nazi organizations.

[48] Throughout the following year, the closure of most of the industry in the east of the country and economic recession - the worst since 1945 - caused a constant increase in unemployment. In May 1994, the conservative, Roman Herzog, backed by Kohl, was designated president of Germany by a special electoral assembly, after defeating the Social Democrat Johannes Rau. In the second half of the year, a cycle of economic expansion began, which allowed a level of 2.8 per cent growth to be reached during the 1994 financial year. Kohl triumphed again in the October general elections, although his majority fell to only 10 seats of the 672 in play.

[49] In 1995, the constant weakening of the FDP in various local elections prompted the resignation of Foreign Minister Klaus Kinkel. On the social front, Parliament adopted a new law which, despite again permitting abortion during the first 12 weeks of pregnancy, was more restrictive than the one annulled in 1993 for being unconstitutional.

[50] The discontent of many foreigners resident in Germany led to the formation of the Democratic Party of Germany, which stood for greater access to the electoral role and citizenship - often restricted to people of German origin - for the children of immigrants.

[51] In 1996, five years after unification and three years after the frontiers fell for workers of the European Union, unemployment stood at around 10.6 per cent on a national level, and up to 16 per cent in the states of the former East Germany. Five million people were out of work.

[52] Racism and anti-Semitism continued to be issues for the Kohl administration. In October 1997, a television broadcast showed an army battalion giving Nazi salutes and shouting anti-Semitic and anti-US slogans. Amnesty International indicated that police abuse to foreigners could not be seen as isolated cases, due to the systematic repetition of the offences.

[53] In early 1998, the Deutsche Bank paid back Jewish organizations the money made from the sale of gold suspected to have been robbed from the Jews by the Nazis. At the same time, a Swiss foundation began to provide economic compensation - although with 'token' sums of money - to Roma (gypsy) residents in Germany who had survived the Nazi holocaust.

[54] The September 1998 elections delivered an overwhelming victory for the Social Democrats and Gerhard Schröder was named Federal Chancellor. The PSD leader Oskar Lafontaine headed the Finance ministry. The former Communists of former East Germany were well supported, winning 36 seats in the Federal Parliament.

[55] In March of the following year, Lafontaine resigned from both posts following discrepancies with the political line of the head of government, in what became a party crisis. A series of defeats in the 1999 local elections put the squeeze on the SPD and it seemed the public had returned to the Christian Democrats.

[56] But the CDU was hit by a corruption scandal in November 1999. Initially, former chancellor Kohl was accused of authorising the sale of armored vehicles to countries at war without parliament knowing, but only a few weeks later it was announced that he had accepted a series of illegal contributions from private donors. Kohl stood down as honorary president of the CDU and was found guilty of handling illegal funds.

[57] In July 2000 talk of "two-speed" Europe emerged again, with Germany and France pressing for closer integration. ∎

Ghana

Ghana

Population: 19,678,000 (1999)
Area: 238,540 SQ KM
Capital: Accra
Currency: New cedi
Language: English

In about 1300, the Akans or Ashantis moved into Ghana from the north. The powerful and organized Fanti State of Denkyira was already established on the coast so the Akans settled in the inland jungles. Here, they founded a series of small cities that paid tribute to the coastal nation.

2   In the 15th century the Ashantis began to trade in the markets of Begho, on the border of present-day Côte d'Ivoire. They traded slaves and gold for fabrics and other goods from North Africa and further afield. An ornate pitcher that had once belonged to Richard II, King of England between 1367 and 1400, was discovered in the treasure of a Kumasi ruler.

3   In the 17th century, new waves of migration threatened the existence of the small jungle states. This crisis forced the Akans to unite in confronting the Doma invaders. The Doma were defeated.

4   With the decline of the Songhai, the Moroccan incursions and the beginning of the Fulah expansion, the North African trade network collapsed with serious repercussions for the inland economy. The Ashanti were also deprived of access to the coastal trading posts as these were in Denkyira Territory. Instead of paying taxes, they declared war on the Denkyira and defeated them. They then organized a centralized state, ruled by the 'Ashantihene' (leader of the Ashanti nation) endowed with a powerful army. By 1700, the Ashanti had control of the slave trade to the coast and the flow of European goods to the interior.

5   When the British stopped trading in slaves, the Ashanti reacted by attempting to seize the shoreline from the Fanti, who had retained a significant share of the coastal trade. English backing of the Fanti led to the Anglo-Ashanti wars, 1806-1816, 1825-28 and 1874. After the last war, the British turned the Fanti territory into a colony.

In 1895 under the pretext of defending the region from Samori Turé (see Guinea) they also proclaimed a protectorate over the northern territories.

6   While the coastal and northern regions were under British rule, the central region belonged to the autonomous Ashanti nation. It did not take long for friction to build up and another Anglo-Ashanti war broke out in 1896. The capital, Kumasi, was razed by cannon fire, and the ruler was deposed and exiled. The Ashanti were then told that they owed 50,000 ounces of gold in compensation for 'war

damages'. An attempt to collect the debt coupled with the British Governor's culturally insensitive desire to sit on the gold throne, led to a general rebellion four years later. This was immediately put down with a great loss of lives. In 1902 the Ashanti state was formally annexed to the Gold Coast Colony.

7   During the first half of the 20th century, a strong nationalist current developed in spite of the ethnic and religious differences within Ghana. Economic opposition to the British also grew at this time both in the north, where the traditional structures had remained intact, and in the south, where a Westernized middle class and a relatively significant working class had developed.

8   Popular pressure on the colonial administration led to political concessions. In 1946, London admitted a few Africans into the colonial administration and in 1949 Kwame Nkrumah formed the Convention People's Party (CCP) to campaign for greater reform.

9   Nkrumah is known as one of the founding fathers of Pan-Africanism and African nationalism. He established a solid rural and urban party structure and, in 1952, he became Prime Minister of the colony. In his inaugural speech, he proclaimed himself a 'socialist, Marxist and Christian', promising to fight against imperialism.

10   Nkrumah represented Ghana at the Bandung Conference in 1955. This conference marked the birth of the Movement of Non-Aligned Countries, and together with Tito, Nasser, Nehru and Sukarno, Nkrumah played an important part. In 1957 he achieved a major victory and Ghana became the first country in West Africa to gain independence. Known as Osagyefo (redeemer), Nkrumah enthusiastically embraced the Pan-African anti-colonialism. He initiated a series of internal changes based on industrialization, agrarian reform and socialist education.

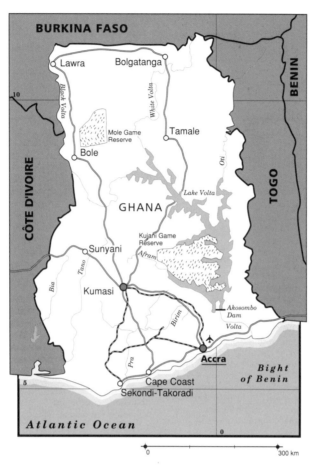

WORKERS

% OF LABOUR FORCE   **1998**

■ FEMALE: 51%   ■ MALE: 49%

1990

■ SERVICES: 27.7%
■ INDUSTRY: 13.0%
■ AGRICULTURE: 59.3%

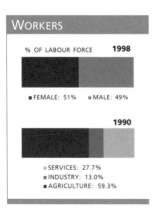

LAND USE

DEFORESTATION: 1.3% annual (1990/95)
IRRIGATED: 0.2% of arable (1993)

1993

■ FOREST & WOODLAND: 33.1%
■ ARABLE: 11.7%
■ OTHER: 55.2%

PUBLIC EXPENDITURE

DEFENCE EXPENDITURE (% of goverment exp.)   **2.4%** (1997)

MILITARY EXPENDITURE (% of health & education)   **12%** (1990/91)

11 These new measures, however, did not suit everybody. Traditional and neo-colonial interests conspired against the Government and Nkrumah was overthrown. The coup leaders drew up a parliamentary constitution and in 1969 held elections for a civilian government. The CPP was not allowed to participate. Nkrumah died in exile in Bucharest in 1972.

12 Also in 1969, Colonel Ignatius Acheampong led a coup replacing the Government of Dr Kofi Busia. Acheampong dropped the ambitious industrialization and development plans, substituting an essentially agrarian policy which favored the owners of large cocoa plantations.

13 Acheampong survived eight coup attempts in five years, but his economic policy was not as successful. In 1977, Ghana had an inflation rate of 36 per cent, an oppressive foreign debt, a devalued currency and hundreds of imprisoned intellectuals and students, condemned for questioning government policy.

14 In July 1977, the so-called revolt of the middle class occurred. The period of social unrest came to a head in July 1978 and Acheampong resigned. A new military regime was established, lead by General William Frederick Akuffo. The opposition claimed this was simply a continuation of the previous government under a different figurehead. On June 4 1979, a coup led by Lt Jerry Rawlings overthrew Akuffo and called fresh elections. The People's National Party, which included Nkrumah's followers, won a large majority. A transitional government took power promising an eventual return to a constitutional system.

15 On October 1 1979, with the acquiescence of the Revolutionary Council of the Armed Forces, Hilla Limann, a PNP leader, took over the presidency. Limann abandoned many of Nkrumah's nationalistic economic policies, replacing them with International Monetary Fund policies, in an attempt to reduce the fiscal deficit. To attract foreign investors and overcome the sharp fall in cocoa export revenues, the Ghanaian Government drastically reduced all imports, including food. As a result, food prices escalated wildly while the purchasing power of workers fell drastically. This inevitably led to a series of strikes in 1980 and 1981.

16 Support for Rawlings remained high among the poor. He accused the Government of being indecisive and preoccupied with foreign capital. Inflation exceeded 140 per cent and the unemployment rate was more than 25 per cent. This created an unstable situation which culminated in a further coup led by Rawlings on January 1 1982.

17 The first concern of the new group of officers was to launch a campaign against corruption in the public sector. They committed themselves to nothing short of a revolution for social justice in the country. Within a few months they were able to increase the amount of taxes collected, and greatly reduce cocoa smuggling (*kalabule*) to neighboring countries. People's Courts were set up to pass judgement on irregularities committed by the authorities of the previous government.

18 To deal with the economic crisis it was necessary to straighten out economic policy, and look for sources of foreign capital. Rawlings had already expressed his willingness to carry out an austerity program dictated by the IMF. He intensified relations with them in 1983, and generous loans were granted to Ghana on the basis that IMF prescriptions would be followed religiously and that Ghana would serve as a model for other countries in the region.

19 To increase national income and bring contraband under control Ghana devalued its currency (the *cedi*). This went from 2.74 per $1 in 1982, to 183 per $1 in 1988. Taxes were increased, subsidies were removed, the Government salaries budget was reduced, financing for inefficient private enterprises was eliminated and the printing of currency was virtually suspended.

20 However there were some positive results. Inflation fell from 200 to 25 per cent, the banking system improved and better prices were obtained for cocoa producers.

21 By applying this economic policy Ghana obtained loans on extremely generous. The major drawback of this scheme was that Ghana's finances were under rigid IMF control. Ghana's foreign debt approached $4 billion and the servicing of the debt used up two-thirds of the country's export earnings.

22 The social cost of this readjustment program was high. Consumer prices rose by some 30 per cent between 1983 and 1987; 45,000 public employees have lived under the constant threat of losing their jobs and there was a general loss of earning power leading to an increase in hunger, infant mortality and illiteracy.

23 In 1900 there were only 8 urban centers in the whole of the country, but by 1984 the number had risen to 180. In the recent years there has been a

PROFILE

ENVIRONMENT

The southern region is covered with dense rainforest, partially cleared to plant cocoa, coffee, banana and oil palm trees. Wide savannahs extend to the north. The rest of the territory is low-lying, with a few high points near the border with Togo. The Volta, Ghana's main river, has an artificial lake formed by the Akosombo dam. The climate is tropical, with summer rains. The subsoil is rich in gold, diamonds, manganese and bauxite. Desertification in the northwest and deforestation are the main environmental problems.

SOCIETY

Peoples: Ghanaians come from six main ethnic groups the Akan (Ashanti and Fanti), 44 per cent, located in the mid southern part of the country; the Ewe, 13 per cent, and Ga-Adangbe, 8 per cent, on both sides of the Volta in southern and southeastern Ghana; the Mole-Dagbane,16 per cent, in the northern savannahs; the Guan, 4 per cent, and the Gurma, 3 per cent, in the valleys and plateaus of the northeastern territory.
Religions: 50 per cent Christian, 32 per cent traditional religions, 13 per cent Muslim.
Languages: English (official); Ga is the main native language, Fanti, Haussa, Fantéewe, Gaadanhe, Akan, Dagbandim and Mampusi are also spoken.
Political Parties: Progressive Alliance, coalition made up of the National Democratic Conference (NDC); the National Convention Party (NCP); and the Every Ghanaian Living Everywhere (EGLE); People's National Convention; National Independence Party (NIP); New Patriotic Party (NPP); People's Heritage Party (PHP).
Social Organizations: Ghana Trade Union Congress.

THE STATE

Official Name: Republic of Ghana.
Administrative divisions: 10 regions, subdivided into 110 districts.
Capital: Accra 1,560,000 people (est 1995).
Other cities: Kumasi 600,000 people; Tamale 265,000 people.
Government: Jerry Rawlings, President since 1981, re-elected in 1996. Legislature: Parliament (single-chamber), with 200 members elected by direct popular vote for 4-year terms.
National Holiday: March 6, independence (1957).
Armed Forces: 7,000.
Other: People's Militia 5,000.

LITERACY
1995
64%

EXTERNAL DEBT
1998
Per capita
US$ 359

FOREIGN TRADE
Millions US$ 1998
IMPORTS
2,732
EXPORTS
2,004

migration towards the major cities, resulting in the creation of shantytowns with no drinking water or sanitation. In the poorest quarters of Takoradi there were only 16 public toilets per 3,250 people. If current rates of rural exodus continue, by the year 2020 over half the population of Ghana will be living in urban centers.

24   The economic upheaval had environmental costs as well. Tropical forest used to cover 34 per cent of the country's surface. This forest is now only a quarter of its original size; and 42 per cent of the area which is officially considered 'forest', is in fact covered with timber plantations, secondary vegetation, or immature trees. For the people who live in the country, and for most of those who live in the cities, forest plants constitute the basis of their traditional medicine. 75 per cent of the population rely on bush meat for their basic source of protein and forests also provide firewood, a basic household necessity.

25   All of these activities are ignored by official plans, which see the forest merely as a source of timber for export. In Ghana at present some 70,000 people are employed in the timber industry.

26   A National Forestry Administration Program (NFAP) was established, supported by international bodies like USAID, the FAO and countries such as Canada and the UK. Such programs however lay the blame for deforestation, desertification and soil degradation on the poor population and its search for new areas of farmland. In this thinking the very people who are the victims of an economic model which encourages exports at any price are held responsible for environmental degradation.

27   Ghana considerably increased its production of cocoa, gold, wood and bauxite, but the fall in the world market price of cocoa generated a loss of $200 million, and many industries were forced to close down. In meetings at the Paris Club in January and February of 1989, further loans of $900 million were granted.

28   In 1990 in, spite of monetary infusions, the hopes of growth collapsed. The GDP growth fell from 6.1 to 2.7 per cent. Inflation at 25 per cent in 1989, went up to 37 per cent. The current account deficit almost doubled and earnings for exports were lower than in 1988. Between 1988 and 1989, around 120 industries closed down because their products could not compete with cheaper and higher-quality goods from China, South Korea, and Taiwan.

29   In December 1991, the World Bank announced that Ghana would receive two more loans, totalling $155 million, for the Government to reform the financial system and improve the rural road network.

30   The Rawlings Government initiated a democratization program and a devolution plan, favoring local administrations. In June 1991, an advisory assembly of 260 members was elected to draft a new constitution. The National Council for Women and Development, a body with ministerial status, won 10 seats and the Organization of Graduate Nurses and Midwives was also represented.

31   In December 1991, Amnesty International denounced the Ghanaian policy of silencing or intimidating its opponents. In view of such serious and constant human rights violations, the Ghana Committee for Human and Popular Rights was created in January 1992, the first such organization in the country.

32   In that year, a new constitution was approved and elections were held. Rawlings took 58.3 per cent of the vote in the November presidential elections and the three parties which supported him took 197 of the 200 seats in the December legislative elections.

33   In spite of alleged election irregularities, 80 countries and international organizations attended Rawlings' investiture in January 1993. This foreign support was attributed to the rigorous application of the IMF imposed structural adjustment plans in the previous decade and the prompt payment of servicing on the foreign debt, which represented some 35 per cent of export earnings.

34   In February 1994, confrontations over land ownership caused the death of more than a thousand people and the migration of 150,000. The Government declared a state of emergency and in June an agreement was reached to bring an end to the violence. The budget for that year had a surplus of $80 million, following two years of deficit. In May, demonstrations against the new value-added tax left five people dead. Economy Minister, Kwesi Botchwey, withdrew the new tax from the budget, and after 13 years in the post - coinciding with the implementation of the IMF plans - resigned from his job.

35   Despite the New Patriotic Party and the People's Convention trying to settle their differences and form an alliance to present a common electoral platform, Rawlings won the December 1996 elections with 57.2 per cent of the vote.

36   The country faced a serious drop in water level in the Akosombo dam, producing a severe energy crisis. In March 1998, the Ministry of Science and Technology said Ghana could not pay the initial investment needed to develop a possible nuclear energy-based project. The crisis was partly resolved with help from Côte d'Ivoire, which increased the amount of electricity supplied to Ghana from 20 to 35 megawatts per day.

37   The police harshly put down a student demonstration in August 1999. The students were protesting against an increase in fees and costs passed by the Government. Finally, the authorities decided to close the University of Ghana temporarily until the demonstrators could be calmed.

38   Vice President John Atta Mills stood as ruling party candidate in elections slated for the end of 2000. ■

STATISTICS

DEMOGRAPHY

Population: 19,678,000 (1999)
Annual growth: 3.0 % (1975/97)
Estimates for year 2015 (million): 29.8 (1999)
Annual growth to year 2015: 2.6 % (1997/2015)
Urban population: 36.8 % (1997)
Urban Growth: 4.3 % (1980/95)
Children per woman: 5.1 (1998)

HEALTH

Life expectancy at birth: 60 years (1998)
male: 58 years (1998)
female: 62 years (1998)
Maternal mortality: 210 per 100,000 live births (1990-98)
Infant mortality: 67 per 1,000 (1998)
Under-5 child mortality: 105 per 1,000 (1998)
Daily calorie supply: 2,560 per capita (1996)
4 doctors per 100,000 people (1993)
Safe water: 65 % (1990/98)

EDUCATION

Literacy: 64 % (1995)
male: 75 % (1995)
female: 53 % (1995)
School enrolment:
Primary total: 76 % (1990/96)
male: 83 % (1990/97)
female: 70 % (1990/97)
Secondary:
male: 45 % (1990/96)
female: 29 % (1990/96)
Tertiary: 1 % (1996)

COMMUNICATIONS

14 newspapers (1996), 238 radios (1997), 41 TV sets (1996) and 4 main telephone lines (1996) per 1,000 people

ECONOMY

Per capita, GNP: $ 390 (1998)
Annual growth, GNP: 4.6 % (1998)
Annual inflation: 28.6 % (1990/98)
Consumer price index: 214.8 (1998)
Currency: 2,314.1 new cedis = $ 1 (1998)
Cereal imports: 458,995 metric tons (1998)
Fertilizer use: 75 kg per ha (1997)
Exports: $ 2,004 million (1998)
Imports: $ 2,732 million (1998)
External debt: $ 6,884 million (1998); $ 359 per capita (1998)
Debt service: 28.4 % of exports (1998)
Development aid received: $ 493 million (1997); $ 32.2 per capita (1997); 7.30 % of GNP (1997)

ENERGY

Consumption: 383.0 Kgs of Oil equivalent per capita yearly (1997); 15.0 % imported (1997)

HDI (rank/value): 133/0.544 (1997)

Greece

Ellás

Population: 10,626,000 (1999)
Area: 131,990 SQ KM
Capital: Athens (Athínai)
Currency: Drachma
Language: Greek

B etween 5,000 and 3,000 BC, the Greek peninsula was inhabited by maritime peoples from Asia. In Thessaly, central Greece and Crete traces have been found of previous inhabitants, nomadic and agricultural peoples. From the second millennium BC the Achaeans, an Indo-European people, started to expand throughout the peninsula.

2 The Achaeans founded Mycenae, Tyrins and Argos, later conquering Athens and the eastern Peloponnese, invading Crete and raiding Troy. They were warriors, with an economy based on agriculture and cattle-breeding. The hierarchical social organization had kings, nobles, and warriors dominating farmers, artisans and peasants.

3 By the first millennium BC, Mycenian civilization had succumbed to Dorian invasions. The Dorians used iron weapons, unknown to the Achaeans, and they soon mixed with the subject population, bringing linguistic unity to the region.

4 The peninsula's topography favored the appearance of city-states (*polis*), ruled by a king or tyrant, supported by the military aristocracy. The peasants were forced to pay tributes in kind, and if they could not produce sufficient crops they became serfs or their whole family was sold into slavery.

5 Despite the social differentiation, the Greeks had an original concept of the human being. All previous civilizations had seen humans as a mere instruments of the will of the gods or the monarchs, whereas in Greek philosophy they acquired the value of individuals. The concept of a citizen, as an individual who belongs to the polis regardless of

nobility, was one Greek culture's main contributions to Western civilization.

6 The city states alternately established alliances and fought each other. However, Hellenic groups started to feel they belonged to a common nationality bound by factors like the Olympic games, and a common religion and language.

7 In the 8th century BC most city-states went through crises, due to the decline in power of the monarchs (who were progressively replaced by magistrates appointed by the nobility), to the lack of fertile soil, and to demographic growth. This produced great social tension spurring the Greeks to colonize the Mediterranean, creating active trade routes and expanding the use

of Greek as the language of commerce.

8 Around 760 BC the Greeks established colonies in southern Italy, in the bay of Naples and in Sicily. The Phoenicians and the Etruscans prevented them from ruling the whole of Sicily and the south of Italy, but their culture was deeply influential in later developments on the Italian peninsula.

9 When colonization started, the social and political structure of the polis underwent transformations. Merchants, wealthy as a result of maritime expansion, were not ready to leave government to the nobility. They joined the peasants in pressing for political participation. Between the 7th and 6th centuries BC, Athens

one of the most prosperous cities in the peninsula started a process of political transformations which led to the gradual democratization of its governmental structures. In 594 BC a reformer called Solon took the first steps in this direction with the establishment of written law, a court of justice and an assembly of 400 members, elected from among the wealthy, which was in charge of legislating on city matters.

10 Sparta, the other great city-state in the region, evolved in a completely different way. It consolidated an oligarchic state, with a strict social and political structure. Spartan society was completely militarized because of the central importance of the army, which had been a determining factor in expansion and annexation of neighboring territories.

11 In 540 BC the Persians started advancing on Asia Minor, conquering some Greek cities. These cities revolted, backed first by Athens and then by Sparta, resulting in several wars until the Persians were defeated around 449 BC. These wars served to consolidate Athenian power in the region, exerting its political and economic influence over the other city-states through the League of Delos.

12 The Athenian triremes (galleys) played a key role in the wars against the Persians. The oarsmen, who belonged to the lowest strata of Athenian society, became an indispensable tool in the defence of Athens, and were thus in a position to demand improvements in their living conditions and increased political rights. In 508 BC, after a period when the Athenian oligarchy had succeeded in recovering its political power, a reformer called Cleisthenes raised the number of assembly members to 500, turning this body into the main governmental structure. Participation in the Assembly was open to all free citizens in the polis. However, these constituted a minority of the population; Athenian prosperity was actually based on the exploitation of huge numbers of slaves. Athenian society of this period is therefore referred to as a 'slave holding democracy' by historians.

13 In 446 BC the *archon* or governor of Athens, Pericles, agreed the Thirty Years' Peace with Sparta, recognizing each city's areas of

WORKERS

1997
UNEMPLOYMENT: 9.6%

% OF LABOUR FORCE **1998**

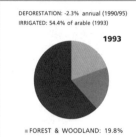

■ FEMALE: 37% ■ MALE: 63%

1990

■ SERVICES: 49.7%
■ INDUSTRY: 27.3%
■ AGRICULTURE: 23.0%

LAND USE

DEFORESTATION: -2.3% annual (1990/95)
IRRIGATED: 54.4% of arable (1993)

1993

■ FOREST & WOODLAND: 19.8%
■ ARABLE: 918.3%
■ OTHER: 61.9%

PUBLIC EXPENDITURE

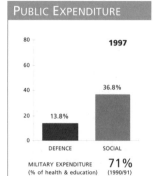

80
1997
60
36.8%
40
20
13.8%
0
DEFENCE   SOCIAL

MILITARY EXPENDITURE **71%**
(% of health & education) (1990/91)

influence in the Athenian League and the League of the Peloponnese.

14 Under Pericles' rule, Athens became the trading, political, and cultural centre of the region. The domination of maritime trade and the prosperity this created enabled Pericles to start new democratic reforms. This was the period of scholars such as Anaxagoras, of dramatists such as Sophocles, Aeschylus, Euripides, Aristophanes, and of sculptors like Phidias. The Greeks achieved great scientific knowledge, much of which has now been altered, particularly in the fields of medicine or astronomy, but their contributions to geometry and mathematics are still indispensable for most of present-day science.

15 A long period of continuous struggles over who should control the region ensued between the Spartans and Athenians. This mutual attrition enabled the Macedonians to conquer this domain under the rule of Philip II, 359-336 BC. Philip's son, Alexander the Great, 336-323 BC, continued to spread Hellenic influence over the north of Africa and the Arabian Peninsula, through Mesopotamia, and as far as India. This empire, built over 11 years, contributed to the dissemination of Greek culture in the East. During the years of conquest, many trading cities were founded. Alexander promoted the fusion of Greek culture with that of the conquered peoples, giving rise to what is known as Hellenism. Upon his death, the Macedonian Empire collapsed and wars and rebellions continued to shake the peninsula.

16 These internal disputes resulted in a decline in the Greek civilization, leading to devastation and impoverishment which enabled the Romans to move in. The Macedonian wars lasted from 215 to 168 BC, ending with the Romans establishing their rule over Greece by 146 BC.

17 Under the Romans, Greece was acquainted with Christianity in the 3rd century, and it became a more rural society which was subjected to several invasions. From 395 to 1204, it belonged to the Eastern Empire, whose domination ended with the formation of the Eastern Roman Empire and the region's division into feudal possessions. In 1054, as a consequence of the Schism of the Roman Church, Greek Christians pledged obedience to the Orthodox Church in Constantinople.

18 The Turks invaded and conquered in 1460, dividing Greece into six provinces which were forced to pay taxes. The Turks kept an army of occupation in the country for 400 years. External attempts to expel the Turks, in particular incursions led by Venice - eager to acquire this strategic territory for trade with the East - and internal revolts all failed. The Peace of Passarowitz incorporated Greece into the Ottoman Empire in 1718.

19 In 1821 a Greek uprising succeeded in freeing Tripolitza, and a national assembly drafted a constitution, declaring independence. In 1825 the attempt ended in a bloodbath when the Turks, aided by Egypt, regained control of the city.

20 In 1827 Russia, France and Britain, eager to keep the Turks away from their borders, signed the Treaty of London, which demanded Greek autonomy. The Turks refused it, and that year the allied fleet defeated the Turkish-Egyptian navy. In 1830, the London Convention declared the total independence of Greece, although the country had to sacrifice the region of Thessaly.

21 In later years the European powers fought to control the peninsula, intervening in its domestic affairs and supporting kings who complied with their interests. Otto of Bavaria, 1831-1862, who favored the Russians, was followed by George I, 1864-1913, who was backed by the British.

22 In 1910, a coup led by Eleutherios Vinizelos resulted in the enactment of a constitution (1911) establishing a parliamentary monarchy. Throughout the two World Wars and the interwar years, subsequent military coups brought sympathizers of each side alternately to power.

23 Once the German occupation was ended in 1944, an important part of the country remained under the control of communist guerrillas. They were led by Markos Vafiades, and had been crucial in resisting the Nazis. The British and Americans supported the Government in repressing the guerrillas until they were totally destroyed in 1949.

24 Greece remained under American influence, becoming a member of the Council of Europe in 1949 and of NATO in 1951. In the 1956 elections women voted for the first time. After the War, Greece experienced political instability.

25 In April 1967, a group of colonels staged a coup. Martial Law was enforced, the Constitution was suspended and democratic movements harshly repressed. Socialist leader Andreas Papandreou was sentenced to nine years' imprisonment. In December the King attempted to oust the military junta, but he failed and fled to Rome. The military appointed General Zoitakis president, and Papadopoulos Prime Minister.

26 The Colonels' regime, as it was known, was supported by the United States and by tycoons such as Onassis and Niarchos. Attempts were made to mask the dictatorship behind a unicameral Parliament in 1968, but in reality the military junta ruled by decree.

27 Between 1973 and 1974 the military government grew weaker. In November, student demonstrations at the Polytechnic University of Athens were harshly repressed, leaving hundreds of casualties, and attracting international condemnation.

PROFILE

ENVIRONMENT

Located at the southeastern end of the Balkan peninsula, in the eastern Mediterranean, the country consists of a continental territory between the Aegean Sea and the Ionian Sea and numerous islands, including the island of Rhodes. Greece is a mountainous country, with a Mediterranean climate of hot, dry summers. It is essentially an agricultural country, producing wine and olives. Goats and sheep are raised in the mountains, where the soil is unfit for agriculture.

SOCIETY

Peoples: Most people are of Greek origin and there is a small Turkish minority (1 per cent).
Religions: Greek Orthodox.
Languages: Greek.
Political Parties: New Democracy; Pan-Hellenic Socialist Movement (PASOK); Communist Party; Political Spring; Progressive Left Coalition.
Social Movements: The General Confederation of Greek Workers.

THE STATE

Official Name: Helleniké Demokratía.
Administrative divisions: 10 regions divided into 51 administrative units.
Capital: Athens/Piraeus 3,150,000 (est 1995).
Other cities: Thessaloniki 384,000 people; Patras 153,000 people (1991).
Government: Kostis Stephanoupoulos, President since March 1995. Kostas Simitis, Prime Minister since January, 1996.
National Holiday: March 25 (Independence)
Armed Forces: 159,300 (1994).
Other: Gendarmerie: 26,500; Coast Guard and customs: 4,000.

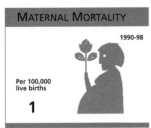

MATERNAL MORTALITY

1990-98

Per 100,000 live births

1

LITERACY

1995

96%

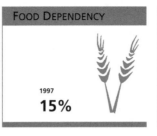

FOOD DEPENDENCY

1997

15%

FOREIGN TRADE

Millions US$ 1997

IMPORTS

28,763

EXPORTS

18,837

28   In July 1974, the junta promoted a coup in Cyprus by collaborating with the Cypriot National Guard. The coup succeeded in deposing president Archbishop Vaneziz Makarios, who was forced into exile in London. A minister in favor of Greek annexation was appointed. The Turkish army immediately invaded Cyprus, allegedly defending the Turkish minority in the country. The Greek military government became even more discredited and internationally condemned, and they relinquished power immediately at the prospect of war with Turkey.

29   In that month, former conservative Prime Minister Konstantin Karamanlis returned from exile and took over the government. In the 1974 elections his party won a parliamentary majority and a later referendum abolished the monarchy. In June 1975, Parliament adopted a new constitution and Konstantinos Tsatsos, a Karamanlis partisan, was elected first president of the republic.

30   From 1974 Greece decided not to take part in NATO military exercises after conflict with Turkey, another member of the Organization.

31   In the 1981 parliamentary elections, Pasok (Pan-Hellenic Socialist Movement) led by Papandreou gained an absolute majority, and the first socialist government in the history of Greece took office. The country also became the 10th member of the European Economic Community (EEC).

32   The socialist government approached Third World countries, in particular the Arab nations, recognized the PLO and led a worldwide campaign in favor of handing back works of art that had been stolen during colonial domination.

33   In 1983, salaries were frozen, provoking a wave of protests and strikes. Trade unions were granted greater participation in the public sector, but their right to strike was curtailed.

34   The 1983 census revealed that women constituted one-third of the economically active population. Most of them worked in the service sector and their pay was lower than that of their male counterparts. Peasant women accounted for 40

per cent of the active female population, not counting the 400,000 women who worked unpaid on family plots.

35   In the 1984 elections the PASOK won again, by an even greater margin than it had held in 1981. The 1986 constitutional amendment gave more power to the parliament at the expense of the President. Successive austerity plans and salary freezes fuelled new protests and strikes.

36   In November 1988, details of embezzlement in the Bank of Crete, involving several government members were disclosed. This scandal caused several ministerial crises. In June of the following year, the Greek Left and the Communist Party formed the Left Alliance.

37   In the 1989 elections PASOK lost its majority, and the conservative New Democracy party received a large part of the vote. As there was no adequate parliamentary majority and no agreement to form a government, the presidency went to the leader of the left-wing coalition, the communist Charilaos Florakis. He formed a temporary government with New Democracy, aiming to investigate the financial scandals.

38   The results of the November 1989 elections subsequent did not give any of the parties a significant majority. This led to coalition government.

39   Between 1983 and 1989, Greece and the United States signed various co-operation agreements including the maintenance of four US military bases in the country, in return for economic and military assistance. This also guaranteed US diplomatic support for Greece in its disputes with Turkey, particularly over Cyprus.

40   In January 1990, Washington and Athens publicized a new agreement, closing two military bases, as part of the US plan to reduce its military presence in the region.

41   On March 7, a law was passed on collective work agreements for the private sector, public companies and services. The new law established free negotiations between workers and bosses, putting an end to 50 years of State intervention, and including norms for the organization of the company and union committees, as

well as worker participation in company decisions.

42   Following Karamanlis' triumph in the April presidential elections, a new government was formed headed by the conservative Constantinos Mitsotakis. In 1991, Mitsotakis promoted public spending cuts, price liberalization and privatizations.

43   The social cost of these measures contributed to the defeat of the conservative government in the 1993 legislative elections. On October 12, Papandreou's PASOK gained the support of 47 per cent of the voters - compared with the 40 per cent of New Democracy - and the absolute majority in Parliament.

44   The public debt and pressures from the European Union for a more 'rigorous' economic policy complicated Papandreou's leadership. In the 1994 European elections PASOK and above all New Democracy lost votes to the smaller parties like Political Spring, the Communist Party and the Progressive Left Coalition.

45   In 1995, amidst permanent rumors of Papandreou's retirement on health grounds and fresh accusations of the misappropriation of public funds against him, Finance Minister Alexandros Papadopoulos implemented unpopular fiscal reforms and launched a policy of 'strict (budgetary) rigour'.

46   Ill, and increasingly criticized even within his own party, Papandreou resigned from his post in January 1996 and was replaced by his former industry minister, Konstantinos Simitis. The veteran leader of Greek Socialism died in June. In September, the Socialist Party, led by the new Prime Minister, won the legislative elections with 41.5 per cent of the vote.

47   The tensions between Greece and Turkey continued, partly as a consequence of the situation in Cyprus. This did not prevent both countries participating in a regional meeting in Athens, along with the rest of the Balkan governments. Simitis said the idea of the summit was to attack the image of 'disorder' which prevented the region from integrating with the rest of Europe.

48   In January 1998, backing its pro-regional integration stance, Athens decided to abolish a discriminatory constitutional article

allowing citizenship to be stripped from 'non-ethnic Greeks' wanting to leave the country. This article had been used mainly against the Muslim minority, mostly of Turkish origin. Some 60,000 people had lost their Greek nationality since this much-criticized measure was imposed under the dictatorship of the colonels.

49   A series of demonstrations and bomb attacks were timed to coincide with a visit by US President Bill Clinton in November 1999. Tension with Washington had increased in preceding months due to US leadership of the bombing in Yugoslavia. Two earthquakes a few weeks apart in 1999, one in Turkey and one in Greece brought solidarity between the two countries, with both sending medical aid and supplies to their neighbor. In November of this year, under the auspices of the UN, the two countries backed a joint resolution for the first time proposing the creation of an emergency aid unit. This rapprochement was also reflected in Greece lifting its veto on Turkish entry to the European Union.

50   In December that year, Athens and Skopje signed a military co-operation treaty, thus bringing years of diplomatic confrontations to a close. Rapprochement with Turkey reached new heights, especially when Turkish Foreign Minister, Ismail Cem, called for the return of works of art taken from the Parthenon and still on exhibition today in the British Museum.

51   Greece requested entry into the Euro zone, the EU single currency, in March 2000.

52   The closest elections in the country's history, in April, gave PASOK the victory over the conservatives led by Costas Caramanlis. Greek electoral laws favor the winner, so despite the 'technical draw', Prime Minister Kostas Simitis has 30 more seats than Caramanlis' defeated New Democracy. But the outcome was a personal defeat for Simitis, who had brought forward the election in the hope of strengthening his mandate, thinking that he would have greater public support given Greece's economic progress.

53   In June 2000 the British defence attache was shot in Athens, allegedly by the terrorist 'November 17' group. ■

Grenada

Grenada

Population: 85,000 (1999)
Area: 340 SQ KM
Capital: St George's
Currency: EC dollar
Language: English

The Carib Indians inhabited Grenada when Christopher Columbus arrived, around 1498, and named the island 'Concepción'. This European visit did not disrupt the island's peace but two centuries later in 1650 the governor of the French possession of Martinique, Du Parquet, decided to occupy the island. By 1674, France had established control over Grenada, despite fierce resistance from the Caribs.

[2] In 1753, French settlers from Martinique had around a 100 sugar mills and 12,000 slaves on Grenada. The indigenous population had been exterminated.

[3] The British took control of the island towards the end of the 18th century and cultivated cocoa, cotton and nutmeg, using slave labor. In 1788 there were 24,000 slaves, a number which remained stable until the abolition of slavery in the following century.

[4] The severe living conditions of workers resulted in the creation of the first union in the mid-20th century, the Grenada Manual and Metal Workers Union. In 1951, a strike broke out and the labor struggle won considerable wage increases. Eric Matthew Gairy, a young adventurer who had lived away from the island most of his life, formed the first local political party, the Grenada United Labor Party (GULP) which favored independence. In 1951, GULP won a legislative election and Gairy became leader of the assembly.

[5] In 1958 Grenada joined the Federation of the British West Indies, which was dissolved in

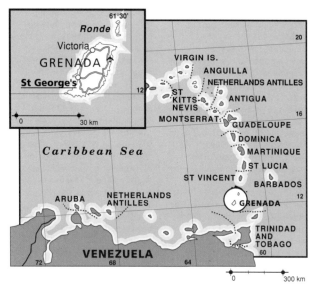

1962. The country became part of the Associated State of the British Antilles in 1967. That year, Gairy was appointed Prime Minister when his party won the August elections. Their main objective was total independence from Britain.

[6] GULP soon obtained semi-independence which gradually led to full independence. By that time, left-wing groups such as the New Jewel Movement (NJM) had appeared on the island, opposing separation from Britain. Though apparently paradoxical, many Grenadians considered that Gairy was seeking independence for his personal benefit, manipulating a politically unprepared population.

[7] In January 1974, an 'anti-independence' strike broke out to prevent Gairy from seizing power. After some weeks of total paralysis of the country 'Mongoose squads', similar to the Haitian Tonton-Macoutes appeared. They were on the Prime Minister's payroll and brutal repression was used to end the strike. Independence was proclaimed the following week.

[8] As feared, Gairy exploited power for his own personal benefit. He distributed government jobs among the members of his party, while promoting the paramilitary squad to the level of a 'Defence Force', making it the only military body on the island. The 'Mongoose Squad' received military training from Chilean advisers and

increased its numbers considerably by incorporating ex-inmates of St George's Prison.

[9] In the December 1976 election, the People's Alliance, made up of the NJM, the National Party of Grenada and the United Popular Party, gained new ground in Parliament, moving from one to six representatives in a total of 15 parliamentary seats. On March 13 1979, while Gairy was out of the country, the opposition carried out a bloodless coup and seized power. Thanks to widespread popular support, they were able to establish a provisional revolutionary government, under the leadership of Maurice Bishop, a lawyer.

[10] In four years, the People's Revolutionary Government stimulated the formation of grass-roots organizations, and they created a mixed economy, expanding the public sector through agro-industries and state farms. Private enterprise was encouraged making Grenada more compatible with global economic policy.

[11] The Government based its foreign policy on the principles of anti-imperialism and non-alignment. Special attention was given to the development of ties with the socialist world. Cuba agreed to collaborate in the construction of an international airport. The project was conceived as a way to stimulate tourism, which employed 25 per cent of the country's work force.

[12] Prime Minister Bishop faced constant pressure from the NJM's extreme left wing. This faction, led by deputy Prime Minister Bernard Coard. On October 10 1983, upon his return from a short state visit to Hungary, Czechoslovakia and Cuba, Bishop was placed under house arrest, while General Hudson Austin, head of the army, seized power. Bishop was freed by a crowd of sympathizers, only to be shot dead by troops. A number of others were killed along with him, including his wife Jacqueline Creft - Minister of Education, the Foreign and Housing Ministers, two union leaders and 13 members of the crowd.

[13] The US then began to take definite steps towards military intervention, a move which had been decided upon and planned for over a year; troop-landing had been rehearsed in manoeuvres. Early in the morning of October 25 1983, 5,000 marines and Green Berets landed on the island. They were followed several hours later by a symbolic contingent of 300 police from six Caribbean countries; Antigua, Barbados, Dominica, Jamaica, St Lucia and St Vincent, who joined the farce of a 'multinational intervention for humanitarian reasons'.

[14] Resistance from the Grenadian militia and some Cuban technicians and workers, meant that the operation lasted much longer than expected. The US suffered combat casualties, and the press was barred from entering Grenada until all resistance had been eliminated. This made it impossible to verify how many civilians had been killed in attacks on a psychiatric hospital and other non-military targets.

[15] While strict US military control continued, Sir Paul Scoon, official British crown representative in Grenada, assumed the leadership of an interim government with the task of organizing an election within a period of 6 to 11 months. Under the discreet surveillance of the invaders, voting was held on December 3 1984 to elect the members of a unicameral parliament. In turn, the representatives appointed Herbert Blaize Prime Minister. Blaize led a coalition of parties

LAND USE

1993

- FOREST & WOODLAND: 8.8%
- ARABLE: 32.4%
- OTHER: 58.8%

that was presented to public opinion as the New National Party (NNP) and received support from the US.

[16] Neither NATO nor the OAS dared to condone the aggression. Twenty days later, Barbados was rewarded for its 'co-operation' in the invasion with a $18.5-million aid program.

[17] The new government reached a classic agreement with the International Monetary Fund including a reduction of the civil service, a wage-freeze and incentives to private enterprise.

[18] The System of Regional Security (SSR) permitting the Prime Minister to call on troops from neighboring Caribbean islands if Grenada was threatened was established by Blaize in December 1986, under the pretext that the trial of those involved in the 1983 coup was coming to an end. Bernard Coard, his wife Phyllis, and former army commander Hudson Austin were sentenced to death, along with 11 soldiers. Three others were tried, receiving prison sentences of 30 to 45 years.

[19] During his first years in government, Blaize achieved considerable economic growth, at between five and six per cent per year, basically from tourism. However, youth unemployment continued to increase, along with crime and drug addiction.

[20] Blaize died in 1989. He was replaced by Ben Jones of the National Party, who was backed by big business and the landowners. On March 13 1990 - the anniversary of the coup which overthre Eric Gairy in 1979 - the general elections were won by Nicholas Braithwaite, member of the NDC and interim head of government after the invasion, and warmly regarded by the United States.

[21] Studies carried out in 1994 revealed unemployment of 30 per cent and a marked pattern of emigration. The fall in international prices of bananas, coconuts, wood and nutmeg influenced this trend. Between March and April 1995, there were strikes in key sectors of the economy, like the hotels, and sugar and cocoa production.

[22] In the June 1995 general elections, the governing NDC was pushed out by Keith Mitchell, former mathematics professor at the Howard University in Washington and leader of the NNP. His victory was attributed to his promise to remove income tax, which had been revoked in 1986 and re-imposed by the NDC in 1994.

[23] Despite the agreement made between Indonesia and Grenada - the leading world nutmeg producer - in 1994, the international prices continued to tumble in 1995.

[24] In early 1996, the ruling NNP objected against the privatization process in the State electricity company alleging 'misuse of funds'.

[25] The Government announced income on cocoa sales had fallen due to a leading US buyer suspending its imports from Grenada.

[26] In May, Grenada signed an extradition and legal co-operation agreement with the United States. The treaties formed part of the campaign against drug-trafficking which Washington was implementing in the region.

[27] In March 1997, the Government rejected a request from the Grenada Conference of Churches to free the two men serving life sentences for the 1993 murder of former Prime Minister Maurice Bishop, his wife and a group of ministers and union leaders.

[28] In April, Grenada and Cuba re-established diplomatic relations, broken off during the invasion of Grenada by US troops in 1983. Prime Minister Keith Mitchell made an official visit to Cuba, during which he signed an economic co-operation agreement.

[29] Mitchell swore he had cleaned up his image, but barely seven weeks later his government collapsed as its members of parliament defected in the face of repeated accusations of governmental corruption from the United Labor Party. In the January 1999 elections, Mitchell's New National Party won all the 15 seats in Parliament.

[30] In November 1999, the First International Bank of Grenada signed an agreement with the Congolese (DR) rebel Ernest Wamba dia Wamba promising to lend a total of $16 million to his group, the Ugandan-backed Congolese Union for Democracy. ∎

PROFILE

ENVIRONMENT

Grenada is the southernmost Windward island of the Lesser Antilles. The island is almost entirely volcanic. Lake Grand Etang and Lake Antoine are extinct volcanic craters. The rainy, tropical, climate, tempered by sea winds, is fit for agriculture which constitutes the country's major source of income. It is famous for its spices, and is known as 'the Spice Island of the West'. The territory includes the islands of Carriacou (34 sq km) and Petite Martinique (2 sq km), which belong to the Grenadines.

SOCIETY

Peoples: Most are descended from African slaves (84 per cent), although there are a large number of mestizos (11 per cent) and European (0.7 per cent) and Indo-Pakistani (3 per cent) minorities.
Religions: Mainly Catholic (53.1 per cent); protestant (38.1 per cent); other (7.4 per cent).
Languages: English (official and predominant). A patois dialect derived from French, and another from English are also spoken.
Political Parties: The National Democratic Congress (NDC). The New National Party (NNP).Grenada United Labor Party (GULP). The Maurice Bishop Patriotic Movement.

THE STATE

Official Name: Grenada.
Administrative divisions: 7 zones.
Capital: St George's 4,361 people (1991).
Government: Queen Elizabeth II, Head of State; Daniel Williams has been the representative of the British Crown since 1996. Keith Mitchell, Prime Minister from June 1995. Legislature: the bicameral Parliament is made up of the 15-member Chamber of Deputies and the 13-member Senate. Deputies are elected by direct popular vote, while 7 of the senators are appointed by the governor, 3 by the prime minister and 3 by the leader of the opposition.
National holiday: February 7, Independence (1974).

STATISTICS

DEMOGRAPHY

Population: 85,000 (1999)
Annual growth: 0.1 % (1975/97)
Estimates for year 2015 (million): 0.1 (1999)
Annual growth to year 2015: 0.4 % (1997/2015)
Urban population: 36.6 % (1997)
Children per woman: 3.6 (1998)

HEALTH

Life expectancy at birth: 72 years (1998)
Maternal mortality: 0 per 100,000 live births (1990-98)
Infant mortality: 23 per 1,000 (1998)
Under-5 child mortality: 28 per 1,000 (1998)
Daily calorie supply: 2,731 per capita (1996)
50 doctors per 100,000 people (1993)

EDUCATION

Literacy: 96 % (1995)
School enrolment:
Primary total: 88 % (1990/96)

COMMUNICATIONS

561 radios (1997) and 243 main telephone lines (1996) per 1,000 people

ECONOMY

Per capita, GNP: $ 3,250 (1998)
Annual growth, GNP: 5.3 % (1998)
Consumer price index: 103.3 (1997)
Cereal imports: 28,184 metric tons (1998)
Food import dependency: 26 % (1997)
Exports: $ 130 million (1998)
Imports: $ 211 million (1998)
External debt: $ 183 million (1998); $ 1,966 per capita (1998)
Development aid received: $ 8 million (1997); $ 85.5 per capita (1997); 2.70 % of GNP (1997)

HDI (rank/value): 52/0.777 (1997)

Guadeloupe

Guadeloupe

Population: 450,000 (1999)
Area: 1,710 SQ KM
Capital: Basse-Terre
Currency: French franc
Language: French

The entire archipelago of present-day Guadeloupe was inhabited by the Caribs. Originally from South America, they dispersed throughout the islands after overpowering the Arawak people. They resisted the Spanish invasion in 1493 but were defeated by the French two centuries later.

2 The French colonizers built the first sugar mill on the island in 1633 and began importing African slave laborers. By the end of the 17th century, Guadeloupe had become one of the world's main sugar producers. The colonists killed the last of the archipelago's surviving Caribs in the early 18th century.

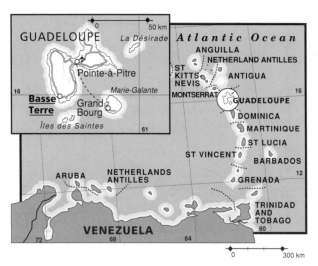

3 With the abolition of the slave trade in 1815, France restructured its formal links with the Caribbean islands, giving them the status of colonies. In 1946, with the initiation of the new French constitution, Guadeloupe achieved greater political autonomy, as an Overseas Department.

4 French Government subsidies increased per capita income and the consumption of imported goods, but ruined the local economy.

5 In 1981, in a country where 90 per cent of the population was of African or racially mixed origin, racism made the social climate more tense.

6 In 1985 there were violent clashes between pro-independence demonstrations and the police. Several disruptive actions led to the imprisonment of members of the Revolutionary Caribbean Alliance (ARC).

7 In the 1988 election, François Mitterrand received 70 per cent of the vote on Guadeloupe, although two-thirds of the voters abstained. In the regional elections of October 1988, the Left already in the majority within the General Council was further strengthened, gaining another seat.

8 In 1989, ARC members sentenced in 1985 were granted amnesty. The ARC took part in the elections for the first time, and their failure was taken as a show of support for the present situation.

9 In 1989 Hurricane Hugo left 12,000 people homeless. The French Government announced that it would freeze the interest on the foreign debt, and would send $5.4 million in aid to the island.

10 In 1992 the European Community decision to reduce banana import quotas from the 'French' Antilles to benefit imports from Africa and Latin America triggered strong protests in Guadeloupe. In the elections for the Regional Council - one of the two main assemblies in the island - the Guadeloupe Federation of the Union for the Republic (RPR) won. The RPR is a conservative, neo-Gaullist party, led by current French president Jacques Chirac. The RPR obtained 15 of the 41 seats, followed by the Socialist Party with 9.

11 In 1993, the reduction in tourism aggravated the economic crisis. The unemployment rate reached 24 per cent of the active population and the informal sector of the economy increased.

12 An important reduction of productive activities increased the trade balance deficit: exports, which represented just 9.9 per cent of imports in 1995, were reduced to 5.2 per cent in 1996. Due to the reduction of external demand and the competition from United States' corporations, banana exports in 1996 fell to half the quantity exported in 1993.

13 In late 1997, a massive strike of banana workers was launched. Union representatives accused plantation owners of creating militias which threatened to kill workers to force them to lift the strike. In February 1998, in a country with 40 per cent of unemployment and increasing social inequalities, the strike extended to other sectors.

14 In September 1999 there were heated confrontations between the police and demonstrators protesting against the arrest of a Union activist accused of wounding two police officers. As a result, six more police were wounded and 70 people were arrested. ∎

PROFILE

ENVIRONMENT

Includes the dependencies of Marie Galante, La Désirade, Les Saintes, Petite-Terre, St Berthélemy and the French section of St Martin forming part of the Windward Islands of the Lesser Antilles. The tropical, rainy climate is tempered by sea winds, and sugarcane is grown.

SOCIETY

Peoples: A majority of descendants of native Africans with a small European minority.
Religions: Mainly Catholic.
Languages: French (official).
Political Parties: Guadeloupe Federation of the Union for the Republic (RPR), and Guadeloupe Federation of the Union in French Democracy (UDF), are the local branches of the colonial parties; Guadeloupe Federation of the Socialist Party (PS); the Communist Party of Guadeloupe (PCG); the Guadeloupe Democrats; the Popular Union for the Liberation of Guadeloupe (UPLG), the largest of the radical pro-independence groups; the Revolutionary Caribbean Alliance (ARC), founded in Point-à-Pitre in 1983, has carried out several armed attacks.
Social Organizations: The Guadeloupe General Labor Confederation, with 15,000 members; the Department Union of Christian Workers' French Confederation, with 3,500 members; the Department Organization of Trade Unions (CGT-FO), with 1,500 members.

THE STATE

Official Name: Département d'Outre-Mer de la Guadeloupe.
Administrative Divisions: 3 Arrondissements, 36 Cantons.
Capital: Basse-Terre 15,000 people (1995).
Government: Jean-François Carenco (since 1999), commissioner appointed by the French Government. Legislative power: a 42-member General Council (chaired by Marcellin Lubeth since 1998), and 41-member regional Council (chaired by Lucette Michaux Chevry since 1992). Guadeloupe has 4 deputies and 2 senators in the French parliament.

DEMOGRAPHY

Population: 450,000 (1999).

Guam

Guam

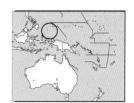

Population: 165,000 (1999)
Area: 550 SQ KM
Capital: Agaña
Currency: US dollar
Language: English

G uam shares a common history with the rest of the Micronesian archipelago (see Micronesia). The population, which settled on the island thousands of years ago, became the victim of extermination campaigns at the hands of Spanish colonizers, between 1668 and 1695.

[2] As a result of armed aggression and epidemics (the people lacked immunity against European illnesses) the population declined from 100,000 at the beginning of the 17th century to fewer than 5,000 in 1741.

[3] The few survivors intermarried with Spanish and Filipino immigrants, producing the Chamorro people who presently populate the island.

[4] For three centuries, Guam was a port of call on the Spanish galleon route between the Philippines and Acapulco (Mexico), a major depot on the trade route to Spain.

[5] Under the terms of the Treaty of Paris of 1898, Guam changed hands from Spain to the United States, together with the Philippines. The island continued to serve as a stopover until it was invaded by the Japanese in 1941. Recovered in 1944, it became a US military base.

[6] Since 1973, the United Nations has unsuccessfully urged Washington to permit the islanders to exercise their right to self-determination. In January 1982, in a plebiscite on self-determination, 75 per cent of the electorate favored a system of association with the United States. As a result of this the UN General Assembly recommended that the US implement Guam's decolonization in December 1984. The UN also reiterated its conviction that military bases are a major obstacle to self-determination and independence, two principles established in the UN Charter.

[7] In February 1987, former governor Ricardo Borballo, who had been elected in 1984, was found guilty of bribery, extortion and conspiracy.

[8] In November 1987, the High Commission initiated a self-determination referendum for Guam, and voters supported negotiation of a new relationship with the US. In February 1988 Guam received US economic aid, or more precisely, disaster relief, to repair the damage done by the typhoon in January.

[9] In November 1994, the democrat Carl Gutiérrez was elected governor with 54.6 per cent of the vote.

[10] Negotiations over political self-determination and the creation of a Free Associated State with the United Nations and the United States were restarted in 1996. A landowners' organization demanded the Government include the territory occupied by the US military in the discussions. Washington considered Guam an extremely important geo-strategical enclave.

[11] In September 1996, the island formed the operations base for US bombers which carried out a 'limited attack' on Iraq.

[12] In the November 1996 legislative elections, the Republican Party took 11 seats in the legislative chamber, while the Democrat Party took 10.

[13] In early 1998, the economy of the country was mainly sustained by middle-class tourism mostly from Japan, South Korea and Taiwan. The tourists spent some $300 million on the island each season. Governor Gutiérrez planned to increase these figures by 50 per cent over the next five years; in 2000 over a million tourists were anticipated. ∎

PROFILE

ENVIRONMENT

Guam is the southernmost island of the Marianas archipelago, located east of the Philippines and south of Japan. Of volcanic origin, its contours are mountainous except for the coastal plain in the northern region. The climate is tropical, rainy from June to November (over 300 mm a month) and drier and colder from December to May. It has rainforest vegetation. One-third of the island is occupied by military installations.

SOCIETY

Peoples: Chamorro indigenous people account for approximately 47 per cent of the population; Filipino, 25 per cent.. US troops and dependents, 10 per cent. Japanese, Chinese, Korean and other, 18 per cent.
Religions: 98 per cent of all Guamanians are Catholic.
Languages: English (official), Chamorro (a dialect derived from Indonesian), and Japanese.
Political Parties: Republican and Democrat, as in the US.

THE STATE

Official Name: Territory of Guam.
Capital: Agaña 10,000 people (est 1995).
Government: Carl T C Gutiérrez, Governor, elected on November 1994. His office reports to the US Interior Department and actually has less autonomy than the local military commander, as one-third of the island is under control of the US Navy and Air force. Although Guamanians formally possess US citizenship they have no representation in the US Congress nor do they participate in the US presidential elections.

STATISTICS

DEMOGRAPHY

Population: 165,000 (1999)

EDUCATION

Tertiary: 66 % (1996)

COMMUNICATIONS

193 newspapers (1996) and 1,408 radios (1997) per 1,000 people

ECONOMY

Cereal imports: 11,989 metric tons (1998)

Guatemala

Guatemala

Population: 11,090,000 (1999)
Area: 108,890 SQ KM
Capital: Guatemala
Currency: Quetzal
Language: Spanish

The Maya civilization flourished during the first ten centuries AD in what is now Guatemala and parts of Mexico, Honduras and El Salvador.

[2] Spanish troops, under the command of Pedro de Alvarado, entered the country in 1524, founding the city of Guatemala and gaining total control over the country two years later. This process was facilitated by the fact that the country was undergoing a gradual transition and readjustment among its various ethnic groups - the K'iche', Kaqchi, Mam, Q'eqchi, Poqomchi', Q'anjob'al, Tz'utujiil and others - all of which stemmed from a common Mayan ancestry. Though the situation favored the invaders, there were nevertheless frequent incidents in which they faced stiff resistance.

[3] On September 15 1821, large landowners and local business interests joined forces with colonial officials, to peacefully proclaim the independence of the Viceroyalty of New Spain, including the five countries of Central America.

[4] The new political and administrative union, called the Federation of Central American States, was dissolved in 1839 as a result of internal struggles prompted by the British policy of 'divide and conquer'.

[5] In 1831, under tremendous debt pressure, the Government yielded large portions of territory to Britain for timber. This later became British Honduras, now the independent nation of Belize.

[6] The discovery of synthetic dyes in Europe in the mid-18th century caused a serious economic crisis in Guatemala, where the main export products were vegetable dyes. Coffee replaced dyes as the country's main cash crop, and plantation owners deprived the indians of most of their communal lands through the Liberal Reform of 1871. During the late 19th century, Guatemalan politics were dominated by the antagonism between liberals and conservatives. German settlers in Guatemala developed ties with German companies and initiated an import-export business which damaged the interests of the incipient national bourgeoisie.

[7] Toward the end of the 19th century, Manuel Estrada Cabrera rose to power and governed Guatemala until 1920. He began an 'open door policy' for US transnationals, who eventually owned the railroads, ports, hydroelectric plants, shipping, international mailing services and the enormous banana plantations of the United Fruit Company (Unifruco).

[8] General Jorge Ubico Castañeda, the last of a generation of military leaders, was elected President in 1931. However, a popular uprising known as the 'October Revolution' toppled him in 1944 calling fresh elections. The winner was reformist Juan José Arévalo, who launched a process of economic and social reform.

[9] Arévalo's government heralded a climate of political and economic liberalization. In 1945, literate women were granted the right to vote. That same year the first *campesino* labor union was formed. The land reform program, under which extensive tracts of unused Unifruco land were expropriated, was considered 'a threat to US interests' by Washington. An aggressive anti-communist campaign was launched, with the sole aim of harassing Arévalo and his successor, President Jacobo Arbenz.

[10] John Foster Dulles, US Secretary of State, but also a United Fruit Company (UFCO) shareholder and company lawyer pressured the Organization of American States (OAS) to condemn the reforms being carried out by Jacobo Arbenz's government. Allen Dulles, director of the CIA and former president of the company organized an invasion carried out by Castillo Armas in June 1954. With the fall of Arbenz, UFCO managed to get back its lands, and subsequently changed its name to United Brands.

[11] Two decades of military regimes followed. Most Guatemalans felt that the four elections which followed, in 1970, 1974, 1978 and 1982, were rigged - with the top military candidates invariably elected.

[12] This kind of political atmosphere bred armed insurgency. The Rebel Armed Forces (FAR) entered the scene in 1962, followed by the Poor People's Guerrilla Army (EGP) and the Organization of the People in Arms (ORPA) in 1975 and 1979 respectively.

[13] According to estimates from several humanitarian organizations, official repression took some 80,000 lives between 1954 and 1982. The Guatemalan National Revolutionary Unity (URNG) was founded in February 1982, uniting the Poor People's Guerrilla Army, the Rebel Armed Forces, the Organization of the People in Arms, and the Guatemalan Labor Party (PGT, National Leadership Committee).

[14] On March 23 1982, only a few days after a rigged election which brought him to power, Lucas Garcia was ousted in a military coup and replaced by General Efraín Ríos Montt.

[15] Ríos Montt's counter-insurgency campaign surpassed that of his predecessor's in terms of ferocity. Over 15,000 Guatemalans were killed in the first year of Ríos Montt's administration. 70,000 took refuge in neighboring countries, especially Mexico, and 500,000 fled to the mountains to escape the army. Hundreds of villages were razed, while the number of 'model hamlets' increased systematically. Peasants were taken by force to these hamlets, where they were required to produce cash crops for export, rather than growing subsistence crops.

WORKERS

% OF LABOUR FORCE — **1998**

- FEMALE: 28%
- MALE: 72%

1990

- SERVICES: 30.1%
- INDUSTRY: 17.5%
- AGRICULTURE: 52.4%

LAND USE

DEFORESTATION: 2.0% annual (1990/95)
IRRIGATED: 9.4% of arable (1993)

1993

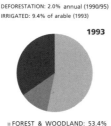

- FOREST & WOODLAND: 53.4%
- ARABLE: 12.2%
- OTHER: 34.4%

PUBLIC EXPENDITURE

DEFENCE EXPENDITURE (% of goverment exp.)	**15%**	(1997)
MILITARY EXPENDITURE (% of health & education)	**31%**	(1990/91)

[16] In August 1983, another coup staged by the CIA deposed Ríos Montt and General Oscar Mejía Víctores came into power, promising a quick return to a democratic system.

[17] An 88-seat Constituent Assembly was elected on July 18 1984, to replace the legal framework in effect since 1965, but annulled after the 1982 coup. The Assembly offered new constitutional guarantees, habeas corpus and electoral regulations. Seventeen parties ran candidates; however lack of guarantees forced the Left to abstain from running yet another time.

[18] The Constituent Assembly approved the right to strike for civil servants, authorized the return from exile of leaders of the Socialist Democratic Party and called for elections in November 1985.

[19] The election, boycotted by the URNG, gave a clear victory to the Christian Democratic candidate, Vinicio Cerezo. One of the first measures was the 'total and definitive' suspension of secret police activities.

[20] In October 1987, representatives of the URNG and Vinicio Cerezo's government met in Madrid, the first direct negotiations between the Government and guerrilla forces in 27 years of conflict. That year, the National Reconciliation Commission (CNR) played a decisive role in the rapprochement process. The commission was created as a result of the Esquipulas II peace plan for Central America, signed by 6 countries in the region.

[21] On March 30, in Oslo, guerrillas and government agreed on an operational pattern for the meetings and the role of CNR and UN mediators. Despite the persistence of political persecution and assassination, on June 1 1990 a basic agreement was signed in Madrid by the National Commission for Reconciliation, the political parties and the URNG. The overall aim of the accord was to continue the search for peace in Guatemala.

[22] During the last few months of 1990, negotiations came to a standstill and a high degree of skepticism developed among voters, which led to a 70 per cent abstention rate in the November 11 1990 presidential elections. During the second round of the elections, held on January 6 1991, Jorge Serrano Elías, of the Solidarity Action Movement (MAS), was elected President.

[23] The Serrano Government and the URNG decided to take up peace negotiations. A fortnight later, in Cuernavaca, Mexico, a three-day meeting was held. After three decades of violence, during which over 100,000 people were murdered and 50,000 went missing, the Government and the guerrillas committed themselves to the negotiation process, attended by top level delegates and with the aim of achieving a firm and lasting peace agreement in the shortest possible time. The agenda included topics such as: democratization, human rights, the strengthening of civil groups, rights of the indigenous peoples, constitutional reforms, the resettlement of the landless, the incorporation of the URNG into legal political life.

[24] In July, the US Senate suspended military aid to Guatemala. The URNG demanded that human rights violations cease immediately. Human rights organizations found that in the first 9 months of Serrano's rule there had been 1,760 human rights violations, 650 of them executions without trial. Several deaths of street children below the age of six were also reported.

[25] Also in September 1991, the Guatemalan president recognized the sovereignty and self-determination of Belize, the former British colony which proclaimed its independence in 1981. The announcement caused the resignation of chancellor Alvaro Arzú, the leader of the National Advancement Party (PAN), and one of the ruling party's main allies.

[26] In 1992, a national debate began on the existence of government armed civilian groups, such as the Civilian Self-Defense Patrols (PAC). The Catholic Church criticized the Government's economic policy and spoke out in favor of agrarian reform. In the meantime, organizations representing the indigenous peoples demanded the ratification of ILO Agreement 169, dealing with indigenous and tribal peoples.

[27] The Government created the 'Hunapú' force, made up of the Army, the National Police and the 'Hacienda Guard', replacing the former PACs. In April, members of the 'Hunapú' provoked an incident during a student demonstration demanding improvements in the education policy. One student was killed and 7 injured. The World Bank, the US Government and the European Parliament urged the Guatemalan government to end political violence.

[28] In October, while the quincentenary of Columbus' arrival on the continent was celebrated by some, Rigoberta Menchú Tum, an indigenous leader from the Quiché ethnic group, won the Nobel Peace Prize. Menchú travelled world-wide, denouncing the situation of her country's indigenous peoples.

[29] On May 25 1993, President Serrano, backed by a group of military officers, carried out a coup themselves, revoking several articles of the constitution and dissolving Congress and the Supreme Court. On June 1, national and international rejection of this measure - including pressure from the United States - forced Serrano from office. On June 6, after several days of uncertainty, former Human Rights attorney Ramiro De León Carpio was elected head of the Executive, to finish Serrano's term.

[30] De León Carpio began by purging the officers that had supported Serrano, changing five military commands. Shortly afterwards, Jorge Carpio Nicolle, leader of the Union of the National Center and the president's cousin, was assassinated.

[31] Despite the intense campaign against the PACs and compulsory military service, President De León Carpio stated that he would maintain both institutions as long as the situation of armed conflict persisted, a U-turn on his previously stated opinion. On August 5, the Government announced that the 'Files' - records kept on citizens considered a 'danger' to State security - had disappeared. However, the loss of these papers also implied the elimination of evidence against those responsible for human rights violations. In November, excavations in several clandestine cemeteries uncovered the remains of 177 women and children assassinated by the military in the 1982 'Rio Negro Massacre'.

[32] The 1994-95 Government Plan, presented in August, reaffirmed the structural adjustment program already in effect, prioritizing the end of state intervention in the economy, along with fiscal reform and the privatization of enterprises.

[33] De León Carpio's stated goal was to fight corruption in the public sector. On August 26, the President called for the resignation of legislative deputies and members of

---

PROFILE

ENVIRONMENT

The Sierra Madre and the Cuchumatanes Mountains cross the country from east to west, and these are the areas of volcanic activity and earthquakes. Between the mountain ranges there is a high plateau with sandy soil and easily eroded slopes. Although the plateau occupies only 26 per cent of the country's territory, 53 per cent of the population is concentrated there. The long Atlantic coastline is covered with forests and is less populated. In the valleys along the Caribbean coast and in the Pacific lowlands there are banana and sugar cane plantations. In 1980, 41.9 per cent of the country's land area was covered by forests; in 1990, that figure had been reduced to 33.8 per cent, threatening the exceptionally diverse ecosystems, with a great variety of species.

SOCIETY

Peoples: Approximately 90 per cent are of Mayan descent. Amid the country's great cultural and linguistic diversity, four major peoples can be distinguished: the Ladino (descendants of Amerindians and Spaniards), the Maya, the Garifuna (of the Caribbean region) and the Xinca.
Religions: Mainly Catholic. In recent years a number of Protestant groups have appeared. The Mayan Religion has also survived.
Languages: Spanish is official but most of the population speak one of the 22 Maya dialects.
Political Parties: National Advancement Party, conservative; Guatemalan Republican Alliance (FRG), ultra-right-wing. Christian Democracy of Guatemala (DCG); Union of the National Center (UCN); New Guatemala Democratic Front, a new left wing coalition; Solidarity Action Movement (MAS). The National Revolutionary Unity of Guatemala (URNG) is a coalition of different armed groups.
Social Organizations: Union of Labor and Popular Associations; National Labor Union Alliance; National Workers' Coordinating Committee; Labor Union of Guatemalan Workers; Committee for Campesino Unity; National Coordinating Committee of Indigenous Campesinos; Communities of Peoples Resistance; Permanent Commissions of Refugees in Mexico; National Commission of Widows of Guatemala; Mutual Support Group; 'Runujel Junam' Council of Ethnic Communities; Office of Human Rights of the Archbishopric; Coordinating Committee of Mayan Women; Academy of Mayan Languages of Guatemala; 'Majawil Q'uij' Coordinating Committee and Council of Mayan Organizations of Guatemala.

THE STATE

Official Name: República de Guatemala.
Administrative Divisions: 22 Departments.
Capital: Guatemala 1,167,495 people (1995).
Other cities: Mixco 436,668 people; Villa Nueva 165,567; Chinautla 61,335 (1995).
Government: Alfonso Portillo Cabrera, President since January 2000.
National Holiday: September 15 (1821), Independence Day.
Armed Forces: 44,200 troops (1994). Other: 10,000 National Police, 2,500 Hacienda Guard; 500,000 Territorial Militia.

MATERNAL MORTALITY

1990-98

Per 100.000
live births

190

LITERACY

1995

65%

FOOD DEPENDENCY

1997

13%

STATISTICS

DEMOGRAPHY

Population: 11,090,000 (1999)
Annual growth: 2.6 % (1975/97)
Estimates for year 2015 (million):
16.4 (1999)
Annual growth to year 2015:
2.5 % (1997/2015)
Urban population: 39.4 % (1997)
Urban Growth: 3.6 % (1980/95)
Children per woman: 4.9 (1998)

HEALTH

Life expectancy at birth: 64 years
(1998)
male: 61 years (1998)
female: 67 years (1998)
Maternal mortality: 190 per
100,000 live births (1990-98)
Infant mortality: 41 per 1,000
(1998)
Under-5 child mortality:
52 per 1,000 (1998)
Daily calorie supply:
2,191 per capita (1996)
90 doctors per 100,000 people
(1993)
Safe water: 68 % (1990/98)

EDUCATION

Literacy: 65 % (1995)
male: 73 % (1995)
female: 58 % (1995)
School enrolment:
Primary total: 84 % (1990/96)
male: 90 % (1990/97)
female: 79 % (1990/97)
Secondary:
male: 26 % (1990/96)
female: 24 % (1990/96)
Tertiary: 8 % (1996)
Primary school teachers:
one for every 35 (1996)

COMMUNICATIONS

33 newspapers (1996), 79 radios
(1997), 122 TV sets (1996) and 31
main telephone lines (1996) per
1,000 people

ECONOMY

Per capita, GNP: $ 1,640 (1998)
Annual growth, GNP: 5.5 % (1998)
Annual inflation: 11.4 % (1990/98)
Consumer price index: 129.8 (1998)
Currency: 6.4 quetzales = $ 1
(1998)
Cereal imports: 702,649 metric
tons (1998)
Food import dependency: 13 %
(1997)
Fertilizer use: 1,571 kg per ha
(1997)
Exports: $ 3,524 million (1998)
Imports: $ 5,101 million (1998)
External debt: $ 4,565 million
(1998); $ 423 per capita (1998)
Debt service: 9.8 % of exports
(1998)
Development aid received: $ 302
million (1997); $ 33.7 per capita
(1997); 1.70 % of GNP (1997)

ENERGY

Consumption: 536.0 Kgs of Oil
equivalent per capita yearly
(1997); 21.0 % imported (1997)

HDI (rank/value): 117/0.624 (1997)

the Supreme Court, causing a confrontation between the President and Congress. This led to a clash of economic and political interests, culminating in the Executive and Congress agreeing on constitutional reform.

[34] A plebiscite was scheduled for January 30 1994, for nation's voters to decide on reforms to public administration and in the constitution.

[35] Following a 22-day occupation of the local OAS office by members of the Committee for Campesino Unity and the National Commission of Widows of Guatemala, some 5,000 members of indigenous groups carried out a march demanding the dissolution of the PACs.

[36] In January 1994, the Government and guerrillas signed agreements for the resettlement of the population displaced by the armed conflict, without a mediated cease fire. As a result of the accords 870 people were able to settle in the zones of Chacula, Nenton and Huehuetenango, but the majority of the resettlement areas were still under army control.

[37] Around the same date, a referendum for constitutional reform registered an abstention rate of 85 per cent. Of those who did vote, 69 per cent supported the moves for a new Congress and a new Supreme Court. In general elections with a similar abstention rate, the Guatemalan Republican Alliance (FRG) led by former dictator Efrain Ríos Montt took the majority. The National Vanguard Party came second.

[38] Monica Pinto, the UN Human Rights observer, recommended the demilitarization of society through the gradual reduction in size of the army, the disbanding of the PACs and the Presidential Staff, along with the creation of a Truth Commission.

[39] Following a prolonged silence in early 1994, the Minister of Foreign Affairs recognized Belize as an independent State, but upheld Guatemala's territorial claim, meaning no frontier could be established.

[40] In March, the Government and the URNG ratified an agreement related to the disbanding of the PACs and the international verification of human rights by the UN. Three days later the President of the Court of Constitutionality,

Epaminondas González, was murdered.

[41] In April, the police evicted 300 rural workers' families from an estate they had occupied in Escuintla. In May a new contingent of nearly 2,000 refugees returned, heading for the Quiche area, which was still occupied by the military.

[42] The URNG and the Government signed a draft agreement for the 'Resettlement of the People Uprooted by the Armed Confrontation', in Oslo, Norway, in June. The Communities of Peoples were recognized as non-fighting civilians and the vital importance of land for these uprooted populations was explicitly stated. The second agreement in Oslo enshrined the principle of not individualizing responsibility for human rights violations as a way of neutralizing the action of sectors opposed to a negotiated outcome.

[43] Income from tourism fell by $100 million due to the hunger strike by a US citizen protesting for the liberty of her husband, who had been detained in 1992 for alleged links with left-wing organizations, and because another US citizen, suspected of involvement in a baby-trafficking network, was brutally flogged before a crowd.

[44] The peace negotiations between the guerrillas and the Government reached stalemate during 1995, due to the elections lack of interest by the army and landowners, and the Government weakness in face of them. The UN mission reported that impunity continued to be the main obstacle to the respect for human rights, and described hundreds of cases of torture, illegal detentions and extrajudicial executions.

[45] In August 1995, Congress leader Efrain Rios Montt and another two members of the FRG lost their legal immunity and were tried by the Supreme Court on charges of bugging telephones, falsifying documents and abuse of power.

[46] In the November general elections, Alvaro Arzú, candidate for the National Progress Party, won over Alfonso Portillo Cabrera of the FRG. Abstention reached a record 63 per cent. In December - first in Europe and then in Mexico and Guatemala - the Government and the URNG signed a series of peace agreements which put an

end to a civil war which had cost more than 100,000 lives. The cease-fire was respected and was followed by a large increase in crime. Around 80 per cent of the population were living below the poverty threshold at this time.

[47] In December 1997, Guatemala was amongst the five Latin American countries most affected by climatic change resulting from El Niño. According to ECLAC preliminary figures Hurricane Mitch's passage through Central America in September 1998 caused damage in the region of $5.36 million and left around 24,000 dead, 256 of them Guatemalan. More than 100,000 people were made homeless and worsening health conditions left the country in a 'state of emergency'.

[48] Investigation of human rights violations during the war produced an avalanche of threats against investigators and members of the judiciary. After presenting a report condemning the armed forces for several massacres, Bishop Juan Gerardi was murdered in 1998. The public prosecutor working on the case fled to the United States where he requested asylum, claiming he had been under heavy pressure and had received several death threats. In October that year, the Government ordered hundreds of bodies to be dug up in the grounds of an elite police unit in the capital. A United Nations report estimated this same year that 96 per cent of the deaths during the war were the responsibility of the army and armed forces.

[49] In the second round of the elections held in late December 1999, Alfonso Portillo of the FRG took 68 per cent of the vote, defeating Oscar Berger of the ruling PAN. Abstention reached 59 per cent, while more than 50 per cent of registered voters had turned out in the first round ballot.

[50] In early 2000, Guatemala lodged a claim for nearly half the territory of the neighboring Belize. The country recognized the independence of the former British colony in 1991, but still claims this part of the territory. Representatives of both parties talked briefly in Miami in February and March 2000, under the auspices of the Organization of American States (OAS). ∎

The colonization of America

The victory of the Spanish invaders over the Inca Empire (Tahuantinsuyo) in the 15th century paved the way in South America for one of the most ferocious colonial regimes, which pillaged precious metals and decimated the native population

At first glance it seems inexplicable how the handful of men arriving in the Peruvian Andes region from Spain in 1532 could come to dominate the Inca empire, but the Spanish had several powerful forces at their command: superior weaponry, gunpowder and iron, and the cavalry - which had an important psychological impact - to name a few.

Their skill at subtle intrigue, using the wiles of Renaissance politics, was also greatly effective. The Spaniards took advantage of internal rivalries, getting local allies to support their intrusion.

When they arrived, Tahuantinsuyo was riven by civil war, with Huascar and Attahualpa at loggerheads, fighting it out to succeed Inca Wayna Qhápaq. Thus the greatest Inca forces were divided into two opposed blocs and at the critical moment they were unable to form a united front.

Similarly, the interpretations of the Inca oracle before the invasion meant the Spaniards were confused with gods expected to return from the sea to start off a new historical cycle. This meant the invaders were given an exceedingly warm welcome, and their real intentions were discovered too late.

Finally, the measles epidemic they provoked wiped out massive numbers of Amerindians, who lacked immune defences to a disease which had hitherto been unknown on the continent. Thus a regime of oppression and cruel exploitation was rapidly installed, and it lasted for nearly 300 years.

THE INTRODUCTION OF MERCANTILISM

The Spanish conquest of the Americas occurred during the time of mercantilism. Villey defined this economic doctrine in the following terms:

'Etymologically [mercantilism] indicates the doctrine which exalts the development of markets, of merchants, of trade. This idea was born at the beginning of the 16th century like a reflection of the sun on the gold of the New World. It was mainly there - in Portugal and Spain - that the gold entered Europe, where the magic of the precious metals was felt, making the accumulation of these the supreme object of the action of individuals, and the politics of the princes.... In these eras the precious metals of the New World came almost exclusively from the Spanish and Portuguese colonies. The other countries did not have gold mines: for them the question was not how to keep hold of gold, but how to attract it. This is what the French mercantilists tried to do, stimulating the production above all of manufactured goods, and the English developing trade.'

The systematic pillaging provided a continuous flow of precious metals (gold and silver) to the colonial centres, a seemingly inexhaustible booty. But this did not benefit Spain as much as the more advanced European countries, which accumulated the capital that would later allow them to undergo industrialization. The resources wrenched out of the Americas in immense quantities barely sufficed to pay for the metropolitan consumption of manufactured and non-manufactured goods from other areas, and to maintain the armies. The sea connection required massive ships and fleets, making dominion of the waves essential.

THE COLONIAL ECONOMY

In return for metal, the colonial élite received luxury articles, but had to pay heavily for them. No interest at all was taken in improving the living conditions of the population who produced the metal.

The indigenous workforce that powered the production of metals received no benefits for their toil. A chain of economic relations was formed between the silver-producing regions of present-day Bolivia, the mercury-producing area of Peru, the Arica region where silver was loaded into ships, the wheat, dried meat and wine supplying regions of Chile and Cordoba and the regions of Tucumán in Argentina which supplied draught animals.

Amongst all the vast silver seams in production, it was Potosí which gained greatest world-wide prestige. In 1772, Potosí's Cerro Rico (Rich Mountain) was described as 'a beehive' of activity. But the technology used was antiquated even for the time. The rise of silver eclipsed gold mining. In the middle of the 17th century, silver made up nearly 99 per cent of exports from Spanish America. This meant the annihilation of the indigenous population in the 5,000 pitheads and foundries of Potosí, which rapidly fell into disuse in the 19th century.

EXPLOITATION OF THE AMERINDIANS

The human resources needed for the mines were obtained through forced labour, known as the *mita*. Sixteen indigenous provinces were obliged to supply the workforce with men aged between 18 and 50 years old.

This term of service lasted a year, to be repeated every seven years. The first work group raised by this system in 1573 by Viceroy Toledo, numbered 13,500. In the following centuries the numbers fell markedly, due mainly to the excessively tough conditions of the *mita* itself. It was almost impossible for any individual to live through three terms of service, as one year in the mines was enough to irreparably ruin the health of any worker.

The indigenous workers ended up physically exhausted and were often plagued by illnesses which killed them. The Imperial Villa of Potosí needed more than 90,000 natives to operate its mines, and simple arithmetic can show us the massive proportions of the undertaking: if we take each of the men to have been the head of a family of five people, then half a million people suffered the consequences of this system.

Descriptions of Potosí in 1603 mention data like the consumption of 1,600,000 bottles of *chicha*, a local alcoholic drink, and 21,900 packs of cards, giving some idea of what the lifestyle of the city was like at the time.

GENOCIDE

Between the time when conquest first began and 1754, the population of Tahuantinsuyo fell by more than 95 per cent, from more than thirteen million to 612,780. An eloquent example of this genocide is that of Tiahuanaco in Bolivia, which had 868 taxpayers in 1583 of which a mere 9 remained by 1658. This drastic reduction of the indigenous population through subhuman working conditions and the spread of epidemics affected mining production, as it became impossible to find workers, causing a terminal decline at the dawn of the 19th century. ■

Guinea

Guinée

Population: 7,359,000 (1999)
Area: 245,860 SQ KM
Capital: Conakry
Currency: Franc
Language: French

Guinea was initially inhabited by pygmies who were driven towards the more inhospitable regions by the Mande peoples. The country was originally connected to the great states of Sudan and their trade system. The Bambuk gold mines that fed the Mediterranean economy for centuries were located on the ridges of the Futa Dyalon massif (see Mali and Morocco). The same region witnessed the rise and fall of the Fulah states between the 16th and 19th centuries.

[2] In 1870, against this background, Samor became the local political and spiritual leader (Almamy) of a state that included the greater part of Guinea and parts of present-day Mali and Côte d'Ivoire. He had first confronted the French troops in 1886, as they were advancing from Senegal, and he had continued to fight constantly until 1898 when he was taken prisoner and exiled to Gabon. He died there two years later.

[3] This episode had been kept alive in the people's memory until 1947 when a small group of activists led by Ahmed Sekou Touré founded the Guinea Democratic Party (GDP). Supported by labor unions, the GDP soon became a very influential political organization.

[4] Overwhelmed by the loss of Indochina in 1954, the independence of Tunisia and Morocco in 1956, and the uprising of Algeria which began in 1954, French President de Gaulle attempted to salvage his interests in West Africa by creating the French Community in 1958. Through agreements and covenants he attempted a neo-colonialist project, to guarantee continued French hegemony in the area, in particular through its large monopolies. When the population of Guinea was consulted, 1,200,000 opposed de Gaulle's proposal for a French Community and only 57,000 supported it.

[5] Four days later, the country proclaimed independence. Sekou Touré stated: 'We'd rather be poor and free than rich and enslaved'. It was the first time that such a thing had happened in 'French' West Africa, and in retaliation, Paris withdrew its technical advisers, paralyzed the few industries that there were, and blocked Guinean trade.

[6] In 1959, the State took over the main economic activities and Guinea immediately created its own currency, becoming independent from the French franc. Industry and farming were diversified in an attempt to attain self-sufficiency, and aluminum production surpassed one million tons per year.

[7] French aggression mounted. In 1965, Guinea's bank accounts in Paris were blocked, large-scale smuggling was fostered and counterfeit currency introduced. In 1970, Portuguese mercenaries invaded the country in an attempt to overthrow the Government and destroy the PAIGC, which was fighting for the independence of neighboring 'Portuguese' Guinea-Bissau. In response to the ever more frequent destabilization campaigns, Local Revolutionary Powers (LRPs) were created in every neighborhood or village with the aim of fighting against corruption, mismanagement and contraband.

[8] In November 1978, the Congress decided to change the country's name to the People's and Revolutionary Republic of Guinea, and to re-open relations with France. After a long period of isolation, Sekou Touré visited African and Arab countries in search of new sources of foreign capital to exploit the country's mineral wealth and to attract investments which might help to pay the foreign debt.

[9] The rapprochement between France and Guinea brought new agreements. The exploitation of the Mount Nimba iron ore reserves was granted to a French firm while the French Oil Company started offshore oil prospecting and the exploitation of rich bauxite deposits discovered in the 1970s. Guinea became the world's second largest bauxite producer. At that time Guinea and Mali signed an agreement envisaging the merger of the two neighbors into an economic and political federation.

[10] At the end of March 1984, Sekou Touré died in a US hospital while undergoing treatment for an old ailment. A week later, Colonel Lansana Conté headed a military coup which overthrew interim president Louis Beavogui.

[11] The new regime dismantled the political structure, the grassroots organizations and the Assembly; the Constitution was abolished too. The Democratic Party of Guinea was banned and the name of the country was changed, eliminating the words 'People's' and 'Revolutionary'. The military government stimulated private enterprise, eliminated mixed companies and applied for economic aid to France, the US and the African States.

[12] Under the burden of an $800 million foreign debt, the Government decreed a 100 per cent devaluation of the *syli* (the national currency), and reduced public expenditure, a precondition of Guinea's entry into the French franc monetary scheme.

[13] In December 1984, the number of cabinet members was reduced, as was the number serving on the Reconstruction Committee. In addition, Colonel Conté consolidated power by simultaneously taking on the positions of head of state, prime minister and minister of defense.

[14] In December 1985, an economic recovery program was introduced, where agriculture, especially the cultivation of rice, was given top priority. Industrial and agricultural enterprises were also to be privatized. Self-sufficiency in food is still an unattained goal.

[15] To meet the country's serious economic problems head-on, in 1987 there were mass dismissals of public officials. In 1988, Conté moved a group of military officers away from the capital, as their discontent over low salaries constituted a threat to his government. In January of the same year, the 80 per cent increase in all salaries caused a price explosion with prices tripling over a few days. The demonstrations which took place at the time forced the Government to freeze the prices of consumer good and rents.

[16] In February 1990 the

WORKERS

% OF LABOUR FORCE **1998**

- FEMALE: 47%
- MALE: 53%

1990

- SERVICES: 10.9%
- INDUSTRY: 1.9%
- AGRICULTURE: 87.2%

LAND USE

DEFORESTATION: 1.1% annual (1990/95)
IRRIGATED: 15.2% of arable (1993)

1993

- FOREST & WOODLAND: 58.8%
- ARABLE: 2.5%
- OTHER: 38.7%

PUBLIC EXPENDITURE

DEFENCE EXPENDITURE (% of goverment exp.)	**8%** (1997)	
MILITARY EXPENDITURE (% of health & education)	**37%** (1990/91)	

Government announced an amnesty for political prisoners and exiles. In December, a referendum approved by a vast majority modified the Constitution and created a Temporary Council for National Development (CTDN) in charge of leading the transition to democracy. President Conté announced that legislative elections would be held in 1992, with the participation of several parties.

[17] The drop in the international price of bauxite, which accounted for 60 per cent of the country's earnings and 96 per cent of its exports, aggravated the state of the economy. According to international credit agencies, official corruption was so widespread that a structural adjustment program would be impossible to implement without first eradicating these practices. In 1992, the World Bank demanded that the Government fire 40,000 civil servants.

[18] Guinea's problems were reflected in the quality of life of its inhabitants. Nutritional deficiencies and diseases resulted in a short life expectancy of 42 years, as well as a high infant mortality rate. The most serious environmental problems were water pollution and the lack of sanitation, which result in the spreading of parasitic diseases like amoebic dysentery.

[19] In 1992, 650,000 refugees crossed the border from Sierra Leone and Liberia, setting up makeshift camps. The Government increased the number of peacekeeping troops sent to both countries by the Southwest African Economic Community, to patrol the borders and prevent more refugees from entering the country.

[20] When the multiparty system was approved, opposition leader Alpha Conde returned from exile and sponsored the creation of the National Democratic Forum (FND) which enclosed 30 opposition groups. However, tension and political persecution continued.

[21] Lansana Conté was re-elected in the December 1993 presidential elections with almost 51 per cent of the vote. Alpha Conde accused him of having staged a coup which led to confrontations between the police and opposition followers. In January 1994, dozens of people died in riots in Macenta near the border with Liberia.

[22] In June 1995, the ruling parties won 76 seats out of 114 in parliamentary elections which the opposition deemed fraudulent. Estimated annual GDP growth reached almost five per cent and, in recognition of what it considered to be good economic results, the Paris Club cancelled $85 million of Guinea's foreign debt, refinancing another $85 million still outstanding.

[23] In February 1996, a sector of the army rebelled when pay increases were not forthcoming. The mutiny ended in an attempt to overthrow the Government. The rebellion was put down in two days despite the fact that the mutineers, around 2,000 troops and some officers, had taken control of the urban center of the capital and used artillery to bombard the presidential palace. Several government officials were accused of encouraging the revolt, and were sent to prison. In July, the economist Sidia Touré was named Prime Minister. Touré announced the government priority would be reactivating the economy.

[24] Sierra Leone's President Ahmad Tejan Kabbah was ousted from power in May 1997 and fled to Guinea with most of the members of his government. The political instability in that country meant thousands of people sought refuge in Guinea, fearing attacks against their towns and villages. Kabbah's restoration in 1998 appeared to boost confidence, but it was feared that this would be short-lived.

[25] AIDS continued to strike the African continent and in November 1997, it was estimated that 1.5 per cent of the Guinean population carried the virus. This percentage, one of the lowest in Africa, was several times higher than that of rich countries like France.

[26] In September 1998, human rights' organizations sent food to the north-east of the country where dozens had died as a result of prolonged drought. In November, Sierra Leone and Liberia signed a non-aggression pact in Conakry, in a meeting mediated by US Reverend Jesse Jackson, special envoy of President Clinton. Both countries accused the other of harbouring and helping various rebel groups.

[27] In the presidential elections of December 13, Lansana Conté was re-elected with 54.1 per cent of the vote, while the Democratic Opposition Co-ordination claimed its lists had not been distributed over national territory and that, with the closure of the frontiers, the Government had prevented its voters from coming in from neighboring countries. The next day, opposition leader and candidate Alphe Conde was arrested for trying to overturn the government in 1993 and for having left the country illegally when he exiled himself.

[28] In February 1999, UN High Commissioner for Refugees, Sadako Ogata, visited the camps holding half a million refugees from Sierra Leone and Liberia. In March, Sidia Touré was ousted with no reason given and he was replaced with Lamine Sidime.

[29] On July 21, French President Jacques Chirac, began an official tour of the West African nations in Guinea and he met with political opponents who asked for his mediation in liberating Alphe Conde. In September, representatives of Guinea, Sierra Leone and Liberia met in Nigeria where they formed a committee to 'reduce the armed conflicts in their border zones'. Guinea and Liberia lodged mutual accusations of maintaining rebel groups.

[30] In November, movements opposed to female genital mutilation stated that after 14 years of fighting against this practice which is a 'violation of human rights', it had managed to convince surgeons they should use suitable instruments and avoid excessive bleeding and infections.

[31] In January 2000, Security Minister, Sekou Koureissy Conde, issued a three-day ultimatum for Muslims and Christians to stop fighting over land in the Balizia region. There had been 30 deaths in less than a week.

[32] On April 21, at a meeting of the Economic Community of West African States (ECOWAS) in Accra, Ghana, Guinea, Nigeria, Sierra Leone, Gambia and Liberia agreed to establish a common currency for the year 2003. ∎

PROFILE

ENVIRONMENT

The central massif of Futa-Dyalon, where cattle are raised, separates a humid and densely populated coastal plain, where rice, bananas and coconuts are grown, from a dryer northeastern region, where corn and manioc/cassava are cultivated. Rainfall reaches 3,000-4,000 mm per year along the coast. The country has extensive iron and bauxite deposits.

SOCIETY

Peoples: Guineans comprise 16 ethnic groups, of which Fulah, Mandingo, Malinke and Sussu are the most numerous. **Religions:** 65 per cent are Muslim, 33 per cent practice traditional religions, and 2 per cent are Christian. **Languages:** French (official). The most widely-spoken local languages are Malinke and Sussu. **Political Parties:** Party for Unity and Progress; Guinean People's Union; Union for National Prosperity; Democratic Party of Guinea/African Democratic Union. **Social Organizations:** National Confederation of Guinean Workers.

THE STATE

Official Name: République de Guinée. **Administrative divisions:** 33 regions. **Capital:** Conakry 1,100,000 people (1995). **Other Cities:** Kankan 60,000 people; Labe; N'Zerekore. **Government:** General Lansana Conté, President since April 1984. Elected in December 1993; reelected in 1998. Lamine Sidime, Prime Minister since March 1999. **National Holiday:** October 2, Republic Day. **Armed Forces:** 9,700 (1996). **Other:** People's Militia: 7,000; Gendarmerie: 1,000; Republican Guard: 1,600.

Guinea-Bissau

Guinea-Bissau

Population: 1,187,000 (1999)
Area: 36,125 SQ KM
Capital: Bissau
Currency: Peso
Language: Portuguese

Guinea-Bissau was the first Portuguese colony to gain independence in Africa. This was achieved even before the fall of the Portuguese dictatorship in Lisbon, in a successful political and military struggle led by Amilcar Cabral's African Party for the Independence of Guinea and Cape Verde (PAIGC).

[2] After belonging to the Mali and Songhai empires, the peoples in the Geba river valley became independent. This independence was soon threatened by the Portuguese, who had been settled on the coast from the end of the 15th century, and by the Fulah, coming from the interior in the 16th century. Inland, the state of Gabu remained autonomous until the 19th century (see Senegal: The Fulah States) while the coastal population suffered the consequences of the slave trade and forced displacement to the Cape Verde Islands (see Cape Verde).

[3] Resistance against the European colonists began in 1500 when the Portuguese arrived in Guinea. At that time, the country was inhabited by several different groups, immigrants from the state of Mali along with the Fulah and Mandingo groups, who lived in organized autocratic societies in the savannahs. During the 17th century Guineans made their first contact with the inhabitants of the Cape Verde islands, a mandatory stopover for the ships carrying slaves to Brazil.

[4] As the country was small and poor the monopoly on trade and agriculture was dealt with by a private company, the Uniao Fabril. Guineans were forced to cultivate export crops while massively reducing the acreage available for subsistence farming. In the 1950s, infant mortality reached the remarkable rate of 600 deaths per 1,000 births. There were only 11 doctors in the country and only one per cent of the rural population was literate. In the early 1960s, only 11 Guineans had completed secondary education.

[5] It was against this setting of misery and exploitation that Amilcar Cabral founded the Athletics and Recreational Association in 1954. This organization developed into the PAIGC two years later. The Party called on all Guineans and inhabitants of Cape Verde to unite in anti-colonial resistance, regardless of color, race or religion. In September 1959, after trying fruitlessly to engage the Portuguese in negotiations for three years, the PAIGC embarked upon guerrilla warfare. The fighting spread quickly and by 1968 the Portuguese were confined to the capital, Bissau, and a few coastal strongholds. Four years later, the PAIGC had taken two-thirds of the nation's territory under their control. In September and October 1972, the first free elections were held in the liberated areas. A Popular National Assembly was elected and a year later on September 24 1973, the 'democratic, anti-imperialist and anti-colonialist republic of Guinea' was proclaimed. Two months later the UN General Assembly recognized the independent state.

[6] Amilcar Cabral was assassinated in Conakry, Guinea, in February 1973, by Portuguese agents. He left many books and studies on the struggles for freedom in the African colonies. His successor, Luis Cabral, set up the Government Council of Guinea-Bissau in a small village called Madina do Boé, in the heart of the liberated area.

[7] The impact of the unilateral independence of Guinea-Bissau and its immediate recognition by the UN shook the infrastructure of Portuguese colonialism. General Spinola, commander of the 55,000 colonial soldiers, came to the realization that his army could not be successful in the war against the PAIGC and argued for political changes in Portugal. It was as a result of these conditions in Bissau that the Captains' Movement was born. This movement later became the Armed Forces' Movement, the group which was responsible for the coup that overthrew the dictatorial regime in Portugal on April 25 1974. Four months after the coup, Portugal recognized the independence of Guinea-Bissau.

[8] The PAIGC Government diversified agriculture giving priority to feeding the population and reducing the emphasis on export crops. Foreign companies were nationalized, agrarian reform was implemented together with a mass literacy campaign. In foreign relations, the new government opted for non-alignment and unconditional support for the struggle against apartheid and colonialism in Africa. The PAIGC congress also gave top priority to economic integration with the archipelago of Cape Verde, with a view towards uniting the two countries.

[9] In 1980, a military conspiracy led by Joao Bernardino (Niño) Vieira, a former guerrilla commander, overthrew Luis Cabral replacing all the government bodies with a centralized Revolutionary Council, headed by himself.

[10] Talks with Cape Verde were cut short while the two countries were discussing a united constitution (See Cape Verde). The new government in Bissau was immediately recognized by the neighboring Republic of Guinea, which had been at loggerheads with the former president Cabral in a dispute over offshore oil rights in an area presumed to be rich in petroleum deposits.

[11] Contact between the two Guineas was intensified in September 1982, and in February 1983 diplomatic missions were exchanged.

[12] The first development plan of 1983-86 proposed an initial investment of $118.6 million, of which 75 per cent would be financed by international funds. In 1984, the construction of five ports was started at an estimated cost of $40 million, and the construction of the Bisalanca Airport was completed. The Government started a campaign against corruption and inefficiency in public administration, and as a result in 1984 Vice-President Victor Saude Maria was asked to resign. Shortly afterwards, the Popular Assembly eliminated the position of prime minister, and the Revolutionary Council became the Council of State.

WORKERS

% OF LABOUR FORCE   **1998**

■FEMALE: 40%   ■MALE: 60%

1990

■SERVICES: 12.8%
■INDUSTRY: 1.9%
■AGRICULTURE: 85.3%

LAND USE

DEFORESTATION: 0.4% annual (1990/95)
IRRIGATED: 5.7% of arable (1993)

1993

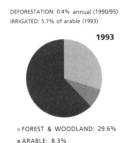

■FOREST & WOODLAND: 29.6%
■ARABLE: 8.3%
■OTHER: 62.1%

PUBLIC EXPENDITURE

DEFENCE EXPENDITURE   **13%**
(% of goverment exp.)   (1997)

[13] In November 1984, the vice-president of the Council of State, Colonel Paulo Correia, led an unsuccessful coup against President Vieira. Correia was executed on July 21 1986.

[14] The 1984 stabilization plan failed, causing further deterioration of the economic and financial situation. The international economic crisis increased, the price of Guinea-Bissau's oil exports lost market value. The Government adopted a 'corrective' policy, including freezing salaries and reducing public investment. This was an attempt to bring it into line with IMF conditions for refinancing the servicing of the foreign debt. The economy was subsequently opened up to foreign capital in the hope of attracting resources from Portugal and France, particularly in the high-priority areas of telecommunications. In 1989, Portugal participated in the creation of a commercial bank.

[15] In 1986, the Government granted an amnesty to political prisoners. Two years later, in June 1988, the Central Committee of the PAIGC began discussing a proposal for separating the executive and legislative powers. At that time Guinea-Bissau spent more on its military budget than on education and health combined.

[16] In February 1991, the PAIGC approved a political reform which anticipated elections for 1992. The IMF cancelled several loans granted to Guinea-Bissau after the resignation of Economy Minister Manuel dos Santos.

[17] Dependence on agricultural exports - especially on peanuts, whose price had fallen abruptly - caused significant social and economic imbalances along with political tensions in 1992 and 1993. The 1992 elections were not held due to a government decision and after the murder in March 1993 of a high military commander they were delayed once more.

[18] Finally, in 1994 João Bernardo Vieira defeated Kumba Iala of the Party for Social Renovation, obtaining 52 per cent of the vote in the second round. During the campaign, Iala accused him of supporting tribalism and racism. In the parliamentary elections, Vieira's PAIGC took 64 of the 100 seats at stake. Believing that the ruling party had 'bought' votes, Iala refused to take part in a national unity government.

[19] In January 1995, the IMF granted a new $14 million loan in support of economic reforms. In June, the visit of Senegalese president Abdou Diouf led to a rapprochement with Dakar after a period of relative hostility. Both countries agreed to exploit joint energy and mineral resources. In August, Iala denounced Vieira's closer ties with France, the rise in the price of basic items like rice, and human rights violations by the government.

[20] In late 1995, Guinea-Bissau ratified the border agreement signed with Senegal in 1993, resetting its maritime frontiers and stipulating the joint exploitation of an area which was supposedly rich in oil.

[21] In August 1996, the Government accepted 44 illegal African immigrants expelled from Spain. The League of Human Rights of Guinea-Bissau said the Government had agreed to the Spanish request in return for payment. In the UN Security Council, Guinea-Bissau supported an air embargo against Sudan for refusing to extradite three individuals suspected of a murder attempt against Egyptian president, Hosni Mubarak.

[22] In 1998, Guinea-Bissau continued to house pro-independence rebels from the Senegalese Movement of Democratic Forces of Casamance (MFDC). However, Guinea-Bissau's military intervention against a refugee camp on the frontier with Senegal in January that year fed rumors of rapprochement between Bissau and Dakar, which led to a more hard-line attitude towards the Casamance refugees.

[23] On May 4, the UN asked 'donor' countries to help Guinea-Bissau recover following eight months of civil war. Three days later however Mané rose up again and Vieira was defeated; he sought political asylum in Portugal. The army accused Vieira of corruption and treason. France condemned the coup and Mané was accused of violating the Abuja and Lomé agreements, signed three months earlier.

[24] In August, the FAO included Guinea-Bissau amongst the 16 African countries with the greatest poverty and food shortages, stating that it was facing a serious emergency.

[25] Five months after the coup, a mass grave was found containing 18 bodies in the town of Portogole, including former vice president Correira. Meanwhile, the military junta presented evidence to Portugal of the 'crimes' committed by Vieira in order to get him repatriated. On November 17, two weeks before the national elections, General Mané stated that 'any president who is elected and does not fulfil his promises will be immediately deposed'. Supporters of the General stated the military junta would be dissolved once the new president was in power.

[26] In the first round ballot on November 28, the PSR took 38 of the 102 seats in the National Assembly and the Resistance of Guinea-Bissau-Bafatá Movement came second with 28 seats. In the second round of presidential elections on January 16 2000,

PROFILE

ENVIRONMENT

The land is flat with slight elevations in the southeast and abundant irrigation from rivers and canals. The coastal area is swampy, suitable for rice. Rice, peanuts, palm oil and cattle are produced in the drier eastern region. The need to increase exports led to over-cultivation of the soil; in addition, rice plantations are replacing part of the coastal woodlands. Slash-and-burn techniques, as well as numerous forest fires, have contributed to deforestation.

SOCIETY

Peoples: Balante 27.2 per cent; Fulani 22.9 per cent; Malinke 12.2 per cent; Mandyako 10.6 per cent; Pepel 10.0 per cent; other 17.1 per cent
Religions: Two-thirds profess traditional African religions; nearly one-third are Muslim and there is a small Catholic minority.
Languages: Portuguese (official). The *crioulo* dialect, a mixture of Portuguese and African languages, is used as the lingua franca. The most widely spoken native languages are Mande and Fulah.
Political Parties: The African Party for the Independence of Guinea and Cape Verde (PAIGC) was the country's sole political party until the end of 1991; since that date 10 political groups were registered, among them the Party for Social Renovation, formed by dissidents from the PAIGC.

THE STATE

Official Name: República da Guiné-Bissau.
Administrative Divisions: 8 Regions and 1 Autonomous Sector.
Capital: Bissau 200,000 people (1995).
Other cities: Bafatá 13,429 people; Gabu 7,803 people (1979).
Government: Kumba Yalá, President since February 2000. Caetano N'Tchama, Prime Minister since February 2000. National People's Assembly, parliament of 100 seats.
National Holiday: September 24 (1973). Independence Day.
Armed Forces: 7,250 (1996). Other: 2,000 Gendarmes.

President Kumba Yalá, of the populist Party for Social Renovation (PSR) was elected with 72 per cent of the vote. The new government was made up of the two parties. Caetano N'Tchama was Prime Minister. ■

Guyana

Guyana

Population: 855,000 (1999)
Area: 214,970 SQ KM
Capital: Georgetown
Currency: Guyana dollar
Language: English

The original inhabitants of what is now Guyana, the Arawaks, were displaced from the area by the Caribs, warriors who dominated the region before moving on to the nearby islands which were later called after them.

[2] Both the Arawaks and the Caribs were nomads. Organized into families of 15 to 20 people, they lived by fishing and hunting. There are thought to have been half a million inhabitants at the time of the arrival of Europeans in Guyana. There are around 45,000 indians, divided into nine ethnic groups, of which seven maintain their cultural identity and traditions.

[3] Led on by the legend of El Dorado, in 1616 the Dutch built the first fort. Guyana was made up of three colonies: Demerara, Berbice and Essequibo. But in 1796, the Dutch colony was taken over by the British, who had already begun a wide-scale introduction of slaves. A slave, Cuffy, led a rebellion in 1763 which was brutally put down. To this day, Cuffy is considered a national hero.

[4] Those slaves that escaped from the plantations went into the forests to live with the indigenous peoples, giving rise to the 'bush blacks'. The English brought in Chinese, Javanese and Indian workers as cheap labor. In the second half of the 20th century, Guyana's population managed to channel independence politics into a single movement, the People's Progressive Party (PPP), with policies of national independence and social improvements, with long-term aims for a socialist country. Cheddi Jagan, the first Prime Minister of the colony, was in power for three successive terms.

[5] After years of struggle and periods of great violence, Britain recognized Guyana's independence within the Commonwealth on May 26 1966. By that time, the PPP had split; the Afro-Guyanese population joined the People's National Congress (PNC), while indigenous people remained loyal to Jagan. Forbes Burnham, leader of the PNC took office, supported by other ethnic minorities.

[6] This process was influenced by ethnic conflict and by foreign interests, particularly from the US, which felt its hegemony in the Caribbean threatened by Jagan's socialism.

[7] Even though Burnham came to power with Washington's blessing, he kept his distance. He declared himself in favor of non-alignment and proclaimed a Cooperative Republic in 1970. The bauxite, timber and sugar industries were nationalized in the first half of the 1970s, and by 1976 the State controlled 75 per cent of the country's economy. At the same time, regional integration was implemented through CARICOM, the Latin American Economic System (SELA), and the Caribbean Merchant Fleet. During the first decade after independence, Burnham and Jagan defended the same political platform.

[8] In May 1976, Cheddi Jagan stated the need to 'achieve national anti-imperialist unity', when disputes broke out with Brazil over the border. The PPP representatives returned to Parliament, from which they had withdrawn three years earlier to protest over electoral corruption. Shortly afterwards, Burnham announced the creation of a Popular Militia.

[9] Elections were postponed in order to hold a constitutional referendum, with Parliament drawing up a new constitution. This gave way to harsh criticism by the PPP, which withdrew from legislative activity for the second time. In 1980 Burnham was elected President. However, according to international observers, the election had been plagued by fraud. In 1980 Burnham granted authorization for transnational corporations to carry out oil and uranium operations. In addition, he turned to the IMF to obtain credit.

[10] In June of the same year, Walter Rodney, the famous Guyanese intellectual and founder of the opposition Working People's Alliance (WPA,) was killed by a car bomb. The culprits were never found.

[11] In the post-election period, border disputes escalated. Venezuela claimed the Essequibo region, approximately 159,000 sq km (three quarters) of Guyanese territory, arguing that British imperialism illegally deprived Venezuela of that area in the 19th century.

[12] In 1983, both countries turned to the UN. In 1985 direct negotiations started again to settle the dispute 'within a framework of cordiality and goodwill'. Negotiations were focused on an outlet to the Atlantic Ocean for Venezuela.

[13] While financial difficulties increased during 1984 and the Government faced a new crisis in its relations with labor unions, Burnham resumed contacts with the IMF to obtain a $150 million loan. Burnham considered the conditions on the loan 'unacceptable'. The American invasion of Grenada - and Guyana's criticism of this action - led to a deterioration of the relations between the two countries. Guyana made overtures to the socialist countries.

[14] Burnham died in August 1985 and was replaced by Desmond Hoyte. The PNC won the general elections that year with 78 per cent of the vote, but the opposition complained of alleged fraud. In

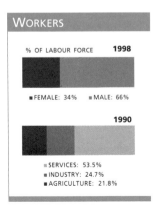

WORKERS

% OF LABOUR FORCE **1998**

■ FEMALE: 34%   ■ MALE: 66%

1990

■ SERVICES: 53.5%
■ INDUSTRY: 24.7%
■ AGRICULTURE: 21.8%

LAND USE

IRRIGATED: 27.1% of arable (1993)

1993

■ FOREST & WOODLAND: 76.8%
■ ARABLE: 2.2%
■ OTHER: 21.0%

PUBLIC EXPENDITURE

DEFENCE EXPENDITURE (% of goverment exp.)	**2.4%**	(1997)
MILITARY EXPENDITURE (% of health & education)	**21%**	(1990/91)

1986, five of the six opposition parties formed the Patriotic Coalition for Democracy, which boycotted the 1986 municipal elections, whereby all the seats went to the PNC. Hoyte, who was chosen President, announced in January 1987 his Government would return to 'Co-operative Socialism'.

[15] Parliament met on December 3 1991, five days after the Government declared a state of emergency in order to postpone the elections planned for that month. The Government ignored the opposition objections and extended the state of emergency until June 1992. On October 5 1992, Cheddi Jagan defeated President Desmond Hoyte (54 per cent to 41 per cent respectively) in the general elections. The Progressive People's Party took 32 seats in the National Assembly, while the PNC took 31.

[16] One of the first Latin American leaders to raise the flag of Marxism in the 1950s, Jagan returned to power, putting an end to 28 years of PNC dominion.

[17] In early 1993, unlike his neighbors including Brazil, President Cheddi Jagan allowed US troops to be deployed for training in the forests. He accepted US military collaboration to combat drug-trafficking and aid to develop sanitation in the interior.

[18] Guyana had frequent border disputes with neighboring Venezuela and Suriname, although it maintained good relations with Brazil, especially on the trade front.

[19] Jagan intended to modify the adjustment plan launched by his predecessor, Desmond Hoyte, in agreement with the IMF. His government defended 'non-conventional' methods of problems solving in land distribution, transport, health, housing and education.

[20] He proposed a market economy strategy to resolve the problem of the poverty of 80 per cent of the population. The emigration rate exceeded the demographic growth index, so that the population diminished from 1,020,000 in 1989 to 808,000 in 1992.

[21] The nation's wealth still remained nearly intact with large reserves of gold, diamonds, bauxite, forests and great agricultural potential. The fiscal deficit, which caused high inflation, was related to the smuggling of minerals, along with the price policy on exports of sugar, rice and other agricultural products.

[22] The celebration of the first anniversary of Jagan's Government was tarnished by a strike in the national electricity company as the Government had failed to implement its promise to increase State workers' pay by 300 per cent. The Government claimed the conditions imposed by the IMF prevented it from being this generous.

[23] In June 1994, Jagan rejected the ambassador to Georgetown nominated by the United States, accusing him of 'subversive activities' during the last few years of British colonial administration.

[24] In 1995, the worst environmental accident in the history of the country occurred, when four million cubic metres of cyanide-contaminated waste fell into the Omai river, a tributary of the Essequibo, the nation's main river.

[25] In February 1996, the human rights organization Amnesty International denounced the use of the death penalty by hanging in Guyana, the first such since 1990. That same year the Government had $500 million - nearly a quarter - of its foreign debt pardoned.

[26] Following Jagan's death in 1997, his wife Janet took over as interim Prime Minister. In the December 15 elections, she was elected President with 55.5 per cent against the 40.6 per cent of Hoyte's PNC. Despite threats of civil disobedience incited by Hoyte, the 77 year-old, US-born Jagan took office on December 19. Sam Hinds was appointed Prime Minister.

[27] In her first months in office, Jagan had to deal with a drought that affected the country's production (especially of gold), reduced trade, created transportation problems and facilitated forest fires. Rising prices triggered protests, the largest of which gathered outside the state telephone company to denounce rate increases of 400 to 1,000 per cent.

[28] After serving just 20 months of her term, Jagan resigned for health reasons. Economy Minister Bharrat Jagdeo - a youngster at 35 - took her place. The National People's Party, mostly made up of Afro-Guyanans, criticised the way the power transition was handled.

[29] In March 2000, Venezuelan President Hugo Chávez reiterated his country's claims to the Essequibo region, but affirmed

that Venezuela would submit to UN arbitration. Chávez also criticized a US company planning to build a rocket-launching site in the area in question. ∎

PROFILE

ENVIRONMENT

90 per cent of the population and most of the country's agriculture are concentrated on the coastal plane which ranges between 15 and 90 km in width. Rice and sugar cane are the main crops. As most of the shore is below sea level, dams and canals have been built to prevent flooding. The inner land consists of a 150 km-wide rainforest where the country's mineral resources are concentrated (bauxite, gold, and diamonds). To the west and south, the rest of the country is occupied by an ancient geological formation, the Guyana mountain range. Guyana is a native word meaning 'land of waters'. There are many rivers, as a result of the tropical climate and year-round rains. In terms of world-wide deforestation, Guyana has suffered little and until 1990, only a small fraction of the extensive forests had been felled. However, foreign companies are pressing for the intensification of lumber exploitation. In some areas, reforestation after logging has not been done, and this has led to soil erosion.

SOCIETY

Peoples: Half the population are descended from Indian indentured workers, one-third from African natives and the rest are native Americans, mixed European and indian descendants, Chinese and Europeans.
Religions: Protestant 34 per cent; Catholic 18 per cent; Hindu 34 per cent; Muslim 9 per cent.
Languages: English is official, Hindi and Urdu are used in religious ceremonies.
Political Parties: People's Progressive Party (PPP); People's National Congress (PNC).
Social Organizations: Trade Union Congress (TUC).

THE STATE

Official Name: Cooperative Republic of Guyana.
Administrative Divisions: 10 Regions.
Capital: Georgetown 248,000 people (1992).
Other cities: Linden 27,200 people; New Amsterdam 17,700.
Government: Bharrat Jagdeo, President and Head of State since August 1999, Samuel Archibald Hinds, Prime Minister and Chief of Goverment since August 1999. Parliament is composed of a unicameral assembly with 65 members, of which 12 are regional representatives and 53 are elected through direct vote and proportional representation.
National Holiday: February 23, Proclamation of the Republic (1970).
Armed Forces: 1,600 (1995). Other: 4,500 People's Militia, national service.

Haiti

Haïti

Population: 8,087,000 (1999)
Area: 27,750 SQ KM
Capital: Port-au-Prince
Currency: Gourde
Language: French and Creole

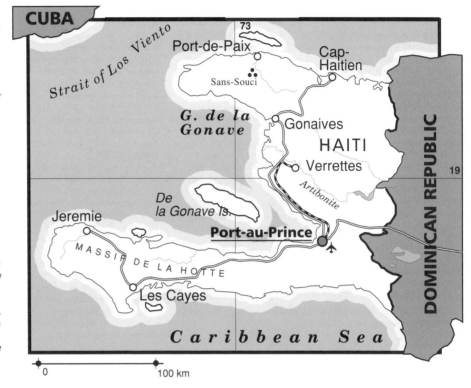

W hen Quisqueya, as the local population named it, was 'discovered' by Christopher Columbus in 1492, the island was inhabited by numerous Arawak peoples. The contact with Europeans was devastating for the Arawaks, who almost entirely disappeared from the island over the next few decades. Spanish colonists, supported by the Dominican missionaries, called the islands after their patron saint, St Dominic (Santo Domingo).

2   The island was later colonized by the French and other European settlers who were attracted by the sugar plantations. Disputes arose among the Europeans and in 1697 Spain ceded the west of the island to France, under the Treaty of Ryswick.

3   After gaining control of the island, France began to exploit it, introducing about 20,000 African slaves per year, leading to rapid racial mixing. Sugar soon became the principal export product of the region, and during the 18th century Haiti became the most important French possession in the Americas.

4   This prosperity was based on African slave labor. By 1789, the number of African slaves in the colony had reached 480,000. There were 60,000 mulattos and free 'colored' people, while the rich land-owning Europeans constituted a minority of no more than 20,000. The Haitians were influenced by the revolutionary movement that had started in the colonial capitals and they waged a revolutionary war, led by former slave Toussaint l'Ouverture. The war lasted from 1791 to 1803 and

ended with the proclamation of the first black republic in the world.

5   Haiti's struggle for independence went through several stages. Initially, the large landowners joined the revolutionary movement, along with the slaves, merchants and poor Europeans (called *petit blancs*), forming a local Assembly to demand an end to colonial rule. In the second stage, the free mulattos supported the French revolution, under the assumption that it would give equal rights to all people, regardless of the color of their skin. However, in 1790

the European planters fiercely rejected the demands of the freed slaves, leaving them no alternative but to ally themselves with the *marrons*, two groups of rebel slaves, a year later.

6   It was l'Ouverture who gave the *marrons* their direction, rallying them to the call of 'general freedom for all', transforming the different groups into a disciplined army. On February 4 1794, taking advantage of the splits in the French colonial system, he succeeded in getting the French National Convention to ratify a decree abolishing slavery in Santo Domingo and appointing himself as a general.

7   After the coup of the Brumaire 18, Napoleon Bonaparte sent a large military expedition to reconquer the colony and re-establish slavery. L'Ouverture responded with a general uprising, but he was imprisoned and died in exile in France in 1803.

8   Jean-Jacques Dessalines took over leadership of the war of independence, aided by Henri Christophe and Alexandre Pétion, who together radicalized L'Ouvertures's legacy. They

succeeded in uniting the Africans and mulattos and after a series of heroic campaigns, they forced the French troops to capitulate. Independence was proclaimed on November 28 1803, and Haiti became the first independent state in Latin America.

9   Dessalines gave his government a strong nationalist direction, trying to consolidate his personal power by creating an autocratic state, similar to the one emerging in France. Like Napoleon, Dessalines proclaimed himself emperor, calling himself Jacques I. Pétion and Christophe immediately started to plot against him, and he was murdered during a revolt in 1806.

10   The east of the island was recovered by the Spaniards under the Treaty of Paris in 1814, while in the west Christophe and Pétion fought for the leadership, dividing the territory. Henri Christophe established a republic in the north, later making it a kingdom with himself as King Henri I from 1811 to 1820. In the south, Alexandre Pétion ruled over a separate republic from 1808 to 1818, supporting Simon Bolívar with weapons and funding. Pétion was convinced

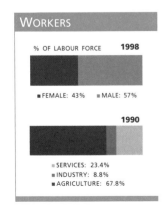

WORKERS

% OF LABOUR FORCE	1998

■ FEMALE: 43%   ■ MALE: 57%

1990

■ SERVICES: 23.4%
■ INDUSTRY: 8.8%
■ AGRICULTURE: 67.8%

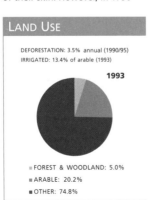

LAND USE

DEFORESTATION: 3.5% annual (1990/95)
IRRIGATED: 13.4% of arable (1993)

1993

■ FOREST & WOODLAND: 5.0%
■ ARABLE: 20.2%
■ OTHER: 74.8%

that only total American independence could guarantee that of Haiti, as the country was being harassed by European powers and the US.

[11] In 1818, JP Boyer was elected president instead of Pétion. Boyer recovered the north of the country in 1820, putting an end to Christophe's monarchic experiment. Two years later he conquered Santo Domingo in the east of the island, thus achieving a fragile reunification, which lasted for a quarter of a century. In 1843, a revolution led by the Santo Domingan Creoles divided the island into two definite, independent States: the Dominican Republic in the east, and the Republic of Haiti in the west.

[12] In spite of the permanent political violence throughout the 19th century, foreign investors gained access to the Haitian market by building ports and railways and by buying profitable plantations. The new transport and communications led to a faster and more effective extraction of the island's riches, with the profits going to the industrialized countries. The unfavorable trading exchange led the country into debt, until it became wholly dependent on its creditors, who were mostly American.

[13] From 1867, a bloody civil war launched a period of political instability and economic crisis which lasted until 1915, when the country was occupied by US marines for non-compliance with 'its commitments'. A year later the US invaded the Dominican Republic, gaining control of the whole island.

[14] The invasion of Haiti was heroically resisted by Charlemagne Péralte's 'Revolutionary Army'. Péralte was treacherously murdered in 1919. The US troops finally defeated the resistance and controlled the country until 1934, turning it into a virtual colony. That year, President Vincent succeeded in getting the US troops to withdraw from the island, but he could not eliminate US influence from the country's domestic affairs.

[15] The national army, or Garde d'Haiti, took a central role in national politics, staging coups against presidents Lescot, 1941-1946; Estime, 1946-1950; and Magloire, 1950-1957. In 1957, François Duvalier, a middle-class doctor, seized power supported by the army and the US.

[16] The elite mestizo group which was in power repressed the African-based culture until François Duvalier recognized the strategic power he could achieve by manipulating it. Over time he succeeded in building two great supports for his domination. The first was voodoo, the syncretic and distinctive religion of Haiti that combines African and Catholic rites. The second was the Tontons-Macoutes, a group of some 300,000 'national security volunteers'.

[17] The army, the commercial bourgeoisie, the ecclesiastic authorities, the state bureaucracy, and the US State Department used Duvalier to control the country for over 30 years. With Washington's backing, Duvalier or 'Papa Doc' proclaimed himself President-for-life in 1964, passing on the title to his son Jean-Claude or 'Baby Doc' on his death in 1971.

[18] Assailed on the international level by continual condemnations of human rights violations, and on the domestic level by active opposition, Jean-Claude Duvalier's government called elections in 1984. Sixty-one per cent of the population abstained. Organizations opposed to Duvalier renewed their underground activities and the opposition grew, organizing itself into parties and trade unions, while the regime was becoming a burden to the US.

[19] Repression grew, and by 1985 it was estimated that Baby Doc's regime had been responsible for 40,000 murders. The country was enveloped by a growing wave of protests and strikes. Duvalier fled the country in a US airforce plane and received temporary asylum in France.

[20] A National Governing Council (CNG) led by General Henri Namphu assumed control of the government, promising 'free and direct' elections by the end of 1987.

[21] The dictator's flight did not end the mobilization of the people. Mass lynching by Tontons-Macoutes forced the National Governing Council to dissolve this repressive force and to free all the prisoners.

[22] In October 1986, the CNG called elections to elect a Constituent Assembly to draw up a new constitution. Less than 10 per cent of the 3 million Haitians participated in the election and, on March 29 1987 a referendum approved the new constitution with 99.8 per cent of the vote. The new constitution limited the presidential term to 5 years, prohibited re-election and divided the power with a prime minister chosen by Parliament.

[23] The elections were to be held in November 1987, but a few hours after the polling stations were opened, they were sabotaged by factions of the armed forces and by former Tontons-Macoutes, and the elections were suspended, finally taking place in January 1988. In a very volatile atmosphere, Leslie Manigat, the 'official' candidate, was elected, only to be deposed in June, in a coup led by General Namphu.

[24] In September 1988, a movement of sergeants and soldiers deposed General

PROFILE

ENVIRONMENT

Haiti occupies the western third of the island of Hispaniola, the second largest of the Greater Antilles. Two main mountain ranges run from east to west, extending along the country's northern and southern peninsulas, contributing to their shape. The hills and river basins in between form the center of Haiti. The flatlands that open up to the sea in the west, are protected from the humid trade winds by the mountains to the north and east. Coffee is the main export product. Copper extraction ceased in 1976 and bauxite deposits are almost exhausted. The northern coastline has the heaviest rainfall and contains the country's most developed area, though the land there is suffering from serious erosion. Forests make up less than 2 per cent of the land area.

SOCIETY

Peoples: Nearly 95 per cent of Haitians are descendants of African slaves. There are also minorities of European and Asian origin, and integration has produced a small mestizo group. Thousands of Haitians have emigrated in recent years, especially to Colombia, Venezuela and the United States.
Religions: Voodoo, a mixture of Christianity and various African beliefs. Catholicism.
Languages: French and Creole. French is spoken by less than 20 per cent of the population. Most people speak Creole, a local language mix of Spanish, English, French and African languages.
Political Parties: National Front for Change and Democracy (FNCD); National Alliance for Democracy and Progress (ANDP); National Committee of the Democratic Movements (Konakom); National People's Assembly (APN); Agricultural Industrial Party (PAIN); Unified Party of Haitian Communists (PUCH) ; Union for National Reconciliation (UNR); Lavalas Political Organization.
Social Organizations: The 'Grassroots' Church groups, of Catholic origin; Movement in Favor of the Creole Language; Solidarity of the Women of Haiti (SOFA).

THE STATE

Official name: Repiblik Dayti.
Administrative divisions: 9 departments.
Capital: Port-au-Prince,1,500,000 people (est. 1995).
Other Cities: Cap-Haitien 100,638; (1995).
Government: René Préval, President since 1996.
National Holiday: January 1, Independence Day (1804).
Armed Forces: None.

LITERACY	EXTERNAL DEBT	FOREIGN TRADE
1995	1998	Millions US$ 1998
	Per capita **US$ 132** 	IMPORTS **1,128** EXPORTS **445**
44%		

Namphu, putting Prosper Avril, the *eminence grise* of the Duvalier period, into power.

25 In March 1990, during a period of intense popular protest, General Avril was ousted by General Abraham, who relinquished control to a provisional civilian government headed by Judge Ertha Pascal-Trouillot, the first woman to occupy the presidency in Haiti. The provisional government created suitable conditions to put the Constitution into practice, and called elections for December 1990.

26 These elections were won by a priest, Jean-Bertrand Aristide, who obtained 67 per cent of the vote as the leader of the National Front for Change and Democracy. He was voted in mostly by the poor urban sectors, and he took office on February 7 1991.

27 Aristide, a Liberation Theology activist, had been censured in 1988 by the church authorities and expelled from the Salesian order. His governmental program was based on a war against corruption and drug trafficking, including a thorough literacy campaign, and a project to move from 'extreme poverty to poverty with dignity'.

28 On September 30, General Raoul Cédras staged a bloody coup. In protest the Organization of American States (OAS) declared a trade embargo, starting diplomatic negotiations in the region and in the UN. Meanwhile, the rebels tried to avoid international isolation by officially recognizing the sovereignty and operation of parliament.

29 In February 1992, OAS representatives, Haitian members of parliament, and the deposed Aristide signed an agreement in Washington to re-establish democracy and reinstate the former president.

30 In January 1993, the de facto government held legislative elections which many people considered illegitimate as they were designed only to partially replace Parliament. Less than 3 per cent of those registered to vote took part. Months later, Marc Bazin resigned as prime minister.

31 On June 27, indirect talks began in New York between General Cédras and ousted president Aristide. Meanwhile, the UN Security Council imposed a financial, oil and arms embargo on Haiti. In July, Aristide and Cédras signed an agreement which guaranteed the return of the President as well as an amnesty for all military leaders involved in the coup. In accordance with the agreement, Aristide named Robert Malval prime minister.

32 However, a new wave of violence soon broke out in Haiti, to prevent the agreement from going into effect. In October, a US warship patrolled the coast near the capital. An armed mob threatened the American troops, so US President Clinton ordered the ship back to US Guantanamo military base in Cuba. In the meantime, the Security Council reinstated the naval embargo.

33 Malval's Justice Minister, Guy Malary, was assassinated. The attack was carried out almost in the same place where Antoine Izmery, a pro-Aristide businessman, had been killed a month earlier. Those responsible for the killings were members of the pro-military Front for the Advancement and Progress of Haiti, who used the same tactics as the Tontons-Macoutes.

34 The UN embargo destroyed the formal economy and increased poverty, although it did not substantially affect the lifestyle of the country's wealthy families. Violence rose: according to a UN report, 426 Aristide supporters were murdered between May 1993 and February 1994.

35 On October 15, Aristide returned after the coup leaders had gone into exile and the country was occupied by a multinational force led by the United States. While in exile, the President had promised to implement a structural adjustment program prescribed by the IMF. In December, troops were demobilized in order to create a new national police force.

36 In spite of meaning to punish those responsible for human rights abuses, Aristide - under sustained pressure from Washington - was forced to offer merely symbolic gestures in most cases, such as a gravestone in memory of the victims of death squads.

37 In 1995, a contingent of UN troops replaced the multinational forces. In November, René Préval, an Aristide supporter, won the elections with 88 per cent of the vote and took office on February 7 1996. Préval requested the UN peace forces to remain for an additional period of time due to the numerous conflicts and acts of violence which involved national police. Kidnappings and murders - including those of eight policemen out of duty - did not stop, while popular uprisings were violently repressed.

38 On July 16 1996, Claude Raymond, a general and minister in Duvalier's cabinet, was arrested for terrorist activities. Four days later, André Armand, former Army sergeant and leader of the retired soldiers lobby group, was killed by unknown assailants after publicly stating that retired army members were plotting to assassinate Préval and former president Aristide. The resignation of Prime Minister Rosny Smarth in 1997 and the President's decision to dissolve Parliament and govern by decree heightened political tensions and confrontation with the opposition. Jacques-Edouard Alexis, of the Lavalas political organization, was named in March 1999 to take over as Prime Minister.

39 In 1997, UN peacekeeping troops were replaced by a 300-member civilian police force, which completed its withdrawal in January 2000. Elections slated for March of that year were postponed in order to resolve voter registration problems. A demonstration of Aristide supporters against election officials led to the deaths of four people in March 2000. ■

DEMOGRAPHY

Population: 8,087,000 (1999)
Annual growth: 2.1 % (1975/97)
Estimates for year 2015 (million): 10.4 (1999)
Annual growth to year 2015: 1.6 % (1997/2015)
Urban population: 33.0 % (1997)
Urban Growth: 3.9 % (1980/95)
Children per woman: 4.3 (1998)

HEALTH

Life expectancy at birth: 54 years (1998)
male: 51 years (1998)
female: 56 years (1998)
Infant mortality: 91 per 1,000 (1998)
Under-5 child mortality: 130 per 1,000 (1998)
Daily calorie supply: 1,855 per capita (1996)
16 doctors per 100,000 people (1993)
Safe water: 37 % (1990/98)

EDUCATION

Literacy: 44 % (1995)
male: 47 % (1995)
female: 41 % (1995)
School enrolment:
Primary total: 56 % (1990/96)
male: 58 % (1990/97)
female: 54 % (1990/97)
Secondary:
male: 23 % (1990/96)
female: 22 % (1990/96)
Tertiary: 1 % (1996)

COMMUNICATIONS

3 newspapers (1996), 55 radios (1997), 5 TV sets (1996) and 8 main telephone lines (1996) per 1,000 people

ECONOMY

Per capita, GNP: $ 410 (1998)
Annual growth, GNP: 3.2 % (1998)
Annual inflation: 23.3 % (1990/98)
Consumer price index: 160.8 (1998)
Currency: 16.8 gourdes = $ 1 (1998)
Cereal imports: 481,009 metric tons (1998)
Fertilizer use: 173 kg per ha (1997)
Exports: $ 445 million (1998)
Imports: $ 1,128 million (1998)
External debt: $ 1,048 million (1998); $ 132 per capita (1998)
Debt service: 8.2 % of exports (1998)
Development aid received: $ 332 million (1997); $ 50.4 per capita (1997); 11.80 % of GNP (1997)

ENERGY

Consumption: 237.0 Kgs of Oil equivalent per capita yearly (1997); 27.0 % imported (1997)

HDI (rank/value): 152/0.430 (1997)

Honduras

Honduras

Population: 6,315,000 (1999)
Area: 112,090 SQ KM
Capital: Tegucigalpa
Currency: Lempira
Language: Spanish

Before the arrival of the Spanish, the region of present-day Honduras was inhabited by Chibcha (see Colombia), Lenca and Maya Indians. In the north of Honduras lies the city of Copan, which belonged to the ancient Mayan Empire. Copan's splendour lasted until the 9th century AD, ending with the downfall of the Mayan Empire.

[2] The first European to reach Honduras appears to have been Amerigo Vespucci in 1498, but Pedro de Alvarado was in charge of the final Spanish conquest of Honduran territory, joining it to the Captaincy-General of Guatemala, despite strong resistance from the Indians led by Lempira.

[3] In 1821, Honduras gained independence from Spain. Together with the other Central American provinces it joined the short-lived Mexican Empire of Iturbide, which collapsed two years later. Francisco Morazán and other Honduran leaders of the last century, sought in vain to set up an independent Central American federation. Their efforts were no match for Britain's 'Balkanization' tactics.

[4] With the liberal reform of 1880, mining became the backbone of the economy. To encourage the development of this sector the country was opened to foreign investment and technology. In 1898, another 'empire' managed to penetrate Honduras: the notorious US United Fruit Company (Unifruco). The Company took over vast tracts of land. It produced almost the entire fruit output of the country, ruled railroads, ships and ports, and dictated many key political decisions.

[5] US Marines invaded Honduras in 1924, imposing a formal democracy and allowing Unifruco to establish a monopoly in banana production by buying out its main competitor, the Cuyamel Fruit Company. Washington eventually handed power over to Tiburcio Carias Andino, who governed Honduras from 1933 to 1949.

[6] Border disputes with Guatemala led to US arbitration in 1930. In 1969, friction developed with El Salvador when the number of Salvadoran peasants emigrating to Honduras reached a critical level. This led to a further war, which was triggered by a soccer game, and was finally ended with mediation by the Organization of American States (see El Salvador).

[7] In 1971, nationalists and liberals signed the Unity Pact. General Osvaldo López Arellano, in power since 1963, permitted elections and Ramón Ernesto Cruz of the National Party, was elected President.

[8] However in 1972 López Arellano overthrew the Cruz administration. He demonstrated his sensitivity to peasant demands for land reform and began to impose controls upon United Brands (as Unifruco was now called). This resulted in López Arellano's resignation and his replacement by Colonel Juan A Melgar Castro.

[9] The army commander-in-chief, General Policarpo Paz García, took power in August 1978. This regime became closely allied to that of the dictator Anastasio Somoza in neighboring Nicaragua. Nicaragua's Sandinista Revolution in 1979 hastened the election of a constituent assembly which promptly ratified Paz García as President. General elections were held in 1981, but leftist parties were banned. Liberal Party candidate, Roberto Suazo Córdova, won the presidency and was inaugurated in January 1982.

[10] The price of consumer goods immediately rose and an anti-terrorist law was passed forbidding strikes as intrinsically subversive. Death squads acted with impunity and opposition political figures disappeared daily.

[11] Honduras tolerated the presence of US troops and the installation of Nicaraguan 'Contras' in its territory. It was estimated that the Pentagon had 1,200 soldiers there in 1983. They participated in some military operations, gave military instruction and logistical support, and established a military infrastructure. The Contras had some 15,000 soldiers within Honduran territory, alongside 'Nica' camps, holding around 30,000 refugees.

[12] In April 1985, 7,000 US soldiers were on maneuvers near the Nicaraguan border. Washington offered the Honduran air force the renewal of all its combat planes. With almost $300 million in military aid, the Honduran army doubled its number of troops and renewed its Air Force combat fleet.

[13] Jose Azcona Hoyo of the Liberal Party won the 1985 elections. The new president requested help from Washington so that the Contras could leave the country; he also tried to stimulate foreign investment.

[14] In 1989 the National Party candidate Rafael Callejas won by a big margin although the elections were marked by fraud. Supported by the US and the business community, Callejas launched an overall liberalization of the economy.

[15] In 1990, after the Sandinista defeat in neighboring Nicaragua's elections, US President Bush's administration made significant cuts in its economic aid to Honduras. Callejas sought closer ties with the armed forces, in the hopes of keeping growing social discontent under control.

[16] In early 1990, the Government raised taxes, increased fuel prices by 50 per cent and devalued the national currency.

[17] In December 1990 the Government extended an amnesty to all political prisoners or victims of political persecution. The anti-terrorism law was abolished and a forum for political discussion was set up, with no group excluded.

[18] On January 12 1991, after eight years in exile, four leftist political leaders returned to Honduras, announcing the end of their armed struggle. In October 1991, the 'Lorenzo Zelaya' People's Revolutionary Forces accepted the government's peace declaration and renounced armed conflict.

[19] Armed forces commander, General Arnulfo Cantarera, accused of human rights violations, was relieved of his command and replaced by General Luis Discua, who favored increased intervention by the military in the country's political life. Political assassination and other abuses committed by the military were denounced by the Honduran Committee for the Defense of Human Rights.

[20] The increase in military power and the country's overall political instability compounded the weakness of the economy, which was suffering the effects of losing dollars previously provided by US military aid.

[21] Voters registered their discontent in the ballots, bringing about the triumph of opposition candidate Carlos Roberto Reina, a social democrat, in the November 1993 elections.

[22] One of the new government's first decisions was the abolition of the mandatory military service. This measure was approved by Parliament in May 1994 and ratified by the legislature in April 1995. However, in August 1994, giving in to pressure from the military the Government agreed to a temporary draft call to fill 7,000 openings in the armed forces. In mid-1994, the Government dissolved the infamous National Bureau of Investigations, which had once been the torture section of the armed forces.

[23] As a result of the fall in banana exports to the EC, the Tela Railroad Company (formerly part of the United Fruit Company) closed four plantations, claiming that they were no longer profitable. They also laid off 3,000 employees for three months. Union workers went on strike and after several days of tension, the Government called off the strike and forced the Company to reopen the banana plantations and

rehire the workers who had been laid off. After negotiating directly with the Union - SITRATERCO - the Company reinstated 1,200 workers, though nearly 1,000 female employees were not re-employed.

[24] As a result of the drought which hit the country during the first half of 1994, 90 villages lost over 60 per cent of their subsistence crops. Given the danger of famine, which threatened more than 1.5 million people, the Government requested aid from the UN's food agency, FAO. The latter provided $900 million for agricultural development of the declared emergency areas. However, 73 per cent of the population of Honduras were still living in conditions of poverty or extreme poverty.

[25] While the armed forces continued with police assignments in the cities, the Legislative Assembly began to work on amendments to the constitution that handed control of public security forces over to civilians. In January 1995 the new Crime Investigations Unit began to act, led by civilians, replacing the secret police that had been dismantled the previous year. The new body,

initially of 1,500 agents, was trained by the Israeli police and the FBI from the US. At that time, more than 50 people were murdered each day in the country.

[26] Senior government officials were imprisoned in 1995 for their involvement in trafficking official passports. The Supreme Court revoked the immunity of former president Callejas to testify on the falsification of documents and the appropriation of public funds. President Reina himself was touched by the offensive against corruption, being investigated for using State funds for private ends.

[27] In early 1996, a 25-per-cent pay rise coincided with a 30-per-cent increase in the cost of basic products. Demonstrations calling for pay increases became increasingly frequent, especially in the public sector. The IMF imposed strict restrictions on state spending. The Government pruned military power with a series of measures - like removing control of the police force from their hands - and downsized the army. A bomb attack on the presidential palace was attributed to grieved military personnel. In July, the Commander in Chief of the armed forces

stopped an attempted military rebellion from occurring.

[28] In October 1997, the police prevented some 400 people erecting a statue of Lempira - the indigenous resistance leader of the Spanish conquest era - in a public thoroughfare in Tegucigalpa. A statue of Christopher Columbus previously on this spot had been pulled off its pedestal and destroyed by demonstrators.

[29] On November 23, the general elections returned the Liberal Party of outgoing President Carlos Reina to power. His successor, Carlos Flores, took 53 per cent of the vote, 11 points more than the ultra-right National Party candidate, Nora Castro. The legislative elections confirmed the exclusion of Left from parliament. Flores announced he would continue with the economic liberalization.

[30] When sworn in, in January 1998, the new President said he was willing to appoint a national unity government and to make a non-aggression pact with the military-linked opposition. Flores took over a country in crisis where 80 per cent of the population lived in extreme poverty and 228 landowners controlled more than 75 per cent of the land. The international financial bodies pressed for the urgent implementation of a new adjustment program.

[31] In September of that year, Hurricane Mitch struck, causing damage calculated at $5.36 billion and an estimated 24,000 deaths throughout Central America - 6,000 in Honduras. More than 1.3 million Hondurans lost their homes and another 8,000 disappeared. One year later, floods killed 35 people and devastated 14,000 hectares of farmland, with losses totaling $20 million. The authorities maintained that if the country had received the aid promised by the industrialized countries after the devastation caused by Mitch, they would have been able to dredge the rivers and prevent the new catastrophe.

[32] The ratification of a border treaty with Colombia in November 1999 sparked a diplomatic dispute with Nicaragua, leading both countries to mobilize troops along their shared frontier. According to the treaty, Honduras recognized Colombian sovereignty over a group of islands off the Nicaraguan coast as a result of setting parallel 15 as the Honduran-Colombian border. Colombian possession of the San Andres and Providencia islands and the establishment of parallel 15 as a border strips Nicaragua of some 130,000 square km of maritime territory. The Foreign Ministers from the two countries signed a framework accord to hold future talks and established a demilitarized zone along the border in February 2000. Within one month after signing the accord,

PROFILE

ENVIRONMENT

80 per cent of the land is covered by mountains and rainforests. Both population and economic activity are concentrated along the Caribbean coast and in the southern highlands, close to the border with El Salvador. The coastal plains have the largest banana plantations in Central America. Coffee, tobacco and corn are grown in the southern part of the country. Deforestation, misuse of the soil and uncontrolled development have led to soil depletion.

SOCIETY

Peoples: Honduran people are of mixed Mayan and European descent. There is a 10 per cent minority of native Americans; 2 per cent are Afro-American. Garifunas, descendants of fugitive slaves and native Americans, live along the Caribbean coast and on the nearby islands, maintaining their traditional lifestyles. **Languages:** Spanish is the official and most widely-spoken language; Garifuna, various indian languages (eg Lenca and Miskito). **Religions:** Roman Catholic 85 per cent; Protestant 10 per cent. **Political Parties:** People's Liberal Alliance (ALIPO), of social democratic orientation; National Party, conservative; Liberal Party; 'Rodista' National Movement (MNR), led by former president Suazo Córdova; Revolutionary Democratic Movement; Innovation and Unity Party (PINU); Christian Democratic Party; Socialist Action Party of Honduras (PASOH); Marxist-Leninist Communist Party (PCML); The Unified National Direction (DNU) is made up of the People's Revolutionary Forces (FPR), the 'Morazanista', Alliance for the Liberation of Honduras, the 'Cinchonero' People's Liberation Movement (MPLC), the United Revolutionary Movement (MUR), the Communist Party of Honduras (PCH), and the Revolutionary Party of Central American Workers of Honduras. **Social Organizations:** The Confederation of Honduran Workers (CTH) founded in 1964 and affiliated to the ORIT (Regional Interamerican Labor Organization), is the only officially-recognized labor federation. The General Workers' Central Union (CGT), Social-Christian; the United Federation of Workers (FUT); the Federation of Honduran Workers' Unions (FESITRAH); the Independent Workers' Federation and the United National Peasants' Front of Honduras (FUNACAMPH).

THE STATE

Official Name: República de Honduras. **Administrative divisions:** 18 Departments. **Capital:** Tegucigalpa 775,300 people (est 1995). **Other cities:** San Pedro Sula 368,500 people; La Ceiba 86,000; El Progreso 81,200; Choluteca 72,800 (1994). **Government:** Carlos Roberto Flores Facussé, President since January, 1998. **National Holiday:** September 15, Independence Day (1821). **Armed Forces:** 18.800 troops, 13.200 conscripts (1995). **Other:** 5,500 members of the Public Security Force.

DEMOGRAPHY

Population: 6,315,000 (1999)
Annual growth: 3.2 % (1975/97)
Estimates for year 2015 (million): 9.0 (1999)
Annual growth to year 2015: 2.3 % (1997/2015)
Urban population: 45.0 % (1997)
Urban Growth: 5.2 % (1980/95)
Children per woman: 4.2 (1998)

HEALTH

Life expectancy at birth: 70 years (1998)
male: 68 years (1998)
female: 72 years (1998)
Maternal mortality: 220 per 100,000 live births (1990-98)
Infant mortality: 33 per 1,000 (1998)
Under-5 child mortality: 44 per 1,000 (1998)
Daily calorie supply: 2,368 per capita (1996)
22 doctors per 100,000 people (1993)
Safe water: 78 % (1990/98)

EDUCATION

Literacy: 70 % (1995)
male: 70 % (1995)
female: 69 % (1995)
School enrolment:
Primary total: 111 % (1990/96)
male: 110 % (1990/97)
female: 112 % (1990/97)
Secondary:
male: 29 % (1990/96)
female: 37 % (1990/96)
Tertiary: 11 % (1996)
Primary school teachers: one for every 35 (1994)

COMMUNICATIONS

55 newspapers (1996), 386 radios (1997), 80 TV sets (1996) and 31 main telephone lines (1996) per 1,000 people

ECONOMY

Per capita, GNP: $ 740 (1998)
Annual growth, GNP: 4.0 % (1998)
Annual inflation: 20.6 % (1990/98)
Consumer price index: 169.2 (1998)
Currency: 13.4 lempiras = $ 1 (1998)
Cereal imports: 162,493 metric tons (1998)
Food import dependency: 18 % (1997)
Fertilizer use: 782 kg per ha (1997)
Exports: $ 2,463 million (1998)
Imports: $ 2,796 million (1998)
External debt: $ 5,002 million (1998); $ 814 per capita (1998)
Debt service: 18.7 % of exports (1998)
Development aid received: $ 308 million (1997); $ 61.3 per capita (1997); 6.70 % of GNP (1997)

ENERGY

Consumption: 532.0 Kgs of Oil equivalent per capita yearly (1997); 37.0 % imported (1997)

HDI (rank/value): 114/0.641 (1997)

patrol boats from both sides exchanged gunfire in the Gulf of Fonseca on the Pacific coast in confrontations that continued throughout March that year. ∎

Hungary

Magyarország

Population: 10,075,000 (1999)
Area: 93,030 SQ KM
Capital: Budapest
Currency: Forint
Language: Hungarian

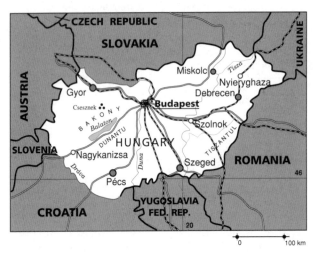

The territory of Hungary belonged to the Roman provinces of Pannonia and Dacia. By the end of the 4th century Rome had lost Pannonia which had been occupied by Germans, Slavs, Huns and Avars. The latter ruled over the Danube basin during the 7th and 8th centuries, until they were conquered by Charlemagne.

[2] Charlemagne's successors set up a series of Duchies in the western and northern parts of the basin, while the southern and eastern parts were under the sphere of influence of the Byzantine Empire and Bulgaria. The Duchy of Croatia became independent in 869 and Moravia put up stiff resistance to the Carolingians until the appearance of the Magyars.

[3] The Magyars had organized a federation of tribes west of the lower Don. These were made up by several clans led by a hereditary chieftain. The federation was called On-Ogur (Ten Arrows); 'Hungarian' is a derivation of this term in the Slav language. In 982 Emperor Rudolf turned to the Magyars to break Moravian resistance.

[4] Led by Arpad, the Magyars crossed the Carpathians and conquered the inhabitants of the central plateau. Moravia was defeated in 906 and Pannonia a year later. The Hungarians then expanded northwards and repeatedly raided the rest of Europe.

[5] The German Emperor Otto I defeated Arpad in 955 and halted Magyar expansion. Arpad's heirs reunified the tribes and adopted Western Christianity. Stephen I was crowned by Rome, subsequently laying the foundations of the Hungarian State.

[6] The question of succession

upon Stephen's death triggered two centuries of instability, but Hungary consolidated its dominions as far as the Carpathian mountains and Transylvania in the north, and the region between the Sava and Drava rivers in the south. In addition, it ruled over Croatia, Bosnia, and Northern Dalmatia (although the latter remained a separate state).

[7] With the Mongol invasion of the 13th century, Hungary lost half of its population. This prompted the Kingdom to reorganize and open its doors to new settlers; however, it had to make important concessions to the Cuman overlords and immigrants, who further weakened the Kingdom. Finally, the succession of foreigner Charles Robert of Anjou to the throne, stabilized the country.

[8] As the struggles between the Holy Roman Empire and the Papacy did not involve Hungary, the 14th century was the country's golden age. The Kingdom established friendly relations with Austria,

Bohemia and Poland, and strong links with Bosnia. However, during this period the country seized Dalmatia from Venice, and other territories from Serbia.

[9] Sigismund of Luxembourg (1387-1437) was both a German and Czech king. His long absences and arbitrary rule enabled the Hungarian Diet (parliament), which was made up of nobles, to expand its power. The Diet's consent was required in order for laws to be passed. Taxes were continually being exacted from the peasants, who started revolts in the north and in Transylvania.

[10] After another controversial succession, Matthias Corvinus of Prague was elected king of Hungary in 1458. He ruled over his country with an iron fist. With the help of the Black Army, an army of mercenaries, Matthias subdued his enemies inside the country and expanded his dominion over Bosnia, Serbia, Walachia, and Moldova. He also carried out a series of campaigns against

Bohemia and Austria.

[11] Upon Matthias' death in 1490 the magnates - the richest nobles - appointed Vladislav II, who was King of Bohemia and whose weak personality was well known. The Black Army was disbanded but the oppressed peasants rebelled again in 1514; the rebellion was ruthlessly put down. Meanwhile, Austria recovered the southern provinces and established its authority over Hungary.

[12] Hungary was conquered by the Ottoman empire in 1526. At first the Sultan supported Zapolya of Hapsburg to succeed the King who had been killed in battle. However, upon Zapoyla's death he occupied Budapest himself, and annexed a large portion to the south and centre of the country. Croatia and the western and northern strip of the country remained under the rule of Ferdinand of Hapsburg, who had to pay tribute to the Turkish Empire.

[13] During the 17th and 18th centuries Hungary was under two empires whose only interest in the country lay in the tributes it paid. The situation became more volatile when the majority of the population embraced the Reformation, while Vienna attempted to re-establish Catholicism. Even the nobles began to react against absolutism, peasant oppression and stagnation.

[14] During the 1848 revolution, the Hungarian Diet passed the April Laws, which brought changes in agricultural and fiscal matters. They reorganized on a more representative basis and proposed the reunification of the country and the creation of a separate administration in Budapest. The reform was met with distrust on the part of large landowners and Serbian, Romanian, and Croatian minorities.

[15] When the revolution was defeated, Austria, aided by Russia, annulled all reforms and regained control over Hungary. When Austria was defeated by Prussia in 1866, Vienna decided to subdivide its empire and accepted Hungary's April Laws. A 'Nationalities Law' guaranteed respect for the rights of minorities, giving way to the establishment of the Austro-Hungarian Empire in 1867.

[16] In the early 20th century, Hungarian politics was still dominated by conservative landowners, as most business people were foreigners, Jewish or German,

WORKERS

1997
UNEMPLOYMENT: 8.7%

% OF LABOUR FORCE **1998**

- FEMALE: 45% ■ MALE: 55%

1990

- SERVICES: 46.9%
- INDUSTRY: 37.9%
- AGRICULTURE: 15.2%

LAND USE

DEFORESTATION: -0.5% annual (1990/95)
IRRIGATED: 4.3% of arable (1993)

1993

- FOREST & WOODLAND: 19.0%
- ARABLE: 51.0%
- OTHER: 30.0%

PUBLIC EXPENDITURE

1997

43.2%

4.3%

DEFENCE   SOCIAL

MILITARY EXPENDITURE **18%**
(% of health & education) (1990/91)

and the majority of the population remained excluded from political activity. Minorities continued to be oppressed and the country lacked a strong sense of autonomy.

[17] With the collapse of the Hapsburg empire during World War I, a provisional government took power and proclaimed the Republic of Hungary. But Serbians, Czechs and Romanians seized two-thirds of the country and the central government was paralyzed. In 1919 a communist rebellion was followed by the formation of a 'Soviet' republic.

[18] Bela Kun's Bolsheviks expected Moscow to support them, but they were forced to flee when the Romanian troops took over the capital. The European powers pushed Romania into withdrawing and installed a provisional government. The 1920 Parliament restored monarchy and appointed Admiral Milkos Horthy as provisional ruler.

[19] In the Trianon Treaty, the victorious allies recognized Hungarian independence, but

MATERNAL MORTALITY

1990-98

Per 100,000
live births

15

LITERACY

1995

99%

EXTERNAL DEBT

1998

Per capita

US$ 2,825

Yugoslavia, Romania, and Czechoslovakia remained in possession of most of the country's territory and 60 per cent of its population. Austria, Poland, and Italy also benefited from the partition of Hungary.

[20] Hungary was forced to pay heavy reparations; its industry and production were left in a shambles. Unemployment rose to unprecedented figures and nearly 400,000 refugees arrived from the territories it had lost. The middle classes and the refugees set up right-wing armed groups, blaming the left for their ruin.

[21] Funds granted by the League

of Nations, followed by private investments and credits, alleviated domestic tension, but the depression of the 1930s had serious effects on Hungary. Horthy formed an extreme-right government which sided with Germany, while anti-Semitism grew within the country.

[22] The alliance with Berlin enabled Budapest to recover part of Slovakia, Ruthenia, and the north of Transylvania. Hungary cooperated in the German attacks on Romania, Yugoslavia and the USSR, but nothing could stop the Red Army counter-offensive. In the Treaty of Paris, Hungary was forced to retreat to the borders fixed in the Treaty of Trianon.

[23] In 1944 a provisional assembly formed a coalition government and took up a program proposed by communist leaders and backed by the USSR. This program included the expropriation of large estates, the nationalization of banking and heavy industry, as well as guarantees for small landowners and private initiative, democratic rights and liberties.

[24] The Communists, at that time represented by the Workers' Party, assumed control of the government. In 1946 the Constitution of the Peoples' Republic of Hungary was established.

[25] In 1948, the Communist Government forcibly collectivized agriculture and started a series of development plans which stressed the development of heavy industry. Upon Stalin's death in 1953, Matyas Rakosi, head of government, was replaced by Imre Nagy, who promised political changes.

[26] In 1955, Nagy was deposed and expelled from the party. Rakosi returned for a short period, until 1956, when he handed power over to Erno Gero, who had similar political views to his own.

[27] Students staged a demonstration in Budapest, and were joined by the rest of the population. Gero reacted harshly: the police were instructed to shoot into the crowd, and the demonstration turned into a popular revolution, backed by the Army. The Government was handed back to Nagy, heading a broad national coalition.

[28] In November 1956, Nagy announced the withdrawal of Hungary from the Warsaw Pact,

and requested that the United Nations recognize its neutrality. The Red Army, which had withdrawn during the revolution, occupied the country again and reinstated the communist government, led by Janos Kadar.

[29] Kadar followed Soviet guidelines, where foreign policy was concerned. As for domestic policy, central planning was partly liberalized from 1968 onwards, the standard of living rose, but bureaucracy and corruption increased.

[30] Sexual discrimination continued on all fronts. In 1981, while women made up 45 per cent of all workers, they were systematically paid less than men and their job opportunities were restricted to specific fields of traditionally female labor.

[31] Kadar was elected First Secretary of the Hungarian Workers' Socialist Party and head of government, and he ruled without serious opposition until March 1986, when a youth protest march was heavily crushed. Two years later some 10,000 people demanded freedom and reforms in a demonstration in Budapest.

[32] The Government relaxed press censorship and permitted the formation of trade unions and independent political groups - such as the newly constituted Hungarian Democratic Forum - to be formed.

[33] Between 1986 and 1988 Hungarian and Austrian environmentalists protested against the construction of a dam on the Danube; part of a Hungarian-Czechoslovakian project supported by Austria. The Budapest Government resisted the pressure but in the end the project was shelved.

[34] In January 1989 Parliament passed a law legalizing strikes, public demonstrations and political associations. Meanwhile, it adopted an austerity plan which reduced subsidies and devalued the currency. Unemployment was expected to rise to 100,000 and annual inflation to 30 per cent.

[35] The Workers' Party also approved the elimination of the single party system and agreed to celebrate Independence Day on March 15, the date of the 1848 revolt against Austria. In March 1989, 100,000 people demonstrated in Budapest, demanding elections and the withdrawal of Soviet troops.

PROFILE

ENVIRONMENT

The country is a vast plain with a maximum altitude of 1,000 m partially ringed by the Carpathian Mountains. The mountainous region has abundant mineral resources (manganese, bauxite, coal). Between the Danube and its tributary, the Tisza, lies a very fertile plain, site of most of the country's farming activity. Cattle are raised on the grasslands east of the Tisza. In the past 30 years there has been rapid industrial expansion, particularly in the production of steel, non-ferrous metals, chemicals and railway equipment. Oil and natural gas deposits have been found in the Szegia and Zala river basins. 41 per cent of the population is exposed to sulfur dioxide and nitrogen dioxide in the air. The sulphurous emissions are greater than in most eastern European countries.

SOCIETY

Peoples: Magyar 92 per cent; Gypsy/Roma 3 per cent; German 1 per cent; Slovak 1 per cent; Jewish 1 per cent; Southern Slav 1 per cent; other 1 per cent.
Religions: Christian 92.9 per cent, of which Roman Catholic 67.8 per cent, Protestant 25.1 per cent; atheist and agnostic 4.8 per cent; other 2.3 per cent.
Languages: Hungarian (official)
Political Parties: Hungarian Socialist Party (HSP); Hungarian Democratic Forum (MDF); Alliance of Free Democrats (SZDSZ); Smallholders' Party; Federation of Young Democrats (FIDESZ); Popular Christian Democratic Party; Social Democratic Party of Hungary; Agrarian Party; Hungarian Socialist Workers' Party (communist).
Social Organizations: Central Council of Hungarian Trade Unions (SZOT); Hungarian Women's Network.

THE STATE

Official Name: Magyar Köztársaság.
Administrative Divisions: 19 Counties and the Capital.
Capital: Budapest 1,909,000 people (1996).
Other cities: Miskolc 180,000; Debrecen 211,000; Szeged 167,000 (1996).
Government: Arpad Göncz, President. Gyula Horn, Prime Minister since June 1994. The single-chamber National Assembly (386 representatives elected for five-year terms) is the supreme authority in the Republic. Eight seats in the Assembly are reserved for each of the country's minorities.
National Holiday: March 15, Independence (1848), April 4, Anniversary of the Liberation (1945).
Armed Forces: 64,300 (1996).
Other: Border Guard, 15,900. Civil Defense Troops, 2,000. Internal Security Troops, 2,500.

36 The opposition candidates won the provincial elections held in 1989. In August, two million workers went on strike, protesting against price increases. In October, after an agreement between the Workers' Party and the opposition, Parliament proclaimed the Republic of Hungary and eliminated the single-party system.

37 Hungary was the first country in the Warsaw Pact to break its Cold War alliances. Within two years, Budapest established relations with Israel, South Korea, and South Africa.

38 By the end of the year, the Workers' Party had become the Hungarian Socialist Party, with one faction deciding to keep its old name. In the 1990 elections, the Hungarian Democratic Front obtained 43 per cent of the vote, forming a coalition government with two smaller parties: the Socialist Party and the Workers' party. These received 10.3 and 3.5 per cent of the vote, respectively.

39 In late 1991, the Hungarian Prime Minister met with the Czechoslovakian and Polish presidents in Krakow, Poland. The three leaders expressed their wish to establish formal relations with NATO and the West European Union. The Krakow declaration also stressed the importance of associating with the European Community.

40 Hungary had a foreign debt of $21 billion, the largest in Europe. Its agricultural and industrial production fell by 10 per cent - a situation aggravated by IMF policies-preventing domestic capital accumulation and favoring foreign investors. In 1990, inflation reached 30 per cent, with the average family spending 75 per cent of its income on basic consumer goods. The following year, the figure was 90 per cent, for the same goods. Of its 10 million inhabitants, 2 million were living below the poverty line.

41 In this new era in Hungary, women's representation in politics declined. In the 1990 elections, women won 7.5 per cent of the seats, while in 1985 they had held 21 per cent. Women constitute 46 per cent of the active workforce, but this began to change with the increasingly popular ideological position of restoring the 'natural order'. The idea of women staying at home clashed with the new economic reality of the country, where two salaries were needed to cover even the most basic needs of a nuclear family.

42 The women's movement was also heavily involved in the abortion issue. Over 4 million legal abortions have been carried out in Hungary over the past 25 years. However, nearly all the current political parties, except for the Federation of Young Democrats and the Free Democrats, have come out against the practice. Meanwhile, the Hungarian Women's Network campaigned against the criminalization of abortion and in defense of the living standards, working rights and health of women.

43 In January 1992, the Government announced its decision to reduce the public deficit, which stood at a level in excess of $900 million in 1991. They hoped to achieve this by imposing a four per cent reduction in public spending. Growing popular discontent, which was reflected in a reduced turn-out for elections and in repeated union strikes, have forced Joszef Lantall's right-of-center government to take a more cautious position.

44 The economic crisis encouraged nationalistic and xenophobic demonstrations, including the notorious publication of a manifesto signed by the writer and vice-president of the Democratic Forum, Istvçn Csurka, blaming the ex-communists, the 'westernized' liberals, the gypsies and the Jews for 'the deterioration of the social climate'.

45 The liberal wing of the MDF immediately repudiated the declaration, and a few days later 70,000 people from various political groups took part in a demonstration - a march for democracy - through the city, to 'chase the ghost of radicalism out of the country'. After this event 48 skinheads were brought to face charges in court.

46 In October 1993 the Prime Minister, Jozef Antall, was hospitalized when he became seriously ill. Minister of the Interior Peter Boross replaced him, later being confirmed in the post upon Antall's death the following December.

47 In the winter of that year, a TV report revealed high levels of air pollution in Budapest over a 10-day period, and recommended that children should not play outside. In March 1994, in the middle of the electoral campaign, the Government sacked 129 radio reporters. This action was condemned by international press and human rights organizations. This measure meant the end of 30 cultural and political programs in the three state radio stations.

48 In the general elections of May 1994, the Hungarian Socialist Party led by Gyula Horn won in the second round. The ex-communists won 54 per cent of the vote and 208 of the 386 seats. In second place came the Free Democrats, with 70 seats compared with 90 in the 1990 election. The Democratic Forum was the largest loser, only retaining 37 of its previous 165 seats.

49 Horn was sworn in as Prime Minister and the electoral supremacy of the former communists was confirmed in local elections toward the end of the year. In March 1995, his 'idyll' with the electorate came to an end, when an unpopular package of economic measures was approved. The Government drastically reduced the education budget, funding for unemployment and maternity benefits, in order to cut back the fiscal deficit.

50 Horn continued his rapprochement with the Western countries and negotiation with neighboring countries in order to help the Hungarian minorities living abroad to 'preserve their cultural identity'. In May 1996, Hungary signed an agreement with Slovakia for the protection of ethnic minorities and, in September that year, a similar accord with Romania was signed.

51 In early 1997, Hungary started negotiating NATO membership. Budapest accepted the installation of nuclear weapons and NATO troops in Hungarian territory as a pre-condition to joining the military alliance. In November, membership was approved in a referendum where 85 per cent of those who voted supported the integration. Half the electorate (around 4 million people) abstained.

52 Bilateral relations with Romania, home to a large Hungarian minority, improved following former communist Ion Iliescu's defeat and the removal of the ultra-nationalist Romanian parties, which were hostile to the Hungarian and Gypsy/Roma minorities. In 1998, Hungary continued to focus its diplomatic efforts on admission into the European Union.

53 Parliament voted overwhelmingly in February 1999 in favor of the country's joining NATO: 330 Deputies supported the decision, while 13 voted against and one abstained. The major force against entering the organization was the extreme right Party for Justice and Life. In March, Hungary, Poland and the Czech republic were admitted into the alliance, one month before initially planned and just two weeks before the NATO bombings against Yugoslavia began.

54 A 100,000 cubic meter cyanide spill - originating at a mining site in Romania - in the Tisza river valley in February 2000 resulted in the region's worst environmental disaster since the Chernobyl nuclear catastrophe in 1986. All life along a 40-km stretch of the river died, from microbes to fish and plants. The river, which flows into the Danube, contaminated an important source of potable water for Yugoslavia, as well as Romania and Hungary. Two smaller acid spills occurred in March 2000, prompting authorities to take legal action against the Romanian mining company, which had filed a bankruptcy claim almost immediately after the first spill. ∎

Iceland

Island

Population: 279,000 (1999)
Area: 103,000 SQ KM
Capital: Reykjavik
Currency: Kronur
Language: Icelandic

In 874, immigrants of European origin began settling in Iceland: Norwegians, Scots and Irish. Iceland was an independent state between 930 and 1264, but under the terms of the 'Old Treaty' of 1263, the country became part of the kingdom of Norway.

2 In 1381, Iceland and Norway were conquered by Denmark, but when Norway separated from the Danish Crown in 1814, Iceland remained under its protection. In 1918, Iceland became an associated state of Denmark, until it recovered its independence and a republic was proclaimed in June 1944.

3 Until the end of the 19th century, Iceland had no roads or bridges in the interior, and trade was entirely in the hands of Danish companies.

4 In 1915, Icelandic women acquired equal rights with men, being granted the right to vote and to hold elected office. This was attained through the same legislation which granted these rights to Danish women, as at the time, the country was a Danish colony.

5 After World War I, local agriculture was revitalized through a series of laws aimed at the agrarian sector, and the introduction of modern equipment. From 1920 onwards, the fishing industry grew steadily. In addition, communication throughout the island improved with the building of a new network of inland roads and bridges, and the creation of a coast guard.

6 Iceland joined the Council of Europe and NATO in 1949. It had no army or navy, and the United States provided the country with defense forces, within NATO's strategic framework. Iceland had only three coast guard ships, one airplane and two helicopters to protect itself against illegal fishing in its territorial waters.

7 In 1952, Iceland founded the Nordic Council, including Sweden, Norway, Finland and Denmark.

8 Due to the importance of fishing for Iceland, and the fear of over-fishing near the island by foreign fleets, Reykjavik extended its territorial waters to 12 nautical miles in 1964, and in 1972 to 50 miles. This triggered two serious conflicts known as the 'cod wars' with the United Kingdom. They were resolved by a treaty signed in 1973.

9 In October 1975, Iceland announced the extension of its territorial waters to 200 nautical miles, citing the protection of the environment and of its economic interests. The failure of the 1973 treaty with the UK, and the impossibility of reaching a new agreement led to the third and most serious 'cod war'.

10 In February 1976, Iceland briefly broke off relations with the UK, the first breaking of diplomatic ties to occur between NATO members. In June, the two countries reached an agreement and in December, English trawlers withdrew from Icelandic waters. In July 1979, Iceland re-affirmed its 200 mile claim.

11 NATO membership became a controversial issue in Iceland in the 1970s. In the 1978 election, the joint victory of the Popular Alliance, who favored renouncing the treaty, and the Social Democratic Party (SDP), who were more moderate, caused a two-month delay in the formation of a new government, which depended upon the alliance of the two political groups.

12 According to 1980 figures, women made up 43.4 per cent of the country's economically active population.

13 In 1980, Vigdis Finnbogadottir, an independent candidate campaigning against the retention of American military bases on the island, won the presidential election with the support of the left, making her the country's first female head of state. This post did not confer the power for her significantly to alter government policy, so she was unable to carry out her campaign commitment. In 1984 she was re-elected with no opposition candidates.

14 A strict austerity plan was implemented in 1983, aimed at reducing inflation. Trade unions accepted the conditions, and the inflation rate consequently fell from 130 per cent at the beginning of the year, to 27 per cent by December.

15 In May 1985, Parliament approved a resolution declaring Iceland a 'nuclear-free zone', thereby prohibiting nuclear weapons from being brought into the country. Iceland was chosen as the site for the important summit meeting between United States president Ronald Reagan and his Soviet counterpart Mikhail Gorbachev in October 1986.

16 Although Iceland's continuing NATO membership has not really been threatened, the air base at Keflavik continued to cause controversy. With 2,200 troops, the base is a part of the US 'early warning' system. In September 1988, Iceland's executive power formally declared that there would be no new military projects initiated in the country.

17 That same year, relations between Reykjavik and Washington became tense. The US claimed that Iceland's decision to catch 80 fin whales and 40 sei whales violated the moratorium imposed by the International Whaling Commission. Iceland replied that it was a scientific program and did not modify its decision.

18 The United States threatened to boycott Icelandic fish products and two Icelandic whaleboats were sunk by ecological activists in Reykjavik Bay. In 1987, Iceland announced the reduction of its catch to 20 whales. The threats of sanctions continued, and the following year it reduced this quota even further.

19 In June 1988, President Finnbogadottir was re-elected for her third four-year term, with the backing of the main parties and a margin of over 90 per cent of the electorate. This victory was obtained in spite of the existence of an electoral rival, who had proposed increasing presidential power during the campaign.

20 In September of 1988, Steingrimur Hermannsson became Prime Minister, as head of a coalition including center and left-wing groups, made up of the SDP and the Popular Alliance. The new government promised to initiate an austerity program for Iceland's economy, which was suffering from

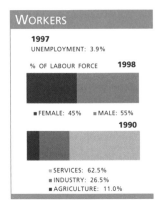

WORKERS

1997
UNEMPLOYMENT: 3.9%

% OF LABOUR FORCE   **1998**

■ FEMALE: 45% ■ MALE: 55%

1990

■ SERVICES: 62.5%
■ INDUSTRY: 26.5%
■ AGRICULTURE: 11.0%

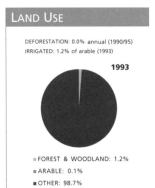

LAND USE

DEFORESTATION: 0.0% annual (1990/95)
IRRIGATED: 1.2% of arable (1993)

1993

■ FOREST & WOODLAND: 1.2%
■ ARABLE: 0.1%
■ OTHER: 98.7%

high inflation and recession, accompanied by currency devaluations.

[21] In August 1989, as a result of growing international pressure, including an international boycott of Icelandic products organized by Greenpeace, Reykjavik announced a two-year suspension of its whale hunting.

[22] In 1989 Iceland faced economic difficulties, like its Arctic neighbors, the Faeroe Islands, Greenland and northern Norway, affected by a sudden reduction in the international price of fish, due to over-production.

[23] As a result of these economic difficulties, the country's labor unions signed a wage agreement for 1990, accepting an eight per cent drop in purchasing power. One indication of the reduction in consumer demand was the fact that the total number of registered motor vehicles - the world's largest in proportion to its population - decreased that year for the first time ever.

[24] In 1990 the Government created the new post of environment minister, and Julius Solnes was appointed.

[25] In the parliamentary elections of April 1991, the majority again went to the center-left coalition of Prime Minister Hermannsson.

[26] From November 1992, discussion of the potential benefits of joining the European market, with its 380 million consumers, divided the political scene. The opposition Popular Alliance, including socialists and dissident Social Democrats, was against joining. Jon Baldvin Hannibalsson, foreign minister and minister of foreign trade, on the other hand, claimed that joining the EC would bring a flow of capital and new foreign investment to the island.

[27] Fishing, the most important source of employment, went into crisis as reserves of certain species, especially cod, suffered from over-fishing. This situation led to new laws restricting the foreign access to territorial waters, causing friction in commercial relations with other countries.

[28] Iceland produces abundant electric power and in the early 1990s it had hoped to develop its non-ferrous metal industry. This sector faced stiff competition from Russia, which depressed prices on the international market.

[29] The tourist industry expanded amid hopes that income from this will entail economic recovery for the island. A series of laws was passed in 1993 to protect polar bears which were being systematically exterminated.

[30] Iceland's entry into the European Union was approved by the *Althing* (parliament) on January 1 1993. The preparations for unification caused excitement during that and the following year. There was a feeling that unification would not be achieved and a debate was triggered on whether joining the European Union was beneficial or not.

[31] In 1994 a number of Iceland's fishing boats entered an area of the Barents sea near Russian and Norwegian territorial waters, causing friction in relations with these two countries. Both nations had undertaken a process to recover fish reserves in the area by reducing capture. By the end of 1995, diplomatic negotiations were considered the only solution for the difference.

[32] In the parliamentary elections of April 8 1995, the Independence Party won 25 of the 63 seats and was forced to create an alliance with the Progress Party - with 15 seats - in order to reach a majority in the *Althing*. The representation of the Popular Alliance and the Women's Alliance dropped, while the new Popular Movement obtained 4 seats.

[33] Iceland's economy managed a slight recovery in 1995 after a slow growth in the previous years. The gross domestic product increased 3 per cent and inflation did not exceed 2 per cent. Unemployment - aggravated by redundancies at the NATO base - reached 5 per cent.

[34] After having governed the country for 16 years, President Vigdis Finnbogadottir did not stand in the June 29 elections in 1996. Olafur Ragnar Grimsson, former finance minister and member of the Popular Alliance, won the election with 41.4 per cent of the vote, taking office on August 1 of that year.

[35] In 1996, marine resources began to be exploited again and fishing quotas were increased after several years of restrictions imposed to preserve the species, and this stimulated economic growth. That year, the GDP increased 5.7 per cent, unemployment fell to 4 per cent and inflation stood at around 3 per cent.

[36] The economy continued to grow in 1997, partly due to expanding internal consumption, as exports increased only 3 per cent on the previous year's figures. The bulk of investments were aimed at aluminum production. Several foreign companies - mostly from Switzerland, the US and Norway - intensified exploitation of this mineral resource.

[37] At the end of that year, Iceland participated in the Kyoto negotiations for reductions in toxic gas emissions in. Because of its economic factors, Iceland, along with Australia and Norway, was authorized to increase emissions, unlike 'highly polluting' countries such as the US or the European Union.

[38] Transparency International's 1998 Perception of Corruption index, based on the statements of investors, financial risk analysts and the public, ranked Iceland among the five least dishonest countries in the world.

[39] In May 1999 the Conservative Party won the *Althing* elections with 26 of the 63 seats, followed by the Alliance made up of feminists, socialists and social democrats, which obtained 17, the Liberal Party (12) and the Green Party (6). ∎

PROFILE

ENVIRONMENT

Located between the North Atlantic and the Arctic Ocean, Iceland is an enormous plateau with an average altitude of 500 meters. A mountain range crosses the country from east to west passing through an extensive ice-covered region; source of the main rivers. The coastline falls sharply from the plateau forming fjords. Most of the population live in the coastal area in the south and west, where ocean currents temper the climate. Reykjavik, the capital and economic center, is located in a fertile plain where the largest cities are found. The northern coast is much colder as a result of Arctic Ocean currents. Geysers and active volcanoes are used as a source of energy. Agricultural output is poor; fishing accounts for 80 per cent of all exports.

SOCIETY

Peoples: 96 per cent of Icelanders are descendants of Norwegian, Scottish and Irish immigrants. **Religions:** Mainly Lutheran (91.5 per cent). Other Protestants 4.3 per cent. Catholics 0.9 per cent.
Languages: Icelandic.
Political Parties: Independence Party, conservative; Popular Alliance, socialist; Progress Party, left-of-center; Social Democratic Party. Other parties with parliamentary representation are the Women's Party and the People's Movement.
Social Organizations: Icelandic Federation of Workers, with 47,000 members.

THE STATE

Official Name: Lydhveldid Island.
Administrative divisions: 7 districts.
Capital: Reykjavik 155,000 people (est 1995).
Other cities: Kopavogur 17,660 people; Hafnarfjordhur 17,538 people (1996).
Government: Olafur Ragnar Grimsson, President and Head of State since August 1st,1996. David Oddson, Prime Minister and Head of Government since September 1991. Unicameral parliament composed of 63 members, elected by popular vote for a 4-year term.
National Holiday: June, 17.
Other: 130 coast guard (1994); 2.200 NATO troops.

India

Bharat

Population: 998,056,000 (1999)
Area: 3,287,588 SQ KM
Capital: New Delhi
Currency: Rupee
Language: Hindi

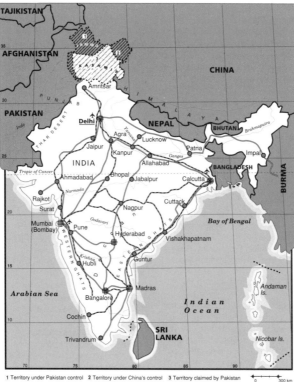

1 Territory under Pakistan control   2 Territory under China's control   3 Territory claimed by Pakistan
0   300 km

A round 3000 BC, the Dravidian inhabitants of the Indus Valley, in present-day Pakistan, built about a hundred cities, erected huge temples in larger urban centers, like Harappa and Mohenjo Daro, created a written language, that has yet to be deciphered, and carved cylindrical seals of rare perfection. With their irrigated agriculture they developed a prosperous economy and maintained active trade from the Indian Ocean to the spurs of the Himalayas, using the Indus River as their main means of communication. Little is known about their culture, their political organization or development except that, after five centuries of existence, invaders devastated the whole region, exterminating the population and destroying their civilization.

2   Towards 1600 BC, waves of Indo-Europeans arrived from Afghanistan, gradually conquering the subcontinent. Armed with iron weapons, protected by armor and using war chariots, they subdued the local population and established numerous states. The civilization they created, later called Vedic, was based on a rigid caste system in which the conquerors constituted the dominant nobility. They were called the *ariana* or *ayriana* - nobility - giving rise to the term Aryan which was later generically used to designate all Indo-Europeans.

3   The Iranian-Greek invasions of the 6th-4th centuries BC (see Iran) did not reach Magadha in the Ganges River valley, the most powerful state in India. Under the rule of Ashoka, 274-232 BC, Magadha occupied the entire subcontinent, except for the extreme south. Indian civilization

proper dates from this period. Ashoka and his descendants were the driving force behind a cultural unification that included the organization and diffusion of Buddhism, based on the preaching of Gautama Siddhartha, who lived from 563 to 483 BC, and was later known as Buddha. Between the 1st and 3rd centuries AD, this civilization began to break up, fragmented by the development of the Seythian Kusana (see Afghanistan) and Ksatrapa states in the northeast.

4   When the Guptas of Magadha seized power in the 3rd-6th

centuries AD, a new process of unification ushered in one of the most brilliant periods of Indian culture. The 8th century spread of Islam failed to take hold in India, but it was more successful four centuries later, when the Turks of Mahmud of Ghazni reintroduced the faith. Successive groups of Islamic migrants from central Asia invaded the subcontinent, ending with the Tatars of Timur Lenk (Tamburlaine). Between 1505 and 1525, one of their descendants, Babur, founded what later came to be known as the Empire of the Grand Mogul, with its capital in Delhi.

5   Babur's descendants consolidated Islam, particularly in the northwest and northeast (see Pakistan and Bangladesh). Culture and the arts developed remarkably - the Taj Mahal was built around 1650 - but the European presence, which had been limited to coastal trading posts, began to mmake a deeper impression. In 1687, the British East India Company settled in Bombay. In 1696, it built Fort William in Calcutta, and throughout the 18th century, the Company's private army waged war against the French competition, emerging victorious in 1784. From 1798, Company troops led by a brother of the Duke of Wellington methodically conquered Indian territory in various campaigns. By 1820, the English were in control of almost all of India, except for the Punjab, Kashmir and Peshawar, which were governed by their Sikh ally, Ranjit Singh. After his death in 1849, the British annexed these territories. The 'loyal allies' retained nominal autonomy and were allowed to keep their courts, great palaces and immoderate luxury, much to the satisfaction of European visitors.

6   The Indian economy was completely dismantled. Its textile industry, whose exports of high-quality cloth had reached half the globe, was an obstacle to the growth of the British cotton industry.

7   The ruin of this industry, based on individual weavers, brought widespread impoverishment to the countryside. Peasants were also hard hit by the reorganization of agriculture for export crops. The early results of British domination were lower incomes and greater unemployment. Public accounts were conveniently arranged. All military spending, including the campaigns in Afghanistan, Burma and Malaya, was covered by the Indian treasury, 70 per cent of whose budget was earmarked for these 'defense expenses'. All British spending, however remotely connected with India, was entered as expenditures of the 'Indian Empire'.

8   'Divide and rule' was a motto of British domination. Mercenaries recruited in one region were used to subdue others. Such was the case with Nepalese Gurkhas and Punjabi Sikhs. Religious strife was also fomented; an electoral reform at

WORKERS

% OF LABOUR FORCE   **1998**

■ FEMALE: 32%   ■ MALE: 68%

1990

■ SERVICES: 20.0%
■ INDUSTRY: 16.0%
■ AGRICULTURE: 64.0%

LAND USE

DEFORESTATION: 0.0% annual (1990/95)
IRRIGATED: 28.9% of arable (1993)

1993

■ FOREST & WOODLAND: 20.8%
■ ARABLE: 50.5%
■ OTHER: 28.7%

PUBLIC EXPENDITURE

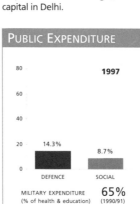

1997

80
60
40
20   14.3%   8.7%
0
        DEFENCE   SOCIAL

MILITARY EXPENDITURE   **65%**
(% of health & education)   (1990/91)

the beginning of the 20th century stated that Muslims, Hindus and Buddhists could each vote only for candidates of their own faiths. Throughout the colonial period all this manipulation generated innumerable uprisings, both large and small, on local and national levels.

9   The most serious of these were the 1857-1858 rebellions by sepoys, Indian soldiers in the British army. These began as a barracks movement, eventually incorporating a range of grievances and growing into a nationwide revolt. Hindus and Muslims joined forces and even proposed the

PROFILE

ENVIRONMENT

The nation is divided into three large natural regions: the Himalayas, along the northern border; the fertile, densely populated Ganges plain immediately to the south, and the Deccan plateau in the center and south. The Himalayas shelter the country from cold north winds. The climate is subject to monsoon influence; hot and dry for eight months of the year, and raining heavily from June to September. Rice is widespread. Coal and iron ore are the main mineral resources. There is a long-standing territorial dispute with Pakistan over Kashmir in the northwest.

SOCIETY

Peoples: The population of India is a multitude of racial, cultural and ethnic groups. Most are descendants of the Aryan peoples who developed the Vedic civilization and created a caste system so robust that it has survived until the present. The influence of Arab invasions, in the 7th and 12th centuries, and Mongolian incursions, in the 13th century, is still felt in the north. Peoples of Dravidian origin still predominate on the Deccan plateau in the center and south of India.
Religions: 83 per cent Hindu, 11 per cent Muslim, 2.5 per cent Sikh. There are Christian and Buddhist minorities. **Languages:** There are 18 officially recognized languages of which Hindi is the most widely spoken. English is an associated language, widely spoken for official purposes. There are 16 official regional languages and infinity of local dialects. **Political Parties:** The Indian National Congress (INC), founded in 1885. Under the leadership of Mahatma Gandhi they fought for independence from Britain. The United Front, former National Front-Left Front. The Bharatiya Janata Party (BJP) is a rightwing nationalist party which supposedly has connections with the Rashtriya Swayan Sevak Sangh (RSSS), a paramilitary communal organization, considered responsible for a series of violent acts, especially against Muslims. The Communist Party of India-Marxist (CPI-M). The Lok Dal claims to be the party of the poor peasants and aims to have considerable influence in northern India. Its main support comes from the middle castes. Amongst the most important regional parties are the all-India Anna Dravida Munetva Kazhagam (AIA-DMK), the National Conference of Jammu and Kashmir, the Asom Ghana Parishad, ruling in Assam, the Telegu Desam, and the Akali Dal which leads a struggle for greater Punjabi autonomy.
Social Organizations: The most important are the Indian National Trade Union Congress (INTUC), with over 4 million members; the Bharatiya Mazdoor Sangh, with approximately 2 million members; the All-India Trade Union Congress (AITUC), with 1.5 million members; and the Center of Indian Trade Unions (CITU), with 1 million members.

THE STATE

Official name: Bharat (Hindi).
Capital: Delhi and New Delhi 10,800,000 people (est 1995).
Other cities: Greater Mumbai/Bombay 15,093,000 people; Calcutta 11,673,000; Madras 5,906,000; Bangalore 4,749,000; Hyderabad 5,343,000 (1995).
Government: Kocheril Raman Narayanan, President since July 1997. Atal Bihari Vajpayee, Prime Minister since March 1998.
National Holidays: August 15, Independence Day (1947); January 26, Day of the Republic (1950).
Armed Forces: 1,145,000 troops (1995). Other: 1,421,800.

restoration of the ancient Moghul empire. This movement demonstrated that the East India Company was incapable of administering such a large domain and led the British crown, after violent repression, to assume direct government of India.

10   The educational system was based on the classic British model and was conceived to train 'natives' for colonial administration in the civil service. However, it did not exactly fulfill this purpose. What it did do was create an intellectual elite fully conversant with European culture and thinking. The British had certainly never planned that the first association of civil servants in India, created in 1876 by Surendranath Banerjee, would take the Italian revolutionary Giuseppe Mazzini as its patron and inspiration and not just quietly follow the Government line. Years later in 1885, it was this intelligentsia that formed the Indian National Congress which included British liberals and, for a long time, limited itself to proposing superficial reforms to improve British administration.

11   When Mohandas K Gandhi, a lawyer educated in England with experience of colonial methods in South Africa, returned to India in 1915, he became aware of the need to break out of the straitjacket of Anglo-Indian 'cooperation'. Gandhi tried to win Muslims over to the inmdependence cause. He reintroduced Hindu teachings that Ram Mohan Roy had reinterpreted in the 19th century, giving particular importance to mass mobilization. His ties with the Indian National Congress strengthened the movement's most radical wing where young Jawaharlal Nehru was an activist. In 1919, the Amritsar massacre occurred; a demonstration was savagely repressed leaving, according to British sources, 380 dead and 1200 wounded. In 1920, in response to the Amritsar massacre, at Gandhi's urging, the Indian Congress launched a campaign which showed the effectiveness of unarmed civilian opposition. The campaign tactics included the boycotting of colonial institutions; non-participation in elections or administrative bodies, non-attendance at British schools, refusal to consume British products, and passive acceptance of the ensuing legal consequences. The movement spread nationwide at all levels. Gandhi came to be called Mahatma (Great Soul) in recognition of his leadership.

12   A new campaign between 1930 and 1934 aimed to attain full independence and denounce the state salt monopoly. This demonstrated Gandhi's ability to combine a key political goal with a specific demand affecting all the

poor; one they would understand and support. For the first time the British saw women flocking to demonstrations. Jails overflowed with prisoners who did not resist arrest posing an immense problem to the colonial authorities. It was impossible not to negotiate with Gandhi, and after World War II the British were left with no option but to rapidly grant independence.

13   With the British withdrawal in 1947, the subcontinent was divided into two states; the Indian Union, and Pakistan, which was created to concentrate the Muslim population into one area (see Pakistan and Bangladesh). This 'Partition' as it was called was a painful and often violent separation. The Indian Union brought together an enormous diversity of ethnic, linguistic, and cultural groups in a single federated state, consolidating the sentiment of national unity forged in the independence struggle that the British had never managed to stifle. The excitement of independence was clouded by the assassination of Gandhi less than a year later, on 30 January 1948.

14   After independence, Prime Minister Jawaharlal Nehru, along with Sukarno of Indonesia, Gamal Abdel Nasser of Egypt and Tito of Yugoslavia, advanced the concept of political non-alignment for newly decolonized countries. In India, he applied development policies based on the notion that the industrialization of the society would bring prosperity.

15   In a few decades India made rapid technological progress, which enabled it to place satellites in orbit and, in 1974, to detonate an atom bomb, making India the first nuclear power in the non-aligned movement. However, the relevance of this kind of project to a country which had yet to feed all its people was widely questioned. Pakistan's civil war and conflict with India over East Pakistan eventually led to the independence of this portion as Bangladesh, in 1971.

16   The Indian economy was severely hit by the oil crisis of the early 1970s as it was dependent on oil imports. Industrial exports could not grow fast enough to offset increases in import prices, nor to meet the demand for food from a population growing at a rate of 15 million per year. In 1975, the economic crisis, and popular resistance to the government's mass sterilization campaigns, led Indira Gandhi, Nehru's daughter, who had taken over as Prime Minister when her father died in 1966) to declare a state of emergency and impose press censorship.

17   Abandoning the Congress Party's traditional populist policies, Mrs Gandhi followed World Bank economic guidelines, losing mass support for the government,

without winning wholehearted backing from business sectors (particularly those linked to foreign capital), which demanded even greater concessions. The British tradition of respect for democratic freedoms instilled in mass organizations, big business and the middle class, led them (for different reasons) to close ranks in opposition and force the Government to call parliamentary elections for March 1977. The Congress Party was roundly defeated by the Janata Party, a heterogeneous coalition formed by a splinter group of rightwing Congress Party members, the Socialist Party headed by trade union leader George Fernandes, and the Congress for Democracy, led by Jagjivan Ram, leader of the *Harijans* (Children of God, as Gandhi had renamed the out-castes or 'untouchables') and former minister in Indira Gandhi's cabinet.

[18] India's foreign policy of non-alignment remained basically unchanged under ageing Prime Minister Morarji Desai. In his time in power he was also unable to fulfill his promises of full employment and economic improvement. By mid-1979, disagreements within the party caused groups led by Charan Singh and Jagjivan Ram to split from the Janata Party. Desai had to resign and, unable to form a cabinet with a stable parliamentary majority, the Prime Minister called early elections, which returned Indira Gandhi to power in January 1980.

[19] Indira's second term was marked by a growing concentration of power, and accusations of unnecessary bureaucracy and corruption in the government, which gradually blemished her image. The problems in the Punjab, where the Government faced increasingly strident demands from Sikh separatists, exemplified regionalism at its worst. Small groups of militant Sikhs harassed Hindus, to drive them out of the Punjab and create an absolute Sikh majority in the province. After that, the next step would be secession and the formation of independent 'Khalistan'. Indira accused 'forces from abroad' (namely Pakistan and the US) of destabilizing the country.

[20] On June 6 1984, the Prime Minister called in the army to evict hundreds of militant Sikhs from their most sacred shrine, the Golden Temple at Amritsar, which they had transformed into a command post for their separatist war. Hundreds of Sikh extremists were killed within the temple, including prominent Sikh leader, Jarnail Singh Bhindranwale. This bloody confrontation left moderate Sikh leaders with no room for negotiation. The atmosphere which prevailed throughout the region after the incident led to Indira Gandhi's assassination by two of her Sikh bodyguards, on October 31 1984.

[21] After the assassination, thousands of Sikhs fell victim to indiscriminate retaliation by Hindu paramilitary groups. Bypassing party and institutional formalities, Indira's son Rajiv was rapidly promoted to the office of Prime Minister and leader of the Congress Party.

[22] Elections in January 1985 gave him overwhelming support: he obtained 401 of Parliament's 508 seats. None of the other parties reached the 50 seats needed to be officially recognized as the opposition. Despite the landslide victory, some strongly regionalist areas such as the states of Karnataka and Andhra Pradesh were influenced by Rama Rao, a charismatic former actor, and turned their backs on Gandhi. Gandhi also lost in Sikkim, a Himalayan kingdom annexed to India in the 1970s, where the separatist Sikkim Sangram Parishad party won.

[23] The new premier took several steps to deal with Punjab's problems. He appointed a conciliatory figure as governor of the area, released political prisoners including opposition leaders, and directed that militants within his own party who had participated in the anti-Sikh violence should be tried and punished. These measures paved the way for dialogue with Akali Dal, the regional majority party of Sikhs and other dissident groups. Some progress was made. The Punjab autonomists proposed that the Indian central government should keep responsibility for defense and foreign affairs, the issuing of currency, mail, highways and telecommunications. Meanwhile, the local government would have greater autonomy than in India's other states.

[24] In 1987, India intervened in the conflict in Sri Lanka, pressing for a cease-fire and an agreement between Sinhalese and Tamils by sending in troops. Three years later, the Indian Peace Forces had to discreetly withdraw, having suffered many casualties.

[25] Rajiv Gandhi was an active participant in the group of six neutral countries (Argentina, India, Sweden, Tanzania, Mexico and Greece) which appealed to the superpowers to curtail the arms race. The Prime Minister announced India would not relinquish nuclear weapons in the future if Pakistan persisted in making the atomic bomb.

[26] India's foreign policy remained loyal to non-alignment but some domestic changes were announced. Rajiv made the personal computer the symbol of his swift 'modernization' policy. He promised the private sector he would lift restrictions on imports and on the purchase of foreign technology, while relaxing fiscal controls. Labor unions feared that sophisticated technology would lead to unemployment and that Indian industry would not survive the competition from foreign products.

[27] Elections in November 1989 were held amidst a violent atmosphere which left more than 100 dead and revealed the opposition's progress. The Congress Party's representation went down to 192 seats while Janata Dal's went up to 141. Although a minority, this party succeeded in forming a government coalition with the National Front which appointed Vishwanath Pratap Singh as Prime Minister. This was possible because of the unusual simultaneous support from the right-wing Bharatiya Janata Party (BJP) and several left-wing groups.

[28] In March 1990, tensions between India and Pakistan mounted as Pakistan increased its support for the Kashmir independence movements. There were fears that, if both countries went to war, one of them could resort to nuclear weapons. In November, confrontations between Hindus and Muslims escalated amidst a general worsening of the economic crisis. Prime Minister Singh was replaced by Chandra Shekhar, also from the Janata Dal.

[29] An election campaign which claimed over 280 lives gave way to parliamentary elections which started on May 20 1991. The following day, they were adjourned following the assassination of Rajiv Gandhi, attacked by the Tamil liberation movement. A week later, Narasimha Rao was appointed Gandhi's successor as leader of the Congress Party. The elections, in which only 53 per cent of those registered voted and which were to become the most violent in India's independent history, were resumed between June 12 and 16. The Congress Party obtained 225 seats followed by the Bharatiya Janata Party with 119.

[30] In August 1991, the new government announced a drastic shift toward liberalism that would change the economic policy in force since independence. This change gave rise to criticism and protests. Already in September of the previous year, 70,000 representatives of tribal groups had met to halt dam constructions on the holy Narmada river, which threatened to flood ancient temples and ancestral lands belonging to the region's peasants. Over 200,000 people driven from their lands by the dams protested in 1991.

[31] This and other infrastructure projects formed part of a tradition of industrial modernization without weighing possible ecological consequences. Safety problems of

the country's seven nuclear reactors remain unsolved and controls over companies which use or emit toxic substances are still insufficient.

[32]   Numerous acts of violence took place in 1992 by Hindu fundamentalists against the Islamic population in the cities of Bombay and Ayodhya. According to Hindu tradition, in the latter - which had a mosque that was built in 1528 - the god Rama had been born. In December, Lal Krishnan Advani, leader of the BJP, ordered his followers to destroy the temple. The following clashes between the two communities left approximately 1,300 dead in several Indian cities and reached neighboring countries such as Pakistan and Bangladesh. In 1995, the Supreme Court was consulted about the possible existence of a Hindu temple in Ayodhya, before the (ruined) Babri mosque was built. The members of the Court unanimously declined to issue an opinion on the matter.

[33]   The reforms planned by Prime Minister Rao, implemented by finance minister Manmohan Singh, included opening up India's market to foreign investment. The state gradually reduced its intervention in the economy, leaving the rupee to fluctuate freely against the dollar, and removing import controls.

[34]   The outcome was reflected in the reduction of inflation (below 10 per cent in 1995) and the fiscal deficit while exports have grown steadily since 1992. The country continues to bear the burden of a foreign debt equal to 38 per cent of the GDP while the per capita income of its over 935 million inhabitants is one of Asia's lowest.

[35]   Economic reforms have triggered protests from several sectors, especially from agriculture. Resistance to multinationals involved in fertilizers and seeds was very strong. As part of the 'green revolution' and a capital-intensive agriculture, the World Bank had granted those subsidies following instructions from the World Bank's structural adjustment plan. The Farmers' Association of the State of Karnataka (KKRS) headed rural protests which were responsible for a number of direct attacks against representatives of multinational corporations since 1991.

[36]   The Government proceeded to eliminate, protests against the

economic reforms and natural disasters - an earthquake killed over 10,000 people in September 1993 - the Government was optimistic in early 1994. However, differences between the states were growing. In the north, Utta Pradesh, home to over 140 million people, showed figures of social development far below the national average. The male population outnumbered that of females - 882 women for every 1,000 men in 1995 - figures which can indicate both female infanticide and reduced nutrition/health care for girls and women. In the southern state of Kerala, where a Communist government had been in power for some years, beggars were less common. In addition, 90 per cent of the State's population could read and write and infant mortality (17 per 1,000) was closer to that of Latvia (16 per 1,000) instead of the rest of India (79 per 1,000).

[37]   At the International Conference on Rights of Third World Farmers held in Bangalore on October 3 and 4, 1993, farmers declared that the 'seeds, plants, biological material and wealth of the Third World form part of the Collective Intellectual Property of the peoples of the Third World'. They pledged to develop these rights in the face of the private patenting system which encourages the spread of monoculture and threatens biodiversity.

[38]   Despite the violence among religious communities significant loans during the 1960s and 1970s for the purchase of hybrid seeds while the Government subsidized farmers.

[39]   In 1994, the Supreme Court of India declared that state governments could lose some powers if they did not enforce religious freedom, which was stipulated in the Constitution. Conflicts between Hindus and Muslims continued in Karnataka. In December, three Cabinet members resigned after being involved in corruption cases related to public security.

[40]   That year India signed two agreements with China: the first one stated a reduction of military troops stationed along the 4,000 km of common borders between the two countries while the other encouraged trade relations. When former Pakistani Prime Minister Nawaz Sharif claimed his country had nuclear weapons, relations

between New Delhi and Islamabad were strained. Pakistan closed its consulate in Bombay.

[41]   During 1995, Prime Minister Narasimha Rao changed his cabinet three times. Elections in several states revealed an increasingly weakened Congress Party, with several internal schisms, and growing support for the Hindu nationalist party Bharatiya Janata (BJP). The new BJP Government in the state of Maharashtra decided to change the name of Bombay to Mumbai.

[42]   Economic stability and assistance schemes announced by Rao, which included a school dinners plan for 110 million children and the construction of 10 million rural homes, were not enough to stop his popularity from plummeting. Rao resigned on May 10 1996, following his party's defeat in the general elections held between April 27 and May 7. The BJP, in alliance with other minor parties, took 187 seats in the lower house, while the Congress Party took 138 and the National Front - Left Front, which changed its name to the United Front, took 117.

[43]   The BJP did not get a big enough parliamentary majority to govern. The new Prime Minister, Atal Bihari Vajpayee, resigned on May 28, 12 days after taking office. President Shankar Dayal Sharma appointed HD Deve Gowda, leader of the United Front, to head the new Government, with Congress Party support.

[44]   An agreement between India and China reduced the number of troops from both countries along the common border. In March 1997, Pakistan's Foreign Minister, Shamshad Ahmad, visited India to reopen negotiations to normalize relations between the two countries.

[45]   Also in March, the Congress Party withdrew support from the Gowda Government, toppling the Prime Minister. Sitaram Kesri, the main force behind the break with the Left, was elected President of the Congress Party in June. Nearly a month after the fall of Gowda, Inder Kumar Gujral, also of the United Front, was appointed Prime Minister. In July, Vice-President KR Narayanan was elected President.

[46]   The Congress Party withdrew its support from the Gujral Government in November when an official commission revealed alleged links between a governing coalition party, the Dravida Munnetra Kazagham (DMK), and Sri Lanka's Tamil guerrillas, a group involved in the murder of former Prime Minister Rajiv Gandhi. Gujral was forced to resign.

[47]   The BJP triumphed in the February 1998 parliamentary elections. The Bharatiya Janata Party and its allies won 251 seats, followed by the Congress Party

(166) and the United Front (96). For the second time in 22 months, Atal Biharia Vajpayee was appointed Prime Minister. In May, a series of nuclear tests in India heightened tensions with Pakistan, giving the neighboring country the pretext to carry out similar tests that same month.

[48]   A legislative bill that would reserve one third of parliamentary seats for women was successively boycotted in Parliament throughout the month of July. The Bill's opponents, led by two socialist parties, staged a protest outside the Parliament and repeatedly interrupted legislative proceedings. According to the opposition, the proposal was unacceptable because it did not include quotas for women from the lower castes. The Bill's principal defenders were the ruling party and the major opposition force, the Indian National Congress Party – in agreement for the first time.

[49]   The Government coalition collapsed in April 1999 when Jayaram Jayalalitha, leader of the Tamil AIA-DMK party, forced two of his ministers to resign after Prime Minister Vajpayee rejected AIA-DMK demands that Defense Minister George Fernandes be removed from office and investigated for having sacked India's Navy Commander, Admiral Vishnu Bhagwat. After Jayalalitha retreated and the opposition parties were unable to put together a coalition to replace the collapsed government, President KR Narayanan dissolved the Lower House so that new elections would be called.

[50]   Armed confrontations with Pakistan erupted in June after Pakistani forces crossed the border set by the United Nations. Some 1,000 people died in the conflicts. The international organization Human Rights Watch reported serious human rights violations on either side of the border, attributed to officials from both governments. India's security forces were accused of carrying out summary executions, rape and torture.

[51]   In October, after five electoral rounds, the BJP once again remained in the Government after the alliance it led won 293 of the 545 parliamentary seats. Despite the coalition's victory, this election also marked a BJP decline that benefited leftist and regional parties. More than half of the legislative seats were no longer controlled by the two major national parties (the BJP and the Congress Party, which suffered the worst defeat of its history, obtaining just 120 seats, 20 fewer than in the previous election). The BJP's dependence on its minor partners foretold another difficult term for the Government. ∎

Indonesia

Indonesia

Population: 209,255,000 (1999)
Area: 1,889,700 SQ KM
Capital: Jakarta
Currency: Rupiah
Language: Bahasa Indonesia

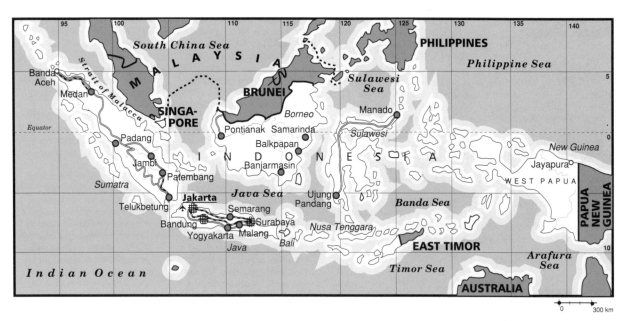

Indonesia has some of the world's earliest homo sapiens remains. The ancestors of the present-day population were Malay immigrants who arrived on the islands of Java and Sumatra around 400 BC. They brought with them the cultural and religious influences of India. Indonesian civilization reached its height in the 15th century when the state of Mojopahit extended far east - beyond Java, Bali, Sumatra, and Borneo - becoming commercially and culturally linked with China.

[2] At the end of the 13th century, through contact with Arab traders, Islam was introduced, rapidly flourishing in the archipelago. Islam was not imposed through conversion campaigns, but was freely adopted because it represented a simple, egalitarian faith suited to local conditions.

[3] When the Muslim traders sent Indonesian spices (from the Moluccas) to Europe, the Europeans' interest was aroused, and they set their colonial sights on the region. In 1511, the Portuguese arrived in Melaka; in 1521, the Spanish reached the Moluccas and in 1595, private Dutch merchants organized their first expedition. The Netherlands had just won its independence from Spain and wanted to secure its own supply of spices. In 1602, the Dutch East India Company was founded, obtaining a trade monopoly, with a colonial mandate from the Governor of the region.

[4] During the 17th and 18th centuries, Indonesia was fought over by Spain, Portugal, the Netherlands and Britain, the latter creating another private company. The Netherlands gained the upper hand and became the colonial power. Cash crops, coffee and sugar were introduced, yielding excellent profits for the European investors but seriously upsetting the local socio-economic organization. This had remained intact until then but was virtually destroyed by the export economy. Anti-colonial revolts broke out. Towards the end of the 19th century, rubber, palm oil and tin became the main export products, though industry only began to develop during World War II, when the Netherlands was unable to meet its production needs at home.

[5] In December 1916, nationalist pressure caused the formation of the *Volksraad* (People's Council), a body designed to defend the rights of the local population. Although its proposals were largely ignored, the Council encouraged political participation among the local population.

[6] In 1939, eight nationalist organizations formed a coalition called the Gabusan Politick Indonesia (GAPI), demanding democracy, autonomy and national unity within the framework of the anti Fascist struggle. GAPI adopted the red and white flag and Bahasa Indonesia as the national language.

[7] After the outbreak of World War II, the Netherlands were invaded by Germany, and Indonesia by Japan in 1942. The Japanese, who claimed to be the 'Asiatic brothers' of the Indonesians, freed nationalist leaders like Achmed Sukarno and Muhammad Hatta who had been imprisoned under Dutch rule. On August 11 1945, just four days prior to the Japanese surrender, they invested Sukarno and Hatta with full powers to establish an autonomous Indonesian government.

[8] Indonesia proclaimed independence on August 17 1945. The Dutch tried to recover the archipelago, forcing the Indonesians to fight back. The Arab and Indian communities actively supported the pro-independence guerrillas, while Britain backed the Netherlands. The US pressed for a negotiated settlement.

[9] Unable to recover military control, the Netherlands was

WORKERS

1996
UNEMPLOYMENT: 4.0%

% OF LABOUR FORCE **1998**

■ FEMALE: 40%   ■ MALE: 60%

1990

■ SERVICES: 31.2%
■ INDUSTRY: 13.6%
■ AGRICULTURE: 55.2%

LAND USE

DEFORESTATION: 1.0% annual (1990/95)
IRRIGATED: 24.3% of arable (1993)

1993

■ FOREST & WOODLAND: 58.7%
■ ARABLE: 9.9%
■ OTHER: 31.4%

PUBLIC EXPENDITURE

1997

DEFENCE 13.1%
SOCIAL 36.2%

MILITARY EXPENDITURE **49%**
(% of health & education) (1990/91)

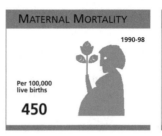

MATERNAL MORTALITY
1990-98

Per 100,000
live births

450

LITERACY
1995

84%

PROFILE

ENVIRONMENT

Indonesia is the largest archipelago-state in the world, made up of approximately 3,000 islands. The most important are Borneo (Kalimantan), Sumatra, Java, Celebes, Bali, the Moluccas, West Papua and Timor. Lying on both sides of the equator, the island group has a tropical, rainy climate and dense rainforest vegetation. The population, the fourth largest in the world, is unevenly distributed: Java has one of the highest population densities in the world, 640 people per sq km, while Borneo has fewer than 10 people per sq km. Cash crops, mainly coffee, tea, rubber and palm oil are cultivated, along with subsistence crops, especially rice. Indonesia is the tenth largest oil producer and the third largest tin producer in the world. Like neighboring Malaysia, Indonesia has suffered deforestation due to the expansion of the paper and lumber-exporting industries.

SOCIETY

Peoples: 90 per cent of Indonesians are of Malay origin, half of whom belong to the Javanese ethnic group. There are also Chinese and Indian minorities.

Religions: Mainly Muslim (86 per cent); 10 per cent are Christian; 2 per cent Hindi; 1 per cent Buddhist.

Languages: Bahasa Indonesia (official), similar to Malay, is the official language. The Governments of Indonesia and Malaysia have agreed to gradual language unification based on Melayu, the common mother tongue. Javanese, native language to 60 million of the country's inhabitants. English, the language of business and commerce. 250 regional languages.

Political Parties: Indonesian Democratic Party; Sekber Golkar, a coalition of various professional and interest groups; United Development Party; National Mandate Party; Indonesian People's Party; Communist Party of Indonesia.
The Free Aceh Movement and the Aceh National Liberation Front, made up of insurgents from the northern region of the island of Sumatra, started attacks on the Government, but they were virtually crushed by the Army.

Social Organizations: All-Indonesian Union of Workers (SPSI), founded in 1973 and renamed in 1985.

THE STATE

Official Name: Republik Indonesia.
Administrative Divisions: 26 Provinces.
Capital: Jakarta, 13,900,000 people (est 1995).
Other cities: Surabaya 2,500,000 people; Bandung 2,000,000; Medan, 1,700,000 (1990).
Government: Abdurraman Wahid, President since October 1999. Legislature, single-chamber, made up of 500 members, 400 elected by direct popular vote, and 100 designated by the President.
National Holiday: August 17, Independence Day (1945).
Armed Forces: 274,000 (1995).
Other: Police, 215,000, Auxiliary Police, (Karma), 1.5 million, Auxiliary Armed Force, in regional commands (Wanra).

forced to surrender in 1949, although it retained partial control through a Dutch-Indonesian confederation.

[10] In 1954, the Dutch-Indonesian Union, which was never fully implemented, was renounced by the Sukarno Government and the archipelago became fully independent. Sukarno's government soon began its own colonial policies in the region. In 1963, reacting to The Hague's refusal to withdraw from the island of New Guinea, Indonesia occupied West Irian (Irian Jaya, now West Papua), the former Dutch colony whose territory took up half of the island. The Indonesian independence process offered an important example for the other Third World countries. Together with other major events of the period - Indian and Pakistani independence, the Cuban Revolution, the nationalization of the Suez Canal in Egypt, and the French defeats in Vietnam and Algeria - it heralded the arrival of the South onto the international political scene. Sukarno was one of the main leaders of the movement for Third World solidarity and in 1955 the Indonesian city of Bandung played host to a meeting of heads of government, giving rise to the Non-Aligned Movement.

[11] The three-million strong Communist Party - the second most powerful in Asia after the Chinese - supported Sukarno. He launched nationalist development programs, aimed at raising the living standards of a population with one of the world's lowest per capita incomes. The country had sizeable petroleum reserves, which provided a strong foundation on which to base economic development. Sukarno created a state petroleum company, PERTAMINA to break the domination of the Anglo-Dutch transnational, Royal Dutch Shell.

[12] In 1965, Indonesian oil deposits were nationalized. In October of that year, a small force of soldiers led by General Suharto seized power under the pretext of stemming the 'communist penetration.' This bloody coup left nearly 700,000 dead, and some 200,000 political activists were imprisoned.

[13] Though deprived of any real power, Sukarno remained the nominal president until 1967, when Suharto was officially named head

of state. Suharto opened the doors to foreign oil companies seeking drilling rights. But with the rise in oil prices, the influx of capital, and a liberal economic policy, the Government also widened the gap between those with the highest and lowest incomes. Living conditions did not improve for millions of rural dwellers, many of whom had to leave their lands joining the shantytowns in the large cities.

[14] In 1971, defying repression, students took to the streets in protest at the 'corrupt generals, Chinese merchants, and Japanese investors' controlling the nation. In an attempt to divert the attention of young officers and neutralize dissent, Suharto invaded East Timor, on that country's independence from Portugal in 1975. US President Gerald Ford visited Jakarta a few hours before the invasion and apparently gave it his blessing. However, from the point of view of the Maubere people of Timor, the Indonesians were not seen as liberators but as new colonists. The unyielding resistance on the island only deepened Indonesia's internal problems.

[15] In May 1977, when elections were held for a portion of the seats in the House of Representatives, discontent surfaced once again. Despite repression, the banning of leftist parties and press censorship, the official Sekber Golkar (Golongan Karya) Party lost in Jakarta to a Muslim coalition which had campaigned against the rampant corruption. The governing party also lost ground in rural areas where it had always previously maintained effective political control.

[16] In the light of this setback, and to ensure victory in the election five years later, the regime clamped down on political activity and reorganized the electoral system, making it dependent on the Ministry of Home Affairs.

[17] On March 10 1983, in spite of growing opposition, the People's Consultative Assembly unanimously re-elected Suharto for a fourth 5-year presidential term.

[18] Indonesia adopted a birth control policy which led to a reduction in the population's growth rate. While figures for the 1984 census revealed an annual increase of 2.34 per cent, the average rate of growth between

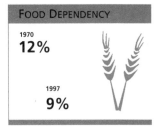

FOOD DEPENDENCY

1970
12%

1997
9%

EXTERNAL DEBT

1998

PER CAPITA
US$ 731

FOREIGN TRADE

Millions US$ 1998

IMPORTS
41,250

EXPORTS
50,755

STATISTICS

DEMOGRAPHY

Population: 209,255,000 (1999)
Annual growth: 1.9 % (1975/97)
Estimates for year 2015 (million): 250.4 (1999)
Annual growth to year 2015: 1.2 % (1997/2015)
Urban population: 37.4 % (1997)
Urban Growth: 4.8 % (1980/95)
Children per woman: 2.5 (1998)

HEALTH

Life expectancy at birth: 65 years (1998)
male: 63 years (1998)
female: 67 years (1998)
Maternal mortality: 450 per 100,000 live births (1990-98)
Infant mortality: 40 per 1,000 (1998)
Under-5 child mortality: 56 per 1,000 (1998)
Daily calorie supply: 2,930 per capita (1996)
12 doctors per 100,000 people (1993)
Safe water: 74 % (1990/98)

EDUCATION

Literacy: 84 % (1995)
male: 90 % (1995)
female: 78 % (1995)
School enrolment:
Primary total: 114 % (1990/96)
male: 117 % (1990/97)
female: 112 % (1990/97)
Secondary:
male: 52 % (1990/96)
female: 44 % (1990/96)
Tertiary: 11 % (1996)
Primary school teachers: one for every 22 (1996)

COMMUNICATIONS

24 newspapers (1996), 156 radios (1997), 232 TV sets (1996) and 21 main telephone lines (1996) per 1,000 people
Books: 3 new titles per 100,000 people (1992/94)

ECONOMY

Per capita, GNP: $ 640 (1998)
Annual growth, GNP: -16.7 % (1998)
Annual inflation: 12.2 % (1990/98)
Consumer price index: 181.7 (1998)
Currency: 10,013.6 rupiahs = $ 1 (1998)
Cereal imports: 2,691,499 metric tons (1998)
Food import dependency: 9 % (1997)
Fertilizer use: 1,373 kg per ha (1997)
Exports: $ 50,755 million (1998)
Imports: $ 41,250 million (1998)
External debt: $ 150,875 million (1998); $ 731 per capita (1998)
Debt service: 33.0 % of exports (1998)
Development aid received: $ 832 million (1997); $ 4.6 per capita (1997); 0.40 % of GNP (1997)

ENERGY

Consumption: 693.0 Kgs of Oil equivalent per capita yearly (1997); -60.0 % imported (1997)

HDI (rank/value): 105/0.681 (1997)

1980 and 1990 was only 1.8 per cent. Even so, demographic pressure, particularly on the island of Java, together with the radical reorientation of the country's economy and commerce toward a world market, coupled with rapid industrialization, have all led to a deterioration in the quality of the environment and the depletion of agricultural lands. From 1979, the Government reacted to this situation with a population transfer project known as *Transmigrasi*, which involved moving 2.5 million Javanese to other less populated islands, causing great social tension, and destroying the lifestyles of the peoples already on these islands.

[19] In the 1980s over 300 ethnic groups saw their standards of living drop sharply. The most energetic protests were those of the inhabitants of West Papua who demanded self-determination and freedom of movement to and from the neighboring territory of Papua New Guinea, with which they had a high degree of cultural and historical affinity.

[20] Suharto was re-elected in 1988, in an election marked by unprecedented discussion of issues in the press.

[21] In 1991 the fighting between the army and the Aceh liberation movements in Sumatra became more acute when the commander of the army called for the annihilation of the insurgents. At the beginning of March 1992, an armed offensive of several separatist groups was started in Irian Jaya province. At the same time the US Government asked Congress to approve $2,300,000 for the training of the official security forces of Indonesia.

[22] In March 1993 the Popular Consultative Assembly chose Suharto as President for the sixth time.

[23] In the 1990s the exports of gas, oil, wood and the new industrial goods, as well as tourism contributed to an annual rate of growth of six to eight per cent. Nevertheless the foreign debt put 27 per cent of Indonesians into conditions of extreme poverty. The compulsive logging and the large infrastructural works resulted in the loss of fertile land and displacement of the peasant population.

[24] * During 1995 the technocrat middle class manifested a growing interest in political openness.

[25] In May, Suharto announced a plan to reduce the seats assigned to the military in Parliament by 1997.

[26] Two years before the campaign for the parliamentary elections of mid-1997, Suharto's Minister of Information, Harmoko, toured Indonesia in support of Golkar, the major political party. The opposition accused the Government of interfering in its activities. Particularly vocal was the Indonesian Democratic Part (PDI), headed by Megawati Sukarnoputri, daughter of Sukarno, the still-respected independence leader.

[27] In 1996 the pre-election debates reached a new low when complaints about the illegal enrichment of the Suharto family and its circle grew. The military saw Islamic groups as well as Sukarnoputri and the PDI as the main threats to Suharto's power. The change of political climate is due partly to a wider circulation of information via the Internet as well as campaigning journalism and vigorous protest about arms sales to Indonesia.

[28] In spite of a climate of political uncertainty, the economy continued to prosper and inflation was kept at bay. However, the trade surplus fell due to the reduction of key exports, such as textiles. Suharto, then 75, had to travel to Germany for a medical check-up, which increased doubts over his government.

[29] In early 1997, the population reached 200 million. The Government announced it would continue its program to transfer the people from 'over-populated' regions to less populated areas.

[30] The ruling Golkar party won the May 1997 parliamentary elections, obtaining 74 per cent of the vote (325 of 400 seats at stake). The new parliament included 12 of President Suharto's relatives - six children, two wives, two son-in-laws, one brother and a cousin - as well as many of the leader's trade partners or cronies. On March 10 1998, Parliament re-elected Suharto for a seventh 5-year term.

[31] A severe stock market crisis in April increased inflation and caused a risk of hyperinflation. The currency had lost 50 per cent of its value since mid-1997. The price rise affected mostly basic goods. Two million workers lost their jobs between October 1997 and March 1998. Widespread social unrest followed, including the looting of

shops and victimization of the Chinese community who were seen as wealthy and therefore supporters of the status quo. Student demonstrations calling for democracy met a brutal response, but Suharto stepped down on 21 May to be succeeded by his Vice-President Jusuf Habibie.

[32] In October 1998, violent student protests to demand democracy and the removal of army chief Wiranto overwhelmed the capital. Five students were killed in confrontations with anti-insurrection forces. Also that month, two civilians died during armed conflicts between separatist rebels and police in Aceh province, the northernmost point of Indonesia, where the army had been accused of committing all kinds of abuses.

[33] Inter-ethnic fighting intensified in Borneo, between the Malay, Bugi, Dayak and Chinese on one side and Maduran immigrants on the other, leading to the deaths of some 70 people in March 1999. In Jakarta the following month, hundreds of Muslims set fire to a community center in retaliation for a bomb explosion at a mosque in Ujung Pandang, the largest in the country and in Southeast Asia.

[34] October elections gave the presidency to Abdurraman Wahid, who until that time was leader of the Nahdlatul Ulama Muslim organization. A Sufi, and a pro-democracy activist during the Suharto regime, Wahid had repeatedly defended the rights of minorities in the country. Political analysts rejected the idea that he would establish a Government based on Islamic law.

[35] One of Wahid's first acts as President was to offer Aceh broad autonomy and an increase in economic support if the province were to remain a part of Indonesia. He set a seven-month deadline to carry out a referendum, similar to the one held in August of that year in East Timor (See East Timor). The plan to retain the province established that 75 per cent of all income produced there would remain in Aceh, one of the country's richest regions in natural resources. The news upset the army chiefs, who indicated that the referendum would lead to the disintegration of the whole country. ■

Iran

Iran

Population: 66,796,000 (1999)
Area: 1,648,000 SQ KM
Capital: Teheran (Tehran)
Currency: Rial
Language: Persian

Shortly before the 18th century BC, nations of the Indo-European area reached the plains of Iran, subduing the shepherds who inhabited the region. More of these people arrived up until the 10th century BC, contributing to the Mesopotamian cultural mix. They later became known by different names: Medes, from the name of the ruling group; Iranians, the name they adopted in Persia and India (from Sanskrit *ayriana* meaning nobles); Persians (a Greco-Latin term alluding to Perseus, the mythological ancestor that the Greeks foisted on Iranians), with its corrupted forms: Parsis, Farsis, Fars, or Parthians (according to the time and source). Whatever their names, they first won control of the mountainous region, then conquered the Mesopotamian plains under the reign of Ciaxares. During the rule of Ciro the Great (559-530 BC), this wave of expansion reached as far west as Asia Minor, and as far east as present-day Afghanistan. These borders were later extended as far as Greece, Egypt, Turkestan and part of India.

2   Towards the end of the 4th century BC, this vast empire fell into the hands of Alexander of Macedonia. Alexander's successors, the Seleucides and Romans (see Syria) lost their hold on the eastern part of the empire to the Persians, who recovered their independence with the Arsacid dynasty (2nd century BC to 3rd AD). They remained independent under the Sassanids until the 7th century, though constantly at war with the Romans and Byzantines.

3   After the Arab conquest reached the region in 641 (see Saudi Arabia), Islamic thought and practices became dominant. Unlike the people in most other provinces of the Arab Empire, they retained their own language and distinctive styles in arts and literature. With the fall of the Caliphate of Baghdad, Persia attained virtual independence, first under the descendants of Tahir, the last Arab viceroy, and later under the Seleucidian Turks and the Persian dynasties. Despite political restlessness, the period was remarkably rich in cultural and scientific progress, personified by the poet, mathematician, philosopher and astronomer, Ummar al-Khayyam.

4   The Mongol invasion led by Hulagu Khan that began in 1258 was an altogether different matter. Three centuries of Mongol domination brought dynastic strife between the descendants of Timur Lenk (Tamburlaine) and the Ottomans. The dispute paved the way for Persian Ismail Shah whose grandson Abbas I (1587-1629) succeeded in uniting the country. He expelled the Turks from the west, the Portuguese from the Ormuz region, and also conquered part of Afghanistan. For a short time Iran ruled a region extending from India to Syria.

5   The weakness of the Persian ruler or Shah during frequent Anglo-Russian interventions in Iran and Afghanistan encouraged a strong nationalist movement, ideologically influenced by Syrian Pan-Islamic intellectuals.

6   A 1909 treaty divided the country into two areas - one of Russian and the other of British economic influence. A British firm was given the opportunity to exploit Iranian petroleum fields. Military occupation by the two powers during World War I, in addition to government corruption

and inefficiency, led to the 1921 revolution headed by journalist Sayyid Tabatabai and Reza Khan, commander of the national guard.

7   Reza, the revolution's war minister, became prime minister in 1923. Two years later, the National Assembly dismissed Tabatabai, and Reza ousted the Shah, occupying the throne himself. Reza repealed all treaties granting extra-territorial rights to foreign powers, abolished the obligatory use of the veil by women, reformed the education and health systems, and cancelled oil concessions that favored the British.

8   His attempt to establish a militarily strong, internationally neutral modern state, that became known as Iran in 1935, met with strenuous resistance from European powers. Reza Shah insisted in maintaining strict neutrality, rejecting a July 1941 ultimatum demanding passage for allied arms to the Soviet Union through Iranian territory. In August, British and Soviet forces invaded, forcing the Iranian army to surrender in September. The Shah was overthrown and sent into exile after abdicating in favor of his son, Muhammad Reza Pahlevi. Educated in Europe and more amenable to European interests, the new ruler governed under Anglo-Soviet tutelage until the end of the war.

9   A 1949 constitution curtailed the Shah's authority, and progressive, nationalist forces won seats in parliament. With their support, Prime Minister Muhammad Mossadegh attempted to nationalize oil reserves and expropriate the Anglo-Iranian Oil Company.

10   Mossadegh maintained that it was 'better to be independent and produce only one ton of oil a year than produce 32 million tons and continue as slaves of England' - despite the fact that Britain had other sources of supply in the Arab states, Venezuela and the US, while Iran had no alternative market. Mossadegh's audacity was met in 1953 by an economic blockade and a coup backed by the US Central Intelligence Agency (CIA) which returned almost absolute power to the Shah. This chain of events was accompanied by the killing of nationalists and left-wing activists. Thousands were imprisoned. Mossadegh remained in prison until his death in 1967.

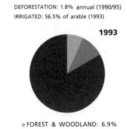

① Neutral Zone ▨ Kurdistan

0   300 km

WORKERS

% OF LABOUR FORCE   **1998**

■ FEMALE: 26%   ■ MALE: 74%

1990

■ SERVICES: 43.0%
■ INDUSTRY: 24.6%
■ AGRICULTURE: 32.4%

LAND USE

DEFORESTATION: 1.8% annual (1990/95)
IRRIGATED: 56.5% of arable (1993)

1993

■ FOREST & WOODLAND: 6.9%
■ ARABLE: 10.1%
■ OTHER: 83.0%

PUBLIC EXPENDITURE

1997

41.1%

11.6%

DEFENCE   SOCIAL

MILITARY EXPENDITURE   **38%**
(% of health & education)   (1990/91)

11 The Shah's power depended principally on the oil economy. He encouraged multinational penetration of Iran, citing 'modernization' which effectively consisted of promoting Western consumer habits.

12 Westernization was resisted by Islamic clergy who feared encroaching secularism, and by those social sectors most affected, notably small farmers and the urban poor. By the end of the 1970s, the growing power of foreign enterprises in the domestic market, plus rapidly changing consumption patterns, had lost the Shah the sympathies of the powerful commercial and industrial élites known locally as the 'bazaar'.

13 Opposition groups included the National Front founded by Mossadegh, the Tudeh Communist Party, and Fedayin (Marxist) and Mujahedin (Islamic) guerrillas - each using a different strategy. The most effective opposition was centered around the Muslim leader Ayatollah Ruhollah Khomeini, exiled in 1964. Khomeini was resident in Iraq for many years until the Shah, irritated by political ferment in Iranian mosques, pressured the Iraqi Government into deporting him to France.

14 The recordings of Khomeini's preaching in Paris became well-known and encouraged the masses to organize. During 1977, demonstrations began in secondary schools and by 1978 became generalized. The Shah was forced to flee in January 1979 and Khomeini made a triumphant return to Iran. On February 11 1979 crowds invaded the imperial palace; the Shah's prime minister resigned, and a divided army accepted the new state of affairs. The Islamic Revolution, seen as a successful alternative to both socialist and capitalist Western models, was welcomed enthusiastically, not only in Iran but throughout the Muslim world.

15 Prime Minister Mehdi Bazargan of the National Front sought to reconcile Muslim traditions with a model of progressive development

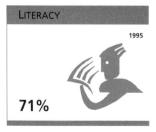

MATERNAL MORTALITY 1990-98

Per 100,000 live births

37

LITERACY 1995

71%

permitting broad participation. However he was supported neither by the revolutionary left nor by the Muslim fundamentalists. The latter, bolstered by the 'revolutionary guards' and Khomeini's popularity, first excluded their former left-wing and right-wing allies and then proceeded to suppress them harshly.

16 In early November 1979, a student group stormed the US embassy in Tehran, taking the diplomatic personnel hostage. Documents found inside provided evidence of CIA involvement in Iranian politics. In April 1980, a US attempt to rescue the hostages was unsuccessful.

17 On July 17 1980, the Shah died in Egypt and lengthy negotiations began for release of the hostages. This was finally accomplished on January 20 1981.

18 In September 1980, Iran and Iraq began a war which lasted for eight years. Iraqi president Saddam Hussein wanted to reassert his country's sovereignty over both banks of the Shatt al-Arab river, which historically had been the border between the two countries. Hussein was also concerned over attempts by Iran's new Islamic revolutionary government to incite rebellion among Iraq's Shi'a majority.

19 The Islamic Revolutionary Party (IRP) won the presidential elections with more than 90 per cent of the vote in 1981. On August 30, violent incidents and bombings caused the death of 72 political leaders, among them President Muhammad Ali Rajai and Prime Minister Muhammad Javad Bahonar. A new president, Ali Khamenei, former secretary-general of the IRP, was elected.

20 The clergy held a favored position, and the Government made widespread use of imprisonment, exile and execution for both political opponents and common criminals. Government sources registered 500 executions in 1989 - mostly for drug trafficking.

21 In 1985, the country made great commercial profits, despite the war with its neighbor. Iran's main clients were West Germany, Japan, Switzerland, Sweden, Italy and the Arab Emirates, with petroleum being the main export product, constituting 98 per cent of exports.

22 Contrary to Western expectations, the death of Ayatollah Khomeini on June 3 1989 did not lead to widespread chaos and instability. As more than 8 million mostly poor mourners gathered to bury Khomeini, President Ali Sayed Khamenei was appointed Iran's spiritual leader by a vote of the Assembly of Experts.

23 In August, new elections gave a landslide victory to Hojatoleslam Ali Akbar Hashemi Rafsanjani, ex-Speaker of Parliament, who became president. The new constitution enhanced the President's role and Rafsanjani took office as a fully empowered executive head of state rather than a ceremonial one. Iran's international image had deteriorated when Khomeini had issued a *fatwa* (death sentence) on Indo-British writer, Salman Rushdie, stating that the writer's book *The Satanic Verses* was blasphemous. Rushdie went into hiding, but in late 1990 he made a few public appearances, reconfirmed his Islamic faith and became reconciled with the main Islamic authorities.

24 In 1990, Iran condemned the Iraqi invasion of Kuwait, taking advantage of the situation to negotiate previous border disputes. Iraq withdrew from 2,600 square kilometers of occupied Iranian territory, prisoners of war were exchanged, and the countries' sovereignty over the Shatt al-Arab canal was divided. Iran remained neutral when hostilities broke out in 1991.

25 Rafsanjani's election as president meant a strengthening of the 'pro-Western' wing in the regime. According to the Iranian Constitution, religious and lay authorities share power. But, unlike his predecessor Ruholah Khomeini, the religious leader Ali Khamenei was appointed supreme leader but not Great Ayatollah. The old ayatollah, Araki, bore that responsibility.

26 Sectors hostile to the West were pre-eminent, but did not have a two-thirds majority in the *Majlis* (Parliament), therefore having no power to change presidential resolutions. The Revolutionary Guards meanwhile were merged into the army, depriving the anti-West sectors of an important pressure group.

27 Iranian neutrality during the Gulf War was designed to gain advantages over Baghdad, but also to gain acceptance in regional and international diplomacy. Diplomatic

EXTERNAL DEBT

1998

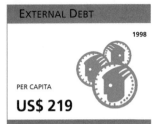

PER CAPITA

US$ 219

FOREIGN TRADE

Millions US$ 1998

IMPORTS

16,750

EXPORTS

14,927

STATISTICS

DEMOGRAPHY

Population: 66,796,000 (1999)
Annual growth: 3.1 % (1975/97)
Estimates for year 2015 (million): 83.1 (1999)
Annual growth to year 2015: 1.4 % (1997/2015)
Urban population: 60.0 % (1997)
Children per woman: 2.8 (1998)

HEALTH

Life expectancy at birth: 69 years (1998)
male: 69 years (1998)
female: 70 years (1998)
Maternal mortality: 37 per 100,000 live births (1990-98)
Infant mortality: 29 per 1,000 (1998)
Under-5 child mortality: 33 per 1,000 (1998)
Daily calorie supply: 2,824 per capita (1996)
Safe water: 95 % (1990/98)

EDUCATION

Literacy: 71 % (1995)
male: 79 % (1995)
female: 63 % (1995)
School enrolment:
Primary total: 90 % (1990/96)
male: 92 % (1990/97)
female: 87 % (1990/97)
Secondary:
male: 79 % (1990/96)
female: 69 % (1990/96)
Tertiary: 18 % (1996)
Primary school teachers: one for every 31 (1996)

COMMUNICATIONS

28 newspapers (1996), 265 radios (1997), 164 TV sets (1996) and 95 main telephone lines (1996) per 1,000 people
Books: 16 new titles per 100,000 people (1992/94)

ECONOMY

Per capita, GNP: $ 1,650 (1998)
Annual growth, GNP: 1.5 % (1998)
Annual inflation: 28.3 % (1990/98)
Consumer price index: 180.3 (1998)
Currency: 1,751.9 rials = $ 1 (1998)
Cereal imports: 6,339,974 metric tons (1998)
Fertilizer use: 649 kg per ha (1997)
Exports: $ 14,927 million (1998)
Imports: $ 16,750 million (1998)
External debt: $ 14,391 million (1998); $ 219 per capita (1998)
Debt service: 20.2 % of exports (1998)
Development aid received: $ 196 million (1997); $ 3.5 per capita (1997); 0.20 % of GNP (1997)

ENERGY

Consumption: 1,777.0 Kgs of Oil equivalent per capita yearly (1997); -108.0 % imported (1997)

HDI (rank/value): 95/0.715 (1997)

relations with Britain were renewed in 1990 and with Saudi Arabia in March 1991, during the Gulf War.

[28] This rapprochement with the West, and the refusal openly to support Iraq during the US offensive, affected relations with other Muslim groups in the region. Iran's lack of support to the Shi'a rebellion in Iraq at the end of the War disappointed those sectors which regarded Tehran as the capital of Shi'a expansion.

[29] The much-desired normalization of relations between Iran and the West was hindered by the use of violence by groups linked to Tehran. The secretary of Chaput Bakhtiar, Shah Reza Pahlevi's former prime minister, was assassinated in April 1991. Bakhtiar himself was killed in May.

[30] With the disintegration of the Soviet Union, a new area of influence lay open to Iran. In 1991, Tehran opened embassies in the Islamic republics of the Caucasus and Central Asia, signing trade and cultural agreements and opening new means of communications with its neighbors.

[31] Iran's biggest step in its rapprochement with the West was the release of ten hostages held by pro-Iranian forces in Lebanon, in a process which lasted throughout 1991.

[32] On April 10 1992, legislative elections were held, with the 'moderates' who supported President Rafsanjani winning a clear victory over the 'radical' candidates.

[33] In July, Iran's spiritual leader Khamenei launched a campaign to 'eradicate Western influence', clashing with Rafsanjani and his more moderate vision of Islam to the extent that the President threatened to resign.

[34] However in June 1993, Rafsanjani was confirmed President by 63 per cent of the vote. The high rate of abstentions - 41 per cent of the country's 29 million voters - was read as a sign of discontent over corruption.

[35] In February 1994 - at a time of great tension among the different leading groups - a failed attempt was made on Rafsanjani's life during the celebration of the 15th anniversary of the Islamic Revolution. Disagreements with Saudi Arabia regarding the Muslims' annual pilgrimage to Mecca - Islam's main holy site, in Saudi territory - affected relations with the government of King Fahd and reflected once more the struggle between the two states for the world leadership of Islamic states.

[36] In the economic field, the results did not turn out as expected. Oil sales between March 1994 and March 1995 amounted to $10.5 billion, compared to $17.7 billion in the previous year. Meanwhile, the Government stopped subsidizing 23 imported products, mostly food and medicine, which led to rising prices .

[37] In July, the US toughened its sanctions against Iran, blaming the country for terrorist actions. The measure proposed was challenged by the international community. At the time, unemployment in Iran reached 10 per cent of the working people.

[38] In the May 23 1997 elections there was a 90 per cent turnout of voters. The winner with 69 per cent of the vote was Mohammad Khatami, regarded as the most pro-Western candidate. A new government took over in August and Khatami announced it would open up the country to the West.

[39] The judicial decision to confiscate the property of influential ayatollah Hussein Ali Montazeri, a presidential ally and critic of Khamenei, revealed the power struggle between Montazeri's followers and those of the spiritual leader. Demonstrations of support for Khamenei were held in several Iranian cities, and he was confirmed in his position. Montazeri had criticized the leader's power to intervene in matters of State.

[40] At the Islamic conference held in Teheran in December 1997, Israel was criticized for its 'expansionist policy'. The declaration also condemned 'terrorism', in what was considered a 'point in favor' of Khatami in the power struggle occurring within Iran.

[41] In March 1998, Masoume Ebtekar, Iran's deputy minister of Environmental Affairs, denounced the oppressive conditions in which the women of Afghanistan were living under the Islamic regime of the Taliban. In Iran, in contrast with other Muslim countries, women have the right to vote and are increasingly found in decision-making positions.

[42] In November of that year, a series of assassinations of writers and political dissidents began. Official investigations showed that members of the Intelligence Ministry were implicated in the murders. This intensified the struggle for power between reformists and the hardliners, and led President Khatami to propose Fiscal General Ali Yunesi as the new Intelligence Minister in February 1999.

[43] In July 1999, after six days of student protests demanding the reopening of a banned newspaper and greater liberalization, the orthodox sectors launched a counter-protest involving hundreds of thousands of people in support of the clerical authorities and 'revolutionary values'. Ali Khamenei sent a message to the demonstrators calling for strong sanctions against the opposition. Hasan Rowhani, a religious leader and parliamentary speaker, stated that those who were arrested in the student protests should face the death penalty. The orthodox sectors accused the United States of being behind the demonstrations.

[44] Days later, at various points on a tour through the nation's interior that he used as a counter-offensive against the orthodoxy, President Khatami affirmed he would keep his electoral promise to defend civil liberties, despite the attacks of the religious hierarchy, which accused him of having provoked the worst social disturbances since the beginning of the Islamic revolution in 1979.

[45] The general elections of February 2000 gave an overwhelming victory to the reformists headed by Khatami, who won 226 of the 290 parliamentary seats. In March, the *Hammihan* newspaper printed an image of the US flag, something that had not occurred in this country since the 1979 revolution. Though there was no law prohibiting the publication of the flag, the *Hammihan* gesture was interpreted as the breaking of a taboo. ■

Iraq

'Iraq

Population: 22,450,000 (1999)
Area: 438,320 SQ KM
Capital: Baghdad
Currency: Dinar
Language: Arabic

The territory of present-day Iraq was the cradle of the Sumerian civilization around 4000 BC. Over the centuries it was the home of a series of prestigious civilizations: the Akkad, Babylonian, and Assyrian or Chaldean. Known as Mesopotamia, from the Greek, 'between rivers', it was a crossroads for innumerable migrations and conquest expeditions. Hittites, Mitannians, Persians, Greeks, Romans and Byzantines all passed through the territory, leaving behind more destruction than cultural heritage.

[2] In the 7th century the Arab conquest transformed Mesopotamia into the center of an enormous empire (see Saudi Arabia). A century later, the new Abbas dynasty decided to move the capital east from Damascus. Caliph al-Mansur built the new capital, Baghdad, on the banks of the Tigris and for three centuries the city of the 'thousand and one nights' was the center of a new culture.

[3] This culture led to the greatest flourishing of the arts and sciences in the Mediterranean region since the days of the Greeks. The empire began to fall apart after the death of Harun al-Raschid. The African provinces were lost (see Tunisia: Islam in North Africa), and the region north and east of Persia won independence under the Tahiris (the Kingdom of Khorasan). The caliphs depended increasingly on armies of slaves or mercenaries (Sudanese or Turks) to retain their grip on an ever-shrinking empire. When the Mongols assassinated the last caliph in Baghdad in 1258, the title had already lost its political meaning. The conquests of Genghis Khan devastated the region's agricultural economy, and the region was subsequently ruled in whole or part by Seleucids,

Ottomans, Turks, Mongols, Turkomans, Tartars, and Kurds. The movement of steppe peoples (see Afghanistan), brought great instability to the fertile crescent, which finally achieved unification under the Ottoman Turks in the 16th century, having repelled an attack by Timur Lenk (Tamburlaine) in the 14th century.

[4] In the early 20th century, Arab Renaissance movements were active in Iraq, paving the way for the rebellion that rocked the Turkish realm during World War I (see Saudi Arabia, Jordan and Syria). The British already had a foothold in the region and were keen to expand their influence. With the defeat of the Turks, Iraq entertained hopes of independence. These however were dashed when the revolutionary Soviet government revealed the

existence of the secret Sykes-Picot treaty (signed in 1916), whereby France and Britain divided the Arab territories between themselves. Faisal, son of the shereef Hussein, had proclaimed himself King of Syria and occupied Damascus. However, since this territory 'belonged' to the French, who had promised nothing to the Arabs, (see Saudi Arabia, Jordan and Syria), he was forcibly evicted. In 1920, Britain was awarded a mandate over Mesopotamia by the League of Nations, triggering a pro-independence rebellion.

[5] In 1921, Emir Faisal ibn Hussain was appointed King of Iraq, in compensation for his previous bad treatment. In 1930, general Nuri as-Said was appointed Prime Minister, signing a treaty of alliance with the British, under which the country would become nominally independent on October 3 1932.

[6] That year, the Baghdad Pact was founded, making Iraq part of a military alliance with Turkey, Pakistan, Iran, Britain and the US. This pact was resisted by Iraqi nationalists. In July 1958, anti-imperialist agitation resulted in a

military coup led by Abdul Karim Kassim, bringing about the execution of the royal family.

[7] In 1959 the regime tried to forge a union with Syria, but the Communist Party - one of the most important in the East - and the democrats, whose model was the European parliamentary system, opposed the move. In July, in an attempt to consolidate the regime, Kassim banned all political parties and proclaimed that the emirate of Kuwait belonged to Iraq. The Arab League, dominated by Egypt, authorized the deployment of British troops to protect the oil rich enclave.

[8] Kassim's over-exaggerated ties with the Soviet Union and China fomented predictions that Iraq could become 'a new Cuba'. In the summer of 1960 the country suddenly moved towards the West. Steps toward economic change were taken, a land reform program was implemented, and the profits of the Iraq Petroleum Company were severely restricted. In 1963, Kassim was deposed by pan-Arabian sectors within the army. Several unstable governments ensued until July 17 1968, when a military coup placed the Ba'ath party in power.

[9] Founded in 1947, the Arab Ba'ath Socialist Party (ba'ath meaning renaissance) was inspired by the ideal of Pan-Arabism, regarding the Arab World as an indivisible political and economic unit where no country 'can be self-sufficient'. The Ba'athists proclaimed that 'socialism is a need which emerges from the very core of Arab nationalism. It is organized on a 'national' (Arab) level, having several 'regional' leaders in each country.'

[10] Iraq nationalized foreign companies, and Baghdad defended the use of oil as a 'political weapon in the struggle against imperialism and Zionism'. It insisted on protected prices and the consolidation of OPEC as an organization which would support the struggle of the Third World for the recovery and enhancement of its natural resources. A land reform program was decreed, and ambitious development plans encouraged the reinvestment of oil money into national industrialization.

[11] In 1970, the Baghdad Government gave the Kurdish language official status, and

MAP

1 Neutral Zone   ///// Kurdistan   0 —— 300 km

WORKERS

% OF LABOUR FORCE   **1998**

■ FEMALE: 19%   ■ MALE: 81%

1990

■ SERVICES: 66.4%
■ INDUSTRY: 17.5%
■ AGRICULTURE: 16.1%

LAND USE

DEFORESTATION: 0.0% annual (1990/95)
IRRIGATED: 48.6% of arable (1993)

1993

■ FOREST & WOODLAND: 0.4%
■ ARABLE: 12.0%
■ OTHER: 87.6%

PUBLIC EXPENDITURE

MILITARY EXPENDITURE   **271%**
(% of health & education)   (1990/91)

granted Kurdistan domestic autonomy. However, abetted by the Shah of Iran, and fearful of land reform, the traditional regional leaders rose in armed confrontation. In March 1975, the Iran-Iraq border agreement deprived the Kurds of their main foreign support and the rebels were defeated. The Baghdad Government decreed the teaching of Kurdish in local schools, greater state investment in the region, and the appointment of Kurds to key administrative positions.

[12] On July 16 1979, President Ahmed Hassan al-Bakr resigned because of ill-health. He was replaced by Vice-President Saddam Hussein.

[13] Saddam Hussein tried to establish himself as leader of the Arab world. He was one of the most outspoken critics of the 1979 Camp David agreements between Egypt, Israel and the US, but Iraqi relations with other Arab countries still worsened. A branch of the Ba'ath party took power in Syria in 1970, but its discrepancies with Baghdad led to rivalry and some border disputes.

[14] Saddam wanted to reassert Iraq's sovereignty over both banks of the Shatt al-Arab waterway that historically had been the border with Iran. He was also concerned about attempts by Iran's new Islamic revolutionary government to incite rebellion among Iraq's Shi'a majority. These issues spurred Saddam to make a preemptive strike on Iran. By attacking when it did, Iraq took advantage of the apparent disorder of Iran's new government and demoralization of its regular armed forces. The Iraqis were confident of a quick victory but in the event the war lasted for 8 years.

[15] During the war, the Saudis and Kuwaitis - like others who had benefited from Iraq acting as a bulwark against Iranian fundamentalism - granted Baghdad many loans which were used both in the conflict and for strengthening the country's infrastructure. An oil pipeline was built through Turkey as an alternative to the one which crossed Syria to the Mediterranean; Syria had closed this in sympathy with Iran. The roads to Jordan were also improved.

[16] In November 1984, 17 years after they had broken off diplomatic relations, official links with the US were re-established.

[17] The 1988 armistice meant that Iraq retained 2,600 square kilometers of Iranian territory with its powerful and skilful army. Neighboring Kuwait was extracting more oil than allowed from deposits under the border and refused to establish export quotas. As the US hinted that they would remain neutral in the event of conflict, Baghdad thought that it would be able to take the neighboring territory and exploit its wealth. On August 2, Iraq invaded Kuwait and took thousands of foreign hostages.

[18] Four days later the UN decided on a total economic and military blockade until Iraq retreated unconditionally from the occupied territory. Withdrawal was rejected, but a proposal for an international conference to discuss the Middle East issue was submitted. When Iraq started to release the hostages and to make new attempts at negotiating, the US refused to talk and demanded an unconditional surrender.

[19] On January 17 1991, an alliance of 32 countries led by the US started the attacks on Iraq. When the land offensive began in March, Saddam Hussein had already announced his unconditional withdrawal. The Iraqi army did not resist the offensive and hardly attempted to stage an organized withdrawal, yet it suffered great losses. The war ended early in March, with the total defeat of the Iraqis.

[20] At the end of the offensive, the US encouraged an internal revolt of the southern Shi'a and of the northern Kurds so that Saddam Hussein would be deposed. However, the political differences between these factions made an alliance impossible, and Washington abandoned the rebels to their own fates, whereupon they were crushed by the still powerful Iraqi army. Over one million Kurds sought refuge in Iran and Turkey to escape the Baghdad forces, and thousands starved or froze to death when winter came.

[21] Between 150,000 and 200,000 people, mostly civilians, died in the war. As a result of the blockade - still in force - some 70,000 more may have died in the first year, among them 20,000 children. At the end of 1991, both the Turkish and Iraqi armies were continuing to harass the Kurds in the border area.

[22] The conditions stipulated for lifting sanctions became even more demanding with the increased determination on the part of the US Government to bring down Hussein. In addition, *The New York Times* and the London *Sunday Telegraph* reported that the United States had introduced huge amounts of counterfeit dinars (Iraq's currency), smuggled across the Jordanian, Saudi Arabian, Turkish and Iranian borders. Baghdad established the

PROFILE

ENVIRONMENT

The Mesopotamian region, between the rivers Tigris and Euphrates (Al-Furat) in the center of the country, is suitable for agriculture, and contains most of the population. In the mountainous areas in the north, in Kurdistan, there are important oil deposits. In Lower Mesopotamia, on the Shatt-al-Arab channel, where the Tigris and the Euphrates merge, 15 million palm trees produce 80 per cent of the world's dates which were sold worldwide, before the blockade. The war's devastation included the destruction of the major part of the country's infrastructure. Tank and troop movements caused profound damage to road surfaces and soil, especially in the environmentally sensitive area along the Saudi Arabian border.

SOCIETY

Peoples: Iraqis are mostly Arab; 20 per cent belong to a Kurdish minority living in the north.
Religions: Mainly Islamic. Most of the Shi'a Muslims (62 per cent) live in the south. In the center, Sunni Arabs predominate, and they share a common religion with the Kurds in the north. 35 per cent of Iraqi population is Sunni.
Languages: Arabic (official and predominant); in Kurdistan it is regarded as a second language, after Kurdish.
Political Parties: The Arab Ba'ath Socialist Party has been in power since 1968; the Kurdistan Democratic Party; the Kurdistan Fatherland Party.
Social Organizations: The General Federation of Trade Unions of Iraq.

THE STATE

Official Name: Al-Jumhuriyah al-'Iraqiyah.
Administrative divisions: 15 provinces and 3 autonomous regions.
Capital: Baghdad 4,900,000 people (1997).
Other cities: Diyala 961,073 people; Al-Basrah 406,296; Arbil 485,968; Mosul (Al-Mawsil) 664,221.
Government: Saddam Hussein, President since July 1979 and Prime Minister since May 1994.
National Holidays: July 14, Proclamation of the Republic (1958); July 17, Revolution Day (1968).
Armed Forces: There are no official figures.

STATISTICS

DEMOGRAPHY

Population: 22,450,000 (1999)
Annual growth: 3.0 % (1975/97)
Estimates for year 2015 (million): 34.1 (1999)
Annual growth to year 2015: 2.7 % (1997/2015)
Urban population: 75.5 % (1997)
Children per woman: 5.2 (1998)

HEALTH

Life expectancy at birth: 63 years (1998)
male: 61 years (1998)
female: 64 years (1998)
Infant mortality: 103 per 1,000 (1998)
Under-5 child mortality: 125 per 1,000 (1998)
Daily calorie supply: 2,252 per capita (1996)
51 doctors per 100,000 people (1993)
Safe water: 81 % (1990/98)

EDUCATION

Literacy: 58 % (1995)
male: 71 % (1995)
female: 45 % (1995)
School enrolment:
Primary total: 85 % (1990/96)
male: 92 % (1990/97)
female: 78 % (1990/97)
Secondary:
male: 51 % (1990/96)
female: 32 % (1990/96)
Tertiary: 11 % (1996)
Primary school teachers: one for every 20 (1995)

COMMUNICATIONS

19 newspapers (1996), 229 radios (1997), 78 TV sets (1996) and 33 main telephone lines (1996) per 1,000 people

ECONOMY

Currency: 0.3 dinars = $ 1 (1998)
Cereal imports: 3,455,169 metric tons (1997)
Fertilizer use: 653 kg per ha (1997)
Development aid received: $ 281 million (1997); $ 15.1 per capita (1997)

ENERGY

Consumption: 1,240.0 Kgs of Oil equivalent per capita yearly (1997); -129.0 % imported (1997)

HDI (rank/value): 125/0.586 (1997)

death penalty for anyone participating in these operations.

[23] Toward the end of 1991, the Iraqi Government authorized UN inspections of military establishments. In 1992, Iraq was found to have a uranium enrichment project, which had been developed using German technology. UN inspection teams destroyed 460 x 122 mm warheads armed with sarin, a poisonous gas. They also dismantled the nuclear complex at al-Athir, the uranium enrichment installations at Ash-Sharqat and Tarmiuah, and the chemical weapons plant at Muthana.

[24] In 1992 and 1993, the United States carried out several missile attacks on military targets and factories near Baghdad. They also bombed Iraqi troops along the border with Kuwait, recovering weapons abandoned by the retreating Iraqis. When Bill Clinton assumed the presidency of the United States, the Iraqi Government asked for a cease-fire. They put no conditions on further UN inspections.

[25] In 1994 a frontier crossing was opened with Turkey to allow certain UN authorized foodstuffs and medicines to enter the country - the only exceptions to the trade embargo. However a few months later in March 1995, Turkish troops invaded Iraqi Kurdistan - under the military protection of 'allied' - basically US - troops to repress members of the Kurdish Workers' Party (PKK) which was launching attacks from there on Turkish troops stationed in Turkish Kurdistan.

[26] The international isolation of Baghdad became yet more serious in 1996 when Jordan distanced itself from Saddam's Government, as King Hussein's relations with Kuwait and Saudi Arabia improved. These two countries continued pressuring the US not to lift the embargo on Iraq, because - amongst other reasons - Saudi oil had replaced Iraq's in several markets. However, the UN Security Council voted for the partial lifting of sanctions, allowing the controlled sale of crude oil, in order to buy the food and medicines needed by the Iraqi population. However many medicines and other necessities do not get through the rigorous vetting by the sanctions committee.

[27] In April 1997, a UN report revealed that the number of people dying from hunger as a result of the embargo had passed the million mark, and 570,000 of these were children. Meanwhile, UNICEF stated 25 per cent of children aged less than five years old were suffering from severe clinical malnutrition.

[28] In October, a new Iraqi crisis erupted as the Security Council threatened to impose further sanctions if a new inspection were not authorized to verify that Saddam was unable to manufacture chemical and biological weapons. Iraq rejected the presence of US inspectors, which led President Clinton to take a hard-line approach. Despite pressures from Washington, the Security Council ruled out the use of force. Accords reached in Baghdad by UN Secretary-General Kofi Annan in March 1998 reduced tensions and allowed new inspections to begin.

[29] Clinton, with the sole backing of British Prime Minister Tony Blair, decided to order missile attacks on several Iraqi cities. This coincided with the beginning of discussions in the US Congress that would result in Clinton's impeachment trial.

[30] Beginning December 16, the 'Operation Desert Fox' bombing campaign killed hundreds of Iraqis, both military troops and civilians. France, Russia and China, all members of the UN Security Council, protested at the US-British offensive and criticized the role played by Richard Butler, head of UNSCOM, the UN commission entrusted with overseeing Iraq's chemical and nuclear disarmament. The UN Secretary-General expressed reservations about the Australian diplomat's negotiating style. The hardline attitude against Iraq that Butler advocated was more important from the publicity point of view than from the perspective of real debilitation of Iraq's military and moral potential.

[31] By a narrow margin, the Security Council approved a measure in December 1999 to renew inspections in Iraq and to suspend economic sanctions if Baghdad were to co-operate. Russia, France, China and Malaysia abstained from voting, which was a sharp blow to US and British interests, as they had intended to send an unequivocal message to Hussein. Among the Security Council's permanent members, the resolution won only a minority of the votes. Iraq, which had already indicated it would reject the resolution, alleging it was a US attempt to impose its 'evil' will upon the Security Council, refused inspection and demanded the sanctions be lifted. The Iraqi refusal presaged the return to conflict. ∎

Kurds: from nomadism to nationalism

The Kurds are an ethnic and linguistic group living mostly in the mountains of Taurus, in eastern Anatolia, in the regions of Zagros and Khorasan (Iran), and in northern Iraq. It is estimated that, including the communities existing in Armenia, Georgia, Kazakhsztan, Lebanon and Syria, they number more than 15 million people. For centuries they have been nomads in the Mesopotamian plains and the mountain regions of Iran and Turkey, raising sheep and goats. Exceptionally, they have also been farmers. After World War I, many were forced to live in urban areas, leaving their traditions behind.

[2] Although they have lived in the same geographic region for a long time, they have never had a national state. The Treaty of Sèvres, which was concluded in 1920 and granted autonomy to Kurdistan, was never ratified. It was followed in 1923 by the Lausanne Treaty, which no longer mentioned Kurdistan nor the Kurds. After the war, the region was engulfed by violence, with the appearance of armed separatist movements .

[3] For centuries, the Kurds had a form of social government which followed the rules of the tribe. The sheikh was the main authority. This holds true even today, although not as much in urban groups which have lost some of their tribal identity while adapting to city life. In some cases, and even when the law does not allow it, as in Turkey, the Kurds practice polygamy.

[4] In Turkey, Government discrimination against the Kurds is widespread. Their identity has been denied by calling them 'mountain Turks', their language is banned (and regarded as a dialect derived from Turkish) as are some of their most typical customs. The Government repressed their political activity in the Eastern provinces and also encouraged their migration to urban areas in the west, in order to disperse Kurds concentrated in mountain areas. In Iran they are subject to strong pressure by the Government to assimilate into the majority culture and religious persecution from the Shiite majority.

[5] In Iraq, when the monarchy was defeated in 1958, the Kurds expected their linguistic status would be acknowledged and thought they would receive more social benefits and greater participation in development projects. However, these expectations were not fulfilled. Instead, the Iraqi Government implemented a policy of displacement, promoted armed conflicts and, in the 1980s, used lethal chemical weapons against whole communities. Over a period of 15 years, more than 400,000 Kurds died in Iraq.

[6] Kurdish nationalism has begun to appear not just as a response to these discriminatory conditions. Its late emergence can perhaps be attributed to their ancient nomadic lifestyle. In a way, this nationalism is prompted by certain Western influences (such as private property), the partition of the Kurdistan region into states, and the appearance of an urban intellectual minority. The interests of some Western countries in the Persian Gulf have played a part as well. ∎

Ireland

Eire

Population: 3,705,000 (1999)
Area: 70,280 SQ KM
Capital: Dublin
Currency: Punt
Language: Irish and English

The religious tensions in Irish history date back to the 17th century when a large number of British Protestants (in particular, Scottish Presbyterians) were encouraged to settle in the province of Ulster in the northern part of the island by the English colonial rulers. They subjugated the native Catholic population, Celtic peoples who had been converted to Christianity in the early 5th century.

[2] By virtue of the 1800 Act of Union, Ireland was incorporated into the United Kingdom. During the 19th century most of the population outside the Protestant-dominated North-east supported independence, which led to the formation of a strong nationalist movement.

[3] In 1916, the republican Easter Rising in Dublin was crushed by the occupying forces but it marked the foundation of the Irish Republican Army (IRA) and the final stage of the long struggle for freedom.

[4] The IRA's campaign of guerrilla warfare forced the British in 1920 to grant independence to the 26 counties with Catholic majorities. Southern Ireland became a self-governing region within the UK. The remaining six north-eastern counties became Northern Ireland, with a devolved government in Belfast and representation in the British parliament in Westminster. In 1922 Southern Ireland had declared independence and become the Irish Free State, a dominion under the British crown. In 1949 the Free State became the Irish Republic, formally breaking its final links with British commonwealth.

[5] The 1937 Irish Constitution considered Ireland to be a single country, where all the inhabitants - North and South - have citizenship rights.

[6] Supported by the Protestant majority, the Ulster Unionist Party always managed to retain control of the Parliament in Belfast. For 50 years, Northern Ireland was ruled exclusively by Unionists, led by the Provincial Prime Minister and a Governor acting as a representative of the British Crown.

[7] The Catholic minority in Northern Ireland was thus excluded from domestic political affairs, and many other fields. This led to the creation of an active civil rights movement in the 1960s.

[8] Although it was non-violent, the civil rights movement was considered a threat to the region's status and their dominant position by Protestant extremists and they reacted to it with violence.

[9] In April 1969, amidst growing disturbances, the Northern Ireland government requested British troops to protect the region's strategic installations. In August, Belfast and London agreed that all the Province's security forces should come under British command.

[10] As a counterpart to the Provisional IRA, the 'loyalists' (loyal to the British crown) formed a number of paramilitary organizations, including the Ulster Volunteer Force and the Ulster Defence Association. Between 1969 and the middle of 1994, more than 3,100 people died at the hands of the Protestant and Catholic paramilitaries, the British army and the Ulster police force, the Royal Ulster Constabulary (RUC). In 1972 political status was given to paramilitary prisoners, but this amendment was abolished in 1976.

[11] The growing violence provoked London to take over full responsibility for law and order in Northern Ireland. The Government in Belfast was abolished and a system of 'direct rule' from Westminster installed. In a plebiscite held in March 1973, 60 per cent of the population of Northern Ireland voted in favor of union with Britain.

[12] At the end of 1973, a Northern Irish Assembly and Executive was created in Belfast in which Protestant and Catholic representatives were supposed to share power.

[13] In December, the London and Dublin governments agreed on the establishment of an Irish Council. Both this agreement and the new power-sharing Assembly were bitterly opposed by most Protestants in Ulster. In 1974, the Protestant Ulster Workers' Council declared a general strike in Northern Ireland. This resulted in the resignation of the Executive and London took over direct rule once more.

[14] In the 1973 election in the Irish Republic, Fianna Fáil - a conservative nationalist party which had been in power for 44 years - was defeated. A coalition between the conservative Fine Gael and the Labour Party took office. This new administration was committed to power-sharing between the two communities in Ulster, but it rejected the immediate withdrawal of British troops from the region.

[15] In 1976, after the IRA murdered the British ambassador in Dublin, the Irish Government took stricter anti-terrorist measures. Fianna Fáil was elected in 1977 and it maintained the friendly relations with London established by the previous administration. Prime Minister Jack Lynch supported the creation of a devolved parliament in the North, instead of total unification.

[16] In August 1979, Dublin agreed to increase border security after the murders, on the same day, of Lord Mountbatten (a prominent British public figure related to the Royal Family) in the Irish Republic, and 18 British soldiers in Warrenpoint, Northern Ireland. In December, Lynch resigned and was replaced by former Prime Minister Charles Haughey, who went back to the old idea of reunification with some form of autonomy in Ulster.

[17] The Irish Council of Womens' Affairs was created in 1972. The weight of Catholic tradition has been a hindrance to women's

WORKERS

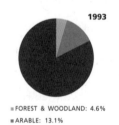

1997
UNEMPLOYMENT: 10.3%

% OF LABOUR FORCE **1998**

■ FEMALE: 34%   ■ MALE: 66%

1990

■ SERVICES: 57.0%
■ INDUSTRY: 28.6%
■ AGRICULTURE: 14.4%

LAND USE

DEFORESTATION: -2.6% annual (1990/95)

1993

■ FOREST & WOODLAND: 4.6%
■ ARABLE: 13.1%
■ OTHER: 82.3%

PUBLIC EXPENDITURE

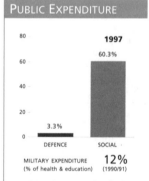

1997
60.3%

3.3%

DEFENCE   SOCIAL

MILITARY EXPENDITURE   **12%**
(% of health & education)   (1990/91)

liberation. In the Irish Republic the sale of contraceptives was limited to licensed outlets.

[18] In 1983, a controversial referendum in the Republic approved the outlawing of abortion under the Irish constitution. The law against divorce, in force for 60 years, was maintained in spite of the Government's proposal to revoke it.

[19] In 1980 there were talks between the heads of the Irish and British governments. This led to the formation of the Anglo-Irish Intergovernmental Council a year later, with the aim of holding ministerial level meetings.

[20] Discussions between the British and Irish governments finally led to the signing of the Anglo-Irish Agreement in 1985, under which the Dublin Government had some influence on the political, legal, security and border affairs of Northern Ireland. A majority of Protestants remained strongly opposed to the Agreement, although it guaranteed that the constitutional position of Northern Ireland was subject to the will of the majority of its population.

[21] In 1988, Dublin and London quarreled over the British Government's refusal to investigate members of the RUC (Royal Ulster Constabulary) accused of shooting at terrorist suspects before attempting to arrest them.

[22] At the same time, an inquest was started in the Ulster Defence Regiment (UDR), a locally-recruited,

part-time British Army regiment, which is dominated by Protestants, over the death of six IRA members in 1982.

[23] During the first months of 1989 a new wave of violence broke out. In April, three members of the paramilitary Ulster Defence Association were arrested in Paris together with a South African diplomat. Pretoria was supposedly supplying them with arms in exchange for secret British missile technology stolen from a Belfast arms production plant.

[24] In September 1989, the Irish Government demanded a complete review of the UDR, in particular of their links with the Protestant paramilitaries and the leaking of intelligence documents on Republican suspects. The United Kingdom accepted the Irish demands and as a result 94 UDR soldiers were arrested.

[25] During the 1980s, unemployment ran high in the Republic- an average of 16.4 per cent between 1983 and 1988 - and so did emigration. The country also faced spiraling inflation and industrial recession. A strict austerity program, implemented since 1987, brought about economic growth, and a significant decrease in inflation.

[26] In May 1987, Ireland reaffirmed its EC commitments through a national referendum. The Single Europe Act was approved by 69.9 per cent of the electorate.

[27] Since joining the EC in 1973, Community aid has played an important role in the economy of the Irish Republic, one of the poorest EC members.

[28] Irish women made up 38.5 per cent of the labor force in 1987; one of the lowest in Western Europe.

[29] In 1990, the General Synod of the Church of Ireland approved the ordination of female priests in the country. This decision placed the Church of Ireland ahead of most other Anglican churches.

[30] In November 1990, academic lawyer Mary Robinson was elected President of the Republic, the first woman to be elected to this post. An independent candidate, supported by the Labour Party, the Political Association of Women and the trade unions, Robinson gained 52 per cent of the vote.

[31] In a country that is predominantly Catholic and overwhelmingly conservative, Mary Robinson spoke out in defense of gay and women's rights and the legal recognition of illegitimate children.

[32] In April 1991, multiparty negotiations began in Belfast, in another attempt to define Northern Ireland's political future. These were the first important talks to be held since 1974. Representatives of Ulster's main 'constitutional' parties participated (Protestant Unionists, Catholic nationalists and the small non-sectarian Alliance Party), as did representatives of the Government in London. Sinn Féin, the political wing of the Provisional IRA, which supported the immediate withdrawal of British troops, the disarming of the RUC and the reunification of Ireland, was excluded from the talks due to their refusal to condemn the IRA's campaign of violence.

[33] Opinion polls released in London at the time of the peace talks showed that most Britons favored the withdrawal of British troops from Ulster.

[34] In January 1992, the IRA launched one of its major offensives, in Ulster and in England. In County Tyrone, Northern Ireland, the IRA killed seven Protestant construction workers, stating that, as they were working on British Army barracks, they were considered to be 'collaborating with the occupiers'. Republicans also carried out a series of arson attacks in Ulster on commercial establishments.

[35] From late 1991, there was a sharp increase in attacks on Catholics by Protestant paramilitary groups. These groups vowed to retaliate for each IRA attack with 'an eye for an eye'.

[36] In response to the demands of Protestant politicians and in order to confront the escalating violence, London sent several hundred

military reinforcements to Ulster. They joined the 11,000 British troops already stationed there, as well as the 6,000 volunteers of the Ulster Defence Regiment, and the 12,000-strong police force.

[37] In March 1992, the issue of abortion hit the headlines. A 14 year-old girl who became pregnant as the result of a rape was forbidden by the High Court from travelling to England for an abortion. It was estimated that up to 4,000 Irish women per year have abortions in Britain as the operation is forbidden under the Irish constitution. The case of the 14 year-old girl went before the Supreme Court, provoking demonstrations from both pro-choice and anti-abortion groups, and calls for another referendum on abortion. The Supreme Court eventually overturned the High Court decision, and the girl was allowed out of the country. The case raised important issues with regards to the relationship between the Irish constitution and European Community law, which guarantees the freedom of movement of EC citizens within member nations.

[38] In mid-July 1992, 69 per cent of the Irish population voted in favor of ratifying the Maastricht Treaty and the further integration of the European Community. This figure exceeded all expectations, with 57 per cent of the electorate participating in the vote.

[39] In January 1993, Albert Reynolds, of Fianna Fail, was confirmed as head of government, despite the fact that his party and the Fine Gael had lost seats to the Labour Party in the previous election.

[40] In the meantime, a referendum was held on the abortion issue. Two-thirds of the voters pronounced themselves in favor of the right to have access to information on methods for interrupting pregnancy, as well as the right to travel abroad for an abortion. However, the electorate voted against legalizing abortion except in cases where the mother's life was in danger.

[41] In 1993, with the reduction in workers in the rural and traditional industry sectors, unemployment reached 20 per cent, while the GDP grew due to an increase in exports, especially high-tech goods.

[42] The Government lifted broadcasting restrictions on the Sinn Féin in early 1994. In August, the IRA declared a complete cessation of military operations, a gesture which enabled political talks to take place on the island.

[43] In November, the Reynolds administration collapsed after the Labour Party withdrew its support following a controversy over long delays in the extradition - to

PROFILE

ENVIRONMENT

The country comprises most of the island of Ireland. The south is made up of rocky hills, none exceeding 1,000 meters in height. The central plain extends from east to west and is irrigated by many rivers and lakes. With a humid ocean climate and poor soil, much of the country is covered with grazing land. Farming is concentrated mainly along the eastern slopes of the hills and the Shannon valleys. The main agricultural products are wheat, barley, oats, potatoes and beet. Meat and milk processing are among the major local industrial activities.

SOCIETY

Peoples: The Irish comprise 94 per cent of the population, with a small English minority. The great famines which struck the island over the last two centuries led to the emigration of about 4 million Irish people, especially to the US. **Religions:** 91.6 per cent Catholic, 2.3 per cent Anglican, 0.4 per cent Presbyterian (1991). **Languages:** Irish and English.
Political Parties: The conservative Fine Gael, linked to the rural population. The nationalist, conservative Fianna Fail. The progressive Democrats. The center-leftist Labour Party; Sinn Féin, socialist and the political wing of the IRA; the Communist Party, and the Workers' Party, socialist. **Social Organizations:** The Irish Congress of Trade Unions, with 600,000 members, amounts to 45 per cent of the economically active population.

THE STATE

Official Name: Poblacht na hÉireann. **Administrative Divisions:** 26 Counties. **Capital:** Dublin 1,021,449 people (city and county) (1996). **Other cities:** Cork 127,092 people; Limerick 52,040; Galway 57,095; Waterford 40,345 (1996). **Government:** Mary McAleese, President since November 1997, elected through direct vote. Prime Minister Bertie Ahern, since June 1997. Bicameral parliament (Oireachtas); 166-member Chamber of Deputies (Dail), 60-member Senate (Seanad).
National Holiday: March 17 (St Patrick's Day). **Armed Forces:** 12,900 (1995).

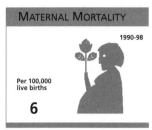

MATERNAL MORTALITY 1990-98

Per 100,000 live births

6

FOREIGN TRADE

Millions US$ 1998

IMPORTS
47,739

EXPORTS
61,457

Northern Ireland - of a pedophile priest. Reynolds was succeeded as Prime Minister by John Bruton from Fine Gael, with support from the Labour Party and the democratic left.

[44] The government coalition achieved political and social stability in 1995. The February budget was advantageous for civil servants, small business and low-waged workers while economic growth amounted to 5.25 per cent.

[45] The Catholic Church continued to be the target of accusations regarding priests who molested children. In Dublin, the archbishop publicly confessed he had used part of the diocese's funds to pay off one of the clergy's victims. Meanwhile, the Supreme Court authorized doctors to inform women about abortion clinics abroad. In a close referendum, the Irish approved (with 50 per cent to 49 per cent of the vote) a constitutional reform which allowed the divorce of couples who had been separated for 4 years.

[46] Bruton established an excellent relationship with British Prime Minister John Major, while also having close ties with Ulster's John Hume, the leader of the Social Democratic and Labour Party (SDLP) leader and Gerry Adams, president of Sinn Féin. Prince Charles' mid-year visit enhanced the need for links between England and Ireland. The opposition limited itself to staging peaceful demonstrations. Late in the year, the visit of United States President Bill Clinton had an encouraging effect on the parties to find a formula which would solve the armed conflict.

[47] The Prime Minister took part in a round of talks in Belfast in June 1996. Bruton supported Britain's initiative to exclude Sinn Féin representatives from the negotiations since both governments believed IRA behavior - which in February had ended the unilateral truce observed since August 1994 with bombings in mainland UK - had made no contributions to peace.

[48] The Irish economy performed well that year, with an increase in consumption, sustained growth and the creation of jobs. The livestock sector was affected by 'mad cow' disease, BSE, which reduced exports to Russia and the Middle East.

[49] In April 1997, a series of attacks announced by the IRA in public

places, train stations and airports upset the British transport system in the middle of the electoral period. Sinn Féin asked the IRA to call another cease-fire, which they did in July. In September, negotiations were restarted with the participation of Sinn Féin.

[50] The legislative election in June 1997 brought Bertie Ahern's Fianna Fáil to power, taking 77 of the 166 seats - followed by the Fine Gael with 54. The Labour Party took 17. The coalition with the Progressive Democrats (4 seats) did not provide the overall majority needed to constitute a center-right government. Meanwhile, Sinn Féin gained one seat in a county in the north of the country. On June 26, Parliament named Ahern Prime Minister.

[51] In September, President Mary Robinson left her post to join the UN. On November 11, Mary McAleese of the Fianna Fáil took over the presidency. Four of the five contenders for the post were women. The economy continued to perform well, and the annual inflation rate was only 1 per cent, the lowest in the European Union.

[52] The abortion debate was reopened at the end of that year, following a ruling by a children's court this time allowing a girl to travel to Britain to terminate a pregnancy resulting from rape.

[53] On April 10 1998, following tough negotiations, Catholic separatists and Protestant unionists reached a peace agreement over Ulster in Belfast. The document, known as the Good Friday Agreement, was negotiated by eight political parties with the backing of London, Dublin and Washington, proposed limited autonomy for Northern Ireland with the creation of a legislative assembly and north-south co-operation bodies. The plan also stipulated the disarmament of the paramilitary organizations represented by political parties in the negotiations, and the freeing of prisoners.

[54] The majority of the political parties, including Sinn Féin, were in favor of the agreement in principle. The pact overcame a first obstacle when the Protestant Unionist leader, David Trimble, secured the agreement of his party, the Ulster Unionists. Only two extremist Protestant parties, the Reverend Ian Paisley's Democratic Unionist Party

and Robert McCartney's UK Unionist Party, were opposed to the move.

[55] At the end of May a referendum ratified the Agreement in both Ulster and Ireland. A month later, the first elections to integrate the Assembly were held, and in February 1999 the new institutions are to be established. The agreement left the door open for the Ulster people to decide the future of the Province in the polls - whether to reunite with Ireland or stay in the UK.

[56] In August 1998 a bomb in Omagh killed about 30 people, causing the fragile peace process to falter.

[57] The December 1999 installation of the first Northern Ireland government in 25 years – though 'trans-border' – confirmed London's return of sovereignty to that territory's inhabitants. This new Government (Executive Council) was comprised of Prime Minister David Trimble, of the Ulster Unionists, Vice-Premier Seamus Mallon, of the Social Democrat and Labour Party (SDLP), and 10 others – three from the pro-British UUP and the moderate Catholic socialist SDLP, and two from Sinn Féin and the Reverend Ian Paisley's radical Protestant Democratic Unionist Party (DUP). This was the first time representatives from these parties took on cooperative political roles.

[58] The DUP announced that, though it rejected the inclusion of Sinn Féin in the Northern Ireland Government, it would assume its two Cabinet posts, but would attempt to block the work of the new executive. The elderly cleric's son warned that the DUP did not plan to join this executive, and that its problems would really begin once operations got underway, as it was a 'road that led to crisis'.

[59] After the new government took office, the Republic of Ireland withdrew its constitutional claims on the whole of the island, included since its independence from the United Kingdom. The declaration, signed by Prime Minister Bertie Ahern, was simultaneous with the creation of trans-border organizations, in which Irish from the north and the south participated. The elimination of Articles 2 and 3 from the Constitution, though it entailed a long debate, was seen as the only possible route toward the unification of the six counties of the north with the independent south.

[60] Though the six northern counties were mainly Protestant, the demographic situation tended to favor the Catholics because, according to forecasts, they would be the majority within 10 years and a future referendum could then consecrate the reunification of the island. ∎

STATISTICS

DEMOGRAPHY

Population: 3,705,000 (1999)
Annual growth: 0.6 % (1975/97)
Estimates for year 2015 (million): 4.2 (1999)
Annual growth to year 2015: 0.7 % (1997/2015)
Urban population: 57.9 % (1997)
Urban Growth: 0.5 % (1980/95)
Children per woman: 1.9 (1998)

HEALTH

Life expectancy at birth: 76 years (1998)
male: 74 years (1998)
female: 79 years (1998)
Maternal mortality: 6 per 100,000 live births (1990-98)
Infant mortality: 6 per 1,000 (1998)
Under-5 child mortality: 7 per 1,000 (1998)
Daily calorie supply: 3,636 per capita (1996)
167 doctors per 100,000 people (1993)

EDUCATION

School enrolment:
Primary total: 103 % (1990/96)
male: 103 % (1990/97)
female: 103 % (1990/97)
Secondary:
male: 111 % (1990/96)
female: 119 % (1990/96)
Tertiary: 41 % (1996)
Primary school teachers: one for every 22 (1996)

COMMUNICATIONS

150 newspapers (1996), 699 radios (1997), 469 TV sets (1996) and 395 main telephone lines (1996) per 1,000 people

ECONOMY

Per capita, GNP: $ 18,710 (1998)
Annual growth, GNP: 9.2 % (1998)
Annual inflation: 2.0 % (1990/98)
Consumer price index: 105.7 (1998)
Currency: 0.7 punts = $ 1 (1998)
Cereal imports: 719,451 metric tons (1998)
Food import dependency: 8 % (1997)
Fertilizer use: 5,026 kg per ha (1997)
Exports: $ 61,457 million (1997)
Imports: $ 47,739 million (1997)

ENERGY

Consumption: 3,412.0 Kgs of Oil equivalent per capita yearly (1997); 77.0 % imported (1997)

HDI (rank/value): 20/0.900 (1997)

Israel

Yisra'el

Population: 6,101,000 (1999)
Area: 21,060 SQ KM
Capital: Jerusalem/Tel Aviv
Currency: New Shekel
Language: Hebrew and Arabic

I n 1896 Viennese journalist Theodor Herzl published a book entitled *The Jewish State*. Influenced by the European nationalism which had engendered the unification of Germany and the Italian Risorgimento, Herzl envisaged a Jewish nation-state which would put an end to anti-Semitic acts, like the Russian pogroms and the Dreyfus Affair (a spy case in France).

[2] This Jewish state was to be established in Palestine, then a Turkish colony. The name 'Palestine' inspired the suffering Jews of Eastern Europe, who dreamed of the return to Zion, the land of the ancient kingdoms of Israel. Zion is the name of a hill in Jerusalem; by extension it became a synonym for Jerusalem itself and then for the whole of Palestine. But the Zionists, as Herzl's followers began to be called, preferred to ignore the fact that half a million Arabs had been living there for over 1,000 years, naturally becoming attached to their land and traditions.

[3] Zionism firmly pursued a policy of forming alliances with the great capitalist powers, denying the peoples of Palestine their national identity - the precise right the Jews claimed for themselves.

[4] During World War I, Britain and France agreed to divide up the remains of the Ottoman Empire in the Middle East. In 1917, British Foreign Secretary Arthur Balfour declared his support for the establishment of a national homeland for the Jewish people in Palestine, although when Prime Minister in 1905 he had opposed Jewish immigration into Britain. The Balfour Declaration stated 'that nothing shall be done which may prejudice the civil and religious rights of existing non-Jewish

communities in Palestine'; these groups made up 90 per cent of the population.

[5] At the end of World War II, the French colonies of Syria and Lebanon and the British colonies of Iraq and Transjordan obtained their independence. But Britain retained control of Palestine, based on its commitment under the Balfour Declaration.

[6] Zionists regarded Jews the world over as exiles, and they organized migration to Israel from all corners of the globe. At the beginning of the 20th century there were 500,000 Arabs and 50,000 Jews living in Palestine. By the 1930s, the number of Jews had risen to 300,000. The anti-Semitic persecutions in Nazi Germany raised immigration above the legally permitted quotas, alarming the British who saw their power in Palestine threatened.

[7] In 1939 London declared that its aim was not to set up a Jewish state but an independent, bi-national Palestinian state with both peoples sharing government. Ships bringing refugees from Hitler's Europe were turned back from Palestinian ports. The Zionists organized acts of sabotage and terrorism, using force to hold Britain to its promise.

[8] Using donations from Jews all over the world, the Zionists purchased Arab lands from wealthy absentee owners living in Beirut or Paris, who cared little about the fate of their tenants, the Palestinian *fellahin* (peasants). The Jews then arrived, deeds in hand, to expel peasant families whose ancestors had lived there for generations. They set up agricultural colonies, kibbutzim, defended by armed Zionist militia.

[9] In February 1947, in view of intensified anti-British attacks, London submitted the Palestinian problem to the United Nations. A special committee recommended partition of the territory into two independent states; one Arab, the other Jewish. Jerusalem would remain under international administration.

[10] The Soviet Union preferred a Jewish state to continued British military presence, and its support was decisive in the creation of Israel. At the same time, London and Washington considered the partition unfeasible. US Secretary of Defense James Forrestal

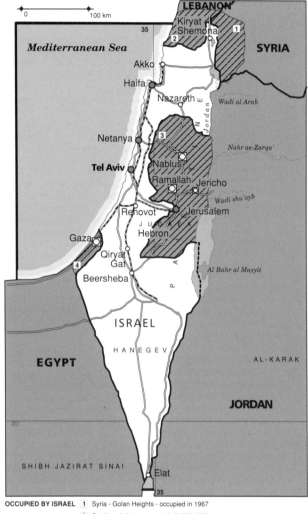

OCCUPIED BY ISRAEL

1	Syria - Golan Heights - occupied in 1967
2	Southern Lebanon - occupied 1983-2000
3	West Bank - occupied in 1967
4	Gaza Strip - occupied 1967-1994
⊙	Recovered by Palestine from 1994: Gaza Strip, Jericho, Nablus, Ramallah

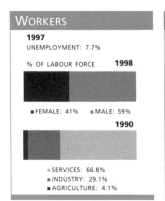

WORKERS

1997
UNEMPLOYMENT: 7.7%

% OF LABOUR FORCE   **1998**

- FEMALE: 41%   ■ MALE: 59%

1990

- SERVICES: 66.8%
- INDUSTRY: 29.1%
- AGRICULTURE: 4.1%

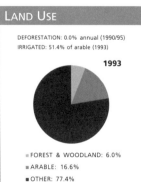

LAND USE

DEFORESTATION: 0.0% annual (1990/95)
IRRIGATED: 51.4% of arable (1993)

1993

- FOREST & WOODLAND: 6.0%
- ARABLE: 16.6%
- OTHER: 77.4%

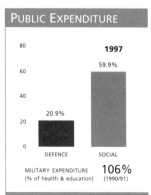

PUBLIC EXPENDITURE

1997

59.9% SOCIAL
20.9% DEFENCE

MILITARY EXPENDITURE   **106%**
(% of health & education)   (1990/91)

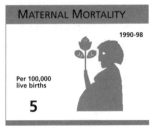

MATERNAL MORTALITY

1990-98

Per 100,000
live births

5

LITERACY

1995

95%

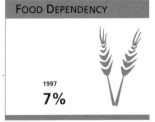

FOOD DEPENDENCY

1997

7%

FOREIGN TRADE

Millions US$ 1998

IMPORTS

43,278

EXPORTS

32,105

proposed that President Harry Truman send troops to impose a UN trusteeship over the territory of Palestine.

11 The UN General Assembly finally approved the partition plan in a 33 to 13 vote, there were 10 abstentions and the Arab countries and India voted against partition. Armed Zionist organizations seized control of major cities and towns and began to expel Palestinians en masse, alleging an imminent attack by Arab armies. This policy culminated in a massacre at the village of Deir Yasin in April 1948, when its entire population was murdered by the Irgun, an extremist group led by Menachem Begin.

12 On May 14 1948, the British high commissioner withdrew from Palestine, and David Ben Gurion proclaimed the state of Israel. The Jordanian, Egyptian, Syrian, Iraqi and Lebanese armies attacked immediately, and the governments of those countries urged the Palestinians to abandon their possessions and take refuge.

13 The war ended with an armistice in January 1949, granting Israel 40 per cent more territory than it had been due under the partition plan. Soviet weapons and aircraft, purchased in Czechoslovakia, proved decisive in the Israeli victory.

14 Israel's government changed sides during the Cold War and formed a permanent strategic alliance with the United States. This alliance was not forged easily nor immediately.

15 In 1956, when Israeli troops backed by France and Britain invaded Egypt in response to the nationalization of the Suez Canal, the United States and the Soviet Union both firmly opposed the move, and the expeditionary force had to be withdrawn.

16 The diaries of former Prime Minister Moshe Sharett, published posthumously, revealed that Israel used Zionist agents to sabotage Western targets in Cairo, forcing US President Dwight Eisenhower to opt for Tel Aviv and not Cairo as its principal Middle East ally. The episode is known as the Lavon affair.

17 In the 1960s, Egyptian President Gamal Abdel Nasser was deprived of US credit and arms, and he turned to the Soviet Union. This was enough to produce closer

relations between Israel and Washington.

18 In the 1967 Six Day War, Israel carried out a lightning strike, using North American weaponry, and seizing the whole of Palestine (the West Bank of the Jordan River), the Syrian Golan Heights and Egyptian Sinai .

19 Paradoxically, this military victory undermined Israel's moral strength; the newborn state was transformed into an expansionist power in control of areas housing thousands of Palestinians.

20 Resolution 242 of the UN Security Council, passed on November 22 1967, called on Israel to withdraw from the occupied territories. Israel refused, claiming that it needed 'secure borders' in order to resist Arab threats to its existence.

21 Armed conflict broke out again in 1973, when Egyptian troops crossed the Suez Canal and ended the myth of Israeli military invincibility. In truth, by the time armistice was decreed, battlefield positions had hardly changed.

22 In 1977, Menachem Begin was elected Prime Minister, breaking with the political and ideological continuity of the previous governments. For the first time in the history of the Israeli state, the Labor Party was not in power.

23 Begin's victory resulted partly from growing social tension between Ashkenazim (economically and culturally privileged Jews of European origin who were traditionally Labor supporters) and Sephardim (Eastern Jews from Arab countries).

24 The oriental Jews, who culturally had more in common with the Arabs than with European Jews, made up 55 per cent of the population, but their average income was just two-thirds that of the Ashkenazis. Their resentment of the Ashkenazim, aggravated to the point of fanaticism, provided the electoral basis for the political right.

25 Begin completely rejected the idea of negotiating with the Palestine Liberation Organization (PLO) and expressed his intention to annex the West Bank. Meanwhile in 1977, the US persuaded Egyptian President Anwar Sadat to sign the Camp

David Agreement, leading to peace between Cairo and Tel Aviv and the return of Sinai to Egypt.

26 From then on, international attention gradually shifted from the issue of secure borders for Israel to the plight of the Palestinians. Changing tactics, the PLO gained sympathy and allies, so that when Jerusalem was declared the capital of Israel in 1980, the move was condemned as an arrogant gesture by many of Israel's supporters.

27 In June 1982, the Israelis launched 'Operation Peace for Galilee', invading Lebanon and devastating Beirut, under the pretext that these were maneuvers to stop infiltration by Palestinian guerrilla groups. PLO combatants agreed to evacuate the city in exchange for the deployment of a joint force of Italians, French, and North Americans to guarantee the security of Palestinian civilians.

28 In spite of the agreement, hundreds of Palestinians in the Sabra and Shatila refugee camps, in Israeli-controlled areas, were murdered by right-wing militia with Israeli complicity. The invasion of Lebanon fomented dissent in Israel, and 400,000 people attended a demonstration sponsored by the group Peace Now. Begin was forced to appoint a commission of inquiry which found Defense Minister Ariel Sharon and other military leaders 'indirectly responsible' for the massacres.

29 After the September 1984 elections, the Labor Party headed by Shimon Peres was able to form a government, though lacking an absolute majority. Its coalition included Likud, and the agreement stipulated that the leader of that party, Yitzhak Shamir, would assume the prime minister's post in 1986.

30 At the end of 1987, several young Palestinians were killed in a clash with Israeli military patrols in the occupied West Bank. The funerals turned into protest demonstrations and led to further confrontations, deaths, and general strikes - civil protests where people refuse to leave their homes. This marked the beginning of the *intifada* or uprising, and Middle Eastern politics were shaken from the least expected quarter - the unarmed grassroots.

31 Images of young Palestinians armed with slingshots confronting the mighty Israeli army were

televised worldwide, ruining Israel's international standing. This development came as a shock for a state founded on the basis of international solidarity.

32 At this time, the most apparent evidence of the challenge to Israeli credibility was the fact that 250,000 young Israelis were leaving the country each year. Negative net migration throughout the 1980s was balanced only in 1989 with the massive immigration of Jews from the Soviet Union. Since its creation as a solution to the Jewish issue, the state of Israel has managed to attract only 20 per cent of the world's Jews.

33 In 1989, during the last National Palestine Congress, the PLO recognized the State of Israel, accepting UN resolutions 242 and 338. According to US sources, Washington's aid to Israel between 1949 and 1991 totaled $53 billion. In the 1979 Camp David Agreements, the figure reached $40 billion, 21.5 per cent of all US foreign aid.

34 In Israel military service is mandatory for both women and men. All men up to the age of 51, and unmarried women up to age 24, belong to the Reserve. The militarization of society also resulted in a high level of State intervention in the economy and in an enormous weight of war industry on the country's production figures.

35 In its search for markets, Israel became an arms exporter involved in dubious deals like the 'Iran-Contras' scandal, supplying arms to Iran. It also provided military training for Colombian drug militias.

36 When Iraq invaded Kuwait on August 2 1990, Israel was excluded from the anti-Iraq coalition led by the United States. This was done on the grounds that if it had participated, the Arab countries would not have joined. Israel made preparations for war regardless, and a state of siege was declared in the occupied territories.

37 On January 17, in answer to the Allied bombing, Iraq launched several missile attacks against Israel. The aim was to try and force Israel to enter the war. However, Israel did not do so, leaving its defense to Patriot anti-missile units operated by American troops.

38 When the war ended in

March 1991, the US presented diplomatic circles with a 'land for peace' proposal. Two months later in Damascus, Syria and Lebanon signed a 'brotherhood, co-operation and co-ordination' treaty. To Israel, this treaty constituted a military threat to 'water tank' - a region in the north containing many important water sources.

[39] Israel asked the United States to approve loans of $10 billion to ease its economic difficulties, caused by the resettling of between 250,000 and 400,000 Soviet Jews from 1989 to 1991.

[40] The Government began transferring immigrants to new settlements on the West Bank where in 1991 unemployment reached 11 per cent, despite efforts to create new jobs for immigrants.

[41] Wishing to launch peace negotiations in the region, the US government imposed the condition that loans granted would not be invested in settlements in occupied territories.

[42] The creation of Jewish settlements and the construction of new housing for Soviet Jews on the West Bank, became a double-edged sword for Shamir's government. The US loans and new settlements were vitally important, but Palestinians and other Arabs demanded that resettlement cease, in order for the peace talks to continue.

[43] On October 30 1991, a Middle-Eastern Peace Conference was held in Madrid, sponsored by the US and the former USSR. Shortly afterwards, hundreds of thousands of Israelis demonstrated, calling upon their government to maintain a dialogue with the Palestinians and Israel's Arab neighbors. Delegations from Jordan, Lebanon, Syria and Israel attended the conference; the Palestinians formed part of the Jordanian delegation, as Israel refused to negotiate directly with Palestinian representatives.

[44] The Arab countries supported the 'land for peace' scheme, though it was rejected by Israel. Israel, in turn, showed itself willing to discuss limited self government by the Palestinian population in the occupied areas, as a provisional solution for a 5-year period. This offer triggered a crisis in the Likud's coalition government, when the Tehiya and Moladet (ultra-right-wing parties) walked out of the coalition, leaving Shamir without a parliamentary majority.

[45] On June 23 1992, Labor won a decisive victory in the general elections and Yitzhak Rabin was nominated prime minister. Construction of housing in the occupied territories came to a sudden standstill, and as a result, the United States removed the embargo on loan guarantees for Israel.

[46] On September 13 1993, after months of secret negotiations in Oslo, Norway, Israeli authorities and PLO leaders signed the Declaration of the Principles of the Interim Self-government Agreement, in Washington. This agreement foresaw the installation of a limited autonomy system for Palestinians in the Gaza Strip and the city of Jericho for a five-year period. This agreement would subsequently be extended to include all of the West Bank.

[47] Hamas and the pro-Iranian Hezbollah, two radical Islamist movements active in many Arab countries, questioned the agreement. Meanwhile, Jewish settlers in the occupied territories - who had been supplied with arms by the Government - rejected the agreement out of hand, as it provided for the withdrawal of settlers and the Israeli army.

[48] It was not long before this situation erupted in violence. On February 25 1994, Baruch Goldstein, a member of Kahane Kach's ultra-right-wing Jewish movement, entered the Tomb of the Patriarchs in Hebron, armed with an M-16 rifle and massacred several dozen Palestinians who were at prayer. He was subsequently beaten to death by Palestinians.

[49] The official investigation of the Hebron massacre revealed that soldiers in the occupied territories had been under orders not to shoot against armed settlers under any circumstances. According to the investigation, several soldiers fired into the crowd, and doors were closed blocking the victims' escape. The PLO withdrew from the negotiations demanding that the settlers turn over their arms immediately, and that the United Nations issue an official condemnation. The latter approved a statement which categorically condemned the massacre and voted for a peacekeeping force to be sent to the occupied territories.

[50] In early May 1994, Israeli Prime Minister Yitzhak Rabin and PLO leader Yasser Arafat signed an agreement in Cairo granting autonomy to Gaza and Jericho. Late that month, the Israeli army withdrew from Gaza, ending 27 years of occupation (see Palestine).

[51] Negotiations with several Arab states progressed, especially with Jordan, which signed an agreement with Tel Aviv in July ending with the 'state of aggression' between the two countries. However, disagreements with Syria continued because, among other reasons, Israel refused to accept a full evacuation of the Golan Heights, occupied since 1967.

[52] 1995 was marked by a growing division of Israeli society

---

PROFILE

ENVIRONMENT

20,770 sq.km, within the pre-1967 borders (see Palestine). These territories are currently occupied, both militarily and with settlements of Jewish colonists: Golan Heights (Syria) 1,150 sq km, West Bank 5,879 sq.km, Gaza Strip 378 sq.km, Greater Jerusalem 70 sq km. The land comprises four natural regions: the coastal plains, with a Mediterranean climate, the country's agricultural center; a central hilly and mountainous region, stretching from Galilee to Judea; the western lowlands, bound on the north by the Jordan River, which flows into the Dead Sea; and the Negev Desert, to the south, which covers half of the total territory. The main agricultural products are citrus fruits for export, grapes, vegetables, cotton, beet, potatoes and wheat. There is considerable livestock production. Industrial production is growing rapidly and there are serious difficulties with water; the country has over 2,000 sq km of irrigated land - part of the Negev has been reclaimed through irrigation. Pollution, caused by both industrial and domestic waste, as well as pesticides, is also an important problem.

SOCIETY

Peoples: Jewish, 81.4 per cent; Arab and other, 18.6 per cent.
Religions: Judaism. Arabs are Muslim and Christian.
Languages: Hebrew and Arabic are official. English is used for business. Native languages of immigrants (notably Yiddish and Russian) are also spoken.
Political Parties: The Zionist left is made up of the Labor Party, and the Meretz (a front which includes three parties). The non-Zionist left is made up of Hadash (formerly Communist) and the Democratic Arab Party. The Zionist right is formed by Likud; the Tehiya (Renaissance); the Tsomet and the Moledet. The religious parties are: the Shas; the Agudat-Israel (the League of Israel); the National Religious Party and the Degel Hatora.
Social Organizations: The Histadrut Haoudim Haleumit (National Labor Federation) is the main trade union.

THE STATE

Official Name: Medinat Yisra'el (Hebrew); Isra'il (Arabic).
Administrative divisions: 6 districts, 31 municipalities, 115 local councils and 49 regional councils.
Capital: In 1980, Jerusalem (591,400 people in 1996) was proclaimed the 'sole and indivisible' capital of Israel. The UN condemned this decision and most diplomatic missions are in Tel Aviv.
Other cities: Haifa 252,300 people; Tel Aviv-Jaffa 355,900; Holon 163,900 (1996).
Government: Esser Weizman, President since March 1993. Ehud Barak, Prime Minister since July 1999. Parliamentary system of government.
National holiday: 7-V, Independence (1948).
Armed Forces: 175,000 (1996). Other: Border Police: 6,000; Coast Guard: 50.

regarding the peace process with the Palestinians. Anti-Rabin demonstrations were frequent and led to the Prime Minister's assassination by a young Israeli member of the far right. Shimon Peres, also from the Labor Party, took Rabin's place but was defeated in the general elections of May 1996 by right-wing leader Binyamin Netanyahu.

[53] The return to power of the conservatives hindered negotiations with Palestine and heightened tensions, putting the country on the brink of a new war in September. In the middle of that month the Government authorized the opening of a tunnel under the Al-Aqsa mosque, the third most sacred place of Islam, violating the status quo maintained since the signing of the peace agreements and provoking a Palestinian reaction. Several Israeli soldiers and dozens of Palestinians died during the disturbances.

[54] Netanyahu, harshly critical of Rabin for having held talks with Arafat and the PLO, ended up meeting with the Palestinian leader on repeated occasions in late 1996 and early 1997 to negotiate the complete withdrawal of Israeli troops from the city of Hebron in the West Bank.

[55] In March, the Government announced its plan to build a new settlement in the Har Homa hills, on the Palestinian outskirts of Jerusalem. The Palestine Authority and the United States rejected the project, considering it contrary to the spirit and letter of the Oslo agreements. Netanyahu's firm decision to go ahead with the settlements stalled the negotiations.

[56] Ehud Barak, a retired general, replaced Peres as leader of the Labor Party and became leader of the opposition. Peres had been party to an agreement with the Likud to form a unity Government which would allow for the reopening of the peace process, suspended in the early months of 1997.

[57] In November, the Israeli Supreme Court authorized the continued detention of 21 Lebanese prisoners (mostly members of Hezbollah) who had already completed their sentences, in retaliation for Israelis kidnapped in Lebanon. Earlier on, 'moderate physical force' had been authorized in the handling of prisoners during interrogation. Judge Aaron Barak even stated that the violation of human rights was 'obligatory' in these cases.

[58] At the end of 1997, a three-day strike, calling for reforms to the welfare system and government-planned privatizations, paralyzed the public sector, transport and financial activity.

[59] In February 1998, Israel tightened its anti-Syrian and Iraqi military alliance with Turkey. In the same month, Lebanon rejected an offer from Netanyahu to negotiate the withdrawal of Israeli troops from Lebanese territory, considering this withdrawal should be made totally unconditionally.

[60] Mordechai Vanunu, the Israeli technician imprisoned for revealing Israel's nuclear secrets, was moved out of solitary confinement in March for the first time in 12 years. He was allowed to leave his cell and talk to other prisoners in the jail. The attitude was credited to international pressures in favor of Vanunu, who had been kidnapped by Israeli agents in London, in 1986, and condemned to 18 years of prison.

[61] The peace process reached its lowest point in June when Israel decided to fill its Civil Guard in the occupied territories with Jewish settlers, who already armed themselves without any restriction. The Labor leader Ehud Barak, alarmed both by the collapse of a mountain caused by Israeli nuclear tests, and also by Netanyahu's delays over the second withdrawal from occupied territory, warned that the region was on the verge of a blood bath. As the Prime Minister refused to call a referendum to decide the issue of withdrawal, President Ezer Weizman urged him to bring forward the elections. This was also rejected by Netanyahu.

[62] However as a result of strong international pressures, Netanyahu accepted the US proposal to seek an accord to restart the peace process and met Clinton and Arafat at the Wye River conference center in the United States. After the meetings it was agreed that Israel would return Palestinian territory in exchange for Arafat's acceptance of supervision by US intelligence organizations in his fight against terrorism by certain Islamic sectors. The accord, which weakened Arafat in the eyes of his internal enemies, also led to the fall of the Likud Government. Labor backed the signing of the accords, but the governing coalition dissolved and several Likud legislators left the party. New general elections were set for May 17 1999.

[63] The elections revealed a highly fragmented electorate and, though Barak was victorious, the sharp polarization between the different groups with parliamentary representation fed predictions that his job as Prime Minister would be a difficult one. In July, Barak was able to form a coalition after the ultra-religious Shas, supported by Labor and its allies, agreed to take part in the new Cabinet. Shas agreed to participate only after clearly defining what its powers would be within the economically powerful Ministry of Finance. To do so it had to negotiate with the National Religious Party, which also hoped to control the ministry. The other Cabinet posts that went to Shas included Labor, Health and Public Works. The 17 seats of the religious party gave the Labor leader a majority with 75 deputies out of a total 120, one of the largest governing party majorities in years.

[64] Shas participation in the coalition complicated Labor's situation with its leftist allies, especially with Meretz, which held 10 seats, but also with the Central Party, an offshoot of the Likud that had six deputies. Both groups demanded that the previous Shas leader, Aryeh Deri, who faced trial for fraud and bribery, retire from the political scene. The acting Shas leader, Rabbi Ovadia Yosef, believed that ceding territory in exchange for peace guarantees was the only way to end violence in the region.

[65] Breaking with a 50-year tradition, in November Israel decided to lift the state of emergency that had been in effect since 1948. The country held the world record for the longest continuous implementation of a state of emergency.

[66] Pope John Paul II visited Jordan and Israel in March 2000. He was the first Pope to recognize Palestinians' 'national rights' and to recognize and establish diplomatic relations with Israel. One month prior to his visit, the Vatican had signed an accord with the PLO about the Christian sanctuaries in Jerusalem that upset the Israeli Government because it charged that Arafat intended to declare the old city of Jerusalem, where Jews plan to build their Third Temple, the capital of a sovereign State in Gaza and the West Bank.

[67] That month, former premier Netanyahu and his wife were accused of corruption. The police also investigated the fate of large sums of money president Ezer Weizman had received from a French millionaire.

[68] In late May, Barak ordered the total withdrawal of troops from Southern Lebanon. The president of the Knesset, Abraham Burg, said that same week that Israel was ready to accept an independent Palestinian State.

[69] Late in September, violence erupted again after the visit by hardliner Ariel Sharon to a shrine in Jerusalem sacred to Jews and Muslims. Some 100 people, mainly Palestinians, died in the following weeks. In October three Israeli soldiers were 'lynched' in Ramallah. Diplomats met in Egypt to try and save the tattered peace process. ∎

DEMOGRAPHY

Population: 6,101,000 (1999)
Annual growth: 2.4 % (1975/97)
Estimates for year 2015 (million): 7.6 (1999)
Annual growth to year 2015: 1.4 % (1997/2015)
Urban population: 90.9 % (1997)
Children per woman: 2.7 (1998)

HEALTH

Life expectancy at birth: 78 years (1998)
male: 76 years (1998)
female: 80 years (1998)
Maternal mortality: 5 per 100,000 live births (1990-98)
Infant mortality: 6 per 1,000 (1998)
Under-5 child mortality: 6 per 1,000 (1998)
Daily calorie supply: 3,272 per capita (1996)
459 doctors per 100,000 people (1993)

EDUCATION

Literacy: 95 % (1995)
male: 97 % (1995)
female: 93 % (1995)
School enrolment:
Primary total: 99 % (1990/96)
male: 96 % (1990/97)
female: 96 % (1990/97)
Secondary:
male: 84 % (1990/96)
female: 89 % (1990/96)
Tertiary: 44 % (1996)

COMMUNICATIONS

290 newspapers (1996), 520 radios (1997), 300 TV sets (1996) and 441 main telephone lines (1996) per 1,000 people
Books: 86 new titles per 100,000 people (1992/94)

ECONOMY

Per capita, GNP: $ 16,180 (1998)
Annual growth, GNP: 3.4 % (1998)
Annual inflation: 11.0 % (1990/98)
Consumer price index: 127.9 (1998)
Currency: 3.8 new shekels = $ 1 (1998)
Cereal imports: 2,734,762 metric tons (1998)
Food import dependency: 7 % (1997)
Fertilizer use: 3,410 kg per ha (1997)
Exports: $ 32,105 million (1998)
Imports: $ 43,278 million (1998)
Development aid received: $ 1,192 million (1997); $ 240.7 per capita (1997); 1.20 % of GNP (1997)

ENERGY

Consumption: 3,014.0 Kgs of Oil equivalent per capita yearly (1997); 97.0 % imported (1997)

HDI (rank/value): 23/0.883 (1997)

Italy

Italia

Population: 57,343,000 (1999)
Area: 301,270 SQ KM
Capital: Rome
Currency: Lira
Language: Italian

In the 13th century BC, ancient central European peoples occupied the northern part of what is now Italy.

2 With the fall of the Hittite empire around 900 BC the Etruscans established themselves to the north of the Tiber River. Their influence extended throughout the Po valley until the end of the 6th century, when the Celts bore down on them, destroying their territorial unity.

3 According to legend, Romulus founded the city of Rome upon the Palatine hill in the year 753 BC. During the following century, this settlement was united with those on the Quirinal, Capitoline and Esquiline hills. The first form of government was an elective monarchy. Its powers were limited by a senate and a people's assembly of clans which held the power of imperium or mandate to govern.

4 There were two social classes: the patricians, who could belong to the Senate, and the plebeians, who had to band together to protect themselves from the abuses of the large landowners.

5 Under King Tarquinius Priscus (616-578), Rome entered the Latin League. The poverty of the plebeians and the system of debt-induced slavery led to the expulsion of the kings in 509. In the 5th century, the traditional laws were written down. This 'Law of the Twelve Tables' extended to the plebeians, who after a lengthy struggle had managed to win some rights.

6 The Punic Wars against Carthage in the 3rd century allowed Rome to increase its possessions once again; in the early 2nd century, after displacing the Macedonians, Greece became a 'protectorate'. Within a few years, Asia Minor, the northeast of Gaul, Spain,

Macedonia and Carthage (including the northern part of Africa) had fallen into Roman hands.

7 Toward the end of the 2nd century, the Gracchi brothers, Tiberius and Gaius - both Roman representatives - were assassinated by the nobles, along with 3,000 followers, for supporting the plebeians.

8 The Roman Empire controlled the land from the Rhine in Germany to the north of Africa, and also included the entire Iberian Peninsula, France, Britain, Central Europe and the Middle East as far as Armenia. The 2nd

century brought internal disputes which plunged Rome into chaos.

9 In 330, the Emperor Constantine transferred the capital of the Empire to Byzantium - called New Rome - and converted to Christianity. In 364, the empire split into two parts: the Western and Eastern Roman Empires.

10 The end of the 5th century was marked by the invasions of the Mongols and other northern tribes, and by the attempts of the Byzantine Empire to recover its lost territories. In the mid-6th century, Italy became a province once again, but the Lombards conquered the northern part of the peninsula.

11 When the capital of the empire had been transferred to Byzantium, the bishops of Rome had presented themselves as an alternative to Byzantine power with a separate power base in Rome. When the Lombard kings began taking up arms in defense of Christianity against Rome's enemies, the

bishops broke the alliance, in order to maintain their temporal power.

12 In 754, Pope Steven II asked for help from Pepin the Short, and in exchange, crowned him King of the Franks. After the defeat of the Lombards, Pepin turned over the center of the peninsula to the Pope. Charlemagne, Pepin's son, was crowned king and emperor of Rome in 800, but the Muslim invasions which took place mid-century once again left the region without government.

13 Between the 9th and 10th centuries, the Church formed Pontifical States in the central region, including Rome itself. In the 12th century, self-government arose in some cities because of the lack of a centralized power.

14 In the 14th century, when the struggle intensified between the Guelfs (those who favored the Pope) and the Ghibellines (the defenders of the German empire), the Holy See was transferred to Avignon, where it remained for the next seven papacies. Two centuries later, the prosperity and stability of cities like Venice, Genoa, Florence and Milan produced the intellectual and artistic flowering or the Renaissance.

15 In the early 16th century, the peninsula was attacked by the French, the Spanish and the Austrians, who all craved control of Italy. In 1794, Napoleon Bonaparte entered the country expelling the Austrians. Four years later, he occupied Rome and created the Roman Republic and the Parthenopean Republic, in Naples. Only the two Italian states of Sicily and Sardinia were not under Napoleon's control, as they were governed by Victor Emmanuel I. The French Emperor rescinded the temporal power of the popes and deported Pius VII to Savona.

16 Before the fall of Napoleon in 1815, Victor Emmanuel II named Camillo Benso di Cavour president of the council of ministers. Cavour was to be the architect of Italian unification, forging a single kingdom of Italy from those of Sardinia and Piedmont, with only Rome and Venice remaining outside the realm. In 1870, the Italians invaded Rome and, given Pope Pius IX's refusal to renounce his temporal power, they confined him to the Vatican, where his successors would remain until 1929. In 1878, the King, Humberto I, brought Italy

WORKERS

1997
UNEMPLOYMENT: 12.5%

% OF LABOUR FORCE **1998**

■ FEMALE: 38% ■ MALE: 62%

1990

■ SERVICES: 60.0%
■ INDUSTRY: 31.4%
■ AGRICULTURE: 8.6%

LAND USE

DEFORESTATION: -0.1% annual (1990/95)
IRRIGATED: 30.0% of arable (1993)

1993

■ FOREST & WOODLAND: 22.5%
■ ARABLE: 30.0%
■ OTHER: 47.5%

PUBLIC EXPENDITURE

DEFENCE EXPENDITURE (% of goverment exp.)	**4.1%** (1997)	
MILITARY EXPENDITURE (% of health & education)	**21%** (1990/91)	

MATERNAL MORTALITY

1990-98

Per 100,000
live births

7

LITERACY

1995

98%

into the Triple Alliance with Austria-Hungary and Germany. Italy's colonial conquest of Eritrea, Ethiopia and Somalia, in eastern Africa, also began.

[17]   In 1872, influenced by the events of the Paris Commune, Italy's first socialist organization was formed, giving rise in 1892 to the Socialist Party (PSI). The encyclical Rerum Novarum (1891) oriented Catholics towards militant unionization and the union movement expanded rapidly. The Italian invasion of Ethiopia in 1896 ended in defeat.

[18]   When World War I broke out, Italy proclaimed its neutrality; however, in the face of growing pressure from nationalist groups on the Left, it ended up declaring war against its former allies of the Triple Alliance.

[19]   Benito Mussolini, who had been expelled from the PSI for supporting Italy's entry into the war, was able to manipulate resentment over the poor outcome. Through a blend of nationalism and pragmatism, he called for the unions to work towards collaboration between capital and labor, in the name of 'the interests of the nation'. In 1921, a group headed by Amadeo Bordiga and Antonio Gramsci split off from the PSI to form the Communist Party (PCI), leaving the PSI without its radical wing.

[20]   Having confronted one government crisis after another, and following Mussolini's impressive march on Rome, Victor Emmanuel III turned over the government to Mussolini. An electoral reform, giving Mussolini's Fascist Party a majority, was denounced by socialist leader Giaccomo Matteotti, who was subsequently assassinated by followers of 'Il Duce' Mussolini in 1924. A new constitution established censorship of the press; in 1929 the Pact of Letran was signed with the Vatican, re-establishing the temporal power of the popes, and thereby gaining Catholic support for the Government.

[21]   Mussolini's foreign policy was directed almost exclusively toward the acquisition of colonies. In 1936, Italy invaded Ethiopia, and a year later the Italian East African Empire was formed. During the Spanish Civil War, closer ties developed with Hitler's Germany, forming the basis for what was to become the Rome-Berlin axis. In April 1939, Italian troops took Albania.

[22]   During World War II, Italy declared war on France and Britain. Its troops were not able to keep the war out of the country and the entire peninsula became a combat zone for Germans and Allies alike. In 1943, the latter defeated Hitler's troops, and Humberto II became king. Italy lost all of its colonies.

[23]   Following a referendum at the end of the war (June 1946), the monarchy was abolished and the republic of Italy was formed. Under the leadership of Alcide de Gasperi, the Christian Democrats (DC) managed to form a minority government. These first elections marked the beginning of the Christian Democrats' hold on power. In May 1948, Luigi Einaudi, also of the DC, was elected Italy's first President.

[24]   The 1946 International Conference authorized Italy to continue administrating Somalia (known as Italian Somaliland), a situation which continued until 1960. During the 1950s, Italy participated in the reconstruction of Europe. In 1957, it became one of the charter members of the Common Market.

[25]   At the same time that the socialists were seeking closer links with the Christian Democrats, the Communist Party (PCI) embarked upon a revision of its political base under the leadership of Palmiro Togliatti. The PCI reaffirmed its belief in a democratic means toward a socialist end. During this period, the Party's influence extended into the labor unions, shaping the power structure of the General Union of Italian Workers (CGIL). The PCI, the country's second strongest electoral force, as well as the second largest Communist Party in the Western world, defined itself in terms of 'Eurocommunism' - Commusim with a European face.

[26]   After successive victories at the polls, in 1961 the DC began opening up to the Left, seeking alliances with the Socialists and Social Democrats. The powerful Communist Party, in spite of its strong electoral presence, was permanently excluded from the Cabinet. The economic and institutional crises which took place during that decade led radical groups from the right and left alike to turn to violence as a means of bringing about change. The far right organized bombings to draw attention to its demands, while the Red Brigades of the Left used political kidnapping as their main tool. In 1978, the kidnapping and assassination of former Prime Minister Aldo Moro sealed their isolation from mainstream politics.

[27]   Between 1952 and 1962, the average income of Italians doubled, as a result of the development of industry, which had come to employ 38 per cent of the national workforce. At the same time, agricultural employment dropped by 11 per cent, triggering migrations from the countryside to the cities, and from the south to the north. The industrial triangle of Milan, Turin and Genoa attracted a concentration of millions of people, living in overcrowded conditions inferior to those of the rest of Europe.

[28]   According to the 1948 constitution the President of the republic, elected every seven years, is the head of state. One of their duties is to select a head of government, the Prime Minister, who will have the support of the bicameral parliament. Until 1978, when socialist Sandro Pertini was elected, all presidents had belonged to the DC. Francesco Cossiga, elected in 1985, returned Italy to the tradition of Christian Democrat presidents.

[29]   Cabinets which take lengthy negotiations to form generally only manage to last a few months. Charges against Christian Democrat Arnaldo Forlani's government - linking his supporters and allies to an organization called 'Propaganda Due'- brought the Government down in May 1981, giving way to just over a year of government led by Republican Giovanni Spadolini.

[30]   The instability of the Government, coupled with astronomical fiscal deficits and the political influence of the Mafia and the 'Camorra' led many to consider the need for constitutional reform.

[31]   In February 1991, the last secretary-general of the PCI proposed that the old name be changed to the Democratic Party of the Left (PDS). Immediately afterwards, the PDS sought admission into the Socialist International. The PDS also called for reunification with the PSI, hoping to heal the split which had taken place 70 years earlier. In December 1991, dissenters from the official party line decided to create the 'Reformed' Communist Party (PRC), using the red flag, hammer and sickle as its symbols.

PROFILE

ENVIRONMENT

The northern region of the country consists of the Po River plains which extend as far as the Alps. It is the center of the country's economic activity, having the main concentration of industry and farming. Cattle are raised throughout the peninsula; important crops include olives and grapes, with vineyards extending along the southern coastal strip. The country includes not only the peninsula - which is divided by the Apennines - but also the islands of Sicily and Sardinia.

SOCIETY

Peoples: Italians 94 per cent. Others, particularly Sardinians and German on Alto Adige and immigrants from Africa.
Religions: Predominantly Catholic. Muslims are about 700,000.
Languages: Italian (official). Several regional languages, like Neapolitan and Sicilian, are widely spoken. French is spoken in Val d'Aosta and German in Alto Adige. Immigrants speak their own languages, particularly African languages. **Political Parties:** L'Ulivo (Olive Tree), center-left electoral coalition led by Romano Prodi, bringing together the Democratic Party of the Left (DPL, former Communist Italian Party), the Italian Party of the People (IPP, former Christian Democrats), Pact for Italy (PI), the Socialist Italian Party (SIP) and the Socialist Democratic Italian Party (SDIP); National Alliance; Forza Italia, led by Silvio Berlusconi; National Alliance, neo-fascist; League of the North, a regional xenophobic party; Reconstructed Communists (RC); Liberal Party (PLI); Republican Party (PRI); Southern Tyrolean Popular Party; National Federation for the Green List, ecologists. **Social Organizations:** Three central unions: the CGIL; the CISL and the UIL.

THE STATE

Official Name: Repubblica Italiana. **Administrative Divisions:** 20 Regions divided into 95 Provinces. **Capital:** Rome (Roma) 3,000,000 people (1998). **Other cities:** Milan (Milano) 3,700,000 people; Naples (Napoli) 1,200,000; Turin (Torino) 992,000; Palermo 734,000 (1994). **Government:** Carlo Azeglio Ciampi, President since May 1999. Massimo D'Alema, Prime Minister, since October 1998. Bicameral parliamentary system. **National Holiday:** June 2, Anniversary of the Republic (1946). **Armed Forces:** 325,150 (1996). **Other:** 111,800 Carabinieri.

32   By the end of 1991, confrontations between DC's Cossiga and the PDS leader, Achille Occhetto worsened. In February 1992, the President and the Prime Minister dissolved Parliament, bringing the legislative elections forward.

33   In the April 1992 elections, the DC did not achieve a parliamentary majority, the first defeat of a Christian Democratic government since 1946. Days afterwards, Prime Minister Giulio Andreotti announced the dissolution of his government and President Cossiga resigned early. At the end of May, Judge Giovanni Falcone - number one enemy of the Mafia - was killed in Sicily. This allowed the election of former president of the chamber of deputies, Oscar Scalfaro.

34   Two months after the assassination of Judge Falcone, the Mafia killed Paolo Borsellino who on Falcone's death had inherited the investigation against organized crime.

35   In October 1992, the Government presented a series of economic adjustment measures. These gave rise to a general strike in protest against the measures, with 10 million workers participating.

36   Attorney General Antonio di Pietro launched an investigation that revealed a complex system of illegal operations which included politicians of all persuasions, entrepreneurs and the mafia. During 1993, more than a thousand political and business leaders were tried under operation 'Clean Hands', including former Prime Ministers Bettino Craxi and Giulio Andreotti.

37   Between 1980 and 1992, corruption deprived State coffers of some $20 billion. Because of illegal payments to officials and politicians, Italian public investments were 25 per cent more expensive than in the rest of the European Community.

38   In April 1993, former Central Bank president, Carlo Azeglio Ciampi, was appointed Prime Minister. A few days later, a plebiscite was held on electoral reform according to which three quarters of the seats in the two chambers - Senate and Deputies - would be awarded by simple majority in the electoral districts. The remaining 25 per cent would be filled by proportional representation.

39   For the March 1994 legislative elections, within a few months, media magnate, Silvio Berlusconi created the 'Forza Italia' party which, allied with Umberto Bossi's federalist Northern League and the Gianfranco Fini's neo-fascist National Alliance (NA), won an absolute majority in Parliament.

40   Berlusconi was appointed Prime Minister in June and consolidated his popularity when 'Forza Italia' triumphed in the European elections. However, relations with the Northern League, which had persistently criticized Berlusconi, and the NA 'fascists', started to complicate government action.

41   In October, the unions opposed retirement pension reforms proposed by the Prime Minister as, in their view, the reforms limited benefits, increased contributions and 'privatized' part of the system. Following a large demonstration in Rome, attended by more than a million people, Berlusconi withdrew his reform bill. In December, Bossi - who despite a poor show in the election had nearly a fifth of the deputies behind him - withdrew his support for the Government and Berlusconi resigned.

42   Scalfaro refused to hold fresh elections, naming Berlusconi's former finance minister Lamberto Dini Prime Minister. Counting on greater support in the international financial organizations than his predecessor - he had worked in the IMF years ago - Dini formed a government of supposedly 'apolitical' technocrats.

43   Support from the Left meant the new Prime Minister was able to reform the pensions system and reduce the public deficit. As occurred with Ciampi - another technocrat Prime Minister who governed between 1993 and 1994 - Dini formed an alliance with the PDS in order to impose economic austerity measures.

44   On April 21 1996, the 'L'Ulivo' (Olive Tree) coalition led by former Democratic Christian Romano Prodi and supported by the PDS, triumphed in the legislative elections. Prodi was named Prime Minister and formed a government made up of prominent PDS leaders as well as well-known independent conservative personalities, like Ciampi or Dini himself. The presence of former communists in the cabinet and the support offered to the Government by the Reconstructed Communists (RC) marked the new period.

45   A serious crisis shook the Government in October 1997. The Communist Party threatened to withdraw support from Prodi and to block approval of the 1998 budget if the Government did not reduce the working week to 35 hours. Parliamentary negotiations ended with the Government committed to a reduction of the current 40 hours per week for companies with more than 15 employees from the year 2001.

46   The triumph of the Olive Tree coalition in the municipal elections the following month consolidated the Government position.

47   The proposed expansion of the Aviano base in southern Italy - the biggest NATO establishment in Europe - became highly controversial after a US plane flew too low and downed a cable car killing 20 people in February 1998.

48   In October 1998 the conflict between the Government and the Reconstructed Communists about the budget was repeated, but this time Prodi was forced to resign. In order to avoid calling new elections, which could put the government in the hands of the right wing, the center-left alliance chose Massimo D'Alema, a former communist and leader of the PDS, to take over as Prime Minister. President Scalfaro confirmed D'Alema as Premier on October 21.

49   Federal prosecutors accused former premier Andreotti in May 1999 of having used his political influence to aid the Mafia, sealing legal proceedings that had already lasted four years. Prosecutor Roberto Scarpinato also requested that Andreotti, age 80 and senator-for-life, be removed from public service. In his closing arguments, Scarpinato said that Andreotti's relationship with the Mafia was not 'accidental', but that the former prime minister had 'performed a service' for the crime organisation.

50   In May 1999, banker and former Economy minister Carlo Azeglio Ciampi, age 78, won the presidency with broad support from both the political left and right. Ciampi won the elections in the first round, marking only the third time in post-war Italy that presidential elections have not gone onto a run-off vote. For many, his easy victory suggested that the center and center-right parties were ready to work together to reform the paralytic political system. The presidency, though it is seen as a mostly ceremonial post in Italy, grants some important powers to whoever serves in that role. The President arbitrates in political crises, decides if it is appropriate to dissolve Parliament and convoke new elections, and designates the candidates who will make up the new Government.

51   In early December, the Olive Tree coalition won in the five legislative elections. The most significant victory was in Bologna, where voters elected a replacement for Romano Prodi, who had been selected to serve as president of the European Commission. Bologna had been the major defeat for the Left in June's municipal elections, at the hands of Berlusconi supporters.

52   On the 22nd of that month, D'Alema had to form his second administration, four days after being forced to resign when he lost the confidence of three small groups within the governing center-left coalition. The new Cabinet included 25 ministries, six headed by women, and remained in the hands of the Democratic Party, which had been created that year by Prodi in order to restart the Olive Tree coalition. Socialist leader Enrico Boselli charged that D'Alema had put together a weak government. ∎

STATISTICS

DEMOGRAPHY

Population: 57,343,000 (1999)
Annual growth: 0.2 % (1975/97)
Estimates for year 2015 (million): 54.4 (1999)
Annual growth to year 2015: -0.3 % (1997/2015)
Urban population: 66.7 % (1997)
Urban Growth: 6.3 % (1980/95)
Children per woman: 1.2 (1998)

HEALTH

Life expectancy at birth: 78 years (1998)
male: 75 years (1998)
female: 81 years (1998)
Maternal mortality: 7 per 100,000 live births (1990-98)
Infant mortality: 6 per 1,000 (1998)
Under-5 child mortality: 6 per 1,000 (1998)
Daily calorie supply: 3,504 per capita (1996)

EDUCATION

Literacy: 98 % (1995)
male: 99 % (1995)
female: 98 % (1995)
School enrolment:
Primary total: 99 % (1990/96)
male: 100 % (1990/97)
female: 99 % (1990/97)
Secondary:
male: 87 % (1990/96)
female: 88 % (1990/96)
Tertiary: 47 % (1996)
Primary school teachers: one for every 11 (1995)

COMMUNICATIONS

104 newspapers (1996), 878 radios (1997), 436 TV sets (1996) and 440 main telephone lines (1996) per 1,000 people
Books: 57 new titles per 100,000 people (1992/94)

ECONOMY

Per capita, GNP: $ 20,090 (1998)
Annual growth, GNP: 1.4 % (1998)
Annual inflation: 4.4 % (1990/98)
Consumer price index: 108.2 (1998)
Currency: 1,736.2 lire = $ 1 (1998)
Food import dependency: 11 % (1997)
Fertilizer use: 2,223 kg per ha (1997)
Exports: $ 312,934 million (1997)
Imports: $ 263,367 million (1997)

ENERGY

Consumption: 2,839.0 Kgs of Oil equivalent per capita yearly (1997); 82.0 % imported (1997)

HDI (rank/value): 19/0.900 (1997)

Jamaica

Jamaica

Population: 2,561,000 (1999)
Area: 10,990 SQ KM
Capital: Kingston
Currency: Jamaica dollar
Language: English

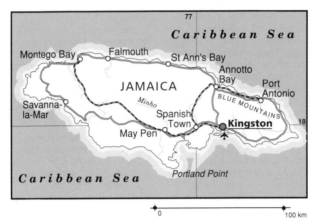

The name Jamaica apparently comes from the Arawak Indian name for the island - Xamayca. The Arawaks had pushed out the Guanahatabey, the original inhabitants, who had come from North America. The name Xamayca means 'land of springs', a reference to the abundant waters of its luxuriant forests. The Arawaks lived in villages of houses made from palm branches and carried out farming and fishing activities.

2 Columbus reached Jamaica on his second voyage to the New World in May 1494, but it was his son, Diego Colon, who conquered the island in 1509. From then on, the number of Arawaks decreased dramatically. Around 1545, Spanish historian Francisco López de Gomara wrote that 'Jamaica resembles Haiti in all respects - here the Indians have also been wiped out'. Some sources believe that prior to the Spanish Conquest, there may have been as many as 60,000 Arawaks.

3 The Spanish, now absolute rulers of the island, began to plant sugarcane and cotton, and to raise cattle. There were incursions by the British in 1596 and 1636, and in 1655, 6,500 British soldiers under the command of William Penn dislodged the 1,500 Spaniards and Portuguese. Jamaica rapidly became a haven for pirates who ravaged Spanish trade in the Caribbean. The last important enemies that the English had to face on the island were the enclaves of rebel slaves or quilombos, hidden in remote areas like the Blue Mountains. In 1760 a general rebellion in the colony was put down, and in 1795 a further revolution shook the island.

4 By the late 19th century there were approximately 800 sugar mills and more than 1,000 cattle ranches

in Jamaica. The economy was built on the labor of 200,000 slaves brought from Africa. Anti-slavery and anti-colonial rebellions of the 18th and 19th centuries were followed by labor union struggles in the first few decades of the 20th century. The two large contemporary political parties, the Labor Party and the People's National Party both grew out of workers' organizations. Independence was proclaimed in 1962, but successive Labor governments failed to rescue the economy from foreign hands.

5 In 1942 rich deposits of bauxite were discovered, and the aluminum transnationals ALCOA, ALCAN, Reynolds and Kaiser quickly established themselves on the island. The sugar industry was virtually replaced by bauxite exploitation.

6 The transnationals exploited Jamaica's bauxite by shipping the raw metal out of the country, making all the decisions on production, and paying minimal customs duties.

7 After independence in 1962, a few plants were built to transform

bauxite into aluminum, but the bulk of the mineral extracted continued to be shipped unprocessed to the US. In 1973, Jamaica was the second largest producer of bauxite in the world. The mineral accounted for half of the country's exports but employed only one per cent of the labor force. Transnationals' earnings were not reinvested in the country. Export and import duties were reduced as the transportation of the mineral was classified as an internal transfer, with preferential taxation rates.

8 The People's National Party (PNP) won the 1972 elections and in 1974 the new Prime Minister, Michael Manley, raised the bauxite export tax. In addition, he began negotiations with the foreign companies to recover the third of the nation owned by them, and to assert greater control over their activities.

9 At the same time, the PNP Government strongly supported Caribbean integration. A bi-national bauxite marketing company was created with Venezuela. Jamaica became a member of the Caribbean Multinational Merchant Fleet with Cuba and Costa Rica. Together, the associates devised ways to prevent penetration by US capital.

10 These progressive measures were resisted by the mining companies and by local conservative forces who sought to upset the December 1976 elections. The PNP

won anyway, with an overwhelming victory at the polls and an increased majority in parliament. Manley advocated socialism within the existing constitutional structure.

11 Jamaica took active part in the Movement of Non-Aligned Countries. It also supported anti-colonial positions at all world forums and proclaimed its unconditional solidarity with all liberation movements, particularly those of southern Africa.

12 This stand strained relations with the US. As a result, the transnational mining companies reduced their production, transferring operations to other countries. Export revenues fell, and with them, funding for government social programs.

13 In 1979, the Government was forced to seek loans from the IMF which imposed harsh conditions. In February 1980, Manley announced that he was suspending negotiations with the Fund since meeting its requirements would mean a drastic reduction in living standards for the population. That year elections were held ahead of schedule, in a climate of destabilization generated by the right-wing opposition, which finally won a landslide victory. The new Labor government, headed by Edward Seaga, expelled the Cuban ambassador and imposed neo-liberal economic policies, opening the country to unconditional foreign investment and even suggesting that it might request Jamaica's admittance to the United States. The results were counterproductive: between 1981 and 1983, unemployment increased, bauxite production continued to decline, inflation rose and the foreign debt doubled.

14 In November 1983, Jamaica was one of the small group of Caribbean countries that gave diplomatic support and symbolic military assistance to the invasion of Grenada. A month later, taking advantage of the favorable political atmosphere, Seaga decided to call early parliamentary elections. The PNP boycotted the elections, accusing the Government of not having fulfilled a previous commitment to update the electoral register and reorganize the system of voter identification, so as to avoid rigging. Only the governing party

WORKERS

1996
UNEMPLOYMENT: 16.0%

% OF LABOUR FORCE **1998**

▪ FEMALE: 46% ▪ MALE: 54%

1990

▪ SERVICES: 52.0%
▪ INDUSTRY: 23.2%
▪ AGRICULTURE: 24.8%

LAND USE

DEFORESTATION: 7.5% annual (1990/95)
IRRIGATED: 22.6% of arable (1993)

1993

▪ FOREST & WOODLAND: 16.8%
▪ ARABLE: 14.1
▪ OTHER: 69.1%

PUBLIC EXPENDITURE

DEFENCE EXPENDITURE (% of goverment exp.)	**2.4%**	(1997)
MILITARY EXPENDITURE (% of health & education)	**8%**	(1990/91)

nominated candidates, thereby winning all 60 seats.

[15] In 1984 the need to negotiate new loans with the IMF and the consequent cuts in public spending aggravated an already critical situation. Inflation soared from 4.7 per cent in 1981 to 32 per cent in 1984. In addition, in 1985 revenues from bauxite production fell and there was a 50 per cent decrease in tourism. Union federations announced that workers' living conditions were being allowed to deteriorate deliberately in order to attract transnationals to the Kingston 'free zone' where workers' rights were not respected.

[16] 96 per cent of the workforce in the 'free zone' were women who bore long working days in unhealthy conditions, with no security and low pay. This affected the situation of the children of Kingston, as 52 per cent of the heads of household were women.

[17] Between 1985 and 1987, the Labor Government adopted a campaign against drug trafficking, in agreement with the United States. Some $750 million worth of marijuana was estimated to enter the United States via Jamaica each year.

[18] In 1989, Michael Manley's PNP came to power again, strengthened by its triumph in the June 1986 municipal elections. He presented a very different program from 1976, based on free enterprise and good relations with the United States. Manley re-established relations with Cuba and stated the agreements with the IMF would be respected, although he made it clear he would not accept conditions which would worsen the social inequalities. His aim was to maintain economic growth, but with better wealth distribution.

[19] In April 1992, Percival Patterson replaced Manley as Prime Minister, as the latter resigned from this post and the presidency of the PNP, following a long period of illness. Patterson, a well-known politician, former senator and minister of several PNP governments, was also elected party president.

[20] In 1992, promising labor guarantees, the Government started the privatization of around 300 State companies and public services classified as unproductive. This package included the entire sugar industry.

[21] In March 1993, the PNP took more than 60 per cent of the vote, confirming Patterson in the post of Prime Minister. The Labor Party - led once again by Edward Seaga - refused to participate in the partial elections in 1994 in order to show their disagreement with the electoral system and lobby for modifications. In October 1995, a group of Seaga's opponents within the Labor Party abandoned the group to found the National Democratic Movement.

[22] Prime Minister Patterson continued in 1995 with the economic and financial liberalization which, amongst other things, made Jamaica's financial sector one of the most prosperous in the country.

[23] In 1997, a committee of political parties, religious representatives and community groups was formed to seek solutions to the internal violence. Pressure from this committee contributed to Jamaica becoming the first country to abandon an agreement, within the framework of the United Nations International Convention on Civil and Political Rights, which made the death penalty more difficult to apply.

[24] The violence during the run-up to the December 18 1997 parliamentary elections led to the mass resignation of candidates. The National Democratic Movement had only 54 candidates for 60 seats. Following the election, the PNP retained the absolute majority, with 50 seats, while the Labor Party took 10.

[25] Jamaica withdrew from the Inter-American Commission on Human Rights of the Organization of American States in 1998 due to the forum's opposition to the death penalty, still used by Jamaica and other Caribbean countries. In June, Jamaica, Barbados, Guyana and Trinidad - all independent nations but with various ties to Britain - announced plans to cut links with the the House of Lords and form their own Caribbean Court of Justice.

[26] After he was made president of the G-15 (a group of 15 developing countries), Prime Minister Patterson declared during the group's February 1999 meeting in Kingston that a lending organization would need to be created as a last resource. Patterson specified that, in his opinion, the IMF was not fit to play that role. ∎

PROFILE

ENVIRONMENT

Jamaica is the third largest of the Greater Antilles. A mountain range, occupying one third of the land area, runs across the island from east to west. A limestone plateau covered with tropical vegetation extends to the west. The plains are good for farming and the subsoil is rich in bauxite. The climate is rainy, tropical at sea level and temperate in the eastern highlands. Soil loss from deforestation and erosion reaches 80 million tons per year. In some metropolitan areas, the lack of sewerage and the dumping of industrial wastes have polluted drinking water supplies, threatening the urban population.

SOCIETY

Peoples: Most Jamaicans are of African descent. There are small Chinese, Indian, Arab and European minorities.
Religions: Protestants 56 per cent; Catholics 5 per cent, Rastafarians 5 per cent.
Languages: English (official). A dialect based on English is also spoken.
Political Parties: People's National Party (PNP); Jamaican Labor Party (JLP); National Democratic Movement; Workers' Party of Jamaica (JWP).
Social Organizations: National Workers Union of Jamaica (NWUJ); Bustamante Industrial Trade Union (BITU).

THE STATE

Official Name: Jamaica.
Administrative Divisions: 13 Districts.
Capital: Kingston 750,000 people (est 1995).
Other cities: Montego Bay 83,500 people; Spanish Town 92,000 people (1991).
Government: Parliamentary monarchy. Head of State: Elizabeth II of Britain. Prime Minister since March 1992: Percival J Patterson. Bicameral Legislature: 21 member Senate, designated by the Governor General; Chamber of Deputies, 60 elected by direct popular vote every 5 years.
National Holiday: First Monday in August, Independence Day (1962).
Armed Forces: 3,350 troops.

Japan

Nihon

Population: 126,505,000 (1999)
Area: 377,800 SQ KM
Capital: Tokyo
Currency: Yen
Language: Japanese

E arliest culture in Japan dates back 10,000 to 30,000 years ago to the Paleolithic Age, known as the Pre-Cambrian era. This was followed by the Jomon Neolithic culture, which lasted until 200-300 BC and extended throughout the Japanese archipelago.

2   The Jomon culture was altered by the arrival of the Yayoi, who probably arrived from the continent at a time when Japan was still linked by land bridges across the straits of Korea, Tsushima, Soya and Tsugaru. The Yayoi introduced rice cultivation, horses and cows, the potter's wheel, weaving, and iron tools.

3   According to Chinese chronicles, at the beginning of the Christian era the Wo region (Wa in Japanese) was divided into more than 100 states. During Himito's reign, some 30 of them were grouped together. The Wa people were divided into social classes and paid taxes, advanced building techniques were known and used, there were large markets and correspondence was exchanged with the continent.

4   From the end of the civil war until Yamato's consolidation as emperor (266-413), the Wa territory was isolated. This led to the unification of the nation by the middle of the 4th century, a prerequisite for further expansion. In the year 369, Yamato subdued the Korean kingdoms of Paekche, Kaya and Sila and established military headquarters from which he could control the region.

5   The Yamato empire suffered a rapid decline, due to both the resistance of its Korean subjects and to internal fighting within the court. During that period, between the years 538 and 552, Buddhism was introduced into the country,

though initially it was merely an object of curiosity and admiration, due to its majestic temples and the magical powers that were attributed to it.

6   The most important traces of Chinese presence in Japanese culture are the grid system for dividing the land, which dates back 1,500 years and is still visible today, the Chinese characters used in the writing system and the Buddhist religion.

7   However, this cultural heritage underwent successive adaptations to the local weather, language, and habits, especially during the 17th and 18th centuries. This was particularly apparent in the

architecture and the language, each of which shows evidence of very different local influences.

8   Japan's first permanent capital was Nara, established in the year 710. In the 9th century, tribal chieftains were replaced by a permanent court with a hereditary right to title. The aristocracy made Buddhism a controlling force, which served to reinforce the power of the state. After several conflicts, Kammu (781-806) re-established the empire's independence and transferred the capital to Heian (Kyoto).

9   In the new capital, the power of the Fujiwara family was consolidated. The Fujiwaras established the regent as the ruling figure, above and beyond the power of the emperor. With imperial approval, two new Buddhist sects - Tendai and Shingon - developed in Heian. They were both seen to be more closely identified with Japanese culture than the previous Buddhist sects, a

fact which brought an end to Nara's religious hegemony.

10   The imperial land tenure system also fell increasingly into private hands. The members of the aristocracy and the religious institutions began taking over large extensions of tax-free land (*shoen*). The nobility organized private armies for themselves, and a rural warrior class - the samurai - emerged.

11   The Taira and Minamoto clans, who were prominent families and local leaders, became involved in a power struggle which led to a number of military confrontations between these two warlords. The Taira were in power from 1156 until their defeat in the Gempei War (1180-85). The shogun (general), Minamoto Yoritomo, founded the Kamakura shogunate, the first of a series of military regimes which ruled Japan until 1868.

12   The Kamakura were put to the test during the Mongol invasions of 1274 and 1281. Aided by providential storms, which were called kamikaze (divine winds), the Japanese defeated the invaders. During this period, several new Buddhist sects emerged, such as Pure Land Buddhism, True Pure Land and Lotus.

13   In the early 14th century, the Kamakura shogunate was destroyed, and Emperor Go-Daigo re-established his authority over the warlords in the Kemmu Restoration. However, a short while later he was expelled from Kyoto and replaced by a puppet emperor, who was controlled by the military clans. Go-Diago established his court in Yoshino, and for 56 years there were two imperial courts operating alongside each other.

14   The Onin War (1467-77), over succession within the Ashikaga shogunate, became a civil war which lasted a hundred years. New military chiefs emerged, independent of imperial or shogun authority. They established themselves and their vassals within fortified cities, leaving the surrounding villages to run themselves, and to pay tribute.

15   In the cities, trade and manufacturing ushered in a new way of life. Portugal began trading with Japan in 1545, and the missionary Francis Xavier introduced Catholicism to the Japanese in 1549. However, Christianity caused conflicts with feudal loyalties, and

WORKERS

1997
UNEMPLOYMENT: 3.4%

% OF LABOUR FORCE   **1998**

FEMALE: 41%   MALE: 59%

1990

SERVICES: 58.5%
INDUSTRY: 34.2%
AGRICULTURE: 7.3%

LAND USE

DEFORESTATION: 0.1% annual (1990/95)
IRRIGATED: 69.1% of arable (1993)

1993

FOREST & WOODLAND: 66.4%
ARABLE: 10.7%
OTHER: 22.9%

PUBLIC EXPENDITURE

DEFENCE EXPENDITURE (% of goverment exp.)	**6.6%**	(1997)
MILITARY EXPENDITURE (% of health & education)	**12%**	(1990/91)

so it was proscribed in 1639. All of the Europeans in Japan, except for the Dutch, were banished from the country.

16 Toward the end of the 16th century, the Japanese warlords isolated themselves from the rest of society, pacifying and uniting the country around a single national authority. To achieve these objectives, the warlords made use of firearms and of military fortresses; in addition, they disarmed the peasants and achieved greater control over the land.

17 During the 17th century, the Tokugawa clan gained supremacy over the entire country. From the city-fortress of Edo (Tokyo), the Tokugawa shogunate governed Japan until 1867. A careful distribution of the land among their relatives and the local chieftains guaranteed them the control of the largest cities, Kyoto, Osaka and Nagasaki, as well as of the most important mines.

18 Local chieftains were compelled to spend half their time on the shogun's affairs while their families remained behind, as hostages. Transformed into military bureaucrats, the samurai were the highest level of a four-class system, followed by the peasants, artisans and traders.

19 A national market arose for textiles, food, handcrafts, books and other products. As of 1639, the Tokugawas implemented a policy of almost total isolation from the outside world. Nagasaki was the only exception; here, the Chinese and the Dutch were allowed to open trading posts, although the latter were restricted to a nearby island.

20 In the 19th century, the old economic and social order went into a state of collapse. Peasant revolts became more and more frequent, and the samurai and local chieftains found themselves heavily in debt with the traders. In 1840, the government tried to carry out a series of reforms, but these failed and weakness allowed the United States to prize open its ports.

21 Japan was forced out of its isolation by Commodore Matthew Perry, using cannon to persuade the Japanese to cooperate with him. The signing of unfavorable trade agreements with the United States and several European countries simply deepened the crisis within the shogunate. The samurai carried out several attacks against the foreigners and then turned against the shogun, forcing him to resign in 1867.

22 Imperial authority was restored with the young Meiji emperor, in 1868. During the Meiji Restoration, Japan's modernization process began, following the Western model. The United States exerted its influence, as did England, France and Germany, in the fields of education, the sciences, communication and Japanese cultural expression.

23 Within less than 50 years, Japan was transformed from a closed, feudal society into an industrialized world power. Western advisers and technology were brought in, for education, trade and industry. An army based on the draft replaced the military authority of the samurai, who were defeated when they tried to rebel, in 1877.

24 In 1889, succumbing to internal political pressure, the emperor approved a constitution which established a constitutional monarchy, with a bicameral legislature (Diet). However, only one per cent of the population was eligible for office, and the prime minister and his cabinet were responsible to the emperor who continued to be seen as a divine figure.

25 Japan defeated China in the war of 1894-95, and maintained control over Korea. Japan's victory in the Russo-Japanese War (1904-5) enabled it to annex the Sajalin Peninsula, with Korea being annexed a few years later (1910). Japan entered World War I as a British ally, as a treaty had been signed to that effect in 1902.

26 The war allowed Japan to gain control of several German possessions in East Asia, including the Chinese territory of Kiaochow. In 1915, Japan forced China to accept the extension of its influence over Manchuria and Inner Mongolia. In 1918, Hara Takashi became the head of the first government to have a parliamentary majority.

27 In 1921-22 Japan signed a naval arms limitation treaty with the US in Washington, replacing an agreement with Britain, and establishing a new balance of power in the Pacific.

28 The economic difficulties caused by the international depression of the 1930s gave the militarists the excuse they were seeking to attack the government. They proposed that the country's problems could only be solved by expanding its military power, and through the conquest of new markets for their products and as sources of raw materials.

29 Within this context, Japanese officers occupied Manchuria in 1931, without government authorization. Unable to deter the military, the government accepted the creation of the puppet state of Manchukuo, in February 1932. Three months later, the country's political leaders were forced to turn the government over to the militarists, who retained power until 1945.

30 In 1940, Japan invaded Indochina hoping to open up a passage through to Southeast Asia. The United States and Britain reacted by imposing a total embargo upon Japanese merchandise. The Japanese attack on Pearl Harbor, in Hawaii, and of the Philippines, Hong Kong and Malaysia, unleashed the war with the United States and opened up a new phase of World War II.

31 Japan surrendered on August 14 1945, after the US had dropped two atomic bombs on Hiroshima and Nagasaki on August 6 and 9. Japan was subsequently occupied by US troops who remained in the country between 1945 and 1952, and was governed by the Supreme Command of the Allied Powers (SCAP) under the leadership of General Douglas MacArthur. SCAP forced Japan to abandon the Meiji institutions, to renounce the emperor's claim to divinity, and transfer the government to a parliament, which was charged with electing the prime minister and to establishing an independent judiciary.

32 Although imposed upon the Japanese from the outside, the principles laid down in the 1947 constitution were accepted by all sectors of society and in 1952 the country recovered its independence. Japanese sovereignty was restored over the Tokara archipelago in 1951, over the Amami islands in 1953, over the Bonin islands in 1968, and over the rest of the Ryukyu, including Okinawa, in 1972.

33 SCAP also took other measures to weaken the hierarchical model of the Meiji family-state. These ranged from giving tenants the right to purchase the land they lived on, and laws aimed at strengthening free trade and preventing the return of monopolies. However, the Japanese financial system remained intact and provided the basis for economic recovery at the end of the occupation.

34 In 1955, opposing the country's conservative and nationalist sectors, which had supported the war policy, the Liberal Democratic Party (LDP) was formed. It was a center-right party, holding a majority in Parliament and has governed the country from its foundation to the present.

35 The 1947 Constitution established restrictions upon the development of Japanese military power. During the postwar period, Japan bowed to US strategy for the region forming alliances with Taiwan and South Korea. In 1956 it joined the UN and re-established relations with the USSR.

36 The return to independence found the Japanese economy in a state of growth and change. Farmers became unable to survive with the traditional methods of small-scale production and left the land in droves, leading to great urban migration. Industrialization and full employment triggered the need for technological innovation in the countryside to increase the food supply.

37 During the 1960s, Japan specialized in the production of high technology products, which made it necessary to establish stable trade relations with more industrialized countries instead of its previous Asian partners. The oil crisis of 1973 did not halt the growth of the Japanese industry, which led the world in steel, ship building, electronics, and automobile manufacturing.

38 Although Prime Minister Kakuei Tanaka's visit to Beijing in 1972 signaled Japanese recognition of the People's Republic of China, it damaged the country's relations with Taiwan. The scandal following the disclosure of the fact that Tanaka had been bribed by the Marubeni Corporation (a representative of the US Lockheed Aircraft Corporation), adversely affected the LDP's popularity and in 1976, for the first time in its history, it lost its absolute majority in parliament.

39 During the 1960s and 1970s, there was a large trade surplus in Japan's favor in its trade with the US. During this period, Japan began ranking first or second with all its trading partners. With direct investment and the establishment of subsidiaries of Japanese companies, Japan expanded worldwide.

40 The Japanese corporate world at the time dominated by the Sogo-Shosha system, huge conglomerates which commercialize virtually all kinds of raw material in almost every country in the world, by means of state-of-the-art information systems capable of supplying data for instantaneous decision-making.

41 The organization of Japanese corporations maintains some principles which are the legacy of Japan's medieval tradition. The worker is bound to the corporation by an allegiance similar to that which bound the medieval peasant to his land and the local warlord. This often results in great company discipline and production efficiency.

42 The impressive development of the Japanese economy was due not only to this efficiency but also to a policy of foreign investment in projects which quickly deplete non-renewable natural resources. This policy has caused irreversible damage to rainforests and serious alterations to the Third World ecosystem.

43 At this time Japan was importing over 16 million cubic meters of tropical timber every year. This has caused a massive deforestation in Malaysia, Thailand, Indonesia, the Philippines, and

Papua New Guinea. Japan has also become a consumer of endangered species and products derived from them, such as ivory and tortoise shells.

[44] Japan makes direct investments in Third World countries and gives credits through its agencies to aid in building roads and in scientific research projects. As with all international aid this assistance is geared toward its own interest in gaining cheap, easy access to the raw materials of those countries.

[45] For some, the pursuit of economic success has become the main objective. Family, leisure, and individual ideals are sacrificed to the factory or the company. Within this system, women play a very subservient role as the pillar of the home and of the children's education.

[46] There is great social pressure for women to get married: 80 per cent of women are married by the age of 30 and 98 per cent are married, widowed, or divorced by the age of 50. Women may work outside the home, generally in second-rate, badly paid jobs.

[47] In spite of this age-old discrimination - a legacy of the country's traditional cultures - Japanese women are active in local movements against the pollution caused by industry and nuclear power plants. They also actively defend the quality of life and of consumer goods.

[48] The traditional full-employment situation in Japan was threatened by two factors: demographic growth and technological modernization which created a labor shortage. Japanese resistance to foreign immigrants and the progressively ageing profile of the population only intensified the problem. In June 1990, an immigration law went into effect opening up the Japanese labor market to foreign workers, for the first time ever.

[49] Although the US at that time gave military support to Japan, Washington started exerting pressure in 1982 so that the country would increase its military expenditure (around 0.9 per cent of its GDP) and assume greater responsibility in regional security in the Western Pacific.

[50] Since the early 1950s, Japan began demanding that the USSR return four small islands which Japan claimed belonged to the Kurile archipelago. Relations between the two countries entered a new era in 1986 with Minister of Foreign Affairs Eduard Shevardnadze's visit to Tokyo. This visit resulted in the decision to hold regular ministerial consultations, and to increase trade.

[51] Prime Minister Yasuhiro Nakasone traveled to Eastern Europe in 1987, in the first such visit by a Japanese head of government. Three years later, Prime Minister Toshiki Kaifu traveled to several European countries and declared his support of the liberalization of Eastern Europe.

[52] The economic and social stability of southeast Asia was of utmost importance for Japan because a growing part of its investments and a third of its foreign trade depended on this region, which provides the country with raw materials vital to its industry.

[53] The death of Emperor Hirohito in January 1989 brought to an end the Showa era, which had begun in 1926. The coronation of his successor, Akihito, in the traditional Japanese style, marked the beginning of the Heisei era (achievement of universal peace). The coronation ceremony was attended by more heads of state than had ever gathered together for any such event. The expense incurred generated internal protests.

[54] Japanese relations with the EC and the US have been strained at times, due to problems of protectionism and a trade imbalance (in Japan's favor). In 1987, Washington protested at Japan's sale of sophisticated submarine technology to the USSR, between 1982 and 1984. Nevertheless in 1989 Naboru Takeshita was the first head of government to be received by newly-elected US president, George Bush. Takeshita resigned in April, as a result of a real estate scandal. He was succeeded by Sosuke Uno, who was forced to resign after less than three months in office after admitting having sexual relations with a geisha woman.

[55] At the end of the Cold War, Japan emerged as one of the three main world economic powers, together with the US and the EC. At present, it is the country with the largest overseas investment. It is a key participant in the world financial system, and is influential in the exchange of Third World debt funds.

[56] On November 5 1991, Prime Minister Toshiki Kaifu presented his resignation, and was replaced by 72-year-old Kiichi Miyazawa who had been elected president of the

Liberal Democratic Party nine days before. Kaifu had been elected in August 1989 because he was one of very few party members who had never been involved in a corruption scandal. His political career rapidly came to an end when he lost the support of the Takeshita clan, the most influential of the official party's five factions, and the one which had backed his election.

[57] The Takeshita clan also backed the next prime minister, Miyazawa, even though he had been forced to resign as minister of finance in December 1988, because of his involvement in the Recruit scandal. (Recruit was a Japanese telecommunications firm that had made large financial contributions to many politicians in the hope of obtaining governmental favours.) In his inaugural speech, Miyazawa outlined the objectives he had set for his administration: to expand relations with, and aid to China; to negotiate with the United States and to normalize relations with the USSR. In addition, he announced his willingness to liberalize the rice market, making concessions similar to those already made by the EC and the United States, to ward off a failure of the Uruguay Round of the GATT.

[58] On November 23, US Defense Secretary Richard Cheney called on Japan to play a more active role in the military and political aspects of world affairs. US military forces currently in Japan consist of three air bases, an aircraft carrier and some 56,000 troops, including a division of Marines.

[59] On February 9 1992, Yukihise Yoshida, an opposition candidate supported by all four opposition parties, defeated the official candidate by 51 per cent to 37 per cent, in the western district of Nara. This outcome was attributed to popular disenchantment with the party in power, because endemic corruption was not only extant, but was very obviously on the increase. Prime Minister Kiichi Miyazawa himself appeared to be entirely surrounded by people with a record of corruption.

[60] On February 10 1992, it was revealed that the minister of postal services, Hideo Watanabe, had admitted to receiving a bribe greater than the $40,000 he had previously admitted to during the Recruit scandal of 1988. On February 14, four people were arrested with relation to another financial scandal, which involved more than 100 members of Miyazawa's government, as well as the mafia group known as Inagawagumi. It was revealed that billions of yen had been siphoned off from party donations making the new case, known as Kyubin, an even more serious breach of conduct than the Recruit scandal.

PROFILE

ENVIRONMENT

The country is an archipelago made up of 3,400 islands, the most important being Hokkaido, Honshu and Kyushu. The terrain is mountainous, dominated by the so-called Japanese Alps, which are of volcanic origin. Since 85 per cent of the land is taken up by high, uninhabitable mountains, 40 per cent of the population lives on only 1 per cent of the land area, in the narrow Pacific coastal plains, where demographic density exceeds 1,000 inhabitants per sq km. The climate is sub-tropical in the south, temperate in the center and cold in the north. Located where cold and warm ocean currents converge, Japanese waters have excellent fishing, and this activity is important to the country's economy. Japan's intensive and highly mechanized farming is concentrated along the coastal plains (rice, soybeans and vegetables). There are few mineral resources. Highly industrialized, the country's economy revolves around foreign trade, exporting manufactured products and importing raw materials. The major environmental problems are air pollution, especially in the major urban areas of Tokyo, Osaka and Yokohama, and acid rain in many parts of the country. One of the world's largest heavy industries has polluted many coastal areas.

SOCIETY

Peoples: The Japanese are culturally and ethnically homogeneous, having their origin in the migration of peoples from the Asian continent. There are Korean, Chinese, Ainu and Brazilian minorities. **Religions:** Buddhism 38.3 per cent and Shintoism 51.3 per cent.
Languages: Japanese. **Political Parties:** The Government coalition is made up of the Liberal Democratic Party (LDP), the Social Democratic Party of Japan (SPDJ) and the New Party Sakigake. The Shinshinto (Japan Renewal Party) has been in the opposition since 1994.
Social Organizations: The General Council of Japanese Trade Unions has 4,500,000 members.

THE STATE

Official Name: Nihon or Nippon **Capital:** Tokyo 11,771,819 people (1995).
Other cities: Yokohama 3,307,408 people; Osaka 2,602,352; Nagoya 2,153,293; Kyoto 1,463,601 (1995). **Government:** Parliamentary constitutional monarchy. Emperor Akihito has been Head of State since 1989, although his official coronation did not take place until November 12 1990. Yoshiro Mori, Prime Minister and head of the Government since April 2000. The Diet (Legislature) is bicameral: House of Representatives, made up of 512 members; House of Counselors, with 252 members, elected by direct popular vote every 4 and 6 years, respectively. **National Holiday:** January 1, New Year's Day. February 11, Founding of the Country (1889). **Armed Forces:** 239,500 (including 8,000 women). **Other:** 12,000 (non-combat Coast Guard, under the jurisdiction of the Ministry of Transport).

61 Toward the middle of the year, after heated debate, a law was passed authorizing troops to be sent abroad for the first time since World War II.

62 In early 1993, Miyazawa promised to broaden the scope of Japanese forces, both in terms of funding and personnel, within the framework of the UN peacekeeping missions.

63 Also in 1993 the Prime Minister was censured by the Diet for failing to carry out electoral reforms needed to end the endemic corruption in Japanese political life. The official party split, losing 54 seats, and elections were moved up to July.

64 The two dissident groups, led by Tsutomu Hata and Masayoshi Takemura, formed new parties; the Reformation Party and the Pioneer Party.

65 Debate intensified in April over whether Japanese troops should be sent abroad, after a civilian and a member of the Japanese police force were killed in Cambodia as members of the UN forces.

66 Diplomatic relations with the Russian Government improved slightly when Japan announced that, while not relinquishing its claim to the Kuril Islands, it would not allow its claim to the islands to prevent economic aid to Russia.

67 On July 18, general elections drew the lowest rate of voter participation since the war (67.3 per cent), a clear sign of the electorate's dissatisfaction with the corrupt state of Japan's political scene.

68 The LDP, in power since 1955, lost its majority in the Kokkai (Diet), obtaining only 228 of the 512 disputed seats in the House of Representatives, compared with 275 in the 1990 election. This result was significant enough to alter the balance of power which had been in effect since World War II.

69 Miyazawa, who had announced his decision to remain in office regardless of the election results, changed his mind. A few days later, he resigned the party presidency, and assumed responsibility for the LDP's defeat. Yohei Kono was named party President.

70 In July, the 'new majority' of the Socialist, Reformation, Komeito (Buddhist), Democratic Socialist, Unified Democratic Socialist and Pioneer parties, agreed to form a new Government, based upon a limited platform which would not attempt any profound changes.

71 Hosokawa, the former governor of the province of Kunamoto, was elected Prime Minister in August. Upon assuming office, he announced a far-reaching political-reform bill, aimed at fighting corruption, putting an end to the recession and modernizing the pension and health systems.

72 In his first speech before the Diet, Hosokawa referred to the aggression with which Japan had treated its Asian neighbors, from the 1930s until the end of World War II. On August 15, the 48th anniversary of Japan's surrender, Hosokawa offered condolences and apologies to the victims of Japanese colonialism.

73 In December 1993, the Japanese Government opened up the rice market, allowing up to 4 per cent of internal consumption, amounting to 10 million tons, to be imported. Many families tend to hoard domestic rice, and shopkeepers speculate with prices. The 'Rice Lord', or *kome*, is a sacred part in Japanese tradition, and is linked to the earth and the ancestors.

74 Japan's enormous trade surplus has been a source of constant tension on the international market, particularly with the United States. This surplus reached $107 billion in 1992, and $150 billion in 1993.

75 Beyond the problems caused by the surplus, the Japanese economy has also suffered the effects of world recession. The most apparent consequence being that of unemployment, which has been on the increase since mid-1992 and reached its peak in 1996 with 3.2 per cent.

76 A corruption scandal among top Government circles had been revealed in 1992 when Shin Kanemaru, historic LDP leader, admitted he had received bribes. Kanemaru was arrested in March 1993 and was granted an amnesty shortly afterward. When Hosokawa succeeded Miyazawa, the Confederation of Industries announced it would discontinue its 'contributions' to the LDP. According to local press versions, these had amounted to $1 billion per year.

77 In August, 165 political leaders and 445 business people were arrested for irregularities committed during the July 1993 election campaign. 5,500 cases were brought to court to deal with electoral fraud. In October, Shinji Kiyoyama - president of Kajima, the country's second largest construction firm - was arrested for paying a bribe in exchange for a building permit.

78 Hosokawa's 'romance' with public opinion, after reaching record levels of popularity, started to cool off in early 1994 as press reports became critical, accusing him of having received huge amounts of money in exchange for favors.

79 Already in February 1994, the Prime Minister had been forced to abandon a scheme which he himself had sponsored, aimed at keeping the Government coalition intact. Worn out by the pressure, he had to issue a self-critique - unpleasant for a head of Government - explaining the reckless manner in which he had handled the situation.

80 A new $140 billion plan to reactivate the economy also drew criticism. Its feasibility was questioned and the press stressed the plan did not address the problems posed by a rapidly ageing population.

81 In March 1994, a summit meeting between Japan and the United States ended in failure. Although Hosokawa showed a willingness to accept opening up the Japanese automobile, telecommunications, medicine and insurance markets, he rejected the US scheme of mandatory quotas. Japanese businessmen disqualified Hosokawa and felt inclined to wage a commercial war with the US before yielding to its pressures. The automobile industry employs 11 per cent of Japan's labor and contributes 30 per cent of the GDP.

82 A new corruption case involved LDP member of parliament Nakamura, who was arrested for accepting bribes from Kajima and other construction firms. Hosokawa was unable to shake off accusations from the opposition about his own involvement in illicit business deals. In April he resigned and asked 'sincerely for forgiveness from the people of Japan'.

83 Tsutomu Hata was nominated Prime Minister and on April 28, Japan's first minority Government in four decades was formed. The socialists had walked out of the Government coalition leaving the Government with only 182 of the 512 seats in the lower house.

84 Hata made official visits to Europe aiming to establish closer trade links with the European Community. He also admitted that Japan's trade surplus had caused the trade crisis with the United States. After an initial agreement was reached between the two countries, Hata launched a scheme to promote economic deregulation.

85 Socialist Tomiichi Murayama was elected Prime Minister on June 29 1994 and took office on July 18. His party, the Social Democratic Party of Japan (SDPJ) did not obtain a majority in parliament but formed an alliance with its traditional rival, the LDP, and with a new party, the Sakigake.

86 The opening of Kansai airport, located on an artificial island, led to a blossoming of island-city projects. The overpopulation of Japan's large cities has led to a permanent real estate development, taking up what little space is available for construction.

87 On January 17 1995, an earthquake hit the area of Hanshin. Over 6,000 died, 100,000 buildings were destroyed in the city of Kobe and over 300,000 were left homeless. The Government's delayed response to the disaster was harshly criticized. The lower house added $10 billion to the budget for the area's recovery.

88 In March, a series of attacks

with poisonous Sarin gas killed 12 people and affected 12,000 others in Tokyo's subways. A similar attack had taken seven lives in Matsumoto in June 1994. Shoko Asahara, the leader of a religious sect called Aum Shinriyko (Supreme Truth), was charged with the attack and arrested along with 16 other leaders from the movement.

89 Murayama was defeated when

Independent Yukio Aoshima was elected governor of Tokyo in the April 9 1995 elections. The Socialists did not obtain favorable returns at the July elections either, which renewed half of the upper house's seats and in which opposition party Sakigake had a significant growth.

90   In January 1996, Ryutaro Hashimoto (LDP president) replaced Murayama as Prime Minister. The new Head of Government called for general elections on October, in which his party won a relative majority in parliament. In November, Hashimoto formed a cabinet with only LDP members.

91   In a referendum held in late 1997, slightly more than half of the Nago population, on Okinawa island, decided against the construction of a US heliport on the island. The United States had been stationed in Okinawa since the Japanese surrender in 1945 and had already built a sophisticated airbase with tens of thousands of soldiers. The Japanese and US governments claimed the construction of the heliport was a step towards the dismantling of the base which apparently did not convince the majority of Noga voters.

92   The financial and economic crisis which struck Southeast Asia in 1997 also affected Japan, the second world power and first creditor of the world. On April 1998, the yen was at its lowest level in the last seven years and the Tokyo Stock Exchange had lost 6 per cent in three days. At an economic level, a reduction of the gross domestic product was expected. Hashimoto stated his country was facing an 'extremely severe' situation, not seen since World War II.

93   Hashimoto resigned in early July after the bitter electoral results for his Liberal Democratic Party (LDP). On July 30, after being defeated in the Upper House of Parliament, former foreign minister Keizo Obuchi, also of the LDP, obtained the necessary votes in the Lower House and was named the new Prime Minister. The greatest challenges facing the new Government were to cut taxes in order to stimulate consumption and to take action against the bad loans that paralysed the Japanese banking system.

94   A major radioactive uranium leak at a JCO company reprocessing plant, just three kilometres from the Tokoaimura nuclear plant north of Tokyo, caused radiation levels to rise to 15,000 times higher than normal. The environmental organization Greenpeace denounced the accident as a symptom of the problems plaguing Japan's nuclear safety system. According to Greenpeace, Japan holds five tonnes of uranium within its territory, in addition to 30 tonnes it has purchased but which remain in Europe.

95   Flourishing right-wing groups enthusiastically applauded the re-adoption, after a 50-year break, of the former imperial flag in August, while dozens of teachers who refused to salute the old imperial symbols of the military era were fired. Growing nationalism was also evident in the armed forces, which began to carry out maneuvers in Japanese waters and achieved their highest levels of recruitment in decades.

96   Following yet another nuclear accident, this time at the Tokaimura plant in September, Obuchi ordered the inspection of all installations using nuclear fuel. The JCO firm, which recycled nuclear material, admitted that for years it had been using procedures that did not comply with the minimum safety requirements established by the Government. Despite the company's self-criticism, the Governor of Ibaraki province and the Mayor of Tokaimura presented complaints to the Prime Minister about the way authorities had responded to the emergency. Greenpeace claimed that the plant continued to emit radiation five times higher than recommended safety levels, while Government officials from the nuclear safety area were criticized for their slowness in measuring the contamination. The Yomiuri newspaper reported that the three operators charged with negligence in the handling of radioactive materials did not even know what a nuclear chain reaction meant.

97   Obuchi, who had worked hard to achieve his country's economic revival fell into a coma in early April 2000, and was immediately replaced by Yoshiro Mori. In May, days before Obuchi's death, the new Prime Minister spoke at a meeting of Shintoist followers (who during World War II worshipped Emperor Hirohito as a living deity). Mori shocked national and international public opinion with his description of Japan as 'a divine nation that has the Emperor at its center'. ■

Divine Shinto and Japanese life

Shinto, the national religion of Japan, is 2,500 years old and has no founder, no official sacred texts in the strict sense of the term, nor set dogmas. The word Shinto, which in the literal sense means 'the way of the kami' (kami means mystical, superior or divine and is applied to the beneficial and harmful principles of earth, water and deified people) is used to differentiate Japanese indigenous beliefs from Buddhism, which was introduced to Japan in the 6th century AD.

Shinto is made up of traditional Japanese religious practices, beliefs and attitudes to life which harmonize with these practices. Today it subsists more as part of the social life of the Japanese and their motivations than as a formal pattern of beliefs or philosophy. It remains closely linked to the Japanese value system and their way of thinking and acting.

Its origins lie in a mixture of tribal religions, each one with its own kami; a system of faith and a stock of ethnic customs, festivals, myths, ancient writings and attitudes relating to the kami.

THE FOUR AFFIRMATIONS

There are four basic affirmations or beliefs to Shintoism:

1. The affirmation of family traditions: these are the vital rites like birth and marriage, and other traditions which have been passed down from generation to generation.

2. The affirmation of the love of nature: nature is sacred; hence contact with nature implies a person is in contact with the gods.

3. The affirmation of personal cleanliness: the worshipper must be clean in the presence of the spirits; anyone who is unclean is disrespectful.

4. Affirmation of the matsuri: the matsuri are festivals in honor of the spirits.

SANCTUARY, SECT AND POPULAR SHINTO

Shinto can be classified in three broad categories: Shinto of the sanctuary (jinja Shinto), Shinto of the sect (kyoha Shinto) and popular Shinto (minzoku Shinto). Jinja Shinto is one of the main currents and includes within its structure the now defunct state Shinto (kokka Shinto). Kyoha Shinto is relatively new and is made up of 13 main sects which originated in Japan in the 19th century as well as many others which arose after World War II. Each of these sects was organized, either by a founder, or a systematizer, as a body of doctrine. Minzoku Shinto is a strain of popular Japanese beliefs and is closely linked to other types of Shinto. It lacks a formal organizational structure and formulated doctrine, but is based on the veneration of small idols by the roadside and the farming rituals of rural families. These three variants are interrelated: popular Shinto exists as a substructure of the Shinto faith, as the follower of sect Shinto is usually a parishioner (ujiko) of a particular sanctuary.

SHINTO SANCTUARIES

There are more than 110,000 Shinto sanctuaries and temples for the kami in Japan. The sanctuaries usually owe their existence to a physical characteristic or historical event. Many are so big that they require a large well-organized staff to serve them. Many Japanese homes contain small house sanctuaries known as kami-dana.

SHINTO AND THE EMPEROR

Shintoists believe the kami created the islands of Japan and that the solar goddess Amaterasu was the mother of the first emperor, who was sent to Earth to found an imperial dynasty. This belief formed the basis of state Shinto. The Emperor became a symbol of the people and of the unity of the nation. This tradition fed respect for state authority, the employer and the family. During the Meiji dynasty (1868-1912), the Government decided to institutionalize Shinto, taking control of the sanctuaries, and it adopted a restrictive policy on other religions. The 1889 Constitution considers obedience to Shinto sanctuaries to be the patriotic duty of all Japanese, thus making Shinto the official religion and using it to justify the cult of the Emperor and Japanese militarism in the early 20th century. Even though the new Constitution drawn up after World War II reduced Shinto to the status of an ordinary sect, more than 90 per cent of Japanese are Shintoist today. As it is not an exclusive religion, people can practice Shinto alongside another faith: most Japanese are also Buddhists. ■

Jordan

Urdunn

Population: 6,483,000 (1999)
Area: 97,740 SQ KM
Capital: Amman
Currency: Dinar
Language: Arabic

In biblical times, when it was divided among the Semitic nations of Gilead, Moab and Edom, the territory of present-day Jordan was central to the development of the region's history. In classical times, the state of Petra was one of the 'desert sentries' allies of the Roman Empire. In the 7th century it was the site of the battle of Yarmuk, in which the Arabs fought Byzantine Emperor Heraclius, winning access to the fertile crescent (see Saudi Arabia), and during the Crusades the western part of the territory served as the operational base to initiate warfare against the European strongholds.

[2] In the 16th century, Turkish domination made the territory part of the district of Damascus, and it remained so until the beginning of World War I in 1914.

[3] The Jordanians participated actively in the Arab rebellion against the Turkish Ottoman Empire. The secret 1916 Sykes-Picot Treaty between France and Britain, later formalized by the League of Nations, gave the French control of Lebanon and Syria and Britain a mandate over Iraq and Palestine (which included present-day Jordan). The British had promised Shereef Hussein of Mecca a unified Arab nation, including these territories, and the Arabian peninsula.

[4] The conflict with Faisal, the Shereef's son, in Syria (see Syria) and his expulsion by the French in 1920, led his brother Prince Abdullah to organize a support force of Jordanian Bedouin. The British persuaded Abdullah that he would be better off accepting the Government of Trans-Jordan.

[5] With this, and the later creation of the state of Iraq, which was granted to Faisal as compensation,

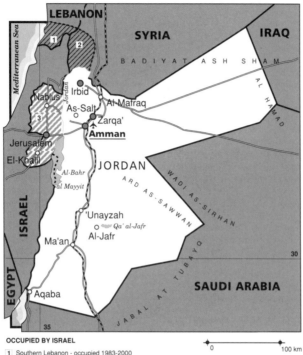

OCCUPIED BY ISRAEL
1. Southern Lebanon - occupied 1983-2000
2. Syria - Golan Heights - occupied in 1967
3. West Bank - occupied in 1967 (some individual towns now have autonomy)

0   100 km

Britain put Shereef Hussein in an awkward position; if he insisted on his Greater Arabia idea, his sons would lose their recently acquired positions as heads of state. Conversely, as Hussein controlled Hidjaz, three parts of the proposed nation were already in the hands of the family, making subsequent unification a possibility. This was not to happen, however. In 1924 the Shereef proclaimed himself Caliph. Emir Ibn Saud, King of Nejd, viewed this as a threat, so he invaded Hidjaz and drove Hussein out of Mecca (see Saudi Arabia).

[6] The emirate of Trans-Jordan remained under British mandate until 1928, when the borders with Palestine were established. Abdullah and his heirs were given legislative and administrative powers. Foreign and military affairs remained in British hands until May 1946, when the Emirate became the 'Hashemite Kingdom of Trans-Jordan'. After the Arab-Israeli War of 1948, King Abdullah annexed Palestinian territories on the West Bank of the Jordan River, calling the new nation Jordan. Palestinian refugees, the legal status of Jerusalem, and the doubling in length of the border with Israel were problems he had to face.

[7] In 1951, Abdullah was assassinated and his son Talal succeeded him. Talal appeared to harbor anti-British sentiments and promised a progressive government, but a year later he was deposed. In 1953, his 17-year-old son Hussein took over the throne.

[8] King Hussein managed to remain in power because of firm US support and the personal devotion of Bedouins, both essential to keep the army under control.

[9] For over 40 years, and particularly after Israel occupied the West Bank, Palestinian immigration has been large. First came those driven from their lands by Israeli occupation troops in 1948, then those expelled from refugee camps in 1967. Palestinians currently make up two-thirds of Jordan's population. Demographic pressure and Hussein's ambition to replace the PLO as spokesperson for the Palestinians, were detonating factors in Black September, the 1970 Jordanian massacre of Palestinians.

[10] After the 1973 Arab-Israeli war, there was a startling change in Jordanian policy and the king re-established relations with the PLO in 1979.

[11] In 1984, Jordan reasserted its position against unilateral negotiations with Israel though closer links with Egypt began. In 1985, King Hussein and PLO leader Yasser Arafat announced a common diplomatic initiative for peace in the Middle East; this failed as Israel refused to negotiate.

[12] In July 1988, Hussein relinquished his claim on the West Bank, and made the PLO legally responsible for the territories under Israeli occupation.

[13] Most international currency came in remittances from migrant workers and the national budget depended on financial aid from Arab countries, estimated at $1 billion in 1989.

[14] A backlog of repayments, and a foreign debt that reached $6 billion in 1989, led the Government to turn to the IMF. Price increases in consumer goods caused a popular revolt in April 1989.

[15] King Hussein gave parliament power over the monarchy, he freed political prisoners and called for democratic elections.

[16] The outbreak of the Gulf crisis, when Iraq invaded Kuwait in August 1990, found the King at the height of popularity, but his position was very difficult. He was surrounded by Israel and Iraq, most of his Palestinian subjects supported the Iraqi leader, Saddam Hussein. Jordan depended on Saudi Arabia financially and on Baghdad for oil.

[17] Jordan joined the trade embargo on Iraq, while opposing the use of military force to enforce the resolutions of the Security Council. The country lost $570 million as a result of the embargo. It also received 40,000 Kurd refugees, more than a million Iraqis and some 300,000 Jordanians of Palestine origin expelled from Kuwait in reprisal for Jordan's support of Iraq.

[18] On June 9 1991, King Hussein and political representatives signed a new Constitution which legalized political parties and extended political rights to women.

[19] In the same month, Taher Al Masri was nominated Prime Minister, substituting Mudar Badram. Al Masri backed Jordanian participation in the Middle East Peace Conference and encouraged rapprochement with the US Bush administration. In November 1991, Taher Al Masri was removed from office following a vote of no confidence by the Islamic fundamentalist bloc in parliament. He was replaced by Sharif Zeid Ibn Shaker.

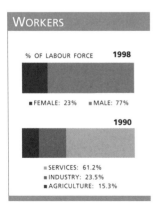

WORKERS

% OF LABOUR FORCE	**1998**

■ FEMALE: 23%   ■ MALE: 77%

1990

■ SERVICES: 61.2%
■ INDUSTRY: 23.5%
■ AGRICULTURE: 15.3%

²⁰ The growth of the Islamic fundamentalist movement was less repressed here than in other countries of the region. The Muslim Brotherhood was authorized to function as a philanthropic organization. It gained prestige in the social welfare area, running hospitals, schools and various Islamic studies centers. The political wing of the Brotherhood was the Islamic Action Front (IAF). Both groups were opposed to Arab-Israeli dialogue. In November 1992, two IAF members of parliament were freed under an amnesty granted to 1,480 political and common prisoners.

²¹ In May 1993, Abdul Salam Madjali, head of the Jordanian delegation in the peace talks with Israel, was appointed Prime Minister. In the first parliamentary elections in November, the television hostess Tuyan Faisal, became the first woman in the country to be elected to parliament.

²² The difficult relations between Islamic groups and the throne obstructed the negotiations with Israel. It was not until July 1994, in Washington, that Jordan and Israel established a schedule to bring the 46 years of war to an end, including the repatriation of nearly 60,000 Palestinian refugees in Jordan.

²³ King Hussein and Israeli Prime Minister Yitzhak Rabin signed a bilateral peace treaty on October 26 1994. Israel handed over 300 square kilometers of desert to Jordan and the frontier was established, but greater significance was given to King Hussein being given custody of the holy Islamic sites in Jerusalem. The Jordanian public was surprised by the speed of the peace agreement and the meager economic benefits for their country.

²⁴ In November 1995, King Hussein visited Jerusalem for the first time since Israel had occupied the city in 1967, to attend the funeral of Yitzhak Rabin. Sharif Zaid ibn Shaker, designated Prime Minister in January 1996, was replaced in February 1996 by Abdul Karim al-Kabariti, also foreign and defense minister.

²⁵ Despite its dependence on Iraqi oil (75,000 barrels at special prices), Jordan decided in 1996 to reduce trade with Baghdad. It dropped exports to that country by 50 per cent and it authorized the United States use of an air base in its territory. Two Iraqi diplomats were expelled from Jordan in August, accused of instigating uprisings following tension generated by the doubling of the cost of bread.

²⁶ Ahmed Yassine, the founder of Hamas (a Palestine resistance group) was freed on October 2 1997, after serving eight an a half years in prison in Israel. Yassine created the organization in 1987 and had been sentenced to life imprisonment in 1989, for his part in numerous operations. His freedom was negotiated in exchange for two Israeli Mossad (secret police) agents arrested in Amman after trying to murder a member of the Hamas political Bureau.

²⁷ Political support for King Hussein strengthened following the parliamentary elections of November 4 1997, where fewer voters turned out than in previous sessions. The so-called tribal chiefs - leaders of nomadic groups living in the desert, mostly loyal to Hussein - took 68 of the 80 seats in the lower house. The other 12 went to traditionalist candidates. The elections were boycotted by the main fundamentalist group - the Islamic Action Front - protesting against restrictions on public freedoms, Hussein's economic policy and the peace agreement with Israel. Abdul Salam Madjali was designated Prime Minister for the second time.

²⁸ In the same month, the Jordanian Government announced it would offer Christian education in the State schools to the children wanting this.

²⁹ In February 1998, under the threat of a US bombardment of Iraq, Jordan prepared to receive a wave of refugees. During the 1991 Gulf War, more than a million Iraqis had sought refuge in Jordan. 150,000 were still in the country in 1998, although only 35,000 had legal residence.

³⁰ After a long and difficult illness, King Hussein died February 7 1999, after appointing Abdullah, 37, his son from his first marriage as his heir, displacing his own brother, former Crown Prince Hassan.

³¹ As Abdullah II took over the throne, Jordan was immersed in a Palestinian-Israeli peace process that had stalled, while neighboring Iraq was being subjected to US bombing attacks. On the internal front, the country faced a serious economic crisis as political parties demanded greater liberalization from the Government. Official unemployment rates rose above 30 per cent, cash reserves were non-existent and the fiscal deficit had jumped from 2 per cent in 1997 to 6 per cent in 1998. Trade, the principal activity of this country with scarce natural resources, was in free fall from the combined effects of the embargo against Iraq and the Asian crisis.

³² Following in the tradition begun by his father, the new monarch toured his kingdom in disguise in order to have firsthand contact with places that are usually beyond the sphere of official politics. Undisguised, during the first part of his reign he made many surprise visits to hospitals, border areas and public services. ■

PROFILE

ENVIRONMENT

75 per cent of the country is a desert plateau, 600 to 900 m. in altitude. The western part of this plateau has a series of cleavages at the beginning of the great Rift Fault, which crosses the Red Sea and stretches into east Africa. In the past, these fissures widened the Jordan River valley and formed the steep depression which is now the Dead Sea. As most of the country is made up of dry steppes, farming is limited to cereals (wheat and rye) and citrus fruits. Sheep and goats are also bred. The shortage of water is the chief environmental problem. Desertification and urban expansion have caused the loss of arable land near the Jordan River.

SOCIETY

Peoples: Most of the population is Palestinian, from Israeli post-war migrations. Native Jordanians are of the 20 large Bedouin ethnic groups of which about one third are still semi-nomadic. There is a Circassian minority from the Caucasus, who now play a major role in trade and administration. **Religions:** 90 per cent of the population are Sunni Muslim but the Shi'a numbers are increasing rapidly. **Languages:** Arabic (official). English is often used. **Political Parties:** By March 1993, the Government recognized nine parties. The most important are: the Islamic Action Front, Shi'a oriented; the Jordanian Communist Party and the Socialist Arab Ba'ath Party of Jordan. **Social Organizations:** The most important labor union is the General Federation of Labor Unions of Jordan. The Union of Jordanian Women has participated in the democratization process and in the defense of the political rights of women.

THE STATE

Official Name: al-Mamlakah al-Urdunniya al-Hashimiyah. **Administrative divisions:** 8 provinces. **Capital:** Amman 2,3000,000 people (est 1995). **Other cities:** az-Zarqa 344,500 people; Irbid 208,200; as-Salt 187,000; ar-Rusayfah 115,500 (1994). **Government:** Abdullah II, King since February 1999. Abd ar-Raouf ar-Rawabdeh, Prime Minister since 1999. Legislative branch: National Assembly (bicameral), with a 40 member Senate appointed by the king, and an 80 member Chamber of Deputies elected by direct popular vote; the latter can be dissolved by the king. **National Holiday:** May 25, Independence Day (1946). **Armed Forces:** 98,650 troops (1996). **Other:** 6,000 soldiers under the authority of the Department of Public Security; 200,000 militia in the 'People's Army'; 3,000 Palestinians in the Palestinian Liberation Army, under the supervision of the Jordanian Army.

Kanaky/
New Caledonia

Kanaky

Population: 211,000 (1999)
Area: 18,580 SQ KM
Capital: Noumea
Currency: CFP franc
Language: French

New Caledonia (Kanaky) was populated by Melanesians (Kanaks) 3,000 years ago. The islands were named by Captain Cook in 1774, as the tree-covered hills reminded him of the Scottish - Caledonian - landscape.

[2] In 1853, the main island was occupied by the French Navy which organized a local guard to suppress frequent indigenous uprisings. Nickel and chrome mining attracted thousands of French settlers. The colonizers pushed out the original inhabitants, and traditional religions, crafts and social organizations were obliterated, and many landless natives were confined to 'reservations', and the system of terraced fields were trodden over by cattle. The last armed rebellion, stifled in 1917, only accelerated European land appropriation.

[3] After Algerian independence, in July 1962, colonization increased with the arrival of pieds-noirs, the former French colonists in Algeria. By 1946, New Caledonia had become a French Overseas Territory, but the resulting political autonomy did not favor the Kanaks, reduced to a minority group in relation to the *caldoches* (descendants of Europeans who had settled a century ago).

[4] The election of President Mitterrand in 1981 rekindled the hopes of the pro-independence parties. The French socialist leader was supported by most Kanaks, who saw independence as a way to end the unfair income distribution on the island. This stood at $7,000 per capita (the highest in the Pacific except for Nauru) but the vast majority of the money was concentrated in the hands of European - mostly French - business people, the *métros,* who enjoyed incredible fiscal benefits, and the *caldoches* who monopolized the most important official positions.

[5] Most of the Kanaks actively supported independence as the bulk of them lived in poverty, with high unemployment rates, and suffered educational discrimination.

[6] In the 1970s, discontent with the economic situation produced by colonial domination caused strikes, land invasions, experiments in cooperative work, and a powerful campaign to restore traditional lands to the local groups. These had been totally occupied by settlers and used mostly as cattle pastures. The rescue of *coutume* (cultural traditions) and the Kanak identity became a priority, and the proposed luxury tourist Club Méditerranée camps were firmly rejected.

[7] Kanak claims were supported by other independent Melanesian countries (Fiji, Solomon, Papua New Guinea and above all Vanuatu), and were put forward at the South Pacific Forum in August 1981. A month later, pro-independence leader Pierre Declercq, a Catholic of European origin, was murdered at his home by right-wing extremists, changing the malaise to a fully-blown political crisis.

[8] Another strong reason why France is hesitant to grant Kanaky independence is that it has the world's second largest nickel deposits, and extensive reserves of other minerals including chrome, iron, cobalt, manganese, and polymetallic nodules, discovered recently on the ocean floor within territorial waters.

[9] Furthermore, the islands' strategic position is of great military value. Its ports, facilities and bases house 6,000 troops and a small war fleet (including a nuclear submarine), considered by the military command as a 'vital point of support' for the French nuclear-testing site on Mururoa atoll.

[10] In July 1984, the French National Assembly passed special bills concerning the colony's autonomy, though it rejected amendments submitted by pro-independence parties, confirming Kanak fears that the socialist government of France had no intention of granting independence. In November, the main opposition force, the Socialist Kanak National Liberation Front (FLNKS) called for a boycott of local Territorial Assembly elections, which were sure to endorse the French government plan of postponing Kanak independence indefinitely.

[11] In December 1984, local government became fully controlled by the caldoches with no indigenous Kanak representation, therefore, the FLNKS unilaterally declared New Caledonia independent, proclaiming a Kanak state. The resulting election boycott involved 80 per cent of the Kanak population, forcing the Government to call off the election, and prepare for negotiations.

[12] On December 5 1984 - immediately after the French Government announced its willingness to talk with the FLNKS - ten Kanak political activists were brutally murdered by right-wing *caldoches.* This incident led to widespread violence which continued throughout the following year, leaving a toll, among Kanak activists, of almost 40 dead and thousands wounded. Security forces sent in by the French Government, far from controlling the situation, were in fact linked to several of the crimes and violent incidents carried out against the independence movement.

[13] In December 1986, the United Nations General Assembly proclaimed the right of the Kanak people to self-determination and independence, proposing that the FLNKS be recognized as their legitimate representative.

[14] One year later a referendum was held to determine whether or not ties with France should be maintained. Voting was open to all

PROFILE

ENVIRONMENT

The territory consists of the island of New Caledonia (16,700 sq km), the Loyalty Islands (Ouvea, Lifou, Maré and Walpole), the archipelagos of Chesterfield, Avon, Huon, Belep, and the island of Noumea. The whole group is located in southern Melanesia, between the New Hebrides (Vanuatu) to the east and Australia to the west. Of volcanic origin, the islands are mountainous with coastal reefs. The climate is rainy, tropical, and suitable for agriculture. The vegetation is dense and the subsoil is rich in nickel deposits.

SOCIETY

Peoples: Indigenous New Caledonians are of Melanesian origin (the Kanaka group), 42.5 per cent; there are French and descendants of French (known as *caldoches*), 37.1 per cent; as well as Wallisian, 8.6 per cent, Vietnamese, Indonesian, Chinese and Polynesian minorities. **Religions:** Roughly 60 per cent Catholic, 16 per cent Protestant and around 5 per cent Muslim. **Languages:** French (official), Melanesian and Polynesian languages. **Political Parties:** Rally for Caledonia within the Republic (RPCR); Kanak Liberation Party (PALIKA); Kanak Socialist National Liberation Front (FLNKS). **Social Organizations:** The Caledonian Workers Confederation (CTC); the Federation of New Caledonian Miners' Unions (FSMNC); the New Caledonian Federation of Laborers' and Employees' Unions (USOENC); and the Union of Exploited Kanak Workers (USTKE).

THE STATE

Official Name: Territoire d'Outre-Mer de la Nouvelle-Calédonie. **Administrative divisions:** Three provinces: Southern, Northern and Islands. **Capital:** Noumea 100,000 people (est. 1994). **Other Cities:** Mont-Doré 16,370 people; Dumbéa 10,052; Poindimié; Koné (1989). **Government:** Dominique Bur, High Commissioner named by Paris, since 1995. 54-member Territorial Assembly. The French President is Head of State. **Armed Forces:** French troops; 3,700 (1993).

residents of the island, even Europeans and immigrants who arrived as recently as three years and, for this reason, the FLNKS boycotted the referendum. According to the opposition and the Australian and New Zealand/ Aotearoan governments, the high abstention rate of around 41.5 per cent invalidated any claim to legitimacy for continued colonial domination.

[15] In May 1988, the FLNKS captured 22 French gendarmes and held them hostage on the island of Ouvea. Their objective was to negotiate their freedom in exchange for a post-electoral agreement with the French Government.

[16] When all attempts at negotiation failed for the Kanaks, the French attacked the island of Ouvéa, killing 19 people, most of whom were apparently executed rather than killed in combat.

[17] In June 1988, FLNKS leader, Jean-Marie Tjibaou, and Jacques Lafleur (leader of the Caledonian Popular Assembly for the Republic and strongly opposed to independence) signed Section 1 of the Matignon Accord, supported by the French prime minister Michel Rocard, in Paris. From July that year direct government over Kanaky was re-established from Paris. Section II of the Accord stipulated the adoption of preparatory measures for voting on self-determination in 1998 and the freezing of electoral roll, to prevent France increasing the number of voters by sending new colonists.

[18] The territory was divided into three regions, two with a majority of Kanak voters. One of the aims of this division was to create a Melanesian (Kanak) political and financial 'élite', taking over power from the pro-independence groups in most of the territory. Other clauses of the agreement planned greater financial support from Paris during the following ten years.

[19] In a first referendum that same year, the agreements were ratified. In May 1989, Tjibaou and another independence leader who supported the Matignon agreements were assassinated in Ouvéa.

[20] In 1991, the trade balance was affected by the fall in international prices for nickel and fish. In the two provinces controlled by the pro-independence parties, a new generation of leaders appeared, but the situation worsened for most of the Melanesian

population. The imbalance of income became pronounced amongst the Kanaks and greater access to material goods distanced many Melanesians from their community structures and traditions.

[21] In the *caldoche* areas, mainly covering the capital Nouméa, social inequalities also increased, partly due to the arrival of Melanesian farmers who built shanty towns on the outskirts of the city, but also due to the impoverishment of some *caldoches*. In a context of increasing social tension, disturbances like those which took place in March 1992 became more common.

[22] The political repercussions of these new social contradictions were reflected in the 1995 provincial elections. The Palika, one of the FLNKS groups, registered separately, criticizing the leadership of the Front representatives in the two provinces controlled by the pro-independence groups. Both political sectors obtained similar results.

[23] On the trade union front, the increasing inequalities showed themselves in the rising number of *caldoches* in the Union of Exploited Kanak Workers (USTKE). Furthermore, this union, the main

'enemy' of the employers' groups, stepped up criticism of the 'technocrats' leading the pro-independence provinces.

[24] Nickel exploitation by the pro-independence groups in the northern province gave outstanding results in the first years of their leadership, allowing them to form an association with the Canadian Falconbridge company. However, the pro-independence groups' attempts to establish a processing plant with the Canadian company were complicated by similar plans in the French State mining company, SLN-Eramet. FLNKS sympathizers protested, blocking access to the French-controlled installations.

[25] Kanaky independence negotiations changed course in April 1998. The FLNKS and Paris established the basis for a general agreement, known as the Noumea Accord. The coexistence of two different systems - one that follows Kanak traditions and the other imposed by France - proved to be the most difficult issue to resolve. The Kanaks wanted respect for their culture and their traditional civil organization. The Nouméa Accord allowed for the transference of powers that would assure a 'nearly sovereign' territory within 15 to 20 years. The Kanaks and the Caldoches agreed to share a common 'citizenship', while France

acknowledged the 'shadows' remaining from the colonial period.

[26] In November, a referendum was held to ratify the Noumea agreements. The Yes-vote was victorious with 69.14 per cent of the vote. In December, the text of the law defined the application of the Noumea Accord. On December 23, the National Assembly voted on the new country's legal foundations, which covered the implementation of new institutions as well as a 'progressive' transfer of state powers. ■

Melanesians: survivors in the Pacific

The peoples of Melanesian origin (from the Greek: 'melas' meaning black and 'nesia', islands) are clustered in a group of South Pacific islands - New Guinea, Kanaky (New Caledonia), Vanuatu, Solomon, Fiji, Santa Cruz, in other smaller islands and in the Bismarck and Louisiade archipelagos. They are an anthropologically unique population. Due to the dark colour of their skin and their curled hair, Melanesians were in the past included in the 'Negroid' group. However, recent studies link them to the Papuans and even to the aboriginal communities living in Australia.

[2] It is also now recognized that

the peoples referred to as Melanesian actually include two distinct communities and cultures.

[3] The first Melanesians arrived, probably from South Asia, some 40,000 years ago. About 9,000 years ago, these communities started growing crops such as sugarcane.

[4] Later they also specialized in trade and shipbuilding, as well as in fishing. They travelled in small groups, living at certain sites depending on the time cycle of crops.

[5] Melanesians speak several languages, including some 400 dialects. The main one, used in Fiji, is spoken by some 334,000 people and used in press and official publications. Other dialects are Motu, Roviana,

Bambatana, Tolai and Yabem.

[6] Christianity gradually replaced traditional religions, although some communities still practice rites of cosmic initiation or sorcery.

[7] Nowadays, Western culture has reached even the remotest villages, where it is possible to see certain types of entrepreneurial and capitalist organization, as well as dependence on imported products. It is in marginal areas where traditional culture survives that resistance to the prevailing culture is greatest. ■

Kazakhstan

Kazajstan

Population: 16,269,000 (1999)
Area: 2,717,299 SQ KM
Capital: Almaty and Astana
Currency: Tengue
Language: Kazakh

In the Bronze Age (about 2000 BC), the territory of Kazakhstan was inhabited by tribes who lived by farming and raising livestock. Around 500 BC, an alliance was formed among the Saka peoples and in the 3rd century BC, the Usune and Kangli tribes - who lived near the Uighur, Chechen and Alan - subdued the other tribes in the area. The region was subsequently occupied by Attila's Huns, until they were expelled by the Turks.

2   In the mid-4th century, the Turkish *Kaganate* (Khanate or kingdom) was formed and later divided into Eastern and Western parts. In the 8th century two states emerged: a Turkish and a Karluk *Kaganate*. The Turkish conquerors built mosques and tried to impose Islam upon the local population. Over the following 300 years scholarship flourished in the area.

3   Between the 9th and 12th centuries, the region was occupied by the Oghuz, Kimak, Kipchak and Karajanid tribes. The Kipchaks never achieved political unity and remained outside the realm of Islamic influence, which was concentrated in the cities along the Caspian Sea. Until the 13th century, successive waves of Seleucid, Kidan and Tatar invasions swept across the great steppes. Kipchak chiefs and Muscovite princes joined together to resist foreign domination, but did not achieve independence until the fall of the Mongols.

4   Most of these peoples were nomads but gradually, settled groups of farmers and artisans were organized, and cities like Otrar, Suyab, Balasagun, Yanguikent, Sauran and Kulan arose. The Silk Road, uniting Byzantium, Iran and China, passed through Kazakhstan. Trade relations developed between the nomads of the steppes and the inhabitants of the oases, which extended as far as Western Europe, Asia Minor and the Far East.

5   By the late 15th century, the Khanate of Kazakh had been formed, disintegrating into three loosely allied but like-minded *yuzos* (hordes). By the 16th century, an ethnic identity had been forged among the Kazakhs. The khans of the Kazakh *yuzos* passed on their power to their heirs, who thought of themselves as descendants of Juchi, the eldest son of Genghis Khan. Below them were the

sultans, with administrative and judicial power, who governed through the *biy* and the local chieftains.

6   In the 17th century, the Khanate of Dzhungar carried out successive raids in the Kazakh region, sometimes looting and other times remaining and occupying the area. Russian colonial expansion from the north began in the 18th century. The Russians built a line of forts and then began working their way southward, creating a line of defense against the Dzhungars. The two smaller hordes or *yuzos* fell under Russian protection eliminating their autonomy in the 1820s because of the frequent rebellions. With the defeat of the Great Horde, annexation of Kazakhstan to the Empire was completed.

7   Russia installed its government institutions, collected taxes, established areas closed to the Kazakhs and built new cities, declaring the entire territory property of the State. As of 1868, there were six provinces under the control of governors general; the sultans and the *biy* became mere state officials. The conquest of Kazakhstan was a long process of wars against local tribes. The Cossack regiments were the vanguard of the Russian army and they overcame the khans of Khiva, Boukhara and Kokand, one by one, defeating the last of these in 1880.

8   The Kazakhs were registered in the censuses as citizens of the State of Russia and were incorporated into the Russian army's foreign

expeditions. Kazakhstan became a place to which Russian deportees were sent, including the Decembrists (aristocrats who had conspired against Czar Nikolai I in 1825), Polish and Ukrainian revolutionaries (including the Ukrainian hero, Taras Shevchenko) and the members of the St Petersburg 'Petrashevski circle', which included the writer Feodor Dostoyevsky.

9   In the late 19th century and early 20th century, Russia built huge railroads (the Trans-Caspian, the Trans-Aralian and the Trans-Siberian), which crossed the region, uniting it with distant urban centers and facilitating the exploitation of Kazakhstan's fabulous mineral wealth. A third of Russia's coal reserves, half its copper, lead and zinc reserves; strategic metals like tungsten and molybdenum; iron, and oil were found in Kazakhstan. Agriculture remained stagnant and attempts to resettle farmers, after the abolition of feudal serfdom in Russia, met with limited success, although there was some development of cotton, wool and traditional Kazakh leather production.

10   At the beginning of the 20th century, a small nationalist movement emerged in Kazakhstan, and after the Russian Revolution of 1905 the Kazakhs had their own representatives to the first and second *Duma* (parliament) convened by the Czar. In 1916, when the czarist regime ordered the mobilization of all men between the age of 19 and 43 for

auxiliary military service, the Kazakhs rebelled, led by Abdulghaffar and Amangeldy Imanov. The revolt was brutally crushed, but in November 1917, after the triumph of the Soviet revolution in Petrograd, the Kazakh nationalists demanded total autonomy for their country. In the early decades of this century, Kazakhstan received massive waves of Ukrainian, Belorusian, German, Bulgarian, Polish, Jewish and Tatar immigrants. A nationalist government was installed in Alma Ata (now Almaty) in 1918, but the country soon became a battleground.

11   Fighting between the Red Army and the White Russians - the latter defending the overthrown regime - lasted until 1920, when the counter-revolution was defeated. The Autonomous Soviet Socialist Republic (ASSR) of Kirghiz was formed, as a part of the Russian Federation; it later became known as the ASSR of Kazakhstan. In 1925, the revision of the borders in Soviet central Asia was completed, and all Kazakh lands were unified. In 1936, Kazakhstan became one of the 15 republics of the USSR and the following year, the local Communist Party was founded.

12   In addition to developing its industrial potential, the Soviet regime increased the amount of land under cultivation. Previously considered not very fertile (in 1913, only 4.2 million hectares were under cultivation), Kazakhstan increased the number of hectares of tilled land to 35.3 million, 15 per cent of all agricultural land in the USSR. Production included wheat, tobacco, mustard, fruit and cattle. Bringing virgin territory under cultivation was an achievement associated with Leonid Brezhnev, during his period as head of the Communist Party of Kazakhstan. Brezhnev replaced Nikita Khrushchev in 1964 as head of the Soviet Party until his death in 1982. Although he proclaimed an era of 'developed socialism', the country's economic and political problems actually worsened during his administration.

13   Until 1985, the person who wielded the power in Kazakhstan was Dinmujamed Kunaev, a member of the Politburo of the Soviet Communist Party Central Committee. In 1989, the forced resignation of Kunaev triggered

student disturbances; the army resorted to violence in dealing with the demonstrators.

[14] After the transformations set in motion in the USSR by President Mikhail Gorbachev, the republic of Kazakhstan declared independence. During this period two social movements arose - Birlik and Zheltoksan - as well as the anti-nuclear movement Semipalatinsk-Nevada. The main test-sites for Soviet nuclear weapons were situated in Kazakhstan, as is the Baykonur cosmodrome for launching Soviet space vehicles. After the failed coup against the Soviet President in August 1991, Nursultan Nazarbayev resigned as head of the Soviet Communist Party, of which he had been a member, in his capacity as president of a Soviet republic.

[15] In September, Kazakhstan presented a seven-point plan for the creation of a new union treaty, which was approved by Gorbachev and ten republics. On December 1 1991, Nazarbayev was elected the first president of an independent Kazakhstan. The Communist Party became the Socialist Party of Kazakhstan. On December 21, in Almaty (Kazak form of Alma Ata), 11 republics signed an agreement which formally dissolved the USSR and created the new Commonwealth of Independent States, whose members applied separately for admission to the UN.

President Nazarbayev's foreign policy envisaged a privileged alliance with Russia and the Islamic republics of the region, as well as closer links with the West.

[16] In 1992, Nazarbayev let the Russian President Boris Yeltsin know that he would not allow the nuclear missiles - installed when Kazakhstan was still part of the USSR - to remain under the exclusive control of Moscow. In 1993, Almaty promised to dismantle these missiles in return for financial aid from the United States.

[17] This same year several political entities were created, like the Socialist Party, the Peoples Congress Party and the ruling Union of National Unity. Nazarbayev also undertook to bring in swiftly a series of privatizations and to stimulate foreign investment.

[18] In March 1994 the first multiparty legislative elections were held, and they were won by Nazarbayev's party. Shortly after the victory, a series of scandals over alleged corruption forced Prime Minister Sergey Tereschenko to resign. He was replaced by Akezhan Kazhegeldin, who immediately announced an acceleration of the economic liberalization process. The Government resolved to transfer the national capital from Almaty to Aqmola over a period of several years.

[19] In April, Kazhegeldin launched a vast privatization plan, including

3,500 state enterprises, that is, 70 per cent of the public companies. The rapid introduction of the market economy and the natural riches of the country attracted a large number of foreign investors in 1995, but the economic liberalization also led to a fall in the standard of living for many Kazakhs.

[20] The Constitutional Court annulled the elections of the previous year and the President said he would govern by decree until new elections were held. Nazarbayev, concerned over widespread discontent and the risk of not being re-elected in elections with various candidates, took advantage of the political crisis suggesting his term be extended by referendum until the year 2000. The official results of this poll, carried out in April, gave the President almost unanimous support.

[21] In March 1996, a customs union was created between Kazakhstan, Kyrgyzstan, Belarus and the Russian Federation, aiming to form a common market for goods, capital and workers. The agreement also included possible integration of transport, energy and data systems.

[22] In April 1997, Kazakhstan, along with Kyrgyzstan and Tajikistan, signed an agreement to demilitarize the frontier and reduce the number of troops. This step followed the agreement between Russia and China, as part of a Russian policy of rapprochement with its Asian neighbors thought up in Gorbachev's time. In October, the Government appointed Nurlan Balgimbayev Prime Minister, replacing Kazhegeldin.

[23] Nazarbayev won the presidential elections in January 1999 with 78 per cent of the vote, while his closest rival, Serkbolsyn Abdildin, a communist party leader, won just 13 per cent of the vote. Despite objections about the lack of transparency, 80 per cent of eligible voters took part in the elections.

[24] A scandal in March about exporting MIG aircraft in poor condition led to the resignations of Defense Minister Mukhtar Altynbayev and president of the National Security Committee, Nurtai Abykayev.

[25] Senate elections were held in September, and the *Mazhilis* (Lower House) elections were in October, with 11 parties registering to participate, the first time such voting would took place on a party basis. Of the seats in the *Mazhilis*, only 10 were elected with party support, while the remaining 67 involved independent candidates.

[26] Because he had received a vote of censure from Parliament when he had tried to push through a budget with deep cuts, Prime Minister Nurlan Balgimbayev resigned on October 1. Former Foreign minister Kasymzhomart Tokayev was appointed the new Prime Minister. ■

PROFILE

ENVIRONMENT

Kazakhstan is bordered to the southeast by China; to the south by Kyrgyzstan; and to the north by the Russian Federation. In the western part of the country lie the Caspian and Turan plains; in the center, the Kazakh plateau; and in the eastern and southeastern regions, the Altai, Tarbagatay, Dzhungarian Alatau and Tien Shan mountains. It has a continental climate, with average January temperatures of 18 degrees below zero in the north, and 3 below zero in the south. In July, the temperature varies from 19 degrees in the north, to 28 degrees in the south. Important rivers include the Ural, Irtysh, Syr Dar'ya, Chu and Ili. There is also Lake Balkhash and the Caspian and Aral Seas. The vegetation is characteristic of the steppes, but vast areas have come under cultivation (wheat, tobacco, etc) or are used for cattle-raising. The region's abundant mineral wealth includes coal, copper, semi-precious stones and gold.

SOCIETY

Peoples: Kazakhs, 46.5 per cent, Russians, 35 per cent, Ukrainians, 5 per cent, Uzbeks 2 per cent, Tatars 2 per cent, **Religions:** Muslim and Christian Orthodox. **Languages:** Kazakh (official), Russian, German, Ugric, Korean, Tatar. **Political Parties:** Union of National Unity, President Nazarbayev's party, moderate; Socialist Party (which replaced the Communist Party); People's Congress; Republican Party, a nationalist party.
Social Organizations: Independent labor unions are in the process of being formed. Birlik Movement, Zheltokso and Semipalatinsk-Nevada, an anti-nuclear movement.

THE STATE

Official Name: Respublika Kazajstan. **Administrative divisions:** 19 regions and 2 cities. **Capitals:** Almaty 1,172,400 people (1995) and Astana 277,000 people.**Other cities:** Karaganda 573,700 people; Semipalatinsk 320,000; Pavlodar 340,700; Kokchetav 127,000 (1995). **Government:** Nursultan Nazarbayev, President since December 1991, confirmed in April, 1995. Kasymzhomart Tokayev, Prime Minister since October 1999. Unicameral legislative power, with 360 members. **National Holiday:** December 16, Independence (1991). **Armed Forces:** 2 regiments of Russian Air Defence.

Kenya

Kenya

Population: 29,549,000 (1999)
Area: 580,370 SQ KM
Capital: Nairobi
Currency: Shilling
Language: English and Swahili

The prosperous city of Malindi was founded in the 10th century on the coast of what is now Kenya. It was the center of a rich African Arab culture (the Zandj Culture), which was destroyed by a Portuguese armed occupation in the 16th century. When they were forced to withdraw in 1698, the Portuguese left behind only a few abandoned forts and economic ruin, ideal conditions for the slave and ivory trades managed by Shirazi merchants from Zanzibar.

2   The inland peoples were mainly Bantu with Nilotic and Somalian groups also present. They did not develop material cultures comparable to those of the coast, nor did they evolve into organized states. It was only in the 19th century that the Masai, Nilotic shepherds, succeeded in establishing a certain degree of authority over other groups in the region. A few decades later when a bovine plague annihilated almost all of their herds and deprived them of their economic mainstay, their power base collapsed.

3   At the end of the 19th century, the Berlin Conference and subsequent German-British agreements delimited spheres of European influence in East Africa. Zanzibar, Kenya and Uganda were assigned to the English who had already settled in Uganda, and who decided to build a railway line from this colony to the coast.

4   White settlers occupied the lands which 'became available' along the railway line after half the local population died in an epidemic of smallpox brought in with Indian laborers. As late as 1948, 4,200 sq km of the approximately 5,000 sq km of fertile land were held between 5,000 European planters, while one

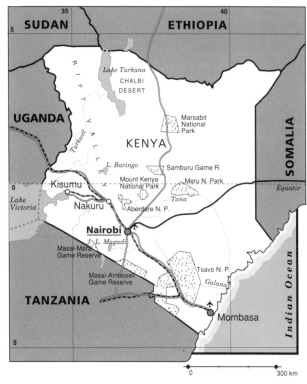

million Kikuyu occupied fewer than 1,000 sq km. There was no indemnity or compensation for this theft.

5   In 1944, the Kenya African Union (KAU) was created to defend Kikuyu interests. Under the leadership of Jomo Kenyatta, KAU organized strikes, farmers' rallies and mass demonstrations.

6   At almost the same time the Mau-Mau, a political and religious group organized as a secret society, launched its first offensive. The Mau-Mau program was both political and cultural. They demanded self-government, restitution of lands, and wage

parity, while rejecting Christianity and other European influences in favor of traditional customs and beliefs.

7   In 1952, in response to increased Mau-Mau attacks on settlers' lives and property, the colonial administration declared a state of emergency, arrested nationalist leaders (Kenyatta among them), dissolved political parties and imprisoned thousands of Kikuyu in concentration camps.

8   After years of bitter repression and indiscriminate killing by colonial governments, KAU was legalized in 1960 as the Kenya African National Union (KANU).

9   KANU found electoral support among leading urban and ethnic communities and, with British encouragement, was able to defeat tribal-based political movements. In 1961, Kenya was freed and in 1962 the Legislative Council was elected. After the May 1963 elections Kenya was granted autonomy. It achieved independence within the Commonwealth on December 12 1963. Kenyatta became Prime Minister, and when his country achieved full independence on December 12 1964, he was elected first president.

10   However, Jomo Kenyatta, a nom de guerre meaning 'Kenya's flaming spear', soon forgot his commitment to the nation as a whole, and began to favor his own ethnic group, the Kikuyu. His government encouraged private enterprise and transnational concerns. Farmers who had won back their lands lost them again under the burden of debt.

11   A black bourgeoisie, largely Kenyatta's family and friends, took over where the former colonists had left off. KANU, once a model for other African parties in the struggle against foreign domination, succumbed to neo-colonialism. It even went so far as to admit British military forces to the port of Mombasa and allowed its own military installations to be used for the notorious Israeli raid on Entebbe, Uganda.

12   This led to a breach of relations between Kenya and Uganda, and tension with Tanzania grew over differences in economic policies. The three countries were unable to consolidate 1967 plans for an East African Economic Community, and this ambitious integration project was finally dropped in 1977.

13   Kenyatta died at the age of 85 in September 1978. He was succeeded by his vice-president, Daniel Arap Moi, a member of the smaller Kalenjin ethnic group.

14   This might have soothed ethnic conflict in Kenya, but penetration by transnationals produced structural imbalances, worsening an already difficult economic situation and aggravating social tensions. Even before Kenyatta's death there was growing distrust between the urban consumer bourgeoisie and the larger rural population. The country people's whole way of life was being steadily degraded, as the market for cash crops undermined traditional communal self-sufficiency.

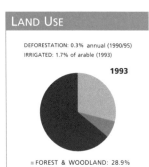

WORKERS

% OF LABOUR FORCE   **1998**

■ FEMALE: 46%   ■ MALE: 54%

1990

■ SERVICES: 13.2%
■ INDUSTRY: 7.3%
■ AGRICULTURE: 79.5%

LAND USE

DEFORESTATION: 0.3% annual (1990/95)
IRRIGATED: 1.7% of arable (1993)

1993

■ FOREST & WOODLAND: 28.9%
■ ARABLE: 6.9%
■ OTHER: 64.2%

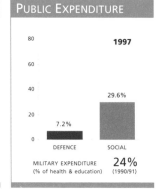

PUBLIC EXPENDITURE

1997

80

60

40

20

0

7.2%
DEFENCE

29.6%
SOCIAL

MILITARY EXPENDITURE   **24%**
(% of health & education)   (1990/91)

MATERNAL MORTALITY
1990-98
Per 100,000
live births
590

LITERACY
1995
77%

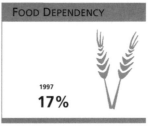

FOOD DEPENDENCY
1997
17%

EXTERNAL DEBT
1998
PER CAPITA
US$ 242

15 Arap Moi was interim president from September 1978 until the general election of November. KANU was the only party authorized to run candidates, and Moi was confirmed as President.

16 In early 1979, President Moi declared an amnesty for political prisoners and launched a campaign against corruption. The first measures of the new administration revealed a technocratic approach which deflated hopes of radical change. One of the outstanding technocrats was Charles Njonjo, appointed minister of home affairs in June 1980.

17 Njonjo played a key role in dissolving the ethnic-based organizations that arose in the early 1970s. The largest of these, GEMA (the Gikuyo, Embu and Meru Association), led by a millionaire, became a powerful pressure group for tribal leaders who were growing rich from business with British and US companies.

18 GEMA opposed Moi's designation, and after the death of Jomo Kenyatta had been indirectly involved in a conspiracy to assassinate all top government officials.

19 Droughts and crop changes led to a drop in the production of corn and other basic consumer goods. Credits supplied by multinational companies encouraged Kenyan farmers to grow flowers and to plant sugarcane, coffee and tea for export under the control of large North American and British firms. As a result, the government had to import huge quantities of corn and wheat from the US and South Africa.

20 These difficulties led President Moi to seek reconciliation with old political rivals who had been excluded from public life. It was a maneuver devised to neutralize potential opposition at a moment of great instability. Former vice-president Oginga Odinga, a veteran nationalist politician who had broken with Kenyatta in 1971 in disagreement with KANU's conciliatory policy, was one of the major beneficiaries of this relaxation of the regime. Odinga had lost his political rights after founding a dissident party, the Kenya Popular Union (KAPU). After 11 years of ostracism, he returned to parliament at the end of 1981.

21 Despite all this reconciliation, the crisis erupted into violence in August 1982, in a military conspiracy that unleashed widespread rioting and looting of shops and public buildings in Nairobi. The coup attempt had been staged by members of the air force, leading to the disbanding of all airforce units after the army had suppressed the rebellion.

22 Repression also affected the university, where dozens of professors and students were detained. Oginga Odinga was placed under house arrest and the university was closed down indefinitely. The frustrated coup precipitated profound changes in Kenyan politics and sowed distrust among the different political elements in KANU.

23 In May 1983, President Moi denounced a conspiracy involving minister Charles Njonjo, supported by Israel and South Africa. In the midst of the confusion, President Moi decided to call general elections, in which his followers won a landslide victory, while Njonjo and his supporters were overwhelmingly defeated.

24 Moi's administration reopened the border with Tanzania in November 1983, after a summit meeting in Arusha with Tanzania's Julius Nyerere and Uganda's Milton Obote. The meeting was a point of departure for gradually renewing economic co-operation between Kenya, Tanzania and Uganda after the failure of the East African Economic Community in 1977.

25 President Arap Moi had extended the executive's jurisdiction to the detriment of the parliament. He made it compulsory for civil servants to join KANU, and replaced secret voting in internal party elections with a public vote making intimidation easier. The moderate women's opposition group, Mandeleo Ya Wanawake, was taken over by the Government in 1986.

26 Reports backed by Amnesty International and other groups implicated the government in torture and the murder of opposition members, especially the 'subversive' Mwakenya group.

27 During October and November 1987, Muslim demonstrations in Mombasa served to justify a further wave of repression in which Nairobi University was once again closed. In December, a series of frontier skirmishes with Uganda, plus the expulsion of Libyan diplomats accused of encouraging civil disorder, seemed to herald new disturbances.

28 Despite harsh 'restructuring' policies imposed by the IMF and World Bank, elections in March 1988 consolidated the position of Moi's followers within both KANU and the Government. By August, Moi had completed his authoritarian reorganization by placing the judiciary directly under his command. He prolonged the period for which detainees may be held without notifying a judge from 24 hours to 14 days.

29 In the years that followed, cases of corruption and human rights violations became more widespread. In April 1989 Vice-President Josephat Karanja lost the confidence of parliament, accused of furthering his interests and those of his own tribe. After he resigned, Karanja was expelled from KANU.

30 Robert Ouko, the Foreign Affairs minister and a harsh critic of corruption in the cabinet was murdered in February 1990. An inquest carried out by Scotland Yard disclosed that the culprits were close advisers of the President. This triggered a new wave of popular anti-government protests.

31 Through the active preaching of the Catholic and Protestant churches, democratization demands spread throughout the country. The suspicious circumstances surrounding the death of a Protestant minister involved in this

PROFILE

ENVIRONMENT

Kenya is located on the east coast of central Africa. There are four main regions, from east to west: the coastal plains with regular rainfall and tropical vegetation; a sparsely populated inland strip with little rainfall which extends towards the north and northwest; a mountainous zone linked to the eastern end of the Rift valley, with a climate tempered by altitude, and volcanic soil fit for agriculture (most of the population and the main economic activities are concentrated here); and the west which is covered by an arid plateau, part of which benefits from the moderating influence of Lake Victoria. The principal environmental problems are soil exhaustion, erosion and desertification; deforestation; pollution of drinking water supplies, especially near such large cities as Nairobi and Mombasa.

SOCIETY

Peoples: Kenyans are descended from the main African ethnic groups: Bantu, Nilo-Hamitic, Sudanese and Cushitic. Numerically and culturally, the most significant groups are the Kikuyu, the Luyia and the Luo. Others include the Kamba, Meru, Gusii and Embu. There are Indian and Arab minorities. **Religions:** 73 per cent of the population are Christian, 6 per cent are Muslim and 20 per cent practice traditional religions.

Languages: English and Swahili are the official ones. The latter is the national language. Kikuyu and Kamba are also spoken.

Political Parties: Kenya African National Union (KANU) founded in 1943 by Jomo Kenyatta. A Constitutional reform allowed the formation of new parties in 1991. Forum for the Restoration of Democracy (FORD), split into two branches in 1992 (FORD-Asili and FORD-Kenya); Democratic Party (DP), Kenya Social Congress (KSC); Kenya National Congress (KNC). **Social Organizations:** Central Organization of Trade Unions (COTU), founded by the Government in 1965.

THE STATE

Official Name: Jamhuri ya Kenya. **Capital:** Nairobi 2,079,000 people (1995). **Other cities:** Mombasa 465,000 people; Kisumu 185,100; Nakuru 162,800; Machakos 92,300 (1989). **Government:** Daniel Arap Moi, President since August 1978, re-elected in 1993 and 1997. Legislature: National Assembly (single-chamber), with 202 members, elected every five years. **National Holiday:** December 12, Independence Day (1963). **Armed Forces:** 24,200 troops. **Other:** 5,000.

democratization movement renewed street protests. The registration of new political parties was also prohibited.

[32] Kenya's diplomatic isolation became more marked during the 1980s, but it decreased after the Persian Gulf war. Kenya's strict alignment with the interests of the US-led coalition enabled the country to receive economic aid from Britain, and military support from Washington.

[33] The permanent deterioration in the human rights situation, however, led to the severing of diplomatic relations with Norway in 1991, and relations with Sudan, Ethiopia, and Uganda also became tense. The governments of Kenya and Sudan accused each other of protecting rebel groups, hostile to Nairobi and Khartoum, operating in the neighboring country. Political differences between Uganda and Kenya have caused permanent conflict since 1986.

[34] The economy has been incapable of achieving growth rates like those of the past decade. According to official estimates, inflation in 1990 amounted to 15 per cent, but all independent sources indicate it was very near to 30 per cent. As a result of the Gulf war oil import expenditure was a great deal higher than expected, and this had a negative effect on the trade balance.

[35] Tourism has dropped sharply in the last few years, and the servicing of the foreign debt accounted for 30 per cent of 1990 exports. Like other countries in the region, Kenya has implemented cuts in public expenditure, which include privatizing state-run companies and not filling vacancies in the public sector. Kenya's economy is heavily dependent on foreign aid.

[36] The KANU called the party Council to discuss the introduction of democratic reforms, including authorization for several national opposition parties. Lobbying groups such as the Forum for the Restoration of Democracy (FORD), led by Oginga Odinga, and the Moral Alliance for Peace (MAP), became fully-fledged parties.

[37] In order to keep the situation under control, the Government continued to imprison opposition leaders. Early in 1992, lawyer James Orengo and environmentalist Wangari Maathai were arrested and accused of 'spreading malicious rumours' that President Moi planned to interrupt the democratization process started in 1991.

[38] In February, 1992, the Democratic Party (PD) was created. It was a new opposition group which proposed the creation of a multiparty democratic system. Meanwhile, women's groups demanded greater participation in politics; they constituted 53 per cent of the electoral roll and 80 per cent of the work force in agriculture, the country's main production sector. That same month a march organized by FORD rallied over 100,000 people in Nairobi demanding the end of repression and press censorship, and a definite date for elections. This was the first authorized anti-government march in the country's 22 years of independent life.

[39] Several Government ministers had resigned in January to form new political parties, and in March, a general strike called by wives of political prisoners was crushed by the government. Further violence occurred in April, when clashes broke out between various tribes in the western part of the country. The Government banned all political meetings and began censoring the press. Nevertheless, the general strike called by the opposition constituted a setback for President Arap Moi.

[40] General elections were held in December. President Arap Moi was re-elected amidst accusations of fraud. His party obtained 95 seats with 36 per cent of the vote, while the opposition had only 88 seats with 60 per cent of the returns.

[41] In February 1993, the IMF considered Kenya's plan to privatize and liberalize foreign trade was insufficient. In April, Sheik Khaled Balala from the opposition's Islamic Party was arrested on charges for the murder of three policemen. In November, international finance organizations lifted the boycott imposed in February, since the government promised to fight against corruption and remove several restrictions on free trade.

[42] Liberalization continued in 1994: Nairobi eliminated exchange controls to attract private investors from Kenya and abroad. An extended drought hit several provinces especially in the eastern side of the country and in the Rift Valley which led the Government to grant urgent assistance to the affected regions. The forced relocation of some 2,000 Kikuyu farmers from the Rift Valley caused serious riots and confrontation with police.

[43] In December, financial organizations and Kenya's creditor countries expressed their satisfaction with the country's economic policy and the introduction of a multiparty system by Nairobi. In 1995, the Government announced the partial privatization of the national airline and other major state companies. However, despite some isolated progress in the field, organizations such as Amnesty International continued to accuse Arap Moi of human rights violations.

[44] In March 1996 the World Bank approved a $115 million loan for road reconstruction. A month later, the IMF paid a $214 million loan, blocked since 1994. Kenya signed an economic cooperation agreement with China and Iran offered its assistance in energy, industry and crops.

[45] Thousands of people were displaced in 1997 due to floods in the northeast. Social and political tension grew significantly throughout the year. In February, thousands of students protested for the murder of a student leader. In late October, an opposition candidate was killed in a shootout between the police and criminals. The Government and part of the opposition initiated talks in Nairobi about the elections.

[46] In November, President Daniel Arap Moi dissolved Parliament and on December 29 was re-elected by 40.1 per cent of the vote. His ruling party obtained 109 of the 202 seats at the National Assembly. In January 1998, the controversial President appointed a new cabinet.

[47] Environmental groups and fishing authorities warned there would be severe environmental damage in the Lake Victoria region - one of the largest fishing reserves in the world - if the Kenyan Government and its Ugandan and Tanzanian colleagues did not find a way to stop the poisoning of fish and the pollution of water sources. Kenyan, as well as Ugandan and Tanzanian fishers, use chemicals to poison the fish, making them easier to catch.

[48] Arap Moi announced his intention to abolish female genital mutilation, a declaration that only led to the intensification of the ritual practice: 'circumcisions' were performed at night and many girls were mutilated at an earlier age than usual. As a countermeasure, a non-governmental organization promoted an alternative rite, known as Ntanira na Mugambo - or 'circumcision through words' - which began to replace the traditional ritual practiced in half of the country's rural districts.

[49] Following the dictates of the March 2000 African summit in Nairobi on the proliferation of firearms, Moi announced a one-month amnesty for those who turned in illegal weapons to the authorities.

[50] That month, news agencies reported that starvation was killing dozens of people in the Wajir area and accused the Government of ignoring the situation. The Government denied that death from starvation was occurring and accused the agencies of 'politicizing the drought', then in its second year. ∎

STATISTICS

DEMOGRAPHY

Population: 29,549,000 (1999)
Annual growth: 3.4 % (1975/97)
Estimates for year 2015 (million): 37.6 (1999)
Annual growth to year 2015: 1.6 % (1997/2015)
Urban population: 30.4 % (1997)
Urban Growth: 7.0 % (1980/95)
Children per woman: 4.4 (1998)

HEALTH

Life expectancy at birth: 52 years (1998)
male: 51 years (1998)
female: 53 years (1998)
Maternal mortality: 590 per 100,000 live births (1990-98)
Infant mortality: 75 per 1,000 (1998)
Under-5 child mortality: 117 per 1,000 (1998)
Daily calorie supply: 1,971 per capita (1996)
15 doctors per 100,000 people (1993)
Safe water: 44 % (1990/98)

EDUCATION

Literacy: 77 % (1995)
male: 86 % (1995)
female: 69 % (1995)
School enrolment:
Primary total: 85 % (1990/96)
male: 85 % (1990/97)
female: 85 % (1990/97)
Secondary:
male: 26 % (1990/96)
female: 22 % (1990/96)
Tertiary: 2 % (1996)
Primary school teachers: one for every 30 (1995)

COMMUNICATIONS

9 newspapers (1996), 104 radios (1997), 19 TV sets (1996) and 8 main telephone lines (1996) per 1,000 people

ECONOMY

Per capita, GNP: $ 350 (1998)
Annual growth, GNP: 2.7 % (1998)
Annual inflation: 15.8 % (1990/98)
Consumer price index: 129.0 (1998)
Currency: 60.4 shillings = $ 1 (1998)
Cereal imports: 931,998 metric tons (1998)
Food import dependency: 17 % (1997)
Fertilizer use: 333 kg per ha (1997)
Exports: $ 2,851 million (1998)
Imports: $ 3,742 million (1998)
External debt: $ 7,010 million (1998); $ 242 per capita (1998)
Debt service: 18.8 % of exports (1998)
Development aid received: $ 457 million (1997); $ 18.8 per capita (1997); 4.60 % of GNP (1997)

ENERGY

Consumption: 494.0 Kgs of Oil equivalent per capita yearly (1997); 18.0 % imported (1997)

HDI (rank/value): 136/0.519 (1997)

Kiribati

Kiribati

Population: 77,000 (1999)
Area: 730 SQ KM
Capital: Bairiki on the island of Tarawa
Currency: Australian dollar
Language: Gilbertese and English

The islands that make up the Republic of Kiribati (formerly known as Gilbert Islands) are inhabited by Micronesian people. In 1764 these islands were visited by and named after British explorer Gilbert.

[2] Missionaries arrived in 1857, and three years later, trade in palm oil and copra began. In 1892 the islands became a British protectorate. In 1915 the islands were annexed to the neighboring Ellice archipelago (now Tuvalu), to form the colony of the Gilbert and Ellice Islands.

[3] In 1916 Banaba Island became part of the colony. At that time, there were large deposits of guano on the island which were exploited by the British Phosphate Commission from 1920, and exported to Australia and New Zealand. The Banabans were evacuated during World War II and resettled on the island of Rabi, 2,600 km from Fiji. They were unable to return to their island because the open-cast mining of guano had made the island uninhabitable.

[4] After discussing different alternatives in 1981 the Banabans obtained an indemnity of £19 million from the British Government. In 1957 Britain, as part of its nuclear armament program, detonated three hydrogen bombs near Christmas Island.

[5] The Polynesian population of the Ellice Islands obtained

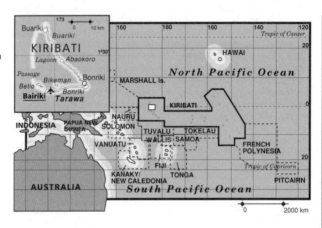

administrative separation in 1975, arguing that the ethnic, historical and cultural differences between them and the Melanesian majority of the Gilbert Islands made secession necessary. Under the name of the Territory of Tuvalu these islands gained independence in 1978.

[6] The inhabitants of the Gilbert Islands proclaimed independence on July 12 1979 adopting the name: Republic of Kiribati (the equivalent of 'Gilbert' in Gilbertan).

[7] As the soil is not suitable for large-scale cultivation, copra and fish are the main exports. Copra production is in the hands of small landowners, while the exportation of the product is handled exclusively by the national trading company. Problems facing copra production include abrupt variations in price.

Fishing is carried out primarily under agreements with Japanese, US, Korean and Taiwanese fishing fleets.

[8] Kiribati also hopes to exploit deep-sea mineral deposits. The manganese discovered is considered the highest-grade deposit of its kind in the world.

[9] In 1986 Kiribati began negotiations with the IMF and was recognized by the UN as one of the world's poorest countries, a fact which gives it access to certain credit and trade advantages.

[10] A 1989 UN report on global warming and the possible rise in sea level said that Kiribati could disappear under the rising sea.

[11] In the 1991 elections, Teatao Teannaki won with 46 per cent of the vote, producing the first change in president since independence.

[12] In a regional meeting attended by representatives of the Asian-Pacific nations in 1993, the Bairiki delegate asked for detailed studies of global warming. Australia promised aid to create a natural disasters prevention centre in Kiribati.

[13] In May 1994, the Government of President Teannaki - accused of poor administration of public funds - lost a vote of confidence in Parliament and was forced to stand down. In July, the opposition coalition Maneaba te Mauri won a parliamentary majority and in the September presidential elections, Teburoro Tito took over as national leader.

[14] The new president abandoned the privatization of state enterprises started by his predecessors, and in 1995 he announced his intention to increase the prices paid to the copra producers and the salaries of civil servants. The Tito government also expressed concern at the passage of Japanese plutonium-loaded vessels

through the region and criticized French nuclear tests in the Pacific.

[15] In 1996 the Government proposed a balanced budget, including a 1.7 per cent rise in public spending. Part of the funds still came out of a reserve fund established from the payment of rights over phosphate mining on the island of Banaba, a resource depleted since 1979.

[16] Also in 1996, Kiribati signed a trade agreement with China, in order to increase commerce between both countries.

[17] In December, at the Conference for an Independent and Nuclear Energy-Free Pacific Ocean, in Fiji, Tito supported this country's proposal intended to definitely ban nuclear weapon tests in the world.

[18] In August 1997, Kiribati signed a friendship treaty with Tuvalu. In September, the Government of Japan contributed $40 million to build the Betio port, one of Kiribati's largest.

[19] Because of the low elevation of the majority of the islands, in the last years of the 1990s the Government and the people became increasingly concerned about the 'greenhouse effect' on the sea level. If this rose the islands would be flooded. ■

PROFILE

ENVIRONMENT

33 islands and coral atolls scattered over 5 thousand million sq km in Micronesia. The climate is tropical and rainy, tempered by the effect of sea winds. The country's large phosphate deposits are now virtually exhausted. Fishing and underwater mineral deposits make up Kiribati's major economic potential.

SOCIETY

Peoples: The population is mostly of Micronesian descent. Kiribati 97.4 per cent; mixed (Kiribati and other) 1.5 per cent; Tuvaluan 0.5 per cent; European 0.2 per cent; other 0.4 per cent. **Languages:** Kiribati and English. **Political Parties:** National Progressive Party and the Maneaban te Mauri. **Social Organizations:** Kiribati General Labor Confederation.

THE STATE

Official Name: Republic of Kiribati. **Capital:** Tarawa, 25,000 people (1995). **Other cities:** Abaiang 5,314 people; Bairiki, 1,800; Tabiteuea 4,600. **Government:** Teburoro Tito, President since October 1994. Parliament is made up of 39 members, elected by direct popular vote, plus one representative of Banaba Island. **National Holiday:** July 12, Independence Day (1979).

Korea

North Korea
South Korea
(see history and statistics
on the following pages)

Korea

The Korean peninsula lies between China and Japan, and this position has shaped the nation's history, and the character of its people. The territory has frequently been the arena of struggles between armies from China, Mongolia and Japan. The peninsula was first inhabited by tribes of the Tungu language which emigrated to Siberia. Between the 10th and 8th centuries BC several tribal states were established, of which the most complex was the one known as Old Choson, in the Taedong river basin. Towards the 4th century BC, Choson developed into a league of tribes grouped between the basins of the Liao and Taedong rivers. At this time, Choson inhabitants used weapons made of iron, harnesses for horses and war carriages. In 108 BC, the Chinese empire defeated the kingdom of Choson and replaced it with four Chinese colonies. During the height of Old Choson, other tribal states flourished in the peninsula: Puyo, in the Manchurian region of the Sungari river basin, and Chin, which during the 2nd century BC appeared to the south of the Han river and was later divided into three tribal states (Mahan, Chinhan and Pyonhan).

2   The different leagues expanded through the peninsula which, as of the 1st century BC, was divided into the rival kingdoms of Koguryo, Paekche and Silla. Koguryo (which in the 6th century covered an area similar to the present North Korea) was founded by Chu-mong in 37 BC. Paekche was founded by Onjo in 19 BC, and Silla by Pak Hyokkose in 57 BC. These three states were consolidated by King Taejo (53-146) in Koguryo, King Koi (204-286) in Paekche and King Naemul (356-402) in Silla. The three kingdoms developed into states through successive wars which led to the organization of centralized military and administrative systems. A powerful aristocracy grew up in all of them, comprised of tribal chiefs from the respective capitals. Another common feature of these kingdoms was that they developed highly sophisticated cultures and produced their own historiographies in order to strengthen the authority of the State.

3   With the support of the T'ang Chinese dynasty, Silla conquered Paekche in the year 660 and Koguryo in 668. However, the survivors of the defeated Koguryo,

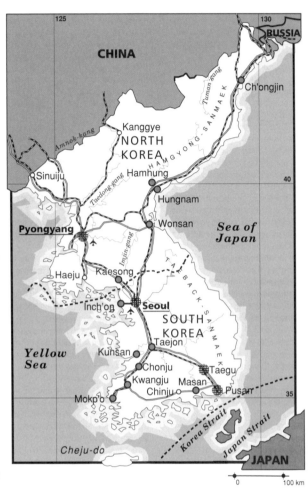

led by General Tae Cho-yang, established the Kingdom of Perhae to the north of present Manchuria and soon, impeded by China from integrating with the other Korean kingdom, entered into direct confrontation with Silla. The peninsula was divided into two states, one in the north and one in the south, both paying taxes to China. Perhae became a very sophisticated state, called 'the prosperous state of the East' by the Chinese, but after it fell into the hands of the Khitan, a nomad people from the north, its territory no longer came into the history of Korea.

4   United Silla became an absolute monarchy, which minimized the influence of the aristocracy. The Chinese variant of Avatamsaka Buddhism offered the ideological base for the monarchy and the aristocracy, while the underprivileged were attracted to

Pure Land Buddhism, which promised redemption in the next world. In the capital (current Kyongju, in South Korea), the monarchs built giant palaces and royal tombs, while the State's administration was divided, following China's example, into provinces, prefectures and counties.

5   The decline of Silla began towards the end of the 8th century, as a result of peasant uprisings and conflicts with the aristocracy, which had abolished royal despotism. A new system was established which increased the power of some landlords. Two provincial leaders, Konhwon and Kungye, established the kingdoms of Late Koguryo and Late Paechke respectively. During this period, known as the Three Late Kingdoms Period, Zen Buddhism was the most popular religion, with emphasis on individual fulfillment through contemplation. This doctrine was much less hierarchical

than that of Avatamsaka Buddhism, and favored individual autonomy.

6   In 918, Wang Kong founded Songak (today's Kaesong, in North Korea) and in 936 he united the peninsula once more, incorporating the survivors of Late Paechke, devastated by the Khitan. Wang Kong proclaimed himself the legitimate succesor of Koguryo and repeatedly confronted the Khitan, expanding Koguryo's territory up to the Yalu river. Wang Kong was the founder of the Koryo dynasty, from which the western name Korea derives. The ruling class of Koryo was made up mainly of provincial lords, owners of castles, and by Silla's old aristocracy. Koryo was ruled by a Supreme State Council, formed by aristocrats, who adopted Buddhism as a religion to achieve spiritual goals and personal happiness, while they practiced the political principles and ethical values of Confucianism.

7   In spite of the practical need to have a strong defensive system, the military were not well treated. This led to a coup in 1170 and, taking advantage of the subsequent chaos, one of the generals, Ch'oe Ch'ung-hon, established a military regime from 1197 to 1258. The Koryo dynasty stayed in power because the Ch'oe family preferred to rule behind the scenes and did not take over the throne. In the 13th. century, Koryo was repeatedly invaded by the Mongols who came to have great influence in the court. In 1392, Confucian master Yi song-gye overthrew the tottering dynasty and founded the Choson (Yi) dynasty, which would last until 1910. In 1394, Yi Song-gye founded Seoul and turned it into the capital of the Kingdom.

8   The territory controlled by the Yi dynasty came to be known as Choson, with the approval of the Emperor of China. The Confucian ethical system was officially adopted and replaced Buddhism, which had become corrupt. Choson was dominated by an hereditary aristocratic class, called yangban, which devoted itself to the study of neo-Confucian doctrines. During the Kingdom of Sejo, the seventh monarch, a government structure emerged, led by the yangban ideology. The country was divided into eight provinces and the central government appointed the administrative chiefs of the state. Legal codes were written and the State Council took charge of the administration. During the 15th

century many teachers were recruited to serve the government. They criticized the bureaucracy and recommended several radical measures to implement the ideas of Confucius. However, these teachers had to leave the administration due to strong pressures.

9	In 1597, Toyotomi Hideyoshi, a Japanese military leader who had just reunited his country, invaded Shohon under the pretext of invading China. The national crisis made people from all spheres of life including Buddhist monks join in the struggle against the invaders. In 1598, with China's help, the Koreans forced the retreat of the aggressors, but most of Shohon was devastated. Many palaces, public buildings and homes were burnt, numerous national treasures destroyed and a large number of crafts people and experts were kidnapped and taken to Japan. In the beginning of the 17th century, nomad Manchurians invaded Shohon, took over the northern part of the territory, and captured Seoul in 1636, demanding the unconditional surrendering of the king. In 1640 the Manchurians overthrew the Ming dynasty in China and replaced it with the Ch'ing dynasty. The taxes Korea paid to the Ming went to the Ch'ing.

10	During the second half of the 17th century and throughout the 18th century, Korean society underwent great changes. Rice became widespread and irrigation systems were improved. Agricultural production was increased and the peasants' standard of living improved. Tobacco and ginseng crops encouraged domestic and foreign trade, thus intensifying contacts with European traders and Catholic priests. Meanwhile, radical ideological changes were taking place in Korea, since many teachers

no longer concerned themselves only with theoretical speculation but also with matters of practical importance. This gave birth to *silhak* or education based on pragmatism, which urged the Government to undergo changes. Also, a school of *silhak* devoted itself to the study of the Korean language and history and facilitated, jointly with the development of popular art, the access of the people to written texts. To the end of the 18th century some teachers of *silhak* had converted to Catholicism, followed by members of the aristocracy. Large sectors of the population, encouraged by the hope of finding equality before God after death, were seduced by the new religion which expanded itself rapidly.

11	The decline of the Yi dynasty was characterized by economic and religious factors, plus outside pressures. The yangban or aristocracy had appropriated public lands and did not pay taxes, which led the Government to increase the taxes on the poor, who could not pay and lost their lands. When the famines came, the Government did not have enough money to alleviate the situation. Also, the State banned Christianity, because of its incompatibility with Confucianism. During the persecutions of 1801, 1839 and 1866, the converted teachers were forced to die or fall into apostasy, while foreign missionaries were beheaded. At the same time, Japan pressed Korea to open its foreign trade and China increased its interference in the peninsula to counterbalance the Japanese influence. In 1860, the scholar Ch'oe-u founded a popular religion called *Tonhak* (oriental teachings) which combined elements of Confucianism, Christianity, Shamanism and

Buddhism. Soon, these new teachings, in the name of resistance against foreigners and corruption, gained a large following among peasants and by 1893 had turned into a political movement. In May 1893, the Tonhak followers took the city of Chonju, in the southwest and the two intervening powers, China and Japan, sent troops to crush them.

12	To justify their military presence in the peninsula, Japan proposed that China carry out a joint reform in Korea, but China's negative reply led to a military conflict which ended with a Japanese victory in 1895. Emboldened by this victory, Japan occupied Korea in 1905 and in 1910 the country was formally annexed, putting an end to the Yi dynasty.

13	Under the Japanese, Korea was exploited as a supplier of foodstuffs and as a source of cheap labor. Japanese landlords and factory owners settled in Korea, with a developed infrastructure merely to extract the wealth of the country. In the 1930s, the northern part of Korea saw industrial development of war materials, to supply Japan's goal of expansion into China.

14	With the defeat of Japan in World War II, Korea was occupied on each side of the 38th parallel: the northern part by Soviet troops and the southern by the United States. Korean hopes for a united, independent country seemed on the verge of being realized but a complex struggle of interests between the two powers made it impossible. The Soviet Union maintained its influence and did not allow general elections in the north of the peninsula. In the south, under the supervision of a United Nations Temporary Commission, elections were held in May 1948 and Syngman Rhee was elected first president of the Republic of Korea, whose capital was established in Seoul. Meanwhile, the Supreme Assembly of the People of North Korea wrote a new constitution, which came into effect in August 1948. Kim Il-Sung was appointed Prime Minister and on September 9 the People's Republic of Korea was proclaimed, with its capital in Pyŏngyang.

15	On October 12, the Soviet Union recognized this state as the only legitimate government of Korea. In December, the General Assembly of the United Nations recognized the exclusive sovereignty of the southern Republic of Korea. Most foreign troops left both countries the following year but US troops remained in the south under the UN flag, then dominated by the United States.

16	In June 1950, North Korea launched a carefully planned offensive against South Korea. The United Nations convened its members, to put a stop to the invasion. In the meantime US President Truman called his army to

assist South Korea, without asking Congress to declare war.

17	Likewise, Truman failed to seek UN permission before sending the US Fleet to the Strait of Formosa to protect one of the US Army's flanks, and also to come to the assistance of Chiang Kai Shek's anti-communist Chinese regime, which had established itself on the island of Formosa (Taiwan). This in turn gave rise to fears in Peking of a nationalist invasion of 'continental' China.

18	In the meantime, the military campaign on the Korean peninsula was turning into a disaster for the South Koreans and US troops, who had arrived hurriedly and poorly equipped, and were forced to retreat nearly as far as Pusan, on the southern coast.

19	Defeat was narrowly avoided by the action of General Douglas MacArthur, who landed some 160 km south of the 38th parallel and managed to divide and defeat North Korean troops.

20	China, concerned over the advancing allied troops, warned that the presence of the US in North Korea would force it to enter the war. MacArthur ignored the warning and in November launched his 'Home by Christmas' offensive.

21	However, China sent 180,000 troops to Korea and by mid-December it had driven US troops back, south of the 38th parallel. On December 31 1951, China launched a second offensive against South Korea, subsequently taking up positions along the former border.

22	After differences of opinion on military strategy, MacArthur was relieved of his command by Truman. It was later revealed that MacArthur had outlined plans to use nuclear weapons against Chinese cities, advocating full-scale war with China.

23	The battle continued up and down the peninsula and the city of Seoul changed hands several times. Up to this point the conflict had left four million dead.

24	After renewed fighting in June 1953, an armistice went into effect the following month. From that time on, Korea was officially separated by the 38th parallel.

25	On August 8 1990, the UN Security Council unanimously approved the admission of both Koreas. On December 13 1991, Prime Ministers Yon Kyong Muk (North Korea) and Chong Won Shik (South Korea) signed a 'Reconciliation, Non-Aggression, Exchange, and Cooperation Agreement'. This has been the most important step towards reunification since 1972. The Korean peninsula is in a strategic region located between the three large powers of Russia, China and Japan. There are currently intense negotiations underway to solve the nuclear question. ∎

PROFILE

ENVIRONMENT

North Korea comprises the northern portion of the peninsula of Korea, east of China, between the Sea of Japan and the Yellow Sea. The territory is mountainous with wooded ranges to the East, along the coast of the Sea of Japan. Rice, the country's main agricultural product, is cultivated on the plains, 90 per cent of the land being worked under a cooperative system. Abundant mineral resources (coal, iron, zinc, copper, lead and manganese). **South Korea** is located in the southern part of the Korean Peninsula, east of China, between the sea of Japan and the Yellow Sea. The terrain is more level than North Korea's and the arable land area, mainly used for rice farming, is larger. Atmospheric pollution first appeared in the 1970s, as did pollution of water supplies, rivers and the sea. The western coast, on the Yellow Sea, is seriously contaminated.

SOCIETY

Peoples: Both north and south Koreans, probable descendants of the Tungu people, were influenced by their Chinese and Mongolian conquerors over many centuries. Homogeneous ethnic and cultural features in Korea stand out in sharp contrast with those of most other Asian countries. There are no distinct minorities. **Religions:** Religious practices are frowned upon. Buddhism, Confucianism (a code of ethics rather than a religion), Chondokio (which combines Buddhist and Christian elements) are practiced throughout the country, while traditional Shamanic cults prevail in the interior. **Languages:** Korean (official).

North Korea

Choson Minjujuui In´min

Population: 23,702,000 (1999)
Area: 120,540 SQ KM
Capital: Pyongyang
Currency: Won
Language: Korean

O n Sept. 9 1948, the People's Republic of Korea was proclaimed in Pyongyang and Kim Il Sung, leader of the Korean Workers Party was elected Prime Minister (see history of Korea).

2 The Kingdom of Koguryo, the equivalent in the 7th century of the present North Korea, had a special way of treating foreign enemies. It avoided direct confrontation and maintained an impressive military capacity within the cities (see history of Korea). North Korea also had a similar strategy since it limited its outer contact and devoted its efforts to achieve considerable military strength. Despite its geographical proximity to the People's Republic of China, North Korea tried to remain neutral in the Sino-Soviet conflict.

3 The Korean Workers Party (KWP) enjoyed uninterrupted power for five decades. The party's philosophy is called Juche, a blend of self-reliance, nationalism and centralized control of the economy.

4 With the establishment of a socialist regime, agrarian reform was carried out, with part of the country's agriculture being collectivized. Industrialization had begun during Japanese occupation, and large textile, chemical and hydroelectric plants were established.

5 With the War behind it (1950-53, see Korea), and armistice signed in Panmunjon, North Korea devoted all its efforts to the reconstruction of the country, which had been devastated by the War. When Syngman Rhee was ousted from office in South Korea (1960), North Korea attempted rapprochement with its neighbor. However, when the military took power in Seoul these overtures were interrupted.

6 The development of industry, expanding rapidly after 1958, was aided by the availability of rich mineral deposits. The Yalu River Hydroelectric Plant was built in conjunction with China.

7 Korea adopted a socialist economy with central planning; 90 per cent of the national industry was in the hands of the State with the remaining 10 per cent organized in cooperatives.

8 Between 1954 and 1961, North Korea signed military assistance treaties with China and the USSR. In 1972, a new constitution was approved, making Kim Il Sung President as well as Prime Minister.

9 Kim Jong Il, Kim Il Sung's son, was named head of the Government in 1980. In 1984, North Korea provided relief to flood victims in South Korea. That same year, the formation of mixed enterprises was authorized in the construction, technology and tourist sectors.

10 In 1988, North Korea began 'ideological rectification' in direct contrast to the Soviet liberalization process introduced by Gorbachev.

11 In 1990, there were massive demonstrations in support of the regime, on Kim Il Sung's 78th birthday. He was re-elected in May 1991. During this period, North and South Korea intensified their efforts toward warmer relations, with an eye to eventual reunification.

12 According to North Korea, any possibility of reunification was to be preceded by a formal peace treaty with the US and removal of their troops from Korean soil. In 1990, North Korea submitted a proposal for denuclearization to the International Agency for Atomic Energy, subject to guarantees from the US that it would not use the 1,000 nuclear bombs it has in South Korea against them.

13 In 1991, the USSR cut Korea's oil quota by half. Signs of the regime's growing economic difficulties began to show. From 1992, Kim Jong Il assumed responsibility for the formulation of the country's foreign policy.

14 In mid-1992, the Government issued a report on the country's nuclear installations, including its Yongbyon plant, to the International Atomic Energy Agency (IAEA). However, in February 1993, North Korea refused to allow the IAEA inspectors access sparking a serious crisis with the West. South Korea denounced the danger posed by North Korean possession of nuclear weapons. Negotiations between the two Koreas came to a halt.

15 Kim Il Sung's death at 82 - officially announced on July 7 1994 - once again complicated talks with the US and deferred the summit planned between the two Koreas. Kim Jong Il succeeded his father without having the same real power as the historical leader of North Korean communism, which gave way for a fight for power among leading cadres.

16 In 1995, widespread floods affected some five million people. One consequence was the loss of the harvests. These losses were calculated at 1.9 million tons of crops, which led the North Korean Government to make an uncommon appeal for foreign aid. Japan, one of its main capitalist trade partners, donated 300,000 tons of rice and South Korea 150,000 tons.

17 The US decided to lift the trade embargo and a delegation of US investors visited the country, while Pyongyang reported it no longer opposed the presence of US troops in South Korea.

18 The food shortage became more serious in 1996, reaching famine proportions in some areas. North Koreans continued to flee to South Korea seeking asylum. The defection of Worker's Party secretary Huang Yang Yop, in February 1997 caused a new political crisis. Returning from a tour of Japan and China, Huang sought asylum in the South Korean embassy in Beijing. Two days later, Prime Minister Kang Song Dan was forced to resign and was replaced by Hong Song Nam. In October, Kim Jong Il, the de facto ruler following the death of his father, was officially appointed head of the Worker'Party. However, due to internal rivalries he was not formally appointed president of the country.

19 In late 1997, the Government proposed tripartheid negotiations between Pyongyang, Seoul and Washington for a definitive peace agreement on the peninsula. In 1998, it was estimated some 100,000 people had died of cold, hunger and lack of medical attention since 1995.

20 The UN World Food Programme (WFP) reported the per person daily ration of rice was only 100 grams. The situation became critical due to the drought which followed the floods, but despite this Pyongyang did not succumb to before political pressure from Seoul. In early 1998, international aid was insufficient. In March, the Government imposed the measures of a 'war economy'.

21 The individual rice ration was only 100 grams per day. The situation entered a critical phase as drought which followed the floods, but in spite of this, Pyongyang did not appear disposed to give in to political pressure from Seoul. In March 1998, the government brought in 'War Economy' measures.

22 In June 1999, tensions with the South increased and confrontations over maritime frontiers led to the sinking of a North Korean ship, and the arrest by the North of a South Korean tourist accused of spying. However, representatives of both parties met in Beijing that same month to discuss various issues, including economic aid to the North and the establishment of liaison offices in the respective capitals.

23 In December, Japan lifted sanctions in place since August 1998 against North Korea, after Pyongyang launched a ballistic missile over Japanese territory. These had included the immediate suspension of food aid, the banning of charter flights to the peninsula and the stoppage of Japanese contributions to the nuclear stations being built to relieve the Korean power shortage. The only pending problem between the two nations now is that North Korea demands an official apology for the atrocities committed before and during the Second World War as a precondition for full diplomatic relations. ∎

PROFILE

SOCIETY

Political Parties: The Korean Workers' Party (KWP), founded in 1945 with Marxist-Leninist orientation, is the dominant political organization. The Democratic People's Republic of Korea is a virtual one-party state, but smaller parties do exist: the Korean Social Democratic Party and the Chondokio Chong-u party, the first being affiliated to the KWP in a National Front for the Reunification of Korea, created in June 1945. Youth and women are organized into the Union of Young Socialist Workers and the Democratic Women's Union.
Social Organizations: The General Federation of Trade Unions is the only workers' organization, while the union of Agricultural Workers is a peasants' association.

THE STATE

Official Name: Tschosson Mintschutschui Inmin Konghwaguk.
Administrative Divisions: 9 Provinces, 1 District.
Capital: Pyongyang 1,600,000 people (est 1997).
Other cities: Hamhung 701,000 people; Chongjin 520,000; Sinuiju 330,000; Kaesong 310,000 (1987).
Government: Kim Jong Il, President of the Republic since July 1994. The supreme body of the state is the People's Assembly, with 541 members.
National Holiday: September 9, Republic Day (1948).
Armed Forces: 1,054,000 (1994).
Other: 3,800,000 Peasant Red Guard, 115,000 Security Troops, of the Ministry of Public Security.

South Korea

Taehaen-Min `Guk

Population: 46,479,000 (1999)
Area: 99,020 SQ KM
Capital: Seoul
Currency: Won
Language: Korean

On August 15 1948, a Republic was established in the southern part of the Korean peninsula, with its capital in Seoul (see Korea). Syngman Rhee was named its first president and, supported by US military, economic and political advisors, he ruled the southern portion of Korea for 14 years. Through constitutional laws giving him indefinite power, he ruled as a constitutional dictator. All opposition forces were controlled by charging them with cooperating with the North at the first signs of dissent.

[2] The US advisers convinced the Rhee regime of the need for a thorough land reform program. They were very much aware of events in China, where the nationalist Kuomintang had been defeated by the communists who promised rural peoples 'land to the tiller'. The US scheme in South Korea allowed for compensation, and land redistribution limited to three hectares per person; former Japanese-owned land was also redistributed. Many of the previous land-owners moved to the cities.

[3] Despite the introduction of a draconian National Security Law in 1958, when many political dissidents were jailed, the regime was unable to suppress opposition completely. Rhee was re-elected in 1952, 1956 and in 1960. The results of the last election were not accepted by the opposition, who claimed there had been fraud. There were protests in Seoul, which were repressed harshly by Government forces. Growing opposition and the danger of a revolution extending to the rest of the country, led Syngman Rhee to resign on April 27 1960. He was succeeded by Huh Chung Tok as interim President.

[4] New elections were held, and Po Sun Yun, a member of the Democratic Party, was elected President. John Chang, who had been named head of the government, attempted to lead the country toward effective economic development and put an end to the corruption and waste which had characterized the previous regime. Some members of his cabinet were in favor of warmer relations with North Korea.

[5] In May 1961 a military coup ousted Chang; a military junta was installed, presided over by General Chan Yung. In July, General Chung Hee Park took command of the junta and proceeded to suspend all democratic freedoms and imprison all members of the previous regime.

[6] The new regime initiated a National Reconciliation policy, including a planned strategy against communism and corruption, and promised a return to civilian government after completion of these 'revolutionary tasks'.

[7] In March 1962, Park took the presidency from Po Sun Yun. In late 1963, Park was confident of power and held elections. He won by a mere 1.4 per cent despite suppression of the opposition. The protests that followed led him to declare martial law, the military retained their political domination and a long, harsh dictatorship ensued.

[8] The military regime established strong centralized economic planning and, with the help of western technocrats, Korea became a prime example of export-oriented development. Imports and exports, domestic prices and access to credit were used as levers to control and guide the economy. Restrictive laws were established governing the right to strike, organize or allow collective bargaining.

[9] From a war-torn, mainly rural, indebted economy, South Korea developed into an industrial economy dominated by large, Korean-owned transnational corporations producing steel, ships, cars and electronics goods.

[10] Villagers, affected by low grain prices, were forced into cities and the urban labor pool, contributing to the 'Korean miracle'. Some of the world's lowest wages, longest hours and most unsafe working conditions are the norm for Korean workers.

[11] Eighteen years after taking power, Park was still president, having won four fraudulent elections.

[12] In October 1979, Park was killed: shot by the director of the hated Korean Central Intelligence Agency, Kim Jae Kiu, in murky circumstances.

[13] Before the end of 1979, General Chun Doo Hwan, head of military intelligence, decided to secure his position, arresting rival. On May 17 1980, martial law was once again established and civilian politicians were arrested, dropping all pretense of civilian rule. Chun resigned from the army and on August 27 became President

[14] The following day, citizens in the southern city of Kwangju took control in protest against the military regime, and particularly the arrest of Kim Daw Jung, a leading opposition figure and a native of Kwangju. The Korean army suppressed the citizens with extreme brutality and 'hundreds lost their lives' with the knowledge and agreement of US military commanders stationed in the country. Although the protest had been carried out as a public reaction to the arrest of Kim Daw Jung, this fact was ignored and Daw Jung was sentenced to life imprisonment, charged with 'instigating' the uprising. The Kwangju incident was used by the military as justification for seizing power and questions were raised as to whether the whole event had been deliberately provoked by the military.

[15] Chun launched a 'purification campaign' of public and private sectors, even setting quotas for singling out the corrupt and 'subversives'. In the same manner as his predecessor, Chun Doo Hwan held elections in an attempt to legitimize and civilianize his rule; he won the elections in 1981.

[16] In October 1983, several members of the South Korean cabinet were killed by a bomb at the Martyrs' Mausoleum in Burma during a state visit; arriving late, President Chun escaped the bomb blast. The Burmese, claiming proof of North Korean involvement, broke off diplomatic relations and rescinded their recognition of the North Korean Government.

[17] Opposition to Chun's regime continued to grow as repression escalated, reminiscent of Park's worst excesses. The US withdrew their support of the Marcos regime in the Philippines, after claims of election fraud and human rights abuses, and a worried Korean regime instituted some reforms. Censorship was lifted somewhat and Kim Daw Jung released from house arrest.

[18] During 1987, hundreds of thousands of Korean workers joined in strikes and factory occupations in an unprecedented wave of protests. Korean workers demanded the right to form democratic unions independent of the government-run Federation of Korean Trade Unions, higher wages, an end to forced overtime and a larger share of the benefits of the nation's spectacular growth.

[19] In July 1987, Chun stepped down and appointed Roh Tae Woo both as his successor and as president of the official Democratic Justice Party. Demonstrations followed amid protests that Roh would continue the dictatorship as a close military colleague of Chun. Demands that Chun face trial for his part in the Kwangju massacre were also voiced.

[20] Faced with the possibility of larger street demonstrations and concern over its international image (South Korea was host of the Olympic Games in 1988) political restrictions were eased during the December, 1987 election campaign.

[21] Polls showed government candidates trailing badly in late November when a Korean Airways passenger jet disappeared near Thailand with 118 passengers aboard. North Korea was again suspected, as in the Burma bombing, but Pyongyang denied any involvement.

[22] In the elections, the newly-freed opposition together polled a majority, but failed to unite the two factions, led by Kim Yong Sam of the Reunification Democratic Party and Kim Dae Jung of the Party for Peace and Democracy. The split enabled the incumbent government, under Roh Tae Woo, to secure power with a majority of 42 per cent.

[23] In January 1990, the most conservative opposition groupings formed a merger with the official Democratic Justice Party, and became the Democratic Liberal Party, controlling 220 seats in the 298-member National Assembly. The Party for Peace and Democracy remained the only real parliamentary opposition.

WORKERS

1997
UNEMPLOYMENT: 2.6%

% OF LABOUR FORCE **1998**

■ FEMALE: 41%   ■ MALE: 59%

1990

■ SERVICES: 46.5%
■ INDUSTRY: 35.4%
■ AGRICULTURE: 18.1%

MATERNAL MORTALITY

1990-98

Per 100,000 live births

20

LITERACY

1995

97%

FOOD DEPENDENCY

1997

6%

24 In the spring of 1990, a new offensive against independent trade unions and labor rights resulted in the arrest of the movement's leaders. In April, police stormed the Hyundai shipyards and arrested over 600 union activists, ending a 72-hour worker occupation protesting the arrest of union leaders. A few days later, 400 striking workers occupying the Korean Broadcasting System's headquarters were also arrested. The resulting nationwide protests precipitated the biggest drop in the history of the Korean stock market.

25 In September 1991, US President George Bush made the decision to withdraw tactical nuclear weapons from South Korea, and in November this was accomplished. This significant step met one of the requirements of North Korea and was necessary for inspections of their territory to be made.

26 In December of that year, Seoul and Pyongyang signed a 'Reconciliation, Non-aggression, Exchange and Cooperation Accord', affecting bilateral relations (see Korea).

27 In the legislative elections of March 1992, both the pro-government groups and the Left suffered a serious setback. The Democratic Liberal Party won 149 of the 299 seats, one short of the

majority. The Democratic Party (DP, formerly the Party for Peace and Democracy) came in second with 30 per cent, followed by the Party of National Unification with 17.4 per cent and 31 seats, a new grouping led by a former corporate leader. The left-wing People's Party (PP) won 1.4 per cent of the vote and no seats.

28 In May, President Roh Tae Woo named Kim Young Sam, who had obtained 41.4 per cent of the returns in the December presidential election, as his successor. Kim's election coincided with a weakening opposition, worsened by the resignation in February 1993 of Chung Ju-Yung, leader of the United People's Party, charged with having accepted illegal contributions from a major corporation during the electoral campaign.

29 Corruption scandals also reached the Government. Choi Ki Son, a close aide of President Kim, admitted he had embezzled $1 million of public funds. Furthermore, Suh Eui Hyun, leader of the country's largest Buddhist order, was accused of accepting $10 million from a businessman to hand them over to Kim Young Sam. This accusation caused confrontations among Buddhist monks which led to 134 arrests.

30 In 1995, two former presidents, Chun Doo Hwan (1979-1988) and Roh Tae Woo (1988-1993), were arrested for their role in the coup which brought Chun to power in December 1979, accused of treason and corruption. In June of this year, the governing party was defeated in the first local and provincial elections not controlled by the Government since 1961. The collapse of the department store Sampoong in Seoul, killing more than 500 people, brought the issue of corruption back to the fore, when it became known local authorities had approved the construction of the fifth floor after being paid hidden commissions.

31 In April 1996, the governing New Korea Party took 139 of the 299 seats in contention. Meanwhile the National Congress for a New Policy took 79 seats and the United Liberal Democrats 50. In December, the Seoul courts sentenced former defence minister Lee Yang-Ho to four years imprisonment for accepting illegal commissions from the Daewoo company, the fourth biggest concern in the country.

32 In June 1997, the Kim Young-Sam Government requested a loan from the IMF, a measure broadly rejected by the public. The December presidential elections were won by Kim Dae Jung, candidate of the opposition Democratic Party (DP), which agreed the liberation of Chu Doo Hwan and Roh Tae Woo and announced an amnesty for political prisoners. When the new President took office in March 1998 Kim Jong Pil became Prime Minister.

33 Despite the armed skirmishes weeks before, representatives of Seoul and Pyongyang met in Beijing to discuss various issues, including economic aid for the North and the possibility of establishing liaison offices in the respective capitals.

34 The government coalition, made up of the Democratic Party of the Millennium (former DP) and The Democratic Liberal Union began to show signs of collapse. In January 2000, Park Tae Joon, member of the latter was appointed new Prime Minister. The new government announced changes tending toward reinforced security and developing an infrastructure capable of withstanding a rapid increase in the number of Internet users. ∎

PROFILE

SOCIETY

Political Parties: Democratic Liberal Party (DLP), in power; the Democratic Party (DP), in opposition; the National Unification Party, opposition; the United People's Party (PP), or Minjung Party constitutes the only left-wing party.

Social Organizations: Legally, all unions must belong to the Government-controlled Federation of Korean Trade Unions (FKTU) which has a persistent reputation for intervening against workers to end industrial action, sometimes violently. In January 1990, democratic trade unions formed by workers since 1987 announced the formation of the Korean Alliance of Genuine Trade Unions (Chonnohyop) claiming affiliation of 600 unions with 190,000 members, according to organization figures.

THE STATE

Official Name: Republic of Korea.
Administrative Divisions: 9 Provinces.
Capital: Seoul 10,229,000 people (1995).
Other cities: Pusan 3,798,000 people, Taegu 2,249,000 people (1995).
Government: Kim Dae Jung, President and head of State, elected in December 1997. Park Tae Joon, Prime Minister and head of Government, named in January 2000. Legislature, single-chamber: National Assembly, with 209 members, elected every 4 years.
National Holiday: August 15, Liberation Day (1945).
Armed Forces: 633,000 (1995). **Other:** 3,500,000 Civil Defence Corps, 4,500 Coast Guard.

STATISTICS

DEMOGRAPHY

Population: 46,479,000 (1999)
Annual growth: 1.2 % (1975/97)
Estimates for year 2015 (million): 51.1 (1999)
Annual growth to year 2015: 0.6 % (1997/2015)
Urban population: 83.5 % (1997)
Urban Growth: 3.5 % (1980/95)
Children per woman: 1.7 (1998)

HEALTH

Life expectancy at birth: 73 years (1998)
male: 69 years (1998)
female: 76 years (1998)
Maternal mortality: 20 per 100,000 live births (1990-98)
Infant mortality: 5 per 1,000 (1998)
Under-5 child mortality: 5 per 1,000 (1998)
Daily calorie supply: 3,336 per capita (1996)
127 doctors per 100,000 people (1993)
Safe water: 93 % (1990/98)

EDUCATION

Literacy: 97 % (1995)
male: 99 % (1995)
female: 95 % (1995)
School enrolment:
Primary total: 94 % (1990/96)
male: 94 % (1990/97)
female: 94 % (1990/97)
Secondary:
male: 102 % (1990/96)
female: 102 % (1990/96)
Tertiary: 68 % (1997)
Primary school teachers: one for every 31 (1996)

COMMUNICATIONS

393 newspapers (1995), 1,033 radios (1997), 326 TV sets (1996) and 430 main telephone lines (1996) per 1,000 people
Books: 77 new titles per 100,000 people (1992/94)

ECONOMY

Per capita, GNP: $ 8,600 (1998)
Annual growth, GNP: -6.6 % (1998)
Annual inflation: 6.4 % (1990/98)
Consumer price index: 117.8 (1998)
Currency: 1,401.4 won = $ 1 (1998)
Cereal imports: 11,993,181 metric tons (1998)
Food import dependency: 6 % (1997)
Fertilizer use: 5,258 kg per ha (1997)
Exports: $ 156,330 million (1998)
Imports: $ 114,879 million (1998)
External debt: $ 139,097 million (1998); $ 5,958 per capita (1998)
Debt service: 12.9 % of exports (1998)
Development aid received: $ -160 million (1997); $ -3.7 per capita (1997)

ENERGY

Consumption: 3,834.0 Kgs of Oil equivalent per capita yearly (1997); 86.0 % imported (1997)

HDI (rank/value): 30/0.852 (1997)

Kuwait

Kuwayt

Population: 1,897,000 (1999)
Area: 17,820 SQ KM
Capital: Kuwait (Al-Kuwayt)
Currency: Dinar
Language: Arabic

In the history of navigation, the voyage of Nearco, one of Alexander of Macedonia's admirals, was a milestone; he sailed from the Indo River to the farthest end of the Gulf of Arabia, ending his voyage in the port of Diridotis, in present-day Kuwait. This was not, however, the first contact between India and Kuwait, which had already been an active trade center for almost 2,000 years. The fate of the country was always intimately linked to that of the Mesopotamian civilizations (see Iraq) but, beginning in the 13th century, after the Mongol invasion caused collapse of the Caliphate, the region entered into a long period of isolation.

[2] After this, new Arab groups began to settle there. In the 18th century, although nominally subject to the Ottoman Empire, the settlements were virtually independent; they decided to elect a shaij (sheikh) to conduct sporadic negotiations with the Turks. In 1756, the leader of the Anaiza tribe, Abdul Rahim al-Sabah, founder of the reigning dynasty, was appointed to this task.

[3] At that time, the place, formerly known as the Qurain (horn) began to be called Kuwait, a diminutive for al-Kout, which is a local Arabic term to describe the fortified houses on the coast.

[4] The weakness of Turkish sultans and the growing British influence in the region were two fundamental factors that encouraged the formation of proto-states, of which the emirate of Najd (see Saudi Arabia) was the most dynamic.

[5] In order to avoid absorption by the Wahabites, the emirs of Kuwait requested support from the British who had moved the East India Company's overland mail terminal from Basra to Kuwait in 1779. The British sent Indian troops to guarantee the autonomy of the Emirate, an initiative which the Turks were helpless to stop. For decades Kuwait was the most prosperous and peaceful part of a region peppered by constant disputes.

[6] In 1892, with Turkish support, the Emir of Najd was deposed and was granted asylum in Kuwait. Sheikh Mubarak al Sabah allowed the territory to be used as a base for their raids against the pro-Turkish Rashidis. Since this implied

IRAQ • IRAN • KUWAIT • Bubiyan Is. • Failaka Is. • Al-Jahrah • Kuwait City • Salmiya • Persian Gulf • Al Ahmadi • Mina al Ahmadi • Wafrah • SAUDI ARABIA

[1] Neutral Zone

0 _____ 100 km

great risks, a treaty was signed with Britain in 1899, whereby the Sheikh undertook not to cede any part of the territory to another country without British consent; in exchange, Britain guaranteed Kuwait's territorial integrity. This treaty, and the subsequent British military presence in the region, frustrated Turkish attempts to expand the Berlin-Baghdad railway to reach the Gulf through Kuwaiti territory.

[7] At the end of World War I, France and Britain divided up the remains of the Ottoman Empire. Kuwait was now considered a British protectorate, separate from the newly-created kingdom of Iraq, which claimed it as a province, alleging the historical subjection of the region to the Government of Baghdad.

[8] In 1938, oil began to flow from the Burgan wells. Ahmad Jabir al-Sabah, the crown prince, opposed the exploitation of the extensive deposits, arguing that a high income and high salaries resulting from the new activity would ruin pearl fishing, until then the country's main economic activity, employing 10,000 sailors as deep-sea divers. After the impasse created by World War II, the emir granted the concession to the Kuwait Oil Company, owned by British BP and US Gulf, with oil first exported in 1946. The large-scale exploitation of these reserves soon turned the small port into a large trading center.

[9] In 1961, independence was negotiated, within the British policy of gradual decolonization. Sheikh Sabah proclaimed himself Emir and took up full powers. Iraq refused to recognize the new state, claiming that it was an artificial creation of the British to maintain access to oil. Consequently, the British troops remained to defend the emirate until they were replaced by troops of the Arab League.

[10] In 1962 a Constitution was enforced creating a National Assembly of 50 members, elected individually by male citizens aged over 21, whose fathers or grandfathers had resided in Kuwait before 1920. None of the candidates belonged to a political party, as these had been made illegal. Thus, out of the 826,500 Kuwaitis who lived in the country in 1990, a minority of the population - only 85,000 - would have been entitled to vote if elections had been called.

[11] In 1966, Kuwait and Saudi Arabia solved their ancient border disputes, and the 'neutral zone' which existed between both countries was divided equally. In 1969 the Central Bank of Kuwait was created, and in 1976 a Social Security Law and a Law of Reserves for Future Generations were passed. The latter established that 10 per cent of the State revenue was to be earmarked for an investment fund.

[12] In a few years, oil entirely changed the country. The Bedouins replaced their camels with luxurious air-conditioned cars. Pearl fishing

disappeared. The entire population settled in brand new cities, where the stylized mosque towers stood side-by-side with shopping centers which replaced the old souks (markets). The population's educational standards and life expectancy rose. All manual labor and work in the oil industry was done by immigrant workers. In 1970 the number of migrants equaled the local population, and by 1985 this figure had almost doubled.

[13] Kuwaiti rulers became concerned that despite so much prosperity in such a poor area its legitimacy could be questioned. In 1961 the Arab Fund for Economic Development was created, in order to channel 'soft' loans and donations to Third World countries. When the Organization of Petroleum Exporting Countries (OPEC) succeeded in raising prices in 1973, Kuwait increased its revenue immensely.

[14] Most of the Third World countries supported OPEC, hoping that they would receive help to establish a 'New International Economic Order', by asking for better prices for the other raw materials that they supply to the Northern countries. However, instead of investing their oil revenues in their own countries or in other Third World nations, the Gulf monarchs placed their fortunes in transnational banks. This further accentuated the excess of liquidity in transnational private banks, which started to grant loans to the Third World quite indiscriminately. This situation was one of the main factors that provoked the 'debt crisis' in 1982.

[15] Within the Gulf area, however, Kuwait was generous with its wealth. By the end of the 1980s, Kuwait had the highest rate of official development assistance in the world, proportional to its gross national product.

[16] Unfortunately, prosperity did not prevent political conflicts. In August 1976, the National Assembly was dissolved by Sheikh Jabir al-Sabah, arguing that it had acted against national interests. In December 1977, the Emir died and the Crown of Kuwait passed to Jabir Al-Sabah, who called national elections in February 1981. Over 500 candidates ran for the 50 seats in the National Assembly and 40 were won by Sunni candidates, loyal to the ruling family. Shi'a candidates won

four seats, and Islamic fundamentalists won six. Only 6.4 per cent of the population was permitted to vote.

[17] When the Iran-Iraq war broke out in 1979, Kuwait officially remained neutral, but in fact supported Iraq with large donations and loans. Kuwait considered Iraq to be a 'first line of defense' against the Iranian Islamic revolution.

[18] In 1985, the National Assembly began to disapprove of governmental measures such as press control, increases in the prices of public services and educational reforms, echoing other accusations that corruption existed within the ruling family. In August 1986, the Emir dissolved the Assembly and began to rule by decree.

[19] In the late 1980s, the Kuwait Investments Office (KIO) had capital assets outside the country estimated at $1 billion, which included hotels, art galleries, European and US real estate, and major shares in large transnational corporations: 10 per cent of British Petroleum, 23 per cent of Hoechst, 14 per cent of Daimler-Benz, and 11 per cent of the Midland Bank.

[20] In 1987, alleging that Iraq was using the port of Kuwait to export oil and import weapons, the Iranian navy attacked Kuwaiti merchant ships. In response, Kuwait requested and obtained permission from the major powers - US, France, Britain, and the USSR - to use their flags for the Kuwait merchant navy. The US and Britain sent their navies to protect Kuwaiti ships in the Gulf.

[21] Once the war between Iran and Iraq ended in 1988, tensions between Kuwait and Iraq started to mount. Kuwait demanded the payment of $15 billion on account of war loans, which Iraq refused to return, alleging that those sums had been used to protect Kuwait. Iraq accused Kuwait of 'stealing' their country's oil, by extracting large amounts of oil from the common deposits which stretch along the border. Iraq claimed that the Emirate was pumping out much more oil than its entitlement, and demanded $2.4 billion in compensation.

[22] In spite of repeated attempts at mediation by Palestinian leader Yasser Arafat, tension rose. On August 2 1990, Iraq invaded Kuwait quickly and decisively. Emir al-Sabah and his family took refuge in Saudi Arabia. Nearly 300,000 Kuwaitis fled the country, to join the other 100,000 who were abroad on their summer vacation. The occupation forces encouraged the exodus, perhaps to 'de-Kuwaitize' the country. A pro-Iraqi provisional government, led by Al Hussein Ali, requested the total fusion of Iraq and Kuwait. A few days later the Emirate was declared an Iraqi province.

[23] Iraq had expected understanding from the US, in exchange for assured oil supplies, but the US reacted very harshly to the invasion and promoted a series of extremely tough measures from the UN Security Council. On August 6, the trading, financial, and military boycott of Iraq was voted through, and on November 29, the use of force against Iraq was approved if the country refused to withdraw from Kuwait before January 15 1991. Only Cuba and Yemen abstained from voting.

[24] When the Emir went into exile in Saudi Arabia he was pressured by the US to promise democratic elections once the country was liberated.

[25] The ensuing Gulf War devastated the country, not so much in terms of lives lost, for most of the fighting was done on Iraqi territory, but the bombings and forced withdrawal of the occupation troops left most of Kuwait's oil wells burning and the country was unable to produce any oil until 1992.

[26] The War also turned Kuwait into an environmental disaster area. The black cloud formed by some 50 burning oil wells, and gigantic oil spills along the coast produced major degradation of the air, marine resources and soil. An enormous mass of oil lined the coasts, posing a threat to birds and other animals. The Gulf's ecosystem was seriously affected, especially fish species which form a staple of the local diet.

[27] It was estimated that the clean-up and reconstruction cost between $150 and 200 billion. On January 9 1991, Britain committed itself to grant a loan of $950 million for reconstruction. Kuwait's debts to allied countries, arising from war costs, rose to more than $22 billion.

[28] After the War was over more than 1,300 people were killed by mines which were laid during the conflict.

[29] On March 18 1991 Amnesty International in London denounced the arbitrary detention and torture of Palestinians residing in Kuwait, carried out by Kuwaiti civilians and military.

[30] Also in March 1991, while US Secretary of State James Baker was visiting Kuwait, the Prince and premier Sheikh Saad al-Abdallah promised to lead the Emirate towards democracy and to reinstate parliament.

[31] On April 1 1991 a group of Kuwaiti citizens demanded freedom of the press, independence of the judiciary, the legalization of political parties, and the implementation of measures to fight corruption.

[32] On April 8, the Emir announced that a new National Assembly would be elected 'when circumstances permitted', but he failed to state a precise date. According to several reports, popular discontent was running high as a consequence of the monarch's delay in returning to the country and the vagueness of his political plans.

[33] In June 1991, Sheikh Jabir al-Sabah called a National Council to discuss the elections, and female and foreign suffrage. The opposition was still demanding the re-establishment

PROFILE

ENVIRONMENT

Nearly all the land is flat, except for a few ranges of dunes. The inland is desert with only one oasis, the Al-Jahrah. The coast is low and uniform. The city and port of Kuwait is located in the only deep-water harbor. The climate is tempered by ocean currents but the temperature is high in summer. Winters are warm with frequent dust and sand storms. Petroleum is the main economic resource, with three refineries in Shuaiba, Mina al-Ahmadi and Mina Abdulla. Tremendous environmental damage was caused by burning oil wells, as a result of the Gulf war in 1991. The country also suffers from a lack of water.

SOCIETY

Peoples: Kuwaitis, of Arab descent, account for less than half of the population, 60 per cent of which is made up of immigrant workers from Palestine, Egypt, Iran, Pakistan, India, Bangladesh, the Philippines and other countries. **Religions:** Muslim 85 per cent, of which Sunni 45 per cent, Shi'ah 30 per cent; other Muslim 10 per cent; other (mostly Christian and Hindu) 15 per cent. **Languages:** Arabic (official). **Political Parties:** Islamic Constitutional Movement, a moderate Sunni group; Kuwaiti Democratic Forum, liberal; Salafeen, a fundamentalist Sunni group. **Social Organizations:** Federation of Unions.

THE STATE

Official Name: Dawlat al-Kuwayt. **Administrative divisions:** 5 governances. **Capital:** Kuwait (Al-Kuwayt) 1,090,000 people (1995). **Other cities:** al-Jahra 139,476 people; as-Salimiyah 116,104; Hawalli 84,478; al-Farwaniyah 47,106 (1993). **Government:** Jabir al-Ahmad al Sabah, Emir, since December 1977; Saad al-Abdullah as-Salim as-Sabah, Prime Minister since February 1978. The National Assembly has 50 members. **National Holiday:** February 25, Independence Day (1961). **Armed Forces:** 15,300 (1996). **Paramilitary:** The National Guard has 5,000 troops.

STATISTICS

DEMOGRAPHY

Population: 1,897,000 (1999)
Annual growth: 2.5 % (1975/97)
Estimates for year 2015 (million): 2.6 (1999)
Annual growth to year 2015: 2.3 % (1997/2015)
Urban population: 97.3 % (1997)
Urban Growth: 0.9 % (1980/95)
Children per woman: 2.9 (1998)

HEALTH

Life expectancy at birth: 76 years (1998)
male: 74 years (1998)
female: 78 years (1998)
Maternal mortality: 5 per 100,000 live births (1990-98)
Infant mortality: 12 per 1,000 (1998)
Under-5 child mortality: 13 per 1,000 (1998)
Daily calorie supply: 3,075 per capita (1996)
178 doctors per 100,000 people (1993)

EDUCATION

Literacy: 79 % (1995)
male: 82 % (1995)
female: 76 % (1995)
School enrolment:
Primary total: 75 % (1990/96)
male: 76 % (1990/97)
female: 74 % (1990/97)
Secondary:
male: 65 % (1990/96)
female: 65 % (1990/96)
Tertiary: 19 % (1996)
Primary school teachers: one for every 14 (1996)

COMMUNICATIONS

374 newspapers (1996), 660 radios (1997), 373 TV sets (1996) and 232 main telephone lines (1996) per 1,000 people
Books: 11 new titles per 100,000 people (1992/94)

ECONOMY

Annual growth, GNP: 6.1 % (1995)
Consumer price index: 104.4 (1998)
Currency: 0.3 dinars = $ 1 (1998)
Cereal imports: 699,307 metric tons (1998)
Food import dependency: 16 % (1997)
Fertilizer use: 2,000 kg per ha (1997)
Exports: $ 11,347 million (1998)
Imports: $ 11,760 million (1998)
Development aid received: $ 2 million (1997); $ 1.5 per capita (1997)

ENERGY

Consumption: 8,936.0 Kgs of Oil equivalent per capita yearly (1997); -618.0 % imported (1997)

HDI (rank/value): 35/0.833 (1997)

of the 1962 constitution and the formation of a democratically elected parliament, though no opposition leaders would be allowed in the Council. Over a thousand people demonstrated in the streets after the Emir made his announcement. Although street demonstrations are illegal in Kuwait, the Government made no attempt to stop the march.

[34] When the war ended, the Emir launched the slogan of 're-Kuwaitizing' Kuwait. The plan included a drastic reduction in the number of foreigners in the country. Over 800,000 people had to leave the country, to comply with the Sheikh's measure. A small number of foreigners were deported, but most have to leave when they fail to find jobs and schools for their children.

[35] In mid-December 1991, Saudi Arabia, the United Arab Emirates, Oman, Qatar, Bahrain, and Kuwait held a summit meeting aimed at creating a collective security mechanism, and establishing a new defensive framework for the region which holds 40 per cent of the world's oil reserves.

[36] After renewing oil production, Kuwait initially accepted the OPEC quota of two million barrels per day. However, in February, it confronted OPEC's other members and unilaterally decided to raise daily production to 2.16 million barrels. The Oil Minister explained that the country had confirmed the existence of new deposits of crude oil in what was formally a 'neutral zone' along the border with Saudi Arabia.

[37] In January, press censorship was lifted. Demonstrations were organized by women's groups demanding the right to vote. Elections for the National Assembly were finally held on October 5, with independent opposition groups winning 31 seats, the fundamentalists 19 and the liberals 12. For the first time ever, the cabinet contained several Members of Parliament elected by direct popular vote.

[38] In early 1993, a financial scandal broke involving the Kuwait Investment Office (KIO), and two members of the royal family were found to have been involved. The personal holdings of high-ranking KIO officials were frozen when $5 billion was discovered to be missing. $1 billion had been diverted to Torras, a Spanish business consortium.

[39] As a result, the Government prohibited the publication of any information on government corruption, without prior official consent. Months later, the British *Financial Times* newspaper accused the KIO of having used $300 million to win the support of several UN diplomats in the military operation against Iraq.

[40] In 1993 the UN finally determined the frontier with Iraq, despite protests by Baghdad. As a response to supposed incursions by Iraqi troops, the US bombed Iraq repeatedly (see Iraq). Washington decided to install missiles in Kuwait and it began building a wall 130 kms long equipped with 1.3 million mines along the new frontier.

[41] In August the ex-chief of the Temporary Free Government imposed by Baghdad, Al-Hussein Ali, was condemned to death, as well as five Kuwaitis and 10 Jordanians accused of collaborating with the Iraqi occupation.

[42] In 1994, several leading officials of Kuwait were accused of corruption. On April, Petroleum minister Ali Ahmad al-Baghli was expelled from the Government, after which he denounced corruption within the Kuwait Petroleum Corp. On June, the Constitutional Court declared itself without jurisdiction on a protest against former Finance minister, sheikh Ali Khalifah as-Sabah, presented by the National Assembly.

[43] In 1995, the Government with the aid of numerous Kuwaiti investors pursued the privatization of state companies and carried out major investments in arms.

[44] In February 1996, Amnesty International denounced summary executions, torture and expulsions without trial. In October, the Government obtained 30 of 50 seats in the National Assembly election. In the same year the economy grew due to the rise of international crude oil prices and new investments, both in the construction and oil sectors.

[45] In November 1997, the Emir ordered the closure of borders with Iraq and bolstered surveillance in several border points, due to the new crisis which erupted between Washington and Baghdad. Kuwait was the only Arab country which supported the US plan to promote a new armed intervention against Iraq. In March 1998, the Emir formed a new government and replaced his Finance Minister.

[46] After several legislators threatened to dismiss the Minister of Muslim Affairs because of mistakes printed in 120,000 copies of the Koran, the Emir dissolved Parliament in May 1999 and called for legislative elections in July, a year and a half ahead of schedule. The deputy Prime Minister, Sheikh Sabah al-Ahmed al-Sabah, had urged legislators not to proceed with the dismissal process.

[45] Even though Kuwaiti women have for decades been directing companies and newspapers, heading diplomatic missions and actively helping in the oil industry, making up approximately 30 per cent of the country's workforce, it was only in 1999 that the Emir gave in to decades of lobbying and made Cabinet approve a bill by which women acquired the right to vote and to stand as parliamentary candidates. The law will become effective in 2003, that is, after two parliamentary elections. ∎

Islamic civilization:

The Arab peninsula, inhabited during the first centuries of the Christian Era by nomad or semi-sedentary Bedouins, was the geographical and human context where Islamic culture and civilization surged. It is said that it was in Mecca, a center of pilgrimage, a city of caravans, and a trade centre of the Medieval world, that Mohammed was born. There truth was revealed to him and there he began his preaching of Islam until in the year 622 - the origin of the Hejira - he sought refuge under menace of death in the city of Medina, and the 30 years that followed Mohammed's death (632-661, during which period the four orthodox caliphs, who accompanied him in his preaching, governed) are considered by the Muslims as the 'golden age' of Islam. Sustained by the inner belief in its message and by the overwhelming strength of the Arabic armies, Islamic expansion defeated the Sasanid and Byzantine empires, as well as the ancient Roman West and built a Muslim Empire which headed world trade and structured a web of major cities.

ISLAMIC CITY AND RELIGIOUS INSTITUTIONS

The Islamic city is a community of people who practise the Islamic religion. It constitutes the 'umma', or nation, in which each Muslim person is included, whether he lives alone or as part of a group, whether peasant or citizen, nomad or settled. A much quoted expression defines it as *Dar al-Islam*, 'the home of Islam', and it limits it to the countries or urban groups which obey the Islamic canonical law, and where its traditional lifestyles are practised. Islam, which signifies 'submission to God', comprises three basic religious institutions: the Koran, the Tradition of the Prophet (*sunna*), and the written and oral teachings of the jurists. Through the double testimony of the faith - 'There is no more God than the One and Only' (Allah); 'Mohammed is the messenger of God' - which declaration confers the condition of Muslim to every person of good will, the Koran proclaims its essential message, *al-tawhid* or 'Divine Unity', which establishes the rights of the Cre-

ator above all contingencies of our earthly existence and it achieves itself in the individual life of everyone who places his/her thoughts and actions nearest to God. With that purpose people are urged to read the Koran, to invoke the names of God, and to fulfill the obligatory practices of prayer, fasting, alms giving, and pilgrimage to Mecca, at least once in a lifetime. The Prophet, providentially 'chosen' in order to communicate Muslim law (*sharia*), became the most exalted person in the Islamic world. The collection of his sayings and advice, his acts and gestures, were gathered during the third century of Hejira, in the *hadits* or traditions, with the purpose of making the transmission and knowledge of them easier for the community of followers. Neither the Koran nor the Sunna, nevertheless, were elaborated as bodies of law. It was a later task of the learned men of Islam to formulate the juridical system that rules and divides the actions of the believers and makes them either compelling, recommended, permissible, damnable or prohibited. Its development led to a divergence between the *sunni* jurisprudence, which does not approve of personal reflection, or of the law being adaptable, or of its possible evolving into something else, and the *shi'a* jurisprudence, which approves of all of that. A wisdom such as the Muslim, which tends to introduce the religious dimension in all aspects of life, takes this divergence as a difference of interpretation which derives, ultimately, from the kindness of God. 'The disagreements between learned men - one of its proverbs declares - are a gift'.

SOCIETY, community, AND INDIVIDUAL

The essential thing about the Islamic city is the 'durable combination of the effort by every man [sic] in order to submit to the will of the divine legislator within the communal framework which is the help and support of his effort'. In Islam, the link between the individual and the social whole is so strong that the task of individual salvation 'includes ipso facto the sacralization of the social'. The salvation of a single man [sic] depends on the people who surround him, as well as on favorable or unfavorable circumstances. Tradition assumes that it was Mohammed himself who formulated the principle of 'iyma' or consensus of believers, which becomes concrete in Muslim law through the form of a collective statute called the 'duty of sufficiency'. It would exonerate a Muslim person of any compelling

origins and foundations

legal duty provided a sufficient number of followers would exonerate him of it. The individual, nevertheless, is not lost in the communal. Islamic law supposes that a person compromises only him/herself through his/her behavior and that, on its own day, s/he alone will appear before the Supreme Judge to respond for her/his behavior. The fact of all people being equal before God, and being also equally dependent on Him/Her, and compelled to obey the law, has given place to the definition of the Muslim community as 'equable theocracy'. The strong sense of social cohesion which accompanied the high degree of integration of traditional Muslim societies is due in a great degree to the socio-religious values which guided the life of its individuals and communities.

GOVERNMENT AND POLITICS: THE ISLAMIC COMMUNITY

The community established in Medina in the first century of Hejira (the 7th century AD), was the prime model of institutional religious organization which ruled in all traditional Muslim societies. Its name being Yatrib before that date, its new name, al-Madina ('the city by excellence'), designated its condition as a center of *umma* and a seat of authority and justice. The caliph or imam, a successor of the Prophet, united in his person the spiritual and the secular authority, and was the supreme chief of the city. He was in charge of creating the conditions for the application of Koranic law, of directing the Holy War (*jihad*), of organizing the army, and of assuring an orderly administration and the security of the countries under its dominion. The caliph designated also, in each city, the ministers or viziers, the governors, the army chiefs, the tax collectors, and even the police corps (*surta*) that maintained order and protected the city from enemies. Justice in the traditional Islamic society was derived from divine mandate. It refers to an original pact through which God designated the people who exercise authority. These must protect the followers, and the followers must obey the authorities. The Platonic ideal of justice and Islam are synonomous: the order decreed by God will only prevail where virtuous people rule, who are capable of uniting their deep knowledge of the divinity to a high moral quality. They have in their hands 'the task of making people, in this life and in this milieu enjoy a maximum of happiness, and also of making them reach the joys of a future life through communal institutions based on justice and brotherhood' (al-Farabi, 4th century of Hejira). Despite the fact that the juridical order of traditional Islamic cities lacked the local and municipal autonomy enjoyed by medieval European cities, its institutions, guided by values that negated racial, religious, or social discrimination, nevertheless stimulated the high degree of integration shared by all cities of the Muslim world from al-Andalus to India. Muslim jurists accepted through the centuries, as source of legislation, the local customs and habits of the different cities. This shows their flexibility and democratic inclinations.

THE ECONOMY IN MEDIEVAL SOCIETY

The economy of traditional Muslim cities was ruled by a corporate system which integrated the people dedicated to production, distribution, and services, whether they were proprietors, employees, home servants, independent workers or government employees, whether they were 'people of high or low condition, Muslim, Christian, or Jew, native or foreign residents, they all belonged to the corporate system'. In the corporations the urban population was gathered according to the profession of each individual; there were artisan, merchant, auctioneer, lender, musician, singer, storyteller, transport, and sailor groups. The members of each corporation were considered also members of the community of believers to which service was specially credited the contribution of each profession and trade. These were learnt through hard work supervised by a master (*sayj*) connected to a chain of corporation masters, linked as well to other corporations, to the Holy Patrons, and even to the Prophet. The corporations were structured according to a conceptual and ritual system transmitted orally from generation to generation and linked to the sufi orders (Islamic loggias). To the acceptance of a young person as an apprentice in a workshop there followed the recitation of the first *azora* (chapter) of the Koran before the masters of the corporation and a period of years of work with low remuneration or lack thereof, compensated by the notion that this was the way of learning and of becoming gradually integrated to the rest of the community. A branch of sweet basil was given on behalf of the master to the young apprentice, signalling the beginning of his initiation. The ceremony, celebrated in the house of a master or in some city garden, was attended by a large group of noble people, who undertook religious and ceremonial rites at the end of which the young person became a member of the brotherhood, under a ritual expression of joy in which several traditions coincided: 'God bless Jesus, Moses, and the ones who embellish their eyes with antimonium*, so that no one can harm us'. The initiation ended with a simple meal called *tamliha* (salad) in memory of the double value of salt, a link between those who share it, and also symbol of craftspeople themselves (known as 'the salt of bazaars' for being seen as the nucleus of people who make a life out of sweat and patience). The initiate entered his own corporation, and through it, the umma. After some years, the execution of a masterpiece as a proof of his refined abilities could elevate the artisan to the position of a master. We should mention in passing that, for Islamic sufism, craftsmanship was synonymous of art and at the same time, it was considered a means of spiritual evolution. In this sense, it was 'an image of the task a man [sic] must undertake on himself and on his soul if he aspires to the contemplation of the divine realities; he is compared to a rough material, without order or form, but potentially noble'.

EDUCATION AND RELIGIOUS INSTRUCTION

Muslim education, initiated at the time of the Prophet in Mecca, was fundamentally given through the mosque, and its content was the *sharia* or Islamic law, whose learning was a 'duty of sufficiency' for the Islamic community. The highest distinction in Islam was to acquire the 'knowledge' - al-'ilm - or the knowledge of revealed law. Memory was a praised gift, and the title of *hafiz* was granted to the person who knew the Koran by heart. Religious instruction was one of the key elements in order to assure the survival of Islamic civilization. A citizen of average education could be a consultant inside the community, as well as conduct the prayers, and practice the Koran law. At the beginning, religious instruction and overall education were the same, but lately there were differences between the two. The first century of Hejira, dedicated to military conquest and to the establishment of political authority in Islam, did not produce a noticeable development of Islamic education. But from the second century onwards - during which the institution of the mosque developed among the conquered territories - and above all from the third century onwards - in which a generation of jurists, theologians, and linguists sought to preserve the language and the traditions of a civilization which had grown far through very diverse cultural areas - education became a foremost preoccupation. During the third and the fourth centuries the mosque was a virtual public university, a center of worship and also a center for social gatherings. But it was then also that the elementary school (*kultab*) appeared, as well as the 'houses of wisdom' or of 'science', exclusively for academic activities. In the fifth century appeared the high school or *madrasa*, fostered by the Government, which was from then on the highest centre of learning in the Muslim world. Towards the ninth century, it was necessary to have finished studies in a madrasa in order to occupy a position in government. It was not only the acquisition of knowledge - which is the means of distinguishing between the prohibited and the praiseworthy - but its transmission also, which became a religious obligation in Islam, anticipating thus the historical effort in order to democratize teaching. 'Islamic society repudiates the *alim* (learned person) who does not transmit his learning to others'. Islam has defended the freedom of thought, and has recognized the limits of reason. It cannot doubt neither divine unity nor the truth of Mohammed's message. From the point of view of Islam, reason can be either inborn - when it is a divine gift, or acquired - when it is the result of individual effort and experience. A valuable contribution of Islam is its recognition of the practical nature of thought and education, evident through a tradition attributed to the Prophet: 'You should acquire all the wisdom of which you are capable! But God will not reward you for all that you have learned until you translate it into action!' ∎

* The custom of painting the eyes with antimonium distinguished the Arabs as such.

Kyrgyzstan

Kyrguyzstan

Population: 4,669,000 (1999)
Area: 198,500 SQ KM
Capital: Bishkek
Currency: Som
Language: Kyrgyz

In the Bronze Age (2000 years BC), the present Kyrgyzstan was inhabited by tribes who farmed and raised livestock. Between the 7th and the 3rd centuries BC the Saks settled in the area, and between the 3rd and 2nd centuries BC, a group of Usun tribes.

[2] From the 1st century BC to the 4th century AD, Kyrgyzstan was a part of the state of Kushan, which disappeared after the nomadic Eufalites invaded. Toward the end of the 4th century, Kyrgyzstan became part of the western region of the Turkish *Kaganate* (Khanate), governed by the brothers Tumin and Istemi.

[3] In the 7th century, Kyrgyz territory was occupied by the Turguesh (under the chieftain Moje-Dajan). Between the 8th and 10th centuries it came under the Karluks who were replaced by the Karahanyds between the 10th and 12th centuries. From the 12th to the 14th century, the Turkish peoples of Kyrgyzstan were absorbed as part of the Mongol Empire, in the ulus (province) of the Chagatai khan.

[4] During this period, Kipchak-Kyrguish tribes in the area between the Irtysh and Yenisey rivers migrated to Tian Shan, where they mixed with the Mongols and local Turkish tribes. In the 15th and 16th centuries, the Kyrgyz people were formed. The Kyrgyz Khanate was established in Tian Shan by Khan Ajmet.

[5] The distinguishing feature of Kyrgyz social organization was the lack of a ruling class of princes or nobles, with authority exercised instead by the *manaps* (elders), whose leadership depended on their personal prestige. The tribes maintained a high degree of cohesion because they were constantly at war against neighboring peoples.

[6] Between the 16th and 18th centuries, the Kyrgyz were subdued by the Oirat-Yungars. In the mid-18th century the Oirat-Yungar State was conquered by Chinese troops. Kyrgyzstan became a protectorate of the Tsin (Chin) Empire. In the early 19th century, Russia began to show interest in the region, which had been conquered by Khan Madali of Kokand.

[7] In 1862, Russian troops supported the Kyrgyz rebellion against the Khanate of Kokand, and took Pishpek. The following year, Kyrgyz representatives from central Tian Shan surrendered to Russia, in the city of Verni (today Alma-Ata). In 1864, Northern Kyrgyzstan joined the Russian Empire, as part of the region of Semirechensk.

[8] In 1867, Czar Alexander II created the Regional Government of Turkistan. Russian colonists began arriving by the thousands, and the Kyrgyz saw their best lands confiscated, and turned over to immigrants for agricultural use.

[9] In 1875 there was an uprising against Khan Jodoyar of Kokand. The Russian Empire leapt in to annex the Khanate of Kokand and Southern Kyrgyzstan. Despite the fact that the major part of its population was Uzbek, the region of Fergana was formed as part of the Province of Turkistan. Kyrgyzstan was divided into three regions - Semirechensk, Syr Darya and Fergana - within the province of Turkistan, with Tashkent as its center.

[10] Friction between the various ethnic groups periodically flared up over the issue of land ownership and mandatory military service, finally triggering a major revolt by the Kyrgyz, which was brutally put down by the czarist regime.

[11] Soviet power was established in the district of Pishpek in December 1917, though there was strong opposition from guerrilla groups in the rest of the country. In 1921 and 1922, agrarian and water reforms were carried out.

[12] In 1924 the Autonomous Region of Kara-Kirghiz was formed, as a part of the Russian Federation. In 1925, its name was changed to the Autonomous Region of Kirghizia, becoming, in 1926, an 'Autonomous Soviet Socialist Republic'. In December 1936, Kyrgyzstan became a federated republic of the Soviet Union (USSR).

[13] Under socialism the Kyrgyz had to change their nomadic way of life radically, joining the new agricultural cooperatives or working in the industries created by the State (textile, leather, tobacco, lumber, metal and hydroelectric power). They also had to change 'Pishpek' to 'Frunze', the name of a

famous Red Army general, and the USSR continued to recruit a major part of its soldiers from among the Kyrgyz.

[14] As a part of the pre-World War II five-year development plans, the USSR built large plants in Kyrgyzstan for the extraction of antimony, as well as the processing of its agricultural products. The first metal-processing plants and modern blast furnaces were set up during this period.

[15] During the War and in the decades which followed, the region's industry underwent further expansion, producing machinery, building materials and electric power.

[16] From 1961 until the end of the Brezhnev era, Turdakun Usubaliev was first secretary of the Kyrgyzstan Communist Party, which functioned as a branch of the CP of the Soviet Union. Kyrgyz writer Chingiz Aytmatov achieved international fame during the 1970s, as the author of a play dealing with the moral compromises made under Stalinism.

[17] From 1986, with the changes put in motion in the USSR by Mikhail Gorbachev, an independence movement developed in Kyrgyzstan. After the failed coup against Gorbachev in August 1991, the republic of Kyrgyzstan decided to separate from the USSR.

[18] On August 31 1991, Kyrgyzstan's Soviet declared the new republic a democratic and independent state. On that occasion, a statement was made in recognition of the three new Baltic states of Estonia, Latvia and Lithuania.

[19] In Kyrgyzstan's first presidential elections, held in October of that year, Askar Akayev, former president of the Academy of Sciences and a physicist of international renown, ran unopposed and was elected. Akayev was among the few leaders - along with Russian President, Boris Yeltsin - who personally resisted the failed coup in August, at the Parliament in Moscow.

[20] Akayev was the first head of state in the former Soviet Union to ban the Communist Party and to proclaim the independence of his republic. In December, Kyrgyzstan signed the founding charter of the Commonwealth of Independent States (CIS) with 10 other ex-Soviet

WORKERS

% OF LABOUR FORCE **1998**

■ FEMALE: 47% ■ MALE: 53%

1990

■ SERVICES: 41.2%
■ INDUSTRY: 26.7%
■ AGRICULTURE: 32.1%

LAND USE

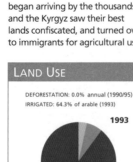

DEFORESTATION: 0.0% annual (1990/95)
IRRIGATED: 64.3% of arable (1993)

1993

■ FOREST & WOODLAND: 3.5%
■ ARABLE: 7.1%
■ OTHER: 89.4%

republics

21 In December 1991, President Akayev had to exercise his veto power over a law approved by the Parliament, establishing the exclusive right of the Kyrgyz to the land. He thus avoided inflaming aggression between the native population and the Uzbeks of Fergana, which could have turned into an even greater conflict with the neighboring republic of Uzbekistan. The previous year, in the region of Os, in the western part of the country, more than 200 Uzbeks were assassinated by bands of young Kyrgyz, manipulated, it was claimed at the time, by agents of the former Soviet secret police (KGB).

22 Kyrgyzstan started to create a National Guard of a thousand troops, and asked CIS forces to remain in its territory. This military presence was justified, for 'security reasons', until the republic was ready for full membership of the international community.

23 In March 1992, Akayev reaffirmed his intention to maintain a strict neutrality, in spite of the attempts of Muslim states like Pakistan, Saudi Arabia or Iran to have closer ties. However, the President of Kyrgyzstan stated he was willing to cultivate closer relations with Turkey.

24 In May 1993, a new constitution was approved while controversies and disagreements between Akayev and Parliament continued, as Parliament was opposed to his economic reform policies. A national currency, the *som*, was introduced that month. In the midst of growing tensions, many Kyrgyz of Russian origin, mainly intellectuals and engineers, began to flee the country.

25 In 1994, Akayev continued his reforms policy recommended by the IMF. After the som's introduction, inflation fell from 40 and 50 per cent per month to 4 per cent, among the lowest in the former Soviet Union. At the same time, national production fell 19 per cent in 1992 and 16 per cent in 1993, imports - especially from Turkey and China - grew rapidly and social inequality was increased.

26 In February 1995, legislative elections did not significantly modify Parliament's opposition to Akayev's economic liberalization policy. The President tried to extend his term through a referendum, but Parliament decided to hold presidential elections in December, which were won by Akayev with 60 per cent of the vote.

27 In February 1996, Akayev held a referendum on constitutional changes giving him greater powers, and most of his proposals were approved. Opponents to the Government, like journalists who criticized Akayev's policies, were persecuted, imprisoned on charges of slander and mistreated, something which was denounced by Amnesty International in its 1997 report.

28 The role played by Kyrgyzstan in the production and trafficking of drugs in the region changed substantially during 1997, going from a country of transit to a nation with an increasing number of processing laboratories.

34 On April 12 1999, Amangeldy Mursadykovich Muraliyev was appointed Premier, succeeding Zhumabek Ibraimov who had died. Muraliyev, who was 52 when he took office, had served as governor of the Osh region in the nation's south.

35 The Government resigned in December 1999 after Akayev accused it of incompetence and of failing to stimulate the frail economy. According to the Government's own data, the economy grew 1.7 per cent in 1998, making Kyrgyzstan one of the few former Soviet republics that did not suffer an economic recession that year. But increased inflation rates, a trade deficit and the ever-weakening national currency led then Prime Minister Kubanychbek Zhumaliyev and his cabinet to resign, following the Security Council president's criticism.

36 The decision to prevent some of the main opposition parties from taking part in the Parliamentary elections in February and March 2000 cast doubts on Kyrgyzstan's democracy. Candidates failed to get the 50 per cent needed to win outright in the first round of voting and the second round was held hours after the Supreme Court upheld a ban preventing leading opposition figure Daniyar Usenov from taking part in the run-off ballot. Hundreds of Usenov's supporters staged a series of demonstrations demanding the Kyrgyz authorities declare the results invalid.

37 In April, a court found Usenov guilty of involvement in a fight with officials at Bishkek airport in 1996. In March another rival of Akayev, the former vice-president, Felix Kulov, had been detained on charges relating to his period as head of the national security ministry in 1997. ■

MATERNAL MORTALITY

1990-98

Per 100,000 live births

65

PROFILE

ENVIRONMENT

Located in the northeastern part of Central Asia, Kyrgyzstan lies in the heart of the Tian Shan mountain range. It is bounded by China and Tajikistan in the south, Kazakhstan in the north, Uzbekistan in the west, the Pamir and Altai mountain ranges in the southwest and the Tian Shan range in the northeast. It has plateaus and valleys: in the north, the Chu and Talas valley; in the south, the Alai Valley; and in the southwest, the Fergana Valley. The climate is continental, with sharp contrasts between day and night temperatures. The eastern part of Tian Shan is dry, while the southwestern slopes of the Fergana range are rainy. The main rivers are the Narym and the Kara-Suu. Lake Issyk-Kul is the most important of the country's lakes. In the mountains there are forests and meadows, while desert and semi-desert vegetation abounds at lower altitudes. Metal deposits include lead and zinc; in addition, there are large coal reserves and some oil and natural gas deposits. Water pollution is a serious problem, since one third of the population obtains its water from rivers, streams, or wells.

SOCIETY

Peoples: Kyrgyz, 52.4 per cent; Russians, 21.5 per cent; Uzbeks, 12.9 per cent; Ukrainians, 2.5 per cent, Germans 2.4 per cent.
Religions: Islam (Sunni) and Christian (Russian Orthodox Church).
Languages: Kyrgyz (official), Russian, Uzbek.
Political Parties: Democratic Movement of Kyrgyzstan, Erkin Kyrgyzstan Democratic Party, Communist Party.

THE STATE

Official Name: Respublika Kyrguyzstan.
Capital: Bishkek 700,000 people (1997).
Other cities: Os 218,700 people; Tokmok 71,200; Kara-Köl 64,300 (1991).
Government: Askar Akayev, President since October 1991, re-elected in 1995. Amangeldy Mursadykovich Muraliyev, Prime Minister since April 1999.
National Holiday: December 15, Independence (1991).
Armed Forces: 7,000.

STATISTICS

DEMOGRAPHY

Population: 4,669,000 (1999)
Annual growth: 1.5 % (1975/97)
Estimates for year 2015 (million): 5.5 (1999)
Annual growth to year 2015: 0.9 % (1997/2015)
Urban population: 39.2 % (1997)
Urban Growth: 1.6 % (1980/95)
Children per woman: 3.2 (1998)

HEALTH

Life expectancy at birth: 68 years (1998)
male: 63 years (1998)
female: 72 years (1998)
Maternal mortality: 65 per 100,000 live births (1990-98)
Infant mortality: 56 per 1,000 (1998)
Under-5 child mortality: 66 per 1,000 (1998)
Daily calorie supply: 2,489 per capita (1996)
310 doctors per 100,000 people (1993)
Safe water: 79 % (1990/98)

EDUCATION

Literacy: 97 % (1995)
male: 99 % (1995)
female: 95 % (1995)
School enrolment:
Primary total: 107 % (1990/96)
male: 108 % (1990/97)
female: 105 % (1990/97)
Secondary:
male: 76 % (1990/96)
female: 85 % (1990/96)
Tertiary: 12 % (1996)
Primary school teachers: one for every 20 (1995)

COMMUNICATIONS

15 newspapers (1996), 112 radios (1997) and 75 main telephone lines (1996) per 1,000 people
Books: 7 new titles per 100,000 people (1992/94)

ECONOMY

Per capita, GNP: $ 380 (1998)
Annual growth, GNP: 4.2 % (1998)
Annual inflation: 157.8 % (1990/98)
Consumer price index: 193.5 (1998)
Currency: 20.8 som = $ 1 (1998)
Cereal imports: 154,532 metric tons (1998)
Food import dependency: 21 % (1997)
Fertilizer use: 230 kg per ha (1997)
Exports: $ 602 million (1998)
Imports: $ 876 million (1998)
External debt: $ 1,148 million (1998); $ 247 per capita (1998)
Debt service: 9.4 % of exports (1998)
Development aid received: $ 240 million (1997); $ 53.9 per capita (1997); 14.10 % of GNP (1997)

ENERGY

Consumption: 603.0 Kgs of Oil equivalent per capita yearly (1997); 50.0 % imported (1997)

HDI (rank/value): 97/0.702 (1997)

Laos

Lao

Population: 5,297,000 (1999)
Area: 236,800 SQ KM
Capital: Vientiane (Viangchan)
Currency: New kip
Language: Lao

In the 14th century Sam Sen Tal, a Burmese ruler united the present northeast Thailand with most of the modern day territory of Laos, founding the flourishing state of Lang Xang, the 'Land of a Million Elephants'. In the late 18th century, the country split into three parts: Champassac, Vientiane and Luang Prabang.

2 By the 19th century, the Thais had established dominion over the land and Tiao Anuvong, Prince of Vientiane, led an ill-fated nationalist rebellion in 1827. In 1892, the French invaded and by 1893 had established a protectorate over Luang Praband, with the rest of the country becoming part of French Indochina.

3 During World War II, Japan occupied Laos and a pro-independence movement arose in Vientiane, led by three princes, Phetsarat, leader of the Free Laos government-in-exile, Suvana Fuma, leader of the National Progressive Party, and his half-brother, Tiao Sufanuvong, head of the Neo Lao Issara (Laos National United Front). In September 1945, Sufanuvong set up a provisional Pathet Lao government, declaring independence and promulgating the constitution of 'independent Laos', in spite of protests from King Sisavang Vong, reigning since 1904.

4 In early 1946, the country was again under French occupation. The Pathet Lao provisional government sought refuge in Bangkok, where the Pathet leaders organized the anti-colonialist struggle through the Lao Issara or 'free Laos' movement.

5 On July 19 1949, the Franco-Laotian Convention recognized Laotian independence 'as part of the French Union'. The Pathet Lao leaders saw this as mere formal independence and refused to recognize it. Suvana Fuma opted for negotiation, but the opposition coalition decided on active resistance; the military victories led to a new treaty in 1953.

6 Differences between the Lao Issara, Suvana Fuma government, and the Pathet Lao were reconciled in November 1957. An agreement was reached, whereby the latter would participate in the political life of the country under the name 'Neo Lao Haksat' (Laotian Patriotic Front), led by Tiao Sufanuvong.

7 The May 1958 elections were won by the Left, worrying the US. Suvana Fuma's ruling party joined forces with the Independent Party to form the so-called Laotian People's Demonstration, together achieving a small majority. They formed a center-left coalition government, led by 'neutralist' Suvana Fuma, with Sufanuvong as planning minister.

8 The US was strongly opposed and threatened to cut economic aid. This destabilized the Government, and in August the leaders of the Committee for the Defence of National Interests took over. A military offensive against the Pathet Lao drove Sufanuvong from the capital, forcing him into guerrilla action in the forests.

9 In 1959, the army gained control, while the Pathet Lao controlled the strategic northern provinces and the central plain of Jars.

10 General Fumi Nosavang, the former defense minister, and his troops seized Vientiane on December 13 1960, driving out Pathet Lao troops. A massive air raid left 1,500 dead and forced Vientiane to surrender.

11 The Thai and US supported Revolutionary Anti-Communist Committee, headed by Fumi Nosavang and Prince Bun Um claimed legitimacy to govern. On December 20 1960, however, Princes Suvana Fuma and Sufanuvong declared their intention of forming a national unity government.

12 The 'neutralists' joined forces with the Pathet Lao and launched successful joint military campaigns.

13 In 1961 in Geneva, Britain and the Soviet Union initiated negotiations for a peaceful solution, and on January 19 1962, a final agreement was signed for a national unity government.

14 Growing US intervention resulted in the internationalization of the Vietnam War. Air raids on Laotian territory increased to 500 missions per day by 1970 and in nine years Laos was subjected to a greater number of bombings than the whole of Europe during World War II.

15 The Pathet Lao declared an armistice in 1973, and the Vientiane Government formed a new cabinet, including Pathet Lao members, with a Council of Ministers headed by Suvana Fuma. After the US defeat in Vietnam, right-wing groups lost the support they had been getting from the US. In 1975, the national unity cabinet gave way to a majority of Neo Lao Haksat ministers, and on December 1, a peaceful movement put an end to the monarchy. A People's Democratic Republic was proclaimed with Sufanuvong as President, led by the Lao People's Revolutionary Party (PPRL). Entrepreneurs and state bureaucrats left the country en masse, ruining the economy and crippling public administration.

16 The Government nationalized banks and reorganized the public sector. Rice production rose from 700,000 tons in 1976 to 1,200,000 in 1981, when grain self-sufficiency was achieved. For access to the sea and to reduce dependence on Thailand, a road was constructed to the Vietnamese port of Danang, and an oil pipeline to Vietnam's refineries.

17 In 1986, Phumi Vengvichit became President. In November, Kaysone Phomvihane was re-elected secretary general of the PPRL, subsequently becoming Prime Minister.

18 A bloody border war with Thailand, at the end of 1987 resulted in a great loss of life, but ended rapidly in a cease-fire.

19 In 1988 diplomatic relations were renewed with China, and in early 1989 cooperation agreements were signed with the US, which granted a symbolic $10 million to combat the cultivation and trafficking of opium.

20 The changes in Eastern Europe resulted in the suspension of all Soviet economic aid to Laos, and trade fell by 50 per cent.

21 In 1991, the poor economic situation was exacerbated by floods and pest infestations in a quarter of the country's farmlands. Consequently, over 200,000 tons of rice were imported to feed the population.

22 Also in 1991, Thailand and Laos agreed to a repatriation plan for 60,000 Laotian refugees by 1994, also signing a Cooperation and Security Treaty. Thai investments were meanwhile concentrated in banking and trade. Laos has also

LAND USE

IRRIGATED: 16.0% of arable (1993)

1993

- FOREST & WOODLAND: 52.8%
- ARABLE: 3.3%
- OTHER: 43.9%

put a lot of effort into establishing closer ties with China.

[23] In September 1991, 70-year-old Kaysone Phomvihane was named President. Upon his death a year later, Prime Minister Khamtay Sifandon assumed interim presidency of the country and the PPRL.

[24] In December 1992, legislative elections were called; only the PPRL and a few independent government-authorized candidates took part. This essentially represented a continuation of the one-party system. Anti-government demonstrations were banned, and scores of government opponents were imprisoned.

[25] The Supreme Assembly of the People met in February 1993, and named Nouhak Phumsavanh president of the republic, and Khamtai Siphandon leader of the PPRL.

[26] Major free-market oriented reforms were introduced, but without drastically changing the political system. In 1993, Prince Suvana Fuma was authorized to return to the country in an unofficial capacity to represent foreign companies.

[27] Following IMF-proposed strategies, the country managed to bring down the inflation rate - averaging 46 per cent in the 1980s - to an annual rate of 10 per cent, meanwhile the GDP grew by 7 per cent. It is estimated that part of that economic 'growth' resulted from the introduction into the market of products and activities previously not accounted for, and not from an actual increase in production.

[28] The US Agency for International Development (USAID) approved a $9.7 million loan to build roads in several regions of the country, arguing that access to markets would improve living conditions.

[29] Deforestation became a serious environmental problem. The timber felled increased from 6,000 cubic meters in 1964 to over 600,000 in 1993. That year, the Government began to restrict timber exports.

[30] As a result of this, there was an increase in the illegal felling of trees, and in 1993 half of all timber was logged illegally. In March 1994, the World Bank extended a loan given to Laos for reforestation, at an initial value of $8.7 million. A number of international environmental organizations criticized the project, as it gave the funds directly to the Government, with little or no participation from the local communities and for placing emphasis on commercial tree plantations, an activity that could further endanger the forests and the livelihood of their inhabitants.

[31] On April 8 1994, the 'Friendship Bridge' over the Mekong was opened, uniting Laos and Thailand. For Laos this reconciliation represented a distancing from Vietnam and marked the way for economic and cultural integration with Thailand - a more prosperous nation. The Thai banks, communication networks, transport companies and factories soon dominated investment in the Laos economy, which had by now abandoned its socialist principles.

[32] A law approved in March that year established the rules for foreign investment, eliminating the remnants of the planned economic system. Another law guaranteed union rights and updated the labor legislation. Political liberalization, however, was not included in this reform: the Government was determined to maintain its Communist identity.

[33] In mid-1995, Laos expressed its desire to become a full member of the Association of South East Asian Nations (ASEAN) within two years. This more liberal attitude was also reflected in the ratification of a border treaty with Myanma/Burma. The United States lifted a veto on the country limiting US economic aid in place since the Vietnam war.

[34] In March 1996, at the Sixth Congress of the Lao People's Revolutionary Party (PPRL), Prime Minister Siphandon confirmed the single party rule, while also insisting on economic liberalization, efficiency and growth.

[35] In December 1997, the PPRL retained its dominion in the parliamentary elections for the 99 posts in the General Assembly. The result however was no surprise as only four of the 159 individuals standing were from outside the single party.

[36] The stock market crisis affecting several countries of the region also struck the economy of Laos. The indirect effects included increased prices on imports and higher prices for consumers, particularly on the basic basket of foodstuffs.

[37] In February 1998, the Supreme Assembly of the People made Prime Minister Siphandon the new President. Sisavat Keobounphan became the new Prime Minister in August. Amnesty International appealed to Laos to release several prisoners of conscience but one of these, Thongsouk Saysangkhi, died in prison.

[38] The Supreme Assembly of the People elected Prime Minister Siphandon as new president in February 1998. Sisavat Keobounphan became the new Prime Minister. Vice-President Oudom Khattigna died on December 1999 aged 69.

[39] Burma/Myanmar, Thailand and Laos agreed in April 1999 to coordinate their fight against the production and export of drugs, particularly opium.

[40] In August 1999, President Siphandon dismissed Finance Minister Kamphoui Keoboualapha and Central Bank governor Cheuang Sombounkham, making them responsible for the steep fall of the *kip* against the dollar (more than 500 per cent in two years). The economy deteriorated towards the latter part of the decade. ∎

PROFILE

ENVIRONMENT

Laos is the only landlocked country in Indochina. The territory is mountainous and covered with rainforests. The Mekong river valley, stretching down the country from north to south, is suited to agriculture, basically rice. It is estimated that 40 per cent of the arable land was left barren as a result of the 25-year independence war. The climate is tropical and the lowlands are prone to disasters such as the 1978 drought and the 1988 flood. The main environmental problem is intense logging and as a result of the this, dwindling water supplies and a loss of 70 per cent of natural habitats.

SOCIETY

Peoples: 60 per cent of Laotians are descendants of the Lao ethnic groups who inhabit the western valleys. The inhabitants of the mountains account for more than one-third of the total population, while 5 per cent are of Chinese and Vietnamese origin. **Religions:** Buddhist 57.8 per cent; traditional religions 33.6 per cent; Christian 1.8 per cent, of which Roman Catholic 0.8 per cent, Protestant 0.2 per cent; Muslim 1.0 per cent; atheist/no religion 4.8 per cent; Chinese folk-religions 0.9 per cent. **Languages:** Lao (official); minor ethnic group languages, and French. **Political Parties:** The Lao People's Revolutionary Party (PPRL), Marxist-Leninist, is in power. It originated in the old Neo Laotian Haksat. **Social Organizations:** The Patriotic Youth and the Association of Patriotic Women. The National Liberation Front, based in the Meo ethnic minority, wages guerrilla warfare and is accused of receiving Chinese support.

THE STATE

Official Name: Sathalanalat Paxathipatai Paxaxon Lao. **Administrative divisions:** 16 provinces, sub-divided into municipalities. **Capital:** Vientiane 528,109 people (1995). **Other cities:** Savannakhét 96,652 people; Louangphrabang 68,399. **Government:** Khamtay Siphandon, President since February 1998. Sisavat Keobunphan, Prime Minister since August 1998. Legislature: Supreme Assembly of the People. **National Holiday:** December 2, Proclamation of the Republic 1975. **Armed Forces:** 37,000 troops (conscripts) (1996). **Other:** 100,000 members of the Self-defense Militia Forces.

STATISTICS

DEMOGRAPHY

Population: 5,297,000 (1999)
Annual growth: 2.3 % (1975/97)
Estimates for year 2015 (million): 7.8 (1999)
Annual growth to year 2015: 2.5 % (1997/2015)
Urban population: 21.8 % (1997)
Urban Growth: 6.3 % (1980/95)
Children per woman: 5.7 (1998)

HEALTH

Life expectancy at birth: 53 years (1998)
male: 52 years (1998)
female: 55 years (1998)
Maternal mortality: 650 per 100,000 live births (1990-98)
Infant mortality: 96 per 1,000 (1998)
Under-5 child mortality: 116 per 1,000 (1998)
Daily calorie supply: 2,143 per capita (1996)
Safe water: 44 % (1990/98)

EDUCATION

Literacy: 57 % (1995)
male: 69 % (1995)
female: 44 % (1995)
School enrolment:
Primary total: 111 % (1990/96)
male: 125 % (1990/97)
female: 97 % (1990/97)
Secondary:
male: 36 % (1990/96)
female: 23 % (1990/96)
Tertiary: 3 % (1996)
Primary school teachers: one for every 30 (1996)

COMMUNICATIONS

4 newspapers (1996), 143 radios (1997), 10 TV sets (1996) and 6 main telephone lines (1996) per 1,000 people
Books: 1 new titles per 100,000 people (1992/94)

ECONOMY

Per capita, GNP: $ 320 (1998)
Annual growth, GNP: 4.0 % (1998)
Annual inflation: 16.3 % (1990/98)
Consumer price index: 275.2 (1998)
Currency: 3,298.3 new kips = $ 1 (1998)
Cereal imports: 100,104 metric tons (1998)
Fertilizer use: 44 kg per ha (1997)
Exports: $ 47 million (1998)
Imports: $ 61 million (1998)
External debt: $ 2,437 million (1998); $ 472 per capita (1998)
Debt service: 6.3 % of exports (1998)
Development aid received: $ 341 million (1997); $ 82.4 per capita (1997); 19.50 % of GNP (1997)

HDI (rank/value): 140/0.491 (1997)

Latvia

Latvija

Population: 2,389,000 (1999)
Area: 64,500 SQ KM
Capital: Riga
Currency: Lat
Language: Latvian

The first inhabitants of present-day Latvia were nomadic tribes of hunters, fishers and gatherers who migrated to the forests along the Baltic coast, after the last glaciers had retreated. Around 2,000 BC, these groups were replaced by the Baltic peoples, Indo-European tribes who began farming and established permanent settlements in Latvia, Lithuania and eastern Prussia.

[2] The ancient Baltic peoples had come into contact with the Roman Empire through the amber trade. This activity, which reached its peak during the first two centuries of the Christian era, was brought to a halt by Slav expansion toward central and eastern Europe. At this time, the Balts' trade and cultural relations turned northward, to their Scandinavian neighbors.

[3] The Danes used the Dvina and Dnepr rivers in their expansion toward the steppes north of the Black Sea, and therefore crossed Latvian territory. The Swedes and the Russians both claimed these lands during the 10th and 11th centuries and in the 12th century, German warriors and missionaries came to the Latvian coast. As it was inhabited at the time by the Livs, the Germans called it Livonia. In 1202, the bishop of the region, under authorization from Rome, established the Order of the Knights of the Sword.

[4] Before becoming the Knights of the Teutonic Order, in 1237, the Germans had subdued and converted the tribal groups of Latvia and Estonia to Christianity. The Teutonic Knights created the so-called Livonian Confederation, consisting of areas controlled by the Church, free cities and regions governed by knights. In the mid-16th century, rivalries within Livonia became more pronounced with the expansion of Protestantism and discontent among the peasants.

[5] During this period, Latvians benefited from Riga's participation in the Hanseatic League, a German mercantile society which attained a high level of prosperity. Nevertheless the Latvians were treated by the Germans like any vanquished people: the local nobility was abolished and the peasants were forced to pay tithes and taxes, paying with labor if they had no money. After being defeated by Lithuania and Poland, the power of the Teutonic Order declined. However, as the knights' power diminished, their exploitation of the Latvians actually increased.

[6] When Russia invaded the region in 1558, to halt Polish-Lithuanian expansion, the Order fell apart and Livonia was partitioned. At the end of the Livonian War in 1583 Lithuania annexed the area north of the Dvina river; the south remained in Polish hands and Sweden kept the north of Estonia. In 1621, Sweden occupied Riga and Jelgava; Estonia and the northern part of Latvia were subsequently ceded to Sweden by the Truce of Altmark (1629).

[7] The region west of Riga, on the Baltic Sea, was organized into the Duchy of Courland, becoming a semi-independent vassal of Poland. In the mid-17th century, Courland became known as a major naval and trade center for northern Europe, and even had colonial aspirations. Duke Jacob led a brief Latvian occupation of Tobago, in the Caribbean, and of another island in the Gambia River delta in Africa. The name Great Courland Bay, in Tobago, dates back to this time.

[8] Sweden kept these territories until the Great Northern War, when it was forced to cede them to Russia under the Peace of Nystad. In 1795, after the three partitions of Poland, Livonia was finally subdivided into three regions within Russia: Estonia (the northern part of Estonia); Livonia (the south of Estonia and north of Latvia) and Courland. The Russian Revolution of 1905 gave rise to the first instances of Latvian national reaffirmation.

[9] The peasants revolted against their German feudal lords, and the Russian rulers. Although the rebellion was put down by czarist troops, it set the stage for the war of independence 13 years later. After the Russian Revolution of 1917, the Latvian People's Council proclaimed the country's independence on November 18 1918. A government led by the leader of the Farmers' Union, Karlis Ulmanis, was formed.

[10] Far from having its desire for independence and sovereignty respected, Latvia was attacked by German troops and by the Red Army. Only in 1920 was Latvia able to sign a peace treaty with the USSR, in which the latter renounced its territorial ambitions. In 1922, a constituent assembly established a parliamentary republic. The international economic crisis of the 1930s, and the polarization of socialists and Nazi sympathizers led to the collapse of the Latvian Government. In 1934, Prime Minister Ulmanis suspended parliament and governed under a state of emergency until 1938.

[11] With the outbreak of World War II, according to the secret Russo-German pact, Latvia remained within the USSR's sphere of influence. In 1939, Latvia was forced to sign a treaty permitting the Soviets to install troops and bases on its soil. In 1940, it was invaded by the Red Army, and a new government was formed, which subsequently requested that the republic be admitted to the USSR.

[12] During the German offensive against the USSR, between 1940 and 1944, Latvia was annexed to the German province of Ostland, and its Jewish population was practically exterminated. The liberation of Latvia by the Red Army meant the re-establishment of Soviet Government. Before the Soviet forces arrived, 65,000 Latvians fled to Western Europe.

[13] In 1945 and 1946, about 105,000 Latvians were deported to Russia, and the far northeastern corner of Latvia - with its predominantly Russian population - was taken away from Latvia to form part of the USSR. In 1949, forced collectivization of agriculture triggered a mass deportation of Latvians, with about 70,000 being sent to Russia and Siberia. In 1959 the President of Latvia's Supreme Soviet, Karlis Ozolins, was dismissed because of his nationalist tendencies.

[14] Armed Latvian resistance to the Soviet regime was finally put down, in 1952. All symbols of Latvian independence - the national anthem, the flag, and national monuments and history - were banned or adapted to the new regime. Russian became the official language, and massive immigration of Russians and other nationalities began. To the nationalists, this was taken to be a deliberate colonization policy, aimed at diminishing the influence of the indigenous population.

[15] Until the 1980s, Latvian resistance was expressed in isolated actions by political and religious dissidents, which were systematically repressed by the regime; in addition, some nationalist campaigns were carried out by exiles. From 1987, the policy of glasnost (openness) initiated by Mikhail Gorbachev in the USSR, gave hope to Latvian aspirations, permitting public political demonstrations, and the reinstatement of the national symbols.

[16] In June 1987 some 5,000 people gathered in front of the Monument to Liberty, in Riga, to honor the victims of the 1941 Soviet deportations. This marked the beginning of increasingly important political agitation, in which independence began to be discussed openly once again. In 1988, the National Independence Movement of Latvia (LNNK) demanded an end to the Russification of the country, and called for freedom of the press and for the formation of independent political parties.

[17] In September 1988, the Environmental Protection Club of Latvia (VAK) organized an ecology-awareness rally, in which 30,000 people joined hands all along a

stretch of the Baltic Sea coast. The following month, the Latvian Communist Party renewed its leadership, incorporating politicians who were identified with the reforms and who had broad popular support. The national flag was legalized, and Latvian was adopted as the country's official language.

[18] In October 1988, close to 150,000 people gathered to celebrate the founding of the Popular Front of Latvia (LTF), which brought together all of Latvia's recently formed social and political groups, as well as militant communists. A month later, for the first time since Soviet occupation, hundreds of thousands of Latvians commemorated the anniversary of the 1918 declaration of independence. The LTF began to have influence with the local government, and with the Moscow authorities.

[19] A year later, the LTF Congress endorsed the country's political and economic independence from the Soviet Union. Despite Moscow's resistance to Latvia's secession, the LTF's policy of carrying out changes peacefully met with widespread popular support, from citizens of Russian or other origins. The LTF program for non-violent change included public demonstrations, free elections and change through parliamentary procedure. Latvia's 1938 constitution went into effect once again, for the first time since the 1940 Soviet occupation.

[20] May 4 1990 marked the Declaration of the Re-establishment of Independence, as well as the reinstatement of the 1922 constitution. In September 1991, the new Council of State of the USSR, in its inaugural session, formally recognized the independence of the Baltic republics. They were also immediately recognized by a number of countries, and admitted as new members to the UN in the General Assembly session held that same month. The three Baltic States initiated negotiations with the European Community (EC), in the areas of trade and financial assistance. In February 1992, Latvia and Russia signed an agreement on the withdrawal of the former USSR's troops, stationed within Latvian territory.

[21] A new parliament was selected in June 1993 which appointed Guntis Ulmanis as President. The beginning of an economic liberalization process caused a sharp rise of unemployment. In 1994, foreign investment grew but the economy was still dependant on Russia, its main supplier of fuel and its first exporting market. Also, in spite of the massive privatization of state companies, the budget and trade balance deficits persisted.

[22] In 1995, lack of controls over commercial banks led to the bankruptcy of several financial institutions. The September legislative elections did not reveal any clear winner since nine parties obtained between 5 per cent and 16 per cent of the vote. An agreement between the conservative National Block and two left-wing parties led to Andris Skele being appointed Prime Minister in December.

[23] Parliament re-elected Guntis Ulmanis as President in June 1996, with 53 votes in 100. Throughout that year, relations with Russia improved slightly. However, Latvia still demanded a boundaries treaty between both countries.

[24] Guntars Krast became Prime Minister in July 1997, replacing Andris Skele, who resigned after being charged with corruption. In November, Russia repeated its opposition to an eventual incorporation of Latvia into NATO. Although Riga was not on the candidate list for entry into the Atlantic alliance, the Latvian Government had on several occasions stated its intention of becoming a member.

[25] During February 1998, in a new attempt to reduce tensions with the Russian minority in the country, Latvia adopted a law allowing the issuing of passports to foreigners residing permanently in the country since 1991.

[26] Juris Dalbinsh, Commander-in-Chief of the armed forces, was given leave in April 1998 to participate in a rally of former SS Latvian members who had fought with Nazi forces against the former USSR. That same week the chief of police in Riga was removed from his post for not providing the necessary protection to a synagogue which was attacked with bombs. That month, Italy warned that the discriminatory treatment given to the Russian minority was inadmissable in a country that intended to join the European Union.

[27] A referendum approved in the October elections reduced the Latvian language requirement for obtaining citizenship, repealing the restrictive law passed in February. The Popular Party defeated the Latvian Path Union party by a margin of 21.2 per cent to 18.1 per cent of the vote. In April 1999, a government commission proposed to pay $2,000 to all those 'non-Latvian' citizens who wished to leave the country.

[28] President Vaira Vike-Freiberga asked former Prime Minister Skele to head the new government. ■

PROFILE

ENVIRONMENT

Latvia's terrain is characterized by softly rolling hills (highest point: Gaizins, 310 m), and by the number of forests, lakes and rivers, which empty into the Baltic Sea and the Gulf of Riga, in the northeastern part of the country. Latvia has a 494 km coastline, with important ports and attractive beaches. The country's most fertile lands lie in the Zemgale Plain, which is known as the country's breadbasket. The plain is located in the south, extending as far as the Lithuanian border. The Highlands, which make up 40 per cent of the land, lie in the western and northern parts of the country, crossing over into Estonia. The climate is humid and cold, due to masses of cold air coming from the Atlantic. Summers are short and rainy, with an average temperature of 17°C; winters last from December to March, with temperatures below zero, sometimes as low as -40°C. Two-thirds of all arable land is used for grain production, and the rest for pasture. The main industries are metal engineering (ships, automobiles, railway passenger cars and agricultural machinery), followed by the production of motorcycles, electrical appliances and scientific instruments. Industrial wastes and the pollution of the country's rivers and lakes are problems which remain to be solved.

SOCIETY

Peoples: Latvians and Lithuanians constitute the two main branches of the Baltic Indo-European peoples, with a distinct language and culture that sets them apart from the Germans and Slavs. Ethnic Latvians make up 52 per cent of the country's population, followed by Russians, 34 per cent; Poles, Belarusians, Ukrainians, Lithuanians and Estonians account for the remaining 14 per cent. **Religions:** The majority is Protestant (Lutheran), followed by Catholics. **Languages:** Latvian (official); Russian and Polish. **Political Parties:** Popular Party; Latvian Path Union; National Bloc; National Conciliation Bloc; Communist Party; Fatherland and Freedom movement.

THE STATE

Official Name: Latvijas Republika. **Capital:** Riga 839,670 people (1995). **Other cities:** Daugavpils 120,152 people; Liepaja 100,271; Jelgava 71,129; Jurmala 59,247. **Government:** Parliamentary republic. Vaira Vike-Freiberga, President, elected in July 1999. Andris Skele, Prime Minister since July 1999. Single-chamber parliament (Saeima), made up of 201 members, elected by direct vote. **National holiday:** November 18, Independence (1918).

Lebanon

Lubnan

Population: 3,236,000 (1999)
Area: 10,400 SQ KM
Capital: Beirut (Bayrut)
Currency: Pound
Language: Arabic

Much of present-day Lebanon corresponds to the ancient land of the Phoenicians, who probably arrived in the region in about 3000 BC. Commercial and religious connections were established with Egypt after about 2613 BC and continued until the end of the Egyptian Old Kingdom and the invasion of Phoenicia by the Amorites (c2200 BC). Other groups invading and periodically controlling Phoenicia included the Hyksos (18th century BC), the Egyptians of the New Kingdom (16th century BC), and the Hittites (14th century BC). Seti I (1290-79 BC) of the New Kingdom reconquered most of Phoenicia, but Ramses III (1187-56 BC) lost it to invaders from Asia Minor and Europe. Between the withdrawal of Egyptian rule and the western advance of Assyria (10th century BC), the history of Phoenicia is primarily the history of Tyre. This city-state rose to hegemony among Phoenician states and founded colonies throughout the Mediterranean region. The Achaemenians, an Iranian dynasty under the leadership of Cyrus II, conquered the area in 538 BC. Sidon, 20 miles (32 km) north of Tyre, became a principal coastal city of this empire. In 332 BC Tyre capitulated to the army of Alexander the Great after resisting for eight months. This event marked the demise of Tyre as a great commercial city, as its inhabitants were sold into slavery. In 64 BC Phoenicia was incorporated into the Roman province of Syria.

[2] Emperors embracing Christianity protected the area during the later Roman and Byzantine periods (c. AD 300-634). A 6th-century Christian group fleeing persecution in Syria settled in what

OCCUPIED BY ISRAEL
1. Southern Lebanon - occupied 1983-2000
2. Syria - Golan Heights - occupied in 1967

0   50 km

is now northern Lebanon, absorbed the native population, and founded the Maronite Church. In the following century, Arab tribes settled in southern Lebanon after the Muslim conquest of Syria. Four hundred years later, many of this Arab group coalesced their beliefs into the Druze faith. In the coastal towns the population became mainly Sunni Muslim. By the end of the 11th century Lebanon had become part of the crusader states, and it later became part of the

Mamluk state of Syria and Egypt. Lebanon was able to evolve a social and political system of its own between the 15th and the 18th century. Throughout this period European, particularly French, influence was growing. In 1516 the Ottoman Turks replaced the Mamluks. The social system came under severe strain as the Christian population grew.

[3] Around 1831 the vigorous Egypt of Muhammed Ali extended its influence northwards

undermining the decadent Turkish empire. The European powers did not want the Turkish Empire to crumble until Europe was in a position to carry off the spoils. They conveniently decided that Christians anywhere in the world could be equated with Europeans, meriting their protection, and they began to support the Maronite Arab Christians against Egypt. Between 1831 and 1834, five powers intervened in the 'Syrian question'. Russia and Austria devoted their efforts exclusively to the Balkans, and France and Britain were left to dispute domination of the Arab countries, laboriously shunting Prussia aside. The Ottoman Turks ended the local rule of the Druze Shihab princes in 1842, exacerbating already poor relations between the Maronites and the Druze. These relations reached a low ebb with the massacre of Maronites by Druze in 1860.

[4] The French intervened on behalf of the Christians, forcing the Ottoman Sultan to form an autonomous province within the Ottoman Empire for the mountainous Christian area, known as Mount Lebanon. In 1919, Syria and Lebanon became French protectorates, while Britain took Egypt, Jordan and Iraq. For administrative purposes, France separated Lebanon from Syria and when the army pulled out in 1947, they left behind two separate states.

[5] Camille Chamoun was elected President in 1952, following a clearly pro-Western foreign policy. The 1957 parliamentary elections were marked by Muslim demonstrations and riots, demanding closer alignment with Egypt and Syria, and rejecting re-election for the Maronite president.

[6] By the following year the rioting had grown into full scale insurrection, pitting Muslims against Christians in a bloody civil war. In July 1958, President Chamoun allowed 10,000 US Marines to disembark in order to 'pacify' the country. The foreign troops remained in Beirut (Bayrut) and in other strategically important Lebanese cities until October of that year.

[7] By the early 1970s, the population had become mostly Muslim, and they began to question the traditional political system which required a Christian president

WORKERS

% OF LABOUR FORCE   **1998**

■ FEMALE: 29%   ■ MALE: 71%

1990

■ SERVICES: 61.7%
■ INDUSTRY: 31.0%
■ AGRICULTURE: 7.3%

LAND USE

DEFORESTATION: 8.1% annual (1990/95)
IRRIGATED: 39.8% of arable (1993)

1993

□ FOREST & WOODLAND: 7.7%
■ ARABLE: 20.8%
■ OTHER: 71.5%

PUBLIC EXPENDITURE

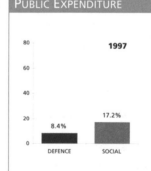

1997

8.4%   17.2%

DEFENCE   SOCIAL

and a Sunni Muslim prime minister in order to maintain a balance between the two communities. The Shi'as had no specified role.

[8] Differences between the various religious and ethnic communities were combined with an eminently unjust social and economic system. Predatory colonial exploitation had exhausted the traditional cedars of Lebanon, leaving the land barren and farmers impoverished. The new distribution of labor and wealth kept trade control for the Maronites, while the Muslims worked as artisans, laborers and farm workers.

[9] These tensions erupted in civil war again, when the Christian right wing used the 'Palestinian problem' as a pretext for conflict in 1975. Lebanon, which had remained neutral in the 1973 Arab-Israeli War, granted refuge to 300,000 Palestinians in the southern part of its territory. Israel used this fact to justify frequent incursions and bombings against civilians. Meanwhile, the Lebanese Christian Phalange militia unleashed its might on the Palestinian refugee camps.

[10] In 1976, Syrian troops, part of an Arab-League peace force, put a stop to the fighting and guaranteed national unity. The underlying causes of the civil war persisted, and Israeli attacks continued. In 1981, Israeli artillery, together with a unit of the former Lebanese commander Saad Haddad, bombarded the cities of Tyre and Sidon (Saida), while Syrian troops installed anti-aircraft missiles in the Bekaa Valley. That July, Israeli jets launched a number of attacks against Palestinian positions, including a wave of air raids on western Beirut; they left 166 dead and 600 wounded.

[11] In June 1982, Israeli troops invaded Lebanon by land, sea and air. Tyre and Sidon were quickly overrun, and Nabataea and Tripoli (Trâblous) were devastated by bombings.

[12] Beirut, one of the most important political and cultural capitals in the Arab world, was virtually destroyed. Thousands of civilians were killed. Bridges, oil pipelines, airports, hospitals, schools, major buildings and modest homes, factories and museums were razed. Eight thousand Palestinians and Lebanese were interned in prison camps.

[13] The PLO finally agreed to pull out of Beirut, providing that the evacuation was carried out under international supervision. US, French and Italian soldiers provided the necessary protection, and the people of West Beirut gave a heroes' farewell to the freedom fighters, who went to seven other Arab countries.

[14] On August 23 1982, what was left of the Lebanese Congress named Israel's nominee, Bashir Gemayel - the sole candidate - to succeed President Elias Sarkis. The Maronite leader did not live to take office, however. He died on September 14 in a dynamite attack on the Phalange's east Beirut command headquarters. No one accepted responsibility for the act.

[15] The following day, Beirut was occupied by Israeli troops. On September 16 1982, a militia group led by former commander Haddad burst into the Palestinian refugee camps of Sabra and Chatila and assassinated hundreds of unarmed civilians, including old people, women and children.

[16] Later investigations left no doubt as to Israel's responsibility for the killings, as Israeli officers had encouraged the right-wing militia to act.

[17] While Israeli troops still held half of Lebanon, Amin Gemayel was elected president under the same conditions as his younger brother Bashir.

[18] The new president was unable to eliminate distrust among the various communities of Lebanon. A majority of the governing Phalange party sought to replace the 1943 National Alliance with a new constitutional dictate to divide the state into districts under a central federal government. This raised the prospect of Lebanon's political division into several religious mini-states. Sunni and Shi'a leaders favored administrative (but not political) decentralization, and the Druze community wanted greater autonomy.

[19] In May 1983 Israel and Lebanon signed an agreement to cease hostilities. Israel promised to withdraw from Lebanese territory, along with the other foreign troops. Lebanon in turn promised not to harbor any armed groups, organizations, bases, offices or structures with the aim of 'carrying out raids on the other party's territory'.

[20] In July 1984 the Lebanese currency, which had remained relatively stable since the beginning of the war in 1975, slumped abruptly, producing unprecedented inflation.

[21] Recession in the Gulf dealt a death blow to Beirut's economy which was already severely weakened by the withdrawal of foreign currency. This caused a balance of payments deficit of over $1.5 billion in 1984.

[22] Before the Israeli army officially withdrew from Lebanon in 1985, it ensured that the Christian militia had displaced the Muslims from southern Lebanon guaranteeing a 'friendly' civilian population in the 10-kilometre security zone they imposed.

[23] In September 1988, pro-Israeli Maronite General Michel Aoun took over the presidency, which had been vacant since Amin Gemayel's constitutional mandate was truncated in a palace coup. The country was now governed by two rival administrations - Aoun's, and that of Muslim Prime Minister Selim al-Hoss.

[24] In October 1989 Lebanon's single chamber parliament met, for the first time since independence, outside the country and under the auspices of the Arab League. The league includes Saudi Arabia, Algeria and Morocco, who acted as intermediaries in negotiations between the Lebanese factions. The meeting in Taif sealed the peace and laid down an alternative to the political system that had been in place since 1943. Under a new constitution, the next president would be elected indirectly by the parliament.

[25] Christian and Muslim Lebanese legislators announced a national reconciliation agreement on October 12, granting greater power to Muslims and providing for the withdrawal of Syrian troops from Lebanon. General Aoun rejected the agreement because it was instituted by Saudi Arabia, and he considered it a 'Syrian trap'.

[26] On November 5 1989, René Moawad, a Maronite Christian sympathetic to Muslim causes, was unanimously elected president. Moawad was killed by a car-bomb scarcely 17 days before taking office.

[27] Elias Hrawi, another Maronite Christian, was elected president on November 24 by a meeting of the parliament at Zahle, in Syrian-controlled territory. General Aoun immediately rejected the election of a new president in an area outside the Christian enclave under his control.

[28] Taking advantage of the new situation created by the Iraqi invasion of Kuwait, the Syrian-backed forces started an offensive against Aoun in October 1990. Lacking international support, as Syria belonged to the anti-Iraq coalition, Aoun was soon defeated and he sought asylum in France.

[29] In December 1990, a national unity government was formed, for the first time since the beginning of the war. It incorporated the Lebanese Forces (Christian), the Amal (Shi'a), the PSP (Druze), and the pro-Syrian parties.

PROFILE

ENVIRONMENT

One of the smallest Middle East countries, Lebanon has a fertile coastal plain where most of the population lives, with a mild Mediterranean climate making it rainy in the winter; two parallel mountain ranges, the Lebanon Mountains (whose highest peak is Sauda, at 3,083 m) and the Anti-Lebanon Mountains, with temperate forests on their slopes, and between the ranges, the fertile Bekaa Valley. The soil is very fertile because of rich alluvial deposits. Along the coast, a dry bush known as maquis grows, while vineyards, and wheat, olives, and oranges are cultivated. Cedar has become a national symbol. This wood was used to build the Phoenician fleet and temples. Nowadays there are little over 400 cedars left, ranging in age between 200 and 800 years old. The war has had disastrous consequences, causing a loss of vegetation and soil erosion.

SOCIETY

Peoples: Mostly Arab. There are also small Armenian, European, Syrian and Kurdish minorities, and a large group of Palestinian refugees.
Religions: 75 per cent are Muslim, with the traditionally powerful Sunni challenged by the militant Shi'a. There is also a large Druze population. 25 per cent are Christian, mostly Maronites; also Catholics and Orthodox Christians.
Languages: Arabic (official and predominant). French is widely spoken, Armenian and English are less common.
Political Parties: There are many political, political-military, political-religious factions and militias in Lebanon. The National Front is an alliance of groups from the left, especially Muslims. The Lebanese Phalange is the most important Maronite Christian party. The Progressive Socialist Party is primarily Druze. The political-military Shi'a organization Amal ('Hope') is pro-Syrian. Hezbollah ('party of God'), Shi'a guerrilla group, pro-Iranian.

THE STATE

Official Name: al-Jumhouriyah al-Lubnaniyah.
Administrative divisions: 6 governmental divisions.
Capital: Beirut (Bayrut) 1,500,000 people (1995).
Other cities: Tripoli (Tarabulus) 240,000 people; Juniyah 100,000; Zahlah 45,000 (1991).
Government: Emile Lahoud, President since November 1998. Rafiq Hariri, Prime Minister since September 2000.
National Holiday: November 22, Independence Day (1943).
Armed Forces: 44,300 troops (1995).
Other: External Security Forces: UN peacekeeping forces 5,000; Syrian army 35,000. Civilian militias: Hezbollah/the Party of God 3,000.

30 The presidents of Lebanon and Syria signed a Brotherhood, Co-operation and Co-ordination Agreement in Damascus, the Syrian capital on May 22 1991. Syria recognized Lebanon as a separate and independent state. The agreement established Syrian-Palestinian co-operation in military, security, cultural and economic matters, and it was ratified by the majority of the Lebanese parliament. The Israeli Government, the Phalangist party and the Lebanese Forces militia (both Christian and traditionally anti-Syrian), opposed the treaty as they believed that it gave Syria control over Lebanon's domestic matters.

31 Early in July, 6,000 soldiers of the Lebanese army took over the territories occupied by the PLO around the port of Sidon, in the south of the country. This offensive forced the PLO out of its main operations base for campaigns against Israel. On July 7, in spite of the apparent defeat of the PLO, Israel stated that it would not withdraw its forces from the security zone.

32 In November, Israel increased its offensive on the security zone, demanding that the Lebanese army should leave the territories within 12 hours. This action caused the massive exodus of nearly 100,000 Shi'a Muslims.

33 In December 1991, Lebanon was granted loans amounting to $700 million, to be used over the next three years for the rehabilitation and reconstruction of the country.

34 On February 16 1992 - eight days before peace talks between Arabs and Israelis were due to resume - an Israeli air raid killed Sheikh Abbas Mussawi, head of the Hezbollah ('The Party of God', an Iranian-backed Islamic group). Six days later, the Shi'a guerrillas suspended attacks against Israel as the result of an agreement between the Hezbollah, Amal (another Islamic grouping) and the representatives of Syrian and Lebanese forces.

35 A general strike against the government's economic policy, accompanied by violent public demonstrations brought about the fall of the pro-Syrian Omar Karame government. President Elias Hrawi designated Rashid Al Sohl, a moderate Sunni, as the new head of government. He formed his cabinet with an equal number of Christians and Muslims. The August parliamentary elections were boycotted by the Christians. The new parliament included Hezbollah and Amal representatives. In October, Rafiq al-Hariri, a nationalized Saudi Arabian millionaire, was named prime minister.

36 In 1993, the World Bank granted a loan for reconstruction and education projects. The currency regained 10 per cent of its value and the country began receiving more foreign investment. The gap between rich and poor widened.

37 Israel continued to bomb Palestinian refugee camps and PLO bases. In August, Lebanese authorities rejected an Israeli proposal for total withdrawal since Israel demanded Hezbollah's total disarmament.

38 Among other terrorist incidents, a bomb killed a top Hezbollah leader, 21 Israeli soldiers died and Christian churches were shelled causing dozens of deaths. In March, the Government suspended private radio and television broadcasting until a new press law had been enacted while it reinstated the death penalty for political murders or crimes.

39 During 1995, government attention was focused on finding a solution to the armed conflict and the reconstruction of Beirut. In January, the UN Security Council decided to extend its intervention in the country. At the beginning of talks between Israel and Palestine in Oslo, Norway, Hezbollah and Southern Lebanon Army resumed their attacks in order to displace Israeli troops and defer negotiations with Syria.

40 On June 24, former Maronite leader Samir Geagea was sentenced to life imprisonment for the murders of his rival Dany Chamoun and his family. Political balance shifted toward the Muslims.

41 Prime Minister al-Hariri promoted the 'Horizon 2000' scheme to deal with Beirut's urban renovation and a constitutional reform which would extend the presidential term from 6 to 9 years to achieve the necessary stability to carry out his project. His goal of reinstating Lebanon as a central financial centre in the Middle East made progress. A plan to reconstruct Beirut's business and residential area was delayed by the discovery of archaeological remains, which led to a debate about their rescue and effect on the costs of urban renovation.

42 The economic situation changed significantly from 1992 to 1996. This was evident among other things, in the reduction of annual inflation from 170 per cent to 10 per cent and in the 200-per-cent increase of foreign currency reserves.

43 In 1997, fighting was renewed between the Lebanese guerrillas and the Israeli army, which still occupied what Tel Aviv called a 'security zone', an area covering 850 square kilometers in southern Lebanon. Israel lost 39 soldiers that year, the highest number since 1985. The rise in the number of victims increased the pressure by Israeli public opinion on its government to put an end to the war.

44 In February 1998, Beirut rejected a proposal from Tel Aviv to start negotiations on an eventual withdrawal of Israeli troops from its territory and demanded the unconditional end of the occupation, based on resolution 425 of the UN Security Council. Israel wanted, in exchange for its withdrawal, a bilateral agreement that would put an end to guerrilla attacks on its territory. However, an agreement between both countries was hardly imaginable without Syria's consent, which seemed hard to obtain. It was thought Damascus preferred the conflict in southern Lebanon to continue in order to strengthen its own position in the negotiations with Tel Aviv to recover the strategic region of the Golan Heights.

45 In 1997 fresh confrontations erupted between the Lebanese guerrillas and the Israeli army, which continued to occupy what Tel Aviv referred to as the 'security zone', 850 km^2 of territory in southern Lebanon. Attempts to negotiate a withdrawal from Lebanon in 1998 failed, but the Israeli government was increasingly convinced that this was necessary.

46 On October 15 1998, the National Assembly elected General Emile Lahoud president. Lahoud had the backing of the Syrian army. Municipal elections that year demonstrated a growth in support for Hezbollah. The Christians took 12 of the 24 seats in the council of Beirut. Salim al-Hoss was elected Prime Minister in December.

47 The change of government in Israel in July 1999 opened new prospects for peace. Ehud Barak had promised a withdrawal from southern Lebanon in his election campaign and in December offered a new plan to leave the Lebanese territory, but final negotiations hung on an agreement with Syria for the return of the Golan Heights.

48 Finally, in March 2000, Israel agreed to withdraw from southern Lebanon before July. At first the Prime Minister welcomed the Israeli decision but called for the withdrawal to be within the framework of a peace accord. President Lahoud emphasised that Israel would not have the security it sought until it returned the Golan Heights to Syria and resolved the problem of the Palestinian refugees in southern Lebanon.

49 Israel withdrew its forces in May. The withdrawal of the pro-Israeli South Lebanon Army (SLA) brought fresh confrontations with Hezbollah.

50 In a surprise result, former Prime Minister Rafiq Hariri returned to power in the September 2000 elections. ■

STATISTICS

DEMOGRAPHY

Population: 3,236,000 (1999)
Annual growth: 0.6 % (1975/97)
Estimates for year 2015 (million): 3.9 (1999)
Annual growth to year 2015: 1.3 % (1997/2015)
Urban population: 88.5 % (1997)
Urban Growth: 3.7 % (1980/95)
Children per woman: 2.7 (1998)

HEALTH

Life expectancy at birth: 70 years (1998)
male: 68 years (1998)
female: 72 years (1998)
Maternal mortality: 100 per 100,000 live births (1990-98)
Infant mortality: 29 per 1,000 (1998)
Under-5 child mortality: 35 per 1,000 (1998)
Daily calorie supply: 3,279 per capita (1996)
191 doctors per 100,000 people (1993)
Safe water: 94 % (1990/98)

EDUCATION

Literacy: 83 % (1995)
male: 91 % (1995)
female: 77 % (1995)
School enrolment:
Primary total: 111 % (1990/96)
male: 113 % (1990/97)
female: 108 % (1990/97)
Secondary:
male: 78 % (1990/96)
female: 85 % (1990/96)
Tertiary: 27 % (1996)

COMMUNICATIONS

107 newspapers (1996), 906 radios (1997), 355 TV sets (1996) and 149 main telephone lines (1996) per 1,000 people

ECONOMY

Per capita, GNP: $ 3,560 (1998)
Annual growth, GNP: 3.0 % (1998)
Annual inflation: 24.0 % (1990/98)
Currency: 1,516.1 pounds = $ 1 (1998)
Cereal imports: 647,704 metric tons (1998)
Fertilizer use: 3,345 kg per ha (1997)
Exports: $ 1,833 million (1998)
Imports: $ 8,796 million (1998)
External debt: $ 6,725 million (1998); $ 2,108 per capita (1998)
Debt service: 18.7 % of exports (1998)
Development aid received: $ 239 million (1997); $ 64.5 per capita (1997); 1.60 % of GNP (1997)

ENERGY

Consumption: 1,265.0 Kgs of Oil equivalent per capita yearly (1997); 96.0 % imported (1997)

HDI (rank/value): 69/0.749 (1997)

Lesotho

Lesotho

Population: 2,108,000 (1999)
Area: 30,355 SQ KM
Capital: Maseru
Currency: Loti
Language: Sotho and English

For most African states, national unity is a task still to be accomplished. In some cases, however, the nation existed before the political state. Lesotho and Swaziland are both examples of this.

2   The Zulu conquests, begun in 1818 by Shaka, affected a large number of Bantu nations, among them the North Sotho or Pedi who occupied a vast area in what became Transvaal. While some withdrew northwards, the head of the Bakwena tribe, Moshoeshoe, brought other Sotho tribes and groups of dissident Zulus together under his command, retreating with them towards the Drakensberg mountains. The lengthy war of resistance fought first against the Zulus, and then against the expansionist Boers, consolidated the bonds between these groups of diverse origin who gave Moshoeshoe the title of 'Great Leader of the Mountain', and called themselves Basothos.

3   The Boers, the Dutch colonizers, tried to use the Basothos as labor. But they soon admitted defeat declaring that 'these savages prefer liberty to slavery'. Some Basothos refused to work on the Europeans' farms, saying 'God created animals to feed men and not men to feed animals'.

4   Until 1867, Dutch colonization in South Africa was tenuous. Then diamonds were discovered. Soon afterwards gold was found, and along with its discovery the British came up from the Cape. In 1868, British missionaries persuaded the Basotho traditional leader Moshoeshoe, that only the 'protection' of the British Crown could save the people from subjection by the Boers. The territory became a protectorate, administered separately from South

Africa even after the Boer War of 1899-1902, when the British took control of the whole country.

5   Britain had promised the South African Government that Basotholand (Lesotho), Bechuanaland (Botswana) and Swaziland, which were all in similar situations, would eventually be integrated into South Africa. However, when the South African Union broke all ties with London in 1961, consolidating its racist policy of apartheid, the British left those countries independent. In 1965, a constitution was promulgated in Basotholand and in 1966 the country proclaimed independence under the name of Lesotho.

6   However, as an enclave within South Africa, Lesotho depended on the surrounding country as an outlet for its products of wheat, asbestos, cattle, and diamonds. The currency was the South African rand and South African companies controlled its economy and communications.

7   Foreign trade was extremely unbalanced, with imports 10 times higher than exports. The difference

was offset by money that the migrant workers sent home. At this time some 45 percent of the labor force worked in the South African gold mines.

8   The difficult economic situation enabled the opposition Congress Party to win a victory in the legislative elections of 1970. Prime Minister Leabua Jonathan engineered a coup, dissolved Parliament, and sent King Moshoeshoe into exile. He was allowed to return on the promise that he would refrain from any political activity.

9   After the 1976 student uprising which took place in Soweto, South Africa, Lesotho opened its doors to thousands of young South African refugees despite the tremendous economic sacrifice this implied for such a poor country. When South Africa began its Bantustan policy, Lesotho, in compliance with the UN resolution condemning this new form of apartheid, refused to recognize the puppet state in Transkei. In early 1977, South Africa closed the Lesotho border in retaliation. This economic aggression endangered the country's survival. Lesotho made dramatic appeals for international solidarity, requesting aid to resist the blockade.

10   After Zimbabwean independence, Lesotho joined the economic integration project

promoted by the Front Line states, strengthening relations with Mozambique.

11   South Africa retaliated by supporting groups opposed to the Jonathan Government. This led the leader to seek help from the United Nations and the European Economic Community. The official Basotho National Party (BNP) also had to face the opposition of groups linked to the Basotho Congress Party (BCP), led by Ntsu Mokhele.

12   Most of the incidents were really caused by South African military groups interested in preventing the anti-apartheid refugees of the African National Congress (ANC) from organizing in Maseru (see South Africa). The most important of these attacks took place in December 1982, when a South African military air raid killed 45 people, 12 of them children, in the outskirts of Maseru. During the attack, three ANC leaders were killed, but the other victims were all bystanders.

13   In 1982, the Government imposed an emergency law allowing the arrest of anyone suspected of illegal activities, without any previous judicial process. The army and the police were reinforced and a paramilitary group known as Koeko violently suppressed BCP supporters in the Drakensberg mountains.

14   In March 1983, there was a border incident between Lesothan and South African troops, when saboteurs tried to enter the country to destroy the principal electric power plant. There was growing South African pressure to sign a non-aggression treaty with Pretoria, similar to the agreements that the apartheid regime had signed with Swaziland and Mozambique. The Prime Minister, Leabua Jonathan was against the treaty, but due to Lesotho's economic dependence on South Africa he was forced to be more flexible.

15   Towards the end of 1984, the South African Government began to prevent products from getting to Lesotho, particularly weapons purchased in Europe, and to delay the remittances sent by almost 400,000 migrant workers. They also delayed plans to build a dam on the Sengu River, on the border between the two countries. South African pressures were directed at intimidating the Lesotho electorate

WORKERS

% OF LABOUR FORCE **1998**

- FEMALE: 37%   ■ MALE: 63%

1990

- ■ SERVICES: 32.1%
- ■ INDUSTRY: 29.8%
- ■ AGRICULTURE: 40.1%

LAND USE

DEFORESTATION: 0.0% annual (1990/95)
IRRIGATED: 0.9% of arable (1993)
ARABLE: 10.5% of total (1993)

and strengthening opposition to the BNP, the conservative Basotho Democratic Party (BDA) and the (ANC-aligned) BCP.

[16] But even these tough measures did not satisfy Pretoria and on January 20 1986, a military coup toppled Leabua Jonathan, and General Justin Lekhanya, head of Lesotho's paramilitary forces, led the Military Committee that replaced him.

[17] In 1988, workers residing in South Africa sent remittances totaling more than $350 million to Lesotho - 500 per cent of the total value of the country's exports.

[18] In March 1990, the military regime exiled King Moshoeshoe, accusing him of being a hindrance to the country's democratization program. His son Bereng Mohato Siisa replaced him as Letsie III. On April 30 1991, the armed forces went on strike for higher salaries, and a bloodless military coup deposed Lekhanya's government, setting up a Council chaired by Colonel Elias P Ramaema.

[19] The South African Government blocked remittances from migrant workers in 1991. In May, a demonstration against foreign interference in the economy ended with 34 people dead and 425 arrests.

[20] A new constitution designated the King head of state in 1993, without giving him either legal or executive powers. The July legislative elections gave all the seats to the BCP. In August the privatization of six state businesses was started with a loan from the IMF.

[21] Erosion affected 58 per cent of the low lying soils. Two thirds of all farming land belonged to migrant laborers, but was worked by their wives and families. Plans were developed to make use of the water from the highlands - the main natural resource of the country - through a hydroelectric project which would change the course of several rivers to feed water to South Africa in return for electricity.

[22] During 1994, the low salaries led to armed confrontations between rival military factions. The government plan to integrate the armed wing of the BCP into the army led to the kidnapping and murder of the finance minister by disgruntled soldiers.

[23] The King dissolved the Government and Parliament. Protests outside the palace were put down by soldiers and police, with at least four people killed. The internal republican opposition and international pressure forced Letsie III to abdicate in favor of his father, King Moshoeshoe II, who was formally restored to the throne in January 1995.

[24] During 1995, the tunnel under the mountains to supply water to the Vaal river valley in South Africa was completed.

[25] In March 1995, members of the National Security Forces kidnapped several high-ranking officers, demanding their immediate withdrawal from the army for their part in assassinations and various sorts of corruption.

[26] In January 1996, the King died in a road accident. The Assembly designated his son Letsie III as his replacement.

[27] The Government took up plans to use the water from the mountains again in 1998, and inaugurated the first stretch, including a dam, in April. The project had been suspended in 1997 following protests from the displaced local populations and accusations of corruption from the opposition. Non-governmental organizations accused the World Bank of violating the human rights of the communities and damaging the environment by funding the construction of hydroelectric dams in Lesotho.

[28] In early 1998, the Catholic Church protested over the inclusion of courses in Islam, Hinduism, Buddhism and Judaism, in schools controlled by Catholics. The Government quashed their complaint saying the Constitution authorized religious diversity.

[29] On March 8, hundreds of women demanded stiffer penalties for those guilty of rape. Official estimates pointed to an average of five women or girls raped every day in Lesotho. A report from the Southern Africa Development Community stressed that in the majority of its 14 member nations - including Lesotho - the legislation on violence against women was not fulfilled. That same month, a new political party, the Democratic Christian Party (DCP), was born of a split in the National Progress Party.

[30] The May 1998 elections were won by the Government, now called Congress for Democracy in Lesotho (CDL). The Opposition, which considered the elections fraudulent, organized demonstrations against the regime. According to electoral authorities, the opposition only won one of the 80 disputed seats. The Government asked South Africa for military assistance in September when a sector of the army joined the protests and the authorities considered the situation was out of control. The South African army calmed the situation through use of force. South Africa charged $1 million for the one-month intervention.

[32] A 24-member body with government and opposition representatives was formed in December that year with the goal of organizing new elections and revising electoral legislation. South

PROFILE

ENVIRONMENT

This small country is an enclave in the foothills of the Drakensberg mountains in southern Africa. Landlocked and mountainous, its only fertile land is located in the west where corn, sorghum and wheat are grown. In the rest of the country cattle is raised. Except for small diamond deposits, there are no mineral resources. Soil erosion is a serious problem.

SOCIETY

Peoples: Ethnically homogeneous, the country is inhabited by the Basotho (Sotho) people (85 per cent) and a Zulu minority (15 per cent). There are small communities of Asian and European origin.
Religions: Mainly Christian. Also traditional African beliefs.
Languages: Sotho and English (officials).
Political Parties: The Basotho Congress Party (BCP), founded in 1952; the Basotho National Party (BNP), founded in 1958; the Lesotho Communist Party (LCP), founded in 1962; the Marematlou Liberation Party, founded in 1962; the National Independence Party (NIP), Christian; and the People's Front for Democracy (PFD), which emerged from a split in the Lesotho Communist Party (LCP); the Kopanang of Basotho Party, Founded in 1992, leading campaigns for women's rights; Democratic Christian Party (DCP), resulting from a split in the National Progress Party (NPP).
Social Organizations: The Lesotho General Workers' Union (LGWU), founded in 1954 is the only central labor organization.

THE STATE

Official Name: Kingdom of Lesotho.
Administrative Divisions: 10 Districts.
Capital: Maseru 170,000 people (est 1995).
Other cities: Mafeteng 12,667 people; Maputsoe 20,000 (1986).
Government: King Letsie III, Chief of State since February 1996. Pakalitha Mosisili, Prime Minister since May 1998. Parliamentary Monarchy.
National Holiday: October 4, Independence Day (1966).
Armed Forces: 2,000 troops (1995).

African troops, along with a small contingent from Botswana, pulled out of the territory by May 1999. ∎

The origins of the Yoruba culture

In the 5th century, iron-working rural communities settled in the forest region of the coastal strip which stretches between Volta and Cameroon, establishing an organized agricultural economy with advanced and stable ways of life. Amongst the largest, and seemingly oldest, of these were the Yoruba communities, found in the Ife, Ilesha and Ekiti regions.

In around the 13th century, a movement outwards by the groups which imposed economic, political and political supremacy on the weaker communities led to the creation of the Yoruba kingdoms. But the idea of a 'kingdom' associated with the traditional African societies is far from the Western view of, for example, the 'kingdom of Louis XVI'.

THE YORUBA KINGDOMS OR STATES

The Yoruba kingdoms - south of modern-day Nigeria - owe their linguistic and cultural homogeneity to this ethnic group, recognizing their roots in these ancestors. The splendor accomplished by the Ife and Oyo kingdoms spread to the traditions of the other areas and overshadowed their own origins.

There is one belief structure which is based on the myth of Ife who created the world in the city of Ife-Ife, and another which attributes the creation to Oyo and says the Yoruba have their origins in a migration movement which came from the east. What is certain, however, is that the life of these kingdoms led to the spread of their institutions and practices amongst the local populations, and that the execution of complex functions - extensive agriculture, long-distance trade, tax systems, military expansion, citizen policies - were possible because of the well-planned and organized states.

Although each king aimed to leave his successor an even bigger kingdom, a policy of tolerance encouraged a certain level of interchange which led to the cultural enrichment of both the stronger communities and those they absorbed. It was this exchange which ultimately explained the heterogeneity of Yoruba civilization: a single culture expressed through differences.

THE ECONOMIC LIFE OF THE YORUBA KINGDOMS

The Yoruba states were generally of a modest size, sometimes covering only a single city and the surrounding villages. The kingdom of Oyo was one important exception, spreading over a vast area and acquiring imperial status in the 17th century. The more common kingdoms consisted of a compact town surrounding the compound of the kings and elders in an area contained by a wall marking the edge of the kingdom. Resources produced from agriculture, a certain amount of mining and craftwork were taken to local markets organized on alternate days in order to prevent competition between markets. However, luxury articles -like the gold paid in tax in the courts, marble, art objects, nuts and others- were the main object of long distance trade, like that with the Hausa states of the eastern zones, to the benefit of the rich-

est strata of society - the kings and their courts, officials, merchants and professionals. In the more developed communities slave ownership was common as a result of crimes or debts, and these people worked as domestic servants or agricultural laborers on the common lands.

There was no slave trade amongst the early traditional Yoruba societies. Historical reports tell of a slave trade which probably began in the 15th century under the kings of Benin, by which time this kingdom had become a powerful expansionist state.

THE YORUBA COSMOVISION

An ancient myth, revealing how mythical time is transposed over historical time, explains how the grandchildren of the mythical founder of Ife - the sacred city - spread out into the surrounding area establishing and naming the first generation of Yoruba states: Owu, Ketu, Benin, Illa, Dave, Popo and Oyo.

The Yoruba belief system is based on the idea of a superior entity made up of three divinities, Olofi, Oloddumare and Olorun. The first of these created the world, which was initially only populated by orixas, or saints. The power, or ache was later divided between the orixas, who from then on were empowered to intervene in human affairs and to represent people to Olofi through the mediation of the supreme judge or main messenger, Obbatala.

As in most of the languages of Black Africa, 'the power' is expressed amongst the Yoruba through the word 'ache' which means 'the force', not in the sense of violence, but as a vital energy which creates a multiplicity of process and determines everything from physical and moral integrity to luck.

The Yoruba cosmovision is prevalent in all the cultural creations of this group of people. As is generally the case with peoples where every action is carried out, interpreted and lived as part of an organic belief system which is not precisely religious, this cosmology includes the idea that the order of the cosmic forces can be upset by immoral actions which have the effect of unbalancing and damaging humanity, nature and the perpetrators themselves.

The unity between nature and ethics in these cultures constitutes a cosmic determination, and along with it, a principle for the exercising of power, a condition for its beneficent application.

COMMUNITY LIFE

The community was of great value in the traditional Yoruba societies. It defined the conception of history - identified with the life of the group in continuous change - and time - conceived of as the social time, lived by the group, which transcends the time of the individual. It is, at the same time, the dimension where people can, and must, incessantly play out their fight against decadence and for the enrichment of their vital energy.

The Yoruba believed that throughout the history lived by the group a certain ache was accumulated incarnated in objects. These objects were sent from the ancestors down through the successive generations via their patriarchs or kings, who were intermediaries between the transcendental and visible worlds, as gifts from the orixas.

Although they were headed by kings, the communities were led by governing councils made up of men of varied standing, where the elders enjoyed their deserved dignity. The Yoruba, as in the majority of traditional African societies, were societies of public opinion, where the conduct of the authorities was monitored, spied on, and the violations of the principles which ruled the community life were always denounced through persistent verbal criticism and rumors which were so wearing that, in time, the subject of these was forced either to explain their actions or stand down.

Women also had a great deal of authority in other aspects of community life.

THE YORUBA RELIGION

The religion of the traditional Yoruba societies is characterized by the cult of God and a group of intermediary divinities, whose intervention and wills rule human life. The orixas were ancestors who accumulated power and knowledge over the forces of nature and humanity during their lifetimes, by virtue of which they one day changed from people into gods. Each one personifies certain forces of nature and is associated with a cult which obliges believers to offer food, sacrifices and prayers in order to escape their wrath and attract their favor.

The Yoruba gods and goddesses occasionally take possession of the faithful, and when this happens the god dances with his devotees in a friendly manner and sometimes speaks, offers advice or gives prophecies. The most well known orixas include: Eleggua, the god who opens paths and is found behind the doors of Yoruba homes; Oggun, the inventor of the forge, god of the minerals and the mountains; Oxosi, the god of hunting; Xango, the god of fire and war; Oxun, the goddess of fresh water, love and all tenderness and Iemanya, the queen of the sea.

YORUBA ART

The art in the most ancient Yoruba communities was distinguished by its sculptures, metalwork and ceramics. Bas reliefs, woodworking, masks and human heads created by the lost-wax method were jealousy guarded as divine heirlooms.

However, Yoruba art is dominated by music. Music is inseparably united to the Yoruba religious cults and liturgy.

The most characteristic musical tradition is the predominance of the drums and especially the presence of the *bata* (family) drums, an exclusive creation of the Yoruba people. This is an orchestra of three drums - *Iya* (the mother), *Itotele* and *Okongolo* played together by three drummers. For the Yoruba 'the batas speak' and each of their blows - be they of the sacred bata or the non sacred bembe - are inspired by legends attributed to the orixas.

The sound and symphonic integrity of the bata (the vegetable sound of the wood of the drums, the animal sound of the skins, and the mineral for the accompanying bells and rattles), along with human voices, obey a magical criteria through which the Yoruba evoke the integrity of the cosmic powers. ∎

Liberia

Liberia

Population: 2,930,000 (1999)
Area: 111,369 SQ KM
Capital: Monrovia
Currency: Liberian dollar
Language: English

The present Liberia was formerly known as the Grain Coast, and was inhabited by 16 different ethnic groups. The Kru speakers lived in the southwest, and the Mande speaking peoples, including the Mandingo, lived in the east and northeast. After the arrival of the Portuguese, Mandingo traders and artisans played an important role as they spread throughout the territory, becoming the principal propagators of Islam.

[2] Long before US President Abraham Lincoln freed the slaves in 1865, during the US civil war, emancipated blacks posed a social problem to US southern slaveholders. As a solution to the 'problem' some were 'repatriated'. On the assumption that blacks would be at home in any part of Africa, it was planned to ship them to the British colony of Sierra Leone.

[3] In 1821, the American Colonization Society purchased a portion of Sierra Leone and founded a city which was named Monrovia after James Monroe, President of the United States.

[4] Only 20,000 US blacks returned to Africa. The native population distrusted these settlers whose language and religion were those of the colonizers. Supported by US Navy firepower, the newcomers settled on the coast and occupied the best lands. For a long time, they refused to mix with the 'junglemals', whom they considered 'savages'. Even today only 15 per cent of the population speak English and practice Christianity.

[5] In 1841, the US Government approved a constitution for the African territory. It was written by Harvard academics, who called the country Liberia. Washington also appointed Liberia's first African governor: Joseph J Roberts. In July 1847, a Liberian Congress representing only the

repatriates from the US, proclaimed independence. Roberts was appointed President and the Harvard-made constitution was kept, along with a flag which resembled that of the United States.

[6] The emblem on the Liberian coat of arms reads: 'Love of liberty brought us here'. However, independence brought little freedom for the original population. For a long time, only landowners were able to vote. Today, the 45,000 descendants of the former US slaves form the core of the local ruling class and are closely linked with transnational capital. One of the principal exports, rubber, is controlled by Firestone and Goodrich under 99-year concessions granted in 1926. The same is true of oil, iron ore and diamonds. Resistance to this situation has been suppressed on several occasions by US Marine interventions to 'defend democracy'.

[7] The discovery of extensive mineral deposits, and the use of the Liberian flag by US ships, fanned a period of economic growth beginning in 1960. This was instantly dubbed an 'economic miracle', but this so-called miracle only reached the American-Liberian sector of the

population, who secured significant increases in income during this period.

[8] The political establishment was shaken in 1979, when the increase in the price of rice triggered demonstrations and unrest. A year later, Sergeant Samuel Doe overthrew the regime of William Tolbert, who was executed, along with other members of his government. These disturbances led to the suspension of the Constitution and the banning of all political parties. In 1980, the beginning of a democratization process was announced, followed by the signing of the first agreement with the International Monetary Fund, that included a strong cut in public spending and the privatization of state owned companies.

[9] Falling exports, increasing unemployment, the reduction of salaries in both public and private sectors, and spiraling foreign debt threw the country into a crisis of substantial proportions.

[10] Popular discontent increased. Between 1980 and 1989 Doe's administration uncovered many new anti-government conspiracies.

[11] Elections were held in 1985. With any viable political opposition banned, and

accusations of fraud and imprisonment of opposition leaders abounding, Doe obtained 50.9 per cent of the vote. The Liberian People's Party (LPP) and United People's Party (UPP), which represented the major opposition forces, were not authorized to participate.

[12] In 1987, most Government financing came directly from the US, a fact related to the vast North American business interests in Liberia. These included $450 million of investments, military bases, a regional Voice of America station, and a communications center for all US diplomatic missions in Africa.

[13] In May 1990, the National Patriotic Front of Liberia (NPFL) launched an attack against the city of Gbarnga, 120 km from the capital. The guerrilla movement rapidly took over several parts of the country.

[14] An NPFL victory, under the leadership of former civil servant Charles Taylor, seemed imminent in June However, in July, when the battle to take Monrovia was just underway, the rebel front split, with one faction forming the Independent Patriotic Front (INPFL), led by Prince Johnson.

[15] On July 31, 200 civilians who had sought refuge in a Lutheran mission, were massacred by Government soldiers.

[16] In September 1990, President Samuel Doe was assassinated by Johnson's troops. In the mêlée which followed, Johnson, Taylor, Amos Sawyer (a civil servant in Doe's government) and Raleigh Seekie (head of the Presidential Guard) all proclaimed themselves 'Interim President'.

[17] In November 1990, Sawyer formed a provisional government, with the support of Cote d'Ivoire, Gambia, Nigeria, Burkina Faso and Togo, the five West African countries that had made up a peacekeeping force.

[18] In 1992, Taylor turned down the vice-presidency which Sawyer had offered him. The NPFL controlled most of the country, through the Government of the Patriotic National Assembly of Reconstruction. In August, 2,000 NPFL troops were killed in an attack upon Tubmanburg, north

WORKERS

% OF LABOUR FORCE **1998**

■ FEMALE: 40%   ■ MALE: 60%

of Monrovia by United Liberian forces (ULIMO).

[19] ULIMO split into two factions in November. Alhaji Kromah, accused of being overly-friendly toward Muslim groups and the Libyan Government, became the leader of the faction that established its headquarters in Tubmanburg. Raleigh Seekie became the leader of the Sierra Leone faction.

[20] In June 1993, ULIMO attacked a refugee camp in Kata. According to the United Nations High Commissioner for Refugees, during the attack 450 people were killed and many of the victims' bodies were mutilated.

[21] US support for an increased UN role in the conflict gave the Security Council the go-ahead to demand a cease-fire and decree an arms embargo, amongst other measures.

[22] The military stalemate and UN participation led to a peace agreement being signed in Geneva, on July 17 1993. The two main armed forces and the provisional Sawyer government agreed a cease-fire in seven months and the calling of general elections.

[23] In August, following the timetable established in Geneva, a transitional Council of State was established with representatives of the NPFL, ULIMO and Sawyer's government.

[24] By 1993, the total of civil war victims had risen to 150,000. Nearly a million Liberians, out of a total population of 2.4 million, had been displaced to another part of the country, or were living as refugees in neighboring countries.

[25] In March 1994, the Council of State took power, but the

formation of a new government was delayed until May due to disagreements between the NPFL, ULIMO and Sawyer's representatives. Meanwhile, the fighting between rival armed groups and the skirmishes between some of them and the recently deployed Economic Community of the West African States (ECOWAS) peace troops continued.

[26] In December, the seven warring groups agreed a cease-fire. In 1995, negotiations between the various bands continued. The composition of the Council of State was broadened, with the entry of Charles Taylor, and a new government was formed.

[27] Civil war broke out again in 1996 with violent clashes, particularly in Monrovia. In September, Ruth Perry took over leadership of the Council of State, with ECOWAS support. The war had seriously affected essential services. In August, the main leaders agreed a new truce. ECOWAS deployed more troops to guarantee the fulfillment of the agreements signed in 1995.

[28] In November, the peace forces started to disarm the rival factions. The war had caused around 200,000 deaths and made refugees of hundreds of thousands of people.

[29] In July 1997, Charles Taylor won the presidential and parliamentary elections with 75.3 per cent of the vote, taking over as President a month later. Taylor's National Patriotic Front took 21 of the 26 posts in the Senate and 49 of the 64 seats in the Chamber of Representatives.

[30] The President approved a law to defend human rights and appointed a commission to monitor the situation. However, Amnesty International called for an impartial tribunal to investigate human rights violations committed during the civil war.

[31] In March 1998, some 480,000 Liberian refugees, in various African countries, started registering for voluntary repatriation. However, the program ran into serious problems due to the lack of funds promised by donor organizations. It had also aimed to help 220,000 internally-displaced Liberians.

[32] President Taylor urged Britain in June 1999 to stop arms shipments to Sierra Leone, arguing that they were a threat to peace in West Africa. Sierra Leone meanwhile claimed that Liberian mercenaries were collaborating with the RUF rebels there. Taylor affirmed that his government did not

support the mercenaries and that they would be arrested if caught. He also denied that Liberia was providing arms to the RUF rebels in the neighboring country, though he acknowledged he was a long-time friend of their leader, Foday Sankoh.

[33] The Government's relations with the Opposition and the media became heated after the closure of two radio stations in March 2000. After shutting down Radio Veritas, the Government allowed it to reopen later that month - but at the same time decreed the closure of Star Radio for having broadcast the statements of diplomats from the US and other countries who criticized Taylor's actions. Eleven opposition parties demanded that the Government lift the ban. The Press Syndicate of Liberia declared an embargo on news about government activities in protest at the 'illegal and arbitrary' closing of the two radio stations, but lifted it soon thereafter. The Syndicate's justification for lifting the embargo was that it 'sought an amicable solution to the tense relations between the independent media and the Government'. ∎

PROFILE

ENVIRONMENT

The country is divided into three geographic regions: the coastal plain contains most of the population, and is low and swampy; the central plateau, crossed by numerous valleys and covered by dense tropical forests; and the mountainous inland area along the border with Guinea. In the fertile coastal areas, rice, coffee, sugar-cane, cocoa and palm oil are produced. American companies own large rubber plantations. Liberia is also the leading African iron ore producer. War, the loss of biodiversity and erosion are the main threats to the environment.

SOCIETY

Peoples: Most Liberians belong to the Mende, Kwa and Vai groups, which are split into nearly 30 ethnic sub groups. Of these, the most significant are the Mandingo, Kpelle, Mendo, Kru, Gola and Bassa (the Vai are renowned for having created one of the few African written languages). The descendants of 'repatriated' US slaves control business and politics, though they constitute only 5 per cent of the population.
Religions: The majority profess traditional African religions. About 15 per cent are Muslim, and slightly fewer Christian. The State, however, is officially Christian.
Languages: English is the official language, though it is spoken by only 15 per cent of the population. The rest speak local languages.
Political Parties: National Patriotic Front of Liberia (NPFL); United Liberation Movement for Democracy in Liberia (Ulimo); Liberia Peace Council (LNC); Ulimo-J and Ulimo-K (both created after the division of the United Liberian Independence Movement).

THE STATE

Official Name: Republic of Liberia.
Administrative divisions: 11 Counties and 2 Territories.
Capital: Monrovia 720,000 people (1996).
Other cities: Harper 60,000; Gbarnga 30,000; Buchanan 25,000; Yekepa 16,000 (1985).
Government: Charles Taylor, President since July 1997.
National Holiday: August 26, Independence Day (1846).
Armed Forces: 3,000 (1996).

Libya

Libiyah

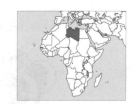

Population: 5,470,000 (1999)
Area: 1,759,540 SQ KM
Capital: Tripoli (Tarabulus)
Currency: Dinar
Language: Arabic

The Socialist People's Libyan Arab Jamahiriya (known as Libya) has always been torn between the different political and economic centers of North Africa. Bordering pharaonic Egypt, Libya shared its culture and two Libyan dynasties ruled Egypt between the 10th and 8th centuries BC. However such influences did not lead to a unified state. The Carthaginian and Roman empires on the western border further stressed this division. After the Arab conquest in the 7th century, Tunisia, Morocco and Egypt became the new power centErs.

[2] The development of maritime trade and the ensuing piracy turned Tripoli into one of the major Mediterranean ports, bringing European involvement which caused further intervention by the Turkish Sultan. In 1551, Suleiman the Magnificent annexed the region to the Ottoman Empire. A weakened central authority gave increasing autonomy to the governors precipitating independence movements. The beginning of the 19th century saw piracy again on Libya's shores; this was used as a pretext for US military intervention and in 1804 US forces attacked Tripoli.

[3] In 1837, Muhammad al-Sanussi founded a clandestine Muslim brotherhood (the Sanussi religious sect) which promoted resistance to Turkish domination, though the Italians really posed a greater threat. With the decline of the Ottoman Empire, Italy declared war on Turkey in 1911 and seized the Libyan coast, the northernmost Turkish possession in Africa. With the outbreak of World War I, the Italian presence was confined to Tripoli and Homs (Al-Khums) while the rest of the territory remained autonomous. At the end of the War Italy attempted

to recover control of the territory but faced resistance for 20 years by Sidi Omar al-Mukhtar's forces. In 1931, al-Mukhtar was captured and executed and the Italians formally annexed the territory.

[4] From Egypt and Tunisia, the Sanussi brotherhood remained active and co-operated with the Allies in World War II. Muhammad Idris al-Sanussi, leader of the brotherhood, was recognized as Emir of Cyrenaica by the British. At the end of the conflict, the country was divided into an British zone (Tripolitania and Cyrenaica) and a French (Fezzan) governed from Chad. In 1949, a UN resolution restored legitimate union to the region and established the independent nation of Libya, with

Idris al-Sanussi as leader for his religious authority.

[5] Idris consolidated his position with support from the powerful Turkish-Libyan families, military advisers from the US and Britain and transnational oil companies. In 1960, foreigners settled in the country, as the oil began to flow in great quantities.

[6] In 1966, Muammar al-Khaddafi, the son of Bedouin nomads, founded the Union of Free Officials in London, where he was studying. He returned to Libya and on September 1 1969 he led an insurrection in Sabha overthrowing the King.

[7] Khaddafi's Revolutionary Council proclaimed itself Muslim, Nasserist and socialist, beginning to eliminate all US and British military bases in Libya, and imposing severe limitations on transnationals operating in the country. The production of petroleum and its derivatives was placed under state control but the Government kept some ties with the foreign companies.

[8] Khaddafi began an ambitious modernization program, with special emphasis on agricultural development. Each rural family was allotted 10 hectares of land, a tractor, a house, tools, and irrigation facilities. Over 1,500 artesian wells were drilled and two million hectares of desert were irrigated and turned into fertile farmland.

[9] Rapid growth meant that immigrant workers and experienced technicians from other Arab countries were needed. In 1973 following publication of Khaddafi's Green Book a complex structure of popular participation was created through people's committees and a People's General Congress.

[10] In the cities, a social security system was created, with free medical assistance and family allowances to encourage large families. Industrial workers were granted 25 per cent participation in the profits of the companies. Industrial investment was 11 times greater than during the monarchy and agricultural investment was 30 times greater. This massive oil-financed reform transformed Libya into the North African Nation with the highest per-capita income on the continent, at $4,000 a year.

[11] In 1977, the country changed its name to the Socialist People's Libyan Arab Jamahiriya (meaning mass state in Arabic). But while Khaddafi achieved ample positive results internally, external relations were dismal. Attempts to unite with Syria and Egypt met with failure, and overtures towards Tunisia came to nothing. Khaddafi became the main critic of the diplomatic rapprochement between Egypt and Israel; he clashed with the Saudi monarchy and the Emirates, and maintained his long-standing antagonism with King Hassan of Morocco. In OPEC, Libya opposed the moderate stand of Saudi Arabia and the Emirates on oil prices, and firmly resisted the pressures and manoeuvres of transnational corporations.

[12] From 1980, Libya became diplomatically active in Sub-Saharan Africa and Latin America. The Government supported the Polisario Front in Western Sahara and participated directly in the civil war in Chad, defending the Transitional Government of National Union, led by Goukouni Oueddei.

[13] US President Reagan

Map

Mediterranean Sea

TUNISIA — Tripoli · Al-Khums · Sabrata · Leptis Magna · Benghazi · Ptolemais · Apolonia · Darnah · Cyrene · Tubruq

Khalij Surt · Qusayr ad-Daffah · Tombs

ALGERIA · Al-Jaghbub

Awbari · Sabha · LIBYA · Germa Jarmah · Waha · Bi'r al-Harash · Al-Khufrah

FEZZAN · EGYPT

Tropic of Cancer · MARZUQ · SAHARA · Ma'tan Bisharah · SUDAN

AS SAHRA AL LIBIYA

NIGER · CHAD

Area claimed by Chad

0 — 300 km

WORKERS

% OF LABOUR FORCE — **1998**

■ FEMALE: 22% ■ MALE: 78%

1990

■ SERVICES: 66.2%
■ INDUSTRY: 22.9%
■ AGRICULTURE: 10.9%

LAND USE

DEFORESTATION: 0.0% annual (1990/95)
IRRIGATED: 25.9% of arable (1993)

1993

■ FOREST & WOODLAND: 0.5%
■ ARABLE: 1.0%
■ OTHER: 98.5%

PUBLIC EXPENDITURE

MILITARY EXPENDITURE   **71%**
(% of health & education)   (1990/91)

undertook a huge international campaign to link the Libyan leader with world terrorism. In August 1981 in the Gulf of Sidra two Libyan planes were shot down by the US Sixth Fleet. Khaddafi skillfully avoided any violent response to the provocation, winning the sympathy of the conservative Arab regimes which had until then been hostile to his government.

[14] In 1983 Libya attempted to resume friendly relations with Morocco, a move which met with success in August 1984 when an agreement was signed. Most North African nations were surprised at the pact, for Moroccans and Libyans held opposite views on practically all political issues. However, the rapprochement could be regarded as a consequence of increasing cooperation between the Algerian, Tunisian and Mauritanian governments. Moreover, Morocco aimed at neutralizing Libyan support of the Polisario Front, while Libya sought to cut off Moroccan aid to Habre's regime in Chad.

[15] In January 1986, the US imposed an economic embargo on Libya, and on April 14 American war planes bombed Tripoli and Benghazi, leaving dozens of civilians dead. Subsequent information revealed the main objective had been to eliminate Colonel Khaddafi.

[16] In November 1991, US and British courts blamed the Khaddafi Government for the bombing of two airplanes: a Pan Am flight over Lockerbie, Scotland, with 270 deaths, of whom 17 were US citizens; and a UTA flight in Nigeria with 170 victims. Interpol issued an international arrest warrant for two people accused of the bombings. In January 1992, Libya expressed willingness to cooperate with the UN in the clarification of both attacks.

[17] Nevertheless Khaddafi rejected a UN extradition order, unsuccessfully proposing that the trial be held in Tripoli.

[18] Libyan inflexibility strengthened UN determination. In February and March the extradition of the accused Libyan agents was again requested. The UN demanded that Libya explicitly renounce terrorism, setting April 15 as the deadline and threatening sanctions, a blockade and even military measures should the ultimatum not be met.

[19] Libya passed the deadline, invoking economic sanctions from the EC and the seven most industrialized countries. Khaddafi took the decision to the International Court of Justice.

[20] In August, when the embargo was renewed, Khaddafi decided on a change of foreign policy and designated as chancellor a 'moderate', able to negotiate Libyan and US positions. In 1993 Tripoli continued a policy of economic liberalization, initiated in 1989, when it broke off relations with Iran.

[21] Libya's isolation increased in 1994. The UN intensified the embargo despite Khaddafi's concessions. In the end he accepted that the two accused be tried in Scotland. Inside the country, the difficult situation made him more popular since at least a section of public opinion held the US responsible for the scarcity of goods and related problems.

[22] Nevertheless, some concessions awoke resistance: in the southern region of Fezzan the population protested when the area of Aouzou was given to Chad following a decision of the International Court of The Hague. On the other hand Tripoli made progress towards achieving an old project by signing an agreement for the building of an aqueduct that would allow water to come from other countries.

[23] In 1995 the country remained isolated despite the ongoing Libyan proposals for a dialogue with the West. This fact did not counter either the growth of the private sector or foreign investment. Several international firms were willing to participate in new projects to exploit oil resources.

[24] In the second half of 1996, the Libyan economy continued to benefit from the near 40 per cent increase in international oil prices despite the embargo. In the same year, part of an aqueduct designed to supply water to isolated desert settlements was opened.

[25] In 1997, Libya began to emerge from international isolation, fighting to get the embargo lifted. Three Security Council member countries, Egypt, Guinea-Bissau and Kenya, asked for a mission to be sent to Tripoli to evaluate the situation for the first time. The Movement of Non-Aligned Nations and the Organization of African Unity backed a Libyan request for the two men suspected of blowing up the Pan Am plane over Lockerbie in 1988 to be tried in a neutral country.

[26] In October, South Africa formally appealed to the UN to end the embargo, following President Nelson Mandela's visit to Libya, in an attempt to mediate on the conflict. Mandela said he supported the Libyan position, but that he would not ask for an 'unconditional' lifting of sanctions. However, the Security Council renewed the measures in November.

[27] In March 1998, Libya saw its first international legal victory when the UN Court of Justice upheld the plea for removal of the economic embargo. The decision caused conflict between the Security Council and the Court within the UN.

[28] After extensive multilateral negotiations, the UK and the US proposed that the two men accused of the Lockerbie bombing be tried in The Hague by Scottish judges under Scottish Law. The proposal was finally accepted in March 1999 and in April the UN Security Council lifted sanctions in place since 1992. In September, more than twenty African and Arab leaders attended a meeting in Tripoli for the 30th anniversary of the Libyan revolution, amongst them the presidents of South Africa, Palestine, Algeria and Zambia. After 15 years of no diplomatic contact, London accredited an ambassador in Tripoli in December 1999.

[29] Libya made the most of the thaw to initiate a diplomatic offensive in the region, offering help as mediator in the conflict in Sudan and reinitiating dialogue with Chad. In March 2000, Washington sent a high-level delegation in to look into lifting sanctions on investment in and travel to Libya, banned since 1981. ∎

PROFILE

ENVIRONMENT

Most of the country is covered by desert. The only fertile lands are located along the temperate Mediterranean coast, where most of the population live. There are no perennial rivers and rain is scarce. The country has major oil reserves. Water is scarce, with most of the supply pumped from underground reserves. The air is polluted by gases given off in the oil refining process and desertification, erosion and the destruction of vegetation are rapidly advancing.

SOCIETY

Peoples: Arabs and Berbers account for 79 per cent of the population. There are Tunisian, Egyptian, Greek and Italian and Chadian minorities (21 per cent). **Religions:** Islam (official), mainly Sunni. There is a small Christian minority. **Languages:** Arabic (official) is predominant. English and Italian are also spoken. **Political Parties:** Socialist People's Libyan Arab Jamahiriya. **Social Organizations:** There are mass organizations of workers, peasants, students and women.

THE STATE

Official Name: al-Jamahiriyah al-'Arabiyah al-Libiyah ash-Sha'biyah al-Ishtirakiyah. **Administrative divisions:** 3 provinces, 10 counties and 1,500 communes. **Capital:** Tripoli (Tarabulus) 1,500,000 people (1994). **Other cities:** Benghazi 750,000 people; Misratah 360,000; az-Zawiyah 300,000 (1994). **Government:** The People's General Congress is the highest Government body. Col. Muammar Khaddafi, leader of the Revolution and commander-in-chief of the People's Armed Forces, is the Head of State since September 1969. **National Holiday:** September 1, Revolution Day (1969). **Armed Forces:** 80,000. **Other:** Revolutionary Guards, 3000.

Lithuania

Lietuva

Population: 3,682,000 (1999)
Area: 65,200 SQ KM
Capital: Vilnius
Currency: Lit
Language: Lithuanian

Lithuanians have lived along the shores of the Baltic Sea since long before the Christian era. Protected by the forests, Lithuanian tribes fiercely resisted German efforts to subdue them in the 13th century, and united under the leadership of Mindaugas, who was crowned king by Pope Innocent IV in 1253.

2 In the 14th century, Lithuania began its eastward and southern expansion, going into Belarusian lands. Gediminas built the Grand Duchy of Lithuania, which extended from the Baltic Sea to the Black Sea, with its capital at Vilnius. In 1386, Jagiello, Gediminas' grandson, married the Queen of Poland, thus uniting the two kingdoms.

3 Lithuania withstood a series of attacks from the Teutonic Order, which continued to combat the Lithuanian-Polish union - despite the fact that the latter were Christian - until the Battle of Tannenberg in 1410, in which they suffered a crushing defeat. This defeat was a harsh blow to German supremacy in the Baltic region. A new pact between Lithuania and Poland, signed in 1413, reaffirmed the principle of union while respecting the autonomy of both States.

4 With the coronation of Ivan III of Muscovy as the sovereign of all Russia, a new and greater threat emerged for historic Lithuania. Nevertheless, the Lithuanian-Polish union reached its peak in the 16th century, when it was unrivalled in Europe as a political system (see Poland), only to fall in the 17th century, in the course of a series of devastating wars with Sweden, Russia and Turkey and the peasant rebellions within.

5 In the 1772 and 1793 partitions of Poland among Russia, Prussia and Austria, Russia kept only Belarus. But the Polish state disappeared in 1795, and all of Lithuania was in Russian hands by 1815. The Congress of Vienna granted the Russian Emperor the additional titles of King of Poland and Grand Prince of Lithuania.

6 Lithuanians were harshly suppressed by the Russians. The czarist regime treated Lithuania as though it were a part of Russia, calling it the Northwest Territory after 1832. Between 1864 and 1905, Russification extended to all aspects of life: books which were printed in Lithuanian had to use the Cyrillic alphabet, and Catholics were persecuted.

7 With the Revolution of 1905, the peoples of the Russian Empire were granted freedom of speech. A congress with some 2,000 delegates called for the demarcation of Lithuania's borders, territorial autonomy and the election of a parliament by democratic means.

8 During World War I, Germany occupied a major part of Lithuania. In 1915, a congress - authorized by the occupying Germans - elected the 20-member Council of Lithuania. The 214 delegates to the congress called for the creation of an independent Lithuanian state within its 'ethnic borders' and with Vilnius as its capital. On February 16 1918, the Council declared Lithuania's independence and terminated all political ties with other nations.

9 In 1919, the Red Army entered Vilnius and formed a communist government, but the Allied powers forced it to withdraw. The new head of the Polish State, Josef Pilsudski, tried to re-establish the former union, but failed due to the resistance of the Lithuanians, Ukrainians and Belarusians. In the end, the League of Nations and the European powers agreed to the separation of Poland and Lithuania in 1923, but Lithuania refused to recognize the line of demarcation (with Poland) which had been established by these powers.

10 In 1926, Lithuania and the Soviet Union signed a non-aggression treaty. A treaty of good will and cooperation was signed in Geneva in 1934 by Lithuania, Latvia and Estonia. As of 1938, relations with Warsaw became tense, due to Poland's claim of sovereignty over Vilnius. Tension increased when a group of Nazis came to power in Klaipeda; they demanded the ceding of that city, which meant the loss of Lithuania's only port on the Baltic.

11 In September 1939, a secret German-Soviet non-aggression treaty brought Lithuania within the USSR's sphere of influence. In October, a mutual assistance treaty was signed in Moscow; according to its terms, Lithuania was forced to accept the installation of Soviet garrisons and air bases on its soil. In 1940, the Soviet Army occupied Lithuania and a number of local political leaders were arrested and deported, while others fled toward Western Europe.

12 The new Prime Minister, Justas Paleckis, and Parliament asked to be admitted to the USSR, a request which was immediately granted by the Supreme Soviet. Lithuania thereby became a constituent republic of the USSR in August 1940. After German occupation in 1941, the Baltic Sates and Belarus became the German province of Ostland.

13 During German occupation, 190,000 Jews were sent to concentration camps. A hundred thousand residents of Vilnius - a third of that city's population, most of them Jews - were killed. Vilnius was known as the 'Jerusalem of Lithuania' and had been considered to be one of the most important centres of Jewish culture in the world. Many non-Jewish Lithuanians throughout the rest of the country were killed, and tens of thousands of young people were sent to Germany to work.

14 Vilnius was reconquered by the Red Army in 1944. Lithuania was once again occupied by the Soviets and a new period of Sovietization began. This included religious persecution and wide-scale deportations to northern Russia and Siberia, amid the forced collectivization of agriculture.

15 Religious persecution continued even after Stalin's death in 1953. Thus the resistance of the Catholic Church became identified with the nationalist movement. In 1972, the 'Lithuanian Catholic Church Chronicle' (banned by the Government) was published by the Lithuanian Movement for Human Rights. That year, a young man set fire to himself; his funeral triggered violent clashes in which 15 people were killed and 3,000 were arrested.

16 With the democratization process initiated by Mikhail Gorbachev in the USSR, Lithuania began a period of intense political agitation. In June, the Lithuanian Movement to Support Perestroika (restructuring) was founded; its Executive Committee adopted the name *Sejm* -the name of the Lithuanian Parliament at the time of independence- also known as 'Sajudis'. The Sajudis installed a kind of 'shadow' government, and demanded a return to the peace

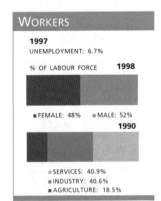

WORKERS

1997
UNEMPLOYMENT: 6.7%

% OF LABOUR FORCE   **1998**

■ FEMALE: 48%   ■ MALE: 52%

1990

■ SERVICES: 40.9%
■ INDUSTRY: 40.6%
■ AGRICULTURE: 18.5%

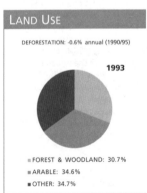

LAND USE

DEFORESTATION: -0.6% annual (1990/95)

1993

■ FOREST & WOODLAND: 30.7%
■ ARABLE: 34.6%
■ OTHER: 34.7%

treaties which recognized the country's independence, stating that Lithuania's admission to the USSR was the result of a secret agreement and therefore had no legal value.

[17] In July, the Lithuanian Freedom League (LFL) emerged from underground activity. The LFL, which dates back to 1978, called for immediate withdrawal of Soviet troops from the country, and the independence of Lithuania. Police brutality toward participants of a demonstration sponsored by the LFL triggered joint protest actions by members of the League and the Sajudis, and led to a crisis within the Lithuanian Communist Party leadership.

[18] The Lithuanian Government opted not to follow the example set by Estonia's Supreme Soviet, which had made a unilateral decision on the question of sovereignty. Instead, Lithuanian authorities began making concessions to local movements, legalizing the use of the flag and the national anthem, designating Independence Day as a holiday and authorizing public commemoration of that day. In addition, Lithuanian was adopted as the country's official language, and the Vilnius Cathedral and other churches were reopened.

[19] In February 1989, the first secretary of the CP and the Sajudis attended the official commemoration of the country's 1918 independence, side by side. In December, Lithuania's Supreme Soviet did away with the article of the constitution which assigned the CP a leading role; the first decision of its kind within the USSR.

[20] In January 1990, Gorbachev announced in Vilnius that the details of a future relation with the Union would be established through legislation. In March, the Lithuanian Parliament proclaimed the nation's independence, to be effected immediately. In September 1991, the new Council of State of the USSR accepted the independence of the three Baltic States, which were immediately recognized by several countries and by the UN.

[21] In August 1991, after the failed coup against Gorbachev in the USSR, the Lithuanian Parliament banned the Communist Party, the Democratic Workers' Party and the Lithuanian Communist Youth organization. The following month, President Vytautas Landsbergis issued a call, before the United Nations, for the withdrawal of 50,000 Soviet troops from Lithuania; they had been stationed in Vilnius since January of that year.

[22] The new constitution was approved by a referendum on October 25 1992. That year, the GNP diminished by 35 per cent and inflation soared to 1,150 per cent.

[23] On February 14 1993, the leader of the former Communist Party, Algirdas Brazauskas, was elected President with 60 per cent of the vote. In 1993 and 1994, Brazauskas continued with the transition policy toward a market economy.

[24] In 1995, around 80 per cent of Lithuanians were estimated to be 'poor', 15 per cent 'middle class', and 5 per cent 'rich'. The accentuation of social inequalities was seen as the key factor in the ruling party defeat in local elections this year.

[25] In February 1996, Prime Minister Adolfas Slezevicius was replaced by Mindaugas Stankevicius, who was replaced by Gediminas Vagnorius in December. During this period, inflation fell from 35 to 14 per cent, and there was 3 per cent growth in the Gross Domestic Product.

[26] The 1996 parliamentary elections brought the opposition to power, allowing Landsbergis to become head of parliament. This cohabiting with the former Communists ended with the 1997-1998 elections, when Valdas Adamkus was elected President in the second round, with a narrow margin of votes above his rival, the former Communist Arturas Paulaskas. Adamkus, a 71-year-old who had lived more than 40 years in the United States, had been a member of the Conservative Party. His campaign was based on the consolidation of a market economy, closer relations with the US and NATO membership for Lithuania.

[27] Finance minister, Jonas Lionginas, and Economy minister, Eugenijus Maldeikis, resigned from their posts in early October 1999, after the Government approved the sale of national oil production to the US company Williams International. The sale granted the foreign company control of the refinery and the export terminal. As a result of the massive demonstrations against the sale, Prime Minister Rolandas Paskas was forced to resign at the end of that month. The President appointed Andrius Kubilius, who had been Vice-President, to replace the Prime Minister and he went ahead with the operation.

[28] That same month Parliament approved a frontier treaty with Russia, the first of the post-Soviet era, concentrating on access to Kaliningrad, a Russian enclave located southeast of Lithuania which has no land access to the rest of the Russian Federation. In December 1999, the European Union decided to include Lithuania on the list of possible entrants, and this was considered a success by the Government. ∎

Luxembourg

Luxembourg

Population: 426,000 (1999)
Area: 2,586 SQ KM
Capital: Luxembourg
Currency: Luxembourg franc
Language: French and German

Luxembourg, Belgium, the Netherlands, and part of northern France constitute the Low Countries, and until 1579 they shared a common history (see the Netherlands).

2 In the war of the Low Countries against Spain, Luxembourg sided with the southern provinces, acknowledging the authority of Philip II. Luxembourg was conquered by France in 1684, but returned to Spain 13 years later, under the Treaty of Rijswijk. In 1713, the Austrian Hapsburgs took control of the country until the Napoleonic invasion in 1795, when the country was annexed to the French Empire.

3 In 1815, after the defeat of Napoleon, the Congress of Vienna handed over the Duchy of Luxembourg to William of Orange. William incorporated the Duchy as his kingdom's eighteenth province. After the Belgian revolt in 1831, Luxembourg was divided again: the largest section was given to Belgium, and the smallest handed over to William as the Grand Duchy of Luxembourg, which he finally accepted in 1839. Thereafter the Duchy was administered independently until 1867. In 1866, the German Confederation was dissolved, the Treaty of London guaranteed the neutrality of the grand duchy giving control to the House of Nassau.

4 Germany invaded the country twice, in 1914 and again during World War II. After the War productivity increased when the country formed an economic alliance with Belgium and the Netherlands called the Benelux, later becoming a member of the EEC.

5 The Christian Social Party, a center-right party, maintained a majority in Parliament from 1919 until 1974. Afterwards a center-left coalition of the Socialist Workers' Party and the Democratic Party took office. The Christian Social Party recovered its majority in 1979, forming alliances with the Parti Socialist Workers' Party and the Democratic Party.

6 In 1949 Luxembourg became a founder member of NATO. In 1986, women were admitted to the armed forces.

7 Women were granted the right to vote in 1919. The female presence in the registered workforce was 25.2 per cent in 1979, increasing to 34 per cent by 1988. In Luxembourg women occupy 74.8 per cent of posts in education, the highest percentage in the European Community.

8 The June 1989 legislative elections reaffirmed the dominance of the Social Christians and Socialists. The PCS took 22 seats, the POS 18 and the Democratic Party 11. The Action Committee, a group created to defend the pension rights of private sector workers, won four seats.

9 In 1990, border controls were abolished with Belgium, France, Germany and the Netherlands. In 1991, a new 'financial scandal' hit the headlines when the International Bank of Credit and Commerce (BCCI) went bankrupt - an institution which was originally from Luxembourg with its headquarters in the Arab Emirates.

10 In 1993, Josée Jacobs became the first woman to hold a cabinet position in the history of the nation, becoming minister of agriculture and viniculture. In 1994, the PCS and the POS, who had governed the country together since 1984, were returned to power in the general elections, allowing Jacques Santer to continue as Prime Minister.

11 In 1995, Santer became President of the European Commission and was replaced as Prime Minister by Jean-Claude Juncker. Luxembourg established itself as one of the main financial markets of the world, especially in the administration of social funds - like pension funds- with an estimated worth of $356 billion.

12 As with the rest of the Union, unemployment rates increased in late 1997, although it continued to be the lowest of the 15 member states (3.7 per cent). In November, some 30,000 people from various European countries demonstrated in Luxembourg for a Europe 'serving employment'.

13 In March 1998, the Government announced it would increase funding for the plan to extend the track for the high speed train (TGV) - initially developed in France - to the east, in order to intensify contact with Eastern Europe.

14 In November 1999, along with Belgium and the other Low Countries, Luxembourg proposed that the European Union should allow some of its members closer association. This would both allow other (new) members to join without having to attain such high levels of economic harmonisation, and also prevent them holding back more advanced economies. Prime Minister Jean-Claude Juncker said the 'two-speed operation' was a necessity.

15 Grand Duke Jean announced in December 1999 that in September 2000 he would abdicate in favour of his son Henri. Jean had been head of state for 35 years. ∎

PROFILE

ENVIRONMENT

Located on the southeastern side of the Ardennes, Luxembourg has two natural regions: the north with valleys and woods, and a maximum altitude of 500 meters, is sparsely populated with potato and grain farming; the south (Gutland) is a low plain and the country's main demographic corridor, with most of the population and cities and major industries (iron, steel and mining), including the capital.

SOCIETY

Peoples: Luxemburger 67.4 per cent; Portuguese 12.1 per cent; Italian 4.8 per cent; French 3.5 per cent; Belgian 2.8 per cent; German 2.3 per cent; other 7.1 per cent. **Religions:** Majority Catholic. (94.9 per cent) **Languages:** Letzebuergish, French, German, Portuguese. **Political Parties:** Christian Social Party; Socialist Workers' Party; Liberal Party; Democratic Party; Communist Party; Green Alternative Party and Ecological Initiative. **Social Organizations:** Luxembourg National Workers' Confederation; National Council of Unions.

THE STATE

Official Names: Grand-Duché de Luxembourg; Grossherzogtum Luxemburg, Groussherzogtum Lëtzebuerg. **Administrative divisions:** 12 cantons. **Capital:** Luxembourg-Ville 76,446 people (1996). **Other cities:** Esch-sur-Alzette 24,255 people; Dudelange 15,883; Differdange 16,950 (1995). **Government:** Constitutional monarchy. Multi-party parliamentary system. Grand Duke Jean, Head of State since 1964; Jean-Claude Juncker, Prime Minister and Chief of Government since 1995. Single-chamber legislature: Chamber of Deputies, with 60 members elected by direct popular vote, every 5 years. **National holiday:** June 23 (National day). **Armed Forces:** 800. **Other:** 560 (Gendarmes).

STATISTICS

Population: 426,000 (1999). **Annual growth:** 0.6 % (1975/97) **Estimates for year 2015 (million):** 0.5 (1999). **Annual growth to year 2015:** 0.6 % (1997/2015). **Urban population:** 90.0 % (1997) **Children per woman:** 1.7 (1998). **Life expectancy at birth:** 77 years (1998). **Male:** 73 years (1998). **Female:** 80 years (1998). **Maternal mortality:** 0 per 100,000 live births (1990-98). **Infant mortality:** 5 per 1,000 (1998). **Under-5 child mortality:** 5 per 1,000 (1998). 213 doctors per 100,000 people (1993). **School enrolment:** Primary total: 99 % (1990/96). Male: 88 % (1990/97). Female: 94 % (1990/97). **Secondary:** Male: 72 % (1990/96). Female: 76 % (1990/96). **Tertiary:** 10 % (1996). 325 **newspapers** (1996), 681 **radios** (1997), 628 **TV sets** (1996) and 592 **main telephone lines** (1996) per 1,000 people. **Books:** 169 new titles per 100,000 people (1992/94). Per capita, **GNP:** $ 45,100 (1998). **Annual growth, GNP:** 5.1 % (1998). **Consumer price index:** 103.8 (1998). **Exports:** $ 16,609 million (1997). **Imports:** $ 13,976 million (1997). **HDI** (rank/value): 17/0.902 (1997)

Macedonia

Makedonija

Population: 2,011,000 (1999)
Area: 25,710 SQ KM
Capital: Skopje
Currency: Denar
Language: Macedonian

Macedonia's ancient cultural history is linked to that of Greece and Anatolia. According to archaeological studies, the ancestors of the Macedonians can be identified in the early Bronze Age. In the year 700 BC, a people calling themselves 'Macedonian' migrated toward the east from their native lands on the banks of the Aliakmon River. Aegae was the capital of the kingdom which, during the reign of Amyntas I, extended to the Axios River and beyond, as far as the Chalcidice Peninsula.

[2] Macedonia reached a position of power and influence within Greece during the reign of Philip II (359-336 BC). Warriors had the power to choose a new king, and also to try cases of high treason. Alexander 'the Great', Philip's son and a student of Aristotle, defeated the Persian Empire and led the Macedonian armies to northern Africa and the Arabic peninsula, crossing Mesopotamia and reaching as far east as India.

[3] The Macedonian Empire, built up over 11 years, contributed to the propagation of Greek culture in the Orient. Alexander the Great founded a large number of cities and was responsible for the fusion of Greek culture with the cultures of the peoples he conquered, giving rise to what is known as Hellenism. His death in 323 BC was followed by a period of internal struggles, though Macedonia maintained the unity of the empire.

[4] Around the year 280 BC, groups of Galatian marauders invaded Macedonia, killing the King. Three years later, Antigonus II defeated the Galatians and was crowned king by an army from Macedonia. Most of the population were farmers, except in urban areas like Beroea and Pella, and the Greek settlements along the coast. The King held exclusive rights to the mines and forests.

[5] During the reign of Philip V (221-179), Macedonia conquered Rome's client-states in Illyria and subsequently turned eastward and to the northeast, subduing the cities of Rhodes and Pergamum. Rome responded by going to war and defeated Philip in 197 adding Macedonia to its kingdom and taking Thessaly away from Macedonia. Philip collaborated with the Romans and consolidated his power. This was a prosperous period for Macedonia, which also managed to recover Thessaly.

[6] From 168 to 146 BC, Macedonia was a Roman province, with four independent administrative sections. Macedonia supervised the Greeks for Rome, keeping watch for rebellions and invasion attempts across the northern border. In the year 27, Macedonia became a senatorial province separate from Greece. By the 4th century AD, most Macedonians had adopted Christianity.

[7] The ethnic composition of the Macedonians was not significantly affected by the Goth, Hun and Avar invasions. However, when Slavs arrived in the Balkans, they established permanent settlements throughout Macedonia. Between the 7th and the 14th centuries, Macedonia was successively subdued by the Bulgarian, Byzantine and Latin empires until they were almost completely dominated by the Serbs, except in the Greek region of Salonika.

[8] Towards the end of the 14th century, Turkey began invading the Balkans. By 1371, it had conquered most of Macedonia and in 1389, inflicted a decisive defeat upon the Serbian Empire at Kosovo. The Ottomans seized the best lands for themselves and established a feudal system. Christian peasants either became vassals of Muslim lords, to whom they paid a tithe, or were driven onto the less fertile lands.

[9] In 1864, the Ottoman Empire divided Macedonia into three provinces: Salonika, Monastir, including parts of Albania, and Kosovo, which extended into 'Old Serbia'. In 1878, Russia forced Turkey into accepting the creation of Bulgaria, which included most of

Macedonia, but the other European powers returned this territory to the Ottomans. During the ensuing years, Bulgaria, Serbia and Greece all continued to lay claim to Macedonia.

[10] Towards the end of the 19th century, a strong nationalist movement emerged in Macedonia. Macedonian Slavs created the VMRO (Vatreshna Makedonska Revolutsionna Organizatsia) in 1893, with the slogan 'Macedonia for the Macedonians'. At the same time, Bulgaria and Greece began sending guerrillas into Macedonia, provoking the Greco-Turkish War of 1897. Turkey supported the Serbs to offset the influence of the VMRO and Bulgarians.

[11] By 1903, the increase in opposition activities by Bulgarians, Greeks, Serbs and Macedonians led Russia and Austria-Hungary to demand that an inspector general be appointed, and that the police force be reorganized. Turkey agreed to meet the demands, but in August there was a general uprising, apparently initiated by Bulgaria. It was ruthlessly put down by the Turks, who destroyed 105 Macedonian-Slav villages.

[12] In 1908, after the fall of the Ottoman Empire, with the 'Young Turks' rebellion, the clamor to divide up Ottoman-Turkish territories in the region culminated in the two Balkan Wars of 1912 and 1913. Bulgaria and Serbia signed a Mutual Assistance Treaty, with Greece and Montenegro subsequently joining the alliance. Russia supported the Balkan League, because of its interest in halting the southeasterly advance of the Austro-Hungarian Empire.

[13] After defeating Turkey in the first war, the allies turned against each other. Bulgaria provoked the second Balkan War, confronting both Greece and Serbia. Romania and Turkey then allied themselves with Greece and Serbia to defeat Bulgaria. The Treaty of Bucharest gave Greece Salonika and most of the Macedonian coastal area, while Serbia was given the center and the northern parts of the territory.

[14] When World War I broke out, Bulgaria saw a chance to reassert its territorial claims over Macedonia. Sofia joined the Central Powers (Austria-Hungary, Germany and Turkey), and occupied all of Serbian Macedonia and also a part of Serbia. The victorious allied powers left the Greco-Macedonian borders as they were, and Yugoslav Macedonia was incorporated into the new Serbian, Croat and Slovenian kingdom.

[15] In the inter-war period, Serbian domination deepened Yugoslav inter-ethnic conflicts. King Alexander, who assumed dictatorial powers in 1929, was assassinated in Marseilles in 1934 by Croatian nationalists. At the beginning of World War II, when Germany invaded Yugoslavia, these internal divisions meant that the invaders met little resistance.

[16] The Yugoslav nationalist struggle intensified during the following years. Guerrillas led by the Yugoslav Communist League (YCL) seized power in May 1945, later proclaiming the Socialist Federal Republic of Macedonia. Yugoslav Macedonia joined the new state as one of its six constituent republics.

[17] In 1947, Yugoslavia declared that Macedonia was the country's least developed region. The federal government subsequently began earmarking funds for industrialization projects, especially in steel, chemical and textile production.

[18] In January, 1990, a special YCL Congress decided to adopt a multiparty system, and eliminate the leadership role which the constitution assigned to the party. However, the motion to grant greater autonomy to YCL branches in the republics was not accepted. After the Congress, the Communist Leagues of Slovenia, Croatia and Macedonia decided to separate from the YCL and call themselves by a new name, the Democratic Renewal Party.

[19] On September 8 1991, in the midst of fighting between the new separate republics of Croatia and Slovenia and the federal army, a plebiscite was held in which Macedonians pronounced themselves in favor of separation from the former Yugoslav Federation. All Macedonian political parties, except for the Albanian ethnic minority, favored independence.

[21] On January 20 1992, Greek and Bulgarian representatives held an informal meeting. Sofia had recognized Macedonia five days previously. From Skopje, the newspaper 'Nova Makedonika' accused the Greek and Bulgarian governments of entertaining territorial designs upon their country.

[22] In a plebiscite held on January 12, Macedonia's Albanian minority voted in favor of having an independent State, but on April 3 1992, the Independent Republic of Ilirida (the republic of the Albanian residents of Yugoslavia) was proclaimed, within Macedonian territory.

[23] The new Yugoslav Federation withdrew its troops from the country. In July, the Cabinet resigned en masse and international recognition was not received. In August, Parliament rejected the EEC proposal to change the country's name.

[24] Social Democrat Branko Crvenkovski became Prime Minister that month, gaining official recognition of the new Macedonian state from Russia, Albania, Bulgaria and Turkey.

[25] In April 1993, the UN Security Council recommended that the country be admitted to the General Assembly, with the provisional name of 'The Former Yugoslav Republic (TFYR) of Macedonia'.

[26] Greece withheld official recognition, fearing Macedonia's growing territorial ambitions on the Greek province of Macedonia.

[27] Athens did everything within its power to complicate Skopje's foreign relations, campaigning to change the country's official name, and to alter Macedonia's 'expansionist' constitution. Athens also pressured Macedonia to adopt a new flag, as the emblem of the Vergana star - associated with Alexander the Great - is revered by the Greeks as a symbol of their own Hellenic culture.

[28] After Macedonia's admittance to the UN, negotiations with Greece began, mediated by Lord Owen (British) and Thornvald Stoltenberg (Swedish), both of whom were already conversant with Balkan politics. Andreas Papandreou's victory in the October 1993 Greek elections helped cool the debate.

[29] The Balkan's War seriously affected the Macedonian economy. Although it maintained international sanctions on the former Yugoslavia, Kiro Gligorov's government was forced to allow trucks to cross its territory, transporting goods to Belgrade. Likewise, the oil-transporting Athens-Belgrade railway continued to operate.

[30] On February 16 1994, over two years after Macedonia's independence, Greece decided on a total economic blockade of the country. Greece still did not recognize the adoption of the Greek name 'Macedonia'. The northern frontier and the port of Salonica, through which 80 per cent of Macedonian exports, and all of its oil went abroad, were closed.

[31] Gligorov was re-elected in October 1994 receiving 52.4 per cent of the votes. The Social Democratic Alliance of Macedonia (ASDM), headed by Prime Minister Branko Crvenkovski decided on a coalition government with the liberals, the Socialist Party, and the Party of Democratic Prosperity, the main Albanian political group. This coalition was called Alliance of Macedonia (AM).

[32] In October 1995, a bomb exploded in Gligorov's car. The President survived and remained in power. That same month, negotiations with Greece led to the lifting of the trade embargo.

[33] In 1996, a privatization plan caused a split in the governing coalition. Crvenkovski sacked four liberal ministers and reformed his cabinet.

[34] The Albanian minority make up more than 20 per cent of the population. Albanian activists continued to campaign for the recognition of their language and culture. Some of these wanted the regions with an Albanian majority to be transferred to Albania.

[35] A new coalition known as the Internal Revolutionary Organization of Macedonia-Democratic Party for Macedonian National Unity (VMRO-DPNME) won a majority in the parliamentary elections in October and November 1998 with 28.1 per cent of the vote. The Social Democratic League won 25.1 per cent, while the Democratic Alternative, with just over 10 per cent, joined the Government coalition. The Party for Democratic Prosperity of Albanians came in third with 19.3 per cent of the vote. Ljubco Georgievski was named Prime Minister in late November.

[36] To avoid problems with the Albanian minority while tensions increased in neighboring Yugoslavia, the Government asked NATO to station troops along the border. According to the Government, the Kosovo Liberation Army (KLA) had units operating in Macedonian territory, prompting Yugoslavia to respond calling the move 'unfriendly'. When bombing missions began in March 1999, thousands of Albanian Kosovars sought refuge in Macedonia, further aggravating internal tensions.

[37] Interior Minister Pavle Trajanov said the KLA's growing influence was destabilizing the country. The World Bank granted a $30-million loan to resolve the crisis triggered by the massive influx of refugees, while Taiwan also pledged economic aid. In June, once the conflict was over, Georgievski threw his support behind the new KLA-leaning Kosovar government.

[38] Tito Petkovski, of the formerly communist Social Democratic Party, won the first round of the 1999 presidential elections with 38 per cent of the vote. But the governing party's Boris Trajkovski won the run-off, though he had received just 25 per cent of the vote in the first round. The opposition and international observers acknowledged that the elections suffered serious irregularities.

[39] During the last months of 1999 and the first part of 2000, the Albanian parties called for more assistance for the refugees and benefits for the areas where Albanians were the majority, and threatened to topple the Government. ∎

PROFILE

ENVIRONMENT

In the south-central part of the Balkan Peninsula, Macedonia, which has no maritime coast, is bounded in the north by Serbia and Kosovo, in the east by Bulgaria, in the south by Greece and in the west by Albania. Two mountain ranges cross the region, the Pindo (a continuation of the Alps) and the Rodope, in the center and the east. With a continental climate, the average temperature in the capital is 1°C in winter, and 24°C in summer. The country's main agricultural activity is centered in the Vardar River basin. In the mountain region, sheep and goats are raised. There are some copper, iron and lead deposits.

SOCIETY

Peoples: Macedonians 66.4 per cent; Albanians 23.1 per cent; Turks 3.9 per cent; Roma 2.3 per cent; Serbs 1.9 per cent; other 2.3 per cent (1994). **Religions:** Christian Orthodox (majority); Muslim. **Languages:** Macedonian (official), Albanian. **Political Parties:** Macedonia's Alliance, a coalition of the Democrat Alliance of Macedonia, liberal, the Socialist Party and the Albanian Party for Democratic Prosperity. The Alliance was founded in 1994 and has been in power since that date.

THE STATE

Official Name: Republika Makedonija. **Administrative divisions:** 30 districts. **Capital:** Skopje 470,000 people (1995). **Other cities:** Bitolj (Bitola) 75,386 people; Prilep 67,371; Kumanovo 66,237; Tetovo 50,376. (1995). **Government:** President: Boris Trajkovski since December 1999. Prime Minister: Ljubco Georgievski since November 1998. **National Holiday:** September 8, Independence (1991). **Armed Forces:** 10,400 (8,000 conscripts). **Other:** 7,500 (police).

Madagascar

Madagasikara

Population: 15,496,000 (1999)
Area: 587,040 SQ KM
Capital: Antananarivo
Currency: Franc
Language: Malagasy and French

About 2,000 years ago, Malay-Polynesian navigators reached the African coast in canoes, voyage which was frequently repeated between the 1st and 5th centuries.
[2] Towards the 14th century, groups of Comoran traders established a series of ports in the northern region. These ports were destroyed by the Portuguese in 1506-1507.
[3] When the Portuguese found no gold, ivory or spices, they lost interest in the territory. By this time the Europeans had introduced firearms to the island in exchange for slaves.
[4] In the 16th century the Sakalawas on the west coast and the Betsilios on the east coast established the first monarchies. In the 17th century the state of Merina or Imerina came into being on the eastern edge of the central plateau. A century later it was the Merinas, under their leader Nampoina, who initiated the process of unification which was completed later by Nampoina's son Radama I (1810-1828).
[5] Contact with the Arabs and Europeans became more frequent. Radama adopted the Latin alphabet for the Malagasy language. He also used their help to create a modern army. However, the untimely death of the ruler and the ensuing conflicts over succession paved the way for European occupation of the island by the end of the century.
[6] The colonials cleared the virgin forests to make way for sugar-cane, cotton, and coffee plantations. They seized the best lands and the peasants were forced to work in conditions of semi-slavery. The struggle for political rights and economic improvement led to a great uprising from 1947 to 1948,

and this was ruthlessly put down by the French army with the loss of thousands of lives.
[7] The failure of the insurrection enabled the colonial administration to control the transition to autonomy. Independence was finally proclaimed in 1960. In the following September the country held it's first elections and the Social Democratic Party (PSD) won by a large margin. Its leader, Philibert Tsiranana, became the Republic's first President, an office to which he was re-elected in 1965 and 1972.
[8] In May 1972, after a series of serious disturbances, Tsiranana was forced to resign; he turned over full presidential powers to General Ramanantsoa, who suspended the National Assembly and the Senate. He also eliminated the presidency and abolished the 1959 Constitution, giving a military

government both executive and legislative power, and creating Institutional and National Councils. In October, he had these measures approved by referendum.
[9] A year later, France decided to withdraw its troops, and the succeeding three years of instability ended in June 1975, when Cdr D Ratsiraka became Prime Minister. He adopted socialist policies, and called a referendum on December 21 1975. His nomination as head of state was overwhelmingly approved, and the Charter of the Madagascan Socialist Revolution was adopted as the basis for a new constitution. On December 30 1975 the State changed the country's name to the 'Democratic Republic of Madagascar'.
[10] In June 1976, the new power structure was put into operation, with a 12-member Supreme Council

of the Revolution and the Government, which was presided over by Col J Rakotomalala. When he died in an airplane accident in July 1976, he was replaced by Justin Rakotoniaina. The legislative function was placed in the hands of a 144-member National Council.
[11] The progressive Malgache parties joined together to form the National Revolutionary Front. AREMA (the Malagasy Revolutionary Vanguard) was the leading party of the Front, and was created in 1975 in support of Ratsiraka's renewal program. The Supreme Council of the Revolution was made up primarily of AREMA members, with members of five other parties ranging in their views from Marxist/Leninist to Christian Democrat. In 1977, Désiré Rakotoarijaona became Prime Minister.
[12] In 1982, the President was re-elected by 80 per cent of the vote while the radical sector - represented by MONIMA - obtained the remaining 20 per cent.
[13] Madagascar has unique ecological characteristics. Plant and animal species extinct in other parts of the world are found here. The island possesses 3 per cent of the world's flora varieties, 53 per cent of the bird species, and 80 per cent of the reptile and amphibian families present on Earth. But this enormous biological reserve is in danger of extinction. Small-scale farmers, pressured by the lack of land, add to the deforestation process by burning pieces of land for cultivation at a greater rate than ever before. Although this form of land-clearing has been practised for centuries, the forest is now being destroyed faster than it can regenerate.
[14] In 1988, Lt-Col Victor Ramahatra succeeded Raotoarijaona as Prime Minister. AREMA, the party in power, won the 1989 elections; Didier Ratsiraka was re-elected President, with 67.2 per cent of the vote. His presidency was characterized by reform, with the restoration of a multiparty system and the inclusion in his cabinet of several opposition members by March 1990.
[15] In 1991, the opposition united around the Committee of Living Forces, made up of 16 organizations. A series of street demonstrations and the taking of the National Radio, led the

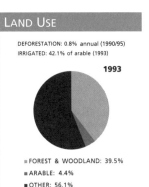

WORKERS

1996
UNEMPLOYMENT: 16.3%

% OF LABOUR FORCE **1998**

■ FEMALE: 45%   ■ MALE: 55%
1990

■ SERVICES: 15.1%
■ INDUSTRY: 6.7%
■ AGRICULTURE: 78.2%

LAND USE

DEFORESTATION: 0.8% annual (1990/95)
IRRIGATED: 42.1% of arable (1993)

1993

■ FOREST & WOODLAND: 39.5%
■ ARABLE: 4.4%
■ OTHER: 56.1%

PUBLIC EXPENDITURE

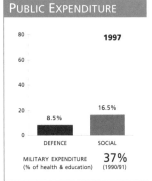

1997

80
60
40
20 8.5%   16.5%
0   DEFENCE   SOCIAL

MILITARY EXPENDITURE   **37%**
(% of health & education)   (1990/91)

STATISTICS

DEMOGRAPHY

Population: 15,496,000 (1999)
Annual growth: 2.9 % (1975/97)
Estimates for year 2015 (million): 23.4 (1999)
Annual growth to year 2015: 2.6 % (1997/2015)
Urban population: 27.6 % (1997)
Urban Growth: 5.7 % (1980/95)
Children per woman: 5.4 (1998)

HEALTH

Life expectancy at birth: 58 years (1998)
male: 56 years (1998)
female: 59 years (1998)
Maternal mortality: 490 per 100,000 live births (1990-98)
Infant mortality: 95 per 1,000 (1998)
Under-5 child mortality: 157 per 1,000 (1998)
Daily calorie supply: 2,001 per capita (1996)
24 doctors per 100,000 people (1993)
Safe water: 40 % (1990/98)

EDUCATION

Literacy: 46 % (1995)
male: 60 % (1995)
female: 32 % (1995)
School enrolment:
Primary total: 73 % (1990/96)
male: 74 % (1990/97)
female: 71 % (1990/97)
Secondary:
male: 13 % (1990/96)
female: 13 % (1990/96)
Tertiary: 2 % (1996)
Primary school teachers: one for every 37 (1995)

COMMUNICATIONS

5 newspapers (1996), 192 radios (1997) and 3 main telephone lines (1996) per 1,000 people
Books: 1 new titles per 100,000 people (1992/94)

ECONOMY

Per capita, GNP: $ 260 (1998)
Annual growth, GNP: 4.9 % (1998)
Annual inflation: 22.1 % (1990/98)
Consumer price index: 132.9 (1998)
Currency: 5,441.4 francs = $ 1 (1998)
Cereal imports: 148,298 metric tons (1998)
Food import dependency: 15 % (1997)
Fertilizer use: 37 kg per ha (1997)
Exports: $ 796 million (1998)
Imports: $ 1,094 million (1998)
External debt: $ 4,394 million (1998); $ 292 per capita (1998)
Debt service: 14.7 % of exports (1998)
Development aid received: $ 838 million (1997); $ 70.5 per capita (1997); 24.30 % of GNP (1997)

HDI (rank/value): 147/0.453 (1997)

Government to declare a state of emergency. The Committee called for Ratsiraka's resignation and, in July, nominated a transition government.

[16] In August, following the detention of two ministers from the transition cabinet, 400,000 people took to the streets and repeated the demand for Ratsiraka's resignation. The demonstration was brutally put down, with 31 people killed and more than 200 injured.

[17] In March 1992, a multiparty forum was created to draw up a new constitution and presidential elections were set for August. In this month, the new document was approved and Albert Zafy was elected President with 66.2 per cent of the vote to Ratsiraka's 33.8.

[18] The economic and social situation of the country, one of the poorest in the world, was considered disastrous. Per capita income barely increased between 1976 and 1992, going from $200 to $230 per year,

while calorie consumption went from 108 per cent of those required in 1964-66, to 95 per cent in 1988-90.

[19] In March 1994, the Government introduced a series of austerity measures recommended by the International Monetary Fund, which increased the social tensions even further. At the end of that year, massive demonstrations were held in opposition to these policies. In January 1995, the governor of the Central Bank abandoned his post on request from the IMF and the World Bank.

[20] In September, the Malagasy people approved increased powers for Zafy in a referendum. The debate over structural adjustment coincided with disagreements over the use of the nation's natural resources, when the mining transnational RTZ proposed opening a mine on the southern coast of the island to extract titanium dioxide. This sparked strong protests by militant ecologists, convinced the project would destroy unique species of the Madagascar flora and fauna.

[21] In May 1996, the National Assembly approved a vote of no confidence in the Government, leading to the formation of a new cabinet. The motion was partly caused by comments made by the IMF director, Michel Camdessus, who said the lack of governmental cohesion meant agreements with the body were not guaranteed.

[22] President Zafy resigned in September, accused of violating the Constitution. In the presidential elections organized at the end of this year, Didier Ratsiraka became the new Madagascan President, taking 65 per cent of the votes.

[23] In 1997, the social and health situation of the nation deteriorated. Illnesses like malaria increased amongst the poorer people. According to the FAO, three quarters of the population were malnourished.

[24] A new Constitution, approved by referendum in March 1998, established greater presidential power and conferred more economic autonomy to the nation's six provinces. The opposition Committee of Living Forces boycotted the referendum, saying the Government had dictatorial aims. Following May's legislative elections, Tantely Andranarivo became the new Prime Minister in July, replacing Pascal Rakotomavo, both members of AREMA. ∎

PROFILE

ENVIRONMENT

Madagascar is one of the world's largest islands, separated from the African continent by the Mozambique Channel. The island has an extensive central plateau of volcanic origin which overhangs the hot and humid coastal plains. These are covered with dense rainforest to the east and grasslands to the west. The eastern side of the island is very rainy, but the rest has a dry, tropical climate. The population is concentrated on the high central plateau. Rice and export products (sugar, coffee, bananas, and vanilla) are cultivated on the coast. Cattle-raising is also important throughout the island. The major mineral resources are graphite, chrome and phosphate. Deforestation is one of the major environmental problems, it is estimated that the destruction of forests affects up to 75 per cent of the island. Only 10 per cent of the rural population has assured access to drinking water. The lack of sewage facilities and concentration of organic wastes have led to the pollution of many watercourses.

SOCIETY

Peoples: The Malagasy population is a broad composite of Malayo-Polynesian, Arab and African ethnic groups. The Merinas are about 20 per cent and the Batsimisaraka 10 per cent. Tiny French, Indian and Chinese minorities.
Religions: Christian 51 per cent (of which Roman Catholic 26 per cent, Protestant 22.8 per cent); traditional beliefs 47.0 per cent; Muslim 1.7 per cent.
Languages: Malagasy and French. Hovba and other local dialects are also spoken.
Political Parties: AREMA, socialist; Committee of Living Forces, an alliance of 16 groups; Militant pro-Socialist Movement.
Social Organizations: Confederation of Malagasy Workers (FMM); Christian Confederation of Trade Unions (SEKRIMA); Federation of Autonomous Trade Unions of Madagascar (USAM); Federation of Workers' Unions of Madagascar (FISEMA).

THE STATE

Official Name: Repoblikan'i Madagasikara. République Démocratique de Madagascar.
Administrative Divisions: 6 provinces, 10 districts, 1,252 sub-districts, and 11,333 towns.
Capital: Antananarivo 1,500,000 people (1995).
Other cities: Toamasina 127,000 people; Mahajanga (Majunga) 100,000; Fianarantsoa 99,000 (1993)
Government: Parliamentary republic. Didier Ratsiraka, President since 1997; Tantely Andranarivo, Prime Minister since 1998. Bicameral Legislature-Senate (2/3 selected by an Electoral College and 1/3 selected by the president) and a National Assembly, whose members are elected directly.
National Holiday: June 26, Independence Day (1960).
Armed Forces: 21,000 (1996)
Other: Gendarmerie: 7,500.

Malawi

Malawi

Population: 10,640,000 (1999)
Area: 118,480 SQ KM
Capital: Lilongwe
Currency: Kwacha
Language: Chewa

The state of Kitwara was part of a small country on the coast of Lake Malawi (previously Nyasa), and had been part of a series of nations related to gold production and ruled by the Monomotapa of Zimbabwe (see Zimbabwe). The decline of this power center allowed the Chewa to enlarge their territory, only to see it reduced again when the Changamira Rotsi restored the predominance of Zimbabwe. Around 1835, Zulu expansion (see South Africa) pushed the Ngoni-Ndwande to the shores of the lake, leading to 60 years of war between the Ngoni and the Chewa and Yao allies.

2 The country was explored by Livingstone in 1859 and it suffered a Portuguese attempt at colonization in 1890 which was ended by an ultimatum from the British Government. Britain wanted to keep the territory which would eventually serve as a link in a continuous chain of colonies joining South Africa to Egypt. In 1891, Cecil Rhodes' British South African Company negotiated the Protectorate of what became Nyasaland.

3 The British idea was to create a Central African Federation embracing present-day Zimbabwe, Malawi and Zambia - regions linked by similarities of people, climate, plains, plateaus and dry forests. Politically this would have meant the extension of a Rhodesian-style white-racist domination to the entire Federation.

4 The Malawi Congress Party (MCP) and the UNIP of Zambia favored a pro-independence stance. They were strongly influenced by Dr Hastings Kamuzu Banda, a doctor who had studied in the US and who was presented as the 'nation's savior'.

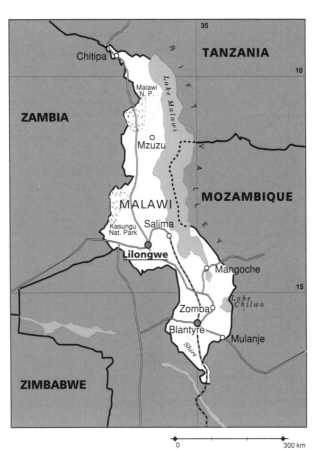

5 Banda's demands for greater power within the Party were granted to prevent internal division. When the colony became independent in 1964, Banda seized control of the MCP and the country. As President he established close economic and diplomatic relations with the racist governments of South Africa and Rhodesia, and with the colonial administration in Mozambique.

6 South Africa became Malawi's main tea and tobacco purchaser while South African investors built roads, railways and a new capital city. South African managers took charge of the airline, information and development agencies and a large part of the state administration.

7 In 1975, Mozambican independence radically changed Banda's situation. He had actively cooperated with the Portuguese in their struggle against FRELIMO. The closure of the Mozambique-Rhodesia border led to a drastic reduction in Malawi's trade with Rhodesia, depriving Ian Smith's racist government of an escape route from the international blockade.

8 In June 1978, Banda held the first election in 17 years. All the candidates had to be MCP members and pass an English test, which immediately excluded the 90 per cent of the population who did not speak English.

9 After 1980, Zimbabwe's independence changed the economic and political situation of Malawi. Banda lost direct communication with South Africa, and was therefore deprived of major support. Consequently the Government drew closer to the Front Line states, joining the SADCC association because of Malawi's dependence on the railway lines through Mozambique and Zimbabwe.

10 The success of neighboring socialist governments strengthened the Socialist League of Malawi (LESOMA) which favored breaking economic and political ties with South Africa, putting an end to Banda's dictatorship and implementing full democracy in the country. In 1980, this party created a guerrilla force, the Malawi Freedom Movement (MAFREMO), led by Orton Chirwa, also gained strength.

11 In 1983, Chirwa and Attati Mpakati, a LESOMA leader, were accused of conspiracy and sentenced to death. Shortly thereafter, Mpakati was assassinated by South African agents while visiting Harare. Chirwa and his wife were kidnapped in Zambia where they lived as exiles, and imprisoned in Blantyre.

12 Banda created a secret police force, called the Special Branch, with South African and Israeli advisers. The president-for-life also personally controlled the economy, owning 33 per cent of all businesses.

13 Between 1987 and 1988, the country received 600,000 refugees from Mozambique, in whose civil war Malawi had supported the counter-revolutionaries of the National Resistance Movement (Renamo). This support was discontinued in 1988, after the visit which Banda received from President Chissano of Mozambique.

14 Also in 1988, Amnesty International denounced the imprisonment of well-known scholars and writers, among them Jack Mapanje, the country's foremost poet. The United States announced the cancellation of $40 million of foreign debt in November 1989.

WORKERS

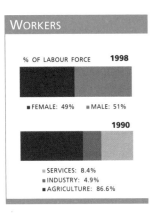

% OF LABOUR FORCE **1998**

- FEMALE: 49% ■ MALE: 51%

1990

- ■ SERVICES: 8.4%
- ■ INDUSTRY: 4.9%
- ■ AGRICULTURE: 86.6%

LAND USE

DEFORESTATION: 1.6% annual (1990/95)
IRRIGATED: 1.7% of arable (1993)

1993

- ■ FOREST & WOODLAND: 31.2%
- ■ ARABLE: 14.1%
- ■ OTHER: 54.7%

PUBLIC EXPENDITURE

DEFENCE EXPENDITURE (% of goverment exp.)	**2.9%**	(1997)
MILITARY EXPENDITURE (% of health & education)	**24%**	(1990/91)

[15] The implementation of an IMF-adjustment program led to a reduction in inflation and in the balance of payments deficit, as well as an increase in investments. However, it also aggravated the situation faced by the poorest sectors of the population.

[16] In 1990 and 1991, earthquakes and floods exacerbated food shortages among the rural population, 90 per cent of the country's total population. The privatization of the maize/corn market benefited a few producers at the expense of the poorest rural sectors.

[17] During the Cold War, Banda was a staunch ally of the West, but the constant human rights violations by his government led to several countries cutting aid to Malawi.

[18] For the first time since independence, the Catholic Church wrote a pastoral letter criticizing the human rights situation, and calling for greater political freedom. This letter was followed by a popular uprising in Blantyre, which was harshly repressed by government forces.

[19] In April 1992, opposition leader Chafuka Chihana of the Alliance for Democracy was caught trying to return to the country, and imprisoned. An international campaign prevented him from being executed.

[20] In May 1992, a general strike called by textile workers was brutally put down, with 38 deaths and hundreds of injuries. In reprisal, the World Bank discontinued part of its financial aid.

[21] The ruling Congress Party of Malawi, the only party to participate in the June general elections, obtained 114 seats in the National Assembly.

[22] In late 1992, news was received of the death of Orton Chirwa of MAFREMO. He had been in prison since 1983, and died under torture. To keep popular indignation from turning violent, Banda announced that a referendum would be held on opening up the political system.

[23] The referendum took place in June 1993. Two thirds of voters chose a multiparty system. That month, Banda promised presidential elections would be held in 1994 and released Vera Chirwa, widow of the assassinated dissident and who by that time had served one of the longest prison terms for political reasons in Africa.

[24] Opposition member Bakili Muluzi was elected President in May 1994. His party, the United Democratic Front (UDF), won 84 of the 177 seats at stake in the legislative elections. In September, having won only 55 seats, Banda decided to retire from political activity.

[25] Malawi suffered the consequences of an intensive drought in 1994 which led to a food shortage. In the midst of a growing difficult social situation, the Government went ahead with its IMF-sponsored policy to cut public spending. In January 1995, ex-president Banda was arrested, charged with the murder of three former ministers. The alleged violation of human rights by Muluzi's government was frequently denounced by opposition members throughout the year.

[26] In January 1996, Malawi entered negotiations to form a free trade area, along with another 11 Southern African nations. The Government announced it would revoke the laws affecting foreign investors in rural areas.

[27] In 1997, the United States started to train Malawian troops with a view to creating an African peacekeeping force.

[28] The drought, which affected vast regions of Africa, almost totally dried up Malawi's Shire river, one of the country's main water courses. International experts recommended a reduction in the amount of water used in agriculture through the importing of food, and the progressive industrialization of the economy. In 1998, it was estimated the underground water reserves of the region would take 1,400 years to recover.

[29] In January 1999, Abdul Pillane, former minister of Public Works, was formally accused of corruption after acknowledging he had accepted money from a South African construction company. In February, reports indicated that the cholera epidemic, which affected some 15,000 people, had left 500 people dead in 1998 and 1999. In April of that year, President Muluzi inaugurated the country's first television station.

[30] After a process plagued with irregularities, President Muluzi was victorious in the June elections, while his party, with 47.3 per cent of the vote, won 93 of the 192 legislative seats. In December, the legislators complained to the Economy Minister that their salaries were extremely low. In late February 2000, the President called for the resignation of his entire Cabinet. Countries providing development aid considered some of the Government ministers untrustworthy, among them Economy Minister Cassim Chilumpha. ∎

PROFILE

ENVIRONMENT

The terrain and the climate are extremely varied. The major geological feature is the great Rift fault that runs through the country from north to south. Part of this large depression is filled by Lake Malawi, which takes up one fifth of the land area. The rest is made up of plateaus of varying altitudes. The most temperate region is the southern part, which is also the highest, containing most of the population and economic activities (basically farming). The lowlands receive heavy rainfall and are covered by grasslands, forests or rainforests, depending on the amount of rainfall they receive. The degradation of the soil and deforestation are the main environmental problems.

SOCIETY

Peoples: Maravi (including Nyanja, Chewa, Tonga, and Tumbuka) 58.3 per cent; Lomwe 18.4 per cent; Yao 13.2 per cent; Ngoni 6.7 per cent.
Religions: Many people follow traditional religions, but they also belong to Christian (64.5 per cent) and Muslim (16.2 per cent) communities.
Languages: Chewa (official) and English; several Bantu languages - other than Chewa - are spoken by their respective ethnic groups.
Political Parties: United Democratic Front (UDF); Alliance for Democracy (Aford); Malawi Congress Party (MCP).
Social Organizations: Trade Union Congress of Malawi.

THE STATE

Official Name: Republic of Malawi.
Administrative divisions: 24 districts.
Capital: Lilongwe 350,000 people (1995).
Other cities: Blantyre 446,800 people; Mzuzu 62,700 (1994).
Government: Presidential republic. Bakili Muluzi, President since May 1994. Legislature: single-chamber: National Assembly, made up of 177 members.
National Holiday: July 6, Independence Day (1964).
Armed Forces: 9,800 (1996).
Other: 1,500.

STATISTICS

DEMOGRAPHY

Population: 10,640,000 (1999)
Annual growth: 3.0 % (1975/97)
Estimates for year 2015 (million): 15.8 (1999)
Annual growth to year 2015: 2.5 % (1997/2015)
Urban population: 14.2 % (1997)
Urban Growth: 6.0 % (1980/95)
Children per woman: 6.7 (1998)

HEALTH

Life expectancy at birth: 39 years (1998)
male: 39 years (1998)
female: 40 years (1998)
Maternal mortality:
620 per 100,000 live births (1990-98)
Infant mortality: 134 per 1,000 (1998)
Under-5 child mortality: 213 per 1,000 (1998)
Daily calorie supply: 2,097 per capita (1996)
2 doctors per 100,000 people (1993)
Safe water: 47 % (1990/98)

EDUCATION

Literacy: 56 % (1995)
male: 72 % (1995)
female: 41 % (1995)
School enrolment:
Primary total: 135 % (1990/96)
male: 142 % (1990/97)
female: 128 % (1990/97)
Secondary:
male: 21 % (1990/96)
female: 12 % (1990/96)
Tertiary: 1 % (1996)
Primary school teachers: one for every 59 (1995)

COMMUNICATIONS

3 newspapers (1995), 249 radios (1997) and 4 main telephone lines (1996) per 1,000 people
Books: 3 new titles per 100,000 people (1992/94)

ECONOMY

Per capita, GNP: $ 210 (1998)
Annual growth, GNP: 1.5 % (1998)
Annual inflation: 33.2 % (1990/98)
Consumer price index: 194.9 (1998)
Currency: 31.1 kwacha = $ 1 (1998)
Cereal imports: 208,558 metric tons (1998)
Fertilizer use: 358 kg per ha (1997)
Exports: $ 515 million (1998)
Imports: $ 740 million (1998)
External debt: $ 2,444 million (1998); $ 236 per capita (1998)
Debt service: 14.7 % of exports (1998)
Development aid received: $ 350 million (1997); $ 40.0 per capita (1997); 14.10 % of GNP (1997)

HDI (rank/value): 159/0.399 (1997)

Malaysia

Malaysia

Population: 21,830,000 (1999)
Area: 329,750 SQ KM
Capital: Kuala Lumpur
Currency: Ringgit
Language: Malay

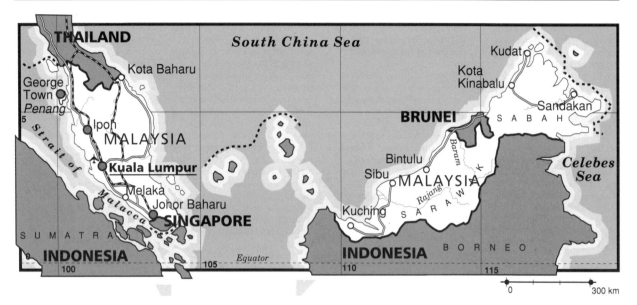

The Malay Peninsula and the Borneo states of Sarawak and Sabah were originally inhabited by native aboriginal peoples, living in the forests.

[2] In the second millennium BC, there was migration from the south of present-day China to present-day Malaysia, Indonesia and the Philippines. Over the millennia, metal-working techniques and agriculture were introduced. Rice farming was not developed until the first millennium AD. Indian influence was all-pervasive, bringing religion, political systems and the Sanskrit language.

[3] The Indianized kingdom of Funan was founded in the Mekong river area in the 1st century AD and Buddhist states eventually developed in the east, trading with China. In the 15th century, the port of Melaka (Malacca) was founded; its rulers were the first in the region to convert to Islam. Trade with Islamic merchants brought prosperity to Melaka. The new faith spread across the rest of present-day Malaysia and Indonesia, replacing Buddhism. At the beginning of the 16th century, Melaka attracted the Portuguese, who were competing with Arab merchants for the Indian Ocean trade routes.

[4] In 1511 the Portuguese viceroy of India, Alfonso de Albuquerque, seized the port by force. It was of vital strategic importance in the Portuguese struggle to maintain their monopoly on the spice-trade from the Moluccas Islands. These spices were exchanged for Indian textiles and Chinese silk and porcelain. In the 17th century, the Dutch formed an alliance with the Sultan of Johor to drive the Portuguese out of Melaka. This alliance between Johor and the Dutch was established in Batavia (present-day Jakarta) and it succeeded in eliminating European and Asian competition for a hundred years.

[5] Meanwhile, the British began to establish back-up points for their trade with China in northern Borneo (Kalimantan), and in 1786 founded the port of Georgetown, on the island of Penang (Pulau-Pinang), off the western coast. The British model of free trade proved more successful than the Dutch trade monopoly and Penang attracted a cosmopolitan population of Malays, Sumatrans, Indians and Chinese. In 1819, the British founded Singapore, but at the time they were more interested in safeguarding shipping than in the local spice trade, as their imports from China were being paid for with opium from India. Nevertheless, the Dutch and the British found it difficult to coexist in the region. A treaty drawn up in 1824 granted control of Indonesia to the Dutch, while Malaya was left in British hands.

[6] The colonies of Penang, Melaka and Singapore became the key points of the British colony. The British encouraged Chinese (and to a lesser degree, Indian) immigration to the ports along the Straits of Malacca, and large numbers of Chinese arrived to work the tin mines and service the urban ports. The Malay peasants and fishing people continued their traditional activities. From 1870, the British began to sign protectorate agreements with the sultans and in 1895 they encouraged them to form a federation, with Kuala Lumpur as its capital. The sultanates of northern Borneo (Brunei, Sabah and Sarawak, the latter ruled by James Brooke, and his heirs) also became British protectorates, administered from Singapore, but without any formal ties with the peninsula.

[7] Towards the end of the 19th century, the British introduced rubber with *Hevea* seeds smuggled from Brazil, so bringing about an end to the rubber boom in the South American Amazon. They encouraged Tamil immigration from southern India, to get workers for the rubber plantations which faced growing demand from the incipient automobile industries.

WORKERS

1996
UNEMPLOYMENT: 2.5%

% OF LABOUR FORCE **1998**

- FEMALE: 37% ■ MALE: 63%

1990

- SERVICES: 49.5%
- INDUSTRY: 23.1%
- AGRICULTURE: 27.3%

LAND USE

DEFORESTATION: 2.4% annual (1990/95)
IRRIGATED: 32.7% of arable (1993)

1993

- FOREST & WOODLAND: 67.6%
- ARABLE: 3.2%
- OTHER: 29.2%

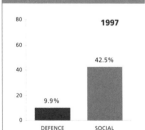

PUBLIC EXPENDITURE

1997

42.5%

9.9%

DEFENCE   SOCIAL

MILITARY EXPENDITURE **38%**
(% of health & education) (1990/91)

8   The colonial administration set up a three band education system that differed for Malays, Indians and Chinese. In the economy, the Malays stayed mainly in rural agriculture, the Chinese worked in tin mines and the urban service sectors, and the Indians worked on the rubber estates. In the first decades of the 20th century, the Malays joined the Islamic reform movements of the Middle East, the Indians supported the struggles of Mahatma Gandhi, and the Chinese were ideologically influenced first by the nationalism of Sun Yat-Sen and then by the Communist Party.

9   In 1942, during World War II, the country was occupied by the Japanese. The Japanese tried to form alliances with local Southeast Asian nationalist movements to gain support against the European powers. The greatest resistance came from the Chinese, especially the Malayan Communist Party, which organized guerrillas to oppose the invading forces.

10   At the end of the war it was clear that British domination could not persist without changes, but the difficulties of diverse ethnic interests, 'protected' sultanates and ports under direct colonial administration, made it difficult to find a suitable political system. The British proposed a Malayan Union with equal citizenship for all. This threatened the position of the Malays, and Malay nationalists gathered around the symbolic figure of the sultans founding the United Malays' National Organization (UMNO), controlled by the dominant class but with popular support.

11   In 1948, there was a communist-led insurrection that was suppressed by British forces. Its failure was partly due to the view of many poor Malays and Indians that the revolt was a Chinese effort and not the action of a unifying, anti-colonial progressive movement. The Marxist parties were outlawed and their leaders jailed. From 1948 until 1960, the Communist Party waged guerrilla warfare in the northern Malayan Peninsula and in Borneo.

12   Journalist and activist Dato Onn made a new attempt at creating a pan-ethnic party. He left UMNO to found the Malayan Independence Party. He was defeated in the 1952 municipal elections by an alliance of UMNO and the Malayan Chinese Association. The alliance was later broadened to include the Indian Malayan Congress, winning nationwide elections, except for Singapore, where Lee Kuan Yew's socialists were victorious.

13   Faced with the threat of an armed communist insurrection, the British decided to negotiate. This resulted in Malayan independence in 1957. Tunku Abdul Rahman, a prince who led the independence movement, became the first prime minister. A federation of 11 states was established with a parliamentary system and a monarch chosen every five years from among nine state sultans. A constitutional bargain was struck by the three communities: citizenship was granted to the non-Malays, but the Malays were recognized as indigenous people. They were accorded special privileges in education and public-sector employment and Malay would be the official language. The country adopted the free market system and a reliance on foreign capital, which had been established under colonialism, remained dominant. Malaya was politically pro-Western.

14   In 1963, the British colonial states of Singapore (south of Malaya), Sabah and Sarawak obtained independence and joined Malaya to form the Federation of Malaysia. There were major disagreements over ethnic policy and Singapore was expelled from the federation in 1965 becoming an independent republic.

15   The conservative Alliance Party ruled with a large majority from 1957, but in the 1969 elections it lost many seats to the Islamic PAS Party, Gerakan and - mostly - to the Chinese-based Democratic Action Party (DAP). Tensions escalated into widespread riots and unrest, largely blamed by the authorities on 'Communist Terrorists'. The parliamentary system was suspended and the country was ruled for two years by a National Operations Council. The Malay population were dissatisfied with their share of corporate equity, because in 1970 they made up over 50 per cent of the population, but had only one per cent of the income. A new economic policy was formulated to deal with this. It set targets to increase the Malay and other 'Bumiputera' ('sons-of-the-soil' [sic] or indigenous people) share to 30 per cent by 1990, while the foreign share would drop from 70 to 30 per cent and the non-Bumiputera (mainly Chinese and Indian) share would be 40 per cent.

16   This policy dominated internal economic policy for the next two decades. The Bumiputera equity share rose to almost 20 per cent by 1989 whilst foreign ownership fell below 40 per cent. Because of these policies, Malaysians of Chinese descent claimed that they faced discrimination at work, in education and elsewhere.

17   Communist guerrilla warfare gradually died out, and the National Front won over two-thirds of the parliamentary seats in elections during the 1970s and 1980s. The present prime minister, Mahathir Mohamad, took office in 1981, and started to develop

PROFILE

ENVIRONMENT

The Federation of Malaysia is made up of Peninsular Malaysia (131,588 sq km), and the states of Sarawak (124,450 sq km) and Sabah (73,711 sq km) in northern Borneo (Kalimantan), 640 km from the peninsula in the Indonesian archipelago. Thick tropical forests cover more than 70 per cent of the mainland area, and a mountain range stretches from north to south across the peninsula. Coastal plains border the hills on both sides. In Sabah and Sarawak, coastal plains ascend to the mountainous interior. There is heavy annual rainfall. Malaysia's economy is export orientated. Tin and rubber, the traditional export products have recently been replaced by petroleum and manufactured goods. Indiscriminate logging and the use of highly toxic herbicides worries ecologists who fear irreparable damage to native species, and the destruction of the few surviving native cultures.

SOCIETY

Peoples: Malays (or Bumiputeras) 60 per cent, Chinese 33 per cent, Indians 10 per cent.
Religions: Islam, the official religion, is practiced by 54 per cent of the populations. Buddhist 17 per cent, Taoist 22 per cent, Hindu, 7 per cent, Christians 7 per cent.
Languages: Malay is the official language, the common language, and the main language of education. Chinese dialects, Tamil and English are also used.
Political parties: Barisan Nasional (National Front), including United Malays National Organisation (UMNO) and Parti Islam SeMalaysia (PAS), People's Party (Parti Rakyat); Alternative Front, including Democratic Action Party (DAP).
Social Organizations: The leading labor organization is the Congress of Malaysia's Unions.

THE STATE

Official Name: Persekutan Tanah Malaysia.
Capital: Kuala Lumpur 3,030,000 people (1994).
Other cities: Ipoh 382,633 people; Johor Baharu 328,646; Melaka 295,999; Petaling Jaya 254,849; Georgetown (Penang) 250,000 (1991).
Government: Constitutional, parliamentary and federal monarchy. Tuanku Salehuddin Abdul Aziz Shah ibni al-Marhum Hisamuddin Alam Shah is the current king or *yang di-pertuan agong* (sovereign), since April 1999. The sovereign is elected every five years from among the nine regents (sultans), and only the sultans can vote. Datuk Seri Mahathir bin Mohamad, Prime Minister since 1981.Central bicameral parliament, 69-member senate, 192-member chamber of deputies, with a constitution and a legislative assembly for every state.
National Holiday: August 31, Independence Day (1957).
Armed Forces: 114,500 (1995).
Other: 21,500 Police, Regular, Sea and Air, Auxiliaries.

FOOD DEPENDENCY	EXTERNAL DEBT	FOREIGN TRADE

FOOD DEPENDENCY

1997
5%

EXTERNAL DEBT

1998

Per capita
US$ 2,091

FOREIGN TRADE

Millions US$ 1998

IMPORTS
67,098

EXPORTS
82,899

Malaysia's industry. In the late 1980s he faced increasing challenges to his leadership from UMNO (the Front's main party). Some of his opponents left to form a new opposition party, Semangat 46. In 1990 they formed a loose opposition coalition with the Islamic PAS, the DAP and the small left-wing People's Party.

[18] The Internal Security Act allowed detention without trial for two years. Under Mahathir at this time, the number of political prisoners declined from over 1,000 to a few hundred. In 1987 a major crackdown led to 150 more detentions, including opposition politicians and leaders of social groups, all of whom were released by 1990.

[19] In 1988, the chief judge and three other Supreme Court judges were sacked following a dispute between the judiciary and the executive. Lawyers and critics accused the Government of threatening the judiciary's independence. There are currently serious limits imposed on the freedom of press and of assembly; permits are required for both newspapers and public meetings.

[20] Malaysian foreign policy moved from its pro-western position in the 1960s through non-alignment in the 1970s to a pro-Third World stance in the 1980s. In 1990, Kuala Lumpur hosted the inaugural summit meeting of 15 Third World countries (including India, Brazil, Indonesia, Mexico, Venezuela, Tanzania and Senegal) aimed at fostering concrete South-South co-operation projects and aiming to reduce Northern dominance of Southern economies. It played a major role in the South Commission and actively supported the Palestine Liberation Organization and South Africa's African National Congress.

[21] The *Sahabat Alam* (Friends of the Earth) Malaysia assisted indigenous groups in Sarawak to defend their forest from loggers in a widely-publicized campaign. The natives (especially nomadic Penan) staged blockades on timber roads to prevent logs leaving the forest. In August 1991 a judge in Sarawak condemned eight protest leaders to nine months in prison.

[22] Malaysia is at this time the major world exporter of tropical wood with a growing demand in the industrialized countries, especially Japan. In 1989 its timber exports earned $ 2.6 billion. More than 80 per cent of this timber comes from Sarawak and Sabah, in Borneo. It is estimated that out of the previous 305,000 square kilometres (sq km) of tropical forests, only 157,000 sq km are left, and the country loses 5,000 sq km of tropical forest each year. Environmental organizations accuse several companies of destroying vast areas of forest, and of causing huge fires to create new areas for cultivation. Alternative development models based on satisfying basic needs and living in harmony with nature are increasingly advocated by social and ecological groups.

[23] In 1991 a dam project on the Pergau river, to be financed by Britain, caused outrage when it was learned that the money was tied to British arms purchases amounting to $1.5 billion. The rapid growth of high-tech industries has led to a shortage of skilled and semi-skilled labour. Wages in the industrial sector have had a significant raise which led to increase social differences.

[24] Tuanku Ja'afar ibni al-Marhum Tuanku Abdul Rahman was elected sovereign in April 1994. Support for Prime Minister Mohamad was apparent in 1995 when his coalition, the National Front, took 162 of the 192 seats in the Chamber of Representatives, and 84 per cent of the vote.

[25] Economic growth continued until 1997, when an unprecedented stock exchange crisis hit the region. The devaluation of the Malaysian currency coincided with a deterioration in the social situation. In early 1998, unemployment already topped a million. The Government tightened up migration policies. In the first three months of that year, 19,000 foreign workers without papers were expelled. The Government revealed a plan to expel a total of 200,000 people, approximately 10 per cent of the foreign workers living in the country.

[26] In early September 1998, after months of debate on how to end the economic crisis, Prime Minister Mahathir removed Economy Minister Anwar Ibrahim from office, accusing him of 'sexual misconduct'. After his dismissal, Anwar led major protests against the Government and was arrested on September 20. The opposition could identify with Anwar, seeing him as a liberal and a champion of foreign investment, and showed its support in protests. After he was imprisoned, the opposition's leadership passed into the hands of his wife, Azizah Ismail. The economy suffered a 7 per cent recession compared to the previous year, and the new Economy Minister called for control over exchange rates and investment in order to stabilize the country.

[27] In April 1999, Anwar was sentenced to six years in prison, charged with 'sexual misconduct' and sodomy. Tens of thousands of demonstrators took to the streets of Kuala Lumpur to express solidarity for Anwar.

[28] The November 1999 legislative elections gave the absolute majority and more than two thirds of the seats to the governing party, allowing Mahathir to continue in power until 2005. The Alternative Front, led by Azizah Ismail, received less than 20 per cent of the vote and complained that the Government had permitted just nine days of political campaigning. Meanwhile, the party of the Prime Minister, UMNO, suffered internal divisions, ceding space to its Islamic partner, PAS.

[29] In January 2000, when the trial against Anwar was reopened, the Government arrested four opposition leaders and the lawyer who had defended the former Economy Minister, sparking a wave of protests both in and outside the country. The accusations against the opposition ranged from sedition to inciting racial violence. In March of that year, the Government limited the publication of *Harakah*, a weekly newspaper, to two editions per month. Harakah had grown a great deal as a publication due to its complete coverage of the Anwar case. In response to criticisms, in April the Government announced the creation of a National Human Rights Commission as an arena where citizens could present their claims. ∎

STATISTICS

DEMOGRAPHY

Population: 21,830,000 (1999)
Annual growth: 2.5 % (1975/97)
Estimates for year 2015 (million): 27.5 (1999)
Annual growth to year 2015: 1.5 % (1997/2015)
Urban population: 55.1 % (1997)
Urban Growth: 4.3 % (1980/95)
Children per woman: 3.1 (1998)

HEALTH

Life expectancy at birth: 72 years (1998)
male: 70 years (1998)
female: 74 years (1998)
Maternal mortality: 39 per 100,000 live births (1990-98)
Infant mortality: 9 per 1,000 (1998)
Under-5 child mortality: 10 per 1,000 (1998)
Daily calorie supply: 2,899 per capita (1996)
43 doctors per 100,000 people (1993)
Safe water: 78 % (1990/98)

EDUCATION

Literacy: 84 % (1995)
male: 89 % (1995)
female: 79 % (1995)
School enrolment:
Primary total: 91 % (1990/96)
male: 90 % (1990/97)
female: 92 % (1990/97)
Secondary:
male: 58 % (1990/96)
female: 66 % (1990/96)
Tertiary: 11 % (1996)
Primary school teachers: one for every 20 (1994)

COMMUNICATIONS

158 newspapers (1996), 420 radios (1997), 228 TV sets (1996) and 183 main telephone lines (1996) per 1,000 people
Books: 21 new titles per 100,000 people (1992/94)

ECONOMY

Per capita, GNP: $ 3,670 (1998)
Annual growth, GNP: -5.8 % (1998)
Annual inflation: 5.1 % (1990/98)
Consumer price index: 111.8 (1998)
Currency: 3.9 ringgits = $ 1 (1998)
Cereal imports: 3,569,469 metric tons (1998)
Food import dependency: 5 % (1997)
Fertilizer use: 6,593 kg per ha (1997)
Exports: $ 82,899 million (1998)
Imports: $ 67,098 million (1998)
External debt: $ 44,773 million (1998); $ 2,091 per capita (1998)
Debt service: 8.7 % of exports (1998)
Development aid received: $ -241 million (1997); $ -12.9 per capita (1997); -0.30 % of GNP (1997)

ENERGY

Consumption: 2,237.0 Kgs of Oil equivalent per capita yearly (1997); -53.0 % imported (1997)

HDI (rank/value): 56/0.768 (1997)

Maldives

Maldives

Population: 278,000 (1999)
Area: 300 SQ KM
Capital: Male
Currency: Rufiyaa
Language: Dhivehi

The Republic of the Maldives consists of an archipelago of more than 1,000 coral islands in the Indian Ocean, southwest of India and Sri Lanka, of which only 192 are permanently inhabited. Maldivans are skilled sailors and fishing people and have always had close contact with the mainland of Asia. It was through this connection that Arab and Muslim influence reached them in the 12th century; the islanders converted to Islam and their ruler took the title of Sultan.

[2] European colonizers came to the Maldives quite early on, as it was a compulsory stopover on the way to the Far East. The local peoples put up tenacious resistance to foreign domination, forcing the Portuguese to seek alternative harbors; hence the foundation of Goa on the west coast of India.

[3] Eventually, the Sultan of the Maldives gave in to the enticing offers of the agents of British imperialism and in 1887 he agreed to place his islands under British 'protection'. The economy was makeshift based on the production of coconut oil, fishing and the cultivation of tropical fruits. On the other hand, the Maldives possessed great strategic value, which was enhanced by the opening of the Suez Canal.

[4] A naval base was set up on Gan Island, on the equator, which became a link in the safety chain that protected navigation from Gibraltar to Hong Kong, via Aden and Singapore.

[5] The local population was of no interest to the authorities even as a source of labor, so very little was done for their education, health or welfare.

[6] This neglect stimulated rebellion against the Sultan, whose position as an intermediary between his people and the colonial capital made him the only person to benefit from this contact. In 1952, a popular revolt overthrew the ruler and a republic was proclaimed. British troops intervened to 'restore order', putting the Sultan back on the throne two years later. In 1957, Britain requested permission to enlarge the Gan naval base and install facilities for fighter planes to land there. The proposal aroused fierce opposition and pro-British Prime Minister Ibrahim Ali Didi was forced to resign. His successor, Amir Ibrahim Nasir, refused permission to build the new facilities claiming that such a project would violate the country's neutrality.

[7] In 1959, rebellion broke out in the southern Maldives, which decided to break away under the name of the Republic of Suvadiva. This autonomy was short-lived, and in 1960, the 20,000 Suvadivan republicans were restored to the sultanate with British help. The colonialists took the opportunity of signing a new agreement with the Sultan extending the protectorate, and maintaining and enlarging the bases.

[8] This time the British paid nothing towards them, only the pay due to the British soldiers and the cost of the ammunition used to stifle the rebellion in the south.

[9] The British Empire was by now in decline. During the 1960s, the British finally decided to withdraw from their strategic positions 'east of Suez', making sure that their interests would continue to be defended by the United States. In 1965, the Maldives chose to become independent, receiving immediate recognition from the United Nations.

[10] The Sultan was unable to survive the withdrawal of foreign support and in 1968 a plebiscite was held which favored the establishment of a republic. Amir Ibrahim Nasir, the Prime Minister, now became President.

[11] The Gan naval base remained in British hands until 1975, when the building of modern US military installations on the neighboring island of Diego Garcia rendered it obsolete.

[12] In March 1975, President Nasir announced that he had uncovered a conspiracy led by Prime Minister Ahmed Zaki; Zaki was exiled to a desert island along with some of his supporters. Nasir's proposal to rent the unused installations on Gan Island to transnational enterprises was rejected by the Majilis (legislative council). Realizing that he had lost support, Nasir ended his second presidential term in 1978, without standing for re-election. The Majilis appointed Maumoon Gayoom, a Muslim intellectual of international prestige, to replace him.

[13] The new president concerned himself with the serious difficulties of the fishing community and set up a state fisheries corporation to control the country's main economic resource from catch to marketing. Gayoom founded schools in 19 of the major atolls and opened up the archipelago to the rest of the world, personally travelling to Europe, the Middle East and the Sixth Summit Conference of the Non-Aligned Movement.

[14] In May 1980, he officially announced that his government had crushed an attempted mercenary invasion of the islands, organized from abroad by Ibrahim Nasir. Nasir's extradition from Singapore was immediately requested.

[15] The Republic of Maldives supported Islamic solidarity, non-alignment, Palestine, the New International Economic Order, disarmament, African solidarity, and demilitarization of the Indian Ocean. In spite of its size, population and resources, its strategic location gave it considerable bargaining power for the country and an independent position in foreign policy. In addition, non-aligned foreign policy provided the basis for assistance and support from all, without

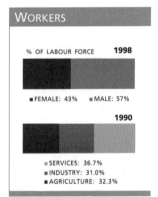

WORKERS

% OF LABOUR FORCE **1998**

■ FEMALE: 43%   ■ MALE: 57%

1990

■ SERVICES: 36.7%
■ INDUSTRY: 31.0%
■ AGRICULTURE: 32.3%

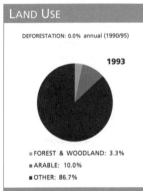

LAND USE

DEFORESTATION: 0.0% annual (1990/95)

1993

■ FOREST & WOODLAND: 3.3%
■ ARABLE: 10.0%
■ OTHER: 86.7%

[Map of Maldives]

Ihavandiffulu Atoll

Indian Ocean

Tiladunmati Atoll

Makunudu Atoll

Miladunmadulu Atoll

North Malosmadulu Atoll

Fadippolu Atoll

Male Atoll

South Malosmadulu Atoll

MALDIVES   Kardiva Channel

Male Atoll

Male Atoll

South Male Atoll

Ari Atoll

Male

North Nilandu Atoll

Felidu Atoll

South Nilandu Atoll

Mulaku Atoll

Kolumadulu Atoll   Veimandu Channel

Haddunmati Atoll

Addu Atoll

Huvadu Atoll

Equator

Gan

Addu Atoll

100 km

sacrificing too much freedom of action.

[16] In April 1980, the Maldives signed a scientific and technological cooperation agreement with the Soviet Union, and in April 1981, a trade agreement with India, which is the country's closest cooperator in the region. In July, 1981, Chinese foreign minister Huang Hua visited Male and signed a technical cooperation agreement.

[17] In July 1982, the Government achieved a major diplomatic victory when the Maldives became the 47th member of the British Commonwealth. This was the second major achievement of Gayoom's government since 1979, when the Maldives had joined the Non-Aligned Movement. The Maldives have, however, refused to join ASEAN as this organization tends to act on bloc decisions agreed by a majority.

[18] Being the country closest to the US naval base at Diego Garcia in the Indian Ocean, Maldivan developments have attracted the interest of other countries. In a referendum held in 1983, Gayoom was elected for another five-year period, with 95.5 per cent of the vote.

[19] In August 1988, three months before being elected President for the third time, Maumoon Gayoom frustrated another coup attempt, allegedly promoted by Amir Nasir. Seventy-five people were arrested, most of them Sri Lankans, of whom 16 were sentenced to death and 59 were given prison sentences.

[20] In 1985, there was a 37 per cent increase in tourism over the 1984 figure, coinciding with the virtual closing down of the Maldivan docks, as a result of the drastic reduction of its imports and the loss of important international markets. In 1986, tourism maintained its economic importance, generating $42 million, close to 17 per cent of the GDP and in 1991 the Maldives had 200,000 tourists who brought $80 million into the country. Fishing continued to be the main activity, employing 45 per cent of the country's workforce and generating 24 per cent of the GDP.

[21] The environmental impact on the Maldives of industrial activity in developed countries, is a major issue. In March, 1990, thousands of schoolchildren demonstrated in the streets of the capital, voicing their concern over the rising sea levels around their tiny archipelago. This phenomenon is attributed to the 'greenhouse effect' which is producing global warming, that will lead to the melting of the polar ice caps, causing the sea level to rise. According to scientific predictions, if present trends continue most of the islands will disappear over the next hundred years.

[22] To counteract the sea rise, large retaining walls were built around the islands. In 1987, gigantic waves flooded two-thirds of the capital, Male, causing damage estimated at $40 million. In June 1991, heavy rainfalls destroyed the homes of over 10 per cent of the population, causing damage for $30 million worth of damage.

[23] Twenty-eight tons of garbage are collected daily in Male, generating serious environmental problems, given the island's small surface area. A UN body determined that the garbage should not be recycled, but should be taken instead to a neighboring island, to be used as filling material to reclaim land from the sea.

[24] The Government of Maldives denied Amnesty International access to prisoners held in the Dhoonidhoo detention center and the Gamadhoo prison, where there had been reports of inhumane treatment. Most political prisoners were sent there under the Prevention of Terrorism Act which, among other measures, authorized detention without trial for up to 45 days.

[25] In 1993 and 1994, the Maldives went through an economic crisis caused by the 1991 monsoons and a chronic trade deficit dating from 1992. The Government sold 25 per cent of the Bank of Maldives' shares and applied a free market economy to all sectors except frozen fish exports.

[26] President Gayoom began his fourth term of office in 1993 and remained as head of the ministries of defense, national security and finance. 27 per cent of the budget was turned over to education, health and social security. The fishing sector received 30 per cent since it employs one fourth of the working population.

[27] $113 million in tourism revenues from 1994 helped in the recovery of the archipelago's economy in 1995.

[28] Although no political parties or an organized opposition are allowed, young Maldivans educated abroad have shown signs of rejecting the system imposed by the President. The spread of religious radicalism throughout the islands was another reason for concern for Gayoom's government.

[29] The Maldives experienced slow but steady economic progress in 1996, and industrial production increased 10 per cent. Education spending increased to 9.2 per cent of the national budget.

[30] At a May 1997 meeting in Male, the Southeast Asian Co-operation Association approved poverty eradication initiatives and, based on studies confirming the rising sea level around the Maldives, instituted environmental protection measures. A new Constitution was approved in November and went into effect January 1 1998, establishing that the legislature would elect the President. Choosing from among five candidates, legislators decided in September to re-elect Gayoom to a fifth term, which was confirmed by referendum in November with 90 per cent of the vote.

[31] Amnesty International (AI) accused the Government of arresting three legislative candidates in the November 1999 elections. According to AI's report, presented in January 2000, the candidates had been accused of 'inciting discontent', which could lead to their 15-year suspension from political activity. The Government had prohibited political parties from campaigning for their candidates, forcing all of them to run as individuals. ∎

PROFILE

ENVIRONMENT

There are nearly 1,200 coral islets in this archipelago, where the land is never more than 3.5 meters above sea level. Vegetation is sparse except for coconut palms which are plentiful. A tropical monsoon climate prevails. There are no mineral or energy resources. Fishing is the economic mainstay.

SOCIETY

Peoples: The population of the archipelago came from migrations of Dravidian, Indo-Aryan and Sinhalese peoples from India, later followed by Arab peoples.
Religions: Muslim (official and proclaimed universal).
Languages: Dhivehi (official), an Indo-Arian language related to Sinhala, English and Arabic are also spoken.
Political Parties: There are no political parties. The *Majilis* or parliament is elected by direct vote and in turn proposes a president whose candidacy is submitted to a plebiscite.

THE STATE

Official Name: Divehi Jumhuriyya (Republic of the Maldives).
Administrative divisions: 20 districts.
Capital: Male 63,000 people (1995).
Government: Presidential republic. Maumoon Abdul Gayoom, President since 1978, re-elected in 1998. Legislative Power; the Citizens' Council, with 48 members, 8 of whom are elected by the President.
National Holiday: July 26, Independence Day (1965).
Armed forces: About 1,000. The force performs both army and police functions.

Mali

Mali

Population: 10,960,000 (1999)
Area: 1,240,190 SQ KM
Capital: Bamako
Currency: CFA franc
Language: French

The empire of Mali, one of the great cultural and commercial centers of Africa was occupied by the French in 1850. Together with what are now Burkina Faso (Upper Volta), Benin and Senegal it was renamed the French Sudan and later French West Africa.

[2] Domination brought about considerable changes. Trade, which traditionally flowed towards the Mediterranean, was turned back towards the Atlantic where Dakar (in Senegal) had become the official trade center of the colony. This in turn caused the decline of the trans-Saharan trade routes. After 1945 the anti-colonial feelings of French Sudan were expressed in the formation of the African Democratic Assembly (RDA), at a conference in Bamako encouraged by the democratic atmosphere that prevailed after World War II. Under the impact of the Dien Bien Phu defeat of French colonialism in Vietnam and the Algerian revolution, Paris embarked on a policy of gradual concessions that would lead to Mali's independence in 1960.

[3] Aware of their limitations, the new states formed the Federation of Mali, but their differences soon caused it to collapse. French Sudan then severed its last remaining ties with France, becoming the Republic of Mali, with Modibo Keita as its first president.

[4] Together with presidents Senghor from Senegal and Houphouët-Boigny from Cote d'Ivoire, Keita belonged to a generation of African leaders educated in France and inspired by social democracy. Unlike his neighbors, the President of Mali did not accept neocolonialism. Instead he pushed for reforms and economic development under the banner of African socialism; moving closer to the views held by Guinea's Sekou Touré and Nkrumah of Ghana.

[5] The economy was nationalized, industrialization stimulated and the proportion of children in school rose from 4 to 20 per cent. His struggle for Pan-Africanism, non-alignment and independent foreign policy earned Keita a good reputation among progressive forces throughout the continent. He was however unable to build a strong political structure and there was a successful coup against him in November 1968.

[6] The Military Committee for National Liberation (CMLN) took over, headed by Moussa Traoré. The Committee promised to straighten out the economy and fight corruption, but the results were exactly the opposite. Grain, which had been produced in sufficient quantities to provide a surplus for export, began to be rationed in the 1970s.

[7] Economic dependence and agricultural intensification geared towards a world market created a large foreign debt for Mali during this decade.

[8] In 1974 seeking to gain political support, the CMLN held a referendum on a new constitution. With the opposition banned and the followers of Keita imprisoned, the Government won a 99.8 per cent majority, too large to be believed. On May 16 1977 Modibo Keita died somewhere in the desert where he had been held prisoner since 1968. The official cause of death was food poisoning, but this was commonly re-interpreted as simply poisoning. In the largest mass demonstration ever seen in Bamako, the people followed Keita's body to the cemetery in open defiance of the military regime.

[9] In 1979, President Moussa Traoré embarked upon an austerity program drawn up by the IMF and the international creditor banks. This naturally stirred up social unrest. In November 1979 students and teachers took to the streets staging rallies and demonstrations which lasted for over a month. Teachers also went on strike. The Government reacted violently. Thirteen students were tortured to death and around 100 were arrested.

[10] After 1983 Mali also drew closer to France. At the same time Traoré distanced himself from the Soviet Union after having received economic and educational aid during the 1970s.

[11] Key sectors such as agriculture continued to decline. A prolonged drought drastically reduced Mali's livestock.

[12] In June 1985, President Traoré was re-elected for a further six years. As the official party's only candidate he received 99.94 per cent of the vote.

[13] In 1988 students, teachers and public employees took to the streets once again. The Government was reorganized and a Social and Economic Council was created, headed by General Amadou Baba Diarra.

[14] The Government faced a foreign debt which amounted to 125 per cent of its GDP, with the servicing of the debt exceeding a quarter of the income earned from exports. Negotiations for an economic adjustment program began with the IMF in 1988. The privatization of Mali's banking system was initiated, financed by an 8,000,000 CFA franc loan from France. At the same time the Government announced a reduction in their number of employees, and the decision to sell off state enterprises.

[15] On April 10 1991, a popular and military revolt against the Traoré regime carried Lt-Col Amadou Toumani Touré to power. He was the leader of the Council of Transition for the Salvation of the People (CTSP), which promised to transfer government to civilians early in 1992.

[16] The CTSP contained many cadres from the previous military dictatorship. Popular distrust of the military led to violent action by student organizations, as buildings associated with the old dictatorial regime were raided.

[17] Old political parties reorganized and new ones appeared. Social organizations demonstrated in favor of several issues, including pay increases, and against the privatization of public companies in the telecommunication, railroad, textile, pharmaceutical and cement sectors.

[18] In June, the rising of the Tuaregs in the north and the Moors in the east increased the state of social unrest. The new president met with his colleagues in Algeria and Mauritania to deal with the Tuareg question.

[19] An attempted coup by some of the armed forces initially led Toumani Touré to grant a salary increase of 70 per cent to the armed forces and civil servants in an effort to avert unrest.

[20] In December 1991, talks were renewed between Mali's authorities and the Tuareg rebels, who accepted a cease-fire in order for prisoners to be exchanged.

[21] In March the next year, with Algerian mediation, the Government of Mali and the Tuaregs reached a new peace agreement. In April a final peace settlement was signed with the Azawad Unified Front and Movements, an organization of four Tuareg opposition groups.

[22] In the March 1992 municipal and legislative elections, the Alliance for Democracy in Mali (ADEMA) won 76 of the 116 seats. The rest were divided up among other political alliances and representatives of the expatriate Mali community.

23   The Malian Government and the Tuareg rebels in the north ratified a 'national peace pact' in April 1992, putting an end to almost two years of armed conflict.

24   On April 26, Alpha Oumar Konaré, leader of ADEMA, was elected President in the first multiparty elections since the country's independence in 1960. His main rival was Tieoule Mamadou Konaté, head of the Sudanese Union-African Democratic Group (US-RDA).

25   Konaré, a teacher by profession, had played a key role in ousting Moussa Traoré's regime in 1991.

26   Konaré and Konaté called for a second ballot, as neither had won an absolute majority in the initial round of voting on April 12, although seven candidates were eliminated in this first round. Both rounds of voting were characterized by a very low voter turnout (only 21 per cent of the voters participated in the second ballot).

27   Most political parties boycotted the parliamentary election and challenged the electoral procedures, this perhaps accounted for the high rate of absenteeism.

28   In its annual report for 1992, Amnesty International condemned the imprisonment of several opposition figures without charges or trial. Fourteen death sentences had also been passed, although these were later commuted to life sentences. Finally, according to the report, several dozen members of the Tuareg community had been executed without trial by the army.

29   A group of students occupied the state radio station in March 1993 and massive demonstrations were held against the Government's economic policy in April. However, with support from international financial organizations, Konaré consolidated the economic liberalization begun by Traoré. The President reformed the tax system, reduced public spending, privatized state companies and eliminated price controls.

30   In February 1994, new demonstrations were staged against the government, and all the education centers except primary schools were closed. Some observers indicated the appearance of underground armed groups determined to attack properties belonging to Mali's major creditor countries.

31   The Government signed an agreement with the MFUA, one of the main groups representing Tuareg rebels. But violent incidents continued to take place and on one occasion, some 200 people, including many women and children, died due to police repression in the cities of Gao and Beher.

32   In 1995, the Government pursued negotiations with other Tuareg rebel groups - likewise with neighboring countries - to organize the relocation of 120,000 Tuareg refugees from Algeria, Burkina Faso, Mauritania and Niger. A three year repatriation scheme was launched in October.

33   The IMF approved the third annual structural adjustment plan after it considered Mali's economic results were good. At the same time, many foreign investors showed a renewed interest in Mali after new gold fields were found in the south.

34   A new peace agreement, signed on March 27 1996, put an end to the conflict with the Tuareg. The Government arranged the return of some 25,000 refugees from Niger. The agreement also included the demobilization of some 2,700 guerrillas.

35   In May 1997, Alpha Oumar Konaré was re-elected President with 95.9 per cent of the valid votes. In the legislative elections of July and August, the governmental ruling ADEMA took 130 seats in the new parliament. In both cases, the opposition boycotted the elections and there was only a minimal turn-out.

36   The opposition boycott coincided with increased violence in the streets, leading to the resignation of Prime Minister Ibrahima Boubacar Keita and his government in late 1997. A group of intellectuals called for the liberation of various opposition leaders to ease the situation. However, the President confirmed the Prime Minister in his post and the latter designated a new government.

37   In March 1998, the Government indefinitely postponed local elections planned for April 19. According to the Government, this measure was imposed to allow the political parties time to prepare, given the announcement of a further boycott by the opposition.

38   After several postponements, the June 1998 local elections were won by the Government. The opposition boycotted the elections, claiming a lack of political freedoms in order to take part. In that year, there was a great increase in rice production. The Government embarked on the privatization of water and electrical power state-owned utilities.

39   Moussa Traore and his wife were charged with unlawful appropriation and breach of trust. They were sentenced to death in January 1999, but the sentence was later commuted to life in prison. Trade unions obtained a 7-per-cent wage raise in August for state employees after a two-day strike in July. A health employees' strike shook the country for several days during October.

40   A coup attempt was foiled in January 2000. A few days later the

PROFILE

ENVIRONMENT

There are three distinct regions: the northern region which is part of the Sahara desert; the central region which consists of the Sahel grasslands, subject to desertification, and finally, the southern region, with humid savannah vegetation, most of the population, and the two major rivers: the Senegal and the Niger. The shortage of water and the over use of forest resources have given rise to further aridity.

SOCIETY

Peoples: There are many ethnic groups, the largest being the Bambara. Other important groups are the Malinke, Songhai, Peul-Fulani, Dogon, Tuareg and Moor. 10 per cent of the population are nomads; they are the most affected by drought. **Religions:** 90 per cent, is Muslim, 9 per cent practice traditional African religions and there is a small Christian minority. **Languages:** French (official). Of the African languages, Bambara is the most widely spoken. Arabic and Tuareg are also spoken in the north. **Political Parties:** Alliance for Democracy in Mali (ADEMA); National Committee for Democratic Initiative (CNID); Sudanese Union-African Democratic Group (US-RDA); National Renaissance Party (PRN); Unified Movements and Fronts of Azawad (MFUA). **Social Organizations:** Workers' Union of Mali; Union of Malian Women (UNFM); National Union of Malian Youth (UNJM); Association of Pupils and Students of Mali (AEEM).

THE STATE

Official Name: République du Mali. **Administrative divisions:** 8 regions and the district of Bamako. **Capital:** Bamako 840,000 people (1994). **Other cities:** Ségou 88,877 people; Mopti 73,979; Sikasso 73,050; Gao 54,874 (1987). **Government:** Parliamentary republic, with strong head of State. Alpha Oumar Konaré, President since April 1992, re-elected in May 1997. Mande Sidibe, Prime Minister since February 2000. Legislature: single-chamber: National Assembly, with 129 members, elected every 5 years. **National Holiday:** September 22, Independence Day (1960). **Armed Forces:** 7,350. **Other:** 7,350 (Gendarmes, Republican Guard, Militia and National Police).

President decided to incorporate military personnel in his cabinet. Prime Minister Ibrahim Boubacar Keita resigned in February 2000, accused by the press of being incapable of eradicating poverty in the country. Mande Sidibe, an economist and former IMF official, was appointed to replace him. ∎

Malta

Malta

Population: 386,000 (1999)
Area: 320 SQ KM
Capital: Valletta
Currency: Liri
Language: Maltese and English

For territorial expansionists, Malta's most valuable asset was probably its geographic location which made it the historical focus of every conflict for domination of the Mediterranean. In ancient times, Phoenicians, Greeks, Carthaginians, Romans and Saracens successively occupied the island.

[2] In 1090, the Normans conquered the island and 300 years later it fell to the Spanish Kingdom of Aragon. In the 16th century, the defense of the island was entrusted to the ancient order of the Knights of St John of the Hospital. Renamed the Knights of Malta, they remained there for another three centuries, until they were driven out by the French in 1798. The Congress of Vienna granted Britain sovereignty over the island, in 1815.

[3] After a popular rebellion in 1921, London agreed to a certain degree of internal autonomy for the islands, which was revoked at the beginning of World War II.

[4] During World War II, Malta suffered greatly; it was used as a base for the Allied counter-offensive against Italy. The heroic struggle of the Maltese raised their national consciousness and in 1947, London restored autonomy to the island.

[5] Independence was formally declared on September 8 1964, but

Britain assumed responsibility for defense and financial support. In 1971, Dominic Mintoff's government established relations with Italy, Tunisia, the USSR and Libya, from whom it received substantial financial assistance. NATO forces left in 1971, and Malta joined the Movement of Non-Aligned Countries two years later. In December 1974, the Republic of Malta was proclaimed.

[6] In 1980, tensions developed in Malta's relations with Libya, primarily over oil explorations. The conflict was eventually turned over

to the International Court of Justice in the Hague, and relations returned to normal.

[7] From the beginning of the Labor administration, measures to reduce the Church's power had been introduced. The bishops owned 80 per cent of all real estate on the island and virtually controlled education. In July 1983, the Government expropriated all Church properties and made secular education obligatory in primary schools. In 1985, the Government and the Church signed an agreement providing for a gradual transition to secular education at the secondary level.

[8] In May 1987, the Liberal Prime Minister, Dr Fenech Adami, initiated a policy of rapprochement towards US policies, favoring EEC membership.

[9] Forecasts of a falling birth rate and the increase in people aged over 60 forced the Government to draw up plans to deal with the problems of the elderly. At that time 7 per cent of those over 65 lived in hospitals.

[10] There was a certain amount of tension with the United States in 1993, when President Bill Clinton accused Malta of violating the UN trade embargo on the Yugoslav Federation.

[11] Tourism was the country's chief economic activity, with one-third of the workforce in this sector and more than one million visitors per year.

[12] In 1993, the EU declared that Malta's democratic stability and its human rights policy were acceptable for its incorporation into the Union. However, its economic

structures were considered 'archaic' and the implementation of 'fundamental economic reforms' was advised.

[13] On January 1 1995 a Value Added Tax came into effect, under criticism from labor unions and shopkeepers.

[14] In the October 1996 elections, the Labor Party took 50.7 per cent of the vote, while the National Party took 47.8 per cent. Alfred Sant became Prime Minister.

[15] Following the elections, the new government withdrew Malta from NATO. Sant said his country would use its constitutional neutrality to promote the stability and security of the Mediterranean region. He also put brakes on the program for entry to the European Union and announced he would be seeking more gradual entry through co-operation or free trade agreements.

[16] The 1997 budget deficit, added to the increased unemployment, forced the Government to plan austerity measures for 1998. But an opposition non-confidence vote brought down Prime Minister Sant and his government in March 1998. Sant had claimed that the approval of a development project with US funds should be considered as a vote of confidence. The opposition Nationalist Party along with several Labor members defeated the government by 35 to 34 votes in Parliament.

[17] After the crisis, new elections were called for September. These were won by the Nationalist Party with 52 per cent of the vote. The first measure taken by the new head of government, Eddie Fenech Adami, was to raise again the issue of incorporation into the EU, which had been put on hold by the 1996 Labor government.

[18] The European Union again formally accepted Malta's application to join at its annual meeting in Brussels, in December 1999. ∎

PROFILE

ENVIRONMENT

Includes five islands, two of which are uninhabited. The inhabited islands are the three largest ones: Malta, where the capital is located, 246 sq km; Gozo, 67 sq km; and Comino, 3 sq km. The archipelago is located in the Central Mediterranean Sea, south of Sicily, east of Tunis and north of Libya. The coast is high and rocky, with excellent natural harbors. The islands' environmental problems are concentrated precisely in these areas. The problems are caused by the encroachment of civilization, the development of tourism, the gradual abandonment of lands devoted to agriculture and the increase in waste. The coastal areas are also polluted by industrial activity.

SOCIETY

Peoples: The Maltese (95.7 per cent) come from numerous ethnic combinations, with strong Phoenician, Arab, Italian and British roots. There is a small British minority (2.1 per cent). **Religions:** mainly Catholic. **Languages:** Maltese and English, both official. **Political Parties:** The Nationalist Party (NP); the Labor Party (LP); Democratic Alternative. **Social Organizations:** The Confederation of Trade Unions.

THE STATE

Official Name: Repubblika ta'Malta. **Capital:** Valletta 210,000 people (1995). **Other cities:** Birkirkara 21,770 people; Qormi 19,904; Hamrun 13,654; Sliema13,514 (1994). **Government:** Guido de Marco, President since April 1999. Eddie Fenech Adami, Prime Minister since September 1998. Parliamentary Republic. **National Holiday:** September 8, Independence day (1964). **Armed Forces:** 1,950 troops (1996).

Marshall Islands

Marshall Islands

Population: 63,000 (1999)
Area: 180 SQ KM
Capital: Majuro
Currency: US dollar
Language: Marshallese and English

The Kwajalein and Bikini atolls of the Marshall Islands were thrust into modern history in February 1944 when heavy bombing by combined US naval and air force units hit the islands. This was followed by a prolonged and bloody battle which ended with the defeat of the Japanese and the occupation of the islands. Countless lives were lost but the military command considered it was a fair price to pay for the islands given their strategic position.

2 In 1979, the US proposed to make an Associated Free State with the four administrative units of the region; the Kwajalein and Bikini atolls, plus the Mariana and Caroline islands which were also trust territories. The Marshall Islands were granted jurisdiction over local and foreign affairs but the US declared the islands military territory for specific use.

3 In 1961, Kwajalein became the Pacific experimental missile target area, especially for intercontinental ballistic missiles launched from California, and early in the 1980s the US chose the atoll as a testing site for its new MX missiles. The local population was evicted and entry was forbidden to civilians.

4 Twenty-three nuclear tests were performed there between 1946 and 1958, including the detonation of the first H-bomb. Despite the legacy of cancer, thyroid diseases and leukemia left behind by the bomb, the inhabitants of the atoll insisted on returning to their homeland after having been transferred to the Rongerik atoll. In 1979, testing revealed that 139 of the total 600 inhabitants living on the Bikini atoll had extremely dangerous levels of plutonium in their bodies.

5 The inhabitants of Bikini, together with those living on Rongelap (also exposed to the radioactivity of the H-bomb dropped on Bikini) sued the US Government for $450 million. Abnormalities already existed in children under 10 years of age and could not be eliminated. The charges were filed together with reports compiled by US Government agencies proving that local people had been intentionally exposed to radioactivity in 1954 in order to study the effects of the bomb on humans. Reports revealed by the US Government in 1995 proved the dangers of exposure

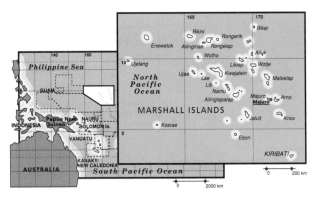

were known but this had never been passed on to the Marshall Islands population.

6 In April 1990, the US announced that it would use the area to destroy all the nerve gas supplies which had been installed in Europe to date. Environmentalists denounced plans to dispose of 25 million tons of toxic waste on one of the archipelago's atolls, between 1989 and 1994.

7 In October 1986, the US and the Marshall Islands signed a pact, whereby the latter became a Free Associated State, responsible for its own internal politics. According to the pact, the US would be responsible for the defense of the new state for a period of 15 years, which would enable the US to have an air base on the island, and entitle the island to US financial aid.

8 In the first elections of the new state, held in 1986, Amata Kabua was elected President.

9 In the years following independence, the Marshall Islands attempted to consolidate diplomatic and commercial relations with most of the neighboring states. In 1988 they were admitted in the South Pacific Agreement on Economic Cooperation and Regional Trade, and in 1989 set up diplomatic relations with Japan and Taiwan.

10 On September 17 1990, during the 46th UN General Assembly, held in New York, the Marshall Islands were accepted as a member state of the organization.

11 Foreign affairs minister Tony de Brun founded the Ralik Ratak Democratic Party in June 1991, after becoming estranged from President Kabua. In the November elections, Kabua was re-elected for his fourth consecutive term.

12 That year, a Hawaiian court ordered the suspension of missile testing until the operations' effects on the environment had been assessed. Two years later, local environmentalists protested against an alternative energy project based on the burning of discarded tyres, considering it a source of atmospheric contamination.

13 The controversy over the use of the Islands resurfaced in 1995 when the Government announced plans to install a nuclear waste dump on Bikini, even though atomic explosions between 1946 and 1958 had made it uninhabitable for a period of 10,000 years.

14 In December 1996, President Amata Kabua died. Kunio Lemari, transport and communication Minister, replaced him as an interim measure. In January 1997, Parliament appointed Imata Kabua, cousin of the late leader, as the new President.

15 Opposition from the United States and ecologist organizations finally led to the suspension of the project to store nuclear waste in June 1997. The Government announced the construction of a massive hotel and casino complex, funded by South Korean capital. This same month, in Majuro, 24 Pacific countries, including the Marshall Islands, signed an agreement to conserve fishery resources.

16 During February 1998, Asian banks expressed their satisfaction with the economic reforms which, according to the Government, were related to the conclusion in 2001 of the Free Associated State status and the end of US financial assistance. Inflation continued to rise, reaching 10 per cent that year. The Government reduced state wages by 12.5 per cent in June, causing widespread protest. The Government was unable to reduce the state budget deficit, one of its main economic problems. ∎

PROFILE

ENVIRONMENT

A total of 1,152 islands grouped in 34 atolls and 870 reefs. The land area covers 180 sq km, but the islands are scattered over a million sq km in the Pacific. The atolls of Mili, Majuro, Maloelap, Wotje and Likiep lie to the north-east. The south-west atolls are: Jaluit, Kwajalein, Rongelap, Bikini and Enewetak among others. The northern islands receive less rainfall than the southern atolls.

SOCIETY

Peoples: Sixty per cent of the population lives on Majuro and Kwajalein. A large part of Kwajalein's residents consist of US military personnel.
Religions: Protestant 90.1 per cent; Roman Catholic 8.5 per cent; other 1.4 per cent.
Languages: Marshallese (kajin-majol), English.
Political Parties: Ralik Ratak Democratic Party, opposition.

THE STATE

Official Name: Republic of the Marshall Islands. **Administrative divisions:** 25 districts. **Capital:** Majuro 24,000 people (est 1997). **Other cities:** Ebeye 10,000 people (1997).
Government: Parliamentary Republic. Kessai H. Note, President of the local Government since January 2000. A High Commissioner Janet McCoy is the US Government delegate and handles security, defense and foreign affairs. The constitution provides for a 33-member parliament which appoints the local President. **National holiday:** 1 May 1979, Proclamation of the Republic of the Marshall Islands.

STATISTICS

Demography: Population: 63,000 (1999). **Health:** Infant mortality: 63 per 1,000 (1998). Under-5 child mortality: 92 per 1,000 (1998). Safe water: 82 % (1990/98). **Education:** Literacy: 91 % (1995). Female: 90 % (1995). School enrolment: Primary total: 95 % (1990/96). **Economy:** Per capita, GNP: $ 1,540 (1998). Annual growth, GNP: -4.3 % (1998).

Martinique

Martinique

Population: 392,000 (1999)
Area: 1,100 SQ KM
Capital: Fort-de-France
Currency: French franc
Language: French

The Carib indians migrated throughout the central and northern parts of the South American continent, and from there to the nearby islands in the Caribbean. They called the largest of the Lesser Antilles 'Madinina', becoming known as Martinique in the colonial period.

2 The Caribs were primarily hunter-gatherers and banded together to form a small group on the island. The French occupied it in 1635, but economic development did not occur until 150 years or so later.

3 Late in the 17th century, sugar cultivation transformed the natural and economic landscape of the island, ending the indians' lifestyle. The system of production changed on the sugarcane plantations. The indigenous population was replaced by African slaves, brought to the island by slave-traders. This monoculture dominated Martinique's economy, reinforcing the colonial ties with France.

4 A minority of 12,000 European land, sugar mill and business owners controlled 93,000 slave laborers, an imbalance that gave rise to countless uprisings, known as *Marronuage* - meaning collective rebellions of slaves. Accounts written in those days recall the existence of quilombos (see Quilombos in Brazil) on the island in 1811, 1822 and 1833: years when rebellions shook Martinique

5 In the early 19th century, unprecedented social disturbances occurred as the traditional plantation system was abandoned without investment in industrialization.

6 In 1937 the formation of Martinique's Central Labor Union prompted social mobilization. In 1945 the leftist Aimé Césaire became mayor of Fort-de-France, and in 1946, a deputy for Martinique in the French National Assembly. Césaire was co-founder with Senegal's Léopold Sédar Senghor of the *Négritude* movement which among other things stood against the imposition of French cultural patterns.

7 In 1946 the French Government revised its approach to colonial relations, creating the Overseas Departments in 1948. At first, the Martinican middle class had hoped to have the same rights as French citizens, but lack of consensus within the anti-colonial movement hampered the achievement of this goal.

8 In the March 1986 elections, the left-wing parties obtained 21 of the 41 seats on the Regional Council. Aimé Césaire, representing the leftist coalition, was re-elected President of the Council. Rodolphe Désiré became Martinique's first left-wing party (PPM) representative in the French Senate. In March 1992 Claude Lise, of the Progressive Party of Martinique, was elected to lead the General Council, one of the nation's two assemblies.

9 In 1993, the establishment of a single European market worsened the island's economic situation. In the elections that year there was a tied vote between the Right on the one side and the pro-independence and Left parties on the other. In the plebiscite to ratify the Maastricht Treaty, the abstention rate was 75 per cent, showing hostility or at least a passive approach toward a deeper integration of the island into the European Union (EU).

10 Other signs of hostility toward the EU were the demonstrations of banana producers, who protested against the opening of the European market to imports from Africa and Latin America, where fruits were cheaper than in the 'French' Antilles. The crisis worsened in 1994 with a 20 per cent increase in unemployment and a noticeable drop in corporate investments.

11 The future of the island caused disagreements between the various Martinican parties and was the object of intense debate during 1995 and 1996. While the Communist Party proposed greater autonomy without attempting to gain independence, the Martinique Independence Movement (MIM) called for negotiations for sovereignty.

12 In 1997, the US continued to favor Central American banana production over that of the Caribbean producers, (including Martinique and Guadeloupe) and called on the European Union to revise its prices in line with increasing production costs.

13 Social tension increased in early 1998. Unemployment affected 40 per cent of the active population, the highest level in national history. Strikes and demonstrations, mainly in the health and transport sectors, followed one after another, calling for employment, pay increases and better working conditions.

14 Lise was re-elected in March 1998; however, the elections showed increased support for the MIM, which became the dominant force in the Council.

15 French President Jacques Chirac visited the island in March 2000. He was confronted by Martinique's increasing demands for greater trade with France. The island also sought more autonomy from the colonial power in order to trade directly, particularly with its Caribbean neighbors. ■

PROFILE

ENVIRONMENT

Martinique is a volcanic island, one of the Windward Islands of the Lesser Antilles. Mount Pelée, whose eruption in 1902 destroyed the city of Saint Pierre is a dominant feature of the mountainous terrain. The fertile land is suitable for agriculture, especially sugar cane. The tropical, humid climate is tempered by sea winds.

SOCIETY

Peoples: Descendants of former enslaved Africans (90 per cent). There is a minority made up of people of European origin (5 per cent). Indian, Lebanese and Chinese (5 per cent).
Religions: Catholic (95 per cent) and traditional African religions (5 per cent).
Languages: French (official), and Creole.
Political Parties: Communist Party of Martinique, (PCM); Progressive Party of Martinique (PPM); Union of Martinican Democrats, (UDM); Socialist Party (SP); National Martinican Front for Autonomy; Democratic Union of Martinique (DUM); Socialist Revolution Group; Martinican Independence Movement (MIM).
Social Organizations: General Confederation of Workers

THE STATE

Official Name: Département d'Outre-Mer de la Martinique.
Capital: Fort-de-France 150,000 people (est 1995).
Other cities: Le Marin; La Trinité.
Government: Jean François Cordet, French appointed commissioner. Claude Lise, re-elected in 1998 as General Council President. The Council's 36 members are elected through universal suffrage for 6-year terms.

DEMOGRAPHY

Population: 392,000 (1999)

Mauritania

Mauritenie

Population: 2,598,000 (1999)
Area: 1,025,520 SQ KM
Capital: Nouakchott
Currency: Ouguiya
Language: Arabic and French

The process of desertification that turned fertile plains into the Sahara desert, would have separated southern Berbers from the Mediterranean coast if camels had not been introduced into the area. The groups that migrated southward in search of pastures kept in touch with their native culture, and later shared the benefits of the Islamic civilization which flourished along the Mediterranean coast.

[2] The southern part of present-day Mauritania was the setting for one of the most peculiar African civilizations. But the Almoravid conquest and later the Fulah migrations stimulated the integration and unification of the population.

[3] In the 14th century, the Beni Hilal, who had invaded North Africa three centuries before, reached Mauritania. For over 200 years, they plundered the region and warred with the Berbers throughout an area including present-day southern Algeria and Sahara. In 1644, all the Berber groups in the region joined to fight the Arabs, but the resulting conflict, the Cherr Baba War, ended 30 years later with the defeat of the Berbers. The Arabs became a warrior caste, known as the Hassani, monopolizing the use of weapons, while trade, education and other civilian activities were left in the hands of the local population. Beneath these two groups came the Haratan, African shepherds from the south, kept as semi-serfs. Though this rigid social stratification weakened

with time, it is still intact among the Arab-Berbers, the Fulah and Soninke.

[4] Towards the end of the 17th century various emirates arose. These were unable to achieve the political organization of the country, due to their internal rivalries and dynastic quarrels. Nevertheless, they provided a minimal degree of order within the region which led in turn to a small revival of trade caravans. These efforts were supported by the cultural unification being carried out by the zuaias. These Berber-Marabouts devised a simple system of Arabic writing, propagating it along with their religious teachings.

[5] In the 19th century, growing trade coincided with a French project to transfer Sudanese commercial activities to Senegal (see Mali), requiring the elimination of trans-Saharan trade and the frequent robberies in Senegal. The French therefore invaded Mauritania in 1858, under General Faidherbe, and the fighting continued until the 20th century. The resistance initially met in the emirates of Trarza and Brakna continued with the Sheikh Ma al-Aini (see Western Sahara), with his sons and later his cousin, Muhammad al-Mamun, the emir of Adrar. Pursued by the French almost one thousand kilometers into the Sahara, Muhammad al-Mamun died in combat in 1934.

[6] After World War II, Mauritania became a French Overseas Province, sending deputies to the French Parliament. Ten years later

internal autonomy was granted and in 1960 independence was gained.

[7] A French transnational company, MIFERMA, was more powerful than the Government. MIFERMA's iron ore mines supplied 80 per cent of the country's exports and employed one in four salaried workers.

[8] In 1965 Mauritania withdrew from OCAM (the Common Afro-Mauritanian Organization), created to maintain French control over their former colonies.

[9] In 1966, the Government set up a state company, SOMITEX, with a monopoly on sugar, rice and tea imports, and a campaign was launched to rekindle the Arab culture. Mauritania set up its own customs system independent from Senegal; the Arab-Mauritanian Bank was granted the monopoly on foreign trade and the country began to issue its own currency.

[10] In 1974 the iron mines were nationalized. The country started to replace French influence by closer links with Muslim countries, and finally became a member of the Arab League. Saudi Arabia, Kuwait, and Morocco supplied economic assistance.

[11] In 1975 Mauritania, fulfilling an old ambition to annex part of Sahara, joined Morocco in an attempt to divide the Spanish possession. With logistic and military support from France, 3,000 Mauritanian soldiers and 10,000 Moroccan troops occupied Western Sahara.

[12] Ould Haidalla's government paid an extremely high price for this aggression. Mauritania soon became the target of violent reprisals by the Polisario Front (see Western Sahara) and was virtually occupied by Moroccan troops.

[13] Economic hardship aroused widespread popular unrest leading to protest rallies and street fighting. Opposition groups condemned Mauritanian interference in the Western Sahara liberation war.

[14] The crisis exploded in 1978 and over the next six years there were five coups. An attempt was made to Arabize

WORKERS

% OF LABOUR FORCE **1998**

- FEMALE: 44%   MALE: 56%

1990

- SERVICES: 34.4%
- INDUSTRY: 10.4%
- AGRICULTURE: 55.2%

LAND USE

DEFORESTATION: 0.0% annual (1990/95)
IRRIGATED: 23.9% of arable (1993)

1993

- FOREST & WOODLAND: 4.3%
- ARABLE: 0.2%
- OTHER: 95.5%

PUBLIC EXPENDITURE

DEFENCE EXPENDITURE (% of goverment exp.)	**9.8%**	(1997)
MILITARY EXPENDITURE (% of health & education)	**40%**	(1990/91)

MATERNAL MORTALITY 1990-98

Per 100,000 live births

550

LITERACY 1995

37%

EXTERNAL DEBT 1998

PER CAPITA

US$ 1,024

FOREIGN TRADE

Millions US$ 1998

IMPORTS

536

EXPORTS

407

the whole population, ignoring the African population (20 per cent), living in the southern part of the country.

[15] Ould Haidalla's government ended the Arabization process of total and also relinquished Mauritania's claim to the Sahara, making peace with the Polisario Front in August 1979. With the support of young officers and intellectuals from the Left, a decree was signed abolishing slavery in Mauritania.

[16] A coup occurred on December 11 1984. Maawiya Ould Sid'Ahmed Taya, an army colonel and chief of staff, ousted Haidallah. The first measures of the new administration were the recognition of the Democratic Saharawi Arab Republic (Western Sahara) and steps to dismantle a growing 'clandestine economy' (only 50 per cent of the firms operating in the country kept legal accounting records).

[17] In April 1985 the IMF announced that a $12 million standby credit had been granted to Mauritania under an agreement to restructure foreign debt. Conditions were particularly harsh for a country with a depleted agrarian economy affected by a persistent process of desertification and an annual grain deficit of 12,000 tons.

[18] The economic and social outlook deteriorated; the southern farming and grazing lands reduced as the desert expanded, and the impoverished nomadic people were driven to the cities.

[19] In the fishing sector the Government adopted a long-term strategy, with two objectives: on the one hand, to save resources, and on the other, to integrate the fishing industry into the rest of the economy. No new licenses are being given to foreign fishing fleets.

[20] Since 1987, a number of incidents have occurred between farmers and cattle herders in the border area along the Senegal River. In Nouakchott, many angry Mauritanians attacked hundreds of unarmed Senegalese with sticks and stones in 1989. In Dakar, Senegalese returning from Mauritania reported assassinations and mutilations of their compatriots in Mauritania. Scores of furious Senegalese reacted by murdering Mauritanian shop-keepers, and looting their shops. Within the country, there have been instances of violence between African Mauritanians from the south and Arabs and Berbers from the rest of the country. Throughout these events, the army supported the Arabs and Berbers, killing hundreds of African Mauritanians.

[21] Repeated border incidents with Senegal, leading to hundreds of victims on both sides, prompted Senegal to break off diplomatic relations in August 1989. Thousands of refugees returned to their country of origin: 170,000 returned to Mauritania.

[22] In July 1991, the Mauritanians approved a referendum that recognized a multiparty system and established a democratic government. The opposition, concentrated in the United Democratic Front (FDU) exerted pressure on the Government to achieve this objective, but by early 1991 the only response from the Government had been increased repression. In spite of the constitutional reform, social tensions caused by the crisis did not decrease. A period of great social conflict ensued, and the majority of the population went on strike.

[23] Six months later, in January 1992, President Maawiya Ould Sid Ahmed Taya was re-elected, in the first multiparty elections to be held. The opposition and numerous international observers suspected a fraud. Taya defeated his main rival, Ahmed Ould Daddah, winning 63 per cent of the vote to Daddah's 33. In March, after two rounds of voting in the legislative election, the DSRP (the official party) achieved an absolute majority in the National Assembly, winning 67 of the 79 disputed seats.

[24] Six opposition groups boycotted the voting and denounced there had been a fraud in the elections. In April, Mauritania re-established diplomatic relations with Senegal and Mali. This allowed to resume negotiations on pending border disputes and to find a possible solution for the situation of Mauritanian refugees in both neighboring countries.

[25] Foreign aid granted by China and France gave new impetus to Taya's discredited government, accused of electoral fraud and of being responsible for the country's difficult social conditions. The application of an IMF-sponsored adjustment plan further aggravated mounting tensions, peaking in October when the prices of basic consumer goods were increased.

[26] Demonstrations were widespread and harshly quelled by the police. In early 1993, Interior minister Ba Aliu Ibra Hasni Uld Dudi was forced to resign and was replaced by a 'moderate'. In January 1994, the ruling party won the local elections, also considered a fraud by opposition members. In May, the Government tried to prevent *Le Calame* newspaper from appearing since it included a report on Mauritania by the Amnesty International, a human rights international association.

PROFILE

ENVIRONMENT

Two thirds of the country is occupied by the Sahara Desert. The terrain consists of rocky, dry plateaus and vast expanses of dunes where extremely dry climate prevails. The desert region reaches into the southern part of the country, the Sahel grasslands, with some rainfall and sparse vegetation. The southwestern region receives slightly more rain and is irrigated by a tributary of the Senegal river. This region holds most of the population and the main economic activities. Nomadic shepherds are scattered throughout the country. Desertification is a serious problem for Mauritania.

SOCIETY

Peoples: Three-fourths of all Mauritanians are descendants of the Moors; a mixture of Arab, Berber and African peoples, nomadic shepherds of north-west Africa. The other 25 per cent are from African groups in the south, the most important being the Peul and the Soninke. There are small groups of Wolof and Bambara.
Religions: Muslim 99.5 per cent (official and predominant), Catholics 0.2 per cent.
Languages: Arabic and French (official). The Moors speak Bassanya, an Arab dialect. In southern Mauritania, Peul-Fulani and Sarakole (of the Soninke) are also spoken.
Political Parties: Democratic and Social Republican Party; Union of Democratic Forces-New Era (UDF-EN); Union for Democracy and Progress (UDP); Movement of Independent Democrats.
Social Organizations: Workers' Union of Mauritania.

THE STATE

Official Name: al-Jumhuriyah al-Islamiyah al-Muritaniyah
Administrative divisions: 12 regions and the district of Nouakchott.
Capital: Nouakchott 800,000 people (1996).
Other cities: Nouadhibou 72,305; Kaédi 35,241; Kiffa 29,300; Rosso 27,783 (1992).
Government: Maawiya Ould Sid'Ahmed Taya, President since 1984, re-elected in December 1997. El Afia Ould Mohamed Khouna, Prime Minister since November 1998.
National Holiday: November 28, Independence Day (1960).
Armed Forces: 15,600.
Other: 6,000 (National Guard and Gendarmes).

27 Sixty Islamic leaders were arrested in October, on charges of creating an atmosphere of fear. Afterward, the Government ordered all 'fundamentalist' militants to cease political activity.

28 In January 1995, thousands of demonstrators rocked Nouakchott, setting cars on fire and looting shops after a new valued added tax caused a rise in prices. In June, Mauritania's creditors accepted a re-negotiation of the public debt which was then partially cancelled.

29 In January 1996, President Taya appointed fisheries minister El Afia Ould Mohamed Khouna as Prime Minister. Most of the opposition boycotted the April elections for a new Senate. The Democratic and Social Republican Party (PRSD), won the majority of the disputed seats in the Senate and, in the October legislative elections, took 71 of the 79 seats in the National Assembly.

30 In June 1996, an agreement with the European Union gave Mauritania access to set figure credits for five years, in return for permission to fish its national waters, considered the richest in the world. International bodies said the nation's macroeconomic performance improved. However, it continued to rank amongst the poorest nations of the world in its social indicators.

31 In December 1997, President Taya was re-elected with nearly 90 per cent of the vote, with Mohamed Lemine Ould Guig as Prime Minister.

32 In April 1998, Human Rights organizations appealed for an end to slavery in Mauritania. Three human rights activists were imprisoned for denouncing cases of slavery.

33 In October, Taya called for Guig's resignation, as he had turned out to be extremely unpopular with Mauritanians, and appointed Sheikh Mohamed Khouna the new prime Minister, and he partially reshuffled the cabinet.

34 The Paris Club agreed to reduce Mauritania's debt by $620 million. The Club justified its decision by stating the country was making great efforts to reform its economy. ∎

Fishing: end of the line?

Four of the 15 main fishing regions of the world have already been decimated, and nine are well on the way to becoming exhausted. The Food and Agriculture Organization (FAO) warns that this crisis is a direct consequence of the over-exploitation of marine resources at the hands of the fishing industry

2 Marine fishing has shot up in the last 50 years. In 1952, 18.5 million tons of fish were extracted, but by the late 1980s this figure had risen to 89 million tons.

3 The commercialization of sea products which has led to this over-exploitation, is threatening to do away with certain species, like Canadian cod, forever. Marine diversity is threatened by this relentless race to satisfy increasing world demand. In the United States alone, according to official figures, 80 per cent of the marine population (of more than 100 species) is in danger of extinction.

4 Millions of people whose way of life depends on fishing (both commercialized and subsistence) are today up against the exhaustion of these resources and extremely unequal competition with an industry supplied by the great fishing fleets.

Commercial competition made the fishing industries increase the volume of catches using equipment so indiscriminate that it kills many species which are not even eaten. Furthermore, enormous drag nets damage the sea bed, destroying marine habitats and coral reefs.

5 The FAO has forecast that if this situation continues, marine resources will soon be insufficient to meet human needs. This threat is especially worrying for the millions of people living along the rivers of the Third World, for whom fish is the main source of protein. ∎

Mauritius

Mauritius

Population: 1,149,000 (1999)
Area: 2,040 SQ KM
Capital: Port Louis
Currency: Rupee
Language: English

According to Portuguese accounts, the island of Mauritius was deserted when they first explored it in the 16th century. The island was immediately coveted by the imperial powers, who fought over it ceaselessly by both diplomatic and military means. Between 1598 and 1710, the Dutch, attracted by the island's ebony, installed themselves and named it Mauritius. In 1715, it was recolonized by the French Bourbons, who renamed it Ile de France. When rivalry between France and Britain recurred over the control of India, the island of Mauritius constituted an important strategic base. The island was used in trade with India, and treaties were signed with Madagascar and Mozambique to use their coasts to expand sugar cane plantations.

[2] During the French Revolution, Mauritius acquired a certain degree of autonomy but in 1810, it fell into British hands. In 1815, after Napoleon's defeat, the Treaty of Paris recognized the status of the island as a British colony. The British introduced sugarcane which became the island's main economic resource right up until the present.

[3] In the 19th century, sugar plantations expanded considerably, but in 1835 the emancipation of slaves, who constituted 70 per cent of the population, caused a serious labor shortage. Emancipation was opposed by the European landowners, who tried to alleviate the situation by importing over 450,000 Indian indentured 'hired' workers over the next 100 years. With the passage of time, the Indians became an increasingly important sector of the Mauritius social and economic structure, and today their descendants constitute the majority of the Mauritius population. Local culture however still bears the mark of French influence.

[4] In 1936, the Labor Party was organized but a series of strikes were brutally repressed, causing the death, imprisonment or exile of most party leaders. Seewooagur Ramgoolam, a doctor, started his political career as the leader of the Advance group. In the late 1940s, encouraged by the colonial administration, he became leader of the Labor Party of Mauritius (PLM).

[5] During World War II, the British were unable to guarantee the security of their colonial dominions, which encouraged the emergence of claims for independence. At the same time, US political and military influence increased. The inhabitants of Mauritius fought for and achieved representation within British colonial government. In 1957, a new government structure was created, giving Mauritius its own Prime Minister. In 1959, the first elections with universal suffrage brought the PLM to power, making Seewooagur Ramgoolam Prime Minister in 1961.

[6] From Mauritius, the British administration ran the islands of Rodrigues, Cargados-Carajos and the Chagos archipelago. In 1965, with the approval of Ramgoolam, Chagos and other islands became the British Indian Ocean Territories, and the United States established a major naval base on one of its islands, Diego García.

[7] Diego García's population was secretly transferred to Mauritius, a move that caused a scandal in Congress when it was later made public. However, the island was not returned to Mauritius and its inhabitants were not granted permission to return home.

[8] Mauritius became independent in 1968, after a long decolonization process. Britain expected it to end with the granting of a very limited autonomy for the island, allowing it merely to run its domestic affairs. The 1958 Constitution, still in force, was created by the Colonial Office following the usual model used in the Commonwealth. Mauritius was a monarchy, ruled by Elizabeth II, and the sovereign was represented by a Governor-General and a High Commissioner. In 1964, the Council of Ministers and the Legislative Assembly were created. The latter appointed the Prime Minister (head of government) and the rest of the ministerial cabinet.

[9] On independence, in 1968, there was an established two-party system in the country. The Labor Party, supported by the Indian population, was the majority party. That year, the French-Mauritians and Creoles gathered in the Social Democratic Party of Mauritius (PSDM), and Muslim groups founded the Muslim Action Committee. During the 1960s, the common struggle for independence drew the Indian Labor groups and Muslims together, and in 1967 they formed an alliance which took them to power. Sir Seegwooagur Ramgoolam was re-elected Prime Minister, and Gaetan Duval, the leader of the PSDM, led the group which opposed independence. In 1969, a coalition government was formed with the Labor Party and the PSDM. Duval, the representative of the French elite and the main opponent to independence, became foreign minister, showing that the British-granted independence was a mere formality.

[10] Internally, the Government was tainted by electoral fraud and trade union repression, and in foreign affairs, it established close links with Israel and South Africa. Pretoria had a free zone in Port Louis which enabled it to trade with the EEC, thus evading international sanctions.

[11] In the 1970s a new opposition group emerged, called the Militant Mauritius Movement (MMM). It denounced the alliance between the Labor Party and the former French settlers. The growth of the MMM and the

---

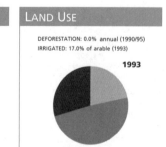

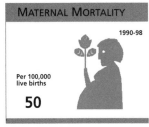

MATERNAL MORTALITY

1990-98

Per 100,000 live births

50

LITERACY

1995

82%

FOOD DEPENDENCY

1997

15%

general deterioration of the political environment led to the legislative elections scheduled for 1972, being postponed until 1976. The MMM was the best supported party in the 1976 elections, but the Labor party succeeded in forming weak alliances with certain minority groups, managing to stay in power. The workers' demonstrations and the social unrest caused by unemployment increased, reaching their peak in 1979.

[12]   In the 1982 elections the MMM allied with the Socialist Party of Mauritius (PSM) and won with a landslide majority. This gave them 62 of the 66 seats and full control of the

Government. Aneerood Jugnauth became Prime Minister. The program of the MMM-PSM alliance promised to increase job opportunities and salaries, nationalize key sectors in the economy, reduce economic links with South Africa, and demand the return of Diego Garcia from the US.

[13]   The increase in the price of oil, coupled with the drop in the world price of sugar, caused a deficit in the balance of payments equal to 12 percent of the gross domestic product. The Government was forced to turn to the IMF which approved five stand-by loans between 1979 and 1985.

[14]   To receive these loans, the

Government had to agree to conditions imposed by the IMF: to adopt austerity measures, to postpone part of the planned salary increase and job creation programs, to relinquish part of its control over public expenditure, to cut subsidies on basic foods and to devalue the Mauritian rupee.

[15]   All these measures led to clashes between the MMM and the socialists, a situation which eventually led to a call for early elections, in August of that year. The MMM was defeated and a new coalition was formed including labor, socialists and Duval's social-democrats. However, this apparent political stability was very weak and was followed by a series of governmental alliances which did not consolidate the coalition's position. Majority parties underwent serious divisions, giving rise to new political groups such as the Mauritius Socialist Movement (MSM), a splinter of the PSM, led by Aneerood Jugnauth.

[16]   The main economic potential lay in manufacture, in particular in textiles. The industrial free zones employ 90,000 people, around 10 per cent of the population, and the per capita income of the population in Mauritius is three or four times higher than the average for other African countries, though inflation is increasing at an annual rate of 16 per cent. The lack of skilled labor on Mauritius could bring a new migratory wave from Madagascar, India, and Kenya.

[17]   In 1988, in agreement with the Organization of African Unity (OAU), Mauritius demanded the devolution of the island of Tromelin, administered by France, and of the Chagos archipelago, along with the demilitarization of the Indian Ocean, which is used for manoeuvres by the superpowers. The claims were supported by environmentalist groups, because of the proliferation of nuclear weapons in the claimed territories.

[18]   In the legislative elections of December, 1987, the coalition of MSM, PSDM and Labor won a very narrow victory, giving it a majority in parliament. Aneerood Jugnauth was re-elected Prime

PROFILE

ENVIRONMENT

This island, located in the Indian Ocean, 800 km east of Madagascar, is 53 km wide and 72 km long. Mauritius also controls several dependencies: Rodrigues Island, 104 sq km with 23,000 inhabitants who farm and fish; Agalega, 69 sq km with 400 inhabitants, producing copra; and Saint Brandon, 22 small islands inhabited by people who fish and collect guano. The islands are of volcanic origin, surrounded by coral reefs. The terrain climbs from a coastal lowland to a central plain enclosed by mountains. Heavy rainfall contributes to the fertility of the red tropical soils. Sugar cane is the main crop. The degradation of the soil, due to monoculture and use of pesticides, and water pollution are the most serious environmental problems.

SOCIETY

Peoples: Indo-Pakistani 68.0 per cent; Creole (mixed Caucasian, Indo-Pakistani, and African) 27.0 per cent; Chinese 3.0 per cent; Illois.
Religions: 50.6 per cent Hindu; 27.2 per cent Christian (mostly Catholic, with an Anglican minority); 16.3 per cent Muslim; 0.3 per cent Buddhist; 2 per cent other.
Languages: English (official) 29.1 per cent. Creole 21.6 per cent. Hindi 18.6 per cent. Bhojpuri (a Hindi dialect), Urdu, Hakka, French, Chinese, Tamil, Arabic, Marati, Telegu, and other languages are also spoken.
Political Parties: Democratic Social Party of Mauritius (PSDM). Mauritius Socialist Movement (MSM); Militant Mauritian Movement - Labor Party (MMM); Mauritian Militant Renaissance (RMM);
Social Organizations: General Workers' Federation (GWF); Mauritian Women's Committee.

THE STATE

Official Name: State of Mauritius.
Administrative divisions: 4 islands and 9 districts.
Capital: Port Louis 460,000 people (1995).
Other cities: Rose Hill 96,621 people; Curepipe 76,610 people; Quatre Bornes 73,500 (1994).
Government: Parliamentary republic. Cassam Uteem, President since 1992, re-elected in June 1997. Navin Ramgoolam, Prime Minister since December 1995. Legislature: single-chamber: National Assembly, with 72 members, elected every 5 years.
National Holiday: March 12, Independence Day (1968).
Armed Forces: non-existent.
Other: 1,300 elite forces.

Minister, and the MMM became the main opposition force.

19   In the legislative elections held in September 1991 the governing MSM succeeded in maintaining Jugnauth in the post of Prime Minister, by reinforcing the traditional alliance with the MMM. In March 1992, Mauritius changed from a constitutional monarchy to a republic, and in June Cassam Uteem became the first President of the country.

20   In August 1993, the Foreign Minister Paul Bérenger of the MMM withdrew from the cabinet, leaving Jugnauth without an absolute majority. In 1994, the island's economic results were still regarded as satisfactory by international agencies such as the World Bank. The foreign debt accounted for 25 per cent of the GDP and the per capita income was $2,740.

21   In January 1995, Jugnauth included representatives of the right-wing Social Democratic Party of Mauritius in his government. In the legislative elections of December, an opposition coalition (the Militant Mauritius Movement-Labor Party) led by Paul Bérenger and Nuvin Rangoolam took two thirds of the seats. Rangoolam became Prime Minister.

22   The social indicators in Mauritius improved in 1996. Life expectancy reached an average of 70 years and literacy reached 81.7 per cent. Most of the population had access to healthcare, and 99 per cent to clean drinking water and drainage.

23   In June 1997, the MMM left the governing coalition. Rangoolam took over the functions of foreign minister when Bérenger abandoned the post. A few days later, Parliament re-elected Cassam Uteem president.

25   The visit of Indian Prime Minister, Atal Behari Vajpayee, in March 2000, which coincided with the celebration of the thirtieth anniversary of the independence of Mauritius, allowed for the signing of several agreements between the two countries on the issues of trade, information technology and coastal patrols. ∎

Diego García

Population: 1,000 (1994)
Area: 52 SQ KM
Language: English

The settlement of Diego García began in 1776 when the French Viscount de Souillac sent a ship there from Mauritius, trying to establish a French presence before the English could get there. French entrepreneurs obtained permission to exploit all of the island's riches: coconuts (for coconut oil), giant tortoises, fish and birds. They also established a leper colony on the island. With the defeat of Napoleon in 1815, the island passed into the hands of the British Crown together with Mauritius' other dependencies. During the 19th century, many workers came from India and Africa.

2   Around 1900, there were approximately 500 inhabitants but the population increased radically over the next decades, with the arrival of Africans, Madagascans and Indians. Once they had settled, they developed a culture of their own. They spoke creole, a mixture of their local languages and they took part in the Tamul rituals (of Madagascan origin) even though they were mostly Roman Catholic. The indigenous Chagos community, the Ilois, lived in their traditional manner more or less unchanged until the 1960s.

3   In 1965, Britain decided to remove Diego García from Mauritius jurisdiction, annexing it to the BIOT (British Indian Ocean Territories). Although this change was condemned by the UN, the British and Mauritius governments made a deal where a large sum changed hands. Two years later, Britain ceded the island to the United States for 50 years in

exchange for a discount on its purchase of nuclear arms. To make way for the construction of important air and naval bases, the Ilois were deported to Mauritius in the early 1970s.

4   The 2,000 or so Ilois were abandoned as soon as they arrived in Mauritius, finding themselves in a situation of total indigence. They had not been allowed to keep their belongings and they suffered the effects of being uprooted. Many died of despair or hunger, and lacked the basic human right of having a nationality. The British Government does not recognize them as subjects, and the Mauritius Government does not consider them to be citizens. Ilois attempts to return to their land became increasingly numerous, as did their demands for a solution to their problems, and they began to receive the support of international opinion. The situation reached the US Senate in 1975, but both the US and British governments continued to ignore the problem, each blaming the other for the situation and both spending intermittent sums of money, which do nothing more than temporarily alleviate the severity of the problem. A report issued by the Mauritius Government in 1981 revealed that 77 per cent of the Ilois wished to return to their homeland.

5   The Government of Mauritius stopped shipping foodstuffs and supplies to Diego García, as way of emphasising its desire to recover the islands.

6   Between 1992 and 1993, the Government issued repeated claims to the Chagos archipelago, including Diego García, before the UN and the International Court of Justice.

In reprisal, Britain cut economic aid to the country.

7   In July 1997, just as the UK returned Hong Kong to Chinese control, Mauritius demanded that the British Prime Minister Tony Blair return Diego Garcia to Mauritius. ∎

PROFILE

ENVIRONMENT

The Chagos Archipelago is located some 1,600 km southwest of India, in the middle of the Indian Ocean. The main islands are Diego García (8 km long by 6 km wide), Chagos, Peros, Banhaus and Solomon. The islands are made up of coral formations and are flat; they have a large number of coconut trees, which grow well here because of the tropical climate and year-round rain.

SOCIETY

Peoples: All the inhabitants are American or British military personnel.
Social Organizations: Lalit, local movement which demands the de-militarization of all the archipelago's islands and the devolution of Diego Garcia to Mauritius.

THE STATE

Government: Rule is nominally exercised by an English commissioner from the Foreign Office in London.
Armed Forces: 25-strong Royal Navy detachment.

DEMOGRAPHY

Population: 1,000 (1994)

Mexico

México

Population: 97,366,000 (1999)
Area: 1,958,200 SQ KM
Capital: Mexico City
Currency: New Peso
Language: Spanish

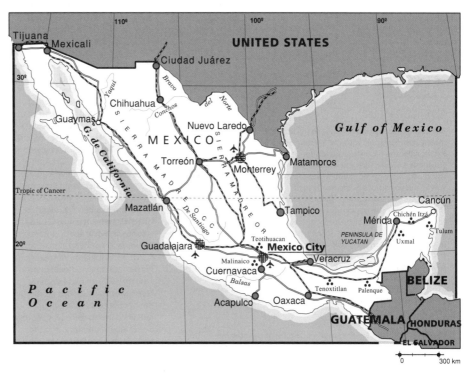

The 20,000-year history of the present Mexican territory includes only 2,000 years of urban life. Over this period, meso-American peoples developed advanced civilizations such as the Olmeca, Teotihuacan, Maya and Mexica. These cultures had complex political and social organizations, and they had advanced artistic, scientific, and technological skills.

2   When the Spaniards arrived, Moctezuma II, Emperor of the Aztecs, ruled over an empire the size of modern Italy, with the capital, Tenochtitlan, under the present Mexico City. The conquest was completed in 1521, when Spanish explorer Hernán Cortés took advantage of internal strife between the ruling Aztecs and other native peoples who paid them tribute. Cortés succeeded in imposing Spanish domination over the local armies and, from then on, the colonials initiated Christianization and Hispanization of the indigenous inhabitants.

3   In the 17th century, the major economic structures of the so-called 'New Spain' were laid down. The *hacienda*, a landed estate, emerged as the basic production unit, and mining became the basis of a colonial economy conceived to meet the gold and silver needs of the Spanish homeland. The American indian population was exploited and decimated by hard labor and disease. By 1800, Mexico had become one of the world's richest countries, but with great poverty also.

4   After almost three centuries of colonial domination, the struggle for independence began in 1810, led by *criollos* (Mexicans of Spanish descent) such as Miguel Hidalgo and José Maria Morelos, two priests. The struggle became a broad-based national movement as indians and mestizos (people of mixed European and indian descent) joined its ranks, but the rebels were soon crushed by the royal army. The liberal revolution in Spain radically changed the situation. Afraid to lose their privileges, the Spanish residents and the conservative clergy came to an agreement with the surviving revolutionaries. This pact became known as the Iguala Plan, trading independence for a guaranteed continuation of Spanish dominance. In 1821 General Iturbide proclaimed himself Emperor, but was rapidly replaced by General Antonio López de Santa Anna.

5   At the time, Mexico was the most extensive Spanish American country, covering 4.6 million square kilometers, including the Central American provinces, but it was also stricken by economic, political and social problems. In 1824, a Constitution was approved establishing a federal republic, made up of 19 states, four regions and a federal district. In 1836, Santa Anna, elected President three years previously, passed a new Constitution which did away with all vestiges of federalism and the Mexican state of Texas, which had been settled by some 30,000 US citizens, called on the United States for support and protection. Santa Anna led his army to victory against the Texans that year at the Alamo, but was defeated by US troops who took him prisoner later releasing him for a large ransom.

6   In 1845, the US annexed Texas, which led to a break in diplomatic relations with Mexico. It also caused a frontier conflict, since the United States claimed that the southern border of Texas was on the Rio Bravo, not the Rio Nueces (further north) as was commonly accepted. In 1846, the US president James Polk tried to force through a frontier agreement and buy the state of California - both moves rejected by Mexico. Polk ordered the US army to occupy the disputed lands between the two rivers, leading to a two-year war which was won by the United States. The victors annexed all Mexican territory north of the Rio Bravo, paying $15 million and taking responsibility for a further $3.5 million to cover US citizens' claims against the Mexican government. More than half of the Mexican territory was controlled by the US at the end of the war.

7   Between 1821 and 1850, Mexico had 50 different governments. As with many other Latin American states, the Mexican bourgeoisie supported two political

WORKERS

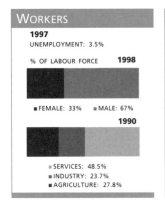

1997
UNEMPLOYMENT: 3.5%

% OF LABOUR FORCE   **1998**

▪ FEMALE: 33%   ▪ MALE: 67%
1990

▪ SERVICES: 48.5%
▪ INDUSTRY: 23.7%
▪ AGRICULTURE: 27.8%

LAND USE

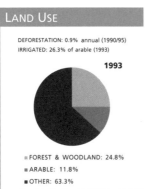

DEFORESTATION: 0.9% annual (1990/95)
IRRIGATED: 26.3% of arable (1993)

1993

▪ FOREST & WOODLAND: 24.8%
▪ ARABLE: 11.8%
▪ OTHER: 63.3%

PUBLIC EXPENDITURE

1997

80

60   50.1%

40

20
6.2%
0
DEFENCE   SOCIAL

MILITARY EXPENDITURE   **5%**
(% of health & education)   (1990/91)

parties: the liberals and the conservatives. A minor conflict between Mexico and France (known as the Pastry War) arose in 1838-39 from the claim of a French pastry cook living in Tacubaya, near Mexico City, that some Mexican army officers had damaged his restaurant. A number of foreign powers had pressed the Mexican government without success to pay for losses that some of their nationals claimed they had suffered during several years of civil disturbances. France decided to back up its demand for $600,000 by sending a fleet to Veracruz. After occupying the city, the French won a guarantee of payment (with Britain's help) and withdrew their fleet. The main result of this conflict was the further enhancement of the prestige and influence of political dictator Antonio López de Santa Anna, who lost a leg in the fighting.

[8] After the Liberals' victory of 1857 Benito Juárez tried to strengthen the republic, instituting a free market economy, prescribing individual rights and guarantees, and expropriating the wealth of the clergy. Juárez - a Zapotec indian educated as a middle-class liberal - and his party, sought to give a juridical base for their reforms by drafting a new constitution. The Constitution of 1857 prohibited slavery and restrictions on freedom of speech or the press. It abolished special courts and prohibited civil and ecclesiastical corporations from owning property, except buildings in use; it eliminated monopolies and prescribed that Mexico was to be a representative, democratic, republican nation. Neither the religious community nor the military accepted this constitution, and both inveighed against the reform, calling for retention of 'religion and *fueros*' (privileges). The church excommunicated all civil officials who swore to support the constitution; civil war erupted and foreign powers became involved in the Mexican struggle. On April 6 1859, the United States recognized the Juárez government, permitted war supplies to be shipped to the liberal forces and encouraged its citizens to serve the liberal cause as volunteers; while Spain, Britain and France favored the conservatives.

[9] President Juárez was successful in re-establishing national unity in January 1861. He was however faced with many serious problems: the opposition's forces still remained intact, the new Congress distrusted its president, and the treasury was virtually empty. As a solution to this latter problem Juárez decided in July 1861 to suspend payment on all foreign debts for two years. France, Britain and Spain invaded Mexico in January, 1862, landing with their troops in Veracruz. But when Britain and Spain realized that Napoleon III intended to conquer Mexico and control it through a puppet, Maximilian of Austria, they withdrew their troops. Despite a major defeat at Puebla on May 5 1862, reinforcements enabled the French to occupy Mexico City in June 1863, and Maximilian - crowned Emperor of Mexico - soon followed to take control of the government. Forced to leave the capital again, Juárez kept himself and his government alive by a long series of retreats that ended only at Ciudad Juárez, on the Mexican-US border. Early in 1867, as a result of continued Mexican resistance, increased US pressure and criticism at home, Napoleon decided to withdraw his troops. Soon afterward, Mexican forces captured Maximilian and executed him.

[10] In 1871, Juan de Wata Rivera started the newspaper *The Socialist*. On September 10, this newspaper published the general statutes of the 1st Marxist International for the first time in Latin America. General Porfirio Díaz, who fought with the Liberals against French intervention, became president in 1876 and remained so until 1911. During the 35 years of his dictatorship, the country opened its doors to foreign investment, the economy was modernized and social inequalities increased.

[11] In 1910, Francisco Madero led the Mexican Revolution under the slogan 'effective suffrage, no re-election'. This was the first popular Latin American revolution of the century. In 1913, US ambassador Henry Lane Wilson participated in a conspiracy, resulting in the assassination of Madero. The people responded by taking up arms more vigorously than before. Peasants joined the revolt, led by Emiliano Zapata and Francisco (Pancho) Villa. The principles of this Revolution were set out in the Constitution of 1917, promulgated by Venustiano Carranza. It was the most socially-advanced constitution of its time and many of the principles are still in force today. However, conflict between the various revolutionary factions continued, resulting in the deaths of the major leaders.

[12] In 1929, under President Plutarco Elias Calles, these factions joined to form the National Revolutionary Party. In 1934, General Lázaro Cárdenas took office. He embodied the continuation of the revolutionary process, and was one of the main driving forces behind its accomplishments. The major reforms included land reform, the nationalization of oil (the founding of PEMEX), the expropriation of oil refineries, incentives for new industries, and a national education system. The 'No re-election' principle became lastingly inscribed in the Mexican Constitution. When Cárdenas was asked to amend the constitution for his own re-election, he refused. The National Revolutionary Party became the Institutional Revolutionary Party (PRI) and the deeply-rooted revolutionary socialist principles were gradually abandoned.

[13] Conditions created by World War II accelerated the first phase of Mexico's industrialization which reached its peak during Miguel Aleman's term of office (1946-1952). The changes that took place during this period altered the former social balance. Mexico's population remained predominantly rural, with only 40 per cent in the cities, but the rapid development was not able to absorb the quickly growing population. Communal land ownership, which had stimulated solidarity and revolutionary feeling among peasants in the 19th century, was gradually replaced by a new type of individual land tenure causing the formation of large estates or *latifundios*.

[14] During the following decade, Cardenas' successors, though not always loyal to his principles,

MATERNAL MORTALITY

1990-98

Per 100,000
live births

48

LITERACY

1995

89%

EXTERNAL DEBT

1998

PER CAPITA

US$ 1,669

STATISTICS

DEMOGRAPHY

Population: 97,366,000 (1999)
Annual growth: 2.1 % (1975/97)
Estimates for year 2015 (million): 119.2 (1999)
Annual growth to year 2015: 1.3 % (1997/2015)
Urban population: 73.8 % (1997)
Urban Growth: 3.0 % (1980/95)
Children per woman: 2.7 (1998)

HEALTH

Life expectancy at birth: 72 years (1998)
male: 70 years (1998)
female: 75 years (1998)
Maternal mortality: 48 per 100,000 live births (1990-98)
Infant mortality: 28 per 1,000 (1998)
Under-5 child mortality: 34 per 1,000 (1998)
Daily calorie supply: 3,137 per capita (1996)
107 doctors per 100,000 people (1993)
Safe water: 85 % (1990/98)

EDUCATION

Literacy: 89 % (1995)
male: 92 % (1995)
female: 87 % (1995)
School enrolment:
Primary total: 115 % (1990/96)
male: 116 % (1990/97)
female: 113 % (1990/97)
Secondary:
male: 61 % (1990/96)
female: 61 % (1990/96)
Tertiary: 16 % (1996)
Primary school teachers: one for every 28 (1996)

COMMUNICATIONS

97 newspapers (1996), 325 radios (1997), 193 TV sets (1996) and 95 main telephone lines (1996) per 1,000 people

ECONOMY

Per capita, GNP: $ 3,840 (1998)
Annual growth, GNP: 4.7 % (1998)
Annual inflation: 19.5 % (1990/98)
Consumer price index: 187.9 (1998)
Currency: 9.1 new pesos = $ 1 (1998)
Cereal imports: 11,621,226 metric tons (1998)
Food import dependency: 6 % (1997)
Fertilizer use: 636 kg per ha (1997)
Exports: $ 122,956 million (1998)
Imports: $ 130,668 million (1998)
External debt: $ 159,959 million (1998); $ 1,669 per capita (1998)
Debt service: 20.8 % of exports (1998)
Development aid received: $ 108 million (1997); $ 1.3 per capita (1997)

ENERGY

Consumption: 1,501.0 Kgs of Oil equivalent per capita yearly (1997); -58.0 % imported (1997)

HDI (rank/value): 50/0.786 (1997)

---

stabilized the system by reinforcing those factors responsible for its success in a continent generally afflicted by underdevelopment and stagnation. Strong governmental influence, involving substantial public investment, kept the economy strong. A reasonable balance was maintained between heavy and light industry, tourism was encouraged and a stable government, seeming to satisfy the people's demands, was in power.

[15] Against the backdrop of the 1968 Mexico Olympics, the students' movement organized protests against the true social situation in the country. A student rally held on the Plaza de las Tres Culturas was dispersed by the army. The order to shoot to kill was given without warning, and hundreds of people died or were injured in the 'Tlatelolco Massacre'.

[16] During the presidency of José Lopez Portillo (1976-1982), important oil deposits were discovered. This bound Mexico, as the main oil supplier, more closely to the US.

[17] In 1982, Miguel de la Madrid assumed the presidency implementing an IMF economic adjustment plan. Cuts in subsidies and public spending, changes in the pattern of public investment, and a dual currency exchange rate caused public discontent and the PRI's first electoral defeat since its foundation.

[18] Under the pressure of foreign debt the trends of 1983 continued: growing inflation; losses in real wages; reductions of public spending; falls in production, and rising unemployment.

[19] In 1985, direct foreign investment increased by $1.5 billion, 66 per cent coming from US investors. However, export profits also increased, totaling $344 million in the first nine months. The $96 billion foreign debt continued to be the main problem, as it required an average annual servicing of $12 billion.

[20] The devastating earthquake of September 1986 which buried more than 20,000 people alive further aggravated an already critical situation. The reduction in the oil quota by the US made it necessary to generate alternative sources of income. One of these was tourism, and another was the *maquiladoras* - foreign companies on the border with the US which are exempt from taxes and from paying their workers social insurance, disposing of the products on the vast domestic market.

[21] The internal situation became more difficult for the PRI and it was accused of rigging the 1986 municipal elections. The formation of an independent Labor Union Negotiation Board posed a threat to the PRI's labor wing, which had traditionally formed a bloc within the Labor Congress, the largest coordinating board of labor federations.

[22] On July 6 1988, several parties gained a significant vote in the national elections, something which had not happened since 1910. Carlos Salinas de Gortari, the PRI candidate, won the ballot with - according to official figures - 50 per cent of the vote (the lowest percentage in party history). The Left emerged for the first time as a real alternative to the PRI. Cuauhtemoc Cárdenas, the son of President Cárdenas, led a coalition of groups operating as a single party, the FDN, representing the masses and opposing the Institutional Revolutionary Party. Cárdenas took second place in an election marked by accusations of fraud and irregularities, obtaining more votes than the conservative PAN (National Action Party. The abstention rate was 49.72 per cent.

[23] In 1989, the FDN split, and Cárdenas founded the Democratic Revolution Party, made up of former members of the PRI, communists and members of smaller organizations. In the meantime, the People's Socialist Party (PPS), the Authentic Party of the Mexican Revolution (PARM) and the Party of the Cardenista Front for National Reconstruction (PFCRN) continued as autonomous organizations which voted with the PRI in Congress.

[24] The PRI administration resolved to open up the country to foreign investment, and also announced a series of measures aimed at controlling inflation. Both these decisions were welcomed by the US Government. Mexico made overtures to the US to sign a free trade agreement, coinciding with Mexico's entry into GATT (now the World Trade Organization - WTO) and the legal authorization for foreign investment in Mexican enterprises to go above the previously stipulated 49 per cent. In May 1990, President Salinas de Gortari privatized the banking system, which had been nationalized eight years earlier.

[25] In the elections of August 18 1991, the PRI proclaimed itself the winner with 61.4 per cent of the vote, amid accusation of fraud. It gained control of the Chamber of Deputies, and power to carry out constitutional reforms.

[26] The President presented an agrarian reform bill on November 8 1991. Approved in December, it granted property rights to *campesinos* (peasants) who farm state lands known as *ejidos* (co-operative farms ceded by the Zapata Revolution in 1917). According to the PRI, the new system was designed to reduce the on an annual 10 million tons of imported food. According to the opposition, the reform - which allowed campesinos to sell their lands - would bring about a transfer of small landholdings to larger investors.

[27] On December 17 1992, the Mexican, US and Canadian governments signed the North American Free Trade Association (NAFTA) Treaty.

[28] During the Salinas administration, inflation was reduced from three figures to a rate of 9 per cent in 1993. Between the end of 1988 and mid-1993, the State received some $21 billion from the privatization of state interests. Private foreign debt increased by $11 billion in 1993, to an accumulated total of $34.265 billion.

[29] In the first quarter of 1994 - as the NAFTA treaty went into effect - trade with the US increased at an unprecedented rate. Mexican sales increased by 22.5 per cent, while US exports to Mexico were up 15.7 per cent on the preceding quarter.

[30] The high interest rates stifled the small and middle-sized businesses. Unemployment and under-employment affected 5 and 12 million people respectively, mostly indigenous people working as street vendors and domestic servants.

[31] On January 1 1994, the previously unknown Zapatista National Liberation Army (EZLN) took three towns in the southern state of Chiapas, declaring them a freed zone. Chiapas was the region where the paramilitary guards contracted by the landowners to

---

expel the indigenous people from their land acted with most impunity. It is one of the states with the largest Maya population, mostly from the Tzotzil group. It also has the highest level of Spanish language illiteracy and the lowest incomes. However, it also has large oil and gas reserves - 21 per cent of the nation's crude oil is extracted in Chiapas.

[32] The Government initially refused to accept the importance of the uprising which spread rapidly, increasing the size of the area under its control, with the rural public and workers of other areas taking up the cause. As a result, a fifth of the army was deployed to the region. When the number of dead rose above a thousand and the complaints of summary executions continued, the Government - at the insistence of Catholic Bishop Samuel Ruíz - agreed to negotiate.

[33] In February, a cease-fire was agreed and negotiations began in San Cristobal de las Casas - the city in the center of the Zapatista area - with the rebels demanding electoral reforms, the creation of new municipal areas, ethnic representation in Congress and the government of Chiapas, schooling in the native languages, health and education infrastructure, along with modifications to the Penal Code and land ownership. The Government accepted half the Zapatista claims, but after consulting with the indigenous communities, the rebels rejected the agreement.

[34] The PRI presidential candidate Luis Donaldo Colosio was murdered on March 23 in Tijuana. Three members of his bodyguard were involved. The PRI nominated Ernesto Zedillo as his replacement for the August 21 elections, and Zedillo was voted in by 49 per cent of the electorate. Both the PRD and the EZLN accused the Government of electoral fraud.

[35] In September, PRI secretary-general Jose Ruiz Massieu was assassinated, and in November his brother Mario resigned from his post as Attorney-General as he believed Party officials were blocking the criminal investigation. His brother's death increased suspicions that leading PRI figures, and perhaps the drug mafia, were also involved in the murders.

[36] The economy continued to grow until, on December 20, the new government abandoned the policy of gradually depreciating the currency because of the acceleration of capital flight. By the end of the year, the peso had lost 42 per cent of its value. Its fall caused the stock market to collapse in an event which came to be known as 'The Tequila effect'.

[37] The Zedillo Government took until March 1995 to put an austerity plan into action, gaining the support of the United States and the IMF, but provoking a deep recession.

[38] During the course of the year, millions of Mexicans joined spontaneous protest movements, like 'El Barzon'. Many of these protests, by the middle classes and the small business sector, were prompted by the increase in debts caused by the devaluation. In August, President Zedillo approved a relief plan which benefited 7.5 million debtors.

[39] In January, Zedillo attempted to achieve a quick, peaceful solution to the situation in Chiapas. Following the failure of his initiative, in February, he launched a military offensive. The investigations of the Colosio and Ruiz Massieu murders had still got nowhere.

[40] Raul Salinas de Gortari, brother of the former president, was arrested in February accused of masterminding the Ruiz Massieu killing. At the same time, the Government called for the extradition of Mario Ruiz Massieu from the United States, on charges of hampering the investigation into his brother's death. Raul Salinas' wife was arrested in Switzerland in November when using false documents to carry out a banking transaction. Mrs Salinas was attempting to transfer funds - presumably from the laundering of drug money - from her husband's account. The former president Carlos Salinas said he was astounded by his brother's illegal wealth.

[41] The PRI and the two leading opposition parties agreed an electoral reform in December, which included establishing an independent control commission and limiting campaign expenditure.

[42] In September 1996, the peace negotiations came to a halt after 16 months when the Zapatistas accused the Government of being arrogant and racist, and insensitive to their claims. Meanwhile, the interior minister declared there was no reason for suspending the talks.

[43] Cuahutémoc Cárdenas was elected the new mayor of Mexico City in July 1997, while in the same elections the Democratic Revolution Party (PRD) became the opposition party with most seats in the chamber of deputies, outdoing the National Action Party (PAN). These two parties, along with the Greens and the Workers Party, announced the creation of an opposition alliance against the PRI, from September 1.

[44] On December 22, in Acteal, Chiapas, 45 Tzotzil indigenous people of the 'Las Abejas' (the bees) pacifist group were massacred by paramilitaries with the compliance of the public security forces. Acting governor of the state, Julio Ruiz Ferro, and his secretary, Emilio Chuayffet were forced to resign.

[45] Even though investigators claimed that Mexico had overtaken Colombia as the main headquarters of the drug cartels, the US certified the nation - meaning it was still able to receive US loans and facilities.

[46] On April 11 1998, on the orders of the new governor of Chiapas, Roberto Albores (appointed by Zedillo following Ruiz Ferro's resignation), hundreds of police officers and soldiers burst into the community of Taniperlas. This had been established the day before as capital of the Ricardo Flores Magón independent municipality to celebrate the 79th anniversary of the death of Zapata. Although the San Andrés agreements were not yet legally applicable, the National Indigenous Congress called for the creation of new municipalities throughout the republic.

[47] Twelve foreigners found operating as observers in Taniperlas were deported under article 33 of the Constitution, accused of encouraging the creation of parallel authorities, and therefore interfering in Mexican politics. This action earned Mexico criticism in both diplomatic circles and from national and international civil society.

[48] The number of deaths of people trying to cross the frontier with the United States increased four times in 1998 compared with the previous year. The crudeness of US anti-immigration forces and increased vigilance in places where illegal immigrants tended to cross forced people to attempt much more dangerous routes. Despite the obstacles, low pay and the lack of work in Mexico make the effort worthwhile, and the number of illegals arriving in California, continued to rise.

[49] In August 1999, Cuauhtémoc Cárdenas's PDR and the right-wing PAN led by Vicente Fox decided to form an alliance to confront PRI dominance, presenting a single candidate for the June 2000 elections.

[50] However, the coalition failed in December after the PAN rejected the proposal of a group of 'notables' on how to elect a common candidate for the coalition. The Right had opposed 25 observations made in a proposal formulated by 14 independent personalities who suggested primary elections and four surveys in order to designate a candidate for the eight opposition parties. A survey published in La Reforma, the week the agreement failed stated that 63 per cent of Mexicans wanted the opposition alliance to challenge the PRI and that 60 per cent of those favored Fox as presidential candidate. Only 19 per cent supported Cárdenas.

[51] In February 2000, acting on instructions from a federal judge, the police stormed UNAM (The Independent University of Mexico, the biggest in Latin America) arresting hundreds of students who had organized a strike and occupied the campus for nine months. The strike began in response to the university proposal to charge fees on courses which had been free. In recent years, UNAM had tried to raise standards by restricting admission and it also reduced the number of years a student could take to complete their course.

[52] The electoral reforms cleared the way for the first really fair elections in the country's history. The PAN finally joined forces with the Green Party and in a landmark election, Fox was elected President in July, ending more than 70 years of PRI power. The partnership also gained control of both chambers. Fox said his government would be open to honest members from all parties, but also warned that corruption would 'no longer be tolerated in Mexico'. ■

Micronesia

Micronesia

Population: 106,000 (1999)
Area: 702 SQ KM
Capital: Palikir
Currency: US dollar
Language: Kosrean, Yapese, Pohnpeian and Trukese

The name Micronesia is derived from the Greek meaning small islands. It refers to the Marshall Islands, the Marianas (including Guam) and the Caroline Islands.

2 In 1531, Ferdinand Magellan named them the Islands of Thieves, but they were later renamed after Queen Mariana of Austria, Spanish regent.

3 In 1885, the Germans tried to impose a protectorate on the islands, but the Spaniards appealed to the Vatican and managed to keep the islands. Guam was annexed to the United States by the Treaty of Paris of December 12 1898, and the rest of the Marianas were sold to Germany.

4 In 1914 Micronesia was occupied by the Japanese who were negotiating the demilitarization of the region with the US. The accord was broken in 1935, and the Japanese launched the attack on Pearl Harbor from Micronesia on December 7 1941, bringing World War II to the Pacific.

5 In 1947, when the fate of the Japanese and German possessions was decided, an agreement between the United Nations Security Council and the US Government assigned the

islands to Washington as a trust territory. Though located 13,000 km from the coast of the United States, they came under Washington's control.

6 A UN mandate obliged the US to develop national consciousness and promote an economy enabling the native population to exercise their right to self determination.

7 This 'Free Associated State' system allowed Washington to keep military bases in such countries, while handling their defense and foreign affairs. In 1975, the Northern Marianas voted for Free Associated State status, and in February 1978, the islands became part of the

United States under a trusteeship agreement.

8 In 1978, another plebiscite led to the creation of the Federated States of Micronesia. Four districts supported the motion, but Palau and the Marshall Islands decided to continue as autonomous states.

9 Before World War II the major Micronesian economic activities were fishing and coconut plantations. After the War, the population increase made this economic base insufficient.

10 Bikini and Eniwetok atolls, where the first hydrogen bomb was tested in 1954, were used as sites for nuclear experiments and the people displaced from these islands have not been able to return. In 1968 the Bikini atoll and 34 neighboring islands were declared suitable for human habitation, but tests carried out in 1977 revealed that water, fruit, and vegetables were still too radioactive for consumption.

11 Several countries dump radioactive waste in the Pacific, turning the ocean into a lethal sewer for industries and nuclear power stations. This situation has drawn strong protests from the local population, who have already had to suffer the consequences of nuclear waste, and displacement from atolls used for US navy and air force target practice.

12 In October 1982, the US signed a Free Association agreement with the Marshall Islands and the Federated States of Micronesia. This meant that all the islands, including the Northern Marianas would manage their own internal affairs, while the US would be responsible for defense and security. In 1983 the agreement was approved in plebiscites, and in October 1986 President Reagan issued a proclamation, formally putting an end to the US administration of Micronesia. However, the US still controls Micronesian foreign affairs.

13 On September 17 1990, the 46th UN General Assembly approved the admission of Micronesia and another six countries, increasing the number of member states from 159 to 166.

14 In the March 1991 legislative elections, President John Haglelgam was defeated, and in May, Bailey Olter was elected President. In June 1993 Micronesia joined the IMF which according to Olter was part of a scheme to solve the country's problems.

15 The President called a national conference in 1994 to analyze the long-term possibilities of the Micronesian economy. One of the issues on was the country's dependence on the US, whose aid equaled about two thirds of the GDP. Participants also referred to problems dealing with fishing, tourism and the country's small industrial sector.

16 In March 1995 Olter won the presidential elections. He began his second term taking no heed of the pressures to establish a rotating system to allow representatives from different regions to become president.

17 In late 1995, some 500 delegates of the Federated States of Micronesia met to discuss economic relations with the US, with a view to the creation of a free association agreement in 2001. The summit proposed fiscal measures, the promotion of the private sector and greater fiscal discipline.

18 In December 1996, a typhoon caused extensive damage to homes and state dependencies, and also ruined the harvests. US President Bill Clinton declared a state of emergency in the region and sent aid.

19 In November, President Olter was replaced by Jacob Nena who was sworn in as President in May 1997. In the March 1997 elections, the ten members of Congress who had finished their terms were all re-elected.

20 The economic difficulties continued all year. The Government tried to produce incentives to encourage 20 per cent of civil servants to retire.

21 Leo A Falcam, who had been Vice-President to Nena, was appointed President in May 1999. In September, Falcam issued an official communiqué repeating and confirming the strong opposition of Micronesia to countries like Britain, France and Japan transporting Plutonium through the region, especially in waters under its jurisdiction. Similarly, he criticized the 'barefaced' contempt of these countries for international maritime law. ∎

PROFILE

ENVIRONMENT

Covers an area of 2,500 sq km, more than half of which is taken up by the island of Pohnpei (called Ponape until 1984). The terrain is mountainous, with tropical climate and heavy rainfall. The Federation is made up of four states, including the Caroline islands, except Palau: Yap,119 sq km; Chuuk, (called Truk before 1990), 127 sq km; Pohnpei, 345 sq km; and Kosrae, 100 sq km.

SOCIETY

Peoples: Trukese 41.1 per cent; Pohnpeian 25.9 per cent; Mortlockese 8.3 per cent; Kosraean 7.4 per cent; Yapese 6.0 per cent; Ulithian, or Woleaian, 4.0 per cent; Pingelapese, or Mokilese, 1.2 per cent; Western Trukese 1.0 per cent; Palauan 0.4 per cent; Filipino 0.2 per cent. **Religions:** Christianity is the predominant religious tradition, with the Kosraeans, Pohnpeians, and Trukese being mostly Protestant and theYapese mostly Roman Catholic. **Languages:** Kosraean, Yapese, Pohnpeian and Trukese. English is a common language.

THE STATE

Official Name: Federated States of Micronesia. **Administrative Divisions:** 4 States. **Capital:** Palikir, on the island of Pohnpei, 5,000 people in 1983. **Other cities:** Weno (Moen) 15,253 people; Tol 6,705; Kolonia 6,169 (1989). **Government:** Leo A Falcam, President since May 1999. Legislature, single-chamber: Congress, with 14 members (10 on 2-year terms, 4 on 4-year terms).

STATISTICS

Demography: Population: 106,000 (1999). Children per woman: 4.0 (1998). **Health:** Life expectancy at birth: 67 years (1998). Infant mortality: 20 per 1,000 (1998). Under-5 child mortality: 24 per 1,000 (1998). Safe water: 22 % (1990/98). **Eucation:** Literacy: 81 % (1995). Female: 79 % (1995). School enrolment: Primary total: 100 % (1990/96). **Comunications:** 73 radios (1996) per 1,000 people. **Economy:** Per capita, GNP: $ 1,800 (1998). Annual growth, GNP: -3.1 % (1998). Cereal imports: 13,973 metric tons (1998).

Moldova

Moldova

Population: 4,379,000 (1999)
Area: 33,700 SQ KM
Capital: Chisinau (Kishinev)
Currency: Moldovan lei
Language: Moldovan

Moldovans are descended from the peoples of the southern part of Eastern Europe who had been subdued, and culturally influenced, by the Roman Empire. The Vlachs were mentioned by Byzantine chronicler, John Skilitsa (976 AD) as the forebears of the Moldovan people. In the mid-14th century, Vlach tribes from the northeast formed their own state, independent of the Hungarian Kingdom, in the territory of South Bukovina. The first *gospodar* (governor) of the Moldovan Principality was Bogdan (1356-1374), although according to legend, it was Dragos who founded the principality.

2   During the second half of the 14th century, the Moldovans freed themselves from Hungarian domination, and from the Tatar khans. By the early 15th century, Moldova's borders were the Dnestr River (to the west), the Black Sea and the Danube (to the south) and the Carpathian mountains (to the west).

3   This small principality found itself subject to the influence and interest of the larger states: Hungary, Poland, the Grand Principality of Lithuania, Turkey and the Crimean Khanate. The principality was alternately a vassal of Hungary, Poland and the Ottoman Empire. The Christian Orthodox Church was the official church, and the language - known as Ecclesiastical Slav - was used for church liturgy, for official documents and education. The first capitals were Baya, Stret and Suchava. Main economic activities included livestock and agriculture, especially wheat and vineyards.

4   The Moldovan Principality achieved its greatest political and economic success under the gospodars Alexander the Good (1400-1432) and Stephen the Great (1457-1504). During this period, Moldova warred against Hungary, Poland and the Crimean Khanate, but its main threat came from the Turks. Turkish expansionism posed a constant danger, Moldova also had to pay tribute to the Porte (the Ottoman Government in Turkey). In 1475, the Turkish army invaded Moldova, suffering a resounding defeat at the Battle of Vaslui. Nevertheless, the Moldovans were no match for the Turks numerically, and in 1484 the Turks stripped Moldova of its territories. The Turks surrounded the fortresses at Kilia and Belgorod and gave them the Turkish name Akkerman; and the *raya* - enclaves ruled over by the Turks - were created.

5   In the early 16th century, Moldova lost its independence as a state, being forced to recognize the power of the Turkish sultan (although still maintaining considerable autonomy within the Ottoman Empire). Turkish domination over Bukovina lasted until 1775, when the latter was incorporated into the Austrian Empire. Bessarabia was under Turkish control until 1812, and the rest of the Moldovan Principality until 1878. Turkey seized one Moldovan territory after another; by the mid-18th century, Moldova had lost half of its lands between the Prut and the Dnestr rivers.

6   Anti-Turkish sentiment increased because of Moldova's territorial losses, by the increase in the tributes paid to the sultans, and invasions by Turkish and Tatar troops, who devastated Moldovan cities and towns. Gospodars Petra Rares (1527-38, 1541-46), Ioann Voda Liuti (1572-74) and Dmitri Kantemir (1710-11) all turned against Turkey. In 1711, Dmitri Liuti and his Moldovan army joined forces with Russian czar, Peter the Great. In its struggle against the Ottomans, Moldova was forced to ally itself with the large powers which had opposed Turkey, signing pacts with Hungary, Austria and Poland. From the end of the 18th century, Moldova began developing closer relations with Russia.

7   Under the Treaty of Jassy (1792), the Russians obtained the left bank of the Dnestr, south of the Yagolik River. During the second partition of Poland between Russia, Prussia and Austria in 1793, Russia obtained the other part of the left bank of the Dnestr. After the Russo-Turkish War of 1806-1812 and the Peace of Bucharest, Russia seized the territory between the Prut and the Dnestr rivers calling it all Bessarabia. The Muslim population was deported, thus putting an end to the Turkish invasions of Bessarabia. At first, this territory was an autonomous region within Russia, with Kishinev (Chisnau) as its capital. However, in 1873 it became a Russian province, subject to all the laws of the Russian Empire.

8   All the wars between Russia and Turkey in the 18th and 19th centuries included Moldova in some way. The Prut expedition undertaken by Peter the Great in 1711 was a failure for Russia and its ally, Moldova, but it demonstrated Moldova's intention of achieving independence by relying upon Russian aid. Distrusting the Moldovans, the Ottomans began putting Greek Phanariotes (from Phanar, a suburb of Istanbul), on the Moldovan throne. They continued to rule over Bessarabia (a region bounded by the Prut and Dniester rivers on the north and east, the Black Sea on the southeast, and the Chilia arm of the Danube River delta on the south). It is until the beginning of the 19th century, and over the rest of the Moldovan Principality until 1821. There were bloody Russo-Turkish wars on Moldovan soil (1735-39; 1768-74; 1787-91), with a considerable number of Moldovan volunteers fighting against the Turks in Russian ranks.

9   During the 19th century, the population of Bessarabia grew from 250,000 to 2,500,000 and by the end of the century, Moldovans made up half of the province's population. There were also a significant number of Ukrainians and Russians, as well as Bulgarians, Germans, Jews and Gagauz (Muslims). In 1812, Kishinev had 7,000 inhabitants; by 1897, it had 109,000. During the Russian-Turkish wars of 1828-29, 1877-78 and the Crimean War (1853-56), Bessarabia acted as a rearguard for the Russian army. Under the Treaty of Paris (1856), the part of Southern Bessarabia next to the Danube and the Black Sea was incorporated into the Moldovan Principality, which joined Walachia in 1859 to form the State of Romania. In 1878, the Treaty of Berlin returned this territory to Russia.

10   Moldovan schools began to be closed in the 1840s, and as of 1866 the Moldovan language was no longer taught. After the Russian Revolution of 1905, the teaching of Moldovan was once again authorized. On December 2, 1917, the People's Republic of Moldova was proclaimed. Romanian troops entered Bessarabia and ousted local Soviet authorities. Between December 1917 and January 1918, first the Soviets and then the Romanians gained control over Moldova. Toward the end of January, the independent Moldovan Republic was proclaimed.

11   In the 1920s and 1930s, the territory of modern Moldova was divided into two unequal parts. Bessarabia was part of the Romanian Kingdom, while the left bank of the Dnestr belonged to the USSR. On October 12 1924, the Autonomous Republic of Moldova was formed, in Ukraine. Its first

capital was Balta, and after 1929, Tiraspol. Moldova made certain gains in industrial and cultural development, while Bessarabia, as part of Romania, remained at a standstill.

[12] On June 28 1940 - with World War II already underway - the Soviet Government issued an ultimatum whereby Romania was forced to accept Soviet annexation of Bessarabia. On August 2, the Federated Republic of Moldova was founded as a part of the USSR, uniting the central part of Bessarabia and the Autonomous Republic of Moldova. The northern and southern parts of Bessarabia, and the eastern region of the Autonomous Republic of Moldova, remained within Ukraine. In June 1941, Nazi troops invaded the USSR. Romania made an alliance with Hitler and recovered all of Bessarabia, as far as the Dnestr and Odessa. Three years later, the Red Army took on a weakened Germany, recovering Bessarabia and northern Bucovina.

[13] Soviet leader Leonid Brezhnev's political career began in Moldova, where he was leader of the local Communist Party. He was later to become Secretary General of the Communist Party of the Soviet Union (CPSU) and President of the USSR, positions which he held simultaneously until 1983.

[14] After the liberalization process initiated by Soviet president, Mikhail Gorbachev, in 1985, political and ethnic problems began to emerge in Moldova. In 1988, the Democratic Movement in Support of Perestroika (restructuring) began demanding the return to the use of the Latin alphabet instead of the Cyrillic alphabet for writing the Moldovan language. Moldovan nationalists called for an end to the political and economic privileges which Russian residents enjoyed, stating that if they could not do without them, they should return to their native land. In July 1989, a violent confrontation was barely avoided between Moldovan nationalists and Russians, who made up 14.2 per cent of the population. In August, some 300,000 Moldovans carrying Romanian flags, demonstrated in Kishinev in favor of Moldovan independence.

[15] On November 10 1989, Parliament approved the Official Language Law, which established Moldovan as the country's official language for political, economic, social and cultural affairs, with Russian to be used only in the press and other means of communication. There was an outbreak of nationalist protests and a strike by some 80,000 Russian workers. In the meantime, separatist activity increased in the Dnestr region, where a large proportion of the population is Russian, and the Gagauz Muslim region.

[16] On August 27 1991, Moldova declared its independence from the USSR. A month later, Dnestr and Gagauz - opposing both Moldova's independence and the possibility of union with Romania - declared themselves independent republics.

[17] After the failed coup against Gorbachev in Moscow in August 1991, the Moldovan Government arrested the leaders of the local separatist movements. In December, the country's first presidential elections were held, with Mircea Snegur winning the election. On March 2 1992, Moldova was admitted to the UN as a new member. Given the continued fighting in Dnestr, President Snegur declared a state of emergency on March 16, and ordered the elimination of the opposition forces fighting in the region.

[18] In June 1992, fighting broke out between the pro-Russian Pridnestrovie government in the Dnestr river basin and the Moldovan army. Pridnestrovie managed to maintain its independence.

[19] In Moldova, the Government's refusal to use force to resolve the conflict marked an important change in policy. The political scene was divided in two camps, one pro-unification with Romania, and the other pro-sovereignty and independence.

[20] In the parliamentary elections, independent parties received widespread support and confirmed Andrei Sangheli as Prime Minister. In August, the new Constitution came into force, declaring the state independent and democratic. Two months later, an agreement was signed with Moscow to begin the withdrawal of Russian troops.

[21] In 1995, Chisinau intensified the privatizations of public enterprises and facilitated the entrance of foreign investment. President Snegur failed to gather much support for his policies and was defeated by Petru Lucinschi in the November-December 1996 elections.

[22] In 1999, with the aim of relieving the deep recession and the pressure of both internal and external debt, Lucinschi started a new stage of privatization. Moldtelecom, the telecommunications monopoly, was put up for sale along with the electricity sector, which was plagued with inefficiencies, insufficiencies and a catastrophic payment level, with tens of thousands of users unaccustomed to paying anything. One part of the country only had electricity for a couple of hours per day, while for the most part power supplies came via a Soviet-era network from the Ukraine, where the electricity was purchased. The tobacco and the wine industries, two objects of national pride, were also put up for sale.

[23] In November, Parliament passed a vote of no confidence in Ion Sturdza, the Prime Minister. After two of his candidates were rejected by Parliament, Lucinschi appointed Dumitru Barghis as the new Premier, and he was approved by the legislators. Barghis took over on December 16. ∎

PROFILE

ENVIRONMENT

Located south of Russia, Moldova is bounded in the west by Romania and the east by Ukraine. Moldova lies at the foot of the Carpathian mountains, and is made up of plateaus of relatively low altitude. The region is drained by the Dnestr and the Prut rivers. The soil is black and very fertile. Average temperature in summer is 19-22°C, and in winter, -3 to -5°C. The country's main economic activities are livestock raising and agriculture - especially vineyards, sugar beets, fruits and vegetables. 40 per cent of the underground waters are contaminated with bacteria and 45 per cent of watercourses and lakes are contaminated with chemicals.

SOCIETY

Peoples: Moldovans, 64 per cent; Russians, 14 per cent; Ukrainians, 13.8 per cent; Gagauz, 3.5 per cent; Bulgarians, 1.5 per cent.
Religions: Christian Orthodox.
Languages: Moldovan (official), Russian, Ukrainian, Gagauz.
Political Parties: Communist Party; Democratic Convention; Movement for a Democratic and Prosperous Moldova, Party of Democratic Forces.

THE STATE

Official Name: Republica Moldova.
Capital: Chisinau 850,000 people (est 1996).
Other cities: Tiraspol 186,000 people; Bel'cy 165,000.
Government: President, Petru Lucinschi, elected in December 1996. Prime Minister, Dumitru Barghis, since December 1999.
National Holiday: August 27 Independence Day.
Armed Forces: 11,900 (1996).
Other: Internal Troops (Ministry of Interior): 2,500.

Mongolia

Mongol Ard Uls

Population: 2,621,000 (1999)
Area: 1,566,500 SQ KM
Capital: Ulaanbaatar (Ulan Bator)
Currency: Tughrik
Language: Khalkha Mongolia

The Mongols constitute one of the principal ethnic groups of northern and eastern Asia, linked by cultural ties and a common language. Dialects vary from one part of the region to another, but few cannot be understood by a Mongolian.

[2] Direct lineage from a male ancestor gives the family or clan its name, though there was an earlier tradition of female lineages. Intermarriage between members of the same clan was forbidden so there was great need for establishing alliances between clans, who formed tribal groups.

[3] The Mongols were mostly nomadic, with the movement of livestock and campsites determined by pasturage needs throughout the year. Animals were owned individually, while the grazing lands were collective property.

[4] The most powerful clans tended to control the tribal groups' activities. The weakest families maintained their own authority and their ownership of the animals, but they were obliged to pay tribute to the dominant clan. They moved, camped, grazed their livestock and went to war under that clan's orders.

[5] Political and military organization was adapted to the needs of each clan or tribe. A person capable of handling a weapon could be a chief or a soldier, according to the needs of the moment. Capturing livestock, women or prisoners from other tribes was a common means of acquiring wealth.

[6] When a tribal group became very powerful, as with that of Genghis Khan in the 13th century, it organized itself in groups of 10, 100, 1,000 or 10,000 soldiers. The leaders of large units were assigned a territory where they could collect tribute and recruit warriors for the supreme leader.

[7] The Siung-nu, or Huns, were the earliest inhabitants of the Selenga valleys, joining Siberia to the heart of Asia, and they are thought to have been settled in this region by 400 BC.

[8] The Huns created a great empire in Mongolia when China was undergoing unification as an imperial state under the Ch'in and Han dynasties (221 BC-220 AD). The Hun Empire warred against China for centuries, until it disintegrated - perhaps due to internal conflicts - around the 4th century.

[9] Some of the southern tribes surrendered to China and settled in Chinese territory, where they were eventually absorbed by the Chinese, while others migrated westward. In the 5th century, Attila's Huns conquered almost all of Europe, reaching Gaul and the Italian peninsula.

[10] The major Hun chieftains set up general headquarters, surrounded by cultivated lands where they bred larger, stronger horses, capable of carrying a warrior in armor.

[11] This led to a differentiation between aristocrats and traditional tribal archers, who rode smaller horses. Agriculture also became more important to the economy. The Huns were subsequently displaced by the Turks, who established themselves throughout the region. The Uigurs, who came to occupy the Orhon valley after the Turks, developed a settlement around an oasis, where agriculture was possible.

[12] The term 'Mongol' first appeared in records of different groups which were written during the T'ang Chinese dynasty. It then disappeared until the 11th century, when the Kidan became the rulers of Manchuria and northern China, controlling almost all of present-day Mongolia.

[13] The Kidan established the Liao dynasty in China (907-1125) and ruled Mongolia, fostering division between the different tribes. Historical records mention the existence of a single Mongol nation, although it did not include all Mongolian-speaking peoples.

[14] The Kidan were succeeded by the Juchen, who were in turn succeeded by the Tatars, before the era of Genghis Khan (Temujin). Born in 1162, Temujin was the grandson of Qabul (Kublai Khan), who had been the Mongols' greatest leader to date. Temujin inherited several fiefdoms that had been seized from his family.

[15] In 1206, because of his political and military prowess, Temujin was recognized as leader of all the Mongols, and given the title of Genghis Khan. His armies invaded northern China, reaching Beijing. By 1215, the Mongolian Empire extended as far as Tibet and Turkistan.

[16] Upon Genghis Khan's death in 1227 disputes among his successors caused the Mongolian Empire to disintegrate, until the Chinese throne was left in the hands of the Ming dynasty in 1368. China invaded Mongolia and destroyed Karakorum, the former imperial capital by fire, though it was unable to bring the territory under control.

[17] In the 15th and 16th centuries, controlling the areas beyond the Great Wall of China demanded military mobilization. In addition, cities were needed to act as centers of trade and serve as market places for food produced by local peasants.

[18] The Oyrat alliance made by groups living in western Mongolia began gaining control of the territory. They added their own mercantile and administrative expertise to the Mongols' tribal organization.

[19] The separation of the Oyrat from the Jaljas began during this period, with the latter forming the core of what was later to become Outer Mongolia. A tribal league was formed between the Khalkhas in the north and the Chahars in the south, while the leadership passed over to the Ordos, during the reign of Altan Khan (1543-83).

[20] To keep their hold on power, the Mongolian princes thought it useful to be backed up by a religious ideology. They adopted the Tibetan Buddhist religion as Tibet posed no cultural threat, and the Tibetan script was easy to use.

[21] Altan Khan proceeded to invite a Tibetan prelate, whom the Mongols called 'Dalai Lama' to lead the state religion. The merging of religious interests with those of the State was accomplished by claiming that an heir to the Khalkhas clan was the first 'reincarnation' of the Living Buddha of Urga.

[22] In 1644, after consolidating their power in Manchuria, the Manchus seized the Chinese throne, with the help of Mongolian tribes from the far east. Before occupying Beijing, the Manchus took control of southern Mongolia, which was henceforth known as Inner Mongolia.

[23] It took China almost a century

WORKERS

% OF LABOUR FORCE **1998**

■ FEMALE: 47%   ■ MALE: 53%

1990

■ SERVICES: 45.5%
■ INDUSTRY: 22.5%
■ AGRICULTURE: 32.0%

LAND USE

DEFORESTATION: 0.0% annual (1990/95)
IRRIGATED: 5.7% of arable (1993)

1993

■ FOREST & WOODLAND: 8.8%
■ ARABLE: 0.9%
■ OTHER: 90.3%

PUBLIC EXPENDITURE

DEFENCE EXPENDITURE
(% of goverment exp.)   **5.1%**
(1997)

to conquer Outer Mongolia. Meanwhile, Inner Mongolia became a part of China, and the Khalkhas' desire to retain power in the south prevented the Oyrats from attaining reunification.

[24] This was the final stage of the great wars among the Mongols; ending in their overall dispersal. Several groups of Khalkhas remained in the south; some Chahars settled in Sinkiang and the Oyrat dispersed in different directions, including czarist Russia.

[25] In the Russo-Japanese War of 1904-05, both armies used Mongolian troops and staff. This served Japanese interests well as a resurgence of Mongolian nationalism could weaken both Russia and China. At the end of the war, Russia secretly recognized Inner Mongolia as belonging to Japan's sphere of influence.

[26] With the outbreak of the Chinese Revolution in 1911, there was a pervading malaise in Mongolia. Until then, the region had been the object of disputes between Russia and Japan. However, the Mongolians' social and political discontent was directed against the Manchus and the local government.

[27] Led by their Buddhist leader, Mongolia proclaimed independence from China and sought Russian support. However, because of its secret treaties with Japan and England, Russia could offer nothing more than mere 'autonomy'. After lengthy negotiations, this status was granted to Outer Mongolia.

[28] This situation continued until the Russian Revolution in 1917. China sent in troops and made the Mongolians sign a request for aid from Beijing. But the region was invaded by retreating czarist troops, who expelled the Chinese and mistreated the Mongolians.

[29] With the traditional leaders discredited because of their poor handling of the Chinese and White Russian interventions, some groups of Mongolian revolutionaries sought help from the Bolsheviks. Russian and Mongolian troops took the capital, Urga, in July 1921.

[30] This was the beginning of the republic, although the first monarchy had the Living Buddha as puppet king, only authorized to endorse the new regime's proposals. Upon his death in 1924, the People's Republic of Mongolia was proclaimed.

[31] The People's Revolutionary Party (MPRP), made up of conservatives and revolutionary nationalists, wavered between Beijing and Moscow until the defeat of the Chinese Revolution, at the hands of Chiang Kai-shek. At this time, Mongolia began to fall increasingly under the influence of the USSR, and Joseph Stalin.

[32] The new republic proclaimed the right for women to vote. The efforts to impose socialism upon Mongolia, which was still feudal in many ways, were marked by even greater excesses than were committed in other republics.

[33] Following the Soviet model, the MPRP Government tried to collectivize the economy in order to break the power of the feudal lords and the Buddhist priests. Between 1936 and 1938, the Mongolian regime purged the party and the army, executing many leaders.

[34] In the 1930s, the MPRP destroyed 750 monasteries and killed over a thousand monks. Mongolia's demographic level had been unchanged for hundreds of years, as a large part of the male population became Buddhist monks.

[35] In 1939, Japan invaded northeastern Mongolia, along the Siberian border. With Soviet help Japan was defeated; a blow to the Axis powers in Berlin and Tokyo. Mongolia and the USSR fought together in the Inner Mongolian and Manchurian campaign, two weeks before the end of World War II.

[36] As part of the Yalta agreement, Chiang Kai-shek agreed to hold a plebiscite in Mongolia. Although the result overwhelmingly favored independence, Mongolia failed to receive diplomatic recognition because of an unresolved territorial dispute. In 1961, Mongolia was admitted to the UN.

[37] In 1960, Government officials in Ulaanbaatar accused the Chinese Government of mistreating Mongolian citizens and of seeking territorial expansion, at Mongolia's expense. In the early 1970s, there were a number of incidents along the border between the two countries, and 2,000 Chinese immigrants were expelled from Mongolia.

[38] Friction continued until 1986, when the Chinese deputy minister of the Council of Ministers visited Mongolia and re-established consular and commercial relations. In 1987, the Soviet Government announced the withdrawal of part of its military forces, as a goodwill gesture aimed at stabilizing the region.

[39] In March 1988, China and Mongolia signed the first treaty ever, aimed at defining the 4,655 km border between the two countries. A year later, during Mongolian premier Tserenpylium Gombasuren's visit, the first in 40 years, relations between the two countries were returned to normal.

[40] In 1989, within the framework of Soviet perestroika (restructuring), Moscow announced that three-quarters of its troops would be withdrawn in 1990. Shortly afterwards, both governments agreed to the complete withdrawal of all Soviet military personnel and equipment from Mongolian territory by the end of 1992.

[41] At the same time, the MPRP leadership admitted that social and economic reforms were not having satisfactory results. The official party adopted changes in its internal elections, making them more democratic, and rehabilitated some figures who had been purged during the 1930s.

[42] In 1989 and 1990, several opposition groups emerged. One of the most active, the Democratic Union of Mongolia, was officially recognized in January 1990. In March of that year, increasingly frequent public demonstrations against the Government triggered a new crisis within the MPRP.

[43] The National Assembly approved a constitutional amendment withdrawing the reference to the MPRP as society's 'prime moving force' and approving new electoral legislation; however, no changes were made with relation to political party activity.

[44] Toward the end of March, demonstrators in the streets of Ulaanbaatar clamored for the dissolution of the National Assembly. Leaders of the opposition stated that the changes which had been proposed were insufficient, and called for legislation allowing all parties to present candidates.

[45] Rich in oil, minerals, livestock, timber and wool, what Mongolia lacked was the money, machinery and specialized personnel to exploit these resources, particularly after the loss of Soviet subsidies and withdrawal of 50,000 Soviet technicians and government advisers.

[46] The legendary figure of Genghis Khan, whose name was forbidden for many years, has begun to be rehabilitated as an authentic expression of Mongolian pride and tradition, sentiments which until recently were condemned as being an expression of a narrow-minded 'nationalism'.

[47] In spite of 65 years of Soviet aid, Mongolia's economy maintained vestiges of nomadism. In the early 1990s, urbanization was just beginning, and half of Ulaanbator's population lived in tents, with rudimentary electric and water supplies.

[48] In the first months of 1991, Mongolia registered a substantial reduction in its foreign trade. Its balance of payments deficit reached $250 million. Shortages of food, medicine and fuel became

---

more acute. The currency suffered devaluation, from 7.1 to 40 *tughrik* per US dollar, and government income declined sharply, while expenditure steadily increased.

49 Prime Minister Dashiun Byambasuren announced a new economic policy which included incentives to attract foreign investment, the establishment of a national stock exchange, the sale of two-thirds of the state's capital goods, deregulation of prices and changes in the banking system. The Government warned that the reform was complex and would take time to implement.

50 The life of most Mongolians, whose median income at this time was $100, became harder than before. The population was not only anxious to see the results of the changes announced by the Government but was also worried about the scandals which affected the administration.

51 After an official investigation, the President of the Central Bank of Mongolia, Zhargalsaikhan, together with a group of new investors, were arrested in December 1991, for a $82 million fraud, money which they had invested in business deals that went wrong. As a result, the country lost the major part of its reserves. At the same time, the deputy Prime Minister, Cabaadorjiyn Ganbold - the highest ranking reform figure in a government dominated by former communists - was accused of secretly authorizing the transfer of 4,400 kg of gold to a branch of Goldman Sachs - a British merchant bank. The gold was collateral for a $46 million loan, apparently earmarked for covering losses. The reform sector said that the minister of finance would try to cover the losses and accused the former communists of using such denunciations to try to discredit the transition toward a market economy.

52 In January 1992, the National Assembly approved a proposed constitutional reform presented to the Government, adopting the official name 'Republic of Mongolia', and dropping the term 'People's'. The reform also established a pluralistic democratic system, replacing the socialist system.

53 The governing People's Revolutionary Party gained more than 70 of the 76 Mongolian parliamentary seats in the June 1992 legislative elections. The opposition democratic coalition only obtained three or four seats according to the Electoral Commission which supervised the count. Over 90 per cent of the electorate voted.

54 In October 1992, after being defeated in the June elections, the Mongolian National Democratic Party (MNDP) became an opposition party. The Social Democrats preferred to remain independent.

55 A scheme was implemented in November 1992 for privatizing 80 per cent of State enterprises involved distributing bonds for the purchase of shares to all of the country's inhabitants. However, it seems that the scheme was not explained fully enough to the largely nomadic population. They appeared not to understand it, and most of the bonds were sold on the black market.

56 In 1992, the withdrawal of Russian troops - begun in 1987 - was completed. Meanwhile, Otchirbat had a rapprochement with the NMDP and the SDP to prepare the presidential elections in June 1993. Thanks to the two groups, which had been previous members of the opposition, the President was re-elected with almost 58 per cent of the vote and announced the 'westernization' of economy.

57 Disagreements between Otchirbat and the former communist majority in parliament were frequent. Poverty and unemployment kept growing and, according to official estimations, 26.5 per cent of the population did not earn the minimum income to subsist.

58 Meanwhile, for the first time since the collapse of the Communist regime, Mongolia saw a 2.5 per cent economic growth in 1994. Differences between the parliament majority and the opposition NMDP and SDP groups diminished, which enabled a deal in 1995 to modify the election system. Thus, it was decided that 24 of the 76 members of parliament would be elected by proportional vote and the majority system would continue for the remaining seats.

59 In the economic field, several international organizations criticized Mongolia's apparent sluggishness in liberalizing its economy and promote the private sector's development.

60 The June 1996 elections marked the end of communist dominion, with victory of the Democratic Union Coalition (DUC), a coalition formed by the Social Democratic party and the Mongolian National Democratic Party. The DA took 50 of the 76 seats, while the former communist bloc shrank from 70 to 25 seats. In July, Parliament accepted Mendsayhany Enkhsaikhan as Prime Minister.

61 After the election, the Government went ahead with reforms to introduce the market economy as fast as possible. This process had a high social cost, increasing unemployment and poverty. This situation added to the damage caused by the lack of technical and economic assistance following the disappearance of the Soviet Union. Around 19.6 per cent of the population were living below the poverty line.

62 In May 1997, Natsagiyn Bagabandi, of the Mongolian People's Revolutionary Party, won the presidential election with 60.8 per cent of the vote. President Punsalmaagiyn Otchirbat, the DUC re-election candidate, took 29.8 per cent. The result was interpreted as a reaction against the 'shock therapy' applied in order to reach a liberal economy.

63 A law introduced in June 1998 required the use of surnames in legal documents. The new legislation, which responded to demands for modernization and greater integration with the rest of the world, caused confusion and concern amongst the people. For centuries, most of the population had been made up of nomadic herders, living in small groups, and for whom surnames were irrelevant.

64 The lack of capacity to confront the economic crisis and strong criticism caused the government to resign, and a new cabinet was established headed by Janlaviin Narantsatsralt. Seven months later, in July 1999, following a dispute related to the privatization of a copper mine co-owned between Mongolia and Russian, Narantsatsralt and his ten ministers all resigned. Parliament appointed a new member of the CUD, economist Rinchinnyamiin Amarjargal as premier.

65 A report issued in January 2000 by non-governmental organizations estimated there were 4,000 street children. According to the National Children's Center, when the country abandoned the Soviet model in 1992 there were only 300 street children. As factories and other workplaces closed, urban poverty increased compounding rural poverty. In a certain type of traditional family, when a family of Mongolian herders could not feed the whole group, it would send one or several children to live in the city. This system, which had worked for hundreds of years, became bankrupt as the urban relatives could not feed the children either. Ill-health is also a serious threat in the winter in Ulanbataar, the coldest capital in the world.

66 Living conditions for the entire population became considerably worse after the winter of 2000 - the coldest in the country for 55 years. The Government declared more than half the country a disaster area. More than two million head of livestock were lost, the equivalent of $1.65 billion. ∎

Montserrat

Montserrat

Population: 11,000 (1998)
Area: 100 SQ KM
Capital: Plymouth
Currency: EC dollar
Language: English

Montserrat was first inhabited by Carib Indians but after being sighted by Columbus in 1493, it shared the history of the other Lesser Antilles.

2   The island was colonized by Irish people, driven out from neighboring St Kitts. Owing to its barren nature and unsuitable coastline, it was never really coveted by Europeans, and apart from sugar cane and cotton, no crops were grown on the Island. In the mid-19th century it had a population of about 10,000 people, including 9,000 slaves.

3   Montserrat was a member of the Federation of the Leeward Islands and later of the West Indies Federation, until the latter was dissolved in 1962. Since 1960 Montserrat's colonial statute has ensured a rather autonomous political organization. The Progressive Democratic Party (PDP) founded by William Bramble and later headed by his son, Austin

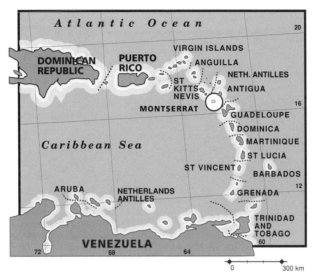

Bramble, refused to change this situation when the group of Associated States of the Antilles was formed in 1967 as a preliminary step towards total independence.

4   Despite its isolation the island felt the influence of the decolonization process. Bramble's party lost all its parliamentary seats in November 1973, driven out by the new People's Liberation Movement (PLM). In 1979, Montserrat's Prime Minister John Osborne announced that the island would attain full independence in 1982, a promise that failed to materialize.

5   Barely a quarter of the country's surface area is agricultural land, and the population density on those lands is very high. Half of the island is suitable for cattle raising, which has been a major source of export for some time. Montserrat has one of the highest swimming-pool counts per capita in the world: 2 per inhabitant. Tourist activity has developed since 1979, largely because of US immigration. Another source of income is international radio stations; Radio Antilles, and the Voice of Germany both broadcast from the island.

6   In August 1987, 11 months late, Osborne called elections. The PLM won four of the seven elective seats, the National Development Party (NDP) two and the PDP one.

7   Tourism revenues and pay sent home from Montserrat workers abroad were insufficient to cover the enormous balance of payments deficit. At that time, Britain made up the balance, and this was the main sustaining argument of those who stood against independence.

8   Relations between the Government and the UK were not good. By early 1989, Montserrat was the accommodation address for 347 offshore banks, though the Government only received about five per cent of the sale of licences. The lack of control over banking gave rise to accusations that the island was used in fraud and in laundering drug money. Since 1990, the new governor, David Pendleton, has encouraged stiffer regulations for offshore companies.

9   In 1989, Hurricane Hugo devastated Montserrat. The British granted $35 million for reconstruction on the island to revive the economy. The tourism sector was one of those which grew most.

10   During 1991, new legislation permitted the re-establishment of the offshore financial activities. Systematic investigations of banking operations in 1992 led the United Kingdom to close 90 per cent of commercial banks and offshore concerns as they were involved in illegal transactions and money laundering of money from drug trafficking. Frank Savage was appointed Governor in February 1993.

11   From 1995 and throughout 1996, the Chances Peak volcano continually spewed out ash. The resulting uncertainty seriously weakened the economy. Prime Minister Bertrand Osborne resigned in August 1997 after residents protested at the way the population evacuation had been handled.

12   The eruption of Soufriere volcano in mid-1997 killed hundreds of people and left most of Montserrat uninhabitable. Thousands of people were evacuated to areas in the north of the island, to other countries in the Caribbean and to the UK. It was hoped that, during the first half of 2000, once the lava flows and the amount of ash in the atmosphere were stabilized, several disaster areas could once again be inhabited. ∎

PROFILE

ENVIRONMENT

Montserrat is one of the Leeward islands in the Lesser Antilles, located 400 km east of Puerto Rico, northwest of Guadeloupe. The terrain is volcanic in origin and quite mountainous, with altitudes of over 1,000 meters. The tropical, rainy climate is tempered by sea winds. The soil of the plains is relatively fertile and suitable for agriculture.

SOCIETY

Peoples: Most of the population is descended from African and European immigrants.
Religions: Mostly Christian; Anglicans, Catholics and Methodists predominate.
Languages: English (official). Most people speak a local dialect.
Political Parties: The People's Progressive Alliance; the Progressive Democratic Party (PDP); the People's Liberation Movement (PLM); the National Development Party (NDP); the National Progressive Party..
Social Organizations: The Montserrat Allied Workers' Union, led by George Irish, has 1,300 members and is the only labor federation. There is also a 120 member Teachers' Union and a 122-member, Seamen and Waterfront Workers' Union.

THE STATE

Official Name: Colony of Montserrat.
Capital: Plymouth 3,900 people (est 1995), before being evacuated in April 1996 after volcanic activity. By the end of 1997, the city had been destroyed.
Government: Anthony John Abbot, Governor appointed by the British Crown, since 1997. David Brandt, Prime Minister since 1997. Legislative Council with seven elected members.

DEMOGRAPHY

Population: 11,000 (1998)

ECONOMY

Cereal imports: 2,184 metric tons (1998)

Morocco

Magreb

Population: 27,866,000 (1999)
Area: 446,550 SQ KM
Capital: Rabat
Currency: Dirham
Language: Arabic

Morocco was the cradle of the two North African empires that dominated the Iberian peninsula. It became one of the power centers of the region because of its geographic location: it was close to Spain, and at the northern end of the trans-Saharan trade routes. Although neither Fés nor Marrakech achieved the academic prestige of Cairo, their political influence was felt as far as Timbuktu and Valencia. Their close ties with Spain were culturally enriching during the Cordovan Caliphate, but they brought negative consequences to Morocco in the final stages of the 'Reconquest'. The war moved into Africa and the Spanish seized strongholds on the coast (Ceuta in 1415, and Tangier in 1471). European naval dominance blocked Mediterranean and Atlantic routes to Morocco causing a decline in trade.

[2] Unlike Algeria and Tunisia, Morocco was not formally annexed to the Ottoman Empire, but it did benefit from the presence of Turkish corsairs who hampered Luso-Spanish expansion. This precarious balance allowed the sultans to remain autonomous until the 20th century. France's policy of economic penetration meant that France was supervising Moroccan finances, aiming to guarantee repayment of the Moroccan foreign debt, while France argued with Germany over who should have political sway over the area. The French finally won, securing agreements with Spain over the borders of the Spanish Sahara, and Sultan Muley Hafid ended

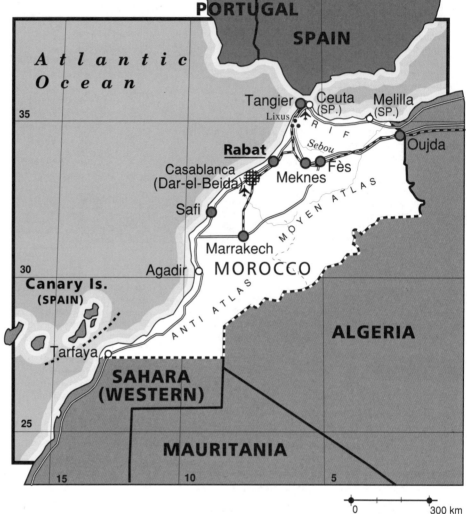

his support of the Saharan rebels (see Sahara, Western). In 1912, an agreement between France, Spain and Britain transformed Morocco into a French protectorate, giving Spain the Rif region, to the north (where Ceuta and Melilla are located), and the Ifni region to the south, near the Sahara. In exchange, Britain obtained French consent for its policies in Egypt and Sudan. The city of Tangier was declared an international free port and the sultan became a figurehead.

[3] The areas under Spanish control became sanctuaries for the nationalists who disagreed with European domination. In 1921, it was on Spanish territory that the Berber revolt led by Emir Abdel Krim (Abd al-Karim al-Khattab) began. Backed by the Third International and the Pan-Islamic Movement, he proclaimed the Republic of the Confederated Tribes of the Rif, induced the inland peoples to rebel, and put Spain on the defensive. The French intervened causing the rebellion to spread throughout the entire country. It took them until 1926 to force the Emir to surrender.

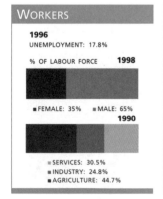

WORKERS

1996
UNEMPLOYMENT: 17.8%

% OF LABOUR FORCE **1998**

■ FEMALE: 35%   ■ MALE: 65%

1990

■ SERVICES: 30.5%
■ INDUSTRY: 24.8%
■ AGRICULTURE: 44.7%

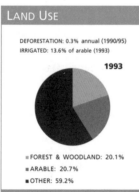

LAND USE

DEFORESTATION: 0.3% annual (1990/95)
IRRIGATED: 13.6% of arable (1993)

1993

■ FOREST & WOODLAND: 20.1%
■ ARABLE: 20.7%
■ OTHER: 59.2%

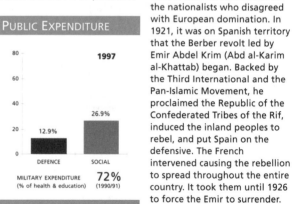

PUBLIC EXPENDITURE

1997

26.9%

12.9%

DEFENCE   SOCIAL

MILITARY EXPENDITURE **72%**
(% of health & education)   (1990/91)

MATERNAL MORTALITY	LITERACY	FOOD DEPENDENCY
 1990-98 Per 100,000 live births **230**	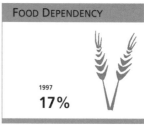 1995 **44%**	1997 **17%**

4   In the south, Spanish rule was nominal, and French pressures to close down this 'sanctuary' for Algerian, Moroccan, Saharan and Mauritanian rebels failed (see Western Sahara).

5   During World War II, there was sustained nationalist agitation. Demands for liberation were so pressing that Sultan Muhammad V himself became the spokesperson for the cause. To calm the people, the French thought they could rely on the prestige of the elderly Emir Abdel Krim who had been deported to Réunion. Unfortunately for them, the veteran fighter took advantage of a stopover in Egypt to escape from the ship, seeking refuge in Cairo where he died in 1963. Growing tension led the French to depose Muhammad V in 1953, but this only succeeded in making the nationalist movement more radical. The nationalists raised an army and fought until they achieved Muhammad's return to power. In 1956, the French were forced to acknowledge Morocco's independence.

6   On April 7 1956, Morocco recovered Tangier, as well as the 'special zones' of Ceuta and Melilla, although the ports of these two cities still remain under Spanish control. Ifni was not returned to Morocco until 1969.

7   The goal set by Muhammad V was 'to move forward slowly' gradually modernizing the country's economic and political structures. But his son, Hassan II, who succeeded him in 1961, had more conservative ideas. His family came from the lineage of Muhammad, the prophet, and his theocratic regime, based on a paternalistic system of favors and duties prevented the development of authentic national commerce. The King also encouraged foreign investment, especially from France, to exploit the nation's natural resources.

8   In 1965, Ben Barka, leader of the powerful National Union of Popular Forces (NUPF) was assassinated on the orders of Hassan II. The NUPF worked for the social and economic welfare of workers and peasants.

9   The death of Ben Barka in Paris was followed by a crackdown on popular organizations. The NUPF split and Ben Barka's followers were banned. Meanwhile, another NUPF faction, headed by Abderrahim Bouabid, changed its name to the Socialist Union and traded Ben Barka's principles for a minority place in parliament. The Istiqlal, who were originally anti-colonialist, became supporters of right-wing nationalist expansionism, fully backing Hassan's dream of restoring 'Greater Morocco' through the annexation of the Western Sahara and, if possible, Mauritania.

10   In 1975, the conflicts underlying Moroccan society surfaced when King Hassan ordered the occupation of Sahara, unleashing a war that has brought about important political changes in North Africa (see Western Sahara).

11   Funds for the military campaign, the fall in the price of phosphates on the international market, and the loss of financial aid from Saudi Arabia - in retaliation for Hassan's support of the Camp David agreements between Israel and Egypt - deepened the economic crisis. The political consequences of the crisis soon appeared. In 1979, students and workers held massive street demonstrations. The withdrawal of Mauritania from the Western Sahara war in July 1980 was a serious blow to the Moroccan Government, which then carried sole responsibility for continuing to fight.

12   Severe drought in 1980 and 1981 drastically reduced food supplies, forcing the Government to increase food imports. This sent the country's foreign debt soaring to intolerable levels. The IMF assisted the monarchy with emergency loans which carried a condition eliminating subsidies on food and housing, a measure which increased the hardships faced by the working classes. The Government failed to achieve its ambitious development aims, and the export of unemployed workers was limited by French immigration restrictions.

13   The situation worsened when several moderate opposition parties decided to break the tacit political truce. The Socialist Union of Popular Forces (USFP) staged anti-government street demonstrations. In June 1981, Casablanca was the scene of bloody repression which left 60 dead, according to official reports, or 637, according to the opposition. Two thousand people were arrested. This 'Casablanca massacre' led to an open conflict between the King and the leftist parties over the high cost of the Sahara war which was swallowing more than $1 million a day.

14   The stalemate on the battlefield caused conflict within the Moroccan armed forces, and in early 1983, they began to show signs of dissent. This tension became evident with the assassination of General Ahmed Dlimi, the supreme commander

of the Royal Armed Forces, who was killed in mysterious circumstances after having secret meetings with European countries over ending the Sahara war.

¹⁵ In 1984, the Saharan Arab Democratic Republic (RASD), proclaimed by the Polisario Front's fighters in the former Spanish Saharan colony, was recognized as a full member of the Organization of African Unity (OAU). Morocco reacted by withdrawing from the pan-African organization.

¹⁶ In his capacity as religious leader, the Moroccan king became worried about the rise of Islamic fundamentalism throughout the Arab world. For this reason, Hassan improved administrative measures for reinforcing the power of the *ulemas* (priests) and other religious representatives.

¹⁷ In 1987, the Moroccan monarch suggested to King Juan Carlos of Spain that both governments form a study group designed to consider the future of Ceuta and Melilla (see boxes). The proposal was not well received in Spain, as there was an insistence on the 'historical nature' of Spain's presence in Ceuta and Melilla.

¹⁸ In May 1988, after 12 years of tension, Morocco and Algeria re-established diplomatic relations, through the mediation of Saudi Arabia and Tunisia. The cause of the disruption in their relations had been the war in the Sahara, as Algeria had openly supported the Saharan nationalists from the beginning.

¹⁹ Better relations between Algeria and Morocco meant that a gas pipeline was built across the Strait of Gibraltar joining the two countries to Europe. From 1995, an Algerian-Moroccan firm based in Rabat would transport between 10 and 15 billion cubic meters of Algerian gas via the line.

²⁰ Urban migration of a million people per year has exacerbated the urban housing situation, putting a strain on sanitation, water and other services. In October 1992, 800 Moroccans were arrested in Tarifa, in the south of Spain, trying to enter the country illegally, while another 35 failed to make it to Spain, drowning in the Mediterranean.

²¹ In March 1992, the Paris Club of creditor nations signed an agreement with Morocco, renegotiating its foreign debt of $21.3 billion. Development credits were renegotiated for 20 years, while other types of credit were extended to 15 years. The economy underwent adjustment. The state deficit was reduced from 10 per cent in the early 1980s to 3.2 per cent in

Ceuta

Population: 71,000 (1994)
Area: 19 SQ KM
Currency: Peseta
Language: Arabic and Spanish

This is an enclave on the Mediterranean coast of Morocco facing Gibraltar (Spain). The climate is Mediterranean with hot summers and moderate winters. There is sparse rainfall in winter.

² Occupied by troops of Portuguese King John in 1415, Ceuta was transferred to Spain in 1688 and retained by the Spanish after Moroccan independence in 1956. Despite many UN backed claims and negotiations, before the United Nations Decolonization Committee, the port is still in Spanish hands. It is used as a harbor, but two thirds of the territory is reserved exclusively for military purposes.

SOCIETY

Peoples: 80 per cent of the population is born in Ceuta. Minorities include Spaniards, Hindu and others (according to 1996 census taken by the Ceuta municipal goverment).
Religions: Catholic (majority), Muslim and others.
Languages: Arabic and Spanish.

THE STATE

Government: Civil authority is exercised by a representative of the Spanish Home Affairs Ministry, who administers it as part of Cádiz Province. Military authority lies in the hands of a General Commander. The territory has one representative in the Spanish parliament.

DEMOGRAPHY

Population: 71,000 (1994)

Melilla

Population: 58,000 (1994)
Area: 12 SQ KM
Currency: Peseta
Language: Arabic and Spanish

Melilla is a small peninsula on the Mediterranean coast of Morocco with two adjacent island groups. The climate is similar to that of Ceuta. Melilla is an ancient walled town built upon a hill with a modern European-style city on the plain. It is an important port which, like Ceuta, hopes to be a tourist attraction.

² Founded by Phoenicians and successively held by Romans, Goths and Arabs, Melilla was occupied by Spain in 1495. It was repeatedly besieged by the Riffs, a Berber group that opposed French and Spanish domination, most recently in 1921. Like Ceuta, it has been claimed by Morocco and it also is a port and a military base; more than half of the territory is used for military purposes.

³ On the northern Moroccan coast the Spanish also hold Peñón (rock) de Vélez de la Gomera, which had 60 inhabitants in 1982; Peñón de Alhucemas with 61 inhabitants in 1982; (with the islets of Mar and Tierra) and the Chafarinas Archipelago (Islands of Congreso, Isabel II and Rey), 1 sq km in area and with a population of 191 inhabitants in 1982.

SOCIETY

Peoples: languages, religions and other features of the population are similar to those of Ceuta.

THE STATE

Government: A representative of the Spanish Government is responsible for administrating the territory's civilian affairs. There is a military command in charge of military affairs. Like Ceuta, Melilla has a representative in Cortes, the traditional Spanish parliament.

DEMOGRAPHY

Population: 58,000 (1994)

1992. The balance of payments has improved and the net reserves have increased.

[22] The United Nations International Council for the Control of Narcotics condemned the fact that many farmers in countries like Morocco have been pressured into cultivating opium and coca, respectively the raw materials for the production of heroin and cocaine.

[23] In Western Sahara, A UN peace plan announced in 1991 resulted in a ceasefire and plans for a referendum in which Saharans would choose either independence or integration with Morocco. But the referendum process fell apart over disagreements as to who should be able to vote - Morocco wanted 120,000 extra voters to be enfranchised so as to increase its chances of victory However, the ceasefire held and the UN presence remained (see Western Sahara).

[24] Torture and disappearances are common both in Sahara and in Morocco itself. In February 1993, the Moroccan Human Rights Association announced the existence of 750 political prisoners - Nubier Amau, secretary general of the Democratic Confederation of Labor, was sentenced to two years imprisonment, for 'defaming' the regime. He was released a few months later, after the opposition's victory in Parliament.

[25] In June 1993, the opposition won in the first parliamentary elections following the 1992 reform of the constitution, taking 99 of the 222 seats, while the ruling party won only 74. Two months later, Hassan held a spectacular inauguration ceremony in the biggest mosque in the world, built in Casablanca at a cost of $536 million.

[26] Despite the constitutional reform, the King continued to dominate national politics, and in May 1994, he appointed one of his relations by marriage, Abd al-Latif Filali as prime minister. In August, the King issued a surprise call for the integration of Berber culture and language into national life.

[27] The economic situation of the country worsened abruptly in 1995, due largely to the lack of rains, resulting in harvests falling to a sixth of the previous year's figures. The GDP, which had grown 12 per cent in 1994, fell 4 per cent in 1995. Following tough negotiations, Morocco and the European Union signed a new association agreement in November.

[28] In early 1996, the Government announced it would submit proposals for constitutional reform to referendum. The changes, which basically aimed at the formation of a bicameral legislature, were approved in September. The King still had the right to dissolve the chambers. The privatization policies continued that year with the sale of several companies.

[29] In 1997 Morocco was forced by UN and US pressure to agree to a series of direct meetings with the Polisario Front which resulted in an agreement to relaunch the peace plan in Western Sahara (see Western Sahara). The long-postponed referendum offering self-determination for the Saharan people was set for December 1998 and a clear timetable laid down for the release of prisoners and return of refugees.

[30] In the November 1997 legislative elections, an opposition coalition made up of four political parties took 102 of the 325 seats in Parliament. The block included the Socialist Union of Popular Forces, which took 57 seats and the Independence Party, with 32. The right-wing and pro-Government Wifaq alliance took 100 seats (including the Constitutional Union, with 50) and its center allies, 97, (including the National Union of Independents, with 46), providing the Government broad parliamentary support.

[31] In February 1998, King Hassan II appointed Abderrahmane El Youssoufi, leader of the Socialist Union of Popular Forces, as Prime Minister. He appointed the new cabinet on March 1998. One year later, In March 1999 after several delays, the Government asked the UN for a further extension to the referendum scheduled for December. The Moroccan authorities suggested a new date: March 2000. After analyzing the situation and the differences between the Moroccan Government and the Polisario Front, the UN Secretary-General proposed to postpone the referendum yet again. It had initially been planned for 1991 but postponed each time the voting date approached. It was now to take place sometime between 2000 and 2002.

[32] The death of Hassan II in July 1999 and the succession of his son, Mohammed IV, as King brought significant political changes to the country. The first move of the new monarch was to liberate some 800 political prisoners. On a television address in August, he pledged to fight social inequalities, domestic violence, unemployment and rural emigration. The Polisario Front welcomed the King's first measures and his decision to go ahead with the Western Sahara self-determination referendum. Mohammed IV announced in November his decision to make some form of self-rule possible for the occupied zone.

[33] That same month, Mohammed IV dismissed Home Minister Driss Basri, who had served throughout King Hassan's reign of almost two decades. The King announced the liberation of another 2,000 political prisoners as a goodwill gesture on January 2000, in order to celebrate the end of Ramadan. The Government's proposals to recognize increasing rights to women caused demonstrations both for and against the measures during March 2000. The plans included the elimination of polygamy, raising the legal age of marriage for women from 14 to 18 and granting 50 per cent of marriage assets to each spouse in the case of divorce. This process would be handled by a judge, and not by the husband as had traditionally been the case. ∎

Mozambique

Moçambique

Population: 19,286,000 (1999)
Area: 801,590 SQ KM
Capital: Maputo
Currency: Metical
Language: Portuguese

The city of Sofa was founded by Shirazis towards the end of the 10th century. It became a point of contact between two of the most flourishing developed cultures in Africa: the commercial, Muslim cultures of the east coast and the metallurgical, animist culture of Zimbabwe. As with other civilizations on the continent, the Portuguese presence on the coast of present-day Mozambique was fatal; they planned to seize control of the Eastern trade which had nourished the two civilizations for centuries. This led to the destruction of the ports and the stifling of Zimbabwean gold exports.

[3] The Portuguese were never able to re-establish this trade to their own benefit, nor were they able to achieve their other goals. The Monomotapa (leaders of the Karanga) became Portuguese subjects in 1629, but these authorities were insignificant figureheads on the coast, and the way to the gold mines was still closed by the Changamiras of Zimbabwe.

[4] When Zanzibar expelled the Portuguese from their area of influence, the colonists turned to the slave trade as a profitable business. Attempts at connecting Mozambique and Angola by land failed repeatedly and European control was confined to a coastal strip where their entire 'administration' was limited to granting *prazos*, concessions of huge areas of land, to Portuguese and Indian adventurers who either plundered the land or searched for natives to enslave. These *prazeiros* became virtually independent of the Portuguese authorities.

[5] In 1890, the English questioned Portuguese control over these lands and threatened to occupy them. The Portuguese Government underwent a long, hard struggle to forcibly subdue the *prazeiros*, and prove their authority over the region. The conquest of the interior, however, was only completed around 1920 when they finally defeated the ruler, Mokombe, in the Tete region.

[6] Mozambique started to supply South African gold mines with migrant workers (up to one million every year) and its ports were open to South African and Rhodesian foreign trade.

[7] Portuguese colonialism controlled the country as an 'Overseas Province', encouraging local group rivalries to prevent nationalist feelings from developing. Split into several movements, the nationalists staged strikes and demonstrations in their struggle for independence.

[8] In 1960, a spontaneous and peaceful demonstration in Mueda was fiercely repressed, leaving over 500 people dead. This convinced many Mozambicans that any peaceful negotiations with colonialism were doomed to failure.

[9] The following year, Eduardo Mondlane, then a United Nations official, visited his home country and persuaded the struggling pro-independence groups that their unity was essential. This was finally achieved on July 25 1962, in Tanzania, with the creation of FRELIMO (the Front for the Liberation of Mozambique). FRELIMO was made up of individuals and organizations from all regions and ethnic groups of Mozambique.

[10] On December 25 1964, after two years of underground activity, FRELIMO started guerrilla warfare to win 'total and complete independence'. By the end of 1965, FRELIMO controlled some areas in Mozambique and by 1969, one-fifth of the country's territory was under their control.

[11] In February of that year, Mondlane was assassinated by colonialist agents. Differences of opinion developed within FRELIMO about the desired form of independence; some wanting a mere 'Africanization' of the established system and others seeking to create a new popular democratic society.

[12] The second faction dominated FRELIMO's second congress, held in the liberated areas, and Samora Machel was elected president of the organization. From then on, the fighting intensified and spread to other areas. The impossibility of winning the colonial wars in Africa led to a military uprising in Lisbon on April 25 1974, ending Salazar and Caetano's regimes.

[13] A transitional government was established in Mozambique and on June 25 1975, the People's Republic of Mozambique was formed, with Samora Machel announcing that 'the struggle will continue' in solidarity with the freedom fighters in Zimbabwe and South Africa.

[14] On the domestic front, the FRELIMO Government nationalized education, health care, foreign banks and several transnational corporations. The Government promoted communal villages, bringing together the scattered rural population and organizing collective production methods.

[15] In 1977, FRELIMO held its third congress in Maputo. Marxist-Leninism was announced as the Front's ideology.

WORKERS

% OF LABOUR FORCE — **1998**

- FEMALE: 48%
- MALE: 52%

1990

- SERVICES: 9.3%
- INDUSTRY: 8.0%
- AGRICULTURE: 82.7%

LAND USE

DEFORESTATION: 0.7% annual (1990/95)
IRRIGATED: 4.0% of arable (1993)

1993

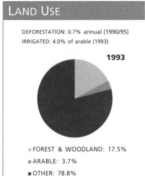

- FOREST & WOODLAND: 17.5%
- ARABLE: 3.7%
- OTHER: 78.8%

PUBLIC EXPENDITURE

DEFENCE EXPENDITURE (% of goverment exp.)	**9.2%**	(1997)
MILITARY EXPENDITURE (% of health & education)	**121%**	(1990/91)

16 Mozambique supported Zimbabwe's independence struggle, blockading the imports and exports of Ian Smith's racist regime despite severe repercussions on the Mozambican economy. Zimbabwean freedom fighters were given permission to set up bases within Mozambican territory; the white minority regimes retaliated with air raids and invasions.

17 Zimbabwe finally gained independence in 1980, altering the political outlook of the region, tightening the circle around apartheid and allowing Mozambique to revitalize its economy through the economic integration of the Front-Line nations (Tanzania, Zambia, Angola and Botswana) and with Zimbabwe, Malawi, Lesotho and Swaziland.

18 In March 1980 President Samora Machel launched a political campaign aimed at eliminating corruption, inefficiency and the increasing bureaucracy of state agencies and companies. A 10-year program for economic development was implemented, calling for investments of $1 billion in agriculture, transport and industry, and the political organization of the country was improved by consolidating FRELIMO, which decided to implement a more representative distribution of political leaders of the Government and the Front.

19 All of these projects were affected by the increasing deterioration of relations with South Africa. In 1981 South African forces invaded Mozambican territory, attacking the Maputo suburb of Matola.

They also backed the anti-government Movement of National Resistance (RENAMO), made up of former Salazar followers and mercenaries. South Africa's terrorism was aimed at their anti-racist refugees living in Mozambique, while RENAMO aimed to sabotage economic objectives and intimidate the rural population.

20 At the end of 1982, the Government cracked down on the black market and launched a major offensive against RENAMO in the Gorongoza region, where RENAMO's armed bands were attacking the communal villages of the interior.

21 At the fourth congress of FRELIMO in April 1983, major changes in the Government's economic program were discussed. One of the main subjects under debate was a proposed reduction in the emphasis given to large agricultural projects, to provide greater incentives for smaller projects.

22 Debate of the 'eight points' of the fourth congress resulted in the wider participation of party members who were called in to supervise the behavior of Government officials more directly. This initiative to refurbish the links between the party leadership and its rank and file, brought a complete change in the make-up of the delegation attending the congress. The overwhelming majority was rural workers and the number of women delegates had more than doubled since the third FRELIMO congress in 1977.

23 The emphasis given to small-scale agriculture and industry was the result of a major reappraisal of all the large state-run farms. These were charged with excessive centralization, bureaucracy and economic inefficiency.

24 1985 marked the beginning of a critical period for Mozambique, with RENAMO terrorist attacks, on the one hand, and a severe drought, on the other. The drought decimated cattle, causing a 70 per cent drop in production, and was also responsible for a 25 per cent reduction in grain production.

25 President Samora Machel denounced South Africa's covert support for RENAMO, saying that it was a violation of the Nkomati agreements of March 1984, when the two countries had signed a treaty of non-aggression.

26 Already tense economic and defense situations were compounded by the death of President Samora Machel on October 19 1986. His plane crashed while returning from a high-level conference in Zambia. At that conference, presidents Kenneth Kaunda of Zambia, Mobutu Sese Seko of Zaire, José Eduardo Dos Santos of Angola and Machel had debated joining forces to confront South Africa's growing aggression toward the independent countries of southern Africa. They wanted to end South African support for UNITA and RENAMO in Angola and Mozambique. It has never been established whether the plane crash in which Machel died was an accident or an act of sabotage.

27 On November 3, the Central Committee of FRELIMO met in a special session where they elected Joaquim Chissano (minister of Foreign Relations) as the new president and Commander-in-Chief of the Armed Forces.

28 In the following year, the Government began to reconsider the economic strategy it had followed since independence in 1975. A more flexible foreign investment policy was adopted and local producers were encouraged to invest more. This was the first step toward the establishment of a mixed economy, a concept adopted by the FRELIMO Congress in July 1989. The party dropped all references to its Marxist-Leninist orientation.

29 Peace negotiations between RENAMO and the Government in Maputo began in 1990. These negotiations were made easier as the new constitution had recently brought in a multiparty system. The continuation of the single-party system had been one of the arguments used by the rebels to justify their terrorist activity.

30 In October 1991 the authorities of Manica province, one of the most fertile regions of the country, declared a state of

PROFILE

ENVIRONMENT

The wide coastal plain, wider in the south, gradually rises to relatively low inland plateaus. The Tropic of Capricorn runs across the country and the climate is hot and dry. Two major rivers cross the country: the Zambeze in the center and the Limpopo in the south. Due to its geographic location, the country's ports are the natural ocean outlets for Malawi, Zimbabwe and part of South Africa. However, trade has been hampered by wars during the past two decades. Mineral resources are important though scarcely exploited. The war devastated the country's entire productive structure, especially in the agricultural sector. The use of its mangrove forests for firewood has caused deforestation.

SOCIETY

Peoples: The Mozambican population is made up of a variety of ethnic groups, mainly of Bantu origin. The main groups are: Makua 47 per cent; Tsonga 23.3 per cent; Malawi 12 per cent; Shona 11.3 per cent; Swahili 9.8 per cent; Yao 3.8 per cent; Makonde 0.6 per cent.
Religions: The rural population practice traditional religions. Most of the urban population is Christian or Muslim. Islam prevails in the north.
Languages: Portuguese (official). Most of the population speak Bantu languages, the main ones being Swahili and Macoa-Lomne.
Political Parties: Mozambique Liberation Front (FRELIMO); National Resistance of Mozambique (RENAMO); Liberal and Democratic Party of Mozambique (PALMO); National Union of Mozambique (UNAMO).
Social Organizations: Organization of Mozambican Women; Mozambican Youth Organization was formed.

THE STATE

Official Name: República de Moçambique.
Administrative divisions: 10 provinces and 1 city (Maputo).
Capital: Maputo-Matola 1,500,000 (est 1995).
Government: Joaquim Chissano, President since November 1986, re-elected in October 1994 and December 1999. Pascoal Mocumbi, Prime Minister since 1996. The People's Assembly is the main political body.
National Holiday: June 25, Independence Day (1975).
Armed Forces: 50,000 (1993).

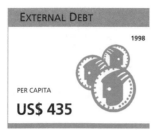

EXTERNAL DEBT

1998

PER CAPITA

US$ 435

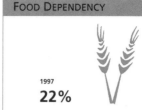

FOOD DEPENDENCY

1997

22%

STATISTICS

DEMOGRAPHY

Population: 19,286,000 (1999)
Annual growth: 2.6 % (1975/97)
Estimates for year 2015 (million):
25.2 (1999)
Annual growth to year 2015:
1.8 % (1997/2015)
Urban population: 36.5 % (1997)
Urban Growth: 8.5 % (1980/95)
Children per woman: 6.2 (1998)

HEALTH

Life expectancy at birth: 44 years
(1998)
male: 44 years (1998)
female: 47 years (1998)
Maternal mortality:
1,100 per 100,000 live births
(1990-98)
Infant mortality: 129 per 1,000
(1998)
Under-5 child mortality:
206 per 1,000 (1998)
Daily calorie supply:
1,799 per capita (1996)
Safe water: 46 % (1990/98)

EDUCATION

Literacy: 38 % (1995)
male: 55 % (1995)
female: 23 % (1995)
School enrolment:
Primary total: 60 % (1990/96)
male: 70 % (1990/97)
female: 50 % (1990/97)
Secondary:
male: 9 % (1990/96)
female: 5 % (1990/96)
Tertiary: 1 % (1996)
Primary school teachers:
one for every 58 (1998)

COMMUNICATIONS

3 newspapers (1996), 40 radios
(1997), 3 TV sets (1996) and 3
main telephone lines (1996) per
1,000 people

ECONOMY

Per capita, GNP: $ 210 (1998)
Annual growth, GNP: 11.8 % (1998)
Annual inflation: 41.1 % (1990/98)
Consumer price index: 153.0
(1997)
Currency: 11,874.6 meticais = $ 1
(1998)
Cereal imports:
523,317 metric tons (1998)
Food import dependency: 22 %
(1997)
Fertilizer use: 22 kg per ha (1997)
Exports: $ 456 million (1998)
Imports: $ 1,186 million (1998)
External debt: $ 8,208 million
(1998); $ 435 per capita (1998)
Debt service: 18.0 % of exports
(1998)
Development aid received: $ 963
million (1997); $ 66.8 per capita
(1997); 37.40 % of GNP (1997)

ENERGY

Consumption: 461.0 Kgs of Oil
equivalent per capita yearly
(1997); 9.0 % imported (1997)

HDI (rank/value): 169/0.341 (1997)

---

emergency because of the drought which destroyed most of the crops. It was considered the worst drought to have affected the area in the last 40 years causing enormous shortages for the 300,000 local inhabitants.

[31] In Rome, in November 1991, a peace protocol was signed by the Government of Mozambique and RENAMO. It foresaw the recognition of the rebel movement as a legal political party. This protocol was considered the forerunner to a peace agreement. In addition to the new laws regulating the political parties, this agreement guaranteed freedom of information, expression and association, and pledged that elections would be held.

[32] The refinancing of the $1.6 billion foreign debt was contingent upon the success of the peace accord. Prime Minister Machungo explained that his country was suffering badly from the effects of the cessation of aid from the former USSR and the Eastern European countries.

[33] When RENAMO activities continued, the elections scheduled for 1991 were postponed. In May 1991, a new opposition party, the Liberal and Democratic Party of Mozambique, was created. The following month, a coup attempt by those opposed to peace negotiations ended in failure. In August, Chissano was re-elected during FRELIMO's 6th Congress, and Feliciano Salamao was named secretary general.

[34] In early 1992, the new political party regulations became one of the major hindrances to peace negotiations in Mozambique. The Chissano Government initially offered RENAMO a special status, guaranteeing their members political rights but the rebels turned down the offer. The armed opposition also refused to accept the terms which stated that they would have to have a minimum of a hundred registered members in each province, as well as in the capital, to qualify as a *bona fide* political party.

[35] On October 4 1992, with Italy as mediator, Chissano and Alfonso Dhlakama (of RENAMO) signed a peace agreement in Rome, putting an end to 16 years of conflict which had caused over a million deaths, and five million refugees.

[36] According to the terms of the agreement, RENAMO and Government troops were confined to pre-established areas, and weapons were to be turned over to UN soldiers charged with disarming both sides within a six-month period.

[37] Zimbabwean troops, who controlled the corridors linking that country with Mozambique's ports, were to be withdrawn. The agreement also provided for the creation of an army of both Government and guerrilla forces.

[38] Differences between the two parties led to direct UN Security Council intervention in December 1992. The Peace Plan approved civilian observers and 7,500 troops being sent into Mozambique.

[39] In February and March 1993, FRELIMO participated in joint military manoeuvres with the United States. This change of attitude was interpreted as an attempt at rapprochement with the West, from whom Mozambique was seeking aid.

[40] The UN decided to postpone elections until October 1994, hoping to overcome the stalemate which was stalling the peace process. After negotiations, RENAMO agreed to take part in the elections. Chissano was re-elected with over 53 per cent of the vote. In the parliamentary elections, FRELIMO won with 44.3 per cent followed by RENAMO with 37.7 per cent.

[41] In March 1995, the Paris Club promised to give Maputo $780 billion for the country's reconstruction. Social conditions after the civil war were disastrous, partly because Mozambique - one of the poorest countries in the world - came out of the strife with a devastated agricultural sector and many fields ridden with landmines.

[42] During 1996, the Government managed to restore old trade links between Johannesburg and Maputo. Investments were desperately needed to revive the ailing economy. An agreement between Chissano and his South African President Nelson Mandela allowed thousands of South African farmers of European origin to settle in 200,000 hectares in the North of the country, as part of a process resisted by the opposition.

[43] The heavy rains of 1997 displaced thousands of people, most of whom sought refuge in Malawi. This water, however, helped maintain cereal production, a family subsistence and main export crop.

[44] The Government privatization program went ahead. By mid-year, more than 900 of the 1,200 State companies had been sold. Inflation reached 5.8 per cent that year, the lowest figure since the World Bank and IMF began to oversee the national economy.

[45] In early 1998, a cholera epidemic killed more than 800 people. The disease spread mostly in the south and the central provinces.

[46] A report from the United Nations published in October established that life expectancy in Mozambique, one of the nine African countries hardest hit by the HIV virus, with more than 10 per cent of adults infected, would fall to 47 years. Had they not suffered the scourge of AIDS, following average global growth, Mozambicans would have had a life expectancy of 64 years.

[47] The opening of trade relations with South Africa made economic growth possible, and in 1999 this was amongst the highest in the world (11 per cent). Expectations were not so high for the following year. The recession indicated that growth for 2000 would be below 10 per cent.

[48] The December legislative and presidential elections saw a FRELIMO win, with Chissano re-elected. The opposition RENAMO lodged complaints of electoral fraud.

[49] In February 2000, several of the nation's biggest approved an 18-month moratorium on debt payments, but following the floods in March 2000 which devastated the country, Germany promoted the measure of cancelling Mozambique's foreign debt of nearly $1.5 billion. More than a million people were displaced and more than 200 killed as a result of the catastrophe. ∎

Myanmar/Burma

Myanmar

Population: 45,059,000 (1999)
Area: 676,580 SQ KM
Capital: Yangon (Rangoon)
Currency: Kyat
Language: Burmese

Inscriptions dating from the 6th century BC testify to the very early establishment of advanced civilizations in Burma. Migrations occurred frequently from north to south and from the mountains to the coast. The people intermingled and occasionally engaged in battles until the 11th century when Burmese conquered the southern Hmong and the northern Kadu, establishing the state of Pagan.

2   The following two centuries were a golden age in Burmese thought and architecture. The Mongols attacked from the North, with aid from the Great Khan in Beijing. In 1283, the Mongol invasion ended the Pagan state and the Mongols remained in power until 1301. Marco Polo, in the service of Kublai Khan, participated in the invasion and is thought to have been the first European to visit the country.

3   Burma remained divided into small ethnic states until the 16th century when Toungoo local leaders reunified the territory. The second of these rulers, Bayinnaung, extended his domain to parts of present-day Laos and Thailand.

4   Extravagance undermined the agricultural foundations of the economy, resulting in an exodus of peasants to neighboring states. The process of fragmentation was hastened by the presence of early European traders and their consequent rivalries.

5   In 1740, a Toungoo ruler again achieved unification, with the help of the British. But when his successors continued the project of national reconstruction, they clashed with British interests in Assam, India, and a confrontation resulted with their former European allies. The Burmese fought three wars against the British throughout the 19th century, in 1820-26, 1852-53 and 1885-86. During the last war, King Thibaw was taken prisoner and Burma was annexed to the British viceroyalty of India.

6   The 1930s began with a rising tide of nationalist movements; that of the Buddhist monk, U Ottama, inspired by Gandhi; Saya San's attempt to restore the monarchy; and uprisings organized by the University of Rangoon, bringing together Buddhists and Marxists. In 1936, a student demonstration became an anti-British national protest, led by Aung San.

7   The anti-colonial movement was not restricted to the urban élites. Heavy taxes and the collapse of the world rice market in 1930 forced thousands of small farmers into debt and ruin at the hands of British banks and Indian moneylenders. Discontent expressed itself as a generalized xenophobia, leading to popular rebellions in 1938 and 1939.

8   When World War II broke out, a group of militant anti-colonialists in Bangkok, known as 'the 30 comrades', including members from the newly-created Communist Party, formed the Burma Independence Army (BIA). They joined the Japanese against the British and invaded the capital on 7 March 1942. Minority groups of Karen, Kachin and Chin organized guerrilla groups to combat both the BIA and the Japanese.

9   The Japanese granted Burma independence on August 1 1943, appointing Ba Maw head of state. The 'national' army was placed under the command of Ne Win. However, friction soon developed between the Japanese and the socialist wing of the '30 comrades'. On March 27 1945, the BIA declared war on Japan and was recognized by the British as the Patriotic Burmese Forces. On May 30, they captured Rangoon, this time with the help of the British. Aung San organized a transition government, and in 1947, a constitution was drafted. On July 19, a military commando assassinated Aung San and several aides in the palace, and U Nu stepped in as premier. On January 4 1948, independence was proclaimed.

10   Several challenges faced the new government: ethnic minorities rebelled; recently-defeated Chinese Kuomintang forces moved into Shan state, where they were also involved in drug trafficking, and Aung San's army, renamed the People's Volunteer Organization and linked to the Communist Party, mounted a further armed insurrection.

11   On May 2 1962, General Ne Win overthrew U Nu, who had been very successful in the 1960 elections. Burma had peacefully settled its border conflicts with India and China, and throughout the war in Southeast Asia Rangoon maintained a policy of non-alignment. Ne Win nationalized the banks, the rice industry (which accounted for 70 per cent of foreign earnings), and the largely Indian controlled trade.

12   In 1972, a new constitution confirmed the governing Burma Socialist Program Party (BSSP) as the only legal political organization.

13   Ne Win's regime declined after the 1973 economic crisis and opponents emphasized the ambiguity of his 'Burmese Socialism'.

14   In 1979, Burma withdrew from the Non-Aligned Movement. In 1981, the National Congress named San Yu as successor to Ne Win, who resigned the presidency but continued as party chairperson and thus maintained control of the country.

WORKERS

% OF LABOUR FORCE — **1998**

▪ FEMALE: 48%   ▪ MALE: 52%

1990

▪ SERVICES: 9.3%
▪ INDUSTRY: 8.0%
▪ AGRICULTURE: 82.7%

LAND USE

DEFORESTATION: 0.7% annual (1990/95)
IRRIGATED: 4.0% of arable (1993)

1993

▪ FOREST & WOODLAND: 17.5%
▪ ARABLE: 3.7%
▪ OTHER: 78.8%

PUBLIC EXPENDITURE

DEFENCE EXPENDITURE (% of goverment exp.) — **9.2%** (1997)

MILITARY EXPENDITURE (% of health & education) — **121%** (1990/91)

15 At the end of 1987, the social and economic situation worsened. In August, Ne Win admitted making mistakes in the economic policy of the previous 25 years. A BSPP ruling congress appointed Sein Lwin as head of state, triggering a new wave of protests. Hundreds of students and Buddhist monks died in the streets, and Lwin - nicknamed 'the butcher of Rangoon' was forced to resign after 17 days, replaced by Dr Maung Maung.

16 The opposition organized for the multiparty elections scheduled for May 1990. The Government changed the country's name to Union of Myanmar and dropped the term 'Socialist'.

17 The National League for Democracy (NLD) won 80 per cent of the vote, while the ruling National Unity Party (ex-BSPP) retained only 10 of the 485 seats. The election results were ignored by the Government who banned opposition activities, imprisoned or banished its leaders, and harshly repressed street demonstrations.

18 In July 1989, the leader of the NLD, Aung San Suu Kyi, the daughter of anti-colonial hero Aung San, was sentenced to house arrest and held incommunicado. She received the Nobel Peace Prize in 1991.

19 The opposition was reinforced by agreements between students, Buddhist monks and some minorities. In March 1992, the UN High Commission for Refugees denounced the massacres carried out against ethnic minorities. All political parties were dissolved or banned.

20 In April, General Than Shwe took power releasing 200 dissidents and permitting 31 universities and schools to reopen. Myanmar returned to the Movement of Non-Aligned Nations. In September, martial law was suspended, but Amnesty International reported the continued use of torture.

21 In January 1993, the military invoked a National Convention to draw up a new constitution. At the end of that year, Amnesty International denounced the imprisonment of over 1,550 opposition figures.

22 An article of the new 1994 constitution stipulated presidential candidates could neither be married to foreigners nor bear children under foreign citizenship and they should have been residing in Myanmar for the last 20 consecutive years. The regulation was custom-made for Suu Kyi who was married to a British subject and lived several years abroad. The military junta met with her in September 1994 for the first time since she was arrested. No agreement was reached regarding the new constitution.

23 In July 1995, Suu Kyi was released from house arrest and called on the State Law and Order Restoration Council (SLORC) to hold a dialogue. The SLORC refused, jailed dozens of dissidents and maintained the ban on political debates.

24 The headquarters of the rebel minority in Manerplaw was taken by the SLORC in January. The fall of Manerplaw was an important defeat for the opposition since it was also an important base for undercover organizations belonging to the rebel armies and democrat activists. In January 1996 through a secret accord the Government achieved the surrender of Khun Sa, known as the 'opium king' and leader of a Shan force.

25 Huge crowds - some of them with up to 10,000 followers - periodically gathered to express support at Suu Kyi's home in May and June 1996 but these demonstrations lost strength due to government repression. In June, the SLORC banned statements against the Government and threatened a complete prohibition of the NLD's activities and the arrest of its members for unlawful association.

26 The SLORC declared 1996 as year of tourism. It promoted the development of public works and the real estate sector - a base for drug-money laundering - with strong participation by the state and foreign investors.

27 In 1996, the military junta ordered the arrest of some 250 members of the NLD, who had planned to celebrate the anniversary of their victory in the 1990 parliamentary elections. The regime also approved a law banning NLD political meetings.

28 Arrests of members of the NLD continued to be arrested in 1996. The Government restricted Suu Kyi's freedom, to the point of banning her use of the telephone.

29 The SLORC, submitted to increasing international pressure, above all from the United States and the European Union, made some concessions in 1997. In September, it allowed the NLD to hold its first congress in seven years, although it only authorized the attendance of half its 600 delegates.

30 In an attempt at renovation, toward the end of 1997, the military junta dissolved itself appointing a State Peace and Development Council (SPDC) in its place a. In July of that year, Myanmar became a member of the Association of Southeast Asian Nations (ASEAN).

31 In early 1998, inflation increased enormously, as a consequence of the stock market crisis in Southeast Asia. In addition, the rice harvest - one of the main crops for internal consumption and export - was far smaller than had been expected.

32 In August the army launched a virulent press campaign against Suu Kyi, who had been arrested when she tried to leave the capital to meet with supporters. The Junta classed Suu Kyi as 'public enemy number one'. The government newspapers added that anyone meeting with her in public would not have 'long to live'.

34 The Government's intimidation policy was kept up over the following months. In March 2000, in a public event celebrating the armed forces, President Than Shwe warned that government opponents would be 'eliminated' if they threatened the 'stability of the country'. Similarly, Than Shwe called for national unity and for the insurgents fighting along the frontiers to sign a cease fire 'and swiftly join hands with the army'.

35 In September 2000 Suu Kyi was under police guard after her 9-day protest against travel restrictions was forcibly ended. ∎

PROFILE

ENVIRONMENT

The country lies between the Tibetan plateau and the Malayan peninsula. Mountain ranges to the east, north and west surround a central valley where the Irrawaddy, Sittang and Salween rivers flow. Most of the population are concentrated in this area where rice is grown. The climate is tropical with monsoon rains between May and October. Rainforests extend over most of the country. Deforestation has been responsible for the destruction of two-thirds of the country's tropical forest.

SOCIETY

Peoples: Burmese 69 per cent; Shan 8.5 per cent; Karen 6.2 per cent; Rakhine 4.5 per cent; Mon 2.4 per cent; Chin 2.2 per cent; Kachin 1.4 per cent.
Religions: Bhuddist 89.1 per cent, Christian 4-9 per cent, Muslim 3.8 per cent; other 2.2 per cent. **Languages:** Burmese (official) and the languages of the ethnic groups. **Political Parties:** National League for Democracy (NLD), League of Shan Nationalities for Democracy; Arakan League for Democracy; the National Unity Party (NUP). **Social Organizations:** The Workers' Organization of Burma; the Peasants' Organization.

THE STATE

Official Name: Pyidaungzu Myanma Naingngnandaw. **Capital:** Yangôn (Rangoon) 3,851,000 people (1995). **Other cities:** Mandalay 533,000 people; Moulmein 220,000; Pegu 150,000; Bassein, 144,100 (1983). **Government:** General Than Shwe, President, Head of state and Government since April 1992. Legislature: suspended since 1988. **National Holiday:** January 4, Independence Day (1948). **Armed Forces:** 286,000 (1995). **Other:** 85,000 (People's Police, People's Militia).

Namibia

Namibia

Population: 1,695,000 (1999)
Area: 824,290 SQ KM
Capital: Windhoek
Currency: Namibian dollar
Language: English

S outhwestern Africa was occupied first by San and Khoikhoi peoples, Ovambo in the north and the Bantu-speaking Herero. Later the Nama, known as the Red Nation, set up lands in the southern part and maintained tight union between their clans and lived from grazing animals. Closely linked to this people were the Damara, coming from Central Africa, who combined herding with hunting and the smelting of copper. In the central and north eastern regions, the Herero built clan alliances, often led by a supreme chief. The Ovambo, farmers who developed several kingdoms along both banks of the Kunene river, were a constant threat for the unity of the Herero.

² Arid and scarcely populated, the territory of the Kalahari desert did not offer great attractions to European colonization. From 1670 onward German missionaries, European traders and Norwegian whalers began to arrive to the coast and some ventured into the hinterland. Traders stimulated conflict between the various clans, which became increasingly destructive and which encouraged the arrival, at the beginning of the 19th century, of the Oorlam-Nama, a tribe from The Cape whose military technology was inspired by that of the Afrikaners. Thanks to these strategies, which included horses, rifles and an organisation model of small commands, they dominated the Nama and the Damara. Half way through the century, a

kingdom was set up by Chief Jonker Afrikaner, of Oorlam and Herero lineage, who had the full backing of the Damara and the Red Nation.

³ In 1870 the British made a treaty with the Herero and flew their flag on the port of Walvis Bay. However, the German Second Reich of Bismarck and William I, launched an occupation of the area through dubious treaties, plunder and the strategy of dividing the African peoples. In 1884, Germany annexed the territory under the name of South West Africa. In 1885, Herero resistance forced the Germans back to Walvis Bay, until the British arrived to support them.

⁴ Toward the end of the century, German colonists arrived and started to build railways from Swakopmund and Luderitz. The country acquired strategic value for the Europeans with the discovery of large reserves of iron, lead, copper and diamonds, which were later augmented by metals of military interest: manganese, tungsten, vanadium, cadmium and great quantities of uranium.

⁵ The great war of resistance from 1904-1907, led by the Herero, almost expelled the Germans, who reacted brutally with mass hangings and enforced detention in concentration camps, which led to a 90 per cent reduction in Herero numbers by 1910. The Nama, who had been slow to enter the conflict, were defeated in 1907. Only a third of the Nama population survived, confined in concentration camps. Despite the rigidity with which the Germans exercised

WORKERS

% OF LABOUR FORCE **1998**

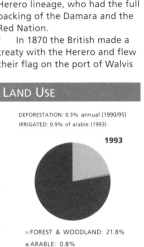

■ FEMALE: 41%   ■ MALE: 59%

1990

■ SERVICES: 35.5%
■ INDUSTRY: 15.4%
■ AGRICULTURE: 49.1%

LAND USE

DEFORESTATION: 0.3% annual (1990/95)
IRRIGATED: 0.9% of arable (1993)

1993

■ FOREST & WOODLAND: 21.8%
■ ARABLE: 0.8%
■ OTHER: 77.4%

PUBLIC EXPENDITURE

DEFENCE EXPENDITURE (% of goverment exp.)	7.3%	(1997)
MILITARY EXPENDITURE (% of health & education)	23%	(1990/91)

their control, this did not extend northwards significantly to trouble the Ovambo.

6   During World War I, the British invaded the German colony from South Africa and took over. At the end of the War, the region became a League of Nations trust territory known as South West Africa, assigned to the Union of South Africa as 'a sacred charge of civilization' to 'promote to the maximum the material and moral well-being of its inhabitants'.

7   The mandate did not help the local African population, who were exploited by the German colonists and South

African *boers*. The territory was unofficially a 'fifth province' of South Africa. The railways were extended to Walvis Bay and Cape Town in order to link South West Africa's economy with South Africa.

8   Local resistance there and elsewhere in South West Africa continued in a sustained and violent manner until the1930s. Through trade union organizing, political and economic resistance began in the 1920s. Despite the efforts of the Afrikaners, the 'province' of South Western Africa was not productive until the end of World War II. Mining production was low

and due to elevated export prices, there was only slight demand for minerals. Pretoria had to fund the survival of the colonists.

9   From 1947, the Namibians started to ask the United Nations to free them from South African domination. On another front, the UN - which inherited responsibility for the colonies in trust from the League of Nations - ignored South African demands to officially annex the territory, arguing that 'the African inhabitants of South West Africa have still not achieved political independence'.

10   Between 1961 and 1968, the United Nations tried to annul the trust mandate and establish the independence of the country. Legal pressure was ineffective and the Namibian people, led by the South West Africa People's Organization (SWAPO) decided to fight for freedom. The fighting broke out on 26 August 1966.

11   In 1968 the UN finally proclaimed that the South African occupation of the country now known as Namibia was illegal. However, attempts by most members of the UN General Assembly to follow this condemnation with economic sanctions systematically came up against the veto of the Western powers. A UN Council was set up as legal representative of the territory until sovereignty could be freely exercised by the people.

12   Angolan independence, declared in 1975, gave SWAPO a supportive rearguard. The guerrilla war intensified despite South African pressure against Angola, and the Western powers started to put pressure on Pretoria to seek a 'moderate' solution before a revolutionary regime could take over the country.

13   In December 1978, South Africa held elections in Namibia with a view to establishing an independent government, presented as a step toward independence. But the poll was carried out without UN observers, with the territory occupied by racist troops and with no SWAPO

participation, leading to a total lack of credibility in the results.

14   The economy had grown in a sustained manner since World War II, reaching a peak of $1,000 per head in the seventies ($20,000 for Europeans and $150 for black Namibians). Even while incomes in the white enclave soared, the salary of black workers was barely enough to live on, at a level of minimal subsistence for one person. It took until half way through this decade for workers to be trained to any significant degree, in qualified tasks.

15   The South-African controlled administration in Windhoek operated along customary colonial lines of dependence. Ninety per cent of the goods consumed in Namibia came from South Africa. The *Odendaal* was a body established by the colonial government to encourage growth along segregationist lines, favoring the elite of professional blacks in the 1980s. During this period the Government increased the salaries of professional blacks - teachers, nurses, administrators and army personnel. However, the vast majority of the black population, which at that time numbered two thirds of the total, were left in conditions of extreme poverty. On another front, employment contracts damaged the social and civil fabric, increasing the number of single female-headed households in rural areas and also in the outlying urban areas.

16   According to the book *To be Born a Nation*, Namibian independence would mean the loss of $240 million in exports and extra costs of $14 million of imports of foreign produce for South Africa. As a result, South Africa upped its military budget by 30 per cent for the conflict against the Namibian People's Liberation Army, SWAPO's armed wing. South Africa made any independence agreement conditional on the withdrawal of Cuban troops from Angola, whilst demanding guarantees that

PROFILE

ENVIRONMENT

Mainly made up of plateaus in the desert region along the Tropic of Capricorn. The Namib desert, along the coast, contains rich diamond deposits and is only populated because of mining activities. To the east, the country shares the Kalahari desert with Botswana, an area populated by shepherds and hunters. The population is densest in the north, and in the central plateau, where rainfall is heaviest. There is a coastal fishing industry which, together with cattle raising, was the mainstay of the economy before mining began in the 1960s. The country has important reserves of copper, lead, zinc, cadmium and uranium.

SOCIETY

Peoples: Ovambo 47.4 per cent; Kavango 8.8 per cent; Herero 7.1 per cent; Damara 7.1 per cent; Nama 4.6 per cent. There is a European minority (4.6 per cent).
Religions: Many people practice traditional African religions although there are a large number of Christians (Lutheran 51.2 per cent, Catholics 19.8 per cent, Anglican 5 per cent).
Languages: English (official), Khoisan, Bantu, German and Afrikaans.
Political Parties: Southwest African People's Organization (SWAPO); Southwest African People's Organization for Justice (SWAPO for Justice); Democratic Turnhalle Alliance (DTA); United Democratic Front; National Christian Action.
Social Organizations: National Union of Workers of Namibia.

THE STATE

Official Name: Republic of Namibia.
Administrative divisions: 13 districts.
Capital: Windhoek 200,000 people (est 1995).
Other cities: Walvis Bay 45,000 people; Swakopmund 15,500; Rundu 15,000; Rehoboth 15,000; Keetmanshoop 25,000.
Government: Sam Nujoma, President since March 1990, re-elected in 1999. Hage Geingob, Prime Minister since 1990. The Constitution established a presidential regime and a multiparty system.
National holiday: March 21 (Independence).
Armed Forces: 8,100.

investments in Namibia would not be touched. SWAPO did not accept the privileges granted to the white population in the draft constitution, nor the limitations to possibilities of future reforms to this. It also insisted that the elections should be supervised by the UN, an idea not accepted by Pretoria.

[17]   In February 1984, representatives of Angola and South Africa met in Zambia's capital, Lusaka, for peace negotiations. They agreed a planned withdrawal of South African troops from Southern Angola, in return for a ceasefire. In May, delegates from SWAPO and other Namibian parties met a South African representative but negotiations failed due to South African intransigence. The South African withdrawal from Angola did not occur within the deadline and the situation was deadlocked again.

[18]   In December 1988, after prolonged US-mediated negotiations, South Africa, Angola and Cuba reached an agreement whereby South African troops would leave Namibia and the Cubans would withdraw their 50,000 soldiers from Angola.

[19]   In November 1989 more than 710,000 Namibians voted for members of the First Constituent Assembly. Ten political parties stood in the UN-supervised elections. SWAPO won a resounding victory with 60 per cent of the poll, and gained control of the Assembly. SWAPO leader, Sam Nujoma, became the first president of Namibia. .

[20]   Independence was proclaimed on 21 March 21 1990. The presidential guard of honor, made up of troops from SWAPO and the SWA Territory Force which had protected the South African regime; both to be integrated into the new National Army of Namibia.

[21]   The new government had to face up to the inequalities inherited from the South African apartheid system, above all in heath and education. Income inequality within the population led economic analysts to classify the nation as having a 'dual economy' as around 70 per cent of the population lived in Third World conditions, 25 per cent within a transition economy and only 5 per cent benefited from economic conditions linked to development.

[22]   Namibia adopted English as its official language replacing Afrikaans at independence. The Government organized a Department of Informal Education to help women learn to read. In collaboration with UNICEF it decided Namibia's women should be taught to read first in their own languages in order to later learn English. As for health, the Government earmarked resources to develop a rehabilitation plan for some 40,000 unemployed - mostly the victims of 23 years of pro-independence guerrilla warfare.

[23]   Prepared to play an important role in Southern Africa, Nujoma donated around $3 million in 1991 to the African National Congress (ANC), then the main black opposition to the minority white government in South Africa - a sum which was handed over to ANC Nelson Mandela on a visit he made to Namibia on January 31.

[24]   In 1992 Namibia and South Africa agreed to return the port of Walvis bay to Windhoek in 1994. One year later the National Council, the upper chamber of Parliament, came into operation. In 1994, the Government approved a land law, which aimed among other things to limit the concentration of wealth. It was estimated that 1 per cent of the population held 75 per cent of the nation's land.

[25]   In December of that year, Nujoma was re-elected president with 70 per cent of popular support. However, in May 1995 his party, SWAPO, split - leading to the creation of the SWAPO for Justice group.

[26]   In mid 1997, a SWAPO Congress proclaimed Nujoma for a third period as president of Namibia. Social protests, above all due to unemployment, were not heeded by the government. A large part of the former SWAPO army was still unemployed.

[27]   The number of HIV-positive and people with AIDS increased alarmingly. In 1997, the illness caused 1,539 deaths, bringing the total registered since 1988 to 3,677. The number of those infected since the same year is 40,629.

[28]   The fishing industry showed signs of recovery and recorded strong growth in 1998. Also that year, in search of new sources of income, the Government began promoting Namibia as a tourist destination, an industry that had not yet been developed in this country.

[29]   After a small band of rebels attempted to take over the town of Katima Mulil in August 1999, some 200 people were detained and tortured until many 'confessed' to being supporters of Caprivi Strip independence, Namibia's panhandle territory several hundred km long but just 40 or 50 km wide that divides Botswana from Angola. Of the 200 detainees, at least 76 were tried for treason and other crimes, while the rest were released without charges. Some 100,000 people inhabit the Caprivi Strip, primarily members of the Iozi ethnic group, who refuse to be led by the country's Ovambo majority, which also dominates SWAPO.

[30]   Despite protests from the opposition, the Constitution was modified so that Nujoma could run for a third presidential term in the 1999 elections, which he won easily with 76 per cent of the vote. Upon taking office in March 2000 the re-elected President declared that the country's goals were to achieve a standard of living similar to the industrialized North by the year 2030 and in the immediate term, to fight HIV, which continued to decimate the Namibian population. ■

Nauru

Nauru

Population: 12,000 (1998)
Area: 20 SQ KM
Currency: Australian dollar
Language: English

Nauru, which lies in the central Pacific, was originally populated by migrating Polynesian, Micronesian and Melanesian people. The British sailor John Fearn was the first European to visit the island, which he named Pleasant Island. Whaling ships often called at Nauru during the 19th century, until it was annexed by the German Second Reich in 1888.

[2] In 1899, Nauru was found to have phosphate-rich rock which made it one of the wealthiest territories in the world. In 1905, an Anglo-German company began mining on the island.

[3] At the beginning of World War I, Nauru came under Australian trusteeship and during World War II, under Japanese control with thousands of Nauruans sent to forced labor camps on the island of Truk (in present-day Micronesia). At the end of the War, only 700 came back alive. Australia recovered the island, and mining was continued by British, Australian and Aotearoan/New Zealand transnational consortia.

[4] The Nauruans did not adjust well to mining and were soon replaced by immigrants, mostly Chinese. Immigrant workers became so numerous that in 1964, the Australian Government officially suggested that Nauruans should accept resettlement on a different island or elsewhere in Australia. Nauruans rejected this, deciding to stay on their island and seek autonomy.

[5] The mining sector was nationalized in 1967, which resulted in a large increase in per capita income. In 1992, the minimum annual salary was $6,500. Nauru declared independence on January 31 1968, rejecting Australian attempts at domination. A year later it became a member of the Commonwealth.

[6] Government expenses and public investment were paid out of a huge legal fund fed by phosphate revenues. Education, medical care and housing are free.

[7] Hammer de Roburt dominated the political scene, and as the first President, he governed continuously until 1976 when he lost the majority to Bernard Dowiyogo, of the Nauru Party. Two years later, De Roburt once again obtained the majority, holding office from 1978 to 1986.

[8] Bernard Dowiyogo returned to the presidency in 1989. His government started a court case against the Australian state for the indiscriminate exploitation of the phosphate mines during the past 50 years. In 1991, Australia recognized Nauru's right to claim compensation. Britain and Aotearoa promised to collaborate with Australia in the payment of $100 million to Nauru.

[9] That year the economy of Nauru registered a budget deficit for the first time in its history. It was estimated that if mining continued at the same rate, the phosphate resources of the island could be exhausted. The dependence on phosphate exports forced islanders to think of conversion. The only apparent viable alternative is fishing, as the land is not fit for agriculture. The production of vegetables and tropical fruits is enough to meet domestic needs.

[10] The Government, led by Lagumot Harris from 1995, invested in developing the nation's airline and fishing fleets. Harris aimed to correct the deficit, reducing spending and increasing taxes, freezing pay for two years, closing some consulates abroad and privatizing some state bodies.

[11] Falling international phosphate prices, the high maintenance costs of the airline, and unprofitable investments, pushed the economy into serious difficulties.

[12] On February 13 1997, Parliament appointed Kinza Godfrey Clodumar the new President, the fourth in only four months. One of his first policies was to try to attract foreign investors, above all Australians. In December, Nauru re-established diplomatic relations with France, suspended since 1995 in protest over the nuclear tests in French Polynesia.

[13] In late 1997, Clodumar called on the world for drastic reductions in the production of greenhouse gases. The leader stressed that Nauru could disappear under the sea as a consequence of global warming.

[14] The Nauruan people, who until recently enjoyed one of the highest per capita incomes in the world, saw their standard of living decline sharply as a result of poor Government investments. Bernard Dowiyogo, Clodumar's successor, lost the Parliament's vote of confidence and, in April 1999, Rene Harris took over as President. The largest problem confronting the island was that its mineral resources, which had been its major source of income, were practically exhausted. Unable to handle the nation's problems, Harris resigned in April 2000.

[15] After Harris' resignation, Parliament reelected Dowiyogo President. ∎

PROFILE

ENVIRONMENT

Nauru is a coral island, 6 km long by 4 km wide, located near Micronesia just south of the Equator. With sandy beaches and a thin belt of fertile land (300 meters wide), the island has a 60-meter high central plateau of guano, rich in phosphoric acid and nitrogen.

SOCIETY

Peoples: Nauruans, are descendants of Polynesian, Micronesian and Melanesian immigrants. There are also Australian, Aotearoan, Chinese, European minorities, and workers from Tuvalu, Kiribati and other neighboring islands. There are two men to every woman.
Religions: Christian.
Languages: English (official) and Nauruan.
Political Parties: Nauru Party (NP). Democratic Party of Nauru.
Social Organizations: There are two organizations: the Nauru Workers Organization (NWO), founded in 1974 and affiliated to the NP; and the Phosphate Workers' Organization (PWO), founded in 1953.

THE STATE

Official Name: Republic of Nauru.
Capital: There are no population centers and so the island has no formal capital. The Government buildings are located opposite the airport in the Yaren district.
Administrative Divisions: 14 districts.
Government: Bernard Dowiyogo, President since April 2000. One-chamber parliament of 18 deputies.
National Holiday: January 31, Independence Day (1968).

DEMOGRAPHY

Population: 12,000 (1998)

HEALTH

Infant mortality: 25 per 1,000 (1998)
Under-5 child mortality: 30 per 1,000 (1998)

Nepal

Nepal

Population: 23,386,000 (1999)
Area: 140,800 SQ KM
Capital: Kathmandu
Currency: Rupee
Language: Nepali

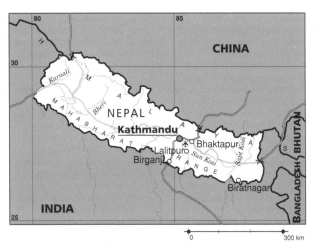

Nepal is a landlocked country in the central Himalayas between two of the world's most densely populated countries; India and China. References to Nepal Valley and Nepal's lower hill areas are found in the ancient Indian classics, suggesting that the Central Himalayan hills were closely connected culturally and politically to the Gangetic Plain at least 2,500 years ago. Lumbini, Gautama Buddha's birthplace in southern Nepal, and Nepal Valley also figure prominently in Buddhist accounts. There is substantial archaeological evidence of early Buddhist influence in Nepal, including a famous column inscribed by Ashoka (Emperor of India, 3rd century BC) at Lumbini and several shrines in the valley.

2 Although there are gaps, the sequence of the Nepal Valley's history can be traced along with the rise of the Licchavi dynasty in the 4th or 5th century AD. While the earlier Kirati dynasty had claimed the status of the Kshatriya caste of rulers and warriors, the Licchavis were probably the first ruling family in that area of plain Indian origin. This set a precedent for what became the normal pattern thereafter - Hindu kings claiming high-caste Indian origin ruling over a population much of which was neither Indo-Aryan nor Hindu.

3 The Licchavi dynastic chronicles, supplemented by numerous stone inscriptions, are particularly detailed from AD 500 to 700. A powerful, united kingdom also emerged in Tibet during this period, and the Himalayan passes to the north of the valley were opened. Extensive cultural, trade and political relations developed across the Himalayas, transforming the valley from a relatively remote backwater into the major intellectual and commercial center between South and Central Asia. Nepal's contacts with China began in the mid-7th century with the exchange of several missions. But intermittent warfare between Tibet and China terminated this relationship; and while there were briefly renewed contacts in subsequent centuries, these were re-established on a continuing basis only in the late 18th century.

4 The middle period in Nepalese history roughly corresponds with the rule of the Malla dynasty (10th-18th century) in Nepal Valley and

surrounding areas. Although most of the Licchavi kings were devout Hindus, they did not impose Brahmanic social codes or values on their non-Hindu subjects. The Mallas perceived their responsibilities differently, however, and the great Malla ruler Jaya Sthiti (reigned c. 1832-95) introduced the first legal and social code strongly influenced by contemporary Hindu principles. His successor Yaksa Malla (reigned 1429-1482) divided his kingdom among his three sons, thus creating the independent principalities of Kathmandu, Patan, and Bhaktpur (Bhagdaon) in the valley. Each of these states controlled territory in the surrounding hill areas, with particular importance attached to the trade routes northward to Tibet and southward to India that were vital to the valley's economy. There were also numerous small principalities in the western and eastern hill areas, whose independence was sustained through a delicate balance of power based upon traditional inter-relationships and in some cases common ancestral origins among the ruling families.

5 In the 16th century virtually all these principalities were ruled by dynasties claiming high-caste Indian origin whose members had left the hills in the wake of Muslim invasions of Northern India. In the early 18th century the principality of Gorkha (or Gurkha) began to assert a predominant role in the hills and even to pose a challenge to Nepal Valley. The Mallas, weakened by familial dissent and widespread social and economic discontent, were no match for the

great Gorkha ruler Prithvi Narayan Shah, who conquered the valley in 1769 and moved his capital to Kathmandu shortly thereafter, providing the foundation of the modern state of Nepal.

6 The Shah (or Sah) rulers faced tremendous and persistent problems in trying to centralize an area long characterized by extreme diversity and ethnic and regional parochialism. They absorbed dominant regional and local elites into the central administration of Kathmandu, thus neutralizing potentially disintegrative political forces and involving them in national politics. However, this also severely limited the centre's authority in outlying areas because local administration was based upon a compromise division of responsibilities between the local elites and the central administration.

7 The British conquest of India in the 19th century posed a serious threat to Nepal and left the country with no real alternative but to seek an accommodation with the British to preserve its independence. This was accomplished by the Rana family regime after 1860. Under this de facto alliance, Kathmandu permitted the recruitment of highly valued Gurkha units for the British Indian Army and also accepted British 'guidance' on foreign policy. In exchange, the British guaranteed the Rana regime protection against both foreign and domestic enemies and allowed it virtual autonomy in domestic affairs. Nepal was also careful to maintain a friendly relationship with China and Tibet, for economic reasons.

8 When the British withdrew from India in 1947, the Ranas were

deprived of a vital external source of support and the regime was exposed to new dangers. Anti-Rana forces, composed mainly of Nepalese residents in India who had served their political apprenticeship in the Indian nationalist movement, formed an alliance with the Nepalese royal family, led by the king. A tripartite agreement between Nepal, India and the UK was signed in Kathmandu in November 1947, and Gurkha troops were used by India in the war against China, in 1961-62; Pakistan in 1965 and 1971, and by the UK against Argentina in 1982.

9 In February 1951, the Nepalese Congress succeeded in overthrowing the Rana regime with support from King Tribhuvan Bir Bikram Shah Deva. From this time until December 1960 a series of democratic experiments took place in Nepal. Political parties were legalized and a general election was held in 1959, based on the Constitution approved by King Mahendra Bir Bikran Shah Deva. On December 15 1960, the first elected Prime Minister, B P Koirala, was arrested. Parliament was dissolved and most of the provisions of the Constitution were suspended. Political parties were outlawed and a non-party system or Panchayat was introduced in December 1962.

10 Nepal became a member of the United Nations in 1955, and it has been an active member of the Non-Aligned Movement since the days of the Bandung Conference. By July 1986, some 75 countries, including the major powers, endorsed a proposal by King Birendra Bir Birkram Shah Dev that Nepal should be declared a peace zone. All of its neighbors except India and Bhutan endorsed the proposal.

11 India is Nepal's major trading partner, and they have signed several treaties on trade and transit routes since 1950. The last treaty expired in 1989, and the two countries became locked in an undeclared trade war. Nepal had earlier India by importing arms from China. India then suspended trade with Nepal, closing 19 of the 21 transit routes from March 1989, seriously affecting the Nepalese economy. Nepal claimed that transit was a basic right for a landlocked country and that India had accepted trade as a separate issue in previous treaties they had agreed on. India threatened to withdraw all special trade facilities and suspended the supply of petroleum products and other essentials.

12 In 1979, student protest movements emerged in Kathmandu

and other cities, challenging the system. King Birendra responded by holding a plebiscite to choose between a multiparty system or a reformed Panchayat. The 1980 referendum frustrated the hopes of a return to a multiparty system as 55 per cent of the electorate voted for continued, reformed, Panchayat rule. The transition to parliamentary democracy with a constitutional monarchy was proclaimed by royal decree in April 1990.

[13] The Birendra monarchy was accused of having one of Asia's worst human rights records. In mid-1989 more than 300 political prisoners were held in Nepalese jails. The King passed laws that contradict the human rights provisions of the country's 1962 constitution.

[14] On April 12 1991, the first free elections were held in Nepal after 32 years of semi-monarchic rule. The Communist Party of Nepal and the Nepalese Congress Party allied for the elections, and other groups joined them. The Communists obtained 4 of the 5 seats in the capital, but the national majority went to the Nepalese Congress Party.

[15] In 1991, the Nepali and Indian governments signed two treaties on trade and transit, both subject to parliamentary approval. The major criticism, from the left and the right alike, was the fact that the 1950 Friendship Treaty was not revised or abrogated. Critics considered it to be a threat to the country's sovereignty, in that it expressly forbid the acquisition of military equipment from countries other than India.

[16] Escaping from the ethnic conflict in Bhutan, 22,000 Bhutanese people of Nepalese origin entered the country in 1992. One month later, a general strike against corruption and price increases paralyzed the nation. The repression of the demonstrations left many people dead.

[17] From 1994 onwards, the Government decided to charge $50,000 to any expedition planning to climb Mount Everest. The rivers flowing from the Himalayas potentially make Nepal one of the world's richer countries; however, the full exploitation of this resource for energy production, flood control and irrigation has been deterred by the lack of agreement between Nepal and India on sharing dam construction costs.

[18] Koirala was unsuccessful in his fight against poverty and illiteracy. The loss of parliamentary support and infighting in the monarchist Nepalese Congress Party (NCP) forced him to resign on July 10 1994. In the November elections, the United Communist Party took 88 seats in the Chamber of Representatives, surpassing the NCP who had 83. Man Mohan Adhikari was nominated Prime Minister. When unable to gain majority political support for his leadership in September 1995, the Communist Prime Minister handed over control to NCP leader, Sher Bahadur Deuba.

[19] Nepal is one of the poorest countries in the world. The annual per capita income stood at $250 in 1995, infant mortality was around 165 per thousand live births, and 71 per cent of the population lived below the poverty line. Conditions in Kathmandu and the provinces are very different, for while life expectancy is 71 years in the capital, in rural areas the average drops to 34.

[20] In early 1996, guerrilla groups describing themselves as Maoist started campaigns to 'eradicate feudalism'. In its 1997 report, Amnesty International denounced the abuses committed, mainly by the Government forces, in armed confrontations with the guerrillas.

[21] In March 1997, Bahadur Deuba resigned and Lokendra Kahadur Chand took over with support from a coalition, including the pro-monarchy Sadbhavana Party of Nepal (SPN) and the United Communist Party (UCPN). In October, Surya Bahadur Thapa took over as Prime Minister, with the support of another fragile coalition, similar to that which had appointed his predecessor. In April 1998, the NPC withdrew its support, forcing him to stand down and pushing through the nomination of Koirala as the new Head of Government.

[22] In January 1999, King Birendra dissolved Parliament on the recommendation of Koirala and announced new elections for May. The Prime Minister announced that the new Government would ensure that the elections were clean and that it would not make any important resolutions while in power.

[23] After the two rounds of elections in May, Krishna Prasad Bhattarai, of the Congress Party, became the new Prime Minister, creating the first single-party government in four years. From the outset, however, Bhattarai faced dissent from within his own party, which accused him of favoring only those who had directly supported him.

[24] Pressure from his party members led the Prime Minister to resign in March of the following year, which prompted the King to name Koirala Prime Minister once again. Once he took office for the third time, Koirala declared that the new Government would seek to put an end to the Maoist insurgency, improve national security, fight corruption and reform the Government's administrative sector. ■

Netherlands

Nederland

Population: 15,735,000 (1999)
Area: 40,844 SQ KM
Capital: Amsterdam
Currency: Guilder
Language: Dutch

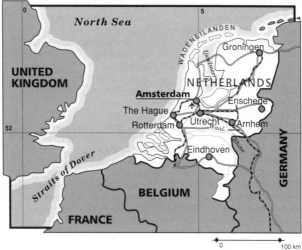

The Netherlands, Belgium, Luxembourg and the northern part of France constitute the region once known as the Low Countries. The first inhabitants of these lands arrived at the end of the last Ice Age, changing over thousands of years from hunter-gathering groups to the more elaborate and hierarchical cultures which the Romans encountered.

[2] When the Romans reached the area in the 1st century BC it was inhabited by Celts and Germanic people. The Empire never managed to occupy the land of the Frisians, in the north above the Rhine, so the Romans settled in the southern delta, where they created the provinces of Belgica and lesser Germanica.

[3] The Frisians lived by fishing and raising cattle, while in the south agriculture was carried on around the villages and towns. By the second half of the 3rd century, the encroaching sea had drastically altered the economic basis of the region.

[4] The strengthening of the Germanic tribes forced Rome to grant them custody of the Empire's borders, as it did with the Franks in Toxandria and Brabant. The line between the Romance and Germanic languages ran across the middle of the Low Countries, coinciding with the borders of the Roman Empire.

[5] The Frisians remained independent until the 7th century, when the Franks and the Catholic Church started a strong offensive. By the end of the century, the region had been subdued by the Franks, under the Pepin and Carolingian dynasties.

[6] The decline of the Carolingian Empire led to a period of instability during the 10th century. Several principalities were formed, with feudal ties to the kingdoms of Germany and France. The Frisians still remained free of sovereign authorities.

[7] The secular principalities of Flanders (Vlaanderen), Hainaut, Namur, Loon, Holland, Zeeland, Guelders, and the duchies of Brabant and Limburg were formed. In the principalities of Utrecht and Liege, the secular and ecclesiastic authorities shared power.

[8] The principalities worked towards greater freedom from royal authority. Flanders was the first to establish an efficient administration, followed by Brabant, Hainaut, and Namur. The appointment of their own bishops marked the end of German influence, and the establishment of closer links between the principalities.

[9] France tried to subdue Flanders but was defeated in the Battle of the Spurs in 1302. In general, France and Britain kept a balance of power, a situation that contributed to preserving the autonomy of the region.

[10] Population pressure led to the creation of new farmlands. On the coast, the Cistercian and Premonstratensian monks (an order founded by St Norbert) constructed many dykes. These were initially built to defend people from the high tides, but they later served to reclaim land.

[11] From the 11th century onwards, the Frisians developed a drainage system which removed the sea-water, providing land for pasturage and arable fields. During the 12th and 13th centuries, a vast peat bog in the Netherlands and Utrecht was reclaimed for agriculture.

[12] This area of *polders* on the coast of Flanders and Friesland became economically very significant. Between the 12th and 14th centuries, the struggle against the sea and inland water became so important that water authorities were created to organize the construction of dykes and the use of water.

[13] This increase in arable land and population brought about growth, not only in agriculture but also in industry and commerce. The new towns gave birth to new social classes who sought autonomy. Merchants in the towns had to swear an oath of co-operation; promising that they would keep law and order.

[14] The towns gradually became independent centers, having the power to sign commercial, political, and military agreements with other towns or with the Prince. The town owned the land within its boundaries and the inhabitants did not rely on any external authorities.

[15] During the second half of the 14th century, the dukes of Burgundy from the French royal house of Valois ruled over most of the Low Countries where they tried to create a centralized state. There was a movement to prevent this centralization, in 1477, but the accession of the Hapsburgs interrupted it.

[16] By virtue of the Hapsburg marriage, the fate of the Low Countries depended on the outcome of the House of Austria's struggle for European domination. This situation intensified in 1504, when King Philip and his wife, Joan, inherited the Spanish Crown. Centralization was on the increase and the Church was no exception. A Papal Bull was issued, creating a Rome-based administration, with three archbishops and 15 bishops. This was deeply resented by the local nobility.

[17] The Lutheran and Anabaptist faiths had difficulty gaining converts in the Low Countries, while Calvinism quickly gained acceptance among the lower classes and the intellectuals. Repression drove many Calvinists into exile, but they still had influence in the 1567 anti-absolutism rebellion.

[18] Popular unrest and the nobility and urban gentry's desire for autonomy led to a successful rebellion in Holland. After the defeat of the Spanish troops, the rebellion extended to all the provinces, ending with the Treaty of Ghent in 1576.

[19] Three years later, for geographic, economic, political, and religious reasons, this union dissolved. The Union of Arras was founded in the south, and the Union of Utrecht in the north, both of these being within the

WORKERS

1997
UNEMPLOYMENT: 5.5%

% OF LABOUR FORCE **1998**

■ FEMALE: 40% ■ MALE: 60%

1990

■ SERVICES: 69.8%
■ INDUSTRY: 25.6%
■ AGRICULTURE: 4.6%

LAND USE

DEFORESTATION: 0.0% annual (1990/95)
IRRIGATED: 61.8% of arable (1993)

1993

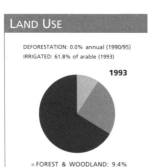

■ FOREST & WOODLAND: 9.4%
■ ARABLE: 24.3%
■ OTHER: 66.3%

PUBLIC EXPENDITURE

1997
63.9%

6.4%

DEFENCE   SOCIAL

MILITARY EXPENDITURE **22%**
(% of health & education) (1990/91)

MATERNAL MORTALITY	FOOD DEPENDENCY	FOREIGN TRADE

1990-98 Per 100,000 live births **7**	1997 **11%**	Millions US$ 1997 IMPORTS **177,838** EXPORTS **203,314**

boundaries of a larger unit led by the States-General.

[20] In 1581, the States-General passed an Act of Abjuration making the Union of Utrecht into a state of Spain, seizing sovereignty from Philip II. The Netherlands was the largest economic and political power within the Union, so all of the union's inhabitants became known as Netherlanders.

[21] During the Twelve Years' Truce with Spain, 1609-21, controversies within the Union grew. The collaboration between the province of Holland and the House of Orange gave way to a growing rivalry. This situation was antagonized by the dispute over Church-State relations.

[22] In 1618, Maurice of Orange, supported by the States-General, executed the leader of the main party in the Netherlands. When war against Spain resumed in 1621, the French and Dutch rivals were forced to reunite until the signing of the Treaty of Utrecht in 1713.

[23] The 17th century is called the golden age in Dutch history, because the country established relations with the great powers of the time. This was viewed as the birth of a great nation, a fact that was only called into question at the end of the 17th century.

[24] Dutch prosperity was not only the result of continental trade, but also of its colonial power. In 1602, the East India Company was created, with bases in South Africa, Ceylon (Sri Lanka), India and Indonesia. The Netherlands had sovereign powers in these colonies, as did the British and French in theirs.

[25] At first the Company only held coastal trading bases, but later on, it started to occupy the hinterland controlling the region and certain commodities. The colonial administration was autonomous, as the Dutch preferred governing through agreements with local leaders.

[26] In 1621, the West Indies Company was founded. It made the bulk of its profits from the slave trade and privateering, it also operated outside Zeeland, a southwestern maritime province, especially against Spanish ships. The Netherlands dominated the slave trade during the 17th century.

[27] In 1648, the Dutch had three large settlements in the Americas: one in the north, for the fur trade; another on the Atlantic coast, with outposts for the slave trade and smuggling with Spanish colonies; and another in what is now Brazil and Suriname (formerly Dutch Guyana). By 1700, they were left with only the trading outposts in Curaçao, St Eustacius and St Martin, the plantations in Guyana, and the slave port of Elmina.

[28] Dutch maritime power weakened in the 18th century, especially after the war against Britain (1708-84). The country used up a portion of its capital to buy bonds in foreign governments. The bankers in Amsterdam were among the most powerful in Europe.

[29] The 1750s saw the emergence of the Patriot movement, a group of factions who had been overlooked in governmental policies: they ranged from bankers and simple artisans, to dissident Protestants and Catholics, unhappy with monarchic abuse of power.

[30] The Patriots went into exile during the Prussian invasion of 1786. Their hopes were rekindled with the French Revolution, but it was not until 1794 that France managed effective opposition to Britain and Prussia, who supported William V. They proclaimed the Republic and started the process of political modernization.

[31] The new republic declared equality among its citizens and changed the institutional framework. It replaced the assembly of States-General for a National Assembly with direct electoral representation, and executive power was separated from the legislative and the judicial.

[32] In 1806, France annexed the state to the Empire under the name of the Napoleonic Kingdom of the Netherlands. Five years later, Bonaparte incorporated the Netherlands into France, until the fall of the Empire. In 1814, King

William I of Orange was chosen by the Dutch leaders, and he restored the monarchy.

[33] In the Congress of Vienna, the victorious powers gave William I sovereignty over the whole of the Low Countries. The Belgian revolution of 1830 broke out during his reign. His successors, William II and William III made the final move towards parliamentary monarchy.

[34] Universal male suffrage was approved in 1917; women were granted the vote in 1922. After decades of debate over the school system, Protestants and Catholics allied themselves against the liberals and, in 1888, the first private denominational schools were opened.

[35] New political parties were founded, based on the religious ideas and ideologies of the time. To the Liberal, Protestant and Catholic parties were added the Protestant Conservative, the Socialist and the Communist parties. As none could obtain a majority, coalitions became commonplace.

[36] During World War I, the Netherlands declared its neutrality and political parties agreed on a truce in order to devote themselves to the domestic economy and trade. The merchant navy had recovered and industry grew, in particular textiles, electronics, and chemicals.

[37] During the postwar period, the Netherlands was a member of the League of Nations, but it re-affirmed its neutrality. Symbolically, The Hague became the seat of the International Court of Justice. During the Versailles negotiations, Belgium tried unsuccessfully to revive an old territorial claim against the Netherlands.

[38] During World War II, Hitler attacked France through the Netherlands, and Queen Wilhelmina formed a government-in-exile in London. All political factions took part in anti-Nazi resistance. German repression was harsh, and by the end of the war the country was on the verge of famine.

[39] In 1945, an agreement was signed by the Government, companies and trade unions. It lasted 20 years and was aimed at controlling prices and salaries. Indonesia became independent in 1945 while Suriname had to wait until 1975. The Netherlands underwent rapid industrialization especially in steel production, electronics and petrochemicals.

PROFILE

ENVIRONMENT

The country is a vast plain and 38 per cent of its territory is below sea level. Intensive agriculture and cattle raising produce high priced milk products and crops (particularly flowers). Population density is amongst the highest in the world. Highly industrialized, the country is the world's third largest producer of natural gas, and is a dominant influence in petroleum activity. It has large refineries in the Antilles and Rotterdam, the world center of the free, or 'spot', crude oil market. As a result of the massive use of pesticides, underground water supplies contain high levels of nitrates. Similarly, the country's main rivers are filled will all kinds of organic and industrial wastes, which often originate in other European countries.

SOCIETY

Peoples: Dutch 95 per cent; Turks 1.3 per cent; Moroccans 1 per cent; Germans 0.3 per cent. **Religions:** 31 per cent Catholic, Dutch Reformed Church 14 per cent; Calvinist 8 per cent; Muslim 3.9 per cent; other 4.1 per cent; no religion 39 per cent. **Languages:** Dutch (official), Turkish, Arab. **Political Parties:** Christian Democratic Appeal; People's Party for Freedom and Democracy, liberal; Democrats 66, liberal; Labor Party, affiliated to the Socialist International; among the minor parties are three religious (Protestant) parties; Green Left, Socialist Party. **Social Organizations:** There are two large central unions: the Federation of Dutch Trade Unions and the Christian National Trade Union.

THE STATE

Official Name: Koninkrijk der Nederlanden. **Administrative Divisions:** 12 Provinces. **Capital:** Greater Amsterdam 1,300,000 people (1997). Although the Government has its seat in The Hague, Amsterdam is still considered the capital. **Other cities:** Rotterdam 599,521 people; The Hague (s'-Gravenhage) 442,105; Utrecht 235,357; Eindhoven, 197,055 (1995). **Government:** Constitutional and parliamentary monarchy. Queen Beatrix, Head of State; Wim Kok, Prime Minister since 1994, re-elected August 1998. Bicameral parliament, with 75 members elected by regional parliaments, and 150-member second chamber **National Holiday:** April 30. **Armed Forces:** 74,400 (1995). **Other:** 3,600 Royal Military Corps. **Dependencies:** See Netherlands Antilles and Aruba.

40 Dutch capital controlled some large transnational corporations such as Royal Dutch Shell, the oil company (jointly a British company). Unilever, the world's largest food and soap manufacturer, had branches all over the world and its products were used by companies everywhere. Other Dutch transnationals included Philips electronics, AKZO, a chemical manufacturer, DSM, Hoogoven Groep and Heineken.

41 In the postwar period, the Government was composed of Labor party (the former socialists) and Catholic coalitions. The Netherlands gave up neutrality, becoming a member of NATO and of the European Economic Community. Also, together with Belgium and Luxembourg it formed an economic alliance known as the Benelux.

42 During the 1960s, youth demonstrations developed into violent riots, the royal marriages also became the subject of public controversy and ideological and religious questioning occurred in all Dutch institutions.

43 In the 1970s, voters favored the center and the left, while the Government reformed the tax system and redistributed income. The most controversial subjects were the defense budget and the installation of NATO atomic missiles within the country.

44 The Netherlands is one of the few OECD countries giving over 0.7 per cent of its GNP for aid to the Third World. It has also maintained a coherent policy on the defense of human rights and against apartheid in South Africa, though links with Israel have tended to estrange it from some Arab countries.

45 In 1989 the Government approved a 0.6 per cent increase in the defense budget for 1990 and 1991, to be followed by a budget suspension until 1995 and the withdrawal of 750 Dutch soldiers posted in West Germany. This Dutch resolution caused much malaise within NATO.

46 In the Netherlands there were some 100,000 farms, with around 4,500,000 head of cattle. The cost to the country of raising and feeding each cow is $2,000 per year, a sum which is higher than the per capita income of many Third World countries. The Dutch export dairy products and flowers, but also import a great amount of raw materials for their agro-industry. Fifteen million hectares of land in other countries (including 5 million in the Third World) is under production for Dutch needs. This is mainly because much of the soy and tapioca that their farm animals eat comes from other countries, mainly Brazil and Thailand. Only 20 per cent of the vegetable protein fed to animals is converted to animal protein. The rest produces 110 million tons of manure a year, of which only half is used in agriculture. The other half ends up polluting the soil, drinking water and the air, where it adds to industrial emissions to cause acid rain. Over 40 per cent of Holland's trees have been irreversibly damaged by acid rain and the country has exceptionally high levels of contamination.

47 Dutch agriculture is also characterized by a high energy consumption (for greenhouses to produce summer crops in winter) and the intensive use of pesticides, at a rate of about 20 kg per hectare per year. These seep into underground water reserves, contaminating drinking water supplies. Likewise, the high level of industrialization and population density have given rise to the presence of heavy metals, nitrates and other organic wastes in the Maas, Rhine and Waal rivers.

48 Due to the high level of consumption which characterizes Dutch society, each person produces an estimated 3,000 kg of refuse per year. In Amsterdam and other cities many apartment buildings are inhabited by people who live alone, a fact which increases the demand for housing.

49 Taking advantage of the fact that the Netherlands was occupying the EU presidency at the time, in December 1991 the Dutch Parliament pressed EU heads of state and governments to condemn all forms of racism in Maastricht. In addition, they urged the adoption of legislation prohibiting xenophobic acts throughout Europe.

50 Despite this official position, the country was beset by growing racism, although to a lesser degree than other European countries. In September 1993 the Netherlands adopted legislation restricting the admission of immigrants from outside the European Union.

51 Government agencies devised economic indicators capable of assessing environmental damage, and methods for calculating national income. In 1992, the Central Office of Statistics announced the 'green gross national product' (GGNP). This indicator evaluates losses in natural resources, according to the capacity for regeneration, and the effect on local communities.

52 The government coalition parties suffered a serious setback in the March 1994 local elections, which showed the growth of the anti-immigration far right. On August 22, Wim Kok became Prime Minister.

53 In 1995, for the second year in a row, the complex hydraulic system failed, causing flooding of vast areas in the south and center.

54 In late 1996, the unemployment rate fell to 6.6 per cent. The GDP grew 2.7 per cent as a result of, among other things, the rise of exports and the recovery of local demand.

55 In March 1998, the European Union demanded 'considerable efforts' – that is, economic 'austerity' policies - from the Netherlands and five more countries to allow for the introduction the European single currency.

56 The elections for the Second Chamber in May 1998 confirmed the Government coalition's popularity among voters. With 29 per cent and 27.7 per cent of the vote respectively, the Labor Party and People's Party for Freedom and Democracy maintained their dominance and reinforced the Government alliance along with the Democrats 66. In the election for the First Chamber in March 1999, the Christian Democrats had the highest ranking as a single party, with 26 per cent of the vote, but the government coalition had a total of 50.6 per cent.

57 A student shot and injured a teacher and three students at a school in Eindhoven in December 1999, causing widespread outcry for stricter measures to control firearms.

58 A parliamentary debate on legalizing euthanasia and assisted suicide was set to continue through to 2001. If the law receives parliamentary approval, the Netherlands would became the first country to decriminalize mercy killings. ■

STATISTICS

DEMOGRAPHY

Population: 15,735,000 (1999)
Annual growth: 0.6 % (1975/97)
Estimates for year 2015 (million): 15.9 (1999)
Annual growth to year 2015: 0.1 % (1997/2015)
Urban population: 89.1 % (1997)
Urban Growth: 0.6 % (1980/95)
Children per woman: 1.5 (1998)

HEALTH

Life expectancy at birth: 78 years (1998)
male: 75 years (1998)
female: 81 years (1998)
Maternal mortality: 7 per 100,000 live births (1990-98)
Infant mortality: 5 per 1,000 (1998)
Under-5 child mortality: 5 per 1,000 (1998)
Daily calorie supply: 3,259 per capita (1996)

EDUCATION

School enrolment:
Primary total: 107 % (1990/96)
male: 108 % (1990/97)
female: 106 % (1990/97)
Secondary:
male: 141 % (1990/96)
female: 133 % (1990/96)
Tertiary: 47 % (1996)

COMMUNICATIONS

306 newspapers (1996), 978 radios (1997), 495 TV sets (1996) and 543 main telephone lines (1996) per 1,000 people
Books: 222 new titles per 100,000 people (1992/94)

ECONOMY

Per capita, GNP: $ 24,780 (1998)
Annual growth, GNP: 3.3 % (1998)
Annual inflation: 2.1 % (1990/98)
Consumer price index: 106.3 (1998)
Currency: 2.0 guilders = $ 1 (1998)
Cereal imports: 5,818,419 metric tons (1998)
Food import dependency: 11 % (1997)
Fertilizer use: 5,567 Kgs per ha (1997)
Exports: $ 203,314 million (1997)
Imports: $ 177,838 million (1997)

ENERGY

Consumption: 4,800.0 Kgs of Oil equivalent per capita yearly (1997); 13.0 % imported (1997)

HDI (rank/value): 8/0.921 (1997)

Netherlands Antilles

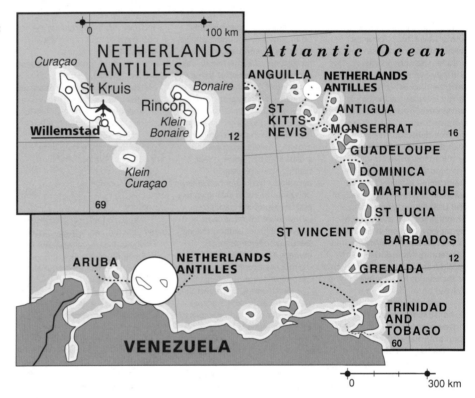

Population: 215,000 (1999)
Area: 800 SQ KM
Capital: Willemstad
Currency: NA guilder
Language: Dutch

Netherlands Antilles

The Caiquetio were the original inhabitants of what today are the islands of Aruba, Bonaire and Curaçao. Soon after the arrival of the Spaniard Alonso de Ojeda in 1499, these local people were enslaved and taken to Hispaniola (present-day Haiti and Dominican Republic). The indians that Columbus found on the 'S Islands' (the Windward Islands) in 1493 met a similar fate.

[2] The conquistadors attached little importance to these islands because they lacked readily exploitable natural resources. However, the Windward Islands (particularly St Martin Island) acquired strategic importance as a port of entry into the Caribbean and also became important for their salt deposits. Ports on the Iberian Peninsula were closed to Holland after the war with Spain and Portugal, so the Dutch were forced to seek alternative sources of salt in the Antilles.

[3] In 1606, the Spanish Crown decided to put a halt to this intense traffic, and prohibited Dutch shipping in the Antilles. Holland retaliated by creating the West Indies Company, which was charged with establishing, managing and defending the colonies. Thus the theft of Spanish ships became one of the main sources of income.

[4] Although salt and Brazilwood were important products, the slave trade became the principal economic activity. In 1634, the stockholders of the Company in Amsterdam decided to invade Curaçao. The Spaniards offered no resistance and Curaçao became a major international slave-trading center.

[5] In 1648, after three centuries of conflict, the Treaty of Westphalia was signed,

granting Holland control over these small islands in the Antilles. The native populations - particularly those of Curaçao and Bonaire - were replaced by African slaves to meet the needs of new agricultural operations, and thus became a minority on these islands. As in the rest of the Antilles, slave rebellions were frequent, culminating in the 18th century with a massacre at the hands of colonial troops.

[6] During the Napoleonic wars at the beginning of the 19th century, the three islands passed into British hands on two different occasions; however, the change failed to produce any improvement in the lives of the local inhabitants. Although the slave trade had been prohibited in 1814, it was not abolished in the Dutch colonies until 1863. Even then, although the slaves were 'free', their lives did not change substantially. Many migrated to the Dominican Republic, Panama, Venezuela and Cuba.

[7] Once slavery was abolished, interest in the islands waned. In 1876, the Dutch parliament proposed to sell them to

Venezuela, but negotiations fell through. With the rise of the oil industry at the beginning of the 20th century, refineries were installed because of the proximity to Lake Maracaibo. From the 1920s onward, this new activity radically changed the colony. The plantations were abandoned and the demand for labor attracted thousands of immigrants from Venezuela, Suriname and the British West Indies.

[8] However, the boom dwindled over time, as automation significantly reduced the number of jobs. On May 30 1969, when unemployment stood at 20 per cent, police broke up a labor demonstration. This sparked large-scale riots which were quelled only by the joint intervention of 300 Dutch marines and some US marines from the American fleet, which happened to be anchored in the archipelago. As a result of these disturbances, Parliament was dissolved.

[9] The islands have been more politically active since 1937 when the first local parties were founded. However, they have

only existed as states since 1948, when the new post-war Dutch constitution renamed what had been known as 'Curaçao and dependencies' as the 'Netherlands Antilles'.

[10] The issue of independence has long been at the center of local political life. In 1954, a new law established the islands' autonomy over their internal affairs. Nevertheless, the People's Electoral Movement (PEM), founded in 1971 in Aruba, maintained that, as the islands were no longer 'Dutch', they have nothing in common (not even a name, because 'Antilles' is the generic designation of the whole region) and each island should be free to choose its own constitution and set itself up as an autonomous republic. Secessionist feeling was strong in Aruba, where a referendum carried out in 1977 for consultation purposes only (ie, not politically binding), showed that the majority wished to separate from the other islands.

[11] The Netherlands however preferred to maintain the political unity of the islands,

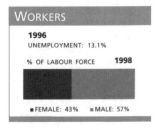

WORKERS

1996
UNEMPLOYMENT: 13.1%

% OF LABOUR FORCE **1998**

■ FEMALE: 43%   ■ MALE: 57%

arguing that this would ensure better economic prospects for the whole group and, above all, more political stability in the turbulent Caribbean region. This difference of opinion, together with the diversity of views held by the local parties on the matter, delayed negotiations for independence.

[12] The delay radicalized the electorate and in 1979 the New Antilles Movement (MAN) achieved a parliamentary majority in Curaçao (7 out of 12 seats). In coalition with the PEM and the UPB (Bonaire Patriotic Union) it formed the first left-of-center government in the history of the islands. The MAN favored a federal formula with considerable autonomy for each of the islands but the PEM insisted on the total separation of Aruba.

[13] In 1980 it was agreed to set independence for 1990, on the condition that each of the six islands submitted the issue to a referendum as soon as possible. Aruba chose to become an individual associated state, breaking away from the federation in January 1986 (see Aruba).

[14] The Netherlands Antilles became modern trading posts, totally dependent on transnational oil companies. Exxon and Royal Dutch Shell (an Anglo-Dutch consortium), maintained a monopoly on all oil refining and processing. They also controlled the petrochemical fertilizer industry and all

transportation and sales. These powerful companies, linked financially and commercially to branches of approximately 2,500 foreign firms registered on the islands, were responsible for 85 per cent of the total imports, 99 per cent of the exports and 50 per cent of the islands' net income.

[15] Despite modest industrial growth and a booming tourist industry, the economy was fragile. This was clearly demonstrated towards the end of 1984, when the transnational oil companies announced their withdrawal from the islands, spreading panic among the people and local political leaders. The conflict was partially resolved in October 1985 with the purchase of the Curaçao refinery by the Antilles Government, which in turn rented the facility to Petroleos de Venezuela SA., an oil company owned by the Venezuelan Government. The deal did not include the Exxon plant on Aruba which closed down.

[16] The separation of Aruba favored the 1984 victory of a right-of-center coalition headed by Maria Liberia Peters of the National People's Party (PNP). This coalition was unable to sustain the minimum consensus necessary to stay in power. Therefore in January 1986, MAN leader, Domenico Martina, became Prime Minister once again. Two years later, Maria Liberia Peters returned to power.

[17] In 1990 the Government renewed its contracts with the Venezuelan oil company and introduced a series of austerity measures designed to cover the deficit generated by the Aruban withdrawal from the federation.

[18] The election of the Island Councils in 1991 was marked by the defeat of the Democratic Party as a result of internal divisions and financial irregularities committed by the administration.

[19] The Netherlands requested that each island make a separate proposal for constitutional reform in 1993. Accordingly, Curaçao received special status, St Martin was made independent, while Bonaire,

STATISTICS

DEMOGRAPHY
Population: 215,000 (1999)

COMMUNICATIONS
337 newspapers (1996) and 996 radios (1997) per 1,000 people

ECONOMY
Consumer price index: 108.2 (1998)
Cereal imports: 195,155 metric tons (1998)

Saba and St Eustatius continued under Dutch control. The constitution also dictated that the Treaty of Strasburg, which predicted complete independence for 1999, would not be applied in the islands.

[20] In a plebiscite held in 1994, the constituent members of the Netherlands Antilles voted to preserve their federation.

[21] That same year, Miguel Pourier was appointed Prime Minister. In 1996, the structural adjustment program caused tensions in the Government, which led to the resignation of the labor minister, Jeffrey Corion. The legislative elections of January 1998, confirmed Pourier in his post. ■

Nicaragua

Nicaragua

Population: 4,938,000 (1999)
Area: 130,000 SQ KM
Capital: Managua
Currency: Córdoba
Language: Spanish

W hat today is Nicaragua was in pre-Colombian times an area of influence for the Chibcha (see Colombia) and the Maya. The Caribbean coast was inhabited by the Miskito and was visited by Christopher Columbus in 1502. By converting local leaders Nicoya and Nicarao to Christianity and crushing the resistance of Diriangen's armies, the conquistadors Gil Gonzales Dávila and Andrés Nino consolidated Spain's hold over the territory. In 1544 it was incorporated into the Captaincy-General of Guatemala.

² In 1821 Nicaragua became independent, together with the rest of Central America, joining the Mexican Empire but subsequently withdrawing in 1824 to form the Federation of the United Provinces of the Center of America.

³ Nicaragua left the Federation in 1839, declaring itself an independent state. The country was divided between two groups: the coffee and sugar oligarchies, and the artisans and small landowners. The former would become the conservatives, and the latter, the liberals who favored free trade.

⁴ In 1856, 120 soldiers landed in Nicaragua under the command of William Walker, an American mercenary. With Washington's tacit support, he proclaimed himself President of Nicaragua. His purpose was to find new territories for slavery which was on the point of being abolished in the Union. Walker was defeated by the allied armies of Central America in 1857, and later executed. Nicaragua's ports were occupied by Germany in 1875 and Britain in 1895. Britain commandeered Nicaragua's Customs in order to collect on unpaid debts.

⁵ After 30 years of conservative rule the Liberal Party came to power in 1893, and José Santos Zelaya

became President. The liberals refused to comply with demands made by the United States so in 1912 the US invaded. After killing the Liberal Party leader, Benjamin Zeledón, the US Marine force remained in Nicaragua until 1925. In 1926 they returned to protect president Adolfo Díaz, who was about to be overthrown.

⁶ This second US occupation was resisted by Augusto C Sandino, who raised and commanded a popular army of about 3,000 troops. For more than six years they held out against 12,000 US marines who were supported by the airforce and ground troops of the local

oligarchy. Sandino promised that he would lay down arms when the last marine left Nicaragua. He carried out his promise in 1933, but was assassinated by US-backed Anastasio Somoza García who, after seizing power, ruled despotically until he was killed by the patriot Rigoberto López Pérez in 1956.

⁷ During two decades of dictatorship, Somoza had achieved almost absolute control of the nation's economy. He was succeeded by his son, engineer Luis Somoza Debayle, who in turn handed the Government on to his son, Anastasio, a West Point graduate.

⁸ Anastasio Somoza outlawed all trade unions, massacred members of peasant movements and banned all opposition parties. In the 1960s the Sandinista National Liberation Front was founded. This organized and developed the guerrilla warfare which lasted for 17 years. When opposition leader Pedro

Joaquín Chamorro, editor of the daily La Prensa, was assassinated on Somoza's orders in January 1978, a nationwide strike was called and there were massive protest demonstrations.

⁹ By March 1979, the Sandinista Front had united its three factions and began to lead the political opposition, the 'Patriotic Front'. In May 1979 the Front launched the 'final offensive', combining a general strike, a popular uprising, armed combat, and intense diplomatic activity abroad. On July 17, Somoza fled the country, bringing an end to a dynasty that had killed 50,000 people. The Junta for National Reconstruction, created a few weeks before in Costa Rica, was installed in Managua two days later.

¹⁰ The victorious revolutionaries nationalized the Somozas' lands and industrial properties, which constituted 40 per cent of the economic resources of Nicaragua. They also replaced the defeated National Guard with the Sandinista Popular Army. The revolutionary government implemented a literacy campaign and began the reconstruction of the devastated economy. Other important policies were non-alignment, a mixed

WORKERS

% OF LABOUR FORCE **1998**

■ FEMALE: 35%   ■ MALE: 65%

1990

■ SERVICES: 44.9%
■ INDUSTRY: 26.5%
■ AGRICULTURE: 28.6%

LAND USE

DEFORESTATION: 2.5% annual (1990/95)
IRRIGATED: 8.0% of arable (1993)

1993

■ FOREST & WOODLAND: 24.6%
■ ARABLE: 8.5%
■ OTHER: 66.9%

PUBLIC EXPENDITURE

DEFENCE EXPENDITURE (% of goverment exp.)	**4.5%** (1997)
MILITARY EXPENDITURE (% of health & education)	**97%** (1990/91)

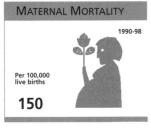

MATERNAL MORTALITY

1990-98

Per 100,000 live births

150

LITERACY

1995

66%

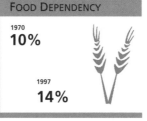

FOOD DEPENDENCY

1970
10%

1997
14%

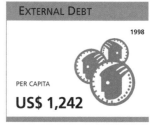

EXTERNAL DEBT

1998

PER CAPITA

US$ 1,242

economy, political pluralism, and respect for individual rights and liberties.

[11] In May 1980 two non-Sandinista members of the Junta, Violeta Barrios de Chamorro and Alfonso Robelo, resigned. The Government avoided a crisis by replacing them with Rafael Córdoba and Arturo Cruz, two 'moderate' anti-Somoza activists.

[12] In 1981, US President Ronald Reagan announced his aim of destroying the Sandinistas. Between April and July 1982 deputy interior minister, Edén Pastora ('Commander Zero'), deserted and announced from Costa Rica that he would drive the Sandinista Front's National Directorate out 'at gunpoint'. Some 2,500 former National Guardsmen, supported by the US, invaded Nicaragua from Honduras. From then on Nicaragua was harassed without respite, forcing the authorities to extend the state of emergency, to institute compulsory military service and to ban pro-American political declarations.

[13] In 1983, President Reagan admitted the existence of secret funds destined for covert CIA operations against Nicaragua. The funds were also used to aid counter-revolutionaries or contras operating from Honduran territory. Reagan referred to the contras as 'freedom fighters'.

[14] Concerned at the serious threat of a war that might escalate throughout Central America, the governments of Colombia, Mexico, Panama and Venezuela began to seek a negotiated settlement to the conflict. As the 'Contadora Group', these countries' foreign ministers advanced peace plans which won great diplomatic support and prevented an invasion by US forces.

[15] Contra attacks intensified steadily with open US backing. Elections were held in November 1984. Candidates were drawn from the Sandinista National Liberation Front (FSLN), the Democratic Conservative Party, the Independent Liberal Party, the Popular Social Christian Party, the Communist Party, the Socialist Party and the Marxist-Leninist People's Action Movement. Over 80 per cent of Nicaragua's 1.5 million registered voters went to the polls and the Sandinista Front Government led by Daniel Ortega obtained 67 per cent of the vote. In November Reagan was re-elected and in April 1985 he declared a trade embargo against Nicaragua and seized its assets.

[16] In 1986, the Assembly discussed the details of a new Constitution, which went into effect in January 1987. It provided for a presidential system, with a president elected by direct vote for a six-year term. Legislators would be elected on the basis of proportional representation.

[17] In 1987, with UN and OAS participation, the Central American presidents met for negotiations in Esquipulas, Guatemala. The Esquipulas II accords stipulated an end to external support for armed opposition groups; the opening of internal dialogue in each of the countries, mediated by the Catholic Church; and an amnesty for those who lay down their arms, with guarantees of political representation.

[18] In Nicaragua a National Reconciliation Commission was formed. Among its most spectacular achievements was the return of contra leader Fernando Chamorro from exile. He was granted an amnesty after he renounced violence. Press censorship was lifted and Violeta Chamorro's opposition daily *La Prensa* reappeared. On October 7, a unilateral cease-fire went into effect in several parts of the country, although contra leaders announced that they would continue hostilities.

[19] Throughout 1988, as US pressure increased the economic situation worsened. A monetary reform and a 10 per cent reduction in the Government budget in February were insufficient to halt spiralling inflation.

[20] In July 1988, the US ambassador to Managua was expelled on the accusation of encouraging anti-Sandinista activities. The US Government responded by expelling Nicaragua's representative in Washington.

[21] The Esquipulas II accords seemed to be doomed, but when the five Central American presidents met at Costa del Sol, El Salvador, in February 1989, President Daniel Ortega embarked on fresh negotiations. The Sandinista proposal was to bring the elections forward to February 1990 and to accept proposed modifications to the 1988 electoral law. The condition was that the contras dismantle their bases in Honduras within three months of an agreement. The US however insisted that the contras continue in Honduras, and President George Bush persuaded Congress to award them $40 million in 'humanitarian aid'.

[22] Daniel Ortega was the FSLN presidential candidate. The National Opposition Union (UNO), a 14-party coalition, nominated Pedro Joaquin Chamorro's widow, Violeta Barrios de Chamorro. Unexpectedly, the UNO won the elections with 55 per cent of the vote against the FSLN's 41 per cent. The Sandinistas accepted defeat and ascribed it to the Nicaraguan people's desperate desire for peace, the dire state of the economy and FSLN overconfidence that victory was assured.

[23] On April 25, before she took office, the President and the FSLN signed a 'Transition Protocol'. This included respecting the standing Constitution and the social achievements of the revolution, and supporting disarmament of the contras. The new president announced that she would personally assume the defence portfolio and maintain the Sandinista General Humberto Ortega as commander of the armed forces. She also indefinitely suspended compulsory military service.

[24] The UNO's Vice-President, Virgilio Godoy, and other members of the coalition withdrew from the Government accusing Chamorro of

PROFILE

ENVIRONMENT

Nicaragua has both Pacific and Caribbean coastlines. It is crossed by two important mountain ranges: the Central American Andes, running from northwest to southeast, and a volcanic chain with several active volcanoes along the western coast. The Managua and Nicaragua lakes lie between the two ranges. On the eastern slopes, the climate is tropical with abundant rainfall, while it is drier on the western side where the population is concentrated. Cotton is the main cash crop in the mountain area, while bananas are grown along the Atlantic coast. Changes in water and soil have affected approximately 40 per cent of the country's territory.

SOCIETY

Peoples: Over 70 per cent of Nicaraguans are mixed descendants of American natives and Spanish colonizers; there are minorities of Europeans, Miskitos, Sunos and Ramas, and African descendents.
Religion: Mainly Catholic.
Languages: Spanish (official and predominant). Miskito, Suno and English are spoken on the Atlantic coast.
Political Parties: Conservative Party of Nicaragua (CPN); Independent Liberal Party (ILP), Nicaraguan Resistance Party (NRC), Liberal Alliance (LA), Party of the Nicaraguan Christian Road (PNCR), Sandinista National Liberation Front (SNLF), Sandinista Renovation Movement (SRM)
Social Organizations: The Nicaraguan Labor Confederation (CTN); the Labor Unity and Action Confederation (CAUS); the Rural Workers' Association (ATC); the Workers' Front (FO); the Unified Labor Confederation (CUS); the National Employees Union (UNE); the National Confederation of Professionals (CONAPRO).

THE STATE

Official Name: República de Nicaragua.
Administrative Division: 16 Departments.
Capital: Managua 819,731 people (1995).
Other cities: León 124,117 people; Masaya 101,900; Chinandega 84,281; Matagalpa 95,300; Granada 74,300 (1995).
Government: President, Arnoldo Alemán, elected in October 1996.
National Holidays: September 15, Independence Day (1821); July 19, Sandinista Revolution Day (1979).
Armed Forces: 17,000 troops (1996).

betraying pre-election agreements by keeping Humberto Ortega in office.

[25] In May 1990, public employees went on strike for wage increases of up to 200 per cent. The Government declared the strike illegal, and revoked the civil service law (under which civil servants could not be fired without just cause) as well as the agrarian reform law passed by the Sandinista Government. Workers responded by extending the strike over the whole country. After a week, the Government partially gave in to the workers' demands, and the strike ended.

[26] In mid-1990, the Government received several offers from international consortia interested in carrying out projects in northern Nicaragua. This area comprises some 270,000 hectares of tropical rain forests, occupying more than half of the country's total land area. The proposals ranged from the creation of landfills for toxic waste, to the exploitation of the region's vast fishing, mineral and forestry resources.

[27] When the Government was accused of carrying out secret negotiations with a Taiwanese enterprise, the existence of large mineral deposits was inadvertently revealed. These included gold, silver, copper, tungsten and Central America's largest deposits of calcium carbonate, a raw material used in cement production.

[28] A partial disarming of the contras was carried out, at the same time that significant reductions in army personnel were announced. In October 1991, a number of former contra commanders founded the Nicaraguan Resistance Party. This new political group rejected the return to violence by other contras - some 600, in all - in the northern part of the country, where civilians were being killed, and farms as well as farm cooperatives were being burned.

[29] In 1991, President Chamorro agreed with the FSLN to recognize agrarian reform and to set aside for the workers at least 25 per cent of shares in state enterprises slated for privatization.

[30] Inflation fell from 7,000 per cent in 1990 to 3.8 per cent in 1992 due to an IMF and World Bank-sponsored adjustment program. Productive investments and spending in education and health were reduced. Unemployment rose to 60 per cent.

[31] Differences between the President and the UNO led them to break in 1993 after which Chamorro received support from the Sandinistas and the UNO's Center Group. The following month, the UNO expelled that group and changed its name to Political Opposition Alliance (APO).

[32] Parliamentary debate on constitutional reform caused the FSLN's orthodox sector, led by former president Daniel Ortega, to exclude former Vice-President Sergio Ramirez, head of the Sandinista parliamentary bloc, from the Front. By-passing the party's leadership, the parliamentary bloc presented its own bill against nepotism which banned presidential re-election and prohibited relatives of the current president from running for president. This clause put an end to the political aspirations of Chamorro's son-in-law, minister Antonio Lacayo.

[33] The economic crisis was intensified by a drought which led to the loss of 80,000 hectares of crops and left 200,000 farmers without food. Child malnutrition affected 300,000 children and some lost their sight through lack of vitamin A.

[34] In January 1994, the UNO, with less than half its founders and unable to obtain the support to set up a constituent assembly, put an end to a year of boycotting the National Assembly. Violence continued between the army, gangs of criminals and small guerrilla groups.

[35] General Humberto Ortega confirmed he would resign after a new military law had been passed. In August the Assembly passed the law which aimed at eliminating political involvement by the Sandinista Popular Army and increasing its dependence on civilian authority, although the power was actually left in the hands of a military council.

[36] The Government signed a 3-year agreement with the IMF which opened the possibility of renegotiating public debt. Unemployment was estimated between 43 per cent and 60 per cent. The per capita GDP dropped for the eleventh year in a row.

[37] Debate on constitutional reform prevailed in 1995. In February, the Assembly proposed to change the army's name, ban compulsory military service and grant guarantees to private property. These measures were supported by President Chamorro but she did not agree with the shift of power from the executive to the legislative branch, regarding the right to raise taxes. The Assembly published the reforms unilaterally in February and began to implement them.

[38] In June, an agreement was reached on a general law for constitutional reforms which stated these had to be supported by a majority of 60 per cent in the Assembly before being signed by the President, who concluded the agreement in July. The National Assembly ratified its choice of judges for the Supreme Court of Justice and a new Supreme Electoral Tribunal was appointed.

[39] The approval of the nepotism law was deferred. President Chamorro's son-in-law remained in the Government, although he announced his resignation to launch his presidential campaign.

[40] Conservative Arnoldo Alemán, ex-mayor of Managua, obtained 49 per cent of the vote in the October 1996 elections. The electoral law established that if any of the candidates obtains more than 45 per cent of the vote, there is no need for a second vote, thus leaving Sandinista ex President Daniel Ortega (with 39 per cent) out of the race. The FSLN suspected a fraud but the Supreme Electoral Court named Alemán president.

[41] On assuming the presidency, Alemán promised to create 500,000 new jobs and launched a plan to relieve the debt of the agricultural sector, estimated at $150 million.

[42] In April 1997, the Government and Opposition accused each other of arming and training paramilitaries. Despite negotiations, no understanding was reached and relations between the ruling party and the Sandinistas remained tense.

[43] In August, the Government announced it would not pass goods confiscated by the Sandinistas in 1979 on to Anastasio Somoza's heirs, in answer to a lawsuit filed by Lilian Somoza, the former dictator's daughter.

[44] According to estimates made in early 1998, the US had once again become Managua's main trade partner. Nicaraguan exports to this country were worth $375 million in 1997, 30 per cent up on two years previously.

[45] Hurricane Mitch struck in November 1998, leaving in its wake 3,000 dead, tens of thousands of people homeless and a devastated economy.

[46] Nicaragua entered into conflict with Honduras at the end of 1999 when Tegucigalpa ratified a border treaty with Colombia that included possession of three groups of Caribbean islands along the Nicaraguan coast and, according to Managua, cut off 30,000 square km of its maritime territory. Both sides accused each other of provoking the conflict, of taking 'bellicose' measures and on two occasions ships from the two countries exchanged gunfire.

[47] Following mediation by the Organization of American States, Nicaragua and Honduras signed an accord on March 8 2000 to prevent the dispute from turning into an armed conflict. Managua and Tegucigalpa agreed to freeze troop movements along their shared land border and to carry out joint patrols until the dispute could be resolved by the International Court of Justice at The Hague. ∎

Niger

Niger

Population: 10,401,000 (1999)
Area: 1,267,000 SQ KM
Capital: Niamey
Currency: CFA franc
Language: French

Fossil remains found in the Niger region indicate that it was inhabited in prehistoric times and later populated by many different nomadic and trading peoples. The Nok Empire, reaching its peak in present-day Nigeria between the 15th century BC and the 5th century AD (see Nigeria) left its mark on this neighboring region.

[2] During the 7th century AD, the western side of the country became part of the Songhai Empire created by the Berber, who were important propagators of Islam from the 11th century onwards.

[3] Between the 14th and 19th centuries the eastern part of the territory belonged to the Kanem-Bornu State, which had been founded by the Kurani in the 8th century. Meanwhile, during the 19th century, the Haussa states flourished in the south (see Nigeria), until conquered by the Fulani.

[4] Throughout the 19th century, the French colonized the territory, making Niger a colony in 1922. Traditional subsistence crops were replaced by cash crops like peanuts and cotton, which were grown for export, causing food shortages in Niger.

[5] In the 1950s, Niger launched its independence movement, led by Hamani Diori. In 1960, the country's first constitution was approved and Niger became an independent state.

[6] When it broke its colonial ties, Niger was the poorest country in French West Africa, with 80 per cent of the population living in rural areas with persistent drought, soil erosion and population pressure which threaten the country's agriculture and ecology.

[7] In 1960 the new republic's first election the Progressive Party's candidate, Hamani Diori, was elected President. The new government maintained deep economic and political ties with France, to the point of allowing French troops to remain within its territory. In the first years of his presidency, Diori banned the opposition Sawaba party, forcing its leader, Djibo Bakari into exile. The Government was accused of corruption and of harsh repression of the growing political opposition.

[8] In the early 1970s, the drought which hit the Sahel region meant that the army was charged with distributing food among the peasants. This brought them into contact with the needs of the rural people for the first time. On April 13 1974, a Supreme Military Committee took power, naming Seyni Kuntch'e as President. Price controls were set on agricultural products, salaries were raised, nepotism was eliminated, investments were reoriented and education and health services were planned. An attempt was made to access underground water sources and incentives were given to set up farming cooperatives.

[9] The new government tried out new ways of organizing the youth to establish the political base which the country lacked. It also expelled Djibo Bakari, who had returned from exile to lend his support to the regime, and signed bilateral agreements with France. These agreements allowed neocolonialism to focus greater attention on the exploitation of Niger's mineral wealth than on traditional colonial products.

[10] During the 1970s the country experienced an economic boom, based on an increase in the international price of uranium. This mineral accounted for 90 per cent of the country's exports in 1980, when the so-called 'miracle' came to an abrupt end.

[11] The foreign debt was $207 million in 1977 and by 1983 it had increased to $1 billion, forcing Kuntch'e to introduce an IMF structural adjustment program, in an attempt to turn the economy around. The hoped-for return of favorable uranium prices did not materialize and, between 1984 and 1985, the perennial drought in the Sahel region worsened. The

Government also confronted political challenges on different fronts: in 1983, it put down an attempted coup by former members of the secret police and it also engaged in combat with the Tuareg people who had resorted to guerrilla warfare.

[12] The economic crisis worsened when Nigeria closed its borders between April 1984 and March 1986 halting traffic between the two countries, including the transportation of cattle and basic foodstuffs. The decision to close the borders was made by authorities in Lagos to carry out a readjustment of their monetary system. An exception was made in 1985, allowing fuel to be transported across the border.

[13] In 1985 there was no change in the situation: the price of uranium fell an additional four points, there was a deficit of 400,000 tons of grain, a growing foreign debt and the increasing cost of servicing this debt.

[14] In 1986 the Government tried changing its policies, but General Kuntch'e had a cerebral hemorrhage, dying in a Paris military hospital 11 months later. The Supreme Military Committee designated Ali Seibou as his successor. Among his first measures as President was the appointment of 10 new ministers, and the declaration of an amnesty which provided for the return of political exiles, including Djibo Bakari and Hamani Diori, who were personally welcomed by the President and were allowed to return to political activity. In April 1989, Diori died in Rabat, Morocco.

[15] In 1988, Seibou was faced with 3,000 protesting students, who boycotted classes for 22 days, until their demands were finally met.

[16] On August 2, the National Movement for a Developing Society (MNSD) was formed as the only government authorized party, and the National Development Council drew up a new constitution, put to the vote and approved by plebiscite in 1989. In December, Seibou was elected President of the Republic by universal suffrage, in the first elections to be held since independence in 1960.

[17] The drought in the Sahel forced the Government to give special attention to agricultural production and to the people in rural areas. During the 1980-90

WORKERS

% OF LABOUR FORCE **1998**

- FEMALE: 44% ■ MALE: 56%

1990

- SERVICES: 6.2%
- INDUSTRY: 3.9%
- AGRICULTURE: 89.9%

LAND USE

DEFORESTATION: 0.0% annual (1990/95)
IRRIGATED: 1.8% of arable (1993)

1993

- FOREST & WOODLAND: 2.0%
- ARABLE: 2.8%
- OTHER: 95.2%

PUBLIC EXPENDITURE

DEFENCE EXPENDITURE (% of goverment exp.)	**6.9%**	(1997)
MILITARY EXPENDITURE (% of health & education)	**11%**	(1990/91)

1990-98

Per 100,000
live births

590

1995

13%

period it invested 32 per cent of the national budget in agriculture. A major part of the environmental problem was that 98 per cent of people use firewood for cooking. In a country facing deforestation and almost permanent drought, this almost exclusive use of wood for household energy is dangerously destructive. Facing the problem head-on, the Government had solar and wind-powered generators installed, developed electric energy and sponsored the manufacture of low-cost energy-saving stoves. With wood consumption at close to two million tons per year, the Government proposed six-fold increases in the cost of wood-cutting permits, in the hope that this would put an end to further deforestation.

[18] The new president had a favorable economic outlook on his side, as there was a grain surplus of 200,000 tons in 1989. He promised that he would initiate a true democratization process, but this did not occur and throughout 1990 there was intense opposition from the political sector, the labor unions and the students, demanding salary increases, the enactment of educational reforms, and the establishment of a multiparty system. Strikes and massive protest demonstrations were organized in support of these demands and these were harshly suppressed by the police.

[19] In 1990, the country's agricultural production dropped by more than 70 per cent, while the population continued to increase at 3 per cent per year. Despite doubling the amount of arable land, food production rose by only one per cent, and the land has lost its fertility through phosphate and nitrogen depletion.

[20] To confront the crisis the Government launched another structural adjustment plan, imposed by the World Bank and the IMF. A two-year freeze on the salaries of public employees was announced as part of the plan. Workers and students reacted by calling a new series of strikes and holding more demonstrations. In late 1990, Seibou publicly announced his commitment to leading the country towards a multiparty democratic system and he created the National Conference, which was charged with organizing the political transformation.

[21] After four months, the National Conference decided to form a transitional government, headed by a new Prime Minister, Amadou Cheffou. André Salifou was named president of the High Council of the Republic, the body holding legislative power during the transition period. However, the country's situation had never been more critical. The State was bankrupt. There was no money to pay the salaries of the public employees, and students did not receive money for their grants.

[22] The economic disaster and its accompanying social crisis could be traced back to the end of the uranium boom. In 1989, this mineral cost Fr 30,000,000 per kilo, dropping to Fr 19,000,000 per kilo in 1991.

[23] In February 1992, Tuareg guerrillas rose up in arms against the Government once more. In December, the new constitution was approved with nearly 90 per cent of the votes in a referendum but two months later in February 1993 the ruling party was defeated in the legislative elections.

[24] In April, Mahamane Ousmane became President of Niger, with 55.4 per cent of the vote in the second round. The efforts to reach an agreement to end the insurrection of the Tuareg guerrillas in the north continued throughout 1990-1994.

[25] In May 1994, 40 people were killed in confrontations between the rebel and Government forces - but the main guerrilla group, the Coordination of Armed Resistance and the Government managed to seal an agreement. Thus, in June, Niamey granted independence to part of the country inhabited by some 750,000 Tuaregs.

[26] Amidst student protests calling for, the payment of money owed in grants, amongst other things, the Government arrested 91 members of the opposition. In September, Prime Minister Mahamadou Issoufou resigned after his party, the Nigerien Party for Democracy and Socialism, withdrew from the Government coalition, leaving it without an absolute majority in Parliament.

[27] In January 1995, an opposition coalition triumphed in the legislative elections and immediately replaced the Prime Minister, Boubacar Cissé Amadou with Hama Amadou. The latter announced that his first move would be to bring in an economic austerity plan, reaching an agreement for settling the payment of overdue civil service salaries.

[28] Tension continued to mount between the new government

PROFILE

ENVIRONMENT

Most of this land-locked country is made up of a plateau at an average altitude of 350 m. The north is covered by the Sahara desert and the south by savannas. There are uranium, iron, coal and tin deposits, and possibly oil. 80 per cent of the population lives in rural areas. There are nomadic shepherds in the center of the country, and peanut, rice and cotton farming in the south. 85 per cent of all energy is provided by firewood. This region is affected by marked desertification. There is also considerable erosion, produced by strong winds. There is air and water pollution primarily in densely populated urban areas.

SOCIETY

Peoples: Among the shepherds of the central steppe, ethnic origins vary from the Berber Tuareg, to the Fulah, including the Tibu (Tubu). In the south there are western African ethnic groups; the Haussa, Djerma (Zarma), Songhai and Kamuri. **Religions:** mostly Muslim; in the south there are traditional African religions and a Christian minority. **Languages:** French (official) and several local languages. **Political Parties:** National Movement for a Developing Society (MNSD); Alliance for Democracy and Progress (AFC). **Social Organizations:** Nigerien National Workers Union (UNTN).

THE STATE

Official Name: République du Niger. **Administrative Divisions:** 7 Départements. **Capital:** Niamey 510,000 people (1995). **Other cities:** Zinder 120,000 people (1981); Maradi 104,000; Tahoua 50,000 (1988). **Government:** Tandja Mamadou, President since November 1999. Hama Amadou, Prime Minister since November 1999. Legislative power. National Assembly, with 883 members. **National Holiday:** August 3, Independence (1960). **Armed Forces:** 5,300. **Other:** 5,400 Gendarmes, Republican Guards and National Police.

DEMOGRAPHY

Population: 10,401,000 (1999)
Annual growth: 3.3 % (1975/97)
Estimates for year 2015 (million): 16.7 (1999)
Annual growth to year 2015: 3.0 % (1997/2015)
Urban population: 19.1 % (1997)
Urban Growth: 7.2 % (1980/95)
Children per woman: 6.8 (1998)

HEALTH

Life expectancy at birth: 49 years (1998)
male: 47 years (1998)
female: 50 years (1998)
Maternal mortality: 590 per 100,000 live births (1990-98)
Infant mortality: 166 per 1,000 (1998)
Under-5 child mortality: 280 per 1,000 (1998)
Daily calorie supply: 2,116 per capita (1996)
3 doctors per 100,000 people (1993)
Safe water: 61 % (1990/98)

EDUCATION

Literacy: 13 % (1995)
male: 21 % (1995)
female: 7 % (1995)
School enrolment:
Primary total: 29 % (1990/96)
male: 36 % (1990/97)
female: 22 % (1990/97)
Secondary:
male: 9 % (1990/96)
female: 5 % (1990/96)
Tertiary: 1 % (1996)
Primary school teachers: one for every 41 (1996)

COMMUNICATIONS

0 newspapers (1996), 69 radios (1997) and 2 main telephone lines (1996) per 1,000 people

ECONOMY

Per capita, GNP: $ 200 (1998)
Annual growth, GNP: 8.4 % (1998)
Annual inflation: 6.8 % (1990/98)
Consumer price index: 113.3 (1998)
Currency: 590.0 CFA francs = $ 1 (1998)
Cereal imports: 98,798 metric tons (1998)
Fertilizer use: 19 kg per ha (1997)
Exports: $ 333 million (1998)
Imports: $ 479 million (1998)
External debt: $ 1,659 million (1998); $ 165 per capita (1998)
Debt service: 18.4 % of exports (1998)
Development aid received: $ 341 million (1997); $ 86.5 per capita (1997); 18.40 % of GNP (1997)

HDI (rank/value): 173/0.298 (1997)

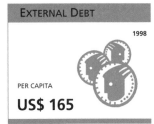
and the President. In January 1996, a military coup toppled Ousmane, who was replaced by the National Salvation Council, headed by Colonel Ibrahim Baré Mainassara, who designated Boukary Adji as Prime Minister. In July, Mainassara was elected President with 52 per cent of the vote. The new 'strongman' dissolved the Independent National Electoral Commission, leading the main opposition parties to boycott the November legislative elections. In December, following the victory of Mainassara's supporters, Boubacar Cissé was made Prime Minister.

[29] In October 1997, Ali Sabo, campaign co-ordinator of the Front for the Restoration and Defense of Democracy was imprisoned. In November 1997, Ibrahim Hassane Mayaki was made Prime Minister, replacing Cissé. A month later in Algiers a ceasefire was agreed between the Government and the Tuareg guerrillas.

[30] In early 1998, Mainassara ordered the arrest of several members of the opposition, including Amadou, accused of an alleged conspiracy. Throughout the year, students, military personnel and public employees led a series of anti-government demonstrations. The Supreme Court annulled the March 1999 election results in some districts and called for a new round of balloting. On April 4, after a tension-filled week in which the opposition called on Mainassara to resign, the presidential guard assassinated him. Coup leader Daouda Malam Wanke was then named President and head of the National Reconciliation Council, which governed the country during the nine-month transition period. Prime Minister Ibrahim Assane Mayaki dissolved the National Assembly, which was dominated by members of Baré's party, and political parties were temporarily suspended.

[31] The international community strongly pressured the country to return to democratic rule. In October Niger held the first round of general elections and, in the second round in November, retired military officer Tandja Mamadou, of the National Movement for a Developing Society (MNSD), was victorious over his rival, former prime minister and parliamentary leader Issoufou Mamadou. President Mamadou took office January 1 2000. ∎

Tuareg: children of the wind and sand

The Tuareg people were originally settled farmers and came from North Africa - the Libya and Algeria of today. This is discovered from fragments of 'tifinar' writing - a style with a Tuareg alphabet differing from the Arabic - dating back to 130 BC. The Tuareg belong to the group of Berber speaking peoples, who number around 12 million in total.

[2] The Tuareg were forced to take up a nomadic lifestyle when they were expelled into the Sahara by the Hilaliana and Arab invasions of the 12th century AD. They adopted some of the ideas of Islam, but only to a degree which suited them - maintaining their original common law and justice system intact, surviving, and eventually getting rich by trading camels and zebu with other peoples of the region.

[3] Their fame as fearless warriors, better armed and trained than any other, stemmed from their systematic sacking of farming settlements and caravans for food and slaves. This plunder allowed them to survive in the Sahara, maintaining a rigid caste structure with separate groups of nobles, clergy, free men and artisans. The political structure consisted of families, councils and heads of councils. Inheritance went down the female line, in the Berber tradition, although daily life was organised in a patriarchal system. Household chores were the mainly in charge of servants, and women spent their time on crafts or composing poetry, whilst the men gained prestige and power within the group in the battles and raids.

[4] For centuries the Tuareg confederations - Ahaggar (also called Hoggar), Azjer (Ajjer), Asben (A´r Tuareg), Ifora, Itesan (Kel Geres), Aulliminden and Kel Tademaket - dominated trade and trade routes. The Tuareg established themselves as the great lords of the desert and savannah. However, the arrival of French colonists in the early 19th century, began to rapidly erode their culture. They made their living by carrying merchandise from west to east, from the Atlantic Ocean to the Mediterranean Sea, and trading or exchanging spices from group to group, travelling in caravans of hundreds of camels.

[5] Once independent from France, newly formed states like Mali, Niger, Mauritania and Chad found their Tuareg inhabitants demanding independence and the return of lands taken by the colonist. However, the governments' need to exploit the large petrol, gold and uranium reserves on these lands to pay off debts to the IMF led to years of battles, persecution and expulsions.

[6] These events led to the appearance of Tuareg guerrilla groups. The civil wars added to the misery of the famines of the1970s and 1980s forcing many Tuareg to flee to refugee camps in neighbouring countries like Burkina Faso, or to urban centres where they settled and took on different values and cultures. The men no longer use the traditional blue veil in front of women, foreigners or the courts - the only known instance of such a practice in the Islamic world. At the same time, the introduction of new means of transport and communication led to the decline of the camel and the Tuareg role as expert guides on the sands of the Sahara. The Tuareg population is currently estimated at around 900,000. ∎

Nigeria

Nigeria

Population: 108,945,000 (1999)
Area: 923,770 SQ KM
Capital: Abuja
Currency: Naira
Language: English

As heirs to the ancient Nok civilization, the Yoruba lived in walled cities with broad avenues. As early as the 11th century they developed a democratic system of urban administration, also producing beautiful ceramics and bronze sculptures (see The origins of the Yoruba culture).

[2] Between the 10th and 11th centuries, Ife, Oyo, Ilorin and Benin (not the present-day nation) were loosely confederated city-states extending their influence from the Niger River in the east to present-day Togo.

[3] Ife always enjoyed a reputation as the main religious center of the nation, and the Oni of Ife is still the High Priest of all Yorubans, whether Nigerian or not.

[4] The city of Oyo, strengthened since the 16th century by the slave trade, had a higher status as a political and economic center, through the Alafin (ruler). The dependence on slavery caused its downfall when that institution was abolished.

[5] The northern part of the country held the Haussa states and was the center of a different culture. A similar group of active Igbo traders emerged in the southeast, but they did not develop urban civilizations like the Yoruba.

[6] The British colonial system disregarded these differences, forcing all the territories under a single administration in 1914, creating an artificial state that has not attained national unity. British interests focused on the exploitation of tin and agricultural and timber resources.

[7] British administration in northern Nigeria was indirect, based on traditional Muslim emirs who acted as go-betweens. Consequently this area, populated by Haussa and Peul, enjoyed greater political autonomy than the other regions.

[8] Independence in 1960 brought the Northern People's Congress to power, in an alliance with the National Council of Nigerian Citizens, an Igbo organization. The country had been divided into a federal structure of four states, and a two-chamber parliament was established, based on the British model.

[9] These political imports proved to be poorly suited to local conditions. Regional governors acquired more power than the President Nnambi Azikiwe. Progressive parties were pushed aside in a succession of electoral frauds, while political leaders lost their national outlook, encouraging ethnic rivalries.

[10] After months of infighting, the military chose General Yacuba Gowon as President. About this time the oil industry began to develop, just as France was inciting the separatist movement among the Igbo, provoking a three-year secessionist civil war in Biafra.

[11] Nigeria became the world's 8th largest oil producer, and Gowon expropriated 55 per cent of the transnational petroleum operations, creating financing for local entrepreneurs.

[12] Real power was vested in the nationalist Supreme Military Council, with different leaders acting as President. The council closed US military and espionage installations. During Olusegun Obasanjo's presidency, Barclays Bank and British Petroleum assets were nationalized as these companies were violating economic sanctions against apartheid South Africa.

[13] In 1978, constitutional reform was proposed, calling for elections and a return to civilian government. The Federal Election Commission authorized only five parties, all representing the traditional financial and political elite. Parties

WORKERS

% OF LABOUR FORCE **1998**

- FEMALE: 36% ■ MALE: 64%

1990

- SERVICES: 50.1%
- INDUSTRY: 6.9%
- AGRICULTURE: 43.0%

LAND USE

DEFORESTATION: 0.9% annual (1990/95)
IRRIGATED: 3.2% of arable (1993)

1993

- FOREST & WOODLAND: 12.2%
- ARABLE: 32.3%
- OTHER: 55.5%

PUBLIC EXPENDITURE

DEFENCE EXPENDITURE (% of goverment exp.) **12.3%** (1997)

MILITARY EXPENDITURE (% of health & education) **33%** (1990/91)

with socialist or revolutionary perspectives were barred from the electoral process, under the pretext of avoiding political fragmentation.

[14] The National Party of Nigeria (NPN) won the election with 25 per cent of the vote, and the Unity Party of Nigeria (UPN) came second, with 20 per cent.

[15] The inauguration of Shagari, who lacked majorities in both legislative chambers, ended 13 years of military rule. He launched a capitalist development plan based exclusively on petrodollars, to transform Nigeria into the development hub of sub-Saharan Africa. His promises included constructing a new capital, doubling primary school attendance and achieving self-sufficiency in food production via controversial 'green revolution' methods.

[16] None of these proposals came to anything. Contraband, large urban concentrations of immigrants and poor peasants, unemployment and poverty all increased.

[17] The International Monetary Fund demanded the refinancing of the foreign debt, putting the country under further pressure. Shagari announced new elections, and took part as the NPN candidate. He was re-elected, amidst accusations of electoral fraud and military conspiracies.

[18] On January 1 1984, Muhamad Buhari staged the fourth coup in the country's republican history. The new leaders accused their predecessors of corruption in the petroleum sector, accounting for 95 per cent of export earnings. Hundreds of people were arrested, and all civilian government officials were replaced by military personnel.

[19] However, the crisis was not checked, and the price of rice quadrupled in a single year. Repression extended to foreigners and 600,000 were expelled, classed as illegal immigrants. These events set the stage for another coup, the country's sixth, on August 26 1985. General Ibrahim Babangida became the new President. That year, the foreign debt reached $15 billion.

[20] In December 1987, local elections were held with 15,000 unaffiliated candidates taking part. A National Election Commission had been appointed to oversee the voting and ensure that the election was clean and free of coercion. The lack of proper preparation for the voting itself, however, led to acts of violence, confusion and subsequent accusations of fraud. The election was finally annulled.

[21] On December 7 1989, the military government announced that the elections, originally scheduled for the end of the month, would be postponed until December 1990. Six months later, President Babangida announced that the ban on political activism had been lifted, in an attempt to monitor the transition from military to civilian government in 1992.

[22] Babangida visited Britain in May 1990. One outcome of the visit was a treaty between the two countries granting Nigeria $100 million in aid. Most of its trade is with the United States, the United Kingdom and France, though it sought more balanced international relations by maintaining relations with all the countries in the world.

[23] Between August and October, the creation of nine new states to separate hostile ethnic groups generated protests which were repressed by the army, causing some 300 deaths according to unofficial figures. The Government imposed a curfew.

[24] Toward the end of 1991, the Government invalidated the allegedly fraudulent internal party elections, held to select government candidates. In November, a new census eliminated 20 million non-existent voters from the electoral register. On December 14, governmental elections were held; the Social Democratic Party (SDP) won in 16 states, and the National Republican Convention (NRC) in 14.

[25] The opposition groups were granted a general amnesty, and 11 dissidents were freed. A law prohibiting former Government officials from running for office was revoked.

[26] Early in 1992, the imprisonment of 263 Muslim militants caused protests in the state of Katsina. During this period, there was also an escalation of inter-ethnic conflict between Haussa and Kataj in the state of Kaduna, and territorial conflict between Tiv and Jukin in the Taraba.

[27] In July 1992, legislative elections were held, but the National Assembly did not convene until December. The SDP won 52 seats in the Senate, and 314 in the Chamber of Representatives. The National Republican Convention obtained 37 seats in the Senate, and 275 in the Chamber of Representatives. Nigeria subsequently began the transition to civilian government, after 23 years of military regimes.

[28] In October, presidential primary elections were held, with candidates from the two main parties, the SDP (left-of-center) and the RNC (right-of-center). Both parties were created by the regime, with nearly indistinguishable manifestos. Another 23 candidates also took part. President Babangida invalidated the election, claiming fraud, stripped the candidates of their authority and ousted the leadership of the SDP and RNC. Later that month, the military government suspended all political activity. These developments halted the democratic transition process, jeopardizing the possibility of a transfer to civilian government in early 1993.

[29] In November Babangida announced that elections slated for January 1993 had been postponed until June. He also ratified the proscription of the 23 1992 presidential candidates. Finally, he postponed the transfer to a democratic regime until August.

[30] On June 12 1993, the first presidential elections since 1983

PROFILE

ENVIRONMENT

The country's extensive river system includes the Niger and its main tributary, the Benue. In the north, the 'harmattan', a dry wind from the Sahara, creates a drier region made up of plateaus and grasslands where cotton and peanuts are grown for export. The central plains are also covered by grasslands, and are sparsely populated. The southern lowlands receive more rainfall, they have dense tropical forests and most of the country's population lives there. Cocoa and oil-palms are grown in this area. The massive delta of the Niger River divides the coast into two separate regions. In the east, oil production is concentrated around Port Harcourt, the homeland of the Igbo, who converted to Christianity and fought to establish an independent Biafra. To the west, the industrial area is concentrated around Lagos and Ibadan. Yoruba are the predominant western ethnic group, and some of them have converted to Islam. Nigeria has lost between 70 and 80 per cent of its original forests.

SOCIETY

Peoples: Nigeria has the largest population in Africa. The 250 or so ethnic groups can be divided into four main groups: the Haussa and Fulani in the north; the Yoruba in the southwest; and the Igbo in the southeast.

Religions: The north is predominantly Muslim, while Christians form the majority in the southeast; Muslims, Christians and followers of traditional African religions can be found in the southwest.

Languages: English (official). Each region has a main language depending on the predominant ethnic group, Hausa, Igbo or Yoruba.

Political Parties: the United Nigerian Congress Party; the Committee for National Consensus; the National Central Party of Nigeria; the Democratic Party of Nigeria and the 'Grassroots' Democratic Movement

Social Organizations: Unified Federation of Nigerian Unions.

THE STATE

Official Name: Federal Republic of Nigeria.
Administrative Divisions: 30 States.
Capital: Abuja 40,000 people (1995 est).
Other cities: Lagos 5,600,000 people (1995); Ibadan 1,295,000; Ogbomosho 660,000; Kano 700,000 (1992).
Government: Olusegun Obasanjo, President from March 1999.
National Holiday: October 1, Independence Day (1960).
Armed Forces: 77,100 troops (1995).
Other: 7,000 National Guard, 2,000 Port Security Police.

were held. The military government did not divulge election results until it had concluded an investigation of alleged fraud. The main contest was between the NCR and SDP candidates, who had been authorized to take part in the election, although the original candidates continued to be proscribed.

[31] Babangida invalidated the election results on June 23, accusing SDP and NCR candidates of 'buying votes'. Abiola, a wealthy Muslim who was the SDP candidate and who had apparently won the June election, left for London to campaign for international condemnation of the Babangida regime.

[32] The US and Britain suspended their economic aid and training of Nigerian military personnel. Abiola launched a civil disobedience campaign and large protests broke out in the streets of Lagos, where at least 25 people were killed by federal troops.

[33] Clashes continued and on August 26 Babangida resigned, leaving the provisional command of the country in the hands of Ernest Shonekan, who promised to hold new elections.

[34] The following month, Abiola returned to London and labor unions called a general strike, demanding he be recognized as Nigerian president. Toward the end of 1993 the Minister of Defense, General Sani Abacha, overthrew Shonekan, dissolved Parliament and banned all political activity.

[35] This new 'strongman' had been a very influential member of the previous military regime and a key figure in the military coup that had ousted the Government in 1983. In one of his first statements, Abacha announced he would abandon some liberal economic reforms adopted in the 1980s.

[36] Interest rates fell and a new foreign exchange control was established, at a time when any possibility of reaching an agreement with the IMF was increasingly remote. Popular support for Abiola mounted; in June 1994, the political leader was arrested, which triggered a 10-day-strike by oil workers, the most important sector in the country.

[37] In November 1994, the execution of nine members of the Movement for the Survival of the Ogoni People, resulted in the isolation of the military regime. Several countries, including the United States, withdrew their ambassadors from Nigeria.

[38] In June 1996 on the basis of a register of political parties drawn up by the National Electoral Commission, Abacha and his military council legalized five political groups: the United Nigerian Congress Party, the Committee for National Consensus, the National Central Party of Nigeria, the Democratic Party of Nigeria and the 'Grassroots' Democratic Movement.

[39] An increase in oil prices stimulated economic growth in 1997. On several occasions, the Government confirmed that this increase had led to improvements in the difficult social situation of the country. However, official data indicated that 80 per cent of the population was living in poverty.

[40] In April 1998, Abacha announced that the August elections were to be replaced by a plebiscite that would determine whether he was to continue in power. The sudden death of the dictator on June 8 led to widespread expressions of happiness and generated expectations of political changes. General Abdusalam Abu-Bakar, appointed by the military junta as new President on June 9, promised to respect the democratic transition, but did not modify the proposal for a referendum.

[41] Local elections in February 1999 ended in victories for the Popular Democratic Party, of General Olusegun Obasanjo - a former military ruler - and the Alliance for Democracy. The Alliance, which primarily represents the Yoruba ethnic group, won the government of the former capital, Lagos, by a broad margin, while the Party of All Peoples, led by supporters of former dictator Sani Abacha, won only the state of Jigawa. The Government set general elections for March 1999.

[42] Obasanjo won the March presidential elections. At first, the opposition attempted to appeal the results before the Electoral Court, but later backed down. The new President promised to re-evaluate the Government's investment policies and to reform the inefficient and corrupt public sector. Upon taking office in May, Obasanjo called upon Nigerians to join him in a three-day fast to seek divine intervention that would ensure his positive presidential performance. One of his first measures was to purge the army ranks, removing 30 military officers. At the same time, he confiscated millions of dollars which he said had been stolen from the public Treasury during previous administrations.

[43] The civilian-led Government improved the country's international image. In October, the United States promised to quadruple its economic aid to Nigeria.

[44] Four days of ethnic fighting between the Ijaw and the Ilaje in Lagos in December left 12 people dead. The conflicts continued and by March 2000, when Obasanjo visited the area and established a peace committee made up of leaders from both communities, hundreds of people had been killed. The committee was able to put an end to the fighting, at least temporarily. ∎

The creation of Africa

A frican peoples have an array of creation myths, stories about the origins of life and the universe. Creation myths provide the model for other stories that refer to the origins of cultural practices.

[2] Konos from Guinea believe the initial force of the world, prior even to God, was Death. The Pangwa from Tanzania claim the world was created out of ant excrement and the Yorubas from Nigeria think God was intoxicated with wine when he created disabled people and albinos.

[3] For the herding tribes of the Peules or Fulanis from Mali, milk is the centre of creation. In the beginning there was a huge drop of milk. Then Doondari came and created the stone, then the stone created steel, and steel created fire, and fire created water, and water created the air. Then Doondari came down for a second time. He took the five elements and with them created man. But man was proud. Then Doondari created blindness and blindness humbled man. But when blindness became too proud, Doondari created dreams, and dreams humbled blindness; but when dreams became too proud, Doondari created grief, and grief humbled dreams, and when grief became too proud, Doondari created death, and death humbled grief, but when death became too proud, Doondari came down for a third time. And he came as Gueno the Eternal. And Gueno conquered death. ∎

STATISTICS

DEMOGRAPHY

Population: 108,945,000 (1999)
Annual growth: 2.8 % (1975/97)
Estimates for year 2015 (million): 153.3 (1999)
Annual growth to year 2015: 2.2 % (1997/2015)
Urban population: 41.3 % (1997)
Urban Growth: 5.6 % (1980/95)
Children per woman: 5.1 (1998)

HEALTH

Life expectancy at birth: 50 years (1998)
male: 49 years (1998)
female: 52 years (1998)
Infant mortality: 112 per 1,000 (1998)
Under-5 child mortality: 187 per 1,000 (1998)
Daily calorie supply: 2,609 per capita (1996)
21 doctors per 100,000 people (1993)
Safe water: 49 % (1990/98)

EDUCATION

Literacy: 57 % (1995)
male: 66 % (1995)
female: 47 % (1995)
School enrolment:
Primary total: 89 % (1990/96)
male: 100 % (1990/97)
female: 79 % (1990/97)
Secondary:
male: 33 % (1990/96)
female: 28 % (1990/96)
Tertiary: 4 % (1996)
Primary school teachers: one for every 37 (1994)

COMMUNICATIONS

24 newspapers (1996), 223 radios (1997), 55 TV sets (1996) and 4 main telephone lines (1996) per 1,000 people
Books: 1 new titles per 100,000 people (1992/94)

ECONOMY

Per capita, GNP: $ 300 (1998)
Annual growth, GNP: 1.1 % (1998)
Annual inflation: 38.7 % (1990/98)
Consumer price index: 154.3 (1998)
Currency: 21.9 nairas = $ 1 (1998)
Cereal imports: 2,955,325 metric tons (1998)
Fertilizer use: 49 kg per ha (1997)
Exports: $ 9,712 million (1998)
Imports: $ 13,115 million (1998)
External debt: $ 30,315 million (1998); $ 285 per capita (1998)
Debt service: 11.2 % of exports (1998)
Development aid received: $ 202 million (1997); $ 25.3 per capita (1997); 11.00 % of GNP (1997)

ENERGY

Consumption: 753.0 Kgs of Oil equivalent per capita yearly (1997); -115.0 % imported (1997)

HDI (rank/value): 146/0.456 (1997)

Northern Marianas

Northern Marianas

Population: 44,000 (1999)
Area: 464 SQ KM
Capital: Saipan
Currency: US dollar
Language: English

In Saipan, the largest island of the Mariana archipelago, evidence has been found of human habitation from 1500 BC.

[2] During his first expedition around the world, Portuguese navigator Ferdinand Magellan sighted the islands in 1521 and claimed them for the Spanish Crown. They were held by the Spanish until ceded to Germany in 1899 as the Spanish empire declined.

[3] During World War I the islands came under the control of Japan, which had an alliance with Britain since 1902. The Japanese occupied the islands until World War II.

[4] In June 1944, after fierce fighting, the US took Saipan and Tinian from the Japanese. The islands were contested because of their strategic location in the North Pacific, on the route between Hawaii and the Philippines. They finally came to form part of the Trust Territory of the Pacific Islands in 1947.

[5] The islands held this status until they became a Free Associated State under a referendum held in 1975. In 1977, US President Jimmy Carter approved the constitution of the Northern Mariana islands. At the end of the year this new constitution brought about elections for posts in the bicameral legislative.

[6] In 1978, the islands began to be administered autonomously. Washington developed a project to turn two-thirds of Tinian into a military air base and an alternative center for the storage of nuclear weapons.

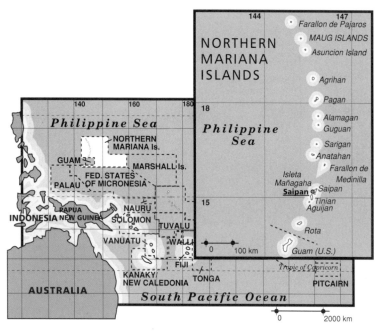

[7] When news leaked out that cement deposits containing radioactive waste from Japanese nuclear plants - cobalt 60, strontium 90 and cesium 137 - had been dumped in this part of the Pacific, the alarm was sounded on similar US projects that would directly affect the Mariana Islands.

[8] In 1984 US President Ronald Reagan granted some civil and political rights to the islands' residents, such as equal employment opportunities in the federal government, the civil service and the US armed forces.

[9] The Northern Marianas were formally admitted to the Commonwealth of the United States in 1986. Mariana inhabitants were granted US citizenship but not the right to vote in presidential elections. They have a representative in the US Congress with no voting rights.

[10] The main economic activities of the country are fishing, agriculture - concentrated in smallholdings - and tourism which employs about 10 per cent of the workforce. Some of these activities have been affected often by the typhoons which the islands suffer in the rainy season: in January 1988 Rota Island was devastated by a typhoon which forced the US to declare a state of emergency there. Two years later, the Koryn typhoon struck the archipelago in January 1990 .

[11] In the local elections held in 1989, Republicans retained the governorship, ousting the Democrat representative from Washington. Larry Guerrero was elected governor after Pedro Tenorio had decided to stand down.

[12] The termination of UN Security Council trusteeship of the islands was approved in 1990. Thus, the Northern Marianas became an independent state, associated to the United States.

[13] The Republican Party won the November 1991 legislative elections by a wide margin. Given this majority, it hoped to modify the islands' status with relation to the US, in order to guarantee control over a 200-mile exclusive economic zone.

[14] In 1992, the US Supreme Court ratified the property ownership system, whereby only nationals could own land. In 1994, Froilan C Tenorio was re-elected governor.

[15] In 1995, there were some 22,600 foreign workers in the country, three times the number of Marianan workers. Unemployment amongst the latter stood at 15 per cent.

[16] In January 1998, Froilan C Tenorio was re-elected again. His victory was questioned by opposition groups, as it was his third period in office following previous terms in 1982 and 1986. ■

PROFILE

ENVIRONMENT

The Marianas archipelago, located in Micronesia, east of the Philippines and south of Japan consists of 16 islands (excluding the island of Guam), of which only six are inhabited. The most important in size and population are: Saipan (122 sq km), Tinian (101 sq km) and Rota (85 sq km). Of volcanic origin, the islands are generally mountainous. The climate is tropical, with rain forest vegetation. In the northernmost islands, however, these conditions shade gradually into a more temperate climate and brush-like, herbaceous vegetation.

SOCIETY

Peoples: The population is mostly indigenous, of Chamorro origin. There are also Japanese, Chinese, Korean, European and Micronesian minorities.
Religions: Catholic. **Languages:** English (official), 55 per cent speak Chamorro. **Political Parties:** Republican Party; Democratic Party.

THE STATE

Official Name: Commonwealth of the Northern Mariana Islands. **Capital:** Saipan 28,000 people (est. 1994). **Other islands:** Rota 2,295 people; Tinian 2,118 people (1990). **Government:** By virtue of the US Commonwealth status, the President of the United States is the Head of State. Froilan C. Tenorio, Governor by direct election, since January 1998. There is a two-chamber legislature with 9 senators and 18 representatives .
National Holiday: Commonwealth Day, January 8 (1986).
Armed forces: The US is in charge of defense.

DEMOGRAPHY

Population: 44,000 (1999)

Norway

Norge

Population: 4,442,000 (1999)
Area: 323,900 SQ KM
Capital: Oslo
Currency: Kroner
Language: Norwegian

The earliest human traces in Norway correspond to the period between the 9th and the 7th millennia BC. Germanic tribes are thought to have emigrated to these areas when glaciers receded from the northern European coasts and mountains. Cave drawings show that navigation was already known to the peoples of the time, as were something like skis, designed for gliding over the snow.

[2] Historians believe that Norwegian nationality and conversion to Christianity began between 800 and 1030 AD. These dates also correspond to the rise of the Vikings, the name given to Scandinavian seafarers, merchants, and above all, raiders, who dominated the northern seas for 200 years. Harald Harfagre is considered to be the founder of the nation, a feat which he accomplished after defeating his rivals in a naval battle at Hafrsfjord, near the city of Stavanger. After this victory, a large part of the country came under his control.

[3] Viking expeditions expanded the Norwegian Empire, reaching Greenland to the west, and Ireland to the south. In 1002, Leif Erikson and his followers were the first Europeans to cross the Atlantic and reach North America, which they named Vinland.

[4] At the end of the Viking era, Norway was an independent kingdom in which four regional peasant assemblies (*lagting*) elected the monarch. Legitimate and illegitimate children of the king had equal rights to succession before the lagtings. In the 10th and 12th centuries it was common for two kings to govern simultaneously without any conflict arising between them.

[5] King Magnus III Barfot (1093-1103) conquered the Scottish Orkney and Hebrides Islands. His three sons governed together: they imposed a tithe, founded the first monasteries and built cathedrals. At the beginning of the 12th century, a hundred-year civil war broke out, as a result of the increased power of the monarchy and also of disputes between the monarchy and the church.

[6] This war continued until the coronation of Haakon IV in 1217. The new king reorganized public administration, imposing a hereditary monarchy. Haakon signed a treaty with Russia over the country's northern border. Greenland and Iceland agreed to a union with the King. With the Scottish islands and the Faeroes included the Norwegian Empire reached its maximum extent.

[7] The Black Death killed close to 50 per cent of Norway's population between 1349 and 1350. The upper classes were decimated; Danes and Swedes were hired to fill the positions left vacant in the higher levels of the Government and the church. However, the King lost control over his dominions and isolated regions organized autonomous administrations.

[8] The ascent of Queen Margaret of Denmark to the throne in 1387 paved the way for the union of the Scandinavian countries. In 1389, she was crowned Queen of Sweden and in 1397 her adopted nephew Erik was elected king of all Scandinavia in Kalmar, Sweden. With the Kalmar union, Norway was gradually subordinated, ultimately becoming a province of Denmark, a situation which lasted for more than 400 years.

[9] After 1523, Norway's administrative council tried to obtain greater independence from Denmark. However, the fact that power lay in the hands of the Catholic bishops made it difficult to gain Swedish support. At the end of the civil war, between 1533 and 1536, the council was abolished. In 1537, the Danish King made the Lutheran religion the country's official religion; the Norwegian Church has been a State church ever since.

[10] During this period, social conditions in Norway were better than in Denmark. There was a class of rich landlords in the countryside which exploited the regional timber resources, as well as a large group of rural wage-earners. Most of Norway's population were peasants and fishing people. Cities were limited to fewer than 15,000 inhabitants.

[11] At the end of the Napoleonic wars, Denmark unilaterally surrendered control of Norway to Sweden. In 1814, Norway's constituent assembly proclaimed national independence. Sweden re-established its dominance over Norway by force, but this union was dissolved once again without bloodshed in 1905, with Norway regaining its sovereignty and with its full previous territories intact.

[12] In spite of its subordination to Sweden, the majority of the laws enacted in 1814 remained in force during this period. The Norwegian constitution is one of the oldest in the world, second only to that of the United States. It is based on the principles of national sovereignty, the separation of powers and the inviolability of human rights.

[13] Under a constitutional amendment in 1884, Norway

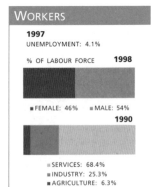

WORKERS

1997
UNEMPLOYMENT: 4.1%

% OF LABOUR FORCE **1998**

■ FEMALE: 46%   ■ MALE: 54%

1990

■ SERVICES: 68.4%
■ INDUSTRY: 25.3%
■ AGRICULTURE: 6.3%

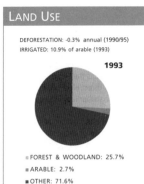

LAND USE

DEFORESTATION: -0.3% annual (1990/95)
IRRIGATED: 10.9% of arable (1993)

1993

■ FOREST & WOODLAND: 25.7%
■ ARABLE: 2.7%
■ OTHER: 71.6%

PUBLIC EXPENDITURE

1997

80
60 — 50.2%
40
20
4.8%
0
DEFENCE   SOCIAL

MILITARY EXPENDITURE **22%**
(% of health & education)   (1990/91)

MATERNAL MORTALITY	FOOD DEPENDENCY	FOREIGN TRADE

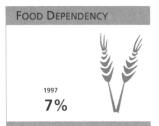

MATERNAL MORTALITY

Per 100,000 live births

1990-98

6

FOOD DEPENDENCY

1997

7%

FOREIGN TRADE

Millions US$ 1997

IMPORTS
63,277

EXPORTS
48,922

adopted a parliamentary monarchy as its system of government. The Danish Prince Carl was elected king of Norway, under the name Haakon VII, in 1905. Up until 1914, the country experienced rapid economic expansion, with the hydroelectric wealth of the region allowing large-scale industrial development.

[14] The sale of a large number of Norwegian water courses with hydroelectric power-generating potential, to foreigners, caused great concern among the population. In 1906, 75 per cent of Norway's hydroelectric dams belonged to foreign investors. In 1909, Parliament passed laws for the protection of the country's natural resources.

[15] Universal suffrage, a term which applied to men only when it was passed in 1898, was extended to women by reforms approved in 1907 and 1913. One consequence of industrialization and universal suffrage was the growth of the Labor Party (LP).

[16] During World War I, Norway tried to remain neutral, but was obliged by the other powers to cut trade with Germany. Anti-German feeling was strong, particularly because of the various accidents caused by German submarines. Price increases provoked by the conflict hit the workers hardest.

[17] Unlike other Western European social democracies, Norway's LP (in which the Left formed the majority) decided to

join the Third Communist International in 1918. However, the Norwegian LP could not agree with the centralization applied by the Soviet Communist Party, and cut its ties with the Comintern in 1923.

[18] Despite economic difficulties and serious labor conflicts (with unemployment reaching 20 per cent in 1938), Norway underwent vigorous industrial expansion in the inter-war years. The Government extended social legislation to include pensions, mandatory leave for workers and unemployment benefits.

[19] In 1940, at the beginning of World War II, Norway was invaded by Germany, which seized control of the country after two months of fighting. King Haakon and the Government went into exile in London, co-ordinating the resistance from there. Norway was liberated in 1945. Haakon died in 1957 and was succeeded by his son Olaf V.

[20] The LP governed continuously between 1935 and 1965, except for a brief one-month period in 1963. In 1965, the LP lost its parliamentary majority and Per Borten, the leader of the Center Party, was named Prime Minister. However, he resigned in 1971 when it was revealed that he had leaked confidential information during EC negotiations.

[21] After the War, Norway abandoned its neutrality policy, joining NATO in 1949. This membership was encouraged by the fear of Soviet expansionism and the unsuccessful attempt to establish a Scandinavian military alliance between Norway, Denmark and Sweden. However, in 1952, the Scandinavian countries established the Nordic Council to deal with their common interests. Norway became a member of the Nordic Council in 1952, and of the European Free Trade Association (EFTA) in 1960. By 1972, the idea of joining the EC had been proposed. The issue divided the population and a plebiscite was held to decide the question; 53 per cent voted against, while 47 per cent were in favor.

[22] Trygve Bratteli, the Labor Prime Minister resigned and a new government was formed by Lars Korvald of the Christian People's Party, to negotiate a trade agreement with the EEC. After this the Labor Party formed a minority

cabinet under Oddvar Nordli, who served until 1981, when the LP appointed Gro Harlem Brundtland, the first woman Prime Minister.

[23] In 1977, Norway extended its territorial waters to 200 miles and designated a protected fishing zone in its territory of Svalbard.

[24] In 1986, the Labor Party formed a minority government, once more under Gro Harlem Brundtland, who appointed 8 women to her 18-member cabinet.

[25] Trade conflicts between Norway and the US have frequently occurred. In 1987, the state-owned Kongsberg Vapenfabrik exported advanced automated machinery to the Soviet Union, violating NATO sales restrictions to Warsaw Pact and Third World countries.

[26] There were also problems with nuclear 'heavy water' exports. Romania and West Germany, had re-sold some to India, but later pledged not to re-sell the material for weapons production without Norwegian authorization. The dispute was not properly resolved until Norway prohibited all 'heavy water' exports in 1988.

[27] In 1988, US threats to impose sanctions were dropped after Norway agreed to limit its whaling quota to scientific studies. In 1990, however, the Government announced its intention to return to commercial whaling.

[28] In 1986, the pollution of rivers and lakes in southern Norway was attributed to acid rain coming from the UK. The British Government announced its intention to reduce emissions by 14 per cent by 1997, but the Norwegians considered this measure to be insufficient. A 60 per cent reduction of emissions within the country since the early 1980s has been insufficient to stop the environmental damage.

[29] The vulnerability of the Norwegian environment to events beyond national borders was underscored in April 1986 when a fire broke out in the Chernobyl nuclear power plant, in the Ukraine. The high levels of radioactivity released into the atmosphere most seriously affected the Sami population in the northern part of the country, and over 70 per cent of all reindeer meat had to be destroyed.

[30] In the early 1970s, Norway and the former USSR were at odds over rights to large parts of the Barents Sea. A temporary agreement signed in 1978 defined a 'grey area' for the joint management of fishing. The unresolved questions continued to create tension until early 1989, when the USSR proposed that they begin negotiations.

[31] Protests have been triggered

PROFILE

ENVIRONMENT

The Scandinavian mountain range runs north-south along the coast of the country. On the western side, glacier erosion has gouged out deep valleys that are way below actual sea level, resulting in the famous 'fjords', narrow, deep inlets walled in by steep cliffs. Maritime currents produce humid, mild winters and cool summers. The population is concentratred in the south, especially round Oslo. Nine tenths of the territory is uninhabited.

SOCIETY

Peoples: Norwegians 96.3 per cent, Danish 0.4 per cent, British 0.3 per cent, Pakistani 0.2 per cent, Iranian 0.2 per cent, others (including 40,000 Sami, an indigenous people who live chiefly in the northern province of Finnmark) 1.9 per cent.
Religions: 88 per cent of the population belongs to the Church of Norway (Lutheran); there are Evangelical and Catholic minorities.
Languages: Two forms of Norwegian are officially recognized; 80 per cent of school children learn the old form 'Bokmal', and 20 per cent learn the neo-Norwegian 'Landsmal'. In the north, the Sami speak their own language.
Political Parties: Labor Party; Conservative Party; Progress Party; Party of the Socialist Left; Christian Democratic Party, Center Party.
Social Organizations: Norwegian Federation of Unions; Organization of Academics (AF); Organization of Trades (YS).

THE STATE

Official Name: Kongeriket Norge.
Administrative divisions: 19 provinces (*Fylker*).
Capital: Oslo 700,000 people (est 1996).
Other cities: Bergen 223,000 people; Trondheim 143,746; Stavanger 104,000 (1996).
Government: Parliamentary constitutional monarchy since 1884; Harald V, King since January 17 1991. Prime Minister: Jens Stoltenberg, since March 2000. Legislative power resides in the *Storting*, the 165-member unicameral parliament.
National Holiday: May 17, Constitution Day (1814).
Armed Forces: 29,000 (1995).

by acid rain emanating from industries on the Kola Peninsula to the east of Norway. Since the fall of the communist regime this situation has changed, and there is growing trade across the border. Norway, Sweden and Finland have joined forces to help Russia solve the immense environmental problems in the area.

[32] Towards the end of 1986, Norway suffered a recession, immediately following a consumer boom which had transformed it into the Scandinavian country with the highest standard of living. There was a large devaluation that year, tax reforms were carried out, and unemployment increased. The Government responded by implementing a harsh austerity plan.

[33] Norway is the world's sixth largest producer of natural gas and crude oil, and the third largest oil exporter. Operating outside the OPEC, oil concessions have always been handled as an economic and political weapon. Although drilling rights are granted to foreign companies, the State looks after its own interests by requiring 50 per cent participation by Statoil, the national oil company, in all operations.

[34] In January 1992, Norway's mission in South Africa was upgraded from a consulate to an embassy, and in the course of 1993,

Norwegian diplomacy gained a great deal of prestige when the minister of foreign affairs, Johan Juergen Holst served as an intermediary in the Israeli-PLO negotiations.

[35] In 1993 the economy picked up, although unemployment remained at 6 per cent. Oil, fishing (with 25,000 employed), the merchant marine (with 1,059 ships and a capacity of 36 million tons) and agriculture play important roles in the country's economy. The Norwegian agricultural system is one of the most heavily subsidized in Europe, but while the country imports fruit, vegetables and cereals, it is self-sufficient in animal products.

[36] Despite serious disagreements among Norwegians, Oslo sought entry to the European Union (EU) in late 1992. The unions considered that joining the former European Community would threaten national sovereignty, while many entrepreneurs - particularly in the export sector - wanted full access to the EU market.

[37] For entry to be effective it had to be approved by a referendum, and a date was set for November 1994. The campaign for this vote largely dominated political life for two years and revolved around three main issues: oil exploitation, the regional policy and the fishing policy.

[38] The social democrats and conservatives supported joining the EU, while all the other opposed the move, leading to an extremely close outcome: 52.4 per cent of the electorate voted against integration, blocking Norway's membership of the bloc.

[39] In 1994, the economy continued to expand and unemployment to fall. In 1995, unemployment reached 4.8 per cent and the trend was expected to continue.

[40] In October 1996, the Labor Party's Thorbjorn Jagland became head of government after Gro Harlem Brundtland resigned.

[41] Following the September 1997 elections, Jagland was forced to stand down. The ruling Labor Party took 35 per cent of the votes and 65 seats out of the total 165 in play. The Prime Minister had announced he would stand down if the party could not equal the 36.9 per cent it had achieved in 1993.

[42] Christian Democrat, Kjell Magne Bondevik was appointed his successor. A coalition of three 'centre' parties took control. These parties held only 43 votes in Parliament. Bondevik started by earmarking part of the oil income for investments in health and education.

[43] In 1997, the economy expanded for the fifth year running. However in early 1998, Norway began to suffer the consequences of falling international crude oil prices, following the stock exchange crash in Southeast Asia - the biggest oil importing market in the world.

[44] A project to install the nation's first natural gas energy plants became the center of a controversy that led Bondevik to lose Parliament's vote of confidence. He resigned in March 2000. Bondevik's minority government maintained that the new energy plants would release too much carbon dioxide into the atmosphere, while the Opposition insisted on becoming less dependent on imported coal-produced energy during dry periods.

[45] Labor deputy leader Jens Stoltenberg took office as the new Prime Minister on March 17. Women were appointed to approximately half of the Cabinet posts.

[46] In August Norway gave assistance in the rescue/salvage of the Russian nuclear submarine *Kursk*. ■

The Sami culture

T he Sami are descendants of nomadic tribes which travelled throughout northern Scandinavia for thousands of years. Presently settled in Norway, they are a small community of some 40,000 people, living in the centre and north of the country (the province of Lapland). Some Sami also live in Russia, Sweden and Finland.

[2] Their origins are uncertain and lost in time. Some claim they are linked to Siberian peoples, others to Alpine communities from Central Europe. The reindeer formed the basis of their economy until a few years ago. However, a more settled existence has substantially altered their traditions.

[3] The last remaining Sami herders accompany the reindeer through valleys with grasslands, while their families live in modern homes. Through the years, their survival has now come to depend on fishing and agriculture.

[4] The use of the Sami language was banned for a long time in schools in Norway. It is composed of three basic dialects: each one with several subtypes and local variations. The number of Sami has increased since the last century, but the number of those that speak the language has decreased. ■

STATISTICS

DEMOGRAPHY

Population: 4,442,000 (1999)
Annual growth: 0.4 % (1975/97)
Estimates for year 2015 (million): 4.7 (1999)
Annual growth to year 2015: 0.4 % (1997/2015)
Urban population: 73.6 % (1997)
Urban Growth: 0.7 % (1980/95)
Children per woman: 1.9 (1998)

HEALTH

Life expectancy at birth: 78 years (1998)
male: 75 years (1998)
female: 81 years (1998)
Maternal mortality: 6 per 100,000 live births (1990-98)
Infant mortality: 4 per 1,000 (1998)
Under-5 child mortality: 4 per 1,000 (1998)
Daily calorie supply: 3,350 per capita (1996)

EDUCATION

School enrolment:
Primary total: 99 % (1990/96)
male: 99 % (1990/97)
female: 99 % (1990/97)
Secondary:
male: 120 % (1990/96)
female: 113 % (1990/96)
Tertiary: 62 % (1996)

COMMUNICATIONS

588 newspapers (1996), 915 radios (1997), 569 TV sets (1996) and 555 main telephone lines (1996) per 1,000 people
Books: 159 new titles per 100,000 people (1992/94)

ECONOMY

Per capita, GNP: $ 34,310 (1998)
Annual growth, GNP: 2.3 % (1998)
Annual inflation: 1.8 % (1990/98)
Consumer price index: 106.2 (1998)
Currency: 7.5 kroner = $ 1 (1998)
Cereal imports: 441,719 metric tons (1998)
Food import dependency: 7 % (1997)
Fertilizer use: 2,308 kg per ha (1997)
Exports: $ 63,277 million (1997)
Imports: $ 52,453 million (1997)

ENERGY

Consumption: 5,501.0 Kgs of Oil equivalent per capita yearly (1997); -778.0 % imported (1997)

HDI (rank/value): 2/0.927 (1997)

Oman

'Uman

Population: 2,460,000 (1999)
Area: 212,460 SQ KM
Capital: Muscat (Masqat)
Currency: Omani rial
Language: Arabic

Sumerian clay tablets from the third century BC mention Oman as one of the outstanding markets in the economy of the Mesopotamian cities. Omani navigators became the lords of the Indian Ocean, connecting the Gulf to India, Indonesia and Indochina. In the 7th century they also played a major role in the peaceful propagation of Islam. Around 690 AD Abd Al-Malik decided to control the expansion of dissident sects. Consequently, some defeated leaders were forced to abandon the country. One of them, Prince Hamza, emigrated to Africa where he founded Zanzibar (see Tanzania: The Zandj Culture) beginning a relationship between Oman and the African coast which would last until the 19th century.

2   Persecution only served to further reinforce Sharite 'heresy'. Towards 751, Oman took advantage of the dynastic strife in Damascus to elect an imam who gradually evolved from a spiritual leader to a temporal sovereign. Omani wealth gave the imam considerable power in the entire Gulf region, but also made Oman the object of successive invasions by the caliphs of Baghdad, the Persians, the Mongols and the local groups of central Arabia. The Portuguese arrived from 1507, destroying the fleet and coastal fortifications, opening the way for the occupation of the principal cities and the control of the Strait of Hormuz. The Portuguese held control of the region for almost 150 years, stifling the Gulf's trade.

3   In 1630, Imam Nasir bin Murshid launched an inland struggle against the invaders. His son, Said, concluded this endeavour in 1650 with the expulsion of the Portuguese from Muscat (Musqat)

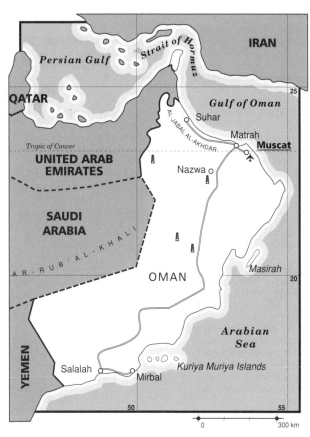

and the recovery of Zanzibar and the African coast of Mombasa in 1698. Thus a powerful state was created which obtained the political unification of the African and Asian territories where a common culture and economy had developed.

4   Sultan Said expanded the African territories and moved the capital to Zanzibar in 1832. At the time of his death in 1856, the British presence was already being strongly felt on both continents. Said's sons argued and as a result, the African and Asian parts of the state were separated: the elder son, Thuwaini, kept the sultanate of Oman while his brother Majid took control of Zanzibar. The 1891 Canning Agreement virtually made Oman a British protectorate.

5   In 1913, inland peoples elected their own imam in opposition to the sultan's hereditary rule. The struggle came to an end only in 1920, when a treaty was signed acknowledging the country's division in two: the Sultanate of Muscat and the Imamate of Oman.

6   Muscat was an extremely poor country, where arable lands accounted for less than one per cent of the total territory. Between 1932 and 1970, it suffered the despotic rule of Sultan Said bin Taimur, who fanatically opposed any foreign influence in the country, even in education and health. This did not prevent him from granting control over the country's oil deposits to Royal Dutch Shell.

7   Imam Ghaleb bin Alim, elected in 1954, proclaimed independence and announced his intention to join the Arab League. In 1955 the British reunited Oman.

8   Taimur was overthrown by his own son Qabus on July 23 1970. Those who expected the young, Oxford-educated monarch to introduce modernizing changes soon realized that British domination was only being replaced by US domination. The US became a net importer of oil and began to develop an active interest in the area.

9   Oil, produced commercially since 1967, provided more than half of the Gross Domestic Product. However more than half of Oman's labor force remained involved in agriculture, in the thin coastal strip that contains the country's only arable land.

10   With US assistance, Qabus organized a mercenary army but when this force proved incapable of smashing the Popular Front for the Liberation of the Gulf, he signed an agreement with Shah Reza Pahlevi to secure Iranian intervention in the conflict.

11   The guerrilla fighters were forced to retreat under the superior firepower of Iranian troops. Iranians also placed the Strait of Hormuz under their jurisdiction.

12   Upon the Shah's downfall, Iranian soldiers were quickly replaced by Egyptian commandos and troops. The Sultan decided to give the US the Masirah island air base, and later the air bases at Ihamrit and Sib and the naval bases at Matrah and Salalah. Two-thirds of the national budget were committed to defense, while the people continue to suffer acute poverty and widespread illiteracy.

13   Oman's strategic importance, with a geographic position giving the country full control over oil routes, led the US to concentrate on the sultanate in efforts to settle in the area.

14   The country's isolation gradually came to an end during the first part of Qabus' rule, but the eager 'opening' towards foreign capital, followed by insignificant action in the education and cultural fields, did not end the extremely authoritarian features of the traditional social system. The only real opposition is the People's Front for the Liberation of Oman (PFLO), which dropped the armed struggle, to create a broad based democratic front. The organization's objectives were to

WORKERS

% OF LABOUR FORCE   **1998**

■ FEMALE: 16%   ■ MALE: 84%

1990

■ SERVICES: 31.5%
■ INDUSTRY: 23.7%
■ AGRICULTURE: 44.7%

LAND USE

DEFORESTATION: 0.0% annual (1990/95)
ARABLE: 0.1% of total (1993)

PUBLIC EXPENDITURE

DEFENCE EXPENDITURE
(% of goverment exp.)   **36.4%**   (1997)

MILITARY EXPENDITURE
(% of health & education)   **293%**   (1990/91)

Maternal Mortality

1990-98

Per 100,000 live births

19

Literacy

1995

64%

Food Dependency

1997

17%

form an alliance with the Arab nationalists, especially the Palestinians, and to expel the foreign troops.

15 In the 1980s, US presence grew in Oman. 10,000 soldiers were stationed in different bases, mainly on the Masira Island base, equipped with nuclear weapons and where the Rapid Intervention Force has operated since 1984 despite violent protests. Oman purchased two F-16 combat aircraft squads with sophisticated equipment.

16 In June 1989, the Petroleum Development of Oman announced the discovery of the most important natural gas deposits found within the last 20 years.

17 In March, Oman adopted a conciliation policy toward Iran, which included an economic cooperation agreement, though this aid was contingent upon efforts to achieve political stability in the Gulf region.

18 In 1991, the Foreign Ministers of Egypt, Syria and the six Arab member States of the Cooperation Council (CGC) signed an agreement with the US in Riyadh, the capital of Saudi Arabia, aimed at maintaining the region's security.

19 Later that year, the Government announced that the democratization process was underway; this included the creation of a parliament directly elected by the country's citizens.

20 Anticipating a depletion of oil reserves before the year 2010, Sultan Qabus launched a plan to diversify the economy, aiming to develop fishing, agriculture and tourism, among other sectors.

21 During the summer of 1994, some 500 dissidents were arrested, including several senior officials and well-known business people, charged with trying to topple the Government 'using Islam as a cover'. The fiscal deficits accumulated by the Government since 1981, regarded as excessive, led the World Bank to warn that the level of State expenditure was 'unsustainable'.

22 Taking heed of the international financial organization's stand, in 1995 the Sultan announced a programme of reforms which included a reduction of state spending, a series of privatizations and measures to attract foreign investment.

23 In 1996, the Government announced a five-year plan to balance the budget by 2000. The project, aiming to free the economy from oil dependence, included privatizations and stimuli to increase foreign investment.

24 That same year, the Sultan established a new succession mechanism. This meant that, if the royal family could not reach agreement on the appointment of a successor within three days of his death, the candidate chosen by the Sultan himself would be accepted.

25 Oman became one of the first Arab countries to establish diplomatic and trade relations with Israel in January 1997. A month later, the rapprochement process came to a halt, when the Arab League questioned the Israeli decision to build new settlements in eastern Jerusalem.

26 In early 1998, Oman, along with all the other Gulf Cooperation Council (GCC) member nations, debated the possibility of freeing its currency from the dollar to prevent the loss of income on oil sales. The six GCC nations controlled 45 per cent of the world's crude oil reserves, but were losing millions of dollars per year due to falling international exchange rates of the US currency.

27 Oman and the United Arab Emirates signed an accord in May 1999 that defined part of the common border with the Abu Dhabi Emirate. Both parties agreed that, eventually, they would have to more exactly delineate the borders between Oman and the other emirates.

28 After an 18-year hiatus, the Government once again began to recruit young people for the Omani army in Makram, an area that belonged to Oman until the end of the 1950s, but which is currently part of Pakistan. Oman had abandoned recruitment measures in 1982 after a recruiting team was attacked by Pakistani troops.

29 During the visit of US President Bill Clinton in March 2000, the Sultan Qabus expressed his approval of the US announcement that it would lift some of its sanctions against Iran. ■

Profile

ENVIRONMENT

With its 2,600 km coastline, Oman occupies a strategic position on the southeastern edge of the Arabian Peninsula and flanking the Gulf of Oman, where oil tankers leave the Persian Gulf. It is separated from the rest of the peninsula by the Rub al Khali desert which stretches into the center of the country. Local nomadic groups now live with petroleum and natural gas exploitation. Favored by ocean currents, the coastal regions enjoy a better climate. Monsoon summer rains fall in the north.

SOCIETY

Peoples: Omani Arab 73.5 per cent; Pakistani (mostly Baluchi) 18.7 per cent; other 5.5 per cent.
Religions: Muslim 86 per cent; Hindu 13 per cent; other 1 per cent.
Languages: Arabic, official and predominant, English, Baluchi and Urdu are also spoken.
Political Parties: There are no legal political parties.

THE STATE

Official Name: Saltanat 'Uman (Sultanate of Oman).
Administrative divisions: 59 Districts.
Capital: Muscat (Masqat) 550,000 people (1995).
Other cities: Nizwa 62,880; Sama'il 44,721; Salalah 10,000.
Government: Qabus ibn Said, Sultan in power since July, 1970.
National Holiday: November 19. The Sultan's birthday.
Armed Forces: 43,500 (1996).
Other: 3,900.

Statistics

DEMOGRAPHY

Population: 2,460,000 (1999)
Annual growth: 4.5 % (1975/97)
Estimates for year 2015 (million): 4.1 (1999)
Annual growth to year 2015: 3.3 % (1997/2015)
Urban population: 79.5 % (1997)
Urban Growth: 8.6 % (1980/95)
Children per woman: 5.8 (1998)

HEALTH

Life expectancy at birth: 71 years (1998)
male: 69 years (1998)
female: 73 years (1998)
Maternal mortality: 19 per 100,000 live births (1990-98)
Infant mortality: 15 per 1,000 (1998)
Under-5 child mortality: 18 per 1,000 (1998)
120 doctors per 100,000 people (1993)
Safe water: 85 % (1990/98)

EDUCATION

Literacy: 64 % (1995)
male: 75 % (1995)
female: 51 % (1995)
School enrolment:
Primary total: 77 % (1990/96)
male: 80 % (1990/97)
female: 75 % (1990/97)
Secondary:
male: 68 % (1990/96)
female: 65 % (1990/96)
Tertiary: 8 % (1997)
Primary school teachers: one for every 26 (1995)

COMMUNICATIONS

29 newspapers (1996), 598 radios (1997), 591 TV sets (1996) and 86 main telephone lines (1996) per 1,000 people
Books: 1 new titles per 100,000 people (1992/94)

ECONOMY

Annual growth, GNP: 3.2 % (1995)
Annual inflation: -2.9 % (1990/98)
Consumer price index: 99.4 (1998)
Currency: 0.4 Omani rials = $ 1 (1998)
Cereal imports: 509,292 metric tons (1998)
Food import dependency: 17 % (1997)
Fertilizer use: 4,438 kg per ha (1997)
External debt: $ 3,629 million (1998); $ 1,523 per capita (1998)
Development aid received: $ 20 million (1997); $ 11.4 per capita (1997)

ENERGY

Consumption: 3,003.0 Kgs of Oil equivalent per capita yearly (1997); -662.0 % imported (1997)

HDI (rank/value): 89/0.725 (1997)

Pakistan

Pakistan

Population: 152,330,000 (1999)
Area: 796,100 SQ KM
Capital: Islamabad
Currency: Rupee
Language: Urdu

1 Claimed by India
2 Claimed by Pakistan

0   300 km

Pakistan means the land of the pure, as it was religion (Islam) that bound together the people of different ethnic communities and languages. Poet-philosopher Mohammed Iqbal articulated the concept of Pakistan in its basic form in 1931 when he proposed a separate state for the Muslims in India.

[2] The first Muslims to arrive in the Indian subcontinent were the traders from Arabia and Persia. A permanent Muslim foothold was achieved with Mohammed bin Qasim's conquest of Sind in 711 AD. It was in the early 13th century that the foundations of Muslim rule in India were laid, establishing borders and a capital in Delhi. The region including the present territory of Pakistan was subsequently ruled by several Muslim dynasties, finishing with the Mughals.

[3] The question of Muslim identity emerged alongside the decline of Muslim power and the rise of the Hindu middle class during British colonialism. In the early years of the 20th century, Muslim leaders became convinced of the need for effective political organization. A delegation of Muslim leaders met the viceroy (the chief representative of the British imperial government in India) in October 1906, demanding the status of a separate electorate for the Muslims. The All India Muslim League (ML) was founded in Dhaka that year with the objective of defending the political rights and interests of Indian Muslims. The British conceded the status of a separate electorate in the Government of India Act of 1909, confirming the ML's status as the representative organization of Indian Muslims.

[4] In the 1930s there was a growing awareness of a separate Muslim identity and a greater desire to preserve it within separate territorial boundaries. Under the leadership of Mohammed Ali Jinnah, ML continued its campaign for Pakistan; a separate homeland in British India. After the general election of April 1946, ML called a convention of the newly-elected ML parliamentarians in Delhi. A motion by Hussain Shaheed Suhrawardi, then chief minister of Bengal, reiterated the demand for a separate state of Pakistan in no uncertain terms.

[5] The Hindu-Muslim relationship had been seriously affected by communal tensions and riots in different parts of India. This convinced the leadership of the Indian National Congress (representing mainly the nationalists) to accept Pakistan as a solution to the problems. A Partition Plan for transfer of power was announced on June 3 1947. Both the ML and the Congress accepted the Plan. On August 14 1947, the new state of Pakistan was born comprising West Punjab, Sind, Baluchistan, North-West Frontier Province and East Bengal. The process of partition was painful and often violent.

[6] Pakistan has suffered numerous political crises. The first constitution was adopted on March 23 1956, but the civilian government was deposed in a coup on October 7 1958. Martial law was proclaimed and the constitution abrogated. On October 27 1958, General Ayub

Khan emerged as the new leading force. He introduced 'basic democracy', a system of local self-government and indirect presidential elections. Martial law was withdrawn in 1962 and a new constitution, granting absolute power to the president, was instituted, with Pakistan being declared an Islamic Republic. Ayub Khan was forced to resign on March 25, 1969, following a popular uprising. Martial law was promulgated again and General Yahya Khan became president.

[7] A general election was held at the end of 1970, the first ever in Pakistan under neutral administration. Two political parties, the Awami League (AL) and the Pakistan People's Party (PPP) emerged victorious in East and West Pakistan, respectively. However, the AL won an absolute majority in the parliamentary election on an all-Pakistan basis, forming the federal government. However, the parliamentary session was postponed, and the people of East Pakistan began the movement for an independent Bangladesh under the leadership of the AL in March 1971. The AL was banned and its leader Sheikh Mujibur Rahman was arrested. A civil war broke out, leading the AL to form a government in exile in India. The Indian army intervened and on December 16 1971, Bangladesh's independence was granted.

[8] Zulfiqar Ali Bhutto, the leader of the PPP, formed a civilian government in 1972 following the resignation of General Yahya Khan. He encouraged strong public sector participation in the economy, followed a non-aligned foreign policy and approved radical land reforms. The PPP was victorious again in the general election of 1977, but the results were rejected by opposition political parties who accused the PPP of vote-rigging. Against this backdrop of political unrest, General Zia-ul Haq ousted the Bhutto government and proclaimed martial law. Bhutto was arrested and later sentenced to death on charge of conspiring to murder an opposition political leader.

[9] General Zia accelerated the process of Islamicization in all

WORKERS

1995
UNEMPLOYMENT: 5.4%

% OF LABOUR FORCE   **1998**

- FEMALE: 28%   ■ MALE: 72%

1990

- SERVICES: 29.7%
- INDUSTRY: 18.5%
- AGRICULTURE: 51.8%

LAND USE

DEFORESTATION: 2.9% annual (1990/95)
IRRIGATED: 82.3% of arable (1993)

1993

- FOREST & WOODLAND: 4.4%
- ARABLE: 26.1%
- OTHER: 69.5%

PUBLIC EXPENDITURE

DEFENCE EXPENDITURE (% of goverment exp.)	**24.5%**	(1997)
MILITARY EXPENDITURE (% of health & education)	**125%**	(1990/91)

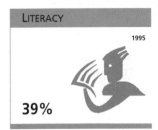

LITERACY

1995

39%

FOOD DEPENDENCY

1970
21%

1997
19%

spheres of political and social life. Many political opponents were harassed and detained. A general election on a non-party basis was held in February 1985 under martial law, and a pro-Zia government was formed. Zia was killed in a mysterious air crash in August 1988. In the general election of November 1988, the PPP were victorious and a government was formed under the leadership of Bhutto's daughter Benazir Bhutto. The democratic system was brought back after an 11 year absence.

[10] Benazir Bhutto became the first woman to serve as head of state of a predominantly Islamic country. One of her first moves was to release all female prisoners charged with crimes other than murder. Many of these had been imprisoned under discriminatory 'Black Laws' passed during Zia's term in office. They included the law of evidence, under which the declaration of one man was given more weight than that of two women in legal proceedings. Zia left a legacy of such laws in the form of constitutional amendments, which required a virtually politically-impossible two-thirds majority to overturn.

[11] The army remained a strong institution in Pakistan. The country became a member of the Southeast Asian Treaty Organization (SEATO) in 1954 and the Central Treaty Organization (CENTO) in 1955, two strong military alliances led by the United States. Although Pakistan later withdrew from these alliances, bilateral relations with the US remained cordial. Pakistan has received military and economic aid from the US.

[12] Relations with India have always been strained. Both countries have territorial claims over the state of Kashmir. India treats it as an integral part of the country, while Pakistan has been demanding a plebiscite there to allow the people of Kashmir to decide their own fate. After wars in 1948, 1965 and 1971, the two states agreed on a cease-fire zone on both sides of the Kashmir border. This meant not only a division of land, but also a separation of the local population. Since then, Kashmiri nationalist groups have demanded the creation of an independent state in the region.

[13] Throughout the 1980s, Pakistan was very vocal in its opposition to the Soviet intervention in Afghanistan (started in December 1979). Pakistan also supported the Mujahedin - Afghan resistance groups based in Pakistan - in their fight against the pro-Soviet regime in Kabul. During the Soviet intervention in Afghanistan, the US used Pakistani territory to supply arms to the rebel groups. This turned Pakistan into a key ally for the US regional policy, and resulted in the granting of significant economic assistance to the country. There were about three million Afghan refugees living in Pakistan in mid-1990.

[14] On August 6 1990, President Ghulam Ishaq Khan dissolved the government of Prime Minister Benazir Bhutto, charging her administration with nepotism and corruption. The President suspended the National Assembly and named Ghulam Mustafa Jatoi, leader of the Combined Opposition Parties (COP) coalition, head of the interim government.

[15] Elections were held on October 24. Nawaz Sharif was elected Prime Minister, with the support of the Muslim League, the main party in the coalition opposing Bhutto. Benazir Bhutto also put forward her candidacy, but her Peoples Party of Pakistan claimed the elections had been rigged and started an intense opposition campaign.

[16] When the Gulf War broke out in January 1991, following the Iraqi invasion of Kuwait, Pakistan quickly aligned with the US and sent troops to Saudi Arabia. Surveys showed that the population had strong pro-Iraqi tendencies, but the Government announced that the country's forces would only defend Islamic holy places, and would not take part in combat or go into Iraqi territory.

[17] Shortly after taking office, Prime Minister Nawaz Sharif, who came from a family of industrialists, implemented an economic reform plan, aimed at encouraging private investment. The plan included a far-reaching privatization process which was strongly resisted by the 300,000 workers in the state-run companies.

[18] Apart from the economic reforms, Sharif's government began a process of strengthening Islam which provoked wide hostility. The plan included the introduction of Sharia or Islamic law. In Sharif's opinion, Benazir Bhutto's term was a period of religious regression. The enforcement of Sharia immediately resulted in setbacks for women's social and legal status. The Government banned the media from making any reference to a woman's right to divorce. The main leaders of the women's movements, who demanded the end of discrimination against women, were harassed by security forces, and some were kidnapped and raped.

[19] On November 22 1990, a serious political and administrative scandal broke out. The opposition accused Nawaz Sharif of embezzling public funds. Sharif was responsible for the bankruptcy of several cooperative credit institutions. Only the unconditional support of President Ishaq Khan prevented the fall of the prime minister and the matter was referred to the judiciary. The scandal triggered a wave of demonstrations led by the PPP, and the Government responded with increased repression.

[20] Apart from the disputes between the government and the opposition, Pakistan has been periodically shaken by inter-ethnic violence, in particular between the Sindhis and the Muhajirs (former Indian refugees). Violence has particularly affected the Sind region and the city of Karachi, the country's main industrial center.

PROFILE

ENVIRONMENT

Pakistan is mountainous and semi-arid, with the exception of the Indus River basin in the east. This is virtually the only irrigated zone in the country, suitable for agriculture and vital to the local economy. The Indus rises in the Himalayas in the disputed province of Kashmir and flows into the Arabian Sea. The majority of the population lives along its banks. The main agricultural products are wheat and cotton, grown under irrigation. The country's main industry is the manufacture of cotton goods. Pakistan suffers from water shortage, soil depletion and deforestation.

SOCIETY

Peoples: Pakistan has a complex ethnic and cultural composition, basically Indo-European combined with Persian, Greek and Arab in the Indus Valley, plus Turkish and Mongolian in the mountainous areas. Much Indian immigration has occurred in recent years.
Religions: Islam is the official religion followed by 97 per cent of the population (most belong to the Sunni sect); 2 per cent are Christian;1.6 per cent are Hindu; the remainder belong to other smaller sects.
Languages: Urdu (official, although it is spoken by only 9 per cent of the population). Other languages are Punjabi, Sindhi, Pashto, Baluchi, English and several dialects.
Political Parties: The Pakistan People's Party (PPP); the Pakistan Muslim League (IJI or IDA).
Social Organizations: The National Pakistan Federation of Unions.

THE STATE

Official Name: Islam-i Jamhuriya-e Pakistan.
Administrative divisions: 4 Provinces.
Capital: Islamabad 350,000 people (est 1996).
Other cities: Karachi 12,000,000 people (est 1998); Lahore 2,952,689; Faisalabad 1,104,209 (1981).
Government: General Pervez Musharraf, Chairman of the National Security Council since October 12 1999. Mohammad Rafiq Tarar, President since January 1998.
National Holidays: August 14, Independence Day (1947); March 23, Proclamation of the Republic (1956).
Armed Forces: 587,000 (1996).
Other: 275,000 (National Guard, Border Corps, Maritime Security, Mounted Police).

21   The end of Soviet intervention in Afghanistan placed Pakistan in a difficult position. From the US viewpoint, Pakistan had lost the key position that it had held during the years of Soviet military intervention. The Islamicization process started by Sharif was also unacceptable to the US, because of the implication of greater cooperation with other Islamic regimes in the area, such as the Taliban in Afghanistan.

22   In February 1992, the ancient dispute over the border territory of Kashmir brought Pakistan and India to the brink of a new armed conflict. The Jammu and Kashmir Liberation Front, a Muslim group demanding the creation of an independent state staged a protest march along the line that divides the country between Pakistan and India. The organizers encouraged thousands of demonstrators on both sides to cross the border. The Pakistan Government ordered the army to shoot at the demonstrators in order to stop the separatist march. Five people died and fifty were injured.

23   Amidst the tension created by the Kashmir border crisis, the differences between Washington and Islamabad became more obvious. When Pakistan announced their nuclear weapon construction project was well under way, the US began to exert pressure on the country. This resulted in the virtual suspension of US economic assistance and arms sales to Pakistan. As a response to the US measures, Pakistan announced that China had guaranteed economic and technological support to continue the nuclear research program.

24   President Ishaq Khan accused Prime Minister Nawaz Sharif of poor administration, corruption and nepotism, forcing him to resign in April 1993. The National Assembly was dissolved and elections were announced for July. Sharif appealed to the Supreme Court and was reinstated in May. The dissolution of the Assembly was revoked and the call for elections cancelled.

25   Sharif's return aggravated the conflict with President Ishaq Khan. Both leaders resigned in July. The interim president, Moin

Kureishi, a former World Bank and IMF official, took unprecedented measures: he abolished the old system whereby members of parliament had received funds for investment in their own districts, a source of endless corruption, and also taxed large property units.

26   Traditionally, powerful landowners had dominated Pakistan's economy and political system and had exempted themselves from paying taxes. Only one per cent of the country's 139 million inhabitants paid taxes, but charges of tax evasion had never been filed.

27   Benazir Bhutto returned to power in the October 6 1993 elections. The PPP won 86 of the Assembly's 217 seats, against 72 obtained by Sharif. Bhutto received the support of minor parties and was confirmed with 121 votes. Her position was strengthened with the election of Faruk Ahmed Leghari (also from the PPP) as president in November.

28   The Prime Minister tried to stimulate the economy and avoided confrontation with the conservative clergy. However, Islamic fundamentalists put a price on the head of the justice minister, who supported a proposal to modify Pakistan's laws on blasphemy. The modification included making false charges of blasphemy as an offence.

29   Bhutto's efforts to bring democracy and equal rights to her country were tainted by political and ethnic violence in 1994 and 1995, the bloodiest years since 1971 when Bangladesh was formed. Karachi and the northern separatist areas were the center of disputes. Over 3,500 people died in confrontations between August 1994 and October 1995.

30   An attempted coup led by fundamentalist military officials was put down by the Government in late 1995.

31   In June 1996, hundreds of people protesting against the proscription of pro-independence candidates in local elections in Azad, Jammu and Kashmir were arrested.

32   One of Benazir Bhutto's main political rivals, her brother Murtaza, died in a confrontation with police on September 20 1996. Murtaza commanded a guerrilla group demanding the prime minister's resignation. The Bhuttos had been rivals since their father was overthrown in 1977.

33   In November 1996, Benazir was forced to resign as Prime Minister, charged with corruption, and new parliamentary elections were held. The Pakistan People's Party was defeated, receiving only 19 seats out of the 217 at stake, compared to the 136 won by the followers of former prime minister Nawaz Sharif. Miraj Khalid led the Government as Deputy Prime Minister until Sharif came to office once again in early 1997.

34   The military confrontations between India and Pakistan continued in Kashmir. Talks held between New Delhi and Islamabad stalled when India began a series of nuclear trials. Pakistan responded with its own tests.

35   Armed confrontations between India and Pakistan continued in the Kashmir region. Negotiations between New Delhi and Islamabad were still at a halt: while India maintained the zone belonged to them and that its future was 'not negotiable', Sharif's government called for a referendum to be held on self-determination. Tension between the two countries worsened in May 1998, when India carried out a series of controlled nuclear explosions and Pakistan responded with its own atomic tests.

36   On October 12 1999, General Pervez Musharraf, who had been in charge of the military operations in Kashmir, led a coup after Prime Minister Sharif ordered that the General be stripped of military power. Sharif was then imprisoned by the army, who accused him of kidnapping, terrorism and attempted murder for endangering the lives of people on board the airplane transporting Musharraf on his return to Islamabad. Pakistan became the first nuclear power to have a military leadership.

37   The military government tried the former Prime Minister, and his lawyers received constant death threats. Leading defense lawyer, Iqbal Raad was murdered inside his own office. While Musharraf blamed the murder on terrorists, Sharif's supporters accused the Government of committing the murder. ■

Palau

Palau

Population: 17,000 (1999)
Area: 459 SQ KM
Capital: Koror
Currency: US dollar
Language: English

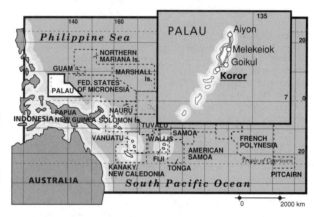

Five thousand years ago, sailors from China peopled the islands of Micronesia, forming highly stratified societies where age, sex and military prowess defined rank and wealth.

[2] European colonization in the 19th century, did not totally eliminate the indigenous peoples of Palau as it had on other islands.

[3] In 1914, the Japanese took the islands from Germany who had bought them from Spain in 1899. During World War II, Japan installed its main naval base in Palau and it soon became the scene of fierce combat when the US recognized its strategic position in relation to the Philippines.

[4] By the end of World War II, the indigenous population of Palau had been reduced from 45,000 to 6,000. Micronesia became a US trust territory. The US used the islands as nuclear testing grounds and reneged on promises of self-government, instead fostering economic dependence.

[5] In 1978, at the beginning of the transition to self-government, the archipelago opted for separation from Micronesia. In January 1979, the new constitution banned all nuclear weapons installations, nuclear waste storage, and foreign land ownership. A further amendment established a 200-mile area of territorial waters under the UN-approved Law of the Sea, which the US tried to veto.

[6] The new constitution received majority approval of assembly members, but the US put pressure on the local parliament to change provisions which would frustrate their attempts to use Palau as a military base. In July 1979, a referendum showed 92 per cent support for an unamended constitution. Bending to US pressure, the local Supreme Court annulled the referendum and entrusted Palau's parliament to draft a 'revised' constitution. In October 1979, this document was rejected by 70 per cent of the voters, and In July 1980, a third referendum ratified the original document by a 78 per cent majority.

[7] US Ambassador Rosemblat declared the Constitution 'incompatible with the system of Free Association' in effect since November 1980 'because it impedes (the US) from exercising its responsibility of defending the territory.

[8] In 1981, International Power Systems (IPESCO) scheduled the installation of a 16-megawatt nuclear power plant in Palau; the scheme was to be financed by the US, subject to amendments to the anti-nuclear constitution.

[9] President Haruo Remliik was persuaded to hold another plebiscite to decide on the IPESCO plan and a 'Compact of Free Association' with the US. The Compact received majority support, but failed to achieve the 75 per cent needed to override the constitution. In 1983, despite this ambiguous ballot, the President signed agreements for a loan totaling $37.5 million. UN intervention was immediately called for by the opposition.

[10] In 1984, the power plant was built and the following year, Remliik refused to call a third referendum when the US proposed to revoke the historic anti-nuclear constitution. A few days later he was assassinated.

[11] The Palau Congress amended the Constitution by a referendum requiring a simple majority, and on August 21 1987, a further plebiscite approved the Compact. However, in April 1988, the constitutional amendment was invalidated by the Supreme Court, stating the 75 per cent majority requirement.

[12] In August 1988, President Salii was found dead with a bullet in his head and a pistol at his side. His death was officially described as suicide.

[13] A new referendum held in February 1989 again did not gain the necessary majority for approval. Moreover, to restrain constant violations of its territorial waters by Indonesian vessels, in early 1992 Palau requested Japanese assistance in monitoring the area, in exchange for fishing rights.

[14] Towards the end of that year, Kuniwo Nakamura was elected President by a narrow margin. At the same time, a plebiscite was supported by 62 per cent of the electorate to reduce the percentage needed to approve the status of Free Associated State of the US to a simple majority in a new referendum.

[15] This eighth referendum on the same issue was held in July 1993. No special majority was required, and therefore the Free Associated State system was approved by 68 per cent of the electorate.

[16] Palau finally became a Free Associated State as of October 1994.

[17] Nakamura tightened links with Japan and increased trade and tourism exchange between the two countries. He visited Tokyo in April 1995, stopping over in Taiwan.

[18] In November 1996, the first presidential elections since independence were held. Nakamura was elected President. Despite Chinese opposition, Palau decided to establish diplomatic relations with Taiwan and to open a consulate in Taipei.

[19] In 1997, the Government of Palau designed an economic plan to diversify income and reduce dependence on tourism.

[20] The Government of Palau opened diplomatic relations with Taiwan in December 1999. This political event coincided with an aggressive Taiwanese policy of gaining the recognition of small Pacific nations in return for economic aid. ∎

PROFILE

ENVIRONMENT

A barrier reef to the west of Palau forms a large lagoon dotted with small islands. Coral formations and marine life in this lagoon are among the richest in the world with around 1,500 species of tropical fish and 700 types of coral and anemones.

SOCIETY

Peoples: Most are of Polynesian origin.
Religions: Catholic.
Languages: English and Palauan.

Political Parties: The Coalition for Open, Honest and Fair Government is opposed to the proliferation of nuclear arms and toxic wastes in the region and rejected the status of Free Associated State; the Palau Party favored it.

THE STATE

Official Name: Republic of Palau (Belu'u er a Belau).
Administrative Divisions: 16 States.
Capital: Koror 10,486 people (1996).
Government: Kumino Nakamura, President, elected in November 1996.

DEMOGRAPHY

Population: 17,000 (1999)

HEALTH

Infant mortality: 28 per 1,000 (1998)
Under-5 child mortality: 34 per 1,000 (1998)
Safe water: 88 % (1990/98)

EDUCATION

Literacy: 98 % (1995)
Female: 97 % (1995)
School enrolment:
Primary total: 103 % (1990/96)

Palestine

Palestine

Population: 3,019,704 (1999)
Area: 6,220 SQ KM
Capital: Jerusalem (Al-Quds Ash Sharif)
Currency: New Israeli shekel
Language: Arabic

A round 4000 BC, the Canaanites, a Semitic people from the inner Arabian peninsula, settled in the land which became known as Canaan and later, Palestine. The Jebusites, one of the Canaanite tribes, built a settlement which they called Urusalim (Jerusalem), meaning 'the city of peace'.

[2] The Egyptian Pharaohs occupied part of Canaan in 3,200 BC, building fortresses to protect their trade routes, but the country kept its independence. Around 2000 BC, another Semitic people, Abraham's Hebrews, passed through Palestine on their way south. Seven centuries later, twelve Hebrew tribes returned from Egypt, following Moses. There was fierce fighting over possession of the land. The Bible records that 'The sons of Judah were unable to exterminate the Jebusites that dwell in Jerusalem' (Joshua 15, 63).

[3] Four centuries later, Isaac's son David managed to defeat the Jebusites and unite the Jewish nation. After the death of his son Solomon the Hebrews split into two states, Israel and Judah. These later fell into the hands of the Assyrians, in 721 BC, and Chaldeans, in 587 BC. It was in 587 that Nebuchadnezzar destroyed Jerusalem and took the Jews into captivity in Babylon.

[4] In 332 BC, Alexander the Great conquered Palestine, but the territory returned to the Egyptian Empire of the Ptolemies soon after his death. The country was subdued by the Seleucids from Syria before a rebellion, headed by Judas Maccabeus, restored the Jewish state in 67 BC.

[5] In 63 BC, the Roman Empire seized Jerusalem, placing the city under its domination. Maccabeans, Zealots and other Jewish tribes resisted the invaders but were fiercely subdued. Solomon's temple was demolished around 70 AD, and the Jews were

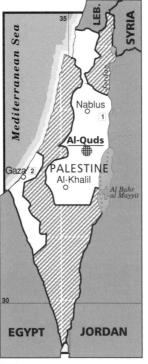

▨	Jewish State, UN Plan, 1947
☐	Arab State, UN Plan, 1947
1	West Bank

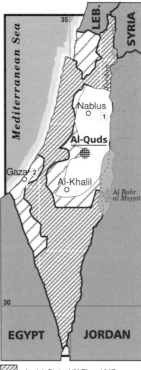

▨	Jewish State, UN Plan, 1947
◪	Annexed to Israel in the 1948 war
2	Gaza Strip

▨	Israel's pre-1967 borders
◪	Occupied by Israel in 1967
▣	Recovered by Palestine from 1994: Gaza Strip, Jericho, Nablus, Ramallah

expelled from Jerusalem around 135 AD.

[6] The Romans gave Palestine its present name, and Roman domination was followed by that of the Byzantine Empire (the Roman Empire in the East), which lasted until 611 when the province was invaded by the Persians. The Arabs, a Semitic people from the inner peninsula, conquered Palestine in 634, and, according to legend, it was in Jerusalem that the prophet Muhammad rose to the heavens. As a result, the city became a holy place for all three monotheistic religions.

[7] The Islamic faith and the Arabic language united all the Semitic peoples except for the Jews. With short intervals of partial domination by the Christian Crusaders and the Mongols in the 11th, 12th and 13th centuries, Palestine had Arab rulers for almost 1,000 years and Islamic governments for 15 centuries.

[8] In 1516, Jerusalem was conquered by the Ottoman

Empire which maintained power until the end of World War I. During this conflict, the British promised Shereef Hussein the independence of the Arab lands in exchange for his cooperation in the struggle against the Turks. At the same time, in 1917, British Foreign Secretary Lord Balfour promised the Zionist Movement the establishment of a 'Jewish National Homeland' in Palestine.

[9] Britain had no power at all over the area, either de facto or de jure, but it soon obtained this right by defeating the Turks, with the help of Arab allies, with a League of Nations mandate in 1922. Massive immigration raised the Jewish population of Palestine from 50,000 at the beginning of the century to 300,000 prior to World War II (see Israel).

[10] The Palestinians staged a general strike in April 1936 in protest against this immigration, which they saw as a threat to their rights. The British put forward a plan for the partition of Palestine into three states:

Jewish in the north, Arab in the south, and a third section under British administration in the Jerusalem-Jaffa (Tel Aviv) corridor. The Arabs rejected the plan and rebellion broke out, lasting until 1939, when London gave up the idea and set limits to immigration.

[11] Once World War II was over, Britain handed the problem over to the newly-established United Nations.

[12] When the UN General Assembly approved a new partition plan (1947) 749,000 Arabs and 9,250 Jews lived in the territory where the Arab State would be set up, while 497,000 Arabs and 498,000 Jews lived in the part which was to become the Jewish state.

[13] To drive the Palestinians from their land, a detachment of the Irgun organization commanded by Menachem Begin raided the village of Deir Yasin on April 9 1948, killing 254 civilians. 10,000 terrified Palestinians left the country.

[14] On May 14 1948, Israel

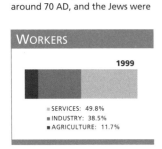

WORKERS

1999

- ■ SERVICES: 49.8%
- ■ INDUSTRY: 38.5%
- ■ AGRICULTURE: 11.7%

unilaterally proclaimed itself an independent country. Neighboring Arab armies immediately attacked, but were unable to prevent the consolidation of the Jewish State. On the contrary, the latter emerged from the 1949 war with a land area larger than that proposed by the United Nations.
[15] More than half of Palestine's inhabitants had abandoned their homes: most of them lived as refugees on the West Bank, a territory which had been annexed by the Hashemite kingdom of Transjordan, and in the Gaza Strip, which was under Egyptian administration.
[16] In the eyes of the United Nations and therefore of international law, the Palestinians were not a people but simply refugees, a 'problem' to be solved.
[17] Political decisions about the Palestinian cause were left entirely in the hands of the Arab governments, who even had the right to appoint the Palestinian representative to the Arab League. At the 1964 Arab summit, Egyptian leader, Gamal Abdel Nasser, asked the League to take on the task of forging a united Palestinian organization.
[18] In Jerusalem, on May 27, the Palestine National Council met for the first time. There were 422 participants, including personalities, business leaders, representatives of the refugee camps, the trade-union organizations, and the young people's and women's groups; they founded the Palestine Liberation Organization (PLO).
[19] Palestinian groups already operating secretly, such as Al Fatah, were wary of this Arab-promoted organization as they distrusted its emphasis on using diplomatic channels for its struggle. They were convinced that their land could only be recovered by military force.
[20] On January 1 1965, the first armed operation took place in Israel. The attacks intensified during the following months, until the outbreak of the Six Day War in 1967, when Israel occupied all of Jerusalem, Syria's Golan Heights, Egypt's Sinai Peninsula, the Palestinian territories of the West Bank and the Gaza strip. The defeat of the regular Arab armies strengthened the conviction that guerrilla warfare was the only path.
[21] In March 1968, during a battle in the village of Al-Karameh, Palestinians forced the Israelis to withdraw. The event passed into folk history as the first victory of the Palestinian force.
[22] With their prestige thus restored, the various armed groups joined the PLO and obtained the support of the Arab governments. In February 1969, Yasser Arafat was elected chairman of the organization.
[23] The growing political and military strength of the Palestinians was seen as a threat by King Hussein of Jordan, who had acted as their representative and spokesman. Tension mounted between the King and the Palestinians eventually reaching explosive proportions. In September 1970, after much bloody fighting, the PLO was expelled from Jordan to set up its headquarters in Beirut.
[24] This new exile reduced the possibility of armed attacks on targets inside Israel, and new radical groups such as 'Black September' directed their efforts towards Israeli institutions and businesses in Europe and other parts of the world. Palestinians, until then regarded by world opinion purely as refugees, quickly came to be identified by some as terrorists.
[25] PLO leaders promptly realized the need to change their tactics and, without abandoning armed struggle, launched a large-scale diplomatic offensive, starting to devote much of their energy to consolidating Palestinian unity and identity. The Algiers Conference of Non-Aligned Countries (1973) identified the Palestine problem, and not Arab-Israeli rivalry, as the key to the conflict in the Middle East for the first time.
[26] In 1974, an Arab League summit conference recognized the PLO as 'the only legitimate representative of the Palestinian people'. In October of the same year the PLO was granted observer status in the UN General Assembly, which recognized the right of the Palestinian people to self-determination and independence, and condemned Zionism as 'a form of racism'.
[27] The PLO program aimed to set up 'a secular and independent state in the whole of the Palestinian territory, where Muslims, Christians and Jews can live in peace, enjoying the same rights and duties'. This necessarily implied the end of the present state of Israel. Without giving up this ultimate goal, the PLO has gradually come to accept the 'temporary solution' of setting up an independent Palestinian state 'in any part of the territory that might be liberated by force of arms, or from which Israel may withdraw'.
[28] In 1980, the Likud prime minister, Menachem Begin and Egyptian president Anwar Sadat signed a peace accord at Camp David, with US mediation. Shortly afterwards, Begin began officially to annex the Arab part of Jerusalem, proclaiming it the 'sole and indivisible capital' of Israel.

PROFILE

ENVIRONMENT

In terms of international law 'Palestine' is the 27,000 sq km territory west of the Jordan River which the League of Nations handed over to Britain's 'mandatory' power in 1918. This territory comprises the area occupied by Israel before 1967, 20,073 sq km; Jerusalem and its surroundings, 70 sq km; the West Bank area, 5,879 sq km and the Gaza Strip, 378 sq km. It is a land of temperate Mediterranean climate, fertile on the coast and in the Jordan Valley. It is surrounded in the south and the northeast by the Sinai and Syrian deserts respectively. The Gaza region suffers from a severe scarcity of water. The accumulation of waste waters and refuse convert the refugee camps into highly contaminated areas. Soil erosion and deforestation are also serious problems.

SOCIETY

Peoples: Palestinians are an Arab people. In 1997 estimates were of near 7 million Palestinians living in Palestine and abroad. There are 700,000 in Israel; 1,500,000 on the West Bank; 800,000 in the Gaza Strip, and the rest spread in Middle Eastern and European countries. 33 per cent of the inhabitants of the occupied territories live in refugee camps. There are large Palestinian populations in US, Chile, Brazil and other countries.
Religions: Most are Muslim (97 per cent), but there are some Christians.
Languages: Palestinians speak Arabic and often also use Hebrew in the occupied territories, a language with the same Semitic root which is more similar to Arabic than to the European languages of immigrants.
Political Parties: The main political organization represented in the PLO is the Al-Fatah National Liberation Movement, founded in 1965 by Yasser Arafat. The Popular Front for the Liberation of Palestine (PFLP), the second party in number, founded in 1967 by George Habash, with a Marxist-Leninist orientation, like the Democratic Front for the Liberation of Palestine (DFLP), led by Nayef Hawatmeth. Al-Saika, led by Zuheir Moshen, has brought in the Palestinians who support the Syrian Ba'ath Party; the Arab Liberation Front, of Abder Rahin Ahmed, hold close links with the Iraqi Ba'ath Party; the General Command-DFLP, a split of the DFLP, led by Ahmed Yabril. Hamas (Islamic Resistance Movement), with great influence in West Bank and the Gaza Strip, opposes autonomy arrangements.

THE STATE

Official name: State of Palestine.
Capital: Jerusalem (Al-Quds Ash Sharif) has traditionally been the capital of Palestine; the Palestine National Authority (PNA) is in Jericho 16,000 people (1993).
Government: Yasser Arafat, President of the Palestine National Authority since July 1994, re-elected in January 1996. The Autonomous Council acts as a Parliament.
Armed Forces: there are no official data available.

Jewish settlements on the West Bank multiplied, using Palestinian lands and increasing tension in the occupied territories. Successive United Nations votes against these measures, or for any action against Israel, were stripped of any practical value by the US using its veto in the Security Council.

29   In July 1982, in an attempted 'final settlement' of the Palestine issue, Israeli forces invaded Lebanon. The intention, as it later became clear, was to destroy the PLO's military structure, capture the greatest possible number of its leaders and combatants, annex the southern part of Lebanon and set up a puppet government in Beirut. Surrounded in Beirut, the Palestinian forces only agreed to withdraw after receiving guarantees of protection for civilians under a French-Italian-North American international peace-keeping force.

30   The massacres that took place at the refugee camps of Sabra and Chatila showed the ineffectiveness of international protection, but the PLO managed to transform what seemed a final defeat into a political and diplomatic victory. The headquarters of the organization were moved to Tunis and Yasser Arafat toured Europe receiving the honors due a head of state in various countries, most notably in the Vatican.

31   The PLO quietly initiated talks with Israeli leaders receptive to a negotiated settlement with the Palestinians. With the invasion of Lebanon, small but active peace groups emerged in Israel, demanding the initiation of a dialogue with the PLO. Palestinian radicals questioned these overtures, breaking with Yasser Arafat's policies. This division of the PLO put its factions at odds with each other, sometimes causing violent confrontations.

32   In 1987, after several years of internal difficulties, the Palestine National Council met in Algiers with representatives from all Palestinian organizations, except those groups that favored direct action, and the internal structure of the PLO was rebuilt.

33   The official answer to the Arab protests was to increase the repression. But unlike what had happened on other occasions, this time the military intervention only managed to increase the number of women, elderly people and children taking part in the demonstrations. The more civilian casualties there were, the greater the hatred grew and the more demonstrations, strikes, and closures occurred. Funerals transformed into acts of open political defiance. This marked the beginning of the *intifada* or rebellion.

34   During the first few months of 1988 many Palestinians with Israeli citizenship participated in the strikes called by the so-called 'United Leadership of the Popular Uprising in the Occupied Territories'. This was the first instance of their joint political expression with Palestinians of the occupied territories.

35   In July 1988, King Hussein of Jordan announced that all economic and political links were being broken with the inhabitants of the West Bank. From that moment on, the PLO assumed sole responsibility for the territory's people.

36   At a meeting in Algeria on November 15 1988, the Palestine National Council proclaimed an independent Palestinian state in the occupied territories, citing Jerusalem as its capital. It also approved UN resolutions 181 and 242, which in effect meant accepting Israel's right to exist. Within the next 10 days, 54 countries around the world recognized the new state.

37   Arafat, elected president, was received in Geneva by the UN General Assembly, which had called a special session in order to hear him. The Palestinian leader repudiated terrorism, accepted the existence of Israel and asked that international forces be sent to the occupied territories. As a result of his speech, US president Ronald Reagan decided to initiate talks with the PLO.

38   When tensions began between Iraq and Kuwait in the second half of 1990, Arafat tried unsuccessfully to start negotiations between the countries. After the invasion, the Palestinian position seemed to strengthen when a parallel could be drawn between Kuwait and Palestine: if Iraq could be forced to submit to UN resolutions, then so could Israel.

39   When the war broke out, it was clear that the Palestine people were pro-Iraqi. This support deprived the PLO of the financial support of the rich Gulf emirates, who opposed the Iraqi regime.

40   In September 1991, in the closing session of the Palestine National Council, Yasser Arafat was confirmed as President of Palestine and of the PLO. The body accepted the resignation of Abu Abbas, the leader of the Palestine Liberation Front. Abbas had been given a life sentence in absentia by an Italian tribunal, for the hijacking of the *Achille Lauro* liner in 1985.

41   Between October 30 and November 4 1991, the first Peace Conference for the Middle East was held in Madrid, with support from the US and the former USSR. The Arab delegations unanimously demanded that the negotiations should be based on resolutions 242 and 338 of the UN Security Council. These resolutions forbade the acquisition of territories by force and recommended the granting of territories in exchange for peace agreements.

42   The Conference for the Middle East continued in Washington in December. No progress was made as far as the Palestinian issue was concerned, as Israel reaffirmed the validity of its own interpretations of the UN resolutions. At the end of the Conference, the Israeli delegation left satisfied because UN resolution 3379, defining Zionism as a form of racism, had been eliminated.

43   Following the Israeli elections of June 1992, the Labor leader and new prime minister Yitzak Rabin froze the settlement of new colonies in the Gaza strip and on the West Bank. However, it was difficult to restart negotiations which had been interrupted by the expulsion of 415 Palestinians from the Hamas group to Lebanon.

44   Secret negotiations between the PLO and Israel, with the active participation of Norwegian diplomats, resulted in mutual recognition in September 1993. The Declaration of Principles on the autonomy of the occupied territories granted limited autonomy to Palestinians in the Gaza strip and the city of Jericho in the West Bank. This autonomy was to be extended to the rest of the West Bank and, five years later, a definite status was to be negotiated for the occupied territories and the part of Jerusalem occupied by Israel since 1967.

45   Hamas and Hezbollah on the Palestinian side, as well as settlers in the occupied territories and far-right parties on the Israeli side, opposed the agreement. In a climate of hostility, Israeli military withdrawal from Gaza and Jericho anticipated for December 13 was postponed.

46   In May, 1994 Rabin and Arafat signed the 'Gaza and Jericho first' autonomy agreement, while Israeli withdrawal continued, enabling the return of several contingents of the Palestinian Liberation Army exiled in Egypt, Yemen, Libya, Jordan or Algeria.

47   Arafat arrived in Gaza in July and took office as head of the Palestine National Authority's Executive Council. The struggle between the PLO leader and his fundamentalist rivals became increasingly violent.

48   Once again, Gaza was on the brink of civil war in April 1995 when an explosion destroyed a building killing 7 people, including Kamal Kaheil, one of the leaders of the Ezzedin-El-Kassam brigades. In retaliation, suicide attacks by Hamas and Islamic Jihad caused the death of 7 Israeli soldiers and a US tourist, leaving 40 wounded. The Jihad's military wing said the attempt

DEMOGRAPHY
Population: 3,019,704 (1999)
Children per woman: 6.0 (1997)

HEALTH
Safe water: 84 % (1997)

EDUCATION
Literacy: 84 % (1995)
male: 92 % (1995)
female: 77 % (1995)

ECONOMY
Per capita, GNP: $ 1,537 (1996)
Per capita, GNP: $ 1,560 (1998)
Annual growth, GNP: 7.0 % (1998)
Annual inflation: 11.0 % (1990/98)
Currency: 4.2 new Israeli shekels = $ 1 (1999)
Exports: $ 693 million (1998)
Imports: $ 2,532 million (1998)

was a 'heroic suicide operation' and a 'gift for the soul of the criminal massacre's martyrs' - referring to the building explosion.

[49] The tension continued, as did negotiations between Islamic fundamentalists and PLO leaders. Among other things, Arafat wanted Hamas to participate in the Palestinian general elections of January 1996, which would have legitimized his leadership. After negotiations, the fundamentalists decided to boycott the elections. Arafat was elected president with 87 per cent of the vote and government candidates won 66 out of the 88 seats.

[50] Binyamin Netanyahu's election as Israeli prime minister (see Israel) in May 1996 aggravated tension between the countries.

[51] The delicate negotiations which finally brought about the withdrawal of Israeli troops from the city of Hebron gave new support to the government led by Yasser Arafat. In January 1997,

the Palestinian President highlighted again that the subject of Jerusalem's status was still pending and that, together with the formation of the Palestinian state, both were the next issues of the political agenda.

[52] The Israeli decision to build a new settlement in the Har Homa hills, within the Palestinian sector in Jerusalem, was firmly rejected by the PNA and Western diplomats. The work started in March 1997, and led to fierce confrontations between Palestinians and the army, stalling the peace process. At the same time, the Israeli Government announced that it was going to return only 2 per cent of the West Bank to the PNA. Israeli President Ezer Weizman met Arafat as a gesture of good will, but he could not change Netanyahu's attitude nor the violent reaction of Palestinians. Soon afterwards, the PNA decided to apply capital punishment to those citizens who sold lands or houses to Israelis.

[53] In November 1997, the commemoration of the second

anniversary of the assassination of prime minister Yitzhak Rabin led to the biggest pro-Peace with Palestine demonstration in recent years.

[54] Arafat and Netanyahu met in London in May 1998 on the invitation of British Prime Minister, Tony Blair, and in the presence of US Secretary of State Madeleine Albright, in an attempt to re-establish the peace process, but negotiations foundered on the issue of the occupied West Bank.

[55] Arafat had threatened to proclaim the Palestinian State on May 4 1999, when the interim peace treaties would expire. However, Arafat himself, along with the Palestine Central Council, deferred the proclamation a year, arguing that the United States had urged them to reach a final negotiated peace within the year. PCC members recognized that, furthermore, the measure tended not to play along with Netanyahu, whose election campaign was in full swing at the time, with him insisting that there

would never be a Palestine state while he was Prime Minister of Israel.

[56] Further delays from Israel - which never fully withdrew from the occupied territories as it had agreed - and the impasse in the new rounds of negotiations led Arafat to suggest greater US participation in the negotiations. In April 2000, the new Israeli Prime Minister Ehud Barak acceded to this suggestion and it was hoped that the agreement to be signed on May 20 that year would pave the way for a final peace treaty.

[57] In May Israel withdrew from southern Lebanon.

[58] Violence flared up in September after Israel's Ariel Sharon visited a shrine in Al Quds/Jerusalem deemed holy to Muslims and Jews. In the following weeks some 100 people died, mainly Palestinians. Three Israeli soldiers were killed in Ramallah in October. Diplomats met in Egypt to try and salvage the peace process. ■

Palestinians: still on the move

The recent history of Palestinians, especially since the 1940s, has been marked by confrontations, enforced segregation, overcrowding and massive geographic displacement throughout several Middle East regions.

[2] Many Palestinians have emigrated to countries such as Iraq, Syria, Lebanon, and several states of the Persian Gulf region in search of better living conditions. Victims of discrimination and police surveillance, few have been granted citizenship in these countries.

[3] Their history has been different in Jordan, where they make up two-thirds of the total population. In the late1940s, the Jordanian monarchy granted them citizenship, in order to carry out its expansionist goals. There were serious confrontations with the recently created state of Israel,

which occupied the West Bank and exerted its control over this Palestinian region. The Jordanian authorities carried out a policy of influence and control to manage the political future of the Palestinians. This Jordan to became the alleged spokesperson of the Palestinian cause.

[4] In May 1950, the United Nations, which had already set up an agency to assist Palestinian refugees, reported the existence of 53 refugee camps in Jordan, the Gaza Strip, Syria and Lebanon. Over 600,000 refugees lived there in difficult conditions, in tents shared by several families, receiving some basic services like water, health and education, but unable to overcome poverty.

[5] The limited avenues of employment open to them depended on the efforts of the United Nations' agency, which attempted to integrate them in countries of the region.

[6] The government of Egypt controlled the Gaza Strip from 1948 to

1967 with repressive and violent policies, denying citizen status to the Palestinians and only granting them a small share of power in the local administration. However, Palestinians were not prevented from attending Egyptian universities.

[7] Presently, most of the territory's inhabitants live in poverty. The area is regarded as one of the most densely populated in the world. The unemployment rate is very high and the refugee camps are overcrowded. The land is depleted due to over-cropping and is completely useless for agricultural purposes.

[8] Arab Israelis - some 150,000 people who, in 1948, chose not to emigrate from the newly created state of Israel - account for one-eighth of the Palestinian diaspora. Since many of their lands had been confiscated, they had to move to towns in Western Galilee and were forced to became unskilled workers - most had been farmers - hired by Israeli con-

struction companies and industries.

[9] In the Sixties, Palestinians witnessed the erosion of some of their traditions due to the exodus towards urban areas. The social system based on a clan led by an elder could not survive these changes.

[10] Palestinians living in Israel were subject to the restraints of a military jurisdiction since 1966. They live under a very severe regime of restrictions which not only hampers political activity, but also harms civil rights and freedom of worship.

[11] Even under these conditions, a number of Palestinians are politically neutral, while others accept the situation taking part in elections, education and the economy. Israeli policies have been aimed at preventing the development of a Palestinian national identity. ■

Panama

Panamá

Population: 2,812,000 (1999)
Area: 75,520 SQ KM
Capital: Panama City
Currency: Balboa
Language: Spanish

The Chibcha civilization was one of America's great cultures, which developed in the Isthmus of Panama. It was a highly stratified society, developed elaborate architecture, crafted gold and had a wide scientific knowledge.

[2] In 1508, Diego de Nicuesa was given the task of colonizing what was known as the Gold Coast (present day Panama and Costa Rica). The enterprise ended in complete failure. In 1513, Vasco Nuñez de Balboa was sent to look for what was assumed to be a 'South Sea', and on the 25th of September he found the Pacific.

[3] The isthmus soon acquired great geopolitical significance. Panama became an important commercial center with merchandise distributed throughout America from San Francisco to Santiago. The Peruvian gold followed the opposite route, and the Ecuadorian straw hats are still called Panama hats because they were transported from there. The concentration of riches attracted English pirates and buccaneers; Francis Drake razed Portobelo in 1596 and Henry Morgan set fire to Panama in 1671.

[4] Panama was dependent upon the viceroyalty of Peru until 1717, when the Bourbons transferred it to the new viceroyalty of Granada, this was later to be a part of Greater Colombia when the country became independent from Spain in 1821.

[5] In 1826, Panama was selected by Simón Bolívar as the site of the Congressional Assembly which was to seal the continent's unity. But the economic decadence of the end of the 18th century, coupled with the change in commercial routes meant that Panama did not maintain its strategic importance after breaking with Spain, and did not become an independent nation with the disintegration of Greater Colombia in 1830.

[6] In 1831 Panama seceded from New Granada for a year, with the intention of forming a Colombian Confederation while maintaining autonomy. The state of Panama was created in 1855 within the Federation of New Granada (present-day Colombia).

[7] The first direct reference to the United States' 'right' of military intervention in Panama, is the Mallarino-Bidlak treaty of 1864 signed by the governments of Washington and Bogota. The document authorized the United States to obtain a faster means of uniting the east coast with the west and to build a railroad across the isthmus; the Atlantic terminal was the Island of Manzanillo in the Bay of Limón. With the railway the US tried to offset British presence in the area, especially in Nicaragua.

[8] On January 1 1880, a French company started to build the Panama Canal. In 1891, the company was accused of fraud in its dealings, causing its eventual bankruptcy, though 33 km of the project had already been completed.

[9] In 1894 the New Panama Canal Company was formed to complete the canal project.

[10] In 1902, the US bought out the French company, and in January 1903, the Hay-Herran Treaty was signed with a representative of the Colombian Government. The treaty spelled out the terms of the construction and administration of the canal, granting the United States the right to rent a 9.5 km-wide strip across the isthmus in perpetuity. The Colombian Senate rejected the treaty unanimously, considering it improper and an affront to Colombia's sovereignty. Only a revolution allowed the United States to remain. The 'revolutionaries', supported by US marines, declared Panama's independence in November 1903, and the US recognized the new state within three days. While Theodore Roosevelt was President, the 'Big Stick' policy of sending troops into Central American states was common practice.

[11] A new treaty, the Hay-Buneau Varilla Treaty, granted the United States full authority over a 16 km-wide strip and the waters at either end of the canal in perpetuity. Buneau Varilla, a former shareholder of the canal company and a French citizen, signed as the official representative of Panama. He received payment for his services in Washington, and did not return to Panama. The canal, covering a distance of 82 km, was officially dedicated on August 15 1914, and from then on was administrated and governed by the United States.

[12] The Canal Zone brought incalculable wealth to the United States, not so much in toll fees but in time and distance saved by vessels traveling between California and the East coast. US military bases in Panama functioned as an effective means of control over Latin America. Against the backdrop of the Cold War, American military instructors lectured Latin American military officers on the National Security Doctrine, a politico-military system which guaranteed loyalty to the US, including when necessary ousting legally constituted governments and replacing them with military dictators. Also, the financial center created in the isthmus became an initial foothold for the expansion of US transnational corporations and money laundering.

[13] In January 1964, 21 students died in an attempt to raise Panama's flag in the Canal Zone, still under US jurisdiction. The sacrifice of these young Panamanians transformed them into national martyrs.

[14] The demand for full sovereignty over the Zone was taken up by the Government of General Omar Torrijos. He rose to power in 1969, upon the dissolution of a three-member Military Junta which had overthrown President Arnulfo Arias in 1968. The diplomatic battle against the colonial enclave was waged in all the international forums and gained the support of the Latin American countries, the Movement of Non-Aligned Countries and the United Nations.

[15] The struggle for sovereignty drew Panamanians closer together stimulating nationalistic feelings

WORKERS

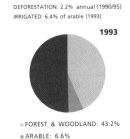

1996
UNEMPLOYMENT: 14.3%

% OF LABOUR FORCE **1998**

■ FEMALE: 35% ■ MALE: 65%

1990

■ SERVICES: 57.7%
■ INDUSTRY: 16.1%
■ AGRICULTURE: 26.2%

LAND USE

DEFORESTATION: 2.2% annual (1990/95)
IRRIGATED: 6.4% of arable (1993)

1993

■ FOREST & WOODLAND: 43.2%
■ ARABLE: 6.6%
■ OTHER: 50.2%

PUBLIC EXPENDITURE

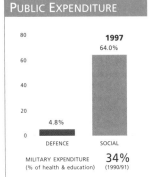

1997
64.0%

4.8%

DEFENCE   SOCIAL

MILITARY EXPENDITURE **34%**
(% of health & education) (1990/91)

MATERNAL MORTALITY
1990-98
Per 100,000 live births
85

LITERACY
1995
91%

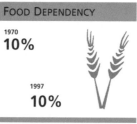

FOOD DEPENDENCY
1970
10%
1997
10%

FOREIGN TRADE
Millions US$ 1998
IMPORTS
3,940
EXPORTS
3,090

submerged by decades of foreign cultural penetration. At the same time, the Torrijos Government initiated a process of transformation aimed at establishing a more equitable social order. The outstanding reforms included agriculture, education, and the exploitation of copper on a nationalized basis. The 'banana war' was also waged against transnational fruit companies like the United Fruit Company to obtain fairer prices.

[16] The US finally agreed to open negotiations in favor of a new canal treaty, as the Panama issue was damaging its image in Latin America. The 1977 Torrijos-Carter Treaty (signed with US President Jimmy Carter) abrogated the previous one and provided for a Panamanian canal from the year 2,000. Amendments introduced by the US Senate, however, added provisions to the treaty that were contrary to Panamanian sovereignty. The United States retained the right to intervene 'in defense of the Canal' even after expiration of the treaty, scheduled for December 31 1999.

[17] On July 31 1981 General Torrijos died in a suspicious airplane accident. Unconfirmed reports suggested that the plane's instruments were interfered with from the ground. President Aristides Royo, who succeeded Torrijos in 1978, lost the support of the National Guard and was forced to resign by his new commander-in-chief, Ruben Paredes. He started realigning the country's policies, adopting a pro-US stance.

[18] The role of the US in the Malvinas (Falklands) War and the Contadora Group, (a meeting of South American heads of states seeking peace in Central America) of which Panama was the first host, led to new friction in the relations between the nations. The island of Contadora had already gained a certain notoriety as the hiding place chosen by the US for the exiled shah of Iran, Reza Pahlevi, after he was overthrown.

[19] In 1983, Paredes was replaced as commander-in-chief of the National Guard by General Manuel Noriega. Presidential and legislative elections were narrowly won by Nicolas Barletta, the candidate of the Democratic Revolutionary Party, which was founded by Torrijos and supported by the armed forces. The opposition, led by veteran politician Arnulfo Arias brought accusations of fraud. Barletta encountered growing opposition to his economic policies, and resigned toward the end of 1985.

[20] He was succeeded by Eric del Valle, but the driving force continued to be General Noriega, whom the US targeted to overthrow. A former protegé of the US Government, Noriega had not been forgiven by them for his unwillingness to collaborate in US plans to invade Sandinista-ruled Nicaragua. A 'settling of accounts' began, in which Noriega was accused of links with drug-traffickers and other crimes. The opposition united behind the National Civil Crusade, made up of parties of the right and center with broad support of the business community.

[21] In 1987 the US withdrew its economic and military aid. In 1988, it froze Panama's assets in the United States and imposed economic sanctions, including the cessation of payments for Canal operations. In March all the Panamanian banks closed for several weeks, provoking a financial crisis. American military presence increased. Del Valle overthrew Noriega, but the National Assembly backed the commander-in-chief and removed the President, replacing him with the Minister of Education, Manuel Solis Palma.

[22] Elections were called for May 5 1989. The official candidate was Carlos Duque and the opposition, the so-called Democratic Alliance of Civilian Opposition, put forward Guillermo Endara. Amid interference from the White House, which discredited the electoral process and its results even before it had taken place, the results of the ballot were kept secret for several days and, because they favored the opposition, the election was declared null and void.

[23] Solis declared that the United States' objective was to set up a puppet government regardless of the election results and retain control of the Canal Zone, going back on the commitments it had assumed through the Torrijos-Carter treaty.

[24] An anti-Noriega uprising by a group of young officers failed in October 1989, and as the climax of a series of economic sanctions which destroyed the country's economy, the US invaded Panama. The attack began at dawn on December 20 1989 without prior declaration of war. Endara was installed as president at Fort Clayton, the American base, at the start of the invasion.

[25] This was the largest American military operation since the Vietnam War (1964-1973), with the mobilization of 26,000 troops. Indiscriminate bombing damaged heavily-populated neighborhoods. The invaders withheld all information concerning the number of people killed or injured, as well as figures for property damage. The number of dead is estimated at between 4,000 and 10,000, and the Chamber of Commerce estimated losses at more than $2 billion.

[26] Panamanian resistance proved to be stronger than the invaders had anticipated, and prolonged the military undertaking. Noriega took refuge within the Vatican Embassy and was later arrested and transferred to the United States. About 5,000 Panamanians were arrested and temporarily imprisoned.

[27] The new government of Guillermo Endara abolished the National Defense Force and replaced it with a minor police agency, called the Public Force. In order to disarm the population, $150 was paid for each weapon

PROFILE

ENVIRONMENT

The country is bordered by the Caribbean in the north and the Pacific in the south. A high mountain range splits the country into two plains, a narrow one covered by rainforest along the Atlantic slopes and a wider one with forests on the Pacific slopes. Panamanians generally say that their main resource is their geographic location, since the canal and the trade activities connected to it constitute the main economic resource of the country. Tropical products are cultivated and copper is mined at the large Cerro Colorado mines. Air and water pollution in both urban and rural areas is significant. 40 million tons of raw sewage are pumped into Panama Bay each year.

SOCIETY

Peoples: 64 per cent of the inhabitants are the result of integration between native Americans and European colonist immigrants. 14 per cent are of African descent. The three main indigenous groups are the Cunas on the island of San Blas in the Caribbean, the Chocoles in the province of Darien and the Guaymies, in the provinces of Chiriqui, Veraguas and Bocas del Toro.
Religions: 80 per cent Catholic, 10 per cent Protestant, 5 per cent Muslim, 1 per cent Baha'i, 0.3 per cent Jewish.
Languages: Spanish, official and spoken by the majority.
Political Parties: Democratic Revolutionary Party (PRD), founded by Omar Torrijos, Liberal Republican Party, Labor Party, Nationalist Republican Liberal Movement, Christian Democrat Party, Authentic Liberal Party.
Social Organizations: The National Council of Workers' Organizations (CONATO); Ishtmenian Central of Workers (CIT)

THE STATE

Official Name: República de Panamá.
Capital: Panama City 948,000 people (1995).
Other cities: San Miguelito 293, 564 people; Colón 54,654; David 50,000 (1990).
Government: Mireya Moscoso, President since May 1999. Single-chamber parliament: Legislative Assembly, made up of 67 members, elected every 5 years by direct vote.
National Holiday: November 3, Independence (1903).
Armed Forces: The National Guard was declared illegal in June 1991.
Other: 11,000 National Police.

that was turned in. American economic aid, which the new government had counted on, did not materialize and Endara himself began a hunger strike in order to obtain it. The Government had to accept the presence of US 'supervisors' in the ministries and the actions of the Southern Commando troops outside the canal zone in order to fight drug trafficking and Colombian guerrilla warfare.

[28] Washington's interest in the region waned after the defeat of the Sandinistas in Nicaragua, and so the economic crisis in Panama at the time of the invasion was never overcome. Independent sources put unemployment at 20 per cent in 1991.

[29] The Organization of American States called the invasion 'deplorable' and called for a vote on the withdrawal of troops; there were 20 votes in favor, one against (the United States) and six abstentions. Britain supported the invasion and France vetoed the UN Security Council denunciation. In Latin America, only El Salvador supported the US invasion.

[30] In spite of this, control of the canal was given to Panama. In March 1991, a Panamanian took over the administration of the canal for the first time.

[31] In April 1991, Endara announced the end of his alliance with the Christian Democrat Party (PDC), dismissing five of their ministers. The Government's precarious stability was shaken by five coup attempts during its first two years. The Democratic Revolutionary Party (PRD), which won a significant victory in the by-elections of January 1991, called for general elections.

[32] In the course of General Noriega's trial, which started late in 1991 in Miami, it was disclosed that the former leader had close connections with the US Drug Enforcement Agency (DEA) and the CIA. That same year it was discovered that President Endara's legal office had connections with 14 companies which laundered drug money. The DEA also disclosed that drug dealings had increased since the American invasion. In June 1992, Noriega was sentenced to 40 years in prison.

[33] The Government suffered a serious setback when, in a plebiscite on constitutional reform on November 15 1992, the people rejected the formal abolition of the Defence Force by 63.5 to 31.5 per cent. The Government was further weakened when the deputy vice-president, Christian Democrat Ricardo Arias Calderón, resigned on December 17 after accusing Endara of failing to deal with the social crisis.

[34] Foreign Minister Julio Linares was forced to resign in August 1993 as he had been involved in the sale of weapons to Serbian forces in Bosnia through the consulate in Barcelona.

[35] Economist Ernesto Pérez Balladares, former minister and admirer of Omar Torrijos, was elected President in 1994 with 34 per cent of the vote. Balladares ran as candidate for the social democratic alliance Pueblo Unido (United People), made up of the PRD, the Liberal Republican Party and the Labor Party. Mireya Moscoso, from the right-wing Democratic Alliance, had 29 per cent and salsa singer Ruben Blades, from the Papa Egoro Movement, had 17 per cent. These were the first general elections held after the US invasion.

[36] In June 1994, the Kuna and Embera indigenous groups rejected the construction of a road through their autonomous territory. They were supported by environmentalist groups and the Catholic Church. The highway was to have crossed the 550,000 hectare rainforest called 'Darien's Barrier', declared a universal heritage by UNESCO. The 108-km highway would link Panama with Colombia. For years, this forest endured illegal logging of oak, cedar and mahogany. Likewise, the area has been devoted to coca cultivation and arms smuggling.

[37] A plan to assassinate Pérez Balladares and several cabinet members was uncovered in January 1995. Ten National Police members were arrested on charges of conspiracy but the investigation was shelved for lack of evidence.

[38] The country continued to have an active role in arms and drug traffic as well as money laundering. The explosion of a package during a routine drug inspection killed three officials and injured 25. The explosives, grenades and ammunitions, were being sent to Ecuador, supposedly to guerrilla groups. Two arms deposits were found in the capital, belonging to a Colombian citizen.

[39] The reform of the labor code, aimed at attracting foreign investment, led to an atmosphere of social violence and strikes, since it would reduce labor security and the freedom to unionize and negotiate collectively. Confrontations between workers and students with the police left 4 dead and 86 injured in August. However, the law was passed.

[40] Talks with the US over the transfer of the sovereignty of the Canal from 1999 seemed to point to the continuation of some form of US presence in Panama. In July 1996, President Pérez Balladares announced that the Howard US Air Force Base would remain, in order to keep drug trafficking under control. The US army spent $319 million in Panama that year (5 per cent of the country's GDP).

[41] The announcement that US troops would remain in Panama was made after it became known Balladares had received money from the Colombian Cali cartel to fund his 1994 election campaign. The President admitted the fact but denied having known of the origin of the funds. This scandal was followed by the forced closure of the Agro-Industrial and Commercial Bank due to its excessive debts and drug money-laundering activities.

[42] In March 1997, the Government decreed price freezes on items like school books, milk, gas, sugar and medicines. The measure was designed to counteract the indiscriminate price increases complained of by the Free Competition Commission.

[43] In September, after 80 years' presence in Panama's territory, the Southern Command headquarters returned to the US, in Miami. The Government released statements guaranteeing that the operation of the Panama Canal would not be affected by its return to national ownership. It also announced plans for building a third set of lock gates in early 2000, due to the increase in traffic and the tonnage of the ships.

[44] After Balladares was defeated in a referendum in which he proposed to change the Constitution to allow for his re-election, the main candidates for the May 1999 elections were Mireya Moscoso, the widow of Arnulfo Arias, and Martín Torrijos, son of General Omar Torrijos. Moscoso won on a manifesto which proposed - as did her opponent's - the avoidance of corruption and politicking in the administration of the Canal and also that both workers and ship owners were to be involved in decisions related to the Canal.

[45] On December 14, a ceremony was held to celebrate the Canal's return to Panamanian jurisdiction. Moscoso and former US President Jimmy Carter - who had signed the treaty agreeing to return the Canal with Omar Torrijos in 1977 - put their seal on diplomatic addenda which ratified this. Carter stated it was 'one of the most important historic occasions in the hemisphere' and that with the vigorous development of trade, Panama now had the chance to 'become the Singapore of the region', making the most of the Canal, and the international financial center, which contained the offices of 120 banks of the world.

[46] Moscoso stated that in the first years of the new millennium Panama would invest a billion dollars to widen the Culebra Cut section of the Canal and to buy equipment, but that international aid would be needed to build the third set of locks. ■

Papua New Guinea

Papua-New Guinea

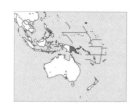

Population: 4,702,000 (1999)
Area: 462,840 SQ KM
Capital: Port Moresby
Currency: Kina
Language: English

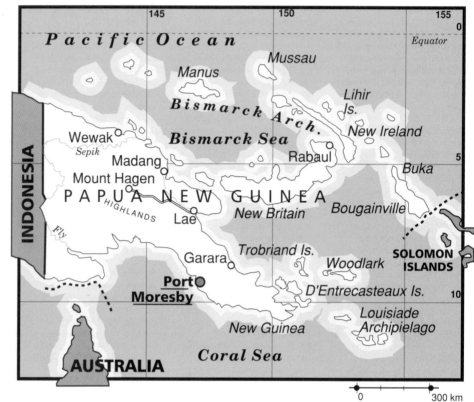

P apua New Guinea (PNG) has been inhabited by Melanesian peoples since 3,000-2,000 BC. Traditionally, its population lived in groups scattered throughout the dense tropical jungle, cut off from the outside world. As a result, over 700 dialects are spoken on the New Guinean island and the smaller islands of the republic. One third of the population lives in the highlands, and many communities there knew neither the wheel, iron implements nor Europeans until the 1930s.

[2] In a short time, PNG has passed from the stone age into the plastic age, and it currently faces an economic boom based on the exploitation of non-renewable natural resources (copper, gold, oil and hardwoods).

[3] The present state of Papua New Guinea was formed when the Territory of Papua, a British protectorate under Australian administration since 1906, was joined with New Guinea, a German colony until World War I. New Guinea was later administered by Australia under mandates, first from the League of Nations and then the United Nations.

[4] The process leading to self-government really began in 1964 and culminated in the proclamation of independence in 1975. That same year, there was an unsuccessful attempt at secession by the island of Bougainville. This island has rich deposits of copper and gold and its population is ethnically closer to the Solomon Islanders than to the Papuans. Australia maintains a strong presence in PNG, providing considerable investment in business, and military and financial assistance.

[5] Papua New Guinea's system of government is currently parliamentary. Each government enjoys a six-month truce period after which it has to submit its actions for parliamentary approval. Political parties form around personalities and regional groups rather than ideological differences. Although this might suggest a tendency to instability, the fact that no single group is dominant has produced a government of political consensus, which in itself has a stabilizing influence.

[6] Papua New Guinea has strong links with Australia and in turn exercises a degree of leadership among South Pacific states. Its military contributed to suppressing a secession attempt by the island of Espiritu Santo (Vanuatu) in 1979, led by Jimmy Stevens, and backed by French authorities and US economic interests.

[7] In May 1988, Papua New Guinea together with Vanuatu and the Solomon Islands signed an agreement to defend and preserve traditional Melanesian cultures. It also expressed support for Kanaky's (New Caledonia) independence. Relations with the Government of Indonesia, which occupies the western portion of the island, West Papua, were troubled. The Free Papua independence movement operated in this province, and Indonesian military operations here in 1984 led 12,000 inhabitants to seek refuge in Papua New Guinea.

[8] In 1989, PNG strengthened its ties with Southeast Asia, signing a friendship and co-operation treaty with ASEAN and opening negotiations with Malaysia. At the same time, it granted the Soviets permission to open an embassy in Port Moresby. In December, a maritime agreement was signed with the Federated States of Micronesia which allowed PNG to take advantage of an existing multilateral fishing agreement between the South Pacific and the US.

[9] Two thirds of the population are subsistence cultivators, and the 0.3 per cent that work with mining concerns generate 66 per cent of export earnings. Mines at Bougainville and Ok Tedi boasted the largest copper deposits in the world and also produce gold. The Porgera gold mine went into production in 1990, soon to be the largest in the world outside South Africa. Another on the island of Lihir may be even larger. The mines are exploited by transnationals, some of them Australian. Sizeable oil deposits have also been found and will be exploited only after a 175-mile oil

LAND USE

DEFORESTATION: 0.4% annual (1990/95)
IRRIGATED: 90.7% of arable (1993)

1993

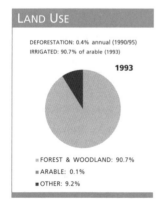

- FOREST & WOODLAND: 90.7%
- ARABLE: 0.1%
- OTHER: 9.2%

WORKERS

% OF LABOUR FORCE **1998**

- FEMALE: 42%   MALE: 58%

PUBLIC EXPENDITURE

DEFENCE EXPENDITURE (% of goverment exp.)	**4.1%**	(1997)
MILITARY EXPENDITURE (% of health & education)	**41%**	(1990/91)

<table>
<tr><td>

MATERNAL MORTALITY

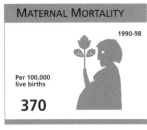

1990-98

Per 100,000 live births

370

</td><td>

LITERACY

1995

72%

</td><td>

FOREIGN TRADE

Millions US$ 1998

IMPORTS

2,630

EXPORTS

2,554

</td></tr>
</table>

pipeline is built, at a cost of $1 billion.

10   Parliament reinstated the death penalty in August 1991, 34 years after it had been abolished. This move was denounced by Christian movements, feminists and human rights organizations. The National Council of Women feared that the reinstatement of the death penalty might lead to a return of 'bounty' payments in assassination cases, as formerly.

11   In June 1992, the Justice Department brought corruption charges against former prime minister Namaliu and his minister of finance, Paul Pora.

12   The new Prime Minister, Palas Wingti pledged to increase the country's participation in joint ventures with foreign capital. This triggered an angry reaction from PJV, an Anglo-Australo-Canadian consortium which controls 90 per

cent of Porgera, the country's largest gold mine.

13   Wingti was replaced in August 1994 by Julius Chan.

14   Chan harshly denounced the French nuclear tests in the Pacific. After the second atomic test was carried out in October 1995, the Prime Minister of Papua New Guinea suspended talks between France and the South Pacific Forum, acting as president of the regional organization.

15   The conflict in Bougainville worsened when Theodore Miriung was assassinated in 1996. He had been the main transitional authority on the island and had promoted a peace agreement. The Prime Minister was accused by a military leader of contracting international mercenaries to quash the secessionist forces and, consequently, representatives of the armed forces called for Chan

to be sacked.

16   Despite having parliamentary backing, the Prime Minister resigned in March 1997, and was replaced by an interim ruler, John Giheno. A few weeks later, Parliament appointed Bill Skate as Head of Government.

17   In July 1997, in Aotearoa/New Zealand, the Government and secessionist rebels brought an end to the Bougainville crisis by signing a definitive peace agreement, including the demilitarization of the island and the deployment of UN peace-keeping troops. Australia promised funds for the rebuilding of Bougainville.

18   The drought in other parts of the country caused extensive fires and also affected coffee production.

19   In February 1998, 13 forestry companies closed down with the loss of 4,000 jobs as an indirect effect of the stock market and financial crisis in other Southeast Asian countries in 1997 and 1998.

20   Skate's announcement of the opening of diplomatic relations with Taiwan, and that country's concession of a soft credit line worth $2.5 billion pushed Parliament into requesting the Prime Minister's resignation in July 1999.

21   Mekere Morauta, leader of the opposition Popular Democratic Movement and former Central Bank governor, took a landslide majority of 99 votes to just 5 against and was appointed Prime Minister. Mekere immediately announced that the agreement with Taiwan, which had exasperated mainland China, would be invalidated.

22   In order to make up for the loss of the Taiwanese loan, Mekere announced he would be appealing to the International Monetary Fund. The economic situation was becoming critical with inflation above 20 per cent per year and a large fiscal deficit. ■

PROFILE

ENVIRONMENT

Located east of Indonesia, just south of the Equator, the country is made up of the eastern portion of the island of New Guinea (the western part is the Indonesian territory of West Papua) plus a series of smaller islands; New Britain, New Ireland and Manus, in the Bismarck archipelago; Bougainville, Buka and Nissau, which form the northern part of the Solomon Islands; the Louisiade and Entrecasteaux archipelagos; and the islands of Trobriand and Woodlark, southeast of New Guinea. The terrain is volcanic and mountainous, except for the narrow coastal plains. The climate is tropical and the vegetation is equatorial rainforest. The country suffers from deforestation, due to large-scale indiscriminate felling.

SOCIETY

Peoples: Papuans 85 per cent; Melanesians 15 per cent.
Religions: Many people follow local traditional religions but they also belong to Catholic (32.8 per cent) and Protestant (58.4 per cent) communities.
Languages: English (official). A local Pidgin, with many English words and Melanesian grammar is widely spoken, as well as 700 other local languages.
Political Parties: Popular Democratic Movement (PDM); Pangu Pati (PP); Popular Action Party; Popular Progressive Party (PPP).

THE STATE

Official Name: Independent State of Papua New Guinea.
Administrative Divisions: 20 Provinces.
Capital: Port Moresby 220,000 people (est 1995).
Other cities: Lae 80,655 people; Madang 27,057; Wewak 23,224; Goroka 17,855 (1990).
Government: Queen Elizabeth II, Head of State, represented by Governor General Silas Atopare. Mekere Morauta, Prime Minister and Head of the Government since July 1999. Single-chamber legislature: Parliament, with 109 members.
National Holiday: September 16, Independence Day (1975).
Armed Forces: 3,700 troops (1996).

STATISTICS

DEMOGRAPHY

Population: 4,702,000 (1999)
Annual growth: 2.3 % (1975/97)
Estimates for year 2015 (million): 6.5 (1999)
Annual growth to year 2015: 2.1 % (1997/2015)
Urban population: 16.6 % (1997)
Urban Growth: 3.6 % (1980/95)
Children per woman: 4.6 (1998)

HEALTH

Life expectancy at birth: 58 years (1998)
male: 57 years (1998)
female: 59 years (1998)
Maternal mortality: 370 per 100,000 live births (1990-98)
Infant mortality: 79 per 1,000 (1998)
Under-5 child mortality: 112 per 1,000 (1998)
Daily calorie supply: 2,253 per capita (1996)
18 doctors per 100,000 people (1993)
Safe water: 41 % (1990/98)

EDUCATION

Literacy: 72 % (1995)
male: 81 % (1995)
female: 63 % (1995)
School enrolment:
Primary total: 80 % (1990/96)
male: 87 % (1990/97)
female: 74 % (1990/97)
Secondary:
male: 17 % (1990/96)
female: 11 % (1990/96)
Tertiary: 3 % (1996)
Primary school teachers: one for every 38 (1995)

COMMUNICATIONS

15 newspapers (1996), 97 radios (1997), 4 TV sets (1996) and 11 main telephone lines (1996) per 1,000 people

ECONOMY

Per capita, GNP: $ 890 (1998)
Annual growth, GNP: 2.3 % (1998)
Annual inflation: 7.1 % (1990/98)
Consumer price index: 131.8 (1998)
Currency: 2.1 kina = $ 1 (1998)
Cereal imports: 320,101 metric tons (1998)
Fertilizer use: 2,167 kg per ha (1997)
Exports: $ 2,554 million (1998)
Imports: $ 2,630 million (1998)
External debt: $ 2,692 million (1998); $ 585 per capita (1998)
Debt service: 8.6 % of exports (1998)
Development aid received: $ 349 million (1997); $ 88.9 per capita (1997); 8.60 % of GNP (1997)

HDI (rank/value): 129/0.570 (1997)

Paraguay

Paraguay

Population: 5,359,000 (1999)
Area: 406,750 SQ KM
Capital: Asunción
Currency: Guaraní
Language: Spanish and Guarani

There were three ethnic groups in the Paraguay River basin in the 16th century: the Guaranís in the center and the Guaycurús and Payaguás in the Chaco region to the south. The Guaranís cultivated cassava, squash, sweet potatoes and corn. They were settled agriculturalists, organized in villages headed by a *tubichá* (chief).

[2] The Payaguás and Guaycurús were nomadic hunters and fishers. They periodically attacked the Guaraní plantations, leading the Guaranís to aid the Spaniards in the conquest of the Chaco area.

[3] Spanish conquistadors sailed up the Paraná River in the mid-16th century, searching for the mythical silver mountains that gave the Rio de la Plata (silver river) region its name. In 1537, Juan de Salazar founded the fort of Nuestra Señora de Asunción. This tiny settlement grew and became capital of the Rio de la Plata Province for over a century.

[4] Having failed to find precious metals in these 'worthless lands', it was only much later that Spanish colonizers were attracted by the wild cattle herds that prospered on the fertile plains of the Banda Oriental (today's Uruguay) and the humid Argentinian Pampas. A powerful oligarchy of trade merchants quickly developed in the ports of Buenos Aires (founded in 1580) and Montevideo (founded in 1726), and the former capital of the province, Asunción, declined.

[5] A pre-capitalist system of large landed estates grew up around Buenos Aires and Montevideo. Meanwhile, in what is now Paraguay, the Jesuits organized a system of agricultural colonies in which the indigenous population worked the land and produced handicrafts on a communal basis.

Private interests and the Spanish administration both resented this system, and the Society of Jesus was finally expelled in 1767. The local people either became slaves on Brazilian sugar cane plantations or peasant laborers on large cattle ranches.

[6] Although the Paraguayan province did not initially join the 1810 Liberal Revolution, the Asunción oligarchy ousted the Spanish Governor Velazco on May 14 1811, demanding free trade for *yerba mate* (a local tea) and tobacco.

[7] This rebellion began a process which concentrated all the power in the hands of Gaspar Rodríguez de Francia, secretary to the junta that had overthrown Spanish rule and

later appointed dictator. He was supported by the peasants, owners of small and medium-sized plots who wanted order and feared the 'anarchy' that was affecting the other provinces of the Río de la Plata Viceroyalty (that had been created in 1776). The oligarchy in Asunción, the new system's only enemy, was eliminated, and Paraguay withdrew into itself. Stimulated by public investment, industry began to develop, laying the foundations for Paraguay's future economic strength.

[8] Paraguay continued to develop under the patriarchal governments of Gaspar Rodríguez de Francia (El Supremo), Carlos Antonio López and his son, Francisco Solano López. It remained cut off from the rest of the world for decades and was untouched by the British influence that was so greatly felt in the other newly independent Rio de la Plata provinces. Left to develop alone, the State assumed an important role in the country's economy, controlling agricultural production (yerba mate and high quality

timber), and the first railroads, telegraph system and steel furnaces in South America.

[9] The leaders of Brazil, Argentina, and Uruguay - Pedro II, Bartolomé Mitre and Venancio Flores respectively - signed the Triple Alliance in 1865. With the support of the British Empire and the Baring Brothers' Bank, they began a 5-year war to eliminate Paraguay on the pretext of frontier disputes.

[10] Sixty-two years later, Paraguay fought a second fratricidal war, this time against Bolivia, orchestrated by rival oil multinationals. The Chaco War (1932-1935) was won, but it cost Paraguay 50,000 lives.

[11] In 31 years, there were 22 presidents, until the 1954 coup which brought General Alfredo Stroessner to power. Descended from Germans, and an admirer of Nazism, he gave refuge to war criminals fleeing Europe. Stroessner had himself re-elected seven times, the last time in February 1988. He allowed only a legal 'opposition', whose leaders he often appointed himself.

[12] By the mid-1980s, the Stroessner regime was showing clear signs of weakening. Democratization processes elsewhere in Latin America doubtless contributed to this. Internal opposition was growing in a variety of forms: an Inter-Union Labor Movement; a Permanent Assembly of Landless Rural Workers (APCT); indigenous peoples' organizations; and the Rural Women's Co-ordination Group. The Catholic church, through the Paraguayan clergy, began to voice the need for change.

[13] On February 3 1989, General Stroessner was overthrown by a coup headed by his son's father-in-law, army commander General Andrés Rodríguez, who immediately called free elections for the following May to elect a government and legislators to see out Stroessner's term.

[14] The elections, held on May 1 1989, were open to all political parties except the still-banned Communist Party. General Rodríguez was elected President with 68 per cent of the vote. The principal opposition group, the Authentic Radical Liberal Party led by Domingo Laíno, took 21 per cent. Despite the presence of foreign observers, voting was

WORKERS

1996
UNEMPLOYMENT: 8.2%

% OF LABOUR FORCE **1998**

- FEMALE: 30%   - MALE: 70%

1990

- SERVICES: 39.1%
- INDUSTRY: 22.0%
- AGRICULTURE: 38.9%

LAND USE

DEFORESTATION: 2.6% annual (1990/95)
IRRIGATED: 3.1% of arable (1993)

1993

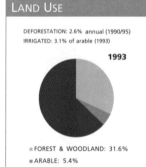

- FOREST & WOODLAND: 31.6%
- ARABLE: 5.4%
- OTHER: 63.0%

PUBLIC EXPENDITURE

DEFENCE EXPENDITURE (% of goverment exp.)	**10.5%**	(1997)
MILITARY EXPENDITURE (% of health & education)	**42%**	(1990/91)

plagued by countless irregularities, attributed to the Colorado Party which was leaving power.
[15] Nevertheless, opposition groups still considered the election to be the start of a democratization process, which was to be completed by 1993, with a Constituent Assembly convened, and a new constitution in place.
[16] Transnationals became involved in the production of soybeans and cotton. At that time, 2 per cent of all landholders had 85 per cent of the land. Most of the companies and foreign settlers congregated along the border with Brazil on a strip of land 2000 km long and 65 km wide. The main language was Portuguese, and the Brazilian *cruzeiro* was common currency. Between 300,000 and 400,000 Brazilians lived in the border districts.
[17] The World Bank-supported Caazapa and Caaguazu rural development projects involved the settlement and ranching of indigenous lands in eastern Paraguay. The indians found themselves restricted to tiny pockets of their former territories. Twelve indigenous communities asked the Unitary Workers' Center (CUT) to represent them in the National Constitutional Assembly. In December 1991, in the first round of elections to appoint representatives to this Assembly, the CUT gave its support to the 'Constitution for All' Movement.
[18] When the huge Itaipú hydroelectric plant on the border with Brazil went into operation, economic ties between the two countries increased.
[19] The first free municipal elections, held in June 1991, were marked by the emergence of the independent Asunción for All movement in the capital. Led by Carlos Filizzola, a 31 year-old doctor, the movement counted on the support of the United Workers Center and various social groups, and was elected with more than 35 per cent of the vote.
[20] In the elections for the National Constituent Assembly in December, the Colorado Party took 60 per cent of the vote. The Authentic Liberal Radical Party (PLRA) of Domingo Laíno came second with 29 per cent and the Constitution for All Movement, led by Filizzola, came third.
[21] The Constitution of June 1992 replaced the one brought in by Stroessner in 1967. The presidents of the Republic, the Supreme Court and Congress did not take part in the public meeting held to announce the new constitution, which included broad dispensations for the protection of human rights and banned the death penalty for common crimes.
[22] The repeated accusations of widespread corruption within the armed forces, including drug trafficking, led to investigations. Warrants were issued for the arrest of leading generals, including the commander-in-chief of the army.
[23] In December 1992, Paraguay signed an agreement for the constitution of a common market. The Mercosur, which would come into operation in 1995, with Argentina, Brazil and Uruguay (see box in Brazil).
[24] Amid allegations of fraud and declarations from the army that it would keep the Colorado Party in power, the ruling party candidate, Juan Carlos Wasmosy took 40 per cent of the vote in the May 1993 elections. Some 75 per cent of the 1.7 million eligible adults voted. However, troops positioned on the borders prevented the entry of citizens resident in Argentina and Brazil. The PLRA took 33 per cent of the vote, and the National Encounter, a pro-business coalition, 25 per cent.
[25] When Wasmosy took over the presidency in August, he became the first elected civilian president in the 182 years since national independence. Congress granted civilian power the control over the military.
[26] In September, the World Jewish Congress asked President Wasmosy for access to the Government archives in order to locate Nazis who took refuge in Paraguay following World War II.
[27] Parliament voted in a law banning members of the military from party politics in May. The Government and the high command immediately started action to declare this law unconstitutional. This attitude led the opposition to abandon the cooperation pact with the Colorados.
[28] Under pressure from the United States, Wasmosy nominated General Ramón Rozas Rodríguez to lead the war on drugs. Rozas was assassinated in 1994, when he was to have presented a report on corruption involving the military hierarchy, including General Lino Oviedo.
[29] Violent confrontations between rural people and the police affected

PROFILE

ENVIRONMENT

A landlocked country in the heart of the Río de la Plata basin, Paraguay is divided into two distinct regions by the Paraguay River. To the east lie fertile plains irrigated by the tributaries of the Paraguay and Paraná rivers, and covered with rainforest. This is the main farming area, producing soybeans (the major export crop), wheat, corn and tobacco. The western region or Northern Chaco is dry savannahs, producing cotton and cattle. Farmers, especially those linked to large agricultural operations, have felled large areas of forest, destroying habitats in the process. Indiscriminate hunting, combined with deforestation, have resulted in 14 species of mammals, 11 birds and 2 reptiles now being in danger of extinction. Large amounts of industrial and domestic waste are dumped into watercourses, and untreated sewage from the capital city flows directly into the Bay of Asunción.

SOCIETY

Peoples: 90 per cent of Paraguayans are of mixed descent from indigenous peoples and Spanish colonizers. The native Guaraní people currently account for only 5 per cent of the population and are threatened with the loss of their cultural identity. There are German, Italian, Argentinian and Brazilian minorities. This last group is expanding along the border between the two countries. One million Paraguayans live abroad, some 200,000 having migrated for political reasons.
Religions: Mainly Catholic, official.
Languages: Spanish and Guaraní (both official); most Paraguayans are bilingual. **Political Parties:** Colorado Party. Electoral Alliance, an electoral coalition made up of the parties led by Laíno and Filizzola (Authentic Radical Liberal Party and National Encounter; the *Febrerista* Revolutionary Party; Colorado Popular Movement (MOPOCO) - which grew from a split within the Colorado Party, in 1959. Christian Democratic Party. Communist Party.
Social Organizations: The Paraguayan Labor Confederation; the United Workers' Center (CUT) founded in 1990, uniting labor unions and the powerful rural workers' movement; the Paraguayan Women's Union.

THE STATE

Official Name: República del Paraguay. **Administrative Divisions:** 19 departments. **Capital:** Asunción 550,000 people (est 1997). **Other cities:** Ciudad del Este 133,900 people (1995); Pedro Juan Caballero 80,000; Encarnación 31,445; Pilar 26,352; Concepción 25,607 (1984). **Government:** Presidential republic, Luis González Macchi, President since March 28 1999. **National Holiday:** May 14, Independence Day (1811). **Armed Forces:** 20,200 (1996).

DEMOGRAPHY

Population: 5,359,000 (1999)
Annual growth: 3.0 % (1975/97)
Estimates for year 2015 (million): 7.8 (1999)
Annual growth to year 2015: 2.4 % (1997/2015)
Urban population: 53.9 % (1997)
Urban Growth: 4.7 % (1980/95)
Children per woman: 4.1 (1998)

HEALTH

Life expectancy at birth: 70 years (1998)
male: 67 years (1998)
female: 72 years (1998)
Maternal mortality: 190 per 100,000 live births (1990-98)
Infant mortality: 27 per 1,000 (1998)
Under-5 child mortality: 33 per 1,000 (1998)
Daily calorie supply: 2,485 per capita (1996)
67 doctors per 100,000 people (1993)
Safe water: 60 % (1990/98)

EDUCATION

Literacy: 92 % (1995)
male: 93 % (1995)
female: 90 % (1995)
School enrolment:
Primary total: 112 % (1990/96)
male: 113 % (1990/97)
female: 110 % (1990/97)
Secondary:
male: 42 % (1990/96)
female: 45 % (1990/96)
Tertiary: 10 % (1996)
Primary school teachers: one for every 21 (1996)

COMMUNICATIONS

43 newspapers (1996), 182 radios (1997), 144 TV sets (1996) and 36 main telephone lines (1996) per 1,000 people
Books: 3 new titles per 100,000 people (1992/94)

ECONOMY

Per capita, GNP: $ 1,760 (1998)
Annual growth, GNP: -0.5 % (1998)
Annual inflation: 14.6 % (1990/98)
Consumer price index: 131.0 (1998)
Currency: 2,755.7 guaraníes = $ 1 (1998)
Cereal imports: 141,669 metric tons (1998)
Food import dependency: 21 % (1997)
Fertilizer use: 155 kg per ha (1997)
Exports: $ 3,871 million (1998)
Imports: $ 4,253 million (1998)
External debt: $ 2,304 million (1998); $ 441 per capita (1998)
Debt service: 5.3 % of exports (1998)
Development aid received: $ 116 million (1997); $ 26.7 per capita (1997); 1.20 % of GNP (1997)

ENERGY

Consumption: 824.0 Kgs of Oil equivalent per capita yearly (1997); -66.0 % imported (1997)

HDI (rank/value): 84/0.730 (1997)

MATERNAL MORTALITY	LITERACY	EXTERNAL DEBT	FOOD DEPENDENCY

MATERNAL MORTALITY

1990-98

Per 100,000 live births

190

LITERACY

1995

92%

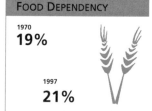

EXTERNAL DEBT

1998

PER CAPITA

US$ 441

FOOD DEPENDENCY

1970

19%

1997

21%

several regions. A hundred demonstrators blocking the access to Asunción were injured by rubber bullets. The farmers were supported by church organizations, unions and opposition parties. A general strike was declared in May to press for pay rises and protest against the privatization of State companies. The Government admitted that purchasing power had fallen by 42 per cent in the previous five years and upped salaries by 35 per cent. In December, all timber exports were suspended with the aim of halting deforestation.

[30] In January 1995, the National Human Rights Commission said that many of the crimes from Stroessner's time had gone unpunished and that rural people continued to be murdered.

[31] The President forced a group of eight high-ranking army officers to retire in April 1996. General Lino Oviedo resisted the order and occupied army barracks along with a group of young officers. Wasmosy took refuge in the US embassy, from where he appointed Oviedo Defense Minister in order to quell the crisis,

later revoking the decision. In May, the Colorado Party and the opposition agreed to ban the serving military from political activity.

[32] In the Colorado Party internal elections in September 1997, Lino Oviedo was elected Presidential candidate with 36.8 per cent of the vote, to the 35 of Luis María Argaña and the 22.5 of Wasmosy's favorite, Carlos Facetti. Oviedo was arrested on sedition charges in October.

[33] Oviedo was sentenced to 10 years' imprisonment by a military tribunal in April 1998, sparking rumors of a coup and the postponement of the presidential election. The political uncertainty compounded the nation's economic crisis, reflected in a 35 per cent drop in value of the national currency, the *guaraní*, against the US dollar in only four months.

[34] In the May 10 elections, with Oviedo in prison, 46.8 per cent of the vote went to the Colorado Party's Raúl Cubas-Luis María Argaña partnership, compared with 38.2 per cent to the Democratic Alliance of Laíno and Filizzola.

Cubas released his mentor Oviedo from prison, but in December the Supreme Court ruled that his release was unconstitutional and that he should be returned to prison. This unleashed a series of confrontations between supporters and opponents of the Cubas Government.

[35] The tension between state authorities worsened and in March 1999 Parliament prepared to vote on a political trial for the President. However, on March 23 unknown soldiers assassinated Vice-President Argaña. After almost a week of confrontations in the streets of Asunción with more victims, Cubas resigned and fled to Brazil, while Oviedo got a safe conduct to Argentina. President of Congress, Luis González Macchi, took over the presidency on March 28 and formed a cabinet of both Colorados and the opposition. According to the Constitution, new elections were to have been held in six months' time.

[36] However a Supreme Court ruling allowed González Macchi to take over his predecessor's

presidential term, so that he would be president until 2003.

[37] The new President had to deal with a wave of strikes and protests against the economic policy by workers, farmers and business people. On another front, the unions of state employees implemented a strong campaign resisting the announced privatizations of the telecommunications and electricity services. In response, González Macchi announced he was prepared to sign a commitment with all sectors to carry forward, the reforms, warning that were he to fail in government this would mean 'the collapse of the Paraguayan ruling class'.

[38] Social tension worsened in March 2000, when groups of farmers held several demonstrations in the capital, calling for greater state support, improvements in credit and higher prices for their produce. In the Northern town of Santa Rosa, some farmers were killed and other seriously wounded in confrontations with the police. ■

The Archives of Terror and Operation Condor

The military dictatorships that governed South America's Southern Cone countries in the 1970s and 1980s coordinated and implemented transborder intelligence and repression through what they called Operation Condor.

[2] For years, human rights organizations, left political parties and social movements in the region denounced the 'anti-subversive' atrocities committed by the armed forces and civilian collaborators in these countries under the National Security Doctrine implemented at the behest of the United States. But the charges - primarily based on testimony from witnesses who had suffered repression, torture or exile - did not take shape in civil society until 1992 because, for the most part, the claims could not be made through official channels.

[3] It was in that year, at a police station in Asuncion, Paraguay, that a human rights lawyer discovered what would later become known as the 'Archives of Terror'. They consist of tens of thousands of documents created by Paraguayan dictator Alfredo Stroessner's staff . For the first time there was official proof of the covert operations carried out by the armed forces against leftist activists and politicians in Chile, Argentina, Paraguay, Brazil and Uruguay, often simply for being *suspected* of subversion.

[4] The Archives of Terror identified when and how Operation Condor had originated and who was involved in orchestrating it: the military intelligence services in each of the participating countries. Once Operation Condor was exposed, political analysts, social activists and independent journalists began to put the facts together and come up with explana-

tions or theories about the disappearances of thousands of people, as well as the attempted murders and international assassinations. The most notorious of these were the assassination of Chilean military official Carlos Pratts in Buenos Aires, that of Chile's ex-Foreign Affairs minister Orlando Lettelier in Washington DC, and of Uruguayan lawmakers Zelmar Michelini and Hector Gutiérrez Ruiz in Buenos Aires.

[5] The Archives of Terror cleared up other suspicions as well. One was that the authorities at the time, under Operation Condor, had designed a sinister plan to 'disappear' the children born to mothers in prison, changing the identities of the minors before they were 'adopted' by military personnel or civilian collaborators.

[6] In recent years, some Argentinian military officers have

asked to be pardoned for the events of the past and others, members of the military 'Junta' are facing trial for a second time. They had been released under an amnesty declared by then-President Carlos Menem. The military officials face charges of detention and disappearance of minors, a crime not covered by the amnesty laws. The discovery of the Archives of Terror and the information gleaned from them led to the arrest of former Chilean dictator, retired general Augusto Pinochet, in London in October 1998, as well as the charges of human rights' violations filed by Spanish judge Baltasar Garzón against Argentinian, Chilean and Uruguayan military officials – many of whom now hesitate to leave their home countries for fear of arrest. ■

Peru

Perú

Population: 25,230,000 (1999)
Area: 1,285,220 SQ KM
Capital: Lima
Currency: New sol
Language: Spanish, Aymara and Quechua

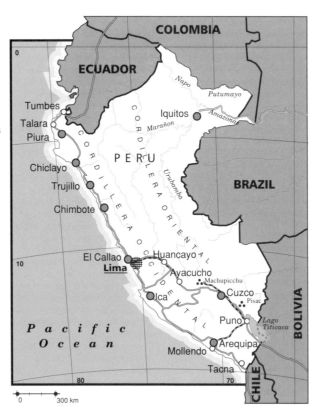

Caves near Ayacucho revealed evidence that humans had lived in Peru for more than 15 thousand years. For millennia complex cultures had settled in the Andean zone. The Chavin civilization excelled at urban planning, reaching its apogee between 1400 and 200 BC. The cultures which followed inherited its knowledge. The Paraca (700 to 100 BC) were the first to carry out brain surgery. The Mochica built great adobe temples in the Mocha valley, and it is thought their direct descendants were the Chimu (1000 to 1400 AD) who were great metalworkers. The Nazca culture (200 BC to 800 AD) developed agriculture with large-scale irrigation systems and built great calendars which can still be seen from the heights. The Tiahuanaco-Huari culture (600 BC to 1000 AD), based in what is now Bolivia, expanded into the Peruvian highlands.

2 The 12th century marked the beginning of the rise of the Inca, who were united the various cultures and languages of the region. As with the rest of the Andean civilizations, the Incas' cultural legacy was preserved down the generations by oral tradition and texts written after the Spanish conquest. According to tradition, the founders of the Inca dynasty, Manco Capac and Mama Oclo, established their tribe in Cuzco, which remained the capital from then on. Up until the 14th century, little distinguished the Incas from the rest of the cultures dominating small territories in the Andes. It was during this century, under the reign of the fourth Emperor (or Inca) Mayta Capac, that the Inca began to attack the neighboring populations.

3 The next in the dynastic line, Capac Yupanqui, was the first to extend the influence of the Inca beyond the Cuzco valley. With the eighth emperor, Viracocha Inca, the Empire began a programme of permanent conquest, establishing garrisons amongst the settlements of the conquered peoples. In 1438, Pachacuti Inca Yupanqui, one of the sons of Viracocha Inca, usurped the throne from his brother Inca Urcon and the Tahuntinsuyu Empire -as it was known-expanded beyond lake Titicaca, subjugating powerful peoples like the Chanca, Quechua and the Chimu and taking over the kingdom of the Shiri in Quito.

4 The Inca began a policy of forced resettlement, thereby assuring the political stability of the Empire. Large numbers of people were taken from their place of origin and redistributed to other points within the Empire. They were forced to live and work alongside other ethnic groups, in order to make the organization of uprisings against the seat of power in Cuzco difficult. Quechua was imposed as the common language across the Empire and during the reign of Topa Inca Yupanqui (1471-1493) the Inca extended their power southwards, towards what is now central Chile. On the death of Topa Inca a war of succession broke out, which was won by Huayna Capac (1493-1525). He extended the northern frontier up to the river Ancasmayo (the current frontier between Ecuador and Colombia) before dying. On his death, Tahuantisuyu, as the Inca state was known, imposed its government over more than 12 million people.

5 The death of Huayna Capac caused a new war of succession between Huscar, who governed in Cuzco, and his younger brother Atahualpa, a son of Huayna Capac and a Shiri princess, who ruled the northern part of the Empire from Quito. In 1532, the scales were tipped in favor of Atahualpa when a group of 180 Spaniards, led by Francisco Pizarro and his lieutenant Diego de Almagro disembarked in Tumbes. The Spanish intervened in the civil war, killing those loyal to Atahualpa but at the same time recognizing him as the legitimate governor of the Empire until they were able to meet him in Cajamarca, kidnap him and demand a large ransom in silver and gold. During his time in captivity, Atahualpa arranged for Huscar to be killed, before being strangled himself in 1533. The news of the death of Atahualpa paralysed the forces of the Empire, allowing the Spanish to reach Cuzco, where they crowned Topa Hualpa, an ally of Huscar. This put the Europeans, who wanted to reign through an Inca emperor, in a difficult situation, as they found themselves committed to the faction they initially did not want to support.

6 Topa Hualpa died some months later and the Spanish reinforced their alliance with the pro-Huscar faction by putting his brother Manco Capac on the throne and helping him to disperse the last of Atahualpa's army. In 1535, Pizarro prohibited Manco Capac from re-establishing control over the dominions along the coast and in the north, which were either still loyal to Atahualpa or lacked central control. Manco Capac then understood that the Spanish were a far greater threat than any of Atahualpa's followers and in 1536 he besieged Cuzco for a year. But his forces were finally disbanded by Diego de Almagro, returning from an expedition to Chile.

7 After his defeat, Manco Capac founded an independent Inca state in the Amazon regions which lasted until 1572, with the death by poisoning of Titu Cusi Yupanqui, the last Inca. The days of the Tahuantisuyu were numbered from the moment Pizarro founded Lima in 1535 on the coast, operating as the center of Spanish power. The Spanish administration radically changed the property and land-use rules; the payment of tributes and forced labor broke up the bases of the old society and the old gods were officially replaced with Catholicism. Even though the official Inca religion was suppressed, an Inkalculable number of cults to minor deities survived amongst the people. Similarly, regions and cities of the old Empire survived beyond the reach of the Spanish Crown for centuries. The most notable example of this was the fortress of Macchu Pichu, 80 kilometres north-east of Cuzco which was only re-discovered in 1911 by Hiram Bingham, a Yale University professor.

8 Conflicts between the *conquistadores* (the Spanish conquerors) meant that the Spanish Crown could not fully establish its authority for decades. Almagro, disillusioned by losing his chances to conquer lands in Chile, besieged Cuzco until he was beaten and executed in 1538. His allies continued conspiring with his son and they attacked Pizarro's palace. Pizarro died in 1541. The Spanish Crown refused to recognize the young Almagro, who was captured and executed in 1542. But the conquistadores, led by Francisco Pizarro's brother Gonzalo, unhappy with the Spanish King's new laws (aiming to impede feudalism, and thereby threatening their wealth and power) rebelled again in 1542, remaining independent from

Spanish control to all intents and purposes until 1544, when Gonzalo Pizarro was defeated and executed.

[9] It was only with the appointment of Viceroy Francisco de Toledo in 1569 that Spain consolidated its dominion over the region. The Andeans' institutions were adapted to the ends of the Spanish authority and for a long time the chiefs of the various Andean nations administered the interests of their communities while taking on responsibility for the collection of tributes and the provision of an indigenous workforce for the mines. In any case, Toledo did not trust the Andeans and when the son of Manco Capac, Tupac Amaru, led the indigenous rural population in an uprising, the Spanish authority had him executed in 1571.

[10] Once Toledo's administration was over, the Viceroyalty in Peru assumed the form it maintained until the 18th century, including all of South America except Venezuela and Brazil. The discovery of the silver mines in Potosí in 1545 was followed by those of Huancavelica in 1563. With the exception of the gold from New Granada (Colombia), mineral production was concentrated in Peru itself, or in Upper Peru (Bolivia). The Spanish Crown prioritized these areas, which became the most developed and rich parts of the continent.

[11] During the 16th and 17th centuries, Lima was the center of power and wealth for all of Spanish-controlled South America. Based on the labor of the indigenous workforce, the Court of Lima - where the King's justice was meted out - attracted not only the rich and powerful but also religious orders, intellectuals and artists. It was in Lima that the tribunals of the Inquisition worked most avidly and cruelly. With the advent of the Bourbon dynasty in 1700, replacing the Hapsburgs as rulers of Spain, measures were taken to promote the development of the colonies and to achieve better government of the continent, something which severely affected Peru. The creation of the Viceroyalty of New Granada meant the Viceroyalty of Peru lost control over the port of Quito as well as the territory constituting modern day Colombia. The creation of the Viceroyalty of the River Plate in 1777 also removed control over Upper Peru and what are today Argentina, Paraguay and Uruguay. Chile, meanwhile, became an independent Captaincy of the Viceroy of Peru.

[12] Reforms to the mercantile system, allowing the Pacific and Atlantic ports to trade directly with Spain, weakened the condition of the Viceroyalty even further. In 1780, the *cacique* (indigenous leader) José Gabriel Condorcanqui had a *corregidor* (chief magistrate) arrested on charges of cruelty. He led a general uprising of indigenous people against the authority of the Viceroyalty in 1781 under the name of Tupac Amaru II, even gaining the support of some *criollos* (descendants of the Spanish). The rebellion, which spread to Bolivia and Argentina lost support when it turned into a violent battle between the indigenous people and the whites. Tupac Amaru II was captured in 1781 and taken to Cuzco where, after being forced to witness the execution of his wife and children, he was quartered and beheaded. The revolution continued, however, until the Spanish Government approved a general pardon for the insurgents.

[13] The effective suppression of the indigenous uprisings, the presence of numerous Spaniards, the concentration of the Crown's military power in Lima and the conservative attitude of the local oligarchy, meant that Peru remained loyal to Spain when the rest of the Hispanic colonies in South America began the fight for independence between 1810 and 1821. The forces which finally expelled the Spanish came from beyond Peruvian borders. General José de San Martín, an Argentinian *criollo*, freed Chile in 1818 and used it as a base to attack Peru by sea with the aim of securing control over the mines of Upper Peru and of assuring independence for the Argentine provinces. In September 1820, San Martín's forces occupied the port of Pisco and the Viceroy withdrew his troops into the interior of the country. San Martín entered Lima and declared independence on July 18 1821.

[14] Lacking sufficient forces to attack the large Spanish contingents in the interior of Peru, San Martín asked for the help of Venezuela's Simón Bolívar, who had liberated the northern part of South America, but Bolívar would not agree to share the leadership. Hence, San Martín withdrew and Bolívar took over in Peru to continue the fight. In the battles of Junín and Ayacucho, in August and December 1824, the Spanish were defeated and effectively Peru became politically independent.

[15] The first years of independence were spent in constant battles between the conservative oligarchy, yearning for the times of the viceroyalty, and the liberals. The wars with Colombia, in 1827, and Bolivia took place against that backdrop. The unification of Peru with Bolivia, attempted by Bolivian President Andrés Santa Cruz in 1835, failed both socially and economically

[16] Marshal Ramón Castilla, who ruled the country from 1845 to 1862, shaped the modern Peru, after abolishing slavery and proclaiming the Constitution.

[17] In 1864, Spain attempted to establish enclaves on the Peruvian coast. Peru, Chile, Bolivia and Ecuador declared war on the country. The Spanish fleet bombarded Valparaiso, Chile, and El Callao in Peru, before being defeated in 1866.

[18] From 1845, with the silver mines exhausted, guano - bird faeces used as fertilizer - became Peru's main export product. When the guano 'boom' was over it was replaced by saltpeter from the southern deserts. The potential wealth to be made from this product brought about the Pacific War (1879-1883). Peru and Bolivia joined forces against Chile, which exploited the saltpeter, with the support of British companies. Peru and Bolivia lost the war and with it the provinces of Arica, Tarapac and Antofagasta.

[19] The early decades of the 20th century marked the beginning of large-scale copper mining, particularly by the North American Cerro de Pasco Copper Corporation. Foreign capital was also involved in oil exploitation in the north, and sugar cane and cotton in the north and center. The anachronistic agrarian structures, however, continued unchanged.

[20] Within this context, the APRA (American Popular Revolutionary Alliance), a Marxist-inspired party committed to Latin Americanism, achieved widespread support. Victor Haya de la Torre, its main leader, was in favor of merging class boundaries and debated with José Carlos Mariteguí, founder of the Peruvian Communist Party (PC). Triumphant in several elections, APRA never actually came to power as it was always prevented by military coups.

[21] APRA dissidents and sectors of the revolutionary left unsuccessfully attempted guerrilla warfare in the 1960s.

[22] In 1968, a military faction headed

PROFILE

ENVIRONMENT

The Andes divide the country into three regions. The desert coastal area, with large artificially irrigated plantations and some natural valleys has historically been the most modern and westernized. Half of the populaton live in the *Sierra* (highlands), between two ranges of the Andes. Numerous peasants here are still organized into *ayllus* (communities) with Incan roots. Subsistence farming of corn and potatoes is practiced, the traditional raising of llamas and alpacas having been forced onto the higher slopes due to the incursions of mining and sheep rearing. The eastern region, comprising the Amazon lowlands, with tropical climate and rainforests, is sparsely populated. Perú is one of the largest producers of coca, a medicinal and energizing plant. Coca - traditionally consumed among indians who chew its leaves - once chemically refined and developed into a different substance, becomes the basis of cocaine. The country suffers from soil depletion, on soils which are poor to begin with. Indiscriminate fishing has endangered some species. The coastal area has been polluted by both industrial and household waste.

SOCIETY

Peoples: Nearly half of all Peruvians are of indigenous American origin, mostly from the Quechua and Aymara ethnic groups living on the *Sierra*. Along the coast, most of the population are mixed descendents of native Indians and Spaniards. There are several indigenous groups in the East Amazon jungle. **Religions:** Catholic (official), with syncretic expressions related to Indian beliefs. **Languages:** Spanish and Quechua, Aymara (all official). **Political Parties:** The Change 90-New Majority, founded in 1989 by Alberto Fujimori. In the 2000 elections the opposition candidate withdrew from the contest in protest. Others are: Popular Action (AP); the Peruvian 'Aprista' Party, founded in 1930; the Christian Popular Party; the United Left (IU), an alliance of the National Workers' and Campesinos' (Farmers') Front, the Peruvian Communist Party and the Union of the Revolutionary Left; the Socialist Left, a splinter group from the IU led by Alfonso Barrantes. There two main guerrilla organizations are the Peruvian Communist Revolutionary Party - Sendero Luminoso (Shining Path) and the Tupac Amaru Revolutionary Movement (MRTA). **Social Organizations:** The Peruvian Workers', General Central Union (CGTP), founded in 1928 and predominantly Communist. The Peruvian Workers' Central Union (CTP), founded in 1944, linked to the APRA. The independent National Worker's Confederation (CNT), founded in 1971. The Workers' Central of the Peruvian Revolution, founded in 1972 by Velasco backers. In March, 1991, the four trade union federations (CGTP, CTP, CTRP, and CNT) created the national Coordinating Body of Trade Union Federations, as a step towards the creation of a single federation. There are two rural organizations: the National Agrarian Confederation (CNA), founded in 1972, and the Peruvian *Campesino* Confederation (CCP), founded in 1974.

THE STATE

Official Name: República del Perú. **Administrative divisions:** 25 Departments, 155 Provinces and 1,586 Districts. **Capital:** Lima 6,022,313 people (1995). **Other cities:** Arequipa 726,000 people; Callao 684,000; Trujillo 627,000; Chiclayo 411,500 (1995). **Government:** Alberto Fujimori, President since July 28 1990, re-elected in April 1995 and May 2000. **National Holiday:** July 28, Independence (1821). **Armed Forces:** 115,000 troops (65,000 conscripts). 188,000 reserves. **Other:** National Police: 60,000 members. Coast Guard: 600 members. Campesino Rounds: the campesino self-defense forces, made up of 2,000 groups mobilized within emergency zones.

by General Juan Velasco Alvarado ousted President Fernando Belaúnde Terry and started a process of change by nationalizing oil production. This also included recovery of the natural resources and fishing, co-operative based agrarian reform, worker participation in company ownership, the creation of socially-owned enterprises, the expropriation of the press - planning to hand this over to organized social sectors - and an independent non-aligned foreign policy.

[23] An ailing Velasco gradually lost control over the process and the trust of his allies. He was overthrown by his Prime Minister, General Francisco Morales Bermúdez, in August 1975. Under pressure from the IMF and an oligarchy keen on regaining power, Morales called elections in 1978. APRA, the Left and the Christian People's Party - the traditional right - took almost equal seats in the Constituent Assembly.

[24] Belaunde's Acción Popular (AP), which had boycotted the constituent elections, triumphed in 1980 presidential elections. Its economic policy followed IMF guidelines with disastrous results: unemployment grew, income became even more concentrated and an unregulated informal economy developed with no social benefits. In 1980, fighting broke out with the Shining Path guerrillas and the Tupac Amaru Revolutionary Movement (MRTA) in 1984.

[25] The United Left (IU), a parliamentary coalition of left-wing parties, won the mayoralty of Lima in the 1982 elections. Faced with increased guerrilla action, the provinces most affected were placed under military control, with a state of emergency declared in 1983.

[26] In the 1985 elections, the APRA candidate Alan García came in first with 46 per cent. When García took power in July 1985, the foreign debt stood at $14 billion, with annual servicing of $3.5 billion. García announced he would limit payments to 10 per cent of the annual export income and would negotiate directly with the creditors, without IMF mediation.

[27] In the second half of 1988, international reserves hit rock bottom and amidst growing inflation and recession the Government began an economic adjustment policy.

[28] In the 1989 general elections, the Democratic Front (Fredemo) with writer Mario Vargas Llosa as its candidate stood against APRA's Luis Alva Castro, the Left with the 'United' Henry Pease and the 'Socialist' Alfonso Barrantes, and Change 90 (Cambio 90), with the unknown outsider, Alberto Fujimori. Fujimori was elected with 56.4 per cent of the vote.

[29] On assuming power in July 1990, Fujimori implemented a severe anti-inflationary plan, or 'Fujishock,' which dropped the standard of living of all Peruvians, leaving more than half in extreme poverty. The four union groups convened a 'march against hunger,' and later united to form the National Co-ordination. When parliamentary opposition got in his way, Fujimori began to govern by decree.

[30] On April 5 1992, Fujimori led a coup claiming that Parliament was corrupt and inoperative and that the judicial system was obstructing national reconstruction.

[31] The United States suspended economic and military aid to Peru, but soon restarted negotiations. In late April, the IMF approved the Peruvian Government's economic and structural reform program.

[32] In September, the imprisonment of Abimael Guzmn, founder and leader of the Shining Path, dealt a major blow to the guerrilla group, which said it was prepared to start peace negotiations. In the election for the Democratic Constituent Congress in November, Fujimori's party took the overall majority, with the absence of the traditional parties.

[33] The economy grew by 6.5 per cent on income from fishing, construction, manufactured goods and the informal economy. Peruvian reluctance over the removal of tariffs obstructed the creation of a common Andean market with Colombia, Venezuela and Bolivia, planned for 1995.

[34] In early 1995, Peru and Ecuador fought an undeclared war on their common frontier in the Condor mountains. The peace negotiations were held under the patronage of the Rio Protocol, with Argentina, Brazil, Chile and the United States as guarantors.

[35] In the April elections, Fujimori was re-elected in a resounding victory. Javier Pérez de Cuéllar, former UN Secretary General, did not get enough votes to enter the second round.

[36] That year, Fujimori granted an amnesty to all military and police personnel convicted for human rights violations during fighting with the guerrillas since 1980. The so-called 'faceless judges', who maintained anonymity during the trials, sentenced more than 2,000 people between 1992 and 1995.

[37] In December 1996, a MRTA group took over the Japanese ambassador's residence in Lima, during a reception for 450 guests, causing national and international commotion. Negotiations led to the freeing of successive groups of hostages. On April 22, 126 days later, a group of army commandos stormed the building. The death toll included 14 MRTA members, one of the remaining 72 hostages, and two soldiers. Fujimori's popularity soared to 65 per cent approval in the polls.

[38] In May 1997 members of the Constitutional Tribunal were sacked after it ruled that Fujimori's standing for re-election would be unconstitutional.

[39] Amnesty International reported some 5,000 Peruvians were arrested and imprisoned under the anti-terrorist laws in the last five years. Some 1,400 of these had been unjustly detained, and 600 were still in prison at the close of 1997.

[40] Defence Minister César Saucedo stated in November 1997 that so far that year the MRTA and the Shining Path had carried out 534 attacks, compared with 660 the previous year, and 4,467 in 1992 - the peak year for guerrilla action in the country. A month later, the Shining Path declared it still maintained the offer of peace made to the Fujimori Government in 1993.

[41] In April 1998, the US anti-drug 'Czar' Barry McCaffrey visited the country and met with General Vladimiro Montesinos, of the national intelligence services. Just days before, it had been reported that the Colombian conflict could overflow into Peru with an 'invasion of guerrilla groups', but in the end nothing happened.

[42] October 23, three years after the armed conflict, Peru and Ecuador agreed to sign a peace accord - to take place one week later in the Brazilian capital - based on a new border proposed by the treaty's guarantor countries: Argentina, Chile, Brazil and the US.

[43] Politically, the year 1999 centered on the President's desire to run for a third consecutive term in office, despite constitutional prohibitions. Fujimori officially announced his electoral bid in December, but on October 12, various indigenous groups had organized and led a national strike in protest of his potential candidacy. According to independent polls, the previously unknown Alejandro Toledo, an independent economist, had a chance of winning the presidency.

[44] Peruvians were disconcerted when they went to the polls on April 9 2000, as the media had reported that Fujimori's political apparatus (Independent Movement Peru 2000) allegedly presented one million false signatures in support of his candidacy. Once the first results were in, Toledo (who obtained 41 per cent of the vote) stated that Fujimori (48.7 per cent) had misappropriated government funds to finance his campaign and had prevented access for Toledo's political organization to the major state-run and private media. That night, Toledo led a strong popular protest in Lima to demand a run-off vote.

[45] On April 26, US President Clinton warned Fujimori that if the run-off vote in May was not 'free and fair', he had the authority to implement economic, political or military sanctions against Peru.

[46] Fujimori 'won' the election on 28 May after Toledo withdrew from the contest citing 'serious irregularities' in the electoral process. ∎

Philippines

Population: 74,454,000 (1999)
Area: 300,000 SQ KM
Capital: Manila
Currency: Peso
Language: Filipino

Pilipinas

The Philippine archipelago was first inhabited in Palaeolithic times, and the Neolithic culture on the islands began around 900 BC with metal working beginning in about the 15th century. Native peoples, such as the Aeta and the Igorot, probably subsisted without being assimilated by the later groups of migrants.

[2] Between the 2nd and 15th centuries AD, migrants from Indonesia and Malaysia settled on the islands, gathering in clans. Unlike the rest of the Malays, they were virtually uninfluenced by the classical Indian culture. Between the 11th and 13th centuries the coastal areas were raided by Muslim, Japanese, and Chinese merchant ships, bringing traders and craftsmen to the islands. The southern islands adopted Islam and sultanates soon appeared.

[3] The archipelago was only 'discovered' by Ferdinand Magellan in 1521 when it was named after the Spanish king Felipe. The explorer was killed on one of its beaches and Spanish possession of the islands, which were also coveted by the British and the Dutch, was not secured until 1564. The Igorot of the Cordillera region and the Islamic population of Mindanao were never fully incorporated by European colonization, and most of the rural population preserved their subsistence economy, never even paying tribute to the Europeans. Several uprisings by these communities and the Chinese were repressed by the Spaniards.

[4] Spanish colonization in the Philippines followed similar patterns to that in America. However, the Philippines had two distinguishing features; they were located on the oceanic trading routes, in a position that received

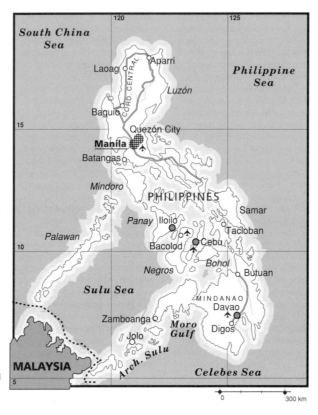

merchandise from all over Southeast Asia on its way to Europe, and they were ruled by the Viceroyalty of Mexico.

[5] Late in the 19th century, a local independence movement developed, led by the native bourgeoisie, who wanted the political power which was barred to them. They were soon followed by the other oppressed sectors. Anti-colonial revolution erupted in 1896 and independence was proclaimed on July 12th. However, the US was attracted by the archipelago's strategic position and vulnerability,

and it immediately stepped in to seize control. This resulted in the signing of the Treaty of Paris, on December 10 1898, ending the Spanish-US war (see history of Cuba and Puerto Rico). In meetings, which barred Filipino delegates, Spain decided to cede the archipelago to the US in exchange for compensation.

[6] Between 1899 and 1911, more than 500,000 Filipinos died in the struggle against occupying troops commanded by US General Arthur MacArthur. During World War II, the archipelago was occupied by

Japan and the Huk Movement, peasant-based and socialist inspired, emerged during the struggle against the invaders. In 1946, after the war had ended, occupation troops returned led by Douglas MacArthur, son of the earlier General MacArthur. The archipelago was eventually granted formal independence but the Philippines have remained under US economic domination ever since.

[7] Nor did independence bring about any social changes. The hacienda system still persists in the country, where large estates are farmed by sharecroppers. More than half the population are peasants, and 20 per cent of the population own 60 per cent of the land. Although the sharecropper is supposed to receive half of the harvest, most of the peasant's actual income goes to paying off the debts incurred with the *cacique*, the landowner. There is almost 9 per cent unemployment and the country suffers from the consequences of a balance of trade deficit, typical of a producer of agricultural commodities.

[8] The Nationalist Party, a conservative party of landowners, was in power until 1972 when Ferdinand Marcos, president since 1965, declared Martial Law. In 1986 a coalition of opposition forces rebelled against the continuous abuses of Ferdinand Marcos. During his presidency repression grew both against armed movements (the Muslim independent groups of Mindanao and the New People's Army led by the Maoist Communist Party), and against political and trade union opposition. This repression often had the military support of the US.

[9] Due to its long presence in the country, the Catholic Church is deeply rooted in Filipino society. This is reflected in the fact that 75 per cent of Filipinos over the age of 10 have learnt to read in institutions dependent on the Church. The Church played an active role in the denunciation of fraud when the 1976 referendum supported the invocation of martial law. Five years later, 45 political and trade union organizations united to boycott the fraudulent and unconstitutional elections that Marcos used to stay in power. In September 1981 thousands of people demonstrated in Manila,

WORKERS

1996
UNEMPLOYMENT: 7.4%

% OF LABOUR FORCE **1998**

■ FEMALE: 38% ■ MALE: 62%
1990

■ SERVICES: 38.9%
■ INDUSTRY: 15.3%
■ AGRICULTURE: 45.8%

LAND USE

DEFORESTATION: 3.5% annual (1990/95)
IRRIGATED: 28.6% of arable (1993)

1993

■ FOREST & WOODLAND: 45.3%
■ ARABLE: 18.4%
■ OTHER: 36.3%

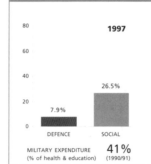

PUBLIC EXPENDITURE

1997

80

60

40

20

0

7.9%
DEFENCE

26.5%
SOCIAL

MILITARY EXPENDITURE
(% of health & education) **41%** (1990/91)

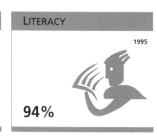
demanding the end of dictatorship and the withdrawal of the US military bases. Since the 19th century, the US army has had its two largest foreign bases in the Philippines.

[10] On August 21 1983, opposition leader Benigno Aquino was murdered at Manila airport as he stepped down from the commercial flight that had brought him back to his country after prolonged exile in the US, a murder which was attributed to Marcos. More than 500,000 mourners followed his coffin to the cemetery, blaming Marcos for the crime. The crowds flooded the streets refusing to go home until the dictator was ousted.

[11] In the May 14 1984 by-elections, the opposition made important progress; for though it lost the elections, it won 78 of the 183 parliamentary seats. In April 1985, the 'Reform of the Army Movement' (RAM) was formed by officers who were opposed to Marcos' interventions in the army.

[12] Amidst a scenario of increased violence and repression, compared by the Church with the dirty war of Argentina in the 1970s, a large section of the population put pressure on Marcos, demanding early elections in 1986, and supporting the candidacy of Corazon Aquino, widow of the assassinated leader.

[13] Elections were held in February 1986, but widespread fraud prevented Cory Aquino from winning, and she subsequently called for civil disobedience. Marcos' Minister of Defense, Juan Ponce Enrile, attempted a coup against the dictator, but failed. A million supporters surrounded the rebels, led by Enrile, in the field where they had taken refuge. The air force refused to bombard their comrades-in-arms and the people who supported them, so Marcos opted for exile and Corazon Aquino assumed the presidency with Enrile as her Minister of Defense.

[14] Aquino faced various attempts at ousting her; the most threatening of which took place in November 1986 and September 1987, both ending in cabinet reshuffles. After the first attempt, Enrile resigned from his post. The breach with the more conservative figures had to be balanced by the removal of several front-line advisors who were directly involved in grassroots movements and the

defense of human rights.

[15] The new constitution was approved by a large majority in the February 1987 plebiscite. The charter granted autonomy to the Mindanao and Cordillera regions, thus paving the way for a truce with guerrilla groups operating in those areas. The New People's Army representatives soon left the negotiating table, after several acts of provocation against mass organizations and attempts on the lives of civilian leaders. Agrarian reform, which should have been the cornerstone of the government's plan for social transformation, was diluted after

going through a legislature where many of the members are landowners. The debate over the future of the Clark and Subic Bay American military bases began in April 1988, as the contracts were due to expire in 1991.

[16] In 1990, 39 per cent of the Filipino population was under the age of 14, and in spite of NGO efforts to alleviate their suffering, only a third of their basic needs were met. A number of government 'internal refugee' camps were created to provide basic assistance to some 1,250,000 homeless people.

[17] The UN has recorded a total of

110 regional and ethnic groups in the Philippines. During 1991 increasing pressure from these groups, the urgent need for better land and wealth distribution and, possibly, the approaching presidential elections of May 1992, led Corazon Aquino to create a Bureau of Northern Communities. The bureau was concerned with the mountain tribes and ethnic groups, particularly in Luzon. There was also a Bureau of Southern Cultural Communities, excluding the Muslims. The staff of those bureaux were recruited from among the communities concerned.

[18] In the Mindanao region there

PROFILE

ENVIRONMENT

Of the 7,000 islands that make up the archipelago, spread over 1,600 km. from north to south, eleven account for 94 per cent of the total area and house most of the population. Luzon and Mindanao are the most important. The archipelago is of volcanic origin, forming part of the 'Ring of Fire of the Pacific'. The terrain is mountainous with large coastal plains where sugar cane, hemp, copra and tobacco are grown. The climate is tropical with heavy rainfall and dense rainforests. The country is the main producer of iron ore in Southeast Asia, there are chrome, copper, nickel, cobalt, silver and gold deposits. Like other countries in the region, it is suffering the effects of rapid deforestation.

SOCIETY

Peoples: Most of the population migrated from Malaysia and Indonesia between the 24th century BC and the 11th. century AD. Native peoples such as the Aetas and the Igorots may have subsisted without being assimilated into the other ethnic groups. In the 15th century, when Islamic communities arrived from Borneo, some 200,000 Chinese traders were already established on the islands. The Spanish arrived in 1521, evangelizing much of the population as they conquered. Some peoples of Malay extraction, were not converted.

Finally, from 1898 onwards, US colonization influenced Filipino culture and society.

Religions: Catholics 83 per cent; Protestants 8 per cent, Muslims 5 per cent, Anglipayans (Independent Filipino Church), 3 per cent; Animists and Buddhists.

Languages: The Philippines presents a complex linguistic map. 55 per cent of the population speaks Filipino (official), based on Tagalog, a language of Malaysian origin. English, spoken by 45 per cent, is obligatory in schools. 90 per cent of the population speaks one of the following: Cebuano (6 million); Hiligayano (3 million); Bikolano (2 million); Waray-Waray (1 million). Spanish and Chinese are minority languages.

Political Parties: Lakas ñg Bansa (The People's Struggle); the Laban Party (The People's Power Movement), founded in 1988 by Benigno Aquino, the Democratic Christian Party; the BISIG, socialist movement of Tagalog speakers; the People's Reform Party founded in 1991; the Liberal Party; the right-wing Nationalist Party. The main leftist opposition force is the National Democratic Front (NDF) which includes mass organizations, religious and cultural groups led by the Philippine Communist Party (PKP) and its military wing, the New People's Army (NPA). In the Cordillera region, an NPA splinter group, the Cordillera People's Liberation Army (CPLA) organized the Cordillera Bodong Association (CBA) which demands full autonomy for the north. In the southern Muslim areas, the Moro

National Liberation Front also demands autonomy. Kababaihan Para Sa Inang Bayan (Women for the Motherland), created in 1986, the first party exclusively for women; the Mindanao Alliance, regional.

Social Organizations: Labor is divided between the left-wing Kihusan Mayo Uno (May Day Confederation) and the Trade Union Congress of the Philippines (TUCP), affiliated with AFL-CIO. The Philippines has over 700 voluntary organizations and church groups, gathered in the 'Green Forum'.

THE STATE

Official Name: Republika ñg Pilipinas.

Capital: Metro Manila 9,280,000 people (1995).

Other cities: Quezon City 1,627,900 people; Davao 867,800; Cebu 641,000; Calaocan 629,500; Zamboanga 453,200 (1991).

Government: Presidential republic. Joseph Estrada, President since May 1998. Bicameral Legislative: Chamber of Deputies (Congress) 250 members, 200 elected by general vote, 50 chosen by the President, and a 24-member Senate. Administrative Divisions: 3 regions, 73 provinces.

National Holiday: July 12th, Independence Day (1946).

Armed Forces: 106,500 troops (1995).

Other: 40,500 National Police (Ministry of the Interior), 2,000 Coastguards.

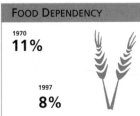
FOREIGN TRADE	
Millions US$	1998
IMPORTS **39,008**	
EXPORTS **36,232**	

has been a Bureau of Muslim Affairs since 1987. Conflict was brewing there, as the 20,000-strong Moro Liberation Front considers that the government has not respected conditions set out in the 1987 Constitution.

[19] In June 1991, the eruption of Mount Pinatubo shook the country, claiming the lives of over 700 Filipinos, flattening entire villages, forcing the evacuation of over 300,000 people, and completely burying the evacuated Clark US airforce base under the ashes.

[20] With its airbase completely unusable, and swamped with difficult negotiations as the contract approached their expiry dates, the US opted to abandon the base of its own accord. On November 26 1991, Clark airbase was formally abandoned. It had employed over 6,000 US military, and over 40,000 Filipinos, most of whom had carried out the menial work. The Aetan people claimed the territory they had been deprived of when the base was installed, and the Philippines Government made plans to build an airport there.

[21] The issue of closing the Subic Bay naval base, with the relocation or loss of around 12,000 personnel, resulted in unease in the Senate because of the economic implications. In October, the Senate voted not to renew the bases' agreement.

[22] The evacuation of Clark base and its relocation on a nearby island outside Filipino sovereignty worried local and international environmental movements. They were concerned that the constant circulation of nuclear weapons may pose a threat to the area.

[23] The forest, which covered 75 per cent of the land in the 1950s, was reduced to 42 per cent by 1990. The effect of natural disasters like typhoon Uring which killed 8,000 in 1991, was magnified by the lack of trees.

[24] Of the 32 million Filipinos entitled to vote, 25 million took part in the May 1992 elections which were considered the calmest and cleanest in the country's history. The winner was Fidel Ramos, former Defense Minister in the Aquino administration. In September, the United States left its naval base at Subic Bay with an infrastructure worth $8 billion. Thousands of rural women who had worked as prostitutes were left unemployed.

[25] In 1993 the Government and Congress tightened their links with Muslim secessionists and the guerrillas in northern Luzon. At the same time, the authorities were charged with torture and 'disappearances'.

[26] In 1994, the Ramos Government had to turn to the opposition's support to control evasion of the 10 per cent VAT tax. This measure won him the IMF's support - including a loan - and enabled a five per cent growth of the GNP. The campaign against crime, now headed by Vice-President Estrada, implicated two per cent of police forces - who were discharged - in criminal activities, while another 5 per cent was kept under investigation. The NPA communist guerrillas lost strength due to an amnesty for its members and to internecine conflicts regarding the amnesty.

[27] In 1995 Imelda Marcos won the elections in the Chamber of Deputies, in spite of being accused of many corruption charges. Swiss banks returned $475 million to the country deposited by Marcos during the dictatorship, but the Government is convinced billions remain in other accounts.

[28] The elimination of restrictions to investments, the reduction in customs barriers and the presence of educated and cheap labor, attracted investors which led to a six-per-cent growth of the GNP. Remittances totaling $2 billion from 4.2 million workers living abroad - mainly housemaids - came into the country in 1995.

[29] In late 1995, there was an unprecedented food crisis, with a 70 per cent increase in rice prices. More than two thirds of the population were estimated to be living below the poverty line. The farmers organizations blamed the government for their incoherent and corrupt agricultural policy, calling for agrarian reform, including the industrialization of rural activity, food self-sufficiency and protection of the environment.

[30] Despite protests from representatives of the Christian Filipinos, who make up the majority of the nation, the Government continued negotiations with the Muslim guerrillas, offering its leaders presence in Congress, the Supreme Court and the cabinet, while incorporating the guerrillas

into the army and police force. The government objective was to pacify the country in order to impose economic reforms and put it in a position to compete with its partners in the Association of Southeast Asian Nations (ASEAN).

[31] On September 30, 1996, the government and the Muslim guerrillas signed a peace agreement. Nur Misuari, leader of the Moro National Liberation Front, became governor of Mindanao, an independent region which covers around a quarter of the national territory. The Christian opposition organized a referendum in 1998 against this agreement. President Ramos also started negotiations with the Communist Party, whose armed wing, the New People's Army, continued to operate in cities and rural towns. In August 1997, Ramos accepted the resignation of his Defense Minister Renato de Villa.

[32] In January 1998, thousands of children from various countries marched through the streets of Manila in protest against exploitative child labor. This sparked a world-wide campaign for better conditions for the world's 250 million working children, employed despite international agreements banning this. 63 per cent of the exploited children are estimated to be living in Asia.

[33] In May, Vice-President Joseph Estrada was elected President with 37 per cent of the votes cast. Buffeted by the Southeast Asian economic crisis, the Government announced it would continue the structural adjustments initiated under the previous administrations at the behest of the World Bank and the IMF. Estrada also ruled out adopting control mechanisms for the national currency or foreign trade.

[34] At the end of that year, the country was listed among the nations that 'concerned' the US because they were considered to be producers of illegal drugs. The Philippines, according to the US report, was a major exporter of marijuana/cannabis.

[35] In 1999, the floods that hit East Asia also affected the Philippines, destroying a large portion of the harvest and displacing thousands from their homes, though the damage was less severe than in China.

[36] Satisfied with the development of the Government's economic programs, in April 2000 President Estrada announced that the year's priority would be to fight corruption in the public administration, primarily targeting bribes and gratuities. To underscore his position, Estrada warned that without exception all officials charged with corruption would face trial. ∎

Pitcairn

Pitcairn

Population: 44 (2000)
Area: 5 SQ KM
Capital: Adamstown
Currency: NZ dollar
Language: English

L ike most of the islands of the region, Pitcairn's first settlers were Polynesians. The first European to visit the island was the English voyager Robert Pitcairn who sailed along its coasts in 1767.

[2] In 1789, part of the crew of HMS Bounty mutinied on their return to Britain from six months in Tahiti. The captain and the rest of the crew were given a small boat and the other men returned to Tahiti. They stayed there a short time and then transferred to Pitcairn Island.

[3] The group, led by Fletcher Christian, was made up of eight crew members, six Tahitian men and twelve women. Ten years later, only one of the mutineers, John Evans, was still alive, with eleven women and 23 children. Purportedly guided by 'apparitions', Adams christened the children and peopled Pitcairn, which later became a British colonial dependency.

[4] The population reached 200 inhabitants in 1937, but decreased in recent times as young islanders emigrated to Aotearoa/New Zealand in search of work.

[5] Pitcairn was under the jurisdiction of the Governor of Fiji between 1952 and 1970. At this time, it became a dependency of the British High Commissioner in Aotearoa, who assumed the functions of a governor, in consultation with the island's Administrative Council.

[6] The island's communications with the outside world were for many years limited to a radio and boats that occasionally anchor off the coast.

[7] Despite the lack of communications, education in the islands was important and primary school was compulsory for all children between the ages of 5 and 15. The sole teacher needed for this is normally appointed for a two-years period and is also responsible for publishing the Pitcairn Miscellany, a four-page bulletin.

[8] The island's Administrative Council is made up of 11 representatives, only 5 of which are chosen from inhabitants over the age of 18 who have lived on the island at least 3 years.

[9] The only national celebration is the Queen's birthday, which is celebrated on the second Saturday in June. The Queen is the Head of State.

[10] The inhabitants work almost exclusively at subsistence fishing and farming. The fertile valleys produce a wide variety of fruit and vegetables, including citrus, sugar cane, watermelons, bananas, potatoes, and beans. However, the island's main source of income is the export of postage stamps for sale to stamp collectors.

[11] The reforestation plan carried out in 1963 increased plantations of the *miro* tree, which provides a kind of wood that can be used for handcrafts.

[12] Since 1987 the Japanese Tuna Fisheries Cooperative Association fleet was allowed to operate within Pitcairn's 200-mile Exclusive Economic Zone.

[13] That same year, the British High Commissioner in Fiji - representing Pitcairn, the UK's last possession in the South Pacific - met representatives of the United States, France, Aotearoa/New Zealand, and six other states of the region, to sign a Regional Convention of the South Pacific for the Protection of the Environment. The aim of this agreement was to put an end to the dumping of nuclear waste in the region.

[14] In 1989, Henderson island, located 68 kilometers northeast of Pitcairn, was listed among the UK property to be preserved as a natural bird reserve. It is home of five unique species. In early 1992, deposits of manganese, iron, copper, zinc, silver and gold were identified in underwater volcanoes within the island's territorial waters.

[15] In 1995, Robert John Alston became the new Governor, replacing David Moss.

[16] The population of Pitcairn has been shrinking in recent years. In January 1998, there were just 30 people, only eight of whom were working. Ten had emigrated the year before.

[17] The survival of the island is dependent on the boats which ship in the necessary goods, as there is no airstrip. The lack of crews for the boats could accelerate depopulation. London aimed to avoid this happening by building an emergency air strip.

[18] The 44 inhabitants of Pitcairn discovered that Britain no longer had any interest in the island in January 2000, when the Crown issued an edict to remove the last subsidies on electricity and the tariffs for unloading provisions, which had allowed the islanders to survive. The population then began to consider the possibility of becoming a French overseas département. ∎

PROFILE

ENVIRONMENT

Four islands of volcanic origin, of which only Pitcairn is inhabited. The others are: Henderson, Ducie and Oeno. The group is located in the eastern extreme of Polynesia, slightly south of the Tropic of Capricorn, east of French Polynesia. The economy is based on subsistence agriculture, fishing, handicrafts, and there are very few export products. The rainy, tropical climate is tempered by sea winds. The islands are subject to typhoons between November and March.

SOCIETY

Peoples: The population consists of descendants of mutineers from HMS Bounty and Polynesian women from Tahiti. **Religion:** Seventh Day Adventist (100 per cent). **Languages:** English (official). **Political Parties:** None.

THE STATE

Official Name: Pitcairn, Henderson, Ducie and Oeno Islands.
Capital: Adamstown. **Government:** Robert John Alston, British High Comissioner in Aotearoa, acting governor of the islands since 1995. Jay Warren, magistrate and president of the Council since 1993. The Council is made up of ten members. In addition to the magistrate who presides over it, one member functions as the Council's secretary. Five members are elected every year and three are named by the Government for a one-year period.

DEMOGRAPHY

Population: 44 (2000)

Poland

Polska

Population: 38,741,000 (1999)
Area: 323,250 SQ KM
Capital: Warsaw (Warzawa)
Currency: Zloty
Language: Polish

The name Poland comes from a Polanian tribe, the Poles, who tilled the soil in the Warta basin region. A region later known as Greater Poland. Their chiefs belonged to the Piast dynasty, descendants of a legendary ancestor, and they lived in the town of Gniezno.

[2] During the 10th century, the Polanians subdued the Kujavians, the Mazovians, the Ledzians, the Pomeranians, the Vistulans, and the Silesians. Mieszko I (960-992) duke of the Piast, founded the first Polish State when he united neighboring tribes under a common state structure. Mieszko was christened in the year 966 establishing the Christian influence in the area.

[3] Poland was a hereditary monarchy until the 12th century. The duke and a group of nobles held power, supported by an army of elite warriors. Free peasants, who constituted the largest and poorest group, were mobilized as they were needed, and paid taxes to support the system.

[4] The greatest dilemma for Poland was what stance to take towards the German Empire and the Pope. As the Empire expanded, Mieszko submitted - in exchange for an acknowledgement of his sovereignty. As compensation, he appealed for Papal protection and in 1,000 AD he founded the first Polish ecclesiastical city state.

[5] From then on, the Roman Catholic Church became a crucial element in the political structure of the Polish State. Poland alternated phases of independence and annexation until the 12th century, when the State began to fragment.

[6] During the feudal period, Poland was subdivided into several duchies, led by the Piasts and some 20 overlords. The nobility and the

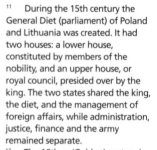

Church became increasingly autonomous as the central power and the dukes lost strength. This was also a period of great demographic growth.

[7] The arrival of German settlers created a new ethnic situation in the country, for up to then the population had been of Slavic stock. From the 13th century, the population of the towns became increasingly German and Jewish. Immigrants brought in their own legal systems, their capital, their crafts and their agricultural skills.

[8] Under the reign of Casimir the Great (1333-70), Poland became a monarchy divided into estates, with the King acting as an arbiter between the nobility, the clergy, the bourgeoisie, and the peasants. The State ceased to be royal property and in 1399 the monarchy became elective.

[9] Through a royal marriage in 1386, Poland joined with Lithuania, and they adopted an organization which respected the differences between the two countries. In 1409, the Teutonic Order attempted to stop Polish-Lithuanian expansion, but it was defeated at Grunwald. The Peace of Torun in 1411, did not end the conflict, and the power of the Order suffered a setback.

[10] In 1466, after a new victory over the Teutons, Poland recovered Pomerania of Gdansk and Malbork, Elblag, and the Land of Chelm; it also gained the territory of Warmia. In recognition of their assistance during the war, Poland granted autonomy to Pomerania and some privileges to the towns. A period of economic prosperity and cultural renaissance began.

[11] During the 15th century the General Diet (parliament) of Poland and Lithuania was created. It had two houses: a lower house, constituted by members of the nobility, and an upper house, or royal council, presided over by the king. The two states shared the king, the diet, and the management of foreign affairs, while administration, justice, finance and the army remained separate.

[12] The 16th or 'Golden' century is also known as the period of the Royal Republic, for the King had to consult the nobles before fixing taxes or declaring war. The reduction of the rights of the bourgeoisie and the peasantry in favor of the nobility and the clergy modified the original monarchy of divided estates.

[13] In 1573, with the end of the Jagiellon dynasty, the Diet approved the free election of the King and guaranteed religious tolerance, which was exceptional in a time when Europe was being shaken by religious wars. King Stephen Bathory (1576-86) gave up his role as arbitrator and the nobility started to elect their own courts.

[14] During the 17th century, international developments were unfavorable for Poland and Lithuania. Sweden fought Poland over the control of the Baltic, and Russia entered into conflict with Lithuania. Turkish and Austrian ambitions in central Europe also exerted pressure on Poland.

[15] On the lower Dnepr, on the border with the Ukraine, free peasants and impoverished nobles became the first Cossacks, warriors who lived by pillaging. In 1648, the Cossacks and the Ukranian peasants started a national revolt. The King made unsuccessful attempts to reach an agreement with the rebels, whose victories weakened the Polish republic.

[16] The Cossacks formed occasional alliances with the Turks and the Russians. In 1654, Russian troops entered Polish territory, and Sweden invaded the rest of the country a year later. King John Casimir fled to Silesia, and Poland was aided by Austria, while the peasants in the provinces organized the first large-scale armed resistance.

[17] The Swedes and the Turks were expelled from the country and the Cossacks were defeated. Russia kept Smolensk and the Ukraine, the left bank of the Dnepr and the city of

WORKERS

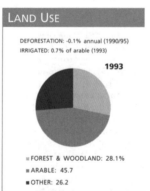

1996
UNEMPLOYMENT: 11.2%

% OF LABOUR FORCE **1998**

■ FEMALE: 46% ■ MALE: 54%

1990

■ SERVICES: 36.7%
■ INDUSTRY: 35.8%
■ AGRICULTURE: 27.5%

LAND USE

DEFORESTATION: -0.1% annual (1990/95)
IRRIGATED: 0.7% of arable (1993)

1993

■ FOREST & WOODLAND: 28.1%
■ ARABLE: 45.7
■ OTHER: 26.2

PUBLIC EXPENDITURE

1997

80 — 71.4%
60
40
20 — 5.6%
0
DEFENCE   SOCIAL

MILITARY EXPENDITURE   **30%**
(% of health & education)   (1990/91)

Kiev. The wars devastated the land, decimated the population and split the republic.

[18] In 1772, Russia, Prussia, and Austria agreed on the territorial partition of Poland. A second partition followed in 1793, after a fresh Russian invasion annulled the 1791 Constitution and put an end to a new Polish attempt to reorganize the State.

[19] A patriotic insurrection was crushed in 1794, and was followed a year later by the third partition of Poland. The Polish State disappeared from the map, but the Polish people retained a sense of national identity.

[20] During the 19th century, the Poles made several attempts to free their homeland. National conscience and Catholicism, both under persecution, became stronger. New political parties appeared: a peasants', a workers', and a national party, and resistance was expressed through culture.

[21] The consolidation of the Russian revolution in 1917 brought Poland the support of Western powers. In 1918 a provisional government was created, led by Jozef Pilsudski. It established an eight-hour working day and equal rights for men and women.

[22] Boundaries could not be moved back, as a sense of national identity had emerged in the Ukraine, Lithuania and Belarus. The creation of a federation failed as a result of the counter-offensive by the Soviet army. The Peace of Riga, signed in 1921, guaranteed the independence of the Baltic states and fixed the eastern border of Poland at Zbrucz.

[23] The 1921 Constitution adopted a parliamentary system. During the years that followed, there was a series of coalition governments, generally between the National and Social Christian parties, which were both conservative, or the Peasants' party, which was moderate.

[24] Political instability, a tariff war against Germany, unemployment and social unrest benefited the Communist Party, which had been banned in 1923. Its main military leader, Jozef Pilsudski, staged a coup in 1926 but the ensuing prosperity was ended by the effects of the 1929 Wall Street crash.

[25] The growing power of Germany and the USSR became a threat to Poland, and Britain and France only gave the country formal support. In a secret agreement, the USSR and Germany divided the Polish territory once more. On September 1 1939, Germany invaded Poland.

[26] Britain and France declared war on Germany. On September 17, the USSR also invaded Poland. In the occupied territories millions of Poles died, especially Jews, some of whom were taken to German concentration camps. Many others starved or were executed.

[27] The Polish government-in-exile led the resistance. A military contingent fought on the western front, while the Home Army carried out subversive actions. After the German invasion, the USSR accepted the creation of a Polish army under its jurisdiction.

[28] The Soviet counter-offensive modified relations with Poland. The government-in-exile demanded an inquiry into the murders of Polish officers, and the USSR broke diplomatic relations. The Red Army invaded Poland and re-established military occupation.

[29] After the defeat of Germany, the allies gathered at Malta and agreed on a Provisional Polish Government of National Unity (made up by representatives from pro-Soviet and exiled groups) which was to call elections. The Government was dominated by the Polish Workers' Party.

[30] In 1945 the provisional government and the USSR signed an agreement establishing the Polish eastern border, along the Curso line. The same year, the allies fixed the eastern border along the Oder-Neisse line of Lusetia.

[31] The Polish Workers' Party and the Socialist Party of Poland constituted the Polish United Workers' Party (PUWP). The Polish Peasants' Party disintegrated, and elections were postponed.

[32] The PUWP governed the country, modeling itself on the Soviet Communist Party (CPSU) in the USSR. Industry and commerce were nationalized, the State built great steel and metal works, and forcibly collectivized agriculture. Women were incorporated into the workforce.

[33] The denunciation of Stalin's crimes during the 20th Congress of the CPSU in 1956 had repercussions on the PUWP. In November of that year Wladyslaw Gomulka was elected party first secretary and promised to take a 'Polish path towards socialism'. Gomulka freed Cardinal Stefan Wyszynski, who was the head of the Catholic Church, and stirred up popular expectations.

[34] In 1968, action taken by an anti-Semitic group within the PUWP forced Jewish groups to leave the country. In a treaty signed in 1970, West Germany recognized the Polish borders established after the War. East Germany had done so in 1950.

[35] In 1970, strikes broke out because of a huge increase in prices. The Government ordered the army to open fire on the workers and started another crisis within the PUWP. Gomulka was replaced by Edward Gierek, but the regime underwent renewed crises over corruption charges and internal fights within the party.

[36] In 1976, new strikes broke out, and this time they were repressed not by the use of firearms but by long prison sentences. In 1979, the Polish Pope John Paul II visited his native land, rekindling the hopes of the population who welcomed him at massive gatherings.

[37] The 1980 strike at Gdansk's Lenin Dockyard was led by trade unionist Lech Walesa. It turned into a general strike and the Government had to negotiate with the strikers. Two months later, the Government was forced to recognize Solidarity, a workers'

PROFILE

ENVIRONMENT

On the extensive northern plains, crossed by the Vistula (Wisla), Warta and Oder (Odra) rivers, there are coniferous woodlands, rye, potato and linen plantations. The fertile soil of Central Poland's plains and highlands yield a considerable agricultural production of beet and cereals. The southern region, on the northern slopes of the Carpathian Mountains, is less fertile. Poland has large mineral resources: coal in Silesia (the world's fourth largest producer); sulfur in Tarnobrzeskie (the world's second largest producer); copper; zinc and lead. Major industries are steel, chemicals and shipbuilding. The country has high levels of air pollution; due to its geographical location in the center of Europe, it absorbs polluted water and air 'in transit' from other countries. Soil depletion has caused extensive erosion, due to the excessive deforestation that has accompanied intensive agriculture.

SOCIETY

Peoples: Polish, 98.7 per cent; Ukrainian, 0.6 per cent; other (Belarusian, German), 0.7 per cent.
Religions: Catholic, 90.7 per cent; Orthodox, 1.4 per cent. Other (7.9 per cent).
Languages: Polish.
Political Parties: Solidarity Electoral Action (SEA); Polish Peasant Party (PPP); Democratic Left Alliance (DLA); Work Union; Reform Support Block; Movement for the Reconstruction of Poland (MRP).
Social Organizations: Central Council of Trade Unions; Central Union of Agricultural Groups; Solidarity.

THE STATE

Official Name: Polska Rzeczpospolita.
Administrative Divisions: 49 provinces.
Capital: Warsaw (Warzawa) 2,120,000 people (est 1996).
Other cities: Lódz 825,000 people; Kraków 745,000; Wroclaw 643,600; Poznan 589,700 (1996).
Government: Aleksander Kwasniewski, Head of State and President since 1995. Jerzy Buzec, Prime Minister since 1997. Legislature, bicameral: Senate and *Sejm*, whose members are elected every four years.
National Holiday: July 22.
Armed Forces: 248,600 (1996).
Other: 23,400 Border Guard, Police, Coast Guard.

EXTERNAL DEBT

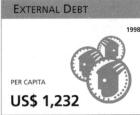

1998

PER CAPITA

US$ 1,232

FOREIGN TRADE

Millions US$ 1997

IMPORTS

42,931

EXPORTS

36,718

union with 10 million members. Rural Solidarity was created, to represent three million peasants.

[38] The PUWP suffered other crises that led to the appointment of Wojciech Jaruzelski, then prime minister, to the post of party first secretary. In December 1981, Jaruzelski declared martial law, Solidarity was banned and its leaders went underground.

[39] Martial law was lifted in 1983, but the Constitution was modified to include a state of emergency. With the Catholic Church acting as a mediator, government and Solidarity representatives went back to negotiations in 1989, while the USSR was embarking on *perestroika* (restructuring).

[40] In the elections in June of that year, the PUWP only obtained the fixed number of representatives that had been agreed on during the negotiations with the opposition. Solidarity rejected General Jaruzelski's proposal to share government with the PUWP. Tadensz Mazowiecki, a journalist and a moderate member of Solidarity, was appointed the first president of a non-communist government in the East European bloc.

[41] Poland re-established diplomatic relations with the Vatican and with Israel. The United States and Germany committed themselves to financial assistance. German reunification caused some alarm, but the Four-Plus-Two negotiations (see Germany) ratified the postwar Polish borders.

[42] In December 1989, the National Assembly approved reinstating the name, the Republic of Poland. In January 1990, the PUWP was dissolved to create another party, but it later split into the Social Democracy of the Republic of Poland and the Polish Social Democratic Union.

[43] In January 1990, the Government started an economic adjustment program agreed with the International Monetary Fund. Poland requested its incorporation to the Council of Europe and established relations with the European Economic Community. The US and the Council of Europe made entry to NATO (the North Atlantic Treaty Organization) dependent on the results of the economic reforms under way and the upgrading of the military warfare to the Alliance's standards.

[44] On May 10 1990, the first strike was held against Mazowiecki's government. This exercise of power hastened the fragmentation of Solidarity. The union became a political party in July 1990, and later divided into several factions.

[45] In December 1990, the first direct presidential elections were held, and Lech Walesa was elected head of state with 75 per cent of the vote. In August 1991, new prime minister Jan Krysztof Bielecki resigned, upsetting the precarious balance of political transition. The former Communist Party and a small peasant party were ready to accept his resignation, but Walesa backed the prime minister and insisted on giving him special powers, by threatening to dissolve the Diet.

[46] In December 1991, the new Diet appointed Jan Olszewski as Prime Minister. He was accepted by President Walesa three days later, but the cabinet was not ratified by the Diet until December 23, and then only by a narrow margin of 17 votes.

[47] As of November 1991, Poland has been the twenty-sixth member country of the European Council, a Western European organization which also includes Turkey, the Czech Republic, and Hungary.

[48] At the end of May, President Walesa asked the *Sjem* (lower house) to form a new Government because of a lack of confidence in Olszewski. In mid-July Parliament accepted Walesa's proposal and appointed Hanna Suchocka Prime Minister, supported by a 7 party coalition.

[49] Suchocka applied strict monetary controls and promoted the privatization of approximately 600 state enterprises with a privatization act in August 1992. Meanwhile, in February 1993 Walesa, under pressure from the Church, made the controversial decision to revoke the law which instituted the right to abortion.

[50] Dissatisfied with Suchocka's social policies, Solidarity sponsored a motion censuring the Government, finally passed by a single-vote majority, forcing the Prime Minister to call early legislative elections.

[51] Elections were held in September and led to the return to power of those political sectors which had supported the communist regime: the Democratic Left Alliance (SLD) and the Polish Peasants' Party (PSL), winning 73 of the 100 seats.

[52] Initially refusing to acknowledge the defeat, Walesa appointed PSL leader Waldemar Pawlack as Prime Minister. Although 1994 featured constant conflicts between the President and the Government, the latter did not significantly modify the economic liberalization policy, despite its attempt to slow the pace of some reforms in order to reduce their social impact.

[53] The former communists' return to power was concluded in November 1995 when Aleksander Kwasniewski defeated Walesa in the second round of presidential elections, with 52 per cent of the vote. The outgoing president had based his election campaign on anti-communism and the support of 'Christian values', insisting on the need to maintain the ban on abortion.

[54] At first, the government of Prime Minister Josef Olesky, who replaced Pawlak, was not altered. However in January 1996, Olesky (former Communist), was forced to resign after the Interior Minister accused him of having been a collaborator with the Soviet KGB. The following month, Olesky was replaced by Wlodzimierz Cimoszweicz.

[55] Right-wing factions of several parties, united by the notion of a conservative social policy and anti-communism, formed a coalition headed by Marian Krzaklewski, called Solidarity Electoral Action (SEA).

[56] In the 1997 parliamentary elections, the SEA defeated the ruling Democratic Left Alliance, with 33.8 per cent of the vote. Jerzy Buzek, a chemical engineer from Silesia, who designed the SEA's economic program, was named Prime Minister.

[57] Poland's entry to NATO was agreed upon in February 1999 by an overwhelming 409 to 7 at the *Sjem*.

[58] Economic reforms carried out by the government to prepare the nation for EU entry left thousands of people out of work and were extremely unpopular. In September, more than 30,000 farmers and workers held a protest march in Warsaw, accusing Buzek of ignoring the economic problems of the country and calling for elections to be brought forward.

[59] Despite Buzek declaring the country had met all the requirements and was ready to enter the EU in April 2000, the ratification process implied that Poland would have difficulty in getting full membership of the community before 2003. ∎

STATISTICS

DEMOGRAPHY

Population: 38,741,000 (1999)
Annual growth: 0.6 % (1975/97)
Estimates for year 2015 (million): 39.3 (1999)
Annual growth to year 2015: 0.1 % (1997/2015)
Urban population: 64.4 % (1997)
Urban Growth: 1.2 % (1980/95)
Children per woman: 1.5 (1998)

HEALTH

Life expectancy at birth: 73 years (1998)
male: 68 years (1998)
female: 77 years (1998)
Maternal mortality: 8 per 100,000 live births (1990-98)
Infant mortality: 10 per 1,000 (1998)
Under-5 child mortality: 11 per 1,000 (1998)
Daily calorie supply: 3,344 per capita (1996)

EDUCATION

Literacy: 100 % (1995)
male: 100 % (1995)
female: 100 % (1995)
School enrolment:
Primary total: 96 % (1990/96)
male: 97 % (1990/97)
female: 95 % (1990/97)
Secondary:
male: 98 % (1990/96)
female: 97 % (1990/96)
Tertiary: 24 % (1996)
Primary school teachers: one for every 15 (1995)

COMMUNICATIONS

113 newspapers (1996), 523 radios (1997), 418 TV sets (1996) and 169 main telephone lines (1996) per 1,000 people
Books: 28 new titles per 100,000 people (1992/94)

ECONOMY

Per capita, GNP: $ 3,910 (1998)
Annual growth, GNP: 4.4 % (1998)
Annual inflation: 26.9 % (1990/98)
Consumer price index: 155.6 (1998)
Currency: 3.5 zlotych = $ 1 (1998)
Cereal imports: 1,405,168 metric tons (1998)
Food import dependency: 8 % (1997)
Fertilizer use: 1,141 kg per ha (1997)
Exports: $ 36,718 million (1997)
Imports: $ 42,931 million (1997)
External debt: $ 47,708 million (1998); $ 1,232 per capita (1998)
Debt service: 9.7 % of exports (1998)
Development aid received: $ 641 million (1997); $ 16.8 per capita (1997); 0.50 % of GNP (1997)

ENERGY

Consumption: 2,721.0 Kgs of Oil equivalent per capita yearly (1997); 4.0 % imported (1997)

HDI (rank/value): 44/0.802 (1997)

Portugal

Portugal

Population: 9,873,000 (1999)
Area: 92,390 SQ KM
Capital: Lisbon
Currency: Escudo
Language: Portuguese

In ancient times Portugal was inhabited by Lusitanians, an Iberian people whose cultural influence extended over a vast area including the whole western shore of the Iberian Peninsula. This area was successively conquered by several Middle Eastern peoples, who only occupied the coastal areas.

2   During the 2nd century BC the Romans settled in the territory, ruling over it until the fall of the Empire around the 5th century AD. Like the rest of Europe, Portugal was invaded by Northern European peoples (generically called Barbarians), who raided the Roman dominions. Among these peoples were the Visigoths. They had a developed culture and settled on the Iberian Peninsula dividing the territory into various kingdoms, and spreading the Christian faith. Their domination over the whole region lasted for nearly six centuries.

3   In the 8th century AD Arab peoples invaded the region imposing their political and cultural domination in spite of resistance from the earlier inhabitants.

4   During the 11th century the reconquest of the Lusitanian territory started, ending with the expulsion of the Arabs a hundred years later. With Muslim domination over, the territory was politically unified and Portugal entered a period of great economic prosperity. This reached its height during the 15th and 16th centuries, with great maritime expeditions and conquests of vast territories in America, Africa, and the Far East.

5   Its maritime superiority enabled Portugal to develop

active worldwide trade and achieve a privileged economic position within Europe. A long time elapsed before other nations like Britain and the Netherlands were in a position to threaten Portugal's naval supremacy.

6   Following a series of dynastic stuggles, in 1580 the country was made subject to Philip II, King of Spain. The two kingdoms remained united until 1688 when Portugal succeeded in having its independence recognized in the Treaty of Lisbon. Unity with Spain brought the decline of Portugal's

power. Most of the maritime empire collapsed, besieged by the British and the Dutch, who started to control most of the trading routes and outposts.

7   By the time Portugal recovered its independence, it had been devastated by three decades of war against Spain. The country was forced to look on while the new maritime powers seized most of its colonies in Africa and Asia. Brazil remained under Portuguese rule. The position of Britain as the leading maritime power became painfully obvious when Portugal was forced to sign the Treaty of Methuen, which established Portugal's political and economic dependence on the British. Pombal, an adviser of Jose I, carried out economic reforms. Like the Spanish Bourbons, Pombal had been influenced by the ideas of the French

Enlightenment and he changed colonial management. The discovery and exploitation of gold mines in Brazil enabled the country to enjoy a period of great economic prosperity. But in spite of Pombal, Portugal finally went into decline.

8   Dependence on Britain was further consolidated when Portugal was forced to seek support to end Napoleonic occupation, which lasted from 1807 to 1811. French domination led to the independence of Brazil; the Portuguese court had fled there in exile. Brazil had enjoyed a significant expansion in trade, in particular with Britain. At the end of the Napoleonic period in Europe, the rising Brazilian bourgeoisie was not ready to be displaced, so in 1821 Brazil declared independence. Meanwhile a civil war broke out in Portugal between those who wanted the restoration of absolutism and liberal groups preferring greater political participation.

9   The economy maintained its traditional agrarian structure. Other countries were embarking on an accelerated industrialization process which would quickly give them economic eminence. Portugal reached the end of the 19th century economically stagnant, deprived of the richest and largest part of its colonial empire, and suffering from acute internal political crisis.

10   The monarchy was incapable of ensuring the stability needed to start economic recovery, and was definitively overthrown by liberal opposition forces in 1910. This started the Republican period. Once they had attained their objective, the alliance of Liberal and Republican groups started to fragment and internal differences prevented them from achieving a common governmental agenda. One of the few things they shared was active opposition to the Church, which had been a traditional ally of the *ancien regime* and had had important privileges and powers, including the control of education. The inefficiency of the Liberals, together with the ruthless persecution of representatives of the *ancien regime*, encouraged the

WORKERS

1996
UNEMPLOYMENT: 7.5%

% OF LABOUR FORCE   **1998**

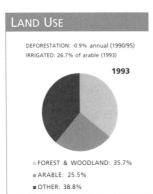

■ FEMALE: 44%   ■ MALE: 56%
1990

■ SERVICES: 48.2%
■ INDUSTRY: 34.0%
■ AGRICULTURE: 17.8%

LAND USE

DEFORESTATION: -0.9% annual (1990/95)
IRRIGATED: 26.7% of arable (1993)

1993

▨ FOREST & WOODLAND: 35.7%
▨ ARABLE: 25.5%
■ OTHER: 38.8%

PUBLIC EXPENDITURE

DEFENCE EXPENDITURE (% of goverment exp.)	**5.9%** (1997)	
MILITARY EXPENDITURE (% of health & education)	**32%** (1990/91)	

MATERNAL MORTALITY

1990-98

Per 100,000
live births

8

LITERACY

1995

90%

FOREIGN TRADE

Millions US$ 1997

IMPORTS

40,642

EXPORTS

31,828

formation of a vast opposition movement.

[11] Portugal sided with Britain in World War I. This only deepened the economic crisis and increased popular discontent. Political instability and economic stagnation were the most salient features of the period. In 1926 this led to a coup bringing a right-wing military group to power. They set up an authoritarian corporatist regime which they called the 'New State'. With a few changes, it was to rule the country for over 40 years. Political opposition was proscribed, with major figures imprisoned or exiled. Trade unions were dissolved and replaced by corporatist organizations similar to those in fascist Italy.

[12] The most significant figure of this period and the true ruler behind the military was economist Antonio de Oliveira Salazar, who occupied various positions and dominated Portuguese political and economic life. The country remained neutral during the Spanish Civil War and World War II which could both have jeopardized its barely stable economy.

[13] The agricultural system remained unchanged throughout the whole period, causing much migration towards the major cities of Portugal and Europe. During the 1950s the decolonization movement started, and the country was faced with the possibility of losing its last dominions in Africa. From that moment on, Salazar's regime fought against the liberation movements emerging in the Portuguese colonies, becoming increasingly isolated from other countries and unpopular at home.

[14] The human and economic cost of these colonial wars accelerated the internal attrition of Salazar's government. Repressive measures had to be increased to halt the growing opposition. Salazar's death in 1970 and the deepening of the economic crisis showed that the end of the regime was close at hand.

[15] In 1974, amidst the opposition of many social groups and political parties, a significant number of dissatisfied army officers gathered under the Armed Forces Movement (Movimento das Forças Armadas-MFA). In April, they staged a coup intending to end the wars in Africa and start the democratization process.

[16] The military government which emerged from the Revolution of the Carnations or Captains' Revolution had vast popular support. This support came out as active encouragement of the progressive tendencies within the MFA. The new government quickly decolonized Angola, Mozambique, and Guinea-Bissau. Meanwhile it actively sought international recognition and attempted to improve the country's image abroad. It legalized left-wing political parties, decreed an amnesty for political prisoners and passed a series of land laws aiming at breaking up large rural estates and modernizing agricultural production.

[17] The Socialist and Communist parties were the main supporters of the new regime, but after a year in office, their alliance began to break up. This slowed the democratization of the country, started in April 1974. In the 1976 general elections, the Socialist Party led by Mario Soares won the majority vote to become Portugal's first democratic constitutional government in the 20th century.

[18] The continuing economic crisis, together with strong political and trade union opposition, wore the Socialist Government down very quickly. This situation was aggravated by Soares' harsh economic adjustment program.

[19] During the 1980s the transition process continued. The electorate approved a new constitution and eliminated all the special bodies created under military rule. Portugal's foreign policy changed, and the country underwent speedy economic and political integration with Europe, including incorporation in NATO and the EEC, in 1986. That year, the Socialist Party lost power again, this time to its one-time ally the center-left Social Democratic Party (PSD).

[20] By the end of the 1980s Portugal was experiencing significant economic growth, but still far below the average level for the rest of Europe. Changes accelerated after the electoral victory of the PSD, which used its ample parliamentary majority to liberalize the economy. The new economic policy received strong opposition, particularly from the workers in the public sector, who make up 5 per cent of the country's active labor force and who saw the PSD's reforms as a threat to their jobs.

[21] The trade union movement brought the country to a complete or partial standstill on several occasions. It opposed the privatization of public companies, the elimination of labor legislation enacted during the 1974 revolution, and the attempt to repeal the 1974 land reform legislation. In 1984 an

PROFILE

ENVIRONMENT

The country includes the Iberian continental territory and the islands of the Azores and Madeira archipelagos. The Tagus, the country's largest river, divides the continental region into two separate areas. The northern region is mountainous, with abundant rains and intensive agriculture: wheat, corn, vines and olives are grown. In the valley of the Douro, the major wine-growing region in the country, large vineyards extend in terraces along the valley slopes. The city of Oporto is the northern economic center. The South, Alentejo, with extensive low plateaus and a very dry climate, has large wheat and olive plantations and sheep farming. The cork tree woods, which made Portugal a great cork producer, are found here. Fishing and shipbuilding are major contributors to the country's economy. Mineral resources include pyrite, tungsten, coal and iron. The effects of erosion are accentuated by the poor quality of the soil. Air pollution levels are significant in urban areas, or near cellulose and cement factories.

SOCIETY

Peoples: The Portuguese (99.5 per cent) came from the integration of various ethnic groups: Celts, Arabs, Berbers, Phoenicians, Carthaginians and others. Immigrants come from Africa (0.2 per cent) and America (Brazilians 0.1 per cent, US Americans 0.1 per cent). There is a great migration of Portuguese towards richer countries in the continent.
Religions: Mainly Catholic. **Language**: Portuguese.
Political Parties: The center-right Social Democratic Party (PSD); the center-left Socialist Party (PS); the Communist Party; the Social Democratic Centre Party, affiliated to the European Union of Christian Democrats. Other minor parties: the right Popular Party; the National Solidarity Party, the Revolutionary Socialist Party, the Greens, the People's Monarchist Party; and the Democratic Renewal Party.
Social Organizations: The General Confederation of Portuguese Workers (CGTP), a nationwide multi-union organization with 287 union members (represents 80 per cent of the organized workers); the General Union of Portuguese Workers (UGTP), which combines 50 unions.

THE STATE

Official Name: República Portuguesa.
Administrative Divisions: 18 districts, 2 autonomous regions.
Capital: Lisbon 2,400,000 people (1997).
Other cities: Oporto 309,500 people; Vila Nova de Gaia 247,500; Amadora 176,100 (1991). **Government**: Jorge Sampaio, President of the Republic since March 1996. Antonio Guterres, Prime Minister since 1995. Legislative power is exercised by a unicameral Assembly, made up of 230 members elected for 4-year terms, through universal suffrage.
National holiday: April 25, Liberty Day. December 1, Restoration of Independence.
Armed Forces: 54,200 (1995). Other: 20,900 Republican National Guard; 20,000 Public Security Police; 8,900 Border Security Guard.

extreme left-wing group, called the Popular Forces of April 25 (FP-25), also started to take action against these measures. The group, which had been very active in recent years, demanded that the parties in power respect the achievements of the 'Revolution of the Carnations'.

[22] In April 1987, the governments of Portugal and the People's Republic of China signed an agreement charging Portugal with the administration of Macau until 1999. Sovereignty is then transferred to China, under the 'one country, two systems' principle (see Macau).

[23] In 1988, after over a month of negotiations, the PSD and the Socialist Party agreed to modify the constitution to allow the re-privatization of various companies nationalized during the 'Revolution of the Carnations' and to further reduce presidential powers. President Mario Soares, former leader of the Socialist Party, opposed these reforms.

[24] Portuguese politics became polarized between the ruling PSD and the PS. The latter was a more viable left-wing alternative after the collapse of real socialism. However, in the October 1991 parliamentary elections, the PSD won over 50 per cent of the vote while the PS did not reach 30 per cent. Cavaco Silva's political victory was due to the social democratic slant with which he disguised his orthodox liberal economic orientation. The right-wing Social Democratic Centre Party received a mere four per cent which led its leader Diego Freitas do Amaral to resign. Support for the Communist Party dropped 3 per cent since 1987.

[25] In January 1992, Portugal took over the presidency of the European Community. The new President, Luis Mira de Amaral, Portuguese minister of industry and energy, announced he would promote industrial cooperation with Latin America, Africa and central Europe. Another of his priorities was the signing of the Maastricht Treaty which entailed political, economic and monetary union between the members of the Community.

[26] In August 1993, the Assembly restricted the right to seek asylum and enabled the

expulsion of foreigners from the country. The legislation was based on the defence of the job market and was opposed by President Soares. Unemployment reached eight per cent but it was set to increase with the privatization or closing of state-run airlines, shipyards and steel industries.

[27] Meanwhile a plan financed by the European Union was approved for the 1993-1997 period for the poorest members, including Portugal, providing investment in education, transport, industrial reconversion and job creation.

[28] Portugal's population was 10 million in 1993, with 4 million workers abroad.

[29] Portuguese politics were rocked by intense student protests against the cost and quality of education, and by strikes for higher wages in the public sector. The 50-per-cent increase in the toll charged at Lisbon's access bridge caused several blockades by transport workers. The Government justified the raise citing the need to finance a new bridge for the last World Expo of the century, held in 1998.

[30] The equilibrium between socialist President Mario Soares and centre-right Prime Minister Cavaco Silva was broken. Soares denounced the excessive power of the Prime Minister and warned of the dangers of a 'dictatorship of the majority'. Prior to the elections, the PSD privatized 28 per cent of Portugal Telecom and 40 per cent of Portucel Industrial.

[31] The October 1995 general elections were won by the Socialist Party which gained an absolute majority at the Assembly. Antonio Guterres was appointed Prime Minister, replacing Anibal Cavaco. After 10 years of PSD dominance, oriented toward European integration and economic liberalism, the PS capitalized on domestic discontent with education and health and assured the financial market it would not interfere with the goals regarding monetary union and privatization.

[32] The Socialist Jorge Sampaio took over the presidency of the country in March 1996, after winning the elections with 54 per

cent of the vote, against the 46 per cent of former Prime Minister Cavaco Silva. The Government brought in an economic plan in line with European Union demands, particularly regarding to the budget deficit.

[33] A successful campaign against tax evasion meant increased spending on health, education and social policies. The privatization program was intensified, selling shares in telecommunications, electricity and roads. Unemployment fell to 6.7 per cent of the active population.

[34] The Socialist Party triumphed in the December 1997 municipal elections, maintaining control over the main cities, Lisbon and Oporto, and beating the conservative Social Democratic Party by an overall margin of five points (38.2 to 33.1 per cent).

[35] In February 1998, Parliament approved a law legalizing abortion up to 10 weeks of pregnancy. Various estimates showed there were around 16,000 illegal abortions carried out each year.

[36] After 442 years' rule, Portugal handed Macao over to China on December 20 1999. President Sampaio was present at the ceremony, along with his Chinese counterpart Jiang Zemin. This act signified the end of the Portuguese empire, as well as the end of all European control in Asia. Portugal, which had been the first European power to control Asian territories, was also the last to withdraw.

[37] Sampaio visited Xanana Gusmão, East Timor's pro-independence leader, in February 2000 and promised to help the Timorese to restore their education system. This was the first visit of a Portuguese head of state since Portugal pulled out of Timor in 1974.

[38] Prime Minister Antonio Guterres took over as President of the European Union until July 2000. His leadership led the EU to impose diplomatic isolation on Austria when the fascist-sympathising Liberty Party, led by Jörg Haider, joined the Austrian governing coalition. ∎

Puerto Rico

Puerto Rico

Population: 3,839,000 (1999)
Area: 8,900 SQ KM
Capital: San Juan
Currency: US dollar
Language: Spanish and English

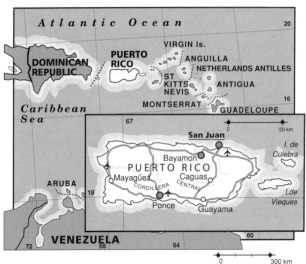

In 1508, fifteen years after Christopher Columbus had arrived on the Caribbean island of Borinquen (now Puerto Rico), that territory came under colonial domination, a status which remains unchanged to this day. Due to its strategic location at the entrance of the Caribbean - Puerto Rico is the easternmost of the Greater Antilles - the island suffered 400 years of Spanish rule, as it also reeled under repeated attacks of pirates and regular naval forces, whether British, Dutch or French, plus US administration after the Spanish-American War of 1898.

2 In the first few decades of the 16th century, a sugar-based economy began to take shape. In some estimates, by 1560 there were already 15,000 slaves on the island. This was however a short-lived period in the island's history; in the latter part of the century leather became the principal product.

3 As in neighboring islands, the local Taino people were exterminated by war, disease and overwork. African slaves were brought in to take their place in the fields where most food supplies for Spanish expeditions into the mainland were produced. Thus, Puerto Rican culture became a blend of its African and Spanish heritage.

4 Spanish rule was continually challenged by external attacks and rebellions by both the Tainos and enslaved African workers. The latter rebelled successively in 1822, 1826, 1843, and 1848. The struggle for independence in the rest of Latin America had its counterpart in Puerto Rico's struggle for administrative reform (1812-1840), but Spanish troops ruthlessly stifled the uprising.

5 In 1868, five years before slavery was finally abolished, a group of patriots led by Ramón Emeterio Betances moved things a step nearer to liberation. In the town of Lares they proclaimed Puerto Rico's independence and took up arms to free the island. Despite their defeat, the Lares revolt signalled the birth of the Puerto Rican nation.

6 The independence movement continued to gain strength in the following years. The Cubans were already up in arms in 1897, led by José Martí in a movement that reached Puerto Rico. US military intervention in the war against Spain, in 1898, hastened European defeat but for Puerto Rico it only meant the imposition of a new ruler.

7 US colonial administrations, first military and then civilian, imposed English as the official language and attempted to turn the island into a sugar plantation and a military base. Puerto Ricans were made US citizens in 1917, though they were given no participation in the island's government. As a result, resistance to colonial rule grew. In 1922 the pro-independence Nationalist Party (PN) was founded. PN-led uprisings in 1930 and 1950 were fiercely put down.

8 The PN leader from 1930 until his death in 1965 was Pedro Albizu Campos, who suffered exile and imprisonment for his anticolonial activities.

9 In 1947, intense internal and international pressure forced the US to allow Puerto Rico to elect its own governor. The 1948 elections gave the post to Luis Muñoz Marín, leader of the Popular Democratic Party (PPD), who favored turning the country into a self-governing, commonwealth, or free associated state. The US Government authorized the drafting of a constitution in 1959, which was approved by a plebiscite and later ratified by the US. Muñoz Marín's program was thus sanctioned.

10 Commonwealth status, still in effect today, leaves defence, financial affairs and foreign relations to Washington, while maintaining common citizenship and currency, as well as free access to the US for Puerto Ricans and vice versa.

11 With the institution of Commonwealth status, US administrations were freed from the obligation of reporting on Puerto Rico's status to the UN Decolonization Committee. Moreover, in this way the UN tacitly endorsed the arrangement declaring the 'end' of colonial rule. Nevertheless in September 1978 the Decolonization Committee reconsidered the situation. In December that year a UN General Assembly resolution once again defined Puerto Rico as a colony and demanded self-determination for its people.

12 Earlier, during World War II, Puerto Rico had again been turned into a military garrison for controlling the Caribbean. The US built seven bases on the island. After an act of Congress of 1950 and adoption of the constitution of 1952, the island was named 'Commonwealth of Puerto Rico', with status of Free Associate State.

13 Muñoz Marín promoted industrialization on the island, through massive US private investment enticed by government tax incentives. During the 1960s, Puerto Rican agriculture was destroyed by an influx of US products, resulting in over 50 per cent of the island's food being imported. The newly-formed labor reserve was more than enough to supply cheap hands for the growing US corporate community, and Puerto Ricans soon began migrating en masse to the US, and especially to New York in search of work. The 1980 US census registered over two million Puerto Ricans living in the United States.

14 With the great social upheavals of the 1960s, the struggle for independence flowered anew on the island. Despite the revival of the independence movement, a 1967 plebiscite confirmed the Commonwealth. Moreover, elections the following year gave the governorship to the New Progressive Party (PNP) which favored making the island the 51st state of the US. Nevertheless after the 1972 elections the PPD returned to power led by Rafael Hernández Colón. In 1976, supporters of the US statehood option returned to the governorship. Carlos Romero Barceló announced that if he was re-elected for a second term, he would call a pro-statehood referendum. Barceló went on to win in 1980, but by such a slim margin that plans for a statehood plebiscite were abandoned, despite encouragement from President Reagan.

15 Puerto Rico has one representative in the US Congress, but with no voting rights other than in committees. US citizenship only gave Puerto Ricans the right to participate in the 1980 presidential elections, although residents in the US are able to vote in all elections.

16 Rafael Hernández Colón was elected President on November 6 1984. He promised a 'four-year term of struggle

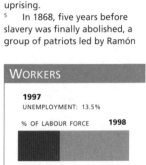

WORKERS

1997
UNEMPLOYMENT: 13.5%

% OF LABOUR FORCE **1998**

■ FEMALE: 26%   ■ MALE: 74%

against corruption and unemployment'. He renewed Puerto Rico's Commonwealth status thus rejecting his predecessor's intention to integrate into the Union.

[17] Hernández Colón was re-elected in November 1988, with 48.7 per cent of the vote, against 45.8 per cent for those in favor of annexation by the United States, and 5.3 per cent for those who favored independence.

[18] In 1989 the Special United Nations Decolonization Committee expressed its wish that the people of Puerto Rico exercise their right to self-determination and independence. The resolution stressed the 'clearly Latin American character and identity of Puerto Rico's people and culture'.

[19] In April 1991, Governor Hernández Colón passed a law granting official status for the Spanish language. A few weeks later, the Puerto Rican people were granted the Prince of Asturias award by the Spanish crown, 'in recognition of the country's efforts to defend the Spanish language'.

[20] In the plebiscite carried out late in 1991, various strategies were proposed to promote development on the island. The governor succeeded in rallying moderate nationalists and supporters of independence, who campaigned together. They were in favor of self-determination, the end of subjection to US jurisdiction, the affirmation of Puerto Rican identity, regardless of any future referendum decisions, and the maintenance of US citizenship. However, all this effort came to nothing in the polls, when 55 per cent of the voters supported the PNP's position that a break with Washington had to be avoided.

[21] Given this result, Hernández's position within his party was weakened, strengthening the hand of more pro-independence sectors and Hernández finally resigned the Popular Democratic Party leadership.

[22] Pedro Rosselló, a supporter of Puerto Rico's integration into the United States, was elected governor in 1992. His plan to make English the only official language on the island - replacing Spanish - caused massive protest demonstrations. Finally in 1993 English was made an official language alongside Spanish.

[23] In November, a referendum was held to decide on the political future of the island. Those wanting to maintain the 'free associated state' status won a narrow victory, with 48.4 per cent of the vote, while the group supporting the transformation of Puerto Rico into the 51st US state took 46.2 per cent. Independence supporters had a mere 4 per cent.

[24] Some pro-independence supporters had agreed to collaborate - in sectors like culture - with the 'pro-annexation' cabinet led by the present governor. However, when Rosselló sacked the director of the Puerto Rico Institute of Culture, Awilda Palau, in May 1995, the possibilities of collaboration were reduced.

[25] In 1996, opposition continued to the US Congress decision to grant tax exemptions to companies established in Puerto Rico, as this was the main fiscal instrument for development on the island. ∎

[26] In January 1997, Rosselló was elected for a second term. In a message for the occasion, US President Bill Clinton promised to promote legislation in Congress allowing Puerto Rico to hold a referendum on its future political status.

[27] In February 1998, Clinton went even further, openly supporting a plebiscite for Puerto Rico, allowing the nationals to choose between total incorporation to the US, independence or maintaining the island as an associated state.

[28] Seven Puerto Rican activists, imprisoned for setting off bombs in the United States and pardoned by US President Bill Clinton, were received as heroes by crowds at San Juan airport on September 12 1999, waving flags and singing nationalist songs. The activists had carried out a terrorist campaign throughout the 1970s and 1980s.

[29] Tens of thousands of people protested in February 200 against renewed military exercises by the US army on the Puerto Rican island of Vieques. This island had been used by the US for military exercises for 50 years, but these had been suspended after the accidental death of a civilian in April 1999. Clinton and Governor Rosselló had made an agreement for training manoeuvres until April 2000, but the church authorities organized a protest group to camp in the target area, thus interrupting the 'war games'. ∎

Qatar

Qatar

Population: 589,000 (1999)
Area: 11,000 SQ KM
Capital: Doha (Ad-Dawhah)
Currency: Riyal
Language: Arabic

In a small desert country without a single river, 400 farms produce almost all the foodstuffs required for domestic consumption. The miracle that changed the desert into a kitchen garden was the advent of oil revenues. Half a million barrels of oil per day, and the successful policies of Amir Khalifa bin Ath-Thanis's government, have helped bring about these achievements.

[2] Like the neighboring island of Bahrain, the Qatar peninsula has participated from ancient times in the Gulf trade between Mesopotamia and India. Islamized in the 7th century (see Saudi Arabia), at the time of the Caliphate of Baghdad, Qatar had already obtained autonomy which was maintained until 1076 when it was conquered by the Emir of Bahrain.

[3] From the 16th century, after a brief period of Portuguese occupation, the country lived in great prosperity due to the development of pearl fishing which attracted immigrants. Settled on the coasts, under the leadership of the Al-Thani family, these settlers succeeded in politically unifying the country in the 18th century, though it remained subject to Bahrain's sovereignty. The process of independence, begun in 1815 by Sheikh Muhammad and his son Jassim, culminated in 1868 with the mediation of the English; the Al-Thanis agreed to end the war in exchange for guaranteed territorial integrity.

[4] The Turkish sultans, nominal sovereigns of the entire Arabian peninsula since the 16th century, did not look favorably upon increasing British penetration in the Gulf. Consequently, they named the reigning Sheikh (Jassim Al-Thani)

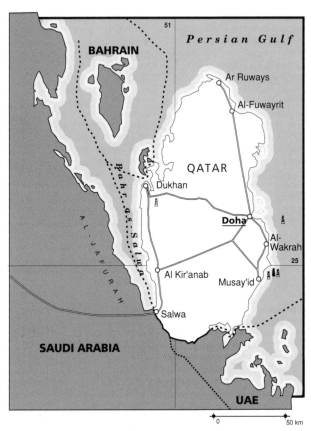

governor of the 'province' of Qatar as a pretext to establishing a small military garrison in Dawhah (Doha). Neither the Qataris nor the British concerned themselves over this formal affirmation of sovereignty and the garrison remained until World War I without the slightest effect on British influence in the region.

[5] In 1930, the price of pearls dropped with the Japanese flooding the market with a cheaper version of cultivated pearls. Consequently Sheikh Abdullah sold all the country's oil prospecting and exploitation rights, and granted a 75-year lease on its territorial waters, for £ 400,000. The Anglo-Iranian Oil Company discovered oil in 1939 but actual production only began after World War II, attracting other companies which purchased parts of the original concession. The

immense wealth obtained by Royal Dutch Shell did not seem to concern Sheikh Ahmad bin Ali Al-Thani as oil and tariff revenues increased his personal fortune by £15 million.

[6] Shortly thereafter, Ahmad was ousted by his own family. They replaced him with his cousin Khalifa, giving him the task of 'removing any elements which are opposed to progress and modernization'.

[7] Sheikh Khalifa created a Council of Ministers and an Advisory Council to share the responsibilities of his absolute power and promised 'a new era of enlightened government, social justice and stability'. Redistributing the oil revenues, he exempted all inhabitants from taxation and provided free education and medical attention. His greatest achievement has perhaps been the

subsidizing and promotion of productive activities not connected with oil prospecting, activities which were symbolically expressed by the first tomato exports at the beginning of his mandate.

[8] To reduce Qatar's dependency on a single product, the fishing industry was revitalized, industrialization was accelerated with new cement and fertilizer plants, plus iron and steel mills. The country took advantage of its strategic position to provide commercial and financial services to the economies of the entire region. In addition, a large part of the country's financial surplus was invested abroad (in Europe and the US). In 1980, it was estimated that income from this 'exportation of capital' would eventually equal all oil revenues. In this way Qatar sought to ensure its future when the oil wells ran dry.

[9] As a tool of control, a state oil company - the Qatar Petroleum Producing Authority (QPPA) - was set up in 1972. By February 1977, all foreign oil installations had been expropriated.

[10] Qatar's economic expansion required the large-scale immigration of foreign technical experts and workers - the former were mainly European and American; the latter Iranian, Pakistani, Indian and Palestinian. Estimates as to the actual number of immigrant workers at this time varied widely, since surveys were not regularly taken. The figure was thought to be approximately 150,000 people, or about 60 per cent of the total population.

[11] To avoid any profound transformation of the local culture, the Government preferred and promoted immigration from other Arab countries. Nevertheless, the advanced systems of social security also protect foreign workers. The local Iranian community lived in better conditions than in any other Gulf emirate and, because of this, Qatar had fewer conflicts with Iran's Khomeini regime than any other country in the region.

[12] Adhering to OPEC policy, in 1982 the country cut crude oil production by 25 per cent. Consequently exports decreased, reflected in a considerable reduction in volume of petrodollars invested in the West, in public spending and in industrial expansion. Nevertheless, Qatar had the infrastructure to face the change. In the industrial center of Umm Said the

WORKERS

% OF LABOUR FORCE   **1998**

■ FEMALE: 14%   ■ MALE: 86%

1990

■ SERVICES: 65.3%
■ INDUSTRY: 32.0%
■ AGRICULTURE: 2.7%

LAND USE

ARABLE: 7.6% of total (1993)

PUBLIC EXPENDITURE

DEFENCE EXPENDITURE (% of goverment exp.)	**27%** (1997)
MILITARY EXPENDITURE (% of health & education)	**192%** (1990/91)

iron and steel plant was producing 450,000 tons a year at the beginning of the decade. A liquid gas plant was also set in full operation and the Government decided to go ahead with a $6 billion natural gas project for use in its energy and desalinization programs.

[13] Qatar's geographical position brought the country both economic benefits and geopolitical worries. Israeli aggression against Lebanon, Syria and Iraq; the lack of solutions to the Palestinian problem; the war between Iran and Iraq, and the US Reagan administration's frightening interest in the region's 'military security' all helped to convince Qatar's rulers of the need to enter new alliances with their neighbors on the Arabian Gulf.

[14] Since 1981, together with Bahrain, Kuwait, Oman, the United Arab Emirates and Saudi Arabia, Qatar has participated in the Gulf Cooperation Council (GCC), an organization designed to coordinate the area's policies in political, economic, social, cultural and military issues. Qatar strongly supported Saudi Arabia's stand regarding the need to reduce and if possible eliminate US troops stationed in the region, mainly in Oman.

[15] In April 1986, tensions flared between Bahrain and Qatar over the artificial island of Fasht ad-Dibal. This conflict was resolved through negotiations sponsored by members of the GCC. In November 1987, the Government renewed diplomatic relations with Egypt.

[16] In March 1991, after the Iraqi invasion of Kuwait, the Gulf Cooperation Council suspended all economic aid to Jordan and the Palestine Liberation Organization.

[17] In the same month, the Foreign Ministers of Egypt, Syria, and the six Arab countries of the GCC gathered in the Saudi capital Riyadh to sign an agreement with the US to preserve security in the region. The plan included four points: a common military strategy between the US and the Arab countries in the anti-Iraqi coalition; mechanisms to avoid arms proliferation; acceptance of a peace treaty by Israel; and a new economic program for the development of the region.

[18] In December, a group of 53 people including some government officials drew up and signed a petition to the Emir of Qatar asking for free parliamentary elections, a written constitution and increased personal and political freedoms. As a result, several citizens were arrested and detained in the Doha Central Prison; they were eventually released several months later.

[19] In addition to this already difficult situation, toward the end of the year Qatar and Bahrain became involved in another territorial dispute over several small islands off the coast of the two emirates: Howard Island, and more especially underground rights to Dibval and Qitat, both potentially rich in oil. Growing tension between the two countries prompted Saudi Arabia to step in and mediate.

[20] In 1993, the fall in the price of oil on the international market triggered an almost 20 per cent decrease in fiscal income.

Furthering his program to develop alternative income sources, in 1994 Doha negotiated new agreements with several Asian companies for the exploitation of natural gas.

[21] In June 1995, heir to the throne Hamad ibn Khalifah ath-Thani overthrew his father to become Emir of Qatar. The new sovereign promised to step up efforts to resolve the territorial disputes with Saudi Arabia and Bahrain. Qatar's membership of the Gulf Cooperation Council was thrown into doubt when its delegation withdrew from a Council meeting in December.

[22] In April 1996, Qatar and Saudi Arabia resolved their territorial disputes on the basis of a previous treaty. A similar dispute between Qatar and Bahrain came to an end in March 1997, when both nations agreed to deal with the issue in the International Courts.

[23] In 1997, Qatar froze relations with Israel, applying the Arab League decision to reactivate the boycott on that country. However it offered its capita Doha as the venue for the Economic Conference of the Middle East and North Africa to be held in November, as part of the peace process. In October, Sheikh Abdullah ibn Khalifa ath-Thani was appointed Prime Minister, a post previously occupied by Emir Hamad.

[24] On March 17 1998, the 25th Conference of Foreign Ministers of the of the Islamic Conference Organization (ICO) closed in Doha. Its resolutions included a call to the Arab states to reconsider relations with Israel. Qatar gratefully received the agreement between Saudi Arabia, Venezuela and Mexico to reduce their respective oil production limits, undertaking to do the same during that year.

[25] In the same month, Qatar and France held joint naval manoeuvres under the title 'Pearl Collection II'. In April, the Emir signed a military co-operation agreement with Russia, including the exchange of specialists and military training projects.

[26] The ban on contracting Egyptian workers was lifted in June 1998 and in November that year a plan for constitutional reform was unveiled, with the goal of creating a parliament elected by direct vote. At this time the emirate was the only Gulf state with an elected parliament, but only men aged over 18 years old were eligible to vote. In the March 1999 local elections, women were allowed the vote for the first time. Despite the impact this created, none of the six female candidates were elected for local posts.

[27] The Emir was increasingly active on the diplomatic front, raising criticism for the US attitude on Iraq and mediating in the dispute over agreements with Iran between the Saudi monarch and the United Arab Emirates. The UAE complained that Saudi Arabia and other members of the Gulf Cooperation Council had improved relations with Iran without considering that they had a territorial dispute with this country. Khalifa al-Thani's proposal led to consensus and the unity of the Council was re-launched.

[28] The 33 rebels responsible for a 1996 coup attempt against the Emir were sentenced to life imprisonment in February 2000. Amongst them was the Emir's cousin, Sheikh Hamad bin Jassem al-Thani, an ally of the deposed father of the current monarch. ∎

PROFILE

ENVIRONMENT

The country consists of the Qatar Peninsula, on the eastern coast of the Arabian Peninsula in the Persian Gulf. The land is flat and the climate is hot and dry. Farming is possible only along the coastal strip. The country's main resource is its fabulous oil wealth on the western coast. Qatar suffered the negative effects of the burning oil wells during the Gulf War.

SOCIETY

Peoples: The native Qatari Arab inhabitants account for 20 per cent of the population. Arabs, though, are a majority thanks to Palestinian, Egyptian and Yemenite immigrants, who account for 25 per cent of the population. The remaining 55 per cent are immigrants, mostly from Pakistan, India and Iran. **Religions:** Muslim (official and predominant). The majority are Sunni, with Iranian immigrants mainly Shi'a. There are also Christian and Hindu minorities. **Languages:** Arabic (official and predominant). Urdu is spoken by Pakistani immigrants, and Farsi by Iranians. English is the business language. **Political Parties:** There are no organized political parties.

THE STATE

Official Name: Dawlat Qatar. **Capital:** Doha (Ad-Dawhah) 400,000 people (est 1995). **Other cities:** Rayyan,100,000 people; Wakrah 26,000; Umm Salal 12,100 (1987). **Government:** Hamad ibn Khalifah ath-Thani, Emir and Head of State since june 1995. Sheikh Abdullah ibn Khalifa ath-Thani, Prime Minister since October 1997. Legislative Power:a Consultative Council with 30 members appointed by the Emir to 3 year-terms. **National Holiday:** September 3, Independence Day (1971). Armed Forces: 11,800 (1996)

Réunion

Réunion

Population: 691,000 (1999)
Area: 2,510 SQ KM
Capital: Saint Denis
Currency: French franc
Language: French

The island of Réunion was uninhabited until the beginning of the 17th century when Arab explorers arrived and called it Diva Margabin. The Portuguese renamed it Ilha Santa Apolonia and the French settlers called it Bourbon. After the French Revolution it was given its current name of Réunion.

[2] The island's four renamings reflect the struggle between the colonial powers for possession of this strategically important point in the Indian Ocean. After decades of fighting, the French finally retained colonial rights over Réunion.

[3] The colonial regime replaced subsistence farming with the export commodities of sugarcane and coffee, and the island's fishing resources were depleted because of the over-exploitation of several species.

[4] Since March 1946, Réunion has been an Overseas Department by the French Government. The local middle-class and the French colonists supported the integration of the island into French territory. Later, conservative political changes in France brought realignment of political forces on the island.

[5] While sectors tied to colonial interests defended the Department status, the Réunion Communist Party (PCR) changed its stance, and in 1959 campaigned for partial autonomy. The PCR suffered the consequences of its about face, and for ten years was the sole supporter of gradual independence.

[6] In July 1978, the UN Decolonization Committee pronounced in favor of full independence for Réunion. The question of independence was now transformed into an international issue.

[7] In 1978, the independence movement made important international contacts in a meeting with other anti-imperialist and anti-colonialist organizations in the Indian Ocean area. At this meeting, a Permanent Liaison Committee was formed in a joint effort against foreign domination. In June 1979, during elections for the European Parliament, Paul Vergés raised the issue of double colonialism, charging that Réunion Island was not only dominated by the French, but forced to serve the interests of the entire European Community.

[8] The production crisis and unemployment were not due to unfavorable climatic conditions (extensive drought, cyclones, etc.) but to the structure of the economy itself. The situation was worsened by the demographic explosion on the island, as the population had increased 20 per cent in the last decade.

[9] Disturbances became more frequent as the social situation deteriorated. In 1991, eight people died in clashes with police in protest over the closure of the pirate television station Tele Free-DOM, directed by the popular Camille Sudre. Sudre, a Frenchman settled in Réunion, formed a political list in record time and won the regional elections in 1992. Support from the PCR enabled him to become leader of the region, one of the two main executive authorities of the island.

[10] However, the main French administrative tribunal annulled the elections for alleged irregularities and banned Sudre from standing again. In fresh elections in 1993, the Free-DOM party, led by Marguerite Sudre, Camille's wife, won again. The new leader formed links with the French Right and was appointed minister in the cabinet of the conservative, Edouard Balladur (in office 1993-1995), in Paris.

[11] Unemployment soared in 1996 to an all-time high of 40 per cent, and it was estimated to be even higher amongst the young. In 1997, the tension and social discontent erupted in constant demonstrations.

[12] In March 1998, Paul Vergés, the CPR leader was elected head of the Regional Council by 24 votes to the 20 of the right wing Union for French Democracy candidate, Jean-Paul Virapoullé. The outcome was due to the support Marguerite Sudre gave Vergés, who had not achieved the 23 vote majority needed for him to stand in the first round. ∎

PROFILE

ENVIRONMENT

Located in the Indian Ocean, 700 km east of Madagascar, Réunion is a volcanic, mountainous island with a tropical climate, heavy rainfall and numerous rivers. These conditions favor the growth of sugarcane, the main economic activity.

SOCIETY

Peoples: Mostly of African descent (63.5 per cent): Europeans 2.2 per cent; Chinese 2.2 per cent; Indian 28.3 per cent. **Religion:** Mainly Catholic (94 per cent). Muslim, Hindu and Buddhist minorities. **Languages:** French (official) and Creole. **Political Parties:** Free-DOM Movement; Communist Party of Reunion (PCR); Union for the Republic (RPR); Union for French Democracy (UDF); Socialist Party.

THE STATE

Official Name: Département d'Outre-Mer de la Réunion. **Administrative Divisions:** 5 Arrondisements. **Capital:** Saint Denis 104,454 people (1994). **Other cities:** St Paul 72,000 people, St Pierre 59,000; Le Tampon 27,300; St André 25,237 (1994). **Government:** Robert Pommies, Prefect appointed by the French Government in 1996. There are two local councils: the 47-member General Council, and the 45 - member Regional Council. The island has 5 representatives and 3 senators in the French parliament. **National Holiday:** December 20, Abolition of slavery (1848). **Armed Forces:** 4,000 French troops.

DEMOGRAPHY

Population: 691,000 (1999)

Romania

România

Population: 22,402,000 (1999)
Area: 238,390 SQ KM
Capital: Bucharest
Currency: Lei
Language: Romanian

The earliest inhabitants of Romania included the Thracians, whose descendants, known as the Getae, established contact with Greek colonies that appeared on the shore of the Black Sea in the 7th century BC. Together with the Dacians, a related people living in the Carpathian Mountains and in Transylvania, the Getae established a distinct society by the 4th century BC.

2 In the first century BC, the Geto-Dacians bitterly resisted conquest by the Romans, who were interested in the region's mineral wealth. Rome finally triumphed over the powerful Dacian kingdom in 106 AD, putting its inhabitants to death or expelling them to the north. According to some Roman sources, most of the males of the conquered area who could not run were put to death or brought to Rome as slaves. However many Dacians ran away from the center of the former kingdom, into vast areas that belonged to the so-called free Dacians, in the north, east and north-east of the Roman province of Dacia.

3 The province was then subdivided into Dacia Superior, Dacia Inferior and Dacia Porolissensis. Emperor Marcus Aurelius abandoned Dacia Superior and Inferior during the period between 271-275. Unwilling to acknowledge before the Senate that he withdrew from such important provinces, he reorganized the province of Moesia Superior at the south of Danube into Dacia Ripensis and Dacia Mediterranea (to keep the name Dacia). The center and east of present Walachia, southern Moldova and Dobrudja were at that time part of the Roman province of Moesia Inferior, which he still occupied. Roman rule left an enduring legacy on the Romanian language which is derived from Latin. This rule continued in the territory of present Romania until the 7th century, when the Byzantine Empire lost its last northern Danubian strongholds to the migratory peoples.

4 Between the 3rd and the 12th centuries, the region underwent successive invasions by Germanic peoples, Slavs, Avars and others. Roman Christianity was brought by Romans during the 2nd and 3rd centuries and spread to the whole region by the 4th century. The Romanian-Bulgarian Empire, which lasted over 200 years, introduced Greek Orthodox Christianity. The Romanian Church adopted the Slavonic language as a result of Bulgarian influence. Towards the end of the 9th century, the Bulgarians were expelled by the Magyars from the Pannonic plains (now Hungary) though they remained in what is today Romania.

5 Transylvania, the cradle of the Romanian nation, was conquered by Hungary during the 10th - 12th century. According to Hungarian sources the existing feudal states in Transylvania put up fierce resistance. The Vlachs from Transylvania reappeared in the 13th century to the south of the Carpathian Mountains, in two separate regions, Walachia and Moldova. Inlanders immediately accepted the newcomers as people with the same origins. The Tatar-Mongol invasion of 1241 produced big losses among the Romanians.

6 The first Romanian state, Walachia, was established south of the Carpathians during the early 14th century and a second, Moldova, was founded in 1349 east of the Carpathians in the Spruth River valley.

7 The principalities of Walachia and Moldova fought for their independence from Hungary, which after conquering Transylvania, tried unsuccessfully to conquer them also. This struggle ended in the first half of the 14th century, when Hungarian invaders were defeated in both areas. By the 15th century the Ottoman Empire began to be a greater threat.

8 After defeating the Serbs in Kosovo in 1389, the Ottoman Empire began closing in on Walachia, with pressure intensifying after the fall of Bulgaria in 1393. Walachia became a vassal state of Sultan Mehmed I in 1417, though Prince Mircea maintained the claim to the throne and the Christian religion remained intact. In 1455 Moldova also became a vassal state.

9 King Mircea's death in 1418 was followed by a rapid succession of princes, until the Turks appointed a Romanian prince of their choice to the throne. Walachia put up resistance, but after the Hungarian defeat at the battle of Mohacs in 1526, Turkish domination became inevitable. The Hungarian kingdom disappeared and was transformed by the Ottomans into a Pashalic. The three Romanian principalities, Walachia, Moldova and Transylvania entered into the sphere of influence of the Ottomans, but kept some indigence by paying a tribute in money.

10 In 1594, the Turkish inhabitants of Walachia were massacred by Prince Michael in alliance with Moldova. He went on to invade Turkish territory, taking several key sites along the banks of the Danube. Faced with the collapse of his counter-offensive, the Sultan had no choice but to recognize the sovereignty of Walachia, which subsequently became linked to Transylvania.

11 Five years later, in 1599, Segismund Bathory of Transylvania abdicated and Michael dethroned Andreas, Segismund's successor. The Vlach peasants in Transylvania rose up against Hungary. Walachia, not wishing to break the alliance, helped put down the rebellion.

12 In 1600, Michael conquered Moldova, proclaiming himself regent. The Austrian Emperor Rudolf II recognized the claim, although he later tried to take over Transylvania and Moldova. Michael the Brave is a national hero because he was the first and the last to unite the Romanians until the modern reunification in 1918.

13 In the 17th and 18th centuries, Walachia and Moldova fell under Turkish rule again. The sultans did not trust the native Romanian princes, so they named either Greek princes from Romania, or Romanian princes from the Greek quarter in Istanbul, Fanar, to rule Walachia and Moldova. Russia occupied the region in 1769, but Austria forced Russia to return the principalities to the sultan in 1774.

14 Russia's power over the area gradually increased, until it included the right to designate the princes. The Sultan ousted these princes, and in 1806, Russia retaliated by invading the region. Under the Treaty of Bucharest in 1812, Russia retained the southeastern part of Moldova - Bessarabia.

15 The Walachian Prince, Ion Caragea, was linked to 'Philiki Etaireia', a Greek revolutionary movement sponsored by Russia. Alexander Ypsilantis, Prince Konstantinos's son and the Czar's aide entered Moldova in 1821, leading the Etaireians, and provoking the Turks.

16 The Sultan managed to divide the Romanians and the Greeks by allowing the principalities to pass laws in their own languages and elect local-born princes. Ion Sandu Sturza and Grigore IV Ghica assumed control of the Government of Moldova and Walachia respectively and both moved closer to Greece and Russia.

17 Another war broke out between Russia and Turkey in 1828. The following year, the Treaty of Adrianopolis maintained the principalities as tributaries of the Sultan, but under Russian occupation. Russian troops remained in the region, and the princes began to be named for life.

18   The local nobility drew up a constitution known as the 'Reglement organique', which was passed in Walachia in 1831 and in Moldova in 1832. This established administrative and legislative bodies made up of people of the principalities. In 1834, after the Sultan's approval of the 'Reglement', Russia withdrew.

19   During the European revolutions of 1848, nationalist sentiment in Moldova and Walachia was stimulated by peasant rebellions. These reached a climax in May with the protests at Blaj, which were put down by Turkish and Russian troops, restoring the 'Reglement organique'. The revolutions were defeated with foreign aid, Ottoman in Walachia, Russian in Moldova, and Austrian and Russian in Transylvania.

20   During the Crimean War, the three Romanian principalities were occupied alternately by Ottoman, Russian and Austrian troops. The Treaty of Paris, 1856, maintained the ancient statutes of the principalities until its revision by a European commission in Bucharest in 1857, with delegates representing the sultan and both principalities.

21   The local delegates made the following proposals: that the provinces be autonomous, joining together under the name 'Romania'; that a foreign king be elected, with the right to hereditary succession; and that the country be neutral. In August 1858, despite the Sultan's opposition, the Treaty of Paris created a commission to carry out the unification process.

22   In 1859, the principalities elected a single prince, Alexandru Ion Cuza, who was recognized by the major powers and by the Sultan in 1861. The Constitution of 1864 established a bicameral legislative body, granting property holders greater electoral power.

23   When the war between Russia and Turkey resumed in 1877, Romania authorized the transit of Russian troops through its territory in April. Moscow declared war on Turkey in May. After suffering heavy losses at Pevna, the Russians asked Prince Carol I of Romania for military support. Romanian troops contributed to the Russian victory against the Turks.

24   The 1878 Treaty of Berlin respected Romania's independence, but failed to return Bessarabia to Romania, instead giving it Dobrudja - without its southern part - and the Danube Delta. In 1881 Romania became a kingdom.

25   When the Balkan War broke out in 1912, tension from territorial disputes in past wars, persisted between Romania and its neighbors. After the first few battles, Bucharest demanded a ratification of its borders in Dobrudja. The St Petersburg Conference of 1913 gave Romania Silistra, much to Bulgaria's displeasure.

26   Romania took advantage of the second Balkan War of 1913 to shore up its position. The Treaty of Bucharest gave Romania the southern part of Dobrudja, which was occupied by Romanian troops. At the beginning of World War I, Romania wavered between taking Bessarabia or Transylvania, finally opting for the latter.

27   In 1916, Romania allied itself with Britain, France, Russia and Italy, declaring war on Austria and Hungary. After the occupation of Bucharest, King Ferdinand and the Romanian Government and army took refuge in Moldova. The defeat of the Central Powers in 1918 made it possible for Romania to double its size, since Transylvania, Bessarabia, Bucovina and Banat expressed their will to belong to Romania through referenda.

28   In 1918 the King approved electoral reforms making voting obligatory for men over the age of 21, and introducing the secret ballot. At the time the peasants made up 80 per cent of the population, and they had their own political party. Conservatives found their position weakened because of having supported Germany, liberals included only people linked to professional and commercial activity, and the socialists carried little weight.

29   Social upheaval, and the landowners' fear of having their lands expropriated, led General Averescu (the hero of two wars and now the head of the government) to take harsh measures. The general strike of 1920 was put down and the Communist Party was declared illegal in 1924.

30   In the 1928 election, the National Peasant Party (NPP) obtained 349 of 387 seats. The Government abolished martial law and press censorship, also decentralizing public administration, an issue supported by the ethnic minorities. It also authorized the sale of land and foreign investment in the country.

31   The council of regency, which had been formed upon Ferdinand's death, was dissolved when King Carol assumed the throne in 1930, a succession agreed on by the major political parties. The economic crisis led to the displacement of the NPP, and the King took advantage of the emergence of the Iron Guard, a fascist Moldovan group similar to those that existed in Germany and Italy, to weaken the traditional parties.

32   In 1938, after a fraudulent plebiscite, Carol passed a new corporative constitution. Seeking closer ties with Germany, he met Hitler in November 1938. Upon his return, he had 13 officials of the Iron Guard assassinated, along with its leader, and Carol founded his own party, the National Renaissance Front (NRF).

33   Carol assured the other powers that he was acting under pressure from Hitler, obtaining French and German assurances of the country's territorial integrity. When Germany and the USSR invaded Poland in 1939, Romania not only renounced the mutual defense treaty which it had signed with Warsaw, but also detained Polish authorities as they fled across Romanian territory.

34   Between June and September of 1940, Romania was forced to turn Bessarabia and Bucovina over to the USSR, north-east Transylvania over to Hungary, and southern Dobrudja to Bulgaria. Because of his disastrous foreign policy, Carol had no choice but to abdicate in September, leaving his son Michael on the throne and turning over the Government of the country to General Antonescu. Romania was occupied by 500,000 German troops, and was proclaimed a 'national legionary state'.

35   Romanian troops cooperated with the abortive German offensive against the USSR, but when the counter-offensive was mounted by the Red Army, Bucharest abruptly changed sides. In June 1944, the Peasant, Liberal, Social Democratic and Communist Parties created the National Bloc and in August, King Michael ousted Antonescu and declared war on Germany.

36   In September, with the major part of its territory occupied since mid-August by Soviet troops, Romania signed an armistice with the Allies. After three short-lived military governments, the USSR intervened in the naming of a new Prime Minister, Petru Groza, leader of the Ploughers' Front, a leftist party which was not a part of the National Bloc.

37   At the Potsdam Conference, the Allies decided to resume relations with Romania, provided its government was 'recognized and democratic'. The USSR granted it immediate recognition while the United States and Britain adopted a 'wait-and-see' attitude. In the 1946 election, the party in power was re-elected, with 71 per cent of the vote.

38   The Government initiated a series of detentions, summary trials and life sentences against the leaders and members of the Social Democratic, the National Liberal and National Peasant parties. In 1947, King Michael was forced to abdicate.

PROFILE

ENVIRONMENT

The country is crossed from north to center by the Carpathian Mountains, the western part of which are known as the Transylvanian Alps. The Transylvanian plateau is contained within the arc formed by the Carpathian Mountains. The Moldavian plains extend to the east, while the Walachian plains stretch to the south, crossed by the Danube, which flows into a large delta on the Black Sea. The mountain forests supply raw material for a well developed timber industry. With abundant mineral resources (oil, natural gas, coal, iron ore and bauxite), Romania has begun extensive industrial development. Its economy still depends to a great extent on the export of raw materials and agricultural products. Romania defines itself as a 'developing country', and is attuned with Third World demands. It is also one of Europe's largest oil producers. Copsa Mica, in the center of Romania, is considered to be one of the areas with the highest levels of industrial pollution in Europe.

SOCIETY

Peoples: Romanian 89.4 per cent, Hungarian 9 per cent, German 0.5 per cent, Ukrainian, Turkish, Greek and Croatian. These official data do not include Romani, which represented between 5 and 10 per cent of the population, but who usually are considered as Romanian in the census.
Religions: Mainly Romanian-Orthodox (86.8 per cent). There are Catholic (5 per cent) and Protestant (3.5 per cent) minorities.
Languages: Romanian (official language, spoken by the majority); ethnic minorities often speak their own languages, particularly Hungarian and Romany. **Political Parties:** Democratic Convention; Social Democrat Union; Hungarian Democratic Union of Romania Party of Social Democracy in Romania. **Social Organizations:** General Confederation of Trade Unions.

THE STATE

Official Name: România. **Administrative Divisions:** 40 Districts and the Municipality of Bucharest. **Capital:** Bucharest 2,375,000 people (1995).
Other cities: Timisoara 327,830 people; Constanza 348,000; Iasi 339,889 (1994). **Government:** Emil Constantinescu, President and Head of State since November 1996. Victor Ciorbea, Prime Minister and Head of Government since 1996. Legislature, bicameral: Senate, 143 members; Deputies, 341 members, 13 representing ethnic minorities.
National holiday: November 1 Union (1947). **Armed Forces:** 228,400 (1996). **Other:** 43,000 Border Guard, Gendarmes, Construction Troops.

39 In 1948, the Communists and some Social Democrats formed the Romanian Workers' Party (RWP) which joined the Ploughers' Front and the Hungarian People's Union to form the People's Democratic Front (PDF). In the March election that year, the PDF won 405 of the 414 seats of the National Assembly.

40 On December 30 1947, the People's Republic of Romania was proclaimed, and a soviet style socialist constitution was adopted. In April, the Government adopted centralized economic planning.

41 Between 1948 and 1949, Bucharest signed friendship and cooperation treaties with the European socialist bloc, and joined the Council for Mutual Economic Assistance (CMEA). In 1955, Romania joined the Warsaw Pact, but in 1963 it began to drift away from the Soviet fold.

42 In 1951 the First Five Year Plan was started, aimed at socialist industrialization of steel, coal, and oil. In 1952, the new regime started to consolidate under President Groza and Prime Minister Gheorghiu-Dej, head of state from 1961.

43 Gheorghe Maurer was appointed Prime Minister in 1961, while Gheorghiu-Dej was President of the republic. Maurer tried to achieve greater economic and political independence, so Romania did not take sides in the Sino-Soviet dispute. In 1962 the economy underwent a series of reforms. The land collectivization policy was finished, and trade with the US, France, and Germany began.

44 In 1965, when Gheorghiu-Dej died, Nicolae Ceausescu was elected First Secretary of the RWP, which subsequently changed its name to the Romanian Communist Party (RCP). The Constitution was reformed, and the name of the country was changed to the Socialist Republic of Romania, by the National Assembly. In 1967, Ceausescu was elected President of the State Council.

45 On the diplomatic front, Ceausescu placed some distance between Romania and the USSR. In 1966, he affirmed that his country was continuing its struggle for independence. Romania established diplomatic relations with West Germany and, unlike other members of the Warsaw Pact, it did not break off relations with Israel in 1967, nor intervene over the Soviet invasions of Czechoslovakia in 1968.

46 Reaffirming Romania's independence from the USSR but not renouncing communism, Ceausescu modified the structure of the RCP and the State.

47 In the 1970s and early 1980s, Ceausescu was re-elected several times, in apparently free elections, as secretary general of the RCP and as president of the country. Despite numerous government reorganizations, economic hardships, accentuated by administrative corruption, led to growing discontent.

48 From 1987, difficult living and labor conditions triggered marches and strikes. These were put down by the security forces. In 1988 and 1989, several government scandals broke out; various cabinet ministers and government authorities were subsequently tried and dismissed.

49 Towards the end of 1989, confrontations between civilians and the army in Timisoara left many dead or injured, the international press spoke of hundreds of deaths, and the news had strong repercussions within Romania.

50 The Government declared a state of emergency, but a faction within the regime carried out a coup with massive popular support. Accused of 'genocide, corruption and destruction of the economy', Ceausescu and his wife were secretly executed by army soldiers. The National Salvation Front (NSF) assumed control of the government.

51 Resistance towards the new government increased, leading to violent confrontations in the streets. In the May 1990 election, the NSF claimed 85 per cent of the vote; but charges of election rigging were confirmed by international observers.

52 In December 1991, 77 per cent of the electorate approved the new constitution which turned Romania into a multiparty presidentialist democracy. In Transylvania, however, the new constitution received scant support.

53 On January 1 1992, the cooperative farming system created by the Ceausescu regime ceased to exist legally, but in fact it was still operating. In the municipal elections of February 1992, incidents occurred in Transylvania when the Magyar Democratic Union candidate was barred from participation.

54 One month before the elections, a new opposition party, the Democratic Convention, was created. It obtained 24.3 per cent of the vote, against the 33.6 per cent of the NSF. Opposed to the First Minister Petre Roman's re-election as party president, Ion Iliescu's faction withdrew from the NSF in March, founding the NSF/22nd of December Group, changing its name in April to the Democratic Front for National Salvation (FDSN).

55 Also in January, Romania and Germany signed a Friendship and Cooperation Treaty. In the meantime, the United States included Romania on the list of 'Most Favored Nations' (MFN), granting preferential treatment in trade. The State privatized 6,000 enterprises in June, selling 30 per cent of the shares to the general public.

56 The World Bank and the IMF granted Romania loans of $400 million for economic reforms. Iliescu won the September and October general elections, but in Parliament, the FDSN obtained a mere 28 per cent of the seats.

57 Western countries and international financial organizations continued to voice their discontent to the Government for its alleged sluggishness in implementing economic reforms. One of the features criticized was land ownership, since 30 per cent still belonged to the State in 1994.

58 1995 was also dominated by disagreement between Bucharest and some of its trade partners, such as the European Union, on the pace of the reforms. Finally, in June, after two years of deliberation, Bucharest passed in June the law to privatize state enterprises.

59 Human rights organizations, such as Amnesty International, also criticized Romania especially for the violence and discrimination often practised against the approximately 500,000 to 2,000,000 Romani (gypsies).

60 After years of attempts, Bucharest and Budapest signed a treaty in September 1996 regarding the 1.6 million Hungarians living in Romania. Hungary had to agree to a commitment to 'guarantee the rights of the minority', leaving aside its demand of 'autonomy' for Transylvanian Hungarians. Although relations with Hungary (which opened a consulate in Cluj, capital of Transylvania) improved after ultranationalist tendencies diminished with the defeat of Iliescu in the November elections, problems arose again when the Romanian senate voted against a university education project for the minorities.

61 The new government of Emil Constantinescu, the President elected in November 1996, announced it would attack corruption and organized crime. Prime Minister Victor Ciorbea implemented an economic and structural adjustment program inspired by IMF prescriptions: balanced state finance, increased privatization and decentralization of the administration.

62 Constant friction between parties of the ruling coalition delayed reforms and the adoption of laws in Parliament. Social unrest with government policies led to a wave of demonstrations which climaxed in October 1997.

63 One of the main goals of Romanian foreign policy in 1998 was to speed up incorporation into NATO and the European Union. ■

Russia

Rossiya

Population: 147,195,000 (1999)
Area: 17,075,400 SQ KM
Capital: Moscow (Moskva)
Currency: Rouble
Language: Russian

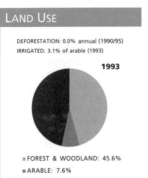

Before the Slavs appeared on the Historical scene, the European territory of the present Russian Federation, Belarus and Ukraine was inhabited by different peoples, and underwent successive invasions by the Huns, Avars, Goths and Magyars. The first mention of the Slavs dates back to the 6th century. Byzantine writers wrote of several Slavic peoples: the Polians (based in Kiev), Drevlians, Dregoviches, Kriviches, Viatiches, Meria and others.

[2] In the 9th century, the first Russian State was formed, known as the Ancient Rus or Kiev Rus. The latter emerged from the struggle against the Khazars of the south, and the Varangians (Scandinavians) of the north. In the 9th century, the route between the Baltic and Black seas, down the Dnepr river, 'the route of the Varangians and the Greeks', became important for European trade.

[3] In 882, Prince Oleg of Novgorod conquered Kiev (in Ukraine) and transferred the center of the Russian State there. In the year 907, Oleg signed a treaty which was to be beneficial for the Rus. During the reign of Sviatoslav, Oleg's grandson, the struggle between Byzantium and Bulgaria intensified. Vladimir (980-1015), Sviatoslav's son and successor, consolidated the judicial, dynastic and territorial organization of the Russian State. To overcome the isolation of the 'pagan' Rus vis-á-vis a monotheistic Europe, Vladimir made Christianity the state religion in 988, adopting the ornate Byzantine ritual.

[4] At the end of Vladimir's reign, strong separatist tendencies were evident within the Principality of Novgorod. Svyatopolk, Vladimir's successor, killed three of his brothers in order to consolidate his own power, but Yaroslav, the fourth brother and prince of Novgorod, ousted Svyatopolk and assumed power in Kiev, granting Novgorod several benefices. After his death, the feudal republic of Novgorod was formed, along with the principalities of Vladimir-Suzdal, Galich-Volin and others. Muscovy (the principality of Rostov-Suzdal) is first mentioned in historical chronicles in 1147.

[5] In 1237, the troops of the Tatar Khan Batu, the grandson of Genghis Khan, invaded the principalities of Riazan and Vladimir, taking Moscow and other Russian cities. From 1239-40, the conquest of Russian principalities continued, followed by two and half centuries of Tatar rule. Apart from the Mongols in the East, the Teutons and the Swedes posed an additional danger in the West. In 1242, Prince Alexander of Novgorod defeated the Teutons in the famous 'battle on ice' on Lake Chudskoye, near the Neva River, obtaining the title 'Prince of Nevsky' as a result of this victory.

[6] The Mongols governed through local princes or Turkish chieftains and Muslim merchants, who were given the authority (*yarlik*) to govern. In the early 14th century, Tver, Moscow, Riazan and Novgorod were the main principalities. Dmitry, grand prince of Moscow began uniting forces in order to expel the Tatars, but ran up against the opposition of the princes of Tver, Nizhni-Novgorod and Riazan. In 1378, the Mamai Khan led an expedition aimed at conquering Russia, but was defeated.

[7] In 1380, Dmitry defeated Mamai in the battle of Kulikov, near the Don river, marking the beginning of Russian liberation from the Tatars. The struggle for liberation lasted a century, and ended in 1480, when Ajmat, the last of the Golden Horde's khans, retreated from a confrontation with the troops of Prince Ivan III, at the Ugra river.

[8] In 1547, Ivan 'the Terrible' came to the throne. In 1552, Ivan IV took Kazan, and annexed the territory of the middle course of the Volga river, inhabited by Tatars, Chuvashes, Mari, Morduins and Udmurts. In 1556, he occupied Astrakhan, while the west continued to war against the Polish-Lithuanian State, trying to gain an outlet to the Baltic Sea. Serfdom was established, with peasants losing the right to leave without the feudal lord's permission. Ivan IV established absolute power by eliminating several upper nobility, boyar clans.

[9] Upon the death of Ivan IV, he was succeeded by his mentally ill son Fyodor in 1584 and power passed to the boyar (lord) Boris Godunov. Godunov conducted a short war against Sweden, signed an alliance with Georgia - which became a Russian protectorate - and annexed the principality of Siberia. On Fyodor's death in 1598, the Council of Territories (Zemski Sodor) elected Boris Godunov as czar. However, the boyar clans of older lineage felt they had a greater claim to the throne, and a period of intrigue and conflict over succession began.

[10] In 1601-2, in the Ukrainian territory - which belonged to Poland - an impostor calling himself 'Prince Dmitry' appeared, claiming to have escaped an attempt on his life by Boris Godunov. Amassing an army, he moved towards Moscow,

WORKERS

1996
UNEMPLOYMENT: 11.3%

% OF LABOUR FORCE **1998**

■ FEMALE: 49%   ■ MALE: 51%

1990

■ SERVICES: 44.6%
■ INDUSTRY: 41.7
■ AGRICULTURE: 13.7%

LAND USE

DEFORESTATION: 0.0% annual (1990/95)
IRRIGATED: 3.1% of arable (1993)

1993

■ FOREST & WOODLAND: 45.6%
■ ARABLE: 7.6%
■ OTHER: 46.8%

PUBLIC EXPENDITURE

1997

80

60

40   30.9%   31.1%

20

0   DEFENCE   SOCIAL

MILITARY EXPENDITURE   **132%**
(% of health & education)   (1990/91)

managing to gain a following among the disaffected members of the population, and eventually seizing the throne. In 1606, the boyars killed the 'False Dmitry' but in 1607 another impostor - a second False Dmitry - appeared, supported by Poles, Lithuanians and Swedes. Polish troops occupied Moscow with the help of turncoat boyar. The Poles were finally expelled from Moscow, and in 1613 the Zemsky Sodor elected Michael Romanov as the new Czar. Between 1654 and 1667, Russia warred against the kingdoms of Sweden and Poland, managing in the process to annex eastern Ukraine.

[11] Under the Romanovs, the Russian State became an absolute monarchy, administrated by an efficient bureaucracy and an oligarchy (made up of nobles, merchants and bishops) which was integrated into the Government structure. The church was reformed and the bible translated into cyrillic script, causing a schism in the Russian church. During the 17th century the economy grew rapidly, as a result of territorial expansion, and the exploitation of Siberia's natural resources. A market also developed for Russia's forest products and semi-manufactured goods, primarily in Britain and Holland.

[12] In 1694, after the accession of Peter I, the Muscovite kingdom became known as the Russian Empire. Peter turned to the West to secure its scientific and technical advances, especially in order to develop the Russian Navy. Allied with Denmark and Poland, Russia successfully intervened in the Great Northern War (1700-21). In 1703, he founded St Petersburg, transferring the capital of his empire there and organizing the Government along a set of strict regulations.

[13] Peter established what amounted to a caste system, as well as an espionage network within his own administration, essential for maintaining his strict autocracy. He put down the boyar in Moscow, and had his own son, Alexei, tortured and executed for joining them.

[14] In 1721, by the Treaty of Nystad, Russia obtained control of the Gulf of Finland and the provinces along the east coast of the Baltic Sea. After winning the war against Persia, Peter extended Russia's southern borders as far as the Caspian Sea. The territorial, economic and commercial expansion which characterized this period made Russia one of the major European powers but also created a mosaic of ethnic and cultural groups which could not easily be assimilated into a single unit.

[15] Peter's sudden death in 1725 ushered in a period of instability, until the accession of Catherine II, in 1762. The Empire's conquests continued, with the occupation of Belarus and the part of Ukraine east of the Dnepr; the partition of Poland between Russia and Prussia; and the annexation of Lithuania and Crimea. Russia also gained control of the northern coast of the Black Sea, penetrating the steppes beyond the Urals and all along the coast, they began exercising an ever-increasing influence over the Balkans.

[16] In the meantime, the impoverishment of the peasants increased. The military democracy of the Ukrainian Cossacks was abolished, and the nationalist sentiment of the subdued peoples began to cause friction.

[17] Toward the end of the 18th century the French Revolution and the fight against absolutism influenced the Russian intelligentsia, which began rebelling against existing social conditions. The accession of Alexander I to the throne brought with it radical changes in the policies of the Russian Empire.

[18] Although Alexander sought peace, Napoleon declared war in 1805 and defeated Russia at Austerlitz. In 1812, Napoleon's troops invaded Russia. The 'War for the Motherland' in which peasant fighters were also involved, ended with the triumph of the Russian army commanded by Marshall Kutuzov. This victory transformed Russia into the continent's major power. In December 1825, after the death of Alexander I, a group of aristocrats later known as 'the Decembrists' attempted a coup in the Senate Square in St Petersburg. When the 1848 revolutions shook Europe, Russia - governed by Nikolai I - remained untouched and used its army to subdue the Hungarians in Transylvania, though it was defeated in the Crimean War against Britain and France (1853-56).

[19] In 1861, Czar Alexander II abolished serfdom. However, freedom was not 'free', as the peasants had to pay their former landlords for the land which they farmed. A system of elected local assemblies was also established, with peasant representation, though the landowners maintained control.

[20] In the 1860s-70s, radical groups emerged whose aims ranged from demanding a constituent assembly to calling for insurrection. Socialist ideas influenced students and intellectuals, who saw in the peasants a revolutionary class. In 1861-62, several different revolutionary groups created an underground association in St Petersburg, called 'Land and Freedom', which existed until 1864. The Polish uprising of 1863 and a failed attempt on the Czar's life in 1866 deepened government repression.

[21] The intellectuals reached the conclusion that they would have to 'go to the people' in order to explain to them who their enemies were. In 1876, another 'Peace and Freedom' underground movement was established. Three years later the group split into three, including the 'People's Will', which assassinated Alexander II in 1881, and whose main leaders were hanged. Alexander III did away with his predecessor's reforms, and increased the power of the autocracy.

[22] In the early 20th century, Russian socialism had two main currents. The socialist revolutionaries promoted the socialization of the land in peasant communities, while the social democrats based socialism upon industrialization and the working class. Within the Social Democratic Worker's Party of Russia (SDWPR), the Bolsheviks, led by Vladimir Ilich Ulyanov (known as 'Lenin') defended the idea of a workers' revolt, while the Mensheviks shared the idea of an evolutionary socialism, put forward by Europe's other social democratic parties.

[23] Russian expansionism in Eastern Asia led to a war with Japan in 1904. The violent repression of a demonstration in Moscow in 1905 unleashed a revolt in both capitals, which was only brought under control by the October 17 Manifesto: Czar Nicholas II's promise to convene a national parliament (Duma). The Bolsheviks boycotted the elections. The first Duma's majority was in the hands of constitutional democrats who were moderate liberals.

[24] The Duma's demands for agrarian reform, equal rights for members of all religions (Russian Orthodoxy was the official religion), an amnesty for political prisoners, and autonomy for Poland were unacceptable to the Czar. The Duma was dissolved and the regime put down the revolt after a long and bloody struggle. In 1907, the second Duma was elected, with the presence of the SDWPR. Both the left and the right wings were reinforced, and the main political issue continued to be land. Prime Minister Stolipin promoted an agrarian reform, in order to create a a class of land-owning peasants and put an end to the traditional communal use of the land.

However, he was unsuccessful and was assassinated. The second Duma was also dissolved. An electoral reform guaranteed that the Duma committees which followed also had a conservative majority.

[25] Russia's entry into World War I precipitated a crisis within the regime. The losses brought about by war, and the lack of food, simply deepened popular discontent. In January 1917, in Petrograd, a Council (Soviet) elected by workers, soldiers and members of the Duma formed a government. In February, Nicholas II abdicated and the Duma committee established a new Provisional Government, while local soviets multiplied. The German Government authorized a group of Bolsheviks, led by Lenin, to pass through German territory, hoping to destabilize the enemy's internal situation. The Bolsheviks returned to Russia in a sealed railway car. Their influence within the soviets began to grow, and a power split emerged between the councils and Alexander Kerensky's Government.

[26] The Bolsheviks launched the slogans 'Peace, land and bread' and 'All power to the soviets', exhorting the people to 'turn the world war into a civil war'. On November 7, Lenin led the uprising which brought down the Government, and the first socialist republic was established. In early 1918, the Bolsheviks dissolved the Constituent Assembly, in which the revolutionary socialists held a majority.

[27] The Soviet Government (Council of People's Commissars) approved a peace 'without annexation or indemnities', the abolition of private ownership of the land and its being turned over to the peasants and the nationalization of the banking system. Other measures were approved, including the control of factories by their workers, the creation of a militia and of revolutionary tribunals, the abolition of the privileges associated with class and of the right of inheritance, the separation of Church and State and equal rights for men and women.

[28] Following Russia's unilateral peace settlement in 1918, Germany, France and Britain sent expeditionary forces to Russia (their former ally), to support the 'White Russians' - the former regime's army forces - and bring down the

MATERNAL MORTALITY

1990-98

Per 100,000 live births

50

EXTERNAL DEBT

1998

PER CAPITA

US$ 1,245

revolutionary government. This foreign intervention force was ousted in 1920, and two years later the civil war ceased, with the triumph of the Red Army. During this period, the Soviet Government's policy of 'war communism' resulted in a maximum centralization of power and a near-collapse of the monetary system.

[29] In December 1922, the Russian Federation, Ukraine, Belarus and the Transcaucasian Federation (Azerbaijan, Armenia and Georgia) established the Union of Soviet Socialist Republics (USSR). During the civil war, the regime had become the official preserve of the Russian (Bolshevik) Communist Party, or R(B)CP.

[30] In 1921, the R(B)CP - faced with the danger of an imminent economic collapse - was forced to do away with its 'war communism' policy, and adopt a New Economic Policy (NEP). This consisted of a return to the laws of a market system and private ownership of small business, while the State took care of infrastructure, heavy industry and general planning. In 1924, the NEP was interrupted by Lenin's death; internal disputes within the R(B)CP came to an end with the triumph of Joseph Stalin, who had become secretary general of the Party in 1922. Trotsky (Lenin's close associate) went into exile and was assassinated under Stalin's orders, in Mexico in 1940.

[31] Stalin re-established the system of centralized planning of the economy, and forcibly imposed the collectivization of agriculture. Opposition figures and dissidents were eliminated through summary trials, like the Great Purge of 1935-38. Official plans cited huge figures for grain harvests as well as the production of electricity and steel, while the secret police held almost absolute power.

[32] At the beginning of World War II, by means of a secret agreement with Germany (the Molotov-Ribbentrop Pact), the USSR occupied part of Poland, as well as Romania, Estonia, Latvia and Lithuania. In 1941, Hitler launched a large attack against Moscow, sending in thousands of troops, as well as German air power. The Nazis took control of many Russian cities; however, at a cost of some 20 million lives, the Soviets were able to repel the German attack. The Red Army liberated several countries, finally taking Berlin in May 1945.

[33] In 1945, at the Yalta conference, the Western powers and the USSR 'carved up' their respective areas of influence. In those countries occupied by the Red Army (Bulgaria, Hungary, Romania, Czechoslovakia, Poland and East Germany), the Communists took power and proclaimed first 'people's republics', then socialist republics, following the model of the Communist Party of the Soviet Union (CPSU).

[34] In 1956, at the 20th Party Congress of the CPSU, Nikita Krushchev began a de-Stalinization process, which abruptly came to an end when Leonid Brezhnev ousted Krushchev in October 1964. Despite difficulties of implementation, 'developed socialism' was proclaimed.

[35] The strategy of the Cold War devised by the United States in the post-war period fuelled the arms race. A by-product of the Cold War was the creation of the Warsaw Pact between the USSR and its Eastern European allies in 1955. The East-West confrontation eventually included nuclear weapons and the control of outer space, where the United States and the USSR actively pursued their own space programs in the 1960s and 1970s, with neither one actually taking a lead.

[36] In 1985, Mikhail Gorbachev became Secretary General of the CPSU and initiated drastic changes to avert a social and economic crisis. Glasnost (transparency) and perestroika (restructuring) - geared to carrying out a series of transformations within the country - unleashed forces which had long been repressed, and brought out into the open the issue of the autonomy of different ethnic groups and nationalities. Changes within the USSR set in motion similar processes in other nations throughout Eastern Europe.

[37] In April 1986, there was a serious accident in one of the reactors of the nuclear power plant at Chernobyl in the Ukraine. Some 135,000 people were evacuated and by 1993 7,000 people had died (see Ukraine).

[38] Gorbachev initiated internal reforms and also made other initiatives in the area of foreign policy, such as the withdrawal of Soviet troops from Afghanistan (where the Soviet army had been involved in a war since 1979). In addition, he was responsible for accords leading to the reduction of nuclear weapons in Europe, and also accepted the reunification of Germany. In 1990, he proposed that the Warsaw Pact and NATO be phased out gradually.

[39] Economic reform, the opening of the country to foreign capital and a return to a free-market economy were all slow in being implemented due to the resistance of the CPSU leadership. After a failed coup, in August, the CPSU was dissolved after 70 years in power. Gorbachev resumed his duties as Soviet president, but his position had become irrevocably weakened. In June 1991, Boris Yeltsin was elected President of Russia.

[40] Trouble broke out in the Chechen-Ingush region (Northern Caucasia). Toward the end of October, parliamentary and presidential elections were held there. General Dzhojar Dudaev, leader of the Chechen nationalist movement, seized power. In early November he proclaimed the independence of the Chechen Republic. An economic embargo was promptly announced by Moscow.

[41] On October 6 1991, Yegor Gaidar was named Deputy Prime Minister, and he launched liberal economic reforms, dubbed 'shock therapy'. On December 8, Boris Yeltsin (Russia), Stanislav Shushkevich (Belarus) and Leonid Kravchuk (Ukraine) revoked the 1922 treaty under which the USSR had been founded, proclaiming the Commonwealth of Independent States (CIS) to take its place (see box on CIS). Russia assumed the formal representation of the former USSR in foreign affairs. Latvia, Estonia and Lithuania withdrew and were recognized as separate countries by the UN.

[42] In early 1992, there was a growing rivalry between the two most important members of the CIS, Russia and Ukraine, revolving around the issue of who controlled the nuclear weapons and navy which had belonged to the former USSR. Relations between them

PROFILE

ENVIRONMENT

The largest country in the world, Russia is divided into five vast regions: the European region, the Ural area, Siberia, Caucasia and the Central Asian region. The European region is the richest of the Russian Federation, and lies between Russia's western border and the Ural Mountains (the conventional boundary between Europe and Asia); it is a vast plain crossed by the Volga, Don and Dnepr rivers. The Urals, which extend from north to south, have important mineral and oil deposits in their outlying areas. The third region, Siberia, lies between the Urals and the Pacific coast. It is rich in natural resources, but sparsely populated because of its rigorous climate. Caucasia is an enormous steppe which extends northward from the mountains of the same name, between the Black and Caspian Seas. Finally, the Central Asian region is an enormous depression of land made up of deserts, steppes and mountains. Grain, potatoes and sugar beet are grown on the plains; cotton and fruit in Central Asia; tea, grapes and citrus fruit in the subtropical Caucasian and Black Sea regions. The country's vast mineral resources include oil, coal, iron, copper, zinc, lead, bauxite, manganese and tin, found in the Urals, Caucasia and Central Siberia. Chelyabinsk, a city which lies south of the Ural Mountains, has high levels of radioactivity, due to leaks in its plutonium plant. Pollution, caused by the dumping of industrial wastes, threatens Lake Baikal. Heavy industry and mining have contributed to increasing contamination of the country's main rivers, air and soil. Other contributing factors include the dependence upon coal in electrical generating plants, defects in nuclear reactors and the abuse of agrochemical products. Deforestation and soil erosion also threaten large areas of the countryside.

SOCIETY

Peoples: Russians, 81.5 per cent; Tatars, 3.8 per cent; Ukrainians, 3 per cent; over 100 other nationalities (1996). **Religions**: Christian Orthodoxy is the main religion. There are also Muslim, Protestant and Jewish minorities. **Languages**: Russian (official). **Political Parties**: Russia Our Home and Option of Russia, both neo-liberal; the Liberal Democratic Party, Nationalist conservative; Communist Party; Democratic Agrarian Party; Yabloko; Congress of Russian Communities. **Social Organizations**: Federation of Independent Labor Unions of Russia (FNPR), with more than 40 million workers; Sotsprof Labor Union Association, with one million affiliates.

THE STATE

Official Name: Rossiyskaya Federatsiya. **Administrative divisions**: The federation is made up of 26 autonomous republics: the republics of Bashkortostan (formerly Bashkir), Chechen-Ingush, Chuvash, Dagestan, Kabardino-Balkar, Kalmykia, Komi, Mari, Mordovia, North Ossetia, Tatar, Tuva and Saja (formerly Yakut); the regions of Adigueya, Gorno-Altai, Hebrea and Karachai-Cherkessk; and the territories of Buryat-Aguin, Buryat-Ust-Ordin, Chukchi, Dolgano-Neneos of Taimir, Evenkos, Janti and Mansi, Koriakos, Neneos and Yamalo-Neneos. **Capital**: Moscow (Moskva) 8,400,000 people (1996). **Other cities**: St Petersburg 4,200,000 people; Nizhny-Novgorod 1,424,600; Novosibirsk 1,418,200; Ekaterinburg (former Sverdlovsk) 1,347,000; Samar 1,522,500; Omsk, 1,116,200; Chelyabinsk 1,124,500; Kazan 1,092,300; Ufa 1,091,800; Perm 1,086,100; Rostov-na-Donu 1,023,200 (1994). **Government**: Vladimir Vladimirovich Putin, President since 1999; Mikhail Mikhaylovich Kasyanov, Prime Minister since May 2000. Parliamentary republic. Legislature, bicameral: Congress of People's Deputies, with 1,068 members elected by direct popular vote; Supreme Soviet, with 252 members appointed from the members of the Congress. **National Holiday**: June 12. **Armed Forces**: 1,270,000 (1996). **Other**: 220,000.

were further complicated by the issue of Crimea's sovereignty. President Yeltsin declared that the United States was no longer a 'strategic rival', and continued the reform of the economy that Gorbachev had begun, including the liberalization of prices, and the privatization of industry, agriculture and trade.

[43] On February 23 1992, violent confrontations broke out between communist and nationalist protesters, and the militia, with several people being killed by the police.

[44] On March 13, the autonomous republics associated to Russia signed the Federation Treaty, except for the Tatar and Chechen republics. A week later, in a referendum in the Tatar republic, the population voted in favor of state sovereignty and the termination of the bilateral treaty with Moscow.

[45] In April 1992, Yeltsin managed to maintain control of his reformist government, despite attacks from the 6th Congress of People's Deputies. In June he threatened to dissolve parliament, which opposed his reforms. In the meantime, the Constitutional Court declared that Yeltsin's decree banning the Communist Party was illegal. On June 12 and 22 there were further clashes between opposition members and the police.

[46] On October 31 a territorial dispute broke out in Northern Caucasia between Ossetia and Ingushetia over part of North Ossetia which had previously been part of Ingushetia. Moscow declared a state of emergency in the region, and after several days, the rebellion was put down.

[47] In early December 1992, the 7th Congress of People's Deputies refused to ratify Boris Yeltsin's choice for Prime Minister, Yegor Gaidar. After exchanging recriminations, the President and Congress agreed to ratify Victor Chernomyrdin in the position.

[48] The arm wrestling between the President and Parliament continued. In March 1993, Congress opposed a referendum proposed by Yeltsin and tried unsuccessfully to limit the powers of the leader. Following further disagreements, Yeltsin took all the power from Parliament, which ousted the President and substituted him with Alexandr Rutskoi. On the same day, September 22, the police surrounded the seat of the legislative power.

[49] The tension continued to increase and on October 4 Parliament was taken by force after having been attacked with tanks. Several opposition leaders, like Rutskoi, vice-president of Congress, and its leader, Ruslan Khasbulatov, were arrested. A few days later, Yeltsin called for new elections and organized a referendum to increase his own powers.

[50] The December elections marked the defeat of those sectors faithful to Yeltsin, but 60 per cent of the voters approved the constitutional reform which granted him greater powers. In February 1994, a bilateral agreement was signed with the Russian republic of Tartarstan and a similar document was expected to be signed with Chechnya. However, the tension between Moscow and the pro-independence groups of this mostly Muslim republic, which had declared independence in 1991, became more serious and in December 1994, Yeltsin ordered military intervention.

[51] Despite protests both within Russia and abroad, the President maintained the military attacks on Grozny, the Chechen capital, which was almost totally destroyed in 1995. In December of that year, the Communist Party led by Zyuganov won the legislative elections with 22.3 per cent, followed by the ultra-right and xenophobic Liberal Democratic Party of Vladimir Zhirinovski, with 11.8 per cent and the Russia Our Home of Prime Minister Viktor Chernomyrdin, with 10.1 per cent.

[52] Fearful of defeat in the July 1996 presidential elections, Yeltsin tried to modify his policies, stopping the privatizations and nominating Yevgeny Primakov - a diplomat from the Soviet era who was an ally of Gorbachev - as foreign minister. In the electoral campaign all the opposition candidates from Gorbachev to the Communists, criticized the unlimited financial speculation, corruption and 'clanishness' of Yeltsin and his allies.

[53] In the second round of the July elections, Yeltsin took 53.8 per cent of the vote and Zyuganov only 40 per cent (4.8 per cent of the voters voted against both). The outgoing president was able to win through an unexpected alliance with Alexandr Lebed, an opposition candidate who had received 11 million votes.

[54] Appointed State security adviser, Lebed immediately started action to end the war in Chechnya, which he stated had caused the deaths of 80,000 people. When it was announced Yeltsin would be undergoing surgery in September, Lebed and Prime Minister Chernomyrdin became the alternative, and opposed, choices should there be a power vacuum.

[55] Yeltsin returned in March 1997, following a long absence. He reformed his cabinet and launched a far-reaching plan to cut back State spending, and privatizations. The living conditions of the population continued to fall. The chaotic change to a market economy damaged the production mechanisms, dismantled the social protection systems, and fed the rise of the mafias. In that year 73 per cent of the banking sector was under mafia control, and one of their most lucrative lines was the trafficking of nuclear material.

[56] On May 12, Yeltsin signed an agreement with Chechnya granting it wide-ranging autonomy. The same day, the Russian Central Bank made an agreement with the Chechen bank similar to that between the US State Bank and the Panamanian bank: Chechnya would provisionally maintain the rouble as its currency, but Moscow would no longer control its bank.

[57] An explosion in the Zeryanovoskaja coal mine in December killed more than 60 people exposing the dreadful safety conditions common in this sector. Some 1,720 miners had died in the five years up to this date.

[58] Chernomyrdin had a brief comeback as Prime Minister during 1998 just after the ruble devaluation and the dismissal of Sergey Kiriyenko. Unable to achieve the support of the Duma, he was substituted by Foreign Affairs Minister Evguenni Primakov, who was voted in September by communists, nationalists and several liberals. Primakov, an economist, managed to reschedule debts with international organizations without promising any concrete changes. Fiscal controls were reintroduced and the Government started to intervene in the economy. At an international level, Primakov introduced a policy less dependent on Washington and clashed with Clinton and Blair over the attacks on Iraq by the US and Great Britain in December 1998. That year inflation reached 84 per cent (from 11 per cent in 1997), the GDP fell by 5 per cent and real income decreased by 15.5 per cent, while the rouble devaluated 74 per cent.

[59] Events in Yugoslavia revealed Moscow's incapacity to prevent NATO incursions into the territory of its historical allies. Russian mediation efforts were not recognized by the alliance. After the bombing was completed, NATO accepted the nominal presence of a Russian 'peacekeeping force'.

[60] Yeltsin felt threatened by the popularity of Primakov and opted for a change of government. During the May bombings in Yugoslavia, he replaced him with Sergei Stepashin. Stepashin in turn was replaced by Vladimir Putin in August.

[61] A guerrilla contingent which crossed the Chechen border advanced into Daguestan during the month of August and took several cities. The Russian army

DEMOGRAPHY

Population: 147,195,000 (1999)
Annual growth: 0.4 % (1975/97)
Estimates for year 2015 (million): 142.9 (1999)
Annual growth to year 2015: -0.2 % (1997/2015)
Urban population: 76.6 % (1997)
Urban Growth: 0.8 % (1980/95)
Children per woman: 1.3 (1998)

HEALTH

Life expectancy at birth: 67 years (1998)
male: 61 years (1998)
female: 73 years (1998)
Maternal mortality: 50 per 100,000 live births (1990-98)
Infant mortality: 21 per 1,000 (1998)
Under-5 child mortality: 25 per 1,000 (1998)
Daily calorie supply: 2,704 per capita (1996)
380 doctors per 100,000 people (1993)

EDUCATION

Literacy: 99 % (1995)
male: 100 % (1995)
female: 99 % (1995)
School enrolment:
Primary total: 108 % (1990/96)
male: 108 % (1990/97)
female: 107 % (1990/97)
Secondary:
male: 84 % (1990/96)
female: 91 % (1990/96)
Tertiary: 41 % (1996)

COMMUNICATIONS

105 newspapers (1996), 418 radios (1997), 386 TV sets (1996) and 175 main telephone lines (1996) per 1,000 people
Books: 20 new titles per 100,000 people (1992/94)

ECONOMY

Per capita, GNP: $ 2,260 (1998)
Annual growth, GNP: -6.6 % (1998)
Annual inflation: 230.9 % (1990/98)
Consumer price index: 216.4 (1998)
Currency: 9.7 roubles = $ 1 (1998)
Cereal imports: 2,016,659 metric tons (1998)
Food import dependency: 19 % (1997)
Fertilizer use: 133 kg per ha (1997)
Exports: $ 87,734 million (1998)
Imports: $ 74,078 million (1998)
External debt: $ 183,601 million (1998); $ 1,245 per capita (1998)
Debt service: 12.1 % of exports (1998)
Development aid received: $ 718 million (1997); $ 4.8 per capita (1997); 0.20 % of GNP (1997)

ENERGY

Consumption: 4,019.0 Kgs of Oil equivalent per capita yearly (1997); -57.0 % imported (1997)

HDI (rank/value): 71/0.747 (1997)

repelled the rebels after some weeks of fighting. A wave of bomb attacks against civilian buildings in Moscow caused scores of deaths and were blamed on Chechen terrorists. The army began a new offensive against the autonomous republic, which had been virtually independent since 1996, although not internationally recognized. The new Prime Minister pledged to 'recover' Chechnya for the Federation. Russia used all disposable means to conquer the territory, but still after eight months of fighting it could barely keep Grozni and the central area in control, while the guerrilla were still strong in the mountains. The forces of President Aslan Maskhadov offered Moscow a truce in April, but were rejected.

[62] Surprisingly, Yeltsin resigned on December 31, leaving Putin in charge of the government. The move confused the Opposition. Primakov, one of the main candidates to the presidency, had to back off after being unable to form a coalition in opposition to Yeltsin's successor. Early elections, held on March 26 2000, gave Putin the victory in the first round, with 52.9 per cent of the vote, leaving Gennadi Zyuganov, the communist candidate, in second place with 29.2 per cent of the vote.

[63] In August 2000 the nuclear submarine *Kursk* sank after an explosion during exercises in the Barents Sea. Some 120 submariners were killed. Rescue attempts came too late and President Putin was criticised for his apparent lack of urgency. That same month four people died in a fire in Moscow's prestigious communications tower building. ∎

National conflicts in the former USSR

Conflicts among different national groups in the former Soviet Union - that gained new strength by its dissolution - are the result, among other things, of the expansionist policy of the Tsarist regime begun in the 18th century and continued by its Soviet successors.

At the time of its break-up in October 1991 the USSR was a vast conglomerate of numerous ethnic groups. This was the result of a long historical process of Tsarist expansion which since the 18th century had transformed Russia. The Tsarist regime implemented a systematic policy of 'Russianis-ation', with the absolute pre-eminence of the Russian language and of the Orthodox Church, as well as obedience to a central power embodied in the Tsar. During the civil wars that followed the October 1917 revolution, the various republics were federated to form the Union of Soviet Socialist Republics.

Soviet policy, unlike the Tsarist one, sought, at least in name, to grant equal rights to the different ethnic groups and political divisions in the State. This implied giving primacy to the central power of the Soviet over land and ethnic conflicts between different regions, the forceful 'sedentarization' of nomadic peoples (such as in Kyrgysztan) and initiatives to fight ethnic divisions which consisted mostly of huge forced migrations from one region to another.

The Baltic republics were annexed to the USSR in 1940, in accordance with a secret agreement signed by Stalin and Hitler in 1939, jointly with the German-Soviet pact signed before World War II. Bukovina and Bessarabia were confiscated from Romania in 1944, which, together with the Autonomous Republic of Moldavia, in Ukranian territory, made up the Socialist Republic of Moldavia (now Moldova).

The USSR consisted of 15 Soviet socialist republics, which were further subdivided into 20 autonomous Soviet socialist republics, 8 autonomous regions (smaller and less populated than the republics) and 10 autonomous districts (for small ethnic groups, mostly nomadic, from Siberia and the Far East).

In 1986, with Mikhail Gorbachev in the Presidential seat, it was clear that the tensions had only been muted (and in some cases increased) by the administrative initiatives of the Communist regime. Several republics demanded their independence, which led to the dissolution of the USSR.

Several regions and districts also demanded their autonomy, leading to armed conflicts. In 1998, some new republics which had declared their sovereignty had not yet resolved their status. These were the Transnitrian Republic of Moldavia (known as Transnitria), the Republic of South Ossetia, the Republic of Nagorno-Karabakh and the People's Republic of Abkhazia.

TRANSNITRIA

The 1989 census revealed that the population of Transnitria was still mostly Slavic (28 per cent Ukranians, 24 per cent Russians), while Moldavians amounted to 40 per cent. However, that year, the Government of Moldavia declared Moldavian as the Republic's sole official language, which led to strikes and social unrest. From January to October 1990, the population of Transnitria organized referenda which decided the creation of the Autonomous Republic of Transnitria. But the Supreme Soviet of the USSR declared these referenda illegal and refused to grant the territory autonomy. In December 1991, after the dissolution of the Soviet Union, Igor Smirnov was chosen first President of Transnitria and a new referendum declared independence. Moldavian police clashed with Transnitrian militias and, in 1992, the Russian Federation and Moldavia signed an agreement to re-establish peace in the region. In 1994, Transnitria and Moldavia (now Moldova) re-established economic relations and 100,000 refugees returned to their homes, although in 1998 the political situation remained uncertain.

SOUTH OSSETIA

Ossetians came to the Caucasus territory in the 13th century. In 1774, Russia annexed the territories held by the Ossetians and, in 1918, created the Autonomous Republic of Ossetia (in the present Federated Republic of Russia). In 1922, the autonomous region of South Ossetia was created in Georgia. In the Eighties, when several movements for self-determination appeared in various parts of the Soviet Union, the idea of joining the Autonomous Republic of Ossetia started to grow in South Ossetia. In September 1990, South Ossetia proclaimed itself a sovereign republic. In December 1990, the parliament of Georgia repealed the status of autonomous region in South Ossetia and declared a state of emergency in the territory, which led to the beginning of armed confrontations. A Russian-Georgian-Ossetian peace force succeeded in putting an end to the fighting in 1992. In 1994, L. Chibirov was elected president of the parliament in South Ossetia and, in 1996, became President of the territory. Since then, several meetings between Georgian and Ossetians authorities failed to reach an agreement on the political status of South Ossetia.

NAGORNO-KARABAKH

Since May 1918, when Moscow's authority was established over Nagorno-Karabakh, it was discussed if the region, mostly populated by Armenians, should belong to Armenia or Azerbaijan. In 1923 the territory became a province of Azerbaijan. The strikes of 1988 in Nagorno-Karabakh were one of the first signs of instability due to nationalist demands in the Soviet Union. In 1991, the Nagorno-Karabakh Parliament not only declared the region's independence, but also annexed the district of Shaumia. Three months later, the majority of the population voted for independence. By then, a full-blown war had erupted between the Karabakhs (supported by Armenia) and Azerbaijan, in which 4,600 Karabakhs and some 30,000 Azerbaijanis died. In 1994, Azerbaijan and Nagorno-Karabakh signed an armistice. The first elections of Nagorno-Karabakh elected Robert Kocharian President in December 1996. In 1997, Kocharian was appointed Prime Minister of Armenia and left Karabakh, being replaced by Arcady Gukassian. In 1998, the creation of Nagorno-Karabakh was still in process and negotiations with Azerbaijan progressed slowly. ∎

Rwanda

Rwanda

Population: 7,235,000 (1999)
Area: 26,340 SQ KM
Capital: Kigali
Currency: Franc
Language: Kinyarwanda, English and French

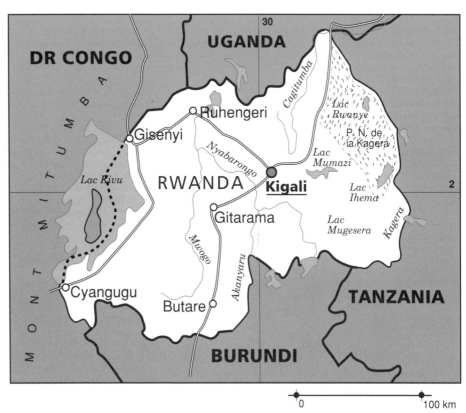

Inhabited since ancient times by the Hutu (Bantus) and Twa (pygmy) ethnic groups, Rwanda's highlands were invaded in the 15th century by the Tutsis (or Watutsis) from Ethiopia. After subduing the local population, the Tutsis set up a stratified society. This social and political organization remained basically unchanged even after German colonization started in the region in 1897. The territory became part of German East Africa, which also included Burundi.

² After World War I, the territory named Rwanda-Urundi was placed under Belgian custody and administered by them from the Congo (today's DR Congo, formerly Zaire). Of the three groups which inhabit the region, the minority - made up of the pastoralist and warrior Tutsis - consolidated its control over the agricultural Hutu and artisan Twa. In 1959, farm workers organized by the Parmehutu (Party of the Hutu Emancipation Movement) revolted against Tutsi rule. A bloody civil war ensued and the Belgian colonial government chose to abandon the territory. The Parmehutu won elections supervised by the United Nations in 1961 and proclaimed a Republic in 1962, autonomous from neighboring Burundi.

³ The power structure favoring Tutsi rulers was abolished and land distributed on the capitalist basis of private ownership. However, this did not lead to true national unity, nor did it settle controversies between ethnic groups. The following year, civil war broke out again. Approximately 20,000 people died and 160,000 Tutsis were expelled from the country.

⁴ Lacking other patterns, the Parmehutu reorganized society according to ethnic group interests: the Twa (40,000 in all) were assigned the crafts industry; the Tutsis, cattle-raising, and land ownership was reserved for the Hutus. The system virtually ignored the possibility of urban development, a fact evidenced by the tiny size of the capital city of Kigali. In order to set an example, President Gregory Kayibanda worked his own piece of land. As a result agriculture was almost entirely reduced to subsistence farming, with little surplus left over for the market.

⁵ In the late 1960s, attempts to increase market production saw a revival of the coffee plantations, burnt down in 1959, in protest against colonial despotism. The new policy however did not solve Rwanda's economic problems but rather exacerbated social tensions as a new group of landowners arose, adding complexity to existing ethnic conflicts, and giving rise to new and violent outbreaks.

⁶ Faced with the threat of a new civil war, Colonel Juvenal Habyarimana overthrew Kayibanda on July 5 1973. Habyarimana, previously defence minister, dissolved the Parmehutu, jailed Kayibanda (who died shortly afterwards) and launched a diplomatic offensive successfully dealing with conflicts which had arisen between Rwanda and neighboring countries during the previous regime.

⁷ The close relationship between Habyarimana and France, and with Zaire's President Mobutu caused disagreements within the governing party, the National Revolutionary Movement for Development (MRND). Progressive factions criticized the situation and Habyarimana's liberal policies. During the 1980 party congress they were expelled. Their leader, labor minister Alexis Kanyarengwe, went into exile in Tanzania to escape prison. Resolutions by the party congress endorsed 'planned liberalism', which resulted in an open-door policy for foreign investments.

⁸ In 1982, Uganda expelled large numbers of Rwandan exiles, who were not allowed back into their own country. Whole towns were burned down by Ugandan troops leaving at least 10,000 people homeless and without food.

⁹ In 1986, the new president of Uganda, Yoweri Museveni, announced that Rwandans who had lived in the country for more than ten years would automatically receive citizenship.

LAND USE

DEFORESTATION: 0.2% annual (1990/95)
IRRIGATED: 0.5% of arable (1993)

1993

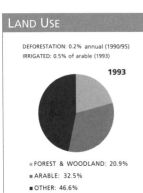

- FOREST & WOODLAND: 20.9%
- ARABLE: 32.5%
- OTHER: 46.6%

WORKERS

% OF LABOUR FORCE **1998**

- FEMALE: 49%   ■ MALE: 51%

PUBLIC EXPENDITURE

DEFENCE EXPENDITURE
(% of goverment exp.)   **22.2%**
(1997)

Relations improved between the two countries; in 1988, both presidents signed a declaration confirming progress in their international policies.

[10] President Habyarimana changed his policies and took firm steps towards establishing a democracy. Initially he set up a National Development Council in an attempt to draw up national policies taking into consideration the country's different social and economic realities. Later, he launched an austerity program, which yielded some positive economic results. He released more than 1,000 political prisoners, and implemented measures to ensure respect for human rights in the prisons.

[11] Habyarimana was re-elected in 1988. On December 26 that year, elections were held to renew one-third of the 70 deputies. Of these, 11 women but only 2 Tutsis were elected. 60,000 Hutu refugees from Burundi entered the country in the course of the year.

[12] On September 30 1990, Fred Rwigyema, an important government official belonging to the Tutsi ethnic group, led an uprising, entering Rwanda from Uganda. President Habyarimana requested help from Belgium, France and Zaire, whose troops played a decisive role in repelling the rebel offensive, although there was also fighting in the capital. In October, a cease-fire was reached between the two parties, through the intervention of Belgian Prime Minister, Wilfried Martens.

[13] At the end of January 1991, some 600 troops belonging to the Rwandan People's Front entered the country from Uganda. In March, a cease-fire was signed. Among its provisions were the liberation of political prisoners and prisoners of war, and a commitment by President Habyarimana to initiate negotiations establishing a more open political atmosphere. In June of that year, the President signed the new constitution, which provided for a multiparty system, creating the post of Prime Minister, guaranteeing freedom of the press, limiting the presidential term to two five-year periods with no further re-election, and establishing a separation of the powers of the state.

[14] In March 1992, at least 300 members of the Tutsi ethnic minority were assassinated, and another 15,000 were forcibly relocated to the region of Bugesera. The leaders of the two principal opposition parties, the Republican Democratic Movement (MDR) and the Liberal Party (PL), blamed the Government for the violence, and especially a militia made up of young Hutus belonging to the MRND.

[15] In early 1993, President Habyarimana rejected the agreement signed in Arusha between the Rwandan delegation - led by Prime Minister Dismas Nsengiyaremye of the Republican Democratic Movement - and the rebels of the Rwandan Patriotic Front (FPR), led by Alex Kanyarengue, made up of Tutsi exiles who had challenged the Hutu domination of their community.

[16] The President refused any form of power-sharing with the FPR, which had demanded five cabinet positions, the incorporation of its soldiers into the regular army and the repatriation of Tutsi refugees from Uganda and Tanzania.

[17] Although both bands had respected the cease-fire which had been in effect since August 1992, the FPR broke off negotiations in February, launching a new offensive which enabled them to gain control over most of the country's territory, and prepare an advance upon the capital.

[18] The death of Presidents of Rwanda, Juvenal Habyarimana, and Burundi, Cyprien Nyataryamira, in an attack on the aeroplane carrying them to Kigali after attending a peace conference in Tanzania on April 6 1994, initiated a new bloodbath which cost the lives of 500,000 people in three months. Both presidents were Hutus.

[19] Given the worsening of the civil war, France, the United States and Belgium decided in April to send in troops to 'guarantee security and evacuate the foreigners'. French troops took control of Kigali airport to oversee the repatriation of 600 French citizens resident in the capital.

[20] The new government tried to revive the Rwandan economy and organize trials for those guilty of what the UN described as 'genocide'. However, the Government did not receive the aid expected from the Western countries and many members of the militias responsible for the massacres continued to operate from their refuge in Zaire (now DR Congo).

[21] During 1995 and 1996 further mass graves were discovered nearly every week, while the violence of the new Rwandan army - formed around a core of FPR fighters - and the militias led to more deaths. Many of the victims of the militias had been witnesses of events in 1994, along with Hutu public officials, accused of 'collaboration'.

[22] Increasing tensions in eastern Zaire and the mass deportations of refugees made violations of human rights more serious. In February 1997, Amnesty International denounced the death of dozens of civilians, both Tutsis and Hutus, and the murder of four UN officials in the city of Cyangugu.

[23] In April 1998, despite the call for clemency made by Pope John Paul II and UN Secretary-General Kofi Annan, 22 of those responsible for the genocide were executed in strategically chosen places, where the largest massacres had taken place. The four executed in Kigali, included Silas Munyagishali (assistant district attorney in Kigali), Froduald Karamira (former vice president of the MDR) and Elie Nhimiyimana (organizer of the

PROFILE

ENVIRONMENT

Known as the country of a thousand hills on account of its geographical location between two mountain ranges, Rwanda lies in the heart of the African continent. The terrain is mountainous and well irrigated by numerous rivers and lakes supporting varied wild life. The population is concentrated in the highlands where the economic mainstay is subsistence agriculture. The lowlands have been eroded and their natural vegetation is disappearing as a result of excessive grazing. 90 per cent of the energy consumed by Rwandans is derived from natural resources, consequently leading to deforestation and erosion.

SOCIETY

Peoples: Rwanda's ethnic composition is the result of close integration between successive migrations and the original pygmy population. Today, 84 per cent are Hutu (a branch of Bantu people), 15 per cent Tutsi (Hamitic) and 1 per cent Twa (descendants of the pygmies). There is a minority of European origin most of whom are Belgian.
Religions: There is no official religion. Most of the population (69 per cent) profess traditional African religions, 20 per cent are Catholic, 10 per cent Protestant and 1 per cent Muslim.
Languages: Kinyarwanda, English and French (the three of them official).
Political Parties: Rwandan Patriotic Front (FPR); National Revolutionary Movement for Development (MRND); Republican Democratic Movement (MDR); Liberal Party (PL).

THE STATE

Official Names: Repubulika y'u Rwanda; République Rwandaise; Republic of Rwanda.
Capital: Kigali 250,000 people (est 1995).
Other cities: Butare 29,000 people; Ruhengeri 30,000; Gisenyi 22,000 (1991).
Government: Paul Kagame, President since March 2000. Bernard Makuza, Prime Minister since March 2000.
National Holiday: July 1, Independence Day (1962).
Armed Forces: 33,000 (1996).

massacre in the Gikondo neighborhood of the capital). Amnesty International classed the executions as 'a brutal parody of justice which jeopardises any hope of reconciliation in Rwanda following the genocide and which will perpetuate the cycle of violence'. Jean Kambanda, former Prime Minister of the Hutu government, decided to plead guilty and collaborate with the International Court, revealing information about his former government colleagues. Kambanda avoided the death penalty and was sentenced to life in prison.
24 Clashes between government troops and Interahamwe Hutu rebel militias on the Northeastern part of the country continued throughout the year causing hundreds of casualties.

25 Prime Minister Pierre Celestin Rwigema, one of few Hutus in government, was accused in October 1999 of channeling hundreds of thousands of international relief dollars into personal projects such as the construction of schools in his home district. Government officials felt 'insulted' by the decision of the international court to free one of the main suspects in the 1994 genocide. In November, the Government denied an entry visa to Carla del Ponte, the court prosecutor. Del Ponte finally entered Rwanda in December. That month the UN asked Rwanda to pardon its inability to prevent the genocide.
26 The allegations against Rwigema created a delicate situation by February 2000: both the press and public opinion

accused him of misappro-priation of funds and of allowing the dumping of toxic waste on the outskirts of Kigali. He was replaced in March by Barnard Makuza, a Hutu from Rwigema's party. That month, President Bizimungu resigned from office after some of his collaborators were not included in the new cabinet. With 81 out of 86 votes, Paul Kagame was elected President by Parliament in April 2000.
27 A UN report released in March 2000 accused Rwanda, Burkina Faso and Togo of assisting UNITA, the Angolan rebel organization. The report also accused Belgium of neglecting to control the traffic of diamonds illegally extracted from Angola into its territory. The Government disagreed with the contents of the report and threatened to sue the UN. ∎

The hidden Twa

The Twa pygmies of Rwanda, Burundi and the Congo were the first to occupy the region lapped by the waters of Lake Kivu, as one member group of the Central African pygmy peoples. They are believed to have originated from deep in the forests and equatorial mountains, where they still live today.
2 The Twa lived more or less alone in this region until the 16th century. They were hunters and potters, with a varied and creative ceramic tradition. Their low numbers and height of just 1.5 meters left them at a disadvantage when Hutu farmers and Tutsi herders led successive invasions into their lands. The invaders swiftly made the Twa their slaves, considering them an inferior ethnic group. All three groups speak the same language.
3 Having neither livestock nor farms, the Twa go unregistered in the statistics of Rwanda and neighboring states, where 90 per cent of the population are farmers. In general they suffer from very poor health, with a high incidence of malaria and various sexually-transmitted diseases. Rwanda is one of the Central African countries with the highest average infant mortality from malnutrition and parasites.
4 In recent decades, reports on Rwanda have also ignored these people, giving priority to the power struggle between the Hutus and Tutsis. Some 85 per cent of the Rwandan population are Hutus and in 1994 they were ousted from government by Tutsi rebels who unleashed a genocidal campaign using machetes to slaughter a million Hutus.
5 While these two ethnic groups fight out their battles, the Twa live quietly away from the large towns, only coming down from the mountains to work as paid laborers in the potato, sorghum and corn plantations when they need supplies or when food is short. ∎

Western Sahara

Sahara Occidental

Population: 284,000 (1999)
Area: 266,000 SQ KM
Capital: L'ayoun
Currency: Moroccan dirham
Language: Arabic and Spanish

From the 5th century, the far west of the Sahara has been populated by Moors, Tuaregs and Tubus. Their presence was shown by the Tassili stone carvings and other sources. But successive waves of migration and conquest have swept across the region over the centuries, as Arabs intermingled with Berbers and black Africans from south of the Sahara. Around the 13th century there was a major migration of people into the area of people from beyond Africa, in Yemen.

[2] By the eighteenth century this particular mix of peoples and cultures had blended into something distinct: a group of nomadic tribes called the Ahl Essahel who shared the same branch of Arabic, Hassania, and the same, tolerant form of Sunni Islam.

[3] Spanish occupation of the Saharan coast was carried out mainly for strategic reasons: to cover the flank of the Canary Islands. The occupation was practically limited to Villa Cisneros (present-day Dakhla) until 1884, when Madrid proclaimed the coastal area between Cape Blanc and Cape Boujdour a 'protectorate', determined that this 'empty space' would not fall to another power.

[4] The borders of the Spanish Sahara were established by agreement with France in 1904 but the local inhabitants, the Saharawis, refused to relinquish their nomadic lifestyle and put up stiff resistance.

[5] In 1895, Sheikh Ma al-Aini founded the Smara citadel and, with the support of the Sultan of Morocco, continued fighting the Franco-Spanish presence until 1910. Under French pressure, the Sultan finally suspended assistance to the rebels, who enlarged their field of action to include Morocco and even threatened Marrakesh. A French counter-attack invaded 'Spanish' territory and occupied Smara in 1913, though resistance continued until 1920.

[6] In 1933 Muhammad al Mamún, the Emir of Adrad and Ma al-Aini's cousin, defeated the French, forcing a change of tactics. France occupied the rebel base at the Tindouf oasis and advanced into Algeria, Mauritania and Morocco, while Spanish troops took Smara, overcoming the rebels and instituting full colonial rule in 1936.

[7] Even then Spain showed little interest in developing the colony until the natural resources of the territory (mainly its phosphates) became evident. It then developed a new capital, L'ayoun, from which phosphates from the mine at Boucraa were exported. The phosphate deposits have been estimated at 1.7 billion tons in the Boucraa area, but there could be another 10 billion tons in other parts of the territory.

[8] Spain's Government, in close association with transnational companies, invested more than $160 million in Sahara, transforming the country, particularly the population distribution. In 1959, L'ayoun had 6,000 inhabitants. In 1974 there were 28,000, while the percentage of nomads decreased from 90 to 16 per cent.

[9] With the progressive abandonment of the nomadic way of life, tribal ties and relationships began to weaken. Over the years, however, a new national identity has slowly been forged, transcending traditional divisions.

[10] In 1966 the UN General Assembly called on Spain to organize a referendum in which Saharawis could exercise their right to self-determination. Locally the Movement for the Liberation of the Sahara was formed in 1967 and organized huge demonstrations before being savagely put down and banned on 17 June 1970.

[11] The repression only increased nationalist aspirations and the Polisario Front (the Popular Front for the Liberation of Saguia el Hamra and Rio de Oro) was formed on 10 May 1973, led by Elwali Mustafa Sayed. This began as a vanguard group committed to armed struggle against colonialism but very quickly became a mass movement.

[12] Spain reluctantly organized a census of the colony in 1974 in preparation for a referendum on self-determination. The census showed that there were 73,497 Saharawis, 20,126 Europeans and 1,396 other Africans living in Western Sahara.

[13] Morocco, however, also claimed sovereignty over Western Sahara. As a result of such claims, the International Court of Justice in The Hague ruled in October 1975 that there were no historic legal ties with Morocco that debarred Western Sahara from decolonization and self-determination.

[14] King Hassan II of Morocco, increasingly beleaguered by bread riots and assassination attempts, seized his chance to unite the nation and organized the so-called 'Green March', a propaganda move which mobilized 350,000 Moroccans to march southward into the Sahara. They crossed the border on November 6 1975.

[15] On November 14, as General Franco lay on his deathbed, Spain signed a secret agreement which handed over the territory to Morocco and Mauritania. A Polisario force which at this stage numbered no more than about 5,000 had no chance against a Moroccan Army which could call in total on 65,000 soldiers.

[16] The Moroccan occupation was already well established by the time the Spanish officially withdrew on February 27 1976, though on the same day Polisario declared the independence of the Saharawi Arab Democratic Republic (SADR).

[17] Thousands of ordinary Saharawis fled the Moroccan invaders into the desert, setting up their own makeshift refugee camps. Many, like the 25,000 which gathered at Guelta Zemmour, were determined to stay on Western Saharan territory but were repeatedly bombed by Moroccan planes which the Red Cross confirmed were using napalm.

[18] In the face of this onslaught, the refugees had to walk hundreds of kilometers across the desert to the Algerian town of Tindouf. Here the Algerian Government ceded control over a portion of its own territory to Polisario, which built and administered its own refugee camps.

[19] Polisario was faced with war on two fronts: against Morocco in the north and Mauritania in the south. The relative weakness of the Mauritanian Army made it the more sensible target and Polisario mounted raids deep into Mauritanian territory, one of which cost the life of the movement's inspirational young leader, Wali Mustafa Sayed.

[20] But on the whole the attacks were successful and in 1979 Mauritania, on the verge of bankruptcy, signed a peace treaty with Polisario. But as Mauritania withdrew Moroccan troops moved in to take over the south, including the city of Dakhla.

[21] The Polisario Front's military victories led to a diplomatic triumph at the June 1980 conference of the Organization for African Unity (OAU) in Freetown, Sierra Leone. Twenty-six African nations officially recognized the RASD as the legitimate title for Western Sahara, and four months later the UN issued a resolution requesting Moroccan withdrawal.

[22] Still vastly outnumbered, Polisario had no chance of regaining and holding major towns by military force. Instead it concentrated on

MOROCCO

ALGERIA

Canary Is. (SPAIN)

Tindouf

Disputed Border

L'ayoun   Smara   Saguia el Hamra   Amgela

Boujdour   Wall

Boucraa   Tifariti

Angra de los Ruivos   Chalwa   Guelta Zemur   25

Dakhla   W E S T E R N   S A H A R A

Tropic of Cancer

A   H   A   R   A

Aoserd   Fortified Wall

Choum

Bou Lanouari

Nouadhibou   **MAURITANIA**   20

15   10

-------------- Fortified Wall

0   300 km

lightning strikes by highly mobile guerrilla units, not least on the longest conveyor belt in the world which carries phosphates from the Boucraa mine to the sea.

23   The Moroccan response from 1980 onwards was to build a fortified wall or *berm*, protected by minefields and artillery. By 1982 the first of these walls was complete, stretching from the border right past Smara to meet the sea south of Boujdour.

24   In the ensuing years further walls were built until by the late 1980s the Wall stretched a full 2,500 kilometres across the desert from the Moroccan border in the north to near the Mauritanian border in the south. The Wall is a vast drain on the Moroccan economy but it now encloses fully three-quarters of Western Sahara.

25   Militarily Morocco was digging in, with significant aid from both France and the US. But in international diplomacy it was losing ground: in 1985 the RASD was welcomed into the Organization of

African Unity, prompting Morocco to leave, and by the end of 1986, 67 countries had recognized the independent Western Saharan state.

26   Through the 1980s Morocco steadfastly refused to debate the issue of Western Sahara in any international forum. But by 1990 diplomatic pressure on Morocco led to a UN peace plan aimed at holding a referendum in which Saharawis could decide their own future. There was to be a cease-fire, repatriation of refugees and the new UN Mission for the Referendum in Western Sahara (MINURSO) would identify legitimate voters. The electoral roll was to be based on the 1974 Spanish census.

27   On April 29 1991, the UN Security Council approved the peace plan. The cease-fire was enforced on September 6, and the referendum was scheduled for January 1992.

28   In the following months, the Moroccan Government settled thousands of Moroccan citizens in the Saharan territory, to ensure their

voter eligibility; furthermore, the cease-fire was ignored, and journalists were hindered. They also banned international observers as repression against the Saharans mounted.

29   The UN Special Representative for the Western Sahara, Johannes Manz, resigned in December 1991, protesting not only at these Moroccan tactics but also at UN Secretary-General Javier Pérez de Cuellar's appeasement of them. The result was stalemate and a vastly expensive UN operation which failed to make Morocco comply with the peace plan

30   Faced with criticism in the US Congress, the UN began to talk about winding up MINURSO and Polisario began to prepare for a return to war. The stalling of the referendum was felt to favor Moroccan authority.

31   At the beginning of 1997, UN withdrawal and a resume of war seemed inevitable. The new UN Secretary-General, Kofi Annan, sought US support for a last attempt to rescue the peace plan and appointed former US Secretary of State James Baker as his Personal Envoy.

32   Baker visited the region then initiated a series of direct talks in Lisbon and London between the Moroccan Government and Polisario - these had never taken place before since Morocco felt they would legitimize Polisario's cause.

33   On September 16 1997 the two parties signed an agreement which established guidelines for voter identification, repatriation of refugees, release of prisoners, troop withdrawal and a code of conduct for the referendum campaign. Voter identification was to be concluded in the first half of 1998 and the referendum to take place on December 7 1998.

34   The key Ministers of Defense, Brahim Gali, and Foreign Relations, Bachir Mustafa Sayed (diplomatic leader for the last 15 years), were replaced in January 1998. The measure was attributed to the Government's wanting to keep its hands free to conduct negotiations over the last phase of the referendum.

35   President Abdelaziz confirmed that, if the Polisario Front were to win, Moroccan citizens would be able to remain in the territory, but the potential offer was not extended to those 'related to

occupation and annexation'.

36   The United Nations' plan for the Morocco and Polisario Front commitment to mutual respect stated that were Morocco to win, the UN would disarm the Saharan fighters, while the opposite outcome would result in the UN supervising the withdrawal of troops and the Moroccan administration in Western Sahara. The resettlement of 200,000 Saharans exiled since the 1970s, particularly in the Algerian city of Tindouf, remained unresolved.

37   The death of Morocco's King Hassan II in July 1999 and his replacement by his son, Mohammed IV, brought enormous political changes in this country. The King issued initial messages of liberalization, including the freeing of political prisoners and a search for solutions to the problem of the Sahara region. The Polisario Front welcomed the new king's opening statements, and his decision to implement a referendum on self-determination in Western Sahara. In November, Mohammed IV announced his decision to bring in some kind of self-rule for the occupied zone.

38   The 10th Congress of the Polisario Front was held in Tindouf in August 1999, and Abdelaziz was re-elected as president of the RASD. In his inaugural speech, Abdelaziz admitted 'deficient management and inadmissible practices' in the Saharan administration, but insisted there were no internal differences over the quest for independence. The President also expressed the hope that the new Moroccan king, Mohammed IV would respect agreements made before the UN.

39   In March 2000 at a meeting of the Polisario Front National Secretariat, in the Saharan government-controlled zone, the Secretariat called on the European Union countries for a firm hand in meeting the official schedule. Before threats of further delays, which would stall the referendum set for July 2000, the Polisario Front National Secretariat expressed its support for Kofi Annan's special envoy, US official James Baker, who negotiated compliance with the agreements. The referendum, which had already been suspended in 1998 due to difficulties in drawing up the draft document, was delayed once again. ■

PROFILE

ENVIRONMENT

The country is almost completely desert and is divided into two regions: Saguia el Hamra in the north and Rio de Oro in the south. It has one of the world's largest fishing reserves, but the principal source of wealth is mining, especially phosphate deposits.

SOCIETY

Peoples: The Polisario Front estimates the dispersed Saharawi population at one million. These are traditionally nomadic groups which differ from the Tuaregs and Berbers in their social and cultural organization.
Religion: Islam.
Languages: Arabic and Spanish (official). Many Saharawi also speak Hassania.
Political Parties: The People's Liberation Front of Saguia al-Hamra and Rio de Oro (Polisario Front) founded on May 10 1973 by Elwali Mustafa Sayed.
Social Movements: The Saguia el Hamra and Rio de Oro General Workers' Union (UGTSARIO).

THE STATE

Official name: Saharawi Arab Democratic Republic.
Capital: L'ayoun.
Other cities: Dakhla, Smara.
Government: Muhammad Abdelaziz, President of the Republic since 1982, is also Secretary-General of the Polisario Front. Ali Beiba, Prime Minister. An elected parliament acts as a check on the executive branch. Polisario is committed to multiparty democracy if it gains independence.
National Holiday: February 27, Proclamation of the Republic (1976).

DEMOGRAPHY

Population: 284,000 (1999)
Urban population: 21.1 % (1997)

St Helena

St Helena

Population: 6,000 (1998)
Area: 210 SQ KM
Capital: Jamestown
Currency: Pound sterling
Language: English

St Helena was uninhabited when Portuguese navigators arrived in 1502. In 1659 an outpost of the British East India Company was established on the islands, and since then St Helena has been an English colony. Of scant economic interest, the island acquired notoriety as the location of Napoleon's second exile, from 1815 until his death in 1821. The Malvinas/Falklands War put it back on the map, a century and a half later.

[2] An English representative stated: 'It was only with the help of Ascension Island and the labor force provided by St Helena, that we could recover the Falklands'. This may justify the expensive maintenance of this British enclave through the Overseas Development Administration. The British could have a shared base like Ascension Island which is a US base and a bridgehead of the Royal Air Force, or they could simply transfer the territory to the US, as they did with Diego Garcia.

[3] The United Nations supports all nations' rights to self-determination and independence, and in December 1984, the UN General Assembly urged Britain to bolster the fishing industry, handcrafts and reforestation on the island and to foster awareness of the right to independence. Washington and London both voted against the resolution. The UN also questioned the existence of the military base on Ascension Island since there should not be any base in non-autonomous territories.

[4] On January 1 1989 a new constitution was instituted conferring greater powers on the members of the Legislative Council and enabling civil servants to become election candidates with the approval of the governor. The new constitution also reduced the voting age to 18.

[5] The island's only export is fish, but there has been a decline in the total catch: 27.2 tons in 1985, and a mere 9.2 tons in 1990.

[6] St Helena is of scientific interest because of the its rare flora and fauna. The island has some 40 plant species unknown in the rest of the world.

[7] In April 1997, two of the five members of the Executive Council resigned from their posts as they disagreed with the budget cuts and, furthermore, with the 'dictatorial' attitude of the Governor, David Smallman. At the same time, unemployment increased to 18 per cent. Part of the local population continued to demand the return of their British citizenship, revoked in 1981.

[8] The announcement in March 1999 that Great Britain was to issue a citizenship charter for inhabitants of the dependent territories was celebrated by people on the island. Governor Smallman said the people of St Helena, previously 'left out in the cold' were now 'going home'. ∎

PROFILE

ENVIRONMENT

Located in the South Atlantic some 2,000 km from the coast of Angola (West Africa), slightly west of the Greenwich meridian. Of volcanic origin, the island is mountainous, has no mineral reserves and industries and the only productive activities are subsistence agriculture and fishing.

SOCIETY

Peoples: The island's population is largely of African descent. Some 6,000 natives of St. Helena have emigrated to South Africa and Great Britain.
Religions: Protestant, Anglican, Baptist, Seventh-Day Adventists, and also Roman Catholic.
Languages: English (official).
Political Parties: St Helena Progressive Party (SHPP), the St Helena Labor Party (SHLP), both inactive since 1976.

THE STATE

Official Name: St Helena Colony with Dependencies.
Capital: Jamestown, 1,744 people (1989). Inland is Longwood, where Napoleon Bonaparte was exiled
Government: David Leslie Smallman, Governor, appointed by the British Crown in 1995. There is an Executive Council and a Legislative Council of 15 seats: twelve members elected by popular vote for a four-year term, the Governor and two former officers.
Armed Forces: Security is the responsibility of the United Kingdom.

DEMOGRAPHY

Population: 6,000 (1998)

ECONOMY

Cereal imports: 533 metric tons (1998)

Ascension Island

Ascension Island is of volcanic origin, covering 88 sq km. Its importance derives from its strategic location in the South Atlantic, 1,200 km northwest of St Helena. It is a communication relay center between South Africa and Europe, and the United States maintains a missile tracking station - Wideawake Airfield - there under an accord with Britain. The island's naval installation and airbase were vital to Britain during the Malvinas Islands/Falklands war (April-June 1982) and afterwards as a base for the ships and planes that supplied the British troops occupying the islands claimed by Argentina.

[2] There is no indigenous population and the majority are employees of the St Helena Government. In 1988, out of the 1,099 inhabitants, 765 were from St Helena, 222 were British, 102 were American and 10 were of other nationalities. These figures do not include British military personnel. The main religion is Protestant and the official language is English. The island's administrator, Brian Connelly, represents the Government of St Helena. ∎

Tristan da Cunha

The most important of a group of South Atlantic islands 2,400 km west of Cape Town, South Africa, and under the administration of St Helena. The islands total 201 sq km (Tristan da Cunha 98 sq km; Inaccessible island 10 sq km, 32 km west of the main island; Nightingale Islands 25 sq km, 32 km south of Tristan da Cunha, and Diego Alvarez or Gough Island 91 sq km, 350 km south of the main island).

[2] The 306 inhabitants (1988) are concentrated in Tristan da Cunha, the majority employed by the Government and in a lobster-processing factory. There were volcanic eruptions in 1961 and the island was evacuated, though the population returned in 1963. On Diego Alvarez there is a small weather station run by the South African Government. The main religion is Protestant and the official language is English. There is an administrator, R Perrys, who represents the Government of St Helena and an advisory council with executive and legislative duties, comprising 8 elected and 3 appointed members.

[3] A 10-year contract to operate Tristan's lucrative lobster-fishing concession, which was awarded in 1996 to a South African firm, went into effect on January 1. The 300 residents of Tristan da Cunha - as those of St Helena did - demanded British citizenship during the annual visit by St Helena's Governor. ∎

St Kitts-Nevis

Saint Kitts-Nevis

Population: 42,000 (1999)
Area: 360 SQ KM
Capital: Basseterre
Currency: EC dollar
Language: English

The island of Liamuiga, or 'fertile land' in the languagE of the Carib Indians who originally lived there, was renamed St Christopher by Columbus on his second voyage to America, in 1493. It was not colonized by Europeans until 1623, when adventurer Thomas Walker established the first English settlement in the Caribbean. The neighboring island of Nevis was colonized five years later. After the rapid extermination of the Caribs, the English started to grow plantation crops, especially sugar cane, for which they used slaves from Africa.

[2] In the 20th century, the decolonization process following World War II gave the islands total internal autonomy, while foreign relations and defenSe were left to the colonial capitals. These islands joined the Associate States of the West Indies. In 1980, Anguilla formally separated from St Kitts and Nevis (see Anguilla), and the islands were then governed by a Prime Minister and a parliament, both elected by universal suffrage.

[3] The Labor Party had been in office since 1967, but suffered a major defeat in the 1980 election, at the hands of an opposition coalition of the People's Action Movement (PAM) and the Nevis Reformation Party (NRP). Kennedy Alphonse Simmonds became Prime Minister. The opposition victory meant that independence, planned for June 1980, had to be postponed as the NRP was opposed to a post-independence federation with St Kitts. The 1976 plebiscite showed that 99.4 per cent of the population of Nevis favored separation.

[4] In the 1984 elections, Kennedy Simmonds and his government increased their parliamentary representation. Simmonds was re-elected in March 1989, in line with the US interests in the region.

[5] In 1990, strikes broke out among agricultural workers who had been refused a 10 per cent wage increase. Sugar companies responded by hiring close to 1,000 workers from St Vincent and the Grenadines, to cut sugarcane. Nevis Prime Minister Daniel Simeon promised that Nevis would secede from St Kitts by the end of 1992.

[6] In June 1992, the Concerned Citizens' Movement, in opposition, won the election in Nevis, obtaining three seats in the Nevis Assembly, ousting the Nevis Reformation Party (NRP) led by Daniel Simeon. Together with the People's Action Movement, the NRP made up the main coalition. Weston Paris, Governor-General Sir Clement Athelston's representative on Nevis, died in unclarified circumstances.

[7] The November 1993 election was inconclusive. Further elections were held in July 1995 in which the St Kitts-Nevis Labor Party, led by Denzil Douglas, came to power.

[8] In mid-1996, a new constitutional crisis arose over the secession of Nevis. Vance Amory, Prime Minister of Nevis, declared that the legal process of secession from the federation had been started. Douglas warned they were running the risk of 'fragmentation'.

[9] Amory's Concerned Citizens' Movement failed in its attempt to achieve independence for the island by not getting the necessary two-thirds of the vote. The election, held in August 1998, ended with 61.2 per cent of votes in favor of secession. Delegations from Caricom member countries, the US and St Kitts came to Nevis to try to restore links damaged by the election campaign.

[10] Hurricane George destroyed or seriously damaged 80 per cent of houses on the islands in September that same year. ■

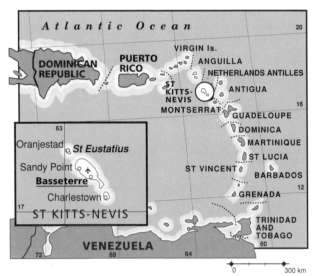

PROFILE

ENVIRONMENT

The territory is divided between St Kitts, 168.4 sq km, and Nevis, 93.2 sq km. The two islands are in the Windward Islands of the Lesser Antilles. They are of volcanic origin, hilly, with a rainy tropical climate, tempered by sea winds which make the land fit for plantation crops, especially sugarcane.

SOCIETY

Peoples: 95 per cent of the population are African descendants and people descended from the integration of African slaves and European colonizers (mulattos). There is a British minority.
Religions: Mainly Protestant (76.4 per cent, of which Anglican 32.3 per cent, Methodist 32.3 per cent); Roman Catholic 10.7 per cent; other 12.9 per cent.
Languages: English (official).
Political Parties: The People's Action Movement (PAM); the Nevis Reformation Party (NRP); the Labor Party (Workers' League); the United National Movement (UNM); and the Concerned Citizens' Movement.

THE STATE

Official Name: Federation of St Christopher (St Kitts) and Nevis.
Capital: Basseterre 18,000 people (1995).
Government: Denzil Douglas, Prime Minister since July 1995; Cuthbert Montroville-Sebastian, Governor-General appointed by the British Crown in 1996. There is a Parliament with 11 members chosen by universal suffrage (8 representatives of St Kitts and 3 of Nevis), and 3 appointed senators.
National Holiday: September 19, Independence (1983).

STATISTICS

DEMOGRAPHY

Population: 42,000 (1999)
Annual growth: -0.6 % (1975/97)
Annual growth to year 2015: -0.5 % (1997/2015)
Urban population: 33.9 % (1997)
Children per woman: 2.4 (1998)

HEALTH

Life expectancy at birth: 70 years (1998)
Maternal mortality: 130 per 100,000 live births (1990-98)
Infant mortality: 30 per 1,000 (1998)
Under-5 child mortality: 37 per 1,000 (1998)
Daily calorie supply: 2,240 per capita (1996)
89 doctors per 100,000 people (1993)
Safe water: 100 % (1990/98)

EDUCATION

Literacy: 90 % (1995)

COMMUNICATIONS

682 radios (1997), 244 TV sets (1996) and 382 main telephone lines (1996) per 1,000 people

ECONOMY

Per capita, GNP: $ 6,190 (1998)
Annual growth, GNP: 3.6 % (1998)
Cereal imports: 4,180 metric tons (1998)
Food import dependency: 19 % (1997)
Fertilizer use: 2,833 kg per ha (1997)
Exports: $ 149 million (1998)
Imports: $ 224 million (1998)
External debt: $ 115 million (1998); Development aid received: $ 7 million (1997); $ 167.5 per capita (1997); 2.70 % of GNP (1997)

HDI (rank/value): 51/0.781 (1997)

St Lucia

St Lucia

Population: 136,000 (1999)
Area: 620 SQ KM
Capital: Castries
Currency: EC dollar
Language: English

Before Christopher Columbus named it Santa Lucia in 1502, the island had already been conquered by the Caribs who had expelled the Arawak indians.

[2] Neither the Spaniards nor the British succeeded in defeating local resistance, and in 1660 the French settled on the island, starting a dispute with Britain which was to last for 150 years. Over this period, the flag of St Lucia changed 14 times.

[3] In 1814, the Treaty of Paris transferred the island from France to Britain, which kept it until 1978. France left the legacy of patois, a pidgin language of mixed African and French.

[4] Under British rule, St Lucia became one big sugarcane plantation populated by African slave laborers. Agriculture is still the main economic resource but 20 years ago sugar gave way to banana cultivation.

[5] The island was part of the Colony of the Windward Islands, and between 1959 and 1962 St Lucia belonged to the West Indies Federation. In 1967 the island became more autonomous and was granted a new constitution as one of the Federate States of the Antilles.

[6] In the first elections held as an independent nation, in July 1979, Prime Minister John G M Compton and his United Workers Party (UWP), who had governed the island since 1964, were beaten. The progressive St Lucia Labor Party (SLP) won.

[7] The new Prime Minister, Allen Louisy, promised to help workers and peasants and to encourage small business as a means of curbing unemployment. George Odlum was Deputy Prime Minister and minister of trade, industry, tourism and foreign affairs. He was also leader of the predominant SLP's 'new left' wing, and he promoted the country's entry to the Non-Aligned Movement and established diplomatic relations with Cuba and North Korea. He also adopted a policy of close collaboration with the neighboring island of Grenada, which had launched its own revolutionary process some months before.

[8] After repeated political crisis, the United Workers' Party won the 1982 and 1987 elections. Compton returned to power with a conservative platform, favoring a market economy and proposing adjustment measures recommended by the IMF. The increase in exports and tourism revenues was not enough to leave economic crisis behind, which continued through the 1990s.

[9] The years 1994 and 1995 were marked by protests from workers on banana plantations - the island's main export - and also by dock employees, demanding higher wages. In 1996, Vaughn Allen Lewis was elected President.

[10] In May 1997, the Labor Party won the elections with 61.3 per cent of the vote. Kenny Anthony took over as Prime Minister. One of his first measures was to form a commission to investigate corruption during the UWP administration.

[11] The summit of Caribbean nations in August 1998 decided to remove border tariffs between member countries to compensate for the reduction of US support. Kenny Anthony issued a statement during the summit which expressed 'deep discomfort' over the US policy of not including Caribbean textile industries into the North American Free Trade Agreement (NAFTA). ∎

LAND USE

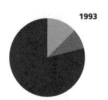

IRRIGATED: 20.0% of arable (1993)

1993

■ FOREST & WOODLAND: 12.9%
■ ARABLE: 8.1%
■ OTHER: 79.0%

PROFILE

ENVIRONMENT

One of the volcanic Windward Islands of the Lesser Antilles, south of Martinique and north of St Vincent. The climate is tropical with heavy rainfall, tempered by ocean currents. The soil is fertile, bananas, cocoa, sugar cane and coconuts are grown.

SOCIETY

Peoples: Most inhabitants are descended from the integration of African slave laborers and European colonists. **Religions:** Roman Catholic 79 per cent; Protestant 15.5 per cent, of which Seventh-day Adventist 6.5 per cent, Pentecostal 3 per cent; other 5.5 per cent. **Languages:** English (official) and a local dialect (Patois) derived from French and African elements. **Political Parties:** The St Lucia Labor Party. The United Workers' Party (UWP). Progressive Labor Party (PLP).The Citizens' Democratic Party.

THE STATE

Official name: St Lucia. **Capital:** Castries 54,000 people (1995). **Government:** Queen Elizabeth II, Head of State; W George Mallet, Governor-General appointed by the British Crown in 1996. Kenny Anthony, Prime Minister since May, 1997. **National Holiday:** 13 December, Independence Day (1978), and discovery by Christopher Columbus.

STATISTICS

DEMOGRAPHY

Population: 136,000 (1999)
Annual growth: 1.4 % (1975/97)
Estimates for year 2015 (million): 0.2 (1999).
Annual growth to year 2015: 1.3 % (1997/2015)
Urban population: 37.3 % (1997)
Children per woman: 2.4 (1998)

HEALTH

Life expectancy at birth: 70 years (1998)
Maternal mortality: 30 per 100,000 live births (1990-98)
Infant mortality: 18 per 1,000 (1998)
Under-5 child mortality: 21 per 1,000 (1998)
Daily calorie supply: 2,822 per capita (1996)
35 doctors per 100,000 people (1993)
Safe water: 85 % (1990/98)

EDUCATION

School enrolment: Primary total: 95 % (1990/96). Primary school teachers: one for every 26 (1996)

COMMUNICATIONS

742 radios (1997), 301 TV sets (1996) and 235 main telephone lines (1996) per 1,000 people

ECONOMY

Per capita, GNP: $ 3,660 (1998)
Annual growth, GNP: 3.0 % (1998)
Consumer price index: 101.0 (1997)
Cereal imports: 20,068 metric tons (1998)
Food import dependency: 26 % (1997)
Fertilizer use: 45,490 kg per ha (1997)
Exports: $ 396 million (1998)
Imports: $ 416 million (1998)
External debt: $ 184 million (1998); Development aid received: $ 24 million (1997); $ 160.0 per capita (1997); 4.10 % of GNP (1997)

HDI (rank/value): 81/0.737 (1997)

St Vincent

St Vincent

Population: 112,000 (1999)
Area: 390 SQ KM
Capital: Kingstown
Currency: EC dollar
Language: English

The first inhabitants were Arawaks who were displaced by the Caribs, the island's inhabitants when Columbus arrived in 1498.

[2] In 1783, St Vincent became a British colony. However, the local people resisted European conquest; the former slaves who had rebelled on the neighboring islands and those who took refuge in St Vincent joined the Caribs to oppose the invaders. In 1796, they were defeated and exterminated or deported.

[3] A plantation economy developed, using slave labor, the chief crops being sugar cane, cotton, coffee and cocoa. In 1833, St Vincent became part of the Windward Islands colony. In 1960, together with the Grenadine Islands, it was granted a new constitution with substantial internal autonomy. It also participated in the West Indies Federation until its dissolution in 1962.

[4] St Vincent became a self-governing state in association with the UK in 1969. The post of head minister - similar to that of Prime Minister, but with more limited powers - was held then by Milton Cato, together with the pro-US St Vincent Labor Party (SVLP). Defence and foreign relations continued to be controlled by Britain, but

independence was declared in October 1979.

[5] The elections in December 1979 reinforced the predominance of the SVLP, and the opposition PPP received only 2.4 percent of the vote.

[6] The new government faced an armed rebellion of Rastafarians led by Lennox 'Bumba' Charles on Union Island. This rebellion was quickly put down by troops from Barbados.

[7] In the early 1980s, the Government faced a serious socio-economic crisis, enabling the popular movements to gain ground. In May 1981, the national Committee in Defense of Democracy was formed, supported by several opposition parties, the labor unions and other organizations. Several days later, the Government attempted to impose repressive legislation designed to maintain 'public order', triggering mass protests.

[8] Cato's government supported the US invasion in Grenada and sent a police detachment to join the occupation forces (see Grenada). Cato called early elections, but the economic crisis and the SVLP's tax policies meant the New Democratic Party (NDP) won the election, while the left found its vote reduced by half, to 7.2 per cent.

[9] In the May 1989 election, James Mitchell (NDP) was re-elected, going on to sign an agreement with the Prime Ministers of Dominica, St Lucia, and Grenada to create a new state of the four islands in 1990 (see Dominica).

[10] In February 1992, the Government of St Vincent adopted the Tlatelolco Treaty to ban nuclear weapons in Latin America and the Caribbean.

[11] Given the Grenadians' secessionist feelings, which had already erupted in violence in 1980, Mitchell created a Ministry of Grenadine Affairs and named Herbert Young, a Grenadian, as Minister of Foreign Affairs.

[12] The SVLP took three of the fifteen seats in Parliament in the early elections held in February 1994, becoming the official opposition to the NDP Government. In August, Mitchell survived a motion of no confidence. The opposition blamed him for the failure to fight the crisis and the fall in banana exports. This product brought in 80 per cent of the income of St Vincent.

[13] Three men accused of murder were hanged in February 1995. The suspension of the moratorium on hanging, in place for many years, was condemned by Amnesty International.

[14] US influence in the region strongly affected the island's economy from 1998 onwards. Pressure from Washington led to the eradication, in December of that year, of marijuana plantations in a 10-day blitz carried out by an Army battalion. In 1999 the cannabis growers - who claimed that the destruction of their plantations left them with no other means of livelihood – added their weight to the protests of the 25,000 banana farmers, producers of the country's main crop. The US measures, which tried to force the World Trade Organization to revoke what the US felt were European privileges, seriously affected this island which depended on the European market. A strong increase in the unemployment rate (already over 30 per cent) was anticipated for 2000. ∎

PROFILE

ENVIRONMENT

Comprises the island of St Vincent (345 sq km) and the northern part of the Grenadines (43 sq km) including Bequia, Canouan, Mustique, Matreau, Quatre, Savan and Union. They are part of the Windward islands of the Lesser Antilles. Of volcanic origin, the islands have fertile rolling hills. The climate, tropical with heavy rainfall and tempered by ocean currents, is fit for plantation crops. St Vincent is a leading arrowroot producer, a plant with starch-rich rhizomes, used in the manufacture of a type of paper used in electronics. The population is concentrated on the island of St Vincent.

SOCIETY

Peoples: Descendants of African slaves 82 per cent, mixed 14 per cent; there are also European, Asian, and indigenous minorities. **Religions:** Anglican and other Protestant; Catholic. **Languages:** English (official); also a local dialect. **Political Parties:** The New Democratic Party (NDP). The St. Vincent Labour Party (SVLP); 2. The National Unity Movement (MNV); the United People's Movement (UPM).

THE STATE

Official name: Commonwealth of St Vincent and the Grenadines. **Capital:** Kingstown 16,132 people (est

1996). **Government:** Charles Antrobus, Governor General appointed by Britain, since 1996. James Fitz-Allen Mitchell, Prime Minister and Head of State since 1984. There are 13 elected representatives in Parliament and a Senate with 6 members. **National Holiday:** October 27, Independence Day (1979).

DEMOGRAPHY

Population: 112,000 (1999). **Annual growth:** 0.9 % (1975/97). **Estimates for year 2015 (million):** 0.1 (1999). **Annual growth to year 2015:** 0.6 % (1997/ 2015). **Urban population:** 50.9 % (1997). **Children per woman:** 2.2 (1998)

HEALTH

Life expectancy at birth: 73 years (1998). **Maternal mortality:** 43 per 100,000 live births (1990-98). **Infant mortality:** 20 per 1,000 (1998). **Under-5 child mortality:** 23 per 1,000 (1998). **Daily calorie supply:** 2,434 per capita (1996). 46 doctors per 100,000 people (1993). **Safe water:** 89 % (1990/98)

EDUCATION

Literacy: 82 % (1995). **School enrolment:** Primary total: 95 % (1990/96)

Samoa

Samoa

Population: 177,000 (1999)
Area: 2,840 SQ KM
Capital: Apia
Currency: Tala
Language: Samoan and English

The archipelago of Samoa has been inhabited since at least 1,000 BC. The people developed a complex social structure. Four of these local groups still hold a privileged position: the Malietoa, the Tamasese, the Mataafa and the Tuimalealiifano.

[2] The Dutch were the first Europeans to visit the islands in 1722, but colonization did not begin until the end of the 19th century.

[3] In 1855, Germany finally occupied the islands. German merchants bought copra with Bolivian and Chilean currency valued at 10 times its real worth. In 1889 a new treaty recognized the US rights over the part of Samoa located east of meridian 171; 'rights' which the US still retains. The western half remained under German rule.

[4] In 1914, upon the outbreak of World War I, New Zealand occupied the German part of the island, which was later granted to Aotearoa (New Zealand) by the League of Nations as a trust territory.

[5] In 1920, an influenza epidemic killed 25 per cent of the population. At about the same time, the 'Mau' movement began to spread throughout the archipelago, preaching resistance to the foreign governments. Samoans carried out a nine-year-long civil disobedience campaign, which eventually became a vigorous pro-independence movement.

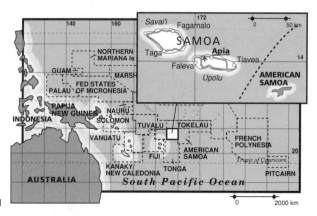

[6] In 1961 after intense protests and pressure from the UN, a plebiscite was held for Samoans to vote on independence. This was achieved the following year, with a Constitution based largely on the traditional social structure and the executive power in the hands of two rulers, Tupua Tamasase Meoble and Malietoa Tanumafili. Only the leading group (*matai*), around 8,500 in all, were eligible to vote.

[7] After being elected Prime Minister in 1970, Tupua Tamasese Lealofi launched a battle against the *matai*. He also backed the establishment of foreign corporations on the archipelago, despite strong opposition.

[8] The 1976 elections were won by the opposition. Tupuola Tais became Prime Minister. In 1979 he retained office by only one vote in parliament. The price of cocoa and copra fell, further aggravating the economic and financial situation, making it necessary for 2,000 Samoans to emigrate each year.

[9] In February 1982, Va'al Kolone, leader of the Party for the Protection of Human Rights, became leader. In September he was removed from government, amid accusations of corruption and abuse of power.

[10] In April 1988, Tofilau Eti Alesana came to power. His political party won an absolute majority in the legislative in the 1985 elections when it obtained 31 of the 47 seats.

[11] At that time, malnutrition was on the increase; one in six pre-school children and 11 per cent of all primary school children were undernourished. The islands have 200,000 hectares of arable land but less than a third of this was cultivated.

[11] The 1991 constitutional reform extended the parliamentary term from three to five years, and increased the number of seats from 47 to 49. Fiame Naomi became minister of education that year, the first woman to be appointed to the cabinet.

[12] Exports suffered a sharp drop in 1993 and 1994. In that year, the country's exports amounted to only 4 per cent of the imports. Remittances from Samoan workers living abroad partially compensated for the gap.

[13] Following recommendations from the US, Samoa opened up to foreign investment with major tourist development projects, which included the construction of hotels and airports.

[14] In 1998 the partial burning of forests by farmers went out of control and destroyed 25 per cent of the natural forests. Prime Minister Tofilau Eti had to resign in November that year due to complications from cancer. He was replaced by Tuilaepa Sailele Malielegaoi.

[15] On April 2000, two ministers were accused of murdering a colleague to prevent disclosures of corruption in which they were involved. Leafa Vitale and Toi Aukuso, Women's Affairs Minister and former Communications Minister respectively, were accused of murdering Public Works Minister Levaula Kamu during a political rally in July 1999. ■

PROFILE

ENVIRONMENT

Includes the islands of Savai'i, 1,690 sq km, 40,000 people; Upolu, 1,100 sq km, 110,000 people, Manono and Apolina, in Polynesia, northeast of Fiji. The eastern portion of the Samoa archipelago is under US administration. The islands are of volcanic origin, mountainous, with fertile soil in the lowland areas. The climate is tropical, tempered by sea winds.

SOCIETY

Peoples: Samoans are mostly Polynesian (92.6 per cent). 'Euronesians' (a result of European and Polynesian integration) make up 10 per cent of the population. There are Europeans and Pacific islanders. **Religions:** Congregational 47.2 per cent; Roman Catholic 22.3 per cent; Methodist 15.1 per cent; Mormon 8.6 per cent; other 6.8 per cent. **Languages:** Samoan and English are the official languages. **Political Parties:** The Human Rights Protection Party (HRPP); the Samoa National Development Party.

THE STATE

Official Name: Samoa i Sisifo. **Capital:** Apia 40,000 people (1995). **Government:** Malietoa Tanumafili II, Head of State for life. Tuilaepa Sailele Malielegaoi, Prime Minister since November 1998. By the 1991 constitutional reform, 2 of the 49 representatives are elected by universal suffrage while the rest are chosen by the Heads of the Samoan clans and families. After the death of Tanumafili II, the President will be elected by direct vote. **National Holiday:** June 10, Independence Day (1962).

American Samoa

American Samoa

Population: 47,000 (1999)
Area: 200 SQ KM
Capital: Pago Pago
Currency: US dollar
Language: Samoan and English

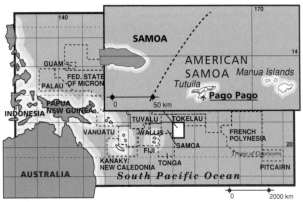

[1] In the 18th century, 150 years after the Europeans had reached the islands, the colonial powers Germany, Britain and the US disputed the possession. The 1899 treaty settled the conflict, granting the United States the seven islands east of Meridian 171. Traditional social structures were maintained but agriculture was not stimulated so the population became totally dependent on the external colonial economy. This situation resulted in an increasing number of emigrants; over half of the Samoan population currently lives in Hawaii and other parts of the United States.

[2] On December 5 1984, the UN General Assembly considered Eastern Samoa's right to self-determination and independence. A unanimous vote reiterated that factors such as territory, geographic location, population and meagre resources should not hinder independence. The US, in its role as administrative power, was urged to implement an educational program to assure Samoans' full awareness of their rights, to hasten the decolonization process. The islanders, however, seemed to be content with their existing status which allowed them to emigrate to the United States without restrictions. There were no organized pro-independence groups.

[3] In 1984, Governor Coleman (elected in the first elections for Governor held in 1977) submitted proposals for a new Constitution in American Samoa for ratification by the US Congress. The proposals were withdrawn in May of the same year, because it was feared that they would be harmful to the interests of US citizens. In November, A P Lutali was elected Governor and Faleomavaega Eni Hunkin became Vice-Governor.

[4] In July 1988, the delegate to the US house of representatives, Fofo Sunia, announced that he would not stand for re-election because he was going to be subjected to official investigations after accusations of financial mismanagement. In October, he was sentenced to a 5 to 15 week term in prison for fraud. Hence, Eni Hunkin replaced Sunia. In November, Coleman was re-elected for his third term and Galeani Poumele replaced Hunkin as Vice-Governor.

[5] In the second half of 1986, the governments of American Samoa and Samoa signed an agreement to create a permanent committee for the development of both countries in tourism, transport, and fishing.

[6] Economic development is dependent on the 90 per cent of Samoan foreign trade going to the US. Tuna fishing and tuna processing plants are the backbone of the private sector economy, with the canneries as the second-largest employers, exceeded only by the Government.

[7] Despite reforms to the 1967 constitution during the 1980s, proposed changes were not ratified by the United States Congress. According to the Constitution currently in effect, in addition to a governor, who is elected for a four-year term, there is also a legislature, or 'Fono' with an 18-member Senate elected every four years by the Matai, or clan heads. There is also a 20-member House of Representatives elected by direct popular vote for two-year terms. Women do not have the right to vote.

[8] After his re-election as Governor in 1992, Lutali took measures to cut public spending, especially by reducing the number of government employees. The projected social security reform in the US and its dependencies led to a debate in the second half of 1996 about the consequences for the inhabitants of American Samoa.

[9] Figures from the archipelago expressed the concern for the reform's effects on American Samoan residents - regarded as US 'nationals' but with fewer rights than the 'citizens' of that country - and on immigrants, specifically those from other Polynesian territories.

[10] In November 1996, Tauese Pita Sunia was elected Governor with 51 per cent of the vote, to replace AP Lutali. Togiola Tulafano became Vice-Governor. Both took office in January 1997.

[11] Later that year, in November, the government in Pago Pago imposed a curfew between 9:00 pm and 6:00 am, after expressing concern over the apparent rise in crime rates. In February 1998, a senior official in the Education Ministry accused the Governor of diverting funds meant for school building improvements in order to install a sauna in his official residence. In September, the opposition tried to challenge the Governor on the charges of 'abuse of power'. Republican Eni Faleomavaega was reelected senator to the US with 86 per cent of the vote during the month of November.

[12] The Government was forced to impose austerity measures in order to reduce the deficit, including a shortened work week, a rise in taxes and cost reductions. ∎

PROFILE

ENVIRONMENT

The island occupies 197 sq km of the eastern part of the Samoan archipelago, located in Polynesia, slightly to the east of the International Date Line, northwest of the Fiji islands. The most important islands are Tutuila (where the capital is located), Tau, Olosega, Ofu, Annuu, Rose and Swains. Of volcanic origin, the islands are mountainous with fertile soil on the plains. The climate is rainy and tropical, tempered by sea winds. There is dense, woody vegetation and major streams of shallow waters. The main export product is fish, especially tuna.

SOCIETY

Peoples: Samoans are mostly Polynesians (89 per cent); Tongans 4 per cent; other 5 per cent.
Religions: Christian (Protestant 50 per cent, Catholic 20 per cent); others 30 per cent.
Languages: Samoan, predominant, and English are the official languages.

THE STATE

Official Name: Territory of American Samoa.
Capital: Pago Pago, on Tutuila, 9,000 people (1994 est).
Government: US President is Head of State. Tauese P. Sunia, Governor since January 1997. There is a bicameral Legislative Power. Samoans are considered US 'nationals', but without the right to vote in presidential elections while living on the islands.

DEMOGRAPHY

Population: 47,000 (1999)

COMMUNICATIONS

84 newspapers (1996) and 955 radios (1997) per 1,000 people

ECONOMY

Cereal imports: 5,084 metric tons (1998)

São Tomé and Príncipe

São Tomé e Príncipe

Population: 127,000 (1999)
Area: 960 SQ KM
Capital: São Tomé
Currency: Dobra
Language: Portuguese

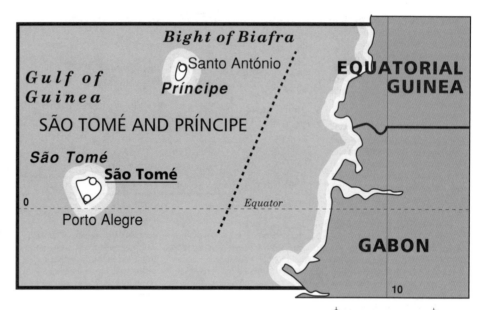

These islands were probably uninhabited when first visited by European navigators in the 1470s. Thereafter, the Portuguese began to settle convicts and exiled Jews there and established sugar plantations, using slave labor from the African mainland. Strategically located 300 kilometers off the African coast, the islands' natural ports were used by the Portuguese as supply stops for ships in the 15th century. Dutch, French, Spanish, British and Portuguese slave traders bought enslaved African laborers to be sold in the American colonies. Some of those slaves remained on the islands, which later became the leading African producers of sugarcane.

[2] Rebellions broke out and after the failure of an insurrection headed by Yoan Gato, a slave named Amador led a revolt that succeeded in taking over two-thirds of the island of São Tomé, where he proclaimed himself ruler.

[3] Soon defeated, the rebels hid in quilombos (guerrilla shelters in the forest) after burning their crops. The Portuguese landlords who moved to Brazil took with them not only their enslaved workers. The slaves carried the seed of insurrection with them, which quickly produced quilombos in Brazil, some of which - such as the Palmares *quilombo* - became true republics and held out for nearly a century.

[4] In São Tomé and Príncipe, agriculture virtually disappeared for three centuries. In the 17th century the island was breifly held by the Dutch. After a period of decline, the colony recovered its prosperity in the late 19th century with the cultivation of cocoa.

[5] Even after abolition was declared in 1869, slavery continued in a disguised manner ('free' workers signed contracts for nine years at fixed salaries), leading to revolts and an international boycott against the 'cocoa slavery' of the Portuguese colony in the early 20th century.

[6] This neo-slavery system continued until the mid-1900s. A Society for Immigration of São Tomé organized the modern slave trade, 'hiring' plantation workers in other Portuguese colonies: Angola, Cape Verde, Guinea and Mozambique. This flow 're-Africanized' the country as the *filhos da terra* (sons of the earth), the result of several centuries of integration between the natives and the Portuguese, mixed with the African immigrants. During the colonial regimes of Salazar and Caetano, repression was particularly harsh. In February 1953, over 1,000 people were killed in Batepá in less than a week.

[7] This massacre revealed the need for the rebels to join forces, and in 1969 the Movement for the Liberation of São Tomé and Príncipe (MLSTP) was founded, with two main objectives: independence and land reform.

[8] Foreign companies owned 90 per cent of the land of São Tomé and despite the fertile soil, most food was imported due to the island's monoculture policy. Rural workers were one of the major pillars of the MLSTP, and held a 24-hour strike in August 1963, which paralyzed all the plantations.

[9] As the island's terrain did not favor guerrilla warfare, the MLSTP launched an intensive underground political campaign that resulted in its recognition by the OAU (Organization of African Unity) and the Non-Aligned Nations. Together with the MPLA of Angola, the PAIGC of Guinea and Cape Verde, and FRELIMO of Mozambique, the MLSTP joined the Conference of National Organizations of the Portuguese Colonies. It was the only legitimate group in existence when, after the 1974 revolution, Portugal began to free its colonies.

[10] The MLSTP joined a transition government in 1974 and in the following year declared independence. Its accomplishments were impressive: banks and farms were nationalized, medicine was socialized, a national currency was created, a major administrative reform was launched to reorganize public administration, and numerous centers of popular culture, based on the culture-building educational methods of Brazilian Paulo Freire, were created as part of a literacy campaign.

[11] Opposing these reforms was a rightist faction led by Health Minister Carlos da Graca, who fled to Gabon to plot a mercenary invasion of the islands in early 1978. The thwarted conspiracy consolidated the unity of the MLSTP, which held its first congress in August 1978. Mass organizations to defend the revolution were fostered and a People's Militia was formed. Miguel Trovoada, Prime Minister since independence was removed thus strengthening the more progressive trends of the Party Coordinating Committee.

[12] In March 1986, two opposition groups based outside the country - the São Tomé e Príncipe Independent Democratic Union (UDISTP) and the more radical São Tomé e Príncipe National Resistance Front (FRNSTP) - founded by Carlos da Graça - announced the formation of an alliance called the Democratic Opposition Coalition. Its aim was to put pressure on the Government to hold free elections. A month later, a fishing vessel with 76 members of the FRNSTP on board arrived in Walvis Bay, the South African enclave in Namibia. They asked the Pretoria Government to supply

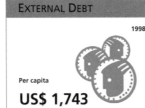
military aid needed to destabilize the São Tomé Government. These events led to Carlos de Graca's resignation as president of the FRNSTP. In May, he announced his willingness to cooperate with the Government, on condition that Cuban and Angolan troops stationed in the country be withdrawn.

[13] In 1985, in the midst of the worst drought in the country's history, the Government sought to open up the economy: new legislation was designed to promote foreign investment and privatize the so-called 'people's stores'. Gradually, the State relinquished economic control, previously heavily dependent upon such key products as cocoa, coffee and bananas. The Government sought ways to attract foreign capital to the agricultural, fishing and tourism sectors.

[14] Late in 1989, the MLSTP leadership discussed reform of the party statutes and of the national constitution. In March 1990, the People's National Assembly approved amendments to the Charter, later to be submitted to a referendum. These changes made possible a move to a multi-party system. Independent candidates were admitted in the legislative elections, and the tenure of the President was limited to no longer than two five-year terms.

[15] The first parliamentary elections after independence were held in January 1991. The opposition Democratic Convergence of Leonel d'Alva was voted into power. In March, the former prime minister Miguel Trovoada returned from exile and was unopposed in the presidential elections.

[16] The heads of state of São Tomé and Principe, Cape Verde, Guinea-Bissau, Mozambique and Angola - all former Portuguese colonies - met in February 1992. After being organized under single party systems, the five countries experienced rapid political change and economic liberalization processes.

[17] The social and economic situation of the country worsened in recent years as the result of an IMF and World Bank imposed austerity plan. Public sector salaries were frozen, a third of all civil servants were dismissed and the local currency was devalued by 80 per cent. While inflation fell, the price of basic foodstuffs quadrupled and unemployment reached 30 per cent.

[18] The island of Principe declared independence on April 29 1995 and established a five-member regional government.

[19] In August, a group of army officers took power in São Tomé in a bloodless coup. Negotiations led to the immediate re-establishment of the legal government.

[20] The General Assembly censured Prime Minister Armindo Vaz D'Almeida, in power since December 31 of the previous year, for 'bad management, inefficiency, incompetence and corruption'.

[21] In November 1998 Manel Pinta da Costa became Prime Minister.

[22] The economy of São Tomé was sustained by international aid in 1997: 60 per cent of the budget was funded by contributions, particularly from Europe. The European Development Fund funded a program to create jobs, set up medical care centers and supply medical equipment. ■

PROFILE

ENVIRONMENT

The country comprises the islands of Sao Tomé (857 sq km) and Principe (114 sq km), and the smaller islands of Rólas, Cabras, Bombom and Bone de Joquei in the Bay of Biafra of the Gulf of Guinea, facing the coast of Gabon. The islands are mountainous, of volcanic origin, with dense rainforests, a tropical climate and heavy rainfall. Cocoa, copra and coffee are the main export crops.

SOCIETY

Peoples: Most are Africans of Bantu origin traditionally classified in five groups formed as a result of different migratory waves: the Filhos da terra (sons of the earth), descendants of the first enslaved workers brought to the islands and intermingled with the Portuguese; the Angolares, believed to descend from Angolans who came to the islands in the 16th Century; the Fôrros, descendants of freed slaves when slavery was abolished; the Serviais, migrant workers from Mozambique, Angola and Cape Verde; and the native Tongas. Since independence, these categories have begun to disappear.
Religions: Roman Catholic, about 80.8 per cent; remainder mostly Protestant, predominantly Seventh-Day Adventist and an indigenous Evangelical Church.
Languages: Portuguese (official); Fôrro; Crioulo, a dialect with Portuguese and African elements, is widely spoken.
Political Parties: Movement for the Liberation of Sao Tomé and Príncipe-Social Democratic Party (MLSTP-PSD), in government; Democratic Convergence Party (PCD); Committee for the Liberation of Sao Tomé and Príncipe (CLSTP); Democratic Coalition, Christian Democratic Front.
Social Organizations: Women's, Youth and Pioneers Organizations linked to the MLSTP.

THE STATE

Official Name: República Democrática de São Tomé e Príncipe.
Capital: Sao Tomé, 42,000 people (1996).
Other cities: Trindade 11,388 people; Santana 6,190; Neves 5,919; Santo Amaro 5,878 (1991).
Administrative Divisions: 7 Districts.
Government: Miguel Trovoada, President, re-elected on July 21 1996; Manuel Pinta da Costa, Prime Minister since November 1998. Legislative: 55-member National People's Assembly.
National Holiday: July 12, Independence Day (1975).

STATISTICS

DEMOGRAPHY

Population: 127,000 (1999)
Annual growth: 2.5 % (1975/97)
Estimates for year 2015 (million): 0.2 (1999)
Annual growth to year 2015: 1.8 % (1997/2015)
Urban population: 44.5 % (1997)
Children per woman: 4.7 (1998)

HEALTH

Life expectancy at birth: 64 years (1998)
Infant mortality: 60 per 1,000 (1998)
Under-5 child mortality: 77 per 1,000 (1998)
Daily calorie supply: 2,156 per capita (1996)
32 doctors per 100,000 people (1993)
Safe water: 82 % (1990/98)

EDUCATION

Literacy: 57 % (1995)

COMMUNICATIONS

275 radios (1997), 165 TV sets (1996) and 20 main telephone lines (1996) per 1,000 people

ECONOMY

Per capita, GNP: $ 270 (1998)
Annual growth, GNP: 1.4 % (1998)
Cereal imports: 9,445 metric tons (1998)
Exports: $ 12 million (1998)
Imports: $ 35 million (1998)
External debt: $ 246 million (1998); $ 1,743 per capita (1998)
Development aid received: $ 34 million (1997); $ 287.3 per capita (1997); 87.50 % of GNP (1997)

HDI (rank/value): 123/0.609 (1997)

Saudi Arabia

Arabiyah as-Sa ' udiyah

Population: 20,899,000 (1999)
Area: 2,149,690 SQ KM
Capital: Riyadh (Ar-Riyad) (royal capital)
Currency: Saudi Arabian riya
Language: Arabic

Arabia was drawn into the orbit of western Asiatic civilization toward the end of the 3rd millennium BC. Caravan trade between south Arabia and the Fertile Crescent began about the middle of the 2nd millennium BC. The domestication of the camel around the 12th century BC made desert travel easier and gave rise to a flourishing society in South Arabia, centred around the state of Saab (Sheila). In eastern Arabia the island of Dolman (Bahrain) had become a thriving entrepot between Mesopotamia, South Arabia, and India as early as the 24th century BC. The discovery by the Mediterranean peoples of the monsoon winds in the Indian Ocean made possible flourishing Roman and Byzantine seaborne trade between the northern Red Sea ports and South Arabia, extending to India and beyond. In the 5th and 6th centuries AD, successive invasions of the Christian Ethiopians and the counter-invasion of the Sasanian kings disrupted the states of South Arabia.

[2] In the 6th century Quraysh - the noble and holy house of the confederation of the Hejaz controlling the sacred enclave of Mecca - contrived a series of agreements with the northern and southern tribes. Under this aegis, caravans moved freely from the southern Yemen coast to Mecca and thence northward to Byzantium or eastward to Iraq. Furthermore, members of the Quraysh house of 'Abd Manaf concluded pacts with Byzantium, Persia, and rulers of Yemen and Ethiopia, promoting commerce outside Arabia. The 'Abd Manaf house could effect such agreements because of Quraysh's superior position with the tribes. Quraysh

had some sanctity as lords of the Meccan temple (the Ka'bah) and were themselves known as the Protected Neighbors of Allah. The tribes on pilgrimage to Mecca were called the Guests of Allah.

[3] In its enclave Quraysh was secure from attack. It arbitrated in tribal disputes, attaining thereby at least a local pre-eminence and seemingly a loose hegemony over many Arabian tribes. The Ka'bah, through the additions of other cults, developed into a pantheon, the cult of other gods perhaps being linked with political agreements between Quraysh - worshippers of Allah - and the tribes.

[4] Mohammed was born in 570 of the Hashimite branch of the noble house of 'Abd Manaf; though orphaned at an early age and in consequence with little influence, he never lacked protection by his clan. Marriage to a wealthy widow

improved his position as a merchant, but he began to make his mark in Mecca by preaching the oneness of Allah. Rejected by the Quraysh lords, Mohammed sought affiliation with other groups; he was unsuccessful until he managed to negotiate a pact with the tribal chiefs of Medina, whereby he obtained their protection and became theocratic head and arbiter of the Medina tribal confederation (*ummah*). Those Quraysh who joined him there were known as *muhajirun* (refugees or emigrants), while his Medina allies were called *ansar* (supporters). The Muslim era dates from the *hijrah* (hegira) - Mohammed's move to Medina in AD 622.

[5] Mohammed's supporters attacked a Quraysh caravan in AD 624, thus breaking the vital security system established by the 'Abd Manaf house, and hostilities broke out against his Mecca kin. In Medina two problems confronted him - the necessity to enforce his role as arbiter and to raise supplies

for his moves against Quraysh. He overcame internal opposition, removing in the process three Jewish tribes, whose properties he distributed among his followers. Externally, his rising power was demonstrated following Quraysh's failure to overrun Medina, when he declared it his own sacred enclave. Mohammed foiled Quraysh offensives and marched back to Mecca. After taking Mecca in AD 630 he became lord of the two sacred enclaves; however, even though he broke the power of some Quraysh lords, his policy thenceforth was to conciliate his Quraysh kin.

[6] After Mohammed's entry into Mecca the tribes linked with Quraysh came to negotiate with him and to accept Islam; this meant little more than giving up their local deities and worshipping Allah alone. They had to pay the tax, but this was not novel because the tribal chiefs had already been taxed to protect the Meccan enclave. Many tribes probably waited to join the winner. From then on Islam was destined for a world role. Under Mohammed's successors the expansionist urge of the tribal groups, temporarily united around the nucleus of the two sacred enclaves, coincided with the weakness of Byzantium and Sasanian Persia. Tribes summoned to the banners of Islam launched a career of conquest that promised to satisfy the mandate of their new faith as well as the desire for booty and lands. With families and flocks, they left the peninsula. Population movements of such magnitude affected all of Arabia; in Hadhramaut they possibly caused neglect of irrigation works, resulting in erosion of fertile lands. In Oman, too, when Arabs evicted the Persian ruling class, its complex irrigation system suffered. Many Omani Arabs about the mid-7th century left for Basra (in Iraq) and formed the influential Azd group there. Arabian Islam replaced Persian influence in the Bahrain district and Al-Hasa province in the northeast, and in Yemen.

[7] As the conquests far beyond Arabia poured loot into the Holy Cities (Mecca and Medina), they became wealthy centres of a sophisticated Arabian culture. Medina became a centre for Qur'anic (Koranic) study, the evolution of Islamic law, and historical record. Under the caliphs - Mohammed's successors - Islam began to assume its characteristic shape. Paradoxically,

LAND USE

DEFORESTATION: 0.8% annual (1990/95)
IRRIGATED: 11.9% of arable (1993)

1993

- FOREST & WOODLAND: 0.8%
- ARABLE: 1.7%
- OTHER: 97.5%

WORKERS

% OF LABOUR FORCE **1998**

- FEMALE: 15%   MALE: 85%

PUBLIC EXPENDITURE

DEFENCE EXPENDITURE (% of goverment exp.)	**35.8%**	(1997)
MILITARY EXPENDITURE (% of health & education)	**151%**	(1990/91)

outside the cities it made little difference to Arabian life for centuries. After the Prophet's death, the second caliph Omar led the Arab conquest. Within ten years the Arabs occupied Syria, Palestine, Egypt and Persia. With Muawiya, the caliphate became hereditary in the family of the Ummaias and the Arabs became a privileged caste which ruled over the conquered nations.

[8] In the 8th century, the borders of the Arabian Empire reached from North Africa and Spain to the west, to Pakistan and Afghanistan in the east. Upon moving the capital to Damascus, Syria became the cultural, political and economic center of the Empire, and it was in Damascus that the foundations of a new culture were laid. Greco-Roman, Persian and Indian components blended into an original combination in which science played an important role. Contrary to Mohammed's expectations, the Arabian peninsula was to remain on the sidelines within the enormous empire, except in religious matters. Mecca, although failing to match Baghdad or Damascus in socio-economic and cultural importance, continued to be the center of Islam and the destination for large pilgrimages from all over the world.

[9] This situation remained unchanged for centuries. The Empire split up; the capital moved to Baghdad and the power of the caliphs passed over to the viziers, while culturally Arabic civilization attained the highest standards in all fields of knowledge and artistic creation. Arabic became the language of scholars from Portugal to India. But little changed in the land that gave birth to all this civilization. Nomadic groups continued to shepherd their flocks, the settled population kept up their commerce, and rivalries between the two were frequently settled through war. As in Mohammed's time, demographic growth was channelled towards conquest, with the emigration of whole communities, such as the Been Hills in the 11th century. Trading caravans carrying supplies to Mecca and stopping points along the way, became much more frequent, while the ports became more active as a result of trade with Africa. The peninsula was governed from Egypt, first by Saladin and later by the Mamelukes. The Turks ruled from the 16th century to the 20th century, without introducing any major changes in the socio-economic pattern of the Arab nation.

[10] Under Turkish rule the provinces of Hidjaz and Asir on the Red Sea had a reasonable degree of autonomy due to the religious prestige of the *shereefs* of Mecca, descendants of Mohammed. The interior, with Riyadh as the main urban center, became the Emirate of Najd at the end of the 18th century, through the efforts of the Saud family supported by the Wahabite sect (known as the Islamic Puritans). In the 19th century, with Turkish assistance, the Rated clan forced Abd al-Rahman bin Saud out of power; the ousted leader sought exile in Kuwait. In 1902, his son Abd al-Aziz, again with the support of the Wahabios, organized a religious-military sect, the Ikhwan, in which he enlisted nearly 50,000 Bedouins in order to reconquer Najd. Twelve years later the Saudis defeated the Rachidis and added the Al-Hasa region on the Gulf until then under direct control of the Turks, against whom the Saudi forces fought during World War I. At the end of the conflict, Britain - the predominant power in the area - faced a difficult situation. In exchange for Abd al-Aziz' continued anti-Turk campaign, Britain had promised to guarantee the integrity of his state. But for the same reason it had also promised to make Hussein bin Ali (the shereef of Mecca) king of a nation that would encompass Palestine, Jordan, Iraq and the Arabian peninsula.

[11] The Emir of Najd waited for some time. It seemed clear to him that Britain would not keep its word to Hussein: such a powerful kingdom, ruled by the Prophet's family with the capital in the holy city, would alter the regional balance of power. But in 1924 Hussein proclaimed himself caliph (see Jordan). Abd al-Aziz invaded his territory immediately, despite English opposition and in January 1926 was declared King of Hidjaz and Sultan of Nadj in the great mosque of Mecca. Six years later the 'Kingdom of Hidjaz, of Nedj and its dependencies' was formally unified under the name of Saudi Arabia.

[12] In 1930, the monarch gave US companies permission to drill for oil. When he died in 1953, his son Saud squandered all the revenues paid into the Kingdom's treasury by the Arab-American Oil Company (Aramco), on palaces, harems, fancy cars and casinos on the French Riviera. In 1964 the country was on the verge of bankruptcy when Saud was ousted by his brother Faisal, an able diplomat who had also proved a valiant soldier in the wars. Monogamous, deeply religious and austere to the point of asceticism, Faisal gave new life to the country's economy and began to invest petrodollars in ambitious development programs, though maintaining the traditional feudal structure headed by the autocratic ruler.

[13] Faisal's religious views led him to bluntly reject the Soviet Union and any other system linked with atheism, including Nasser's nationalism in Egypt, as well as Iraqi or Syrian Ba'athism. His strategic alliance with the United States was seen as 'natural', but was disturbed by US support of Israel after the war of 1967. Faisal used to say that his only dream was to be able to pray one day in Omar's mosque, in a freed Jerusalem and rivalries with neighboring Iran, which under the Shah Pahlevi also played watchdog for Washington's interests in the Gulf.

[14] During the 1973 Arab-Israeli war, Faisal supported an oil embargo on the countries backing Israel, including the US. The sudden oil shortage allowed OPEC countries to increase oil prices in a short space of time, heralding a new era in international relations. On March 25 1975, Faisal was murdered by an apparently insane nephew. His brother Khaled, almost paralyzed by a rheumatic illness, was named as his successor. However, due to his paralysis, the governing duties in an era of superabundance fell to his brother, Crown Prince Fahd ibn Abd al-Aziz.

[15] The oil revenue, which amounted to $500 million a year when Faisal was crowned in 1964, had gone up to almost $30 billion when he died. That same year the Bank of America closed its balance with assets of $57.5 billion, and West Germany's exports amounted to $90 billion. These figures revealed that, when compared with other major economic powers, Saudi economic power was overrated. But these were staggering figures for the Third World: three times the income of Egypt, whose population was eight times bigger.

[16] New cities, universities, hospitals, freeways and mosques sprouted up everywhere. Yet there was surplus money available. Instead of planning oil production to meet the country's needs, which would have avoided the fall in prices and the weakening of OPEC during the 1980s, fortunes accumulated in western banks. Thus, Saudi Arabia tied its future more closely with the industrialized capitalist world. In addition it created a surplus of money in circulation, which the banks lent to Third World countries in some irresponsible ventures. This gave rise to the 1984-85 foreign debt crisis, with a rise in interest rates.

[17] The Muslim fundamentalist groups denounced the Saudi dynasty for allegedly betraying Islam, leading to several violent confrontations with government forces. The theological basis which legitimised the ruling autocracy may be undermined by the progressive rise to power of new members of the ruling family, trained in European and US universities and military academies, rather than in the traditional desert-tent Koranic schools.

[18] After the overthrow of the Shah of Iran, the Saudi Government drew closer to the US. With King Khaled's death, on June 13 1982, his brother Fahd - the architect of Saudi Arabia's foreign policy - became king.

[19] The year before, the new monarch had created a peace plan for the Middle East which had been approved by several Arab countries, the PLO and the US, though the plan collapsed in August, 1981 due to Israeli opposition. This plan proposed the creation of a Palestinian State with Jerusalem as its capital, the withdrawal of Israel from the occupied Arab territories, and the dismantling of the Jewish colonies set up in 1967, as well as the recognition of the right of every state in the region to live peaceably. On September 26 1982, during the Haj or pilgrimage to Mecca, the King condemned Israeli intervention in Lebanon, which he called criminal aggression. He also criticized Soviet intervention in Afghanistan, accused Ayatollah Khomeini of attempting to destabilize the regime through sabotage, and generally condemned the 'influence of great powers' in the Muslim world.

[20] Naval bases in Jubail and Jeddah were built under the supervision of the US Army. Also, investments and bank deposits by the Saudi State and nobility were closely linked with the performance of the US economy: two-thirds of the huge amount of Saudi petrodollars invested abroad went into corporation stocks, treasury bonds and bank deposits in the US.

[21] The official development plans established an industrial policy to reduce dependency from oil resources. Priority was given to the petrochemical industry, and there was a proliferation of steel mills, mechanical manufacturing plants, heavy industry, and others.

[22] The industrial infrastructure is concentrated in two new cities: Jubail on the shores of the Gulf and Yanbu on the Red Sea. They are connected with the eastern hydrocarbon deposits through gas and oil pipelines.

[23] The 1985-89 five-year plan promised a 'wide income redistribution'. Yet that intention coincided with the first signs of economic trouble in the Kingdom. In 1984, due to another drop in the price of crude, the official budget closed with a deficit for the first time. The Minister of Industry, Ghazi Al Gosaibi, was forced to resign after writing a poem which made reference to corruption.

[24] Million-dollar investments in all kinds of mainly US weapons continued, aiming to secure the Gulf coast against the potential Iranian aggression and satisfying the ambitions of an increasingly powerful and influential army.

[25] During the Iran-Iraq war, Saudi Arabia backed Iraq financially, afraid that the Iranian Islamic revolution might spread over the Gulf. Fahd changed his title of King to Guardian of the Holy Sites, but every year the pious pilgrims to Mecca protested more loudly, angry about the alliance between Riyadh and Washington and by what they considered a commercialization and westernization of the sacred places, surrounded today by shopping centers, highways and other symbols of transnational culture. On August 1 1987, a march by Iranian women and disabled war veterans in Mecca was fired upon by Saudi police. Hundreds of pilgrims were killed. In retaliation, the embassies of Saudi Arabia and Kuwait in Tehran were attacked and burned, and relations between both countries grew very tense.

[26] In early 1990 Amnesty International disclosed 'a clear pattern of human rights violations, including torture' of political opposition and labor leaders, belonging primarily to the Shi'a sect.

[27] After the Iraqi invasion of Kuwait in August 1990 Saudi Arabia was the scene of a huge military deployment by a multinational coalition led by the United States. Apart from the loss of human lives, the war caused a huge ecological disaster.

[28] In March 1992, King Fahd issued several decrees aimed at decentralizing political power. This legislation, of 83 articles, is called 'The Basic System of Government'. Amongst other amendments, it established an Advisory Council, with the right to review all matters of national policy. However, the ultimate decision-making power remained with the King.

[29] The royal decrees also created the *mutawein*, religious police, whose mandate is to ensure the observance of Islamic customs. The home is defined as a sacred place, and therefore the state (the religious police) may enter without legal authorization. This situation has led to the detention of several alleged violators of the law.

[30] The Iraqi invasion of Kuwait, and the subsequent crisis in the Persian Gulf, exposed the Kingdom's political and military dependence on the US. It also served as a catalyst for political reform within Saudi Arabia itself.

[31] In 1992, Fahd, who was suffering minor health problems, confirmed his brother Abdullah ibn Abd al-Aziz al-Saud as heir to the throne. Human rights organizations, such as Amnesty International, expressed their concern throughout 1993 over the arbitrary arrest of mainly Christians and Shi'a Muslims, but also Sunnis.

[32] In the economic field, Fahd announced in May 1994 his goal to implement a program to privatize large state enterprises, such as the national airline and telephone companies. Despite a small rise in the price of oil in 1995, the King decreed significant reductions of public spending, which amounted to 20 per cent in the education sector.

[33] According to several observers, growing social differentiation aggravated tensions among Saudis themselves, regarded as privileged compared to the millions of foreign workers living in the country. The attack on the offices of US advisers in Riyadh in November, killing at least 6 people, was seen as proof of those tensions.

[34] Fahd's illness became more serious toward the end of 1995, and he was forced to withdraw from the political scene until the second half of 1996. Hostility toward the US became stronger in one part of the population, reaching crisis point with the attack on the US El Khobar base on June 25 1996. A 2,200 kilogram bomb left 19 soldiers dead and hundreds injured. The United States applied extreme security measures and demanded investigations to find those responsible, as it feared violence would break out again.

[35] That same year, Saudi Arabia was highlighted as one of the world's biggest arms purchasers. Internal battles over who would succeed the 70-year-old king continued at the heart of the royal family, while the social crisis led to the radicalization of Islamic sectors hostile to Fahd's pro-US policy.

[36] In 1997, tension between Washington and Baghdad weakened the alliance with the US. Saudi Arabia warned President Bill Clinton that the contrast between the US' 'hard line' policy against Iraq and the 'soft' policy with Israel could exasperate the region's Arab population. At the end of that year, 2,000 immigrants without papers were expelled, marking a U-turn in migration policy.

[37] The border conflict with Yemen, which has dragged on since 1930, re-ignited in 1999 with the expulsion of some Yemeni citizens. In December of that year the Yemeni authorities called for a plans to settle the issue, but a week later Riyadh expelled 300 more Yemenis for 'violating immigration laws'.

[38] In January 2000, Saudi Arabia

signed an economic co-operation agreement with Iran, thus bringing years of poor diplomatic relations to a close. ∎

Senegal

Sénégal

Population: 9,240,000 (1999)
Area: 196,720 SQ KM
Capital: Dakar
Currency: CFA franc
Language: French

The banks of the Senegal River have been inhabited for many centuries by peoples who had been Islamicized through contact with neighboring Arab countries. This group of countries make up the region known as the Sahel. The Wolof (who constitute more than a third of the population), Fulani, Pulaar and other peoples, all lived within the area of modern Senegal.

[2] When the French occupied the area during the 17th century, they incorporated it into the triangular world trade pattern of the time: European manufactured goods were exchanged for slaves, sold in the Antilles, where colonial European powers produced rum and sugar, which were sold back in Europe.

[3] After slavery was abolished by the French revolution of 1848, the Senegalese became 'second class citizens' of the French Empire, with one political representative in Paris. At this time Senegal exported thousands of tons of peanuts per year and supplied the French army with soldiers.

[4] During the second half of the 19th century, there were frequent rebellions among the Muslim leaders, and it was only in 1892 that the French managed to fully 'pacify' the country.

[5] The Pan-African movement inspired Senegalese Leopold Sédar Senghor and Martinique's Aimé Césaire, and together in Paris, they created the concept of *négritude*, an idea first presented to public opinion in 1933. *Négritude* stood against the imposition of French cultural patterns, which were enforced throughout the colonies. The concept was designed to serve as 'an effective liberation tool'. In Senghor's view, it had to escape 'peculiarism' and find a place within contemporary movements of solidarity, that is, to achieve a definite political profile.

[6] Senghor had been a member of the French *maquis* (resistance) during World War II, he had fought against fascism and was elected representative to the French National Assembly in 1945. Three years later, he brought about the foundation of the Senegalese Progressive Union, which demanded greater autonomy for the colonies, though not independence.

[7] Finally, on April 4 1960, Senegal declared independence, and on September 5 adopted a republican system. Senghor was elected President and through successive re-elections he stayed in power for two decades. He was finally replaced by Abdou Diouf on January 1 1981.

[8] The ideology of African socialism promoted by Senghor was based on the premise that traditional African agrarian society had always been essentially collectivist. Senghor believed that socialism already existed on the continent and therefore did not need to be imposed. This 'collectivism' actually mainly served to provide cheap labor for the export-oriented production of peanuts and cotton. 82 per cent of the nation's industry was French-controlled.

[9] In an effort to keep up with political changes in France, Senghor requested membership of the Socialist International. To this end he pushed through a constitutional reform restricting political representation to three political parties: a 'liberal democratic' party (the Senegalese Democratic Party), a Marxist-Leninist party (the African Party for Independence) and a 'social democratic' party (his own, renamed the Senegalese Socialist Party).

[10] In the 1980s Diouf brought flexibility to the rigid political system he inherited from his predecessor. This prevented the major political adversary Abdoulaye Wade's Democratic Party of Senegal (PDS), from uniting all the Government opposition forces. In 1982, in the southern province of Casamance, on the border with Guinea-Bissau, there was a resurgence of separatist activity, leading to the creation of the Casamance Movement of Democratic Forces (MFDC) led by an abbot, Austin Diamacoune Senghor.

The people of Casamance are primarily from the Diole ethnic group, animists who have prided themselves on their independence and resistance to the Islamic hierarchical societies of the north. In December 1983, after successive confrontations with the Senegalese police forces, many leaders of the MFDC were detained, among them Abbot Diamacoune.

[11] The country faced a series of serious droughts over the last 20 years. These were seen as part of the desertification process caused by climatic conditions and the French-imposed substitution of export crops for traditional food crops,. In the early 1980s the Government gave in to pressure from the US, France, the World Bank and the IMF to accept a structural adjustment plan. The elimination of agricultural subsidies triggered a rise in production costs and the prices of basic consumer goods.

[12] The drought afflicting the country since ruined peanut production (peanuts represent over one third of total exports), and the food deficit required the import of 400,000 tons of rice.

[13] In 1988 the Socialist Party (PS) won another victory in the national elections, obtaining 72.3 per cent of the vote, while the Senegalese Democratic Party (PDS) won only 25.8 per cent. After the legitimacy of the election was called into question by various groups, government troops were mobilized to keep the peace. In the aftermath, hundreds of people were arrested, and the PDS candidate, Abdoulaye Wade, was forced to go into exile, only returning to Senegal in March 1989.

[14] A month later a border conflict broke out with Mauritania triggered by violent altercations between peasants and farmers, causing hundreds of casualties and forcing some 70,000 refugees to enter Senegal.

[15] In January 1991, Amnesty International accused the Senegalese Government of human rights violations, on account of the tortures and murders committed in the Casamance region. Late in May, the Government announced its intention to free political prisoners, including MFDC leader, Abbot Diamacoune Senghor as part of an amnesty settlement.

[16] This conflict affected the planned Senegambian integration, as Diouf criticized Gambian tolerance of the

WORKERS

% OF LABOUR FORCE **1998**

- FEMALE: 43% MALE: 57%

1990

- SERVICES: 15.8%
- INDUSTRY: 7.5%
- AGRICULTURE: 76.7%

LAND USE

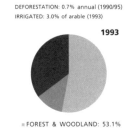

DEFORESTATION: 0.7% annual (1990/95)
IRRIGATED: 3.0% of arable (1993)

1993

- FOREST & WOODLAND: 53.1%
- ARABLE: 11.8%
- OTHER: 35.1%

PUBLIC EXPENDITURE

DEFENCE EXPENDITURE (% of goverment exp.)	**8.5%**	(1997)
MILITARY EXPENDITURE (% of health & education)	**33%**	(1990/91)

Cutting controversy: female genital mutilation

Reaching puberty is a challenging time. But for many young people, it is not simply their bodies changing as the hormones surge which marks the change to adulthood. There may also be circumcision. For girls, Female Genital Mutilation (FGM) is part of an initiation rite in which a girl or adolescent enters maturity. For the cultures that practice it, it means the passage from childhood to adulthood. For its detractors, usually from the West, it is an abuse of human rights.

2   There are many cultures of Africa, the Middle East and Asia that for centuries have performed clitoridectomy as it is known, which consists of removal of a woman's clitoris and often the inner labia and a major portion of the outer labia as well. Some of the countries where this procedure is done are Guinea, Senegal, Ethiopia, Egypt, Burkina Faso, Mali, Gambia, Eritrea, Sudan, Somalia, Nigeria, India, as well as some cultures in the Middle East.

3   It is the community that decides when a young woman can procreate. The initiation rite is a deeply rooted ceremony that serves to reinforce the social and political fabric of the community. Initially, FGM was practiced to protect virginity, and to prevent masturbation and pleasure during sex. It has also been reported that in some of these cultures girls grow up hearing that if they do not undergo circumcision all sorts of punishments will befall them.

4   In recent decades, various human rights groups, including some feminist organizations, put the issue on the Western agenda and began denouncing FGM while educating people about it and attempting to eradicate female circumcision. The reasons for fighting the practice are several. Firstly of course it is painful, requiring the cutting of flesh, and this produces excessive bleeding. Often infections such as tetanus arise from an unclean knife or the dirty water used to clean the wound. There can also be trauma and physical malformations leading to a life of health and reproductive problems. And the critics tend to target female 'surgeons' who are trusted members of society but generally not trained in medicine and hygiene.

5   Circumcision is also condemned because it can lead to the death of the initiates - a fairly common occurrence, usually as a result of infection. Other critics, such as some humanitarian organizations, maintain that the aim of female circumcision is to prevent women from feeling sexual pleasure. They argue that denying women enjoyment of sex is part of the continued subjugation of women to men and their power or supremacy in the political, social and cultural life of the community.

6   However Dr Nahid Toubia, from Sudan, an advisor to various UN agencies such as UNESCO which are studying the issue, feels that these societies circumcise women as part of a positive cultural rite. The intention is not to mutilate for the sake of mutilation, even though the practice causes injury. Toubia affirms that in 'the West they want to change things, but they will not be able to. Only

African women can change their cultures'. And she points out that the only way to help them is through obtaining greater power within the community. Though testimonies about female genital mutilation have become increasingly common in recent years, no systematic study of the issue exists. There has been a veil of silence because the people affected must overcome several obstacles, including cultural issues, to come forward and tell their stories.

7   In May 2000 in Guinea, after years of effort and disseminating information, a group of women opposed to female circumcision scored a victory by convincing the 'surgeons' who perform the procedure to use appropriate medical instruments and disinfectants. But groups in Tanzania, meanwhile, reported that the practice has become more frequent since the government made it illegal and began prosecuting those who performed the circumcisions. Some Masai reached an agreement with their opponents so that they continue performing the ceremony but not the surgery.

8   New revelations about the female circumcision situation continue to shock. Certain women's groups in Guinea for example were charged with using funds from institutions which opposed the practice to continue circumcisions in secret, in a sort of private club. This shows how some were able to take advantage of the system that condemned and persecuted them and reveals the obstacles for human rights groups and their activists, who often are in conflict with the community and national authorities.

9   One important fact is that, in the series of national and international forums on the issue, those who have most vigorously defended the practice have been circumcised women. Some have stated, for example, that 'in our societies and in our lives there are tremendous problems and this, female circumcision, is not a priority issue for us'. Or they may say 'How can we leave our daughters uncircumcised? The Government can do what it wants, but we will continue to circumcise our daughters, we do not fear the punishment'. According to a study by the Egyptian Government, in 1997, 97 per cent of the 14,779 women surveyed were circumcised, and 80 per cent of them said they were content with the results. However, women often internalize the values of their male-dominated communities which ostracize uncircumcised women and make it impossible for them to marry and be part of the community.

10   Another issue is the criticism that most human rights groups fight FGM from the feminist perspective only. If the practice is to be condemned for the excessive bleeding, infections and deaths it causes, then male circumcision should be condemned as well, say FGM defenders. And there are many who would agree with them, arguing that both male and female circumcision is unnecessary and dangerous. But there is a qualitative difference between male and female circumcision. Male circumcision is not bound up with gender relations of dominance. Circumcised men do not lose sexual pleasure, nor are their reproductive capacities affected. ∎

Casamance guerrillas and the signing of a mutual defense treaty with Nigeria.

[17] In July 1991, Diouf was elected President of the ECOWAS (Economic Community of the Western African States), which included 16 countries of the region.

[18] In September, the US Government cancelled $42 million of the Senegalese debt in recognition of the country's support for the allies during the Gulf War and for its contribution to the 'peace troops' stationed in Liberia. The IMF approved a fresh $57.2 million loan.

[19] In 1991, a series of political and institutional changes was launched. The office of Prime Minister was restored and members of opposition parties were named to two cabinet posts. In September 1991, after three months of negotiations with opposition parties, a consensus was reached to reform the electoral laws. The conflict with the Casamance separatist movement (MFDC) resumed in 1992, after a truce.

[20] On February 21 1993, amid denunciations of widespread fraud, President Diouf won the presidential elections on the first ballot, with 58.4 per cent of the vote. In the May legislative elections, his PSS party maintained control of the National Assembly, with 84 of the 120 seats. The main opposition party - the PDS - won 27 seats.

[21] The economic and financial situation of Senegal became more difficult during 1993, amongst other things because the international prices of the Senegalese export products fell considerably. This made the trade deficit worse, which was compensated by new loans which took the foreign debt to $3.5 billion, more than 60 per cent of the GDP.

[22] The 100 per cent devaluation of the CFA franc decided by France and the IMF accentuated the social tensions in early 1994. The opposition Coordination of Democratic Forces organized an anti-government demonstration on February 16, which ended in confrontations with the police. Six police officers died and dozens of people were injured.

[23] Some 180 people were arrested with supposed responsibility for the disturbances, including the opposition leaders, Abdoulaye Wade and Landing Savané, who were declared innocent and freed in July. The repressive policy of the Senegalese Government was criticized by the human rights organizations, the

European Parliament and US Congress.

[24] Wade began negotiations with the Government, which led to him entering Diouf's cabinet in March 1995. The President received the clear support of the international funding organizations, when he announced legislative modifications to encourage foreign investment and accelerate privatization.

[25] Despite support from Paris and Washington, the Government offensives did not achieve any decisive advantage over the Casamance guerrillas. According to some observers, the popularity of the MFDC amongst the Casamance youth, along with the geography of the region, ruled out any possibility of military victory for Dakar. The adoption of a 'regionalization' project in the nation, in 1996, did not produce any political solution to the conflict either.

[26] Following relative calm, in 1997 fresh guerrilla action led to the mobilisation of 2,500 soldiers against the MFDC bases, along the frontier with Guinea-Bissau.

[27] In March, Senegal extended its protocol with the European Union for four more years, under which it would receive nearly $11 million per year in compensation, an increase of 33 per cent.

[28] In early 1998, Amnesty International denounced the reigning 'terror' in Casamance, due to conflict which was decimating a population mainly made up of farmers and ruining an area considered prosperous before the outbreak of war.

[29] During his visit to Dakar in April 1998, US President Bill Clinton proposed the creation of a continental African peace-keeping force.

[30] After 40 years of one-party rule, Wade won the March 2000 elections based on campaign promises denouncing the corruption and inefficiency of the Socialist government. He called for a change appealing to Senegalese youth, the most affected by unemployment. The operation of new independent radio stations which monitored the voting allowed this to be one of the most transparent and peaceful elections the region had ever known.

[31] Upon his appointment in April, Wade appointed a former opposition veteran, Musfafa Niasse, as his Prime Minister. Although the new president promised that the main priority of his government would be to stop the separatist conflict by peaceful means, violence increased in Casamance that same month with successive attacks by some MFDC factions opposed to the conciliatory stance of some of their leaders. ∎

PROFILE

ENVIRONMENT

Located on the west coast of Africa, embracing Gambia, its northern border formed by the Senegal River, the country's population is concentrated in the less arid western part, close to Dakar. The Senegal Valley is still under-populated as a result of slave trade which was very intense in this region. Senegal is undergoing an acute deforestation and desertification process. A project which is currently underway for building a hydroelectric dam in the Senegal River valley in the north poses a threat to the local environment.

SOCIETY

Peoples: Wolof 42 per cent; Peul- (Fulani-) Tukulor 9.3 per cent; Serer 14.9 per cent; Diola 5.3 per cent; Malinke (Mandingo) 3.6 per cent. Approximately 3 per cent are immigrants from non-African countries, mainly France, Lebanon and Syria.
Religions: 94 per cent Muslim, 5 per cent Christian, traditional African religions and others one per cent.
Languages: French (official). The most widely spoken indigenous languages are Wolof, Peul and Ful.
Political Parties: Socialist Party; Senegalese Democratic Party. There are several other minor parties and a coalition of opposition groups, the Coordination of Democratic Forces.
Social Organizations: National Federation of Senegalese Workers (CNTS); Union of Free Senegalese Workers (UTLS).

THE STATE

Official Name: République du Sénégal.
Administrative Divisions: 10 Districts.
Capital: Dakar 1,986,000 people (1995).
Other cities: Thies 216,400 people; Kaolack 193,115; Ziguinchor 161,680; Saint-Louis 132,444 (1994).
Government: Abdoulaye Wade, President since April 2000. Moustapha Niasse, Prime Minister since April 2000. 120-member single-chamber Legislative Power.
National Holiday: April 4, Independence Day (1960).
Armed Forces: 13,400, and 1,200 French troops.

Seychelles

Seychelles

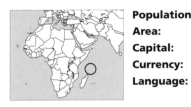

Population: 76,000 (1999)
Area: 450 SQ KM
Capital: Victoria
Currency: Rupee
Language: English and French

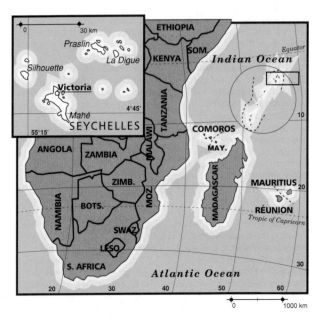

During the 18th century, the French and British colonists fought violently over this Indian Ocean colony. After expelling the French in 1794, the British paid little attention to it, and it was governed from the island of Mauritius until 1903. During the World Wars, the Seychelles archipelago gained strategic significance.

2 The Seychelles People's United Party (SPUP) founded in 1964 gave the local population - most of them descendants of enslaved Africans and Indian workers - a new sense of nationalism. The Party proved its strength during the general strikes of 1965 and 1966, and in the mass demonstrations of 1972. The colonial interests were opposed to the SPUP and independence, and they organized themselves into the Seychelles' Taxpayers Association. It was later renamed the Seychelles Democratic Party, led by James Mancham.

3 In the legislative elections of April 1974, the SPUP won 47.6 per cent of the vote. However, the peculiar colonial 'democratic' system awarded the Party only 2 of the 15 seats and Mancham remained the Prime Minister. In spite of this, it was too late to stem the tide of nationalism and in 1976 Mancham agreed to the British Foreign Office's suggestion that he become the first president of the Republic of Seychelles. Shortly before independence, he had agreed to 'return' the strategic British Indian Ocean Territory (BIOT) islands to Britain; they had been administered from Mahé since 1967. The British in turn passed them on to the United States

which built the important Diego Garcia naval base there.

4 Aware that the people would not accept this deal, Mancham postponed the elections until 1979, arguing that they were not necessary as all of the parties were in favor of independence.

5 Mancham's foreign policy was directed at cementing a strong alliance with South Africa, the source of most of the tourists, while domestic policy destroyed tea and coconut plantations to make room for new five-star hotels, owned by foreign companies. Entire islands were sold off to foreigners like Harry Oppenheimer, the South African gold magnate, and the actor Peter Sellers.

6 In 1977, while Mancham was manoeuvring to postpone the elections yet again, the SPUP took over the country 'with the collaboration of the local police force' while Mancham was out of the country. Accused of 'leading a wasteful life while his people worked hard', Mancham was replaced by SPUP leader Albert René.

7 René renewed his support for the Non-Aligned Movement, which had recognized the SPUP as the country's sole legitimate liberation movement prior to independence. He also strengthened the Seychelles' ties with left-wing countries and

movements around the Indian Ocean. The new government turned to socialism, promising to reorganize tourism, give priority to self-sufficiency in agriculture and fishing, increase education, and cut the high level of unemployment which was affecting nearly half of the working population.

8 In mid-1978, in order to meet the new political situation, the SPUP became the Seychelles People's Progressive Front (SPPF). In June 1979, the SPPF won the national elections with 98 per cent of the vote, in elections where the abstention rate was a mere 5 per cent. After the victory, President René announced his decision to close down the American satellite tracking station on the archipelago and demanded that the US base on Diego Garcia be closed, with the island returning to Mauritius.

9 In August 1978, he launched a land reform program calling for the expropriation of all uncultivated land. He also nationalized the water and electricity services, the construction industry and transportation. Controls were placed on food prices and an obligatory literacy program was introduced. These measures led to a rapid economic recovery in the Seychelles, and by 1979-80, on account of mineral and petroleum wealth, they had the

largest per capita income of any of the islands in the region. The national currency was also revalued, something virtually unheard of in the Third World.

10 This economic growth was encouraged and supported by tourism and effective administration. At this time the Seychelles received an average of 80,000 tourists a year. Under the Mancham Government, most of them were South Africans, but after René took over more Europeans came, especially British. The Seychelles received funding for the expansion of several quays from the African Development Bank, aiming to increase the country's fishing activity.

11 The opponents of Albert René, mainly the South African apartheid regime, did not give up their efforts to overthrow the socialist government of the Seychelles. In November 1981, a group of 45 mercenaries led by former colonel Mike Hoare tried to invade the island and oust the Government. The plot had been hatched in London by former president Mancham, with South African assistance. The attempted coup failed and the mercenaries had to hijack an Indian airliner to escape to South Africa. After the unsuccessful invasion, the Seychelles Government declared a state of emergency and imposed a curfew. The popular militia proved effective in neutralizing conspiracies and tightening controls on all foreigners.

12 The failed invasion and the economic recession in Europe caused tourism to decline by approximately 10 per cent. In August 1982, the situation deteriorated further when military personnel plotted an unsuccessful rebellion, strengthening rumors of another approaching mercenary conspiracy, and European conservative groups organized a smear campaign to support these rumours. In June 1984, Albert René was re-elected with 93 per cent of the vote, and the last political prisoner was released immediately after the elections. The country's greater political stability allowed the President to adopt a more pragmatic policy.

13 In 1986, the Seychelles and

LAND USE

DEFORESTATION: 0.0% annual (1990/95)

1993

- FOREST & WOODLAND: 11.1%
- ARABLE: 2.2%
- OTHER: 86.7%

LITERACY	FOOD DEPENDENCY	EXTERNAL DEBT	FOREIGN TRADE

1995

84%

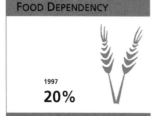

1997

20%

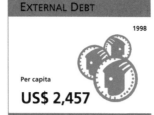

1998

Per capita

US$ 2,457

Millions US$ 1998

IMPORTS

468

EXPORTS

376

the US renegotiated their treaty, originally signed in 1976 and renewed in 1981, allowing a US satellite tracking station to be stationed on Mahé.

[14] In September 1986, there was another coup attempt. Albert René, who was in Zimbabwe participating in a Non-Aligned Countries summit conference, returned immediately and put down the rebellion. Most of those responsible for the coup were arrested, among them the main leader of the conspiracy, Minister of Defense Colonel Ogilvy Berlouis.

[15] The Seychelles Government promoted the creation of a peace zone in the Indian Ocean. It required all warships wanting to call at its ports to be 'nuclear-free', and as a result the US and British naval fleets stopped calling at the archipelago. The Seychelles established diplomatic relations with Comoros and Mauritius in 1988, and with Morocco and Côte d'Ivoire in 1989.

[16] In the presidential elections of June 1989, Albert René was the only candidate and was re-elected for a third term, with 96 per cent of the vote, according to final election returns. After the election, the President announced that he was reorganizing his cabinet. He personally took charge of the ministry of industry and amalgamated the ministries of planning, foreign affairs, finance and tourism into a single cabinet post.

[17] In September 1989, Indian President Ramaswamy Venkataraman carried out a three-day visit to Victoria, signing a cultural exchange agreement. In January 1990, the Seychelles established diplomatic relations with Kenya.

[18] The opposition forced President René to accept a multiparty system. The first experiment was carried out in July 1992, when a commission was elected to draw up the new constitution. The People's Progressive Front of Seychelles (FPPS), the ruling party, took 13 of the 23 seats. The Democratic Party (PD) of former president Mancham won eight seats.

[19] The Government continued its authoritarian ways. The PD soon withdrew from the commission and the first draft constitution was rejected. The project was suspended until the PD returned to the commission in June 1993, and the text was written with support from both parties; 73.6 per cent of the voters approved the new constitution.

[20] This document made official the multiparty system, the 33-member National Assembly and a five year presidential term. The President can be re-elected twice. René won the July 1993 elections and his party took the absolute majority in the National Assembly.

[21] Tourism continued to be the main source of income for the nation. The annual number of visitors was higher than the national population in 1993 and 1994. Oil derivatives and tinned tuna made up more than 80 per cent of the islands' exports during this period. Despite unemployment running at 22 per cent, the gross national product of the Seychelles reached $6,680 per head in 1994. Most people have access to drinking water and 100 per cent can meet their basic nutritional needs.

[22] There was moderate economic growth during 1995 and 1996. Various projects were funded with international aid which totaled $13 million in 1996, especially focusing on the preservation of the environment and improvements to the road infrastructure.

[23] In 1997, only one per cent of the budget was dependent on international contributions, although some forms of technical assistance were maintained.

[24] Although according to the United Nations Development Program (UNDP) Seychelles figured in 1998 as the African country with the highest human development index, on a world scale it only reached 56th place.

[25] During the April 2000 South-South Summit held in Havana, Vice-President James Michell gained recognition for the special problems and the vulnerability of small island countries such as Seychelles. He also proposed the setting up of a vulnerability index by no later than the year 2001. ∎

PROFILE

ENVIRONMENT

An archipelago of 92 islands. Mahé, Praslim, and La Digue are the largest islands, made of granite; the rest are coralloid. The climate is tropical with plentiful vegetation and heavy rainfall. Only the largest islands are inhabited, but some economic use is made of the other islands.

SOCIETY

Peoples: Most residents of the Seychelles are descendants of mixed African and European origin; most of them live on the island of Mahé. There are minorities of European, Chinese and Indian origin.
Religions: Roman Catholic 88.6 per cent; other Christian (mostly Anglican) 7.7 per cent; Hindu 0.7 per cent; other, 3 per cent (1996).
Languages: English and French (official); most of the population speak Creole, a local dialect with European and African influences.
Political Parties: The People's Progressive Front of Seychelles (FPPS; Seychelle Movement for Democracy; Christian Democratic Party/ Encounter of the People of Seychelles for Democracy.
Social Organizations: The National Workers' Union.

THE STATE

Official Name: Repiblik Sesel.
Capital: Victoria 64,900 people (est 1995).
Government: France-Albert René, President since 1977. Legislature, single-chamber: National Assembly, with 33 members.
National Holiday: June 28, Independence Day (1976).
Armed Forces: 800 (1994).
Other: 1,300 National Guard.

STATISTICS

DEMOGRAPHY

Population: 76,000 (1999)
Annual growth: 1.1 % (1975/97)
Estimates for year 2015 (million): 0.1 (1999)
Annual growth to year 2015: 1.0 % (1997/2015)
Urban population: 56.1 % (1997)
Children per woman: 2.1 (1998)

HEALTH

Life expectancy at birth: 71 years (1998)
Infant mortality: 14 per 1,000 (1998)
Under-5 child mortality: 18 per 1,000 (1998)
Daily calorie supply: 2,424 per capita (1996)
104 doctors per 100,000 people (1993)

EDUCATION

Literacy: 84 % (1995)
male: 83 % (1995)
female: 86 % (1995)
School enrolment:
Primary total: 102 % (1990/96)
Primary school teachers: one for every 17 (1996)

COMMUNICATIONS

39 newspapers (1996), 545 radios (1997), 191 TV sets (1996) and 196 main telephone lines (1996) per 1,000 people

ECONOMY

Per capita, GNP: $ 6,420 (1998)
Annual growth, GNP: -1.7 % (1998)
Consumer price index: 102.1 (1998)
Cereal imports: 17,450 metric tons (1998)
Food import dependency: 20 % (1997)
Exports: $ 376 million (1998)
Imports: $ 468 million (1998)
External debt: $ 187 million (1998); $ 2,457 per capita (1998)
Development aid received: $ 15 million (1997); $ 212.0 per capita (1997); 2.80 % of GNP (1997)

HDI (rank/value): 66/0.755 (1997)

Sierra Leone

Sierra Leone

Population: 4,717,000 (1999)
Area: 71,740 SQ KM
Capital: Freetown
Currency: Leone
Language: English

The majority of the population in Sierra Leone are Temne and Mende people. Minority groups of Lokko, Sherbo, Limba, Sussu Fulani, Kono, and Krio also exist.

[2] When Britain faced a 'demographic problem' with runaway slaves in the 1800s, the Government decided to 'return' them to Africa. They had come to London hoping to benefit from a court ruling that had abolished slavery in the city of London. Abolitionist leader Granville Sharp purchased an area of 250 sq km for £ 60 from the local rulers in 1792, organizing an agricultural society based on democratic principles. However, this society was quickly transformed into a colonial company involved in the British conquest of the entire country.

[3] Tossed into a land where they had no roots, the 'creoles' sought to emulate European culture and considered themselves superior to the 'savages' of the interior, acting as brokers for British colonialism.

[4] Yet the 'savages' resisted strongly. In 1898 Bai Buré rallied most of the inland people, already angered by a British tax on their dwellings. However, after nearly a year of resistance, British military superiority overwhelmed and stifled the opposition.

[5] In 1960, the British wanted to withdraw from Sierra Leone, and an agreement was negotiated with the traditional leaders to protect their interests. In 1961, Sir Milton Margai, secretary general of Sierra Leone People's Party (SLPP), became the first prime minister of an independent Sierra Leone.

[6] The creoles, together with British and Syrian-Lebanese merchants, held the colony's economic power. Although removed from political power, they maintained significant influence over the Margai Government.

[7] When Margai died in 1964, he was succeeded by his brother Albert and the situation quickly deteriorated. Corruption and gambling became so widespread that it was compared to the Batista period in Cuba. The diamond trade gave birth to a chain of smuggling operations and crime became a main source of income.

[8] In 1967 the All People's Congress (APC) party led by Syaka Stevens won the elections, signaling the possibility for change; however, the conservative creoles, the traditional leaders, and the neo-colonialist British united to prevent Stevens from taking control of the country as they considered him 'dangerously progressive'. As a result, Stevens was overthrown by a military coup and forced into exile in Conakry (Guinea).

[9] In April 1968, a group of low-ranking officers took power through the so-called Sergeants' Revolt. They brought back Stevens who in 1971 broke all ties with Britain and declared Sierra Leone a republic, becoming its first President.

[10] Important goals were achieved in the first years: the lumber industry was nationalized and the State seized majority control of the mining firm, which controlled the diamond trade. To protect the prices of iron ore and bauxite, Sierra Leone joined the associations of iron and bauxite producing countries.

[11] Stevens called for a plebiscite to establish a one-party system in 1978 in an attempt to appease the opposition. His proposal was approved and the APC incorporated prominent members of the SLPP within its ranks, granting them posts within the Government.

[12] In 1979, President Stevens' popularity began to ebb as a result of worsening living conditions, growing inflation, authoritarian measures, government corruption, a fall in exports and the increasing foreign debt.

[13] Popular unrest reached its climax in September 1981 when the Sierra Leone Labor Congress (SLLC) declared a general strike, demanding immediate changes in economic policy. The strike spread throughout the country and nearly toppled the Government, which had to make several concessions.

[14] In urban areas, the scarcity of staple foods - particularly rice - as well as periodic fuel shortages became chronic. Inflation and the high cost of living reduced the purchasing power of salaried workers by 60 per cent, and the late payment of salaries became normal. Members of parliament were paid with sacks of rice which were later sold on the black market at a large profit.

[15] The powerful Lebanese traders controlled the unofficial market and more than 70 per cent of the country's exports. Gold and diamond smuggling was estimated at nearly $150 million per year while official exports dropped from $80 million to barely $14 million between 1980 and 1984.

[16] In November 1985, Syaka Stevens handed over the presidency to Joseph Momoh, a member of his cabinet, changing nothing in the political and social condition of the country.

[17] The scale of the crisis culminated in the Government's declaration of a state of economic emergency in 1987. This measure included granting the State the sole right to commercialize gold and diamonds, a 15 per cent surcharge on imports, and the reduction of salaries of public employees.

[18] In March 1991, rebel forces operating from Liberia occupied two border towns. Guerrilla groups from Burkina Faso, Liberia, and Sierra Leone joined them, occupying one third of the country.

[19] A referendum approved held in August a new constitution establishing a multiparty system. However, the economic crisis continued alongside ever increasing corruption.

[20] In 1992, the Government launched a structural adjustment program which had been imposed by the International Monetary Fund. James Funa, a former World Bank executive, was named minister of finance.

[21] On April 29, Captain Valentine Strasser seized power through a coup. After suspending the constitution he

WORKERS

% OF LABOUR FORCE **1998**

■ FEMALE: 37%   ■ MALE: 63%

1990

■ SERVICES: 17.3%
■ INDUSTRY: 15.3%
■ AGRICULTURE: 67.4%

LAND USE

DEFORESTATION: 3.0% annual (1990/95)
IRRIGATED: 6.0% of arable (1993)

1993

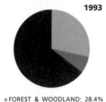

■ FOREST & WOODLAND: 28.4%
■ ARABLE: 6.8%
■ OTHER: 64.8%

PUBLIC EXPENDITURE

DEFENCE EXPENDITURE (% of goverment exp.)	**33%**	(1997)
MILITARY EXPENDITURE (% of health & education)	**23%**	(1990/91)

created the National Provisional Governing Council, prohibiting all political activity, and confirmed the Minister of Finance in his post. In June, all civilian members of the Governing Council were expelled and its name was changed to 'Supreme Council of State'. Press censorship began.

[22] The eastern part of the country was occupied at the time by the United Movement for Liberian Liberation and Democracy, which used Sierra Leone as a base from which to carry out attacks against Charles Taylor's forces (see Liberia). In the meantime, the Revolutionary United Front of Sierra Leone (RUF) was operating in the southeast.

[23] The regions affected by warfare were also the country's richest, where gold and diamond deposits and the main agricultural production area were located. Guerrilla activity led to an abrupt decline in mining activity; the percentage represented by diamonds in the country's exports dropped from 54.7 per cent in 1987 to a mere 7 per cent in 1990. The per capita GDP dropped from $320 in 1980 to $210 in 1991.

[24] Extreme poverty gave rise to the trafficking of children and young people. Under an unusual sort of contract, Lebanese traders in Sierra Leone took the daughters of poor families to Lebanon to work as household servants for five-year periods. However, the traders frequently failed to keep their part of the bargain, and the girls never returned.

[25] Those who managed to escape from the system described the verbal and physical abuse to which they were subjected. Although it was estimated that hundreds of girls and children were involved, no government action was taken against the influential Lebanese community.

[26] The Government promise to organize elections did not convince the RUF, which continued with the armed struggle. The rebels had a series of military victories in early 1994, which left a total of 150 civilians dead.

[27] The World Bank expressed its 'satisfaction' with the economic policies of the country which amongst other things had managed to reduce inflation from 120 per cent in 1991 to 15 per cent in 1994.

[28] In early 1995 the war extended over nearly all the country. Government forces recovered the Sierra Rutile titanium mine, which produced 50 per cent of Freetown's foreign trade. However, despite dedicating 75 per cent of the national budget to the war, and having increased the size of the army to 13,000 troops, the Government did not appear in a position to defeat the guerrillas.

[29] In January 1996, following a bloodless coup, Strasser was replaced by a close former ally, Brigadier-General Julius Maada Bio. The presidential elections held in February as planned were won by Ahmad Tejan Kabbah of the Sierra Leone People's Party (SLPP) in the second round with nearly 60 per cent of the vote.

[30] Rebel troops led by Major-General Johnny Paul Koroma ousted President Kabbah on May 25 1997. The Organization of African Unity, meeting in Namibia, criticized the coup and began negotiations to make the leaders abandon power.

[31] In September 1997, former president Tejan Kabbah asked the UN's General Assembly for help to re-establish his government.

[32] In February 1998, the UN ECOMOG troops - paradoxically mostly Nigerians who at that time were ruled by the dictator Sani Abacha (see Nigeria) - took the main cities and regions of Sierra Leone, forcing out Koroma and his military junta. Kabbah's return to government was not seen as a guarantee of the rapid re-establishment of peace in a country riddled with corruption.

[33] The Kabbah administration achieved some stability and in March 1998 it ordered an end to gold and diamond mining which had been controlled by foreigners for the previous 60 years, allowing Sierra Leone citizens with valid licenses to mine these minerals. But the stability was short-lived, since in the last months of the year another rebel offensive took control of more than half of the capital. The arrival of Nigerian troops balanced the conflict which led to the signing of a cease fire by both sides in January 1999.

[34] Foday Sankoh, the new rebel leader, signed a peace treaty with the Government in July. Under the treaty, Sankoh was appointed Director of the Strategic Minerals Commission and Vice-President in the government, although a 1998 UN resolution had banned him from travelling without its authorization.

[36] The following months saw continuous tension with the UN which had deployed 11,000 peacekeeping troops to supervise the ceasefire and watch over the disarmament of the rebels. The rebels repeatedly violated the ceasefire while Sankoh, besides travelling often - according to the monitors, to sell diamonds - accused the peace force of being a 'threat to the security of the population of Sierra Leone'.

[37] The UN estimated in early 2000 that only half of the 45,000 rebel soldiers had disposed of their weapons. In May, the RUF launched a major offensive and captured 500 ECOWAS troops. As the UN soldiers could not prevent civilian casualties and stop the rebels, the UK sent troops in to expel the RUF from the outskirts of Freetown. Sankoh was captured in May but the rebels continued to hold a large part of the country, including the mining areas.

[38] In August, Johnny Koroma's 'Westside Boyz' took 11 British soldiers hostage. ■

PROFILE

ENVIRONMENT

The country is divided into three regions. The coastal strip, nearly 100 kilometers long, is a swampy plain that includes the island of Sherbo. Several rivers drain the inner tropical forest, mostly cleared for agricultural exploitation. The eastern plateau contains the country's diamond mines. Deforestation is very severe, 85 per cent of all natural habitat has been destroyed.

SOCIETY

Peoples: The Temne and Mende account for nearly one-third of the population. Lokko, Sherbo, Limba, Sussu, Fulah, Kono and Krio are other important groups. The Krio - whose name is from the English word 'creole' - are descendants of African slaves freed in the 19th century who settled in Freetown. There is also an Arab minority.
Religions: Most of the people profess traditional African religions; nearly one third are Muslims, concentrated in the north; the Christian minority is located in the capital.
Languages: English (official). The most widely spoken native languages are Temne, Mende and Krio. The latter serves as the commercial language in the capital.
Political Parties: All Peoples' Congress (APC); Sierra Leone Peoples Party (SLPP); United Political Movements Front; Revolutionary United Front (RUF).
Social Organizations: Sierra Leone Labor Congress.

THE STATE

Official Name: Republic of Sierra Leone.
Capital: Freetown 80,000 people (est 1996), down from 800,000 in 1995. 40 per cent of the population left the country in 1996.
Other cities: Koidu 80,000 people; Bo 26,000; Kenema 13,000 (1985).
Government: Ahmad Tejan Kabbah, President elected in March 1996, ousted by Major General Paul Koroma in May 1997 and re-installed in Government after UN-Ecomog forces seized control of Sierra Leone in February 1998.
National Holiday: April 19, Republic Day (1971).
Armed Forces: 13,000 troops (1995).

Singapore

Singapore

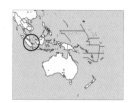

Population: 3,522,000 (1999)
Area: 620 SQ KM
Capital: Singapore
Currency: Singapore dollar
Language: English, Malay, Chinese (Mandarin) and Tamil

Singapore's original name was Temasek, meaning 'people of the sea' in Sanskrit. Later on, the city was named Singa-Pura, the 'city of the lion', after a visiting prince experienced a vision.

2   Singapore was founded in 1297 and destroyed 100 years later. From 1819 onwards, it became an extremely important base for the British; Sir Thomas Stamford Raffles established the local headquarters of the British East India Company there.

3   In 1824, the island of Singapore and the adjacent islets were purchased as a single lot by Raffles from the Sultan of Johore (see Malaysia). The Company appointed Prince Hussein as the new ruler of Singapore. In gratitude, he granted the Company royal authorization to improve the port. Chinese immigrants soon constituted the majority of the local population.

4   Singapore was part of the British colony called 'the Straits Settlements', together with the ports of Penang and Melaka (Malacca). In 1946, Penang and Melaka joined the Malayan Union and Singapore became a crown colony.

5   At one point during World War II the Japanese dominated the whole of southeast Asia. They conquered Singapore in 1942 but were later defeated. Their defeat was partly due to a strong internal resistance group, organized by a revolutionary movement and led by the Communist Party of Malaya (CPM). The name Malaya included both Singapore and the Malay peninsula; the separation of the latter was always questioned by the Left.

6   Once the war was over, the Malay sultanates and the former Straits Settlements attempted to form a union or federation, with a view to attaining independence for the territory. However, the

conflicting interests of the Chinese and Malay communities, and the conservative and progressive forces, made progress difficult. In January 1946, the Singapore Labor Union declared a general strike and in 1948 the Communist Party led an anti-colonial uprising which failed, as it failed to gain the support of the Malays and the poorer sectors of the Indian population. Marxist parties were outlawed and had to move into the forests, where they resorted to guerrilla warfare.

7   As the first step towards the self-government of the city-state, municipal elections were held in 1949. Only English-speaking people were allowed to vote until 1954, when the People's Action Party (PAP) was founded. The anti-imperialism advocated by the PAP

brought citizens of British and Chinese backgrounds together for the first time. In 1959, the Chinese were allowed to vote; full internal autonomy was granted, and the PAP obtained an overwhelming victory. Lee Kuan Yew, founder of the party, became Prime Minister, campaigning on a platform of social reforms and independence. He planned a federation with Malaya, which had been independent since 1957.

8   The PAP split into a socialist faction, led by Lim Chin Siong, and the 'moderates' of Lee Kuan Yew, who encouraged the promotion of private enterprise and foreign investment

9   In 1961, the left wing of the PAP founded Barisan Sosialis (the Socialist Front), which opposed the

prospect of uniting Singapore and Malaya under British control. In September 1963, the Federation of Malaysia, consisting of Singapore, the Malay peninsula, Sarawak and Sabah (both in the north and northeast of Borneo) was set up, after those opposed to the Federation had been conveniently purged.

10   As a Federation member, Singapore depended heavily on the peninsula; even its water supply came from there. Integration at that time was not feasible because of profound disagreements between Singapore's Chinese community and the Malay community of the rest of the Federation. On August 9 1965, after several ethnic conflicts, Prime Minister Lee decided to withdraw from the Federation.

11   In 1965, serious internal conflicts were caused by the mistreatment of the Malay population and other ethnic minorities. There were also intense struggles with the left-wing opposition, which the Government classified as 'communist subversives'. The island became an independent republic, and a Commonwealth member. A mutual assistance and defence treaty was signed with Malaysia, and on October 15 of the same year Singapore became a member of the United Nations.

12   The first years of independence witnessed substantial economic growth. The island was turned into an 'enclave' for the export of products manufactured by transnationals, and into an international financial center which controlled the regional economy.

13   The situation turned gloomy in 1974, when the oil crisis upset Singapore's export scheme. Singapore was the fourth largest port in the world, with the second highest per capita income in Asia, after Japan. The ensuing economic deterioration brought about public demonstrations by students and workers. These protests were fiercely controlled, reaching such proportions that the Socialist International expelled the PAP from its ranks in 1975.

14   In order to placate criticism from the opposition, the regime approved a reform which allowed the entering of two representatives of the Worker's Party and the Democratic Party of Singapore, respectively.

15   Despite the sustained economic growth since 1987, the Government

WORKERS

1997
UNEMPLOYMENT: 2.4%

% OF LABOUR FORCE   **1998**

■ FEMALE: 39%   ■ MALE: 61%
                                  1990

■ SERVICES: 64.0%
■ INDUSTRY: 35.6%
■ AGRICULTURE: 0.4%

LAND USE

DEFORESTATION: 0.0% annual (1990/95)

1993

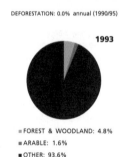

■ FOREST & WOODLAND: 4.8%
■ ARABLE: 1.6%
■ OTHER: 93.6%

PUBLIC EXPENDITURE

1997

19.4%   23.2%

DEFENCE   SOCIAL

MILITARY EXPENDITURE   **129%**
(% of health & education)   (1990/91)

expelled thousands of Thai and Filipino workers blaming them for taking over the jobs of the natural citizens.

[16] The decision to prohibit the circulation of foreign publications judged detrimental by the Government, the imprisonment of opposition members and a Security Law that allows indefinite imprisonment without trial for two renewable years each time, raised countless denunciations of violations of human rights.

[17] In the 1988 elections the opposition vote grew, but due to the mechanisms of the electoral system its parliamentary representation diminished. In 1991, the PAP again won an overwhelming majority of seats. In November, Goh Chok Tong replaced Lee Kuan Yew as Prime Minister, but the latter nevertheless retained considerable political weight. At his initiative, Singapore offered Washington the possibility of installing bases in the country when the Filipino Congress decided to close US military bases in the Philippines.

[18] As an exporter of high technology goods, Singapore's industry was only marginally affected by the recession of its main partners, the US, Japan, and the European Union. In order to expand its activity, the Government started a policy of 'regionalization' increasing its investments in Indonesia and Malaysia. The investments in China surpassed $1 billion per year, and Singapore became the main commercial partner of Vietnam. From 1993 on, annual growth was over eight per cent.

[19] Between 1994 and 1995 relations were strained between the Government and the US, Philippines, and Holland. The hanging of a Dutch engineer accused of heroin trafficking, the sentencing of a young US citizen to be hit with a rattan cane for vandalism, and the execution of a Filipino maid accused of murdering a fellow servant were the reasons for this diplomatic stress. In the case of the maid, the crime was proved and diplomatic relations were re-established. Concerning the young American, the number of blows and months in prison were reduced at the behest of President Clinton.

[20] On domestic affairs, an employee, two economists, and two journalists were sent to prison for braking a law which protected state secrets. Their crime was to publish the economic growth forecast before its official publication.

[21] In June 1996, the 'Speak Mandarin Campaign' was challenged by the ethnic minorities, concerned by the fact that this language became a requirement when applying for a job. The Government - while exhorting the Chinese to have more children - responded that minorities have to be tolerant with the population's majority.

[22] Droughts and changes in wind systems caused by the 'El Niño' climatic phenomenon in late 1997 led to serious losses in agriculture and tourism. The winds carried dense clouds of smoke from the forest fires in the neighboring Indonesia, affecting the health of the population, forcing schools and businesses to close and flights to be cancelled.

[23] In January 1998, the depreciation of the Singapore dollar against the US currency continued in free fall as part of the Asian financial crisis. In April, Singapore took part in a meeting in Washington, organized by President Clinton, along with the Group of Seven and some Southeast Asian, Latin American and Southern African nations, in an attempt to 'strengthen the international financial system'.

[24] Concerned about the decline in the standard of English spoken by the population, the Government launched a 'Speak Proper English' campaign in 1999 against *singlish*, the local version of English which reflects the multiracial community of a country combining colonial English mixed with Malaysian, Tamil and Hokien languages.

[25] During that year, Singapore played a key role in underpinning the region's faltering economy (after the 1997 financial crisis), dedicating part of its huge reserves and surplus in its trade balance to uphold the *baht* and the *rupiah*, the Thai and Indonesian currencies respectively.

[26] Only Sellapan Ramanathan Nathan, PAP candidate, was declared eligible during the August 1999 presidential elections. He took office in September.

[27] The Government set out to transform the country into an 'Asian Silicon Valley'. During a trip to India in January 2000, Premier Goh Chok Tong urged Indian technology and information experts to move to Singapore and boost its economy. ■

PROFILE

ENVIRONMENT

Singapore consists of one large island and 54 smaller adjacent islets. The country is connected to Malaysia by a causeway across the Johore Strait. The terrain, covered by swampy lowlands, is not conducive to farming and the population traditionally works in business and trade. The climate is tropical with heavy rainfall. In its strategic geographical location, central to the trade routes between Africa, Asia and Europe, the island has become a flourishing commercial center. Economically, the main resources of the country have been its port, the British naval base and, more recently, industrial activity; textiles, electronic goods and oil refining. Industrialization has caused severe air and water pollution.

SOCIETY

Peoples: 76 per cent of Singaporeans are of Chinese origin. Malaysians account for 15 per cent and 6 per cent are from India and Sri Lanka.
Religions: Buddhist 28 per cent; Christian 19 per cent; Islam 13 per cent; Taoist 13 per cent; Hindu 5 per cent. There are Sikh and Jewish minorities.
Languages: Malay, English, Chinese (Mandarin) and Tamil are the official languages. Malay is viewed as the national language, but English is spoken in the public administration and serves as a unifying element for the communities. Various Chinese dialects are spoken, with Punjabi, Hindi, Bengali, Telegu and Malayalam in the Indian communities.
Political Parties: The People's Action Party (PAP; Singapore Democratic Party; the Workers' Party; Barisan Sosialis (the Socialist Front); the Singapore Justice Party; the United People's Front and the Singapore United Front.
Social Organizations: The major national trade union is the Congress of Singapore Labor Unions.

THE STATE

Official Name: Hsin-chia-p'o Kung-ho-kuo (Mandarin); Republik Singapura (Bahasa Malaysia); Singapore Kudiyarasu (Tamil); Republic of Singapore. **Capital:** Singapore 2,848,000 people (1995).
Government: Parliamentary republic. Sellapan Ramanathan Nathan, President since August 1999. Goh Chok Tong, Prime Minister since November 1991. Legislature, single-chamber, made up of 81 members, dominated since independence by the official Popular Action Party, which obtained 77 seats in 1991. **National Holiday:** August 9, Independence Day (1965). **Armed Forces:** 55,500, inc. 34,800 conscripts.
Other: 11,600 Police and Maritime Police (estimate). 100,000 Civil Defense Force.

Slovakia

Slovenska

Population: 5,381,000 (1999)
Area: 49,010 SQ KM
Capital: Bratislava
Currency: Koruny
Language: Slovak

B etween the years 500 and 100 BC, a Celtic tribe from western Europe, the Cotini, settled in the territory of present-day Slovakia. Later, from the year 100 BC to 400 AD, the Quadi, a Germanic tribe, formed satellite states of the Roman Empire north of the Danube (the 'Limes Romanum'). Both the Hadi and the Marcomani, their Germanic neighbors in Bohemia, were pushed out by the Huns led by Attila.

2   The Slovaks, a Slav tribe from the eastern region of the Vistula and closely related to the Czechs, started to settle in the territory between the sixth and seventh centuries. They soon had to defend themselves from the Avars, nomads from lower Panonia, until the Frankish trader Samo united the Slav tribes and was chosen as their King. In 805, the Frankish King Charlemagne, expanding his Christian empire, formed an alliance with the Czech leaders of Bohemia and Moravia to defeat the Avars once and for all. In return for their help, Charlemagne distributed dukedoms amongst the Czechs, who took control over the regions of Moravia, Bohemia and Slovakia. The kingdom of Moravia, which included Bohemian and Slovakian territories, was thus established. The first Moravian monarch, Mojmir I, ruled from 830 to 846, and Christianity was adopted under his rule.

3   The nephew who succeeded him, Rotislav I (ruling from 846 to 870), expanded the kingdom to include all of Bohemia and founded Great Moravia, unifying the Slav territories of the region for the first time. Rotislav consolidated relations with the Frankish Empire, which answered to Rome, and maintained constant contact with the Byzantine Empire. In 863, answering a request from Rotislav, the Byzantine Emperor sent Constantine and Methodius, leading a group of missionaries. The monks translated the gospels and designed the first Slav alphabet (see Czech Republic).

4   During the reign of Svatopluc (870-894) the Moravian frontiers extended to include the western part of present-day Hungary and southern Poland. Svatopluc abandoned relations with the Byzantine Emperor, and Methodius' disciples were forced to abandon the kingdom and take refuge in the Balkans.

5   Great Moravia came to an end in 906, when it was destroyed by the German king Arnulf in alliance with the Magyars, a nomadic tribe from the Upper Volga who controlled most of the territories of modern-day Hungary. The western part of the old kingdom remained in the possession of the Czech dukes of Bohemia, while the area between the Carpathians and the Danube - the Slovakia of today - was occupied by the Magyars. Despite repeated attempts to take control of Slovak territory by the dukes of Bohemia, it continued as a dependency of the Hungarian Kings for ten centuries.

6   The Slovaks never lost their language and cultural characteristics, retaining their links with the Czechs. During the 15th century, the University of Prague exercised considerable influence over the Slovaks. The Hussites of Bohemia repeatedly invaded Hungary, bringing the custom of reciting the liturgy in the national language instead of Latin to Slovakia.

7   The Hussite incursions prepared the ground for the later reception of Protestantism, based on the teaching of the Kralice Bible translated by the Bohemian Brethren. In the early 16th century most of the Slovaks had adopted Calvinism. However, when Hungary was invaded by the Ottoman Empire in 1525, Slovakia was governed by the House of Austria, which strengthened the Counter-reformation throughout the region. This dependence on the House of Austria Germanized Slovak culture to a large extent.

8   In 1620, the Czech nobles were beaten by the Magyars, and Slovakia once again formed part of the Kingdom of Hungary. The conquest of central Hungary by the Ottoman Empire increased Magyar influence in Slovakia. Hungarian nobles fleeing Turkish power settled in Slovak villages and initiated Hungarian customs.

9   In the 17th century Turkish dominion in Hungary was replaced by the House of Hapsburg. At the end of the 18th century the Emperor Joseph II changed the Kingdom of Hungary by Germanizing the bureaucracy and limited the power of the Hungarian authorities. This helped the Slovaks hark back to their Slav origin and their cultural links with the Czechs.

10   The nationalist fever which ran across Europe following the Napoleonic Wars also reached the territories dominated by the Austrian Crown. Slovak and Hungarian nationalism came into conflict. In 1834, Magyar replaced Latin as the legal language. In 1848, the Slovaks, allied with Czechs and German Republicans rose up in arms against the Magyars, who had in turn rebelled against the Austrians. Within this period, the Slovaks took over control of their secondary education and founded their first scientific society, the Matica Slovaka.

11   In the late 19th century, the Hungarian authorities banned the Slovak language from public life, replacing it with Magyar. Slovak leaders, especially editors of journals, were persecuted and many were imprisoned. In 1907, the Appony law made Slovak-speaking primary schools adopt Magyar.

12   In 1914, World War I presented the Slovaks with the chance to embrace the cause of the Allies fighting the Austro-Hungarian Empire. Tens of thousands of Slovak soldiers forced to serve in the Hungarian army joined the Allies. In 1915, the Czech Alliance and the Slovak League (of the United States) reached an agreement in Cleveland proclaiming the liberation of the Czech and Slovak nations and their federate union, with complete independence for Slovakia. It would have its own parliament and administration with Slovak as its official State language.

13   Once the War had ended with the Allied victory in 1918, the nationalist efforts of the Slovak doctor Thomas G Masaryk (the son of a Slovak coachman and a German-Moravian mother), the scientist Milan Stefanik (a Slovak living abroad), and the Czech Eduard Benes, working with the opposition forces in Czech and Slovak lands, led to the creation of the Republic of Czecho-Slovakia on October 28 of that year.

14   In November, Masaryk, who had promised to respect the rights of the Germanic and Hungarian minorities, was elected President of the new Republic, a position he was to maintain until 1935 (see Czech Republic). During his term in government - and also that of his successor, Benes - the Slovaks felt they were relegated within a State controlled by the Czechs, without fair participation.

15   The German occupation of the Sudetenland in 1938 forced Benes into exile in London, and the occupation of Czechoslovakia by Nazi troops in 1939 put the history of the Republic on hold. Czechoslovakia was dismembered. Bohemia became a German province and Carpathian Russia was taken by the Hungarians. In March 1939, Slovak independence was proclaimed, making it a free state on paper, with Hitler's puppet President Joseph Tiso in power.

16   After the allied victory in 1945, with the support of Soviet presence in the territory, the Czecho-Slovak republic returned to its former shape. The exiled Eduard Benes returned from abroad and continued in power. The integrity of the Republic was guaranteed by its membership of the Soviet bloc until, in 1991, with the fall of the Soviet regime and the system of alliances, the Czech and Slovak peoples divided to develop separate political lives.

[17] On February 15 1993 Michal Kovac was elected President of the new Republic of Slovakia. Vladimir Meciar, leader of the Movement for a Democratic Slovakia (MED) and the architect of Czechoslovakian separation, was named Prime Minister.

[18] Meciar's administration was marked by controversy and accusations of authoritarianism, from the opposition. He re-nationalized the newspaper *Smena*, and created a compulsory television slot for the broadcasting of government news and propaganda.

[19] Separation from the Czech Republic proved detrimental to the Slovakian economy, which lost nearly $1 billion in bilateral trade. The country suffered more severely than the Czech Republic, because of dependence upon the Socialist bloc. In the first half of 1993, according to the Organization for Economic Co-operation and Development, 500,000 jobs were lost and inflation rose by 18 per cent.

[20] In April, the Confederation of Slovakian Labor Unions mobilized a demonstration of workers through the streets of the capital, to protest the lack of any concrete action on the part of Government authorities.

[21] Pressure from environmental groups forced Hungarian authorities to abandon plans for an important bilateral hydroelectric plant, which had been approved and signed in conjunction with the former Czechoslovakia. This project would have constructed two large dams, diverting the Danube River. The decision led to a distinct cooling of relations between the two governments.

[22] Another cause of friction was the treatment of the Hungarian minority in Slovakia, which was demanding greater cultural autonomy. While in June the Slovakian Parliament approved a law allowing the Hungarian language to be taught in schools, Meciar also called for the enforcement of an old law, which had fallen into disuse, making it mandatory for Hungarian women to add the Slav feminine suffix 'ova' to their last names.

[23] Jozef Moravcik was named Prime Minister in March 1994, after long negotiations between the parties which had ousted the regime of Vladimir Meciar Moravcik announced the formation of a government of national salvation and urgent economic measures.

[24] The new government, with the participation of the Democratic Left Party and Alternative for Real Democracy (both consisting of former MED allies) and the right-wing Christian Democratic Movement was built upon two objectives: to keep Meciar out of power and to accept the general principles of European democracy.

The internal differences in the coalition weakened the Government and made it impracticable as a long-term alternative.

[25] Meciar won 35 per cent of the vote in the 1994 elections. The coalition parties suffered a tough defeat and the parties of the Hungarian minorities formed a coalition which emerged as the third force in Parliament. Meciar became Prime Minister again and immediately put the privatization initiative, started by his predecessor, into reverse, stressing nationalism.

[26] The Meciar Government took various measures to limit the rights of the Hungarians, without those supporting a more open policy towards minorities being able to prevent him. A campaign to avoid Slovak being imposed as the only official language of the country did not get sufficient support. The US and the European Union warned Meciar his nationalist policy could lead the country into isolation.

[27] Despite falling inflation and unemployment, Slovakia left the list of countries with the greatest chances of entering the European Union and NATO in 1997. In May, a referendum on joining NATO was boycotted by 90 per cent of the electorate, after an opposition proposal to consult voters on the issue of direct presidential elections via the same ballot papers was turned down.

[28] Five opposition parties founded the Slovak Democratic Coalition (SDK) and signed a coexistence pact late that year. President Kovac, whose relationship with Meciar was already strained after siding with critics of the Prime Minister and urging him in January 1998 to improve relations with the United States and the European Union, resigned.

[29] Meciar's party received 27 per cent of the vote during the August parliamentary elections, more than any other party, but the coalition won only 45 of the 150 available seats while the opposition parties won 93 seats in total. The Prime Minister resigned when the new Parliament was sworn in.

[30] The two main opposition parties, Slovak Democratic Opposition and Democratic Left, formed a new government in October with Mikulás Dzurinda as Prime Minister.

[31] Claiming discrimination, about one thousand gypsy Slovaks requested asylum in Finland in July 1999. President Schuster acknowledged the claim was legitimate. The Government took immediate precautions to improve this minority's situation and avoid a massive exodus.

[32] The Czech and Slovak governments reached an agreement in November which put an end to the financial differences brought about by the division. Prague promised to deliver four and a half tons of gold to Bratislava and acknowledged its debt to Slovakia of $1.5 billion. ∎

Slovenia

Slovenija

Population: 1,989,000 (1999)
Area: 20,250 SQ KM
Capital: Ljubljana
Currency: Tolar
Language: Slovene

One of the southern Slav groups, the Slovenes occupied what is now Slovenia and the land to the north of this region in the 6th century AD. Subdued by the Bavarians around the year 743, they were later incorporated into the Frankish Empire of the Carolingians.

[2] With the division of the Empire in the 9th century, the region was given to the Germans. The Slovenes were reduced to serfdom and the region north of the Drava River was completely dominated by the Germans.

[3] The Slovene people preserved their cultural identity because of the educational efforts of their native intelligentsia who were mostly Catholic monks and priests. The House of Austria gradually established itself in the region, from the latter part of the 13th century onwards.

[4] Between the 15th and 16th centuries, the Slovenes participated in several peasant revolts - some, like the 1573 revolt, in conjunction with the Croats - leading the Hapsburgs to improve the system of land tenure.

[5] After 1809, a large part of Slovene territory fell within the Napoleonic Empire's Illyrian provinces. After Napoleon's defeat in 1814, Hapsburg (House of Austria) rule was restored within the region. With the 1848 Revolution, the Slovenes called for the creation of a united Slovene province within the Austrian Empire. The first glimmer of hope for a union of southern Slavs (Slavs, Serbs and Croats) emerged in the 1870s.

[6] In the 1890s, the Slovene People's Party (Catholic), and the Progressive (Liberal) and Socialist parties were formed. Members of the Catholic clergy also promoted a large-scale organization of peasants and artisans into cooperatives.

[7] In 1917 the Austrian Parliament, representing Slovenes and other southern Slav peoples, defended the unification of these territories into a single autonomous political entity, within the Hapsburg realm.

[8] At the end of World War I, amid widespread enthusiasm over the fall of the Austro-Hungarian Empire, Slovene leaders supported the creation of a kingdom of Serbs, Croats and Slovenes. In 1919, the new state adopted the name Yugoslavia (land of the southern Slavs). Nevertheless at the Paris Peace Conference the victorious powers handed Gorica to Italy despite the presence of a large Slovene population.

[9] The St Germain Treaty, signed between the victorious powers and Austria, gave Yugoslavia only a small part of southern Carintia. Two plebiscites were announced, to define the future of the rest of Carintia. However, when the southern region opted to join Austria in 1920, the second plebiscite was not held, and both regions remained part of Austria.

[10] Serbian hegemony within the Yugoslav kingdom gave rise to a certain resentment among Slovenes. This feeling never reached the extremes that characterized Croat feelings and which led to a strong anti-Serbian movement there.

[11] In World War II, Slovenia was partitioned between Italy (the southwest), Germany (the northeast) and Hungary (a small area north of the Mura River). The most prominent group within the Slovene resistance movement was the Liberation Front, led by the Communists.

[12] The communist guerrillas fought on two fronts at the same time: against the foreign invaders and against their internal enemies (especially groups belonging to the Slovene People's Party). The occupiers, in turn, organized anti-communist military units, with the participation of the local population. After the defeat of the Axis (Germany, Italy and Japan), the major part of old Slovenia was returned to Yugoslavia.

[13] Upon the foundation of the Federated People's Republic of Yugoslavia, in 1945, Slovenia became one of the Federation's six republics, with its own governing and legislative bodies. Legislative power was made up of a republican council, elected by all citizens, and the council of producers, elected from among Slovenian industrial workers and officials.

[14] Although such entities did not add up to an autonomous government, Slovenia managed to maintain a high degree of cultural and economic independence through this self-management brand of socialism (led by the Yugoslav League of Communists). In 1974, changes in the Yugoslavian federal constitution made Slovenia a Socialist Republic.

[15] Slovenia became one of the most industrialized of the Federation's republics, especially in the area of steel production and the production of heavy equipment. Yugoslavia's first nuclear power plant was completed in 1981 in Krsko, with the assistance of a private US firm.

[16] During the socialist period, Slovenia was first or second among the Yugoslav republics with regard to family income, leading the table for economically active population outside the rural sector. Slovenia also produced both agricultural produce and cattle.

[17] In the late 1980s, influenced by the changes in Eastern Europe, Slovenia evolved toward a multiparty political system. In January 1989, the Slovene League of Social Democrats was founded, the country's first legal opposition party, and in October Slovenia's National Assembly approved a constitutional amendment permitting Slovenia to secede from Yugoslavia.

[18] The Slovene League of Communists left the Yugoslav League in January 1990, becoming the Democratic Renewal Party. In April, in the first multiparty elections to be held in Yugoslavia since World War II, the Demos coalition came out victorious. This coalition's members represented a broad political spectrum - including several communists - united in their aim of achieving Slovenian separation from the federation.

[19] Slovenia and Croatia declared their independence on June 25, 1991. In the hours which followed, central government tanks flocked to Slovenia's Austrian, Hungarian and Italian borders; 20,000 federal troops stationed within the republic were mobilized. After fierce fighting and the bombing of the Ljubljana airport, Belgrade announced that it controlled the federation's borders.

[20] A cease-fire went into effect on July 7 1991, following negotiations held on the Yugoslav island of Brioni between federal and Slovene authorities, with the mediation of the European Community. The agreement resulting from the negotiations reaffirmed the sovereignty of Yugoslav peoples and postponed Slovenian independence for a three-month period. At the same time, the federal president's authority over the army was recognized, and the Slovene police authority over Slovenia's borders.

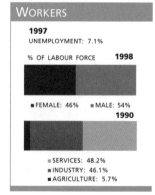

WORKERS

1997
UNEMPLOYMENT: 7.1%

% OF LABOUR FORCE **1998**

FEMALE: 46%   MALE: 54%
1990

SERVICES: 48.2%
INDUSTRY: 46.1%
AGRICULTURE: 5.7%

21 According to the Brioni compromise, customs tariffs along Slovenia's borders remained in the hands of Slovene police, although the income generated was to go into a joint account belonging to the various Yugoslav republics. The federal army was to remain in the green area (free of border controls) during the three-month period established for jurisdiction to be turned over to Slovene authorities.

22 In order for the cease-fire to be enforced, the agreement established an unconditional return of federal army units to army barracks, and the demobilization of the Slovene territorial defense forces. Likewise, directives were established for clearing the highways and freeing prisoners on both sides.

23 Within the following three months, Slovenia strengthened its separatist resolve, while federal troops gradually withdrew from the territory. Only hours before the three-month period was to expire, Slovene authorities announced the creation of a new national currency, the *tolar*, which was to replace the Yugoslavian *dinar*. On October 8 1991,

Slovenia's declaration of independence went into effect.

24 When it was part of Yugoslavia, the population of Slovenia was only 8 per cent of the total (approx. 1.9 million inhabitants). Yet its industrial production accounted for 25 per cent.

25 Between 1991 and January 1992, the EC countries recognized Slovenia and Croatia as independent states, although civil war continued in the latter. The EC threatened to apply economic sanctions to Belgrade unless fighting stopped. The homogeneity of the Slovenian population made its secession the least painful in the Yugoslavian dissolution process.

26 Slovenia's recognition was also one of the most clear-cut cases for the international community, as it controlled its own borders, maintained its own armed forces, and had already issued its own currency. After the withdrawal of Yugoslavian troops, the Government, headed by Milan Kucan, undertook the task of economic reconstruction, with practically no interference from the former Yugoslav government.

27 In April 1992, the center candidate Janez Drnovsek was appointed Prime Minister. In the

December elections, the majority was taken by the Liberal Democratic Party, led by Drnovsek, which formed a coalition government with the Democratic Christians, the second biggest political force in the nation.

28 Slovenia began to define itself as a 'European, not Balkan' State in 1993. Good trade relations with the European Union (EU) and the Slovenian authorities' willingness to open up markets led the country to seek association into the EU. The growth of tourism and the *tolar*'s stability - convertible since September 1995 - enabled Slovenia's exports and gross domestic product to increase.

29 Italy opposed Slovenia's association with the EU. Italian authorities demanded compensation for the nationalization of property belonging to 150,000 Italians between 1945 and 1972. The Catholic Church also demanded the return of property which had been nationalized by the communist regime.

30 The European Commission approved Slovenia's request in May 1995 but Italian opposition continued. In late 1995, Croatia and Slovenia had not reached an agreement regarding the sovereignty of the waters of Piran bay. The destination of Croatian funds deposited in Slovenia's main bank, the Ljubljanska Banka, prior to the break-up of former Yugoslavia, was also discussed.

31 In June 1996 Slovenia signed an association agreement with the EU as a formal step prior to its incorporation as a full member in 2001. One condition set out by the EU - urged by Italy in particular - in order to achieve the agreement was the incorporation of a provision in the Slovenian constitution allowing foreigners to acquire property in the country. Economic policies took into consideration new EU demands, specially with respect to the budget.

32 In September 1998, the Slovenian economy was considered by many Western European countries to be one of the most suitable for incorporation into the EU. Later in November, however, a European Commission report stated that the country had slowed its preparations to become a fully-fledged member of the EU - a comment which surprised the Slovenians.

33 The first visit of Croatian President Stipe Mesic to Ljubljana on March 2000 strengthened relations between the two former Yugoslav republics. Common issues were discussed, particularly integration into the EU and border delimitation. ∎

PROFILE

ENVIRONMENT

Bordered in the west by Italy, in the north by Austria, in the northeast by Hungary and in the south and southeast by Croatia, Slovenia is characterized by mountains, forests and deep, fertile valleys. The Sava River flows from the Julian Alps (highest peak: Mt Triglav, 2,864 meters), in the northwest of the country, to the southeast, crossing the coal-mining region. The Karavanke mountain range is located along the northern border. The region lying between the Mura, Drava, Savinja and Sava rivers is known for its vineyards and wine production. To the west and southwest of Ljubljana, all along the Soca river (known as 'Isonzo' on the Italian side), the climate is less continental, and more Mediterranean. The capital has an average annual temperature of 9°C, with an average of -1°C in the winter and 19°C in summer. The country's main mineral resources are coal and mercury, which contribute to the country's high level of industrialization.

SOCIETY

Peoples: Slovene 87.8 per cent; Croat 2.8 per cent; Serb 2.4 per cent; Bosnian 1.4 per cent; Magyar 0.4 per cent; other 5.2 per cent.
Religions: Mostly Catholic (83.6 per cent); Traditional Catholic Slovene Church and Orthodox 16.4 per cent.
Languages: Slovene, official; Serbo-Croat.
Political Parties: Demos, a right-of-center coalition. Slovene League of Social Democrats. Party of Democratic Renewal (formerly the Slovene League of Communists). People's Party (right wing, conservative).

THE STATE

Official Name: Republika Slovenija.
Administrative Divisions: 62 Districts.
Capital: Ljubljana, 276,119 people (1995).
Other cities: Maribor 139,979 people; Celje 50,155; Kranj 51,602; Velenje 33,436 (1995).
Government: President, Milan Kucan, since April 1990; re-elected in November 1997. Janez Drnovsek, Prime Minister since April 22 1992; re-elected in January 1997. Bicameral legislature:90-member National Assembly, and 40-member National Council.
National Holiday: June 25, Independence (1991).
Armed Forces: 9,550 (1996). Other: 4,500 Police (1994).

Solomon Islands

Solomon Islands

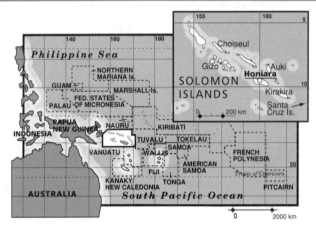

Population: 430,000 (1999)
Area: 28,900 SQ KM
Capital: Honiara
Currency: Solomon Islands dollar
Language: English

The earliest known occupation of the Solomon Islands is circa 28,000 BC by Australoid hunter-gatherers. Today the Islands have a complex social organization based on the *wantok* or extended family system

[2] The Spaniard Alvaro de Mendaña arrived in 1567, searching for El Dorado - land of gold. In the 18th and 19th centuries, the islands were used as a source of slave labor for the sugar plantations of Fiji and Australia.

[3] The Solomon Islands were declared a British protectorate in 1893. They were taken over by the Japanese in 1942. After World War II, the archipelago was recovered and divided in two. The northern part, some 14,000 sq km, was placed under Australian administration, and later annexed to Papua New Guinea.

[4] On May 21 1975, Britain agreed to independence claims. The Islands were granted internal autonomy in 1976, and independence was finally declared on July 7 1978.

[5] The financial system and the Solomons' land holdings, the main center of production, were under foreign control. Although efforts have been made at economic diversification, the Solomon Islands remained dependent almost entirely on external markets.

[6] Solomon Mamaloni was elected Prime Minister in August 1981, after the Islands' parliament censured Kenilorea. He banned nuclear-powered ships and planes, or those carrying nuclear weapons, from the Islands' territorial waters and air space.

[7] In the 1984 election, a coalition worked together to achieve the re-election of Kenilorea as Prime Minister. He patched up relations with the United States and in 1986, named Ezekiel Alebua as his successor. After taking office, Alebua followed Kenilorea's policies faithfully.

[8] In 1989, Mamaloni was re-elected Prime Minister.

[9] Mamaloni's government was subjected to parliamentary investigation in 1992 because of irregularities in the sale of the National Fishing Development Company, a Canadian enterprise.

[10] The Islands' relations with Papua New Guinea deteriorated as a result of the conflict in the secessionist island of Bougainville. Two Solomon Islanders had been killed in an armed confrontation there in September 1992. In April 1993, after attempts at defusing the situation, Papuan troops carried out several incursions into Solomon Island territory (see Papua New Guinea).

[11] Francis Billy Hilly was elected Prime Minister in June 1994 but on October 31 was forced to step down after a vote of no confidence from Parliament. Billy Hilly denounced accusations that the logging industry was a source of government corruption. The new Prime Minister, Mamaloni, did not pursue the conservationist policy. In 1995, the Government ordered the felling of all the trees on Pavuvu island and its inhabitants were transferred to other islands.

[12] In September 1997 Bartholomew Ulufa'alu was appointed Prime Minister. The new government announced the nationalization of the logging industry and ordered an investigation into the use of development funds by the previous administration. In December, the national currency was devalued by 20 per cent and commodity prices rose.

[13] In the first half of 1999, long simmering disputes over land ownership and access to education, employment and economic development erupted into armed conflict around Honiara on Guadalcanal.

[14] The Isatabu Freedom Movement (IFM) - representing Guadalcanal interests - demanded compensation for the use of their land for the national capital and extensive areas of plantations. When the compensation payment was not forthcoming, the IFM forcibly evicted people squatting on their land and forced businesses to close. The group most affected were islanders from Malaita, who hold most of the jobs and who control the power structures. The Malaitans retaliated by forming a private army, the Malaita Eagle Force (MEF), which seized arms and gunboats from the SI Police Force. Prime Minister Ulufa'alu, a Malaitan, offered to pay over $500,000 to the Guadalcanal Provincial Government as compensation. However counter-claims for compensation by Malaitans have further confused the dispute.

[15] In May 2000, the MEF, supported by some members of the SI Police Force, took Prime Minister Ulufa'alu and other government officials hostage. They also occupied key installations in Honiara, including police stations and the telecommunications centre. Ulufa'alu was forced to resign. In July 2000, Opposition leader Manasseh Sogavare was elected Prime Minister. ∎

PROFILE

ENVIRONMENT

Comprises most of the island group of the same name, except for those in the northwest which belong to Papua-New Guinea, the archipelago of Ontong Java (Lord Howe Atoll), the Rennell Islands and the Santa Cruz Islands. The Solomon Islands are part of Melanesia, east of New Guinea. The major islands, of volcanic origin, are: Guadalcanal (with the capital), Malaita, Florida, New Georgia, Choiseul, Ysabel and Makira. The land is mountainous and there are several active volcanoes. Fishing and subsistence agriculture are the traditional economic activities. Ninety per cent of Solomon Islanders live as subsistence farmers in village communities of 100 to 1,000 people. Deforestation is severe. Heavy rains cause soil erosion, particularly in exposed areas.

SOCIETY

Peoples: Most of the population is of Melanesian origin (94 per cent). There are also Polynesians (4 per cent), Micronesians (1.4 per cent) and some Chinese and Europeans. **Religions:** Christian 96.7 per cent, of which Protestant account for 77.5 per cent and Roman Catholic for 19.2 per cent; Baha'i 0.4 per cent; traditional beliefs 0.2 per cent; other and no religion 2.7 per cent.
Languages: English (official), Pidgin (local dialect derived from English) and over 80 dialects. **Political Parties:** Solomon Islands National Unity, Reconciliation and Progressive Party (SINURPP) - formerly party for the Alliance of the People; People's Alliance Party; National Action Party of the Solomon Islands; Solomon Islands Labor Party; United Party. **Social Organizations:** The Solomon Islands Council of Trade Unions (SICTU), formed in 1986, made up of 6 trade unions.

THE STATE

Official Name: Solomon Islands. **Administrative Divisions:** 9 Provinces and the Capital. **Capital:** Honiara 35,288 people (1994). **Other cities:** Gizo 3,727 people; Auki 3,262; Kira Kira 2,585; Buala 1,913.
Government: Queen Elizabeth II, Head of State; Moses Pitakaka, Governor-General since June 1994, appointed by the British Government. Manassah Sogovare, Prime Minister since July 2000.
National Holiday: July 7, Independence Day (1978).

Somalia

Somaliya

Population: 9,672,000 (1999)
Area: 637,660 SQ KM
Capital: Mogadishu (Muqdisho)
Currency: Shilling
Language: Somali and Arabic

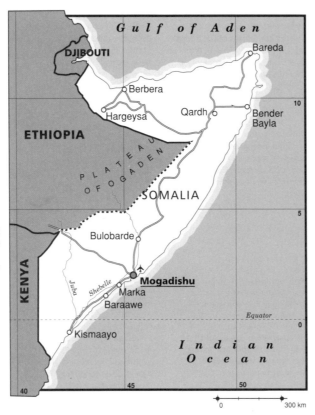

The region of Somalia, called 'the land of Punt' by the Egyptians thousands of years ago, was an Egyptian trading partner. Centuries later, the Romans called it 'the land of aroma' because of the incense produced there.

2   This ancient commercial tradition took on new dimensions from the eighth century when Arab refugees founded a series of commercial settlements on the coast.

3   In the 13th century, Islamicized and led by Yemeni immigrants, Somalians founded a state which they called Ifat, with its principal center in Zeila. Tribute was initially paid to the Ethiopian Empire but Ifat quickly entered into conflict with the Abyssinians and succeeded in consolidating its independence. New territories were annexed and a new name adopted: the Sultanate of Adal.

4   Ties established with Arab markets and the southern part of the coast of Zandj contributed to develop intense commercial activity. At the same time, the sultans tried to enlarge their dominion, at the expense of the none too stable Ethiopian Empire.

5   However, it was not until 1541 that the Portuguese Government, having acquired a clearer knowledge of Indian Ocean trade, sent its fleet. Backed up by the Ethiopian army, the latter razed the city of Zeila, going on to destroy Mogadishu (Muqdisho), Berbera and Brava.

6   The Portuguese destroyed but did not occupy the area, though the presence of their armada hindered economic reconstruction. Adal declined, and was divided into a series of minor sultanates, the northern ones controlled by the Ottoman Empire, while the ones in the south accepted the sovereignty of the Sultan of Zanzibar after the expulsion of the Portuguese in 1698.

7   The Suez Canal gave new strategic value to the region. In 1862, the French bought the port of Obock, leading to the creation of present-day Djibouti and in 1869 the Italians settled in Aseb and later extended their control over Eritrea.

8   In 1885 the British, who had already occupied Aden on the Arabian peninsula, took the Egyptian settlements in Zeila and Berbera. In 1906, in compensation for their defeat in Ethiopia, the Italians obtained Somalia's southern coast.

9   The British colony was the leading center of resistance to foreign domination. Sheikh Muhammad bin Abdullah Hassan organized an Islamic revolutionary movement, which defeated the British troops on four occasions between 1900 and 1904. The British finally gained control of the territory in 1920.

10   On July 1 1960, with decolonization in Africa underway, the British and Italian regions became independent and were merged as the Republic of Somalia. The new republic adopted a parliamentary system, until October 21 1969, when a group of officers led by General Said Barre seized power and proclaimed a socialist regime.

11   In July 1976, the Front for the Liberation of Western Somalia initiated a military offensive in the Ogaden supported by the Somali Government. The invasion was repelled by the Ethiopian army, supported by Cuban troops and backed by most African nations who opposed changes in colonial frontiers. The country broke off relations with Cuba and ended its military agreements with the Soviet Union.

12   The war against Ethiopia caused serious difficulties to Somalia's fragile economy; prices of fuel and grain increased and a severe drought affected most of the country in 1978-79 bringing the Barre Government to the brink of collapse. A group of army officers unsuccessfully attempted to overthrow the government in April 1978. In October 1980 Barre declared a state of emergency and reinstated the Supreme Revolutionary Council which had ceased functioning in 1976.

13   Although the northeastern province of Kenya was historically been claimed by Somalia, relations with Kenya improved since 1984, through commercial and technical cooperation agreements.

14   Problems with Ethiopia recurred sporadically because of the dispute over the Ogaden plains and the steady flow of Ethiopian refugees into Somali camps. In 1988 alone the number of refugees was estimated at 840,000.

15   Said Barre was re-elected in December 1986 by 99 per cent of the vote. In February 1989, he sent Prime Minister Ali Samater to London and Washington, to announce the amnesty and commuting of sentences for 400 political prisoners.

16   Western credits and investments were drastically reduced and exports to Saudi Arabia, the principal market for its cattle, stopped almost completely.

17   In January 1991, the opposition formed the United Somali Congress (USC) and ousted the President, replacing him with Ali Mahdi Mohammed, leader of the USC and representing business interests.

18   After bloody confrontations between the two factions of the USC, President Mahdi fled Mogadishu in November 1991. The capital remained in the hands of General Mohamed Farah Aideed, leader of the military wing of the USC.

19   The two rival factions of the United Somali Congress were made up of members of different sub-groups of the Hawiye clan, led by Farah Aideed and Ali Mahdi, respectively.

20   Since the beginning of the war between the rival clans, 300,000 Somali children have died, and 1.5 million inhabitants - a quarter of the total population - have left the country.

21   On March 9 1991, taking advantage of a ceasefire, 100,000 women and children held a peaceful march through Mogadishu. Nine tribal leaders of the Hiraan region met to discuss how to bring about peace in their country. It was the first meeting of *ugas* or kings in more than a hundred years.

22   In 1993, after two years of civil war and total anarchy, Somalia still had no central governmental structures. The traditional authorities, unable to handle the unprecedented conditions, had abandoned their normal functions, leaving clans and sub-clans unrestrained. In some regions, though, the local population still respected the traditional authority of the tribal elders. However, in the vacuum created by the absence of central administration, power remained in the hands of the warlords and of heavily armed bands of looters.

23   Under pressure from the United States, the UN sent 28,000 troops to assist. This was the first time the world organization had intervened militarily in the internal affairs of a nation.

[24] At the suggestion of the UN, in March 1993 military chiefs, councils of elders and prominent citizens agreed to create a provisional government and a National Transition Council. Aideed's forces confronted the UN blue helmets with losses on both sides. The elite US Rangers failed in their attempt to capture Aideed. In March 1994, the UN withdrew 10,000 European troops, leaving 19,000, mostly Africans and Indians. The peace efforts did not prosper, despite a meeting organized in Nairobi,

Kenya, between the main opponents: Aideed and Ali Mahdi. The last contingent of UN troops left the country in March, protected by a force of 1,800 marines. And even though the regional conflicts continued, the civil war did not spread and economic life seemed to recover.

[25] The Republic of Somaliland broke away from Somalia and declared independence in 1994. The fledgling republic - comprising about 30 per cent of Somalia's territory - was not officially recognized. The port of Berbere, on the Gulf of Aden, formed its economic base. With the economy in ruins, it sheltered a million people displaced from the southern zone (Somalia).

[26] Divided and still without international recognition, the Republic of Somaliland continued to function in 1995. In Somalia the factions regrouped around the Somali Salvation Front (SSF), of Ali Mahdi Mohammed, and the Somali National Alliance (SNA) led by Farah Aideed, both self-proclaimed governments. Farah Aideed died from gunshot wounds in August 1996 and was succeeded by his son Hussein. Osman Hassan Ali ('Ato'), Farah's former right-hand man, emerged as a new force but in association with Ali Mahdi.

[27] In January 1997 in Sodere, Ethiopia, 26 political leaders affiliated to the SSF, with the support of the Organization of African Unity, decided to establish a National Salvation Council empowered to organize a transition government. Hussein Aideed and Mohammed Ibrahim Egal, re-elected President of Somaliland in March, refused to recognize this decision.

[28] The floods of November and December 1997 left 230,000 Somalis stranded in the southern regions of the nation. The UN began a refugee aid program air dropping tons of food over the Garbahari and Gedo districts, alongside the Juba river.

[29] In April 1998, at fresh meetings in Nairobi, Kenya, the military chiefs - Ali Mahdi Mohammed, Hussein Aideed, Osman Hassan Ali and Mohamed Kanyere - declared their commitment to peace for the Somali people. Meanwhile, the devastated economy suffered another downturn following a ban on imports of Somali livestock imposed by Saudi Arabia.

[30] With the objective of forming a new administration called Puntland, a conference of 300 Northeastern leaders held in June at the Garowe district, elected Coronel Abdullah Yussuf Ahmed as President and Mohamed Abdi Hashi as Vice-President. Puntland would include the cattle-raising areas of Garowe, Bari and Galkayo. The nominal founding leaders of the new administration were considering Garowe as the capital.

[31] Tens of thousands of people died in the famine caused by the drought that hit southern Somalia late that year.

[32] A peace conference was scheduled for April 2000 in Djibouti between the different Somali warring factions. In March, a large demonstration was held against Abdullah Yussuf's declaration that Puntland would not participate in the conference. Clashes between forces loyal to the leaders of Puntland and the demonstrators caused many deaths.

[33] Somaliland also opposed the conference, and its representative was expelled from Djibouti in April. The Government formally accused Somaliland of closing the shared border. Meanwhile, the authorities of Puntland arrested three of the peace conference organizers, who were later released. ■

PROFILE

ENVIRONMENT

Somalia is a semi-desert country with a large population of nomads. The north is mountainous, descending gradually from the Galia-Somali plateau to the coastal strip bathed by the Gulf of Aden. The south is almost entirely desert with the exception of a fertile area crossed by two rivers originating in Ethiopia, the Juba and Shebeli. Drought, endemic in this region, has been exacerbated by overgrazing. A drastic increase in livestock has led to desertification. Fishing using explosive charges has damaged coral reefs and aquatic vegetation. The destruction of these fish habitats may have put stocks and future catches of many species at risk. There are 74 endangered species, including mammals, plants and birds.

SOCIETY

Peoples: The Somali people are Hamitic and the most important ethnic groups (Isaq, Dir and Digil) have linguistic and cultural unity, a relatively unusual situation in Africa.
Religions: Islam (official), mostly the orthodox Sunni version. There are a few Christians in Mogadishu.
Languages: Somali and Arabic (official).
Political Parties: There is confrontation between rival factions of the various clans. Major groupings of clans include the United Somali Congress (USC), the Somali Salvation Alliance (SSA) and the Somali National Alliance (SNA). The United Somali Congress (USC), created in 1991, led by Osman Ali Atto. The Somali National Alliance (SNA), made up of Siad Barre's former troops, (formerly loyal to Farah Aideed, but ousted him in 1995). The USC and SNA then formed an alliance. The Somali Salvation Alliance (SSA), Ali Mahdi Mohammed's party. The Somali Patriotic Movement (SPM, Darod clan). The Somali Salvation Democratic Front (SSDF, Majertein clan) in the south. The Somali Democratic Alliance (SDA, Gadabursi clan) and the United Somali Front (USF, Issa clan) in the north.
Social Organizations: The General Federation of Somali Trade Unions, created in 1977.

THE STATE

Official Name: Jamhuriaydda Soomaliya.
Administrative divisions: Somalia is divided into 18 regions or provinces.
Capital: Mogadishu 750,000 people (1994).
Government: Neither the Government nor the public administration have functioned since November 1991, when Ali Mahdi Mohammed fled the capital.
National Holiday: July 1, Independence Day (1960).
Armed Forces: Regular armed forces have not existed since rebel forces ousted the Government in 1991.

STATISTICS

DEMOGRAPHY

Population: 9,672,000 (1999)
Children per woman: 7.2 (1998)

HEALTH

Life expectancy at birth: 47 years (1998)
male: 45 years (1998)
female: 49 years (1998)
Infant mortality: 125 per 1,000 (1998)
Under-5 child mortality: 211 per 1,000 (1998)
Safe water: 31 % (1990/98)

EDUCATION

Literacy: 24 % (1995)
male: 36 % (1995)
female: 14 % (1995)
School enrolment:
Primary total: 11 % (1990/96)
male: 15 % (1990/97)
female: 8 % (1990/97)
Secondary:
male: 9 % (1990/96)
female: 5 % (1990/96)
Tertiary: 2 % (1996)

COMMUNICATIONS

1 newspapers (1996) and 46 radios (1997) per 1,000 people

ECONOMY

Cereal imports:
127,638 metric tons (1998)
Fertilizer use: 5 kg per ha (1997)
External debt: $ 2,635 million (1998); $ 285 per capita (1998)

South Africa

South Africa

Population: 40,583,573 (1996)
Area: 1,221,037 SQ KM
Capital: Pretoria
Currency: Rand
Language: Afrikaans, English + 9 African languages

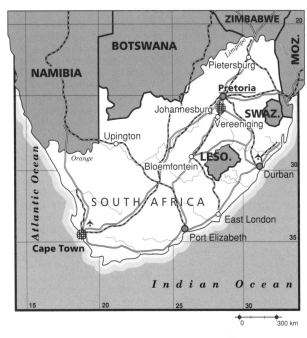

The first Dutch settlers arrived at Cape Town in 1652, more than 150 years after the Portuguese sailor Vasco de Gama rounded the Cape of Good Hope. The Portuguese, more interested in India, showed little desire to confront the Khoikhoi peoples who had been in the region for more than a thousand years and were hostile to the foreign navigators.

2   Jan van Rebeck was the first of the Dutch to challenge the Khoikhoi. He landed in Cape Town and established a colony providing crops and livestock to supply ships on their way to Indonesia. In 1688, nearly 600 farmers had settled there, dividing their energies between farming and the war against the Khoikhoi. Being such a small minority, the first Dutch colonists were fiercely united and aggressive, two characteristics which pervaded *boer* (farmer) society in southern Africa.

3   The Dutch were not typical colonists. They worked for the Dutch East Indies Company, were not allowed to trade with the local people and had to deliver all their production to the Company's ships. They gradually came into conflict with their overseas bosses, who would not loosen the grip of their monopoly. The Dutch won the dispute, and towards the end of the 17th century the so-called free colonists or *burghers* were in the majority. The population of European origin split: some continued to be linked to foreign trade and others moved inland in search of new lands.

4   In 1806, with the Dutch colonial empire on the wane, the British settled in Cape Town. They moved ahead on agreements to trade goods, incorporated the African leaders into intermediaries and end slavery. This rapidly led to conflict with the intransigent Boers, who had begun calling themselves *Afrikaners*, to distinguish themselves from the more recent colonists. In 1834, nearly 14,000 of them emigrated to the interior, starting the Great Trek which would take them to what became Transvaal, the Orange Free State and Natal (now the provinces of Gauteng, Free State and KwaZulu-Nata). They established the state of Transvaal in 1852 and the Orange Free State in 1854. These regions were already occupied by African people who fiercely resisted the new settlers.

5   The British recognized the independence of the two regions, as the settling of new lands by Europeans contributed to Cape Town's security. In their expansion northward, the Afrikaners confronted Xhosas and Zulus. The latter had earlier been led by military genius Shaka, who died in 1828. The resistance blocked the colonists' advance over a period of 50 years. The great empire of the Zulus collapsed shortly before the Great Trek, due to internal strife over royal succession.

6   Conflict between the Boers and the British Crown erupted in the late 19th century when rich gold and diamond fields were discovered in the interior. Realization that the region great economic and strategic value induced Britain to propose a federation between the Cape Colony the Transvaal (the South African Republic) and the Orange Free State. The Boers rejected the idea and war broke out in 1899. Britain was supported by most of its colonies, while the Boers had German backing. After three years of war, with nearly 50,000 Afrikaners dead and double that number confined to concentration camps, the Boers surrendered, accepting British domination, while maintaining a certain independence for its regions. The British victory in the Boer or South African War in 1902 signaled the end of the hegemony of landed Boer farmers in the Orange Free State and Transvaal and the beginning of mining's importance in the economy.

7   For some Boers, the African peoples were 'savages' who had to be forcibly tamed. White supremacy and racial segregation were established to justify the subjugation of the black population and to guarantee a supply of cheap farm labor from tenants. Boer farms in the interior were backward and unprofitable compared with the farming practiced in the Cape and Natal.

8   The British focus on trade and liberalism led them to consider slavery a restraint on the creation of consumer markets. This did not prevent them from erecting rigid barriers to exclude black South Africans from economic and social advancement. The labor legislation from 1809 imposed severe controls on worker mobility. With the 1843 Master and Servant Act, along with later decrees, made it a criminal act to break a work contract.

9   In the 19th century, the British also contracted black workers in the territories of present-day Mozambique, Lesotho, Botswana, as well as Indians and Chinese. These 'imported' workers were not allowed to bring their families; pay was poor and they had to return to their own countries if they lost their jobs.

10   Both in the Cape and Natal hut and poll taxes were introduced, designed to force Africans to work for a salary far lower than that paid to those of European origin. Another law applied to peasants: an annual tax, paid in cash, which they could only get by selling their produce to the Europeans. This destroyed the traditional African ways of life and at the same time salaries could be kept low.

11   When the gold and diamond mines began to be exploited, the European capitalists had to employ qualified white workers. Most of them were former Boer farmers who had lost everything in the war. Others came from Europe attracted by the 'gold fever'. Both of these groups, used to the workings of the industrial capitalist system, made demands for better pay and

WORKERS

1996
UNEMPLOYMENT: 5.1%

% OF LABOUR FORCE   **1998**

■ FEMALE: 38%   ■ MALE: 62%
1990

■ SERVICES: 54.5%
■ INDUSTRY: 32.0%
■ AGRICULTURE: 13.5%

LAND USE

DEFORESTATION: 0.2% annual (1990/95)
IRRIGATED: 10.3% of arable (1993)

1993

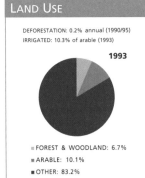

■ FOREST & WOODLAND: 6.7%
■ ARABLE: 10.1%
■ OTHER: 83.2%

PUBLIC EXPENDITURE

DEFENCE EXPENDITURE (% of goverment exp.)	**5.6%** (1997)	
MILITARY EXPENDITURE (% of health & education)	**41%** (1990/91)	

LITERACY	FOOD DEPENDENCY

LITERACY
1995
83%

FOOD DEPENDENCY
1970
5%
1997
6%

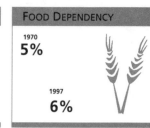

conditions. The mining companies promised benefits to these white workers as long as they fell in with the exploitation of the black workforce.

[12] In 1896, the so-called color bar was in placein the mining sector and in the urban centers where the British were in the majority. In 1910, the Constitution of the Union of South Africa - a federation of Cape Province, Natal, the Orange Free State and Transvaal - deprived most black people of the right to vote or to own land.

[13] From 1910, the segregationist legislation increased. The Native Labor Act pushed urban workers into a system of submission similar to that operating on rural estates. The 1913 Nativse Land Act, earmarked 7 per cent of national territory for the blacks as reserves which became home to 35-40 per cent of the population. Much of the remaining land was reserved for whites who only made up 20 per cent of the population. In the overcrowded black reservations subsistence agriculture was the main activity. The rest, under white control, was intensively farmed with the reserves providing a permanent source of cheap labor. The 1923 Native Urban Act, tightly regulated blacks' lives in cities which were considered white strongholds.

[14] Until 1984, political participation was limited very largely to whites. Most black Africans, almost two thirds of the population, were denied the right to vote. Constitutional Reform in 1984 extended the vote to the Asians - mainly Indians - and the 'Colored' or mixed race groups.

[15] At the outset of World War I, the white economy was based on mining and intensive agriculture. The post-war recession pushed the large mining companies into hiring blacks, which led to racial confrontations within the work force. The Rand strike in 1922 was harshly put down by the Government. Most of the strikers were poor whites, descendants of both English and Boers. Frustrated by their defeat in the war and the loss of their lands, with no easy way of entering the nascent industrial structure, Afrikaners were attracted by the ultra-nationalist propaganda of the far Right.

[16] The Nationalists, triumphant in the 1924 elections along with their English-speaking allies, broke with the traditional liberal economic policy and imposed protectionism. State capitalism promoted by the Nationalists - with steel works, railways and electricity - made rapid national growth possible, something many saw as an 'economic miracle'.

[17] Toward the end of the 1920s the falling gold price on the international market forced the Nationalists into another alliance. They joined forces with traditionally despised foreign capital and maintained the racial segregation system which guaranteed cheap workers. The ensuing industrial take-off brought with it an increased number of blacks employed in industry and this led to racial conflict. A secret society, the Afrikaner Broeder Bond - Brotherhood - became the bastion of white right-wing politics.

[18] The recession following World War II led to a repeat of events: poor whites, threatened by unemployment, rebelled. Racism flourished under the slogan 'Gevaar KKK' (Beware blacks, Indians and communism - Kafir, Koelie, Komunism). In 1948, the Nationalists formed a government by themselves and imposed even harsher restrictions on the black population.

[19] The first national political organization of South African blacks had appeared in 1912. The African National Congress (ANC) was created by a group of former students from schools run by missionaries. Among its founders were also people who had studied or gained degrees in North American and European universities. They believed the Afrikaners could be persuaded of the unfairness of the racial segregation laws and that the Anglophile liberals would allow blacks to participate in politics. Their hopes were dashed in 1920 when the black mine workers strike was crushed and segregation entrenched.

[20] In the 1940s the ANC adopted a strategy of non-violent resistance to the race laws. In 1955, the anti-racist front was broadened with the Freedom Charter, proclaimed at a multiracial gathering in Kliptown. The Charter included a radical denunciation of apartheid (separatenss) and called for its abolition, along with wealth redistribution.

[21] In 1958, sectors of the ANC who disagreed with the multiracial policy of the movement created the Pan African Congress (PAC), which in 1960 held a demonstration in the city of Sharpeville to protest against the pass law which restricted the movement of black workers in areas reserved for whites. The march was brutally repressed, leaving 70 dead.

[22] Following this incident, the PAC, ANC and the Communist Party were all outlawed. The African National Congress (ANC) formed an armed group, the Umkhonto we Sizwe (Spear of the Nation), while the PAC set up another, Poqo (Only Us). In 1963, the main leaders of the ANC were arrested; Nelson Mandela was sentenced to life imprisonment and Oliver Tambo, in exile, took over leadership of the movement. The Government's repressive violence and the lack of supply bases in neighboring countries - dominated by regimes allied to the Afrikaners - prevented the guerillas from making progress necessary to attract greater numbers of recruits.

[23] The racist system was largely upheld by the interests of international capitalism in the region, attracted by the great pool of cheap labor. Foreign investments, especially from the US, increased five times in value between 1958 and 1967. The Afrikaners' protectionist policies created the infrastructure necessary for large industries to be set up, with the aim of developing an industrial center capable of supplying all southern Africa.

[24] The 1960s saw an increasing flow of rural workers to the cities fuelled by the poverty of the 'Homelands' or Bantustans, some with poor quality soils, and the lack of social services. This population movement affected the expectations of other urban sectors, such as the Coloured people, who saw their hopes of integration into the white economy threatened.

[25] In 1976, the black community in the suburbs of Johannesburg erupted. The youth rebellion in Soweto - the South West Township - made the whites realize the crisis had reached their own cities where they had previously felt safe. In 1970, 75 per cent of workers in agriculture, mining or the services were black, and the participation of non-whites in specialized jobs had

tripled over the last 20 years though blacks earned 5-10 times less than whites for the same work. The ruling white minority, dependent on black labor, proposed some reforms to apartheid, with a view to preventing further social crises amongst migrant workers in the cities.

[26] The Pretoria regime declared four Bantustans - Transkei, Ciskei, Venda and Bophuthatswana - as 'independent states' in an effort to prevent the internal migration of the unemployed. Eight million people were thus deprived of their South African nationality and converted into foreigners by decree. However very few countries recognized these newly 'independent states'.

[27] The independence of Angola and Mozambique in 1975 and that of Zimbabwe in 1980 radically changed the situation in southern Africa. The ANC found in these countries the support bases it desperately needed - and in the other Frontline states of Botswana, Tanzania and Zambia. South Africa, with an economy three times bigger than that of those independent countries combined, initiated a destabilization campaign which included economic pressure, sabotage, support for rebel movements and invasion. All this to force the Frontline states to deny support to the anti-apartheid movement and the block attempts by the newly independent countries to escape South African domination.

[28] Tone of the main arenas of the conflict in southern Africa was in Namibia, a former German colony which South Africa occupied during World War I and later annexed. In 1966, the UN ruled that South Africa had to grant Namibia its independence - a demand which the Organization of African Unity (OAU) and Frontline countries continued to make, despite the delaying tactics of South Africa and the Western powers. It took until March 21 1990 for Namibia to become independent.

[29] The support received from the US and Europe was crucial for South Africa in imposing its economic and military strength on southern Africa. Approximately 400 US companies had interests in the country, and US capital and technology were vital for the developing its industrial and military might.

30 On the domestic front, PW Botha, Prime Minister from 1978 to 1989, began reforming to the apartheid system. Between 1982 and 1984, he brought in constitutional reform granting the vote to Indians and colored people and creating two more chambers in parliament for these groups. Blacks were still excluded, with their participation limited to a local level. Many non-whites boycotted the reform, abstaining from voting.

31 The gradual liberalization of apartheid promised by Botha was widely opposed. Repression against blacks did not diminish; it was merely complicated by inter-ethnic confrontations. In July 1985, the Government declared a state of emergency in 36 districts. By the end of 1986, more than 750 had died and several thousands of the Government's opponents were in prison.

32 Pressure from public opinion in the US and Europe forced Western governments and an increasing number of companies and banks to limit their activities in South Africa. The US Congress lifted the veto imposed by President Reagan on economic sanctions, forcing a change in its policy of constructive engagement. Within South Africa, political opposition led to the creation of the United Democratic Front (UDF) which brought together more than 600 organizations working together within the law.

33 From early 1988 the Botha Government came down more heavily on the opposition, outlawing all the constituent groups and detaining religious leaders opposed to apartheid, including Archbishop Desmond Tutu, Nobel Peace Prize winner.

34 In August 1989, cornered by an internal crisis in his party - which had now been in power for 41 years - Botha resigned. He was replaced by FW De Klerk, who was aware of the need to change South Africa's racist image. In September, parliamentary elections were held under the State of Emergency which had been operating since 1986.

35 The Mass Democratic Movement (MDM), an anti-apartheid coalition of legal organizations, called a general strike. Despite police raids and threats, three million black South Africans stopped work in the largest protest ever held there. The growing momentum was accompanied by repression and killings. But by now an increasing number of the white minority was joining the protests.

36 The opposition met in the University of the Witwatersrand (Johannesburg) for a Conference for a Democratic Future in December 1989, agreeing to establish the principle of 'one person, one vote' for any negotiations with the Government.

37 In February 1990, De Klerk legalized the ANC and other opposition groups. Nelson Mandela was released on February 11 after 27 years in prison. A period of negotiations began. Mandela took back his role as leader of the black majority, a post not without its difficulties. Some were related to confrontations - which caused 5,000 deaths since 1986 - between the ANC and members of the Zulu Inkatha movement. Inkatha had government backing in arms, funds and training.

38 In May, Mandela announced an agreement between the ANC and the Government in order to bring an end to the violence and bring political life back to normal. He called on the international community to maintain economic sanctions and other forms of pressure on the South African Government. The Government renounced its policy of creating Bantustans - it had set up ten so far - and abolished racial segregation in hospitals. In December ANC president Oliver Tambo returned to the country after more than 30 years of exile.

39 Mid-way through April 1991, the European Community (EC) began to consider lifting the economic blockade and set June 30 as the deadline for starting democratization. The same day, the Government abolished the Population Registration Act and the Land Acts, which had prevented blacks from owning land. De Klerk also promised to begin negotiations for a new Constitution. The US went ahead and lifted the blockade. The EC planned to do the same, but Denmark and Spain, which had received a visit from Mandela, vetoed the move.

40 In 1993 the Inkatha Freedom Party (IFP), the Afrikaner National

PROFILE

ENVIRONMENT

Located on the southern tip of the African continent, with a coastline on the Indian and Atlantic Oceans, South Africa has several geographic zones. A narrow strip of lowland lies along the east coast, with a hot and humid climate, large sugar cane plantations. In the Cape region are vineyards and *fynbos* vegetation. The vast semi-arid and arid Karoo, with cattle and sheep ranching, makes up over 40 per cent of the total territory, extending inland. The Highveld extends to the north and is the richest arable area. It surrounds the Witwatersrand, a mining area in the Transvaal where large cities and industries are found. The country's economic base lies in the exploitation of mineral resources: South Africa is the world's largest producer of gold and diamonds; the second largest producer of manganese; and the eighth largest producer of coal. The country's water resources are overtaxed, salinization is the main threat in dry areas. Soil erosion is a serious problem, particularly in the former Bantustans (homelands).

SOCIETY

Peoples: Over 76 per cent of the population is of African origin, of which Zulu 22 per cent, Xhosa 18 per cent, Pedi 9 per cent, Sotho 7 per cent, Tswana 7 per cent, Tsonga 3.5 per cent, Swazi 3 per cent, Ndebele 2 per cent, and Venda 2 per cent. There are also Coloured (descendants of whites, slaves and Khoisan). European descendants account for 13 per cent of the total. Asian groups, predominantly Hindu, make up less than 3 per cent of the total population.

Religions: Christianity predominant (68 per cent) including African independent churches. African religions are also followed.

Languages: 11 official languages: Afrikaans, English, isi Ndebele, Sepedi, Sesotho, siSwati, Xitsonga, Setswana, Tshivenda, isi Xhosa, isi Zulu.

Political Parties: African National Congress (ANC); National Party (NP); Inkatha Freedom Party (IFP); Freedom Front (FF); Democratic Party (DP); Pan Africanist Congress (PAC); African Christian Democratic Party (ACDP); African Muslim Party (AMP); Dikwankwetla Party; Federal Party; African Democratic Movement; Ximoko Progressive Party (XPP); Football Party.

Social Organizations: South African Students' Congress (SASCO), the Congress of South African Trade Unions (COSATU), the National Congress of Trade Unions.

THE STATE

Official Name: Republiek van Suid-Afrika, Republic of South Africa.

Administrative Divisions: Nine Provinces.

Capital: Pretoria (administrative capital) 1,080,200 people; Cape Town (legislative capital) 2,671,000 people (1995); Bloemfontein (judicial capital).

Other cities: Johannesburg/Soweto 8,400,000 people; Durban 1,137,400; Port Elizabeth, 853,200 people (1991).

Government: Thabo Mbeki, President since June 1999. Legislature is made up of the Senate and the National Assembly.

National Holiday: 27 April, Freedom Day (1994).

Armed Forces: 136,900 (1995).

Front (NFA) and the Conservative Party left negotiations on the Constitution and decided to abandon boycott the electoral process. Bophuthatswana president Lucas Mangope - in the midst of a strike by public employees - declared he would join the boycott and received military support from the ultra-right Afrikaner Resistance Movement (AWB). The resistance of black civilians and local forces obliged them to withdraw. Mangope was deposed and the South African army took control.

[41] Meanwhile Inkatha boycotted ANC activities and clashed with Mandela's supporters. Buthelezi finally agreed to participate in the elections after the constitution finally recognized his nephew Goodwill Zweletini as king of the Zulus.

[42] In October, the UN lifted sanctions against the South African regime. The United States immediately withdrew its financial restrictions.

[43] The provisional Constitution created a 400-seat National Assembly and a Senate with 90 members. The President would be elected by the Assembly for a 5-year term. The country was newly divided into nine provinces, each with a governor and legislature, absorbing the ten abolished Bantustans.

[44] The first multiracial elections in South Africa were held between April 26-29 1994. Some 87 per cent of registered voters turned out. The ANC won 63 per cent of the vote, De Klerk's NP 20 per cent and Inkatha 10 per cent. The right, the Freedom Front, came in with 2 per cent.

[45] The Government of National Unity (GNU) included members of the NP and IFP. The minister of finance and the governor of the South African Reserve Bank from the previous government kept their posts.

[46] Despite the removal of the barriers of apartheid, economic and cultural obstacles remained. Black workers earned nine times less than whites and unemployment was 33 per cent and 3 per cent respectively. The overall infant mortality is 50 per 1,000 lives births (1998) but the rate for blacks is far higher.

[47] The May 1994 constitution was radical in tone. Among the measures to be applied at the beginning of his term, Mandela proposed free health care for children aged under six and for pregnant women, a basic diet for schoolchildren and the provision of electricity to 350,000 homes. New legal education guidelines were established. In October it was announced that 3.5 million people would be given access to water services over the next 18 months.

The first GNU budget gave 47 per cent to social services, education took 26 per cent, investment in housing doubled and military spending was reduced.

[48] Ambitious land reform was implemented by Derek Hanekom, a farmer. A labor relations act was approved, guaranteeing the right to strike. There were far fewer strikes than in previous years.

[49] In January, the ANC withdrew immunity guaranteed before the elections to two former cabinet ministers and 3,500 police officers who were to be investigated by the Truth and Reconciliation Committee (TRC). The trial of a former police colonel for 121 murders, kidnappings and frauds, provided new evidence of police incitement of political violence during the former regime. Prominent Inkatha leaders appeared implicated in payments made to the security police. A report by the Goldstone Commission was presented to De Klerk in 1994, listing these charges. In June, the under-secretary of the IFP was arrested for murders committed in 1987.

[50] The local elections of November 1995 favored the ANC throughout the country. In May 1996, the NP left the Government to join the opposition, for the first time since 1948.

[51] The National Assembly approved a new Constitution which, in the Government's opinion consolidated the transition to democracy. During the production of the new text, demonstrations attended by thousands of workers and businesspeople led to the elimination of a clause in the final text which gave the bosses the right to close their factories.

[52] In 1996 the Truth and Reconciliation Commission was set up, under the presidency of former Archbishop Desmond Tutu, and began to collect evidence of human rights violations committed between 1960 and 1993. The investigations uncovered many crimes. Several police officers admitted the use of torture in the 1980s and the hiring of mercenaries. Those responsible were offered an amnesty provided they clarified their part in the events.

[53] The Government announced a new macro-economic strategy aimed at creating 800,000 jobs by the year 2000. Throughout 1996, GDP grew 3 per cent. By the end of November, some two million hectares of land had been redistributed under the Government agrarian reform program.

[54] In October 1997, Mandela visited Libya to mediate in the conflict between Tripoli,

Washington and London over the 1992 embargo against Libya resulting from the Lockerbie airplane bombing (see Libya). Mandela said he supported Libya's stance in calling for a trial in a neutral country, although he made it clear he did not back the unconditional lifting of the embargo.

[55] In the face of rising crime, in April 1998 Mandela suggested the possibility of imposing a curfew on some regions of the country in order to maintain law and order.

[56] During his June 1998 farewell message at the Organization of African Unity, Mandela demanded 'the right and the duty to intervene whenever behind sovereign borders people are being massacred to protect tyranny'. These statements contradicted the founding principle of the OAU of non-intervention in the internal affairs of member countries.

[57] That year, during hearings of the Truth and Reconciliation Commission, it emerged that there had been a plan by apartheid scientists to undermine Mandela's health when he was imprisoned. The plan also included the development of diseases which would attack the black population as well as fertility-inhibiting chemical agents.

[58] Attacks against white farmers returned as the black population began to express its anger over the slow changes. During the ANC congress, Mandela and his deputy, Thabo Mbeki, warned that the formal reconciliation era would come to an end with the end of Mandela's term of office. A second ANC government would take tougher measures to improve the lives of the millions of black people marginalized by the apartheid regime.

[59] In April 1999, Russia and South Africa, two of the biggest gold and diamond producers in the world, signed a declaration pledging to further economic cooperation in that area of production.

[60] Although the June 1999 elections gave the ANC solid control of Parliament, it did not reach the two-thirds needed to unilaterally amend the constitution. The opposition leadership in the National Assembly fell into the hands of the mainly white Democratic Party. Thabo Mbeki became the new President and appointed Jacob Zuma, also ANC, as deputy President.

[61] By 2000 South Africa had one of the fastest-growing rates of HIV-AIDS in the world. President Mbeki became embroiled in a public debate when he disputed the connection between HIV and AIDS, citing poverty as the cause. ∎

African cultures before colonization

Until a comparatively short time ago, Europeans knew little about Africa. Scholars of the 15th century summed up their knowledge of that continent writing on the maps 'Ibi sunt leones' (Here there are lions). The 19th century philosopher Hegel, described blacks as a childish race, and Africa as 'the unhistorical spirit, the non-developed spirit, still submerged in the conditions of the natural... situated on the threshold of the history of the world'.

[2] Such notions corresponded with a lack of knowledge about the continent, and the subordination of its peoples to subjugation and slavery. But decolonization in the second half of the 20th century opened a period in which African peoples were confronted with the complex tasks of social and cultural change and development. Part of it consists of a reassessment and a revaluing of the African past. 'The history of Africa', Ki Zerbo has said, 'is the history of the awakening of its consciousness'.

[3] The knowledge that the West has accumulated about Africa is littered with myths. Among them, the myth of the impossibility of a scientific history, or the myth of the inaccessibility of its past, or the myth of the absence of written testimonies and writing itself, or the myth of the stagnation of the black peoples - which reduced historical interest about Africa to its connections with the Mediterranean world and to isolated subjects, such as Egypt, the Maghreb, or Christian Ethiopia.

[4] If these myths are not overturned, the true history of Africa cannot be born. The task involves the double operation of deconstructing traditional African history - written under the light of the prejudices of a domineering Eurocentric perspective - and of critically investigating an ample and ignored past.

[5] In any case, the object of study should not be to wonder about the fate of Africa if colonialism had not existed, but to consider its autonomous contribution to the history of human culture and its promise for the future.

[6] Charles Darwin wrote: 'It is likely that our first fathers had lived in Africa more than anywhere else'. This intuition is apparently being confirmed by contemporary science. Present research supports the view that conditions favourable for the essential phases in the evolution to the human form existed. Africa supposedly holds the most complete spectrum of prehistorical human remains.

[7] Archaeological discoveries indicate the pre-eminence of African prehistory over the prehistory of other civilizations. Advanced techniques of toolmaking - quarries and workshops, manufacture of double-edged axes, the use of stones as heat accumulators, and pottery making - became differentiated as they extended over wider geographical areas, but 'the initiative, the great tradition, and the 'fashion' came from Africa'.

[8] The Neolithic era began in Africa three thousand years earlier than in Europe. Not in Egypt as has been supposed, but in the Sahara, which was then an attractive area with wide rivers and abundant vegetation. The exchange of techniques between different communities made possible diversified agricultural activities. Corn, barley, sorghum, millet, palms, textile plants and so on, were cultivated. There were modest improvements in cattle-breeding. These practices evolved in an autonomous and parallel way to those of other Asian and Indo-American peoples.

[9] Neolithic African peoples of the Sahara created one of the first technical revolutions through their agricultural practices. This allowed them to lead stable lives and to carry on technical and cultural exchanges with peoples from other areas. The development came from the south upwards through the communities living in the Sahara and then reached the north of Africa. The civilization which flourished later in the Nile valley cannot be accounted for solely as a result of the changes that were made possible there because of the extraordinary fertility of the land, and the population pressure which finally led to the desertification of the Sahara. The cultural riches created and transmitted by the black peoples of the South were also a factor in this process. The Egyptians recognized that those peoples shared their ancestry.

[10] The Egyptians organized an agricultural civilization with artisanal skills and a consistent governing and military structure which triumphed over the neighbouring populations, among them the kingdoms of Nubia. They developed commercial relations along the river, and exported towards the south bronze manufactures and other products. They also invented their own writing. They drew hieroglyphs on papyrus, which evolved and became partly alphabetical.

[11] Women had a significant role in Egyptian civilization. The mother figure was foremost in their culture. There was also a female clergy. Landed property was inherited by women, and a dowry was given to the parents of the wife. Their imposing works of art had a profound religious inspiration. Their worldview did not underline the value of progress but rather of equilibrium and peace in opposition to the forces of decay and chaos.

[12] In the centuries immediately before and after the first century AD, migration and mingling took place among the peoples established south of the Sahara. Several languages were born then, and achievements include an indigenous iron culture which had a revolutionary impact. Iron was abundant in the region. The making of iron tools augmented the productive abilities and the military capabilities of those peoples, and allowed their expansion and their subjugation of less advanced groups. Ironsmiths and craftspeople gained the uppermost positions in these societies. This is the origin of a tradition which recognizes the king-smiths as the African ancestors. From the point of view of social organization, this era represents the passage from clan organization to the formation of kingdoms.

[13] Between the 7th and the 12th Centuries the majority of the bigger African kingdoms were founded. The Arab-Muslim conquest of North Africa began in the 7th Century. From then on commerce through the Sahara became easier, as did commerce from the coasts towards the kingdoms of sub-Saharan Africa. The Arabs acted as intermediaries.

[14] The empires of Ghana and Awdaghost to the west, and those of Nubia and Aksum to the north-east dominated several other kingdoms and won territories rich in gold mines. Thanks to the commerce in gold and slaves, they acquired considerable economic power. They created cities as market centres for agricultural products and cattle. Courts headed by black kings admitted civilian councils which, more frequently than not, included Muslim ministers, because of their technical competence. Powerful armies were organized for campaigns of expansion which led either to success, or the decline of those kingdoms.

[15] Today it is recognized that the period between the 12th and the 16th centuries were the 'great centuries' of Black Africa. African countries reached well-balanced positions, were socio-politically well integrated and developed strong economies. The strongest were the empires of Mali, which at the time of Mahmud Ali had 400 cities in what is now west Sudan; the states of Hausa, Yoruba and Benin, respectively towards the south-east and the south-west of Nigeria; the Bantu Kingdom and the Kongo in Central Africa; and the Zimbabwe and Monomotapa in the South.

[16] These empires derived revenue from taxes on harvests and cattle, from tributes, customs houses, gold nuggets (which were by law the property of the government), and war booty. They integrated politically different peoples through a government compounded of high officers whose competence was either functional - such as the ministers - or territorial - the chiefs who controlled the provinces - and whose mandates were revocable, not hereditary. Almost all of them had professional armies. Their lands were worked by peasants, compelled to pay a tribute, and by slaves. There was a distinction between war slaves and house slaves, who respectively served in the court and in households, and who had certain civil rights, and were eligible for eventual emancipation. But in some communities and ethnic groups, such as those of Equatorial Africa, there were no slaves.

[17] Sometimes, as in Timbuktu, cities had centres of religious studies which evolved into universities of sorts. The empires fostered art and architecture, such as the prodigious buildings of Great Zimbabwe, which were heard about in Europe through reports by the Portuguese colonists.

[18] From the 16th century onwards the independent life of the African empires began to be eroded. The Muslim states were not happy with being mere intermediaries anymore, and they launched expansionist policies which demolished the inner empires. In this they were gradually replaced by the Europeans who, after initial exploration, organized slave traffic in order to satisfy the needs of the New World for cheap manual labour. The slave trade was organized from coastal stations and involved a total of some 10-15 million slaves. Some African kings and leaders collaborated.

[19] The economic involvement of Europe was not limited to the slave trade. An economy based on the export of grain was developed, but it did not include, at least at the beginning, direct political control, or the loss of sovereignty on the part of the African states.

[20] These decisive historical changes entrenched a situation of general dependency and contributed to the later underdevelopment of Africa. In the 20 years between 1890 and 1910, the European powers conquered, occupied and finally subjugated a continent whose territory (or rather 80 per cent of it) had been previously governed by autonomous leaders. Most of them resisted this imposition in order to defend their sovereignty and independence, their religions, and their traditional lifestyles.

[21] Despite this resistance, colonization destroyed the social and cultural balance of subjugated countries and established relationships of dependence. European capital and a world economy robbed African peoples of their resources through mining firms, commercial and financial institutions, compelling them to work for European development.

[22] However, these cultures did not disappear. Today, African traditions have not only helped to shape the culture of the European countries which once subjugated them, but also have seen a renaissance in their own native soil over the last years. ∎

Spain

España

Population: 39,633,000 (1999)
Area: 504,780 SQ KM
Capital: Madrid
Currency: Peseta
Language: Spanish

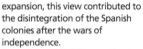

Between the 9th and the 8th century BC Celtic peoples started to settle in the center and west of the Iberian peninsula. Later, during the 6th and 5th centuries BC, the Iberian culture developed in the south of the peninsula. The fusion of these two cultures gave rise to what is known as the Celt-Iberian peoples. The peninsula was colonized by the Phoenicians, the Greeks, and the Romans in succession.

[2] The fall of the Roman Empire coincided with the spread of Christianity and, more importantly, with the invasion of the northern peoples who raided Europe. The Iberian peninsula was occupied by the Visigoths who ruled over the area for 300 years.

[3] In 700 AD the peninsula was invaded by Arabs who defeated Rodrigo, the last Visigoth king, thus starting a period of Muslim domination. The descendants of the Visigoths lived in the north of the territory and set up kingdoms like Castille, Catalonia, Navarre, Aragon, Leon and Portugal. Over the centuries they underwent a slow unification process, which consolidated when they started fighting against the Arabs.

[4] The Arabs called the lands in the south of the Iberian peninsula Al-Andalus, a region that reached its peak during the 10th century. In contrast with the rest of impoverished rural Europe, its cities - and Cordoba in particular - prospered through active trade with the East. Religious tolerance enabled Muslims, Jews, and Christians to live side by side, and science, medicine, and philosophy developed. Copies and translations of the Greek classics were made, paving the way for the 15th century European Renaissance.

[5] In 1492, a triple process of national unification took place in Spain, through the marriage of Isabel of Castille and Fernando of Aragon, the expulsion of the Moors, and the conquest and subsequent colonization of the new American territories. The unification of the country's political power and the creation of the Kingdom of Spain were carried out at the expense of the Jews (and members of other cultures) who were expelled from Spain after having lived there for many centuries. Both the Inquisition and centralized power were institutionalized under the new system, while the new American colonies supplied precious metals, sustaining three centuries of economic bonanza. The indigenous people in America had Christianity imposed upon them by the Crown,

and the exploitation they were subject to through forced labor was responsible for decimating many of their populations.

[6] The economic prosperity provided by the colonies was reflected in a period of great cultural development in Spain. Literature in particular developed extensively during the 16th and 17th centuries, which were dubbed the Spanish Golden Age. Portugal was joined to the Spanish Kingdom for the period 1580-1688.

[7] In the 18th century, the Bourbons came to the Spanish throne. They reorganized domestic and colonial administration, ruling in accordance with the principles of Enlightenment, as the liberal ideas of the French Revolution spread throughout Europe and America. Combined with Napoleonic

expansion, this view contributed to the disintegration of the Spanish colonies after the wars of independence.

[8] At the end of the Napoleonic era, there was great conflict between the liberal sectors seeking political and economic modernization, and the absolutists who wished to preserve the traditional order. The disputes between groups weakened the power of the Empire, making way for revolutions in Spanish America.

[9] By the end of the 19th century Spain had renounced its last American territories and had come to terms with the loss of its privileges.

[10] At the beginning of the 20th century, Spain was plunged into a deep political, social, and economic crisis, exacerbated by World War I. Within an atmosphere of extreme polarization, Primo de Rivera's dictatorship which resulted from the 1923 coup attempted to halt any further increase in demands from workers or regional groups seeking autonomy. The dictatorship, closely resembling the Italian fascist model, retained power until 1931. Its eventual loss of power was a result of existing contradictions within the Church, the armed forces and industry, who were all fascist supporters, and not to the continuous opposition from political and labor organizations. The end of the dictatorship marked the end of the monarchy, and the dawn of a new republican era.

[11] The 'Second Republic' was born in the midst of a series of extremely complex political and economic difficulties. In 1936, after two moderate governments, the People's Front, formed with socialists, republicans, communists and anarchists, gained a narrow electoral triumph, causing much friction with their political opponents.

[12] Immediately after the elections, the army, the Church, and powerful sectors of the Spanish economy started to plot to overthrow the Government. The deep contradictions within the Front and the incessant opposition led to the rise of an important faction of the army, led by Francisco Franco, which provoked the Spanish Civil War lasting for three years. The republican government waited in vain for assistance from the European democracies, but they

WORKERS

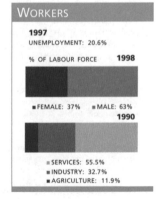

1997
UNEMPLOYMENT: 20.6%

% OF LABOUR FORCE **1998**

■ FEMALE: 37% ■ MALE: 63%

1990

■ SERVICES: 55.5%
■ INDUSTRY: 32.7%
■ AGRICULTURE: 11.9%

LAND USE

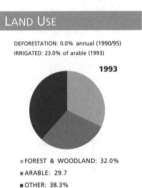

DEFORESTATION: 0.0% annual (1990/95)
IRRIGATED: 23.0% of arable (1993)

1993

■ FOREST & WOODLAND: 32.0%
■ ARABLE: 29.7
■ OTHER: 38.3%

PUBLIC EXPENDITURE

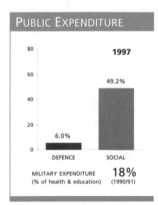

1997

49.2%

6.0%

DEFENCE   SOCIAL

MILITARY EXPENDITURE **18%**
(% of health & education) (1990/91)

had decided not to intervene in the conflict. The Soviet Union was the only state which provided material support to the republican government, while a large number of volunteers from America and Europe also joined the republican army.

[13] Franco won in March 1939, assisted by internal divisions within the republican forces, the military superiority of the troops loyal to him, and German and Italian support.

[14] When the civil war ended, Franco became head of the new state. He set up an authoritarian regime along fascist lines, with a corporatist state, a personality cult, and extreme nationalism. Franco ruled over a deeply divided society and an economy that had been virtually devastated by the civil war.

[15] From the beginning of the Cold War, the US tried to secure Spanish support and Spain became a member of the United Nations in 1955, confirming a change in Franco's foreign policy, which was becoming preoccupied with improving the international image.

[16] In the 1960s, Franco opened parliament to other groups and movements. During those years key figures of the Opus Dei, an ultra-conservative Catholic movement, occupied important posts in government and changed the country's economic policies.

[17] Spain rid itself of economic isolation and liberalized its economy by eliminating many mechanisms of state control. The urban middle classes enjoyed a substantial improvement in their standard of living, which allowed a significant political relaxation. However, the peasants were still extremely poor and many emigrated to the major Spanish and European cities.

[18] Franco died in 1975, and power was handed to his successor, the heir to the Spanish throne, Juan Carlos I of Bourbon. The new monarch immediately started negotiations with the political opposition to re-establish the democratic system overthrown in 1939.

[19] Between 1976 and 1981 Adolfo Suarez, the leader of the Center Democratic Union (UCD), was Prime Minister. In December 1978 during his term in office, a plebiscite was held which turned Spain into a parliamentary monarchy, re-establishing political freedom, and guaranteeing the right of autonomy to some Spanish regions. Several politicians, intellectuals, and artists were able to return to the country after up to 40 years in exile.

[20] In February 1981, a group of Civil Guard officers took the Cortes (parliament) by force. The firm reaction of all the democratic political groups and in particular of King Juan Carlos, who had the support of the army, guaranteed the failure of the coup and the consolidation of the democratization process.

[21] The Spanish Socialist Workers' Party (PSOE) won the October 1982 elections, with a solid majority in the Cortes. Felipe González became President of the Government, the equivalent of Prime Minister in other countries. He was subsequently re-elected in 1988 and 1993.

[22] Despite some setbacks, the parliamentary majority of the PSOE was able to enforce an ambitious adjustment and growth plan which deeply transformed the Spanish economy and gave vast social sectors access to unprecedented levels of consumption. However, this modernization resulted in high unemployment and tensions which led to a split between the Government and the UGT, the trade union which had supported the PSOE.

[23] ETA, the Basque separatist group which many times has used violent means to achieve its political goals, suffered serious setbacks in 1993. Co-operation between French and Spanish security forces led to the arrest of some of its leaders, and the discovery in Bayonne, France, of the organization's main weapons deposit.

[24] The Spanish Government was active in international affairs, joining the European Economic Community and NATO in 1986. Membership of NATO had been opposed by the PSOE while it was in opposition, but once in power the party defended the decision and confirmed it through consultation with the people.

[25] Spain has a long-standing dispute with Britain over the possession of Gibraltar, which has been under British control since 1704. Spain maintains control of Ceuta and Melilla, which are claimed by Morocco.

[26] In 1990, Felipe Gonzalez' government started negotiations with the US to reduce US military presence in Spain. Despite the agreements, some of the B-52 bombers that raided Iraqi territory during the Gulf War took off from the US air bases in Spain.

[27] In 1992 Spain spent $10 billion on the celebration to mark the 500 years since the conquest of Latin America. At the same time the country made political moves towards Europe. The demands of the European policy resulted in a weakening of Spain's traditional links with Latin America.

[28] The moves to align the country with European standards led the Government to cut defence and public spending, and subsidies for the industrial sector. In November, Parliament ratified the Maastricht treaty. The legal proposal to facilitate the dismissal and redeployment of workers caused a general strike in January 1994, but the measure was approved anyway with the argument that it was necessary to make the nation competitive. Unemployment reached 22 per cent, the highest in the European Union.

[29] Many of the Socialist Party leaders were implicated in fraud investigations. The former governor of the Bank of Spain was imprisoned along with the former director of the Madrid Exchange Reserve, and the financier Mario Conde, who had supervised the sale of the Spanish Credit Bank (Banesto).

[30] Due to the numerous scandals, the Socialist Government lost a key part of its parliamentary support in 1995. The Catalan nationalist group Convergence and Union withdrew their support in July and voted in the budget with the right-wing

PROFILE

ENVIRONMENT

Spain comprises 82 per cent of the Iberian Peninsula and includes the Balearic and Canary Islands. The center of the country is a plateau which rises to the Pyrenees in the north, forming a natural border with France. The Betica mountain ranges extend to the South. Inland the Central Sierras separate the plateaus of Nueva and Vieja Castilla. In the Ebro River basin, to the north, lie the prairies of Cataluña, Valencia, and Murcia, and the Guadalquivir River basin, to the south, forms the plains of Andalucía. The climate is moderate and humid in the north and northwest, where there are many woodlands. In the interior, the climate is dry in the south and east. 40 per cent of the land is arable. Approximately 5 per cent of the total land area is under environmental protection. Natural resources include coal, some oil and natural gas, uranium and mercury. Industry is concentrated in Cataluña and the Basque Provinces. Per capita emissions of air and water pollutants exceed Western European averages. Since 1970, the use of nitrogen fertilizers has doubled. Nitrate concentrations in the Guadalquivir River are 25 per cent above 1975 levels. The percentage of the population serviced by sewage systems rose from 14 per cent in 1975, to 48 per cent in the late 1980s. This fact, together with industrial wastes from oil refining plants and natural gas production, has raised the level of pollution of the Mediterranean. The Government has implemented a reforestation program to increase production of timber and prevent further erosion. Many seedlings have been lost in recent years to forest fires. An additional problem is the fact that the large-scale planting of single species, such as eucalyptus, does not take bio-diversity into account. Approximately 22 per cent of Spain's forests have suffered some degree of defoliation.

SOCIETY

Peoples: Castillians, Asturians, Andalucians and Valencians, Catalans, Basques and Galicians, descended from a fusion of the Iberian people of the Mediterranean, the Celts of Central Europe and the Arabs of North Africa.
Religion: Catholicism is the religion of the vast majority of the Spanish people (95.2 per cent). Muslims 1.2 per cent.
Languages: Spanish or Castillian (official national); there are also official regional languages, such as Basque, Catalan, Valencian IS THAT CORRECT? and Galician.
Political Parties: Peoples' Party, rightist. Spanish Socialist Workers' Party (PSOE); United Left; Convergence and Union; Basque Nationalist Party, as well as other regionalist parties.
Social Organizations: There are several national workers' organizations: the General Union of Workers (socialist tendency); the Workers' Commissions (communist tendency); the National Confederation of Labor (anarchist tendency); the Workers' Trade Union (of social democratic tendency).

THE STATE

Official Name: Estado Español.
Administrative Divisions: Spain is divided into 17 autonomous regions: the Basque Country, Catalonia, Galicia, Andalucia, the Principality of Asturias, Cantabria, La Rioja, Murcia, Valencia, Aragon, Castilla, La Mancha, the Canaries, Navarre, Extremadura, the Balearic Islands, Madrid and Castilla León. Each one has its own institutional system, a local leader in executive power and a unicameral legislative.
Capital: Madrid 6,261,000 people (1998).
Other cities: Barcelona, 4,000,000 people (1994); Valencia 777,427; Seville 704,857; Zaragoza 622,371 (1996).
Government: Hereditary monarchy, with King Juan Carlos I de Borbon y Borbon as Head of State. Prime Minister: José María Aznar since April 1996; re-elected in March 2000. The parliament, las Cortes, consists of two bodies: the Senate, with 255 members, and the Chamber of Deputies with 350 members elected by proportional representation.
National Holiday: October 12
Armed Forces: 206,000 (1995). Other: Guardia Civil: 66,000 (3,000 conscripts); Guardia del Mar: 340.

People's Party (PP). Whilst defending his action and that of his government, Gonzalez moved the elections forward a year.

[31] The imminent electoral success of the Right led ETA to change its strategy. In January they assassinated the PP leader in the province of Guipuzcoa, and in April tried to kill the PP candidate for Prime Minister, Jose Maria Aznar. In the May regional elections, the PP comfortably won 10 of the 13 areas at stake.

[32] A former security chief and a socialist official were tried for their connections with the anti-terrorist Liberation Groups (GALs), which legal investigations had linked to the security forces. One of them told the Court that Felipe Gonzalez had been responsible for the GALs, which had killed 27 people on the frontier with France in the so-called 'dirty war' against ETA. A former interior minister was also investigated for paying French officials to collaborate in the persecution of the Basque separatists.

[33] Fishing conflicts set Spain at odds with Canada and Morocco. Both ended with the European Union mediating in agreements limiting their action in the territorial waters of the other nations. Spain took over the presidency of the European Union from July 1 1995, and held several international summits. The opposition, however, questioned the government's ability to fulfil the necessary requirements for integration to European Monetary Union planned for 1997.

[34] The People's Party won the March 1996 parliamentary elections with 38.9 per cent of the vote. The PSOE came second with 37.5 per cent. The IU (Izquierda Unida, United Left) took 10.6 per cent. On April 5, PP leader José Maria Aznar became Prime Minister.

[35] At an international level, the Aznar administration decided to bolster Cuba's isolation, by proposing that the EU impose sanctions on the island, and suspending the loans Spain had promised to the Castro Government.

[36] In August 1997, ETA kidnapped and murdered Miguel Angel Blanco, PP supporter and councillor of a small town in the Basque Country. This unleashed immediate protests throughout the country.

The Government and the opposition, excluding the Herri Batasuna (HB) political group linked to ETA, signed an agreement against violence, while millions of people marched on the streets to condemn the murder. The demonstrations were attended by more people than at any other Spanish political event in the second half of the century.

[37] On December 1 1997, the Spanish Supreme Court sentenced 23 HB leaders to seven years in prison for 'collaborating' in the broadcast of an ETA television commercial during the electoral campaign in 1996. In early 1998, new trials were begun against former Socialist ministers José Barrionuevo and Rafael Vera, for their supposed connections to the GAL.

[38] ETA declared a cease-fire on September 1998. The HB used the name Heuskal Herittarok and adopted new ways of representation among the voters during the Basque elections. All Basque nationalist sectors, including the Basque National Party and former members of the Herri Batasuna party, signed the Estrella Pact, an alliance of Basque parties that achieved the objective of making 'Basques govern themselves' after winning the 1999 local elections.

[39] The Constitutional Court released 23 members of HB in July 1999. This was interpreted as a step forward towards the consolidation of the truce since it was one of the main demands of the terrorists in order to engage in conversations with the authorities. But ETA resumed its armed actions in September - setting off various bombs and killing three people - breaking the Estrella Pact.

[40] More than 100,000 police and civil guards were mobilized in March 2000 to prevent disruptions during the election which was carried out without incident. Euskal Eritarrok had called for people to abstain from voting but the abstention rate was less than the 12 per cent which traditionally supports the Basque political force.

[41] Unemployment reduction brought about by the economic measures of the Aznar Government and Spain's adoption of the single European currency (the Euro) explained the support for the PP in the surveys prior to the elections. The result was surprising nevertheless since the PP won an absolute majority in Parliament which enabled it to rule without the need of coalitions. The left-of-center opposition controlled by the PSOE found its parliamentary participation slashed from 141 to 125 seats, one of the lowest ever. The leader of the PSOE, Joaquín Almunia, resigned his post to force fundamental change in the Socialist Party. ∎

Gibraltar

Population: 28,000 (1998)
Area: 10 SQ KM
Capital: Gibraltar
Currency: Gibraltar pound
Language: English and Spanish

Peninsula on the southern coast of Spain, only 32 km from Morocco, Gibraltar's strategic position allows it to control maritime trade between the Mediterranean and the Atlantic ocean.

[2] Gibraltar was occupied by England in 1704 and ceded by Spain in 1714, following the Treaty of Utretcht. Since 1964 Spain has tried to regain political control of the area. In 1967, a plebiscite opted for continued colonial dependency. In 1968 the UN voted in favor of the Spanish re-incorporation of Gibraltar. Since 1972, the two countries have started negotiations several times, but no significant progress has yet been made.

PROFILE

Peoples: Most of the permanent population is of British origin. The non-permanent population are mainly Spanish workers. **Religions:** Anglican and Catholic. **Languages:** English (official) and Spanish. **Official Name:** Gibraltar. **Government:** Non-autonomous territory, subject to UN control. **Administrative power:** United Kingdom. General Governor named by the British crown: Admiral Sir Richard Luce, since February 1997. Chief minister: Peter Caruana, since 17 May 1996, appointed by the 15-member advisory council. In the council's last election, held in May 1996, the Social Democrat Party obtained 53 per cent of the vote, while the second political force, the Socialist Labor Party, was supported by 42 per cent of the electorate. Britain has made Gibraltarian independence dependent upon an agreement with Spain. In September 1996, the NATO Headquarters acknowledged that in the future the military control over the peninsula would be exercised by Spain. **Population:** 28,000 (1998)

Sri Lanka

Sri Lanka

Population: 18,639,000 (1999)
Area: 65,610 SQ KM
Capital: Colombo
Currency: Rupee
Language: Sinhalese

The island of Ceylon was populated by the Vedda in ancient times, it was then successively invaded by the Sinhalese, Indo-Europeans and Tamils, who laid the foundations of an advanced civilization. When the Portuguese arrived in 1505, the island was divided into seven autonomous local societies.

² The Dutch expelled the Portuguese from their coastal trading posts 150 years later, but it was the British - who had already taken possession of neighboring India - who finally made the island a colony in 1796. Even then, it took them until 1815 to subdue all the local governments who fought hard to remain autonomous. The British then introduced new export crops such as coffee and tea - products which gave Ceylon a worldwide reputation because of their excellent quality.

³ In the 20th century, a strong nationalist movement developed. In 1948, Ceylon became independent and joined the British Commonwealth. Under the leadership of Sir John Kotelawala and Prime Minister Bandaranaike, the country pursued a vigorous anti-colonial foreign policy. In August 1954, Bandaranaike met in Colombo with India's Nehru, Muhammad Ali of Pakistan, U Nu of Burma and Indonesia's Sastroamidjojo. The meeting was of great political importance as it led to the 1955 summit conference of Afro-Asian countries in Bandung, heralding the Movement of Non-Aligned Countries.

⁴ In the late 1950s, the Tamil minority staged a series of secessionist uprisings and in September 1959 the Prime Minister was assassinated. His widow Sirimavo Bandaranaike led the Sri Lanka Freedom Party to electoral victory at the beginning of 1960, although she had no previous political experience. She became the first woman in the world to head a government. Governing in coalition with the Communist and Trotskyist parties, in 1962 she nationalized various US oil and other companies. In 1965, she was defeated by a right-wing coalition but regained power in 1970, in a landslide election victory.

⁵ She was faced with a 'Guevarist' (after Che Guevara) guerrilla uprising which she then had forcibly crushed. She never gave up her anti-imperialist stand and in 1972 declared Sri Lanka a republic, cutting all ties with the British Commonwealth

⁶ A land reform program nationalized British-owned plantations but had little effect on the standard of living of the bulk of the rural population.

⁷ Conflict between the Sinhalese majority and the Tamil minority, descended from the Dravidians of South India, has persisted throughout most of the island's history. The Sinhalese account for 74 per cent of the country's population, while the Tamils comprise 22 per cent and are divided into two groups: the Sri Lankan Tamils and the Indian Tamils. The Sri Lankan Tamils reached the island approximately 2,000 years ago and settled principally in the northern and eastern provinces, while the Indian Tamils are more recent immigrants. Both groups possess common ethnic characteristics and seek regional autonomy or even the formation of a separate Tamil nation. The Tamil United Liberation Front (TULF) founded on May 4 1972, resulted from the fusion of three Tamil parties: the Federal Party, the Tamil Congress and the pro-Indian Ceylon Workers Congress.

⁸ Bandaranaike's main achievement was probably her appointment as president of the Non-Aligned Movement in 1976, at the Conference in Colombo. However, accusations of nepotism, and reaction from the country's intellectuals to the censorship of the press and to emergency measures in force since 1971, caused Bandaranaike to lose the July 1977 election.

⁹ The United National Party, led by Junius Jayewardene, won a comfortable parliamentary majority, with the Tamil Liberation Front coming second. In spite of his socialist leanings, the new prime minister's economic policy exposed the country to transnational capital.

¹⁰ A constitutional reform in 1978 made Jayewardene Sri Lanka's first president. In November 1980, a series of International Monetary Fund (IMF)-approved economic measures began to be applied, with disastrous consequences for the country. A month earlier, Bandaranaike had been expelled from Parliament and deprived of her political rights for seven years. A presidential commission had found her guilty of 'abuse of authority' during her coalition government, between 1970 and July 1977.

¹¹ An IMF package of measures went into effect. There was a general strike against these and the new economic policy, and 44,000 civil servants lost their jobs in the summer of 1980. In 1981 the Government received substantial US aid, supplied with the alleged purpose of stabilizing the region. The same argument was used to justify increasingly frequent visits by US naval ships to the port of Colombo.

¹² Sri Lanka's first presidential election in October 1982, gave Jayewardene a clear victory, with 52.5 per cent of the vote. His campaign was backed by the state apparatus and benefited from the division and internal strife of the Freedom Party. In some parts of the country, the political upheaval meant that elections had to be held under state of emergency conditions.

¹³ The project to turn Sri Lanka into an export center like Hong Kong or Taiwan led to the creation of a free zone in Latunyabe where foreign investment has increased since 1978.

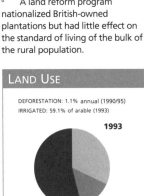

WORKERS

1996
UNEMPLOYMENT: 11.3%

% OF LABOUR FORCE **1998**

■ FEMALE: 36%   ■ MALE: 64%

1990

■ SERVICES: 30.6%
■ INDUSTRY: 20.9%
■ AGRICULTURE: 48.5%

LAND USE

DEFORESTATION: 1.1% annual (1990/95)
IRRIGATED: 59.1% of arable (1993)

1993

■ FOREST & WOODLAND: 32.0%
■ ARABLE: 14.2%
■ OTHER: 53.8%

PUBLIC EXPENDITURE

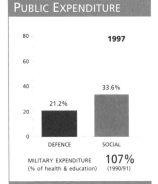

1997

21.2% DEFENCE
33.6% SOCIAL

MILITARY EXPENDITURE **107%**
(% of health & education) (1990/91)

[14] In early 1982, in spite of earlier denials and the Government's outspoken commitment to non-alignment, the US Navy was granted permission to use Sri Lanka's refuelling facilities in Trincomalee, a vital spot linking eastern and western sea routes through the Suez Canal.

[15] Early in 1983, ethnic conflict worsened. It reached crisis point in July and August, leaving hundreds dead and wounded and thousands more homeless. More than 40,000 Sri Lankan Tamils fleeing the conflict sought refuge in Tamil Nadu. President Jayewardene's refusal to negotiate with the Tamil minority led the Indian Government to withdraw its attempts at mediation.

[16] In 1984, Jayewardene made overtures toward the Israeli Government which had offered him help to bring the rebel minorities under control. A diplomatic mission was set up in Colombo with the support of the US embassy. However, Secretary of State Douglas Liyanage was forced to resign in September 1984, after violent demonstrations following a government visit to Tel Aviv. The protesters were mainly from the Muslim community.

[17] The ethnic war became more bitter during 1985, discouraging foreign investors. However tourism remains one of the main sources of income of this 'fiscal paradise'.

PROFILE

ENVIRONMENT

An island in the Indian Ocean, southeast of India, separated from the continent by the Palk Channel. The land is flat, except for a central mountainous region. These mountains divide the island into two distinct regions and also block the monsoon winds which are responsible for the tropical climate. The southwest area receives abundant rainfall, and the remainder of the island is drier. Large tea plantations cover the southern mountain slopes, and other major crops are rice, for domestic consumption, and rubber, coconuts and cocoa, for export. Deforestation and soil erosion are important environmental problems. Likewise, air pollution is on the increase, due to industrial gas emissions.

SOCIETY

Peoples: 82.7 per cent of Sri Lankans are Sinhalese; Tamils are the largest minority group, 8.9 per cent, and there is a small Arab minority (7.7 per cent).
Religions: 69 per cent Buddhist; 15 per cent Hindu; 8 per cent Christian; 7 per cent Muslim; and 1 per cent other religions.
Languages Sinhalese (official). Also Tamil and English.
Political Parties: The United National Party (Siri Kotha; the Sri Lanka Freedom Party; the United Democratic National Front; the Tamil United Liberation Front (TULF); the Communist Party; the Equal Society Party (Lanka Sama Samaja); the People's Democratic Party (Mahajana Prajathantra); the People's Liberation Front (Janata Vimuktui Peramuna); and the Popular Alliance coalition.
Social Organizations: Workers' Congress; Trade Union Federation; Trade Union Council; the Labor Federation.

THE STATE

Official Name: Sri Lanka Prajathanthrika Samajavadi Janarajaya.
Administrative Divisions: 9 Provinces, 24 Districts.
Capital Colombo 3,620,000 people (est 1995).
Other cities Dehiwala-Mount Lavinia 196,000 people; Moratuwa 170,000; Jaffna 151,000; Kandy 122,000 (1994).
Government: Chandrika Kumaratunga Bandaranaike, President and Head of State since November 1994, re-elected in December 1999. Sirimavo Bandaranaike, Prime Minister since 1994. Unicameral Parliament with 225 members.
National Holiday: February 4, Independence Day (1948).
Armed Forces: 126,000 (1994)
Other: 70,000 Police Force, National Guard, Private Guard.

[18] Peace talks between the Tamils and Sinhalese took place throughout 1986. The efforts included a meeting of the leaders of seven southeast Asian countries in Bangalore, India, all of whom were concerned about the civil war that had shaken Sri Lanka.

[19] In late July 1987, presidents Rajiv Gandhi (of India) and Junius Jayewardene finally signed an accord in Colombo granting a certain autonomy to the Tamil minority of the northern and eastern provinces of Sri Lanka. The accord provided for the merger of the two provinces under a single government, and gave Tamil the status of a national language. India guaranteed the agreement and sent troops - the India Peace Keeping Force - to ensure that its terms were complied with. These terms were to be ratified by the parliaments of India and Sri Lanka, and approved by the main guerrilla group, the Liberation Tigers of Tamil Eelam (LTTE) known as the Tamil Tigers.

[20] These efforts did not succeed in pacifying the country, and the Indian military presence - far from guaranteeing peace - became a further cause for irritation and renewed confrontations. Inter-ethnic violence worsened as the Tamil Tigers rejected the 1987 accords.

[21] In November 1988, the official party's hold on power was ratified by 50.4 per cent of the votes. Jayewardene, at the age of 82, ceded his post to the former prime minister Ranasinghe Premadasa. Political violence was so pervasive that only 53 per cent of the electorate actually went to the polling stations to vote. Elections were boycotted, by both the Tamil guerrillas and the Popular Liberation Front (made up of Sinhalese who were violently opposed to any kind of concessions to ethnic minorities). Political opposition to the Government increased, partly fuelled by a strong student movement which was eventually harshly repressed in early 1989.

[22] In early 1990, the Indian Government withdrew the last of its 60,000 peacekeeping force, which had been stationed in Sri Lanka since 1987. More than 1,000 troops had died on the island. Amnesty International announced that, in 1990, the Government had killed thousands of civilians in the region.

[23] In May 1991, the Tamil Tigers were accused of murdering Rajiv Gandhi in a suicide mission. Rajiv had become an enemy of the Tigers after the Indian peace forces in Sri Lanka had attacked the rebels. The Tigers denied any involvement in the attempt. Their guerrilla group was considered the most efficient and best armed in the world. It was financed by expatriate Tamils who make annual donations of millions of dollars. The guerrilla leader, Velupillai Prabhakaran, had his general headquarters in the north of the country, hidden in the jungle.

[24] The next phase of the war against the Tigers started in June 1991, when they broke off talks with the Government after 13 months. Since then, thousands more people have died in combat, and many civilians have taken refuge in the south or in India. In August, according to official estimates, over 2,000 guerrillas and 170 Sri Lankan soldiers died in an attack on the strategic Elephant Pass which was under government control.

[25] In spite of the war, the country was visited by some 300,000 tourists in 1990. In some western countries the island is promoted for its countless brothels. The number of prostitutes in the capital is put at 50,000, with over 10,000 young boys and girls in the business. One reason for the extremely high number is that half of the population in the country live in extreme poverty.

[26] Nearly two decades after the large tea plantations were nationalized, the Government decided to hand management over to private companies, while maintaining state ownership. It was estimated that the state companies which managed these plantations, employing over 400,000 people (mostly Tamil), had accumulated debts of $128.1 million by the end of 1989. Agriculture was the main source of revenue, with 36.3 per cent of the exports coming from tea, rubber, and coconuts at this time.

[27] In August 1991, President Premadasa, who had been accused of violating the constitution and other crimes - such as treason, embezzlement, corruption, abuse of power, and moral depravity - suspended parliamentary sessions to avoid being censured. He also faced major confrontations within his party and the hostility of the opposition, led by Sirimavo Bandaranaike, who demanded democratization and the end of the presidential system.

[28] In negotiations observed by the UN, LTTE supremo Velupillai Prabhakaran declared his desire for a peaceful end to the conflict in February 1992. Prabhakaran stated that he wanted an agreement based on the recognition of a

degree of autonomy for the northern and eastern provinces, where most of the Tamils live. President Premadasa expressed an interest in the proposed solution.

[29] A year later, Prabhakaran expressed his willingness to accept a negotiated settlement to resolve the federalist issue. The Government rejected his request for a lifting of the economic blockade of the Tamil region of Jaffna (decreed in February 1992 and subsequently extended in January 1993). However, Parliament began discussing the terms of such an agreement.

[30] The issue of human rights violations by both sides complicated the negotiations. In October 1992, the Tamil Tigers had massacred 170 Muslims in the village of Polonnarua, in the northeastern part of the country. The following month, a car-bomb had killed a high-ranking naval officer in Colombo. In April 1993, the Government required that all property owners in the capital provide a list of tenants, as a way of monitoring activist movement. That same month former cabinet minister Lalith Athulathmudali, president of the United National Democratic Front (split from the UNP in 1991) was assassinated.

[31] On May 1 1993, during the Labor Day parade in Colombo, President Premadasa was assassinated by a suicide attacker, who threw himself upon the presidential entourage with a bomb tied to his body. The Government accused the Tamil separatists of carrying out the assassination, but spokespersons for the rebels denied responsibility for the attack. Thousands of Tamils fled the capital, fearing government reprisals.

[32] On May 7, Prime Minister Dingiri Banda Wijetunge was named president. Wijetunge promised to continue the political agenda established by his predecessor. A few days later, police identified the presidential assassin as a Tamil from Jaffna.

[33] In the November 1994 presidential elections, the Popular Alliance candidate Chandrika Bandaranaike Kumaratunga won with 63 per cent of the vote. Kumaratunga had been appointed Prime Minister following the parliamentary elections in August and now became the first woman president of Sri Lanka. Her mother, Sirimavo Bandaranaike succeeded her as Prime Minister.

[34] The Government and the Tigers agreed to start negotiations in January 1995, but the pact was broken by the Tamils. The guerrillas initiated a new series of attacks against government forces in April.

[35] Kumaratunga presented a plan for state reform in August. The proposal, supported by the Tamil parliamentarians, included transforming Sri Lanka into a federation of eight regions. The central government was to keep control over defense, foreign relations and international economic relations.

[36] This project required the support of two-thirds of Parliament followed by approval by referendum before it could come into action. The negotiations between the various parties were slow and the increasing military action prevented it being completed.

[37] The city of Jaffna, on the peninsula of the same name, was at the center of the fighting from October 1995. Government forces occupied the city on December 5. Only 400 of the 140,000 people who lived there stayed throughout the fighting. By mid-1996, half the peninsula's Tamil population had returned to their homes.

[38] An attack on the Central Bank in downtown Colombo killed 84 people in February 1996. This led to fears of more widespread inter-ethnic conflict. The Tigers' attacks continued in the streets and trains of Colombo.

[39] In early 1997, the Tigers destroyed an army garrison in Paranthan, in the north of the country. All the military personnel - an estimated 1,200 troops - were killed. Government forces' land and air reprisals led to great losses for the LTTE.

[40] In May, the army deployed some 20,000 troops in the biggest offensive since the outbreak of war. The government forces were able to capture strategic positions and roads, pushing the guerrilla into the jungle. The LTTE responded with a series of bomb attacks in the main tourist centers.

[41] The government offensive destroyed of a large proportion of Sri Lanka's paddy fields, affecting international rice prices and forcing the country to start importing rice. The social situation on the island worsened during the years of conflict. One example of this was the number of very young people involved in prostitution. According to United Nations estimates, around two thirds of all prostitutes were under the age of consent.

[42] The Government offered to suspend the military offensive and discuss proposals to increase the autonomy of regional councils administered by Tamils and Muslims. However, it continued to demand the surrender of the LTTE as a pre-condition for negotiations, something the guerrillas considered unacceptable. In April, the Government and the main opposition group, the United National Party, agreed to form a united front in any negotiations with the LTTE.

[43] Despite efforts at mediation, the civil war worsened in March 1998, with dozens killed on both sides. In April, the Government promised to publish the result of investigations into the disappearance of some 700 people reported in Jaffna. At that time an estimated 50,000 people had died since the war broke out.

[44] Government troops carried out a major offensive in December 1998, forcing the Tamil United Liberation Front (TULF) to retreat to inhospitable areas and abandon several Northern cities.

[45] Clashes between government troops and Tamil rebels intensified during the last quarter of 1999. The TULF took control of the important Northern city of Oddusudan in November, from which it had had to withdraw during the December 1998 government offensive.

[46] In December, President Chandrika Kumaratunga was reelected for a new term, just four days after escaping an assassination attempt. She beat her main rival, Ranil Wickremesinghe, from the UNP, by eight points. The high turnout (70 per cent of 11.5 million registered) surprised political analysts who expected a higher level of abstention due to the TULF attacks days before the election which had caused 33 dead and more than 130 injured – one of them Kamaratunga herself.

[47] Both the President and Wickremesinghe promised during their campaign to put an end to the 16-year-old civil war that by then had caused more than 60,000 deaths. Although Tamil voters had supported Kamaratunga in her 1994 victory, this time they followed TULF's recommendation to vote for Wickremesinghe.

[48] Kumaratunga and Wickremesinghe met on March 2000 to discuss a possible political agreement to put an end to the ethnic conflict. While the talks were taking place, Tamil rebels captured a key government position on the Jaffna peninsula after a 12-hour battle.

[49] The TULF openly rejected the government peace plan, but agreed to take part in conversations if Norway acted as mediator. The Sri Lankan political class considered in turn that, before any negotiation with the rebels took place, a comprehensive agreement between the main political parties was needed to enact a new constitution.

[50] The rebels launched a new offensive byin mid-April, and by May they had practically all Jaffna under control. Lack of commitment by government forces was one of the reasons cited for their repeated defeats in the peninsula – a key area for the Tigers in their independence demands. The Tigers perceive the peninsula as their home and the right place to form their independent state. ■

STATISTICS

DEMOGRAPHY

Population: 18,639,000 (1999)
Annual growth: 1.4 % (1975/97)
Estimates for year 2015 (million): 21.9 (1999)
Annual growth to year 2015: 1.0 % (1997/2015)
Urban population: 22.6 % (1997)
Urban Growth: 1.6 % (1980/95)
Children per woman: 2.1 (1998)

HEALTH

Life expectancy at birth: 73 years (1998)
male: 71 years (1998)
female: 75 years (1998)
Maternal mortality: 60 per 100,000 live births (1990-98)
Infant mortality: 17 per 1,000 (1998)
Under-5 child mortality: 19 per 1,000 (1998)
Daily calorie supply: 2,263 per capita (1996)
23 doctors per 100,000 people (1993)
Safe water: 57 % (1990/98)

EDUCATION

Literacy: 90 % (1995)
male: 94 % (1995)
female: 87 % (1995)
School enrolment:
Primary total: 109 % (1990/96)
male: 110 % (1990/97)
female: 108 % (1990/97)
Secondary:
male: 71 % (1990/96)
female: 78 % (1990/96)
Tertiary: 5 % (1996)
Primary school teachers: one for every 28 (1996)

COMMUNICATIONS

29 newspapers (1996), 209 radios (1997), 82 TV sets (1996) and 14 main telephone lines (1996) per 1,000 people
Books: 17 new titles per 100,000 people (1992/94)

ECONOMY

Per capita, GNP: $ 810 (1998)
Annual growth, GNP: 4.6 % (1998)
Annual inflation: 9.7 % (1990/98)
Consumer price index: 138.9 (1998)
Currency: 64.6 rupees = $ 1 (1998)
Cereal imports: 1,131,842 metric tons (1998)
Fertilizer use: 2,429 kg per ha (1997)
Exports: $ 5,648 million (1998)
Imports: $ 6,661 million (1998)
External debt: $ 8,526 million (1998); $ 462 per capita (1998)
Debt service: 6.6 % of exports (1998)
Development aid received: $ 345 million (1997); $ 20.0 per capita (1997); 2.30 % of GNP (1997)

ENERGY

Consumption: 386.0 Kgs of Oil equivalent per capita yearly (1997); 39.0 % imported (1997)

HDI (rank/value): 90/0.721 (1997)

Sudan

Sudan

Population: 28,882,000 (1999)
Area: 2,505,810 SQ KM
Capital: Khartoum (Al-Khartum)
Currency: Pound
Language: Arabic

A round 3000 BC, the region called Kush by the Egyptians and Nubia by the Greeks was in the ambit of Pharaonic Egypt, a fact which considerably delayed the formation of an organized state. The Pharaohs favored disparate groups under their rule. Consequently, the state of Napata did not come into being until the 8th century when Egypt's decline gave foreign dynasties the opportunity to take over the country. The last of these was Sudanese. The rulers of Napata conquered Egypt in 730 BC and reigned as pharaohs until the Assyrian conquest in 663 BC, when the ruling family was ousted. The country disintegrated, though it was not occupied. Shortly afterwards, the three 'waterfall states', which would last over 20 centuries, rose in its place: Nobatia, Dongola and Alodia.

[2] While Egypt was ruled by Persians, Greeks, Romans and Arabs in succession, the waterfall states maintained their political and cultural autonomy. This was due to their position as trade intermediaries between the Mediterranean market and the sources of slaves, ivory, skins, and other goods in equatorial Africa. They were converted to Christianity in the 6th century under Ethiopian influence. A century later, the Arabs invaded, forcing the ruler of Dongola to give financial aid to Arab merchants and to allow Muslim preaching in exchange for preservation of the territorial integrity of Dongola and Alodia. This treaty remained in effect for over 600 years.

[3] Egyptian Mamelukes destroyed Dongola and Alodia in the 14th century. Raids grew more frequent despite the emergence of new

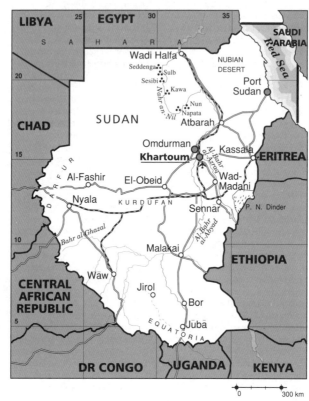

Islamic states: Sennar, on the Blue Nile; Kordofan to the west, and Darfur in the desert.

[4] Intent on exterminating Egyptian soldiers, Pasha Muhammad Ali (see Egypt) entered Sudan in 1820. The Egyptian forces set up permanent quarters in Khartoum, controlling the entire country by 1876. Foreign military occupation brought radical changes: the country was united, limiting the autonomy of various small local governments; the introduction of foreign religious rites (even within the dominant Orthodox Sunni community) upset

established religious communities. Under British pressure, slavery was abolished, undermining the influence of powerful slave dealers. In addition, the burden of heavy taxes - particularly for farmers and cattle raisers - contributed to a general atmosphere of discontent.

[5] In 1881 Muhammad Ahmad proclaimed himself Mahdi, meaning saviour or redeemer, and launched a crusade to restore Islam. He rapidly gained support, especially among the Arabized population in the North. The British, having occupied Egypt in 1882, intervened militarily but were unable to change the course of the conflict. In 1885 Mahdi occupied Khartoum, defeated General Gordon's troops, and established the first national government, which was to last 13 years. The existence of the state threatened the British plan to unite all the territory from Cairo to Cape Town under their rule. In 1898,

Egyptian troops moved in from Uganda and Kenya, attacking Mahdi on both fronts.

[6] The French, with their own east-west transcontinental designs, were also interested in Sudan, and sent troops into the area. This three-pronged attack defeated Mahdi, Khalifa Abdulahi, in September 1898. The colonial armies met in Fachoda, with small skirmishes between the French and British, but France finally recognized British predominance over the Nile basin. In 1899, Sudan was jointly administered by Britain and Egypt. This three-pronged attack defeated

[7] Egypt sought to achieve unity of the Nile by joining Cairo and Khartoum politically, and Britain was determined to prevent this. The British Empire threatened to grant 'federated independence' to the southern population, who were animists and Christians, but not to the Arabic and Muslim north. To make their threat effective, the British started a policy of 'closed districts', which prevented any contact between north and south.

[8] A self-governing statute obtained by Sudan in 1953 was followed by the election of an all-Sudanese parliament in 1955 and the declaration of independence on January 1 1956. However, southerners charged that they had been politically marginalized, and five months before independence a civil war broke out and lasted for 16 years.

[9] In 1969, General Gaafar al-Nimeiry seized power through a coup. He dissolved Parliament, proclaimed the creation of the Sudanese Democratic Republic, and set up a one-party system, the Sudanese Socialist Union. The new government promised to support reconstruction and the development of the southern territories, offering them a certain degree of administrative autonomy.

[10] After coming to power, Nimeiry changed course; he broke with the Sudanese Socialist Union and drew closer to conservative Arab regimes, never fulfilling his promise of greater autonomy for the South.

[11] Nimeiry was forced to sign an agreement with the guerrillas in 1972. This agreement granted autonomy to the southern provinces, while the guerrillas were incorporated into the regular army.

WORKERS

% OF LABOUR FORCE **1998**

- FEMALE: 29%   ■ MALE: 71%

1990

- SERVICES: 22.1%
- INDUSTRY: 8.4%
- AGRICULTURE: 69.5%

LAND USE

DEFORESTATION: 0.8% annual (1990/95)
IRRIGATED: 15.1% of arable (1993)

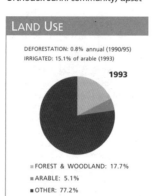

1993

- FOREST & WOODLAND: 17.7%
- ARABLE: 5.1%
- OTHER: 77.2%

PUBLIC EXPENDITURE

DEFENCE EXPENDITURE (% of goverment exp.)	**53.8%** (1997)
MILITARY EXPENDITURE (% of health & education)	**44%** (1990/91)

¹² In 1976, Sudan signed a mutual defense pact with Egypt and initially the Nimeiry government backed the Camp David accords signed by Egypt, Israel and the US. However when it became clear that this position would isolate Sudan from the Arab world, Nimeiry distanced himself from Cairo and drew closer to Saudi Arabia. Nimeiry stressed the Islamic nature of his regime, arousing opposition in the non-Muslim south.

¹³ In May 1977, Nimeiry was re-elected for a six-year term. Shortly afterwards the Government announced a 'national reconciliation' process which enabled exiled political leaders to return and paved the way for the rehabilitation of former opponents of the ruling Umma Party. However, the Sudanese Communist Party and former Finance Minister Shereef al-Hindi's National Front, were ignored.

¹⁴ Nimeiry was re-elected to a third six-year term in 1983, amid widespread accusations of electoral fraud. In September, he suddenly imposed Islamic law (the Sharia) on the whole country. This measure triggered a general protest among the animists and Christians in the South, and recharged the guerrilla movement.

¹⁵ A revolt broke out in the city of Bor, where the Sudanese Popular Liberation Movement (SPLM) arose. This political and military organization gave the southern guerrilla movement a new ideological foundation, with the objectives of achieving national unity and establishing socialism, while respecting southern autonomy and religious freedom.

¹⁶ In the north, Nimeiry was severely criticized by the Muslim Brotherhood and opposition parties for using Islamic law as a tool of repression against dissidents. The financial community also exerted pressure on the Sudanese president to limit the application of the Sharia in business as it stood in opposition to IMF policies.

¹⁷ Sudan's external debt rapidly rose to $8 billion. Debt servicing was systematically delayed until early 1984, with the country considered bankrupt on at least two occasions.

¹⁸ In 1985 the US suspended all credit and the IMF forced the Government to raise food prices. Rebellion broke out, quickly reaching to the capital. Nimeiry visited the US in search of backing, but was unable to return as Abdul Rahman Suwar al-Dahab, minister of defense and army chief of staff, had seized power in his absence after a popular uprising.

¹⁹ The coup did not have much of an effect on the political scenario. The Islamic bourgeoisie in the north made deals with the Government, while the SPLM continued its activities in the south, as the political and economic discrimination against the region continued. Political parties were dissolved and the previous government's subdivision of the south was revoked. The new government promised to review the application of the Sharia, and Dahab promised elections in 1986.

²⁰ The elections were held in April 1986, and Sadiq al-Mahdi, from the Party of the People (UMMA), based on the Koran and on Islamic tradition, was elected Prime Minister.

²¹ Thirty-seven representatives were not elected because of the war in the southern provinces. The SPLM's 12,000 guerrillas besieged government garrisons in the southern provinces, practically splitting Sudan in two, and the south suffered from food shortages as a result of an insurgent blockade. However, the guerrillas agreed to let through airborne food and medical supplies sent by the UN to besieged cities.

²² In June, 1989 the war between the SPLM and the army continued, the foreign debt reached $12 billion and the social tension increased, exacerbated by price increases. Also in June, Major-General Omar al-Bashir ousted the President, blaming his government for the political and economic crisis. Bashir dissolved political parties and created a 15-member military junta, promising to bring the war to an end.

²³ Ten months after the military government took office, there was a coup attempt by a faction of army officials. Ethiopia, Kenya, Uganda, Zaire (now DR Congo), and the US all attempted mediation and all failed. Peace negotiations failed, and southern people continued to suffer at the hands of government troops and Arab paramilitary groups armed by Bashir's predecessors.

²⁴ On February 4 1991, the Government established a federal system in the country. According to the decree, Sudan would be divided into nine states, each administered by a governor and a ministerial cabinet. On January 31 of that year, general Omar Bashir's government had also signed a new criminal code based on the Sharia, only to be implemented in the north of the country, where Islam is predominant.

²⁵ With the People's Liberation Army, led by John Garang, operating in the south, and the Nasir rebel group - a splinter group of the SPLA led by Riak Mashar - operating in the north, the Government lost control. This led to violent government repression against its opponents in urban areas, and against rural communities which supported the guerrillas in the countryside.

²⁶ Negotiations held in Abuja, Nigeria in May 1992, sponsored by Nigeria's president, ended in June with the issuing of an ambiguous communiqué. International pressure forced Omar Bashir to revoke the ban on airplane movements to the south of the country, which had kept food and medicine from being transported. In February of that same year, 60,000 people had died of hunger in Parayang, 800 kilometers southeast of Khartoum.

²⁷ In January 1993, disagreements among high-ranking members of the Government led to a cabinet shake-up, aimed at bringing government policies into line with the IMF and World Bank objectives. However, both international agencies found the reforms insufficient; especially as the debt had not been serviced. The financing for infrastructure projects was consequently discontinued in April. In the meantime, $2 million a day was being spent on defense.

²⁸ In February 1993, the SPLA and the Government resumed negotiations in Entebbe, Uganda. These were boycotted by Mashar, who was in Nairobi trying to speed up negotiations to merge with another SPLA splinter group, led by William Nyuon. This alliance, signed in April, paved the way for a cease-fire, and the promise to carry on with the talks initiated in Nigeria. Disagreements between Garang and Bashir, in Abuja, over the devolution of power to the provinces, caused the talks to flounder in June 1993, and the impasse remained until the end of the year.

²⁹ In May 1994, the Government signed a protocol for humanitarian aid with both rebel factions in order to provide relief for villages cut off by the conflict. Their situation continued to worsen and humanitarian organizations voiced their denunciations. In July 1995, the African Rights organization charged Khartoum of being responsible for the 'genocide' of the Nuba ethnic group.

³⁰ In the March 1996 elections, Bashir was re-elected with 76 per cent of the vote. The possibilities of coexistence between the 'theocrats' of the north and the rebels of the south appeared increasingly remote. The 12 years of war left a million dead and three million refugees.

³¹ In November 1997, disputes with Egypt over administration of the Halaib triangle - rich in phosphates, manganese and, supposedly, oil - led to Sudan asking for intervention from the Arab

PROFILE

ENVIRONMENT

The largest African country, Sudan has three distinct geographic regions: the barren deserts of Libya and the Sahara in the north, the flatlands of the central region and the dense rainforests of the south. Most of the population lives along the Nile, where cotton is grown. Port Sudan, on the Red Sea, handles all of the country's foreign trade. Desertification has affected nearly 60 per cent of the territory. Industrial waste has contaminated coastal areas and some rivers.

SOCIETY

Peoples: The country has a wide ethnic spectrum with over 570 groups. Arabs, who live in the center and north of the country, together with Nubians, account for nearly half of the population. Among the other groups, the most important are the Nilote, Nilo-Hamitic and a few Bantu groups. In the south there are nearly 400,000 refugees from neighboring nations (Chad, Uganda, Ethiopia and Eritrea).
Religions: Islam is the predominant religion among Arabs and Nubians with a majority of Sunni Muslims. In the south, traditional African religions are practiced and there are Christian communities in both north and south.
Languages: Arabic (official and spoken by most of the population); the different ethnic groups speak over 100 different languages.
Political parties: Political parties were dissolved after the 1989 coup. The leading parties based on the 1986 electoral results were: the Umma Party; the Democratic Unionist Party (DUP); the National Islamic Front. Opposition separatist movements in the south include the Sudan People's Liberation Movement (SPLM).

THE STATE

Official Name: Jumhuriyat as-Sudan.
Administrative Divisions: 9 states, 66 Provinces and 281 Local Government Areas.
Capital: Khartoum (Al-Khartum) 2,700,000 people (est 1995).
Other cities: Kassala 234,270 people; Port Sudan (Bur Sudan) 305,385 people (1993).
Government: General Omar al-Bashir, Head of State since June 1989, re-elected in March 1996.
National Holiday: January 1, Independence Day (1956).
Armed Forces: 118,500 (1995). **Other:** 30,000-50,000 People's Defense Force.

League. Under an agreement made in 1899, Halaib belonged to Egypt, but under a newer agreement of 1905, it had been awarded to Sudan.

[32] In January 1998, the United States announced an economic embargo on Sudan, alleging it had supported international terrorism, training opposition groups from neighboring countries in order to destabilize them, and lacking respect for human rights.

[33] A month later, the UN appealed to the international community for more than $100 million to aid 4 million victims of war and drought in Sudan.

[34] Vice-President Al Zubair Mohamed Saleh was killed in February. According to observers, the Christian PLA rebels had been given US support in return for collaboration with Uganda, Ethiopia and Eritrea. The Catholic Church of Sudan decided to take part in peace talks between the Islamic Government and the military Sudanese Peoples Liberation Army faction prepared for dialogue.

[35] In August 1998, the Shifa pharmaceutical plant was destroyed by US missiles in retaliation for the bombing of US embassies in Kenya and Tanzania. The factory was said to be linked with the World Islam Front led by Saudi millionaire and former US ally against communism, Osama bin Laden.

[36] A meningitis epidemic ravaged the country in March 1999. Thirty people died daily in Khartoum alone, the most affected areas being the outskirts of the city.

[37] With a $3 billion investment Sudan managed to inaugurate a 1,500 km oil pipeline in June. This is to allow the development of several oil deposits neglected during the war and the political problems. By late September 1999, 150,000 barrels of oil were produced daily, a figure which was planned to go up to 250,000. Because of the large investment, Sudan would only begin to benefit from it in the year 2003.

[38] War and famine were still haunting the country. Between 1,000-2,000 displaced people per day continued to take refuge in the centers where the international relief organizations operate. ∎

Kanem-Bornu

Where the Bilma trade route neared Lake Chad, there lived, according to oral tradition, communities of 'small red men' who must have given rise, between the first and fifth centuries of our era, to the so-called Civilization of Chad, known for its high-quality artistic and metallurgical production. The Sao probably arrived towards the 10th century. They were a Nilotic nation, noted for their great size. They exterminated the 'little red men' and established a confederation of groups to the southeast of the lake. On the other side of the lake, communities of shepherds related to the Tibu (autochthonous nomads from the Tibesti mountains) had settled around the eighth century. These shepherds were the Kanuri who, after subduing the local population, set up the state of Kanema, ruled by a military caste. Converted to Islam in the 11th century, they cultivated close ties with the Arab world, based on the slave trade.

[2] The capture of slaves frequently took the Kanuri to Sao territory which they eventually conquered. Thereafter, the Saif (Kanuri ruling family) came to be called 'the rulers of Kanem, the masters of Bornu' and their nation was known by this compound name.

[3] The most outstanding period was during Dunama Dibalim's rule. Between 1220 and 1260 Dibalim ruled over the territory that extended from the banks of Lake Chad to Fezzan (Libya) in the north, and from the Haussa states in the west to Ouaddai (border of present-day Sudan) in the east.

[4] The flourishing traffic allowed him to maintain a standing army of 30,000 horsemen. He also built a large residence in Cairo (Al Qahirah) for the young Kanuri who studied at the famous Al Azhar University.

[5] However, total dominion over the other nations did not occur: the Sao, Tibu and Bulala (to the southeast) shook the 14th and 15th centuries with frequent rebellions, forcing the Saifs to leave Kanem and to move their capital.

[6] Idris Alaoma (1571-1603) decided to solve these problems drastically; he bought muskets, hired instructors in Tunis and modernized the army to confront his enemies one by one.

[7] The Sao, long considered rebellious, were completely exterminated in a campaign that razed all their towns. The Tibu were forced to abandon their mountains and settle in Bornu where they were easier to control. To subdue the Bulala he had to conquer the north of what is now Cameroon.

[8] Paradoxically, this 'putting things in order' did not benefit the Kanuri economically. Although the Haussa merchants yielded to Idris' military drive, and eventually paid tribute to the Kanem-Bornu rulers, they succeeded in gaining control of the slave trade, thus benefitting from the 'peace' obtained with so much blood.

[9] This situation remained more or less stable until the 19th century, when the Fulani invasion forced the king of Bornu to turn for help to Mahamad Al-Kanemi, a military chieftain. Al-Kanemi repulsed the invaders, but stayed and became the real power behing the throne, even though the crisis was over. This dual situation lasted until 1846, when the last of the Saifs, Ibrahim, was executed by Omar, al-Kanemi's son.

[10] In 1893, Omar's successor was deposed by Rabah, a Sudanese guerrilla who had fought alongside the Mahdi (see Sudan). The new ruler extended the boundaries of Kanem-Bornu to Sudan. After several years of fighting against the French who wanted to seize control of the territory, Rabah was defeated by the joint action of three colonial armies coming from Algeria, Congo and Mali. His death signaled the end of resistance to colonial penetration. ∎

Suriname

Suriname

Population: 416,000 (1999)
Area: 163,270 SQ KM
Capital: Paramaribo
Currency: Guilder
Language: Dutch
and Spanish

The Caribs settled along the Atlantic coasts of Central and South America. The original groups gradually dispersed; some inland, and others to the islands that lie off the coast of the continent. They lived in small communities where they existed by hunting, fishing and small-scale farming. They were also able warriors.

[2] In the early 17th century Dutch colonists founded a settlement in Guyana and began to trade in slaves.

[3] In 1863, when slavery was abolished in Dutch territories it was replaced by another source of cheap labor, Asian Indian and Javanese immigrants. This gave rise to a complex ethnic structure in the Guyana region. Asian Indians formed one of the largest groups, the most resistant to intermarriage and most strongly attached to their cultural heritage. Then came the Creoles or Afro-Americans, the Javanese, the 'bush people' whose ancestors had rebelled against slavery and fled the plantations, indigenous people and a small European minority.

[4] These ethnic, cultural and linguistic differences hindered the development of a national identity. Political movements tended to represent individual ethnic communities, especially as these broadly corresponded to social divisions. The Creoles formed the NPK (National Party Combination), a coalition of four center-left parties, and they led the fight for independence after World War II. Jaggernauth Lachmon's Vatan Hitakarie represented the Indian population of shop owners and business people, and they sought to postpone independence.

[5] Since 1954, local government had enjoyed a degree of autonomy and, in October 1973, the independence faction won the legislative elections. Liberal Hanck Arron, NPS (National Surinamese Party) leader was appointed Prime Minister.

[6] Arron and Lachmon reached an agreement, and independence was finally proclaimed in 1975. Many middle-income Surinamese took advantage of their status as Dutch citizens to emigrate to the ex-colonial power. Nearly a third of the population, mostly Asian Indian, left and caused a serious shortage of technical, professional and administrative personnel. The country lost much-needed qualified labor with only SURALCO and Billiton, the two transnationals which monopolized local bauxite mining, surviving the exodus. Economic activity decreased and agriculture declined to dangerous levels. In this difficult situation, Arron and his group of politicians were repeatedly accused of corruption and complicity with foreign companies.

[7] On February 25 1980, the premier was overthrown by a coup which had begun as a protest by the sergeants' union for better working conditions. The National Military Council (NMC) summoned opposition leaders to form a government and several leftwing politicians accepted cabinet posts.

[8] The Military Council, led by Lt-Colonel Desi Bouterse, took power from the politicians on February 4 1981, accusing the administration of corruption and underhand dealings with the Netherlands and the United States. This new government established relations with Cuba, in the face of opposition from the major internal parties, from the US and from the Netherlands. Brazil came to its aid on more than one occasion.

[9] In January 1983, Bouterse formed a new government, which appointed Errol Halibux, a nationalist and member of the Farmers' and Labor Union, as Prime Minister. After the American invasion of Grenada, the Suriname Government did an about-face in its relations with Cuba, asking Havana to recall its ambassador and suspending all agreements for cooperation between the countries.

[10] In late 1983 and early 1984, there was a series of strikes by bauxite workers - a product which accounted for 80 per cent of the country's exports - who were joined by power, water and transport workers. Bouterse attributed it to errors by the Prime Minister and the entire cabinet automatically resigned. Bouterse proceeded to eliminate all fiscal restrictions by presidential decree, and appointed two union leaders to the new cabinet.

[11] An effort was made to reduce Suriname's isolation and diversify its foreign relations, which were excessively dependent on Holland. To accelerate this process, the Government began to pursue a more aggressive foreign policy, joining CARICOM (Caribbean Community and Common Market) as an observer and establishing relations with Cuba, Grenada, Nicaragua, Brazil and Venezuela. It also became a member of SELA (Latin American Economic System), the OAS (Organization of American States) and the Amazon Pact.

[12] In mid-1986, former soldier Ronnie Brunswijk, aided by foreign mercenaries and funded by the Netherlands, began a campaign of harassment from bases in French Guyana.

[13] In April 1987, the 33-member National Assembly (of whom 11 were labor union representatives) unanimously approved a draft constitution providing for a return to institutional government. The draft was supported by the three main political parties.

[14] The coalition United Front for Democracy and Development won. On July 21 1989, President Ramsewak Shankar granted an amnesty to the still-active guerrilla movement, allowing them to hold on to their weapons as long as they were in the forests. Bouterse and the NDP opposed this agreement,

WORKERS

1996
UNEMPLOYMENT: 10.9%

% OF LABOUR FORCE **1998**

■ FEMALE: 33%   ■ MALE: 67%

1990

■ SERVICES: 61.0%
■ INDUSTRY: 17.8%
■ AGRICULTURE: 21.2%

LAND USE

DEFORESTATION: 0.1% annual (1990/95)

1993

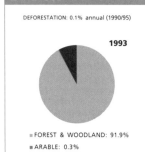

■ FOREST & WOODLAND: 91.9%
■ ARABLE: 0.3%
■ OTHER: 7.8%

PUBLIC EXPENDITURE

DEFENCE EXPENDITURE (% of goverment exp.)	**2.6%**	(1997)
MILITARY EXPENDITURE (% of health & education)	**27%**	(1990/91)

arguing that it legalized an autonomous military force and encouraged the division.

[15] In December 1990, another coup deposed Ramsewak Shankar, who had been the constitutional president since January 1988. Colonel Desi Bouterse, who had resigned a week prior to the coup, resumed his leadership of the army on December 30. The National Assembly, which had been set up in September 1987 for a period of five years appointed the NPS's Johan Draag as provisional president.

[16] During 1991, Dutch and US sources accused the top military echelons of Bouterse's regime of being involved in drug trafficking.

[17] The May elections were held to choose the National Assembly, and the New Front (NF) won - a broad coalition of civilian parties and ethnic groups oppose to the military government. The NF proposed the re-establishment of relations with the Dutch Government and the tightening of economic and political links with the former colonizer.

[18] Fresh elections in May 1991 elected a new government. Spokespeople in The Hague and Washington independently announced their intentions of a military intervention in the country 'should the new government

request it'. International observers warned about the threat implicit in these announcements, in the light of the recent experiences in Grenada and Panama.

[19] In September, Ronald Venetiaan of the NF was elected President. The new head of state launched a 50 per cent cut in defence spending and a peace process, including a UN-sponsored guerrilla disarmament, under the supervision of Brazil and Guyana. In June 1992, a cooperation agreement was signed with the Netherlands, and a year later, a severe structural adjustment program was adopted, which gave rise to discontent among the population.

[20] Poverty and unemployment in the rural agricultural communities formed the background for the occupation of the Afobakka dam, 100 kilometers south of Paramaribo, in March 1994. The rebels, who called for the resignation of the government, were expelled by government troops, after a four-day occupation. Another important movement took place in rural areas in 1995, when representatives of Indians and *Cimarrons* (runaway slaves living in the forest in their own communities) gathered to protest for the environmental damage

caused by a Canadian mining company and an Indonesian timber company.

[21] In September 1996, Parliament elected Jules Wijdenbosch as President, thus blocking Venetiaan's re-election. In April 1997, the Netherlands issued an international warrant for former dictator Besi Bouterse, suspected of links with drug-trafficking. In response, Wijdenbosch appointed the former dictator State Councillor, granting him diplomatic immunity.

[22] Toward the end of that year, a failed coup ended in the arrest of 17 low-ranking officers. The army called for better pay and greater investment in equipment and weapons. The strength of the army had declined since the late 1980s when the Bouterse regime had fought the guerrilla groups. The coup attempt was related to the working conditions of the troops, which had deteriorated, with low salaries and outdated equipment.

[23] Price hikes, an 80-per-cent currency devaluation and demands in wage increases led to a difficult situation in Parliament which had voted itself salary increases both in February and November 1998. This caused deep social discontent. Teachers and civil servants carried out a series of strikes demanding salary increases which would enable them to regain their purchasing power.

[24] Social unrest and an unprecedented economic crisis intensified during the first months of 1999, leaving the country almost at a standstill. Several political groups had blocked parliament in February leaving the legislative body without the necessary quorum, and obstructing the passage of any bill. The guilder, the national currency, had been devaluated by 200 per cent. Inflation reached 20 per cent and the state health system had been left virtually bankrupt. There were constant protests from various social sectors, in particular from state employees. The state employed one out of every ten people in the country.

[25] Amongst the items that Parliament was not able to discuss were the 1999-2003 budget, a national development scheme and a plan to attract foreign investment. Discussion of the development plan had been postponed seven times in six months because the opposition just signed the attendance roll to ensure the payment of their salaries but ignored daily business. Due to a large state debt with the health system, private hospital doctors refused to treat patients with state health insurance. The Government hired 52 Cuban doctors and nine specialists to work in the areas their Surinamese colleagues neglected.

PROFILE

ENVIRONMENT

The coastal plain, low and subject to floods, is suitable for agriculture. Rice, sugar and other crops are grown. Land has been reclaimed from the sea through drainage and dykes. Inland, the terrain is hilly with dense tropical vegetation, rich in bauxite deposits. Year-round heavy rainfall feeds an important system of rivers, some of which are used to generate hydro-electric power for the aluminum industry.

SOCIETY

Peoples: Suriname Creole 30 per cent; Indo-Pakistani 33 per cent; Javanese 16 per cent; 'Bush people' 10 per cent; Amerindian 3 per cent; other 3 per cent.
Religions: Christian 44 per cent (21.6 per cent Catholic, 18 per cent Protestant); Muslim 18.6 per cent; Hinduism 26 per cent; other 15.8 per cent.
Languages: Dutch (official). English (for business), Hindi, Javanese, and a form of Creole are spoken. The Creole, called either Taki-Taki or Senango-Tongo, is based on African languages mixed with Dutch, Spanish and English.
Political Parties: New Front for Democracy and Development (NF) comprised of four parties: Progressive Reform Party (VHP), Suriname National Party (NPS), Javanese Farmers' Party (KPTI) and the National Democratic Party NPD), Democratic Alternative, Jungle Commando, Angola, Mandela Liberation Movement, Tucaya.
Social Organizations: Suriname Trade Union Federation; Central Organization of Civil Servants.

THE STATE

Official Name: Republiek Suriname.
Administrative Divisions: 9 Districts.
Capital: Paramaribo 220,000 people (est 1995).
Other cities: Nieuw Nickerie 6,078 people; Meerzorg 5,355; Marienburg 3,633.
Government: Parliamentary Republic. President, Jules Wijdenbosch since September 1996. Prime Minister, Pretaapnarian Radhakishun since September 1996. 51-member unicameral parliament.
National Holiday: November 25, Independence Day (1975).
Armed forces: 1,800 (1996).

[26] Parliament was rudely awakened by the largest general strike in Suriname's history. There were also huge demonstrations in Paramaribo that went on for several months without any solution in sight. The Wijdenbosch cabinet was dismissed by Parliament in June, accused of the economic collapse of the country.

[27] Although Parliament intended to dismiss him also, Wijdenbosch managed to survive and appointed nine ministers. In spite of this, the cabinet resigned in December after corruption charges involving several of its members. ∎

Swaziland

Swaziland

Population: 980,000 (1999)
Area: 17,360 SQ KM
Capital: Mbabane
Currency: Emalangeni
Language: English

Like Lesotho, Swaziland achieved centralized administration when groups of very different origins joined to form a nation. The danger posed by Zulu expansion, (see South Africa) led Sobhuza, head of the Dlamini local groups, to bring together the remains of several groups split apart by Shaka, including Zulu deserters and Bushmen or San who remained in the region. They became a powerful force in the northeastern part of the present-day South African province of Natal. Sobhuza died shortly after the Zulu defeat by the Boers (1839) leaving his son, Mswati, the task of keeping the nation together, in the face of constant threats from the Afrikaners. The nation was named after its king who led the nation in 30 years of resistance - aside from a period of alliance with the Boers against the Pedi - allying with the British shortly before his death so as to avoid defeat by the Boers.

[2] In 1867, Swaziland formally became a British protectorate, like Basutoland (Lesotho) and Bechuanaland (Botswana).

[3] When Britain defeated the Boers in 1902 and imposed its dominion over the whole of South Africa, these countries remained under separate colonial administrations, though South African settlers attempted to establish claims over the territories. Native authorities were formally recognized according to British criterion of making use of 'local' intermediaries to facilitate colonial administration.

[4] In 1961, when the Union of South Africa broke off relations with Britain and toughened racial segregation policies, London accelerated the decolonization process in the region. Swaziland

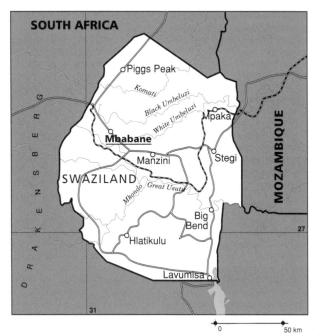

was granted internal autonomy in 1967 and formal independence the following year. Sobhuza II was recognized as head of state and governed with two legislative chambers. On April 12 1973, he dissolved Parliament, claiming that it contained 'destructive elements' and proclaimed himself absolute monarch, banning all political parties and activities.

[5] In the event, Sobhuza II placed himself in the service of the South African colonizers against whom his grandfather had fought. Communications, the postal service, transport, currency and the Bank of Swaziland all became completely dependent on South Africa. South African companies exploited the country's asbestos and iron ore and South African experts ran the state's

public administration - guaranteeing efficient control - and supervised agricultural production. Cotton, the main export product, was marketed by South African merchants and white South Africans opened brothels and cabarets which the strict 'puritanical' official morality prohibited in their own country.

[6] At that time due to the lack of job opportunities, thousands of workers emigrated every year to work in the South African gold mines. The money they send home to their families accounted for 25 per cent of Swaziland's foreign currency earnings. In October 1977, teachers went on strike for better salaries and were supported by students. The following year, the Swazi Liberation Movement (Swalimo) was founded, led by Dr Swane, who managed to escape from prison in the capital, Mbabane. The strengthening of the opposition was accompanied by a rapid growth of the armed forces, from 1,000 in 1975 to more than 5,000 in 1979, and the police force was considerably reinforced.

[7] Mounting opposition inside the country was encouraged by the consolidation of a socialist regime in Mozambique, amongst other things. Increasing tension in Swaziland also led the Government to develop closer military relations with South Africa and Israel; Sobhuza II was one of only three African rulers who

never severed diplomatic relations with the Government of Tel Aviv.

[8] After the 1977 strikes, the Government severely repressed all opposition, invoking a special law allowing detention without charges for up to 60 days.

[9] The Constitution was suspended in 1973 and a reformed version was introduced in 1978 without approval from or consultation with the electorate. Following tribal rules, the process of approval consisted of consultation with the heads of the 40 clans a fortnight before the enactment of the new constitutional draft. It banned opposition parties and established a parliament with little decision-making power.

[10] After 1980, the economic situation in Swaziland was affected by the world recession. The post-independence boom period came to an end with an increase in the prices of imported goods and a drop in prices for corn, sugar and wood exports. Inflation climbed, and a deficit appeared in the balance of payments, the rate of investment fell radically, and the GNP dropped by 4 per cent. Mineral exports fell from 40 per cent of total exports to only 10 per cent due to the depletion of iron ore reserves. Various new coal deposits were discovered in 1980 but their exploitation has been slow due to legal difficulties and the lack of adequate transport facilities.

[11] In August 1982, King Sobhuza died at the age of 83 when his successor, Prince Makhosetive was only 15 years old. The lack of effective government sparked a power struggle between several princes and Prince Mabandla Dlamini was deposed from his position as Prime Minister. He was succeeded by Bhekimpi Dlamini, a pro-South African conservative, who began his reign by persecuting South African refugees.

[12] In August 1983, Ntombi, one of Sobhuza's widows, overthrew the reigning Queen and took power, strengthening the conservative faction. Two months later, 200,000 of the country's 760,000 people voted for a new parliament through a complicated indirect electoral system called *tinkhundla*. As expected, Prince Bhekimpi Dlamini was successful in an electoral contest where no political parties participated.

WORKERS

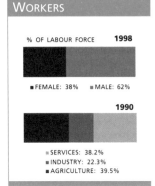

% OF LABOUR FORCE **1998**

■ FEMALE: 38%   ■ MALE: 62%

1990

■ SERVICES: 38.2%
■ INDUSTRY: 22.3%
■ AGRICULTURE: 39.5%

LAND USE

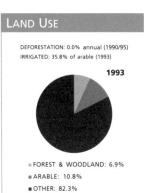

DEFORESTATION: 0.0% annual (1990/95)
IRRIGATED: 35.8% of arable (1993)

1993

■ FOREST & WOODLAND: 6.9%
■ ARABLE: 10.8%
■ OTHER: 82.3%

[13] The election resulted in closer ties with South Africa. The repression of anti-apartheid militants increased in 1984, with detention and return to the Pretoria Government becoming the norm.

[14] During the second half of 1984, a student protest led the Government to close down the university. Prime Minister Bhekimpi Dlamini's authoritarianism stimulated the revival of the Swazi Liberation Movement, which resumed its activities in January 1985. This movement was led by Prince Clement Dumisa Dlamini, who was the former secretary-general of the Progressive Party and a well-known nationalist leader. He was later exiled to England.

[15] On April 25 1986, Prince Makhosetive was crowned, taking the name King Mswati III. His inaugural address reflected his conservative stance. In May he dissolved the Liqoqo (an assembly of local group leaders acting as Supreme State Council), consolidating his power and that of his ministers. Prime Minister Bhekimpi was relieved of his post and replaced by Sotsha Dlamini. In September 1987, King Mswati dissolved Parliament, announcing elections for November, a year ahead of schedule. The 40 members of Parliament and 10 senators were elected by an electoral college. The King however disputed the election of the senators, demanding that the process be repeated in a more satisfactory manner.

[16] Relations with South Africa had not changed with the change of king. The Government condemned economic sanctions against the Pretoria regime and continued to harass anti-apartheid militants.

[17] Since the late 1980s the country's economic situation had improved noticeably. The economy grew and foreign investment continued. A significant part of the food produced was sold to the European Community. This improvement, a direct consequence of trade sanctions against South Africa, allowed the manufacturing sector to increase - contributing 20 per cent of the GDP by 1991 - and helped the country raise its economic growth rate to 3.5 per cent per year.

[18] In 1992, a significant part of the opposition joined the Popular United Democratic Movement (PUDEMO) and lobbied for the King to accept a multiparty system. Discontent mounted in 1993, as a prolonged drought destroyed the corn crop and generated further unemployment.

[19] According to some studies carried out in 1994, even though calorie consumption was slightly higher than the basic minimum, the country still had a high child mortality rate - 107 per 1,000 - and only 30 per cent of the population had access to drinking water. Moreover, Swaziland was still dependent on South Africa, the source of 90 per cent of imports.

[20] Protests against Mswati III continued. After the deliberate fire of February 1995 in the seat of parliament, for which the Swaziland Youth Congress claimed responsibility, 40,000 people took part in a demonstration in support of a two-day general strike. Nelson Mandela's new government in Pretoria pressed the King, and in February 1996 he expressed his willingness to authorize political parties, amidst rumors of possible intervention from the South African army.

[21] The Swaziland Federation of Trade Unions called for an end to the absolute monarchy and the establishment of a multiparty regime. Violent clashes between demonstrators and the security forces caused at least three deaths.

[22] Mid-year, the King called for an end to the upheaval, repeating he would reconsider the banning of the political parties. He also said the citizens would be given the opportunity to participate in drawing up a new Constitution. In May, he sacked Prime Minister Mbilini Dlamini and appointed Barnabas Sibusiso Dlamini as his replacement in July.

[23] The political situation did not change substantially in 1997. In March the King let down the opposition by not sending delegates to the agreed negotiations. In July, he created a 30-member committee, charged with drafting a Constitution, asking for all related initiatives be referred to this body.

[24] These delaying tactics intensified the protests. The King reacted, ordering the security forces to fire live ammunition on demonstrators. The clashes produced large numbers of wounded and several union leaders were arrested. In October 1997, fresh strikes broke out in strategic areas, like the sugar sector. The unions also called for the Constitutional Revision Committee to be dissolved.

[25] In April 1998, the King put an 'environmental conservation' plan into action, with public and private sector participation. Five critical areas were identified. At the same time, bidding was opened on large-scale public works projects including bridges, the re-routing of major water courses, and irrigation structures for vast areas hit by drought.

[26] There were parliamentary elections in October in spite of the ban on political parties. Few voters registered due to a boycott called by trade unions and the opposition. The Government raided the homes of many opposition union leaders in return.

[27] Several prominent lawyers and politicians, including the former justice minister who was one of the King's advisers, were accused of government fraud.

[28] Prime Minister Barnabas Dlamini was involved in an adultery scandal. He was accused by the former husband of a Bank Vice-President as responsible for the break-up of his marriage.

[29] The permanent displacements the citizens had to undergo were detrimental to farmers and caused the winds of public opinion to favor changes in the administration of justice, royal rights and land resettlement policies. A Ministry of Economic Development report showed that mistaken or unplanned farmer relocation was the main cause of rural poverty. Some communities opposed to the relocations clashed with the royal authorities during January 2000. ∎

PROFILE

ENVIRONMENT

The country is divided into three distinct geographical regions known as the high, middle and low veld (plain) all approximately the same size. The western region is mountainous with a central plateau and flatlands to the east. The main crops are sugar cane, citrus fruits and rice (irrigated), cotton, corn (the basic foodstuff), sorghum and tobacco. In the lower veld, infections caused by polluted water are responsible for the high mortality rate. Wildlife was exterminated by European hunters in the first half of this century.

SOCIETY

Peoples: 84.3 per cent of the population belong to the Swazi ethnic group. Zulu account for 9.9 per cent; Tonga and Shangaan another 3 per cent; there are Indian (0.8 per cent), Pakistani (0.8 per cent) and Portuguese (0.2 per cent) minorities. **Religions:** 77 per cent of the population are Christian, the rest follow traditional African religions. **Languages:** Swazi and English (official); ethnic minorities speak their own languages. **Political Parties:** Popular United Democratic Movement (PUDEMO); Swaziland Democratic Alliance; National Congress of Ngwane Liberation. **Social Organizations:** Swaziland Federation of Trade Unions (SFTU); Swaziland Youth Congress.

THE STATE

Official Name: Umbuso weSwatini. **Administrative Divisions:** 210 Tribal Areas, including 40 traditional communities. **Capital:** Mbabane 46,000 people (1990). **Other cities:** Manzini 53,000 people (1990). **Government:** King Mswati III, crowned on April 25 1986. Prime Minister: Barnabas Sibusiso Dlamini since July 1996. **National holiday:** September 6 (Independence Day). **Armed Forces:** 2,657 (1983).

Sweden

Sverige

Population: 8,892,000 (1999)
Area: 449,960 SQ KM
Capital: Stockholm
Currency: Kronor
Language: Swedish

According to archaeological research, the first inhabited area in Sweden is thought to have been the southern part of the country, with occupation dating back to 10,000 years BC. Between 8,000 and 6,000 BC, the region was inhabited by peoples who made a living by hunting and fishing, using simple stone tools. The Bronze Age (1,800-500 BC) brought with it cultural development, reflected in particular in the richness of the tombs of that period.

[2] In 500 AD, in Lake Malaren valley, the Sveas created the first important center of political power. From the 6th century BC until the year 800 the population went through a migration period, later becoming settled, with agriculture becoming the basis of economic and social activities.

[3] Between the 9th and 11th centuries, the Swedish vikings reached the Baltic shores on trade expeditions as well as pirate raids and also went as far as what is now Russia, reaching the Black and Caspian Seas. There they established relations with the Byzantine and Arab empires.

[4] During the same period, Christian missions from the Carolingian empire (led by the missionary, Ansgar) converted most of Sweden. However, the gods of the ancient local mythologies survived into the 12th century. Sweden had its first archbishop in 1164.

[5] From the middle of the 12th century, Sverker and Erik's respective fiefdoms fought against each other to gain control of the Swedish kingdom, alternating in power between 1160 and 1250. The feudal chieftains remained relatively autonomous until the second half of the 13th century, when the King enforced nationwide laws and annexed Finland.

[6] The Black Death brought the country's growth to a standstill in 1350, and it remained so until the second half of the 15th century. In that period the foundries in the central region became important.

During the 15th and 16th centuries the German Hanseatic League dominated Swedish commerce and encouraged the foundation of several cities.

[7] In 1397, the royal power of Norway, Sweden and Denmark was handed over to the Danish queen Margaret, who proclaimed the Union of Kalmar. The ensuing conflicts between the central Danish power and the rebellious Swedish nobility, townspeople and peasants ended in 1523, with the accession of Gustav Vasa to the throne of Sweden.

[8] Under the reign of Vasa, the monarchy ceased to be elected by the nobility and became hereditary. A German administrative model was adopted and the foundations were laid for a nation state. The possessions of the Church went to the state, with the Protestant Reformation following hot on its heels. From then on, Sweden aspired to becoming the main power in the Baltic region.

[9] In 1630, after intervening successfully in the Thirty Years' War, Sweden waged two more wars to conquer the Danish regions of Skane, Halland, Blekinge, and the Baltic island of Gotland, as well as the Norwegian islands of Bohuslan, Jamtland, and Harjedalen.

[10] Sweden thus became a great power in northern Europe, as it now ruled over Finland, several northern German provinces, and the Baltic provinces of Estonia, Latvia and Lithuania. However, the country was still basically rural and lacked resources to maintain its position or power indefinitely.

[11] After its defeat in the Great Northern War (1700-21), the Swedish Empire lost most of the provinces to the south and east of the Gulf of Finland. It was reduced to the territories roughly corresponding to modern Sweden and Finland, with Finland being ceded to Russia during the Napoleonic Wars.

[12] In 1718, after the death of Charles XII, a parliament (Riksdag) made up of nobles did away with the monarchy, assuming power itself. However, the new king Gustav II staged a coup in 1772, gradually claiming more and more power, and finally re-establishing full monarchic powers in 1789.

[13] In compensation for the losses incurred during the Napoleonic Wars, Norway was ceded to King Charles XIV, who had become king in 1810. After a short war, it was forced to join Sweden in 1814. Nevertheless, after a series of conflicts, the union dissolved peacefully in 1905.

[14] In the second half of the 19th century, Sweden continued to be a poor country, with 90 per cent of

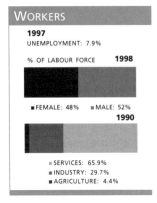

WORKERS

1997
UNEMPLOYMENT: 7.9%

% OF LABOUR FORCE **1998**

■ FEMALE: 48% ■ MALE: 52%
1990

■ SERVICES: 65.9%
■ INDUSTRY: 29.7%
■ AGRICULTURE: 4.4%

LAND USE

IRRIGATED: 4.1% of arable (1993)

1993

■ FOREST & WOODLAND: 62.2%
■ ARABLE: 6.2%
■ OTHER: 31.6%

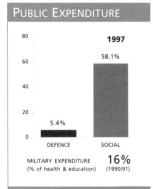

PUBLIC EXPENDITURE

1997
58.1%

5.4%

DEFENCE   SOCIAL

MILITARY EXPENDITURE **16%**
(% of health & education) (1990/91)

MATERNAL MORTALITY
1990-98
Per 100,000 live births
5

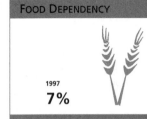

FOOD DEPENDENCY
1997
7%

FOREIGN TRADE
Millions US$ 1997
IMPORTS
83,758
EXPORTS
99,727

the population engaged in agriculture. At this point, a great emigration movement began: one million out of a total of 5 million Swedes left, mainly for North America.

[15] During this period the liberal majority in parliament, supported by King Oscar I, established universal education (1842), the free enterprise system and the liberalization of foreign trade (1846). Legislation was also passed establishing sexual equality in inheritance law (1845), the rights of unmarried women (1858), and religious freedom (1860).

[16] Important social movements such as the temperance league, free churches, women's advancement, and especially the workers' movement emerged, growing with industrialization and influencing the government through social democracy.

[17] From 1890 onwards, with the support of foreign capital, the process of industrialization accelerated in Sweden. The country had one of the most thriving economies in that part of Europe. Finished products using Swedish technical innovations quickly became the country's main exports.

[18] Universal male suffrage has been in force since 1908, a state old-age pension system was adopted in 1913, and in 1918 the 8-hour working day was established by law. That same year, the vote was extended to women.

[19] The parliamentary system has been in effect since 1918. The Social Democrats came to power in 1932; their policies fostered understanding between workers and industrialists, which was enshrined in the 1938 Pact of Salsboejaden.

[20] Sexual equality was achieved earlier in Sweden than in other industrialized countries, through the efforts of feminists and state campaigns against social and sexual prejudice.

[21] The country's educational system - from primary onwards - sought to eliminate sexism by teaching both girls and boys how to keep house, take care of babies, do woodwork and metalwork.

[22] Abortion is available on demand to women up to the third month of pregnancy. The law concerning rape states that there are no extenuating circumstances to be considered in the man's case, and there are also stiff sentences for rape within marriage.

[23] Women can take on any profession, with the exception of the army. However, the female population is still concentrated in the lowest income groups. In general their earnings are 20 per cent lower than those of their male counterparts for similar jobs. In 1981, over 50 per cent of all married women were economically active outside the home.

[24] Within the civil service, there is an official position of Ombudsman, whose role is to investigate cases of abuse of authority, breach of ethics, and ethnic or sexual discrimination in state agencies and private companies.

[25] Since World War I, Sweden has refused to take part in peacetime alliances in order to stay neutral in times of war. This policy relies on Sweden's strong defense system and compulsory national service for men.

[26] Trade routes were disrupted during World War II, which caused serious food shortages in the country. For security reasons Sweden is almost self-sufficient, with up to 80 per cent of its agricultural produce produced internally. The Government maintains a protectionist policy on agricultural imports, which means that food prices are higher than those on the international market.

[27] Sweden favored a thaw in East-West relations during the Cold War, and worked actively for international disarmament. One of the cornerstones of its foreign policy is its support for the UN.

[28] During four decades in power from 1932 to 1976, under the leadership of Tage Erlander, the Social Democrats established

conditions which made it possible to combine rapid economic and industrial growth with a redistribution of wealth through direct taxation. Thus, a costly social welfare system was established, using the framework of a capitalist economy with strong state intervention.

[29] There are a number of Swedish corporations among the largest transnationals in the world, including Stora Kopparberg, Skf, Trelleborg, Ikea, Aga, Procordia, Modo, Sandvik, Esselte, Saab and Svensk stål.

[30] In the 1970s there was a slow-down of economic growth, due partly to the increasing cost of oil imports to satisfy half the country's energy needs. Of the other 50 per cent 15 came from nuclear reactors and 7 per cent from coal and coke.

[31] From 1981 onwards, relations between Sweden and the USSR were affected by the incursion of Soviet submarines into Swedish waters and the effects of the Chernobyl disaster.

[32] Atomic radiation from the Soviet Chernobyl nuclear plant affected northern and central Sweden, as well as the south of Lapland in 1986. The two main subsistence activities of the Sami people there, reindeer-herding and fishing, were badly affected by radiation, which contaminated all animal life in the area.

[33] Sweden was the first Western state to officially recognize North Vietnam (1969). The country's Prime Minister Olof Palme also acted as a mediator in the conflict between Iran and Iraq in 1982, and Sweden sponsored a meeting between Palestinians and American Jews in 1988.

[34] After the 1976 elections, amid an incipient economic crisis, the moderate, liberal and conservative parties formed a coalition. Six years later, the Social Democrats returned to power. In 1986, charismatic leader Olof Palme was shot dead in a murder case that has still not been solved. Ingvar Carlsson succeeded him as prime minister.

[35] In the years that followed, Parliament investigated an alleged case of bribery - involving the Government and Bofors, an arms manufacturing company - in connection with the sale of weapons to the Middle East and India. The country's laws forbade such conduct, as well as trade with

PROFILE

ENVIRONMENT

Sweden lies on the eastern part of the Scandinavian Peninsula. In the wooded northern area are iron mines and paper mills. The central region has fertile plateaus and plains. The main industrial area is located in the southern part of the country which is also productive agriculturally with wheat, potatoes and sugar-beet as well as cattle. The southern area is also the most densely populated.

SOCIETY

Peoples: Swedes 89.4 per cent; Finn and Lapp minorities; plus refugees from around the world.
Religion: Lutheran (official) 89 per cent; Catholics 1.8 per cent; Pentecostal Church 1.1 per cent. Other 10.6 per cent. Languages: Swedish (official); Finnish and Lapp.
Political Parties: The left-of-center Social Democratic Labor Party; the Center Party; the Moderate Party (conservative); the Green Party; the right-wing Liberal Party;). the Christian Democratic Party (center-right) and the Leftwing-Party (formerly Communist Party).
Social Organizations: Confederation of Swedish Trade Unions, Confederation of Professional Associations, Central Wage Earners' Organization.

THE STATE

Official Name: Konungariket Sverige. Administrative divisions: 24 provinces.
Capital: Stockholm 1,060,000 people (est 1995).
Other cities: Göteborg 444,553 people; Malmö 242,706; Uppsala 181,191 (1995).
Government: Hereditary constitutional monarchy. Sovereign: Carl XVI Gustaf (since September 15, 1973). Prime Minister: Göran Persson, since March 1996. The single-chamber Parliament (Riksdag) has 349 members. National Holiday: June 6, Swedish Flag Day.
Armed Forces: 64,000 (1994). Other: Coast Guard: 600 (1993).

areas where there are military tensions or with countries that are at war.

36   The social service and welfare system established in Sweden by the Social Democrats was aimed at ensuring a minimum level of assistance and a more egalitarian wealth redistribution, through graduated taxation of the highest income groups.

37   In spite of the important benefits obtained by the Swedish population, the largest taxpayers managed to evade taxation. On Carlsson's initiative, Parliament approved a fiscal reform in 1989, but it was considered too liberal and divided the Social Democrats.

38   Under this new law, citizens with incomes below a certain level paid the same rate of tax, at 30 per cent. The rate for incomes above this limit went down from 72 to 50 per cent, while capital started to be taxed directly.

39   Toward the end of the 1980s, the prospect of the European Union rekindled debate in Sweden over relations with its main trading partners. Until that time, Sweden had been a member of OECD, the Council of Europe and EFTA (European Free Trade Association). It was also on the Nordic Council, which had created a common labor market and had achieved a high degree of uniformity in legislation among the five member countries.

40   In 1990 negotiations were held in order to create a 'European economic space' and in June 1991 Sweden - represented by the Carlsson Government - applied for entry to the EC.

41   In the September 1991 elections, the Social Democrats lost their parliamentary majority. A coalition of the Moderate, Liberal, Center, and Christian Democratic parties appointed Carl Bildt, the leader of the Moderates, as prime minister. The new government promised to speed up Swedish membership of the EC, and the liberalization of the country's economy.

42   By the end of 1991, unemployment in Sweden hit a record 160,000, doubling figures for the previous year. An additional 83,000 people were receiving vocational training, and 14,000 had been absorbed by government unemployment schemes.

43   In 1991 and 92, the economic crisis served as the background for a

wave of xenophobia and attacks against foreigners, phenomena which had previously been non-existent in a country that had had liberal immigration and asylum policies throughout the 1960s and 1970s.

44   The government budget for the 1992-93 fiscal year involved serious cuts in public spending. This refuelled the controversy over the Swedish model, whose main features were a strong public sector and heavy taxation. In late January, for the first time in 35 years, thousands of Swedish construction workers held demonstrations, demanding jobs.

45   On August 26 1993, the King opened a new parliament for the Sami population of Lapland. At that time there were 17,000 Sami in Lapland, of a total population of 60,000 living in Norway (40,000), Finland, Russia and Sweden. Most of the people herd reindeer, with 10 per cent living by hunting deer. A major dispute with the government arose over the abolition of the Sami's exclusive hunting rights over their lands.

46   Sami children are given two weeks off in the autumn and spring in order for them to learn about pasturing reindeer. In 1971, the law regulating reindeer-raising recognized special Sami rights over the lands and watercourses where this is practiced.

47   After a contentious electoral campaign, in a referendum held in November 1994, 52 per cent of voters approved Sweden's entry into the European Union (EU). A significant part of the political establishment and a number of entrepreneurs supported entry, while left-wing groups and environmentalists were against it. There were also 'geographical' disagreements, since the majority of southern urban population voted for it and rural and northern inhabitants voted against it. Sweden joined the EU on January 1 1995.

48   Relations with France, one of the 15 members of the EU, became complicated because Stockholm openly criticized Paris' decision to hold further nuclear tests in late 1995 and 1996. In the domestic field, the Social Democrats continued their policy of reducing public deficit by increasing taxes and cutting state expenditure, which earned the confidence of

the so-called 'international financial markets'.

49   In May 1996, Minister of Finance Göran Persson replaced Carlsson and became head of a government that included 11 women and 10 men.

50   In September, the Prime Minister announced measures aimed at making the labor market more 'flexible'. The powerful Confederation of Swedish Unions considered the proposals an attack on worker security. Furthermore, it accused the Government of 'swerving to the right' and threatened to withhold its annual contribution to the Social Democratic Party funds.

51   In August 1997 it was revealed that some 60,000 people, mostly women, had been sterilized between 1935 and 1976, as part of a government plan to prevent 'inferior human beings from multiplying'. The concept of the 'purity' of the Swedish race had been defined in 1922 by the Uppsala Institute of Racial Biology. The Government authorized a parliamentary investigation into the issue.

52   At the end of the year, with a healthier economic situation - with lower unemployment (achieved, some believed, by government short-term programs which masked the real situation) the Government announced it would not be part of the monetary union with other EU nations, saying the project was 'highly dubious'.

53   The Government issued a formal apology to the Sami population in August 1998 due to the 'injustices they had borne through the years' because of the colonization of Northern regions which expelled the Samis from their lands.

54   Even though the Social Democrats had their worst election result in history at the September elections (with just 36.6 per cent of the vote), they managed to retain power due to a parliamentary majority supported by the Green Party and the former Socialist Party.

55   However, this was not a comfortable majority for the Social Democrats. They considered the political platforms of the other two parties to be unrealistic. In turn, the other two parties were against joining the European single currency system. ∎

STATISTICS

DEMOGRAPHY

Population: 8,892,000 (1999)
Annual growth: 0.4 % (1975/97)
Estimates for year 2015 (million): 9.1 (1999)
Annual growth to year 2015: 0.1 % (1997/2015)
Urban population: 83.2 % (1997)
Urban Growth: 0.4 % (1980/95)
Children per woman: 1.6 (1998)

HEALTH

Life expectancy at birth: 79 years (1998)
male: 76 years (1998)
female: 81 years (1998)
Maternal mortality: 5 per 100,000 live births (1990-98)
Infant mortality: 4 per 1,000 (1998)
Under-5 child mortality: 4 per 1,000 (1998)
Daily calorie supply: 3,160 per capita (1996)
299 doctors per 100,000 people (1993)

EDUCATION

School enrolment:
Primary total: 105 % (1990/96)
male: 105 % (1990/97)
female: 106 % (1990/97)
Secondary:
male: 126 % (1990/96)
female: 147 % (1990/96)
Tertiary: 50 % (1996)
Primary school teachers: one for every 1 (1996)

COMMUNICATIONS

445 newspapers (1996), 932 radios (1997), 476 TV sets (1996) and 682 main telephone lines (1996) per 1,000 people
Books: 158 new titles per 100,000 people (1992/94)

ECONOMY

Per capita, GNP: $ 25,580 (1998)
Annual growth, GNP: 2.8 % (1998)
Annual inflation: 2.4 % (1990/98)
Consumer price index: 100.9 (1998)
Currency: 7.9 kronor = $ 1 (1998)
Cereal imports: 211,917 metric tons (1998)
Food import dependency: 7 % (1997)
Fertilizer use: 1,104 kg per ha (1997)
Exports: $ 99,727 million (1997)
Imports: $ 83,758 million (1997)

ENERGY

Consumption: 5,869.0 Kgs of Oil equivalent per capita yearly (1997); 36.0 % imported (1997)

HDI (rank/value): 6/0.923 (1997)

Switzerland

Schweiz / Confederatio Helvetica

Population: 7,345,000 (1999)
Area: 41,284 SQ KM
Capital: Bern
Currency: Swiss franc
Language: German, French and Italian

Some Celtic tribes occupied the territory of Switzerland before Roman colonization. The most important of these were the Helvetians, who settled in the Alps and the Jura mountains. The area was strategically important for Rome, with access to its dominions. Consequently, the Alpine valleys north of the Italian peninsula were conquered by Julius Caesar in 58 BC.

[2] The Germanic tribes north of the Rhine invaded from the year 260 onwards. Between the 5th and 6th centuries the Germans established permanent settlements in the region east of the Aar river, together with Burgundian and Frankish groups. By 639 they had founded the kingdoms that would later become France.

[3] The Christian survivors from Roman times had completely disappeared when St Columba and St Gall arrived in the 6th century. These missionaries created the dioceses of Chur, Sion, Basel, Constance and Lausanne. Monasteries were built, in Saint-Gall, Zurich, Disentis and Romainmotier.

[4] Until the partition of Verdun in 843 these territories belonged to Charlemagne's empire. Thereafter, the region west of the Aar was allotted to Lothair, while the east remained in the hands of Louis the German. The French and German influence formed a peculiar blend with the Latin tradition of the Roman Catholic Church.

[5] Around 1033, for dynastic and political reasons, Helvetia became a part of the Holy Roman Empire, remaining so during the Middle Ages. In the 11th century the region was divided after the re-establishment of imperial authority and its disputes with the Papacy. Dukes, counts, and bishops exerted virtually autonomous local power.

[6] Walled cities served as administrative and commercial centers, and protected powerful families seeking to expand their possessions through wars against other lords and kingdoms. In the 13th century, Rudolf IV of Hapsburg conquered most of the territories of Kyburg and became the most powerful lord in the region.

[7] In the cities independence gradually developed in opposition to the nobility. Meanwhile the peasant communities in the most inaccessible valleys practiced economic cooperation to survive the harsh conditions, rejecting forced labor and payment of tithes in cash or kind.

[8] In 1231 the canton (area) of Uri fell under the authority of the Holy Roman Empire, and in 1240 Schwyz and Nidwald were subjected to Emperor Frederick II, although retaining the right to choose their own magistrates.

[9] The Hapsburg overlords questioned this freedom and uncertainty remained until Rudolf of Hapsburg was crowned king of Germany in 1273. He exercised his imperial rights in Uri and inherited rights over Schwytz and Unterwald until his death in 1291. These regions thereafter constituted the Perpetual League.

[10] As with other circumstantial alliances among the regions, the Perpetual League constituted an agreement for dispute arbitration, putting law above armed strength. The honorary magistrates had to be residents of those cantons.

[11] The league of the Uri, Schwyz, and Unterwald cantons was joined by the city of Zurich, constituting the first historic antecedent of the Swiss Confederation. This confederation was consolidated

with the victory of Margarten in 1315, defeating an army of knights sent to impose imperial law in the region by the Hapsburgs.

[12] The Confederation was supported by new alliances. In 1302 the League signed a pact with the city of Luzern, previously dependent on Vienna. In 1315 Zurich reaffirmed its union and in 1353 it was joined by Bern. The Glarus and Zug cantons joined later, forming the core of an independent state within the Germanic Empire.

[13] During the second half of the 14th century, the rural oligarchy was defeated, and their lands and laws given over to city councils. This democratic rural movement gave birth to the 'Landesgemeinde', a sovereign assembly of canton inhabitants and a similar movement was led by the city guilds.

[14] The Confederation soon launched into territorial conquest. During the 15th century the union grew to 13 cantons, it made alliances with other states, and the institution of government known as the Diet was formed where each canton was represented by two seats and one vote.

[15] In 1516, after the defeat of the Helvetians, the King of France forced a peace treaty with the cantons. In 1521 an alliance gave France the right to recruit Swiss soldiers. Only Zurich refused to sign this alliance, maintaining military and economic links with the Old Confederation until its end in 1798.

[16] The Reformation came to Switzerland with Huldrych Zwingli, a priest who preached against the mercenary service and the corruption and power of the clergy. Popular support for Zwingli strengthened the urban bourgeoisie. The Reformation became more radical in rural areas where harsh repression re-established the domination of cities over peasants.

[17] Zwingli's attempt to alter the federal alliance to benefit the reformed cities was frustrated by the military victory of the Catholic rural areas. The second national peace of Kappel, signed in 1531 gave the Catholic minority advantages over the Protestant majority.

[18] The areas where both religions coexisted were subject to constant tension, but cooperation was required to preserve the union of

WORKERS

1997
UNEMPLOYMENT: 4.1%

% OF LABOUR FORCE **1998**

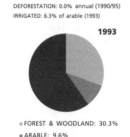

■ FEMALE: 40% ■ MALE: 60%
1990

■ SERVICES: 59.8%
■ INDUSTRY: 34.7%
■ AGRICULTURE: 5.5%

LAND USE

DEFORESTATION: 0.0% annual (1990/95)
IRRIGATED: 6.3% of arable (1993)

1993

FOREST & WOODLAND: 30.3%
ARABLE: 9.6%
OTHER: 60.1%

PUBLIC EXPENDITURE

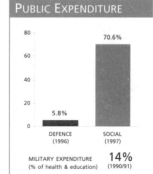

70.6%

5.8%

DEFENCE (1996)   SOCIAL (1997)

MILITARY EXPENDITURE **14%**
(% of health & education)   (1990/91)

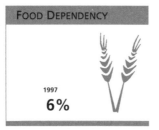
the federation. In Catholic regions agriculture prevailed, while in Protestant areas trade and industry flourished, aided by French, Italian and Dutch refugees.

[19] Popular consultation disappeared in the 17th century. The power of the cities caused uprisings, such as the great peasant revolt of 1653, which were harshly repressed. Three years later when a further war ensued the prerogatives of the Catholic cantons were re-established.

[20] During the European conflicts of the 17th and 18th centuries Switzerland remained neutral because of its religious division and its mercenary armies. Neutrality became a condition for the Confederation's existence. The policy of armed neutrality, which still holds, was first formulated by the Diet in 1674.

PROFILE

ENVIRONMENT

A small landlocked state in continental Europe, Switzerland is a mountainous country made up of three natural regions. To the northwest, on the French border, are the massive Jura mountains, an agricultural and industrial area. Industry is concentrated in the Mitteland, a sub-Alpine depression between the Jura and the Alps, with numerous lakes of glacial origin. It is also an agricultural and cattle-raising region. The Alps cover more than half of the territory and extend in a west-east direction with peaks of over 4,000 meters. The main activities of this region are dairy farming and tourism. The country's ecosystem is currently threatened by acid rain.

SOCIETY

Peoples: Two-thirds of the population are of German origin, while 18 per cent and 13 per cent are French and Italian, respectively. 17.1 per cent of the country's citizens or permanent residents are Italian, Yugoslav, Portuguese, German, Turkish or other nationalities.
Religions: 47.6 per cent Catholic, 44.3 per cent Protestant, 2.2 per cent Muslim, 1 per cent Orthodox Christian.
Languages: German, French and Italian. A very small minority (0.4 per cent) in certain parts of the Grisons canton to the east speak Rhaeto-Romanic (or Romansch), of Latin origin.
Political Parties: Major political parties are: the Social Democrats; the center-right Radical Party; the center-right Christian Democratic Party; the center-left Swiss People's Party; the center left Socialist Party; the Democratic Union of the Center, the right-wing Liberal Party; the Independent Party; and the leftist Labor Party. The ecologist Greens.
Social Organizations: The Swiss Federation of Trade Unions, with 480,000 members; the Confederation of Christian Trade Unions, with 110,000 members; the Federation of Swiss Employees' Societies with 160,000 members.

THE STATE

Official Name: Confederatio Helvetica (Romansche); Schweizerische Eidgenossenschaft (German); Confédération Suisse (French); Confederazione Svizzera (Italian).
Administrative Divisions: 20 Cantons, 6 Sub-Cantons.
Capital: Bern (administrative) 300,000 people; Lausanne (judicial) 117,553 (est 1995).
Other cities: Zurich 342,872 people; Basel 175,561; Geneva 172,737; Lausanne 117,153 (1995).
Government: Adolf Ogi, President of the Confederation since January 2000. Parliamentary republic with strong direct democracy. The legislative power is exercised by a federal assembly, with two bodies: the State Council, with 46 members, and the National Council, with 200 members. The executive power is in the hands of the Federal Council, with 7 members elected by parliament for 4-year terms.
National Holiday: August 1.
Armed Forces: 3,400 regular troops (1995) 28,000 annual conscripts (15 week courses).
Other: 480,000 Civil Defense.

[21] In 1712 the Protestant victory in the second battle of Villmergen ended religious struggles, ensuring the hegemony of cities which were undergoing industrial expansion. Switzerland became the most industrialized country in Europe. Industry was based on labor at home, completely transforming work in the countryside.

[22] Throughout the 18th century, a series of popular revolts against the urban oligarchy called for the reform of the Swiss Constitution. In March 1798, the Old Confederation fell under pressure from Napoleon's army. The Helvetic Republic was proclaimed 'whole and indivisible' with sovereignty for the people.

[23] Between the unitary Republic and the 1848 Federal Constitution, Switzerland was shaken by coups, popular revolts, and civil wars. The new federal pact marked a final victory for liberalism in the country. Two legislative bodies were established guaranteeing the rights of the small Catholic cantons.

[24] A state monopoly was created for custom duties and coin minting, while weights and measures were standardized, so satisfying the industrial and commercial bourgeoisie's economic requirements. The 1848 Constitution thus removed the obstacles to capitalist expansion.

[25] Nepotism and the concentration of capital benefited only the few and fuelled growing opposition to the institutional system. The 1874 Constitution partially addressed these issues, and introduced the mechanism of referendum as an element of direct democracy.

[26] Expansion of the home labor system delayed organization of the Swiss workers' movement in relation to the country's industrialization. The Swiss Workers' Federation, created in 1873 had only 3,000 members, and the Swiss Workers' Union, which replaced it in 1880, only exceeded this figure ten years later.

[27] The first achievement of the workers' movement was factory legislation, passed by parliament in 1877. The working day was limited to 11 hours with improved working conditions. In 1888 the Socialist Party was formed to give workers a political voice.

[28] In 1910, 15 per cent of the workers in Switzerland were foreign. Many were anarchists and socialists who had suffered persecution in their own countries and they consequently encouraged radical positions in the workers' movement. The Swiss Workers' Union took up a platform of 'proletarian class struggle', and the Socialist Party was inspired by the Second International's Marxism.

[29] World War I brought great internal tensions to Switzerland, especially between the French- and German-speaking regions. Under the leadership of Ulrich Wile, the Swiss army cooperated with Germany. Tension only decreased after the French victory, when Switzerland formally approached the allies and became a member of the League of Nations.

[30] Clashes between trade unions and employers echoed the tensions between the different language regions. The 1918 general strike, although lifted three days later under pressure from the armed forces, led the bourgeoisie to form an anti-Socialist bloc. That year proportional representation was introduced.

[31] The elections in 1919 marked the end of the liberal hegemony, in place since 1848. The Socialists obtained 20 per cent of the vote, leading liberals to ally with the peasants who had 14 per cent, while the conservatives became the second power in the Federal Council.

[32] These changes produced noticeable consequences during the following years. The 48-hour week was included in factory legislation, while in 1925 an article on old-age pensions was added to the constitution. Assistance to the unemployed improved and collective work contracts became more common.

[33] In the years before World War II, the Socialist Party was threatened by foreign and national fascism, and a sector split to form the Communist Party. The socialists were forced to include formal recognition of the state and national defence in their policies.

[34] During World War II, European powers recognized Swiss armed neutrality, but the country still suffered strong pressure from Nazi Germany. Throughout the war Switzerland maintained a delicate balance between accepting Hitler's advances and defending its independence; a strategy that kept them out of the conflict.

35 After the war, the West resented Switzerland's relations with Germany, and the USSR refused to re-establish diplomatic relations, broken off 1918. However, the country's financial power paved the way for its return to the international community. During the Cold War, Switzerland sided with the West but did not join the UN, in order to preserve its neutrality.

36 The Swiss economy expanded greatly during the postwar period. The chemical, food, and machinery exporting industries became great transnational corporations. In 1973 Switzerland was placed fourth in direct foreign capital investments, after the US, France, and Britain.

37 Switzerland's main transnational corporation, the food and babymilk manufacturer Nestlé AG, had 196,940 workers worldwide and sales worth $29.36 billion in 1989.

38 The Swiss economic expansion attracted workers from Italy, Spain and other southern European countries. Between 1945 and 1974 the number of immigrants rose from 5 to 17 per cent. Several referenda called for an end to immigration forced thousands of people back to their countries.

39 Due to its political neutrality, Switzerland did not join the European Economic Community in 1957. However, it has been a member of EFTA (European Free Trade Association) since 1960.

40 In 1959, after 10 years of voluntary absence, the socialists joined the Federal Council with two representatives. The Executive consisted of two Radicals, two Christian Democrats, two Socialists, and a peasants' representative. This meant that 80 per cent of the electorate was represented in government.

41 Women gained the right to vote in 1971, but some cantons retained male-only suffrage until 1985. In 1984, the first woman minister was elected when Elisabeth Kopp was made minister for justice and police.

42 Switzerland is governed by consensus, but the population has increasingly abstained in referendums. In the 1979 elections participation was lower than 50 per cent for the first time.

43 During the 1980s new opposition groups appeared, some feminist, some opposed to nuclear plants, and some youth groups fighting against the consumer society. A referendum in 1981 added a clause on equal rights to the Constitution.

44 According to 1981 statistics, male students outnumbered female by three to one in Switzerland. Women accounted for no more than 32.5 per cent of the economically active population, while men made up 63.9 per cent.

45 Since 1986 environmental problems have become more serious and the Government has taken measures to curb pollution, especially acid rain and pollution of the Rhine. In 1987 France, Germany and the Netherlands received compensation for damage caused by an accident in the Swiss chemical industry.

46 Another serious problem is the damage to the Alpine ecosystem. The rapid growth of cities in this area, and the increased transit of heavy trucks, have contributed to regional desertification. As a direct result, so-called natural disasters, such as floods and avalanches of rock, mud and snow have increased; events that would be less likely to occur if the area still had the protection offered by its natural tree coverage.

47 The 1986 Chernobyl disaster had greatly concerned the Swiss population and in 1989, a series of demonstrations took place. A referendum proposed the gradual elimination of existing nuclear power plants, and the Federal Parliament cancelled the construction of a sixth nuclear station.

48 Increasing social problems and the presence of immigrants have given encouragement to the Swiss extreme right. Although being small, the Swiss Democratic Party and the Party of Drivers xenophobic and opposed to social security policies, have both gained support since the fall of the Berlin Wall.

49 Switzerland's integration into the IMF was approved by a plebiscite in May 1992. In June 1993, Parliament approved the incorporation of Swiss troops into the United Nations peacekeeping forces. This represented an important change in Switzerland's traditional policy of neutrality. However, most of the Swiss voted against this proposal in a referendum in 1994.

50 One of the main obstacles to Swiss integration into the European Union was the objection to the free movement of workers between countries. A referendum in the same year approved an anti-racism law which punished discrimination while another granted the police powers to use greater 'severity' against illegal immigrants committing crimes within the country. This measure was widely criticized and considered a violation of the Swiss Constitution and the European Human Rights Convention.

51 In the general elections of October 22 1995, the Social Democrats took 54 seats, the Radicals 45, the Christian Democrats, 34, the Swiss People's Party 29 and the Greens 9.

52 In July 1997, Swiss banks - sued internationally by individuals - released a list of names of account-holders with funds untouched since World War II. Most of these were Jews later exterminated by the Nazis. The World Jewish Congress, the main plaintiff, said this presentation was only a symbolic gesture, as the banks had taken advantage of the funds for over 50 years.

53 In September 1997, 50.8 per cent of voters in a referendum rejected the reduction in unemployment benefit proposed by the Government. Observers claimed this could complicate the planned economic austerity measures.

54 The Government suspended the military intelligence chief on charges of having masterminded the operation leading to a multimillion dollar embezzlement by a former intelligence officer with the purpose of creating an underground army. The Minister of Defense, Adolf Ogi, who was in charge of the investigation, became a prominent political figure.

55 The Democratic Union won the October elections under Ogi's leadership. He became President on January 2000.

56 A 1998 government report established that anti-Semitism had flared up in Switzerland due to the controversy over its relations with Nazi Germany and also over the question of what Swiss banks had done with accounts belonging to Holocaust victims. A study sponsored by the US revealed in January 2000 that 16 per cent of the Swiss population had anti-Semitic feelings, and that this had increased during the 1990s. ∎

Syria

Suriyah

Population: 15,725,000 (1999)
Area: 185,180 SQ KM
Capital: Damascus (Dimashq)
Currency: Pound
Language: Arabic

Syria was once the name for the entire region between the peninsulas of Anatolia (Turkey) and Sinai, including the fertile crescent. Ancient civilizations coveted the territory: the Egyptians wanted it as a port, while the Persians considered the region a bridge to their plans of a universal empire.

[2] Between the 12th and 7th centuries BC, the Phoenician civilization developed on the central coastal stretch of the territory; a society of sailors and traders without expansionist aims. Phoenician cities were always independent, although some exercised temporary hegemony over others, and they developed the world's first commercial economy.

[3] The Phoenicians invented the alphabet, constructed ocean-going ships, practised large-scale ceramic and textile manufacturing, expanded and systematized geography, sailing around the coast of Africa. The propagation of these throughout the Mediterranean helped form what would be later called 'Western civilization', of which the Greeks were the main exponents.

[4] The territory came under the control of Alexander of Macedonia (also known as Alexander the Great) during the 4th century BC. After Alexander's death, his vast empire was divided and Syria became the center of a Seleucidan state (named for Seleucus Nicator, one of Alexander's generals) that initially stretched as far as India. The eastern part was later lost to the Parthians. In the Roman era the province of Syria was a border zone constantly shaken by

OCCUPIED BY ISRAEL
1 Southern Lebanon 1983-2000
2 Syria - Golan Heights 1967
3 West Bank 1967 (some towns now have autonomy)
Kurdistan
0 100 km

fierce local wars and resistance. One example of the latter was Queen Zenobia, whom the Romans finally managed to defeat in 272 AD.

[5] The Arabization of the territory was carried out by the Ummaia Caliphs, who, between the years 650 and 750, turned Damascus (Dimashq) into the capital of the empire (see Saudi Arabia), and fostered a strong national spirit. When the Ummaias were defeated by the Abbas, the capital was transferred to Baghdad, where the new caliphs enjoyed greater support. Although still economically and culturally important, the loss of political power proved significant: in the 11th century when Europeans invaded during the Crusades, the caliphs of Baghdad reacted with

indifference. Local emirs were left to their own resources, and disagreements among them allowed a small Christian force to conquer the area, leading to 200-years of occupation.

[6] The Egyptians initiated the process to drive out the Europeans. One result was that Syria became a virtual Egyptian province and center stage for a confrontation with Mongol invaders. In the 16th century, the country became a part of the Ottoman Empire.

[7] The Crusaders left behind a significant Christian community, especially with the Maronites, serving as sufficient cause for European interference from the 17th century onwards. The Egyptian Khedive Muhammad (Mehemet) Ali conquered Syria in 1831, and heavy taxes and

compulsory military service provoked revolt among both Christian and Muslim communities. The European powers, concerned with propping up the Turkish Empire to stave off the potential emergence of a more aggressive power like Egypt, used the repression of Christians as an excuse for intervention. Ali's offensive was suppressed and the 'protection of Syrian Christians' was entrusted to the French. A withdrawal of Egyptian troops took place in 1840, along with the restoration of Ottoman domination and the establishment of Christian missions and schools subsidized by Europeans.

[8] However, the scene was set for confrontation and in 1858, Maronite Christians gathered in the mountainous region between Damascus and Jerusalem rebelled against the ruling class and eliminated the traditional system of land ownership. Their Muslim neighbors, particularly the Druze, moved to repress the movement before it spread further, triggering a conflict that culminated in the deaths of a large number of Christians in June 1860.

[9] A month later, French troops disembarked in Beirut, ostensibly to protect the Christian community, and forcing the Turkish Government to create a separate province called 'Little Lebanon'. This was to be governed by a Christian appointed by the Sultan but with the approval of the European powers, with its own police force, and traditional privileges were abolished in the territory. The social conflict thus became a confrontation between confessional groups with the Christians in 'Little Lebanon' placed in a position of superiority over the local Muslim population, providing firm roots for the politico-religious conflict that has marked Lebanese history ever since.

[10] When an Arab rebellion broke out during World War I (see Saudi Arabia, Jordan and Iraq), Emir Faisal was proclaimed king of Syria. At the time French and British intentions were unknown, but the Sykes-Picot agreement divided the fertile crescent giving Syria (with

WORKERS

% OF LABOUR FORCE **1998**

■ FEMALE: 26% ■ MALE: 74%

1990

■ SERVICES: 42.9%
■ INDUSTRY: 24.0%
■ AGRICULTURE: 33.1%

LAND USE

DEFORESTATION: 2.2% annual (1990/95)
IRRIGATED: 17.7% of arable (1993)

1993

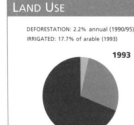

■ FOREST & WOODLAND: 3.5%
■ ARABLE: 27.6%
■ OTHER: 68.9%

PUBLIC EXPENDITURE

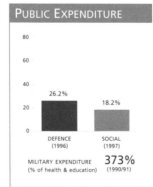

26.2% DEFENCE (1996)
18.2% SOCIAL (1997)

MILITARY EXPENDITURE
(% of health & education)
373%
(1990/91)

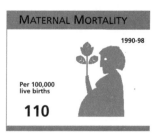
Lebanon) to France, and Palestine (including Jordan) and Iraq to Britain.

[11] In 1920 France occupied Syria forcing Faisal to retreat. Two months later, Syria was divided into five states: Greater Lebanon (adding other regions to the province of 'Little Lebanon'), Damascus, Aleppo, Djabal Druza and Alawis (Latakia). The latter four were reunified in 1924.

[12] Throughout 1932, Syria experienced a period of relative stability, and independence seemed imminent. A Syrian president and parliament were elected that year, but France made it clear that autonomy was unacceptable. This attitude engendered political agitation and confrontation, which only ended with a 1936 agreement with the French. France recognized certain Syrian demands, chiefly reunification with Lebanon. However, the French Government never ratified the agreement, and this led to new waves of violence, which culminated in the 1939 resignation of the Syrian President and a French order to suspend the 1930 constitution that governed both Syria and Lebanon.

[13] In 1941, French and British troops occupied the region to flush out Nazi collaborators. In 1943 Chikri al-Quwatli was elected president of Syria and Bechara al-Kuri president of Lebanon. Bechara al-Kuri proposed elimination of the mandate provisions from the constitution; however, he and his cabinet members were imprisoned by the ever-present French troops. Violent demonstrations followed in both Lebanon and Syria, and the British pressed for withdrawal of the French. In March 1946, the United Nations finally ordered the European forces to withdraw. This was completed in 1947 and the end of the French mandate was officially declared.

[14] In 1948 Syrian troops fought to prevent the partition of Palestine, and in 1956 joined Egypt in the battle against Israeli, French and British aggression. This aggression was the answer to Egyptian President Gamal Abdel Nasser's decision to nationalize the Suez Canal.

[15] In 1958, Syria joined Egypt in founding the United Arab Republic, but Nasser's ambitious integration project collapsed in 1961. Ten years later the scheme was reactivated, with greater flexibility and the Federation of Arab Republics was created including Libya.

[16] In 1963, after a revolution, the Ba'ath Arab Socialist Party came to power. Their main tenet was that the Arab countries were merely 'regions' of a larger Arab Nation. In November 1970, General Hafez al-Assad became president. He launched a modernization campaign, including a series of social and economic changes. The subsequent party congress named Assad party leader and proposed 'accelerating the stages towards socialist transformation of different sectors'. This guideline was adopted and became part of the new constitution which was approved in 1973.

[17] Syria took an active part in the Arab-Israeli wars of 1967 and 1973, during which Israeli troops occupied the Golan Heights. Syria also resisted US efforts to impose a 'settlement' in the Middle East, together with Algeria, Iraq, Libya, Yemen and the Palestine Liberation Organization (PLO). They also opposed the Camp David agreement (see Egypt).

[18] Syrian troops formed a major part of the Arab Deterrent Force that intervened in Lebanon in 1976 to prevent partition of the country by right-wing Lebanese factions allied with Israel.

[19] In 1978, the Syrian and Iraqi branches of the Ba'ath Party drew closer, but negotiations for creation of a single state disintegrated. In late 1979, at the congress of the Syrian branch of the Ba'ath Party, the Muslim Brotherhood (a right-wing Islamic movement) was harshly censured and were labeled 'Zionist agents'.

[20] In 1980, the Government set a September deadline giving brotherhood members the opportunity to surrender before capital punishment was enforced for acts of sabotage.

[21] Brotherhood attacks continued. In 1982 the army launched a full offensive which resulted in thousands of casualties. The Syrian Government blamed Iraq for arming the rebels, and closed the border between the two countries in April 1982. Iraq retaliated by closing the oil pipeline connecting Kirkuk, Iraq, to the Syrian port of Banias.

[22] The virtual alliance formed in 1980 between Saudi Arabia, Iraq and Jordan and tensions between those three countries and Syria were exacerbated by the outbreak of the Iran-Iraq War. Assad charged Iraq as the aggressor and diverted attention from what he called the major regional issue - the Palestinian question. Toward the end of the year, Syrian accusations of Jordanian support for the Brotherhood brought the two countries to the verge of war. The mediation of Saudi prince Abdalla Ibn Abdul-Aziz averted armed conflict.

[23] In 1981 the 'missile crisis' broke out in Syria, when the Christian Phalangist Movement sought to extend their area of authority to include the area around the Lebanese city of Zahde. An Arab Deterrent Force, organized and commanded by Syria, attempted to prevent the advance. Syria installed Soviet surface-to-air SAM-9 missiles, triggering an Israeli reaction. The crisis was finally averted, but in 1982 Israel invaded Lebanon, and destroyed the bases of Syrian missiles.

[24] In mid-1983 there was a crisis between the Syrian authorities and the PLO leadership. This encouraged Syria to support the Palestinian groups opposed to Yasser Arafat's leadership, until

PROFILE

ENVIRONMENT

To the west, near the sea, lies the Lebanon mountain range. To the south there are semi-desert plateaus and to the north low plateaus along the basin of the Euphrates River. Farming - grains, grapes and fruit - is concentrated in the western lowlands that receive adequate rainfall. In the south, the volcanic plateaus of the Djebel Druze are extremely fertile farmlands, some as the oases surrounding the desert, the main one being that of Damascus. Cotton and wool are exported. Exploitation of oil fields is the country's chief industry. The dumping of toxic substances from the extraction of crude is responsible for the high levels of pollution of Syria's waters.

SOCIETY

Peoples: Syrians are mostly Arabs, with minority ethnic groups in the north: Kurds, Turks and Armenians. There are few statistics on the number of Palestinian refugees (they were around 200,000 in 1977), and the Jewish population was authorized to emigrate in 1992.
Religions: Mainly Muslims, mostly Sunni, followed by Alamites, Shi'a and Ismailites. Also minor communities of eastern Christian religions.
Languages: Arabic (official). Minority groups speak their own languages.
Political Parties: The Ba'ath Arab Socialist Party, founded in Damascus in 1947 by Michel Aflaq, including the National Progressive Front and other minor parties. The armed political-religious opposition is represented by the Muslim Brotherhood, a fundamentalist Sunni sect.
Social Organizations: The General Federation of Labor Unions unites ten workers' federations representing different sectors of the economy.

THE STATE

Official Name: Al-Jumhouriya al Arabiya as-Suriya.
Administrative Divisions: 14 Districts.
Capital: Damascus (Dimashq) 3,000,000 people (est 1995).
Other cities: Aleppo (Halab) 1,591,000 people; Homs (Hims) 644,000; Latakia 306,500; Hamah 229,000 (1994).
Government: Bashar al-Assad, President since June 2000; Muhammad Mustafa Miro, Prime Minister since March 2000. The People's Council (a unicameral legislature) has 195 members.
National Holidays: April 17, Independence Day (1946); November 16, Revolution Day (1978).
Armed Forces: 421,000 troops (1996). **Other:** 8,000 Gendarmes.

the division ended in 1987. The fall in oil prices further aggravated the economic problems caused by the war and the Government set up strict austerity measures in 1984: financial activities were tightly controlled, borders were closed to the illegal trafficking of merchandise, previously tolerated, and public expenditure was substantially reduced.

[25] In 1985, President Assad won a new seven-year term. In 1987, Prime Minister Abdul Rauf al-Kassem was forced to resign amid charges of corruption, following the resignation of four other ministers. In November 1987, Mahmoud Az-Zoubi, president of the People's Assembly, was chosen as Prime Minister.

[26] In April 1987, at a summit meeting of Arab countries, most nations sought alignment with Syria in exchange for economic assistance, and condemned Iranian prolongation of the war. Syria maintained its position on Iran, and vetoed the motion for Egypt's re-entry into the Arab League.

[27] In October 1986, the British Government accused Syria of supporting a terrorist attempt against an Israeli plane at London airport. In November most of the EEC countries broke off diplomatic relations with Syria, although there were disagreements from some countries. In July 1987 all the EEC countries except for Britain re-established relations with Syria, when the Syrian Government withdrew support of the Al-Fatah Revolutionary Council, a Palestinian organization which opposed Yasser Arafat. In May 1990, Syria finally re-established diplomatic relations with Egypt.

[28] When Iraq invaded Kuwait, Syria immediately sided with the anti-Iraqi alliance and sent troops to Saudi Arabia. Diplomatic relations with the US improved noticeably. During the crisis Syria increased its influence over Lebanon and strengthened the allied government in that country; they were also successful in disarming most of the autonomous militias.

[29] In May 1991 Syria and Lebanon signed a cooperation agreement whereby Syria recognized Lebanon as an independent and separate state, for the first time since both countries gained independence from France.

[30] In December 1991, al-Assad was re-elected for the fourth time, by 99.98 per cent of the vote, in elections which had him as sole candidate. That month, the Government announced the pardon of 2,800 political prisoners, members of the Muslim Brotherhood.

[31] In 1992, the Government abolished the death penalty and allowed the emigration of 4,000 Jews. On the economic front GNP grew 7 per cent and exports of oil and its by-products amounted to $2 billion. New legislation favored investments in the private sector, which saw significant growth between 1991 and 1993.

[32] Syria stayed away from the first stages of the regional peace process, which facilitated the establishment of a limited autonomy for Palestine and the signing of agreements between Israel and Jordan in July 1994. In January, a 'historic' meeting took place between US President Bill Clinton and Assad in Geneva and in September, the Syrian minister of foreign affairs was interviewed for the first time on Israeli television. However, Damascus maintained its refusal to negotiate officially with Israel, due to the murder of 29 Palestinians in Hebron committed by an Israeli settler in February.

[33] In the domestic field, the death of Basel al-Assad, eldest son and supposed successor of the Syrian President, increased uncertainty regarding the country's political future. In August, the ruling National Progressive Front won the general elections but only 49 per cent of registered voters took part.

[34] In June 1995, official negotiations with Israel failed to return the Golan Heights to Syria as Tel Aviv wanted, to maintain limited military presence in the region indefinitely. In October, a Hezbollah ambush of Israeli troops in southern Lebanon complicated negotiations again. In mid 1996, al-Assad participated in a meeting of Arab countries to co-ordinate a common strategy for negotiation with Israel.

[35] As part of a policy to stimulate the Syrian economy private sector, key state sectors, including electricity generation, cement production and pharmaceuticals were opened up to private capital.

[36] In November 1997, Damascus unexpectedly strengthened relations with Baghdad at the threat of fresh US military intervention in Iraq - a strategy designed to work against the rapidly consolidating Turkish-Israeli alliance. Given the situation of the Golan Heights, militarily Syria would remain in the middle of this new bloc. If Iraq were to be beaten, new states could emerge on the basis of linguistic or religious criteria, with Turkey possibly gaining control of the oil fields of Iraqi Kurdistan.

[37] The threat presented by the Turkish-Israeli military bloc - which planned to produce a thousand new tanks for its armed forces - forced Iran to join the Syrian-Iraqi negotiations on security issues in April 1998.

[38] Al-Assad was re-elected for his seventh consecutive five-year presidential period in 1999. The President stated during his electoral speech that the Government needed 'new blood' to push ahead economic reforms.

[40] All 37 of Prime Minister Mahmoud el-Zouebi's cabinet members resigned in March 2000. Mohamed Mustafa Miro, a veteran leader of the Ba'ath party and governor of Aleppo province, was appointed the new Premier.

[41] Israel withdrew from Southern Lebanon in May 2000 but this was not matched by a parallel withdrawal from the Golan Heights.

[42] Al-Assad's sudden death in June 10 plunged the country into mourning for the only leader most Syrians had ever known. Moves to install his 34-year-old son Bashar as the new president started at once. Parliament voted to amend the constitution to lower the minimum age for being president from 40 to 34. The the next day, Bashar was declared commander of the armed forces and nominated party president. ∎

Tajikistan

Tadzhikistan

Population: 6,104,000 (1999)
Area: 143,100 SQ KM
Capital: Dushanbe (Dusanbe)
Currency: Rouble
Language: Tajik

A round 500 BC, Central Asia and southern Siberia's first centers of settled civilization arose in what is now Tajikistan. The Bactrian State was located in the upper tributaries of the Amu Darya. Likewise, in the Zeravshan river basin and the Kashkadarya river valley lay the nucleus of another State, Sogdiana. The inhabitants of these early civilizations built villages, with adobe and stone houses all along the rivers which they used for irrigating their crops. These included wheat, barley and millet, and a variety of fruits. Navigation was well developed and the cities which lay along the route of the caravans uniting Persia, China and India became important trading centers.

[2] In the 6th century BC these lands were annexed by the Persian Achaemenid Empire. In the 4th century BC, Alexander the Great conquered Bactria and Sogdiana. With the fall of his empire in the 3rd century, the Greco-Bactrian State and the Kingdom of Kushan emerged, and subsequently fell to the onslaught of the advancing Yuechzhi and Tojar steppe tribes. In the 4th and 5th centuries AD, Sogdiana and its surrounding regions were invaded by the Eftalites, and in the 6th and 7th centuries, by Central Asian Turkish peoples. In the 7th century, Tajikistan became a part of the Arab Caliphate, along with other Central Asian regions. After its demise, the region was incorporated into the Tahirid and Samanid kingdoms. In the 9th and 10th centuries, the Tajik people emerged as an identifiable ethnic group.

[3] From the 10th to the 13th centuries AD, Tajikistan formed part of the Gaznevid and Qarakhanid empires, as well as the realm of the Shah of Khwarezm. In the early 13th century, Tajikistan was conquered by Genghis Khan's Mongol Tatars. In 1238, Tarabi, a Tajik artisan, led a popular revolt. From the 14th to the 17th centuries, the Tajiks were under the control of the Timurids and the Uzbek Shaybanid dynasty. From the 17th to the 19th centuries, there were small fiefdoms throughout Tajikistan whose chieftains alternately submitted to or revolted against the khans of Bukhara.

[4] In the 1860s and 1870s, the Russian Empire conquered Central Asia, and the northern part of Tajikistan was annexed by Russia. The Khanate of Bukhara however maintained a relationship of sovereignty rather than annexation with Russia. The Tajik population of Kuliab, Guissar, Karateguin and Darvaz was incorporated into the Khanate as the province of Eastern Bukhara. Oppression by the Russian bureaucracy and the local feudal lords triggered a wave of peasant revolts toward the end of the 19th century and beginning of the 20th century. The most important of these was the 1885 uprising led by Vose.

[5] In 1916, during World War I, the local populations of Central Asia and Kazakhstan revolted over the mobilization of their people for rearguard duty with the retreating Russian army. After the triumph of the Bolshevik revolution in St Petersburg in October 1917, Soviet power was established in Northern Tajikistan. In April 1918, this territory became a part of the Autonomous Soviet Socialist Republic of Turkistan. Nevertheless, a large number of Tajiks remained under the power of the Emirate of Bukhara, which existed until 1921. In early 1921, the Red Army took Dushanbe, but in February it was forced to withdraw from Eastern Bukhara.

[6] Having broken Alim Khan's resistance in 1921-22, Soviet power was proclaimed throughout the entire territory of Tajikistan. In 1924, the Soviet Socialist Republic of Uzbekistan was formed, of which the Autonomous Soviet Socialist Republic of Tajikistan was a part. In January 1925, the Autonomous Region of Gorno-Badakhshan was established, high up in the Pamir range. On November 16 1929, Tajikistan became a federated republic of the Soviet Union. In the 1920s and 1930s, land and water reforms were carried out. The collectivization of agriculture was followed by industrialization, and the so-called 'cultural revolution' campaign.

[7] After World War II, the Soviet regime carried out a series of large construction projects, including a system of canals and reservoirs linking up with water projects in the neighboring republic of Uzbekistan. The purpose of this irrigation network was to develop the region's agricultural potential, especially for the cultivation of cotton. In the 1970s and 1980s, the effects of mismanagement and economic stagnation were felt in Tajikistan, one of the poorest regions in the USSR, with a high rate of unemployment, especially among the young, who made up most of the population.

[8] From 1985 onwards, the changes promoted by President Mikhail Gorbachev made the democratization process possible, which in turn gave way to the expression of long-suppressed ethnic and religious friction in Tajikistan. In February 1990, there were violent incidents between Tajiks and Russians in the capital, with more than 30 people killed and scores injured. The Government decreed a state of emergency, which remained in effect during that year's Supreme Soviet (Parliament) elections, in which the Communist Party won 90 per cent of the available seats. The opposition attributed the February events to provocation by the former Soviet secret police (KGB), aimed at discrediting Gorbachev's reforms and suppressing nationalist tendencies. Muslims and Democrats called for the dissolution of the Soviet, because the elections had been held while a state of emergency was in effect.

[9] In August1990, Parliament passed a vote of no-confidence in President Majkamov, accusing him of supporting those responsible for the Moscow coup, and forcing him to resign. He was succeeded by Kadridin Aslonov as interim president of the republic.

[10] Aslonov's decision to ban the Communist Party (CP) of Tajikistan, announced after the coup attempt against Gorbachev in August 1991, was not supported by Parliament. Dominated by hardline communists, Parliament forced Aslonov to resign, naming Rajmon Nabiev to take his place as interim president. Nabiev had been First Secretary of the local CP until ousted by Gorbachev in 1985. In mid-September 1991, Parliament approved the Declaration of Independence and the new constitution, decreeing a state of emergency and banning the Islamic Renaissance Party.

[11] Tajikistan's religious revival has been stronger than in the rest of the former Soviet Union republics. In the early 1980s, there were 17 mosques; 10 years later, as a result of the liberalization promoted by Moscow, there were 128 large mosques, 2,800 places of prayer, an Islamic institute and five centers offering religious instruction. According to unofficial estimates, at this time between 60 and 80 per cent of the population were practising Muslims. The Islamic Renaissance Party proposed that the state allow political and religious freedom, but that it be based on Islam, with Sharia (Islamic law) as the law of the land. In 1991, the Tajik Government instituted the celebration of several important Muslim holy days.

[12] The mobilization of pro-Islamic forces, on the one hand, and mediation by Moscow, on the other, led to the state of emergency and the Communist Party ban being lifted in early October. Two months later, in the first presidential elections in November 1991, Nabiev was confirmed in his post by 58 per cent of the voters.

[13] On December 21 Tajikistan entered the Commonwealth of Independent States (CIS). At the same time, the Autonomous Region of Gorno-Badakhshan, high in the Pamir mountains, asked to be granted the status of an autonomous republic. Like neighboring Afghanistan, the majority of this region's inhabitants are Shi'a Muslims.

[14] During his visit to Dushanbe, in February 1992, US Secretary of State James Baker expressed the West's concern over the region's uranium deposits. Tajikistan, together with Turkmenistan and Uzbekistan, have important deposits of this mineral, which is crucial to the development of nuclear weapons.

[15] Outside Dushanbe there was violence from both pro-government and opposition forces, causing a conflict of civil-war proportions. Another protest demonstration against Nabiev led to his resignation on September 8. A private pro-communist army in the northern part of the country, far from accepting this state of affairs, launched a major offensive. The attack ended in December, with the fall of the capital and the formation of a new government controlled by the Popular Front.

[16] Some 300,000 people fled to other CIS republics and Afghanistan. As of February 1993, the persecution and massacre of members of the opposition began to diminish.

[17] The Russian Government of President Boris Yeltsin was the first to recognize the new regime, led by Imamali Rajmonov, whom Yeltsin considered ideal for keeping the Islamic groups under control. In March, bombing started from Afghanistan, followed by incursions of opposition troops across the Russian-controlled frontier.

[18] Following nine months of confrontations, in April 1994, representatives of the Government and the Islamic and liberal opposition met in Moscow, at a time when Tajikistan was more dependent than ever on Russian aid, both military and economic. Rajmonov proposed a new constitution, approved in November by referendum. The outgoing president was also re-elected in the presidential elections which accompanied the referendum, but the Islamic opposition accused the Government of fraud.

[19] In February 1996, Prime Minister Jamshed Karimov resigned and was replaced by Yakhyo Azimov. Two ceasefires, sponsored by the United Nations, and an agreement signed in Moscow late that year, failed to stop the fighting. Also, the Government was weakened after the rebellion of two of its main military leaders. The crisis was settled after a compromise was reached with both.

[20] The civil war ended officially on June 27 1997 with the signing in Moscow of a peace agreement between the Government and the opposition, grouped in the so-called Tajik Opposition Union (TOU). The agreement secured 30 per cent of cabinet positions for the opposition, places in the justice system and an amnesty for those accused of war crimes.

[21] The agreement failed to stop the violence or the activity of armed bands in major cities. The Islamic opposition blamed the attack on TOU splinter groups. Various smaller armed groups, excluded from the peace process, made their presence felt with attacks against the Government and the opposition.

[22] In February 1998, the Government announced the intensification of a privatization program to attract investments. The four year war had taken the lives of tens of thousands and more than 600,000 were displaced within the country, while another 300,000 fled to Afghanistan, Russia and other CIS countries.

[23] The peace process gained momentum after Akbar Turajonzoda, second in the UTO hierarchy, returned from his exile in Iran to become the first deputy prime minister. One of his first proposals was to admit the Islamic Renaissance Party (IRP) with all its rights into the political arena, allowing it to take part in the elections. Parliament passed a bill banning the creation of religious parties. Although the president vetoed the bill, he stated he would not allow an Islamic government in the country.

[24] Elections called for November 1999 were held in spite of strong protests by Usmon, the only opposition candidate. According to the opposition, other candidates were not able to collect the signatures required to run for office due to governmental pressure. Several groups called for boycotting the elections because of these irregularities, but the measure was lifted hours before the ballot. President Rakhmonov obtained 96 per cent of the vote, which represented 98 per cent of the electoral roll of 2.8 million.

[25] A car bomb killed the deputy secretary of security Shamsullo Dzhabirov, two weeks before the February 2000 parliamentary elections. The results gave the victory to the ruling party with 64.5 per cent of the vote. The Communist Party was in second place, with 20 per cent. Muslim groups obtained 7.5 per cent of the ballots in an election considered acceptable by all. Usmon was dismissed as Minister of the Economy two weeks after the elections. ∎

PROFILE

ENVIRONMENT

The Tian Shan, Guissaro-Alai and Pamir mountains occupy more than 90 per cent of Tajikistan's territory. This republic is located in the southeastern part of Central Asia between the Syr Darya River and the Fergana Valley in the north, the Pamir and Paropaniz mountain ranges in the south, the Karakul lake and the headwaters of the Murgab in the east, and the Guissar and Vakhsh valleys in the southwest. The Turkistan, Alai and Zeravshan mountains cross Tajikistan from north to south, joining the Pamir plateau. The highly cultivated valleys (lying at an altitude of 1000-2000 meters) have a warm, humid climate. Lower mountains and valleys, located in northern and southeastern Tajikistan, have an arid climate. It is bounded by Kyrgyzstan in the north, Uzbekistan in the west, China in the southeast and Afghanistan in the southwest. Abundant mineral resources include iron, lead, zinc, antimony and mercury, as well as important uranium deposits. Since 1960, land under irrigation has increased by 50 per cent, but as in other countries where cotton is the sole crop, the salinity of the soil has increased. Due to the lack of adequate sewage systems, and insufficient supplies of drinking water, a high proportion of Tajik infants suffer from diarrhea, the main cause of the country's high infant mortality rate.

SOCIETY

Peoples: Tajik 63.8 per cent; Uzbek 24.0 per cent; Russian 6.5 per cent; Tatar 1.4 per cent; Kyrgyz 1.3 per cent; Ukrainian 0.7 per cent; German,0.3 per cent; other 2.0 per cent. **Religions:** Muslim (Sunni 80 per cent; Shi'a 5 per cent). **Languages:** Tajik (official), Uzbek, Russian. **Political Parties:** Communist Party; Socialist Party; Rastokhez People's Movement; Islamic Renaissance Party; Democratic Party. **Social Organizations:** Union Federation of Tajikistan.

THE STATE

Official Name: Yumhuri Tochikiston. **Administrative Divisions:** 3 Regions, 57 Districts. **Capital:** Dushanbe (Dusanbe) 720,000 people (est 1995). **Other cities:** Khujand (formerly Leninabad) 164,500 people; Kulob 79,300; Oürghonteppa 58,400; Uroteppa 47,700. **Government:** Inomali Rakhmonov, President since 1994. Akil Akilov, Prime Minister since December 1999. **National Holiday:** September 9, Independence (1991). **Armed Forces:** 7,000; 6,000 Russian troops (1996).

STATISTICS

DEMOGRAPHY

Population: 6,104,000 (1999)
Annual growth: 2.5 % (1975/97)
Estimates for year 2015 (million): 7.8 (1999)
Annual growth to year 2015: 1.5 % (1997/2015)
Urban population: 32.4 % (1997)
Children per woman: 4.1 (1998)

HEALTH

Life expectancy at birth: 67 years (1998)
male: 64 years (1998)
female: 70 years (1998)
Maternal mortality: 65 per 100,000 live births (1990-98)
Infant mortality: 55 per 1,000 (1998)
Under-5 child mortality: 74 per 1,000 (1998)
Daily calorie supply: 2,129 per capita (1996)
210 doctors per 100,000 people (1993)
Safe water: 60 % (1990/98)

EDUCATION

Literacy: 99 % (1995)
male: 99 % (1995)
female: 98 % (1995)
School enrolment:
Primary total: 93 % (1990/96)
male: 95 % (1990/97)
female: 92 % (1990/97)
Secondary:
male: 81 % (1990/96)
female: 72 % (1990/96)
Tertiary: 20 % (1996)
Primary school teachers: one for every 24 (1996)

COMMUNICATIONS

20 newspapers (1996), 142 radios (1997), 279 TV sets (1996) and 42 main telephone lines (1996) per 1,000 people
Books: 4 new titles per 100,000 people (1992/94)

ECONOMY

Per capita, GNP: $ 370 (1998)
Annual growth, GNP: 15.2 % (1998)
Annual inflation: 300.0 % (1990/98)
Currency: 776.6 roubles = $ 1 (1998)
Fertilizer use: 834 kg per ha (1997)
Exports: $ 1,918 million (1995)
Imports: $ 1,907 million (1995)
External debt: $ 1,070 million (1998); $ 178 per capita (1998)
Debt service: 13.7 % of exports (1998)
Development aid received: $ 101 million (1997); $ 18.5 per capita (1997); 5.00 % of GNP (1997)

ENERGY

Consumption: 562.0 Kgs of Oil equivalent per capita yearly (1997); 63.0 % imported (1997)

HDI (rank/value): 108/0.665 (1997)

Tanzania

Tanzania

Population: 32,792,000 (1999)
Area: 883,749 SQ KM
Capital: Dodoma
Currency: Shilling
Language: Swahili and English

The oldest fossils of the human race were found in the Olduvai gorge, in the north of Tanzania. These remains date from millions of years ago, yet little is known about life on most of modern Tanzania's mainland before the 7th century.

[2] A mercantile civilization, heavily influenced by Arab culture, flourished in this region between 695 and 1550 (See The Zandj Culture in East Africa) but it was eventually destroyed by Portuguese invaders. One hundred and fifty years later, under the leadership of the Sultan of Oman, the Arabs succeeded in driving out the remaining Portuguese, but the rich cultural and commercial life of past times did not return. As the slave trade grew, Kilwa and Zanzibar became the leading trade centers.

[3] Between 1698 and 1830, Zanzibar and the coast were under the rule of the Oman Sultanate, with the Sultan living in Zanzibar. His sons, under British pressure, later split the inherited domain, dividing the old Sultanate in two.

[4] At the end of the 19th century a German adventurer, claiming rights over Tanzania, based on treaties signed by local Tanganyika leaders set up a company which immediately received imperial endorsement, leasing out the mainland coastal strip to the sultan of Zanzibar. The British had also made a similar deal, so the Berlin Conference, where the European powers distributed Africa among themselves, was obliged to recognize the claims of both powers. The European powers eventually agreed upon the 'cession of German rights' in favor of Britain.

[5] The areas of influence were delimited in 1886. Tanganyika, Rwanda and Burundi were recognized as German possessions while Zanzibar formally became a British protectorate in 1890. German troops and British warships joined efforts to stifle a Muslim rebellion on the coast of Tanganyika in 1905.

[6] After the defeat of Germany in World War I, the League of Nations placed Tanganyika under British mandate, while Rwanda-Burundi was handed over to the Belgians.

[7] Nationalist feelings were later channelled into TANU (Tanganyikan African National Union), a party founded in 1954 by Julius Nyerere, a primary school teacher known by the people as Mwalimu, the teacher.

[8] After seven years of organizing and fighting against racial discrimination and the appropriation of lands by European settlers, independence was achieved in 1961, and Nyerere became President, elected by an overwhelming majority.

[9] Meanwhile, in Zanzibar, two nationalist organizations, which had been active sporting and cultural institutions since the 1930s, merged to form the Afro-Shirazi Party in February 1957. In December 1963, the British transferred power to the Arab minority, and a month later this government was overthrown by the Afro-Shirazi. In April, Tanganyika and Zanzibar formed the United Republic of Tanzania, though the island maintained some autonomy.

[10] Under Nyerere's leadership, Tanzania based its foreign policy on non-alignment, standing for African unity, providing unconditional support to liberation movements, particularly FRELIMO in neighboring Mozambique.

[11] In February 1967, TANU issued the Arusha Declaration proclaiming socialism as its objective. The declaration laid down the principle of self-sufficiency and gave top priority to the development of agriculture, on the basis of communal land ownership, a traditional system known in Swahili as ujamaa, which means community.

[12] Ten years later TANU and the Afro-Shirazi Party merged into the Chama Cha Mapinduzi (CCM), which officially incorporated the aim of building socialism on the basis of self-sufficiency.

[13] In October 1978, Tanzania was invaded by Ugandan troops in an attempt by dictator Idi Amin to distract attention from his internal problems. At the same time he sought to divert Tanzanian energies from supporting the liberation struggles in Southern Africa. The aggression was repelled in a few weeks, and Tanzanian troops co-operated closely with the Ugandan National Liberation Front to overthrow Idi Amin.

[14] The cost of mobilizing the army and maintaining troops to prevent chaos in Uganda weighed heavily on the State budget, which was facing serious difficulties by the end of the 1970s. The falling price of Tanzania's main exports; coffee, spices, cotton, pyrethrum and cashew nuts, plus the growing cost of imported products, caused serious financial imbalances and forced cutbacks in the program to expand the ujamaa villages.

[15] These villages were conceived as the nucleus of the Tanzanian economy and were designed to be self-sufficient. To achieve autonomy, they received sizeable initial investments from the Government. Despite Nyerere's enormous efforts, various factors hindered the progress of ujamaa which grew slowly when compared with small and medium-sized private farms. They continued to depend upon imported foodstuffs and as the Government aid was cut, many of them collapsed.

[16] At the end of 1982, the CCM held its second general congress. A new generation of young leaders, most of them strongly committed to the development of

WORKERS

% OF LABOUR FORCE **1998**

■ FEMALE: 49% ■ MALE: 51%

1990

■ SERVICES: 10.7%
■ INDUSTRY: 4.9%
■ AGRICULTURE: 84.4%

LAND USE

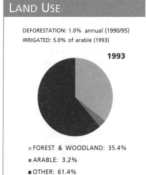

DEFORESTATION: 1.0% annual (1990/95)
IRRIGATED: 5.0% of arable (1993)

1993

■ FOREST & WOODLAND: 35.4%
■ ARABLE: 3.2%
■ OTHER: 61.4%

PUBLIC EXPENDITURE

DEFENCE EXPENDITURE (% of goverment exp.)	**10.7%**	(1997)
MILITARY EXPENDITURE (% of health & education)	**77%**	(1990/91)

the socialist project were appointed to key posts within both the Government and the party.

[17] Edward Sokoine was appointed Prime Minister and immediately launched a campaign against corruption while adopting a more flexible policy towards foreign investment. Sokoine also arranged for Tanzania and Kenya to resume relations which had broken down in 1977 when the East African Economic Community of Tanzania, Kenya and Uganda was dissolved.

[18] After his death, his successor Salim Ahmed Salim from Zanzibar continued along the same lines.

[19] A national debate was organized to discuss constitutional reform to reorganize the executive power, grant greater political participation to women, strengthen democracy along CCM lines and prohibit more than two successive presidential terms.

[20] On November 5 1985, after 24 years as head of state, President Julius Nyerere passed power on to Ali Hassan Mwinyi, winner of the October 27 election, gaining 92.2 per cent of the vote. Nyerere took on a new post, presiding over the South-South Commission, an organization based in Geneva, working to strengthen Third World unity and its negotiating capacity with the North.

[21] In 1986, an economic recovery plan went into effect, following IMF and World Bank guidelines. The measures emphasized the reduction of tariff barriers and included incentives for private capital.

[22] Agricultural production improved and some industrial enterprises increased their profits.

[23] In the meantime, the crisis surrounding the *ujamaa* model intensified, partly due to its poor results and partly to the growing resistance of the population towards the resettlement of entire villages, especially when carried out by force. The recovery of the economy depended on the credit promised by international agencies, which would only be granted when the required structural modifications had been introduced.

[24] The development of private capital and incentives to create such capital have caused new problems. According to UNICEF studies, half the children in the country at that time were malnourished. Tanzania remained among the 30 poorest countries in the world, although it has managed to escape the famine which has hit other Central African nations.

[25] Agricultural tasks have traditionally been carried out chiefly by women. While nearly half the workforce in the economy as a whole is made up of women, 85 per cent of all agricultural work is performed by them. In the outlying areas around the major cities, the female population is increasingly opting for work in the underground economy.

[26] Economic data for 1989 revealed that the agricultural sector accounts for 51 per cent of the GDP, industry 10.2 per cent, trade 13.3 per cent and services 25 per cent. With only 10 per cent of the employed work force, the latter was the most competitive sector. Agriculture, in turn, was the least capital-intensive but the most labor-intensive, with 85.6 per cent of the total work force.

[27] At the beginning of 1990, former president Julius Nyerere said that he was not opposed to a multiparty democracy in his country. According to Nyerere, the absence of an opposition party contributed to the fact that the CCM had abandoned its program and its commitments, straying from its commitment to the masses.

[28] In February 1991, under the leadership of Abdullah Fundikira, a commission was formed to oversee the country's transition period.

[29] In its 1991 report, Amnesty International disclosed the existence of 120 prisoners on the island of Zanzibar, of which at least 40 were presumed to be political prisoners. Mwinyi's government denied that any political arrests had been made, and invited the human rights organization to prove its charges.

[30] In March 1991, the Tanzanian Workers' Organization (JUWATA) broke its ties with the CCM.

[31] In December, after a 23-year exile in England, opposition leader Oscar Kambona announced his plan to return to Tanzania and lead the fight for a multiparty system.

PROFILE

ENVIRONMENT

The country is made up of the former territory of Tanganyika plus the islands of Zanzibar and Pemba. The offshore islands are made of coral. The coastal belt, where a large part of the population live, is a flat lowland along the Indian Ocean with a tropical climate and heavy rainfall. To the west lies the central plateau, dry and riddled with tsetse flies. The north is a mountainous region with slopes suited for agriculture. Around Lake Victoria, a heavily populated area, there are irrigated farmlands. Large plantations of sisal and sugar cane stretch along the coastal lowlands. Mount Kilimanjaro, the highest peak in Africa at 6,000 m is located in the northern highlands. The need to increase exports has led to intensification of agricultural production in semi-arid areas, leading, in turn, to further soil erosion. Indiscriminate cutting of forests has continued.

SOCIETY

Peoples: Most Tanzanians are of Bantu origin, split into around 120 ethnic groups. In the western region of the mainland there are Nilo-Hamites; in Zanzibar there is a Shirazi minority, of Persian origin. In both regions there are small groups of Arabs, Asians and Europeans.
Religions: Muslim 35 per cent; traditional religions 35 per cent; Christian 30 per cent.
Languages: Swahili and English are the official ones. Several local languages are spoken.
Political Parties: Revolutionary Party of Tanzania (CCM-Chama Cha Mapinduzi); Party for Democracy and Progress (CHADEMA); Civic United Front (CUF); National Convention for Construction and Reform-Mageuzi (NCCR-Mageuzi); Movement for a Democratic Alternative (MDA), of Zanzibar.
Social Organizations: Union of Tanzanian Workers (JUWATA), Youth League (VIJANZ), Union of Women of Tanzania (UWT), Co-operative Union of Tanzania (WASHIRICA).

THE STATE

Official Name: Jamhuri ya Muungano wa Tanzania.
Administrative Divisions: 25 Divisions.
Capital: Dodoma 150,000 people (est 1996).
Other cities: Dar es Salaam 1,540,000 people; Mwanza 1,700,000; Tanga 187,000; Zanzibar and Pemba 680,189 (1994).
Government: Benjamin Mkapa, President, and Frederick Sumaye, Prime Minister since October 1995. Unicameral Legislature: 291-member Assembly, 216 elected by direct popular vote.
National Holiday: April 26, Union Day (1964).
Armed Forces: 34,600 (1996). Other: 1,400 Rural Police, 85,000 Militia.

AIDS in Africa: pandemic of the poor

Of all the people in the world who are infected with HIV or have contracted AIDS - an estimated 33.4 million people - 63 per cent are found in Africa.

[2] The statistics are chilling, the stories and images even more so. The future of African countries, which also face profound social, economic, political and military crises, is truly discouraging. According to the latest reports from the United Nations AIDS Program (UNAIDS), some 33.4 million people worldwide are infected with the virus that causes AIDS and of that total some 27.6 million were infected in 1999 alone.

[3] But when these same studies show that 95 per cent of all infected people live in developing countries, and 63 per cent live in Africa, the problem shows its true character. The HIV-AIDS pandemic has hit hardest those countries which are extremely indebted. The economies of these nations depend structurally on international financial organizations, primarily the World Bank and the International Monetary Fund (IMF).

[4] According to these organizations, the combined debt of all African countries amounts to some $350,000 million. This sum does not take into account the payments already made, in some form or another, and which far surpass this total, which is impossible for the African nations to pay. When it comes to AIDS, for example, the World Bank says it has already helped with $1,000 million for dozens of projects in various African countries since 1986. According to Dr Dorothy Logie, from a London-based medical organization, the 'AIDS crisis prospers amid poverty, with social disintegration and ignorance. The debt and adjustments have been instrumental in creating this situation, to the detriment of education and prevention'. In other words, some African nations earmark resources to refinance their debts rather than to directly combat HIV-AIDS and ensure access to health services and education for their citizens.

[5] The sub-Saharan African countries are home to 63 per cent of all cases of HIV infection in the world, and are where 83 per cent of AIDS-related deaths have occurred since 1980 - at least 6 million people. In addition, 95 per cent of children who have lost one or both parents to the disease in the last 20 years live in this part of Africa. In Uganda alone, there are 1.7 million AIDS-orphaned children.

[6] The HIV-AIDS epidemic has taken on new dimensions. In Zimbabwe, 26 per cent of adults are infected with the virus, and life expectancy has fallen by 23 years. The Zimbabwean Government estimates that within five years, 60 per cent of its health budget will be spent on HIV-AIDS research and prevention. In Botswana, 25 per cent of all adults are infected -a similar trend is found in Swaziland, Namibia and Zambia.

[7] United Nations Secretary-General Kofi Annan made an illustrative comparison in May 2000 when he stated in London that more people have died in Africa from AIDS than from armed conflict there in the last two decades, citing the cases of Sierra Leone, Angola, Ethiopia, Eritrea, the Democratic Republic of Congo, Congo and Somalia.

[8] Yet this comparison gives only a limited perspective of the dimension of the HIV catastrophe in the region. The drastic reduction of life expectancy in these countries due to AIDS shows only too clearly that all the misfortunes afflicting sub-Saharan Africa - poverty, starvation, war, various pandemics – none gets near the scale of destruction of this virus. ∎

---

[32] The opposition leader announced the founding of the Democratic Alliance of Tanzania party. However, the national elections held in April 1993 confirmed yet again the predominance of the Chama Cha Mapinduzi, the party in power, which obtained 89 per cent of the vote.

[33] The Government pledged to the IMF it would implement a harsh program of economic adjustment which, among other measures, included the elimination of 20,000 public sector jobs and a reduction of the budget deficit. It thus reduced education pending from 30 per cent in 1960 to 5 per cent of total public expenditure and in February 1994, authorized a 68 per cent raise in electricity bills and 233 per cent increase of several local taxes.

[34] In March, the World Bank praised Tanzania considering it the second-best African student after Ghana. The country's harsh social conditions were aggravated by a massive influx of Rwandan refugees, fleeing from massacres which killed over 500,000 in the neighboring country.

[35] 1995 was dominated by the multiparty legislative and presidential elections held in October, where the CCM triumphed again due to Nyerere's support. Benjamin Mkapa became the new President and appointed Frederick Sumaye Prime Minister.

[36] In December 1996, the Government decided to expel the majority of the 540,000 Rwandan refugees from the country. Most of them faced deaths, coming up against the same conflicts they had fled three years previously. Tanzania still had 230,000 Hutu refugees from Burundi, and some 50,000 from the Democratic Republic of Congo (formerly Zaire).

[37] Production of the nation's leading exports, coffee and cotton, fell again in 1997. Benjamin Mkapa called for international aid, stating that 13 of the nation's 20 productive zones were unable to meet the basic needs of the population due to the destructive effects of drought caused by the 'El Niño' weather phenomenon.

[38] In 1998, Tanzania's parliament began discussion of the Sexual Offences Law, proposing harsher sentences for sexual abuses committed against children aged under 18 years old. Poverty, child abuse and sex tourism were considered the main causes of the increase in child prostitution in the country.

[39] A bomb at the US embassy in Dar es Salaam killed several people in August. It was thought to be linked with the global Islam network of Osama bin Laden, based in Afghanistan.

[40] Political tensions between the capital and the Civic United Front of Zanzibar marked the first months of 1998. The opposition group protested about electoral fraud in 1995 and the subsequent repression of those who spoke out against the government.

[41] A bomb planted in the US embassy in Dar es Salaam killed 11 and left another 80 injured in December 1998.

[42] The death of Julius Nyerere in October 1999 raised response from political leaders world-wide. A proposal for semi-autonomous local government for the mainland territory, presented in December, which would be in addition to the government of the Union - as the national government is known - and that of Zanzibar, unleashed a furious wave of attacks between the President and those in favor of the project. The idea of a federation of independent zones had been attacked by Nyerere, but his death prompted the idea again, as this would balance the rights of the mainland dwellers and those of the island who already have their own semi-independent government.

[43] Heightened fighting in Burundi in early 2000 upped the number of refugees coming into Tanzania, creating complications in health care and food supplies for Burundians.

[44] A series of constitutional reforms implemented in February 2000 were criticized by Fatma Maghimbi, leader of the opposition. Maghimbi said withdrawing the requirement of one and a half votes to win the presidential election and presidential authorization in appointing his cabinet was dangerous and tailor-made for the present ruling party. ∎

Thailand

Prathet Thai

Population: 60,856,000 (1999)
Area: 513,120 SQ KM
Capital: Bangkok (Krung Thep)
Currency: Baht
Language: Thai or Siamese

Archaeological evidence indicates almost continuous human occupation of Thailand for the last 20,000 years. Thai-speaking peoples migrated southward from China around the 10th century AD. During the 13th century two Thai states emerged. The Sukhothai Kingdom was founded about 1220 after a successful revolt against the Khmer kingdom. Chiang Mai was founded in 1296. In 1350 the Thai kingdom of Aytthaya succeeded the state of Sukhotai and devastated the declining Khmer kingdom.

² The Myanmar (Burmese) were the most powerful rival of the Aytthaya kingdom, and in 1569 they defeated Aytthayan forces, occupied their capital, and ruled the kingdom for 15 years. In 1767 the Myanmar again occupied the Thai capital and ended the Ayutthayan rule.

³ In 1782, Rama I founded the Chakri dynasty that still rules the country, with its capital in Bangkok (Krung Thep). Rama III extended the Thai Empire south along the Malay Peninsula, north into Laos and southeast into Cambodia.

⁴ Throughout the 19th century, control of Siam (as Thailand was called) was disputed by the French and the British. In 1896, the two powers agreed to leave the state formally independent, but continued to compete for control over its flourishing agricultural resources. In World War I, Siam fought alongside the Allies and later joined the League of Nations.

⁵ On June 24 1932, a coup curtailed the power of the monarchy, creating a parliament elected by universal suffrage. The democratic experience was short-lived and in 1941, during World War II, the Bangkok Government allowed Japan to use its territory,

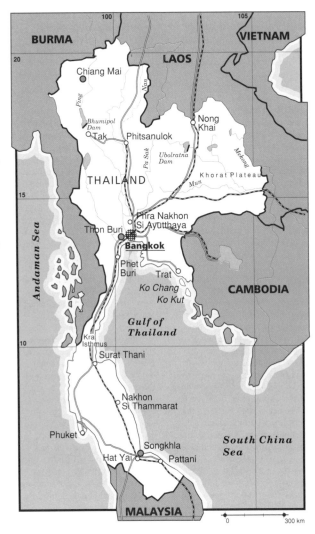

becoming a virtual satellite of that country. During the conflict, Siamese troops occupied part of Malaysia, but was forced to abandon it in 1946, after the allied victory.

⁶ In June of that year, King Ananda Mahidol was assassinated in mysterious circumstances. US manoeuvring succeeded in putting his brother, Rama IX, into power. Born in the United States, the new king had never hidden his pro-US leanings. Since then, Thailand has remained under Washington's patronage.

⁷ US interests in Thailand were essentially strategic as its geographical location and plans for a projected channel through the Kra Isthmus made the country critical to US military policy in the area. In 1954, the Southeast Asian Treaty Organization (SEATO), a military pact designed to counterbalance the growing power of revolutionary forces in the region, established its headquarters in Bangkok.

⁸ In 1961, large numbers of US troops entered the country in reaction to an insurrection in Laos. The US military maintained its presence in Thailand for 14 years, resulting in strong ties being forged between the Thai and US armed forces. In exchange for their participation in the anti-communist struggle, the Thai military enjoyed greater political influence and impunity from their corrupt activities, which included control of the drug trade from the famous 'golden triangle' in the north.

⁹ Between 1950 and 1975, US support of military regimes in Thailand cost it over $2 billion. On October 14 1973, a popular uprising by students brought down the government. As a result in 1975 the first civilian government in 20 years was formed. Elections brought Prince Seni Pramoj to power. He demanded the immediate withdrawal of US troops, the dismantling of military bases and an improvement of relations with neighboring revolutionary governments.

¹⁰ The Thai military disagreed with the new government, and in October 1976 Pramoj was overthrown in a bloody coup planned by right-wing navy officers. Thousands of students and intellectuals joined a guerrilla struggle led by the Communist Party in the rural areas, and Thai relations with neighbors became extremely tense. Finally, in October 1977, a second coup brought the 'civilized right wing' of the military to power. They took a liberal line in policy-making as they were eager to attract new transnational investments. In 1979, Thailand granted asylum to Cambodian refugees. Refugee camps along the border became the rearguard of

---

WORKERS

1997
UNEMPLOYMENT: 0.9%

% OF LABOUR FORCE   **1998**

■ FEMALE: 46%   ■ MALE: 54%

1990

■ SERVICES: 21.9%
■ INDUSTRY: 14.0%
■ AGRICULTURE: 64.1%

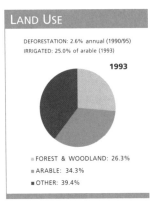

LAND USE

DEFORESTATION: 2.6% annual (1990/95)
IRRIGATED: 25.0% of arable (1993)

1993

■ FOREST & WOODLAND: 26.3%
■ ARABLE: 34.3%
■ OTHER: 39.4%

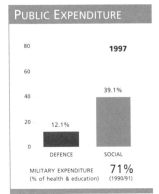

PUBLIC EXPENDITURE

1997

DEFENCE 12.1%
SOCIAL 39.1%

MILITARY EXPENDITURE **71%**
(% of health & education) (1990/91)

MATERNAL MORTALITY	LITERACY	FOOD DEPENDENCY	EXTERNAL DEBT

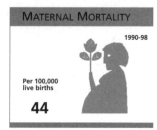

MATERNAL MORTALITY 1990-98

Per 100,000 live births

44

LITERACY 1995

94%

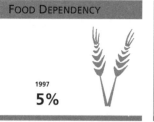

FOOD DEPENDENCY 1997

5%

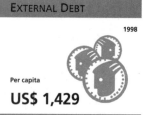

EXTERNAL DEBT 1998

Per capita

US$ 1,429

Cambodian strongman Pol Pot's Khmer Rouge guerrillas; a large part of international humanitarian aid was unwittingly channeled to them. Thailand thus served US interests in the region, as a base for new attacks against communist Vietnam which supported the anti-Khmer forces.

[11] On April 1 1981, another military coup shook Bangkok. This time it was led by General Sant Chitpatima with the support of young middle-ranking officers demanding institutional democracy and social change. The King and Prime Minister General Prem had been asked to lead the coup and had apparently accepted. However, they finally opposed the uprising, and it was put down after three days of great tension. The young officers' revolt, rooted within the military establishment, was at base a reaction to government measures bringing in forced retirement for certain senior generals. Nevertheless, the short-lived coup gained unusually strong support from trade unions and student groups - and this support in itself was extraordinary since the coup was instigated by the military.

[12] At the same time, the left-wing opposition was severely weakened by an internal split in the Communist Party into the pro-Vietnamese and pro-Chinese factions.

[13] On April 20 1983, elections were held and General Prem Tinsulanonda was appointed Prime Minister for a second successive term.

[14] Towards the end of 1984, the currency was sharply devalued, sparking discontent from General Arthit Kamlang-Ek and other hardline generals, who threatened to withdraw military support for Prem. Some timely political manoeuvring by the prime minister, offering incentives to the officers for their support, allowed Prem to isolate Arthit. After a further coup attempt in September 1985, Prem relieved Arthit of his command and designated General Chaovalit Yongchaiyut as the head of the armed forces.

[15] Political instability continued in Bangkok, with several cabinet changes and requests for early legislative elections on two separate occasions. In May 1986, the Democrat Party obtained enough of a majority to form a coalition,

presided over once again by General Prem as Prime Minister. While General Chaovalit's stature continued to grow, enhanced by his forceful attacks on corruption, the Government called for early elections in April 1988, to avoid the censure of Prem. The main criticisms of his administration were his questionable management of public funds and overall incompetence, particularly in the handling of the border war with Laos several months earlier, which had escalated from a dispute over the control of three villages.

[16] In the first general election since 1976, amid massive vote-buying campaigns (a practice considered normal by almost all candidates), the Thai Nation Party won the election. King Bhumibol Adulyahed asked General Chatichai Choonhavan to form a new government, which he did by arranging a six-party coalition.

[17] Thailand's new leading force and a successful entrepreneur, Chatichai introduced important policy changes, breaking with the traditional focus on internal affairs and security. His main idea was to convert what had once been the Indochinese battlefield into a huge regional market. Tempted by the possibility of Cambodia and Laos opening up their markets, he invested considerably in those countries. This formula further fuelled the Thai economy, and in 1989 the growth rate exceeded 10 per cent. Thailand then challenged Western Europe and its subsidy policies for agricultural export products. There were also disagreements with the United States over Bangkok's refusal to accept North American trade criteria on intellectual property, especially with regard to computer programs.

[18] Chatichai's government made foreign policy one of its main priorities, while failing to pay sufficient attention to serious domestic problems such as the deterioration and pollution of the environment, and the extreme poverty of the majority of the population. In 1989, rapid deforestation contributed to serious flooding as the regulatory effect of the forests on the water cycle was altered. Trees had been removed from river banks, where they had formed natural dikes.

[19] Charges of corruption and nepotism leveled against the Chatichai government grew as quickly as the economy. General Chaovalit, a political 'rising star', was named minister of defense in 1990, to lend an air of honesty to the government.

[20] In March 1991, the military carried out another coup led by General Sunthorn Kongsompong, who presented King Bhumibol Adulyahed with a draft for a new constitution. The latter approved the draft, and justified the military coup on the grounds of 'growing corruption' within the civilian government. The King also agreed with the military on the need for calling new elections. As an indirect result of the military coup in Thailand, peace negotiations in neighboring Cambodia came to a standstill, with the Cambodian Government denouncing Thailand for its renewed support of the Cambodian armed opposition.

[21] Throughout 1991, Thailand remained under the command of the Council for the Maintenance of National Peace (NPKC), a body of the military commanded by Sunthorn. In December, the King approved the new constitution which stipulated that elections to replace the NPKC Government would be held within 120 days. However, the military junta reserved the right to directly appoint 270 senators out of a total of 360, giving it total control over the new government.

[22] In elections held on March 22 1992, the majority of votes went to the opposition. There were 15 parties, with a total of 2,740 candidates, and 32 million out of 57 million Thais turned out to vote. In early April, General Suchinda Kraprayoon, commander-in-chief of the army at the time became Prime Minister, backed by a small majority made up of five pro-military parties. On his 49-member cabinet, Suchinda included 11 former ministers who had been accused of embezzlement during Chatichai's government.

[23] At the end of May, what began as an anti-government demonstration ended in a massacre, with hundreds of people killed and injured. Army troops fired into a crowd gathered at the Democracy Monument and political leaders such as Chamlong Srimuang were imprisoned. The protests continued

until an unexpected television appeal for national reconciliation from the Thai king. Suchinda, in the meantime, announced his support of a constitutional amendment whereby the Prime Minister would have to be an elected member of Parliament, a clause which would disqualify even Suchinda from holding the post. Srimuang was subsequently freed, and an amnesty announced for those who had been arrested. With a curfew still in effect in Bangkok, Parliament initiated discussion of the constitutional amendment and the King appointed General Pren Tinsulanonda to supervise the process.

[24] On May 24, Suchinda resigned and his Vice President, Mitchai Ruchuphan, became interim president. Constitutional amendments approved in June reduced military participation in the government and King Bhumibol named Anand Panyarachun Prime Minister. Panyarachun, who enjoyed a great deal of prestige in Thailand, had been prime minister after the 1991 military coup.

[25] Parliament accepted the King's nomination of Panyarachun, who appointed a number of technocrats to cabinet positions and requested the resignations of the 12 military officers responsible for the May massacre.

[26] On June 29, the Prime Minister dissolved Parliament and announced elections for September. The Democratic Party (DP) won the election, obtaining 79 seats in the Chamber of Representatives. On September 23, a parliamentary majority made up of the DP, the Palang Dharma (PD) and the New Aim Party (NAP) emerged, holding 177 seats, and anti-military political leader Chuan Leekpai was elected Prime Minister. Shortly afterwards, the pro-military New Aim Party joined the coalition.

[27] Several violent incidents motivated by religious sensitivities took place in 1993. Concerned with his country's role in the region, Chuan strengthened ties with China and Indonesia and in October officially terminated the support which Thailand had provided to Cambodia's Khmer Rouge since 1979. Cambodian authorities accused Thailand of supporting the 'Pol Potists' after 14 Thais were arrested during a thwarted coup attempt in Phnom Penh.

28 The Government approved a reform to liberalize the banking system in January 1994. Among other things, the reform permitted the opening of branches of foreign banks in various Thai cities.

29 A proposal for a constitutional reform generated a long debate in Parliament. The new project envisaged a reduction of the size and power of the Senate and lowered the voting age to 18 years. The subject remained unresolved due to mutual accusations by the different parties and the parliamentary changes which took place in 1995.

30 Although in 1994 the economy of Thailand was among those that grew most, its economic stability did not spread to the political sphere. The first parliamentary session of 1995 brought an exchange of accusations and the tense political atmosphere led to the dissolution of Parliament. On July 2 early elections took place. The Thai Nation Party obtained 25 per cent of the seats and the Democrats 22 per cent. Banham Silapa-archa, leader of the winning party, formed a government supported by several small parties.

31 In 1995, inflation reached 6.5 per cent. It was considered 'manageable' by the Central Bank. With an annual population growth rate of 1.5 per cent and a growth in the economy of over 8 per cent, Thailand remained on the list of countries with sustained economic success.

32 In November 1996, Chavalit Yonchaiyudh (NAP) was elected Prime Minister, with 125 of the 393 seats in the Chamber of Representatives. Chuan Leekpai's DP, took 123 seats. A coalition with the Chart Pattana (52), Social Action (20), Prachakorn Thai (18) plus two minor parties, allowed Chavalit to obtain the majority weeks later.

33 Thailand was hit by a financial crisis in 1997, exacerbated by scandals and attempts to salvage the banks - leading to the resignation of the economy minister and the closure of businesses - and by Chavalit's proposal for constitutional reform in order to lift a vote of no confidence lodged by the opposition.

34 In August 1997, the constitutional reform project was completed. It aimed to limit corruption, put citizens' rights into the legislation and eliminate army influence from the Senate. Alarmed by the perceived loss of power, the governing parties initially rejected this project, but they were forced to accept it given the agreement between the army and King Bhumibol. The new Constitution was passed in a General Assembly on October 11.

35 When the new prime minister Chuan Leekpai took office in November 1997, the Thai currency, the baht, had devaluated 37 per cent. The crisis lasted throughout the following year, which closed with an 8 per cent drop in Gross National Product. Unemployment affected 1.8 million people (6 per cent) of the population, while the government proposed making 200,000 of its 1.5 million employees redundant. The $17.2-billion loan granted by the IMF involved a series of counterpart demands. As well as redundancies in the state sector, the Government put 59 state companies up for sale, including those in telecommunications, electricity, petrochemicals and finances.

36 In March the Prime Minister survived a vote of no confidence and even extended his base of his alliance, by incorporating Chart Pattana, which had 51 votes in parliament, into the government. The Government decided not to renew the work permits of half a million immigrant workers, but finally gave in to pressure from rice-growers and other entrepreneurs who employ cheap labor, granting 95,000 new permits.

37 After months of tension with political refugees from Burma (Myanmar), the Government demanded they register with the UN High Commissioner for Refugees' office in order to be relocated. Deportations continued throughout 1999, and in November of that year the Government reported it still hoped to expel another 700,000 foreign workers in order to give their jobs to unemployed Thais. In January 2000, under pressure from the business sector, the authorities once again allowed foreigners in as seasonal workers.

38 The March 2000 elections for the direct appointment of senators were plagued with irregularities. The electoral authority disqualified 78 of the 200 legislators elected, accusing them of corruption and fraud. Two of the disqualified senators were wives of the Interior and Justice ministers. It was the first time senators had been elected by popular vote. ∎

PROFILE

ENVIRONMENT

Thailand is located in central Indochina. From the mountain ranges in the northern and western zones, the Ping and Nan Rivers flow down to the central valley through extensive deltas, into the Gulf of Thailand. The plains are fertile with large commercial rice plantations. The southern region occupies part of the Malay Peninsula. Severe deforestation of the area resulted in decreased production of rubber and timber, and has been responsible for migration of part of the native population. Pollution has increased massively through a number of ways: vehicle emissions in the cities, industrial pollution, lack of waste disposal, unrestricted industrial development, etc.

SOCIETY

Peoples: The Thai group constitutes the majority of the population. The most important minority groups are the Chinese, 12 per cent and, in the south, the Malay, 13 per cent. Other groups are Khmer, Karen, Indians and Vietnamese.

Religions: Most people (94 per cent) practice Buddhism. Muslims, concentrated in the south, make up about 4 per cent of the population. There is a Christian minority.

Languages: Thai or Siamese (official). Minority groups speak their own languages.

Political Parties: Thai Nation Party, in power, formed a coalition with Chart Thai Party, New Aim Party, Righteous Force Party.

THE STATE

Official Name: Muang Thai, or Prathet Thai (Kingdom of Thailand).

Administrative Division: 5 regions and 73 provinces.

Capital: Bangkok (Krung Thep) 6,566,000 people (1995).

Other cities: Chiang Mai 161,541 people; Thon Buri, 264,20; Songkhla 172,604; Ratchasima 202,503; Khon Kaen 131,478; Nakhon Pathom 37,200 (1991).

Government: King Bhumibol Adulyade, Head of State. Chuan Leekpai, Prime Minister and Head of Government since November 1997. Legislative, bicameral: Senate, with 279 members; House of Representatives, with 360 members.

National Holiday: December 5, the King's birthday (1927).

Armed Forces: 254,000 troops (1996).

Other: 141,700 (National Security Volunteer Force, Air Police, Frontier Police Patrols, Province Police and 'Hunter Soldiers').

STATISTICS

DEMOGRAPHY

Population: 60,856,000 (1999)
Annual growth: 1.7 % (1975/97)
Estimates for year 2015 (million): 68.9 (1999)
Annual growth to year 2015: 0.8 % (1997/2015)
Urban population: 20.6 % (1997)
Urban Growth: 2.6 % (1980/95)
Children per woman: 1.7 (1998)

HEALTH

Life expectancy at birth: 69 years (1998)
male: 66 years (1998)
female: 72 years (1998)
Maternal mortality: 44 per 100,000 live births (1990-98)
Infant mortality: 30 per 1,000 (1998)
Under-5 child mortality: 37 per 1,000 (1998)
Daily calorie supply: 2,334 per capita (1996)
24 doctors per 100,000 people (1993)
Safe water: 81 % (1990/98)

EDUCATION

Literacy: 94 % (1995)
male: 96 % (1995)
female: 92 % (1995)
School enrolment:
Primary total: 88 % (1990/96)
male: 99 % (1990/97)
female: 96 % (1990/97)
Secondary:
male: 38 % (1990/96)
female: 37 % (1990/96)
Tertiary: 21 % (1996)

COMMUNICATIONS

63 newspapers (1996), 232 radios (1997), 167 TV sets (1996) and 70 main telephone lines (1996) per 1,000 people
Books: 13 new titles per 100,000 people (1992/94)

ECONOMY

Per capita, GNP: $ 2,160 (1998)
Annual growth, GNP: -7.7 % (1998)
Annual inflation: 4.8 % (1990/98)
Consumer price index: 120.8 (1998)
Currency: 41.4 baht = $ 1 (1998)
Cereal imports: 1,016,104 metric tons (1998)
Food import dependency: 5 % (1997)
Fertilizer use: 866 kg per ha (1997)
Exports: $ 65,593 million (1998)
Imports: $ 47,219 million (1998)
External debt: $ 86,172 million (1998); $ 1,429 per capita (1998)
Debt service: 19.2 % of exports (1998)
Development aid received: $ 626 million (1997); $ 11.1 per capita (1997); 0.40 % of GNP (1997)

ENERGY

Consumption: 1,319.0 Kgs of Oil equivalent per capita yearly (1997); 42.0 % imported (1997)

HDI (rank/value): 67/0.753 (1997)

Togo

Togo

Population: 4,512,000 (1999)
Area: 56,790 SQ KM
Capital: Lomé
Currency: CFA franc
Language: French

T ogo was peopled by the Ewe (of the same origin as the Igbo and Yoruba of Nigeria and the Ashanti of Ghana), who make up over a third of its population. The Ewe were a relatively poor and peaceful people with simple social structures like the Dagomba kingdoms in the north.

2 The slave trade gave the region the name of Slave Coast, and millions of people were shipped to slavery in the US between the 16th and 19th centuries.

3 Togo became a German colony in 1884 under 'treaties' signed with local chieftains. Occupied by Anglo-French troops during World War I, the territory was divided between the two powers with the endorsement of the League of Nations. The western part was annexed to Ghana in 1956, after a British-organized plebiscite, while the eastern part remained under French rule.

4 In 1958, Sylvanus Olympio, (a member of the Togolese Unity party) won the elections. His program was pro-independence, but moderate. The 1960 proclamation of independence seemed to overlook a contract signed in 1957 with the Benin Mines Company, in which the French consortium had seized control of Togo's phosphate reserves, its main natural resource, thus compromising independence. When Olympio confronted this situation in 1963, proposing a series of basic reforms - doubtlessly influenced by Nkrumah's radical pro-independence program in neighboring Ghana - he was assassinated in a military revolt, allegedly involving a young military officer, Eyadéma.

5 Olympio's successor, the neo-colonialist Nicholas Grunitzky, from

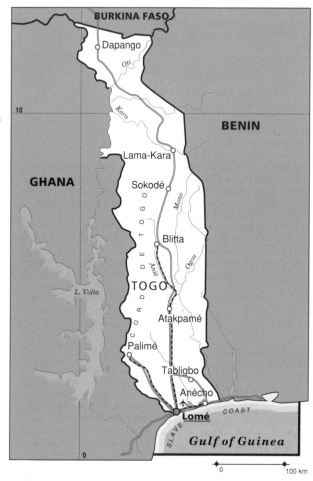

the opposition Togolese Progress Party, was overthrown by a further coup in 1967, led by General Gnassingbé Eyadéma, who became the new head of state.

6 In 1969, Eyadéma's Togo Peoples' Group (RPT) brought in a one-party system. In 1972 a law gave the state 35 per cent of shares of the mining company, which was

raised to 51 per cent in 1975 and in 1976 the production and export of phosphate was nationalized.

7 On December 30 1979, a constitution was approved and Eyadéma was re-elected President for a 7-year term. His government was confident of improving the economy, basing its optimism on tourism, oil and a rise in world phosphate prices. However in 1981 phosphate prices dropped by 50 per cent and a worldwide economic recession reduced the number of European tourists. A serious balance of payments deficit increased the foreign debt to $1 billion.

8 In June 1984 a refinancing agreement with stringent

conditions, was reached with the Paris Club and the IMF. Consequently, there were salary freezes, reduction of government investments and high taxes levied to increase government funds, including a so-called 'solidarity tax' which took 5 per cent of the population's incomes.

9 In January 1985 the Lomé III agreements were signed in Togo, regulating cooperation between ACP (Africa, Caribbean and Pacific) countries and the EEC.

10 In January 1986 Eyadéma was re-elected for 7 years, with 99.95 per cent of the vote. Consultation with the IMF resumed and new agreements were planned in 1988. In 1990, adjustment programs were initiated, including denationalization, on account of trade deficits and a public deficit of $1.27 billion. Meanwhile food production rose slightly.

11 In 1991, more than 10,000 peasants in the northern district of Keran Oti lost their lands to create an 80 sq km game reserve for hunting.

12 In early April 1991, there were pro-democracy demonstrations throughout the country, and on April 8 more than a thousand people took over one of Lomé's neighborhoods, setting up barricades and demanding Eyadéma's resignation. The police reacted violently, killing more than thirty people and injuring many more. However on April 12, opposition parties were legalized and Eyadéma announced an amnesty for political prisoners, and liberalization of the political system.

13 On August 28 1991, a National Conference named Kokou Koffigoh - president of Togo's Bar Association and a recognized human rights leader - as provisional Prime Minister. A legislative assembly was established which ousted Eyadéma as head of the armed forces and blocked his candidacy in the upcoming 1992 elections.

14 The dissolution of the RPT on November 26 1991, prompted a military coup. Two days later, the armed forces took over the government, dissolved the legislative assembly and kidnapped Koffigoh for several hours. The perpetrators of the coup claimed that the legislative assembly was made up of extremists, whose aim was to 'disrupt the army and discredit the military regime and its achievements'. Political parties and other opposition organizations cooperated together within the

WORKERS

% OF LABOUR FORCE **1998**

- FEMALE: 40%   ■ MALE: 60%

1990

- SERVICES: 24.4%
- INDUSTRY: 10.1%
- AGRICULTURE: 65.5%

LAND USE

DEFORESTATION: 1.4% annual (1990/95)
IRRIGATED: 0.3% of arable (1993)

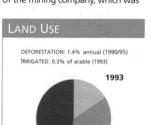

1993

- FOREST & WOODLAND: 15.8%
- ARABLE: 36.5%
- OTHER: 47.7%

PUBLIC EXPENDITURE

DEFENCE EXPENDITURE (% of goverment exp.)	**11.6%**	(1997)
MILITARY EXPENDITURE (% of health & education)	**39%**	(1990/91)

MATERNAL MORTALITY

1990-98

Per 100,000 live births

480

LITERACY

1995

51%

EXTERNAL DEBT

1998

Per capita

US$ 329

DEMOGRAPHY

Population: 4,512,000 (1999)
Annual growth: 2.9 % (1975/97)
Estimates for year 2015 (million): 6.7 (1999)
Annual growth to year 2015: 2.6 % (1997/2015)
Urban population: 31.7 % (1997)
Urban Growth: 5.0 % (1980/95)
Children per woman: 6.0 (1998)

HEALTH

Life expectancy at birth: 49 years (1998)
male: 48 years (1998)
female: 50 years (1998)
Maternal mortality: 480 per 100,000 live births (1990-98)
Infant mortality: 81 per 1,000 (1998)
Under-5 child mortality: 144 per 1,000 (1998)
Daily calorie supply: 2,155 per capita (1996)
6 doctors per 100,000 people (1993)
Safe water: 55 % (1990/98)

EDUCATION

Literacy: 51 % (1995)
male: 67 % (1995)
female: 35 % (1995)
School enrolment:
Primary total: 119 % (1990/96)
male: 140 % (1990/97)
female: 99 % (1990/97)
Secondary:
male: 40 % (1990/96)
female: 14 % (1990/96)
Tertiary: 4 % (1996)
Primary school teachers: one for every 51 (1995)

COMMUNICATIONS

4 newspapers (1996), 218 radios (1997), 14 TV sets (1996) and 6 main telephone lines (1996) per 1,000 people

ECONOMY

Per capita, GNP: $ 330 (1998)
Annual growth, GNP: -1.0 % (1998)
Annual inflation: 8.8 % (1990/98)
Consumer price index: 114.4 (1998)
Currency: 590.0 CFA francs = $ 1 (1998)
Cereal imports: 134,403 metric tons (1998)
Fertilizer use: 67 kg per ha (1997)
Exports: $ 509 million (1998)
Imports: $ 610 million (1998)
External debt: $ 1,448 million (1998); $ 329 per capita (1998)
Debt service: 5.7 % of exports (1998)
Development aid received: $ 124 million (1997); $ 34.1 per capita (1997); 8.60 % of GNP (1997)

HDI (rank/value): 143/0.469 (1997)

---

framework of the National Resistance Committee, and encouraged people to resist a return to dictatorship.

[15]   Togo's complicated political scenario was compounded by economic, social and ethnic problems. Eyadéma came from the southern Kabye group, which provided the majority of the country's 12,000 troops. Meanwhile, Koffigoh was a member of the Ewe tribe. Negotiations began between those who favored the military regime and the opposition, aimed at precipitating the transition to civilian government by 1992. That year, a timetable was established for a return to democracy, and all citizens were re-registered to vote.

[16]   In June, opposition leader Tavio Komlavi was assassinated. After an attempt upon the life of Mining Minister Joseph Yao Amefia, Eyadéma took advantage of the incident to have his powers restored by the High Council of the Republic (the interim legislature).

Eyadéma proceeded to pack the cabinet with his supporters. In the face of widespread protests from the opposition, the Government postponed elections indefinitely. The unions, in reprisal, called a long-term general strike.

[17]   The opposition split from Koffigoh in January 1993, after which they met in Benin and nominated a government in exile. In this same month the presidential guard killed some hundred demonstrators in Lomé, which led to thousands of people fleeing to Ghana and Benin.

[18]   Eyadéma agreed to organize elections for August. In an atmosphere of civil war, he won with 96.5 per cent of the vote, in a poll classed as 'fraudulent' by the opposition. The protests in the streets intensified, and in January 1994, Eyadéma was unharmed in a foiled assassination attempt - carried out by around a hundred armed attackers - which left 67 people dead.

[19]   The opposition won the February legislative elections, but Eyadéma did not allow one of its leaders, Edem Kodjo, to form a government without members of the ruling parties. The Action Committee for Renewal, which included the opposition groups, decided to boycott Parliament, paralyzing government for a large part of the year.

[20]   On another front, widespread floods in Lomé left 150,000 people homeless in July. In September three weeks of heavy rains destroyed whole villages, roads and bridges, particularly in the northern and central regions of the nation, leaving 21,000 people destitute.

[21]   In August 1996, Kodjo resigned as prime minister and was substituted by Kwassi Klutse, from the Rally of the Togolese People (RTP).

[22]   In July 1997, the opposition increased efforts to become united managing to defeat Eyadéma. The President, in power since 1967, was even pressured to liberalize the political system by elements within the military itself.

[23]   The European Union agreed to provide the Government with $30 million in aid for public health, education and the building of rural roads.

[24]   During 1998, the legislative assembly approved a new press bill banning the arbitrary arrest of journalists, as well as other police abuses, such as night 'visits' without judicial authorization. The June presidential elections were harshly criticized by the opposition which considered them a fraud. Eyadéma won with 52 per cent of the vote, defeating Gilchrist Olympio, son of the assassinated president. During the following months the capital was rocked by constant demonstrations by the opposition against the fraud.

[25]   In November 1999, thousands of students and teachers flouted a ban and took part in a demonstration demanding back-payment of wages and improvement of education standards. However, in spite of isolated cases of discontent, in time the situation returned to normal.

[26]   The meeting of the West African Francophone nations held in March 2000 was a diplomatic success for the Eyadéma regime as Benin, Niger, Burkina Faso and Côte d'Ivoire attended, and Togo opened up to its neighbors. ∎

PROFILE

ENVIRONMENT

The country is a long, narrow strip of land with distinct geographical regions. In the south, a low coastline with lakes, typical of the Gulf of Guinea; a highly populated plain where manioc, corn, banana and palm oil are grown. In the north, subsistence crops are gradually giving way to coffee and cocoa plantations. The Togo Mountains run through the country from northeast to southwest.

SOCIETY

Peoples: The main ethnic groups are the Ewe (43.1 per cent), Kabye (26.7 per cent), Gurma (16.1 per cent), Kebu (3.8 per cent) and Ana (Yoruba, 3.2 per cent). The descendants of formerly enslaved Africans who returned to Togo from Brazil are called Brazilians. They form a caste with great economic and political influence. The small European minority (0.3 per cent) is concentrated in the capital.
Religions: The majority profess traditional African religions (50 per cent). There are Christian (35 per cent) and Muslim (15 per cent) minorities. Languages: French (official). The main local languages are Ewe, Kabye, Twi and Hausa.
Political Parties: Rally of the Togolese People; Union for Justice and Democracy; Action Committee for Renewal.
Social Organizations: National Confederation of Togolese Workers (CNT).

THE STATE

Official Name: République Togolaise.
Administrative Divisions: 5 Regions and 21 Prefectures.
Capital: Lomé 810,000 people (1995).
Other cities: Sokodé 48,098 people; Kpalimé 27,700 people (1983).
Government: Gnassingbé Eyadéma, President since January 1967; Koffi Eugene Adoboli, Prime Minister since May 1999. Unicameral 79-member Legislative Assembly.
National Holiday: April 27, Independence Day (1960).
Armed Forces: 6,950 (1997). Other: 750 Gendarmes.

Tonga

Tonga

Population: 98,000 (1999)
Area: 750 SQ KM
Capital: Nuku'alofa
Currency: Pa'anga
Language: Tongan and English

The original inhabitants of Tonga, which means 'south' in several Polynesian languages, immigrated from Fiji and Samoa over 1,000 years ago. Tongans developed a complex social organization, with a traditional leader in charge. According to oral tradition, the first Tui Tonga (ruler, Son of the Creator) of the islands was Aholitu in the second half of the 10th century. Towards the 15th century, religious and social roles were assigned to different leaders and this system of double leadership continued until the Dutch came to the islands in 1616. English explorer Captain James Cook, visited them in 1775 and named them the 'Friendly Islands'.

[2] The archipelago only achieved political reunification in the mid-19th century, in a civil war, under the leadership of Taufa'ahau Tupou, ruler of the island of Haapai from 1820 onwards. Converted to Christianity and subsequently backed by European missionaries, Taufa'ahau Tupou seized Vavau and Tongatopu, securing control over the whole of the territory which he ruled under the Christian name of George I until 1893. The King introduced a parliamentary system including the local leaders, and an agrarian reform which granted each adult male in the country 3.3 ha of arable land. This ensured social stability and agricultural self-sufficiency.

[3] In 1889, Britain and Germany signed a treaty which gave Britain a free hand in its relations with Tonga. The following year the archipelago was made a 'protectorate' of the British crown, though the monarchy was kept with limited powers.

[4] Queen Salote, great-grand-daughter of George I was crowned in 1918. In 1960, she gave women the right to vote in legislative elections.

[5] The British transformed the country's agriculture, which was reoriented towards the export crops of copra and bananas.

[6] Present King Taufa'ahau Tupou IV was crowned in 1967, and three years later Tonga obtained independence. The high international market prices for copra and bananas helped Tonga to develop a wide-ranging social security system which included free education and medical services for all the inhabitants of the islands.

[7] In the mid-1970s welfare programs suffered because of the drop in fruit prices, and about 10,000 Tongans emigrated to Aotearoa/New Zealand. Tonga's economy suffers from serious inflation, with a high level of unemployment, despite emigration, and a substantial trade deficit. It has also suffered from the whims of nature; in 1982 Hurricane Isaac destroyed a number of plantations.

[8] In February 1990, reformists announced the creation of the first political party in the Kingdom. The King accused the leader of the movement, Akalisi Pohiva, of Marxist tendencies.

[9] The UN questioned Tonga about the absence of trade unions in the country, in spite of there being over 3,000 civil servants. The Government of Tonga explained that there were no trade unions because they were unnecessary. The UN dismissed the Tongan response.

[10] The Crown Prince and Prime Minister since 1965, Fatafehi Tu'ipelehake, was replaced by Baron Vaea in 1991. In 1992, opposition groups founded the Pro-Democracy Movement which won 6 of the 9 seats in the National Assembly in February 1993 elections.

[11] However, power continued to be controlled by the King, subjects named by him to high posts in the Government and a small group belonging to the royalty. In September 1994, the Pro-Democracy Movement became the Tonga Democratic Party, led by 'Akilisi Pohiva.

[12] The King continued to promote a multiparty system but did not modify his quasi-monopolistic grip on power. As tourism had a significant growth of 11.3 per cent in 1994, Tonga refused to authorize Tokyo's request to fish for whales in its territorial waters.

[13] Along with other countries from the South Pacific Forum, Nuku'alofa denounced French nuclear testing in the Polynesian atolls of Mururoa and Fangataufa in 1995 and 1996.

[14] In January 1996, the Party of the People won six of the nine seats held by elected deputies in the Legislative Assembly.

[15] In that year, prolonged drought seriously affected the economy, in particular agriculture. Products from the agricultural sector made up 80 per cent of the total exports.

[16] Demands for political liberalization continued in 1997. Several political leaders and journalists were arrested that year.

[17] In March 1998, the aristocrat Fakafanua who was the Minister of Lands and also son-in-law of the King, was arrested and accused of mishandling public funds and accepting bribes. A court rejected his incarceration and freed him a few days later, although banning him from leaving the country. ∎

PROFILE

ENVIRONMENT

This archipelago is also known as 'Friendly Isles' and is located in western Polynesia, east of the Fiji Islands, slightly north of the Tropic of Capricorn. It comprises approximately 169 islands, only 36 of which are permanently inhabited. It includes three main groups of islands: Tongatapu, the southernmost group where more than half of the population live; Vavau, to the north, and Haapai in between. The volcanic islands are mountainous while the coral ones are flat. The climate is mild and rainy with very hot summers. The fertile soil is suitable for growing banana, copra and coconut trees.

SOCIETY

Peoples: Tongans are Polynesian people. It is estimated that 20 per cent of them now live abroad. **Religions:** Free Wesleyan, 43.6 per cent; Roman Catholic, 16.0 per cent; Mormon, 12.1 per cent; Free Church of Tonga, 11.0 per cent. **Languages:** Tongan and English are official. **Political Parties:** Tonga Democratic Party.

THE STATE

Official Names: Pule'anga Fakatu'i 'o Tonga. Kingdom of Tonga. **Administrative Divisions:** 23 Districts. **Capital:** Nuku'alofa 32,000 people (1994). **Other cities:** Neiafu 15,170 people; Haveluloto 3,070; Vaini 2,697; Tofoa-Koloua 2,298. **Government:** Taufa'ahau Tupou IV, King since 1967; Lavaka'ata Ulukalala, Prime Minister since 2000. **National Holiday:** June 4, Independence Day (1970). **Armed Forces:** There is no army in Tonga. 300 National Police (1991).

STATISTICS

Demography: Population: 98,000 (1999). Children per woman: 3.6 (1998). **Health:** Life expectancy at birth: 71 years (1998). Infant mortality: 19 per 1,000 (1998). Under-5 child mortality: 23 per 1,000 (1998) Safe water: 95 % (1990/98) **Education:** Literacy: 99 % (1995) female: 99 % (1995). School enrolment: Primary total: 98 % (1990/96) **Communications:** 617 radios (1997) per 1,000 people **Economy:** Per capita, GNP: $ 1,750 (1998). Annual growth, GNP: -1.5 % (1998). Consumer price index: 108.6 (1998). Cereal imports: 8,333 metric tons (1998). External debt: $ 65 million (1998); $ 660 per capita (1998)

Trinidad and Tobago

Trinidad and Tobago

Population: 1,288,000 (1999)
Area: 5,130 SQ KM
Capital: Port of Spain
Currency: Trinidad dollar
Language: English

Although Trinidad and Tobago currently form a single nation, the two islands have different histories. Trinidad, 12 kilometres from the mouth of the Orinoco River, was claimed by Columbus in 1498 for Spain. Tobago had been inhabited by Carib indians, but when the Dutch arrived in 1632, apparently they found it uninhabited. Shortly thereafter, Spanish troops invaded to prevent the Dutch from using Tobago as a base for exploring the Orinoco, where there was thought to be gold.

2   The islands suffered a succession of invasions by the Dutch, French and British. In 1783, three centuries after the arrival of the first Europeans, the local population comprised 126 people of European origin, 605 of African origin including 310 slaves, and 2,032 Amerindians. Trinidad finally became a British colony in 1802, and Tobago in 1814.

3   The local economy was based on sugar. Once slavery was abolished in 1834, most Africans moved to the cities and were replaced on the plantations by workers from India and some Chinese. These changes defined the islands' current ethnic and social composition. The Africans were mostly urban workers, while the Indians constituted the large rural working class. Nonetheless, some African workers remained in the countryside, where they survived by a system of mutual aid called *gayap*.

4   In 1924, the first moves towards autonomy were made and the colonial administration was reformed, allowing elections for certain secondary positions although suffrage was limited. The newly-organized trade unions also raised the issue of independence. In 1950 internal autonomy was granted, and the People's National Movement (PNM) won the elections. Dr Eric Williams became Prime Minister, a post which he held until his death in 1981. In 1962, after a brief period as part of the West Indies Federation (1958-62), Trinidad and Tobago became fully independent. On August 31 1976, a new constitution proclaimed the republic.

5   In the early 1900s sugar production began to decline and was gradually replaced by oil; by 1940, the latter had become the principal economic activity. Between 1972 and 1982, there was a five-fold increase in earnings from petroleum, as well as in government expenditure. Unemployment was reduced to less than 10 per cent and imports (primarily of luxury items) increased eleven-fold. Trinidad had the highest per capita income in Central and South America, and began to take on the aspect of a 'consumer society'. In the meantime, President Williams' PNM Government initiated nationalization of the oil industry and adapted pricing policies to those established by OPEC, while encouraging investment from transnational corporations.

6   However, during the 1970s there was social unrest. In 1975, a number of strikes occurred and oil workers of African origin and Asian Indian plantation hands fought together for better conditions. The strike movement finally foundered when the PAM government called in the army and gave it the responsibility of gasoline distribution.

7   The over-dependence on oil caused serious problems and instability from 1982. This was due to a number of reasons: the international recession and the fall in oil prices, as well as factors linked specifically to the oil industry; the decrease in the demand for heavy oil, competition from major refineries which had been installed along the southern and eastern coasts of the United States, and a decline in production rates.

8   In 1983, the economy took a downturn. A 26-per-cent decrease in oil revenues was predicted, leading to an actual net loss of 5.2 per cent of the GNP. The Government was able to control this situation by eliminating subsidies, reducing public investment and holding down public salaries.

9   In October 1983, the Government led by George Chambers opposed the US invasion of Grenada and did not provide troops for the expeditionary force from six Caribbean countries. Chambers' government faced growing social and political unrest. The opposition reformed as the National Alliance for Reconstruction (NAR) and won elections in December 1986, taking 33 of the 36 parliamentary seats to end 30 years of PNM government.

10   Arthur Napoleon Robinson's new government proposed a five year 'readjustment' plan, effective as of December 1990, designed to accelerate the process of integration with other CARICOM members (Caribbean Community and Common Market). This project entailed eliminating protection for the textile industry, developing tourism and new industrial projects, such as methane and natural gas refineries.

11   The Government applied austerity measures agreed with the IMF, from which it received $110 million in 1988, as well as a $128 million standby loan in 1989. There were a number of strikes in the oil industry, including a general strike in March 1989.

12   The Robinson administration committed itself to reducing inflation to 5 per cent a year, restructuring state-owned companies, limiting the number of public employees and further liberalizing the economy. To achieve these goals, the Government abolished export licences, liberalized the national price system (while maintaining control over basic food products and pharmaceuticals), and decreed a 10 per cent reduction in the salaries in the public sector.

13   On July 27 1990, Trinidad and Tobago suffered their first coup attempt since winning independence from Britain in 1962. One hundred Muslims of African origin occupied Parliament and took hostages. They demanded that Prime Minister Arthur Jay Robinson resign and call elections. On August 1, after freeing all the hostages, the group surrendered unconditionally.

14   The 1990 balance-sheet showed a slight economic recovery, achieved through an increase in oil

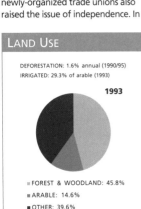

LAND USE

DEFORESTATION: 1.6% annual (1990/95)
IRRIGATED: 29.3% of arable (1993)

1993

- FOREST & WOODLAND: 45.8%
- ARABLE: 14.6%
- OTHER: 39.6%

WORKERS

1996
UNEMPLOYMENT: 16.2%

% OF LABOUR FORCE   **1998**

- FEMALE: 34%   MALE: 66%

PUBLIC EXPENDITURE

DEFENCE EXPENDITURE (% of goverment exp.)	**5.4%**	(1997)
MILITARY EXPENDITURE (% of health & education)	**9%**	(1990/91)

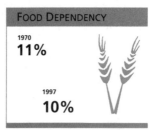
and petrochemical exports, which had increased as a result of the Gulf crisis. This enabled the Government to avoid enforcing the 10-per-cent reduction in salaries.

[15] In December 1991, the PNM won the general elections with 46 per cent of the vote, and obtained 20 of the 36 parliamentary seats. The United National Congress (UNC) obtained 26 per cent and Robinson's NAR, 20 per cent. Abstentions were considerably higher than before.

[16] The main obstacles facing the new government, led by Patrick Manning, were a foreign debt amounting to $2.51 billion, and 24 per cent unemployment in a 460,000-strong workforce.

[17] The Government's economic adjustment and privatization plans sparked protest demonstrations in January 1993. The civil servants also demanded the payment of overdue backpay. Manning called the army in to 'control' the situation given the increasing agitation.

[18] Partial parliamentary elections in 1994 showed the increasing unpopularity of Manning, as the governing PNM lost two of the three contested seats.

[19] On another front, the amnesty decreed by then Prime Minister Robinson on the 114 members of the Jamaat-al-Muslimeen Islamic group responsible for the July 1990 coup attempt, was annulled. However, this was a symbolic measure, as the court decided the accused would be neither arrested nor taken to trial.

[20] Faced with what he considered a more favorable economic and political situation, Manning decided to call elections in November 1995, a year early. However, he had miscalculated, for the PNM took only 17 seats, as did the opposition UNC, led by Basdeo Panday.

[21] After making an alliance with the NAR, Panday became the first Asian to be head of government in Trinidad and Tobago.

[22] In 1996, the governing coalition approved a balanced budget which reduced spending. The Government granted permission to a consortium, including a British company, to build a natural gas plant to supply the United States and Spain, to come into operation in 1999.

[23] In early 1997, the opposition reduced its presence in the Chamber of Representatives even further, when two of its members joined the governing coalition as 'independents'. This desertion left it with only 15 seats to the ruling party's 21.

[24] On February 14, ruling party candidate and former Prime Minister AN Robinson was elected President, when he received 46 votes in the electoral college. The opposition candidate, Anthony Lucky, took 18. Robinson officially took office on March 19.

[25] In March 1988, new tensions arose with the Islamic Jamaat-al-Muslimeen group which had led an attempted coup in 1990. The Government repeated its demand for a piece of land occupied by the fundamentalists to be returned. The group claimed it owned the land, while the Government insisted the Islamic group had taken it illegally.

[26] That same year, oil corporation Amoco Trinidad discovered significant hydrocarbon resources in the sea bed. The Government signed treaties with various foreign companies to tap these resources. Another US firm announced in July it had found the largest-ever natural gas deposit near Trinidad's southern coast.

[27] In May, British judicial authorities prevented the hanging of nine people accused of murders committed in 1996; the intervention caused discontent on the islands. Although Trinidad and Tobago had been independent since 1976, the British Privy Council is the last appeals court of its justice system. According to local surveys, 80 per cent of the population favors the death penalty for murders and crimes related with drug trafficking.

[28] The visit of Prince Charles during February 2000 offered an opportunity to test the ties between the UK and its former colony. The Prince was received with music in the streets and there were no demonstrations. ∎

PROFILE

ENVIRONMENT

The country is an archipelago located near the Orinoco River delta off the Venezuelan coast in the southern portion of the Lesser Antilles in the Caribbean. Trinidad, the largest island (4,828 sq km), is crossed from East to West by a mountain range which is an extension of the Andes. One-third of the island is covered with sugar and cocoa plantations. Petroleum and asphalt are also produced. Tobago, 300 sq km with a small, central, volcanic mountain range, is flanked by Little Tobago (1 sq km), the islet of Goat and the Bucco Reef. In the archipelago the prevailing climate is tropical with rains from June to December, but tempered by the sea and east trade winds. Rivers are scarce, but dense forest vegetation covers the mountains. Its geographical proximity to the main sea route linking the Caribbean to the Atlantic, has led to pollution of the islands' coasts.

SOCIETY

Peoples: There is a large minority of African origin (39.6 per cent), and a slight majority descended from Asian Indians (40.3 per cent) brought during the 19th century as contract workers. European (0.6 per cent) and Chinese (0.4 per cent) groups make up a small minority.
Religions: Catholic 29.4 per cent. Protestant 29.7 per cent; Hindu 23.7 per cent; Muslim 5.9 per cent; other 11.3 per cent..
Languages: English (official). Hindi, Urdu, French and Spanish.
Political Parties: The People's National Movement (PNM); National Alliance for Reconstruction (NAR); United National Congress (UNC); National Joint Action Committee (NJAC).
Social Organizations: Trinidad and Tobago Labor Congress (TTLC); Jamaat-al-Muslimeen.

THE STATE

Official Name: Republic of Trinidad and Tobago.
Administrative Divisions: 7 Counties, 4 Cities with own government, 1 semi-autonomous island, Tobago.
Capital: Port of Spain 200,000 people (1993). Scarborough is the main town on Tobago.
Other cities: San Fernando 30,000 people; Arima 29,483; Point Fortin 20,025 (1990).
Government: Arthur N Robinson, President since March 1997. Basdeo Panday, Prime Minister since 1995.
National Holiday: August 31, Independence Day (1962).
Armed Forces: 2,100 (1996).
Other: 4,800 Police.

STATISTICS

DEMOGRAPHY

Population: 1,288,000 (1999)
Annual growth: 1.1 % (1975/97)
Estimates for year 2015 (million): 1.4 (1999)
Annual growth to year 2015: 0.6 % (1997/2015)
Urban population: 72.7 % (1997)
Urban Growth: 1.6 % (1980/95)
Children per woman: 1.6 (1998)

HEALTH

Life expectancy at birth: 74 years (1998)
male: 72 years (1998)
female: 76 years (1998)
Infant mortality: 16 per 1,000 (1998)
Under-5 child mortality: 18 per 1,000 (1998)
Daily calorie supply: 2,751 per capita (1996)
90 doctors per 100,000 people (1993)
Safe water: 97 % (1990/98)

EDUCATION

Literacy: 98 % (1995)
male: 99 % (1995)
female: 97 % (1995)
School enrolment:
Primary total: 96 % (1990/96)
male: 91 % (1990/97)
female: 102 % (1990/97)
Secondary:
male: 66 % (1990/96)
female: 79 % (1990/96)
Tertiary: 8 % (1996)
Primary school teachers: one for every 25 (1996)

COMMUNICATIONS

123 newspapers (1996), 534 radios (1997), 318 TV sets (1996) and 168 main telephone lines (1996) per 1,000 people
Books: 2 new titles per 100,000 people (1992/94)

ECONOMY

Per capita, GNP: $ 4,520 (1998)
Annual growth, GNP: 6.2 % (1998)
Annual inflation: 6.9 % (1990/98)
Consumer price index: 113.2 (1998)
Currency: 6.3 Trinidad dollars = $ 1 (1998)
Cereal imports: 232,915 metric tons (1998)
Food import dependency: 10 % (1997)
Fertilizer use: 1,413 kg per ha (1997)
Exports: $ 2,638 million (1998)
Imports: $ 3,598 million (1998)
External debt: $ 2,193 million (1998); $ 1,710 per capita (1998)
Debt service: 10.2 % of exports (1998)
Development aid received: $ 33 million (1997); $ 26.5 per capita (1997); 0.60 % of GNP (1997)

ENERGY

Consumption: 6,414.0 Kgs of Oil equivalent per capita yearly (1997); -66.0 % imported (1997)

HDI (rank/value): 46/0.797 (1997)

Tunisia

Tunisie

Population: 9,460,000 (1999)
Area: 163,610 SQ KM
Capital: Tunis
Currency: Dinar
Language: Arabic

From the 12th century BC the Phoenicians had a series of trading posts and ports of call on the North African coast. Carthage was founded in the 8th century BC in the general vicinity of present-day Tunis, and by the 6th century the Carthaginian kingdom encompassed most of present-day Tunisia. Carthage became part of Rome's African province in 146 BC after the Punic Wars. Roman rule endured until the Muslim Arab invasions in the mid-7th century AD. In Tunisia, the Arabs met the strongest resistance to their westward advance, but this region eventually became one of the best cultivated and developed of their cultural centers; the city of Kairuan is associated with some of the most outstanding names in Islamic architecture, medicine and historiography. During the dissolution of the Almohad Empire (see Morocco: Almoravids and Almohads) the region of Tunisia attained independence under the Berber dynasty of the Haffesides who, between the 13th century and the beginning of the 16th century extended their power over the Algerian coast.

2   The development of European maritime trade attracted Turkish corsairs. The most famous, Khayr ad-Din (known as Red Beard), set up his headquarters in Tunisia, placing the Tunisian-Algerian coast under the domination of the Ottoman sultans. The inland regions, however, remained in the hands of the Berbers. The need to work with them, coupled with the distance from Istanbul, allowed the *Bey* (designated governor) to attain a large degree of autonomy and in practice, become a hereditary ruler. The Murad family ruled between 1612 and 1702, and from 1705 until

after independence in 1957, this role was filled by the Husseinite family.
3   After the French occupation of Algeria, European economic penetration became increasingly evident and with it came increasing debts. In 1869 the burden of the foreign debt forced the Bey to allow an Anglo-French-Italian commission to supervise the country's finances. Foreign interference increased until 1882, when 30,000 French soldiers invaded the country, under an agreement whereby Britain, which had just occupied Egypt,

'transferred its rights' to Tunisia, to compensate France for its loss of control over the Suez Canal.
4   In 1925, the Tunisians launched a campaign for a new Constitution (Destur 1), which would bring autonomy to the country. After World War II, the pro-independence Neo-Destur party grew considerably, and a series of demonstrations and anti-colonial uprisings led to armed struggle between 1952 and 1955. In March 1956, France recognized the sovereignty and independence of the country under the Bey's regime. The new ruler was a direct heir of the sovereign under whom the

country had become a French Protectorate in 1882. However the Bey was +deposed on July 25 1957 by a constituent assembly controlled by 'Desturians'. A republic was proclaimed and the leader of the party, Habib Bourguiba, was elected President. Bourguiba started an energetic campaign against the French presence at the Bizerta naval base, finally dislodging them in 1964. Also in 1964 the New Destur Party became the Destur Socialist Party (PSD) and until 1981 was the only legal political organization.
5   Between 1963 and 1969, minister of finance Almed Ben Salah undertook a program of collectivization of small farms and trading companies, and nationalized foreign enterprises.
6   In 1969, following Ben Salah's arrest and subsequent deportation, government social and economic policy changed direction. The collectivization process was aborted and the economy thrown open to foreign investment. A 1972 law practically turned the whole country into a duty-free zone for export industries. Habib Bourguiba, the 'Supreme Combatant', was appointed president for life.
7   Towards the end of the 1970s, the economy suffered the effects of declining phosphate exports, and protectionist measures by the EEC against Tunisia's substantial textile industry. In January 1978, the UGTT (General Union of Tunisian Workers) called a general strike against wage controls and the repression of unions. The Government declared a state of emergency and street fighting left dozens dead. The union leaders, including the President Habib Achour, were arrested.
8   Appointed Prime Minister in 1980, Mohammed Mzali initiated a program of political liberalization. One year later, political parties were allowed to reorganize and trade union elections were held to renew the UGTT. General elections were held in November 1981 and, despite the vitality of the opposition parties, the ruling National Front won 94 per cent of the vote and all of the seats. Numerous irregularities were reported.
9   In January 1984, the Government decided to end several food subsidies. The price of bread rose 115 per cent and violent demonstrations left more than 100 dead. President Bourguiba cancelled the price increases. In 1985, there was further trade unrest and the UGTT was placed under government

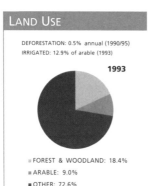

WORKERS

% OF LABOUR FORCE   **1998**

■ FEMALE: 31%   ■ MALE: 69%

1990

■ SERVICES: 39.1%
■ INDUSTRY: 32.8%
■ AGRICULTURE: 28.1%

LAND USE

DEFORESTATION: 0.5% annual (1990/95)
IRRIGATED: 12.9% of arable (1993)

1993

■ FOREST & WOODLAND: 18.4%
■ ARABLE: 9.0%
■ OTHER: 72.6%

PUBLIC EXPENDITURE

1997

46.6%

5.3%

DEFENCE   SOCIAL

MILITARY EXPENDITURE   **31%**
(% of health & education)   (1990/91)

control. There were also violent confrontations with the emerging illegal Islamic fundamentalist movement which ended with hundreds of arrests and some death sentences.

[10] During the period dominated by Bourguiba, Tunisia had developed as the most westernized of Arab societies. From 1986 onwards, the Fundamentalist reaction confronted the public with the issues of religion in the life of the individual and the community, and Tunisia's identity as an Arab-Muslim country. Female emancipation and European tourism were brought into question.

[11] In 1985, Colonel (later General) Zina El Abidine Ben Ali rose to power. In 1987, he was appointed Prime Minister and, in November, he dislodged president-for-life Bourguiba whom a medical board declared mentally and physically unfit to govern. This marked the start of a period of national reconciliation, meaning greater press freedom and the liberation of hundreds of political prisoners and Islamic militants. The PSD was renamed the Constitutional Democratic Grouping (RSD) without losing political dominance.

[12] The presidential and legislative elections of April 2 1989, were considered by observers to be the most free and fair since independence, even though 1,300,000 citizens were not registered to vote. The electorate split between the Government RSD (with 80 per cent of the vote and all the seats) and the Hezb Ennahda Islamic movement, whose independent candidates won 15 per cent. Center and left-wing opposition parties trailed as tiny minorities. President Ben Ali was elected by 99 per cent of voters.

[13] After distancing itself from the Arab League during the 1970s, Tunisia denounced the Camp David accords between Israel and Egypt, and became host to the PLO after its eviction from Beirut. Although President Ben Ali made overtures toward Islam during his first few years in office, he later unleashed a repressive campaign against the outlawed Hezb Ennahda movement and other opposition groups.

[14] In June 1990, Amnesty International published a report on Tunisia which included detailed accounts of torture and mistreatment of prisoners, including solitary confinement. The organization called for the death sentences of two prisoners to be commuted. The first of the two was executed in November of that year. In mid-1991, political figures urged their fellow-citizens to support the student movement, and asked the international community to offer the solidarity necessary to 'sustain the Tunisian people in their struggle for liberation, democracy, progress and the respect for human rights'.

[15] In reply to the mobilization, Ben Ali continued to reinforce repressive legislation. A restrictive Law of Association was passed in March 1992 and in July, members of the Islamic Hezb Ennahda were sentenced to life in prison. Unofficially, representatives from Western countries suggested the risk of expansion of Islamic fundamentalism in Tunis could justify Ben Ali's policy.

[16] In the meantime, human rights organizations continued to denounce Tunis for torture. In November 1993, Ben Ali enacted a further law restricting basic liberties. Against this background the President was re-elected with 99 per cent of the vote in the March 1994 general elections, the ruling party having obtained the control of 88 per cent of parliamentary seats.

[17] The leader continued his hard line economic policies. The opposition leader Mohamed Moada was sentenced to 11 years in prison in October 1995, for publishing a document discussing the curtailment of liberties in Tunisia and maintaining secret contacts with 'a foreign power' - Libya.

[18] President of the World Bank, James Wolfensohn, visited Tunisia in April 1996, and classed it as 'the World Bank's best student in the region.' However, the increasing economic liberalization was expected to destroy a third of all Tunisian businesses and increase the income inequalities amongst the population.

[19] In June 1997, the IMF called on the Government to accelerate economic reforms - in particular, the privatizations. The organization also stated the 15 per cent unemployment level was too high. At the end of that year, Parliament adopted a law allowing the Head of State to amend the Constitution by referendum.

[20] The free trade agreement between Tunisia and the European Union, in force since January 1998, gave better access to European markets for Tunisian products. Similar treaties were signed with Egypt, Libya and Morocco. The fall of customs collection was compensated with a rise in value-added-tax. The opening to regional markets and fast process of privatization led the IMF to maintain support for the government.

[21] The first multiparty elections held in October 1999 gave an overwhelming victory to President Al-Abidine Ben Ali, who received 99.4 per cent of the vote. His party, the Constitutional Democratic Group (RCD), was left with 148 of the 182 seats at stake, while the 34 seats reserved for the Opposition went to six other parties. One of the first measures taken by the new government was the liberation of some 600 political prisoners, mostly from the Al-Nahda Movement and the Workers' Communist Party.

[22] The death of Habib Bourguiba, in April 2000, was mourned by political leaders from Europe and the Arab countries. Presidents Jacques Chirac of France, Abdelaziz Bouteflika of Algeria, and Yasser Arafat of Palestine were present at the burial, carried out at the birthplace of the former president, Monastir. ∎

PROFILE ·

ENVIRONMENT

Tunisia is the northernmost African state. The eastern coastal plains are heavily populated and intensively cultivated with olives, citrus fruit and vinyards. The interior is dominated by the mountainous Tell and Aures regions populated by nomadic shepherds. The Sahara desert, in the south, has phosphate and iron deposits, while dates are cultivated in the oases.

SOCIETY

Peoples: 93 per cent of Tunisians are Arab, 5 per cent are Berber and 2 per cent European.
Religions: 99.4 per cent Islam, Sunni. There are also Jewish and Catholic groups. Languages: Arabic (official). French, Berber.
Political Parties: Constitutional Democratic Assembly; Democratic Socialist Movement; Communist Workers Party; Hezb Ennahda. Social Organizations: General Union of Tunisian Workers (UGTT).

THE STATE

Official Name: Al-Jumhuriyah at-Tunisiyah. Administrative Divisions: 25 Government Regions.
Capital: Tunis 674,100 people (1994).
Other cities: Safaqis (Sfax) 230,000 people; Aryanah 152,700; Ettadhamen 149,000; Sousse 125,000.
Government: Zine al-Abidine Ben Ali, President since 1987, re-elected in 1994 and 1999. Mohamed Ghannouchi, Prime Minister since November 1999. 163-member unicameral parliament.
National Holiday: June 1, Independence (1957).
Armed Forces: 35,500 (1997). Other: 13,000, National Police; 10,000, National Guard.

Turkey

Türkiye

Population: 65,546,000 (1999)
Area: 774,815 SQ KM
Capital: Ankara
Currency: Lire
Language: Turkish

The region of Anatolia has been inhabited for thousands of years. In the 8th century BC the Greeks founded the city of Byzantium on the strategic strait of Bosphorus, controlling traffic between the Black Sea and the Mediterranean. The city was conquered by the Romans in 96 AD and Emperor Constantine had it rebuilt. Under the new name of Constantinople, it became the capital of the Eastern Roman Empire, which outlived the Barbarian destruction of Rome and the Western Roman Empire by a hundred years.

[2] Constantinople was seized by the Turks in 1453 and renamed Istanbul. It became the capital of the flourishing Ottoman Empire. In the 16th century, the domains of Suleyman the Magnificent reached from Algeria to the Caucasus and from Hungary to the southern end of the Arabian Peninsula, populated by 50 million people (ten times the population of contemporary England). Western visitors marvelled at the efficiency and prosperity of the Government, and the respect shown for the rights of the peasants. This may explain why more than once the Christian peasants of the Balkans fought alongside the 'infidel' Muslim, against Christian nobles and clergy.

[3] From the 17th century, the Empire fell behind the impressive technological advance of western Europe and its aggressive trade expansion. The route to the East round the Cape of Good Hope, opened by the Portuguese, slowly deprived the Ottoman Empire of its trade monopoly between Europe and eastern Asia. The very borders of the Empire gave way to the thrust of European traders, whose companies introduced French, British and Dutch products in the eastern Mediterranean region.

[4] The fate of Turkey foreshadowed the course of events that later affected the great civilizations of China and India. They all became peripheral markets where Europeans imposed the sale of their manufactured goods and collected the food and raw materials for their own workforce and industries. Turkish artisans went bankrupt, the local textile industry failed to compete with British technology and the peasants grew increasingly poor, having to pay the price of imported goods.

[5] In the 19th century, a modernizing movement known as *Tanzimat* tried to impose European patterns and to build a centralized state, using modern technology, the telegraph and railways. New accords were signed with Britain and Germany but the influx of capital and goods further deepened Turkish dependency on Europe. One of the outstanding consequences was a large external debt which turned Turkey into 'the sick man of Europe'.

[6] At the beginning of the 20th century, a clandestine organization started to emerge from the discontent with the autocratic government. The 'Young Turks' formed within the universities and military academies. In July 1908, they led a rebellion in Macedonia, and within a few days Sultan Abdul Hamid yielded to their demand for a constitution limiting his power. The following year he was forced to abdicate in favor of Muhammad V, who bestowed real power on the Young Turks. They followed a nationalistic policy opposed to foreign suppliers, and various ethnic minorities, in particular the Greeks and Armenians.

[7] In World War I, Turkey sided with the second German Empire and the Austro-Hungarian Empire, and it was defeated along with them. The Ottoman Empire was torn apart and many small autocratic states rose on the Arabian Peninsula and in the Balkan region. The ethnic minority groups which remained within Turkish borders were ruthlessly repressed. In 1915 approximately 800,000 Armenians were killed in an episode that went down in history as 'the first genocide of the 20th century'.

[8] The conditions imposed on Turkey by the Treaty of Sèvres (1920) were so humiliating that military leader Mustafa Kemal (later known as Kemal Ataturk) deposed Sultan Muhammad VI, who had signed the accord, and launched a national liberation war. He finally succeeded in negotiating a new treaty, signed in Lausanne in 1923. Turkey was relieved of paying war reparations, and the privileges enjoyed by foreign traders (capitulations) were annulled. In exchange, the Bosphorus straits giving access to the Black Sea were declared international waters, open to all ships regardless of nationality in times of peace.

[9] Ataturk proclaimed a republic and had a new constitution approved. The Government initiated a process of rapid modernization. State and church separated, the Muslim Friday ceased to be the weekly holiday, replaced by Sunday, the Latin alphabet replaced Arab notation, and women were urged to stop wearing veils.

[10] After Ataturk's death in 1938, the military remained very influential in Turkish politics. The Government crushed the leftist groups which had grown under the influence of the neighboring Soviet revolution and during the fight against neo-colonialism. Eventually, Turkey signed a non-agression agreement with Nazi Germany in 1941 and kept neutrality until February 1945, when the Government decided to back the Allies.

[11] After World War II, Turkey now a US ally, became an anti-Soviet bastion. The growing influence of its northern neighbor led to stronger links with the US, which began to send military aid in 1947. The US built major military bases in Turkey and military doctrine was gradually replaced by the Pentagon's concept of 'national security'. With US influence Turkey adopted a multiparty system and gave incentives to foreign investors. Although the economy was still dependent upon agricultural exports, rural areas no longer provided enough jobs and young people emigrated to the cities or to western European countries, particularly West Germany. The country sent troops to Korea and in 1952 joined NATO.

WORKERS

1997
UNEMPLOYMENT: 6.4%

% OF LABOUR FORCE **1998**

■ FEMALE: 37%   ■ MALE: 63%
1990

■ SERVICES: 28.3%
■ INDUSTRY: 18.1%
■ AGRICULTURE: 53.6%

LAND USE

DEFORESTATION: 0.0% annual (1990/95)
IRRIGATED: 15.0% of arable (1993)

1993

■ FOREST & WOODLAND: 25.9%
■ ARABLE: 31.4%
■ OTHER: 42.7%

PUBLIC EXPENDITURE

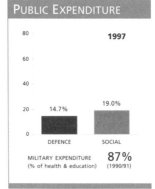

1997

80
60
40
20   14.7%   19.0%
0   DEFENCE   SOCIAL

MILITARY EXPENDITURE   **87%**
(% of health & education)   (1990/91)

MATERNAL MORTALITY	LITERACY	EXTERNAL DEBT	FOREIGN TRADE
1990-98	1995	1998	Millions US$ 1998
			IMPORTS
			56,129
Per 100,000 live births		Per capita	EXPORTS
130	**82%**	**US$ 1,583**	**49,229**

12 Turkish military intervention in Cyprus caused that island to split in 1974, provoking the resignation of Turkey's Prime Minister Bulent Ecevit, a social democrat. Conservative Suleyman Demirel succeeded Ecevit but the rivalry between these two leaders prevented the formation of a stable government for the rest of the decade.

13 Demirel was ousted by the military in 1980 and General Kenan Evren became President. A new accord changed the conditions of the military bases, and Turkey started to receive US$1 billion per year for leasing them. Labor unions and political parties were banned and the Government was accused of systematic human rights violations.

14 In 1983, a new constitution heralded a period of political liberalization designed to soothe western European critics. The new government program aimed at gaining access to the European Economic Community, giving new vigor to modernization, moving away from the old nationalistic policies and embracing economic liberalism.

15 In 1987, rivalries between the main opposition groups, formed by the followers of Demirel and Ecevit, enabled the Motherland Party (ANAP) to win the elections.

16 Prime Minister Turgut Ozal embarked enthusiastically on a policy of privatization, economic liberalization and promotion of exports, following International Monetary Fund and World Bank guidelines. His willingness to adopt these policies was based on the assurance that they would lead to prosperity and to admittance into the European Community, an undeniably popular goal in a country where nearly all families had at least one relative working in Western Europe. However, political freedoms were not liberalized to the same extent and the Community postponed considering the Turkish bid until 1993, alleging that its high rates of inflation and unemployment, the lack of a concrete social policy and Turkey's conflict with Greece made its incorporation into the Community untenable.

17 Accused of nepotism, corruption and a lack of sensitivity over the social impact of his economic policy, Ozal suffered a total defeat in the March 1989 municipal elections. However, as a result of successful political manoeuvering, he managed to get Parliament to name him President in October of the same year. In 1990, his government was confronted by the growing activism of the Kurd separatists in the southeast of the country, where the PKK (Kurdish Workers' Party) was taking military action.

18 In August 1990, when Iraq was blockaded after the invasion of Kuwait, Turkey interrupted the flow of Iraqi oil to the Mediterranean by blocking the pipeline through the country. Although it did not send troops, Turkey authorized the use of its military airports and US bases for the massive bombings of Iraq. The opposition questioned these measures, arguing that they would affect relations with a neighboring country in an area already made unstable by Kurdish independence movements.

19 Ankara feared that the independence of Iraqi Kurdistan might affect the Turkish Kurds. The 19 million Kurds live in a territory divided between four countries: Turkey, Syria, Iran, and Iraq. They are the world's largest ethnic minority without a territory of their own. For several decades, Turkey had a policy of virtual cultural annihilation against the Kurds, giving them few rights to use their language and express their identity.

20 In October 1991, the Turkish army entered northern Iraq in order to attack PKK bases, supported by aircraft and helicopters. Kurdish representatives accused the Turkish Government of bombing the civilian population.

21 The parliamentary elections of October 20 were won by Suleyman Demirel's True Path Party (DYP), which obtained 27 per cent of the vote, gaining 178 of the 450 parliamentary seats. This narrow majority forced Demirel to seek alliances with Erdal Inonu's Social Democratic Populist Party (SHP), which came in third with 21 per cent of the vote. The Motherland Party (ANAP), which obtained 24 per cent of the vote, formed the opposition.

22 Demirel faced a budget deficit of US$6 billion, a foreign debt of US$44 billion, and an annual inflation rate of 70 per cent. Apart from the fundamentalist movements, all the other political parties agreed that Turkey's main priority was to gain entrance to the European Economic Community.

24 In mid-March 1992, the banned PKK announced the formation of a war government and a national assembly in the territory which they claimed formed the core of Kurdistan, the internationally unrecognized Kurdish state. A few days later, coinciding with the Kurdish new year, there was an uprising in the southeastern provinces with violent action between the guerrillas and the Turkish security forces, especially in Cizre. In April, the Turkish Interior Minister, Ismet Sezgin, visited Damascus in Syria and Turkey announced an agreement to fight against the Kurdish 'terrorist organizations'. Under the agreement, the Syrian Government stated that it would close the PKK training camps and carry out stricter controls along its borders.

25 In 1992, the Council of Europe urged the Government to reduce repression against the Kurdish community. The Turkish authorities

PROFILE

ENVIRONMENT

The country is made up of a European part, Eastern Thrace, and an Asiatic part, the peninsula of Anatolia and Turkish Armenia, separated by the Dardanelles, the Sea of Marmara and the Bosphorus. Eastern Thrace, located in the extreme southeast of the Balkan Peninsula, makes up less than one-thirtieth of the country's total land area including an arid steppe plateau, the Istranca mountains to the east, and a group of hills suitable for farming. Anatolia is a mountainous area with many lakes and wetlands. The Ponticas range in the north and the Taurus range in the south form the natural boundaries for the Anatolian plateau, which extends eastward to form the Armenian plateaus. The far east is filled by the Armenian Massif, centered around the lake region of Van, where there is a great deal of volcanic activity and occasional earthquakes. Parallel to the Taurus there are a number of ranges known as Anti-Taurus, which run along the border of the Georgia, together with the Armenian mountains. The country is mainly agricultural. The lack of natural resources, and absence of capital and appropriate infrastructure, have been major obstacles to industrialization. The air in the area surrounding Istanbul contains high levels of sulphur dioxide and the Marmara Sea is contaminated with mercury.

SOCIETY

Peoples: Turkey's people are descendants of ethnic groups from Central Asia that began to settle in Anatolia in the 11th century. There are Kurdish, 12 per cent, Arab, 1 per cent, Jewish, Greek, Georgian and Armenian minorities, whose cultural autonomy, including teaching in their respective languages, is severely limited.
Religions: Mainly Islamic. Sunni Muslims represent about 80 per cent of the population and Alevi (non-orthodox Shi'a) almost 20 per cent.
Languages: Turkish (official), Kurdish and other minority languages.
Political Parties: True Path Party (DYP); Motherland Party (ANAP); Social Democratic Populist Party (SHP); Party of the Democratic Left (DSP); Nationalist Action Party; Republican People's Party (CHP); Socialist Party; Welfare Party; Democracy Party; Kurdish Workers' Party (PKK). Social Organizations: Confederation of Turkish Trade Unions; Confederation of Progressive Trade Unions of Turkey.

THE STATE

Official Name: Türkiye Cumhuriyeti.
Administrative Divisions: 74 Provinces.
Capital: Ankara 2,900,000 people (est 1994)
Other cities: Istanbul 12,000,000 people; Izmir (Smyrna) 2,800,000; Adana 1,100,000; Bursa 1,016,760; Gaziantep 730,435; Konya 584,783 (1994).
Government: Ahmet Necdet Sezer, President since May 5, 2000. Bülent Ecevit, Prime Minister since January 1999.
Armed Forces: 639,000 troops (1996). Other: 70,000 Gendarmes-National Guard, 50,000 Reserves.

subsequently granted an amnesty to 5,000 political prisoners and authorized the circulation of two Kurdish-language newspapers. In November, the EC set 1996 as the date for Turkish admission to the European Customs Union, a first step toward eventual membership of the EU.

²⁶ Upon the death of President Turgut Ozal in April 1993, Prime Minister Demirel was elected to be his successor. Tansu Ciller, minister of economic affairs, assumed the leadership of the DYP and was named Prime Minister. Ciller, the first woman to head a government in Turkey, presented her program which was approved by Parliament in July. It included an accelerated privatization program - to be carried out by decree - as well as fiscal reform. In order to stem the growing budget deficit, which stood at $9.4 billion, there would be a moratorium on public investment. In July, public employees carried out strikes and demonstrations to protest the massive loss of jobs which would be brought about by privatization. Some 700,000 people participated in the protests, which took place over a two-day period in Ankara, Istanbul and Izmir.

²⁷ The PKK ordered a cease-fire and offered to withdraw demands for the formation of an independent state in Kurdistan, in return for the initiation of formal negotiations with the Government. At the end of May 1993, government evasiveness led the guerrillas to declare an 'all-out war' on Ankara and to take action in European cities, especially in Germany, accused of giving military support to Turkey.

²⁸ The army extended its offensive during 1994, forcing the inhabitants of hundreds of Kurd villages to leave their homes while it bombed Iraqi Kurdistan to destroy PKK bases.

²⁹ The growth of Islamic fundamentalism in Turkey was apparent in 1995, in the run-up to the December elections. Its main representative, the Welfare Party, pledged during the election campaign to form Islamic organizations to compensate for the influence of NATO and the European Union. The party became Turkey's main political group winning 158 of the 550 seats.

³⁰ Prime Minister Ciller's DYP and the ANAP, overcame their differences to prevent Islamic fundamentalists from coming to power and formed an unexpected government coalition, led by Mesul Yilmaz from the ANAP, who took office in March 1996. However, the alliance was swiftly dissolved and the DYP chose to rule with the fundamentalists. Necmettin Erbakan became head of government in June.

³¹ At an international level, the signing of a military agreement with Israel in April further complicated Turkey's relations with several Arab countries, such as Syria. Tension mounted on the April 24, when Ankara decided temporarily to shut off the supply of water from its controversial dams on the Euphrates river for 'technical reasons', forcing Syrian authorities to ration water in Damascus, shortly before Muslim Aid el Adha (the sacrifice) festivities.

³² The year 1997 was marked by the confrontation between the Erbakan administration and the army-backed secularist opposition. The army gave evidence linking the DYP with Islamic organizations made illegal by the previous government and now working underground, stating they were more dangerous than the PKK separatist Kurds. The President replaced Erbakan with Mesut Yilmaz in June, and the Constitutional Court - the most important Turkish legal entity - accused him of bringing the country 'to the brink of civil war and conspiring against the secular regime'.

³³ In September, around 20,000 Turkish troops and 100 tanks crossed over the frontier with Iraq into Kurdistan to dismantle the military bases of the PKK. The Turkish soldiers, backed by Iraqi Kurds from the Democratic Party of Kurdistan (KDP), surrounded PKK bases close to the frontier with Iran.

³⁴ Although Turkey was one of the 11 countries on the European Union waiting list, and had already been in the application process for 10 years, it did not attend the conference in London in March 1998 where the other 10 met up with the EU's 15 members. The Ankara Government said its absence was due to the veto imposed on its entry by Germany.

³⁵ In April that year Semdin Sakik, the best-known commander of the PKK, gave himself up to the forces of Iraqi Kurd leader Barzani, in northern Iraq. He alleged that he feared being killed by Abdullah Ocalan, leader of his party. Sakik had been relieved of his command in Southeastern Turkey, in the Tuncelli mountains region.

³⁶ The Government used the celebrations in October that year of the 75th anniversary of the Republic and the commemoration of the 60 years since the death of Kemal Atatürk to strengthen the centralized politics of the secular state. The offensive against Islamic forces had begun on January, when the Constitutional Court dissolved the Welfare Party and banned Nmettin Erbakan and other leaders from politics during five years. The Party of Virtue (PV) was immediately established to replace the banned Welfare Party. In

September, an appeals court confirmed the ten month prison sentence to Recep Tayyip Erdogan, the Muslim mayor of Istanbul.

³⁷ The denial of political asylum to Abdullah Ocalan in late 1998 and his detention in February 1999 as he sought refuge at the Greek embassy in Kenya sparked fresh controversy. Kurds throughout Europe protested angrily at the extradition allowed to Turkey. Kurdish demonstrators occupied several Greek embassies in Europe in protest at the handing over of their leader. After a long process, Ocalan was sentenced to death in June despite of his pleas for mercy and his suggestions that a pardon by the court could open the way to political understanding between Kurds and Ankara. However, the military weakness of the PKK led the court to ratify the death sentence in November.

³⁸ The Party of the Democratic Left (DSP) obtained a relative majority in the April 1999 elections, having won 22.3 per cent of the vote and 136 seats, ahead of the National Movement which received 18.1 per cent of the vote and 129 seats. The Islamic Party of Virtue were third with 15.5 per cent, defeating the Motherland Party, which ended up with 13.3 per cent, and the True Path Party, with 12.1 per cent.

³⁹ By an overwhelming majority, in June Parliament approved the creation of a new government committed to crushing the Kurdish guerrillas in the Southeastern region of the country. The new administration included the DSP of Prime Minister Bulent Ecevit, the ultra-right National Movement and a small right of center party.

⁴⁰ Greek cooperation in the detention of Ocalan and the assistance received from Greece after the August 1999 earthquake served to improve relations between Athens and Ankara. The Greek Government lifted its veto on the incorporation of Turkey into the EU and on talks about the incorporation of Cyprus. After having waited for 36 years, Turkey was invited to join the EU in December 1999.

⁴¹ Ocalan's death sentence was put on hold in January 2000 awaiting guidance from the European Human Rights Court. A PKK congress announced in February it was abandoning armed struggle and presented a seven-point plan to become a political party. During the third round of voting in May, Parliament elected Ahmet Necdet Sezer as President. Sezer, a well-known democratic rights advocate, was expected to give momentum to the reforms demanded by the EU as a prerequisite to Turkey's membership. ∎

STATISTICS

DEMOGRAPHY

Population: 65,546,000 (1999)
Annual growth: 2.1 % (1975/97)
Estimates for year 2015 (million): 80.3 (1999)
Annual growth to year 2015: 1.3 % (1997/2015)
Urban population: 71.9 % (1997)
Urban Growth: 5.3 % (1980/95)
Children per woman: 2.5 (1998)

HEALTH

Life expectancy at birth: 69 years (1998)
male: 67 years (1998)
female: 72 years (1998)
Maternal mortality: 130 per 100,000 live births (1990-98)
Infant mortality: 37 per 1,000 (1998)
Under-5 child mortality: 42 per 1,000 (1998)
Daily calorie supply: 3,568 per capita (1996)
103 doctors per 100,000 people (1993)
Safe water: 49 % (1990/98)

EDUCATION

Literacy: 82 % (1995)
male: 92 % (1995)
female: 72 % (1995)
School enrolment:
Primary total: 105 % (1990/96)
male: 107 % (1990/97)
female: 102 % (1990/97)
Secondary:
male: 67 % (1990/96)
female: 45 % (1990/96)
Tertiary: 21 % (1996)
Primary school teachers:one for every 28 (1994)

COMMUNICATIONS

111 newspapers (1996), 180 radios (1997), 309 TV sets (1996) and 224 main telephone lines (1996) per 1,000 people
Books: 8 new titles per 100,000 people (1992/94)

ECONOMY

Per capita, GNP: $ 3,160 (1998)
Annual growth, GNP: 3.9 % (1998)
Annual inflation: 79.4 % (1990/98)
Consumer price index: 618.5 (1998)
Currency: 260,724.3 lire = $ 1 (1998)
Cereal imports: 2,970,779 metric tons (1998)
Food import dependency: 5 % (1997)
Fertilizer use: 687 kg per ha (1997)
Exports: $ 49,229 million (1998)
Imports: $ 56,129 million (1998)
External debt: $ 102,074 million (1998); $ 1,583 per capita (1998)
Debt service: 21.2 % of exports (1998)
Development aid received: $ -1 million (1997)

ENERGY

Consumption: 1,140.0 Kgs of Oil equivalent per capita yearly (1997); 61.0 % imported (1997)

HDI (rank/value): 86/0.728 (1997)

Turkmenistan

Turkmenistán

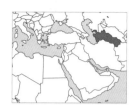

Population: 4,384,000 (1999)
Area: 488,100 SQ KM
Capital: Ashkhabad (Aschabad)
Currency: Manat
Language: Turkmen

From 1000 BC onwards, the area now known as Turkmenistan was part of several large states: the Persian Empire (controlled by the Achaemenid dynasty) and later, the empire of Alexander the Great. In the third century AD, Turkmenistan was conquered by the Sassanids, an Iranian dynasty. Between the 5th and 8th centuries, there were successive invasions by the Eftalites, the Turks and the Arabs.

[2] From the 6th to the 8th century, the entire area adjacent to the Caspian Sea was under the Arab Caliphate, and when the latter dissolved in the 9th and 10th centuries, the territory became a part of the Tahirid and Sassanid states. In the mid-11th century, the Seljuk Empire was formed in Turkmenistan, and towards the end of the 12th century it was conquered by the dynasty of the Shah of Khwarezm (Anushteguinidas).

[3] During the Seljuk period the Turkmens formed as an ethnic group through the fusion of Oguz Turks and local tribes. This was a gradual process which was completed by the 15th century. In the early 13th century, Turkmenistan was invaded by Genghis Khan, whose heirs divided up the country. A large part of the territory was incorporated into the State of Hulagidas, and the northern regions were overrun by the Golden Horde of the Mongol Tatars. In the 14th and 15th centuries, the country fell under the Timurids, who were succeeded by the Uzbek khans of the Shaybani dynasty. From the 16th to the 18th century, Turkmenistan belonged to the *khanates* of Khiva and Bukhara, and the Iranian state of the Safavids, successively.

[4] In the 1880s, Turkmenia - as it was then known - was conquered by the Russian army. The major part of its territory lay within the Trans-Caspian region and the province of Turkistan, but the lands inhabited by the Turkmens passed into the hands of Khiva and Bukhara, which were Russian protectorates. There was strong resistance to Russian domination in Turkmenia until the Battle of Geok-Tepe in 1881, in which the last of the rebels were defeated. The Turkmens were active participants in the 1916 uprising against the Czar. The most violent revolt was in the city of Tedzhen, where several Russian residents and government officials were executed by the local population.

[5] The fall of the Czar in February 1917, led to the creation of soviets (councils of workers, peasants and soldiers) throughout the empire. The Trans-Caspian region fell under the control of the Russian Provisional Government. In December 1917, after the Bolshevik (socialists in favor of the revolution) take-over in St Petersburg, Soviet power was proclaimed. In July 1918, the English expeditionary forces re-established the Provisional Government in Trans-Caspia. After two years of civil war, Soviet power was reinstated in 1920 and on February 14 1924, the Soviet Socialist Republic of Turkmenistan was founded (joining the USSR, at the same time).

[6] Up until that time, Turkmenistan had never known even nominal national political unity. Tribal organization was the only form of social organization, and most of the population was nomadic. For this reason, the Soviet regime resorted to repressive techniques in order to impose industrialization and collective agriculture upon the local population.

[7] After World War II, Turkmenistan entered a period of economic growth, accompanied by increases in oil and gas production. In addition, gains were made in the area of cotton farming. But during Leonid Brezhnev's administration from 1963-83, political problems worsened and the economy entered a period of stagnation. In those republics where the Soviets had adopted a monocropping policy, as in the case of Turkmenistan with the cultivation of cotton, agriculture was more vulnerable to the effects of the recession.

[8] As of 1985, the changes promoted in the USSR by President Mikhail Gorbachev vitalized political life in Turkmenistan. There was also an Islamic religious rebirth, expressed through the construction of a number of mosques.

[9] After the coup attempt in the USSR in August 1991, the Communist Party of Turkmenistan lost its legitimacy to govern. Communist leader Saparmurad Niyazov declared the need to restore state sovereignty and in October, a plebiscite brought in a presidential system. In November, Turkmenistan joined the Commonwealth of Independent States (CIS), which replaced the former USSR, and the Communist Party changed its name to the Democratic Party. The sovereignty of Turkmenistan was internationally recognized.

[10] President Saparmurad Niyazov, former secretary of the Turkmen Communist Party, visited Ankara and Teheran. Niyazov stated that he would give priority to the country's relations with Turkey, given the cultural proximity between the two countries.

[11] In Teheran, Niyazov signed trade agreements, giving joint top priority to exploration for natural gas and the construction of a transportation network. He also expressed the need to integrate the Turkish and Turkmen banking systems.

PROFILE

ENVIRONMENT

Turkmenistan is in an arid zone, with dry continental climate, located in the southeastern part of Central Asia between the Caspian Sea to the west, the Amu Darya River to the east, the Ustiurt mountains to the north and the Kopet-Dag and Paropamiz mountain ranges to the south. The land is flat and most of the territory (80 per cent) lies within the Kara-Kum desert. Topographically, 90 per cent of Turkmenistan is sandy plain. On the eastern shore of the Caspian Sea lie the Major and Minor Balkan ranges, of relatively low altitude. The Amu Darya river crosses Turkmenistan from east to west. The Kara-Kum Canal diverts the waters of the Amu Darya to the irrigation systems of the Murgab and Tedzhen oases, as well as those of the Mary and Ashkhabad areas. Turkmenistan is bounded by Kazakhstan to the northwest, Uzbekistan to the east; and Afghanistan and Iran, to the south. There are rich mineral deposits, including natural gas and oil.

SOCIETY

Peoples: Turkmenis 77 per cent; Russians 6.7 per cent; Uzbeks 9.2 per cent, Kazakhs 2 per cent; Tatars 0.8 per cent. Other 6.6 per cent. (1996).
Religions: Mainly Sunni Muslim (87 per cent); Russian Orthodox 6.4 per cent. Other 6.6 per cent. **Languages:** Turkmen (official), Russian. Political Parties: Democratic Party; Socialist Party; Agzibirlik (Unity); Party for Democratic Development.

THE STATE

Official Name: Türkmenistan Jumhuriyäti. **Administrative divisions:** 3 provinces and 1 'Dependent Region' (Ashkhabad). **Capital:** Ashkhabad (Aschabad) 480,000 people (est 1995). **Other cities:** Chardzhou (Cardzou) 166,000 people. **Government:** Saparmurád A. Niyazov, President and Head of State and Government since November 1991, re-elected in 1992 and 1994. Legislative: Islamic Assembly with 50 members elected by direct vote each five years. **National Holiday:** May 18 (Independence Day). **Armed Forces:** 18,000 (1997).

[12] In early 1992, the new constitution was approved, granting Niyazov the dual powers of head of state and head of government, and abolishing the vice-presidency, establishing instead the Mechlis (Islamic parliament) and a People's Council. Niyazov rejected a free-market economy and the privatization of state-owned enterprises. In January, the Government reduced the price of bread and other staples, and stopped the liberalization program which had been initiated during the Gorbachev era.

[13] Under Niyazov's presidency, Turkmenistan joined the European Conference for Security and Cooperation (ECSC) and in March 1992, became a member of the United Nations.

[14] Niyazov was re-elected in June 1992 with 99.5 per cent of the votes. Without distancing himself from Russia, which signed a series of trade agreements in 1993, Turkmenistan drew closer to Iran, through the construction of the Ashkhabad-Teheran railway, amongst other things. It also achieved the status of most favored nation with the US.

[15] Niyazov was reconfirmed in his post by 99.9 per cent of the vote in the January 1994 referendum. The President continued with his 'hard handed' policy against the opposition, which led several opposition leaders to take refuge in Moscow.

[16] In January 1995, Turkmenistan, Turkey, Iran, Kazakhstan and Russia signed an agreement to fund an oil pipeline which would allow Ashkhabad to export its natural gas to Eastern Europe through Iran and Turkey.

[17] Despite attempts to reconcile its openness to Iran - and its reticence at becoming fully involved in the Community of Independent States - with a 'balanced' policy towards Moscow, the Russian Government was obviously uneasy about Niyazov's rapprochement with Tehran.

[18] Russian observers claimed the July 1995 demonstrations against the Turkmeni President - where between 300 and 500 people protested against the 'dictatorship' - were organized with Moscow's support.

[19] In December 1997, the first oil pipeline was opened between Turkmenistan and Iran, to export Turkmeni oil and gas to the countries of the Mediterranean and the Persian Gulf. The Government now had to negotiate with the United States over the non-application of the 1996 Iran Sanctions Act, which punished companies, subsidiaries and citizens investing more than $40 million per year in the Iranian oil or gas industries.

[20] In February 1998 Niyazov announced his plans to give Parliament more authority and less to the executive branch, which was regarded as a token gesture prior to the meeting with US President Bill Clinton. After the visit to Washington on April, Niyazov declared that discussions over constitutional changes would take place after the December 1999 parliamentary elections.

[21] Only the ruling DP party was allowed to present candidates in the parliamentary elections, causing the Organization for Security and Cooperation in Europe (OSCE) to withdraw its offer to supervise the elections. The Government claimed there were two or more candidates in almost all electoral areas. After the elections, in which 95 per cent of the registered voters participated, Niyazov asked Parliament not to name him president for life. He also passed a law abolishing the death penalty, making Turkmenistan the first of the five former USSR Asian republics to eliminate capital punishment.

The OSCE reported the February 2000 arrests of two opposition activists who were condemned to five years in prison.

[22] Niyazov decided not to attend a summit of Asian Turkish-speaking countries including Turkey, Uzbekistan, Kazakhstan, Kyrgyzstan and Tajikistan, and which was held in Azerbaijan during April 2000. The meeting was conceived as a way of uniting those countries, but the dispute with Azerbaijan over the Caspian Sea oil-pipe prevented the Turkmenistan President from attending. ∎

STATISTICS

DEMOGRAPHY

Population: 4,384,000 (1999)
Annual growth: 2.4 % (1975/97)
Estimates for year 2015 (million): 5.6 (1999)
Annual growth to year 2015: 1.5 % (1997/2015)
Urban population: 45.0 % (1997)
Children per woman: 3.6 (1998)

HEALTH

Life expectancy at birth: 66 years (1998)
male: 62 years (1998)
female: 69 years (1998)
Maternal mortality: 110 per 100,000 live births (1990-98)
Infant mortality: 53 per 1,000 (1998)
Under-5 child mortality: 72 per 1,000 (1998)
Daily calorie supply: 2,563 per capita (1996)
353 doctors per 100,000 people (1993)
Safe water: 74 % (1990/98)

EDUCATION

Literacy: 98 % (1995)
male: 99 % (1995)
female: 97 % (1995)
Tertiary: 20 % (1996)

COMMUNICATIONS

276 radios (1997), 163 TV sets (1996) and 74 main telephone lines (1996) per 1,000 people
Books: 14 new titles per 100,000 people (1992/94)

ECONOMY

Per capita, GNP: $ 650 (1997)
Annual growth, GNP: -24.0 % (1997)
Annual inflation: 663.4 % (1990/98)
Currency: 5,277.0 manat = $ 1 (1998)
Cereal imports: 755,159 metric tons (1998)
Fertilizer use: 883 kg per ha (1997)
External debt: $ 2,266 million (1998); $ 526 per capita (1998)
Debt service: 42.0 % of exports (1998)
Development aid received: $ 11 million (1997); $ 2.9 per capita (1997); 0.40 % of GNP (1997)

ENERGY

Consumption: 2,615.0 Kgs of Oil equivalent per capita yearly (1997); -54.0 % imported (1997)

HDI (rank/value): 96/0.712 (1997)

Chechnya and Abkhazia

Unlike former Soviet republics, which already had a degree of autonomy within the Soviet Union, the 'autonomous regions' such as Chechnya and Abkhazia did not obtain the independence demanded by some of their inhabitants. In 1922, Chechnya became an autonomous region of the Socialist Federate Soviet Republic of Russia. In 1936, along with Ingushetia, it became the Autonomous Republic of Checheno-Ingush. Chechens and Ingush were deported by Stalin in 1944 to Kazakhstan and Kyrgysztan and when Nikita Krushchev allowed them to return in 1957, the Autonomous Republic was re-established.

[2] In late 1990, the Chechnya National Congress declared the sovereignty of the Republic of Chechen-Ingush. The first presidential elections were held in November 1991 and Dzojar Dudayev was elected President. Dudayev declared the Chechen Republic's independence from the Russian Federation. Russia launched a war against the Chechens to regain control over the territory and, after three months of fighting, took control of the devastated capital, Grozny. In 1995, the first Russian-Chechen armistice was signed, but fighting continued. In spite of the death of Dudayev, killed by a Russian missile, Chechen forces recovered the capital in August 1996. That same month, the first agreements between the Russian Federation and the Chechen Republic were signed. In January 1997, Aslan Mashadon was elected President.

[3] Early in 2000, the new Russian President Vladimir Putin proposed an end to the conflict which was crushing the Chechens with a massive deployment of Russian troops. However, just as it seemed Moscow would achieve its objective, the war appeared to veer off in a different direction when the Russian Government threatened to attack Afghanistan, believing that the Taliban regime there was supporting the Chechen rebels. According to some analysts, Moscow's campaign was merely a front for a war 'against Islam'.

[4] In 1810, Abkhazia, then under Ottoman rule, was annexed to Russia, followed by decades of dispute. In 1878, more than half the Abkhazian population was forcefully displaced to Turkey and Abkhazia became colonized by Armenians, Megrels and Russians. In 1921 the Socialist Soviet Republic of Abkhazia was proclaimed, but soon the region became a part of Georgia, as an autonomous province. In the early 1930s, Georgian settlers started to arrive in the region and would later become the largest ethnic group in Abkhazia. In the late 1980s, Abkhazian Georgians demanded secession, while the rest of the population preferred to remain within the Soviet Union. In August 1992, Georgia sent troops to control the region, with frequent armed conflicts. By October 1993, the Georgian forces had been defeated and most of the local Georgians had become refugees. In June 1994, a 24-kilometre border zone was established, patrolled by Russian peace forces. The Republic of Abkhazia was declared a sovereign and democratic state that same year. In 1997, the population of Abkhazia voted for a new parliament, but Georgia declared both the new constitution and the new parliament illegal. In 1998, a solution to the conflict was nowhere in sight, in spite of border restraints imposed by Russia in order 'to lead the Abkhazian Government towards peace'. ∎

Turks and Caicos

Turks and Caicos Islands

Population: 16,000 (1998)
Area: 430 SQ KM
Capital: Cockburntown
Currency: US dollar
Language: English

Turks and Caicos were first inhabited by Arawak peoples. Some researchers claim it was on East Caicos or Grand Turk that Columbus first set foot on New World soil in 1492. The first Europeans to settle on the islands were salt-rakers from Bermuda in 1678.

[2] During the following century, Turks and Caicos faced several invasions by both French and Spanish forces. The islands were a refuge during this period for both pirates and their merchant-vessel victims, Spanish galleons carrying American wealth to Europe. By 1787, colonial settlers had established cotton plantations and imported African slaves, and British domination was consolidated. Both archipelagos remained British colonies.

[3] Turks and Caicos were administered from the Bahamas until the Separation Act of 1848. After 1874, the islands were annexed to Jamaica, remaining a dependency until independence in 1962, when they again became a separate colony. During World War II, the United States built an airstrip on South Caicos and in 1951 the islands' authorities signed an agreement permitting the US to establish a missile base and a Navy base on Grand Turk island.

[4] After the Bahamas'

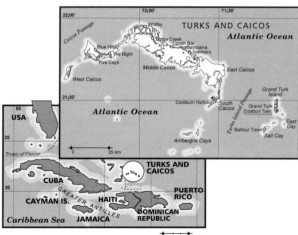

independence in 1972, Turks and Caicos received their own governor. Further autonomy achieved through the 1976 constitution, provided for a Governor, a Legislative Council, a Supreme Court and a Court of Appeals.

[5] In the 1976 elections, the pro-independence People's Democratic Movement (PDM), led by JAFS McCartney, won over the pro-US Progressive National Party (PNP). The PDM favored a new constitution which granted internal autonomy as a step towards eventual independence.

[6] In 1980, election year, Britain showed an interest in granting

independence to the islands, which receive $2 million a year in aid. The overwhelming electoral triumph of the PNP was attributed to the failure of the PDM to solve the country's economic crisis, including a 30 per cent unemployment rate and the local population's fears that the economy could worsen with independence.

[7] The new head minister, entrepreneur Norman Saunders, convinced Britain to shelve the idea of independence. He concentrated on bringing new business to the islands: tourism talks with the French Club Mediterranée; the development of light industry and offshore banking; and finally an agreement with BCM Ltd, for construction of an oil refinery with a capacity of 125,000 barrels per day.

[8] Internal differences arose within the Government with regard to economic policy. However, these differences were quickly forgotten when Saunders and Stafford Missik, his development minister and a key opposition figure within the government, were arrested in Miami. They were in the process of creating an international drug network, using the islands as a bridge between the US and South America.

[9] Saunders was released after paying an apparently exorbitant sum of bail money, and immediately resigned his post. His successor was Nathaniel Francis of the PDM, also forced to resign a year later together with the entire cabinet after accusationsn of 'unconstitutional behavior and mismanagement'. The British Government suspended the ministerial system until 1988, when a general election was held. PDM's Oswald Skippings won the election, with 11 of the 13 parliamentary seats

going to his party. The election marked the end of direct British administration of the islands.

[10] The Government declared the objective of achieving financial independence within four years, and political independence before 1998.

[11] Unemployment reached 12 per cent of the active population in 1992. In 1993 imports cost $42.8 million and exports were worth $6.8 million.

[12] Martin Bourke was appointed Governor in 1993, and Derek H Taylor became Prime Minister in 1995.

[13] Tourism registered a 10 per cent increase in the first three months of 1995 compared with the same period of 1994. Some 70 per cent of the total 60,000 tourists were US citizens. The economy of the islands was also supported by fishing and international financial services.

[14] During 1996, the Government and the opposition parties tried unsuccessfully to persuade Britain to remove Governor Martin Bourke. This hostility towards Bourke was due to his abuse of power and lack of respect for the people of the island. In September, when his term of office came to an end, John Kelly was appointed the new Governor.

[15] Haitian refugee ships reaching the islands in 1998 and 1999 were systematically rejected by the archipelago maritime authorities. One of these ships was sunk in June 1998 and six people died as a result of a confrontation with the coastguards. The survivors accused the coastguards of firing without previous warning.

[16] The December 1999 elections for the Legislative Council gave the majority to the People's Democratic Movement which obtained 52.8 per cent of the vote and nine representatives. The Progressive National Party obtained 40.3 per cent of the vote and 4 of the 13 elected legislators. Mervyn Jones was appointed Governor in January 2000.

[17] A new financial scandal arose in April 2000 when a lawyer vanished leaving no traces of the money from the Christian foundation which he controlled. There are some 7,000 financial companies registered on the islands which do business considered shady by other countries. The UK, US and some European countries complained about the financial system which allows the daily laundering of millions of dollars derived from drug trafficking and other illegal activities. ■

PROFILE

ENVIRONMENT

An archipelago of more than thirty islands comprising the southeastern part of the Bahamas. Only eight are inhabited: Grand Turk, Salt Cay, South Caicos, Central Caicos, North Caicos, Providenciales, Pine Cay and Parrot Cay. The climate is tropical with heavy rainfall, moderated by ocean currents. The islands are on the hurricane path and were particularly devastated in 1928, 1945 and 1960. Fishing is the main economic activity.

SOCIETY

Peoples: The majority are of African descent. There is a Caucasian minority and a significant number of Haitian immigrants. **Religions:** Baptists 41.2 per cent; Methodists 18.9 per cent; Anglicans 18.3 per cent; Adventists of the Seventh Day 1.7 per cent. Other 19.9 per cent. **Languages:** English. **Political Parties:** Progressive National Party (PNP); the People's Democratic Movement (PDM); and the National Democratic Alliance (NDA).

THE STATE

Official Name: Turks and Caicos Islands. **Capital:** Cockburntown on Grand Turk Island 3,761 people (1995). **Other cities:** The population is distributed as follows: Grand Turk 3,098; South Caicos 1,380; Central Caicos 396; North Caicos 1,278; Providenciales 977; Salt Cay 284. (1980). **Government:** Roman, serif'>Mervyn Jones, Governor, appointed by Britain, since January 2000. Derek H Taylor, Prime Minister since 1995. **Armed Forces:** Defense is responsibility of the United Kingdom.

Tuvalu

Tuvalu

Population: 10,000 (1998)
Area: 30 SQ KM
Capital: Fongafale
Currency: Australian dollar
Language: Tuvaluan and English

Around 30,000 BC, the peoples from South East Asia, ancestors of the aborigines, started their expansion toward the Pacific islands. By the 19th century AD, they had spread throughout practically all of Polynesia. The inhabitants of the archipelago then known as 'Funafuti' came there from the islands of Samoa and Tonga.

2   In the 16th century the Europeans reported seeing the islands but did not settle on them due to the lack of exploitable resources. Years later, a European named the atolls the Ellice Islands.

3   Between 1850 and 1875, thousands of islanders were captured by slave traders and sent to the phosphate (guano) works in Peru and the saltpeter mines in Chile. Within a few years, the population had shrunk from 20,000 to 3,000 inhabitants. As a source of slave labor, the Polynesian islands offered direct access to markets on the Pacific coast.

4   A new wave of invasions began in 1865, with the arrival of British and North American missionaries. By 1892 the islands had become a British protectorate. In 1915, with their neighbors, the Gilbert Islands (see Kiribati), the British formed the Colony of the Gilbert and Ellice Islands.

5   This arbitrary merger was decided on administrative grounds and had little to do with other factors. In a referendum of 1974, 90 per cent of the Ellice islanders voted in favor of separate administrations, after having attained relatively autonomous local government.

6   The split became official in October 1975, and the first elections in independent Tuvalu were held in August 1977. Toaripi Lauti was named Prime Minister.

7   The archipelago became independent on October 1 1978, adopting the name Tuvalu, which in the local language means 'united eight', symbolizing the eight inhabited islands which make up the country. The islands became autonomous from London, but they fell under the economic influence of Australia, which had already started to hold considerable sway on the economy; the Australian dollar is used as the local currency.

8   Under a friendship treaty of 1979 Washington relinquished its claim over the islands of Nurakita, Nukulaelae, Funafuti, and Nukufetau.

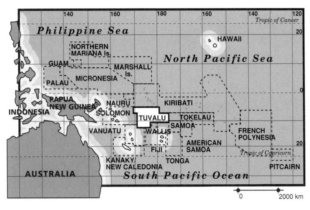

9   On December 8 1981, Lauti was succeeded by Tomasi Puapua.

10   In September 1985, general elections were held for the third time in the archipelago's history. Dr Tomasi Puapua was re-elected Prime Minister. In February 1986, the Government showed its opposition to French nuclear weapon testing in Mururoa, Polynesia, by denying entry to a French warship which was on a 'goodwill' mission.

11   Tuvalu is the smallest of the Lesser Developed Countries, in both population and land area. One of its main sources of foreign exchange is the sale of stamps, which are valuable collectors' items, and the granting of fishing licenses to foreign fleets which earns some $100,000 per year.

12   A United Nations report on pollution-induced global warming and the subsequent rise in sea levels, stated that Tuvalu could be completely submerged, unless severe measures are taken.

13   Faced with a lack of natural resources, a sparse population, and an almost total lack of internal sources of savings or investment, the country depends heavily on foreign aid, of which Australia is the principal source, to finance its regular budget and its development budget. In 1989, the State was able to meet about 10 per cent of its expenses. Most of this money was sent home by the quarter of the islands' population, mostly young people, who reside in neighboring islands working in the phosphate mines in the early 1990s.

14   The situation of the archipelago worsened as citizens returning from abroad look for jobs, competing with young people just finishing school. Only 30 per cent of school-leavers were successful in finding employment.

15   In 1993, Kamuta Laatasi became Prime Minister. His government dismissed Governor-General Tomu Sione in 1994, arguing that he was a political appointee of the previous regime.

16   In the independence day celebrations, in October 1995, a new flag was hoisted, replacing the British Union Jack. In 1996, the new Prime Minister, Bikenibeu Paeniu once again made the British flag official.

17   Former Prime Minister Kamuta Latasi lost his seat in the March parliamentary elections, and Paeniu was confirmed in his place. In August the Government sold its Internet website (identified with the letters 'tv'), to a Canadian television corporation for $50 million and future shares in the utilities.

18   A high tide with strong winds and waves caused floods in most of the Funafuti island area as well as other islands during February 2000. The situation brought the global warming issue to the forefront once more, the consequences of which could mean the complete disappearance of Tuvalu and other islands.

19   A fire which swept through a residential village for students in Vaitupu island, causing the death of 18 girls and their supervisor in March 2000. The girls' doors had been locked to 'protect' the young women from male students. The Prime Minister condemned this custom. Since then, the girls have been protected instead by gates which keep them in at the nights - and presumably keep men out. ∎

PROFILE

ENVIRONMENT

Tuvalu is distributed over the Funafuti, Nanumanga, Nanumea, Niutao, Nui, Nukufetau, Nukulaelae, Nurakita and Vaitupu coral atolls, known as the Ellice Islands, within an ocean area of 1,060,000 sq km. The archipelago is situated slightly south of the equator, 4,000 km northeast of Australia, south of the Gilbert Islands, between Micronesia and Melanesia. The climate is tropical with heavy rainfall. The islands are completely flat with a thin layer of topsoil suffering from severe erosion. Fishing and coconut farming are traditional activities.

SOCIETY

Peoples: Tuvaluans are mainly Polynesians. **Religion:** Church of Tuvalu (Congregational) 96.9 per cent; Seventh-Day Adventist 1.4 per cent; Baha'i 1 per cent; Roman Catholic 1.4 per cent; other 0.5 per cent.
Languages: Tuvaluan and English. **Political Parties:** Prominent families control Tuvalu's politics. They are not formally organized in parties.

THE STATE

Official Name: Tuvalu. **Capital:** Fongafale on Funafuti's atoll, 4,000 people (1985). **Other atolls:** Vaitupu 1.231 people; Niutao 904; Nanumea 879; Nukufetau 694 (1985). **Government:** Tulaga Manuella, Governor-General and Chief of State, since 1994; Ionatana Ionatana, Prime Minister since April 1999. Tuvalu has a parliamentary government modeled on the British system. Parliament has twelve members. **National Holiday:** October 1, Independence Day (1978).

STATISTICS

Demography: Population: 10,000 (1998). **Health:** Infant mortality: 40 per 1,000 (1998). Under-5 child mortality: 56 per 1,000 (1998). Safe water: 100 % (1990/98). **Education:** Literacy: 99 % (1995). School enrolment: Primary total: 101 % (1990/96). **Economy:** Cereal imports: 1,522 metric tons (1998)

Uganda

Uganda

Population: 21,143,000 (1999)
Area: 241,038 SQ KM
Capital: Kampala
Currency: Shilling
Language: Swahili

In present-day Uganda the large mud walls of Bigo state are evidence of urban civilizations dating from the 10th century.

[2] Various places in Uganda still bear the ruins of sizeable hilltop fortresses, overlooking the surrounding territory. Built with earthen walls, moats and trenches, these fortifications mark the lines of Bacwezi penetration. Around the 13th century, the Bacwezi, a nation of Nilotic herders, arrived from the north and subdued the Bantu inhabitants of the area. Their characteristic fortresses -in some cases up to 300 meters in diameter-, were built to protect themselves and their cattle - their main source of wealth and status symbols. The fortresses were gradually abandoned, and the conquerors mixed with the conquered and adopted Bantu languages. The descendants of the Bacwezi, who preserved their nomadic herding lifestyle, intermingled less with the local population though they also adopted a Bantu language, and came to be called Bahima.

[3] The peoples of Bunyoro, Buganda, Busoga and Ankole were connected to the eastern coast and the Sudanese slave trade; they consolidated their national unity between the 17th and 18th centuries. A supremacy dispute arose between Bunyoro, supported by the Sudanese traders, and Buganda, linked to the 'Shirazis' of Zanzibar. At the beginning of the 19th century, Bunyoro was already losing ground, and when some of their allies defected to form the independent state of Toro the predominance of Buganda became inevitable.

[4] Buganda was governed by Kabakas or traditional leaders, who were in theory absolute rulers but

in practice were limited by the Lukiko, a council representing the higher castes. In the mid-19th century, Buganda maintained a standing army which was enough to guarantee their autonomy from the regional powers: Egypt and Zanzibar. It had a balanced society in which caste privileges were more honorary and political than economic and a sound agricultural economy which allowed Buganda to overcome the decline of the slave trade.

[5] The first contact with Europe occurred in 1862. The second contact had more far-reaching results. HM Stanley, adventurer and journalist, arrived in 1875. He vociferously denounced the spread of Islam in the region and announced an alleged 'request' made by Kabaka Mutesa I asking Europe to send missionaries to check Egyptian-Sudanese religious infiltration.

[6] These missionaries soon arrived: English Protestants in 1877 and French Catholics in 1879. They quickly converted part of the Bugandese hierarchy, splitting the power elite into three parties. Two of these reflected the rivalry between missionaries, in local dialect the 'Franza' and 'Ingleza' parties, while the third took the role of defending national interests, as they were moderate and Islamic.

[7] The main consequence of this conflict was the consolidation of European presence. The missionaries succeeded in deposing the Moslem Kabaka, Mwanga in 1888, and swift on their heels came the Imperial British East Africa Company (IBEA), a typical colonial trading company, followed by the British Government.

[8] The 1886 Anglo-German agreements had delimited areas of influence and the states of the lakes

area went to the British who established a Protectorate over them in 1893.

[9] The other organized local groups did not have governmental institutions similar to those of Buganda's but these were imposed on them as the British thought that the Lukiko resembled their own parliamentary system.

[10] With the intention of developing a ruling elite to serve as intermediaries to the colonial power, the British undertook 'land reform'. This consisted of distributing communally-owned land to select individuals, depriving the rural population of their legitimate property to benefit the bureaucracy that sat in the Lukiko.

[11] The severe disruption of production caused by this confiscation was aggravated by the introduction of cash crops for export (including cotton, coffee and tea) in the post-World War II period. These crops were alien to the agricultural traditions of the region, and their production resulted in a deterioration in the living conditions of most of the inhabitants.

[12] There was no way of changing this state of affairs until the 1960s when the decolonization movement led to the independence of Uganda. Kabaka Mutesa II of Buganda was the first President of the new republic and the Prime Minister was Dr Milton Obote.

[13] In 1965, Obote succeeded in reforming the Constitution and he assumed greater powers, eliminating the federal system imposed by the British, which had created various relatively autonomous territorial sub-divisions. He also adopted a policy that favored the most impoverished sectors.

[14] This aroused fierce opposition among the Asian bourgeoisie; a minority of 40,000 people who controlled almost all the commercial activity in the country. Since the Asians held British passports, they had resisted total integration into the new nation.

[15] Obote decisively supported regional economic integration with Tanzania and Kenya to counterbalance the effects of Uganda's lack of access to the coast. This led to the formation of the East African Community.

[16] In January 1971, Obote was overthrown in a bloody coup led by

WORKERS

% OF LABOUR FORCE **1998**

■ FEMALE: 48% ■ MALE: 52%

1990

■ SERVICES: 10.7%
■ INDUSTRY: 4.7%
■ AGRICULTURE: 84.5%

LAND USE

DEFORESTATION: 0.9% annual (1990/95)
IRRIGATED: 0.2% of arable (1993)

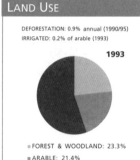

1993

■ FOREST & WOODLAND: 23.3%
■ ARABLE: 21.4%
■ OTHER: 55.3%

PUBLIC EXPENDITURE

DEFENCE EXPENDITURE (% of goverment exp.)	**23.9%**	(1997)
MILITARY EXPENDITURE (% of health & education)	**18%**	(1990/91)

former paratroop sergeant and boxing champion Idi Amin Dada. The economic base of the deposed government had been seriously shaken by a series of destabilization manoeuvres by the Asian minority and interests connected to transnationals. Idi Amin quickly demonstrated his authoritarianism. In 1972 he ordered the extensive expulsion of the Asians.

[17]   Although he came to power with the support of the 'élite' of the business community, Amin's attitudes and measures were very controversial: he maintained commercial relations with the United States and Britain, also cultivating good relations with the socialist world. Similarly, while he supported several African liberation movements, he opposed Angola's bid for membership to the Organization of African Unity (OAU) and was permanently hostile to Nyerere's government in Tanzania. Finally, although he had been trained as a paratrooper in Israel, he expropriated the lands and other properties of members of the Jewish community and made overtures toward the Arab countries.

[18]   Amin declared himself President-for-Life. In 1978, he exacerbated tensions with Tanzania by annexing its northern territories. In April 1979, war between the two countries ended Amin's regime and he was forced to flee Kampala, after a joint offensive launched by Tanzanian troops and opposition activists united in the Ugandan National Liberation Front (FNLU).

[19]   The new government's main body was a National Advisory Council led by Yusuf Lule, a politically inexperienced university professor with conservative tendencies. 68 days later, Lule was replaced by the FNLU's powerful Godfrey Binaisa.

[20]   The Front was a frail, eclectic movement, founded merely on joint efforts aimed at ending the terror imposed by Idi Amin. As expected, Binaisa was unable to conciliate the conflicting tendencies within his movement. He was even less capable of confronting the growing prestige of Milton Obote whose Uganda People's Congress party (UPC) continued to be very popular.

[21]   The President brought forward the elections scheduled for 1981, and tried to ban Obote's candidacy. This fuelled a crisis that exploded in May 1980 when the army, on the pretext of preventing the implementation of the Government's policies, forced him to resign.

[22]   The President was replaced by a Military Commission entrusted with maintaining the electoral schedule and enforcing the democratic principles of the movement that had overthrown Amin. The Commission, under the orders of General David Oyite Ojok, supervised the elections in December 1980, and the UPC won the predicted overwhelming majority.

[23]   Obote's party won 73 of the 126 seats in the new parliament. The legitimacy of the election was questioned, but an international commission of 60 members confirmed that, given the constraints of the country, minimum standards had been complied with.

[24]   Obote inherited a bankrupt country. Copper mines had not been worked for several years and corruption and speculation were commonplace. Despite the reaffirmation support for Obote in the elections, in 1981 the defeated conservative groups initiated an intense destabilization campaign that gradually became an openly anti-government guerrilla movement.

[25]   In spite of the guerrilla presence, Obote authorized the return of Asian businesses, regulated the participation of foreign capital and undertook the reorganization of the economy, fighting corruption and speculation. Despite the intensification of political violence in 1985, Obote requested and obtained the withdrawal of Tanzanian troops who had been in Uganda since the fall of Amin.

[26]   By early 1982, coffee exports had been resumed, international trade was returning to normal and negotiations to restructure the foreign debt; largely inherited from Amin's period, had been initiated with the IMF.

[27]   In 1983, Obote and his party were re-elected, gaining 90 seats compared with the 35 of the Democratic Party. Shortly before the elections, the UPC had achieved another major goal: the revival of the East African Community, dissolved in 1977. The Community slowly and steadily gained in strength.

[28]   Between 1981 and July 1985, 16 major military offensives were launched against the main strongholds of opposition guerrillas. These groups included; the National Resistance Army (NRA), the military wing of the National Resistance Movement (NRM) founded by former president Yusuf Lule and led by Yoweri Museveni; the Uganda National Rescue Front, led by retired Brigadier Moses Ali (one of

MATERNAL MORTALITY

1990-98

Per 100,000 live births

510

Idi Amin's former associates); and Lt-Colonel George Nleawanga's Federal Democratic Movement (FEDEMU).

[29]   Civil warfare displaced 100,000 people. In 1981, the Government took steps to prevent cattle smuggling by the nomadic peoples across the Kenyan border, causing starvation among thousands in the province of Karamoja.

[30]   In spite of the guerrilla activity, Uganda's economy had grown an average 5 per cent yearly since 1982, and, according to the World Bank, exports had increased 45 per cent since 1983. Food was available and gasoline no longer rationed.

[31]   Nevertheless, the floating exchange rate system introduced in 1981 accentuated inflation, the most serious problem, causing a 1,000 per cent devaluation of the Ugandan shilling, and the price of bread increased 5,000 per cent between 1979 and 1984.

[32]   General elections were scheduled for December 1985, and a UPC victory was expected. However, in late July 1985, General Bazilio Olara Okello led a military coup putting an end to Obote's government. General Tito Okello, not related to the rebel leader, was appointed President. Within 12 months, he called elections to form a broad-based government. The Okellos belonged to the northern Ajuli ethnic group and Obote, member of the Langis, was accused of favoritism towards his own people.

[33]   After the coup, the National Resistance Army intensified its action, occupying Kampala, the capital, in January 1986. After a bloody fight, Okello was ousted, and on January 30, NRA leader Yoweri Museveni assumed the presidency. The northern town of Gulu, the last bastion of forces loyal to Okello, finally fell in March of that year.

[34]   Museveni was faced with the reconstruction of a country virtually destroyed by a series of authoritarian regimes which had left almost a million dead, two million refugees, 600,000 injured and incalculable property damage.

[35]   Resources are scarce in a country with a fertility rate of 7.0 (1995) children per woman, and a life expectancy of not more than 41 years. This difficult situation has been aggravated by an extremely high incidence of AIDS, which is said

PROFILE

ENVIRONMENT

The land is made up of a number of plateaus, gently rolling towards the northwest where the Nile River flows. There are volcanic ranges and numerous rivers, the largest of which is the Nile. Nearly 18 per cent of the territory is taken up by rivers, great lakes and swamps. The climate is tropical tempered by altitude. Lumber is taken from the rainforest which covers 6.2 per cent of the land. In addition to subsistence farming of rice and corn, the cash crops are coffee, cotton, tea and tobacco. Lake Victoria is one of the largest fish reservoirs in the world. Swampland is being drained indiscriminately for agricultural use.

SOCIETY

Peoples: Most Ugandans come from the integration of various African ethnic groups, mainly the Baganda, Bunyoro and Batoro, and to a lesser extent, the San/Bushmen, Nile-Hamitic, Sudanese, and Bantu. Some have distinct physical traits typical of the northern Nile, Hamitic groups, but they speak Bantu languages. There are also minorities of Indian and European origin.
Religions: More than half of the people are Christian (62 per cent), 19 per cent practice traditional religions and there are 15 per cent of Muslims. Others, 1 per cent.
Languages: English, the official language, is spoken by a minority. Of the native languages, Swahili and Luganda are the most widely spoken.
Political Parties: National Resistance Movement (NRM), led by President Museveni. All other parties have been disenfranchised by the government; the most important among them are the Ugandan People's Congress (UPC); the Democratic Party (DP), the Ugandan Freedom Movement (UFM); the Conservative Party (CP); the Nationalist Liberal Party; the Ugandan Democratic Alliance; the Ugandan Revolutionary Movement for Independence; the Ugandan United Nationalist Movement; and the Ugandan Patriotic Movement.
Social Organizations: National Organization of Trade Unions (NOTU).

THE STATE

Official Name: Republic of Uganda.
Capital: Kampala 850,000 people (1996).
Other cities: Jinja 61,000 people; Mbale 54,000 people (1996).
Government: Yoweri Museveni, President since January 30 1986, re-elected in May 1996. Apolo Nsibambi (NRM), Prime Minister since 1999.
National Holiday: October 9, Independence Day (1962).
Armed Forces: 55,000 (1997).

to have achieved epidemic proportions in some parts of the country.

[36] Uganda's foreign debt rose to $1.2 billion in 1987. To solve this, Museveni resorted to exchange arrangements with other African countries.

[37] The country attempted to establish its economic independence, avoiding the International Monetary Fund (IMF). This led to some problems with Western countries, who did not approve of Uganda's relations with Cuba and Libya. The United States pressed Tanzania and Rwanda into ending the exchange operations which they had organized with Uganda.

[38] In 1991, the Ugandan Government banned logging in the east of the country to try to prevent further environmental destruction. Although this measure has caused significant economic losses in the short term, the Government announced that it would stop the timber exports.

[39] In various regions throughout the country, local elections were scheduled for March 1992. The supporters of former president Milton Obote announced their decision to boycott these.

[40] Meanwhile, President Museveni ordered the imprisonment of several journalists who reported human rights violations committed by the army in the north and northeast of the country. He also passed a law granting the Government controlling power over the local press.

[41] In February 1992, local human rights organizations accused Museveni of harassing his political opponents and of not allowing the establishment of a multiparty democracy in the country. The Government replied that it preferred to build a democracy based on traditional tribal structures, and that political parties were therefore unnecessary.

[42] But pressure from the opposition and some international agencies led President Museveni to authorize the election of a Constituent Assembly, which would be announced in February 1993 and established in 1995, charged with studying a draft of the new constitution. Nevertheless, the text drafted by the Government was criticized by the opposition (Democratic Party and the UPC) for maintaining the partial ban on political parties for a seven-year period.

[43] In February, Pope John Paul II visited Uganda and urged the population to practice sexual abstinence, to prevent the spread of AIDS. This advice caused grave concern in a country where over 20 per cent of the population are HIV-carriers.

[44] As part of a policy aimed at winning the support of the Baganda people, Museveni authorized the restoration of the monarchy. During Prince Ronald Muenda Mutebi's coronation ceremony as Kabaka, on July 31, authorities returned all royal property, which had been confiscated during former president Obote's administration.

[45] On another front, Museveni was accused by the opposition of having ordered the assassination of opposition leader Amon Bazira in Kenya in August. In the March 1994 elections the supporters of the Ugandan President took around half the seats, but the direct appointed of some of the posts gave Museveni a broad majority in the new assembly.

[46] Continuing with his policy of restoring the local authorities, the leader once again authorized the Nioros, a people in the north of the country, to have their own kingdom, and this decision was implemented in June.

[47] The discussion of a multiparty system continued throughout 1995. Museveni continued to claim the authorization of several parties would only make the 'tribal divisions' more serious. On another front, the international funding organisations said they were satisfied with the economic performance of Uganda. Foreign investments grew, but budget cuts worsened the situation of most of the population as they already lived in poverty.

[48] On May 9 1996, Museveni was re-elected by more than 75 per cent of the electorate, with a 72.6 per cent turnout, defeating Paul Semogerere and Muhammad Mayanja. The President was victorious again in the May legislative elections, as his party took 156 of the 196 seats at stake. The new Government was appointed in July, with Kintu Musoke as Prime Minister.

[49] The economic reforms carried out by Museveni with loans and aid from international creditors, meant Uganda topped the list in the World Bank project to help out 20 debtor countries in 1997. However, half the population was living below the poverty line, leading to estimates that $24 million would be needed to relieve the hunger in this country. The Franco-Australian LaSource company paid Uganda for the right to exploit its cobalt mines, and the nation received loans from the European Union and North Korea for the construction of a hydroelectric plant.

[50] Disputes between Uganda and Sudan continued throughout the year. The two governments armed and supported their respective guerrilla groups, causing tens of thousands of deaths and large numbers of refugees. Uganda received aid from the United States, both in weaponry and military training, in return for its efforts against Sudan and the ousted Mobutu Sese Seko regime in the Zaire.

[51] In mid-1998, the Ugandan army entered neighboring Democratic Republic of Congo (DRC, formerly Zaire) and joined the rebels fighting President Laurent Kabila. On October 18 1999, Ugandan Defense Minister, Stephen Kavuma, stated that his troops would remain in DRC until peace was restored.

[52] On November 12 1999, seventy independent and state journalists marched through the streets of Kampala to denounce official persecution and the systematic abuse of freedom of speech. They also demanded the repeal of the so-called 'sedition act'. On November 30, in the Tanzanian city of Arusha, the Presidents of Kenya, Tanzania, and Uganda signed a treaty which established the Economic Union of Eastern Africa. On December 11, the International Monetary Fund granted Uganda a $12 million loan for its efforts to 'combat poverty', according to Shigemistsu Sugisaki, IMF deputy director. Sugisaki suggested that the Ugandan Government invest less in national defense. However, several days later, Museveni met in Kampala with Rwandan President Pasteur Bisimungu to discuss their military alliance.

[53] On February 1 2000, Museveni accused Sudan of breaking the pact signed two months earlier which would restore diplomatic relations - broken off in 1995 - and initiate an exchange of prisoners. Days later, UN officials in Uganda started to investigate the alleged involvement of the country in supplying weapons to UNITA, the rebel group in Angola. Meanwhile, combat between government troops and the Lord's Resistance Army, in the north of the country, continued taking civilian lives and delaying a solution. On March 18, communal graves were found in the village of Kanungu with hundreds of bodies belonging to followers of the Christian cult 'Restoration of the 10 Commandments of God', who had committed collective suicide.

[54] On April 4, in Kampala, senior Ugandan army officers met with their rebel allies from the DR Congo to implement, the UN-sponsored cease-fire agreed a few days before in the country. On May 2, the IMF - with the support of the World Bank and the African Development Bank - wrote off $640 million of Ugandan debt as a result of its reputation as a 'safe state for foreign investment'. The initiative was made public a few weeks after it was known that President Museveni had spent $35 million on a private jet. ∎

Ukraine

Ukrayina

Population: 50,658,000 (1999)
Area: 603,700 SQ KM
Capital: Kiev (Kijef)
Currency: Grivna
Language: Ukranian

Between the 9th and 12th centuries AD, most of the present Ukraine belonged to the Kievan (Kijef) Rus, which grouped together several alliances of Eastern Slavic peoples. Its nucleus was the Russian alliance, with its capital at Kiev. The ancient Russian people gave rise to the three main eastern Slav nations: Russia, Ukraine and Belarus. In the 12th century, the Kievan Rus separated into the principalities of Kiev, Chernigov, Galich and Vladimir-Volynski, all in what is now Ukrainian territory. In the 14th century, the Grand Principality of Lithuania annexed the territories of Chernigov and Novgorod-Severski, Podolia, Kiev and a large part of Volin. The Khanate of Crimea emerged in the southern part of Ukraine and Crimea, and expanded into Galicia and Podolia. After the 11th century, Hungary began seizing the Transcarpathian territories.

2   The Ukrainians emerged, as an identifiable people, in the 15th century. Their name was derived from krai, meaning border, which in 1213 was the name given to the territories along the Polish border. In the 16th century, the use of the name was extended to the entire Ukrainian region. Historically, there were close ties between Ukrainians and Russians, they had fought together against the Polish and Lithuanian feudal kingdoms and against the Tatars in Crimea. The Ukrainian territories (Volin, eastern Podolia, Kiev and part of the left bank of the Dnepr) were incorporated into the Rzecz Pospolita (the union of Poland and Lithuania), which imposed Roman Catholicism.

3   During the first half of the 17th century, the struggle for independence from Poland and Lithuania intensified. The Khmelnytsky insurrection (1648-1654) under Bohdan Khmelnytsky ended with the unification of Ukraine and Russia, approved by the Rada (council) of Pereyaslav. In March 1654, Ukrainian autonomy within the Russian Empire was ratified. The region along the right bank of the Dnepr and Galicia remained under Polish jurisdiction. Ukrainian colonization of what is now Kharkov (Char'cov) began in the 17th century.

4   In 1783, the Khanate of Crimea - home of the Tatars - was annexed by Russia. After the partition of Poland among Russia, Prussia and Austria (1793-95), the right bank of the Dnepr became a part of Russia and Ukraine's autonomy was abolished at the end of the 18th century. In 1796, the left bank of Ukraine became the Province of Malo-Rossiya (Little Russia).

5   After the end of czarism in 1917, a dual system emerged in Ukraine, with power being divided between the Provisional Government of Saint Petersburg and the Ukrainian Central Rada (council) in Kiev. In December, after the Bolshevik Revolution, a Ukrainian Soviet government was formed in Kharkov. The Ukrainian Central Rada supported the Austro-German troops which invaded the country in the spring of 1918. In December, the Ukrainian Directorate, led by Symon Petlyura, seized power. Between 1918 and 1920, Ukraine was the scene of major fighting between the Soviets and their internal and external enemies. In December 1922, Ukraine attended the first All-Union Congress of the Soviets, held in Moscow, where the Treaty and Declaration of the Founding of the Union of Soviet Socialist Republics (USSR) was ratified.

6   In the period between the world wars, the Soviet Government carried out rapid industrialization and collectivization of agriculture.

7   The secret clauses of the 1939 Soviet-German non-aggression pact incorporated western Ukraine into the USSR. In 1940, the Ukrainian Soviet Socialist Republic was enlarged through the addition of Bessarabia and Northern Bukovina. Germany attacked the Soviet Union in 1941, a strong guerrilla offensive began and by the end of World War II, all areas inhabited by ethnic Ukrainians became part of the USSR. Ukraine participated in the founding of the UN as a charter member.

8   In 1954, Crimea - which had formerly belonged to the Russian Federation - was turned over to Ukraine, by the Soviet centralized authority. The leader of the Soviet Communist Party at the time was Nikita Krushchev, former first secretary of the Ukrainian CP.

9   On April 26 1986, the nuclear plant at Chernobyl - 130 kilometres north of Kiev - was the scene of the worst nuclear accident in history when one of its reactors exploded. The explosion affected an area inhabited by 600,000 people; 135,000 were evacuated and by 1993, 7,000 had died of radiation-related diseases.

10   In 1985 within the framework of the reforms in the USSR, Communist leaders and Ukrainian nationalists founded the Ukrainian People's Movement for Perestroika (restructuring) (RUKH), which demanded greater political and economic autonomy. In the March 1990 legislative elections, RUKH candidates received massive support from the population. On July 16 1990, the Ukrainian Supreme Soviet (Parliament) proclaimed the sovereignty of the republic. On August 24 1991, the Ukrainian Parliament approved the republic's independence, and convened a plebiscite to ratify or reject the decision.

11   Leonid Kravchuk, former first secretary of the Ukrainian Communist Party, was elected President, with 60 per cent of the vote. Russia, Canada, Poland and Hungary immediately recognized Ukrainian independence, underscoring the failure of Gorbachev's attempt to reach a new union treaty, within the USSR.

12   On December 8 1991, the presidents of Ukraine, the Russian Federation and Belarus pronounced the end of the USSR, founding the Commonwealth of Independent States (CIS). Ukraine declared itself a neutral and nuclear-free country, and stated its willingness to participate in the process of European integration. A few days later, 7 former republics of the USSR joined the CIS, but differences among them kept them from defining the scope of the new alliance.

13   In the first months of 1992, the Ukrainian Government declared the end of the fixed prices system; created a new currency, and called for bids to build arms factories, announcing incentives for attracting foreign investment.

14   On May 5, the Crimea peninsula declared independence, but it was vetoed by the Ukrainian Parliament. Crimea yielded and withdrew the declaration. Russia reacted to the situation in June, annulling the 1954 decree by which it had ceded Crimea to Ukraine, demanding that it be returned. Kiev refused, but granted Crimea economic autonomy. After the dissolution of the USSR, Crimea became one of the chief sources of conflict between the Kiev and Moscow governments.

15   In March 1993, Ukraine suspended the transfer of tactical nuclear weapons to the Russian Federation, claiming there were no guarantees that these would actually be destroyed.

16   The four CIS States with nuclear arms (Russia, Ukraine, Belarus and Kazakhstan) subsequently agreed to form an international commission to supervise the withdrawal and destruction of the nuclear weapons sited on Ukrainian soil.

17   Prime Minister Vitold Fokin resigned in September over the failure of his economic policies. He was replaced by Leonid Kuchma, former president of the Union of Industrialists and Entrepreneurs.

18   The liberal policies of the new government and its privatization scheme soon came up against the dual obstacles of the Supreme Council - dominated by former communists - and worker resistance.

Kuchma presented his resignation on May 21, but it was not accepted.

[19] In June, in a direct challenge to Kravchuk's moderate foreign policy, the Supreme Council announced the appropriation of the entire ex-USSR nuclear arsenal in Ukraine. With the disintegration of the Soviet Union, Ukraine became the world's third most important nuclear power.

[20] Finding himself politically vulnerable, in September 1993 Kravchuk ceded the part of the Black Sea fleet belonging to Ukraine to Russia, in compensation for debts incurred through oil and gas purchases from Moscow. In addition, he accepted help from Russia in dismantling the 46 intercontinental SS24 missiles which Ukraine had wanted to keep as a last bastion against any possible future expansionist schemes on the part of Russia. However, opposition in Kiev led to the invalidation of the settlement.

[21] In the meantime, the economy went out of control -with inflation reaching 100 per cent per month and Kuchma resigned.

[22] In November 1993, the Council ratified the START-1 strategic weapons limitation treaty, and agreed to the gradual dismantling of 1656 nuclear warheads.

[23] The first presidential elections of the post-Soviet era took place in June and July 1994. Former Prime Minister Leonid Kuchma defeated Kravchuk with 52 per cent of the vote, after which he declared his intention to strengthen links with Russia and enter fully into the Commonwealth of Independent States (CIS).

[24] The tenth anniversary of the Chernobyl accident, in April 1996, sparked an international campaign against the nuclear plants of the former soviet countries. According to studies, a million people were directly affected by the radiation, 2.4 million lived within affected regions and 12 per cent of the farming land in the country was contaminated.

[25] In September 1997, the United States, Belarus, Russia, Kazakhstan and Ukraine signed disarmament agreements which would end the suspension of the nuclear arms reduction treaty, Start 2, signed in 1993.

[26] The Communist Party of Ukraine (KPU) obtained 113 seats (24.7 per cent) during the March 1998 parliamentary elections, effectively becoming a left and center-left parliamentary majority. The rehabilitation of a Chernobyl nuclear reactor was announced in April.

[27] President Leonid Kuchma, an independent, was reelected with 56 per cent of the vote on December 14 1999, in the second round of the presidential elections. Petro Symonenko, the KPU candidate, took 38 per cent of the vote. Kuchma promised to continue with market reforms and pro-Western policies: better ties with Eastern Europe, the United States and NATO. Symonenko, on the other hand, based his campaign on deepening relations with Russia. International observers pointed out that the elections were far from free and fair.

[28] On November 26, and faithful to his promises, Kuchma exhorted the European Union (EU) to take Ukraine into account when the bloc discussed expansion plans in December. As the Ukrainian ambassador at the EU said, the incorporation into the bloc could become a reality once the country fulfilled the necessary political and economic prerequisites. In late December, after striking a deal with the opposition, Kuchma appointed Viktor Yuschenko, then head of the National Bank of Ukraine, as Prime Minister.

[29] During January 2000, eleven moderate right-wing parties formed a coalition supporting Kuchma with the intention of stopping the "conservative" left, as they called it. A month later, while on visit to London, Prime Minister Yuschenko announced his country had plans to restructure its foreign debt with tougher fiscal policies and a massive privatization plan. The President banned the death penalty on March 22, following European Council demands. On April 16, 90 per cent of the population backed via referendum the alliance and reform initiatives proposed by Kuchma, who will now be able to dissolve Parliament if he does not have the expected majority. The opposition claims the Ukraine is heading towards a dictatorship.

[30] On April 18, while in the Ukrainian city of Sebastopol, on the Black Sea, Ukrainian and Russian Presidents Leonid Kuchma and Vladimir Putin agreed to increase technological and military cooperation. However, this was just protocol, since the division of the Black Sea fleet was still on the agenda and Russia is ever more present in Crimea, a province mainly populated by Russians.

[31] On April 25, the International Labor Organization (ILO) warned Ukraine that - although the Government claimed unemployment figures reached just 5 per cent - the country was falling into a deep economic crisis with poverty levels below the minimum standards accepted by the United Nations. The ILO recommended reforms in the labor market to halt the fall of the economy. ∎

PROFILE

ENVIRONMENT

Ukraine is bounded by Poland, Czechoslovakia, Hungary, Romania and Moldavia in the west and southwest; by Belarus in the north and Russia in the east and northeast. The Black Sea and the Sea of Azov (Acovsko More) are located in the south. Ukraine is mostly made up of flat plains and plateaus, with the Carpathian Mountains (max. altitude, 2061 m) along the country's southwestern borders, and the Crimean Mountains (max. altitude, 1545 m) in the south. The climate is moderate and mostly continental. There is black soil; both wooded and grassy steppes in the south. Much of the north is made up of mixed forest areas (such areas occupy 14 per cent of the republic's total land surface). Pollution of the country's rivers and air has reached significant levels. Approximately 2,800,000 people currently live in areas contaminated by the Chernobyl disaster.

SOCIETY

Peoples: Ukrainians, 72.7 per cent; Russians, 22.1 per cent; Belarusians, 0.9 per cent; Moldovans, 0.6 per cent, Poles, 0.4 per cent.
Religions: Mainly Christian Orthodox.
Languages: Ukrainian (official), Russian.
Political Parties: The Communist Party; The Christian Democratic Party; the Social Democratic Party; the National Party; the Republican Party; the People's Democratic Party; the Democratic Peasant Party; the Green Party; the Democratic Renaissance Party; the Democratic Party.
Social Organizations: Unions are being reorganized after recent institutional changes.

THE STATE

Official Name: Ukrayina.
Administrative Divisions: 25 Regions, the Republic of Crimea has special status as well as great internal autonomy.
Capital: Kiev (Kijef) 3,130,000 people (est 1996).
Other cities: Kharkov (Char'cov) 1,555,100 people; Dnipropetrovsk 1,162,000; Doneck 1,147,000; Odessa 1,046,400 (1996).
Government: Leonid Kuchma, President and Head of State since November 1999. Viktor Yushchenko, Prime Minister since December 1999. Legislature, single-chamber:Supreme Council, with 450 members.
National Holiday: August 24, Independence (1991).
Armed Forces: 387,400 (1997). **Other:** 72,000 National Guard and Border Guard.

United Arab Emirates

Ittihad al-Imarat al-' Arabiyah

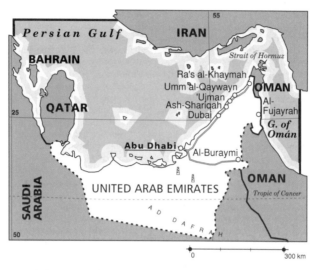

Population: 2,397,000 (1999)
Area: 83,600 SQ KM
Capital: Abu Dhabi (Abu Zaby)
Currency: Dirham
Language: Arabic

In the southeastern corner of the Arab peninsula, between the Jabal Ajdar mountain range in Oman and the rocky steppe of Najd extending from the center of the peninsula to the Gulf shores (al-Hasa), is the Rub al-Khali desert taking up part of the territory of present-day Saudi Arabia and almost the entire United Arab Emirates.

2 Toward the 6th century the oases which were spread over the land supplied enough water to the small stable population, enabling them to farm regular crops. The residents of the area spoke different Arabian dialects and shared diverse lifestyles. Some were grain growers, others were merchants or craftspeople from small villages and others, still usually known as 'Bedouins' were nomads who raised camels, sheep and goats, making the most of the desert's scant water resources. Along with these activities, the coastal peoples also fished in Gulf waters.

3 Despite being a minority, the nomads - taking advantage of their condition as a mobile and armed group - and together with the merchants, dominated farmers and craftspeople. Gathered around relatively stable family chiefs, they had a typically tribal organization.

4 Among shepherds and farmers, religion had become another type of social control but it appeared not to have a defined form. Local gods were identified with the heavenly bodies and could incarnate into rocks, trees or animals. Some families, claiming they had the power to understand the language of the gods, managed to control the others.

5 Until the 7th century, Byzantine and Sassanid empires waged a long war with constant comings and goings which involved the peninsula, although not directly the land of the present-day Emirates. Likewise, such activity and opening of trade routes brought immigrants (mostly merchants, dealers and craftspeople) who shared their culture and knowledge of the foreign world.

6 Islam was peacefully adopted in the area during the prophet Muhammad's lifetime. Tribal chiefs secured their power but the lifestyle of the few inhabitants did not change significantly.

7 Upon the Prophet's death, various groups appeared which disputed his spiritual inheritance. One of them, the Ibadis (who claimed to be his direct descendants), created the Uman (Oman) imanate in mid-8th century. It lasted to the 9th century when it was suppressed by the Abassids, caliphs who claimed a universal authority and whose main capital was in Baghdad.

8 After the 11th century, the Sunni form of Islam gradually spread from being the ruling groups' religion to reach the population at large. The Ibadis communities continued until the 15th century, exerting strong religious authority.

9 The Gulf ports were already of significant importance for the traffic of commodities which came from China (textiles, glass, porcelain and spices), and were transported to the Red Sea through an oasis chain.

10 During the 17th and 18th centuries, the Ottoman Empire occupied a large area of the peninsula but had not reached the Gulf coast in the southeastern region. The Ibadis had reinstated their *imanate* under a Yaribi dynasty. Further to the north, Bahrain was under Iranian domain.

11 Beyond the reach of the Ottomans (occupied with constant wars in Europe, Africa and Asia), the southeastern region of the peninsula thrived on trade. Ruling families linked directly with merchants appeared and piracy developed, benefiting from the natural advantages of the indented coasts. The area came to be known as 'Pirate Coast'.

12 An important change was introduced when European fleets increasingly used the maritime route round the Cape. British influence grew gradually, since they used the Gulf ports as a stop on the way to India, and helped to combat piracy.

13 At the beginning of the 19th century, Britain held complete control over the region, obtained through agreements reached with the local chiefs and small governors of the ports. Since then, the Pirate Coast became the Trucial States, which included Abu Dhabi, Dubai and Sharja. Relations with Britain continued in the same way until the first decades of the 20th century.

14 Around 1914, the Saudi state re-emerged as a great force in Central Arabia, becoming a threat even for the Ottoman power. Russia, France and Germany also sought to intensify their presence in the area. This led the British to formalize relations with the Trucial States of Bahrain, Oman and Kuwait, which let the Government in London handle their affairs with the rest of the world.

15 World War I, which led to the end of the Ottoman Empire and the independence of several Arab peninsula states, did not alter the relations between Britain and the Trucial States. London was the real power behind the puppet Abd al-Aziz in the new kingdom of Saudi Arabia, who controlled the southern and southeastern coasts of the peninsula. Furthermore, air routes were beginning to develop and the Gulf's airfields along with those in Egypt, Palestine and Iraq had an important role in the Middle East.

16 During the inter-war period, England focused its attention onto Egypt and Iraq (where oil fields were already being exploited). After World War II, relations among Arab countries changed. The League of Arab States was formed in 1945 by those countries which had some form of independence.

17 At the beginning of the 1960s, the Middle East's oil deposits were known to be among the largest in the world. The United States joined Britain in keeping their control over the Gulf States, which received almost 100 per cent of their revenues from oil.

18 The growing influence of Gamal Abdel Nasser in the Arab world led Britain to allow greater local participation in the governments of several states of the protectorate. In 1968, it decided to withdraw all its military forces from the region. That same year, the OPEAC was created - a branch of OPEC - formed exclusively by oil-exporting Arab states.

19 In 1971, upon Britain's withdrawal, Abu Dhabi began a

WORKERS

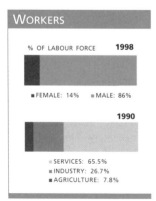

% OF LABOUR FORCE **1998**

- FEMALE: 14%   MALE: 86%

1990

- SERVICES: 65.5%
- INDUSTRY: 26.7%
- AGRICULTURE: 7.8%

LAND USE

DEFORESTATION: 0.0% annual (1990/95)
IRRIGATED: 17.2% of arable (1993)
ARABLE: 0.3% of total (1993)

PUBLIC EXPENDITURE

DEFENCE EXPENDITURE (% of goverment exp.) **46.5%** (1997)

MILITARY EXPENDITURE (% of health & education) **44%** (1990/91)

large-scale exploitation of its oil wells. The clear establishment of borders within the territories became indispensable. Under British influence, the United Arab Emirates were created that year without participation of Qatar or Bahrain.

[20] Immediately after its formation, the new state had to face a conflict with Iran which, claiming historical rights, occupied the islands of Abu Mussa, Tunb al-Cubra and Tunb al-Sughra on the Strait of Hormuz. During the first decade, oil production rose mainly in the three most important emirates: Abu Dhabi with 79 per cent of the total, Dubai and Sharjah. National participation in the control of oil exploitation also grew.

[21] When the oil-exporting countries, through OPEC, decided in 1973 to raise the price of the barrel by 70 per cent and reduce supply by 5 per cent, a new era in the relations with the industrialized world began. The results of this policy were explosive. From the rock-bottom price of $1.50 a barrel of crude oil in the early 1960s, it rose to $10 in 1973 and to $34 between 1979 and 1980. The Emirates' annual growth rate in the 1970s was over 10 per cent due to oil revenues.

[22] This led to two immediate effects: a rapid growth of cities with state-of-the-art highways, oil pipelines and banks, and many immigrants attracted by the region's economic possibilities. Little was left of the ancient pursuits of fishing or collecting of pearls on the coast.

[23] The 1980s began with the Iran-Iraq war. Although the Emirates maintained an apparently neutral stand, they gave economic support to Iraq to avoid a possible 'Iranization' of the region. Once the conflict had ended, the Arab Emirates had become the Middle East's third biggest oil producer, after Saudi Arabia and Libya.

[24] Although since 1981 the Government has tried to develop other industrial fields, technological differences with other countries and a small domestic market limited possible industrial diversification which would reduce dependence on oil production.

[25] The UAE was a member of the Non-Aligned Movement and supported Palestinian claims. In late 1986, diplomatic relations were established with the Soviet Union and the People's Republic of Benin. In 1987, relations with Egypt were reinstated, broken after the Camp David agreements with Israel.

[26] During the Gulf War, the Emirates made financial contributions to the fight against Iraq. Once the conflict had ended, the policy to diversify the economy seemed to gather strength when the free port of Jabel Ali was opened to over 260 foreign companies.

[27] In March 1991, the Gulf Cooperation Council signed an agreement with the US to preserve security in the region, which included a common military strategy and mechanisms to prevent arms proliferation, among other items.

[28] In 1992, with Syrian mediation, Iran restricted the claims it had over the islands of the Strait of Hormuz, occupied since the 1970s. Tehran claimed sovereignty over Abu Mussa and has allowed expelled Arab residents to return. The conflict was, by pressure from the Emirates, under international arbitration.

[29] Successive immigration waves have formed a very heterogeneous population. According to 1993 figures, the Arab population in the country amounts to barely one quarter, half of it coming from other countries (mainly Egypt). The rest of the population is made up by immigrants from Bangladesh, Pakistan, Sri Lanka, Iran and other Asian or African states.

[30] The influence of Islamic fundamentalism increased in the Emirates between 1993 and 1996. Sheikh Zaid, President of the Union, has often made it understood - as in a speech at the end of Ramadan in 1993 - that official circles were concerned about the spread of Muslim 'radicalism'. In February 1994, Zaid decided to extend Islamic law to many criminal cases which had previously been dealt with by civil courts.

[31] In 1995, new talks were held in an attempt to solve the dispute with Iran over the Strait of Hormuz islands, without any results. In 1997, in view of the US' threat of an armed intervention in Iraq, Sheikh Zaid stated that the Iraqi people deserved a 'new chance'. Afterwards, he added that a measure of this type would be 'unacceptable and loathsome'.

[32] At the domestic level, the Head of State continued the economic liberalization policy which led in 1998, among other things, to the creation of a free trade area in the city of Ra's al-Khaymah, the first in the Middle East. Meanwhile, reports of human rights violations continued while the Government increasingly curtailed the rights of foreigners, in a country where three-quarters of the population is made up of immigrants.

[33] The drop in the price of oil led the Government to try to moderate the spending habits of the population. Within this framework, in late 1999 the Kingdom started to organize public weddings at a cost of $16,000, one third the cost of private weddings.

[34] Following the introduction of shari'a or Islamic law in February 2000, a criminal court from the Eastern emirate of Fujairah condemned an Indonesian woman to be stoned to death, a punishment not often applied in the country.

[35] The only states that recognized the Taliban regime in Afghanistan were the United Arab Emirates, Saudi Arabia and Pakistan. ■

PROFILE

ENVIRONMENT

Located in the southeastern part of the Arabic peninsula, stretching from the Qatar peninsula toward the strait of Hormuz, the land is mostly desert with few oases and *wadis* (dry and rocky river beds). The coastal areas are very hilly lowlands with coral islands offshore and sand dunes. Most of the oil fields are located in these areas.

SOCIETY

Peoples: Arabs 25 per cent, of which 13 per cent come from other Arab countries (mainly Egypt) and 12 per cent from the Emirates themselves. Population includes large immigrant component. From Bangladesh, India, Pakistan, Sri Lanka (45 per cent), Iran (17 per cent) and other Asian and African countries 8 per cent (1993). Europeans and US 5 per cent. 80 per cent live in Dubai, attracted by the oil wealth.
Religions: Muslim 94.9 per cent (Sunni 80 per cent, Shi'a 20 per cent); Christian 3.8 per cent; others 1.3 per cent.
Languages: Arabic (official). English is used among immigrants and in business.
Political Parties: There are neither political parties nor trade unions.

THE STATE

Official name: Daulat al-Imarat al-'Arabiyah al-Muttahidah.
Administrative divisions: 7 emirates Abu Dhabi, Dubai, Sharjah, Ras al-Khaimah, Ajman, Fujairah and Umm al-Qaiwain.
Capital: Abu Dhabi (Abu Zaby) 980,002 people (est 1995).
Other cities: Dubayy 585,189 people; Al-'Ayn 176,411; Ash-Shariqah 125,000; Ra's al-Khaymah 42,000 (1989).
Government: Parliamentary Republic with a president of the federation as a Head of State (Sheikh Zaid ibn Sultan al-Nuhayyan, Emir of Abu Dhabi, since 1971); a Vice President and Prime Minister (Sheikh Rashid ibn Said al-Maktum, Emir of Dubai, since 1990) and a National Federal Council with 40 members appointed by the emirs, serves as the legislative body.
National Holiday: December 1. Proclamation of the Union (1971)
Armed Forces: 64,500 (1997)

United Kingdom

United Kingdom

Population: 58,744,000 (1999)
Area: 244,100 SQ KM
Capital: London
Currency: Pound sterling
Language: English

The first known inhabitants of what is now Britain were paleolithic hunters, following herds of wild animals. After the final ice age, agriculturalists began to settle on the island. Over thousands of years, these people and the many others who migrated from the continent, evolved increasingly complex social systems. By the final millennium BC, Britain was dominated by Celtic tribes who used iron tools and had extensive contact with the European mainland.

2 In 44 AD the Romans invaded southern Britain. In 90 AD they created the province of Britannia, and founded London between 70 and 100 AD. In the early 5th century they abandoned the island, leaving it largely defenseless against the raids of Angles, Saxons and Jutes. These Germanic peoples pushed the Celts westwards, taking over the southern part of the island and establishing Anglo-Saxon kingdoms.

3 During the 5th century, the inhabitants of Ireland and Wales adopted Christianity. In the 7th century, the British church came under the power of Rome.

4 During the 7th and 9th centuries Danish invaders overran the eastern part of England. In the 11th century, the Normans, led by William the Conqueror, invaded England and secured the throne. Successive Anglo-Norman kings maintained their power by establishing various forms of vassalage over the feudal lords.

5 The prestige which Richard the Lion-Heart (1189-99), one of the leaders of the Third Crusade, gained for the English Crown was lost under the reign of his successor, King John (1199-1216). Under John, England lost its French territories,

and the barons, in alliance with the clergy, were able to restrict the power of the monarchy through the Magna Carta, signed in 1215.

6 The Magna Carta laid the foundations for the British parliamentary system. It also marked the beginning of a continuous power struggle between the monarchy and the nobility. The growing power of the land-owning class and later the bourgeoisie eventually led to the consolidation of a parliamentary monarchy.

7 Frequent dynastic conflicts, disputes over territories in France belonging to the English Crown, commercial rivalry between England and France in Flanders, and French aid to Scotland in its wars with England paved the way for the Hundred Years' War (1337-1453), which culminated in the loss of the English possessions on the continent.

8 The negative effects of the War increased the unpopularity of the monarchy which faced at the same

time an anti-Papal movement led by the followers of Wycliffe (a precursor of Luther) and a peasant rebellion. The peasants, led by Wat Tyler, rose up against the payment of tribute and the power of the feudal lords. In 1381, Tyler and his followers managed to enter London and negotiate directly with the King. The Peasants' Revolt was unsuccessful however and Tyler was later executed.

9 The period following the Hundred Years' War was dominated by a long struggle for control of the throne between the royal Houses of Lancaster and of York. This led to the War of the Roses which ended with the coming to power of the Welsh House of Tudor in 1485. The Tudor period is considered the beginning of the modern British state. One of the Tudor kings, Henry VIII (1509-47) broke away from the Church of Rome, confiscating all its monasteries and founding the Anglican Church. The desire to extend English authority and the religious Reformation to Ireland led to the subjugation of Ulster by Henry's successor Elizabeth I (1558-1603). Tudor involvement in Ireland laid the foundations of centuries of religious and political conflict in the country.

10 Under the reign of Elizabeth I (1558-1603), poetry and the theatre flourished with playwrights such as Ben Jonson, Marlowe and Shakespeare. Industry and trade developed, and the country embarked upon its 'colonial adventure', the beginning of its future empire. After defeating the Spanish fleet - the 'Invincible Armada' - in 1588, the British Navy 'ruled the waves', with no other fleet capable of opposing it.

11 British merchant ships involved in the slave trade, or laden with colonists or belonging to pirates and privateers sailed the oceans freely. Markets multiplied, demand grew rapidly, and producers were forced to seek new techniques in order to accelerate production. It was a prelude to the industrial revolution which was to arise in the country at the beginning of the 18th century.

12 In 1603, the crowning of James I (James VI of Scotland) put an end to the independent Scottish monarchy. The religious intolerance of James' son Charles I, led to a Scottish uprising and increasing discontent in England. The

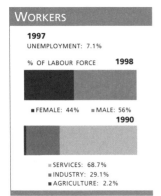

WORKERS

1997
UNEMPLOYMENT: 7.1%

% OF LABOUR FORCE **1998**

■ FEMALE: 44%   ■ MALE: 56%

1990

■ SERVICES: 68.7%
■ INDUSTRY: 29.1%
■ AGRICULTURE: 2.2%

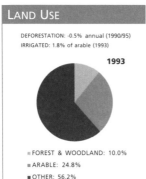

LAND USE

DEFORESTATION: -0.5% annual (1990/95)
IRRIGATED: 1.8% of arable (1993)

1993

■ FOREST & WOODLAND: 10.0%
■ ARABLE: 24.8%
■ OTHER: 56.2%

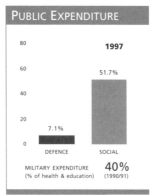

PUBLIC EXPENDITURE

1997

51.7%

7.1%

DEFENCE   SOCIAL

MILITARY EXPENDITURE   **40%**
(% of health & education)   (1990/91)

deteriorating political situation led to the Puritans forming an army supported by Parliament; led by Oliver Cromwell, they defeated the royal forces in 1642. In 1649, Parliament sentenced the King to death and proclaimed Cromwell 'Lord Protector', establishing a republic known as the Commonwealth. After Cromwell's death, in 1658, the monarchy was restored with Charles II.

[13] The priorities of the new regime were the colonization of North America and trade with America, the Far East and the Mediterranean. The slave trade - the kidnapping, trafficking and selling of slaves from Africa to buyers in America and other places - which had started in the 16th century, became one of the main sources of income for the empire.

[14] The absolutism of James II and his espousal of Catholicism were opposed by the Protestant Parliament which deposed James through the 'Glorious Revolution'. Parliament invited the Dutch prince William of Orange to assume the English throne. William was forced to sign the Declaration of Rights (1689), limiting royal powers and guaranteeing the supremacy of Parliament.

[15] In this period John Locke summarized revolutionary ideals, proposing that human beings have basic natural rights: to property, life, liberty and personal security. Government, created by society to protect these rights, must fulfil its mission; if it fails to do so, the people have the right to resist its authority.

[16] In 1707, the parliaments of Scotland and England were joined together, creating the United Kingdom of Great Britain. Britain intervened in the war of succession in Spain, obtaining Minorca, Gibraltar and Nova Scotia through the Treaty of Utrecht (1713). In 1765, increased taxes imposed by the Stamp Act triggered the rebellion and secession of the American colonies, who declared their independence in 1776.

[17] During this period, the two large political parties were formed: the Conservatives (Tories), representing the interests of the large landowners, and the Liberals (Whigs), representing the merchant class. The ideas forming the basis of economic liberalism were developed at this time by Adam Smith. The liberal doctrine provided the political ideology for British imperialism, which used the concept of 'free trade' as a justification for forcing open the ports and markets of the Third World, often with the use of naval force. Perhaps the most notorious examples of this were the Opium Wars fought against China in the mid-19th century.

[18] After the crushing of a nationalist rebellion in Ireland in 1798, the United Kingdom of Great Britain and Ireland was created in 1801 with the dissolution of the Irish Parliament.

[19] The 18th century gave rise to the agricultural 'revolution', which introduced important innovations in farming techniques, as well as major changes in land tenure. The large landowners enclosed their properties, eliminating communal lands which had hitherto been used by small farmers, and introducing a more capitalist agricultural economy.

[20] At the same time, the industrial revolution began, with the textile manufacturers being the first to confront the problem of meeting a growing demand for fabric overseas. The introduction of machinery changed the way in which work was done, and the medieval shop was replaced by the factory. On the heels of the textile industry came mining and metallurgy. The mechanization process was consolidated with the invention of the steam engine, the use of coal as a fuel and the substitution of first iron, then steel, for wood in construction.

[21] This period was characterized by population growth (up from 10,900,000 in 1801 to 21,000,000 in 1850), increasing demand and expanding trade, improvements in the transport system, capital accumulation, the creation of a vast colonial empire, scientific advances and the golden age of the bourgeoisie. Britain became the world's premier manufacturing nation. Its colonial policy helped to prevent competition for its factories; for example it established regulations which destroyed the Indian textile industry.

[22] The United Kingdom obtained new territories from its different wars with France, and its triumph over Napoleon at Waterloo (1815).

[23] One result of the industrial revolution was growing discontent among the rapidly increasing working class, due to low salaries, unhealthy working conditions, unsatisfactory housing, malnutrition, job insecurity and the long and tiring working days to which men, women and children were subjected. In many cases, popular uprisings were characterized by violence, and were met with equally violent repression.

[24] In the early stages of the industrial revolution, spontaneous movements arose, like the 'Luddites' - textile workers who destroyed machinery to prevent it from destroying their cottage industry. Trade unions began to appear later.

[25] In 1819 a demonstration in Manchester was ruthlessly put down, and repressive legislation followed, limiting the right of association and freedom of the press. Nevertheless, resistance movements continued their activity. One of the main movements of this period was the nationalist Irish Association led by Daniel O'Connell.

[26] The most important of the mass movements was the Chartist Movement, made up primarily of workers. It took its name from the People's Charter, published in 1838 at a mass assembly in Glasgow, Scotland. This movement brought a number of issues to the fore, both political - universal suffrage, use of the secret ballot, reform of voting registers - and social - better salaries and better working conditions. After its demonstrations and strikes, 'Chartism' faded away. However, it had a far-reaching influence and its grievances were subsequently taken up by some members of parliament.

[27] Robert Owen (1771-1858), considered to be the founder of socialism and the English co-operative movement, argued that the predominance of individual interests led to the impoverishment of the masses. From 1830 on, he devoted himself to the establishment of co-operatives and the organization of labor into trade unions.

[28] During the long reign of Queen Victoria (1837-1901), the traditional nobility strengthened its alliance with the industrial and mercantile bourgeoisie. Trade unions were legalized in 1871 and shortly afterwards some labor legislation was approved.

[29] Beginning in 1873, the rising population numbers led to a food shortage, making imports necessary. At the same time industry began to feel the competition from the US and Germany. Britain increased its imperial activities in Africa, Asia and Oceania, not only for economic reasons, but also because of the political ambition to build a great empire. The Boer or South African War (1899-1902), fought to secure

PROFILE

ENVIRONMENT

The country consists of Britain (England, Scotland, Wales and Northern Ireland) and several smaller islands. The Pennines, a low mountain range, runs down the northern centre of England. The Grampian mountains are located in Scotland and the Cambrian mountains in Wales. The largest plains are in the southeast, around London. The climate is temperate. Farming is highly mechanized and is now a secondary activity. The huge coal and iron ore deposits, which made the Industrial Revolution possible, have nearly run out, but gas and oil finds in the North Sea have turned the United Kingdom into an exporter of these products. The country is highly industrialized and environmental pollution, especially air pollution, poses a serious problem. The nuclear reprocessing plant at Seascale in the north west of England appeared to be linked to the high incidence of leukemia in areas along both coastlines.

SOCIETY

Peoples: English, Scots, Welsh and Irish. Minorities including Pakistanis, Indians and Afro-Caribbeans form about 6 per cent of the population.
Religions: Protestant, 53.4 per cent (Anglican 43.5 per cent; Presbyterian 4.5 per cent; Methodist 2.2 per cent); Roman Catholic 9.8 per cent; Orthodox 1 per cent; other Christians 1.7 per cent; Islam 2.6 per cent; Hindu 0.6 per cent, Sikh 0.5 per cent; Jewish 0.5 per cent; other/no religion 29.9 per cent.
Languages: English (official), Welsh and Gaelic.
Political Parties: Labour Party (social democrat), led by Tony Blair, in government. Conservative Party in opposition. Liberal Democrat Party, center. Green Party. The Republican Party Sinn Féin in Northern Ireland gained two seats in the last elections.
Social Organizations: Trade Union Congress (TUC), with 12 million affiliates.

THE STATE

Official Name: United Kingdom of Great Britain and Northern Ireland.
Administrative Divisions: 39 Counties and 7 Metropolitan Districts.
Capital: London 7,230,000 people (est 1995).
Other cities: Birmingham 1,017,500 people, Leeds 725,000, Glasgow 674,800, Sheffield 528,500, Bradford 482,700, Liverpool 470,800, Edinburgh 447,600, Manchester 432,600, Bristol, 400,700 (1995).
Government: Queen Elizabeth II, Head of State. Tony Blair, Prime Minister since May 2 1997. Parliamentary monarchy. Legislative Power: a House of Lords, with 1,197 life members, recently reformed to reduce the number of hereditary peers; and a House of Commons, with 659 members elected every five years.
Armed Forces: 213,800 (1996).
Dependencies: See Gibraltar (Spain), Malvinas/Falklands (Argentina), Montserrat, Virgin Islands, Cayman Islands, Turks and Caicos, Bermuda, St Helena, British Indian Ocean Territory (Mauritius), and Pitcairn (Oceania).

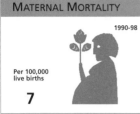

MATERNAL MORTALITY

1990-98

Per 100,000
live births

7

FOOD DEPENDENCY

1997

9%

FOREIGN TRADE

Millions US$ 1997

IMPORTS

374,045

EXPORTS

367,971

control over southern Africa, was the most expensive regional conflict of the 19th century.

30   The first quarter of the 20th century saw the birth of the women's liberation movement. The militancy of the suffragettes led to some women obtaining the right to vote in 1917. The most famous example of their militancy was the suicide of Emily Davison, who threw herself in front of the King's horse during a race in 1913.

31   In Ireland, the majority Catholic population were stripped of their lands, restricted in their civil rights because of their religion, and deprived of their political autonomy. Millions emigrated, and political unrest periodically resulted in violent uprisings. Not until 1867 were the privileges of the Anglican Church eliminated; at the same time, measures were taken to improve the situation of the peasants. The 1916 Easter Rising in Dublin was ruthlessly put down by the British, but the Crown forces were unable to win the ensuing guerrilla war which began in 1918, and Britain finally granted Ireland independence in 1921. Six counties in the north-east, with Protestant majorities, remained under British control with a devolved administration in Belfast.

32   Economic and political rivalry between the European powers led to the outbreak of World War I (1914-18). The Central Powers of Austro-Hungary and Germany, joined subsequently by Turkey and Bulgaria, fought against the Allied powers of France, Britain, Russia, Serbia and Belgium, with Italy, Japan, Portugal, Romania, the United States and Greece joining during the course of the War.

33   Despite its victory, Britain emerged from the War weakened. It had invested $40 billion in military expenditure, mobilized 7,500,000 troops, suffered a loss of 1,200,000 soldiers and acquired an enormous foreign debt. The deep economic depression in the post-War years led to renewed unrest among workers, which reached its height in the General Strike of 1926. The Conservative Government declared the strike illegal, but did not take any measures to revive British industry. In the elections of 1929, the Labour Party (formed in 1924) came to power for the first time.

34   The United Kingdom supported the US proposal to create the League of Nations. In 1931, the British Community of Nations (Commonwealth) was established under the Statute of Westminster. This formally recognized the independence of Canada, Australia, New Zealand and South Africa.

35   On September 1 1939, Germany invaded Poland and two days later Britain declared war on Germany, marking the beginning of its participation in World War II (1939-45). In May 1940 a coalition cabinet was formed, with Winston Churchill as Prime Minister. From 1939 to 1941, Britain and France were ranged against Germany which was joined by Italy in 1940. Hungary, Romania, Bulgaria and Yugoslavia participated in the war as 'lesser' allies of the Nazis.

36   In 1941, the Soviet Union, Japan and the US entered the conflict. On May 8 1945, Germany surrendered. The UK, US and the USSR emerged as the major victors from the war. However, the British Empire was eclipsed by the rising power of the US, which became the undisputed economic, technological and military leader.

37   In May 1945, the Labour Government of Clement Attlee, who won the elections with the slogan 'We won the war, now we will win the peace', nationalized the coal mines, the Bank of England and the iron and steel industries.

38   Pakistan was formed and India became independent in 1947, although both remained members of the British Commonwealth. During the following decade, most of Britain's overseas colonies obtained their independence. Britain was a founder member of NATO in 1949.

39   The Franco-British military intervention in the Suez Canal Zone in 1956, which failed due to a lack of US support, was met by strong criticism from both inside and outside Britain (see Egypt). The following year, the UK detonated its first hydrogen bomb in the Pacific Ocean.

40   The general election of 1964 was won by the Labour Party under the leadership of Harold Wilson. His government faced serious problems, such as the declaration of independence by Southern Rhodesia (today Zimbabwe), and the severing of diplomatic relations with nine other African countries.

41   In 1967, having been denied entry to the Common Market, and faced with rapidly increasing unemployment, Wilson withdrew British troops from South Yemen, evacuated all bases east of Suez except for Hong Kong, discontinued arms purchases from the US and implemented a savage austerity budget.

42   In Northern Ireland in 1969, the latent conflict erupted. A number of people were killed and wounded in riots between Catholics and Protestants. The Catholics demanded equal political rights, and better access to housing, schools and social security. The Protestant-controlled Northern Irish Government responded by sending in their armed police reserves against the Catholic demonstrators. The British Government sent in their troops to separate the two sides and took control of police and reserve forces away from the Belfast Government.

43   In August 1971, Prime Minister of Northern Ireland Brian Faulkner opened internment camps and authorized the detention of suspects without trial. Protests against these measures resulted in more than 25 deaths. On January 30 1972, 'Bloody Sunday', British soldiers opened fire on a peaceful protest march in Derry (Londonderry), killing 13 Catholics and injuring hundreds more. The Irish Republican Army (IRA) responded with numerous assassinations.

44   In March 1973, the people of Northern Ireland voted in a referendum to remain within the United Kingdom rather than join a united Ireland. Voting was characterized by a high rate of abstentions of 41.4 per cent, and the Protestant majority voted to stay in the UK.

45   In the 1970s, social conflict in Britain intensified, and Edward Heath's Conservative Government was faced with strikes in key public enterprises. The dockers, coal miners and railway workers all went on strike. Inability to deal with this labour unrest led to his resignation in 1974, and the Labour Party won the following elections. Amid a complex situation on the domestic front, in January 1973 a majority of the electorate voted in favour of entering the EEC. A policy of progressive integration with Europe began, as well as a search for new markets for ailing British industry.

46   A new divorce law was passed in 1975. The same year, feminists campaigned successfully against restrictions being added to the 1967 abortion law.

47   In 1979, voters in Scotland and Wales turned down autonomy for their regions in referenda organized by James Callaghan's Labour Government.

48   In May of that year, after the 'winter of discontent', characterized by strikes, the Conservative Party won the election, with Margaret Thatcher as its leader. The new Prime Minister brought in a severe monetarist policy to bring down inflation. She began to reverse the nationalization process carried out under Labour, and returned to a free market policy.

49   In 1981, a group of IRA prisoners began a hunger strike as part of their campaign to win recognition as political prisoners. The Government refused to accept the prisoners demands. The strike resulted in 12 deaths.

50   In April 1982, Thatcher sent a Royal Navy force, including aircraft carriers and nuclear submarines, to the Malvinas islands (Falklands) which had been occupied by troops from the military junta in Argentina. After 45 days of fighting the British recovered the islands for the Crown (see Argentina).

51   In October 1983, the British Government decided to withdraw its troops from Belize. The following year, in agreement with a treaty dating back to the First Opium War, Britain ceded sovereignty over Hong Kong to the People's Republic of China, with effect from June 1997.

52   During the Thatcher administration, the trade union movement suffered serious setbacks, with the loss of local affiliates in the industrial sector, itself in decline. The 1984/85 miners' strike culminated in defeat for the union after a year of violent internal strife and confrontation with the police.

53   In 1987, Thatcher was elected to her third consecutive term in office. She continued her policies as before: radical economic liberalization, privatization of state corporations, and opposition to union demands. In foreign affairs, Britain opposed greater European Community integration and continued to align itself closely with the US.

54   In mid-1989, after several years of growth, inflation reached high levels, unemployment continued to rise steeply, productive investments fell and the balance of payments deficit grew. At the same time, the introduction of a new Poll Tax and other projected reforms produced strong popular resistance.

55   In February 1990, the United Kingdom and Argentina renewed diplomatic relations and their representatives met in Madrid to negotiate the issue of the return of the Malvinas/Falklands.

56 In November 1990 Thatcher was replaced as head of the Government and Tory leader by her former minister, John Major. Upon taking office, Major declared himself to be in favor of capitalism with a human face, thus setting himself apart from the reality of the 'Iron Lady's' harsh capitalism.

57 In 1991, Major announced that the Poll Tax would be replaced, and promoted the adoption of a bill of rights for the sick, for working women, the consumer and the family, among other social categories. However, Major continued most of Thatcher's reforms, including that of the health system and the selling-off of nationalized industries such as the railways.

58 In European affairs, the Prime Minister distanced himself from his predecessor. In 1991, London gave its backing to European agreements on monetary union. However, the fidelity which British diplomacy showed towards the US remained unaltered, as proven by British aid to the US in the Gulf War.

59 The Government managed to bring down inflation (which dropped from 10 per cent to 3.8 per cent between 1990 and 1991) and interest rates (which decreased from 15 per cent to 9.5 per cent), but economic activity remained stagnant. In 1991, industrial production declined and numerous small businesses failed. Unemployment continued to rise (over 9 per cent by late 1991), and now affected white-collar workers and professionals, groups which had supported Thatcher's neo-liberal policies.

60 Within this context, Major's personal popularity (the highest in British history since Winston Churchill) did not translate itself into a similar level of support for his party. In the local elections held at the end of April 1991, the Tories lost 800 council seats and several of its traditional districts, while Labour gained more than 400 council seats. In these elections, the Liberal Democratic Party also made important gains.

61 In September 1991, frustration with high unemployment and cuts in social spending erupted in a wave of urban violence not seen since 1976. Demonstrations - specially by young people - took place in cities as far apart as Cardiff, Newcastle, Birmingham and Oxford. At the same time, racist violence had significantly increased, according to Scotland Yard.

62 In 1992, the Conservatives won parliamentary elections for the fourth consecutive time with 336 seats out of 651 giving them an overall majority. Shortly after the voting in which Gerry Adams, President of Sinn Féin - the political wing of the Irish Republican Army (IRA) - lost his seat, several high-powered bombs went off in London.

63 As of 1993, the Conservatives suffered a series of setbacks at the polls in local elections, in the middle of an economic recession and high unemployment affecting some 3 million. On December 15, London signed a joint declaration with Dublin regarding the situation in Northern Ireland, which paved the way for peace talks (see Ireland).

64 In spite of a more favorable economic context, the Conservative Government was not able to recover its popularity during 1994. The GDP grew 3 per cent and unemployment went down to 2.5 million (9 per cent of the working population) but a series of scandals, such as the illegal financing of a dam in Malaysia, further tarnished the Tories' image. Meanwhile, Parliament decided to lower the legal age of consent for homosexual intercourse from 21 to 18, refusing to put it on the same level as heterosexual intercourse, where the age of consent is 16.

65 The Labour Party, led by Tony Blair since July 1994, pursued its 'modernization' program, eliminating Clause Four of the Party's constitution which aimed at 'the common ownership of the means of production, distribution and exchange'.

66 Labour won a landslide victory in the May 1997 general elections, and Tony Blair took office as Prime Minister. The Conservatives suffered a crushing defeat, taking only 30 per cent of the vote to Labour's 43.1 - a difference unprecedented so far this century - forcing changes in its leadership. However, the new government kept to spending limits planned by the Conservatives, keeping nurses and other public-sector workers on their low pay. The Government also adopted right-of-center policies on law and order, defense and social welfare.

67 In June, Blair announced a new round of negotiations on Northern Ireland. The Prime Minister gave Sinn Féin permission to participate, once the IRA had called a cease-fire. This happened on July 20 and Sinn Féin joined talks opening on September 15.

68 Chancellor Gordon Brown told Parliament in October that the country would not be adopting the Euro (common currency unit within the EU) in January 1999, but would consider joining after the next general election. Denmark and the UK were the only European countries granted a special clause exempting them from the monetary union.

69 Referenda held in Wales and Scotland in 1997 came out in favour of greater independent powers for the regions. In early 1998, negotiations on Northern Ireland allowed a new peace formula to be drawn up. Submitted to referendum in May, the proposal gained more than 70 per cent approval in the province. That same month,

Londoners approved an amendment allowing direct election of the mayor of London. Abstention ran at 66 per cent, but 72 per cent of those who did vote approved the change, making the post of mayor of London the first executive post to be filled by direct vote in the country.

70 Under the 'Good Friday Agreement', Northern Ireland would have a legislative assembly, directly elected by the people, the same as Wales and Scotland. Alongside this, a referendum in Ireland brought 95 per cent support for ending any territorial claim over Northern Ireland, leaving the way clear for the people of Ulster to decide on their own. The nomination of Northern Ireland members of parliament David Trimble (Ulster Unionist) and John Hume (SDLP) for the Nobel Peace Prize in October 1998 helped create a feeling of common cause between the Protestant and Catholic communities.

71 That same month Scotland Yard arrested General Augusto Pinochet on request by the Spanish courts for extradition. The former Chilean dictator was in a London hospital recovering from an operation on his back. After 18 months of legal wrangling he was freed. Home Secretary Jack Straw concluded Pinochet was too physically unwell to withstand the strain of extradition to Spain and the ensuing trial.

72 During 1999 the Northern Irish Loyalist and Nationalist parties made commitments to joint government, which culminated with the establishment of an executive in December. The two-community cabinet was to operate under the leadership of David Trimble as First Minister and included Sinn Féin: Gerry Adams and Martin McGuinness of Sinn Féin were on the executive until January 2000 when it was suspended after the Unionists withdrew. Sovereignty went back to London until May.

73 The Labour Party selection process for its candidate for the Mayor of London resulted in a split with MP Ken Livingstone, the most popular candidate according to all surveys. Livingstone, bastion of the old Labour left, accused Tony Blair of imposing an anti-democratic system for selecting Labour's mayoral candidate. The Labour Party expelled the rebel in March 2000. The break with the Labour Party did not affect Livingstone's campaign. He was elected mayor in May 2000.

74 The Labour Government's commitment to high taxes on fuel, to reduce vehicle use and emissions, was challenged when oil prices escalated in September 2000. Farmers and hauliers blockaded oil depots, reducing fuel supplies. ■

United States

United States

Population: 276,219,000 (1999)
Area: 9,363,520 SQ KM
Capital: Washington
Currency: Dollar
Language: English

The continental territory occupied by the United States was inhabited 30,000 years before the arrival of the Europeans by peoples who came from the northwest, probably from Asia across the Bering Strait. Among the most significant were those who became the Apache, Arapaho, Cherokee, Cheyenne, Chippewa, Crow, Comanche, Hopi, Iroquois, Lakota, Navajo, Nez Percé, Oglala Sioux, Pawnee, Pueblo, Seminole, Shawnee, Shoshone and the Ute native Americans.

[2] In the deserts and on the plains, they were primarily hunters and gatherers, living in small tribes with a simple social structure. Where the lands were more fertile, agriculture developed and relatively large towns were established. The first and largest of these, Cahokia, close to what is now St Louis, is thought to have had a population of 40,000 in the year 1000 AD.

[3] The religious beliefs of these peoples were rooted in a cosmic conception of the Earth - that as it belongs to the Universe, it belongs to no one. The Earth is considered a living being, with both material and spiritual powers. American Indian religious leaders or *shamans* have the power to call upon the forces of this sacred Universe, either to foretell the future, to lead their people, or to heal the sick.

[4] The first Europeans to come to America were Viking sailors from Greenland, but they did not settle permanently in the region. After the voyage of Christopher Columbus in 1492, the Spaniards established the colonies of St Augustine in Florida, and Santa Fe in New Mexico; in addition, they

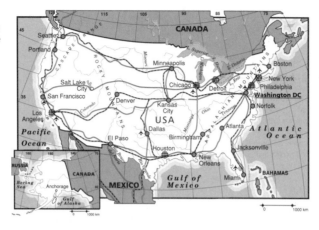

explored both Texas and California. After the Spanish came the British, French and Dutch, all bent on territorial conquest.

[5] In 1540, Hernando De Soto wrote in his journals of having found among the Cherokee an advanced agricultural society, linked to the peoples of the Ohio, the Mississippi and even the Aztecs. Europeans introduced firearms, which significantly altered life among the American peoples, and ultimately established domination by white people.

[6] There were an estimated 1,500,000 Native Americans in the 15th century. Two centuries later, the large plantations of the South began buying slaves, and by 1760 there was a total of 90,000 Africans - twice the number of whites in that part of the country. The total number of British settlers on the Atlantic coast at the time was 300,000, far outnumbering the French in the Mississippi Valley.

[7] Most British immigrants left their country fleeing from

poverty, religious persecution and political instability. Yet the birth of the colonies was marked by war against the native peoples, whose culture and way of life were systematically destroyed, and against other European colonists. By 1733, there were 13 English colonies, whose chief economic activities were agriculture, fishing and trade.

[8] In 1763, with the 17th and 18th century European imperial wars behind them, France ceded its colonies east of the Mississippi to Britain, while its possessions west of that river went to Spain.

[9] War with England broke out in 1775. The Declaration of Independence, which marked the birth of the United States, was signed on July 4 1776. The war continued, but in the end the United States won (aided by its ally, France), with American sovereignty finally being recognized by England in 1783.

[10] In 1787, the Philadelphia Constitutional Convention drew up the first federal constitution, which went into effect the

following year. George Washington, commander of the Continental Army, was elected President in April 1789. In 1791, ten amendments dealing with individual freedoms and 'states' rights' were added to the original constitution.

[11] The prime attraction of the West was the possibility of acquiring land and wealth without previous ownership, simply by staking a claim. The presidents in power at the time justified this 'Empire of Freedom': it was the United States' 'Manifest Destiny' to occupy the entire continent, in order to become a great nation.

[12] In 1803, the Louisiana purchase (from the French) doubled the size of the Union. Between 1810 and 1819, the US went to war against Spain in order to annex Florida. In 1836, the Texans rebelled against Mexico and set up a republic, subsequently joining the Union in 1845. The United States declared war on Mexico, taking over vast areas of Mexican territory. California became a state in 1850, and Oregon in 1853.

[13] Westward expansion meant not only a change of 'ownership', but also still another tragedy for the original inhabitants of the region, decimated by successive waves of land and gold fever. Treaties were signed then ignored as thousands of new settlers poured onto native lands. On occasion new treaties were imposed by force. In 1838, 14,000 Cherokee people were forced off their lands by the army, 4,000 perishing in a march to their new territory.

[14] The Civil War (or War of Secession), from 1861-65 revolved around the question of the preservation of slavery, but it was in fact a struggle between the two economic systems prevailing in the country. While the industrial North sought to free an important source of labor, and protect the domestic market, the slave-owning and agricultural South's interest was to maintain its cheap force of labor and continue to enjoy free access to foreign markets.

[15] In 1850, of the six million inhabitants of European origin in the South, only 345,525 were slave owners. However most

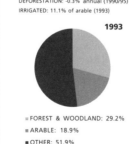

WORKERS

1997
UNEMPLOYMENT: 4.9%

% OF LABOUR FORCE **1998**

■ FEMALE: 46%   ■ MALE: 54%
1990

■ SERVICES: 71.2%
■ INDUSTRY: 26.0%
■ AGRICULTURE: 2.8%

LAND USE

DEFORESTATION: -0.3% annual (1990/95)
IRRIGATED: 11.1% of arable (1993)

1993

■ FOREST & WOODLAND: 29.2%
■ ARABLE: 18.9%
■ OTHER: 51.9%

PUBLIC EXPENDITURE

1997

80

60 — 53.5%

40

20 — 16.3%

0
DEFENCE   SOCIAL

MILITARY EXPENDITURE **46%**
(% of health & education) (1990/91)

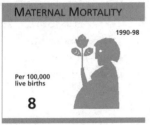

MATERNAL MORTALITY
1990-98
Per 100,000 live births
8

LITERACY
1995
99%

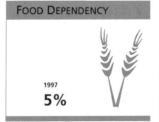

FOOD DEPENDENCY
1997
5%

FOREIGN TRADE
Millions US$ 1997
IMPORTS
1,058,800
EXPORTS
948,600

PROFILE

ENVIRONMENT

There are four geo-economic regions. The East includes New England, the Appalachian Mountains, part of the Great Lakes and the Atlantic coast, a sedimentary plain which stretches from the mouth of the Hudson River to the peninsula of Florida. To the west are the Appalachian mountains, where mineral deposits (iron ore and coal) abound. This is the most densely populated and industrialized area. A highly technological agriculture provides food for the large cities. The Midwest stretches from the western shores of Lake Erie to the Rocky Mountains and is the country's largest agricultural area. Horticulture and milk production predominate in the north, while wheat, corn and other cereals are cultivated in the south, and cattle raised. Major industrial centers are located near the Great Lakes, near the area's agricultural production and large iron ore and coal deposits. The South is a subtropical flatland area, comprising the south of the Mississippi plain, the peninsula of Florida, Texas and Oklahoma. Large plantations, (cotton, sugarcane, rice) predominate here, while there is extensive cattle-raising in Texas. The region is also rich in mineral deposits (oil, coal, aluminum, etc.). The West is a mountainous, mineral-rich area (oil, copper, lead, zinc). There is horticultural production in the fertile valleys of the Sacramento and San Joaquin rivers in California. Large industrial centers are located along the Pacific coast. The US has two states outside its contiguous area: Alaska, on the continent's northwest where Mt McKinley is located (Mt 'Denali', in the indigenous Atabasco language), the highest peak in North America, and Hawaii, an archipelago in the Pacific Ocean. The US is the main producer of gases - principally carbon dioxide - which are responsible for the greenhouse effect.

SOCIETY

Peoples: There are 1.9 million Native Americans, half of whom live in 300 reservations. The white population came originally from immigrant Europeans including English, Germans, Irish, Russian and Italian, now mixed with immigrants from all parts of the world. The largest minorities are of African origin, 11 per cent of the total population; Hispanic 10 per cent; and Asian 8 per cent.
Religions: There is a Protestant majority (58 per cent), which encompasses several denominations. There are also a considerable number of Catholics (21 per cent). Other Christians 6.4 per cent; Jewish 2 per cent; Muslims 2 per cent.
Languages: English; Spanish; Native American Languages and those of each immigrant group.
Political Parties: Democratic Party; Republican Party.
Social Organizations: The American Federation of Labor-Congress of Industrial Organizations (AFL-CIO) is the country's largest workers' organization, with 13,500,000 members. Many of the country's rural laborers, especially those of Mexican origin, are organized in the United Farm Workers (UFW) labor union, founded by César Chávez.

THE STATE

Official Name: United States of America.
Administrative Divisions: Federal State, 50 States and 1 Federal District, Columbia.
Capital: Washington, DC 5,600,000 people (est 1997).
Other cities: New York 7,380,906 people; Los Angeles 3,553,638; Chicago 2,721,547; Houston 1,744,058; Philadelphia 1,478,002 (1996).
Government: Al Gore, George W. Bush presidential candidates for 2000 election. William Clinton, President since 1992, re-elected in 1996. Presidential government, federal system (50 states). There is a bicameral Congress where each state has two senators and a number of representatives proportional to its population.
National Holiday: July 4, Independence (1776).
Armed Forces: 1,547,300 (1995).
Other: 68,000 Civil Air Control.

whites were pro-slavery, remembering the slave rebellions which had taken place in South Carolina (1822) and Virginia (1800 and 1831).

[16] The election of Abraham Lincoln in 1860 precipitated a conflict: before he had even been inaugurated as president, the Southern states seceded. Committed to preserving the Union, and with a superior industrial base and superior weapons, the North finally triumphed over the South in the Civil War, although a million people were killed on both sides. Slavery was abolished, but ill-feeling between the two regions continued to exist.

[17] After the War, the Native Americans of the Great Plains, especially the Sioux, launched repeated wars of defense. The treaties of 1851 and 1868, which had granted them sovereignty over their tribal lands were ignored after the discovery of gold in the area. The gradual occupation of their territory was completed by 1890, when the Sioux were defeated for the last time.

[18] In the 1880s, the remaining Native Americans were confined to reservations most of which were on arid, barren lands. Years later, when uranium, coal, oil, natural gas and other minerals were discovered on some of the reservations, mining companies became interested in developing these mineral resources. This triggered the question of 'rights' to even the marginal land on which the reservations were located.

[19] Between 1870 and 1920, the population of the United States grew from 38 to 106 million, and the number of states increased from 37 to 48. It was a period of rapid capitalist expansion, triggered by the growth of the railroads as huge companies. By the turn of the century, what had been essentially an agrarian country was transformed into an industrial society.

[20] By the end of the 19th century, a two-party system of government had been established, with the Republican and Democratic parties alternately in power. Despite their different traditions, both parties have historically maintained a large degree of consensus on major national and international issues, a fact which led to a highly coherent foreign policy. The long struggle for women's suffrage began in 1889, being achieved in 1920.

[21] Having dealt with its principal domestic problems, the US ventured onto the international scene. The Spanish-American War in 1898, fought in Cuba and the Philippines, marked the beginning of a US imperial era. The occupation of Panama, and subsequent construction of the Panama Canal and a series of military bases turned Central America - an area of 'vital security interest' to the US - into a kind of protectorate.

[22] The United States justified its interventions with the Monroe Doctrine, and former-President Monroe's slogan 'America for the Americans'. France was forced to withdraw its troops from Mexico (where they were protecting Emperor Maximilian) and Britain had to drop a territorial dispute with Venezuela. In 1890, the first Pan-American conference was held, paving the way for the inter-American system later set up.

[23] When World War I broke out in 1914, the United States declared its neutrality. However in 1917 it declared war on Germany, Austria and Turkey. In 1918, President Woodrow Wilson was one of the architects of the Treaty of Versailles, which established the framework for a new European peace. However in 1920 US entry into the League of Nations was blocked by Congress.

[24] The United States emerged from the War more powerful than ever, but the Great Crash on Wall Street (the US Stock Exchange) shook the country in 1929. In its wake, many banks failed, industry and trade were severely affected and unemployment figures rose to 11 million. Under Franklin Roosevelt's presidency (1933-45), the Government managed to bring the financial crisis under control.

[25] While Europe headed steadily toward another war, Congress passed a law in 1935 proclaiming US neutrality. Roosevelt's 'New Deal' established a limited welfare state to protect the poor.

But in 1941, the Japanese attack on the US military base at Pearl Harbor in Hawaii precipitated the US entry into the World War II.

26 The War acted as a dynamo for the entire American economy. With 15 million Americans at the Front, employment grew from 45,500,000 to 53,000,000, as workers churned out more supplies and arms for the war effort. To meet the demand for workers, six million people migrated from the countryside to the cities. On the labor front, in spite of a labor 'truce' in support of the war effort, there were 15,000 strikes during the War, a fact which led Congress to pass a law limiting the right to strike.

27 With Germany defeated on the European front, President Harry Truman (who had assumed the presidency upon Roosevelt's death) unleashed the United States' new military might upon Japan. On August 6 and 9, 1945 he gave the order for history's first atomic bombs to be dropped on the cities of Hiroshima and Nagasaki, wiping them out. That same year, at Yalta and Potsdam, Britain, the United States and the Soviet Union spelled out the terms for peace, and divided up the areas which would come under their respective spheres of influence.

28 Truman presided over the opening of the United Nations in 1945, and was re-elected President in 1948. As the number one Western power, the United States was in firm opposition to the USSR and its communist system. Soon a 'Cold War' developed as the two superpowers confronted each other in Eastern Europe and jousted for allies throughout the Third World. Within this framework, the Inter-American Treaty of Reciprocal Assistance was signed, and the North Atlantic Treaty Organization (NATO) was created.

29 The United States took it upon itself to safeguard the global capitalist system, with the support of such international institutions as the World Bank and the IMF, as well as armed intervention by its troops all around the world.

30 In 1952, General Dwight Eisenhower, commander-in-chief of American forces in Europe during the War and head of NATO, was elected President of the United States. The events of this period - the Korean War (1950-53), the partition of Germany, popular uprisings in Poland and Hungary, the delicate balance of nuclear weapons between the superpowers and the space race - all served to maintain the tension in US-Soviet relations. In 1960, a summit meeting between Eisenhower and Soviet leader Khruschev was cancelled when an American U-2 spy plane flying over Soviet territory was brought down.

31 In the 1950s, the US economy grew steadily, as did its population, leading to a sense of over-all prosperity and contentment. The 'American way of life' was exported to the rest of the world, hand-in-hand with American investments abroad. In 1956, the US offered South Vietnam's anti-communist puppet government military support. Labor conflict increased; in 1959, Congress passed a law aimed at curbing corruption in the labor unions.

32 The election of Democratic presidential candidate John F Kennedy in 1960 reflected the US people's desire for relief from domestic and foreign tensions. However, the President supported the abortive Bay of Pigs invasion of Cuba in 1961, initiated the economic blockade of Cuba and presided over the Cuban Missile Crisis. In 1963, the assassination of President Kennedy in Dallas, Texas, underscored the violence in American society.

33 In Latin America, President Kennedy launched the Alliance for Progress in Uruguay in 1961, in an attempt to stem the influence of the Cuban Revolution throughout the hemisphere. However, the funds earmarked for this project were insufficient to effect real change, serving merely to expose the region's problems. Faced with growing guerrilla activity in the region, the US decided to support official regional armies and their 'counterinsurgency' programs.

34 Lyndon Johnson, elected in 1964, launched the 'Great Society'. However, the country was brought face to face with new frustrations. The war in Vietnam escalated and then became a stalemate, causing a wave of protests throughout the US. This led the Government to initiate a withdrawal from Vietnam, a blow to the American psyche. The War ended in 1975. Racial segregation led to increasing confrontation. In 1968, violent protests in black neighborhoods in urban areas were sparked off by the assassination of black Civil Rights leader, Dr Martin Luther King. Richard Nixon became President.

35 That same year, the American Indian Movement (AIM) was founded by two Chippewa leaders. In 1969, AIM occupied the abandoned prison on Alcatraz Island in San Francisco to call attention to its demands and denounce the mistreatment of their people, which was followed by similar actions elsewhere.

36 Richard Nixon was re-elected President in 1972 and visited Moscow and Beijing in 1973. In 1974, he signed the final withdrawal of US troops from Vietnam but was forced to resign that same year, after the discovery that Republicans had spied on Democrat election campaign headquarters located in the Watergate Hotel.

37 In 1978, thousands of Native Americans demanding action on their grievances, carried out 'The Longest March', descending on Washington DC from the official 'Indian reservations' throughout the country. In 1982, AIM occupied the Black Hills in South Dakota, a site sacred to the Sioux, to protest against the mining operations of some 30 multinational companies, in that area.

38 American transnational companies spread around the world. These included Ford and General Motors (with more than a million workers combined), the oil companies Exxon and Mobil Oil, International Business Machine (IBM), ITT, General Electric and Philip Morris, amongst others.

39 The conservative Republican administration of Ronald Reagan (1980-88) reduced taxes on wealth and state social assistance, while increasing defense expenditure. The military-industrial complex energized the whole economy and partly made up for lagging behind Japan and Western Europe on other fronts.

40 The Hispanic proportion of the population increased by 53 per cent in the 1980s, reaching more than 22 million. The proportion of Asian-Americans grew even more.

41 In the 1980s the US emitted 25 per cent of the world total of carbon dioxide, (compared with the 13 per cent for the European Community which had a similar sized industrial sector) and refused to establish a deadline for reducing this. In 1991, the US was the biggest user of most forms of energy. It was also number one producer of nuclear energy and liquid gas, the number two producer of coal, hydroelectric power and natural gas, and the third largest oil producer. It was also the main consumer.

42 In February 1991, the US led the multinational force which confronted Iraq. The Gulf War demonstrated US military supremacy and allowed Republican President George Bush to propose a new world order under the hegemony of his country.

43 In 1991, 15 per cent of the population lived below the

poverty line. Those most affected were the US citizens of African (33 per cent) and Latin American (29 per cent) origins.

[44] Bill Clinton, Democrat Governor of Arkansas, was elected President in November 1992, and the Democratic Party also gained the majority in the House of Representatives. Clinton promised to concentrate on domestic problems, to move the greatest income tax burden on to the richer sectors, and to meet the health needs of all citizens. The health system reform, conducted by the nation's First Lady Hillary Clinton in 1994, was rejected by Congress after a vigorous campaign by private health providers.

[45] The North American Free Trade Agreement (NAFTA) with Mexico and Canada went into operation in January 1994. The measures aiming at the globalization of the economy were criticized for giving other countries the jobs lost internally, both in the public and private sectors. The feeling of rejection grew amongst the immigrant workers, especially when California approved a state law reducing education rights for children of illegal immigrants.

[46] Although the crime rate fell, the US citizens called for increasingly tougher punishment for offenders. The prisons overflowed as the number of inmates doubled and even tripled the figures of 10 years earlier. In 1994, civilians were banned from using assault weapons, a measure which was questioned by gun rights advocates.

[47] The summit between Clinton and Russian president Boris Yeltsin in Moscow in January that year marked the end of the threat of nuclear war between the two superpowers after the dismantling of the USSR.

[48] The economy recovered and unemployment fell. Consumption remained high despite increased interest rates, only falling towards the end of the year. The social security reform included cuts in benefits to the poor, betraying traditional democratic values.

[49] The Democrats lost the majority in the House of Representatives in the mid-term elections of 1994, for the first time in 40 years. The discontent also showed in 1995 with the formation of right-wing paramilitary organizations who refused to recognize federal authority. In one extreme case two right-wing paramilitaries exploded a car bomb outside a federal office in Oklahoma.

[50] Relying on foreign policy which bolstered his image as world leader, in the year before the elections Clinton pushed a military intervention in Bosnia-Herzegovina and signed the Dayton (Ohio) Accords in November 1995. In October 1996 he sponsored a round of Israeli-Palestinian talks in Washington and one month later he was re-elected with 49.2 per cent of the vote.

[51] In May 1997, the administration obtained one of its most significant diplomatic victories after signing an agreement with Russia on the expansion of NATO into Eastern Europe.

[52] At home, the enforcement of Affirmative Action laws aiming to place visible minorities in decision-making positions was restricted in Texas and California. Over 80 prisoners were executed in 1997 - the highest number since the death penalty was reinstated in 1976.

[53] In October 1997, Resolution 1134 of the UN Security Council threatened to impose new sanctions on Iraq if Baghdad did not authorize the inspection of all potential weapons-manufacturing facilities. President Clinton then tried to reorganize the multinational alliance (which in 1991 had confronted the Iraqi Government) to carry out a new attack against Iraq. However, in November, the Security Council dismissed a new armed intervention which allowed negotiations to take place. In February 1998, thousands of US residents demonstrated against Clinton's policy: 'We don't want your racist war', said the banners. The CIA spent over $100 million in a period of six years in attempts to oust Iraqi president Saddam Hussein.

[54] President Clinton had to refute accusations of perjury by independent investigator Kenneth Starr during 1998. Assigned to investigate a possible real estate fraud, Starr concluded that Clinton had lied about having sexual relations with a White House employee. The President's popularity was not affected by the charges and the Democratic Party obtained a significant victory in the congressional elections of November 3. Nevertheless, Starr presented proof of presidential perjury and the Senate decided in December to start impeachment proceedings.

[55] Two days before the impeachment vote in the Senate, Clinton decided, with the support of British Prime Minister Tony Blair, to bomb Baghdad and other Iraqi cities.

The attacks, in which more missiles were fired than in the 1991 Gulf War, caused hundreds of civilian deaths.

[56] In the Senate vote of February 1999, two-thirds of the vote were necessary to impeach the President, but the Republicans could not even get a simple majority. The charge of perjury was lost by 55 to 45 and the charge of obstruction of justice received 50 votes in favor to 50 against.

[57] The strained relationship with Cuba came to light again in November 1999 with the case of Elián González, the child who was one of three survivors of a Cuban boat that sunk en route to Miami. Opposing pronouncements by the Department of Justice and the Attorney-General in favor of the child being reunited with his father in Cuba,

Republicans led by senator Dan Burton - who had drafted the Helms-Burton law strengthening the embargo on Cuba - asked Congress to grant the child American citizenship. But the child was later returned to Cuba.

[58] By the year 2000, economic growth had continued for the longest period in the country's history. Since the 1996 incorporation of a new social security system, unemployment continued to decline and the number of families on social assistance also diminished. However, unlike previous periods, growth did not result in more equity nor social integration. The gap between the rich and poor widened, putting pressure on the middle class. ∎

US DEPENDENCIES

JOHNSTON:

Coral atoll of 2.6 sq km, made up of the Johnston island and the Sand, East and North islets, located approximately 1,150 km west-southwest of Honolulu (Hawaii). With an Air Force base the population (all military) is approximately 1,000. The atoll was uninhabited when it was discovered by British Captain Johnston in 1807. In 1858, Hawaii claimed sovereignty, but that same year US companies started exploitation of phosphate. Since 1934, the atoll has been administered by the US Navy. Civilians are not admitted.

Midway:

A round atoll which comprises two islands: Sand and Eastern, with 5 sq km of total area and 2,300 inhabitants (1985) almost exclusively military. In 1867, they were annexed by the US and are currently administered by its Navy. The islands are used for military purposes and operate as a refueling base for trans-Pacific flights. In 1942 during World War II, an important sea battle took place here.

WAKE:

Together with neighboring Wilkes and Peale, they make up an atoll with an area of 6.5 sq km and an estimated population of 1,600 inhabitants, mainly military personnel. Located between Midway and Guam, the island was seized by the United States during the 1898 war with Spain. It has a large airport which used to be a stopover for trans-Pacific flights, but nowadays it is not used for business purposes. Since 1972 it has been administered by the Air Force which now uses it as a missile testing station.

HOWLAND, JARVIS & BAKER:

Located in central Polynesia, in the Equatorial Pacific they were occupied by the US in the middle of the 19th century. The islands have been uninhabited since the end of World War II as major phosphate deposits had been depleted. There is a lighthouse in Howland. The islands are administered by the US Fishing and Wild Life Service.

PALMIRA & KINGMAN:

The northernmost islands of the Line archipelago. Palmira is an atoll surrounded by more than fifty coral islets covered with exuberant tropical vegetation. It was annexed in 1898 during the war with Spain and is now a private property, dependent on the US Department of the Interior. Kingman is a reef, located north of Palmira, annexed by the US in 1922. The total area of both islands is 7 sq km. Although uninhabited, the US-Japanese project to turn them into deposits of radioactive waste raised protests throughout the Pacific region in the 1980s.

Uruguay

Uruguay

Population: 3,313,000 (1999)
Area: 177,410 SQ KM
Capital: Montevideo
Currency: Peso
Language: Spanish

The range lands and forests of the eastern shore of the Uruguay River have been inhabited for at least 10,000 years. By the beginning of the 16th century there were three major cultural groups: the Charrúa, the Chaná and the Guaraní. The Charrúa were hunters, while the Chaná developed a rudimentary form of agriculture along the banks of the Uruguay River. Eventually the Guaraní developed some agricultural skills, mastered ceramics and navigation of the river in canoes.

2 In 1527, Sebastián Cabot was the first European to sail up the rivers Paraná and Uruguay, where he established the first Spanish settlement in the territory. The settlers ignored the east bank of the Uruguay river for over a century, until cattle were brought in by the governor of Asunción, Hernando Arias de Saavedra (Hernandarias) in 1611.

3 Good pasture and a moderate climate were conducive to large-scale cattle rearing. This attracted the *faeneros*, the Río de la Plata equivalent of cowboys, from Brazil and Buenos Aires. The indian culture was totally transformed by the introduction of beef in their diet, and the horse as a means of obtaining it. Through intermarriage with the indians these 'cowboys' -hunters of wild cattle, not cattle tenders- gave rise to the *gaucho*. Not all the *gauchos* were mestizos (people of mixed European and Indian ancestry). Sometimes they were white, black or 'mulatto' (of mixed black and white ancestry). In the 18th century, cattle-raising led to the extinction of some indigenous mammals, a reduction of plant diversity and soil degradation. By the mid-19th century the American indians who could not adapt to this new life were killed or displaced and

moved to the Jesuit missions further north.

4 In search of cattle and to gain control of the rivers which led to the interior regions of the Río de la Plata basin, the Portuguese advanced on the Banda Oriental (East Bank), an area approximately equivalent to that of present-day Uruguay, and founded Colonia del Sacramento on the shore opposite Buenos Aires in 1680. This settlement caused constant friction between Portugal and Spain. In 1724, Spain ordered the Governor of Buenos Aires, Bruno Mauricio de Zabala, to cross the Río de la Plata and establish a fort in the Bay of Montevideo.

5 Montevideo came under the Viceroyalty of Peru until 1776, as did Buenos Aires. That year, the Bourbon reforms decreed the creation of the Viceroyalty of the Río de la Plata, with Buenos Aires as the capital, and Montevideo as a naval station.

6 The May Revolution which broke out in Buenos Aires in 1810 was rejected by the Montevideans, who profited from the monopoly on trade with Spain. But it found support in the countryside among small and medium-scale producers and the landless people, led by the popular *caudillo* (leader) José Artigas. A Federal League was created with what is now Uruguay

and the Argentine provinces of Cordoba, Corrientes, Entre Ríos, Misiones and Santa Fe.

7 Uruguay was invaded by the Portuguese in 1816, with the tacit approval of Buenos Aires, whose government was alarmed by events known as the 'Artigan chaos'. In 1820, Artigas fought his way to Paraguay, where he remained until his death in 1850. Portugal ruled over the Uruguayan territory until 1823 when Brazil became independent. Uruguay became the Brazilian Cisplatine Province. In 1825 the 'orientales' renewed their campaign against the Brazilian Empire, and one of its objectives was to return to the United Provinces of the Río de la Plata. On August 25 1825, independence was declared and the decision made to reunite with the territories of the former Viceroyalty.

8 The country was eventually granted independence in 1828, through an agreement between Buenos Aires and Brazil mediated by Britain. The 1830 Constitution created a republic for the elite: only independently wealthy males of European origin could vote or be eligible for office. The 19th century was riven by civil wars and witnessed the formation of two political parties: the Blanco (White) or National Party, linked to Argentine leader Juan Manuel de Rosas, and the Colorado (Red but not communist), linked to European capital and liberal ideas.

9 In 1865, Colorado dictator Venancio Flores signed an agreement with Brazil and Argentina and created the Triple Alliance, breaking Paraguayan isolation - with European support - and forcing the country to open its borders to foreign trade (see Paraguay).

10 Between 1876 and 1879, under the dictator Colonel Lorenzo Latorre, the countryside was enclosed by fences. The implications of this were far-reaching: the land was completely appropriated by the private sector, production was geared to the capitalist market (over which Britain held undisputed control) and the countryside was 'organized' leaving no space for the *gaucho*, who was transformed into a hired hand.

11 In 1903 the Colorado José Batlle y Ordoñez assumed the presidency. The following year he fought and defeated Aparicio

WORKERS

1995
UNEMPLOYMENT: 10.2%

% OF LABOUR FORCE   **1998**

▪ FEMALE: 41%   ▪ MALE: 59%

1990

▪ SERVICES: 58.5%
▪ INDUSTRY: 27.2%
▪ AGRICULTURE: 14.3%

LAND USE

DEFORESTATION: 0.0% annual (1990/95)
IRRIGATED: 11.1% of arable (1993)

1993

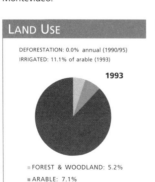

▪ FOREST & WOODLAND: 5.2%
▪ ARABLE: 7.1%
▪ OTHER: 87.7%

PUBLIC EXPENDITURE

	1997	74.6%
DEFENCE 4.4%		SOCIAL

MILITARY EXPENDITURE   **38%**
(% of health & education)   (1990/91)

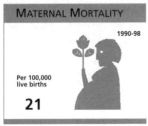

MATERNAL MORTALITY

1990-98

Per 100,000
live births

21

LITERACY

1995

97%

EXTERNAL DEBT

1998

Per capita

US$ 2,311

FOREIGN TRADE

Millions US$ 1998

IMPORTS

4,620

EXPORTS

4,512

Saravia - the last rural caudillo of the Blancos. With the ideological influence of European social-democracy, and the support of immigrants, Batlle laid the foundations for the modern Uruguayan state. The high rate of productivity of extensive cattle-raising generated such a surplus that, without changing the land ownership structure of large units in the hands of a few, the State was able to redistribute wealth in the form of welfare, education, and protection of local industry oriented toward domestic consumption.

[12] The country underwent rapid urbanization. Commerce and services expanded quickly, with the State as the main employer. A large liberal middle-class developed, educated in State schools with Europeanized curricula.

[13] The Church and the State were separated and divorce legalized. A collegiate system of government was introduced in 1917 to avoid power accumulation. This open legislation earned the country the title 'the Switzerland of South America'. Urban migration and European immigration enlarged the cities, but the birth-rate dropped. Abortion was the major birth-control technique, becoming so common that it was legal between 1933 and 1935, although made illegal again after political negotiations with Catholic authorities. In 1934, women were granted the right to vote.

[14] Uruguayan exports grew during both World Wars. Meat and its products were supplied first to the Allies, who were fighting against Nazism and Fascism in Europe, and later to US troops fighting in Korea.

[15] Trade balance surpluses secured the country large foreign currency reserves. The welfare policy of subsidies encouraged the emergence of relatively strong import-substitution industries. Meanwhile, a prosperous building industry helped maintain high employment.

[16] Instead of reinvesting their profits, land owners invested capital abroad, engaging in financial speculation and superfluous consumption. This inevitably led to inflation, corruption and the exacerbation of social conflict. In the mid-1950s, the industrial sector stagnated - a situation that proved impossible to reverse.

[17] The first Blanco Government of the century, which came to power in 1959, accepted IMF economic guidelines which accelerated the recession causing a strong reaction among workers. The situation became critical in 1968 when Jorge Pacheco Areco's government, yielding to IMF prescriptions, curtailed the purchasing power of wage-earners and aimed to eliminate the bargaining power of trade unions. The National Workers' Convention and the student organizations opposed such policies. At the same time the Tupamaro (MLN) guerrilla movement was active throughout the country. In 1971 the Broad Front (Frente Amplio), a left-wing coalition, was founded. It promoted a progressive government program, and nominated a retired general, Liber Seregni, in the presidential elections of that year.

[18] Juan Maria Bordaberry, the Colorado nominee, won the elections, which the Blanco National Party denounced as fraudulent. During that regime, the military took up the fight against the guerrilla movement, backed by parliament's declaration of a state of civil war. In 1972 the Tupamaros were defeated. A campaign including the systematic use of torture rapidly dismantled the clandestine organization. On June 27 1973, President Bordaberry and the armed forces staged a coup. Parliament was dissolved, and a civilian-military government was formed. Local trade unions resisted the coup with a 15-day strike.

[19] The Uruguayan military set up a regime based on the National Security Doctrine, a system learnt in US training academies. Economically, the neo-liberal theories of US Professor Milton Friedman were applied, favoring the concentration of wealth in transnational corporations. Salaries lost 50 per cent of their purchasing power, whilst foreign debt reached $5 billion. During this period, all public and private institutions, political parties and unions were banned, people disappeared and torture and arbitrary detentions were commonplace.

[20] The economic situation deteriorated and the civilian population systematically rebuffed efforts to legalize the police state, voting overwhelmingly against the draft of a new constitution that would support this. The Uruguayan generals had no alternative but to work out a timetable for reinstating an institutionally legitimate government.

[21] In April 1983, the Inter-union Plenary of Workers (PIT) was formed and May Day was celebrated for the first time since the coup. The three political parties recognized as legal by the military government took up the banner for the labor movement and the causes espoused prior to the dictatorship. They also demanded the release of all political prisoners. The Broad Front, whose president had been in prison since 1973, was excluded from political activity.

[22] Protests against the military regime intensified as a result of the break-down in negotiations. Women's groups defied the Government's prohibition of street demonstrations. After a successful 24-hour general strike called by the PIT, talks between the political parties and the military were resumed in January 1984, this time

PROFILE

ENVIRONMENT

Uruguay has a gently rolling terrain, crossed by characteristic low hills - an extension of Brazil's southern plateau - belonging to the old Guayanic-Brazilian massif. Its average altitude is 300 meters above sea level. This, together with its location and latitude, determines its temperate, subtropical, semi-humid weather, with rainfall throughout the year. The vegetation is made up almost entirely of natural grasslands, suitable for cattle and sheep raising. The territory is well irrigated by many rivers, and has over 1,100 km of navigable waterways, in particular on the rivers Negro and Uruguay, and on the Plata estuary. The coast is made up of many sandy beaches which attract tourists from the neighboring countries. There is increasing pollution in the northern departments as a result of emissions from a thermoelectric plant in Candiota (Brazil), while rivers and streams suffer from the use of poisonous agricultural chemicals. A growing loss of ecosystems on the plains and in the eastern wetlands has been observed, due to monoculture of wood and rice, respectively. Large infrastructure projects (e.g. the Buenos Aires-Colonia bridge, and connecting highway to Sao Paulo, Brazil) pose an additional threat to the environment.

SOCIETY

Peoples: Most Uruguayans are descendants of Spanish, Italian and other European immigrants. The native population was annihilated in the mid-19th century. Afro-American descendants make up about 8 per cent of today's population.
Religions: Catholics 66 per cent; Protestants 2 per cent. Afro-Brazilian cults are also practiced.
Languages: Spanish.
Political Parties: Colorado Party (Red); National Party (Blanco/White); Broad Front (Frente Amplio/Encuentro Progresista); Nuevo Espacio (New Space); Unión Cívica (Civic Union).
Social Organizations: PIT-CNT (Inter-Union Workers' Bureau - National Workers' Convention). FUCVAM (Uruguayan Federation of Housing Construction by Mutual Help). Federation of University Students (FEUU).

THE STATE

Official Name: República Oriental del Uruguay.
Administrative Divisions: 19 Departments
Capital: Montevideo 1,800,000 people (1997).
Other cities: Salto 81,600 people; Paysandú 79,100; Las Piedras 68,400; Rivera 59,700; Maldonado 40,700.
Government: Jorge Batlle, President since November 1999. Presidential system, with a bicameral legislative. A 99-member House of Representatives and a 30-member House of Senators, chosen by proportional representation. Luis Hierro López, Vice-president since November 1999, chairs the Senate.
National Holidays: August 25, Independence (1825); July 18, Constitution (1830).
Armed Forces: 25,600 (1994).
Other: 700 Metropolitan Guard, 500 Republican Guard.

with the participation of representatives of the Broad Front.

23 The National Party leader Wilson Ferreira Aldunate was arrested on his return to the country after an 11-year exile. He was not permitted to run as a candidate in the 1984 election. General Líber Seregni and hundreds of others were also proscribed as candidates.

24 Under the slogan of *cambios en paz* (peaceful change), the leader of the Colorado Party, Julio Maria Sanguinetti, won the national election. During the new government's first month in power, an amnesty law was approved whereby all political prisoners were freed.

25 President Sanguinetti supported many international diplomatic moves in Latin America. The first two years of his term coincided with a favorable international situation, but he returned to the neo- liberal policies of the previous government, which were strongly resisted by the population.

26 In 1986, under pressure from the President and the armed forces, Parliament approved an amnesty for military personnel accused of violations of human rights, by 3 to 1. A referendum in April 1988 ratified the law, with 56 per cent in favor, while 42 per cent wanted to try the military for their crimes.

27 In May 1989, the Government signed a secret structural adjustment agreement with the World Bank, in exchange for rescheduling Uruguay's debt. The Government committed itself to reduce expenditure on social security; to privatize bankrupt banks absorbed by the State, and to reform public companies making them profitable and attractive for privatization.

28 In the November 1989 election the Blanco/National Party under Luis Alberto Lacalle inflicted a severe electoral defeat upon the Colorado Party, taking 17 of the country's 19 departments. The Broad Front won in Montevideo with its candidate Tabaré Vázquez. The Left assumed responsibility for municipal administration for the first time in the history of the country. Six women were elected to the Chamber of Deputies and another seven to the Municipal Council (legislative) of the capital.

29 The associations of pensioners succeeded in bringing about constitutional reform - contra to the agreement with the World Bank - and pensions were readjusted, in line with the salaries of civil servants. This legislation was approved in a referendum.

30 Lacalle carried out his neo-liberal policy: taxes were increased and the privatization of state-run companies was encouraged. Salaries lost over 15 per cent of their purchasing power during the first year of his term, while inflation rose from 90 to 130 per cent at the end of his term. In March 1991, Argentina, Brazil and Paraguay approved the Mercosur agreement (see box in Brazil).

31 A commission convened by the labor union movement, constituted by members of several parties, presented a petition requesting a plebiscite on a privatization law. In December 1992, 72 per cent of the population voted to repeal the law. However, the Government managed to privatize certain state enterprises, including the national airline, the gasworks and the sugarcane plantations in the north of the country.

32 The mayor of Montevideo had approval ratings higher than the electoral support which he had received during his first four years in office. He decentralized the departmental government into 18 zones, within which local voters could elect their own representatives.

33 In the general and regional elections of November 27 1994, Colorado Party candidate Julio Maria Sanguinetti was elected once again by a small majority.

34 The Progressive Encounter - made up of the Broad Front, the Christian Democrats and other sectors which had split from the traditional parties - won the mayoralty of the capital for the second time

35 Sanguinetti took office on March 1 1995, two months after Mercosur came into force, and proposed political and economic reforms. The fall in inflation and the loss of jobs - mainly among the construction and industrial sectors - were the outcome of austerity measures implemented by Economy Minister Luis Mosca.

36 In October, Uruguay became the first country for two decades officially to receive Cuban President Fidel Castro. Sanguinetti rejected Castro's invitation to visit Cuba in September 1996, considering the time was not right.

37 The wife of former President Lacalle and several of his closest aides were accused of corruption which rocked the foundations of the political parties in mid-1996. A system of social security by savings accounts was implemented that year, in line with reforms previously carried out in Argentina and Chile.

38 In 1996, Parliament discussed a constitutional reform which entailed difficult political negotiations. The main goal of the reform was the electoral system, establishing the ballot system to elect the president. The Broad Front voted against, arguing that it was conceived to prevent the left from winning the presidency, but the reform was approved with 50.6 per cent of the vote

39 Unemployment reached 11.5 per cent in early 1999, but inflation was driven down to 4 per cent, the lowest it had been for 30 years. In September that year, Uruguay rejected the extradition to Paraguay of former Paraguayan Defense Minister José Segovia. He was granted political asylum in Uruguay while being sought by the Paraguayan justice system on charges of fraud against the State. Segovia was a close associate of Lino Oviedo who had sought political asylum in Argentina following the murder of then vice-president José María Argaña.

40 In October, Argentinian poet Juan Gelman requested Sanguinetti to investigate the disappearance of his daughter-in-law María Claudia García in December 1976 in Montevideo. Gelman also asked him to investigate the whereabouts of the child María Claudia had given birth to at the military hospital before 'disappearing' - the same happened to Gelman's son - at the hands of identified army personnel. Sanguinetti told him that no information had been found which could confirm nor deny Gelman's accusations, and that therefore the case was closed. In support of Gelman's case, hundreds of intellectuals, artists and journalists throughout the world sent letters to the President asking him to follow up the investigations in his role as 'Commander in Chief of the Armed Forces'.

41 During the October presidential elections, the Encuentro Progresista was the majority political party with 40.1 per cent of the vote, 12 senators and 40 representatives. Since no party reached the required minimum to win the presidency, the two front-runners Tabaré Vázquez (Broad Front/EP) and Jorge Batlle (Colorado Party) started their campaigns for the second round. To prevent a victory of the left, the National party allied itself with the Colorado party and voted for Batlle. Jorge Batlle was elected president in the November 28 elections with 52 per cent of the vote.

42 During his inaugural speech on March 1 2000, Batlle declared that 'achieving peace between Uruguayans ... belongs to all of us', clearly referring to the Gelman and other 'disappeared' cases. Over a month later, the President informed Gelman, who was in Uruguay at the time, that he had found his daughter-in-law's 'baby' (now 23 years old) - much to to surprise of Gelman and his supporters worldwide. The news confirmed the involvement of the armed forces in 'Operation Condor' (see p 434), and the kidnapping and disappearance of children born to mothers in detention in Uruguay, something denied by Sanguinetti during his last two terms of office. ■

DEMOGRAPHY

Population: 3,313,000 (1999)
Annual growth: 0.7 % (1975/97)
Estimates for year 2015 (million): 3.7 (1999)
Annual growth to year 2015: 0.7 % (1997/2015)
Urban population: 90.7 % (1997)
Urban Growth: 1.0 % (1980/95)
Children per woman: 2.4 (1998)

HEALTH

Life expectancy at birth: 74 years (1998)
male: 70 years (1998)
female: 78 years (1998)
Maternal mortality: 21 per 100,000 live births (1990-98)
Infant mortality: 16 per 1,000 (1998)
Under-5 child mortality: 19 per 1,000 (1998)
Daily calorie supply: 2,830 per capita (1996)
309 doctors per 100,000 people (1993)

EDUCATION

Literacy: 97 % (1995)
male: 97 % (1995)
female: 98 % (1995)
School enrolment:
Primary total: 113 % (1990/96)
male: 113 % (1990/97)
female: 112 % (1990/97)
Secondary:
male: 77 % (1990/96)
female: 92 % (1990/96)
Tertiary: 30 % (1996)
Primary school teachers: one for every 20 (1996)

COMMUNICATIONS

293 newspapers (1996), 607 radios (1997), 305 TV sets (1996) and 209 main telephone lines (1996) per 1,000 people

ECONOMY

Per capita, GNP: $ 6,070 (1998)
Annual growth, GNP: 3.9 % (1998)
Annual inflation: 40.5 % (1990/98)
Consumer price index: 170.4 (1998)
Currency: 10.5 pesos = $ 1 (1998)
Cereal imports: 125,009 metric tons (1998)
Food import dependency: 10 % (1997)
Fertilizer use: 1,022 kg per ha (1997)
Exports: $ 4,512 million (1998)
Imports: $ 4,620 million (1998)
External debt: $ 7,600 million (1998); $ 2,311 per capita (1998)
Debt service: 23.5 % of exports (1998)
Development aid received: $ 57 million (1997); $ 18.2 per capita (1997); 0.30 % of GNP (1997)

ENERGY

Consumption: 883.0 Kgs of Oil equivalent per capita yearly (1997); 62.0 % imported (1997)

HDI (rank/value): 40/0.826 (1997)

Uzbekistan

Uzbekistan

Population: 23,941,000 (1999)
Area: 447,400 SQ KM
Capital: Tashkent
Currency: Som-Kupon
Language: Uzbek

S everal ancient agricultural centers developed in what is now Uzbekistan, including Khwarezm, Ma Wara an-Nahr and the Fergana Valley. The population and the languages of the first states to emerge in the 10th century BC were Indo-European. Between the 6th and 7th centuries AD, these states formed part of the Persian Achaemenid empire, the empire of Alexander the Great, the Greco-Bactrian kingdoms, and that of Kusha, the white Hun or Eftalite state.

[2] Turkish nomads defeated the Eftalites and brought the major part of Central Asia into their empire, the Turkish *kaganate* (Khanate), between the 6th and 8th centuries. During this period, Turkish-speaking peoples began coming to the region and integrating with the local population. In the mid-8th century, the country was conquered by the Arabs. Islam spread quickly, particularly in the cities.

[3] When the power of the Arab caliphs declined, during the reign of the local Samanid and Karajanid dynasties, and under the shahs of Khwarezm (9th to early 13th centuries), an Islamic civilization developed. Agriculture was its main activity, made possible by a highly developed irrigation system. This culture was also noted for its artisans. The cities of Bukhara, Samarkand and Urgenca became prosperous trading centers for the caravans that crossed the Great Silk Route, from China to Byzantium.

[4] From 1219-1221, the state ruled over by the shahs of Khwarezm was overrun by the Tatars, and completely devastated. Khwarezm was turned over to the Golden Horde, under the leadership of Genghis Khan's oldest son. Ma Wara an-Nahr and Fergana went to the second son, Chagatai; the inhabitants of the area began calling themselves Chagatais. Turkish and Mongol tribes moved into the steppes, and in the second half of the 14th century, Timur, the head of one of these tribes, settled in Ma Wara an-Nahr, making Samarkand the capital of his empire. Later, Samarkand became the residence of Ulug Beg, the grandson of Timur Lenk (Tamburlaine), a Khan and an astronomer.

[5] The union of nomad tribes who called themselves Uzbeks was achieved in the 15th century, in Central Kazakhstan. During the second half of the century, the great Uzbek poet and thinker Ali Shir Navai, who lived at the court of one of Timur's descendants, became a world-renowned figure. The leader of the Uzbeks, Muhammad Shaybani, conquered Ma Wara an-Nahr at the beginning of the 16th century, and the Uzbek immigrants gave their name to all the country's inhabitants. After dissolving the State of Shaybani, Uzbek Khanates emerged in the region. In 1512, the Khanate of Khiva was formed; its military elite belonged to the Kungrats, an Uzbek people. In 1806 Muhammad Amin, head of the Kungrats, founded the dynasty which was to rule over Khiva until 1920.

[6] The Khanate of Bukhara was formed in the mid-16th century. Its military elite belonged to the Uzbek Manguite people. Muhammad Rajim, leader of the Manguites, founded his dynasty in 1753; it also lasted until 1920. The Khanate of Bukhara reached its apogee at the time of Nasrula, a Khan who ruled from 1826-1860. In the early 19th century, the Emirs of Fergana (of the Ming dynasty) created the Khanate of Kokand. These feudal theocracies were populated by Uzbeks, as well as Turkmens, Tajiks, Kyrgyz and Karakalpaks, who were in constant conflict.

[7] None of these states had definite boundaries, nor were they capable of exacting absolute loyalty from their chieftains. The Emirs of Khiva and Bukhara exercised only nominal sovereignty over the Turkmen tribes of the Kara Kum Desert, who were slave traders in Iranian territory. Although the three Uzbek Khanates reached their highest level of organization during this period, they were not prepared to face the imminent European expansion. In Central Asia, Russian and British colonial interests clashed over the cotton market.

[8] In 1860, the Russian offensive against the Khanates began, though it was impeded by their geographical isolation, particularly in the case of Khiva which was surrounded by desert. In 1867, the Czar created the province of Turkistan, with its center in Tashkent. Although it belonged to Kokand, it was officially annexed in 1875. By the end of the 19th century, the province included the regions of Samarkand, Syr Darya and Fergana. On August 12 1873, the Khan of Khiva signed a peace treaty with Russia, accepting protectorate status, as did the Khan of Bukhara in September of the same year. The difficult living conditions imposed on the people by czarist Russia triggered several uprisings, including Andizhan in 1898, and Central Asia in 1916.

[9] With the fall of the Czar in February 1917, power was shared by the committee of the Provisional Government, and the Soviets (councils) of workers and soldiers. After the triumph of the October Revolution in St Petersburg power was concentrated in the hands of the Tashkent Soviet. In 1918, Red Army units crushed both the attempt to form an autonomous Muslim government in Kokand and an anti-Bolshevik uprising in Turkistan. The Red Army occupied Khiva in April 1920, and entered Bukhara in September. Land and water reform began in spring 1921, with military operations continuing until mid-1922, when the implementation of the reforms left the rebels without a cause.

[10] In 1924, the Soviet Government reorganized Central Asian borders along ethnic lines, and proclaimed the Soviet Socialist Republic (SSR) of Uzbekistan. In May 1925, Uzbekistan became a federated republic of the Soviet Union. The Autonomous Soviet Socialist Republic of Tajikistan was a part of Uzbekistan until 1929, when it joined the USSR. During the Great Purge of 1937-38, a number of Uzbeks including the prime minister, Fayzullah Khodzhayev and the first secretary of the Uzbek Communist Party, Akmal Ikramov, were sentenced to death. In Moscow In 1953, both leaders were rehabilitated.

[11] The socialist reforms were aimed primarily at taking advantage of the region's agricultural potential. Huge mechanized irrigation systems, including the Great Fergana, North Fergana and Tashkent canals, were constructed by the State, as were reservoirs like the Kattakurgan on the Zeravshan River (the Uzbek Sea), the Kuyumazar and the Akhangaran (the Tashkent Sea). Between 1956 and 1983, when Sharaf Rashidov was first secretary of the Communist Party, the Republic's economy revolved around cotton. National industry was geared toward producing machines and heavy equipment for cotton cultivation, harvesting and processing. Uzbekistan became the USSR's largest cotton producer and the third largest in the world.

[12] In the 1940s, the population increased; Kurds and Mesketian Turks, who had been deported from the Caucasus, came to Uzbekistan, and all was stable until the 1980s. When Leonid Brezhnev became head of the Communist Party of the USSR in 1983 he changed the Uzbek authorities. The new first secretary of the local CP, Inamjon Ousmankhodjaev, revealed that official cotton production statistics had been systematically falsified by his predecessor.

[13] The Uzbek corruption case was the biggest scandal in the Soviet Union at the time, and triggered many arrests, lawsuits against 4,000 civil servants and expulsions from the Party. However, this turned out to be just another political purge as it did not bring about any substantial changes.

[14]   From 1985 onward, the changes initiated by President Mikhail Gorbachev, the deterioration of the economic situation and the weakening of the Soviet Communist Party's centralized authority gave rise to increased ethnic and religious conflicts in Uzbekistan. The Uzbeks, predominantly Sunni Muslims, resisted the Party's anti-clerical campaigns.

[15]   The USSR's intervention in Afghanistan against fellow-Sunni Muslims only worsened the situation, and all these factors combined to create a hostile climate toward Moscow and the Russian minority residing in Uzbekistan. The most serious consequence was the conflict in the region of Fergana in June 1989, and conflicts in Namangan, in December 1990.

[16]   In August 1991, the Uzbek Soviet (Parliament) approved the Law of Independence. On December 12, in Alma Ata (Kazakhstan), the Uzbek delegation signed the agreement creating the Commonwealth of Independent States (CIS), which marked the end of the USSR.

[17]   On 29 August, presidential elections were held with a referendum supporting independence. Islam Karimov, the former first secretary of the Uzbek Communist Party, was elected president.

[18]   In January 1992, students demonstrating in Tashkent against the shortage of bread and the high price of staple goods were fired upon by police; six people were killed and many were injured. The Uzbekistan Government gradually started to liberalize the economy by deregulating some prices, following the example of other former Soviet republics. In an attempt to reduce the tension, authorities announced an increase in student grants.

[19]   At the same time, a leadership struggle in the upper echelons of the religious (Islamic) hierarchy, reinforced the secular power of the President.

[20]   Karimov imposed a harsh, authoritarian style in an attempt to maintain the country's political stability. When the deregulation of prices resulted in student protests, the Government responded with severe repressive measures. One such demonstration resulted in two students being killed and several injured.

[21]   In March, arrests were made in the city of Namangan, a bastion of Muslim opposition. The Islamic center was attacked; with several leaders of the Birlik Democratic Party and other religious leaders being arrested. That same month Uzbekistan was admitted to the UN as a new member.

[22]   In June 1992, Karimov defined a new economic course for Uzbekistan, based upon the Southeast Asian model: eliminating dissidence and modernizing the economy by adopting free-market policies. The opposition went underground.

[23]   The deregulation of prices, privatization and financial and fiscal reforms which have been implemented since 1992, have been far less drastic in Uzbekistan than in other former Soviet republics.

[24]   During 1993, Uzbekistan strengthened political links with other former soviet republics in Central Asia, establishing diplomatic relations with Hungary and signing bilateral agreements with Turkey, Afghanistan and Pakistan.

[25]   Several Central Asian countries tried to design a program to protect the environment in Aral Sea region. However, in order to prevent the drying up of the lake, according to Western experts, the flow of water to irrigate cotton crops in Uzbekistan would have to be reduced.

[26]   On a diplomatic front, the country aimed to contain the Russian and Iranian influences in the region, particularly from 1995 onwards. Karimov actively supported the US embargo on Iran, calling for the creation of a common Turkmenistan between the nations of the region, making it understood that it was threatened by the 'imperialist' tendencies of Russia.

[27]   In 1996, for the first time, Parliament admitted human rights abuses had been committed in the past and approved new legislation on the issue. Two official visits by the Uzbek President, to France and the United States, in April and June respectively, ratified Uzbekistan's rapprochement with the Western countries.

[28]   In June, Uzbekistan refused to sign a peace agreement formally putting an end to the civil war in Tajikistan, stating this would provoke political instability, as the process overlooked several of the warring groups.

[29]   Uzbekistan was one of three countries - along with Israel and the US - that in late 1997 voted against the lifting of the Cuban economic embargo at the UN general assembly (a majority of 143 countries voted in favor of the resolution).

[30]   During early 1998, Tashkent showed concern for the Muslim advance in Tajikistan and for the actions of the Wahhabi sect, in the Fergana valley, a densely populated area belonging to Uzbekistan, Tajikistan and Kyrgyzstan.

[31]   On May 25 1999, the US promised President Karimov a $33-million loan to keep implementing economic reforms. Four days later, the World Bank (WB) gave $25 million to the Central Bank to enhance its supervision duties. Since 1992, the WB has injected $444 million into the country.

[32]   Six men were sentenced to death on June 28 accused of car bombings in the capital in February which had killed 16 people and injured more than 100. According to human rights groups, the Government used the 'threat' of a Muslim fundamentalist uprising to curtail religious and political rights. Government repression increased and some thousand people fled to neighboring Tajikistan while the Government requested their extradition under charges of involvement. A UN mission was sent to that country on July 12 to verify the refugee situation.

[33]   On September 17, Minister of Foreign Affairs Abdulaziz Komilov accused Tajikistan of supporting Muslim fundamentalists operating in neighboring Kyrgyzstan. Tajik opposition declared that by these actions the minister 'worsened the situation in the region'

[34]   In November, President Karimov backed Russia in its war against Chechnya - an anti-Islamic war in the eyes of some people. Political analysts said the measure was typical of the élites of former Soviet republics who, ironically, seek to end Islamic funda-mentalism in largely Muslim countries.

[35]   Karimov was reelected on January 9 2000 with 92 per cent of the vote. James Rubin, spokesperson from the US State Department, stated the elections had been neither 'free nor fair' since the population had no 'alternatives'. He also recalled that the only opposition leader, Abulchafiz Dzjalalov - who received 4 per cent of the vote - had declared 'even I voted for Karimov'. For similar reasons, the Organization for the Cooperation and Security of Europe (OCSE) did not send observers.

[36]   On March 28 2000, Human Rights Watch condemned the Government for carrying out a 'brutal campaign' against religious activists. Three weeks later, while visiting the country, US Secretary of State Madeleine Albright offered a $3- million package to fight drug trafficking and terrorism. With this support, President Karimov requested - while in Delhi - the cooperation of India to fight international terrorism in Afghanistan and other Central Asian countries. ∎

PROFILE

ENVIRONMENT

Uzbekistan is bordered in the north and northwest by Kazakhstan, in the southeast by Tajikistan, in the northeast by Kyrgyzstan and in the south by Afghanistan. Part of its terrain is flat, while the rest is mountainous. There are two main rivers and more than 600 streams, some of which are diverted for irrigation, while others are utilized for hydroelectric projects. The plains are located in the northwest and the center (the Ustyurt Plateau, the Amu Darya Valley and the Kyzylkum desert), while the mountains are in the southeast (the Tien-Shan and Gissar and Alay ranges). It has a hot, dry climate on the plains, and is more humid in the mountains. There are large deposits of natural gas, oil and coal. Among the most pressing environmental problems are the salinization of the soil as a result of monoculture, desertification, drinking water and air contamination.

SOCIETY

Peoples: Uzbeks 75.8 per cent; Russians 6 per cent; Tajiks 4.8 per cent; Kazakhs 4.1 per cent, Kyrgyz 0.9 per cent; Ukranians 0.6 per cent; Turks 0.6 per cent; other 7.2 per cent (1995).
Religions: Muslim (Sunni), 88 per cent: Orthodox, 1 per cent. Other (mostly non-religious), 11 per cent.
Languages: Uzbek (official), Russian, Tajik.
Political Parties: People's Democratic Party; National Progress Party; Birlik Democratic Party; Islamic Renaissance Party.

THE STATE

Official Name: Uzbekistan Jumhuriyati.
Capital: Tashkent 2,400,000 people (1997).
Other cities: Samarkand 362,000 people; Namangan 333,000; Andizhan 313,000; Bukhara 235,000 (1995).
Government: Islam Karimov, President since December, 1991. Reelected in January 2000. Otkir Sultonov, Prime Minister since 1995. Sultonov was confirmed in January 2000. Legislature: Supreme Assembly, (single-chamber), with 250 members: 83 elected by direct popular vote every five years and 167 elected by locals councils.
National Holiday: September 1, Independence (1991).
Armed Forces: 65,000 (1995).
Other: (National Guard) 700.

Vanuatu

Vanuatu

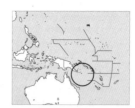

Population: 186,000 (1999)
Area: 12,190 SQ KM
Capital: Vila
Currency: Vatu
Language: Bislama, English and French

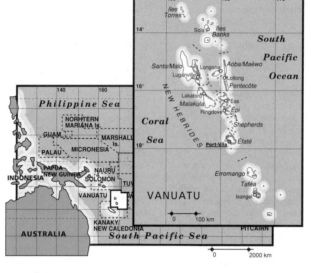

The first colonization of Polynesia is still a mystery to anthropologists and historians. Thor Heyerdahl's highly publicized Kon Tiki expedition tried to demonstrate that people could have reached the South Pacific islands from America. But linguistic, cultural and agricultural similarities relate Melanesians to Indonesians.

[2] Sailing westwards, Polynesians reached Vanuatu around 1400 BC. These navigators crossed and populated the entire Pacific Ocean from Antarctica to Hawaii and as far as Easter Island on the eastern edge of the Pacific Ocean. Their culture was highly developed, Polynesians domesticated animals and developed some subsistence crops; they manufactured ceramics and textiles, organized their societies with a caste system and, in some cases, possessed a historical knowledge which had been orally transmitted down the generations for centuries.

[3] On April 29 1605 the Portuguese-Spanish navigator, Pedro Fernandez de Quiros, was the first European to sight mountains which he believed to be part of the Great Southern Continent for which he was searching; he named the place, Tierra del Espíritu Santo (Land of the Holy Spirit). A century and a half later, Frenchman Louis Antoine de Bougainville, sailed around the region and demonstrated that it was not part of Australia but rather a series of islands. In 1774, James Cook drew the first map of the archipelago, calling it the New Hebrides after the Scottish Hebrides Islands.

[4] Shortly thereafter traders arrived and felled all the aromatic sandalwood forests. Lacking other attractive natural resources, the islands became the source of a semi-enslaved labor force. The workers were either taken by force or purchased from local leaders in exchange for tobacco, mirrors and firearms.

[5] Popular resentment of this plundering caused the murders of more European missionaries in the New Hebrides than in any other area of the Pacific.

[6] During almost all of the 19th century, the archipelago was on the dividing line between the French (in New Caledonia) and British (in the Solomon islands) zones of influence, and the two nations finally decided to share the islands instead of fighting over them. In 1887, a Joint Naval Commission was established, and in 1906, the Condominium was formalized. The native islanders soon referred to it as the 'pandemonium'.

[7] The formula of shared domination envisaged the joint provisions of some basic services; the post, radio, customs, public works, but left each power free to develop other services. Consequently, there were two police forces, two monetary systems, two health services and two school systems ruled by two representatives on the islands.

[8] Melanesians were relegated to being 'stateless' in their own country, and they were not considered citizens until a legislative assembly was established in the territory in 1974. Until then only British or French people were entitled to citizenship or land ownership.

[9] Most of the neighboring archipelagos achieved independence in the 1970s. This encouraged the foundation of the National Party of the New Hebrides (the Vanuatu Party, VP) in 1971. The Party organized grassroots groups on all of the islands on the basis of the Protestant parochial structure. The Party became the country's leading political force and demanded total independence, in opposition to various 'moderate' pro-French parties that preferred to maintain the colonial status. When the Party won two-thirds of the vote in 1979 this convinced the British that independence could no longer be postponed. The British also carried out a vigorous anti-nuclear policy and turned Vanuatu into the only nation among the Pacific islands to become a member of the Non-Aligned Movement.

[10] During that period French agents and US business encouraged the growth of the Na Griamel separatist group in Espíritu Santo. This group began as a popular protest movement against the sale of property to North American hotels. The group's leader, Jimmy Stevens, received $250,000, arms and a radio from the Phoenix Foundation, an ultra-right US organization, in return for concessions to install a casino and, allegedly, cover for illicit activities from Stevens' 'Republic of Vemarana'.

[11] Stevens visited France to obtain the support of President Giscard d'Estaing, and the French police did nothing to prevent the rebellion and expulsion of Vanuatu Party followers from the island. Meanwhile francophone support of the other islands encouraged small 'moderate' pro-French parties to oppose the VP government of Walter Lini, who was accused of being authoritarian, too centralist and too close to Britain and Australia.

[12] Finally, Lini, supported by forces from Papua New Guinea, managed to disarm the separatists, deporting Stevens and his followers, who were granted asylum in Kanaky/New Caledonia.

[13] Vanuatan independence was declared on July 30 1980. Measures were immediately taken to return the land held by foreigners to the Melanesians; the school system was unified and a national army was created.

[14] In February 1981, the newly-arrived itinerant ambassador of Vanuatu, Barak Sope, was refused entry at Nouméa airport by the French Government, to prevent his participation in the Melanesian Independence Front Congress in New Caledonia (Kanaky). Retaliation was immediate; Lini's government declared the French ambassador persona non grata and requested that the French diplomatic mission be reduced to five members. This incident delayed the cooperation program between the governments.

[15] At this time government revenues depended heavily on foreign aid and the country's exports covered only half of the cost of its imports. Since the country was a tax haven with more than 60 banks established in Vila there was no firm strategy raise taxes. One project called for opening the country to international maritime registration under Vanuatu's flag.

[16] In February 1984, President Ati George Sokomanu resigned, claiming that the constitution did not adequately protect the head of state or his ministers, or guarantee 'coherent management'. However, he later agreed to participate in the March 1984 elections, and was re-elected.

[17] The second Vanuatu Development Plan (1987-1991) to ensure balanced regional and rural development, to take better advantage of the country's natural resources, to provide for the faster development of human resources

LAND USE

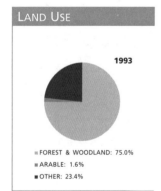

1993

- FOREST & WOODLAND: 75.0%
- ARABLE: 1.6%
- OTHER: 23.4%

and to promote development of the private sector. The plan suffered a serious set-back in February 1987, with Hurricane Ulna, which caused an estimated $36 million damage and affected about 34 per cent of the population.

[18] In the December 1987 elections, Lini won over Barak Sope, who attempted an unsuccessful challenge for the party leadership. Barak Sope accepted the cabinet post of minister of tourism and immigration, but in May 1988 he was relieved of his responsibilities by Lini, due to violent demonstrations by his followers. Finally, Sope split from the ruling party and founded his own political group, the Melanesian Progressive Party.

[19] In 1988, former president Sokomau, together with Barak Sope, tried unsuccessfully to oust Prime Minister Walter Lini. They were both arrested and imprisoned. Fred Timakata was appointed president.

[20] On August 7 1991, the ruling party of Vanuatu voted in favor of deposing Walter Lini as Prime Minister. The minister of foreign affairs, Donald Kalpokas, was appointed to this post.

[21] In October, Walter Lini founded the United National Party. The Union of Moderate Parties, led by Maxime Carlot Korman, won the elections held on December 2.

[22] In January 1992, Carlot Korman formed a coalition with the UNP.

Lini's sister Hilda was named minister of health, occupying the cabinet position to which the UNP - as a member of the coalition - was entitled. At this time, French was re-established as an official language. Minister of Finance Willy Jimmy's economic plan established a series of priorities, including exports, foreign investment, agrarian reform and free primary education.

[23] Carlot Korman launched a program to diversify agriculture in 1993, a year after Hurricane Betsy had destroyed 30 per cent of the harvest. In 1994 the Government decided to cut 200 of the 4,800 public sector posts. They justified this by pointing to the large increase since 1985, when there had been only 3,300.

[24] On the international front, Vanuatu was the only country of the South Pacific Forum which did not join this organization's protests against French nuclear tests in Polynesia, in September 1995.

[25] Carlot Korman was forced to resign in February 1996 and Serge Vohor became Prime Minister. In August 1996, the Vanuatu Mobile Force (VMF), a paramilitary group, declared a strike over unpaid wages. Three months later, its officers were arrested by the police and freed once they had sworn their loyalty.

[26] In 1997, against a background of political instability, caused partly by constant rumors of a new VMF uprising, the Asian Development Bank agreed a $14 million loan for the economic reform program brought in by the Government.

[27] In early 1998, the Court of Appeal confirmed the dissolution of Parliament called for by President Jean-Marie Leye.

[28] In early 1998, the Court of Appeals confirmed the dissolution of the Parliament of the Republic, requested by President Jean-Marie Leye. In the ensuing elections, held in March, the Vanua'aku Unity Front (UF) won 18 of the 52 seats in play, followed by the Union of Moderate Parties (UMP), with 12 and the United National Party (UNP) with 11. The other seats were distributed amongst various minor groups. Donald Kalpokas, former vice president and leader of the UF, formed an unstable alliance with the UNP, which collapsed a few months later and once again formed a cabinet with the UMP.

[29] Growing corruption in

government spheres was cited by Ombudsman Marie-Noelle Ferrieux-Patterson, who presented reports denouncing the diversion of funds meant for cyclone victim aid, the issuing of false passports and the misappropriation of monies from pensions funds. These accusations provoked street demonstrations and the Government declared a state of emergency to bring the disturbances under control.

[30] The Government was unable to stabilize the situation and in November 1999 Barak Sopé, of the Melanesian Progressive Party, was asked to form a new cabinet. ∎

PROFILE

ENVIRONMENT

Vanuatu is a Melanesian archipelago of volcanic origin, comprising more than 70 islands and islets many of them uninhabited. It stretches for 800 km, in a north-south direction in the South Pacific about 1,200 km east of Australia. Major islands are: Espiritu Santo, Malekula, Epi, Pentecost, Aoba, Maewa, Paama, Ambrym, Efate, Erromango, Tanna and Aneityum. Active volcanoes are found in Tanna, Ambrym and Lopevi and the area is subject to earthquakes. The land is mountainous and covered with dense tropical forests. The climate is tropical with heavy rainfall, moderated by the influence of the ocean. The subsoil of Efate is rich in manganese and the soil is suitable for farming. Fishing is a traditional economic activity. The land tenure system has contributed to general soil depletion (deforestation, erosion). Rising sea levels - a 20 cm increase in Vanuatu's tides has been estimated for the next four decades - will affect both inhabited and uninhabited coastal areas. There is also a risk that salt water (from rising tides) will seep into ground water, threatening water supplies

SOCIETY

Peoples: Most people are Melanesian (98 per cent), with 1 per cent European (British and French) and smaller groups from Vietnam, China and other Pacific islands.
Religions: Mainly Christian (77 per cent).
Languages: Bislama, English and French are official. Other Melanesian languages are also spoken.
Political Parties: Union of Moderate Parties; National United Party; People's Democratic Party; Unity Front; Tan Union, Frei Melanesio and Na Griamel. Social Organizations: Vanuatu Trade Union Congress (VTUC).

THE STATE

Official Name: Ripablik blong Vanuatu. République de Vanuatu, Republic of Vanuatu.
Capital: Vila, on Efate Island, 30,000 people (1992).
Other cities: Luganville (Santo) 6,900 people; Port Olry 884; Isangel 752 (1989).
Administrative Divisions: 11 Government Regions, 2 Municipalities.
Government: John Bernard Bani, President since March 1999; Barak Sopé, Prime Minister since November 1999. The unicameral Representative Assembly is made up of 46 representatives elected every 4 years.
National Holiday: July 30, Independence Day (1980).

Venezuela

Venezuela

Population: 23,706,000 (1999)
Area: 912,050 SQ KM
Capital: Caracas
Currency: Bolívar
Language: Spanish

Cumanagotos, Tamaques, Maquiritares, Arecunas, and other Carib groups inhabited the northern tip of South America when the Spanish arrived on these shores in 1498. Local buildings, constructed on poles, reminded the Spaniards of the appearance of Venice, so they named the country Venezuela.

[2] During the colonial period, Venezuela was organized as a Captaincy General of the Viceroyalty of New Granada, and in the 18th century it became the most important farming colony, producing mainly cocoa. A local aristocracy of *mantuanos* developed, a landowning class of European extraction, who used African slave labor on their plantations. The *pardos* (blacks) who constitute the overwhelming majority of the population are descended from the slaves.

[3] Two of the greatest leaders of the Latin American independence movement were born in the Captaincy: Francisco de Miranda and Simón Bolívar. On April 19 1810, the wars of independence broke out after the constitution of a *Cabildo* or Assembly. Miranda became the commander of the army, envisaging a vast American Confederacy to be known as Colombia, which would crown an Inca emperor. His dreams did not however come to fruition as he was captured by the Spaniards in 1811 and later died in prison.

[4] Bolívar took up Miranda's project for American liberation and was backed, in principle, by the mantuano oligarchy. In a swift campaign (1812-13) he took over the country, and was able to install a government in Caracas. His plans for independence did not include changes in social structure, and he

was not supported by the masses who lived in the plains (*llaneros*), most of whom were mulattos living under the severe repression of white creoles whom they hated. Their liberation movement was led by the Spanish loyalist General José Tomás Boves, who defeated Bolívar in 1814. Boves abolished slavery and redistributed the land among the people.

[5] Having lost the first republic, Bolívar went into exile, working closely with the Haitian President, Alexandre Sabés Petión, who helped him add a social dimension to his American revolutionary project. Bolívar returned to Venezuela and, championing popular demands, he won mass support.

[6] Accompanied by other important military leaders like

Antonio José de Sucre, Mariño, José A Páez and Arismendi, he carried out successful military campaigns in the northern half of the continent. He subsequently founded Bolivia in what had hitherto been known as 'Upperu'.

[7] In 1819, the Angostura Congress created the new republic of 'Gran Colombia', uniting Colombia, Ecuador, Panama and Venezuela. In 1830, after Bolívar's death, General José Antonio Páez declared Venezuela's secession from Gran Colombia, establishing it as an independent nation.

[8] For decades, Venezuelan politics revolved around the *caudillo* or leader, Páez. His political successor, Antonio Guzmán Blanco, was determined to modernize Venezuela. He succeeded to a certain extent, introducing new technology, new means of communication, and reforming the country's legal code.

[9] Juan Vicente Gómez took power in 1908 ruling for 17 years, and his government made an attempt to eliminate the caudillo system. He gave free access to the multinational oil companies, which

set up oil extracting operations primarily on the Lake Maracaibo oil fields.

[10] In 1935 Gómez' former aide, General Eleazar López Contreras, took office. He was succeeded in 1941 by General Isaías Medina Angarita, who laid the foundations for greater political activity by legalizing the Democratic Action Party (AD).

[11] It was a long time before majority demands were met, however, and this situation was aggravated by the unrest within the army. A civilian-military movement took power, led by Rómulo Betancourt, the leader of AD, and General Marcos Pérez Jiménez, and they held the country's first free elections in 1947. The writer Rómulo Gallegos of the AD was elected President only to be overthrown in 1948 by yet another military coup, installing the harsh dictatorship of Marcos Pérez Jiménez.

[12] Ten years later, in January 1958, Pérez Jiménez was overthrown by a popular revolt and he fled the country. Venezuela then entered a stable democratic period under a coalition government formed by Democratic Action, COPEI (the Christian Democrats) and the Republican Democratic Union (URD). This stability was largely achieved because of massive oil revenues, improved relations with the US, and expanded political rights. Unfortunately, the ensuing economic growth brought little change to the lives of the poor majority. Popular discontent resulted in guerrilla warfare led by the Communist Party, the Movement of the Revolutionary Left (which split from AD), and other groups.

[13] In 1960, Venezuela sponsored the formation of the Organization of Petroleum Exporting Countries (OPEC). Sixteen years later, during the presidency of social democrat Carlos Andrés Pérez, Venezuelan reserves of oil and iron were nationalized. Pérez also supported the creation of the Latin American Economic System (SELA) and argued in favor of a New International Economic Order.

[14] At this time, Venezuela was the world's third largest oil exporter and received its highest prices during the governments of Pérez and Christian Democrat Luis Herrera Campins. It had the highest per

WORKERS

1995
UNEMPLOYMENT: 10.3%

% OF LABOUR FORCE **1998**

■ FEMALE: 34%   ■ MALE: 66%
1990

■ SERVICES: 60.7%
■ INDUSTRY: 27.3%
■ AGRICULTURE: 12.0%

LAND USE

DEFORESTATION: 1.1% annual (1990/95)
IRRIGATED: 5.9% of arable (1993)

1993

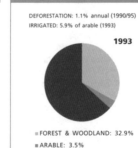

■ FOREST & WOODLAND: 32.9%
■ ARABLE: 3.5%
■ OTHER: 63.5%

PUBLIC EXPENDITURE

DEFENCE EXPENDITURE (% of goverment exp.)	**9.8%**	(1997)
MILITARY EXPENDITURE (% of health & education)	**33%**	(1990/91)

MATERNAL MORTALITY 1990-98
Per 100,000 live births
65

LITERACY 1995
91%

FOOD DEPENDENCY
1970 **10%**
1997 **16%**

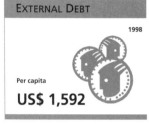

EXTERNAL DEBT 1998
Per capita
US$ 1,592

capita income in Latin America, but the Government was unable to manage the enormous amounts of money coming into the country. Huge state-run companies were created for the manufacture of iron ore, aluminum, cement, and for hydroelectric power, while most private companies were being subsidized. The Venezuelan state obtained 95 per cent of the country's revenues from oil exports and was by far its largest business owner.

¹⁵ Long-standing border disputes between Venezuela and its neighbors flared up again in 1981 and 1982. Disputes with Colombia over the Guajira peninsula, and with Guyana over the Essequibo region, continued. Meanwhile, after holding many conferences to discuss the issue of national waters, Venezuela established its territorial rights over huge areas of the Caribbean sea.

¹⁶ In 1982, a sharp decrease in oil revenues, foreign debt, and a flight of private capital abroad, forced the Government to take control of exchange rates and foreign trade. The foreign debt grew while inflation, unemployment, and housing shortages started to rise, and critical poverty rose.

¹⁷ Charges of government corruption contributed to the victory of the AD's Jaime Lusinchi in the December 1983 elections where he gained 56 per cent of the vote, defeating COPEI's Rafael Caldera.

¹⁸ The population continued to support Lusinchi for some time, but when the June 1983 economic collapse proved impossible to halt, Venezuela had to suspend $5 billion in service payments on its $37 billion debt, and the ensuing difficulties resulted in a drop in his popularity.

¹⁹ In response to the economic problems, Lusinchi's policy comprised an austerity plan which gave meagre results, and a flawed 'social pact' between employers and unions and, towards the end of his term, increasing state control over the economy.

²⁰ In its foreign relations, Venezuela resumed its active role in the Contadora Group, but dealt with the IMF and US in a 'traditional' way. In January 1986, Venezuela rescheduled nearly two thirds of its foreign debt over ten years, but falling oil prices forced the Government to renegotiate a year later. Before leaving office, Lusinchi announced a moratorium to obtain a further rescheduling.

²¹ The AD's candidate for the December 1988 elections was former president Carlos Andrés Pérez. Backed by the Confederation of Venezuelan Workers (CTV), he took 54.5 per cent of the vote, and Eduardo Fernández, the COPEI candidate, took 41.7 per cent.

²² Social tension increased and 25 days later the most underprivileged sectors responded with a wave of riots and looting. Police repression left more than 1,000 dead (246 according to the government), and 2,000 wounded or jailed.

²³ The populist tone was dropped, and IMF-backed economic restructuring measures were initiated. In December 1989, these policies were blamed for abstention rates of nearly 70 per cent and broad gains by the Christian Democrats and left-wing parties, when Venezuelans elected their 20 state governors and 369 mayors for the first time.

²⁴ Ten AD governors were elected, and COPEI had four, with the AD losing seats in many of its traditional strongholds. Most remarkable were the left-wing victories in three states: in Bolívar, the trade union leader Andrés Velázquez of the Popular Cause party was elected; in Aragua, the Movement Toward Socialism (MAS) won; and Anzoátegui elected a leader of the People's Electoral Movement (MEP).

²⁵ In the early 1990s, Venezuela's indigenous population totaled around 200,000 - approximately one per cent of the population, but their future survival was threatened. Despite the fact that the Government has clearly recognized Yanomami land rights, there has not been adequate protection of the indigenous population. They suffer persecution from landowners, farmers and government officials, while Brazilian miners continue to invade their land prospecting for gold within Venezuelan territory.

²⁶ The immigration rate has fallen, but between 1950 and 1980 it was very high. Most of the present immigrants are from Colombia and there are smaller numbers of Ecuadorans, Peruvians, and Dominicans.

²⁷ Early in 1992, the popularity of the Pérez Government was at its lowest, with the AD party distancing itself from imposing further economic measures. Congress exercised its controlling function by investigating crimes, but due to the corruption and inefficiency of the Judiciary these investigations very rarely led to prosecutions.

²⁸ On February 4 1992, a group of colonels staged a coup against the President. The group was led by Francisco Arias and while the attempt failed, it re-emphasized the fact that administrative corruption and the economic crisis were the causes of instability. Arias and parachute commander Hugo Chavez, both belonging to the Bolívar-200 Military Movement, were arrested. This coup attempt caused several dozen civilian and military casualties.

PROFILE

ENVIRONMENT

The country comprises three main regions. In the north and west, the Andes and other mountain chains, and high mountains to the south. The central Orinoco Plains are a livestock farming area. In the southeast, highlands of ancient rock and sandstone extend to the borders with Brazil and Guyana, forming Venezuelan Guyana. It is a sparsely inhabited area with thick forests, savannas, rivers, and some peculiar features: the 'tepuyes' or plateau mountains, and the rare Sarisarinama depths. Most of the population lives in the hilly north. The oil-rich Maracaibo lowlands and Gulf of Paria are on the coast. The country produces oil, iron ore, manganese, bauxite, tungsten and chrome, gold and diamonds. Among the country's most important environmental problems are deforestation and the degradation of the soil. In addition, the lack of sewage treatment facilities in the main urban and industrial centers has increased pollution in the country's rivers and the Caribbean Sea.

SOCIETY

Peoples: Venezuelans come from the integration of indigenous peoples, Afro-Caribbeans and European settlers. Today, indigenous peoples and Afro-Caribbeans each account for less than 7 per cent of the population. In recent times, Venezuela has received more immigrants than any other South American country.
Religions: Mainly Catholic, 92.7 per cent.
Languages: Spanish, official and predominant; 31 native languages are spoken.
Political Parties: Patriotic Pole, led by Hugo Chávez. Democratic Action (AD), member of the Socialist International; the Social Christian Party (COPEI), a member of the Christian Democrat International; the Movement Toward Socialism (MAS), founded in 1970; Radical Cause; Convergence, created in 1993 by Christian Democratic splinter groups; the People's Electoral Movement (MEP); the Venezuelan Communist Party (PCV); the New Democratic Generation, linked to the Liberal International; Intergration, Representation, New Hope (IRENE), founded in 1997 by independent mayor of Chacao, Irene Saez.
Social Organizations: The Venezuelan Confederation of Workers (CTV) is the main trade union, and is controlled by AD. There are other trade unions which are clearly linked to political parties.

THE STATE

Official Name: República Bolivariana de Venezuela.
Administrative divisions: 21 states with partial autonomy (including the Federal District), 2 Federal territories.
Capital: Caracas 3,400,000 people (1996).
Other cities: Maracaibo 1,249,670 people; Valencia 1,034,033 people; Barquisimeto 692,600 people; Guyana City 523,580 people (1990).
Government: Hugo Rafael Chávez Frías, President since February 1999, re-elected August 2000. Presidential system, Congress with Chamber of Deputies and Senate (201 and 49 members respectively).
National Holiday: July 5, Independence Day (1811).
Armed Forces: 79,000, including 18,000 conscripts (1997).
Other: Cooperation Army, 23,000.

FOREIGN TRADE

Millions US$ 1998

IMPORTS

19,083

EXPORTS

19,030

29   On the day of the attempted coup, the Venezuelan President suspended all constitutional rights. This emergency measure - ratified by Congress - banned meetings, limited the freedom of press and movement and made it possible to arrest citizens without a warrant. An agreement was reached with the teachers' trade unions, putting an end to a fortnight of strikes and police repression of students and teachers.

30   In early April, a 'National Civic Strike' was organized by students, labor unions and other organizations, to put pressure on the President to resign. The strike's organizers also demanded the release of the military officers who had been arrested for participating in the February 4 coup attempt.

31   While demonstrations against Pérez continued to increase throughout the country, AD and COPEI reached an agreement in late May to form an alliance which they believed would reinforce the stability of Venezuela's democratic system.

32   Another coup attempt took place on November 27 1992. The air force played a key role in controlling the rebels. The ruling party only won in 7 of the 22 states where elections for governors, mayors, regional legislative assemblies and municipal councils were held.

33   President Pérez was suspended from office on May 21 1993, charged with the misappropriation of funds. He was provisionally replaced by Ramón Velázquez.

34   Rafael Caldera, President between 1969 and 1974 from the Social Christian Party, won the general elections on December 5 1993. He was supported by a wide range of sectors and political parties, with the backing of Convergencia and MAS being the most important factors in his success. Abstention reached 40 per cent as only around 5 million voted.

35   According to official statistics, the annual rate of inflation reached nearly 40 per cent in 1993 and almost half of the population was living below the poverty line.

36   Another source of social unrest was the repeated violation of human rights, both of ethnic minorities and of inmates in several prisons. On August 21 the murder of 16 Yanomami close to the Brazilian border at the hands of the *garimpeiros* - Brazilian gold prospectors - was reported. Several members of the Yupca people were murdered by landowners in the state of Zulia.

37   The repression of a riot in a Maracaibo jail by the security forces caused 122 deaths on January 3 1994. Built to accommodate 1,500, the prison housed 2,500 inmates.

38   Because of his age - over 75 - former president Carlos Andrés Pérez was sentenced to house arrest. In his opulent residence overlooking Caracas, Pérez concluded his sentence in September 1996 and returned to the political scene, affirming he would be president once more. During his 'confinement', Pérez was accused of having traveled abroad.

39   At the end of the 1980s, Caracas had become one of Latin America's most violent cities. A feeling of insecurity prevailed as the number of murders rose. In 1995 it was estimated that 10 per cent of Caracas residents carried a weapon.

40   The economic crisis worsened after 1994. The banks' collapse began in February 1993 with the fall of the Banco Latino, the country's second commercial bank. In August 1995, 18 out of the 41 private banks had been investigated and 70 per cent of the deposits were being managed by the Government.

41   President Caldera suspended constitutional guarantees regarding real estate, private property and business. He also restricted trips abroad, meetings and the immunity against arbitrary arrests. Despite Congress' vote to reinstate these rights, the President restricted them once more to prevent speculation and capital flight.

42   In April 1996, Caldera announced new liberalizing economic measures that enabled him to receive a $1.4 billion loan from the IMF, suspended since July 1995.

43   In 1997 the divisions both between and within the political parties interrupted parliamentary analysis of the 'Agenda Venezuela' reform project promoted by the government. This was to include privatization of the electricity, aluminium and iron industries; reform of the judicial system and the reorganization of public finances. With less than 10 per cent of the seats, Caldera's party had to seek alliances in various sectors in order to get the reforms approved. Democratic Action demanded a greater economic liberalization in return for its support.

44   On December 6 1998, the leader of the 1992 coup attempts, Hugo Chávez, was elected constitutional president with 56.5 per cent of the vote. In his inaugural speech, Chávez announced he would replace what he described as a 'dead' constitution through a 'peaceful revolution' to fight poverty and restructure foreign debt, standing at more than $23 billion. In order to do this there would be a National Constituent Assembly (NCA) which would draw up a new constitution in six months.

45   In early 1999, Chávez publicized his 'peaceful revolution' through his diplomatic corps and through a television program which received and directly 'resolved' the concerns of the public. On July 25, in elections for the NCA, 75 per cent of the population voted for the Chavez's Patriotic Pole, giving it the absolute majority in the body.

46   In September, the country hosted the second meeting between Colombia's National Liberation Army (ELN) and the Colombian governmental authorities. Chávez, who started to play an important role in the Colombian conflict turned down a US request to use his air bases to 'combat drug trafficking' there. It was widely believed the US aimed to invade Colombia and suppress insurgent groups.

47   In a referendum on December 15, 70 per cent of the Venezuelans who turned out to vote - half the electoral roll - approved a new constitution which named the country the 'Bolivarian Republic of Venezuela' and dissolved Congress. The high abstention rate was due, amongst other factors, to floods which plagued the country and killed 50,000 people.

48   On January 30 2000, the National Constituent Assembly was dissolved after new presidential and parliamentary elections were slated for May 28. Claudio Fermin (National Meeting) and Francisco Arias (independent) presented candidacies on a 'get Chávez out' ticket.

49   On March 20, Venezuela's energy minister, Ali Rodríguez, announced from Kuwait that the countries of the Organization of Petroleum Exporting Countries (OPEC) would increase daily production in order to reduce prices which had tripled in the previous year.

50   In August, Chávez was re-elected as President. ∎

Vietnam

Viêt-nam

Population: 78,705,000 (1999)
Area: 331,690 SQ KM
Capital: Hanoi
Currency: Dong
Language: Vietnamese

The Vietnamese nation was established after centuries of struggle against more powerful peoples. In the ninth century, they defeated the Chinese Han dynasty, ending nearly a thousand years of subjugation. In the 11th and 12th centuries, the Vietnamese succeeded in fighting off the Chams. They repulsed Genghis Khan, his Mongol hordes, and later his grandson Kublai Khan, when these were conquering the Asian world in the 18th century. In the 15th and 18th centuries the Vietnamese were victorious over the Ming and Ching Chinese dynasties, and in the 18th century they drove back the Khmers.

[2] In 1860, the French began to occupy Indochina, meeting with spontaneous, disorganized and badly armed resistance which, nonetheless, took them three decades to overcome. By 1900 the French had consolidated their domination over the region. Vietnam was divided into three parts: Tonkin in the north, Annam in the center and Cochinchina in the south. To eliminate Chinese cultural influence, the French taught Quoc Ngu, a Romanized writing script of the Vietnamese language. The French did not intend to help Vietnam's nationalists in the renewal and dissemination of national culture, but this system of notation facilitated reading and lowered printing costs when compared with the formerly used Chinese ideograms.

[3] In the 1920s, the first nationalist organizations were created. Marxist-Leninist parties appeared in different parts of Vietnam in 1929, achieving unity as the Indochina Communist Party the following year. This was founded by a patriot called Nguyen Ai Quoc,

who adopted the name Ho Chi Minh. The Party later decided that it would be more effective if it was split into three different national sections, for Cambodia, Laos and Vietnam respectively. The latter was known as the Workers' Party until

its 4th Congress in 1976, when it became the Communist Party of Vietnam once again.

[4] During World War II, the country was occupied by Japan. Vietnam's communists organized the resistance from the start, cooperating with the allies but staying true to their intent to defeat colonialism. In 1941, Ho Chi Minh founded the Viet Minh or League for the Independence of Viet Nam, conceived as a broad unity front to include workers, peasants, the petit-bourgeoisie and the nationalist bourgeoisie. By the

time of the Japanese surrender, the Viet Minh army had become a powerful force with widespread popular support in the northern part of the country. On August 18 1945, Ho Chi Minh launched a general insurrection in the north. Within two weeks the revolutionary forces took control of the entire country, and an independent republic was declared. Emperor Bao Dao abdicated and offered to cooperate in advising the new regime.

[5] Negotiations between the French - who seized the southern part known as Cochinchina - and Ho Chi Minh led to an agreement in March 1946 that appeared to promise a peaceful solution. Under the agreement France would recognize the Viet Minh government and give Vietnam the status of a free state within the French Union. However, the French aimed to re-establish colonial rule, while Hanoi wanted total independence. Georges-Thierry d'Angelieu, the High Commissioner for Indochina, proclaimed Cochinchina an autonomous republic in June 1946. The French reunited Cochinchina with the rest of Vietnam in 1949 and proclaimed the Associated State of Vietnam, appointing former emperor Bao Dao as chief of state. The Viet Minh did not surrender and waged an increasingly successful guerrilla war, aided after 1949 by the new Communist Government of China. After nine years of fighting, the Vietnamese were finally victorious when they captured the garrison of Dien Bien Phu, in the north, on May 7 1954.

[6] The 1954 Geneva Agreements stipulated the withdrawal of the French and directed the Vietnamese to hold general elections in 1956. Viet Minh troops were to withdraw north of the 17th parallel. The United States set up the Ngo Dinh Diem regime in Saigon (present-day Ho Chi Minh City), dividing the country and violating the Geneva agreements, as elections were prevented. In 1960, the organizations hostile to Diem's regime (democratic, socialist, nationalist and Marxist forces) became the National Liberation Front, led by lawyer Nguyen Huu Tho. The 'second resistance' was then launched, this time against the successive military governments based in Saigon and above all

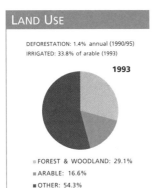

WORKERS

% OF LABOUR FORCE   **1998**

- FEMALE: 49%   - MALE: 51%

1990

- SERVICES: 14.7%
- INDUSTRY: 14.0%
- AGRICULTURE: 71.3%

LAND USE

DEFORESTATION: 1.4% annual (1990/95)
IRRIGATED: 33.8% of arable (1993)

1993

- FOREST & WOODLAND: 29.1%
- ARABLE: 16.6%
- OTHER: 54.3%

PUBLIC EXPENDITURE

DEFENCE EXPENDITURE
(% of goverment exp.)   **11.1%**
(1997)

MATERNAL MORTALITY 1990-98

Per 100,000 live births

160

LITERACY 1995

91%

EXTERNAL DEBT 1998

Per capita

US$ 288

FOREIGN TRADE

Millions US$ 1997

IMPORTS

13,625

EXPORTS

11,480

against the United States, the true supporter, arms-supplier and policy-maker. US aid was initially limited to a handful of advisors. Then troops were sent to bolster the Diem regime - a process that escalated until, by 1969, 580,000 US troops were in Vietnam. A larger tonnage of bombs was dropped in Vietnam than during the whole of World War II, and terrible chemical and biological weapons were used.

[7] The US spent $150 billion in Vietnam, destroyed 70 per cent of the northern villages and left 10 million hectares of productive land barren. Despite their efforts, Saigon was finally liberated by the Viet Cong on April 30 1975. On July 2 1976, Vietnam was reunited under the name of the Socialist Republic of Vietnam.

[8] Since then Vietnam has not enjoyed stable peace. In January 1979, it went to war against Pol Pot's regime in Cambodia. Pol Pot had claimed vast portions of Vietnamese territory. No sooner had the Cambodian regime been overthrown, than China invaded Vietnam on its northern border as a punitive measure. China, in the meantime, had been a staunch ally of the ousted Cambodian regime. Subsequent clashes along the border in 1980 underscored the military superiority of the Vietnamese, but the border between the two countries remained unchanged.

[9] Vietnam considered Cambodia's union with the other Indochinese states to be essential for its security. Vietnam's support of the Heng Samrin Government against the Khmer Rouge, Prince Sihanouk, and the National Liberation Front entailed costly military efforts and a drain on Vietnam's resources, particularly in terms of food, which was already scarce. China launched a brief but fierce punitive invasion along the Sino-Vietnamese border in early 1979 in response to Vietnamese actions in Cambodia. During the month-long war the Chinese destroyed major Vietnamese towns and inflicted heavy damage in the frontier zone, but also suffered heavy casualties from the Vietnamese defenders. Also, from 1978 to 1981, Vietnam suffered floods, typhoons and droughts.

[10] After 1981, Vietnam faced active hostility from the Reagan administration in the US, which stopped grain shipments provided by an American charity and blocked a Vietnamese aid program organized by the United Nations Development Program (UNDP).

[11] In April 1985, several political prisoners were freed, and diplomatic ties with ASEAN countries and the United States were intensified in an effort to reach negotiated settlements for Indochina. Arrangements were made to cooperate with the US to search for the corpses of missing soldiers as well as to allow people loyal to the former government to leave the country, and to permit the exit of children of US servicemen.

[12] Le Duan, Secretary-General of the Communist Party of Vietnam since 1969 and a close collaborator of Ho Chi Minh, died on July 11 1986. The Congress designated 71 year-old Nguyen Van Linh, a former Viet Cong strategist, as the new Secretary-General.

[13] Toward the end of 1988, the Government adopted austerity measures to combat inflation, including a marked devaluation of the *dong* (national currency) against the dollar. In the process, many businesses were forced to close down and the already high unemployment rate reached almost 30 per cent, while lack of food led to popular protests.

[14] The political changes in Eastern Europe at the end of the 1980s were not well-received by Vietnamese communists since these had local repercussions, specifically growing demands for a multiparty political system. In the absence of such a system, dissenting voices sought expression within the Vietnamese Communist Party (VCP) itself. Some sectors of the Party demanded change toward a multiparty, parliamentary political system.

[15] In August, the Central Committee of the VCP accused the West of trying to destroy the socialist world. Nguyen Van Linh urged his fellow-citizens to reject bourgeois liberalization, multiparty politics and opposition parties, whose aims were to make them renounce socialism. Even so, the participation of non-communist candidates was authorized in the 1989 National Assembly elections, and a year later, the Government authorized the formation of the Vietnam Veterans Association. However, this liberalization was accompanied by a reaffirmation of the dominant role of the VCP, with the arrest of a number of campaigners for multiparty politics, and the dismissal of 18,000 public employees accused of corruption.

[16] During the 1980s, 'illegal emigration' - the flight of Vietnamese toward neighboring countries - continued. The reluctance of Western countries to receive them has indefinitely prolonged their stays in overpopulated refugee centers. This was especially true in Hong Kong; the British Government began deporting them from there in December 1989, though this operation was later suspended because of international pressure.

PROFILE

ENVIRONMENT

A long and narrow country covering the eastern portion of Indochina along the Gulf of Tongkin and the South China Sea. The monsoon influenced climate is hot and rainy. Rainforests predominate and there is a well-supplied river system. The northern region is comparatively higher. There are two river deltas: the Song Koi in the north, and the Mekong in the south. Most of the population are farmers, and rice is the main crop. The north is rich in anthracite, lignite, coal, iron ore, manganese, bauxite and titanium. Textile manufacture, food products and mining are the major economic activities. The felling of trees for domestic use (firewood) and construction have contributed to deforestation. However, the most significant losses - particularly in the northern part of the country - are a result of the Vietnam War, specifically from the use of such chemical defoliants like 'Agent Orange'. Vietnamese Government policy - started after 1975 and reaching its peak in the mid-1980s - that moved millions of former North Vietnamese to what was thought to be the relatively underpopulated central highlands took a heavy toll on the environment, including wide-scale deforestation on the highlands.

SOCIETY

Peoples: Most are native Vietnamese. Mountain groups of different ethnic origins from southern Asia - Tho, Hoa, Tai, Khmer, Muong, Nung - and descendants of the Chinese form the rest of the population.
Religions: Mainly Buddhist; traditional religions. There are some 2 million Catholics and 3 million followers of the Hoa-Hao and Cao-Dai sects.
Languages: Vietnamese (official) and languages of the ethnic minorities.
Political Parties: The Vietnamese Communist Party (Dan Cong San Vietnam), according to the constitution 'the leading organization of society', founded by Ho Chi Minh in 1931; the Democratic Party and the Socialist Party of Vietnam, founded respectively in 1944 and 1946, organized intellectuals and the national bourgeoisie for the anti-colonialist struggle.
Social Organizations: The Federation of Unions of Vietnam (Tong Cong Doan Vietnam), founded in 1946, is the only union confederation and a WFTU member; the Vietnamese Women's Union, founded in 1930.

THE STATE

Official Name: Nu'ó'c Công Hòa Xã' Hôi Chu' Nghĩ'a Viêt Nam.
Administrative Divisions: 39 Provinces, including the urban areas of Hanoi, Haiphong and Ho Chi Minh.
Capital: Hanoi (Hanoi), 3,057,000 people (est 1997).
Other cities: Ho Chi Minh City (formerly Saigon), 3,555,000 people (1995); Haiphong 1,573,000; Da-Nang 381,410 (1993).
Government: Tran Duc Luong, President and Head of State, elected in September 1997. Phan Van Khai, Prime Minister and Head of Government, elected in September 1997. The National Assembly is made up of 496 members elected by universal suffrage; it elects the members of the Council of State. The Executive Power is exercised by a Council of Ministers.
National Holiday: September 2, Independence Day (1945).
Armed Forces: 572,000 troops (1995).
Other: 5,000,000 (Urban Defense Units, Rural Defense Units).

17   The 8th VCP Congress held in June 1991, agreed to continue the process of building socialism, a path considered to be 'the only correct choice'. Van Linh was replaced as the party's general secretary by Du Muoi, who continued with the renewal process which had been initiated in 1986 (called *Doi Moi*). Tron My Moa, the first woman member of the country's new leadership, became a member of the 9-member Secretariat of the Central Committee.

18   The VCP confirmed the continuance of a single-party system. The first step toward renewal and reform was a more flexible economic policy - specifically a change to a mixed economy. This implied allowing private enterprise and foreign investment within pre-established parameters.

19   In October 1991, the initiation of negotiations between the four Cambodian factions opened the way for the normalization of Sino-Vietnamese relations.

20   In November 1991, the British Government with the support of the US began the forcible repatriation of 64,000 Vietnamese exiles from refugee camps within Hong Kong, a British dependency.

21   The new constitution approved in April 1992 authorized independent candidates to run for election, but in the July legislative elections 90 per cent of the candidates belonged to the VCP. In September the new Assembly elected General Le Duc Anh president, known ally of Prime Minister Vo Van Kiet. In November, a commission of US senators visited the country to discuss the issue of the missing remains of over 2,000 US military killed in action.

22   At the beginning of the 1990s Vietnam decided to follow the example of its neighbors, the so-called 'Asian tigers'. Privatization and the liberalization of foreign investment led to an 8.3 per cent increase in the GDP in 1992. For 1993 and 1994, 8 and 9 per cent increases respectively were achieved. In the meantime, the volume of exports rose 20 per cent per year since 1991. However, the 'economic takeoff' also brought a number of negative results. Vietnamese workers were among the lowest paid in Asia, while economic growth put growing pressure on the environment, particularly in the cities.

23   As for foreign trade, Vietnam depended primarily on two products: rice and, to a lesser extent, oil. In 1989, Vietnam became the world's third largest exporter of rice, after Thailand and the United States.

24   According to Vietnamese standards, a poor family is one that can not afford 13 kg of rice person each month. A hungry family is one that can not afford 8 kg of rice person each month.

25   The south has been the main beneficiary of the rice production and export boom in the Mekong delta. This has underscored the structural inequality between the two parts of the country. With more than five million inhabitants - almost double the size of Hanoi, the capital city - Ho Chi Minh City (formerly Saigon) is the country's economic capital, adapting itself far better to the new era than the north.

26   This expansion of trade is taking place in what is primarily an agricultural country. Around 57 million of the 70 million Vietnamese depend upon agriculture, the backbone of the economy and of Vietnamese society. As a result, the Government has granted a number of benefits to farmers, such as loans and long-term land leases, tax cuts and the right to inherit up to three hectares of land. However, total private land ownership has not yet been authorized (for instance, farmers enjoy what is called *Land Use Rights*, under which they can sell, transfer or will land).

27   The effects of several decades of war are still evident, especially in the economic structure which was tailored to the demands of war. The devastation remains visible in a large part of the country, as a result of the use of lethal weapons like napalm or Agent Orange, a powerful defoliant. The country's infrastructure, in general - telecommunications, highways and energy production - slowly began to recover as a result of projects financed by the World Bank and Asian Development Bank loans.

28   In 1993, the per capita GDP was among the lowest in Asia. Between $230 and $350 per year, it was roughly equivalent to one-sixth of Thailand's GDP, and one-twentieth of South Korea's. Unemployment and underemployment, taken together, continue to stand at 30 per cent, while the underground economy and contraband are on the increase.

29   The Communist Party continued to oppose political and economic liberalization, and was cautious on economic liberalization, fearing a massive return of emigrants and the ensuing Western influence. However, Prime Minister Vo Van Kiet forced his government officials to learn foreign languages, especially English.

30   Vietnam and the US established formal diplomatic relations in August 1995. President Clinton stated his concern for the 2,200 US soldiers still considered to be lost in action in Southeast Asia.

31   The rapprochement between Hanoi and Washington did not lead to a rush of US firms, although many multinational corporations showed interest in the liberalization of the Vietnamese economy.

32   In September, Tran Duc Luong and Phan Van Khai, were elected as new President and Prime Minister, respectively. Observers said the former would maintain his predecessor's economic policy and 'rejuvenate' the party leadership. In December, the VCP Central Committee decided to replace three of its leading figures. Former president Le Duc Anh and former prime minister Vo Van Kiet went and the civilian Le Kha Phieu was appointed Secretary General, replacing veteran leader Du Muoi.

33   In April 1998, the drought which had affected the southern province since January destroyed some 7,000 hectares of coffee plantations, while a further 40,000 (out of a total of 160,000) were threatened. Vietnam had increased its plantations from 15,000 to 260,000 hectares since the economic liberalization of the 1980s, exporting the product mainly to Europe and the US.

34   The economic crisis which affected the region in 1998 barely touched Vietnamese growth, which fell from 8.8 per cent in 1997 to 6.1per cent this year. But in order to maintain competitive edge as an exporter, the government devalued the currency twice. Direct foreign investment fell 70 per cent in respect to the previous year. In September Vietnam joined as a full member of the Asia Pacific Economic Co-operation (APEC).

35   A typhoon and violent rains in 1998 and the floods in 1999 - the worst in decades - left hundreds dead, with a knock-on effect on the national economy. Several environmental organizations complained the effects of the floods had been worsened due to indiscriminate commercial felling of forests. In a speech to parliament in November this year, Prime Minister Khai stressed that the crisis had been influenced by low consumption demand, increasing stocks of unsold products and the inefficiency of state companies.

36   The VCP demanded the resignation of deputy prime minister Ngo Xuan Loc, and former governor of the central bank, Cao Sy Kiem, was sanctioned; both had been accused of corruption and embezzlement.

37   According to both governments, the signing of a frontier treaty with China in December 1998 opened 'a new era' in relations between the two countries. The agreement ended 8 years of negotiations, leaving the resolution of maritime issues for a later stage.

45   Ousted former deputy prime minister Ngo Xuan Loc returned to the cabinet as the Prime Minister's advisor on manufacture, construction and transport in April 2000. ∎

DEMOGRAPHY

Population: 78,705,000 (1999)
Annual growth: 2.1 % (1975/97)
Estimates for year 2015 (million): 96.6 (1999)
Annual growth to year 2015: 1.3 % (1997/2015)
Urban population: 19.5 % (1997)
Urban Growth: 2.7 % (1980/95)
Children per woman: 2.6 (1998)

HEALTH

Life expectancy at birth: 68 years (1998)
male: 65 years (1998)
female: 70 years (1998)
Maternal mortality: 160 per 100,000 live births (1990-98)
Infant mortality: 31 per 1,000 (1998)
Under-5 child mortality: 42 per 1,000 (1998)
Daily calorie supply: 2,502 per capita (1996)
Safe water: 45 % (1990/98)

EDUCATION

Literacy: 91 % (1995)
male: 95 % (1995)
female: 88 % (1995)
School enrolment:
Primary total: 114 % (1990/96)
male: 106 % (1990/97)
female: 100 % (1990/97)
Secondary:
male: 44 % (1990/96)
female: 41 % (1990/96)
Tertiary: 7 % (1996)

COMMUNICATIONS

4 newspapers (1996), 107 radios (1997), 180 TV sets (1996) and 16 main telephone lines (1996) per 1,000 people
Books: 8 new titles per 100,000 people (1992/94)

ECONOMY

Per capita, GNP: $ 350 (1998)
Annual growth, GNP: 5.8 % (1998)
Annual inflation: 18.5 % (1990/98)
Currency: 11,359.4 dong = $ 1 (1998)
Cereal imports: 697,580 metric tons (1998)
Fertilizer use: 2,773 kg per ha (1997)
Exports: $ 11,480 million (1997)
Imports: $ 13,625 million (1997)
External debt: $ 22,359 million (1998); $ 288 per capita (1998)
Debt service: 8.9 % of exports (1998)
Development aid received: $ 997 million (1997); $ 14.7 per capita (1997); 4.10 % of GNP (1997)

ENERGY

Consumption: 521.0 Kgs of Oil equivalent per capita yearly (1997); -11.0 % imported (1997)

HDI (rank/value): 110/0.664 (1997)

Virgin Is. (US)

Virgin Islands

Population: 102,000 (1999)
Area: 347 SQ KM
Capital: Charlotte Amalie
Currency: US dollar
Language: English

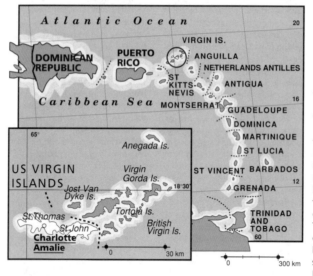

A s is the case in other Caribbean islands, the Virgin Islands were originally inhabited by Carib and Arawak Indians. The only gold on the islands was seen in the ornaments worn by the inhabitants and was of little economic interest. From the time of Columbus' arrival in 1493 onwards, the local population was persecuted and massacred and also was destroyed by the second half of the 16th century.

[2] The western part of the archipelago was claimed by other countries after the departure of the Spaniards. The Netherlands gained control in the 18th century and organized crop cultivation; first of sugar cane and then of cotton. They imported African slave workers as in many other parts of Latin America and the Caribbean. At the height of Dutch colonization, there were 40,000 African slaves on the islands.

[3] During Abraham Lincoln's second presidential term, the United States failed to acquire the islands. But in 1917, after World War 1 when the US wanted to consolidate its presence in the area, $25 million was paid to the Dutch for the islands and the 26,000 African former slaves who inhabited them.

[4] From that time on, the US initiated a series of changes in the territorial administration, ranging from the continuation of the legislation established by the Dutch, to the new law approved in 1969. This instituted the election of a Governor and Vice-Governor, the election of a non-voting Congressional delegate and the right of its inhabitants to vote in American elections. In a 1981 referendum, a proposed Constitution was voted against by 50 per cent of the registered voters. In December 1984, the UN General Assembly reiterated the right of the islands to self-determination, and urged the local population to exercise their right to independence.

[5] The local economy still depended on the US. It largely revolved around an oil refinery owned by US-Ameranda Hess Corporation on the island of St

Croix. The company's influence on local politics was very important, as it had 1,300 permanent and 1,700 temporary employees. The Corporation also supplied all the islands' energy needs. In spite of this, tourism was still the island's main source of income.

[6] A referendum scheduled for November 1989 was to decide the future status of the islands. However, it was not held because in September 1989 the islands were severely damaged by Hurricane Hugo. According to official estimates, 80 per cent of the buildings were destroyed. The disaster caused an outbreak of looting and unrest. Armed bands wandered the streets; some members of the police and National Guard also took part in the pillaging. The US sent more than 1,000 troops to the area, but the disturbances had virtually ceased by the time they arrived. In the words of local people, there was nothing left to steal.

[7] The US Government declared the islands a disaster area and granted $500 million in humanitarian aid. However, damages were estimated at $1 billion.

[8] An aluminum oxide plant, which had been closed in 1985, was purchased in 1989 by an international group trading in raw materials. The plant has a capacity for an annual production of 700,000 metric tons. Shipments to the US and Europe began in 1990.

[9] Alexander A Farrelly, who had governed the islands since 1987, left his post in 1995 and was replaced by Roy L Schneider. In the following elections, in November 1998 Charles Turnbull won with 58.9 per cent of the vote, while Schneider took the remaining 41.1 per cent. In elections for the senate, Turnbull's Democrat Party took 6 seats while the Republicans kept 2 and the pro-region Independent Citizens' Movement took one seat. The independents drew even with the Democrats, holding six seats.

[10] Hurricane Lenny lashed the islands in November 1999 causing four deaths in St Croix and serious damage to buildings and roads. ■

PROFILE

ENVIRONMENT

It comprises the western area of the Virgin Islands, east of Puerto Rico. The territory includes three main islands - St Thomas, St John and St Croix - and approximately 50 uninhabited small islands. The mountainous terrain is of volcanic origin. The climate is tropical, but irregular rainfall makes farming difficult. A small amount of fruit and vegetables are grown in St Croix and St Thomas. Tourism is an important economic activity. There is a large oil refinery in St Croix, supplying the US market.

SOCIETY

Peoples: Most of the population is English-speaking and of African origin with a small Spanish-speaking Puerto Rican minority. 35 to 40 per cent of the inhabitants are from other Caribbean islands; 10 per cent from the US.
Religions: Protestant and Catholic.
Languages: English, official; also Spanish and Creole.
Political Parties: There are local representatives of the US Republican and Democrat parties and an Independent Citizens Movement (ICM).

THE STATE

Official Name: Virgin Islands of the United States.
Capital: Charlotte Amalie 60,000 people (est 1995).
Government: Roy L Schneider, Governor since July 1995. The unicameral legislature is made up of 15 representatives (7 from St Thomas, 7 from St Croix and 1 from St John).
Armed Forces: The US is responsible for the defense of the islands. The naval bases have been under local jurisdiction since 1967, but the US retains the right to occupy them at any moment, as well as to recruit local residents for US armed forces.

DEMOGRAPHY

Population: 102,000 (1999)

COMMUNICATIONS

1,000 **radios** (1997) per 1,000 people

ECONOMY

Fertilizer use: 2,600 kg per ha (1997)

Virgin Is. (British)

British Virgin Islands

Population: 20,000 (1998)
Area: 150 SQ KM
Capital: Road Town
Currency: US dollar
Language: English

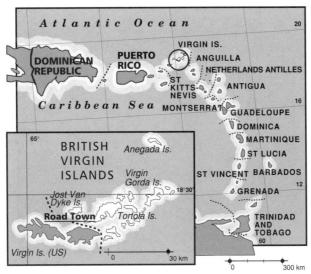

The Virgin Islands, were named by Christopher Columbus in 1493 in honour of St Ursula. At that time the islands were inhabited by Caribs and Arawaks, but by the mid-16th century they had all been exterminated by the Europeans.

[2] In the 18th century, the English gained control of the easternmost islands of the archipelago and, using African slave labor, they began cultivating sugar cane, indigo and cotton. By the mid-18th century, the islands' slave population had reached 7,000, outnumbering the European colonists 6 to 1. Slavery was eventually abolished there in the 1830s.

[3] From 1872 the islands joined the British colony of the Leeward Islands, which were administered under a federal system. This federation was dissolved in July 1956, but the Governor of the Leeward Islands continued to be responsible for the administration of the Virgin Islands until 1960. In that year direct control over the islands passed into the hands of an administrator designated by the British Crown. Unlike the Leeward Islands, the British Virgin Islands did not belong to the East Indies Federation, which existed between 1958 and 1962, preferring to develop links with the American Virgin Islands, under US control.

[4] Constitutional reform required elections to fill the seats of the Legislative Council. They were held in November 1979. Independent candidates won five of the nine seats and the Virgin Islands Party (VIP) won the remaining four. Five years later, the independent candidates only retained one seat; however, by forming an alliance with the United Party (UP), they managed to have one of their members appointed Prime Minister.

[5] The colony has been governed under several constitutions this century, and the ministerial form of government began in 1967 with the first open elections. In 1977 the Constitution was modified, granting greater autonomy and carrying out changes in the electoral system. The responsibility for defense, internal security and foreign affairs remained in the hands of the British-appointed governor.

[6] In the 1980s tourism accounted for 45 per cent of the national income, while fishing was the traditional economic activity. Gravel and sand were important exports, and a 'tax-haven' banking facility has been established.

[7] In August 1986, the British Government dissolved the Legislative Council, calling a new election several days after the opposition presented a vote of no-confidence in the Prime Minister. In September the VIP won 5 of the 9 seats and the UP won 2. Lavity Stott, the VIP leader, was named chief minister.

[8] In March 1988, Chief Minister Omar Hodge resigned under accusations of corruption, and was replaced by Ralph O'Neal. Hodge denied the charges against him, and in March 1989 he created a new party, the Independent People's Movement and in early 1990 was cleared of the charges against him.

[9] In the November elections, the VIP increased its majority to 6 seats, while the IPM obtained 1 seat, and the independents 2. Stott maintained his post as chief minister, and O'Neal was re-elected Prime Minister.

[10] Due to the increase in drug trafficking, and following recommendations by the British Government, legislation was introduced to control the operations of international financial companies. These would need a licence to operate on the islands and their activities would be subject to periodic inspections, as the authorities believed most of the investments were coming from the drug trade.

[11] In October 1991, Peter Alfred Penfold was named Governor.

[12] As a result of tourism in coastal areas, environmental degradation grew, particularly on the coral reefs.

[13] In the legislative elections of February 1995, the VIP took 6 seats, the IPM 3, the Movement of Concerned Citizens (CCM) took 2, as did the UP. On May 15 1995, following the death of H Lavity Stott, Ralph O'Neal took over as chief minister. In June 1995, David Mackilligin was appointed Governor.

[14] In 1995, unemployment affected three per cent of the population, growth reached four per cent and per capita annual income stood at $10,200.

[15] In July 1997, the Government approved a three-year development plan, which included a $2 million plan to extend the port and the construction of two tourist centers.

[16] The British Crown appointed Frank Savage governor in 1998, and in the May 1999 elections the VIP took 8 seats with 38 per cent of the vote. The National Democratic Party took 5 with 36.9 per cent of the vote, while the remainder went to the Concerned Citizens' Movement (4 per cent). Independent candidates took 13.4 per cent of the vote, but none had enough support to get into the Legislative Council. ∎

PROFILE

ENVIRONMENT

The eastern portion of the Virgin Islands comprises 36 islands and reefs, 16 of which are inhabited. The larger ones are Tortola, Anegada, Virgin Gorda and Jost Van Dyke, which hold most of the population. The islands' rolling terrain is of volcanic origin. Agricultural production is limited to fruit and vegetables as a result of erratic rainfall. The major economic activities are fishing and tourism. The coral reefs are threatened by tourist activities.

SOCIETY

Peoples: Most are descendants of African slaves. There is also a small British minority. 86 per cent of the population are concentrated on Tortola Island, 9 per cent live on Virgin Gorda, 3 per cent on Anegada and 2 per cent on Jost Van Dyke. **Religions:** Mainly Protestant (45 per cent Methodist, 21 per cent Anglican, 7 per cent Church of God, 5 per cent Seventh-Day Adventists, 4 per cent Baptist, 2 per cent Jehova Witnesses, 2 per cent others); 6 per cent Roman Catholic; 6 per cent others (1981). **Languages:** English (official).
Political Parties: The Virgin Islands Party (VIP), of Ralph T O'Neal; the Independent People's Movement (IPM), of Omar Hodge and Allen O'Neal; the United Party (UP), of Conrad Maduro; the Concerned Citizens Movement (CCM), of E Walwyln Brewley.

THE STATE

Official Name: British Virgin Islands. **Capital:** Road Town 6,330 people (est 1995). **Government:** Frank Savage, British-appointed Governor since 1998. Ralph O'Neal is the Chief Minister since May 1995. There is a Legislative Council of 9 elected and 4 appointed members.
Armed Forces: The United Kingdom is responsible for defense.

DEMOGRAPHY

Population: 20,000 (1998)

ECONOMY

Cereal imports: 278 metric tons (1998)

Yemen

Yaman

Population: 17,488,000 (1999)
Area: 527,970 SQ KM
Capital: Sana´a
Currency: Rial
Language: French

When the Cretan civilization reached its highest point, another trade culture was flourishing on the Arabian peninsula which rapidly led to the appearance of numerous cities. Ma'in, Marib, Timna, and Najzan were the principle cities of the interior, along the caravan routes that brought aromatic fragrances from Dhufar (presently part of Oman) and Punt (Somalia). These extensive trade routes continued along the coast of the Red Sea as far as the Mediterranean markets, and from Taima on towards Mesopotamia.

[2] These cities were united and ruled by whichever trade center held greatest power at the time, first Mina and later the better-known Saba, cited in the Bible. The latter's ties with the African coast dated from the founding of the Ethiopian state of Axum (see Ethiopia).

[3] In spite of the rudimentary state of their fleet, Saban merchants kept close links with Africa for centuries, and as a result Christianity was propagated among the Yemenis through the teachings of Ethiopian preachers during the fourth century. Shortly thereafter, the Himyarites (a Hebrew sect) took control in Southern Arabia, establishing Judaism as the official religion and provoking a series of conflicts between the groups.

[4] Ethiopians conquered the country in 525 AD and were driven out by the Persians in 570. At this time the Persians established their first contact

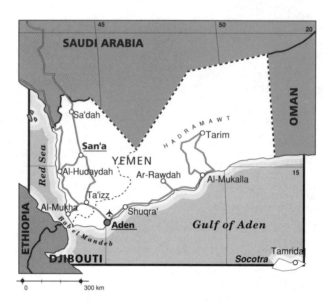

with southern African trade, which was renewed centuries later when the Persians settled in Africa.

[5] By the time of Muhammad and the ensuing Arab unification, the region had suffered almost three centuries of conflict and invasions, resulting in the loss of much of its splendor. Even the Marib Dam, a monumental construction forming the center of the agricultural irrigation system, had collapsed from lack of maintenance. The downfall of this civilization triggered great population migrations towards Africa and the eastern part of the peninsula.

[6] By the end of the 8th century the borders of the Arabian Empire reached from north Africa and Spain in the west, to Pakistan and

Afghanistan in the east. Damascus in Syria became the capital of the empire, where the foundations of a new culture were laid. Greco-Roman, Persian and Indian components blended to form the new dominant culture, with the Arabs reaching high levels of scholarship and philosophy. The Arabs formed the social elite, the ruling class, though little changed in the lives of the Yemenis and other subject peoples.

[7] Then, in the 16th century, the Ottoman expansion started. The Turks occupied a few of the coastal areas of the Red Sea, leaving inland areas and the southern coast independent, governed by an *imam* (priest).

[8] In 1618, the British arrived in the area and established the East India Company in the port

of Mukha (Mocha: origin of the name for a type of coffee).

[9] In the 19th century they expanded their presence. As a consequence of Muhammad Ali's conquest of the country, the British occupied the entire extreme south-western region (see Egypt) and took Aden, the best harbor in the region, to discreetly monitor Turkish activities. Meanwhile the Turks consolidated their inland dominion, which was finally achieved in 1872. Concessions were made to allow the imam to retain his position and also make the post hereditary rather than elective.

[10] Towards 1870, with the opening of the Suez Canal and the consolidation of Turkish domination over the northern part of Yemen, the Aden settlement acquired new importance in British global strategy; it was a key port on the Red Sea and ultimately gave them access to the new canal. Friendship and protectorate treaties were gradually signed with local leaders, but it was a slow process, only completed in 1934 when the British gained control of the entire territory, as far as the border with Oman.

[11] In 1911, Imam Yahya Ad-Din led a nationalist rebellion; and two years later the Turks recognized the imam's full authority over the territory in exchange for the formal acceptance of Turkish sovereignty. After World War I Yahya proclaimed himself independent sovereign of the whole of Yemen, and conflicts arose with the Saudi Emir of Najd and with the British, in Aden.

[12] After uniting Hidjaz with his nation, leader Ibn Saud launched a rapid military offensive against Yahya. In the 1934 peace treaty, Yahya accepted the loss of territory in the northern part of the country in return for the cessation of aggression. The British stopped before the actual declaration of war, but internal rivalries were fuelled and groups actively opposed to the imam were encouraged; the imam was assassinated in 1948.

WORKERS

% OF LABOUR FORCE **1998**

■FEMALE:28% ■MALE: 72%

1990

■ SERVICES: 22.2%
■ INDUSTRY: 16.8%
■ AGRICULTURE: 61.0%

LAND USE

DEFORESTATION: 0.0% annual (1990/95)
IRRIGATED: 26.2% of arable (1993)

1993

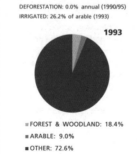

■ FOREST & WOODLAND: 18.4%
■ ARABLE: 9.0%
■ OTHER: 72.6%

PUBLIC EXPENDITURE

1997

80

60

40

20

0

17.4% DEFENCE

19.4% SOCIAL

MILITARY EXPENDITURE
(% of health & education)

197%
(1990/91)

---

13 In 1958, his successor Ahmad joined the United Arab Republic formed by Egypt and Syria but he later withdrew in 1961. He was succeeded in 1962 by his son Muhammad Al Badr, who was later deposed by the Nasserist military in September of that year. The former imam received both Saudi and British support, initiating a long civil war against the republican government, which lasted until 1970.

14 The new People's Democratic Republic of Yemen closed all the British bases in 1969, nationalized the banking system, took charge of foreign trade and the shipbuilding industry and initiated agrarian reform.

15 In October 1972, despite ideological and political differences between North and South Yemen, Al Iryani signed a treaty with the revolutionary government of the People's Democratic Republic of Yemen

(South Yemen) for a future merger of the two states.

16 This ran counter to Saudi strategy and, in June 1974 Colonel Ibrahim al-Hamadi forced Al Iryani to resign and installed himself as ruler in San'a. Although initially accepted by Saudi's King Faisal, the young officer made a powerful enemy when he challenged the landlords of the north in an effort to centralize power. He survived three assassination attempts, but was finally killed on October 11 1977 together with his brother, Lt-Colonel Abdallah Muhammad al Hamdi.

17 A junta led by Lt-Colonel Ahmed al-Gashmi, with Prime Minister Abdelaziz Abdul Ghani and Major Abdul al-Abdel Aalim, took power vowing to continue their predecessor's policies. This action cost al-Gashmi his life as he died in a bomb attack in June 1978.

18 When South Yemen claimed territorial rights over the areas where the Algerian state-owned oil enterprise had discovered large deposits, Saudi Arabia intensified hostilities and the US military presence in Saudi Arabia added to tensions in the area.

19 Major Ali Abdullah Saleh was appointed President in 1978 but was unable to prevent internal dissent leading to armed conflict in January 1979. The National Democratic Front, which included the nation's progressive sectors, was on the brink of taking power, so with Saudi provocation the conflict was diverted into a war with Democratic Yemen. Syria, Iraq and Jordan intervened and their mediation led to a cease-fire and negotiations for the unification of the two Yemeni states, which had been suspended since 1972.

20 In February 1985, the People's Supreme Council made President Ali Nasser Muhammad step down as prime minister, appointing Haider Abu Bakr Al-Atlas as his successor. Nasser Muhammad resented the loss of power and conspired to recover his position. On January 13, a counter-coup led to a brief but

intense armed confrontation leaving 10,000 dead. Nasser Muhammad was ousted and Haider Abu Bakr Al-Atlas was appointed president. The new head of state pledged to maintain the alliance with Ethiopia and Syria.

21 President Saleh's successful efforts to balance internal and external pressures resulted in more favourable conditions for rapid reunification.

22 Finally, on May 22 1990, the Republic of Yemen was proclaimed, with the political capital in San'a (former capital of the Arab Republic of Yemen) and the economic capital in Aden (former capital of the Democratic Republic of Yemen).

23 In a joint session of the Legislative Assemblies of the two states, held in Aden, a Presidential Council was elected, made up of General Ali Abdullah Saleh (ex-president of North Yemen), Kadi Abdul Karim al-Arshi, Salem Saleh Mohammed and Abdul Aziz Abdel Ghani. The members of the Council elected Ali Abdullah Saleh president of the united republic. Ali Al Beid was vice-president and General Haidar Abu Bakr Al-Atlas, ex-president of South Yemen, was also given a post in the new government.

24 In May 1991, the Constitution was ratified in a national referendum: an overwhelming majority voted for freedom of expression and political pluralism. Islamic fundamentalist groups opposed to unification called for a boycott, finding the absence of the principles of *sharia* (law based on the Koran) unacceptable, including, among other things, the introduction of voting rights for women.

25 As a consequence of the Gulf War, a million Yemenis were expelled from Saudi Arabia and other countries of the region in retaliation for Yemen's pro-Iraqi stance during the Gulf War. However, Yemen made proposals to Saudi Arabia to settle border disputes, which had existed since 1930 when Saudi Arabia had annexed three Yemeni provinces.

26 At the same time, another million Yemenis returned to the country from Africa, mainly from

PROFILE

ENVIRONMENT

The Republic of Yemen is formed by the union of Democratic and Arab Yemen. North Yemen has the most fertile lands of the Arabian Peninsula. For that reason the country, together with the Hadhramaut Valley, used to be called 'Happy Arabia'. Beyond a semi-desert coastal strip along the Red Sea, lies a more humid mountainous region where the agricultural lands are found (sorghum is grown for internal consumption and cotton for export). The traditional coffee crop has been replaced by qat, a narcotic herb. The climate is tropical with high temperatures especially in Tihmah - where rainfall is heavy - and in the eastern region. The country has no mineral resources. The southern territory is dry, mountainous and lacks permanent rivers. Two-thirds of its land area is either desert or semi-desert. Agriculture is concentrated in the valleys and oases (1.2 per cent of the territory). Fishing is an important commercial activity. The country's boundaries include the island of Socotra, which due to its location at the entrance to the Gulf of Aden, has important strategic value. This island, which became part of South Yemen in 1967, has 17,000 inhabitants spread over 3,626 sq.km. The use of ground water beyond its capacity to regenerate has caused a decline in its levels.

SOCIETY

Peoples: Nearly all Arab. A small Persian minority lives along the sea coast.
Religions: Islam, official (Shi'a, 53 per cent and Sunni, 46.9 per cent).
Languages: Arabic, official.
Political Parties: General Congress of the People; the Yemenite Socialist Party; the Islah Party.

THE STATE

Official Name: Al-Jumhouuriya al-Jamaniya.
Administrative Divisions: 16 Provinces.
Political Capital: San'a 1,000,000 people (est 1997).
Other cities: Aden 562,000 people; Al-Hudaydah (Hodeida) 246,000; Taiz 290,107 (1995).
Government: Ali Abdallah Saleh al-Hashidi, President since May 1990. Abdel Karim al-Iriani, Prime Minister since April 1998. Since unification of the Yemen Arab Republic (North) and the People's Democratic Republic of Yemen (South) in May 1990, Presidential Council made up of 5 members (3 from the North, 2 from the South). Single-chamber Parliament, with 301 members (159 northern deputies, 111 from the south, 31 non-elected members).
National Holiday: May 22, unification (1990).
Armed Forces: 66,300 (1997).
Other: 20,000 (Central Organization for Security); 20,000 (tribal forces).

Somalia. The sudden arrival of such a large number of people from abroad had a negative impact on the economic situation within Yemen. Unemployment at this time stood at over two million in a total population 10.5 million. The returning workers, especially from Saudi Arabia, also deprived Yemen of an important source of foreign currency which came from their remittances.

[27] In response to the measures adopted by Saudi Arabia, the Yemeni Government withdrew the contracts of thousands of foreign workers, including approximately ten thousand Saudi citizens employed as teachers. This economic crisis resulted in spiraling inflation and the rapid growth of the black market.

[28] After unification, in the middle of the crisis triggered by the Gulf War, the San'a Government was not able to begin the project to convert the old capital of South Yemen into a center of economic development. Strikes and demonstrations revealed the social tension which the Government tried to control under the conviction that stability would bring about an immediate increase in foreign investment.

[29] The War also resulted in the suspension of refining in Aden, as the crude oil normally came from Iraq and Kuwait. US economic aid dropped from $22 million to $2.9 million. Saudi Arabia was even harsher on the country, simply suspending their grant of $70 million to the Yemeni Government.

[30] Thirty-six per cent unemployment and price increases in basic consumer goods led to a series of demonstrations in late 1992 and early 1993. At the same time, Islamic fundamentalism - strongly supported by the poorest sectors of the population - was blamed for a series of attacks against politicians from South Yemen.

[31] In March 1993, Saleh's General Congress of the People won the elections and obtained 122 seats, followed by the fundamentalist Reform (Islah) Party, with 62. The Socialist Party of then vice-president Salem El Baidh came in third place, with 56 seats. In order to weaken unified Yemen, a hypothetical 'bad example' to the region's monarchies, Saudi Arabia supported the fight for secession led by El Baidh.

[32] In May 1994, once again secessionists proclaimed the creation of a southern Yemen democratic republic and requested diplomatic support from Saudi Arabia and the Gulf states. However, they were defeated by forces loyal to the Government. In July, the council of ministers adopted a plan of general amnesty in order to protect political pluralism. Furthermore, the Government named Aden as the country's economic capital, which was regarded as a gesture towards southern Yemenites.

[33] In September, Socialist Party members were forced to leave the government, while Islah obtained six new places in the cabinet. The Constitution was modified, stating that *sharia* law would be the source of all Yemenite legislation.

[34] In February 1995, 11 parties formed a new alliance, the Opposing Democratic Coalition, seeking to obtain the power. The Government signed an agreement draft with Saudi Arabia in which both states express their will to set permanent common borders and promote bilateral relations.

[35] The landing of Eritrean forces on the Hanish Islands in the Red Sea in December was considered an act of aggression by the Yemeni Government, causing a war. Egypt's President Hosni Mubarak offered to mediate and in March 1996 Yemen and Eritrea accepted international arbitration to resolve the disagreement. At the end of that year, however, the key points had still not been resolved.

[36] On April 27 1997, the GCP won the parliamentary elections, taking 187 of the 301 seats, followed by the Islamic Islah party, with 53. The Socialist Party, after extensive internal debate, boycotted the elections.

[37] On May 15, the new Prime Minister, Faraj Said Ibn Ghanem formed a 28-member government, including 24 GCP representatives. That year the Government implemented a structural adjustment plan to revive an economy suffering the effects of civil war and the reduction of aid from many Western and Arab nations. The economic reforms, especially the privatizations, earned the Government funding from the World Bank and the International Monetary Fund.

[38] According to Amnesty International, Yemen was one of the five countries still applying the death penalty to offending minors in 1998, along with Iran, Pakistan, Saudi Arabia and the United States.

[39] Abdel Karim al-Iriani took over as prime minister in May 1998, a post he had held from 1980 to 1983 in the north. A Saudi attack on a Yemeni detachment on the island of Duwaima, in the Red Sea, in July, further worsened relations between the two neighbors. In October the international court in the Hague ruled in favor of Yemeni ownership of the Hanish islands, also claimed by Eritrea.

[40] The September 1999 elections gave a clear victory to Ali Abdullah Saleh, who was re-elected with 96.3 per cent of the vote.

[41] The abduction of 28 mostly British tourists in December 1998 raised controversy over the method used by some clans to make their claims known to the central authorities. Kidnapping was becoming a common practice in order to get government attention and to force it to give in to local petitioners. In the 1990s some 200 tourists or executives from European or US companies were taken in this manner. In February 2000, a new law was introduced making the abduction of foreigners a capital offence. A month later a group kidnapped the Polish ambassador in Yemen, freeing him four days later. ■

Yugoslavia, Fed. Rep.

Yugoslavija

Population: 10,637,000 (1999)
Area: 102,170 SQ KM
Capital: Belgrade
Currency: New dinar
Language: Serb

In the 4th century BC, the Balkan Peninsula and the Adriatic coast were inhabited by Illyrian, Thracian and Panonian tribes, and they were also the site of Greek colonies. In the mid-2nd century, Rome defeated the alliance of the Illyrian peoples and began colonizing the new province of Illyria. Important Roman cities developed, such as Emona (now Ljubljana), Mursa (Osijek) and Singidunum (Belgrade). When the Roman Empire split into Eastern and Western regions, the border between the two ran straight through what is now Yugoslavian territory. Towards the end of Roman domination, Christianity was established in the region.

[2] In the 5th and 6th centuries AD, these territories were invaded by a number of nomadic tribes: Visigoths, Huns, Ostrogoths, Avars, Bulgars and Slavs. They imposed their own religious beliefs upon the people, but Christianity gradually took hold again between the 9th and 11th centuries. From the 7th to the 13th centuries there were several feudal states. The Serbs were separate from these states, although they were unable to resist external pressure. Bosnia was subdued by Hungary, and the rest of the territory, as far as the state of Ducla, by Byzantium. Macedonia was divided up between Byzantium and Bulgaria (see Bosnia and Herzegovina, and Croatia).

[3] In the mid-11th century, under the reign of Stephen Nemanja (1168-1196), Serbia freed itself from Byzantine domination. The Serbian rulers of the Nemanja dynasty fought against the non-Christian religions which had been spread by the Bulgars. They received a royal title from the Pope in 1217, but the hoped-for propagation of the Catholic faith did not follow. In 1219, the Serbian Orthodox Church was founded, and mass began to be celebrated in Serbian. Under the reign of Stefan Dusan (1331-1355) the medieval Serbian State reached

its apogee when it occupied Albania and Macedonia.

[4] The Ottoman Empire began its conquest of the Balkans in the mid-14th century, after the Battle of Kosovo in 1389. In the 14th and 15th centuries, the first of a series of migrations began from Serbia and Bosnia to neighboring Slav regions and ultimately to Russia. In 1395, all of Macedonia came under the Ottoman Empire. Bosnia which had been a part of the Hungarian kingdom since the 12th century was conquered in 1463. The Slav population of Bosnia became Muslim within a relatively short period of time. In 1465, the Turks occupied Herzegovina. By this time, Venetia had annexed the territories of Neretva and Zetina, along the coast. The city-state of Dubrovnik came under Hungarian control, and then, after 1526, became a part of the Ottoman Empire for 489 years.

[5] Between the 16th and 18th centuries, all of Yugoslavia's territories had been divided up. Serbia, Bosnia, Herzegovina, Montenegro and Macedonia belonged to the Ottoman Empire; Croatia, Slovenia, Slavonia, part of Dalmatia and Vaivodina belonged to the Hapsburgs; and Istria and Dalmatia belonged to the Venetian Republic. After the 1690 revolution was put down in Old Serbia, some 70,000 people took refuge in the

Hapsburg Empire. The Ottoman Empire transferred Albanian Muslims to the abandoned territories of Kosovo and Motojia.

[6] After the Russo-Turkish war of 1768-74, Russia obtained the right to sponsor the Orthodox population of the Ottoman Empire, through the Treaty of Kuchuk-Kainardzhi. Austria seized the Balkans in 1797, as a result of the Napoleonic Wars, The Balkan *pashalik* (the north of Serbia), which belonged to the Ottoman Empire after the first Serbian uprising (1804-13), the Russo-Turkish war (1806-12) and the second Serbian uprising (1815), was granted internal autonomy. The political and military leaders Gueorgui Cherny (Karadjordje) and Milos Obrenovic founded Serbia's ruling dynasties. In 1829, Serbia became an independent principality within the Ottoman Empire, with Milos Obrenovic as its prince.

[7] In the 1878 Congress of Berlin, the Great Powers recognized the full independence of Serbia and Montenegro, which became kingdoms in 1882 and 1905 respectively. In the first Balkan war in 1912, Serbia, Montenegro, Greece, Romania and Bulgaria formed an alliance. In the second, in 1913, they warred against each other over the Ottoman Empire's domains. The end result was

Macedonia's partition between Serbia, Greece and Bulgaria, while Serbia and Montenegro expanded their territories.

[8] Serbian resistance to the Austro-Hungarian Empire led to the assassination of the Austrian archduke Franz Ferdinand in 1914, in Sarajevo, the event that marked the beginning of World War I. After the War, which saw an end to Austria-Hungary's empire, a kingdom of Serbs, Croats and Slovenes was founded, including Serbia, Montenegro and the territories of Slovenia, Croatia, Slavonia, Bosnia and Herzegovina.

[9] In 1929, the nation began to be called Yugoslavia: the land of the southern Slavs. The Government remained in the hands of Serbians, and under the reign of Alexandr Karagueorgevich, it became an absolute monarchy. The regime's exclusivist policies gave rise to a strong anti-Serbian movement among Croats and other ethnic minorities, which led to the King's assassination in Marseilles in 1934.

[10] At the beginning of World War II, Yugoslavia was neutral. In 1941, when Hitler attacked Yugoslavia, the country was so divided internally that it was easily subdued within a few days. The King and the members of the government fled the country, and the German Command carried out a policy of extermination against the Serbian and Muslim population.

[11] Two groups which were hostile towards each other launched the resistance movement: the nationalists loyal to the King - called *chetniks* - led by Draza Mihajlovic, and the partisans under the leadership of Josip Brozxz, a Croat better known by his *nom de guerre*, Tito. This group was made up of communists in favor of a united Yugoslavia, and anti-Nazi forces from all the republics with the exception of Serbia; it later became the Yugoslav League of Communists (YLC).

[12] After bloody fighting against occupation troops and the Croatian *ustasha* (fascist) movement allied to the Germans, Tito emerged victorious. After the liberation of the country in May 1945, a Provisional Government was formed led by Tito and supported by the Soviet Union and Britain.

[13] During the War 2,000,000 Yugoslavians were killed and 3,500,000 were left homeless. When

WORKERS

% OF LABOUR FORCE **1998**

■ FEMALE: 43%   ■ MALE: 57%

the War finally ended, the country was in ruins.

[14] On November 29 1945, a Constituent Assembly abolished the monarchy, proclaiming a federation of six republics: Slovenia and Croatia in the North, Serbia in the East, Bosnia-Herzegovina and Montenegro at the center, and Macedonia in the South. It also founded two autonomous provinces: Vojvodina and Kosovo, to the northeast and southeast of Serbia, respectively.

[15] The YLC joined the Cominform (Communist and Workers' Parties' Information Bureau) in 1947, but withdrew in the Spring of 1948 over disagreements with the Soviet CP leadership. The USSR initiated an embargo against Yugoslavia, which

led to the strengthening of its ties with the West and the Third World.

[16] After a phase of economic centralization including the forced collectivization of agriculture in 1950, Tito introduced the concept of 'self-management'. Its goals were to ensure workers direct, democratic participation in all decision-making processes concerning their living and working conditions, and to protect social democracy against the distortions and abuses of 'statism' - bureaucracy and technocracy. The system was based on social (not state) ownership of the means of production and natural resources, managed directly by workers in their own and the community's interest. Similar forms of self-

management were developed for trade and services.

[17] Tito was one of the founders of the Non-Aligned Movement. The Yugoslav leader defined non-alignment as the process whereby countries which were not linked to political or military blocs could take part in international issues, without being satellites of the major powers.

[18] The Yugoslavian leadership was charged with revisionism and isolated from the international Communist movement because of its neutral foreign policy and heterodox model of social and economic organization. Relations with the USSR slowly returned to normal after Stalin's death in 1953.

[19] That same year, an Agrarian Reform Law was approved authorizing private farming, and 80 per cent of the land returned to private hands. The combination of private economic activity and the self-management system led to average annual GNP growth rates of 8.1 per cent, between 1953 and 1965. In 1968, industrial production was 12 times greater than in 1950, the year in which the self-management system was first introduced. Likewise, industrial production was three times as important as agricultural production, in its impact upon the national economy. As a result, Yugoslavia's social and economic model was of great interest to the European left.

[20] The country's growth rate declined slightly toward the end of the 1960s. Even so, until the end of the 1970s, the annual growth rate exceeded 5 per cent.

[21] President Tito was aware of the inter-ethnic tensions in the Yugoslavia of his day, as well as the sharp contrasts between the socio-economic situation of the industrialized north and that of the underdeveloped south. In 1970, he announced that after he stepped down, the country's leadership should be exercised by a body made up of the federated republics and the autonomous provinces.

[22] In 1971 and 1972, ethnic conflicts worsened especially between Serbs and Croats, and Croatia presented a formal complaint against the confederated system. After 1974, there was an increase in separatist activity by Kosovo's Albanian majority.

[23] After Tito's death in April 1980, the executive power was vested in a collective presidential body, made up of a representative of each republic and autonomous province, and the president of the YLC with a rotating annual presidency. The new regime ratified Tito's policies of self-management socialism and non-alignment.

[24] Despite a strong economic position during the 1960s, both Serbia and Croatia became exporters of labor. Yugoslavia continued to export labor, and cash remittances from Yugoslavian workers in Western Europe together with revenues from tourism constituted an essential source of foreign currency to improve the balance of payments. This became more important in 1980 when the economic situation worsened.

[25] In March and April 1981, there were riots in the autonomous province of Kosovo (bordering on Albania) and these recurred in 1988 and 1990. In Kosovo, 90 per cent of the population (1.9 million) at this time was of Albanian origin. It was the poorest region of Yugoslavia, with unemployment reaching 50 per cent in 1990, with a per capita GNP of $730 while Serbia's was $2,200.

[26] According to the federal government, Kosovo housed nationalist forces and separatist extremists inspired and instigated from abroad, whose final objective was secession from Serbia and Yugoslavia. Many Serbs and Montenegrins left the area. Repression of the uprisings in Kosovo, which left a number of people dead and injured, led to mutual diplomatic recrimination between Belgrade and Tirana (the Albanian capital) and the resignation of Kosovo's governor, Jusuf Zejnullahu, in March 1990. There was also tension in other republics due to the growth of militant Muslim and Catholic groups.

[27] Ethnic conflicts - coupled with inflation, which reached 90 per cent in 1986 and four figures in 1989 - were considered by the central committee of the Communist League to be rooted in deeper contradictions. During these years, several lawsuits dealing with government corruption exposed the fact that the system was crumbling. The Communist parties of Slovenia and Croatia announced their withdrawal from the YLC. In its January 1990 congress, the Yugoslavian League of Communists renounced its constitutional single-party role, and called on parliament to draft a new constitution, eliminating the leading role assigned to the League in all spheres of Yugoslav life.

[28] In April of the same year, in the first multiparty elections to be held in Yugoslavia since World War II,

PROFILE

ENVIRONMENT

Most of the country is taken up by mountain ranges, leaving one important plain north of the Sava River, a tributary of the Danube, where agricultural activities are concentrated. The climate is continental in this area, and Mediterranean along the coast. Rich deposits of bauxite, coal, lead, copper and zinc in the mountains, together with tourism in the Adriatic coast of Montenegro are major sources of income.

SOCIETY

Peoples: Thirteen distinct ethnic groups are represented in the Yugoslav population. The major ones are Serbs and Montenegrans. In Kosovo, up to 90 per cent of the population is of Albanian origin.
Religions: 65 per cent Serb-Orthodox, 19 per cent Muslim, 4 per cent Catholic.
Languages: Serb (official), Albanian, Montenegran, Hungarian.
Political Parties: Socialist Party of Serbia (SPS), nationalist; Serbian Radical Party; Reformist Party, neo-liberal; Democratic Movement of Serbia; Socialist Party of Vojvodina; Hungarian Democratic League of Vojvodina; Green Party, among others.
Social Organizations: League of Unions.

THE STATE

Official name: Savezna Republika Jugoslavija (Federal Republic of Yugoslavia).
Capital: Belgrade 1,470,000 people (1995).
Other cities: Novi Sad 179,626 people; Nis 175,391; Krusevac 146,607; Pristina 108,020; Subotica 100,386 (1991).
Government: Federal parliamentary republic, made up of the republics of Serbia and Montenegro. President, Vojislav Kostunica, since September 2000. Parliament, bicameral: citizens' assembly, with 138 members (Serbia: 108, Montenegro: 30), and assembly of the republics, with 40 members (20 from each republic). President of Serbia, Milan Milutinovic since 1997; President of Montenegro, Milo Djukanovic since December 1997. Kosovo and Vojvodina are provinces within Serbia that were autonomous until 1990 and 1989, respectively. The province of Kosovo is under an international protectorate presided over by the French diplomat Bernard Kouchner, in office since June 30, 1999.
National Holiday: November 29, Proclamation of the Republic (1945).
Armed Forces: 126,500 (60,000 recruits) (1995).

nationalist groups demanding either secession or a confederated structure won in all of the republics except Serbia and Montenegro.

29 In 1989, Yugoslavia's last socialist prime minister, Ante Markovic - a Croat and a neo-liberal - launched a series of structural reforms in order to put an end to the crisis.

30 Yugoslavia had hoped that Western Europe's renewed interest in the countries of Eastern Europe (since the demise of Communism in the former Soviet Union) would lead to a liberalization of its economy. However throughout 1989 Yugoslavia did not receive a single dollar in foreign aid. In fact during the same period it paid between $3.7 and $3.8 billion to its creditors.

31 As of 1990, the situation began to deteriorate even further, with the exception of foreign trade which began registering negative figures a year later. Industrial production fell by 18-20 per cent in Serbia and 13 per cent in Montenegro - while the gross foreign debt of the Federation as a whole reached $16.295 million. Of this, more than $5.5 million arose from Serbia and Montenegro.

32 With mounting social pressures because of the economic situation and the disintegrating state, Yugoslavian politics were polarized by two fundamentally opposed concepts. Kucan in Slovenia argued for decentralization to relieve the wealthier regions of the obligation to subsidize the more backward areas, while Slobodan Milosevic, charismatic president of the Serbian Communist League, proposed greater centralization and solidarity in the Federation.

33 In December 1990, the Croatian Parliament adopted a new constitution which established the right to withdraw from the Federation. At the same time, a referendum in Slovenia endorsed independence. In the following months, disagreement over the reform of the federal system and the designation of the presidency gave rise to an insoluble crisis within Yugoslavia's collective leadership.

34 On September 8 1991, Croatia and Slovenia declared their independence from the Federation, and the Serbian population within Croatia declared its intention of separating from Croatia. The federal army, whose officials answered primarily to Serbia, intervened in Slovenia and Croatia, stating that separation was a threat to Yugoslavia's integrity. War broke out, with many victims on both sides (see Croatia).

35 War led to the destruction by federal troops of entire cities - like Osijek, Vukovar and Karlovac - as well as the occupation of nearly a fourth of Croatia's total land area.

Areas affected included the territories of West and East Slavonia, as well as the area known as Krajina, which toward the end of 1991 proclaimed itself the 'Republic of Serbian Krajina'.

36 In December, both the president of the governing council, Stjepan Mesic, and Prime Minister Markovic resigned, the last representatives of a united government. Markovic - like Mesic, a Croat - was unwilling to present the preliminary legislation for the 1992 budget, believing it to be biased against Croatia (81 per cent of the projected budget was earmarked for the federal army). By the end of 1991, there was a total of 550,000 refugees, 300,000 of them from occupied areas of Croatia.

37 In 1992, within the territory which still defined itself as Yugoslavia, Serbian president Milosevic shored up his position by retiring 70 generals and admirals of the federal armed forces whose loyalty to him was in question. He also won Montenegrin support for his plan to establish a unified Yugoslavia with its capital in Belgrade, through a plebiscite in that republic. The March 1 referendum was boycotted by the opposition.

38 On January 15 1992, the European Community recognized Croatia and Slovenia as sovereign states. On April 27, the parliament of Serbian and Montenegrin deputies announced the foundation of the new Federal Republic of Yugoslavia, a federation between Serbia and Montenegro, with a parliamentary system of government.

39 In the meantime, fighting continued in the regions characterized by inter-ethnic strife. Since April 1992, the heart of the fighting had been the republic of Bosnia-Herzegovina, which was recognized by the EC on April 7. In order to divest itself of responsibility for the aggression in Croatia and Bosnia-Herzegovina, in early May Belgrade announced that it was no longer in control of troops from what had formerly been the federal army, now fighting in the independent republics. Far from having the desired effect, Serbia's position led the EC to declare a trade embargo against Yugoslavia on May 28.

40 However, the general elections held in the new federation on May 31 served to further strengthen Milosevic's position. His Socialist Party of Serbia (SPS) won 70.6 per cent of the vote in Serbia, while the Socialist Democratic Party of Montenegro won 76.6 per cent. The democratic opposition, as well as the Albanian minorities and the Muslims of Sandchak, boycotted the elections; only 56 per cent of the electorate participated.

41 With the election of Dobrica Cosic, a writer, as federal president on June 15, and Milan Panic, a businessman, as prime minister on July 14 Serbia's leaders projected an image of a greater willingness to negotiate. Unlike Milosevic, Panic agreed with the London peace proposals of August 26 and 27. Nevertheless, this new development did not prevent the intensification of Serbian aggression in Bosnia.

42 In the presidential elections held in Serbia on December 20, Panic was defeated by Milosevic, and Radoje Kontic succeeded Panic as prime minister on February 9. A series of purges began within Serbian government institutions, in which more than a thousand state radio and television employees - as well as dissident intellectuals and professors - lost their jobs. Finally, on June 25 federal president Cosic was replaced by Zoran Lilic, a member of Milosevic's inner circle.

43 The intransigence of the Serbian government was evident in Kosovo, where any attempt at independence, even in the cultural scene, was met with repression.

44 As Milosevic and the ruling SPS party grew more authoritarian, international pressure increased and the social and economic crisis deepened. In 1993, 80 per cent of the federal budget was earmarked for the armed forces, and 20 per cent of the country's GNP went to supporting the Serbs in Bosnia and Croatia.

45 Consequently, by the end of 1993, unemployment had reached 50 per cent. Given the fact that 80 per cent of the country's public spending was being financed by uncontrolled printing of currency, inflation shot up from 100 per cent in January to 20,190 per cent in November. The monthly minimum wage was approximately $1.50, enough to feed a family of four for 3 days.

46 The power of Milosevic's SPS party increased from 1994 onwards. After the parliamentary elections of December 1993 they held 123 of the 250 seats in the Assembly and had formalized alliances with eight opposition deputies, gaining the majority in the chamber. Milosevic imprisoned his most important political rivals and tried to take a less central role in the war. This line of action included selective collaboration with the war crimes trials in The Hague.

47 Milosevic's main aim was that the UN should suspend its sanctions on Yugoslavia from May 1992. On September 24 1994, the international organization decided to partially lift the measures for 100 days, allowing international flights, and cultural and sporting exchanges. This diplomatic coup by Milosevic - who was previously accused of being the main

instigator of the war in the Balkans - contributed to his increasing popularity in the Federation.

48 The Yugoslav President, Zoran Lilic, continued to play an important role in the peace process in Bosnia-Herzegovina during 1995. The political distancing between Yugoslavia and the Bosnian Serb leaders Radovan Karadzic and Ratko Mladic was at odds with the attitude adopted on the military front.

49 Belgrade continued to supply arms and troops to the Serbian Republic of Krajina in Croatia, during the first half of the year. However, Yugoslavia did not intervene when the Croats invaded the territory of Krajina in August. Some Serbian refugees were authorized to enter Yugoslavia and were housed in the province of Kosovo, amongst a majority Albanian population, along with groups of Hungarians and Croats expelled from Vojvodina.

50 The popularity of Milosevic soared again following the signing of the peace agreement in Dayton, Ohio, though his major triumph came on December 14 1995 when the United States suspended the

sanctions on Yugoslavia as a result of the signing of the Paris agreement. During the embargo, per capita income had fallen to half the previous amount and more than one and a half million people were unemployed.

[51] The year 1997 was marked by confrontations between the federal army and the population of Kosovo (90 per cent of Albanian origin). Milosevic called a referendum, in all of Serbia, on the need for foreign mediation on this conflict. This move was rejected by 75 per cent of the voters (with a boycott by the Albanian-speaking population of Kosovo).

[52] In April 1998, Yugoslav army soldiers killed two Albanian citizens trying to enter the Federation, claiming they were 'terrorists'. This aggravated tension between Yugoslavia and Albania - accused by Belgrade of arming the Kosovan Liberation Army (KLA). A week later, members of the 'contact group', the US, France, Italy, Germany, Russia and Britain, meeting in Rome to agree a common stance, confirmed they would seek dialogue between the parts. The US stated its support for a fresh embargo on Belgrade if Milosevic refused dialogue, including a ban on weapons deliveries and a ban on

investments. This proposal was not accepted by Russia.

[53] Later confrontations in Kosovo in June 1998 led Britain and other NATO member countries to issue a call for intervention in the region. After a brief truce in the second half of this year, which the KLA forces used to establish an independent policy of persecuting the Serb minority, the Yugoslav army re-entered the territory. The failure of a round of negotiations held in Rambouillet, France, through which the European countries and the US wanted to make Yugoslavia a protectorate, paved the way for war. Yugoslavia, presented as the party guilty of failing to agree the accords in Rambouillet, remained under NATO observation and isolated from its old ally, Russia.

[54] In March, 1999 the Alliance launched a series of air raids against Yugoslav targets in Serbia, Montenegro and the province of Kosovo. The UK and the US, the main military forces, also had air, naval and logistical support from Germany, Italy, France and Turkey amongst others. Bombardments, practiced at a height beyond the reach of anti-aircraft fire, caused hundreds of deaths amongst Kosovans and Serbs. The air attack unleashed a campaign of revenge attacks against Kosovars, who had

to flee in tens of thousands to neighboring countries and Montenegro. NATO air attacks with 'intelligent' bombs destroyed hundreds of civilian buildings, including a State TV station, schools, a hospital and the Chinese embassy in Belgrade. The violence between Serb and Kosovan civilians grew from the initiation of the bombardments.

[55] At the beginning of June, the Group of Eight richest countries sent former Russian prime minister Viktor Chernomyrdin and former Finnish president Martti Ahtisaari to negotiate conditions for a cease fire. The proposal was less severe than that of Rambouillet, but implied the creation of a NATO protectorate, with the symbolic presence of Russian troops in the province. The bombardment ended on June 10 and after negotiating with NATO commanders, the Yugoslav forces accepted the stationing of a UN force, KFOR, made up of some 35,000 troops. According to the agreement, Yugoslav sovereignty was recognized over the province, but in practice it was a protectorate under NATO military control and the political aegis of the UN.

[56] Ethnic cleansing of Serbs and Gypsies led to dozens of deaths after KFOR arrived, and the force

was unable to totally disarm the KLA, integrating this into the police force. Several thousand members of these communities had to move from their homes, while a large number of Kosovan refugees returned to the province.

[57] The Serb opposition was unable to unite against Milosevic, and despite demonstrations after the arrival of KFOR troops in which up to 10,000 people demanded his resignation, the movement split.

[58] The railway from Montenegro to Serbia was reopened in October 1999, while the ban on commercial flights between third countries and Yugoslavia was lifted in February 2000. In November 1999, Montenegro adopted the German mark as its currency, and remained at loggerheads with Belgrade.

[59] Arkan - real name Zeljko Raznjatovic - one of the Serb paramilitary leaders and president of the Serbian Unity Party, was assassinated in January 2000 in Belgrade. This prompted a spate of political killings which also killed the Defense Minister, the Montenegran Pavle Bulatovic in February.

[60] The opposition united behind Vojislav Kostunica for the September 2000 presidential elections. ∎

Gypsies and the world

According to Iranian historiography, the true legend of the old Gypsy homeland was only known by Gypsies living on the island of Leinos in the Aegean Sea. The same sources claim the Gypsies - now known derogatively as 'lurios' or 'nutters' in Iran - came to Persia in the third century AD and were known as 'Sindis' or 'Hindis' after the river which gave its name to India, the original homeland of the Gypsies.

They reached the Mediterranean and Greece in the 11th century, where they were known as 'Egyptians' - as they were believed to have come from Egypt - a term which later became 'Gypsies'. They have been present in Macedonia, Croatia and Romania since the 14th century and in Slovenia and Ireland since the 15th.

Dispersed across Asia, Europe and even South America (where their presence has been recorded since 1581), these nomadic peoples have been given endless names. In Turkey, Macedonia and Russia, they are known as 'Cigani', in Kurdistan as 'Luri' and in India as 'Banjar'. Depending on the country or the tasks they carry out, they are also known as 'Farao Nerek', 'Bohemians', 'Gypsy', 'Romany', 'Manush', 'Sinti', 'Kale', 'Kalderash', 'Burugoti', and by several other names.

But despite the varied names, one common feature in Europe is that throughout history they have almost always been discriminated against and persecuted. This reached an extreme with the systematic extermination of Gypsies under the Nazi regime during World War II, but the limitation of the rights of Gypsies dates back much further. There was active persecution in France, Spain, the Netherlands and Germany in the 16th century. In the 17th century, a law was passed in England saying it was a serious crime to come into contact with Gypsies, and similar laws came into being in Switzerland at around the same time. In the first half of this century of 'enlightenment', in Austria and Germany alone, 68 laws were passed to persecute Gypsies. In Ireland, legal discrimination began in 1541 - in 1596, a group of 198 Gypsies were sentenced to death for being 'unemployed' - and the persecution continued without a break until the 18th century.

THE QUEST FOR RIGHTS

There are far too many examples of persecution to list, and even though active persecution has reduced, Gypsy rights have not improved greatly during the 20th century. The progress which has been made, however limited, has been the fruit of hard work by international organisations lobbying for the rights of Gypsies within countries in which they live

or travel, and the efforts of the Gypsy communities themselves which, in recent decades have tried to recover their cultural values and identity.

In the 1970s, organizations came into being to defend the political rights of Gypsies. In London, the first Gypsy Congress in 1971 established a Gypsy anthem and flag. The first International Gypsy Festival took place in India in 1976. In 1977, following an Indian proposal, the United Nations commissions for the Prevention of Discrimination and the Protection of Minorities issued a call asking all countries with Gypsy populations to respect their rights.

In 1978, the Second Gypsy World Congress was held in Genoa (followed by a third in Sweden in 1981, and a fourth in Poland in 1990). Apart from strengthening the ethnic and cultural identity of the Gypsies in the countries where they live, these Congresses also tried to support their access to education. In present-day Europe, Gypsies have political parties in the Czech Republic, Croatia and Yugoslavia, and there are important institutions working to improve the legal, economic, cultural and social rights of Gypsies in other countries (like France, Britain, Hungary, Italy and India). In Macedonia, they have three political parties, two representatives in Parliament, one mayor, and radio and television channels in their language. ∎

Zambia

Zambia

Population: 8,976,000 (1999)
Area: 752,618 SQ KM
Capital: Lusaka
Currency: Kwacha
Language: English

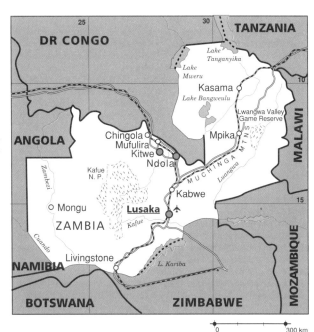

Archaeological evidence suggests that early humans roamed present-day Zambia between 2,000,000 and 1,000,000 years ago. Stone Age sites and artifacts are found in many areas. Early Iron Age peoples settled in the region with their agriculture and domesticated animals about 2,000 years ago. Ancestors of the modern Tonga tribe reached the region early in the 2nd millennium AD, but other modern peoples reached the country only in the 17th and 18th centuries from Zaire (D.R.Congo) and Angola. Portuguese trading missions were established early in the 18th century at the confluence of the Zambezi and Luangwa rivers. The mighty state of Lunda began to lose power towards the end of the 18th century. The slave trade declined in the 19th century, weakening the authority of the Mwata Yambo (traditional Lunda leaders). This, coupled with the growing autonomy of Kazembes (provincial governors), gave rise to small local autocratic states. In 1835 a group of Bantu-speaking Ngoni settled in the Lake Nyasa-Luangwa watershed. The Sotho people, the Kololo (Makololo), crossed the upper Zambezi and in 1835 took control of what became Barotseland.

[2] In 1851, David Livingstone, a British missionary, followed the Zambezi river as far as Victoria Falls. Later came merchants and explorers in the service of British-born millionaire Cecil Rhodes, who owned a vast fortune in South Africa and wanted to expand northwards. In 1889 the British Crown granted Rhodes, and his British-South Africa Company exclusive rights to establish a mining and trade monopoly in the Katanga area in present-day D R Congo (formerly Zaire). A year later Cecil Rhodes signed a treaty with the Barotse ruler Lewanika and this protectorate was soon followed by colonial domination which created Northern Rhodesia (Zambia).

[3] The British-South Africa Company kept control of this territory in order to prevent the Portuguese from achieving their plan of joining Angola and Mozambique. In 1909, a railway line was built to the coast of the Indian Ocean and in 1924, Britain assumed direct control of the region, developing arable and livestock farms along the railway. South African and US mining companies increased their investment in copper, and 13 years later nearly 40,000 Africans worked in the mines which made massive profits as the labor was cheap. The miserable conditions of the miners led to protest campaigns and stimulated the formation of workers unions; the Northern Rhodesia African National Congress (NRANC), linked to South Africa's African National Congress (ANC), was born in this era. In 1952, Kenneth Kaunda, a primary school teacher, became NRANC secretary-general with Harry Nkumbula as president. Kaunda was to be Zambia's main leader in the independence struggle.

[4] In 1953, the British engineered a federation which threatened to serve white settler interests alone. The Federation comprised Northern Rhodesia (Zambia), Southern Rhodesia (Zimbabwe) and Nyasaland (Malawi), assigning Zambia mining production and Zimbabwe, agricultural. The ANC had just launched its struggle for independence and against racial discrimination. When Nkumbula hesitated before a constitutional project designed to institutionalize European domination, Kaunda chose to leave the NRANC, founding the African National Council of Zambia (ANCZ) and boycotting the elections.

[5] The ANCZ was promptly outlawed and Kaunda was arrested in 1959. Undaunted, his followers created the United National Independence Party (UNIP), which Kaunda chaired when he was released in 1960.

[6] The UNIP was outlawed a few months later when the British recognized the existence of popular support for the Party's nationalist platform. In 1961, repression and marginalization of the majority led to an outbreak of violence in Zambia. By October 1964, the Federation was dissolved, UNIP candidates had won the general election and proclaimed independence.

[7] Zambia actively supported liberation movements in Angola and Mozambique. It nationalized its copper reserves, acted as a founding member of OCEC (Organization of Copper Exporting Countries), sometimes referred to as the 'copper OPEC', and served as host for the 3rd Summit Meeting of the Non-Aligned Countries Movement in 1970.

[8] In 1974, with the inauguration of the Tan-Zam Railway, Zambia gained access to an ocean outlet not dominated by colonial forces. In the same year, Angolan and Mozambican independence brought about a complete turnaround in the regional balance of power.

[9] Zimbabwean independence in 1980 was welcomed by Zambia. However, forces from the South

African army made incursions into Zambia, attacking Namibian refugee camps. In October, a coup against Kaunda, supported by the South African regime, failed.

[10] The situation forced the Government to decree a state of emergency and curfew.

[11] President Kaunda tried to surround himself with former comrades-at-arms, generating friction with the younger sectors, who felt that after Zimbabwe's independence, they no longer needed to live in a climate of war. They even questioned the one-party system. This inter-generational conflict diminished after the October 1983 election, where President Kenneth Kaunda won 93 per cent of the votes, 10 per cent more than in 1978.

[12] In 1984, Zambia faced drought, the worsening of the economic crisis, and trade union demands for wage-increases. Severe food shortages affected 300,000 people. The constant deterioration of world copper prices led the Government to announce a price rise of up to 70 per cent on basic foodstuffs in July 1984 as part of an IMF-adjustment-programme.

[13] The rising cost of living led Zambian trade unions to protest against IMF impositions. Various strikes broke out in early 1985 and were suppressed by security forces.

[14] Toward the end of that year, IMF conditions for a $200 million credit for the 1986-87 period led to a decision to increase the price of corn meal. This caused violent protests in the mining region in the northern part of the country. Three days of protests and looting left 15 people dead and $90 million of damage done. In May 1987 Kaunda changed his policy towards the IMF and limited debt servicing to 10 per cent of the country's foreign exchange.

[15] With 45 per cent abstention, Kaunda was re-elected in 1988. The following elections were brought forward 2 years to 1991, because of the critical economic situation. That time, Kaunda was defeated by Frederick Chiluba, a former union leader who gained 81 per cent of the vote, and 125 of the 150 seats in Parliament. Kaunda resigned as UNIP party leader in January 1992.

[16] The new government restructured the economy, privatized state enterprises and doubled the price of corn meal and

other basic consumer goods. In December 1992, the Government adopted the IMF and the World Bank recommendations, devaluing the country's currency by 29 per cent, freeing the exchange market and deregulating foreign trade. In early 1992, Southern Africa experienced the worst drought of the century, resulting in widespread food shortages.

[17] A meeting of Western countries called by the World Bank granted $400 million of food aid to Zambia, and the Paris Club agreed to restructure its debt.

[18] President Chiluba declared Christianity the official religion and banned the formation of a fundamentalist party. The Muslim religious authorities estimated there were around 1.2 million Shi'a believers and more than one million Sunnis in the country.

[19] In March 1993, a state of emergency was called in an attempt to undermine a campaign of civil disobedience. Several members of UNIP - who admitted there had been a plot - were imprisoned. The state of emergency was lifted at the end of the month.

[20] Inflation reached 140 per cent in 1993. The Government had to reduce public spending, promote the privatization of companies and fight drug trafficking in order to get the aid asked of the Paris Club in 1994.

[21] The University of Zambia was closed in April 1994, when 300 teachers and researchers were dismissed for striking over pay claims. The reduction of spending on public schools led to constant teachers strikes.

[22] Accusations of corruption and of the lack of agricultural policy in 1995 led President Chiluba to ask his minister of lands to resign, and the others to declare their incomes. Shortly afterwards he sacked the governor of the Bank of Zambia when the local currency, the *kwacha*, was suddenly devalued by 20 per cent. Chiluba attributed the crisis to the foreign debt-servicing this ate up 40 per cent of GDP. The Trade minister admitted in July that 5.5 of the 9.5 million Zambians live in extreme poverty.

[23] In March 1996, the Paris Club cancelled 67 per cent of Zambia's debt. The implementation of the structural adjustment programme dictated by the IMF and the World Bank in 1997 led to increased poverty amongst the rural population and redundancies for at least 150,000 workers with the privatization of the State companies.

[24] A controversial bill in May 1996, passed by the President, amended the Constitution to state that presidential candidates must be second-generation Zambians. Chiluba was re-elected in November 1996.

[25] In November 1997, a month after a failed coup attempt, several people - including former president Kaunda, disqualified from standing for re-election by the constitutional amendment - were arrested for alleged links with the rebel troops. Representatives of the opposition and human rights organizations said that the failed coup became a pretext for summary arrests and torture.

[25] The Government imposed a state of emergency for three months, but it continued until March 1998. In June Kaunda was freed from house arrest and the charges against him were dropped. Meanwhile, the former president announced his retirement from leadership of the United National Independence Party.

[26] Falling international copper prices blocked the sale of the Nkana and Nchanga mines called for by potential aid donors, complicating the government situation. At the end of the year, droughts and floods combined in different regions, disbanding the national economy. The UN World Food Program sent aid worth $17 million toward the end of this year. In November, a few months after being forced to resign, former economy minister Ronald Penza was assassinated.

[27] The advance of rebel troops in the Democratic Republic of Congo and the army in Angola brought waves of refugees into Zambia. In May of that year the UN and the Organization for African Unity looked into claims of Zambian collaboration with the Angolan UNITA. Leaders of the Congolese opposition arrived in Lusaka in September to sign a peace agreement with the Angolan government, but their differences were too great to be overcome.

[28] The Angolan army concentrated troops on the frontier with Zambia in January 2000 in order to combat the remaining UNITA guerrillas, causing concern amongst the Zambian armed forces. The mass of Angolan refugees in Zambian territory grew so much that life in the camps became endangered. The UN was obliged to send food aid in order to supplement that sent by the government in Lusaka. In February, Chiluba refused Angolan troops permission to enter Zambian territory and he moved troops into the zone to ensure there was no unauthorized entry. In April, the Government declared it would be prepared to receive the white farmers expelled by violence in neighboring Zimbabwe. ∎

PROFILE

ENVIRONMENT

A high plateau extends from Malawi on the east to the swamp region along the border with Angola in the west. The Zambezi River flows from north to south and provides hydroelectric power at the Kariba Dam. The climate is tropical, tempered by altitude. Mining is the main economic activity, as there are large copper deposits. Mining has had a bad effect upon the environment. Soil erosion and loss of fertility are associated with the overuse of fertilizers. Shanty towns account for 45 per cent of the housing in Lusaka, linked with problems like the lack of drinking water and adequate health care, factors which contributed to the 1990 and 1991 cholera epidemics. Wildlife is threatened by poaching, and a lack of resources with which to maintain wildlife reserves.

SOCIETY

Peoples: 98 per cent of Zambians are descendants of successive waves of Bantu migrants, currently divided into 73 ethnic groups. There are approximately 70,000 inhabitants of European descent and 15,000 Asians. **Religions:** Traditional African religions are practiced. There are Christians and Muslim and Hindu minorities. **Languages:** English (official). Of the many Bantu languages, five are officially used in education and administration; Nyanja, Bemba, Lozi, Luvale and Tonga. **Political Parties:** The United National Independence Party (UNIP), was the sole party until 1991. In the 1991 elections, the Movement for a Multiparty Democracy (MMD) won 81 per cent of the votes and 125 of the 150 contested parliamentary seats; UNIP obtained 25 seats. **Social organizations:** The Trade Union Congress of Zambia comprises 16 unions. The newly-created Workers Trade Union has 2 million members.

THE STATE

Official Name: Republic of Zambia. **Capital:** Lusaka 1,327,000 people (1997). **Other cities:** Ndola 376,300 people; Kitwe 348,600; Mufulira 175,000 (1990). **Government:** Frederick Chiluba, President, re-elected November 1996. Legislative power: National Assembly, single-chamber, with 150 members, of which 10 are appointed directly by the President. **National Holiday:** October 24, Independence Day (1964). **Armed Forces:** 21,600 (1997). **Other:** Police Mobile Unit (PMU):700; Police Paramilitary Unit (PPMU): 700.

Zimbabwe

Zimbabwe

Population: 11,529,000 (1999)
Area: 390,760 SQ KM
Capital: Harare
Currency: Zimbabwe dollar
Language: English

B etween the Zambezi and Limpopo rivers one can find, in the words of French historian Pierre Bertaux, 'thousands of abandoned mines; cultivated terraces that covered entire mountains, irrigation canals, paths, and wells 12 meters deep excavated in rock..'..

[2] Among the ruins scattered over an extensive region including nearly 300 archaeological sites, the most important cities were Khami, Naletali, DhloDhlo, Mapungubwe and the better known Zimbabwe with its high-walled enclosure. The Karangas, members of the present-day Shona people built these walls in the 10th century.

[3] The Bantu ironworkers who settled in the region in the 5th century also discovered gold, copper and tin deposits. In a few centuries they developed sophisticated techniques for working these metals. In the 8th century, the rise of Arab-influenced trade centers on the coast provided a market for their goods, and the growth of trade resulted in a great expansion of this culture. When the Shirazis founded Sofala (in present-day Mozambique) in the 10th century, the Karanga state acquired an export market for its mining production. The 'Monomotapa', the Karanga leader, imposed a tributary relation on the neighboring Muslim nation as he had done with other minor cultures of the area. Thus, Karangan supremacy was established over a region including parts of present-day Malawi.

[4] This civilization established important trading connections with Asia and continued to develop until the mid-15th century when the Rotsi, a southern people belonging to the Shona, the same ethnic group as the Karanga, forced the Monomotapa to withdraw towards

the north and the coast. The Zimbabwe citadel and palace were taken over by the Rotsi, whose Changamira (king) extended his control over the mining area. He did not however succeed in controlling an area as vast as the ancient Karanga had done.

[5] Portuguese presence brought about the end of the prosperous trade with the east and a consequent economic decline. Also, in reaction to the Europeans' greed for gold, the Shona miners filled in their mines, keeping only their ironworks functioning.

[6] In 1834, the Zulus devastated the region. The Rotsi emigrated westwards; cities and farmlands, palaces and irrigation canals were abandoned and grass began to grow over the ancient walls of Zimbabwe. In the first half of the

19th century, the territory was divided between the Shona peoples in the northeast, and the Zulu kingdom of Ndebele in the southeast. In 1889, Lobenguela, the Ndebele ruler, received a visit from Charles Rudd, envoy of the wealthy English adventurer-entrepreneur Cecil Rhodes. In exchange for arms and a life pension, Lobenguela granted exclusive rights for the exploitation of the country's mineral resources to Rhodes' British-South Africa Company (BSA).

[7] The British Government gave the BSA control over trade, immigration, communications and the police in the Ndebele territory. Since Matabeleland, as the British called it, was an independent state, the concession of these privileges granted by a foreign government, needed 'formal and free' approval from ruler Lobenguela who lived in Bulawayo. After Rhodes took control, British settlers were established in the Shona territory. They were protected by 700 police officers and were authorized to live there, founding a fortified camp which they called Salisbury. The settlers had no legal title deeds to

the land, just the backing of the British Government.

[8] Lobenguela withheld his approval for the BSA's activities. So Rhodes' agents created conflictual situations with him to provide a 'reason' to depose him. In 1895, under the pretext of arresting some Ndebele who had stolen cattle from the Shona, Rhodes's 'police' attacked Bulawayo, Lobenguela's central town. The ruler was driven into the bush and his nation and the Shona territory fell under BSA domination, under the name of Southern Rhodesia.

[9] In 1960, settlers of European origin accounted for barely five per cent of the population but owned more than 70 per cent of the arable land. When the decolonization process began in Africa, Zambia and Malawi, formerly part of a federation with Southern Rhodesia, resisted further European domination and gained independence in 1964. In Rhodesia, the African National Congress (ANC) also intensified the struggle for independence. The colonial government of Prime Minister Ian Smith reacted declaring a 'state of emergency' in November 1965. The British Government urged Southern Rhodesia to transfer power gradually to the African native majority. Smith flatly refused and proclaimed independence on November 11 1965 in order to remain in power with his segregationist Rhodesian Front.

[10] The rebel regime faced an embargo declared by the United Nations, though the blockade was systematically violated by the western powers. Guerrilla warfare organized by ZAPU (Zimbabwe African People's Union) and ZANU (Zimbabwe African National Union), was launched. The armed struggle grew increasingly intense and the Smith regime bombarded Zambia and Mozambique. These countries together with Angola, Botswana and Tanzania, formed the group of Front Line Countries to fight racism. In Zimbabwe, ZAPU and ZANU joined to form the Patriotic Front under the joint leadership of Joshua Nkomo and Robert Mugabe.

[11] In 1978 Smith and some African leaders opposed to the Patriotic Front signed an 'internal agreement', which legalized their own political parties. In 1979, after fraudulent elections, Bishop Abel

WORKERS

% OF LABOUR FORCE **1998**

■ FEMALE: 44% ■ MALE: 56%

1990

■ SERVICES: 23.5%
■ INDUSTRY: 8.3%
■ AGRICULTURE: 68.2%

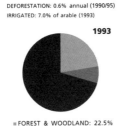

LAND USE

DEFORESTATION: 0.6% annual (1990/95)
IRRIGATED: 7.0% of arable (1993)

1993

■ FOREST & WOODLAND: 22.5%
■ ARABLE: 7.0%
■ OTHER: 70.5%

PUBLIC EXPENDITURE

DEFENCE EXPENDITURE (% of goverment exp.) **11.9%** (1997)

MILITARY EXPENDITURE (% of health & education) **66%** (1990/91)

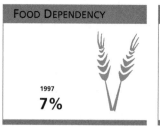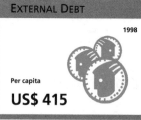
Muzorewa became premier and changed the name of the country to ZimbabweRhodesia. With the majority of parliamentary seats, the racist minority had the power to control the socio-economic and political system.

[12] However, guerrilla pressure was mounting, and finally the white government and its African allies were forced to negotiate. The British Government agreed to supervise free elections arranged for February 1980, when Robert Mugabe's ZANU party won a landslide victory. By the Lancaster House agreements, signed on April 18 1980, Britain held power temporarily before transferring to the ZANU Party. Although the white Zimbabweans maintained some economic and political privileges, they lost their veto over possible constitutional changes.

[13] Meanwhile, because of war,

the country's cattle herd had shrunk to a third of its previous size; many roads had been rendered useless, and some schools had remained closed for seven years. The medical and sanitary systems were also in serious disrepair and diseases such as malaria were increasingly in evidence among the population.

[14] Prime Minister Robert Mugabe offered generous cabinet participation to the ZAPU leadership, also calling in segregationist politicians to form the government team. These steps were aimed at preventing old rivalries from interfering with national reconstruction, especially the ambitious National Development Plan. The gross national product grew by seven per cent, farm production broke all records, and consumption reached higher levels than expected. However, Robert Mugabe had to

face two major difficulties: South Africa's blockade on Zimbabwe's agricultural exports and political dissent between ZANU and ZAPU. In 1981 this led the Prime Minister to remove Nkomo from the home affairs ministry, though maintaining his ministerial rank.

[15] Political differences intensified. In 1982, Nkomo's followers created an armed movement called 'Super-ZAPU'. Growing political tension coincided with the start of the great drought which was responsible for a drop in agricultural production.

[16] Pressure from African farmers, who had hoped for a true agrarian reform after independence, clashed with the limitations imposed by the Lancaster House agreement. This treaty impeded the expropriation of European land-holdings and the British and Americans avoided giving Zimbabwe the resources promised for the purchase and distribution of land. In Matabeleland, Nkomo's followers explained that the difficulties stemming from the drought and lack of funds were anti-Ndebele schemes of Mugabe's, aimed at repressing the country's second largest ethnic group after the Shona, and that they were all elements designed to create inter-tribal animosity.

[17] Towards the end of June 1985, Mugabe's ZANU-PF obtained a comfortable victory in parliamentary elections throughout the country, except in Matabeleland, while the majority of whites voted for the Rhodesian Front, created by Ian Smith, a fact which led the President to remind them that the privileges granted to former colonists under the Lancaster House agreement should not be considered unalterable.

[18] The political privileges enjoyed by whites were subsequently eliminated, though there were extensive privileges in other areas. These were evident by figures in a technical report on Zimbabwe's land tenure system: 4,500 farmers (most of them white) owned 50 per cent of the country's productive land while the 4.5 million peasants lived in communally-owned rural areas - known as 'tribal lands', where the black population were moved to during the colonial era.

[19] The Commercial Farmers' Union (CFU) of white farmers blocked many initiatives for rural relocation. They controlled 90 per

cent of all agricultural production, paid a third of the country's salaries and exported 40 per cent of the country's goods. This situation existed despite the fact that a third of the properties belonging to members were not exploitable, and that productivity could be increased, and that the great efficiency of the farmers was due to state support rather than the managerial talent of the farmers themselves.

[20] Two constitutional reforms were carried out in September 1987. Previously, 20 seats of the Assembly and 10 in the Senate had been reserved for whites, but this practice was abolished. In addition, an executive authority was assigned to the President, elected by Parliament for a six-year period.

[21] Mugabe played an important role in the summit of the Movement of Non-Aligned Countries held in September in Harare, where he enthusiastically promoted the widespread adoption of sanctions against South Africa. In addition, Zimbabwe supported the Government of Mozambique against the counter-revolutionaries of the National Resistance of Mozambique (RENAMO). In May 1987, some 12,000 Zimbabwean troops were stationed in Mozambique, while RENAMO led incursions into Zimbabwean territory during 1987 and 1988.

[22] In December 1987, Mugabe and Nkomo reached reconciliation, and the two major political parties agree to unification. This agreement was ratified in April 1988 creating the Patriotic Front of the Zimbabwe African National Union (ZANU-PF). Subsequently, with the help of the alliance of several white deputies within ZANU, the country oriented itself, against the general trend in Africa, toward a one-party system.

[23] In the March 1990 elections, ZANU-PF obtained 116 of the 119 parliamentary seats. Mugabe interpreted the results as a mandate in favor of a one-party system. Nevertheless, only 54 per cent of the people went to the polls and the newly organized Zimbabwe Unity Movement obtained 15 per cent of the votes. In Harare and other urban centers, the opposition obtained almost 30 per cent of the votes, while ZAPU held its ground in rural areas.

[24] In an economy with an average

PROFILE

ENVIRONMENT

The country consists mainly of a high rolling plateau. Most of the urban population live in the High Veld, an area of fertile land, with moderate rainfall and mineral wealth. The climate is tropical, tempered by altitude. Soil depletion is very severe, above all on communal farms, where subsistence agriculture is practised.

SOCIETY

Peoples: The majority of Zimbabweans, 94 per cent, are of Bantu origin from the Shona (founders of the first nation in the region) and the Ndebele group (a Zulu people arrived in the 19th century).
Religions: Most of the population are Christian (45 per cent), predominantly Anglican. Also African traditional beliefs are followed.
Languages: English, official. Most of the people speak their own Bantu languages.
Political Parties: Zimbabwe African National Union-Patriotic Front (ZANU-PF), emerged from the 1987 fusion of the Zimbabwe African National Union (ZANU), led by Mugabe, and the Zimbabwe People's Union (ZAPU) in 1987; Movement for Democratic Change (MDC); Zimbabwe Unity Movement (ZUM); Regional ZANU-Ndonga party, of right-wing nationalist Ndabaningi Sithole; Emmanuel Magoche's Democratic Party split from the ZUM in 1991.
Social Organizations: Organization of Rural Associations for Progress (ORAP).

THE STATE

Official Name: Republic of Zimbabwe.
Administrative Divisions: 8 Provinces.
Capital: Harare 1,520,000 people (est 1995).
Other cities: Bulawayo 620,900 people; Chitungwiza 274,000; Mutare 131,800; Gweru 124,700 (1992).
Government: Robert Mugabe, President since 1987, re-elected in April 1996. There is a bicameral parliament with a 40-member Senate and a House of Assembly with 100 seats elected through universal suffrage.
National Holiday: April 18, Independence Day (1980).
Armed Forces: 39,000 (1997).
Other:15,000 Republican Police Force, 2,000 Police Support Unit, 4,000 National Militia.

FOREIGN TRADE

Millions US$ 1998

IMPORTS

3,027

EXPORTS

2,911

annual growth of 4 per cent, the share of agriculture in the GNP was 14 per cent in 1980, and rose to 20 per cent in 1990. That same year, Parliament approved land reform authorizing the Government to expropriate land held by Europeans, at a price fixed by the State, and to redistribute it among the poor. The majority of the African population supported the law, deeming it an act of racial and economic justice. The white farmers, on the other hand, supported by legal experts, criticized it as a violation of the civil and human rights established under the Constitution.

25   In June 1991, the ruling ZANU-PF decided to relinquish its Marxist-Leninist doctrine, eliminating all references to this and scientific socialism from its programme. Mugabe appealed for the doctrine of pure socialism to be abandoned, in favor of social democracy and a mixed economy.

26   In October 1991, the Zimbabwean Unity Movement split, creating the Democratic Party led by Emmanuel Magoche, the former president of the ZUM.

27   In January 1992, the Government announced that a five-year reform plan would be implemented. Its aim would be to liberalize the economy, bring the budget deficit down to 5 per cent of the GNP, and to substantially increase job opportunities.

28   Within the framework of public spending cuts in May, the Government reduced the education budget and announced that tertiary education would no longer be free. As a result, massive student protests broke out, culminating in the expulsion of 10,000 students from the University of Zimbabwe in June. Demonstrations repudiating this measure were harshly repressed by the police. The Labor Union Congress declared a general strike, protesting the government's economic policies.

29   The countries that gave Zimbabwe economic assistance gathered in Paris in March 1995, a month later than planned, because Mugabe's government did not have its finance books in good order. Despite some local fear of reprisals for not having carried on the financial reforms demanded by the IMF 'in due time', the country received a larger amount

than the figure initially announced. Zimbabwe's foreign debt was equal to the GDP, so that 23 per cent of the national budget was earmarked for servicing the debt.

30   In October 1995, Ndabaningi Sithole, leader of the ZANU-Ndonga, and one of the two members of the Assembly not belonging to the ZANU-PF, was arrested for allegedly planning the assassination of the President. Mugabe's opponents attributed the arrest to Sithole's announcement of his candidacy for the presidency.

31   With the abstention of 68 per cent of the voters, the April 1996 elections resulted in Mugabe's victory with 93 per cent of the votes. Several opposition parties boycotted the elections since they questioned the electoral procedures.

32   In August a civil servants' strike was declared as salaries had fallen 40 per cent in the last six years. The Government proposed a 9 per cent increase but the conflict continued until a 20 per cent increase was accepted. In 1997, 62 per cent of the population lived below the poverty line, compared with 25 per cent in the 1980s.

33   In January 1998, a price increase in basic goods led thousands of residents in Harare's suburbs to raid shops and businesses, until the army was called in to recover order. The price hike was seen as a consequence of November's devaluation of the Zimbabwe dollar. However, Information Minister Chen Mutengwende accused white traders of deliberately raising prices to provoke a revolt against the government. Unemployment of more than 45 per cent of the active population had been feeding fears of a social explosion for some months.

34   Due to pressure from his followers on one side and the European Union and IMF on the other - Mugabe's plan to confiscate the farms of some 1,500 white owners oscillated. From January to March, Mugabe blew hot and cold on the idea. In June, some landless war veterans took over six farms to the east of Harare and in July the Government announced a new plan to set up 100,000 families on five million hectares to be bought from white farmers. The IMF and the EU, whilst recognizing the need for land reform, rejected Mugabe's plan, considering this too ambitious, and agreed to support only a two year pilot program. Mugabe changed his mind again in November, ordering the expropriation of 841 white-owned farms. The 4,000 white

farms took approximately a third of the productive land.

35   In October 1999 a special tax was implemented charging 3 per cent on salaries. According to the Government, the money raised was to be used to deal with AIDS, in a nation where 25 per cent of the adult population carries the virus. However, the measure was interpreted by many as a cover scheme to raise funds for the 11,000 troops Mugabe had sent in to back the Laurent Kabila regime in the Democratic Republic of Congo.

36   In order to strengthen government authority and to continue the confiscation of land from white farmers without paying compensation, Mugabe suggested a change to the Constitution, which was put to the public in a referendum in February 2000. The change was rejected by 55 per cent of voters - a result which was interpreted as a reprimand for poor government performance. Unemployment affected 50 per cent of the economically active population and inflation was flying high at 70 per cent per year.

37   In March, 420 white farms were occupied by war veterans. The Commercial Farmers Union accused Mugabe of orchestrating the occupations as a smokescreen to hide the failure of land distribution projects. It reminded everyone that the government owns nearly two million acres of farm land which have not been used for resettlement and which are kept fallow - some owned by Mugabe's cronies and political allies. Mugabe countered that the country could not pay for the division of land into smaller plots nor to provide even minimal infrastructure, such as plumbing and roads.

38   Violent occupations of white farms continued throughout the following months and dozens of people were killed - black opposition activists and some farmworkers and white farmers. Lender organizations and countries like the US and the UK increased pressure for the expropriation process to be stopped. In May, Mugabe launched a manifesto in which he announced he would not give in to international pressure and reverse the land invasions. The parliamentary elections in June saw the opposition Movement for Democratic Change (MDC) led by Morgan Tsvangírai take 57 seats and so deny Mugabe's Zanu-PF of the two-thirds majority needed to change the constitution. ∎

STATISTICS

DEMOGRAPHY

Population: 11,529,000 (1999)
Annual growth: 2.8 % (1975/97)
Estimates for year 2015 (million): 13.6 (1999)
Annual growth to year 2015: 1.1 % (1997/2015)
Urban population: 33.2 % (1997)
Urban Growth: 5.7 % (1980/95)
Children per woman: 3.8 (1998)

HEALTH

Life expectancy at birth: 44 years (1998)
male: 44 years (1998)
female: 45 years (1998)
Maternal mortality: 400 per 100,000 live births (1990-98)
Infant mortality: 59 per 1,000 (1998)
Under-5 child mortality: 89 per 1,000 (1998)
Daily calorie supply: 2,083 per capita (1996)
14 doctors per 100,000 people (1993)
Safe water: 79 % (1990/98)

EDUCATION

Literacy: 85 % (1995)
male: 90 % (1995)
female: 80 % (1995)
School enrolment:
Primary total: 113 % (1990/96)
male: 115 % (1990/97)
female: 111 % (1990/97)
Secondary:
male: 52 % (1990/96)
female: 44 % (1990/96)
Tertiary: 7 % (1996)
Primary school teachers: one for every 39 (1997)

COMMUNICATIONS

19 newspapers (1996), 93 radios (1997), 29 TV sets (1996) and 15 main telephone lines (1996) per 1,000 people
Books: 2 new titles per 100,000 people (1992/94)

ECONOMY

Per capita, GNP: $ 620 (1998)
Annual growth, GNP: 0.5 % (1998)
Annual inflation: 21.9 % (1990/98)
Consumer price index: 190.1 (1998)
Currency: 23.7 Zimbabwe dollars = $ 1 (1998)
Cereal imports: 294,435 metric tons (1998)
Food import dependency: 7 % (1997)
Fertilizer use: 588 kg per ha (1997)
Exports: $ 2,911 million (1998)
Imports: $ 3,027 million (1998)
External debt: $ 4,716 million (1998); $ 415 per capita (1998)
Debt service: 38.2 % of exports (1998)
Development aid received: $ 327 million (1997); $ 32.6 per capita (1997); 3.90 % of GNP (1997)

ENERGY

Consumption: 866.0 Kgs of Oil equivalent per capita yearly (1997); 18.0 % imported (1997)

HDI (rank/value): 130/0.560 (1997)

Bibliography

ABDEL-MALEK, A., ed.- Contemporary Arab Political Thought. London, Zed, 1983.

AGUILAR DERPICH, J.- Guyana: Otra vía al socialismo. Caracas, El ojo del camello, 1973.

ALGERIE: Guide economique et social. Dely, ANEP, 1987.

ALIANZAS políticas y procesos revolucionarios. Mexico, SEPLA, 1979.

ALMANAQUE BRASIL 1995/1996. Editora Terceiro Mundo, Rio de Janeiro, 1995.

AMARASINGAM, SP.- The Industrialized Nations of the West and the Third World. Colombo, Tribune, 1982.

AMIN, S., et al.- Nuevo Orden Internacional. Mexico, Nueva Política, 1977.

AMNESTY INTERNATIONAL.- Contra la pena de muerte. Madrid, 1992.

AMNESTY INTERNATIONAL.- Guía de la Carta Africana de los derechos humanos y de los pueblos. Madrid, 1991.

AMNESTY INTERNATIONAL.- Informes 1984-1996. Madrid, 1996.

AMNESTY INTERNATIONAL.- Reino Unido: desigualdad ante la ley. Madrid, 1991.

ANUARIO del Centro de Investigaciones para la Paz 1988/1989: Paz, militarización y conflictos. Madrid, IEPALA, 1989.

ANNUAIRE Geopolitique Mondial. Paris, Hachette, 1989. (Suppl. de Politique International.)

ARNOLD, M.- The Testimony of Steve Biko. Suffolk, Granada Publ., 1979.

ARRUDA, M., et al.- Transnational Corporations: A Challenge for Churches and Christians. Geneva, World Council of Churches, 1982.

ASIA 1990 Yearbook. Hong Kong, Dai Nippon, 1990.

ATLAS Barsa. Rio de Janeiro, Encyclopaedia Britannica, 1980.

ATLASECO du Monde 1997. Paris, Les Editions EOC, 1996.

ATLAS de L'humanité. Paris, Solar, 1983.

AZIZ, T.- Reflexions sur les relations Arabo-Iraniennes. Baghdad, 1980.

BARDINI, R.- Belice:historia de una nación en movimiento. Tegucigalpa, Universitaria, 1978.

BARDINI, R.- El Frente Polisario y la lucha del pueblo saharaui. Tegucigalpa, CIPAAL, 1979.

BARRACLOUGH, G.- Introducción a la Historia Contemporánea. Barcelona, Anagrama, 1975.

BASSOLS BATALLA, A.- Geografía, subdesarrollo y regionalización. Mexico, Nuestro Tiempo, 1976.

BASSOLS BATALLA, A.- Los recursos naturales. Mexico, Nuestro Tiempo, 1974.

BASTIDE, R.- Las Américas negras. Madrid, Alianza, 1969.

BECKFORD, G.- Persistent Poverty, Underdevelopment in Plantations of the Third World. 2a.ed. London, 1983.

BEDJAQUI, M.- Towards a new International Economic Order. Paris, UNESCO, 1979.

BELFRACE, C & ARONSON, J.- Something to Guard. New York, Columbia Univ. Press, 1978.

BELLER, WS., ed.- Environmental and Economic Growth in the Smaller Caribbean Island. Washington, Department of State, 1979.

BENOT, I.- Ideologías de las independencias africanas. Barcelona, 1973.

BENZ, W.- El siglo XX: Problemas mundiales entre los dos bloques de poder. Madrid, Siglo XXI, 1984.

BERGER, J. & MOHR, J.- A seventh man. Middlesex, 1975.

BIANCO , L.- Asia contemporánea. Mexico, Siglo XXI, 1980.

BILAN Economique et Social 1984-1989-1991. Le Monde; Dossiers et Documents; Paris, 1992.

BOUSTANI, R & FARGUES, P.- Atlas du Monde Arabe. Géopolitique et Societé. Paris, Bordas, 1990.

BRANDT, W.et al.- Das Ueberleben sichern. Kiepenheur y Witsch, Koln, 1980.

BRITTAIN, V., & SIMMONS, M.- Third World Review. London, Guardian, 1987.

BROWN, L.- Food or Fuel: New Competition for the Worlds Cropland. Washington, Worldwatch Institute, 1980.

BRUBAKER, S.- Para vivir en la tierra. Mexico, Pax, 1973.

BRUHAT, J.- Historia de Indonesia. Buenos Aires, EUDEBA, 1964.

BUETTNER, T., et al.- Afrika: Geschichte von den Anfaengen bis zur Gegenwart. Koln, Pahl-Rugenstein, 1979.

BURCHETT, WG.- Otra vez Corea. Mexico, ERA, 1968.

BURGER, J.- The Gaia Atlas of first peoples. A future for the indigenous world. London, Gaia, 1990.

CALCAGNO, AE & JAKOBOWICZ, JM.- El monólogo Norte-Sur y la explotación de los países subdesarrollados. México, Siglo XXI, 1981.

CALCHI NOVATI, G.- La revolución argelina. Barcelona, Bruguera, 1970.

CALDWELL, M.- The Wealth of Some Nations. London, Zed, 1977.

CARATINI, R.- Dictionnaire des nationalités et des minorités en URSS. Paris, Larousse, 1990.

CARRERAS, J.- Historia de Jamaica. Havana, Ed.Ciencias Sociales, 1984.

CARTA africana de Derechos Humanos y de los pueblos. Nairobi, 1981.

Adoptada por la Decimoctava Conferencia de Jefes de Estado y de Gobierno de la Organización de la Unidad Africana.

CASTRO, F.- La crisis económica y social del mundo. Havana, OPCE, 1983.

CAVALLA, A.- Geopolítica y Seguridad Nacional en América. Mexico, UNAM, 1979.

CEPAL.- Anuario estadístico de América Latina. Santiago de Chile, 1981.

CEPAL.- Estudio económico de América Latina y el Caribe. Santiago de Chile, 1984.

CEPAL.- Notas sobre la economía y el desarrollo. Santiago de Chile, 1985.

CEPAL.- La evolución de la economía de América Latina en 1983. Santiago de Chile, 1984.

CHALIAND, G.- Revolution in the Third World. Middlesex, Penguin, 1979.

CHEE, Y.- How big powers dominate the Third World. Penang, Third World Network, 1987.

CHOMSKY, N., STEELE, J. & GITTINGS, J.- Super Powers in Collision. Penguin, 1984.

CHRISTENSEN, Ch.- The Right to Food: how to guarantee. New York, 1978.

CINCO conferencias Cumbres de los Países No Alineados. Havana, 1979.

CIPOLLA, C.- La explosión demográfica (entrevista). Barcelona, Salvat, 1973.

CLAIRMONTE, FF & CAVANAGH, H.- Transnational Corporations and Services: The final frontier. Geneva, UNCTAD, 1984.

CLARK, C.- Crecimiento demográfico y utilización del suelo. Madrid, 1968.

COLCHESTER, M & LOHMANN, L.- The tropical forestry action plan;what progress? 1990.

COMANDANTE de los pobres: testimonios sobre Omar Torrijos. Madrid, Centro de Estudios Torrijistas, 1984.

COMISION INTERNACIONAL SOBRE PROBLEMAS DE LA COMUNICACION.- Un solo mundo, voces múltiples. Mexico, Fondo de Cultura, 1980.

CONNELL-SMITH, G.- Los Estados Unidos y la América Latina. Mexico, 1977.

CONSTANTINO, R.- The Philippines:A past revisited. Manila, 1975.

CONTRERAS, M.& SOSA, I.-Latinoamérica en el siglo XX. Mexico, UNAM, 1973.

CORDOVA, A., et alii.- El Imperialismo. Mexico, Nuestro Tiempo, 1979.

CORM, G.- Le Proche-Orient éclaté. Paris, La Découverte, 1983.

Le COURIER des Pays de l'est. Paris, 1986.

CUEVA, A.- El proceso de dominación política en el Ecuador. Quito, Critica, 1973.

DAVIDSON, B.- The Liberation of Guiné. Middlesex, Penguin, 1971.

DAWISHA, K.- Eastern Europe, Gorbachev and reform: the great challenge. 2a.ed. New York, Cambridge Univ., 1990.

DEBRAY, R.-La crítica de la armas. Madrid, Siglo XXI, 1975.

DECRAENE, P.- El Panafricanismo. Bs.As., EUDEBA, 1962.

DEGENHARDT, H, comp.- Political dissention international guide to dissent, extraparliamentary, guerrillas and illegal political movements. London, Longman, 1983.

DE LA COURT, T; PICK, D & NORDQUIST, D.- The nuclear fix. A guide to nuclear activities in the Third World. Amsterdam, Wise, 1982.

DENVERS, A.- Points choc:l'environnement dans tous ses états. Editions 1, 1990.

DE SOUZA, H.- El capital mundial. Montevideo, CUI, 1987. v.1.

DER FISCHER WELT ALMANACH 1993. Fischer Taschenbuch Verlag. Bonn, 1992.

DIFRIERI, H., et al.- Geografía Universal. Bs.As., ANESA, 1971.

DORE, F.- Los regímenes políticos en Asia. Mexico, Siglo XXI, 1976.

DRECHSLER, H.-Africa del Sudoeste bajo la dominación colonial alemana. Berlin, Verlag, 1986.

DREIFUSS, R.-A Internacional capitalista. Rio de Janeiro, Espaço e Tempo, 1986.

ECE.- Economic Bulletin for Europe. New York, 1991.

ECE.- Economic Survey of Europe in 1988-1989. New York, 1989.

ECE.- Economic Survey of Europe in 1989-1990. New York, 1990.

ECE.- Economic Survey of Europe in 1990-1991. New York, 1991.

ECKHOLM, E.- The dispossessed of the earth: Land reform and Sustainable Development. Washington, Worldwatch Institute, 1979.

L'ECONOMIE de la drogue. Le Monde; Dossiers et Documents; Paris, feb.1990.

L'ECONOMIE de l'Espagne. Le Monde; Dossiers et Documents; Paris, Jan.1990.

ELLIOT, F.- A Dictionary of Politics. Middlesex, Penguin, 1974.

EMMANUEL, A., AMIN, S, et al.- Imperialismo y comercio Internacional.(El intercambio desigual). Madrid, Siglo XXI, 1977.

El EMPUJE del Islam. Madrid, IEPALA, 1989. (Africa Internacional, 7)

El SALVADOR. Alianzas políticas y proceso revolucionario. Mexico, SEPLA, 1979.

ENTRALGO, A., ed.- Africa. Havana, Ed.Ciencias Sociales, 1979.

ENZENSBERG, H.-Zur Kritik der politischen Okologie. Berlin, Kursbuch, 1973.

L'ETAT du Monde 1989-1990. Annuaire économique et géopolitique mondial. Paris, La Découverte, 1989.

L'ETAT des religions dans le Monde. Paris, La Découverte, 1987.

L'ETAT du Monde. Paris, La Découverte, 1996 and 1997.

L'ETAT du Tiers Monde. Paris, La Découverte, 1989.

The EUROPA Yearbook. London, Europa Pub., 1984.

FABER, G.- The Third World and the EEC. Netherlands, 1982.

FAHRNI, D.- Historia de Suiza. Ojeada a la evolución de un peque–o país desde sus orígenes hasta nuestros días. 2a.ed. Zurich, Pro Helvetia, 1984.

FALK, R & WAHL, P.- Befreiungsbewegungen in Afrika. Pahl-Rugenstein, Koln, 1986.

FANON, F.- Os condenados da Terra. Rio de Janeiro, Civilizaçao Brasileira, 1979.

FAO.- Estado mundial de la agricultura y la alimentación. Rome, 1983.

FAO.- Production Yearbook. Rome, 1993.

FERNANDEZ, W.- El gran culpable.La responsabilidad de los Estados Unidos en el proceso militar uruguayo. Montevideo, Atenea, 1986.

FIELDHOUSE, DK.- The Colonial Empires.A comparative survey from the eighteenth century. 2a.ed. London, MacMillan1982.

FIGUEROA ALCACES, E, ed.- Antología de geografía histórica moderna y contemporánea. Mexico, UNAM, 1974.

FISHLOW, A, et al.- Rich and Poor Nations in the World Economy. New York, McGraw Hill, 1978.

FORDHAM, P.- The geography of African Affairs. Middlesex, Penguin.

FOREST Resources crisis in the Third World, Malaysia, Sep.1986. Proceeding. Malaysia, 1987.

FRENTE POLISARIO.-VII Anniversaire du Declenchement de la Lutte de Liberation nationale. Dep. Informations, 1980.

FRETLIN Conquers the Right to Dialogue. London, 1978.

GALEANO, E.- As Véias Abertas de América Latina. Rio de Janeiro, Vozes, 1979.

GALTUNG, J. & O'BRIEN, P, et al.- Self-reliance. A Strategy for development. London, IDS, 1980.

GANDHI, MK.- An autobiography. Boston, Beacon Press, 1957.

GATT International trade 1981-1982. New York, 1982.

GAZOL SANTAGE, A.- Los países pobres. México, FCE, 1987.

GENOUD, R.- Sobre las revoluciones parciales del Tercer Mundo. Barcelona, Anagrama, 1974.

GEORGE, P.- Geografía económica. Barcelona, Ariel, 1976.

GEORGE, P.- Panorama del mundo actual. Barcelona, Ariel, 1970.

GEORGE, P.- Geografía y medio ambiente, población y economía. Mexico, UNAM, 1979.

GEORGE, S.- How the Other Half Dies. Middlesex, Penguin, 1980.

GEZE, F., et al.- L'Etat du Monde-1982. Paris, Maspero, 1982.

GOUROU, P.- L'Afrique. Paris, Hachette, 1970.

GRANT, JP.- Situaçao Mundial da Infancia. New York, UNICEF, 1984.

GREENBERG, S, ed.- Guinness book of Olympic Records. Bantam, 1988.

GREINER, B.- Amerikanische Aussenpolitik von Truman bis heute. Koln, Pahl-Rugenstein, 1980.

GROUSSET, R.- Historia de Asia. Buenos Aires, EUDEBA, 1962.

GUIA CIUDADANA sobre el Banco Mundial y el Banco Interamericano de Desarrollo, Red Bancos, Instituto del Tercer Mundo, Montevideo, 1996.

GRUNEBAM, GE, ed.- El Islam. Desde la caída de Constantinopla hasta neustros días. Mexico, Siglo XXI, 1975.

GUIM, JB.- Compendio de geografía Universal. Mexico, Bouret, 1875.

HALLIDAY, F.- Arabia without Sultans. Middlesex, Penguin, 1974.

HALPERIN DONGHI, T.- Historia contemporánea de América Latina. Madrid, Alianza, 1983.

HAMELINK, C.- The Corporate Village. Rome, IDOC, 1977.

HANDWÖRTERBUCH INTERNATIONALE POLITIK. Wichard Woyke (Hrsg.). Leske Budrich. 1993.

HAYES, MD.- Dimensiones de seguridad de los intereses de Estados Unidos en América Latina. Mexico, CIDE, 1981.

HERRERA, L & VAYRYNEN, R, ed.- Pace, development and New International Economic Order. Tampere, IPRA, 1979.

HUIZER, G.- El potencial revolucionario del campesino en América Latina. Mexico, Siglo XXI, 1974.

HUMAN Rights Newsletter. 1991.

HUMANN, K. & BRODERSEN, I.- Welt Aktuell'86. Hamburg, Roro, 1985.

IBGE.- Tabulaçoes Avançadas do Censo Demográfico. Rio de Janeiro, 1982.

IDB.- External Debt and Economic Development in Latin America. Washington, 1984.

IDB.- Progreso económico y social en América Latina. Washington, 1984.

ILO.- Yearbook of Labour Statistics/Anuario de Estadísticas del Trabajo. Geneva, 1997.

IIED.- World Resources 1986. New York, 1986.

INDEX on Censorship. London. 1991-1992

INSTITUTE OF RACE RELATIONS.- Patterns of Racism. London, 1982.

INSTITUTO GEOGRAFICO DE AGOSTINI.- Atlas Universal Geo-económico. Barcelona, Teide, 1977.

INTERNATIONAL INSTITUTE FOR STRATEGIC STUDIES.- The Military Balance 1993-94. London, Brassey's, 1993.

INTERNATIONAL INSTITUTE FOR STRATEGIC STUDIES.- Strategic Survey 1982-1983. London, 1983.

INTERNATIONAL COMMISSION OF JURISTS AND CONSUMERS'ASSOCIATION OF PENANG.- Rural development and Human Rights in South East Asia. Penang, 1982.

INTERNATIONAL MONETARY FUND.- Directory of Regional Economic Organizations and Intergovernmental Commodity Organizations. Washington, 1979.

INTERNATIONAL MONETARY FUND.- Estadísticas Financieras Internacionales. Washington, 1985.

JALEE, P.- El Tercer Mundo en la economía Mundial. Mexico, Siglo XXI, 1980.

JAULIN, R.- La des-civilización. Política y práctica del etnocidio. Mexico, Nueva Imagen, 1979.

JONAS, S.& TOBIS, D.-Guatemala. New York, NACLA, 1974.

JOYAUX, F.- L'année internationale 1990. Paris, Hachette, 1989. Annuaire géopolitique de la Revue Politique Internationale.

KAPLAN, L.- Revoluciones. Mexico, Extemporáneos, 1973.

K+K...NEN, J.- The Mechanics of Neo-Colonialism. M+ntt+, Finnish Peace Research Association, 1974.

KENT, G.- Food Trade: The Poor Feed the Rich en the Ecologist Ecosystem. United Kingdom, 1985.

KETTANI, M.- Ali, the Muslim Minorities. Leicester, Islamic Foundation, 1979.

KHADAFI, M.- O livro verde. Tripoli, EPOEPD.

KHOR, K.P.- Recession and the Malaysian Economy. Penang, Masyarakat, 1983.

KIDROM, M & SEGAL, R.- The State of the World Atlas. London, Pan Books, 1981.

KINDER, H. & HILGEMANN, W.- The Penguin Atlas of World History. New York, 1978.

KI-ZERBO, J.- Historia del Africa Negra. Madrid, Alianza, 1980.

KLAINER, R, LOPEZ, D & PIERA, V.- Aprender con los chicos:propuesta para una tarea docente fundada en los Derechos Humanos. Buenos Aires, MEDH, 1988.

KLARE, M, et al.- Supplying Repression. Washington, IPS, 1981.

KUPER, L.- Genocide: Its political use in the Twentieth Century. Middlesex, Penguin, 1981.

LACOSTE, Y.-Geografía del subdesarrollo. Barcelona, Ariel, 1982.

LACOSTE, Y.-Los países subdesarrollados. Buenos Aires, EUDEBA, 1965.

LAINO, D.- Paraguai: Fronteiras e penetraçao brasileira. Sao Paulo, Global, 1979.

LEBEDEV, N.- La URSS en la política mundial. Moscow, Progreso, 1983.

LEGER SIVARD, R.- World Military and Social Expenditures 1986. Washington, 1986.

LEGER SIVARD, R.- World Military and Social Expenditures 1989. Washington, 1989.

LEWIS, DE.- Reform and revolution in Grenada:1950-1981. Havana, Casa de las Américas, 1984.

LEWYCKY, D.& WHITE, S.- An African abstract;Council for International Cooperation. Manitoba, 1979.

LICHTHEIM, G.- Imperialism. Middlesex, Penguin, 1974.

LINHARES, MY.- A luta contra a metrópole (Asia e Africa). Sao Paulo, Brasilense, 1981.

LINIGER GOUMAZ, M.- Guinée Equatoriale: de la Dictadure des Colons á la Dictadure des Colonels. Geneva, Ed.Temps, 1982.

LINIGER GOUMAZ, M.- De la Guinée Equatoriale Nguemiste. Geneva, Ed.Temps, 1983.

LINTER, B.- OUTRAGE: Burma's struggle for democracy. Hong Kong, Review Publ., 1989.

LIPSCHUTZ, A.-El problema racial en la conquista de América. Mexico, Siglo XXI, 1963.

LUNA, J.-Granada, la nueva joya del Caribe. Havana, Ciencias Sociales, 1982.

McCOY, A.& JESUS, EDC.- Philippine Social History. Manila, ASSA, 1982.

McEVEDY, C.& JONES, R.-Atlas of world Population History. Kerala, 1986. Middlesex, Penguin, 1978

MAGDOFF, H.- La empresa multinacional en una perspectiva histórica. Barcelona, 1980.

MAHAHTIR BIN MOHAMED.- The Malay dilema. Selangor, 1982.

MANORAMA Yearbook 1986. Kerala, 1986.

MASUREL, E.- L'année 1989 dans le Monde:les principaux evénements en France et a la l'etranger. Paris, Gallinard, 1990.

MAX-NEEF, M.- La economía descalza. Lima, 1985.

MAYOBRE MACHADO, J.- Información dependencia y desarrollo;la prensa y el nuevo orden económico internacional. Caracas, Monte Avila, 1978.

MEILE, P.- Historia de la India. Buenos Aires, EUDEBA, 1962.

MEJIA RICART, T.- Breve historia dominicana. Santa Dominica, 1982.

MENENDEZ DEL VALLE, E.- Angola, imperialismo y guerra civil. Barcelona, Akal, 1976.

MICHELINI, Z.- Uruguay vencerá. Barcelona, Laja, 1978.

MOITA, L. Os Congressos da Frelimo do PAIGC e do MPLA, CIDAC. Lisbon, 1979.

MOORE LAPPE, F & COLLINS, J.-El hambre en el mundo. Diez mitos. Mexico, COPIDER/FONAPAS, 1980.

MOREIRA, N.- Modelo peruano. Rio de Janeiro, Paz e Terra, 1975.

MOREIRA, N.- El Nasserrismo y la revolución del Tercer Mundo. Montevideo, EBO, 1970.

MPLA.- Historia de Angola. Porto, Afrontamento, 1975.

MYERS, N., ed.- The Gaia Atlas of Planet Management. London, Pan Books, 1985.

MYERS, N.- The Gaia Atlas of future worlds: challenge and opportunity in age of change. London, Gaia, 1990.

MYLLYMAKI, E.& DILLINGER, B.- Dependency and Latin American Development. Finnish Peace Research Asociation. Tampere, 1977.

El NACIMIENTO de una nación: la lucha por la liberación de Namibia. London, Zed, 1985.

NKRUMAH, K.- I Speak of Freedom. New York, Praeger, 1961.

NKRUMAH, K.- Africa debe unirse. Buenos Aires, EUDEBA, 1965

NEARING, S & FREEMAN, J.- La diplomacia del dólar. Mexico, SELFA, 1926.

NEDJATIGIL, ZM.- The Cyprus Conflict. Nicosia, A-Z Publ., 1981.

NYERERE, JK.- El reto del Sur; informe de la Comisión Sur.

NYERERE, JK.- Freedom and Socialism. London, Oxford Univ.Press, 1968.

NEWLAND, K.- The Sisterhood of Man. New York, WW Norton, 1979.

OECD.- Geographical Distribution of Financial Flows to Developing Countries. Paris, 1982.

OMAR TORRIJOS imágenes y voz. Panama, CET, 1981.

O MUNDO HOJE/93. Anuario Economico e Geopolitico Mundial. Ensaio, Sao Paulo, 1993.

ORTIZ MENA, A.-América Latina en desarrollo. Washington, IDB, 1980.

ORTIZ QUESADA, F.- Salud en la pobreza. Mexico, CEESTEM-Nueva Imagen, 1982.

OSBORNE, M.- Region of Revolt. Focus of Southeast Asia. Middlesex, Penguin, 1970.

OSMANCZYK, EJ.-Enciclopedia Mundial de relaciones internacionales y Naciones Unidas. Madrid, Fondo de Cultura, 1976.

PAIGC.- História da Guiné e Ilhas de Cabo Verde. Porto, Afrontamento, 1974.

PAISES NO ALINEADOS, Los. Mexico, Diogenes, 1976.

PAISES NO ALINEADOS, Los. Prague, Prensa Latina-Orbis, 1979.

PALOMINO, E.- Qosqo, Centro del Mundo, Perú, Municipalidad Provincial del Qosqo, 1993.

PAQUE, R., ed.- Afrika antwortet Europa. Berlin, Ullstein, 1976.

PEASE GARCIA, H., ed.- América Latina 80: Democracia y movimiento popular. Lima, DESCO, 1980.

PERROT, D.& PREISWEK, R.- Etnocentrismo e Historia. Mexico, Nueva Imagen, 1979.

Le PETROLE, les matières de base et le développment. Algeria, Sonatrach, 1974.

PIACENTINI, P.- O Mundo do petróleo. Lisbon, Tricontinental, 1984.

PONCE SANGINES, C.- La cultura nativa en Bolivia, La Paz, Ed. Amigos del Libro, 1992.

PIERRE-CHARLES, G.- El caribe contemporáneo. Mexico, Siglo XXI, 1981.

PUTZGER, FW.- Historicher Weltatlas. Berlin, Velhagen, 1961.

Quality of Life, from a common people's point of view, by PapyRossa Verlags GmbH & Co. KG, K+ln & World Data Research Center, Ernst Fidel FŸrntratt-Kloep, 1995, Hackús, Sweden.

QUIROGA SANTA CRUZ, M.- El saqueo de Bolivia. Buenos Aires, Crisis, 1973.

RAGHAVAN, Ch.- Un GATT sin cascabel. La Ronda Uruguay, una sigilosa reconquista del tercer Mundo. Montevideo, Red del Tercer Mundo, 1990

RAGHAVAN, Ch.- Recolonization. GATT, the Uruguay round and the Third World. Penang, Third World Network, 1990

RAHMAN, MA.- Grass-Roots Participation and self-reliance: experiences in South and South East. Asia, ILO, 1984.

RAMA, C.- Historia de América Latina. Barcelona, Bruguera, 1978.

REFORMS in foreigns economic relations of Eastern Europe and the Soviet Union. Proceedings. New York, ECE, 1991. (Economic Studies, 2)

RETURN to the good earth. Third World Network Dossier, Penang, 1983.

REYES MATTA, F, ed.- La noticia internacional. Mexico, ILET, 1977.

RIBEIRO, D.- Las Américas y la civilización. Buenos Aires, Centro Editor, 1973.

RIBEIRO, S.- Sobre a unidade no pensamento de Amilcar Cabral. Lisbon, Tricontinental, 1983.

RODNEY, W.- How Europe Underdeveloped Africa. Washington, Howard Univ., 1974.

RODRIGUEZ, M.- Haití, un pueblo rebelado. Mexico, 1982.

ROGER, M.- Timor - hier la colonisation portugaise, aujourd'hui la résistance. Paris, L'Harmattan, 1977.

SAID, E.- Orientalism. Middlesex, Penguin, 1985.

SALAS, RM.- Estado de la población mundial. Barcelona, FNUA, 1983.

SARKAR, S, - Modern India 1885-1947. Madras, McMillan India, 1985.

SCHLESINGER, R.-La Internacional Comunista y el Problema Colonial. Mexico, Pasado y Presente, 1974.

SCHMIEDER, O.- Geografía de América Latina. Mexico, FCE, 1975.

SCHUON, F.- Understanding Islam. London, Mandala Books, 1979.

SEAGER, J & OLSON, A.- Women in the world. An International Atlas. London, Pan Books, 1986.

SECRETARIA DE AGRICULTURA (MEXICO).- El desarrollo Agroindustrial y la Economía Internacional. 1979.

SEGAL, G.- The world affairs companion. New York, Touchstone, 1991.

SELSER, G.- Apuntes sobre Nicaragua. Mexico, CESTEM, 1981.

SERRYN, P.- le Monde d'aujourd'hui. Paris, Bordas, 1981.

SHINNIE, M.- Ancient African Kingdoms. New York, Mentor, 1980.

SHIVA, V.- The violence of the green revolution, ecological degradation and political conflict in Punjab. India, 1989.

SITUACION en el mundo 1991, La. Buenos Aires, Sudamericana, 1991.

SIVARD, RL.- World Military and Social Expeditures. Virginia, World Priorities, 1979.

SOCIAL WATCH - The Starting Point, N° 1 and N° 2, Instituto del Tercer Mundo, Montevideo, 1996, 1997 and 1998.

SOMALIA.MINISTRY OF INFORMATION.- The Arab World. Magdishn, 1975.

SOY un soldado de América Latina. Panama, CET, 1981.

STANLEY, D.- Eastern Europe on a shoestring. Australia, Lonely Planet, 1989.

STANLEY, D.- South Pacific Handbook. Hong Kong, Moon Publ., 1982.

STATE OF THE WORLD 1991-1996. World Watch Institute, New York, Norton & Company, 1996.

STAVRIANOS, LS.- Global Rift.The Third World Comes of Age. New York, William Morow, 1981.

SUAREZ, L.- Los Países No Alineados. Mexico, FCE, 1975.

SUB-SHARAN AFRICA: From crisis to sustainable growth, a long-term perspective study. Washington, World Bank, 1989.

SUTER, K.- West Irian, East Timor and Indonesia. London, 1979.

SWEEZY, P.- Teoria do Desenvolvimento Capitalista. Sao Paulo, Abril, 1983.

TERRE DES FEMMES. Panorama de la situation des femmes dans le monde. Paris, La Découverte, 1982.

THE STATE of the World's Refugees 1995, United Nations High Commissioner for Refugees-UNHCR, New York, 1995.

THE UNIVERSAL ALMANAC 1994. Wright, John W. USA, 1993.

THIRD WORLD FOUNDATION.- Third World Affairs 1987. London, 1987.

THOMAS, EJ., ed.- Les travailleurs immigrés en Europe: quel status? Paris, UNESCO, 1981.

TIMERMAN, J.- Israel: La Guerra más larga. Madrid, Mochnik, 1983.

TITO, JB.- La misión histórica del Movimiento de No Alineación. Beograd, CAS, 1979.

TOMLINSON, A. & WHANNEL, G., ed.- Five-ring circus: Money, power and politics at the Olympic Games. London, Pluto Press, 1984.

TORRIELLO GARRIDO, G.- Tras la Cortina de Banano. Havana, Ciencias Sociales, 1979.

TORRIJOS, O.- La quinta frontera. Costa Rica, Ed.Univ.Centroamericana, 1981.

TORRIJOS, O.- Figura, tiempo, faena. Panama, Lotería Nacional, 1981.

TOWARDS Socialist Planning. Tanzania, UCHEMI, 1980.

TRIBUNAL PERMANENTE DOS POVOS. Sessao sobre Timor-Leste. Lisbon, 1981.

TUNBULL, M.- A Short History of Malaysia, Singapore and Brunei. Singapore, Graham Brash, 1980.

UL HAQ, M.- La cortina de la pobreza. Mexico, FCE, 1978.

UN.- ABC das Nacoes Unidas. New York, 1982.

UN.- Concise Report on the World Population situation. New York, 1979.

UN.- Demographic Yearbook. New York, 1984.

UN.- Efectos de la empresas multinacionales en el desarrollo. New York, 1974.

UN.- Final documents of the Eighth Conference of Heads of States or Government of Non-Aligned Countries. New York, 1986.

UN.- A guide to the New Low of the Sea. New York, 1979.

UN.- Informe del Comité Especial sobre descolonización. New York, 1975.

UN.- Monthly Bulletin of Statistics. New York.

UN.- Resolutions and Decisions. General Assembly. New York, 1995.

UN.- Resolutions on the Palestine question. Beirut

UN.- Statistical Yearbook, 41st issue. New York, 1997.

UN.- Statistical Yearbook for Asia and the Pacific. New York, 1980.

UN.- Terminology Bulletin. New York, 1979.

UN.- A trust betrayed: Namibia. New York, 1974.

UN.- UNCTAD VII. Actas. Geneva 1987.

UNCTAD.- Handbook of International Trade and Development Statistics 1995. New York, 1997.

UNESCO.- Geografía de América Latina. Barcelona, 1975.

UNESCO.- Historia General de Africa. UNESCO-Tecnos, 1987.

UNESCO.- Recherches en matière du relations raciales. Paris, 1965.

UNESCO.- Résumé statistique. Paris, 1982.

UNESCO.- Yearbook 1984. Paris, 1985.

UNDP.- Human Development Reports 1980-1996. New York, 1996.

UNICEF.- The State of the World's Children Report 1998. New York 1998.

URSS Anuario 1991. Moscow, Novosti.

US ARMS CONTROL AND DISARMAMENNT AGENCY.- World Military Expenditure and Arms Transfer 1972-1982. Washington, 1982.

VALDES VIVO, R.- Etiopía: la Revolución desconocida. Havana, Ciencias Sociales, 1977.

VARELA BARRAZA, H.- Africa:Crisis del poder político. Mexico, CEESTEM, 1981.

VARGAS, JA.- Terminología sobre Derecho del Mar. Mexico, CEESTEM, 1979.

VENTURA, J.- El Poder Popular en El Salvador. Mexico, SALPRESS, 1983.

VERDIEU, E & BWATSHIA, K.- Les Eglises face au Nouvel Ordre Economique National e International. Quebec, CECI, 1980.

VERDIEU, E & BWATSHIA, K.- Cooperation Technique des Pays en Development;est-ce Possible? Quebec, CECI, 1980.

VERDIEU, E & BWATSHIA, K.- Liberation et Autonomie Collectives. Québec, CECI, 1980.

VERLAG DIE WIRTSHAFT.- L+nder der Erde. Koln, Pahl- Rugenstein, 1982.

VIEL, B.- La explosión demográfica. Mexico, PAX, 1974.

VILLALOBOS, J.- Por qué lucha el FMLN. Radio Venceremos, 1983.

VILLEGAS QUIROGA, C & AGUIRRE BADANI, A.- Estudio de la crisis y la nueva política económica en Bolivia. Bolivia, Centro de Estudios para el Desarrollo Laboral y Agrario.

VISION de Belice. Havana, Casa de las América, 1982.

VIVO ESCOTO, JA.- Geografía Humana y Económica. Mexico, Patria, 1975.

WEISSMAN, S. et al.- The Trojan Horse. A radical Look at Foreign Aid. San Francisco, Ramparts, 1974.

WETTSTEIN, G.- Subdesarrollo y geografía. Mérida, Universida de los Andes, 1978.

WHANNEL, G.- Blowing the whistle: The politics of sport. London, Pluto, 1983.

WIENER, D.- Shalom, Israels Friedensbewegung. Hamburg, Rowohlt, 1984.

WILLIAMS, N.- Chronology of the modern World 1763-1965. Middlesex, Penguin, 1975.

WOLFE, A.et al.- La cuestión de la Democracia. Mexico, UILA, 1980.

WORLD DEBT TABLES 1996. External debt of developing countries. Washington, 1996.

WORLD BANK.- Atlas 1996. New York, 1996.

WORLD BANK.- Energy in the Developing Countries. Washington, 1980.

WORLD BANK.- World Development Indicators 1998. Washington, 1998.

WORLD FACTS and MAPS. Rand McNally. USA, 1994.

WORLD OF INFORMATION: The Africa Review 1999; The Americas Review 1999; The Asia and Pacific Review 1999; The Europe Review 1999; The Middle East Review 1999 - Walden Publishing Ltd, Saffron Walden, UK, 1999.

WORLD Military Expenditure and Arms Transfer 1972-1982. Washington,1984.

WORLD RESOURCES INSTITUTE.- The Environmental Almanac 1993. Houghton Mifflin Company, Boston & New York, 1992.

WORLD RESOURCES INSTITUTE.- World Resources 1990-91. A guide to the global environment. New York, Oxford Univ., 1991.

WORLD RESOURCE INSTITUTE.- World Resources 1986. New York, Basic Books, 1986.

WORSLEY, P.- El tercer Mundo: una nueva fuerza en los asuntos internacionales. Mexico, Siglo XXI, 1978.

ZERAOUI, Z.- El mundo arabe: imperialismo y nacionalismo. Mexico, CEESTEM-Nueva Imágen, 1981.

ZERAOUI, Z.- Irán-Iraq: guerra política y sociedad. Mexico, Nueva Imágen, 1982.

ZIEGLER, J.- Main Basse sur l'Afrique. Paris, Du Seuil, 1978.

PERIODICALS

Africa News, Durham, NC, EUA

Afrique Mass-Media, Budapest, Hungary

Afrique Nouvelle, Dakar, Senegal

Afrique-Asie, Paris, France

ALAI, Montreal, Canada

ALDHU, Quito, Ecuador

Altercom, Mexico,

AMPO Japan-Asia Quarterly Review, Tokyo,

Análisis, Santiago de Chile,

APSI, Santiago de Chile, Chile

AQUI, La Paz, Bolivia

Barricada Internacional, Managua, Nicaragua

Bohemia, La Habana, Cuba

Boletín de Namibia, UNITED NATIONS, New York

Bulletin of Concerned African Scholars, Charlemont, MA, EUA

Caribbean Monthly, Río Piedras, Puerto Rico

CEAL, Brussels, Belgium

Central America Update, Toronto, Canada

CERES, Rome, Italy

CILA, Mexico

Comercio Exterior, Mexico,

Contextos, Mexico,

Counterspy, Washington, DC, EUA

CovertAction, Washington, EUA

CRIE, Mexico,

Cuadernos del Tercer Mundo, Brasil,

Descolonización, UNITED NATIONS, New York

Diálogo Social, Panama,

Documentos FIPAD, Ginebra, Switzerland

Economie et Politique, Paris, France

El Caribe Contemporáneo, Mexico,

Eritrea in Struggle, New York, EUA

Facts & Reports, Amsterdam, Netherlands

Far Eastern Economic Review, Asia 1990, Yearbook. Japan

Fortune International, Los Angeles, CA, EUA

Freedomways, New York, EUA

Gombay, Belize

IFDA, Nyon, Switzerland

Informe R - CEDOIN , Bolivia.

Indian and Foreign Review, New Delhi, India

Internews, Berkeley, EUA

Isis, Rome, Italy

Ko-Eyú, Caracas, Venezuela

L'Economiste du Tiers Monde, Paris, France

Lateinamerika Nachrichten, Berlin

Latin America Weekly Report, London, United Kingdom

Le Monde Diplomatique, Paris, France

Monthly Review, New York, US

Mujer-Fempress, Santiago, Chile.

Multinational Monitor, Washington, US

NACLA Report on the Americas, New York, US

New Outlook, Dar-es-Salaam, Tanzania

New Internationalist, Oxford, UK

Newsfront International, Oakland, US

Noticias Aliadas, Lima, Peru

Novembro, Luanda, Angola

O Correio da UNESCO, Paris-Rio de Janeiro,

Onze Wereld, Den Haag, Netherlands

Palestine, Beirut, Lebanon

Pensamiento Propio, Managua, Nicaragua

Philippine Liberation Courier, Oakland, US

Política Internazionale, Rome, Italy

Política Internacional, Belgrade, Yugoslavia

Resister (Bulletin of the Committee on South African War Resistance), London, UK

Revista del Centro de Estudios del Tercer Mundo, Mexico.

Revista del Sur, ITeM, Montevideo, Uruguay.

Sharing, Geneva, Switzerland

SIAL, Italy

Soberanía, Managua, Nicaragua

Southern Africa, New York, US

Statesman's Yearbook, 1988-1989.

Tempo, Maputo, Mozambique

Tercer Mundo Económico, ITeM, Montevideo, Uruguay

The Black Scholar, Sausalito, CA, US

The Ecologist, United Kingdom.

The CTC Reporter, UNITED NATIONS, New York.

Third World Quarterly, London, United Kingdom.

Third World Resurgence, Penang, Malaysia.

Tiempos Nuevos, Moscow

Tigris, Madrid, Spain

Tribune, Sri Lanka

Tricontinental, Havana, Cuba

Two Thirds, A journal of underdevelopment studies, Toronto, Canada

WISE (World Information Service on Energy), Netherlands

YEKATIT Quarterly, Addis Ababa, Ethiopia

NEWS AGENCIES

Interpress - IPS, INA, WAFA, SALPRESS, ANN, Prensa Latina, Angop, AIM, Shihata.

ALAI (Agencia Latinoamericana de Información).

SEM (Servicio Especial de la Mujer).

ELECTRONIC SOURCES

Rulers: http://www.geocities.com/Athens/1058/rulers.html

Le Monde Diplomatique online: http://www.ina.fr/CP/MondeDiplo/Thesaurus/thesaurus.fr.html

Folha de S‹o Paulo: http://www.uol.com.br/fsp/

OneWorld News Service: http://www.oneworld.org/news/index.html

Fourth World Documentation Project: http://www.halcyon.com/FWDP/fwdp.html

Banco Interamericano de Desarrollo: http://www.iadb.org/

OMRI Daily Digest: http://www.omri.cz/Publications/Digests/DigestIndex.html

Il Manifesto in Rete: http://www.mir.it/mani/index.html

Electric Library: http://www.elibrary.com/id/2525/

United Nations: http://www.un.org/

The Washington Report's Resources Page: http://www.washington-report.org/links.html

Foundation for Middle East Peace: http://www2.ari.net/fmep/

Institute of Latin American Studies: http://lanic.utexas.edu/

New Internationalist magazine: http://www.newint.org

Index

The world in figures

2001/2002

Countries	Area (square km) [1]	Total population (Thousands) [2]	Demographic growth to year 2015 (%) [3]	Population estimate for year 2015 (million) [3]	Total fertility rate (children per woman) [4]	Infant mortality rate (per 1,000 live births) [4]	Under-5 mortality rate (per 1,000 live births) [4]	Life expectancy at birth (years) [4]	% of population with access to health services [5]	Literacy (total adult literacy rate %) [4]
	1998	1999	1997/2015	1999	1998	1998	1998	1998	1990/96	1995
Afghanistan	652,090	21,923	..	..	6.8	165	257	46	29	32
Albania	28,750	3,113	0.6	3.5	2.5	30	37	73	..	..
Algeria	2,381,740	30,774	1.9	41.2	3.8	35	40	69	98	58
Andorra	450	64	..	..	..	5	6	..	..	..
Angola	1,246,700	12,478	2.9	19.7	6.7	170	292	47	..	42
Anguilla	96	8e	..	..	..	..	..	..	..	..
Antigua	440	69	0.5	0.1	1.7	17	20	76	..	95
Aotearoa/N.Zealand	270,534	3,828	0.8	4.4	2.0	5	6	77	..	..
Argentina	2,766,889	36,577	1.1	43.5	2.6	19	22	73	71	96
Armenia	29,800	3,525	0.4	3.8	1.7	25	30	71	..	100
Aruba	190	84	..	..	..	..	..	..	..	..
Australia	7,741,220	18,705	0.9	21.5	1.8	5	5	78	..	..
Austria	83,859	8,177	0.2	8.3	1.4	5	5	77	..	..
Azerbaijan	86,600	7,697	0.8	8.8	2.0	36	46	70	..	100
Bahamas	13,880	301	1.4	0.4	2.6	18	21	74	..	96
Bahrain	694	607	1.5	0.8	2.8	16	20	73	..	85
Bangladesh	144,000	126,948	1.5	161.5	3.1	79	106	58	45	38
Barbados	430	269	0.4	0.3	1.5	13	15	76	..	97
Belarus	207,600	10,275	-0.3	9.8	1.4	22	27	68	..	99
Belgium	30,519	10,152		10.1	1.6	6	6	77	..	..
Belize	22,696	235	2.0	0.3	3.6	35	43	75	..	70
Benin	112,620	5,937	2.6	8.9	5.8	101	165	53	18	32
Bermuda	53	60	..	..	..	..	..	..	..	..
Bhutan	47,000	2,064	2.6	3.1	5.5	84	116	61	65	42
Bolivia	1,098,580	8,142	2.1	11.2	4.3	66	85	62	67	82
Bosnia-Herz.	51,130	3,838	..	..	1.4	16	19	73	..	..
Botswana	581,730	1,597	1.4	2.0	4.3	38	48	47	..	73
Brazil	8,511,969	167,988	1.1	200.7	2.3	36	42	67	..	83
Brunei	5,770	321	1.6	0.4	2.8	8	9	76	..	89
Bulgaria	110,910	8,280	-0.6	7.5	1.2	14	17	71	..	98
Burkina Faso	274,000	11,616	2.8	18.1	6.5	109	165	45	90	19
Burundi	27,830	6,565	2.2	9.5	6.2	106	176	43	80	42
Cambodia	181,040	10,946	1.8	14.4	4.6	104	163	53	53	65
Cameroon	475,440	14,710	2.4	21.5	5.3	94	153	55	80	63
Canada	9,970,609	30,857	0.9	35.3	1.6	6	6	79	..	97
Cape Verde	4,030	418	2.1	0.6	3.5	54	73	69	..	69
Cayman Is.	260	34e	..	..	..	..	..	..	..	..
Central African Rep.	622,980	3,549	1.9	4.8	4.9	113	173	45	52	40
Ceuta	19	71a	..	..	..	..	..	..	..	..
Chad	1,284,000	7,458	2.6	11.2	6.0	118	198	47	30	48
Chile	756,950	15,019	1.1	17.9	2.4	11	12	75	97	95
China	9,559,867	1,266,838	0.7	1,417.7	1.8	38	47	70	88	80
Christmas Is.	135	2,5	..	..	..	..	..	..	..	..
Cocos	14	0.6	..	..	..	..	..	..	..	..
Colombia	1,138,910	41,564	1.6	53.2	2.8	25	30	71	81	90
Comoros	2,230	676	2.5	1.0	4.8	67	90	59		57
Congo D.R.	2,344,860	50,336	2.9	80.3	6.4	128	207	51	26	77
Congo R.	342,000	2,864	2.8	4.4	6.0	81	108	49	83	74
Cook Is.	230	19	..	..	..	26	30	..	..	99
Costa Rica	51,100	3,933	1.9	5.2	2.8	14	16	76	..	95
Croatia	56,540	4,477	-0.2	4.3	1.6	8	9	73	..	97
Cuba	110,860	11,160	0.3	11.6	1.6	7	8	76	100	96
Cyprus	9,250	779	0.7	0.9	2.0	8	9	78	..	95
Côte d'Ivoire	322,460	14,527	2.0	20.0	5.0	90	150	47	..	40
Denmark	43,090	5,283	0.1	5.3	1.7	5	5	76	..	..
Diego García Is.	..	1a	..	..	..	..	..	..	..	..
Djibouti	23,200	629	1.9	0.9	5.3	111	156	51	..	46
Dominica	750	75	0.1	0.1	1.9	17	20	76	..	..
Dominican Rep.	48,730	8,365	1.3	10.3	2.8	43	51	71	78	82

Burma - see Myanmar/Burma

Countries	Primary pupil to teacher ratio [6]	Newspapers per 1,000 people [6]	TV sets per 1,000 people [3]	Radios per 1,000 people [6]	Books (titles published per million people) [7]	GNP per capita ($) [6]	GNP, annual growth (%) [6]	Average annual inflation (%) [6]	Exports of goods and services (current millions dollars) [6]	Imports of goods and services (current millions dollars) [6]
	1998	1996	1996	1997	1992/94	1998	1998	1990/98	1998	1998
Afghanistan	..	5	..	124	..	..	..	..	..	..
Albania	18[b]	36	161	217	..	810	7.9	51.5	289	980
Algeria	27[c]	38	68	241	1	1,550	5.8	21.1	11,083	11,045
Andorra	..	..	..	216	..	..	..	..	..	..
Angola	..	11	51	54	..	380	19.8	924.3	3,874	3,113
Anguilla	..	..	..	..	..	..	..	..	..	..
Antigua	..	91	412	510	..	8,450	3.7	..	461	512
Aotearoa/NZ	18[d]	216	517	990	..	14,600	-0.6	1.6	18,768[d]	18,345[d]
Argentina	17[d]	123	345	681	26	8,030	3.9	7.8	31,019	38,494
Armenia	19[c]	23[b]	217	224	6	460	3.4	349.1	360	990
Aruba	..	..	..	552	..	..	..	..	..	..
Australia	18[c]	293	666	1,376	61	20,640	5.6	1.7	84,100[d]	86,400[d]
Austria	12[c]	296	496	753	100	26,830	3.3	2.5	87,234[d]	88,418[d]
Azerbaijan	20[c]	27[b]	212	23	5	480	9.9	322.3	963	2,312
Bahamas	22[c]	99	233	744	..	..	3.0	..	..	..
Bahrain	20[a]	112	429	545	..	7,640	2.1	..	6,357[d]	4,370[d]
Bangladesh	..	9	7	50	..	350	5.9	3.6	5,885	8,058
Barbados	..	200	287	891	..	..	4.4	..	1,484	1,475
Belarus	20[a]	174[b]	292	296	32	2,180	10.5	449.9	13,984	15,332
Belgium	..	160	464	793	..	25,380	3.0	2.3	176,844[d]	165,856[d]
Belize	26[a]	..	180	594	34	2,660	3.0	..	330	363
Benin	52[b]	2	73	108	2	380	4.7	10.1	537	740
Bermuda	12[c]	274	..	1,323	..	35,590[d]	3.1[d]	..	..	..
Bhutan	..	..	19	60	..	470	5.5	..	132	170
Bolivia	..	55	202	675	..	1,010	5.1	9.9	1,693	2,480
Bosnia-Herz.	..	152[b]	..	248	..	..	..	..	..	..
Botswana	25[c]	27	27	156	..	3,070	3.7	10.3	1,705	1,646
Brazil	23[a]	40	289	444	14	4,630	-0.0	347.4	57,826	78,557
Brunei	15[b]	70	417	303	16	27,270[d]	0.4	..	5,542	5,671
Bulgaria	17[c]	257	361	543	69	1,220	4.4	116.9	5,542	5,671
Burkina Faso	50[b]	1	6	33	..	240	6.3	6.6	356	775
Burundi	50[b]	3	2	71	..	140	4.7	11.8	72	174
Cambodia	46[d]	2	9	127	..	260	-0.1	32.8	978	1,251
Cameroon	..	7	..	163	..	610	6.7	6.1	2,305	2,176
Canada	16[b]	159	709	1,077	76	19,170	2.9	1.4	247,047[d]	237,088[d]
Cape Verde	..	..	45	180	..	1,200	5.2	..	124	282
Cayman Is.	..	..	..	984	..	..	..	..	..	..
Central African Rep.	..	2	5	83	..	300	4.5	5.4	168	264
Ceuta	..	..	..	..	..	..	..	..	..	..
Chad	67[c]	..	2	242	..	230	8.4	8.3	327	537
Chile	30[c]	98	277	354	13	4,990	8.7	9.3	21,680	22,730
China	24[c]	..	252	333	8	750	7.4	9.7	207,595	165,906
Christmas Is.	..	..	..	..	..	..	..	..	..	..
Cocos	..	..	..	..	..	..	..	..	..	..
Colombia	25[c]	46	185	581	..	2,470	-0.6	21.5	14,337	20,159
Comoros	52[b]	..	4	138	..	370	0.0	..	33	82
Congo D.R.	45[a]	3	41	375	..	110	4.0	1,423.1	1,463[d]	1,350[d]
Congo R.	70[b]	8[b]	7	124	..	680	11.4	7.1	1,236	1,409
Cook Is.	..	..	..	..	..	..	..	..	..	..
Costa Rica	29[d]	94	221	271	29	2,770	4.7	17.6	5,132	5,326
Croatia	19[c]	115	267	336	59	4,620	1.8	131.2	8,707	10,666
Cuba	12[c]	118	199	353	9	..	..	..	..	..
Cyprus	15[c]	114	146	459	142	11,920	5.0	..	4,127[c]	4,703[c]
Czech Republic	19[b]	254	406	803	91	5,150	-2.2	13.7	33,817	34,610
Côte d'Ivoire	..	..	58	..	..	..	..	8.7	..	..
Denmark	..	309	533	1,141	230	33,040	2.7	1.6	61,158[d]	55,463[d]
Diego García Is.	..	..	..	..	..	..	..	..	..	..
Djibouti	34[c]	..	73	84	..	..	..	..	207[d]	285[d]
Dominica	..	..	183	613	..	3,150	4.1	..	138	151
Dominican Rep.	..	52	84	178	..	1,770	6.8	10.6	4,849	6,264

Burma - see Myanmar/Burma

Countries	Area (square km) [1]	Total population (Thousands) [2]	Demographic growth to year 2015 (%) [3]	Population estimate for year 2015 (million) [3]	Total fertility rate (children per woman) [4]	Infant mortality rate (per 1,000 live births) [4]	Under-5 mortality rate (per 1,000 live births) [4]	Life expectancy at birth (years) [4]	% of population with access to health services [5]	Literacy (total adult literacy rate %) [4]
	1998	1999	1997/2015	1999	1998	1998	1998	1998	1990/96	1995
East Timor	14,870	871	..	..	..	..	..	..	..	..
Ecuador	283,560	12,411	1.6	15.9	3.1	30	39	70	..	89
Egypt	1,001,450	67,226	1.5	85.2	3.3	51	69	67	99	51
El Salvador	21,040	6,154	1.7	8.0	3.1	30	34	69	40	76
Equatorial Guinea	28,050	442	2.4	0.6	5.5	108	171	50	..	78
Eritrea	117,600	3,720	2.7	5.5	5.7	70	112	51	..	..
Estonia	45,100	1,412	-0.9	1.2	1.3	18	22	69	..	98
Ethiopia	1,104,300	61,095	2.5	90.9	6.3	110	173	43	46	33
Faeroe Is.	1,400	48e	..	..	..	..	..	..	..	..
Fiji	18,270	806	1.3	1.0	2.7	19	23	73	..	91
Finland	338,130	5,165	0.1	5.3	1.7	4	5	77	..	..
France	551,500	58,886	0.2	61.1	1.7	5	5	78	..	..
French Guiana	90,000	115	..	..	..	..	..	..	..	..
French Polynesia	4,000	231	..	..	..	..	..	..	..	..
Gabon	267,670	1,197	2.1	1.7	5.4	85	144	52	..	63
Gambia	11,300	1,268	2.4	1.8	5.2	64	82	47	93	39
Georgia	69,700	5,005	..	5.1	1.9	19	23	73	..	99
Germany	356,733	82,177	..	81.6	1.3	5	5	77	..	..
Ghana	238,540	19,678	2.6	29.8	5.1	67	105	60	60	64
Gibraltar	10	28e	..	..	..	..	..	..	..	..
Greece	131,990	10,626	-0.1	10.4	1.3	6	7	78	..	96
Greenland	2,175,600	59e	..	..	..	..	..	..	..	..
Grenada	340	85	0.4	0.1	3.6	23	28	72	..	96
Guadeloupe	1,710	450	..	..	..	..	..	..	..	..
Guam	550	165	..	..	..	..	..	..	..	..
Guatemala	108,890	11,090	2.5	16.4	4.9	41	52	64	57	65
Guinea	245,860	7,359	2.0	10.5	5.5	124	197	47	80	36
Guinea-Bissau	36,125	1,187	2.0	1.6	5.7	130	205	45	40	31
Guyana	214,970	855	0.7	1.0	2.3	58	79	65	..	98
Haiti	27,750	8,087	1.6	10.4	4.3	91	130	54	60	44
Honduras	112,090	6,315	2.3	9.0	4.2	33	44	70	69	70
Hungary	93,030	10,075	-0.4	9.4	1.4	10	11	71	..	99
Iceland	103,000	279	0.8	0.3	2.1	5	5	79	..	..
India	3,287,588	998,056	1.3	1,211.7	3.1	69	105	63	85	50
Indonesia	1,889,700	209,255	1.2	250.4	2.5	40	56	65	93	84
Iran	1,648,000	66,796	1.4	83.1	2.8	29	33	69	88	71
Iraq	438,320	22,450	2.7	34.1	5.2	103	125	63	93	58
Ireland	70,280	3,705	0.7	4.2	1.9	6	7	76	..	..
Israel	21,060	6,101	1.4	7.6	2.7	6	6	78	..	95
Italy	301,270	57,343	-0.3	54.4	1.2	6	6	78	..	98
Jamaica	10,990	2,561	0.9	2.9	2.5	10	11	75	90	85
Japan	377,800	126,505	..	126.1	1.4	4	4	80	..	..
Jordan	97,740	6,483	2.7	9.9	4.8	30	36	70	97	86
Kanaky/New Caled.	18,580	211	..	..	..	..	..	..	..	..
Kazakhstan	2,717,299	16,269	0.2	16.9	2.3	36	43	68	..	100
Kenya	580,370	29,549	1.6	37.6	4.4	75	117	52	77	77
Kiribati	730	77	..	..	4.5	54	74	60	..	93
Korea, North	120,540	23,702	..	..	2.0	23	30	72	..	..
Korea, South	99,020	46,479	0.6	51.1	1.7	5	5	73	100	97
Kuwait	17,820	1,897	2.3	2.6	2.9	12	13	76	100	79
Kyrgyzstan	198,500	4,669	0.9	5.5	3.2	56	66	68	..	97
Laos	236,800	5,297	2.5	7.8	5.7	96	116	53	67	57
Latvia	64,500	2,389	-1.0	2.1	1.3	18	22	69	..	100
Lebanon	10,400	3,236	1.3	3.9	2.7	29	35	70	95	83
Lesotho	30,355	2,108	2.0	2.9	4.7	94	136	56	80	81
Liberia	111,369	2,930	..	..	6.3	157	235	48	39	45
Libya	1,759,540	5,470	2.1	7.6	3.8	20	24	70	95	74
Liechtenstein	160	28	..	..	..	10	11	..	..	100
Lithuania	65,200	3,682	-0.3	3.5	1.4	19	23	70	..	99
Luxembourg	2,586	426	0.6	0.5	1.7	5	5	77	..	..

Countries	Primary pupil to teacher ratio [6]	Newspapers per 1,000 people [6]	TV sets per 1,000 people [3]	Radios per 1,000 people [6]	Books (titles published per million people) [7]	GNP per capita ($) [6]	GNP, annual growth (%) [6]	Average Annual inflation (%) [6]	Exports of goods and services (current millions dollars) [6]	Imports of goods and services (current millions dollars) [6]
	1998	1996	1996	1997	1992/94	1998	1998	1990/98	1998	1998
East Timor	..	..	..	..	..	..	..	..	..	..
Ecuador	25[c]	70	148	419	..	1,520	4.2	32.0	4,988	6,311
Egypt	23[c]	40	126	324	5	1,290	6.3	9.7	13,932	19,274
El Salvador	33[c]	48	250	464	..	1,850	3.3	8.9	2,738	4,239
Equatorial Guinea	..	5	98	429	..	1,110	34.7	10.1	465	791
Eritrea	44[c]	..	7	91	3	200	-4.0	10.1	129	583
Estonia	17[b]	174	449	693	152	3,360	5.7	75.4	4,149	4,651
Ethiopia	43[c]	1	4	195	..	100	-1.8	8.0	1,034	1,810
Faeroe Is.	..	..	..	594	..	..	..	..	..	..
Fiji	..	52	94	640	52	2,210	-4.2	..	1,041	1,021
Finland	18[c]	455	605	1,496	247	24,280	6.7	1.7	47,709[d]	37,106[d]
France		218	598	937	78	24,210	3.2	1.7	371,529[d]	316,618[d]
French Guiana	..	..	..	..	..	..	..	..	..	..
French Polynesia	14[b]	109	..	564	..	18,050[d]	2.5[d]	..	..	..
Gabon	51[b]	29	76	183	..	4,170	5.7	7.2	2,823	2,220
Gambia	30[b]	2	..	168	2	340	5.0	4.4	213	258
Georgia	18[c]	..	474	555	6	970	2.7	709.3	720	1,437
Germany	17[b]	311	493	948	87	26,570	2.8	2.2	560,414[d]	528,778[d]
Ghana	..	14	41	238	..	390	4.6	28.6	2,004	2,732
Gibraltar	..	..	..	..	..	..	..	..	..	..
Greece	14[c]	153[b]	442	477	..	11,740	3.3	11.0	18,837[d]	28,763[d]
Greenland	18	..	481	..	..	..	..	..	..	..
Grenada	..	..	..	561	..	3,250	5.3	..	130	211
Guadeloupe	..	..	..	..	..	..	..	..	..	..
Guam	..	193	..	1,408	..	..	..	..	..	..
Guatemala	35[c]	33	122	79	..	1,640	5.5	11.4	3,524	5,101
Guinea	49[d]	..	8	47	..	530	3.9	6.7	777	841
Guinea-Bissau	..	5	..	44	..	160	-28.9	41.8	31	72
Guyana	29[c]	50	42	498	4	780	0.8	..	690	774
Haiti	..	3	5	55	..	410	3.2	23.3	445	1,128
Honduras	35[a]	55	80	386	..	740	4.0	20.6	2,463	2,796
Hungary	11[a]	186	442	689	100	4,510	4.2	22.0	23,814	25,037
Iceland	..	537	447	953	537	27,830	5.9	..	2,693[d]	2,647[d]
India	64[a]	..	64	121	1	440	6.2	8.9	47,419	59,138
Indonesia	22[c]	24	232	156	3	640	-16.7	12.2	50,755	41,250
Iran	31[c]	28	164	265	16	1,650	1.5	28.3	14,927	16,750
Iraq	20[b]	19	78	229	..	..	..	..	..	..
Ireland	22[c]	150	469	699	..	18,710	9.2	2.0	61,457[d]	47,739[d]
Israel	..	290	300	520	86	16,180	3.4	11.0	32,105	43,278
Italy	11[b]	104	436	878	57	20,090	1.4	4.4	312,934[d]	263,367[d]
Jamaica	..	62	326	480	..	1,740	0.9	29.1	3,166	4,007
Japan	19[a]	578	700	955	28	32,350	-2.7	0.2	465,591[d]	415,867[d]
Jordan	21[b]	58	..	287	10	1,150	3.3	3.3	3,636	5,200
Kanaky/New Caled.	..	122	..	544	..	..	..	..	..	..
Kazakhstan	..	..	275	384	7	1,340	-2.2	330.7	6,735	7,716
Kenya	30[b]	9	19	104	..	350	2.7	15.8	2,851	3,742
Kiribati	24[d]	..	..	211	..	1,170	15.3	..	..	..
Korea, North	..	199	..	147	..	..	..	..	..	..
Korea, South	31[c]	393[b]	326	1,033	77	8,600	-6.6	6.4	156,330	114,879
Kuwait	14[c]	374	373	660	11	..	6.1[b]	..	11,347	11,760
Kyrgyzstan	20[b]	15	..	112	7	380	4.2	157.8	602	876
Laos	30[c]	4	10	143	1	320	4.0	16.3	47	61
Latvia	13[c]	247	598	710	65	2,420	3.4	71.1	3,053	3,899
Lebanon	..	107	355	906	..	3,560	3.0	24.0	1,833	8,796
Lesotho	47[c]	8	13	49	..	570	-3.1	7.7	265	988
Liberia	..	12	..	274	..	..	..	..	..	..
Libya	..	14	143	233	..	..	..	..	..	..
Liechtenstein	..	..	..	669	..	..	..	..	..	..
Lithuania	16[c]	93	376	513	77	2,540	4.8	111.5	5,071	6,348
Luxembourg	..	325	628	681	169	45,100	5.1	..	16,609[d]	13,976[d]

Countries	Area (square km) [1]	Total population (Thousands) [2]	Demographic growth to year 2015 (%) [3]	Population estimate for year 2015 (million) [3]	Total fertility rate (children per woman) [4]	Infant mortality rate (per 1,000 live births) [4]	Under-5 mortality rate (per 1,000 live births) [4]	Life expectancy at birth (years) [4]	% of population with access to health services [5]	Literacy (total adult literacy rate %) [4]
	1998	1999	1997/2015	1999	1998	1998	1998	1998	1990/96	1995
Macedonia, TFYR	25,710	2,011	0.5	2.2	2.1	23	27	73	..	..
Madagascar	587,040	15,496	2.6	23.4	5.4	95	157	58	38	46
Malawi	118,480	10,640	2.5	15.8	6.7	134	213	39	35	56
Malaysia	329,750	21,830	1.5	27.5	3.1	9	10	72	..	84
Maldives	300	278	2.6	0.4	5.3	62	87	65	..	95
Mali	1,240,190	10,960	2.6	16.7	6.5	144	237	54	40	32
Malta	320	386	0.6	0.4	1.9	6	7	77	..	91
Malvinas/Falklands	12,170	2ᵉ	..	..	..	..	..	..	..	..
Marshall Is.	180	63	..	..	..	63	92	..	..	91
Martinique	1,100	392	..	..	..	..	..	..	..	..
Mauritania	1,025,520	2,598	2.6	3.9	5.5	120	183	54	63	37
Mauritius	2,040	1,149	0.8	1.3	1.9	19	23	72	100	82
Mayotte Is.	375	149	..	..	..	..	..	..	..	..
Melilla	12	58ᵃ	..	..	..	..	..	..	..	..
Mexico	1,958,200	97,366	1.3	119.2	2.7	28	34	72	93	89
Micronesia	702	106	..	..	4.0	20	24	67	..	81
Moldova	33,700	4,379	0.1	4.5	1.7	28	35	68	..	98
Monaco	1	30	..	..	..	5	5	..	..	..
Mongolia	1,566,500	2,621	1.5	3.3	2.6	105	150	66	95	83
Montserrat	100	11ᵉ	..	..	..	..	..	..	..	..
Morocco	446,550	27,866	1.4	34.8	3.0	57	70	67	70	44
Mozambique	801,590	19,286	1.8	25.2	6.2	129	206	44	39	38
Myanmar/Burma	676,580	45,059	1.1	53.5	2.4	80	113	60	60	83
Namibia	824,290	1,695	1.3	2.0	4.9	57	74	51	59	78
Nauru	20	12ᵉ	..	..	25	30	..	..	..	..
Nepal	140,800	23,386	2.1	32.7	4.4	72	100	58	..	36
Netherlands	40,844	15,735	0.1	15.9	1.5	5	5	78	..	..
Netherlands Antilles	800	215	..	..	..	..	..	..	..	..
Nicaragua	130,000	4,938	2.5	7.3	4.4	39	48	68	83	66
Niger	1,267,000	10,401	3.0	16.7	6.8	166	280	49	99	13
Nigeria	923,770	108,945	2.2	153.3	5.1	112	187	50	51	57
Niue	260	2ᵉ	..	..	..	..	..	..	99	..
Norfolk Is.	36	2	..	..	..	..	..	..	..	..
Northern Marianas	464	44	..	..	..	..	..	..	..	..
Norway	323,900	4,442	0.4	4.7	1.9	4	4	78	..	..
Oman	212,460	2,460	3.3	4.1	5.8	15	18	71	96	64
Pakistan	796,100	152,330	2.4	222.6	5.0	95	136	64	55	39
Palau	459	17	..	..	..	28	34	..	..	98
Palestine	6,220	3,019,704	..	..	5.9	..	..	71	..	84
Panama	75,520	2,812	1.3	3.5	2.6	18	20	74	70	91
Papua New Guinea	462,840	4,702	2.1	6.5	4.6	79	112	58	96	72
Paraguay	406,750	5,359	2.4	7.8	4.1	27	33	70	63	92
Peru	1,285,220	25,230	1.5	31.9	2.9	43	54	68	44	88
Philippines	300,000	74,454	1.7	96.7	3.6	32	44	68	71	94
Pitcairn	5	0.07ᶜ	..	..	..	..	..	..	..	..
Poland	323,250	38,741	0.1	39.3	1.5	10	11	73	..	100
Portugal	92,390	9,873	-0.1	9.7	1.4	8	9	75	..	90
Puerto Rico	8,900	3,839	..	..	..	..	..	..	..	..
Qatar	11,000	589	1.4	0.7	3.7	15	18	72	..	79
Réunion	2,510	691	..	..	..	..	..	..	..	..
Romania	238,390	22,402	-0.4	21.1	1.2	21	24	70	..	98
Russia	17,075,400	147,195	-0.2	142.9	1.3	21	25	67		99
Rwanda	26,340	7,235	3.2	10.5	6.1	105	170	41	80	60
Sahara (Western)	266,000	284	..	..	..	..	..	..	..	..
Samoa	2,840	177	1.8	0.2	4.1	22	27	71	..	98
Samoa, American	200	47	..	..	..	..	..	..	..	..
San Marino	60	25	..	..	..	6	6	..	..	..
São Tomé and Príncipe	960	127	1.8	0.2	4.7	60	77	64	..	57
Saudi Arabia	2,149,690	20,899	2.9	32.6	5.7	22	26	72	97	71
Senegal	196,720	9,240	2.5	13.7	5.5	70	121	53	90	33
Seychelles	450	76	1.0	0.1	2.1	14	18	71	..	84

New Zealand - see Aotearoa/New Zealand

Countries	Primary pupil to teacher ratio [6]	Newspapers per 1,000 people [6]	TV sets per 1,000 people [3]	Radios per 1,000 people [3]	Books (titles published per million people) [7]	GNP per capita ($) [6]	GNP, annual growth (%) [6]	Average annual inflation (%) [6]	Exports of goods and services (current millions dollars) [6]	Imports of goods and services (current millions dollars) [6]
	1998	1996	1996	1997	1992/94	1998	1998	1990/98	1998	1998
Macedonia, TFYR	19[c]	21	170	200	31	1,290	3.1	17.9	1,021	1,412
Madagascar	37[b]	5	..	192	1	260	4.9	22.1	796	1,094
Malawi	59[b]	3[b]	..	249	3	210	1.5	33.2	515	740
Malaysia	20[a]	158	228	420	21	3,670	-5.8	5.1	82,899	67,098
Maldives	..	20	39	125	..	1,130	7.1	..	..	..
Mali	80[c]	1	11	54	..	250	4.3	9.3	636	928
Malta	19[b]	129	497	673	115	10,100	5.3[b]	3,071	..	3,259
Malvinas/Falklands	..	..	..	..	..	..	..	..	..	..
Marshall Is.	..	..	..	..	..	1,540	-4.3	..	..	..
Martinique	..	..	..	..	..	..	..	..	..	..
Mauritania	50[c]	..	82	151	..	410	4.3	5.3	407	536
Mauritius	24[c]	75	219	368	8	3,730	5.1	6.2	2,723	2,727
Mayotte Is.	..	..	..	..	..	..	..	..	..	..
Melilla	..	..	..	..	..	..	..	..	..	..
Mexico	28[c]	97	193	325	..	3,840	4.7	19.5	122,956	130,668
Micronesia	..	..	..	73[c]	..	1,800	-3.1	..	..	..
Moldova	23[c]	60	307	740	18	380	-9.5	173.9	752	1,216
Monaco	19[b]	..	..	..	..	..	..	..	..	..
Mongolia	31[c]	27	63	151	12	380	3.5	78.2	516	577
Montserrat	..	..	..	..	..	..	..	..	..	..
Morocco	28[c]	26	..	241	1	1,240	7.0	3.5	6,421	9,251
Mozambique	58[e]	3	3	40	..	210	11.8	41.1	456	1,186
Myanmar/Burma	..	10	7	95	8	..	-20.0	25.9	..	..
Namibia	..	19	29	144	..	1,940	1.2	9.5	1,951	1,956
Nauru	..	..	..	..	..	..	..	..	..	..
Nepal	..	11	4	38	..	210	2.7	8.9	1,107	1,644
Netherlands	..	306	495	978	222	24,780	3.3	2.1	203,314[d]	177,838[d]
Netherlands Antilles	..	337	..	996	..	..	..	..	..	..
Nicaragua	38[b]	30	170	285	..	370	6.1	45.5	785	1,434
Niger	41[c]		..	69	..	200	8.4	6.8	333	479
Nigeria	37[a]	24	55	223	1	300	1.1	38.7	9,712	13,115
Niue	..	..	..	..	..	..	..	..	..	..
Norfolk Is.	..	..	..	..	..	..	..	..	..	..
Northern Marianas	..	..	..	..	..	..	..	..	..	..
Norway	..	588	569	915	159	34,310	2.3	1.8	63,277[d]	52,453[d]
Oman	26[b]	29	591	598	1	..	3.2[b]	-2.9	..	..
Pakistan	..	23[b]	24	98	..	470	3.0	11.1	10,017	12,818
Palau	..	..	..	..	..	..	..	..	..	..
Palestine	..	..	..	..	..	3,097[c]	7.0	11.0	693	2,532
Panama	..	62	229	299	..	2,990	2.5	2.2	3,090	3,940
Papua New Guinea	38[b]	15	4	97	..	890	2.3	7.1	2,554	2,630
Paraguay	21[c]	43	144	182	3	1,760	-0.5	14.6	3,871	4,253
Peru	28[b]	..	142	273	9	2,440	-1.6	33.7	7,506	10,483
Philippines	35[c]	79	125	159	2	1,050	0.1	8.5	36,232	39,008
Pitcairn	..	..	..	..	..	..	..	..	..	..
Poland	15[b]	113	418	523	28	3,910	4.4	26.9	36,718[d]	42,931[d]
Portugal	..	75	367	304	68	10,670	3.9	5.8	31,828[d]	40,642[d]
Puerto Rico	..	126	..	753	..	8,200[d]	3.2	3.7	..	..
Qatar	6[b]	130	538	450	69	12,000[b]	-2.1[b]	..	..	..
Reunion	..	..	..	..	..	..	..	..	..	..
Romania	20[c]	300[a]	226	319	18	1,360	-8.3	113.8	9,801	13,037
Russia	..	105	386	418	20	2,260	-6.6	230.9	87,734	74,078
Rwanda	..	..	..	102	..	230	9.9	18.1	110	464
Sahara (Western)	..	..	..	..	..	..	..	..	..	..
Samoa	24[b]	..	45	1,047	..	1,070	1.3	..	..	..
Samoa, American	..	84	..	955	..	..	..	..	..	..
San Marino	..	..	..	..	..	..	..	..	..	..
São Tomé and Príncipe	..	..	165	275	..	270	1.4	..	12	35
Saudi Arabia	13[c]	57	263	321	..	6,910	2.3	1.4	46,275	39,546
Senegal	56[d]	5	38	142	..	520	6.7	5.6	1,559	1,780
Seychelles	17[c]	39	191	545	..	6,420	-1.7	..	376	468

New Zealand - see Aotearoa/New Zealand

Countries	Area (square km) [1]	Total population (Thousands) [2]	Demographic growth to year 2015 (%) [3]	Population estimate for year 2015 (million) [3]	Total fertility rate (children per woman) [4]	Infant mortality rate (per 1,000 live births) [4]	Under-5 mortality rate (per 1,000 live births) [4]	Life expectancy at birth (years) [4]	% of population with access to health services [5]	Literacy (total adult literacy rate %) [4]
	1998	1999	1997/2015	1999	1998	1998	1998	1998	1990/96	1995
Sierra Leone	71,740	4,717	2.3	6.7	6.0	182	316	38	38	31
Singapore	620	3,522	0.9	4.0	1.7	4	5	77	..	91
Slovakia	49,010	5,381	0.1	5.5	1.4	9	10	73	..	..
Slovenia	20,250	1,989	-0.2	1.9	1.3	5	5	74	..	100
Solomon Is.	28,900	430	2.8	0.7	4.8	22	26	72	..	62
Somalia	637,660	9,672	..	..	7.2	125	211	47	..	24
South Africa	1,221,037	39,900	0.6	43.4	3.2	60	83	54	..	83
Spain	504,780	39,633	-0.2	38.5	1.1	6	6	78	..	97
Sri Lanka	65,610	18,639	1.0	21.9	2.1	17	19	73	..	90
St Helena	210	6[e]	..	..	..	..	..	..	..	..
St Kitts-Nevis	360	42	-0.5	..	2.4	30	37	70	..	90
St Lucia	620	136	1.3	0.2	2.4	18	21	70	..	..
St Pierre and Miq.	242	7[e]	..	..	..	..	..	..	..	..
St Vincent	390	112	0.6	0.1	2.2	20	23	73	..	82
Sudan	2,505,810	28,882	2.0	39.8	4.6	73	115	55	70	51
Suriname	163,270	416	0.8	0.5	2.2	28	35	70	..	93
Swaziland	17,360	980	2.6	1.5	4.7	64	90	60	..	76
Sweden	449,960	8,892	0.1	9.1	1.6	4	4	79	..	..
Switzerland	41,284	7,345	0.3	7.6	1.5	5	5	79	..	..
Syria	185,180	15,725	2.3	22.6	4.0	26	32	69	90	70
Taiwan	36,000	21,804[e]	..	..	..	..	..	..	..	..
Tajikistan	143,100	6,104	1.5	7.8	4.1	55	74	67	..	99
Tanzania	883,749	32,792	2.3	47.2	5.4	91	142	48	42	69
Thailand	513,120	60,856	0.8	68.9	1.7	30	37	69	90	94
Togo	56,790	4,512	2.6	6.7	6.0	81	144	49	..	51
Tokelau	10	2[e]	..	..	..	..	..	..	..	..
Tonga	750	98	..	..	3.6	19	23	71	..	99
Trinidad and Tobago	5,130	1,288	0.6	1.4	1.6	16	18	74	100	98
Tunisia	163,610	9,460	1.3	11.6	2.5	25	32	70	..	65
Turkey	774,815	65,546	1.3	80.3	2.5	37	42	69	..	82
Turkmenistan	488,100	4,384	1.5	5.6	3.6	53	72	66	100	98
Turks and Caicos	430	16[e]	..	..	..	..	..	..	..	..
Tuvalu	30	10[e]	..	..	40	56	..	..	99	..
Uganda	241,038	21,143	3.1	34.5	7.1	84	134	40	49	62
Ukraine	603,700	50,658	-0.4	47.9	1.4	18	22	69	..	99
United Arab Emir.	83,600	2,397	1.5	3.0	3.4	9	10	75	99	79
United Kingdom	244,100	58,744	0.1	59.6	1.7	6	6	77	..	..
United States	9,363,520	276,219	0.7	307.7	2.0	7	8	77	..	99
Uruguay	177,410	3,313	0.7	3.7	2.4	16	19	74	82	97
Uzbekistan	447,400	23,941	1.4	29.9	3.4	45	58	68	..	100
Vanuatu	12,190	186	2.3	0.3	4.3	38	49	68	..	64
Vatican	0.4	0.8	..	..	..	..	..	..	..	..
Venezuela	912,050	23,706	1.7	30.9	3.0	21	25	72	..	91
Vietnam	331,690	78,705	1.3	96.6	2.6	31	42	68	90	91
Virgin Is. (Am.)	347	102	..	..	..	..	..	..	..	..
Vírgin Is. (Br.)	150	20[e]	..	..	..	..	..	..	..	..
Wallis and Futuna Is.	200	15[e]	..	..	..	..	..	..	..	..
Yemen	527,970	17,488	3.4	29.6	7.5	87	121	58	38	40
Yugoslavia Fed. Rep.	102,170	10,637	..	..	1.8	18	21	73	..	98
Zambia	752,618	8,976	2.3	12.8	5.5	112	202	40	..	78
Zimbabwe	390,760	11,529	1.1	13.6	3.8	59	89	44	85	85

Data refers to:

a. 1994
b. 1995
c. 1996
d. 1997
e. 1998

1. UNCTAD - Handbook of Statistics, 2000
2. Population Division, Web site, United Nations, 1999
3. Human Development Report 1999, UNDP, 1999
4. The State of the World's Children 2000, UNICEF, 2000
5. The State of the World's Children 1997, UNICEF, 1997
6. World Development Indicators 2000, World Bank, 2000
7. Human Development Report 1997, UNDP, 1997

Countries	Primary pupil to teacher ratio [6]	Newspapers per 1,000 people [6]	TV sets per 1,000 people [3]	Radios per 1,000 people [6]	Books (titles published per million people) [7]	GNP per capita ($) [6]	GNP, annual growth (%) [6]	Average annual inflation (%) [6]	Exports of goods and services (current millions dollars) [6]	Imports of goods and services (current millions dollars) [6]
	1998	1996	1996	1997	1992/94	1998	1998	1990/98	1998	1998
Sierra Leone	..	4	17	253	..	140	-0.7	32.5	142	203
Singapore	22[b]	360	361	822	..	30,170	1.5	2.1	128,706	113,699
Slovakia	19[c]	185	384	580	65	3,700	4.2	11.4	12,965	15,239
Slovenia	14[c]	199	375	406	151	9,780	3.9	27.0	11,068	11,351
Solomon Is.	24[a]	..	7	141	..	760	-7.0	..	..	..
Somalia	..	1	..	46	..	..	..	..	..	..
South Africa	36[b]	32	123	317	11	3,310	0.5	10.6	34,384	32,733
Spain	17[b]	100	509	333	112	14,100	3.7	4.2	150,984[d]	144,605[d]
Sri Lanka	28[c]	29	82	209	17	810	4.6	9.7	5,648	6,661
St Helena	..	..	..	..	..	..	..	..	..	..
St Kitts-Nevis	..	..	244	682	..	6,190	3.6	..	149	224
St Lucia	26[c]	..	301	742	..	3,660	3.0	..	396	416
St Pierre and Miq.	..	..	..	..	..	..	..	..	..	..
St Vincent	..	..	234	690	..	2,560	5.2	..	159	226
Sudan	29[c]	27	80	271	..	290	5.0	74.4	..	..
Suriname	..	122	208	686	..	1,660	2.8	..	..	..
Swaziland	34[d]	26	96	164	..	1,400	1.8	..	1,239	1,155
Sweden	1[c]	445	476	932	158	25,580	2.8	2.4	99,727[d]	83,758[d]
Switzerland	..	337	493	1,000	217	39,980	1.8	1.7	101,826[d]	90,492[d]
Syria	23[c]	20	91	278	4	1,020	0.2	8.9	5,049	6,994
Taiwan	..	..	..	..	..	..	..	..	..	..
Tajikistan	24[c]	20	279	142	4	370	15.2	300.0	1,918[b]	1,907[b]
Tanzania	37[d]	4	..	279	..	220	6.5	24.3	1,474	2,004
Thailand	..	63	167	232	13	2,160	-7.7	4.8	65,593	47,219
Togo	51[b]	4	14	218	..	330	-1.0	8.8	509	610
Tokelau	..	..	..	..	..	..	..	..	..	..
Tonga	..	..	..	617	..	1,750	-1.5	..	..	..
Trinidad and Tobago	25[c]	123	318	534	2	4,520	6.2	6.9	2,638	3,598
Tunisia	24[c]	31	156	223	6	2,060	5.5	4.8	8,464	9,103
Turkey	28[a]	111	309	180	8	3,160	3.9	79.4	49,229	56,129
Turkmenistan	..	..	163	276	14	650[d]	-24.0[d]	663.4	..	..
Turks and Caicos	..	..	..	..	..	..	..	..	..	..
Tuvalu	..	..	..	..	..	..	..	..	..	..
Uganda	35[b]	2	26	128	2	310	5.7	15.3	697	1,335
Ukraine	..	54	341	884	10	980	-2.4	440.0	17,365	18,687
United Arab Emir.	16[c]	156	282	345	14	17,870	-5.7	2.4	..	..
United Kingdom	..	329	612	1,436	164	21,410	2.1	3.0	367,971[d]	374,045[d]
United States	16[b]	215	806	2,146	20	29,240	2.5	1.9	948,600[d]	1,058,800[d]
Uruguay	20[c]	293	305	607	..	6,070	3.9	40.5	4,512	4,620
Uzbekistan	21[a]	3	190	465	6	950	5.2	356.7	4,529	4,578
Vanuatu	..	..	13	348	..	1,260	2.1	..	..	..
Vatican	..	..	..	..	..	..	..	..	..	..
Venezuela	21[c]	206	180	468	17	3,530	-0.4	49.2	19,030	19,083
Vietnam	..	4	180	107	8	350	5.8	18.5	11,480[d]	13,625[d]
Virgin Is. (Am.)	..	..	..	1,000	..	..	..	..	..	..
Vírgin Is. (Br.)	..	..	..	..	..	..	..	..	..	..
Wallis and Futuna Is.	..	..	..	..	..	..	..	..	..	..
Yemen	..	15	278	64	..	280	7.3	24.2	1,489	2,315
Yugoslavia Fed. Rep.	..	107	..	297	..	..	..	..	..	..
Zambia	39[b]	12	80	121	..	330	-1.9	63.5	984	1,286
Zimbabwe	39[d]	19	29	93	2	620	0.5	21.9	2,911	3,027

Also from New Internationalist Publications

The A-Z of World Development

A major reference book on global issues for the new century.

by Andy Crump and Wayne Ellwood

The A-Z of World Development is a first-rate reference book on key themes and ideas of global development. The book combines the authority of a comprehensive reference work with the unique political and economic analysis for which the *New Internationalist* is famous.

◆ The book contains over 700 entries covering essential items as well as the eclectic. The listings vary in length from the short and snappy to longer definitions of a few hundred words.

◆ Entries are compiled in an alphabetical format but with a mix ranging from acronym, ideas and concepts through to individuals and events.

◆ Sample listings include the UNITED NATIONS, STRUCTURAL ADJUSTMENT and ORAL REHYDRATION THERAPY but also include RASTAFARIANISM, INDIRA GANDHI and the CHIPKO MOVEMENT.

◆ Additional information to some of the main entries are in sidebars or boxes. These contain factual information or brief, colourful, atmospheric vignettes in the form of quotes or anecdotes.

The book is handsomely visual: three to four colour images per spread including colour photos, historical line-work drawings, colour illustrations, design motifs as well as charts, graphs and cartoons.

The A-Z of World Development book and accompanying CD-ROM is ideal for teachers and students at high school, college and university levels, as well as for home reference. It meets the strong public appetite for factual reference works and appeals to the many active supporters of human rights, social justice and Third World development organizations.

About the Authors:

Andy Crump has written *The Dictionary of Environment and Development* and works with the World Health Organization.

Wayne Ellwood is one of the staff editors of the *New Internationalist* magazine and works out of Toronto, Canada.

Format: Large paperback 274 mm × 216 mm (11" × 8½") 294 pages, full colour throughout. Also available on CD-ROM.

'Thanks to the A-Z of World Development for guiding us on our way to better understanding the world. A rattling good book!'

Professor Norman Myers,
Editor of The Gaia Atlas of Planet Management

The A-Z of World Development CD-ROM

This CD-ROM of the book includes some 250 pictures, 140 charts, graphs and maps. Also the most comprehensive collection of UN statistical information PLUS UNICEF's Progress of Nations and The State of the World's Children (statistics). All exportable to reports, lectures, articles and essays.

The No-Nonsense Guides...
the series that makes sense of the world

A new series of handy reference books that makes sense of the most complex global issues, such as **Global Economy**, **Fair Trade** or **Climate Change** - the first titles in the series.

In each pocket-sized book are facts, charts/graphs, information and analysis to give you easy access to the important issues about each topic. And that's not all: each book is fully indexed to make finding a topic easy. There's a bibliography to spur follow-up reading plus an Action Section so that you can find out who's doing what on the campaigning side - and join in!

Upcoming titles planned are **The No-Nonsense Guide to Democracy**, **The No-Nonsense Guide to Aid Projects**, **The No-Nonsense Guide to Sexual Minorities** and **The No-Nonsense Guide to World History**.

Contact details:
New Internationalist Publications, 55 Rectory Road, Oxford OX4 1BW, UK.
e-mail: jol@newint.org OR your national distributor.
Visit the NI website at: www.newint.org

The World Guide CD-ROM

This completely revised and updated edition, **The World Guide 2001/2002**, is a biennially updated database packed with key information on every country in the world.

This CD-ROM is a major reference guide with a big difference: there are *three* major works on it. They each emphasise priorities that are not reflected in standard texts, such as:

◆ Human Rights

◆ Environment

◆ Indigenous People

◆ Militarism

◆ Sexual and Racial discrimination

◆ Perspective of people in the countries portrayed.

The biggest single work on this CD-ROM is **The World Guide 2001/2002** compiled by the Third World Institute in Montevideo, Uruguay, with a wide network of contributors around the world.

The other two works on the disk are the **Amnesty Annual Report** on each country and **Social Watch**, a review of how each country is faring on key social development targets.

Using The World Guide 2001/2002

This new edition of **The World Guide** has been designed with ease of use in mind. Six menu buttons at the top of each screen give single-click access to all other areas of the CD. Select:

◆ Themes - for a fascinating overview of some major development topics

◆ Countries - for a particular country to study, including its historical overview, profile, location map, country map, key statistics, flag and anthem.

◆ Tables - to review indicators for each country such as the literacy rate or the debt burden.

◆ Amnesty - for the latest Amnesty Annual Report on human rights.

◆ Social Watch - for the rating on each country's social development progress.

◆ Graphics - to present your chosen information in graphic format, with data for several selected countries side by side.

Use the forward and back buttons on the toolbar to move easily back and forth to specific areas you have visited or wish to see.

All this adds up to a unique package of alternative and highly relevant material on the world, unavailable elsewhere. It is exportable from the CD-ROM for your reports, essays, lectures, articles and research papers.

Site licences available.
Contact your national distributor or see below.

Contact details:
New Internationalist Publications, 55 Rectory Road, Oxford OX4 1BW, UK.
e-mail: jol@newint.org OR your national distributor.
Visit the NI website at: www.newint.org

AOTEAROA/New Zealand
New Internationalist Aotearoa
PO Box 4499
Christchurch
Tel: 00 64 (0) 33 656 153
Fax: 00 64 (0) 3 365 6153
E-mail: newint@chch.planet.org.nz

AUSTRALIA
New Internationalist Australia
28 Austin Street
Adelaide
SA 5000
Tel: 00 61 (0) 8 8232 1563
Fax: 00 61 (0) 8 8232 1887
E-mail: helenp@newint.com.au

For book shop distribution:

Bush Books
PO Box 1370
Gosford South
NSW 2250
Tel: 04 323 3274
Fax: 02 9212 2468
E-mail: bushbook@ozemail.com.au

BELGIUM
11.11.11
Vlasfabriekstraat 11
1060 Brussel
Tel: 322 539 2620
Fax: 322 539 1343

CANADA
New Internationalist Canada
1011 Bloor Street West
Toronto
Ontario M6H 1M1
Tel: 001 416 588 6478
Fax: 001 416 537 6435
E-mail: reidmill@web.net

For book shop distribution:

Garamond Press
63 Mahogany Court
Aurora
Ontario L4G 6M8
Tel: 905 841 1460
Fax: 905 841 3031
E-mail: garamond@web.net

DENMARK
Mellemfolkeligt Samvirke
Borgergade 14
1300 Copenhagen
Tel: 3332 6244
Fax: 3315 6243
E-mail: avillums@ms-dan.dk

GERMANY
Lamuv Verlag
Postfach 2605
D-37016 Gottingen
Tel: 551 44024
Fax: 551 41392

NETHERLANDS
Novib Publications
Mauritskade 9
PO Box 30919
2500 GX
The Hague
Tel: 31 70 342 1610
Fax: 31 70 361 4461
E-mail: uschi.bevers@novib.nl

NEW ZEALAND see Aotearoa/New Zealand

NORWAY
Arning Publications
Postboks 1706
Sentrum
7416 Trondheim
Tel: 73 53 60 70
Fax: 73 53 6071
E-mail: arning@arning.no

SOUTH AFRICA
David Philip Publishers
PO Box 23408
Claremont 7735
Fax: 21 64 3358
E-mail: kieran.mckenna@dpp.co.za

UNITED KINGDOM
New Internationalist Publications
55 Rectory Road
Oxford OX4 1BW
Tel: 01865 728181
Fax: 01865 793152
E-mail: ni@newint.org

For book shop distribution:

Central Books
99 Wallis Road
Hackney
London E9 5LN
Tel: 020 8986 4854
Fax: 020 8533 5821
E-mail: orders@centbks.demon.co.uk

UNITED STATES
Stylus Publishing
22883 Quicksilver Drive
Sterling
VA 20166
Tel: 703 661 1500
Fax: 703 661 1501

URUGUAY
Instituto del Tercer Mundo
Juan D. Jackson 1136
CP 11200, Montevideo
Tel: 8 2409 6192
Fax: 8 2401 9222
E-mail: item@chasque.net